THE NORTON ANTHOLOGY OF DRAMA

Third Edition

VOLUME 2: THE NINETEENTH CENTURY TO THE PRESENT

THE NORTON ANTHOLOGY OF DRAMA

Third Edition

J. ELLEN GAINOR
CORNELL UNIVERSITY

STANTON B. GARNER JR.
UNIVERSITY OF TENNESSEE

MARTIN PUCHNER
COLUMBIA UNIVERSITY

VOLUME 2: THE NINETEENTH CENTURY TO THE PRESENT

W. W. NORTON & COMPANY
NEW YORK · LONDON

W. W. Norton & Company has been independent since its founding in 1923, when William Warder Norton and Mary D. Herter Norton first published lectures delivered at the People's Institute, the adult education division of New York City's Cooper Union. The firm soon expanded its program beyond the Institute, publishing books by celebrated academics from America and abroad. By midcentury, the two major pillars of Norton's publishing program—trade books and college texts—were firmly established. In the 1950s, the Norton family transferred control of the company to its employees, and today—with a staff of four hundred and a comparable number of trade, college, and professional titles published each year—W. W. Norton & Company stands as the largest and oldest publishing house owned wholly by its employees.

Editor: Peter Simon
Associate Editor: Gerra Goff
Managing Editor, College: Marian Johnson
Project Editor: Linda Feldman
Electronic Media Editor: Carly Fraser Doria
Marketing Manager, Literature: Kimberly Bowers
Production Manager: Ashley Horna
Photo Editor: Nelson Colón
Permissions Manager: Megan Schindel
Permissions Clearing: Nancy Rodwan
Text Design: Rubina Yeh
Art Director: Trish Marx

Composition: Westchester Book Composition
Manufacturing: LSC Communications—Crawfordsville, IN

978-0-393-28348-8

W. W. Norton & Company, Inc., 500 Fifth Avenue, New York, NY 10110-0017
wwnorton.com
W. W. Norton & Company Ltd., 15 Carlisle Street, London W1D 3BS

2 3 4 5 6 7 8 9 0

Contents

COLOR INSERT

*Plays in Performance: *Hedda Gabler*
*Plays in Performance: *A Streetcar Named Desire*
*Plays in Performance: *A Raisin in the Sun*
*Plays in Performance: *Angels in America, Part I*

Preface

D RAMA, one of the oldest of the arts, is also the most multifaceted. Grounded in the different mediums of writing and performance, it offers pleasures both to live audiences and to the solitary reader. In preparing the third edition of *The Norton Anthology of Drama*, the editors have continued to follow our guiding principle that drama is at once a literary document, speaking to us across a vast expanse of time and space, and a live event, taking place in the here and now. Most of the plays collected here can be experienced in theaters today, or can at least be seen in a filmed performance. But even those that are rarely performed in the contemporary era are presented in *The Norton Anthology of Drama* with considerable attention to their life on the stage.

This third edition builds on the strengths that distinguish *The Norton Anthology of Drama* from other available drama anthologies. Its plays and their presentation reflect a commitment to the richness and internationality of the dramatic tradition and to the dialogues that mark dramatic performance across languages, borders, and periods. Most anthologies organize their plays into historical and geographical units with such headings as "Greek Drama," "Renaissance Drama," and "Contemporary Drama." One of the chief results of this kind of demarcation is a hard line of separation between Western traditions and non-Western ones. We, on the other hand, rely on chronology to organize our plays (using actual or estimated dates of first performance, and substituting publication or composition dates for those plays not originally written for performance or plays whose performance was significantly delayed). This decision reflects our belief that theater is historically and geographically more fluid than traditional organizational structures imply. We believe, too, that what we call "Western" and "non-Western" texts are marked by concurrent developments across cultures and by similarities of form, subject, and even performance conditions that traditional theatrical and dramatic histories neglect. Chronological presentation allows surprising juxtapositions: Zeami's noh masterpiece *Atsumori* with *The Second Shepherds' Play*, Racine's *Phèdre* with Sor Juana's *Loa to the Divine Narcissus*, or Arthur Miller's *Death of a Salesman* with Tawfiq al-Hakim's *Song of Death*. It also enhances flexibility of course development and organization—*The Norton Anthology of Drama* makes possible many different courses while mandating no specific approach. Nonetheless, those who desire a presentation of theatrical history that emphasizes historical periods and national traditions will find this structure in the anthology's Introduction.

In determining the table of contents for this anthology, the editors were guided by the desire to select the most thematically rich, performatively engaging, and pedagogically compelling plays available—plays that respond to the historical, cultural, literary, and theatrical contexts in which they were written in new, often groundbreaking, ways. To ensure that reading classic plays written in languages other than English is a lively experience for students, we have selected vibrant translations that speak in a modern idiom while respecting the spirit and sense of the original. When no existing version satisfied us, we commissioned a new one. Whether commissioned specifically for *The Norton Anthology of Drama* or published previously, the translations in this anthology are all not only engaging and accessible on the page but also eminently performable. In balancing the literary with the theatrical, we have designed an anthology that will work in both English and theater classrooms. For the instructor of dramatic literature courses at the introductory and advanced levels, the plays in *The Norton Anthology of Drama* reward textual attention of a literary kind while also encouraging analysis of the play's performance possibilities. For the theater instructor, the anthology provides theatrically vibrant texts in actable editions and translations. Students encountering drama for the first time will discover how powerfully the language of these plays comes alive on the tongue, and experienced and inexperienced students alike will find the versions here to be ideal for in-class performance as well as for line and scene reading. The teaching of drama can be conducted through a range of classroom activities, and *The Norton Anthology of Drama* has been designed to facilitate as many as possible. Not only does this edition of *The Norton Anthology of Drama* offer more plays (sixty-four) than any other available drama anthology, but it also provides instructors with a fuller range of periods, texts, and playwrights from which to choose. Those familiar with the second edition will notice a number of additions to the third. Whereas the enhancements to the selection of plays in the second edition focused on the first volume as well as the second, our attention in the third edition

was dedicated to making the second volume as teachable and attractive to instructors and students as possible. In response to reviews and comments from hundreds of teachers, we have added plays that have proven to be popular with students and teachers alike. Eugene O'Neill's *The Hairy Ape*, one of the finest examples of expressionism in the American theater, explores the transformative and dislocating effects of industrialism in the First Machine Age. Edward Albee's one-act play *The Zoo Story* is a riveting portrait of alienation, encounter, and responsibility in a contemporary urban setting. Lorraine Hansberry's *A Raisin in the Sun*, one of the most requested plays by our survey respondents, addresses issues of race and aspiration that resonate as much today as they did at the dawn of the Civil Rights Era. Paula Vogel's *How I Learned to Drive* probes deeply controversial questions of sexuality and abuse through innovative theatrical means, while Lynn Nottage's award-winning play *Ruined* captures the pain and trauma, but also the resilience and hope, of African women grappling with the horrors of the ongoing conflict in the Democratic Republic of the Congo. All of the works we're including in this edition demonstrate the vital role that drama and theatrical performance play in addressing our world's most pressing political, social, and human issues.

Like the Norton anthologies of British, American, and world literatures; *The Norton Anthology of Theory and Criticism*; and the other anthologies with which Norton has shaped classroom teaching over the years, *The Norton Anthology of Drama* provides students and instructors with a wealth of introductory and editorial support. The substantial Introduction opens by exploring the relationship between dramatic literature and theatrical performance, and it concludes with a discussion of the challenges and opportunities of reading plays as scripts for performance. This final section— "Reading Drama, Imagining Theater"— is designed to give students approaching drama for the first time the tools they need to understand this uniquely hybrid form. The "Short History of Theater," which makes up the central part of the Introduction, provides a detailed yet brisk overview of the political, social, and theatrical contexts within which drama has been embedded through the ages and across the globe. We illustrate this history—and the headnotes that accompany each play—with vivid images of theaters, playwrights, actors, and audiences; manuscript pages, woodcuts, early printings, and other illustrations representing the importance of manuscript and print culture to the development and dissemination of drama; pictures from acting manuals; and other images related to theatrical production. The performance dimension of the plays included in this anthology is further enlivened by new headnote photographs of legendary or contemporary performances of the plays under discussion and by the "Plays in Performance" feature, which highlights the issues involved in bringing eight classic plays to the contemporary stage. These color inserts (one set per volume) expand students' understanding of the complex decision-making that informs the production of a play, and they give students a glimpse of the creative work performed by actors and directors as they reframe and reimagine plays onstage. They also include examples of critical responses to the productions selected for discussion.

New to this edition is a "Critical Perspective" feature that provides students with a taste of important documents in drama criticism and theory. Beginning with a generous selection from Aristotle's seminal treatise *The Poetics*, these eight readings—four in each volume—provide touchstones for reading and discussion. In addition to selecting readings that illuminate the plays they accompany, preference was given to documents that raise questions of broader aesthetic, historical, and theoretical concern: the concept of *yūgen*, or "grace," that underpins Japanese noh drama; the medieval preoccupation with mortality; neoclassic theory and its critics in the seventeenth and eighteenth centuries; and the philosophical foundation of absurdism in postwar Europe. Students can explore the issue of reception in Samuel Johnson's reading of Shakespeare and Shaw's reading of Ibsen, and they can discover continuities and contrasts between readings: Aristotle, Johnson, Arthur Miller, and Martin Esslin on tragedy; Shaw and August Wilson on theater and social institutions. The editors have written short

headnotes for these critical texts and annotated them as necessary to help students understand unfamiliar terms and references. Students reading these documents—and everything else in the anthology—will also find an extensive glossary of terms related to the study of drama, which is included for the first time in this edition.

Supplemented by the substantial yet concise historical survey that opens the anthology, the headnotes that accompany each selection offer detailed, accessible introductions to the plays. These headnotes include summaries of the author's life and career, the specific historical and cultural contexts of the play in question, production information (where pertinent), and consideration of the play's importance in terms of its historical period and the broader history of drama and theater. The headnotes also include a discussion of the plays themselves, though we have taken care not to "explain" the plays to students, instead raising issues that will enable them to interpret the works on their own. For those interested in delving more deeply into the subject matter, we provide a carefully chosen and annotated bibliography of books and articles on each play and author. Throughout the headnote and bibliography, the editors have emphasized usefulness, readability, and student interest.

Similar care has been taken with the dramatic texts and their annotations. We have done everything possible to ensure that the texts in *The Norton Anthology of Drama* are the most authoritative ones available; if competing versions of these texts exist, we have selected the ones that are endorsed by contemporary scholarly consensus. In cases in which there is more than one version of a play—Marlowe's *Doctor Faustus*, Shaw's *Pygmalion*, and Shepard's *Buried Child*, for instance—we have usually selected the text that reflects the playwright's earliest theatrical vision. Our edition of *Hamlet*—a play with one of the most complicated and contested textual histories in world drama—is accompanied by a brief summary of that textual history, an overview of recent attempts to establish or resist an "authoritative" text, and a rationale for the version of the text included here. At the levels of selection and copyediting, we have devoted an exceptional amount of attention to ensuring that the text as it appears here is the most correct published version available. Whereas other drama anthologies occasionally present historically and linguistically challenging plays without any annotations at all, *The Norton Anthology of Drama* provides footnotes and marginal glosses whenever an unfamiliar word, phrase, or historical/cultural reference risks interfering with a student's understanding of the text. We have tried to avoid cluttering plays with such material—we assume that students have access to a dictionary—but we have worked to annotate those words and references whose significance is obscured or hidden by historical remoteness.

Comprehensive anthologies of drama, students and instructors have long agreed, are unwieldy affairs, encompassing as they do twenty-five centuries of drama in phonebook-size volumes. *The Norton Anthology of Drama*, by contrast, has been published in two companion volumes that fit comfortably in the hand and on a lap, with the play-texts appearing on easy-to-read, single-column pages. Students can carry one volume at a time to class, and the anthology as a whole is an attractive addition to a bookshelf. There are pedagogical reasons for the two-volume choice as well. The first volume ("Antiquity through the Eighteenth Century") contains the periods that typically make up the first half of a two-semester history of theater or drama course, and the second volume ("The Nineteenth Century to the Present") lends itself to the second semester of such courses. Because of their rich historical coverage of specific periods, the two volumes can also be used—together or separately—for advanced courses in Renaissance drama, modern drama, American drama, contemporary drama, script analysis, dramaturgy, tragedy, comedy, and the like and for courses that include extended units in these and other areas. So that the users of the single volumes can have the fullest possible exposure to theatrical antecedents, crosscurrents, and historical developments, the Introduction has been included in full in each volume.

Finally, the many resources in *The Norton Anthology of Drama*—the Introduction, individual headnotes, bibliographies,

and textual annotations—are complemented by resources available on the third edition's much improved companion site (digital.wwnorton.com/drama3). Among the resources available there is an Instructor's Manual by Zander Brietzke, written in consultation with the editors, that provides valuable material for teaching both large survey courses and smaller lectures and seminars. This guide presents the most important topics that might be covered in a lecture on a given play; it also suggests creative classroom exercises for students who want to explore the complexities of a scene by performing it in class. Topics and exercises focus on particular passages and scenes, yet also cover larger themes, as do the handy paper topics provided for each play. Teachers will also find a list of prominent productions in this Instructor's Manual, along with a list of the best film adaptations that might be used in class or for further study. Other resources for instructors found on the companion site are lecture PowerPoints, displayable digital files of all images included in the anthology, and links to online videos of notable performances.

The online companion site also offers resources to help students write critically about drama and theater. A short ebook, *Writing About Drama*, provides clear advice about academic writing in general as well as specific guidance for the student of drama. A digital collection of 35 readings in criticism and theory expands upon the "Critical Perspective" pieces in the anthology itself, and gives students a rich sampling of the wide variety of critical and theoretical writing about drama and theater. The editors have written short headnotes for these critical texts and annotated them where appropriate. Finally, the companion site offers short quizzes for every play and introduction in the anthology, each one offering feedback that points students back to the text when necessary.

Coming from performing arts and literature departments, the editors of *The Norton Anthology of Drama* bring the perspectives of these overlapping disciplines to dramatic history and performance and to the project of compiling a comprehensive anthology of dramatic literature. We have been aided in our efforts by a number of contributing editors, who have taken responsibilities for plays and playwrights that require special expertise. Numerous other scholars have lent knowledge and experience to this project—reading drafts of the headnotes and Introduction; clarifying points of fact and interpretation; providing nuance, when needed, to prevent historical overgeneralization; and helping us track down and identify historical images for the anthology. *The Norton Anthology of Drama*, in short, has been a deeply collaborative process, in which scholars from a number of areas have pooled their expertise to produce the most complete, informative, and engaging anthology of its kind.

Acknowledgments

A project of this magnitude cannot reach its final form without the help and encouragement of many people beyond those whose names appear on the book's cover. Given our appreciation of and love for the collaborative art of theater, we editors of *The Norton Anthology of Drama* are especially sensitive to the countless ways in which we have been helped and inspired by others.

CONTRIBUTING EDITORS

First, we would like to acknowledge the following scholars, who lent us their expertise by editing and introducing specific plays and critical perspectives:

- **Dina Ahmed Amin (University of Cairo)**, *Song of Death*
- **Art Borreca (University of Iowa)**, *The Homecoming; Angels in America: Millennium Approaches*
- **Karen Brazell (late of Cornell University)**, *Atsumori*
- **Thomas Cartelli (Muhlenberg College)**, *The Tragical History of Doctor Faustus*
- **Sudipto Chatterjee (Loughborough University)**, *The Little Clay Cart*

- **Heather Hirschfeld (University of Tennessee)**, *The Spanish Tragedy; The Duchess of Malfi*
- **Ivo Kamps (University of Mississippi)**, *Hamlet; Twelfth Night*
- **Rebecca Kastleman (Harvard University)**, *Poetics; The Quintessence of Ibsenism; The Theatre of the Absurd*
- **Evan Darwin Winet (independent scholar, Berkeley, California)**, *Snow in Midsummer*

Each of these scholars has played a critical role in making the anthology what it is, and we are grateful to have had the opportunity to collaborate with them.

TRANSLATORS

Some of the texts in *The Norton Anthology of Drama* are plays in translation that were commissioned specifically for the anthology. We thank the following translators whose skillful work has provided our readers with new translations that are both readable and performable:

- **Sudipto Chatterjee (Loughborough University)**, *The Little Clay Cart*
- **Constance Congdon (Amherst College)**, *Tartuffe*

- **Gregary Racz (Long Island University)**, *Life Is a Dream; Fuenteovejuna*
- **David Ball (Smith College)**, *Ubu the King*

We remain grateful to all those who offered support and assistance with previous editions of the anthology. We would like to acknowledge here the following people and institutions who provided us with advice, encouragement, administrative support, research assistance, and constructive critiques as we prepared the third edition: Zander Brietzke, Judith Byfield, Amanda Claybaugh, Honey Crawford, David, St. John, and Loie Faulkner, Helene Foley, Coralyn Foults, Mary Gainor, Alison Maerker Garner, Helen Elizabeth Garner, Amy Gillingham, Lyonette Louis-Jacques, Shilo McGiff, Meagan Michelson, Fred Muratori and the Reference and Interlibrary Loan Staff of Cornell University Libraries, Sabine Sörgel, Erin Stoneking, Aoise Stratford, Thomas Robert Travers, and the staff of the University of Tennessee Library Interlibrary Loan and Library Express departments.

Finally, the publisher and editors are grateful to all of the educators who responded to surveys, questionnaires, and review requests during the planning stages of this edition. The anthology continues to be a popular and useful text in large part because of the good suggestions offered by the following people: Guilherme Almeida, Claudia Barnett, Lawrence Blackwell, Kurt Blaugher, Shane Breaux, Steve Burch, Terry Burnsed, Patrick Byanne, David Carter, Brandon Chitwood, Claudia Clausius, Tom Connolly, Kerri Ann Considine, Terence Cranendonk, Ruthann Curry Browne, Stephen Di Benedetto, Lofton Durham, Ashley Edwards, James J. Fallon, Laura Fox, C. David Frankel, Becky Goldberg, M. Scott Grabau, Martine Green-Rogers, Juliet Guzzetta, Peter Hadorn, Steven Hardy, Randy Holmes, Victor Holtcamp, Lori Isbell, Timothy James Gilbreath, Susan Kattwinkel, Ali Kiani, Frederick Kiefer, Douglas King, Kenneth Krauss, Ralph Leary, Robert Lublin, Tony R. Magagna, Paulette Marty, Julia Matthews, Janet E. McLean, Donald McManus, Jeffrey S. Miller, Derek Miller, Marja Mogk, Chris Nelson, Deirdre O'Boy, John O'Connor, Claudia Orenstein, Eleanor Owicki, Laura Pattillo, Anthony Pearson, James Pecora, Christopher Petty, Paul Prece, Christine Prestash, Katherine Profeta, Tom Provenzano, Jason Radalin, Ingrid Ranum, Robert S. Rennicks, Kenneth Robbins, Tom Robson, Dale Rose, Maria Scott, Sarah S. Shaver, Yu-Li Alice Shen, Janet Smarr, Lee Stille, Janet Sussman, Theresa Trela, Nathaniel Wallace, Ariel Watson, Brenda Wentworth, and Philip Winters.

Thank you, one and all.

THE NORTON ANTHOLOGY OF DRAMA

Third Edition

VOLUME 2: THE NINETEENTH CENTURY TO THE PRESENT

Introduction

DRAMA AND THEATER

Audiences gather in a hillside amphitheater under the eastern Mediterranean sun to watch the impersonated figures of Greek myth play out their heroic, terrifying stories. In Kyoto, Japan, the sweep of robes on a railed wooden bridge announces the entry of a masked noh actor, who moves and gestures in front of his aristocratic audience with stylized precision. In London, a group of traveling players are given advice on acting by a Danish prince while the spectators who crowd the theater—aldermen, midwives, apprentices—enjoy the irony of actors meditating on their craft. In Paris, two tramps sitting by a tree on a country road share conversation and stage routines that barely conceal their anguish; an audience, seated in the dark, bears witness to their starkly contemporary situation.

The history of theater and dramatic performance is, in many ways, the history of moments such as these. The collaborative product of actors, playwrights, designers, directors, and spectators, theater achieves its magic in the live moment, rich with its sounds, sights, and feelings. The immediacy of the audience-stage encounter renders the act of theater-making magical and unique. Like other

art forms—such as novels, paintings, and movies—theater constructs imaginative worlds that we can marvel at, be moved by, and learn from. Unlike these other forms, however, theater puts its worlds into live motion, in real time. In a kind of alchemy, theater takes the realm of fiction and brings it to life with living beings whose interactions take place before our eyes. At the same time, it takes the experiences of everyday life and transforms them through the magic of performance into something more powerful, deeply felt, and artful than the daily exchanges we witness and participate in. The actor stands in for us, embodies our hopes and fears, boldly enacts what is forbidden or only dreamed of. And like the theater itself, the actor introduces us to the pleasures inherent in recognition, imitation, and the intensity of a life passionately observed and lived.

Theater is the art of the moment, and its ability to captivate us with its illusion is linked to its magical but always precarious sleight of hand. Theater is the most ephemeral of vehicles—a performance, once finished, is lost to time—and the unrepeatability of its accomplishments is a major source of its power. Unlike film, which fixes action in celluloid or other media, theater takes place in the actual, in the here and now that it shares with its spectators, and its illusions are inseparable from its precariousness. Not surprisingly, the most memorable playgoing experiences are often those when something goes wrong—a stage chair collapses, a piece of stage machinery fails, an understudy is rushed on during the middle of a performance when the main actor falls ill—and the carefully constructed dramatic illusion hangs in the balance.

Central to the act of theater-making is the dramatic text, play-text, or script, which serves as the fictional and narrative foundation of the theatrical event. Whether these texts are loosely sketched, as in the improvisational performances of the Renaissance commedia dell'arte, or highly detailed in plot, setting, characterization, and dialogue, the use of scripted narratives is one of the principal features distinguishing theater from other performance types. With the invention of writing, these texts became artworks in and of themselves, and drama assumed its place as the first "literary" form, no longer exclusively dependent on performance for its realization. Plays were available in manuscript form to the educated elite of ancient Greece and Rome; classical India, China, and Japan; and medieval Europe; and after the invention of the printing press in the fifteenth century, they became available to an expanding popular readership. The plays of WILLIAM SHAKESPEARE and TENNESSEE WILLIAMS share space on twenty-first-century bookstore shelves with the novels of Jane Austen and Cormac McCarthy. But the literary dimension of dramatic works remains inseparable from performance—actual, possible, historical, imagined—with the result that drama has different aims and reference points than do more exclusively literary forms. To read a novel is to project characters, actions, and locations within an imaginative realm that is guided and limited by the words on the page; it is to undertake a mental and emotional activity that resembles dreaming more than it does the actions we engage in daily. To read a play, in contrast, is to encounter a text whose primary purpose, with rare

exceptions, is to make something happen in real space and time with actors whose bodies and voices are the drama's principal instruments. In this sense, a play resembles a symphonic score, whose printed notations are directions for the production of musical sound. Even those plays that we refer to as "closet dramas," which were usually not performed when written—whether because of political, technical, or cultural barriers or because their authors preferred them to be read or recited rather than subjected to the stage's inherent limitations—often seem to have been created with some ideal performance in mind.

As the final section of this introduction ("Reading Drama, Imagining Theater") will discuss in more detail, drama invites the reader to put her- or himself in the position of a theater artist, alive to the possibilities and choices that bring a play to life, imagining the different ways that a scene, line, or gesture might look, sound, and feel when performed. Being attentive to the conditions of performance allows one to appreciate the features that characterize drama as a literary and theatrical form: the necessary economy of its action, setting, and characterization, which are denied the leisure of novelistic description; the centrality of spoken language, which provides access to offstage and subjective worlds; and the preoccupation with questions of role-playing, impersonation, and the many ways in which we perform for the benefit of others and ourselves. In the absence of an omniscient narrator or other guiding authorial consciousness, drama emerges through the interplay of its characters, who enact their stories in the theater and on the imagined stage of one's reading. The power of these stories resides in the immediacy of the actors and their interactions with the theater environment, which of course includes the audience.

Humans have always told each other stories. From the earliest times for which we have physical or documentary evidence, we have acted our stories for each other. We donned costumes and masks, wielded props, and later created designated places—theaters—where we use the immediacy of live performance to communicate the powerful experiences that have

Spectators watch a performance of Anton Chekhov's *Three Sisters* at the Guthrie Theater in Minneapolis, 1963.

shaped us. Like other forms of organized social performance—games, festivities, storytelling, athletic displays, civic ceremonies, political events, and rituals—these encounters are deeply embedded in specific historical, social, and cultural contexts. To study the history of theater and drama is to confront a range of historical junctures, social and institutional practices, and cultural forms. It is also to encounter one of the most enduring of human activities: make-believe, the act of making oneself other than oneself for purposes of entertainment, commemoration, communication, or devotion.

Through performance and its rituals, we confirm our shared humanity—we acknowledge the importance of each other's existence and suggest that our lives are of value. Collectively, we generate forms of community while articulating the meanings that lend shape to our lives. The sense of communion and reciprocal awareness engendered by live performance, and the dramatic texts written for it, transcends cultures and history; it is foundational to who we are as living beings. As prehistoric cave paintings indicate, imitation and ritual were part of the earliest human societies. We are performers by nature. Although theater and drama are relative latecomers to human history (having been around for a mere 2,500 years), the activities they draw on are as old as humanity itself.

A SHORT HISTORY OF THEATER

The origins of theater—and hence of drama—have long been a subject of scholarly debate. We possess little material evidence concerning the development of theatrical activity in most cultures, and what generalizations we might draw from it are complicated by the fact that the earliest forms of theater were the product of a variety of social, political, and religious forces. However, those studying different dramatic traditions have found theater to be closely connected to hunting, fertility, and other rituals in those early societies where it emerged. The nature of this connection has been debated by scholars, but the consensus view is that theatrical activity represented an extension of ritual's symbolic forms of representation into nonritual contexts. The rituals of early societies involved the enactment of religious and mythic narratives by privileged participants—shaman, priest, ruler, sacrificial victim—and these performances could become quite elaborate. In Egypt, rituals commemorating the death and resurrection of Osiris, a god associated with fertility, took place at the sacred site of Abydos as early as 2500 B.C.E. Evidence suggests that the dramatic events of Osiris's life may have been performed by priests and that these performances were accompanied by lavish spectacle.

Ritual differs from theater, of course, in that its prescribed actions, passed down from generation to generation, are designed to effect change in the natural or spiritual worlds. The ritual performances of Egypt remained tied to their religious and dynastic functions and never developed in the direction of theater. In those cultures in which theater did emerge, symbolic performance asserted itself as an object of interest in its own right, thereby paving the way for institutions, practitioners, and audiences who conceived of theater as a communal artistic activity. The earliest of these transitions—and one of the most important for the subsequent history of theater and drama—occurred in Greece in the fifth century B.C.E.

Greek Theater

ORIGINS OF GREEK THEATER

The theater of classical Greece looms large in the history of Western theater. Not only did the emergence of theater as an institution in Athens during the fifth century B.C.E. establish the world's first theatrical culture, but the characters who confronted their fate on the Greek stage—Orestes, Oedipus, Antigone, Medea—remain among the most imposing characters in the dramatic repertoire. Yet despite the importance of Greek theater to the history of Western drama, little is known about its origins. Scholars have depended, for the most part, on the scattered remarks of later classical writers who were themselves speculating about events hundreds of years in the past. Archaeological findings, the history of words associated with the theater, and vase paintings have since provided additional hints as to how the first Greek theaters came into existence. Most scholars subscribe to the notion that the origins of Greek theater lie in religious rituals. Ancient Greek religious life included many different types of ceremonies and public performances: funeral services, festivals celebrating the seasons or individual gods, processions and competitions. But which of these performances provided the decisive impulse is much harder to pinpoint. The Greek word for tragedy, tragōidia, originally meant "goat song" and therefore seems to associate tragedy with ritual practices involving the killing of a goat. Other theories hold that theater emerged from rituals performed at the tombs of heroes.

Though we know little about either the goat song or the ritual performances at tombs, other cultural practices that aided the development of theater are much better documented. Among them are the public performances of storytellers, or rhapsōidoi, who recited stories of gods and mythical humans to large audiences. The first theorist of theater, the philosopher Plato (ca. 427–ca. 347 B.C.E.), emphasized the similarities between public recitations of epic poetry and simple dramatic performances. What is still the most convincing theory about the origin of Greek theater was developed by Aristotle (384–322 B.C.E.), who wrote a generation after his teacher Plato. Aristotle claimed that theater emerged from a specific ceremony honoring Dionysus, a god associated with fertility, agriculture, wine, and (by extension) physical and spiritual intoxication. During the Attic ceremony honoring him, a chorus and a chorus leader (koryphaios) sang and danced a hymn composed in a particular form known as the dithyrambos. According to Aristotle, these ritual performances formed the basis for later dramatic performance. The Greek language reinforces Aristotle's claim, for

This image, a detail from a *kylix* (a wine cup) painted by the so-called Brygos Painter in the early fifth century B.C.E., depicts a devotee (a *bacchante* or *maenad*) of the god Dionysus performing a ritualized dance. In her right hand is a *thrysus*, an ivy-covered staff that was an important part of sacred rituals.

the choral performers of dithyrambs were called *tragōidoi*, pointing once again to the later word for tragedy.

The association of theater with the dithyrambs performed in the honor of Dionysus makes sense for many reasons. The first Greek playwright, Thespis (sixth century B.C.E.), whose plays have all been lost, is credited with adding an individual performer to the dithyrambic chorus and chorus leader, and thus enabling dramatic interaction to emerge. Because Thespis himself is said to have performed this newly individual role, he is considered by many to be the world's first actor, and his name has given us the word *thespian*. From this point on the chorus (or chorus leader) was not limited to reciting a hymn but could impersonate an imaginary figure by engaging in a dialogue with the newly introduced actor. The Greek word for actor, *hypokritēs*, by the way, still exists in the English word *hypocrite*, whose now largely negative meaning underscores that acting involves imitation

and pretense. Subsequent playwrights added more actors to increase the possibilities for dialogue between individuals, although the chorus remained an important component of Greek, and subsequently of Roman, theater.

Another reason for associating theater with the Dionysian dithyrambs is that the first known Greek plays were performed at the City Dionysia, one of four Athenian festivals (another was the Rural Dionysia) held during the winter in honor of the god. Over the course of the fifth century B.C.E., when Greek theater was at its height, other festivals incorporated dramatic performances, but the City Dionysia remained the most important event for theater. The City Dionysia, which attracted many visitors from other city-states and from outside Greece, was a multiday affair, whose focus was various competitions. The first was a competition of dithyrambs, first organized around 600 B.C.E., among the four (later ten) "tribes" (*phylai*)—the administrative and military divisions to which all Athenian citizens belonged. Each tribe sponsored two choruses, one consisting of fifty men, the other of fifty boys. Although these dithyrambic performances centered on the worship of Dionysus, they soon included other gods and myths as well. As early as 534 B.C.E., when Thespis became the first recorded winner of the prize for tragedy, plays were added to the program. By the beginning of the fifth century B.C.E, a system was in place: each dramatist had to compose three tragedies, which were followed by the performance of a short satirical work (called a *satyr play*). Somewhat later, around 486 B.C.E., another type of drama was added: comedy. The City Dionysia held a competition among the different playwrights for first prize, an honor that helped spark the explosive growth in the number of plays written for the occasion and raising the status of theater more generally.

GREEK TRAGEDY

One development necessary for drama to emerge from these various rituals and performances was the invention of writing and the spread of literacy. Greek rituals did not include written scripts but were instead based on formulaic and orally transmitted incantations, hymns, and performances. Likewise, dithyrambic and epic poems were originally memorized and improvised by the performers, but not composed as literature. The first epics to be preserved in writing were those attributed to Homer (ca. 750–700 B.C.E.), the *Iliad* and the *Odyssey*; and in the late seventh century B.C.E., Arion (active 628–625 B.C.E.) was apparently the first to write down his own dithyrambs (none of which have survived). Consequently, Homer and Arion are considered by some to be the first tragedians, though they did not actually write plays.

The earliest extant tragedies all date from the fifth century B.C.E. and were written by three playwrights: AESCHYLUS (ca. 525–456 B.C.E.), SOPHOCLES (ca. 496–406 B.C.E.), and EURIPIDES (ca. 480–406 B.C.E.). These plays are set in a mythical past (with one exception—Aeschylus's *Persians*, which takes place during the Persian Wars), using the stories of gods and heroic humans that had been transmitted orally by the early epic poets and subsequently written down. Because Greek audiences already knew the broad outlines of the stories dramatized on the stage, they were able to notice and appreciate subtle differences in the treatments of given myths.

At the center of tragedy is a conflict that eventually results in the downfall of a larger-than-life character. The protagonists of tragedy are socially and morally elevated beings, and the destruction they undergo results, in part, from what Aristotle called *hamartia*; though the term has sometimes been translated as "tragic flaw," it is more accurately understood as referring to a mistaken action or error of judgment. That tragic protagonists bear responsibility for their fate does not mean that they deserve the destruction inflicted on them, however, for their fate is also determined by forces, circumstances, and dilemmas outside their control. For example, while the decision of Antigone (in Sophocles' play of the same name) to bury her brother Polyneices follows the religious imperative, obeying that imperative brings her into conflict with her uncle Creon, the king of Thebes, who has declared him a traitor and therefore has forbidden his burial. Faced with this set of forces not of her making—one, a social and religious mandate; the other, a legal prohibition—Antigone has no alternative but to choose her tragic fate. Similarly, the protagonist of Sophocles' *OEDIPUS THE KING* (ca. 428 B.C.E.), who unknowingly killed his father and married his mother, must accept punishment for deeds performed not with malicious intent but with an overweening pride and belief in his own invulnerability. Ironically, the man of action and the solver of the Sphinx's riddle proves rash in his actions and blind to fate's riddle in his own life. Virtues and flaws, the notion of *hamartia* may also suggest, are intimately tied up in each other: we can trust our talents and strengths too much and learn, in the outcome of our actions, that they are both the reason for our good fortune and the cause of our demise.

As these tragic conflicts unfold, the protagonists find themselves in another contentious relation, namely with the chorus. Not surprisingly, given its origins in choral dithyrambs, tragedy retained the chorus as an important element. Reflecting the perspective of the community, this body observes and comments on the actions and entanglements of the protagonists, trying to rein in their excesses and restore order to the civic realm. The chorus also reminds the audience of the background story of a given myth and often engages the protagonists in a dialogue that draws out the motives of their actions. In keeping with the evolving nature of Greek tragedy during the fifth century B.C.E., the role of the chorus underwent changes. As dramatic characters grew in number, complexity, and importance, the role of the chorus lessened.

The complexity of the relations between individual actors and the chorus shaped the typical structure of Greek tragedy. Greek tragedies begin either with a prologue that sets the scene or with the entrance—*parodos*—of the chorus. The main body of the tragedy is then composed of a sequence of episodes—*epeisodia*, scenes in which the main actors talk to one another or to the chorus—and choral songs without dialogue, *stasima*. At the end of the play, the characters and the chorus leave the stage in what is called the *exodos*. Greek tragedy, in other words, was a highly structured and formalized art form in which dialogue between two individual actors, today the main component of drama, was relatively unimportant. Instead, choral lyrics and the dialogue between chorus and protagonist took up most of the play. Playwrights used different styles of language and meter to distinguish between the different sections of tragedy. Choral lyrics were a form of poetry highly elevated in diction and intricately composed, while the exchanges between the chorus and individual characters, though still quite stylized, were more conversational. The dialogues in iambic meter between the individual characters, though they too were artfully wrought, were closer still to everyday speech. Such differentiation can clearly be seen in the works of Euripides, who, writing slightly later than Aeschylus and Sophocles, attempted to bring the language of tragedy nearer to the language actually spoken by the audience.

As noted above, in its mature form the City Dionysia included a competition in

This detail from the so-called Pronomos Vase, painted in the late fifth century B.C.E., depicts actors preparing for a satyr play.

which each dramatist presented three tragedies followed by a satyr play. Unfortunately, because only one complete satyr play has survived—Euripides' *Cyclops*—it is difficult to generalize about the genre. The plays seem to have dealt with the same mythical and heroic figures and stories as tragedies but irreverently, as burlesque. Accordingly, their language was apparently more colloquial than that of tragedy. The satyr play remained closely connected to Dionysus, for in Greek mythology satyrs were half-human and half-bestial creatures who formed part of his retinue, and the leader of the chorus in satyr plays was Silenus, a satyr who was a constant companion of the god. The satyr play provided the audience with comic relief at the end of a daylong performance of tragedies.

GREEK COMEDY

The satyr play, despite its comic elements, belonged to a genre distinct from comedy. Although comedies had not originally been part of festival competitions, they were incorporated into the City Dionysia festival around 486 B.C.E. The origins of comedy also lie in ritual, most likely in rites that featured groups of men wearing representations of large *phalloi* (male sexual organs) and animal masks. A second source for Greek comedy was a form of mime—short, improvised sketches treating everyday situations humorously. These foundations are visible in what is called Old Comedy, which developed in the fifth century B.C.E.; its only remaining examples are the plays of ARISTOPHANES (ca. 450–ca. 385 B.C.E.), although the names of other comic playwrights are known to us, including Magnes (active 472 B.C.E.) and Aristophanes' main rival, Eupolis (ca. 445–ca. 411 B.C.E.). The choruses of comedy may well represent animals or inanimate objects—Aristophanes' plays have such titles as *The Frogs*, *The Wasps*, and *The Clouds*—and they often treat explicitly sexual themes. In contrast to both tragedy and the satyr play, comedies take as their subject matter not the gods and heroes of Greek mythology but rather the everyday life of contemporary Athenians, and the topics they engage range from the long Peloponnesian War with Sparta (which provides the background to *LYSISTRATA* [411 B.C.E.], Aristophanes' best-known play) to public personalities such as the philosopher Socrates. Like tragedy, Old Comedy begins with a prologue, which is followed by the entry of the chorus; it contains passages of dialogue; and it concludes with the exit of all the characters. It also features an added element: a section called the *parabasis* (literally, "digression") in which the chorus addresses the audience directly, discussing political and social problems and sometimes praising the playwright. In the *parabasis* and throughout each play, classical comedy engages with political and social issues much more directly than tragedy, although it does so comically, drawing on fantasy, humor that frequently is ribald, and farce.

THE GREEK STAGE

The main performance venue for Athenian theater was the Dionysus theater, located in the hill just below the Acropolis, an elevated area on which stood the Parthenon and which served as the city's religious and political center. Given the elaborate nature of later Greek and Roman theaters, the Dionysus theater in the fifth century B.C.E. was surprisingly simple. A large *amphitheatron*, holding between 14,000 to 17,000 audience members, was built into the hillside, with seating provided by temporary wooden benches. At the center of the amphitheater was the *orchēstra* (or "dancing place"), a semicircle in whose middle stood the *thymelē*, a raised stone used as an altar or a table. Behind the *orchēstra* stood a wooden structure, the *skēnē*, which served as a place where actors could change masks and costumes and, through one or more doors, appear and disappear from the stage. The area in front of the *skēnē* would later be known as the *paraskēnion*, a term from which the modern word *proscenium* derives. On either side of the *skēnē* were passageways.

This physical arrangement was used by the Greek dramatists in increasingly complex ways. The passageways aided the elaborate entrances and exits of the chorus, while the *orchēstra* was the place where the dances performed by the chorus and the interaction between chorus and individual actors took place. The altar or table could be used by individual actors to hide and suddenly appear. The *skēnē* at the back of the performance area provided even more theatrical possibilities. For example, playwrights placed messengers and other figures on its roof, where they could be on the lookout and describe battles and other scenes they pretended to see on its other side (a stage device called *teichoskopeia*, or "watching from a wall"). The doors in the *skēnē* were used not only to aid entrances and exits but also to suddenly reveal characters. To heighten the effect of the doors, a rolling platform, or *ekkyklēma*, was employed to roll the body of a killed character in front of the audience or to make other dramatic disclosures. Such a device was especially important since almost all physical violence—the blinding of Oedipus, for example, or Medea's murder of her children—occurred offstage, often (the audience was led to believe) within the scene building. A second mechanism became increasingly popular: a crane called a *mēchanē*, which could move characters through the air into the space in front of the scene building. Euripides, in particular, used such cranes to introduce gods, who would resolve the plot and mete out punishment at the end of his tragedies; this device became well-known by its Latin name, *deus ex machina* (god from a machine). Various forms of painted panels were probably employed on the stage as well, though little is known about their appearance and function.

Because theater was an integral part of civic and religious festivals, an elaborate system of rules and practices governed the production of plays. A leading figure of the Athenian government, an *archōn eponymos*, selected from among the wealthy citizens a *chorēgos*, or producer, who would provide the funds for the chorus, while the city government provided the funds for the playwright and the leading actors.

The playwrights were responsible for rehearsals and sometimes even performed in their own plays. The number of performers was strictly limited. The chorus probably contained twelve to fifteen members, although as many as fifty may have appeared in some early plays of Aeschylus. The number of individual actors was even more crucial, because it directly affected how many characters were available to the playwright. Aeschylus's early plays used two actors, who could take on different roles over the course of a play—but obviously, no more than two speaking parts could be present simultaneously. Either Aeschylus or, more likely, his younger rival Sophocles took the decisive step of introducing a third actor, thereby expanding the playwright's options considerably.

One reason why actors could change so easily from one role to the next was the relative simplicity of their costumes. A thick, richly colored garment covered their bodies; large, high boots made them appear larger than life; and a mask made from either fabric or wood covered their entire face. Given the size of the theater and the bulkiness of their costumes, the actors had

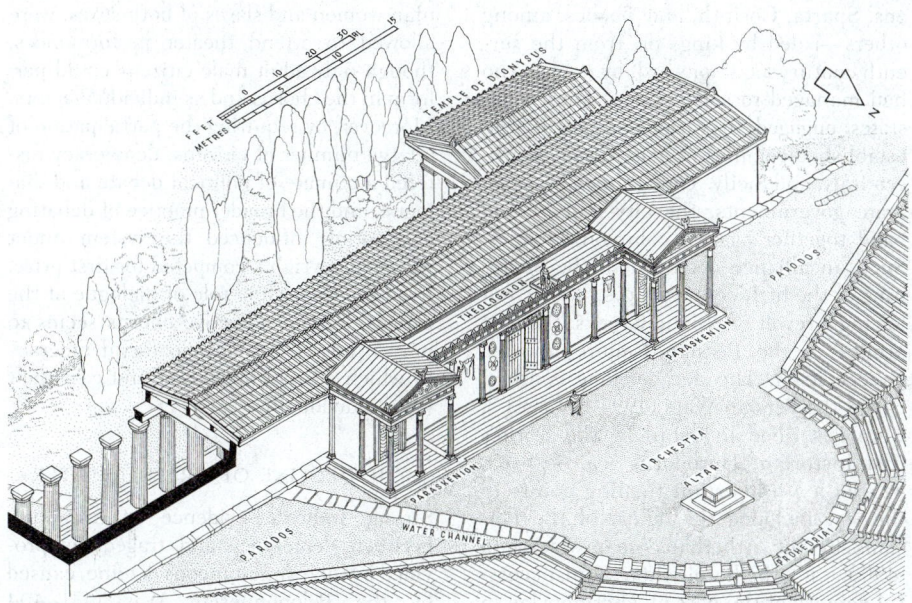

A reconstruction of the Dionysus theater by the theater and architectural scholar Richard Leacroft. An actor stands in the *orchēstra*, while another stands on the roof of the *skēnē*.

to rely on large gestures rather than on small, intimate reactions, and in masks they lacked any recourse to facial expressions. Scenes of dialogue alternated with the elaborate dances of the chorus. The performance of Greek plays was accompanied by music, provided mainly by the flute—it was a flute player who led the entrance of the chorus at the beginning of the play—but various other wind and percussion instruments were employed as well. Today's audiences and readers can easily overlook the significance of music, which is generally little used in contemporary revivals of Greek plays, but the scholars and artists who attempted to revive Greek tragedy during the European Renaissance were very conscious of its importance. Indeed, this awareness led to the creation of opera, a form of theater that relies primarily on music and song and only secondarily on spoken dialogue.

THEATER AND ATHENIAN DEMOCRACY

The emergence and rise of Greek theater is intimately tied to the political history of Greece. Greece was not a unified nation but rather a network of city-states—Athens, Sparta, Corinth, and Thebes, among others—ruled by kings or, from the seventh century B.C.E. onward, by nobles who had managed to seize power. These city-states engaged in various alliances and established colonies in Asia Minor, southern Italy, and Sicily. Though they had separate governments, the city-states could band together against common enemies. Such an alliance occurred in the beginning of the fifth century B.C.E., when, following a revolt of Asiatic Greeks, the vast armies of the Persian Empire invaded Greece itself. The decades-long conflict, called the Persian Wars (499–449 B.C.E.), were described in detail by the world's first historian, Herodotus (ca. 484–ca. 425 B.C.E.). Important turning points in the war included the defeat of the Persians by the Athenians near Marathon (490 B.C.E.), the heroic though unsuccessful defense of the pass of Thermopylae in central Greece by a small Spartan force (480 B.C.E.), and the destruction of the Persian fleet by Athens at Salamis (480 B.C.E.), a battle that was critical to Persia's subsequent defeat.

The crucial role of Athens in winning this victory led to its increasing dominance over the rest of Greece, and it built a largely seaborne empire consisting of allies, dependent states, and colonies. It was during this time of military dominance that Athens became a cosmopolitan center for the arts—the birthplace of Greek theater and the center of many other intellectual and cultural pursuits, such as philosophy (although many philosophers living in Athens were foreign-born). Equally important was the development in Athens of an early form of democracy that involved all adult male citizens in the governance of the Athenian empire, serving in the courts, military offices, and other administrative posts. Women, slaves, and foreigners, it is important to note, were not considered citizens. Moreover, though it was a predecessor of modern democracies, Athenian democracy included many features that might strike today's citizens as odd, such as the choosing of important positions by lot (to avoid favoritism). Many scholars consider the rise of Athenian theater and of democracy to be related developments. It is likely that most of the city's inhabitants, including Athenian women and slaves of both sexes, were allowed to attend theater performances, though only adult male citizens could perform in the chorus and as individual actors. Moreover, by requiring the participation of a large number of citizens, democracy fostered a climate of political debate and dialogue, and the broader practice of debating and voting influenced the system under which playwrights competed for first prize. Even the increasing role of dialogue at the expense of the collective chorus seems to mirror the rise of a participatory democracy in which citizens speak out and cast their votes individually.

THE DECLINE OF GREEK THEATER

Strong indirect evidence of the link between democracy and tragedy is provided by their simultaneous decline, caused by the Peloponnesian War (431–404 B.C.E.)—the long conflict between Athens and Sparta described by the Athenian historian Thucydides (ca. 455–ca. 400 B.C.E.).

The ruins of the theater at Epidaurus, Greece. The theater was built in the middle of the fourth century B.C.E.

By the war's end, Athens had lost its empire and, at least temporarily, its democracy. Though Greek theater continued to develop—chiefly through the emergence, in the following century, of New Comedy, whose main practitioner was the playwright Menander (ca. 342–ca. 292 B.C.E.) and whose plays depended much less on fantastic plots and conceits than had their Old Comedy predecessors—by the end of the fifth century B.C.E. the most important era of Greek theater had come to an end.

GREEK THEORIES OF DRAMA

The fourth century B.C.E.'s contribution to theater history was the work of two authors who together provided the first written theories of drama: Plato and Aristotle. Though Plato did not take up the subject separately, his philosophy as a whole is deeply engaged with the theater as medium and institution. All of his works were written as dialogues, and although there is no evidence of their performance before large audiences, they may have been recited by students in his Academy, the school that he founded (which took its name from its site, a park sacred to the legendary hero Academus). In these dialogues, Plato—or, more precisely, his main character, Socrates—is often critical of tragedy and comedy as well as of actors, arguing that drama and other works of art offer mere representations of the world and therefore stand in the way of the pursuit of truth, which consists of knowledge of the things themselves. Drawn to the exchange of ideas but suspicious of the seductions of theatrical performance, Plato offered his own philosophical dialogues as an alternative form of drama.

Plato's student Aristotle, by contrast, devoted an entire treatise to the subject of tragedy, describing its classifications, elements, and structure and examining its effect on spectators. In his widely influential *Poetics*, probably composed around 330 B.C.E., Aristotle discusses the origin of tragedy in dithyrambic hymns, the nature of the heroic protagonist, the function of the chorus, and what he considers to be the six crucial elements of theater: plot, character, thought, diction, music, and spectacle (the last is accorded a marginal position in his descriptive hierarchy). He also emphasizes certain plot elements, such as sudden reversals (*peripeteiai*) and the moment of recognition (*anagnōrisis*), and insists that unlike epic poetry, with its meandering plots, tragedy should present a single, unified action. This focus mandates that the action of tragedy be confined to short periods of time, typically one day, and to a single place. Renaissance commentators on the *Poetics* turned these recommendations into the three unities—of time, place, and action—that, according to the strictures of what became known as neoclassical theory, must be maintained by playwrights.

In response to Plato's attack on theatrical representation, Aristotle defended actors by arguing that the drive to imitate, *mimēsis*, was a common human trait and served as a source of pleasure. Perhaps the most influential term introduced in this treatise was *katharsis*, the purging or cleansing of emotions that was the desired effect of tragedy on the audience. Whereas Plato had argued that the extreme emotions depicted in tragedy could have adverse effects on the audience and therefore recommended that playwrights, like other artists, be banished from his ideal republic, Aristotle held that tragedy provided a release, a *katharsis*, of those stirred-up emotions—particularly fear and pity—and that dramatic art thus served a socially therapeutic function. The disagreement between Plato and Aristotle about the value of theater, the reaction of the audience, and the status of actors has persisted to the present—in our debates, for instance, about depictions of violence onstage and on the screen. Much as the playwrights of the fifth century B.C.E. have continued to influence theater history, so the philosophers of the fourth century still shape our thinking about theater.

Roman Theater

The decline of Athens, which at its height had dependent colonies in Italy (where Greeks from several city-states had settled as early as the eighth century B.C.E.), coincided with the rise and expanding influence of Rome. By the middle of the third century B.C.E., the city-state of Rome had managed to unify most of Italy under its leadership, and its victory over its North African rival, Carthage, in the First Punic War (264–241 B.C.E.) enabled Rome to extend its hegemony over Sicily as well as parts of Greece itself. One hundred years later, Rome had absorbed the entire Greek world on its way to becoming one of the largest empires ever created.

Even though Rome was a rising military power, its art, literature, philosophy, and theater remained heavily influenced by those of Greece. Like Greek theater, Roman theater was performed in the context of civic festivals, here called *ludi*, which by 240 B.C.E. included both tragedies and comedies. The most important of these festivals were the *Ludi Romani*, which honored not Dionysus (or his Roman counterpart, Bacchus) but Jupiter, chief of the gods. This and other festivities differed from their Greek counterparts in significant ways. Influenced by the earlier performance practices of the Etruscans, who belonged to an earlier civilization (centered in present-day Tuscany and part of Umbria) that reached its height in the sixth century B.C.E., the festivities of early Rome included

Roman masks—one tragic, one comic—as depicted in a wall mosaic from the first century B.C.E.

a variety of nondramatic entertainments—chariot races, prizefighting, dance, farce—that vied with dramatic performance for the spectators' attention. Relatively few early Roman tragedies and comedies survive, although it is clear that most were adaptations of existing Greek plays, which were introduced to Rome in 240 B.C.E. The first known dramatists in Rome, Livius Andronicus (ca. 284–ca. 204 B.C.E.) and Gnaeus Naevius (ca. 270–201 B.C.E.), adapted both Greek tragedies and comedies into Latin, while later playwrights, including the tragedians Quintus Ennius (239–169 B.C.E.) and Lucius Accius (170–ca. 86 B.C.E.), specialized in one or the other genre. Even though Roman tragedies were mostly versions of Greek ones, Roman playwrights introduced considerable alterations, changes, and innovations; far from being a sign of unoriginality, adaptation thus became a special art form. Whereas the Greek playwrights had used known stories and characters in composing their plays, Roman playwrights perfected a more elaborate technique of imitation by working from established dramatic models.

ROMAN COMEDY

Though both tragedies and comedies were performed in Roman theaters, comedy was the genre in which Roman playwrights excelled. Roman comedians could look back at a long tradition of farce, and they drew especially on Atellan farce, a burlesque form based on improvisation and a small set of stock characters that took its name from Atella, a town near Naples in southern Italy. These improvised sketches and stock characters remained popular throughout the history of Rome and beyond, influencing such later theater traditions as Italy's commedia dell'arte. At the same time, a more literary form of comedy, based on Greek Old and New Comedy, was developing. The two most famous Roman playwrights—TITUS MACCIUS PLAUTUS (ca. 254–ca. 184 B.C.E.) and Terence (Publius Terentius Afer, ca. 190–159 B.C.E.)—were authors of such comedies. The most important changes Plautus and Terence made to their Greek models were eliminating the chorus and significantly expanding the use of music, thereby turning their comedies into a kind of musical theater.

EMPIRE AND SPECTACLE

The height of Roman drama, as represented by Plautus and Terence, occurred under the Roman Republic, a political system that allowed a limited number of citizens to participate in government and prevented any single individual from gaining supreme power. It was under the Republic that Rome established its dominance through the Second Punic War with Carthage (218–201

This detail from a Roman mosaic depicts a *venation*—a battle between a leopard and a gladiator.

B.C.E.) and finally defeated and destroyed Carthage in 146 B.C.E. at the end of the Third Punic War (149–146 B.C.E.). Rome now dominated not only Italy and Greece but also large parts of northern Africa. The resulting flow of wealth and power to Rome increasingly undermined republican institutions, and the Republic gave way to an empire with an absolute ruler. Under the emperors—beginning with Augustus (63 B.C.E.–14 C.E.)—Rome expanded its empire as far as England, Germany, France, Spain, and the Balkans and controlled the entire Mediterranean basin.

The increasing scale of the Roman Empire, and the unheard-of concentration of wealth and power in Rome itself, fueled a tendency toward expensive and lavish spectacles, comparable perhaps to blockbuster Hollywood action films today. These nondramatic varieties of performance, most of them significantly more spectacular than anything seen on the dramatic stage, came to overshadow tragedy and comedy. Among these new public entertainments were chariot races held in sizable arenas, the largest of which, the Circus Maximus in Rome, accommodated more than 60,000 spectators. Other spectacles included elaborately orchestrated, and often lethal, sea battles, which sometimes involved thousands of participants; contests called *venationes*, in which wild animals fought against one another or against humans; and of course the most emblematic and notorious of Roman spectacles—gladiatorial contests, which featured hand-to-hand combat to the death. Although their appetite for staged (but real) violence was voracious, Romans weren't entirely bloodthirsty in their entertainment preferences; pantomime and short comic sketches of mime performances were also very popular.

CLOSET TRAGEDY

The overwhelming popularity of nondramatic entertainments led to a decline of traditional dramatic forms, especially tragedy and comedy. Writers with literary ambitions therefore began to create "closet dramas," plays designed to be recited at small, private gatherings or to be read in private. In fact, the most famous Roman tragic dramatist, Lucius Annaeus Seneca (4 B.C.E.–65 C.E.), wrote only closet dramas, and his plays were never performed on the great Roman stages of the time. Modeled on Greek tragedy, Seneca's tragedies are composed in an intricate, literary Latin that became a model for many subsequent writers. That these dramas were not written to be performed did not make them less violent. Indeed, unlike Greek tragedy, which had hidden most of its violence offstage, Seneca required that the audience or readers envision it as happening in their "sight." Though few in his own time would have known of his plays, they proved enormously influential on later playwrights, including the Elizabethan playwrights THOMAS KYD and William Shakespeare.

THE ROMAN STAGE

Although plays had been written in Latin since the third century B.C.E., the first permanent theater—erected at Pompeii—was not built until 55 B.C.E. Before that time, temporary stages (often quite stable and elaborate) were used for dramatic and other performances. Modeled on their Greek predecessors, Roman theaters included large amphitheaters for the audience; these could be built into hills, like Greek theaters, or erected on level ground. The amphitheater formed a semicircle similar to the Greek *orchēstra*, which was closed on one side by a building, the *scaena*, which was the counterpart of the Greek *skēnē*. In their adaptation from one society to another, however, the function and proportions of these elements changed significantly. For example, the *orchēstra* was used by the chorus, but its Roman equivalent was occupied—as it is in today's theaters—by the most privileged of the audience members. The action of the play took place on a raised stage, or *pulpitum*, located in front of the scene building, which was significantly larger and more elaborate than its Greek predecessor. Supported by several sets of columns and often ornately decorated, the scene building could be many stories high—a change that had profound implications. Unlike the audience of Greek theater, whose view of the stage was framed by landscape and sky, the Roman audience looked entirely at the artificial world created on a stage.

A digital reconstruction of the interior of the theater of Pompey in Rome. This image—based on a collaborative research project by Richard Beacham, James E. Packer, and John Burge—was generated by the King's Visualization Lab and is copyright © King's College London.

Even as playwrights such as Seneca withdrew from the stage, the Roman taste for spectacle—races, parades, festivals, and staged battles—led to the development of elaborate stage machinery. Roman theater producers not only instituted the stage curtain but also invented sliding panels, cranes, and a type of elevator with which actors or animals could be lifted onto the stage from below. They also introduced more complex, three-dimensional stage decorations, extensive stage props, and even live animals. The actors, called *histriones* in Latin, were not, as had originally been the case in Greece, talented citizen amateurs; instead, they were theater professionals, some of whom were slaves. Their acting style ranged from burlesque and conversational for comedy to more formal and declamatory for tragedy. Costumes and masks were mostly fashioned on Greek models.

THE DECLINE AND INFLUENCE OF ROMAN THEATER

Roman theater declined significantly with the rise of Christianity, which won official toleration in 313 C.E. when the emperor Constantine I issued the Edict of Milan; it soon became the dominant religion in the Roman Empire. Christian clergy were highly critical of theater and in particular its actors, declaring the attendance of theater cause for excommunication and denying actors the holy sacraments (a practice that remained in place in some parts of Europe well into the modern era). Yet despite the theater's waning under Christianity, the influence of classical theater would reverberate through the centuries. The architecture of Roman theater buildings helped shape Renaissance stage design, for example, and Roman comedy and tragedy were important models for English Renaissance playwrights, who often knew of Greek works only through their Roman adaptations and translations. Equally vital for Renaissance theater was Rome's most significant critic, the poet Quintus Horatius Flaccus, known as Horace (65–8 B.C.E.), whose *Ars Poetica* (*The Art of Poetry* [ca. 10 B.C.E.]) discusses the origins, forms, and ends of drama. Recommending such formal practices as the division of plays into five acts, Horace also offered a powerfully moral conception of drama's function. Not only should playwrights cater to their audiences, he asserted, they should also serve as moral instructors: their works, in other words, should prove useful (*utile*) as well as pleasing (*dulce*). In keeping with this conception of theater's social role, he argued against the more fantastic, spectacular, and violent aspects of Roman theater. Like those of Aristotle, his views on drama were taken up by later theorists of drama and theater.

Although Roman theater was in many ways derivative, the influence of its drama, architecture, and practice on subsequent theater history was even greater than that of its Greek predecessor and model. The plays of Plautus, Terence, and Seneca inspired the work of later playwrights, and Roman theater technology—much of it described in *De Architectura* (*On Architecture*), written in the first century B.C.E. by the architect and engineer Vitruvius—made important contributions to theater design during the European Renaissance. One of the most lasting legacies of Roman theater may be the division it opened up between drama as a literary genre and stage as a site of spectacle. In later centuries, in the great ages of world theater, drama and theater have often worked hand in hand; but at times they have become estranged, leading to forms of literary drama disconnected from a theater system mainly interested in extravagant spectacle. To the extent that this division still informs our theater today—when, for example, lavish Broadway spectacles divert attention from serious plays—we are still in the process of working through the inheritance of Roman theater.

Classical Indian Theater

During the millennium after Greece and Rome established the outlines of European theatrical culture, the foundations were being laid for separate traditions in Asia. The earliest, and arguably the most influential, form of Asian theater emerged in India, home to one of the world's oldest civilizations. By 2500 B.C.E. the Indus Valley civilization had introduced city-states and a technologically advanced agricultural society in northwestern and western India. Its decline was caused in part by internal weakness and in part by the incursions of the Aryans, a nomadic people from northern Iran or central Asia. By 1500 B.C.E., the Indian subcontinent had been settled by

the Aryans, who developed the Vedic civilization that would subsequently shape Indian history and culture. Central to this culture were the Vedas, or scriptures, that constituted the founding texts of Hinduism (the earliest of these, the *Rig-Veda*, was composed between 1500 and 1000 B.C.E.). Written in Sanskrit, these texts inspired a number of further writings; among them were two epic poems, the *Mahabharata* and the *Ramayana* (both written between 500 and 200 B.C.E.), which exerted a vast influence on later literature and theater in India and Southeast Asia. The Aryans also introduced the system of caste, or social stratification, that divided Indian society into four groups: priests, warriors and rulers, traders and merchants, and workers and peasants. The caste system, which provided the social framework of classical Indian drama and the audience that attended it, remains influential in today's India despite laws mandating equality of treatment for all members of society.

ORIGINS OF INDIAN THEATER

The scarcity of available historical evidence prevents us from knowing much about the origins of Indian, or Sanskrit, theater. In some Vedic rituals priests performed symbolic gestures, and these actions occasionally involved impersonating a represented figure, but it is impossible to tell whether these rites were the seeds of a more purely theatrical tradition. The *Mahabharata* makes references to performers (*nata*), though it is not known if actors were among them. Unlike Greece, India has no surviving theater structures from this period. The earliest plays extant, which date from the first century C.E., display a sophistication that suggests a long period of prior development, but there is no way of determining when a literary theater was first established. What evidence we do have concerning the Sanskrit theater comes from the plays that have survived from later centuries and from the *Natyasastra* (*The Art of Theater*), a compendious treatise on the nature and purpose of dramatic performance ascribed to Bharata Muni and written sometime between 300 B.C.E. and 200 C.E. Longer and more detailed than Aristotle's *Poetics*, the *Natyasastra* includes information concerning acting, theater and stage structures, theater organization, music, dance, playwriting, and aesthetics.

AUDIENCE, PLAYHOUSE, AND ACTORS

Theatrical performances during the classical age of Sanskrit theater (100–900 C.E.) apparently were offered on occasions ranging from sacred festivals to the coronation of kings, marriages, births, or the return of travelers. Although Bharata writes that the ideal spectator for such performances was learned and of high birth, members of all four castes (seated separately) seem to have attended. The *Natyasastra* describes three types of playhouses (square, triangular, and rectangular) and three sizes that these buildings could assume (small, medium-sized, and large), but focuses mainly on a rectangular building measuring 96 by 48 feet. Such a playhouse should resemble a cave, so that the actors' voices would resonate. Its interior was divided into two equal areas, with one half (called the *prekshagriha*) devoted to seating an audience that would have probably included no more than 500 spectators. The other half was itself divided in two: its back half (the *nepathya*) served as a backstage and dressing room,

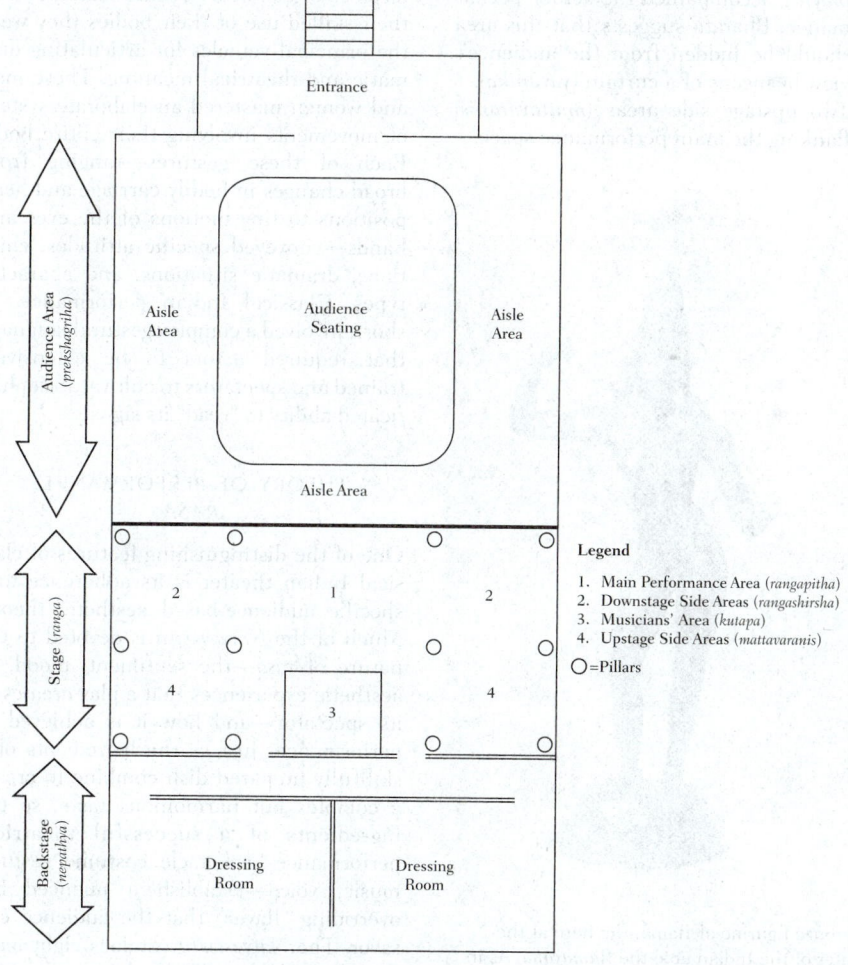

The Classical Indian Stage

A diagram of the Sanskrit stage, based on descriptions in the *Natyasastra* by Bharata.

and its front half (the *ranga*) represented the performance area. The performance area, in turn, contained a number of distinct zones:

1. The main performance space (*rangapitha*) at the center of the stage.
2. The upstage area (*rangashirsha*), which stretched across the width of the performance space, between the back wall and the front performance area. Demarcating the back of this area was an ornamented curtain, possibly held by two attendants, with two openings, one for entrances and the other for exits.
3. The space between these openings (the *kutapa*), an area for musicians, whose playing accompanied the actors' performance. Bharata suggests that this area should be hidden from the audience's view by means of a curtain (*yavanika*).
4. Two upstage side areas (*mattavaranis*) flanking the main performance space.

A bronze figurine of Rama, the hero at the center of the Indian epic the *Ramayana*. As in performance, the gestures and attitudes portrayed in Indian sculpture are highly stylized.

These separate but contiguous acting areas made possible the fluid narrative structure of Sanskrit drama, in which dramatic action shifts between different locations and events and encounters can be staged simultaneously.

Apart from general decorations, which could serve a symbolic function, there were few props and no scenery on the classical Indian stage. Location and specific actions were indicated through a fixed repertoire of highly stylized movements. Actors walked around the stage in a circle to indicate a journey, for example, and mimed actions such as stepping into and out of a carriage. To an even greater degree than most other theatrical traditions, actors were the centerpiece of classical Indian theater, and in their skilled use of their bodies they were the principal vehicles for articulating dramatic and theatrical meaning. These men and women mastered an elaborate system of movements involving their entire body. Each of these gestures—ranging from broad changes in bodily carriage and head positions to tiny motions of the eyes and hands—conveyed specific attitudes, emotions, dramatic situations, and character types. Classical Indian performance, in short, involved a complex gestural language that required actors to be extensively trained and spectators to cultivate a sophisticated ability to "read" its signs.

THEORY OF PERFORMANCE: *RASA*

One of the distinguishing features of classical Indian theater is its adherence to a specific audience-based aesthetic theory. Much of the *Natyasastra* is devoted to the nature of *rasa*—the sentiment, mood, or aesthetic experiences that a play creates in its spectator—and how it is achieved in performance. Just as the ingredients of a skillfully prepared dish combine to create a complex but harmonious taste, so the ingredients of a successful theatrical performance—spectacle, costume, gesture, music, voice—establish a nuanced but overriding "flavor" that the audience can savor. The *Natyasastra* catalogs eight basic *rasas* (a ninth was added by later commentators) and associates these with eight permanent (and thirty-three transitory) human emotions, or *bhavas*. As actors portray these emotions, the spectator experiences the corresponding *rasa*. The effect, akin to that of any good meal, is a sense of aesthetic fullness and satisfaction.

CLASSICAL INDIAN DRAMA

About two dozen Sanskrit plays have survived to the present day, and they demonstrate the formal richness of classical Indian drama. Though Bharata describes ten major categories of play, two types were dominant on the classical Indian stage: *nataka* plays, whose stories are drawn from mythology or history, deal with exploits of kings and heroes; and *prakarana* plays are characterized by invented stories and less exalted characters. All plays combine a central story with numerous subsidiary plots, interweaving the serious and the comic. Indian dramatists employed both verse and prose in their plays and a mixture of Sanskrit and the popular dialects collectively known as Prakrit. The former is reserved for characters of high social standing, whereas the latter is spoken by characters of lesser station.

Most of the finest Sanskrit plays were written during the Gupta dynasty (ca. 320–ca. 550 C.E.), a period that witnessed a golden age of science, mathematics, literature, and philosophy in India. Major playwrights during this period include Bhasa, the author of thirteen surviving plays; Kalidasa, whose epic romance *Shakuntala* is considered by many to be the finest Sanskrit play; and SHUDRAKA, whose lengthy masterpiece THE LITTLE CLAY CART (ca. 100–300 C.E.) is excerpted in this anthology. Important Sanskrit drama continued to be written through the seventh century. Subsequent Indian history was marked by political instability as the court culture that helped sustain Sanskrit drama was threatened by a series of invasions by Muslim armies from the north from the tenth century onward. Sanskrit theater had largely disappeared as a cultural form by 1000 C.E.

Classical Chinese Theater

ORIGINS OF CHINESE THEATER

China, another of the world's oldest civilizations, has one of its richest performance and theater histories. Ancient Chinese scholars described performances synthesizing dance, music, and poetry as early as the reign of the legendary sage-ruler Yu Shun (2300–2205 B.C.E.), and shamanistic and court rituals involving dance and music were attributed to the Shang dynasty (1600–1045 B.C.E.). There are records dating to the first millennium B.C.E. of court entertainments—performed by jesters and others—that included music, dance, and mime. The integration of various activities in these earliest Chinese performances anticipates the capacious scope of later Chinese theater. The Chinese word that would later be used for "play" (*xi*) also meant "game," and it could be used to describe acrobatics, sports, and other kinds of entertainment. This highly theatrical synthesis of performance forms has flourished in Chinese theater to the present day, as the popularity of Beijing opera—a style of theater combining dance, music, storytelling, acrobatics, and martial arts—demonstrates.

THEATER DURING THE TANG AND SONG DYNASTIES

Theater and other forms of entertainment thrived during the Tang and Song dynasties, whose rulers held power in China between the seventh and thirteenth centuries C.E. During the Tang dynasty (618–907 C.E.), dance stories, skits, shadow and puppet plays, and a popular genre of play satirizing corrupt officials thrived at court and in the marketplace, as did circuslike performances and other forms of staged spectacle. Storytelling flourished as well, in forms that included the oral presentation of religious and secular stories by preachers attempting to disseminate Buddhism to nonliterate audiences. It was during the Tang period that Emperor Minghuang—considered the patron of Chinese theater—established the Pear Orchard Conservatory, the first academy in China devoted to the training of actors and other performers.

During the Song dynasty (960–1279), a period that saw a rise in commerce and the growth and social diversification of Chinese urban centers, amusement centers called "tile districts" (*wazi*) were organized in major cities. These centers, which provided a wide variety of entertainment, included theaters—as many as fifty in the tile districts of the northern capital Bianliang (modern-day Kaifeng)—that could seat up to several thousand spectators. The most accomplished players also performed at the emperor's palace, while itinerant players performed in villages and elsewhere on temporary stages. In addition to viewing such activities as tightrope walking, storytelling, and puppetry, audiences in the tile districts of northern China (a region that was taken over from the Song emperor by invaders from Manchuria in 1127 and ruled thereafter by the Jin dynasty) were entertained by the performance of *zaju*: variety shows that featured dramatic sketches accompanied by musical performance, comic routines, dancing, and acrobatics. In the southern provinces (which remained under Song rule), a separate form of theater known as *nanxi* developed during this period. Longer than their counterparts presented in the north and more intricate in story lines, *nanxi* made use of folk music and an array of familiar character types that influenced subsequent Chinese drama.

YUAN DRAMA: *ZAJU*

Though *nanxi* and the *zaju* have clear dramatic elements, it was not until the Yuan dynasty (1234–1368), when first part and later all of China was under Mongol occupation, that drama flourished as a literary genre. As the Venetian explorer Marco Polo (1254–1324) reported during his travels to the court of Kublai Khan (1215–1294), greatest of the Mongol emperors, China during the Yuan dynasty was a land of prosperity and cultural achievement, enjoying the fruits of increased trade and cultural exchange with western Asia and Europe. Contemporary records mention the titles of some 700 plays written during this period—of which 163 have been preserved, many of them in collections compiled during the late Ming dynasty (1368–1644)—and the names of roughly 550 dramatists, including GUAN HANQING (ca. 1245–ca. 1322), the most prolific and best known of the Yuan playwrights. In its quantity and sophistication, Yuan drama has often been compared to

that of Elizabethan and Jacobean England. One of the reasons for its flourishing is that Chinese scholars, who had traditionally served in government posts, found themselves excluded from civil service under Mongol rule; they therefore turned their attention to other careers, such as writing. To appeal to a popular audience, these scholars abandoned the classical Chinese of Confucius (Kong Fuzi, ca. 551–479 B.C.E.)—whose ethical teachings constituted a pillar of traditional Chinese society—and helped develop the vernacular as a dramatic language. The result was a richly poetic drama, literary in conception yet deeply grounded in the performance traditions of Chinese theater.

Most of this drama is referred to as "Yuan *zaju*," to distinguish it from the earlier form of northern theater. These plays treated subjects ranging from the historical, legendary, and supernatural to the contemporary. They told stories of love, war, political intrigue, adventure, religious conversion, domestic drama, crime, and judicial punishment. Their characters—covering a broad spectrum, from gods, emperors, and generals to hermits, outlaws, concubines, and ordinary people—derive from an array of popular types. Yuan *zaju* plays are typically four acts long, though shorter wedge acts (*xiezi*) may be added when additional plot material is required, and they include from ten to twenty songs, all performed by the main character. These songs, often of great poetic beauty, are the lyrical center of *zaju* plays. The remainder of the dramatic action is conveyed through speech and dialogue. In keeping with the Confucian emphasis on right and wrong and on the importance of correct conduct, *zaju* plays end with justice served, even when (as in Guan Hanqing's SNOW IN MIDSUMMER) a play's hero or heroine dies.

ACTORS AND STAGE

Yuan acting troupes included men and women performers, and both men and women played male and female roles. From the scattered evidence we possess—including a fourteenth-century colored mural from a temple in the northern province of Shanxi that depicts a Yuan acting

Yuan troupe onstage, from a 1324 temple wall painting in the northern Chinese province of Shanxi.

troupe onstage—we know that actors wore ornate, colorful costumes and highly stylized makeup. Though the physical structure of the stage most likely varied with the venue and performance occasion, the stage depicted in the Shanxi mural—consisting of a bare tile floor with entrances on either side of a decorative wall painting in the rear—was probably typical. There was no formal scenery on the Yuan stage and props were minimal. Musicians performed onstage, and their instruments included the flute, gong, clapper, drum, and a lute-like instrument known as a *pipa*. The audience of these Yuan performers seems to have represented a wide range of Chinese society, from the Mongol emperors and their courts down to merchants, peasants, and poor laborers. Yuan *zaju* was a drama that appealed to educated and uneducated spectators alike.

THE RISE OF *NANXI*

Zaju continued to be popular into the Ming dynasty, which assumed power in 1368 after a rebellion drove the Yuan from power, but in the fourteenth century it was rivaled and eventually eclipsed by the reemergence of *nanxi* drama in the southern provinces and its development into a form markedly different from the theater found in the north. *Nanxi* plays are longer than *zaju* plays, and they contain a variable number of acts (as many as fifty or more, each with its own title). Singing is not restricted to a single character; instead, songs are performed by two or more singers, and sometimes by choruses. Acted to the accompaniment of a bamboo flute, *nanxi* plays drew on folk music, and their overall atmosphere in performance was elegiac. Although *zaju* is considered China's premier classical drama, the development of a "southern style" of drama proved to be more influential. A number of the distinctive character types of *nanxi* drama, in fact, remain popular on today's Chinese stage.

Classical Japanese Theater

When Westerners think of Asian theater, it is the theater of Japan that most often comes to mind. In part, this can be explained by the cultural distinctiveness of Japan's theatrical and dramatic traditions: the meditative dance theater of noh, the stylized acrobatics of kabuki, the sophisticated gestures of bunraku puppet theater. But it also has to do with the preservation of such theatrical traditions through centuries of political and social change. In a country devoted to ritual, ceremony, and other forms of tradition, theatrical practices have been handed down with the formal exactitude of the tea ceremony. As a result, we can come to understand the development of Japanese theater not only by reading histories of theater but also by attending live performances.

ORIGINS OF JAPANESE THEATER

Although archaeologists have uncovered clay representations of singers, dancers, and musical instruments from as early as the third century B.C.E., the earliest manifestations of what we would consider theater in Japan were dance-based ritual celebrations collectively known as *kagura*. These performances were connected with Shintoism, a prehistoric religion devoted to the worship of gods and spirits who represented aspects of the natural world. Versions of *kagura* were performed at Shinto shrines by shamanistic priestesses, at the imperial court, and in villages during harvest and other annual festivals. Other theatrical forms emerged in the centuries after Buddhism was introduced to Japan between 538 and 552 C.E., a period during which continental Asian culture was embraced by the imperial court. In the seventh and eighth centuries, two forms of dance theater came from China via Korea: *gigaku*, a Buddhist dance play in which masked figures moved in procession, and *bugaku*, a stately court entertainment that eventually included dances from India, Tibet, and Vietnam in addition to those from China and Korea.

Other popular forms of entertainment also flourished during this time, involving music, dance, masked pantomime, and in some instances acrobatics, juggling, and tightrope walking. Several of these traditions had dramatic components, including *sarugaku* (monkey entertainment), a form of variety theater containing comic dialogues and short skits that came to be performed at Buddhist temples. By the thirteenth century, the dramatic and performance elements of these entertainments had become increasingly sophisticated, and the form was given the name *sarugaku noh*. The term *noh*, which means "skill" or "craft," eventually stood alone as a theatrical category.

THE EMERGENCE OF NOH THEATER: KANAMI AND ZEAMI

The emergence of noh theater reflected the political and social changes that Japan had undergone during the previous two centuries. In 1192 the Japanese emperor relinquished rule of the country to samurai generals, whose rising military and economic power had made them the country's dominant social class. These generals, who gave themselves the title *shogun*, presided over wealthy courts in Kamakura and later Kyoto and established a feudal society with rigidly demarcated social strata. Although many cultural forms that had found favor in the imperial court fell out of fashion, the shoguns patronized the arts, including the theater of *sarugaku noh*. In 1374, Kanami Kiyotsugu (1333–1384), head of one of the country's *sarugaku noh* troupes, performed before the young shogun Ashikaga Yoshimitsu (1358–1408). So impressed was the shogun that he became Kanami's patron and took the performer's son, ZEAMI MOTOKIYO (1363–1443), who was also an accomplished actor, as his companion and lover.

It was through the efforts of Kanami and Zeami that noh became an autonomous form. An innovator by temperament, Kanami combined elements of existing performance traditions into a dramatic form adapted to the tastes of the shogunate and lower warrior classes. Kanami amalgamated popular songs, dance, music, and poetry within an aesthetic of meditative deliberateness and restraint drawn from Zen Buddhism. Limiting his plays to a single protagonist, he advocated a style of acting based on authenticity of physical and vocal characterization. After Kanami's death, Zeami, who would become one of the most important figures in the history of Japanese theater, extended and refined his father's theatrical innovations. In a number of theoretical writings, including the seven-volume *Kadensho* (1400–02), Zeami discussed the intricacies of noh acting, the relationship of noh theater to its audience, and the aesthetic concepts underlying noh performance, such as *yūgen*, which denotes suggestive beauty, gracefulness, and an awareness of life's impermanence. In addition to being noh's chief theoretician and one of its greatest actors, Zeami was also its most accomplished playwright, authoring nearly half of the 240 surviving plays that constitute the noh repertoire.

NOH DRAMA

The stories of noh plays are drawn from mythology, legend, and history, particularly (as in Zeami's ATSUMORI [ca. 1400]) the twelfth-century civil war between rival samurai clans. The main character (or *shite*) is often a ghost, demon, or tormented person who cannot find rest because of his or her past deeds. In the typical two-act structure, the central character appears disguised in the first act and is revealed in the second. He or she speaks an elevated, highly literary verse and frequently quotes classical Chinese and Japanese poetry. Other established roles include the main character's companion (*tsure*); a third party (*waki*), frequently a priest, who encounters the main character in the first act; and a servant or commoner (*kyogen*), whose language is colloquial and who often provides a narrative summary in the interlude between acts. An onstage chorus sings many of the characters' lines and narrates events within the dramatic action, while three or four onstage musicians accompany the play with drums and

The *shite*, or primary actor, in a contemporary performance of the noh drama *The Lady Aoi*. Note the mask, costume, folding fan, and stylized gesture of the performer. In the background sit the *hayashi-kata*, or musicians.

flute. The climax of a noh play takes the form of a ritualized dance.

Noh dramas fall into five categories: plays about gods; warrior plays; plays about women, or "wig plays"; miscellaneous plays, including plays about madness and plays about the present time; and demon plays, in which the main character is a good or evil supernatural being. In a traditional noh program, plays from each of these categories were performed, in the order given. Between the plays, farcical sketches known as *kyogen* (wild words) were performed by the same actors who took the colloquial roles in the noh drama. A *nohgaku* program (the term refers to the combination of *noh* and *kyogen* in performance) took seven or eight hours to complete.

ACTORS

The actors of noh drama, who were male—a tradition maintained in all but a few noh companies today—were dressed in elaborate, highly formal silk costumes. These costumes, which included kimonos for male characters, involved variously layered inner and outer garments. Actors were usually wigged. Among the most celebrated features of noh theater are the masks that the main character and his or her companion wore. Treasured for their craftsmanship and elegant yet simple design, these masks offered stylized representations of the established noh character types: male and female, old and young, human and supernatural. Actors in other roles wore masklike makeup. In contrast to the richness of visual presentation that characterized the actors thus attired, the physical setting and props in noh performance were minimal. Movable structures were used to represent a hut, boat, mountain, and other features, while handheld props served to represent emotional states and a range of other objects. A folding fan, for instance, one of the main props in noh theater, could be used to stand for a sword, a flute, or other item. The handling of physical objects formed part of the broader choreography of noh performance, which involved slow, deliberate movement and symbolic, meditative gestures. The acts of walking and dancing, for example, called for painstaking control of body position and motion, and years of training were required for the actor to master such simple gestures as lifting an arm or raising a hand to the eyes, the symbol of weeping.

THE NOH STAGE

Drawn to its formal precision and ceremonial nature, later dramatists and theater artists have sought to appropriate elements of the noh for the modern theater (*Four Plays for Dancers*, published in 1921 by the Irish playwright and poet William Butler Yeats, represents one such attempt). To an extent unrivaled in world theater, however, traditional noh performance is inseparable from the stage for which it was written. The configuration, dimensions, and materials of this stage were standardized during the seventeenth century and have remained unchanged in noh theaters to the present day. The main stage, roughly 18 feet square and raised about $2\frac{1}{2}$ feet above the ground, consists of a polished surface of Japanese cypress with four pillars, roughly 15 feet high, that support a temple-like roof. The audience sits in front of and to the left of this stage. A visible backstage area, at the front of which the musicians sit, features a wooden wall with painted pine trees, while an area to the audience's right of the main acting area is occupied by the chorus, who sit in two rows facing the stage.

One of the most characteristic features of the noh stage is the *hashigakiri*, a railed passageway or bridge that extends from the side of the backstage area on the audience's left to a dressing (or "mirror") room, from which actors make their entrances and to which they exit. A secondary exit to the right of the backstage area is used by the chorus and stage attendants. Reverberating jars are placed under the main stage, backstage, and bridge to provide additional resonance and to amplify the sound of characters walking and stomping their feet. Specific areas of the stage are associated with individual characters and with conventionally assigned functions. The pillar that stands where the bridge meets the stage, for instance, known as the *shite* pillar, is where the main character stops to announce his name upon entering the stage area.

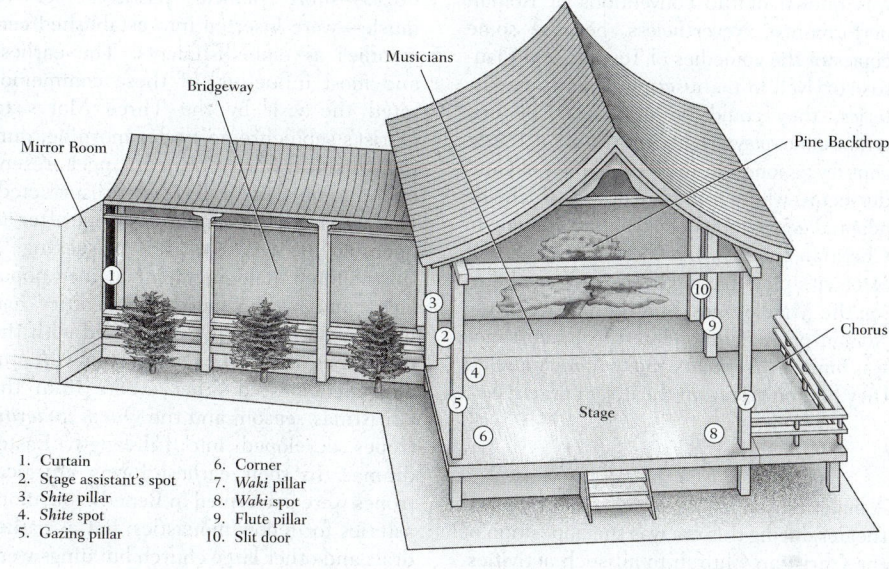

- Mirror Room
- Bridgeway
- Musicians
- Pine Backdrop
- Chorus
- Stage
- Audience

1. Curtain
2. Stage assistant's spot
3. *Shite* pillar
4. *Shite* spot
5. Gazing pillar
6. Corner
7. *Waki* pillar
8. *Waki* spot
9. Flute pillar
10. Slit door

LATER NOH THEATER

The conventions of modern-day noh theater were standardized during the Tokugawa shogunate (1603–1867), a period when the center of government was moved to Edo (modern-day Tokyo) and the hierarchies of Japanese society were institutionalized to a greater extent. Noh theater companies assumed their modern form as hereditary heads (*iemoto*) were made responsible for preserving the traditions of the major schools of noh. Rooted in the practices and accomplishments of its early masters, noh became an art for connoisseurs; although amateur noh companies found support among the commoners, its principal audience was courtly and upper-class.

KABUKI AND BUNRAKU

By the early seventeenth century, other theatrical forms had emerged to satisfy the tastes of a rising urban middle class. Kabuki—a form of dramatic theater involving music, dance, and acrobatics; ornate costumes and makeup; extensive scenery; and spectacular tricks of stage technology—developed in the early decades of the 1600s from the lively, often erotic, dances that temple maidens performed at religious shrines. The performance of kabuki, which was restricted to adult males in 1653, became a highly conventional and stylized art, and its practitioners—including the popular *onnagata*, or actor of female roles—require decades of training. Bunraku, an elaborate form of puppet (or doll) theater that developed out of earlier puppet and storytelling traditions, also became popular during this period. Like noh, which can be seen in specially built theaters throughout Japan, these centuries-old theater forms remain popular on today's stage.

Medieval European Theater

EUROPE AFTER THE ROMAN EMPIRE

The disintegration of the Roman Empire between the fifth and sixth centuries C.E. marked the end of organized theatrical activity in western and central Europe as it had been practiced in classical Rome. Itinerant groups of performers traveled through southern Europe offering such entertainments as storytelling, juggling, tumbling, and jesting; local popular festivals, many with origins in pagan rites surrounding the winter solstice and the earth's return to fertility in spring, contained a variety of performative elements. But although the abandoned amphitheaters across Europe gave evidence of an earlier theatrical culture, after the sixth century little to nothing was known of the conventions of Roman performance. Nevertheless, because some copies of the comedies of Terence and Plautus survived in manuscripts held in monasteries, they could be drawn on by one remarkable playwright: HROTSVIT, a tenth-century canoness at the Saxon abbey of Gandersheim, who wrote six plays in which she adapted conventions of Terentian comedy to Christian subjects. But there is no record of Hrotsvit's plays having been performed during the Middle Ages, and the impact of the Roman playwrights before the Renaissance was limited to scholars and to literary circles; they had no effect on theatrical practice.

EARLY CHURCH DRAMA

A major reason for the absence of organized theater during this era was the opposition of the Christian Church to all such activities. Throughout the Middle Ages (and much of the early modern period), church authorities and moralists denounced theater and other forms of spectacle and impersonation as idolatrous, obscene, and dangerous in their effects on the audience members' passions. Ironically, this same church served as the major site for the reemergence of theater in medieval Europe—but perhaps not surprisingly, since the Catholic liturgy is itself a performed spectacle. During the medieval mass, priests wearing ornate robes officiated before spectators gathered in designated locations within enclosed structures. Processions and other forms of ceremony marked holy days throughout the year, while each day's canonical "offices" or "hours" (such as matins and vespers) were marked by services of their own. Chanting during the liturgy was often antiphonal—with passages sung alternately by two choirs, much like dialogue—and singer-performers often gave voice to the words of Christ and others in the Bible. Individual dates throughout the Christian calendar commemorated biblical events and the figures who participated in them, and thus were inherently associated with a rich trove of narrative and potentially dramatic material.

But ritual and ceremony are not the same as drama, and the latter could emerge only when liturgical celebration gave way to a wider range of characters and actions. This shift took place in the tenth century, when *tropes*—short biblical passages set to music—were inserted into established ceremonies as embellishments. The earliest and most influential of these commemorated the visit by the Three Marys to Christ's sepulchre on Easter morning, during which they learn from an angel present at the tomb that he has been resurrected. Known as the *Quem quaeritis* trope after its opening line ("Whom are you seeking?"), this chanted dialogue rapidly gained popularity and by the late tenth century had inspired similar tropes connected with the Christmas liturgy. The connections eventually encompassed other events from the Christmas season, and the *Quem quaeritis* tropes developed into full-length Easter dramas. In their earliest forms liturgical tropes were performed in Benedictine monasteries for fellow monastics; but as cathedrals and other large church buildings were constructed in the eleventh and twelfth centuries, the lay congregations became audiences for these religious performances.

By the twelfth century, church drama had so expanded in scope and complexity that some works—the Christmas and Passion plays from the Benediktbeuern Abbey in Bavarian Germany, for example—were performed outside the context of the liturgy. Eventually, as part of this natural progression, the plays came to be performed outside the context of the church. The range of suitable dramatic subjects grew to include figures and events from the Old and the New Testaments: the raising of Lazarus, Daniel in the lion's den, and the conversion of St. Paul, to name a few. Plays commemorating the lives of saints—often called "miracle plays" because they recounted the miracles or martyrdoms that led to the protagonist's conversion—mixed narratives of conflict and romantic adventure with moral exemple. Versions of these saints' plays were written and performed into the late Middle Ages.

CORPUS CHRISTI CYCLES

In a parallel development, religious plays began to be written in the national languages of central and western Europe (rather than the Latin of the church), and during the fourteenth and fifteenth centuries these vernacular forms developed into elaborate dramatic cycles of short plays, or pageants. The most notable of these cycle plays were performed in conjunction with the Feast of Corpus Christi (literally, "The Body of Christ"), a holy day—proposed by Pope Urban IV in 1264 and instituted by the church in 1311—celebrating the redemptive presence of the Holy Eucharist. This feast day, which occurred in late spring or early summer, included an outdoor procession in which the host was displayed; eventually, taking advantage of the generally favorable weather and the longer period of daylight, performers took an entire day and sometimes more to mount plays dramatizing events from biblical history. Though more limited versions of these cycles were performed on the Continent, the best-known achievements in this extended dramatic form were England's Corpus Christi plays, which dramatized the history of the world from the fall of the angels and the creation to the Last Judgment. Local records and the manuscripts of individual plays note performances in London, Coventry, Norwich, Newcastle-on-Tyne, and elsewhere in England, but the great majority of the surviving cycle plays come from just four towns, apparently all in the north: York, Wakefield, Chester, and N Town (where N stands for *nomen*—Latin for "name"—suggesting that this cycle was performed by touring players who would insert whatever name was appropriate as they traveled across the countryside). These cycles are quite extensive, containing between twenty-five pageants (the Chester cycle) to forty-eight (the York cycle). Although English cycle drama was performed as early as 1376, most Corpus Christi plays date from the fifteenth century. This distinctive form of drama continued to be performed—scholars have speculated that as a youth, William Shakespeare may have seen a performance of the Coventry cycle; by the late sixteenth century, however, it was effectively suppressed by the newly established Church of England.

The development of theatrical activity on such a scale was made possible by the growth of medieval towns and the formation of guilds: that is, associations governing the practice of individual crafts and trades, which participated in town government and played a major role in both the religious and nonreligious aspects of civic life. In northern England, guilds assumed primary responsibility for the production of the Corpus Christi plays, which therefore are also called "mystery cycles" (the word *mystery*, derived from the Latin *mysterium*, referred to a craft, trade, or profession known only to a few). This arrangement indicates that the cycle plays performed a civic as well as religious function. Given responsibility for individual pageants, guilds provided actors, scenery, costumes, props, and other theatrical elements and materials. In some cases guilds were assigned plays for which they seemed particularly suited: the shipwrights would be given the Noah plays, for instance, while the goldsmiths produced plays about the Three Kings.

STAGING

The manner in which individual Corpus Christi cycles were staged remains a matter of debate. Although practice varied from town to town, there is evidence of two forms of staging: processional and fixed. In certain cities, such as York and Coventry, plays were mounted on pageant wagons that performed, in procession, before spectators gathered at designated viewing sites throughout the town. Scholars disagree on the structure and appearance of these wagons: some speculate that they had two levels (the lower serving as a dressing room), while others argue for a single-platform structure. In addition to the acting area, performers occasionally acted in the street surrounding the pageant wagon; in the Nativity pageant, one of two surviving plays from Coventry, the actor playing Herod "rages in the pagond [pageant wagon] and in the street also." In the alternative staging method, all plays were performed at stationary locations. It is also possible that some combination of processional and fixed staging was practiced: for instance, pageant wagons may have paraded through the town with the actors arranged in tableaux, then gathered in a circle at an open place where they could serve as stages for an audience that stood within the circle's periphery and moved from play to play.

Whether presented on pageant wagons or at fixed locations, the Corpus Christi cycles drew on a staging convention that had characterized medieval drama since its liturgical beginnings. The acting area had two components: one or more structures called *sedes* (mansions) and a non-localized playing space adjacent to these that was known as the *platea* (courtyard, or place). The former, usually represented by decorative booths, oriented the dramatic action to specific locations (Heaven, Hell, palace, house, manger), while the latter allowed for extensions of the action into more indeterminate spaces beyond the *sedes*. Financed by prosperous guilds and engineered by skilled craftsmen, Corpus Christi performances could be awe-inspiring affairs, with special effects and elaborate technical devices. Cranes enabled characters to ascend, descend, and fly between locations, while the Hell's Mouth through which sinners were dragged relied on an elaborate contraption of pulleys and smoke-ejecting bellows. Costumes included everyday medieval garments, ecclesiastical vestments, and—in the case of heavenly beings, who wore gilded masks, and devils, who were given the features of grotesque animals—nonnaturalistic adornments.

DRAMATIC TEXTS

Individual plays, or pageants, within specific cycles vary in length, structure, and style. Some are very formal and rely heavily on long-standing conventions, while others combine biblical narratives with scenes and characters from medieval life. Because the authors of these plays often embellished the biblical accounts with more realistic incidents and characterizations, the Corpus Christi cycles established links between sacred history and the world of their audiences. Indeed, the plays reveal as much about the medieval world as they do about the biblical episodes they take as their subjects. Among the greatest of these works blending the sacred and everyday is by an author whom later scholars call the WAKEFIELD MASTER. This unidentified playwright, whose plays display a command of vernacular dialects, complex characterization, and realistic situations, wrote THE SECOND SHEPHERDS' PLAY (ca. 1475), which parallels and contrasts the scene of the Nativity with a

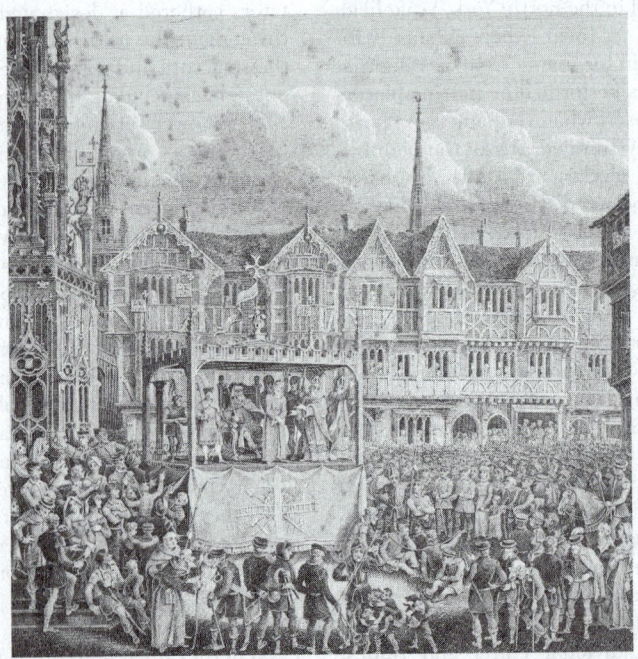

This engraved illustration from Thomas Sharp's *Dissertation on the Pageants Anciently Performed at Coventry* (1825) presents an imaginative reconstruction of the performance of a pageant play in Coventry, England.

rustic sheep-stealing episode. By counter-pointing the mystery of Christ's Incarnation with the earthiness of fallen humanity, this widely known play demonstrates the use of comedy in Corpus Christi drama. Its folk elements remind us of popular forms of entertainment and celebration—folk festivals, songs and stories, mummers' plays (i.e., seasonal folk plays)—and of the drama that emerged from them in the later Middle Ages. In this tradition are the farces of the German poet and dramatist Hans Sachs (1494–1576), written for the festivities of Shrovetide, the three days preceding Lent.

MORALITY PLAYS

At the same time that the mystery cycles were being organized in the late fourteenth century, a different form of religious drama was emerging in England and France: the morality play. Like the Corpus Christi pageants, this drama was concerned with human salvation—but rather than exploring sin and redemption across the vast landscape of human and divine history, as did the cycles, morality plays focused on the moral life of the individual Christian. Written in the mode of allegory, in which abstract ideas and categories of individuals are given concrete form, morality drama featured a representative figure of humanity—Mankind, Everyman, Well-Advised, Ill-Advised—whose identity is universal rather than historical, biblical, or individual. This character interacts with figures personifying virtues and vices, who typically seek to win his soul in a battle between temptation and spiritual obedience. Whereas Corpus Christi plays occasionally employed allegorical characters, morality drama derived neither from these plays nor from the liturgical drama that preceded them. In addition to reflecting the general fondness for allegory in the Middle Ages—Prudentius's poem *Psychomachia* (fourth century C.E.), which introduced the competition of virtues and vices, was widely influential throughout the medieval period—morality drama likely drew on Pater Noster (or Lord's Prayer) plays; these were dramatizations of the seven deadly sins, performed in England during the fourteenth and fif-teenth centuries. Since no Pater Noster plays have survived, specific relationships between the two dramatic forms cannot be established.

The oldest extant English morality play is a dramatic fragment titled *The Pride of Life* (ca. 1350). Only a few plays from the following 160 years have survived, but they indicate the drama's variety of forms and staging practices. The longest and most complex of the English moralities, *The Castle of Perseverance* (ca. 1405–25), presents the life of its protagonist Mankind from birth to death, the struggle over his soul by virtues and vices, a debate between Body and Soul, the parliament of heaven, and the final judgment on Mankind's soul. The manuscript for this play, which includes a diagram, offers particular insight into its staging. Located outdoors, the performance area of *The Castle of Perseverance* consisted of a circular playing space with a structure indicating Mankind's castle in the center and five mansions on the periphery. The later *Mankind* (ca. 1465–70), by contrast, was performed before rural audiences by an itinerant group of professional or semiprofessional actors. The staging requirements were necessarily simple—a few props, a small booth for entrances and exits—and the play could be staged both in an open courtyard and indoors. The play itself combines the story of the farmer Mankind's temptation, fall, and repentance with wide-ranging comic business, most having to do with the devil and his attendant mischief-figures. Finally, the best known of the moralities, EVERYMAN (ca. 1510, translated from a 1495 Dutch original), eschews the drama of temptation for the more somber story of Everyman's journey to death and final judgment. Although textual evidence suggests that the play was written for a playing area with fixed structures, there are no records of its actual performance.

During the sixteenth century, morality drama became broadly popular with audiences across the social spectrum. A growing number of morality plays were performed in public and private venues throughout England by troupes of professional actors—the direct precursors of the acting companies of Shakespeare's time.

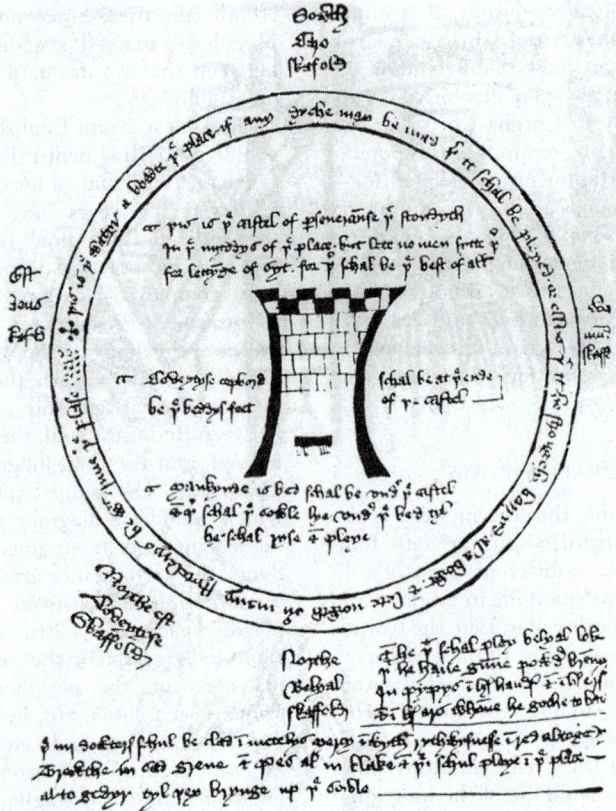

Diagram for staging *The Castle of Perseverance*, from a fifteenth-century manuscript.

As the intellectual and religious climate of England changed in response to Renaissance humanism (a revival in the study of classical literature, science, and philosophy) and to the Reformation (a movement to reform the Catholic Church that led to the founding of Protestant religious denominations), morality drama evolved in its subject matter as well as its ideological function. In the hands of such Tudor humanist writers as Henry Medwall (1462–1501?) and John Skelton (ca. 1460–1529), morality plays engaged with increasingly secular subjects, addressing issues of philosophy, social relations, and politics in addition to moral and religious questions. In this form they frequently resembled Tudor interludes (indoor dramatic entertainments that were usually performed in noble households, guild halls, and schools).

During the religious controversies of the English Reformation, morality drama was employed by Catholics and Protestants to dramatize their doctrinal and political divisions. Even more profoundly than the Corpus Christi cycles, which were cumbersome in structure and rooted in a medieval religious consensus that no longer applied in sixteenth-century England, morality plays helped shape subsequent English drama. Because their allegorical conventions were adaptable to a range of issues and ideologies, these plays provided a dramatic structure for such Elizabethan and Jacobean plays as CHRISTOPHER MARLOWE'S *DOCTOR FAUSTUS* (ca. 1588). Certainly, the legacy of the Vice characters, with their conniving but theatrically appealing horseplay, can be seen clearly in such later dramatic masterpieces as BEN JONSON'S *VOLPONE* (1606).

Theater in Early Modern Europe, 1500–1700

As European theater developed between 1500 and 1700, it was affected by a range of political, economic, social, artistic, and religious changes that were transforming the region and its relationship to the rest of the world. The term *early modern*, which is often used to designate the period in European history between the end of the Middle Ages and the beginning of the Industrial Revolution, focuses attention on those developments that inaugurated the world we know today: the rise of science and accelerating technological innovation, the growth of cities and the emergence of mercantile economies, New World exploration and colonization, and the transformations of church and state through reformation, absolutism, and revolution. But as the competing term *Renaissance*—applied to the fifteenth and sixteenth centuries—suggests, this period is also characterized by a powerful look backward to the classical era of Greece and Rome and to the social, artistic, and intellectual values that scholars, newly given access to many of its rediscovered texts, found there. As they combined the new and the old in fruitful, and also volatile, ways, the years 1500–1700 were a period of unprecedented discovery and rediscovery in the visual, plastic, architectural, and musical arts. But arguably it was theater—where audiences in England, Spain, France, and elsewhere in Europe saw their world represented in action—that witnessed the greatest accomplishments during this extraordinary period.

THE EUROPEAN RENAISSANCE: HUMANISM AND THE CLASSICAL PAST

The European Renaissance played a crucial role in the transformations that Europe underwent in the fifteenth and sixteenth centuries. The term *Renaissance,* which means "rebirth," was first used in 1550 by the artist and critic Giorgio Vasari (1511–1574) to refer to the rediscovery of classical values—which, he claimed, had been eclipsed during the Middle Ages by Christianity and the "barbarian" cultures of northern Europe—in the paintings of Giotto (ca. 1267–1337) and later Florentine artists. This view of medieval civilization as a dark age compared to the civilizations of Greece and Rome is, of course, inaccurate, as is any absolute demarcation between the later Middle Ages and the Renaissance. Europe in the 1500s remained in many ways medieval. But the turn to the classical world represented a driving force behind humanism, the dominant intellectual movement in Renaissance Europe, and it effected a profound shift of cultural direction. Convinced that the civilizations of Greece and Rome represented the highest point of human achievement and that modern Europe should cultivate their ideals and emulate their accomplishments, scholars devoted themselves to the rediscovery, translation, and textual study of classical works, many of which had been preserved in European monasteries and in the libraries of the Byzantine Empire and Islamic Spain. The invention of the printing press in 1450 by Johann Gutenberg (ca. 1400–1468) accelerated the process by which these texts and Renaissance commentaries on them were disseminated.

The deepening understanding of Greek and Roman writers, and of classical civilization as a whole, revolutionized the fields of literature and the arts. The Italian writers Petrarch (Francesco Petrarca, 1304–1374) and Giovanni Boccaccio (1313–1375) urged their peers to study Greek and Roman writers, and the influence of authors, literary forms, historical subjects, and mythological characters from the classical period was widespread in the literature of the next three centuries. Though it is a mistake to see this expanding interest as a departure from the religious concerns of medieval literature—most Renaissance writers explored classical materials in the context of Christian belief—an intensifying concern with human experience and the things of the world makes itself felt throughout the literature of this period, including its finest: the essays of Michel de Montaigne (1533–1592), for example, and the picaresque fiction of Miguel de Cervantes (1547–1616). A similar interest in the world as it is lived and observed is apparent in the work of Leonardo da Vinci (1452–1519), Michelangelo (1475–1564), and other Renaissance artists, who abandoned the flat, often ornamental surfaces of medieval art for more lifelike representations of the human figure and the visible world.

PATRONAGE

The Renaissance as a cultural phenomenon was closely linked to the increasing urbanization and the changing economic and political landscapes of European society. The movement began in the city-states of Italy, where rulers competed with each other to be patrons of scholarship, literature, and the other arts. Here, as elsewhere in Europe, wealth and power were increasingly concentrated in the hands of princes and other monarchs, civic authorities, and an expanding merchant class, and these groups sought to enhance their prestige by funding art, architecture, literature, music, and lavish spectacles. The most prominent of the Italian cultural centers was Florence, which served—under the rule of Lorenzo de' Medici (1449–1492), "the Magnificent"—as a home for humanists, artists, poets, and philosophers. Later centers of patronage included the courts of England's Elizabeth I and James I, Spain's Philip II, and France's Louis XIV. Acting companies, whose members had previously operated on the margins of society, also benefited from the patronage system during the sixteenth and seventeenth centuries. Even as it earned money from the London playgoing public, for instance, the company to which William Shakespeare belonged—the Lord Chamberlain's Men, later renamed the King's Men—enjoyed the support, protection, and legitimation conferred by courtly patronage.

SCIENCE AND THE "NEW PHILOSOPHY"

As Renaissance humanism reevaluated medieval learning in light of earlier classical traditions, it profoundly altered established fields of knowledge and inquiry. In the field of political philosophy, for instance, the Italian theorist Niccolò Machiavelli (1469–1527) proposed a view of politics and government in which the maintenance and exercise of power, not moral authority, were the ultimate justification for political action. So controversial were these ideas that his very name became synonymous with cunning and ruthless self-interest. The argument between older and newer conceptions of the world was a defining feature of the scientific revolution that took place during the sixteenth and seventeenth centuries. In 1543 Nicolaus Copernicus (1473–1543) published his treatise demonstrating that the earth orbited the sun, thereby refuting the geocentric model that had dominated classical and medieval understanding of the heavens.

Further astronomical discoveries were made by Galileo Galilei (1564–1642), who relied on an improved version of the recently invented telescope to make direct celestial observations. The use of empirical observation, experimentation, and inductive reasoning (i.e., drawing general conclusions from data) represented a shift from the more abstract procedures applied by medieval scholars of the natural world. While Aristotle and classical authorities continued to influence Renaissance science and its social practice—the theories of human physiology set forth by the Greek physician Galen (129–ca. 199 C.E.) remained popular during the period, for example—and while most early modern scientists reconciled their scientific methods and discoveries with a literal belief in the Bible, the scientific method worked to undermine traditional notions of authority. As the poet John Donne wrote of recent scientific discoveries in 1611, "[T]he new Philosophy calls all in doubt."

REFORMATION AND COUNTER-REFORMATION

By 1600, the spirits of inquiry and individualism had challenged the authority of the Catholic Church and, in the process, redrawn the political and religious map of Europe. The Protestant Reformation began as a call for reform within the church in 1517, when Martin Luther (1483–1546) wrote a series of theses protesting the sale of indulgences (the remission of temporal punishment for sins) on behalf of the pope. Luther's opposition to the abuses of the Catholic Church quickly expanded to include a broader challenge to its authority. Believing that the church had lost contact with the fundamental truths of Christianity, Luther rejected the doctrine that salva-

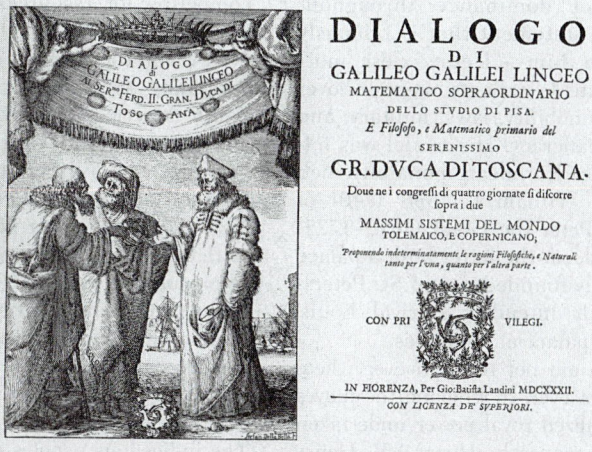

The title page and engraved frontispiece of Galileo's *Dialogue Concerning the Two Chief World Systems*, published in Florence in 1632. In the book, Galileo argued in favor of Copernicus's model of the solar system, in which the planets revolve around the sun, and against the older Ptolemaic system, which placed the earth at the center of the known universe. The engraving shows Aristotle (left), Ptolemy (center), and Copernicus (right).

tion required the intercession of a religious clergy, arguing instead that salvation was a function of faith alone and that the Bible was the sole authority on spiritual matters.

With the help of the newly invented printing press, Luther's ideas were widely disseminated throughout Europe, and other Protestant movements followed. Protestantism was adopted by states in Germany, Scandinavia, and elsewhere in northern Europe, many of which took advantage of this opportunity to assert their independence from Catholic Rome; the Church of England, for example, was established as a Protestant church under the head of Henry VIII (1491–1547) when the king broke from Rome in 1534 for political reasons. Italy, Spain, the Holy Roman Empire (which included much of central Europe), and eventually France remained within a reviving Catholicism that consolidated its doctrine at the Council of Trent (1545–63) and extended its authority through the Counter-Reformation that followed. Wars, rebellions, and the persecution of religious minorities within states swept across Europe as Catholics, state-sponsored Protestant majorities, and more radical Protestant sects confronted each other over

matters of faith, doctrine, and religious and social hierarchy. The conflict between nations that resulted from the Reformation would not begin to be resolved until the Peace of Westphalia, which ended Europe's devastating Thirty Years' War (1618–48).

MONARCHY AND GOVERNMENT

Religious controversy and the political turmoil it precipitated contributed to the changing shapes of monarchy and government during the early modern period. In the late sixteenth and early seventeenth centuries, power was increasingly centralized in the hands of monarchs, who justified this movement toward absolutism by invoking the doctrine of the divine right of kings—the right to rule by virtue of birth, a right bestowed by God alone. France offers the most striking example of this development. Following the religious wars that divided the country in the 1500s and the continuation of civil disturbances and political intrigues in the first half of the 1600s, Louis XIV (1638–1715), the "Sun King," assumed the throne in 1643 and began a seventy-two-year reign that saw France and the French court achieve a position of dominance throughout Europe. The statement that is famously attributed to him—"L'état, c'est moi" ("I am the state")—reflects his power over the country's nobility, laws, military, and growing bureaucracy. His model was followed by other European monarchs such as Frederick William I (1688–1740) of Prussia and Peter the Great (1672–1725) of Russia; indeed, the latter built a palace in the recently founded city of St. Petersburg explicitly intended to rival Louis' monumental palace at Versailles.

Absolutism did not triumph everywhere in Europe, however. In England the moves toward centralized royal power undertaken by the Tudor monarchs Henry VII, Henry VIII, and Elizabeth I were checked by Parliament in the 1600s: the Stuart king Charles I (1600–1649) was beheaded in 1649 during the English Civil War, and for the following eleven years—a period divided into the Commonwealth and the Protectorate—England was subject to parliamentary and military rule. The Stuart monarchy was restored in 1660 with the crowning of Charles II (1630–1685), but the next forty years, known as the Restoration, witnessed the overthrow of his brother and successor, the Catholic James II (1633–1701), as a result of conflicts with his Protestant Parliament. Similar clashes awaited European monarchs in the eighteenth century.

NEW WORLD ENCOUNTERS

No overview of early modern Europe would be complete that failed to acknowledge the profound shift in European consciousness brought about by the encounter with the Western Hemisphere. In the Middle Ages Europeans had traveled through Asia by land as far east as Kublai Khan's China, and by 1500 the Portuguese had explored the west coast of Africa. But the "discovery" of an inhabited land across the ocean by the Italian-born Spanish explorer Christopher Columbus (1451–1506), who landed in the Caribbean in 1492 while seeking a western sea route to Asia, had consequences that reached much further. The success of this and subsequent expeditions prompted a race for conquest and settlement of the Americas by Spain and other European powers competing for resources, territorial possessions, and prestige. Over the next hundred years, the Spanish colonized an area stretching from eastern and southern South America to what is today Mexico and much of the United States, while Portugal, the Netherlands, France, and England also established colonies in the New World. The first permanent English settlement was Jamestown (located in the colony of Virginia) in 1607, and by the end of the seventeenth century England's colonial holdings encompassed a good deal of eastern North America.

The history of European colonialism in the Americas is, without doubt, a dark one. The indigenous peoples of South, Central, and North America suffered violence, exploitation, death by disease, and forced conversions, and the relationships between colonizer and colonized were shaped by military power, economic interests, and the religious fervor of missionaries. Europe's colonization of the New World inaugurated a transatlantic system of trade that would eventually bring African slaves to the Americas as part of a highly organized exchange of labor, resources, and commodities. At the same time, even as New World settlers may have sought to Europeanize the indigenous peoples and societies they encountered, their own world was transformed by the contact. Materially, Europe benefited from the introduction of new commodities, such as tobacco, corn, and previously unknown medications. But as Renaissance travel literature reveals, the encounter with the New World also fundamentally changed Europeans' awareness of their recently expanded world. When four delegates (or "kings," as they were called) from the Iroquois Confederacy visited London and Queen Anne's court in 1710, they inspired a fascination whose intensity reveals how deeply their newly discovered hemisphere had penetrated the early modern imagination.

PROFESSIONAL THEATER, 1500–1700

Theater played an important part in the emergence of early modern Europe. As a medium of impersonation and display, theater spoke to a deeply theatricalized society where power was asserted through spectacles, performances, and rituals of display. The spirits of individualism and inquiry found a natural home in an art form in which characters grappled with their destinies on a public stage, and spectators who flocked to attend these performances saw the concerns of their world illuminated and explored. As defenders and critics debated its moral authority, European theater during this period exerted unprecedented social influence.

The years 1500–1700 saw wide-ranging developments in the institution and practices of theater. In addition to those performances that took place in court, private, and university settings, the first professional theaters, public and private, opened in Europe during the second half of the sixteenth century. Paris had the Hôtel de Bourgogne, built in 1548; London the short-lived Red Lion, in 1567; and Madrid the Corral de la Cruz, in 1579; and by 1600 these major cities—and several in Italy— had become thriving theatrical centers. Many of these early theater buildings employed staging arrangements used in courtyard and other outdoor performance venues—the major public theaters of London, such as the Globe, were open-air theaters and contained stages that extended into the audience. But the development of theater architecture and scenic practices during this period was also influenced by the rediscovery of the treatise on architecture by the Roman engineer and architect Vitruvius. Italian architects and theorists drew on it in determining the theater's shape, the relationship between stage and auditorium, and the design of tragic, comic, and pastoral scenes. During the seventeenth and eighteenth centuries, Italian stage design became influential throughout Europe, as such innovations were introduced as the use of perspective, a form of visual representation that creates the impression of three-dimensionality and distance. As it gained popularity, the simultaneous staging that characterized the medieval period and continued into early modern production was replaced by a spatially unified visual field. Italian designers also pioneered the use of the proscenium, an archway or a frame that would become characteristic of European stage design from the late sixteenth to nineteenth centuries.

As the sophistication of theater technology grew, stage design and scenic effects became increasingly elaborate. The spectacular staging for which the theaters of seventeenth-century Italy, France, and Spain became particularly well-known— multiple scenery changes, flying chariots, hidden grottoes, lavish pictorial effects—

An engraving from the mid-1600s showing actors onstage at the Hôtel de Bourgogne.

were manifestations of the baroque style that dominated European arts during this period. The baroque, which stresses exuberance, monumentality, and ornateness, achieved its highest realization in court performances, when royalty spent large sums for the work of Italy's leading designers and those who studied their innovations. This movement toward greater spectacle was accelerated by the development of opera during the 1600s.

COMMEDIA DELL'ARTE

The establishment of theater as a public, private, and courtly institution was paralleled by the professionalization of actors and others involved in theatrical productions. Acting companies operated in England and on the Continent throughout the sixteenth century, and these troupes often performed in other countries in addition to their own. The most widely known were the *commedia dell'arte* (literally, "comedy of art") players who emerged in Italy in the mid-1500s, performed throughout Europe, and occupied an important place in European theatrical history into the eighteenth century. These troupes—which consisted of ten to twelve actors, both male and female—presented comic scenarios centering on love and intrigue. While the narrative outlines of these scenarios were established in advance, their performance depended on improvisation and the use of comic routines or improvisational asides known as *lazzi*. Popular with audiences, *lazzi* were often ingenious bits of comic business that players used to enliven their performances, such as using a wooden arm to slip away from a beating or engaging in acrobatic contortions in order to catch a flea. Commedia dell'arte actors portrayed a range of stock characters—some masked and some unmasked—that included lovers, masters, and servants (known as *zanni*). Among the best known of the masked characters are Pantalone, a rich miser, and Arlecchino (or Harlequin), an acrobatic servant with a distinctive motley-colored costume.

Commedia dell'arte companies were organized on the sharing plan, an arrangement that enabled performers to share in the risks and profits of their companies. It was just one of the forms of economic organization that acting companies throughout Europe used as actors, managers, playwrights, and others participated in the expanding business of theater. Performing at Europe's courts (often under the patronage of royalty and nobility) while also operating within a newly established network of public and private playhouses, theater companies in the late 1500s and 1600s began to enjoy some measure of economic security. At the same time, the life of theater professionals remained a hard one, with actors and playwrights often living on the edge of poverty and under the threat of debtors' prison. Theater and the profession of acting were regarded with the social ambivalence and antitheatrical prejudice that early modern Europe inherited from the medieval period. In Catholic and Protestant countries alike, the theater was regularly associated with immorality, and such charges came from secular as well as religious sources. Relationships with state and civic authorities were often equally fraught. Dramatic censorship was instituted in Spain and England, and the theater was subject to a range of restrictive laws throughout Europe. Although the licensing of theaters that took place during the 1600s conferred greater legitimacy on the companies that gained state approval, the implementation of such policies had the effect of bringing theatrical activity even more firmly under government control.

THE DRAMA OF EARLY MODERN EUROPE

The profound changes in Europe between 1500 and 1700 and the accompanying theatrical developments helped ensure that the era would become one of the most prominent in the creation of dramatic literature. The rediscovery, translation, and publication of Greek and Roman plays spurred widespread interest in classical drama, and the translation into Italian of Aristotle's *Poetics* in 1549 helped ignite a debate over Aristotelian dramatic theory that lasted into the eighteenth century. Through the efforts of sixteenth-century Italian and French commentators, Aristotle's treatise was interpreted and codified into neoclassical precepts concerning

Riciulina. Metzetin

A sixteenth-century engraving of two commedia actors dancing.

decorum, verisimilitude, dramatic probability, concentrated action, and uniformity of subject and tone. The dramatic unities of time, place, and action, for example, dictated that the playwright not strain a spectator's credulity by having events take place over more than one day and in more than one location and that the play be restricted to a single, focused plotline. Noble characters were appropriate to tragedy, while those of lower social station belonged to the domain of comedy. Neoclassical theory had its greatest impact on the drama of Italy and France; but even in England and Spain, where dramatists generally eschewed its precepts for more episodic, stylistically varied dramatic styles, debates over classical authority took place.

Early in the sixteenth century, comedy, tragedy, tragicomedy, pastoral, and dramatic satire were strongly influenced by classical models. But as the academic performance of plays in Latin gave way to plays written in the vernacular, the drama of early modern Europe began drawing more strongly on native performance traditions inherited from the Middle Ages. The result was a rich tapestry of dramatic styles, ranging from the multiple, episodic plots of Elizabethan and Jacobean English

drama to the classical simplicity of the plays of JEAN RACINE (1639–1699). As part of a larger theatrical field that included religious performances, royal pageants, civic commemorations, and such popular forms as mumming, drama during the period 1500–1700 entertained a variety of spectators in numerous venues. Concentrated in Europe's major cities, this drama reflected a lively urban culture and the early stirrings of national self-awareness. And although many of its most enduring technological, performative, and theoretical innovations arose in Italy, the theater of early modern Europe found its highest dramatic achievement in England, Spain, and France.

English Theater, 1576–1642

In 1576, when the actor, manager, and theatrical entrepreneur James Burbage (1531–1597) built the Theatre in Shoreditch (an area to the northeast of the City of London), the commercial theater was in its infancy in England. The performance of plays and other theatrical activity had, of course, enjoyed popularity earlier in the sixteenth century. Dramatists influenced by Renaissance humanism wrote comedies, tragedies, and moral interludes that made use of classical and medieval models alike; they were performed in a variety of places, including at court and in noble households, schools, universities, and London's legal societies, the Inns of Court. Among the best known of these earlier plays are *Ralph Roister Doister* (ca. 1553) and *Gammer Gurton's Needle* (1552–53), two early English comedies, and Thomas Norton and Thomas Sackville's *Gorboduc* (1561), generally considered the first English tragedy. Traveling actors brought mummings, farces, and other forms of popular dramatic entertainment to local communities, and Corpus Christi plays continued to be staged throughout England until the 1570s, when their performance was effectively halted by royal edict. But the expansion of dramatic activity that would make London one of the most vibrant theatrical centers in Europe did not occur until the commercial theater was established during the century's final quarter.

PUBLIC AND PRIVATE THEATERS

In England, as elsewhere in Europe, the construction of theater buildings was essential to the institutionalization of theater. Theater buildings in London were of two kinds: public and private. Burbage's Theatre established the model for subsequent public theaters. Polygonal in shape, it contained three tiers of audience galleries surrounding a roughly circular, unroofed yard. We have sufficient information about this and other public theaters built between 1577 and 1623—notably the Swan, the Rose, the Fortune, and the Globe, which was built in Southwark (on the southern side of the Thames) with timber from the dismantled Theatre in 1599—to know that the stage for these theaters extended into the yard at a height of approximately 5 feet. Partly roofed, this stage featured a structure at the rear known as the *tiring house,* which included two doors for entrances and exits and one or two balcony levels that could be used for audience seating, music, and scenes requiring actors to perform above stage level (the so-called balcony scene in Shakespeare's *Romeo and Juliet* [1595], for example). A trapdoor on the stage floor

allowed ghosts and other characters to ascend from a darkened cellar (sometimes referred to as *hell*), while pulleys on the underside of the stage roof made it possible to raise and lower actors and stage properties. The audience to which these public theaters catered represented a cross section of London society; it included men and women, from apprentices and tradespeople to the gentry and nobility. Those who paid a penny for admission, known as *groundlings*, stood in the yard surrounding the stage, while those who paid two or three pennies sat on benches in the covered galleries.

Because theaters were banned within the City of London itself, the Theatre, the Globe, and other public theaters were built in the suburbs to the north and south, where they could operate beyond the reach of municipal law. Most of London's private theaters, in contrast, were built within city limits on properties known as *liberties* that were exempt from municipal control. The most famous of these, the Blackfriars, was built and subsequently rebuilt on the grounds of a former Dominican monastery that had been closed by Henry VIII in 1538. With substantially higher admission charges than the public theaters, private theaters entertained a more socially homogeneous body of spectators. Smaller than the public playhouses, these indoor theaters were designed as long rooms with a stage at one end, benches for seating on the main floor, and galleries along the side walls. Unlike the open-air theaters, which were lit by natural light, private theaters were illuminated by candlelight. Until 1609, performances at London's private theaters were given exclusively by companies of boy actors; originally formed at choir schools, they became popular at court and on the London stage during the late 1500s and early 1600s but subsequently fell out of favor.

ACTING COMPANIES

An essential contribution to the rise of professional theater in late sixteenth-century England was a legal shift in the status of actors. In 1572 the government of Elizabeth I passed a law decreeing that itinerant actors and entertainers be arrested

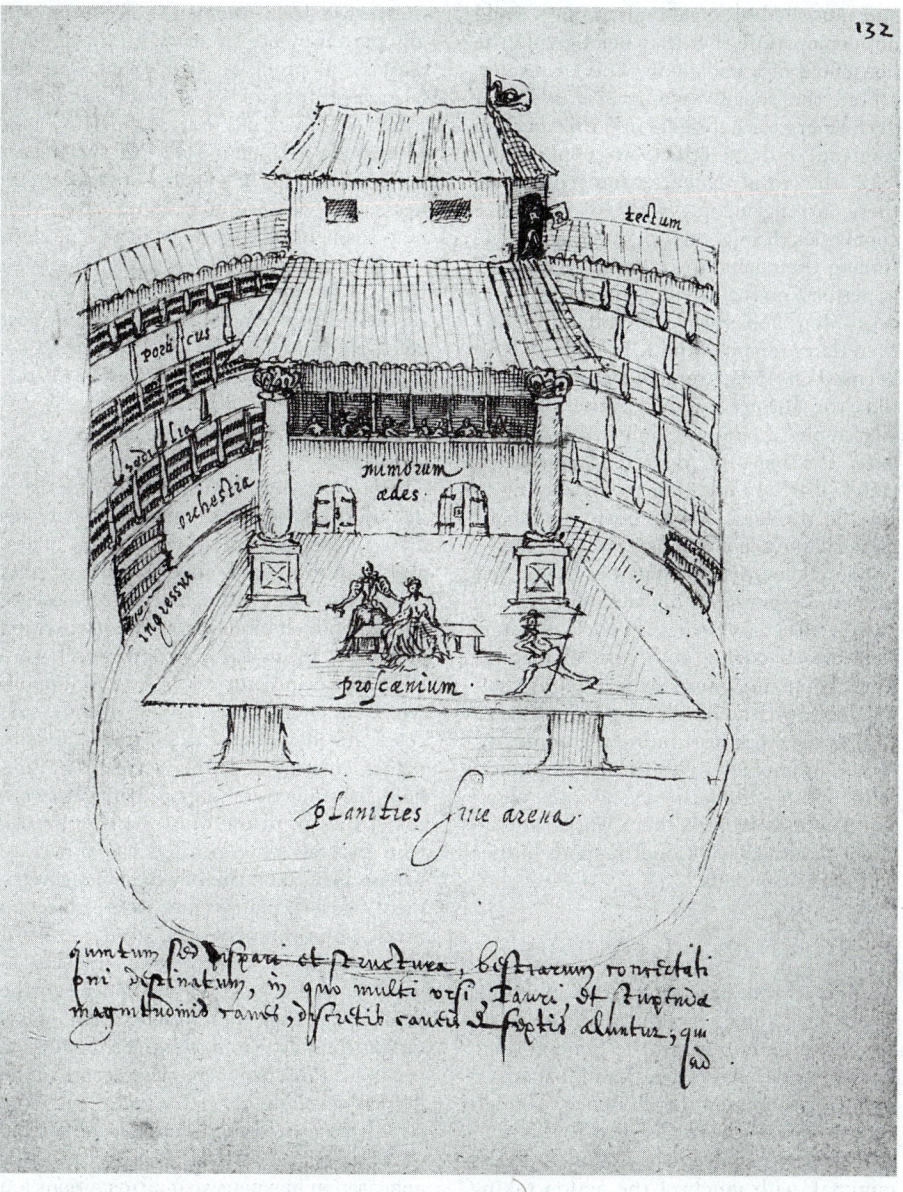

This sketch of the Swan Theater—a copy of an original by a late sixteenth-century Dutch visitor to London named Johannes de Witt—is the only surviving contemporary likeness of the inside of an Elizabethan theater. Latin words or phrases identify the major parts of the theater: the *proscaenium* (the flat, open stage); the *mimorum aedes* (a dressing room for the actors); the *planities sive arena* (the "yard," in which spectators could stand in front of the stage); the *tectum* (the roof); the *porticus* (covered gallery); the *sedilia* (seats); the *orchestra* (seats for important spectators); and the *ingressus* (the entry into the various galleries).

and punished as vagabonds if they could not demonstrate that they belonged to the household of a nobleman. The law underscored the socially marginal world that performers inhabited in Elizabethan England, but its effect—in conjunction with the royal patents that confirmed these arrangements—was to legitimize companies through aristocratic patronage. Among the companies that were licensed to perform on the London stage, the Admiral's Men and the Lord Chamberlain's Men (later renamed the King's Men), both licensed in 1594, were the most influential; the former produced the plays of Christopher Marlowe (1564–1593) and the latter the plays of William Shakespeare (1564–1616). In addition to performing in specific theaters—Shakespeare's company played at the Globe and, later, Blackfriars—London theatrical companies also performed at court and on tours outside the city (a necessity when London theaters were closed during outbreaks of plague). Adult companies were structured as sharing plans, with actors sharing the profits as well as the work of running the company. As a shareholder in the Lord Chamberlain's Men, Shakespeare wrote plays, acted in his own and others' works, and no doubt assumed additional responsibilities within the company.

PROPERTIES AND COSTUMES

As befit the design of theater buildings where spectators surrounded the stage on three or even four sides, the London stage was presentational rather than illusionistic in how it addressed the audience. Though stage properties were clearly a part of theatrical performance, they tended to be minimal, with much of the action taking place on an undefined area of the stage reminiscent of the *platea* of medieval drama. Setting, when it was specified, was established more through verbal description than through stage properties. Costumes, on the other hand, were often quite elaborate, with visually luxurious pieces provided by the nobility or purchased by the companies themselves. Whereas actresses were allowed to perform on the Continent, only male actors performed on the London stage before the closing of the theaters in 1642. Women's roles were usually played by boy actors within the companies, a practice that Shakespeare's Cleopatra (played by a boy) alludes to when she imagines her story being performed on a Roman stage: "I shall see / Some squeaking Cleopatra boy my greatness / I'th' posture of a whore." But what may seem like limitations to the modern eye were opportunities for exceptional displays of acting skill by the period's many renowned performers, including the most celebrated actor of his day, Richard Burbage (James Burbage's son, 1568–1619).

PLAYWRIGHTS AND PLAYS

The proliferation of theaters and the rising demand for theatrical entertainment created intense competition for new plays, and a professional class of playwrights emerged to meet this demand. Shakespeare earned enough money from his playwriting and other theatrical efforts to purchase a large house and property in Stratford-upon-Avon, but not all playwrights had equal success, and they often turned their hands to pamphleteering and other activities in London's booming print market. Forced to work under the eye of the Master of the Revels, who in 1581 was granted the power to license plays (and thereby to act as government censor), playwrights were subject to arrest, imprisonment, and even torture if they addressed controversial subjects in their plays. Because plays belonged to the companies that purchased them, playwrights had no rights over their production or publication. Nor were plays accorded the literary standing of poetry and other more strictly literary forms. Company-authorized and pirated versions of plays occasionally appeared in inexpensive quarto editions (on small-sized paper), but it wasn't until 1616, when Ben Jonson (1572–1637) published his plays under the title *The Works of Benjamin Jonson*, that a dramatist presumed to accord his works the status of literary art. Like most of his contemporary dramatists, Shakespeare showed little interest in the publication of his plays, and it was only in 1623, seven years after his death, that two of his colleagues published his plays in a large-format edition, subsequently known as the First Folio.

The drama of Renaissance England was rich and varied, combining the eloquence of dramatic poetry with the vibrant particularity of contemporary life. During the 1580s and 1590s, the London stage offered a wealth of plays in the genres of comedy, tragedy, dramatic pastoral, and history play. With THE SPANISH TRAGEDY (1587), Thomas Kyd (1558–1594) inaugurated the genre of revenge tragedy that was to prove popular during the reigns of Elizabeth and James, and before his premature death (in 1593) Marlowe wrote a half-dozen or so tragedies and history plays that remain among the finest of their age. Elizabethan comedy ranged from the pastoral and romantic plays of Robert Greene (1558–1592) to Jonson's early satiric comedies. The exuberance that characterizes much of this drama reflected the optimism of an England that was asserting itself as a European power (the English defeat of the Spanish Armada occurred in 1588). This attitude changed in the years preceding Elizabeth's death in 1603, and the drama of the early seventeenth century was marked by a darkening of tone and subject matter. Shakespeare's greatest tragedies were written during this period, as were the plays of JOHN WEBSTER (1579–1630s?) and other tragic dramatists. In the area of comedy, the closing years of the sixteenth century and the first quarter of the seventeenth saw the sharpening of dramatic satire; a proliferation of city comedies (plays whose characters are drawn from London's urban classes) in the drama of Thomas Middleton (1580–1627), Thomas Dekker (ca. 1572–1632), and others; and the popularity of a hybrid genre—tragicomedy—in the plays of Francis Beaumont (ca. 1584–1616) and John Fletcher (1579–1625). The years of Charles I's reign (1625–49) saw the tragedies of John Ford (1586–1639?) and the genteel comedies of James Shirley (1596–1666).

COURT THEATER: MASQUES

The early seventeenth century also witnessed a flowering of theatrical activity in the courts of James I and Charles I. The Stuart court masque was an elaborate form of entertainment that featured lavish spectacle, music, singing, dance, and alle-

Inigo Jones's costume design of a fiery spirit in Thomas Campion's *Lord's Masque* (1613).

gorical or mythological plots celebrating monarchical authority. Jonson was the leading writer of masques during this period, and he worked in collaboration with the architect and stage designer Inigo Jones (1573–1652), who introduced important aspects of Italian stage design to the English theater. Like the court ballets that were performed in France during the reign of Louis XIV later in the century, the Stuart masques reflect the profound relationship between theatricality and the performance of power in the early modern state.

CIVIL WAR, COMMONWEALTH, AND THE CLOSING OF THE THEATERS

This relationship came to an end during the English Civil War (1642–49), which was followed by the Commonwealth and the Protectorate (1649–60); those eighteen years witnessed the overthrow of the English monarchy by a Puritan-dominated Parliament and the closing of the theaters by parliamentary decree in

1642. The Globe was torn down in 1644 to make room for tenements, and other theaters were subsequently dismantled or allowed to fall into disrepair. Theatrical activity was not entirely eliminated during these years—dramatic performances were given at private houses and other nontheatrical venues, and in the 1650s the musical dramas of William Davenant (1606–1668) marked the beginning of English opera—but the great age of Tudor and Stuart theater had come to a decisive end.

Spanish Theater, 1580–1700

During the sixteenth and seventeenth centuries, a period known as the "Golden Age" of Spanish literature and art, dramatic theater in Spain achieved a level of excellence that rivaled that of Shakespeare's England. The rise of theater and the distinctive shapes it assumed reflected the history of Spain's emergence as a European and global power. During the medieval period much of Spain was under Muslim rule, and the slow reconquest of the Iberian peninsula by Christian armies was not completed until the Battle of Granada in 1492. The kingdoms of Aragon and Castile were joined by the marriage of Ferdinand II (1452–1516) and Isabella I (1451–1504) in 1469, and the resultant unified Spain extended its power through further dynastic alliances and an overseas empire that included vast areas of North, Central, and South America.

While other areas of Europe were feeling the initial shocks of the Protestant Reformation, the Catholic Church consolidated its authority in Spain and, through the office of the Spanish Inquisition, kept religious division beyond its borders. Spain's unique history strongly affected its theatrical development. The centuries of Muslim occupation gave Spanish drama and Spanish literature as a whole their most distinctive theme— that of honor; at the same time, the pervasive Catholicism of Spanish life during the later period ensured that the religious and secular theaters, which were diverging elsewhere in Europe, remained unusually close.

RELIGIOUS DRAMA: THE *AUTO SACRAMENTALE*

The most widely produced form of religious drama in sixteenth- and seventeenth-century Spain was the *auto sacramentale*. Performed, like the earlier mystery cycles throughout Europe, on the Feast of Corpus Christi, *autos sacramentales* celebrated the mystery of the Eucharist in stories mixing the human, the supernatural, and the allegorical. To put on the *autos*, the players used two-story *carros*, or wagons, which were first paraded through Madrid and other cities and towns as part of the Corpus Christi procession and then positioned behind a portable or fixed outdoor stage. Two *carros* were used for each performance until the mid-1600s, when the number was expanded to four (and later to eight). Early *autos* were produced by trade guilds, but by the mid-sixteenth century the responsibility had passed to municipal authorities, who often spent considerable amounts to stage them. Enormously popular events that brought together civic and church authority, *autos sacramentales* were performed by professional acting troupes hired specifically for these occasions, and they commanded the talents of Spain's leading dramatists.

PUBLIC THEATER: THE *CORRALES*

Although there was dramatic and theatrical activity—including the performance of secular plays for academic, aristocratic, and popular audiences—in the early and mid-sixteenth century, it was not until the 1570s that a professional public theater was fully established in Spain's major cities. Not surprisingly, the country's theatrical center was Madrid, which in 1561 became the capital under Philip II (1527–1598). The Corral de la Cruz, Madrid's first permanent theater, was built in 1579; it was followed by the Corral del Príncipe in 1583. Like the open-air theaters of Elizabethan England, the design of the *corrales*, or Spanish public theaters, derived from courtyard performances. The *corrales* were constructed within square or rectangular courtyards enclosed on three sides by buildings. A raised stage with permanent

The Corral de Comedias de Almagro, built in 1628 and restored in the 1950s, is the only surviving *corral*. Seats for the audience are positioned in an enclosed courtyard, while the rows of seats known as *gradas* ascend on either side.

backdrop and upper levels was placed on one end of the courtyard, and an open space, or *patio,* for standing spectators was located directly in front of it. In the seventeenth century several rows of benches or stools (called *taburetes*) were installed immediately in front of the stage on a raised platform. On either side of the patio, a section of seats in ascending rows known as the *gradas* extended to the second story. Above the *alojería* (refreshment booth) at the end of the courtyard facing the stage, galleries accommodated additional spectators. The first of these, the *cazuela,* provided seating for women, while higher galleries accommodated officials from the city of Madrid and the Council of Castile and (above them) clergymen and intellectuals. The windows of buildings above the *gradas* served as box seats (*aposentos*), and additional levels of box seats or open galleries were available at the third- and fourth-floor levels. The lively, sometimes unruly, audiences who attended performances in the *corrales* represented a cross section of Madrid society.

From its inception the public theater in Madrid was embedded in the city's institutional structures. The *corrales* were originally licensed to confraternities, or charitable organizations, which used theatrical performance as a means of raising money to support hospitals and aid the poor. This arrangement lasted until 1615, when the city of Madrid assumed control of the theaters and the distribution of their revenues for charitable purposes. The theatrical companies it hired—consisting of actor-managers (*autores*), actors, apprentices, and others involved in the productions—were subject to government regulation. After 1603 only licensed companies could operate in Spain, and the number of licenses was limited. Actors who were not hired by these companies joined *compañías de la legua* (companies of the road), which performed throughout the countryside. No company was allowed to perform in any one place for more than two months of the year, and only one could perform there at any one time (more were permitted in Madrid and Seville). As a result, even licensed companies regularly traveled between cities. Women actors were licensed to perform in 1587, but this practice sparked such controversy that a royal decree was issued in 1599 stipulating that only those women married to members of the company perform and that male and female actors not dress in the clothing of the opposite sex. Compromises in response to this final restriction were frequent, however, and actresses who played women disguised as men regularly wore male clothing down to the waist with a skirt below.

THEATER AT COURT

Court performances, which had been infrequent in Spain during the sixteenth century, began to be mounted in the seventeenth century with a splendor that rivaled that displayed in Italy and France. During the reign of Philip III (r. 1598–1621), professional productions and masque-like entertainments involving elaborate settings, costumes, and special effects were given in one of the halls in the Alcázar (the royal palace). When a new palace, the Buen Retiro, was completed on the outskirts of Madrid in 1633, it became the center for court entertainments, which reached their high point during the reign of Philip IV (r. 1621–65). Under the supervision of Italian set designers who were brought to the Spanish court to oversee and engineer these performances, spectacular entertainments were staged both within the palace—a permanent theater, the Coliseo, was constructed there in 1640—and outdoors on the palace grounds. For a 1635 production of *Love Is the Greatest Enchantment* by PEDRO CALDERÓN DE LA BARCA (1600–1681), the Tuscan hydraulics engineer, scenographer, and landscape designer Cosimo (Cosme) Lotti (d. 1643) built a special stage above the waters of a lake, managed to have a silver chariot drawn across the water's surface by two large fish, and transformed a mountain into a palace.

SPANISH GOLDEN AGE DRAMA

The drama of Spain's Golden Age represents one of the period's greatest achievements. Those plays that were performed by early professional troupes in Spain were written by actor-managers for the companies they ran—hence, these versatile men of the theater were given the full title *autores de comedias*. By the 1590s, a class of professional dramatists had emerged to satisfy the increasing demand for original dramatic scripts. The *comedia nueva* (new drama)—or *comedia*, as it became known less formally—proved to be the most popular and enduring dramatic form written during the Spanish Golden Age. Consisting of three-act plays in varying verse forms, *comedia nueva* mixed high and low, tragedy and comedy, in plots that were drawn from history, mythology, legend, Italian *novelle* and other literary sources, the Bible, popular ballads, and the everyday life of country and town. Among its specialized subgenres were the *comedias de capa y espada* (cape and sword plays), which featured stories of romance and intrigue, and *comedias de costumbres* (comedies of manners). Popular character types in the *comedia* included the *cabellero* (gentleman), *galán* (cavalier or gallant), *dama* (lady), and *gracioso* (comic character, or fool, whose actions often parallel the actions of those of superior rank).

Of the many playwrights who contributed to the *comedia nueva*, none played a greater role in its development and success than LOPE DE VEGA (1562–1635), a towering figure in Spanish Golden Age drama and one of the most prolific dramatists ever to write for the stage. He wrote as many as 1,500 plays (of which 470 have survived), and his output included *comedias*, *autos sacramentales*, and *loas* (prologues) and *entremeses* (interludes), which were performed before and between the acts of plays, respectively. In *The New Art of Writing Plays* (1609), his treatise on dramatic theory, Lope defended his disregard for the classical rules of playwriting in favor of variety and "the likeness of truth." Other dramatists followed in his footsteps—including Tirso de Molina (Gabriel Téllez, ca. 1584–1648), whose play *The Trickster of Seville* is the earliest known version of the Don Juan story—but none achieved a more prominent position in seventeenth-century Spanish theater than Pedro Calderón de la Barca. Calderón—whose plays are marked by meticulous craftsmanship, linguistic complexity, and richness of metaphor—became a leading figure in the *corrales* and in the court of Philip IV, where much of his dramatic activity was concentrated. He also became the leading author of *autos sacramentales*; so exceptional was his mastery of this form that between 1647 and 1681 he wrote all of the *autos* produced in Madrid.

THE LEGACY OF GOLDEN AGE DRAMA

Calderón's death is generally considered to mark the end of Spanish Golden Age drama. Those dramatists who followed in his footsteps conformed to established models rather than pursuing innovation. While spectacular productions continued to be undertaken at court through the end of the century, the heyday of both the court theater and public *corrales* had passed. In their decline they mirrored the condition of Spain itself, which had been weakened and demoralized by a century of wars, declining wealth, and waning influence. Yet during its Golden Age, Spain had achieved one of Europe's most vibrant theatrical cultures, and its dramatic legacy was felt throughout the Continent (particularly in France) and in the world beyond its shores. Colonizing armies and Spanish missionaries brought drama and theatrical performance to the Philippines and the Americas, and the colonial drama that appeared there retained its Spanish heritage (the Philippine vernacular drama known as *komedya,* for instance, derived from European romances brought to the islands by Spanish soldiers). The more developed colonial societies produced dramatists who worked within the forms and conventions of Golden Age drama. The Mexican scholar, poet, and nun SOR JUANA INÉS DE LA CRUZ (1648?–1695), one of the finest writers of the Spanish Golden Age, composed nearly thirty *autos sacramentales,* comedies, and *loas.* The theater of sixteenth- and seventeenth-century Spain, in other words, provided the world with its first truly global drama.

French Theater, 1630–1700

THEATER IN PARIS

During the second half of the seventeenth century, France established one of the most admired and emulated dramatic traditions in Europe. Yet the theatrical institutions needed to underpin this achievement developed significantly later there than they did in Italy, England, and Spain. The delay was largely attributable to external factors, most importantly the Wars of Religion between Catholics and French Protestants (known as Huguenots) that paralyzed the country from 1562 to 1598. The early history of the public theater in Paris certainly did not bode well for establishing an urban theatrical culture. The Hôtel de Bourgogne, Paris's first public theater, was built in 1548 by the Confrérie de la Passion, an association of Paris merchants and tradesmen that had been organized in 1402 to produce religious plays and thereafter held a monopoly on theatrical productions of all kinds in Paris. By the end of the century the Confrérie had ceased to perform plays and was leasing its theater for short periods to theater companies from outside Paris. But traveling companies often avoided Paris, because the cost of renting the Hôtel de Bourgogne was substantial, and because the Confrérie enforced its monopoly by charging a fee to companies who chose to perform elsewhere in the city. The capital lacked a resident theater company until 1629, when a permanent company was allowed to occupy the Hôtel de Bourgogne. In 1634 a second theater—the Théâtre de Marais—opened in a converted tennis court (the sport, popular among the nobility, was played on enclosed courts with a gallery for spectators; these structures often served as theaters in the seventeenth century). It housed a second permanent company, and after a fire in 1644 the theater was rebuilt with many technical improvements. Though Paris had not been without theatrical entertainment during the early decades of the 1600s—commedia dell'arte troupes performed in the city, farce was widely popular, and the foundations of a French dramatic tradition were laid by Alexandre Hardy (ca. 1572–1632), who composed hundreds of tragedies, tragicomedies, and pastoral plays—it was not until the 1630s that the theater became a regular pastime for Paris's middle and upper classes.

STATE PATRONAGE

The growing status of French theater during this time owed much to the support of those in positions of power. Cardinal Richelieu (1585–1642), chief minister to Louis XIII (1601–1643) and one of the figures most responsible for the centralization of power in the French monarchy, was a strong supporter of the arts, and under his patronage the theater acquired a legitimacy it had previously lacked. Richelieu awarded a subsidy to the theater company that occupied the Marais, inaugurating the practice whereby all major French companies received government subsidies. In addition, he had a theater built in his private palace, the Palais Cardinal (renamed the Palais Royal when the palace came under the control of the crown); it was the first in France to include the proscenium arch and side wings characteristic of Italian stage design. The strong link between theater and the French state that Richelieu helped establish was a defining feature of the reigns of Louis XIII and Louis XIV—and this link achieved its clearest institutional expression in 1680, when the latter merged Paris's two leading theater companies to form Europe's first national theater, the Comédie Française.

THEATERS AND AUDIENCE

Like the indoor tennis courts that preceded them and continued to be used as venues for theatrical productions, the public theaters of Paris were rectangular structures, typically long and narrow, with an auditorium for the public and a stage that included room, as the century progressed, for increasingly sophisticated technical machinery. The main floor of the auditorium consisted of a pit (*parterre*) for standing spectators with benches along the wall. The side and rear walls contained three rows of galleries, the first two of which were divided into boxes (*loges*). At the rear of the *parterre* and below the boxes rose the *amphithéâtre*, a section whose rows were raked to provide a better angle for viewing the stage. Both stage and auditorium were illuminated by candlelight. For much of the first half of the seventeenth century, scenic practice followed the conventions of medieval drama, with dramatic locales represented by the separate scenic structures called *mansions*. But as Italian scene design was adopted in the public theaters, the Parisian stage incorporated the spatially unifying principles of perspective staging. Any increase in dramatic illusion that might have resulted from perspective staging, though, was offset by the lively presence of the spectators, whose appearance and behavior in the Paris theater often constituted a performance in their own right. Perhaps more distracting to the actors than the unruly occupants of the *parterre* were those spectators who were allowed to sit onstage during performances. A cross section of Paris society, including the nobility and, on occasion, the king himself, made up the audience.

NEOCLASSICISM AND FRENCH DRAMA

The triumph of Italian scene design, with its concentration on single locations, was aided by the growing influence of neoclassicism on seventeenth-century French drama. During the 1630s and 1640s a number of French authors and intellectu-

An engraving from 1641 showing the stage, complete with proscenium arch and perspectival stage scenery in the background, of the Palais Cardinal.

als championed the "rules" that earlier Renaissance commentators had drawn from Aristotle's *Poetics,* and the principles advocated by neoclassical theory (including the dramatic unities) were given official sanction by the newly formed Académie Française. The authority and validity of neoclassicism were fiercely debated, particularly as its strictures might apply to the genre of tragedy. The most passionately argued of these debates concerned *Le Cid* (1636–37), a tragedy written by France's leading playwright at the time, Pierre Corneille (1606–1684). Those who attacked Corneille's play for not observing the principles of verisimilitude, decorum, and purity of genre were supported by the Académie, which entered the debate at the request of Richelieu. Although some writers continued to resist, the principles of neoclassical theory became widely adopted by French playwrights. That these principles could be artistically enabling as well as prescriptive is demonstrated by the formally elegant, psychologically complex plays of Jean Racine (1639–1699), France's greatest tragic dramatist.

French comedy also attained a pinnacle of excellence in the later seventeenth century, chiefly through the plays of JEAN-BAPTISTE POQUELIN (1621?–1673), better known by his stage name, MOLIÈRE. Like Shakespeare, Molière was a man of the theater as well as a writer, and his career as a dramatist is intertwined with the professions of actor and company manager. After years touring the French provinces, the theatrical troupe that Molière had helped found in 1643 settled in the French capital. By the 1660s the company had established itself in the Palais Royal, had been awarded an annual subsidy from Louis XIV, and was performing to great acclaim at court and before the Parisian public. Much of this acclaim resulted from Molière's dramatic contributions: farces influenced by the commedia dell'arte, court spectacles, ballets, and, most of all, the comedies of manners in which Molière offered lively and satirical portraits of French society. These plays were not without their controversies—*TARTUFFE* (1664–69), Molière's comic investigation of religious hypocrisy, was attacked on religious grounds and banned from

An engraving showing the performance of Molière's *The Imaginary Invalid*, in 1664, before Louis XIV and his court.

performance for five years—but they quickly became standards of the classical French repertoire.

THE DECLINE OF COURT INFLUENCE

By the end of the seventeenth century, Paris had established itself as the theatrical capital of Europe. The Comédie Française was the leading theatrical company of its time, and under the influence of Jean-Baptiste Lully (1632–1687) French opera had become equally renowned. The brilliance of the theatrical arts in seventeenth-century France owed much to the splendor of the French court, which displayed its power through the culture of spectacle. After Louis XIV moved his court and France's nobility outside Paris to the newly built Palace of Versailles in 1682, however, the role in French theater of the court and its literary tastes declined. As in England at the turn of the eighteenth century, in France public theater was left to thrive on its own terms. That Paris continued to exert a strong influence on European theater in the centuries that followed is powerful testimony to the theater that Corneille, Racine, and Molière helped build.

English Theater, 1660–1700

RESTORATION AND THEATER

When Charles II, eldest son of the executed Charles I, made his triumphant return in 1660 after eighteen years of parliamentary rule, both the monarchy and the public theater were reestablished in England. But the intervening years ensured that both institutions looked very different than they had before the Civil War. Restoration theater (1660–1700) was the product of a largely aristocratic culture, and it catered to a much narrower audience than had the theater of Elizabeth I and James I. Rejecting the Puritanism of the Commonwealth and Protectorate, upper-class Restoration London was an intensely social world, and the licentiousness, materialism, social competition, and love of wit for which the elite society of this period is notorious found ample representation onstage.

An early nineteenth-century engraving of the interior of the Duke's Theatre in Lincoln's Inn Fields during the reign of Charles II.

The emergence of this theater owes much to broader European theatrical developments. During their exile in France, Charles II and members of his court grew familiar with the theatrical culture that flourished under Louis XIV, and the theater that they helped establish upon their return reflected their taste for Continental stagecraft. Shortly after Charles II was restored to the throne, he issued royal patents to William Davenant (1606–1668) and Thomas Killigrew (1612–1683) to form theatrical companies and purchase or build theaters. Because the few theaters that survived the Civil War were unable to meet the technical requirements of Italian scenic innovations—sliding upstage shutters and side wings that made possible rapid scene changes, trapdoors, and flying machinery, for instance—new theaters were built to accommodate the new technology. The King's Company (managed by Killigrew and sponsored by Charles II himself) first used an indoor tennis court but soon was performing at the newly built Theatre Royal on Bridges Street; when this burned down in 1672 they performed at a new structure on the same site, the Drury

Lane Theatre. The Duke's Company (managed by Davenant and sponsored by the duke of York, the future king James II) used the Lincoln's Inn Fields Theatre (a converted tennis court) and, after 1671, the Dorset Garden Theatre. Given that the patented companies held a monopoly over theatrical production in London—merging in 1682 (after the King's Company fell into dire financial straits) to form the United Company, an arrangement that lasted until 1695—these buildings were the center of London's theatrical life.

PLAYHOUSES, AUDIENCE, AND ACTORS

Restoration playhouses were small structures when compared with the open-air theaters that were built in London in the late sixteenth century. The stage featured a proscenium arch with a curved apron (or open floor) extending into the audience and to the side. The main floor of the auditorium (or pit) contained benches, and these were surrounded on the side and rear by box seats and galleries. The play-watching experience in this setting was intimate. Restoration theaters accommodated no more than 600 spectators, and all were seated within 35 feet or so of the stage. Boxes allowed spectators to sit above the sides of the stage (and hence be prominently displayed to the rest of the audience), and by the end of the century spectators were routinely seated onstage. Auditorium and stage were both lit by candelabra, with the result that actors and their spectators were equally illuminated. Restoration actors often played on the forestage (near the audience), and they delivered their lines as much to the spectators as to the play's other characters. It was not uncommon for spectators, who could be quite unruly in the Restoration theater, to interrupt a play by addressing the actors themselves.

As these practices and behaviors begin to suggest, the relationship between Restoration spectators and the performances they attended was marked by mutual interaction and display. Attending the theater was a popular activity for the upper classes of London society and for the king, and the theater became a microcosm of this aristocratic world, its relationships (overt and covert), and its social distinctions. Men and women came to the theater arrayed in the latest fashions, and the theater became an arena for displaying symbols of social distinction. Women—some of them prostitutes—often wore masks (or *vizards*) to disguise their identities, and the rendezvous that were arranged through this and other stratagems mirrored the sexual intrigue being performed onstage. The introduction of women actors for the first time on the English stage contributed to the sexually charged atmosphere of Restoration theaters. Charles II, who had seen actresses perform on the Continent, justified their inclusion in the name of moral reformation, since their presence would eliminate transvestism—boys dressing as women. But the theatrical display of female bodies onstage became an erotic attraction in its own right, particularly when women actors dressed as men, donning tight-fitting, knee-length pants in what were called *breeches roles*. Contemporary moralists viewed actresses as a symbol of the theater's licentiousness; and while their general accusation was unfair, it was certainly true that some actresses did have affairs with theatergoers. Charles II, a well-known libertine, numbered the actress Nell Gwynn (1650–1687) among his many mistresses.

RESTORATION DRAMA

The drama of Restoration England assumed a number of characteristic forms. Even the revivals of English plays written before the Civil War—chiefly, the works of Beaumont and Fletcher, Shakespeare, and Jonson—were often adapted to reflect contemporary tastes and conventions. During this period heroic tragedy flourished; it featured larger-than-life characters, exotic locales, and elevated—occasionally ranting—dramatic verse. Other tragedies written during this time observed the principles of French neoclassicism, such as the concentration of dramatic action according to the dramatic "unities." Adherence to these principles was not as strict in England as it was in France, however, and Restoration tragedy continued to be influenced by Shakespeare and by earlier English dramatic conventions. In his 1668 *An Essay of Dramatic Poesy*, the period's most significant work of dramatic theory, John Dryden (1611–1700)—a leading writer of tragic and other drama—defended "the honour of our *English* writers" against those who overvalued French dramatic models.

But it was in comedy that the Restoration's achievements were most dazzling. Set in contemporary London, the Restoration comedy of manners featured gallants (or rakes), ladies, jealous husbands, cast-off mistresses, unsophisticated country visitors, fops, and clever servants engaged in often predatory games of intrigue and seduction. The wit and wordplay that characterize these plays reflect the importance of language, innuendo, and verbal disguise to Restoration stage interactions. Many of the plays contain a secondary plot involving conventional lovers, but the theatrical energies of the finest Restoration comedies—THE COUNTRY WIFE (1675), by WILLIAM WYCHERLEY (1641–1716); *The Man of Mode* (1676), by George Etherege (1636–1692); THE ROVER (written in two parts, 1677, 1681), by APHRA BEHN (1640–1689), England's first professional woman playwright; and *The Way of the World* (1700), by William Congreve (1670–1729)—are located in the central, equally matched "wit" couple. The lens provided by these interactions enabled playwrights to investigate fashion, marriage as a social contract, authenticity, masculinity, and social difference. By the end of the century, however, Restoration comedy faced opposition from a growing middle-class audience that rejected its libertinism, amorality, and elitism. When Jeremy Collier (1650–1726), an English clergyman, published *A Short View of the Immorality and Profaneness of the English Stage* in 1698, his attack hastened the end of a comic form that had outlived the courtly world of Charles II.

Eighteenth-Century Theater

The eighteenth century in Europe was characterized by stability and change; it was a period when the new rubbed uncomfortably against the old, and the outlines of the modern world began to emerge with unprecedented clarity. Throughout the century many of the artistic forms that had traditionally been preferred by the social elite continued to thrive. However, the social and economic transformations that would lead, by century's end, to the beginning of the Industrial Revolution hastened the growth of a middle class with its own interests, moral expectations, and tastes. Neoclassicism retained considerable authority on the Continent throughout the century, and the influence of classical ideals was evident in movements in literature, art, architecture, and music late in the century, but these were countered by the growing middle-class demand for nonelite literary and cultural forms such as the novel, which—with the help of an expanding popular press—by 1800 had become a literary form in its own right.

THE ENLIGHTENMENT

The eighteenth century was also the period of the Enlightenment, a philosophical movement centered in France that stressed the authority of reason and universally valid principles in human affairs. While some of the age's thinkers approved of the authoritarian rule of such "enlightened despots" as Frederick the Great (1712–1786) of Prussia and Catherine the Great (1729–1796) of Russia, the Enlightenment's main proponents challenged arbitrary authority and advocated limits to state power. The writings of such theorists as Jean-Jacques Rousseau (1712–1778), who argued that a social contract between individuals constitutes the only legitimate form of political order, established the foundations of modern democracy and were an important influence on the American Revolution (1775–83), the French Revolution (1789–99), and the Latin American revolutions of the early nineteenth century.

THEATERS AND ACTORS

The public theaters of eighteenth-century Europe offered a variety of entertainments—pantomime, comic opera, burlesque, and other popular performance forms in addition to serious and comic drama—to an audience whose numbers grew through-

A painting by William Hogarth of a scene from John Gay's popular ballad opera *The Beggar's Opera*. Note the audience members onstage in boxes.

out the century. To accommodate this increase in spectators and keep up with the latest trends in stage design and technology, the major theaters of the period were expanded, renovated, and sometimes replaced by newer, larger buildings. Established theaters and theatrical companies continued to dominate theatrical life in Europe's capitals, usually as a result of government licensing, though theatrical activity beyond these theaters enjoyed periods of popularity. In London (the capital of what was now known as Great Britain, following the union of England and Scotland in 1707), a number of unlicensed theaters operating in the 1720s and 1730s contributed to a lively theatrical scene that produced the long-running ballad opera *The Beggar's Opera* (1728), by John Gay (1685–1732), and satirical burlesques directed at the government of Sir Robert Walpole (1676–1745), who was in effect Britain's prime minister (a title not yet in official usage). In part as a reaction to this satirical

activity, the Theatrical Licensing Act, which confirmed the Drury Lane and Covent Garden as London's only licensed theaters and empowered the Lord Chamberlain to approve plays for performance, was passed in 1737. In Paris, the monopoly of the Comédie Française and the Opéra was challenged by nonlicensed troupes that performed as part of the city's seasonal fairs. These troupes, which presented comic operas, pantomimes, and (by the end of the century) comic and noncomic drama, eventually established themselves as year-round companies housed on the fashionable Boulevard du Temple.

Although theater as an institution changed less in the eighteenth century than in earlier centuries, scenic practice underwent a number of modifications designed to intensify the stage's visual realism. The symmetries of classical perspective were relinquished in favor of angled perspectives, which allowed the scene to be viewed from varying points of view, and mid- and late-century designers introduced picturesque landscapes, historical and exotic locales, and increasingly sophisticated atmospheric settings made possible, in part, by advances in lighting and sound effects. Another development that reinforced the increasing illusionism of the eighteenth-century stage in London and Paris was the removal from it of spectators, a change that was complete by the middle of the century.

Although by modern standards eighteenth-century acting remained stylized in gesture and vocal delivery, in this area, too, practitioners shifted toward realism—and away from rhetorical modes of delivery. David Garrick (1717–1779), the century's greatest English actor, was praised for his natural style of acting, and similar advances in realistic performance took place on the Continent. To be sure, these efforts to bring the stage closer to life were limited in their aspirations and accomplishments. But though realism would not become a fully formed theatrical aesthetic until the nineteenth century, the first steps toward it were taken in the eighteenth.

EIGHTEENTH-CENTURY DRAMA

In the eighteenth century, the genres of tragedy and comedy underwent a number of important modifications that reflected the tastes of a growing middle-class audience and its largely conservative moral outlook. Tragedy, which had traditionally been concerned with actions of the ruling classes, set in historical and mythological locales, was expanded to include the events and scenes of ordinary life. The pioneering play in the subgenre of domestic tragedy was *The London Merchant* (1731), by the English playwright George Lillo (1693–1739), which centered on the downfall and moral reclamation of a London apprentice. Comedy was similarly modified as the values of wit, ingenuity, and sexual titillation gave way to noble feeling, moral elevation, and what Sir Richard Steele (1672–1729), one of the new subgenre's earliest champions, called "a joy too exquisite for laughter." Sentimental comedy (known in France as *comédie larmoyante,* or "tearful comedy") became popular throughout Europe during the eighteenth century.

Traditional tragedy and comedy had their supporters and practitioners as well. For example, the French philosopher and writer Voltaire (François-Marie Arouet, 1694–1778) wrote intricate tragedies in the elevated style, and the Irish-born London playwrights Oliver Goldsmith (ca. 1730–1774) and RICHARD BRINSLEY SHERIDAN (1751–1816) championed "laughing comedy" against the drama of sentimentality. In Italy Carlo Goldoni (1707–1793) reformed Italian comedy by transforming the improvisational drama of the commedia dell'arte into a literary genre. While eliminating the bawdiness and nonrealistic devices of the commedia, he nonetheless succeeded in preserving the tradition's comic spirit. Overall, though, sentimental drama and the century's other dramatic innovations crossed and, because of their popularity, undermined the boundaries between the traditional genres. In the 1750s Denis Diderot (1713–1784), one of the leading figures of the French Enlightenment, advocated a genre midway between tragedy and comedy: the *drame bourgeois*, which would take the social and familial problems of the middle class as its subject. Though it produced few plays of note during the late eighteenth century, the *drame bourgeois* was an important precursor to the social problem plays of HENRIK IBSEN (1828–1906) and later modern dramatists.

GERMAN THEATER AND DRAMA

One of the most important theatrical developments in the eighteenth century was the rise of established theater beyond its traditional centers in Italy, Spain, England, and France. This expansion was most striking in the German states of northern and central Europe. Although Vienna was one of the leading centers of opera in the late seventeenth century and troupes of professional actors performed at courts and in public settings throughout German-speaking Europe, an organized German theater did not develop until the eighteenth century. The Thirty Years War, which was fought largely on German soil, had devastated the region in the seventeenth century, and the territories that in the late nineteenth century would become modern Germany consisted of numerous small states within a declining

Holy Roman Empire. With the region's resources scattered over a large area rather than concentrated in a capital or in other urban centers, it fell to the individual states to establish and support public theaters. The Hamburg National Theater, established in 1767, was a short-lived venture that paved the way for state-subsidized theaters elsewhere in German-speaking Europe. The Gotha Court Theater was founded in 1775, the Imperial and National Theater of Vienna in 1776, and the Court and National Theater of Mannheim in 1779. Of the numerous state theaters that followed these, the most significant were the Royal National Theater, established in Berlin in 1786, and the Weimar Court Theater (1791), which produced plays by two of the century's greatest dramatists, JOHANN WOLFGANG VON GOETHE (1749–1832) and Friedrich von Schiller (1759–1805). Though these theaters operated independently of each other, their founding reflected a broad cultural concern with the expression of German national identity.

Despite being a relative newcomer to the European dramatic tradition, German drama of the mid- and late eighteenth century was significant in its experimentation and the range of its literary achievement. Gotthold Ephraim Lessing (1729–1781), an early advocate of sentimental drama, wrote plays that dealt with national, social, and philosophical themes and was instrumental in freeing German drama from the influence of French neoclassicism. His *Hamburg Dramaturgy,* a series of essays published in 1767 and 1768, was one of the century's most important works of dramatic theory. A more radical break with neoclassicism was achieved by the playwrights of the *Sturm und Drang* (storm and stress) movement, a revolt against Enlightenment rationalism that flourished between the late 1760s and early 1780s. The drama written as part of this movement—including early plays by Goethe and Schiller—explored intense emotion, nature, rebellion against society, and violent action in irregular, often episodic plots.

Goethe and Schiller eventually rejected *Sturm und Drang* for the "Weimar classicism" of their work created between the former's visit to Italy in 1786–88 and the latter's death in 1805. Ranging over mod-

An illustration of a scene from one of Schiller's *Sturm und Drang* dramas, *Kabale und Liebe* (1784).

ern European history, classical mythology, and philosophy, the plays of this period pursued the values of harmony, wholeness, and aesthetic distance. This desire to provide Germany with a classical tradition reflected a revived interest in the classical world in late eighteenth-century Europe—the ruins of Herculaneum and Pompeii, which offered Europeans a mesmerizing portrait of Roman life preserved in the ashes of Mount Vesuvius's eruption of 79 C.E., were discovered in Italy in 1709 and 1748. The resultant drama embodied the aesthetic values of beauty, harmony, and form rather than the prescriptive neoclassicism of earlier centuries. At the same time, this drama drew its subjects from a Europe facing a period of political and aesthetic changes. Indeed, Goethe's masterpiece, the poetic drama FAUST (written in two parts, 1808, 1831), owes as much to the Romanticism that flourished in the next century as it does to the classical past.

Romanticism and Melodrama, 1800–1880

THE AGE OF REVOLUTION

At the end of the eighteenth century, two events fundamentally changed the political and cultural landscape of the Western world: the American Revolution and the French Revolution. The American Revolution severed England from its most prosperous colony and launched a radical experiment in democracy in the New World. A few years later, the French Revolution showed that even in Europe the old order was not impervious to change. Begun as a relatively modest revolt against the excesses of a king seeking absolute power, the French Revolution became radical when the lower orders and their revolutionary leaders turned against the aristocracy with increasing violence. The twin revolutions had far-reaching consequences, as neighboring countries watched them and their aftermaths with astonishment, enthusiasm, and fear. Soon, they would be directly affected as well, when Napoleon Bonaparte (1769–1821) rose from the French revolutionary forces to conquer much of Europe, propelled by a powerful army and the promise of freedom from local tyranny. Even after Napoleon had been defeated and the political map of Europe reordered in 1815 at the Congress of Vienna, what historians now term the Age of Revolution would continue well into the second half of the nineteenth century.

ROMANTICISM AND THE THEATER

The two revolutions changed more than the political order of two countries: they also altered how Western societies thought about themselves, with marked effects on cultural institutions and the arts. The French and the American revolutions had been inspired by Enlightenment philosophers such as Voltaire (François-Marie Arouet, 1694–1778), Immanuel Kant (1724–1804), and Thomas Jefferson (1743–1826), who had advocated new social organizations based not on religious beliefs but on rational planning and thought. But as the social upheavals of these revolutions grew more and more violent and unsettling, the Enlightenment insistence on pure reason lost some of its currency. Reflecting these changing historical and intellectual currents, the generation of writers, artists, and thinkers following the revolutions articulated the movement known as Romanticism. The Romantics did not reject the Enlightenment and its social experiments entirely, but they considered its more extreme claims with skepticism. They consequently placed greater emphasis on subjective experience and even on irrational desires and beliefs, which had been rejected by the Enlightenment. By the same token, they turned against the restrained, rational movement in the arts known as classicism. Whereas artists adhering to classicism respected the boundaries between styles and poetic forms, the Romantics created unusual mixtures and sometimes left their works deliberately in fragments. Ruins of medieval architecture were prized over classical buildings, and folk arts such as fairy tales or rustic idylls over Greek and Roman models.

These developments changed the face of drama and theater as well. Indeed, the battles between the advocates of classicist theater and those of the new Romantic theater were often fierce. The French writer Victor Hugo (1802–1885), whose preface to the play *Cromwell* (1827) served as a manifesto of Romanticism, aroused the ire of traditionalists by rejecting the unities of time and place, advocating the use of historically accurate stage settings, and calling for a theatrical art that included the sublime and the grotesque. So intense were the passions of classicists and romanticists over the future of French theater that the performances of Hugo's play *Hernani* (1830) at the Comédie Française were interrupted by sustained outbursts by supporters and detractors.

Like many of their contemporaries, Romantic playwrights developed an ambivalent attitude toward the French Revolution. In the early nineteenth century GEORG BÜCHNER (1813–1837) wanted to bring the legacy of the French Revolution to Germany, where the political system was especially hierarchical and repressive. He even wrote a tragedy about one of the leaders of the French Revolution—*Danton's Death* (1835), a sympathetic portrait of Georges-Jacques Danton (1759–1774).

An illustration, by Jean Albert Grand-Carteret, of the audience disturbances that followed the final scene of Victor Hugo's *Hernani* at its premiere in 1830.

the great Romantic writers either were not performed during their lifetimes or received limited, private performances or readings. Such plays written for reading only, or *closet dramas*, form the most significant genre of dramatic literature during the Romantic era. Among them are *The Borderers* (1796), by Wordsworth; *The Death of Empedocles* (1798; unfinished), by Friedrich Hölderlin (1770–1843); *Remorse* (1813), by Coleridge; *Manfred* (1817), by Lord Byron (1788–1824); *The Cenci* (1819), by Percy Bysshe Shelley (1792–1822); and the plays of Alfred de Musset (1810–1857). The two plays from this era collected in the *Norton Anthology of Drama*—Goethe's *Faust* (part 1, 1808) and Büchner's WOYZECK (1836)—are closet dramas as well.

THEATERS AND ACTORS

The increasing division between dramatic literature and theatrical performance had to do both with the preferences of writers and with the state of the theater industry. Poets distrusted theater managers and actors, choosing instead to write for the reading public only. At the same time, theaters—which, throughout Europe, continued to expand in size during the nineteenth century—catered to the tastes of the general public by putting on lavish spectacles. (When a similar estrangement between dramatic authors and theater managers had occurred in imperial Rome, Seneca likewise wrote only for readers or small recitations and left the theater to the popular entertainments then dominating the stage.) The demand for such spectacles drove innovation, and thus nineteenth-century theater history is dominated by a series of technical developments—including the use of gaslights (first introduced around 1825) and limelights, an early form of spotlight that greatly enhanced designers' ability to create theatrical illusions and effects. The public also desired equestrian as well as nautical plays, as new traps, elevators, moving panoramas, and, later on, revolving stages expanded the range of theatrical possibilities. Other developments were more in tune with cultural tastes and ideas dominant in the Romantic era. As

Other Romantics, such as William Wordsworth (1770–1850) and Samuel Taylor Coleridge (1772–1834), became much more disenchanted with the French Revolution, foregrounding not its social gains but its violence. But though they were divided in their attitudes toward the political and social upheavals of their time, the Romantics could agree on many other things. One was the eminence of William Shakespeare, which led to a revival of the playwright across Europe; French and German Romantics treated the Elizabethan playwright as their most important predecessor. What the Romantics admired in Shakespeare was precisely what classicism had rejected: namely, the mixing of high and low characters and of comedy and tragedy, as well as the fantastic events depicted in Shakespeare's romances.

CLOSET DRAMA

Despite the fascination with theater in general and Shakespeare in particular, Romantic drama was characterized by an increasing distance from the theater audience. Although plays such as Hugo's *Hernani* enjoyed controversy and success on the popular stage, many dramas written by

general interest in the distant past grew, audiences began to pay more attention to historically accurate costumes and sets. At the same time, celebrated actors such as England's Edmund Kean (1787–1833)—famous for his interpretation of Shakespeare—and France's Frédérick Lemaître (1800–1876) developed a Romantic acting style based on the expression of strong emotions. Such performances may have seemed spontaneous and authentic, but in fact many Romantic actors, who were given little time for rehearsal, followed manuals of gesture and expression.

MELODRAMA

Though most poets refused to write plays for the stage, a second group of writers were only too willing to supply the theaters of Europe with the popular drama they needed. The most popular type of play during this period was melodrama, which suited the public's taste for spectacle, music, and easily digestible characters and plots. The term *melodrama* is taken from the French *melodrame*, which joins the Greek word for music (*melos*) to drama; it was first applied in the late eighteenth century to plays with musical interludes that employ an easily recognizable dramatic formula and unambiguous moral contrasts. Drawing on a set of stock characters—the villain, the hapless maiden in distress, and the hero—melodramatic plots involve extraordinary coincidences and hinge on sudden revelations and encounters. France was the birthplace of melodrama, and its king was René-Charles Guilbert de Pixérécourt (1773–1844). Another prominent author of melodrama was the Irish writer Dion Boucicault (1820?–1890). Boucicault not only wrote popular plays set in Ireland, such as *The Colleen Bawn* (1860), but after spending several years in the United States he set several notable plays there as well, including *The Octoroon; or, Life in Louisiana* (1859).

Both in England and in France, many melodramas were produced by adapting novels to the stage. It was a time when the novel experienced an unprecedented rise in status and appeal, and many of the era's most accomplished writers turned their hands to fiction. Prime candidates for adaptation were the immensely popular novels of Charles Dickens (1812–1870). In France, novels by Alexandre Dumas père (1802–1870) and his son, Alexandre Dumas fils (1824–1895), were adapted by the two authors themselves, among them the former's *The Three Musketeers* (1844) and *The Count of Monte Christo* (1845) and the latter's *La Dame aux camélias* (in English known as *Camille*; 1848), which also became the libretto for Giuseppe Verdi's opera *La Traviata* (1853). Because of Paris's dominant cultural position, nineteenth-century French melodramas were imported into many European countries and more distant lands.

THE WELL-MADE PLAY

Alongside melodrama, French playwrights perfected another, related form of drama, the so-called *well-made play* (a name borrowed from the French *pièce bien-fait*). The well-made play was based not on spectacle and music but on complicated, intricately constructed plots. Playwrights relied on well-known techniques such as overheard conversations, mistaken identities, sudden appearances and disappearances, and other forms of confusion that culminated in the main scene of the play—the confrontation of the main antagonists—followed by the final resolution. Because everything in a well-made play led up to such a scene, it was called *scène à faire*, the obligatory scene that "had to be done." Masters of the well-made play included Augustin-Eugène Scribe (1791–1861), who wrote more than 300 plays, and the even more popular Victorien Sardou (1831–1908), who composed several plays specifically for the greatest star of the French nineteenth-century stage, Sarah Bernhardt (1844–1923). Sardou so dominated the second half of the nineteenth century that GEORGE BERNARD SHAW (1856–1950), a radical reformer of the well-made play, referred to his drama as "sardoodledom." Like melodrama, the well-made play was an extremely popular export, imitated everywhere.

Sarah Bernhardt in the title role of Victorien Sardou's *Theodora* (1884).

EUROPE AT MIDCENTURY

The ever-more-sophisticated spectacles, melodramas, and well-made plays were created in the context of Europe's larger economic and political developments. The Age of Revolution had come to a second climax with the Europe-wide revolution of 1848, during which the countries of Continental Europe suffered through protests, strikes, and overturned governments. The revolution of 1848 gave expression to the social consequences of rapid, though uneven, industrialization in various regions of Europe, including the large-scale movements of people to urban centers, the emergence of an industrial proletariat, and the triumph of a bourgeois class. What followed was a period of political reaction and a new focus on economic gains. It was a time when England and France in particular secured and expanded their empires, and from those holdings outside Europe they drew enormous resources. The financial speculation that attended such enterprises as the building of the railroads led a fortunate few to amass unheard-of for-

tunes, especially in the 1870s and 1880s. This new accumulation of wealth contributed to the development of extravagant and lavish spectacles, the expansion of theaters, and an emphasis on technical developments.

NATIONALISM AND THE THEATER

The nineteenth century was also the century of nationalism, as growing numbers of countries attempted to establish and affirm their own native traditions and values. Nationalists called for national theaters to showcase the new (or old) national self-consciousness, on the model of the Comédie Française, the foremost theater of France. Theatrically the most remarkable of those efforts was undertaken by Richard Wagner (1813–1883) in Germany. Wagner sought to integrate dramatic literature, music, and acting, as well as all the other components of theater such as set design and lighting, into a new and complete synthesis—what he labeled the *Gesamtkunstwerk* (total work of art). Single-handedly, he wrote the libretti, composed the music, and influenced the staging of his operas, which he called music-dramas, at the opera house in Bayreuth newly built under his supervision, the Festspielhaus (Festival Theater). Because Wagner wanted to immerse his spectators in the power of theatrical illusion, he inaugurated what are today common theatrical methods such as dimming the light in the auditorium and hiding the orchestra to encourage the audience to focus exclusively on the stage. Though Wagner himself relied on Romantic plots and folktales, many later theater practitioners, such as the Swiss designer Adolphe Appia (1862–1928), took their inspiration from him as they attempted to create a new and modern theater.

THEATER IN THE UNITED STATES, 1800–1900

The quest for national identity was no less urgent in the United States, but it took a very different form. Theatrical activity in colonial America was recorded in the 1600s, and the first theater was built in

The Astor Place Riot, New York City, 1849.

Williamsburg, Virginia, in 1716. Even after the American Revolution was over and independence from England had been won, many economic and cultural ties between the newly formed United States of America and its former mother country remained in place. One particularly strong connection was their theaters. In the United States in the late eighteenth century, theatrical activity was largely restricted to the cities of Philadelphia, New York, Boston, and Charleston, South Carolina, and the small but growing number of resident professional companies was dominated by English-born actors and actors who had been trained in England. While the United States produced its own playwrights—including Mercy Otis Warren (1728–1814) and Royall Tyler (1757–1826)—English plays constituted most of the dramatic repertoire well into the nineteenth century.

During the nineteenth century, a new and genuinely American theater culture appeared, owing in no small part to the country's first native-born acting star. Edwin Forrest (1806–1872) established an American school of acting based on a heroic style that relied on grand, physical gestures and speech that appealed to popular audiences. While Forrest stayed in America, Charlotte Cushman (1816–1876), the first famous American actress, moved to England once she had become well known, proving that England still had greater cachet and rewards for an ambitious actor. In 1849 the relation between the United States and England, and more specifically the difference between the English and the more physical American acting schools, led to violence. In New York City, both Forrest and the visiting English actor William Charles Macready (1793–1873) were playing Macbeth. The two men were longtime rivals, and when thousands of followers of Forrest invaded the Astor Place Opera House to stop Macready's performance, with thousands more outside, the mayor called out the National Guard. Guardsmen fired into the crowd, and at least twenty-two died in what has become known as the Astor Place Riot.

STAGING RACE

While Americans were fighting for cultural independence, there emerged in the United States another type of theater not found in England or any other part of Europe: the minstrel show. Initially its players were white performers in blackface, their skins darkened with burnt cork or shoe polish, but African American minstrel troupes soon appeared as well. Musicians and singers would form a semicircle, and they would alternate between songs, dances, and short bits of dialogue, mostly between two characters—Tambo (a player of the tambourine) and Bones (a player of the bones, a clacking folk instrument made of bones or wood)—seated at either end of the semicircle, or between them and an interlocutor who sat in the middle. The minstrel show relied on racial stereotypes, for whether whites represented African Americans, as was most often the case, or African Americans made up the troupe, they had to conform to the stereotyped routines that were initially established by white performers and demanded by the predominantly white audiences. In this way, the minstrel show, America's most popular form of theatrical entertainment in the nineteenth century, was part of the fabric of American racism even as it established an American, and especially an African American, performance tradition.

America's most popular play of the nineteenth century also dealt with race relations. Harriet Beecher Stowe's (1811–1896) immensely influential novel *Uncle Tom's Cabin* (1851–52), which some have credited with having helped to start the U.S. Civil War (1861–65) through its moving depiction of the plight of slaves, inspired numerous dramatic adaptations; the most famous was an 1852 version by George L. Aiken (1830–1876), which had the longest run—more than 300 performances—of any single production in nineteenth-century America. Aiken's dramatization was largely faithful to Stowe's antislavery stance, but many other adaptations simply reverted to racial stereotypes. These adaptations, known as Tom shows, helped establish "Uncle Tom" as a derogatory label for African Americans who appeared to make their peace with slavery and suppression rather than rebelling against them. While minstrel shows and the dramatizations of *Uncle Tom's Cabin* played a central role in nineteenth-century American theater, other representations of black life or slavery rarely appeared onstage. As so often in the history of drama, dramatists at odds with popular taste had to write for a smaller reading public instead, as the African American writer and former slave William Wells Brown (1814–1884) did with his play *The Escape; or, A Leap for Freedom* (1858).

Modern Theater, 1880–1945

THEATER AND THE MODERN WORLD

In the era of Romanticism, theatrical performance and dramatic literature had increasingly drifted apart. During the last two decades of the nineteenth century, however, serious writers were finally drawn to the theater once more. This did not mean that they sought to please the tastes of popular audiences. Indeed, modern drama was often characterized by a tension, even antagonism, between dramatists and audiences, an antagonism sometimes provoked by the playwrights themselves. Riling up audiences had been part of theater history for some time, as demonstrated by various nineteenth-century clashes in theaters, but now an adversarial relationship between producers and consumers became expected. The history of modern drama frequently involved confrontations between supporters of innovation and hostile audiences unprepared for new subjects, dramatic structures, and theatrical techniques. Whether by design or not, being controversial became the very condition for being modern.

Many modern dramatists earned their notoriety by engaging and often confronting audiences with challenging subjects and unusual forms. They wanted to restore theater's serious, moral function and to challenge, rather than please, their audience. To that end, they depicted the most vexing moral problems and dilemmas of their time. During the late nineteenth and early twentieth centuries, Europe and North America underwent a number of profound changes: new technologies, scientific advancement, urbanism, the proliferation of nationalist movements, changing class relationships, an accelerating economic transition from agriculture to industry, and new theories of human nature (including Marxism, Darwinism, and Freudianism).

Challenging the conventions and complacency of late nineteenth and early twentieth century society, modern playwrights addressed the impact of these and other changes. The Norwegian dramatist Henrik Ibsen (1828–1906) depicted public hypocrisy, restrictive social conventions, and such taboo subjects as hereditary syphilis. His play A DOLL HOUSE (1879), which exposes the hypocrisies and inequalities of Victorian marriage, was denounced in newspapers, sermons, and books. George Bernard Shaw (1856–1950), who championed his Norwegian contemporary in *The Quintessence of Ibsenism* (1891), wrote about prostitution and woman's emancipation in *Mrs. Warren's Profession* (1893) and expressed his idiosyncratic form of socialism in such plays as *Man and Superman* (1903). The German writer Gerhart Hauptmann (1862–1946) used his play *The Weavers* (1892) to call attention to the degrading conditions of weavers, while the Swedish playwright AUGUST STRINDBERG (1849–1912) depicted the ruthless battle between the sexes in MISS JULIE (1888). Even OSCAR WILDE (1854–1900), who delighted audiences with THE IMPORTANCE OF BEING EARNEST (1895) and other social comedies, violated conventional expectations with *Salomé* (1894), a play based on a sexually charged episode in the New Testament that describes the decapitation of St. John the Baptist. What united these playwrights was that all struggled with official censors; many of their plays could be presented only to small, private audiences because they were banned.

Though provocative themes and characters drew the most immediate hostile reaction, dramatists also deviated radically from the established rules governing dramatic forms. Many modernists criticized and ridiculed the most popular nineteenth-century dramas, such as melodramas and well-made plays. Ibsen and Shaw borrowed the conventions of the well-made play but interrupted its smooth, technically structured plots with lengthy dialogues, set speeches, and other devices that shifted dramatic attention from incidents to social and psychological issues. In such later plays as *The Dream Play* (1902) and *The Ghost Sonata* (1907), Strindberg abandoned dramatic rules for the logic of dreams. Seeking to capture the nuances of everyday life, ANTON CHEKHOV (1860–1904) rejected the stock characters and heightened dramatic incidents of the contemporary Russian theater for a drama of understatement, indirection, and psychological nuance. Traditional forms, when they were used, were adapted to new purposes, and new forms were developed to respond to a changing modern world.

THE INDEPENDENT THEATER MOVEMENT: NATURALISM

These modern playwrights could present their work to the public because of the opening of small, independent theaters intended to provide an alternative to the larger commercial theaters. Particularly important in this respect was André Antoine's (1858–1943) Théâtre Libre in Paris, which introduced the plays of Ibsen, among others. In London the Independent Theatre, founded by J. T. Grein (1862–1935), was devoted to the same task, and later Shaw and Harley Granville-Barker (1877–1946) would find a home at the Court Theatre. In Berlin it was the Freie Bühne of Otto Brahm (1856–1912) and in Moscow the Moscow Art Theater of Konstanin Stanislavsky (1863–1938) that made available performance venues for modern drama. All the theaters named above were associated with naturalism, a movement that originated in France in the 1860s and advocated that literature and art must faithfully present reality, with the writer and artist assuming the position of an objective scientist.

In its concern with the accurate portrayal of human beings and the external world, naturalism represented an extension of the realist movement that came to dominate European and North American art and literature during the middle of the nineteenth century and remains a powerful aesthetic current in today's theater. A reaction against the idealizing tendencies of Romanticism, realism seeks to depict contemporary life and society directly, unmediated by art's distorting conventions. The plays of Ibsen and Chekhov and the early plays of Shaw, which address social realities in recognizably contemporary settings, fall under this rubric. Naturalism differs from realism in that it relies on a more scientifically grounded understanding of the relation between individuals and their environment. Inspired by Charles Darwin (1809–1882) and his theory of natural selection, naturalists believed that humans are not free

Eleonora Duse as Rebecca in the 1906 production of Ibsen's *Rosmersholm* at the National Theater of Christiania. Rebecca rejects not only the Christian religion but also the entire structure of Christian ethics.

agents choosing their own destiny but rather are creatures determined by their environment, their physiology, and the social conditions under which they live. In the arts, the chief proponent of naturalism was Émile Zola (1840–1902), who influenced Antoine, Grein, Brahm, and other directors associated with naturalism in the theater. Dramatists who were strongly affected by naturalism include Strindberg and Hauptmann.

MODERN ACTING

Naturalism changed not only the nature of plays but also the modes of staging them. The movement led to an increased emphasis on realistic stage props and décor and a rejection of the histrionic acting practiced in the nineteenth-century commercial theater. The Russian actor and director Kon-

stantin Stanislavsky, for example, pioneered a new acting system based on the actor's psychology and emotions. For performances of Ibsen, he even imported Norwegian furniture to help the actors merge with their roles. What Stanislavsky did for individual roles, George II, the duke of Saxe-Meiningen (1826–1914), did for groups, introducing new systems of ensemble acting and bringing vivid crowds to the stage. Modern plays, with their new and daring female roles, also made it possible for a new generation of female stars to emerge and contribute to a truly modern acting style. Among them were Eleonora Duse (1958–1924) in Italy, Elizabeth Robins (1862–1952) in England, and Eva Le Gallienne (1899–1991) in the United States. In developing their signature roles, many of these actresses chose characters from Ibsen's plays.

AESTHETICISM AND SYMBOLISM

Naturalism was not the only movement that sought to break with the conventions of nineteenth-century theater. Indeed, the rapidity with which such movements followed one another, and their strenuous and public efforts to present a distinctive rationale for artistic innovation, became a distinctive feature of modernism. Aestheticism, which advocated the primacy of beauty over values such as social or political utility, was particularly associated with Oscar Wilde (although Wilde himself was well aware of the importance of societal forces; he expressed a commitment to socialism and suffered prosecution as a homosexual). Symbolism focused on rarified meanings, subjectivity, and suggestion rather than common idioms or everyday speech. Symbolist playwrights included Maurice Maeterlinck (Belgium, 1862–1949), Madame Rachilde (France, 1860–1953), William Butler Yeats (Ireland, 1865–1939), and Aleksandr Blok (Russia, 1880–1921). Symbolism also entailed a return to exalted and poetic speeches and a preference for simple, symbolic designs over the cluttered stage sets of naturalism. Symbolist design was championed especially in Paris, in Aurélien Lugné-Poe's (1869–1940) Théâtre de l'Œuvre. In England, the abstract sets of Edward Gordon Craig (1872–1966) had many affinities with symbolism, as did the monumental and abstract designs of Adolphe Appia (1862–1928).

THEATER AND THE AVANT-GARDE

The battles between different movements became more pronounced and complicated in the first decades of the twentieth century. A host of "isms," often announced through manifestos and declarations, emerged virtually overnight, and many disappeared as quickly. Among those that made a mark was expressionism, which arose in Germany at the start of the century. Expressionists, who advocated the externalization of psychic states instead of the realistic representation of life, critiqued the dehumanizing forces of industrialization in distorted, often nightmarish form.

Prominent expressionistic dramatists included Georg Kaiser (1878–1945), Oskar Kokoshka (1886–1980), and Ernst Toller (1893–1939). These and other writers championed technological advances that supported their artistry, especially in scenic design and stage lighting, as well as through the expanding medium of cinema. *The Cabinet of Dr. Caligari* (1920) was an especially influential expressionistic film. In the late 1910s and 1920s, expressionism also had an influence on such American playwrights as EUGENE O'NEILL (1888–1953), SUSAN GLASPELL (1876–1948), and SOPHIE TREADWELL (1885–1970).

A very different movement was futurism, which was initiated by F. T. Marinetti (1876–1944) and flourished largely in Italy and Russia. Inspired by an enthusiasm for technology and machines—the products of a belated but rapid industrialization in northern Italy—Marinetti sought to banish the human actor from the theater, relying instead on puppets, machines, and other inanimate objects. He also rejected well-structured plays in favor of short episodes of discontinuous actions and effects. Futurism was followed by Dadaism, which pushed the anarchic provocations of the futurists to an extreme. In the Cabaret Voltaire, which flourished in Zurich during World War I (1914–18), Tristan Tzara (1896–1963) and other Dadaists presented nonsense poems, manifestos, musical pieces, and masked performances of various kinds, often simultaneously. Like futurism, Dadaism quickly became an international movement with followers in the major European cities and beyond. When Dadaism declined in Paris in the early twenties, many of its adherents joined the movement of surrealism, which was led by André Breton (1896–1966). Influenced by the psychoanalytic theory of Sigmund Freud (1865–1939), surrealism focused on spontaneous associations, drifting thoughts, and dream images. The surrealists were also interested in earlier writers who shared their concerns, including the provocateur ALFRED JARRY (1873–1907), who had written crude and funny plays violating almost all strictures of decency and proper form. His scatological, grotesque, and irreverent play *UBU THE KING* (1896) became an icon of the

A photograph of the original 1935 production of Antonin Artaud's *Les Cenci*. Based on an Italian story of incest, torture, and patricide adapted by English poet Percy Bysshe Shelley, the play embodies the Theater of Cruelty that Artaud espoused in *The Theater and Its Double*. Artaud, in the role of Count Cenci, stands in front.

surrealist movement. The most influential theater maker associated with surrealism (even though he left the movement after a quarrel with Breton) was Antonin Artaud (1896–1948), who, under the name Theater of Cruelty, advocated a primal, physical theater inspired not just by ancient rituals but also by the slapstick comedy of the Marx Brothers. Artaud's writings on theater, which were published in 1938 under the title *The Theater and Its Double*, drew on images such as the plague, primitive myths, and the "animated hieroglyphics" of Balinese theater to establish theater as an antidote to the decadence of modern life.

The increasingly strident movements of the early twentieth century are often grouped together under the classification *avant-garde*. Originally a military term used to designate the advance corps of an army, in the early nineteenth century avant-garde became a political label applied to radical and advanced groups seeking social change. It was only in the second half of the nineteenth century that the notion of the avant-garde infiltrated the arts, allowing artists of various movements to present themselves as ahead of everyone else. Yet because the avant-garde groups maintained ties to their political roots, their formation must be understood in the context of the political history of the early twentieth century, and they often strongly promoted socialism, anarchism, or, as in the case of the Italian futurists, fascism. Indeed, the Futurists were extreme Italian nationalists, advocating war as an end in itself as well as a form of self-aggrandizement. The Dadaists, by contrast, formed in opposition to World War I and came to embrace an international socialism as a way to destroy the old class-based societies. They shared that aim with surrealists, many of whom joined various communist parties. Even more closely linked to socialism were the Russian futurists, who participated in the Russian October Revolution of 1917 and strove through artistic means to help it succeed.

POLITICAL THEATER: BRECHT

Socialism had an immense effect on many artists and thinkers of the first half of the twentieth century and later, including

A scene from the original 1928 production of *The Threepenny Opera*, a collaboration between the composer Kurt Weill and Bertolt Brecht.

those not associated with the more extreme avant-garde movements. The most influential political playwright was BERTOLT BRECHT (1898–1956), who developed a new form of drama and performance called Epic Theater, which relied on a number of techniques meant to interrupt the flow of plot and acting. Brecht believed that such interruptions would ensure that audiences actively ponder, rather than passively consume, the theatrical spectacle. He had also learned from the director Erwin Piscator (1893–1966) the value of bringing many art forms, including film (still relatively new at the time), into the theater, and he collaborated with composers such as Kurt Weill (1900–1950) on new, presentational forms of opera and other forms of musical theater. Brecht, Piscator, and Weill, together with many other European writers and theater makers, fled to the United States during the Nazi era and exerted considerable influence on theater and music there. Besides these émigrés, the best-known political writer in the United States was Clifford Odets (1906–1963), whose plays depicted the plight of working-class families and often included rousing calls for a socialist society.

CULTURAL RENEWAL: IRELAND AND THE UNITED STATES

Not all theaters in the early twentieth century were dominated by avant-garde and socialist plays. The Abbey Theatre (1904) in Dublin, for example, was devoted to gaining the cultural independence of Ireland, which for centuries had been under England's control; it thus followed the nineteenth-century movement for national theaters in European countries other than those—England, France, Spain, and Italy—that had traditionally dominated theater. One of its founding members, Lady Augusta Gregory (1852–1932), advocated a return to the Irish language, which had long been marginalized by English colonizers and settlers. The playwrights associated with the theater took varied approaches to drama. While Ireland's leading poet William Butler Yeats composed dense, difficult plays filled with highly poetic language and mostly set in a mythical past, JOHN MILLINGTON SYNGE

A photograph of the Provincetown Players' original production of Eugene O'Neill's *All God's Chill'un Got Wings* (1924). Paul Robeson, seated, played the lead role.

(1871–1909) wrote in a more colloquial, highly lyrical idiom. His plays, which undercut romanticized views of the Irish peasantry, proved controversial with the theatergoing Dublin public; so jarring was his presentation of rural Ireland in *The Playboy of the Western World* (1907) that it sparked theatrical riots and a long dispute that threatened the existence of the Abbey Theatre and the Irish Theatre Movement of which it was part.

Cultural independence was also the purpose of the Provincetown Players in the United States, a small theater troupe devoted to presenting new and challenging plays by American playwrights such as Susan Glaspell and Eugene O'Neill. Founded in Cape Cod and then moved to New York City, the company was part of the so-called Little Theatre Movement of the 1910s and 1920s in the United States. This movement, which was inspired by Europe's alternative theater movement of the late nineteenth century, provided the space for staging new and experimental plays without the financial constraints of the commercial theater, which by the late nineteenth century was dominated by New York's Broadway theaters and by touring productions of

successful shows that took star performers to theaters in an extensive network across the United States. Some modern playwrights, such as O'Neill, both participated in the Little Theatre Movement and managed to have their plays performed on Broadway, where the largest and most elegant commercial theaters were located. Broadway still retains its unique status, as demonstrated by the distinction drawn today between Broadway, off-Broadway, and even off-off-Broadway theaters.

TRAGEDY, METATRAGEDY, METATHEATER

While the era of modern drama saw an unprecedented explosion of new forms of drama and theater, a number of playwrights also sought to return to one of the oldest dramatic forms: tragedy. In the eyes of Ibsen, the bourgeois family and its struggle against the overwhelming power of the past created the conditions for modern tragedy to take place. A similar view led Eugene O'Neill to adapt Greek tragedies to contemporary America, as in *Mourning Becomes Electra* (1931), and to write new tragedies based on his own family, as in *Long Day's Journey into Night* (written 1941; produced 1956). Other playwrights in the United States followed his lead: such dramatists as Tennessee Williams (1911–1983), ARTHUR MILLER (1915–2005), SAM SHEPARD (b. 1943), DAVID MAMET (b. 1947), and EDWARD ALBEE (1928–2016) have all explored the intersection of the tragic and the everyday in American life, as characters grapple with the economic, social, and personal challenges of their modern world. Another set of playwrights turned to remote, rural settings in search of appropriate material for modern tragedies. The Spaniard FEDERICO GARCÍA LORCA (1898–1936), for example, set such tragedies as *THE HOUSE OF BERNARDA ALBA* (1936) in Andalusia, and Synge turned to the remote western coast of Ireland for *RIDERS TO THE SEA* (1904), a play that was later adapted by the Caribbean writer Derek Walcott (1930–2017) in *The Sea at Dauphin* (1957).

A second group of modern playwrights were also drawn to tragedy but did not believe that it was suitable for the modern world. Instead, they wrote plays *about* tragedy—what they called metatragedy or *metatheater*—that focused on the nature of role-playing and the relationship between reality and theatrical illusion. The best-known writer of metatragedies was the Italian LUIGI PIRANDELLO (1867–1936), whose plays—such as the influential *SIX CHARACTERS IN SEARCH OF AN AUTHOR* (1921)—are mirrored cabinets in which characters adopt roles, pretend to be mad, or philosophize, in self-referential ways, about the nature of theater itself. Another prominent writer of metatragedies was the French JEAN GENET (1910–1986). Originally a novelist, Genet turned to the theater because of his fascination with costumes and role-playing, and his plays create intricate layers of pretense that are never entirely peeled back. The turn to metatheater proved influential throughout modern and contemporary drama—nontragic as well as tragic—and a self-conscious awareness of theatrical reality is an important part of the twentieth- and early twenty-first-century stage.

WAR, REVOLUTION, AND DEPRESSION: 1900–1945

The explosion of forms, the emergence of politically driven avant-gardes, the return to tragedy, and the rise of metatheater were all responses to the unprecedented turmoil of the first half of the twentieth century in Europe and elsewhere. Nineteenth-century industrialization had effected profound changes in how people lived and worked, leading scores of men and women who formerly had labored in agriculture or trades to join the urban proletariat. The revolutions and wars of the first half of the twentieth century were fueled by these changes. Social unrest was everywhere, even in the relatively stable United States, and the Russian Revolution of 1917 was only one of its most striking manifestations. The unforeseen horrors of World War I, in which the European nations brought on themselves incalculable loss of life, showed once and for all the destructive potential of advances in technology and industrialization. European self-confidence, as well as the belief in

progress and the upward course of civilization more generally, was dashed. Peace brought only short-lived relief, as the worldwide stock market crash of 1929 and the depression that followed it threw the global economy into a crisis—one that, unlike the war, affected the United States as much as it did Europe. Faced with the Great Depression, President Franklin Delano Roosevelt (1882–1945) undertook, as part of his New Deal, an ambitious public works program, which included unprecedented sponsorship of the theater. During its brief existence (1935–39), the Federal Theatre Project rejuvenated theatrical activity across the country and pioneered such innovative forms as the "living newspaper," which addressed social and political issues in innovative, multimedia productions. Other changes affected the theater arts as well. Economic turmoil and racism in the South encouraged the great migration of African Americans to northern cities, which helped make New York's Harlem a cultural center for the arts in the 1910s and 1920s. African American musicians and jazz flourished, and so did such writers, intellectuals, and playwrights of the Harlem Renaissance as Zora Neale Hurston (1891–1960) and Langston Hughes (1902–1967).

In Europe of the twenties and thirties, fascism and Nazism were on the rise, and soon England and the Continent, the United States, and the world as a whole would be plunged into another and even bloodier war. The cataclysm of World War II (1939–45) brought to a close the era of modern drama that began with Ibsen and other groundbreaking figures of the later nineteenth century, and it cleared the way for new movements and playwrights who would explore the emerging outlines of the contemporary world. The period 1880–1945—which opened with Thomas Edison's first public demonstration of the incandescent lightbulb on December 31, 1879, and ended with the atomic bombing of Hiroshima and Nagasaki in August 1945—was a time of profound and unsettling changes that inevitably affected playwrights. They participated in the political, ideological, and social movements and changes around them, contributing with their plays and performances to

Figures silhouetted by the U.S. Constitution in a production of
Triple-A Plowed Under sponsored by the Federal Theatre Project
during the 1930s. This play, one of the earliest and best-known of the
"living newspapers," addressed the plight of American farmers during
the Depression.

urgent debates, problems, and opportunities. They responded to these unsettling times in their stark and jagged plays, in which all the old forms, structures, and certainties seemed to have fallen apart. In the process, they gave rise to the most innovative and influential era of theatermaking since the Renaissance. The varied forms of dramatic art that they introduced would influence the shape of theater for generations.

Postwar Theater, 1945–1970

THE POSTWAR WORLD

In political, social, and cultural terms, the latter half of the twentieth century was shaped by the second of two global wars and by the geopolitical changes that followed in its wake. World War II, which was fought between the Axis powers (Germany, Italy, and Japan) and the Allies (Britain, France, the Soviet Union, the United States, and China), claimed 60 million military and civilian lives, including 11 million who died in German-controlled concentration camps (6 million of them Jews killed in the Holocaust) and

as many as 200,000 who died as a result of the atomic bombs that the United States dropped on the Japanese cities of Hiroshima and Nagasaki. With much of Europe and parts of Asia devastated by warfare, the United States emerged from World War II as the world's dominant military, industrial, and economic power, though its unilateral supremacy proved to be short-lived. The Soviet Union, which successfully tested its own atomic bomb in 1949, established its influence over the countries of Eastern Europe, while the revolution led by Mao Zedong (1893–1976) ended with a communist government ruling mainland China. By 1950 the international landscape had been redrawn between two competing economic and ideological blocs—a capitalist "West" and a communist "East"—and the cold war that would dominate the world for the next forty years was well under way. Although the United States and the Soviet Union avoided direct military confrontation during this period, their struggle for ideological supremacy played itself out in a series of regional wars—notably in Korea, Vietnam, and Afghanistan—and in the internal politics of countries throughout Asia, Africa, and Latin America. They competed as well in the fields of science, technology, culture, and sports. No symbol was more resonant of this bipolar world than the city of Berlin, which was divided into western and eastern sectors by the Berlin Wall, a literal version of the "Iron Curtain" that divided not just Germany but Europe as a whole.

The 1950s inaugurated a period of prosperity for North America, Western Europe, and Japan, and the middle class established itself more firmly as the arbiter of social values. After years of wartime austerity, many in the West began to enjoy the benefits of a thriving consumer-oriented economy that catered to domestic households and an emergent youth subculture. On the surface, the 1950s was a decade of materialism and conformity, a period during which social stability was reinforced—particularly in the United States, where a new "Red Scare," like the one that had followed the Russian Revolution, inflamed anticommunist sentiment in the late 1940s and early 1950s—by the fears of enemy infiltration and nuclear war. Yet many of the social problems that would erupt in the following decade were already visible. The civil rights movement on behalf of African Americans took definitive shape in the United States in the mid-1950s, and London was the site of clashes between white youths and West Indian immigrants in the Notting Hill race riots of 1958. In 1954 France became involved in a war in Algeria that ended eight years later with the independence of its oldest major colony. Decolonization was under way around the globe, as the former holdings of European empires became newly independent countries in what was soon being called the Third World. Even in those nations under Soviet control—the Warsaw Pact countries of Eastern Europe—there were disturbances, as citizens in client states sought more autonomy. In 1956 the Soviet Union brutally suppressed the Hungarian Revolution, as it would Czechoslovakia's "Prague Spring" in 1968.

Driven by these and other impulses for change, an increasing number of challenges arose in the 1960s to the social consensus that had largely prevailed in the United States and Western Europe since the end of World War II. A growing number of intellectuals and activists condemned the inequalities of Western capitalism from the points of view of Marxism/socialism and anarchism, and to their social critique were added the voices of radical trade unionists, an emerging youth subculture, Black Power advocates in the United States, and members of such issue-specific movements as the Campaign for Nuclear Disarmament in Britain and the international protests against the United States' war in Vietnam (1961–73). These movements came to a head in Paris in May 1968, when an escalating series of strikes by students and workers brought France to a standstill and nearly toppled the government of Charles de Gaulle (1890–1970). Similar uprisings took place elsewhere, and it seemed—for the moment, at least—as if capitalism itself was under siege.

POSTWAR THEATER: EXPANSION, CONTINUITY, AND INNOVATION

During the years 1945–70 theater and drama underwent their own changes, many of which intensified trends that had emerged earlier in the century—while others signaled important new directions for the late twentieth-century stage. Even as London, Paris, Berlin, Moscow, New York, Toronto, and other major cities continued to serve and grow as important theatrical centers, more theaters were built and more residential theater companies formed outside these cities. Regional and provincial theaters were established, a number of annual theatrical festivals—such as those in Avignon, France; Edinburgh, Scotland; and Stratford, Ontario—were founded and expanded, and smaller theaters were opened in cities to provide opportunities for productions that the larger commercial theaters were unwilling or unable to undertake. The period also saw the founding of a number of state-sponsored theaters and theater companies, such as London's National Theatre, which was established in 1963. Like other new theaters and companies, these venues opened the way for new kinds of techniques, performance aesthetics outside the mainstream, and unconventional dramatic texts.

Though new theatrical theorists emerged, much of the innovation of these years reflected the influence of two earlier writers: Bertolt Brecht and Antonin Artaud. Brecht's Epic Theater—specifically, its presentational devices and acting style, as well as its view of theater as a medium for social analysis and intervention—maintained a powerful hold on European political theater, while Artaud's conception of a total theater that would surround its audience and address it on a visceral level had a profound impact on the environmental theater movements of the 1960s and the pioneering work of the Polish director Jerzy Grotowski (1933–1999). Both of these traditions helped the theater of the mid-twentieth century to meet one of its greatest challenges: rediscovering its performative uniqueness during an age when competition from film, radio, and television was increasing.

POSTWAR FRENCH THEATER: ABSURDISM

The psychological and social impact of World War II on midcentury drama was felt most immediately in France, where the absurdists established themselves as one of the most important groups of postwar dramatists. The term *absurdism* was not coined until 1961, when the critic and scholar Martin Esslin (1918–2002) published his influential study *The Theater of the Absurd*, and the dramatists who were included under this label are as notable for their differences as for their similarities. But the word does underscore a shared rejection of conventional dramatic structures and a skepticism toward rationality, language, and the coherent subject of traditional philosophy and drama. As they confronted a universe apparently bereft of meaning, divine or otherwise, they echoed the assumptions of Jean-Paul Sartre (1905–1980), Albert Camus (1913–1960), and other proponents of philosophical existentialism, while the dramatic features that defined their plays—nonlinearity, antirealism, lack of traditional coherence, nonsensical language, metadramatic awareness, and the mixture

of tragedy, comedy, and farce in a modern form of tragicomedy—owed much to the experiments of Dada, surrealism, and other avant-garde movements earlier in the century. Eugène Ionesco (1909–1994) and Jean Genet (1910–1986) are among the most prominent of the playwrights whose works show the influence of absurdism, though no figure in this tradition had a greater impact on the drama that followed than the Irish-born playwright SAMUEL BECKETT (1906–1989), whose play *WAITING FOR GODOT* (1952)—first performed in Paris in 1953—changed the landscape of postwar theater. Although it originated in France, absurdism exerted a pronounced influence on international drama during the 1950s and 1960s. Its challenge to arbitrary forms of order lent itself to social and political critique in the hands of Eastern European dissidents such as the Czech playwright Václav Havel (1936–2011) and dramatists living under repressive regimes throughout the Third World.

POSTWAR GERMAN THEATER: THE BRECHTIAN LEGACY

Postwar drama followed a different trajectory in Germany and the other German-speaking countries of central Europe. Most of Germany's theaters had been destroyed during the war, and the governments of both West Germany and East Germany embarked on major efforts to rebuild their countries' cultural infrastructure. The drama that was written for these theaters in the 1950s dealt mainly with social and political issues, and the subjects of guilt and responsibility loomed particularly large for a people confronting their collective role in World War II. Aiding the development of political theater were Bertolt Brecht's return to East Germany after his self-imposed exile during the Nazi period and the founding of the Berliner Ensemble in 1949 by Brecht and his wife, the actress Helene Weigel (1900–1971). The Berliner Ensemble put Brecht's theories of rehearsal and production into practice and in performing to audiences at home and abroad established Brecht's plays and the "Brechtian style" as major forces in the contemporary theater. In the German-speaking theater Brecht's influence was

In Eugène Ionesco's *The Bald Soprano*, a classic example of Theater of the Absurd, characters engage in nonsensical banter that calls into question the nature of communication in modern society. Pictured here is the 1950 production at the Théâtre Noctambules in Paris, directed by Nicolas Bataille.

manifest in the drama of a new generation of playwrights, many of whom adopted the Brechtian focus on social and political issues and employed Brechtian techniques, though usually without the doctrinaire and, at times, utopian Marxism that often shaped Brecht's plays. The Swiss playwright Friedrich Dürrenmatt (1921–1990) made Brechtian and absurdist techniques part of his pessimistic dramatic vision of humanity in the postwar world, while the German playwright Peter Weiss (1916–1982) brought elements of Artaud's Theater of Cruelty to a Brechtian concern with history. Weiss's dramas of the mid- and late 1960s—such as *The Investigation* (1965), which examines the Holocaust through the theatrical re-creation of war crimes testimony—were written in the style of documentary theater, a genre that other dramatists embraced during the decade.

POSTWAR BRITISH THEATER: THE WELFARE STATE AND ITS DISCONTENTS

In the ten years immediately following the war, the theater in Britain gave little evidence of the important role it would play in the history of contemporary drama. The country itself was undergoing historic changes: in 1945 Clement Attlee's (1883–1967) Labour Party achieved a landslide victory over the incumbent prime minister and wartime hero Winston Churchill (1874–1965), and the following six years saw the establishment of the British welfare state. One sign of the increasing role of government in society was the creation of the Arts Council of Great Britain, an independent, government-funded body that—for the first time in Britain—provided state subsidies for the arts. But these changes in society left little mark on the London theater, which for the most part was sustaining itself on an uninspiring diet of West End productions. Two events caused a seismic shift. In 1955 Beckett's *Waiting for Godot* was given its London premiere, and in the following year *Look Back in Anger*, by the playwright John Osborne (1929–1994), electrified the theater world; it was produced by the London Stage Company, a noncommercial company specifically formed to support new playwrights. Osborne's play expressed the

Jimmy Porter (played by Kenneth Haigh) plays his trumpet to distract himself from his cramped quarters and the complacency of postwar Britain in the original 1956 Royal Court production of John Osborne's *Look Back in Anger*.

restlessness and anger of a generation at odds with the materialism and oppressive class structure of Britain in the mid-1950s, and it reflected the disillusionment permeating an imperial power in the twilight of its ascendancy. Along with the work of the Theatre Workshop—a company in a working-class area in East London that, under the leadership of Joan Littlewood (1914–2002), produced plays by such working-class playwrights as Shelagh Delaney (1939–2011)—*Look Back in Anger* opened the door for a new generation of dramatists grappling with social class and other issues central to British national identity.

The subsequent development of social and political theater in Britain was influenced by Brecht's theories and practices; indeed, over the next two decades Brechtian dramaturgy and stagecraft found their widest application outside Germany in British theater. The Berliner Ensemble visited London in 1956 (the year of Brecht's death) and 1965, and its epic style influenced a number of left-wing directors, designers, and playwrights. John Arden (1930–2012) and Edward Bond (b. 1934) belong to the first generation of British dramatists who employed the strategies and techniques of Brechtian theater to strikingly original ends. The Brechtian turn in British drama received greater impetus in the aftermath of 1968, when a new generation of socialist playwrights—inspired by the revolutionary events in Paris and elsewhere and aided by the abolition of government censorship, which had been in effect since the Theatrical Licensing Act of 1737—made Brechtian devices a cornerstone of their more radical political drama. John McGrath (1935–2002), Howard Brenton (b. 1942), and David Hare (b. 1947) are only a few of the many dramatists who drew on Brecht in the 1970s and early 1980s. Among the women playwrights who sought to adapt Brecht within the politics of an emerging feminist movement, CARYL CHURCHILL (b. 1938)—whose plays range with deliberate abandon through space and time in treating their historical and contemporary subjects—is the most accomplished and widely known. This intensification of political playwriting after the events of 1968 was matched by a proliferation of radical (or "fringe") theater groups throughout Britain and Northern Ireland.

PINTER, STOPPARD, ORTON

Other playwrights and dramatic currents helped define postwar British theater. The influence of Samuel Beckett was apparent in the drama of HAROLD PINTER (1930–2008) and Tom Stoppard (b. 1937), two of the country's leading contemporary playwrights. Pinter combined the indeterminacy and linguistic evasions of Beckettian drama with the often gritty realism of interactions within the lower, middle, and upper strata of Britain's class-based society. Stoppard, who was born in Czechoslovakia, drew on Beckett in a technically virtuosic, philosophically sophisticated drama that also has more than a passing kinship to GEORGE BERNARD SHAW's "drama of ideas." Joining Stoppard in reworking the English comic tradition was Joe Orton (1933–1967), whose plays of the mid-1960s exploited the farcical, the macabre, and the surface gentility of English drawing-room comedy within an anarchic drama of sexual desire pursued across boundaries of gender, sexual identity, and class.

Director Elia Kazan and playwright Arthur Miller sitting on Jo Mielziner's set for the 1949 Broadway production of *Death of a Salesman*.

POSTWAR AMERICAN THEATER: EXPRESSIVE REALISM, METHOD ACTING

Theater in the United States achieved one of its greatest flowerings in the years immediately following World War II. While Europe found it necessary to revive—and in many cases, rebuild—its theatrical institutions, the Broadway theaters that represented the center of theatrical life in the United States had been left relatively untouched by the war. But with few exceptions—the plays of Thornton Wilder (1897–1975), for instance—this theater had produced little of substance since the mid-1930s. The rebirth of American theater that followed the end of the war resulted from the collaboration between a group of visionary theatrical practitioners and two emerging dramatists—Tennessee Williams (1911–1983) and Arthur Miller (1915–2005)—whose innovative dramaturgy was put to work in plays that captured the aspirations and anxieties of postwar America. The designer Jo Mielziner (1901–1976) pioneered an expressive or "subjective" stage realism that presented the theatrical categories of present and past, here and there, exterior and interior with poetic fluidity. Using the stage designs of Mielziner and under the direction of Elia Kazan (1909–2003), such plays as Williams's *A STREETCAR NAMED DESIRE* (1947) and Miller's *DEATH OF A SALESMAN* (1949) explored the shifting landscapes of memory and desire on a stage where the external world was at once materially real and evanescent. Such plays created a need for performers to convey greater psychological complexity, and it was met by contemporary developments in American acting. Continuing the interest in Konstantin Stanislavsky's psychological approach to acting that had marked the work of the Group Theater in the 1930s, the Actors Studio (founded in 1947 by members of the earlier company) promoted method acting, a performance style that emphasized psychological motivation, intention, and the importance of subtext in the presentation of dramatic characters. This approach, perhaps most famously realized in the theatrical and film performances of Marlon Brando (1924–2004), dominated American acting through the 1950s.

OFF-BROADWAY AND OFF-OFF-BROADWAY THEATER

Even as Broadway played a central role in presenting a revitalized American drama, its historically dominant role in American theater was challenged during the postwar years. In an attempt to diversify and expand theatrical activity outside the city of New York, a number of regional theaters were formed with resident companies presenting an annual season of plays. Among the most prominent of these are the Alley Theatre (Houston, 1947), the Arena Stage (Washington, 1950), and the Guthrie Theater (Minneapolis, 1963). Within New York, the increasing conservatism of Broadway theaters in the face of rising production costs led to the opening of off-Broadway theaters. Like the Little Theater Movement of the 1910s, off-Broadway theater involved smaller buildings that often were some distance from the main commercial theater district, and because these spaces served smaller audiences—between 100 and 499 spectators—they could be used to produce plays that the larger Broadway houses found too risky. European writers such as Beckett and Ionesco saw the first New York productions of their plays in off-Broadway theaters, as did a number of new American playwrights, including Edward Albee (1928–1916), whose play THE ZOO STORY (1959) became one of the defining off-Broadway works of its era. Off-Broadway also played a significant role in the careers of more established American playwrights. The 1956 production of *The Iceman Cometh* by Circle in the Square, one of the decade's most important off-Broadway theaters, revived interest in the plays of Eugene O'Neill (1888–1953) and thus helped lead to the Broadway premiere of *Long Day's Journey into Night* that same year.

But by the end of the 1950s, off-Broadway theaters were themselves dealing with rising costs; they therefore became more reluctant to gamble on experimental plays or on unproven writers and increasingly reliant on productions whose commercial success seemed guaranteed. In response, off-off-Broadway theaters were founded throughout New York. These low-budget theaters—which were located in coffeehouses, church buildings, various basements, and wherever else space was available—provided opportunities for a generation of younger dramatists with

Playwright Luis Valdez, right, founder of El Teatro Campesino, with the United Farm Workers president, Cesar Chavez, in front of New York's Winter Garden Theater in 1979. *Zoot Suit*, by Valdez, was the first Chicano play to be performed on Broadway.

strong antiestablishment leanings and experimental creative interests. During the 1960s—in Caffe Cino (1958), La MaMa Experimental Theatre Club (1961), Judson Poets' Theater (1961), and elsewhere—they launched the careers of such prominent contemporary playwrights as MARIA IRENE FORNES (b. 1930) and Sam Shepard (b. 1943). The often radical plays produced in these venues took part in the experimentation more broadly under way in 1960s American theater. For example, under the leadership of Joseph Chaikin (1935–2003), the Open Theater rejected the psychological realism of method acting for a form of acting rooted in improvisation, role-playing, and transformation. Communal theater groups, such as the Living Theater (which had been founded as an off-Broadway company in 1947), explored a radically participatory theater in which the division between performer and audience became almost imperceptible. Other theater groups—the Free Southern Theater, the Bread and Puppet Theater, and El Teatro Campesino, to name a few—used agitprop techniques, puppetry, and populist theater traditions to engage with social issues such as civil rights, the conditions of migrant farmworkers, and the Vietnam War.

AFRICAN AMERICAN THEATER

The years 1945–70 also saw the rise of contemporary African American drama. Drama and theater, of course, had played a central role in the Harlem Renaissance during the 1920s and 1930s, most notably in the plays of Langston Hughes (1902–1967), and the government-funded Federal Theatre Project of the 1930s had provided work for African American theater professionals through the "Negro units" that were established in New York and other cities. But it was not until LORRAINE HANSBERRY's (1930–1965) play *A RAISIN IN THE SUN*, which had an acclaimed run on Broadway in 1959, that serious African American drama claimed the attention of mainstream audiences. A product of the 1950s civil rights movement, the play also anticipated the more radical political and cultural movements of the decade that followed. African American theater of the 1960s reflected a deepening militancy; the plays

of Amiri Baraka (1934–2014), for instance, reveal the author's growing separatism and revolutionary convictions, while the Black Arts Repertory Theatre (1965) that Baraka helped establish in Harlem was at the forefront of the militant Black Arts Movement. These and other dramatists of the 1950s and 1960s laid the groundwork for such later African American playwrights as Ntozake Shange (b. 1948), AUGUST WILSON (1945–2005), LYNN NOTTAGE (b. 1964), and SUZAN-LORI PARKS (b. 1964).

Contemporary Theater

THE CONTEMPORARY WORLD

The term *contemporary*, always imprecise, is particularly elusive when applied to today's historical moment. In a world of accelerated change—where international events, technological developments, and cultural trends follow each other with dizzying speed—the past of even a few years ago can seem like another age. Much has transpired during the period from the end of the 1960s through the second decade of the twenty-first century, and these years could be subdivided into smaller segments, each with its defining issues and preoccupations. Over the time since 1970, a world has emerged markedly different from that of the postwar years, and the overall trends and transformations of those decades have led to a present whose outlines we are still coming to understand.

In the past fifty years a number of pivotal events have remapped the international geopolitical landscape, and two have been particularly important in their immediate and long-range consequences. As the result of intensifying pressure from the outside and the weaknesses of their own economic and social systems, which were unable to adapt to a changing global economy, the Soviet Union and its satellite states rejected communism in favor of Western-style capitalist economies in the years 1989–91, thereby bringing an end to the cold war that had defined international relations since the end of World War II. The fall of the Berlin Wall in November 1989 was the most visual symbol of this rapid change that took the form of peaceful and violent revolutions throughout the former Eastern Bloc, the unification of Germany, the dissolution of the Soviet Union in 1991, and the wars among the newly independent states of the former Yugoslavia. The second major shift was the rise of Islamist militancy as a social and political force. Islamic fundamentalists in Iran overthrew the monarchy of the shahs in 1979, replacing it with a revolutionary Islamic republic; in the 1980s, foreign volunteers joined an Afghan national resistance movement in what they viewed as a fight for Islam and drove the Soviet Union out of Afghanistan (1979–89). Such successes helped foster the growth of organized terrorist organizations, leading to the attacks on the World Trade Center and the Pentagon on September 11, 2001, and the subsequent wars in Afghanistan and Iraq.

THEATER AND GLOBALIZATION

Even more important in shaping the contemporary world than these geopolitical and ideological changes have been developments in the transnational spheres of capital and finance, corporate organization, information, communications, and culture. The world's economy has become literally global: the flow of goods, services, money, and information is increasingly unfettered, as traders move currencies and corporations reconfigure labor forces, production networks, management operations, and marketing strategies without respect to national borders. This process of globalization has been supported by innovations in information and communications technology—most notably, personal and network computing, cellular and electronic communications, and the rapid expansion of the Internet, which has made possible unprecedented access to information. Culture and the arts also show the effects of the global economy, as the products of high, popular, and mass (or commercial) culture reflect an ever-richer dialogue between the local and global. American teenagers read graphic novels that borrow from the latest in Japanese anime, while fans in Asia, Europe, and South America follow the steadily internationalizing game of American basketball. Music and other cultural products circulate between societies, and these encounters generate hybrid forms that draw on and transform both national and more localized styles and traditions.

British director Peter Brook's 1985 production of the *Mahabharata*, a Sanskrit epic, at Avignon.

Not surprisingly, the field of theater has adapted itself to—and been shaped by—this globalizing, technological world. Though one can still speak of national theaters, the activities of theater and drama have become increasingly internationalized over the twentieth and early twenty-first centuries. The 1913 Nobel Prize in Literature was won by the Indian poet and playwright Rabindranath Tagore (1861–1941), whose play *The Post Office* had been performed by Dublin's Abbey Theatre earlier that year; the 2000 prize was awarded to the Chinese playwright and novelist Gao Xingjian (b. 1940). Playwrights, theatrical companies, and productions cross borders with ease, and the encounter of cultural traditions has become both a subject and a collaborative aesthetic of theatrical production. The 1985 theatrical adaptation of the Hindu epic the *Mahabharata* by the British director Peter Brook (b. 1925) was produced at the Avignon Festival in France with actors from sixteen countries; over the next four years it toured internationally. More recently, the French Canadian director, writer, and performer Robert Lepage (b. 1957) has produced a number of theatrical pieces that combine international performance styles in narratives about history, migration, and cultural identity that span the globe. These, too, have been performed around the world. Other prominent contemporary directors—such as Ariane Mnouchkine (b. 1939), Robert Wilson (b. 1941), and Ivo van Hove (b. 1958)—similarly are international theater figures.

THEATER AND MEDIA

One reason for the internationalism of contemporary theater is the shifting relationship of the performing arts to the expanding field of media technologies. For much of the twentieth century, theater was forced to compete with a series of emerging media: film, radio, tape recording, and television. In a number of cases, it responded by incorporating these technologies into its repertoire of staging practices: onstage projections in Brechtian theater, for example, and the disembodied voices of Beckett's late plays. In the century's final decades, the line separating theater from film and other media continued to blur. The American playwright Sam Shepard's (b. 1943) reputation owes as much to his work as a film actor as it does to his theater work, while David Mamet (b. 1947) writes as frequently for cinema as he does for the stage. Plays are regularly adapted for film and television—vastly more people saw TONY KUSHNER'S (b. 1956) *ANGELS IN AMERICA* (1991–92) on HBO in 2003 than saw it in the theater—and videos of noteworthy productions of such plays as Chekhov's *Uncle Vanya* are widely available. As it becomes less reliant on specific performance sites, in other words, theater is more transportable than it has ever been.

The shifting boundary between theater and other media—and the resultant blurring of the distinction between elite and mass culture—is also reflected in the influence of postmodernism on contemporary theater and drama. *Postmodernism*, a term most frequently applied to developments in architecture, the visual arts, and literature in the second half of the twentieth century, denotes a style (or set of styles) that challenges the Enlightenment and modernist belief in metanarratives (i.e., overarching frameworks of meaning) and abandons historical analysis in favor of juxtaposing historical and contemporary elements in the mode of quotation or pastiche.

The theater has also responded to competing media technologies by asserting its uniqueness in the actuality of the theatrical moment and the proximity of live actor to spectator. This impulse, which marked the activities of theater groups influenced by Artaud and the performances of the Living Theater and other communal theater groups of the 1960s, manifested itself in the work of performance artists who began presenting their work in the United States during the 1970s. These artists, often working solo, appeared at a range of locations inside and outside the theater; their performances, which could be scripted or unscripted, often involved the performer's body in situations or encounters that addressed various issues pertaining to social representation, politics, and other matters. By the 1980s, though, even these artists were engaging with contemporary media culture in their performances.

INTERNATIONAL THEATER

In keeping with the overall trend of globalization, in the twentieth and early twenty-first centuries the importance of theater outside Europe and the United States has increased. The rise of national theaters outside Italy, Britain, France, Spain, and Germany is connected to the political and cultural nationalisms that gathered force in Europe and other areas of the world in the late nineteenth and twentieth centuries. From Mexico to Ireland to Egypt, plays were produced that embraced newly emerging cultural identities, often within theaters that were built and designated as national sites. The dramatists who helped drive these movements frequently were influenced by traditional and modern European dramatic forms, and in this sense their dramatic writing represented an attempt to bring Western modernity to local theatrical cultures. This pattern can be observed in Japan, China, and India, where Western-influenced plays entered ancient theatrical traditions. Many of the most influential figures in international theater during the past century brought Western traditions into dialogue with indigenous theatrical, dramatic, and narrative forms. The Egyptian playwright TAWFIQ AL-HAKIM (1898–1987), for instance—who lived in Paris for several years during the 1920s—helped establish an Arabic literary dramatic tradition by applying Western dramatic forms and techniques to traditional Arabic story material (such as *The Thousand and One Nights*). Al-Hakim's plays after 1950, like those of playwrights who followed in his footsteps, addressed the political and social issues of the contemporary Arab world.

POSTCOLONIAL THEATER

The internationalization of drama after the end of World War II received a strong impetus from the decolonization movements that led to the dismantling of Europe's global empires. India achieved its independence from Great Britain in 1947, and by 1970 all but a few of the British, French, and other European colonies in Africa, Asia, and the Caribbean had followed suit. In most cases independence followed intense campaigns by nationalist groups, such as the Viet Minh (the full form of its name means "League for the Independence of Vietnam") of Ho Chi Minh (1890–1969) in French Indochina and the Mouvement National Congolais of Patrice Lumumba (1925–1961) in the Belgian Congo. The newly independent countries faced their own formidable challenges: poverty and underdevelopment; corrupt, often repressive governments; outside political interference; economic exploitation; and tribal, ethnic, and sectarian divisions, in addition to the pervasive political, social, and economic legacies of colonial rule. The unbalanced power relations between indigenous peoples and long-established populations of white settlers caused wide economic disparities, which had political consequences. For example, in South Africa, which became independent of Great Britain in 1910, a system known as *apartheid* (an Afrikaans word that means "separate") restricted political power to citizens of British and Dutch ancestry and legally classified all persons within the country into one of four racial groups. Until it was abolished in 1994, black citizens were forced to live and work in so-called homelands (only those with a work permit could live in a city), were forced into a separate education system, and were compelled to carry government-issued passes for identification. Other former colonies, as well as those nation-states that achieved independence when the Soviet Union dissolved in 1991, have had to deal with their own legacies of colonial suppression.

The term *postcolonial* is frequently used in discussions of national identity in a world still coming to terms with the effects of colonialism—or, according to some, now living under a neocolonial system of new economic and cultural dependencies. The term is often applied to literature and other cultural forms—such as theater—within those nations previously subjected to colonial rule. *Postcolonial*, in this sense, refers less to the historical period after colonialism than it does to the inheritance of a

Actor-playwrights Percy Mtwa and Mbongeni Ngema in *Woza Albert!*, a play about apartheid performed in 1983 at the Market Theater in Johannesburg.

system whose tensions and contradictions—social, psychological, and cultural—remain very much alive. Postcolonial writers and other artists address the metropolitan centers that historically dominated their nations and societies (most prominently, London and Paris), but they do so as subjects who have been partly formed by those centers and their language, educational system, social structures, and culture. Literature, theater, and other postcolonial art forms establish relationships between native and colonial traditions; explore the influence of imperial ideologies, power structures, and discourses on contemporary perceptions and relations; and look for ways in which those who live in postcolonial societies can achieve new forms of identity and cultural resistance.

Postcolonial dramatists, whose work represents one of the most vibrant and important currents in contemporary theater, have been at the forefront of those seeking to rewrite the received traditions of Western culture from a postcolonial point of view. The Nigerian playwright WOLE SOYINKA (b. 1934), who studied in England and worked with the Royal Court Theatre in London before returning to his native country in the late 1950s, draws on the rituals and festivals of Nigeria's Yoruba culture as well as on European dramatic models in plays that address the impact of colonialism and the tyranny of oppressive regimes that followed in its wake. The West Indian playwright Derek Walcott (1930–2017) has also sought fusions of Western and indigenous performance forms, drawing on Caribbean folklore, dance, storytelling, and linguistic patois while celebrating the hybridization of the region's multiple cultures. Because language was central to the dynamics of colonial subjugation—local languages were usually subordinated to an "official" tongue and, in some countries, were even outlawed—the politics of language is an important subject of postcolonial drama. Many of these plays include non-European languages—Gaelic, Zulu, Bengali—within a broadened field of linguistic interaction.

The term *postcolonial* is also used to refer to playwrights who live in the former "settlement colonies," predominantly English-speaking countries where white settlers adopted their own version of British culture and whose relations with London, for most of the colonial period, were largely autonomous. In Canada, which became a dominion in 1867 and achieved legislative independence in 1931, drama challenging the dominant Anglo-Canadian culture has been produced by the country's French-speaking minority—including the leading Quebecois playwright, Michel Tremblay (b. 1942)—and such Native American playwrights as Tomson Highway (Cree, b. 1951) and DANIEL DAVID MOSES (Delaware, b. 1952). In Australia, which was settled as a British penal colony in the late eighteenth century, a national history that includes the displacement of the indigenous population has been explored by such writers as the Aboriginal playwright Jack Davis (1917–2000) and the white Australian Louis Nowra (b. 1950). And no postcolonial drama is more socially urgent than that which was produced within apartheid South Africa by writers such as ATHOL FUGARD (b. 1932), Zakes Mda (b. 1948), and Maishe Maponya (b. 1951), many of them associated with the pioneering multiracial Market Theatre in Johannesburg (established 1976).

THEATER AND DIVERSITY

The social, cultural, and psychological changes associated with postcolonialism, it is important to note, extend beyond the nations that had been imperial holdings. Many former colonial subjects were among the immigrants who streamed into Europe to work in the decades after World War II, and this growing population of naturalized citizens—South Asians, West Indians, and Africans in Britain; North Africans in France; Turks in West Germany—has redrawn the racial profile of societies that once were homogeneous. Throughout western Europe, cities have become more cosmopolitan—a cosmopolitanism deepened at the end of the twentieth century and the beginning of the twenty-first by the economic integration of nations within the European Union and the liberalization of economies in Eastern Europe. The effects on the contemporary theater of Britain, Ireland, and the Continent have been profound. Second- and third-generation writers

from immigrant populations—Hanif Kureishi (b. 1954) and Ayub Khan-Din (b. 1961) in Britain, for instance—who find themselves between two cultures and belonging completely to neither, have created plays that explore their often conflicted position, while playwrights from culturally dominant racial groups have produced a drama increasingly concerned with the changing face of nationhood.

A different version of this cultural evolution is evident in the United States, where immigration has been central to national self-definition since the metaphor of the "melting pot" was first used in 1782. Though it has traditionally been assumed that immigrants and their descendents would surrender their particular racial and ethnic differences for a dominant, shared "Americanness," this stance has been replaced in recent decades by an embrace of cultural uniqueness and ethnic/racial identity. Following the development of a contemporary African American drama in the 1950s and 1960s, the American theater has seen the emergence of Asian American drama in the work of DAVID HENRY HWANG (b. 1957) and others, Chicano/a drama, and—since the 1990s—Arab American drama. The growing political and cultural assertiveness of the continent's original inhabitants has also produced an impressive body of Native American drama. This drama is sometimes the product of theater groups, such as the U.S.-based Spiderwoman Theater, that draw on Native American storytelling and performance traditions.

More broadly, the theater has begun to include a wider range of voices and experiences that traditionally have been marginalized within, or excluded from, the stage. The roots of this expansion lie in the "identity" or "liberation" movements that have gathered strength in recent decades in Europe, North America, and other areas of the world. The contemporary women's movement, for example, which burgeoned in the 1970s, has produced a rich body of drama concerned with women's experience, the meaning of "woman" in traditional representations, and the changing manifestations of gender in the late twentieth and early twenty-first centuries. This drama has often formed part of an explicit feminist project to challenge male-directed theatrical practices, institutions, and notions of authorship, and it has sometimes been produced by companies employing newer, more collaborative forms of theatrical practice. Within the traditional theater, women playwrights have continued to explore new dramatic styles and subjects. Among those who have brought their voices to urgent contemporary issues are PAULA VOGEL (b. 1951) and Lynn Nottage (b. 1964).

Gay and lesbian drama has also gained a prominent voice in the contemporary theater. Though homosexual rights groups existed in Europe and the United States earlier in the century, agitation for the rights and recognition of gay, lesbian, bisexual, and transgendered individuals did not come to the attention of the general public until the late 1960s. The Sexual Offenses Act of 1967 decriminalized most sexual acts between adults in Britain, and the 1969 Stonewall riots in New York galvanized the gay liberation movement in the United States. Perhaps because of its interest in role-playing and its tolerance for unconventional identities, the modern theater has attracted an impressive number of homosexual and bisexual playwrights, including Oscar Wilde (1854–1900), Gertrude Stein (1874–1946), Federico García Lorca (1898–1936), Tennessee Williams (1911–1983), Jean Genet (1910–1986), Lorraine Hansberry (1930–1965), Edward Albee (1928–2016), and Joe Orton (1933–1967). Yet only in the 1970s did an openly gay and lesbian drama emerge in its own right. Among the leading writers of this drama is the American playwright Tony Kushner, whose two-part dramatic fantasia *Angels in America* was one of a number of plays during the 1980s and 1990s that addressed the AIDS epidemic. Important authors of lesbian drama include the playwright and performance artists Holly Hughes (b. 1955) and Lisa Kron (b. 1961), as well as Paula Vogel, whose most influential play to date is *HOW I LEARNED TO DRIVE* (1997).

THEATER IN THE TWENTY-FIRST CENTURY

As the works of these and other contemporary playwrights indicate, theater remains deeply responsive to social movements, cultural developments, and historical shifts and transformations. As the twenty-first century unfolds, theater—a medium at once traditional and new—offers a unique perspective on the issues and preoccupations of a changing world. One of the oldest of the arts, theater brings nearly 2,500 years of performance forms and dramatic texts to the current historical moment. At the same time, theater is one of the most immediate of the representational arts, grounded in the physical presence of the actor's body and the irreproducible occasion of live performance. Old plays are performed in new contexts, and the resulting dialogue frames both present and past in mutually illuminating ways. *HAMLET* (1600–01) has been performed thousands of times, but every time the Danish prince picks up Yorick's skull—a stage prop—he does it for different audiences in a performance interaction that changes from moment to moment. Its sensitivity to audience and occasion makes theater exceptionally responsive to the complex web of issues, relationships, and interactions that make up the present moment. For this reason, many of the contemporary theater's most important activities have taken place not in traditional theater buildings but in the squares, community centers, and other sites where people gather and work. Health and theater workers have used theater as a vehicle for vaccination campaigns in South America, AIDS education in Africa, and trauma therapy for those victimized by violence around the world. In these and other forms, theater remains deeply important in regions that may not have access to other media, in cultures that rely for education less on print than on oral modes of transmitting information, and with marginalized social groups in other societies.

Theater is more international than it has ever been, and in its emerging and time-honored forms it constitutes an important part of the global cultural landscape. As the expansion and proliferation of media continue in this digitalizing age of multiple entertainment sources, theater and drama carry on traditions that have been handed down for centuries, reworking these conventions in often striking ways and making them responsive to a new century's changing realities.

READING DRAMA, IMAGINING THEATER

For those of us who are used to reading novels and short stories, opening the text of a play can come as something of a surprise. Characters are identified before the story ever begins, in a listing (often labeled *dramatis personae*) that seems more like the entries in an address book than the stuff of literature. Instead of the designations "he said" or "she said" that embed what these characters say within a novel's or short story's unfolding narrative, dialogue is presented directly, with the speakers' names indicated on the left-hand margin. Stage directions indicate when characters enter or exit the dramatic scene, how they move around in relation to each other, and how they handle the objects of their material world. The very world they inhabit feels constrained—even claustrophobic—next to the expansive, shifting settings of *Don Quixote* or *War and Peace*.

Features such as these point to the essential difference between drama and more strictly literary forms such as fiction and poetry. While the term *playwright* means "maker of plays," the written text that we pick up to read provides only a part of the larger phenomenon we call *performance*. Its meanings, in other words, are not limited to the private worlds created by readers as they encounter words on a page. Rather, the printed play is a blueprint for something that happens in real time and space before an audience. The dramatic text in performance thus depends not on a single literary author but on the collective artistry of actors, designers, directors, and others involved in theatrical production. Even those plays—known as "closet dramas"—that were written with the expectation that they would never (or could never) be performed in an actual theater generate imaginative scenarios that have more in common with an audience's experience of watching a play than with a solitary reader's enjoyment. The fact that plays are written with some form of theater in mind—that they exist as dramatic scripts as well as literary works—ensures that the pleasures associated with dramatic art are rich and complex.

As a consequence, to read drama well requires a theatrical imagination attuned to the possible realizations of the dramatic script onstage. The first time we encounter an unfamiliar play, we seek and respond to its narrative—the story it is telling us. But we cannot fully appreciate the impact of such a play unless we consider *how* that story is told and what kind of performance it suggests. Reading plays is an active process—a creative collaboration with the dramatist that takes place in the mind of the reader. As a way of conceiving the dramatic world of a play, it may be helpful to start by envisioning its physical environment, or setting. Where and when is the play set? What and where are the key markers in that location (a door, for example, or a throne)? Some playwrights—particularly those who write under the influence of theatrical realism—include a great deal of information about the play's physical environment, making the stage materialize by supplying a wealth of particular detail. Other dramatic texts provide minimal, or no, setting specifications; for example, Samuel Beckett's *Waiting for Godot* (1952) includes the famously minimalist direction "A country road. A tree. Evening." Plays written before the nineteenth century often lack place descriptions and depend on the dramatic action and dialogue to establish what is onstage. The settings of Sanskrit drama, for instance, are suggested through dialogue and mimed actions, as when the courtesan Vasantasena mimes stepping into a carriage in Shudraka's *The Little Clay Cart* (ca. 100–300 C.E.), while the plays of Shakespeare and his contemporaries establish location through economical, highly evocative verbal description. Knowing something about the production conventions in use during specific periods can help you re-create how a play might have looked to its original audience, but it should not limit your imagination. As the history of theatrical performance indicates, plays are adaptable to other kinds of theaters, stage resources, and production practices.

When visualizing this physical environment, you may wish to make a rough sketch of the scenic environment (or environ- ments) indicated within the dramatic text, so that you can visualize how the characters and locale interact in each scene. Some theatrical terminology is useful here. In many theatrical traditions, locations and movement onstage are designated by a gridlike pattern. The section farthest away from the audience is considered *upstage*, while the area closest to them is *downstage*. Unless otherwise indicated, the sides of the stage are noted from the actor's per- spective; hence, *stage right* will be to the actor's right, and *stage left* will be to the actor's left. The midpoint of the stage is called its *center*. Thus, for example, an actor might be told to enter through a door up right and to move (or "cross") to sit on a chair down left. When imagining the layout of a particular scene, it is impor- tant to be aware of who is onstage and where at all times, even when these char- acters participate only silently in what is going on. Though the presence of such characters may be easy to forget, they may prove pivotal to the action of individual scenes.

Try to envision each character's appear- ance, as well as how much flexibility there may be in matching the bodily reality of a given actor to the physical description of the character. At some times and in some places, the correspondence between bodily appearance and role has been fairly conventionalized, with recognizable "types" recurring in similar dramatic per- formances. But even such roles can be taken by actors who vary in appearance, bearing, age, and manner, or even play against type. Throughout theater history, for example, what we now call cross- gender casting and cross-racial casting have been important elements of perfor- mance. As part of your effort to visualize the play in performance, you might cast known actors in your imaginary staging to make it more vivid, then substitute others to see how different personalities and styles of acting might shape a role differ- ently. Here, too, the text can be your guide. Is the performance required by the text naturalistic or stylized, comic or seri- ous? In some cases—the stylized theater of Japanese noh, for example—the answer is clear, and by imposing antithetical act-

ing styles you may violate the play's aes- thetic underpinnings. In most cases, however, access to a range of acting styles can liberate possibilities within the dra- matic text, offering new perspectives and opening it up to new theatrical energies.

In addition, it is useful to pay close attention to what characters say and how they say it. Language is the playwright's principal means for revealing characters and their dramatic world, and the play relies mainly on the spoken word to com- municate with its audience. Dramatic speech often reveals important informa- tion about the characters, including their class position, geographic origin (espe- cially through dialect), and personality. In the absence of a narrator who might make known to us a character's inner thoughts and feelings, speech is the conduit through which the play's figures disclose their hopes, fears, and intentions. Such characterization rests not simply on what a specific character says but also on what is said about him or her. Indeed, the richness of a dramatic portrait is often the product of multiple—and differing—accounts, observations, and perspectives offered by a play's characters.

Language, of course, is more than information, and nowhere is this truer than in the theater, where language exists not to be read but to be spoken. The words on the page of a dramatic text are designed for the mouth, and as chosen by the best dramatists their sounds fill and guide the mouth, position the body in specific atti- tudes, and occupy the stage with their acoustic power. When the playwright John Millington Synge wrote that "in a good play every speech should be as fully flavored as a nut or apple," he was refer- ring not just to his own use of Irish dialect but also to the linguistic and syntactical richness that makes all great dialogue a kind of vocal music. When bringing a play to theatrical life in your mind, read its lines aloud, feel the emotions they stir in your body, and enjoy the music that they create within your room. By yourself or with a friend, read some of the dialogue, noticing the contrapuntal rhythms that characters establish when they speak together. Even when reading translations—such as the ones included in this anthology, which were selected with vocal and other forms of performability in mind—you can feel such cadences and musicality. Along with the other sounds that a play may require—the ritualized foot stamping of the noh actor, the swish of regal costumes, Feste's lute in Shakespeare's TWELFTH NIGHT (1600–01)—the spoken word makes up the soundscape of dramatic performance. Reading with an awareness of this aural power can enhance your understanding and appreciation of drama.

While noting that the spoken language is a primary determinant of dramatic and theatrical meaning, we must not ignore the other elements that reinforce or complicate the acts of expression, communication, and signification. Three texts, in fact, work together in performance: the spoken text, the action text, and the subtext. Whereas the *spoken text*, or dialogue, is what the characters say to each other (or to the audience) during the play, the *action text*—whether scripted by the playwright or created by the director, the actors, or both—is the physical language of the play: the gestures and movements that significantly shape our understanding of the story. In highly conventionalized theater cultures, such as those of classical India and Japan, the actors' movements and gestures become intricate languages in their own right, signifying to an audience that understands their meaning specific relationships, emotions, and attitudes. But directors and actors of all eras have used the action text as a way of communicating meaning, even when the effect of such gestures and movements may be to undermine the sentiments expressed in the spoken text (as when the villain of nineteenth-century melodrama winks at the audience while professing his sincerity to an onstage character). *Subtext* consists of the unspoken thoughts, feelings, and intentions of the characters that underlie and prompt the action and spoken texts. The relationship between the subtext and its manifestation in word and action is as variable in the theater as it is in life. Sometimes language and gesture express the inner life directly and fully. "Language most shows the man; speak that I may see thee," wrote Ben Jonson in a prose collection published shortly after his death. But as *Volpone* (1606) and other plays by Jonson demonstrate, drama concerns itself more frequently with the discrepancy between private intention and public expression. Characters hide their meanings from others (and occasionally from themselves), feign indifference when they feel love, say only part of what they mean, pursue their designs under the unsuspecting eyes of those they interact with. Even silence—the choice not to speak—plays an important role in conveying contextual meaning.

The dynamic interplay of these three texts—and their interaction with set design, lighting, and the other elements of production—creates the depth and complexity of live theater. When we speak of an actor's interpretation of a role, or a director's concept for a production, we are thinking about the myriad choices that artists make, using these intersecting texts, to develop fully realized characters and to communicate with the audience through the play and its performance. The key word here is "interpretation," for the dramatic text as it exists on its own is fundamentally incomplete, suspended between possible realizations. Because plays are designed for performance, they depend on the activities of actors, directors, designers, stage managers, musicians, and the other theatrical practitioners who have served in different periods to usher them into life. And every choice that is made by these practitioners helps to realize, or interpret, the play in light of its possible range of meanings. Because the combinations of such choices are infinite, no two productions of a play are ever the same, and a great work of dramatic art has an endless capacity to surprise us with new experiences and insights whenever it is performed.

Because reading drama can and should resemble the process of actual production, you should approach the dramatic text as if you were a theater professional. Instead of reading a play to discern preexisting meanings, look for the places where a role, a scene, or a verbal exchange may be performed in different ways, and make choices as to how such components might be interpreted in the theater of your mind. What happens if an actor dwells on certain words in a speech as opposed to others? Where might he or she pause when delivering the lines, and what would be the effect of such vocal punctuation? What subtextual meanings do you see behind words and actions, and how might your actors bring them out? Consider the other elements of production as well. How would you light a production of your play, and what would be the effect of your decisions? How do the meaning and dynamics of a scene change if you focus your light on certain characters rather than others? What costumes do you imagine for your actors, and what would these tell us about the characters they play? Where would you position actors on the stage, and how would they move in relation to each other? Is the stage busy or relatively still during individual scenes? In those plays that lack detailed set descriptions, what theatrical environment do you envision for the action that takes place? Conversely, with plays that have extensive directions, what specific fixtures and objects might you choose to realize the desired effect? Although some dramatists have indicated that they expect their directions be followed exactly in production, would you want to modify the given directions in any way, either to accommodate different kinds of stages or to offer a more radical vision of the play and its dramatic possibilities? As you imagine your play in the theater, you can also consider how much—if any—of the direction provided by the playwright to employ and what possible impact on an audience such changes in direction might have. Finally, what stage might you choose for a production of your play: a traditional stage, with the audience seated directly in front of the action (the proscenium stage, for instance), or a different stage arrangement, such as

one in which the audience is seated on three sides (i.e., "in the round")? How do the meanings and implications of your play change when the spectators are so close to the actors and can see each other as they look at the stage?

Though reading a play in this way does not require extensive familiarity with the theater, your ability to appreciate the theatrical possibilities of a given play will be greatly enriched by the experience of seeing plays performed onstage. Go to the theater when you can; immerse yourself in the moment when the audience grows quiet, the actors enter, and the stage is taken over by a spectacle that is illusory but feels, in its most powerful moments, more real than life itself. And while attending the theater will enhance your reading of dramatic texts, the reverse is also true. Readers who imagine the theater as part of their reading become more informed and responsive audience members, actively aware of the choices the artists have made in interpreting dramatic texts and better able to evaluate their effectiveness. One of the many pleasures of reading drama is measuring your interpretation against actual performances of the play and comparing those individual performances with each other. Like the aficionados of other arts, you may develop, over a lifetime, your own repertoire of remembered performances and texts. And as you deepen your awareness of the relationship between what is written and what takes place onstage, you may fall under the spell of drama, which—whether enacted in the theater or in your own mind—is timeless yet always new.

THE PLAYS

THE PLAYS

GEORG BÜCHNER

1813–1837

WHEN Georg Büchner died of typhus at the age of twenty-three, he was known as a political activist and as a lecturer in anatomy but not as a playwright. Only one major play, *Danton's Death* (1835), had been published during his lifetime, along with his translations of two plays by Victor Hugo. Indeed, Büchner was doomed to obscurity for the greater part of the nineteenth century, as few knew his other dramatic works, which had never been staged. All this changed in the late nineteenth century, when the writer and editor Karl Emil Franzos rediscovered Büchner and made his works available, many for the first time. In the following decades these works, especially the unfinished *WOYZECK*, were greeted with enthusiasm and astonishment by many playwrights, who hailed Büchner as a fellow modernist ahead of his time. Unknown or overlooked for half a century, Büchner's plays eventually came to be seen as the hidden starting point of modern drama. Because *Woyzeck* seems oddly disconnected from its original context, it must be understood within the evolution of Büchner as an author who produced an astonishingly heterogeneous body of work ranging from medical tracts to political pamphlets. *Woyzeck* remains a singular play, but it is also the logical culmination of Büchner's unusual career as a thinker, researcher, political activist, and writer.

Büchner was born into a family of doctors, and after completing high school in Darmstadt he set out to follow in the footsteps of his father. He enrolled in the medical faculty at Strasbourg and quickly excelled in his studies even as he pursued many other interests. He continued to work as a researcher in Strasbourg and Giessen and completed a dissertation on the nervous system of a fish. Finally, he was invited to Zurich, where in 1836 he obtained a teaching post in anatomy. His medical work on the nerves of the human skull not only made a significant contribution to anatomical studies but also displayed considerable philosophical ambition, especially in its detailed discussion of philosophers such as Descartes and Spinoza. For Büchner, as for many of his contemporaries, the fields of philosophy and science were intimately related. Consequently, he did not hesitate to use his findings in science to critique philosophy. Büchner strongly believed in materialism—the notion that the world is composed only of matter and can be explained only through observation, experiment, and empirical evidence—and he shunned speculative philosophies of all kinds. His materialism, his work on the nervous system, and his skill in anatomy are central for understanding the power and peculiar force of his literary work.

More than his academic career impelled Büchner's move to Switzerland: he was a fugitive from the German police. During his student days, Büchner had become a political activist. He had been associated with several secret student organizations, inspired by the French Revolution, that demanded the unification of the scattered German small states, the overthrow of the monarchy, and the foundation of a republic. The brutality of the French government against striking workers in Lyon in the early 1830s radicalized him, and he came to believe that to create a just society would require completely overturning the existing laws and social structures. In 1834 he founded the Society for Human Rights and began to agitate on behalf of peasants and workers, whom he saw as exploited by a small leisure class of aristocrats. It was during this time that Büchner wrote the text that first gained the attention of his contemporaries and that caused him to flee from the police: *The Hessian Courier* (1834). In this pamphlet mixing cold analysis and impassioned prose, Büchner described how the tax and political system of his day—and even the rule of law—systematically exploited the many in favor of the few. The text was coauthored with the pastor Dr. Friedrich Ludwig Weidig, who tried to tone down those passages that seemed to call for an all-out class war. A precursor of Marx and Engels's *Communist Manifesto* (1848), *The Hessian Courier* also provides an essential context for understanding Büchner's later focus on class differences, exploitation, and oppression—especially in his last play, *Woyzeck*.

Weidig's changes were not enough. Betrayed by a police spy, the group around Weidig and Büchner was discovered, several members were arrested, and Büchner fled back to Darmstadt. Weidig died in prison two years later, probably as a result of torture. During this unsettled time, Büchner began to work on his first play, clearly inspired by *The Hessian Courier*: *Danton's Death*. Now a revolutionary writer himself, Büchner turned to the French Revolution for inspiration, but he did so with a critical edge. *Danton's Death* evokes the immense promise of the French Revolution but also its growing violence, indeed its violent self-destruction. The figure responsible for this self-destruction—representing the increasingly violent and radical wing of the revolution—is Robespierre, who finally wins out over the more moderate Danton. In Büchner's play, this battle over the course of the revolution is fought primarily through long political speeches, delivered both to small groups of revolutionaries and to the more public assembly. A number of these speeches are transcribed more or less directly from the historical record. In a letter, Büchner defined the role of the literary writer as an extension of that of the historian.

Büchner would publish no other play in his lifetime, although we have polished drafts of his final dramatic work and masterpiece, *Woyzeck*. Like *Danton's Death*, *Woyzeck* relies on historical sources. It is based on the criminal case of Johann Christian Woyzeck, a schizophrenic soldier who had killed his lover in a fit of jealousy. The main question in the case, and in Büchner's play, is what drove the lowly soldier to commit this crime. Woyzeck's public trial brought to the forefront the relation between law, oppression, and medical psychiatry, which had always been of special interest to Büchner. He was fascinated by the psychiatric diagnoses, the medical language used to describe the soldier's breakdown, but he was also intrigued by the moral and philosophical consequences of that breakdown. The play Büchner forged from the public record is a medical, literary, and philosophical inquiry into madness, devoted to analyzing the different phases of its protagonist's path toward a final, culminating crisis.

The play offers very little continuous action and instead sketches a character portrait of Woyzeck and his estranged relation to Marie, to his fellow soldiers, and to the world at large. Woyzeck is a low character, the quintessential victim who is driven to commit a crime. Büchner preserved the main motivation of the historical case, jealousy: spurred as Marie gradually falls for the better-positioned Drum Major, it ultimately drives Woyzeck to murder. But Büchner also added dramatic material to the case, paying special attention to the relation between Woyzeck and his superior, the Captain. The Captain

A production of *Woyzeck* at the Betty Nansen Theater, Copenhagen, in 2000, directed and designed by Robert Wilson and featuring music by Tom Waits.

demands many kinds of services from his subaltern even as he repeatedly scolds Woyzeck for having fathered an illegitimate child. The Captain couches his domination over Woyzeck in moral and religious terms. Such morality is too costly for the likes of Woyzeck, however; the soldier's poverty is a constant underlying theme of his existence. Like Büchner's other plays, *Woyzeck* details the psychology of exploitation: it depicts the reactions of the common soldier who suffers small affronts, constant degradation, and finally the humiliation of seeing the mother of his son fall for a rival.

There is a second mode of exploitation at work in this play as well. In order to earn extra cash, Woyzeck lets a local doctor experiment on him. As he follows a strict and cruel diet consisting of nothing but peas, medicine becomes another mode of oppression and of analysis. In the hands of the doctor, Woyzeck becomes nothing but a disposable guinea pig. Throughout the play, Woyzeck is being observed, measured, and observed. More humiliating

still, the doctor exhibits the increasingly feeble Woyzeck to medical students as if he were one of the performing animals that he and Marie had earlier seen at the carnival. Theatrical display, in *Woyzeck*, becomes one more instrument of degradation.

Woyzeck thrives on the collisions between characters and their styles of speaking. Each character employs a different idiom, ranging from Woyzeck's own heavy local dialect to the somewhat more standard speech of his army superiors to the Latinate vocabulary of the doctor. Büchner's language oscillates between abstract nouns such as "nature," "morality," and "necessity" and minute descriptions of corporeal symptoms charted by the doctor, including sexual drive, the consumption of food, and pissing. To this mix is added a metaphorical language of violence: at one point, Woyzeck compares the moon to a "bloody blade," anticipating the murder he will eventually commit with an old knife purchased for the purpose.

In attempting to dramatize the case of Woyzeck, Büchner drew on a number of his previous works. From *Danton's Death*, Büchner took an interest in theater and theatrical modes of display. Much as *Danton's Death* portrays the French Revolution as a kind of theater, complete with public beheadings, *Woyzeck* features the daily humiliation and display of its protagonist. From his minor early play *Leonce and Lena* (written 1836), Büchner drew a tendency toward social satire. A play loosely based on SHAKESPEARE's *As You Like It* (1599), *Leonce and Lena* is full of spoiled and irresponsible characters whose main motivation is boredom; at the same time, we see the people, hungry and desolate, forced to line up to cheer their hollow and often idiotic leaders. In *Woyzeck,* Büchner made profitable use of these overdrawn satirical characters, now transposed from satire into the dark key of tragedy. Finally, to capture mental illness Büchner drew on his novella, *Lenz* (written 1835). Similarly unfinished and unpublished in Büchner's lifetime, *Lenz* tells the case of a minor eighteenth-century poet, Jakob Michael Reinhold Lenz, who moves to a remote mountain village and suffers a breakdown caused by schizophrenia. The breakdown is described in ruthless detail, mixing medical language with poetic expression—as does *Woyzeck*. The novella tries to capture schizophrenia subjectively, focusing on the distorted perceptions and manic thoughts racing through the protagonist's head. In *Woyzeck*, Büchner tackles the same problem in a dramatic and therefore less subjective form: we, along with Woyzeck's superiors, observe the protagonist from the outside.

Even as it draws on Büchner's previous literary experiments, *Woyzeck* is a startlingly original play, for Büchner did nothing less than invent a new dramatic form, one suited to representing the tragedy of exploitation, humiliation, and mental instability. Its organization into short and stark scenes, loosely connected, is one of the most remarkable features of *Woyzeck*, and it anticipates early twentieth-century episodic drama. That Büchner never finished readying this play for publication has added to the confusion about the precise sequence and nature of these scenes.

While they form a marked trajectory—a downward spiral leading to Woyzeck's final breakdown—they are also disjointed and fragmentary, a series of brief episodes without transitions. This peculiar structure offers a formal analogue of Woyzeck's confusion, his inability to draw logical conclusions and to act rationally. As his mind focuses on single encounters, objects, and figures, so the play as a whole presents isolated moments rather than tightly interconnected scenes. In effect, Büchner applied a subjective narrative technique, such as that used in *Lenz*, to drama. Theorists of modern drama sometimes speak of the intrusion of epic or narrative modes into the theater, and *Woyzeck* is a fine case in point. In this sense, too, *Woyzeck* can be considered ahead of its time, blazing the way for twentieth-century epic and expressionist theaters that would showcase similar forms.

Woyzeck has had enormous influence on modern and contemporary drama. It inspired many writers and artists in the late nineteenth and the twentieth centuries, including the naturalist playwright Gerhart Hauptmann, who was fascinated by Büchner's revolutionary method of portraying mental collapse; the expressionist Frank Wedekind, who echoed Büchner's sexualized language of violence in his own work; and BERTOLT BRECHT, who took from *Woyzeck* its episodic structure and the technique of sketching characters with sharp contours. Many acclaimed directors, both in Europe and in America, have staged *Woyzeck*; notable productions include that of the Bread and Puppet Theater, a company that uses large puppets to stunning aesthetic and political effect. Heightening the influence of this play in the twentieth century was its borrowing by Alban Berg, one of the pioneers of modernist music, who used *Woyzeck* as the libretto for his best-known opera, *Wozzeck* (1925). This operatic tradition extends to the early twenty-first century, when the American director Robert Wilson and the musician Tom Waits created a new musical version of *Woyzeck* (2000) to critical acclaim. Equally important has been a film version of the play (1979), directed by Werner Herzog, with Klaus Kinski in the title role. These adaptations testify to the power that this fragmentary play still holds over contemporary theater.

Woyzeck remains one of the most unusual cases in theater history. Written by a twenty-two-year-old lecturer in anatomy, it lay dormant for many decades; once it came to light, it belatedly became a touchstone of modern drama. With its fragmentary, episodic structure, interest in mental instability, and detached, medical precision, it is now seen as the harbinger of modern drama, composed many decades before the plays of HENRIK IBSEN or AUGUST STRINDBERG. Indeed, because *Woyzeck* is more daring and radical than almost all examples of late nineteenth-century modernism, it thwarts all attempts to tell a linear history of modern drama. Somehow, Büchner anticipated what would become routine only much later. *Woyzeck*, like the few extant Greek tragedies, has survived to be read and performed because of lucky accidents—accidents on which theater history, both ancient and modern, often depends.   M.P.

Woyzeck[1]

CHARACTERS

FRANZ WOYZECK	ANNOUNCER	GRANDMOTHER
MARIE	OLD MAN	FIRST CHILD
CAPTAIN	CHILD	SECOND CHILD
DOCTOR	JEW	FIRST PERSON
DRUM MAJOR	INNKEEPER	SECOND PERSON
SERGEANT	FIRST APPRENTICE	COURT CLERK
ANDRES	SECOND APPRENTICE	JUDGE
MARGRET	KARL, an idiot	Soldiers, Students, Young
BARKER	KATEY	Men, Girls, Children

4,1

[SCENE: *Open field. The town in the distance.*]

[WOYZECK *and* ANDRES *are cutting branches in the bushes.*]

WOYZECK   Yes, Andres—that stripe there across the grass, that's where heads roll at night; once somebody picked one up, he thought it was a hedgehog. Three days and three nights, and he was lying in a coffin. [*Softly*] Andres, it was the Freemasons,[2] that's it, the Freemasons—shh!

1. Translated by Henry J. Schmidt. Büchner left no definitive version of the play, and even the ordering of its scenes is disputed. All versions of the text are therefore reconstructions; the following is based on the reconstruction by Walter Hinderer and Henry J. Schmidt. The numbers at the beginning of each scene indicate which of Büchner's four drafts supplied the text and, after the comma, the scene in that draft.

2. Members of a secret association, founded in its modern form in England in the early 18th century to promote Enlightenment ideals such as brotherly love and charity. Its secret hierarchies and rituals have long made Freemasonry a target for conspiracy theories.

ANDRES [*sings*]

5
        I saw two big rabbits
        Chewing up the green, green grass . . .

WOYZECK   Shh! Something's moving!

ANDRES

        Chewing up the green, green grass
        Till it was all gone.

10 WOYZECK   Something's moving behind me, under me. [*Stamps on the ground.*] Hollow—you hear that? It's all hollow down there. The Freemasons!

ANDRES   I'm scared.

WOYZECK   It's so strangely quiet. You feel like holding your breath.

15   Andres!

ANDRES   What?

WOYZECK   Say something! [*Stares off into the distance.*] Andres! Look how bright it is! There's fire raging around the sky, and a noise is coming down like trumpets. It's coming closer! Let's go! Don't look back! [*Drags him into the bushes.*]

20 ANDRES [*after a pause*]   Woyzeck! Do you still hear it?

WOYZECK   Quiet, it's all quiet, like the world was dead.

ANDRES   Listen! They're drumming. We've got to get back.

4,2

[SCENE: *The town.*]

      [MARIE *with her* CHILD *at the window.* MARGRET. *A military patrol goes by, the* DRUM MAJOR *leading.*]

MARIE [*rocking the* CHILD *in her arms*]   Hey, boy! Ta-ra-ra-ra! You hear it? They're coming.

MARGRET   What a man, like a tree!

MARIE   He stands on his feet like a lion.

      [*The* DRUM MAJOR *greets them.*]

5 MARGRET   Say, what a friendly look you gave him, neighbor—we're not used to that from you.

MARIE [*sings*]

        A soldier is a handsome fellow . . .

MARGRET   Your eyes are still shining.

MARIE   So what? Why don't you take *your* eyes to the Jew[3] and have them
10 polished—maybe they'll shine enough to sell as two buttons.

MARGRET   What? Why, Mrs. Virgin, I'm a decent woman, but you—you can stare through seven pairs of leather pants!

MARIE   Bitch! [*Slams the window shut.*] Come, my boy. What do they want from us, anyway? You're only the poor child of a whore, and you make your
15 mother happy with your bastard face. Ta-ta!

      [*Sings.*]

---

3. That is, the pawnbroker (historically, moneylending and pawnbroking were among the few professions open to Jews).

Maiden, now what's to be done?
You've got no ring, you've a son.
Oh, why worry my head,
I'll sing here at your bed:
20   Rockabye baby, my baby are you,
Nobody cares what I do.

Johnny, hitch up your six horses fleet,
Go bring them something to eat.
From oats they will turn,
25   From water they'll turn,
Only cool wine will be fine, hooray!
Only cool wine will be fine.

[*A knock at the window.*]

MARIE   Who's that? Is that you, Franz? Come on in!
WOYZECK   I can't. Have to go to roll call.
30 MARIE   What's the matter with you, Franz?
WOYZECK [*mysteriously*]   Marie, there was something out there again—a lot.
Isn't it written: "And lo, the smoke of the country went up as the smoke of
a furnace"?[4]
MARIE   Man alive!
35 WOYZECK   It followed me until I reached town. What's going to happen?
MARIE   Franz!
WOYZECK   I've got to go.
[*He leaves.*]

MARIE   That man! He's so upset. He didn't look at his own child. He'll go
crazy with those thoughts of his. Why are you so quiet, son? Are you
40   scared? It's getting so dark, you'd think you were blind. Usually there's a
light shining in. I can't stand it. I'm frightened.
[*Goes off.*]

4,3

[SCENE: *Carnival booths. Lights. People.*]

OLD MAN; DANCING CHILD

How long we live, just time will tell,
We all have got to die,
We know that very well!

[WOYZECK]   Hey! Whee! Poor man, old man! Poor child! Young child! Hey,
5   Marie, shall I carry you? . . . Beautiful world!
CARNIVAL BARKER [*in front of a booth*]   Gentlemen! Gentlemen! [*Points to a
monkey.*] Look at this creature, as God made it: he's nothing, nothing at all.
Now see the effect of art: he walks upright, wears coat and pants, carries a
sword! Ho! Take a bow! Good boy. Give me a kiss! [*Monkey trumpets.*]
10   The little dummy is musical!

---

4. Genesis 19.28 (describing the destruction of the cities of Sodom and Gomorrah).

Ladies and gentlemen, here is to be seen the astronomical horse and the little cannery-birds[5]—they're favorites of all potentates of Europe and members of all learned societies. They'll tell you everything: how old you are, how many children you have, what kind of illnesses. [*Points to the monkey.*] He shoots a pistol, stands on one leg. It's all a matter of upbringing; he has merely a beastly reason, or rather a very reasonable beastliness— he's no brutish individual like a lot of people, present company excepted. Enter! The presentation will begin. The commencement of the beginning will start immediately.

Observe the progress of civilization. Everything progresses—a horse, a monkey, a cannery-bird. The monkey is already a soldier—that's not much, it's the lowest level of the human race!

[WOYZECK]   Want to?

MARIE   All right. It ought to be good. Look at his tassels, and the woman's got pants on!

[SERGEANT. DRUM MAJOR. MARIE. WOYZECK.]

SERGEANT   Hold it! Over there. Look at her! What a piece!

DRUM MAJOR   Damn! Good enough for the propagation of cavalry regiments and the breeding of drum majors.

SERGEANT   Look how she holds her head—you'd think that black hair would pull her down like a weight. And those eyes, black . . .

DRUM MAJOR   It's like looking down a well or a chimney. Come on, after her!

MARIE   Those lights!

WOYZECK   Yeah, like a big black cat with fiery eyes. Hey, what a night!

[*Inside the booth.*]

CARNIVAL ANNOUNCER [*presenting a horse*]   Show your talent! Show your beastly wisdom! Put human society to shame! Gentlemen, this animal that you see here, with a tail on his body, with his four hooves, is a member of all learned societies, is a professor at our university, with whom the students learn to ride and fight duels. That was simple comprehension! Now think with double *raison*.[6] What do you do when you think with double *raison*? Is there in the learned *société*[7] an ass? [*The horse shakes its head.*] Now you understand double *raison*! That is beastiognomy. Yes, that's no brutish individual, that's a person! A human being, a beastly human being, but still an animal, a *bête*.[8] [*The horse behaves improperly.*] That's right, put *société* to shame! You see, the beast is still nature, unspoiled nature! Take a lesson from him. Go ask the doctor, it's very unhealthy! It is written: man, be natural; you were created from dust, sand, dirt.[9] Do you want to be more than dust, sand, dirt? Observe his power of reason! He can add, but he can't count on his fingers—why is that? He simply can't express himself, explain himself—he's a transformed person! Tell the gentlemen what time it is. Who among the ladies and gentlemen has a watch—a watch?

DRUM MAJOR   A watch! [*Slowly and grandly he pulls a watch out of his pocket.*] There you are, sir.

---

5. Canaries, perhaps; the German word used here, *Kanaillevögele*, literally means "riffraff birds."
6. Reason (French).

7. Society (French).
8. Beast, animal (French).
9. For the creation of man from dust, see Genesis 2.7.

MARIE This I've got to see.

    [*She climbs into the first row. The* DRUM MAJOR *helps her.*]

4,4

[SCENE: *Room.*]

    [MARIE *sits with her* CHILD *on her lap, a piece of mirror in her hand.*]

MARIE [*looks at herself in the mirror*] These stones really sparkle! What kind are they? What did he say?—Go to sleep, son! Shut your eyes tight. [*The* CHILD *covers his eyes with his hands.*] Tighter—stay quiet or he'll come get you.

    [*Sings.*]

5

Close up your shop, fair maid,
A gypsy boy's in the glade.
He'll lead you by the hand
Off into gypsyland.

[*Looks in the mirror again.*] It must be gold. The likes of us only have a little
10 corner in the world and a little piece of mirror, but I have just as red a mouth as the great ladies with their mirrors from top to toe and their handsome lords who kiss their hands. I'm just a poor woman. [*The* CHILD *sits up.*] Shh, son, eyes shut—look, the sandman! He's running along the wall. [*She flashes with the mirror.*] Eyes shut, or he'll look into them, and you'll go blind.

    [WOYZECK *enters behind her. She jumps up with her hands over her ears.*]

15 WOYZECK What's that you got there?

MARIE Nothing.

WOYZECK Something's shining under your fingers.

MARIE An earring—I found it.

WOYZECK I've never found anything like that. Two at once.

20 MARIE What am I—a whore?

WOYZECK It's all right, Marie.—Look, the boy's asleep. Lift him up under his arms, the chair's hurting him. There are shiny drops on his forehead; everything under the sun is work—sweat, even in our sleep. Us poor people! Here's some more money, Marie, my pay and some from my captain.

25 MARIE Bless you, Franz.

WOYZECK I have to go. See you tonight, Marie. Bye.

MARIE [*alone, after a pause*] What a bitch I am. I could stab myself.—Oh, what a world! Everything goes to hell anyhow, man and woman alike.

4,5

[*The* CAPTAIN. WOYZECK.]

    [*The* CAPTAIN *in a chair,* WOYZECK *shaves him.*]

CAPTAIN Take it easy, Woyzeck, take it easy. One thing at a time; you're making me quite dizzy. You're going to finish early today—what am I supposed to do with the extra ten minutes? Woyzeck, just think, you've still got a good thirty years to live, thirty years! That's 360 months, and days, hours,
5 minutes! What are you going to do with that ungodly amount of time? Get organized, Woyzeck.

WOYZECK Yes, Cap'n.

CAPTAIN I fear for the world when I think about eternity. Activity, Woyzeck,
activity! Eternal, that's eternal, that's eternal—you realize that, of course.
10 But then again it's not eternal, it's only a moment, yes, a moment.—Woyzeck,
it frightens me to think that the earth rotates in one day—what a waste of
time, what will come of that? Woyzeck, I can't look at a mill wheel any more
or I get melancholy.

WOYZECK Yes, Cap'n.

15 CAPTAIN Woyzeck, you always look so upset. A good man doesn't act like
that, a good man with a good conscience. Say something, Woyzeck. What's
the weather like today?

WOYZECK It's bad, Cap'n, bad—wind.

CAPTAIN I can feel it, there's something rapid out there. A wind like that
20 reminds me of a mouse. [*Cunningly*] I believe it's coming from the
south-north.

WOYZECK Yes, Cap'n.

CAPTAIN Ha! Ha! Ha! South-north! Ha! Ha! Ha! Oh, are you stupid, terribly
stupid. [*Sentimentally*] Woyzeck, you're a good man, a good man—[*with
25 dignity*] but Woyzeck, you've got no morality. Morality—that's when you are
moral, you understand. It's a good word. You have a child without the blessing of the church, as our Reverend Chaplain says, without the blessing of
the church—*I* didn't say it.

WOYZECK Cap'n, the good Lord isn't going to look at a poor little kid only
30 because amen was said over it before it was created. The Lord said: "Suffer
little children to come unto me."[1]

CAPTAIN What's that you're saying? What kind of a crazy answer is that?
You're getting me all confused with your answer. When I say *you,* I mean
you—you!

35 WOYZECK Us poor people. You see, Cap'n—money, money. If you don't
have money. Just try to raise your own kind on morality in this world. After
all, we're flesh and blood. The likes of us are wretched in this world and in
the next; I guess if we ever got to Heaven, we'd have to help with the
thunder.

40 CAPTAIN Woyzeck, you have no virtue, you're not a virtuous person. Flesh
and blood? When I'm lying at the window after it has rained, and I watch
the white stockings as they go tripping down the street—damn it, Woyzeck,
then love comes all over me. I've got flesh and blood, too. But Woyzeck,
virtue, virtue! How else could I make time go by? I always say to myself:
45 you're a virtuous man, [*sentimentally*] a good man, a good man.

WOYZECK Yes, Cap'n, virtue! I haven't figured it out yet. You see, us common
people, we don't have virtue, we act like nature tells us—but if I was a
gentleman, and had a hat and a watch and an overcoat and could talk
refined, then I'd be virtuous, too. Virtue must be nice, Cap'n. But I'm just
50 a poor guy.

CAPTAIN That's fine, Woyzeck. You're a good man, a good man. But you
think too much, that's unhealthy—you always look so upset. This discus-

---

1. That is, allow infants to be brought to receive Jesus's blessing (Luke 18.16; see also Matthew
19.14; Mark 10.14).

sion has really worn me out. You can go now—and don't run like that! Slow, nice and slow down the street.

4,6

[MARIE. DRUM MAJOR.]

DRUM MAJOR   Marie!

MARIE [*looking at him expressively*]   Go march up and down for me.—A chest like a bull and a beard like a lion. Nobody else is like that.—No woman is prouder than me.

5 DRUM MAJOR   Sundays when I have my plumed helmet and my white gloves— goddamn, Marie! The prince always says: man, you're quite a guy!

MARIE [*mockingly*]   Aw, go on! [*Goes up to him.*] What a man!

DRUM MAJOR   What a woman! Hell, let's breed a race of drum majors, hey?

[*He embraces her.*]

MARIE [*moody*]   Leave me alone!

10 DRUM MAJOR   You wildcat!

MARIE [*violently*]   Just try to touch me!

DRUM MAJOR   Is the devil in your eyes?

MARIE   For all I care. What does it matter?

4,7

[MARIE. WOYZECK.]

WOYZECK [*stares at her, shakes his head*]   Hm! I don't see anything, I don't see anything. Oh, I should be able to see it; I should be able to grab it with my fists.

MARIE [*intimidated*]   What's the matter, Franz? You're out of your mind, 5 Franz.

WOYZECK   A sin so fat and so wide—it stinks enough to smoke the angels out of Heaven. You've got a red mouth, Marie. No blister on it? Good-bye, Marie, you're as beautiful as sin.—Can mortal sin be so beautiful?

MARIE   Franz, you're delirious.

10 WOYZECK   Damn it!—Was he standing here like this, like this?

MARIE   As the day is long and the world is old, lots of people can stand on one spot, one after another.

WOYZECK   I saw him.

MARIE   You can see all sorts of things if you've got two eyes and aren't blind, 15 and the sun is shining.

WOYZECK   [With my own eyes!]

MARIE [*fresh*]   So what!

4,8

[WOYZECK. *The* DOCTOR.]

DOCTOR   What's this I saw, Woyzeck? A man of his word!

WOYZECK   What is it, Doctor?

DOCTOR   I saw it, Woyzeck—you pissed on the street, you pissed on the wall like a dog. And even though you get two cents a day. Woyzeck, that's bad. 5 The world's getting bad, very bad.

WOYZECK   But Doctor, the call of nature . . .

DOCTOR   The call of nature, the call of nature! Nature! Haven't I proved that the *musculus constrictor vesicae*[2] is subject to the will? Nature! Woyzeck, man is free; in man alone is individuality exalted to freedom. Couldn't hold
10   it in! [*Shakes his head, puts his hands behind his back, and paces back and forth.*] Did you eat your peas already, Woyzeck?—I'm revolutionizing science, I'll blow it sky-high. Urea ten per cent, ammonium chloride, hyperoxidic.[3] Woyzeck, don't you have to piss again? Go in there and try.

WOYZECK   I can't, Doctor.

15   DOCTOR [*with emotion*]   But pissing on the wall! I have it in writing, here's the contract. I saw it all, saw it with my own eyes—I was just holding my nose out the window, letting the sun's rays hit it, so as to examine the process of sneezing. [*Starts kicking him.*] No, Woyzeck, I'm not getting angry; anger is unhealthy, unscientific. I am calm, perfectly calm—my pulse is
20   beating at its usual sixty, and I'm telling you this in all cold-bloodedness! Who on earth would get excited about a human being, a human being! Now if it were a Proteus lizard[4] that were dying! But you shouldn't have pissed on the wall . . .

WOYZECK   You see, Doctor, sometimes you've got a certain character, a certain
25   structure.—But with nature, that's something else, you see, with nature—[*He cracks his knuckles.*] that's like—how should I put it—for example . . .

DOCTOR   Woyzeck, you're philosophizing again.

WOYZECK [*confidingly*]   Doctor, have you ever seen anything of double nature? When the sun's standing high at noon and the world seems to be
30   going up in flames, I've heard a terrible voice talking to me!

DOCTOR   Woyzeck, you've got an *aberratio*![5]

WOYZECK [*puts his finger to his nose*]   The toadstools, Doctor. There—that's where it is. Have you seen how they grow in patterns? If only someone could read that.

35   DOCTOR   Woyzeck, you've got a marvelous *aberratio mentalis partialis*, second species,[6] beautifully developed. Woyzeck, you're getting a raise. Second species: obsession with a generally rational condition. You're doing everything as usual—shaving your captain?

WOYZECK   Yes, sir.

40   DOCTOR   Eating your peas?

WOYZECK   Same as ever, Doctor. My wife gets the money for the household.

DOCTOR   Going on duty?

WOYZECK   Yes, sir.

DOCTOR   You're an interesting case. Subject Woyzeck, you're getting a raise.
45   Now behave yourself. Show me your pulse! Yes.

4,9

[CAPTAIN. DOCTOR.]

CAPTAIN   Doctor, I'm afraid for the horses when I think that the poor beasts have to go everywhere on foot. Don't run like that! Don't wave your cane

---

2. The muscle that controls the urethral sphincter (Latin).
3. Apparently an analysis (though a somewhat nonsensical one) of Woyzeck's urine.
4. A kind of large, rare salamander, found in
Austria (also called an olm).
5. Aberration (Latin).
6. Distinct class. *Aberratio mentalis partialis*: partial mental aberration (Latin).

around in the air like that! You'll run yourself to death that way. A good man with a good conscience doesn't go so fast. A good man. [*He catches the* DOC-
5 TOR *by the coat.*] Doctor, allow me to save a human life. You're racing . . .

Doctor, I'm so melancholy, I get so emotional, I always start crying when I see my coat hanging on the wall—there it is.

DOCTOR Hm! Bloated, fat, thick neck, apoplectic constitution. Yes, Captain, you might be stricken by an *apoplexia cerebralis.*[7] But you might get it just
10 on one side and be half paralyzed, or—best of all—you might become mentally affected and just vegetate from then on: those are approximately your prospects for the next four weeks. Moreover, I can assure you that you will be a most interesting case, and if, God willing, your tongue is partially paralyzed, we'll make immortal experiments.

15 CAPTAIN Doctor, don't frighten me! People have been known to die of fright, of pure, sheer fright.—I can see them now, with their hats in their hands— but they'll say, he was a good man, a good man.—You damn coffin nail!

DOCTOR [*holds out his hat*] What's this, Captain? That's brainless!

CAPTAIN [*makes a crease*] What's this, Doctor? That's in-crease!

20 DOCTOR I take my leave, most honorable Mr. Drillprick.

CAPTAIN Likewise, dearest Mr. Coffin Nail.

4,10

[SCENE: *The guardroom.*]

[WOYZECK. ANDRES.]

ANDRES [*sings*]

> Our hostess has a pretty maid,
> She's in her garden night and day,
> She sits inside her garden . . .

WOYZECK Andres!

5 ANDRES Huh?

WOYZECK Nice weather.

ANDRES Sunday weather. There's music outside town. All the broads are out there already, everybody's sweating—it's really moving along.

WOYZECK [*restlessly*] A dance, Andres, they're dancing.

10 ANDRES Yeah, at the Horse and at the Star.

WOYZECK Dancing, dancing.

ANDRES Big deal.

[*Sings.*]

> She sits inside her garden,
> Until the bells have all struck twelve,
15 > And stares at all the soo-ooldiers.

WOYZECK Andres, I can't keep still.

ANDRES Fool!

WOYZECK I've got to get out of here. Everything's spinning before my eyes. How hot their hands are. Damn it, Andres!

20 ANDRES What do you want?

WOYZECK I've got to go.

7. Cerebral apoplexy (Latin); that is, cerebral hemorrhage, stroke.

ANDRES   With that whore.
WOYZECK   I've got to get out. It's so hot in here.

4,11

[SCENE: *Inn.*]

[*The windows are open, a dance. Benches in front of the house.* APPRENTICES.]

FIRST APPRENTICE

This shirt I've got, I don't know whose,
My soul it stinks like booze . . .

SECOND APPRENTICE   Brother, shall I in friendship bore a hole in your nature? Dammit, I want to bore a hole in your nature. I'm quite a guy, too, you
5   know—I'm going to kill all the fleas on his body.
FIRST APPRENTICE   My soul, my soul it stinks like booze.—Even money eventually decays. Forget-me-not! Oh, how beautiful this world is. Brother, I could cry a rain barrel full of tears. I wish our noses were two bottles and we could pour them down each other's throats.
OTHERS [*in chorus*]

10

A hunter from the west
Once went riding through the woods.
Hip-hip, hooray! A hunter has a merry life,
O'er meadow and o'er stream,
Oh, hunting is my dream!

[WOYZECK *stands at the window.* MARIE *and the* DRUM MAJOR *dance past without seeing him.*]

15   MARIE [*dancing by*]   On! and on, on and on!
WOYZECK [*chokes*]   On and on—on and on! [*Jumps up violently and sinks back on the bench.*] On and on, on and on. [*Beats his hands together.*] Spin around, roll around. Why doesn't God blow out the sun so that everything can roll around in lust, man and woman, man and beast. Do it in broad
20   daylight, do it on our hands, like flies.—Woman!—That woman is hot, hot! On and on, on and on. [*Jumps up.*] The bastard! Look how he's grabbing her, grabbing her body! He—he's got her now, [*like I used to have her.*]
FIRST APPRENTICE [*preaches on the table*]   Yet when a wanderer stands leaning against the stream of time or gives answer for the wisdom of God, ask
25   ing himself: Why does man exist? Why does man exist?—But verily I say unto you: how could the farmer, the cooper, the shoemaker, the doctor exist if God hadn't created man? How could the tailor exist if God hadn't given man a feeling of shame? How could the soldier exist, if men didn't feel the necessity of killing one another? Therefore, do not ye despair, yes,
30   yes, it is good and pleasant, yet all that is earthly is passing, even money eventually decays.—In conclusion, my dear friends, let us piss crosswise so that a Jew will die.

4,12

[SCENE: *Open field.*]

WOYZECK   On and on! On and on! Shh—music. [*Stretches out on the ground.*] Ha—what, what are you saying? Louder, louder—stab, stab the bitch to

death? Stab, stab the bitch to death. Should I? Must I? Do I hear it over there too, is the wind saying it too? Do I hear it on and on—stab her to
5 death, to death.

4,13

[SCENE: *Night.*]

[ANDRES *and* WOYZECK *in a bed.*]

WOYZECK [*shakes* ANDRES] Andres! Andres! I can't sleep—when I close my eyes, everything starts spinning, and I hear the fiddles, on and on, on and on. And then there's a voice from the wall—don't you hear anything?

ANDRES Oh, yeah—let them dance! God bless us, amen. [*Falls asleep again.*]
5 WOYZECK And it floats between my eyes like a knife.

ANDRES Drink some brandy with a painkiller in it. That'll bring your fever down.

4,14

[SCENE: *Inn.*]

[DRUM MAJOR. WOYZECK. *People.*]

DRUM MAJOR I'm a man! [*Pounds his chest.*] A man, I say. Who wants to start something? If you're not drunk as a lord, stay away from me. I'll shove your nose up your ass. I'll . . . [*To* WOYZECK] Man, have a drink. A man gotta drink. I wish the world was booze, booze.

WOYZECK [*whistles*]
5 DRUM MAJOR You bastard, you want me to pull your tongue out of your throat and wrap it around you? [*They wrestle,* WOYZECK *loses.*] Shall I leave you as much breath as an old woman's fart? Shall I?

[WOYZECK *sits on the bench, exhausted and trembling.*]

DRUM MAJOR He can whistle till he's blue in the face. Ha!

Oh, brandy, that's my life,
10 Oh, brandy gives me courage!

A PERSON He sure got what was coming to him.

ANOTHER He's bleeding.

WOYZECK One thing after another.

4,15

[WOYZECK. THE JEW.]

WOYZECK The pistol costs too much.

JEW Well, do you want it or don't you?

WOYZECK How much is the knife?

JEW It's good and straight. You want to cut your throat with it? Well, how
5 about it? I'll give it to you as cheap as anybody else; your death'll be cheap, but not for nothing. How about it? You'll have an economical death.

WOYZECK That can cut more than just bread.

JEW Two cents.

WOYZECK There!

[*Goes off.*]
10 JEW There! Like it was nothing. But it's money! The dog.

4,16

[MARIE. KARL, *the idiot.* CHILD.]

MARIE [*leafs through the Bible*] "And no guile is found in his mouth"[8] . . . My God, my God! Don't look at me. [*Pages further.*] "And the scribes and Pharisees brought unto him a woman taken in adultery, and set her in the midst . . . And Jesus said unto her, 'Neither do I condemn thee: go, and sin
5 no more.'"[9] [*Clasps her hands together.*] My God! My God! I can't. God, just give me enough strength to pray. [*The* CHILD *snuggles up to her.*] The boy is like a knife in my heart. [Karl! He's sunning himself!]

KARL [*lies on the ground and tells himself fairy tales on his fingers*] This one has a golden crown—he's a king. Tomorrow I'll go get the queen's child.
10 Blood sausage says, come, liver sausage! [*He takes the* CHILD *and is quiet.*]

[MARIE] Franz hasn't come, not yesterday, not today. It's getting hot in here. [*She opens the window.*] "And stood at his feet weeping, and began to wash his feet with tears, and did wipe them with the hairs of her head, and kissed his feet, and anointed them with ointment."[1] [*Beats her breast.*] It's
15 all dead! Savior, Savior, I wish I could anoint your feet.

4,17

[SCENE: *The barracks.*]

[ANDRES. WOYZECK *rummages through his things.*]

WOYZECK This jacket isn't part of the uniform, Andres; you can use it, Andres. The crucifix is my sister's, and the little ring. I've got an icon, too— two hearts and nice gold. It was in my mother's Bible, and it says:

May pain be my reward,
5   Through pain I love my Lord.
Lord, like Thy body, red and sore,
So be my heart forevermore.

My mother can only feel the sun shining on her hands now. That doesn't matter.
10 ANDRES [*blankly, answers to everything*] Yeah.

WOYZECK [*pulls out a piece of paper*] Friedrich Johann Franz Woyzeck, enlisted infantryman in the second regiment, second battalion, fourth company, born . . . Today I'm thirty years, seven months, and twelve days old.

ANDRES Franz, you better go to the infirmary. You poor guy—drink brandy
15 with a painkiller in it. That'll kill the fever.

WOYZECK You know, Andres, when the carpenter nails those boards together, nobody knows who'll be laying his head on them.
[*End of Büchner's revision.*]

[*Scenes from the First Draft:*]

---

8. A close echo of 1 Peter 2.22, where Jesus is described as a model of patient suffering.
9. John 8.3, 11.

1. Luke 7.38; the "she" is a woman described in the preceding verse as "a sinner."

1,14

[SCENE: *Street.*]

> [MARIE *with girls in front of the house door.* GRANDMOTHER. *Then* WOYZECK.]

GIRLS

> How bright the sun on Candlemas Day,[2]
> On fields of golden grain.
> As two by two they marched along
> Down the country lane.
> The pipers up in front,
> The fiddlers in a chain.
> Their red socks . . .

FIRST CHILD   That's not nice.

SECOND CHILD   What do you want, anyway?

[OTHERS]   Why'd you start it?

> Yeah, why?

I can't.

> Because!

Who's going to sing?

> Why because?

Marie, you sing to us.

MARIE   Come, you little shrimps.

> [*Children's games: "Ring-around-a-rosy" and "King Herod."*]

Grandmother, tell a story.

GRANDMOTHER   Once upon a time there was a poor child with no father and no mother, everything was dead, and no one was left in the whole world. Everything was dead, and it went and searched day and night. And since nobody was left on the earth, it wanted to go up to the heavens, and the moon was looking at it so friendly, and when it finally got to the moon, the moon was a piece of rotten wood and then it went to the sun and when it got there, the sun was a wilted sunflower and when it got to the stars, they were little golden flies stuck up there like the shrike sticks 'em on the blackthorn and when it wanted to go back down to the earth, the earth was an overturned pot and was all alone and it sat down and cried and there it sits to this day, all alone.

WOYZECK   Marie!

MARIE [*startled*]   What is it?

WOYZECK   Marie, we have to go. It's time.

MARIE   Where to?

WOYZECK   How do I know?

1,15

> [MARIE *and* WOYZECK.]

MARIE   So the town is over there—it's dark.

WOYZECK   Stay here. Come on, sit down.

---

2. The Roman Catholic celebration (February 2) of the day on which Jesus first came to the temple and was blessed (see Luke 2.22).

MARIE   But I have to get back.

WOYZECK   You won't get sore feet.

5 MARIE   What's gotten into you!

WOYZECK   Do you know how long it's been, Marie?

MARIE   Two years since Pentecost.[3]

WOYZECK   And do you know how long it's going to be?

MARIE   I've got to go, the evening dew is falling.

10 WOYZECK   Are you freezing, Marie? But you're warm. How hot your lips
are!—Hot, the hot breath of a whore—and yet I'd give heaven and earth to
kiss them once more. And when you're cold, you don't freeze any more. The
morning dew won't make you freeze.

MARIE   What are you talking about?

15 WOYZECK   Nothing. [*Silence.*]

MARIE   Look how red the moon is.

WOYZECK   Like a bloody blade.

MARIE   What are you up to? Franz, you're so pale. [*He pulls out the knife.*]
Franz—wait! For God's sake—help!

20 WOYZECK   Take that and that! Can't you die? There! There! Ah—she's still
twitching—not yet? Not yet? Still alive? [*Stabs once again.*] Are you dead?
Dead! Dead!

[*People approach, he runs off.*]

1,16

[*Two people.*]

FIRST PERSON   Wait!

SECOND PERSON   You hear it? Shh! Over there.

FIRST PERSON   Ooh! There! What a sound.

SECOND PERSON   That's the water, it's calling. Nobody has drowned for a long
5 time. Let's go—it's bad to hear things like that.

FIRST PERSON   Ooh! There it is again. Like someone dying.

SECOND PERSON   It's weird. It's so fragrant—some gray fog, and the beetles
humming like broken bells. Let's get out of here!

FIRST PERSON   No—it's too clear, too loud. Up this way. Come on.

1,17

[SCENE. *The inn.*]

[WOYZECK. KATEY. KARL. INNKEEPER. *People.*]

WOYZECK   Dance, all of you, on and on, sweat and stink—he'll get you all in
the end.

[*Sings.*]

> Our hostess has a pretty maid,
> She's in her garden night and day,
> She sits inside her garden,
> Until the bells have all struck twelve,
> And stares at all the soldiers.

5

3. A Christian festival celebrated seven weeks after Easter commemorating the descent of the
Holy Spirit upon the apostles.

[*He dances.*] Come on, Katey! Sit down! I'm hot! Hot. [*He takes off his jacket.*] That's the way it is: the devil takes one and lets the other go. Katey, you're hot! Why? Katey, you'll be cold someday, too. Be reasonable. Can't you sing something?

[KATEY]

> For Swabian[4] hills I do not yearn,
> And flowing gowns I always spurn,
> For flowing gowns and pointed shoes
> A servant girl should never choose.

[WOYZECK]   No, no shoes—you can go to hell without shoes, too.

[KATEY]   For shame, my love, I'm not your own,
        Just keep your money and sleep alone.

[WOYZECK]   Yes, that's right, I don't want to make myself bloody.

KATEY   But what's that on your hand?

WOYZECK   Who? Me?

KATEY   Red! Blood!

   [*People gather around.*]

WOYZECK   Blood? Blood?

INNKEEPER   Ooh, blood.

WOYZECK   I guess I must have cut myself, there on my right hand.

INNKEEPER   But how'd it get on your elbow?

WOYZECK   I wiped it off.

INNKEEPER   What, with your right hand on your right elbow? You're talented.

KARL   And then the giant said: I smell, I smell, I smell human flesh. Phew! That stinks already.

WOYZECK   Damn it, what do you want? What's it got to do with you? Get away, or the first one who—damn it! You think I killed someone? Am I a murderer? What are you staring at? Look at yourselves! Out of my way!

   [*He runs out.*]

1,18

[*Children.*]

FIRST CHILD   Come on! Marie!

SECOND CHILD   What is it?

FIRST CHILD   Don't you know? Everybody's gone out there already. Someone's lying there!

SECOND CHILD   Where?

FIRST CHILD   To the left through the trench, near the red cross.

SECOND CHILD   Let's go, so we can still see something. Otherwise they'll carry her away.

1,19

[WOYZECK *alone.*]

WOYZECK   The knife? Where's the knife? Here's where I left it. It'll give me away! Closer, still closer! What kind of a place is this? What's that I hear?

4. Of Swabia, a mountainous region of southwestern Germany.

Something's moving. Shh! Over there. Marie? Ah—Marie! Quiet. Everything's quiet! Why are you so pale, Marie? Why is that red thread around
your neck? Who helped you earn that necklace, with your sins? They made
you black, black! Now I've made you white. Why does your black hair hang
so wild? Didn't you do your braids today? Something's lying over there!
Cold, wet, still. Got to get away from here. The knife, the knife—is that it?
There! People—over there.

[He runs off.]

1,20

[WOYZECK at a pond.]

WOYZECK   Down it goes! [He throws the knife in.] It sinks into the dark water
like a stone! The moon is like a bloody blade! Is the whole world going to
give me away? No, it's too far in front—when people go swimming—[He
goes into the pond and throws it far out.] All right, now—but in the summer,
when they go diving for shells—bah, it'll rust. Who'll recognize it? I wish
I'd smashed it! Am I still bloody? I've got to wash myself. There's a spot[5]—
and there's another.

1,21

[COURT CLERK. BARBER. DOCTOR. JUDGE.]

[CLERK]   A good murder, a real murder, a beautiful murder—as good a murder as you'd ever want to see. We haven't had one like this for a long time.

3,1[6]

[SCENE: *The PROFESSOR's courtyard.*]

[*Students below, the PROFESSOR at the attic window.*]

[PROFESSOR]   Gentlemen, I am on the roof like David when he saw Bathsheba,[7] but all I see is underwear on a clothesline in the garden of the girls'
boarding house. Gentlemen, we are dealing with the important question of
the relationship of subject to object. If we take only one of the things in
which the organic self-affirmation of the Divine manifests itself to a high
degree, and examine its relationship to space, to the earth, to the planetary
system—gentlemen, if I throw this cat out of the window, how will this
organism relate to the *centrum gravitationis*[8] and to its own instinct? Hey,
Woyzeck. [Shouts.] Woyzeck!

WOYZECK   Professor, it bites!

PROFESSOR   The fellow holds the beast so tenderly, like it was his grandmother!

WOYZECK   Doctor [sic], I've got the shivers.

DOCTOR [elated]   Say, that's wonderful, Woyzeck! [Rubs his hands. He takes
the cat.] What's this I see, gentlemen—a new species of rabbit louse, a
beautiful species, quite different, deep in the fur. [He pulls out a magnify-
ing glass.] Ricinus,[9] gentlemen! [The cat runs off.] Gentlemen, that animal

---

5. A phrase that recalls the attempts of
Shakespeare's sleepwalking Lady Macbeth to
cleanse her hands after committing murder
(*Macbeth* [1606] 5.1).
6. The first of two optional scenes.

7. David, king of Israel (ca. 1010–970
B.C.E.), was said to have seen the beautiful
Bathsheba bathing herself (2 Samuel 11.2).
8. Center of gravity (Latin).
9. Tick (Latin); that is, the louse.

has no scientific instinct. Ricinus—the best examples—bring your fur collars. Gentlemen, instead of that you can see something else: take note of this man—for a quarter of a year he hasn't eaten anything but peas. Notice
20 the result—feel how uneven his pulse is. There—and the eyes.

WOYZECK   Doctor, everything's getting black.

　　　　[*He sits down.*]

DOCTOR   Courage, Woyzeck—just a few more days, and then it'll be all over. Feel him, gentlemen, feel him.

　　　　[*Students feel his temples, pulse, and chest.*]

Apropos, Woyzeck, wiggle your ears for the gentlemen; I meant to show it
25 to you before. He uses two muscles. Come on, hop to it!

WOYZECK   Oh, Doctor!

DOCTOR   You dog, shall I wiggle them for you, are you going to act like the cat? So, gentlemen, this represents a transition to the donkey, frequently resulting from being brought up by women and from the use of the mother
30 tongue. How much hair has your mother pulled out for a tender memory? It's gotten very thin in the last few days. Yes, the peas, gentlemen.

3,2[1]

　　　　[KARL, *the idiot. The* CHILD. WOYZECK.]

KARL [*holds the* CHILD *on his lap*]   He fell in the water, he fell in the water, he fell in the water.

WOYZECK   Son—Christian![2]

KARL [*stares at him*]   He fell in the water.

5 WOYZECK [*wants to caress the* CHILD, *who turns away and screams*]   My God!

KARL   He fell in the water.

WOYZECK   Christian, you'll get a hobbyhorse. Da-da! [*The* CHILD *resists. To* KARL] Here, go buy the boy a hobbyhorse.

KARL [*stares at him*]

WOYZECK   Hop! Hop! Horsey!

10 KARL [*cheers*]   Hop! Hop! Horsey! Horsey!

　　　　[*Runs off with the* CHILD.]

1. The second of two optional scenes.　　　　2. That is, baptized by the water.

AUGUST STRINDBERG

1849–1912

WHEN scholars try to decide who invented modern drama, their arguments focus on two Scandinavian playwrights: the Norwegian HENRIK IBSEN and the Swede Johan August Strindberg. Ibsen is the more classical writer of the two: his plays are tightly constructed, formally controlled, and carefully paced. Strindberg, by contrast, is a modernist rebel: his plays are flights of fancy, manifestations of a wild imagination that created characters engaged in a perpetual struggle of wills and desires. Strindberg refused to have anything to do with inherited forms of drama. Instead, he reinvented drama from scratch. In order to find new models for his plays, he turned to the most unlikely places. He read contemporary philosophy—for example, the German philosopher Friedrich Nietzsche. He explored the logic of dreams. He studied Eastern religions such as Hinduism. At the same time, he made a name for himself as a painter and wrote a voluminous geographical and cultural history of Sweden as well as a large number of essays, pamphlets, and books on a great variety of subjects, including the occult, magic, and science. Strindberg's career was littered with ill-conceived and quixotic projects, such as his attempts to synthesize gold, which nearly cost him his sanity. Even more disturbing, and notorious, were his anti-Semitic pamphlets and his attacks on

the women's rights movement. But somehow out of this volatile life and mind emerged a number of modernism's most compelling and revolutionary plays.

Strindberg was born into a lower-middle-class family, but his mother had been a servant. The stigma attached to this parentage, which Strindberg captured and exaggerated in his first autobiographical novel, *The Son of a Servant* (1886), continued to haunt him to the end of his life. So did his lack of economic resources. He was financially dependent on his friends as early as his student days in Upsala, and even after he had established himself as a writer he could barely make ends meet. His precarious finances forced him to give up his university studies and take jobs as a teacher and also, briefly, as an actor. Eventually he landed a somewhat more secure position as a librarian, which allowed him enough free time to start his career as a writer. But the uneventful and quiet periods in Strindberg's life were few, in part because of his difficult relations with women. His first marriage—to Siri von Essen, an independent and freethinking Finnish aristocrat—lasted for seven tumultuous years and became the subject of his autobiographical novel *A Madman's Defense* (1888). At the same time, his professional life was in almost as much turmoil. Some of his early plays were staged with relative success, but Strindberg felt attacked by critics and ignored by the theater establishment, a sense that persisted throughout his life. This perceived lack of appreciation was also why he left Sweden in 1883, beginning a long self-imposed exile in France, Germany, Switzerland, and Denmark, interrupted only briefly by returns home.

Many of Strindberg's best-known plays, including *The Father* (1887) and *MISS JULIE* (1888), were first produced outside Sweden, where he first achieved fame as a dramatist. Most of the important influences on Strindberg were likewise European. He engaged in a long correspondence with the influential Danish critic and philosopher Georg Brandes and had less extensive exchanges with Friedrich Nietzsche and Émile Zola. While living in Berlin, he met the director Max Reinhardt, who produced several of Strindberg's plays to great acclaim. Strindberg made friends, but he had a greater talent for making enemies, and he often broke with friends and supporters for no good reason. One of the targets of Strindberg's ire was Ibsen, the older and more established of the two Scandinavian playwrights.

Even though Strindberg had been a professed atheist for much of his life, in the 1890s he increasingly turned to religion, occultism, and pseudoscience. This period also coincided with the end of his volatile second marriage, to Frida Uhl, an Austrian writer. In 1895, after separating from her, he found himself in desolate circumstances in Paris and stopped writing literature entirely. Instead he spent his scant funds purchasing chemical equipment with which he attempted to produce gold. Paranoid delusions, illness, and failed experiments, together with the mystical writings of Emanuel Swedenborg (1688–1772), fueled his mental instability. The autobiographical *Inferno* (ca. 1898) and his *Occult Diary* (written 1896–1908) sadly testify to this physical and mental decline. In 1897, when he was close to fifty years old, he finally returned permanently to Sweden.

Upon his return to Sweden, Strindberg started to write plays again but in a very different mode. Whereas his earlier plays had concentrated on single events and

encounters, these new, symbolist and expressionist plays, including *The Road to Damascus* (1898) and *The Dream Play* (1901), unfold in loosely connected scenes and episodes. Characters are fluid and shifting, mysterious encounters lead to unforeseen consequences, and the dialogue is infused with religious figures and expressions. These later plays—which also include his so-called chamber plays, among them *The Ghost Sonata* (1907) and *The Pelican* (1907)—revolve around suffering, sin, and redemption. Back in Stockholm Strindberg had also gotten married a third time, to Harriet Bosse, an actress much younger than he. But this marriage was brief, and Strindberg spent his last years alone, in a modest apartment in Stockholm known as the Blue Tower. He never became popular, but in the last years of his life he achieved something of a literary reputation. Although he failed to win the Nobel Prize in Literature—one of the five prizes endowed by the final bequest of the Swedish chemist and armaments manufacturer Alfred Nobel, first awarded in 1901—he was finally honored with a state pension and a so-called Anti-Nobel Prize, a large sum raised by national subscription, one year before his death.

Miss Julie belongs to Strindberg's naturalist period, which also includes *The Father* and *Creditors* (1889). Naturalist drama was a rebellion against the bombastic history plays of Romanticism, the simplistic division between good and evil characters in melodrama, and the neatly constructed drawing-room comedies that flourished in the middle of the century. Naturalism, by contrast, privileged contemporary, and particularly lower-class, settings, which had rarely been seen on the stage except for comic effect. Strindberg's naturalist plays are interested in class differences, especially their effect on the relations between men and women. Like his autobiographical novels and short stories, Strindberg's naturalist plays depict the sexes as engaged in an all-out war. Whether vampires or degenerate creatures, women are always seeking the subjection of men. *The Father* pushes such irrational misogyny to an extreme: it portrays a man who, surrounded by his wife, daughter, mother-in-law, and old nurse, is slowly but surely being driven mad by these vengeful women; finally, he collapses dead in the arms of his nurse. The dramatist's autobiographical novels, as well as his letters and essays, suggest that Strindberg experienced his own marriages as similarly assaultive. But in his plays, at least, he was able to treat his own bitter experiences and paranoid obsessions with more detachment, thereby turning them into more compelling artistic forms.

Miss Julie strives for verisimilitude in its form. The play, confined to a single setting and one long act, represents a single, continuous action that lasts precisely as long as the play itself; it thus strictly obeys the neo-Aristotelian unities of time, place, and action. It is set not in some elaborate drawing room but in the kitchen of an estate, the domain of a cook and her apparent fiancé, another servant in the house in which a count lives with his daughter. Though its opening scene depicts the two servants, the play soon turns to its primary interest: the relation between the emancipated and freethinking mistress of the house, Miss Julie, and the ambitious, virile valet, Jean. The play describes a simple dramatic arc. At first Miss Julie has the upper hand. She flirts with her servant and finally persuades him to dance with her. After a sexual encounter, the dynamics change: now the servant is the dominant one. The play shows in detail the shifting power balance as Jean suggests to Miss Julie that they flee together and fantasizes about setting up a hotel in Italy. But nothing comes of the plan: they are trapped in the kitchen and trapped by their deed. Miss Julie finds herself in the hands of a power-hungry but volatile man, and by the end of the play she has lost her social position and her honor and has nowhere to turn.

As is to be expected from a self-declared opponent of the New Woman such as Strindberg, Miss Julie does not fare well in this play precisely because she is too emancipated. In keeping with naturalist doctrine, her stance is caused by her parents' corrupting influence; one sign of their moral failings is their initial refusal to be lawfully wedded. Her mother's descent into adultery and arson also helps explain the transformation of the seem-

ingly self-confident and articulate mistress into a moral wreck. Nowhere is Strindberg's reactionary view on marriage and emancipation clearer than in the backstory of Miss Julie, which serves to justify her ultimate downfall. Like many other naturalists, Strindberg was deeply influenced by "social Darwinists," who misapplied evolutionary theory to explain and justify social inequities; here, bad parentage necessarily dooms her. Such plots of social rising and falling are common in naturalist novels and plays alike.

Even though the emancipated aristocrat Miss Julie may in some ways be reminiscent of Strindberg's first wife, the play itself is based not on his own marriage but rather on an account Strindberg had heard of a servant who ended up dominating his former mistress both sexually and socially. In Strindberg's moral universe, the degenerate aristocrat must ultimately be brought down, just as the servant Jean, of humble birth but possessing a forceful will, must rise. The relation between Miss Julie and Jean, couched in a language of dominance,

Siri von Essen, Strindberg's first wife and the first to play the lead role in the 1889 production of *Miss Julie* at the Scandinavian Experimental Theater.

servitude, and struggle, is indebted to Nietzsche, especially those aspects of his philosophy that now seem most troubling.

All the characters in *Miss Julie* are measured in terms of their power and their will to dominate others, but the backdrop of their struggle for dominance is a fixed class structure. Even though in the second part of the play Jean presents himself as the strong servant who will triumph over his mistress, he wavers between arrogance and submission, falling into the latter attitude especially toward Miss Julie's absent father. Throughout the play, the count's return is expected and with it the resumption of Jean's duties, epitomized in the task of polishing his master's shoes. Miss Julie, too, fears the return of her father, who has wholly rejected his former liberal attitudes and now rules sternly and justly, conforming to Strindberg's own conservative ideal. The battle between Jean and Miss Julie is waged in the oppressive atmosphere of the servants' quarters, a setting that underscores the constant threat of retribution. Despite Strindberg's belief in social Darwinism and the survival of the stronger, the determining power of social class can never be entirely overcome in *Miss Julie*: the play and its protagonist remain mired in class resentment. Jean may despise Miss Julie and manage to bring her into his power, but part of him remains a servant.

The oscillation between dominance and subservience within an individual is part of the theory of characterization that Strindberg articulates in his famous preface to the play. He rejects the traditional stage characters, who often manifest a single dominant trait—such stock figures as the hapless victim, the scheming villain, and the trusted friend. Clear motivations and distinct types may be useful in the construction of plots, but in Strindberg's view they fail to represent the conflicted and shifting forces that actually drive human action. Like modernist novelists such as James Joyce and Virginia Woolf, Strindberg wanted to replicate the irregular workings of the human mind. While other naturalists placed great emphasis on external detail of costume and dialect, Strindberg was more interested in interiority and psychology. His characters change their minds constantly, and when they express their thoughts, they are allowed to be inconsistent, shifting, and inarticulate. Strindberg also insisted on abolishing many of the artificial aspects

Aisling O'Sullivan as Miss Julie and Christopher Eccleston as Jean in the 2000 Theatre Royal Haymarket (London) production of *Miss Julie*.

of stagecraft, including painted scenes, makeup, unnatural lighting effects such as those caused by footlights, and the practice of playing to the audience. At the same time, he made no attempt to do away with all elements of theatrical artifice. Even in his naturalist plays, he included theatrical set pieces such as dance, music, and ballet. They often take the place of crowd scenes, which Strindberg did not believe could be staged naturalistically in the theater. He thus pragmatically opted for established theatrical techniques when necessary.

Miss Julie has remained a central play in the canon of modern drama. Early productions were mounted in Copenhagen, Berlin, and, most famously, Paris at André Antoine's Théâtre Libre in 1893, a production that confirmed Strindberg's standing as a leading naturalist playwright. In Sweden, the play was not produced until 1906, when it was staged at the Intima Teater. Upon his return to Sweden, Strindberg had founded this theater with the director August Falck, and many of his late chamber plays were written for it. Decorated in green and white draperies, with a bust of Strindberg in the small foyer, the Intima Teater was in fact modeled on Antoine's Théâtre Libre. But even though Strindberg had control over this theater, he was never entirely content with its productions of his plays. The quality of the acting was mixed, and the theater was under constant financial strain. In 1910 it had to be closed for good. Despite his efforts, Strindberg thus never found a company that could adequately translate his theories and plays into theatrical reality. And not until shortly before his death did he receive the enthusiastic support from the press, publishers, and the theatergoing public that had eluded him for decades.

Strindberg's life was a struggle against the world and against himself. His plays, likewise, are full of struggles among characters, even as they fight for a new type of drama. While Strindberg's struggles were mostly destructive in his life, they were immensely productive in his art. His plays never take anything for granted, and in each play he sought to invent drama anew. In the process, he first created an unusual form of naturalism; then, in his later work, he pioneered what would be known as expressionism—plays full of enigmatic characters, religious language, and episodic plots. But neither label can entirely capture the essence of Strindberg's plays, which are among the most personal and singular in the history of modern drama. Even though readers today are, if anything, more shocked than his contemporaries at his racist, misogynist, and strange religious opinions, Strindberg's unusual plays have continued to compel generations of readers, theatergoers, and critics, and his varied and rich work remains one of the pillars of modern drama.

M.P.

Miss Julie[1]

Preface

Like the arts in general, the theater has for a long time seemed to me a *Biblia Pauperum*,[2] a picture Bible for those who cannot read, and the playwright merely a lay preacher who hawks the latest ideals in popular form, so popular that the middle classes—the bulk of the audiences—can grasp them without racking their brains too much. That explains why the theater has always been an elementary school for

1. Translated by Evert Sprinchorn. 2. Bible of the Poor (Latin).

youngsters and the half-educated, and for women, who still retain a primitive capacity for deceiving themselves and for letting themselves be deceived, that is, for succumbing to illusions and responding hypnotically to the suggestions of the author. Consequently, now that the rudimentary and undeveloped mental processes that operate in the realm of fantasy appear to be evolving to the level of reflection, research, and experimentation, I believe that the theater, like religion, is about to be replaced as a dying institution for whose enjoyment we lack the necessary qualifications. Support for my view is provided by the theater crisis through which all of Europe is now passing, and still more by the fact that in those highly cultured lands which have produced the finest minds of our time—England and Germany—the drama is dead, as for the most part are the other fine arts.

Other countries, however, have thought to create a new drama by filling the old forms with new contents. But since there has not been enough time to popularize the new ideas, the public cannot understand them. And in the second place, controversy has so stirred up the public that they can no longer look on with a pure and dispassionate interest, especially when they see their most cherished ideals assailed or hear an applauding or booing majority openly exercise its tyrannical power, as can happen in the theater. And in the third place, since the new forms for the new ideas have not been created, the new wine has burst the old bottles.

In the play that follows I have not tried to accomplish anything new—that is impossible. I have only tried to modernize the form to satisfy what I believe up-to-date people expect and demand of this art. And with that in mind I have seized upon—or let myself be seized by—a theme that may be said to lie outside current party strife, since the question of being on the way up or on the way down the social ladder, of being on the top or on the bottom, superior or inferior, man or woman, is, has been, and will be of perennial interest. When I took this theme from real life—I heard about it a few years ago and it made a deep impression on me—I thought it would be a suitable subject for a tragedy, since it still strikes us as tragic to see a happily favored individual go down in defeat, and even more so to see an entire family line die out. But perhaps a time will come when we shall be so highly developed and so enlightened that we can look with indifference upon the brutal, cynical, and heartless spectacle that life offers us, a time when we shall have laid aside those inferior and unreliable mechanical apparatuses called emotions, which will become superfluous and even harmful as our mental organs develop. The fact that my heroine wins sympathy is due entirely to the fact that we are still too weak to overcome the fear that the same fate might overtake us. The extremely sensitive viewer will of course not be satisfied with mere expressions of sympathy, and the man who believes in progress will demand that certain positive actions be taken for getting rid of the evil, a kind of program, in other words. But in the first place absolute evil does not exist. The decline of one family is the making of another, which now gets its chance to rise. This alternate rising and falling provides one of life's greatest pleasures, for happiness is, after all, relative. As for the man who has a program for changing the disagreeable circumstance that the hawk eats the chicken and that lice eat up the hawk, I should like to ask him why it should be changed. Life is not prearranged with such idiotic mathematical precision that only the larger gets to eat the smaller. Just as frequently the bee destroys the lion (in Aesop's[3] fable)—or at least drives him wild.

If my tragedy makes most people feel sad, that is their fault. When we get to be as strong as the first French Revolutionists were, we shall be perfectly content and happy to watch the forests being cleared of rotting, superannuated trees that have stood too long in the way of others with just as much right to grow and flourish for a while—as content as we are when we see an incurably ill man finally die.

---

3. Greek storyteller (early 6th c. B.C.E.), known especially for his moralizing animal fables (Strindberg is here apparently thinking of "The Gnat and the Lion").

Recently my tragedy *The Father*[4] was censured for being too unpleasant—as if one wanted merry tragedies. "The joy of life" is now the slogan of the day. Theater managers send out orders for nothing but farces, as if the joy of living lay in behaving like a clown and in depicting people as if they were afflicted with St. Vitus's dance[5] or congenital idiocy. I find the joy of living in the fierce and ruthless battles of life, and my pleasure comes from learning something, from being taught something. That is why I have chosen for my play an unusual but instructive case, an exception, in other words—but an important exception of the kind that proves the rule—a choice of subject that I know will offend all lovers of the conventional. The next thing that will bother simple minds is that the motivation for the action is not simple and that the point of view is not single. Usually an event in life—and this is a fairly new discovery—is the result of a whole series of more or less deep-rooted causes. The spectator, however, generally chooses the one that puts the least strain on his mind or reflects most credit on his insight. Consider a case of suicide. "Business failure," says the merchant. "Unhappy love," say the women. "Physical illness," says the sick man. "Lost hopes," says the down-and-out. But it may be that the reason lay in all of these or in none of them, and that the suicide hid his real reason behind a completely different one that would reflect greater glory on his memory.

I have motivated the tragic fate of Miss Julie with an abundance of circumstances: her mother's basic instincts, her father's improper bringing-up of the girl, her own inborn nature, and her fiancé's sway over her weak and degenerate mind. Further and more immediately: the festive atmosphere of Midsummer Eve, her father's absence, her period, her preoccupation with animals, the erotic excitement of the dance, the long summer twilight, the highly aphrodisiac influence of flowers, and finally chance itself, which drives two people together in an out-of-the-way room, plus the boldness of the aroused man.

As one can see, I have not been entirely the physiologist, not been obsessively psychological, not traced everything to her mother's heredity, not found the sole cause in her period, not attributed everything to our "immoral times," and not simply preached a moral lesson. Lacking a priest, I have let the cook handle that.

I am proud to say that this complicated way of looking at things is in tune with the times. And if others have anticipated me in this, I am proud that I am not alone in my paradoxes, as all new discoveries are called. And no one can say this time that I am being one-sided.

As far as the drawing of characters is concerned, I have made the people in my play fairly "characterless" for the following reasons. In the course of time the word *character* has acquired many meanings. Originally it probably meant the dominant and fundamental trait in the soul complex and was confused with temperament. Later the middle class used it to mean an automaton. An individual who once and for all had found his own true nature or adapted himself to a certain role in life, who in fact had ceased to grow, was called a man of character, while the man who was constantly developing, who, like a skillful sailor on the currents of life, did not sail with close-tied sheets but who fell off before the wind in order to luff again, was called a man of no character—derogatorily of course, since he was so difficult to keep track of, to pin down and pigeonhole. This middle-class conception of a fixed character was transferred to the stage, where the middle class has always ruled. A character there came to mean someone who was always one and the same, always drunk, always joking, always melancholy, and who needed to be characterized only by some physical defect such as a club foot, a wooden leg, or a red nose, or by the repetition of some such phrase as, "That's capital," or "Barkis is willin'."[6] This uncomplicated

---

4. Published one year earlier, in 1887.
5. Chorea, a disease characterized by involuntary spasmodic movements.
6. A phrase repeated by Mr. Barkis, a character in Charles Dickens's *David Copperfield*

(1849–50), to indicate his desire to marry Clara Peggotty; that novel, like many other works by Dickens, was successfully adapted to the stage.

way of viewing people is still to be found in the great Molière. Harpagon[7] is nothing but a miser, although Harpagon could have been both a miser and an exceptional financier, a fine father, and a good citizen. Worse still, his "defect" is extremely advantageous to his son-in-law and his daughter, who will be his heirs and who therefore should not find fault with him, even if they do have to wait a while to jump into bed together. So I do not believe in simple stage characters. And the summary judgments that writers pass on people—he is stupid, this one is brutal, that one is jealous, this one is stingy, and so on—should not pass unchallenged by the naturalists who know how complicated the soul is and who realize that vice has a reverse side very much like virtue.

Since the persons in my play are modern characters, living in a transitional era more hectic and hysterical than the previous one at least, I have depicted them as more unstable, as torn and divided, a mixture of the old and the new. Nor does it seem improbable to me that modern ideas might also have seeped down through newspapers and kitchen talk to the level of the servants. Consequently the valet may belch forth from his inherited slave soul certain modern ideas. And if there are those who find it wrong to allow people in a modern drama to talk Darwin and who recommend the practice of Shakespeare to our attention, may I remind them that the gravedigger in *Hamlet* talks the then-fashionable philosophy of Giordano Bruno (Bacon's philosophy),[8] which is even more improbable, seeing that the means of spreading ideas were fewer then than now. And besides, the fact of the matter is that Darwinism has always existed, ever since Moses' history of creation[9] from the lower animals up to man, but it was not until recently that we discovered it and formulized it.

My souls—or characters—are conglomerations from various stages of culture, past and present, walking scrapbooks, shreds of human lives, tatters torn from old rags that were once Sunday best—hodgepodges just like the human soul. I have even supplied a little source history into the bargain by letting the weaker steal and repeat words of the stronger, letting them get ideas (suggestions as they are called) from one another, from the environment (the songbird's blood), and from objects (the razor). I have also arranged for *Gedankenübertragung*[1] through an inanimate medium to take place (the count's boots, the servant's bell). And I have even made use of "waking suggestions" (a variation of hypnotic suggestion), which have by now been so popularized that they cannot arouse ridicule or skepticism as they would have done in Mesmer's[2] time.

I say Miss Julie is a modern character not because the man-hating half-woman has not always existed but because she has now been brought out into the open, has taken the stage, and is making a noise about herself. Victim of a superstition (one that has seized even stronger minds) that woman, that stunted form of human being, standing with man, the lord of creation, the creator of culture, is meant to be the equal of man or could ever possibly be, she involves herself in an absurd struggle with him in which she falls. Absurd because a stunted form, subject to the laws of propagation, will always be born stunted and can never catch up with the one who has the lead. As follows: A (the man) and B (the woman) start from the same point C, A with a speed of let us say 100 and B with a speed of 60. When will B overtake A?

---

7. The protagonist in *The Miser* (1668), a play by the French dramatist Molière (1622–1673).
8. Perhaps a reference to the extreme logical precision of the gravedigger's wordplay in Shakespeare's *Hamlet* (1600–01), 5.1. Francis Bacon (1561–1626), an English philosopher and essayist, promoted the use of the inductive method of modern science; Bruno (1548–1600), an Italian philosopher, challenged dogmatism (he was burned at the stake for heresy). The major idea of the English

naturalist Charles Darwin (1809–1882)—the theory of evolution through natural selection, or Darwinism—was gaining wider acceptance at the end of the 19th century.
9. That is, the account given in Genesis, whose authorship was traditionally ascribed to Moses.
1. Telepathy (German).
2. Franz Anton Mesmer (1734–1815), German physician who devised a therapeutic technique, based on "animal magnetism," that was developed into hypnosis.

Answer: never. Neither with the help of equal education or equal voting rights—nor by universal disarmament and temperance societies—any more than two parallel lines can ever meet. The half-woman is a type that forces itself on others, selling itself for power, medals, recognition, diplomas, as formerly it sold itself for money. It represents degeneration. It is not a strong species for it does not maintain itself, but unfortunately it propagates its misery in the following generation. Degenerate men unconsciously select their mates from among these half-women, so that they breed and spread, producing creatures of indeterminate sex to whom life is a torture, but who fortunately are overcome eventually either by a hostile reality, or by the uncontrolled breaking loose of their repressed instincts, or else by their frustration in not being able to compete with the male sex. It is a tragic type, offering us the spectacle of a desperate fight against nature; a tragic legacy of romanticism, which is now being dissipated by naturalism—a movement that seeks only happiness, and for that strong and healthy species are required.

Miss Julie, however, is also a vestige of the old warrior nobility that is now being superseded by a new nobility of nerve and brain. She is a victim of the disorder produced within a family by a mother's "crime," of the mistakes of a whole generation gone wrong, of circumstances, of her own defective constitution—all of which put together is equivalent to the fate or universal law of the ancients. The naturalists have banished guilt along with God, but the consequences of an act—punishment, imprisonment, or the fear of it—cannot be banished for the simple reason that they remain whether or not the naturalist dismisses the case from his court. Those sitting on the sidelines can easily afford to be lenient; but what of the injured parties? And even if her father were compelled to forgo taking his revenge, Miss Julie would take vengeance on herself, as she does in the play, because of that inherited or acquired sense of honor that has been transmitted to the upper classes from—well, where does it come from? From the age of barbarism, from the first Aryans,[3] from the chivalry of the Middle Ages. And a very fine code it was, but now inimical to the survival of the race. It is the aristocrat's form of hara-kiri, a law of conscience that bids the Japanese to slice his own stomach when someone else dishonors him. The same sort of thing survives, slightly modified, in that exclusive prerogative of the aristocracy, the duel. (Example: the husband challenges his wife's lover to a duel; the lover shoots the husband and runs off with the wife. Result: the husband has saved his *honor* but lost his wife.) Hence the servant Jean lives on; but not Miss Julie, who cannot live without honor. The advantage that the slave has over his master is that he has not committed himself to this defeatist principle. In all of us Aryans there is enough of the nobleman, or of the Don Quixote,[4] to make us sympathize with the man who takes his own life after having dishonored himself by shameful deeds. And we are all of us aristocrats enough to be distressed at the sight of a great man lying like a dead hulk ready for the scrap pile, even, I suppose, if he were to raise himself up again and redeem himself by honorable deeds.

The servant Jean is the beginning of a new species in which noticeable differentiation has already taken place. He began as a child of a poor worker and is now evolving through self-education into a future gentleman of the upper classes. He is quick to learn, has highly developed senses (smell, taste, sight), and a keen appreciation of beauty. He has already come up in the world, for he is strong enough not to hesitate to make use of other people. He is already a stranger to his old friends, whom he despises as reminders of past stages in his development, and whom he fears and avoids because they know his secrets, guess his intentions, look with envy on his rise and with joyful expectation toward his fall. Hence his character is unformed and

3. Hypothetical ancient speakers of Indo-European, progenitors of European (especially the Germanic) peoples.
4. The eponymous hero of Miguel de Cer-

vantes's novel (1605, 1615), here invoked as a symbol of unflagging devotion to chivalric ideals.

divided. He wavers between an admiration of high positions and a hatred of the men who occupy them. He is an aristocrat—he says so himself—familiar with the ins and outs of good society. He is polished on the outside, but coarse underneath. He wears his frock coat with elegance but offers no guarantee that he keeps his body clean.

Although he respects Miss Julie, he is afraid of Christine, because she knows his innermost secrets. Yet he is sufficiently hard-hearted not to let the events of the night upset his plans for the future. Possessing both the coarseness of the slave and the toughmindedness of the born ruler, he can look at blood without fainting, shake off bad luck like water, and take calamity by the horns. Consequently he will escape from the battle unwounded, probably ending up as proprietor of a hotel. And if he himself does not get to be a Rumanian count, his son will doubtless go to college and possibly end up as a government official.

Now his observations about life as the lower classes see it, from below, are well worth listening to—that is, they are whenever he is telling the truth, which is not too often, because he is more likely to say what is advantageous to him than what is true. When Miss Julie supposes that everyone in the lower classes must feel greatly oppressed by the weight of the classes above, Jean naturally agrees with her since he wants to win her sympathy. But he promptly takes it all back when he finds it expedient to separate himself from the mob.

Apart from the fact that Jean is coming up in the world, he is also superior to Miss Julie in that he is a man. In the sexual sphere, he is the aristocrat. He has the strength of the male, more highly developed senses, and the ability to take the initiative. His inferiority is merely the result of his social environment, which is only temporary and which he will probably slough off along with his livery.

His slave nature expresses itself in his awe of the count (the boots) and his religious superstitions. But he is awed by the count mainly because the count occupies the place he wants most in life; and this awe is still there even after he has won the daughter of the house and seen how empty that beautiful shell was.

I do not believe that any love in the "higher" sense can be born from the union of two such different souls; so I have let Miss Julie's love be refashioned in her imagination as a love that protects and purifies, and I have let Jean imagine that even his love might have a chance to grow under other social circumstances. For I suppose love is very much like the hyacinth that must strike roots deep in the dark earth *before* it can produce a vigorous blossom. Here it shoots up, bursts into bloom, and turns to seed all at once. Such plants can only be short-lived.

Christine—finally to get to her—is a female slave, spineless and phlegmatic after years spent at the kitchen stove, bovinely unconscious of her own hypocrisy, and with a full quota of moral and religious notions that serve as scapegoats and cloaks for her sins—which a stronger soul does not require since he is able either to carry the burden of his own sins or to rationalize them out of existence. She attends church regularly where she deftly unloads unto Jesus her household thefts and picks up from him another load of innocence. She is only a secondary character, and I have deliberately done no more than sketch her in—just as I treated the country doctor and parish priest in *The Father* where I only wanted to draw ordinary everyday people such as most country doctors and parsons are. That some have found my minor characters one-dimensional is due to the fact that ordinary people while at work are to a certain extent one-dimensional and do lack an independent existence, showing only one side of themselves in the performance of their duties. And as long as the audience does not feel it needs to see them from different angles, my abstract sketches will pass muster.

Now as far as the dialogue is concerned, I have broken somewhat with tradition in refusing to make my characters into interlocutors who ask stupid questions to elicit witty answers. I have avoided the symmetrical and mathematical design of the artfully constructed French dialogue and have let minds work as irregularly as they do in real life, where no subject is quite exhausted before another mind engages at random some cog in the conversation and governs it for a while. My dialogue wanders here and there, gathers material in the first scenes which is later picked up, repeated, reworked, developed, and expanded like the theme in a piece of music.

The action of the play poses no problem. Since it really involves only two people, I have limited myself to these two, introducing only one minor character, the cook, and keeping the unhappy spirit of the father brooding over the action as a whole. I have chosen this course because I have noticed that what interests people most nowadays is the psychological action. Our inveterately curious souls are no longer content to see a thing happen; we want to see how it happens. We want to see the strings, look at the machinery, examine the double-bottom drawer, put on the magic ring to find the hidden seam, look in the deck for the marked cards.

In treating the subject this way I have had in mind the case-history novels of the Goncourt brothers,[5] which appeal to me more than anything else in modern literature.

As far as play construction is concerned, I have made a stab at getting rid of act divisions. I was afraid that the spectator's declining susceptibility to illusion might not carry him through the intermission, when he would have time to think about what he has seen and to escape the suggestive influence of the author-hypnotist. I figure my play lasts about ninety minutes. Since one can listen to a lecture, a sermon, or a political debate for that long or even longer, I have convinced myself that a play should not exhaust an audience in that length of time. As early as 1872 in one of my first attempts at the drama, *The Outlaw,* I tried out this concentrated form, although with little success. I had finished the work in five acts when I noticed the disjointed and disturbing effect it produced. I burned it, and from the ashes there arose a single, complete reworked act of fifty pages that would run for less than an hour. Although this play form is not completely new, it seems to be my special property and has a good chance of gaining favor with the public when tastes change. My hope is to educate a public to sit through a full evening's show in one act. But this whole question must first be probed more deeply. In the meantime, in order to establish resting places for the audience and the actors without destroying the illusion, I have made use of three arts that belong to the drama: the monologue, the pantomime, and the ballet, all of which were part of classic tragedy, the monody having become the monologue and the choral dance, the ballet.

The realists have banished the monologue from the stage as implausible. But if I can motivate it, I make it plausible, and I can then use it to my advantage. Now it is certainly plausible for a speaker to pace the floor and read his speech aloud to himself. It is plausible for an actor to practice his part aloud, for a child to talk to her cat, a mother to babble to her baby, an old lady to chatter to her parrot, and a sleeping man to talk in his sleep. And in order to give the actor a chance to work on his own for once and for a moment not be obliged to follow the author's directions, I have not written out the monologues in detail but simply outlined them. Since it makes very little difference what is said while asleep, or to the parrot or the cat, inasmuch as it does not affect the main action, a gifted player who is in the midst of the situation and mood of the play can probably improvise the monologue better than the author, who cannot estimate ahead of time how much may be said and for how long before the illusion is broken.

Some theaters in Italy have, as we know, returned to the art of improvisation[6] and have thereby trained actors who are truly inventive—without, however, violating the intentions of the author. This seems to be a step in the right direction and possibly the beginning of a new, fertile form of art that will be genuinely *creative.*

In places where the monologue cannot be properly motivated, I have resorted to pantomime. Here I have given the actor even more freedom to be creative and win

5. Edmond de Goncourt (1822–1896) and Jules de Goncourt (1830–1870), coauthors of six novels set in 18th-century France.

6. That is, the commedia dell'arte, which relies on improvisation by stock characters along conventional plotlines.

honor on his own. Nevertheless, not to try the audience beyond its limits, I have relied on music—well motivated by the Midsummer Eve dance—to exercise its hypnotic powers during the pantomime scene. I beg the music director to select his tunes with great care, so that associations foreign to the mood of the play will not be produced by reminders of popular operattas or current dance numbers or by folk music of interest only to ethnologists.

The ballet that I have introduced cannot be replaced by a so-called crowd scene. Such scenes are always badly acted, with a pack of babbling fools taking advantage of the occasion to "gag it up," thereby destroying the illusion. Inasmuch as country people do not improvise their taunts but make use of material already to hand by giving it a double meaning, I have not composed an original lampoon but have made use of a little-known round dance that I noted down in the Stockholm district. The words do not fit the situation exactly, which is what I intended, since the slave in his cunning (that is, weakness) never attacks directly. At any rate, let us have no comedians in this serious story and no obscene smirking over an affair that nails the lid on a family coffin.

As far as the scenery is concerned, I have borrowed from impressionistic painting the idea of asymmetrical and open composition, and I believe that I have thereby gained something in the way of greater illusion. Because the audience cannot see the whole room and all the furniture, they will have to surmise what's missing; that is, their imagination will be stimulated to fill in the rest of the picture. I have gained something else by this: I have avoided those tiresome exits through doors. Stage doors are made of canvas and rock at the slightest touch. They cannot even be used to indicate the wrath of an angry father who storms out of the house after a bad dinner, slamming the door behind him "so that the whole house shakes." (In the theater it sways and billows.) Furthermore, I have confined the action to one set, both to give the characters a chance to become part and parcel of their environment and to cut down on scenic extravagance. If there is only one set, one has a right to expect it to be as realistic as possible. Yet nothing is more difficult than to make a room look like a room, however easy it may be for the scene painter to create waterfalls and erupting volcanos. I suppose we shall have to put up with walls made of canvas, but isn't it about time that we stopped painting shelves and pots and pans on the canvas? There are so many other conventions in the theater that we are told to accept in good faith that we should be spared the strain of believing in painted saucepans.

I have placed the backdrop and the table at an angle to force the actors to play face to face or in half profile when they are seated opposite each other at the table. In a production of *Aida*[7] I saw a flat placed at such an angle, which led the eye out in an unfamiliar perspective. Nor did it look as if it had been set that way simply to be different or to avoid those monotonous right angles.

Another desirable innovation would be the removal of the footlights. I understand that the purpose of lighting from below is to make the actors look more full in the face. But may I ask why all actors should have full faces? Doesn't this kind of lighting wipe out many of the finer features in the lower part of the face, especially around the jaws? Doesn't it distort the shape of the nose and throw false shadows above the eyes? If not, it certainly does something else: it hurts the actor's eyes. The footlights hit the retina at an angle from which it is usually shielded (except in sailors who must look at the sunlight reflected in the water), and the result is the loss of any effective play of the eyes. All one ever sees on stage are goggle-eyed glances sideways at the boxes or upward at the balcony, with only the whites of the eyes being visible in the latter case. And this probably also accounts for that tiresome fluttering of the eyelashes that the female performers are particularly guilty of. If an actor nowadays wants to express something with his eyes, he can only do it looking right at the

7. An Italian opera by Giuseppe Verdi (1871), set in ancient Egypt.

audience, in which case he makes direct contact with someone outside the proscenium arch—a bad habit known, justifiably or not, as "saying hello to friends."

I should think that the use of sufficiently strong side lights (through the use of reflectors or something like them) would provide the actor with a new asset: an increased range of expression made possible by the play of the eyes, the most expressive part of the face.

I have scarcely any illusions about getting actors to play for the audience and not directly at them, although this should be the goal. Nor do I dream of ever seeing an actor play through all of an important scene with his back to the audience. But is it too much to hope that crucial scenes could be played where the author indicated and not in front of the prompter's box as if they were duets demanding applause? I am not calling for a revolution, only for some small changes. I am well aware that transforming the stage into a real room with the fourth wall missing and with some of the furniture placed with backs to the auditorium would only upset the audience, at least for the present.

If I bring up the subject of makeup, it is not because I dare hope to be heeded by the ladies, who would rather be beautiful than truthful. But the male actor might do well to consider if it is an advantage to paint his face with character lines that remain there like a mask. Let us imagine an actor who pencils in with soot a few lines between his eyes to indicate great anger, and let us suppose that in that permanently enraged state he finds he has to smile on a certain line. Imagine the horrible grimace! And how can the old character actor wrinkle his brows in anger when his false bald pate is as smooth as a billiard ball?

In a modern psychological drama, in which every tremor of the soul should be reflected more by facial expressions than by gestures and grunts, it would probably be most sensible to experiment with strong side lighting on a small stage, using actors without any makeup or a minimum of it.

And then, if we could get rid of the visible orchestra with its disturbing lights and the faces turned toward the public; if the auditorium floor could be raised so that the spectator's eyes are not level with the actor's knees; if we could get rid of the proscenium boxes and their occupants, arriving giggling and drunk from their dinners; and if we could have it dark in the auditorium during the performance; and if, above everything else, we could have a *small* stage and an *intimate* auditorium—then possibly a new drama might arise and at least one theater become a refuge for cultured audiences. While we are waiting for such a theater, we shall have to write for the dramatic stockpile and prepare the repertory that one day shall come.

Here is my attempt. If I have failed, there is still time to try again!

CHARACTERS

MISS JULIE, twenty-five years old

JEAN, valet, thirty years old

CHRISTINE, cook, thirty-five years old

THE CHORUS, a party of country folk

The scene is a country estate in Sweden.

The time: A Midsummer Night in the 1880s. The hours after midnight, June 24, St. John the Baptist's Day.

The Set

The scene is the kitchen of the estate belonging to the count, MISS JULIE's father. It is a large kitchen, situated along with the servants' quarters in the basement of the manor house. The side walls and the ceiling of the kitchen are masked by the tormentors[8] and borders of the set. The rear wall runs obliquely upstage from the left. On this wall to the left are two shelves with pots and pans of copper, iron, and pewter. The shelves are decorated with goffered[9] paper. A little to the right can be seen three-fourths of a deep arched entry with two glass doors, and through them can be seen a fountain with a statue of a cupid,[1] lilac bushes in bloom, and the tops of some Lombardy poplars.

From the left of the stage the corner of a large, Dutch-tile kitchen stove protrudes with part of the hood showing.

Projecting from the right side of the stage is one end of the servants' dining table of white pine, with a few chairs around it.

The stove is decorated with branches of birch leaves; the floor is strewn with juniper twigs.

On the end of the table is a large Japanese spice jar filled with lilacs.

An icebox, a sink, a washbasin.

Over the door a big old-fashioned bell; and to the left of the door the gaping mouth of a speaking tube.[2]

———————

[CHRISTINE *is standing at the stove, frying something in a pan. She is wearing a light-colored cotton dress and an apron.*]

[JEAN *enters, dressed in livery and carrying a pair of high-top boots with spurs. He sets them where they are clearly visible.*]

JEAN   What a night! She's wild again! Miss Julie's absolutely wild!

CHRISTINE   You sure took your time getting back!

JEAN   I took the count down to the station, and on my way back, I passed the barn and went in for a dance. And there was Miss Julie leading the dance
5   with the game warden. Then she noticed me. And she ran right into my arms and chose me for the ladies' waltz. And she's been dancing ever since like—like I don't know what. Wild, I tell you, absolutely wild!

CHRISTINE   That's nothing new. But she's been worse than ever during the last two weeks, ever since her engagement was broken off.

10 JEAN   Yes. I never did hear all there was to that. He was a good man, too, even if he wasn't rich. Well, they've got such crazy ideas. [*He sits down at the end of the table.*] Tell me, isn't it strange that a young girl like her—all right, young woman—prefers to stay home here with the servants rather than go with her father to visit her relatives?

15 CHRISTINE   I suppose she's ashamed to face them after that fiasco with her young man.

JEAN   No doubt. He wouldn't take any nonsense from her. Do you know what happened, Christine? I saw the whole thing. Of course, I didn't let on.

CHRISTINE   You were there? I don't believe it.

20 JEAN   Well, I was. They were in the stable yard one evening—and she was training him, that's what she called it. Do you know what? She was making him jump over her riding whip—training him like a dog. He jumped over

---

8. Curtains or doors on the sides of a stage set that hide the wings from the view of the audience.
9. Embossed to produce patterns of raised figures.

1. A representation of the Roman god of love.
2. A hollow pipe connecting two cones, used in businesses and upper-class homes in the 19th century for communicating over distances.

twice, and she whipped him both times. But the third time, he grabbed
the whip from her, [scratched her face with it—long scratch on her left
25   cheek;]³ then broke it in a thousand pieces—and walked off.

CHRISTINE   I don't believe it! What do you know!

JEAN   Yes, that put an end to that affair. —What have you got for me that's
really good, Christine?

CHRISTINE [*serving him from the frying pan*]   Just a little bit of kidney. Cut it
30   from the veal roast.

JEAN [*smelling it*]   Wonderful! One of my special *délices*!⁴ [*Feeling the plate*]
Hey, you didn't warm the plate!

CHRISTINE   You're more fussy than the count himself when you set your
mind to it. [*She rumples his hair affectionately.*]

35 JEAN [*irritated*]   Cut it out! Don't muss up my hair. You know how particular
I am!

CHRISTINE   Oh, don't get mad. Can I help it if I like you?

[JEAN *eats.* CHRISTINE *gets out a bottle of beer.*]

JEAN   Beer on Midsummer Eve! No thank you! I've got something much better than that. [*He opens a drawer in the table and takes out a bottle of red
40   wine with a gold seal.*] Do you see that? Gold Seal. Now give me a glass.

[*She hands him a tumbler.*]

—No, a wineglass of course. This has to be drunk properly. No water.

CHRISTINE [*goes back to the stove and puts on a small saucepan*]   Lord help
the woman who gets you for a husband. You're an old fussbudget!

JEAN   Talk, talk! You'd consider yourself lucky if you got yourself a man as
45   good as me. It hasn't done you any harm to have people think I'm your
fiancé. [*He tastes the wine.*] Very good. Excellent. But warmed just a little
too little. [*Warming the glass in his hands*] We bought this in Dijon. Four
francs a liter, unbottled—and the tax on top of that. . . . What on earth are
you cooking? It stinks like hell!

50 CHRISTINE   Some damn mess that Miss Julie wants for her Diana, that damn
dog of hers.

JEAN   You should watch your language, Christine. . . . Why do you have to
stand in front of the stove on a holiday, cooking for that mutt? Is it sick?

CHRISTINE   Oh, she's sick, all right! She sneaked out to the gatekeeper's pug
55   and—got herself in a fix. And you know Miss Julie, she can't stand anything
like that.

JEAN   She's too stuck-up in some ways and not proud enough in others. Just
like her mother. The countess felt right at home in the kitchen or down in
the barn with the cows, but when she went driving, one horse wasn't
60   enough for her, she had to have a pair. Her sleeves were always dirty, but
her buttons had the royal crown on them. As for Miss Julie, she doesn't
give a hoot in hell how she looks and acts. I mean, she's not really refined,
not really. Just now, down at the barn, she grabbed the game warden right
from under Anna's eyes and asked him to dance. You wouldn't see anybody
65   in our class behaving like that. But that's what happens when the gentry try
to act like the common people—they become common! . . . However, I'll

---

3. The passage in brackets was deleted in
Strindberg's manuscript, probably by Strind-

berg himself [translator's note].
4. Pleasures, delights (French).

say one thing for her: she *is* beautiful! Statuesque! Ah, those shoulders—
those—and so forth, and so forth!

CHRISTINE   Oh, don't exaggerate. Clara tells me all about her, and Clara
70   dresses her.

JEAN   Clara, pooh! You women are always jealous of each other. I've been out
riding with her. . . . And how she can dance . . . !

CHRISTINE   Listen, Jean, you *are* going to dance with me, aren't you, when
I'm finished here?

75   JEAN   Certainly! Of course I am.

CHRISTINE   Promise?

JEAN   Promise! Listen—if I say I'm going to do a thing, I do it. . . . Christine,
I thank you for a delicious meal. Superb! [*He shoves the cork back into the
bottle.*]

[MISS JULIE *appears in the entry, talking to someone outside.*]

MISS JULIE   I'll be right back. Don't wait for me.

[JEAN *slips the bottle into the table drawer quickly and rises respectfully.*
MISS JULIE *comes in and crosses over to* CHRISTINE, *who is at the stove.*]

80   MISS JULIE   Did you get it ready?

[CHRISTINE *signals that* JEAN *is present.*]

JEAN [*polite and charming*]   Are you ladies sharing secrets?

MISS JULIE [*flipping her handkerchief in his face*]   Don't be nosy!

JEAN   Oh, that smells good! Violets.

MISS JULIE [*flirting with him*]   Don't be impudent! And don't tell me you're
85   an expert on perfumes, too. I love the way you dance!—No, mustn't look!
Go away!

JEAN [*cocky but pleasant*]   What are the ladies cooking up? A witches' brew
for Midsummer Eve? So they can tell the future?[5] Read what's in the cards
for them, and see who they'll marry?

90   MISS JULIE [*curtly*]   You'd have to have good eyes to see that. [*To* CHRISTINE]
Pour it into a small bottle, and seal it tight. . . . Jean, come and dance a
schottische[6] with me.

JEAN [*hesitating*]   I hope you don't think I'm being rude, but I've already
promised this dance to Christine.

95   MISS JULIE   She can always find someone. Isn't that so, Christine? You don't
mind if I borrow Jean for a minute, do you?

CHRISTINE   It ain't up to me. If Miss Julie is gracious enough to invite you, it
ain't right for you to say no, Jean. You go on, and thank her for the honor.

JEAN   Frankly, Miss Julie, I don't want to hurt your feelings, but I wonder if
100   it's wise—I mean for you to dance twice in a row with the same partner.
Especially since the people around here love to talk.

MISS JULIE [*bridling*]   What do you mean? What kind of talk? What are you
trying to say?

JEAN [*retreating*]   I wish you wouldn't misunderstand me, Miss Julie. It just
105   doesn't look right for you to prefer one of your servants to the others who
are hoping for the same unusual honor.

MISS JULIE   Prefer! What an idea! I'm really surprised. I, the mistress of
the house, am good enough to come to their dance, and when I feel like

5. In Swedish folklore, Midsummer Eve is a
time of fortune-telling.

6. Literally, "Scottish" (German), a country
dance similar to the polka.

110 dancing, I want to dance with someone who knows how to lead. After all I don't want to look ridiculous.

JEAN As you wish, Miss Julie. I am at your orders.

MISS JULIE [*gently*] Don't take it as an order. Tonight we're all just having a good time. There's no question of rank. Now give me your arm. —Don't worry, Christine. I won't run off with your boyfriend.

> [JEAN *gives her his arm and leads her out.*]

Pantomime Scene

This should be played as if the actress were actually alone. She turns her back on the audience when she feels like it; she does not look out into the auditorium; she does not rush through the scene as if afraid the audience will grow impatient.

CHRISTINE *alone. In the distance the sound of the violins playing the schottische.* CHRISTINE, *humming in time with the music, cleans up after* JEAN, *washes the dishes, dries them, and puts them away in a cupboard. Then she takes off her apron, takes a little mirror from one of the table drawers, and leans it against the jar of lilacs on the table. She lights a tallow candle, heats a curling iron, and curls the bangs on her forehead. Then she goes to the doorway and stands listening to the music. She comes back to the table and finds the handkerchief that* MISS JULIE *left behind. She smells it, spreads it out, and then, as if lost in thought, stretches it, smooths it out, and folds it in four.*

> [JEAN *enters alone.*]

JEAN Wild! I told you she was wild! You should have seen the way she was dancing. Everyone was peeking at her from behind the doors and laughing at her. What's the matter with her, Christine?

CHRISTINE You might know it's her monthlies, Jean. She always acts peculiar 5 then. . . . Well, are you going to dance with me?

JEAN You're not mad at me because I broke my promise?

CHRISTINE Of course not. Not for a little thing like that, you know that. I know my place.

JEAN [*grabs her around the waist*] You're a sensible girl, Christine. You're 10 going to make somebody a good wife—

> [MISS JULIE, *coming in, sees them together. She is unpleasantly surprised.*]

MISS JULIE [*with forced gaiety*] Well, aren't you the gallant beau—running away from your partner!

JEAN On the contrary, Miss Julie. As you can see, I've hurried back to the partner I deserted.

15 MISS JULIE [*changing tack*] You know, you're the best dancer I've met. — Why are you wearing livery on a holiday? Take it off at once.

JEAN I'd have to ask you to leave for a minute. My black coat is hanging right here—[*He moves to the right and points.*]

MISS JULIE You're not embarrassed because I'm here, are you? Just to 20 change your coat? Go in your room and come right back again. Or else stay here and I'll turn my back.

JEAN If you'll excuse me, Miss Julie.

> [*He goes off to the right. His arm can be seen as he changes his coat.*]

MISS JULIE [*to* CHRISTINE] Tell me something, Christine. Is Jean your fiancé? He acts so familiar with you.

25 CHRISTINE Fiancé? I suppose so. At least we say we are.

MISS JULIE What do you mean?

CHRISTINE   Well, Miss Julie, you have had fiancés yourself, and you know—

MISS JULIE   But we were properly engaged—!

CHRISTINE   I know, but did anything come of it?

[JEAN *comes back, wearing a black cutaway coat and derby.*]

30   MISS JULIE   *Très gentil, monsieur Jean! Très gentil!*

JEAN   *Vous voulez plaisanter, madame.*

MISS JULIE   *Et vous voulez parler français!*[7] Where did you learn to speak French?

JEAN   In Switzerland. I was *sommelier*[8] in one of the biggest hotels in
35   Lucerne.

MISS JULIE   My! but you look quite the gentleman in that coat! *Charmant!*[9]

[*She sits down at the table.*]

JEAN   Flatterer!

MISS JULIE [*stiffening*]   Who said I was flattering you?

JEAN   My natural modesty would not allow me to presume that you were
40   paying sincere compliments to someone like me, and therefore I could only
assume that you were exaggerating, which, in this case, means flattering
me.

MISS JULIE   You certainly have a way with words. Where did you learn to talk
like that? Seeing plays?

45   JEAN   And other places. You don't think I stayed in the house for six years
when I was a valet in Stockholm, do you?

MISS JULIE   I thought you were born in this district. Weren't you?

JEAN   My father worked as a farmhand on the district attorney's estate, next
door to yours. I used to see you when you were little. Of course you didn't
50   notice me.

MISS JULIE   Did you really?

JEAN   Yes. I remember one time in particular—. But I can't tell you about
that!

MISS JULIE   Of course you can. . . . Oh, come on. Just this once—for me.

55   JEAN   No. No, I really couldn't. Not now. Some other time maybe.

MISS JULIE   Some other time? That means never. What's the harm in telling
me now?

JEAN   There's no harm. I just don't feel like it. —Look at her.

[*He nods at* CHRISTINE, *who has fallen asleep in a chair by the stove.*]

MISS JULIE   Won't she make somebody a pretty wife! I'll bet she snores, too.

60   JEAN   No, she doesn't. But she talks in her sleep.

MISS JULIE [*archly*]   Now how could you know she talks in her sleep?

JEAN [*coolly*]   I've heard her . . .

[*Pause. They look at each other.*]

MISS JULIE   Why don't you sit down?

JEAN   I wouldn't take the liberty in your presence.

65   MISS JULIE   Not even if I ordered you?

JEAN   Of course I'd obey.

MISS JULIE   Well then: sit down. —Wait a minute. Could you get me something to drink?

---

7. "Very nice, Mister Jean! Very nice!" "You
are trying to flatter me, madam." "And you
are trying to speak French!" (French).

8. Wine steward.

9. Charming (French).

JEAN   I don't know what there is in the icebox. Only beer, I suppose.

70   MISS JULIE   Only beer?! I have simple tastes. I prefer beer to wine.

> [JEAN *takes a bottle of beer from the icebox and opens it. He looks in the cupboard for a glass and a plate, and serves her.*]

JEAN   At your service, *mademoiselle.*[1]

MISS JULIE   Thank you. What about you?

JEAN   I'm not much of a beer-drinker, thank you, but if it's your wish—

MISS JULIE   My wish! I should think a gentleman would want to keep his lady
75   company.

JEAN   A point well taken! [*He opens another bottle and takes a glass.*]

MISS JULIE   Now drink a toast to me!

> [JEAN *hesitates.*]

You're not shy, are you? A big, strong man like you?

> [*Playfully,* JEAN *kneels and raises his glass in mock gallantry.*]

JEAN   To my lady's health!

80   MISS JULIE   Bravo! Now you have to kiss my shoe, too. Then you will have hit
it off perfectly.

> [JEAN *hesitates, then boldly grasps her foot and touches it lightly with his lips.*]

Superb! You should have been an actor.

JEAN [*rising*]   This has got to stop, Miss Julie! Someone might come in and
see us.

85   MISS JULIE   So what?

JEAN   People would talk, that's what! If you knew how their tongues were
wagging out there just a few minutes ago!

MISS JULIE   What did they say? Tell me. Sit down and tell me.

JEAN   I don't want to hurt your feelings. . . . They used expressions that—
90   that hinted at certain—you know what I mean. You're not a child. And
when they see a woman drinking, alone with a man—and a servant at
that—in the middle of the night—well . . .

MISS JULIE   Well what?! Besides, we're not alone. Christine is here.

JEAN   Sleeping!

95   MISS JULIE   I'll wake her up. [*She goes over to* CHRISTINE.] Christine! Are you
asleep? [CHRISTINE *babbles in her sleep.*] Christine! —My, how sound she
sleeps!

CHRISTINE [*talking in her sleep*]   Count's boots are brushed . . . put on the
coffee . . . right away, right away, right . . . mm—mm . . . poofff . . .

> [MISS JULIE *shakes* CHRISTINE.]

100   MISS JULIE   Wake up, will you!

JEAN [*sternly*]   Let her alone! Let her sleep!

MISS JULIE [*sharply*]   What?

JEAN   She's been standing over the stove all day. She's worn out when night
comes. Anyone asleep is entitled to some consideration.

105   MISS JULIE [*changing her tone*]   That's a very kind thought. It does you credit,
Jean. You're right, of course. [*She offers* JEAN *her hand.*] Now come on out
and pick some lilacs for me.

---

1. Miss (French).

[*During the following,* CHRISTINE *wakes up and, drunk with sleep, shuffles off to the right to go to bed. A polka can be heard in the distance.*]

JEAN   With you, Miss Julie?

MISS JULIE   Yes, with me.

110 JEAN   That's no good. Absolutely not.

MISS JULIE   I don't know what you're thinking. Aren't you letting your imagination run away with you?

JEAN   No. Other people are.

MISS JULIE   How? Imagining that I'm—*verliebt*[2] with a servant?

115 JEAN   I'm not conceited, but it's been known to happen. And to these people nothing's sacred.

MISS JULIE   "These people!" Why, I do believe you're an aristocrat!

JEAN   Yes, I am.

MISS JULIE   I'm climbing down—

120 JEAN   Don't climb down, Miss Julie! Take my advice. No one will believe that you climbed down deliberately. They'll say you fell.

MISS JULIE   I have a higher opinion of these people than you do. Let's see who's right! Come on! [*She gives him a long, steady look.*]

JEAN   You know, you're very strange.

125 MISS JULIE   Perhaps. But then so are you. . . . Besides, everything is strange. Life, people, everything. It's all scum, drifting and drifting on the water until it sinks—drowns. There's a dream I have every now and then. It's coming back to me now. I'm sitting on top of a pillar. I've climbed up it somehow and I don't know how to get back down. When I look down I get

130 dizzy. I have to get down but I don't have the courage to jump. I can't hold on much longer and I want to fall; but I don't fall. I know I won't have any peace until I get down; no rest until I get down, down on the ground. And if I ever got down on the ground, I'd want to go farther down, right down into the earth. . . . Have you ever felt anything like that?

135 JEAN   Never! I used to dream that I'm lying under a tall tree in a dark woods. I want to get up, up to the very top, to look out over the bright landscape with the sun shining on it, to rob the bird's nest up there with the golden eggs in it. And I climb and I climb, but the trunk is so thick, and so smooth, and it's such a long way to that first branch. But I know that if I could just

140 reach that first branch, I'd go right to the top as if on a ladder. I've never reached it yet, but someday I will—even if only in my dreams.

MISS JULIE   Here I am talking about dreams with you. Come out with me. Only into the park a way. [*She offers him her arm, and they start to go.*]

JEAN   Let's sleep on nine midsummer flowers, Miss Julie, and then our

145 dreams will come true![3]

[MISS JULIE *and* JEAN *suddenly turn around in the doorway.* JEAN *is holding his hand over one eye.*]

MISS JULIE   You've caught something in your eye. Let me see.

JEAN   It's nothing. Just a bit of dust. It'll go away.

MISS JULIE   The sleeve of my dress must have grazed your eye. Sit down and I'll help you. [*She takes him by the arm and sits him down. She takes his*

2. In love (German).

3. A girl would pick in silence on Midsummer Eve nine different sorts of flowers, make a bouquet of them, and place them under her pillow. The man who appeared in her dreams would be the man she would marry [translator's note].

head and leans it back. With the corner of her handkerchief she tries to get
150 *out the bit of dust.*] Now sit still, absolutely still. [*She slaps his hand.*] Do as
you're told. Why, I believe you're trembling—a big, strong man like you.
[*She feels his biceps.*] With such big arms!

JEAN [*warningly*] Miss Julie!

MISS JULIE Yes, *Monsieur Jean?*

155 JEAN *Attention! Je ne suis qu'un homme!*[4]

MISS JULIE Sit still, I tell you! . . . There now! It's out. Kiss my hand and
thank me!

JEAN [*rising to his feet.*] Listen to me, Miss Julie—Christine has gone to
bed! —Listen to me, I tell you!

160 MISS JULIE Kiss my hand first!

JEAN Listen to me!

MISS JULIE Kiss my hand first!

JEAN All right. But you'll have no one to blame but yourself.

MISS JULIE For what?

165 JEAN For what! Are you twenty-five years old and still a child? Don't you
know it's dangerous to play with fire?

MISS JULIE Not for me, I'm insured!

JEAN [*boldly*] Oh, no, you're not! And even if you are, there's inflammable
stuff next door.

170 MISS JULIE Meaning you?

JEAN Yes. Not just because it's me, but because I'm young and—

MISS JULIE And irresistibly handsome? What incredible conceit! A Don Juan,
maybe! Or a Joseph![5] Yes, bless my soul, that's it: you're a Joseph!

JEAN You think so?!

175 MISS JULIE I'm almost afraid so!

[JEAN *boldly steps up to her, grabs her around the waist, tries to kiss her.*
She slaps his face.]

None of that!

JEAN More games? Or are you serious?

MISS JULIE I'm serious.

JEAN Then you must have been serious a moment ago, too! You take your
180 games too seriously; that's dangerous. Well, I'm tired of your games, and if
you'll excuse me, I'll return to my work. [*Takes up the boots and starts to*
brush them.] The count will be wanting his boots on time, and it's long past
midnight.

MISS JULIE Put those boots down.

185 JEAN No! This is my job. It's what I'm here for. I never undertook to be your
playmate. That's something I could never be. I consider myself too good for
that.

MISS JULIE You are proud.

JEAN In some ways. Not in others.

190 MISS JULIE Have you ever been in love?

---

4. Be careful! I am just a man! (French).
5. In the Bible, a son of Jacob: after Joseph
was sold into slavery by his brothers, his good
looks led his master's wife to make sexual
advances toward him; when he refused her,
she falsely accused him of rape (Genesis
39.6–18). *Don Juan:* the legendary Spanish
seducer of women, whose story is told in a
number of European dramas and in Mozart's
opera *Don Giovanni* (1787).

JEAN We don't use that word around here. But I've hankered after some girls, if that's what you mean. . . . I even got sick once because I couldn't have the one I wanted—really sick, like the princes in the Arabian Nights[6]—who couldn't eat or drink for love.

195 MISS JULIE Who was she?

[JEAN *does not reply.*]

Who was the girl?

JEAN You can't get that out of me.

MISS JULIE Even if I ask you as an equal—ask you—as a friend? . . . Who was she?

200 JEAN You.

MISS JULIE [*sitting down*] How—amusing . . .

JEAN Yes, maybe so. Ridiculous. . . . That's why I didn't want to tell you about it before. Want to hear the whole story? . . . Have you any idea what you and your people look like from down below? Of course not. Like hawks
205 or eagles, that's what: you hardly ever see their backs because they're always soaring so high up. I lived with seven brothers and sisters—and a pig—out on the wasteland where there wasn't even a tree growing. But from my window I could see the wall of the count's garden with the apple trees sticking up over it. That was the Garden of Eden for me, and there
210 were many angry angels with flaming swords standing guard over it.[7] But in spite of them, I and the other boys found a way to the Tree of Life. . . . How contemptible, that's what you're thinking.

MISS JULIE For stealing apples? All boys do that.

JEAN That's what you say now. All the same, you think me contemptible.
215 Never mind. One day I went with my mother into this paradise to weed the onion beds. Next to the vegetable garden stood a Turkish pavilion, shaded by jasmine and hung all over with honeysuckle. I couldn't imagine what it was used for; I only knew I had never seen such a beautiful building. People went in, and came out again. And then one day the door was left open.
220 I sneaked in. The walls were covered with portraits of kings and emperors, and the windows had red curtains with tassels on them. —Recognize it? Yes, the count's private privy. . . . I— [*He breaks off a lilac and holds it under* MISS JULIE's *nose.*] I had never been inside a castle, never seen anything besides the church. This was more beautiful. And no matter what I
225 tried to think about, my thoughts always came back—to that little pavilion. And little by little there arose in me a desire to experience just for once the whole pleasure of—. *Enfin,*[8] I sneaked in, looked about, and marveled. And just then I heard someone coming! There was only one way out—for the upper-class people. But for me there was one more—a lower one.[9] And I
230 had no other choice but to take it. [MISS JULIE, *who has taken the lilac from* JEAN, *lets it fall to the table.*] Then I began to run like mad, plunging through the raspberry bushes, plowing through the strawberry patches, and came up on the rose terrace. And there I caught sight of a pink dress and a pair of white stockings. You! I crawled under—well, you can imagine

6. *The Thousand and One Nights*, a collection of ancient tales in Arabic, arranged in its present form in the 15th century.
7. See Genesis 3.24.

8. Finally (French).
9. That is, through the pit or trench under the outhouse.

235 what it was like—under thistles that pricked me and wet dirt that stank to high heaven. And all the while I could see you walking among the roses. I said to myself, "If it's true that a thief can enter heaven and be with the angels,[1] isn't it strange that a poor man's child here on God's green earth can't enter the count's park and play with the count's daughter."

240 MISS JULIE [*sentimentally*]   Do you think all poor children have felt that way?

JEAN [*hesitatingly at first, then with mounting conviction*]   If all poor ch—? Yes—yes, naturally. Of course!

MISS JULIE   It must be terrible to be poor.

JEAN [*with exaggerated intensity*]   Oh, Miss Julie! You don't know! A dog can
245 lie on the sofa with its mistress; a horse can have its nose stroked by the hand of a countess; but a servant—! [*Changing his tone*] Of course, now and then you meet somebody with guts enough to work his way up in the world, but how often? —Anyway, you know what I did afterward? I threw myself into the millstream with all my clothes on. Got fished out and spanked. But the
250 following Sunday, when Pa and everybody else in the house went to visit Grandma, I arranged things so I'd be left behind. Then I washed myself all over with soap and warm water, put on my best clothes, and went off to church—just to see you there once more. I saw you, and then I went home determined to die. But I wanted to die beautifully and comfortably, without
255 pain. I remembered some stories I had heard about how fatal it was to sleep under an elderberry bush. And we had a big one that had just blossomed out. I stripped it of every leaf and blossom it had and made a bed of them in a bin of oats. Have you ever noticed how smooth oats are? As smooth to the touch as human skin. . . . So I pulled the lid of the bin shut and closed my eyes.
260 Fell asleep. And when they woke me I was really very sick. However, I didn't die, as you can see. —What was I trying to prove? I don't know. There was no hope of winning you. It was just that you were a symbol of the absolute hopelessness of my ever getting out of the class I was born in.

MISS JULIE   You know, you have a real gift for telling stories. Did you go to
265 school?

JEAN   A little. But I've read a lot of novels and gone to the theater. And I've also listened to educated people talk. That way I learned the most.

MISS JULIE   You mean to tell me you stand around listening to what we're saying!

270 JEAN   Certainly! And I've heard an awful lot, I can tell you—sitting on the coachman's seat or rowing the boat. One time I heard you and a girlfriend talking—

MISS JULIE   Really? . . . And just what did you hear?

JEAN   Well, now, I don't know if I can repeat it. I can tell you I was a little
275 amazed. I couldn't imagine where you had learned such words. Maybe at bottom there isn't such a big difference as you might think, between people and people.

MISS JULIE   How vulgar! At least people in my class don't behave like you when we're engaged.

280 JEAN [*looking her in the eye*]   Are you sure? —Come on now, it's no use playing the innocent with me.

---

1. According to 1 Corinthians 6.9–10, the thief cannot enter heaven.

MISS JULIE   He was a beast. The man I offered my love was a beast.

JEAN   That's what you all say—afterward.

MISS JULIE   All?

285 JEAN   I'd say so. I've heard the same expression used several times before in similar circumstances.

MISS JULIE   What kind of circumstances?

JEAN   The kind we're talking about. I remember the last time I—

MISS JULIE [*rising*]   That's enough! I don't want to hear any more.

290 JEAN   How strange! Neither did she! . . . Well, now if you'll excuse me, I'll go to bed.

MISS JULIE [*softly*]   Go to bed on Midsummer Eve?

JEAN   That's right. Dancing with that crowd up there really doesn't amuse me.

295 MISS JULIE   Jean, get the key to the boathouse and row me out on the lake. I want to see the sun come up.

JEAN   Do you think that's wise?

MISS JULIE   You sound as if you were worried about your reputation.

JEAN   Why not? I don't particularly care to be made ridiculous, or to be 300 kicked out without a recommendation just when I'm trying to establish myself. Besides, I have a certain obligation to Christine.

MISS JULIE   Oh, I see. It's Christine now.

JEAN   Yes, but I'm thinking of you, too. Take my advice, Miss Julie. Go up to your room.

305 MISS JULIE   When did you start giving me orders?

JEAN   Just this once. For your own sake! Please! It's very late. You're so tired, you're drunk; you don't know what you're doing. Go to bed, Miss Julie. — Besides, if my ears aren't deceiving me, they're coming this way, looking for me. If they find us here together, you're done for!

THE CHORUS [*is heard coming nearer, singing*]

310   Said Jill to Jack, "Soil needs a tilling."
           Tri-di-ri-di-ralla, tri-di-ri-di-ra.
           Said Jack to Jill, "Time's a-spilling."
           Tri-di-ri-di-ralla-la.
           Said Jill to Jack, "Gold's a-hoarding."
315   Tri-di-ri-di-ralla, tri-di-ri-di-ra.
           Said Jack to Jill, "Tell not my lording."
           Tri-di-ri-di-ralla-la.
           Said Jill to Jack, "Hair is for plaiting."
           Tri-di-ri-di-ralla, tri-di-ri-di-ra.
320   "But Jill for Jack is not waiting."
           Tri-di-ri-di-ralla-la![2]

MISS JULIE   I know these people. I love them just as they love me. Let them come. You'll see.

JEAN   Oh, no, Miss Julie, they don't love you! They take the food you give 325 them, but they spit on it as soon as your back is turned. Believe me! Just listen to them. Listen to what they're singing. —No, you'd better not listen.

---

2. A peasants' folk song.

MISS JULIE [*listening*]   What are they singing?

JEAN   A nasty song—about you and me!

MISS JULIE   How disgusting! Oh, what cowardly, sneaking—

330 JEAN   That's what the mob always is—cowards! You can't fight them; you can only run away.

MISS JULIE   Run away? Where? There's no way out of here. And we can't go in to Christine.

JEAN   What about my room? What do you say? Rules don't count in a situa-
335   tion like this. You can trust me. —You said, let's be friends. Remember? Well, I'm your friend—your true, devoted, respectful friend.

MISS JULIE   But suppose—suppose they looked for you there?

JEAN   I'll bolt the door. If they try to break it down, I'll shoot. Come, Miss Julie! [*On his knees*] Please, Miss Julie!

340 MISS JULIE [*meaningfully*]   You promise me that you won't—

JEAN   I swear to you!

[MISS JULIE *goes out quickly to the right. Jean follows her impetuously.*]

The Ballet

The country people enter in festive costumes, with flowers in their hats. The fiddler is in the lead. A keg of small beer and a little keg of liquor, decorated with greenery, are set up on the table. Glasses are brought out. They all drink. Then they form a circle and sing "Said Jill to Jack," dancing the round dance as they sing. At the end of the dance, they all leave singing.

MISS JULIE *comes in alone; looks at the devastated kitchen; clasps her hands together; then takes out a powder puff and powders her face.* JEAN *enters. He is in high spirits.*

JEAN   You see! You heard them, didn't you? You've got to admit it's impossible to stay here.

MISS JULIE   No, I don't. But even if I did, what could we do?

JEAN   Go away, travel, get away from here!

5 MISS JULIE   Travel? Yes—but where?

JEAN   Switzerland, the Italian lakes. You've never been there?

MISS JULIE   No. Is it beautiful?

JEAN   Eternal summer, oranges, laurel trees, ah . . . !

MISS JULIE   What do we do when we get there?

10 JEAN   I'll set up a hotel—a first-class hotel with a first-class clientele.

MISS JULIE   Hotel?

JEAN   I tell you that's the life! Always new faces, new languages. Not a min-
ute to think about yourself or worry about your nerves. No looking for something to do. The work keeps you busy. Day and night the bells ring,
15   the trains whistle, the buses come and go. And all the while the money comes rolling in. I tell you it's the life!

MISS JULIE   Yes, that's the life. But what about me?

JEAN   The mistress of the whole place, the star of the establishment! With your looks—and your personality—it can't fail. It's perfect! You'll sit in the
20   office like a queen, setting your slaves in motion by pressing an electric but-
ton. The guests will file before your throne and timidly lay their treasures on your table. You can't imagine how people tremble when you shove a bill in their face! I'll salt the bills and you'll sugar them with your prettiest smile. Come on, let's get away from here—[*He takes a timetable from his pocket.*]—

25 right away—the next train! We'll be in Malmö at six-thirty, Hamburg eight-forty in the morning; Frankfurt to Basel in one day, and to Como[3] by way of the Gotthard tunnel in—let me see—three days! Three days!

MISS JULIE   You make it sound so wonderful. But, Jean, you have to give me strength. Tell me you love me. Come and put your arms around me.

30 JEAN [*hesitates*]   I want to . . . but I don't dare. Not any more, not in this house. I do love you—without a shadow of a doubt. How can you doubt that, Miss Julie?

MISS JULIE [*shyly, very becomingly*]   You don't have to be formal with me, Jean. You can call me Julie. There aren't any barriers between us now. Call
35 me Julie.

JEAN [*agonized*]   I can't! There are still barriers between us, Miss Julie, as long as we stay in this house! There's the past, there's the count. I've never met anyone I feel so much respect for. I've only got to see his gloves lying on a table and I shrivel up. I only have to hear that bell ring and I shy like a fright-
40 ened horse. I only have to look at his boots standing there so stiff and proud and I feel my spine bending. [*He kicks the boots.*] Superstitions, prejudices that they've drilled into us since we were children! But they can be forgotten just as easily! Just get us to another country where they have a republic! They'll crawl on their hands and knees when they see my uniform. On their
45 hands and knees, I tell you! But not me! Oh, no. I'm not made for crawling. I've got guts, backbone. And once I grab that first branch, you just watch me climb. I may be a valet now, but next year I'll be owning property; in ten years, I'll be living off my investments. Then I'll go to Rumania, get myself some decorations, and maybe—notice I only say maybe—end up as a count!

50 MISS JULIE   How wonderful, wonderful.

JEAN   Listen, in Rumania you can buy titles. You'll be a countess after all. My countess.

MISS JULIE   But I'm not interested in that. I'm leaving all that behind. Tell me you love me, Jean, or else—or else what difference does it make what
55 I am?

JEAN   I'll tell you a thousand times—but later! Not now. And not here. Above all, let's keep our feelings out of this or we'll make a mess of everything. We have to look at this thing calmly and coolly, like sensible people. [*He takes out a cigar, clips the end, and lights it.*] Now you sit there and I'll sit here,
60 and we'll talk as if nothing had happened.

MISS JULIE [*in anguish*]   My God, what are you? Don't you have any feelings?

JEAN   Feelings? Nobody's got more feelings than I have. But I've learned to control them.

MISS JULIE   A few minutes ago you were kissing my shoe—and now—!

65 JEAN [*harshly*]   That was a few minutes ago. We've got other things to think about now!

MISS JULIE   Don't speak to me like that, Jean!

JEAN   I'm just trying to be sensible. We've been stupid once; let's not be stupid again. Your father might be back at any moment, and we've got to decide our
70 future before then. —Now what do you think about my plans? Do you approve or don't you?

---

3. A city on the southwest end of Lake Como, in northern Italy; Jean outlines the journey there from Sweden through Germany and Switzerland.

MISS JULIE   I don't see anything wrong with them. Except one thing. For a big undertaking like that, you'd need a lot of capital. Have you got it?

JEAN   [*chewing on his cigar*]   Have I got it? Of course I have. I've got my knowledge of the business, my vast experience, my familiarity with languages. That's capital that counts for something, let me tell you.

MISS JULIE   You can't even buy the railway tickets with it.

JEAN   That's true. That's why I need a backer—someone to put up the money.

MISS JULIE   Where can you find him on a moment's notice?

JEAN   You'll find him—if you want to be my partner.

MISS JULIE   I can't. And I don't have a penny to my name.

    [*Pause.*]

JEAN   Then you can forget the whole thing.

MISS JULIE   Forget—?

JEAN   And things will stay just the way they are.

MISS JULIE   Do you think I'm going to live under the same roof with you as your mistress? Do you think I'm going to have people sneering at me behind my back? How do you think I'll ever be able to look my father in the face after this? No, no! Take me away from here, Jean—the shame, the humiliation. . . . What have I done? Oh, my God, my God! What have I done! [*She bursts into tears.*]

JEAN   Now don't start singing that tune. It won't work. What have you done that's so awful? You're not the first.

MISS JULIE   [*crying hysterically*]   Now you think me contemptible—I'm falling, falling!

JEAN   Fall down to me, and I'll lift you up again!

MISS JULIE   What awful hold did you have over me? What drove me to you? The weak to the strong? The falling to the rising! Or maybe it was love? Love? This? You don't know what love is!

JEAN   Want to bet? Did you think I was a virgin?

MISS JULIE   You're coarse—vulgar! The things you say, the things you think!

JEAN   That's the way I was brought up. It's the way I am! Now don't get hysterical. And don't play the fine lady with me. We're eating off the same platter now. . . . That's better. Come over here and be a good girl and I'll treat you to something special. [*He opens the table drawer and takes out the wine bottle. He pours the wine into two used glasses.*]

MISS JULIE   Where did you get that wine?

JEAN   From the wine cellar.

MISS JULIE   My father's burgundy!

JEAN   Should be good enough for his son-in-law.

MISS JULIE   I was drinking beer and you—!

JEAN   Shows I have better taste than you.

MISS JULIE   Thief!

JEAN   You going to squeal on me?

MISS JULIE   Oh, God! Partner in crime with a petty house thief! I must have been drunk; I must have been walking in my sleep. Midsummer Night! Night of innocent games—

JEAN   Yes, very innocent!

MISS JULIE   [*pacing up and down*]   Is there anyone here on earth as miserable as I am?

120 JEAN   Why be miserable? Look at the conquest you've made! Think of poor
Christine in there. Don't you think she's got any feelings?

MISS JULIE   I thought so a while ago; I don't now. A servant's a servant—

JEAN   And a whore's a whore!

MISS JULIE [*falls to her knees and clasps her hands together*]   Oh, God in
125   heaven, put an end to my worthless life! Lift me out of this awful filth I'm
sinking in! Save me! Save me!

JEAN   I feel sorry for you, I have to admit it. When I was lying in the onion
beds, looking up at you on the rose terrace, I—I'm telling you the truth
now—I had the same dirty thoughts that all boys have.

130 MISS JULIE   And you said you wanted to die for me!

JEAN   In the oat bin? That was only a story.

MISS JULIE   A lie, you mean.

JEAN [*getting sleepy*]   Practically. I think I read it in a paper about a chimney
sweep who curled up in a wood-bin with some lilacs because they were
135   going to arrest him for nonsupport of his child.

MISS JULIE   Now I see you as you really are.

JEAN   What did you expect me to do? It's always the fancy talk that gets the
women.

MISS JULIE   You dog!

140 JEAN   You bitch!

MISS JULIE   Well, now you've seen the eagle's back—

JEAN   Wasn't exactly its back—!

MISS JULIE   I was going to be the window dressing for your hotel—!

JEAN   And I the hotel—!

145 MISS JULIE   Sitting at the desk, attracting your customers, padding your
bills—!

JEAN   I could manage that myself—!

MISS JULIE   How can a human soul be so dirty and filthy?

JEAN   Then why don't you clean it up?

150 MISS JULIE   You lackey! You shoeshine boy! Stand up when I talk to you!

JEAN   You lackey lover! You bootblack's tramp! Shut your mouth and get out
of here! Who do you think you are telling me I'm coarse? I've never seen
anybody in my class behave as crudely as you did tonight. Have you ever
seen any of the girls around here grab at a man like you did? Do you think
155   any of the girls of my class would throw themselves at a man like that? I've
never seen the like of it except in animals and prostitutes!

MISS JULIE [*crushed*]   That's right! Hit me! Walk all over me! It's all I deserve.
I'm rotten. But help me! Help me to get out of this—if there is any way out
for me!

160 JEAN [*less harsh*]   I'd be doing myself an injustice if I didn't admit that part of
the credit for this seduction belongs to me. But do you think a person in
my position would have dared to look twice at you if you hadn't asked for
it? I'm still amazed—

MISS JULIE   And still proud.

165 JEAN   Why not? But I've got to confess the victory was a little too easy to give
me any real thrill.

MISS JULIE   Go on, hit me again!

JEAN [*standing up*]   No. . . . I'm sorry I said that. I never hit a person who's
down, especially a woman. I can't deny that, in one way, it was good to find

170 out that what I saw glittering up above was only fool's gold, to see that the eagle's back was as gray as its belly, that the smooth cheek was just powder, and that there could be dirt under the manicured nails, that the handkerchief was soiled even though it smelled of perfume. But, in another way, it hurts to find that everything I was striving for wasn't very high above me
175 after all, wasn't even real. It hurts me to see you sink far lower than your own cook. Hurts, like seeing the last flowers cut to pieces by the autumn rains and turned to muck.

MISS JULIE   You talk as if you already stood high above me.

JEAN   Well, don't I? Don't forget I could make you a countess but you can
180 never make me a count.

MISS JULIE   I have a father for a count. You can never have that!

JEAN   True. But I might father my own counts—that is, if—

MISS JULIE   You're a thief! I'm not!

JEAN   There are worse things than being a thief. A lot worse. And besides,
185 when I take a position in a house, I consider myself a member of the family—in a way, like a child in the house. It's no crime for a child to steal a few ripe cherries when they're falling off the trees, is it? [He begins to feel passionate again.] Miss Julie, you're a beautiful woman, much too good for the likes of me. You got carried away by your emotions and now you want
190 to cover up your mistake by telling yourself that you love me. You don't love me. Maybe you were attracted by my looks—in which case your kind of love is no better than mine. But I could never be satisfied to be just an animal for you, and I could never make you love me.

MISS JULIE   How do you know that for sure?

195 JEAN   You mean there's a chance? I could love you, there's no doubt about that. You're beautiful, you're refined—[He goes up to her and takes her hand.]—educated, lovable when you want to be, and once you set a man's heart on fire, I'll bet it burns forever. [He puts his arm around her waist.] You're like hot wine with strong spices. One of your kisses is enough to—

[He attempts to lead her out, but she rather reluctantly breaks away from him.]

200 MISS JULIE   Let me go. You don't get me that way.

JEAN   Then how? Not by petting you and not with pretty words, not by planning for the future, not by saving you from humiliation! Then how, tell me how?

MISS JULIE   How? How? I don't know how! I don't know at all! —I hate you
205 like I hate rats, but I can't get away from you.

JEAN   Then come away with me!

MISS JULIE   [pulling herself together]   Away? Yes, we'll go away! —But I'm so tired. Pour me a glass of wine, will you?

[JEAN pours the wine, MISS JULIE looks at her watch.]

Let's talk first. We still have a little time. [She empties the glass of wine and holds it out for more.]

210 JEAN   Don't overdo it. You'll get drunk.

MISS JULIE   What difference does it make?

JEAN   What difference? It looks cheap. —What did you want to say to me?

MISS JULIE   We're going to run away together, right? But we'll talk first—that is, I'll talk. So far you've done all the talking. You've told me your life, now

215 I'll tell you mine. That way we'll know each other through and through before we become . . . traveling companions.

JEAN Wait a minute. Are you sure you won't regret this afterward—surrendering your secrets to me?

MISS JULIE I thought you were my friend.

220 JEAN I am—sometimes. Just don't count on it.

MISS JULIE You don't mean that. Anyway, everybody knows my secrets. —My mother's parents were very ordinary people, just commoners. She was brought up, according to the theories of her time, to believe in equality, the independence of women, and all that. And she had a strong aversion to

225 marriage. When my father proposed to her, she swore she would never become his wife but that she might possibly consent to become his mistress. So he told her he didn't want to see the woman he loved enjoy less respect than he did. But she said she didn't care what the world thought—and he, believing that he couldn't live without her, accepted her condi-

230 tions. That did it. From then on he was cut off from his old circle of friends and left without anything to do in the house, which couldn't have kept him occupied anyway. Then I came into the world—against my mother's wishes, as far as I can make out. My mother decided to bring me up as a nature child. And on top of that I had to learn everything a boy learns, so I could

235 be living proof that women were just as good as men. I had to wear boy's clothes, learn to handle horses—but not to milk the cows! Girls did that! I was made to groom the horses and harness them, and learn farming and go hunting—I even had to learn how to slaughter the animals. It was disgusting. Awful! And on the estate all the men were set to doing women's chores,

240 and the women to doing men's work—with the result that the whole place fell to pieces, and we became the local laughing-stock. Finally, my father must have come out of his trance. He rebelled, and everything was changed according to his wishes. They got married—very quietly. Then my mother got sick. I don't know what kind of sickness it was, but she often had con-

245 vulsions, and she would hide herself in the attic or in the garden, and sometimes she would stay out all night. Then there occurred that big fire you've heard about. The house, the stables, the cowsheds, all burned down—and under very peculiar circumstances that led one to suspect arson. You see, the accident occurred the day after the insurance expired,

250 and the premiums on the new policy, which my father had sent in, were delayed through the messenger's carelessness, and didn't arrive in time. [*She refills her glass and drinks.*]

JEAN You've had enough.

MISS JULIE Who cares! —We were left without a penny to our name. We had to sleep in the carriages. My father didn't know where to turn for money to

255 rebuild the house. Then Mother suggested to him that he might try to borrow money from an old friend of hers, who owned a brick factory not far from here. Father took out a loan, but there wasn't any interest charged, which surprised him. So the place was rebuilt. [*She drinks some more.*] Do you know who set fire to the place?

260 JEAN Your honorable mother!

MISS JULIE Do you know who the brick manufacturer was?

JEAN Your mother's lover?

MISS JULIE   Do you know whose money it was?

JEAN   Let me think a minute. . . . No, I give up.

265 MISS JULIE   It was my mother's!

JEAN   The count's, you mean. Or was there a marriage settlement?[4]

MISS JULIE   There wasn't a settlement. My mother had a little money of her own which she didn't want under my father's control, so she invested it with her—friend.

270 JEAN   Who pinched it!

MISS JULIE   Right! He kept it for himself. Well, my father found out what happened. But he couldn't go to court, couldn't pay his wife's lover, couldn't prove that it was his wife's money. That was how my mother got her revenge because he had taken control of the house. He was on the verge of
275 shooting himself. There was even a rumor that he tried and failed. But somehow he took a new lease on life and he forced my mother to pay for her mistakes. Can you imagine what those five years were like for me? I loved my father, but I took my mother's side because I didn't know the whole story. She had taught me to hate all men—I'm sure you've heard how
280 she hated men—and I swore to her that I'd never be slave to any man.

JEAN   You got engaged to the attorney, didn't you?

MISS JULIE   Only to make him my slave.

JEAN   I guess he didn't go for that, did he?

MISS JULIE   Oh, he wanted to well enough. I didn't give him the chance. I got
285 bored with him.

JEAN   Yes, so I noticed—in the stable yard.

MISS JULIE   What did you notice?

JEAN   I saw how he—. [Still see it on your cheek.

MISS JULIE   What!

290 JEAN   The stripe on your cheek.][5] He broke it off.

MISS JULIE   It's a lie! I broke it off! Did he tell you that? He's beneath contempt!

JEAN   Come on now, as bad as that? So you hate men, hm?

MISS JULIE   Yes, I do. . . . Most of the time. But sometimes, when I can't help
295 myself—oh . . . [She shudders in disgust.]

JEAN   Then you hate me, too?

MISS JULIE   You have no idea how much! I'd like to see you killed like an animal—

JEAN   Like when you're caught having sex with an animal: you get two years at hard labor and the animal is killed. Right?

300 MISS JULIE   Right.

JEAN   But there's no one to catch us—and no animal!—So what are we going to do?

MISS JULIE   Go away from here.

JEAN   To torture ourselves to death?

305 MISS JULIE   No. To enjoy ourselves for a day or two, or a week, for as long as we can—and then—to die—

JEAN   Die? That's stupid! I've got a better idea: start a hotel!

---

4. An agreement, made before a marriage, to transfer some property to the wife.
5. The passage in brackets was deleted in Strindberg's manuscript, probably by Strindberg himself [translator's note].

MISS JULIE [*continuing without hearing* JEAN]   —on the shores of Lake Como, where the sun is always shining, where the laurels bloom at Christmas, and
310   the golden oranges glow on the trees.

JEAN   Lake Como is a stinking wet hole, and the only oranges I saw there were on the fruit stands. But it's a good tourist spot with a lot of villas and cottages that are rented out to lovers. Now there's a profitable business. You know why? They rent the villa for the whole season, but they leave
315   after three weeks.

MISS JULIE [*naively*]   Why after only three weeks?

JEAN   Because that's about as long as they can stand each other. Why else? But they still have to pay the rent. You see? Then you rent it out again to another couple, and so on. There's no shortage of love—even if it doesn't
320   last very long.

MISS JULIE   Then you don't want to die with me?

JEAN   I don't want to die at all! I enjoy life too much. And moreover, I consider taking your own life a sin against the Providence that gave us life.

MISS JULIE   You believe in God? You?

325 JEAN   Yes, certainly I do! I go to church every other Sunday—. Honestly, I've had enough of this talk. I'm going to bed.

MISS JULIE   Really? You think you're going to get off that easy? Don't you know that a man owes something to the woman he's dishonored?

JEAN [*takes out his purse and throws a silver coin on the table*]   There you are.
330   I don't want to owe anybody anything.

MISS JULIE [*pretending not to notice*]   Do you know what the law says—?

JEAN   Lucky for you the law says nothing about women who seduce men!

MISS JULIE [*as before*]   What else can we do but go away from here, get married, and get divorced?

335 JEAN   Suppose I refuse to enter into this *mésalliance?*[6]

MISS JULIE   *Mésalliance?*

JEAN   For me! I've got better ancestors than you. I don't have a female arsonist in my family.

MISS JULIE   You can't prove that.

340 JEAN   You can't prove the opposite—because we don't have any family records—except in the police files. But I've read the whole history of your family in that peerage book in the drawing room. Do you know who the founder of your family line was? A miller—who let his wife sleep with the king one night during the Danish war.[7] I don't have any ancestors like that.
345   I don't have any ancestors at all! But I can become an ancestor myself.

MISS JULIE   This is what I get for baring my heart and soul to someone too low to understand, for sacrificing the honor of my family—

JEAN   Dishonor! —I warned you, remember? Drinking makes one talk, and talking's bad.

350 MISS JULIE   Oh, how sorry I am! . . . If only it had never happened! . . . If only you at least loved me!

JEAN   For the last time—what do you want me to do? Cry? Jump over your whip? Kiss you? Lure you to Lake Como for three weeks and then—? What

6. Literally, "misalliance" (French), an ill-advised marriage.
7. That is, the war begun by Denmark in 1657

that ended with the Treaty of Copenhagen (1660), which restored to Sweden its southern provinces.

am I supposed to do? What do you want? I've had more than I can take.
355 This is what I get for involving myself with women. . . . Miss Julie, I can
see that you're unhappy; I know that you're suffering; but I simply cannot
understand you. My people don't behave like this. We don't hate each
other. We make love for the fun of it, when we can get any time off from
our work. But we don't have time for it all day and all night like you do. If
360 you ask me, you're sick, Miss Julie. Your mother's mind was affected, you
know. There are whole counties affected with pietism. That was your
mother's trouble—pietism. It's spreading like the plague.

MISS JULIE   You can be understanding, Jean. You're talking to me like a human
being now.

365 JEAN   Well, be human yourself. You spit on me, but you don't let me wipe it
off—on you.

MISS JULIE   Help me, Jean. Help me. Tell me what I should do, that's all—
which way to go.

JEAN   For Christ's sake, if only I knew myself!

370 MISS JULIE   I've been crazy—I've been out of my mind—but does that mean
there's no way out for me?

JEAN   Stay here as if nothing had happened. Nobody knows anything.

MISS JULIE   Impossible! Everybody who works here knows. Christine knows.

JEAN   They don't know a thing. Anyhow they'd never believe it.

375 MISS JULIE [slowly, significantly]   But . . . it might happen again.

JEAN   That's true!

MISS JULIE   And one time there might be . . . consequences.

JEAN [stunned]   Consequences!! What on earth have I been thinking of!
You're right. There's only one thing to do: get away from here! Immediately!
380 I can't go with you—that would give the whole game away. You'll have to go
by yourself. Somewhere—I don't care where!

MISS JULIE   By myself? Where? —Oh, no, Jean, I can't. I can't!

JEAN   You've got to! Before the count comes back. You know as well as I do
what will happen if you stay here. After one mistake, you figure you might
385 as well go on—the damage is already done. Then you get more and more
careless until—finally you're exposed. I tell you, you've got to get out of the
country. Afterward you can write to the count and tell him everything—
leaving me out, of course. He'd never figure it was me. He wouldn't even
let himself think it was me.

390 MISS JULIE   I'll go—if you'll come with me!

JEAN   Lady, are you out of your mind? "Miss Julie elopes with her footman."
The day after tomorrow it would be in all the papers. The count would
never live it down.

MISS JULIE   I can't go away. I can't stay. Help me. I'm so tired, so awfully
395 tired. . . . Tell me what to do. Order me. Start me going. I can't think any
more, can't move any more . . .

JEAN   Now do you realize how weak you all are? What gives you the right to
go strutting around with your noses in the air as if you owned the world?
All right, I'll give you your orders. Go up and get dressed. Get some travel-
400 ing money. And come back down here.

MISS JULIE [almost in a whisper]   Come up with me!

JEAN   To your room? . . . You're going crazy again! [He hesitates a moment.]
No! No! Go! Right now! [He takes her hand and leads her out.]

MISS JULIE [*as she is leaving*]   Don't be so harsh, Jean.

405 JEAN   Orders always sound harsh. You've never had to take them.

> [JEAN, *left alone, heaves a sigh of relief and sits down at the table. He takes out a notebook and a pencil and begins to calculate, counting aloud now and then. The pantomime continues until* CHRISTINE *enters, dressed for church, and carrying* JEAN's *white tie and shirtfront in her hand.*]

CHRISTINE   Lord in Heaven, what a mess! What on earth have you been doing?

JEAN   It was Miss Julie. She dragged the whole crowd in here. You must have been sleeping awfully sound if you didn't hear anything.

410 CHRISTINE   I slept like a log.

JEAN   You already dressed for church?

CHRISTINE   Yes, indeed. Don't you remember you promised to go to communion with me today?

JEAN   Oh, yes. Of course, I remember. I see you've brought my things. All

415 right. Come on, put it on me. [*He sits down, and* CHRISTINE *starts to put the white tie and shirtfront on him. Pause.*]

JEAN [*yawning*]   What's the lesson for today?

CHRISTINE   The beheading of John the Baptist, what else? It's Midsummer. It's his feast day.

JEAN   My God, that will go on forever. —Hey, you're choking me! . . . Oh,

420 I'm so sleepy, so sleepy.

CHRISTINE   What were you doing up all night? You look green in the face.

JEAN   I've been sitting here talking with Miss Julie.

CHRISTINE   That girl! She doesn't know how to behave herself!

> [*Pause.*]

JEAN   Tell me something, Christine . . .

425 CHRISTINE   Well, what?

JEAN   Isn't it strange when you think about it? Her, I mean.

CHRISTINE   What's so strange?

JEAN   Everything!

> [*Pause.* CHRISTINE *looks at the half-empty glasses on the table.*]

CHRISTINE   Have you been drinking with her?

430 JEAN   Yes!

CHRISTINE   Shame on you! —Look me in the eyes! You haven't . . . ?

JEAN   Yes!

CHRISTINE   Is it possible? Is it really possible?

JEAN [*thinking about it*]   Yes. It is.

435 CHRISTINE   Oh, how disgusting! I could never have believed anything like this would happen! No. No. This is too much!

JEAN   Don't tell me you're jealous of her?

CHRISTINE   No, not of her. If it had been Clara—or Sophie—I would have scratched your eyes out! But her—? That's different. I don't know why. . . .

440 But it's still disgusting!

JEAN   You're not mad at her?

CHRISTINE   No. Mad at you. You were mean and cruel to do a thing like that, very mean. The poor girl! . . . Let me tell you, I'm not going to stay in this house a moment longer, not when I can't have any respect for my employers.

445 JEAN   Why do you want to respect them?

CHRISTINE   Don't try to be smart. You don't want to work for people who behave like pigs, do you? Well, do you? If you ask me, you'd be lowering yourself by doing that.

JEAN   Oh, I don't know. I think it's rather comforting to find out that they're not one damn bit better than we are.

CHRISTINE   Well, I don't. If they're not any better, there's no point in us trying to be like them. —And think of the count. Think of all the sorrows he's been through in his time. My God! I won't stay in this house any longer. . . . Imagine! You, of all people! If it had been the attorney fellow; if it had been somebody respectable—

JEAN   Now just a minute—!

CHRISTINE   Oh, you're all right in your own way. But there's a big difference between one class and another. You can't deny that. —No, this is something I can never get over. She was so proud, and so sarcastic about men, you'd never believe she'd go and throw herself at one. And at someone like you! And she was going to have Diana shot because the poor thing ran after the gatekeeper's mongrel! —Well, I tell you, I've had enough! I'm not going to stay here any longer. When my term's up, I'm leaving.

JEAN   Then what'll you do?

CHRISTINE   Well, since you brought it up, it's about time that you got yourself a decent place, if we're going to get married.

JEAN   Why should I go looking for another place? I could never get a job like this if I'm married.

CHRISTINE   Well, I know that! But you could get a job as a porter, or maybe try to get a government job as a caretaker somewhere. A square deal and a square meal, that's what you get from the government—and a pension for the wife and children.

JEAN [wryly]   Fine, fine! But I'm not the kind of guy who thinks about dying for his wife and children this early in the game. Let me tell you, I've got slightly bigger plans than that.

CHRISTINE   Plans! Ha! What about your obligations? You'd better start giving them a little thought!

JEAN   Don't start nagging me about obligations! I know what I have to do without you telling me. [He hears a sound upstairs.] Anyhow, we'll have plenty of chance to talk about this later. You just go and get yourself ready, and we'll be off to church.

CHRISTINE   Who is that walking around up there?

JEAN   I don't know. Clara, I suppose. Who else?

CHRISTINE [starting to leave]   It can't be the count, can it? Could he have come back without anybody hearing him?

JEAN [frightened]   The count? No, it can't be. He would have rung.

CHRISTINE [leaving]   God help us! I've never heard the like of this.

[The sun has now risen and strikes the tops of the trees in the park. As the scene progresses, the light shifts gradually until it is shining very obliquely through the windows. JEAN goes to the door and signals. MISS JULIE enters, dressed for travel, and carrying a small birdcage, covered with a towel. She sets the cage down on a chair.]

MISS JULIE   I'm ready now.

JEAN   Shh! Christine's awake.

MISS JULIE [extremely tense and nervous during the following]   Did she suspect anything?

JEAN   She doesn't know a thing. —My God, what happened to you?

MISS JULIE   What do you mean? Do I look so strange?

JEAN   You're white as a ghost, and you've—excuse me—you've got dirt on your
495   face.

MISS JULIE   Let me wash it off. [*She goes over to the washbasin and washes her
face and hands.*] There! Do you have a towel? . . . Oh, look, the sun's coming up!

JEAN   That breaks the magic spell!

500   MISS JULIE   Yes, we were spellbound last night, weren't we? Midsummer
madness . . . Jean, listen to me! Come with me. I've got the money!

JEAN [*suspiciously*]   Enough?

MISS JULIE   Enough for a start. Come with me, Jean. I can't travel alone today.
Midsummer Day on a stifling hot train, packed in with crowds of people, all
505   staring at me—stopping at every station when I want to be flying. I can't,
Jean, I can't! . . . And everything will remind me of the past. Midsummer
Day when I was a child and the church was decorated with leaves—birch
leaves and lilacs . . . the table spread for dinner with friends and relatives . . .
and after dinner, dancing in the park, with flowers and games. Oh, no mat-
510   ter how far you travel, the memories tag right along in the baggage car . . .
and the regrets and the remorse.

JEAN   All right, I'll go with you! But it's got to be now—before it's too late!
This very instant!

MISS JULIE   Hurry and get dressed! [*She picks up the birdcage.*]

515   JEAN   No baggage! It would give us away.

MISS JULIE   Nothing. Only what we can take to our seats.

JEAN [*as he gets his hat*]   What in the devil have you got there? What is that?

MISS JULIE   It's only my canary. I can't leave it behind.

JEAN   A canary! My God, do you expect us to carry a birdcage around with
520   us? You're crazy. Put that cage down!

MISS JULIE   It's the only thing I'm taking with me from my home—the only
living thing who loves me since Diana was unfaithful to me! Don't be cruel,
Jean. Let me take it with me.

JEAN   I told you to put that cage down! —And don't talk so loud. Christine
525   can hear us.

MISS JULIE   No, I won't leave it with a stranger. I won't. I'd rather have you
kill it.

JEAN   Give it here, the little pest. I'll wring its neck.

MISS JULIE   Oh, don't hurt it. Don't—. No, I can't do it!

530   JEAN   Don't worry, I can. Give it here.

[MISS JULIE *takes the bird out of the cage and kisses it.*]

MISS JULIE   Oh, my little Serena, must you die and leave your mistress?

JEAN   You don't have to make a scene of it. It's a question of your whole life
and future. You're wasting time!

[JEAN *grabs the canary from her, carries it to the chopping block, and
picks up a meat cleaver.* MISS JULIE *turns away.*]

You should have learned how to kill chickens instead of shooting revolvers—
535   [*He brings the cleaver down.*]—then a drop of blood wouldn't make you
faint.

MISS JULIE [*screaming*]   Kill me too! Kill me! You can kill an innocent creature without turning a hair—then kill me. Oh, how I hate you! I loathe you!

There's blood between us. I curse the moment I first laid eyes on you! I
540 curse the moment I was conceived in my mother's womb.

JEAN   What good does your cursing do? Let's get out of here!

MISS JULIE [*approaches the chopping block, drawn to it against her will*].   No,
I don't want to go yet. I can't. —I have to see. —Shh! [*She listens but
keeps her eyes fastened on the chopping block and cleaver.*] You don't think
545 I can stand the sight of blood, do you? You think I'm so weak, don't you?
Oh, how I'd love to see your blood, your brains on that chopping block. I'd
love to see the whole of your sex swimming in a sea of blood just like that.
I could drink blood out of your skull. Use your chest as a foot bath, dip my
toes in your guts! I could eat your heart roasted whole! —You think I'm
550 weak! You think I loved you because my womb hungered for your semen.
You think I want to carry your brood under my heart and feed it with my
blood? Bear your child and take your name? —Come to think of it, what is
your name? I've never even heard your last name. I'll bet you don't have
one. I'd be Mrs. Doorman or Madame Garbageman. You dog with *my*
555 name on your collar—you lackey with *my* initials on your buttons! Do you
think I'm going to share you with my cook and fight over you with my
maid?! Ohh! —You think I'm a coward who's going to run away! No, I'm
going to stay—come hell or high water. My father will come home—find
his desk broken into—his money gone. He'll ring—on that bell—two rings
560 for the valet. And then he'll send for the sheriff—and I'll tell him everything. Everything! Oh, what a relief it'll be to have it all over . . . over and
done with . . . if only it will be over. . . . He'll have a stroke and die . . .
and there'll be an end to all of us. There'll be peace . . . and quiet . . .
forever. . . . The coat of arms will be broken on his coffin; the count's line
565 will be extinct—while the valet's breed will continue in an orphanage, win
triumphs in the gutter, and end in jail!

[CHRISTINE *enters, dressed for church and with a hymnbook in her hand.*
MISS JULIE *rushes over to her and throws herself into her arms as if seeking protection.*]

MISS JULIE   Help me, Christine! Protect me against this man!

CHRISTINE [*cold and unmoved*]   This is a fine way to behave on a holy day!
[*She sees the chopping block.*] Just look at the mess you've made there!
570 How do you explain that? And what's all this shouting and screaming
about?

MISS JULIE   Christine, you're a woman, you're my friend! I warn you, watch
out for this—this monster!

JEAN [*feeling awkward*]   If you ladies are going to talk, you won't want me
575 around. I think I'll go and shave. [*He slips out to the right.*]

MISS JULIE   You've got to understand, Christine! You've got to listen to me!

CHRISTINE   No, I don't. I don't understand this kind of shenanigans at all.
Where do you think you're going dressed like that? And Jean with his hat
on? —Well? —Well?

580 MISS JULIE   Listen to me, Christine! If you'll just listen to me, I'll tell you
everything.

CHRISTINE   I don't want to know anything.

MISS JULIE   You've got to listen to me—!

CHRISTINE   What about? About your stupid behavior with Jean? I tell you
585 that doesn't bother me at all, because it's none of my business. But if you

have any silly idea about talking him into skipping out with you, I'll soon put a stop to that.

MISS JULIE [*extremely tense*]   Christine, please don't get upset. Listen to me. I can't stay here, and Jean can't stay here. So you see, we have to go away.

590 CHRISTINE   Hm, hm, hm.

MISS JULIE [*suddenly brightening up*]   Wait! I've got an idea! Why couldn't all three of us go away together?—out of the country—to Switzerland—and start a hotel? I've got the money, you see. Jean and I would be responsible for the whole affair—and Christine, you could run the kitchen, I thought.

595 Doesn't that sound wonderful! Say you'll come, Christine, then everything will be settled. Say you will! Please! [*She throws her arms around* CHRISTINE *and pats her.*]

CHRISTINE [*remaining aloof and unmoved*]   Hm. Hm.

MISS JULIE [*presto tempo*[8]]   You've never been traveling, Christine. You have to get out and see the world. You can't imagine how wonderful it is to travel by

600 train—constantly new faces, new countries. We'll go to Hamburg, and stop over to look at the zoo—it's famous, has everything—you'll love that. And we'll go to the theater and the opera. And then when we get to Munich, we'll go to the museums, Christine. They have Rubenses and Raphaels there—those great painters, you know. Of course you've heard about

605 Munich where King Ludwig[9] lived—you know, the king who went mad. And then we can go and see his castles—they're just like the ones you read about in fairy tales. And from there it's just a short trip to Switzerland—with the Alps. Think of the Alps, Christine, covered with snow in the middle of summer. And oranges grow there, and laurel trees that are green the whole year

610 round—

> [JEAN *can be seen in the wings at the right, sharpening his straight razor on a strop held between his teeth and his left hand. He listens to* MISS JULIE *with a satisfied expression on his face, now and then nodding approvingly.* MISS JULIE *continues tempo prestissimo.*[1]]

—and that's where we'll get a hotel. I'll sit at the desk while Jean stands at the door and receives the guests, goes out shopping, writes the letters. What a life that will be! The train whistle blowing, then the bus arriving, then a bell ringing upstairs, then the bell in the restaurant rings—and I'll be making

615 out the bills—and I know just how much to salt them—you can't imagine how timid tourists are when you shove a bill in their face! —And you, Christine, you'll run the whole kitchen—there'll be no standing at the stove for you—of course not. If you're going to talk to the people, you'll have to dress. And with your looks—I'm not trying to flatter you, Christine—you'll run off

620 with some man one fine day—a rich Englishman, that's who it'll be, they're so easy to—[*Slowing down*]—to catch. —Then we'll all be rich. —We'll build a villa on Lake Como. —Maybe it does rain there sometimes, but—[*More and more lifelessly*]—the sun has to shine sometimes, too—even if it looks

---

8. Quick time (Italian), a musical direction.
9. King Ludwig II of Bavaria (1845–1886; r. 1864–86), known as "the Fairy-Tale King," built several extravagant palaces—most famously Neuschwanstein, the so-called Cinderella castle; he was declared insane in

1886. Peter Paul Rubens (1577–1640) was a Flemish baroque painter; Raphael (Raffaello Sanzio, 1483–1520), a master of the Italian Renaissance.
1. At a very rapid tempo (Italian).

cloudy. —And—then . . . or else we can always travel some more—and come

625 back . . . [*Pause*]—here . . . or somewhere else . . .

CHRISTINE   Do you really believe a word of that yourself, Miss Julie?

MISS JULIE [*completely beaten*]   Do I believe a word of it myself?

CHRISTINE   Do you?

MISS JULIE [*exhausted*]   I don't know. I don't believe anything any more. [*She sinks down on the bench and lays her head between her arms on the table.*]

630 Nothing. Nothing at all.

CHRISTINE [*turns to the right and faces* JEAN]   So! You were planning to run away, were you?

JEAN [*taken aback, lays his razor down on the table*]   We weren't exactly going to run away! Don't exaggerate. You heard Miss Julie's plans. Even if she's

635 tired now after being up all night, her plans are perfectly practical.

CHRISTINE   Well, just listen to you! Did you really think you could get me to cook for that little—!

JEAN [*sharply*]   You keep a respectful tongue in your mouth when you talk to your mistress! Understand?

640 CHRISTINE   Mistress!

JEAN   Yes, mistress!

CHRISTINE   Well of all the—! I don't have to listen—

JEAN   Yes, you do! You need to listen more and blabber less. Miss Julie is your mistress. Don't you forget that! And if you're going to despise her for what

645 she did, you ought to despise yourself for the same reason.

CHRISTINE   I've always held myself high enough to—

JEAN   High enough to make you look down on others!

CHRISTINE   —enough to keep from lowering myself beneath my station. Don't you dare say that the count's cook has ever had anything to do with

650 the stable groom or the swineherd. Don't you dare!

JEAN   Yes, you got yourself a decent man. Lucky you!

CHRISTINE   What kind of a decent man is it who sells the oats from the count's stables?

JEAN   Listen to who's talking! You get the gravy on the groceries and take

655 bribes from the butcher!

CHRISTINE   How dare you say a thing like that!

JEAN   And you say you can't respect your employers. You of all people! You!

CHRISTINE   Are you going to church or aren't you? You need a good sermon after your great exploits.

660 JEAN   No, I'm not going to church! Go yourself. Go tell God how bad you are.

CHRISTINE   Yes, I'll do just that. And I'll come back with enough forgiveness for your sins, too. Our Redeemer suffered and died on the cross for all our sins, and if we come to Him in faith and with a penitent heart, He will take

665 all our sins upon Himself.

JEAN   Rake-offs[2] included?

MISS JULIE   Do you really believe that, Christine?

CHRISTINE   With all my heart, as sure as I'm standing here. It was the faith I was born into, and I've held on to it since I was a little girl, Miss Julie.

670 Where sin aboundeth, there grace aboundeth also.[3]

---

2. Cuts; money or goods skimmed off the top.   3. Romans 5.20.

MISS JULIE If I had your faith, Christine, if only—

CHRISTINE But you see, that's something you can't have without God's special grace. And it is not granted to everyone to receive it.

MISS JULIE Then who receives it?

675 CHRISTINE That's the secret of the workings of grace, Miss Julie, and God is no respecter of persons. With Him the last shall be first[4]—

MISS JULIE In that case, he does have respect for the last, doesn't he?

CHRISTINE [*continuing*] —and it is easier for a camel to go through the eye of a needle than for a rich man to enter the kingdom of God.[5] That's how

680 things are, Miss Julie. I'm going to leave now—alone. And on my way out I'm going to tell the stable boy not to let any horses out, in case anyone has any ideas about leaving before the count comes home. Goodbye.

[*She leaves.*]

JEAN She's a devil in skirts! —All because of a canary!

MISS JULIE [*listlessly*] Never mind the canary. . . . Do you see any way out of

685 this, any end to it?

JEAN [*after thinking for a moment*] No.

MISS JULIE What would you do if you were in my place?

JEAN In your place? Let me think. . . . An aristocrat, a woman, and— fallen. . . . I don't know. —Or maybe I do.

690 MISS JULIE [*picks up the razor and makes a gesture with it*] Like this?

JEAN Yes. But I wouldn't do it, you understand. That's the difference between us.

MISS JULIE Because you're a man and I'm a woman? What difference does that make?

695 JEAN Just the difference that there is—between a man and a woman.

MISS JULIE [*holding the razor in her hand*] I want to! But I can't do it. My father couldn't do it either, that time when he should have.

JEAN No, he was right not to. He had to get his revenge first.

MISS JULIE And now my mother is getting her revenge again through me.

700 JEAN Didn't you ever love your father, Miss Julie?

MISS JULIE Yes, enormously. But I must have hated him too. I must have hated him without knowing it. It was he who brought me up to despise my own sex, to be half woman and half man. Who's to blame for what has happened? My father, my mother, myself? Myself? I don't have a self

705 that's my own. I don't have a single thought I didn't get from my father, not an emotion I didn't get from my mother. And that last idea—about all people being equal—I got that from him, my fiancé. That's why I say he's beneath contempt. How can it be my own fault? Put the blame on Jesus, like Christine does? I'm too proud to do that—and too intelligent,

710 thanks to what my father taught me. . . . A rich man can't get into heaven? That's a lie. But at least Christine, who's got money in the savings bank, won't get in. . . . Who's to blame? What difference does it make who's to blame? I'm still the one who has to bear the guilt, suffer the consequences—

715 JEAN Yes, but—

[*The bell rings sharply twice.* MISS JULIE *jumps up.* JEAN *changes his coat.*]

4. Matthew 19.30, 20.16; Luke 13.30; Mark 10.31.   5. Matthew 19.24.

JEAN   The count's back! What if Christine—[*He goes to the speaking tube, taps on it, and listens.*]

MISS JULIE   Has he looked in his desk yet?

JEAN   This is Jean, sir! [*Listens. The audience cannot hear what the count says.*] Yes, sir! [*Listens.*] Yes, sir! Yes, as soon as I can. [*Listens.*] Yes, at once,
720   sir! [*Listens.*] Very good, sir! In half an hour.

MISS JULIE [*trembling with anxiety*]   What did he say? For God's sake, what did he say?

JEAN   He ordered his boots and his coffee in half an hour.

MISS JULIE   Half an hour then! . . . Oh, I'm so tired. I can't bring myself to do
725   anything. Can't repent, can't run away, can't stay, can't live . . . can't die. Help me, Jean. Command me, and I'll obey like a dog. Do me this last favor. Save my honor, save his name. You know what I ought to do but can't force myself to do. Let me use your willpower. You command me and I'll obey.

JEAN   I don't know—. I can't either, not now. I don't know why. It's as if this
730   coat made me—I can't give you orders in this. And now, after the count has spoken to me, I—I can't really explain it—but—I've got the backbone of a damned lackey! If the count came down here now and ordered me to cut my throat, I'd do it on the spot.

MISS JULIE   Then pretend you're him. Pretend I'm you. You were such a good
735   actor just a while ago, when you were kneeling before me. You were the aristocrat then. Or else—have you been to the theater and seen a hypnotist?

[JEAN *nods.*]

He says to his subject, "Take this broom!" and he takes it. He says, "Now sweep!" and he sweeps.

JEAN   The person has to be asleep!

740 MISS JULIE [*ecstatic, transported*]   I'm already asleep. The whole room has turned to smoke. You seem like an iron stove, a stove that looks like a man in black with a high hat. Your eyes are glowing like fading coals in a dying fire. Your face is a white smudge, like ashes.

[*The sun is now shining in on the floor and falls on JEAN.*]

It's so good and warm—[*She rubs her hands together as if warming them at
745   a fire.*]—and so bright—and so peaceful.

JEAN [*takes the razor and puts it in her hand*]   There's the broom. Go now, when the sun is up—out into the barn—and—[*He whispers in her ear.*]

MISS JULIE [*waking up*]   Thanks! I'm going to get my rest. But tell me one thing. Tell me that the first can also receive the gift of grace. Tell me that,
750   even if you don't believe it.

JEAN   The first? I can't tell you that. —Wait a moment, Miss Julie. I know what I can tell you. You're no longer one of the first. You're one of—the last.

MISS JULIE   That's true! I'm one of the last. I am the very last! —Oh! —Now
755   I can't go! Tell me just once more, tell me to go!

JEAN   Now I can't either. I can't!

MISS JULIE   And the first shall be the last . . .

JEAN   Don't think—don't think! You're taking all my strength from me. You're making me a coward. . . . What?! I thought I saw the bell move. No. . . .
760   Let me stuff some paper in it. —Afraid of a bell! But it isn't just a bell. There's somebody behind it. A hand that makes it move. And there's some-

thing that makes the hand move. —Stop your ears, that's it, stop your ears! But it only rings louder. Rings louder and louder until you answer it. And then it's too late. Then the sheriff comes—and then—[*There are two sharp rings on the bell.* JEAN *gives a start, then straightens himself up.*] It's horrible! But there's no other way for it to end. —Go!

    [MISS JULIE *walks resolutely out through the door.*]

HENRIK IBSEN

1828–1906

WRITING in an era when the theater had become a second-rate occupation, with most gifted writers turning instead to novels or poetry, Henrik Johan Ibsen restored to drama its prestige and relevance. During the nineteenth century, the invention of new theatrical machinery and techniques had turned theater into spectacle. Producers spent their time and money on special effects, dazzling audiences with lighting, horses, or even sea battles to add to—and sometimes replace—the appeal of popular actors. Nineteenth-century theater was in some ways comparable to present-day Hollywood and its focus on blockbuster action movies filled with special effects and big-name stars. Ibsen showed Europe that drama could be more than just spectacle: it could be an art form addressing the most serious moral and social questions of the time. The theatergoing public was first shocked, and later thrilled, to have controversial figures and themes presented on the stage, in plays that relied not on special effects but on carefully drawn characters and well-constructed dramatic situations. Honing his dramatic technique over half a century, Ibsen almost single-handedly brought a new seriousness to drama, and in doing so he won enduring acclaim as the originator of modern drama.

Ibsen achieved his unparalleled success against all odds. He was born in Skien, a small town in Norway, far removed from the cultural centers of Europe both physically and linguistically. When Ibsen left his provincial home at the age of fifteen, he was apprenticed to a pharmacist for more than six years; during that time he began to write occasional pieces, including his first play, *Catiline* (written 1848–49). Only at the age of twenty-two was he able to free himself from his apprenticeship—as well as from a liaison with a maid that had resulted in an illegitimate child—and move to the capital, Christiania (now Oslo), to study for the university entrance exam, which he failed. His efforts as a dramatist were better received, as one of his plays—the one-act *The Burial Mound* (1850)—was performed. The true beginning of his career occurred several years later, however, when he moved to Bergen to take his first job in the theater. After a few years spent learning the craft, he assumed positions of greater responsibility—as artistic director and dramatist—at a theater back in Christiania, where in 1857 he also married and had another child. By the time Ibsen was thirty-five, the foundation for his subsequent success as a dramatist had been laid.

While working at the theaters in Bergen and Christiania, Ibsen got to know the standard dramatic form of the time, the so-called well-made play (a literal translation of the French *pièce bien-fait*). Popularized by the French playwrights Victorien Sardou (1831–1908) and Augustin-Eugène Scribe (1791–1861), well-made plays were formulaic dramas focused less on well-developed characters than on complicated plots and well-timed confrontations. They offered fast-moving action, intrigues, alliances, and sudden revelations. Immensely popular at the time, the genre was also attacked by proponents of modern drama for favoring cheap suspense and empty entertainment over social relevance and meaningful art.

Ibsen's own drama can be viewed as an evolving series of reactions to the well-made play, beginning with *Brand* (1866) and *Peer Gynt* (1867). They mark Ibsen's rejection not only of the well-made play but also of the theater as such, for they were "dramatic poems"—plays written exclusively to be read, not performed. All the rules that governed stage action, the rules of the well-made play, could thus be ignored entirely. Both plays were built around a single character on a singular and willful mission. *Brand* is the more tragic of the two; it presents a fanatical preacher who seeks to impose an uncompromising religion on his small parish high up in the Norwegian mountains, demanding increasingly large sacrifices of his congregants and of himself until he finally dies in utter isolation. In *Peer Gynt*, the protagonist's quest is cast in a more satirical form. The adventures of the title character, a notorious liar, take him from the fairy-tale realm of the Norwegian mountain trolls to the Moroccan desert and then back to Norway, where he dies not as a hero but as a mediocrity, even in his sinning. Drawing on literary models such as GOETHE'S *FAUST* (1808, 1832) and Byron's *Don Juan* (1819–24), *Peer Gynt* freely mixes fantasy and reality, conjuring mountain trolls, mad German philosophers, and the devil himself.

By the time he wrote *Brand* and *Peer Gynt*, Ibsen had left Norway. He would spend twenty-seven years on the Continent, mostly in Italy and Germany, before returning to his homeland in 1891, at the age of sixty-three. Exile became the condition in which he thrived and from which he suffered. After *Brand* and *Peer Gynt*

had secured his reputation, Ibsen started writing for the stage once more, but in an entirely different style. Whereas his earliest dramas had dealt with history, he now chose to write, once and for all, about the contemporary world he knew best—namely, the contemporary Norwegian middle class—in prose, not verse. His single purpose was to lay bare the ugly reality behind the facade of middle-class respectability, to expose the lies of bourgeois characters and indeed of bourgeois society as a whole. The five plays of this period—*The Pillars of Society* (1877), *A DOLL HOUSE* (1879), *Ghosts* (1881), *An Enemy of the People* (1882), and *The Wild Duck* (1884)—made Ibsen notorious throughout Europe and established him as an author of shock, confrontation, and revolt: in short, as a modern. With these plays, Ibsen struck a nerve and secured his place in the pantheon of world drama.

The main cause of audiences' consternation also explains why these plays are now seen as the beginning of modern drama: they introduced realism, long established in the novel, to the theater. Using idiomatic language, Ibsen created a drama devoted to unveiling hidden motives and past misdeeds so that the truth would shine forth on the stage. In this way, Ibsen campaigned not only against a theater of special effects but also against a theater of convention. Realism, for Ibsen, required a theater of emotional and moral truth, a theater centered on understanding the subjective experience and objective conditions of modern life.

A DOLL HOUSE

Within this group of plays, *A Doll House* made the biggest splash. Its initial sales in Scandinavia numbered in the thousands and led to theatrical productions both there and abroad, including Germany and the United States; soon the play was translated into many other languages, inaugurating an unparalleled global career. One reason for this success was the play's notorious ending, which violated nineteenth-century views of marriage and the family. Nora is oppressed by a domineering husband who belittles her from the very opening lines of the play and who is revealed as callous at a moment of crisis. In response, Nora leaves him and her children, banging the door behind her. Her husband and contemporary audiences were shocked. This unexpected turn of events alone sufficed to establish Ibsen as a bold critic of gender relations or, in the views of his growing number of enemies, as a muckraker singularly intent on assaulting audiences with indecency. So unusual was this ending that GEORGE BERNARD SHAW even coined a new term, "discussion play," to capture how this plot-driven drama suddenly changes course and engages in a lengthy discussion about marriage before the final bang. With a single stroke, Ibsen had scandalized Europe and the United States and turned himself into a controversial public figure.

Shortly after the play's publication, a German theater manager decided the play's ending was more than his audience could stomach and had Nora return to her husband in remorse; he even managed to force Ibsen into writing the bowdlerized ending himself. Ibsen probably wanted to do damage control, fearing that a hack writer would do worse. More recently, a new production has Nora return to her husband as

well, but only to shoot him with a pistol. Through eccentric decisions like these, the play's ending has remained the most famous in theater history.

Given all this notoriety, it may be surprising to recognize that for the most part, the play is quite conventionally and carefully crafted. It is driven forward by a blackmail plot and includes all the tricks of the trade for creating suspense that Ibsen had learned from French well-made plays during his long apprenticeship in the theater, including the gradual revelation of secrets, overheard threats, and surprising revelations about past events; we even have the blackmail letter waiting in a mailbox right onstage, threatening to reveal Nora's secret, while she desperately tries to distract her husband, hoping to keep him from opening it.

But beyond its plot devices, the enduring power of this play is due to the skill with which Ibsen weaves together several threads and themes that give nuance to its abrupt ending. Ibsen is an expert at handling stage props, beginning with the macaroons that Nora secretly savors and that are also harbingers of other, more

Hattie Morahan as Nora Helmer and Dominic Rowan as Torvald Helmer in the 2012 production at the Young Vic Theatre, London, directed by Carrie Cracknell.

consequential, secrets. The Christmas tree that greets us in the first scene with a homey atmosphere soon gives way to an excessive Tarantella dance, suggesting that the play will spiral out of control. The nicely set-up home is nothing but a doll's house that will end up being utterly destroyed.

Like Ibsen's other famous plays, *A Doll House* is set among the bourgeoisie, the world of lawyers, doctors, architects, professors, and above all, bankers. Torvald is a banker, and Ibsen never lets us forget it. The questions Ibsen wants us to ask are specific to this social group: What kind of houses do they live in? Did they borrow money to buy them? Can they meet their mortgage payments? How about the furniture: did they buy that on credit as well? In order to get credit, or to advance in the banking business, the characters in this world must inspire trust. Trust in turn requires them to keep up appearances, both financial and moral. As soon as Torvald sees his appearance threatened, he begins to treat Nora with unvarnished roughness, ultimately causing Nora's departure. Keeping up appearances is not just a matter of social respectability but goes to the heart of bourgeois life. In peeling back layer after layer of pretense, Ibsen's plays aim at this heart with surgical precision.

Ibsen's greatest topic is inheritance. This theme, too, is tied to money and credit, but in keeping with the spirit of the time, Ibsen pursues it much further. Inspired by lively scientific debates about evolution and inheritance, Ibsen has his characters inherit medical diseases that turn out to be moral ones as well, as with Dr. Rank in *A Doll House*, who is the family friend and commentator on the action almost in the manner of a Greek chorus. Moral and immoral features are passed down through the generations, and Ibsen's characters often struggle in vain to rid themselves of these various inheritances.

By weaving together questions of credit, trust, appearance, and inheritance, Ibsen became the great dramatist of the bourgeoisie, the poet of bourgeois capitalism. No one managed to capture the fears, but also the fantasies, of the bourgeoisie quite like him.

While the ending of the play continues to be its most famous feature, it has long ceased to be shocking. Ibsen's scandalous reputation, his apparent embrace of radical projects such as women's liberation, placed him in the company of political radicals, some of whom, like the British playwright and pamphleteer George Bernard Shaw, were eager to adopt him in their cause. But Ibsen did not seek to replace the world of bourgeois capitalism with a socialist system. Rather, he became an expert at diagnosing the bourgeoisie. It is to this diagnosis that *A Doll House* owes its enduring power and significance.

HEDDA GABLER

After winning fame and some infamy with his realist plays, Ibsen changed course once more as he attempted to write modern versions of Greek tragedy. In this last phase of his career, he managed to give definite shape to the tragedy of modern middle-class life. *HEDDA GABLER* (1890) is the most compelling and famous of the plays from this period, but it shares many features with the others—*Rosmersholm* (1886), *Lady from the Sea* (1888), *The Master Builder* (1892), *Little Eyolf* (1894), *John Gabriel Borkman* (1896), and *When We Dead Awaken* (1899). All are set in the same bourgeois milieu as his realist plays, but they are less concerned with social deceptions and pretense. Instead, they are interested in the bourgeois characters themselves, presented as complex figures with hidden yearnings and fantasies that take them outside of the constricted worlds in which they live.

The title character of *Hedda Gabler* is the daughter of a general; she has married an aspiring scholar (Tesman) waiting for his university post. As the play begins, upon the couple's return from their honeymoon, we see almost immediately that the marriage is an unequal, and unsettled, one. Tesman is eager to start his new life, and he is clearly proud of his beautiful wife. Hedda, by contrast, is dismissive of both his affectionate tone and his values. She snubs him, is impatient, abruptly changes the topic of conversation, and sulks. The class difference between the upper-middle-class Hedda and lower-middle-class Tesman is starkly drawn, as the collision between Hedda's and Tesman's respective classes, expectations, and attitudes occurs in and in fact centers on the bourgeois home. Like many of Ibsen's late plays, the home in *Hedda Gabler* bears and reveals the contradictions of bourgeois life. While Tesman thinks he has provided an ideal house, his wife from the bottom of her heart despises it and the life it offers. Gradually we learn that Hedda married Tesman and encouraged his purchase of the house only out of boredom and because she felt that her time and options were running out. But now she finds herself trapped in her marriage, and in the house.

For that reason, Ibsen has Hedda focus her scorn on the house and its furnishings, as the play revolves around what they represent: class and taste. Hedda Gabler demands a new piano because her old one does not "fit in" with the "other things" in this house, and she expects to have horses so that she can keep up the lifestyle to which she is accustomed. At the same time, she despises those objects associated with Tesman and his class—the déclassé hat of one of his aunts and his old and worn slippers, which his other aunt has hand embroidered. She admires the remnants of her former life, preserved in the towering portrait of the general and his set of pistols. Tesman's scholarly area is the handicrafts of the Middle Ages. What he does not see is that around him a battle is occurring over a different set of objects, which become the game pieces in a struggle of two classes and two wills.

Hedda Gabler, bored and without a function except to bear children—a thought she rejects with horror—manipulates everyone around her in order to exert control. Her coaxing Tesman to get a house he cannot afford is just the beginning. Hedda is equally calculating in her dealings with the other characters, from Tesman's aunt to Løvborg and his companion, Mrs. Elvsted, whom she knew as a schoolgirl. She gets them to do her bidding through force, lies, flattery, and utter ruthlessness. As the play progresses, we find her destroying careers and lives without blinking an eye; she lacks any moral compass beyond her own will. Although her actions at times seem to have some motive, they more often have no apparent goal. Hedda seems to value power as an end in itself.

The main victim of Hedda's plotting is Tesman's rival, Løvborg, who not only has published a well-received history of civilization but has just completed a book about the future. At an earlier moment in his career, Ibsen might have shown interest in the content of Løvborg's ideas, as he had done in examining the idealist drive for truth in *The Wild Duck*, for example, or in discussing marriage in *A Doll House*; here, the ideas are reduced to their container, Løvborg's manuscript, which becomes a central plot device. Ibsen had learned from the well-made play how to weave objects and characters into suspenseful plots. But these props also convey something important about those who possess them: they are multifaceted devices that take on a life of their own.

Hedda may be a manipulator, but she is a manipulator with a vision. She is driven by her hunger for a more fulfilling, ideal, and beautiful life. She fantasizes about acts of heroism and beauty, which she tries to bring about by assigning roles to the people around her as if she were the director of a play. Hedda shares her desire for a better life with many tragic characters of Ibsen's later plays, characters who cannot rid themselves of the chains that bind them to their houses, their objects, their habits, their class, and their past. The architect Solness falls from the tower of his final house in the play *The Master Builder*, and the sculptor Rubek, in *When We Dead Awaken*, climbs higher and higher into the dangerous mountains with his former love only to be killed by an avalanche. Ibsen's attitude toward his characters' desire for beauty is ambivalent. On the one hand, he sympathizes with them—even the cold-hearted Hedda Gabler. On the other hand, his plays show that the single-minded desire to achieve an ideal life wreaks destruction. Hedda Gabler's vision is an escape fantasy, the stuff of historical and idealist plays of the kind Ibsen had written in his youth. Ibsen perceived and understood both the desire for ideals and their destructive effects.

Ibsen is a dramatist of singular importance in part because he has consistently inspired the most important actors and directors. In England, Ibsen initially owed his influence to George Bernard Shaw and William Archer, writers who led what some have called the Ibsen campaign. Shaw's defense of Ibsen against the scornful reception given his drama in the popular press

Elizabeth Robins as Hedda. Robins was the first actress to play
Hedda in English, at the Vaudeville Theatre in London in 1891.

and Archer's translations and productions of Ibsen's plays turned the Norwegian into the most important figure in British modern drama. Directors and playwrights elsewhere soon championed Ibsen as well. André Antoine, whose Théâtre Libre had pioneered a naturalist style of acting and design, played Oswald in *Ghosts* in 1890, and the influential Russian director Konstantin Stanislavski, whose Moscow Art Theater promoted an acting style based on authentic emotional responses, played Doctor Stockman in *An Enemy of the People* in 1900. Ibsen's later plays, including *Hedda Gabler*, attracted a different set of directors, more interested in symbolism and poetry than in naturalism and truth. Aurélien Lugné-Poe, who had attacked realist drama and instead pioneered a symbolist theater full of ominous allusions and hieratic moods, staged *Rosmersholm* (1893) and *The Master Builder* (1894) in Paris, and directors interested in surrealism and suggestive stagecraft, such as Ingmar Bergman, have continued to be attracted first and foremost to Ibsen's late plays.

Ibsen is acknowledged as a founder of modern drama, but his place in theater history is full of enigmas and contradictions. He started his career with historical dramas that were typical nineteenth-century fare, yet he became the herald of modern drama. Rather than simply rejecting the dramatic techniques of his time, he transformed them into a drama that seemed new, shocking, and modern to his audience. He received the most attention for his realist plays but later turned realism in a more poetic and symbolist direction. In the end, Ibsen created a dramatic oeuvre of variety and complexity. His plays could be many things to many people, viewed as stirring manifestos against social injustice or modern tragedies of striking poetic and dramatic force. This versatility, more than anything else, is responsible for Ibsen's having remained one of the most popular dramatists of all time. Today, he ranks second only after SHAKESPEARE as the world's most-performed playwright, a position that testifies to Ibsen's dramatic art: shocking and novel when it was first presented to audiences, it has stood the test of time. To learn more about the staging of *Hedda Gabler* and to view photographs from select performances of the play, see the "Plays in Performance" color insert near the center of this volume.   M.P.

A Doll House[1]

CHARACTERS

TORVALD HELMER, a lawyer

NORA, his wife

DR. RANK

MRS. LINDE

NILS KROGSTAD, a bank clerk

THE HELMERS' THREE SMALL CHILDREN

ANNE-MARIE, their nurse

HELENE, a maid

A DELIVERY BOY

Act 1

A comfortable, tasteful, but not expensively furnished room. A door to the right in the back wall leads out to the hall; another door to the left leads in to Helmer's study. Between these doors is a piano. In the middle of the left wall, a door, and farther back, a window. Near the window a round table with armchairs and a small sofa. In the right wall, upstage, a door and, on this same side nearer the foreground, a porcelain stove with a pair of armchairs and a rocking chair. Between the stove and the door, a little table. Engravings on the walls. An étagère[2] with porcelain figures and other small art objects; a small bookcase with books in rich bindings. Carpet on the floor; the fire burns in the stove. A winter's day.

> [*A bell rings in the hallway; soon after, we hear the door being opened. Nora, cheerfully humming, enters the room; she is dressed in outdoor clothes and carries a great number of packages, which she sets down on the table, right. She lets the door to the hall stand open and we see a Porter carrying a Christmas tree and a basket, which he hands to the Maid, who had opened the door for them.*]

NORA Be sure you hide the tree, Helene. We can't let the children see it before it's decorated tonight. [*To the Porter as she takes out her purse.*] How much—? Oh yes, I know, half a krone—here's one—no, keep the change.

> [*The Porter thanks her and leaves. Nora closes the door. She continues laughing softly to herself while she takes off her outdoor clothes. She takes a bag of macaroons from her pocket and eats a couple; then she walks cautiously and listens outside her husband's door.*]

He's home, all right.

> [*Humming again, she goes over to the table, right.*]

5 HELMER [*From within the study.*] Do I hear a skylark singing out there?

NORA [*Busy opening some packages.*] Yes, you do.

HELMER Is there by any chance a squirrel rummaging around?

NORA Yes!

HELMER When did the squirrel get home?

---

1. Translated by Rick Davis and Brian Johnston.

2. A shelf for the display of objects.

10 NORA   Just this second. [*She puts the bag of macaroons in her pocket and wipes her mouth.*] Come out here, Torvald, and look at what I've bought.

HELMER   Can't be disturbed! [*After a moment, he opens the door and looks in, his pen in his hand.*] Did you say bought? All that? Has the little spendthrift been out wasting money again?

15 NORA   Oh, Torvald—this year we really ought to let ourselves go a little bit. It's the first Christmas we haven't had to watch our money.

HELMER   But we still can't go around wasting it, you know.

NORA   Yes, Torvald, now we can afford to waste a little bit here and there. Isn't that right? Just a teeny little bit. Now that you've got such a big salary
20   and we've got heaps and heaps of money coming in?

HELMER   Yes, after New Year's. And then it's three whole months before the first paycheck.

NORA   Fuff! We can borrow till then.

HELMER   Nora! [*Goes over to her and takes her playfully by the ear.*] Is that
25   dizzy little head of yours spinning around again? Suppose I borrowed a thousand today, and you wasted it all on Christmas, and then on New Year's Eve I got hit in the head by a falling brick and lay there—

NORA   [*Covering his mouth.*]   Ugh! Don't say awful things like that!

HELMER   Well, suppose it happened—what then?

30 NORA   If anything that awful happened, some silly loan would be the least of my worries.

HELMER   What about the people I'd borrowed from?

NORA   Them? Who cares about them! They're only strangers.

HELMER   Nora, Nora, you are such a woman! Seriously, Nora, you know
35   what I think about these things. No debts! Never borrow! Some freedom's lost, and because of that some beauty too, from a home that's built on borrowing and debt. The two of us have managed to hold out bravely until now; and we'll stay the course for the little time remaining.

NORA   [*Goes over to the stove.*]   All right, Torvald, whatever you want.

40 HELMER   [*Following.*]   Now, now; the little songbird mustn't droop its wings. Right? Is the squirrel standing there sulking? [*Taking out his wallet.*] Nora, guess what I have?

NORA   [*Turning quickly.*]   Money!

HELMER   There, see? [*Handing her some bills.*] For heaven's sake, I know
45   how much a house goes through at Christmastime.

NORA   [*Counting.*]   Ten—twenty—thirty—forty—Oh, thank you, thank you, Torvald. This will help me no end.

HELMER   It had certainly better.

NORA   Yes, yes, I'll make sure it does. But come here so I can show you what
50   I've bought. And so cheap! Look—new clothes for Ivar, also a sword. Here's a horse and trumpet for Bob. And for Emmy, a doll and a doll bed. They're pretty plain, but she'll just tear them to pieces anyway before you know it. And here's some dress material and some handkerchiefs for the maids— even though old Anne-Marie really deserves a little more.

55 HELMER   And what's in that package there?

NORA   [*With a cry.*]   No, Torvald! Not till tonight!

HELMER   Aha! But tell me, you little spendthrift, what did you think of for yourself?

NORA   For me? Oh, I don't need anything.

60 HELMER   You most certainly do. Tell me what you'd like most of all—within reason.

NORA   Oh, I really don't know. Yes—listen, Torvald—

HELMER   Well?

NORA [*Fumbling with his button; not looking at him.*]   If you want to give me
65 something, you could—you could—

HELMER   Well, say it.

NORA [*Quickly.*]   You could give me money, Torvald. Only what you can spare; then one of these days I could buy something with it.

HELMER   No, but Nora—

70 NORA   Yes, do it, Torvald, darling. I'm begging you. And I'll hang the money in pretty gilt paper on the tree. Wouldn't that be lovely?

HELMER   What do we call those little birds that are always spending their money?

NORA   Spendthrifts—yes, I know, I know. But let's do what I say, Torvald;
75 then I'll have time to think about what I really need. That's pretty practical, isn't it?

HELMER [*Smiling.*]   Absolutely—if you could only hold on to the money I give you, and if you actually bought something for yourself with it. But it will go for the house, for a lot of things we don't need, and I'll just have to
80 shell out again.

NORA   Oh, Torvald—

HELMER   Can't be denied, my dear little Nora. [*Puts his arm around her waist.*] Spendthrifts are sweet; but they go through an awful lot of money. It's unbelievable how expensive it is to keep a spendthrift.

85 NORA   Oh, fuff—how can you say that? I save absolutely everything I can.

HELMER [*Laughing.*]   Yes, that's true—everything you *can*. But the trouble is, you *can't*.

NORA [*Humming and smiling with quiet complacency.*]   Hmm. You just can't imagine what kinds of expenses larks and squirrels have, Torvald.

90 HELMER   You are a strange little one. Just like your father was. You'll try anything you can think of to get hold of some money; but the moment you get some, it slips through your fingers. You never know what you've done with it. But you are what you are. It's in your blood—these things are hereditary, Nora.

NORA   I wish I'd inherited a lot of Papa's qualities.

95 HELMER   Well I don't want you to be anything but what you are: my sweet little songbird. But listen—I'm getting the distinct impression—you've got a sort of a—what can I call it—a kind of a guilty look today.

NORA   I do?

HELMER   You certainly do. Look me straight in the eye.

100 NORA [*Looking at him.*]   Well?

HELMER [*Wagging his finger.*]   Our sweet tooth wouldn't have been running wild in town today, would it?

NORA   No, what makes you think that?

HELMER   You're sure that sweet tooth didn't make a little stop at the
105 bakery?

NORA   No, Torvald, I swear—

HELMER   Didn't nibble a little candy?

NORA   No, absolutely not.

HELMER   Not even munched on a macaroon or two?

110 NORA   No, Torvald, honestly, I promise—

HELMER   Now, now—of course I'm only joking.

NORA [*Going to the table, right.*]   I'd never dream of going against you.

HELMER   No, I know that. And after all, you've given me your word. [*Goes to her.*] Well, you keep your little Christmas secrets to yourself, then, my
115 dearest Nora. I guess everything will be revealed this evening when we light the tree.

NORA   Did you remember to invite Doctor Rank?

HELMER   No—there's no need; it's taken for granted. But I'll ask him again when he stops in this morning. I've ordered the very best wine. Nora, you
120 can't imagine how excited I am about tonight.

NORA   Me too! And the children are just going to love it!

HELMER   Ah, it's so marvelous to have a secure position and a comfortable income. Isn't it fun just to think about that?

NORA   Oh, it's wonderful!

125 HELMER   Do you remember last Christmas? Three whole weeks beforehand, you locked yourself up every evening, till way past midnight, making flowers for the Christmas tree, and all the other little surprises you had for us. Uch—I've never been so bored in my whole life.

NORA   I wasn't bored at all.

130 HELMER [*Smiling.*]   But it didn't amount to much after all, Nora.

NORA   Oh, are you going to tease me with that again? I couldn't help it that the cat came in and tore everything to bits.

HELMER   No, that's right, you couldn't, my poor little Nora. You worked so hard to make us happy, that's the main thing. But it's good that those hard
135 times are behind us.

NORA   Yes, it's really wonderful.

HELMER   Now I don't have to sit here all alone boring myself, and you don't have to torture your precious eyes and your delicate little fingers—

NORA [*Clapping her hands.*]   No, is that true, Torvald, I really don't have to?
140 How wonderful to hear that! [*Takes his arm.*] Now I'll tell you what I thought we should do—as soon as Christmas is over—[*The doorbell rings.*] Oh, that doorbell. [*Tidying up the room.*] That means a visitor—what a bore!

HELMER   I'm not at home to visitors, remember that.

145 MAID [*In the doorway.*]   Madam, there's a strange lady here to see you.

NORA   Show her in.

MAID [*To Helmer.*]   And the Doctor arrived at the same time.

HELMER   He went straight to my study?

MAID   Yes, sir, he did.

[*Helmer goes into his room. The Maid shows Mrs. Linde, dressed in traveling clothes, into the room and closes the door after her.*]

150 MRS. LINDE [*Timidly and somewhat hesitantly.*]   Good day, Nora.

NORA [*Uncertainly.*]   Good day—

MRS. LINDE   You don't recognize me.

NORA   No; I don't know—I think—[*Bursting out.*] Kristine! Is it really you?

MRS. LINDE   Yes, it is.

155 NORA   Kristine! How could I not recognize you? But then how could I—? [*Quieter.*] You've changed, Kristine.

MRS. LINDE   Yes, I expect I have. In nine—ten—long years—

NORA Is it that long? Yes, that's right. Oh, the last eight years have been
happy ones, believe me. And now you've come to town as well. Made the
160 long trip in winter. That was brave.

MRS. LINDE I just got here this morning on the steamer.

NORA To enjoy yourself at Christmas, of course. That's a lovely idea! Yes,
enjoy ourselves—we will certainly do that. But take off your coat. You're
not too cold? [*Helps her.*] That's it; now let's settle down and be cozy here
165 by the stove. No, take the armchair there. I'll sit here in the rocking chair.
[*Gripping her hands.*] Yes, now you look more like yourself again; it was just
those first few moments—you have gotten a bit paler, Kristine—and maybe
a little thinner.

MRS. LINDE And much, much older, Nora.

170 NORA Well, maybe a little older, a tiny little bit; but not too much. [*Drawing
back, suddenly serious.*] Oh, I can't believe how thoughtless I am, sitting
here chattering—Kristine, can you forgive me?

MRS. LINDE What do you mean, Nora?

NORA [*Quietly.*] Poor Kristine, you're a widow.

175 MRS. LINDE Yes, for three years now.

NORA I knew it of course, I read it in the paper. Oh, Kristine, you have to
believe me, I was always going to write you at the time, but I kept putting
it off, and things kept getting in the way.

MRS. LINDE Nora, dear, I understood completely.

180 NORA No, it was horrible of me. You poor thing, it must have been so hard
for you—and he didn't leave you anything to live on?

MRS. LINDE No.

NORA And no children?

MRS. LINDE No.

185 NORA So, nothing at all.

MRS. LINDE No—not even a sense of grief to hold on to.

NORA [*Looking at her in disbelief.*] Kristine, how is that possible?

MRS. LINDE [*Smiles sadly, stroking Nora's hair.*] Ah, sometimes it happens
that way, Nora.

190 NORA So completely alone. That must be terribly sad for you. I have three
lovely children—you can't see them right now, they're out with Anne-
Marie. But now you have to tell me everything.

MRS. LINDE No, no, I'd rather hear about you.

NORA No, you have to go first. Today I'm not going to be selfish. Today I'm
195 only going to think about you. But I have to tell you *one* thing. Did you
hear about the great luck we just had?

MRS. LINDE No, what is it?

NORA My husband has been made manager of the Bank.

MRS. LINDE Your husband? That is lucky!

200 NORA Isn't it? The law is such a chancy business, especially when you won't
take the ugly cases. Torvald would never do that, of course, and I agree
with him completely. So you can imagine how happy we are! He starts at
the Bank right after New Year's, and then he'll be getting a huge salary and
lots of commissions. From now on we'll be able to live quite differently—we
205 can actually do what we want. Oh, Kristine, I feel so light and happy! Isn't
it lovely to have lots of money, and not have to worry about anything?

MRS. LINDE It's lovely just to have enough.

NORA No, not just enough, but lots and lots of money!

MRS. LINDE [*Smiling.*] Nora, Nora, haven't you gotten over that yet? You
210 were such a spendthrift in school.

NORA [*Laughing softly.*] Yes, Torvald still says the same thing. [*Wagging her
finger.*] But "Nora, Nora" hasn't been as wild as you all think. We haven't
exactly been in a position where I could waste any money. We've both had
to work.

215 MRS. LINDE You too?

NORA Yes, odd jobs—sewing, embroidery, work like that—[*Casually.*] and also
other things. You know Torvald left the government when we got married;
he saw he'd never be promoted, and he needed to earn more money than
before. In that first year he worked himself to the bone, always looking for
220 extra income, day and night. But he couldn't keep it up, and he got deathly
sick. The doctor said he absolutely had to move south.

MRS. LINDE Didn't you stay a whole year in Italy?

NORA That's right. It wasn't that easy to get away, as you can imagine. Ivar
had just been born. But we had to go, there was no question about it. Ah,
225 it was a wonderful trip, and it saved Torvald's life. But it was incredibly
expensive.

MRS. LINDE I believe you.

NORA Four thousand, eight hundred kroner. That's a lot of money.

MRS. LINDE It's just lucky you had it when the emergency came up.

230 NORA Well, I can tell you, we had to get it from Papa.

MRS. LINDE So that's how. That was about the time your father died, I think.

NORA Yes, Kristine, it was right then. Just think, I couldn't go and be with
him. I stayed right here and waited every day for little Ivar to come into the
world. And I had my poor, sick Torvald to take care of. Dear, sweet Papa!
235 I never saw him again, Kristine. That was the saddest time in my whole
marriage.

MRS. LINDE I know how much he meant to you. But then you left for Italy?

NORA Yes, we had the money then, and the doctors insisted. So we left in a
month.

240 MRS. LINDE And your husband came back completely cured?

NORA Right as rain!

MRS. LINDE But—the doctor—?

NORA What do you mean?

MRS. LINDE I thought the maid said the man who came in with me was a
245 doctor.

NORA Yes, Doctor Rank. He's not here on a house call, he's our best
friend—he comes by at least once a day. No, Torvald hasn't been sick a day
since then. And the children are strong and sound and so am I. [*Jumping
up and clapping her hands.*] Oh God, oh God, Kristine, it's so wonderful to
250 live and be happy! But I'm being hateful here, only talking about myself.
[*Sits on a stool close by Kristine and lays her arms on her knees.*] Please don't
be mad at me! Tell me something—is it really true that you didn't love your
husband? So why did you marry him?

MRS. LINDE My mother was still alive, but she was bedridden and couldn't
255 take care of herself; and I also had to look after my two younger brothers.
I couldn't justify refusing his offer.

NORA No, no, you were right. He was rich at the time, wasn't he?

MRS. LINDE   He was pretty well-off, I think. But the business wasn't very solid, Nora: when he died it all went to pieces, nothing was left.

260   NORA   And then—?

MRS. LINDE   Well, I had to do what I could for myself—a little shop, a few students, whatever else I could find. These last three years have been like one long workday without a break. But now it's over, Nora. My poor mother doesn't need me any more, she's gone. And the boys are working now,
265   they're on their own.

NORA   You must feel such relief—

MRS. LINDE   No, not at all. Only inexpressibly empty. Nothing more to live for. [*Stands uneasily.*] So I couldn't stand it any longer out in that little backwater. It's got to be easier here to find something to do, something to
270   keep my mind working. If only I could be lucky enough to find a steady job, some office work—

NORA   But Kristine, that's so exhausting, and you're tired enough to begin with. You'd be better off if you could get away to a spa for a while.

MRS. LINDE   [*Going over to window.*]   I don't have a papa to send me on a trip,
275   Nora.

NORA   [*Getting up.*]   Oh, don't be mad at me!

MRS. LINDE   Nora, dear, don't you be mad at me. That's the worst thing about this situation of mine; it leaves you with so much bitterness. You've got nothing to work for, but you still have to watch out for every opportu-
280   nity. You have to live, so you become selfish. When you told me your news, I was more excited for my own sake than yours.

NORA   Why? Oh, I see—you mean maybe Torvald can do something for you.

MRS. LINDE   That's exactly what I was thinking.

NORA   And so he will, Kristine! Leave it to me—I'll suggest it so beautifully,
285   so beautifully—find something charming that he'll really appreciate. Oh, I can't wait to help you.

MRS. LINDE   You're so kind, Nora, to take such an interest in me—doubly kind, since you don't know much about life's hardships yourself.

NORA   I—? Don't know much—?

290   MRS. LINDE   [*Smiling.*]   Well, good Lord, a little sewing and things like that— you're such a child, Nora.

NORA   [*Tosses her head, walks across the room.*]   You shouldn't be so sure about that.

MRS. LINDE   Oh?

295   NORA   You're like everyone else. You all think I'm not capable of anything serious—

MRS. LINDE   Now, now—

NORA   That I've never been put to the test in the cold, hard world.

MRS. LINDE   Nora, you've just been telling me all about your troubles.

NORA   Fuff! Trifles! [*Quietly.*] I haven't told you the big thing.

300   MRS. LINDE   What big thing? What do you mean?

NORA   You look down on me an awful lot, Kristine, but you really shouldn't. You're proud that you've worked so hard for your mother all these years.

MRS. LINDE   I don't look down on anyone. But it's true that I'm proud—and happy—that I was given the chance to ease my mother's sorrow in her last
305   days.

NORA   And when you think about what you've done for your brothers, you're proud of that as well.

MRS. LINDE   I think I'm entitled to that.

NORA   So do I. But now you'll hear, Kristine. I also have something to be
310   proud and happy about.

MRS. LINDE   I don't doubt it. But how do you mean?

NORA   Let's talk quietly. What if Torvald heard? He mustn't, not for anything
in the world. Nobody can find out about this, nobody but you.

MRS. LINDE   What is it?

315   NORA   Come over here. [*Pulls her down on the sofa beside her.*] Now then:
here's what I have to be proud and happy about. I saved Torvald's life.

MRS. LINDE   Saved—? How did you save—?

NORA   I told you about the trip to Italy. Torvald would never have survived if
he hadn't gone down there—

320   MRS. LINDE   Yes, well, your father gave you all the money you needed—

NORA [*Smiling.*]   Yes, that's what Torvald and everyone else believe, but—

MRS. LINDE   But—?

NORA   Papa never gave anything. I got the money myself.

MRS. LINDE   You? That was a lot of money.

325   NORA   Four thousand, eight hundred kroner. What do you say to that?

MRS. LINDE   But Nora, how was that possible? Did you win the lottery?

NORA [*Disdainfully.*]   The lottery. [*Snorting.*] What kind of art would *that*
have taken?

MRS. LINDE   Then where did you get it from?

330   NORA [*Humming and smiling secretively.*]   Hmm; tra la la la la!

MRS. LINDE   Because you certainly couldn't have borrowed it.

NORA   Oh? Why not?

MRS. LINDE   No, a wife can't get a loan without her husband's permission.

NORA [*Tossing her head.*]   Well, but a wife with a head for business, a wife
335   who knows how to be a little clever—

MRS. LINDE   Nora, I just don't understand—

NORA   And you don't need to. Nobody said anything about *borrowing* the
money. Maybe I got it some other way. [*Throwing herself back on the sofa.*]
Maybe I got it from one of my admirers. When you're as alluring as I am—

340   MRS. LINDE   You're crazy.

NORA   I've got you really curious now, haven't I?

MRS. LINDE   Listen to me, Nora: you haven't done anything foolish, have you?

NORA [*Sitting up again.*]   Is it foolish to save your husband's life?

MRS. LINDE   I think it's foolish that without his knowledge you—

345   NORA   But that's just it—he mustn't know anything! Good Lord, can't you
see that? He can never know how bad off he was. The doctors came to *me*
to say his life was in jeopardy—that only a trip south could save him. At
first I tried to coax him into it—I told him how lovely it would be to take a
trip abroad like other young wives—then I begged and cried—I said he
350   should be kind and indulge a woman in my condition—and I hinted that he
could easily take out a loan. That really set him off, Kristine. He told me I
was being frivolous, and that it was his duty as a husband not to indulge my
every whim and caprice—I think that's what he called them. Well, well, I
thought, saved you must be and saved you shall be—and that's when I came
355   up with my plan.

MRS. LINDE   Didn't your husband ever find out that the money wasn't your
father's?

NORA   Never. Papa died right after that. I thought about letting him in on it and asking him not to say anything. But with him lying there so sick—and finally it wasn't necessary.

MRS. LINDE   And you've never confided in your husband?

NORA   No, for heaven's sake, how can you even imagine that? He's so strict about those things. And besides, Torvald's a man—he'd be so humiliated if he knew he owed me anything. It could even spoil our relationship; it would be the end of our beautiful, happy home.

MRS. LINDE   So you'll never tell him?

NORA   [*Reflectively, half-smiling.*]   Yes, maybe someday; years from now, when I can't count on my looks any more. Don't laugh! I mean when Torvald's not as attracted to me as he is now—when my dancing and dressing-up and reciting for him don't interest him any more. Then it'll be good to have something to fall back on. [*Breaking off.*] Dumb, dumb, dumb! That'll never happen. So what do you think of my big secret, Kristine? I can do things after all, can't I? But as you can imagine, it's been a big worry for me. It hasn't been that easy to make the payments on time. So I had to save a little, here and there, whenever I could. I couldn't really take anything out of the housekeeping budget, because Torvald has to live in a certain style. And I couldn't scrimp on the children's clothes; I used up whatever I got for them—the angels!

MRS. LINDE   Poor Nora! So it came out of your allowance?

NORA   Yes, of course. But then it was mostly my problem. Whenever Torvald gave me money for new clothes or whatever, I'd only use half; I always bought the simplest, cheapest things. I'm lucky that everything looks good on me, so Torvald never noticed. But it made me sad sometimes, Kristine—because it's so nice to dress up now and then, isn't it?

MRS. LINDE   Yes it is.

NORA   But I found other ways to make some money too. Last winter I was lucky enough to get a big copying job to do. So I shut myself in and wrote every evening till late at night. Ah, I'd get so tired, so tired—but it was also great fun, sitting and working and earning money like that. Almost like being a man.

MRS. LINDE   How much have you managed to pay off like that?

NORA   Well, I can't really say exactly. This kind of account is very hard to keep track of. I only know that I've paid back everything I can scrape together. A lot of times I didn't know which way to turn. [*Smiling.*] I'd sit here and imagine that a rich old man had fallen in love with me.

MRS. LINDE   What? Which man?

NORA   Oh, come on! And that he'd just died and when they read his will, there it was in big letters: "My entire fortune is to be paid in cash, immediately, to the delightful Mrs. Nora Helmer."

MRS. LINDE   But Nora, who is he?

NORA   Good Lord, don't you get it? There never was any such person; it was just something I'd sit here and dream about when I couldn't think of any other way to get the money. But now it doesn't matter, the old bore can go back where he came from; I don't need him or his will, because my troubles are over. Oh, God, it's so lovely to think of, Kristine! Carefree! To be carefree, completely carefree! To run around and play with the children; to

make everything in the house warm and beautiful, just the way Torvald
likes it! Then maybe we can travel a little. Maybe I'll get down to the ocean
410 again. Oh yes, it is so wonderful to live and be happy!

[*The bell rings in the hallway.*]

MRS. LINDE [*Rising.*]   The bell—maybe I should go.

NORA   No, stay here. It won't be for me. It's probably for Torvald.

MAID [*From the hall doorway.*]   Excuse me, ma'am. There's a gentleman here
to speak with the lawyer.

415 NORA   With the Bank Manager, you mean.

MAID   Yes, with the Bank Manager. But I didn't know if—since the Doctor's
in there—

NORA   Who is the gentleman?

KROGSTAD [*From the doorway.*]   It's me, Mrs. Helmer.

[*Mrs. Linde starts, checks herself, and turns toward the window.*]

420 NORA [*A step towards him, tense, in a low voice.*]   You? What is it? What do
you want to talk to my husband about?

KROGSTAD   Bank matters—more or less. I have a minor position on the bank
staff, and I hear your husband is our new chief.

NORA   And so it's—

425 KROGSTAD   Just dry business, Mrs. Helmer. Absolutely nothing else.

NORA   Then would you please be good enough to step into his study?

[*She nods indifferently and shuts the hallway door; then she goes and
tends the stove.*]

MRS. LINDE   Nora—who was that man?

NORA   That was a lawyer named Krogstad.

MRS. LINDE   So it really was him.

430 NORA   Do you know that man?

MRS. LINDE   I used to know him—a long time ago. He was a law clerk for a
while up in our area.

NORA   Yes, that's right, he was.

MRS. LINDE   He certainly has changed.

435 NORA   He had a very unhappy marriage.

MRS. LINDE   And now he's a widower?

NORA   With several children. There we go, now it's burning. [*She closes the
stove door and moves the rocking chair a little to the side.*]

MRS. LINDE   He's got himself involved in all kinds of businesses, they say.

NORA   Oh yes? Probably; I really wouldn't know. But let's not think about
440 business—it's so boring!

[*Doctor Rank comes out from Helmer's study.*]

RANK [*Still in the doorway.*]   No, no, Torvald: I don't want to be in the way;
I'd just as soon go talk to your wife for a while. [*Closing the door and noticing Mrs. Linde.*] I'm sorry—I'm in the way here too.

NORA   You certainly are not. [*Introducing him.*] Doctor Rank, Mrs. Linde.

445 RANK   Aha! That's an oft-mentioned name in this house. I think I passed you
on the stairs when I arrived.

MRS. LINDE   Yes, I don't handle stairs very well.

RANK   Aha—are you having some kind of trouble?

MRS. LINDE   Probably just overwork.

450 RANK   Nothing more? So you've probably come to town to catch your breath
in the holiday parties.

MRS. LINDE   I'm looking for a job.

RANK   Is that the prescription for overwork?

MRS. LINDE   One has to live, Doctor.

455 RANK   Yes, there's general agreement on that point.

NORA   Oh, come on now, Doctor Rank, you want to live as much as anyone.

RANK   Yes, I really do. Wretched as I am, I really want to stretch my torment
to the limit. All my patients feel the same way. And it's the same with the
morally diseased—right now there's a terminal moral case in there with
460   Helmer—

MRS. LINDE [*Quietly.*]   Ah—!

NORA   Who's that?

RANK   Oh, just a certain lawyer Krogstad, no one you'd know anything about.
His character, my ladies, is rotten right down to the roots—but even he
465   began making speeches—as if it were self-evident—that he had to *live.*

NORA   Oh? What did he want to talk to Torvald about?

RANK   I don't know for sure. All I heard was something about the bank.

NORA   I didn't know Krog—that this lawyer Krogstad had anything to do with
the bank.

470 RANK   Yes, he's got some kind of position down there. [*To Mrs. Linde.*] I don't
know if you have, in your part of the country, any of these moral detectives,
these investigators who go around sniffing out moral corruption and then
get their victims into a safe place where they can keep them under constant surveillance—it's a lucrative business these days. The healthy ones
475   get left out in the cold—no room for them!

MRS. LINDE   And yet it's the sick ones who need to be brought inside.

RANK [*Shrugs his shoulders.*]   There you have it. That's the philosophy that's
turning our whole world into a hospital.

> [*Nora, lost in thought, breaks into quiet laughter, clapping her hands.*]

RANK   Why do you laugh? Do you really know what the world is?

480 NORA   What do I care about the boring old world? I was laughing at something else—something terribly funny. Tell me, Doctor Rank, all those people
who work at the bank—are they all under Torvald now?

RANK   Is *that* what's so terribly funny to you?

NORA [*Smiling and humming.*]   Never mind! Never mind! [*Walking around
485   the room.*] Yes, it is extremely amusing that we—that Torvald has so much
influence over so many people. [*Takes a bag from her pocket.*] Doctor Rank,
how about a little macaroon?

RANK   Aha! Macaroons! I thought they were illegal here.

NORA   Yes, but Kristine gave me these—

490 MRS. LINDE   What? I—?

NORA   Now, now, now, don't worry. How could you know that Torvald made a
law against them? You see, he's afraid they'll rot my teeth. But, fuff—just
this once—don't you agree, Doctor Rank? There you are! [*She pops a macaroon into his mouth.*] You too, Kristine. And I'll have one too, just a little
495   one—or two at the most. [*Walking around again.*] Yes, now I am really tremendously happy. There's just one last thing in the world I have a tremendous desire to do.

RANK   Oh? What's that?

NORA   I have this tremendous desire to say something so that Torvald can
500   hear it.

RANK   So why can't you say it?

NORA   No, I don't dare. It's too horrible.

MRS. LINDE   Horrible?

RANK   Well, then, maybe you'd better not. But with us—can't you? What do
505   you want to say so Torvald can hear?

NORA   I have a tremendous desire to say: To hell with everything!

RANK   Are you crazy?

MRS. LINDE   For heaven's sake, Nora.

RANK   Say it—here he is.

510   NORA [Hiding the macaroons.]   Shh, shh, shh!

[Helmer enters from his study, hat in hand and overcoat on his arm.]

NORA   Well, my dear, are you through with him?

HELMER   Yes, he just left.

NORA   Let me introduce you—this is Kristine, who's just come to town.

HELMER   Kristine? I'm sorry, but I don't know—

515   NORA   Mrs. Linde, Torvald dear, Mrs. Kristine Linde.

HELMER   Oh, I see. A childhood friend?

MRS. LINDE   Yes, we knew each other back then.

NORA   And just think, she made the long trip here just to talk to you.

MRS. LINDE   Well, actually, I didn't—

520   NORA   Kristine, you see, is extremely good at office work, and so she's tremendously eager to place herself under the direction of a capable man so
that she can learn even more than she—

HELMER   Very sensible, Mrs. Linde.

NORA   So that when she heard you'd been made bank manager—there was a
525   bulletin about it in all the papers—she started out as fast as she could,
and—it's true, isn't it, Torvald? You could do something for Kristine for my
sake, yes?

HELMER   It's not completely out of the question. You are, I suppose, a widow?

MRS. LINDE   Yes.

530   HELMER   And you have experience in office work?

MRS. LINDE   Yes, quite a bit.

HELMER   Well then, it's entirely possible that I can offer you a position—

NORA [Clapping her hands.]   You see, you see!

HELMER   You appeared at a lucky moment, Mrs. Linde.

535   MRS. LINDE   How can I thank you—

HELMER   Not at all necessary. [Puts on overcoat.] But today I'll have to ask
you to excuse me—

RANK   Wait—I'll go with you.

[Rank gets his fur coat from the hall and warms it at the stove.]

NORA   Don't be out long, Torvald my dear.

540   HELMER   Just an hour, no more.

NORA   Are you leaving too, Kristine?

MRS. LINDE [Putting on her outdoor things.]   Yes, now I've got to find myself
a room.

HELMER   Then maybe we can all walk together for a while.

545   NORA [Helping her.]   It's so boring that we don't have space here, but it's just
impossible for us to—

MRS. LINDE   Don't even think of it! Goodbye, Nora, and thank you for
everything.

NORA   Goodbye for now. But I'll see you again this evening. You too, Doctor
550   Rank. What? If you feel well? Of course you will! Wrap yourself up nice
and warm.

[*They all go out together into the hall. Children's voices are heard on the
stairs.*]

NORA   There they are! There they are!

[*She runs to open the front door. Anne-Marie, their nanny, enters with
the children.*]

NORA   Come in, come in! [*Bends down and kisses them.*]
Oh, you sweet little darlings! Look at them, Kristine, aren't they lovely!
555   RANK   No loitering out here in the draft!
HELMER   Let's go, Mrs. Linde; this place is unbearable now for anyone but
mothers.

[*Doctor Rank, Helmer, Mrs. Linde go down the stairs. The nursemaid
goes into the living room with the children. Nora goes in also, after shut-
ting the door to the hallway.*]

NORA   You look so clean and healthy! Your cheeks are all red! Like apples and
roses. [*The children chatter away to her throughout the following.*] Was it
560   fun? That's great. Really? You pulled both Emmy and Bob on the sled? My
goodness, both of them together! You're a clever boy, Ivar. Here, let me
hold her for a little while, Anne-Marie. My sweet little doll-baby! [*Takes the
smallest child from Anne-Marie and dances with her.*] Yes, yes, Mommy will
dance with Bob too. What? A snowball fight? Oh, I wish I was there with
565   you! No, don't bother, I'll undress them myself, Anne-Marie. Yes, let me do
it, it's so much fun. Go in for a while—you look frozen. There's warm coffee for you on the stove. [*Anne-Marie goes into the room on the left. Nora
takes off the children's outdoor clothes and throws them around while the
children all talk at the same time.*] Is that so? A great big dog came running
after you? But it didn't bite? No, dogs never bite lovely little doll-babies.
570   Stop peeking into the packages, Ivar! What is it? Oh, wouldn't you like to
know? No, it's something awful! Well? Do you want to play? What'll we
play? Hide-and-seek. Yes, let's play hide-and-seek. Bob, you hide first. Me?
All right, I'll hide first.

[*She and the children play, laughing and shouting, in the living room
and the adjoining room to the right. At last Nora hides under the table;
the children come storming in, searching, not finding her; then, hearing
her muffled laughter, rush to the table, lift the tablecloth, and discover
her. A storm of delight. Meanwhile, there has been a knocking at the
front door; no one has noticed it. Now the door half opens, and Krogstad
appears. He waits a little while the game continues.*]

KROGSTAD   I beg your pardon, Mrs. Helmer.
575   NORA [*Turns, with a stifled cry, half jumps up.*]   Ah! What do you want?
KROGSTAD   Excuse me. The front door was open—somebody must have for-
gotten to shut it.
NORA [*Rising.*]   My husband's not here, Mr. Krogstad.
KROGSTAD   I know that.
580   NORA   Well—what do you want?
KROGSTAD   A word with you.
NORA   With—? [*To the children, quietly.*] Go in with Anne-Marie. No, the
strange man won't hurt Mama. When he's gone we can play some more.

[*She leads the children in to the room on the left and closes the door after them. Now, tense and nervous.*] You want to speak with me?

585 KROGSTAD Yes, I do.

NORA Today—? But it's not the first of the month yet—

KROGSTAD No, it's Christmas Eve. It's up to you how much Christmas cheer you'll have.

NORA What do you want? Today I can't possibly—

590 KROGSTAD We won't talk about that right now. It's something else. I suppose you have a moment?

NORA Well, yes; all right—though—

KROGSTAD Good. I was sitting over at Olsen's Restaurant and I saw your husband going down the street—

595 NORA Oh yes.

KROGSTAD With a lady.

NORA So?

KROGSTAD I wonder if you'll allow me to ask if that lady was Mrs. Linde?

NORA Yes.

600 KROGSTAD Just arrived in town?

NORA Yes, today.

KROGSTAD She's a good friend of yours?

NORA Yes, she is. But I can't see—

KROGSTAD I also knew her at one time.

605 NORA I'm aware of that.

KROGSTAD Really? That's what I thought. Well, then, let me get right to the point: Is Mrs. Linde getting a job at the bank?

NORA Why do you think you can cross-examine me, Mr. Krogstad? You, who's just one of my husband's employees? But since you ask, you might as

610 well know: yes, Mrs. Linde got a job. And I arranged it all for her, Mr. Krogstad. Now you know.

KROGSTAD As I thought.

NORA [*Pacing the floor.*] Oh, I should hope that one always has a little bit of influence. Just because one is a woman, it doesn't follow that—when one

615 is in an inferior position, Mr. Krogstad, one ought to be very careful with somebody who—

KROGSTAD Who has influence?

NORA Exactly.

KROGSTAD [*Changing tone.*] Mrs. Helmer, would you be good enough to use

620 your influence on my behalf?

NORA What? What do you mean?

KROGSTAD Would you be kind enough to make sure that I keep my inferior position at the bank?

NORA What do you mean? Who's trying to take it away from you?

625 KROGSTAD Oh, you don't have to play the innocent with me. I understand perfectly well that your friend doesn't want to run the risk of seeing me again; and now I also understand who to thank for being let go.

NORA But I promise you—

KROGSTAD Yes, yes, yes. But here's the point: there's still time, and I'd advise

630 you to use your influence to prevent it.

NORA But, Mr. Krogstad, I have no influence at all.

KROGSTAD No? I thought a minute ago you said—

NORA   I didn't mean it that way. What makes you think I've got any sort of influence over my husband in things like that?

635 KROGSTAD   Oh, I've known your husband since we were students together—and I don't believe our Bank Manager has any more willpower than any other married man.

NORA   You talk like that about my husband and I'll show you the door.

KROGSTAD   The lady has courage.

640 NORA   I'm not afraid of you any more. Soon after New Year's I'll be done with the whole business.

KROGSTAD   Now listen to me, Mrs. Helmer. If it becomes necessary, I'll fight to the death for my little job at the bank.

NORA   Yes, it looks that way.

645 KROGSTAD   And not just for the money—that's the least of my concerns. It's something else—well, all right—you know, of course, like everyone else, that some years ago I was guilty of an indiscretion.

NORA   I think I heard something about it.

KROGSTAD   The case never came to trial, but even so every door was closed to 650 me. So I had to go into the sort of business you're familiar with. I had to find something—and I think I can say that I've been far from the worst in that line of work. But now I want to put all of it behind me. My sons are growing up. For their sake I want to win back as much respect as I can in the community. That position in the bank was the first rung in the ladder 655 for me. Now your husband wants to kick me right back off the ladder and into the mud again.

NORA   But for God's sake, Mr. Krogstad, it's just not in my power to help you.

KROGSTAD   That's because you don't have the will to do it—but I can force you to.

660 NORA   You wouldn't tell my husband that I owe you money?

KROGSTAD   Hmm—what if I did?

NORA   That would be shameful. [*Choking with tears.*] That secret—my pride and my joy—if he learned about it in such a horrible way—learned it from you—. You'd put me through such an incredibly unpleasant scene—

665 KROGSTAD   Only unpleasant?

NORA   [*Vehemently.*]   Just try it! It'll only be worse for you. Because then my husband will really get to see what kind of man you are, and you'll have no chance of keeping your job.

KROGSTAD   I asked you if all you were afraid of was this unpleasant scene 670 here at home?

NORA   If my husband finds out about it, of course he'll pay you off immediately, and we'd have nothing more to do with you.

KROGSTAD   [*A step nearer.*]   Listen, Mrs. Helmer: either you've got a terrible memory or a very shaky grasp of business. Let me get a few facts straight 675 for you.

NORA   How do you mean?

KROGSTAD   When your husband was sick, you came to me for four thousand, eight hundred kroner.

NORA   I didn't know where else to go.

680 KROGSTAD   I promised to get it for you—

NORA   And you did.

KROGSTAD   I promised to get it for you on certain conditions. At the time you were so wrapped up in your husband's illness that I suppose you didn't

think through all the details. Maybe I'd better remind you of them. Now:
685   I promised to get you the money based on a note that I drafted.

NORA   Yes, which I signed.

KROGSTAD   Very good. But below your signature I added some lines to the effect that your father would guarantee the loan. Your father was to sign there.

NORA   Was to—? He signed it.

690 KROGSTAD   I left out the date. Your father was supposed to date his own signature. Do you remember that?

NORA   Yes, I think so—

KROGSTAD   Then I handed the note over to you so you could mail it to your father. Isn't that the case?

695 NORA   Yes.

KROGSTAD   And of course you did that right away—because only about five, six days later, you brought me the note, with your father's signature. And then you got your money.

NORA   Well? Haven't I been meeting my payments?

700 KROGSTAD   Yes, more or less. But to return to the question: that was a difficult time for you, wasn't it, Mrs. Helmer?

NORA   Yes, it was.

KROGSTAD   Your father was very ill, I believe.

NORA   He was very near the end.

705 KROGSTAD   He died soon after that?

NORA   Yes.

KROGSTAD   Tell me, Mrs. Helmer, do you by any chance recall the date of your father's death? Which day of the month, I mean.

NORA   Papa died on the twenty-ninth of September.

710 KROGSTAD   Quite correct; I've already confirmed that. That brings us to an oddity that I simply cannot account for.

NORA   What kind of oddity? I don't understand—

KROGSTAD   Here's the oddity, Mrs. Helmer: your father countersigned the note three days after his death.

715 NORA   How? I don't understand—

KROGSTAD   Your father died on the twenty-ninth of September. But look at this. Here your father has dated his signature "October 2nd." Isn't that odd, Mrs. Helmer? [*Nora is silent.*] Can you explain it to me? [*Nora remains silent.*] Here's another remarkable thing: the date "October 2nd" and the
720 year are not written in your father's hand, but in a hand that I ought to know. Now, that could be explained; your father forgot to date his signature, and someone else did it for him, somewhat carelessly, before anyone knew of his death. Nothing wrong with that. Everything hinges on the signature. And that *is* genuine, isn't it, Mrs. Helmer? It really was your father
725 himself who signed his name there?

NORA [*After a short silence, throws back her head and looks firmly at him.*]   No, it wasn't. *I* signed Papa's name.

KROGSTAD   Listen, Mrs. Helmer—do you understand that this is a dangerous confession?

730 NORA   Why? You'll get your money soon enough.

KROGSTAD   Can I ask you—why didn't you send the note to your father?

NORA   Impossible. Papa was so sick. If I had asked him for his signature, I'd have had to tell him what the money was for. I just couldn't tell him, in his condition, that my husband was dying. It was just impossible.

735 KROGSTAD   Then it would have been better for you to give up the trip.

NORA   No, impossible again. That trip was to save my husband's life. I couldn't give that up.

KROGSTAD   But didn't it occur to you that you were committing a fraud against me?

740 NORA   I couldn't worry about that. I certainly wasn't concerned about you. I could hardly stand you, making up all those cold conditions when you knew perfectly well how much danger my husband was in.

KROGSTAD   Mrs. Helmer, you obviously don't have any idea what you've implicated yourself in. But let me tell you this: what I once did was nothing

745 more, and nothing worse, and it destroyed me.

NORA   You? Are you trying to get me to believe that you risked everything to save your wife?

KROGSTAD   Laws don't much care about motives.

NORA   Then they must be very bad laws.

750 KROGSTAD   Bad or not, if I produce this paper in court, you'll be judged by those laws.

NORA   I don't believe it. Doesn't a daughter have the right to spare her dying father from worry and anxiety? Shouldn't a wife have the right to save her husband's life? I don't know the law very well, but I'm sure it must say

755 somewhere in there that these things are legal. You must be a very bad lawyer, Mr. Krogstad.

KROGSTAD   Maybe so. But business—this kind of business we're in—don't you think I know something about that? Good. Do what you want. But hear this: if I get thrown down a second time, you're coming with me. [*He bows and goes out through the hall door.*]

760 NORA   [*Stands for a moment, reflecting, then tosses her head.*]   Nonsense! He's trying to frighten me! I'm not all that naïve. [*Starts gathering up the children's clothes, but soon stops.*] But—? No, impossible. I did it out of love.

CHILDREN   [*In the doorway, left.*]   Mama, the strange man's going down the street.

765 NORA   Yes, I know. But don't mention the strange man to anyone. You hear? Not even Papa.

CHILDREN   No, Mama. Now can we play again?

NORA   No, no. Not now.

CHILDREN   But Mama, you promised.

770 NORA   Yes, but right now I can't. Go inside; I've got too much to do. Go in, go in, my dear, sweet little ones. [*She herds them carefully into the room and closes the door after them. She sits on the sofa, takes up her embroidery, makes some stitches, but soon stops.*] Helene! Let me have the tree in here. [*Goes to the table at left and opens a drawer, pauses again.*] No, that's completely impossible!

775 MAID   [*With the spruce tree.*]   Where should I put it, Ma'am?

NORA   There—in the middle of the floor.

MAID   Anything else?

NORA   No, thank you. I have what I need.

[*The Maid, having set the tree down, goes out.*]

NORA   [*Busy decorating the tree.*]   Candles here, flowers here—that horrible

780 man! Talk, talk, talk. Nothing's going to happen. The Christmas tree will be just lovely. I'll do anything you want me to, Torvald—I'll sing for you, dance for you—

[*Helmer, with a packet of papers under his arm, comes in through the hall.*]

NORA   Ah! Back already?

HELMER   Yes. Has someone been here?

785 NORA   Here? No.

HELMER   That's strange. I just saw Krogstad going out the door.

NORA   Really? Oh, of course. Krogstad was here for a moment.

HELMER   Nora, I can see it in your eyes, he's been here asking you to put in a good word for him.

790 NORA   Yes.

HELMER   And you were going to pretend it was your own idea. You'd pretend he'd never been here. Did he ask you to do that as well?

NORA   Yes, Torvald, but—

HELMER   Nora, Nora, you could go along with that? Do business with that sort
795   of person, and make promises to him? And then, on top of it all, tell me a lie!

NORA   A lie?

HELMER   Didn't you tell me no one had been here? [*Wagging his finger.*] My little songbird mustn't ever do a thing like that again. A songbird needs a clean beak to chirp with. No false notes. [*Takes her by the waist.*] Isn't that
800   the way it should be? Yes, of course it is. So let's not talk about it any more. [*Sits by the stove.*] Ah, it's so snug and cozy here.

NORA   [*Working on the tree; after a short pause.*]   Torvald!

HELMER   Yes?

NORA   I'm terribly excited about the Stenborg's party the day after tomorrow.

805 HELMER   And I'm terribly curious to see what you'll surprise me with.

NORA   Oh, that stupid nonsense!

HELMER   What?

NORA   I can't find anything I like; everything seems so pointless, so idiotic.

HELMER   Is that what little Nora thinks?

810 NORA   [*Behind his chair, her arms on its back.*]   Are you very busy, Torvald?

HELMER   Well—

NORA   What are those papers?

HELMER   Bank business.

NORA   Already?

815 HELMER   I've convinced the retiring manager to give me full authority to make changes in personnel and procedure. I'll have to use Christmas week for that. I want everything in order for the New Year.

NORA   So that's why this poor Krogstad—

HELMER   Hm.

NORA   [*Still leaning on the back of his chair, stroking the hair on his neck.*]
820   If you weren't so busy, I would ask you for a terribly big favor.

HELMER   Let's hear it. What can it be?

NORA   No one has your good taste. I really want to look my best at the costume party. Torvald, couldn't you take over from me and advise me what to wear and how to design my costume?

825 HELMER   So our little rebel's ready for a cease-fire?

NORA   Yes, Torvald. I can't get anywhere without your help.

HELMER   All right. I'll think about it. We'll come up with something.

NORA   How sweet of you! [*Goes over to the Christmas tree; pause.*] These red flowers are so pretty—But tell me, was what that Krogstad did really such
830   a crime?

HELMER He forged people's names. Do you know what that means?

NORA Maybe he did it out of need.

HELMER Yes, or thoughtlessness, like so many others. And I wouldn't condemn a man categorically because of one isolated incident.

835 NORA No, you wouldn't, would you, Torvald?

HELMER Men can often redeem themselves by openly confessing their guilt
and accepting their punishment.

NORA Punishment?

HELMER But Krogstad didn't do that. He got himself off the hook with tricks
840 and loopholes. That's what's corrupted him.

NORA Do you think that would—?

HELMER Imagine what life is like for a man like that: he has to lie and dis-
semble and cheat everyone he meets—has to wear a mask in front of his
nearest and dearest—yes, even his wife and children. And the children—-
845 that's the most terrible part of it.

NORA Why?

HELMER Because an atmosphere so filled with lies brings pestilence and
disease into every corner of a home. Every breath the children take carries
the infection.

850 NORA [Closer behind him.] Are you sure about that?

HELMER Ah, my dear, I'm a lawyer—I've seen it often enough. Almost everyone who turns bad as a youth has had a compulsive liar for a mother.

NORA Why just—a mother?

HELMER Usually you can trace it to the mother, but fathers have the same
855 effect; it's something every lawyer knows. And yet this Krogstad has been
living at home, poisoning his children with lies and deceit; that's why I
call him morally corrupt. And that's why my sweet little Nora must promise
me not to plead his case. Your hand on that. Now, now, what's this?
Give me your hand. There. That's settled. And let me tell you, it would be
860 impossible for me to work with him; I literally feel sick when I'm around
someone like that.

NORA [Withdraws her hand and goes over to the other side of the Christmas
tree.] It's so hot in here! And I've got so much to pull together!

HELMER [Rising and gathering his papers.] Yes, I've got to try to get through
some of these before dinner. I'll also give some thought to your costume.
865 And I might also be thinking about something to hang on the tree in gilt
paper—. [Lays his hand on her head.] Oh, my sweet little songbird. [He goes
into his room and closes the door.]

NORA [Softly, after a silence.] No, no! It's not true. It's impossible. It just
can't be possible.

ANNE-MARIE [In doorway, left.] The children are asking if they can come in
870 to Mama.

NORA No, no, no, don't let them in here with me! You stay with them,
Anne-Marie.

ANNE-MARIE Very well, Ma'am.

NORA [Pale with terror.] Harm my children—! Poison my home? [Short
875 pause; she tosses her head.] It's not true. It could never be true!

Act 2

The same room in the corner by the piano stands the Christmas tree, stripped, bedraggled, with its candle-stumps all burned down. Nora's outdoor clothing lies on the sofa.

> [*Nora, alone, walks restlessly around the room. Finally she stands by the sofa and picks up her coat.*]

NORA [*Dropping the coat again.*]   Somebody's coming! [*Goes to the door, listens.*] No, nobody there. Naturally—nobody's coming on Christmas Day—or tomorrow either. But maybe— [*She opens the door and looks out.*] No, nothing in the mailbox—perfectly empty: [*Comes forward.*] Oh, nonsense!
5   Of course he wasn't serious about it. Nothing like that could happen. After all, I have three small children.

> [*Anne-Marie, carrying a large carton, comes in from the room on the left.*]

ANNE-MARIE   Well, I finally found the box of masquerade costumes.

NORA   Thanks. Put it on the table.

ANNE-MARIE [*Does so.*]   But it's a terrible mess.

10   NORA   Ah, I wish I could rip them into a million pieces.

ANNE-MARIE   Lord bless us—they can be fixed up again. Just have a little patience.

NORA   Yes, I'll go and get Mrs. Linde to help.

ANNE-MARIE   You're not going out again now? In this horrible weather? Mrs.
15   Nora will catch cold—get sick.

NORA   Worse things could happen. How are the children?

ANNE-MARIE   The poor little things are playing with their Christmas presents, but—

NORA   Are they always asking for me?

20   ANNE-MARIE   They're so used to having their Mama with them.

NORA   Yes, Anne-Marie, but I can't be with them as much as before.

ANNE-MARIE   Well, little children get used to anything.

NORA   Do you think so? Do you think they'd forget their mama if she were really gone?

25   ANNE-MARIE   Lord help us—gone?

NORA   Listen—tell me, Anne-Marie—I've wondered about this a lot—how could you ever, in your heart of hearts, stand to give your child away to strangers?

ANNE-MARIE   But I just had to when I became little Nora's wet nurse.

30   NORA   Yes, but how could you actually do it?

ANNE-MARIE   When I could get such a good place? A poor girl in trouble has to jump at a chance like that. Because that slick good-for-nothing wouldn't do anything for me.

NORA   But your daughter's completely forgotten you.

35   ANNE-MARIE   Oh no, not really. She wrote to me when she was confirmed, and when she got married.

NORA [*Clasps her around the neck.*]   Dear old Anne-Marie—you were a good mother for me when I was little.

ANNE-MARIE   Poor little Nora, with me as her only mother.

40   NORA   And if my little ones didn't have a mother, I know that you—stupid, stupid, stupid! [*Opening the carton.*] Go to them. Right now I have to—tomorrow you'll see how beautiful I look.

ANNE-MARIE   Yes, Mrs. Nora will be the most beautiful woman at the party.

[*Anne-Marie goes into the room on the left.*]

NORA [*Begins to unpack the box, but soon throws the whole thing aside.*]   Ah,
if I had the nerve to go out. If only nobody would come. If only nothing
happened here at home in the meantime. Stupid talk; nobody's coming.
Just don't think. I have to brush out this muff. Beautiful gloves, beautiful
gloves. Get it out, get it out! One, two, three, four, five, six, [*Screams.*] Oh,
here they come. [*Goes toward the door, but stops, irresolute. Mrs. Linde
comes in from the hall where she has removed her outdoor clothes.*] So it's
you, Kristine. No one else out there? I'm glad you're here.

MRS. LINDE   I heard you were asking for me.

NORA   Yes, I happened to be passing by. I need your help with something.
Come sit with me by the sofa. Look at this. There's going to be a costume
party tomorrow over at Consul Stenborg's, and Torvald wants me to go as a
Neapolitan³ fisher girl and dance the tarantella⁴—I learned it in Capri.⁵

MRS. LINDE   Well, well—you're giving a real performance?

NORA   Yes, Torvald says I should. Look—here's my costume. Torvald had it
made for me down there. But it's all torn now and I just don't know—

MRS. LINDE   We'll get that fixed up in no time; the trimmings are just coming
loose here and there, that's all. Needle and thread? There, now we have
what we need.

NORA   This is so nice of you.

MRS. LINDE [*Sewing.*]   So you're going in disguise tomorrow, Nora? You know
what? I'll come by for a minute and look at you when you're all dressed up.
You know I've completely forgotten to thank you for the lovely evening
yesterday.

NORA [*Gets up and crosses the floor.*]   Oh, I don't think it was as nice yesterday as it usually is. You should have gotten here a little earlier, Kristine.
Torvald really knows how to make a home charming and elegant.

MRS. LINDE   So do you, just as much, I'd say. You're not your father's daughter for nothing. Tell me—is Doctor Rank always so depressed?

NORA   No, yesterday he was particularly low. But he's got a very serious
illness—tuberculosis of the spine, poor man. You know his father was a
disgusting creature who kept mistresses and things like that—that's how
poor Doctor Rank got to be so sickly.⁶

MRS. LINDE [*Dropping her sewing to her lap.*]   Nora, my dear, how do you
know about these things?

NORA [*Walking around.*]   Fuff. When you've had three children you end up
meeting some women who know a little about medicine, and they tell you
a few things.

MRS. LINDE [*Sewing again, short silence.*]   Does Doctor Rank come to the
house every day?

NORA   Every single day. He's Torvald's best friend ever since they were children, and he's my good friend too. Doctor Rank sort of belongs to the
house.

---

3. An inhabitant of Naples, a city in southern
Italy.
4. An Italian folk dance named after the
tarantula, a venomous spider. It was believed
that victims of the bite needed to keep danc-

ing to stay alive.
5. An island off the coast of Italy, near Naples.
6. Nora expresses the popular, but false, belief
that immoral conduct leads to the disease.

MRS. LINDE   But tell me this—is he honest? I mean, doesn't he like to tell people what they want to hear?

NORA   No, not at all. What makes you think that?

90 MRS. LINDE   When you introduced us yesterday he said he'd heard my name here so often—but then I noticed that your husband didn't have any idea who I was. So how could Doctor Rank—

NORA   That's right, Kristine. Torvald is so unbelievably devoted to me—he says he wants me all to himself. When we were first married he'd get
95 jealous if I so much as mentioned any of my old friends from back home. So, of course, I stopped. But with Doctor Rank I can talk about all those things, because he enjoys hearing about them.

MRS. LINDE   Listen to me, Nora: in many ways you're still a child. I'm quite a bit older than you and I have a little more experience. Let me tell you
100 something: you should put an end to all this with Doctor Rank.

NORA   What should I put an end to?

MRS. LINDE   All of it, I think. Yesterday you said something about a rich admirer who was going to give you money—

NORA   Yes, but unfortunately he doesn't exist. So what?

105 MRS. LINDE   Is Doctor Rank rich?

NORA   Yes.

MRS. LINDE   No one to care for?

NORA   No, no one—but—?

MRS. LINDE   And he comes by every day?

110 NORA   Yes, that's what I told you.

MRS. LINDE   How can such a cultivated man be so obvious?

NORA   I really don't understand you.

MRS. LINDE   Don't play games, Nora. Don't you think I know who lent you the money?

115 NORA   Are you out of your mind? How can you even think that? A good friend of ours, who comes over here every single day! That would have been horrible!

MRS. LINDE   So it really wasn't him?

NORA   No, I promise you. I would never have thought of that—anyway, he
120 didn't have any money to lend back then—he inherited it all later.

MRS. LINDE   Well, that was just as well for you, I think.

NORA   No, I would never have thought of asking Doctor Rank. Even though I'm sure that if I did—

MRS. LINDE   But of course you wouldn't.

125 NORA   No, of course not. I can't imagine how it would be necessary. On the other hand, I'm sure that if I even mentioned it to him—

MRS. LINDE   Behind your husband's back?

NORA   I've got to get out of this other thing—that's also behind his back. I've really got to get out of that.

130 MRS. LINDE   Yes, that's what I said yesterday. But—

NORA [Walking up and down.]   A man can deal with these things so much better than a woman—

MRS. LINDE   Your own husband can, yes.

NORA   Nonsense. [Stopping.] When you pay back everything you owe you get
135 your note back.

MRS. LINDE   That's right.

NORA   And you can tear it up in a hundred thousand pieces and burn it—that disgusting piece of paper!

MRS. LINDE [*Looking straight at her, putting the sewing down, rising slowly.*]   Nora—you're hiding something from me.

140 NORA   Can you see that?

MRS. LINDE   Something's happened since yesterday morning. Nora, what is it?

NORA [*Going to her.*]   Kristine! [*Listens.*] Ssh! Torvald's home. Look—go in there with the children for a while. Torvald can't stand to see people sewing. Let Anne-Marie help you.

145 MRS. LINDE [*Gathering some of her things.*]   Yes, all right, but I'm not leaving before we talk all this through. [*She goes into the room at left; at the same time, Helmer comes in from the hall.*]

NORA [*Goes to meet him.*]   Oh, I've been waiting for you, Torvald my dear.

HELMER   Was that the dressmaker?

NORA   No, it's Kristine; she's helping me with my costume. You know, I think 150 I'm going to outdo myself this time.

HELMER   Yes, that was a pretty good idea I had, wasn't it?

NORA   Brilliant. But wasn't it also nice of me to agree to it?

HELMER [*Taking her under the chin.*]   Nice of you? Agreeing with your husband? All right, you crazy thing, I know you didn't mean it that way. But I 155 don't want to disturb you; I suppose you'll want to try it on.

NORA   Will you be working?

HELMER   Yes. [*Shows her a bundle of papers.*] See. I've been down to the bank— [*He is about to go into his study.*]

NORA   Torvald.

160 HELMER   Yes.

NORA   If your little squirrel were to beg you ever so nicely for something—?

HELMER   Well?

NORA   Would you do it?

HELMER   First, of course, I'd need to know what it is.

165 NORA   The squirrel would romp around and do tricks if you'd be sweet and say yes.

HELMER   Come on, what is it?

NORA   The lark would sing high and low in every room—

HELMER   So what, she does that anyway.

170 NORA   I'd pretend I was a fairy child and dance for you in the moonlight, Torvald.

HELMER   Nora, I hope this isn't that same business from this morning.

NORA [*Coming closer.*]   Yes, Torvald, please, I beg you!

HELMER   You really have the nerve to drag that up again.

175 NORA   Yes, yes, you've got to do what I say; you've got to let Krogstad keep his job in the bank.

HELMER   But Nora, I'm giving his job to Mrs. Linde.

NORA   That's very sweet of you; but can't you get rid of another clerk, someone besides Krogstad?

180 HELMER   I can't believe how stubborn you're being! Just because you went ahead and made a foolish promise to speak up for him, now I'm supposed to—

NORA   That's not why, Torvald. It's for your own sake. That man writes articles for some horrible newspapers; you've said so yourself. He can do you an awful lot of harm. I'm scared to death of him—

185 HELMER   Aha—I understand. You're frightened of the old memories.

NORA   What do you mean by that?

HELMER   You're thinking about your father.

NORA   That's right. Remember how those horrible people wrote about Papa in the papers and slandered him so terribly. I believe they'd have gotten
190   him fired if the government hadn't sent you up there to investigate and if you hadn't been so kind and fair to him.

HELMER   My little Nora, there is a considerable difference between your father and me. Your father's public life was not exactly beyond reproach—but mine is. And that's how I plan to keep it for as long as I hold my position.

195 NORA   Oh, you can never tell what spiteful people might do. It could be so nice and quiet and happy in our home—so peaceful and carefree—you and me and the children, Torvald—

HELMER   And precisely by continuing to plead for him like this you're making it impossible for me to keep him on. It's already known around the
200   bank that I'm letting Krogstad go. What if the rumor got around that the new bank manager was letting himself be overruled by his wife—

NORA   Yes, so what?

HELMER   Oh, of course—as long as our little rebel here gets her way—I should make myself look silly in front of my whole staff—make people think I can be
205   influenced by all kinds of outside pressures—you can bet that would come back to haunt me soon enough. Besides—there's one thing that makes it impossible to have Krogstad in the bank as long as I'm the manager.

NORA   What's that?

HELMER   I might be able to overlook his moral failings if I had to—

210 NORA   Yes, Torvald, isn't that right?

HELMER   And I hear he's quite good at his job too. But he was a boyhood friend of mine—one of those stupid friendships you get into without thinking, and end up regretting later in life. I might just as well tell you—we're on a first-name basis. And that tactless idiot makes no secret of it in front
215   of people. The opposite, in fact—he thinks it entitles him to take a familiar tone with me, so he's always coming out with "Hey, Torvald—Torvald, can I talk to you, Torvald—" and I can tell you I find it excruciating. He'll make my life at the bank completely intolerable.

NORA   Torvald, you can't be serious.

220 HELMER   Oh? Why not?

NORA   No, because these are such petty things.

HELMER   What are you saying? Petty? Do you think I'm petty?

NORA   Not at all, Torvald, and that's just the reason—

HELMER   All right; you call me petty, I might as well be just that. Petty!
225   Very well! Now we'll put a stop to all of this. [*Goes to the door and calls.*] Helene!

NORA   What are you doing?

HELMER   [*Searching through his papers.*]   A decision. [*The Maid enters.*] See this letter? Find a messenger right away and have him deliver it. Quickly.
230   The address is on the envelope. There—here's some money.

MAID   Yes sir. [*She leaves with the letter.*]

HELMER   [*Tidying up his papers.*]   So that's that, my little Miss Stubborn.

NORA   [*Breathless.*]   Torvald, what was that letter?

HELMER   Krogstad's notice.

235 NORA   Get it back, Torvald! There's still time. Oh, Torvald, get it back! Do it for my sake—for your own sake—for the children's sake! Listen, Torvald, do it! You don't realize what can happen to all of us.

HELMER   Too late.

NORA   Yes, too late.

240 HELMER   Nora, I forgive you for being nervous about this, even though you're really insulting me. Yes, you are. Isn't it insulting to think that *I* would be afraid of what some hack journalist might do for revenge? But I forgive you, all the same, because it shows so beautifully how much you love me. That's how it should be, my own darling Nora. Come what may! 245 When things get tough, I've got the courage—and the strength, you can believe it. I'm the kind of man who can take it all on himself.

NORA [*Terrified.*]   What do you mean by that?

HELMER   The whole thing, like I said.

NORA [*Resolutely.*]   You'll never have to do that, never.

250 HELMER   Good—so we'll share it, Nora, as man and wife. That's the way it should be. [*Fondling her.*] Happy now? Well, well, well—enough of those frightened dove's eyes. It's nothing but empty fantasy. Now you should run through your tarantella and try the tambourine. I won't hear a thing in the office, so you can make all the noise you want. [*Turning in the doorway.*] 255 And when Rank comes, tell him where he can find me. [*He nods to her, goes to his study with his papers, and closes the door behind him.*]

NORA [*Distracted with fear, standing as though glued to the spot, whispering.*] He's really going to do it. He will do it. He'll do it in spite of everything—No, never, never in this world! Anything but that—escape! A way out—[*The bell rings in the hall.*] Doctor Rank! Anything but that! Whatever else happens!

[*She brushes her hands over her face, pulls herself together and goes to open the door in the hall. Doctor Rank is standing outside hanging up his fur coat. During the following, it begins to grow dark.*]

NORA   Doctor Rank, I recognized your ring. But you can't see Torvald quite 260 yet; I think he's busy.

RANK   And you?

NORA [*While he comes into the room and she closes the door after him.*]   Oh, as you know perfectly well, I always have an hour to spare for you.

RANK   Thanks. I shall make use of it as long as I can.

265 NORA   What do you mean? As long as you can?

RANK   Yes, does that worry you?

NORA   Well, it's such a strange way to talk. Is anything going to happen?

RANK   Something that I've been expecting for a long time. But I didn't think it would come so soon.

270 NORA [*Gripping his arm.*]   What have you found out? Doctor Rank, you have to tell me!

RANK [*Sitting by the stove.*]   It's all over. There's no point in lying to myself.

NORA [*Breathing easier.*]   Is it you—?

RANK   Who else? I'm the worst of all my patients, Mrs. Helmer. Over the last 275 few days I've done a general audit of my internal account. Bankrupt. Within a month I'll probably be rotting in the churchyard.

NORA   Oh, really. What a horrible thing to say.

RANK   It *is* a horrible thing. But the worst of it all is the horror beforehand. There's one more examination to go; when I've done that I'll know when

280 the disintegration will begin. There is something I want to ask you. Helmer
is so sensitive; he can't stand to be around anything ugly. I won't let him
come to my sickroom.

NORA Oh, but Doctor Rank—

RANK I won't allow him in there. Under any circumstances. I'll lock the door
285 to him. As soon as I'm absolutely certain of the worst, I'll send you my card
with a black cross on it; then you'll know that it's begun.

NORA No, you are completely unreasonable today. And I especially wanted
you to be in a really good mood.

RANK When I hold death in my hands? And to suffer like this for someone
290 else's guilt? Is there any justice in that? In every family—every single one—
somehow this inexorable retribution is taking its course.

NORA [Stopping her ears.] La la la la la! Cheer up! Cheer up!

RANK Yes, finally even I can only laugh at the whole thing. My poor, innocent back has to pay for my father's career as a lascivious lieutenant.

295 NORA [By the table to the left.] Was he that addicted to asparagus and paté
de foie gras?[7]

RANK Yes, and truffles.

NORA Truffles, yes. And also oysters, I believe.

RANK Yes, oysters, oysters, of course.

300 NORA And port and champagne too. It's so sad that all these delicious things
have to go and attack our bones.

RANK Especially when they attack the unfortunate bones that never got the
slightest pleasure from them.

NORA Ah, yes—that's the greatest sadness of all.

305 RANK [Looks searchingly at her.] Hmm—

NORA [Shortly after.] Why did you smile?

RANK No, no—you laughed.

NORA No, you smiled, Doctor Rank!

RANK [Getting up.] You're an even bigger flirt than I thought!

310 NORA I'm full of crazy ideas today.

RANK So it seems.

NORA [With both hands on his shoulders.] Dear, dear Doctor Rank: for Torvald and me, you simply will not die.

RANK Oh, you'll soon get over that loss. Those who go away are soon
315 forgotten.

NORA [Looking anxiously at him.] Do you think so?

RANK You make new relationships, and then—

NORA Who makes new relationships?

RANK Both you and Helmer will, after I'm gone. You're well on your way
320 already, I'd say. What was that Mrs. Linde doing here last night?

NORA Come on now—you're not telling me you're jealous of poor Kristine?

RANK Yes I am. She'll be my successor here in this house. When my time is
up, I'll bet that woman will—

NORA Ssh—don't talk so loud—she's in there.

325 RANK Again today! There, you see?

NORA She's just fixing my costume. Good Lord, you're unreasonable today.
[Sits on the sofa.] Now be nice, Doctor Rank. Tomorrow you'll see how

---

7. French. A paté made from goose liver.

beautifully I'll dance—and you can imagine I'm doing it just for you—yes, for Torvald too, of course. [*Takes various things out of a carton.*] Doctor
330 Rank, sit here. I want to show you something.

RANK [*Sitting.*]   What is it?

NORA   Look here. Look!

RANK   Silk stockings.

NORA   Flesh-colored. Lovely, aren't they? It's so dark in here now, but in the
335 morning—no, no, no, only the feet. Oh, well, you might as well go ahead and look higher up.

RANK   Hmm.

NORA   What's this critical stare? Don't you think they'll fit?

RANK   I couldn't possibly have an accurate opinion on that.

340 NORA. [*Glancing at him for a moment.*]   Shame on you. [*Hits him lightly on the ear with the stockings.*] That's what you get. [*Puts them away again.*]

RANK   And what other splendors do I get to see?

NORA   Not a thing—you're being bad. [*She hums a little and rummages through her things.*]

RANK [*After a short pause.*]   When I'm sitting here like this, so close to you,
345 I can't imagine—I can't begin to comprehend—what would have become of me if I had never found my way to this house.

NORA [*Smiling.*]   Yes, I believe you really enjoy being here with us.

RANK [*Quietly, looking ahead.*]   And to have to leave it all behind—

NORA   Nonsense, you're not leaving us behind.

350 RANK [*As before.*]   And to think that nothing remains after you're gone—no little gesture of gratitude—hardly even a passing regret—just a vacant place that the first person who comes along can fill.

NORA   And what if I were to ask you now for—? No—

RANK   For what?

355 NORA   For a great proof of your friendship.

RANK   Yes, yes?

NORA   I mean a tremendously big favor—

RANK   Would you really let me be so happy, just this once?

NORA   You have no idea what it is.

360 RANK   All right—so tell me.

NORA   No, Doctor Rank, I can't. It's too big, too unreasonable. It's advice, and help, and a great service too.

RANK   So much the better. I can't imagine what you mean. But keep talking. Don't you have confidence in me?

365 NORA   Yes, in you before anyone else. You're my best and truest friend, you know that. That's why I can tell you. All right, Doctor Rank: there's something you've got to help me prevent. You know how intensely, how indescribably deeply Torvald loves me—he'd give his life for my sake without a moment's thought.

370 RANK [*Bending toward her.*]   Nora—do you think he's the only one?

NORA [*With a slight start.*]   Who—?

RANK   Who would gladly give his life for you?

NORA [*Heavily.*]   I see.

RANK   I promised myself that you'd know before the end. I'll never find a bet-
375 ter chance than this. Yes, Nora, now you know. And you also know that you can trust me like nobody else.

NORA [*Rises and speaks, evenly and calmly.*]   Let me through.

RANK [*Makes way for her, but remains seated.*]   Nora—

NORA [*In the hall doorway.*]   Helene, bring in the lamp. [*She goes over to the*
380 *stove.*] Ah, dear Doctor Rank, that was really awful of you.

RANK [*Rising.*]   That I've loved you just as much as anyone? Was *that* awful?

NORA   No, but that you felt you had to tell me. That was just not necessary.

RANK   What do you mean? You mean that you knew—?

[*The Maid enters with the lamp, sets it on the table, and goes out again.*]

RANK   Nora—Mrs. Helmer—I'm asking you. Did you know?

385 NORA   Oh, how do I know what I knew or didn't know? I can't say. How
could you be so clumsy, Doctor Rank! When everything was so nice.

RANK   Well, in any case now you know that I'm at your service with body and
soul. So please go on.

NORA [*Looking at him.*]   After this?

390 RANK   Please, please tell me what it is.

NORA   Now I can't tell you anything.

RANK   Yes, yes. Don't torment me like this. Let me do whatever is humanly
possible for you.

NORA   You can't do anything for me now. In fact, I really don't need any help.
395 You'll see—it was just my imagination. It really is. Of course! [*Sits in the
rocking chair, looks at him, smiling.*] Well, you are a piece of work, Doctor
Rank. Don't you think you should be a little ashamed, now that the lamp is
here?

RANK   No, not really. But maybe I'd better go—for good?

400 NORA   No, you certainly will not do that. Of course you'll keep coming here
just like before. You know perfectly well that Torvald can't do without you.

RANK   Yes, but what about you?

NORA   Oh, I always enjoy your visits very much.

RANK   That's exactly what set me off on the wrong track. You're an enigma to
405 me. I've often felt you'd almost rather be with me than with Helmer.

NORA   Well, you see, there are the people you love the most, and the people
you'd almost rather be with.

RANK   Ah yes, you're on to something there.

NORA   When I was at home, of course I loved Papa the most. But I always
410 had the most fun sneaking into the maids' rooms, because they never tried
to teach me anything and they always had so much fun talking to each
other.

RANK   Ah—so *they're* the ones that I've replaced.

NORA [*Jumping up and going to him.*]   Oh, dear Doctor Rank, I didn't mean
415 that at all. But you can see that with Torvald it's a lot like it was with Papa—

[*The Maid enters from the hall.*]

MAID   Ma'am. [*Whispers and hands Nora a card.*]

NORA [*Glancing at the card.*]   Ah! [*Puts it in her pocket.*]

RANK   Something wrong?

NORA   No, no, not at all. It's just—it's about my new costume.

420 RANK   How could that be? Your costume's in there.

NORA   Oh, yes—that one. But this is a different one, I ordered it—Torvald
can't find out—

RANK   Aha—there's our great secret.

NORA   That's right. Go on in to him. He's working in the inner room. Keep
425   him there as long as—
RANK   Don't worry—he won't get by me. [*He goes into Helmer's study.*]
NORA [*To the Maid.*]   And he's waiting in the kitchen?
MAID   Yes, he came up the back stairs.
NORA   Did you tell him somebody was here?
430 MAID   I did, but that didn't help.
NORA   He won't go away?
MAID   No, he won't leave until he's talked to you.
NORA   Let him come in then; but quietly. Helene, not a word of this to any-
one; it's a surprise for my husband.
435 MAID   Oh, yes, I understand. [*She goes out.*]
NORA   This terrible thing is really happening. It's coming no matter what.
No, no, no. It can't happen. It must not happen.
        [*She goes and bolts Helmer's door. The Maid opens the hall door for Krog-
        stad and closes it after him. He's dressed in traveling clothes, a fur coat,
        overshoes, and a fur cap.*]
NORA [*Goes toward him.*]   Talk quietly—my husband's home.
KROGSTAD   I don't care.
440 NORA   What do you want from me?
KROGSTAD   Some answers.
NORA   Quick, then. What?
KROGSTAD   You know, of course, I got my notice.
NORA   I couldn't stop it, Mr. Krogstad. I fought for you as hard as I could,
445   but it was no use.
KROGSTAD   Does your husband really love you so little? He knows what I can
do to you, and he still dares—
NORA   How can you imagine he knows about it?
KROGSTAD   No, I didn't think he did. It's not like my fine Torvald Helmer to
450   show that kind of strength.
NORA   Mr. Krogstad, I demand respect for my husband.
KROGSTAD   Good Lord, of course, all due respect. But since the lady has kept
all this so carefully hidden, might I ask if you've also come to understand a
little better than yesterday what you've actually done?
455 NORA   Better than you could ever teach me.
KROGSTAD   Yes, I'm such a terrible lawyer—
NORA   What do you want with me?
KROGSTAD   Just to see how things are with you, Mrs. Helmer. I couldn't stop
thinking about you all day. A cashier, a hack journalist, a—well, a man like
460   me also has a little of what is commonly called heart, you know.
NORA   Then show it. Think of my little children.
KROGSTAD   Have you or your husband given any thought to mine? But
that's not the issue right now. I just wanted to tell you that you don't need
to take this business too seriously. For the time being I'm not taking any
465   action.
NORA   Oh, that's true, I was sure of it.
KROGSTAD   The whole thing can be settled amicably. No one else needs to
know about it, just the three of us.
NORA   My husband can never find out.
470 KROGSTAD   How can you stop that? Can you pay off the balance?

NORA   No, not right now.

KROGSTAD   Maybe you can find a way to raise the money in a few days?

NORA   No way that I'd use.

KROGSTAD   Well, it wouldn't do you any good anyway. Even if you were standing
475   there with a pile of cash in your hands you still wouldn't get your note back.

NORA   Tell me what you're going to do with it.

KROGSTAD   Just keep it—just hold it in my custody. No one else needs to
know anything about it. So if you happen to be thinking of some desperate
remedy—

480 NORA   Which I am.

KROGSTAD   If you're thinking of running away from home—

NORA   Which I am.

KROGSTAD   Or something worse—

NORA   How did you know?

485 KROGSTAD   Then give it up right now.

NORA   How could you know I was thinking of *that*?

KROGSTAD   Most of us think of *that* to begin with. I thought about it too—
but I didn't have the courage.

NORA [*Lifelessly.*]   I don't either.

490 KROGSTAD [*Relieved.*]   That's true?

NORA   I don't have it; I don't have it.

KROGSTAD   It'd be pretty silly anyway. As soon as the first big storm blows
over—I have here in my pocket a letter to your husband—

NORA   Which tells everything?

495 KROGSTAD   As nicely as possible.

NORA [*Quickly.*]   He must never get that letter. Tear it up. I'll get the money
somehow.

KROGSTAD   Excuse me, Mrs. Helmer, but I think I just told you—

NORA   I'm not talking about what I owe you. Just let me know how much you
500   demand from my husband and I'll get you the money.

KROGSTAD   I'm not demanding any money from your husband.

NORA   So what then?

KROGSTAD   I'll tell you. I want to get back on my feet, Mrs. Helmer; I want to
move up. And your husband is going to help me. For the last year and a half
505   I haven't gone near anything disreputable—all the time fighting to make
ends meet—but I was happy to work my way up, step by step. Now I'm
being driven out again and I'm not in a very forgiving mood, I'm ready to
climb, I tell you. I'll get back in the bank, and in a higher position than
before. Your husband will set me up.

510 NORA   He'll never do that!

KROGSTAD   He'll do it. I know him; he won't even dare to argue. And once I'm
in there with him, you'll see how it goes. In a year I'll be the manager's right-
hand man. Nils Krogstad will be running that bank, not Torvald Helmer.

NORA   You'll never live to see that.

515 KROGSTAD   You think you might—

NORA   Now I have the courage.

KROGSTAD   Forget it—a pampered, spoiled woman like you?

NORA   You'll see—you'll see.

KROGSTAD   Under the ice, maybe? Down in the freezing black water? Float-
520   ing up in the spring, ugly, unrecognizable, your hair falling out—

NORA   You don't frighten me.

KROGSTAD   You don't frighten me either. People don't do such things, Mrs. Helmer. Besides, what would be the point? I'd have him in my pocket just the same.

525 NORA   After—? Even when I'm no longer—?

KROGSTAD   Are you forgetting? In that case I'll be in charge of your reputation. [*Nora stares speechless at him.*] Well, I've warned you. Don't do anything stupid. When Helmer gets my letter, I'll wait for a word from him. Just keep in mind that it's your husband who has forced me back onto

530   these old roads of mine. I'll never forgive him for that. Goodbye, Mrs. Helmer. [*He goes out through the hallway.*]

NORA [*Goes to the hall door, opens it a fraction, and listens.*]   Gone. He didn't leave the letter. No, no, no, that would be impossible! [*Opening the door farther.*] What? He's waiting outside. Not going downstairs. Changing his

535   mind? Maybe he'll—?

> [*A letter drops into the mailbox; then Krogstad's footsteps are heard receding as he walks downstairs. Nora, with a stifled cry, runs across the room to the sofa table; short pause.*]

NORA   In the mailbox. [*Creeps cautiously to the hall door.*]   Lying there. Torvald, Torvald—no saving us now!

> [*Mrs. Linde enters with the costume from the room at the left.*]

MRS. LINDE   Well, I think that's it for the repairs. Should we try it—

NORA [*In a low, hoarse voice.*]   Kristine, come here.

540 MRS. LINDE [*Throws the dress onto the sofa.*]   What's the matter—you're upset!

NORA   Come here. See that letter? There—see it, through the window in the mailbox?

MRS. LINDE   Yes, I see it.

NORA   It's from Krogstad.

545 MRS. LINDE   Nora—Krogstad's the one who lent you the money!

NORA   Yes. And now Torvald will know everything.

MRS. LINDE   Believe me, Nora, that's best for both of you.

NORA   There's more to it. I forged a signature.

MRS. LINDE   Oh for heaven's sake—

550 NORA   I'm just telling you this, Kristine, so that you can be my witness.

MRS. LINDE   What do you mean, witness? How can I—?

NORA   If I were to lose my mind—that could easily happen—

MRS. LINDE   Nora!

NORA   Or if anything else happened to me, if I couldn't be here—

555 MRS. LINDE   Nora, you're beside yourself!

NORA   And if someone wanted to try to take the whole thing onto himself, all the blame, you see—

MRS. LINDE   Yes, but how can you think—

NORA   You've got to swear it isn't true, Kristine. I'm in my perfect mind; I

560   understand exactly what I'm saying; and I'm telling you: no one else knew about it. I did it all alone. Remember that.

MRS. LINDE   I will. But I don't understand any of it.

NORA   How could you understand? A wonderful thing is about to happen.

MRS. LINDE   Wonderful?

565 NORA   Yes, a wonderful thing. But also terrible, Kristine, and it just can't happen, not for all the world.

MRS. LINDE   I'm going to talk to Krogstad right away.

NORA   Don't: he'll only hurt you some way.

MRS. LINDE   Once upon a time he'd have gladly done anything for me.

570 NORA   Him?

MRS. LINDE   Where does he live?

NORA   How should I know? Wait—[*Searches her pocket.*] Here's his card. But what about the letter, the letter—?

HELMER [*In his study, knocking on the door.*]   Nora!

575 NORA [*Screams in panic.*]   What is it? What do you want?

HELMER   Now, don't be frightened. We're not coming in. The door's locked; are you trying on your costume?

NORA   Yes, I'm trying it on. I'm going to be so beautiful, Torvald.

MRS. LINDE [*Having read the card.*]   He lives right around the corner.

580 NORA   Yes, but that's no help. We're lost. The letter's in the box.

MRS. LINDE   Your husband has the key?

NORA   Always.

MRS. LINDE   Krogstad will have to ask for his letter back unopened—he'll have to find some excuse—

585 NORA   But this is the time when Torvald usually—

MRS. LINDE   Stall him. Go in there and stay with him. I'll get back as fast as I can. [*She goes out hurriedly through the hall door. Nora goes to Helmer's door and opens it, looking in.*]

NORA   Torvald!

HELMER   Well—can I finally come back into my own living room? Come on, 590 Rank, now we'll get to see— [*In the doorway.*] But—?

NORA   What, Torvald my dear?

HELMER   Rank had me all set for a great dress parade.

RANK [*In the doorway.*]   That's what I was expecting, but I guess I was wrong.

NORA   No one gets to bask in my full glory until tomorrow.

595 HELMER   But Nora, you look so tired. Have you been practicing too hard?

NORA   No, I haven't practiced at all yet.

HELMER   You know it's essential—

NORA   Absolutely essential. But I can't possibly do it without your help; I've forgotten everything.

600 HELMER   We'll get it back quick enough.

NORA   Yes, take care of me right to the end, Torvald. Do you promise? Ah, I'm so nervous. That big party—you have to give up everything for me tonight. Not one bit of business, don't even go near your work. All right, Torvald. Promise?

605 HELMER   I promise. Tonight I'll be completely at your service—you helpless little thing. Hmm—just one item to take care of first—[*Goes toward the hall door.*]

NORA   What do you want out there?

HELMER   Just seeing if there's any mail.

NORA   No, no, Torvald, don't do that!

610 HELMER   What now?

NORA   Torvald, please, there's nothing there.

HELMER   Just let me have a look. [*About to go; Nora, at the piano, plays the opening notes of the tarantella. Helmer stops at the door.*]

NORA   I can't dance tomorrow if I don't rehearse with you.

HELMER [*Going to her.*]   Nora, are you really so frightened of it?

615 NORA   Tremendously frightened. Let's rehearse right now; there's still time before dinner. Oh, Torvald, sit down and play for me. Show me how it goes; direct me, like you always do.

HELMER   I'd be glad to, if you want.

[*Nora snatches the tambourine out of the box, and also a long, multicolored shawl which she drapes around herself; then she springs forward and calls out.*]

NORA   Play for me! Now I'll dance!

[*Helmer plays and Nora dances; Doctor Rank stands behind Helmer and watches.*]

620 HELMER [*Playing.*]   Slower, slower—

NORA   I can't help it.

HELMER   Not so violent, Nora!

NORA   That's how it has to be.

HELMER [*Stopping.*]   No, no—that's not it at all.

625 NORA [*Laughing, swinging the tambourine.*]   What did I tell you?

RANK   Let me play for her.

HELMER [*Getting up.*]   Yes, good idea. That way I can be a better teacher.

[*Rank sits at the piano and plays. Nora dances with increasing wildness. Helmer has placed himself by the stove, continually directing dancing instructions to her; she seems not to hear him; her hair loosens and falls over her shoulders; she doesn't notice, but keeps on dancing. Mrs. Linde enters.*]

MRS. LINDE [*As though spellbound in the doorway.*]   Ah—!

NORA [*Still dancing.*]   See, Kristine, what fun!

630 HELMER   But Nora, you're dancing as if your life were at stake.

NORA   It is, it is!

HELMER   Rank, stop. This is absolute madness. Stop it!

[*Rank stops playing and Nora suddenly comes to a halt.*]

HELMER [*Goes to her.*]   I would never have believed this—you've forgotten everything I taught you.

635 NORA [*Throwing down the tambourine.*]   As you can see.

HELMER   Some extra work's in order here.

NORA   Yes, you see how important it is. You've got to keep teaching me right up to the last minute. Promise, Torvald?

HELMER   Depend on it.

640 NORA   You can't even think—today or tomorrow—about anything but me— don't open any letters, don't even touch the mailbox—

HELMER   Ah—you're still afraid of that man.

NORA   Yes, yes, that too.

HELMER   Nora, I can see it in your face, there's a letter from him out there.

645 NORA   I don't know. I think there is. But you can't read things like that now; there can't be anything horrible between us till all this is over.

RANK [*Softly to Helmer.*]   You shouldn't go against her.

HELMER   The child will have its way. But tomorrow night—after you've danced—

NORA   Then you're free.

650 MAID [*In the doorway, right.*]   Ma'am, dinner's on the table.

NORA   We'll have champagne, Helene.

MAID   Very good, ma'am. [*Goes out.*]

HELMER   Hey, hey—a whole banquet?

NORA   Yes—a champagne supper right through till dawn! [*Calling out.*] And
655   some macaroons, Helene—lots of them—just this once.

HELMER   [*Taking her hands.*]   There, there, there—not so wild, not so
scared—be my little skylark again.

NORA   Oh, yes, I certainly will. But go to dinner—you too, Doctor Rank.
Kristine, I need you to help me with my hair.

660   RANK   [*Softly as they go.*]   There wouldn't be anything—anything on the way?

HELMER   No, my friend, not a thing; nothing more than these silly fears I've
been telling you about. [*They go out, right.*]

NORA   Well?

MRS. LINDE   Gone to the country.

665   NORA   I saw it in your face.

MRS. LINDE   He gets back tomorrow night. I left him a note.

NORA   You shouldn't have done that. You can't stop it now. Behind it all
there's this great joy—waiting for a wonderful thing to happen.

MRS. LINDE   What are you waiting for?

670   NORA   You can't understand that. Go in with them—I'll be there in a minute.

> [*Mrs. Linde goes into the dining room. Nora stands for a moment as if to
> compose herself; then she looks at her watch.*]

NORA   Five. Seven hours to midnight. Then twenty-four hours to the next
midnight. Then the tarantella will be done. Twenty-four plus seven—
thirty-one hours to live.

HELMER   [*In the doorway, right.*]   What happened to the skylark?

675   NORA   [*Going to him with open arms.*]   Here's your skylark!

Act 3

*Same room. The sofa-table, with chairs around it, has been moved to the middle of
the room. A lamp is burning on the table. The door to the hall stands open. Dance
music can be heard from the apartment above.*

> [*Mrs. Linde is sitting by the table, desultorily turning the pages of the
> book; she attempts to read but seems unable to fix her attention. Once or
> twice she listens, tensely, for a sound at the door.*]

MRS. LINDE   Not here yet. And it's now or never. If he'd only—[*Listens again.*]
Ah—there he is. [*She goes out into the hall and cautiously opens the outer
door; quiet footsteps are heard on the stairs. She whispers.*] Come in. Nobody's
here.

5   KROGSTAD   [*In the doorway.*]   I found a note from you at home. What does it
mean?

MRS. LINDE   I had to talk to you.

KROGSTAD   Oh yes? And it had to be here, in this house?

MRS. LINDE   My place is impossible—there's no private entrance to my room.
10   Come in; we're all alone. The maid's asleep and the Helmers are at a party
upstairs.

KROGSTAD   [*Comes into the room.*]   Well, well, well—so the Helmers are
dancing tonight. How about that?

MRS. LINDE   Why shouldn't they?

15   KROGSTAD   True enough—why shouldn't they.

MRS. LINDE   Well, Krogstad, let's talk.

KROGSTAD   Do the two of us have anything more to talk about?

MRS. LINDE We have a lot to talk about.

KROGSTAD I wouldn't have thought so.

20 MRS. LINDE No, because you've never really understood me.

KROGSTAD What was there to understand, more than the usual thing? A heartless woman sends a man packing as soon as she gets a better offer.

MRS. LINDE Do you think I'm that heartless? Do you think it was easy for me to break up with you?

25 KROGSTAD Wasn't it?

MRS. LINDE Krogstad, did you really think that?

KROGSTAD Then how could you have written to me that way?

MRS. LINDE I couldn't do anything else. If I had to make the break, it was my duty to try to stamp out whatever feelings you had for me.

30 KROGSTAD [Clenching his hands.] So that was it! And this—all this for money's sake!

MRS. LINDE Don't forget that I had a helpless mother and two little brothers. We couldn't wait for you, Krogstad; your prospects were so cloudy then.

35 KROGSTAD Maybe. But you had no right to abandon me for somebody else's sake.

MRS. LINDE Yes—I don't know. I've asked myself over and over if I had any right to do that.

KROGSTAD [More quietly.] When I lost you I felt the ground dissolve under
40 my feet. Look at me: I'm a man adrift on a wreck.

MRS. LINDE Help could be close by.

KROGSTAD It was—until you appeared and blocked the way.

MRS. LINDE I didn't know, Krogstad. I only learned today that I'm replacing you at the bank.

45 KROGSTAD Since you say so, I believe it. But now you know—so won't you pull out?

MRS. LINDE No, because that wouldn't do you the least bit of good.

KROGSTAD Oh, who cares? I'd do it anyway.

MRS. LINDE I've learned to act rationally. Life and bitter necessity have
50 taught me that.

KROGSTAD And life has taught me not to believe in empty phrases.

MRS. LINDE Then life has taught you a very rational lesson. But you do believe in deeds, don't you?

KROGSTAD What do you mean?

55 MRS. LINDE You said that you were like a man adrift, standing on a wreck.

KROGSTAD I said that with good reason.

MRS. LINDE Well I'm a woman adrift; I'm hanging on to a wreck as well.

KROGSTAD That was your choice.

MRS. LINDE There was no other choice at the time.

60 KROGSTAD So?

MRS. LINDE Krogstad, what if these two shipwrecks could reach across to one another?

KROGSTAD What are you saying?

MRS. LINDE Two on one raft stand a better chance than each one alone.

65 KROGSTAD Kristine!

MRS. LINDE Why do you suppose I came to town?

KROGSTAD Were you really thinking about me?

MRS. LINDE   For me to go on living, I need to work. All my life, as long as I
can remember, I've worked—it's given me my only real joy. But now I'm
70   completely alone in the world, completely empty and desolate. Working for
yourself—well, there's no joy in that. Krogstad: give me someone and
something to work for.

KROGSTAD   I don't believe all this. This is just some hysterical feminine urge
for self-sacrifice.

75   MRS. LINDE   Have you ever known me to be hysterical?

KROGSTAD   Can you really mean all this? Do you know about my past—the
whole story?

MRS. LINDE   Yes.

KROGSTAD   And you know what people think of me here?

80   MRS. LINDE   You hinted just now that you thought you could have been a different person with me.

KROGSTAD   I know that for sure.

MRS. LINDE   Couldn't it still happen?

KROGSTAD   Kristine—you're serious about this? Yes, you are. I can see it in
85   you. Do you have the courage as well?

MRS. LINDE   I need someone to be a mother to, and your children need a
mother. The two of us need each other. Krogstad, I have faith in you, in
what's there deep down in your heart. I could risk anything together with
you.

90   KROGSTAD [*Seizing her hands.*]   Thank you, Kristine, thank you—now I know
I can bring myself up in people's eyes—ah, I forgot—

MRS. LINDE [*Listening.*]   The tarantella! Go, go, go!

KROGSTAD   What's going on?

MRS. LINDE   Do you hear the music up there? When it's over, they'll be
95   down.

KROGSTAD   All right, I'll go. It's all pointless. Of course you don't know what
I've done with the Helmers.

MRS. LINDE   Yes, Krogstad, I know all about it.

KROGSTAD   And you still have the courage to—

100   MRS. LINDE   I know very well how far despair can drive a man like you.

KROGSTAD   If I could only undo what I've done!

MRS. LINDE   That's easy. Your letter's still in the mailbox.

KROGSTAD   Are you sure?

MRS. LINDE   Absolutely. But—

105   KROGSTAD [*Looks searchingly at her.*]   Is that what this is all about? Would you
save your friend at any price? Tell me honestly, tell me straight—is that it?

MRS. LINDE   Krogstad: when you've sold yourself *once* for someone else's
sake, you don't do it a second time.

KROGSTAD   I'll demand my letter back.

110   MRS. LINDE   No, no.

KROGSTAD   Yes, of course I will. I'll stay here until Helmer comes down; I'll
tell him to give me back my letter—that it's only about my dismissal—that
he shouldn't read it.

MRS. LINDE   No, Krogstad. Don't take back your letter.

115   KROGSTAD   But wasn't that exactly why you got me over here?

MRS. LINDE   Yes, in the first panic. But in the twenty-four hours between then
and now, I've seen some incredible things in this house. Helmer has to learn

everything; this awful secret has to come to light; those two have to come
to a clear understanding—they can't go on with all this hiding, all these
120   lies.

KROGSTAD   Well, if you're willing to take the risk—. But there's one thing I
can do right away.

MRS. LINDE [*Listening.*]   Hurry! Go, go! The dance is over. We're not safe
another second!

125 KROGSTAD   I'll wait for you downstairs.

MRS. LINDE   Yes, do that. You'll have to see me home.

KROGSTAD   This incredible happiness—I've never felt anything like it!

[*He goes out by the front door; the door between the living room and the
hall stays open.*]

MRS. LINDE [*Tidies the room a little and gets her outer garments ready.*]   What
a change! What a change! People to work for, to live for—a home to make.
130   That's something worth doing. If only they'd come soon. [*Listens.*] Ah—
there they are. Get dressed.

[*Helmer's and Nora's voices are heard outside; a key is turned and
Helmer leads Nora almost forcibly into the hall. She is wearing the Italian costume with a large black shawl over it; he is in evening dress with
an open black domino[8] over it.*]

NORA [*Still in the doorway, resisting.*]   No, no, no, not in there! I'm going up
again. I don't want to leave so early!

HELMER   But Nora, my dearest—

135 NORA   Oh, I beg you, I implore you, from the bottom of my heart Torvald—
just one more hour!

HELMER   Not another minute, Nora, my sweet. You know we had an agreement. Come on now, into the drawing room; you're catching cold out here.
[*He leads her gently into the drawing room against her resistance.*]

MRS. LINDE   Good evening.

140 NORA   Kristine!

HELMER   Well, Mrs. Linde—here so late?

MRS. LINDE   Yes, forgive me. I really wanted to see Nora in her costume.

NORA   So you've been sitting here waiting for me?

MRS. LINDE   Yes, I didn't get here in time—you'd all gone upstairs. And I just
145   thought I couldn't leave without seeing you.

HELMER [*Taking off Nora's shawl.*]   Well, get a good look at her. I think she's
worth looking at. Isn't she lovely, Mrs. Linde?

MRS. LINDE   Yes, I have to say—

HELMER   Isn't she incredibly lovely? That was the general consensus at the
150   party, too—but also incredibly stubborn, the sweet thing. What to do about
that? Would you believe it, I almost had to use force to get her down here.

NORA   Ah, Torvald, you're going to regret that you didn't let me have my way
just a half-hour more.

HELMER   Hear that, Mrs. Linde? She danced her tarantella to thunderous
155   applause—well-deserved applause, too—even though there was something
a little too naturalistic about the whole thing—I mean, something that
went beyond the strict requirements of art. But so what? The main thing is,
she was a success—a tremendous success. Should I let her stay around

8. A hooded robe usually worn to a costume party.

after that? Spoil the effect? No, thank you! I took my lovely Capri girl—my
160 capricious little Capri girl, I could say—on my arm; made a quick trip
around the ballroom—a curtsy to all sides—and as they say in novels, the
lovely apparition vanished. Exits are tremendously important, Mrs. Linde—
they should always be effective; but that's what I can't get Nora to see.
Uch, it's hot in here. [*Throws his domino on a chair and opens the door to*
165 *his room.*] What? it's dark—oh, yes, of course—excuse me—[*Goes in and*
lights candles.]

NORA [*Whispering quickly and breathlessly.*] Well?

MRS. LINDE [*Quietly.*] I talked to him.

NORA And—?

MRS. LINDE Nora, you have to tell your husband everything.

170 NORA [*Dully.*] I knew it.

MRS. LINDE You've got nothing to worry about from Krogstad—but you have
to speak out.

NORA I won't do it.

MRS. LINDE Then the letter will.

175 NORA Thank you, Kristine. Now I know what I have to do. Sssh!—

HELMER [*Coming in again.*] Now, Mrs. Linde—have you had a chance to
admire her?

MRS. LINDE Yes, and now I'll say good night.

HELMER So soon? Is this yours, this knitting?

180 MRS. LINDE [*Taking it.*] Oh yes.

HELMER So you also knit.

MRS. LINDE Yes.

HELMER Know what? You should embroider instead.

MRS. LINDE Really? Why?

185 HELMER Much prettier. Want to see? You hold the embroidery like this with
your left hand, and guide the needle with your right—like this—lightly, in
and out, in a sweeping curve—right?

MRS. LINDE I suppose so—

HELMER Now knitting, on the other hand—so ugly to watch—see here, the
190 arms jammed together, the needles going up and down—there's something
Chinese about it. Ah—that was a tremendous champagne up there.

MRS. LINDE Well, Nora, good night! And no more stubbornness!

HELMER Well said, Mrs. Linde!

MRS. LINDE Good night, Mr. Helmer.

195 HELMER [*Following her to the door.*] Good night, good night. I hope you're
all right getting home. I would, of course—but you don't have far to go.
Good night, good night. [*She leaves; he closes the door after her and comes*
in again.] Well, well. We finally got her out the door. What an incredible
bore that woman is.

200 NORA Aren't you tired, Torvald?

HELMER No, not a bit.

NORA Not sleepy at all?

HELMER Absolutely not—in fact, I'm exhilarated! You, on the other hand,
are looking very tired and sleepy.

205 NORA Yes, I'm tired. I'll get to sleep soon.

HELMER See, see! I was right! It was time to go home.

NORA Oh, everything you do is right.

HELMER [*Kisses her on the brow.*]   Now my little lark is talking like a real person. Say—did you notice how lively Rank was tonight?

210 NORA   Was he? I didn't get to talk to him.

HELMER   I barely did myself, but I haven't seen him in such a good mood in a long time. [*Looks at Nora a while, then comes closer to her.*] Hmm—my God, it's glorious to be back in our own home again, completely alone with you—you enchanting young woman!

215 NORA   Don't look at me like that, Torvald!

HELMER   Shouldn't I look at my most precious possession? All this magnificence, and it's mine, mine alone, completely and utterly mine!

NORA   You shouldn't talk this way to me tonight.

HELMER [*Following her.*]   The tarantella's still in your blood. I understand.
220   And that makes me want you even more. Listen! Now the guests are beginning to leave. [*More softly.*] Nora—soon the whole house will be silent.

NORA   I hope so.

HELMER   Yes, my own darling Nora, that's right. Ah—do you know why,
225   whenever I'm out at a party with you—do you know why I barely speak to you, why I keep my distance, hardly even shoot you a stolen glance? Do you know why I do that? Because I'm imagining you're my secret lover, my young, secret sweetheart, and that no one in the room guesses there's anything going on between us.

230 NORA   Oh yes, yes, yes—I know you're always thinking of me.

HELMER   And when it's time to go, and I place the shawl over your smooth young shoulders, around this wonderful curve of your neck—then I pretend you're my young bride, that we've come straight from the wedding, that I'm bringing you home for the first time, alone with you for the first
235   time, completely alone with you, you young, trembling, delicious—ah, I've done nothing but long for you all night! When I saw you doing the tarantella—like a huntress, luring us all to your trap—my blood started to boil. I couldn't stand it any longer. That's why I got you down here so early—

NORA   Get away, Torvald! Please get away from me. I don't want all this.

240 HELMER   What are you saying? Still playing the lark with me, Nora? You want, you don't want? Aren't I your husband?

[*There's a noise outside.*]

NORA [*Startled.*]   Did you hear that?

HELMER [*Going to the door.*]   Who's there?

RANK [*Outside.*]   Just me. May I come in for a moment?

245 HELMER [*Softly, irritated.*]   What can he possibly want now? [*Aloud.*] Just a second. [*Goes to the door and opens it.*] I'm so glad you didn't pass us by on your way out.

RANK   I thought I heard voices, and I really wanted to stop in. [*Looking around.*] Oh, yes—the old haunts. What a warm little nest you've got here.

250 HELMER   Speaking of which, you were having a pretty warm time upstairs—almost hot, I'd say.

RANK   Absolutely. And why not? You have to get the most out of life—everything you can, anyway, for as long as you can. That was excellent wine.

HELMER   And the champagne!

255 RANK   You thought so too? My thirst for it was amazing—even to me.

NORA   Torvald also had his share of champagne tonight.

RANK Oh yes?

NORA Yes, and that makes him so entertaining.

RANK And why shouldn't you enjoy an evening like this after a productive
260 day?

HELMER Productive? I can't exactly say that for myself.

RANK [*Slaps him on the back.*] Ah, but you see, I can!

NORA Doctor Rank, it sounds like you've done some medical research today.

RANK That's right.

265 HELMER Oh come on—here's little Nora talking about medical research!

NORA And may I congratulate you on the results?

RANK Yes indeed.

NORA Were they good?

RANK The best kind—for doctor and patient alike—certainty.

270 NORA [*Quickly, inquisitively.*] Certainty.

RANK Absolute certainty. So haven't I earned a festive night out?

NORA Yes, Doctor Rank, you have.

HELMER I'm all for that—as long as the morning after's not too bad.

RANK Well, you never get something for nothing in this world.

275 NORA Doctor Rank, do you like masquerade balls?

RANK Oh yes—especially when the disguises are good and strange—

NORA So tell me. At the next one, how should the two of us appear?

HELMER You little noodlehead! You're already on to the next one?

RANK The two of us? I can tell you that: you'll go as Charmed Life—

280 HELMER All right, but what's the costume for that?

RANK Your wife can go just as she always is.

HELMER Well said. Now have you decided on something for yourself?

RANK Yes, Helmer, my mind's made up.

HELMER Well?

285 RANK At the next masquerade, I will be—invisible.

HELMER That's pretty funny.

RANK I hear there's a hat—a huge, black hat—called the Hat of Invisibility.
You put it on, and no one on earth can see you.

HELMER [*Stifling a grin.*] Oh, yes, of course.

290 RANK But I've forgotten what I really came for. Helmer, how about a cigar—a
dark Havana.

HELMER With pleasure. [*Holds out the case to him.*]

RANK Thanks. [*Takes one and cuts the tip.*]

NORA Let me give you a light.

295 RANK Thank you. [*She holds the match as he lights the cigar.*] Now,
goodbye.

HELMER Old friend—goodbye, goodbye.

NORA Sleep well, Doctor.

RANK Thank you for that wish.

300 NORA Now wish me the same.

RANK Wish you?—All right, if you want—sleep well. And thanks for the
light. [*He exits, nodding to both of them.*]

HELMER [*Quietly.*] He's drunk.

NORA [*Vaguely.*] Maybe.

[*Helmer takes his keys from his pocket and goes out into the hall.*]

305 NORA What are you doing, Torvald?

HELMER   I've got to empty the mailbox—it's so full, there's no room for the morning papers.

NORA   Are you working tonight?

HELMER   You know I'm not. What's this? Someone's been fiddling with the

310   lock.

NORA   The lock?

HELMER   Yes, definitely. Who could it be? I can't believe the maids—? Wait, here's a broken hairpin—Nora, this is yours—

NORA [*Quickly.*]   Then it must be the children.

315   HELMER   Well you've really got to break them of that. Hmm—there we go, finally got it open. [*Takes out the contents and shouts into the kitchen.*] Helene? Helene—put out the hall lamp. [*He comes back into the room and shuts the door. He holds the letters in his hand.*] Look—see how it piled up? [*Sorts through them.*] What's this?

320   NORA [*By the window.*]   The letter! No, no, Torvald!

HELMER   Two cards, from Rank.

NORA   From Doctor Rank?

HELMER [*Looking at them.*]   Doctor Rank, Physician and Surgeon. They were on top. He must have dropped them in as he left.

325   NORA   Is there anything on them?

HELMER   There's a black cross over the name. Look. That's gruesome. It's like he's announcing his own death.

NORA   That's exactly what he's doing.

HELMER   What? Did he tell you anything?

330   NORA   Yes. He said that when these cards arrived, it meant he's saying goodbye to us. Now he'll shut himself in and die.

HELMER   My poor friend. Of course I knew I wouldn't have him for long. But so soon—and now he's hiding himself away like a wounded animal.

NORA   If it has to happen, it's best to let it happen quietly. Isn't that right,

335   Torvald?

HELMER [*Pacing up and down.*]   He'd grown to be a part of us. I don't think I can imagine myself without him. His loneliness—his suffering was like a cloudy background to our sunlit happiness. Well, maybe it's best this way—at least for him. [*Stands still.*] And maybe for us too, Nora. Now we

340   only have each other. [*Puts his arms around her.*] Ah, you—my darling wife. I don't think I'll ever be able to hold you close enough. You know, Nora—so many times I've wished that you were in some terrible danger, so I could risk my life, my blood, everything, everything for you.

NORA [*Tears herself free and says firmly and resolutely.*]   Read your mail now,

345   Torvald.

HELMER   No, not tonight. Tonight I want to be with you—

NORA   With your friend's death on your mind?

HELMER   You're right. We're both a little shaken by this. This ugliness has come between us—thoughts of death and decay. We have to try to get rid of

350   them; until then, we go our separate ways.

NORA [*Her arms around his neck.*]   Torvald—good night! Good night!

HELMER [*Kissing her forehead.*]   Good night, little songbird. Sleep well, Nora. Now I'll read the mail. [*He goes in with the letters, shuts the door behind him.*]

[*Nora, with wild eyes, fumbles around, seizes Helmer's domino, wraps it around herself, and whispers quickly, hoarsely, spasmodically.*]

NORA   Never see him again—never, never, never. [*Throws the shawl over her head.*] Never see the children again either—not even the children—never, never—the icy black water—the bottomless—that—if only it weren't all over—now he has it, he's reading it now—no, no, not yet. Torvald, good-bye, children, good-bye—

[*She starts to go into the hall; at the same moment Helmer flings open his door and stands there, an open letter in his hand.*]

HELMER   Nora!

NORA [*Screams.*]   Ahh—!

HELMER   What is this? Do you know what's in this letter?

NORA   Yes. Yes I know. Let me go. Let me out!

HELMER [*Holding her back.*]   Where are you going?

NORA [*Trying to break loose.*]   Don't try to save me, Torvald!

HELMER [*Staggers back.*]   It's true?! What he said is the truth? Horrible! No—it's impossible—this can't be true.

NORA   It is true. I have loved you more than anything in the world.

HELMER   Don't start with your silly excuses.

NORA [*Taking a step toward him.*]   Torvald!

HELMER   You miserable—what have you done?

NORA   Let me go. You won't have to take the blame for me. You're not going to take it on yourself.

HELMER   No more playacting! [*Locking the hall door.*]   You'll stay right here and explain yourself. Do you understand what you've done? Answer me! Do you understand?

NORA [*Looking fixedly at him, her face hardening.*]   Yes. Now I'm beginning to understand everything.

HELMER [*Pacing up and down.*]   Ah!—what a rude awakening for me! For eight years—my pride and joy, a hypocrite, a liar,—even worse, a criminal! There's so much ugliness at the bottom of all this—indescribable ugliness! Uccch! [*Nora remains silent, looking fixedly at him.*] I should have seen it coming. Every one of your father's disgusting values—quiet!—every disgusting value is coming out in you. No religion, no morals, no sense of duty—this is my punishment for being so easy on him up there. I did it for your sake; and you repay me like this!

NORA   Yes, like this.

HELMER   You've destroyed my happiness. My whole future—thrown away! It's horrible when you think about it. I'm totally at the mercy of some amoral animal who can do whatever he wants with me—demand anything he wants, order me around, command me however he pleases, and I can't so much as squeak in protest. And this is how I'll go down, right to the bottom, all for the sake of some frivolous woman.

NORA   When I'm gone from this world, then you'll be free.

HELMER   Stop playacting! You sound like your father—he always had one of those phrases on the tip of his tongue. How would it help me if you were gone from this world, as you put it? Not in the least. He can still reveal everything, and if he does I'd be suspected of being an accomplice to your crimes! People might think I was behind it all, that it was my idea! And I have you to thank

for all this—after I've carried you along, taken you and led you by the hand
400 ever since we were married. Do you understand what you have done to me?

NORA [*Coldly and calmly.*]   Yes.

HELMER   I can't grasp this—it's just unbelievable to me. But we have to try to
set things right. Take off that shawl. I said take it off! I've got to find some
way to appease him—this thing has to be covered up, whatever it costs. As
405 for you and me, things will seem just like before. For public consumption
only, of course. You'll stay in the house, that's understood. But I can't trust
you to bring up the children. Oh God—to have to say that to the one
I—even now—well, that's over. After today there's no happiness, only holding the wreckage together, the scraps and shards—[*The doorbell rings.*
410 *Helmer starts.*] What's that? It's so late! Is this it? Is he going to—? Nora,
hide yourself! Say you're sick. [*Nora stands motionless. Helmer goes and
opens the hall door.*]

MAID [*Half-dressed in the hall doorway.*]   A letter for Mrs. Helmer.

HELMER   Give it here. [*Takes the letter and closes the door.*] Yes, it's from him.
You're not getting it. I'll read it myself.

415 NORA   Read it.

HELMER [*By the lamp.*]   I hardly dare. It could be the end for both of us. I've
got to know. [*Tears open the letter; scans a few lines; looks at an enclosed
paper and gives a cry of joy.*] Nora! [*Nora looks enquiringly at him.*] Nora!
No, let me read it again—yes, yes, it's true. I'm saved! Nora, I'm saved!

420 NORA   And I?

HELMER   You too, of course. We're both saved, both of us. See? He sent you
back your note—he writes that he's sorry and ashamed—that a happy
change in his life—oh, what does it matter what he writes? We're saved,
Nora! Now no one can hurt you. Oh, Nora, Nora—no: first, let's get all this
425 ugliness out of here. Let me see. [*Glances at the note for a moment.*] No, I
won't look at it. It'll be nothing more than a dream I had. [*He tears both letters in pieces and throws them both into the stove, watching them burn.*] So,
nothing left. He wrote that ever since Christmas Eve—God, these must
have been three terrible days for you, Nora.

430 NORA   I have fought a hard battle these last three days.

HELMER   And suffered, not seeing any way out but—no, we won't think
about this ugly thing any more. We'll just rejoice and keep telling ourselves
"it's over—it's all over." Do you hear me, Nora? It seems like you haven't
quite got it yet—it's over! What's this about, this cold stare? Ah, poor little
435 Nora, I understand—you can't bring yourself to believe I've forgiven you.
But I have, Nora, I swear. I've forgiven everything. I know perfectly well
that you did all this out of love for me.

NORA   That's true.

HELMER   You've loved me like a wife should love her husband. You just
440 couldn't judge how to do it. But do you think that makes me love you any
the less, because you couldn't manage by yourself? No, no—just lean on
me. I'll counsel you, I'll direct you. I wouldn't be much of a man if this
female helplessness didn't make you doubly attractive to me. Forget
what I said in those first few terrible moments, when I thought I was
445 going to lose everything. I've forgiven you, Nora—I swear, I've forgiven
you.

NORA   Thank you for your forgiveness. [*She goes out through the door on the
right.*]

HELMER   No, stay—[*Looking in.*] What are you doing?

NORA   Taking off my costume.

450 HELMER [*By the open door.*]   Yes, do that. Try to calm down, collect your thoughts, my little, shivering songbird. If you need protection, I have broad wings to shelter you with. [*Walks around near the door.*] Oh, Nora—our home is so snug, so cozy. This is your nest, where I can keep you like a dove that I've snatched, unharmed, from the falcon's claws; I'll bring peace and
455 rest to your beating heart. Little by little it will happen, Nora, believe me. Tomorrow, this will all seem different to you; and soon everything will be back to normal. I won't need to keep saying I forgive you—you'll feel it, you'll know it's true. How could you ever think I could bring myself to disown you, or even punish you? You don't know how a man's heart works,
460 Nora. There's something indescribably sweet and satisfying for a man in knowing he's forgiven his wife—forgiven her from the bottom of his heart. It's as if he possesses her doubly now—as if she were born into the world all over again—and she becomes, in a way, his wife and his child at the same time. And that's what you'll be for me from now on, you little, help-
465 less, confused creature. Don't be frightened of anything—just open your heart to me and I'll be both your conscience and your will. What's this—? You've changed your dress?

NORA   Yes, Torvald, I've changed my dress.

HELMER   But why now, so late?

470 NORA   I'm not sleeping tonight.

HELMER   But Nora, dear—

NORA [*Looking at her watch.*]   It's not all that late. Sit down, Torvald. We have a great deal to talk about together. [*She sits at one end of the table.*]

HELMER   Nora—what's going on? That hard expression—

475 NORA   Sit down. This will take time. I have a lot to say to you.

HELMER [*Sits at table directly opposite her.*]   You're worrying me, Nora. I don't understand you.

NORA   No, that's just it. You don't understand me. And I have never understood you—not until tonight. No—no interruptions. You have to hear me
480 out. We're settling accounts, Torvald.

HELMER   What do you mean by that?

NORA [*After a short silence.*]   Doesn't *one* thing strike you about the way we're sitting here?

HELMER   What might that be?

485 NORA   We've been married for eight years. Doesn't it strike you that this is the first time that the two of us—you and I, man and wife—have ever talked seriously?

HELMER   Well—"seriously"—what does that mean?

NORA   In eight whole years—no, longer—right from the moment we met, we
490 haven't exchanged one serious word on one serious subject.

HELMER   Should I constantly be involving you in problems you couldn't possibly help me solve?

NORA   I'm not talking about problems. I'm saying that we've never sat down together and seriously tried to get to the bottom of anything.

495 HELMER   But Nora, dearest—would you have wanted that?

NORA   Yes, of course, that's just it. You've never understood me. A great wrong has been done me, Torvald. First by Papa, then by you.

HELMER What! By us—who've loved you more than anyone in the world.

NORA [*Shaking her head.*] You've never loved me. You just thought it was a
500 lot of fun to be in love with me.

HELMER Nora, how can you say that?

NORA It's a fact, Torvald. When I was at home with Papa, he told me all his
opinions; so of course I had the same opinions. And if I had any others, I
kept them hidden, because he wouldn't have liked that. He called me his
505 doll-child, and he played with me like I played with my dolls. Then I came
to your house—

HELMER What kind of way is that to describe our marriage?

NORA [*Undisturbed.*] I mean, I went from Papa's hands into yours. You set
up everything according to your taste; so of course I had the same taste, or
510 I pretended to, I'm not really sure. I think it was half-and-half, one as
much as the other. Now that I look back on it, I can see that I've lived like
a beggar in this house, from hand to mouth; I've lived by doing tricks for
you, Torvald. But that's how you wanted it. You and Papa have committed a
great sin against me. It's your fault that I've become what I am.

515 HELMER Nora—this is unreasonable, and it's ungrateful! Haven't you been
happy here?

NORA No, never. I thought so, but I never really was.

HELMER Not—not happy!

NORA No, just having fun. You've always been very nice to me. But our home
520 has never been anything but a playpen. I've been your doll-wife here, just
like I was Papa's doll-child at home. And my children, in turn, have been
my dolls. It was fun when you came and played with me, just like they had
fun when I played with them. That's what our marriage has been, Torvald.

HELMER There's some truth in this—as exaggerated and hysterical as it is.
525 But from now on, things will be different. Playtime is over: now the teaching begins.

NORA Who gets this teaching? Me or the children?

HELMER Both you and the children, my dearest Nora.

NORA Ah, Torvald: you're not the man to teach me how to be a good wife to you.

530 HELMER You can say that!

NORA And me—how can I possibly teach the children?

HELMER Nora!

NORA Didn't you say that yourself, not too long ago? You didn't dare trust
them to me?

535 HELMER In the heat of the moment! How can you take that seriously?

NORA Yes, but you spoke the truth. I'm not equal to the task. There's another
task I have to get through first. I have to try to teach myself. And you can't
help me there. I've got to do it alone. And so I'm leaving you.

HELMER [*Springing up.*] What did you say?

540 NORA If I'm going to find out anything about myself—about everything out
there—I have to stand completely on my own. That's why I can't stay with
you any longer.

HELMER Nora, Nora!

NORA I'll leave right away. Kristine can put me up for tonight—

545 HELMER You're out of your mind! I won't allow it—I forbid you!

NORA It's no use forbidding me anything any more. I'll take what's mine with
me. I won't take anything from you, now or later.

HELMER   What kind of madness is this?

NORA   Tomorrow I'm going home—back to my old hometown, I mean. It'll
be easier for me to find something to do up there.

HELMER   You blind, inexperienced creature!

NORA   I have to try to get some experience, Torvald.

HELMER   Abandon your home, your husband, your children! Do you have
any idea what people will say?

NORA   I can't worry about that. I only know what I have to do.

HELMER   It's grotesque! You're turning your back on your most sacred duties!

NORA   What do you think those are—my most sacred duties?

HELMER   I have to tell you? Aren't they to your husband and children?

NORA   I have other duties, equally sacred.

HELMER   No, you don't! Like what?

NORA   Duties to myself.

HELMER   You're a wife and mother, first and foremost.

NORA   I don't believe that any more. I believe that, first and foremost, I'm a
human being—just as much as you—or at least I should try to become one.
I'm aware that most people agree with you, Torvald, and that your opinion
is backed up by plenty of books. But I can't be satisfied any more with what
most people say, or what's written in the books. Now I've got to think these
things through myself, and understand them.

HELMER   What don't you understand about your place in your own home?
Don't you have an infallible teacher for questions like this? Don't you have
your religion?

NORA   Oh, Torvald, I really don't know what religion is.

HELMER   What are you saying?

NORA   I only know what Pastor Hansen said when I was confirmed. He told
me that religion was this and that and the other thing. When I get away
from here, when I'm alone, I'll look into that subject too. I'll see if what
Pastor Hansen said is true—or at least, if it's true for me.

HELMER   These things just aren't right for a young woman to be saying. If
religion can't get through to you, let me try your conscience. You do have
some moral feeling? Or—answer me—maybe not?

NORA   Well, Torvald, it's not easy to answer that. I really don't know. I'm
actually quite confused about these things. I only know that my ideas are
totally different from yours. I find out that the law is not what I thought it
was—but I can't get it into my head that the law is right. A woman has no
right to spare her dying father's feelings, or save her husband's life! I just
can't believe these things.

HELMER   You're talking like a child. You don't understand the society you
live in.

NORA   No, I don't. But now I'm going to find out for myself. I've got to figure
out who's right—the world or me.

HELMER   You're ill, Nora—you have a fever. I almost think you're out of your
mind.

NORA   I've never been so clear—and so certain—about so many things as I am
tonight.

HELMER   You're clear and certain that you'll desert your husband and children?

NORA   Yes, I will.

HELMER   There's only one explanation left.

NORA   What is it?

HELMER   You no longer love me.

600   NORA   No. That's precisely it.

HELMER   Nora!—you can say that!

NORA   Oh, it hurts so much, Torvald. Because you've always been so kind to me. But I can't help it. I don't love you any more.

HELMER [*Struggling to control himself.*]   Are you also clear and certain about
605   that?

NORA   Yes, absolutely clear and certain. That's why I can't live here any more.

HELMER   Can you tell me how I lost your love?

NORA   Yes, I can. It was this evening, when the wonderful thing didn't happen—then I saw that you weren't the man I thought you were.

610   HELMER   Say more—I'm not following this.

NORA   I've waited so patiently for ten years now—good Lord. I know that these wonderful things don't come along every day. Then this disaster broke over me, and I was absolutely certain: now the wonderful thing is coming. While Krogstad's letter was lying out there, I never imagined you'd
615   give in to his terms, even for a minute. I was so certain you'd say to him: tell your story to the whole world! And when that was done—

HELMER   Yes, then what? When I'd given my wife up to shame and disgrace—!

NORA   When that was done, I was completely certain that you would step
620   forward and take everything on yourself—you'd say "I am the guilty one."

HELMER   Nora!

NORA   You're thinking that I'd never accept such a sacrifice from you? No, of course I wouldn't. But what good would my protests be over yours? *That* was the wonderful thing I was hoping for, and in terror of. And to prevent
625   it, I was willing to end my life.

HELMER   I'd work for you night and day, Nora—gladly—suffer and sacrifice for your sake. But no one gives up his honor even for the one he loves.

NORA   That's exactly what millions of women have done.

HELMER   Oh—! You're thinking and talking like an ignorant child.

630   NORA   Maybe. But you don't think—or talk—like the man I could choose to be with. When your big fright was over—not the danger I was in, but what might happen to you—when that threat was past, then it was like nothing happened to you. I was just what I was before, your little songbird, your doll, and you'd have to take care of it twice as hard as before, since it was
635   so frail and fragile. In that moment, Torvald, it dawned on me that I'd been living with a stranger—that I'd borne three children with him—. Aah—I can't stand the thought of it! I could tear myself to pieces.

HELMER [*Heavily.*]   I see. I see. A gulf has really opened up between us. But Nora, can't we fill it in somehow?

640   NORA   The way I am now, I'm no wife for you.

HELMER   I can transform myself—I have the strength for it.

NORA   Maybe—if your doll is taken away from you.

HELMER   To live without—without you! Nora, I can't bear the thought of it!

NORA   All the more reason it has to happen. [*Having gone in to the right, she returns with her outdoor clothes and a little traveling bag, which she sets on a chair by the table.*]

645   HELMER   Nora, Nora, not now! Wait until tomorrow.

NORA [*Puts on her coat.*]   I can't spend the night in a strange man's house.

HELMER   Can't we live here like brother and sister?

NORA [*Tying her hat.*]   You know very well how long that would last. [*Throws her shawl around her.*] Good-bye, Torvald. I won't see the children. They're
650   in better hands than mine, that much I know. The way I am now, I can't do anything for them.

HELMER   But some day, Nora—some day—?

NORA   How do I know? I have no idea what will become of me.

HELMER   But you're my wife, right now and always, no matter what becomes
655   of you.

NORA   Listen, Torvald; when a wife deserts her husband's house, as I'm doing now, I've heard that the law frees him from any responsibility to her. And anyway, I'm freeing you. From everything. Complete freedom on both sides. See, here's your ring. Give me mine.

660 HELMER   Even that.

NORA   Even that.

HELMER   Here it is.

NORA   So. Well, now it's finished. I'm putting the keys here. As far as the household goes, the maids know all about it—better than I do. Tomorrow,
665   after I'm gone, Kristine will come and pack the things I brought from home. I'll have them sent.

HELMER   All finished, all over! Nora—will you never think about me after this?

NORA   Of course I'll think about you often—and the children, and the
670   house—.

HELMER   Could I write to you, Nora?

NORA   No, never. You can't do that.

HELMER   But I'll have to send you—

NORA   Nothing; nothing.

675 HELMER   —help you, if you need—

NORA   No. I'm telling you, I accept nothing from strangers.

HELMER   Nora—can't I ever be anything more than a stranger to you?

NORA [*Taking her traveling bag.*]   Oh, Torvald—not unless the most wonderful thing of all were to happen—

680 HELMER   Name it—what is this most wonderful thing?

NORA   It's—both you and I would have to transform ourselves to the point that—oh, Torvald, I don't know if I believe in it any more—

HELMER   But I will. Name it! Transform ourselves to the point that—

NORA   That our living together could become a marriage. Good-bye. [*She goes through the hall door.*]

HELMER [*Sinking down into a chair by the door and burying his face in his
685   hands.*]   Empty. She's not here. [*A hope flares up in him.*]
The most wonderful thing of all—?

        [*From below, the sound of a door slamming shut.*]

Hedda Gabler[1]

CHARACTERS

GEORGE TESMAN, research fellow in
  cultural history
HEDDA TESMAN, his wife
MISS JULIANE TESMAN, his aunt
MRS. ELVSTED

JUDGE BRACK
EILERT LØVBORG
BERTA, the maid to the Tesmans

The action takes place in the fashionable west side of Christiania, Norway's capital.

Act 1

A large, pleasantly and tastefully furnished drawing room, decorated in somber tones. In the rear wall is a wide doorway with the curtains pulled back. This doorway leads into a smaller room decorated in the same style. In the right wall of the drawing room is a folding door leading into the hall. In the opposite wall, a glass door, also with its curtains pulled back. Outside, through the windows, part of a covered veranda can be seen, along with trees in their autumn colors. In the foreground, an oval table surrounded by chairs. Downstage, near the right wall, is a broad, dark porcelain stove, a high-backed armchair, a footstool with cushions and two stools. Up in the right-hand corner, a corner-sofa and a small round table. Downstage, on the left side, a little distance from the wall, a sofa. Beyond the glass door, a piano. On both sides of the upstage doorway stand shelves displaying terra cotta and majolica objects. By the back wall of the inner room, a sofa, a table and a couple of chairs can be seen. Above the sofa hangs the portrait of a handsome elderly man in a general's uniform. Above the table, a hanging lamp with an opalescent glass shade. There are many flowers arranged in vases and glasses all around the drawing room. More flowers lie on the tables. The floors of both rooms are covered with thick rugs.

Morning light. The sun shines in through the glass door.

> [*Miss Julie Tesman, with hat and parasol, comes in from the hall, followed by Berta, who carries a bouquet wrapped in paper. Miss Tesman is a kindly, seemingly good-natured lady of about sixty-five, neatly but simply dressed in a gray visiting outfit. Berta is a housemaid, getting on in years, with a homely and somewhat rustic appearance.*]

MISS TESMAN [*Stops just inside the doorway, listens, and speaks softly.*] Well—I believe they're just now getting up!

BERTA [*Also softly.*] That's what I said, Miss. Just think—the steamer got in so late last night, and then—Lord, the young mistress wanted so much unpacked before she could settle down.

---

1. Translated by Rick Davis and Brian Johnston.

MISS TESMAN   Well, well. Let them have a good night's sleep at least. But—
they'll have some fresh morning air when they come down. [*She crosses to
the glass door and throws it wide open.*]

BERTA [*By the table, perplexed, holding the bouquet.*] Hmm. Bless me if I
can find a spot for these. I think I'd better put them down here, Miss. [*Puts
the bouquet down on the front of the piano.*]

10 MISS TESMAN   So, Berta dear, now you have a new mistress. As God's my witness, giving you up was a heavy blow.

BERTA   And me, Miss—what can I say? I've been in yours and Miss Rina's
service for so many blessed years—

MISS TESMAN   We must bear it patiently, Berta. Truly, there's no other way.
15 You know George has to have you in the house with him—he simply has to.
You've looked after him since he was a little boy.

BERTA   Yes, but Miss—I keep worrying about her, lying there at home—so
completely helpless, poor thing. And that new girl! She'll never learn how
to take care of sick people.

20 MISS TESMAN   Oh, I'll teach her how soon enough. And I'll be doing most
of the work myself, you know. Don't you worry about my sister, Berta
dear.

BERTA   Yes, but there's something else, Miss. I'm so afraid I won't satisfy the
new mistress—

25 MISS TESMAN   Ffft—Good Lord—there might be a thing or two at first—

BERTA   Because she's so particular about things—

MISS TESMAN   Well, what do you expect? General Gabler's daughter—the
way she lived in the general's day! Do you remember how she would go
out riding with her father? In that long black outfit, with the feather in
30 her hat?

BERTA   Oh, yes—I remember that all right. But I never thought she'd make a
match with our Mr. Tesman.

MISS TESMAN   Neither did I. But—while I'm thinking about it, don't call
George "Mister Tesman" any more. Now it's "Doctor Tesman."

35 BERTA   Yes—that's what the young mistress said as soon as they came in last
night. So it's true?

MISS TESMAN   Yes, it's really true. Think of it, Berta—they've made him a
doctor. While he was away, you understand. I didn't know a thing about it,
until he told me himself, down at the pier.

40 BERTA   Well, he's so smart he could be anything he wanted to be. But I never
thought he'd take up curing people too!

MISS TESMAN   No, no, no. He's not that kind of doctor. [*Nods significantly.*]
As far as that goes, you might have to start calling him something even
grander soon.

45 BERTA   Oh no! What could that be?

MISS TESMAN [*Smiling.*] Hmm—wouldn't you like to know? [*Emotionally.*]
Oh, dear God . . . if our sainted Joseph could look up from his grave and
see what's become of his little boy. [*She looks around.*] But, Berta—what's
this now? Why have you taken all the slipcovers off the furniture?

50 BERTA   The mistress told me to. She said she can't stand covers on chairs.

MISS TESMAN   But are they going to use this for their everyday living room?

BERTA   Yes, they will. At least she will. He—the doctor—he didn't say
anything.

[*George Tesman enters, humming, from the right of the inner room, carrying an open, empty suitcase. He is a youthful-looking man of thirty-three, of medium height, with an open, round, and cheerful face, blond hair and beard. He wears glasses and is dressed in comfortable, somewhat disheveled clothes.*]

MISS TESMAN Good morning, good morning, George!

55 TESMAN Aunt Julie! Dear Aunt Julie! [*Goes over and shakes her hand.*] All the way here—so early in the day! Hm!

MISS TESMAN Yes, you know me—I just had to peek in on you a little.

TESMAN And after a short night's sleep at that!

MISS TESMAN Oh, that's nothing at all to me.

60 TESMAN So—you got home all right from the pier, hm?

MISS TESMAN Yes, as it turned out, thanks be to God. The Judge was kind enough to see me right to the door.

TESMAN We felt so bad that we couldn't take you in the carriage—but you saw how many trunks and boxes Hedda had to bring.

65 MISS TESMAN Yes, it was amazing.

BERTA [*To Tesman.*] Perhaps I should go in and ask the mistress if there's anything I can help her with.

TESMAN No, thank you, Berta. You don't have to do that. If she needs you, she'll ring—that's what she said.

70 BERTA [*Going out to right.*] Very well.

TESMAN Ah—but—Berta—take this suitcase with you.

BERTA [*Takes the case.*] I'll put it in the attic.

TESMAN Just imagine, Auntie. I'd stuffed that whole suitcase with notes—just notes! The things I managed to collect in those archives—really incred-

75 ible! Ancient, remarkable things that no one had any inkling of.

MISS TESMAN Ah yes—you certainly haven't wasted any time on your honeymoon.

TESMAN Yes—I can really say that's true. But, Auntie, take off your hat—Here, let's see. Let me undo that ribbon, hm?

80 MISS TESMAN [*While he does so.*] Ah, dear God—this is just what it was like when you were home with us.

TESMAN [*Examining the hat as he holds it.*] My, my—isn't this a fine, elegant hat you've got for yourself.

MISS TESMAN I bought it for Hedda's sake.

85 TESMAN For Hedda's—hm?

MISS TESMAN Yes, so Hedda won't feel ashamed of me if we go out for a walk together.

TESMAN [*Patting her cheek.*] You think of everything, Auntie Julie, don't you? [*Putting her hat on a chair by the table.*] And now—let's just settle down

90 here on the sofa until Hedda comes. [*They sit. She puts her parasol down near the sofa.*]

MISS TESMAN [*Takes both his hands and gazes at him.*] What a blessing to have you here, bright as day, right before my eyes again, George. Sainted Joseph's own boy!

TESMAN For me too. To see you again, Aunt Julie—who've been both father

95 and mother to me.

MISS TESMAN Yes, I know you'll always have a soft spot for your old aunts.

TESMAN But no improvement at all with Rina, hm?

MISS TESMAN Oh dear no—and none to be expected, poor thing. She lies
there just as she has all these years. But I pray that Our Lord lets me keep
her just a little longer. Otherwise I don't know what I'd do with my life,
George. Especially now, you know—when I don't have you to take care of
any more.

TESMAN [*Patting her on the back.*] There. There. There.

MISS TESMAN Oh—just to think that you've become a married man, George.
And that you're the one who carried off Hedda Gabler! Beautiful Hedda
Gabler. Imagine—with all her suitors.

TESMAN [*Hums a little and smiles complacently.*] Yes, I believe I have quite a
few friends in town who envy me, hm?

MISS TESMAN And then—you got to take such a long honeymoon—more
than five—almost six months . . .

TESMAN Yes, but it was also part of my research, you know. All those archives
I had to wade through—and all the books I had to read!

MISS TESMAN I suppose you're right. [*Confidentially and more quietly.*]
But listen, George—isn't there something—something extra you want to
tell me?

TESMAN About the trip?

MISS TESMAN Yes.

TESMAN No—I can't think of anything I didn't mention in my letters. I was
given my doctorate—but I told you that yesterday.

MISS TESMAN So you did. But I mean—whether you might have any—any
kind of—prospects—?

TESMAN Prospects?

MISS TESMAN Good Lord, George—I'm your old aunt.

TESMAN Well of course I have prospects.

MISS TESMAN Aha!

TESMAN I have excellent prospects of becoming a professor one of these
days. But Aunt Julie dear, you already know that.

MISS TESMAN [*With a little laugh.*] You're right, I do. [*Changing the subject.*]
But about your trip. It must have cost a lot.

TESMAN Well, thank God, that huge fellowship paid for a good part of it.

MISS TESMAN But how did you make it last for the both of you?

TESMAN That's the tricky part, isn't it?

MISS TESMAN And on top of that, when you're traveling with a lady! That's
always going to cost you more, or so I've heard.

TESMAN You're right—it was a bit more costly. But Hedda just had to have
that trip, Auntie. She really had to. There was no choice.

MISS TESMAN Well, I suppose not. These days a honeymoon trip is essential,
it seems. But now tell me—have you had a good look around the house?

TESMAN Absolutely! I've been up since dawn.

MISS TESMAN And what do you think about all of it?

TESMAN It's splendid! Only I can't think of what we'll do with those two
empty rooms between the back parlor and Hedda's bedroom.

MISS TESMAN [*Lightly laughing.*] My dear George—when the time comes,
you'll think of what to do with them.

TESMAN Oh, of course—as I add to my library, hm?

MISS TESMAN That's right, my boy—of course I was thinking about your
library.

TESMAN   Most of all I'm just so happy for Hedda. Before we got engaged
she'd always say how she couldn't imagine living anywhere but here—in
150   Prime Minister Falk's house.

MISS TESMAN   Yes—imagine. And then it came up for sale just after you left
for your trip.

TESMAN   Aunt Julie, we really had luck on our side, hm?

MISS TESMAN   But the expense, George. This will all be costly for you.

155   TESMAN [*Looks at her disconcertedly.*]   Yes. It might be. It might be, Auntie.

MISS TESMAN   Ah, God only knows.

TESMAN   How much, do you think? Approximately. Hm?

MISS TESMAN   I can't possibly tell before all the bills are in.

TESMAN   Luckily Judge Brack lined up favorable terms for me—he wrote as
160   much to Hedda.

MISS TESMAN   That's right—don't you ever worry about that, my boy. All this
furniture, and the carpets? I put up the security for it.

TESMAN   Security? You? Dear Auntie Julie, what kind of security could you
give?

165   MISS TESMAN   I took out a mortgage on our annuity.

TESMAN   What? On your—and Aunt Rina's annuity!

MISS TESMAN   I couldn't think of any other way.

TESMAN [*Standing in front of her.*]   Have you gone completely out of your
mind, Auntie? That annuity is all you and Aunt Rina have to live on.

170   MISS TESMAN   Now, now, take it easy. It's just a formality, you understand.
Judge Brack said so. He was good enough to arrange it all for me. Just a
formality, he said.

TESMAN   That could very well be, but all the same . . .

MISS TESMAN   You'll be earning your own living now, after all. And, good
175   Lord, so what if we do have to open the purse a little, spend a little bit at
first? That would only make us happy.

TESMAN   Auntie . . . you never get tired of sacrificing yourself for me.

MISS TESMAN [*Rises and lays her hands on his shoulders.*]   What joy do I have
in the world, my dearest boy, other than smoothing out the path for you?
180   You, without a father or mother to take care of you . . . but we've reached
our destination, my dear. Maybe things looked black from time to time.
But, praise God, George, you've come out on top!

TESMAN   Yes, it's really amazing how everything has gone according to plan.

MISS TESMAN   And those who were against you—those who would have
185   blocked your way—they're at the bottom of the pit. They've fallen, George.
And the most dangerous one, he fell the farthest. Now he just lies there
where he fell, the poor sinner.

TESMAN   Have you heard anything about Eilert—since I went away, I
mean?

190   MISS TESMAN   Nothing, except they say he published a new book.

TESMAN   What? Eilert Løvborg? Just recently, hm?

MISS TESMAN   That's what they say. God only knows how there could be anything to it. But when *your* book comes out—now that will be something
else again, won't it, George? What's it going to be about?

195   TESMAN   It will deal with the Domestic Craftsmanship Practices of Medieval
Brabant.[2]

2. A province of central Belgium.

MISS TESMAN   Just think—you can write about that kind of thing too.

TESMAN   However, it might be quite a while before that book is ready. I've got all these incredible collections that have to be put in order first.

200 MISS TESMAN   Ordering and collecting—you're certainly good at that. You're not the son of sainted Joseph for nothing.

TESMAN   And I'm so eager to get going. Especially now that I've got my own snug house and home to work in.

MISS TESMAN   And most of all, now that you've got her—your heart's desire,
205   dear, dear George!

TESMAN   [Embracing her.]   Yes, Auntie Julie! Hedda . . . that's the most beautiful thing of all! [Looking toward the doorway.] I think that's her, hm?

> [Hedda comes in from the left side of the inner room. She is a lady of twenty-nine. Her face and figure are aristocratic and elegant. Her complexion is pale. Her eyes are steel-gray, cold and clear. Her hair is an attractive medium brown but not particularly full. She is wearing a tasteful, somewhat loose-fitting morning gown.]

MISS TESMAN   [Going to meet Hedda.]   Good morning, Hedda, my dear. Good
210   morning.

HEDDA   [Extending her hand.]   Good morning, Miss Tesman, my dear. You're here so early. How nice of you.

MISS TESMAN   [Looking somewhat embarrassed.]   Well now, how did the young mistress sleep in her new home?

215 HEDDA   Fine thanks. Well enough.

TESMAN   [Laughing.]   Well enough! That's a good one, Hedda. You were sleeping like a log when I got up.

HEDDA   Yes, lucky for me. But of course you have to get used to anything new, Miss Tesman. A little at a time. [Looks toward the window.] Uch! Look
220   at that. The maid opened the door. I'm drowning in all this sunlight.

MISS TESMAN   [Going to the door.]   Well then, let's close it.

HEDDA   No, no, don't do that. Tesman my dear, just close the curtains. That gives a gentler light.

TESMAN   [By the door.]   All right, all right. Now then, Hedda. You've got both
225   fresh air and sunlight.

HEDDA   Yes, fresh air. That's what I need with all these flowers all over the place. But Miss Tesman, won't you sit down?

MISS TESMAN   No, but thank you. Now that I know everything's all right here, I've got to see about getting home again. Home to that poor dear who's
230   lying there in pain.

TESMAN   Be sure to give her my respects, won't you? And tell her I'll stop by and look in on her later today.

MISS TESMAN   Yes, yes I'll certainly do that. But would you believe it, George? [She rustles around in the pocket of her skirt.] I almost forgot. Here, I
235   brought something for you.

TESMAN   And what might that be, Auntie, hm?

MISS TESMAN   [Brings out a flat package wrapped in newspaper and hands it to him.]   Here you are, my dear boy.

TESMAN   [Opening it.]   Oh my Lord. You kept them for me, Aunt Julie. Hedda, isn't this touching, hm?

240 HEDDA   Well, what is it?

TESMAN   My old house slippers. My slippers.

HEDDA   Oh yes, I remember how often you talked about them on our trip.

TESMAN   Yes, well, I really missed them. [*Goes over to her.*] Now you can see them for yourself, Hedda.

245 HEDDA [*Moves over to the stove.*]   Oh, no thanks, I don't really care to.

TESMAN [*Following after her.*]   Just think, Aunt Rina lying there embroidering for me, sick as she was. Oh, you couldn't possibly believe how many memories are tangled up in these slippers.

HEDDA [*By the table.*]   Not for me.

250 MISS TESMAN   Hedda's quite right about that, George.

TESMAN   Yes, but now that she's in the family I thought—

HEDDA   That maid won't last, Tesman.

MISS TESMAN   Berta—?

TESMAN   What makes you say that, hm?

255 HEDDA [*Pointing.*]   Look, she's left her old hat lying there on that chair.

TESMAN [*Terrified, dropping the slippers on the floor.*]   Hedda—!

HEDDA   What if someone came in and saw that.

TESMAN   But Hedda—that's Aunt Julie's hat.

HEDDA   Really?

260 MISS TESMAN [*Taking the hat.*]   Yes, it really is. And for that matter it's not so old either, my dear little Hedda.

HEDDA   Oh, I really didn't get a good look at it, Miss Tesman.

MISS TESMAN [*Tying the hat on her head.*]   Actually I've never worn it before today—and the good Lord knows that's true.

265 TESMAN   And an elegant hat it is too. Really magnificent.

MISS TESMAN [*She looks around.*]   Oh that's as may be, George. My parasol? Ah, here it is. [*She takes it.*] That's mine too. [*She mutters.*] Not Berta's.

TESMAN   A new hat and a new parasol. Just think, Hedda.

HEDDA   Very charming, very attractive.

270 TESMAN   That's true, hm? But Auntie, take a good look at Hedda before you go. Look at how charming and attractive she is.

MISS TESMAN   Oh my dear, that's nothing new. Hedda's been lovely all her life. [*She nods and goes across to the right.*]

TESMAN [*Following her.*]   Yes, but have you noticed how she's blossomed, 275 how well she's filled out on our trip?

HEDDA   Oh, leave it alone!

MISS TESMAN [*Stops and turns.*]   Filled out?

TESMAN   Yes, Aunt Julie. You can't see it so well right now in that gown—but I, who have a little better opportunity to—

280 HEDDA [*By the glass door impatiently.*]   Oh you don't have the opportunity for anything.

TESMAN   It was that mountain air down in the Tyrol.[3]

HEDDA [*Curtly interrupting.*]   I'm the same as when I left.

TESMAN   You keep saying that. But it's true, isn't it Auntie?

285 MISS TESMAN [*Folding her hands and gazing at Hedda.*]   Lovely . . . lovely . . . lovely. That's Hedda. [*She goes over to her and with both her hands takes her head, bends it down, kisses her hair.*] God bless and keep Hedda Tesman for George's sake.

---

3. A region of the eastern Alps, mainly in western Austria but partly in northern Italy.

HEDDA [*Gently freeing herself.*] Ah—! Let me out!

290 MISS TESMAN [*With quiet emotion.*] I'll come look in on you two every single day.

TESMAN Yes, Auntie, do that, won't you, hm?

MISS TESMAN Good-bye, good-bye.

[*She goes out through the hall door. Tesman follows her out. The door remains half open. Tesman is heard repeating his greetings to Aunt Rina and his thanks for the slippers. While this is happening, Hedda walks around the room raising her arms and clenching her fists as if in a rage. Then she draws the curtains back from the door, stands there and looks out. After a short time, Tesman comes in and closes the door behind him.*]

TESMAN [*Picking up the slippers from the floor.*] What are you looking at,
295 Hedda?

HEDDA [*Calm and controlled again.*] Just the leaves. So yellow and so withered.

TESMAN [*Wrapping up the slippers and placing them on the table.*] Yes, well—we're into September now.

300 HEDDA [*Once more uneasy.*] Yes—It's already—already September.

TESMAN Didn't you think Aunt Julie was acting strange just now, almost formal? What do you suppose got into her?

HEDDA I really don't know her. Isn't that the way she usually is?

TESMAN No, not like today.

305 HEDDA [*Leaving the glass door.*] Do you think she was upset by the hat business?

TESMAN Not really. Maybe a little, for just a moment—

HEDDA But where did she get her manners, flinging her hat around any way she likes here in the drawing room. People just don't act that way.

310 TESMAN Well, I'm sure she won't do it again.

HEDDA Anyway, I'll smooth everything over with her soon enough.

TESMAN Yes, Hedda, if you would do that.

HEDDA When you visit them later today, invite her here for the evening.

TESMAN Yes, that's just what I'll do. And there's one more thing you can do
315 that would really make her happy.

HEDDA Well?

TESMAN If you just bring yourself to call her Aunt Julie, for my sake, Hedda, hm?

HEDDA Tesman, for God's sake, don't ask me to do that. I've told you that
320 before. I'll try to call her Aunt[4] once in a while and that's enough.

TESMAN Oh well, I just thought that now that you're part of the family . . .

HEDDA Hmm. I don't know—[*She crosses upstage to the doorway.*]

TESMAN [*After a pause.*] Is something the matter, Hedda?

HEDDA I was just looking at my old piano. It really doesn't go with these
325 other things.

TESMAN As soon as my salary starts coming in, we'll see about trading it in for a new one.

---

4. In the original Norwegian text, Tesman has asked his wife to address his aunt with the familiar *du* (thou), used only by intimate friends and family, rather than with the formal *De* (you). Hedda refuses but suggests the compromise of calling her "Aunt."

HEDDA   Oh, no, don't trade it in. I could never let it go. We'll leave it in the back room instead. And then we'll get a new one to put in here. I mean, as
330   soon as we get the chance.

TESMAN [*A little dejectedly.*]   Yes, I suppose we could do that.

HEDDA [*Taking the bouquet from the piano.*]   These flowers weren't here when we got in last night.

TESMAN   I suppose Aunt Julie brought them.

335   HEDDA [*Looks into the bouquet.*]   Here's a card. [*Takes it out and reads.*] "Will call again later today." Guess who it's from.

TESMAN   Who is it, hm?

HEDDA   It says Mrs. Elvsted.

TESMAN   Really. Mrs. Elvsted. She used to be Miss Rysing.

340   HEDDA   Yes, that's the one. She had all that irritating hair she'd always be fussing with. An old flame of yours, I've heard.

TESMAN [*Laughs.*]   Oh, not for long and before I knew you, Hedda. And she's here in town. How about that.

HEDDA   Strange that she should come visiting us. I hardly know her except
345   from school.

TESMAN   Yes, and of course I haven't seen her since—well God knows how long. How could she stand it holed up out there so far from everything, hm?

HEDDA [*Reflects a moment and then suddenly speaks.*]   Just a minute, Tes-
350   man. Doesn't he live out that way, Eilert Løvborg, I mean?

TESMAN   Yes, right up in that area.

[*Berta comes in from the hallway.*]

BERTA   Ma'am, she's back again. The lady who came by with the flowers an hour ago. [*Pointing.*] Those you've got in your hand, Ma'am.

HEDDA   Is she then? Please ask her to come in.

[*Berta opens the door for Mrs. Elvsted and then leaves. Mrs. Elvsted is slender with soft, pretty features. Her eyes are light blue, large, round and slightly protruding. Her expression is one of alarm and question. Her hair is remarkably light, almost a white gold and exceptionally rich and full. She is a couple of years younger than Hedda. Her costume is a dark visiting dress, tasteful but not of the latest fashion.*]

355   HEDDA [*Goes to meet her in a friendly manner.*]   Hello my dear Mrs. Elvsted. So delightful to see you again.

MRS. ELVSTED [*Nervous, trying to control herself*]   Yes, it's been so long since we've seen each other.

TESMAN [*Shakes her hand.*]   And we could say the same, hm?

360   HEDDA   Thank you for the lovely flowers.

MRS. ELVSTED   I would have come yesterday right away but I heard you were on a trip—

TESMAN   So you've just come into town, hm?

MRS. ELVSTED   Yesterday around noon. I was absolutely desperate when I
365   heard you weren't home.

HEDDA   Desperate, why?

TESMAN   My dear Miss Rysing—I mean Mrs. Elvsted.

HEDDA   There isn't some sort of trouble—?

MRS. ELVSTED   Yes there is—and I don't know another living soul to turn to
370   here in town.

HEDDA [*Sets the flowers down on the table.*]   All right then, let's sit down here on the sofa.

MRS. ELVSTED   Oh no, I'm too upset to sit down.

HEDDA   No you're not. Come over here. [*She draws Mrs. Elvsted to the sofa and sits beside her.*]

375 TESMAN   Well, and now Mrs.—

HEDDA   Did something happen up at your place?

MRS. ELVSTED   Yes—That's it—well, not exactly—Oh, I don't want you to misunderstand me—

HEDDA   Well then the best thing is just to tell it straight out, Mrs. Elvsted—

380 TESMAN   That's why you came here, hm?

MRS. ELVSTED   Yes, of course. So I'd better tell you, if you don't already know, that Eilert Løvborg is in town.

HEDDA   Løvborg?

TESMAN   Eilert Løvborg's back again? Just think, Hedda.

385 HEDDA   Good Lord, Tesman, I can hear.

MRS. ELVSTED   He's been back now for about a week. The whole week alone here where he can fall in with all kinds of bad company. This town's a dangerous place for him.

HEDDA   But my dear Mrs. Elvsted, how does this involve you?

390 MRS. ELVSTED [*With a scared expression, speaking quickly.*]   He was the children's tutor.

HEDDA   Your children?

MRS. ELVSTED   My husband's. I don't have any.

HEDDA   The stepchildren then?

395 MRS. ELVSTED   Yes.

TESMAN [*Somewhat awkwardly.*]   But was he sufficiently—I don't know how to say this—sufficiently regular in his habits to be trusted with that kind of job, hm?

MRS. ELVSTED   For the past two years no one could say anything against him.

400 TESMAN   Really, nothing. Just think, Hedda.

HEDDA   I hear.

MRS. ELVSTED   Nothing at all I assure you. Not in any way. But even so, now that I know he's here in the city alone and with money in his pocket I'm deathly afraid for him.

405 TESMAN   But why isn't he up there with you and your husband, hm?

MRS. ELVSTED   When the book came out he was too excited to stay up there with us.

TESMAN   Yes, that's right. Aunt Julie said he'd come out with a new book.

MRS. ELVSTED   Yes, a major new book on the progress of civilization—in its
410   entirety I mean. That was two weeks ago. And it's been selling wonderfully. Everyone's reading it. It's created a huge sensation—

TESMAN   All that, really? Must be something he had lying around from his better days.

MRS. ELVSTED   From before, you mean?

415 TESMAN   Yes.

MRS. ELVSTED   No, he wrote the whole thing while he was up there living with us. Just in the last year.

TESMAN   That's wonderful to hear, Hedda. Just think!

MRS. ELVSTED   Yes, if only it continues.

420 HEDDA   Have you met him here in town?

MRS. ELVSTED   No, not yet. I had a terrible time hunting down his address but this morning I finally found it.

HEDDA [*Looks searchingly.*]   I can't help thinking this is a little odd on your husband's part.

425 MRS. ELVSTED [*Starts nervously.*]   My husband—What?

HEDDA   That he'd send you to town on this errand. That he didn't come himself to look for his friend.

MRS. ELVSTED   Oh no, no, no. My husband doesn't have time for that. And anyway I had to do some shopping too.

430 HEDDA [*Smiling slightly.*]   Oh well, that's different then.

MRS. ELVSTED [*Gets up quickly, ill at ease.*]   And now I beg you, Mr. Tesman, please be kind to Eilert Løvborg if he comes here—and I'm sure he will. You were such good friends in the old days. You have interests in common. The same area of research, as far as I can tell.

435 TESMAN   Yes, that used to be the case anyway.

MRS. ELVSTED   Yes, that's why I'm asking you—from the bottom of my heart to be sure to—that you'll—that you'll keep a watchful eye on him. Oh, Mr. Tesman, will you do that—will you promise me that?

TESMAN   Yes, with all my heart, Mrs. Rysing.

440 HEDDA   Elvsted.

TESMAN   I'll do anything in my power for Eilert. You can be sure of it.

MRS. ELVSTED   Oh, that is so kind of you. [*She presses his hands.*] Many, many thanks. [*Frightened.*] Because my husband thinks so highly of him.

HEDDA [*Rising.*]   You should write to him, Tesman. He might not come to

445 you on his own.

TESMAN   Yes, that's the way to do it, Hedda, hm?

HEDDA   And the sooner the better. Right now, I think.

MRS. ELVSTED [*Beseechingly.*]   Yes, if you only could.

TESMAN   I'll write to him this moment. Do you have his address, Mrs.

450 Elvsted?

MRS. ELVSTED   Yes. [*She takes a small slip of paper from her pocket and hands it to him.*] Here it is.

TESMAN   Good, good. I'll go write him—[*Looks around just a minute.*] —Where are my slippers? Ah, here they are. [*Takes the packet and is about to leave.*]

455 HEDDA   Make sure your note is very friendly—nice and long too.

TESMAN   Yes, you can count on me.

MRS. ELVSTED   But please don't say a word about my asking you to do it.

TESMAN   Oh, that goes without saying.

[*Tesman leaves to the right through the rear room.*]

HEDDA [*Goes over to Mrs. Elvsted, smiles and speaks softly.*]   There, now we've

460 killed two birds with one stone.

MRS. ELVSTED   What do you mean?

HEDDA   Didn't you see that I wanted him out of the way?

MRS. ELVSTED   Yes, to write the letter—

HEDDA   So I could talk to you alone.

465 MRS. ELVSTED [*Confused.*]   About this thing?

HEDDA   Yes, exactly, about this thing.

MRS. ELVSTED [*Apprehensively.*]   But there's nothing more to it, Mrs. Tesman, really there isn't.

HEDDA   Ah, but there is indeed. There's a great deal more. I can see that
much. Come here, let's sit down together. Have a real heart-to-heart talk.
[*She forces Mrs. Elvsted into the armchair by the stove and sits down herself on one of the small stools.*]

MRS. ELVSTED   [*Nervously looking at her watch.*]   Mrs. Tesman, I was just thinking of leaving.

HEDDA   Now you can't be in such a hurry, can you? Talk to me a little bit about how things are at home.

MRS. ELVSTED   Oh, that's the last thing I want to talk about.

HEDDA   But to me? Good Lord, we went to the same school.

MRS. ELVSTED   Yes, but you were one class ahead of me. Oh, I was so afraid of you then.

HEDDA   Afraid of me?

MRS. ELVSTED   Horribly afraid. Whenever we'd meet on the stairs you always used to pull my hair.

HEDDA   No, did I do that?

MRS. ELVSTED   Yes, you did—and once you said you'd burn it off.

HEDDA   Oh, just silly talk, you know.

MRS. ELVSTED   Yes, but I was so stupid in those days, and anyway since then we've gotten to be so distant from each other. Our circles have just been totally different.

HEDDA   Well let's see if we can get closer again. Listen now, I know we were good friends in school. We used to call each other by our first names.[5]

MRS. ELVSTED   No, no, I think you're mistaken.

HEDDA   I certainly am not. I remember it perfectly and so we have to be perfectly open with each other just like in the old days. [*Moves the stool closer.*] There now. [*Kisses her cheek.*] Now you must call me Hedda.

MRS. ELVSTED   [*Pressing and patting her hands.*]   Oh, you're being so friendly to me. I'm just not used to that.

HEDDA   There, there, there. I'll stop being so formal with you and I'll call you my dear Thora.

MRS. ELVSTED   My name is Thea.

HEDDA   That's right, of course, I meant Thea. [*Looks at her compassionately.*] So you're not used to friendship, Thea, in your own home?

MRS. ELVSTED   If I only had a home, but I don't. I've never had one.

HEDDA   [*Glances at her.*]   I suspected it might be something like that.

MRS. ELVSTED   [*Staring helplessly before her.*]   Yes, yes, yes.

HEDDA   I can't exactly remember now, but didn't you go up to Sheriff Elvsted's as a housekeeper?

MRS. ELVSTED   Actually I was supposed to be a governess but his wife—at that time—she was an invalid, mostly bedridden, so I had to take care of the house too.

HEDDA   So in the end you became mistress of your own house.

MRS. ELVSTED   [*Heavily.*]   Yes, that's what I became.

HEDDA   Let me see. How long has that been?

MRS. ELVSTED   Since I was married?

---

5. In the original Norwegian text, Hedda claims that they used to address each other with the familiar *du*. Not used to this level of intimacy, Mrs. Elvsted will slip back into the formal *De* before adopting *du*.

HEDDA Yes.

MRS. ELVSTED Five years now.

515 HEDDA That's right, it must be about that.

MRS. ELVSTED Oh these five years—! Or the last two or three anyway—! Ah, Mrs. Tesman, if you could just imagine.

HEDDA [*Slaps her lightly on the hand.*] Mrs. Tesman; really, Thea.

MRS. ELVSTED No, no, of course, I'll try to remember. Anyway, Hedda, if you 520 could only imagine.

HEDDA [*Casually.*] It seems to me that Eilert Løvborg's been living up there for about three years, hasn't he?

MRS. ELVSTED [*Looks uncertainly at her.*] Eilert Løvborg? Yes, that's about right.

525 HEDDA Did you know him from before—from here in town?

MRS. ELVSTED Hardly at all. I mean his name of course.

HEDDA But up there he'd come to visit you at the house?

MRS. ELVSTED Yes, every day. He'd read to the children. I couldn't manage everything myself, you see.

530 HEDDA No, of course not. And what about your husband? His work must take him out of the house quite a bit.

MRS. ELVSTED Yes, as you might imagine. He's the sheriff so he has to go traveling around the whole district.

HEDDA [*Leaning against the arm of the chair.*] Thea, my poor sweet Thea— 535 You've got to tell me everything just the way it is.

MRS. ELVSTED All right, but you've got to ask the questions.

HEDDA So, Thea, what's your husband really like? I mean, you know, to be with? Is he good to you?

MRS. ELVSTED [*Evasively.*] He thinks he does everything for the best.

540 HEDDA I just think he's a little too old for you. He's twenty years older, isn't he?

MRS. ELVSTED [*Irritatedly.*] There's that too. There's a lot of things. I just can't stand being with him. We don't have a single thought in common, not a single thing in the world, he and I.

545 HEDDA But doesn't he care for you at all in his own way?

MRS. ELVSTED I can't tell what he feels. I think I'm just useful to him, and it doesn't cost very much to keep me. I'm very inexpensive.

HEDDA That's a mistake.

MRS. ELVSTED [*Shaking her head.*] Can't be any other way, not with him. He 550 only cares about himself and maybe about the children a little.

HEDDA And also for Eilert Løvborg, Thea.

MRS. ELVSTED [*Stares at her.*] For Eilert Løvborg? Why do you think that?

HEDDA Well, my dear, he sent you all the way into town to look for him. [*Smiling almost imperceptibly.*] And besides, you said so yourself, to 555 Tesman.

MRS. ELVSTED [*With a nervous shudder.*] Oh yes, I suppose I did. No, I'd better just tell you the whole thing. It's bound to come to light sooner or later anyway.

HEDDA But my dear Thea.

560 MRS. ELVSTED All right, short and sweet. My husband doesn't know that I'm gone.

HEDDA What, your husband doesn't know?

MRS. ELVSTED   Of course not. Anyway he's not at home. He was out traveling. I just couldn't stand it any longer, Hedda, it was impossible. I would
565   have been so completely alone up there.

HEDDA   Well, then what?

MRS. ELVSTED   Then I packed some of my things, just the necessities, all in
secret, and I left the house.

HEDDA   Just like that?

570   MRS. ELVSTED   Yes, and I took the train to town.

HEDDA   Oh, my good, dear Thea. You dared to do that!

MRS. ELVSTED [*Gets up and walks across the floor.*]   Well, what else could I do?

HEDDA   What do you think your husband will say when you go home again?

MRS. ELVSTED [*By the table looking at her.*]   Up there, to him?

575   HEDDA   Of course, of course.

MRS. ELVSTED   I'm never going back up there.

HEDDA [*Gets up and goes closer to her.*]   So you've really done it? You've really
run away from everything?

MRS. ELVSTED   Yes, I couldn't think of anything else to do.

580   HEDDA   But you did it—so openly.

MRS. ELVSTED   Oh, you can't keep something like that a secret anyway.

HEDDA   Well, what do you think people will say about you, Thea?

MRS. ELVSTED   They'll say whatever they want, God knows. [*She sits tired and
depressed on the sofa.*] But I only did what I had to do.

585   HEDDA [*After a brief pause.*]   So what will you do with yourself now?

MRS. ELVSTED   I don't know yet. All I know is that I've got to live here where
Eilert Løvborg lives if I'm going to live at all.

HEDDA [*Moves a chair closer from the table, sits beside her and strokes her
hands.*]   Thea, my dear, how did it come about, this—bond between you
and Eilert Løvborg?

590   MRS. ELVSTED   Oh, it just happened, little by little. I started to have a kind of
power over him.

HEDDA   Really?

MRS. ELVSTED   He gave up his old ways—and not because I begged him to. I
never dared do that. But he started to notice that those kinds of things
595   upset me, so he gave them up.

HEDDA [*Concealing an involuntary, derisive smile.*]   So you rehabilitated him,
as they say. You, little Thea.

MRS. ELVSTED   That's what he said, anyway. And for his part he's made a real
human being out of me. Taught me to think, to understand all sorts of
600   things.

HEDDA   So he read to you too, did he?

MRS. ELVSTED   No, not exactly, but he talked to me. Talked without stopping
about all sorts of great things. And then there was that wonderful time
when I shared in his work, when I helped him.

605   HEDDA   You got to do that?

MRS. ELVSTED   Yes. Whenever he wrote anything, we had to agree on it first.

HEDDA   Like two good comrades.

MRS. ELVSTED [*Eagerly.*]   Yes, comrades. Imagine, Hedda, that's what he
called it too. I should feel so happy, but I can't yet because I don't know
610   how long it will last.

HEDDA   Are you that unsure of him?

MRS. ELVSTED [*Dejectedly.*]   There's the shadow of a woman between Eilert
    Løvborg and me.

HEDDA [*Stares intently at her.*]   Who could that be?

615 MRS. ELVSTED   I don't know. Someone from his past. Someone he's never
    really been able to forget.

HEDDA   What has he told you about all this?

MRS. ELVSTED   He's only talked about it once and very vaguely.

HEDDA   Yes, what did he say?

620 MRS. ELVSTED   He said that when they broke up she was going to shoot him
    with a pistol.

HEDDA [*Calm and controlled.*]   That's nonsense, people just don't act that
    way here.

MRS. ELVSTED   No they don't—so I think it's got to be that red-haired singer
625   that he once—

HEDDA   Yes, that could well be.

MRS. ELVSTED   Because I remember they used to say about her that she went
    around with loaded pistols.

HEDDA   Well, then it's her, of course.

630 MRS. ELVSTED [*Wringing her hands.*]   Yes, but Hedda, just think, I hear this
    singer is in town again. Oh, I'm so afraid.

HEDDA [*Glancing toward the back room.*]   Shh, here comes Tesman. [*She
    gets up and whispers.*] Now, Thea, all of this is strictly between you and me.

MRS. ELVSTED [*Jumping up.*]   Oh yes, yes, for God's sake!

[*George Tesman, a letter in his hand, comes in from the right side of the
inner room.*]

635 TESMAN   There now, the epistle is prepared.

HEDDA   Well done—but Mrs. Elvsted's got to leave now, I think. Just a min-
    ute, I'll follow you as far as the garden gate.

TESMAN   Hedda dear, do you think Berta could see to this?

HEDDA [*Takes the letter.*]   I'll instruct her.

[*Berta comes in from the hall.*]

640 BERTA   Judge Brack is here. Says he'd like to pay his respects.

HEDDA   Yes, ask the Judge to be so good as to come in, and then—listen here
    now—Put this letter in the mailbox.

BERTA [*Takes the letter.*]   Yes, ma'am.

[*She opens the door for Judge Brack and then goes out. Judge Brack is
forty-five years old, short, well built and moves easily. He has a round face
and an aristocratic profile. His short hair is still almost black. His eyes are
lively and ironic. He has thick eyebrows and a thick moustache, trimmed
square at the ends. He is wearing outdoor clothing, elegant, but a little too
young in style. He has a monocle in one eye. Now and then he lets it drop.*]

BRACK [*Bows with his hat in his hand.*]   Does one dare to call so early?

645 HEDDA   One does dare.

TESMAN [*Shakes his hand.*]   You're welcome any time. Judge Brack, Mrs. Rysing.
    [*Hedda sighs.*]

BRACK [*Bows.*]   Aha, delighted.

HEDDA [*Looks at him laughing.*]   Nice to see you by daylight for a change, Judge.

BRACK   Do I look different?

650 HEDDA   Yes, younger.

BRACK   You're too kind.

TESMAN   Well, how about Hedda, hm? Doesn't she look fine? Hasn't she filled out?

HEDDA   Stop it now. You should be thanking Judge Brack for all of his hard
655   work—

BRACK   Nonsense. It was my pleasure.

HEDDA   There's a loyal soul. But here's my friend burning to get away. Excuse me, Judge, I'll be right back.

[*Mutual good-byes. Mrs. Elvsted and Hedda leave by the hall door.*]

BRACK   Well, now, your wife's satisfied, more or less?

660   TESMAN   Oh yes, we can't thank you enough. I gather there might be a little more rearrangement here and there and one or two things still missing. A couple of small things yet to be procured.

BRACK   Is that so?

TESMAN   But nothing for you to worry about. Hedda said that she'd look for
665   everything herself. Let's sit down.

BRACK   Thanks. Just for a minute. [*Sits by the table.*] Now, my dear Tesman, there's something we need to talk about.

TESMAN   Oh yes, ah, I understand. [*Sits down.*] Time for a new topic. Time for the serious part of the celebration, hm?

670   BRACK   Oh, I wouldn't worry too much about the finances just yet—although I must tell you that it would have been better if we'd managed things a little more frugally.

TESMAN   But there was no way to do that. You know Hedda, Judge, you know her well. I couldn't possibly ask her to live in a middle-class house.

675   BRACK   No, that's precisely the problem.

TESMAN   And luckily it can't be too long before I get my appointment.

BRACK   Well, you know, these things often drag on and on.

TESMAN   Have you heard anything further, hm?

BRACK   Nothing certain. [*Changing the subject.*] But there is one thing. I've
680   got a piece of news for you.

TESMAN   Well?

BRACK   Your old friend Eilert Løvborg's back in town.

TESMAN   I already know.

BRACK   Oh, how did you find out?

685   TESMAN   She told me, that lady who just left with Hedda.

BRACK   Oh, I see. I didn't quite get her name.

TESMAN   Mrs. Elvsted.

BRACK   Ah yes, the sheriff's wife. Yes, he's been staying up there with them.

TESMAN   And I'm so glad to hear that he's become a responsible person again.

690   BRACK   Yes, one is given to understand that.

TESMAN   And he's come out with a new book, hm?

BRACK   He has indeed.

TESMAN   And it's caused quite a sensation.

BRACK   It's caused an extraordinary sensation.

695   TESMAN   Just think, isn't that wonderful to hear. With all his remarkable talents, I was absolutely certain he was down for good.

BRACK   That was certainly the general opinion.

TESMAN   But I can't imagine what he'll do with himself now. What will he live on, hm?

[*During these last words, Hedda has entered from the hallway.*]

700 HEDDA [*To Brack, laughing a little scornfully.*] Tesman is constantly going around worrying about what to live on.

TESMAN My Lord, we're talking about Eilert Løvborg, dear.

HEDDA [*Looking quickly at him.*] Oh yes? [*Sits down in the armchair by the stove and asks casually.*] What's the matter with him?

705 TESMAN Well, he must have spent his inheritance a long time ago, and he can't really write a new book every year, hm? So I was just asking what was going to become of him.

BRACK Perhaps I can enlighten you on that score.

TESMAN Oh?

710 BRACK You might remember that he has some relatives with more than a little influence.

TESMAN Unfortunately they've pretty much washed their hands of him.

BRACK In the old days they thought of him as the family's great shining hope.

715 TESMAN Yes, in the old days, possibly, but he took care of that himself.

HEDDA Who knows? [*Smiles slightly.*] Up at the Elvsteds' he's been the target of a reclamation project.

BRACK And there's this new book.

TESMAN Well, God willing, they'll help him out some way or another. I've
720 just written to him, Hedda, asking him to come over this evening.

BRACK But my dear Tesman, you're coming to my stag party this evening. You promised me on the pier last night.

HEDDA Had you forgotten, Tesman?

TESMAN Yes, to be perfectly honest, I had.

725 BRACK For that matter, you can be sure he won't come.

TESMAN Why do you say that, hm?

BRACK [*Somewhat hesitantly getting up and leaning his hands on the back of his chair.*] My dear Tesman, you too, Mrs. Tesman, in good conscience I can't let you go on living in ignorance of something like this.

TESMAN Something about Eilert, hm?

730 BRACK About both of you.

TESMAN My dear Judge, tell me what it is.

BRACK You ought to prepare yourself for the fact that your appointment might not come through as quickly as you expect.

TESMAN [*Jumps up in alarm.*] Has something held it up?

735 BRACK The appointment might just possibly be subject to a competition.

TESMAN A competition! Just think of that, Hedda!

HEDDA [*Leans further back in her chair.*] Ah yes—yes.

TESMAN But who on earth would it—surely not with—?

BRACK Yes, precisely, with Eilert Løvborg.

740 TESMAN [*Clasping his hands together.*] No, no, this is absolutely unthinkable, absolutely unthinkable, hm?

BRACK Hmm—well, we might just have to learn to get used to it.

TESMAN No, but Judge Brack, that would be incredibly inconsiderate. [*Waving his arms.*] Because—well—just look, I'm a married man. We went and
745 got married on this very prospect, Hedda and I. Went and got ourselves heavily into debt. Borrowed money from Aunt Julie too. I mean, good Lord, I was as much as promised the position, hm?

BRACK Now, now, you'll almost certainly get it but first there'll have to be a contest.

750 HEDDA [*Motionless in the armchair.*]   Just think, Tesman, it will be a sort of match.

TESMAN   But Hedda, my dear, how can you be so calm about this?

HEDDA   Oh I'm not, not at all. I can't wait for the final score.

BRACK   In any case, Mrs. Tesman, it's a good thing that you know how mat-
755 ters stand. I mean, before you embark on any more of these little purchases I hear you're threatening to make.

HEDDA   What's that got to do with this?

BRACK   Well, well, that's another matter. Good-bye. [*To Tesman.*] I'll come by for you when I take my afternoon walk.

760 TESMAN   Oh yes, yes, forgive me—I don't know if I'm coming or going.

HEDDA [*Reclining, stretching out her hand.*]   Good-bye, Judge, and do come again.

BRACK   Many thanks. Good-bye, good-bye.

TESMAN [*Following him to the door.*]   Good-bye, Judge. You'll have to excuse me.

[*Judge Brack goes out through the hallway door.*]

765 TESMAN [*Pacing about the floor.*]   We should never let ourselves get lost in a wonderland, Hedda, hm?

HEDDA [*Looking at him and smiling.*]   Do you do that?

TESMAN   Yes, well, it can't be denied. It was like living in wonderland to go and get married and set up housekeeping on nothing more than prospects.

770 HEDDA   You may be right about that.

TESMAN   Well, at least we have our home, Hedda, our wonderful home. The home both of us dreamt about, that both of us craved, I could almost say, hm?

HEDDA [*Rises slowly and wearily.*]   The agreement was that we would live in society, that we would entertain.

775 TESMAN   Yes, good Lord, I was so looking forward to that. Just think, to see you as a hostess in our own circle. Hm. Well, well, well, for the time being at least we'll just have to make do with each other, Hedda. We'll have Aunt Julie here now and then. Oh you, you should have such a completely different—

780 HEDDA   To begin with, I suppose I can't have the liveried footmen.

TESMAN   Ah no, unfortunately not. No footmen. We can't even think about that right now.

HEDDA   And the horse!

TESMAN [*Horrified.*]   The horse!

785 HEDDA   I suppose I mustn't think about that any more.

TESMAN   No, God help us, you can see that for yourself.

HEDDA [*Walking across the floor.*]   Well, at least I've got one thing to amuse myself with.

TESMAN [*Beaming with pleasure.*]   Ah, thank God for that, and what is that,
790 Hedda?

HEDDA [*In the center doorway looking at him with veiled scorn.*]   My pistols, George.

TESMAN [*Alarmed.*]   Pistols?

HEDDA [*With cold eyes.*]   General Gabler's pistols.

[*She goes through the inner room and out to the left.*]

795 TESMAN [*Running to the center doorway and shouting after her.*]   No, for the love of God, Hedda, dearest, don't touch those dangerous things. For my sake, Hedda, hm?

Act 2

The Tesmans' rooms as in the first act except that the piano has been moved out and an elegant little writing table with a bookshelf has been put in its place. Next to the sofa a smaller table has been placed. Most of the bouquets have been removed. Mrs. Elvsted's bouquet stands on the larger table in the foreground. It is afternoon.

> [*Hedda, dressed to receive visitors, is alone in the room. She stands by the open glass door loading a pistol. The matching pistol lies in an open pistol case on the writing table.*]

HEDDA [*Looking down into the garden and calling.*]   Hello again, Judge.

BRACK [*Is heard some distance below.*]   Likewise, Mrs. Tesman.

HEDDA [*Raises the pistol and aims.*]   Now, Judge Brack, I am going to shoot you.

5   BRACK [*Shouting from below.*]   No, no, no. Don't stand there aiming at me like that.

HEDDA   That's what you get for coming up the back way. [*She shoots.*]

BRACK   Are you out of your mind?

HEDDA   Oh, good Lord, did I hit you?

10   BRACK [*Still outside.*]   Stop this nonsense.

HEDDA   Then come on in, Judge.

> [*Judge Brack, dressed for a bachelor party, comes in through the glass doors. He carries a light overcoat over his arm.*]

BRACK   In the devil's name, are you still playing this game? What were you shooting at?

HEDDA   Oh, I just stand here and shoot at the sky.

15   BRACK [*Gently taking the pistol out of her hands.*]   With your permission, ma'am? [*Looks at it.*] Ah, this one. I know it well. [*Looks around.*] And where do we keep the case? I see, here it is. [*Puts the pistol inside and shuts the case.*] All right, we're through with these little games for today.

HEDDA   Then what in God's name am I to do with myself?

20   BRACK   No visitors?

HEDDA [*Closes the glass door.*]   Not a single one. Our circle is still in the country.

BRACK   Tesman's not home either, I suppose.

HEDDA [*At the writing table, locks the pistol case in the drawer.*]   No, as soon
25   as he finished eating he was off to the aunts. He wasn't expecting you so early.

BRACK   Hmm, I never thought of that. Stupid of me.

HEDDA [*Turns her head, looks at him.*]   Why stupid?

BRACK   Then I would have come a little earlier.

30   HEDDA [*Going across the floor.*]   Then you wouldn't have found anyone here at all. I've been in my dressing room since lunch.

BRACK   Isn't there even one little crack in the door wide enough for a negotiation?

HEDDA   Now that's something you forgot to provide for.

35   BRACK   That was also stupid of me.

HEDDA   So we'll just have to flop down here and wait. Tesman won't be home any time soon.

BRACK   Well, well, Lord knows I can be patient.

> [*Hedda sits in the corner of the sofa. Brack lays his overcoat over the back of the nearest chair and sits down, keeps his hat in his hand. Short silence. They look at each other.*]

HEDDA So?

40 BRACK [*In the same tone.*] So?

HEDDA I asked first.

BRACK [*Leaning a little forward.*] Yes, why don't we allow ourselves a cozy little chat, Mrs. Hedda.[6]

HEDDA [*Leaning further back in the sofa.*] Doesn't it feel like an eternity
45 since we last talked together? A few words last night and this morning, but I don't count them.

BRACK Like this, between ourselves, just the two of us?

HEDDA Well, yes, more or less.

BRACK I wished you were back home every single day.

50 HEDDA The whole time I was wishing the same thing.

BRACK You, really, Mrs. Hedda? Here I thought you were having a wonderful time on your trip.

HEDDA Oh yes, you can just imagine.

BRACK But that's what Tesman always wrote.

55 HEDDA Yes, him! He thinks it's the greatest thing in the world to go scratching around in libraries. He loves sitting and copying out old parchments or whatever they are.

BRACK [*Somewhat maliciously.*] Well, that's his calling in the world, at least in part.

60 HEDDA Yes, so it is, and no doubt it's—but for me, oh dear Judge, I've been so desperately bored.

BRACK [*Sympathetically.*] Do you really mean that? You're serious?

HEDDA Yes, you can imagine it for yourself. Six whole months never meeting with a soul who knew the slightest thing about our circle. No one we could
65 talk with about our kinds of things.

BRACK Ah no, I'd agree with you there. That would be a loss.

HEDDA Then what was most unbearable of all.

BRACK Yes?

HEDDA To be together forever and always—with one and the same person.

70 BRACK [*Nodding agreement.*] Early and late, yes, night and day, every waking and sleeping hour.

HEDDA That's it, forever and always.

BRACK Yes, all right, but with our excellent Tesman I would have imagined that you might—

75 HEDDA Tesman is—a specialist, dear Judge.

BRACK Undeniably.

HEDDA And specialists aren't so much fun to travel with. Not for the long run anyway.

BRACK Not even the specialist that one loves?

80 HEDDA Uch, don't use that syrupy word.

BRACK [*Startled.*] Mrs. Hedda.

HEDDA [*Half laughing, half bitterly.*] Well, give it a try for yourself. Hearing about the history of civilization every hour of the day.

BRACK Forever and always.

---

6. Although Brack uses the playful "Mrs. Hedda" when they are alone, in Ibsen's original Norwegian text he addresses her with the formal *De* throughout the play.

85 HEDDA   Yes, yes, yes. And then his particular interest, domestic crafts in the Middle Ages. Uch, the most revolting thing of all.

BRACK [*Looks at her curiously.*]   But, tell me now, I don't quite understand how—hmmm.

HEDDA   That we're together? George Tesman and I, you mean?

90 BRACK   Well, yes. That's a good way of putting it.

HEDDA   Good Lord, do you think it's so remarkable?

BRACK   I think—yes and no, Mrs. Hedda.

HEDDA   I'd danced myself out, dear Judge. My time was up. [*Shudders slightly.*] Uch, no, I'm not going to say that or even think it.

95 BRACK   You certainly have no reason to think it.

HEDDA   Ah, reasons—[*Looks watchfully at him.*] And George Tesman? Well, he'd certainly be called a most acceptable man in every way.

BRACK   Acceptable and solid, God knows.

HEDDA   And I can't find anything about him that's actually ridiculous, can you?

100 BRACK   Ridiculous? No—I wouldn't quite say that.

HEDDA   Hmm. Well, he's a very diligent archivist anyway. Some day he might do something interesting with all of it. Who knows.

BRACK [*Looking at her uncertainly.*]   I thought you believed, like everyone else, that he'd turn out to be a great man.

105 HEDDA [*With a weary expression.*]   Yes, I did. And then when he went around constantly begging with all his strength, begging for permission to let him take care of me, well, I didn't see why I shouldn't take him up on it.

BRACK   Ah well, from that point of view . . .

HEDDA   It was a great deal more than any of my other admirers were
110   offering.

BRACK [*Laughing.*]   Well, of course I can't answer for all the others, but as far as I'm concerned you know very well that I've always maintained a certain respect for the marriage bond, that is, in an abstract kind of way, Mrs. Hedda.

115 HEDDA [*Playfully.*]   Oh, I never had any hopes for you.

BRACK   All I ask is an intimate circle of good friends, friends I can be of service to in any way necessary. Places where I am allowed to come and go as a trusted friend.

HEDDA   Of the man of the house, you mean.

120 BRACK [*Bowing.*]   No, to be honest, of the lady. Of the man as well, you understand, because you know that kind of—how should I put this—that kind of triangular arrangement is really a magnificent convenience for everyone concerned.

HEDDA   Yes, you can't imagine how many times I longed for a third person on
125   that trip. Ach, huddled together alone in a railway compartment.

BRACK   Fortunately, the wedding trip is over now.

HEDDA [*Shaking her head.*]   Oh no, it's a very long trip. It's nowhere near over. I've only come to a little stopover on the line.

BRACK   Then you should jump out, stretch your legs a little, Mrs. Hedda.

130 HEDDA   I'd never jump out.

BRACK   Really?

HEDDA   No, because there's always someone at the stop who—

BRACK [*Laughing.*]   Who's looking at your legs, you mean?

HEDDA   Yes, exactly.

135 BRACK   Yes, but for heaven's sake.

HEDDA [*With a disdainful gesture.*] I don't hold with that sort of thing. I'd rather remain sitting, just like I am now, a couple alone. On a train.

BRACK But what if a third man climbed into the compartment with the couple?

140 HEDDA Ah yes. Now that's quite different.

BRACK An understanding friend, a proven friend—

HEDDA Who can be entertaining on all kinds of topics—

BRACK And not a specialist in any way!

HEDDA [*With an audible sigh.*] Yes, that would be a relief.

145 BRACK [*Hears the front door open and glances toward it.*] The triangle is complete.

HEDDA [*Half audibly.*] And there goes the train.

[*George Tesman in a gray walking suit and with a soft felt hat comes in from the hallway. He is carrying a large stack of unbound books under his arm and in his pockets.*]

TESMAN [*Goes to the table by the corner sofa.*] Phew—hot work lugging all these here. [*Puts the books down.*] Would you believe I'm actually sweating,

150 Hedda? And you're already here, Judge, hm. Berta didn't mention anything about that.

BRACK [*Getting up.*] I came up through the garden.

HEDDA What are all those books you've got there?

TESMAN [*Stands leafing through them.*] All the new works by my fellow spe-

155 cialists. I've absolutely got to have them.

HEDDA By your fellow specialists.

BRACK Ah, the specialists, Mrs. Tesman. [*Brack and Hedda exchange a knowing smile.*]

HEDDA You need even more of these specialized works?

TESMAN Oh, yes, my dear Hedda, you can never have too many of these. You

160 have to keep up with what's being written and published.

HEDDA Yes, you certainly must do that.

TESMAN [*Searches among the books.*] And look here, I've got Eilert Løvborg's new book too. [*Holds it out.*] Maybe you'd like to look at it, Hedda, hm?

HEDDA No thanks—or maybe later.

165 TESMAN I skimmed it a little on the way.

HEDDA And what's your opinion as a specialist?

TESMAN I think the argument's remarkably thorough. He never wrote like this before. [*Collects the books together.*] Now I've got to get all these inside. Oh, it's going to be such fun to cut the pages.[7] Then I'll go and

170 change. [*To Brack.*] We don't have to leave right away, hm?

BRACK No, not at all. No hurry at all.

TESMAN Good, I'll take my time then. [*Leaves with the books but stands in the doorway and turns.*] Oh, Hedda, by the way, Aunt Julie won't be coming over this evening.

175 HEDDA Really? Because of that hat business?

TESMAN Not at all. How could you think that of Aunt Julie? No, it's just that Aunt Rina is very ill.

HEDDA She always is.

---

7. When books are published, four or eight pages are usually printed on one sheet, which is subsequently folded to properly order the leaves; formerly, books were often sold with the outer edges of the folded pages left uncut.

TESMAN Yes, but today she's gotten quite a bit worse.

180 HEDDA Well, then it's only right that the other one should stay at home with her. I'll just have to make the best of it.

TESMAN My dear, you just can't believe how glad Aunt Julie was, in spite of everything, at how healthy and rounded out you looked after the trip.

HEDDA [*Half audibly getting up.*] Oh, these eternal aunts.

185 TESMAN Hm?

HEDDA [*Goes over to the glass door.*] Nothing.

TESMAN Oh, all right. [*He goes out through the rear room and to the right.*]

BRACK What were you saying about a hat?

HEDDA Oh, just a little run-in with Miss Tesman this morning. She'd put her 190 hat down there on that chair [*Looks at him smiling.*] and I pretended I thought it was the maid's.

BRACK [*Shaking his head.*] My dear Mrs. Hedda, how could you do such a thing to that harmless old lady.

HEDDA [*Nervously walking across the floor.*] Oh, you know—these things just 195 come over me like that and I can't resist them. [*Flings herself into the armchair by the stove.*] I can't explain it, even to myself.

BRACK [*Behind the armchair.*] You're not really happy—that's the heart of it.

HEDDA [*Staring in front of her.*] And why should I be happy? Maybe you can tell me.

200 BRACK Yes. Among other things, be happy you've got the home that you've always longed for.

HEDDA [*Looks up at him and laughs.*] You also believe that myth?

BRACK There's nothing to it?

HEDDA Yes, heavens, there's something to it.

205 BRACK So?

HEDDA And here's what it is. I used George Tesman to walk me home from parties last summer.

BRACK Yes, regrettably I had to go another way.

HEDDA Oh yes, you certainly were going a different way last summer.

210 BRACK [*Laughs.*] Shame on you, Mrs. Hedda. So you and Tesman . . .

HEDDA So we walked past here one evening and Tesman, the poor thing, was twisting and turning in his agony because he didn't have the slightest idea what to talk about and I felt sorry that such a learned man—

BRACK [*Smiling skeptically.*] You did . . .

215 HEDDA Yes, if you will, I did, and so just to help him out of his torment I said, without really thinking about it, that this was the house I would love to live in.

BRACK That was all?

HEDDA For that evening.

220 BRACK But afterward?

HEDDA Yes, dear Judge, my thoughtlessness has had its consequences.

BRACK Unfortunately, our thoughtlessness often does, Mrs. Hedda.

HEDDA Thanks, I'm sure. But it so happens that George Tesman and I found our common ground in this passion for Prime Minister Falk's villa. And 225 after that it all followed. The engagement, the marriage, the honeymoon and everything else. Yes, yes, Judge, I almost said: you make your bed, you have to lie in it.

BRACK   That's priceless. Essentially what you're telling me is you didn't care about any of this here.

230 HEDDA   God knows I didn't.

BRACK   What about now, now that we've made it into a lovely home for you?

HEDDA   Ach, I feel an air of lavender and dried roses in every room—or maybe Aunt Julie brought that in with her.

BRACK [*Laughing.*]   No, I think that's probably a relic of the eminent prime
235 minister's late wife.

HEDDA   Yes, that's it, there's something deathly about it. It reminds me of a corsage the day after the ball. [*Folds her hands at the back of her neck, leans back in her chair and gazes at him.*] Oh, my dear Judge, you can't imagine how I'm going to bore myself out here.

240 BRACK   What if life suddenly should offer you some purpose or other, something to live for? What about that, Mrs. Hedda?

HEDDA   A purpose? Something really tempting for me?

BRACK   Preferably something like that, of course.

HEDDA   God knows what sort of purpose that would be. I often wonder if—
245 [*Breaks off.*] No, that wouldn't work out either.

BRACK   Who knows. Let me hear.

HEDDA   If I could get Tesman to go into politics, I mean.

BRACK [*Laughing.*]   Tesman? No, you have to see that politics, anything like that, is not for him. Not in his line at all.

250 HEDDA   No, I can see that. But what if I could get him to try just the same?

BRACK   Yes, but why should he do that if he's not up to it? Why would you want him to?

HEDDA   Because I'm bored, do you hear me? [*After a pause.*] So you don't think there's any way that Tesman could become a cabinet minister?

255 BRACK   Hmm, you see my dear Mrs. Hedda, that requires a certain amount of wealth in the first place.

HEDDA [*Rises impatiently.*]   Yes, that's it, this shabby little world I've ended up in. [*Crosses the floor.*] That's what makes life so contemptible, so completely ridiculous. That's just what it is.

260 BRACK   I think the problem's somewhere else.

HEDDA   Where's that?

BRACK   You've never had to live through anything that really shakes you up.

HEDDA   Anything serious, you mean.

BRACK   Yes, you could call it that. Perhaps now, though, it's on its way.

265 HEDDA [*Tosses her head.*]   You mean that competition for that stupid professorship? That's Tesman's business. I'm not going to waste a single thought on it.

BRACK   No, forget about that. But when you find yourself facing what one calls in elegant language a profound and solemn calling—[*Smiling.*] a new calling, my dear little Mrs. Hedda.

270 HEDDA [*Angry.*]   Quiet. You'll never see anything like that.

BRACK [*Gently.*]   We'll talk about it again in a year's time, at the very latest.

HEDDA [*Curtly.*]   I don't have any talent for that, Judge. I don't want anything to do with that kind of calling.

BRACK   Why shouldn't you, like most other women, have an innate talent for
275 a vocation that—

HEDDA [*Over by the glass door.*]   Oh, please be quiet. I often think I only have one talent, one talent in the world.

BRACK [*Approaching.*]   And what is that may I ask?

HEDDA [*Standing, staring out.*]   Boring the life right out of me. Now you
280   know. [*Turns, glances toward the inner room and laughs.*] Perfect timing;
here comes the professor.

BRACK [*Warning softly.*]   Now, now, now, Mrs. Hedda.

> [*George Tesman, in evening dress, carrying his gloves and hat, comes in
> from the right of the rear room.*]

TESMAN   Hedda, no message from Eilert Løvborg?

HEDDA   No.

285   BRACK   Do you really think he'll come?

TESMAN   Yes, I'm almost certain he will. What you told us this morning was
just idle gossip.

BRACK   Oh?

TESMAN   Yes, at least Aunt Julie said she couldn't possibly believe that he
290   would stand in my way any more. Just think.

BRACK   So, then everything's all right.

TESMAN [*Puts his hat with his gloves inside on a chair to the right.*]   Yes, but
I'd like to wait for him as long as I can.

BRACK   We have plenty of time. No one's coming to my place until seven or
295   even half past.

TESMAN   Meanwhile, we can keep Hedda company and see what happens,
hm?

HEDDA [*Sets Brack's overcoat and hat on the corner sofa.*]   At the very worst,
Mr. Løvborg can stay here with me.

300   BRACK [*Offering to take his things.*]   At the worst, Mrs. Tesman, what do you
mean?

HEDDA   If he won't go out with you and Tesman.

TESMAN [*Looking at her uncertainly.*]   But, Hedda dear, do you think that
would be quite right, him staying here with you? Remember, Aunt Julie
305   can't come.

HEDDA   No, but Mrs. Elvsted will be coming and the three of us can have a
cup of tea together.

TESMAN   Yes, that's all right then.

BRACK [*Smiling.*]   And I might add, that would be the best plan for him.

310   HEDDA   Why so?

BRACK   Good Lord, Mrs. Tesman, you've had enough to say about my little
bachelor parties in the past. Don't you agree they should be open only to
men of the highest principle?

HEDDA   That's just what Mr. Løvborg is now, a reclaimed sinner.

> [*Berta comes in from the hall doorway.*]

315   BERTA   Madam, there's a gentleman who wishes to—

HEDDA   Yes, please, show him in.

TESMAN [*Softly.*]   It's got to be him. Just think.

> [*Eilert Løvborg enters from the hallway. He is slim and lean, the same
> age as Tesman, but he looks older and somewhat haggard. His hair and
> beard are dark brown. His face is longish, pale, with patches of red over
> the cheekbones. He is dressed in an elegant suit, black, quite new, dark
> gloves and top hat. He stops just inside the doorway and bows hastily. He
> seems somewhat embarrassed.*]

320

325

330

335

340

345

350

355

360

365

TESMAN [*Goes to him and shakes his hands.*]   Oh my dear Eilert, we meet again at long last.

LØVBORG [*Speaks in a low voice.*]   Thanks for the letter, George. [*Approaches Hedda.*] May I shake your hand also, Mrs. Tesman?

HEDDA [*Takes his hand.*]   Welcome, Mr. Løvborg. [*With a gesture.*] I don't know if you two gentlemen—

LØVBORG [*Bowing.*]   Judge Brack, I believe.

BRACK [*Similarly.*]   Indeed. It's been quite a few years—

TESMAN [*To Løvborg, his hands on his shoulders.*]   And now Eilert, make yourself completely at home. Right, Hedda? I hear you're going to settle down here in town, hm?

LØVBORG   Yes, I will.

TESMAN   Well, that's only sensible. Listen, I got your new book. I haven't really had time to read it yet.

LØVBORG   You can save yourself the trouble.

TESMAN   What do you mean?

LØVBORG   There's not much to it.

TESMAN   How can you say that?

BRACK   But everyone's been praising it so highly.

LØVBORG   Exactly as I intended—so I wrote the sort of book that everyone can agree with.

BRACK   Very clever.

TESMAN   Yes, but my dear Eilert.

LØVBORG   Because I want to reestablish my position, begin again.

TESMAN [*A little downcast.*]   Yes, I suppose you'd want to, hm.

LØVBORG [*Smiling, putting down his hat and pulling a package wrapped in paper from his coat pocket.*]   But when this comes out, George Tesman— this is what you should read. It's the real thing. I've put my whole self into it.

TESMAN   Oh yes? What's it about?

LØVBORG   It's the sequel.

TESMAN   Sequel to what?

LØVBORG   To my book.

TESMAN   The new one?

LØVBORG   Of course.

TESMAN   But my dear Eilert, that one takes us right to the present day.

LØVBORG   So it does—and this one takes us into the future.

TESMAN   The future. Good Lord! We don't know anything about that.

LØVBORG   No, we don't—but there are still one or two things to say about it, just the same. [*Opens the package.*] Here, you'll see.

TESMAN   That's not your handwriting, is it?

LØVBORG   I dictated it. [*Turns the pages.*] It's written in two sections. The first is about the cultural forces which will shape the future, and this other section [*Turning the pages.*] is about the future course of civilization.

TESMAN   Extraordinary. It would never occur to me to write about something like that.

HEDDA [*By the glass door, drumming on the pane.*]   Hmm, no, no.

LØVBORG [*Puts the papers back in the packet and sets it on the table.*]   I brought it along because I thought I might read some of it to you tonight.

TESMAN   Ah, that was very kind of you, Eilert, but this evening [*Looks at Brack.*] I'm not sure it can be arranged—

LØVBORG   Some other time then, there's no hurry.

BRACK   I should tell you, Mr. Løvborg, we're having a little party at my place
370   this evening, mostly for Tesman, you understand—

LØVBORG [*Looking for his hat.*]   Aha, well then I'll—

BRACK   No, listen, why don't you join us?

LØVBORG [*Briefly but firmly.*]   No, that I can't do, but many thanks just the same.

375   BRACK   Oh come now, you certainly can do that. We'll be a small, select circle and I guarantee we'll be "lively," as Mrs. Hed—Mrs. Tesman would say.

LØVBORG   No doubt, but even so—

BRACK   And then you could bring your manuscript along and read it to Tesman at my place. I've got plenty of rooms.

380   TESMAN   Think about that, Eilert. You could do that, hm?

HEDDA [*Intervening.*]   Now, my dear, Mr. Løvborg simply doesn't want to. I'm quite sure Mr. Løvborg would rather settle down here and have supper with me.

LØVBORG [*Staring at her.*]   With you, Mrs. Tesman?

385   HEDDA   And with Mrs. Elvsted.

LØVBORG   Ah— [*Casually.*] I saw her this morning very briefly.

HEDDA   Oh did you? Well, she's coming here; so you might almost say it's essential that you stay here, Mr. Løvborg. Otherwise she'll have no one to see her home.

390   LØVBORG   That's true. Yes, Mrs. Tesman, many thanks. I'll stay.

HEDDA   I'll go and have a word with the maid.

[*She goes over to the hall door and rings. Berta enters. Hedda speaks quietly to her and points toward the rear room. Berta nods and goes out again.*]

TESMAN [*At the same time to Løvborg.*]   Listen, Eilert, your lecture—Is it about this new subject? About the future?

LØVBORG   Yes.

395   TESMAN   Because I heard down at the bookstore that you'd be giving a lecture series here this fall.

LØVBORG   I plan to. Please don't hold it against me.

TESMAN   No, God forbid, but—?

LØVBORG   I can easily see how this might make things awkward.

400   TESMAN [*Dejectedly.*]   Oh, for my part, I can't expect you to—

LØVBORG   But I'll wait until you get your appointment.

TESMAN   You will? Yes but—yes but—you won't be competing then?

LØVBORG   No. I only want to conquer you in the marketplace of ideas.

TESMAN   But, good Lord, Aunt Julie was right after all. Oh yes, yes, I was
405   quite sure of it. Hedda, imagine, my dear—Eilert Løvborg won't stand in our way.

HEDDA [*Curtly.*]   Our way? Leave me out of it.

[*She goes up toward the rear room where Berta is placing a tray with decanters and glasses on the table. Hedda nods approvingly, comes forward again. Berta goes out.*]

TESMAN [*Meanwhile.*]   So, Judge Brack, what do you say about all this?

BRACK   Well now, I say that honor and victory, hmm—they have a powerful
410   appeal—

TESMAN Yes, yes, I suppose they do but all the same—

HEDDA [*Looking at Tesman with a cold smile.*] You look like you've been struck by lightning.

TESMAN Yes, that's about it—or something like that, I think—

415 BRACK That was quite a thunderstorm that passed over us, Mrs. Tesman.

HEDDA [*Pointing toward the rear room.*] Won't you gentlemen go in there and have a glass of punch?

BRACK [*Looking at his watch.*] For the road? Yes, not a bad idea.

TESMAN Wonderful, Hedda, wonderful! And I'm in such a fantastic mood now.

420 HEDDA You too, Mr. Løvborg, if you please.

LØVBORG [*Dismissively.*] No, thank you, not for me.

BRACK Good Lord, cold punch isn't exactly poison, you know.

LØVBORG Maybe not for everybody.

HEDDA Then I'll keep Mr. Løvborg company in the meantime.

425 TESMAN Yes, yes, Hedda dear, you do that.

[*Tesman and Brack go into the rear room, sit down and drink punch, smoking cigarettes and talking animatedly during the following. Eilert Løvborg remains standing by the stove and Hedda goes to the writing table.*]

HEDDA [*In a slightly raised voice.*] Now, if you like, I'll show you some photographs. Tesman and I—we took a trip to the Tyrol on the way home.

[*She comes over with an album and lays it on the table by the sofa, seating herself in the farthest corner. Eilert Løvborg comes closer, stooping and looking at her. Then he takes a chair and sits on her left side with his back to the rear room.*]

HEDDA [*Opening the album.*] Do you see these mountains, Mr. Løvborg? That's the Ortler group. Tesman's written a little caption. Here. "The Ortler
430   group near Meran.[8]"

LØVBORG [*Who has not taken his eyes off her from the beginning, says softly and slowly.*] Hedda Gabler.

HEDDA [*Glances quickly at him.*] Shh, now.

LØVBORG [*Repeating softly.*] Hedda Gabler.

435 HEDDA [*Staring at the album.*] Yes, so I was once, when we knew each other.

LØVBORG And from now—for the rest of my life—do I have to teach myself never to say Hedda Gabler?

HEDDA [*Turning the pages.*] Yes, you have to. And I think you'd better start practicing now. The sooner the better, I'd say.

440 LØVBORG [*In a resentful voice.*] Hedda Gabler married—and then—with George Tesman.

HEDDA That's how it goes.

LØVBORG Ah, Hedda, Hedda—how could you have thrown yourself away like that?[9]

445 HEDDA [*Looks sharply at him.*] What? Now stop that.

LØVBORG Stop what, what do you mean?

HEDDA Calling me Hedda and—

[*Tesman comes in and goes toward the sofa.*]

---

8. Merano, a district of northeastern Italy on the southern slope of the Alps.

9. When addressing Hedda, Løvborg uses the familiar *du* in the first part of this scene; here, he reverts to the formal *De*. However, he calls her by her first name throughout. Hedda, by contrast, addresses him as "Mr. Løvborg" and uses only the formal *De*.

HEDDA [*Hears him approaching and says casually.*] And this one here, Mr.
Løvborg, this was taken from the Ampezzo Valley.[1] Would you just look at
450 these mountain peaks. [*Looks warmly up at Tesman.*] George, dear, what
were these extraordinary mountains called?

TESMAN Let me see. Ah, yes, those are the Dolomites.

HEDDA Of course. Those, Mr. Løvborg, are the Dolomites.

TESMAN Hedda, dear, I just wanted to ask you if we should bring some
455 punch in here, for you at least.

HEDDA Yes, thank you my dear. And a few pastries perhaps.

TESMAN Any cigarettes?

HEDDA No.

TESMAN Good.

[*He goes into the rear room and off to the right. Brack remains sitting,
from time to time keeping his eye on Hedda and Løvborg.*]

460 LØVBORG [*Quietly, as before.*] Then answer me, Hedda—how could you go
and do such a thing?

HEDDA [*Apparently absorbed in the album.*] If you keep talking to me that
way, I just won't speak to you.

LØVBORG Not even when we're alone together?

465 HEDDA No. You can think whatever you want but you can't talk about it.

LØVBORG Ah, I see. It offends your love for George Tesman.

HEDDA [*Glances at him and smiles.*] Love? Don't be absurd.

LØVBORG Not love then either?

HEDDA But even so—nothing unfaithful. I will not allow it.

470 LØVBORG Answer me just one thing—

HEDDA Shh.

[*Tesman, with a tray, enters from the rear room.*]

TESMAN Here we are, here come the treats. [*He places the tray on the table.*]

HEDDA Why are you serving us yourself?

TESMAN [*Filling the glasses.*] I have such a good time waiting on you, Hedda.

475 HEDDA But now you've gone and poured two drinks and Mr. Løvborg definitely does not want—

TESMAN No, but Mrs. Elvsted's coming soon.

HEDDA Yes, that's right, Mrs. Elvsted.

TESMAN Did you forget about her?

480 HEDDA We were just sitting here so completely wrapped up in these. [*Shows
him a picture.*] Do you remember this little village?

TESMAN Yes, that's the one below the Brenner Pass.[2] We spent the night there—

HEDDA —and ran into all those lively summer visitors.

TESMAN Ah yes, that was it. Imagine—if you could have been with us, Eilert,
485 just think. [*He goes in again and sits with Brack.*]

LØVBORG Just answer me one thing—

HEDDA Yes?

LØVBORG In our relationship—wasn't there any love there either? No trace?
Not a glimmer of love in any of it?

490 HEDDA I wonder if there really was. For me it was like we were two good
comrades, two really good, faithful friends. [*Smiling.*] I remember you
were particularly frank and open.

1. A valley in northern Italy in the Dolomites, a section of the Tyrolean Alps.

2. One of the main passes in the Alps, between Austria and Italy.

LØVBORG That's how you wanted it.

HEDDA When I look back on it, there was something really beautiful—
495   something fascinating, something brave about this secret comradeship,
this secret intimacy that no living soul had any idea about.

LØVBORG Yes, Hedda, that's true isn't it? That was it. When I'd come to your
father's in the afternoon—and the General would sit in the window reading
his newspaper with his back toward the room—

500 HEDDA And us on the corner sofa.

LØVBORG Always with the same illustrated magazine in front of us.

HEDDA Instead of an album, yes.

LØVBORG Yes, Hedda—and when I made all those confessions to you—
telling you things about myself that no one else knew in those days. Sat
505   there and told you how I'd lost whole days and nights in drunken frenzy,
frenzy that would last for days on end. Ah, Hedda—what kind of power was
in you that drew these confessions out of me?

HEDDA You think it was a power in me?

LØVBORG Yes. I can't account for it in any other way. And you'd ask me all
510   those ambiguous leading questions—

HEDDA Which you understood implicitly—

LØVBORG How did you sit there and question me so fearlessly?

HEDDA Ambiguously?

LØVBORG Yes, but fearlessly all the same. Questioning me about—About
515   things like that.

HEDDA And how could you answer them, Mr. Løvborg?

LØVBORG Yes, yes. That's just what I don't understand any more. But now
tell me, Hedda, wasn't it love underneath it all? Wasn't that part of it? You
wanted to purify me, to cleanse me—when I'd seek you out to make my
520   confessions. Wasn't that it?

HEDDA No, no, not exactly.

LØVBORG Then what drove you?

HEDDA Do you find it so hard to explain that a young girl—when it becomes
possible—in secret—

525 LØVBORG Yes?

HEDDA That she wants a glimpse of a world that—

LØVBORG That—

HEDDA That is not permitted to her.

LØVBORG So that was it.

530 HEDDA That too, that too—I almost believe it.

LØVBORG Comrades in a quest for life. So why couldn't it go on?

HEDDA That was your own fault.

LØVBORG You broke it off.

HEDDA Yes, when it looked like reality threatened to spoil the situation.
535   Shame on you, Eilert Løvborg, how could you do violence to your comrade
in arms?

LØVBORG [Clenching his hands together.] Well, why didn't you do it for real?
Why didn't you shoot me dead right then and there like you threatened to?

HEDDA Oh, I'm much too afraid of scandal.

540 LØVBORG Yes, Hedda, underneath it all, you're a coward.

HEDDA A terrible coward. [Changes her tone.] Lucky for you. And now
you've got plenty of consolation up there at the Elvsteds'.

LØVBORG   I know what Thea's confided to you.

HEDDA   And no doubt you've confided to her about us.

545 LØVBORG   Not one word. She's too stupid to understand things like this.

HEDDA   Stupid?

LØVBORG   In things like this she's stupid.

HEDDA   And I'm a coward. [*Leans closer to him without looking him in the eyes and says softly.*] Now I'll confide something to you.

550 LØVBORG   [*In suspense.*]   What?

HEDDA   My not daring to shoot you—

LØVBORG   Yes?!

HEDDA   —that wasn't my worst cowardice that evening.

LØVBORG   [*Stares at her a moment, understands and whispers passionately.*]   Ah,
555   Hedda Gabler, now I see the hidden reason why we're such comrades. This craving for life in you—

HEDDA   [*Quietly, with a sharp glance at him.*]   Watch out, don't believe anything of the sort.

[*It starts to get dark. The hall door is opened by Berta.*]

HEDDA   [*Clapping the album shut and crying out with a smile.*]   Ah, finally.
560   Thea, darling, do come in.

[*Mrs. Elvsted enters from the hall. She is in evening dress. The door is closed after her.*]

HEDDA   [*On the sofa, stretching out her arms.*]   Thea, my sweet, you can't imagine how I've been expecting you.

[*Mrs. Elvsted, in passing, exchanges a greeting with the gentlemen in the inner room, crosses to the table, shakes Hedda's hand. Eilert Løvborg has risen. He and Mrs. Elvsted greet each other with a single nod.*]

MRS. ELVSTED   Perhaps I should go in and have a word with your husband.

HEDDA   Not at all. Let them sit there. They'll be on their way soon.

565 MRS. ELVSTED   They're leaving?

HEDDA   Yes, they're going out on a little binge.

MRS. ELVSTED   [*Quickly to Løvborg.*]   You're not?

LØVBORG   No.

HEDDA   Mr. Løvborg . . . he'll stay here with us.

570 MRS. ELVSTED   [*Takes a chair and sits down beside him.*]   It's so nice to be here.

HEDDA   No, you don't, little Thea, not there. Come right over here next to me. I want to be in the middle between you.

MRS. ELVSTED   All right, whatever you like. [*She goes around the table and sits on the sofa to the right of Hedda. Løvborg takes his chair again.*]

LØVBORG   [*After a brief pause, to Hedda.*]   Isn't she lovely to look at?

575 HEDDA   [*Gently stroking her hair.*]   Only to look at?

LØVBORG   Yes. We're true comrades, the two of us. We trust each other completely and that's why we can sit here and talk so openly and boldly together.

HEDDA   With no ambiguity, Mr. Løvborg.

LØVBORG   Well—

580 MRS. ELVSTED   [*Softly, clinging to Hedda.*]   Oh, Hedda, I'm so lucky. Just think, he says I've inspired him too.

HEDDA   [*Regards her with a smile.*]   No, dear, does he say that?

LØVBORG   And she has the courage to take action, Mrs. Tesman.

MRS. ELVSTED   Oh God, me, courage?

585 LØVBORG   Tremendous courage when it comes to comradeship.

HEDDA   Yes, courage—yes! That's the crucial thing.

LØVBORG   Why is that, do you suppose?

HEDDA   Because then—maybe—life has a chance to be lived. [*Suddenly changing her tone.*] But now, my dearest Thea. Why don't you treat yourself
590   to a nice cold glass of punch?

MRS. ELVSTED   No thank you, I never drink anything like that.

HEDDA   Then for you, Mr. Løvborg.

LØVBORG   No thank you, not for me either.

MRS. ELVSTED   No, not for him either.

595   HEDDA [*Looking steadily at him.*]   But if I insisted.

LØVBORG   Doesn't matter.

HEDDA [*Laughing.*]   Then I have absolutely no power over you? Ah, poor me.

LØVBORG   Not in that area.

HEDDA   But seriously now, I really think you should, for your own sake.

600   MRS. ELVSTED   No, Hedda—

LØVBORG   Why is that?

HEDDA   Or to be more precise, for others' sakes.

LØVBORG   Oh?

HEDDA   Because otherwise people might get the idea that you don't, deep
605   down inside, feel really bold, really sure of yourself.

LØVBORG   Oh, from now on people can think whatever they like.

MRS. ELVSTED   Yes, that's right, isn't it.

HEDDA   I saw it so clearly with Judge Brack a few minutes ago.

LØVBORG   What did you see?

610   HEDDA   That condescending little smile when you didn't dare join them at
the table.

LØVBORG   Didn't dare? I'd just rather stay here and talk with you, of course.

MRS. ELVSTED   That's only reasonable, Hedda.

HEDDA   How was the Judge supposed to know that? I saw how he smiled and
615   shot a glance at Tesman when you didn't dare join them in their silly little
party.

LØVBORG   Didn't dare. You're saying I don't dare.

HEDDA   Oh, I'm not. But that's how Judge Brack sees it.

LØVBORG   Well let him.

620   HEDDA   So you won't join them?

LØVBORG   I'm staying here with you and Thea.

MRS. ELVSTED   Yes, Hedda, you can be sure he is.

HEDDA [*Smiling and nodding approvingly to Løvborg.*]   What a strong foundation you've got. Principles to last a lifetime. That's what a man ought to
625   have. [*Turns to Mrs. Elvsted.*] See now, wasn't that what I told you when
you came here this morning in such a panic—

LØVBORG [*Startled.*]   Panic?

MRS. ELVSTED [*Terrified.*]   Hedda, Hedda, no.

HEDDA   Just see for yourself. No reason at all to come running here in mortal
630   terror. [*Changing her tone.*] There, now all three of us can be quite jolly.

LØVBORG [*Shocked.*]   What does this mean, Mrs. Tesman?

MRS. ELVSTED   Oh God, oh God, Hedda. What are you doing? What are you
saying?

HEDDA   Keep calm now. That disgusting Judge is sitting there watching you.

635   LØVBORG   In mortal terror on my account?

MRS. ELVSTED [*Quietly wailing.*]   Oh, Hedda—

LØVBORG [*Looks at her steadily for a moment; his face is drawn.*]   So that, then, was how my brave, bold comrade trusted me.

MRS. ELVSTED [*Pleading.*]   Oh, my dearest friend, listen to me—

LØVBORG [*Takes one of the glasses of punch, raises it and says in a low, hoarse
640   voice.*]   Your health, Thea. [*Empties the glass, takes another.*]

MRS. ELVSTED [*Softly.*]   Oh Hedda, Hedda—how could you want this to happen?

HEDDA   Want it? I want this? Are you mad?

LØVBORG   And your health too, Mrs. Tesman. Thanks for the truth. Long
645   may it live. [*He drinks and goes to refill the glass.*]

HEDDA [*Placing her hand on his arm.*]   That's enough for now. Remember, you're going to the party.

MRS. ELVSTED   No, no, no.

HEDDA   Shh. They're watching us.

650 LØVBORG [*Putting down the glass.*]   Thea, be honest with me now.

MRS. ELVSTED   Yes.

LØVBORG   Was your husband told that you came here to look for me?

MRS. ELVSTED [*Wringing her hands.*]   Oh, Hedda, listen to what he's asking me!

LØVBORG   Did he arrange for you to come to town to spy on me? Maybe he
655   put me up to it himself. Aha, that's it. He needed me back in the office again. Or did he just miss me at the card table?

MRS. ELVSTED [*Softly moaning.*]   Oh, Løvborg, Løvborg—

LØVBORG [*Grabs a glass intending to fill it.*]   Skøal to the old Sheriff too.

HEDDA [*Preventing him.*]   No more now. Remember, you're going out to read
660   to Tesman.

LØVBORG [*Calmly putting down his glass.*]   Thea, that was stupid of me. What I did just now. Taking it like that I mean. Don't be angry with me, my dear, dear comrade. You'll see. Both of you and everyone else will see that even though I once was fallen—now I've raised myself up again, with your help, Thea.

665 MRS. ELVSTED [*Radiant with joy.*]   Oh God be praised.

[*Meanwhile Brack has been looking at his watch. He and Tesman get up
and come into the drawing room.*]

BRACK [*Taking his hat and overcoat.*]   Well, Mrs. Tesman, our time is up.

HEDDA   Yes, it must be.

LØVBORG [*Rising.*]   Mine too.

MRS. ELVSTED [*Quietly pleading.*]   Løvborg, don't do it.

670 HEDDA [*Pinching her arm.*]   They can hear you.

MRS. ELVSTED [*Crying out faintly.*]   Ow.

LØVBORG [*To Brack.*]   You were kind enough to ask me along.

BRACK   So you're coming after all.

LØVBORG   Yes, thanks.

675 BRACK   I'm delighted.

LØVBORG [*Putting the manuscript packet in his pocket and saying to
Tesman.*]   I'd really like you to look at one or two things before I send it off.

TESMAN   Just think, that will be splendid. But, Hedda dear, how will you get Mrs. Elvsted home?

680 HEDDA   Oh, there's always a way out.

LØVBORG [*Looking at the ladies.*]   Mrs. Elvsted? Well, of course, I'll come back for her. [*Coming closer.*] Around ten o'clock, Mrs. Tesman, will that do?

HEDDA   Yes, that will be fine.

TESMAN   Well, everything's all right then; but don't expect me that early, Hedda.

685 HEDDA   No dear, you stay just as long—as long as you like.

MRS. ELVSTED [*With suppressed anxiety.*]   Mr. Løvborg—I'll stay here until you come.

LØVBORG [*His hat in his hand.*]   That's understood.

BRACK   All aboard then, the party train's pulling out. Gentlemen, I trust it
690   will be a lively trip, as a certain lovely lady suggested.

HEDDA   Ah yes, if only that lovely lady could be there—invisible, of course.

BRACK   Why invisible?

HEDDA   To hear a little of your liveliness, Judge, uncensored.

BRACK [*Laughing.*]   Not recommended for the lovely lady.

695 TESMAN [*Also laughing.*]   You really are the limit, Hedda. Think of it.

BRACK   Well, well, my ladies. Good night. Good night.

LØVBORG [*Bowing as he leaves.*]   Until ten o'clock, then.

[*Brack, Løvborg and Tesman leave through the hall door. At the same time Berta comes in from the rear room with a lighted lamp which she places on the drawing room table, going out the way she came in.*]

MRS. ELVSTED [*Has gotten up and wanders uneasily about the room.*]   Oh, Hedda, where is all this going?

700 HEDDA   Ten o'clock—then he'll appear. I see him before me with vine leaves in his hair,[3] burning bright and bold.

MRS. ELVSTED   Yes, if only it could be like that.

HEDDA   And then you'll see—then he'll have power over himself again. Then he'll be a free man for the rest of his days.

705 MRS. ELVSTED   Oh God yes—if only he'd come back just the way you see him.

HEDDA   He'll come back just that way and no other. [*Gets up and comes closer.*] You can doubt him as much as you like. I believe in him. And so we'll see—

MRS. ELVSTED   There's something behind this, something else you're trying to do.

710 HEDDA   Yes, there is. Just once in my life I want to help shape someone's destiny.

MRS. ELVSTED   Don't you do that already?

HEDDA   I don't and I never have.

MRS. ELVSTED   Not even your husband?

715 HEDDA   Oh yes, that was a real bargain. Oh, if you could only understand how destitute I am while you get to be so rich. [*She passionately throws her arms around her.*] I think I'll burn your hair off after all.

MRS. ELVSTED   Let me go, let me go. I'm afraid of you.

BERTA [*In the doorway.*]   Tea is ready in the dining room, Madam.

720 HEDDA   Good. We're on our way.

MRS. ELVSTED   No, no, no! I'd rather go home alone! Right now!

HEDDA   Nonsense! First you're going to have some tea, you little bubble-head, and then—at ten o'clock—Eilert Løvborg—with vine leaves in his hair! [*She pulls Mrs. Elvsted toward the doorway almost by force.*]

3. That is, adorned like Dionysus, the Greek god of wine, whose worship is associated with mad frenzy (his rites were called orgies) and with the origins of Greek tragedy.

Act 3

The room at the Tesmans'. The curtains are drawn across the center doorway and also across the glass door. The lamp covered with a shade burns low on the table. In the stove, with its door standing open, there has been a fire that is almost burned out.

> [*Mrs. Elvsted, wrapped in a large shawl and with her feet on a footstool, sits sunk back in an armchair. Hedda, fully dressed, lies sleeping on the sofa with a rug over her.*]

MRS. ELVSTED [*After a pause suddenly straightens herself in the chair and listens intently. Then she sinks back wearily and moans softly.*]   Still not back . . . Oh God, oh God . . . Still not back.

> [*Berta enters tiptoeing carefully through the hall doorway; she has a letter in her hand.*]

MRS. ELVSTED   Ah—did someone come?

BERTA   Yes, a girl came by just now with this letter.

5 MRS. ELVSTED [*Quickly stretching out her hand.*]   A letter? Let me have it.

BERTA   No ma'am, it's for the doctor.

MRS. ELVSTED   Oh.

BERTA   It was Miss Tesman's maid who brought it. I'll put it on the table here.

10 MRS. ELVSTED   Yes, do that.

BERTA [*Puts down the letter.*]   I'd better put out the lamp; it's starting to smoke.

MRS. ELVSTED   Yes, put it out. It'll be light soon anyway.

BERTA [*Putting out the light.*]   Oh, ma'am, it's already light.

15 MRS. ELVSTED   So, morning and still not back—!

BERTA   Oh, dear Lord—I knew all along it would go like this.

MRS. ELVSTED   You knew?

BERTA   Yes, when I saw a certain person was back in town. And then when he went off with them—oh we'd heard plenty about that gentleman.

20 MRS. ELVSTED   Don't speak so loud, you'll wake your mistress.

BERTA [*Looks over to the sofa and sighs.*]   No, dear Lord—let her sleep, poor thing. Shouldn't I build the stove up a little more?

MRS. ELVSTED   Not for me, thanks.

BERTA   Well, well then. [*She goes out quietly through the hall doorway.*]

25 HEDDA [*Awakened by the closing door, looks up.*]   What's that?

MRS. ELVSTED   Only the maid.

HEDDA [*Looking around.*]   In here—! Oh, now I remember. [*Straightens up, stretches sitting on the sofa and rubs her eyes.*] What time is it, Thea?

MRS. ELVSTED [*Looks at her watch.*]   It's after seven.

30 HEDDA   What time did Tesman get in?

MRS. ELVSTED   He hasn't.

HEDDA   Still?

MRS. ELVSTED [*Getting up.*]   No one's come back.

HEDDA   And we sat here waiting and watching until almost four.

35 MRS. ELVSTED [*Wringing her hands.*]   Waiting for him!

HEDDA [*Yawning and speaking with her hand over her mouth.*]   Oh yes—we could have saved ourselves the trouble.

MRS. ELVSTED   Did you finally manage to sleep?

HEDDA   Yes, I think I slept quite well. Did you?

40 MRS. ELVSTED   Not a wink. I couldn't, Hedda. It was just impossible for me.

HEDDA [*Gets up and goes over to her.*]   Now, now, now. There's nothing to worry about. I know perfectly well how it all turned out.

MRS. ELVSTED   Yes, what do you think? Can you tell me?

HEDDA   Well, of course they dragged it out dreadfully up at Judge Brack's.

45   MRS. ELVSTED   Oh God yes—that must be true. But all the same—

HEDDA   And then you see, Tesman didn't want to come home and create a fuss by ringing the bell in the middle of the night. [*Laughing.*] He probably didn't want to show himself either right after a wild party like that.

MRS. ELVSTED   For goodness sake—where would he have gone?

50   HEDDA   Well, naturally, he went over to his aunts' and laid himself down to sleep there. They still have his old room standing ready for him.

MRS. ELVSTED   No, he's not with them. A letter just came for him from Miss Tesman. It's over there.

HEDDA   Oh? [*Looks at the inscription.*] Yes, that's Aunt Julie's hand all right.

55   So then, he's still over at Judge Brack's and Eilert Løvborg—he's sitting—reading aloud with vine leaves in his hair.

MRS. ELVSTED   Oh, Hedda, you don't even believe what you're saying.

HEDDA   You are such a little noodlehead, Thea.

MRS. ELVSTED   Yes, unfortunately I probably am.

60   HEDDA   And you look like you're dead on your feet.

MRS. ELVSTED   Yes, I am. Dead on my feet.

HEDDA   And so now you're going to do what I tell you. You'll go into my room and lie down on my bed.

MRS. ELVSTED   Oh no, no—I couldn't get to sleep anyway.

65   HEDDA   Yes, you certainly will.

MRS. ELVSTED   But your husband's bound to be home any time now and I've got to find out right away—

HEDDA   I'll tell you as soon as he comes.

MRS. ELVSTED   Promise me that, Hedda?

70   HEDDA   Yes, that you can count on. Now just go in and sleep for a while.

MRS. ELVSTED   Thanks. At least I'll give it a try. [*She goes in through the back room.*]

> [*Hedda goes over to the glass door and draws back the curtains. Full daylight floods the room. She then takes a small hand mirror from the writing table, looks in it and arranges her hair. Then she goes to the hall door and presses the bell. Soon after Berta enters the doorway.*]

BERTA   Did Madam want something?

HEDDA   Yes, build up the stove a little bit. I'm freezing in here.

BERTA   Lord, in no time at all it'll be warm in here. [*She rakes the embers
75   and puts a log inside. She stands and listens.*] There's the front doorbell, Madam.

HEDDA   So, go answer it. I'll take care of the stove myself.

BERTA   It'll be burning soon enough. [*She goes out through the hall door.*]

> [*Hedda kneels on the footstool and puts more logs into the stove. After a brief moment, George Tesman comes in from the hall. He looks weary and rather serious. He creeps on tiptoes toward the doorway and is about to slip through the curtains.*]

HEDDA [*By the stove, without looking up.*]   Good morning.

80   TESMAN [*Turning around.*]   Hedda. [*Comes nearer.*] What in the world—Up so early, hm?

HEDDA   Yes, up quite early today.

TESMAN   And here I was so sure you'd still be in bed. Just think, Hedda.

HEDDA   Not so loud. Mrs. Elvsted's lying down in my room.

85 TESMAN   Has Mrs. Elvsted been here all night?

HEDDA   Yes. No one came to pick her up.

TESMAN   No, no, they couldn't have.

HEDDA [*Shuts the door of the stove and gets up.*]   So, did you have a jolly time at the Judge's?

90 TESMAN   Were you worried about me?

HEDDA   No, that would never occur to me. I asked if you had a good time.

TESMAN   Yes, I really did, for once, in a manner of speaking—Mostly in the beginning, I'd say. We'd arrived an hour early. How about that? And Brack had so much to get ready. But then Eilert read to me.

95 HEDDA [*Sits at the right of the table.*]   So, tell me.

TESMAN   Hedda, you can't imagine what this new work will be like. It's one of the most brilliant things ever written, no doubt about it. Think of that.

HEDDA   Yes, yes, but that's not what I'm interested in.

TESMAN   But I have to confess something, Hedda. After he read—something horrible came over me.

HEDDA   Something horrible?

TESMAN   I sat there envying Eilert for being able to write like that. Think of it, Hedda.

HEDDA   Yes, yes, I'm thinking.

105 TESMAN   And then, that whole time, knowing that he—even with all the incredible powers at his command—is still beyond redemption.

HEDDA   You mean he's got more of life's courage in him than the others?

TESMAN   No, for heaven sakes—he just has no control over his pleasures.

HEDDA   And what happened then—at the end?

110 TESMAN   Well, Hedda, I guess you'd have to say it was a bacchanal.

HEDDA   Did he have vine leaves in his hair?

TESMAN   Vine leaves? No, I didn't see anything like that. But he did make a long wild speech for the woman who had inspired him in his work. Yes— that's how he put it.

115 HEDDA   Did he name her?

TESMAN   No, he didn't, but I can only guess that it must be Mrs. Elvsted. Wouldn't you say?

HEDDA   Hmm—where did you leave him?

TESMAN   On the way back. Most of our group broke up at the same time and Brack came along with us to get a little fresh air. And you see, we agreed to follow Eilert home because—well—he was so far gone.

HEDDA   He must have been.

TESMAN   But here's the strangest part, Hedda! Or maybe I should say the saddest. I'm almost ashamed for Eilert's sake—to tell you—

125 HEDDA   So?

TESMAN   There we were walking along, you see, and I happened to drop back a bit, just for a couple of minutes, you understand.

HEDDA   Yes, yes, good Lord but—

TESMAN   And then when I was hurrying to catch up—can you guess what I found in the gutter, hm?

HEDDA   How can I possibly guess?

TESMAN   Don't ever tell a soul, Hedda. Do you hear? Promise me that for Eilert's sake. [*Pulls a package out of his coat pocket.*] Just think—this is what I found.

135 HEDDA That's the package he had with him here yesterday, isn't it?

TESMAN That's it. His precious, irreplaceable manuscript—all of it. And he's lost it—without even noticing it. Oh just think, Hedda—the pity of it—

HEDDA Well, why didn't you give it back to him right away?

TESMAN Oh, I didn't dare do that—The condition he was in—

140 HEDDA You didn't tell any of the others that you found it either?

TESMAN Absolutely not. I couldn't, you see, for Eilert's sake.

HEDDA So nobody knows you have Eilert's manuscript? Nobody at all?

TESMAN No. And they mustn't find out either.

HEDDA What did you talk to him about later?

145 TESMAN I didn't get a chance to talk to him any more. We got to the city limits, and he and a couple of the others went a different direction. Just think—

HEDDA Aha, they must have followed him home then.

TESMAN Yes, I suppose so. Brack also went his way.

HEDDA And, in the meantime, what became of the bacchanal?

150 TESMAN Well, I and some of the others followed one of the revelers up to his place and had morning coffee with him—or maybe we should call it morning-after coffee, hm? Now, I'll rest a bit—and as soon as I think Eilert has managed to sleep it off, poor man, then I've got to go over to him with this.

HEDDA [*Reaching out for the envelope.*] No, don't give it back. Not yet, I

155 mean. Let me read it first.

TESMAN Oh no.

HEDDA Oh, for God's sake.

TESMAN I don't dare do that.

HEDDA You don't dare?

160 TESMAN No, you can imagine how completely desperate he'll be when he wakes up and realizes he can't find the manuscript. He's got no copy of it. He said so himself.

HEDDA [*Looks searchingly at him.*] Couldn't it be written again?

TESMAN No, I don't believe that could ever be done because the inspiration—

165 you see—

HEDDA Yes, yes—That's the thing, isn't it? [*Casually.*] But, oh yes—there's a letter here for you.

TESMAN No, think of that.

HEDDA [*Hands it to him.*] It came early this morning.

170 TESMAN From Aunt Julie, Hedda. What can it be? [*Puts the manuscript on the other stool, opens the letter and jumps up.*] Oh Hedda—poor Aunt Rina's almost breathing her last.

HEDDA It's only what's expected.

TESMAN And if I want to see her one more time, I've got to hurry. I'll charge

175 over there right away.

HEDDA [*Suppressing a smile.*] You'll charge?

TESMAN Oh, Hedda dearest—if you could just bring yourself to follow me. Just think.

HEDDA [*Rises and says wearily and dismissively.*] No, no. Don't ask me to do

180 anything like that. I won't look at sickness and death. Let me stay free from everything ugly.

TESMAN Oh, good Lord, then— [*Darting around.*] My hat—? My overcoat—? Ah, in the hall—Oh, I hope I'm not too late, Hedda, hm?

HEDDA Then charge right over—

[*Berta appears in the hallway.*]

185 BERTA   Judge Brack is outside.

HEDDA   Ask him to come in.

TESMAN   At a time like this! No, I can't possibly deal with him now.

HEDDA   But I can. [*To Berta.*] Ask the Judge in.

[*Berta goes out.*]

HEDDA [*In a whisper.*]   The package, Tesman. [*She snatches it off the stool.*]

190 TESMAN   Yes, give it to me.

HEDDA   No, I'll hide it until you get back.

[*She goes over to the writing table and sticks the package in the book-case. Tesman stands flustered, and can't get his gloves on. Brack enters through the hall doorway.*]

HEDDA [*Nodding to him.*]   Well, you're an early bird.

BRACK   Yes, wouldn't you say. [*To Tesman.*] You're going out?

TESMAN   Yes, I've got to go over to my aunt's. Just think, the poor dear is dying.

195 BRACK   Good Lord, is she really? Then don't let me hold you up for even a moment, at a time like this—

TESMAN   Yes, I really must run—Good-bye. Good-bye. [*He hurries through the hall doorway.*]

HEDDA [*Approaches.*]   So, things were livelier than usual at your place last night, Judge.

200 BRACK   Oh yes, so much so that I haven't even been able to change clothes, Mrs. Hedda.

HEDDA   You too.

BRACK   As you see. But, what has Tesman been telling you about last night's adventures?

205 HEDDA   Oh, just some boring things. He went someplace to drink coffee.

BRACK   I've already looked into the coffee party. Eilert Løvborg wasn't part of that group, I presume.

HEDDA   No, they followed him home before that.

BRACK   Tesman too?

210 HEDDA   No, but a couple of others, he said.

BRACK [*Smiles.*]   George Tesman is a very naïve soul, Mrs. Hedda.

HEDDA   God knows, he is. But is there something more behind this?

BRACK   I'd have to say so.

HEDDA   Well then, Judge, let's be seated. Then you can speak freely. [*She sits*
215 *to the left side of the table, Brack at the long side near her.*] Well, then—

BRACK   I had certain reasons for keeping track of my guests—or, more precisely, some of my guests' movements last night.

HEDDA   For example, Eilert Løvborg?

BRACK   Yes, indeed.

220 HEDDA   Now I'm hungry for more.

BRACK   Do you know where he and a couple of the others spent the rest of the night, Mrs. Hedda?

HEDDA   Why don't you tell me, if it can be told.

BRACK   Oh, it's certainly worth the telling. It appears that they found their
225 way into a particularly animated soirée.

HEDDA   A lively one?

BRACK   The liveliest.

HEDDA   Tell me more, Judge.

BRACK   Løvborg had received an invitation earlier—I knew all about that.
230 But he declined because, as you know, he's made himself into a new man.

HEDDA   Up at the Elvsteds', yes. But he went just the same?

BRACK   Well, you see, Mrs. Hedda—unfortunately, the spirit really seized him at my place last evening.

HEDDA   Yes, I hear he was quite inspired.

235 BRACK   Inspired to a rather powerful degree. And so, he started to reconsider, I assume, because we men, alas, are not always so true to our principles as we ought to be.

HEDDA   Present company excepted, Judge Brack. So, Løvborg—?

BRACK   Short and sweet—He ended up at the salon of a certain Miss Diana.

240 HEDDA   Miss Diana?

BRACK   Yes, it was Miss Diana's soirée for a select circle of ladies and their admirers.

HEDDA   Is she a redhead?

BRACK   Exactly.

245 HEDDA   A sort of a—singer?

BRACK   Oh, yes—She's also that. And a mighty huntress—of men,[4] Mrs. Hedda. You must have heard of her. Eilert Løvborg was one of her most strenuous admirers—in his better days.

HEDDA   And how did all this end?

250 BRACK   Apparently less amicably than it began. Miss Diana, after giving him the warmest of welcomes, soon turned to assault and battery.

HEDDA   Against Løvborg?

BRACK   Oh, yes. He accused her, or one of her ladies, of robbing him. He insisted that his pocketbook was missing, along with some other things. In

255 short, he seems to have created a dreadful spectacle.

HEDDA   And what did that lead to?

BRACK   A regular brawl between both the men and the women. Luckily the police finally got there.

HEDDA   The police too?

260 BRACK   Yes. It's going to be quite a costly little romp for Eilert Løvborg. What a madman.

HEDDA   Well!

BRACK   Apparently, he resisted arrest. It seems he struck one of the officers on the ear, and ripped his uniform to shreds, so he had to go to the police

265 station.

HEDDA   How do you know all this?

BRACK   From the police themselves.

HEDDA [Gazing before her.]   So, that's how it ended? He had no vine leaves in his hair.

270 BRACK   Vine leaves, Mrs. Hedda?

HEDDA [Changing her tone.]   Tell me now, Judge, why do you go around snooping and spying on Eilert Løvborg?

BRACK   For starters, I'm not a completely disinterested party—especially if the hearing uncovers the fact that he came straight from my place.

275 HEDDA   There's going to be a hearing?

BRACK   You can count on it. Be that as it may, however—My real concern was my duty as a friend of the house to inform you and Tesman of Løvborg's nocturnal adventures.

HEDDA   Why, Judge Brack?

4. Diana was the Roman virgin goddess of the hunt.

280 BRACK   Well, I have an active suspicion that he'll try to use you as a kind of
  screen.

HEDDA   Oh! What makes you think that?

BRACK   Good God—we're not that blind, Mrs. Hedda. Wait and see. This
  Mrs. Elvsted—she won't be in such a hurry to leave town again.

285 HEDDA   If there's anything going on between those two, there's plenty of
  places they can meet.

BRACK   Not one single home. Every respectable house will be closed to Eilert
  Løvborg from now on.

HEDDA   And mine should be too—Is that what you're saying?

290 BRACK   Yes. I have to admit it would be more than painful for me if this man
  secured a foothold here. If this—utterly superfluous—and intrusive
  individual—were to force himself into—

HEDDA   Into the triangle?

BRACK   Precisely! It would leave me without a home.

295 HEDDA [*Looks smilingly at him.*]   I see—The one cock of the walk—That's
  your goal.

BRACK [*Slowly nodding and dropping his voice.*]   Yes, that's my goal. And it's a
  goal that I'll fight for—with every means at my disposal.

HEDDA [*Her smile fading.*]   You're really a dangerous man, aren't you—when
300 push comes to shove.

BRACK   You think so?

HEDDA   Yes, I'm starting to. And that's all right—just as long as you don't
  have any kind of hold on me.

BRACK [*Laughing ambiguously.*]   Yes, Mrs. Hedda—you might be right
305 about that. Of course, then, who knows whether I might not find some
  way or other—

HEDDA   Now listen, Judge Brack! That sounds like you're threatening me.

BRACK [*Gets up.*]   Oh, far from it. A triangle, you see—is best fortified by free
  defenders.

310 HEDDA   I think so too.

BRACK   Well, I've had my say so I should be getting back. Good-bye, Mrs.
  Hedda. [*He goes toward the glass doors.*]

HEDDA   Out through the garden?

BRACK   Yes, it's shorter for me.

315 HEDDA   And then, it's also the back way.

BRACK   That's true. I have nothing against back ways. Sometimes they can
  be very piquant.

HEDDA   When there's sharpshooting.

BRACK [*In the doorway, laughing at her.*]   Oh, no—you never shoot your tame
320 cocks.

HEDDA [*Also laughing.*]   Oh, no, especially when there's only one—
  [*Laughing and nodding they take their farewells. He leaves. She closes
  the door after him. Hedda stands for a while, serious, looking out. Then
  she goes and peers through the curtains in the back wall. She goes to the
  writing table, takes Løvborg's package from the bookcase, and is about to
  leaf through it. Berta's voice, raised in indignation, is heard out in the
  hall. Hedda turns and listens. She quickly locks the package in the
  drawer and sets the key on the writing table. Eilert Løvborg, wearing his
  overcoat and carrying his hat, bursts through the hall doorway. He looks
  somewhat confused and excited.*]

LØVBORG [*Turned toward the hallway.*]   And I'm telling you, I've got to go in! And that's that! [*He closes the door, sees Hedda, controls himself immediately, and bows.*]

HEDDA [*By the writing table.*]   Well, Mr. Løvborg, it's pretty late to be calling for Thea.

325

LØVBORG   Or a little early to be calling on you. I apologize.

HEDDA   How do you know that she's still here?

LØVBORG   I went to where she was staying. They told me she'd been out all night.

330 HEDDA [*Goes to the table.*]   Did you notice anything special when they told you that?

LØVBORG [*Looks inquiringly at her.*]   Notice anything?

HEDDA   I mean—did they seem to have any thought on the subject—one way or the other?

335 LØVBORG [*Suddenly understanding.*]   Oh, of course, it's true. I'm dragging her down with me. Still, I didn't notice anything. Tesman isn't up yet, I suppose?

HEDDA   No, I don't think so.

LØVBORG   When did he get home?

HEDDA   Very late.

340 LØVBORG   Did he tell you anything?

HEDDA   Yes. I heard Judge Brack's was very lively.

LØVBORG   Nothing else?

HEDDA   No, I don't think so. I was terribly tired, though—

[*Mrs. Elvsted comes in through the curtains at the back.*]

MRS. ELVSTED [*Runs toward him.*]   Oh, Løvborg—at last!

345 LØVBORG   Yes, at last, and too late.

MRS. ELVSTED [*Looking anxiously at him.*]   What's too late?

LØVBORG   Everything's too late. I'm finished.

MRS. ELVSTED   Oh no, no—Don't say that!

LØVBORG   You'll say it too, when you've heard—

350 MRS. ELVSTED   I won't listen—

HEDDA   Shall I leave you two alone?

LØVBORG   No, stay—You too, I beg you.

MRS. ELVSTED   But I won't listen to anything you tell me.

LØVBORG   I don't want to talk about last night.

355 MRS. ELVSTED   What is it, then?

LØVBORG   We've got to go our separate ways.

MRS. ELVSTED   Separate!

HEDDA [*Involuntarily.*]   I knew it!

LØVBORG   Because I have no more use for you, Thea.

360 MRS. ELVSTED   You can stand there and say that! No more use for me! Can't I help you now, like I did before? Won't we go on working together?

LØVBORG   I don't plan to work any more.

MRS. ELVSTED [*Desperately.*]   Then what do I have to live for?

LØVBORG   Just try to live your life as if you'd never known me.

365 MRS. ELVSTED   I can't do that.

LØVBORG   Try, Thea. Try, if you can. Go back home.

MRS. ELVSTED [*Defiantly.*]   Where you are, that's where I want to be. I won't let myself be just driven off like this. I want to stay at your side—be with you when the book comes out.

370 HEDDA [*Half aloud, tensely.*]   Ah, the book—Yes.

LØVBORG [*Looking at her.*]   Mine and Thea's, because that's what it is.

MRS. ELVSTED   Yes, that's what I feel it is. That's why I have a right to be with you when it comes out. I want to see you covered in honor and glory again, and the joy. I want to share that with you too.

375 LØVBORG   Thea—our book's never coming out.

HEDDA   Ah!

MRS. ELVSTED   Never coming out?

LØVBORG   It can't ever come out.

MRS. ELVSTED [*In anxious foreboding.*]   Løvborg, what have you done with
380 the manuscript?

HEDDA [*Looking intently at him.*]   Yes, the manuscript—?

MRS. ELVSTED   What have you—?

LØVBORG   Oh, Thea, don't ask me that.

MRS. ELVSTED   Yes, yes, I've got to know. I have the right to know.

385 LØVBORG   The manuscript—all right then, the manuscript—I've ripped it up into a thousand pieces.

MRS. ELVSTED [*Screams.*]   Oh no, no!

HEDDA [*Involuntarily.*]   But that's just not—!

LØVBORG [*Looking at her.*]   Not true, you think?

390 HEDDA [*Controls herself.*]   All right then. Of course it is, if you say so. It sounds so ridiculous.

LØVBORG   But it's true, just the same.

MRS. ELVSTED [*Wringing her hands.*]   Oh God—oh God, Hedda. Torn his own work to pieces.

395 LØVBORG   I've torn my own life to pieces. I might as well tear up my life's work too—

MRS. ELVSTED   And you did that last night!

LØVBORG   Yes. Do you hear me? A thousand pieces. Scattered them all over the fjord. Way out where there's pure salt water. Let them drift in it. Drift
400 with the current in the wind. Then, after a while, they'll sink. Deeper and deeper. Like me, Thea.

MRS. ELVSTED   You know, Løvborg, all this with the book—? For the rest of my life, it will be just like you'd killed a little child.

LØVBORG   You're right. Like murdering a child.

405 MRS. ELVSTED   But then, how could you—! That child was partly mine, too.

HEDDA [*Almost inaudibly.*]   Ah, the child—

MRS. ELVSTED [*Sighs heavily.*]   So it's finished? All right, Hedda, now I'm going.

HEDDA   You're not going back?

410 MRS. ELVSTED   Oh, I don't know what I'm going to do. I can't see anything out in front of me. [*She goes out through the hall doorway.*]

HEDDA [*Standing a while, waiting.*]   Don't you want to see her home, Mr. Løvborg?

LØVBORG   Through the streets? So that people can get a good look at us
415 together?

HEDDA   I don't know what else happened to you last night but if it's so completely beyond redemption—

LØVBORG   It won't stop there. I know that much. And I can't bring myself to live that kind of life again either. Not again. Once I had the courage to live
420 life to the fullest, to break every rule. But she's taken that out of me.

HEDDA [*Staring straight ahead.*]   That sweet little fool has gotten hold of a
human destiny. [*Looks at him.*] And you're so heartless to her.

LØVBORG   Don't call it heartless.

HEDDA   To go and destroy the thing that has filled her soul for this whole
425   long, long time. You don't call that heartless?

LØVBORG   I can tell you the truth, Hedda.

HEDDA   The truth?

LØVBORG   First, promise me—Give me your word that Thea will never find
out what I'm about to confide to you.

430   HEDDA   You have my word.

LØVBORG   Good. Then I'll tell you—What I stood here and described—It
wasn't true.

HEDDA   About the manuscript?

LØVBORG   Yes. I haven't ripped it up. I didn't throw it in the fjord, either.

435   HEDDA   No, well—so—Where is it?

LØVBORG   I've destroyed it just the same. Utterly and completely, Hedda!

HEDDA   I don't understand any of this.

LØVBORG   Thea said that what I'd done seemed to her like murdering a
child.

440   HEDDA   Yes, she did.

LØVBORG   But killing his child—that's not the worst thing a father can do to it.

HEDDA   Not the worst?

LØVBORG   No. And the worst—that is what I wanted to spare Thea from
hearing.

445   HEDDA   And what is the worst?

LØVBORG   Imagine, Hedda, a man—in the very early hours of the morning—
after a wild night of debauchery, came home to the mother of his child and
said, "Listen—I've been here and there to this place and that place, and I
had our child with me in this place and that place. And the child got away
450   from me. Just got away. The devil knows whose hands it's fallen into, who's
got a hold of it."

HEDDA   Well—when you get right down to it—it's only a book—

LØVBORG   All of Thea's soul was in that book.

HEDDA   Yes, I can see that.

455   LØVBORG   And so, you must also see that there's no future for her and me.

HEDDA   So, what will your road be now?

LØVBORG   None. Only to see to it that I put an end to it all. The sooner the
better.

HEDDA [*Comes a step closer.*]   Eilert Løvborg—Listen to me now—Can you
460   see to it that—that when you do it, you bathe it in beauty?

LØVBORG   In beauty? [*Smiles.*] With vine leaves in my hair, as you used to
imagine?

HEDDA   Ah, no. No vine leaves—I don't believe in them any longer. But in
beauty, yes! For once! Good-bye. You've got to go now. And don't come here
465   any more.

LØVBORG   Good-bye, Mrs. Tesman. And give my regards to George Tesman.
[*He is about to leave.*]

HEDDA   No, wait! Take a souvenir to remember me by.

[*She goes over to the writing table, opens the drawer and the pistol case.
She returns to Løvborg with one of the pistols.*]

LØVBORG [*Looks at her.*]   That's the souvenir?

HEDDA [*Nodding slowly.*] Do you recognize it? It was aimed at you once.

470 LØVBORG You should have used it then.

HEDDA Here, you use it now.

LØVBORG [*Puts the pistol in his breast pocket.*] Thanks.

HEDDA In beauty, Eilert Løvborg. Promise me that.

LØVBORG Good-bye, Hedda Gabler. [*He goes out the hall doorway.*]

[*Hedda listens a moment at the door. Afterward, she goes to the writing table and takes out the package with the manuscript, looks inside the wrapper, pulls some of the pages half out and looks at them. She then takes it all over to the armchair by the stove and sits down. She has the package in her lap. Soon after she opens the stove door and then opens the package.*]

475 HEDDA [*Throws one of the sheets into the fire and whispers to herself.*] Now, I'm burning your child, Thea—You with your curly hair. [*Throws a few more sheets into the fire.*] Your child and Eilert Løvborg's. [*Throws in the rest.*] Now I'm burning—burning the child.

Act 4

The same room at the Tesmans'. It is evening. The drawing room is in darkness. The rear room is lit with a hanging lamp over the table. The curtains are drawn across the glass door.

[*Hedda, dressed in black, wanders up and down in the darkened room. Then she goes into the rear room, and over to the left side. Some chords are heard from the piano. Then she emerges again, and goes into the drawing room. Berta comes in from the right of the rear room, with a lighted lamp, which she places on the table in front of the sofa, in the salon. Her eyes show signs of crying, and she has black ribbons on her cap.[5] She goes quietly and carefully to the right. Hedda goes over to the glass door, draws the curtains aside a little, and stares out into the darkness. Soon after, Miss Tesman enters from the hallway dressed in black with a hat and a veil. Hedda goes over to her and shakes her hand.*]

MISS TESMAN Yes, here I am, Hedda—in mourning black. My poor sister's struggle is over at last.

HEDDA As you can see, I've already heard. Tesman sent me a note.

MISS TESMAN Yes, he promised he would but I thought I should bring the
5 news myself. This news of death into this house of life.

HEDDA That was very kind of you.

MISS TESMAN Ah, Rina shouldn't have left us right now. Hedda's house is no place for sorrow at a time like this.

HEDDA [*Changing the subject.*] She died peacefully, Miss Tesman?

10 MISS TESMAN Yes, so gently—Such a peaceful release. And she was happy beyond words that she got to see George once more and could say a proper good-bye to him. Is it possible he's not home yet?

HEDDA No. He wrote saying I shouldn't expect him too early. But, please sit down.

15 MISS TESMAN No, thank you, my dear—blessed Hedda. I'd like to, but I have so little time. She'll be dressed and arranged the best that I can. She'll look really splendid when she goes to her grave.

HEDDA Can I help you with anything?

5. Worn to signify mourning.

MISS TESMAN   Oh, don't even think about it. These kinds of things aren't for
20   Hedda Tesman's hands or her thoughts either. Not at this time. No, no.
HEDDA   Ah—thoughts—Now they're not so easy to master—
MISS TESMAN [*Continuing.*]   Yes, dear God, that's how this world goes. Over
at my house we'll be sewing a linen shroud for Aunt Rina, and here there
will be sewing too, but of a whole different kind, praise God.

[*George Tesman enters through a hall door.*]

25   HEDDA   Well, it's good you're finally here.
TESMAN   You here, Aunt Julie, with Hedda. Just think.
MISS TESMAN   I was just about to go, my dear boy. Well. Did you manage to
finish everything you promised to?
TESMAN   No, I'm afraid I've forgotten half of it. I have to run over there
30   tomorrow again. Today my brain is just so confused. I can't keep hold of
two thoughts in a row.
MISS TESMAN   George, my dear, you mustn't take it like that.
TESMAN   Oh? How should I take it, do you think?
MISS TESMAN   You must be joyful in your sorrow. You must be glad for what
35   has happened, just as I am.
TESMAN   Ah, yes. You're thinking of Aunt Rina.
HEDDA   You'll be lonely now, Miss Tesman.
MISS TESMAN   For the first few days, yes. But that won't last long, I hope. Our
sainted Rina's little room won't stand empty. That much I know.
40   TESMAN   Really? Who'll be moving in there, hm?
MISS TESMAN   Oh, there's always some poor invalid or other who needs care
and attention, unfortunately.
HEDDA   You'd really take on a cross like that again?
MISS TESMAN   Cross? God forgive you child. It's not a cross for me.
45   HEDDA   But a complete stranger—
MISS TESMAN   It's easy to make friends with sick people. And I so badly need
someone to live for. Well, God be praised and thanked—there'll be a thing
or two to keep an old aunt busy here in this house soon enough.
HEDDA   Oh, please don't think about us.
50   TESMAN   Yes. The three of us could be quite cozy here if only—
HEDDA   If only—?
TESMAN [*Uneasily.*]   Oh, it's nothing. Everything'll be fine. Let's hope, hm?
MISS TESMAN   Well, well, you two have plenty to talk about, I'm sure. [*Smil-
ing.*] And Hedda may have something to tell you, George. Now it's home to
55   Rina. [*Turning in the doorway.*] Dear Lord, isn't it strange to think about.
Now Rina's both with me and our sainted Joseph.
TESMAN   Yes, just think, Aunt Julie, hm?

[*Miss Tesman leaves through the hall door.*]

HEDDA [*Follows Tesman with cold, searching eyes.*]   I think all this has hit you
harder than your aunt.
60   TESMAN   Oh, it's not just this death. It's Eilert I'm worried about.
HEDDA [*Quickly.*]   Any news?
TESMAN   I wanted to run to him this afternoon and tell him that his manuscript was safe—in good hands.
HEDDA   Oh? Did you find him?
65   TESMAN   No, he wasn't home. But later I met Mrs. Elvsted, and she told me
he'd been here early this morning.

HEDDA   Yes, just after you left.

TESMAN   And apparently he said that he'd ripped the manuscript up into a thousand pieces, hm?

70 HEDDA   That's what he said.

TESMAN   But, good God, he must have been absolutely crazy. So you didn't dare give it back to him, Hedda?

HEDDA   No, he didn't get it back.

TESMAN   But, you told him we had it?

75 HEDDA   No. [*Quickly.*]   Did you tell Mrs. Elvsted?

TESMAN   No, I didn't want to. But you should have told him. What would happen if in his desperation he went and did something to himself? Let me have the manuscript, Hedda. I'll run it over to him right away. Where did you put it?

80 HEDDA [*Cold and impassively leaning on the armchair.*]   I don't have it any more.

TESMAN   Don't have it! What in the world do you mean?

HEDDA   I burned it up—every page.

TESMAN [*Leaps up in terror.*]   Burned? Burned? Eilert's manuscript!

85 HEDDA   Don't shout like that. The maid will hear you.

TESMAN   Burned! But good God—! No, no, no—That's absolutely impossible.

HEDDA   Yes, but all the same it's true.

TESMAN   Do you have any idea what you've done, Hedda? That's—that's criminal appropriation of lost property. Think about that. Yes, just ask

90 Judge Brack, then you'll see.

HEDDA   Then it's probably wise for you not to talk about it, isn't it? To the Judge or anyone else.

TESMAN   How could you have gone and done something so appalling? What came over you? Answer me that, Hedda, hm?

95 HEDDA [*Suppressing an almost imperceptible smile.*]   I did it for your sake, George.

TESMAN   My sake?

HEDDA   Remember you came home this morning and talked about how he had read to you?

100 TESMAN   Yes, yes.

HEDDA   You confessed that you envied him.

TESMAN   Good God, I didn't mean it literally.

HEDDA   Nevertheless, I couldn't stand the idea that someone would overshadow you.

105 TESMAN [*Exclaiming between doubt and joy.*]   Hedda—Oh, is this true?— What you're saying?—Yes, but. Yes, but. I never noticed that you loved me this way before. Think of that!

HEDDA   Well, you need to know—that at a time like this— [*Violently breaking off.*] No, no—go and ask your Aunt Julie. She'll provide all the details.

110 TESMAN   Oh, I almost think I understand you, Hedda. [*Clasps his hands together.*] No, good God—Can it be, hm?

HEDDA   Don't shout like that. The maid can hear you.

TESMAN [*Laughing in extraordinary joy.*]   The maid! Oh, Hedda, you are priceless. The maid—why it's—why it's Berta. I'll go tell Berta myself.

115 HEDDA [*Clenching her hands as if frantic.*]   Oh, I'm dying—Dying of all this.

TESMAN   All what, Hedda, what?

HEDDA [*Coldly controlled again.*]   All this—absurdity—George.

TESMAN   Absurdity? I'm so incredibly happy. Even so, maybe I shouldn't say anything to Berta.

120 HEDDA   Oh yes, go ahead. Why not?

TESMAN   No, no. Not right now. But Aunt Julie, yes, absolutely. And then, you're calling me George. Just think. Oh, Aunt Julie will be so happy—so happy.

HEDDA   When she hears I've burned Eilert Løvborg's manuscript for your
125 sake?

TESMAN   No, no, you're right. All this with the manuscript. No. Of course, nobody can find out about that. But, Hedda—you're burning for me—Aunt Julie really must share in that. But I wonder—all this—I wonder if it's typical with young wives, hm?

130 HEDDA   You'd better ask Aunt Julie about that too.

TESMAN   Oh yes, I certainly will when I get the chance. [*Looking uneasy and thoughtful again.*] No, but, oh no, the manuscript. Good Lord, it's awful to think about poor Eilert, just the same.

> [*Mrs. Elvsted, dressed as for her first visit with hat and coat, enters through the hall door.*]

MRS. ELVSTED   [*Greets them hurriedly and speaks in agitation.*]   Oh, Hedda,
135 don't be offended that I've come back again.

HEDDA   What happened to you, Thea?

TESMAN   Something about Eilert Løvborg?

MRS. ELVSTED   Oh yes, I'm terrified that he's had an accident.

HEDDA   [*Grips her arm.*]   Ah, do you think so?

140 TESMAN   Good Lord, where did you get that idea, Mrs. Elvsted?

MRS. ELVSTED   I heard them talking at the boarding house—just as I came in. There are the most incredible rumors about him going around town today.

TESMAN   Oh yes, imagine, I heard them too. And still I can swear he went
145 straight home to sleep. Just think.

HEDDA   So—What were they saying at the boarding house?

MRS. ELVSTED   Oh, I couldn't get any details, either because they didn't know or—or they saw me and stopped talking. And I didn't dare ask.

TESMAN   [*Uneasily pacing the floor.*]   Let's just hope—you misunderstood.

150 MRS. ELVSTED   No, I'm sure they were talking about him. Then I heard them say something about the hospital—

TESMAN   Hospital?

HEDDA   No—That's impossible.

MRS. ELVSTED   I'm deathly afraid for him, so I went up to his lodgings and
155 asked about him there.

HEDDA   You dared to do that?

MRS. ELVSTED   What else should I have done? I couldn't stand the uncertainty any longer.

TESMAN   You didn't find him there either, hm?

160 MRS. ELVSTED   No. And the people there didn't know anything at all. They said he hadn't been home since yesterday afternoon.

TESMAN   Yesterday? How could they say that?

MRS. ELVSTED   It could only mean one thing—Something terrible's happened to him.

165 TESMAN   You know, Hedda—What if I were to go into town and ask around at different places—?

HEDDA   No! You stay out of this.

[*Judge Brack, carrying his hat, enters through the hall door, which Berta opens and closes after him. He looks serious and bows in silence.*]

TESMAN   Oh, here you are, Judge, hm?

BRACK   Yes, it was essential for me to see you this evening.

170 TESMAN   I see you got the message from Aunt Julie.

BRACK   Yes, that too.

TESMAN   Isn't it sad, hm?

BRACK   Well, my dear Tesman, that depends on how you look at it.

TESMAN [*Looks at him uneasily.*]   Has anything else happened?

175 BRACK   Yes, it has.

HEDDA [*Tensely.*]   Something sad, Judge Brack?

BRACK   Once again, it depends on how you look at it, Mrs. Tesman.

MRS. ELVSTED [*In an uncontrollable outburst.*]   It's Eilert Løvborg.

BRACK [*Looks briefly at her.*]   How did you guess, Mrs. Elvsted? Do you
180   already know something—?

MRS. ELVSTED [*Confused.*]   No, no, I don't know anything but—

TESMAN   Well, for God's sake, tell us what it is.

BRACK [*Shrugging his shoulders.*]   Well then—I'm sorry to tell you—that Eilert Løvborg has been taken to the hospital. He is dying.

185 MRS. ELVSTED [*Crying out.*]   Oh God, oh God.

TESMAN   Dying?

HEDDA [*Involuntarily.*]   So quickly—?

MRS. ELVSTED [*Wailing.*]   And we were quarrelling when we parted, Hedda.

HEDDA [*Whispers.*]   Now, Thea—Thea.

190 MRS. ELVSTED [*Not noticing her.*]   I'm going to him. I've got to see him alive.

BRACK   It would do you no good, Mrs. Elvsted. No visitors are allowed.

MRS. ELVSTED   At least tell me what happened. What—?

TESMAN   Yes, because he certainly wouldn't have tried to—hm?

HEDDA   Yes, I'm sure that's what he did.

195 TESMAN   Hedda. How can you—

BRACK [*Who is watching her all the time.*]   Unfortunately, Mrs. Tesman, you've guessed right.

MRS. ELVSTED   Oh, how awful.

TESMAN   To himself, too. Think of it.

200 HEDDA   Shot himself!

BRACK   Right again, Mrs. Tesman.

MRS. ELVSTED [*Tries to compose herself.*]   When did this happen, Mr. Brack?

BRACK   Just this afternoon, between three and four.

TESMAN   Oh, my God—Where did he do it, hm?

205 BRACK [*Slightly uncertain.*]   Where? Oh, I suppose at his lodgings.

MRS. ELVSTED   No, that can't be. I was there between six and seven.

BRACK   Well then, some other place. I don't know precisely. All I know is that he was found—he'd shot himself—in the chest.

MRS. ELVSTED   Oh, how awful to think that he should die like that.

210 HEDDA [*To Brack.*]   In the chest?

BRACK   Yes, like I said.

HEDDA   Not through the temple?

BRACK   The chest, Mrs. Tesman.

HEDDA   Well, well. The chest is also good.

215 BRACK   What was that, Mrs. Tesman?

HEDDA [*Evasively.*]   Oh, nothing—nothing.

TESMAN   And the wound is fatal, hm?

BRACK   The wound is absolutely fatal. In fact, it's probably already over.

MRS. ELVSTED   Yes, yes, I can feel it. It's over. It's all over. Oh, Hedda—!

220 TESMAN   Tell me, how did you find out about all this?

BRACK [*Curtly.*]   From a police officer. One I spoke with.

HEDDA [*Raising her voice.*]   Finally—an action.

TESMAN   God help us, Hedda, what are you saying?

HEDDA   I'm saying that here, in this—there is beauty.

225 BRACK   Uhm, Mrs. Tesman.

TESMAN   Beauty! No, don't even think it.

MRS. ELVSTED   Oh, Hedda. How can you talk about beauty?

HEDDA   Eilert Løvborg has come to terms with himself. He's had the courage to do what had to be done.

230 MRS. ELVSTED   No, don't ever believe it was anything like that. What he did, he did in a moment of madness.

TESMAN   It was desperation.

MRS. ELVSTED   Yes, madness. Just like when he tore his book in pieces.

BRACK [*Startled.*]   The book. You mean his manuscript? Did he tear it up?

235 MRS. ELVSTED   Yes, last night.

TESMAN [*Whispering softly.*]   Oh, Hedda, we'll never get out from under all this.

BRACK   Hmm, that's very odd.

TESMAN [*Pacing the floor.*]   To think that Eilert Løvborg should leave the world this way. And then not to leave behind the work that would have

240 made his name immortal.

MRS. ELVSTED   Oh, what if it could be put together again.

TESMAN   Yes—just think—what if it could? I don't know what I wouldn't give—

MRS. ELVSTED   Maybe it can, Mr. Tesman.

TESMAN   What do you mean?

245 MRS. ELVSTED [*Searching in the pocket of her skirt.*]   See this? I saved all the notes he dictated from.

HEDDA [*A step closer.*]   Ah.

TESMAN   You saved them, Mrs. Elvsted, hm?

MRS. ELVSTED   Yes, they're all here. I brought them with me when I came to

250 town, and here they've been. Tucked away in my pocket—

TESMAN   Oh, let me see them.

MRS. ELVSTED [*Gives him a bundle of small papers.*]   But they're all mixed up, completely out of order.

TESMAN   Just think. What if we could sort them out. Perhaps if the two of us

255 helped each other.

MRS. ELVSTED   Oh yes. Let's at least give it a try—

TESMAN   It will happen. It must happen. I'll give my whole life to this.

HEDDA   You, George, your life?

TESMAN   Yes, or, anyway, all the time I have. Every spare minute. My own

260 research will just have to be put aside. Hedda—you understand, don't you, hm? I owe this to Eilert's memory.

HEDDA   Maybe so.

TESMAN   Now, my dear Mrs. Elvsted, let's pull ourselves together. God knows there's no point brooding about what's happened. We've got to try to find

265 some peace of mind so that—

MRS. ELVSTED   Yes, yes, Mr. Tesman. I'll do my best.

TESMAN   Well. So, come along then. We've got to get started on these notes right away. Where should we sit? Here? No. In the back room. Excuse us, Judge. Come with me, Mrs. Elvsted.

270 MRS. ELVSTED   Oh God—if only it can be done.

> [*Tesman and Mrs. Elvsted go into the rear room. She takes her hat and coat off. Both sit at the table under the hanging lamp and immerse themselves in eager examination of the papers. Hedda goes across to the stove and sits in the armchair. Soon after, Brack goes over to her.*]

HEDDA [*Softly.*]   Ah, Judge—This act of Eilert Løvborg's—there's a sense of liberation in it.

BRACK   Liberation, Mrs. Hedda? Yes, I guess it's a liberation for him, all right.

275 HEDDA   I mean, for me. It's a liberation for me to know that in this world an act of such courage, done in full, free will, is possible. Something bathed in a bright shaft of sudden beauty.

BRACK [*Smiles.*]   Hmm—Dear Mrs. Hedda—

HEDDA   Oh, I know what you're going to say, because you're a kind of spe-
280 cialist too, after all, just like—Ah well.

BRACK [*Looking steadily at her.*]   Eilert Løvborg meant more to you than you might admit—even to yourself. Or am I wrong?

HEDDA   I don't answer questions like that. All I know is that Eilert Løvborg had the courage to live life his own way, and now—his last great act—
285 bathed in beauty. He—had the will to break away from the banquet of life—so soon.

BRACK   It pains me, Mrs. Hedda—but I'm forced to shatter this pretty illusion of yours.

HEDDA   Illusion?

290 BRACK   Which would have been taken away from you soon enough.

HEDDA   And what's that?

BRACK   He didn't shoot himself—so freely.

HEDDA   Not freely?

BRACK   No. This whole Eilert Løvborg business didn't come off exactly the
295 way I described it.

HEDDA [*In suspense.*]   Are you hiding something? What is it?

BRACK   I employed a few euphemisms for poor Mrs. Elvsted's sake.

HEDDA   Such as—?

BRACK   First, of course, he's already dead.

300 HEDDA   At the hospital?

BRACK   Yes. And without regaining consciousness.

HEDDA   What else?

BRACK   The incident took place somewhere other than his room.

HEDDA   That's insignificant.

305 BRACK   Not completely. I have to tell you—Eilert Løvborg was found shot in—Miss Diana's boudoir.

HEDDA [*About to jump up but sinks back again.*]   That's impossible, Judge. He can't have gone there again today.

BRACK   He was there this afternoon. He came to demand the return of
310 something that he said they'd taken from him. He talked crazily about a lost child.

HEDDA   Ah, so that's why—

BRACK I thought maybe he was referring to his manuscript but I hear he'd already destroyed that himself so I guess it was his pocketbook.

315 HEDDA Possibly. So—that's where he was found.

BRACK Right there, with a discharged pistol in his coat pocket, and a fatal bullet wound.

HEDDA In the chest, yes?

BRACK No—lower down.

320 HEDDA [*Looks up at him with an expression of revulsion.*] That too! Oh absurdity—! It hangs like a curse over everything I so much as touch.

BRACK There's still one more thing, Mrs. Hedda. Also in the ugly category.

HEDDA And what is that?

BRACK The pistol he had with him—

325 HEDDA [*Breathless.*] Well, what about it?

BRACK He must have stolen it.

HEDDA [*Jumping up.*] Stolen? That's not true. He didn't.

BRACK There's no other explanation possible. He must have stolen it—Shh.

[*Tesman and Mrs. Elvsted have gotten up from the table in the rear room and come into the living room.*]

TESMAN [*With papers in both hands.*] Hedda, my dear—I can hardly see any-
330 thing in there under that lamp. Just think—

HEDDA I'm thinking.

TESMAN Do you think you might let us sit a while at your desk, hm?

HEDDA Oh, gladly. [*Quickly.*] No, wait. Let me just clean it up a bit first.

TESMAN Oh, not necessary, Hedda. There's plenty of room.

335 HEDDA No, no, I'll just straighten it up, I'm telling you. I'll just move these things here under the piano for a while.

[*She has pulled an object covered with sheet music out of the bookcase. She adds a few more sheets and carries the whole pile out to the left of the rear room. Tesman puts the papers on the desk and brings over the lamp from the corner table. He and Mrs. Elvsted sit and continue their work.*]

HEDDA Well, Thea, my sweet. Are things moving along with the memorial?

MRS. ELVSTED [*Looks up at her dejectedly.*] Oh, God—It's going to be so difficult to find the order in all of this.

340 TESMAN But it must be done. There's simply no other choice. And finding the order in other people's papers—that's precisely what I'm meant for.

[*Hedda goes over to the stove and sits on one of the stools. Brack stands over her, leaning over the armchair.*]

HEDDA [*Whispers.*] What were you saying about the pistol?

BRACK [*Softly.*] That he must have stolen it.

HEDDA Why stolen exactly?

345 BRACK Because there shouldn't be any other way to explain it, Mrs. Hedda.

HEDDA I see.

BRACK [*Looks briefly at her.*] Eilert Løvborg was here this morning, am I correct?

HEDDA Yes.

350 BRACK Were you alone with him?

HEDDA Yes, for a while.

BRACK You didn't leave the room at all while he was here?

HEDDA No.

BRACK Think again. Weren't you out of the room, even for one moment?

355 HEDDA   Yes. Perhaps. Just for a moment—out in the hallway.

BRACK   And where was your pistol case at that time?

HEDDA   I put it under the—

BRACK   Well, Mrs. Hedda—

HEDDA   It was over there on the writing table.

360 BRACK   Have you looked since then to see if both pistols are there?

HEDDA   No.

BRACK   It's not necessary. I saw the pistol Løvborg had, and I recognized it immediately from yesterday, and from before as well.

HEDDA   Have you got it?

365 BRACK   No, the police have it.

HEDDA   What will the police do with that pistol?

BRACK   Try to track down its owner.

HEDDA   Do you think they can do that?

BRACK [*Bends over her and whispers.*]   No, Hedda Gabler, not as long as I
370 keep quiet.

HEDDA [*Looking fearfully at him.*]   And what if you don't keep quiet—then what?

BRACK   Then the way out is to claim that the pistol was stolen.

HEDDA   I'd rather die.

BRACK [*Smiling.*]   People make those threats but they don't act on them.

375 HEDDA [*Without answering.*]   So—let's say the pistol is not stolen and the owner is found out? What happens then?

BRACK   Well, Hedda—then there'll be a scandal.

HEDDA   A scandal?

BRACK   Oh, yes, a scandal. Just what you're so desperately afraid of. You'd
380 have to appear in court, naturally. You and Miss Diana. She'd have to detail how it all occurred. Whether it was an accident or a homicide. Was he trying to draw the pistol to threaten her? Is that when the gun went off? Did she snatch it out of his hands to shoot him, and then put the pistol back in his pocket? That would be thoroughly in character for her. She's a feisty
385 little thing, that Miss Diana.

HEDDA   But all this ugliness has got nothing to do with me.

BRACK   No. But you would have to answer one question. Why did you give the pistol to Eilert Løvborg? And what conclusions would people draw from the fact that you gave it to him?

390 HEDDA [*Lowers her head.*]   That's true. I didn't think of that.

BRACK   Well. Fortunately you have nothing to worry about as long as I keep quiet.

HEDDA [*Looking up at him.*]   So I'm in your power now, Judge. You have a hold over me from now on.

395 BRACK [*Whispering more softly.*]   Dearest Hedda—Believe me—I won't abuse my position.

HEDDA   But in your power. Totally subject to your demands—And your will. Not free. Not free at all. [*She gets up silently.*] No, that's one thought I just can't stand. Never!

400 BRACK [*Looks mockingly at her.*]   One can usually learn to live with the inevitable.

HEDDA [*Returning his look.*]   Maybe so. [*She goes over to the writing table, suppressing an involuntary smile and imitating Tesman's intonation.*] Well, George, this is going to work out, hm?

405 TESMAN   Oh, Lord knows, dear. Anyway, at this rate, it's going to be months of work.

HEDDA [*As before.*]   No, just think. [*Runs her fingers lightly through Mrs. Elvsted's hair.*] Doesn't it seem strange, Thea. Here you are, sitting together with Tesman—just like you used to sit with Eilert Løvborg.

410 MRS. ELVSTED   Oh, God, if only I could inspire your husband too.

HEDDA   Oh, that will come—in time.

TESMAN   Yes, you know what, Hedda—I really think I'm beginning to feel something like that. But why don't you go over and sit with Judge Brack some more.

415 HEDDA   Can't you two find any use for me here?

TESMAN   No, nothing in the world. [*Turning his head.*] From now on, my dear Judge, you'll have to be kind enough to keep Hedda company.

BRACK [*With a glance at Hedda.*]   That will be an infinite pleasure for me.

HEDDA   Thanks, but I'm tired tonight. I'll go in there and lie down on the
420 sofa for a while.

TESMAN   Yes, do that, Hedda, hm?

[*Hedda goes into the rear room and draws the curtains after her. Short pause. Suddenly she is heard to play a wild dance melody on the piano.*]

MRS. ELVSTED [*Jumping up from her chair.*]   Oh—what's that?

TESMAN [*Running to the doorway.*]   Oh, Hedda, my dear—Don't play dance music tonight. Just think of poor Aunt Rina and of Eilert Løvborg too.

425 HEDDA [*Putting her head out from between the curtains.*]   And Aunt Julie and all the rest of them too. From now on I shall be quiet. [*She closes the curtains again.*]

TESMAN [*At the writing table.*]   This can't be making her very happy—Seeing us at this melancholy work. You know what, Mrs. Elvsted—You're going to move in with Aunt Julie. Then I can come over in the evening, and we can
430 sit and work there, hm?

MRS. ELVSTED   Yes, maybe that would be the best—

HEDDA [*From the rear room.*]   I can hear you perfectly well, Tesman. So, how am I supposed to get through the evenings out here?

TESMAN [*Leafing through the papers.*]   Oh, I'm sure Judge Brack will be good
435 enough to call on you.

BRACK [*In the armchair, shouts merrily.*]   I'd be delighted, Mrs. Tesman. Every evening. Oh, we're going to have some good times together, the two of us.

HEDDA [*Loudly and clearly.*]   Yes, that's what you're hoping for, isn't it, Judge? You, the one and only cock of the walk—

[*A shot is heard within. Tesman, Mrs. Elvsted and Brack all jump to their feet.*]

440 TESMAN   Oh, she's playing around with those pistols again.

[*He pulls the curtains aside and runs in. Mrs. Elvsted follows. Hedda is stretched out lifeless on the sofa. Confusion and cries. Berta comes running in from the right.*]

[*Shrieking to Brack.*] Shot herself! Shot herself in the temple! Just think!

BRACK [*Half prostrate in the armchair.*]   But God have mercy—People just don't act that way!

CRITICAL PERSPECTIVE

---◆---

GEORGE BERNARD SHAW

The Irish playwright, philosopher, and polemicist George Bernard Shaw (1856–1950) is one of the most significant names in modern drama. A fervent socialist who was fiercely devoted to issues of social justice and equality, Shaw was known for his biting wit, and was especially gifted in using comedy and satire to call attention to Victorian social ills. Many of his theatrical works grapple directly with social and political concerns.

Shaw's critical analysis *The Quintessence of Ibsenism* (1891) celebrates the plays of Henrik Ibsen, the realistic Norwegian dramatist whose reception in Victorian England had been marked by scandal. Here Shaw provides a reading of Ibsen's A DOLL HOUSE that emphasizes the psychological and moral complexity of the work. By describing the process through which Nora Helmer's enchanting illusions about her domestic life are painfully unraveled, Shaw calls the reader's attention to a central aim of dramatic realism: to unmask the fantasies of bourgeois life and enable the spectator to gain perspective on life as it really is.

M.P.

---

from *The Quintessence of Ibsenism*

---◆---

A DOLL'S HOUSE[1]

Unfortunately, *Pillars of Society*,[2] as a propagandist play, is disabled by the circumstance that the hero, being a fraudulent hypocrite in the ordinary police-court sense of the phrase, is not accepted as a typical pillar of society by the class which he represents. Accordingly, Ibsen took care next time to make his idealist irreproachable from the standpoint of the ordinary idealist morality. In the famous *Doll's House*, the pillar of society who owns the doll is a model husband, father, and citizen. In his little household, with the three darling children and the affectionate little wife, all on the most loving terms with one another, we have the sweet home, the womanly woman, the happy family life of the idealist's dream.

1. Here under the alternate title.
2. An 1877 play by Ibsen.

Mrs Nora Helmer is happy in the belief that she has attained a valid realization of all these illusions—that she is an ideal wife and mother, and that Helmer is an ideal husband who would, if the necessity arose, give his life to save her reputation. A few simply contrived incidents disabuse her effectually on all these points. One of her earliest acts of devotion to her husband has been the secret raising of a sum of money to enable him to make a tour which was necessary to restore his health. As he would have broken down sooner than go into debt, she has had to persuade him that the money was a gift from her father. It was really obtained from a money-lender, who refused to make her the loan unless she induced her father to endorse the promissory note. This being impossible, as her father was dying at the time, she took the shortest way out of the difficulty by writing the name herself, to the entire satisfaction of the moneylender, who, though not at all duped, knows that forged bills are often the surest to be paid. Then she slaves in secret at scrivener's[3] work until she has nearly paid off the debt. At this point Helmer is made manager of the bank in which he is employed; and the moneylender, wishing to obtain a post there, uses the forged bill to force Nora to exert her influence with Helmer on his behalf. But she, having a hearty contempt for the man, cannot be persuaded by him that there was any harm in putting her father's name on the bill, and ridicules the suggestion that the law would not recognize that she was right under the circumstances. It is her husband's own con-temptuous denunciation of a forgery formerly committed by the money-lender himself that destroys her self-satisfaction and opens her eyes to her ignorance of the serious business of the world to which her husband belongs—the world outside the home he shares with her. When he goes on to tell her that commercial dishonesty is generally to be traced to the influence of bad mothers, she begins to perceive that the happy way in which she plays with the children, and the care she takes to dress them nicely, are not sufficient to constitute her a fit person to train them. In order to redeem the forged bill, she resolves to borrow the balance due upon it from a friend of the family. She has learnt to coax her husband into giving her what she asks by appealing to his affection for her: that is, by playing all sorts of pretty tricks until he is wheedled into an amorous humour. This plan she has adopted without thinking about it, instinctively taking the line of least resistance with him. And now she naturally takes the same line with her husband's friend. An unexpected declaration of love from him is the result; and it at once explains to her the real nature of the domestic influence she has been so proud of. All her illusions about herself are now shattered: she sees herself as an ignorant and silly woman, a dangerous mother, and a wife kept for her husband's pleasure merely; but she only clings the harder to her illusion about him: he is still the ideal husband who would make any sacrifice to rescue her from ruin. She resolves to kill herself rather than allow him to destroy his own career by taking the forgery on himself to save her reputation. The final disillusion

3. A person employed in secretarial or administrative duties related to reading and writing.

comes when he, instead of at once proposing to pursue this ideal line of conduct when he hears of the forgery, naturally enough flies into a vulgar rage and heaps invective on her for disgracing him. Then she sees that their whole family life has been a fiction—their home a mere doll's house in which they have been playing at ideal husband and father, wife and mother. So she leaves him then and there in order to find out the reality of things for herself, and to gain some position not fundamentally false, refusing to see her children again until she is fit to be in charge of them, or to live with him until she and he become capable of a more honourable relation to one another than that in which they have hitherto stood. He at first cannot understand what has happened, and flourishes the shattered ideals over her as if they were as potent as ever. He presents the course most agreeable to him—that of her staying at home and avoiding a scandal—as her duty to her husband, to her children, and to her religion; but the magic of these disguises is gone; and at last even he understands what has really happened, and sits down alone to wonder whether that more honourable relation can ever come to pass between them.

* * *

OSCAR WILDE

1854–1900

Oscar Wilde cut a remarkable figure within the literary, cultural, and theatrical worlds of late nineteenth-century Britain. Dandy, man of letters, public speaker, proponent of aestheticism (the movement championing "Art for Art's Sake"), and prolific author of poetry, fiction, essays, children's stories, criticism, and drama, he entertained London high society with his epigrammatic wit even as he flouted some of the most deeply held values of late-Victorian society. His 1890 novel, *The Picture of Dorian Gray*, scandalized many of its readers with its decadence and perceived amorality, and his society comedies of the early 1890s both entertained and satirized their West End audience. Something of an outsider by virtue of his Irishness and homosexuality, he fashioned a distinctly modern form of celebrity that challenged the norms of Victorian respectability. But Wilde's position in the society of his day was, it turned out, a precarious one. In 1895, even as two of his dramas played on the West End, he was convicted and imprisoned on the charge of "gross indecency" after three sensational trials that represent, to this day, a landmark in the public perception of homosexuality. "I'll be a poet, a writer, a dramatist," he wrote to a friend before leaving Oxford University in 1878. "Somehow or other, I'll be famous, and if not famous, notorious."

One of the most accomplished writers for the theater in fin de siècle London, Oscar Wilde became, in the end, his own greatest drama.

Oscar Fingal O'Flahertie Wills Wilde was born in Dublin on October 16, 1854, to William Wilde, an eye and ear surgeon, and the former Jane Francesca Elgee, who wrote Irish Nationalist poetry under the pseudonym "Speranza." After graduating from Portora Royal School in Enniskillen, he attended Trinity College, Dublin, where he distinguished himself as a student of the classics; he won a number of awards, including the prestigious Berkeley Prize for Greek. In 1874 he was awarded a scholarship to Magdalen College, Oxford, which he attended for the next four years. Wilde later referred to two great turning points in his life: "the first when my father sent me to Oxford, the second when Society sent me to prison." At Oxford Wilde studied with John Ruskin and Walter Pater, two leading scholars of aesthetics. Pater exerted the most lasting influence on the young Irishman. In his recently published *Studies in the History of the Renaissance* (1873), Pater celebrated "poetic passion, the desire for beauty, and the love of art for art's sake." Wilde, who had been attracted to aestheticism even before he arrived in Oxford, adopted the movement's beliefs, manners, and poses. He wore his hair long, dressed flamboyantly, and decorated his room in the aesthetic mode, with such accessories as lilies (associated with the Pre-Raphaelite painters) and studiously artistic furnishings. "I find it harder and harder every day to live up to my blue china," he famously stated, and the mannered self-consciousness of such sentiments would make him one of England's most visible aesthetes. During this time Wilde also wrote many of the poems that would appear in an 1881 collection of verse.

When Wilde moved from Oxford to London in 1878, he quickly established himself in high society through his brilliant conversation and wit. Within two years the newspaper *Punch* was regularly caricaturing him as a figurehead of the aesthetic movement, and in 1881 W. S. Gilbert and Sir Arthur Sullivan's comic opera *Patience* satirized aestheticism through the "perfectly precious" Wilde-like character Bunthorne. When the producer of *Patience* took the opera on tour in the United States and Canada the following year, Wilde accompanied the production as a lecturer and representative aesthete. Wilde traveled from coast to coast; met Ulysses S. Grant, Walt Whitman, and other prominent Americans; and registered his impressions of the New World in such epigrams as this: "When good Americans die they go to Paris; when bad Americans die they stay in America." Back in England, Wilde toured the British Isles as lecturer, worked as a journalist and book reviewer, and assumed the editorship of *Woman's World*, a popular late-Victorian periodical. In 1884 Wilde married Constance Mary Lloyd, with whom he had two sons over the next two years. But while Wilde continued to entertain the fashionable society of London with his witty conversation, and while his marriage established a degree of social respectability, he was known for little beyond being a celebrity. That began to change in 1888 with the publication of *The Happy Prince and Other Tales*, the first of two collections of original fairy tales. Over the next seven years, Wilde published a collection of critical essays (which included "The Artist as Critic" [1890]); two additional collections of stories; *The Picture of Dorian Gray*, his novel about a hedonistic aristocrat that shocked the Victorian public; and his five major plays.

An avid theatergoer since his college days and a friend of such theater luminaries as the actresses Lillie Langtry and Sarah Bernhardt, Wilde first tried his hand at drama with *Vera; or, The Nihilists* and *The Duchess of Padua*, which were written in the early 1880s and given short runs in New York. In 1891 Wilde agreed to write a social comedy for George Alexander, manager of the St. James's Theatre, and it was this play that would catapult him to the forefront of the London theater scene. *Lady Windermere's Fan*, produced in 1892, uses the narrative frame of the "problem play"—a nineteenth-century dramatic genre that dealt with controversial social issues—but deploys provocative social commentary and witty epigram to undermine the comfortable moral conclusions that plays in this genre frequently adopted. The play was widely popular, and the attention it received was intensified by Wilde himself, who strolled onstage, cigarette in hand, to greet the opening night applause and congratulate the audience for thinking as highly of his play as he did. *Lady Windermere's Fan* was followed by three more extremely successful social comedies: *A Woman of No Importance* (1893), *An Ideal Husband* (1895), and—Wilde's greatest play—THE IMPORTANCE OF BEING EARNEST (1895). *Salomé*, which Wilde wrote in 1891, dramatized the love of Salomé, Herodias's daughter, for John the Baptist (or Iokanaan) and her incantatory dance with his severed head. Deeply influenced by the symbolist drama of Stéphane Mallarmé (1842–1898) and Maurice Maeterlinck (1862–1949), *Salomé* was refused production by the Lord Chamberlain, who invoked a centuries-old law that prohibited the theatrical depiction of biblical figures. Wilde's poetic tragedy would not be seen on the English stage until after the playwright's death.

But even as Wilde was establishing himself as London's leading literary figure, the elements of his precipitous change in fortune were being set in place. In 1891 he met Lord Alfred Douglas, third son of the ninth marquess of Queensberry, and the two became inseparable. It is not clear when Wilde first became involved in homosexual relationships, but by the 1890s he was leading an active hidden life in London and abroad. The antagonism of Douglas's father toward what he understood to be a scandalous connection came to a head in February 1895 when Queensberry delivered a card to the London club of which Wilde was a member with the inscription "To Oscar Wilde, posing Somdomite [sic]." Wilde took out a warrant charging Queensberry with criminal libel, and in April the case went to trial. When Queensberry presented a list of male prostitutes who would testify concerning Wilde's illegal activities, however, Wilde withdrew the prosecution and the marquess was acquitted. Wilde, who was quickly arrested, now found himself the defendant, and after two trials (the first ended with a hung jury), he was sentenced to two years' hard labor for homosexual conduct. Over the next twenty-four months he suffered the misery and deprivations of the Victorian prison system. Initially allowed only a Bible, hymnbook, and prayerbook, he was eventually able to obtain other books and writing materials. Under these somewhat more lenient conditions he wrote *De Profundis* (published in part in 1905; unexpurgated, in 1962), a book-length letter to Douglas that included a meditation on his own life and fate. When Wilde was released from prison in May 1897, he left for France and never again set foot in England. In 1898 Wilde published *The Ballad of Reading Gaol*—inspired by his experience in prison—but his career as a writer was effectively over. He died in Paris on November 30, 1900, at the age of forty-six.

In *De Profundis*, which became his own eulogy, Wilde summed up what he felt to be the nature of his contribution to the cultural and philosophical life of his times:

> I made art a philosophy, and philosophy an art: I altered the minds of men and the colors of things: there was nothing I said or did that did not make people wonder: I took the drama, the most objective form known to art, and made it as personal a mode of expression as the lyric or the sonnet, at the same time that I widened its range and enriched its characterization. . . . I treated Art as the supreme reality, and life as a mere mode of fiction: I awoke the imagination of my century so that it created myth and legend around me: I summed up all systems in a phrase, and all existence in an epigram.

Wilde's conception of art resists both the moral seriousness of much nineteenth-century literature and what he considered to be the Philistine tendencies of the Victorian middle and upper classes. Writing that "all art is quite useless," he sought to dissociate artistic creation from traditional notions of social usefulness and moral edification. The result of this creative principle was a sophisticated manipulation of literary and social form. Indeed, Wilde became one of his age's most visible celebrities by also serving as its most clever critic. Even as his writing detailed the rituals and conventions of Victorian high society, Wilde subverted the hierarchy of values that structured this world.

Nowhere is this transgressive impulse more evident than in the famous Wildean epigrams, which invert traditional platitudes through clever turns of phrase. Take one example: "Ignorance is like a delicate exotic fruit; touch it and the bloom is gone." The immediate effect of such a remark is studied frivolity: as Algernon says of another epigram, similarly found in *The Importance of Being Earnest*, "It is perfectly phrased! and quite as true as any observation in civilized life should be." At the same time, the line offers a pointed commentary on those segments of the British upper class who value privilege over education. Wilde's plays draw on the manners tradition of social comedy, but in their boundary-assaulting wit they bear more than passing kinship to the more explicitly political drama of his fellow Irishman GEORGE BERNARD SHAW.

The Importance of Being Earnest, which opened to widespread acclaim at the St. James's Theatre on February 14, 1895, is the epitome of Wilde's subversive mode of playwriting. Its philosophy, as Wilde defined it, is straightforward: "That we should treat all the trivial things of life seriously, and all the serious things of life with sincere and studied triviality." Unlike

Wilde's earlier comedies, which borrowed the situations and plot devices of contemporary popular drama and were occasionally marred by the uneasy blend of melodrama and wit, *The Importance of Being Earnest* embraces the logic of a thoroughly stylized world in which action borders on farce, epigram rules the day, and even the butler speaks with exceptional propriety. Its world is ruthlessly superficial—"In matters of grave importance," Gwendolen insists, "style, not sincerity is the vital thing"—and its irreverent wit satirizes the institutions and ideals of Victorian society: marriage, religion, gender roles, family, the class system, colonialism, English country living, science, education, romantic idealism, and (of course) earnestness, the habit of taking oneself and one's cherished beliefs quite seriously.

Algernon and Jack, the play's central male characters, pursue a life of leisure and pleasure untroubled by the codes of respectability and responsibility that govern the society around them. Wilde's audience would have recognized them as "dandies" within a nineteenth-century tradition of mannered individualism that included the fashionable man-about-town Beau Brummell (1778–1840). The dandy, as Alan Sinfield observes, rejected the middle-class values of work and purity through a display of "conspicuous idleness, moral skepticism, and effeminacy." As much an attitude toward life as a manner and style of dress, dandyism called attention to its originality even as it embraced the outward forms of aristocratic society. Unlike Wilde's earlier comedies, which introduce dandy characters in conventional social settings, *The Importance of Being Earnest* presents a world in which wit, pleasure, and studied superficiality are the moral norm. It is a world of erased distinctions and inverted expectations, where smoking

Allan Aynesworth as Algernon and George Alexander as Jack in the original 1895 production of *The Importance of Being Earnest*.

is as good an occupation for a man as any other and the most important thing to do in a moment of crisis is eat a muffin in the proper manner. Even Lady Bracknell, that most formidable representative of British social propriety, carries the observance of appearance and form to a dandiacal level of irreverence: "To lose one parent may be regarded as a misfortune—to lose *both* seems like carelessness."

In "The Critic as Artist" Wilde wrote: "Man is least himself when he talks in his own person. Give him a mask, and he will tell you the truth." Few characters in *The Importance of Being Earnest* are what they appear. Jack Worthing takes on his alter ego, Ernest, when he slips away to the city to see his nonexistent brother, and Algernon assumes the same name when he visits Cecily on the pretense of visiting his imaginary friend Bunbury. Gwendolen hides the secret of her romance with Jack from her mother, Cecily creates an imaginary engagement, and Lady Bracknell's authoritarian manner hides the fact that she married into her social position from decidedly nonaristocratic origins. Even Lane, the butler, and Miss Prism, the governess, have their secrets. In a play that pivots on the question of who one is, "Bunburying" becomes a metaphor for more fundamental shifts of identity. As Neil Sammells points out, *The Importance of Being Earnest* is obsessed with public and private documents—letters, diaries, birth certificates, Army Lists, novels—and with "their fallibility as a means of establishing 'authenticity,' whether of person or incident." But in "an age of surfaces" (the phrase belongs to Lady Bracknell), such categories as truth and identity remain elusive, caught in the play of social conventions and outward forms. The play on the word "Earnest" in the comedy's title reflects a society where who one is may hinge on a name and where Sincerity is the stepchild of Accident. "It is a terrible thing," Jack laments, "for a man to find out suddenly that all his life he has been speaking nothing but the truth."

In the end, Victorian earnestness had its revenge, and for those who know the playwright's biography it is hard not to view Wilde's final comedy in light of the events that followed shortly upon its premiere. When Wilde was arrested after the first trial, his name was taken off the billboards for *The Ideal Husband* and *The Importance of Being Earnest*, and in view of the author's sudden notoriety the two productions were soon canceled. The Bunburying in which Wilde's protagonists engage must have felt, to many in his audience, uncomfortably close to the secret life

David Suchet as Lady Bracknell in the 2015 production of *The Importance of Being Earnest* at the Vaudeville Theatre, London.

of which he was accused and for which he was convicted. In fact, the connections are more than coincidental. As recent scholars have demonstrated, Wilde wove a series of homosexual allusions within the play: in addition to its other meanings, for instance, *earnest* was a Victorian code word for homosexual. But though *The Importance of Being Earnest* engages and is framed by the trenchant realities of late nineteenth-century society, its strategy of taking seriousness lightly and lightness seriously ensures that its world maintains the studied refinement for which Wilde strove. Dandyism, Wilde wrote, "is the assertion of the absolute modernity of beauty." What dominates this greatest of nineteenth-century comedies— "written by a butterfly for butterflies" (as Wilde wrote a friend)—is the power of wit, satire, and unscrupulous elegance.   s.g.

The Importance of Being Earnest
A Trivial Comedy for Serious People

CHARACTERS

JOHN WORTHING, J.P.[1]
ALGERNON MONCRIEFF
REV. CANON CHASUBLE, D.D.[2]
MERRIMAN, butler
LANE, manservant

LADY BRACKNELL
HON. GWENDOLEN FAIRFAX
CECILY CARDEW
MISS PRISM, governess

Time
The Present.

First Act

[SCENE: *Morning-room in Algernon's flat in Half Moon Street.*[3] *The room is luxuriously and artistically furnished. The sound of a piano is heard in the adjoining room.*]

[LANE *is arranging afternoon tea on the table, and after the music has ceased,* ALGERNON *enters.*]

ALGERNON   Did you hear what I was playing, Lane?

LANE   I didn't think it polite to listen, sir.

ALGERNON   I'm sorry for that, for your sake. I don't play accurately—anyone can play accurately—but I play with wonderful expression. As far as the piano is concerned, sentiment is my forte. I keep science for Life.

LANE   Yes, sir.

ALGERNON   And, speaking of the science of Life, have you got the cucumber sandwiches cut for Lady Bracknell?

LANE   Yes, sir. [*Hands them on a salver.*]

1. Justice of the Peace.
2. Doctor of Divinity.
3. Located off Piccadilly Street in Mayfair, a fashionable district of London's West End.

Morning-room: an informal room for receiving morning visitors. Later visitors would be received in the more formal drawing room.

10 ALGERNON [*inspects them, takes two, and sits down on the sofa*]   Oh! . . . by
the way, Lane, I see from your book that on Thursday night, when Lord
Shoreham and Mr Worthing were dining with me, eight bottles of champagne are entered as having been consumed.

LANE   Yes, sir; eight bottles and a pint.

15 ALGERNON   Why is it that at a bachelor's establishment the servants invariably drink the champagne? I ask merely for information.

LANE   I attribute it to the superior quality of the wine, sir. I have often observed
that in married households the champagne is rarely of a first-rate brand.

ALGERNON   Good Heavens! Is marriage so demoralizing as that?

20 LANE   I believe it *is* a very pleasant state, sir. I have had very little experience
of it myself up to the present. I have only been married once. That was in
consequence of a misunderstanding between myself and a young person.

ALGERNON [*languidly*]   I don't know that I am much interested in your family
life, Lane.

25 LANE   No, sir; it is not a very interesting subject. I never think of it myself.

ALGERNON   Very natural, I am sure. That will do, Lane, thank you.

LANE   Thank you, sir.   [LANE *goes out.*]

ALGERNON   Lane's views on marriage seem somewhat lax. Really, if the lower
orders don't set us a good example, what on earth is the use of them? They
30   seem, as a class, to have absolutely no sense of moral responsibility.

[*Enter* LANE.]

LANE   Mr Ernest Worthing.

[*Enter* JACK.]   [LANE *goes out.*]

ALGERNON   How are you, my dear Ernest? What brings you up to town?

JACK   Oh, pleasure, pleasure! What else should bring one anywhere? Eating
as usual, I see, Algy!

35 ALGERNON [*stiffly*]   I believe it is customary in good society to take some slight
refreshment at five o'clock. Where have you been since last Thursday?

JACK [*sitting down on the sofa*]   In the country.

ALGERNON   What on earth do you do there?

JACK [*pulling off his gloves*]   When one is in town one amuses oneself. When
40   one is in the country one amuses other people. It is excessively boring.

ALGERNON   And who are the people you amuse?

JACK [*airily*]   Oh, neighbours, neighbours.

ALGERNON   Got nice neighbours in your part of Shropshire?[4]

JACK   Perfectly horrid! Never speak to one of them.

45 ALGERNON   How immensely you must amuse them! [*Goes over and takes
sandwich.*] By the way, Shropshire is your county, is it not?

JACK   Eh? Shropshire? Yes, of course. Hallo! Why all these cups? Why
cucumber sandwiches? Why such reckless extravagance in one so young?
Who is coming to tea?

50 ALGERNON   Oh! merely Aunt Augusta and Gwendolen.

JACK   How perfectly delightful!

ALGERNON   Yes, that is all very well; but I am afraid Aunt Augusta won't quite
approve of your being here.

JACK   May I ask why?

4. A county of England in the west Midlands, adjoining the Welsh border (about 150 miles
northwest of London).

55 ALGERNON My dear fellow, the way you flirt with Gwendolen is perfectly disgraceful. It is almost as bad as the way Gwendolen flirts with you.

JACK I am in love with Gwendolen. I have come up to town expressly to propose to her.

ALGERNON I thought you had come up for pleasure? . . . I call that business.

60 JACK How utterly unromantic you are!

ALGERNON I really don't see anything romantic in proposing. It is very romantic to be in love. But there is nothing romantic about a definite proposal. Why, one may be accepted. One usually is, I believe. Then the excitement is all over. The very essence of romance is uncertainty. If ever I

65 get married, I'll certainly try to forget the fact.

JACK I have no doubt about that, dear Algy. The Divorce Court was specially invented for people whose memories are so curiously constituted.

ALGERNON Oh! there is no use speculating on that subject. Divorces are made in Heaven——[JACK *puts out his hand to take a sandwich.* ALGERNON

70 *at once interferes.*] Please don't touch the cucumber sandwiches. They are ordered specially for Aunt Augusta. [*Takes one and eats it.*]

JACK Well, you have been eating them all the time.

ALGERNON That is quite a different matter. She is my aunt. [*Takes plate from below.*] Have some bread and butter. The bread and butter is for Gwendo-

75 len. Gwendolen is devoted to bread and butter.

JACK [*advancing to table and helping himself*] And very good bread and butter it is too.

ALGERNON Well, my dear fellow, you need not eat as if you were going to eat it all. You behave as if you were married to her already. You are not married

80 to her already, and I don't think you ever will be.

JACK Why on earth do you say that?

ALGERNON Well, in the first place girls never marry the men they flirt with. Girls don't think it right.

JACK Oh, that is nonsense!

85 ALGERNON It isn't. It is a great truth. It accounts for the extraordinary number of bachelors that one sees all over the place. In the second place, I don't give my consent.

JACK Your consent!

ALGERNON My dear fellow, Gwendolen is my first cousin. And before I allow

90 you to marry her, you will have to clear up the whole question of Cecily. [*Rings bell.*]

JACK Cecily! What on earth do you mean? What do you mean, Algy, by Cecily? I don't know anyone of the name of Cecily.

[*Enter LANE.*]

ALGERNON Bring me that cigarette case Mr Worthing left in the smoking-room the last time he dined here.

95 LANE Yes, sir.   [LANE *goes out.*]

JACK Do you mean to say you have had my cigarette case all this time? I wish to goodness you had let me know. I have been writing frantic letters to Scotland Yard[5] about it. I was very nearly offering a large reward.

ALGERNON Well, I wish you would offer one. I happen to be more than usu-

100 ally hard up.

5. The headquarters of the London Metropolitan Police Force.

JACK   There is no good offering a large reward now that the thing is found.

> [*Enter* LANE *with the cigarette case on a salver.* ALGERNON *takes it at once.* LANE *goes out.*]

ALGERNON   I think that is rather mean of you, Ernest, I must say. [*Opens case and examines it.*] However, it makes no matter, for, now that I look at the inscription inside, I find that the thing isn't yours after all.

105 JACK   Of course it's mine. [*Moving to him*] You have seen me with it a hundred times, and you have no right whatsoever to read what is written inside. It is a very ungentlemanly thing to read a private cigarette case.

ALGERNON   Oh! it is absurd to have a hard-and-fast rule about what one should read and what one shouldn't. More than half of modern culture
110   depends on what one shouldn't read.

JACK   I am quite aware of the fact, and I don't propose to discuss modern culture. It isn't the sort of thing one should talk of in private. I simply want my cigarette case back.

ALGERNON   Yes; but this isn't your cigarette case. This cigarette case is a
115   present from someone of the name of Cecily, and you said you didn't know anyone of that name.

JACK   Well, if you want to know, Cecily happens to be my aunt.

ALGERNON   Your aunt!

JACK   Yes. Charming old lady she is, too. Lives at Tunbridge Wells.[6] Just give
120   it back to me, Algy.

ALGERNON   [*retreating to back of sofa*]   But why does she call herself little Cecily if she is your aunt and lives at Tunbridge Wells. [*Reading*] 'From little Cecily with her fondest love.'

JACK   [*moving to sofa and kneeling upon it*]   My dear fellow, what on earth is
125   there in that? Some aunts are tall, some aunts are not tall. That is a matter that surely an aunt may be allowed to decide for herself. You seem to think that every aunt should be exactly like your aunt! That is absurd! For Heaven's sake give me back my cigarette case. [*Follows* ALGERNON *round the room.*]

ALGERNON   Yes. But why does your aunt call you her uncle? 'From little
130   Cecily, with her fondest love to her dear Uncle Jack.' There is no objection, I admit, to an aunt being a small aunt, but why an aunt, no matter what her size may be, should call her own nephew her uncle, I can't quite make out. Besides, your name isn't Jack at all; it is Ernest.

JACK   It isn't Ernest; it's Jack.

135 ALGERNON   You have always told me it was Ernest. I have introduced you to everyone as Ernest. You answer to the name of Ernest. You look as if your name was Ernest. You are the most earnest looking person I ever saw in my life. It is perfectly absurd your saying that your name isn't Ernest. It's on your cards. Here is one of them. [*Taking it from case*] 'Mr Ernest Worthing, B. 4, The
140   Albany.'[7] I'll keep this as a proof that your name is Ernest if ever you attempt to deny it to me, or to Gwendolen, or to anyone else. [*Puts the card in his pocket.*]

JACK   Well, my name is Ernest in town and Jack in the country, and the cigarette case was given to me in the country.

ALGERNON   Yes, but that does not account for the fact that your small Aunt
145   Cecily, who lives at Tunbridge Wells, calls you her dear uncle. Come, old boy, you had much better have the thing out at once.

---

6. A fashionable spa town in Kent, about 30 miles southeast of London.

7. Popular bachelors' quarters near Piccadilly Street, in central London.

JACK   My dear Algy, you talk exactly as if you were a dentist. It is very vulgar to talk like a dentist when one isn't a dentist. It produces a false impression.

ALGERNON   Well, that is exactly what dentists always do. Now, go on! Tell me the whole thing. I may mention that I have always suspected you of being a confirmed and secret Bunburyist, and I am quite sure of it now.

JACK   Bunburyist? What on earth do you mean by a Bunburyist?

ALGERNON   I'll reveal to you the meaning of that incomparable expression as soon as you are kind enough to inform me why you are Ernest in town and Jack in the country.

JACK   Well, produce my cigarette case first.

ALGERNON   Here it is. [*Hands cigarette case.*] Now produce your explanation, and pray make it improbable. [*Sits on sofa.*]

JACK   My dear fellow, there is nothing improbable about my explanation at all. In fact it's perfectly ordinary. Old Mr Thomas Cardew, who adopted me when I was a little boy, made me in his will guardian to his grand-daughter, Miss Cecily Cardew. Cecily who addresses me as her uncle from motives of respect that you could not possibly appreciate, lives at my place in the country under the charge of her admirable governess, Miss Prism.

ALGERNON   Where is that place in the country, by the way?

JACK   That is nothing to you, dear boy. You are not going to be invited. . . . I may tell you candidly that the place is not in Shropshire.

ALGERNON   I suspected that, my dear fellow! I have Bunburyed all over Shropshire on two separate occasions. Now, go on. Why are you Ernest in town and Jack in the country?

JACK   My dear Algy, I don't know whether you will be able to understand my real motives. You are hardly serious enough. When one is placed in the position of guardian, one has to adopt a very high moral tone on all subjects. It's one's duty to do so. And as a high moral tone can hardly be said to conduce very much to either one's health or one's happiness, in order to get up to town I have always pretended to have a younger brother of the name of Ernest, who lives in the Albany, and gets into the most dreadful scrapes. That, my dear Algy, is the whole truth pure and simple.

ALGERNON   The truth is rarely pure and never simple. Modern life would be very tedious if it were either, and modern literature a complete impossibility!

JACK   That wouldn't be at all a bad thing.

ALGERNON   Literary criticism is not your forte, my dear fellow. Don't try it. You should leave that to people who haven't been at a University. They do it so well in the daily papers. What you really are is a Bunburyist. I was quite right in saying you were a Bunburyist. You are one of the most advanced Bunburyists I know.

JACK   What on earth do you mean?

ALGERNON   You have invented a very useful younger brother called Ernest, in order that you may be able to come up to town as often as you like. I have invented an invaluable permanent invalid called Bunbury, in order that I may be able to go down into the country whenever I choose. Bunbury is perfectly invaluable. If it wasn't for Bunbury's extraordinary bad health, for instance, I wouldn't be able to dine with you at Willis's[8] tonight, for I have been really engaged to Aunt Augusta for more than a week.

8. A fashionable restaurant on King Street, near Piccadilly, frequented by Wilde and his companion Alfred Lord Douglas.

195 JACK I haven't asked you to dine with me anywhere tonight.

ALGERNON I know. You are absurdly careless about sending out invitations. It is very foolish of you. Nothing annoys people so much as not receiving invitations.

JACK You had much better dine with your Aunt Augusta.

200 ALGERNON I haven't the smallest intention of doing anything of the kind. To begin with, I dined there on Monday, and once a week is quite enough to dine with one's own relations. In the second place, whenever I do dine there I am always treated as a member of the family, and sent down[9] with either no woman at all, or two. In the third place, I know perfectly well

205 whom she will place me next to, tonight. She will place me next Mary Farquhar, who always flirts with her own husband across the dinner-table. That is not very pleasant. Indeed, it is not even decent . . . and that sort of thing is enormously on the increase. The amount of women in London who flirt with their own husbands is perfectly scandalous. It looks so bad.

210 It is simply washing one's clean linen in public. Besides, now that I know you to be a confirmed Bunburyist I naturally want to talk to you about Bunburying. I want to tell you the rules.

JACK I'm not a Bunburyist at all. If Gwendolen accepts me, I am going to kill my brother, indeed I think I'll kill him in any case. Cecily is a little too

215 much interested in him. It is rather a bore. So I am going to get rid of Ernest. And I strongly advise you to do the same with Mr . . . with your invalid friend who has the absurd name.

ALGERNON Nothing will induce me to part with Bunbury, and if you ever get married, which seems to me extremely problematic, you will be very glad

220 to know Bunbury. A man who marries without knowing Bunbury has a very tedious time of it.

JACK That is nonsense. If I marry a charming girl like Gwendolen, and she is the only girl I ever saw in my life that I would marry, I certainly won't want to know Bunbury.

225 ALGERNON Then your wife will. You don't seem to realize, that in married life three is company and two is none.

JACK [*sententiously*] That, my dear young friend, is the theory that the corrupt French Drama[1] has been propounding for the last fifty years.

ALGERNON Yes; and that the happy English home has proved in half the time.

230 JACK For heaven's sake, don't try to be cynical. It's perfectly easy to be cynical.

ALGERNON My dear fellow, it isn't easy to be anything nowadays. There's such a lot of beastly competition about. [*The sound of an electric bell is heard.*] Ah! that must be Aunt Augusta. Only relatives, or creditors, ever ring in that Wagnerian[2] manner. Now, if I get her out of the way for ten

235 minutes, so that you can have an opportunity for proposing to Gwendolen, may I dine with you tonight at Willis's?

JACK I suppose so, if you want to.

9. Directed to accompany someone to dinner. Victorian dinner guests would gather upstairs in the drawing room, and then gentlemen would escort ladies to the dining room in arranged couples.
1. Because its plots frequently involved adul-

tery and infidelity, French drama was often viewed by the English as immoral.
2. Loud and imposing, like the operas of the German composer Richard Wagner (1813–1883).

ALGERNON   Yes, but you must be serious about it. I hate people who are not serious about meals. It is so shallow of them.

[*Enter* LANE.]

240 LANE   Lady Bracknell and Miss Fairfax.

[ALGERNON *goes forward to meet them. Enter* LADY BRACKNELL *and* GWENDOLEN.]

LADY BRACKNELL   Good afternoon, dear Algernon, I hope you are behaving very well.

ALGERNON   I'm feeling very well, Aunt Augusta.

LADY BRACKNELL   That's not quite the same thing. In fact the two things
245 rarely go together. [*Sees* JACK *and bows to him with icy coldness.*]

ALGERNON [*to* GWENDOLEN]   Dear me, you are smart![3]

GWENDOLEN   I am always smart! Aren't I, Mr Worthing?

JACK   You're quite perfect, Miss Fairfax.

GWENDOLEN   Oh! I hope I am not that. It would leave no room for develop
250 ments, and I intend to develop in many directions. [GWENDOLEN *and* JACK *sit down together in the corner.*]

LADY BRACKNELL   I'm sorry if we are a little late, Algernon, but I was obliged to call on dear Lady Harbury. I hadn't been there since her poor husband's death. I never saw a woman so altered; she looks quite twenty years younger. And now I'll have a cup of tea, and one of those nice cucumber
255 sandwiches you promised me.

ALGERNON   Certainly, Aunt Augusta. [*Goes over to tea-table.*]

LADY BRACKNELL   Won't you come and sit here, Gwendolen?

GWENDOLEN   Thanks, mamma, I'm quite comfortable where I am.

ALGERNON [*picking up empty plate in horror*]   Good heavens! Lane! Why are
260 there no cucumber sandwiches? I ordered them specially.

LANE [*gravely*]   There were no cucumbers in the market this morning, sir. I went down twice.

ALGERNON   No cucumbers!

LANE   No, sir. Not even for ready money.[4]

265 ALGERNON   That will do, Lane, thank you.

LANE   Thank you, sir.   [*Goes out.*]

ALGERNON   I am greatly distressed, Aunt Augusta, about there being no cucumbers, not even for ready money.

LADY BRACKNELL   It really makes no matter, Algernon. I had some crumpets
270 with Lady Harbury, who seems to me to be living entirely for pleasure now.

ALGERNON   I hear her hair has turned quite gold from grief.

LADY BRACKNELL   It certainly has changed its colour. From what cause I, of course, cannot say. [ALGERNON *crosses and hands tea.*] Thank you. I've quite a treat for you tonight, Algernon. I am going to send you down with Mary
275 Farquhar. She is such a nice woman, and so attentive to her husband. It's delightful to watch them.

ALGERNON   I am afraid, Aunt Augusta, I shall have to give up the pleasure of dining with you tonight after all.

---

3. Neatly stylish in appearance.
4. Immediate cash payment (the well-off often bought goods on credit).

LADY BRACKNELL [*frowning*] I hope not, Algernon. It would put my table
completely out.[5] Your uncle would have to dine upstairs. Fortunately he is
accustomed to that.

ALGERNON It is a great bore, and, I need hardly say, a terrible disappointment to me, but the fact is I have just had a telegram to say that my poor
friend Bunbury is very ill again. [*Exchanges glances with* JACK.] They seem
to think I should be with him.

LADY BRACKNELL It is very strange. This Mr Bunbury seems to suffer from
curiously bad health.

ALGERNON Yes; poor Bunbury is a dreadful invalid.

LADY BRACKNELL Well, I must say, Algernon, that I think it is high time that
Mr Bunbury made up his mind whether he was going to live or to die. This
shilly-shallying with the question is absurd. Nor do I in any way approve of
the modern sympathy with invalids. I consider it morbid. Illness of any kind
is hardly a thing to be encouraged in others. Health is the primary duty of
life. I am always telling that to your poor uncle, but he never seems to take
much notice . . . as far as any improvement in his ailments goes. I should be
much obliged if you would ask Mr Bunbury, from me, to be kind enough not
to have a relapse on Saturday, for I rely on you to arrange my music for me.
It is my last reception, and one wants something that will encourage conversation, particularly at the end of the season[6] when everyone has practically
said whatever they had to say, which, in most cases, was probably not much.

ALGERNON I'll speak to Bunbury, Aunt Augusta, if he is still conscious, and I
think I can promise you he'll be all right by Saturday. Of course the music is
a great difficulty. You see, if one plays good music, people don't listen, and if
one plays bad music people don't talk. But I'll run over the programme I've
drawn out, if you will kindly come into the next room for a moment.

LADY BRACKNELL Thank you, Algernon. It is very thoughtful of you. [*Rising, and following* ALGERNON] I'm sure the programme will be delightful,
after a few expurgations. French songs I cannot possibly allow. People
always seem to think that they are improper, and either look shocked,
which is vulgar, or laugh, which is worse. But German sounds a thoroughly respectable language, and indeed, I believe is so. Gwendolen, you
will accompany me.

GWENDOLEN Certainly, mamma.

[LADY BRACKNELL *and* ALGERNON *go into the music-room,* GWENDOLEN
remains behind.]

JACK Charming day it has been, Miss Fairfax.

GWENDOLEN Pray don't talk to me about the weather, Mr Worthing. Whenever people talk to me about the weather, I always feel quite certain that
they mean something else. And that makes me so nervous.

JACK I do mean something else.

GWENDOLEN I thought so. In fact, I am never wrong.

JACK And I would like to be allowed to take advantage of Lady Bracknell's
temporary absence . . .

---

5. That is, ruin the seating arrangement, which
was always carefully planned to balance male
and female guests.
6. That is, the social season in London, which

began in May and lasted through July; during
this time fashionable society attended balls,
dinners, and other entertainments.

GWENDOLEN   I would certainly advise you to do so. Mamma has a way of coming back suddenly into a room that I have often had to speak to her about.

JACK [*nervously*]   Miss Fairfax, ever since I met you I have admired you more
325   than any girl . . . I have ever met since . . . I met you.

GWENDOLEN   Yes, I am quite aware of the fact. And I often wish that in public, at any rate, you had been more demonstrative. For me you have always
had an irresistible fascination. Even before I met you I was far from
indifferent to you. [JACK *looks at her in amazement.*] We live, as I hope you
330   know, Mr Worthing, in an age of ideals. The fact is constantly mentioned
in the more expensive monthly magazines, and has reached the provincial
pulpits I am told: and my ideal has always been to love some one of the
name of Ernest. There is something in that name that inspires absolute
confidence. The moment Algernon first mentioned to me that he had a
335   friend called Ernest, I knew I was destined to love you.

JACK   You really love me, Gwendolen?

GWENDOLEN   Passionately!

JACK   Darling! You don't know how happy you've made me.

GWENDOLEN   My own Ernest!

340   JACK   But you don't really mean to say that you couldn't love me if my name
wasn't Ernest?

GWENDOLEN   But your name is Ernest.

JACK   Yes, I know it is. But supposing it was something else? Do you mean to
say you couldn't love me then?

345   GWENDOLEN [*glibly*]   Ah! that is clearly a metaphysical speculation, and like
most metaphysical speculations has very little reference at all to the actual
facts of real life, as we know them.

JACK   Personally, darling, to speak quite candidly, I don't much care about
the name of Ernest . . . I don't think the name suits me at all.

350   GWENDOLEN   It suits you perfectly. It is a divine name. It has a music of its
own. It produces vibrations.

JACK   Well, really, Gwendolen, I must say that I think there are lots of other
much nicer names. I think Jack, for instance, a charming name.

GWENDOLEN   Jack? . . . No, there is very little music in the name Jack, if any
355   at all, indeed. It does not thrill. It produces absolutely no vibrations. . . . I
have known several Jacks, and they all, without exception, were more than
usually plain. Besides, Jack is a notorious domesticity[7] for John! And I pity
any woman who is married to a man called John. She would probably never
be allowed to know the entrancing pleasure of a single moment's solitude.
360   The only really safe name is Ernest.

JACK   Gwendolen, I must get christened at once—I mean we must get married at once. There is no time to be lost.

GWENDOLEN   Married, Mr Worthing?

JACK [*astounded*]   Well . . . surely. You know that I love you, and you led me
365   to believe, Miss Fairfax, that you were not absolutely indifferent to me.

GWENDOLEN   I adore you. But you haven't proposed to me yet. Nothing has
been said at all about marriage. The subject has not even been touched on.

JACK   Well . . . may I propose to you now?

---

7. A domestic or familiar expression.

GWENDOLEN   I think it would be an admirable opportunity. And to spare you
370   any possible disappointment, Mr Worthing, I think it only fair to tell you
quite frankly beforehand that I am fully determined to accept you.

JACK   Gwendolen!

GWENDOLEN   Yes, Mr Worthing, what have you got to say to me?

JACK   You know what I have got to say to you.

375   GWENDOLEN   Yes, but you don't say it.

JACK   Gwendolen, will you marry me? [*Goes on his knees.*]

GWENDOLEN   Of course I will, darling. How long you have been about it! I am
afraid you have had very little experience in how to propose.

JACK   My own one, I have never loved anyone in the world but you.

380   GWENDOLEN   Yes, but men often propose for practice. I know my brother
Gerald does. All my girl-friends tell me so. What wonderfully blue eyes you
have, Ernest! They are quite, quite, blue. I hope you will always look at me
just like that, especially when there are other people present.

[*Enter* LADY BRACKNELL.]

LADY BRACKNELL   Mr Worthing! Rise, sir, from this semi-recumbent posture.
385   It is most indecorous.

GWENDOLEN   Mamma! [*He tries to rise; she restrains him.*] I must beg you
to retire. This is no place for you. Besides, Mr Worthing has not quite finished yet.

LADY BRACKNELL   Finished what, may I ask?

390   GWENDOLEN   I am engaged to Mr Worthing, mamma. [*They rise together.*]

LADY BRACKNELL   Pardon me, you are not engaged to anyone. When you do
become engaged to some one, I, or your father, should his health permit
him, will inform you of the fact. An engagement should come on a young
girl as a surprise, pleasant or unpleasant, as the case may be. It is hardly a
395   matter that she could be allowed to arrange for herself. . . . And now I have
a few questions to put to you, Mr Worthing. While I am making these
inquiries, you, Gwendolen, will wait for me below in the carriage.

GWENDOLEN [*reproachfully*]   Mamma!

GWENDOLEN   In the carriage, Gwendolen! [GWENDOLEN *goes to the door. She
and* JACK *blow kisses to each other behind* LADY BRACKNELL's *back.* LADY
BRACKNELL *looks vaguely about as if she could not understand what the noise
400   was. Finally turns round.*] Gwendolen, the carriage!

GWENDOLEN   Yes, mamma.   [*Goes out, looking back at* JACK.]

LADY BRACKNELL [*sitting down*]   You can take a seat, Mr Worthing.

[*Looks in her pocket for note-book and pencil.*]

JACK   Thank you, Lady Bracknell, I prefer standing.

LADY BRACKNELL [*pencil and note-book in hand*]   I feel bound to tell you that
405   you are not down on my list of eligible young men, although I have the
same list as the dear Duchess of Bolton has. We work together, in fact.
However, I am quite ready to enter your name, should your answers be
what a really affectionate mother requires. Do you smoke?

JACK   Well, yes, I must admit I smoke.

410   LADY BRACKNELL   I am glad to hear it. A man should always have an occupation of some kind. There are far too many idle men in London as it is. How
old are you?

JACK   Twenty-nine.

LADY BRACKNELL A very good age to be married at. I have always been of
opinion that a man who desires to get married should know either everything or nothing. Which do you know?

JACK [after some hesitation] I know nothing, Lady Bracknell.

LADY BRACKNELL I am pleased to hear it. I do not approve of anything that
tampers with natural ignorance. Ignorance is like a delicate exotic fruit;
touch it and the bloom is gone. The whole theory of modern education is
radically unsound. Fortunately in England, at any rate, education produces
no effect whatsoever. If it did, it would prove a serious danger to the upper
classes, and probably lead to acts of violence in Grosvenor Square.[8] What
is your income?

JACK Between seven and eight thousand[9] a year.

LADY BRACKNELL [makes a note in her book] In land, or in investments?

JACK In investments, chiefly.

LADY BRACKNELL That is satisfactory. What between the duties expected of
one during one's lifetime, and the duties exacted from one after one's death,[1]
land has ceased to be either a profit or a pleasure. It gives one position, and
prevents one from keeping it up. That's all that can be said about land.

JACK I have a country house with some land, of course, attached to it, about
fifteen hundred acres, I believe; but I don't depend on that for my real
income. In fact, as far as I can make out, the poachers are the only people
who make anything out of it.

LADY BRACKNELL A country house! How many bedrooms? Well, that point
can be cleared up afterwards. You have a town house, I hope? A girl with a
simple, unspoiled nature, like Gwendolen, could hardly be expected to
reside in the country.

JACK Well, I own a house in Belgrave Square,[2] but it is let by the year to Lady
Bloxham. Of course, I can get it back whenever I like, at six months' notice.

LADY BRACKNELL Lady Bloxham? I don't know her.

JACK Oh, she goes about very little. She is a lady considerably advanced in
years.

LADY BRACKNELL Ah, nowadays that is no guarantee of respectability of
character. What number in Belgrave Square?

JACK 149.

LADY BRACKNELL [shaking her head] The unfashionable side. I thought there
was something. However, that could easily be altered.

JACK Do you mean the fashion, or the side?

LADY BRACKNELL [sternly] Both, if necessary, I presume. What are your
politics?

JACK Well, I am afraid I really have none. I am a Liberal Unionist.[3]

LADY BRACKNELL Oh, they count as Tories. They dine with us. Or come in
the evening, at any rate. Now to minor matters. Are your parents living?

JACK I have lost both my parents.

8. A Mayfair neighborhood east of Speakers'
Corner in Hyde Park.
9. That is £7,000 to £8,000, roughly equivalent to $1 million today.
1. That is, inheritance taxes, a play on the
secondary meaning of "duties."
2. The center of Belgravia, a fashionable neigh-

borhood just west of Buckingham Palace.
3. The Liberal Unionists were a splinter
group of the Liberal Party that joined with
the Conservatives (known as the Tories) to
defeat William Gladstone's Home Rule Bill of
1886, which would have granted political
autonomy to Ireland.

LADY BRACKNELL   Both? To lose one parent may be regarded as a misfortune—to lose *both* seems like carelessness. Who was your father? He was evidently a man of some wealth. Was he born in what the Radical papers call
460   the purple of commerce, or did he rise from the ranks of the aristocracy?

JACK   I am afraid I really don't know. The fact is, Lady Bracknell, I said I had lost my parents. It would be nearer the truth to say that my parents seem to have lost me . . . I don't actually know who I am by birth. I was . . . well, I was found.

465   LADY BRACKNELL   Found!

JACK   The late Mr Thomas Cardew, an old gentleman of a very charitable and kindly disposition, found me, and gave me the name of Worthing, because he happened to have a first-class ticket for Worthing in his pocket at the time. Worthing is a place in Sussex.[4] It is a seaside resort.

470   LADY BRACKNELL   Where did the charitable gentleman who had a first-class ticket for this seaside resort find you?

JACK   [*gravely*]   In a hand-bag.

LADY BRACKNELL   A hand-bag?

JACK   [*very seriously*]   Yes, Lady Bracknell. I was in a hand-bag—a somewhat
475   large, black leather hand-bag, with handles to it—an ordinary hand-bag in fact.

LADY BRACKNELL   In what locality did this Mr James, or Thomas, Cardew come across this ordinary hand-bag?

JACK   In the cloak-room at Victoria Station.[5] It was given to him in mistake
480   for his own.

LADY BRACKNELL   The cloak-room at Victoria Station?

JACK   Yes. The Brighton line.[6]

LADY BRACKNELL   The line is immaterial. Mr Worthing, I confess I feel somewhat bewildered by what you have just told me. To be born, or at any rate
485   bred, in a hand-bag, whether it had handles or not, seems to me to display a contempt for the ordinary decencies of family life that reminds one of the worst excesses of the French Revolution. And I presume you know what that unfortunate movement led to? As for the particular locality in which the hand-bag was found, a cloak-room at a railway station might serve to
490   conceal a social indiscretion—has probably, indeed, been used for that purpose before now—but it could hardly be regarded as an assured basis for a recognized position in good society.

JACK   May I ask you then what you would advise me to do? I need hardly say I would do anything in the world to ensure Gwendolen's happiness.

495   LADY BRACKNELL   I would strongly advise you, Mr Worthing, to try and acquire some relations as soon as possible, and to make a definite effort to produce at any rate one parent, of either sex, before the season is quite over.

JACK   Well, I don't see how I could possibly manage to do that. I can produce the hand-bag at any moment. It is in my dressing-room at home. I really
500   think that should satisfy you, Lady Bracknell.

---

4. Wilde, who frequently named characters after places, wrote *The Importance of Being Earnest* while vacationing with his family in the coastal town of Worthing. Sussex is a county south of London.

5. One of London's main rail stations, located in Belgravia.

6. The rail line to Brighton, a popular seaside resort in Sussex on England's south coast.

LADY BRACKNELL   Me, sir! What has it to do with me? You can hardly imagine that I and Lord Bracknell would dream of allowing our only daughter—a girl brought up with the utmost care—to marry into a cloak-room, and form an alliance with a parcel? Good morning, Mr Worthing!

[LADY BRACKNELL *sweeps out in majestic indignation.*]

505 JACK   Good morning! [ALGERNON, *from the other room, strikes up the Wedding March.*[7] JACK *looks perfectly furious, and goes to the door.*] For goodness' sake don't play that ghastly tune, Algy! How idiotic you are!

[*The music stops, and* ALGERNON *enters cheerily.*]

ALGERNON   Didn't it go off all right, old boy? You don't mean to say Gwendolen refused you? I know it is a way she has. She is always refusing people.
510   I think it is most ill-natured of her.

JACK   Oh, Gwendolen is as right as a trivet.[8] As far as she is concerned, we are engaged. Her mother is perfectly unbearable. Never met such a Gorgon[9] . . . I don't really know what a Gorgon is like, but I am quite sure that Lady Bracknell is one. In any case, she is a monster, without being
515   a myth, which is rather unfair . . . I beg your pardon, Algy, I suppose I shouldn't talk about your own aunt in that way before you.

ALGERNON   My dear boy, I love hearing my relations abused. It is the only thing that makes me put up with them at all. Relations are simply a tedious pack of people, who haven't got the remotest knowledge of how to live, nor
520   the smallest instinct about when to die.

JACK   Oh, that is nonsense!

ALGERNON   It isn't!

JACK   Well, I won't argue about the matter. You always want to argue about things.

525 ALGERNON   That is exactly what things were originally made for.

JACK   Upon my word, if I thought that, I'd shoot myself . . . [*A pause*] You don't think there is any chance of Gwendolen becoming like her mother in about a hundred and fifty years, do you Algy?

ALGERNON   All women become like their mothers. That is their tragedy. No
530   man does. That's his.

JACK   Is that clever?

ALGERNON   It is perfectly phrased! and quite as true as any observation in civilized life should be.

JACK   I am sick to death of cleverness. Everybody is clever nowadays. You
535   can't go anywhere without meeting clever people. The thing has become an absolute public nuisance. I wish to goodness we had a few fools left.

ALGERNON   We have.

JACK   I should extremely like to meet them. What do they talk about?

ALGERNON   The fools? Oh! about the clever people, of course.

540 JACK   What fools!

ALGERNON   By the way, did you tell Gwendolen the truth about your being Ernest in town, and Jack in the country?

---

7. The recessional often played at weddings, from Felix Mendelssohn's *A Midsummer Night's Dream* (1842).
8. Proverbial expression for steadiness; a trivet is a three-footed stand used to support cooking vessels over a fire.
9. In Greek mythology, one of three snake-haired sisters, the sight of whom turned all who looked at them to stone.

JACK [*in a very patronizing manner*]   My dear fellow, the truth isn't quite the sort of thing one tells to a nice sweet refined girl. What extraordinary ideas
545 you have about the way to behave to a woman!

ALGERNON   The only way to behave to a woman is to make love to her,[1] if she is pretty, and to someone else if she is plain.

JACK   Oh, that is nonsense.

ALGERNON   What about your brother? What about the profligate Ernest?

550 JACK   Oh, before the end of the week I shall have got rid of him. I'll say he died in Paris of apoplexy. Lots of people die of apoplexy, quite suddenly, don't they?

ALGERNON   Yes, but it's hereditary, my dear fellow. It's a sort of thing that runs in families. You had much better say a severe chill.

JACK   You are sure a severe chill isn't hereditary, or anything of that kind?

555 ALGERNON   Of course it isn't!

JACK   Very well, then. My poor brother Ernest is carried off suddenly in Paris, by a severe chill. That gets rid of him.

ALGERNON   But I thought you said that . . . Miss Cardew was a little too much interested in your poor brother Ernest? Won't she feel his loss a
560 good deal?

JACK   Oh, that is all right. Cecily is not a silly romantic girl, I am glad to say. She has got a capital appetite, goes on long walks, and pays no attention at all to her lessons.

ALGERNON   I would rather like to see Cecily.

565 JACK   I will take very good care you never do. She is excessively pretty, and she is only just eighteen.

ALGERNON   Have you told Gwendolen yet that you have an excessively pretty ward who is only just eighteen?

JACK   Oh! one doesn't blurt these things out to people. Cecily and Gwendo-
570 len are perfectly certain to be extremely great friends. I'll bet you anything you like that half an hour after they have met, they will be calling each other sister.

ALGERNON   Women only do that when they have called each other a lot of other things first. Now, my dear boy, if we want to get a good table at Willis's,
575 we really must go and dress. Do you know it is nearly seven?

JACK [*irritably*]   Oh! it always is nearly seven.

ALGERNON   Well, I'm hungry.

JACK   I never knew you when you weren't. . . .

ALGERNON   What shall we do after dinner? Go to a theatre?

580 JACK   Oh no! I loathe listening.

ALGERNON   Well, let us go to the Club?[2]

JACK   Oh, no! I hate talking.

ALGERNON   Well, we might trot round to the Empire[3] at ten?

JACK   Oh no! I can't bear looking at things. It is so silly.

585 ALGERNON   Well, what shall we do?

JACK   Nothing!

ALGERNON   It is awfully hard work doing nothing. However, I don't mind hard work where there is no definite object of any kind.

[*Enter* LANE.]

---

1. That is, flirt with her, court her.
2. Any one of a number of exclusive, members-only clubs for men.

3. The Empire Theatre of Varieties, a well-known music hall in Leicester Square, a center of entertainments in London's West End.

LANE   Miss Fairfax.

[*Enter* GWENDOLEN. LANE *goes out.*]

590   ALGERNON   Gwendolen, upon my word!

GWENDOLEN   Algy, kindly turn your back. I have something very particular to say to Mr Worthing.

ALGERNON   Really, Gwendolen, I don't think I can allow this at all.

GWENDOLEN   Algy, you always adopt a strictly immoral attitude towards life.
595   You are not quite old enough to do that.

[ALGERNON *retires to the fireplace.*]

JACK   My own darling!

GWENDOLEN   Ernest, we may never be married. From the expression on mamma's face I fear we never shall. Few parents nowadays pay any regard to what their children say to them. The old-fashioned respect for the young
600   is fast dying out. Whatever influence I ever had over mamma, I lost at the age of three. But although she may prevent us from becoming man and wife, and I may marry someone else, and marry often, nothing that she can possibly do can alter my eternal devotion to you.

JACK   Dear Gwendolen!

605   GWENDOLEN   The story of your romantic origin, as related to me by mamma, with unpleasing comments, has naturally stirred the deeper fibres of my nature. Your Christian name has an irresistible fascination. The simplicity of your character makes you exquisitely incomprehensible to me. Your town address at the Albany I have. What is your address in the country?

610   JACK   The Manor House, Woolton, Hertfordshire.[4]

[ALGERNON, *who has been carefully listening, smiles to himself, and writes the address on his shirt-cuff. Then picks up the Railway Guide.*]

GWENDOLEN   There is a good postal service, I suppose? It may be necessary to do something desperate. That of course will require serious considera-tion. I will communicate with you daily.

JACK   My own one!

615   GWENDOLEN   How long do you remain in town?

JACK   Till Monday.

GWENDOLEN   Good! Algy, you may turn round now.

ALGERNON   Thanks, I've turned round already.

GWENDOLEN   You may also ring the bell.

620   JACK   You will let me see you to your carriage, my own darling?

GWENDOLEN   Certainly.

JACK [*to* LANE, *who now enters*]   I will see Miss Fairfax out.

LANE   Yes, sir.

[JACK *and* GWENDOLEN *go off.*]

[LANE *presents several letters on a salver to Algernon. It is to be surmised that they are bills, as* ALGERNON, *after looking at the envelopes, tears them up.*]

ALGERNON   A glass of sherry, Lane.

625   LANE   Yes, sir.

ALGERNON   Tomorrow, Lane, I'm going Bunburying.

LANE   Yes, sir.

---

4. A rural county just northeast of London.

ALGERNON   I shall probably not be back till Monday. You can put up my dress clothes, my smoking jacket,[5] and all the Bunbury suits . . .

630 LANE   Yes, sir. [*Handing sherry*]

ALGERNON   I hope tomorrow will be a fine day, Lane.

LANE   It never is, sir.

ALGERNON   Lane, you're a perfect pessimist.

LANE   I do my best to give satisfaction, sir.

[*Enter* JACK. LANE *goes off.*]

635 JACK   There's a sensible, intellectual girl! the only girl I ever cared for in my life. [ALGERNON *is laughing immoderately.*] What on earth are you so amused at?

ALGERNON   Oh, I'm a little anxious about poor Bunbury, that is all.

JACK   If you don't take care, your friend Bunbury will get you into a serious 640 scrape some day.

ALGERNON   I love scrapes. They are the only things that are never serious.

JACK   Oh, that's nonsense, Algy. You never talk anything but nonsense.

ALGERNON   Nobody ever does.

[JACK *looks indignantly at him, and leaves the room.* ALGERNON *lights a cigarette, reads his shirt-cuff, and smiles.*]

Act Drop.[6]

Second Act

[SCENE: *Garden at the Manor House. A flight of gray stone steps leads up to the house. The garden, an old-fashioned one, full of roses. Time of year, July. Basket chairs, and a table covered with books, are set under a large yew tree.*]

[MISS PRISM *discovered seated at the table.* CECILY *is at the back watering flowers.*]

MISS PRISM [*calling*]   Cecily, Cecily! Surely such a utilitarian occupation as the watering of flowers is rather Moulton's duty[7] than yours? Especially at a moment when intellectual pleasures await you. Your German grammar is on 5 the table. Pray open it at page fifteen. We will repeat yesterday's lesson.

CECILY [*coming over very slowly*]   But I don't like German. It isn't at all a becoming language. I know perfectly well that I look quite plain after my German lesson.

MISS PRISM   Child, you know how anxious your guardian is that you should 10 improve yourself in every way. He laid particular stress on your German, as he was leaving for town yesterday. Indeed, he always lays stress on your German when he is leaving for town.

CECILY   Dear Uncle Jack is so very serious! Sometimes he is so serious that I think he cannot be quite well.

15 MISS PRISM [*drawing herself up*]   Your guardian enjoys the best of health, and his gravity of demeanour is especially to be commended in one so comparatively young as he is. I know no one who has a higher sense of duty and responsibility.

CECILY   I suppose that is why he often looks a little bored when we three are 20 together.

5. A loose-fitting casual jacket worn at home, usually in the evening. *Put up:* pack.
6. The painted curtain lowered to indicate divisions between acts or scenes.
7. The gardener Moulton appears in Wilde's earlier, four-act version of the play.

MISS PRISM   Cecily! I am surprised at you. Mr Worthing has many troubles in his life. Idle merriment and triviality would be out of place in his conversation. You must remember his constant anxiety about that unfortunate young man his brother.

25 CECILY   I wish Uncle Jack would allow that unfortunate young man, his brother, to come down here sometimes. We might have a good influence over him, Miss Prism. I am sure you certainly would. You know German, and geology, and things of that kind influence a man very much. [CECILY *begins to write in her diary.*]

MISS PRISM [*shaking her head*]   I do not think that even I could produce any
30 effect on a character that according to his own brother's admission is irretrievably weak and vacillating. Indeed I am not sure that I would desire to reclaim him. I am not in favour of this modern mania for turning bad people into good people at a moment's notice. As a man sows so let him reap.[8] You must put away your diary, Cecily. I really don't see why you should
35 keep a diary at all.

CECILY   I keep a diary in order to enter the wonderful secrets of my life. If I didn't write them down I should probably forget all about them.

MISS PRISM   Memory, my dear Cecily, is the diary that we all carry about with us.

40 CECILY   Yes, but it usually chronicles the things that have never happened, and couldn't possibly have happened. I believe that Memory is responsible for nearly all the three-volume novels that Mudie[9] sends us.

MISS PRISM   Do not speak slightingly of the three-volume novel, Cecily. I wrote one myself in earlier days.

45 CECILY   Did you really, Miss Prism? How wonderfully clever you are! I hope it did not end happily? I don't like novels that end happily. They depress me so much.

MISS PRISM   The good ended happily, and the bad unhappily. That is what Fiction means.

50 CECILY   I suppose so. But it seems very unfair. And was your novel ever published?

MISS PRISM   Alas! no. The manuscript unfortunately was abandoned. I use the word in the sense of lost or mislaid.[1] To your work, child, these speculations are profitless.

55 CECILY [*smiling*]   But I see dear Dr Chasuble coming up through the garden.

MISS PRISM [*rising and advancing*]   Dr Chasuble! This is indeed a pleasure.

[*Enter* CANON CHASUBLE.]

CHASUBLE   And how are we this morning? Miss Prism, you are, I trust, well?

CECILY   Miss Prism has just been complaining of a slight headache. I think it would do her so much good to have a short stroll with you in the Park,
60 Dr Chasuble.

MISS PRISM   Cecily, I have not mentioned anything about a headache.

---

8. A New Testament proverb: "Be not deceived; God is not mocked: for whatsoever a man soweth, that shall he also reap" (Galatians 6.7).

9. Charles Edward Mudie (1818–1890), an English publisher who in 1842 founded a lending library that charged subscribers to borrow books; most Victorian fiction was published in three volumes (a practice that benefited for-fee libraries).

1. That is, not in the sense of "licentious" or "unrestrained."

CECILY   No, dear Miss Prism, I know that, but I felt instinctively that you had a headache. Indeed I was thinking about that, and not about my German lesson, when the Rector came in.

65 CHASUBLE   I hope Cecily, you are not inattentive.

CECILY   Oh, I am afraid I am.

CHASUBLE   That is strange. Were I fortunate enough to be Miss Prism's pupil, I would hang upon her lips. [MISS PRISM *glares.*] I spoke metaphorically.—My metaphor was drawn from bees.[2] Ahem! Mr Worthing I suppose, has not

70 returned from town yet?

MISS PRISM   We do not expect him till Monday afternoon.

CHASUBLE   Ah yes, he usually likes to spend his Sunday in London. He is not one of those whose sole aim is enjoyment, as, by all accounts, that unfortunate young man his brother seems to be. But I must not disturb Egeria

75 and her pupil any longer.

MISS PRISM   Egeria? My name is Lætitia,[3] Doctor.

CHASUBLE   [*bowing*]   A classical allusion merely, drawn from the Pagan authors. I shall see you both no doubt at Evensong?[4]

MISS PRISM   I think, dear Doctor, I will have a stroll with you. I find I have a

80 headache after all, and a walk might do it good.

CHASUBLE   With pleasure, Miss Prism, with pleasure. We might go as far as the schools and back.

MISS PRISM   That would be delightful. Cecily, you will read your Political Economy in my absence. The chapter on the Fall of the Rupee[5] you may

85 omit. It is somewhat too sensational. Even these metallic problems have their melodramatic side. [*Goes down the garden with* DR CHASUBLE.]

CECILY   [*picks up books and throws them back on table*]   Horrid Political Economy! Horrid Geography! Horrid, horrid German!

[*Enter* MERRIMAN *with a card on a salver.*]

MERRIMAN   Mr Ernest Worthing has just driven over from the station. He

90 has brought his luggage with him.

CECILY   [*takes the card and reads it*]   'Mr Ernest Worthing, B.4 The Albany, W.' Uncle Jack's brother! Did you tell him Mr Worthing was in town?

MERRIMAN   Yes, Miss. He seemed very much disappointed. I mentioned that you and Miss Prism were in the garden. He said he was anxious to speak to

95 you privately for a moment.

CECILY   Ask Mr Ernest Worthing to come here. I suppose you had better talk to the housekeeper about a room for him.

MERRIMAN   Yes, Miss.   [MERRIMAN *goes off.*]

CECILY   I have never met any really wicked person before. I feel rather fright-

100 ened. I am so afraid he will look just like everyone else.

[*Enter* ALGERNON, *very gay and debonnair.*]

He does!

ALGERNON   [*raising his hat*]   You are my little cousin Cecily, I'm sure.

---

2. A reference to the honey of Miss Prism's instruction.

3. A Latin name (literally, "beauty, grace, joy"). *Egeria*: in Roman mythology, one of the Camenae (prophetic nymphs), said to have counseled Numa Pompilius, the legendary second

king of Rome; thus, any female adviser or patron.

4. Evening church services.

5. India's currency had been declining in value for a number of years. *Political Economy*: that is, an economics textbook.

CECILY   You are under some strange mistake. I am not little. In fact, I believe I am more than usually tall for my age. [ALGERNON *is rather taken aback.*]
105   But I am your cousin Cecily. You, I see from your card, are Uncle Jack's brother, my cousin Ernest, my wicked cousin Ernest.

ALGERNON   Oh! I am not really wicked at all, cousin Cecily. You mustn't think that I am wicked.

CECILY   If you are not, then you have certainly been deceiving us all in a
110   very inexcusable manner. I hope you have not been leading a double life, pretending to be wicked and being really good all the time. That would be hypocrisy.

ALGERNON   [*looks at her in amazement*]   Oh! Of course I have been rather reckless.

115   CECILY   I am glad to hear it.

ALGERNON   In fact, now you mention the subject, I have been very bad in my own small way.

CECILY   I don't think you should be so proud of that, although I am sure it must have been very pleasant.

120   ALGERNON   It is much pleasanter being here with you.

CECILY   I can't understand how you are here at all. Uncle Jack won't be back till Monday afternoon.

ALGERNON   That is a great disappointment. I am obliged to go up by the first train on Monday morning. I have a business appointment that I am
125   anxious . . . to miss.

CECILY   Couldn't you miss it anywhere but in London?

ALGERNON   No: the appointment is in London.

CECILY   Well, I know, of course, how important it is not to keep a business engagement, if one wants to retain any sense of the beauty of life, but still
130   I think you had better wait till Uncle Jack arrives. I know he wants to speak to you about your emigrating.

ALGERNON   About my what?

CECILY   Your emigrating. He has gone up to buy your outfit.

ALGERNON   I certainly wouldn't let Jack buy my outfit. He has no taste in
135   neckties at all.

CECILY   I don't think you will require neckties. Uncle Jack is sending you to Australia.[6]

ALGERNON   Australia! I'd sooner die.

CECILY   Well, he said at dinner on Wednesday night, that you would have to
140   choose between this world, the next world, and Australia.

ALGERNON   Oh, well! The accounts I have received of Australia and the next world, are not particularly encouraging. This world is good enough for me, cousin Cecily.

CECILY   Yes, but are you good enough for it?

145   ALGERNON   I'm afraid I'm not that. That is why I want you to reform me. You might make that your mission, if you don't mind, cousin Cecily.

CECILY   I'm afraid I've no time, this afternoon.

ALGERNON   Well, would you mind my reforming myself this afternoon?

CECILY   It is rather Quixotic[7] of you. But I think you should try.

---

6. While Australia was no longer a penal colony in Wilde's day, it was still widely seen as a place where disreputable family members might be sent.

7. Impulsively idealistic, like the hero of Miguel de Cervantes's *Don Quixote* (1605, 1615).

150 ALGERNON   I will. I feel better already.

CECILY   You are looking a little worse.

ALGERNON   That is because I am hungry.

CECILY   How thoughtless of me. I should have remembered that when one is going to lead an entirely new life, one requires regular and wholesome
155   meals. Won't you come in?

ALGERNON   Thank you. Might I have a buttonhole[8] first? I never have any appetite unless I have a buttonhole first.

CECILY   A Maréchal Niel?[9] [*Picks up scissors.*]

ALGERNON   No, I'd sooner have a pink rose.

160 CECILY   Why? [*Cuts a flower.*]

ALGERNON   Because you are like a pink rose, Cousin Cecily.

CECILY   I don't think it can be right for you to talk to me like that. Miss Prism never says such things to me.

ALGERNON   Then Miss Prism is a short-sighted old lady. [CECILY *puts the rose*
165   *in his buttonhole.*] You are the prettiest girl I ever saw.

CECILY   Miss Prism says that all good looks are a snare.

ALGERNON   They are a snare that every sensible man would like to be caught in.

CECILY   Oh! I don't think I would care to catch a sensible man. I shouldn't know what to talk to him about.

[*They pass into the house.* MISS PRISM *and* DR CHASUBLE *return.*]

170 MISS PRISM   You are too much alone, dear Dr Chasuble. You should get married. A misanthrope I can understand—a womanthrope, never!

CHASUBLE [*with a scholar's shudder*]   Believe me, I do not deserve so neologistic a phrase.[1] The precept as well as the practice of the Primitive Church was distinctly against matrimony.[2]

175 MISS PRISM [*sententiously*]   That is obviously the reason why the Primitive Church has not lasted up to the present day. And you do not seem to realize, dear Doctor, that by persistently remaining single, a man converts himself into a permanent public temptation. Men should be more careful; this very celibacy leads weaker vessels astray.

180 CHASUBLE   But is a man not equally attractive when married?

MISS PRISM   No married man is ever attractive except to his wife.

CHASUBLE   And often, I've been told, not even to her.

MISS PRISM   That depends on the intellectual sympathies of the woman. Maturity can always be depended on. Ripeness can be trusted. Young
185   women are green.[3] [DR CHASUBLE *starts.*] I spoke horticulturally. My metaphor was drawn from fruits. But where is Cecily?

CHASUBLE   Perhaps she followed us to the schools.

[*Enter* JACK *slowly from the back of the garden. He is dressed in the deepest mourning, with crape hat-band[4] and black gloves.*]

---

8. A flower worn in the lapel of a man's jacket.

9. A fragrant yellow rose, developed in France and first grown in England in 1864; it was named after Adolphe Niel, marshal of France under Napoleon III.

1. Chasuble is pained by the illogical coinage "womanthrope," which mixes Old English and Greek roots.

2. That is, the marriage of clergy (permitted in the Church of England). *The Primitive Church*: the Early Christian church. As his comment on celibacy indicates, the High Church Anglicanism practiced by Chasuble—whose name evokes a vestment worn during services—saw itself as maintaining that tradition.

3. Unripe, and thus inexperienced, easily deceived; understood by Chasuble as suffering from greensickness, an anemic condition found especially in adolescent girls and long believed to be caused by celibacy.

4. A band of crepe material, worn to signify mourning.

MISS PRISM   Mr Worthing!

CHASUBLE   Mr Worthing?

190 MISS PRISM   This is indeed a surprise. We did not look for you till Monday afternoon.

JACK [*shakes* MISS PRISM'*s hand in a tragic manner*]   I have returned sooner than I expected. Dr Chasuble, I hope you are well?

CHASUBLE   Dear Mr Worthing, I trust this garb of woe does not betoken
195 some terrible calamity?

JACK   My brother.

MISS PRISM   More shameful debts and extravagance?

CHASUBLE   Still leading his life of pleasure?

JACK [*shaking his head*]   Dead!

200 CHASUBLE   Your brother Ernest dead?

JACK   Quite dead.

MISS PRISM   What a lesson for him! I trust he will profit by it.

CHASUBLE   Mr Worthing, I offer you my sincere condolence. You have at least the consolation of knowing that you were always the most generous
205 and forgiving of brothers.

JACK   Poor Ernest! He had many faults, but it is a sad, sad blow.

CHASUBLE   Very sad indeed. Were you with him at the end?

JACK   No. He died abroad; in Paris, in fact. I had a telegram last night from the manager of the Grand Hotel.[5]

210 CHASUBLE   Was the cause of death mentioned?

JACK   A severe chill, it seems.

MISS PRISM   As a man sows, so shall he reap.

CHASUBLE [*raising his hand*]   Charity, dear Miss Prism, charity! None of us are perfect. I myself am peculiarly susceptible to draughts. Will the inter-
215 ment take place here?

JACK   No. He seemed to have expressed a desire to be buried in Paris.

CHASUBLE   In Paris! [*Shakes his head.*] I fear that hardly points to any very seri-ous state of mind at the last. You would no doubt wish me to make some slight allusion to this tragic domestic affliction next Sunday. [JACK *presses his*
220 *hand convulsively.*] My sermon on the meaning of the manna in the wilder-ness[6] can be adapted to almost any occasion, joyful, or, as in the present case, distressing. [*All sigh.*] I have preached it at harvest celebrations, chris-tenings, confirmations, on days of humiliation and festal days. The last time I delivered it was in the Cathedral, as a charity sermon on behalf of the Soci-
225 ety for the Prevention of Discontent among the Upper Orders. The Bishop, who was present, was much struck by some of the analogies I drew.

JACK   Ah! that reminds me, you mentioned christenings I think, Dr Chasu-ble? I suppose you know how to christen all right? [DR CHASUBLE *looks astounded.*] I mean, of course, you are continually christening, aren't you?

230 MISS PRISM   It is, I regret to say, one of the Rector's most constant duties in this parish. I have often spoken to the poorer classes on the subject. But they don't seem to know what thrift is.

CHASUBLE   But is there any particular infant in whom you are interested, Mr Worthing? Your brother was, I believe, unmarried, was he not?

235 JACK   Oh, yes.

---

5. A luxurious Paris hotel.
6. The food said to have miraculously fallen

from heaven for the hungry Israelites when they wandered in the wilderness (Exodus 16).

MISS PRISM [*bitterly*]   People who live entirely for pleasure usually are.

JACK   But it is not for any child, dear Doctor. I am very fond of children. No! the fact is, I would like to be christened myself, this afternoon, if you have nothing better to do.

240 CHASUBLE   But surely, Mr Worthing, you have been christened already?

JACK   I don't remember anything about it.

CHASUBLE   But have you any grave doubts on the subject?

JACK   I certainly intend to have. Of course I don't know if the thing would bother you in any way, or if you think I am a little too old now.

245 CHASUBLE   Not at all. The sprinkling, and, indeed, the immersion of adults is a perfectly canonical practice.

JACK   Immersion!

CHASUBLE   You need have no apprehensions. Sprinkling is all that is necessary, or indeed I think advisable. Our weather is so changeable. At what
250   hour would you wish the ceremony performed?

JACK   Oh, I might trot round about five if that would suit you.

CHASUBLE   Perfectly, perfectly! In fact I have two similar ceremonies to perform at that time. A case of twins that occurred recently in one of the outlying cottages on your own estate. Poor Jenkins the carter, a most hard-
255   working man.

JACK   Oh! I don't see much fun in being christened along with other babies. It would be childish. Would half-past five do?

CHASUBLE   Admirably! Admirably! [*Takes out watch.*] And now, dear Mr Worthing, I will not intrude any longer into a house of sorrow. I would
260   merely beg you not to be too much bowed down by grief. What seem to us bitter trials are often blessings in disguise.

MISS PRISM   This seems to me a blessing of an extremely obvious kind.

[*Enter* CECILY *from the house.*]

CECILY   Uncle Jack! Oh, I am pleased to see you back. But what horrid clothes you have got on! Do go and change them.

265 MISS PRISM   Cecily!

CHASUBLE   My child! my child!

[CECILY *goes towards* JACK; *he kisses her brow in a melancholy manner.*]

CECILY   What is the matter, Uncle Jack? Do look happy! You look as if you had toothache, and I have got such a surprise for you. Who do you think is in the dining-room? Your brother!

270 JACK   Who?

CECILY   Your brother Ernest. He arrived about half an hour ago.

JACK   What nonsense! I haven't got a brother.

CECILY   Oh, don't say that. However badly he may have behaved to you in the past he is still your brother. You couldn't be so heartless as to disown
275   him. I'll tell him to come out. And you will shake hands with him, won't you, Uncle Jack?   [*Runs back into the house.*]

CHASUBLE   These are very joyful tidings.

MISS PRISM   After we had all been resigned to his loss, his sudden return seems to me peculiarly distressing.

280 JACK   My brother is in the dining-room? I don't know what it all means. I think it is perfectly absurd.

[*Enter* ALGERNON *and* CECILY *hand in hand. They come slowly up to* JACK.]

JACK   Good heavens! [*Motions* ALGERNON *away.*]

ALGERNON   Brother John, I have come down from town to tell you that I am
very sorry for all the trouble I have given you, and that I intend to lead a
285   better life in the future.

[JACK *glares at him and does not take his hand.*]

CECILY   Uncle Jack, you are not going to refuse your own brother's hand?

JACK   Nothing will induce me to take his hand. I think his coming down here
disgraceful. He knows perfectly well why.

CECILY   Uncle Jack, do be nice. There is some good in everyone. Ernest has
290   just been telling me about his poor invalid friend Mr Bunbury whom he
goes to visit so often. And surely there must be much good in one who is
kind to an invalid, and leaves the pleasures of London to sit by a bed of pain.

JACK   Oh! he has been talking about Bunbury has he?

CECILY   Yes, he has told me all about poor Mr Bunbury, and his terrible state
295   of health.

JACK   Bunbury! Well, I won't have him talk to you about Bunbury or about
anything else. It is enough to drive one perfectly frantic.

ALGERNON   Of course I admit that the faults were all on my side. But I must
say that I think that Brother John's coldness to me is peculiarly painful. I
300   expected a more enthusiastic welcome, especially considering it is the first
time I have come here.

CECILY   Uncle Jack, if you don't shake hands with Ernest I will never forgive
you.

JACK   Never forgive me?

305 CECILY   Never, never, never!

JACK   Well, this is the last time I shall ever do it. [*Shakes hands with* ALGER-
NON *and glares.*]

CHASUBLE   It's pleasant, is it not, to see so perfect a reconciliation? I think
we might leave the two brothers together.

MISS PRISM   Cecily, you will come with us.

310 CECILY   Certainly, Miss Prism. My little task of reconciliation is over.

CHASUBLE   You have done a beautiful action today, dear child.

MISS PRISM   We must not be premature in our judgments.

CECILY   I feel very happy.

[*They all go off.*]

JACK   You young scoundrel, Algy, you must get out of this place as soon as
315   possible. I don't allow any Bunburying here.

[*Enter* MERRIMAN.]

MERRIMAN   I have put Mr Ernest's things in the room next to yours, sir. I
suppose that is all right?

JACK   What?

MERRIMAN   Mr Ernest's luggage, sir. I have unpacked it and put it in the
320   room next to your own.

JACK   His luggage?

MERRIMAN   Yes, sir. Three portmanteaus, a dressing-case,[7] two hat-boxes,
and a large luncheon-basket.

ALGERNON   I am afraid I can't stay more than a week this time.

---

7. A case for toiletries.

325 JACK   Merriman, order the dog-cart[8] at once. Mr Ernest has been suddenly called back to town.

MERRIMAN   Yes, sir.   [*Goes back into the house.*]

ALGERNON   What a fearful liar you are, Jack. I have not been called back to town at all.

330 JACK   Yes, you have.

ALGERNON   I haven't heard anyone call me.

JACK   Your duty as a gentleman calls you back.

ALGERNON   My duty as a gentleman has never interfered with my pleasures in the smallest degree.

335 JACK   I can quite understand that.

ALGERNON   Well, Cecily is a darling.

JACK   You are not to talk of Miss Cardew like that. I don't like it.

ALGERNON   Well, I don't like your clothes. You look perfectly ridiculous in them. Why on earth don't you go up and change? It is perfectly childish to
340   be in deep mourning for a man who is actually staying for a whole week with you in your house as a guest. I call it grotesque.

JACK   You are certainly not staying with me for a whole week as a guest or anything else. You have got to leave . . . by the four-five train.

ALGERNON   I certainly won't leave you so long as you are in mourning. It
345   would be most unfriendly. If I were in mourning you would stay with me, I suppose. I should think it very unkind if you didn't.

JACK   Well, will you go if I change my clothes?

ALGERNON   Yes, if you are not too long. I never saw anybody take so long to dress, and with such little result.

350 JACK   Well, at any rate, that is better than being always over-dressed as you are.

ALGERNON   If I am occasionally a little over-dressed, I make up for it by being always immensely over-educated.

JACK   Your vanity is ridiculous, your conduct an outrage, and your presence in my garden utterly absurd. However, you have got to catch the four-five,
355   and I hope you will have a pleasant journey back to town. This Bunburying, as you call it, has not been a great success for you.   [*Goes into the house.*]

ALGERNON   I think it has been a great success. I'm in love with Cecily, and that is everything.

[*Enter* CECILY *at the back of the garden. She picks up the can and begins to water the flowers.*]

But I must see her before I go, and make arrangements for another Bun-
360   bury. Ah, there she is.

CECILY   Oh, I merely came back to water the roses. I thought you were with Uncle Jack.

ALGERNON   He's gone to order the dog-cart for me.

CECILY   Oh, is he going to take you for a nice drive?

365 ALGERNON   He's going to send me away.

CECILY   Then have we got to part?

ALGERNON   I am afraid so. It's a painful parting.

CECILY   It is always painful to part from people whom one has known for a very brief space of time. The absence of old friends one can endure with

---

8. A light, two-wheeled open carriage, originally designed with a small rear compartment to hold sportsmen's dogs.

370   equanimity. But even a momentary separation from anyone to whom one
has just been introduced is almost unbearable.

ALGERNON   Thank you.

        [*Enter* MERRIMAN.]

MERRIMAN   The dog-cart is at the door, sir.

        [ALGERNON *looks appealingly at* CECILY.]

CECILY   It can wait, Merriman . . . for . . . five minutes.

375 MERRIMAN   Yes, Miss.   [*Exit* MERRIMAN.]

ALGERNON   I hope, Cecily, I shall not offend you if I state quite frankly and
openly that you seem to me to be in every way the visible personification of
absolute perfection.

CECILY   I think your frankness does you great credit, Ernest. If you will allow

380   me I will copy your remarks into my diary. [*Goes over to table and begins
writing in diary.*]

ALGERNON   Do you really keep a diary? I'd give anything to look at it. May I?

CECILY   Oh no. [*Puts her hand over it.*] You see, it is simply a very young girl's
record of her own thoughts and impressions, and consequently meant for
publication. When it appears in volume form I hope you will order a copy.

385   But pray, Ernest, don't stop. I delight in taking down from dictation. I have
reached 'absolute perfection'. You can go on. I am quite ready for more.

ALGERNON [*somewhat taken aback*]   Ahem! Ahem!

CECILY   Oh, don't cough, Ernest. When one is dictating one should speak
fluently and not cough. Besides, I don't know how to spell a cough. [*Writes
as* ALGERNON *speaks.*]

390 ALGERNON [*speaking very rapidly*]   Cecily, ever since I first looked upon your
wonderful and incomparable beauty, I have dared to love you wildly, passionately, devotedly, hopelessly.

CECILY   I don't think that you should tell me that you love me wildly, passionately, devotedly, hopelessly. Hopelessly doesn't seem to make much

395   sense, does it?

ALGERNON   Cecily!

        [*Enter* MERRIMAN.]

MERRIMAN   The dog-cart is waiting, sir.

ALGERNON   Tell it to come round next week, at the same hour.

MERRIMAN [*looks at* CECILY, *who makes no sign*]   Yes, sir. [MERRIMAN *retires.*]

400 CECILY   Uncle Jack would be very much annoyed if he knew you were staying on till next week, at the same hour.

ALGERNON   Oh, I don't care about Jack. I don't care for anybody in the whole
world but you. I love you, Cecily. You will marry me, won't you?

CECILY   You silly boy! Of course. Why, we have been engaged for the last

405   three months.

ALGERNON   For the last three months?

CECILY   Yes, it will be exactly three months on Thursday.

ALGERNON   But how did we become engaged?

CECILY   Well, ever since dear Uncle Jack first confessed to us that he had a

410   younger brother who was very wicked and bad, you of course have formed
the chief topic of conversation between myself and Miss Prism. And of
course a man who is much talked about is always very attractive. One feels
there must be something in him after all. I daresay it was foolish of me, but
I fell in love with you, Ernest.

415 ALGERNON   Darling! And when was the engagement actually settled?

CECILY   On the 14th of February last.[9] Worn out by your entire ignorance of my existence, I determined to end the matter one way or the other, and after a long struggle with myself I accepted you under this dear old tree here. The next day I bought this little ring in your name, and this is the

420 little bangle with the true lovers' knot I promised you always to wear.

ALGERNON   Did I give you this? It's very pretty, isn't it?

CECILY   Yes, you've wonderfully good taste, Ernest. It's the excuse I've always given for your leading such a bad life. And this is the box in which I keep all your dear letters. [*Kneels at table, opens box, and produces letters tied up with blue ribbon.*]

425 ALGERNON   My letters! But my own sweet Cecily, I have never written you any letters.

CECILY   You need hardly remind me of that, Ernest. I remember only too well that I was forced to write your letters for you. I wrote always three times a week, and sometimes oftener.

430 ALGERNON   Oh, do let me read them, Cecily?

CECILY   Oh, I couldn't possibly. They would make you far too conceited. [*Replaces box.*] The three you wrote me after I had broken off the engagement are so beautiful, and so badly spelled, that even now I can hardly read them without crying a little.

435 ALGERNON   But was our engagement ever broken off?

CECILY   Of course it was. On the 22nd of last March. You can see the entry if you like. [*Shows diary.*] 'Today I broke off my engagement with Ernest. I feel it is better to do so. The weather still continues charming.'

ALGERNON   But why on earth did you break it off? What had I done? I had

440 done nothing at all. Cecily, I am very much hurt indeed to hear you broke it off. Particularly when the weather was so charming.

CECILY   It would hardly have been a really serious engagement if it hadn't been broken off at least once. But I forgave you before the week was out.

ALGERNON [*crossing to her, and kneeling*]   What a perfect angel you are, Cecily.

445 CECILY   You dear romantic boy. [*He kisses her, she puts her fingers through his hair.*] I hope your hair curls naturally, does it?

ALGERNON   Yes, darling, with a little help from others.

CECILY   I am so glad.

ALGERNON   You'll never break off our engagement again, Cecily?

450 CECILY   I don't think I could break it off now that I have actually met you. Besides, of course, there is the question of your name.

ALGERNON   Yes, of course. [*Nervously*]

CECILY   You must not laugh at me, darling, but it had always been a girlish dream of mine to love some one whose name was Ernest. [ALGERNON *rises,*

455 CECILY *also.*] There is something in that name that seems to inspire absolute confidence. I pity any poor married woman whose husband is not called Ernest.

ALGERNON   But, my dear child, do you mean to say you could not love me if I had some other name?

460 CECILY   But what name?

9. Valentine's Day, also the date when *The Importance of Being Earnest* premiered at St. James's Theatre in 1895.

ALGERNON   Oh, any name you like—Algernon—for instance . . .

CECILY   But I don't like the name of Algernon.

ALGERNON   Well, my own dear, sweet, loving little darling, I really can't see
why you should object to the name of Algernon. It is not at all a bad name.
465   In fact, it is rather an aristocratic name. Half of the chaps who get into the
Bankruptcy Court are called Algernon. But seriously, Cecily . . . [*Moving to
her*] . . . if my name was Algy, couldn't you love me?

CECILY [*rising*]   I might respect you, Ernest, I might admire your character,
but I fear that I should not be able to give you my undivided attention.

470   ALGERNON   Ahem! Cecily! [*Picking up hat*] Your Rector here is, I suppose,
thoroughly experienced in the practice of all the rites and ceremonials of
the Church?

CECILY   Oh yes. Dr Chasuble is a most learned man. He has never written a
single book, so you can imagine how much he knows.

475   ALGERNON   I must see him at once on a most important christening—I mean
on most important business.

CECILY   Oh!

ALGERNON   I shan't be away more than half an hour.

CECILY   Considering that we have been engaged since February the 14th,
480   and that I only met you today for the first time, I think it is rather hard that
you should leave me for so long a period as half an hour. Couldn't you
make it twenty minutes?

ALGERNON   I'll be back in no time.   [*Kisses her and rushes down the garden.*]

CECILY   What an impetuous boy he is! I like his hair so much. I must enter
485   his proposal in my diary.

[*Enter* MERRIMAN.]

MERRIMAN   A Miss Fairfax has just called to see Mr Worthing. On very
important business Miss Fairfax states.

CECILY   Isn't Mr Worthing in his library?

MERRIMAN   Mr Worthing went over in the direction of the Rectory some
490   time ago.

CECILY   Pray ask the lady to come out here; Mr Worthing is sure to be back
soon. And you can bring tea.

MERRIMAN   Yes, Miss.   [*Goes out.*]

CECILY   Miss Fairfax! I suppose one of the many good elderly women
495   who are associated with Uncle Jack in some of his philanthropic work in
London. I don't quite like women who are interested in philanthropic
work. I think it is so forward of them.

[*Enter* MERRIMAN.]

MERRIMAN   Miss Fairfax.

[*Enter* GWENDOLEN.]   [*Exit* MERRIMAN.]

CECILY [*advancing to meet her*]   Pray let me introduce myself to you. My
500   name is Cecily Cardew.

GWENDOLEN   Cecily Cardew? [*Moving to her and shaking hands*] What a very
sweet name! Something tells me that we are going to be great friends. I like
you already more than I can say. My first impressions of people are never
wrong.

505   CECILY   How nice of you to like me so much after we have known each other
such a comparatively short time. Pray sit down.

GWENDOLEN [*still standing up*]   I may call you Cecily, may I not?

CECILY   With pleasure!

GWENDOLEN   And you will always call me Gwendolen, won't you.

510 CECILY   If you wish.

GWENDOLEN   Then that is all quite settled, is it not?

CECILY   I hope so.

[*A pause. They both sit down together.*]

GWENDOLEN   Perhaps this might be a favourable opportunity for my mentioning who I am. My father is Lord Bracknell. You have never heard of
515 papa, I suppose?

CECILY   I don't think so.

GWENDOLEN   Outside the family circle, papa, I am glad to say, is entirely unknown. I think that is quite as it should be. The home seems to me to be the proper sphere for the man.[1] And certainly once a man begins to neglect
520 his domestic duties he becomes painfully effeminate, does he not? And I don't like that. It makes men so very attractive. Cecily, mamma, whose views on education are remarkably strict, has brought me up to be extremely short-sighted; it is part of her system; so do you mind my looking at you through my glasses?

525 CECILY   Oh! not at all, Gwendolen. I am very fond of being looked at.

GWENDOLEN [*after examining* CECILY *carefully through a lorgnette*]   You are here on a short visit I suppose.

CECILY   Oh no! I live here.

GWENDOLEN [*severely*]   Really? Your mother, no doubt, or some female rela-
530 tive of advanced years, resides here also?

CECILY   Oh no! I have no mother, nor, in fact, any relations.

GWENDOLEN   Indeed?

CECILY   My dear guardian, with the assistance of Miss Prism, has the arduous task of looking after me.

535 GWENDOLEN   Your guardian?

CECILY   Yes, I am Mr Worthing's ward.

GWENDOLEN   Oh! It is strange he never mentioned to me that he had a ward. How secretive of him! He grows more interesting hourly. I am not sure, however, that the news inspires me with feelings of unmixed delight. [*Ris-
540 ing and going to her*] I am very fond of you, Cecily; I have liked you ever since I met you! But I am bound to state that now that I know that you are Mr Worthing's ward, I cannot help expressing a wish you were—well just a little older than you seem to be—and not quite so very alluring in appearance. In fact, if I may speak candidly——

545 CECILY   Pray do! I think that whenever one has anything unpleasant to say, one should always be quite candid.

GWENDOLEN   Well, to speak with perfect candour, Cecily, I wish that you were fully forty-two, and more than usually plain for your age. Ernest has a strong upright nature. He is the very soul of truth and honour. Disloyalty
550 would be as impossible to him as deception. But even men of the noblest possible moral character are extremely susceptible to the influence of the physical charms of others. Modern, no less than Ancient History, supplies

---

1. The 19th-century doctrine of separate spheres divided life into two domains: public (male) and private (female).

us with many most painful examples of what I refer to. If it were not so, indeed, History would be quite unreadable.

555 CECILY   I beg your pardon, Gwendolen, did you say Ernest?

GWENDOLEN   Yes.

CECILY   Oh, but it is not Mr Ernest Worthing who is my guardian. It is his brother—his elder brother.

GWENDOLEN [sitting down again]   Ernest never mentioned to me that he had
560   a brother.

CECILY   I am sorry to say they have not been on good terms for a long time.

GWENDOLEN   Ah! that accounts for it. And now that I think of it I have never heard any man mention his brother. The subject seems distasteful to most men. Cecily, you have lifted a load from my mind. I was growing almost
565   anxious. It would have been terrible if any cloud had come across a friendship like ours, would it not? Of course you are quite, quite sure that it is not Mr Ernest Worthing who is your guardian?

CECILY   Quite sure. [A pause] In fact, I am going to be his.

GWENDOLEN [enquiringly]   I beg your pardon?

570 CECILY [rather shy and confidingly]   Dearest Gwendolen, there is no reason why I should make a secret of it to you. Our little county newspaper is sure to chronicle the fact next week. Mr Ernest Worthing and I are engaged to be married.

GWENDOLEN [quite politely, rising]   My darling Cecily, I think there must be
575   some slight error. Mr Ernest Worthing is engaged to me. The announcement will appear in the 'Morning Post'[2] on Saturday at the latest.

CECILY [very politely, rising]   I am afraid you must be under some misconception. Ernest proposed to me exactly ten minutes ago. [Shows diary.]

GWENDOLEN [examines diary through her lorgnette carefully]   It is certainly
580   very curious, for he asked me to be his wife yesterday afternoon at 5.30. If you would care to verify the incident, pray do so. [Produces diary of her own.] I never travel without my diary. One should always have something sensational to read in the train. I am so sorry, dear Cecily, if it is any disappointment to you, but I am afraid I have the prior claim.

585 CECILY   It would distress me more than I can tell you, dear Gwendolen, if it caused you any mental or physical anguish, but I feel bound to point out that since Ernest proposed to you he clearly has changed his mind.

GWENDOLEN [meditatively]   If the poor fellow has been entrapped into any foolish promise I shall consider it my duty to rescue him at once, and with
590   a firm hand.

CECILY [thoughtfully and sadly]   Whatever unfortunate entanglement my dear boy may have got into, I will never reproach him with it after we are married.

GWENDOLEN   Do you allude to me, Miss Cardew, as an entanglement? You are presumptuous. On an occasion of this kind it becomes more than a
595   moral duty to speak one's mind. It becomes a pleasure.

CECILY   Do you suggest, Miss Fairfax, that I entrapped Ernest into an engagement? How dare you? This is no time for wearing the shallow mask of manners. When I see a spade I call it a spade.

GWENDOLEN [satirically]   I am glad to say that I have never seen a spade. It is
600   obvious that our social spheres have been widely different.

_____

2. The London Morning Post, a conservative daily newspaper.

[*Enter* MERRIMAN, *followed by the footman. He carries a salver, table cloth, and plate stand.* CECILY *is about to retort. The presence of the servants exercises a restraining influence, under which both girls chafe.*]

MERRIMAN Shall I lay tea here as usual, Miss?

CECILY [*sternly, in a calm voice*] Yes, as usual.

> [MERRIMAN *begins to clear table and lay cloth. A long pause.* CECILY *and* GWENDOLEN *glare at each other.*]

GWENDOLEN Are there many interesting walks in the vicinity, Miss Cardew?

CECILY Oh! yes! a great many. From the top of one of the hills quite close
605 one can see five counties.

GWENDOLEN Five counties! I don't think I should like that. I hate crowds.

CECILY [*sweetly*] I suppose that is why you live in town?

> [GWENDOLEN *bites her lip, and beats her foot nervously with her parasol.*]

GWENDOLEN [*looking round*] Quite a well-kept garden this is, Miss Cardew.

CECILY So glad you like it, Miss Fairfax.

610 GWENDOLEN I had no idea there were any flowers in the country.

CECILY Oh, flowers are as common here, Miss Fairfax, as people are in
London.

GWENDOLEN Personally, I cannot understand how anybody manages to exist
in the country, if anybody who is anybody does. The country always bores
615 me to death.

CECILY Ah! This is what the newspapers call agricultural depression,[3] is it
not? I believe the aristocracy are suffering very much from it just at present. It is almost an epidemic amongst them, I have been told. May I offer
you some tea, Miss Fairfax?

620 GWENDOLEN [*with elaborate politeness*] Thank you. [*Aside*] Detestable girl!
But I require tea!

CECILY [*sweetly*] Sugar?

GWENDOLEN [*superciliously*] No, thank you. Sugar is not fashionable any
more.

> [CECILY *looks angrily at her, takes up the tongs and puts four lumps of sugar into the cup.*]

625 CECILY [*severely*] Cake or bread and butter?

GWENDOLEN [*in a bored manner*] Bread and butter, please. Cake is rarely
seen at the best houses nowadays.

CECILY [*cuts a very large slice of cake, and puts it on the tray*] Hand that to
Miss Fairfax.

> [MERRIMAN *does so, and goes out with footman.* GWENDOLEN *drinks the tea and makes a grimace. Puts down cup at once, reaches out her hand to the bread and butter, looks at it, and finds it is cake. Rises in indignation.*]

630 GWENDOLEN You have filled my tea with lumps of sugar, and though I asked
most distinctly for bread and butter, you have given me cake. I am known
for the gentleness of my disposition, and the extraordinary sweetness of my
nature, but I warn you, Miss Cardew, you may go too far.

CECILY [*rising*] To save my poor, innocent, trusting boy from the machina-
635 tions of any other girl there are no lengths to which I would not go.

---

3. British agriculture had been in an economic slump since the 1870s.

GWENDOLEN   From the moment I saw you I distrusted you. I felt that you were false and deceitful. I am never deceived in such matters. My first impressions of people are invariably right.

CECILY   It seems to me, Miss Fairfax, that I am trespassing on your valuable
640   time. No doubt you have many other calls of a similar character to make in the neighbourhood.

[*Enter* JACK.]

GWENDOLEN [*catching sight of him*]   Ernest! My own Ernest!

JACK   Gwendolen! Darling! [*Offers*[4] *to kiss her.*]

GWENDOLEN [*drawing back*]   A moment! May I ask if you are engaged to be
645   married to this young lady? [*Points to* CECILY.]

JACK [*laughing*]   To dear little Cecily! Of course not! What could have put such an idea into your pretty little head?

GWENDOLEN   Thank you. You may! [*Offers her cheek.*]

CECILY [*very sweetly*]   I knew there must be some misunderstanding, Miss
650   Fairfax. The gentleman whose arm is at present round your waist is my dear guardian, Mr John Worthing.

GWENDOLEN   I beg your pardon?

CECILY   This is Uncle Jack.

GWENDOLEN [*receding*]   Jack! Oh!

[*Enter* ALGERNON.]

655   CECILY   Here is Ernest.

ALGERNON [*goes straight over to* CECILY *without noticing anyone else*]   My own love! [*Offers to kiss her.*]

CECILY [*drawing back*]   A moment, Ernest! May I ask you—are you engaged to be married to this young lady?

660   ALGERNON [*looking round*]   To what young lady? Good heavens! Gwendolen!

CECILY   Yes, to good heavens, Gwendolen, I mean to Gwendolen.

ALGERNON [*laughing*]   Of course not! What could have put such an idea into your pretty little head?

CECILY   Thank you. [*Presenting her cheek to be kissed*] You may.

[ALGERNON *kisses her.*]

665   GWENDOLEN   I felt there was some slight error, Miss Cardew. The gentleman who is now embracing you is my cousin, Mr Algernon Moncrieff.

CECILY [*breaking away from* ALGERNON]   Algernon Moncrieff! Oh!

[*The two girls move towards each other and put their arms round each other's waists as if for protection.*]

CECILY   Are you called Algernon?

ALGERNON   I cannot deny it.

670   CECILY   Oh!

GWENDOLEN   Is your name really John?

JACK [*standing rather proudly*]   I could deny it if I liked. I could deny anything if I liked. But my name certainly is John. It has been John for years.

CECILY [*to* GWENDOLEN]   A gross deception has been practised on both of us.

675   GWENDOLEN   My poor wounded Cecily!

CECILY   My sweet wronged Gwendolen!

GWENDOLEN [*slowly and seriously*]   You will call me sister, will you not?

4. Attempts.

[*They embrace.* JACK *and* ALGERNON *groan and walk up and down.*]

CECILY [*rather brightly*]   There is just one question I would like to be allowed to ask my guardian.

680 GWENDOLEN   An admirable idea! Mr Worthing, there is just one question I would like to be permitted to put to you. Where is your brother Ernest? We are both engaged to be married to your brother Ernest, so it is a matter of some importance to us to know where your brother Ernest is at present.

JACK [*slowly and hesitatingly*]   Gwendolen—Cecily—it is very painful for me 685 to be forced to speak the truth. It is the first time in my life that I have ever been reduced to such a painful position, and I am really quite inexperienced in doing anything of the kind. However I will tell you quite frankly that I have no brother Ernest. I have no brother at all. I never had a brother in my life, and I certainly have not the smallest intention of ever having 690 one in the future.

CECILY [*surprised*]   No brother at all?

JACK [*cheerily*]   None!

GWENDOLEN [*severely*]   Had you never a brother of any kind?

JACK [*pleasantly*]   Never. Not even of any kind.

695 GWENDOLEN   I am afraid it is quite clear, Cecily, that neither of us is engaged to be married to anyone.

CECILY   It is not a very pleasant position for a young girl suddenly to find herself in. Is it?

GWENDOLEN   Let us go into the house. They will hardly venture to come 700 after us there.

CECILY   No, men are so cowardly, aren't they?

[*They retire into the house with scornful looks.*]

JACK   This ghastly state of things is what you call Bunburying, I suppose?

ALGERNON   Yes, and a perfectly wonderful Bunbury it is. The most wonderful Bunbury I have ever had in my life.

705 JACK   Well, you've no right whatsoever to Bunbury here.

ALGERNON   That is absurd. One has a right to Bunbury anywhere one chooses. Every serious Bunburyist knows that.

JACK   Serious Bunburyist! Good heavens!

ALGERNON   Well, one must be serious about something, if one wants to have 710 any amusement in life. I happen to be serious about Bunburying. What on earth you are serious about I haven't got the remotest idea. About everything, I should fancy. You have such an absolutely trivial nature.

JACK   Well, the only small satisfaction I have in the whole of this wretched business is that your friend Bunbury is quite exploded. You won't be able to 715 run down to the country quite so often as you used to do, dear Algy. And a very good thing too.

ALGERNON   Your brother is a little off colour,[5] isn't he, dear Jack? You won't be able to disappear to London quite so frequently as your wicked custom was. And not a bad thing either.

720 JACK   As for your conduct towards Miss Cardew, I must say that your taking in a sweet, simple, innocent girl like that is quite inexcusable. To say nothing of the fact that she is my ward.

5. That is, in poor health.

ALGERNON   I can see no possible defence at all for your deceiving a brilliant, clever, thoroughly experienced young lady like Miss Fairfax. To say nothing
725   of the fact that she is my cousin.

JACK   I wanted to be engaged to Gwendolen, that is all. I love her.

ALGERNON   Well, I simply wanted to be engaged to Cecily. I adore her.

JACK   There is certainly no chance of your marrying Miss Cardew.

ALGERNON   I don't think there is much likelihood, Jack, of you and Miss
730   Fairfax being united.

JACK   Well, that is no business of yours.

ALGERNON   If it was my business, I wouldn't talk about it. [*Begins to eat muffins.*] It is very vulgar to talk about one's business. Only people like stockbrokers do that, and then merely at dinner parties.

735 JACK   How you can sit there, calmly eating muffins when we are in this horrible trouble, I can't make out. You seem to me to be perfectly heartless.

ALGERNON   Well, I can't eat muffins in an agitated manner. The butter would probably get on my cuffs. One should always eat muffins quite calmly. It is the only way to eat them.

740 JACK   I say it's perfectly heartless your eating muffins at all, under the circumstances.

ALGERNON   When I am in trouble, eating is the only thing that consoles me. Indeed, when I am in really great trouble, as anyone who knows me intimately will tell you, I refuse everything except food and drink. At the
745   present moment I am eating muffins because I am unhappy. Besides, I am particularly fond of muffins. [*Rising*]

JACK [*rising*]   Well, that is no reason why you should eat them all in that greedy way. [*Takes muffins from* ALGERNON.]

ALGERNON [*offering tea-cake*]   I wish you would have tea-cake instead. I
750   don't like tea-cake.

JACK   Good heavens! I suppose a man may eat his own muffins in his own garden.

ALGERNON   But you have just said it was perfectly heartless to eat muffins.

JACK   I said it was perfectly heartless of you, under the circumstances. That
755   is a very different thing.

ALGERNON   That may be. But the muffins are the same. [*He seizes the muffin-dish from* JACK.]

JACK   Algy, I wish to goodness you would go.

ALGERNON   You can't possibly ask me to go without having some dinner. It's absurd. I never go without my dinner. No one ever does, except vegetarians
760   and people like that. Besides I have just made arrangements with Dr Chasuble to be christened at a quarter to six under the name of Ernest.

JACK   My dear fellow, the sooner you give up that nonsense the better. I made arrangements this morning with Dr Chasuble to be christened myself at 5.30, and I naturally will take the name of Ernest. Gwendolen would
765   wish it. We can't both be christened Ernest. It's absurd. Besides, I have a perfect right to be christened if I like. There is no evidence at all that I ever have been christened by anybody. I should think it extremely probable I never was, and so does Dr Chasuble. It is entirely different in your case. You have been christened already.

770 ALGERNON   Yes, but I have not been christened for years.

JACK   Yes, but you have been christened. That is the important thing.

ALGERNON   Quite so. So I know my constitution can stand it. If you are not quite sure about your ever having been christened, I must say I think it rather dangerous your venturing on it now. It might make you very unwell. You can hardly have forgotten that someone very closely connected with you was very nearly carried off this week in Paris by a severe chill.

JACK   Yes, but you said yourself that a severe chill was not hereditary.

ALGERNON   It usen't to be, I know—but I daresay it is now. Science is always making wonderful improvements in things.

JACK [*picking up the muffin-dish*]   Oh, that is nonsense; you are always talking nonsense.

ALGERNON   Jack, you are at the muffins again! I wish you wouldn't. There are only two left. [*Takes them.*] I told you I was particularly fond of muffins.

JACK   But I hate tea-cake.

ALGERNON   Why on earth then do you allow tea-cake to be served up for your guests? What ideas you have of hospitality!

JACK   Algernon! I have already told you to go. I don't want you here. Why don't you go!

ALGERNON   I haven't quite finished my tea yet! and there is still one muffin left.

[JACK *groans, and sinks into a chair.* ALGERNON *still continues eating.*]

Act Drop.

Third Act

[SCENE: *Morning-room at the Manor House.*]

[GWENDOLEN *and* CECILY *are at the window, looking out into the garden.*]

GWENDOLEN   The fact that they did not follow us at once into the house, as anyone else would have done, seems to me to show that they have some sense of shame left.

CECILY   They have been eating muffins. That looks like repentance.

GWENDOLEN [*after a pause*]   They don't seem to notice us at all. Couldn't you cough?

CECILY   But I haven't got a cough.

GWENDOLEN   They're looking at us. What effrontery!

CECILY   They're approaching. That's very forward of them.

GWENDOLEN   Let us preserve a dignified silence.

CECILY   Certainly. It's the only thing to do now.

[*Enter* JACK *followed by* ALGERNON. *They whistle some dreadful popular air from a British Opera.*[6]]

GWENDOLEN   This dignified silence seems to produce an unpleasant effect.

CECILY   A most distasteful one.

GWENDOLEN   But we will not be the first to speak.

CECILY   Certainly not.

GWENDOLEN   Mr Worthing, I have something very particular to ask you. Much depends on your reply.

CECILY   Gwendolen, your common sense is invaluable. Mr Moncrieff, kindly answer me the following question. Why did you pretend to be my guardian's brother?

6. Possibly a reference to the comic operas of W. S. Gilbert (1836–1911) and Sir Arthur Sullivan (1842–1900), whose 1881 *Patience* satirized Wilde and the aesthetic movement.

ALGERNON   In order that I might have an opportunity of meeting you.

CECILY [*to* GWENDOLEN]   That certainly seems a satisfactory explanation, does it not?

GWENDOLEN   Yes, dear, if you can believe him.

25   CECILY   I don't. But that does not affect the wonderful beauty of his answer.

GWENDOLEN   True. In matters of grave importance, style, not sincerity is the vital thing. Mr Worthing, what explanation can you offer to me for pretending to have a brother? Was it in order that you might have an opportunity of coming up to town to see me as often as possible?

30   JACK   Can you doubt it, Miss Fairfax?

GWENDOLEN   I have the gravest doubts upon the subject. But I intend to crush them. This is not the moment for German scepticism.[7] [*Moving to* CECILY] Their explanations appear to be quite satisfactory, especially Mr Worthing's. That seems to me to have the stamp of truth upon it.

35   CECILY   I am more than content with what Mr Moncrieff said. His voice alone inspires one with absolute credulity.

GWENDOLEN   Then you think we should forgive them?

CECILY   Yes. I mean no.

GWENDOLEN   True! I had forgotten. There are principles at stake that one
40   cannot surrender. Which of us should tell them? The task is not a pleasant one.

CECILY   Could we not both speak at the same time?

GWENDOLEN   An excellent idea! I nearly always speak at the same time as other people. Will you take the time from me?

45   CECILY   Certainly.

[GWENDOLEN *beats time with uplifted finger.*]

GWENDOLEN and CECILY [*speaking together*]   Your Christian names are still an insuperable barrier. That is all!

JACK and ALGERNON [*speaking together*]   Our Christian names! Is that all? But we are going to be christened this afternoon.

50   GWENDOLEN [*to* JACK]   For my sake you are prepared to do this terrible thing?

JACK   I am.

CECILY [*to* ALGERNON]   To please me you are ready to face this fearful ordeal?

ALGERNON   I am!

GWENDOLEN   How absurd to talk of the equality of the sexes! Where ques-
55   tions of self-sacrifice are concerned, men are infinitely beyond us.

JACK   We are. [*Clasps hands with* ALGERNON.]

CECILY   They have moments of physical courage of which we women know absolutely nothing.

GWENDOLEN [*to* JACK]   Darling!

60   ALGERNON [*to* CECILY]   Darling! [*They fall into each other's arms.*]

[*Enter* MERRIMAN. *When he enters he coughs loudly, seeing the situation.*]

MERRIMAN   Ahem! Ahem! Lady Bracknell!

JACK   Good heavens!

[*Enter* LADY BRACKNELL. *The couples separate in alarm.*]

[*Exit* MERRIMAN.]

LADY BRACKNELL   Gwendolen! What does this mean?

7. German biblical scholars of the 19th century were notorious among the British for their skepticism toward scriptural authority and claims of divine revelation.

GWENDOLEN   Merely that I am engaged to be married to Mr Worthing,
65   mamma.

LADY BRACKNELL   Come here. Sit down. Sit down immediately. Hesitation of
any kind is a sign of mental decay in the young, of physical weakness in the
old. [*Turns to* JACK.] Apprised, sir, of my daughter's sudden flight by her
trusty maid, whose confidence I purchased by means of a small coin, I fol-
70   lowed her at once by a luggage train.[8] Her unhappy father is, I am glad to
say, under the impression that she is attending a more than usually lengthy
lecture by the University Extension Scheme[9] on the Influence of a permanent income on Thought. I do not propose to undeceive him. Indeed I have
never undeceived him on any question. I would consider it wrong. But of
75   course, you will clearly understand that all communication between yourself and my daughter must cease immediately from this moment. On this
point, as indeed on all points, I am firm.

JACK   I am engaged to be married to Gwendolen, Lady Bracknell!

LADY BRACKNELL   You are nothing of the kind, sir. And now, as regards Alger-
80   non! . . . Algernon!

ALGERNON   Yes, Aunt Augusta.

LADY BRACKNELL   May I ask if it is in this house that your invalid friend Mr
Bunbury resides?

ALGERNON [*stammering*]   Oh! No! Bunbury doesn't live here. Bunbury is
85   somewhere else at present. In fact, Bunbury is dead.

LADY BRACKNELL   Dead! When did Mr Bunbury die? His death must have
been extremely sudden.

ALGERNON [*airily*]   Oh! I killed Bunbury this afternoon. I mean poor Bunbury died this afternoon.

90   LADY BRACKNELL   What did he die of?

ALGERNON   Bunbury? Oh, he was quite exploded.

LADY BRACKNELL   Exploded! Was he the victim of a revolutionary outrage? I
was not aware that Mr Bunbury was interested in social legislation. If so,
he is well punished for his morbidity.

95   ALGERNON   My dear Aunt Augusta, I mean he was found out! The doctors
found out that Bunbury could not live, that is what I mean—so Bunbury died.

LADY BRACKNELL   He seems to have had great confidence in the opinion of his
physicians. I am glad, however, that he made up his mind at the last to some
definite course of action, and acted under proper medical advice. And now
100   that we have finally got rid of this Mr Bunbury, may I ask, Mr Worthing,
who is that young person whose hand my nephew Algernon is now holding
in what seems to me a peculiarly unnecessary manner?

JACK   That lady is Miss Cecily Cardew, my ward.

[LADY BRACKNELL *bows coldly to* CECILY.]

ALGERNON   I am engaged to be married to Cecily, Aunt Augusta.

105   LADY BRACKNELL   I beg your pardon?

CECILY   Mr Moncrieff and I are engaged to be married, Lady Bracknell.

LADY BRACKNELL [*with a shiver, crossing to the sofa and sitting down*]   I do not
know whether there is anything peculiarly exciting in the air of this particular part of Hertfordshire, but the number of engagements that go on
110   seems to me considerably above the proper average that statistics have laid

---

8. Freight train.
9. An extramural education program in which

university instructors delivered lectures to
students not pursuing regular degrees.

down for our guidance. I think some preliminary enquiry on my part would not be out of place. Mr Worthing, is Miss Cardew at all connected with any of the larger railway stations in London? I merely desire information. Until yesterday I had no idea that there were any families or persons whose

115 origin was a Terminus.[1]

[JACK *looks perfectly furious, but restrains himself.*]

JACK [*in a clear, cold voice*] Miss Cardew is the granddaughter of the late Mr Thomas Cardew of 149, Belgrave Square, S.W.; Gervase Park, Dorking, Surrey; and the Sporran, Fifeshire, N.B.[2]

LADY BRACKNELL That sounds not unsatisfactory. Three addresses always

120 inspire confidence, even in tradesmen. But what proof have I of their authenticity?

JACK I have carefully preserved the Court Guides[3] of the period. They are open to your inspection, Lady Bracknell.

LADY BRACKNELL [*grimly*] I have known strange errors in that publication.

125 JACK Miss Cardew's family solicitors are Messrs[4] Markby, Markby, and Markby.

LADY BRACKNELL Markby, Markby, and Markby? A firm of the very highest position in their profession. Indeed I am told that one of the Mr Markbys is occasionally to be seen at dinner parties. So far I am satisfied.

130 JACK [*very irritably*] How extremely kind of you, Lady Bracknell! I have also in my possession, you will be pleased to hear, certificates of Miss Cardew's birth, baptism, whooping cough, registration, vaccination, confirmation, and the measles; both the German and the English variety.[5]

LADY BRACKNELL Ah! A life crowded with incident, I see; though perhaps

135 somewhat too exciting for a young girl. I am not myself in favour of pre-mature experiences. [*Rises, looks at her watch.*] Gwendolen! the time approaches for our departure. We have not a moment to lose. As a matter of form, Mr Worthing, I had better ask you if Miss Cardew has any little fortune?

140 JACK Oh! about a hundred and thirty thousand pounds in the Funds.[6] That is all. Goodbye, Lady Bracknell. So pleased to have seen you.

LADY BRACKNELL [*sitting down again*] A moment, Mr Worthing. A hundred and thirty thousand pounds! And in the Funds! Miss Cardew seems to me a most attractive young lady, now that I look at her. Few girls of the present day

145 have any really solid qualities, any of the qualities that last, and improve with time. We live, I regret to say, in an age of surfaces. [*To* CECILY] Come over here, dear. [CECILY *goes across.*] Pretty child! your dress is sadly simple, and your hair seems almost as Nature might have left it. But we can soon alter all that. A thoroughly experienced French maid produces a really marvellous

150 result in a very brief space of time. I remember recommending one to young Lady Lancing, and after three months her own husband did not know her.

1. The station at the end of a railway line.
2. That is, with residences in Belgravia, in a county south of London, and in Scotland ("North Britain").
3. Annual publications listing the names and addresses of those presented at court—that is, the British nobility, gentry, and anyone else of social importance.

4. The plural of "Mister." *Solicitors:* British lawyers who advise and represent clients but do not argue cases in court.
5. That is, both rubeola and rubella.
6. Interest-bearing government bonds—and a considerable fortune (roughly equivalent to $20 million today).

JACK [*aside*]   And after six months nobody knew her.[7]

LADY BRACKNELL [*glares at* JACK *for a few moments. Then bends, with a practised smile, to* CECILY]   Kindly turn round, sweet child. [CECILY *turns completely round.*] No, the side view is what I want. [CECILY *presents her profile.*] Yes,
155 quite as I expected. There are distinct social possibilities in your profile. The two weak points in our age are its want of principle and its want of profile. The chin a little higher, dear. Style largely depends on the way the chin is worn. They are worn very high, just at present. Algernon!

ALGERNON   Yes, Aunt Augusta!

160 LADY BRACKNELL   There are distinct social possibilities in Miss Cardew's profile.

ALGERNON   Cecily is the sweetest, dearest, prettiest girl in the whole world. And I don't care twopence about social possibilities.

LADY BRACKNELL   Never speak disrespectfully of Society, Algernon. Only
165 people who can't get into it do that. [*To* CECILY] Dear child, of course you know that Algernon has nothing but his debts to depend upon. But I do not approve of mercenary marriages. When I married Lord Bracknell I had no fortune of any kind. But I never dreamed for a moment of allowing that to stand in my way. Well, I suppose I must give my consent.

170 ALGERNON   Thank you, Aunt Augusta.

LADY BRACKNELL   Cecily, you may kiss me!

CECILY [*kisses her*]   Thank you, Lady Bracknell.

LADY BRACKNELL   You may also address me as Aunt Augusta for the future.

CECILY   Thank you, Aunt Augusta.

175 LADY BRACKNELL   The marriage, I think, had better take place quite soon.

ALGERNON   Thank you, Aunt Augusta.

CECILY   Thank you, Aunt Augusta.

LADY BRACKNELL   To speak frankly, I am not in favour of long engagements. They give people the opportunity of finding out each other's character
180 before marriage, which I think is never advisable.

JACK   I beg your pardon for interrupting you, Lady Bracknell, but this engagement is quite out of the question. I am Miss Cardew's guardian, and she cannot marry without my consent until she comes of age. That consent I absolutely decline to give.

185 LADY BRACKNELL   Upon what grounds may I ask? Algernon is an extremely, I may almost say an ostentatiously, eligible young man. He has nothing, but he looks everything. What more can one desire?

JACK   It pains me very much to have to speak frankly to you, Lady Bracknell, about your nephew, but the fact is that I do not approve at all of his moral
190 character. I suspect him of being untruthful.

[ALGERNON *and* CECILY *look at him in indignant amazement.*]

LADY BRACKNELL   Untruthful! My nephew Algernon? Impossible! He is an Oxonian.[8]

JACK   I fear there can be no possible doubt about the matter. This afternoon, during my temporary absence in London on an important question of
195 romance, he obtained admission to my house by means of the false pretence of being my brother. Under an assumed name he drank, I've just been

---

7. Acknowledged her socially (i.e., her behavior had become scandalous).

8. A student at or graduate of Oxford University.

informed by my butler, an entire pint bottle of my Perrier-Jouet, Brut, '89;[9] a wine I was specially reserving for myself. Continuing his disgraceful deception, he succeeded in the course of the afternoon in alienating the affections

200 of my only ward. He subsequently stayed to tea, and devoured every single muffin. And what makes his conduct all the more heartless is, that he was perfectly well aware from the first that I have no brother, that I never had a brother, and that I don't intend to have a brother, not even of any kind. I distinctly told him so myself yesterday afternoon.

205 LADY BRACKNELL   Ahem! Mr Worthing, after careful consideration I have decided entirely to overlook my nephew's conduct to you.

JACK   That is very generous of you, Lady Bracknell. My own decision, however, is unalterable. I decline to give my consent.

LADY BRACKNELL [to CECILY]   Come here, sweet child. [CECILY goes over.]

210 How old are you, dear?

CECILY   Well, I am really only eighteen, but I always admit to twenty when I go to evening parties.

LADY BRACKNELL   You are perfectly right in making some slight alteration. Indeed, no woman should ever be quite accurate about her age. It looks so

215 calculating. . . . [In a meditative manner] Eighteen, but admitting to twenty at evening parties. Well, it will not be very long before you are of age and free from the restraints of tutelage. So I don't think your guardian's consent is, after all, a matter of any importance.

JACK   Pray excuse me, Lady Bracknell, for interrupting you again, but it is

220 only fair to tell you that according to the terms of her grandfather's will Miss Cardew does not come legally of age till she is thirty-five.

LADY BRACKNELL   That does not seem to me to be a grave objection. Thirty-five is a very attractive age. London society is full of women of the very highest birth who have, of their own free choice, remained thirty-five for

225 years. Lady Dumbleton is an instance in point. To my own knowledge she has been thirty-five ever since she arrived at the age of forty, which was many years ago now. I see no reason why our dear Cecily should not be even still more attractive at the age you mention than she is at present. There will be a large accumulation of property.

230 CECILY   Algy, could you wait for me till I was thirty-five?

ALGERNON   Of course I could, Cecily. You know I could.

CECILY   Yes, I felt it instinctively, but I couldn't wait all that time. I hate waiting even five minutes for anybody. It always makes me rather cross. I am not punctual myself, I know, but I do like punctuality in others, and wait-

235 ing, even to be married, is quite out of the question.

ALGERNON   Then what is to be done, Cecily?

CECILY   I don't know, Mr Moncrieff.

LADY BRACKNELL   My dear Mr Worthing, as Miss Cardew states positively that she cannot wait till she is thirty-five—a remark which I am bound to

240 say seems to me to show a somewhat impatient nature—I would beg of you to reconsider your decision.

JACK   But my dear Lady Bracknell, the matter is entirely in your own hands. The moment you consent to my marriage with Gwendolen, I will most gladly allow your nephew to form an alliance with my ward.

245 LADY BRACKNELL [rising and drawing herself up]   You must be quite aware that what you propose is out of the question.

9. A particularly fine vintage of dry champagne.

JACK   Then a passionate celibacy is all that any of us can look forward to.

LADY BRACKNELL   That is not the destiny I propose for Gwendolen. Algernon, of course, can choose for himself. [*Pulls out her watch.*] Come, dear; [GWENDOLEN *rises.*] we have already missed five, if not six, trains. To miss any more might expose us to comment on the platform.

[*Enter* DR CHASUBLE.]

CHASUBLE   Everything is quite ready for the christenings.

LADY BRACKNELL   The christenings, sir! Is not that somewhat premature?

CHASUBLE [*looking rather puzzled, and pointing to* JACK *and* ALGERNON]   Both these gentlemen have expressed a desire for immediate baptism.

LADY BRACKNELL   At their age? The idea is grotesque and irreligious! Algernon, I forbid you to be baptized. I will not hear of such excesses. Lord Bracknell would be highly displeased if he learned that that was the way in which you wasted your time and money.

CHASUBLE   Am I to understand then that there are to be no christenings at all this afternoon?

JACK   I don't think that, as things are now, it would be of much practical value to either of us, Dr Chasuble.

CHASUBLE   I am grieved to hear such sentiments from you, Mr Worthing. They savour of the heretical views of the Anabaptists,[1] views that I have completely refuted in four of my unpublished sermons. However, as your present mood seems to be one peculiarly secular, I will return to the church at once. Indeed, I have just been informed by the pew-opener[2] that for the last hour and a half Miss Prism has been waiting for me in the vestry.

LADY BRACKNELL [*starting*]   Miss Prism! Did I hear you mention a Miss Prism?

CHASUBLE   Yes, Lady Bracknell. I am on my way to join her.

LADY BRACKNELL   Pray allow me to detain you for a moment. This matter may prove to be one of vital importance to Lord Bracknell and myself. Is this Miss Prism a female of repellent aspect, remotely connected with education?

CHASUBLE [*somewhat indignantly*]   She is the most cultivated of ladies, and the very picture of respectability.

LADY BRACKNELL   It is obviously the same person. May I ask what position she holds in your household?

CHASUBLE [*severely*]   I am a celibate, madam.

JACK [*interposing*]   Miss Prism, Lady Bracknell, has been for the last three years Miss Cardew's esteemed governess and valued companion.

LADY BRACKNELL   In spite of what I hear of her, I must see her at once. Let her be sent for.

CHASUBLE [*looking off*]   She approaches; she is nigh.

[*Enter* MISS PRISM *hurriedly.*]

MISS PRISM   I was told you expected me in the vestry, dear Canon. I have been waiting for you there for an hour and three quarters. [*Catches sight of* LADY BRACKNELL *who has fixed her with a stony glare.* MISS PRISM *grows pale and quails. She looks anxiously round as if desirous to escape.*]

---

1. Members of a radical Protestant sect, established in Germany in the 16th century, that advocated the baptism only of adult believers (*Anabaptist* literally means "one who baptizes over again"); the label was sometimes applied pejoratively to Baptists or to others who rejected Anglican doctrine.
2. An usher who unlocked the private pews provided by many churches.

LADY BRACKNELL [*in a severe, judicial voice*]   Prism! [MISS PRISM *bows her head in shame.*] Come here, Prism! [MISS PRISM *approaches in a humble*
290 *manner.*] Prism! Where is that baby? [*General consternation. The* CANON *starts back in horror.* ALGERNON *and* JACK *pretend to be anxious to shield* CECILY *and* GWENDOLEN *from hearing the details of a terrible public scandal.*] Twenty-eight years ago, Prism, you left Lord Bracknell's house, Number 104, Upper Grosvenor Street, in charge of a perambulator[3] that contained a baby, of the male sex. You never returned. A few weeks later, through the elaborate investigations of the Metropolitan police, the peram-
295 bulator was discovered at midnight, standing by itself in a remote corner of Bayswater.[4] It contained the manuscript of a three-volume novel of more than usually revolting sentimentality. [MISS PRISM *starts in involuntary indignation.*] But the baby was not there! [*Everyone looks at* MISS PRISM.] Prism! Where is that baby? [*A pause.*]

300 MISS PRISM   Lady Bracknell, I admit with shame that I do not know. I only wish I did. The plain facts of the case are these. On the morning of the day you mention, a day that is for ever branded on my memory, I prepared as usual to take the baby out in its perambulator. I had also with me a somewhat old, but capacious hand-bag in which I had intended to place the
305 manuscript of a work of fiction that I had written during my few unoccupied hours. In a moment of mental abstraction, for which I never can forgive myself, I deposited the manuscript in the bassinette, and placed the baby in the hand-bag.

JACK [*who has been listening attentively*]   But where did you deposit the
310 hand-bag?

MISS PRISM   Do not ask me, Mr Worthing.

JACK   Miss Prism, this is a matter of no small importance to me. I insist on knowing where you deposited the hand-bag that contained that infant.

MISS PRISM   I left it in the cloak-room of one of the larger railway stations in
315 London.

JACK   What railway station?

MISS PRISM [*quite crushed*]   Victoria. The Brighton line. [*Sinks into a chair.*]

JACK   I must retire to my room for a moment. Gwendolen, wait here for me.

GWENDOLEN   If you are not too long, I will wait here for you all my life.

[*Exit* JACK *in great excitement.*]

320 CHASUBLE   What do you think this means, Lady Bracknell?

LADY BRACKNELL   I dare not even suspect, Dr Chasuble. I need hardly tell you that in families of high position strange coincidences are not supposed to occur. They are hardly considered the thing.

[*Noises heard overhead as if someone was throwing trunks about. Everyone looks up.*]

CECILY   Uncle Jack seems strangely agitated.

325 CHASUBLE   Your guardian has a very emotional nature.

LADY BRACKNELL   This noise is extremely unpleasant. It sounds as if he was having an argument. I dislike arguments of any kind. They are always vulgar, and often convincing.

CHASUBLE [*looking up*]   It has stopped now. [*The noise is redoubled.*]

330 LADY BRACKNELL   I wish he would arrive at some conclusion.

---

3. Baby carriage (pram).
4. A fashionable residential area of west Lon-   don, north of Kensington Gardens.

GWENDOLEN   This suspense is terrible. I hope it will last.

[*Enter* JACK *with a hand-bag of black leather in his hand.*]

JACK [*rushing over to* MISS PRISM]   Is this the hand-bag, Miss Prism? Examine it carefully before you speak. The happiness of more than one life depends on your answer.

335 MISS PRISM [*calmly*]   It seems to be mine. Yes, here is the injury it received through the upsetting of a Gower Street omnibus[5] in younger and happier days. Here is the stain on the lining caused by the explosion of a temperance beverage, an incident that occurred at Leamington.[6] And here, on the lock, are my initials. I had forgotten that in an extravagant mood I had had
340 them placed there. The bag is undoubtedly mine. I am delighted to have it so unexpectedly restored to me. It has been a great inconvenience being without it all these years.

JACK [*in a pathetic voice*]   Miss Prism, more is restored to you than this hand-bag. I was the baby you placed in it.

345 MISS PRISM [*amazed*]   You?

JACK [*embracing her*]   Yes . . . mother!

MISS PRISM [*recoiling in indignant astonishment*]   Mr Worthing! I am unmarried!

JACK   Unmarried! I do not deny that is a serious blow. But after all, who has
350 the right to cast a stone[7] against one who has suffered? Cannot repentance wipe out an act of folly? Why should there be one law for men, and another for women. Mother, I forgive you. [*Tries to embrace her again.*]

MISS PRISM [*still more indignant*]   Mr Worthing, there is some error. [*Pointing to* LADY BRACKNELL] There is the lady who can tell you who you really are.

355 JACK [*after a pause*]   Lady Bracknell, I hate to seem inquisitive, but would you kindly inform me who I am?

LADY BRACKNELL   I am afraid that the news I have to give you will not altogether please you. You are the son of my poor sister, Mrs Moncrieff, and consequently Algernon's elder brother.

360 JACK   Algy's elder brother! Then I have a brother after all. I knew I had a brother! I always said I had a brother! Cecily—how could you have ever doubted that I had a brother. [*Seizes hold of* ALGERNON.] Dr Chasuble, my unfortunate brother. Miss Prism, my unfortunate brother. Gwendolen, my unfortunate brother. Algy, you young scoundrel, you will have to treat
365 me with more respect in the future. You have never behaved to me like a brother in all your life.

ALGERNON   Well, not till today, old boy, I admit. I did my best, however, though I was out of practice. [*Shakes hands.*]

GWENDOLEN [*to* JACK]   My own! But what own are you? What is your Christian
370 name, now that you have become someone else?

JACK   Good heavens! . . . I had quite forgotten that point. Your decision on the subject of my name is irrevocable, I suppose?

GWENDOLEN   I never change, except in my affections.

CECILY   What a noble nature you have, Gwendolen!

---

5. Public carriage (bus). *Gower Street*: a street in the Bloomsbury section of central London (where the University of London and the British Museum are located).
6. Royal Leamington Spa, in Warwickshire, about 100 miles northwest of London. *Tem-*

perance beverage: in the 1890s, carbonated soda drinks were marketed as wholesome alternatives to alcohol.
7. That is, condemn a sinner—in the phrase's original context, a woman caught committing adultery (see John 8.7).

375 JACK Then the question had better be cleared up at once. Aunt Augusta, a moment. At the time when Miss Prism left me in the hand-bag, had I been christened already?

LADY BRACKNELL Every luxury that money could buy, including christening, had been lavished on you by your fond and doting parents.

380 JACK Then I was christened! That is settled. Now, what name was I given? Let me know the worst.

LADY BRACKNELL Being the eldest son you were naturally christened after your father.

JACK [*irritably*] Yes, but what was my father's Christian name?

385 LADY BRACKNELL [*meditatively*] I cannot at the present moment recall what the General's Christian name was. But I have no doubt he had one. He was eccentric, I admit. But only in later years. And that was the result of the Indian climate, and marriage, and indigestion, and other things of that kind.

JACK Algy! Can't you recollect what our father's Christian name was?

390 ALGERNON My dear boy, we were never even on speaking terms. He died before I was a year old.

JACK His name would appear in the Army Lists[8] of the period, I suppose, Aunt Augusta?

LADY BRACKNELL The General was essentially a man of peace, except in his 395 domestic life. But I have no doubt his name would appear in any military directory.

JACK The Army Lists of the last forty years are here. These delightful records should have been my constant study. [*Rushes to bookcase and tears the books out.*] M. Generals . . . Mallam, Maxbohm, Magley, what ghastly 400 names they have—Markby, Migsby, Mobbs, Moncrieff! Lieutenant 1840, Captain, Lieutenant-Colonel, Colonel, General 1869, Christian names, Ernest John. [*Puts book very quietly down and speaks quite calmly.*] I always told you, Gwendolen, my name was Ernest, didn't I? Well, it is Ernest after all. I mean it naturally is Ernest.

405 LADY BRACKNELL Yes, I remember now that the General was called Ernest. I knew I had some particular reason for disliking the name.

GWENDOLEN Ernest! My own Ernest! I felt from the first that you could have no other name!

JACK Gwendolen, it is a terrible thing for a man to find out suddenly that all 410 his life he has been speaking nothing but the truth. Can you forgive me?

GWENDOLEN I can. For I feel that you are sure to change.

JACK My own one!

CHASUBLE [*to* MISS PRISM] Lætitia! [*Embraces her.*]

MISS PRISM [*enthusiastically*] Frederick! At last!

415 ALGERNON Cecily! [*Embraces her.*] At last!

JACK Gwendolen! [*Embraces her.*] At last!

LADY BRACKNELL My nephew, you seem to be displaying signs of triviality.

JACK On the contrary, Aunt Augusta, I've now realized for the first time in my life the vital Importance of Being Earnest.

Tableau.[9]

Curtain.

---

8. The official lists of all the commissioned officers in the army.
9. That is, a tableau vivant: having characters freeze in a final pose as the curtain fell was a vogue in 19th-century theater.

ALFRED JARRY

1873–1907

THOUGH Alfred Jarry composed a large variety of works during his short life, his name is linked almost exclusively with that of the title character of his best-known play: *UBU THE KING* (1896). Even before the play was first performed, it had become notorious. At the dress rehearsal, Jarry had given a rousing curtain speech that, together with the play that followed, managed to enrage the audience. By the time the play opened officially, word had gotten around that a young and hitherto unknown playwright was intent on violating all rules of decency. *Ubu the King* begins with the word "merdre"—an almost imperceptible distortion of *merde*, the French word for "shit." Fecal expressions dominate the play, in which toilet brushes are thrown onto dinner tables and dishes such as "cauliflower à la shitsky" are served with glee. At the opening, conservative detractors and a small number of supporters started to riot as soon as the offensive word was uttered. A quarter hour of pandemonium ensued, with the two factions outdoing one another in booing, cheering, whistling, and shouting. Somehow, the performance continued, but with frequent interruptions and disturbances. Although the Ubu riot, as it came to be known, led to the immediate closing of the play, it also ensured *Ubu the King*'s place in the mythology of modernism. The riot shored up Jarry's credentials as a daring rebel willing to affront his audience. Offending the audience became the hallmark of modernist playwrights, and no one pursued the practice more avidly than Jarry.

Jarry was born in the provincial town of Laval, in northwest France, but before he was six his mother took him and his older sister to Saint-Brieuc, where they lived with her father. In 1888 they moved to the larger town of Rennes. There Alfred attended high school—an experience that proved crucial for his later career, for it provided the foundation of the figure of Ubu, first conceived as a satirical portrait of his physics teacher, Félix Hébert. Jarry subsequently transformed this character, but all his later Ubu plays retain an element of the sophomoric humor of the initial caricature.

To prepare for the demanding nationwide entrance exam for France's elite university, the École Normale Supérieur, Jarry enrolled in the famous Lycée Henri IV in Paris. Distracted by life in the capital, he failed the exam three years in a row and eventually abandoned the effort. Instead, he devoted himself to café society and artistic circles. During the early 1890s, he wrote poetry and short prose in the symbolist style that dominated the literary and theatrical arts in Paris at the time; he managed to place his pieces in the main symbolist journals such as the *Mercure de France*, whose editor, Alfred Vallette, and his wife, Rachilde, took a liking to Jarry and supported his career whenever they could. Representative of this period is Jarry's *Caesar-Antichrist* (1895), a play populated by biblical figures including Saint Peter and Christ, fantasy creatures such as unicorns and five-winged animals, and the play's title character, the Antichrist. Jarry adds to the standard repertoire of symbolism—rarified poetic expressions and religious, metaphysical topics—some peculiar and unusual elements, including the rude character from his school days, Ubu. The result is an odd mixture, a symbolist play with a crude interlude dominated by Jarry's unseemly protagonist.

Symbolism, the aesthetic doctrine favoring refined poetry over base realism, continued to be important for Jarry throughout his life. In his narrative satire *Exploits and Opinions of Dr. Faustroll, Pataphysician* (published posthumously in 1911), he dedicated each section to a symbolist poet or artist, including Stéphane Mallarmé (1842–1898), Aubrey Beardsley (1872–1898), and Rachilde (1860–1953). Whether imitating their style or otherwise reacting to their work, these sections can be seen as Jarry's most programmatic engagement with symbolism, a retrospective account of the movement that had taught him how to become a writer.

Even more important than symbolist poetry for Jarry's artistic formation was symbolist theater, especially its unrivaled center: Aurélien Lugné-Poe's Théâtre de l'Œuvre. Not much older than Jarry, Lugné-Poe had produced such symbolist playwrights as Maurice Maeterlinck (1862–1949) as well as a wide range of other international playwrights—among them HENRIK IBSEN, AUGUST STRINDBERG, and OSCAR WILDE, whose play *Salomé*, which was banned in England, he had staged to critical acclaim in 1896. Jarry did not just admire this theater from afar but began to seek a more active role in it. In 1896 he became a sort of manager with some artistic responsibilities. At the same time, he began to lobby Lugné-Poe to produce his play *Ubu the King*. After some hesitation and delays, Lugné-Poe gave in

and scheduled the opening for later that year. It proved to be a decision with consequences. The ensuing Ubu riot almost ruined the Théâtre de l'Œuvre, though the uproar ultimately contributed to its place in theater history.

Ubu the King is a strange mixture of styles. The plot and language seem borrowed from a historical play in the manner of SHAKESPEARE, and there are direct Shakespearean echoes as well. The play begins when Ubu's wife, Mama Ubu, apparently imitating Lady Macbeth, incites her husband to kill the King of Poland and usurp his rule. Once the king is killed and Ubu is installed on the throne, he turns more violent, killing nobles, raising taxes, and amassing great wealth. He personally goes out to extract heavy taxes from the impoverished and starving peasants. When he is finally faced with a popular uprising, led by the surviving son of the former king and an army raised in Russia, he flees and is eventually vanquished in battle.

This rough description may capture the play insofar as it resembles a historical drama, but history was the last thing Jarry cared about. He conducted no historical research and did not seek to re-create life in Poland at some remote time. In fact, the opening stage direction gives the place of the action as "*Poland—in other words, nowhere.*" The setting and the characters' bombastic phrases serve only as a foil for the deliberate crudity and vulgarity of the play. Ubu's main feature is extreme childishness, manifest in part in a complete lack of moral introspection. He is motivated to act by hunger and greed, and only fear deters him from following his instincts. In battle, the smallest opposition has him fleeing like Falstaff, the drinker and coward who is Prince Hal's companion in Shakespeare's *Henry IV*. Whether driven by greed or by fear, Ubu acts entirely without forethought or reflection. His impulsive and repulsive behavior has no redeeming features, not even dramatic ones. He is no evil genius whose plots, however objectionable, we can admire. He simply acts randomly from moment to moment, without plan, without a conscience, without a moment of hesitation or doubt. The only thing in which he reliably shows interest is consuming food. He

Poster art by Jarry for a performance of *Ubu the King*.

is persuaded to kill the king when his wife points out that once on the throne, he could "eat stuffed sausages all the time." It was Ubu's fixation on food and excretion that put the play most directly at odds with symbolism and with his audience's expectations. Jarry deliberately violated the most elevated and refined ideals of symbolism, which had sought to ignore everything having to do with the corporeal. In *Ubu the King*, Jarry confronted symbolist audiences with the most unseemly aspects of life.

As if its vulgarity were not upsetting enough, the play exhibits another feature designed to provoke the ire of audiences used to the conventions of symbolism. Its gratuitous violence, so at odds with the refined symbolist plays that Jarry helped produce at the Théâtre de l'Œuvre, reflects a very different theatrical tradition: the puppet theater of Punch and Judy. Jarry had experimented with marionettes and puppets as a teenager, and in fact the early versions of Ubu plays that he created with his classmates had been written for such theaters. One distinctive trait of the Punch and Judy show is that violence never leads to real-life consequences—characters can be hit on the head with a hammer and suffer no injury. In *Ubu the King*, too, characters are run through with sabers, and Ubu himself is perforated by bullets, only to walk away without much difficulty. By the same token, this cartoonish violence in *Ubu* is never cause for tragedy. When Ubu kills the entire nobility to increase his revenue, the murders are accomplished with a simple mechanical device: each noble in turn is pushed through a trapdoor and then "disembrained." At moments in the play, violence seems lamentable—but the mode of inconsequential and exaggerated carnage quickly returns.

The puppet theater was also an important inspiration for Jarry's stage design. His characters were written to be one-dimensional and simple, an effect that Jarry enhanced with the actors' costumes and style of acting and speaking. He created full-body costumes and masks that significantly reduced the mobility of those wearing them. Ubu's entire body was covered by an egg-shaped, stiff costume, eliminating the actor's ability to convey subtle points with facial expressions, gestures, or poses. To make the performance even more stylized, Jarry also instructed his actors to speak unnaturally. For this purpose, he created what he called an acoustic mask, demanding that Ubu deliver his lines in a staccato fashion, giving each syllable equal emphasis. The appearance, movements, and speech of Ubu were thus reduced to a set of mechanical expressions. Ubu was no longer a character taken from life; he was a plainly artificial and crude creation.

For all of its particular use of vulgarity and violence—or because of them—*Ubu the King* is best understood as farce: that is, as a form that turns vulgarity and violence into laughter. The theorist of laughter most useful for explaining Jarry's combination of vulgarity, verbal tics, violence, and puppet-like characters is the turn-of-the-century philosopher Henri Bergson (1859–1941). Indeed, Bergson's influence on Jarry was direct, since the playwright was one of his students at the Lycée Henri IV, where Bergson taught parts of what would become his famous essay on comedy, *Laughter* (1900). In its most basic form, Bergson's theory holds that laughter is provoked by the imposition of something mechanical (i.e., nonliving) onto a living organism. The strength of this theory lies in its ability to work on many levels. In the realm of language, Bergson identifies moments of the mechanical in the form of linguistic tics. *Ubu the King* is full of recurring nonsense phrases such as "by my green candlestick." At the same time, Jarry demanded mechanical repetitions of single characteristic gestures, such as tapping oneself on the head. Bergson's theory also describes the type of violence at work in *Ubu the King*. As king, Ubu treats other characters as if they were mere machines: everywhere, human bodies are penetrated and taken apart, only to be reassembled with ease. From this perspective, *Ubu the King* is a compilation of techniques meant to create laughter.

The daring mixture of pseudohistorical language and vulgarity, violence and laughter, made Jarry famous overnight. Through countless interviews, features, articles, and commentaries following the Ubu riot, Jarry became a notorious figure in the Parisian cultural world. Exploiting this position to the full, he published different versions of the text of *Ubu the King* and wrote new plays based on the Ubu figure. The title character in *Ubu Cocu* (*Ubu Cuckolded*, published posthumously in 1944) is by and large the same; he relies on gratuitous acts of violence to take possession of the house of a scholar of geometrical shapes. From time to time, a character called Conscience appears, only to be dismissed. Another Ubu play, called *Ubu in Chains* (1899), is set after Ubu flees Poland at the end of *Ubu the King*, seeking exile in France. Whereas in *Ubu the King* Ubu had been hungry for power and ready to use all means available to obtain it, in *Ubu in Chains* he insists on becoming a slave. However, the main features associated with this character—wanton violence, abrupt changes, and motiveless decisions—remain the same. Several years later, Jarry wrote a final Ubu play, *Ubu sur la Butte* (*Ubu on the Mound*, 1901), which includes a prologue about theater and, like *Ubu Cuckolded*, many songs and musical interludes, an element absent from the original *Ubu the King*. In addition, Jarry published different kinds of Ubu paraphernalia, including an Ubu *Almanach* (1901). None of these texts and publications repeated the success of *Ubu the King*, in part because none managed to replicate its juxtaposition of high and low, symbolism and farce, or repeat the imaginative implementation of Bergson's theory of laughter that had turned *Ubu the King* into a succès de scandale.

What the various Ubu publications did accomplish was to keep the figure of Ubu alive. Making this achievement all the more important was that Jarry had begun to imitate Ubu's character in his own life. Jarry spoke like Ubu, sometimes acted like Ubu, and more generally turned his own life into a kind of Ubu performance piece. He lived in extremely strange quarters—a room with a half-height ceiling, which allowed him, but few of his guests, to stand without stooping—and cultivated other peculiar habits. He also began to drink excessively, especially absinthe. He became a self-stylized figure of the Parisian bohemia, well-known enough that André Gide, France's most famous novelist of the early twentieth century, modeled a character on Jarry in his novel *The Counterfeiters* (1926). Ubu, Jarry's earliest creation, thus also became a kind of curse. None of Jarry's other artistic endeavors ever came close to having the impact of *Ubu the King*, although *Exploits and Opinions of Dr. Faustroll, Pataphysician* has received scholarly attention and is in some ways a more rewarding artistic achievement. But notoriety prevented Jarry from moving beyond *Ubu the King* and the scandals it had caused.

In fact, it was the reaction to the play more than the play itself that turned *Ubu*

the King into the harbinger of a new phase of modern drama, which became an aggressive, shocking type of avant-garde art. After the Ubu scandal, radical artists in France and elsewhere tried to elicit a similar response to their own work. Provocation, shock, deliberate attacks on the audience—these became the ingredients of a new brand of shrill theater. The audience was turned into the natural enemy of the artist: to establish one's credentials as an avant-garde artist, it was necessary to provoke a riot. Many twentieth-century artists followed suit, among them Antonin Artaud (1896–1948), who named his own short-lived theater Théâtre Alfred Jarry. After Jarry, modern drama had become an art of scandal.   M.P.

Ubu the King[1]

CHARACTERS

PAPA UBU
MAMA UBU
CAPTAIN BARBAGE
KING WENCESLAS, QUEEN ROSEMONDE,
    and their sons: BOLESLAS, LADISLAS,
    BUGGERLAS

COUNCILLORS
GENERAL LASKY
STANISLAS LECZINSKY
JOHANNES SOBIESKY
NICHOLAS RENSKY
CZAR ALEXIS
TAILS
HEADS
The Disembraining Machine
COTISE
Conspirators and Soldiers
Scribes

Crowds
MICHAEL FEDOROVITCH
NOBLES
JUDGES

FINANCIERS
Lackeys of Phynance
Peasants

The Whole Russian Army
The Whole Polish Army
Mama Ubu's Guards
A CAPTAIN
A Bear
The Phynancial Horse
Knighties
The Crew
The Ship's CAPTAIN

---

1. Translated by David Ball.

The play takes place in Poland—in other words, nowhere.[2]

1.1

[PAPA UBU, MAMA UBU.]

PAPA UBU   Shitsky![3]

MAMA UBU   Oh! such language! Papa Ubu, thou art a big bad boy.

PAPA UBU   What stoppeth me from slaying thee, Mama Ubu?

MAMA UBU   It is not I, Papa Ubu, it is someone else who should be assassinated.

5 PAPA UBU   By my green candlestick, I understand not.

MAMA UBU   What, Papa Ubu, are you happy with your lot?

PAPA UBU   By my green candlestick, shitsky! my dear, verily, verily, I am happy. A man could be happy with less: captain of the Dragoons, an officer with the confidence of King Wenceslas, decorated with the Order of the Red Eagle of Poland, and former King of Aragon,[4] what more could you want?

10

MAMA UBU   What! You, who were once King of Aragon, now you think it's good enough to march in a parade at the head of forty attendants armed with cabbage-cutters when after the crown of Aragon you could place the crown of Poland on your noggin?

15 PAPA UBU   Ah! Mama Ubu, I can't understand a word you say.

MAMA UBU   You're so dumb!

PAPA UBU   By my green candlestick, King Wenceslas is still very much alive; and even assuming he dies, does he not have swarms of children?

MAMA UBU   What's stopping you from massacrating the whole family and taking their place?

20

PAPA UBU   Ah! Mama Ubu, you are insulting me and you will soon get dumped in the lobster pot.

MAMA UBU   Ah! miserable wretch, if I got dumped in the lobster pot, who then would mend the seat of your pants?

25 PAPA UBU   Hey, come on! don't I have an ass like everybody else?

MAMA UBU   If I were you, it's that very ass I'd want to put on a throne. You could get infinitely rich, eat stuffed sausage all the time, and drive through the streets in a horse and carriage.

PAPA UBU   If I were king, I'd have me a big cape made like the one I had in Aragon, the one those rascally Spaniards impudently stole from me.

30

MAMA UBU   You could also get an umbrella and a big pea jacket that goes all the way down to your heels.

PAPA UBU   Oh! I'll give in to the temptation. For shitsky's sakesky, for sakesky's shitsky, if I ever meet him somewhere in the woods, he'll have a hard time of it.

35

MAMA UBU   Oh good! Papa Ubu, now you have become a real man.

PAPA UBU   Oh no! a Captain of the Dragoons massacrating the King of Poland! Never! I'd die first!

MAMA UBU [*aside*]   Oh, shitsky! [*To* UBU] So, you will remain poor as a church rat, Papa Ubu.

40

---

2. Even though most places mentioned in this play actually exist, Jarry uses place-names irreverently and inconsistently, with no regard for geographic specificity.

3. In Jarry's original French text, the play's first word is *Merdre,* a distortion of *merde* (shit).
4. A kingdom in northeast Spain (united with Castile in 1479).

PAPA UBU   Oddsbellyzooks! by my green candlestick, I'd rather be poor as a
good thin rat than rich as a wicked fat cat.

MAMA UBU   What about the cape? And the umbrella? And the great big pea
jacket?

45 PAPA UBU   Well! what about them, Mama Ubu? Who needs them?

[*He exits, slamming the door.*]

MAMA UBU   Crapsky, shitsky, he was an old meanie, but crapsky, shitsky, I
do think I have shaken him. Thank God! and myself. In a week I may be
Queen of Poland.

1.2

[SCENE: *The stage represents a room in* PAPA UBU's *house where a splendid table
is laid.*]

[PAPA UBU, MAMA UBU.]

MAMA UBU   Oh, our guests are really late.

PAPA UBU   Yes, by my green candlestick. I'm dying of hunger. Mama Ubu,
you are quite ugly today. Could it be because we're having guests for
dinner?

5 MAMA UBU [*shrugging*]   Shitsky.

PAPA UBU [*grabbing a roast chicken*]   Hey, I'm hungry. I am going to bite into
this bird. It is a chicken, I believe. . . . Hey! this isn't bad!

MAMA UBU   What are you doing, you wretch? What will our guests eat?

PAPA UBU   There will be quite enough for them. I won't touch another thing.

10   Mama Ubu, go to the window and see if our guests are coming.

MAMA UBU [*going there*]   I don't see anything. [*Meanwhile* PAPA UBU *filches a
slice of veal.*]

MAMA UBU   Ah! here are Captain Barbage and his followers. What are you
eating, Papa Ubu?

PAPA UBU   Nothing—a little veal.

15 MAMA UBU   Oh, the veal! the veal! veal! He ate the veal! Help!

PAPA UBU   By my green candlestick, I'm going to scratch thine eyes out!

[*The door opens.*]

1.3

[PAPA UBU, MAMA UBU, CAPTAIN BARBAGE, *and his followers.*]

MAMA UBU   Good evening, gentlemen. We have been waiting for you most
eagerly. Do be seated.

CAPTAIN BARBAGE   Good evening, Madam. But where is Papa Ubu?

PAPA UBU   Here I am, here I am! Gadzookspot, by my green candlestick, I'm
5   fat enough to be visible.

CAPTAIN BARBAGE   Good day, Papa Ubu. Be seated, men. [*They all sit down.*]

PAPA UBU   Whew! I almost went right through my chair.

CAPTAIN BARBAGE   Hey, Ubu! what've you got that's good today?

MAMA UBU   Here's the menu.

10 PAPA UBU   Ah! this is interesting.

MAMA UBU   Polish soup, ratsky cutlets, veal, chicken, dog paté, turkey rumps,
charlotte russe.

PAPA UBU   Hey! that's quite enough, it seems to me. Is there more?

MAMA UBU [*continuing*]   Ice pudding,[5] salad, fruit, dessert, oatmeal, Jerusa-
15 lem artichokes, cauliflower à la shitsky.

PAPA UBU   Hey! what do you think I am to spend that much, the Emperor of
the Orient?

MAMA UBU   Don't listen to him, he's a half-wit.

PAPA UBU   Oh! I'm going to sharpen my teeth against your calves.

20 MAMA UBU   Have dinner instead, Papa Ubu. Here's some of the Polish.

PAPA UBU   Buggersky! it's terrible!

CAPTAIN BARBAGE   Indeed, it is not good.

MAMA UBU   You barbarians, what more do you want?

PAPA UBU [*striking his forehead*]   Ah! I have an idea. I'll be back in a minute.

[*He leaves.*]

25 MAMA UBU   Gentlemen, we are going to sample the veal.

CAPTAIN BARBAGE   It's very good, I'm done.

MAMA UBU   Not the rumps.

CAPTAIN BARBAGE   Exquisite, exquisite! Long live Mama Ubu!

ALL   Long live Mama Ubu.

30 PAPA UBU [*coming back onstage*]   And soon you'll shout, "Long live Papa
Ubu." [*He is holding an incredibly disgusting toilet brush that he throws into
the midst of the banquet.*]

MAMA UBU   Wretch, what have you done?

PAPA UBU   Just taste that! [*Several guests taste it and fall, poisoned.*] Mama
Ubu, pass me the ratsky cutlets so that I can serve them.

35 MAMA UBU   Here they are.

PAPA UBU   Everybody, out! . . . Captain Barbage, I'd like to have a few words
with you.

THE OTHERS   Hey, we haven't had dinner.

PAPA UBU   What do you mean, you haven't had dinner! Everybody out! Stay,
40 Barbage. [*Nobody moves.*]

PAPA UBU   You still haven't left? By my green candlestick, I'm going to knock
you out with ratsky cutlets. [*He starts throwing some at them.*]

ALL   Oh! help! Defend us! Alas, I am dead!

PAPA UBU   Shitsky, shitsky, shitsky. Out! . . . I'm really making a hit.

45 ALL   Every man for himself! Wretched Papa Ubu! The traitor, the beggarly
ruffian!

PAPA UBU   Ah! they're gone. I can breathe again, but I have dined most exe-
crably. Come, Barbage.

[*They exit with* MAMA UBU.]

1.4

[PAPA UBU, MAMA UBU, CAPTAIN BARBAGE.]

PAPA UBU   Well! Captain, have you dined well?

CAPTAIN BARBAGE   Quite well, sir, except for the shitsky.

PAPA UBU   Hey! the shitsky wasn't bad.

MAMA UBU   To each his own.

5 PAPA UBU   Captain Barbage, I have decided to make you Duke of Lithuania.

CAPTAIN BARBAGE   What? I thought you were poor as a beggar, Papa Ubu.

5. That is, a frozen pudding.

PAPA UBU   In a few days, if you wish, I shall reign over Poland.

CAPTAIN BARBAGE   You're going to kill Wenceslas?

PAPA UBU   He's no dumbbell, the little bugger, he guessed it.

10 CAPTAIN BARBAGE   If it's a matter of killing Wenceslas, count me in. I am his mortal enemy, and I'll answer for my men.

PAPA UBU [*throwing himself on him to embrace him*]   Oh! oh! I love you dearly, Barbage!

CAPTAIN BARBAGE   Hey, you stink, Papa Ubu. Don't you ever wash?

15 PAPA UBU   Rarely.

MAMA UBU   Never!

PAPA UBU   I'm going to stamp on thy toes!

MAMA UBU   You big shitsky!

PAPA UBU   All right, Barbage, I have finished talking to you. But by my
20   green candlestick, I swear on Mama Ubu here I'll make you Duke of Lithuania.

MAMA UBU   But . . .

PAPA UBU   Be still, my child.

[*They exit.*]

1.5

[PAPA UBU, MAMA UBU, *a* MESSENGER.]

PAPA UBU   Sirrah,[6] what would you? Beat it, scram! you're getting on my nerves.

MESSENGER   Sir, you are summoned by the King.   [*He exits.*]

PAPA UBU   Oh! shitsky, oddsbellyzooksy, by my green candlestick, I am dis
5   covered, I am going to be beheaded! Alas, alas!

MAMA UBU   What a milksop! And time presses.

PAPA UBU   Oh! I have an idea! I'll say it was Mama Ubu and Barbage.

MAMA UBU   Ah, Big Ubu, if you do that . . .

PAPA UBU   Hey! I'm going there right away.   [*He exits.*]

10 MAMA UBU   Oh, Papa Ubu, Papa Ubu, *I'll* give you stuffed sausage . . .

[*She exits.*]

PAPA UBU [*from the wings*]   Oh! shitsky! you're a fine stuffed sausage yourself!

1.6

[SCENE: *The* KING's *palace.*]

[KING WENCESLAS, *surrounded by his officers;* BARBAGE; *the* KING's *sons:* BOLESLAS, LADISLAS, *and* BUGGERLAS. *Then,* PAPA UBU.]

PAPA UBU [*entering*]   Oh! you know, I didn't do it, it was Mama Ubu and Barbage.

THE KING   What's the matter, Papa Ubu?

BARBAGE   He has had too much to drink.

5 THE KING   So did I, this morning.

PAPA UBU   Yes, I'm drunk; that's because I drank too much French wine.

THE KING   Papa Ubu, I wish to reward you for your many services as Captain of the Dragoons, and I hereby name you Count of Sandomir.[7]

---

6. An archaic form of address to male social inferiors.

7. A city in southeast central Poland (Sandomierz).

PAPA UBU   Oh! Mr. Wenceslas, I hardly know how to thank you.
10 THE KING   Do not thank me, Papa Ubu; but do appear in our grand review
   tomorrow morning.
PAPA UBU   I'll be there, but do accept, I beg of you, this little party noisemaker. [*He presents a coiled-up noisemaker to the* KING.]
THE KING   At my age, what do you expect me to do with a noisemaker? I'll
15   give it to Buggerlas.
YOUNG BUGGERLAS   Man! is that Papa Ubu dumb!
PAPA UBU   And now, I'm gonna split. [*As he turns around, he falls down.*] Oh!
   ow! help! By my green candlestick, I broke my intestine and split my
   bagpipe!
20 THE KING [*helping him up*]   Papa Ubu, art thou hurt?
PAPA UBU   Yea, verily, and I'm sure I'm going to drop dead. Oh! what will
   become of Mama Ubu?
THE KING   We shall provide for her.
PAPA UBU   You are kind indeed.   [*He exits.*]
25   Yes, but, King Wenceslas, you shall be massacrated all the same.

1.7

[SCENE: PAPA UBU'*s house.*]

      [TAILS, HEADS, COTISE, PAPA UBU, MAMA UBU, *Conspirators and Soldiers,*
      CAPTAIN BARBAGE.]

PAPA UBU   Hey! my dear friends, it is high time we drew up the plan for our
   conspiracy. Let each man give his opinion. First I'll give mine, if you will.
CAPTAIN BARBAGE   Speak, Papa Ubu.
PAPA UBU   Well, friends, my opinion is we just poison the King by stuffing
5   some arsenic into his lunch. When he begins to graze on it he'll drop dead
   and so I'll be king.
EVERYBODY   Fie on you, you big ape! Fie, fie!
PAPA UBU   So, you don't like that? Then let Barbage give his opinion.
CAPTAIN BARBAGE   My opinion is, to take a big sword and slit him from his
10   guggle to his zatch.
EVERYBODY   Yes! that is noble and valiant.
PAPA UBU   And what if he kicks you? Now I seem to remember that for his
   reviews, he puts on iron shoes that really hurt. If I thought that's what you
   were going to do, I'd get out of this dirty business, run to him and turn you
15   in. And I think he'd also give me back some change.
MAMA UBU   Oh! the traitor, the coward, the villainous downright miser.
EVERYBODY   Booo, Papa Ubu!
PAPA UBU   Now, gentlemen, be still, if you don't want to pay a visit to my
   pockets. All right, I agree to put myself in danger for you. So, Barbage,
20   you'll take care of slitting the King from one end to the other.
CAPTAIN BARBAGE   And wouldn't it be better if we all jumped on him at the
   same time, yelling and screaming? That way we have a chance of getting
   his troops to go along with us.
PAPA UBU   OK, here goes. I'll try to step on his toes, he'll jump, then I'll say
25   to him: SHITSKY! That's the signal for all of you to jump him.
MAMA UBU   Yes, and as soon as he's dead you'll take his scepter and his
   crown.
CAPTAIN BARBAGE   And I'll go after the royal family with my men.

PAPA UBU   Yes, and I especially recommend young Buggerlas to your
30   attention.

[*They exit.*]

PAPA UBU [*running after them and making them come back*]   Gentlemen, we
have forgotten an indispensable ceremony; we must vow to fight valiantly.

CAPTAIN BARBAGE   How can we do that? We don't have a priest.

PAPA UBU   Mama Ubu will fill in.

35   EVERYBODY   So be it.

PAPA UBU   So, you swear to really kill the king?

EVERYBODY   Yes we do. Long live Papa Ubu!

End of the First Act.

2.1

[SCENE: *The* KING's *palace.*]

THE KING   Mr. Buggerlas, this morning you were quite rude to Mr. Ubu,
Knight of my Orders and Count of Sandomir. That is why I am forbidding
you to appear in my review.

THE QUEEN   But Wenceslas, even your whole family might not be enough to
5   defend you.

THE KING   Madam, I never go back on my word. I'm tired of your
nonsense.

YOUNG BUGGERLAS   I submit, Sire.

THE QUEEN   Sire, are you still set on going to that review?

10   THE KING   Why not, Madam?

THE QUEEN   Must I tell you again, did I not see him in a dream striking you
with his mace and throwing you into the Vistula,[8] and an eagle like the one
in the royal arms of Poland putting a crown on his head?

THE KING   On whose head?

15   THE QUEEN   On Papa Ubu's head.

THE KING   What folly. Monsieur de Ubu is a fine gentleman, who would let
himself be drawn and quartered to serve me.

THE QUEEN and BUGGERLAS   What a mistake.

THE KING   Be quiet, you young ape. And you, Madam, to show you how little
20   I fear Monsieur Ubu, I shall go to the review just as I am, without a
weapon, without a sword.

THE QUEEN   O fatal imprudence! I shall never see you alive again.

THE KING   Come, Ladislas, come, Boleslas.

[*They exit. The* QUEEN *and* BUGGERLAS *go to the window.*]

THE QUEEN and BUGGERLAS   May God and Saint Nicholas preserve you!

25   THE QUEEN   Buggerlas, come to the chapel with me to pray for your father
and your brothers.

2.2

[SCENE: *The reviewing grounds.*]

[*The Polish Army, the* KING, BOLESLAS, LADISLAS, PAPA UBU, CAPTAIN
BARBAGE *and his men,* TAILS, HEADS, COTISE.]

---

8. The principal river of Poland.

THE KING   Noble Papa Ubu, come next to me with your suite to inspect the troops.

PAPA UBU [*to his followers*]   Careful, men. [*To the* KING] We're coming, Sire, we're coming. [PAPA UBU's *men surround the* KING.]

5 THE KING   Ah! here is the regiment of the Danzig Horse Guards. My word, they are gallant-looking lads indeed.

PAPA UBU   You think so? They don't look so hot to me. Look at this one. [*To the soldier*] How long has it been since you've washed, you beastly rogue?

10 THE KING   But this soldier is quite clean. What can be the matter with you, Papa Ubu?

PAPA UBU   There, take that! [*He stamps on his foot.*]

THE KING   Miserable wretch!

PAPA UBU   SHITSKY!! follow me, men!

15 BARBAGE   Hurrah! Forward! [*They all strike the* KING; *a Knightie explodes.*]

THE KING   Oh! Help! Help! By the Blessed Virgin, I am dead.

BOLESLAS [*to* LADISLAS]   What's this? Let us draw!

PAPA UBU   Ah! I've got the crown! On to the others, now!

CAPTAIN BARBAGE   Death to the traitors!!

> [*The* KING's *sons flee; they all run after them.*]

2.3

[*The* QUEEN *and* BUGGERLAS.]

THE QUEEN   At last my misgivings are beginning to fade.

BUGGERLAS   You have no reason to fear.

> [*A frightful clamor is heard outside.*]

BUGGERLAS   Ah! what do I see? My two brothers pursued by Papa Ubu and his men.

5 THE QUEEN   Oh my God! Blessed Virgin, they're losing, they're losing ground!

BUGGERLAS   The whole army is following Papa Ubu. The King is no longer there. Horrors! Help!

THE QUEEN   Now Boleslas is dead! He has been shot.

10 BUGGERLAS   Hey! [LADISLAS *turns around.*] Defend yourself! Hurrah for Ladislas!

THE QUEEN   Oh! he is surrounded.

BUGGERLAS   It's all over for him. Barbage has just sliced him in half like a sausage.

15 THE QUEEN   Ah! Alas! those madmen are entering the palace, they are coming up the stairs.

> [*The clamor increases.*]

THE QUEEN and BUGGERLAS [*kneeling*]   Oh Lord, help us.

BUGGERLAS   Oh, that Papa Ubu! The villain, the wretch, if I had him . . .

2.4

[*The* QUEEN, BUGGERLAS. *The door is smashed in;* PAPA UBU *and his frenzied followers enter.*]

PAPA UBU   Hey, Buggerlas! what would you do with me?

BUGGERLAS   Good God! I shall defend my mother to the death! The first one who moves is a dead man.

PAPA UBU   Oh, Barbage! I'm afraid! Get me out of here.

5   A SOLDIER [*advancing*]   Surrender, Buggerlas!

BUGGERLAS   Here, you thug, take that! [*He smashes in his skull.*]

THE QUEEN   Hold fast, Buggerlas, hold fast!

SEVERAL [*coming forward*]   Buggerlas, we promise to spare your life.

BUGGERLAS   Rapscallions, wine bags, mercenary monkeys!

[*Twirling his sword around his head, he mows them down with it.*]

10   PAPA UBU   Oh, I'll get the best of you anyhow!

BUGGERLAS   Flee, Mother, escape through the secret stairway!

THE QUEEN   And you, my son, what about you?

BUGGERLAS   I shall follow.

PAPA UBU   Try to catch the Queen. Ah! she's gone. As for you, you wretch!
15   . . . [*He advances on* BUGGERLAS.]

BUGGERLAS   Ah! sweet God, here is my vengeance! [*With a terrible blow of his sword,* BUGGERLAS *slits his begizzard.*] Mother, I follow!

[*He disappears through the secret stairs.*]

2.5

[SCENE: *A cavern in the mountains.*]

[*Young* BUGGERLAS *followed by* QUEEN ROSEMONDE]

BUGGERLAS   We'll be safe here.

THE QUEEN   Yes, I think so! Buggerlas, sustain me! [*She falls on the snow.*]

BUGGERLAS   Ah! what ails thee, Mother?

THE QUEEN   I am very ill, believe me, Buggerlas. I have but two hours left to
5   live.

BUGGERLAS   What! have you been struck by the cold?

THE QUEEN   How can I possibly bear up under so many blows? The King massacrated, our family struck down, and you, a representative of the noblest race ever to carry a sword, forced to flee into the mountains like a
10   smuggler.

BUGGERLAS   And forced by whom, great God! by whom? By a vulgar Papa Ubu, an adventurer sprung from the Lord knows where, a vile scoundrel, a shameful vagabond! And to think that my father decorated him and made him a count, and the very next day that villain blushed not to raise his hand
15   against him.

THE QUEEN   O Buggerlas! When I recall how happy we were before the coming of that Papa Ubu! But now, alas! everything has changed!

BUGGERLAS   What can we do? Let us wait in hope and never give up our rights.

20   THE QUEEN   I wish it so for you, my dear child, but as for me, I shall never see that happy day.

BUGGERLAS   Ah! what ails thee? She pales, she falls, o help! But I am in the wilderness! O my God! her heart is no longer beating. She is dead! Can such things be? Another victim of Papa Ubu! [*He hides his face in his*
25   *hands and cries.*] O my God! how sad it is to be alone at the age of fourteen with a terrible vengeance to pursue! [*He falls prey to the most violent despair.*]

[*Meanwhile the souls of* WENCESLAS, BOLESLAS, LADISLAS, *and* ROSE-MONDE *have entered the grotto; their ancestors accompany them and fill up the cave. The oldest goes over to* BUGGERLAS *and gently wakes him.*]

BUGGERLAS Eh! what do I see? My whole family, my ancestors . . . Through what miracle?

30 THE SHADE Learn, Buggerlas, that during my life I was Lord Mathias of Königsberg,[9] the first king and founder of your house. I entrust you with the task of avenging us. [*He gives him a large sword.*] And may the sword I am giving you know no rest till it has struck the usurper dead.

2.6

[SCENE: *The* KING's *palace.*]

[PAPA UBU, MAMA UBU, CAPTAIN BARBAGE.]

PAPA UBU No, I won't! I won't! Do you want to ruin me with all this foodsky?

CAPTAIN BARBAGE But, Papa Ubu, can't you see that the people expect the gift of the happy accession?

5 MAMA UBU If you don't distribute meat and gold, you'll be overthrown within two hours.

PAPA UBU Meat, OK! gold, never! Slaughter three old horses. That's quite good enough for apes like these.

MAMA UBU Ape yourself! Who ever built me an animal like that?

10 PAPA UBU I tell you again, I want to get rich, I'm not gonna give up a red cent.

MAMA UBU When he has all the treasures of Poland in his hands!

CAPTAIN BARBAGE Yes, I know there's a huge treasure in the chapel. We'll distribute it to the people.

15 PAPA UBU You wretch, if you do that . . . !

CAPTAIN BARBAGE But, Papa Ubu, if you don't distribute some things, the people won't want to pay their taxes.

PAPA UBU Is that really true?

MAMA UBU Yes, yes!

20 PAPA UBU Oh, in that case I agree to everything. Get a hold of three million, cook a hundred and fifty oxen and sheep—especially since I'll have some too!

[*They exit.*]

2.7

[SCENE: *The courtyard of the palace, full of people.*]

[PAPA UBU, *crowned,* MAMA UBU, CAPTAIN BARBAGE, *lackeys laden with meat.*]

PEOPLE There's the King! Long live the King! Hurray!

PAPA UBU [*throwing food to the people*] Here, there's something for everyone. I had no desire to give you any money, but you know, Mama Ubu wanted me to. At least promise me to pay your taxes.

9. The former capital of East Prussia, a port on the Baltic Sea (north of Poland). Part of the German Empire during Jarry's lifetime, it was annexed by the Soviet Union in 1945 and renamed Kaliningrad in 1946.

5 EVERYBODY   Yes, yes!

CAPTAIN BARBAGE   Look, Mama Ubu, look how they're fighting for the gold! What a battle!

MAMA UBU   It really is horrible. Feh! there's a man with his skull split open.

10 PAPA UBU   What a fine sight! Bring in more chests full of gold.

CAPTAIN BARBAGE   Let's have a race.

PAPA UBU   Yes, good idea. [*To the people*] My friends, you see this chest full of gold; it contains three hundred thousand pink nobles in gold, in good Polish money. Let those who wish to run go to the end of the courtyard. 15 You will start when I wave my handkerchief and the first one there will get the chest. Those who do not win will have a consolation prize: this other chest, which will be distributed among them.

EVERYBODY   Yes! Long live Papa Ubu! What a good king! There was nothing like this in the days of Wenceslas.

20 PAPA UBU [*to* MAMA UBU, *happily*]   Just listen to them!

[*All the people go line up at the end of the courtyard.*]

PAPA UBU   One, two, three! Are you ready?

EVERYBODY   Yes, yes!

PAPA UBU   Go!

[*They begin to run, tripping all over each other. Shouts, tumult.*]

CAPTAIN BARBAGE   They're coming closer, they're coming closer!

25 PAPA UBU   Hey! the leader is losing ground.

MAMA UBU   No, he's winning again now.

CAPTAIN BARBAGE   Oh! he's losing, he's losing! It's over! The other one won! [*The man who was second comes in first.*]

EVERYBODY   Long live Michael Fedorovitch! Long live Michael Fedorovitch!

MICHAEL FEDOROVITCH   Sire, I really don't know how to thank your 30 Majesty . . .

PAPA UBU   Oh! my dear friend, it's really nothing. Take the chest home with you, Michael, and you others, share this other chest between you, take a coin each until there is no more.

EVERYBODY   Long live Michael Fedorovitch! Long live Papa Ubu!

35 PAPA UBU   And you, my friends, come dine with me! Today the doors of my palace are open to you: pray come honor my table!

PEOPLE   In we go! Long live Papa Ubu! the noblest of monarchs!

[*They go into the palace. We hear the noise of an orgy, which will continue till the next day. The curtain falls.*]

End of the Second Act.

3.1

[SCENE: *The palace.*]

[PAPA UBU, MAMA UBU.]

PAPA UBU   By my green candlestick, now I am king in this country. I already got indigestion and now they're gonna bring me my big cape.

MAMA UBU   What is it made of, Papa Ubu? For we may be kings, but still we must be economical.

5 PAPA UBU   Madam my Female, it is made of sheepskin, with stitching and reins of dogskin.

MAMA UBU   That is fine, but it is finer still to be kings.

PAPA UBU   Yes, you are right, Mama Ubu.

MAMA UBU   We are extremely grateful to the Duke of Lithuania.

10 PAPA UBU   Who's that?

MAMA UBU   Hey, Captain Barbage.

PAPA UBU   I pray thee, Mama Ubu, speak to me not of that buggersky. Now that
I no longer need him, he can go jump in the lake, he won't have his dukedom.

MAMA UBU   You are making a great mistake, Papa Ubu, he will turn against
15   you.

PAPA UBU   Oh! I'm really sorry for that little man. I'm worried about him
about as much as I am about Buggerlas.

MAMA UBU   And you think you have heard the last of Buggerlas, eh?

PAPA UBU   By my Financial Saber, of course I do! What do you think he can
20   do to me, that little ape of fourteen?

MAMA UBU   Papa Ubu, heed what I say. Believe me, try to win over Buggerlas
with your generosity.

PAPA UBU   Give away more money? Hey, no way! you've already made me
waste twenty-two million.

25 MAMA UBU   Just do whatever you want, Papa Ubu, and your goose will be
cooked.

PAPA UBU   Well, you'll be in the pot with me.

MAMA UBU   Listen, I'll tell you once again: I'm sure that young Buggerlas will
triumph, for he has right on his side.

30 PAPA UBU   Ah, you filthy wretch! Isn't the wrong side as good as the right?
Ah! you are insulting me, Mama Ubu, and I'm going to rip you to bits.

[MAMA UBU *runs out, followed by* PAPA UBU.]

3.2

[SCENE: *The great hall of the palace.*]

[PAPA UBU, MAMA UBU, *Officers and Soldiers,* TAILS, HEADS, COTISE,
NOBLES *in chains,* FINANCIERS, JUDGES, *Scribes.*]

PAPA UBU   Bring in the Noble Chest and the Noble Hook and the Noble
Knife and the Noble Book! Then bring forth the Nobles.

[*The* NOBLES *are brutally pushed forward.*]

MAMA UBU   I pray thee, take it easy, Papa Ubu.

PAPA UBU   I am pleased to inform you that in order to enrich the kingdom,
5   I am going to execute all the Nobles and take their property.

NOBLES   Horrors! soldiers and people, follow us!

PAPA UBU   Bring up the first Noble and pass me the Noble Hook. Those who
receive the death penalty will be pushed through the trapdoor; they'll fall
into the cellars of Pig-Pincher and Penny-Chamber, where they'll be dis-
10   embrained. [*To the* NOBLE] Who are you, you buggersky?

THE NOBLE   Count of Vitebsk.[1]

PAPA UBU   What is your income?

THE NOBLE   Three million rixdalers.[2]

---

1. A city in northeastern Belarus (east of
Poland).
2. That is, rix-dollars: silver coins. This was
a denomination used in keeping accounts in
a number of European countries (from the
older Dutch *rijcksdaler,* "kingdom's dollar").

PAPA UBU   Guilty! [*He spikes him with the hook and pushes him into the hole.*]

15 MAMA UBU   What base ferocity!

PAPA UBU   Second Noble, who are you? [*The* NOBLE *does not reply.*] Will you answer, you buggersky?

THE NOBLE   The Grand Duke of Posen.[3]

PAPA UBU   Fine! fine! That's all I need to know. Into the trapdoor with him.

20   Third Noble, who are you? You have an ugly face.

THE NOBLE   Duke of Curland, of the cities of Riga, Revel, and Mitau.[4]

PAPA UBU   Good! good! You don't have anything else?

THE NOBLE   Nothing.

PAPA UBU   OK, down the trapdoor. Fourth Noble, who are you?

25 THE NOBLE   The Prince of Poxdolia.[5]

PAPA UBU   What is your revenue?

THE NOBLE   Alas, I am ruined!

PAPA UBU   For that bad word, you go through the trapdoor. Fifth Noble, who are you?

30 THE NOBLE   Margrave of Thorn,[6] Palatine of Polack.

PAPA UBU   That's not much. You don't have anything else?

THE NOBLE   That was enough for me.

PAPA UBU   Well, better little than nothing. Into the trapdoor. What're you crying about, Mama Ubu?

35 MAMA UBU   You are too fierce, Papa Ubu.

PAPA UBU   Hey! I'm getting rich. I'm going to read out MY List of MY Property. Clerk, read us MY List of MY Property.

CLERK   County of Sandomir.

PAPA UBU   Begin by the Principalities, you dumb bugger!

40 CLERK   Principality of Poxdolia, Grand Duchy of Posen, Duchy of Curland, County of Sandomir, County of Vitebsk, Palatinate of Polack, Margraviate of Thorn.

PAPA UBU   And then what?

CLERK   That's it.

45 PAPA UBU   Whaddya mean, that's it? In that case, Nobles, forward, march! And since I'm going to get rich endlessly I'm going to have all the Nobles executed so I'll get all their vacant property. Come on, throw the Nobles into the trapdoor. [*The* NOBLES *are piled into the trapdoor.*] Hurry up, faster, I want to make some laws now.

50 SEVERAL   We'll see about that.

PAPA UBU   First I'm going to reform the legal system, then we'll proceed to state finance.

SEVERAL JUDGES   We are opposed to any changes.

PAPA UBU   Shitsky. First of all judges will no longer be paid.

55 JUDGES   And what will we live on? We are poor.

PAPA UBU   You'll have the fines you give out and the property of the people who get the death penalty.

---

3. Poznań, a city in west central Poland.

4. Curland is a region that corresponds to western Latvia. Riga is now the capital of Latvia; Revel is the former name of Tallinn, now the capital of Estonia (more than 100 miles from Curland); Mitau is the former name of Jelgava, in Latvia.

5. Podalia is a historical region in western Ukraine.

6. A province in northern Poland (Toruń).

A JUDGE   Horrors!

SECOND   Infamous.

60 THIRD   Scandalous.

FOURTH   An indignity.

ALL   We refuse to judge under such conditions.

PAPA UBU   Down the trapdoor with the judges! [*They struggle in vain.*]

MAMA UBU   Oh! what are you doing, Papa Ubu? Who will deliver judgments
65   now?

PAPA UBU   Hey! I will! You'll see, it'll go great.

MAMA UBU   Sure, it will be a real joy.

PAPA UBU   Come on, be quiet, you buggeress. Now, gentlemen, we shall proceed to the finances of the state.

70 FINANCIERS   There is nothing to change.

PAPA UBU   Whaddya mean? I want to change everything. First of all I want to
keep half the taxes for myself.

FINANCIERS   Makes himself right at home.

PAPA UBU   Gentlemen, we shall establish a tax of ten percent on property,
75   another on commerce and industry, a third on weddings, and a fourth one
on deaths, fifteen francs each.

FIRST FINANCIER   But that's idiotic, Papa Ubu.

SECOND FINANCIER   It's absurd.

THIRD FINANCIER   That is absolutely senseless.

80 PAPA UBU   What are you, kidding?! Down the trapdoor with the financiers!
[*The* FINANCIERS *are shoveled in.*]

MAMA UBU   Now come on, Papa Ubu, what kind of king are you? You're massacrating everybody.

PAPA UBU   Oh, shitsky!

MAMA UBU   No more judges, no more financiers.

85 PAPA UBU   Fear nothing, my child, I shall go from village to village myself and
collect the taxes.

3.3

[SCENE: *A farmhouse near Warsaw. Several* PEASANTS *are gathered there.*]

A PEASANT [*entering*]   Did you hear the news? The King is dead, so are the
Dukes, and young Buggerlas ran away into the mountains with his mother.
What's more, Papa Ubu has taken over the throne.

ANOTHER PEASANT   I know a lot more. I come from Cracow,[7] where I saw the
5   bodies of more than three hundred nobles and five hundred judges carried
away—they'd been killed. And it seems they're going to double the taxes
and Papa Ubu's going to come get them himself.

ALL   Great God! what will become of us? Papa Ubu is a horrible baboon and
it is said that his family is absolutely abominable.

10 A PEASANT   But listen, wouldn't you say someone is knocking at the door?

A VOICE [*outside*]   Oddsbellikins! open, by my shitsky, by Saint John, Saint
Peter, and Saint Nicholas! Open, by my Financial Saber, my Financial
Horn, I've come to get the taxes! [*The door is smashed in and* PAPA UBU
enters, followed by a legion of lackeys.]

---

7. The city in southern Poland where the kings of Poland lived (14th–16th centuries) and were
crowned (until the 18th century).

3.4

PAPA UBU   Who's the oldest one here? [*A peasant steps forward.*] What is your
name?

THE PEASANT   Stanislas Leczinsky.

PAPA UBU   Well, oddsbellikins, listen carefully, or else these gentlemen will
5   cut your earies off. Look, are you going to listen to me? Will you listen?!

STANISLAS   But your Excellency hasn't said anything yet.

PAPA UBU   Whaddya mean, I've been talkin' for an hour. Think you that I
have come here to preach in the desert?

STANISLAS   Far be it from me to have such a thought.

10   PAPA UBU   So. I have come to tell you, order you, and announce to you that
you must promptly produce and exhibit your Finance, or else you will be
massacrated. Come, my Lords Sonsabiddies of Finance, wagon the Phy-
nance[8] Wagonette over here. [*The wagonette is brought in.*]

STANISLAS   Sire, we are only registered for one hundred and fifty two rixdalers
15   that we have already paid, about two weeks ago on Saint Matthew's Day.[9]

PAPA UBU   That is quite possible, but I've changed the government and I had
the newspapers announce that taxes will be paid twice—and three times
for the ones that can be levied later by decree. With this system I'll get rich
quick, then I'll kill everybody and get the hell out.

20   PEASANTS   Papa Ubu, we beg of you, have pity on us. We are poor citizens.

PAPA UBU   I don't give a damn. Pay up.

PEASANTS   I cannot, we have paid.

PAPA UBU   Pay up! Or I'll put you in my pocket with torture and chopping off
of neck and head! Oddshornikins, I'm the King, aren't I?

25   ALL   Ah! so that's the way it is! To arms! Long live Buggerlas, by God's grace
King of Poland and Lithuania!

PAPA UBU   Forward, Gentlemen of Finance, do your duty.

[*There is a struggle, the house is destroyed, and old* STANISLAS *flees alone
across the plain.* PAPA UBU *remains to pick up the Finance.*]

3.5

[SCENE: *A bunker in the fortifications of Thorn.*]

[CAPTAIN BARBAGE *in chains,* PAPA UBU.]

PAPA UBU   So! citizen, you see how it is, you wanted me to pay you what I
owed you, I didn't want to, you conspired, and now here you are in the
slammer. Oddsfinancesky, that's what you get, and it's such a good trick
that you should appreciate it yourself.

5   CAPTAIN BARBAGE   Take care, Papa Ubu. In the five days you have been king,
you have committed more murders than it would take to damn all the
saints in heaven. The blood of the King and his nobles cries for vengeance
and their cries will be heard.

PAPA UBU   Well! my fine-feathered friend, you speak very freely indeed. I
10   have no doubt that there might well be complications if you escaped, but I
don't think the bunkers of Thorn have ever released a single one of the

8. Jarry coined the words "phynance" and
"phynancial," playing on "finance" and
"financial"; all are used to characterize some

of his possessions and other objects.
9. September 21.

honest lads who were turned over to them. That's why, good night, and I suggest you sleep tight, though the rats do dance a fine saraband in these cellies.

[*He exits. The lackeys come in and lock up all the doors.*]

3.6

[SCENE: *The Moscow palace.*]

[CZAR ALEXIS *and his Court,* BARBAGE.]

CZAR ALEXIS   Was it you, you infamous adventurer, who cooperated in the death of our cousin Wenceslas?

BARBAGE   Sire, forgive me, I was carried away by Papa Ubu despite myself.

ALEXIS   Oh! what a frightful liar. Well, what do you want?

5 BARBAGE   Papa Ubu had me thrown in jail on the pretext of conspiracy. I succeeded in escaping and I galloped for five days and five nights across the steppes to come and beg Your gracious mercy.

ALEXIS   What do you bring me as a token of your surrender?

BARBAGE   My adventurer's sword and a detailed map of the city of Thorn.

10 ALEXIS   I accept the sword, but by Saint George, burn this map; I do not wish to owe my victory to an act of treachery.

BARBAGE   One of the sons of Wenceslas is still alive—young Buggerlas. I will do anything to restore him to his throne.

ALEXIS   What was your rank in the Polish army?

15 BARBAGE   I commanded the Fifth Regiment of Vilna Dragoons and a Company of Freebooters in the service of Papa Ubu.

ALEXIS   All right, I name you Second Lieutenant in the Tenth Regiment of Cossacks, and woe betide you if you betray me. If you fight well, you will be rewarded.

20 BARBAGE   Courage is not a thing I lack, Sire.

ALEXIS   All right, vanish from my presence.

[BARBAGE *exits.*]

3.7

[SCENE: UBU's *Council Room.*]

[PAPA UBU, MAMA UBU, *Finance* COUNCILLORS.]

PAPA UBU   Gentlemen, the session is opened. Listen up and try to be quiet. First we are going to tackle the finance question, next we will talk about a little system I've dreamed up to bring good weather and prevent rain.

A COUNCILLOR   Very good, Mr. Ubu.

5 MAMA UBU   What a blockhead.

PAPA UBU   Madame of my shitsky, watch out! for I won't stand for your nonsense. . . . As I was saying, gentlemen, our finances are doing reasonably well. A large number of woolstocking dogs go out into the streets every morning, and the Sonsabiddies are doing wonders. On every side, all you can see is

10 burned-down houses and people crushed under the weight of our phynances.

THE COUNCILLOR   How about the new taxes, Mr. Ubu, are they doing well?

MAMA UBU   Absolutely not. The tax on weddings has only yielded eleven cents, even though Papa Ubu goes running after people everywhere to force them to get married.

15 PAPA UBU   By my Financial Saber, gads of my oddzooks, Madame Financier, I have earies for talking and you have a mouth to hear me with. [*Bursts of laughter.*] Oh, no! you're making me make a mistake and you're the reason why I'm being stupid! But, by Ubu's oddsbelly . . .

[*A messenger enters.*]

OK, OK, what's wrong with *him?* Get out of here, you baboon, or I'll
20   pocket you, with decapitation and twisting of the legs.

MAMA UBU   OK, he's gone, but there's a letter.

PAPA UBU   Read it. I think I'm losing my mind, or I don't know how to read. Hurry up, you buffoodsky, it must be from Barbage.

MAMA UBU   Exactly. He says the czar gave him a warm welcome, he's going to
25   invade your states to bring back Buggerlas, and you'll be killed.

PAPA UBU   Oh! oh! I'm scared! I'm scared! Ah! I think I'm dying. Oh, what a poor man I am. Good God, what will become of me? That wicked man will kill me. Saint Anthony[1] and all the saints, protect me, I will give you phy-nance and I'll burn candles for you. Lord, what will become of me? [*He weeps and sobs.*]

30 MAMA UBU   There is only one course to take, Papa Ubu.

PAPA UBU   Which, my love?

MAMA UBU   War!!!

ALL   God be praised! How noble!

PAPA UBU   Yeah, and I'll get beat up again.

35 FIRST COUNCILLOR   Quick, let us hasten to organize the army.

SECOND   And stock up on food.

THIRD   And prepare the artillery and the fortresses.

FOURTH   And get the money for the troops.

PAPA UBU   Hell no! I'll *kill* you, I don't want to give away any money. Money!
40   now there's good one! I was paid to make war and now I have to do it at my own expense. No, by my green candlestick, we'll make war, since you're so enraged, but we will not spend a red cent.

ALL   Three cheers for war!

3.8

[SCENE: *The camp near Warsaw.*]

SOLDIERS and KNIGHTIES   Three cheers for Poland! Three cheers for Papa Ubu!

PAPA UBU   Ah! Mama Ubu, give me my armor and my little piece of wood. Soon I'll be so heavily loaded down I won't be able to walk if I am
5   pursued.

MAMA UBU   Fie, what a coward.

PAPA UBU   Ah! the Shitsky Saber is getting away and the Financial Hook's coming loose!!! I'll never get out of this, and the Russians are advancing and they'll kill me.

10 A SOLDIER   My Lord Ubu, the Earie Scissors are falling.

PAPA UBU   I keel you weez ze Shitsky Hook and ze Face Knife.

MAMA UBU   How handsome he is with his helmet and his armor; he looks like an armed pumpkin.

1. St. Anthony of Padua (1195–1231), a great miracle worker.

PAPA UBU   Ah! now I shall mount my steed. Gentlemen, bring in the Phynan-
15   cial Horse.

MAMA UBU   Papa Ubu, your horse can no longer carry you; he hasn't had
anything to eat for five days and he's almost dead.

PAPA UBU   Now there's a good one! They charge me twelve cents a day for
this nag and he can't carry me any more. Are you kidding me, by Ubu's
20   horn, or . . . what if you're robbing me? [MAMA UBU *blushes and lowers
her eyes.*] Well then, bring me in another horse, I'm not going to walk,
oddshornikins!

[*An enormous horse is brought in.*]

PAPA UBU   I'm going to mount. Oh! down, horsie, down! for I am going to
fall. [*The horse takes off.*] Ah! stop this beast. Good God, I'm going to fall
25   down and be dead!!!

MAMA UBU   He's a real imbecile. Ah! now he's gotten up again. But he fell
down.

PAPA UBU   Physical horn, I'm half dead! But that's all right, I'm going off to
war and I'll kill everybody. Whoever doesn't walk the straight and narrow,
30   look out! I poot heem in my pock*ett* with twisting of nose and teeth and
extraction of tongue.

MAMA UBU   Good luck, Mr. Ubu.

PAPA UBU   I forgot to tell you—I'm giving you the regency. But I'm keeping
my book of finances on me, and it'll be too bad for you if you cheat me.
35   I leave you Knightie Lap to aid and assist you. Farewell, Mama Ubu.

MAMA UBU   Farewell, Papa Ubu. Have a good czar-killing.

PAPA UBU   For sure. Twisting of the nose and teeth, extraction of the tongue
and driving of the little piece of wood into his earies.

[*The army goes off, to the sound of fanfares.*]

MAMA UBU   [*alone*]   Now that that fat puppet has departed, let us attend to
40   our own business, kill Buggerlas and seize the treasure.

End of the Third Act.

4.1

[SCENE: *The crypt of the ancient kings of Poland in the Warsaw cathedral.*][2]

MAMA UBU   Where the devil is that treasure? Not one stone slab has
sounded hollow. Yet I did count thirteen stones after the tomb of Ladislav
the Great following the wall, and nothing's there. They must have fooled
me. But here: the stone sounds hollow. Let's get to work, Mama Ubu.
5   Courage, let us unseal this stone. It's holding firm. We'll take this end of
the Financial Hook; it will perform its office once again. There! here's the
gold, in the midst of the bones of kings. Into our bag now, all of it! Hey!
what is that sound? Could there still be living souls in these old vaults?
No, it's nothing, let us hurry. We'll take everything. This money will be
10   better in the light of day than in the midst of the tombs of ancient
princes. Let us replace the stone. My presence in this place inspires me
with a strange fear. I'll take the rest of this gold another time; I'll come
back tomorrow.

---

2. The ancient kings of Poland are actually buried in Kraków.

A VOICE [*coming from the tomb of John Sigismund*[3]]   Never, Mama Ubu!

[MAMA UBU *runs away, terrified, carrying off the stolen gold through a secret door.*]

4.2

[SCENE: *The Warsaw palace.*]

[BUGGERLAS *and his followers, People and Soldiers, then* GUARDS, MAMA UBU, KNIGHTIE LAP.]

BUGGERLAS   Forward, my friends! Long live Wenceslas and Poland! That old rascal Papa Ubu is gone, all that's left is that witch Mama Ubu with her Knightie. I offer to march at your head and reestablish the race of my fathers.

5 EVERYONE   Long live Buggerlas!

BUGGERLAS   And we will do away with all the taxes raised by that frightful Papa Ubu.

EVERYONE   Hurray! forward! Let us run to the palace and massacrate that breed.

10 BUGGERLAS   Hey! there's Mama Ubu coming out with her guards on the palace steps!

MAMA UBU   What do you want, gentlemen? Ah! it's Buggerlas.

[*The crowd throws stones.*]

FIRST GUARD   All our windows are broken.

SECOND GUARD   By Saint George, I am knocked out.

15 THIRD GUARD   Oddshornikins, I am dying.

BUGGERLAS   Throw stones, my friends.

KNIGHTIE LAP   So! that's the way it is! [*He unsheathes his sword and rushes forward, causing frightful carnage.*]

BUGGERLAS   I'll take you on! Defend yourself, you cowardly little pistol.

[*They fight.*]

KNIGHTIE LAP   I am dead!

20 BUGGERLAS   Victory, my friends! On to Mama Ubu, let her have it!

[*Trumpets are heard.*]

BUGGERLAS   Ah! the Nobles are coming. Run, let's get that evil harpy!

EVERYONE   And then we'll strangle the old bandit!

[MAMA UBU *runs off, followed by all the Poles. Rifle shots, hail of stones.*]

4.3

[*The Polish army marching through Ukraine.*]

PAPA UBU   Oddshornikins, godsleggikins, by the cow's head! we shall perish, for we are dying of thirst and are tired. Sire Soldier, be good enough to wear our Financial Helmet, and you, Sire Lancer, take up the Shitsky Scissors and the Physical Stick to ease our person, for, I repeat, we are tired.

5   [*The soldiers obey.*]

HEADS   Eh! Meesterr! it is astonishing that ye Russians appear not.

---

3. Prince-elector of the Margraviate of Brandenburg and a duke of Prussia (1572–1619).

PAPA UBU   It is regrettable that the state of our finances does not allow us to have a coach of our size; for, out of fear of demolishing our steed, we have walked all the way, leading our horse by the bridle. But with our knowl-
10   edge of physics and the help of the wisdom of our councillors, when we are back in Poland, we will dream up a wind-driven coach to transport the whole army.

COTISE   Here's Nicholas Rensky running up to us.

PAPA UBU   What's the matter with that boy?

15   RENSKY   All is lost, Sire, the Poles have revolted, Lap is killed, Mama Ubu has taken flight in the mountains.

PAPA UBU   You wretched beast, you night bird, you owl with spats! Where'd you get that garbage? There's a good one! And who did it? Buggerlas, I'll bet. Where are you coming from?

20   RENSKY   From Warsaw, my noble lord.

PAPA UBU   Boy of my shitsky, if I believed you I'd have the whole army do an about-face. But, my lord boy, you have more plumes than brains on your shoulders and you have dreamed up a lot of nonsense. Go to the outposts, my boy, the Russians are not far and soon we will have to thrust with our
25   weapons, both shitskied and phynancials—and physicals.

GENERAL LASKY   Papa Ubu, do you not see the Russians in the plain?

PAPA UBU   It's true, the Russians! Now I'm really in for it. At least if there were some way of getting out of here, but no, we're on a height and we'll be perfect targets.

30   THE ARMY   The Russians! The enemy!

PAPA UBU   Come, gentlemen, let us draw up our plans for the battle. We shall remain on the hill and will not commit the blunder of descending below. I shall stay in the middle like a living fortress and you people will gravitate around me. I must enjoin you to insert into your rifles as many
35   bullets as they can hold, for eight bullets can kill eight Russians and that makes so many more off my back. We'll station the infantrymen at the bottom of the hill to receive the Russians and kill them a bit, the horsemen behind to throw themselves into the confusion, and the artillery around ye windmill here to fire into the crowd. As for us, we shall remain in the wind
40   mill and shall shoot through the window with the Phynancial Pistol, across the door we shall place the Physical Stick, and if anyone tries to get in, watch out for the Shitsky Hook!!!

OFFICERS   Sire Ubu, your orders will be carried out.

PAPA UBU   Ha! that's good, we shall be victorious. What time is it?

45   GENERAL LASKY   Eleven A.M.

PAPA UBU   Well then, let us have lunch, for the Russians will not attack before noon. Lord General, tell the soldiers to relieve themselves and to strike up the Finance Song.

[LASKY *leaves.*]

SOLDIERS and KNIGHTIES   Long live Papa Ubu, our great Financier! Ting,
50   ting, ting; ting, ting, ting; ting, ting, ta-ting!

PAPA UBU   O what fine soldiers, I love them. [*A Russian cannonball comes in and breaks the sail of the windmill.*] Oh! I am afraid, Sire God, I am dead! And yet no, I'm quite all right.

4.4

[*The same, a* CAPTAIN, *then the Russian Army.*]

A CAPTAIN [*entering*]   Sire Ubu, the Russians are attacking.

PAPA UBU   So what do you want me to do about it? *I* didn't tell them to do it! Still, Gentlemen of Finance, let us prepare for combat.

GENERAL LASKY   A second cannonball.

5 PAPA UBU   Ah! I can stand no more. It is raining lead and fire and we might damage our precious person. Let us go down the hill.

[*They all race down. The battle has just begun. They disappear in torrents of smoke at the foot of the hill.*]

A RUSSIAN [*striking*]   For God and the Czar!

RENSKY   Ah! I am dead.

PAPA UBU   Forward! Ah! you, Sir, let me get a hold of you, for you hurt me, do

10 you hear! you wine bag! with your piece that can't fire.

THE RUSSIAN   Ah! watch this. [*He fires a revolver shot at him.*]

PAPA UBU   Ah! Oh! I am wounded, I am punctured, I am perforated, I am administrated, I am cremated. Ah, still and all, ah! I've got him. [*He rips him apart.*] There! Will you start up again now?

15 GENERAL LASKY   Forward, push ahead vigorously, over the ditch, victory is ours.

PAPA UBU   Think so? Up to here I feel more bumps than laurels[4] on my brow.

RUSSIAN HORSEMEN   Hurrah! Make way for the Czar!

[*The* CZAR *enters, accompanied by* BARBAGE *in disguise.*]

A POLE   Ah! Lord! Every man for himself, here comes the Czar!

20 ANOTHER   Oh! my God! he has crossed the ditch.

ANOTHER   Bing! Bang! there go four soldiers, struck down by that big bugger of a lieutenant.

BARBAGE   Ah! it's not over yet for you! Here, Johannes Sobiesky, now you're going to get yours. [*He strikes him down.*] Now for the others! [*He makes a massacre of the Poles.*]

25 PAPA UBU   Forward, my friends! Get that good-for-nothing! Make applesauce out of those Muscovites! Victory is ours. Long live the Red Eagle!

EVERYONE   Forward! Hurrah! Godsleg! Get the big bugger.

BARBAGE   By Saint George, I have fallen.

PAPA UBU [*recognizing him*]   Ah! it's you, Barbage! Aha! my friend. We are

30 quite happy to meet you once again. So is the whole Company. I am going to cook you over a slow fire. Gentlemen of Finance, light the fire. Oh! Ah! Oh! I am dead. I've been hit by a cannon shot at the very least. Ah! God, forgive me my sins. Yes, it is a cannon shot.

BARBAGE   It's a shot from a pistol loaded with powder.

35 PAPA UBU   Ah! you're kidding me! Again! Into my poke-et!

[*He charges at him and rips him apart.*]

GENERAL LASKY   Papa Ubu, we are advancing on all fronts.

PAPA UBU   I can see that very well, I can't take any more, I've been kicked all over, I would like to sit down upon the ground . . . Oh! my bottle.

GENERAL LASKY   Go take the Czar's, Papa Ubu.

---

4. Symbolic of victory in battle.

40 PAPA UBU   Hey! I'm going for it right away. Let's go! Shitsky Saber, do your
duty, and you, Financial Hook, do not remain behind. Let the Physical
Stick work with generous emulation and share with the little wedge of
wood the honor of massacrating, gouging out, and exploiting the Musco-
vite Czar. Forward, Sir Horse of Finance!

[*He charges at the* CZAR.]

45 A RUSSIAN OFFICER   On guard, Your Majesty!
PAPA UBU   Here's for you! Oh! Ouch! Come *on!* Ah! excuse me, sir, do leave
me alone. Oh! really, I didn't do it on purpose!

[*He runs away. The* CZAR *follows him.*]

PAPA UBU   Blessed Virgin, that madman is following me! Great God, what
have I done! Ah! OK, we've still got the ditch to cross over again. Ah! I
50 can feel him behind me, and the ditch ahead! Courage, let us close our
eyes.

[*He jumps the ditch. The* CZAR *falls into it.*]

THE CZAR   Well, I'm in it.
POLES   Hurrah! the Czar is down!
PAPA UBU   I hardly dare turn around! He's in it. Ah! and a good thing too, and
55 they're beating on him. Come on Poles, give it to him good, he has a broad
back, that wretch! *I* don't dare look at him! And yet our prediction has
come completely true, the Physical Stick has wrought marvels, and there is
no doubt that I would have killed him completely if terror had not inexplicably come in to combat and nullify in us the effects of our courage. But
60 we were obliged suddenly to turn turncoat, and we were obliged to owe our
salvation solely to our skill as a horseman as well as to the legs of our
Financial Horse—whose rapidity is only equaled by his stability and whose
lightness is justly celebrated—as well as to the depth of the ditch that quite
luckily happened to be under the feet of the enemy of Us, the present-and-
65 accounted-for Master of Phynances. Now this is all very well, but no one is
listening to me. . . . Uh oh! here we go again!

[*The Russian Dragoons make a charge and deliver the* CZAR.]

GENERAL LASKY   This time, we're in a general rout.
PAPA UBU   Ah! here's a chance to bust outta here. And now, good Polish
Lords, forward! Or rather, backward!
70 POLE   Every man for himself!
PAPA UBU   Come on, let's get going! What a lot of people, what a stampede,
what a multitude, how can I get out of this mess? [*He is roughly jostled.*]
Hey, you! watch out, or you will feel the burning valor of the Master of
Finances. Ah! he has gone, let us get out of here, and fast, while Lasky can't
75 see us.

[*He exits. Then the* CZAR *goes by, and the Russian Army pursuing the*
Poles.]

4.5

[SCENE: *A cavern in Lithuania (it is snowing).*]

[PAPA UBU, HEADS, COTISE.]

PAPA UBU   Ah! what filthy weather, it's cold enough to split rocks, and the
person of the Master of Finances has been quite damaged by it.

HEADS Oh! Milaird Ubu, have you recovered from your terror and your flight?

5 PAPA UBU Yes! I'm not scared any more, but I've still got the flights.

COTISE [*aside*] What a pig.

PAPA UBU Hey! Sire Cotise, how is the health of your earie?

COTISE Milaird, it's as good as it can be seeing as it's bad. Quinsecontly, the lead makes it lean toward the earth and I have not been able to extract the 10 bullet.

PAPA UBU Well! you asked for it! You're one of those guys who always wanted to beat up on other people. As for me, I displayed the greatest valor, and without exposing myself at all I massacrated four enemies with my own hand, not counting all the ones who were already dead that we finished off.

15 COTISE Heads, do you know what happened to little Rensky?

HEADS He was shot in the head.

PAPA UBU AS the wild poppy and the dandelion in their prime are scythed down by the pitiless scythe of the pitiless scyther who pitilessly scythes their pitiful noggins, EVEN SO has little Rensky played poppy; he did fight 20 well however, but also there were too many Russians.

HEADS and COTISE Ooh, Milaird!

AN ECHO Ooooh!

HEADS What have we here? Let us arm ourselves with our bladies.

PAPA UBU Not on your life! I'll bet it's the Russians again, for Godsakes. I'm 25 sick and tired of this! Well, the hell with it, if they get me I sticka dem inna de pocket.

4.6[5]

[SCENE: *The same.*]

> [*Enter a bear.*]

COTISE Yoo-hoo, Milaird of Finances!

PAPA UBU Oh, hey! look at the little doggie. My word, but he's cute.

HEADS Watch out! Ah! what a huge bear: my cartridges!

PAPA UBU A bear! Ah! what a horrible beast. Oh! poor man, I am eaten alive. 5 God protect me. And he's coming right at me. No, he's got Cotise. Ah! I can breathe again.

> [*The bear jumps on* COTISE. HEADS *attacks it with his knife.* UBU *takes shelter on a rock.*]

COTISE To me, Heads! Help, Milaird Ubu!

PAPA UBU Nothing doing! You can shift for yourself, my friend; for the moment, we are reciting an Our Father.[6] Everybody has to take his turn at 10 being eaten.

HEADS I've got him, I've got him.

COTISE Hold firm, friend, he's beginning to let go.

PAPA UBU Hallowèd be thy name.

COTISE Let go, you bugger!

---

5. This scene, adapted from an intermezzo in one of Molière's minor plays, was cut when *Ubu* was first performed in Paris [translator's note].

6. That is, the Lord's Prayer, which begins "Our Father which art in heaven" (Matthew 6.9–13). Ubu continues to quote from this prayer through "But deliver us from evil."

15 HEADS   Ah! he's biting me! Oh good Lord, save us, I am dead.

PAPA UBU   Thy will be done.

COTISE   Ah! I've succeeded in wounding him.

HEADS   Hurray! he's losing blood.

> [*In the midst of the shouting Knighties, the bear bellows with pain and* UBU *continues to mutter.*]

COTISE   Hold on to him, so I can let loose an explosive punch.

20 UBU   Give us this day our daily bread.

HEADS   Do you have him, for godsakes, I can't take any more.

PAPA UBU   Forgive us our debts, as we forgive our debtors.

COTISE   Ah! I've got him.

> [*An explosion rings out and the bear falls, dead.*]

HEADS and COTISE   Victory!

25 PAPA UBU   But deliver us from evil. Well, is he good and dead? Can I come down from my rock?

HEADS [*scornfully*]   As much as you like.

PAPA UBU [*climbing down*]   You may rest assured that if you are still alive and still treading the snow of Lithuania, you owe it to the magnanimous virtue

30 of the Master of Finances, who wore his throat, his back, and his self to a frazzle reciting Our Fathers for your safety and salvation, and who was as brave in wielding the spiritual sword of prayer as you were skillful with the temporal one of the present-and-accounted-for-Knightie Heads's explosive punch. We even went still further in our devotion, for we did not hesitate

35 to climb an extremely high rock so that our prayers would have less distance to travel up to heaven.

HEADS   You disgusting jackass.

PAPA UBU   Now here's a fat beast. Thanks to me, you have something for supper. What a belly, gentlemen! The Greeks would have had more room in it

40 than inside the wooden horse,[7] and, my dear friends, we very nearly went and verified its inner capacity with our own eyes.

HEADS   I'm dying of hunger. What can we eat?

COTISE   The bear!

PAPA UBU   Hey! you poor fools, are you going to eat it raw? We have nothing

45 to make fire with.

HEADS   Have we not the flints from our muskets?

PAPA UBU   Huh! that's true. And then it seems to me that not far from here there is a little wood where there should be some dry branches. Go get some, Sire Cotise.

> [COTISE *goes off through the snow.*]

50 HEADS   And now, Sire Ubu, go cut up the bear.

PAPA UBU   Oh no! he might not be dead. Whereas you, who are already half eaten and bitten all over, it's just your kind of job. I'll light a fire while we wait for him to bring wood.

> [HEADS *begins to cut up the bear.*]

---

7. That is, the Trojan Horse. According to legend, the Trojan War was finally brought to an end when the Trojans were tricked into pulling this hollow construction—filled with the best Greek warriors—within the city walls.

PAPA UBU   Oh! watch out! he moved.

55 HEADS   But Sire Ubu, he is already quite cold.

PAPA UBU   What a shame, it would have been better to eat him hot. This will cause indigestion in the Master of Finances.

HEADS [*aside*]   This is revolting. [*Aloud*] Give us a hand, Mr. Ubu, I can't do the whole job.

60 PAPA UBU   No, I don't wanna do a thing! I'm tired, of course!

COTISE [*entering*]   What snow, my friends, one would think we were in Spain or at the North Pole. Night is beginning to fall. In an hour it will be dark. Let us hurry so that we can still see clearly.

PAPA UBU   Yes, do you hear, Heads? Hurry. Both of you, hurry up! Spit the
65   beast, cook the beast, I'm hungry!

HEADS   Ah! this is really too much! You'll have to work or you won't get a thing, do you hear, you glutton!

PAPA UBU   Oh! I don't care, I'd just as soon eat it raw, you're the ones who'll be sorry. And anyway, I'm sleepy!

70 COTISE   What can we do, Heads? Let's make dinner all by ourselves. He won't get any, that's all. Or else we can give him the bones.

HEADS   Fine. Ah! there's the fire flaming up.

PAPA UBU   Oh! that's nice, it's warm now. But I see Russians everywhere. What a rout, good God! Ah! [*He falls asleep.*]

75 COTISE   I wonder if what Rensky said is true, if Mama Ubu has really lost her throne. It does not sound impossible.

HEADS   Let's finish making supper.

COTISE   No, we have more important things to talk about. I think it would be good to inquire as to the veracity of that bit of news.

80 HEADS   That's true; should we abandon Papa Ubu or stay with him?

COTISE   The night brings counsel. Let us sleep, tomorrow we shall see what we must do.

HEADS   No, it's better to take advantage of the night to get out of here.

COTISE   In that case, let us go.

[*They go.*]

4.7

[PAPA UBU *talking in his sleep.*]

PAPA UBU   Ah! Sire Russian Dragoon, be careful, don't shoot this way, there are people here. Ah! here's Barbage, how bad-natured he is, you'd think he was a bear. And Buggerlas coming right at me! The bear, the bear! Ah! he's down! good God, he's tough! I don't want to do anything! Get out of here,
5   Buggerlas! Do you hear, you idiot? Now here's Rensky and the Czar! Oh! they're going to beat me. And Mabubu. Where did you get all that gold? You took my gold, you wretch, you went and rummaged around in my tomb which is in the Warsaw Cathedral, near the moon. I've really been dead for a long time, Buggerlas is the one who killed me, and I'm buried in Warsaw
10   near Vladislas the Great, and also in Cracow near John Sigismund and also in Thorn in the bunker with Barbage! Here he comes again. Would you get out of here, you beastly bear. You look like Barbage. Do you hear, you damned beast? No, he can't hear, the Sonsabiddies have cut his earies off.

De-brain 'em, kill 'em, cut all their earies off, rip out the finance and drink
15 to the death, that's the life for Sonsabiddies, and for the Master of Finances,
that's what makes his day.

[*He stops talking and sleeps.*]

End of the Fourth Act.

5.1

[*Night.* PAPA UBU *is asleep. Enter* MAMA UBU, *who does not see him. Total
darkness.*]

MAMA UBU Shelter at last. I am alone here, and none too soon, but what a
mad race: crossing all of Poland in four days! Every misfortune assailed me
at once. As soon as that fat jackass had left, I went to the crypt to get rich.
Right after that I almost got stoned to death by Buggerlas and his madmen.
5 I lost my Knightie—Lap, who was so in love with my charms that he
swooned with pleasure when he saw me, and even (so I have been assured)
when he didn't see me, which is the height of love. He would have cut himself in two for me, poor boy. The proof of that is, he was cut in four by Buggerlas. Slish slash slish! . . . Ah! I thought I would die. So then I ran away,
10 pursued by the angry crowd. I left the palace, I reached the Vistula, all the
bridges were guarded. I swam across the river, hoping to wear out my per-
secutors. On all sides the nobility assembled and pursued me. A thousand
times I almost perished, smothered in a circle of Poles determined to end
my days. At last I got the better of their rage, and after four days of racing
15 through the snow of what was once my kingdom I managed to find shelter
here. I have neither eaten nor drunk these four days, Buggerlas was on my
heels . . . Well! at last I am safe. Ah! I am dying of weariness and cold. But
I *would* like to know what happened to my fat puppet, I mean my dear husband. Boy, did I take finance from him! Did I ever steal rixdalers from him!
20 Did I ever ever get his carrots! And his Financial Horse that was dying of
hunger: he didn't see oats very often, the poor devil. Ah! what a story. But
alas! I have lost my treasure! It is in Warsaw, and he who wants may seek it.
PAPA UBU [*beginning to wake up*] Get Mama Ubu, cut her earies off!
MAMA UBU Oh, God! where am I? I'm losing my mind. Oh, no, Lord!

25   Put out the light, and then put out the light.
      Without quenching thee, thou flaming minister,
      I see again my former Ubu sleep . . .

      . . . Let's act nice. Well, has Mama's big boy had a good sleep?
PAPA UBU A very bad one! That bear was tough as hell! A battle of the raven-
30 ous against the cavernous, but the ravenous have completely eaten up and
devoured the cavernous, as you will see when daylight comes—do you
hear, noble Knighties!
MAMA UBU What's he jabbering about? He's even dumber than when he left.
Who's he mad at?
35 PAPA UBU Cotise, Heads, answer me, you shitsky-bags! Where are you? Ah!
I'm scared. But someone spoke. Who spoke? It can't be the bear. Shitsky!
Where are my matches? Ah! I lost them in the battle.

MAMA UBU [*aside*]   Let us take advantage of the situation and the night, let
us simulate a supernatural apparition and make him promise to forgive us
40   our theft.

PAPA UBU   Oh! by Saint Anthony! someone's talking. Godslegs! well, blow me
down!

MAMA UBU [*amplifying her voice*]   Yes, Mr. Ubu, someone is talking indeed,
and the trumpet of the archangel who will pull the dead from the ashes
45   and the final dust would speak no other way! Listen to that severe voice. It
is the voice of Saint Gabriel[8] who can only give you good advice.

PAPA UBU   Oh sure! *that* he can give!

MAMA UBU   Don't interrupt me or I'll be quiet and that'll be the end of your
bogsbelliskin!

50   PAPA UBU   Ah! my godsbellysky! I'll be quiet, I say no more. Continue,
Madam Apparition!

MAMA UBU   We were saying, Mr. Ubu, that you were a big, big boy.

PAPA UBU   Very big, indeed, this is true.

MAMA UBU   Shut up, for God's sake!

55   PAPA UBU   Oh! angels don't swear!

MAMA UBU [*aside*]   Shitsky! [*Continuing*] You are married, Mr. Ubu.

PAPA UBU   Absolutely, to the worst shrew in the world!

MAMA UBU   You mean she's a charming woman.

PAPA UBU   She's horrible. She has claws everywhere, there's no way of han-
60   dling her.

MAMA UBU   Handle her with gentleness, Sire Ubu, and if you handle her like
that you will see that she is at least the equal of the Venus of Milo.[9]

PAPA UBU   Who's that you say should be in a silo?

MAMA UBU   You are not listening, Mr. Ubu; lend us a more attentive ear.
65   [*Aside*] But let us hasten, for day is going to break—Mr. Ubu, your wife is
adorable and delightful, she does not have one single fault.

PAPA UBU   You're wrong, there's not one fault she doesn't have.

MAMA UBU   Silence, I say! your wife is not unfaithful to you!

PAPA UBU   I'd really like to know who could possibly fall in love with her.
70   She's a harpy!

MAMA UBU   She doesn't drink!

PAPA UBU   Ever since I took the key to the wine cellar. Before that, she was
drunk at seven in the morning and the perfume she used was pure booze.
Now the perfume she uses is heliotrope and she smells a lot better. I don't
75   care. But now I'm the only one who's drunk!

MAMA UBU   Silly fool!—Your wife doesn't take your gold.

PAPA UBU   No she doesn't—*that's* funny!

MAMA UBU   She doesn't swindle you out of a cent!

PAPA UBU   Witness our noble and unfortunate Phynancial Horse, who, since
80   he had not been fed for three months, was obliged to go through the whole
campaign led across Ukraine by the bridle. And so he died in harness, poor
beast!

8. According to legend, the archangel Gabriel
is the seventh angel who, in the book of Revelation (11.15), sounds the final trumpet that
announces Judgment Day.
9. An ancient Greek statue of Aphrodite, the
goddess of love; its arms have been lost.

MAMA UBU   That's all a pack of lies, your wife is a model wife and as for you,
you're a monster!

85 PAPA UBU   That's all true, my wife is a rascal, and as for you, you're a natter-
ing ninny!

MAMA UBU   Beware, Papa Ubu, beware!

PAPA UBU   Ah, that's true, I forgot who I was talking to. OK, no, I didn't say
that!

90 MAMA UBU   You killed Wenceslas.

PAPA UBU   That's not *my* fault, of course. Mama Ubu's the one who wanted
to do that.

MAMA UBU   You put Boleslas and Ladislas to death.

PAPA UBU   Too bad for them! They wanted to borrow from me!

95 MAMA UBU   You did not keep your promise to Barbage and later you killed
him.

PAPA UBU   I'd rather it be me than he who reigns in Lithuania. For the
moment it's neither one of us. So you can see it's not me.

MAMA UBU   There is only one way for you to be forgiven for all your evil
100   deeds.

PAPA UBU   What way? I am quite ready to become a holy man; I want to be a
bishop and see my name in the calendar.

MAMA UBU   You must forgive Mama Ubu for having embezzled a little money.

PAPA UBU   Well, there you are! I'll forgive her when she has given enough
105   back to me and when she has been soundly beaten. And when she has
brought my Financial Horse back to life.

MAMA UBU   God, he's crazy about his horse! . . . Ah! I am lost, day is
breaking.

PAPA UBU   At any rate, I am glad to have learned with certainty that my dear
110   wife was stealing from me. Now I have it from a good source. *Omnis a Deo
scientia*, which means: *Omnis*—all; *a Deo*—knowledge; *scientia*—comes
from God.[1] There's the explanation of the phenomenon. But Madame the
Apparition isn't saying anything any more. Would that I could offer her
something to comfort her. What she was saying was very amusing. Hey, it's
115   broad daylight! Oh, good God, by my Financial Horse . . . it's Mama Ubu!

MAMA UBU [*brazenly*]   That's not true, I'll excommunicate you.

PAPA UBU   Ah! you animal!

MAMA UBU   What impiety.

PAPA UBU   Oh! this is too much. I can see it's you, you stupid shrew! What
120   the devil are you doing here?

MAMA UBU   Lap is dead and the Poles threw me out.

PAPA UBU   On my side, it's the Russians who threw me out. Great minds
meet.

MAMA UBU   Let's say a great mind has met a jackass!

125 PAPA UBU   Oh! well, now it's going to meet a palmiped![2] [*He throws the bear
at her.*]

MAMA UBU [*falling crushed under the weight of the bear*]   Ah! good God! how
horrible! Ah! I am dying! I am smothering! He's biting me! He's swallowing
me! He's digesting me!

---

1. Ubu's translation is accurate, but his explanation reverses the meanings of *a Deo* (from
God) and *scientia* (knowledge).
2. A web-footed bird.

PAPA UBU He's dead! you grotesque woman, you. . . . Uh oh! or maybe not!
130 Lord! he's not dead, let's get out of here. [*Climbing back on his rock*] Our
Father who art . . .

MAMA UBU [*extricating herself*] Hey! where is he?

PAPA UBU Oh, Lord! here she is again! The stupid beast, there's no way of
getting rid of her. Is the bear dead?

135 MAMA UBU Of course he is, you stupid donkey, he's already stone cold. How
did he get here?

PAPA UBU [*embarrassed*] I don't know. Oh yes, I do! He wanted to eat Heads
and Cotise and I killed him with one stroke of my Lord's Prayer.

MAMA UBU Heads, Cotise, Lord's Prayer. What *is* all this? He's crazy, that
140 Finance of mine!

PAPA UBU It's true, it's true, what I'm tellin' you! And you're an idiot, Bogsbelliskin of mine!

MAMA UBU Tell me about your campaign, Papa Ubu.

PAPA UBU Oh! for heaven's sake, no! It's too long. All I know is that despite
145 my incontrovertible valiance everybody beat me.

MAMA UBU What! even the Poles?

PAPA UBU They shouted: Long live Wenceslas and Buggerlas. I thought they
wanted me drawn and quartered. Oh! the madmen! And then they went
and killed Rensky.

150 MAMA UBU I don't care! You know, Buggerlas killed Knightie Lap!

PAPA UBU I don't care! And then they went and killed poor Lasky!

MAMA UBU I don't care!

PAPA UBU Oh! not *that*! Get over here, you animal! Fall on your knees before
your master [*He grabs her and throws her to her knees.*], you are going to
155 pay the ultimate penalty.

MAMA UBU Oh, oh, Mr. Ubu!

PAPA UBU Oh! oh! oh! so, have you finished? Now *I'll* start: twisting of the
nose, pulling out of the hair, penetration of the little piece of wood into the
earies, extraction of the brain by the heels, laceration of the posterior, par-
160 tial or even total suppression of the spine marrow (if only that would get rid
of her spiny character!), not to forget opening of the swimming bladder and
finally renewal of the great decapitation of Saint John the Baptist,[3] all
adapted from the very holy Scriptures, both from the Old and New Testament, arranged, corrected, and perfected by the present-and-accounted-for
165 Master of Finances!

[*He tears her apart.*]

MAMA UBU Mercy, Mr. Ubu!

[*Loud noise at the entrance of the cavern.*]

5.2

[*The same, with* BUGGERLAS, *charging into the cavern with his
Soldiers.*]

BUGGERLAS Forward, my friends! Long live Poland!

---

3. See Matthew 14.1–12 (a similar account appears in the other three Gospels).

PAPA UBU   Oh! oh! just you wait, Mr. Polesky. Just wait till I've finished with
   Madame my Better Half!
BUGGERLAS [*striking him*]   There, you coward, you blackguard, you beggar,
5   you infidel, you moslem!
PAPA UBU [*riposting*]   There! You Polesky, drunksky, bastardsky, troopsky,
   Turksky, kibumsky, snoopsky, doopsky, Commie!
MAMA UBU [*also beating him*]   There, you chicken, piggen, felon, bacon, vil-
   lain, slattern, Polen!
        [*The Soldiers charge at the* UBUS, *who defend themselves as best they can.*]
10 PAPA UBU   Ye gods! what reenfortments!
MAMA UBU   We've got feet, Sir Poles.
PAPA UBU   By my green candlestick, will it never end, finally? Another one!
   Ah! if only I had my Phynancial Horse here!
BUGGERLAS   Hit, and keep hitting.
15 VOICE OUTSIDE   Long live Papa Ubu, our great financier!
PAPA UBU   Ah! there they are. Hurrah! there are the Papa Ubus. Forward,
   come on, we need you, gentlemen of the Finance.
        [*Enter the Knighties, who throw themselves into the fray.*]
COTISE   Out with the Poles!
TAILS   Ooh! we are together again, Ghentlemen of the Finance. Forward,
20   thrust vigorously, gain the door; once outside all we'll have to do is run
   away.
PAPA UBU   Oh! there, that's my strongest. O how he can hit.
BUGGERLAS   God! I am wounded.
STANISLAS LECZINSKY   It is nothing, Sire.
25 JOHANNES SOBIESKY   Hit, keep hitting, they are gaining the door, the beggars.
COTISE   We're drawing near, follow the people. In consequence of whyche, I
   can see ye sky.
HEADS   Courage, Sire Ubu.
PAPA UBU   Ah! I'm doing number one in my pants. Forward, oddsbellikins!
30   kiddiddle 'em, blideedle 'em, skin 'em, massmur-murder 'em, by Ubu's horn!
   Ah! there are less of 'em now!
COTISE   There are only two left guarding the door.
PAPA UBU [*knocking them down with blows of the bear*]   One down, two to
   go! Whew! I'm out! Let's get out of here! The rest of you, follow me, and
35   fast!

5.3

[SCENE: *The stage represents the Province of Livonia covered with snow.*]
        [*The* UBUS *and their suite in flight.*]
PAPA UBU   Ah! I think they've given up trying to catch us.
MAMA UBU   Yes, Buggerlas has gone to be crowned.
PAPA UBU   He can keep it; I don't envy him his crown.
MAMA UBU   You are absolutely right, Papa Ubu.
        [*They disappear in the distance.*]

5.4

[SCENE: *The deck of a ship sailing close to the wind on the Baltic.*]

[*On the deck* PAPA UBU *and his whole band.*]

THE CAPTAIN   Ah! what a fine breeze.

PAPA UBU   It is a fact that we are sailing with a speed that borders on the prodigious. We must be going a million knots an hour, and the good thing about those knots is that once they're done, they don't come undone. It is
5   true we have the wind behind us.

TAILS   What a sorry imbecile.

[*A squall blows up, the ship tilts sharply and whitens the sea.*]

PAPA UBU   Oh! ah! God! we've capsized! Why, your boat's all crooked, it's going to fall.

THE CAPTAIN   All hands to the leeward, haul in the foresail!

10   PAPA UBU   Oh! no, for heaven's sake! Don't all stand on the same side! That's really reckless. And just suppose the wind should change sides: everybody would go straight to the bottom and fish will eat us.

THE CAPTAIN   Don't bear down, furl sails, close and hard!

PAPA UBU   No, no, bear down, unfurl those sails, I'm in a hurry! We'll never
15   get there, you brute of a Captain, and it's all your fault! We should be there already. OK, if that's the way it is, I'll take the command! Get ready to veer about! Farewell. Drop anchor, veer wind ahead, veer wind behind. Raise sails, furl sails, tiller up, tiller down, tiller sideways. See, we're going along just fine. Go broadside to the wave and then it'll be perfect.

[*Everyone twists and turns, the breeze freshens.*]

20   THE CAPTAIN   Take in the main jib, reef in the sails!

PAPA UBU   That's not bad, in fact it's good! Listen up, Mr. Crew! "Take a plain rib, beef with ales!"

[*A few collapse with laughter. A wave comes in.*]

PAPA UBU   Oh! what a flood! This is an effect of the maneuvers he ordered.

MAMA UBU and TAILS   Navigation is a delightful thing.

[*Second wave pours in.*]

25   TAILS [*drenched*]   Beware of Satan and all his works.

PAPA UBU   Sire waiter, bring us something to drink.

[*They all sit down to drink.*]

MAMA UBU   Ah! what a pleasure to see fair France again soon, our old friends, and our castle of Mondragon!

PAPA UBU   Hey! we'll be there soon. In a minute we'll be coming in under the
30   castle of Elsinore.[4]

TAILS   My spirits revive at the thought of seeing my beloved Spain again.

COTISE   Yes, and we'll dazzle our friends with tales of our wonderful adventures.

PAPA UBU   Oh, you bet! And I'll get myself appointed Master of Finances
35   in Paris.

MAMA UBU   That's right! . . . Ah! what a jolt!

COTISE   It's nothing, we've just passed the Point of Elsinore.

---

4. On the east coast of Denmark (Hilsingør), the setting of Shakespeare's *Hamlet* (1600–01).

TAILS   And now our noble ship skims rapidly over the darkening waves of the North Sea.

40 PAPA UBU   A wild and inhospitable sea that washes the shores of a land called Germania, so named because the comments of its inhabitants are all germane.

MAMA UBU   Now there's scholarship for you. They say that country is quite beautiful.

45 PAPA UBU   Ah, gentlemen! Beautiful as it may be, it cannot compare to Poland. If there were no Poland, there would be no Poles!

End.[5]

---

5. The original edition ends here. Jarry added a "Disembraining Song" when he put on an earlier version of the play [translator's note].

ANTON CHEKHOV

1860–1904

Anton Chekhov, who died four years after the dawn of the new century, casts a long shadow over the history of modern theater. The greatest dramatist the Russian stage has ever seen, he stands as a central figure in the emergence of twentieth-century drama. At first glance, Chekhov may seem an unlikely candidate for this historical role. Inheriting a tradition of Russian fiction that included such literary monuments as Fyodor Dostoevsky's novel *Crime and Punishment* (1866) and Leo Tolstoy's *War and Peace* (1865–89), Chekhov achieved his initial literary reputation through the writing of novellas and short stories rather than drama. Of the dozen and a half plays that he wrote, the majority are comic one acts, and those on which his reputation chiefly rests—*The Seagull*, *Uncle Vanya*, *The Three Sisters*, and *THE CHERRY ORCHARD*—are only four in number and were written relatively late in his career. In Chekhov's case, though, numbers are misleading, for the dramatic terrain that these plays opened up proved so innovative that their influence can be felt more than a century after his death. Rewriting the aesthetic of theatrical realism through a drama of understatement, indirection, and psychological nuance, Chekhov's major plays offer a new vision of the relationship between theater and everyday life.

Chekhov was born on January 17, 1860, in Taganrog, a small seaport on the Sea of Azov (a northern arm of the Black Sea) in southern Russia. His father was a merchant and his paternal grandfather a serf who had purchased his freedom and that of his family in 1841. Only one generation removed from serfdom, Chekhov remained acutely aware of his background: in an autobiographical letter to his friend and publisher Alexei Suvorin in 1889, he described an imaginary character who, after squeezing the slave blood out of himself "drop by drop," awakes one day to find that "the blood coursing through his veins is no longer that of a slave but that of a real human being." After attending local schools, he graduated in 1879 with a scholarship for university study. Chekhov's father had moved the rest of his family to Moscow three years earlier in order to escape debtor's prison, and when Anton joined them he enrolled at the Moscow University School of Medicine, from which he earned a degree at the age of twenty-four. Although Chekhov soon gave up private practice to focus on writing, his medical training remained an essential part of his personal and professional identity. "Medicine is my lawful wife and literature is my mistress," he later commented. "When I get tired of one I go to the other." He continued to treat patients, often for free, and he demonstrated a lifelong interest in matters of public health. During the famine and cholera epidemic of 1892–93, he served as head of a district sanitary committee and treated many of the epidemic's poorest victims.

Chekhov began writing in his teens. He edited a school newspaper and, encouraged by his older brothers, wrote humorous anecdotes and sketches. By the time he graduated from medical school, he was publishing comic sketches, parodies, dialogues, and short stories in small-press periodicals. As the popularity of his fiction grew, Chekhov's stories began appearing in more established periodicals and newspapers, and in 1884 he published his first collection of short stories, *Fairy Tales of Melpomene*. Dmitri Grigorovich, a leading short-story writer and a prominent figure in Russia's literary establishment, praised Chekhov as the most talented writer of his generation; the young writer's accomplishment was given official recognition when his second collection of stories, *In the Twilight*, was awarded the Pushkin Prize by the Imperial Academy of Science in 1888. Although Chekhov attempted unsuccessfully to write a novel, he was attracted—and his artistic temperament was suited—to more condensed fictional forms. Focusing on the particularities of character, social class, and setting while maintaining the authorial objectivity for which he became renowned, he developed the short story into a vehicle of unprecedented psychological complexity and acute social observation. His finest stories—such as "Ward No. 6" (1892), "My Life" (1896), and "Peasants" (1897)—are considered masterpieces of the genre.

Chekhov's interest in the theater also developed at an early age. As a schoolboy, he participated in amateur theatrical skits with his siblings (he had four brothers and one sister), and he and his friends saw professional plays at the Taganrog theater. In his late teens he composed two plays that have not survived, a one-act farce and a full-length drama titled *Fatherlessness*, and during his first two years of medical school he produced a cumbersome four-act drama that may have been a reworked version of the latter play. Though he subsequently destroyed this play, a copy was discovered after his death and has been published under the title *Platonov*. Chekhov's first theatrical production did not occur until 1887, when *Ivanov*, a play about a bored and disillusioned landowner, premiered in Moscow to critical and popular acclaim. It was followed in 1889 by *The Wood Demon*, a full-length comedy, and by a series of one-act comedies that Chekhov wrote between 1887 and 1901. Conceived in the tradition of vaudeville farce, these "airy trifles" (as Chekhov called them) were little more than curtain-raisers, though *The Bear* (1888) proved popular throughout Russia and *The Proposal* (1889) entertained a St. Petersburg audience that included Czar Alexander III.

A gap of five years separates this early drama from the earliest of the four mature plays that figure so prominently in the history of modern drama. In 1895 Chekhov wrote *The Seagull*, a play about art, disappointed love, and the psychology of survival. Set, like his other major plays, on a provincial Russian estate, it explores the shifting relationships in a quartet of central characters: Arkádina, an aging actress; her son Tréplev, an avant-garde writer; Trigórin, an established novelist; and Nína, a young actress whose aspirations, hardships, and disappointments identify her with a seagull that Tréplev has shot. At the play's premiere in St. Petersburg on October 17, 1896, the audience responded so negatively that Chekhov fled the auditorium during the second act and vowed never to write another play. However, when Konstantin Stanislavsky and Vladimir Nemirovich-Danchenko, founders of the newly formed Moscow Art Theatre, revived *The Seagull* two years later, the play proved so popular that the theater company adopted its title bird as their emblem. With Stanislavsky as director, the MAT staged the Moscow premieres of Chekhov's remaining plays: *Uncle Vanya*, a reworked version of *The Wood Demon*, in 1899; *The Three Sisters* in 1901; and *The Cherry Orchard* in 1904. Six months after *The Cherry Orchard* opened, Chekhov died of tuberculosis at the age of forty-four.

The innovations of dramaturgy and stagecraft in these plays are both subtle and wide-ranging. Late nineteenth-century Russian theater was dominated by farce and melodrama, genres that relied on stock characters and heightened dramatic incident. Reacting against these theatrical conventions, Chekhov insisted that drama imitate the textures, issues, and actions of everyday life and that its characters reflect the complexity of human experience. In a statement of his artistic principles, Chekhov wrote:

> The demand is made that the hero and heroine should be dramatically effective. But in life people do not shoot themselves, or hang themselves, or fall in love, or deliver themselves of clever sayings every minute. They spend most of their time eating, drinking, running after women or men, talking nonsense. It is therefore necessary that this should be shown on the stage. A play ought to be written in which the people should come and go, dine, talk of the weather, or play cards, not because the author wants it but because that is what happens in real life. Life on the stage should be as it really is, and the people, too, should be as they are and not on stilts.

In order to accomplish this objective, Chekhov reduced the importance of traditional dramatic climaxes by minimizing their impact or eliminating them altogether. His characters resist dramatic stereotype, and the stage they occupy generates multiple points of attention rather than central protagonists and antagonists. These characters talk, do ordinary things, and are defined more by the actions they don't take than those they do. In keeping with Chekhov's belief that a dramatist's job is not to judge the characters created but to present them in the light of dispassionate observation, his plays give little evidence of their author's point of view. The result is a drama of understatement, indirection, and nuance, where action and emotion lie beneath the words. Chekhov famously observed: "People are having a meal, just having a meal, but at the same time their happiness is being created, or their lives are being destroyed."

The Cherry Orchard is one of the finest examples of Chekhov's "drama of the undramatic" (in the critic Richard Gilman's phrase). Its plot hinges on the fate of the Ranyévskaya estate, famed for its beautiful cherry orchard but no longer able to support its occupants or their privileged lifestyle. Its threatened sale is the stuff of French "mortgage melodramas," which often hinged on the possible or actual loss of property at the hands of a villainous manipulator; but the climactic event of Chekhov's play—the auction at which the estate is sold—occurs offstage, and its outcome is recounted after the fact. In a similar undermining of expectations, the participants in this crisis do not fit the moral categories of conventional melodrama. Liubóv (Madame Ranyévskaya) and her brother Gáyev, who cling to their childhood memories of the orchard, lose the estate through a mixture of paralysis and fecklessness, not victimization; indeed, their inaction in the face of the imminent loss of their property is the play's most sustained narrative thread. For his part, Lopákhin—the former serf who eventually buys the estate—is a far cry from the stock villain of melodrama. He urges Liubóv and Gáyev to sell the orchard as a way of saving the estate, and in the giddiness of having bought the property he speaks movingly (if somewhat thoughtlessly) about his social transformation. In terms of dramatic technique, the moment in act 3 when he delivers this speech is a rare example in Chekhov's play of a character's dominating the stage and claiming attention. The rest of the time characters engage in conversation with each other, sometimes listening, sometimes not. In keeping with its muted sphere of action, *The Cherry Orchard* opens with the arrival of characters and ends with their departure.

Chekhov wrote *The Cherry Orchard* while living as a semi-invalid in Yalta, and its composition was long and difficult. Yet the play is the most comic of his mature dramas. In September 1903 he wrote to his wife, Olga Knipper, who would play the role of Madame Ranyévskaya, "My play . . . hasn't turned out as a drama, but as a comedy, at times almost a farce." Subtitling his play "A Comedy in Four Acts," Chekhov insisted on this view of the play throughout its rehearsals and found himself in frequent disagreement

The Moscow Art Theater's original 1904 production of *The Cherry Orchard*, directed by Constantin Stanislavsky. Stanislavsky, who performed the role of Gayev in this production, is on the far left, gesturing toward the bookcase.

with his director, Stanislavsky, who considered the play a tragedy and accentuated the atmosphere of pathos and loss. In Chekhov's hands, comedy is central to the play's mixture of tones. In addition to the obvious moments of slapstick—Liubóv's adopted daughter Várya swings a stick at the accountant Yepikhódov in anger but hits Lopákhin instead, while "the eternal student" Trofímov falls noisily down the stairs after an argument with Liubóv—Chekhov employs comedy as a vehicle of irony and distance. His use of comedy is particularly evident in those moments when the physical world intrudes on private emotion and in those tics and mannerisms that signal a character's self-absorption. When the governess Carlotta laments that she doesn't own a birth certificate at the start of the play's second act—"Where I'm from . . . who I am . . . no idea"—the painful undertones of her meditation are deflected when she reaches into her pocket and absentmindedly takes a bite out of a cucumber pickle. And when Gáyev plays his imaginary billiards game or delivers an oration to the family bookcase, these humorous moments measure the extent to which he, like all the play's characters, inhabits a world of his own.

The problem in Stanislavsky's "tearful" direction of *The Cherry Orchard*, in other words, was that he sought to reveal the play's emotions through overt gesture rather than through the ironic counterpoint of surface activity and emotional undercurrents. In Chekhovian drama the weight of emotion lies in what is not said, as when the forced gaiety of the ball in act 3 is undercut by the audience's awareness

that the auction is taking place offstage. And few scenes in all of Chekhov's plays hold the emotional power of Várya's exchange with Lopákhin near the play's end, when the two exchange small talk while failing to address the life-deciding issue that hangs over them.

As elsewhere in Chekhov's writing, individual psychology in *The Cherry Orchard* is deeply embedded within the social, economic, and political landscape of turn-of-the-century Russia. In the sale of the Ranyévskaya estate, Chekhov dramatizes the historical eclipse of the landowning class that had formed the historical pillar of feudal Russia. Semyónov-Píshchik, a neighboring landowner, must borrow money from Liubóv to meet his financial needs, and he pays her back only after selling the rights to extract the white clay that

has been discovered on his property. In Lopákhin's plan to cut down the cherry orchard and build vacation homes we feel the emerging class of others, like him, who have grown prosperous through acquired wealth. Social mobility defines *The Cherry Orchard*, and as the contrasting destinies of Chekhov's central characters demonstrate, this mobility extends in both directions. Beyond the circle of property and money, of course, is the vast number of Russia's poor and uneducated. Firs, the family's aging house servant, recalls the emancipation of the serfs in 1861, and Chekhov's play provides ample evidence of the poverty and social dislocation that this class has had to endure. Indigent peasants have been staying in the old servants' quarters, and a homeless man intrudes upon the pastoral quiet of act 2. The student

Trofímov addresses this poverty and its history in a speech to Liubóv's daughter Ánya: "Your grandfather, and his father, and his father's fathers, they *owned* the people who slaved away for them all over this estate, and now the voices and faces of human beings hide behind every cherry in the orchard, every leaf, every tree trunk." Envisioning a future of happiness and social justice, he calls on Ánya to devote her life to working in the cause of human progress. "This whole country is our orchard," he proclaims, widening the scope of the play's issues to include czarist Russia as a whole.

In view of subsequent Russian history—in 1917 the Communist-led Russian Revolution overthrew Czar Nicholas II and proclaimed an era of social equality—Trofímov's speeches in act 2 have sometimes been taken as Chekhov's own call for transformative social change. Not surprisingly, Soviet productions of *The Cherry Orchard* made Trofímov the herald of a new revolutionary order. To be sure, Chekhov's Trofímov articulates the revolutionary sentiment that had gained increasing force in Russia by the turn of the century. Universities were major sites of antigovernment agitation, and (as Chekhov indicated in a letter to his wife) Trofímov's extended career as a graduate student reflects the fact that he has been expelled more than once for political reasons. At the same time, though Trofímov's rhetoric is stirring, his vision of a future that will redeem the present resembles the beautiful dreams that other Chekhov characters use to escape the drabness and disappointment of their lives. Trofímov does little to translate language into action, and this character who likes the sound of his own voice cuts a somewhat ridiculous figure at times. The optimism of his predictions exist in ironic counterpoint with the present, just as the historical evolution represented by change in *The Cherry Orchard* coexists with the painfulness of individual loss. To push the tone of *The Cherry Orchard* in one direction at the expense of another—to stress its resignation or its desire for something better, its comedy or its tears—is to deny the multiple perspectives that Chekhov so masterfully calls into play.   S.G.

The Cherry Orchard
A Comedy in Four Acts[1]

CHARACTERS

LIUBÓV RANYÉVSKAYA [Lyúba, Liúba Andréyevna], who owns the estate
ÁNYA, her daughter, seventeen years old
VÁRYA, her adopted daughter, twenty-four years old
LEONÍD GÁYEV [Lonya, Lyónya Andréyich], Liubóv's brother
YERMOLÁI LOPÁKHIN [Yermolái Alexéyich], a businessman
PÉTYA TROFÍMOV, a graduate student
BORÍS SEMYÓNOV-PÍSHCHIK, who owns land in the neighborhood

CARLOTTA, the governess
SEMYÓN YEPIKHÓDOV, an accountant
DUNYÁSHA [Avdótya Fyódorovna, Dunyásha Kozoyédov], the maid
FIRS, the butler, eighty-seven years old
YÁSHA, the valet
A HOMELESS MAN
The STATIONMASTER
The POSTMASTER
Guests, servants

---

1. Translated by Paul Schmidt.

The action takes place on Ranyévskaya's estate.

Act 1

[*A room they still call the nursery. A side door leads to* ÁNYA's *room. Almost dawn; the sun is about to rise. It's May; the cherry orchard is already in bloom, but there's a chill in the air. The windows are shut. Enter* DUNYÁSHA *with a lamp, and* LOPÁKHIN *with a book in his hand.*]

LOPÁKHIN   The train's finally in, thank God. What time is it?

DUNYÁSHA   Almost two. [*She blows out the lamp.*] It's getting light.

LOPÁKHIN   How late is the train this time? Must be at least two hours. [*He yawns and stretches.*] That was dumb. I came over on purpose just to meet
5   them at the station, and then I fell asleep. Sat right here and fell asleep. Too bad. You should have woke me up.

DUNYÁSHA   I thought you already left. [*She listens.*] Listen, that must be them.

LOPÁKHIN   [*he listens*]   No, they still have the luggage to get, and all that. [*Pause*] She's been away five years now; no telling how she's changed. She
10   was always a good person. Very gentle, never caused a fuss. I remember one time when I was a kid, fifteen or so, they had my old man working in the store down by the village, and he hit me, hard, right in the face; my nose started to bleed. And we had to come up here to make a delivery or something; he was still drunk. And Liubóv Andréyevna—she wasn't much
15   older than I was, kind of thin—she brought me inside the house, right into the nursery here, and washed the blood off my face for me. "Don't cry," she told me. "Don't cry, poor boy; you'll live long enough to get married." [*Pause*] Poor boy . . . Well, my father was poor, but take a look at me now, all dressed up, brand-new suit and tan shoes. Silk purse out of a sow's ear,
20   I guess . . . I'm rich now, got lots of money, but when you think about it, I guess I'm still a poor boy from the country. [*He flips the pages of the book.*] I tried reading this book, couldn't figure out a word it said. Put me to sleep. [*Pause.*]

DUNYÁSHA   The dogs were barking all night long; they know their mistress is coming home.

25   LOPÁKHIN   Don't be silly.

DUNYÁSHA   I'm so excited I'm shaking. I may faint.

LOPÁKHIN   You're getting too full of yourself, Dunyásha. Look at you, all dressed up like that, and that hairdo. You watch out for that. You got to remember who you are.

[*Enter* YEPIKHÓDOV *with a bunch of flowers; he wears a jacket and tie and brightly polished boots, which squeak loudly. As he comes in, he drops the flowers.*]

30   YEPIKHÓDOV   [*picking up the flowers*]   Here. The gardener sent these over; he said put them on the dining room table. [*He gives the flowers to* DUNYÁSHA.]

LOPÁKHIN   And bring me a beer.

DUNYÁSHA   Right away. [*She goes out.*]

YEPIKHÓDOV   It's freezing this morning—it must be in the thirties—and
35   the cherry blossoms are out already. I cannot abide the climate here. [*He*

sighs.] I never have abided it, ever. [*Beat*]² Yermolái Alexéyich, would you examinate something for me, please? Day before yesterday I bought myself a new pair of boots, and listen to them squeak, will you? I just cannot endear it. Do you know anything I can put on them?

40 LOPÁKHIN   Will you shut up? You drive me crazy.

YEPIKHÓDOV   Every day something awful happens to me. It's like a habit. But I don't complain. I just try to keep smiling.

[*Enter* DUNYÁSHA; *she brings* LOPÁKHIN *a beer.*]

YEPIKHÓDOV   I'm going. [*He bumps into a chair, which falls over.*] You see? [*He seems proud of it.*] You see what I was referring about? Excuse my
45   expressivity, but what a concurrence. It's almost uncanny, isn't it?

[*He leaves.*]

DUNYÁSHA   You know what? That Yepikhódov proposed to me!

LOPÁKHIN   Oh?

DUNYÁSHA   I just don't know what to think. He's kind of nice. . . . He's a real quiet boy, but then he opens his mouth, and you can't ever understand
50   what he's talking about. I mean, it sounds nice, but it just doesn't make any sense. I do like him, though. Kind of. And he's crazy about me. It's funny, you know, every day something awful happens to him. People around here call him Double Trouble.

LOPÁKHIN [*he listens*]   That must be them.

55 DUNYÁSHA   It's them! Oh, I don't know what's the matter with me! I feel so funny; I'm cold all over.

LOPÁKHIN   It really is them this time. Let's go; we should be there at the door. You think she'll recognize me? It's been five years.

DUNYÁSHA [*excited*]   Oh, my God! I'm going to faint! I think I'm going to
60   faint!

[*The sound of two carriages outside the house.* LOPÁKHIN *and* DUNYÁSHA *hurry out. The stage is empty. The sound outside gets louder.* FIRS, *leaning heavily on his cane, crosses the room, heading for the door; he wears an old-fashioned butler's livery and a top hat; he says something to himself, but you can't make out the words. The offstage noise and bustle increases. A voice: "Here we are . . . this way." Enter* LIUBÓV ANDRÉYEVNA, ÁNYA, *and* CARLOTTA, *dressed in traveling clothes.* VÁRYA *wears an overcoat, and a kerchief on her head.* GÁYEV, SEMYÓNOV-PÍSHCHIK, LOPÁKHIN, DUNYÁSHA *with a bundle and an umbrella, Servants with the luggage— all pass across the stage.*]

ÁNYA   Here we are. Oh, Mama, do you remember this room?

LIUBÓV ANDRÉYEVNA   The nursery!

VÁRYA   It's freezing; my hands are like ice. We kept your room exactly as you left it, Mama. The white and lavender one.

65 LIUBÓV ANDRÉYEVNA   The nursery! Oh, this house, this beautiful house! I slept in this room when I was a child. . . . [*She weeps.*] And I feel like a child again! [*She hugs* GÁYEV, VÁRYA, *then* GÁYEV *again.*] And Várya hasn't changed at all—still looks like a nun! And Dunyásha dear! Of course I remember you! [*She hugs* DUNYÁSHA.]

70 GÁYEV   The train was two hours late. What kind of efficiency is that? Eh?

CARLOTTA   And my dog loves nuts.

---

2. Pause.

SEMYÓNOV-PÍSHCHIK   Really! I don't believe it!

[*Everyone leaves, except* ÁNYA *and* DUNYÁSHA.]

DUNYÁSHA   We've been up all night, waiting. . . . [*She takes* ÁNYA'*s coat and hat.*]

ÁNYA   I've been up for four nights now. . . . I didn't sleep the whole trip. And
75   now I'm freezing.

DUNYÁSHA   When you went away it was still winter, it was snowing, and now look! Oh, sweetie, you're back! [*She laughs and hugs Ánya.*] I've been up all night, waiting to see you. Sweetheart, I just can't wait—I've got to tell you what happened. I can't wait another minute!

80   ÁNYA [*wearily*]   Now what?

DUNYÁSHA   Yepikhódov proposed the day after Easter! He wants to marry me!

ÁNYA   That's all you ever think about. . . . [*She fixes her hair.*] I lost all my hairpins. . . .

DUNYÁSHA   I just don't know what to do about him. He really, really loves me!

85   ÁNYA [*looking through the door to her room*]   My own room, just as if I'd never left. I'm back home! Tomorrow I'll get up and go for a walk in the orchard. I just wish I could get some sleep. I didn't sleep the whole trip, I was so worried.

DUNYÁSHA   Pétya's here. He got here day before yesterday.

90   ÁNYA [*joyfully*]   Pétya!

DUNYÁSHA   He's staying out in the barn. Said he didn't want to bother anybody. [*She looks at her watch.*] He told me to get him up, but Várya said not to. You let him sleep, she said.

[*Enter* VÁRYA. *She has a big bunch of keys attached to her belt.*]

VÁRYA   Dunyásha, go get the coffee. Mama wants her coffee.

95   DUNYÁSHA   Oh, I forgot!

[*She goes out.*]

VÁRYA   You're back. Thank God! You're home again! [*She embraces Ánya.*] My angel is home again! My beautiful darling!

ÁNYA   You won't believe what I've been through!

VÁRYA   I can imagine.

100   ÁNYA   I left just before Easter; it was cold. Carlotta never shut up the whole trip; she kept doing those silly tricks of hers. I don't know why you had to stick me with her.

VÁRYA   Darling, you couldn't go all that way by yourself! You're only seventeen!

105   ÁNYA   We got to Paris, it was cold and snowy, and my French is just awful! Mama was living in this fifth-floor apartment, we had to walk up, we get there and there's all these French people, some old priest reading some book, and it was crowded, and everybody was smoking these awful cigarettes—and I felt so sorry for Mama, I just threw my arms around her
110   and couldn't let go. And she was so glad to see me, she cried—

VÁRYA [*almost crying*]   I know, I know . . .

ÁNYA   And she sold the villa in Mentón,[3] and the money was already gone, all of it! And I spent everything you gave me for the trip; I haven't got a thing left. And Mama still doesn't understand! We have dinner at the

3. A resort town on the French Mediterranean coast.

115   train station, and she orders the most expensive things on the menu, and then she tips the waiters a ruble[4] each! And Carlotta does the same! And Yásha expects the same treatment—he's just awful. You know, Yásha, that flunky of Mama's—he came back with us.

VÁRYA   I saw him, the lazy good-for-nothing.

120 ÁNYA   So what happened? Did you get the interest paid?

VÁRYA   With what?

ÁNYA   Oh, my God, my God . . .

VÁRYA   The place goes up for sale in August.

ÁNYA   Oh, my God.

      [LOPÁKHIN *sticks his head in the doorway and makes a mooing sound, then goes away.*]

125 VÁRYA   Oh, that man! I'd like to—[*She shakes her fist.*]

ÁNYA [*she hugs her*]   Várya, did he propose yet? [VÁRYA *shakes her head no.*] But you know he loves you! Why don't the two of you just sit down and be honest with each other? What are you waiting for?

VÁRYA   I don't think anything will ever come of it. He's always so busy, he
130   never has time for me. He just isn't interested! It's hard for me when I see him, but I don't care any more. Everybody talks about us getting married, people even congratulate me, but there's nothing. . . . I mean, it's all just a dream. [*A change of tone*] Oh, you've got a new pin, a little bee. . . .

ÁNYA [*with a sigh*]   I know. Mama bought it for me. [*She goes into her room*
135   *and starts to giggle, like a little girl.*] You know what? In Paris I went for a ride in a balloon!

VÁRYA   Oh, darling, you're back! My angel is home again!

      [DUNYÁSHA *comes in, carrying a tray with coffee things, and begins setting them out on the table.* VÁRYA *stands at the doorway and talks to* ÁNYA *in the other room.*]

You know, dear, I spend the livelong day trying to keep this house going, and all I do is dream. I want to see you married off to somebody rich, then
140   I can rest easy. And I think then I'll go away by myself, maybe live in a convent, or just go traveling: Kiev, Moscow . . . spend all my time making visits to churches. I'd start walking and just go and go and go. That would be heaven!

ÁNYA   Listen to the birds in the orchard! What time is it?

145 VÁRYA   It must be almost three. You should get some sleep, darling. [*She goes into* ÁNYA'S *room.*] Yes, that would be heaven!

      [*Enter* YÁSHA *with a suitcase and a lap robe. He walks with an affected manner.*]

YÁSHA   I beg pardon! May I intrude?

DUNYÁSHA   I didn't even recognize you, Yásha. You got so different there in France.

150 YÁSHA   *I'm* sorry—who are you exactly?

DUNYÁSHA   When you left, I wasn't any higher than this. [*She holds her hand a distance from the floor.*] I'm Dunyásha. You know, Dunyásha Kozoyédov. Don't you remember me?

---

4. Roughly equivalent to $20 today.

YÁSHA   Well! You sure turned out cute, didn't you? [*He looks around carefully, then grabs and kisses her; she screams and drops a saucer;* YÁSHA *leaves in a hurry.*]

155   VÁRYA [*at the door, annoyed*]   Now what happened?

DUNYÁSHA [*almost in tears*]   I broke a saucer.

VÁRYA [*ironically*]   Well, isn't that lucky!

ÁNYA [*entering*]   Somebody should let Mama know Pétya's here.

VÁRYA   I told them to let him sleep.

160   ÁNYA [*lost in thought*]   Father died six years ago, and a month later our little brother, Grísha, drowned. Sweet boy, he was only seven. And Mama couldn't face it, that's why she went away, just went away and never looked back. [*Shivers.*] And I understand exactly how she felt. I wish she knew that.

[*Pause.*]

And Pétya Trofímov was Grísha's tutor. He might remind her . . .

[*Enter* FIRS *in his old-fashioned butler's livery. He crosses to the table and begins looking over the coffee things.*]

165   FIRS   The missus will have her breakfast here. [*He puts on a pair of white gloves.*] Is the coffee ready? [*To* DUNYÁSHA, *crossly*] Where's the cream? Go get the cream!

DUNYÁSHA   Oh, my God, I'm sorry. . . .

[*Hurries off.*]

FIRS [*he starts fussing with the coffee things*]   Young flibbertigibbet . . . [*He mumbles to himself.*] They're all back from Paris. . . . In the old days they went to Paris too . . . had to go the whole way in a horse and buggy. [*He laughs.*]

VÁRYA   Firs, what are you talking about?

FIRS   Beg pardon? [*Joyfully*] The missus is home! Going to see her at last! Now I can die happy. . . . [*He starts to cry with joy.*]

[*Enter* LIUBÓV, GÁYEV, LOPÁKHIN, *and* SEMYÓNOV-PÍSHCHIK, *who wears a crumpled linen suit. As* GÁYEV *enters, he gestures as if he were making a billiard shot.*]

175   LIUBÓV ANDRÉYEVNA   How did it go? I'm trying to remember. . . . Yellow ball in the side pocket! Bank shot off the corner!

GÁYEV   And right down the middle! Oh, sister, sister, just think . . . when you and I were little we used to sleep in this room, and now I'm almost fifty-one! Strange, isn't it?

180   LOPÁKHIN   Time sure passes. . . .

GÁYEV [*beat*]   Say again?

LOPÁKHIN   I said, time sure passes.

GÁYEV [*looking at* LOPÁKHIN]   Who's wearing that cheap cologne?

ÁNYA   I'm going to bed. Good night, Mama. [*She kisses her mother.*]

185   LIUBÓV ANDRÉYEVNA   Oh, my darling little girl, my baby! Are you glad you're home? I still can't quite believe I'm here.

ÁNYA   Good night, Uncle.

GÁYEV [*he kisses her*]   God bless you, dear. You're getting to look so much like your mother! Liúba, she looks just like you when you were her age. She

190   really does.

[ÁNYA *says good night to* LOPÁKHIN *and* PÍSHCHIK, *goes into her room, and closes the door behind her.*]

LIUBÓV ANDRÉYEVNA   She's tired to death.

PÍSHCHIK   Well, that's such a long trip!

VÁRYA   Gentlemen, please. It's almost three; time you were going.

LIUBÓV ANDRÉYEVNA [*laughs*]   You're the same as ever, Várya. [*Hugs and kisses*
195   *her.*] Just let me have my coffee, then we'll all be going.

[FIRS *puts a pillow beneath her feet.*]

Thank you, dear. I've really gotten addicted to coffee; I drink it day and
night. You old darling, you! Thank you.

VÁRYA   I'll just go make sure they've got everything unloaded.

[*Goes out.*]

LIUBÓV ANDRÉYEVNA   I can't believe I'm really here! [*Laughs.*] I feel like
200   jumping up and waving my arms in the air! [*Covers her face with her
hands.*] It's still like a dream. I love this country, really I do, I adore it. I
started to cry every time I looked out the train windows. [*Almost in tears*]
But I do need my coffee! Thank you, Firs, thank you, darling. I'm so glad
you're still alive.

205   FIRS   Day before yesterday.

GÁYEV   He doesn't hear too well any more.

LOPÁKHIN   Time for me to go. I have to leave for Hárkov[5] at five. I'm really
disappointed; I was looking forward to seeing you, have a chance to
talk. . . . You look wonderful, just the way you always did.

210   PÍSHCHIK [*breathes hard*]   Better than she always did. That Paris outfit. . . .
She makes me feel young again!

LOPÁKHIN   Your brother here thinks I'm crude, calls me a money grubber.
That doesn't bother me; he can call me whatever he wants. I just hope
you'll trust me the way you used to, look at me the way you used to. . . . My
215   God, my father slaved for your father and grandfather, my whole family
worked for yours; but you, you treated me different. You did so much for
me I forgot about all that. Fact is, I . . . I love you like you were family . . .
more, even.

LIUBÓV ANDRÉYEVNA   I can't sit still; I'm just not in the mood! [*Gets up excit-
220   edly, moves about the room.*] I'm so happy I could die! I know I sound stupid—
go ahead, laugh. . . . Dear old bookcase. . . . [*Kisses the bookcase.*] My little
desk . . .

GÁYEV   Did I tell you Nanny died while you were away?

LIUBÓV ANDRÉYEVNA [*sits back down and drinks her coffee*]   Yes, you wrote
225   me. God rest her.

GÁYEV   Stásy died too. And Petrúsha Kosói quit and moved into town; he
works at the police station. [*Takes out a little box of hard candies and puts
one in his mouth.*]

PÍSHCHIK   Dáshenka—you remember Dáshenka? My daughter? Anyway, she
sends her regards. . . .

230   LOPÁKHIN   Well, I'd like to give you some very good news. [*Looks at his
watch.*] Afraid there's no time to talk now, though; I've got to go. Well, just
to make it short, you know you haven't kept up the mortgage payments
on your place here. So now they foreclosed and your estate is up for sale.
At auction. They set a date already, August twenty-second, but don't you
235   worry, you can rest easy. We can take care of this—I've got a great idea.

5. That is, Kharkov, the second-largest city in Ukraine (then part of the Russian Empire).

Now listen, here's how it works: your place here is fifteen miles from town, and it's only a short drive from the train station. All you've got to do is clear out the old cherry orchard, plus that land down by the river, and subdivide! You lease the plots, build vacation homes, and I swear that'll bring you in
twenty-five thousand[6] a year, maybe more.

GÁYEV   What an outrageous thing to say!

LIUBÓV ANDRÉYEVNA   Excuse me . . . Excuse me, I don't think I quite understand. . . .

LOPÁKHIN   You'll get at least twenty-five hundred an acre! And if you start
advertising right away, I swear to God come this fall you won't have a single plot left. You see what I'm saying? Your troubles are over! Congratulations! The location is terrific; the river's a real selling point. Only thing is, you've got to start clearing right away. Get rid of all the old buildings. This house, for instance, will have to go. You can't get people to live in a barn like this
any more. And you'll have to cut down that old cherry orchard.

LIUBÓV ANDRÉYEVNA   Cut down the cherry orchard? My dear man, you don't understand! Our cherry orchard is a landmark! It's famous for miles around!

LOPÁKHIN   The only thing famous about it is how big it is. You only get cher-
ries every two years, and even then you can't get rid of them. Nobody buys them. It's just not a commercial crop.

GÁYEV   Our cherry orchard is mentioned in the encyclopedia![7]

LOPÁKHIN [looks at his watch]   We have to think of something to do and then do it. Otherwise the cherry orchard will be sold at auction on August
twenty-second, this house and all the land with it. Make up your minds! Believe me, I've thought this through; there isn't any other way to do it. There just isn't.

FIRS   Back in the old days, forty, fifty years ago, they used to make dried cherries, pickled cherries, preserved cherries, cherry jam, and sometimes—

GÁYEV   Oh, Firs, just shut up.

FIRS   —sometimes they sent them off to Moscow by the wagonload. People paid a lot for them! Back then the dried cherries were soft and juicy and sweet, and they smelled just lovely; back then they knew how to fix them. . . .

LIUBÓV ANDRÉYEVNA   Does anybody know how to fix them nowadays?

FIRS   Nope. They all forgot.

PÍSHCHIK   Tell us about Paris. What was it like? Did you eat frogs?

LIUBÓV ANDRÉYEVNA   I ate crocodiles.

PÍSHCHIK   Crocodiles? Really! I don't believe it!

LOPÁKHIN   You see, it used to be out here in the country there were only land-
lords and poor farmers, but now all of a sudden there are summer people moving in; they want vacation homes. Every town you can name is sur-rounded by them—it's the coming thing. In twenty years they'll expand and multiply! Right now maybe they're only places to relax on the weekend, but
I bet you eventually people will put down roots out here, they'll create neighborhoods, and then your cherry orchard will blossom and bear fruit once again—and even bring in a profit!

6. Roughly equivalent to $500,000 today (all references to money are in rubles).
7. Probably a reference to the *Great Russian*

Encyclopedic Dictionary (1890–1906), an authoritative 86-volume reference work pub-lished by F. A. Brockhaus and I. A. Efron.

GÁYEV [*indignantly*]   That's outrageous!
    [*Enter* VÁRYA *and* YÁSHA.]

285 VÁRYA   Mama, a couple of telegrams came for you. [*Takes a key and opens the old bookcase; the lock creaks.*] Here they are.

LIUBÓV ANDRÉYEVNA   They're from Paris. [*She tears them up without opening then.*] I'm through with Paris.

GÁYEV   Liúba, have you any idea how old this bookcase is? Last week I pulled out the bottom drawer, and there was the date on the back, burned right 290 into the wood. A hundred years! This bookcase is exactly a hundred years old! What do you say to that, eh? We should have a birthday celebration. Of course, it's an inanimate object, any way you look at it, but still, it's a . . . well, it's a . . . a bookcase.

PÍSHCHIK   A hundred years old! Really! I don't believe it!

295 GÁYEV   Yes, yes, it is. [*He caresses the bookcase.*] Dear old bookcase! Wonderful old bookcase! I rejoice in your existence. For a hundred years now you have borne the shining ideals of goodness and justice, a hundred years have not dimmed your silent summons to useful labor. To generations of our family [*Almost in tears*] you have offered courage, a belief in a better future, 300 you have instructed us in ideals of goodness and social awareness. . . .
    [*Pause.*]

LOPÁKHIN   Right. Well . . .

LIUBÓV ANDRÉYEVNA   Oh, Lonya, you're still the same as ever!

GÁYEV [*somewhat embarrassed*]   Yellow ball in the side pocket! Bank shot off the center!

305 LOPÁKHIN   Well, I've got to be off.

YÁSHA [*gives* LIUBÓV *a pillbox*]   Isn't it perhaps time for your pills?

PÍSHCHIK   No, no, no, dear lady! Never take medicine! Won't do any good! Won't do any harm either, though. Watch! [*Takes the pillbox, dumps the contents into his hand, puts them in his mouth, and swallows them with a swig of beer.*] There! All gone!

310 LIUBÓV ANDRÉYEVNA [*alarmed*]   Are you out of your mind?

PÍSHCHIK   I have just taken all your pills for you.

LOPÁKHIN   What a glutton.
    [*Everybody laughs.*]

FIRS   He was here over the holidays, ate half a crock of pickles. . . . [*Mumbles.*]

LIUBÓV ANDRÉYEVNA   What's he mumbling about?

315 VÁRYA   He's been going on like that for the last three years. We're used to it by now.

YÁSHA   He's getting senile.
    [*Enter* CARLOTTA, *in a white dress with a lorgnette on a chain. She starts to cross the room.*]

LOPÁKHIN   Oh, excuse me, Carlotta, I didn't get a chance to say hello yet. [*Tries to kiss her hand.*]

CARLOTTA [*takes her hand away*]   I let you kiss my hand, first thing I know, 320 you'll want to kiss my elbow, then my shoulder . . .

LOPÁKHIN   This isn't my lucky day.
    [*Everybody laughs.*]
Carlotta, show us a trick!

LIUBÓV ANDRÉYEVNA   Yes, do, Carlotta—show us a trick!

CARLOTTA Not now. I'm off to bed.

> [*Leaves.*]

325 LOPÁKHIN Well, I'll see you in three weeks. [*Kisses* LIUBÓV's *hand.*] Goodbye now. I've got to be off. [*To* GÁYEV] Goodbye. [*Hugs* PÍSHCHIK.] So long. [*Shakes hands with* VÁRYA, *then with* FIRS *and* YÁSHA.] I sort of hate to leave. [*To* LIUBÓV] Think over what I said about subdividing the place. You decide to do it, let me know, and I'll take care of everything. I'll get you a loan of
330 fifty thousand. Think it over now, seriously.

VÁRYA [*angry*] Will you please just go?

LOPÁKHIN I'm going, I'm going.

> [*Leaves.*]

GÁYEV What a bore. Oh, excuse me, *pardon,*[8] I forgot—that's Várya's boyfriend. He's going to marry our Várya.

335 VÁRYA Uncle, will you please not talk nonsense?

LIUBÓV ANDRÉYEVNA Oh, but Várya, that's wonderful! He's a fine man!

PÍSHCHIK One of the finest, in fact . . . the very, very finest . . . My Dáshenka always says . . . she says . . . she says a lot of things. [*Snores, but immediately wakes up.*] Dear lady, yes, always respected you, hmm. . . . You think
340 you could lend me, say, two hundred and forty rubles? Mortgage payment, you know, due tomorrow . . .

VÁRYA [*terrified*] We can't; we don't have any!

LIUBÓV ANDRÉYEVNA I'm afraid that's the truth. We haven't any money.

PÍSHCHIK I'll get it somewhere. [*Laughs.*] I never give up hope. There was
345 that time I thought I was finished, it was all over, and all of a sudden—boom! The railroad cut across some of my land and paid me for it. You'll see, something will turn up tomorrow or the next day. Dáshenka will win two hundred thousand in the lottery; she just bought a ticket.

LIUBÓV ANDRÉYEVNA Well, the coffee's gone. We might as well go to bed.

350 FIRS [*takes out a clothes brush and brushes* GÁYEV's *clothes; scolds him*] You've got on the wrong trousers again. What am I supposed to do with you?

VÁRYA [*softly*] Ánya's asleep. [*Quietly opens the window.*] The sun's coming up; it's not as cold as it was. Look, Mama, what wonderful trees! Smell the perfume! Oh, Lord! And the orioles are singing!

355 GÁYEV [*opens another window*] The whole orchard is white. You remember, Liúba? That long path, stretched out like a ribbon, on and on, the way it used to shine in the moonlight? You remember? You haven't forgotten?

LIUBÓV ANDRÉYEVNA Oh, my childhood! My innocence! I slept in this room, I could look out over the orchard, when I woke up in the morning I was
360 happy, and it all looked exactly the same as this! Nothing has changed! [*Laughs delightedly.*] White, white, all white! My whole orchard is white! Autumn was dark and drizzly, and winter was cold, but now you're young again, flowering with happiness—the angels of heaven have never abandoned you. If only I could shake off this weight I've been carrying so long.
365 If only I could forget my past!

GÁYEV Yes, and now they're selling the orchard to pay our debts. Strange, isn't it?

---

8. Gáyev's interjection of the French word *pardon* (excuse me) is typical of the upper classes, who in pre-Soviet Russia spoke French as a second language.

LIUBÓV ANDRÉYEVNA Look! There . . . in the orchard . . . it's Mother! In her white dress! [*Laughs delightedly.*] It's Mother!

370 GÁYEV Where?

VÁRYA Oh, Mama, for God's sake . . .

LIUBÓV ANDRÉYEVNA It's all right; I was just imagining things. There to the right, by the path to the summerhouse, that little white tree all bent over . . . it looked just like a woman.

[*Enter* TROFÍMOV. *He is dressed like a student and wears wire-rimmed glasses.*]

375 What a glorious orchard! All those white blossoms, and the blue sky—

TROFÍMOV Liubóv Andréyevna!

[*She turns to look at him.*]

I don't mean to disturb you; I just wanted to say hello. [*Shakes her hand warmly.*] They told me to wait until later, but I couldn't. . . .

[LIUBÓV *stares at him, bewildered.*]

VÁRYA It's Pétya Trofímov. . . .

380 TROFÍMOV Pétya Trofímov—I was your little boy Grísha's tutor. . . . Have I really changed all that much?

[LIUBÓV *embraces him and begins to weep softly.*]

GÁYEV [*embarrassed*] Liúba, that'll do, that'll do. . . .

VÁRYA [*weeps*] Oh, Pétya, I told you to wait till tomorrow.

LIUBÓV ANDRÉYEVNA Grísha . . . my little boy. Grísha . . . my son . . .

385 VÁRYA Oh, Mama, don't; it was God's will.

TROFÍMOV [*gently, almost in tears*] There, there . . .

LIUBÓV ANDRÉYEVNA [*weeps softly*] My little boy drowned, lost forever . . . Why? What for? My dear boy, why? [*Quiets down.*] Ánya's asleep, and here I am carrying on like this. . . . Pétya, what's happened to you? You used to be such a nice-looking boy. What happened? You look dreadful. You've
390 gotten so old!

TROFÍMOV Some lady on the train called me a high-class tramp.

LIUBÓV ANDRÉYEVNA You were only a boy then, just out of high school, you were adorable, and now you've got glasses and you're losing your hair. And
395 haven't you graduated yet? [*Goes to the door.*]

TROFÍMOV I suppose I'm what you'd call a permanent graduate student.

LIUBÓV ANDRÉYEVNA [*kisses* GÁYEV, *then* VÁRYA] Time for bed. You've gotten old too, Leoníd.

PÍSHCHIK [*follows* LIUBÓV] Time for bed, time to go . . . Ooh, my gout! I'd
400 better stay the night. Now, dear, look, look . . . Liubóv Andréyevna, tomorrow morning I need . . . two hundred and forty rubles. . . .

GÁYEV He never gives up, does he?

PÍSHCHIK Two hundred and forty rubles; my mortgage payment due. . . .

LIUBÓV ANDRÉYEVNA Darling, I simply have no money.

405 PÍSHCHIK But, dear, I'll give it right back. . . . It's such a *trivial* amount. . . .

LIUBÓV ANDRÉYEVNA Oh, all right. Leoníd will get it for you. Leoníd, you give him the money.

GÁYEV I should give him money? That'll be the day.

LIUBÓV ANDRÉYEVNA We have to give it to him; he needs it. He'll give it back.

[*Exit* LIUBÓV, TROFÍMOV, PÍSHCHIK, *and* FIRS. GÁYEV, VÁRYA, *and* YÁSHA *remain.*]

410   GÁYEV   She still thinks money grows on trees. [*To* YÁSHA] My good man, will you leave us, please? Go back to the barn, where you belong.

YÁSHA [*smiles*]   Leoníd Andréyich, you're the same as you always were.

GÁYEV   What say? [*To* VÁRYA] What did he just say?

VÁRYA [*to* YÁSHA]   Your mother came in from the country to see you. She's
415   been sitting in the kitchen for two days now, waiting.

YÁSHA   Oh, for God's sake, can't she leave me alone?

VÁRYA   You are really disgraceful!

YÁSHA   That's all I need right now. Why couldn't she wait till tomorrow?
      [*Goes out.*]

VÁRYA   Mama hasn't changed; she's the same as she always was. If it were up
420   to her, she'd give away everything.

GÁYEV   Yes. . . . [*Pause*] Someone gets sick, you know, and the doctor tries one thing after another, that means there's no cure. I've been thinking and thinking, racking my brains, I come up with one thing, then another, but the truth is, none of them will work. It would be wonderful if somebody left
425   us a lot of money, it would be wonderful if we could marry off Ánya to somebody with a lot of money, it would be wonderful if we could go see Ánya's godmother in Yároslavl,[9] try to borrow the money from her. She's very, very rich.

VÁRYA [*weeps*]   If only God would help us!

430   GÁYEV   Oh, stop crying. She's very, very rich, but she doesn't like us. Because in the first place, my sister married a mere lawyer instead of a man with a title. . . .
      [ÁNYA *appears in the doorway.*]

She married a lawyer, and then her behavior has not been—how shall I put it?—particularly exemplary. She's a lovely woman, goodhearted, charming,
435   and of course she's my sister and I love her very much, and there are extenuating circumstances and such, but the fact is, she's what you'd have to call a . . . a loose woman. And she doesn't care who knows it; you can feel it in every move she makes.

VÁRYA [*whispers*]   Ánya's here.

440   GÁYEV   What say? [*Pause*] Funny, I must have gotten something in my eye: I can't see too well. . . . Did I tell you what happened Thursday, when I was at the county courthouse?
      [ÁNYA *comes into the room.*]

VÁRYA   Why aren't you asleep?

ÁNYA   I tried. I couldn't sleep.

445   GÁYEV   Kitten . . . [*Kisses* ÁNYA'*s cheek, then her hands.*] My dear child . . . [*Almost in tears*] You're more than just my niece, you're my angel, you know that? You're my whole world, believe me, believe me. . . .

ÁNYA   I believe you, Uncle. And I love you; we all love you. . . . But, Uncle dear, you should learn not to talk so much. The things you were saying
450   just now about Mama, about your own sister . . . What were you saying all that for?

GÁYEV   I know, I know. . . . [*Covers his face with her hand.*] It's awful, I know. My God, a few minutes ago I made a speech to a piece of furniture. . . . It

---

9. A city on the Volga River, about 160 miles northeast of Moscow.

was so stupid! The thing is, I never realize how stupid I sound until I'm
455 done.

VÁRYA She's right, Uncle. You just have to learn to keep still, that's all.

ÁNYA If you do, you'll feel much better about yourself, you know you will. . . .

GÁYEV I will, I will, I promise. [*Kisses* ÁNYA's *and* VÁRYA's *hands.*] I'll keep still.
Only right now I have to talk a little more. Business! On Thursday I was
460 at the county courthouse; there was a group of us talking—just this and
that—and it turns out I might be able to arrange a promissory note for
enough money to pay off the mortgage.

VÁRYA If only God would help us!

GÁYEV I'm going in on Tuesday, I'll talk to them again. [*To* VÁRYA] Don't
465 whine! [*To* ÁNYA] Your mother will talk to Lopákhin; he can't refuse to help
her. And you, as soon as you're rested, you go to Yároslavl, go talk to your
godmother. There. We'll be operating on three fronts at once; we're sure to
succeed. We *will* pay off this mortgage, I know we will. . . . [*He pops a hard
candy into his mouth.*] I swear by my honor, I swear by anything you want,
470 the estate will not be sold! [*Excitedly*] I swear by my own happiness! Here,
you have my hand on it. You may call me . . . dishonorable, call me anything you will, if I ever let this estate go on the auction block! I swear by my
entire existence!

ÁNYA [*her calm mood has returned; she is happy*] You're so smart, Uncle!
475 You're such a wonderful man! [*Hugs* GÁYEV.] Now I feel better! So much
better! I'm happy again!

[*Enter* FIRS.]

FIRS [*reproachfully*] Leoníd Andréyich, why aren't you in bed, like decent
God-fearing people?

GÁYEV I'm coming, I'm coming. You go to bed, Firs. I can get undressed by
480 myself. All right, children, nighty-night. We can talk about the details
tomorrow, now it's time for bed. [*Kisses* ÁNYA *and* VÁRYA.] I am a man of the
eighties, you know. People don't think much of that era now, but I can tell
you frankly that I have had the courage of my convictions and often had to
pay the price.[1] But these local peasants all love me. You have to get to know
485 them, that's all. You have to get to know them, and—

ÁNYA Uncle. You're at it again.

VÁRYA Just be quiet, Uncle.

FIRS [*angrily*] Leoníd Andréyich!

GÁYEV I'm coming, I'm coming. . . . Go to bed now. Yellow ball in the side
490 pocket! Clean shot!

[*Goes out;* FIRS *follows him, limping.*]

ÁNYA I feel much better. I don't much want to go to Yároslavl, I don't like my
godmother, but I feel better now. Thanks to Uncle [*Sits down.*]

VÁRYA We've got to get some sleep. I'm going to bed. Oh, there's something
came up since you left. You know we've got all those old retired servants liv-
495 ing out back—Paulina, old Karp, and the rest of them. And what happened,
they started inviting people in to spend the night. Well, it's annoying, but I
never said a thing. Then what happened was, they started telling everybody
all they were getting to eat was beans. Because I was so cheap, you see. It

---

1. When Alexander III (1845–1894) became czar in 1881, he initiated a series of repressive measures designed to combat liberal and revolutionary elements in Russian society.

was that old Karp was doing it. So I said to myself, All right, that's the way
you want it, all right, just wait, and I sent for him [*Yawns*], and in he comes,
so I say, Karp, you're such an idiot—[*Looks at* ÁNYA.] Ánya!

       [*Pause.*]

She's asleep. [*Lifts* ÁNYA *by the arms.*] Come on, time for bed. . . . Come on,
let's go. . . . [*Leads her off.*] My angel fell asleep! Come on. . . . [*They start
out.*]

       [*In the distance, beyond the orchard, a shepherd plays a pipe.* TROFÍMOV
       enters, sees ÁNYA *and* VÁRYA, *stops.*]

VÁRYA   Shh! She's asleep. . . . Come on, darling, let's go. . . .

ÁNYA [*softly, half asleep*]   I was so tired. . . . All those bells . . . Uncle dear . . .
and Mama. Uncle and Mama.

VÁRYA   Come on, darling, come on. . . .

       [*They go off into* ÁNYA's *room.*]

TROFÍMOV [*deeply moved*]   My sunshine! My springtime!

             Curtain.

Act 2

       [*An open space. The overgrown ruin of an abandoned chapel. There is a
well beside it and some large stones that must once have been grave
markers. An old bench. Beyond, the road to the Gáyev estate. On one side
a shadowy row of poplar trees; they mark the limits of the cherry orchard.
A row of telegraph poles, and on the far distant horizon, on a clear day,
you can just make out the city. It's late afternoon, almost sunset.* CAR-
LOTTA, YÁSHA, *and* DUNYÁSHA *are sitting on the bench;* YEPIKHÓDOV *stands
nearby, strumming his guitar; each seems lost in his own thoughts.* CAR-
LOTTA *wears an old military cap and is adjusting the strap on a hunting
rifle.*]

CARLOTTA [*meditatively*]   I haven't got a birth certificate, so I don't know how
old I really am. I just think of myself as young. When I was a little girl,
Mama and my father used to travel around to fairs and put on shows, good
ones. I did back flips, things like that. And after they died this German
woman brought me up, taught me a few things. And that was it. Then I
grew up and had to go to work. As a governess. Where I'm from . . . who
I am . . . no idea. Who my parents were—maybe they weren't even married—no idea. [*Takes a large cucumber pickle out of her pocket and takes a
bite.*] No idea at all.

       [*Pause.*]

And I feel like talking all the time, but there's no one to talk to. No one.

YEPIKHÓDOV [*plays the guitar and sings*]

       "What do I care for the rest of the world,
       or care what it cares for me . . ."[2]

Very agreeable, playing a mandolin.

DUNYÁSHA   That's not a mandolin, it's a guitar. [*Takes out a compact with a
mirror and powders herself.*]

YEPIKHÓDOV   When a man is madly in love, a guitar is a mandolin.

---

2. Words from a popular turn-of-the-century ballad.

[*Sings.*]

"As long as my heart is on fire with love,
and the one I love loves me."

[YÁSHA *sings harmony.*]

CARLOTTA   Oof! You people sound like hyenas.

DUNYÁSHA   But it must have been just lovely, being in Europe.

20   YÁSHA   Oh, it was. Quite, quite lovely. I have to agree with you there. [*Yawns, then lights a cigar.*]

YEPIKHÓDOV   That's understandable. In Europe, things have already come to a complex.

YÁSHA [*beat*]   I suppose you could say that.

YEPIKHÓDOV   I'm a true product of the educational system; I read all the
25   time. All the right books too, but I have no chosen directive in life. For me, strictly speaking, it's live or shoot myself. That's why I always carry a loaded pistol. See? [*Takes out a revolver.*]

CARLOTTA   All done. Time to go. [*Slings the rifle over her shoulder.*] You're a very smart man, Yepikhódov, and a very scary one. Ooh! The women must
30   adore you. [*Starts off.*] They're all so dumb, these smart boys. Never anyone to talk to . . . Always alone, all by myself, no one to talk to . . . and I still don't know who I am. Or why. No idea.

[*Walks slowly off.*]

YEPIKHÓDOV   I should explain, by the way, for the sake of expressivity, that fate has been, ah, *rigorous* to me. I am, strictly speaking, tempest-tossed.
35   Always have been. Now, you may say to me, Oh, you're imagining things, but then why, when I wake up this morning—here's an example—and I look down, why is there this spider on my stomach? Detrimentally large too. [*Makes a circle with his two hands.*] Big as that. Or take a beer, let's say. I go to drink it, what do I see floating around in it? Something highly
40   unappreciative, like a cockroach.

[*Pause.*]

Have you ever read Henry Thomas Buckle?[3]

[*Pause.*]

May I design to disturb you, Avdótya Fyódorovna, with something I have to say?

DUNYÁSHA   So say it.

45   YEPIKHÓDOV   Preferentially alone. [*Sighs.*]

DUNYÁSHA [*embarrassed*]   All right. . . . Only first get me my wrap; it's by the kitchen door. It's getting kind of damp.

YEPIKHÓDOV   Ah, I see. Yes, get the wrap, of course. Now I know what to do with my gun.

[*Takes his guitar and goes off, strumming.*]

50   YÁSHA   Double Trouble. He's an idiot, if you ask me. [*Yawns.*]

DUNYÁSHA   I hope to God he doesn't shoot himself.

[*Pause.*]

I get upset over every little thing any more. Ever since I started working for them here, I've gotten used to their *lifestyle.* Just look at my hands. Look at

3. English historian (1821–1862), author of *History of Civilization in England* (1857–61), an unfinished attempt to present history as an exact science.

how white they are, just like I was rich. I'm different now from like I was.
55 I'm more delicate, I'm more sensitive; everything upsets me. . . . It's just
awful how things upset me. So if you cheat on me, Yásha, I may just have a
nervous breakdown.

YÁSHA [kisses her] Oh, you little cutie! Just remember, though: a girl has to
watch her step. What I'm after is a *nice* girl.

60 DUNYÁSHA I really love you, Yásha, I really do. You're so smart, you know so
many things. . . .

[Pause.]

YÁSHA [yawns] Yeah. . . . But my theory is, a girl says she loves you, she's not
a nice girl.

[Pause.]

Nothing like smoking a cigar out here in the fresh air. . . . [Listens.] Some-
65 body's coming. . . . It's them. . . .

[DUNYÁSHA hugs him impulsively.]

YÁSHA Go on back to the house. Go back the other way, make believe
you've been swimming down by the river, so they don't think we've
been . . . we've been getting together out here like this. I don't want them
to think that.

70 DUNYÁSHA [a little cough] That cigar smoke is giving me a headache. . . .

[Goes out.]

[YÁSHA sits beside the chapel wall. Enter LIUBÓV, GÁYEV, and LOPÁKHIN.]

LOPÁKHIN You have to make up your mind one way or the other; time's running out. There's no argument left. You want to subdivide or don't you? Just
give me an answer, one word, yes or no.

LIUBÓV ANDRÉYEVNA Who's been smoking those cheap cigars? [Sits down.]

75 GÁYEV Everything's so convenient, now that there's the railroad. We went
into town just to have lunch. Yellow ball in the side pocket! What do
you say—why don't we go back to the house, eh? Have ourselves a little
game . . .

LIUBÓV ANDRÉYEVNA Let's wait till later.

80 LOPÁKHIN Just one word! [Imploringly] Why don't you give me an answer?

GÁYEV [yawns] To what?

LIUBÓV ANDRÉYEVNA [rummages in her purse] Yesterday I had a lot of money,
today it's all gone. My poor Várya feeds us all on soup to economize, the
poor old people get nothing but beans, and I just spend and spend. . . .

85 [Drops her purse; gold coins spill out.] Oh, I've spilled everything. . . .

YÁSHA Here, allow me. [Picks up the money.]

LIUBÓV ANDRÉYEVNA Oh, please do, Yásha; thank you. And why I had to go
into that town for lunch—that stupid restaurant of yours, those stupid
musicians, those stupid tablecloths; they smelled of soap. . . . Why do we
90 drink so much, Lyónya? And eat so much? Why do we talk so much? The
whole time we were in the restaurant, you kept talking, and none of it
made any sense. Talking about the seventies, about Symbolism.[4] And to
who? The waiters! Talking about Symbolism to waiters!

---

4. A movement in literature and art that
began in France in the last third of the 19th
century; it emphasized the evocation of subjective emotion, via symbol and metaphor,
rather than objective description, and it had
its greatest influence in Russia in the 1880s.
The seventies: a time of widespread populist
agitation among Russia's peasant population.

LOPÁKHIN Yes.

95 GÁYEV [*makes a deprecating gesture*] I'm incorrigible, I suppose. . . . [*To* YÁSHA, *irritably*] What are *you* doing here? Why are you always underfoot every time I turn around?

YÁSHA [*laughs*] Because every time I hear your voice it makes me laugh.

GÁYEV Either he goes or I do!

100 LIUBÓV ANDRÉYEVNA Yásha, please . . . just go 'way, will you?

YÁSHA [*gives* LIUBÓV *her purse*] I'm going. Right now. [*Barely containing his laughter*] Right this very minute . . .

[*Goes out.*]

LOPÁKHIN You know who Derigánov is? You know how much money he has? You know he's planning to buy your property? They say he's coming to the
105 auction himself.

LIUBÓV ANDRÉYEVNA Who told you that?

LOPÁKHIN Everybody in town knows about it.

GÁYEV The old lady in Yároslavl promised to send money. . . . But when, and how much, she didn't say.

110 LOPÁKHIN How much will she send? A hundred thousand? Two hundred?

LIUBÓV ANDRÉYEVNA Ten or fifteen thousand. And we're lucky to get that much.

LOPÁKHIN Excuse me, but you people . . . I have never met anyone so unbusinesslike, so impractical, so . . . so *crazy* as the pair of you! Somebody tells
115 you flat out your land is about to be sold, you don't even seem to understand!

LIUBÓV ANDRÉYEVNA But what should we do? Just tell us what we should do!

LOPÁKHIN I tell you every day what you should do! Every day I come out here and say the same thing. The cherry orchard and the rest of the land
120 has to be subdivided and developed for leisure homes, and it has to be done right away. The auction date is getting closer! Can't you understand? All you have to do is make up your mind to subdivide, you'll have more money than even you can spend! Your troubles will be over!

LIUBÓV ANDRÉYEVNA Subdivide, leisure homes . . . excuse me, but it's all so
125 hopelessly vulgar.

GÁYEV I couldn't agree more.

LOPÁKHIN You people drive me crazy! Another minute, I'll be shouting my head off! Oh, I give up, I give up! Why do I even bother? [*To* GÁYEV] You're worse than an old lady!

130 GÁYEV What say?

LOPÁKHIN I said you're an old lady! [*Starts to leave.*]

LIUBÓV ANDRÉYEVNA [*fearfully*] No, no, no, please, my dear, don't go. Please. I'm sure we'll think of something.

LOPÁKHIN What's there to think of?

135 LIUBÓV ANDRÉYEVNA Please. Don't go. Things are easier when you're around. . . .

[*Pause.*]

I keep waiting for something to happen. It's as if the house were about to fall down around our ears or something. . . .

GÁYEV [*meditatively*] Yellow ball in the side pocket . . . Clean shot down the
140 middle . . .

LIUBÓV ANDRÉYEVNA We're guilty of so many sins, I know—

LOPÁKHIN Sins? What are you talking about?

GÁYEV [*pops a hard candy into his mouth*] People say I've eaten up my entire inheritance in candy. [*Laughs.*]

145 LIUBÓV ANDRÉYEVNA All my sins . . . I've always wasted money, just thrown it away like a madwoman, and I married a man who never paid a bill in his life. He was an alcoholic; he drank himself to death—on champagne. And I was so unhappy I fell in love with another man, *unfortunately,* and had an affair with him, and that was when—that was the first thing, my first punishment,

150 right down there, in the river, my little boy drowned, and I left, I went to France, I left and never wanted to come back, I never wanted to see that river again, I just closed my eyes and *ran,* forgot about everything, and that man followed me. He just wouldn't let up. And he was so mean to me, so cruel! I bought a villa in Mentón because he got sick while we were there,

155 and for the next three years I never had a moment's peace, day or night. He tormented me from his sickbed. I could feel my soul dry up. And last year I couldn't afford the villa any more, so I sold it and we moved to Paris, and once we were in Paris he took everything I had left and ran off with another woman, and I tried to kill myself. It was so stupid, and so shameful! Finally

160 all I wanted was to come back home, to where I was born, to my daughter. [*Wipes away her tears.*] Oh, dear God, dear God, forgive me! Forgive me my sins! Don't punish me again! [*Takes a telegram from her purse.*] This came today, from Paris. . . . He says he's sorry, he wants me back. . . . [*Tears up the telegram.*] Where's [*Listens.*] . . . where's that music coming from?

165 GÁYEV That's our famous local orchestra. Those Jewish musicians, you remember? Four fiddles, a clarinet, and a double bass.

LIUBÓV ANDRÉYEVNA Are they still around? We should have them over some evening and throw a party.

LOPÁKHIN [*listens*] I don't hear anything. [*Sings to himself.*]

170 "Ooh-la-la . . .
Just a little bit of money
makes a lady very French . . ."

[*Laughs.*] I went to the theater last night, saw this musical. Very funny.

LIUBÓV ANDRÉYEVNA I doubt there was anything funny about it. You ought to

175 stop going to see playacting and take a good look at your own reality. What a boring life you lead! And what uninteresting things you talk about.

LOPÁKHIN Well . . . yeah, there's some truth to that. It is a pretty dumb life we lead. . . .

[*Pause.*]

My father was a . . . he was a dirt farmer, an idiot, never understood me,

180 never taught me anything, just got drunk and beat me up. With a stick. Fact is, I'm not much better myself. Never did well in school, my writing's terrible, I'm ashamed if anybody sees it. I write like a pig.

LIUBÓV ANDRÉYEVNA My dear man, you should get married.

LOPÁKHIN Yes. . . . Yes, I should.

185 LIUBÓV ANDRÉYEVNA And you should marry our Várya. She's a wonderful girl.

LOPÁKHIN She is.

LIUBÓV ANDRÉYEVNA Her people were quite ordinary, but she works like a dog, and the main thing is, she loves you. And you like her, I know you do. You always have.

190 LOPÁKHIN   Look, I've got nothing against it. I . . . She's a wonderful girl.

　　　　[*Pause.*]

GÁYEV   They offered me a position at the bank. Six thousand a year. Did I tell you?

LIUBÓV ANDRÉYEVNA   Don't be silly! You stay right here where you belong.

　　　　[*Enter* FIRS, *carrying an overcoat.*]

FIRS   Sir, sir, please put this on. It's getting damp.

195 GÁYEV [*puts it on*]   Firs, you're getting to be a bore.

FIRS   That so? Went out this morning, didn't even tell me. [*Tries to adjust* GÁYEV's *clothes.*]

LIUBÓV ANDRÉYEVNA   Poor Firs! You've gotten so old!

FIRS   Beg pardon?

LOPÁKHIN   She said you got very old!

200 FIRS   I've lived a long time. They were trying to marry me off way back before your daddy was born. [*Laughs.*] By the time we got our freedom back,[5] I was already head butler. I had all the freedom I needed, so I stayed right here with the masters.

　　　　[*Pause.*]

I remember everybody got all excited about it, but they never even knew
205 what they were getting excited about.

LOPÁKHIN   Oh, sure, things were wonderful back in the good old days! They had the right to beat you if they wanted, remember?

FIRS [*doesn't hear*]   That's right. Masters stood by the servants, servants stood by the masters. Nowadays it's all mixed up; you can't tell who's who.

210 GÁYEV   Shut up, Firs. . . . I have to go into town tomorrow. A friend promised to introduce me to someone who might be able to arrange a loan. Some general.

LOPÁKHIN   That's never going to work. Trust me, you won't get enough even for the interest payments.

215 LIUBÓV ANDRÉYEVNA   He's imagining things. There's no general.

　　　　[*Enter* ÁNYA, VÁRYA, *and* TROFÍMOV.]

GÁYEV   Here come our young people.

ÁNYA   Mama's resting.

LIUBÓV ANDRÉYEVNA [*tenderly*]   Here we are, dears, over here. [*Kisses* ÁNYA *and Várya.*] If you only knew how much I love you both. Come sit here by
220 me . . . that's right.

　　　　[*They all sit down.*]

LOPÁKHIN   Our permanent graduate student seems to spend all his time studying the ladies.

TROFÍMOV   Mind your own business.

LOPÁKHIN   Almost in his fifties, he's still in school.

225 TROFÍMOV   Just stop the silly jokes, will you?

LOPÁKHIN   Oh, the *scholar* is losing his temper!

TROFÍMOV   Will you please just leave me alone?

LOPÁKHIN [*laughs*]   Let me ask you a question: You look at me, what do you see?

---

5. That is, 1861, when the serfs—feudal agricultural workers bound to their lord's land, who made up one-third of Russia's total population—were freed by Alexander II's Edict of Emancipation.

230 TROFÍMOV When I look at you, Yermolái Alexéyich, what I see is a rich man. One who will soon be a millionaire. You are as necessary a part of the evolution of the species as the wild animal that eats up anything in its path.

[*Everybody laughs.*]

VÁRYA Forget biology, Pétya. You should stick to counting stars.

LIUBÓV ANDRÉYEVNA I want to hear more about what we were talking about
235 last night.

TROFÍMOV What were we talking about?

GÁYEV About human dignity.

TROFÍMOV We talked about a lot last night, but we never got anywhere. You people talk about human dignity as if it were something mystical. I suppose
240 it is, in a way, for you anyway, but when you really get down to it, what have humans got to be proud of? Biologically we're pretty minor specimens— besides which, the great majority of human beings are vulgar and unhappy and totally *un*dignified. We should stop patting ourselves on the back and get to work.

245 GÁYEV You still have to die.

TROFÍMOV Who says? Anyway, what does that mean, to die? Maybe we have a hundred senses, and all we lose when we die are the five we're familiar with, and the other ninety-five go on living.

LIUBÓV ANDRÉYEVNA Oh, Pétya, you're so smart!

250 LOPÁKHIN [*with irony*] Oh, yes, very.

TROFÍMOV Remember, human beings are constantly progressing, and their power keeps growing. Things that seem impossible to us nowadays, the day will come when they're not a problem at all, only we have to work toward that day. We have to seek out the truth. We don't do that, you
255 know. Most of the people in this country aren't working toward anything. People I come in contact with—at the university, for instance—they're supposed to be educated, but they're not interested in the truth. They're not interested in much of anything, actually. They certainly don't *do* much. They call themselves intellectuals and think that gives them the
260 right to look down on the rest of the world. They never read anything worthwhile, they're completely ignorant where science is concerned, they talk about art and they don't even know what it is they're talking about. They take themselves so seriously, they're full of theories and ideas, but just go look at the cities they live in. Miles and miles of slums, where
265 people go hungry and where they live packed into unheated tenements full of cockroaches and garbage, and their lives are full of violence and immorality. So what are all the theories for? To keep people like us from seeing all that. Where are the day-care centers they talk so much about, and the literacy programs? It's all just talk. You go out to the parts of town
270 where the poor people live, you can't find them. All you find is dirt and ignorance and crime. That's why I don't like all this talk, all these theories. Bothers me, makes me afraid. If that's all our talk is good for, we'd better just shut up.

LOPÁKHIN I get up at five and work from morning to night, and you know,
275 my business involves a lot of money, my own and other people's, so I see lots of people, see what they're like. And you just try to get anything accomplished: you'll see how few decent, honest people there really are. Sometimes at night I can't sleep, and I think: Dear God, you gave us this

beautiful earth to live on, these great forests, these wide fields, the broad
280 horizons . . . by rights we should be giants.

LIUBÓV ANDRÉYEVNA   What do you want giants for? The only good giants are
in fairy tales. Real ones would scare you to death.

[*Upstage,* YEPIKHÓDOV *strolls by, playing his guitar.*]

[*Dreamily*] There goes Yepikhódov. . . .

ÁNYA [*dreamily*]   There goes Yepikhódov. . . .

285 GÁYEV   The sun, ladies and gentlemen, has just set.

TROFÍMOV   Yes.

GÁYEV [*as if reciting a poem, but not too loud*]   O wondrous nature, cast upon
us your eternal rays, forever beautiful, forever indifferent. . . . Mother, we
call you; life and death reside within you; you bring forth and lay waste—

290 VÁRYA [*pleading*]   Uncle, please!

ÁNYA   Uncle, you're doing it again.

TROFÍMOV   We'd rather have the yellow ball in the side pocket.

GÁYEV   Sorry, sorry. I'll keep still.

[*They all sit in silence. The only sound we hear is old* FIRS *mumbling.
Suddenly a distant sound seems to fall from the sky, a sad sound, like a
harp string breaking. It dies away.*]

LIUBÓV ANDRÉYEVNA   What was that?

295 LOPÁKHIN   Can't tell. Sounds like it could be an echo from a mine shaft. But
it must be far away.

GÁYEV   Or some kind of bird . . . like a heron.

TROFÍMOV   Or an owl.

LIUBÓV ANDRÉYEVNA [*shivers*]   Makes me nervous.

[*Pause.*]

300 FIRS   It's like just before the trouble started. They heard an owl screech, and
the kettle wouldn't stop whistling. . . .

GÁYEV   Before what trouble?

FIRS   The day we got our freedom back.

[*Pause.*]

LIUBÓV ANDRÉYEVNA   My dears, it's getting dark; we should be going in.
305 [*To* ÁNYA] You've got tears in your eyes, darling. What's the matter? [*Hugs*
ÁNYA.]

ÁNYA   Nothing, Mama. It's all right.

TROFÍMOV   Someone's coming.

[*Enter a* HOMELESS MAN *in a white cap and an overcoat; he's slightly
drunk.*]

HOMELESS MAN   Can anyone please tell me, can I get to the train station this
way?

310 GÁYEV   Of course you can. Just follow this road.

HOMELESS MAN   Much obliged. [*Bows.*] Wonderful weather we're having . . .
[*Recites.*] "Behold one of the poor in spirit, just trying to inherit a little of
the earth. . . ."[6] [*To* VÁRYA] Listen, you think you could spare some money
for a hungry man?

---

6. An allusion to two of the beatitudes from Jesus's Sermon on the Mount: "Blessed are the poor in spirit, for theirs is the kingdom of heaven. . . . Blessed are the meek, for they shall inherit the earth" (Matthew 5.3, 5).

[VÁRYA *is terrified; she screams.*]

315 LOPÁKHIN [*angrily*]   Now hold on just a minute!

LIUBÓV ANDRÉYEVNA [*panicked*]   Here . . . here . . . take this. [*Fumbles in her purse.*] Oh, I don't seem to have anything smaller. Here, take this. [*Gives him a gold piece.*]

HOMELESS MAN   Very much obliged!

[*Goes out.*]

[*Everybody laughs.*]

VÁRYA   Get me out of here! Oh, please get me out! Mama, how could you!
320   We can't even feed the servants, and you go and give him a gold piece!

LIUBÓV ANDRÉYEVNA   I know, darling, I'm just stupid about money. When we get home I'll give you whatever I've got left; you can take care of it. Yermolái Alexéyich, can you lend me some money?

LOPÁKHIN   Of course.

325 LIUBÓV ANDRÉYEVNA   My darlings, it really is time to go in. Várya dear, we've just gotten you engaged. Congratulations.

VÁRYA [*almost in tears*]   Mama, that's nothing to joke about!

LOPÁKHIN   Amelia, get thee to a nunnery![7]

330 GÁYEV   Look how my hands shake. I don't know if I could play billiards any more. . . .

LOPÁKHIN   Nymph, in thy horizons be all my sins remembered!

LIUBÓV ANDRÉYEVNA   Please, let's go. It's almost suppertime.

VÁRYA   He scared me half to death. I can feel my heart pounding.

LOPÁKHIN   But keep in mind, the cherry orchard is going to be sold. On
335   August twenty-second! You hear what I'm saying? You've got to think about this! You've got to!

[*They all go off except* ÁNYA *and* TROFÍMOV.]

ÁNYA [*laughs*]   I'm so glad that tramp scared Várya off. Now we can be alone.

TROFÍMOV   Várya's afraid we're going to fall in love; that's why she never leaves us alone. She's so narrow-minded; she simply can't understand that
340   we are above love. Our goal is to get rid of the silly illusions that keep us from being free and happy. We are moving forward, toward the future! Toward one bright star that burns ahead of us! Forward, friends! Come join us in our journey!

ÁNYA [*claps her hands*]   Oh, you talk so beautifully!

[*Pause.*]

345   It's just heavenly out here today!

TROFÍMOV   Yes, the weather's been really good lately.

ÁNYA   I don't know what it is you've done to me, Pétya, but I don't love the cherry orchard any more, not the way I used to. I used to think there was no place on earth like our orchard.

350 TROFÍMOV   This whole country is our orchard. It's a big country and a beautiful one; it has lots of wonderful places in it.

[*Pause.*]

Just think, Ánya: your grandfather, and his father, and his father's fathers, they *owned* the people who slaved away for them all over this estate, and

---

7. Hamlet's charge to Ophelia in Shakespeare's *Hamlet* (1600–01; 3.1.122). Lopákhin's next line also quotes Hamlet though he substitutes "horizons" for "orisons" 3.1.91–92).

now the voices and faces of human beings hide behind every cherry in the
355 orchard, every leaf, every tree trunk. Can't you see them? And hear them?
And owning human beings has left its mark on all of you. Look at your
mother and your uncle! They live off the labor of others, they always have,
and they've never even noticed! They owe their entire lives to those other
people, people they wouldn't even let walk through the front gate of their
360 beloved cherry orchard! This whole country has fallen behind; it'll take us
at least two hundred years to catch up. The thing is, we don't have any real
sense of our own history; all we do is sit around and talk, talk, talk, then
we feel depressed, so we go out and get drunk. If there's one thing that's
clear to me, it's this: if we want to have any real life in the present, we
365 have to do something to make up for our past, we have to get over it, and
the only way to do that is to make sacrifices, get down to work, and work
harder than we've ever worked before. Do you understand what I mean,
Ánya?

ÁNYA   The house we live in isn't our house any more. It hasn't ever been,
370   really. And I'll leave it all behind, I promise you I will.

TROFÍMOV   Yes, you will! Throw away your house keys and go as far away as
you can! You'll be free as the wind.

ÁNYA [*radiant*]   I love the way you say things!

TROFÍMOV   You have to understand me, Ánya. I'm not thirty yet, I'm still
375   young; I may still be in school, but I've learned a lot. Winter comes, sometimes I get cold and hungry, or sick and upset, I don't have a cent to my
name; things work out or they don't. . . . But no matter what, my heart and
soul are always full of feelings, all kinds . . . I can't even explain them. And
I feel happiness coming, Ánya, I can feel it, I can almost see it—

380 ÁNYA [*dreamily*]   Look, the moon's rising.

[*The sound of* YEPIKHÓDOV's *guitar, still playing the same mournful song.
The moon rises. Somewhere beyond the poplar trees,* VÁRYA *can be heard
calling.*]

VÁRYA [*off*]   Anya! Ánya, where are you?

TROFÍMOV   Yes, the moon is rising.

[*Pause.*]

It's happiness, that's what it is: it's rising, it's coming closer and closer, I
can hear it. And even if we miss it, if we never find it, that's all right!
385   Someone will!

VÁRYA [*off*]   Ánya! Ánya, where are you?

TROFÍMOV [*angrily*]   That Várya! Why won't she let us alone!

ÁNYA   Don't let her bother you. Let's take a walk by the river. It's so nice
there.

390 TROFÍMOV   All right, let's go.

[*They leave. The stage is empty.*]

VÁRYA [*off*]   Ánya! Ánya!

Curtain.

Act 3

[*A sitting room, separated from the ballroom in back by an archway. The
chandeliers are lit. From the entrance hall comes the sounds of an
orchestra, the Jewish musicians* GÁYEV *mentioned in Act 2. Evening. In
the ballroom, everyone is dancing a grande ronde.* SEMYÓNOV-PÍSHCHIK's

*voice is heard calling the figures of the dance: "Promenade à une paire!"[8]
The dancers dance through the sitting room in pairs in the following
order:* PÍSHCHIK *and* CARLOTTA, TROFÍMOV *and* LIUBÓV ANDRÉYEVNA, ÁNYA
and the POSTMASTER, VÁRYA *and the* STATIONMASTER, *etc.* VÁRYA *is in
tears, which she tries to wipe away as she dances. The final pair includes*
DUNYÁSHA. *As the dancers return to the ballroom,* PÍSHCHIK *calls out:
"Grande ronde, balancez!" and "Les cavaliers à genoux et remercier vos
dames."[9]* FIRS *in his butler's uniform crosses the stage, carrying a seltzer
bottle on a tray.* PÍSHCHIK *and* TROFÍMOV *come into the sitting room.*]

PÍSHCHIK   I'm prone to strokes, already had two of 'em, I really shouldn't be
dancing, but you know what they say: When in Rome. Besides, I'm really
strong as a horse. Speaking of Romans, my father—what a joker he was—he
used to claim our family was descended from the emperor Caligula's
5   horse—you know, the one he made a senator?[1] [*Sits down.*] The only problem is we have no money. [*His head nods, he snores, then immediately wakes
up.*] So the only thing I ever think about is money.

TROFÍMOV   Your father was right. You do look a little like a horse.

PÍSHCHIK   Nothing wrong with horses. Wonderful animals. If I had one, I
10   could sell it. . . .
[*From the adjacent billiard room come the sounds of a game.* VÁRYA
appears in the archway.]

TROFÍMOV [*teases her*]   Mrs. Lopákhin! Mrs. Lopákhin!

VÁRYA [*angrily*]   High-class tramp!

TROFÍMOV   Yes, I'm a high-class tramp, and I'm proud of it!

VÁRYA [*bitterly*]   We've hired an orchestra! And what are we supposed to pay
15   them with?
[*Goes out.*]

TROFÍMOV [*to* PÍSHCHIK]   All the energy you've used trying to find money to
pay your mortgage, if you'd spent that energy on something else, you could
have moved the world.

PÍSHCHIK   Nietzsche,[2] you know, the philosopher—a great thinker, Nietz-
20   sche, a man of genius, one of the great minds of the century—now Nietzsche,
you know, says, in his memoirs, that counterfeit money's just as good as
real. . . .

TROFÍMOV   I didn't know you'd read Nietzsche.

PÍSHCHIK   Well . . . actually, Dáshenka told me. And I'm desperate enough.
25   I'm ready to start counterfeiting. I need three hundred and ten rubles, day
after tomorrow. All I've got so far is a hundred and thirty. . . . [*He feels in
his pockets anxiously.*] It's gone! My money's gone! [*Almost in tears*] I've lost
my money! [*Joyfully*] Oh, here it is! It slipped down into the lining of my
coat! God, I'm all in a sweat!
[*Enter* LIUBÓV *and* CARLOTTA.]

30   LIUBÓV ANDRÉYEVNA [*she hums a dance tune*]   Why is it taking so long?
What's Leoníd doing all this time in town? He should be back by now.

---

8. "Promenade with your partner!" (French).
9. "Large circle, swing with your arms!";
"Gentlemen, kneel down and thank your
ladies" (French).
1. According to the Roman historian Sueto-
nius, the emperor Caligula (r. 37–41 C.E.)

considered making his favorite racehorse a
consul; the version in popular lore is that he
appointed the animal a senator.
2. Friedrich Nietzsche (1844–1900), German
philosopher who was among the most influential of modern thinkers.

[*Calls to* DUNYÁSHA *in the ballroom.*] Dunyásha, tell the musicians they can take a break.

TROFÍMOV   They probably postponed the auction.

35 LIUBÓV ANDRÉYEVNA   I suppose it was a mistake to hire an orchestra. Or to have a party in the first place. Oh, well . . . what difference does it make? [*Sits down and hums quietly.*]

CARLOTTA [*hands* PÍSHCHIK *a deck of cards*]   Here's the deck. Pick a card, any card. . . . No, no, just think of one.

PÍSHCHIK   All right, I'm thinking of one.

40 CARLOTTA   Good. Now shuffle the deck. Very good. Now give it to me. Observe, my dear Píshchik! *Eins, zwei, drei!*[3] Now look in your jacket pocket, and you will find your card.

PÍSHCHIK [*takes a card from his jacket pocket*]   That's it, the eight of spades! [*Amazed*] Really! I don't believe it!

45 CARLOTTA [*holds out the deck to* TROFÍMOV]   Quick, what's the top card?

TROFÍMOV   The top card? Oh . . . uh . . . the queen of spades.

CARLOTTA   Correct! [*To* PÍSHCHIK] Now which card's on top?

PÍSHCHIK   Ace of hearts!

CARLOTTA   Correct! [*Claps her hands, and the deck disappears.*] Well, isn't this
50 a lovely day we're having?

[*A mysterious woman's voice answers; it seems to come from the floor-boards: "A lovely day indeed. I couldn't agree more."*]

Whoever you are, I adore you!

[*The voice: "I adore you too!"*]

STATIONMASTER [*applauds*]   Bravo! A lady ventriloquist!

PÍSHCHIK [*amazed*]   Really! I don't believe it! Carlotta, you are amazing! I'm completely in love with you!

55 CARLOTTA   In love? [*Shrugs her shoulders.*] What do you know about love? *Guter Mensch aber schlechter Musikant.*[4]

TROFÍMOV [*slaps* PÍSHCHIK *on the shoulder*]   You're just an old horse!

CARLOTTA   All right, everybody, watch closely! One more trick! [*Takes a lap robe from a chair.*] See, what a lovely blanket! I'm thinking of selling it.
60 [*Shakes out the lap robe and holds it up.*] Who wants to buy?

PÍSHCHIK [*amazed*]   Really! I don't believe it!

CARLOTTA   *Eins, zwei, drei!* [*Quickly raises the lap robe.*]

[ÁNYA *appears behind the lap robe; she curtsies, runs to her mother and kisses her, then runs back into the ballroom. General applause and cries of delight.*]

LIUBÓV ANDRÉYEVNA [*applauding*]   Bravo! Bravo!

CARLOTTA   Now one more! *Eins, zwei, drei!*

[*She raises the lap robe;* VÁRYA *appears; she takes a bow.*]

65 PÍSHCHIK   Really! I don't believe it!

CARLOTTA   That's all. The show is over.

[*Throws the lap robe to* PÍSHCHIK, *takes a bow, goes through the ballroom and out.*]

PÍSHCHIK [*goes after her*]   Enchanting! What a woman! What a woman! [*Goes out.*]

3. One, two, three! (German).
4. A good man but a bad musician (German); that is, an incompetent.

LIUBÓV ANDRÉYEVNA   Leoníd still isn't back from town yet. I don't understand what could be taking him so long! It's got to be all over by now: either the
70   estate has been sold or they've postponed the auction. Why does he have to keep us in suspense like this?

VÁRYA [tries to comfort her]   Uncle bought the estate, I'm sure he has.

TROFÍMOV [ironically]   Oh, I'm sure.

VÁRYA   Ánya's godmother sent him a power of attorney to buy the estate in
75   her name; she agreed to take over the mortgage. She did it for Ánya. So God has helped us. Uncle has saved the estate.

LIUBÓV ANDRÉYEVNA   The old lady in Yároslavl sent us fifteen thousand to buy the place in her name—she doesn't trust us—but that's not even enough to pay the interest. [Covers her face with her hands.] My fate . . .
80   my entire life . . . It's all being decided today.

TROFÍMOV [teases VÁRYA]   Mrs. Lopákhin! Mrs. Lopákhin!

VÁRYA [angrily]   And you're a permanent graduate student! Who's been suspended twice!

LIUBÓV ANDRÉYEVNA   Don't get so angry, Várya; he's only teasing you. What's
85   wrong with that? And what's wrong with Lopákhin? If you want to marry him, do; he's a nice man. Interesting, even. If you don't want to marry him, don't; nobody's forcing you.

VÁRYA   It's not a joking matter, Mama, believe me. I'm serious about him. He is a nice man, and I like him.

90   LIUBÓV ANDRÉYEVNA   Then go ahead and marry him! I don't understand what you're waiting for!

VÁRYA   Mama, I can't propose to him myself! For two years now everybody's been telling me to marry him, everybody, but he never mentions it. Or he jokes about it! Look, I understand, he's busy getting rich, he doesn't have
95   time for me. Oh, if I had just a little money—I don't care how much, even a couple of hundred—I'd get out of here and go someplace far away. I'd go join a convent.

TROFÍMOV   Now, there's an exalted idea!

VÁRYA [to TROFÍMOV]   I thought students were supposed to be smart! [Her
100   tone softens; almost crying.] Oh, Pétya, you used to be so nice-looking, and now you're getting old! [To LIUBÓV, in a normal tone] It's just that I need something to do all the time, Mama; it's the way I am. I can't sit around and do nothing.

[Enter YÁSHA.]

YÁSHA [barely controlling his laughter]   Yepikhódov broke a billiard cue!
[Goes out.]

105   VÁRYA   What is Yepikhódov doing here? Who asked him to come? And what's he doing playing billiards? I just don't understand these people. . . .
[Goes out.]

LIUBÓV ANDRÉYEVNA   Pétya, don't tease her like that; you can see she's upset already.

TROFÍMOV   Oh, she's such a busybody, always poking her nose into other
110   people's business. She hasn't left Ánya and me alone the whole summer; she's afraid we're having a . . . an affair. What business is it of hers? Besides, it's not true. I'd never do anything so sordid. We're above love!

LIUBÓV ANDRÉYEVNA   And I, I suppose, am beneath love. [Upset] Why isn't Leoníd back yet? I just want to know: has the estate been sold or not? The

115 whole disaster seems so impossible to me, I don't know what to think, or
do. . . . Oh, God, I'm losing my mind! I want to scream, or do something completely stupid . . . Help me, Pétya! Save me! Say something, say
something!

TROFÍMOV Whether they sell it or not, does it make any difference really?
120 You can't go back to the past. Everything here came to an end a long time
ago. Try to calm down. You can't go on deceiving yourself; at least once in
your life you have to look the truth straight in the eye.

LIUBÓV ANDRÉYEVNA What truth? You seem so sure what's truth and what
isn't, but I'm not. I've lost any sense of it, I've lost sight of the truth. You're
125 so sure of yourself, aren't you, so sure you have all the answers to everything, but darling, have you ever really had to live with one of your answers?
You're too young. Of course *you* look into the future and see a brave new
world, you don't expect any difficulties, but that's because you know nothing about life! Yes, you have more courage than my generation has, and
130 better morals, and you're better educated, but for God's sake have a little
sense of what it's like for me, and be easier on me. Pétya, I was born here!
My parents lived here all their lives; so did my grandfather. I love this
house! Without the cherry orchard my life makes no sense, and if you have
to sell it, you might as well sell me with it. [*She embraces* TROFÍMOV *and*
135 *kisses his forehead.*] And it was here my son drowned, you know that. . . .
[*Weeps.*] Have some feeling for me, Pétya, you're such a good, sweet boy.

TROFÍMOV I pity you. [*Beat*] I do, from the bottom of my heart.

LIUBÓV ANDRÉYEVNA You should have said that differently, just a little differently. . . . [*Takes out her handkerchief; a telegram falls to the floor.*] You can't
140 imagine how miserable I am today. All this noise, and every new sound
makes me shake. I can't get away from it, but then when I'm alone in my
room I can't stand the silence. Don't judge me, Pétya! I love you like one of
my own family; I'd be very happy to see you and Ánya married, you know I
would, only, darling, you must finish school first! You have *got* to graduate!
145 You don't do anything except drift around from place to place—what kind
of life is that? It's true, isn't it? Isn't that the truth? And we have to do
something about that beard of yours; it's so scraggly. . . . [*Laughs.*] You've
gotten so funny-looking!

TROFÍMOV [*picks up the telegram*] I have no desire to be good-looking.

150 LIUBÓV ANDRÉYEVNA The telegram's from Paris. I get a new one every day.
One yesterday, now again today. That madman is sick again and in trouble. . . . He wants me to forgive him, he wants me back . . . and I suppose I
should go back to Paris to be with him. Now see, Pétya, you're giving me
that superior look, but darling, what am I supposed to do? He's sick, he's
155 alone, he's unhappy, and who has he got to look after him? To give him his
medicine and keep him out of trouble? And I love him—why do I have to
pretend I don't, or not talk about it? I love him. That's just the way it is: I
love him. I love him! He's a millstone around my neck, and he'll drown me
with him, but he's *my* millstone! I love him and I can't live without him!
160 [*Grabs* TROFÍMOV's *hand.*] Don't judge me, Pétya, don't think badly of me,
just don't say anything, please just don't say anything. . . .

TROFÍMOV [*almost in tears*] But for God's sake, you have to face the facts! He
robbed you blind!

LIUBÓV ANDRÉYEVNA   No, no, please, you mustn't say that, you mustn't—

165 TROFÍMOV   He doesn't care a thing for you—you're the only person who doesn't seem to understand that! He's rotten!

LIUBÓV ANDRÉYEVNA [*gets angry but tries to control it*]   And you, you're what? Twenty-six, twenty-seven? Listen to you: you sound like you'd never even graduated to long pants!

170 TROFÍMOV   That's fine with me!

LIUBÓV ANDRÉYEVNA   You're supposed to be a man; at your age you ought to know something about love. You ought to be in love yourself! [*Angrily*] Really! You think you're so smart, you're just a kid who doesn't know the first thing about it, you're probably a virgin, you're ridiculous, you're

175 grotesque—

TROFÍMOV [*horrified*]   What are you saying!

LIUBÓV ANDRÉYEVNA   "I'm above love!" You're not above love; you've just never gotten down to it! You're all wet, like Firs says. At your age, you ought to be sleeping with someone!

180 TROFÍMOV [*horrified*]   What a terrible thing to say! That's terrible! [*He runs toward the ballroom, covering his ears.*] That's just horrible. . . . I can't listen to that; I'm leaving. [*Goes out, but reappears immediately.*] All is over between us!

[*Goes out into the entrance hall.*]

LIUBÓV ANDRÉYEVNA [*calls after him*]   Pétya, wait a minute! Come back! I was

185 just joking, Pétya, don't be so silly! Pétya!

[*A great clatter from the entrance hall; someone has fallen downstairs. ÁNYA and VÁRYA scream.*]

What happened?

[*ÁNYA and VÁRYA suddenly howl with laughter.*]

ÁNYA [*runs in, laughing*]   Pétya just fell headfirst down the stairs!

[*Runs out.*]

LIUBÓV ANDRÉYEVNA   Oh, what a silly boy!

[*The STATIONMASTER in the ballroom gets on a chair and begins declaiming the opening lines of "The Magdalen" by Alexei Tolstoy.*[5]]

STATIONMASTER   "The splendid ballroom gleams with gold and candles,
190 a crowd of dancers whirls around the room;
and there apart, an empty glass beside her,
behold the fallen beauty, the lost, the doomed.

Her lavish gown and jewels make all eyes wonder,
her shameless glance bespeaks a life of sin;
195 young men and old cast longing glances at her—
see, how her fatal beauty draws them in!"

[*Everyone gathers to listen, but soon the orchestra returns and the strains of a waltz are heard from the entrance hall. The reading breaks off, and everybody begins to dance. TROFÍMOV, ÁNYA, and VÁRYA come in from the entrance hall.*]

5. Russian novelist, poet, and playwright (1817–1875), a distant relative of the more famous novelist Leo Tolstoy. "The Magdalen" is sometimes translated "The Sinful Woman" (a *magdalen* is a reformed prostitute).

LIUBÓV ANDRÉYEVNA   Pétya . . . oh, darling, I'm *so* sorry. . . . You sweet thing, please forgive me. . . . Come on, let's dance. [*Dances with* TROFÍMOV.]

> [ÁNYA *and* VÁRYA *dance together.* FIRS *enters, leans his walking stick against the side door.* YÁSHA *appears and stands watching the dancers.*]

YÁSHA   What's the matter, pops?

200 FIRS   I don't feel so good. The old days, we had a dance, we had generals and barons and admirals; nowadays we have to send out for the postmaster and the stationmaster. And they're none too eager to come, either. Oh, I'm getting old and feeble. The old master, their grandfather, anybody got sick, he used to dose 'em all with sealing wax. Didn't matter what they had, they all
205 got sealing wax. I've been taking sealing wax myself now for nigh onto twenty years. Take some every day. That's probably why I'm still alive.

YÁSHA   You're getting boring, pops. [*Yawns.*] Time for you to crawl off and die.

FIRS   Oh, you . . . you young flibbertigibbet. [*Mumbles.*]

> [TROFÍMOV *and* LIUBÓV *dance through the ballroom, into the sitting room.*]

210 LIUBÓV ANDRÉYEVNA   *Merci.*[6] I need to sit down and rest a bit. . . . [*Sits.*] I'm so tired.

> [*Enter* ÁNYA.]

ÁNYA [*upset*]   There was a man in the kitchen just now, he said the cherry orchard's already been sold!

LIUBÓV ANDRÉYEVNA   Who bought it?

215 ÁNYA   He didn't say. And he's gone now. [*Dances with* TROFÍMOV; *they dance off across the ballroom.*]

YÁSHA   That was just some old guy talking crazy. It wasn't anybody from around here.

FIRS   And Leoníd Andréyich still isn't back. All he had on was his topcoat; you watch, he'll catch cold. He's all wet, that one.

220 LIUBÓV ANDRÉYEVNA   I'll never live through this. Yásha, go out and see if anybody knows who bought it.

YÁSHA   It was just some old guy. He left long ago. [*Laughs.*]

LIUBÓV ANDRÉYEVNA [*somewhat annoyed*]   What are you laughing at? What's so funny?

225 YÁSHA   That Yepikhódov. What a dope. Old Double Trouble.

LIUBÓV ANDRÉYEVNA   Firs, suppose the estate is sold—where are you going to go?

FIRS   I'll go wherever you tell me to.

LIUBÓV ANDRÉYEVNA   What's the matter? Your face looks so funny. . . . Are
230 you sick? You should go to bed.

FIRS   Yes . . . [*Smirks.*] Yes, sure, go to bed, and then who'll take care of things? I'm the only one you've got.

YÁSHA   Liubóv Andréyevna, there's a favor I have *got* to ask you; it's very important. If you go back to Paris, please take me with you. Please! You've
235 got to! I positively cannot stay around here. [*Looks around, lowers his voice.*] You can see for yourself this place is hopeless. The whole country's a mess, nobody has any culture, it's boring, the food is lousy, and there's

---

6. Thank you (French).

that old Firs drooling all over the place and talking like an idiot. Please, take me with you—you've just got to!

[*Enter* PÍSHCHIK.]

240 PÍSHCHIK   Beautiful lady, what about a waltz? Just one little waltz! [LIUBÓV *crosses to him.*] You dazzler, you! And what about a loan, just one little loan, just a hundred and eighty, that's all I need. [*They begin to dance.*] Just a hundred and eighty . . .

[*They dance off into the ballroom.*]

YÁSHA [*sings to himself*]   "Can't you see my heart is breaking . . ."

[*In the ballroom, a figure appears dressed in checkered trousers and a gray top hat, jumping and waving its arms. We hear shouts of "Bravo, Carlotta!"*]

245 DUNYÁSHA [*stops to powder her nose*]   The missus told me to dance—there's too many gentlemen and not enough ladies—so I did, I've been dancing all night and my heart won't stop beating, and you know what, Firs? Just now, the postmaster, you know? He said something almost made me faint.

[*The orchestra stops playing.*]

FIRS   What did he say?

250 DUNYÁSHA   That I was like a flower. That's what he said.

YÁSHA [*yawns*]   What does he know about it?

[*Goes out.*]

DUNYÁSHA   Just like a flower. I'm a very romantic girl, really. I just adore that kind of talk.

FIRS   You're out of your mind.

[*Enter* YEPIKHÓDOV.]

255 YEPIKHÓDOV [*to* DUNYÁSHA]   Why are you deliberating not to notice me? You act as if I wasn't here, like I was a bug or something [*Sighs.*] Ah, life!

DUNYÁSHA   Excuse me?

YEPIKHÓDOV   Of course, you may be right. [*Sighs.*] But if you look at it, let's say, from a . . . a point of view, then you're the faulty one—excuse my
260   expressivity—because you led me on. Into this predictament. Look at me! Every day something awful happens to me. It's like a habit. But I can look disaster in the face and keep smiling. You gave me your word, you know, and you even—

DUNYÁSHA   Do you mind? Let's talk about it later. Right now I'd rather be left
265   alone. With my dreams. [*Plays with a fan.*]

YEPIKHÓDOV   Every day. Something awful. But all I do—excuse my expressivity—is try to keep smiling. Sometimes I even laugh.

[*Enter* VÁRYA *from the ballroom.*]

VÁRYA [*to* YEPIKHÓDOV]   Are you still here? I thought I told you to go home. Really, you have no consideration. [*To* DUNYÁSHA] Dunyásha, go back to
270   the kitchen! [*To* YEPIKHÓDOV] You come in here and start playing billiards, you break one of our cues, now you hang around in here as if we'd invited you.

YEPIKHÓDOV   Excuse my expressivity, but you have no right to penalize me.

VÁRYA   I'm not penalizing you, I'm telling you! All you do here is wander
275   around and bump into the furniture. You're supposed to be working for us, and you don't do a thing. I don't know why we hired you in the first place.

YEPIKHÓDOV [*offended*]   Whether I work or not or wander around or not or play billiards or not is none of your business! You do not have the know-it-all to make my estimation!

280 VÁRYA   How dare you talk to me like that! [*In a rage*] How dare you! What do you mean, I don't have the know-it-all? You get yourself out of here right this minute! Right this minute!

YEPIKHÓDOV [*apprehensively*]   I wish you wouldn't use language like that—

VÁRYA [*beside herself*]   Get out of here right this minute! Out! [*He goes to the*
285 *door; she follows him.*] Double Trouble! I don't want to see hide or hair of you, I don't want to lay eyes on you ever again! [YEPIKHÓDOV *goes out; from behind the door we hear him screech: "I'll call the police on you!"*] Oh, you coming back for more? [*Grabs the stick that* FIRS *has left by the door.*] Come on . . . Come on . . . Come on, I'll show you! All right, all right, you asked
290 for it—[*Swings the stick; the door opens, and she hits* LOPÁKHIN *over the head as he enters.*]

LOPÁKHIN   Thanks a lot.

VÁRYA [*still angry, sarcastic*]   Oh, I'm so sorry!

LOPÁKHIN   S'all right. Always appreciate a warm welcome.

VÁRYA   I don't need appreciation. [*Walks off, then turns and asks gently.*] I
295 didn't hurt you, did I?

LOPÁKHIN   No, I'm fine. Just a whopping big lump, that's all.

> [*Voices from the ballroom: "Lopákhin! Lopákhin's here! He's back! Lopákhin's back!" People crowd into the sitting room.*]

PÍSHCHIK   The great man in person! [*Hugs* LOPÁKHIN.] Is that cognac I smell? It is! You've been celebrating! Well, so have we. Join the party!

LIUBÓV ANDRÉYEVNA   It's you, Yermolái Alexéyich. Where have you been all
300 this time? Where's Leoníd?

LOPÁKHIN   He's coming; we took the same train.

LIUBÓV ANDRÉYEVNA   What happened? Did they have the auction? Tell me!

LOPÁKHIN [*embarrassed, afraid to show his joy*]   The auction was all over by four this afternoon, but we missed the train. We had to wait for the nine-
305 thirty. [*Exhales heavily.*] Oof! My head is really spinning. . . .

> [*Enter* GÁYEV; *he holds a wrapped package in one hand, wipes his eyes with the other.*]

LIUBÓV ANDRÉYEVNA   Lyónya, what's the matter? Lyónya! [*Impatiently, beginning to cry*] For God's sake, what happened!

GÁYEV [*weeps and can't answer her; makes a despairing gesture with his free hand and turns to* FIRS]   Here, take these . . . some anchovies . . . imported. I haven't eaten a thing all day. You have no idea what I've been through! [*The door to the billiard room is open; we hear the click of billiard balls and* YÁSHA's *voice: "Seven ball in the left pocket!"* GÁYEV's *expression changes; he*
310 *stops crying.*] I'm all worn out. Firs, come help me get ready for bed.

> [*Goes through the ballroom and out;* FIRS *follows him.*]

PÍSHCHIK   What about the auction? Tell us what happened!

LIUBÓV ANDRÉYEVNA   Is the cherry orchard sold?

LOPÁKHIN   It's sold.

LIUBÓV ANDRÉYEVNA   Who bought it?

315 LOPÁKHIN   I did.

[*Pause.* LIUBÓV *is overcome; she would fall, if she weren't standing beside a table and the armchair.* VÁRYA *takes the keys from her belt, throws them on the floor, crosses the room, and goes out.*]

I did! I bought it! No, wait, don't go, please. I'm still a little mixed up about it, I can't talk yet. . . . [*Laughs.*] We get to the auction, and there's Derigánov, all ready and waiting. Leoníd Andréyich only had fifteen thousand, so right away Derigánov raises the bid to thirty, that's on top of the balance on the mortgage. So I see what he's up to, and I bid against him. Raise it to forty. He bids forty-five. I bid fifty-five. See, he was raising by five, and I double him, I raise him ten each time. Anyway, finally it's all over, and I got it! Ninety thousand plus the balance on the mortgage.[7] And now the cherry orchard is mine! Mine! [*A loud laugh*] My God, the cherry orchard belongs to me! Tell me I'm drunk, tell me it's all a dream, I'm making this up—[*Stomps on the floor.*] And don't anybody laugh! My God, if my father and my grandfather could be here now and see this, see *me*, their Yermolái, the boy they beat, who went barefoot in winter and never went to school, see how that poor boy just bought the most beautiful estate in the whole world! I bought the estate where my father and my grandfather slaved away their lives, where they wouldn't even let them in the kitchen! My God, I must be dreaming—I can't believe all this is happening! [*Picks up* VÁRYA's *keys; smiles gently.*] See, she threw away her keys; she knows she isn't running the place any more. . . . [*Jingles the keys.*] Well, that's all right.

[*The orchestra starts tuning up again.*]

That's it, let's have some music—come on, I want to hear it! Everybody come watch! Come on and watch what I do! I'm going to chop down every tree in that cherry orchard, every goddamn one of them, and then I'm going to develop that land! Watch me! I'm going to do something our children and grandchildren can be proud of! Come on, you musicians, play!

[*The orchestra begins to play.* LIUBÓV *curls up in the armchair and weeps bitterly.*]

LOPÁKHIN [*reproachfully*]   Oh, why didn't you listen to me? You dear woman, you dear good woman, you can't ever go back to the past. [*With tears in his eyes*] Oh, if only we could change things, if only life were different, this unhappy, messy life . . .

PÍSHCHIK [*takes his arm; quietly*]   She's crying. Come on, we'll go in the other room, leave her alone for a while. Come on. . . . [*Leads him into the ballroom.*]

LOPÁKHIN   What's the matter? Tell the band to keep playing! Louder! [*Ironic*] It's my house now! The cherry orchard belongs to me! I can do what I want to! [*Bumps into a small table, almost knocking over a candlestick.*] Don't worry about that: I can pay for it! I can pay for everything!

[*Goes out with* PÍSHCHIK.]

[*The sitting room is empty except for* LIUBÓV, *who sits tightly clenched and weeping bitterly. The orchestra plays softly. Suddenly* ÁNYA *and*

---

7. The winning bid for the estate was equivalent to nearly $2 million today—about twice what Lopákhin had offered to lend Liubóv and her family to save the estate (act 1).

TROFÍMOV *enter.* ÁNYA *goes and kneels before her mother.* TROFÍMOV *remains by the archway.*]

ÁNYA Mama! Mama, you're crying. Mama dear, I love you, I'll take care of you. The cherry orchard is sold, it's gone now, that's the truth, Mama, that's the truth, but don't cry. You still have your life to lead, you're still a
355 good person. . . . Come with me, Mama, we'll go away, someplace far away from here. We'll plant a new orchard, even better than this one, you'll see, Mama, you'll understand, and you'll feel a new kind of joy, like a light in your soul. . . . Let's go, Mama. Let's go!

Curtain.

Act 4

[*The same room as Act 1. The curtains have been taken down, the pictures are gone from the walls, and there are only a few pieces of furniture shoved into a corner, as if for sale. The place feels empty. By the doorway, a pile of trunks, suitcases, etc. The door on the right is open; we hear* ÁNYA *and* VÁRYA *talking in the room beyond.* LOPÁKHIN *stands waiting. Beside him,* YÁSHA *holds a tray of glasses filled with champagne. Through the door we see* YEPIKHÓDOV *in the front hall, fastening the straps on a trunk. The sound of murmured voices offstage; some of the local people have come to say goodbye.* GÁYEV's *voice: "Thank you all, good people, thanks, thanks very much for coming."*]

YÁSHA It's some of these poor yokels, come to say goodbye. I'm of the opinion, you know, these people around here . . . ? They're okay, but they're . . . they're just a bunch of know-nothings.

[*The murmur of voices dies away.* LIUBÓV *and* GÁYEV *come in from the entrance hall; she has stopped crying, but she is shaking slightly, and her face is pale. She cannot speak.*]

GÁYEV You gave them all the money you had, Liúba. You can't do that! You
5 can't do that any more!

LIUBÓV ANDREYÉVNA I couldn't help it! I just couldn't help it!

[*They both go out.* LOPÁKHIN *follows them to the door.*]

LOPÁKHIN Wait, please. How about a little glass of champagne, just to celebrate? I forgot to bring some from town, but I got this one bottle at the station. It was all they had.

[*Pause.*]

10 No? What's the matter, don't you want any? [*Comes back from the door.*] If I'd known that, I wouldn't have bought it. I don't feel like any myself.

[YÁSHA *carefully puts the tray down on a chair.*]

Go on, Yásha, you might as well have one.

YÁSHA *Bon voyage!* And here's to the girls we leave behind! [*Drinks.*] This is not your real French champagne, I can tell.

15 LOPÁKHIN Cost me enough.

[*Pause.*]

It's cold as hell in here.

YÁSHA They figured they were going away today anyway—they decided not to heat the place. [*Laughs.*]

LOPÁKHIN What's with you?

20 YÁSHA   I'm laughing because everything worked out just the way I wanted.

LOPÁKHIN   It's October already, but the sun's out; it feels like summer. Good weather for home builders. [*Looks at his watch, then at the door.*] Listen, everybody, you got forty-six minutes till train time! And it's twenty minutes from here to the station, so you better get a move on.

[*Enter* TROFÍMOV *from outside; he's wearing an overcoat.*]

25 TROFÍMOV   It must be time to go. The carts are here. Where the hell are my galoshes? I've lost them somewhere. [*At the door*] Ánya, where are my galoshes? I can't find them anyplace!

LOPÁKHIN   I'm off to Hárkov. I'll be taking the same train as you. Off to Hárkov, spend the winter there. I've been hanging around here too long, 30 doing nothing; I can't stand that. I got to keep working, otherwise I don't know what to do with my hands; if they're not doing something, they feel like they don't belong to me.

TROFÍMOV   So. We're leaving, and you're going back to your useful labors in the real world.

35 LOPÁKHIN   Have a glass of champagne.

TROFÍMOV   No, thanks.

LOPÁKHIN   So you're off to Moscow?

TROFÍMOV   Yes. I'll go into town with them today, and then leave tomorrow for Moscow.

40 LOPÁKHIN   Sure. I'll bet all those professors are waiting for you to show up, wouldn't want to start their lectures without you!

TROFÍMOV   Mind your own business.

LOPÁKHIN   How long you say you've been at that university?

TROFÍMOV   Come on! Think up something new, will you? You're getting bor-
45 ing. [*Pokes around, looking for his galoshes.*] You know, we probably won't ever see each other again, so you mind my giving you a little advice? As a farewell present? Don't wave your arms around so much. Bad habit. And this development you're putting in out here—you think that's going to improve the world? You think your leisure home buyers are going to turn 50 into yeoman farmers? That's a lot of arm waving too. Well, what the hell. I like you anyway. You've got nice hands. Gentle and sensitive. You could have been an artist. And you're like that inside too—gentle and sensitive.

LOPÁKHIN [*hugs him*]   Goodbye, boy. Thanks for everything. Here, let me give you a little money. You may need it for the trip.

55 TROFÍMOV   What for? I don't need money!

LOPÁKHIN   What *for?* You don't have any!

TROFÍMOV   I do too. Thanks all the same. I got paid for a translation I did. I have money right here in my pocket. [*Worried*] I just wish I could find my galoshes!

60 VÁRYA [*from the next room*]   Here they are! The smelly things . . . [*Throws a pair of galoshes into the room.*]

TROFÍMOV   What are you always getting mad for? Hmm . . . These aren't my galoshes.

LOPÁKHIN   This past spring I planted a big crop of poppies. Three hundred acres. Sold the poppy seed, made forty thousand clear. And when those 65 poppies were all in flower, what a picture that was! So look, I just made forty thousand, I can afford to loan you some money. Why turn up your nose at it? Because you think I'm just a dirt farmer?

TROFÍMOV   So your father was a dirt farmer. Mine worked in a drugstore. What does that prove?

[LOPÁKHIN *takes out his wallet.*]

70   Forget it, forget it. Look, you could give me a couple of hundred thousand, I still wouldn't take it. I'm a free man. And you people, everything you think is so valuable, it doesn't mean a thing to me. I don't care whether you're rich or poor; you've got no power over me. I can do without you, I can go right on past you, because I am proud and I am strong. Humanity is
75   moving onward, toward a higher truth and a higher happiness, higher than anyone can imagine. And I'm ahead of the rest!

LOPÁKHIN   You think you'll ever get there?

TROFÍMOV   I'll get there.

[*Pause.*]

I'll get there. Or I'll make sure the rest of them get there.

[*From the orchard comes the sound of axes; they've started chopping down the cherry trees.*]

80   LOPÁKHIN   Well, boy, goodbye. Time to go. You and I don't see eye to eye, but life goes on anyway. Whenever I work real hard, round the clock practically, that clears my mind somehow, and for a minute I think maybe I know what we're all here for. But God, boy, think of the thousands of people in this country who don't know what they're doing or why they're doing it.
85   But . . . I guess that doesn't have much to do with the price of eggs. They told me Leoníd Andréyich got a job at the bank, six thousand a year. He won't last; he's too lazy.

ÁNYA [*at the door*]   Mama asks you to please wait until she's gone before you start cutting down the orchard.

90   TROFÍMOV   I agree. That isn't very tactful, you know.

[*Goes out into the front hall.*]

LOPÁKHIN   All right, all right, I'll take care of it. God, these people . . .

[*Goes out after him.*]

ÁNYA   Have they taken Firs to the nursing home?

YÁSHA   I told them about it this morning. So I imagine they have.

ÁNYA [*to* YEPIKHÓDOV, *who crosses the room*]   Yepikhódov, could you please go
95   and make sure they've taken Firs to the nursing home?

YÁSHA [*offended*]   I already told them this morning! Why keep asking?

YEPIKHÓDOV   The aged Firs, in my ultimate opinion, is beyond nursing. They ought to take him to the cemetery. And I can only envy him. [*Sets a suitcase down on a cardboard hatbox and crushes it.*] There. Finally. Wouldn't you
100   know.

[*Goes out.*]

YÁSHA [*snickers*]   Old Double Trouble.

VÁRYA [*from the next room*]   Have they taken Firs to the nursing home?

ÁNYA   They took him this morning.

VÁRYA   Then why didn't they take the letter for the doctor?

105   ÁNYA   They must have forgotten. We'll have to send someone after them with it.

VÁRYA   Where's Yásha? Tell him his mother is here; she wants to say goodbye.

YÁSHA [*with a dismissive gesture*]   What a bore! Why can't she just leave me alone?

[DUNYÁSHA *has been drifting in and out, fussing with the baggage; now that she sees* YÁSHA *alone, she goes to him.*]

110 DUNYÁSHA Oh . . . oh, Yásha, why won't you even look at me? You're going away . . . you're leaving me behind. . . . [*Starts to cry and throws her arms around his neck.*]

YÁSHA What are you crying about? [*Drinks some champagne.*] Six days from now, I'll be back in Paris. Tomorrow we get on the express train, and we're off! And that's the last you'll ever see of me! I can't hardly believe it myself.
115 *Vive la France!*[8] I can't live around here any more; it's just not my kind of place. They're all so ignorant, and I can't stand that. [*Drinks more champagne.*] What are you crying about? If you'd been a nice girl, you wouldn't have anything to cry about.

DUNYÁSHA [*powders her nose in a mirror*] Don't forget to send me a letter
120 from Paris. Because I loved you, Yásha, I really did. I'm a very sensitive person, Yásha, I really am—

YÁSHA Watch it, someone's coming. [*He starts fussing with the luggage, whistling quietly.*]

[*Enter* LIUBÓV, GÁYEV, ÁNYA, *and* CARLOTTA.]

GÁYEV We should be going. We're already a little late. [*Looks at* YÁSHA.] Who smells like herring?

125 LIUBÓV ANDRÉYEVNA We've only got ten minutes; then we absolutely must start out. [*Glances around the room.*] Goodbye, house! Wonderful old house! Winter's almost here, and come spring you'll be gone. They'll tear you down. Think of everything these walls have seen! [*Kisses* ÁNYA *with great feeling.*] My treasure, look at you! You're radiant today! Your eyes are
130 shining like diamonds! Are you happy? Really happy?

ÁNYA Oh, yes, Mama, really! We're starting a new life!

GÁYEV She's right—everything worked out extremely well. Before the cherry orchard was sold we were at our wit's end—remember how painful it was?—and now everything's finally settled, once and for all, no turning
135 back, and see? We've all calmed down. We're even rather happy. I'm going to work at the bank, I'm about to become a financier! Yellow ball in the side pocket . . . And you look better than you have in a long time, Lyúba; you do, you know.

LIUBÓV ANDRÉYEVNA I know. My nerves have quieted down. You're quite
140 right.

[*Someone holds out her hat and coat.*]

And I sleep much better now. Take my things, Yásha, will you? It's time to go. [*To* ÁNYA] Darling, we'll see each other soon enough. I'm off to Paris—I kept the money your godmother in Yároslavl sent to buy the estate. [*A hard laugh*] Thank God for the old lady! That ought to get me through the
145 winter at least. . . .

ÁNYA And you'll come back soon, won't you? You promise? I'll study hard and get my diploma, and then I'll get a job and help you out. We can read together the way we used to, can't we? [*Kisses her mother's hands.*] We'll spend long autumn evenings together; we'll read lots of books and learn all
150 about the wonderful new world of the future. . . . [*Dreamily*] Don't forget, Mama, you promised. . . .

8. Long live France! (French).

LIUBÓV ANDRÉYEVNA   I will, my angel, I promise. [*Embraces her.*]

    [*Enter* LOPÁKHIN. CARLOTTA *hums a tune under her breath.*]

GÁYEV   Carlotta must be happy; she's singing!

CARLOTTA [*picks up a bundle that looks like a baby in swaddling clothes*] Here's my little baby. Bye, bye, baby . . .

    [*We hear a baby's voice: "Wah! Wah!"*]

155   Shh, baby, shh, shh . . . good little children don't cry. . . .

    [*Again: "Wah! Wah!"*]

I feel so sorry for the poor thing. [*Hurls the bundle to the floor.*] You will find me a job, won't you? I can't go on like this any more.

LOPÁKHIN   Don't worry, Carlotta; we'll take care of you.

GÁYEV   Everybody's just thrown us away. Várya's leaving. . . . All of a sudden
160   we're useless.

CARLOTTA   How can I live in that town of yours? There must be someplace I can go. . . . [*Hums.*] What difference does it make . . . ?

    [*Enter* PÍSHCHIK.]

LOPÁKHIN   Here comes the wonder boy.

PÍSHCHIK [*panting*]   Ooh, give me a minute . . . I'm all worn out. Good
165   morning, good morning, good morning. Could I get a drink of water?

GÁYEV [*sarcastic*]   You're sure it isn't money you want? You'll all have to excuse me if I remove myself from the approaching negotiations.

    [*Goes out.*]

PÍSHCHIK   I'm so glad to see you all. . . . Dear lady . . . I've been a stranger, I know. [*To* LOPÁKHIN] And you're here too. Delighted, delighted, a man I
170   admire, always have. . . . Here. Here. This is for you. [*Gives* LOPÁKHIN *money.*] Four hundred. And I still owe you eight hundred and forty.

LOPÁKHIN [*a bewildered shrug*]   I must be dreaming. Where did you get money?

PÍSHCHIK   Wait a minute; let me cool off. Well, it was an absolutely extra-
175   ordinary thing. These Englishmen showed up, they poked around on my land, found some kind of white clay. . . . [*To* LIUBÓV] Here . . . Here's the four hundred. You've been so kind . . . so sweet . . . [*Gives her money.*] And you'll have the rest before you know it. [*Takes a drink of water.*] You know, there was a young man on the train just now, he was saying . . . there was
180   this philosopher, he said, who wanted us all to jump off the roof. "Jump!" he said. "Jump!" That was his whole philosophy. [*Amazed*] Really! I don't believe it! Give me some more water. . . .

LOPÁKHIN   What Englishmen are you talking about?

PÍSHCHIK   I gave them a lease on the land, the place where the clay is, a
185   twenty-four-year lease. And now excuse me, but I'm off. Lots of people to see, pay back what I owe. I owe money all over the place. [*Takes a drink of water.*] Well, I just wanted to say hello. I'll come by again on Thursday.

LIUBÓV ANDRÉYEVNA   But we're leaving for town today. And tomorrow I'm going back to Paris.

190 PÍSHCHIK   What? [*Astonished*] Leaving for town? Oh, my . . . Oh, of course; the furniture's gone. And all these trunks. I didn't realize. [*Almost in tears*] I didn't realize. Great thinkers, these English . . . God bless you all. And be happy. I didn't realize. Well, all things must come to an end. [*Kisses* LIUBÓV's *hand.*] I'll come to an end myself one of these days. And when I do, I want

195 you all to say: "Semyónov-Píshchik . . . he was a good old horse. God bless him." Wonderful weather we're having. Yes. . . . [*Starts out, overcome with emotion, stops in the doorway and turns.*] Oh, by the way, Dáshenka says hello.

[*Goes out.*]

LIUBÓV ANDRÉYEVNA Now we can go. There are just two things still on my
200 mind. The first is old Firs. [*Looks at her watch.*] We've still got five minutes. . . .

ÁNYA Mama, they took Firs to the nursing home this morning. Yásha took care of it.

LIUBÓV ANDRÉYEVNA . . . And then there's our Várya. She's used to getting
205 up early and working around here all day long, and now she's . . . out of a job. Like a fish out of water. Poor thing—she's so nervous, she cries, she's losing weight . . .

[*Pause.*]

You know, Yermolái Alexéyich—well, of course you know—I'd always dreamed . . . always dreamed she'd marry you; you know we all think it's
210 a wonderful idea. . . . [*Whispers to* ÁNYA, *who nods to* CARLOTTA; *they both leave.*] She loves you, you like her. . . . I don't know why, I just don't know why the two of you keep avoiding the issue. Really!

LOPÁKHIN I don't know why either. It's all a little funny. Well, I don't mind. If there's still time, I'll do it. . . . All right, *basta*,[9] let's just get it over with.
215 But I don't know, I don't think I can propose without you—

LIUBÓV ANDRÉYEVNA Of course you can. All it takes is a minute. I'll send her right in. . . .

LOPÁKHIN We've even got some champagne all ready. [*Looks at the tray of empty glasses.*] Or at least we did. Somebody must have drunk it all up.

[YÁSHA *coughs.*]

220 Guzzled it down, I should say.

LIUBÓV ANDRÉYEVNA Wonderful! We'll leave you alone. Yásha, *allez!*[1] I'll go call her. [*At the door*] Várya, leave that alone; come here a minute, will you? Come on, dear!

[*Goes out with* YÁSHA.]

LOPÁKHIN [*looks at his watch*] Well . . .

[*Pause. A few stifled laughs and whispers behind the door. Finally* VÁRYA *enters.*]

225 VÁRYA [*examines the luggage; takes her time*] That's funny, I can't find them. . . .

LOPÁKHIN What are you looking for?

VÁRYA I packed them myself, and now I don't remember where.

[*Pause.*]

LOPÁKHIN What . . . ah . . . where are you off to, Várya?

VÁRYA Me? I'm going to work for the Ragúlins. I talked to them about it
230 already; they need a housekeeper. And look after things, you know. . . .

LOPÁKHIN All the way over there? That's fifty miles away.

[*Pause.*]

Well, looks like this is the end of things around here. . . .

9. Enough (Italian).   1. Go on! (French).

VÁRYA [*still examining the luggage*] Where are they . . . ? Or maybe I put
them in the trunk. You're right: this is the end of things here. The end of
235 one life—

LOPÁKHIN I'm going too. To Hárkov. Taking the same train, actually. I've got
a million things waiting for me. I'm leaving Yepikhódov, though. Hired him
to take charge here.

VÁRYA You hired *who*?

240 LOPÁKHIN Last year this time it was snowing already, remember? Today it's
still sunny. Nice day. A little chilly, though . . . It was freezing this morning;
must have been in the thirties.

VÁRYA I didn't notice.

[*Pause.*]

Anyway, the thermometer's broken.

[*Pause. A voice from outside calls: "Lopákhin!"*]

245 LOPÁKHIN [*as if he'd been waiting for the call*] I'm coming!

[*Goes out.*]

[VÁRYA *sits down on the floor, leans her head on a bundle of dresses, and
cries. The door opens;* LIUBÓV *enters carefully.*]

LIUBÓV ANDRÉYEVNA Well?

[*Pause.*]

We have to go.

VÁRYA [*already stopped crying, wipes her eyes*] Right, Mama, we have to go.
I can get to the Ragúlins' today, if I don't miss the train.

250 LIUBÓV ANDRÉYEVNA Ánya, get your coat on.

[*Enter* ÁNYA, GÁYEV, CARLOTTA. GÁYEV *wears a winter overcoat. Servants
and drivers come in to pick up the luggage.* YEPIKHÓDOV *directs the
operation.*]

Well, we're ready to start.

ÁNYA [*joyfully*] Ready to start!

GÁYEV My dear friends, my very dear friends! On this occasion, this farewell
to our beloved house, I cannot keep still. I feel I must say a few words to
255 express the emotion that overwhelms me, overwhelms us all—

ÁNYA [*pleads*] Uncle, please!

VÁRYA That's enough, Uncle.

GÁYEV [*crushed*] All right . . . Yellow ball in the side pocket . . . I'll keep still.

[*Enter* TROFÍMOV, *then* LOPÁKHIN.]

TROFÍMOV Ladies and gentlemen, time to go! You'll be late!

260 LOPÁKHIN Yepikhódov, get my coat.

LIUBÓV ANDRÉYEVNA Let me stay a little minute longer. I never really noticed
these walls before, or the ceilings. I want a last look, one last long look. . . .

GÁYEV I remember when I was six, I was watching out that window, right
over there. It was a holy day, Trinity Sunday,[2] I think, and I saw Father on
265 his way to church. . . .

LIUBÓV ANDRÉYEVNA Have we got everything?

---

2. A celebration of the Christian doctrine of
the Trinity (the belief that the Father, Son,
and Holy Spirit exist together in God); in
Eastern Christianity it falls on Pentecost
(seven weeks after Easter).

LOPÁKHIN I guess so. [*To* YEPIKHÓDOV, *who helps him on with his coat*] You
keep an eye on things, Yepikhódov.

YEPIKHÓDOV [*loud, businesslike tone*] You can count on me, Yermolái
270 Alexéyich!

LOPÁKHIN Why are you talking like that all of a sudden?

YEPIKHÓDOV I just had a drink—water. . . . It went down the wrong way.

YÁSHA [*with contempt*] Dumb hick!

LIUBÓV ANDRÉYEVNA We're all going away. There won't be a soul left on the
275 place. . . .

LOPÁKHIN But wait till you see what happens here come spring!

[VÁRYA *grabs an umbrella from the luggage, as if she were going to hit*
him. LOPÁKHIN *pretends to be terrified.*]

VÁRYA Don't get excited. It was just a joke.

TROFÍMOV You've all got to get moving! It's time to go! You'll miss your train!

VÁRYA Here's your galoshes, Pétya, behind this suitcase. [*With tears in her*
280 *eyes*] Smelly old things . . .

TROFÍMOV [*puts them on*] It's time to go!

GÁYEV [*deeply moved, afraid he'll start crying*] Yes, the train . . . mustn't miss
the train . . . Yellow ball in the side pocket, white in the corner . . .

LIUBÓV ANDRÉYEVNA Let's go!

285 LOPÁKHIN Everybody here? Nobody left? [*Closes and locks the door, left.*]
Got to lock up; I've got a few things stored here. All right, let's go!

ÁNYA Goodbye, house! Goodbye, old life!

TROFÍMOV No, hello, new life!

[*Goes out with Ánya.*]

[VÁRYA *looks around the room again; she's not eager to go.* YÁSHA *goes out*
with CARLOTTA *and her little dog.*]

LOPÁKHIN So. Until next spring. Come on, let's go, everybody. Goodbye!

[LIUBÓV *and* GÁYEV *are left alone. It's as if they'd been waiting for this*
moment. They throw their arms around each other and burst out crying,
but try to keep the others outside from hearing.]

290 GÁYEV [*in despair*] Oh, sister, sister . . .

LIUBÓV ANDRÉYEVNA Oh, my orchard, my beautiful orchard! My life, my
youth, my happiness, goodbye! Goodbye! Goodbye!

[ÁNYA's *voice, joyful:* "Mama!" TROFÍMOV's *voice, joyful, excited:*
"Yoo-hoo!"]

These walls, these windows, for the last time . . . And Mama loved this
room . . .

295 GÁYEV Oh, sister, sister . . .

[ÁNYA: "Mama!" TROFÍMOV: "Yoo-hoo!"]

LIUBÓV ANDRÉYEVNA We're coming!

[*They leave.*]

[*The stage is empty. We hear the sound of the door being locked, then the*
carriages as they drive away. It grows very quiet. In the silence, we hear
the occasional sound of an ax chopping down the cherry trees, a mourn-
ful, lonely sound. Then we hear steps. Enter FIRS *from the door, right. He*
wears his usual butler's livery, but with bedroom slippers. He's very ill.]

FIRS [*goes to the door, tries the handle*] Locked. They're gone. [*Sits on the*
sofa.] They forgot about me. That's all right; I'll just sit here for a bit. . . .

300 And Leoníd Andréyich probably forgot his winter coat. [*A worried sigh*] I should have looked. . . . He's still all wet, that one. . . . [*Mumbles something we can't make out.*] Well, it's all over now, and I never even had a life to live. . . . [*Lies back.*] I'll just lie here for a bit. . . . No strength left, nothing left, not a thing . . . Oh, you. You young flibbertigibbet. [*Lies there, no longer moving.*]

> [*In the distance we hear a sound that seems to come from the sky, a sad sound, like a string snapping. It dies away. Everything grows quiet. We can hear the occasional sound of an ax on a tree.*]
>
> *Curtain.*

JOHN MILLINGTON SYNGE

1871–1909

IRELAND, which has spent much of the past five hundred years under the political and cultural domination of its larger neighbor, has played an important role in the modern English theater. William Congreve (1670–1729), RICHARD BRINSLEY SHERIDAN (1751–1816), Oliver Goldsmith (1730–1774), OSCAR WILDE (1854–1900), and GEORGE BERNARD SHAW (1856–1950) were all raised in Ireland before making their fortunes on the London stage. But although Dublin had long been an important theatrical center, Ireland did not achieve a truly national drama until the Irish Renaissance of the late nineteenth century. This movement, which brought to culture and the arts the same drive for self-determination that marked Irish nationalism in the political arena, was distinguished by a reaction against the English literary tradition, an interest in Irish folklore and the Gaelic language, and a focus on Irish themes and topics. Though the Irish Renaissance saw remarkable achievements in poetry and the other arts, some of its most enduring contributions were in drama and theater. In 1899 the Irish poet William Butler Yeats, Lady Augusta Gregory, and Edward Martyn formed the Irish Literary Theatre "to bring upon the stage the deeper thoughts and emotions of Ireland." Their vision of a native Irish theater was soon realized. The Abbey Theatre, which opened in Dublin in 1904, became one of the leading theaters of the twentieth century, and its actors were quickly recognized as forming one of the premier English-speaking companies of their time. In conjunction with these theatrical developments, the Irish Renaissance witnessed a flourishing of dramatic writing as authors availed themselves of a medium newly dedicated to Irish subjects. In one of these writers—John Millington Synge—Ireland produced one of the greatest playwrights of the modern stage. Embracing the poetic as well as the ironic, Synge challenged the theatrical assumptions of his contemporaries with a drama of exceptional vitality, lyricism, and satiric power.

Synge's reputation rests on six plays written between 1902 and 1909. With the exception of *Deirdre of the Sorrows* (1909), which dramatizes a tragic story from Celtic mythology, these plays are set in the hills and hearths of contemporary rural Ireland. In Wicklow, Galway, Kerry, Mayo, and the Aran Islands—regions of the country that he visited throughout his life—Synge found a natural world characterized by beauty and elemental power and a people steeped in folklore and tradition. The Irish peasants also spoke poetic, syntactically rich dialects of English that set them apart from the metropolitan inhabitants of Dublin and cities elsewhere in the British Isles. In his preface to *The Playboy of the Western World* (1907), Synge contrasted the natural poetry of rural speech with the language of cities and towns, and he set himself against HENRIK IBSEN (1828–1906), Émile Zola (1840–1902), and other proponents of dramatic naturalism who dealt with the reality of life "in joyless and pallid words." Arguing that every speech in a good play should be "as fully flavored as a nut or apple," Synge justified his dramatic use of this dialect: "In Ireland, for a few years more, we have a popular imagination that is fiery and magnificent, and tender; so that those of us who wish to write start with a chance that is not given to writers in places where the springtime of the local life has been forgotten, and the harvest is a memory only, and the straw has been turned into bricks."

The beliefs and concerns expressed in Synge's preface were not new, of course. European Romantic writers had celebrated nature and its rural inhabitants since the early nineteenth century, and the study of folklore and popular legends and mythology had been central to Romantic nationalism since Johann Gottfried von Herder first advocated preserving indigenous folk material in the eighteenth century. In Ireland, amateur and professional ethnographers began conducting fieldwork in the western counties in the 1890s, and the Gaelic League was founded in Dublin in 1893 "for the purpose of keeping the Irish language spoken in Ireland." But though Synge's interest in rural Ireland may have been inspired by these broader intellectual and cultural currents, his plays refuse to idealize or sentimentalize the primitive life he found there. While Synge's drama captures the traditions and lyricism of the Irish peasantry, it also portrays the harsher side of its behaviors and beliefs. In his essay "J. M. Synge and the Ireland of His Time," published two years after the playwright's death, Yeats wrote: "He loves all that has edge, all that is salt in the mouth, all that is rough to the hand, all that heightens the emotions by contrast, all that stings into life the sense of tragedy." Deeply ironic, even satiric at times, plays such as *In the Shadow of the Glen* (1903) and *The Playboy of the Western World* juxtapose poetic celebration with bitter comedy and a tragic sense of loss. Given how deeply his Dublin audience was invested in heroic or nostalgic images of the Irish peasantry during a time of intense nationalism, it should come as no surprise that this greatest of Irish playwrights was harshly criticized by many of his contemporaries.

Edmund John Millington Synge (the name is pronounced "sing") was born on April 16, 1871, in Rathfarnham, a suburb south of Dublin, to landowning Anglo-Irish parents of Protestant descent. A sickly child whose early years were solitary, he eventually was tutored at home in lieu of attending school. Having discovered a love for taking long walks in the Irish countryside, he developed an early interest in natural history; he later would join the Dublin Naturalists' Field Club. When, at the age of fourteen, he read *The Descent of Man* (1871) by Charles Darwin, Synge underwent a crisis of faith that led him, three years later, to renounce Christianity. Turning his attention from science to the arts, he began studying the violin at the age of sixteen. While enrolled at Trinity College in Dublin, where he studied Gaelic and Hebrew, he also attended the Royal Irish Academy of Music; upon receiving a B.A. from Trinity he continued his musical studies in Germany. Synge lacked the temperament to be a professional musician, however, and in 1894 he moved to Paris to study language and literature at the Sorbonne and support himself teaching English. He had been composing poems for several years and was determined to launch a career as a writer and critic.

During the years in which he distanced himself from his Protestant family upbringing, Synge had grown increasingly engaged with Irish culture. "Everything Irish became sacred," he later wrote, "and had a charm that was neither quite human nor divine." At the Sorbonne, he attended lectures on Celtic civilization; and in 1896 he met Yeats and Maud Gonne, who were at the center of a circle of revolutionary nationalists living in Paris. It was Yeats who advised him to abandon the self-consciously modern poetry he had been writing and to embrace the life of one of

Ireland's most primitive regions: "Give up Paris, you will never create anything by reading Racine and Arthur Symons will always be a better critic of French literature. Go to the Aran Islands. Live there as if you were one of the people themselves; express a life that has never found expression." The Aran Islands (Inishmore, Inishmaan, and Inisheer) are located 30 miles off the west coast of Ireland in Galway Bay; bearing the brunt of the North Atlantic, they are characterized by harsh conditions and a rugged, treeless beauty. Following Yeats's advice, Synge spent two weeks on the islands in 1898, the first of five such visits he would make over the next four and a half years. He stayed with the Aran Islanders, who spoke Gaelic (and only occasionally English); observed their lives, customs, and speech; and listened to their stories and other lore. In Aran, he wrote, he felt in touch with a "world of inarticulate power." While Synge gathered his notes into a book titled *The Aran Islands* (published in 1907), his observations and experiences in Aran (and elsewhere in Ireland) would find their fullest artistic form in the drama they inspired.

Synge's earliest attempt at playwriting was *When the Moon Has Set* (written 1901), a melodramatic, loosely autobiographical drama that Yeats and Lady Gregory rejected for production by the Irish Literary Theater on artistic grounds. It was not until 1902 that Synge abandoned autobiography and wrote two one-act plays set in the communities of rural Ireland. *In the Shadow of the Glen*, produced in October 1903 by the newly formed Irish National Theatre Society at Molesworth Hall, also established his turbulent relationship with the Dublin theatergoing public. The story of a Wicklow man who feigns death in order to catch his wife in an act of infidelity, *In the Shadow of the Glen* was condemned by many of its reviewers as an attack on Irish womanhood and the institution of marriage. RIDERS TO THE SEA, which opened on February 25, 1904, at Molesworth, received scattered criticism, though its tragic beauty was also recognized, and it quickly became Synge's most acclaimed play. Other plays soon followed, including *The Well of the Saints*, produced at the recently opened Abbey

Theatre in February 1905. This play, about a blind couple who have their sight miraculously restored but eventually choose to return to blindness, was attacked by many as un-Irish. *The Tinker's Wedding*, which Synge wrote between 1902 and 1906, is the story of an indigent couple who try to trick a priest into marrying them; broadly comic, it was considered so inflammatory that it was not staged in Ireland until after Synge's death.

Nothing in the critical responses to these earlier plays, contentious though they often were, could have prepared Synge and his colleagues at the Irish National Theatre Society for the uproar that greeted his three-act play *The Playboy of the Western World* in January 1907 (in 1905 Synge had become the company's co-director; it had replaced the Irish Literary Theatre). Based on a tale that Synge heard in the Aran Islands, *Playboy* is the story of villagers on the coast of Mayo who take in a fugitive claiming to have murdered his father. The young man, named Christy, captivates his protectors with his tale of heroic transgression, and he woos the tavern keeper's daughter, Pegeen Mike, with his poetic speech. After his father unexpectedly shows up, though, wounded but not dead, the villagers turn on Christy—and when he tries in earnest to kill his father they set about to lynch him in a scene of jarring cruelty. With the lines between comedy and the noncomic blurred beyond recognition, Christy and his father depart, cursing the villagers for their villainy.

"The Playboy Riots," as the play's initial performances have come to be known, were among the most violent in the history of the modern theater. The play's opening-night audience sat through the first two acts in relative, if ominous, calm; but when one of the play's characters used the word "shift" (i.e., a woman's undergarment) in the third act, an uproar ensued. At performances over the following week, police were repeatedly called in as audience members grew increasingly violent in their attempts to shout down the actors. Yeats stood up and lectured the audience on their obligation to let the play be heard. Those in the audience who rioted were clearly outraged at Synge's portrayal of rural Ireland, a representation at odds with the idealized images championed by Irish nationalism. One reviewer called *The Playboy of the Western World* "an unmitigated, protracted libel upon Irish peasant men and, worse still, upon Irish peasant girlhood." That Synge himself had come from the Anglo-Irish ruling class only fanned the resentment of his audience. Though the play drew favorable attention when it was performed in London one year later, its Dublin reception guaranteed its notoriety in Ireland for decades.

Riders to the Sea, considered by many to be the finest one-act play ever written, is an exception among Synge's mature plays. Lacking the satiric realism of the later comedies, it resembles the drama of AESCHYLUS and SOPHOCLES in its simplicity of action and its atmosphere of tragic inevitability. Its world is harsh, elemental, and marked by hardship and loss but also given to moments of intense lyricism. *Riders* opens in the Aran cottage of Maurya, who has lost her husband and four of six sons to the sea. The setting is stark: nets, oilskins, a spinning wheel, and a pot-oven for cooking bread on the fire are among the few props. Several new boards stand by the wall, purchased (it turns out) to furnish a coffin for her son Michael, who is presumed to be lost at sea. Cathleen and Nora, Maurya's daughters, have been given articles of clothing found on a drowned man in Donegal, and they hide these from their mother until they have the chance to positively identify them as Michael's. Before they can do so, Maurya's youngest son, Bartley, announces that he will travel by sea in order to sell horses at the Galway fair. She pleads with him not to go, but he dismisses her concerns and leaves before she gives him her blessing. When Maurya follows Bartley to provide that blessing and some bread for his journey, she has a vision that foretells his death: as Bartley rides by the spring well on his red mare, she sees Michael riding in fine clothes on the gray pony that follows him. This fatal omen is shortly fulfilled, and the remainder of Synge's play deals with the aftermath of such irrevocable loss.

Synge drew extensively on his experiences in the Aran Islands when writing *Riders to the Sea*: riding in a curragh on a turbulent sea, attending the burial and funeral of a young man who had drowned, listening to stories like one about a woman who had a vision of her dead son riding a horse. For the original Irish National Theatre Society production, Synge insisted the play's realistic elements be recognized: the actors were shod in authentic pampooties (a form of footwear used on the slippery rocks of the Aran Islands), and they were taught how to deliver the funeral keen by a woman from Galway. But realism in *Riders to the Sea* continually drifts into the mythic and the supernatural. Maurya and her two daughters recall Clotho, Lachesis, and Atropos, the three Fates of Greek mythology, who determine human life and death. Maurya's name echoes *moira* (the Greek word for fate or destiny), and the prominent spinning wheel suggests the wheel on which Clotho spins the thread of life. The death of Bartley recalls that of Hippolytus, dragged along the seacoast by his horses, as told in EURIPIDES' *Hippolytus* (428 B.C.E.) and RACINE's *PHÈDRE* (1677). There is Christian imagery, as well: the bread that Maurya forgets to give to her son resembles the Eucharist, and the gray horse with its ghostly rider recalls the book of Revelation: "And I saw, and behold, a pale horse, and its rider's name was Death." Finally, the action of *Riders to the Sea* is also shaped by Irish folk beliefs and traditions. The gray horse bears traces of the *púca*, a malevolent fairy spirit of Irish myth that takes the form of a horse and lures people to their death.

In part because of these mythic elements, the play's characters and actions acquire a quality of timelessness: present and past give way to a vision of universal loss that transcends time and place. In *The Aran Islands* Synge describes sitting with a group of fishermen on the shore: "I could not help feeling that I was talking with men who were under a judgment of death." The sense of fatality that permeates *Riders to the Sea* derives from a tragic loss enacted over and over again. This inevitability is conveyed in the play's language, which moves in cadences and participial phrases that interrupt linear sequence and bring the past into the present: "I'm after seeing him this day, and he riding and galloping." Individual words and phrases, such as Cathleen's descrip-

Brigit O'Dempsey, Sara Algood, and Maire O'Neill in the 1906 production of *Riders to the Sea*.

tion of string tied around a bundle of clothes as "perished with the salt water," have a fatalistic resonance. When Maurya delivers her powerful laments at the end of the play, surrounded by the women who represent the island community, she speaks not only of individual loss but of a condition. Religion—represented by the young priest who assures Nora that God would not leave her mother destitute "with no son living"—offers little solace in this case. The afterlife of Christian faith is decidedly absent from Synge's play. As in the tragedies of Sophocles or the elegies of Anglo-Saxon England, the mood is much darker. Writing of the play, Yeats observed, "The old woman in *Riders to the Sea*, in mourning for her six fine sons, mourns for the passing of all beauty and strength."

The years after Synge's early plays were themselves shadowed by mortality. In 1906 Synge became engaged to Molly Allgood, an actress of the Abbey company who would play the role of Pegeen Mike in *The Playboy of the Western World*. Because of Synge's deteriorating health, though, they never married. Swelling in his neck, which had first troubled him in 1897, confirmed that he had Hodgkin's disease, and a tumor discovered in his side in 1908 proved inoperable. Synge died in a Dublin nursing home on March 24, 1909. *Deirdre of the Sorrows*, which Synge left incomplete at his death, was arranged into an acting version by Yeats, Lady Gregory, and Allgood and performed at the Abbey Theatre the following year. A story of tragic love, the play is set in the world of Irish mythology with its kings, bards, warriors, and maidens. In dramatizing this world *Deirdre of the Sorrows* recalls the work of others in the Irish Renaissance, such as Yeats, who wrote about the heroic age of Irish myth and legend. But as one contemporary reviewer noted, Synge's concern in working with this mythological material was less to celebrate this age, ethereal and remote, than "to wrest the legend from its exalted plane and breathe the commonplaces of everyday life into it." In that effort, Synge's unfinished drama achieves what *Riders to the Sea* and his other plays do so notably: it brings the ordinary and the poetic together in new, deeply theatrical ways.

S.G.

Riders to the Sea

CHARACTERS

MAURYA, an old woman
BARTLEY, her son
CATHLEEN, her daughter

NORA, a younger daughter
MEN and WOMEN

SCENE: *An island off the West of Ireland.*[1]

> [*Cottage kitchen, with nets, oilskins, spinning-wheel, some new boards standing by the wall, etc.* CATHLEEN, *a girl of about twenty, finishes kneading cake, and puts it down in the pot-oven*[2] *by the fire; then wipes her hands, and begins to spin at the wheel.* NORA, *a young girl, puts her head in at the door.*]

NORA [*in a low voice*]   Where is she?

CATHLEEN   She's lying down, God help her, and maybe sleeping, if she's able.

> [NORA *comes in softly, and takes a bundle from under her shawl.*]

[*Spinning the wheel rapidly*] What is it you have?

5 NORA   The young priest is after bringing them. It's a shirt and a plain stocking were got off a drowned man in Donegal.[3]

> [CATHLEEN *stops her wheel with a sudden movement, and leans out to listen.*]

We're to find out if it's Michael's they are, some time herself will be down looking by the sea.

---

1. Synge's play is set on Inishmore, the largest of the three Aran Islands, located about 15 miles off the west coast of Ireland.
2. A heated iron plate, made into an oven by being covered by a pot on which embers are

heaped; it was used to bake "cake," a small, flattened form of bread.
3. A county on the northwest coast of Ireland, more than 100 miles north of the Aran Islands. *After*: to have just (done something).

10 CATHLEEN How would they be Michael's, Nora? How
      would he go the length of that way to the far north?
    NORA The young priest says he's known the like of it. 'If
      it's Michael's they are,' says he, 'you can tell herself he's
      got a clean burial, by the grace of God; and if they're not
15   his, let no one say a word about them, for she'll be get-
      ting her death,' says he, 'with crying and lamenting.'
              [*The door which* NORA *half closed is blown open by a*
              gust of wind.]
    CATHLEEN [*looking out anxiously*]   Did you ask him would
      he stop Bartley going this day with the horses to the Gal-
      way[4] fair?
20 NORA 'I won't stop him,' says he; 'but let you not be afraid.
      Herself does be saying prayers half through the night,
      and the Almighty God won't leave her destitute,' says he,
      'with no son living.'
    CATHLEEN Is the sea bad by the white rocks, Nora?
25 NORA Middling bad, God help us. There's a great roaring
      in the west, and it's worse it'll be getting when the tide's
      turned to° the wind. [*She goes over to the table with the*   against
      bundle.] Shall I open it now?
    CATHLEEN Maybe she'd wake up on us, and come in before
30   we'd done. [*Coming to the table*] It's a long time we'll be,
      and the two of us crying.
    NORA [*goes to the inner door and listens*] She's moving
      about on the bed. She'll be coming in a minute.
    CATHLEEN Give me the ladder, and I'll put them up in the
35   turf loft,[5] the way° she won't know of them at all, and   so that
      maybe when the tide turns she'll be going down to see
      would he be floating from the east.
              [*They put the ladder against the gable of the chim-*
              ney; CATHLEEN *goes up a few steps and hides the*
              bundle in the turf loft. MAURYA *comes from the inner*
              room.]
    MAURYA [*looking up at* CATHLEEN *and speaking querulously*]
      Isn't it turf enough you have for this day and evening?
    CATHLEEN There's a cake baking at the fire for a short
40   space [*throwing down the turf*], and Bartley will want it
      when the tide turns if he goes to Connemara.[6]
              [NORA *picks up the turf and puts it round the pot-oven.*]
    MAURYA [*sitting down on a stool at the fire*] He won't go this
      day with the wind rising from the south and west. He
      won't go this day, for the young priest will stop him surely.
45 NORA He'll not stop him, mother; and I heard Eamon
      Simon and Stephen Pheety and Colum Shawn saying he
      would go.

4. A county and town on the west coast of   as fuel for fires.
Ireland, northeast of the Aran Islands.   6. A mountainous peninsula on the Galway
5. Loft for storing turf (peat), which was used   coast, north of the Aran Islands.

MAURYA   Where is he itself?°   (*i.e, himself*)

NORA   He went down to see would there be another boat
50   sailing in the week, and I'm thinking it won't be long till
he's here now, for the tide's turning at the green head,
and the hooker's[7] tacking from the east.

CATHLEEN   I hear someone passing the big stones.

NORA [*looking out*]   He's coming now, and he in a hurry.

BARTLEY [*comes in and looks round the room. Speaking sadly*
55   *and quietly*]   Where is the bit of new rope, Cathleen,
was bought in Connemara?

CATHLEEN [*coming down*]   Give it to him, Nora; it's on a
nail by the white boards. I hung it up this morning, for
the pig with the black feet was eating it.

60 NORA [*giving him a rope*]   Is that it, Bartley?

MAURYA   You'd do right to leave that rope, Bartley, hanging
by the boards. [BARTLEY *takes the rope.*] It will be wanting
in this place, I'm telling you, if Michael is washed up tomorrow morning, or the next morning, or any morning
65   in the week; for it's a deep grave we'll make him, by the
grace of God.

BARTLEY [*beginning to work with the rope*]   I've no halter
the way I can ride down on the mare, and I must go now
quickly. This is the one boat going for two weeks or
70   beyond it, and the fair will be a good fair for horses, I
heard them saying below.

MAURYA   It's a hard thing they'll be saying below if the body
is washed up and there's no man in it to make the coffin,
and I after giving a big price for the finest white boards
75   you'd find in Connemara. [*She looks round at the boards.*]

BARTLEY   How would it be washed up, and we after looking each day for nine days, and a strong wind blowing a
while back from the west and south?

MAURYA   If it isn't found itself, that wind is raising the sea,
80   and there was a star up against the moon, and it rising in
the night. If it was a hundred horses, or a thousand
horses you had itself, what is the price of a thousand
horses against a son where there is one son only?

BARTLEY [*working at the halter, to* CATHLEEN]   Let you go
85   down each day, and see the sheep aren't jumping in on
the rye, and if the jobber° comes you can sell the pig   livestock dealer
with the black feet if there is a good price going.

MAURYA   How would the like of her get a good price for a pig?

BARTLEY [*to* CATHLEEN]   If the west winds holds with the
90   last bit of the moon let you and Nora get up weed enough
for another cock for the kelp.[8] It's hard set we'll be from
this day with no one in it but one man to work.

---

7. A light single-masted fishing vessel. *Green*
head: grassy headland or promontory.

8. That is, gather enough kelp (used as fertil-
izer) to form another cone-shaped mound.

MAURYA   It's hard set we'll be surely the day you're drowned
with the rest. What way will I live and the girls with me,
95   and I an old woman looking for the grave?

> [BARTLEY *lays down the halter, takes off his old coat,
> and puts on a newer one of the same flannel.*]

BARTLEY [*to* NORA]   Is she coming to the pier?

NORA [*looking out*]   She's passing the green head and letting fall her sails.

BARTLEY [*getting his purse° and tobacco*]   I'll have half an   money bag
100   hour to go down, and you'll see me coming again in two
days, or in three days, or maybe in four days if the wind
is bad.

MAURYA [*turning round to the fire, and putting her shawl
over her head*]   Isn't it a hard and cruel man won't hear
a word from an old woman, and she holding him from
105   the sea?

CATHLEEN   It's the life of a young man to be going to the
sea, and who would listen to an old woman with one
thing and she saying it over?

BARTLEY [*taking the halter*]   I must go now quickly. I'll ride
110   down on the red mare, and the grey pony 'ill run behind
me. . . . The blessing of God on you.   [*He goes out.*]

MAURYA [*crying out as he is in the door*]   He's gone now,
God spare us, and we'll not see him again. He's gone
now, and when the black night is falling I'll have no son
115   left me in the world.

CATHLEEN   Why wouldn't you give him your blessing and
he looking round in the door? Isn't it sorrow enough is
on every one in this house without your sending him out
with an unlucky word behind him, and a hard word in
120   his ear?

> [MAURYA *takes up the tongs and begins raking the fire
> aimlessly without looking round.*]

NORA [*turning towards her*]   You're taking away the turf
from the cake.[9]

CATHLEEN [*crying out*]   The Son of God forgive us, Nora,
we're after forgetting his bit of bread. [*She comes over to
the fire.*]

125   NORA   And it's destroyed° he'll be going till dark night, and   exhausted
he after eating nothing since the sun went up.

CATHLEEN [*turning the cake out of the oven*]   It's destroyed
he'll be surely. There's no sense left on any person in a
house where an old woman will be talking for ever.

> [MAURYA *sways herself on her stool.*]

[*Cutting off some of the bread and rolling it in a cloth; to*
MAURYA.]

---

9. That is, preventing the bread from baking.

130   Let you go down now to the spring well and give him this
and he passing. You'll see him then and the dark word
will be broken, and you can say 'God speed you,' the way
he'll be easy in his mind.

MAURYA [*taking the bread*]   Will I be in it° as soon as   *there*
135   himself?

CATHLEEN   If you go now quickly.

MAURYA [*standing up unsteadily*]   It's hard set I am to walk.

CATHLEEN [*looking at her anxiously*]   Give her the stick,
Nora, or maybe she'll slip on the big stones.

140 NORA   What stick?

CATHLEEN   The stick Michael brought from Connemara.

MAURYA [*taking a stick* NORA *gives her*]   In the big world
the old people do be leaving things after them for their
sons and children, but in this place it is the young men
145   do be leaving things behind for them that do be old.

        [*She goes out slowly.* NORA *goes over to the ladder.*]

CATHLEEN   Wait, Nora, maybe she'd turn back quickly.
She's that sorry,° God help her, you wouldn't know the
thing she'd do.

NORA   Is she gone round by the bush?

150 CATHLEEN [*looking out*]   She's gone now. Throw it down
quickly, for the Lord knows when she'll be out of it
again.

NORA [*getting the bundle from the loft*]   The young priest
said he'd be passing tomorrow, and we might go down
155   and speak to him below if it's Michael's they are surely.

CATHLEEN [*taking the bundle*]   Did he say what way they
were found?

NORA [*coming down*]   'There were two men,' said he, 'and
they rowing round with poteen[1] before the cocks
160   crowed, and the oar of one of them caught the body, and
they passing the black cliffs of the north.'

CATHLEEN [*trying to open the bundle*]   Give me a knife,
Nora; the string's perished with° the salt water, and   *destroyed by*
there's a black knot on it you wouldn't loosen in a week.

165 NORA [*giving her a knife*]   I've heard tell it was a long way
to Donegal.

CATHLEEN [*cutting the string*]   It is surely. There was a man
in here a while ago—the man sold us that knife—and he
said if you set off walking from the rocks beyond, it would
170   be in seven days you'd be in Donegal.

NORA   And what time would a man take, and he floating?

        [CATHLEEN *opens the bundle and takes out a bit of a*
        shirt and a stocking. They look at them eagerly.]

CATHLEEN [*in a low voice*]   The Lord spare us, Nora! isn't
it a queer hard thing to say if it's his they are surely?

---

1. Literally, "small pot" (Irish; pronounced *puh-cheen*); illegal whiskey, often made from potatoes.

NORA   I'll get his shirt off the hook the way we can put the
175   one flannel on the other. [*She looks through some clothes
      hanging in the corner.*] It's not with them, Cathleen, and
      where will be it?
CATHLEEN   I'm thinking Bartley put it on him in the
      morning, for his own shirt was heavy with the salt in it.
180   [*Pointing to the corner*] There's a bit of a sleeve was of
      the same stuff. Give me that and it will do.

>   [NORA *brings it to her and they compare the flannel.*]

It's the same stuff, Nora; but if it is itself, aren't there great
rolls of it in the shops of Galway, and isn't it many another
man may have a shirt of it as well as Michael himself?
185   NORA [*who has taken up the stocking and counted the
      stitches, crying out*]   It's Michael, Cathleen, it's Michael;
      God spare his soul, and what will herself say when she
      hears this story, and Bartley on the sea?
CATHLEEN [*taking the stocking*]   It's a plain stocking.
190   NORA   It's the second one of the third pair I knitted, and I
      put up three-score stitches, and I dropped four of them.
CATHLEEN [*counts the stitches*]   It's that number is in it.
      [*Crying out*] Ah, Nora, isn't it a bitter thing to think of
      him floating that way to the far north, and no one to keen
195   him but the black hags[2] that do be flying on the sea?
NORA [*swinging herself half round, and throwing out her
      arms on the clothes*]   And isn't it a pitiful thing when
      there is nothing left of a man who was a great rower and
      fisher but a bit of an old shirt and a plain stocking?
CATHLEEN [*after an instant*]   Tell me is herself coming,
200   Nora? I hear a little sound on the path.
NORA [*looking out*]   She is, Cathleen. She's coming up to
      the door.
CATHLEEN   Put these things away before she'll come in.
      Maybe it's easier she'll be after giving her blessing to
205   Bartley, and we won't let on we've heard anything the
      time he's on the sea.
NORA [*helping* CATHLEEN *to close the bundle*]   We'll put
      them here in the corner.

>   [*They put them into a hole in the chimney corner.*
>   CATHLEEN *goes back to the spinning-wheel.*]

Will she see it was crying I was?
210   CATHLEEN   Keep your back to the door the way the light'll
      not be on you.

>   [NORA *sits down at the chimney corner, with her back
>   to the door.* MAURYA *comes in very slowly, without
>   looking at the girls, and goes over to her stool at the
>   other side of the fire. The cloth with the bread is still
>   in her hand. The girls look at each other, and* NORA
>   points to the bundle of bread.*]

---

2. That is, cormorants, black diving birds with hooked beaks. *Keen:* lament bitterly; specifically,
utter the traditional Irish wail of lamentation for the dead.

[*After spinning for a moment*] You didn't give him his bit
of bread?

> [MAURYA *begins to keen softly, without turning round.*]

Did you see him riding down?

> [MAURYA *goes on keening.*]

215 [*A little impatiently*] God forgive you; isn't it a better
thing to raise your voice and tell what you seen, than to
be making lamentation for a thing that's done? Did you
see Bartley, I'm saying to you?

MAURYA [*with a weak voice*]   My heart's broken from this
220 day.

CATHLEEN [*as before*]   Did you see Bartley?

MAURYA   I seen the fearfullest thing.

CATHLEEN [*leaves her wheel and looks out*]   God forgive
you; he's riding the mare now over the green head, and
225 the grey pony behind him.

MAURYA [*starts so that her shawl falls back from her head and
shows her white tossed hair. With a frightened voice*] The
grey pony behind him. . . .

CATHLEEN [*coming to the fire*]   What is it ails you at all?

MAURYA [*speaking very slowly*]   I've seen the fearfullest
230 thing any person has seen since the day Bride Dara seen
the dead man with the child in his arms.

CATHLEEN *and* NORA   Uah.[3]

> [*They crouch down in front of the old woman at the
> fire.*]

NORA   Tell us what it is you seen.

MAURYA   I went down to the spring well, and I stood there
235 saying a prayer to myself. Then Bartley came along, and
he riding on the red mare with the grey pony behind
him. [*She puts up her hands, as if to hide something from
her eyes.*] The Son of God spare us, Nora!

CATHLEEN   What is it you seen?

240 MAURYA   I seen Michael himself.

CATHLEEN [*speaking softly*]   You did not, mother. It wasn't
Michael you seen, for his body is after being found in the
far north, and he's got a clean burial, by the grace of God.

MAURYA [*a little defiantly*]   I'm after seeing him this day,
245 and he riding and galloping. Bartley came first on the red
mare, and I tried to say 'God speed you,' but something
choked the words in my throat. He went by quickly; and
'The blessing of God on you,' says he, and I could say
nothing. I looked up then, and I crying, at the grey pony,
250 and there was Michael upon it—with fine clothes on
him, and new shoes on his feet.

CATHLEEN [*begins to keen*]   It's destroyed we are from this
day. It's destroyed, surely.

---

3. They are keening.

NORA   Didn't the young priest say the Almighty God won't
leave her destitute with no son living?

MAURYA [*in a low voice, but clearly*]   It's little the like of
him knows of the sea. . . . Bartley will be lost now, and let
you call in Eamon and make me a good coffin out of the
white boards, for I won't live after them. I've had a husband, and a husband's father, and six sons in this house—six
fine men, though it was a hard birth I had with every one of
them and they coming into the world—and some of them
were found and some of them were not found, but they're
gone now the lot of them. . . . There were Stephen and
Shawn were lost in the great wind, and found after in the
Bay of Gregory[4] of the Golden Mouth, and carried up the
two of them on one plank, and in by that door.

> [*She pauses for a moment; the girls start as if they
> heard something through the door that is half open
> behind them.*]

NORA [*in a whisper*]   Did you hear that, Cathleen? Did you
hear a noise in the north-east?

CATHLEEN [*in a whisper*]   There's someone after crying out
by the seashore.

MAURYA [*continues without hearing anything*]   There was
Sheamus and his father, and his own father again, were
lost in a dark night, and not a stick or sign was seen of
them when the sun went up. There was Patch after was
drowned out of a curragh[5] that turned over. I was sitting
here with Bartley, and he a baby lying on my two knees,
and I seen two women, and three women, and four
women coming in, and they crossing themselves and not
saying a word. I looked out then, and there were men
coming after them, and they holding a thing in the half
of a red sail, and water dripping out of it—it was a dry
day, Nora—and leaving a track to the door.

> [*She pauses with her hand stretched out towards the
> door. It opens softly and old women begin to come in,
> crossing themselves on the threshold, and kneeling
> down in front of the stage with red petticoats over
> their heads.*]

[*Half in a dream, to* CATHLEEN] Is it Patch, or Michael, or
what is it at all?

CATHLEEN   Michael is after being found in the far north,
and when he is found there how could he be here in this
place?

---

4. Gregory Sound, which separates the islands
of Inishmore and Inishmaan (the name is perhaps derived from the legend that Saint Gregory I, credited with inventing Gregorian chant,
was buried on the Aran Islands after his coffin
miraculously floated there from Rome).
5. Literally, "little ship" (Irish; pronounced *kur-
uh*); a lightweight boat, made of hide or tarred
canvas stretched over a wood or wicker work
frame, common on the west coast of Ireland.

MAURYA   There does be a power of young men floating
290   round in the sea, and what way would they know if it was
Michael they had, or another man like him, for when a
man is nine days in the sea, and the wind blowing, it's hard
set his own mother would be to say what man was in it.
CATHLEEN   It's Michael, God spare him, for they're after
295   sending us a bit of his clothes from the far north.

> [*She reaches out and hands* MAURYA *the clothes that
> belonged to* MICHAEL. MAURYA *stands up slowly, and
> takes them in her hands.* NORA *looks out.*]

NORA   They're carrying a thing among them, and there's
water dripping out of it and leaving a track by the big
stones.
CATHLEEN   [*in a whisper to the women who have come in*]
Is it Bartley it is?
300   ONE OF THE WOMEN   It is, surely, God rest his soul.

> [*Two younger women come in and pull out the table.
> Then men carry in the body of* BARTLEY, *laid on a
> plank, with a bit of a sail over it, and lay it on the
> table.*]

CATHLEEN   [*to the women as they are doing so*]   What way
was he drowned?
ONE OF THE WOMEN   The grey pony knocked him over into
the sea, and he was washed out where there is a great
305   surf on the white rocks.

> [MAURYA *has gone over and knelt down at the head of
> the table. The women are keening softly and swaying
> themselves with a slow movement.* CATHLEEN *and*
> NORA *kneel at the other end of the table. The men
> kneel near the door.*]

MAURYA   [*raising her head and speaking as if she did not see
the people around her*]   They're all gone now, and there
isn't anything more the sea can do to me. . . . I'll have no
call now to be up crying and praying when the wind
breaks from the south, and you can hear the surf is in
310   the east, and the surf is in the west, making a great stir
with the two noises, and they hitting one on the other.
I'll have no call now to be going down and getting Holy
Water in the dark nights after Samhain,⁶ and I won't
care what way the sea is when the other women will be
315   keening. [*To* NORA] Give me the Holy Water, Nora;   *sip, mouthful*
there's a small sup° still on the dresser.

> [NORA *gives it to her.*]

[*Drops* MICHAEL's *clothes across* BARTLEY's *feet, and sprin-
kles the Holy Water over him.*] It isn't that I haven't
prayed for you, Bartley, to the Almighty God. It isn't that

---

6. Literally, probably "Summer's End" (Irish; pronounced _sah-win_); November 1, in the Christian calendar All Saints' Day, originally celebrated as the end of the harvest and the beginning of winter.

I haven't said prayers in the dark night till you wouldn't
320   know what I'd be saying; but it's a great rest I'll have
now, and it's time, surely. It's a great rest I'll have now,
and great sleeping in the long nights after Samhain, if
it's only a bit of wet flour we do have to eat, and maybe a
fish that would be stinking.

> [*She kneels down again, crossing herself, and saying
> prayers under her breath.*]

325 CATHLEEN [*to an old man*]   Maybe yourself and Eamon
would make a coffin when the sun rises. We have fine
white boards herself bought, God help her, thinking
Michael would be found, and I have a new cake you can
eat while you'll be working.

330 THE OLD MAN [*looking at the boards*]   Are there nails with
them?

CATHLEEN   There are not, Colum; we didn't think of the
nails.

ANOTHER MAN   It's a great wonder she wouldn't think of
335   the nails, and all the coffins she's seen made already.

CATHLEEN   It's getting old she is, and broken.

> [*MAURYA stands up again very slowly and spreads out
> the pieces of MICHAEL's clothes beside the body, sprin-
> kling them with the last of the Holy Water.*]

NORA [*in a whisper to CATHLEEN*]   She's quiet now and
easy; but the day Michael was drowned you could hear
her crying out from this to the spring well. It's fonder she
340   was of Michael, and would any one have thought that?

CATHLEEN [*slowly and clearly*]   An old woman will be soon
tired with anything she will do, and isn't it nine days herself is after crying and keening, and making great sorrow
in the house?

MAURYA [*puts the empty cup mouth downwards on the table,
345   and lays her hands together on BARTLEY's feet*]   They're
all together this time, and the end is come. May the
Almighty God have mercy on Bartley's soul, and on
Michael's soul, and on the souls of Sheamus and Patch,
and Stephen and Shawn [*bending her head*]; and may He
350   have mercy on my soul, Nora, and on the soul of every
one is left living in the world.

> [*She pauses, and the keen rises a little more loudly
> from the women, then sinks away.*]

[*Continuing*]   Michael has a clean burial in the far
north, by the grace of the Almighty God. Bartley will
have a fine coffin out of the white boards, and a deep
355   grave surely. What more can we want than that? No man
at all can be living for ever, and we must be satisfied.

> [*She kneels down again and the curtain falls slowly.*]

GEORGE BERNARD SHAW

1856–1950

In the history of English drama, George Bernard Shaw stands second only to SHAKESPEARE as the playwright with the most profound influence on his own era and beyond. Winner of the Nobel Prize for Literature in 1925, Shaw was not only the most famous author of his time but also a highly regarded social critic, routinely sought after for his responses to world events and political issues. Although in the latter part of his career he was best known globally as a public intellectual, his theatrical writing was responsible for his place, long after his death in 1950, as one of the leading cultural forces of the twentieth century. Shaw's plays are still regularly revived and continue to strike audiences as relevant and compelling. This "timeliness" in his work in part reflects how little has changed at the very core of modern civilization over the past century; Shaw's tireless dissection of social ills and insightful grasp of human motivations and foibles also enable his plays to speak to each generation anew. Yet the truthfulness and acuity of his vision would not matter much to audiences if the plays themselves were not such exemplars of theatrical craftsmanship. Shaw's ability to interweave captivating narratives and memorable characters with social critique and, above all, humor sets him apart in the pantheon of modern drama. PYGMALION (1913) is one of the most popular, and arguably among the very finest, of Shaw's comedies. Gently poking fun at the pretensions of the lower class, and the idiosyncrasies of the upper class, *Pygmalion* entrances us with fairy-tale transformations and the possibility of romance; at the same time, it exposes the very real economic and gender inequities that continue to plague our modern world.

Shaw was born in 1856 to an Irish Protestant family that had more aspirations to social position than their father's income—reduced by his alcoholism—could sustain. George Carr Shaw cut short his son's formal education at age fifteen and sent him to work to help support his mother and two older sisters. Shaw spent five years as a clerk in a land agency, experience he would later use in his first play, *Widowers' Houses* (1892), which considers the hypocrisies of slum landlords. Shaw's mother, Lucinda Elizabeth Gurly Shaw, a talented singer, focused much of her time and energy on her music and, apparently, on her voice teacher, George J. Vandeleur Lee, with whom she may have been romantically involved. In 1873, Shaw's mother followed Lee to London, taking her two daughters with her. Shaw joined them in 1876. His first employment there was as a ghostwriter of music reviews for Lee, and he parlayed what he learned into lifelong journalistic work as a music, art, theater, and social critic. But Shaw desired a literary career, and he drafted a novel, *Immaturity* (written 1879), that he hoped would establish him both professionally and financially. Over the next four years, he composed four additional novels, only one of which, *Cashel Byron's Profession* (1886; rev. ed., 1901), saw any real success.

In 1884, Shaw discovered the newly organized Fabian Society, a socialist organization named after the Roman general Fabius Cunctator (the Delayer); its guiding principle was the idea that the best way to accomplish political and social reform was through the calculated, gradual infiltration of established channels of power. In the late nineteenth century and into the first decades of the twentieth, the Fabian Society came to have increasing influence on English politics, attracting into its ranks some of the foremost figures of the era—including its leaders, Sidney and Beatrice Webb, and the novelist H. G. Wells. Through the Fabians Shaw also met Charlotte Payne Townshend, whom he married in 1898. Shaw's writing skills and lecturing acumen soon made him the most visible member of this elite group dedicated to the pursuit of what Shaw deemed its "Socialist and Democratic objects."

In 1890, Shaw began to draw together his passionate commitment to the arts and to socialism by delivering a series of lectures for the Society on HENRIK IBSEN, whose dramas had recently been translated into English by Shaw's friend William Archer. As these plays began to be produced on the London stage, they galvanized broader public debate, especially about marriage and the role of women in modern society. Shaw published his talks the following year as *The Quintessence of Ibsenism*, and his analysis of these pioneering works of the modern theater helped him discover his own vocation as a dramatist.

The timing of these events could not have been more auspicious. Shaw emerged as a playwright just as theatrical modernism was beginning to coalesce as a movement across Europe. Shaw championed the arrival of the "New Drama" in England, leading a theatrical revolution that sought to replace formulaic native melodrama and Continental well-made plays with works closely engaged with the pressing issues of

the day. Shaw also quickly learned that humor was a highly effective vehicle for social critique, and he exploited its didactic potential throughout his career. A remarkably prolific author, Shaw generated new plays and essays annually through the early 1920s and was still writing steadily through World War II.

Pygmalion brings together many of Shaw's lifelong concerns: class and economic structures, shifting gender roles, and England's global influence and power, among others. The play's opening scene, set in London's Covent Garden, provides an opportunity for Shaw to introduce a cross section of character types and ranks in English society. As members of the upper class search for taxis to take them home from an evening at the theater, a "poor girl," Eliza Doolittle, tries to earn her meager income selling bunches of flowers to the passersby. Henry Higgins, a professor of phonetics who frequents the area to study its range of English idioms, hears Eliza, whose Cockney speech interests him. Quite by accident, he also encounters an amateur linguist, Colonel Pickering, an expert in Indian dialects who has come to London to meet him, and Higgins invites Pickering to his home. Eliza overhears Higgins giving out his address, and she shows up the next day to ask Higgins to teach her "genteel" speech so that she will be qualified to work in a flower shop instead of on the streets. Higgins bets Pickering that he can teach Eliza convincingly to speak as a member of the upper class and comport herself as a duchess. But what will it mean for Eliza to appear to be what she is not? What happens when one is removed from one's "natural" place in the social order? While in its plot *Pygmalion* echoes such tales as "The Ugly Duckling," Shaw's transformation narrative also reflects the real and pressing concerns faced by working-class women with severely limited financial options to improve their lives.

Shaw took his title from a classical myth, best known today in the version that appears in book 10 of Ovid's *Metamorphoses*. Pygmalion, "revolted by the many faults which nature has implanted in the female sex," carves a statue "lovelier than any woman born." He promptly falls in love with his creation and prays to the goddess of love for a wife like his "ivory maid" (translation by Mary M. Innes). Venus brings the statue to life, and Pygmalion immediately marries and impregnates Galatea. Such stories of male construction of idealized womanhood pervade Western literature, and Shaw could have drawn on many versions of this myth, including W. S. Gilbert's theatrical extravaganza *Pygmalion and Galatea* (1871). Higgins's claim "I said I'd make a woman of you; and I have," coupled with his assertion (also in act 5) that he has "created this thing out of the squashed cabbage leaves of Covent Garden," indisputably connects him to this tradition. Shaw's rendition may also have been influenced by even darker variants of such tales, such as Mary Shelley's gothic novel *Frankenstein* (1818), which depicts the uncontrollability of creations once they are brought to life. Echoing Shelley's label for Frankenstein's monster, Higgins refers to Eliza as "the creature," ultimately damning his "own folly in having lavished hard-earned knowledge and the treasure of [his] regard" on her.

Shaw weaves together this creation myth with another equally powerful narrative, a tale of a girl magically transformed, as was Cinderella, from rags to riches. By assert-ing that he can make a "duchess" from a "draggle-tailed guttersnipe," Higgins presents himself as the modern-day fairy godfather who will provide Eliza with clothes fit for an ambassador's party and with rides in a taxi, almost as magical to her as a pumpkin coach. But here, too, Shaw introduces a darker tone by also depicting Higgins as the evil stepfather/witch out of a story like "Snow White," tempting Eliza with sweets and munching on an apple taken from the same dessert stand.

For audiences *Pygmalion*'s enduring appeal clearly lies in part in the teasingly undefined and unresolved relationship of Higgins and Eliza. Shaw builds the comedy, which he subtitled a "A Romance in Five Acts," around Higgins's disavowals of romantic interest in Eliza as well as Eliza's need for "a little kindness" and her "right to be loved." Eliza maintains that "the sort of feeling" she wants from Higgins is not the same as that experienced by men such as the poor but aristocratic Freddy Eynsford Hill, who writes "sheets and sheets" of love letters to her. Shaw always insisted that his subtitle should suggest an older sense of the term *romance*—the sense in which it is applied to the late plays of Shakespeare, which similarly depict mythic transfor-

Left to right: Edmund Gurney as Alfred Doolittle, Stella Campbell as his daughter, Eliza Doolittle, and Herbert Beerbohm Tree as Professor Henry Higgins in the original 1914 production of *Pygmalion*.

mations and adventures beyond the everyday. Nevertheless, the agonistic dynamic between Higgins and Eliza has struck many audiences and critics as the verbal equivalent of sexual foreplay, in the tradition of Beatrice and Benedick in Shakespeare's *Much Ado about Nothing* (ca. 1598) or Mirabel and Millimant in William Congreve's *The Way of the World* (1700). From the first production of *Pygmalion* forward, Shaw had to fight both actors' inclinations and audiences' expectations that the comedy end conventionally, in marriage. In that legendary first staging, Herbert Beerbohm Tree (Higgins) got around Shaw by tossing flowers to Stella Campbell (Eliza) right before the final curtain to signal the pair's ultimate union. Well aware of theatergoers' delight at this gesture, Tree told the irate Shaw, "My ending makes money; you ought to be grateful." Shaw responded, "Your ending is damnable: you ought to be shot."

The critical and theatrical controversy that erupted over the play's lack of narrative closure has perennially overshadowed explorations of other social and political issues raised in the play. It is certainly possible that Shaw perceived the amatory dynamic at work in *Pygmalion* but actively sought to expose the darker realities behind such romantic fantasies. Shortly before Shaw conceived the play, the London periodical *Pall Mall Gazette* featured an exposé of white slavery that prompted a public debate over sexual predation and may have contributed to the drama's aura of barely disguised sexual threat. The journal's revelations of the sexual availability and vulnerability of young working-class women, and their exploitation by men in more economically privileged positions, would certainly have been familiar to Shaw's audiences. That Stella Campbell, for whom Shaw created the role of Eliza, was already known to audiences through her prior star turns in highly sexualized "fallen woman" roles, such as in Arthur Pinero's *The Second Mrs. Tanqueray* (1893), only complicated their perception of her and the reception of *Pygmalion*.

Shaw uses details of language—what he calls "phonetics"—to explore class boundaries and their potential malleability. He overtly links economics with dialect and grammar by suggesting that class position is culturally bound to speech. Through Higgins (whom Shaw partly modeled on Henry Sweet, a noted philologist he had met in 1880), Shaw states that the lower class's acquisition of "new speech"—by which he means what came to be known as Standard British English—can "fil[l] up the deepest gulf that separates class from class and soul from soul." He sets up this major arc of the play in act 1, when Higgins remarks: "You see this creature with her kerbstone English: the English that will keep her in the gutter to the end of her days. . . . [I]n three months I could pass that girl off as a duchess. . . . I could even get her a place as lady's maid or shop assistant, which requires better English." In Higgins's idealized vision, once the marker of lower-class status is removed from speech, individuals not only will be able to move upward through social ranks, they will also be able to realize their full potential economically, intellectually, and spiritually.

The juxtaposition of two branches of linguistic inquiry undertaken by Higgins and Pickering—one rooted in the British class system, the other emerging from its imperial endeavors—cannot be accidental. Shaw had already anonymously written the manifesto *Fabianism and the Empire* (1900) for the Fabian Society and had dramatized the familiar parallel of the British and Roman empires in *Caesar and Cleopatra* (written 1898). In *Pygmalion* Shaw demonstrates how language can be used either to perpetuate or to level social distinctions both at home and, by extension, in the colonies. He combines the established idea that British English should be the vehicle for the education and enculturation of colonized natives with social reformers' notions that Britain's underclass had much in common with its colonial "Others."

Shaw uses a streamlined version of the Elizabethan dramatic structure of main plot and comic subplot to develop his themes of language and class. Eliza's willing transfiguration through speech has its comic counterpart in her father's resistance to his removal from the legions of "the undeserving poor" and forced embrace of "middle-class morality" when he unexpectedly receives a sizable legacy. The character of Alfred Doolittle owes much to earlier Victorian literature, especially the novels of Charles Dickens (1812–1870) and the dramas of T. W. Robertson (1829–1871), with their depictions of colorful laggards and other lowlifes. These Victorian characterological influences emerged in Shaw's earliest plays—including *Widowers' Houses*, which featured the rent collector Lickcheese; in *Pygmalion* Shaw more fully and pointedly uses Doolittle to expose the hypocrisy and pretensions of elevated class position through the resolutely unreformed dustman's lectures on "Moral Reform"—lectures that, under the terms of the will that irrevocably changes his social position, he must deliver.

Some critics have contrasted the "human" comedy of Eliza to the "social" comedy of her father, claiming that only the latter is about class. But Shaw's grounding in socialism was too thorough to allow him to separate an understanding of modern humanity from individuals' placement in a class system. Rather, through the triangulated relations of Eliza, Pickering, and Higgins, we come to realize that class position has both external markers and intrinsic qualities. Eliza learns that "apart from the things anyone can pick up (the dressing and the proper way of speaking, and so on), the difference between a lady and a flower girl is not how she behaves, but how shes treated." Henry's mother sees Eliza's transformation from still another perspective: the tension between the appearance of elevated class position and the economic realities of women's lives. Mrs. Higgins questions her son's having taught Eliza "the manners and habits that disqualify a fine lady from earning her own living without giving her a fine lady's income." Eliza pointedly comes to understand the price of class standing for women without independent means—the necessity of finding a husband in a society that still saw marriage as the only "profession" appropriate to real ladies: "I sold flowers. I didnt sell myself. Now youve made a lady of me I'm not fit to sell anything else."

Though Shaw's postscript spells out Eliza's later career in some detail, his play's intentionally ambiguous ending leaves unclear whether she will marry the impecunious Freddy Eynsford Hill, "as soon as hes able to support me," or teach phonetics. It could well be that the financial and emotional independence she craves if she "cant have kindness" proved too threatening to dramatize fully at that time. Tree's conventionally romantic gesture at the final curtain reassured his audiences—members of a society that could not yet accept women's suffrage and other struggles for human equality—that the social problems Shaw placed within the spotlight could be easily resolved. Yet the continued theatrical appeal of *Pygmalion* suggests that the issues Shaw depicts are with us still. Not only can we appreciate the value of complexity and indeterminacy, but such ambiguity may well affirm, better than any pat ending, the realities of our lives.

J.E.G.

Pygmalion
A Romance in Five Acts

CHARACTERS

CLARA EYNSFORD HILL	MRS. PEARCE
MRS. EYNSFORD HILL	ALFRED DOOLITTLE
FREDDY EYNSFORD HILL	MRS. HIGGINS
ELIZA DOOLITTLE	
COLONEL PICKERING	A PARLOR-MAID
HENRY HIGGINS	BYSTANDERS

Act 1

[*Covent Garden*[1] *at 11.15 p.m. Torrents of heavy summer rain. Cab whistles blowing frantically in all directions. Pedestrians running for shelter into the market and under the portico of St. Paul's Church, where there are already several people, among them a lady and her daughter in evening dress. They are all peering out gloomily at the rain, except one man with his back turned to the rest, who seems wholly preoccupied with a notebook in which he is writing busily.*

The church clock strikes the first quarter.]

THE DAUGHTER [*in the space between the central pillars, close to the one on her left*]   I'm getting chilled to the bone. What can Freddy be doing all this time? Hes[2] been gone twenty minutes.

THE MOTHER [*on her daughter's right*]   Not so long. But he ought to have got us a cab by this.

5 A BYSTANDER [*on the lady's right*]   He wont get no cab not until half-past eleven, missus, when they come back after dropping their theatre fares.

THE MOTHER   But we must have a cab. We cant stand here until half-past eleven. It's too bad.

THE BYSTANDER   Well, it aint my fault, missus.

10 THE DAUGHTER   If Freddy had a bit of gumption, he would have got one at the theatre door.

THE MOTHER   What could he have done, poor boy?

THE DAUGHTER   Other people got cabs. Why couldnt he?

[FREDDY *rushes in out of the rain from the Southampton Street side, and comes between them closing a dripping umbrella. He is a young man of twenty, in evening dress, very wet around the ankles.*]

THE DAUGHTER   Well, havnt you got a cab?

15 FREDDY   Theres not one to be had for love or money.

---

1. The site of London's main produce and flower market from the 1600s until 1974, in Westminster; also the site of major entertainment venues, including the Royal Opera House and the Drury Lane Theatre.

2. An example of one of the spelling reforms advocated by Shaw, who argued that the apostrophe was unnecessary in most contractions (he also insisted on dropping the final *e* from Shakespeare).

THE MOTHER   Oh, Freddy, there must be one. You cant have tried.

THE DAUGHTER   It's too tiresome. Do you expect us to go and get one ourselves?

FREDDY   I tell you theyre all engaged. The rain was so sudden: nobody was
20   prepared; and everybody had to take a cab. Ive been to Charing Cross one way and nearly to Ludgate Circus the other;[3] and they were all engaged.

THE MOTHER   Did you try Trafalgar Square?[4]

FREDDY   There wasnt one at Trafalgar Square.

THE DAUGHTER   Did you try?

25   FREDDY   I tried as far as Charing Cross Station. Did you expect me to walk to Hammersmith?[5]

THE DAUGHTER   You havnt tried at all.

THE MOTHER   You really are very helpless, Freddy. Go again; and dont come back until you have found a cab.

30   FREDDY   I shall simply get soaked for nothing.

THE DAUGHTER   And what about us? Are we to stay here all night in this draught, with next to nothing on. You selfish pig—

FREDDY   Oh, very well: I'll go, I'll go.

[*He opens his umbrella and dashes off Strandwards,*[6] *but comes into collision with a flower girl, who is hurrying in for shelter, knocking her basket out of her hands. A blinding flash of lightning, followed instantly by a rattling peal of thunder, orchestrates the incident.*]

THE FLOWER GIRL   Nah then, Freddy: look wh' y' gowin, deah.

35   FREDDY   Sorry.

[*He rushes off.*]

THE FLOWER GIRL [*picking up her scattered flowers and replacing them in the basket*]   Theres menners f' yer! Te-oo banches o voylets trod into the mad.

[*She sits down on the plinth of the column, sorting her flowers, on the lady's right. She is not at all an attractive person. She is perhaps eighteen, perhaps twenty, hardly older. She wears a little sailor hat of black straw that has long been exposed to the dust and soot of London and has seldom if ever been brushed. Her hair needs washing rather badly: its mousy color can hardly be natural. She wears a shoddy black coat that reaches nearly to her knees and is shaped to her waist. She has a brown skirt with a coarse apron. Her boots are much the worse for wear. She is no doubt as clean as she can afford to be; but compared to the ladies she is very dirty. Her features are no worse than theirs; but their condition leaves something to be desired; and she needs the services of a dentist.*]

THE MOTHER   How do you know that my son's name is Freddy, pray?

THE FLOWER GIRL   Ow, eez ye-ooa san, is e? Wal, fewd dan y' de-ooty bawmz a mather should, eed now bettern to spawl a pore gel's flahrzn than ran awy
40   athaht[7] pyin. Will ye-oo py me f'them? [*Here, with apologies, this desperate*

---

3. Freddy has walked more than a half mile in different directions: first southwest to Charing Cross, the busy intersection of a number of major Westminster thoroughfares, and then east to Ludgate Circus, near the entrance to the old City of London.
4. A large plaza near Charing Cross.

5. The westernmost of the inner London boroughs, several miles beyond Charing Cross.
6. That is, toward the Strand, a street in Westminster south of Covent Garden where many theaters were located.
7. Without. *Fewd dan y' de-ooty bawmz:* if you'd done your duty by him.

attempt to represent her dialect without a phonetic alphabet must be abandoned as unintelligible outside London.][8]

THE DAUGHTER Do nothing of the sort, mother. The idea!

THE MOTHER Please allow me, Clara. Have you any pennies?

THE DAUGHTER No. Ive nothing smaller than sixpence.[9]

THE FLOWER GIRL [*hopefully*] I can give you change for a tanner,[1] kind lady.

45 THE MOTHER [*to* CLARA] Give it to me. [CLARA *parts reluctantly.*] Now [*To the* GIRL] This is for your flowers.

THE FLOWER GIRL Thank you kindly, lady.

THE DAUGHTER Make her give you the change. These things are only a penny a bunch.

50 THE MOTHER Do hold your tongue, Clara. [*To the* GIRL] You can keep the change.

THE FLOWER GIRL Oh, thank you, lady.

THE MOTHER Now tell me how you know that young gentleman's name.

THE FLOWER GIRL I didnt.

55 THE MOTHER I heard you call him by it. Dont try to deceive me.

THE FLOWER GIRL [*protesting*] Whos trying to deceive you? I called him Freddy or Charlie same as you might yourself if you was talking to a stranger and wished to be pleasant. [*She sits down beside her basket.*]

THE DAUGHTER Sixpence thrown away! Really, mamma, you might have

60 spared Freddy that. [*She retreats in disgust behind the pillar.*]

[*An elderly gentleman of the amiable military type rushes into shelter, and closes a dripping umbrella. He is in the same plight as* FREDDY, *very wet about the ankles. He is in evening dress, with a light overcoat. He takes the place left vacant by the daughter's retirement.*]

THE GENTLEMAN Phew!

THE MOTHER [*to the* GENTLEMAN] Oh, sir, is there any sign of its stopping?

THE GENTLEMAN I'm afraid not. It started worse than ever about two minutes ago. [*He goes to the plinth beside the flower girl; puts up his foot on it; and stoops to turn down his trouser ends.*]

65 THE MOTHER Oh, dear! [*She retires sadly and joins her daughter.*]

THE FLOWER GIRL [*taking advantage of the military gentleman's proximity to establish friendly relations with him*] If it's worse it's a sign it's nearly over. So cheer up, Captain; and buy a flower off a poor girl.

THE GENTLEMAN I'm sorry, I havnt any change.

THE FLOWER GIRL I can give you change, Captain.

70 THE GENTLEMAN For a sovereign?[2] Ive nothing less.

THE FLOWER GIRL Garn![3] Oh do buy a flower off me, Captain. I can change half-a-crown. Take this for tuppence.[4]

THE GENTLEMAN Now dont be troublesome: theres a good girl. [*Trying his pockets*] I really havnt any change—Stop: heres three hapence,[5] if thats

75 any use to you. [*He retreats to the other pillar.*]

---

8. Shaw's note.
9. That is, six pennies, roughly equivalent in value to $2 today. Before the decimalization of U.K. currency in 1971, the pound was worth twenty shillings, and each shilling was worth twelve pence.
1. Nickname for a sixpence coin.

2. A coin worth one pound, roughly equivalent to $80 today.
3. Go on!
4. Two pence (a single coin). *Half-a-crown:* a coin worth two and a half shillings, roughly equivalent to $10 today.
5. Half-penny coins.

THE FLOWER GIRL [*disappointed, but thinking three halfpence better than nothing*]   Thank you, sir.

THE BYSTANDER [*to the girl*]   You be careful: give him a flower for it. Theres a bloke[6] here behind taking down every blessed word youre saying. [*All turn to the man who is taking notes.*]

THE FLOWER GIRL [*springing up terrified*]   I aint done nothing wrong by speaking to the gentleman. Ive a right to sell flowers if I keep off the kerb.[7] [*Hysterically*] I'm a respectable girl: so help me, I never spoke to him except to ask him to buy a flower off me. [*General hubbub, mostly sympathetic to the FLOWER GIRL, but deprecating her excessive sensibility. Cries of* Dont start hollerin. Whos hurting you? Nobody's going to touch you. Whats the good of fussing? Steady on. Easy, easy, *etc.,* come from the elderly staid spectators, who pat her comfortingly. Less patient ones bid her shut her head,[8] or ask her roughly what is wrong with her. A remoter group, not knowing what the matter is, crowd in and increase the noise with question and answer:* Whats the row? What she do? Where is he? A tec[9] taking her down. What! him? Yes: him over there: Took money off the gentleman, *etc. The FLOWER GIRL, distraught and mobbed, breaks through them to the gentleman, crying wildly.*] Oh, sir, dont let him charge me. You dunno what it means to me. Theyll take away my character[1] and drive me on the streets for speaking to gentlemen. They—

THE NOTE TAKER [*coming forward on her right, the rest crowding after him*]   There, there, there, there! whos hurting you, you silly girl? What do you take me for?

THE BYSTANDER   It's all right: hes a gentleman: look at his boots. [*Explaining to the NOTE TAKER*] She thought you was a copper's nark, sir.

THE NOTE TAKER [*with quick interest*]   Whats a copper's nark?

THE BYSTANDER [*inapt at definition*]   It's a—well, it's a copper's nark, as you might say. What else would you call it? A sort of informer.

THE FLOWER GIRL [*still hysterical*]   I take my Bible oath I never said a word—

THE NOTE TAKER [*overbearing but good-humored*]   Oh, shut up, shut up. Do I look like a policeman?

THE FLOWER GIRL [*far from reassured*]   Then what did you take down my words for? How do I know whether you took me down right? You just shew[2] me what youve wrote about me. [*The NOTE TAKER opens his book and holds it steadily under her nose, though the pressure of the mob trying to read it over his shoulders would upset a weaker man.*] Whats that? That aint proper writing. I cant read that.

THE NOTE TAKER   I can. [*Reads, reproducing her pronunciation exactly.*] "Cheer ap, Keptin; n' baw ya flahr orf a pore gel."

THE FLOWER GIRL [*much distressed*]   It's because I called him Captain. I meant no harm. [*To the GENTLEMAN*] Oh, sir, dont let him lay a charge agen[3] me for a word like that. You—

THE GENTLEMAN   Charge! I make no charge. [*To the NOTE TAKER*] Really, sir, if you are a detective, you need not begin protecting me against molestation by young women until I ask you. Anybody could see that the girl meant no harm.

6. Man.
7. Curb.
8. That is, shut up.
9. Detective (slang).
1. Testimony about an employee's qualities, provided by the employer; more generally, reputation. A woman who lost her reputation, and who therefore was unable to find legal work, was in danger of being driven into prostitution ("on the streets").
2. Show.
3. Against.

THE BYSTANDERS GENERALLY [*demonstrating against police espionage*]   Course
they could. What business is it of yours? You mind your own affairs. He
wants promotion, he does. Taking down people's words! Girl never said a
word to him. What harm if she did? Nice thing a girl cant shelter from the
rain without being insulted, etc., etc., etc. [*She is conducted by the more
sympathetic demonstrators back to her plinth, where she resumes her seat
and struggles with her emotion.*]

THE BYSTANDER   He aint a tec. Hes a blooming busybody: thats what he is. I
tell you, look at his boots.

THE NOTE TAKER [*turning on him genially*]   And how are all your people down
at Selsey?[4]

THE BYSTANDER [*suspiciously*]   Who told you my people come from Selsey?

THE NOTE TAKER   Never you mind. They did. [*To the* GIRL] How do you come
to be up so far east? You were born in Lisson Grove.[5]

THE FLOWER GIRL [*appalled*]   Oh, what harm is there in my leaving Lisson
Grove? It wasnt fit for a pig to live in; and I had to pay four-and-six[6] a week.
[*In tears*] Oh, boo—hoo—oo—

THE NOTE TAKER   Live where you like; but stop that noise.

THE GENTLEMAN [*to the* GIRL]   Come, come! he cant touch you: you have a
right to live where you please.

A SARCASTIC BYSTANDER [*thrusting himself between the* NOTE TAKER *and the*
GENTLEMAN]   Park Lane, for instance. Id like to go into the Housing
Question[7] with you, I would.

THE FLOWER GIRL [*subsiding into a brooding melancholy over her basket, and
talking very low-spiritedly to herself*]   I'm a good girl, I am.

THE SARCASTIC BYSTANDER [*not attending to her*]   Do you know where *I* come
from?

THE NOTE TAKER [*promptly*]   Hoxton.[8]

[*Titterings. Popular interest in the* NOTE TAKER'S *performance increases.*]

THE SARCASTIC ONE [*amazed*]   Well, who said I didnt? Bly me![9] You know
everything, you do.

THE FLOWER GIRL [*still nursing her sense of injury*]   Aint no call to meddle
with me, he aint.

THE BYSTANDER [*to her*]   Of course he aint. Dont you stand it from him. [*To
the* NOTE TAKER] See here: what call have you to know about people what
never offered to meddle with you? Wheres your warrant?

SEVERAL BYSTANDERS [*encouraged by this seeming point of law*]   Yes: wheres
your warrant?

THE FLOWER GIRL   Let him say what he likes. I dont want to have no truck
with him.

THE BYSTANDER   You take us for dirt under your feet, dont you? Catch you
taking liberties with a gentleman!

---

4. A town on the coast of England, directly
south of London.
5. A district of northwest London notorious in
Shaw's day for slums, crime, and prostitution.
6. That is, four shillings and sixpence (the
standard form of expressing amounts of these
currencies).
7. The early twentieth-century debate over
the need to provide adequate, affordable

housing for the working classes. *Park Lane*:
one of the most fashionable streets in London, about a mile west of Covent Garden.
8. A district of central London known for its
theaters and music halls as well as its over-
crowding and slums.
9. That is, blimey, a shortened form of "gor-
blimey" (God blind me!), an exclamation of
surprise.

THE SARCASTIC BYSTANDER   Yes: tell him where he come from if you want to go fortune-telling.

THE NOTE TAKER   Cheltenham, Harrow, Cambridge, and India.[1]

THE GENTLEMAN   Quite right. [*Great laughter. Reaction in the* NOTE TAKER's *favor. Exclamations of* He knows all about it. Told him proper. Hear him tell the toff[2] where he come from? *etc.*] May I ask, sir, do you do this for your living at a music hall?

THE NOTE TAKER   Ive thought of that. Perhaps I shall some day.

[*The rain has stopped; and the persons on the outside of the crowd begin to drop off.*]

THE FLOWER GIRL [*resenting the reaction*]   Hes no gentleman, he aint, to interfere with a poor girl.

THE DAUGHTER [*out of patience, pushing her way rudely to the front and displacing the* GENTLEMAN, *who politely retires to the other side of the pillar*]   What on earth is Freddy doing? I shall get pneumonia if I stay in this draught any longer.

THE NOTE TAKER [*to himself, hastily making a note of her pronunciation of "monia"*]   Earlscourt.[3]

THE DAUGHTER [*violently*]   Will you please keep your impertinent remarks to yourself?

THE NOTE TAKER   Did I say that out loud? I didnt mean to. I beg your pardon. Your mother's Epsom,[4] unmistakeably.

THE MOTHER [*advancing between her* DAUGHTER *and the* NOTE TAKER]   How very curious! I was brought up in Largelady Park, near Epsom.

THE NOTE TAKER [*uproariously amused*]   Ha! ha! What a devil of a name! Excuse me. [*To the* DAUGHTER] You want a cab, do you?

THE DAUGHTER   Dont dare speak to me.

THE MOTHER   Oh, please, please Clara. [*Her* DAUGHTER *repudiates her with an angry shrug and retires haughtily.*] We should be so grateful to you, sir, if you found us a cab. [*The* NOTE TAKER *produces a whistle.*] Oh, thank you. [*She joins her* DAUGHTER.]

[*The* NOTE TAKER *blows a piercing blast.*]

THE SARCASTIC BYSTANDER   There! I knowed he was a plain-clothes copper.

THE BYSTANDER   That aint a police whistle: thats a sporting whistle.

THE FLOWER GIRL [*still preoccupied with her wounded feelings*]   Hes no right to take away my character. My character is the same to me as any lady's.

THE NOTE TAKER   I dont know whether youve noticed it; but the rain stopped about two minutes ago.

THE BYSTANDER   So it has. Why didnt you say so before? and us losing our time listening to your silliness. [*He walks off towards the Strand.*]

THE SARCASTIC BYSTANDER   I can tell where you come from. You come from Anwell. Go back there.

---

1. In effect, a summary of the gentleman's life: born in Cheltenham, a town in Gloucestershire, west of London; educated first at Harrow, a prestigious private school for boys in a borough of London, and then at Cambridge University, in Cambridge; and finally embarked on a career in India, which, as a large part of the British Empire, required the services of many British army officers and administrators.

2. Slightly derogatory slang term for a well-dressed gentleman.

3. That is, Earls Court, a well-to-do section of west London.

4. A suburb on the western periphery of greater London, known for horseracing.

180 THE NOTE TAKER [*helpfully*] Hanwell.[5]

THE SARCASTIC BYSTANDER [*affecting great distinction of speech*] Thenk you, teacher. Haw haw! So long.

[*He touches his hat with mock respect and strolls off.*]

THE FLOWER GIRL Frightening people like that! How would he like it himself.

185 THE MOTHER It's quite fine now, Clara. We can walk to a motor bus. Come.

[*She gathers her skirts above her ankles and hurries off towards the Strand.*]

THE DAUGHTER But the cab—[*Her mother is out of hearing.*] Oh, how tiresome!

[*She follows angrily.*]

[*All the rest have gone except the* NOTE TAKER, *the* GENTLEMAN, *and the* FLOWER GIRL, *who sits arranging her basket, and still pitying herself in murmurs.*]

THE FLOWER GIRL Poor girl! Hard enough for her to live without being worried and chivied.[6]

190 THE GENTLEMAN [*returning to his former place on the* NOTE TAKER'S *left*] How do you do it, if I may ask?

THE NOTE TAKER Simply phonetics. The science of speech. Thats my profession: also my hobby. Happy is the man who can make a living by his hobby! You can spot an Irishman or a Yorkshireman by his brogue. *I* can place any

195 man within six miles. I can place him within two miles in London. Sometimes within two streets.

THE FLOWER GIRL Ought to be ashamed of himself, unmanly coward!

THE GENTLEMAN But is there a living in that?

THE NOTE TAKER Oh yes. Quite a fat one. This is an age of upstarts. Men

200 begin in Kentish Town with £80 a year, and end in Park Lane with a hundred thousand.[7] They want to drop Kentish Town; but they give themselves away every time they open their mouths. Now I can teach them—

THE FLOWER GIRL Let him mind his own business and leave a poor girl—

205 THE NOTE TAKER [*explosively*] Woman: cease this detestable boohooing instantly; or else seek the shelter of some other place of worship.

THE FLOWER GIRL [*with feeble defiance*] Ive a right to be here if I like, same as you.

THE NOTE TAKER A woman who utters such depressing and disgusting sounds

210 has no right to be anywhere—no right to live. Remember that you are a human being with a soul and the divine gift of articulate speech: that your native language is the language of Shakespear and Milton and The Bible;[8] and dont sit there crooning like a bilious pigeon.

5. Dropped *h*s are typical of Cockney pronunciation. Hanwell, a working-class precinct of western London, contained a lunatic asylum founded in 1831.

6. That is, worried and hounded.

7. That is, men rise from grim working-class beginnings (Kentish Town is in northwest London) to become millionaires.

8. Three of the greatest literary influences on the English language: the playwright William Shakespeare (1564–1616), the poet John Milton (1608–1674), and the translation of the Bible commissioned by King James (1611).

THE FLOWER GIRL [*quite overwhelmed, and looking up at him in mingled wonder and deprecation without daring to raise her head*] Ah-ah-ah-ow-ow-ow-oo!

THE NOTE TAKER [*whipping out his book*] Heavens! what a sound! [*He writes; then holds out the book and reads, reproducing her vowels exactly.*] Ah-ah-ah-ow-ow-ow-oo!

THE FLOWER GIRL [*tickled by the performance, and laughing in spite of herself*] Garn!

THE NOTE TAKER You see this creature with her kerbstone English: the English that will keep her in the gutter to the end of her days. Well, sir, in three months I could pass that girl off as a duchess at an ambassador's garden party. I could even get her a place as lady's maid or shop assistant, which requires better English. Thats the sort of thing I do for commercial millionaires. And on the profits of it I do genuine scientific work in phonetics, and a little as a poet on Miltonic lines.

THE GENTLEMAN I am myself a student of Indian dialects; and—

THE NOTE TAKER [*eagerly*] Are you? Do you know Colonel Pickering, the author of Spoken Sanscrit?

THE GENTLEMAN I am Colonel Pickering. Who are you?

THE NOTE TAKER Henry Higgins, author of Higgins's Universal Alphabet.

PICKERING [*with enthusiasm*] I came from India to meet you.

HIGGINS I was going to India to meet you.

PICKERING Where do you live?

HIGGINS 27A Wimpole Street.[9] Come and see me tomorrow.

PICKERING I'm at the Carlton.[1] Come with me now and lets have a jaw over some supper.

HIGGINS Right you are.

THE FLOWER GIRL [*to PICKERING, as he passes her*] Buy a flower, kind gentleman. I'm short for my lodging.

PICKERING I really havnt any change. I'm sorry.

[*He goes away.*]

HIGGINS [*shocked at girl's mendacity*] Liar. You said you could change half-a-crown.

THE FLOWER GIRL [*rising in desperation*] You ought to be stuffed with nails, you ought. [*Flinging the basket at his feet*] Take the whole blooming basket for sixpence.

[*The church clock strikes the second quarter.*]

HIGGINS [*hearing in it the voice of God, rebuking him for his Pharisaic[2] want of charity to the poor girl*] A reminder.

[*He raises his hat solemnly; then throws a handful of money into the basket and follows PICKERING.*]

THE FLOWER GIRL [*picking up a half-crown*] Ah-ow-ooh! [*Picking up a couple of florins*] Aaah-ow-ooh! [*Picking up several coins*] Aaaaaah-ow-ooh! [*Picking up a half-sovereign*][3] Aaaaaaaaaaaah-ow-ooh!!!

---

9. A street in Westminster; its most famous resident was Elizabeth Barrett, who eloped with Robert Browning from her family's home at 50 Wimpole St. in 1846.
1. An elegant London hotel on Haymarket, near Piccadilly Circus.
2. That is, self-righteous and hypocritical, like the Pharisees as depicted in the New Testament.
3. A half-pound coin. *Florins:* two-shilling coins.

250 FREDDY [*springing out of a taxicab*] Got one at last. Hallo! [*To the* GIRL] Where are the two ladies that were here?

THE FLOWER GIRL They walked to the bus when the rain stopped.

FREDDY And left me with a cab on my hands. Damnation!

THE FLOWER GIRL [*with grandeur*] Never you mind, young man. I'm going
255 home in a taxi. [*She sails off to the cab. The driver puts his hand behind him and holds the door firmly shut against her. Quite understanding his mistrust, she shews him her handful of money.*] Eightpence aint no object to me, Charlie. [*He grins and opens the door.*] Angel Court, Drury Lane,[4] round the corner of Micklejohn's oil shop. Lets see how fast you can make her hop it.[5] [*She gets in and pulls the door to with a slam as the taxicab starts.*]
260 FREDDY Well, I'm dashed![6]

Act 2

[*Next day at 11 a.m.* HIGGINS's *laboratory in Wimpole Street. It is a room on the first floor, looking on the street, and was meant for the drawing-room. The double doors are in the middle of the back wall; and persons entering find in the corner to their right two tall file cabinets at right angles to one another against the walls. In this corner stands a flat writing-table, on which are a phonograph, a laryngoscope,[7] a row of tiny organ pipes with a bellows, a set of lamp chimneys for singeing flames with burners attached to a gas plug in the wall by an indiarubber tube, several tuning-forks of different sizes, a life-size image of half a human head, showing in section the vocal organs, and a box containing a supply of wax cylinders for the phonograph.*

Further down the room, on the same side, is a fireplace, with a comfortable leather-covered easy-chair at the side of the hearth nearest the door, and a coal-scuttle. There is a clock on the mantelpiece. Between the fireplace and the phonograph table is a stand for newspapers.

On the other side of the central door, to the left of the visitor, is a cabinet of shallow drawers. On it is a telephone and the telephone directory. The corner beyond, and most of the side wall, is occupied by a grand piano, with the keyboard at the end furthest from the door, and a bench for the player extending the full length of the keyboard. On the piano is a dessert dish heaped with fruit and sweets, mostly chocolates.

The middle of the room is clear. Besides the easy-chair, the piano bench, and two chairs at the phonograph table, there is one stray chair. It stands near the fireplace. On the walls, engravings; mostly Piranesi[8] and mezzotint portraits. No paintings.

PICKERING *is seated at the table, putting down some cards and a tuning-fork which he has been using.* HIGGINS *is standing up near him, closing two or three file drawers which are hanging out. He appears in the morning light as a robust, vital, appetizing sort of man of forty or thereabouts, dressed in a professional-looking black frock-coat with a white linen collar and black silk tie. He is of the energetic, scientific type, heartily, even violently interested in everything that can be studied as a scientific subject, and careless about himself and other people, including their feelings. He is, in fact, but for his years and size, rather like a very impetuous baby "taking notice"[9] eagerly and loudly, and requiring almost as much watching to keep him out of unintended mischief. His manner varies from genial bullying when he is*

---

4. A street close to Covent Garden; once fashionable, by the nineteenth century it became one of London's worst slums.
5. Go away quickly.
6. That is, "I'll be damned!"
7. An instrument for examining the larynx, invented in the mid-19th century.

8. Reproductions of works by Giovanni Battista Piranesi (1720–1778), an Italian print-maker known for his depictions of classical and contemporary Roman sites.
9. Showing signs of intelligent observation (a phrase used specifically of babies).

in a good humor to stormy petulance when anything goes wrong; but he is so entirely frank and void of malice that he remains likeable even in his least reasonable moments.]

HIGGINS [*as he shuts the last drawer*]   Well, I think thats the whole show.

PICKERING   It's really amazing. I havnt taken half of it in, you know.

HIGGINS   Would you like to go over any of it again?

PICKERING [*rising and coming to the fireplace, where he plants himself with his back to the fire*]   No, thank you; not now. I'm quite done up for this
5   morning.

HIGGINS [*following him, and standing beside him on his left*]   Tired of listening to sounds?

PICKERING   Yes. It's a fearful strain. I rather fancied myself because I can pronounce twenty-four distinct vowel sounds; but your hundred and thirty
10   beat me. I cant hear a bit of difference between most of them.

HIGGINS [*chuckling, and going over to the piano to eat sweets*]   Oh, that comes with practice. You hear no difference at first; but you keep on listening, and presently you find theyre all as different as A from B. [MRS. PEARCE *looks in: she is* HIGGINS's *housekeeper.*] Whats the matter?

15   MRS. PEARCE [*hesitating, evidently perplexed*]   A young woman wants to see you, sir.

HIGGINS   A young woman! What does she want?

MRS. PEARCE   Well, sir, she says youll be glad to see her when you know what shes come about. Shes quite a common girl, sir. Very common indeed. I
20   should have sent her away, only I thought perhaps you wanted her to talk into your machines. I hope Ive not done wrong; but really you see such queer people sometimes—youll excuse me, I'm sure, sir—

HIGGINS   Oh, thats all right, Mrs. Pearce. Has she an interesting accent?

MRS. PEARCE   Oh, something dreadful, sir, really. I dont know how you can
25   take an interest in it.

HIGGINS [*to* PICKERING]   Lets have her up. Shew her up, Mrs. Pearce. [*He rushes across to his working table and picks out a cylinder to use on the phonograph.*]

MRS. PEARCE [*only half resigned to it*]   Very well, sir. It's for you to say.

[*She goes downstairs.*]

HIGGINS   This is rather a bit of luck. I'll shew you how I make records. We'll set her talking; and I'll take it down first in Bell's Visible Speech, then in
30   broad Romic,[1] and then we'll get her on the phonograph so that you can turn her on as often as you like with the written transcript before you.

MRS. PEARCE [*returning*]   This is the young woman, sir.

[*The* FLOWER GIRL *enters in state. She has a hat with three ostrich feathers, orange, sky-blue, and red. She has a nearly clean apron, and the shoddy coat has been tidied a little. The pathos of this deplorable figure,*

---

1. The system of phonetic notation—a precursor of the International Phonetic Alphabet (IPA) used today—devised by Henry Sweet (1845–1912), a linguist on whose career Shaw drew in creating Higgins and who defined a "broad" transcription as less detailed (and less scientific) than a narrow one. Bell's

Visible Speech: a system of notation created a decade earlier than Sweet's by the educator Alexander Melville Bell (1819–1905), the father of the inventor Alexander Graham Bell; it attempts to represent the position of the vocal organs as individual sounds are produced.

with its innocent vanity and consequential air, touches PICKERING, *who has already straightened himself in the presence of* MRS. PEARCE. *But as to* HIGGINS, *the only distinction he makes between men and women is that when he is neither bullying nor exclaiming to the heavens against some featherweight cross, he coaxes women as a child coaxes its nurse when it wants to get anything out of her.*]

HIGGINS [*brusquely, recognizing her with unconcealed disappointment, and at once, babylike, making an intolerable grievance of it*]   Why, this is the girl I jotted down last night. Shes no use: Ive got all the records I want of the Lisson Grove lingo; and I'm not going to waste another cylinder on it. [*To the* GIRL] Be off with you: I dont want you.

THE FLOWER GIRL   Dont you be so saucy. You aint heard what I come for yet. [*To* MRS. PEARCE, *who is waiting at the door for further instruction*] Did you tell him I come in a taxi?

MRS. PEARCE   Nonsense, girl! what do you think a gentleman like Mr. Higgins cares what you came in?

THE FLOWER GIRL   Oh, we are proud! He aint above giving lessons, not him: I heard him say so. Well, I aint come here to ask for any compliment; and if my money's not good enough I can go elsewhere.

HIGGINS   Good enough for what?

THE FLOWER GIRL   Good enough for ye-oo. Now you know, dont you? I'm come to have lessons, I am. And to pay for em too: make no mistake.

HIGGINS [*stupent*][2]   Well ! ! ! [*Recovering his breath with a gasp*] What do you expect me to say to you?

THE FLOWER GIRL   Well, if you was a gentleman, you might ask me to sit down, I think. Dont I tell you I'm bringing you business?

HIGGINS   Pickering: shall we ask this baggage to sit down or shall we throw her out of the window?

THE FLOWER GIRL [*running away in terror to the piano, where she turns at bay*] Ah-ah-ah-ow-ow-ow-oo! [*Wounded and whimpering*] I wont be called a baggage when Ive offered to pay like any lady.

[*Motionless, the two men stare at her from the other side of the room, amazed.*]

PICKERING [*gently*]   What is it you want, my girl?

THE FLOWER GIRL   I want to be a lady in a flower shop stead of selling at the corner of Tottenham Court Road.[3] But they wont take me unless I can talk more genteel. He said he could teach me. Well, here I am ready to pay him—not asking any favor—and he treats me as if I was dirt.

MRS. PEARCE   How can you be such a foolish ignorant girl as to think you could afford to pay Mr. Higgins?

THE FLOWER GIRL   Why shouldnt I? I know what lessons cost as well as you do; and I'm ready to pay.

HIGGINS   How much?

THE FLOWER GIRL [*coming back to him, triumphant*]   Now youre talking! I thought youd come off it when you saw a chance of getting back a bit of what you chucked at me last night. [*Confidentially*] Youd had a drop in,[4] hadnt you?

2. In a state of stupefied amazement.
3. A busy central London shopping street, within a half mile of Covent Garden.
4. That is, you'd had something to drink.

70 HIGGINS [*peremptorily*] Sit down.

THE FLOWER GIRL Oh, if youre going to make a compliment of it—

HIGGINS [*thundering at her*] Sit down.

MRS. PEARCE [*severely*] Sit down, girl. Do as youre told. [*She places the stray chair near the hearthrug between* HIGGINS *and* PICKERING, *and stands behind it waiting for the girl to sit down.*]

THE FLOWER GIRL Ah-ah-ah-ow-ow-oo! [*She stands, half rebellious, half bewildered.*]

75 PICKERING [*very courteous*] Wont you sit down?

THE FLOWER GIRL [*coyly*] Dont mind if I do. [*She sits down.* PICKERING *returns to the hearthrug.*]

HIGGINS Whats your name?

THE FLOWER GIRL Liza Doolittle.

HIGGINS [*declaiming gravely*]

      Eliza, Elizabeth, Betsy and Bess,

80   They went to the woods to get a birds nes':

PICKERING   They found a nest with four eggs in it:

HIGGINS   They took one apiece, and left three in it.

    They laugh heartily at their own wit.

LIZA Oh, dont be silly.

MRS. PEARCE You mustnt speak to the gentleman like that.

85 LIZA Well, why wont he speak sensible to me?

HIGGINS Come back to business. How much do you propose to pay me for the lessons?

LIZA Oh, I know whats right. A lady friend of mine gets French lessons for eighteenpence an hour from a real French gentleman. Well, you
90 wouldnt have the face to ask me the same for teaching me my own language as you would for French; so I wont give more than a shilling. Take it or leave it.

HIGGINS [*walking up and down the room, rattling his keys and his cash in his pockets*] You know, Pickering, if you consider a shilling, not as a simple shilling, but as a percentage of this girl's income, it works out as fully
95 equivalent to sixty or seventy guineas[5] from a millionaire.

PICKERING How so?

HIGGINS Figure it out. A millionaire has about £150 a day. She earns about half-a-crown.

LIZA [*haughtily*] Who told you I only—

100 HIGGINS [*continuing*] She offers me two-fifths of her day's income for a lesson. Two-fifths of a millionaire's income for a day would be somewhere about £60. It's handsome. By George, it's enormous! it's the biggest offer I ever had.

LIZA [*rising, terrified*] Sixty pounds! What are you talking about? I never
105 offered you sixty pounds. Where would I get—

HIGGINS Hold your tongue.

LIZA [*weeping*] But I aint got sixty pounds. Oh—

MRS. PEARCE Dont cry, you silly girl. Sit down. Nobody is going to touch your money.

5. Roughly equivalent to $6,000 today; a guinea is a gold coin worth twenty-one shillings.

110 HIGGINS   Somebody is going to touch you, with a broomstick, if you dont stop snivelling. Sit down.

LIZA [*obeying slowly*]   Ah-ah-ah-ow-oo-o! One would think you was my father.

HIGGINS   If I decide to teach you, I'll be worse than two fathers to you. Here! [*He offers her his silk handkerchief.*]

LIZA   Whats this for?

115 HIGGINS   To wipe your eyes. To wipe any part of your face that feels moist. Remember: thats your handkerchief; and thats your sleeve. Dont mistake the one for the other if you wish to become a lady in a shop.

[LIZA, *utterly bewildered, stares helplessly at him.*]

MRS. PEARCE   It's no use talking to her like that, Mr. Higgins: she doesnt understand you. Besides, youre quite wrong: she doesnt do it that way at 120 all. [*She takes the handkerchief.*]

LIZA [*snatching it*]   Here! You give me that handkerchief. He give it to me, not to you.

PICKERING [*laughing*]   He did. I think it must be regarded as her property, Mrs. Pearce.

125 MRS. PEARCE [*resigning herself*]   Serve you right, Mr. Higgins.

PICKERING   Higgins: I'm interested. What about the ambassador's garden party? I'll say youre the greatest teacher alive if you make that good. I'll bet you all the expenses of the experiment you cant do it. And I'll pay for the lessons.

LIZA   Oh, you are real good. Thank you, Captain.

130 HIGGINS [*tempted, looking at her*]   It's almost irresistible. Shes so deliciously low—so horribly dirty—

LIZA [*protesting extremely*]   Ah-ah-ah-ah-ow-ow-oo-oo!!! I aint dirty: I washed my face and hands afore I come, I did.

PICKERING   Youre certainly not going to turn her head with flattery, Higgins.

135 MRS. PEARCE [*uneasy*]   Oh, dont say that, sir: theres more ways than one of turning a girl's head; and nobody can do it better than Mr. Higgins, though he may not always mean it. I do hope, sir, you wont encourage him to do anything foolish.

HIGGINS [*becoming excited as the idea grows on him*]   What is life but a series 140 of inspired follies? The difficulty is to find them to do. Never lose a chance: it doesnt come every day. I shall make a duchess of this draggle-tailed guttersnipe.

LIZA [*strongly deprecating this view of her*]   Ah-ah-ah-ow-ow-oo!

HIGGINS [*carried away*]   Yes: in six months—in three if she has a good ear 145 and a quick tongue—I'll take her anywhere and pass her off as anything. We'll start today: now! this moment! Take her away and clean her, Mrs. Pearce. Monkey Brand,[6] if it wont come off any other way. Is there a good fire in the kitchen?

MRS. PEARCE [*protesting*]   Yes; but—

150 HIGGINS [*storming on*]   Take all her clothes off and burn them. Ring up Whiteley[7] or somebody for new ones. Wrap her up in brown paper til they come.

LIZA   Youre no gentleman, youre not, to talk of such things. I'm a good girl, I am; and I know what the like of you are, I do.

---

6. A popular brand of scouring soap.   7. A large department store in London.

155 HIGGINS   We want none of your Lisson Grove prudery here, young woman.
Youve got to learn to behave like a duchess. Take her away, Mrs. Pearce. If
she gives you any trouble wallop her.

LIZA [*springing up and running between* PICKERING *and* MRS. PEARCE *for protection*]   No! I'll call the police, I will.

MRS. PEARCE   But Ive no place to put her.

160 HIGGINS   Put her in the dustbin.

LIZA   Ah-ah-ah-ow-ow-oo!

PICKERING   Oh come, Higgins! be reasonable.

MRS. PEARCE [*resolutely*]   You must be reasonable, Mr. Higgins: really you
must. You cant walk over everybody like this.

> [HIGGINS, *thus scolded, subsides. The hurricane is succeeded by a zephyr
> of amiable surprise.*]

165 HIGGINS [*with professional exquisiteness of modulation*]   I walk over everybody! My dear Mrs. Pearce, my dear Pickering, I never had the slightest
intention of walking over anyone. All I propose is that we should be kind to
this poor girl. We must help her to prepare and fit herself for her new station in life. If I did not express myself clearly it was because I did not wish

170 to hurt her delicacy, or yours.

> [LIZA, *reassured, steals back to her chair.*]

MRS. PEARCE [*to* PICKERING]   Well, did you ever hear anything like that, sir?

PICKERING [*laughing heartily*]   Never, Mrs. Pearce: never.

HIGGINS [*patiently*]   Whats the matter?

MRS. PEARCE   Well, the matter is, sir, that you cant take a girl up like that as

175 if you were picking up a pebble on the beach.

HIGGINS   Why not?

MRS. PEARCE   Why not! But you dont know anything about her. What about
her parents? She may be married.

LIZA   Garn!

180 HIGGINS   There! As the girl very properly says, Garn! Married indeed! Dont
you know that a woman of that class looks a worn out drudge of fifty a year
after shes married.

LIZA   Whood marry me?

HIGGINS [*suddenly resorting to the most thrillingly beautiful low tones in his
best elocutionary style*]   By George, Eliza, the streets will be strewn with

185 the bodies of men shooting themselves for your sake before Ive done with
you.

MRS. PEARCE   Nonsense, sir. You mustnt talk like that to her.

LIZA [*rising and squaring herself determinedly*]   I'm going away. He's off his
chump, he is. I dont want no balmies[8] teaching me.

HIGGINS [*wounded in his tenderest point by her insensibility to his elocution*]

190 Oh, indeed! I'm mad, am I? Very well, Mrs. Pearce: you neednt order the
new clothes for her. Throw her out.

LIZA [*whimpering*]   Nah-ow. You got no right to touch me.

MRS. PEARCE   You see now what comes of being saucy. [*Indicating the door*]
This way, please.

195 LIZA [*almost in tears*]   I didnt want no clothes. I wouldnt have taken them.
[*She throws away the handkerchief.*] I can buy my own clothes.

---

8. Crazies, madmen (slang). *Off his chump*: out of his senses (*chump* is slang for "head").

HIGGINS [*deftly retrieving the handkerchief and intercepting her on her reluc-tant way to the door*]   Youre an ungrateful wicked girl. This is my return for offering to take you out of the gutter and dress you beautifully and make a lady of you.

200 MRS. PEARCE   Stop, Mr. Higgins. I wont allow it. It's you that are wicked. Go home to your parents, girl; and tell them to take better care of you.

LIZA   I aint got no parents. They told me I was big enough to earn my own living and turned me out.

MRS. PEARCE   Wheres your mother?

205 LIZA   I aint got no mother. Her that turned me out was my sixth stepmother. But I done without them. And I'm a good girl, I am.

HIGGINS   Very well, then, what on earth is all this fuss about? The girl doesnt belong to anybody—is no use to anybody but me. [*He goes to* MRS. PEARCE *and begins coaxing.*] You can adopt her, Mrs. Pearce: I'm sure a daughter

210 would be a great amusement to you. Now dont make any more fuss. Take her downstairs; and—

MRS. PEARCE   But whats to become of her? Is she to be paid anything? Do be sensible, sir.

HIGGINS   Oh, pay her whatever is necessary: put it down in the housekeeping

215 book. [*Impatiently*] What on earth will she want with money? She'll have her food and her clothes. She'll only drink if you give her money.

LIZA [*turning on him*]   Oh you are a brute. It's a lie: nobody ever saw the sign of liquor on me. [*She goes back to her chair and plants herself there defiantly.*]

PICKERING [*in good-humored remonstrance*]   Does it occur to you, Higgins,

220 that the girl has some feelings?

HIGGINS [*looking critically at her*]   Oh no, I dont think so. Not any feelings that we need bother about. [*Cheerily*] Have you, Eliza?

LIZA   I got my feelings same as anyone else.

HIGGINS [*to* PICKERING, *reflectively*]   You see the difficulty?

225 PICKERING   Eh? What difficulty?

HIGGINS   To get her to talk grammar. The mere pronunciation is easy enough.

LIZA   I dont want to talk grammar. I want to talk like a lady.

MRS. PEARCE   Will you please keep to the point, Mr. Higgins. I want to know on what terms the girl is to be here. Is she to have any wages? And what is

230 to become of her when youve finished your teaching? You must look ahead a little.

HIGGINS [*impatiently*]   Whats to become of her if I leave her in the gutter? Tell me that, Mrs. Pearce.

MRS. PEARCE   Thats her own business, not yours, Mr. Higgins.

235 HIGGINS   Well, when Ive done with her, we can throw her back into the gut-ter; and then it will be her own business again; so thats all right.

LIZA   Oh, youve no feeling heart in you: you dont care for nothing but your-self. [*She rises and takes the floor resolutely.*] Here! Ive had enough of this. I'm going. [*Making for the door*] You ought to be ashamed of yourself, you ought.

HIGGINS [*snatching a chocolate cream from the piano, his eyes suddenly begin-

240 ning to twinkle with mischief*]   Have some chocolates, Eliza.

LIZA [*halting, tempted*]   How do I know what might be in them? Ive heard of girls being drugged by the like of you.

[HIGGINS *whips out his penknife; cuts a chocolate in two; puts one half into his mouth and bolts it; and offers her the other half.*]

HIGGINS   Pledge of good faith, Eliza. I eat one half: you eat the other. [LIZA
opens her mouth to retort: he pops the half chocolate into it.] You shall have
245   boxes of them, barrels of them, every day. You shall live on them. Eh?

LIZA [*who has disposed of the chocolate after being nearly choked by it*]   I
wouldnt have ate it, only I'm too ladylike to take it out of my mouth.

HIGGINS   Listen, Eliza. I think you said you came in a taxi.

LIZA   Well, what if I did? Ive as good a right to take a taxi as anyone else.

250   HIGGINS   You have, Eliza; and in future you shall have as many taxis as you
want. You shall go up and down and round the town in a taxi every day.
Think of that, Eliza.

MRS. PEARCE   Mr. Higgins: youre tempting the girl. It's not right. She should
think of the future.

255   HIGGINS   At her age! Nonsense! Time enough to think of the future when
you havnt any future to think of. No, Eliza: do as this lady does: think of
other people's futures; but never think of your own. Think of chocolates,
and taxis, and gold, and diamonds.

LIZA   No: I dont want no gold and no diamonds. I'm a good girl, I am. [*She
sits down again, with an attempt at dignity.*]

260   HIGGINS   You shall remain so, Eliza, under the care of Mrs. Pearce. And you
shall marry an officer in the Guards, with a beautiful moustache: the son
of a marquis, who will disinherit him for marrying you, but will relent when
he sees your beauty and goodness—

PICKERING   Excuse me, Higgins; but I really must interfere. Mrs. Pearce is
265   quite right. If this girl is to put herself in your hands for six months for an
experiment in teaching, she must understand thoroughly what shes doing.

HIGGINS   How can she? Shes incapable of understanding anything. Besides,
do any of us understand what we are doing? If we did, would we ever do it?

PICKERING   Very clever, Higgins; but not sound sense. [*To* ELIZA] Miss
270   Doolittle—

LIZA [*overwhelmed*]   Ah-ah-ow-oo!

HIGGINS   There! Thats all you get out of Eliza. Ah-ah-ow-oo! No use explaining. As a military man you ought to know that. Give her her orders: thats
what she wants. Eliza: you are to live here for the next six months, learning
275   how to speak beautifully, like a lady in a florist's shop. If youre good and do
whatever youre told, you shall sleep in a proper bedroom, and have lots to
eat, and money to buy chocolates and take rides in taxis. If youre naughty
and idle you will sleep in the back kitchen among the black beetles, and be
walloped by Mrs. Pearce with a broomstick. At the end of six months you
280   shall go to Buckingham Palace in a carriage, beautifully dressed. If the
King finds out youre not a lady, you will be taken by the police to the Tower
of London, where your head will be cut off as a warning to other presumptuous flower girls. If you are not found out, you shall have a present of
seven-and-sixpence to start life with as a lady in a shop. If you refuse this
285   offer you will be a most ungrateful and wicked girl; and the angels will
weep for you. [*To* PICKERING] Now are you satisfied, Pickering? [*To* MRS.
PEARCE] Can I put it more plainly and fairly, Mrs. Pearce?

MRS. PEARCE [*patiently*]   I think youd better let me speak to the girl properly
in private. I dont know that I can take charge of her or consent to the
290   arrangement at all. Of course I know you dont mean her any harm; but
when you get what you call interested in people's accents, you never think
or care what may happen to them or you. Come with me, Eliza.

HIGGINS   Thats all right. Thank you, Mrs. Pearce. Bundle her off to the bath-room.

295 LIZA [*rising reluctantly and suspiciously*]   Youre a great bully, you are. I wont stay here if I dont like. I wont let nobody wallop me. I never asked to go to Bucknam Palace, I didnt. I was never in trouble with the police, not me. I'm a good girl—

MRS. PEARCE   Dont answer back, girl. You dont understand the gentleman.

300 Come with me. [*She leads the way to the door, and holds it open for* ELIZA.]

LIZA [*as she goes out*]   Well, what I say is right. I wont go near the king, not if I'm going to have my head cut off. If I'd known what I was letting myself in for, I wouldnt have come here. I always been a good girl; and I never offered to say a word to him; and I dont owe him nothing; and I dont care;

305 and I wont be put upon; and I have my feelings the same as anyone else—

> [MRS. PEARCE *shuts the door; and* ELIZA's *plaints are no longer audible.* PICKERING *comes from the hearth to the chair and sits astride it with his arms on the back.*]

PICKERING   Excuse the straight question, Higgins. Are you a man of good character where women are concerned?

HIGGINS [*moodily*]   Have you ever met a man of good character where women are concerned?

310 PICKERING   Yes: very frequently.

HIGGINS [*dogmatically, lifting himself on his hands to the level of the piano, and sitting on it with a bounce*]   Well, I havnt. I find that the moment I let a woman make friends with me, she becomes jealous, exacting, suspicious, and a damned nuisance. I find that the moment I let myself make friends with a woman, I become selfish and tyrannical. Women upset everything.

315 When you let them into your life, you find that the woman is driving at one thing and youre driving at another.

PICKERING   At what, for example?

HIGGINS [*coming off the piano restlessly*]   Oh, Lord knows! I suppose the woman wants to live her own life; and the man wants to live his; and each

320 tries to drag the other on to the wrong track. One wants to go north and the other south; and the result is that both have to go east, though they both hate the east wind. [*He sits down on the bench at the keyboard.*] So here I am, a confirmed old bachelor, and likely to remain so.

PICKERING [*rising and standing over him gravely*]   Come, Higgins! You know

325 what I mean. If I'm to be in this business I shall feel responsible for that girl. I hope it's understood that no advantage is to be taken of her position.

HIGGINS   What! That thing! Sacred, I assure you. [*Rising to explain*] You see, she'll be a pupil; and teaching would be impossible unless pupils were sacred. Ive taught scores of American millionairesses how to speak English:

330 the best looking women in the world. I'm seasoned. They might as well be blocks of wood. *I* might as well be a block of wood. It's—

> [MRS. PEARCE *opens the door. She has* ELIZA's *hat in her hand.* PICKERING *retires to the easy-chair at the hearth and sits down.*]

HIGGINS [*eagerly*]   Well, Mrs. Pearce: is it all right?

MRS. PEARCE [*at the door*]   I just wish to trouble you with a word, if I may, Mr. Higgins.

335 HIGGINS   Yes, certainly. Come in. [*She comes forward.*] Dont burn that, Mrs. Pearce. I'll keep it as a curiosity. [*He takes the hat.*]

MRS. PEARCE   Handle it carefully, sir, please. I had to promise her not to burn it; but I had better put it in the oven for a while.

HIGGINS [*putting it down hastily on the piano*]   Oh! thank you. Well, what
340   have you to say to me?

PICKERING   Am I in the way?

MRS. PEARCE   Not at all, sir. Mr. Higgins: will you please be very particular what you say before the girl?

HIGGINS [*sternly*]   Of course. I'm always particular about what I say. Why do
345   you say this to me?

MRS. PEARCE [*unmoved*]   No, sir: youre not at all particular when youve mislaid anything or when you get a little impatient. Now it doesnt matter before me: I'm used to it. But you really must not swear before the girl.

HIGGINS [*indignantly*]   I swear! [*Most emphatically*] I never swear. I detest
350   the habit. What the devil do you mean?

MRS. PEARCE [*stolidly*]   Thats what I mean, sir. You swear a great deal too much. I dont mind your damning and blasting, and what the devil and where the devil and who the devil—

HIGGINS   Mrs. Pearce: this language from your lips! Really!

355   MRS. PEARCE [*not to be put off*]   —but there is a certain word I must ask you not to use. The girl has just used it herself because the bath was too hot. It begins with the same letter as bath.[9] She knows no better: she learnt it at her mother's knee. But she must not hear it from your lips.

HIGGINS [*loftily*]   I cannot charge myself with having ever uttered it, Mrs.
360   Pearce. [*She looks at him steadfastly. He adds, hiding an uneasy conscience with a judicial air.*] Except perhaps in a moment of extreme and justifiable excitement.

MRS. PEARCE   Only this morning, sir, you applied it to your boots, to the butter, and to the brown bread.

365   HIGGINS   Oh, that! Mere alliteration, Mrs. Pearce, natural to a poet.

MRS. PEARCE   Well, sir, whatever you choose to call it, I beg you not to let the girl hear you repeat it.

HIGGINS   Oh, very well, very well. Is that all?

MRS. PEARCE   No, sir. We shall have to be very particular with this girl as to
370   personal cleanliness.

HIGGINS   Certainly. Quite right. Most important.

MRS. PEARCE   I mean not to be slovenly about her dress or untidy in leaving things about.

HIGGINS [*going to her solemnly*]   Just so. I intended to call your attention to
375   that. [*He passes on to* PICKERING, *who is enjoying the conversation immensely.*] It is these little things that matter, Pickering. Take care of the pence and the pounds will take care of themselves is as true of personal habits as of money. [*He comes to anchor on the hearthrug, with the air of a man in an unassailable position.*]

MRS. PEARCE   Yes, sir. Then might I ask you not to come down to breakfast in
380   your dressing-gown, or at any rate not to use it as a napkin to the extent you do, sir. And if you would be so good as not to eat everything off the same plate, and to remember not to put the porridge saucepan out of your

9. That is, "bloody," a colloquial intensifier that came to be considered highly offensive and profane (folk etymology linked it to the oath "God's blood!").

hand on the clean tablecloth, it would be a better example to the girl. You know you nearly choked yourself with a fishbone in the jam only last week.

385 HIGGINS [*rounded from the hearthrug and drifting back to the piano*]   I may do these things sometimes in absence of mind; but surely I dont do them habitually. [*Angrily*] By the way: my dressing-gown smells most damnably of benzine.[1]

MRS. PEARCE   No doubt it does, Mr. Higgins. But if you will wipe your
390 fingers—

HIGGINS [*yelling*]   Oh very well, very well: I'll wipe them in my hair in future.

MRS. PEARCE   I hope youre not offended, Mr. Higgins.

HIGGINS [*shocked at finding himself thought capable of an unamiable sentiment*]   Not at all, not at all. Youre quite right, Mrs. Pearce: I shall be particularly careful before the girl. Is that all?

395 MRS. PEARCE   No, sir. Might she use some of those Japanese dresses you brought from abroad? I really cant put her back into her old things.

HIGGINS   Certainly. Anything you like. Is that all?

MRS. PEARCE   Thank you, sir. Thats all. [*She goes out.*]

HIGGINS   You know, Pickering, that woman has the most extraordinary ideas
400 about me. Here I am, a shy, diffident sort of man. Ive never been able to feel really grown-up and tremendous, like other chaps. And yet shes firmly persuaded that I'm an arbitrary overbearing bossing kind of person. I cant account for it.

[MRS. PEARCE *returns.*]

MRS. PEARCE   If you please, sir, the trouble's beginning already. Theres a
405 dustman[2] downstairs, Alfred Doolittle, wants to see you. He says you have his daughter here.

PICKERING [*rising*]   Phew! I say! [*He retreats to the hearthrug.*]

HIGGINS [*promptly*]   Send the blackguard up.

MRS. PEARCE   Oh, very well, sir. [*She goes out.*]

410 PICKERING   He may not be a blackguard, Higgins.

HIGGINS   Nonsense. Of course hes a blackguard.

PICKERING   Whether he is or not, I'm afraid we shall have some trouble with him.

HIGGINS [*confidently*]   Oh no: I think not. If theres any trouble he shall have
415 it with me, not I with him. And we are sure to get something interesting out of him.

PICKERING   About the girl?

HIGGINS   No. I mean his dialect.

PICKERING   Oh!

420 MRS. PEARCE [*at the door*]   Doolittle, sir. [*She admits* DOOLITTLE *and retires.*]

[ALFRED DOOLITTLE *is an elderly but vigorous dustman, clad in the costume of his profession, including a hat with a back brim covering his neck and shoulders. He has well marked and rather interesting features, and seems equally free from fear and conscience. He has a remarkably expressive voice, the result of a habit of giving vent to his feelings without reserve. His present pose is that of wounded honor and stern resolution.*]

1. A solvent used to remove grease spots.   2. Garbage collector.

DOOLITTLE [*at the door, uncertain which of the two gentlemen is his man*] Professor Higgins?

HIGGINS   Here. Good morning. Sit down.

DOOLITTLE   Morning, Governor. [*He sits down magisterially.*] I come about a very serious matter, Governor.

425 HIGGINS [*to* PICKERING]   Brought up in Hounslow.[3] Mother Welsh, I should think. [DOOLITTLE *opens his mouth, amazed.* HIGGINS *continues.*] What do you want, Doolittle?

DOOLITTLE [*menacingly*]   I want my daughter: thats what I want. See?

HIGGINS   Of course you do. Youre her father, arnt you? You dont suppose
430 anyone else wants her, do you? I'm glad to see you have some spark of family feeling left. Shes upstairs. Take her away at once.

DOOLITTLE [*rising, fearfully taken aback*]   What!

HIGGINS   Take her away. Do you suppose I'm going to keep your daughter for you?

435 DOOLITTLE [*remonstrating*]   Now, now, look here, Governor. Is this reasonable? Is it fairity[4] to take advantage of a man like this? The girl belongs to me. You got her. Where do I come in? [*He sits down again.*]

HIGGINS   Your daughter had the audacity to come to my house and ask me to teach her how to speak properly so that she could get a place in a flower-
440 shop. This gentleman and my housekeeper have been here all the time. [*Bullying him*] How dare you come here and attempt to blackmail me? You sent her here on purpose.

DOOLITTLE [*protesting*]   No, Governor.

HIGGINS   You must have. How else could you possibly know that she is here?

445 DOOLITTLE   Dont take a man up like that, Governor.

HIGGINS   The police shall take you up. This is a plant—a plot to extort money by threats. I shall telephone for the police. [*He goes resolutely to the telephone and opens the directory.*]

DOOLITTLE   Have I asked you for a brass farthing?[5] I leave it to the gentleman here: have I said a word about money?

HIGGINS [*throwing the book aside and marching down on* DOOLITTLE *with a
450 poser*]   What else did you come for?

DOOLITTLE [*sweetly*]   Well, what would a man come for? Be human, Governor.

HIGGINS [*disarmed*]   Alfred: did you put her up to it?

DOOLITTLE   So help me, Governor, I never did. I take my Bible oath I aint
455 seen the girl these two months past.

HIGGINS   Then how did you know she was here?

DOOLITTLE [*"most musical, most melancholy"*[6]]   I'll tell you, Governor, if youll only let me get a word in. I'm willing to tell you. I'm wanting to tell you. I'm waiting to tell you.

460 HIGGINS   Pickering: this chap has a certain natural gift of rhetoric. Observe the rhythm of his native wood-notes wild.[7] "I'm willing to tell you: I'm

---

3. A working-class suburb west of central London.

4. Fair (Doolittle's fanciful coinage).

5. An expression equivalent to "one red cent"; a farthing is one-quarter of a penny, and "brass" here is emphatic.

6. From John Milton's poem "Il Penseroso" (ca. 1631), line 62.

7. A quotation from Milton's "L'Allegro" (ca. 1631), line 134; in the poem (a companion piece to "Il Penseroso"), the phrase refers to Shakespeare.

wanting to tell you: I'm waiting to tell you." Sentimental rhetoric! thats the
Welsh strain in him. It also accounts for his mendacity and dishonesty.

PICKERING   Oh, please, Higgins: I'm west country[8] myself. [*To* DOOLITTLE]
How did you know the girl was here if you didnt send her?

DOOLITTLE   It was like this, Governor. The girl took a boy in the taxi to give
him a jaunt. Son of her landlady, he is. He hung about on the chance of her
giving him another ride home. Well, she sent him back for her luggage
when she heard you was willing for her to stop here. I met the boy at the
corner of Long Acre and Endell Street.

HIGGINS   Public house.[9] Yes?

DOOLITTLE   The poor man's club, Governor: why shouldnt I?

PICKERING   Do let him tell his story, Higgins.

DOOLITTLE   He told me what was up. And I ask you, what was my feelings
and my duty as a father? I says to the boy, "You bring me the luggage," I says—

PICKERING   Why didnt you go for it yourself?

DOOLITTLE   Landlady wouldnt have trusted me with it, Governor. Shes that
kind of woman: you know. I had to give the boy a penny afore he trusted me
with it, the little swine. I brought it to her just to oblige you like, and make
myself agreeable. Thats all.

HIGGINS   How much luggage?

DOOLITTLE   Musical instrument, Governor. A few pictures, a trifle of jewelry,
and a bird-cage. She said she didnt want no clothes. What was I to think
from that, Governor? I ask you as a parent what was I to think?

HIGGINGS   So you came to rescue her from worse than death, eh?

DOOLITTLE   [*appreciatively: relieved at being so well understood*]   Just so, Governor. Thats right.

PICKERING   But why did you bring her luggage if you intended to take her
away?

DOOLITTLE   Have I said a word about taking her away? Have I now?

HIGGINS   [*determinedly*]   Youre going to take her away, double quick. [*He
crosses to the hearth and rings the bell.*]

DOOLITTLE   [*rising*]   No, Governor. Dont say that. I'm not the man to stand in
my girl's light. Heres a career opening for her, as you might say; and—

[MRS. PEARCE *opens the door and awaits orders.*]

HIGGINS   Mrs. Pearce: this is Eliza's father. He has come to take her away.
Give her to him. [*He goes back to the piano, with an air of washing his hands
of the whole affair.*]

DOOLITTLE   No. This is a misunderstanding. Listen here—

MRS. PEARCE   He cant take her away, Mr. Higgins: how can he? You told me
to burn her clothes.

DOOLITTLE   Thats right. I cant carry the girl through the streets like a blooming monkey, can I? I put it to you.

HIGGINS   You have put it to me that you want your daughter. Take your
daughter. If she has no clothes go out and buy her some.

DOOLITTLE   [*desperate*]   Wheres the clothes she come in? Did I burn them or
did your missus here?

---

8. The southwestern counties of England—
Somerset, Dorset, Devon, and Cornwall. The
inhabitants of Cornwall and Wales are connected by their related languages, and the

English long regarded (and often denigrated)
them as separate cultural groups.
9. That is, a pub.

505 MRS. PEARCE   I am the housekeeper, if you please. I have sent for some
clothes for your girl. When they come you can take her away. You can wait
in the kitchen. This way, please.

> [DOOLITTLE, *much troubled, accompanies her to the door; then hesitates;
> finally turns confidentially to* HIGGINS.]

DOOLITTLE   Listen here, Governor. You and me is men of the world, aint we?

HIGGINS   Oh! Men of the world, are we? Youd better go, Mrs. Pearce.

510 MRS. PEARCE   I think so, indeed, sir.

> [*She goes, with dignity.*]

PICKERING   The floor is yours, Mr. Doolittle.

DOOLITTLE [*to* PICKERING]   I thank you, Governor. [*To* HIGGINS, *who takes
refuge on the piano bench, a little overwhelmed by the proximity of his visitor; for* DOOLITTLE *has a professional flavor of dust about him*] Well, the truth
is, Ive taken a sort of fancy to you, Governor; and if you want the girl, I'm
515 not so set on having her back home again but what I might be open to an
arrangement. Regarded in the light of a young woman, shes a fine handsome girl. As a daughter shes not worth her keep; and so I tell you straight.
All I ask is my rights as a father; and youre the last man alive to expect me
to let her go for nothing; for I can see youre one of the straight sort, Gov-
520 ernor. Well, whats a five pound note to you? And whats Eliza to me? [*He
returns to his chair and sits down judicially.*]

PICKERING   I think you ought to know, Doolittle, that Mr. Higgins's intentions are entirely honorable.

DOOLITTLE   Course they are, Governor. If I thought they wasnt, Id ask fifty.

HIGGINS [*revolted*]   Do you mean to say, you callous rascal, that you would
525 sell your daughter for £50?

DOOLITTLE   Not in a general way I wouldnt; but to oblige a gentleman like
you I'd do a good deal, I do assure you.

PICKERING   Have you no morals, man?

DOOLITTLE [*unabashed*]   Cant afford them, Governor. Neither could you if
530 you was as poor as me. Not that I mean any harm, you know. But if Liza is
going to have a bit out of this, why not me too?

HIGGINS [*troubled*]   I dont know what to do, Pickering. There can be no
question that as a matter of morals it's a positive crime to give this chap a
farthing. And yet I feel a sort of rough justice in his claim.

535 DOOLITTLE   Thats it, Governor. Thats all I say. A father's heart, as it were.

PICKERING   Well, I know the feeling; but really it seems hardly right—

DOOLITTLE   Dont say that, Governor. Dont look at it that way. What am I,
Governors both? I ask you, what am I? I'm one of the undeserving poor:
thats what I am. Think of what that means to a man. It means that hes up
540 agen[1] middle class morality all the time. If theres anything going, and I put
in for a bit of it, it's always the same story: "Youre undeserving; so you cant
have it." But my needs is as great as the most deserving widow's that ever
got money out of six different charities in one week for the death of the
same husband. I dont need less than a deserving man: I need more. I dont
545 eat less hearty than him; and I drink a lot more. I want a bit of amusement,
cause I'm a thinking man. I want cheerfulness and a song and a band when
I feel low. Well, they charge me just the same for everything as they charge

---

1. Against.

the deserving. What is middle class morality? Just an excuse for never giving me anything. Therefore, I ask you, as two gentlemen, not to play that game on me. I'm playing straight with you. I aint pretending to be deserving. I'm undeserving; and I mean to go on being undeserving. I like it; and thats the truth. Will you take advantage of a man's nature to do him out of the price of his own daughter what hes brought up and fed and clothed by the sweat of his brow until shes growed big enough to be interesting to you two gentlemen? Is five pounds unreasonable? I put it to you; and I leave it to you.

HIGGINS [*rising, and going over to* PICKERING]   Pickering: if we were to take this man in hand for three months, he could choose between a seat in the Cabinet and a popular pulpit in Wales.

PICKERING   What do you say to that, Doolittle?

DOOLITTLE   Not me, Governor, thank you kindly. Ive heard all the preachers and all the prime ministers—for I'm a thinking man and game for politics or religion or social reform same as all the other amusements—and I tell you it's a dog's life anyway you look at it. Undeserving poverty is my line. Taking one station in society with another, it's—it's—well, it's the only one that has any ginger in it, to my taste.

HIGGINS   I suppose we must give him a fiver.

PICKERING   He'll make a bad use of it, I'm afraid.

DOOLITTLE   Not me, Governor, so help me I wont. Dont you be afraid that I'll save it and spare it and live idle on it. There wont be a penny of it left by Monday: I'll have to go to work same as if I'd never had it. It wont pauperize me, you bet. Just one good spree for myself and the missus, giving pleasure to ourselves and employment to others, and satisfaction to you to think it's not been throwed away. You couldnt spend it better.

HIGGINS [*taking out his pocket book and coming between* DOOLITTLE *and the piano*]   This is irresistible. Lets give him ten. [*He offers two notes to the dustman.*]

DOOLITTLE   No, Governor. She wouldnt have the heart to spend ten; and perhaps I shouldnt neither. Ten pounds is a lot of money: it makes a man feel prudent like: and then good-bye to happiness. You give me what I ask you, Governor: not a penny more, and not a penny less.

PICKERING   Why dont you marry that missus of yours? I rather draw the line at encouraging that sort of immorality.

DOOLITTLE   Tell her so, Governor: tell her so. I'm willing. It's me that suffers by it. Ive no hold on her. I got to be agreeable to her. I got to give her presents. I got to buy her clothes something sinful. I'm a slave to that woman, Governor, just because I'm not her lawful husband. And she knows it too. Catch her marrying me! Take my advice, Governor: marry Eliza while shes young and dont know no better. If you dont youll be sorry for it after. If you do, she'll be sorry for it after; but better you than her, because youre a man, and shes only a woman and dont know how to be happy anyhow.

HIGGINS   Pickering: if we listen to this man another minute, we shall have no convictions left. [*To* DOOLITTLE] Five pounds I think you said.

DOOLITTLE   Thank you kindly, Governor.

HIGGINS   Youre sure you wont take ten?

DOOLITTLE   Not now. Another time, Governor.

HIGGINS [*handing him a five-pound note*]   Here you are.

DOOLITTLE   Thank you, Governor. Good morning.

[*He hurries to the door, anxious to get away with his booty. When he opens it he is confronted with a dainty and exquisitely clean young Japanese lady in a simple blue cotton kimono printed cunningly with small white jasmine blossoms. MRS. PEARCE is with her. He gets out of her way deferentially and apologizes.*]

Beg pardon, miss.

THE JAPANESE LADY   Garn! Dont you know your own daughter?

600 DOOLITTLE ⎫
HIGGINS   ⎬ *exclaiming*   ⎰ Bly me! it's Eliza!
PICKERING ⎭ *simultaneously* ⎱ Whats that! This!
                               ⎣ By Jove!

LIZA   Dont I look silly?

HIGGINS   Silly?

MRS. PEARCE [*at the door*]   Now, Mr. Higgins, please dont say anything to
605   make the girl conceited about herself.

HIGGINS [*conscientiously*]   Oh! Quite right, Mrs. Pearce. [*To* ELIZA] Yes: damned silly.

MRS. PEARCE   Please, sir.

HIGGINS [*correcting himself*]   I mean extremely silly.

610 LIZA   I should look all right with my hat on. [*She takes up her hat; puts it on; and walks across the room to the fireplace with a fashionable air.*]

HIGGINS   A new fashion, by George! And it ought to look horrible!

DOOLITTLE [*with fatherly pride*]   Well, I never thought she'd clean up as good looking as that, Governor. Shes a credit to me, aint she?

LIZA   I tell you, it's easy to clean up here. Hot and cold water on tap, just as
615   much as you like, there is. Woolly towels, there is; and a towel horse[2] so hot, it burns your fingers. Soft brushes to scrub yourself, and a wooden bowl of soap smelling like primroses. Now I know why ladies is so clean. Washing's a treat for them. Wish they saw what it is for the like of me!

HIGGINS   I'm glad the bath-room met with your approval.

620 LIZA   It didnt: not all of it; and I dont care who hears me say it. Mrs. Pearce knows.

HIGGINS   What was wrong, Mrs. Pearce?

MRS. PEARCE [*blandly*]   Oh, nothing, sir. It doesnt matter.

LIZA   I had a good mind to break it. I didnt know which way to look. But I
625   hung a towel over it, I did.

HIGGINS   Over what?

MRS. PEARCE   Over the looking-glass, sir.

HIGGINS   Doolittle: you have brought your daughter up too strictly.

DOOLITTLE   Me! I never brought her up at all, except to give her a lick of a
630   strap now and again. Dont put it on me, Governor. She aint accustomed to it, you see: thats all. But she'll soon pick up your free-and-easy ways.

LIZA   I'm a good girl, I am; and I wont pick up no free and easy ways.

HIGGINS   Eliza: if you say again that youre a good girl, your father shall take you home.

635 LIZA   Not him. You dont know my father. All he come here for was to touch you for some money to get drunk on.

---

2. A towel rack, in this case apparently a metal pipe filled with hot water (usually such racks were made of wood).

DOOLITTLE   Well, what else would I want money for? To put into the plate in church, I suppose. [*She puts out her tongue at him. He is so incensed by this that* PICKERING *presently finds it necessary to step between them.*] Dont you give me none of your lip; and dont let me hear you giving this gentleman any of it neither, or youll hear from me about it. See?

HIGGINS   Have you any further advice to give her before you go, Doolittle? Your blessing, for instance.

DOOLITTLE   No, Governor: I aint such a mug[3] as to put up my children to all I know myself. Hard enough to hold them in without that. If you want Eliza's mind improved, Governor, you do it yourself with a strap. So long, gentlemen. [*He turns to go.*]

HIGGINS   [*impressively*]   Stop. Youll come regularly to see your daughter. It's your duty, you know. My brother is a clergyman; and he could help you in your talks with her.

DOOLITTLE   [*evasively*]   Certainly. I'll come, Governor. Not just this week, because I have a job at a distance. But later on you may depend on me. Afternoon, gentlemen. Afternoon, maam.

> [*He takes off his hat to* MRS. PEARCE, *who disdains the salutation and goes out. He winks at* HIGGINS, *thinking him probably a fellow-sufferer from* MRS. PEARCE's *difficult disposition, and follows her.*]

LIZA   Dont you believe the old liar. He'd as soon you set a bull-dog on him as a clergyman. You wont see him again in a hurry.

HIGGINS   I dont want to, Eliza. Do you?

LIZA   Not me. I dont want never to see him again, I dont. Hes a disgrace to me, he is, collecting dust, instead of working at his trade.

PICKERING   What is his trade, Eliza?

LIZA   Talking money out of other people's pockets into his own. His proper trade's a navvy;[4] and he works at it sometimes too—for exercise—and earns good money at it. Aint you going to call me Miss Doolittle any more?

PICKERING   I beg your pardon, Miss Doolittle. It was a slip of the tongue.

LIZA   Oh, I dont mind; only it sounded so genteel. I should just like to take a taxi to the corner of Tottenham Court Road and get out there and tell it to wait for me, just to put the girls in their place a bit. I wouldnt speak to them, you know.

PICKERING   Better wait til we get you something really fashionable.

HIGGINS   Besides, you shouldnt cut[5] your old friends now that you have risen in the world. Thats what we call snobbery.

LIZA   You dont call the like of them my friends now, I should hope. Theyve took it out of me often enough with their ridicule when they had the chance; and now I mean to get a bit of my own back. But if I'm to have fashionable clothes, I'll wait. I should like to have some. Mrs. Pearce says youre going to give me some to wear in bed at night different to what I wear in the daytime; but it do seem a waste of money when you could get something to shew. Besides, I never could fancy changing into cold things on a winter night.

MRS. PEARCE   [*coming back*]   Now, Eliza. The new things have come for you to try on.

---

3. Fool.
4. An unskilled laborer who digs earth.

5. Break off acquaintance with; pretend not to know.

LIZA Ah-ow-oo-ooh!

> [*She rushes out.*]

MRS. PEARCE [*following her*] Oh, dont rush about like that, girl.

> [*She shuts the door behind her.*]

HIGGINS Pickering: we have taken on a stiff job.

PICKERING [*with conviction*] Higgins: we have.

Act 3

[*It is* MRS. HIGGINS's *at-home day.*[6] *Nobody has yet arrived. Her drawing-room, in a flat on Chelsea Embankment,*[7] *has three windows looking on the river; and the ceiling is not so lofty as it would be in an older house of the same pretension. The windows are open, giving access to a balcony with flowers in pots. If you stand with your face to the windows, you have the fireplace on your left and the door in the right-hand wall close to the corner nearest the windows.*

MRS. HIGGINS *was brought up on Morris and Burne Jones,*[8] *and her room, which is very unlike her son's room in Wimpole Street, is not crowded with furniture and little tables and nicknacks. In the middle of the room there is a big ottoman; and this, with the carpet, the Morris wall-papers, and the Morris chintz windows curtains and brocade covers of the ottoman and its cushions, supply all the ornament, and are much too handsome to be hidden by odds and ends of useless things. A few good oil-paintings from the exhibitions in the Grosvenor Gallery thirty years ago (the Burne Jones, not the Whistler side of them)*[9] *are on the walls. The only landscape is a Cecil Lawson on the scale of a Rubens.*[1] *There is a portrait of* MRS. HIGGINS *as she was when she defied fashion in her youth in one of the beautiful Rossettian*[2] *costumes which, when caricatured by people who did not understand, led to the absurdities of popular estheticism in the eighteen-seventies.*

In the corner diagonally opposite the door MRS. HIGGINS, *now over sixty and long past taking the trouble to dress out of the fashion, sits writing at an elegantly simple writing-table with a bell button within reach of her hand. There is a Chippendale*[3] *chair further back in the room between her and the window nearest her side. At the other side of the room, further forward, is an Elizabethan chair roughly carved in the taste of Inigo Jones.*[4] *On the same side a piano in a decorated case. The corner between the fireplace and the window is occupied by a divan cushioned in Morris chintz.*

It is between four and five in the afternoon.

The door is opened violently; and Higgins enters with his hat on.]

6. In middle- and upper-class society, a set time each week for receiving visitors.

7. A roadway along the north bank of the Thames in central London, developed in the late 19th century with residences for the well-to-do.

8. Two highly influential Victorian artists and designers, who were friends and colleagues. William Morris (1834–1896), associated with the Pre-Raphaelites, was one of the founders of the Arts and Crafts movement and is especially well-known for his wallpaper and fabric designs; Edward Burne-Jones (1833–1898), known for his medieval-style paintings, came under the influence of the Pre-Raphaelites at about the same time as Morris.

9. An allusion to an 1877 exhibition; the painting by the American artist James McNeill Whistler (1834–1903) was so severely attacked in a review by John Ruskin (who praised Burne-Jones's work) that Whistler sued for libel.

1. Peter Paul Rubens (1577–1640), a Flemish artist identified with the baroque style and known for very large paintings. Lawson (1851–1882), an English landscape painter whose early works included a number of studies of Chelsea.

2. In the style of Dante Gabriel Rossetti (1828–1882), an English poet and painter who was a founding member of the Pre-Raphaelite Brotherhood; many of his works depict idealized, sensuous women in flowing garments.

3. A popular 18th-century furniture style, graceful and often ornate; it was named for the English cabinetmaker Thomas Chippendale (1718–1779).

4. The founder of English classical architecture (1573–1652); he designed stage sets as well as buildings.

MRS. HIGGINS [*dismayed*]   Henry! [*Scolding him*] What are you doing here
to-day? It is my at-home day: you promised not to come. [*As he bends to kiss
her, she takes his hat off, and presents it to him.*]

HIGGINS   Oh bother! [*He throws the hat down on the table.*]

MRS. HIGGINS   Go home at once.

5   HIGGINS [*kissing her*]   I know, mother. I came on purpose.

MRS. HIGGINS   But you mustnt. I'm serious, Henry. You offend all my friends:
they stop coming whenever they meet you.

HIGGINS   Nonsense! I know I have no small talk; but people dont mind. [*He
sits on the settee.*]

MRS. HIGGINS   Oh! dont they? Small talk indeed! What about your large talk?
10   Really, dear, you mustnt stay.

HIGGINS   I must. Ive a job for you. A phonetic job.

MRS. HIGGINS   No use, dear. I'm sorry; but I cant get round your vowels; and
though I like to get pretty postcards in your patent shorthand, I always
have to read the copies in ordinary writing you so thoughtfully send me.

15   HIGGINS   Well, this isnt a phonetic job.

MRS. HIGGINS   You said it was.

HIGGINS   Not your part of it. Ive picked up a girl.

MRS. HIGGINS   Does that mean that some girl has picked you up?

HIGGINS   Not at all. I dont mean a love affair.

20   MRS. HIGGINS   What a pity!

HIGGINS   Why?

MRS. HIGGINS   Well, you never fall in love with anyone under forty-five.
When will you discover that there are some rather nice-looking young
women about?

25   HIGGINS   Oh, I cant be bothered with young women. My idea of a loveable
woman is something as like you as possible. I shall never get into the way
of seriously liking young women: some habits lie too deep to be changed.
[*Rising abruptly and walking about, jingling his money and his keys in his
trouser pockets*] Besides, theyre all idiots.

MRS. HIGGINS   Do you know what you would do if you really loved me, Henry?

30   HIGGINS   Oh bother! What? Marry, I suppose?

MRS. HIGGINS   No. Stop fidgeting and take your hands out of your pockets.
[*With a gesture of despair, he obeys and sits down again.*] Thats a good boy.
Now tell me about the girl.

HIGGINS   Shes coming to see you.

35   MRS. HIGGINS   I dont remember asking her.

HIGGINS   You didnt. *I* asked her. If youd known her you wouldnt have asked
her.

MRS. HIGGINS   Indeed! Why?

HIGGINS   Well, it's like this. Shes a common flower girl. I picked her off the
40   kerbstone.

MRS. HIGGINS   And invited her to my at-home!

HIGGINS [*rising and coming to her to coax her*]   Oh, thatll be all right. Ive
taught her to speak properly; and she has strict orders as to her behavior.
Shes to keep to two subjects: the weather and everybody's health—Fine
45   day and How do you do, you know—and not to let herself go on things in
general. That will be safe.

MRS. HIGGINS Safe! To talk about our health! about our insides! perhaps about our outsides! How could you be so silly, Henry?

HIGGINS [*impatiently*] Well, she must talk about something. [*He controls himself and sits down again.*] Oh, she'll be all right: dont you fuss. Pickering is in it with me. Ive a sort of bet on that I'll pass her off as a duchess in six months. I started on her some months ago; and shes getting on like a house on fire. I shall win my bet. She has a quick ear; and shes been easier to teach than my middle-class pupils because shes had to learn a complete new language. She talks English almost as you talk French.

MRS. HIGGINS Thats satisfactory, at all events.

HIGGINS Well, it is and it isnt.

MRS. HIGGINS What does that mean?

HIGGINS You see, Ive got her pronunciation all right; but you have to consider not only how a girl pronounces, but what she pronounces; and thats where—

[*They are interrupted by the* PARLOR-MAID, *announcing guests.*]

THE PARLOR-MAID Mrs. and Miss Eynsford Hill.

[*She withdraws.*]

HIGGINS Oh Lord! [*He rises; snatches his hat from the table; and makes for the door; but before he reaches it his mother introduces him.*]

[MRS. *and* MISS EYNSFORD HILL *are the mother and daughter who sheltered from the rain in Covent Garden. The mother is well bred, quiet, and has the habitual anxiety of straitened means. The daughter has acquired a gay air of being very much at home in society: the bravado of genteel poverty.*]

MRS. EYNSFORD HILL [*to* MRS. HIGGINS] How do you do? [*They shake hands.*]

MISS EYNSFORD HILL How d'you do? [*She shakes.*]

MRS. HIGGINS [*introducing*] My son Henry.

MRS. EYNSFORD HILL Your celebrated son! I have so longed to meet you, Professor Higgins.

HIGGINS [*glumly, making no movement in her direction*] Delighted. [*He backs against the piano and bows brusquely.*]

MISS EYNSFORD HILL [*going to him with confident familiarity*] How do you do?

HIGGINS [*staring at her*] Ive seen you before somewhere. I havnt the ghost of a notion where; but Ive heard your voice. [*Drearily*] It doesnt matter. Youd better sit down.

MRS. HIGGINS I'm sorry to say that my celebrated son has no manners. You mustnt mind him.

MISS EYNSFORD HILL [*gaily*] I dont. [*She sits in the Elizabethan chair.*]

MRS. EYNSFORD HILL [*a little bewildered*] Not at all. [*She sits on the ottoman between her daughter and* MRS. HIGGINS, *who has turned her chair away from the writing-table.*]

HIGGINS Oh, have I been rude? I didnt mean to be.

[*He goes to the central window, through which, with his back to the company, he contemplates the river and the flowers in Battersea Park on the opposite bank as if they were a frozen desert.*]

[*The* PARLOR-MAID *returns, ushering in* PICKERING.]

THE PARLOR-MAID Colonel Pickering.

[*She withdraws.*]

PICKERING How do you do, Mrs. Higgins?

MRS. HIGGINS So glad youve come. Do you know Mrs. Eynsford Hill—Miss Eynsford Hill? [*Exchange of bows. The* COLONEL *brings the Chippendale chair a little forward between* MRS. HILL *and* MRS. HIGGINS, *and sits down.*]

PICKERING Has Henry told you what weve come for?

85 HIGGINS [*over his shoulder*] We were interrupted: damn it!

MRS. HIGGINS Oh Henry, Henry, really!

MRS. EYNSFORD HILL [*half rising*] Are we in the way?

MRS. HIGGINS [*rising and making her sit down again*] No, no. You couldnt have come more fortunately: we want you to meet a friend of ours.

90 HIGGINS [*turning hopefully*] Yes, by George! We want two or three people. Youll do as well as anybody else.

[*The* PARLOR-MAID *returns, ushering* FREDDY.]

THE PARLOR-MAID Mr. Eynsford Hill.

HIGGINS [*almost audibly, past endurance*] God of Heaven! another of them.

FREDDY [*shaking hands with* MRS. HIGGINS] Ahdedo?[5]

95 MRS. HIGGINS Very good of you to come. [*Introducing*] Colonel Pickering.

FREDDY [*bowing*] Ahdedo?

MRS. HIGGINS I dont think you know my son, Professor Higgins.

FREDDY [*going to Higgins*] Ahdedo?

HIGGINS [*looking at him much as if he were a pickpocket*] I'll take my oath
100 Ive met you before somewhere. Where was it?

FREDDY I dont think so.

HIGGINS [*resignedly*] It dont matter, anyhow. Sit down.

[*He shakes* FREDDY'S *hand, and almost slings him on the ottoman with his face to the windows; then comes round to the other side of it.*]

HIGGINS Well, here we are, anyhow! [*He sits down on the ottoman next* MRS. EYNSFORD HILL, *on her left.*] And now, what the devil are we going to talk
105 about until Eliza comes?

MRS. HIGGINS Henry: you are the life and soul of the Royal Society's[6] soirées; but really youre rather trying on more commonplace occasions.

HIGGINS Am I? Very sorry. [*Beaming suddenly*] I suppose I am, you know. [*Uproariously*] Ha, ha!

110 MISS EYNSFORD HILL [*who considers* HIGGINS *quite eligible matrimonially*] I sympathize. *I* havnt any small talk. If people would only be frank and say what they really think!

HIGGINS [*relapsing into gloom*] Lord forbid!

MRS. EYNSFORD HILL [*taking up her daughter's cue*] But why?

115 HIGGINS What they think they ought to think is bad enough, Lord knows; but what they really think would break up the whole show. Do you suppose it would be really agreeable if I were to come out now with what *I* really think?

MISS EYNSFORD HILL [*gaily*] Is it so very cynical?

120 HIGGINS Cynical! Who the dickens said it was cynical? I mean it wouldnt be decent.

MRS. EYNSFORD HILL [*seriously*] Oh! I'm sure you dont mean that, Mr. Higgins.

5. That is, "How do you do?"
6. An independent academy of science in the United Kingdom (formally named in its 1663 charter "The Royal Society of London for Improving Natural Knowledge").

HIGGINS   You see, we're all savages, more or less. We're supposed to be civilized and cultured—to know all about poetry and philosophy and art and
125   science, and so on; but how many of us know even the meanings of these names? [*To* MISS HILL] What do you know of poetry? [*To* MRS. HILL] What do you know of science? [*Indicating* FREDDY] What does he know of art or science or anything else? What the devil do you imagine I know of philosophy?

130   MRS. HIGGINS [*warningly*]   Or of manners, Henry?

THE PARLOR-MAID [*opening the door*]   Miss Doolittle. [*She withdraws.*]

HIGGINS [*rising hastily and running to* MRS. HIGGINS]   Here she is, mother. [*He stands on tiptoe and makes signs over his mother's head to* ELIZA *to indicate to her which lady is her hostess.*]

[ELIZA, *who is exquisitely dressed, produces an impression of such remarkable distinction and beauty as she enters that they all rise, quite fluttered. Guided by* HIGGINS's *signals, she comes to* MRS. HIGGINS *with studied grace.*]

LIZA [*speaking with pedantic correctness of pronunciation and great beauty of tone*]   How do you do, Mrs. Higgins? [*She gasps slightly in making sure of the H in Higgins, but is quite successful.*] Mr. Higgins told me I might come.

135   MRS. HIGGINS [*cordially*]   Quite right: I'm very glad indeed to see you.

PICKERING   How do you do, Miss Doolittle?

LIZA [*shaking hands with him*]   Colonel Pickering, is it not?

MRS. EYNSFORD HILL   I feel sure we have met before, Miss Doolittle. I remember your eyes.

140   LIZA   How do you do? [*She sits down on the ottoman gracefully in the place just left vacant by* HIGGINS.]

MRS. EYNSFORD HILL [*introducing*]   My daughter Clara.

LIZA   How do you do?

CLARA [*impulsively*]   How do you do? [*She sits down on the ottoman beside* ELIZA, *devouring her with her eyes.*]

FREDDY [*coming to their side of the ottoman*]   Ive certainly had the pleasure.

145   MRS. EYNSFORD HILL [*introducing*]   My son Freddy.

LIZA   How do you do?

[FREDDY *bows and sits down in the Elizabethan chair, infatuated.*]

HIGGINS [*suddenly*]   By George, yes: it all comes back to me! [*They stare at him.*] Covent Garden! [*Lamentably*] What a damned thing!

MRS. HIGGINS   Henry, please! [*He is about to sit on the edge of the table.*]
150   Dont sit on my writing-table: youll break it.

HIGGINS [*sulkily*]   Sorry.

[*He goes to the divan, stumbling into the fender[7] and over the fire-irons on his way; extricating himself with muttered imprecations; and finishing his disastrous journey by throwing himself so impatiently on the divan that he almost breaks it. Mrs. Higgins looks at him, but controls herself and says nothing.*]

[*A long and painful pause ensues.*]

MRS. HIGGINS [*at last, conversationally*]   Will it rain, do you think?

LIZA   The shallow depression in the west of these islands is likely to move slowly in an easterly direction. There are no indications of any great
155   change in the barometrical situation.

---

7. A low metal fire screen.

FREDDY   Ha! ha! how awfully funny!

LIZA   What is wrong with that, young man? I bet I got it right.

FREDDY   Killing!

MRS. EYNSFORD HILL   I'm sure I hope it wont turn cold. Theres so much
160   influenza about. It runs right through our whole family regularly every
spring.

LIZA [*darkly*]   My aunt died of influenza: so they said.

MRS. EYNSFORD HILL [*clicks her tongue sympathetically*]   !!!

LIZA [*in the same tragic tone*]   But it's my belief they done the old woman in.

165   MRS. HIGGINS [*puzzled*]   Done her in?

LIZA   Y-e-e-e-es, Lord love you! Why should she die of influenza? She come
through diphtheria right enough the year before. I saw her with my own
eyes. Fairly blue with it, she was. They all thought she was dead; but my
father he kept ladling gin down her throat til she came to so sudden that
170   she bit the bowl off the spoon.

MRS. EYNSFORD HILL [*startled*]   Dear me!

LIZA [*piling up the indictment*]   What call would a woman with that strength
in her have to die of influenza? What become of her new straw hat that
should have come to me? Somebody pinched it; and what I say is, them as
175   pinched it done her in.

MRS. EYNSFORD HILL   What does doing her in mean?

HIGGINS [*hastily*]   Oh, thats the new small talk. To do a person in means to
kill them.

MRS. EYNSFORD HILL [*to ELIZA, horrified*]   You surely dont believe that your
180   aunt was killed?

LIZA   Do I not! Them she lived with would have killed her for a hat-pin, let
alone a hat.

MRS. EYNSFORD HILL   But it cant have been right for your father to pour spirits down her throat like that. It might have killed her.

185   LIZA   Not her. Gin was mother's milk to her. Besides, he'd poured so much
down his own throat that he knew the good of it.

MRS. EYNSFORD HILL   Do you mean that he drank?

LIZA   Drank! My word! Something chronic.

MRS. EYNSFORD HILL   How dreadful for you!

190   LIZA   Not a bit. It never did him no harm what I could see. But then he did
not keep it up regular. [*Cheerfully*] On the burst,[8] as you might say, from
time to time. And always more agreeable when he had a drop in. When he
was out of work, my mother used to give him fourpence and tell him to go
out and not come back until he'd drunk himself cheerful and loving-like.
195   Theres lots of women has to make their husbands drunk to make them fit
to live with. [*Now quite at her ease*] You see, it's like this. If a man has a bit
of a conscience, it always takes him when he's sober; and then it makes
him low-spirited. A drop of booze just takes that off and makes him happy.
[*To FREDDY, who is in convulsions of suppressed laughter*] Here! what are you
200   sniggering at?

FREDDY   The new small talk. You do it so awfully well.

LIZA   If I was doing it proper, what was you laughing at? [*To HIGGINS*] Have I
said anything I oughtnt?

---

8. A bout of drunkenness; a binge.

MRS. HIGGINS [*interposing*]   Not at all, Miss Doolittle.

205 LIZA   Well, thats a mercy, anyhow. [*Expansively*] What I always say is—

HIGGINS [*rising and looking at his watch*]   Ahem!

LIZA [*looking round at him; taking the hint; and rising*]   Well: I must go. [*They all rise.* FREDDY *goes to the door.*] So pleased to have met you. Good-bye. [*She shakes hands with* MRS. HIGGINS.]

210 MRS. HIGGINS.   Good-bye.

LIZA   Good-bye, Colonel Pickering.

PICKERING   Good-bye, Miss Doolittle. [*They shake hands.*]

LIZA [*nodding to the others*]   Good-bye, all.

FREDDY [*opening the door for her*]   Are you walking across the Park, Miss
215 Doolittle? If so—

LIZA   Walk! Not bloody likely. [*Sensation*] I am going in a taxi. [*She goes out.*]

> [PICKERING *gasps and sits down.* FREDDY *goes out on the balcony to catch another glimpse of* ELIZA.]

MRS. EYNSFORD HILL [*suffering from shock*]   Well, I really cant get used to the new ways.

CLARA [*throwing herself discontentedly into the Elizabethan chair*]   Oh, it's all
220 right, mamma, quite right. People will think we never go anywhere or see anybody if you are so old-fashioned.

MRS. EYNSFORD HILL   I daresay I am very old-fashioned; but I do hope you wont begin using that expression, Clara. I have got accustomed to hear you talking about men as rotters, and calling everything filthy and beastly;
225 though I do think it horrible and unladylike. But this last is really too much. Dont you think so, Colonel Pickering?

PICKERING   Dont ask me. Ive been away in India for several years; and manners have changed so much that I sometimes dont know whether I'm at a respectable dinner-table or in a ship's forecastle.

230 CLARA   It's all a matter of habit. Theres no right or wrong in it. Nobody means anything by it. And it's so quaint, and gives such a smart emphasis to things that are not in themselves very witty. I find the new small talk delightful and quite innocent.

MRS. EYNSFORD HILL [*rising*]   Well, after that, I think it's time for us to go.

> [PICKERING *and* HIGGINS *rise.*]

235 CLARA [*rising*]   Oh yes: we have three at-homes to go to still. Good-bye, Mrs. Higgins. Good-bye, Colonel Pickering. Good-bye, Professor Higgins.

HIGGINS [*coming grimly at her from the divan, and accompanying her to the door*]   Good-bye. Be sure you try on that small talk at the three at-homes. Dont be nervous about it. Pitch it in strong.

CLARA [*all smiles*]   I will. Good-bye. Such nonsense, all this early Victorian
240 prudery!

HIGGINS [*tempting her*]   Such damned nonsense!

CLARA   Such bloody nonsense!

MRS. EYNSFORD HILL [*convulsively*]   Clara!

CLARA.   Ha! ha!

> [*She goes out radiant, conscious of being thoroughly up to date, and is heard descending the stairs in a stream of silvery laughter.*]

245 FREDDY [*to the heavens at large*]   Well, I ask you—[*He gives it up, and comes to* MRS. HIGGINS]. Good-bye.

MRS. HIGGINS [*shaking hands*]   Good-bye. Would you like to meet Miss Doolittle again?

FREDDY [*eagerly*]   Yes, I should, most awfully.

250 MRS. HIGGINS   Well, you know my days.

FREDDY   Yes. Thanks awfully. Good-bye. [*He goes out.*]

MRS. EYNSFORD HILL   Good-bye, Mr. Higgins.

HIGGINS   Good-bye. Good-bye.

MRS. EYNSFORD HILL [*to* PICKERING]   It's no use. I shall never be able to bring
255   myself to use that word.

PICKERING   Dont. It's not compulsory, you know. Youll get on quite well without it.

MRS. EYNSFORD HILL   Only, Clara is so down on me if I am not positively
reeking with the latest slang. Good-bye.

260 PICKERING   Good-bye. [*They shake hands.*]

MRS. EYNSFORD HILL [*to* MRS. HIGGINS]   You mustnt mind Clara. [PICKERING,
*catching from her lowered tone that this is not meant for him to hear, dis-
creetly joins* HIGGINS *at the window.*] We're so poor! and she gets so few
parties, poor child! She doesnt quite know. [MRS. HIGGINS, *seeing that her
eyes are moist, takes her hand sympathetically and goes with her to the door.*]
But the boy is nice. Dont you think so?

265 MRS. HIGGINS   Oh, quite nice. I shall always be delighted to see him.

MRS. EYNSFORD HILL   Thank you, dear. Good-bye.

> [*She goes out.*]

HIGGINS [*eagerly*]   Well? Is Eliza presentable? [*He swoops on his mother and
drags her to the ottoman, where she sits down in* ELIZA's *place with her son on
her left.*]

> [PICKERING *returns to his chair on her right.*]

MRS. HIGGINS   You silly boy, of course shes not presentable. Shes a triumph
of your art and of her dressmaker's; but if you suppose for a moment that
270   she doesnt give herself away in every sentence she utters, you must be perfectly cracked about[9] her.

PICKERING   But dont you think something might be done? I mean something
to eliminate the sanguinary element[1] from her conversation.

MRS. HIGGINS   Not as long as she is in Henry's hands.

275 HIGGINS [*aggrieved*]   Do you mean that my language is improper?

MRS. HIGGINS   No, dearest: it would be quite proper—say on a canal barge;
but it would not be proper for her at a garden party.

HIGGINS [*deeply injured*]   Well I must say—

PICKERING [*interrupting him*]   Come, Higgins: you must learn to know your
280   self. I havnt heard such language as yours since we used to review the volunteers[2] in Hyde Park twenty years ago.

HIGGINS [*sulkily*]   Oh, well, if you say so, I suppose I dont always talk like a
bishop.

MRS. HIGGINS [*quieting* HENRY *with a touch*]   Colonel Pickering: will you tell
285   me what is the exact state of things in Wimpole Street?

---

9. Infatuated with.
1. That is, the word "bloody."
2. Inspect the troops. Hyde Park, a large park

in central London northwest of Buckingham
Palace, was frequently used for large-scale
military reviews in the 19th century.

PICKERING [*cheerfully: as if this completely changed the subject*]   Well, I have come to live there with Henry. We work together at my Indian Dialects; and we think it more convenient—

MRS. HIGGINS   Quite so. I know all about that: it's an excellent arrangement. But where does this girl live?

HIGGINS   With us, of course. Where would she live?

MRS. HIGGINS   But on what terms? Is she a servant? If not, what is she?

PICKERING [*slowly*]   I think I know what you mean, Mrs. Higgins.

HIGGINS   Well, dash me if *I* do! Ive had to work at the girl every day for months to get her to her present pitch. Besides, shes useful. She knows where my things are, and remembers my appointments and so forth.

MRS. HIGGINS   How does your housekeeper get on with her?

HIGGINS   Mrs. Pearce? Oh, shes jolly glad to get so much taken off her hands; for before Eliza came, she used to have to find things and remind me of my appointments. But shes got some silly bee in her bonnet about Eliza. She keeps saying "You dont think, sir": doesnt she, Pick?

PICKERING   Yes: thats the formula. "You dont think, sir." Thats the end of every conversation about Eliza.

HIGGINS   As if I ever stop thinking about the girl and her confounded vowels and consonants. I'm worn out, thinking about her, and watching her lips and her teeth and her tongue, not to mention her soul, which is the quaintest of the lot.

MRS. HIGGINS   You certainly are a pretty pair of babies, playing with your live doll.

HIGGINS   Playing! The hardest job I ever tackled: make no mistake about that, mother. But you have no idea how frightfully interesting it is to take a human being and change her into a quite different human being by creating a new speech for her. It's filling up the deepest gulf that separates class from class and soul from soul.

PICKERING [*drawing his chair closer to* MRS. HIGGINS *and bending over to her eagerly*]   Yes: it's enormously interesting. I assure you, Mrs. Higgins, we take Eliza very seriously. Every week—every day almost—there is some new change. [*Closer again*] We keep records of every stage—dozens of gramophone disks and photographs—

HIGGINS [*assailing her at the other ear*]   Yes, by George: it's the most absorbing experiment I ever tackled. She regularly fills our lives up; doesnt she, Pick?

PICKERING   We're always talking Eliza.

HIGGINS   Teaching Eliza.

PICKERING   Dressing Eliza.

MRS. HIGGINS   What!

HIGGINS   Inventing new Elizas.

HIGGINS	[*speaking together*]	You know, she has the most extraordinary quickness of ear:
PICKERING		I assure you, my dear Mrs. Higgins, that girl
HIGGINS		just like a parrot. Ive tried her with every
PICKERING		is a genius. She can play the piano quite beautifully.
HIGGINS		possible sort of sound that a human being
		can make—

PICKERING	We have taken her to classical concerts and to music
HIGGINS	Continental dialects, African dialects, Hottentot
335 PICKERING	halls; and it's all the same to her: she plays every-
	thing
HIGGINS	clicks,[3] things it took me years to get hold of; and
PICKERING	she hears right off when she comes home, whether
	it's
340 HIGGINS	she picks them up like a shot, right away, as if she
	had
PICKERING	Beethoven and Brahms or Lehar and Lionel
	Monckton;[4]
HIGGINS	been at it all her life.
345 PICKERING	though six months ago, she'd never as much as
	touched a piano—

MRS. HIGGINS [*putting her fingers in her ears, as they are by this time shouting one another down with an intolerable noise*] Sh-sh-sh—sh! [*They stop.*]

PICKERING I beg your pardon. [*He draws his chair back apologetically.*]

HIGGINS Sorry. When Pickering starts shouting nobody can get a word in
350 edgeways.

MRS. HIGGINS Be quiet, Henry. Colonel Pickering: dont you realize that when Eliza walked into Wimpole Street, something walked in with her?

PICKERING Her father did. But Henry soon got rid of him.

MRS. HIGGINS It would have been more to the point if her mother had. But
355 as her mother didnt something else did.

PICKERING But what?

MRS. HIGGINS [*unconsciously dating herself by the word*] A problem.

PICKERING Oh, I see. The problem of how to pass her off as a lady.

HIGGINS I'll solve that problem. Ive half solved it already.

360 MRS. HIGGINS No, you two infinitely stupid male creatures: the problem of what is to be done with her afterwards.

HIGGINS I dont see anything in that. She can go her own way, with all the advantages I have given her.

MRS. HIGGINS The advantages of that poor woman who was here just now!
365 The manners and habits that disqualify a fine lady from earning her own living without giving her a fine lady's income! Is that what you mean?

PICKERING [*indulgently, being rather bored*] Oh, that will be all right, Mrs. Higgins. [*He rises to go.*]

HIGGINS [*rising also*] We'll find her some light employment.

370 PICKERING Shes happy enough. Dont you worry about her. Good-bye. [*He shakes hands as if he were consoling a frightened child, and makes for the door.*]

HIGGINS Anyhow, theres no good bothering now. The things done. Good-bye, mother. [*He kisses her, and follows* PICKERING.]

3. *Hottentot clicks:* implosive consonant sounds used in a number of languages of southern Africa.
4. Examples of composers featured in classical concerts—the Germans Ludwig van Beethoven (1770–1827) and Johannes Brahms (1833–1897)—and those celebrated for more popular fare, the Hungarian Franz Lehár (1870–1948), known for his operettas, and the English Lionel Monckton (1861–1924), who wrote many hit songs for musical theater.

PICKERING [*turning for a final consolation*] There are plenty of openings. We'll do whats right. Good-bye.

375 HIGGINS [*to* PICKERING *as they go out together*] Let's take her to the Shake-spear exhibition at Earls Court.

PICKERING Yes: lets. Her remarks will be delicious.

HIGGINS She'll mimic all the people for us when we get home.

PICKERING Ripping.

[*Both are heard laughing as they go downstairs.*]

MRS. HIGGINS [*rises with an impatient bounce, and returns to her work at the writing-table. She sweeps a litter of disarranged papers out of her way; snatches a sheet of paper from her stationery case; and tries resolutely to write. At the third line she gives it up; flings down her pen; grips the table angrily and*
380 *exclaims.*] Oh, men! men!! men!!!

Act 4

[*The Wimpole Street laboratory. Midnight. Nobody in the room. The clock on the mantelpiece strikes twelve. The fire is not alight: it is a summer night.*

Presently HIGGINS *and* PICKERING *are heard on the stairs.*]

HIGGINS [*calling down to* PICKERING] I say, Pick: lock up, will you. I shant be going out again.

PICKERING Right. Can Mrs. Pearce go to bed? We dont want anything more, do we?

5 HIGGINS Lord, no!

[ELIZA *opens the door and is seen on the lighted landing in opera cloak, brilliant evening dress, and diamonds, with fan, flowers, and all accessories. She comes to the hearth, and switches on the electric lights there. She is tired: her pallor contrasts strongly with her dark eyes and hair; and her expression is almost tragic. She takes off her cloak; puts her fan and flowers on the piano; and sits down on the bench, brooding and silent.* HIGGINS, *in evening dress, with overcoat and hat, comes in, carrying a smoking jacket[5] which he has picked up downstairs. He takes off the hat and overcoat; throws them carelessly on the newspaper stand; disposes of his coat in the same way; puts on the smoking jacket; and throws himself wearily into the easy-chair at the hearth.* PICKERING *similarly attired, comes in. He also takes off his hat and overcoat, and is about to throw them on* HIGGINS's *when he hesitates.*]

PICKERING I say: Mrs. Pearce will row[6] if we leave these things lying about in the drawing-room.

HIGGINS Oh, chuck them over the bannisters into the hall. She'll find them there in the morning and put them away all right. She'll think we were drunk.

10 PICKERING We are, slightly. Are there any letters?

HIGGINS I didnt look. [PICKERING *takes the overcoats and hats and goes down-stairs. Higgins begins half singing half yawning an air from La Fanciulla del Golden West.[7] Suddenly he stops and exclaims*] I wonder where the devil my slippers are!

---

5. A casual jacket worn at home, usually in the evening.
6. That is, start a quarrel.

7. That is, *La Fanciulla del West* (*The Girl of the Golden West,* 1910), an opera by Giacomo Puccini.

[ELIZA *looks at him darkly; then rises suddenly and leaves the room.*]

[HIGGINS *yawns again, and resumes his song.*]

[PICKERING *returns, with the contents of the letter-box in his hand.*]

PICKERING   Only circulars, and this coroneted billet-doux[8] for you. [*He throws the circulars into the fender, and posts himself on the hearthrug, with his back to the grate.*]

15 HIGGINS [*glancing at the billet-doux*]   Money-lender. [*He throws the letter after the circulars.*]

> [ELIZA *returns with a pair of large down-at-heel slippers. She places them on the carpet before* HIGGINS, *and sits as before without a word.*]

HIGGINS [*yawning again*]   Oh Lord! What an evening! What a crew! What a silly tomfoolery! [*He raises his shoe to unlace it, and catches sight of the slippers. He stops unlacing and looks at them as if they had appeared there of their own accord.*] Oh! theyre there, are they?

PICKERING [*stretching himself*]   Well, I feel a bit tired. It's been a long day.
20 The garden party, a dinner party, and the opera! Rather too much of a good thing. But youve won your bet, Higgins. Eliza did the trick, and something to spare, eh?

HIGGINS [*fervently*]   Thank God it's over!

> [ELIZA *flinches violently; but they take no notice of her; and she recovers herself and sits stonily as before.*]

PICKERING   Were you nervous at the garden party? *I* was. Eliza didnt seem a
25 bit nervous.

HIGGINS   Oh, she wasnt nervous. I knew she'd be all right. No: it's the strain of putting the job through all these months that has told on me. It was interesting enough at first, while we were at the phonetics; but after that I got deadly sick of it. If I hadnt backed myself to do it I should have chucked
30 the whole thing up two months ago. It was a silly notion: the whole thing has been a bore.

PICKERING   Oh come! the garden party was frightfully exciting. My heart began beating like anything.

HIGGINS   Yes, for the first three minutes. But when I saw we were going to
35 win hands down, I felt like a bear in a cage, hanging about doing nothing. The dinner was worse: sitting gorging there for over an hour, with nobody but a damned fool of a fashionable woman to talk to! I tell you, Pickering, never again for me. No more artificial duchesses. The whole thing has been simple purgatory.

40 PICKERING   Youve never been broken in properly to the social routine. [*Strolling over to the piano*] I rather enjoy dipping into it occasionally myself: it makes me feel young again. Anyhow, it was a great success: an immense success. I was quite frightened once or twice because Eliza was doing it so well. You see, lots of the real people cant do it at all: theyre such fools that
45 they think style comes by nature to people in their position; and so they never learn. Theres always something professional about doing a thing superlatively well.

HIGGINS   Yes: thats what drives me mad: the silly people dont know their own silly business. [*Rising*] However, it's over and done with; and now I can go
50 to bed at last without dreading tomorrow.

8. A love letter on fine stationery (coronets signify nobility).

[ELIZA's *beauty becomes murderous.*]

PICKERING   I think I shall turn in too. Still, it's been a great occasion: a triumph for you. Good-night.

[*He goes.*]

HIGGINS [*following him*]   Good-night. [*Over his shoulder, at the door*] Put out the lights, Eliza; and tell Mrs. Pearce not to make coffee for me in the
55   morning: I'll take tea.

[*He goes out.*]

[ELIZA *tries to control herself and feel indifferent as she rises and walks across to the hearth to switch off the lights. By the time she gets there she is on the point of screaming. She sits down in* HIGGINS's *chair and holds on hard to the arms. Finally she gives way and flings herself furiously on the floor raging.*]

HIGGINS [*in despairing wrath outside*]   What the devil have I done with my slippers? [*He appears at the door.*]

LIZA [*snatching up the slippers, and hurling them at him one after the other with all her force*]   There are your slippers. And there. Take your slippers; and may you never have a day's luck with them!

60 HIGGINS [*astounded*]   What on earth—! [*He comes to her.*] Whats the matter? Get up. [*He pulls her up.*] Anything wrong?

LIZA [*breathless*]   Nothing wrong—with you. Ive won your bet for you, havnt I? That enough for you. *I* dont matter, I suppose.

HIGGINS   You won my bet! You! Presumptuous insect! *I* won it. What did you
65   throw those slippers at me for?

LIZA   Because I wanted to smash your face. I'd like to kill you, you selfish brute. Why didnt you leave me where you picked me out of—in the gutter? You thank God it's all over, and that now you can throw me back again there, do you? [*She crisps*[9] *her fingers frantically.*]

70 HIGGINS [*looking at her in cool wonder*]   The creature is nervous, after all.

LIZA [*gives a suffocated scream of fury, and instinctively darts her nails at his face*]   !!

HIGGINS [*catching her wrists*]   Ah! would you? Claws in, you cat. How dare you shew your temper to me? Sit down and be quiet. [*He throws her roughly into the easy-chair.*]

LIZA [*crushed by superior strength and weight*]   Whats to become of me?
75   Whats to become of me?

HIGGINS   How the devil do I know whats to become of you? What does it matter what becomes of you?

LIZA   You dont care. I know you dont care. You wouldnt care if I was dead. I'm nothing to you—not so much as them slippers.

80 HIGGINS [*thundering*]   Those slippers.

LIZA [*with bitter submission*]   Those slippers. I didnt think it made any difference now.

[*A pause.* ELIZA *hopeless and crushed.* HIGGINS *a little uneasy.*]

HIGGINS [*in his loftiest manner*]   Why have you begun going on like this? May I ask whether you complain of your treatment here?

85 LIZA   No.

HIGGINS   Has anybody behaved badly to you? Colonel Pickering? Mrs. Pearce? Any of the servants?

9. Curls.

LIZA   No.

HIGGINS   I presume you dont pretend that *I* have treated you badly.

90 LIZA   No.

HIGGINS   I am glad to hear it. [*He moderates his tone.*] Perhaps youre tired after the strain of the day. Will you have a glass of champagne? [*He moves towards the door.*]

LIZA   No. [*Recollecting her manners*] Thank you.

HIGGINS [*good-humored again*]   This has been coming on you for some days.

95   I suppose it was natural for you to be anxious about the garden party. But thats all over now. [*He pats her kindly on the shoulder. She writhes.*] Theres nothing more to worry about.

LIZA   No. Nothing more for you to worry about. [*She suddenly rises and gets away from him by going to the piano bench, where she sits and hides her face.*] Oh God! I wish I was dead.

100 HIGGINS [*staring after her in sincere surprise*]   Why? in heaven's name, why? [*Reasonably, going to her*] Listen to me, Eliza. All this irritation is purely subjective.

LIZA   I dont understand. I'm too ignorant.

HIGGINS   It's only imagination. Low spirits and nothing else. Nobody's hurt-
105   ing you. Nothing's wrong. You go to bed like a good girl and sleep it off. Have a little cry and say your prayers: that will make you comfortable.

LIZA   I heard your prayers. "Thank God it's all over!"

HIGGINS [*impatiently*]   Well, dont you thank God it's all over? Now you are free and can do what you like.

110 LIZA [*pulling herself together in desperation*]   What am I fit for? What have you left me fit for? Where am I to go? What am I to do? Whats to become of me?

HIGGINS [*enlightened, but not at all impressed*]   Oh, thats whats worrying you, is it? [*He thrusts his hands into his pockets, and walks about in his usual manner, rattling the contents of his pockets, as if condescending to a trivial
115   subject out of pure kindness.*] I shouldnt bother about it if I were you. I should imagine you wont have much difficulty in settling yourself some-where or other, though I hadnt quite realized that you were going away. [*She looks quickly at him: he does not look at her, but examines the dessert stand on the piano and decides that he will eat an apple.*] You might marry, you know. [*He bites a large piece out of the apple, and munches it noisily.*]
120   You see, Eliza, all men are not confirmed old bachelors like me and the Colonel. Most men are the marrying sort (poor devils!); and youre not bad-looking; it's quite a pleasure to look at you sometimes—not now, of course, because youre crying and looking as ugly as the very devil; but when youre all right and quite yourself, youre what I should call attractive. That is, to
125   the people in the marrying line, you understand. You go to bed and have a good nice rest; and then get up and look at yourself in the glass; and you wont feel so cheap.

[ELIZA *again looks at him, speechless, and does not stir.*]

[*The look is quite lost on him: he eats his apple with a dreamy expression of happiness, as it is quite a good one.*]

HIGGINS [*a genial afterthought occurring to him*]   I daresay my mother could find some chap or other who would do very well.

130 LIZA   We were above that at the corner of Tottenham Court Road.

HIGGINS [*waking up*]   What do you mean?

LIZA   I sold flowers. I didnt sell myself. Now youve made a lady of me I'm not fit to sell anything else. I wish youd left me where you found me.

HIGGINS [*slinging the core of the apple decisively into the grate*]   Tosh, Eliza.
135   Dont you insult human relations by dragging all this cant about buying and selling into it. You neednt marry the fellow if you dont like him.

LIZA   What else am I to do?

HIGGINS   Oh, lots of things. What about your old idea of a florist's shop? Pickering could set you up in one: hes lots of money. [*Chuckling*] He'll
140   have to pay for all those togs you have been wearing today; and that, with the hire of the jewellery, will make a big hole in two hundred pounds. Why, six months ago you would have thought it the millennium to have a flower shop of your own. Come! youll be all right. I must clear off to bed: I'm devilish sleepy. By the way, I came down for something: I forget what it was.

145   LIZA   Your slippers.

HIGGINS   Oh yes, of course. You shied them at me. [*He picks them up, and is going out when she rises and speaks to him.*]

LIZA   Before you go, sir—

HIGGINS [*dropping the slippers in his surprise at her calling him Sir*]   Eh?

LIZA   Do my clothes belong to me or to Colonel Pickering?

HIGGINS [*coming back into the room as if her question were the very climax of
150   unreason*]   What the devil use would they be to Pickering?

LIZA   He might want them for the next girl you pick up to experiment on.

HIGGINS [*shocked and hurt*]   Is that the way you feel towards us?

LIZA   I dont want to hear anything more about that. All I want to know is whether anything belongs to me. My own clothes were burnt.

155   HIGGINS   But what does it matter? Why need you start bothering about that in the middle of the night?

LIZA   I want to know what I may take away with me. I dont want to be accused of stealing.

HIGGINS [*now deeply wounded*]   Stealing! You shouldnt have said that, Eliza.
160   That shews a want of feeling.

LIZA   I'm sorry. I'm only a common ignorant girl; and in my station I have to be careful. There cant be any feelings between the like of you and the like of me. Please will you tell me what belongs to me and what doesn't?

HIGGINS [*very sulky*]   You may take the whole damned houseful if you like.
165   Except the jewels. Theyre hired. Will that satisfy you? [*He turns on his heel and is about to go in extreme dudgeon.*]

LIZA [*drinking in his emotion like nectar, and nagging him to provoke a further supply*]   Stop, please. [*She takes off her jewels.*] Will you take these to your room and keep them safe? I dont want to run the risk of their being missing.

HIGGINS [*furious*]   Hand them over. [*She puts them into his hands.*] If these
170   belonged to me instead of to the jeweler, I'd ram them down your ungrateful throat. [*He perfunctorily thrusts them into his pockets, unconsciously decorating himself with the protruding ends of the chains.*]

LIZA [*taking a ring off*]   This ring isnt the jeweler's: it's the one you bought me in Brighton.[1] I dont want it now. [*Higgins dashes the ring violently into the fireplace, and turns on her so threateningly that she crouches over the piano with her hands over her face, and exclaims.*] Don't you hit me.

---

1. A seaside resort on the English Channel, about 50 miles south of London.

175 HIGGINS   Hit you! You infamous creature, how dare you accuse me of such a thing? It is you who have hit me. You have wounded me to the heart.

LIZA [*thrilling with hidden joy*]   I'm glad. Ive got a little of my own back, anyhow.

HIGGINS [*with dignity, in his finest professional style*]   You have caused me to

180 lose my temper: a thing that has hardly ever happend to me before. I prefer to say nothing more tonight. I am going to bed.

LIZA [*pertly*]   Youd better leave a note for Mrs. Pearce about the coffee; for she wont be told by me.

HIGGINS [*formally*]   Damn Mrs. Pearce; and damn the coffee; and damn you;

185 and damn my own folly in having lavished hard-earned knowledge and the treasure of my regard and intimacy on a heartless guttersnipe.

[*He goes out with impressive decorum, and spoils it by slamming the door savagely.*]

[ELIZA *smiles for the first time; expresses her feelings by a wild pantomime in which an imitation of* HIGGINS's *exit is confused with her own triumph; and finally goes down on her knees on the hearthrug to look for the ring.*]

Act 5

[*Mrs.* HIGGINS's *drawing-room. She is at her writing-table as before. The* PARLOR-MAID *comes in.*]

THE PARLOR-MAID [*at the door*]   Mr. Henry, mam, is downstairs with Colonel Pickering.

MRS. HIGGINS   Well, shew them up.

THE PARLOR-MAID   Theyre using the telephone, mam. Telephoning to the

5 police, I think.

MRS. HIGGINS   What!

THE PARLOR-MAID [*coming further in and lowering her voice*]   Mr. Henry's in a state, mam. I thought I'd better tell you.

MRS. HIGGINS   If you had told me that Mr. Henry was not in a state it would

10 have been more surprising. Tell them to come up when theyve finished with the police. I suppose hes lost something.

THE PARLOR-MAID   Yes, mam. [*Going*]

MRS. HIGGINS   Go upstairs and tell Miss Doolittle that Mr. Henry and the Colonel are here. Ask her not to come down till I send for her.

15 THE PARLOR-MAID   Yes, mam.

[HIGGINS *bursts in. He is, as the* PARLOR-MAID *has said, in a state.*]

HIGGINS   Look here, mother: heres a confounded thing!

MRS. HIGGINS   Yes, dear. Good-morning. [*He checks his impatience and kisses her, whilst the* PARLOR-MAID *goes out.*] What is it?

HIGGINS   Eliza's bolted.

20 MRS. HIGGINS [*calmly continuing her writing*]   You must have frightened her.

HIGGINS   Frightened her! nonsense! She was left last night, as usual, to turn out the lights and all that; and instead of going to bed she changed her clothes and went right off: her bed wasnt slept in. She came in a cab for her things before seven this morning; and that fool Mrs. Pearce let her

25 have them without telling me a word about it. What am I to do?

MRS. HIGGINS   Do without, I'm afraid, Henry. The girl has a perfect right to leave if she chooses.

HIGGINS [*wandering distractedly across the room*]   But I cant find anything. I dont know what appointments Ive got. I'm—— [PICKERING *comes in.* MRS. HIGGINS *puts down her pen and turns away from the writing-table.*]

30 PICKERING [*shaking hands*]   Good-morning, Mrs. Higgins. Has Henry told you? [*He sits down on the ottoman.*]

HIGGINS   What does that ass of an inspector say? Have you offered a reward?

MRS. HIGGINS [*rising in indignant amazement*]   You dont mean to say you have set the police after Eliza?

35 HIGGINS   Of course. What are the police for? What else could we do? [*He sits in the Elizabethan chair.*]

PICKERING   The inspector made a lot of difficulties. I really think he suspected us of some improper purpose.

MRS. HIGGINS   Well, of course he did. What right have you to go to the police and give the girl's name as if she were a thief, or a lost umbrella, or some-
40 thing? Really! [*She sits down again, deeply vexed.*]

HIGGINS   But we want to find her.

PICKERING   We cant let her go like this, you know, Mrs. Higgins. What were we to do?

MRS. HIGGINS   You have no more sense, either of you, than two children.
45 Why——

[*The* PARLOR-MAID *comes in and breaks off the conversation.*]

THE PARLOR-MAID   Mr. Henry: a gentleman wants to see you very particular. Hes been sent on from Wimpole Street.

HIGGINS   Oh, bother! I cant see anyone now. Who is it?

THE PARLOR-MAID   A Mr. Doolittle, sir.

50 PICKERING   Doolittle! Do you mean the dustman?

THE PARLOR-MAID   Dustman! Oh no, sir: a gentleman.

HIGGINS [*springing up excitedly*]   By George, Pick, it's some relative of hers that shes gone to. Somebody we know nothing about. [*To the* PARLOR-MAID] Send him up, quick.

55 THE PARLOR-MAID   Yes, sir.

[*She goes.*]

HIGGINS [*eagerly, going to his mother*]   Genteel relatives! now we shall hear something. [*He sits down in the Chippendale chair.*]

MRS. HIGGINS   Do you know any of her people?

PICKERING   Only her father: the fellow we told you about.

60 THE PARLOR-MAID [*announcing*]   Mr. Doolittle.

[*She withdraws.*]

[DOOLITTLE *enters. He is brilliantly dressed in a new fashionable frock-coat, with white waistcoat and grey trousers. A flower in his buttonhole, a dazzling silk hat, and patent leather shoes complete the effect. He is too concerned with the business he has come on to notice* MRS. HIGGINS. *He walks straight to* HIGGINS, *and accosts him with vehement reproach.*]

DOOLITTLE [*indicating his own person*]   See here! Do you see this? You done this.

HIGGINS   Done what, man?

DOOLITTLE   This, I tell you. Look at it. Look at this hat. Look at this coat.

65 PICKERING   Has Eliza been buying you clothes?

DOOLITTLE   Eliza! not she. Not half. Why would she buy me clothes?

MRS. HIGGINS   Good-morning, Mr. Doolittle. Wont you sit down?

DOOLITTLE [*taken aback as he becomes conscious that he has forgotten his hostess*]   Asking your pardon, maam. [*He approaches her and shakes her proffered hand.*] Thank you. [*He sits down on the ottoman, on Pickering's right.*]
70   I am that full of what has happened to me that I cant think of anything else.

HIGGINS   What the dickens has happened to you?

DOOLITTLE   I shouldnt mind if it had only happened to me: anything might happen to anybody and nobody to blame but Providence, as you might say. But this is something that you done to me: yes, you, Henry Higgins.

75   HIGGINS   Have you found Eliza? Thats the point.

DOOLITTLE   Have you lost her?

HIGGINS   Yes.

DOOLITTLE   You have all the luck, you have. I aint found her; but she'll find me quick enough now after what you done to me.

80   MRS. HIGGINS   But what has my son done to you, Mr. Doolittle?

DOOLITTLE   Done to me! Ruined me. Destroyed my happiness. Tied me up and delivered me into the hands of middle class morality.

HIGGINS [*rising intolerantly and standing over Doolittle*]   Youre raving. Youre drunk. Youre mad. I gave you five pounds. After that I had two conversa-
85   tions with you, at half-a-crown an hour. Ive never seen you since.

DOOLITTLE   Oh! Drunk! am I? Mad! am I? Tell me this. Did you or did you not write a letter to an old blighter in America that was giving five millions to found Moral Reform Societies all over the world, and that wanted you to invent a universal language for him?

90   HIGGINS   What! Ezra D. Wannafeller![2] Hes dead. [*He sits down again carelessly.*]

DOOLITTLE   Yes: hes dead; and I'm done for. Now did you or did you not write a letter to him to say that the most original moralist at present in England, to the best of your knowledge, was Alfred Doolittle, a common dustman.

HIGGINS   Oh, after your last visit I remember making some silly joke of the
95   kind.

DOOLITTLE   Ah! you may well call it a silly joke. It put the lid on me right enough. Just give him the chance he wanted to shew that Americans is not like us: that they recognize and respect merit in every class of life, however humble. Them words is in his blooming will, in which, Henry Higgins,
100   thanks to your silly joking, he leaves me a share in his Pre-digested Cheese Trust worth three thousand a year[3] on condition that I lecture for his Wannafeller Moral Reform World League as often as they ask me up to six times a year.

HIGGINS   The devil he does! Whew! [*Brightening suddenly*] What a lark!

105   PICKERING   A safe thing for you, Doolittle. They wont ask you twice.

DOOLITTLE   It aint the lecturing I mind. I'll lecture them blue in the face, I will, and not turn a hair. It's making a gentleman of me that I object to. Who asked him to make a gentleman of me? I was happy. I was free. I touched pretty nigh everybody for money when I wanted it, same as I
110   touched you, Henry Higgins. Now I am worrited; tied neck and heels; and everybody touches me for money. It's a fine thing for you, says my solicitor.

---

2. Shaw conflates the names of two actual American millionaires, the merchant John Wanamaker (1838–1922) and the industrial-

ist John D. Rockefeller (1839–1937).
3. Roughly equivalent to $250,000 today.

Is it? says I. You mean it's a good thing for you, I says. When I was a poor man and had a solicitor once when they found a pram in the dust cart, he got me off, and got shut of[4] me and got me shut of him as quick as he could. Same with the doctors: used to shove me out of the hospital before I could hardly stand on my legs, and nothing to pay. Now they finds out that I'm not a healthy man and cant live unless they looks after me twice a day. In the house I'm not let do a hand's turn for myself: somebody else must do it and touch me for it. A year ago I hadnt a relative in the world except two or three that wouldnt speak to me. Now Ive fifty, and not a decent week's wages among the lot of them. I have to live for others and not for myself: thats middle class morality. You talk of losing Eliza. Dont you be anxious: I bet shes on my doorstep by this: she that could support herself easy by selling flowers if I wasnt respectable. And the next one to touch me will be you, Henry Higgins. I'll have to learn to speak middle class language from you, instead of speaking proper English. Thats where youll come in; and I daresay thats what you done it for.

MRS. HIGGINS   But, my dear Mr. Doolittle, you need not suffer all this if you are really in earnest. Nobody can force you to accept this bequest. You can repudiate it. Isnt that so, Colonel Pickering?

PICKERING   I believe so.

DOOLITTLE [*softening his manner in deference to her sex*]   Thats the tragedy of it, maam. It's easy to say chuck it; but I havent the nerve. Which of us has? We're all intimidated. Intimidated, maam: thats what we are. What is there for me if I chuck it but the workhouse in my old age? I have to dye my hair[5] already to keep my job as a dustman. If I was one of the deserving poor, and had put by a bit, I could chuck it; but then why should I, acause[6] the deserving poor might as well be millionaires for all the happiness they ever has. They dont know what happiness is. But I, as one of the undeserving poor, have nothing between me and the pauper's uniform but this here blasted three thousand a year that shoves me into the middle class. (Excuse the expression, maam: youd use it yourself if you had my provocation.) Theyve got you every way you turn: it's a choice between the Skilly of the workhouse and the Char Bydis of the middle class;[7] and I havnt the nerve for the workhouse. Intimidated: thats what I am. Broke. Bought up. Happier men than me will call for my dust, and touch me for their tip; and I'll look on helpless, and envy them. And thats what your son has brought me to. [*He is overcome by emotion.*]

MRS. HIGGINS   Well, I'm very glad youre not going to do anything foolish, Mr. Doolittle. For this solves the problem of Eliza's future. You can provide for her now.

DOOLITTLE [*with melancholy resignation*]   Yes, maam: I'm expected to provide for everyone now, out of three thousand a year.

HIGGINS [*jumping up*]   Nonsense! he cant provide for her. He shant provide for her. She doesnt belong to him. I paid him five pounds for her. Doolittle: either youre an honest man or a rogue.

---

4. Rid of.
5. That is, to keep from being fired because of his advancing age (no laws prevented such firing).
6. Because.

7. That is, between two equal dangers. In Greek mythology, Scylla and Charybdis are two monsters (who become a rock and whirlpool, respectively) that endanger sailors between Sicily and Italy.

DOOLITTLE [*tolerantly*]   A little of both, Henry, like the rest of us: a little of both.

HIGGINS   Well, you took that money for the girl; and you have no right to
160   take her as well.

MRS. HIGGINS   Henry: dont be absurd. If you really want to know where Eliza is, she is upstairs.

HIGGINS [*amazed*]   Upstairs!!! Then I shall jolly soon fetch her downstairs. [*He makes resolutely for the door.*]

MRS. HIGGINS [*rising and following him*]   Be quiet, Henry. Sit down.

165   HIGGINS   I—

MRS. HIGGINS   Sit down, dear; and listen to me.

HIGGINS   Oh very well, very well, very well. [*He throws himself ungraciously on the ottoman, with his face towards the windows.*] But I think you might have told me this half an hour ago.

170   MRS. HIGGINS   Eliza came to me this morning. She passed the night partly walking about in a rage, partly trying to throw herself into the river and being afraid to, and partly in the Carlton Hotel. She told me of the brutal way you two treated her.

HIGGINS [*bounding up again*]   What!

175   PICKERING [*rising also*]   My dear Mrs. Higgins, shes been telling you stories. We didnt treat her brutally. We hardly said a word to her; and we parted on particularly good terms. [*Turning on* HIGGINS] Higgins: did you bully her after I went to bed?

HIGGINS   Just the other way about. She threw my slippers in my face. She
180   behaved in the most outrageous way. I never gave her the slightest provocation. The slippers came bang into my face the moment I entered the room—before I had uttered a word. And used perfectly awful language.

PICKERING [*astonished*]   But why? What did we do to her?

MRS. HIGGINS   I think I know pretty well what you did. The girl is naturally
185   rather affectionate, I think. Isnt she, Mr. Doolittle?

DOOLITTLE   Very tender-hearted, maam. Takes after me.

MRS. HIGGINS   Just so. She had become attached to you both. She worked very hard for you, Henry! I dont think you quite realize what anything in the nature of brain work means to a girl like that. Well, it seems that when
190   the great day of trial came, and she did this wonderful thing for you without making a single mistake, you two sat there and never said a word to her, but talked together of how glad you were that it was all over and how you had been bored with the whole thing. And then you were surprised because she threw your slippers at you! *I* should have thrown the fire-
195   irons at you.

HIGGINS   We said nothing except that we were tired and wanted to go to bed. Did we, Pick?

PICKERING [*shrugging his shoulders*]   That was all.

MRS. HIGGINS [*ironically*]   Quite sure?

200   PICKERING   Absolutely. Really, that was all.

MRS. HIGGINS   You didn't thank her, or pet her, or admire her, or tell her how splendid she'd been.

HIGGINS [*impatiently*]   But she knew all about that. We didnt make speeches to her, if thats what you mean.

205   PICKERING [*conscience stricken*]   Perhaps we were a little inconsiderate. Is she very angry?

MRS. HIGGINS [*returning to her place at the writing-table*]   Well, I'm afraid she wont go back to Wimpole Street, especially now that Mr. Doolittle is able to keep up the position you have thrust on her; but she says she is
210   quite willing to meet you on friendly terms and to let bygones be bygones.

HIGGINS [*furious*]   Is she, by George? Ho!

MRS. HIGGINS   If you promise to behave yourself, Henry, I'll ask her to come down. If not, go home; for you have taken up quite enough of my time.

HIGGINS   Oh, all right. Very well. Pick: you behave yourself. Let us put on
215   our best Sunday manners for this creature that we picked out of the mud. [*He flings himself sulkily into the Elizabethan chair.*]

DOOLITTLE [*remonstrating*]   Now, now, Henry Higgins! have some consideration for my feelings as a middle class man.

MRS. HIGGINS   Remember your promise, Henry. [*She presses the bell-button on the writing-table.*] Mr. Doolittle: will you be so good as to step out on
220   the balcony for a moment. I dont want Eliza to have the shock of your news until she has made it up with these two gentlemen. Would you mind?

DOOLITTLE   As you wish, lady. Anything to help Henry to keep her off my hands. [*He disappears through the window.*]

[*The* PARLOR-MAID *answers the bell.* PICKERING *sits down in Doolittle's place.*]

MRS. HIGGINS   Ask Miss Doolittle to come down, please.

225   THE PARLOR-MAID   Yes, mam. [*She goes out.*]

MRS. HIGGINS   Now, Henry: be good.

HIGGINS   I am behaving myself perfectly.

PICKERING   He is doing his best, Mrs. Higgins.

[*A pause.* HIGGINS *throws back his head; stretches out his legs; and begins to whistle.*]

MRS. HIGGINS   Henry, dearest, you dont look at all nice in that attitude.

230   HIGGINS [*pulling himself together*]   I was not trying to look nice, mother.

MRS. HIGGINS   It doesnt matter, dear. I only wanted to make you speak.

HIGGINS   Why?

MRS. HIGGINS   Because you cant speak and whistle at the same time.

[HIGGINS *groans. Another very trying pause.*]

HIGGINS [*springing up, out of patience*]   Where the devil is that girl? Are we
235   to wait here all day?

[ELIZA *enters, sunny, self-possessed, and giving a staggeringly convincing exhibition of ease of manner. She carries a little work-basket, and is very much at home.* PICKERING *is too much taken aback to rise.*]

LIZA   How do you do, Professor Higgins? Are you quite well?

HIGGINS [*choking*]   Am I— [*He can say no more*].

LIZA   But of course you are: you are never ill. So glad to see you again, Colonel Pickering. [*He rises hastily; and they shake hands.*] Quite chilly this
240   morning, isnt it? [*She sits down on his left. He sits beside her.*]

HIGGINS   Dont you dare try this game on me. I taught it to you; and it doesnt take me in. Get up and come home; and dont be a fool.

[ELIZA *takes a piece of needlework from her basket, and begins to stitch at it, without taking the least notice of this outburst.*]

MRS. HIGGINS Very nicely put, indeed, Henry. No woman could resist such an invitation.

245 HIGGINS You let her alone, mother. Let her speak for herself. You will jolly soon see whether she has an idea that I havnt put into her head or a word that I havnt put into her mouth. I tell you I have created this thing out of the squashed cabbage leaves of Covent Garden; and now she pretends to play the fine lady with me.

250 MRS. HIGGINS [*placidly*] Yes, dear; but youll sit down, wont you?

[HIGGINS *sits down again, savagely.*]

LIZA [*to* PICKERING, *taking no apparent notice of* HIGGINS, *and working away deftly*] Will you drop me altogether now that the experiment is over, Colonel Pickering?

PICKERING Oh dont. You mustnt think of it as an experiment. It shocks me, somehow.

255 LIZA Oh, I'm only a squashed cabbage leaf—

PICKERING [*impulsively*] No.

LIZA [*continuing quietly*] —but I owe so much to you that I should be very unhappy if you forgot me.

PICKERING It's very kind of you to say so, Miss Doolittle.

260 LIZA It's not because you paid for my dresses. I know you are generous to everybody with money. But it was from you that I learnt really nice manners; and that is what makes one a lady, isnt it? You see it was so very difficult for me with the example of Professor Higgins always before me. I was brought up to be just like him, unable to control myself, and using

265 bad language on the slightest provocation. And I should never have known that ladies and gentlemen didnt behave like that if you hadnt been there.

HIGGINS Well!!

PICKERING Oh, thats only his way, you know. He doesnt mean it.

270 LIZA Oh, *I* didnt mean it either, when I was a flower girl. It was only my way. But you see I did it; and thats what makes the difference after all.

PICKERING No doubt. Still, he taught you to speak; and I couldnt have done that, you know.

LIZA [*trivially*] Of course: that is his profession.

275 HIGGINS Damnation!

LIZA [*continuing*] It was just like learning to dance in the fashionable way: there was nothing more than that in it. But do you know what began my real education?

PICKERING What?

280 LIZA [*stopping her work for a moment*] Your calling me Miss Doolittle that day when I first came to Wimpole Street. That was the beginning of self-respect for me. [*She resumes her stitching.*] And there were a hundred little things you never noticed, because they came naturally to you. Things about standing up and taking off your hat and opening door—

285 PICKERING Oh, that was nothing.

LIZA Yes: things that shewed you thought and felt about me as if I were something better than a scullery-maid; though of course I know you would have been just the same to a scullery-maid if she had been let in the drawing-room. You never took off your boots in the dining room when I was

290 there.

PICKERING You mustnt mind that. Higgins takes off his boots all over the place.

LIZA I know. I am not blaming him. It is his way, isnt it? But it made such a difference to me that you didnt do it. You see, really and truly, apart from the things anyone can pick up (the dressing and the proper way of speaking, and so on), the difference between a lady and a flower girl is not how she behaves, but how shes treated. I shall always be a flower girl to Professor Higgins, because he always treats me as a flower girl, and always will; but I know I can be a lady to you, because you always treat me as a lady, and always will.

MRS. HIGGINS Please dont grind your teeth, Henry.

PICKERING Well, this is really very nice of you, Miss Doolittle.

LIZA I should like you to call me Eliza, now, if you would.

PICKERING Thank you. Eliza, of course.

LIZA And I should like Professor Higgins to call me Miss Doolittle.

HIGGINS I'll see you damned first.

MRS. HIGGINS Henry! Henry!

PICKERING [*laughing*] Why dont you slang back[8] at him? Dont stand it. It would do him a lot of good.

LIZA I cant. I could have done it once; but now I cant go back to it. Last night, when I was wandering about, a girl spoke to me; and I tried to get back into the old way with her; but it was no use. You told me, you know, that when a child is brought to a foreign country, it picks up the language in a few weeks, and forgets its own. Well, I am a child in your country. I have forgotten my own language, and can speak nothing but yours. Thats the real break-off with the corner of Tottenham Court Road. Leaving Wimpole Street finishes it.

PICKERING [*much alarmed*] Oh! but youre coming back to Wimpole Street, arnt you? Youll forgive Higgins?

HIGGINS [*rising*] Forgive! Will she, by George! Let her go. Let her find out how she can get on without us. She will relapse into the gutter in three weeks without me at her elbow.

[DOOLITTLE *appears at the centre window. With a look of dignified reproach at* HIGGINS, *he comes slowly and silently to his daughter, who, with her back to the window, is unconscious of his approach.*]

PICKERING Hes incorrigible, Eliza. You wont relapse, will you?

LIZA No: Not now. Never again. I have learnt my lesson. I dont believe I could utter one of the old sounds if I tried. [DOOLITTLE *touches her on her left shoulder. She drops her work, losing her self-possession utterly at the spectacle of her father's splendor.*] A-a-a-a-a-ah-ow-ooh!

HIGGINS [*with a crow of triumph*] Aha! Just so. A-a-a-a-ahowooh! A-a-a-a-ahowooh! A-a-a-a-ahowooh! Victory! Victory! [*He throws himself on the divan, folding his arms, and spraddling arrogantly.*]

DOOLITTLE Can you blame the girl? Dont look at me like that, Eliza. It aint my fault. Ive come into some money.

LIZA You must have touched a millionaire this time, dad.

DOOLITTLE I have. But I'm dressed something special today. I'm going to St. George's,[9] Hanover Square. Your stepmother is going to marry me.

8. That is, respond with equal abuse.
9. A church in Mayfair, a fashionable area of Westminster.

LIZA [*angrily*] Youre going to let yourself down to marry that low common
335 woman!

PICKERING [*quietly*] He ought to, Eliza. [*To* DOOLITTLE] Why has she changed
her mind?

DOOLITTLE [*sadly*] Intimidated, Governor. Intimidated. Middle class morality claims its victim. Wont you put on your hat, Liza, and come and see me
340 turned off?

LIZA If the Colonel says I must, I—I'll [*Almost sobbing*] I'll demean myself.
And get insulted for my pains, like enough.

DOOLITTLE Dont be afraid: she never comes to words with anyone now, poor
woman! respectability has broke all the spirit out of her.

345 PICKERING [*squeezing* ELIZA's *elbow gently*] Be kind to them, Eliza. Make the
best of it.

LIZA [*forcing a little smile for him through her vexation*] Oh well, just to shew
theres no ill feeling. I'll be back in a moment. [*She goes out.*]

DOOLITTLE [*sitting down beside* PICKERING] I feel uncommon nervous about
350 the ceremony, Colonel. I wish youd come and see me through it.

PICKERING But youve been through it before, man. You were married to
Eliza's mother.

DOOLITTLE Who told you that, Colonel?

PICKERING Well, nobody told me. But I concluded—naturally—

355 DOOLITTLE No: that aint the natural way, Colonel: it's only the middle class
way. My way was always the undeserving way. But dont say nothing to
Eliza. She dont know: I always had a delicacy about telling her.

PICKERING Quite right. We'll leave it so, if you dont mind.

DOOLITTLE And youll come to the church, Colonel, and put me through
360 straight?

PICKERING With pleasure. As far as a bachelor can.

MRS. HIGGINS May I come, Mr. Doolittle? I should be very sorry to miss your
wedding.

DOOLITTLE I should indeed be honored by your condescension,[1] maam; and
365 my poor old woman would take it as a tremenjous compliment. Shes been
very low, thinking of the happy days that are no more.

MRS. HIGGINS [*rising*] I'll order the carriage and get ready. [*The men rise,
except* HIGGINS.] I shant be more than fifteen minutes. [*As she goes to
the door* ELIZA *comes in, hatted and buttoning her gloves.*] I'm going to the
370 church to see your father married, Eliza. You had better come in the
brougham[2] with me. Colonel Pickering can go on with the bridegroom.

[MRS. HIGGINS *goes out.* ELIZA *comes to the middle of the room between
the centre window and the ottoman.* PICKERING *joins her.*]

DOOLITTLE Bridegroom! What a word! It makes a man realize his position,
somehow. [*He takes up his hat and goes towards the door.*]

PICKERING Before I go, Eliza, do forgive him and come back to us.

375 LIZA I dont think papa would allow me. Would you, dad?

DOOLITTLE [*sad but magnanimous*] They played you off very cunning, Eliza,
them two sportsmen. If it had been only one of them, you could have
nailed him. But you see, there was two; and one of them chaperoned the

---

1. Here, courteous disregard of differences in
rank (without the negative connotation common in today's usage).

2. A one-horse closed carriage, which holds
two or four.

other, as you might say. [*To* PICKERING] It was artful of you, Colonel; but I
bear no malice: I should have done the same myself. I been the victim of
one woman after another all my life; and I dont grudge you two getting the
better of Eliza. I shant interfere. It's time for us to go, Colonel. So long,
Henry. See you in St. George's, Eliza.

> [*He goes out.*]

PICKERING [*coaxing*]   Do stay with us, Eliza.

> [*He follows* DOOLITTLE.]

> [ELIZA *goes out on the balcony to avoid being alone with* HIGGINS. *He
> rises and joins her there. She immediately comes back into the room and
> makes for the door; but he goes along the balcony quickly and gets his
> back to the door before she reaches it.*]

HIGGINS   Well, Eliza, youve had a bit of your own back, as you call it. Have
you had enough? and are you going to be reasonable? Or do you want any
more?

LIZA   You want me back only to pick up your slippers and put up with your
tempers and fetch and carry for you.

HIGGINS   I havnt said I wanted you back at all.

LIZA   Oh, indeed. Then what are we talking about?

HIGGINS   About you, not about me. If you come back I shall treat you just as
I have always treated you. I cant change my nature; and I dont intend
to change my manners. My manners are exactly the same as Colonel
Pickering's.

LIZA   Thats not true. He treats a flower girl as if she was a duchess.

HIGGINS   And I treat a duchess as if she was a flower girl.

LIZA   I see. [*She turns away composedly, and sits on the ottoman, facing the
window.*] The same to everybody.

HIGGINS   Just so.

LIZA   Like father.

HIGGINS [*grinning, a little taken down*[3]]   Without accepting the comparison
at all points, Eliza, it's quite true that your father is not a snob, and that he
will be quite at home in any station of life to which his eccentric destiny
may call him. [*Seriously*] The great secret, Eliza, is not having bad manners
or good manners or any other particular sort of manners, but having the
same manner for all human souls: in short, behaving as if you were in
Heaven, where there are no third-class carriages, and one soul is as good as
another.

LIZA   Amen. You are a born preacher.

HIGGINS [*irritated*]   The question is not whether I treat you rudely, but
whether you ever heard me treat anyone else better.

LIZA [*with sudden sincerity*]   I dont care how you treat me. I dont mind your
swearing at me. I dont mind a black eye: Ive had one before this. But
[*Standing up and facing him*] I wont be passed over.[4]

HIGGINS   Then get out of my way; for I wont stop for you. You talk about me
as if I were a motor bus.

LIZA   So you are a motor bus: all bounce and go, and no consideration for
anyone. But I can do without you: dont think I cant.

HIGGINS   I know you can. I told you you could.

---

3. Humbled.   4. Ignored.

LIZA [*wounded, getting away from him to the other side of the ottoman with her face to the hearth*]   I know you did, you brute. You wanted to get rid of me.

HIGGINS   Liar.

LIZA   Thank you. [*She sits down with dignity.*]

HIGGINS   You never asked yourself, I suppose, whether *I* could do without
425   you.

LIZA [*earnestly*]   Dont you try to get round me.[5] Youll have to do without me.

HIGGINS [*arrogant*]   I can do without anybody. I have my own soul: my own
    spark of divine fire. But [*With sudden humility*] I shall miss you, Eliza. [*He
    sits down near her on the ottoman.*] I have learnt something from your idi-
430   otic notions: I confess that humbly and gratefully. And I have grown accus-
    tomed to your voice and appearance. I like them, rather.

LIZA   Well, you have both of them on your gramophone and in your book of
    photographs. When you feel lonely without me, you can turn the machine
    on. It's got no feelings to hurt.

435 HIGGINS   I cant turn your soul on. Leave me those feelings; and you can take
    away the voice and the face. They are not you.

LIZA   Oh, you are a devil. You can twist the heart in a girl as easy as some
    could twist her arms to hurt her. Mrs. Pearce warned me. Time and again
    she has wanted to leave you; and you always got round her at the last
440   minute. And you dont care a bit for her. And you dont care a bit for me.

HIGGINS   I care for life, for humanity; and you are a part of it that has come
    my way and been built into my house. What more can you or anyone ask?

LIZA   I wont care for anybody that doesnt care for me.

HIGGINS   Commercial principles, Eliza. Like [*Reproducing her Covent Gar-*
445   *den pronunciation with professional exactness*] s'yollin voylets [selling vio-
    lets], isnt it?

LIZA   Dont sneer at me. It's mean to sneer at me.

HIGGINS   I have never sneered in my life. Sneering doesnt become either the
    human face or the human soul. I am expressing my righteous contempt for
450   Commercialism. I dont and wont trade in affection. You call me a brute
    because you couldnt buy a claim on me by fetching my slippers and finding
    my spectacles. You were a fool: I think a woman fetching a man's slippers is
    a disgusting sight: did I ever fetch your slippers? I think a good deal more
    of you for throwing them in my face. No use slaving for me and then saying
455   you want to be cared for: who cares for a slave? If you come back, come
    back for the sake of good fellowship; for youll get nothing else. Youve had a
    thousand times as much out of me as I have out of you; and if you dare to
    set up your little dog's tricks of fetching and carrying slippers against my
    creation of a Duchess Eliza, I'll slam the door in your silly face.

460 LIZA   What did you do it for if you didnt care for me?

HIGGINS [*heartily*]   Why, because it was my job.

LIZA   You never thought of the trouble it would make for me.

HIGGINS   Would the world ever have been made if its maker had been afraid
    of making trouble? Making life means making trouble. Theres only one
465   way of escaping trouble; and thats killing things. Cowards, you notice, are
    always shrieking to have troublesome people killed.

LIZA   I'm no preacher: I dont notice things like that. I notice that you dont
    notice me.

5. That is, don't try to deceive or outsmart me.

HIGGINS [*jumping up and walking about intolerantly*]   Eliza: youre an idiot. I
waste the treasures of my Miltonic mind by spreading them before you.
Once for all, understand that I go my way and do my work without caring
twopence what happens to either of us. I am not intimidated, like your
father and your stepmother. So you can come back or go to the devil: which
you please.

LIZA   What am I to come back for?

HIGGINS [*bouncing up on his knees on the ottoman and leaning over it to her*]
For the fun of it. Thats why I took you on.

LIZA [*with averted face*]   And you may throw me out tomorrow if I dont do
everything you want me to?

HIGGINS   Yes; and you may walk out tomorrow if I dont do everything you
want me to.

LIZA   And live with my stepmother?

HIGGINS   Yes, or sell flowers.

LIZA   Oh! if I only could go back to my flower basket! I should be independent of both you and father and all the world! Why did you take my independence from me? Why did I give it up? I'm a slave now, for all my fine
clothes.

HIGGINS   Not a bit. I'll adopt you as my daughter and settle money on you if
you like. Or would you rather marry Pickering?

LIZA [*looking fiercely round at him*]   I wouldnt marry you if you asked me;
and youre nearer my age than what he is.

HIGGINS [*gently*]   Than he is: not "than what he is."

LIZA [*losing her temper and rising*]   I'll talk as I like. Youre not my teacher
now.

HIGGINS [*reflectively*]   I dont suppose Pickering would, though. Hes as confirmed an old bachelor as I am.

LIZA   Thats not what I want; and dont you think it. Ive always had chaps
enough wanting me that way. Freddy Hill writes to me twice and three
times a day,[6] sheets and sheets.

HIGGINS [*disagreeably surprised*]   Damn his impudence! [*He recoils and finds
himself sitting on his heels.*]

LIZA   He has a right to if he likes, poor lad. And he does love me.

HIGGINS [*getting off the ottoman*]   You have no right to encourage him.

LIZA   Every girl has a right to be loved.

HIGGINS   What! By fools like that?

LIZA   Freddy's not a fool. And if hes weak and poor and wants me, may be
hed make me happier than my betters that bully me and dont want me.

HIGGINS   Can he make anything of you? Thats the point.

LIZA   Perhaps I could make something of him. But I never thought of us
making anything of one another; and you never think of anything else. I
only want to be natural.

HIGGINS   In short, you want me to be as infatuated about you as Freddy? Is
that it?

LIZA   No I dont. Thats not the sort of feeling I want from you. And dont you
be too sure of yourself or of me. I could have been a bad girl if I'd liked. Ive
seen more of some things than you, for all your learning. Girls like me can

---

6. At the time, most places in England had two or three mail deliveries daily, and London had
even more.

515   drag gentlemen down to make love to[7] them easy enough. And they wish
each other dead the next minute.

HIGGINS   Of course they do. Then what in thunder are we quarrelling about?

LIZA [*much troubled*]   I want a little kindness. I know I'm a common ignorant girl, and you a book-learned gentleman; but I'm not dirt under your
520   feet. What I done [*Correcting herself*] what I did was not for the dresses
and the taxis: I did it because we were pleasant together and I come—
came—to care for you; not to want you to make love to me, and not forgetting the difference between us, but more friendly like.

HIGGINS   Well, of course. Thats just how I feel. And how Pickering feels.
525   Eliza: youre a fool.

LIZA   Thats not a proper answer to give me. [*She sinks on the chair at the
writing-table in tears.*]

HIGGINS   It's all youll get until you stop being a common idiot. If youre going
to be a lady, youll have to give up feeling neglected if the men you know
dont spend half their time snivelling over you and the other half giving you
530   black eyes. If you cant stand the coldness of my sort of life, and the strain
of it, go back to the gutter. Work til you are more a brute than a human
being; and then cuddle and squabble and drink til you fall asleep. Oh, it's a
fine life, the life of the gutter. It's real: it's warm: it's violent: you can feel it
through the thickest skin: you can taste it and smell it without any training
535   or any work. Not like Science and Literature and Classical Music and Philosophy and Art. You find me cold, unfeeling, selfish, dont you? Very well:
be off with you to the sort of people you like. Marry some sentimental hog
or other with lots of money, and a thick pair of lips to kiss you with and a
thick pair of boots to kick you with. If you cant appreciate what youve got,
540   youd better get what you can appreciate.

LIZA [*desperate*]   Oh, you are a cruel tyrant. I cant talk to you: you turn
everything against me: I'm always in the wrong. But you know very well all
the time that youre nothing but a bully. You know I cant go back to the gutter, as you call it, and that I have no real friends in the world but you and
545   the Colonel. You know well I couldnt bear to live with a low common man
after you two; and it's wicked and cruel of you to insult me by pretending I
could. You think I must go back to Wimpole Street because I have nowhere
else to go but father's. But dont you be too sure that you have me under
your feet to be trampled on and talked down. I'll marry Freddy, I will, as
550   soon as hes able to support me.

HIGGINS [*sitting down beside her*]   Rubbish! you shall marry an ambassador.
You shall marry the Governor-General of India or the Lord-Lieutenant of
Ireland, or somebody who wants a deputy-queen. I'm not going to have my
masterpiece thrown away on Freddy.

555 LIZA   You think I like you to say that. But I havnt forgot what you said a minute ago; and I wont be coaxed round as if I was a baby or a puppy. If I cant
have kindness, I'll have independence.

HIGGINS   Independence? Thats middle class blasphemy. We are all dependent on one another, every soul of us on earth.

560 LIZA [*rising determinedly*]   I'll let you see whether I'm dependent on you. If
you can preach, I can teach. I'll go and be a teacher.

---

7. To pay amorous attention to, to court.

HIGGINS Whatll you teach, in heaven's name?

LIZA What you taught me. I'll teach phonetics.

HIGGINS Ha! Ha! Ha!

565 LIZA I'll offer myself as an assistant to Professor Nepean.

HIGGINS [*rising in a fury*] What! That impostor! that humbug! that toadying ignoramus! Teach him my methods! my discoveries! You take one step in his direction and I'll wring your neck. [*He lays hands on her.*] Do you hear?

LIZA [*defiantly non-resistant*] Wring away. What do I care? I knew youd 570 strike me some day. [*He lets her go, stamping with rage at having forgotten himself, and recoils so hastily that he stumbles back into his seat on the ottoman.*] Aha! Now I know how to deal with you. What a fool I was not to think of it before! You cant take away the knowledge you gave me. You said I had a finer ear than you. And I can be civil and kind to people, which is more than you can. Aha! Thats done[8] you, Henry Higgins, it has. Now I 575 dont care that [*Snapping her fingers*] for your bullying and your big talk. I'll advertize it in the papers that your duchess is only a flower girl that you taught, and that she'll teach anybody to be a duchess just the same in six months for a thousand guineas. Oh, when I think of myself crawling under your feet and being trampled on and called names, when all the 580 time I had only to lift up my finger to be as good as you, I could just kick myself.

HIGGINS [*wondering at her*] You damned impudent slut, you! But it's better than snivelling; better than fetching slippers and finding spectacles, isnt it? [*Rising*] By George, Eliza, I said I'd make a woman of you; and I have. I like 585 you like this.

LIZA Yes: you turn round and make up to me now that I'm not afraid of you, and can do without you.

HIGGINS Of course I do, you little fool. Five minutes ago you were like a millstone round my neck. Now youre a tower of strength: a consort[9] battle- 590 ship. You and I and Pickering will be three old bachelors together instead of only two men and a silly girl.

[MRS. HIGGINS *returns, dressed for the wedding.* ELIZA *instantly becomes cool and elegant.*]

MRS. HIGGINS The carriage is waiting, Eliza. Are you ready?

LIZA Quite. Is the Professor coming?

MRS. HIGGINS Certainly not. He cant behave himself in church. He makes 595 remarks out loud all the time on the clergyman's pronunciation.

LIZA Then I shall not see you again, Professor. Good-bye. [*She goes to the door.*]

MRS. HIGGINS [*coming to* HIGGINS] Good-bye, dear.

HIGGINS Good-bye, mother. [*He is about to kiss her, when he recollects something.*] Oh, by the way, Eliza, order a ham and a Stilton cheese, will you? 600 And buy me a pair of reindeer gloves, number eights, and a tie to match that new suit of mine, at Eale & Binman's. You can choose the color. [*His cheerful, careless, vigorous voice shows that he is incorrigible.*]

LIZA [*disdainfully*] Buy them yourself.

[*She sweeps out.*]

---

8. Defeated.   9. A ship sailing in company with another.

MRS. HIGGINS   I'm afraid youve spoiled that girl, Henry. But never mind, dear: I'll buy you the tie and gloves.

605 HIGGINS [*sunnily*]   Oh, dont bother. She'll buy em all right enough. Goodbye.

[*They kiss.* MRS. HIGGINS *runs out.* HIGGINS, *left alone, rattles his cash in his pocket; chuckles; and disports himself in a highly self-satisfied manner.*]

* * * * *

The rest of the story need not be shown in action, and indeed, would hardly need telling if our imaginations were not so enfeebled by their lazy dependence on the ready-mades and reach-me-downs of the ragshop[1] in which Romance keeps its stock of "happy endings" to misfit all stories. Now, the history of Eliza Doolittle, though called a romance because of the transfiguration it records seems exceedingly improbable, is common enough. Such transfigurations have been achieved by hundreds of resolutely ambitious young women since Nell Gwynne[2] set them the example by playing queens and fascinating kings in the theatre in which she began by selling oranges. Nevertheless, people in all directions have assumed, for no other reason than that she became the heroine of a romance, that she must have married the hero of it. This is unbearable, not only because her little drama, if acted on such a thoughtless assumption, must be spoiled, but because the true sequel is patent to anyone with a sense of human nature in general, and of feminine instinct in particular.

Eliza, in telling Higgins she would not marry him if he asked her, was not coquetting: she was announcing a well-considered decision. When a bachelor interests, and dominates, and teaches, and becomes important to a spinster, as Higgins with Eliza, she always, if she has character enough to be capable of it, considers very seriously indeed whether she will play for becoming that bachelor's wife, especially if he is so little interested in marriage that a determined and devoted woman might capture him if she set herself resolutely to do it. Her decision will depend a good deal on whether she is really free to choose; and that, again, will depend on her age and income. If she is at the end of her youth, and has no security for her livelihood, she will marry him because she must marry anybody who will provide for her. But at Eliza's age a good-looking girl does not feel that pressure: she feels free to pick and choose. She is therefore guided by her instinct in the matter. Eliza's instinct tells her not to marry Higgins. It does not tell her to give him up. It is not in the slightest doubt as to his remaining one of the strongest personal interests in her life. It would be very sorely strained if there was another woman likely to supplant her with him. But as she feels sure of him on that last point, she has no doubt at all as to her course, and would not have any, even if the difference of twenty years in age, which seems so great to youth, did not exist between them.

As our own instincts are not appealed to by her conclusion, let us see whether we cannot discover some reason in it. When Higgins excused his indifference to young women on the ground that they had an irresistible rival in his mother, he gave the clue to his inveterate old-bachelordom. The case is uncommon only to the extent that remarkable mothers are uncommon. If an imaginative boy has a sufficiently rich mother who has intelligence, personal grace, dignity of character without harshness, and a cultivated sense of the best art of her time to enable her to make her house beautiful, she sets a standard for him against which very few women can struggle, besides effecting for him a disengagement of his affections, his sense of beauty, and his idealism from his specifically sexual impulses. This makes him a standing puzzle to the huge number of uncultivated people who have been brought up in tasteless

---

1. That is, a shop selling cheap mass-produced and secondhand clothing ("ready-mades and reach-me-downs").

2. Eleanor Gwynn (1650–1687), one of the first prominent English actresses and a mistress of King Charles II.

homes by commonplace or disagreeable parents, and to whom, consequently, literature, painting, sculpture, music, and affectionate personal relations come as modes of sex if they come at all. The word passion means nothing else to them; and that Higgins could have a passion for phonetics and idealize his mother instead of Eliza, would seem to them absurd and unnatural. Nevertheless, when we look round and see that hardly anyone is too ugly or disagreeable to find a wife or a husband if he or she wants one, whilst many old maids and bachelors are above the average in quality and culture, we cannot help suspecting that the disentanglement of sex from the associations with which it is so commonly confused, a disentanglement which persons of genius achieve by sheer intellectual analysis, is sometimes produced or aided by parental fascination.

Now, though Eliza was incapable of thus explaining to herself Higgins's formidable powers of resistance to the charm that prostrated Freddy at the first glance, she was instinctively aware that she could never obtain a complete grip of him, or come between him and his mother (the first necessity of the married woman). To put it shortly, she knew that for some mysterious reason he had not the makings of a married man in him, according to her conception of a husband as one to whom she would be his nearest and fondest and warmest interest. Even had there been no mother-rival, she would still have refused to accept an interest in herself that was secondary to philosophic interests. Had Mrs. Higgins died, there would still have been Milton and the Universal Alphabet. Landor's[3] remark that to those who have the greatest power of loving, love is a secondary affair, would not have recommended Landor to Eliza. Put that along with her resentment of Higgins's domineering superiority, and her mistrust of his coaxing cleverness in getting round her and evading her wrath when he had gone too far with his impetuous bullying, and you will see that Eliza's instinct had good grounds for warning her not to marry her Pygmalion.

And now, whom did Eliza marry? For if Higgins was a predestinate old bachelor, she was most certainly not a predestinate old maid. Well, that can be told very shortly to those who have not guessed it from the indications she has herself given them.

Almost immediately after Eliza is stung into proclaiming her considered determination not to marry Higgins, she mentions the fact that young Mr. Frederick Eynsford Hill is pouring out his love for her daily through the post. Now Freddy is young, practically twenty years younger than Higgins: he is a gentleman (or, as Eliza would qualify him, a toff), and speaks like one; he is nicely dressed, is treated by the Colonel as an equal, loves her unaffectedly, and is not her master, nor ever likely to dominate her in spite of his advantage of social standing. Eliza has no use for the foolish romantic tradition that all women love to be mastered, if not actually bullied and beaten. "When you go to women," says Nietzsche, "take your whip with you."[4] Sensible despots have never confined that precaution to women: they have taken their whips with them when they have dealt with men, and been slavishly idealized by the men over whom they have flourished the whip much more than by women. No doubt there are slavish women as well as slavish men; and women, like men, admire those that are stronger than themselves. But to admire a strong person and to live under that strong person's thumb are two different things. The weak may not be admired and hero-worshipped; but they are by no means disliked or shunned; and they never seem to have the least difficulty in marrying people who are too good for them. They may fail in emergencies; but life is not one long emergency: it is mostly a string of situations for which no exceptional strength is needed, and with which even rather

---

3. The English poet Walter Savage Landor (1775–1864); in "Roger Ascham and the Lady Jane Grey," in *Imaginary Conversations of Literary Men and Statesmen* (1824), he wrote, "Love is a secondary passion in those who love most, a primary in those who love least."

4. Spoken by a fictional old woman in *Thus Spoke Zarathustra* (1883), by the German philosopher Friedrich Nietzsche (1844–1900).

weak people can cope if they have a stronger partner to help them out. Accordingly, it is a truth everywhere in evidence that strong people, masculine or feminine, not only do not marry stronger people, but do not shew any preference for them in selecting their friends. When a lion meets another with a louder roar "the first lion thinks the last a bore."[5] The man or woman who feels strong enough for two, seeks for every other quality in a partner than strength.

The converse is also true. Weak people want to marry strong people who do not frighten them too much; and this often leads them to make the mistake we describe metaphorically as "biting off more than they can chew." They want too much for too little; and when the bargain is unreasonable beyond all bearing, the union becomes impossible: it ends in the weaker party being either discarded or borne as a cross, which is worse. People who are not only weak, but silly or obtuse as well, are often in these difficulties.

This being the state of human affairs, what is Eliza fairly sure to do when she is placed between Freddy and Higgins? Will she look forward to a lifetime of fetching Higgins's slippers or to a lifetime of Freddy fetching hers? There can be no doubt about the answer. Unless Freddy is biologically repulsive to her, and Higgins biologically attractive to a degree that overwhelms all her other instincts, she will, if she marries either of them, marry Freddy.

And that is just what Eliza did.

Complications ensued; but they were economic, not romantic. Freddy had no money and no occupation. His mother's jointure, a last relic of the opulence of Largelady Park, had enabled her to struggle along in Earlscourt with an air of gentility, but not to procure any serious secondary education for her children, much less give the boy a profession. A clerkship at thirty shillings a week was beneath Freddy's dignity, and extremely distasteful to him besides. His prospects consisted of a hope that if he kept up appearances somebody would do something for him. The something appeared vaguely to his imagination as a private secretaryship or a sinecure of some sort. To his mother it perhaps appeared as a marriage to some lady of means who could not resist her boy's niceness. Fancy her feelings when he married a flower girl who had become déclassée under extraordinary circumstances which were now notorious!

It is true that Eliza's situation did not seem wholly ineligible. Her father, though formerly a dustman, and now fantastically disclassed, had become extremely popular in the smartest society by a social talent which triumphed over every prejudice and every disadvantage. Rejected by the middle class, which he loathed, he had shot up at once into the highest circles by his wit, his dustmanship (which he carried like a banner), and his Nietzschean transcendence of good and evil.[6] At intimate ducal dinners he sat on the right hand of the Duchess; and in country houses he smoked in the pantry and was made much of by the butler when he was not feeding in the dining-room and being consulted by cabinet ministers. But he found it almost as hard to do all this on four thousand a year as Mrs. Eynsford Hill to live in Earlscourt on an income so pitiably smaller that I have not the heart to disclose its exact figure. He absolutely refused to add the last straw to his burden by contributing to Eliza's support.

Thus Freddy and Eliza, now Mr. and Mrs. Eynsford Hill, would have spent a penniless honeymoon but for a wedding present of £500[7] from the Colonel to Eliza. It lasted a long time because Freddy did not know how to spend money, never having had any to spend, and Eliza, socially trained by a pair of old bachelors, wore her

---

5. Shaw slightly misquotes the popular comic opera *Bombastes Furioso* (1810), by English dramatist William Barnes Rhodes: "So have I heard on Afric's burning shore / Another lion give a grievous roar; / And the first lion thought the last a bore."

6. A well-known work by Nietzsche is titled *Beyond Good and Evil* (1886).

7. Roughly equivalent to $40,000 today.

clothes as long as they held together and looked pretty, without the least regard to their being many months out of fashion. Still, £500 will not last two young people for ever; and they both knew, and Eliza felt as well, that they must shift for themselves in the end. She could quarter herself on Wimpole Street because it had come to be her home; but she was quite aware that she ought not to quarter Freddy there, and that it would not be good for his character if she did.

Not that the Wimpole Street bachelors objected. When she consulted them, Higgins declined to be bothered about her housing problem when that solution was so simple. Eliza's desire to have Freddy in the house with her seemed of no more importance than if she had wanted an extra piece of bedroom furniture. Pleas as to Freddy's character, and the moral obligation on him to earn his own living, were lost on Higgins. He denied that Freddy had any character, and declared that if he tried to do any useful work some competent person would have the trouble of undoing it: a procedure involving a net loss to the community; and great unhappiness to Freddy himself, who was obviously intended by Nature for such light work as amusing Eliza, which, Higgins declared, was a much more useful and honorable occupation than working in the city.[8] When Eliza referred again to her project of teaching phonetics, Higgins abated not a jot of his violent opposition to it. He said she was not within ten years of being qualified to meddle with his pet subject; and as it was evident that the Colonel agreed with him, she felt she could not go against them in this grave matter, and that she had no right, without Higgins's consent, to exploit the knowledge he had given her; for his knowledge seemed to her as much his private property as his watch: Eliza was no communist. Besides, she was superstitiously devoted to them both, more entirely and frankly after her marriage than before it.

It was the Colonel who finally solved the problem, which had cost him much perplexed cogitation. He one day asked Eliza, rather shyly, whether she had quite given up her notion of keeping a flower shop. She replied that she had thought of it, but had put it out of her head, because the Colonel had said, that day at Mrs. Higgins's, that it would never do. The Colonel confessed that when he said that, he had not quite recovered from the dazzling impression of the day before. They broke the matter to Higgins that evening. The sole comment vouchsafed by him very nearly led to a serious quarrel with Eliza. It was to the effect that she would have in Freddy an ideal errand boy.

Freddy himself was next sounded on the subject. He said he had been thinking of a shop himself; though it had presented itself to his pennilessness as a small place in which Eliza should sell tobacco at one counter whilst he sold newspapers at the opposite one. But he agreed that it would be extraordinarily jolly to go early every morning with Eliza to Covent Garden and buy flowers on the scene of their first meeting: a sentiment which earned him many kisses from his wife. He added that he had always been afraid to propose anything of the sort, because Clara would make an awful row about a step that must damage her matrimonial chances, and his mother could not be expected to like it after clinging for so many years to that step of the social ladder on which retail trade is impossible.

This difficulty was removed by an event highly unexpected by Freddy's mother. Clara, in the course of her incursions into those artistic circles which were the highest within her reach, discovered that her conversational qualifications were expected to include a grounding in the novels of Mr. H. G. Wells.[9] She borrowed them in various directions so energetically that she swallowed them all within two months. The result was a conversion of a kind quite common today. A modern Acts of the Apostles would fill fifty whole Bibles if anyone were capable of writing it.

8. That is, working in London's finance district.
9. The English writer Herbert George Wells (1866–1946), a prominent member of the socialist Fabian Society and the author not only of science-fiction novels such as The War of the Worlds (1898) but also novels of social criticism such as Tono-Bungay (1908).

Poor Clara, who appeared to Higgins and his mother as a disagreeable and ridiculous person, and to her own mother as in some inexplicable way a social failure, had never seen herself in either light; for, though to some extent ridiculed and mimicked in West Kensington[1] like everybody else there, she was accepted as a rational and normal—or shall we say inevitable?—sort of human being. At worst they called her The Pusher;[2] but to them no more than to herself had it ever occurred that she was pushing the air, and pushing it in a wrong direction. Still, she was not happy. She was growing desperate. Her one asset, the fact that her mother was what the Epsom greengrocer called a carriage lady had no exchange value, apparently. It had prevented her from getting educated, because the only education she could have afforded was education with the Earlscourt greengrocer's daughter. It had led her to seek the society of her mother's class; and that class simply would not have her, because she was much poorer than the greengrocer, and, far from being able to afford a maid,[3] could not afford even a housemaid, and had to scrape along at home with an illiberally treated general servant. Under such circumstances nothing could give her an air of being a genuine product of Largelady Park. And yet its tradition made her regard a marriage with anyone within her reach as an unbearable humiliation. Commercial people and professional people in a small way were odious to her. She ran after painters and novelists; but she did not charm them; and her bold attempts to pick up and practise artistic and literary talk irritated them. She was, in short, an utter failure, an ignorant, incompetent, pretentious, unwelcome, penniless, useless little snob; and though she did not admit these disqualifications (for nobody ever faces unpleasant truths of this kind until the possibility of a way out dawns on them) she felt their effects too keenly to be satisfied with her position.

Clara had a startling eyeopener when, on being suddenly wakened to enthusiasm by a girl of her own age who dazzled her and produced in her a gushing desire to take her for a model, and gain her friendship, she discovered that this exquisite apparition had graduated from the gutter in a few months' time. It shook her so violently, that when Mr. H. G. Wells lifted her on the point of his puissant pen, and placed her at the angle of view from which the life she was leading and the society to which she clung appeared in its true relation to real human needs and worthy social structure, he effected a conversion and a conviction of sin comparable to the most sensational feats of General Booth or Gypsy Smith.[4] Clara's snobbery went bang. Life suddenly began to move with her. Without knowing how or why, she began to make friends and enemies. Some of the acquaintances to whom she had been a tedious or indifferent or ridiculous affliction, dropped her: others became cordial. To her amazement she found that some "quite nice" people were saturated with Wells, and that this accessibility to ideas was the secret of their niceness. People she had thought deeply religious, and had tried to conciliate on that tack with disastrous results, suddenly took an interest in her, and revealed a hostility to conventional religion which she had never conceived possible except among the most desperate characters. They made her read Galsworthy;[5] and Galsworthy exposed the vanity of Largelady Park and finished her. It exasperated her to think that the dungeon in which she had languished for so many unhappy years had been unlocked all the time, and that the impulses she had so carefully struggled with and stifled for the sake of keeping well with society, were precisely those by which alone she could have come into any sort of sincere human contact. In the radiance of these discoveries, and the tumult of

---

1. An area of London at the western edge of the inner suburbs.
2. That is, The Social Climber.
3. A personal attendant, as distinct from a general servant who does housework.
4. That is, feats of religious conversion. William Booth (1829–1912), a Methodist revivalist, founded the Salvation Army; Rodney

Smith (1860–1947), briefly a captain in the Salvation Army, became an internationally renowned evangelist.
5. John Galsworthy (1867–1933), an English playwright and novelist whose writings cast a realistic and critical light on the upper middle class.

their reaction, she made a fool of herself as freely and conspicuously as when she so rashly adopted Eliza's expletive in Mrs. Higgins's drawing-room; for the new-born Wellsian had to find her bearings almost as ridiculously as a baby; but nobody hates a baby for its ineptitudes, or thinks the worse of it for trying to eat the matches; and Clara lost no friends by her follies. They laughed at her to her face this time; and she had to defend herself and fight it out as best she could.

When Freddy paid a visit to Earlscourt (which he never did when he could possibly help it) to make the desolating announcement that he and his Eliza were thinking of blackening the Largelady scutcheon[6] by opening a shop, he found the little household already convulsed by a prior announcement from Clara that she also was going to work in an old furniture shop in Dover Street, which had been started by a fellow Wellsian. This appointment Clara owed, after all, to her old social accomplishment of Push. She had made up her mind that, cost what it might, she would see Mr. Wells in the flesh; and she had achieved her end at a garden party. She had better luck than so rash an enterprise deserved. Mr. Wells came up to her expectations. Age had not withered him, nor could custom stale his infinite variety in half an hour.[7] His pleasant neatness and compactness, his small hands and feet, his teeming ready brain, his unaffected accessibility, and a certain fine apprehensiveness which stamped him as susceptible from his topmost hair to his tipmost toe, proved irresistible. Clara talked of nothing else for weeks and weeks afterwards. And as she happened to talk to the lady of the furniture shop, and that lady also desired above all things to know Mr. Wells and sell pretty things to him, she offered Clara a job on the chance of achieving that end through her.

And so it came about that Eliza's luck held, and the expected opposition to the flower shop melted away. The shop is in the arcade of a railway station not very far from the Victoria and Albert Museum; and if you live in that neighborhood you may go there any day and buy a buttonhole[8] from Eliza.

Now here is a last opportunity for romance. Would you not like to be assured that the shop was an immense success, thanks to Eliza's charms and her early business experience in Covent Garden? Alas! the truth is the truth: the shop did not pay for a long time, simply because Eliza and her Freddy did not know how to keep it. True, Eliza had not to begin at the very beginning: she knew the names and prices of the cheaper flowers; and her elation was unbounded when she found that Freddy, like all youths educated at cheap, pretentious, and thoroughly inefficient schools, knew a little Latin. It was very little, but enough to make him appear to her a Porson or Bentley,[9] and to put him at his ease with botanical nomenclature. Unfortunately he knew nothing else; and Eliza, though she could count money up to eighteen shillings or so, and had acquired a certain familiarity with the language of Milton from her struggles to qualify herself for winning Higgins's bet, could not write out a bill without utterly disgracing the establishment. Freddy's power of stating in Latin that Balbus built a wall and that Gaul was divided into three parts[1] did not carry with it the slightest knowledge of accounts or business: Colonel Pickering had to explain to him what a cheque book and a bank account meant. And the pair were by no means easily teachable. Freddy backed up Eliza in her obstinate refusal to believe that they could save money by engaging a bookkeeper with some knowledge of the business. How, they argued, could you possibly save money by going to extra expense when you already could not make both ends meet? But the Colonel, after making the ends meet over and over again, at last gently insisted; and Eliza, humbled to the dust by

---

6. Reputation (literally, a heraldic shield).
7. An allusion to the description of Cleopatra in Shakespeare's *Antony and Cleopatra* (1606–07): "Age cannot wither her, nor custom stale / Her infinite variety" (2.2.240–41).
8. A flower worn in the buttonhole of a lapel.

9. A great classicist, such as the English scholars Richard Porson (1759–1808) and Richard Bentley (1662–1742).
1. Phrases from standard Latin exercise books (the second is the opening of Caesar's *Gallic War* [ca. 50 B.C.E.]).

having to beg from him so often, and stung by the uproarious derision of Higgins, to whom the notion of Freddy succeeding at anything was a joke that never palled, grasped the fact that business, like phonetics, has to be learned.

On the piteous spectacle of the pair spending their evenings in shorthand schools and polytechnic classes, learning bookkeeping and typewriting with incipient junior clerks, male and female, from the elementary schools, let me not dwell. There were even classes at the London School of Economics, and a humble personal appeal to the director of that institution to recommend a course bearing on the flower business. He, being a humorist, explained to them the method of the celebrated Dickensian essay on Chinese Metaphysics by the gentleman who read an article on China and an article on Metaphysics and combined the information.[2] He suggested that they should combine the London School with Kew Gardens. Eliza, to whom the procedure of the Dickensian gentleman seemed perfectly correct (as in fact it was) and not in the least funny (which was only her ignorance) took his advice with entire gravity. But the effort that cost her the deepest humiliation was a request to Higgins, whose pet artistic fancy, next to Milton's verse, was caligraphy, and who himself wrote a most beautiful Italian hand, that he would teach her to write. He declared that she was congenitally incapable of forming a single letter worthy of the least of Milton's words; but she persisted; and again he suddenly threw himself into the task of teaching her with a combination of stormy intensity, concentrated patience, and occasional bursts of interesting disquisition on the beauty and nobility, the august mission and destiny, of human handwriting. Eliza ended by acquiring an extremely uncommercial script which was a positive extension of her personal beauty, and spending three times as much on stationery as anyone else because certain qualities and shapes of paper became indispensable to her. She could not even address an envelope in the usual way because it made the margins all wrong.

Their commercial school days were a period of disgrace and despair for the young couple. They seemed to be learning nothing about flower shops. At last they gave it up as hopeless, and shook the dust of the shorthand schools, and the polytechnics, and the London School of Economics from their feet for ever. Besides, the business was in some mysterious way beginning to take care of itself. They had somehow forgotten their objections to employing other people. They came to the conclusion that their own way was the best, and that they had really a remarkable talent for business. The Colonel, who had been compelled for some years to keep a sufficient sum on current account at his bankers to make up their deficits, found that the provision was unnecessary: the young people were prospering. It is true that there was not quite fair play between them and their competitors in trade. Their week-ends in the country cost them nothing, and saved them the price of their Sunday dinners; for the motor car was the Colonel's; and he and Higgins paid the hotel bills. Mr. F. Hill, florist and greengrocer (they soon discovered that there was money in asparagus; and asparagus led to other vegetables), had an air which stamped the business as classy; and in private life he was still Frederick Eynsford Hill, Esquire. Not that there was any swank about him: nobody but Eliza knew that he had been christened Frederick Challoner. Eliza herself swanked like anything.

That is all. That is how it has turned out. It is astonishing how much Eliza still manages to meddle in the housekeeping at Wimpole Street in spite of the shop and her own family. And it is notable that though she never nags her husband, and frankly loves the Colonel as if she were his favorite daughter, she has never got out of the habit of nagging Higgins that was established on the fatal night when she won his bet for him. She snaps his head off on the faintest provocation, or on none. He no longer dares to tease her by assuming an abysmal inferiority of Freddy's mind to his own. He storms and bullies and derides; but she stands up to him so ruthlessly that the Colonel has to ask her from time to time to be kinder to Higgins; and it is the

2. An allusion to *The Pickwick Papers* (1836–37), a novel by Charles Dickens.

only request of his that brings a mulish expression into her face. Nothing but some emergency or calamity great enough to break down all likes and dislikes, and throw them both back on their common humanity—and may they be spared any such trial!—will ever alter this. She knows that Higgins does not need her, just as her father did not need her. The very scrupulousness with which he told her that day that he had become used to having her there, and dependent on her for all sorts of little services, and that he should miss her if she went away (it would never have occurred to Freddy or the Colonel to say anything of the sort) deepens her inner certainty that she is "no more to him than them slippers," yet she has a sense, too, that his indifference is deeper than the infatuation of commoner souls. She is immensely interested in him. She has even secret mischievous moments in which she wishes she could get him alone, on a desert island, away from all ties and with nobody else in the world to consider, and just drag him off his pedestal and see him making love like any common man. We all have private imaginations of that sort. But when it comes to business, to the life that she really leads as distinguished from the life of dreams and fancies, she likes Freddy and she likes the Colonel; and she does not like Higgins and Mr. Doolittle. Galatea never does quite like Pygmalion: his relation to her is too god-like to be altogether agreeable.[3]

---

3. In classical mythology, Pygmalion was a legendary king of Cyprus who fell in love with an ivory statue of a woman that he had carved. In answer to his prayers, Aphrodite (called Venus by the Romans), the goddess of love, gave it life and they married; the most familiar version of the story is found in Ovid, *Metamorphoses* (ca. 10 C.E.), 10.243–97.

SUSAN GLASPELL

1876–1948

T HE rediscovery of Susan Glaspell's writing by feminist critics and theater artists has, over the past few decades, exposed new generations of readers and audiences to this groundbreaking American playwright, novelist, and short story author, who received the Pulitzer Prize for drama in 1931. Glaspell came of age in the late nineteenth century, during the heyday of the "local color" movement in American literature. Works in this tradition—such as those of Glaspell's fellow Davenport, Iowa, resident Alice French (writing as Octave Thanet, 1850–1934)—celebrated regional American life and exposed its idiosyncrasies. By the early twentieth century, however, writers were increasingly focusing on the cultural, economic, and political differences growing between the country's burgeoning urban centers and its established rural locales. Glaspell and her contemporaries felt compelled to share with the nation their large and probing questions about American beliefs, values, and goals. In their creative endeavors, they framed these questions through the lenses of the Progressive era and their modern age, most notably the recent discoveries about human psychology. Glaspell's writing—especially her plays—reflects her keen engagement with the pressing issues of her day: how to foster a democratic and equitable society, what to think about the evolving roles of men and women, and how to honor the

nation's founding principles while embracing the spirit of modernism. Artists like Glaspell were also engaged in formal experimentation, and their works reveal a sense of creative excitement as they sought new ways, structurally and aesthetically, to represent these cogent contemporary themes. Glaspell's 1916 play *TRIFLES* has emerged as a canonical text precisely because it exemplifies these intertwining artistic and social goals within American modernism.

Like many American modernists, Glaspell grew up in the nation's heartland. Her father, Elmer Glaspell, was a feed dealer; her mother, born Alice Keating, had been a schoolteacher before her marriage. Glaspell began her career as a journalist, writing a society column for her local paper before leaving home to attend Drake University. After graduation, she secured a post with the *Des Moines Daily News* as a statehouse and legislative reporter, but after two years, she decided to devote herself to fiction. She quickly had success writing short stories, which she placed in such national magazines as *McClure's* and *Harper's*. Following in the local-color tradition, Glaspell based many of her narratives on her experiences growing up in and around Davenport. But she interlaced these intimate portraits of midwestern life with the sharper edge of social critique that epitomizes her evolution as a Progressive and modernist artist. She published her first novel in 1909 and her second in 1911, as she continued to write short fiction. Following her marriage to George Cram "Jig" Cook in 1913, she and her new husband moved to Greenwich Village, as did many other young writers and artists of their generation. They were drawn to New York's bohemian lifestyle and creative freedom, which they felt were unattainable in the Midwest.

During this early twentieth-century moment, a growing number of American modernists recognized the potential of the stage to convey vivid images of life in the contemporary United States and, even more important, to engage audiences directly with larger social concerns. Eschewing the commercial theater and its devotion to profit-making entertainment, they sought to create a new kind of theater that would foster the development of a distinctly American culture. As a cofounder of the influential Provincetown Players—the company originally based in Provincetown, Massachusetts, that first produced the work of EUGENE O'NEILL during summer vacations—Glaspell played a central role in this movement. With Cook and other friends and colleagues such as John Reed, Djuna Barnes, Edna St. Vincent Millay, Theodore Dreiser, and Wallace Stevens, Glaspell participated in establishing a national theater dedicated to artistically innovative and political drama reflecting the explosive arrival of modernism in the United States.

For financial, practical, and philosophical reasons, most of the works produced by the Provincetown Players in their early years were one acts. Having been influenced by a U.S. tour of what was still called the Irish Players—the group founded in 1899 by the poet William Butler Yeats, Lady Gregory, and others that in 1904 became the Abbey Theatre—Cook believed that their repertoire of one-act plays had great impact as both artistic and nationalist creations, and he encouraged the Provincetown dramatists to use this form. Glaspell wrote eleven plays, seven of which were one acts (two written with Cook), for the Provincetown group between 1915 and 1922. Glaspell and Cook then departed from New York for Greece, leaving the

Provincetown Players to reconfigure themselves under others' leadership. After Cook died unexpectedly in 1924, Glaspell chose to return to their home on Cape Cod rather than renew her life in the bohemian Greenwich Village milieu. She also chose to return to her first creative form, fiction, producing six new novels and a children's tale. Glaspell did not abandon the theater however. With her new companion Norman Matson, with whom she lived until 1932, Glaspell wrote *The Comic Artist* (1927); soon thereafter she composed *Alison's House* (1930), based on the life and family of Emily Dickinson, for which she won the Pulitzer Prize. From 1936 to 1938 she lived in Chicago, serving as the director of the Midwest Play Bureau of the Federal Theater Project. Glaspell wrote one additional play, *Springs Eternal* (written 1944), which was neither published nor produced. She died in Provincetown in 1948.

Glaspell's first play, *Trifles*, was quickly identified by critics as an exemplar of one-act dramaturgy, and it was soon both widely produced and anthologized. Although Glaspell had initially conceived the piece as another short story, her husband persuaded her to write it first as a play; its short story version, "A Jury of Her Peers," was equally praised on its publication the following year. *Trifles* established Glaspell as a dramatist of real power; like all her short dramatic pieces, it displays her skill at constructing tight plots and using distinctive images in the service of theme. Like her American modernist contemporaries, Glaspell experimented freely with the various "isms" that defined the period, including realism, symbolism, and expressionism, often combining these approaches to achieve a specific thematic or stylistic effect. She demonstrated the effectiveness of both comedy and tragedy as vehicles for social critique. And she capitalized on the power of live theater to examine issues of particular concern to women, placing female characters and their struggles at the center of her dramaturgy. *The Outside* (1917), set in a lifesaving station on Cape Cod, epitomizes her method of integrating the symbolism of her setting with the play's action, as she portrays characters literally and figuratively in need of salvation. Such one acts as *Woman's Honor*

(1918) showcase Glaspell's gifts as a comic playwright, particularly her ability to depict the foibles of all her characters equally, as she introduces a group of allegorical women responding to what they take to be a demonstration of chivalry. This evenhandedness in her dramaturgical technique gives her plays a sense of balance, which is especially important when her theme is politically charged. Her ability to represent differing ideological perspectives is clearly displayed in *Inheritors* (1921), a full-length play that explores the Espionage Act (1917) and the Sedition Act (1918), which were intended to silence opposition to U.S. involvement in World War I. Other longer dramas, such as her highly regarded *The Verge* (1921), feature Glaspell's engagement with questions of gender identity and feminist consciousness as well as stylistic experimentation with realism and expressionism. Though some earlier critics faulted Glaspell for what they perceived as inconsistencies in style or thematic focus, more recently this variety and breadth have been championed as integral to the modernist movement in America and its willingness to engage with many facets of contemporary life.

Between December 1900 and April 1901, while working as a journalist, Glaspell had written a series of articles on the murder case that became the genesis for *Trifles:* the story of an Iowa farmer named Hossack whose wife was accused of killing him with an axe, and her subsequent trial and conviction. Glaspell transformed the details disclosed in the trial into a dramatic work of remarkable power, economy, and artistry. *Trifles* is set in the kitchen of "the now abandoned farmhouse" of John and Minnie Wright. We soon learn that shortly after the murder, a neighbor, Lewis Hale, discovered John strangled in his bed upstairs and Minnie dazedly rocking in her kitchen. With the body removed and the accused wife in jail, the play opens with the arrival of Hale; the sheriff, Henry Peters; and the county prosecutor, George Henderson, to inspect the crime scene. The wives of the sheriff and the neighbor, Mrs. Peters and Mrs. Hale, remain in the kitchen area to collect a few things Minnie has requested from prison. Glaspell's

choice to identify them only by their married names underscores the traditional assumption that women have significance only through their relation to their husbands. Once the men leave the room, however, the women begin to explore the domestic space on their own. As they interact with the stage environment, the two women discover clues to the couple's personalities as well as potential evidence in the case. Despite their absence from the scene, Minnie and John Wright become vivid figures for us via the dialogue and actions of Mrs. Hale and Mrs. Peters. Glaspell's technique of building a plot around these absent centers is a hallmark of her dramaturgy, recurring in *Bernice* (1919) and *Alison's House*, among other plays. This device enables her to show that identity is as much constructed as innate. Moreover, it creates a distance between the audience and these characters that thwarts identification, thus making it possible for theatergoers to see them and their reported actions from multiple points of view. The irony that Glaspell emphasizes throughout the play (and in its very title) is the inconsequentiality—to the men who are empowered to solve the crime—of the domestic details these women embrace. The "trifles" of women's lives and work that the men dismiss hold great significance for the women who understand how to read their import empathically. Although the women do not really know each other at the beginning of the play, they come to find they have much in common, just as they do with the absent Minnie. Recognizing a sense of responsibility for and community with this other woman, Mrs. Hale exclaims: "I might have known she needed help! I know how things can be—for women. . . . We all go through the same things—it's all just a different kind of the same thing."

By reversing the narrative conventions that place men at the center of a plot as figures of power and knowledge, Glaspell guides her audience toward the recognition that different perspectives and values are essential to appreciate women's lives. The short story's title, "A Jury of Her Peers," adds another layer of irony by highlighting the impossibility of a woman facing such a jury at a time when women were

The 1916 production of *Trifles* by the Washington Square Players at the Comedy Theater. Pictured, from left to right, are Marjorie Vonnegut (Mrs. Peters), Elinor M. Cox (Mrs. Hale), John King (Lewis Hale), Arthur E. Hohl (Henry Peters), and T. W. Gibson (George Henderson).

systematically denied the right to be jurors. In effect, Mrs. Peters and Mrs. Hale (played by Glaspell in the first production) try Minnie Wright in an alternative venue, using a process that reveals details of her experience and possible motives—aspects of the case that the men's investigation will never discover. While Minnie's ultimate fate is left unresolved at the play's end, we sense that these women have come to their own verdict, one that exonerates Minnie and makes the audience wonder who in the couple was the victim.

Part of the ongoing appeal of *Trifles* surely stems from its reliance on the conventions of the murder mystery. Glaspell capitalized on the growing interest in this form of narrative, a genre that was popularized first in the United States by Edgar Allan Poe (1809–1849) and that gained an even wider readership with the Sherlock Holmes stories of England's Arthur Conan Doyle (1859–1930). Like many writers of mysteries, Glaspell uses amateur detectives—the two women—who turn out to be more perceptive than the male

experts investigating the case. Glaspell involves her audience in the process of discovery and deduction intrinsic to the form. Her employment of the mystery genre thus advances her feminist agenda: all members of the audience, regardless of sex, come to understand each piece of the puzzle through the perspectives of the women sleuths as they grapple with the evidence. As feminist critics point out, Glaspell's play teaches its viewers to see as women, to resist the conventions that have dominated the Western theater since its inception.

Glaspell's deft layering of imagery, her poignant representation of her midwestern locale, and the specificity of her characterizations and dialect in such a brief work all point to her mastery of the one-act form and her significance as an American dramatist. During her period of greatest productivity, she was considered by many to be one of the country's two most important dramatists—O'Neill being the other. The prominent cultural critic Ludwig Lewisohn wrote in 1932, "Susan Glaspell was followed by Eugene O'Neill.

The rest was silence; the rest is silence still." Though recent critical attention has focused on Glaspell primarily as a feminist writer, her dramatic work reflects a number of compelling aesthetic and political concerns. She made important contributions to the development of American modernism, and her writing reflects a forceful commitment to the country's foundational principles of democracy and personal liberty. For those wishing to grasp essential nuances of our cultural and political heritage, Susan Glaspell provides eloquent renditions of our nation a century ago.   J.E.G.

Trifles
A Play in One Act

CHARACTERS

GEORGE HENDERSON, county attorney
HENRY PETERS, sheriff

LEWIS HALE, a neighboring farmer
MRS. PETERS
MRS. HALE

SCENE: *The kitchen in the now abandoned farmhouse of* JOHN WRIGHT, *a gloomy kitchen, and left without having been put in order—unwashed pans under the sink, a loaf of bread outside the breadbox, a dish towel on the table—other signs of incompleted work.*

[*At the rear the outer door opens and the* SHERIFF *comes in followed by the* COUNTY ATTORNEY *and* HALE. *The* SHERIFF *and* HALE *are men in middle life, the* COUNTY ATTORNEY *is a young man; all are much bundled up and go at once to the stove. They are followed by the two women—the* SHERIFF's *wife first; she is a slight wiry woman, a thin nervous face.* MRS. HALE *is larger and would ordinarily be called more comfortable[1] looking, but she is disturbed now and looks fearfully about as she enters. The women have come in slowly, and stand close together near the door.*]

COUNTY ATTORNEY [*rubbing his hands*]   This feels good. Come up to the fire, ladies.

MRS. PETERS [*after taking a step forward*]   I'm not—cold.

SHERIFF [*unbuttoning his overcoat and stepping away from the stove as if to mark the beginning of official business*]   Now, Mr. Hale, before we move
5   things about, you explain to Mr. Henderson just what you saw when you came here yesterday morning.

COUNTY ATTORNEY   By the way, has anything been moved? Are things just as you left them yesterday?

SHERIFF [*looking about*]   It's just the same. When it dropped below zero last
10   night I thought I'd better send Frank out this morning to make a fire for us—no use getting pneumonia with a big case on, but I told him not to touch anything except the stove—and you know Frank.

---

1. That is, appearing more relaxed.

COUNTY ATTORNEY Somebody should have been left here yesterday.

SHERIFF Oh—yesterday. When I had to send Frank to Morris Center for
that man who went crazy—I want you to know I had my hands full yesterday. I knew you could get back from Omaha by today and as long as I went
over everything here myself—

COUNTY ATTORNEY Well, Mr. Hale, tell just what happened when you came
here yesterday morning.

HALE Harry and I had started to town with a load of potatoes. We came
along the road from my place and as I got here I said, "I'm going to see if I
can't get John Wright to go in with me on a party telephone."[2] I spoke to
Wright about it once before and he put me off, saying folks talked too
much anyway, and all he asked was peace and quiet—I guess you know
about how much he talked himself; but I thought maybe if I went to the
house and talked about it before his wife, though I said to Harry that I
didn't know as what his wife wanted made much difference to John—

COUNTY ATTORNEY Let's talk about that later, Mr. Hale. I do want to talk
about that, but tell now just what happened when you got to the house.

HALE I didn't hear or see anything; I knocked at the door, and still it was all
quiet inside. I knew they must be up, it was past eight o'clock. So I
knocked again, and I thought I heard somebody say, "Come in." I wasn't
sure, I'm not sure yet, but I opened the door—this door [*indicating the
door by which the two women are still standing*] and there in that rocker—
[*pointing to it*] sat Mrs. Wright.

    [*They all look at the rocker.*]

COUNTY ATTORNEY What—was she doing?

HALE She was rockin' back and forth. She had her apron in her hand and
was kind of—pleating it.

COUNTY ATTORNEY And how did she—look?

HALE Well, she looked queer.

COUNTY ATTORNEY How do you mean—queer?

HALE Well, as if she didn't know what she was going to do next. And kind of
done up.[3]

COUNTY ATTORNEY How did she seem to feel about your coming?

HALE Why, I don't think she minded—one way or other. She didn't pay
much attention. I said, "How do, Mrs. Wright, it's cold, ain't it?" And she
said, "Is it?"—and went on kind of pleating at her apron. Well, I was surprised; she didn't ask me to come up to the stove, or to set down, but just
sat there, not even looking at me, so I said, "I want to see John." And then
she—laughed. I guess you would call it a laugh. I thought of Harry and the
team outside, so I said a little sharp: "Can't I see John?" "No," she says,
kind o' dull like. "Ain't he home?" says I. "Yes," says she, "he's home."
"Then why can't I see him?" I asked her, out of patience. "'Cause he's
dead," says she. "*Dead?*" says I. She just nodded her head, not getting a bit
excited, but rockin' back and forth. "Why—where is he?" says I, not knowing what to say. She just pointed upstairs—like that [*himself pointing to the
room above*]. I got up, with the idea of going up there. I walked from there
to here—then I says, "Why, what did he die of?" "He died of a rope round
his neck," says she, and just went on pleatin' at her apron. Well, I went out

2. That is, a single telephone line shared by   3. Worn out.
two or four households.

60 and called Harry. I thought I might—need help. We went upstairs and there he was lyin'—

COUNTY ATTORNEY   I think I'd rather have you go into that upstairs, where you can point it all out. Just go on now with the rest of the story.

HALE   Well, my first thought was to get that rope off. It looked . . . [*Stops, his*
65 *face twitches.*] . . . but Harry, he went up to him, and he said, "No, he's dead all right, and we'd better not touch anything." So we went back down stairs. She was still sitting that same way. "Has anybody been notified?" I asked. "No," says she, unconcerned. "Who did this, Mrs. Wright?" said Harry. He said it business-like—and she stopped pleatin' of her apron. "I
70 don't know," she says. "You don't *know*?" says Harry. "No," says she. "Weren't you sleepin' in the bed with him?" says Harry. "Yes," says she, "but I was on the inside." "Somebody slipped a rope round his neck and stran-gled him and you didn't wake up?" says Harry. "I didn't wake up," she said after him. We must 'a looked as if we didn't see how that could be, for after
75 a minute she said, "I sleep sound." Harry was going to ask her more ques-tions but I said maybe we ought to let her tell her story first to the coroner, or the sheriff, so Harry went fast as he could to Rivers' place, where there's a telephone.

COUNTY ATTORNEY   And what did Mrs. Wright do when she knew that you
80 had gone for the coroner?

HALE   She moved from that chair to this one over here [*pointing to a small chair in the corner*] and just sat there with her hands held together and looking down. I got a feeling that I ought to make come conversation, so I said I had come in to see if John wanted to put in a telephone, and at that
85 she started to laugh, and then she stopped and looked at me—scared. [*The* COUNTY ATTORNEY, *who has had his notebook out, makes a note.*] I dunno, maybe it wasn't scared. I wouldn't like to say it was. Soon Harry got back, and then Dr. Lloyd came, and you, Mr. Peters, and so I guess that's all I know that you don't.

90 COUNTY ATTORNEY [*looking around*]   I guess we'll go upstairs first—and then out to the barn and around there. [*To the* SHERIFF] You're convinced that there was nothing important here—nothing that would point to any motive.

SHERIFF   Nothing here but kitchen things.

[*The* COUNTY ATTORNEY, *after again looking around the kitchen, opens the door of a cupboard closet. He gets up on a chair and looks on a shelf. Pulls his hand away, sticky.*]

COUNTY ATTORNEY   Here's a nice mess.

[*The women draw nearer.*]

95 MRS. PETERS [*to the other woman*]   Oh, her fruit; it did freeze. [*To the* LAW-YER] She worried about that when it turned so cold. She said the fire'd go out and her jars would break.

SHERIFF   Well, can you beat the women! Held for murder and worryin' about her preserves.

100 COUNTY ATTORNEY   I guess before we're through she may have something more serious than preserves to worry about.

HALE   Well, women are used to worrying over trifles.

[*The two women move a little closer together.*]

COUNTY ATTORNEY [*with the gallantry of a young politician*]   And yet, for all their worries, what would we do without the ladies? [*The women do not unbend. He goes to the sink, takes a dipperful of water from the pail and*

pouring it into a basin, washes his hands. Starts to wipe them on the roller
105   *towel, turns it for a cleaner place.*] Dirty towels! [*Kicks his foot against the*
      pans under the sink.] Not much of a housekeeper, would you say, ladies?

MRS. HALE [*stiffly*]   There's a great deal of work to be done on a farm.

COUNTY ATTORNEY   To be sure. And yet [*with a little bow to her*] I know there
      are some Dickson county farmhouses which do not have such roller
110   towels.

            [*He gives it a pull to expose its full length again.*]

MRS. HALE   Those towels get dirty awful quick. Men's hands aren't always as
      clean as they might be.

COUNTY ATTORNEY   Ah, loyal to your sex, I see. But you and Mrs. Wright were
      neighbors. I suppose you were friends, too.

115   MRS. HALE [*shaking her head*]   I've not seen much of her of late years. I've
      not been in this house—it's more than a year.

COUNTY ATTORNEY   And why was that? You didn't like her?

MRS. HALE   I liked her all well enough. Farmers' wives have their hands full,
      Mr. Henderson. And then—

120   COUNTY ATTORNEY   Yes—?

MRS. HALE [*looking about*]   It never seemed a very cheerful place.

COUNTY ATTORNEY   No—it's not cheerful. I shouldn't say she had the home-
      making instinct.

MRS. HALE   Well, I don't know as Wright had, either.

125   COUNTY ATTORNEY   You mean that they didn't get on very well?

MRS. HALE   No, I don't mean anything. But I don't think a place'd be any
      cheerfuller for John Wright's being in it.

COUNTY ATTORNEY   I'd like to talk more of that a little later. I want to get the
      lay of things upstairs now.

            [*He goes to the left, where three steps lead to a stair door.*]

130   SHERIFF   I suppose anything Mrs. Peters does'll be all right. She was to take
      in some clothes for her, you know, and a few little things. We left in such a
      hurry yesterday.

COUNTY ATTORNEY   Yes, but I would like to see what you take, Mrs. Peters,
      and keep an eye out for anything that might be of use to us.

135   MRS. PETERS   Yes, Mr. Henderson.

            [*The women listen to the men's steps on the stairs, then look about the*
            kitchen.]

MRS. HALE   I'd hate to have men coming into my kitchen, snooping around
      and criticising.

            [*She arranges the pans under sink which the* LAWYER *had shoved out of*
            place.]

MRS. PETERS   Of course it's no more than their duty.

MRS. HALE   Duty's all right, but I guess that deputy sheriff that came out to
140   make the fire might have got a little of this on. [*Gives the roller towel a*
      pull.] Wish I'd thought of that sooner. Seems mean to talk about her for
      not having things slicked up when she had to come away in such a hurry.

MRS. PETERS [*who has gone to a small table in the left rear corner of the room,*
      and lifted one end of a towel that covers a pan]   She had bread set.

            [*Stands still.*]

MRS. HALE [*Eyes fixed on a loaf of bread beside the bread box, which is on a low*
      shelf at the other side of the room. Moves slowly toward it.]   She was going

145 to put this in there. [*Picks up loaf, then abruptly drops it. In a manner of returning to familiar things.*] It's a shame about her fruit. I wonder if it's all gone. [*Gets up on the chair and looks.*] I think there's some here that's all right, Mrs. Peters. Yes—here; [*holding it toward the window*] this is cherries, too. [*Looking again*] I declare I believe that's the only one. [*Gets down,*
150 *bottle in her hand. Goes to the sink and wipes it off on the outside.*] She'll feel awful bad after all her hard work in the hot weather. I remember the afternoon I put up my cherries last summer.

> [*She puts the bottle on the big kitchen table, center of the room. With a sigh, is about to sit down in the rocking chair. Before she is seated realizes what chair it is; with a slow look at it, steps back. The chair which she has touched rocks back and forth.*]

MRS. PETERS   Well, I must get those things from the front room closet. [*She goes to the door at the right, but after looking into the other room, steps back.*] You coming with me, Mrs. Hale? You could help me carry them.

> [*They go in the other room; reappear, MRS. PETERS carrying a dress and skirt, MRS. HALE following with a pair of shoes.*]

155 MRS. PETERS   My, it's cold in there.

> [*She puts the clothes on the big table, and hurries to the stove.*]

MRS. HALE [*examining the skirt*]   Wright was close.[4] I think maybe that's why she kept so much to herself. She didn't even belong to the Ladies Aid. I suppose she felt she couldn't do her part, and then you don't enjoy things when you feel shabby. She used to wear pretty clothes and be lively, when
160 she was Minnie Foster, one of the town girls singing in the choir. But that—oh, that was thirty years ago. This all you was to take in?

MRS. PETERS   She said she wanted an apron. Funny thing to want, for there isn't much to get you dirty in jail, goodness knows. But I suppose just to make her feel more natural. She said they was in the top drawer in this
165 cupboard. Yes, here. And then her little shawl that always hung behind the door. [*Opens stair door and looks.*] Yes, here it is.

> [*Quickly shuts door leading upstairs.*]

MRS. HALE [*abruptly moving toward her*]   Mrs. Peters?

MRS. PETERS   Yes, Mrs. Hale?

MRS. HALE   Do you think she did it?

170 MRS. PETERS [*in a frightened voice*]   Oh, I don't know.

MRS. HALE   Well, I don't think she did. Asking for an apron and her little shawl. Worrying about her fruit.

MRS. PETERS [*starts to speak, glances up, where footsteps are heard in the room above. In a low voice*]   Mr. Peters says it looks bad for her. Mr. Henderson is awful sarcastic in a speech and he'll make fun of her sayin' she didn't
175 wake up.

MRS. HALE   Well, I guess John Wright didn't wake when they was slipping that rope under his neck.

MRS. PETERS   No, it's strange. It must have been done awful crafty and still. They say it was such a—funny way to kill a man, rigging it all up like that.

180 MRS. HALE   That's just what Mr. Hale said. There was a gun in the house. He says that's what he can't understand.

MRS. PETERS   Mr. Henderson said coming out that what was needed for the case was a motive; something to show anger, or—sudden feeling.

4. Stingy.

MRS. HALE [*who is standing by the table*]   Well, I don't see any signs of anger
185   around here. [*She puts her hand on the dish towel which lies on the table,
stands looking down at table, one half of which is clean, the other half messy.*]
It's wiped to here. [*Makes a move as if to finish work, then turns and looks at
loaf of bread outside the breadbox. Drops towel. In that voice of coming back
to familiar things*] Wonder how they are finding things upstairs. I hope she
had it a little more red-up⁵ up there. You know, it seems kind of *sneaking*.
Locking her up in town and then coming out here and trying to get her own
190   house to turn against her!
MRS. PETERS   But Mrs. Hale, the law is the law.
MRS. HALE   I s'pose 'tis. [*Unbuttoning her coat*] Better loosen up your things,
Mrs. Peters. You won't feel them when you go out.
          [MRS. PETERS *takes off her fur tippet, goes to hang it on hook at back of
          room, stands looking at the under part of the small corner table.*]
MRS. PETERS   She was piecing a quilt.
          [*She brings the large sewing basket and they look at the bright pieces.*]
195   MRS. HALE   It's log cabin pattern. Pretty, isn't it? I wonder if she was goin' to
quilt it or just knot it?
          [*Footsteps have been heard coming down the stairs. The* SHERIFF *enters
          followed by* HALE *and the* COUNTY ATTORNEY.]
SHERIFF   They wonder if she was going to quilt it or just knot it!
          [*The men laugh, the women look abashed.*]
COUNTY ATTORNEY [*rubbing his hands over the stove*]   Frank's fire didn't do
much up there, did it? Well, let's go out to the barn and get that cleared up.
          [*The men go outside.*]
200   MRS. HALE [*resentfully*]   I don't know as there's anything so strange, our
takin' up our time with little things while we're waiting for them to get the
evidence. [*She sits down at the big table smoothing out a block with decision.*] I don't see as it's anything to laugh about.
MRS. PETERS [*apologetically*]   Of course they've got awful important things
205   on their minds.
          [*Pulls up a chair and joins* MRS. HALE *at the table.*]
MRS. HALE [*examining another block*]   Mrs. Peters, look at this one. Here,
this is the one she was working on, and look at the sewing! All the rest of it
has been so nice and even. And look at this! It's all over the place! Why, it
looks as if she didn't know what she was about!
          [*After she has said this they look at each other, then start to glance back
          at the door. After an instant* MRS. HALE *has pulled at a knot and ripped
          the sewing.*
210   MRS. PETERS   Oh, what are you doing, Mrs. Hale?
MRS. HALE [*mildly*]   Just pulling out a stitch or two that's not sewed very
good. [*Threading a needle*] Bad sewing always made me fidgety.
MRS. PETERS [*nervously*]   I don't think we ought to touch things.
MRS. HALE   I'll just finish up this end. [*Suddenly stopping and leaning for-
215   ward*] Mrs. Peters?
MRS. PETERS   Yes, Mrs. Hale?
MRS. HALE   What do you suppose she was so nervous about?

5. Tidied up.

MRS. PETERS   Oh—I don't know. I don't know as she was nervous. I sometimes
sew awful queer when I'm just tired. [MRS. HALE *starts to say something, looks*
220   *at* MRS. PETERS, *then goes on sewing.*] Well I must get these things wrapped
up. They may be through sooner than we think. [*Putting apron and other*
things together] I wonder where I can find a piece of paper, and string.
MRS. HALE   In that cupboard, maybe.
MRS. PETERS [*looking in cupboard*]   Why, here's a bird-cage. [*Holds it up.*]
225   Did she have a bird, Mrs. Hale?
MRS. HALE   Why, I don't know whether she did or not—I've not been here for
so long. There was a man around last year selling canaries cheap, but I
don't know as she took one; maybe she did. She used to sing real pretty
herself.
230 MRS. PETERS [*glancing around*]   Seems funny to think of a bird here. But she
must have had one, or why would she have a cage? I wonder what happened to it.
MRS. HALE   I s'pose maybe the cat got it.
MRS. PETERS   No, she didn't have a cat. She's got that feeling some people
235   have about cats—being afraid of them. My cat got in her room and she was
real upset and asked me to take it out.
MRS. HALE   My sister Bessie was like that. Queer, ain't it?
MRS. PETERS [*examining the cage*]   Why, look at this door. It's broke. One
hinge is pulled apart.
240 MRS. HALE [*looking too*]   Looks as if someone must have been rough with it.
MRS. PETERS   Why, yes.

[*She brings the cage forward and puts it on the table.*]

MRS. HALE   I wish if they're going to find any evidence they'd be about it. I
don't like this place.
MRS. PETERS   But I'm awful glad you came with me, Mrs. Hale. It would be
245   lonesome for me sitting here alone.
MRS. HALE   It would, wouldn't it? [*Dropping her sewing*] But I tell you what I
do wish, Mrs. Peters. I wish I had come over sometimes when *she* was here.
I—[*looking around the room*]—wish I had.
MRS. PETERS   But of course you were awful busy, Mrs. Hale—your house and
250   your children.
MRS. HALE   I could've come. I stayed away because it weren't cheerful—and
that's why I ought to have come. I—I've never liked this place. Maybe
because it's down in a hollow and you don't see the road. I dunno what it
is, but it's a lonesome place and always was. I wish I had come over to see
255   Minnie Foster sometimes. I can see now—[*Shakes her head.*]
MRS. PETERS   Well, you mustn't reproach yourself, Mrs. Hale. Somehow we
just don't see how it is with other folks until—something comes up.
MRS. HALE   Not having children makes less work—but it makes a quiet
house, and Wright out to work all day, and no company when he did come
260   in. Did you know John Wright, Mrs. Peters?
MRS. PETERS   Not to know him; I've seen him in town. They say he was a
good man.
MRS. HALE   Yes—good; he didn't drink, and kept his word as well as most, I
guess, and paid his debts. But he was a hard man, Mrs. Peters. Just to pass
265   the time of day with him— [*Shivers.*] Like a raw wind that gets to the bone.
[*Pauses, her eye falling on the cage.*] I should think she would 'a wanted a
bird. But what do you suppose went with it?

MRS. PETERS   I don't know, unless it got sick and died.

[*She reaches over and swings the broken door, swings it again, both women watch it.*]

MRS. HALE   You weren't raised round here, were you? [MRS. PETERS *shakes her*
270   *head.*] You didn't know—her?

MRS. PETERS   Not till they brought her yesterday.

MRS. HALE   She—come to think of it, she was kind of like a bird herself—real sweet and pretty, but kind of timid and—fluttery. How—she—did—change. [*Silence; then as if struck by a happy thought and relieved to get
275   back to everyday things.*] Tell you what, Mrs. Peters, why don't you take the quilt in with you? It might take up her mind.

MRS. PETERS   Why, I think that's a real nice idea, Mrs. Hale. There couldn't possibly be any objection to it, could there? Now, just what would I take? I wonder if her patches are in here—and her things.

[*They look in the sewing basket.*]

280   MRS. HALE   Here's some red. I expect this has got sewing things in it. [*Brings out a fancy box.*] What a pretty box. Looks like something somebody would give you. Maybe her scissors are in here. [*Opens box. Suddenly puts her hand to her nose.*] Why—[MRS. PETERS *bends nearer, then turns her face away.*] There's something wrapped up in this piece of silk.

285   MRS. PETERS   Why, this isn't her scissors.

MRS. HALE [*lifting the silk*]   Oh, Mrs. Peters—it's—

[MRS. PETERS *bends closer.*]

MRS. PETERS   It's the bird.

MRS. HALE [*jumping up*]   But, Mrs. Peters—look at it! It's neck! Look at its neck! It's all—other side *to.*[6]

290   MRS. PETERS   Somebody—wrung—its—neck.

[*Their eyes meet. A look of growing comprehension, of horror, Steps are heard outside.* MRS. HALE *slips box under quilt pieces, and sinks into her chair. Enter* SHERIFF *and* COUNTY ATTORNEY. MRS. PETERS *rises.*]

COUNTY ATTORNEY [*as one turning from serious things to little pleasantries*]   Well, ladies, have you decided whether she was going to quilt it or knot it?

MRS. PETERS   We think she was going to—knot it.

COUNTY ATTORNEY   Well, that's interesting, I'm sure. [*Seeing the birdcage*]   Has the bird flown?

295   MRS. HALE [*putting more quilt pieces over the box*]   We think the—cat got it.

COUNTY ATTORNEY [*preoccupied*]   Is there a cat?

[MRS. HALE *glances in a quick covert way at* MRS. PETERS.]

MRS. PETERS   Well, not *now*. They're superstitious, you know. They leave.

COUNTY ATTORNEY [*to* SHERIFF PETERS, *continuing an interrupted conversation*]   No sign at all of anyone having come from the outside. Their own rope.
300   Now let's go up again and go over it piece by piece. [*They start upstairs.*] It would have to have been someone who knew just the—

[MRS. PETERS *sits down. The two women sit there not looking at one another, but as if peering into something and at the same time holding back. When they talk now it is in the manner of feeling their way over*

6. Twisted around.

strange ground, as if afraid of what they are saying, but as if they cannot
help saying it.]

MRS. HALE   She liked the bird. She was going to bury it in that pretty box.

MRS. PETERS [in a whisper]   When I was a girl—my kitten—there was a boy
took a hatchet, and before my eyes—and before I could get there—[covers
her face an instant] If they hadn't held me back I would have—[catches
herself, looks upstairs where steps are heard, falters weakly.]—hurt him.

MRS. HALE [with a slow look around her]   I wonder how it would seem never
to have had any children around. [Pause] No, Wright wouldn't like the
bird—a thing that sang. She used to sing. He killed that, too.

MRS. PETERS [moving uneasily]   We don't know who killed the bird.

MRS. HALE   I knew John Wright.

MRS. PETERS   It was an awful thing was done in this house that night, Mrs.
Hale. Killing a man while he slept, slipping a rope around his neck that
choked the life out of him.

MRS. HALE   His neck. Choked the life out of him.

[Her hand goes out and rests on the birdcage.]

MRS. PETERS [with rising voice]   We don't know who killed him. We don't
know.

MRS. HALE [her own feeling not interrupted]   If there'd been years and years
of nothing, then a bird to sing to you, it would be awful—still, after the
bird was still.

MRS. PETERS [something within her speaking]   I know what stillness is. When
we homesteaded in Dakota, and my first baby died—after he was two years
old, and me with no other then—

MRS. HALE [moving]   How soon do you suppose they'll be through, looking
for the evidence?

MRS. PETERS   I know what stillness is. [Pulling herself back] The law has got
to punish crime, Mrs. Hale.

MRS. HALE [not as if answering that]   I wish you'd seen Minnie Foster when
she wore a white dress with blue ribbons and stood up there in the choir
and sang. [A look around the room] Oh, I wish I'd come over here once in a
while! That was a crime! That was a crime! Who's going to punish that?

MRS. PETERS [looking upstairs]   We mustn't—take on.

MRS. HALE   I might have known she needed help! I know how things can
be—for women. I tell you, it's queer, Mrs. Peters. We live close together
and we live far apart. We all go through the same things—it's all just a different kind of the same thing. [Brushes her eyes, noticing the bottle of fruit,
reaches out for it.] If I was you I wouldn't tell her her fruit was gone. Tell
her it ain't. Tell her it's all right. Take this in to prove it to her. She—she
may never know whether it was broke or not.

MRS. PETERS [Takes the bottle, looks about for something to wrap it in; takes
petticoat from the clothes brought from the other room, very nervously begins
winding this around the bottle. In a false voice.]   My, it's a good thing the
men couldn't hear us. Wouldn't they just laugh! Getting all stirred up over
a little thing like a—dead canary. As if that could have anything to do
with—with—wouldn't they laugh!

[The men are heard coming down stairs.]

MRS. HALE [under her breath]   Maybe they would—maybe they wouldn't.

345 COUNTY ATTORNEY No, Peters, it's all perfectly clear except a reason for doing it. But you know juries when it comes to women. If there was some definite thing. Something to show—something to make a story about—a thing that would connect up with this strange way of doing it—

[*The women's eyes meet for an instant. Enter* HALE *from outer door.*]

HALE Well, I've got the team around. Pretty cold out there.

350 COUNTY ATTORNEY I'm going to stay here a while by myself. [*To the* SHERIFF] You can send Frank out for me, can't you? I want to go over everything. I'm not satisfied that we can't do better.

SHERIFF Do you want to see what Mrs. Peters is going to take in?

[*The* LAWYER *goes to the table, picks up the apron, laughs.*]

COUNTY ATTORNEY Oh, I guess they're not very dangerous things the ladies
355 have picked out. [*Moves a few things about, disturbing the quilt pieces which cover the box. Steps back.*] No, Mrs. Peters doesn't need supervising. For that matter, a sheriff's wife is married to the law. Ever think of it that way, Mrs. Peters?

MRS. PETERS Not—just that way.

360 SHERIFF [*chuckling*] Married to the law. [*Moves toward the other room.*] I just want you to come in here a minute, George. We ought to take a look at these windows.

COUNTY ATTORNEY [*scoffingly*] Oh, windows!

SHERIFF We'll be right out, Mr. Hale.

[HALE *goes outside. The* SHERIFF *follows the* COUNTY ATTORNEY *into the other room. Then* MRS. HALE *rises, hands tight together, looking intensely at* MRS. PETERS, *whose eyes make a slow turn, finally meeting* MRS. HALE'S. *A moment* MRS. HALE *holds her, then her own eyes point the way to where the box is concealed. Suddenly* MRS. PETERS *throws back quilt pieces and tries to put the box in the bag she is wearing. It is too big. She opens box, starts to take bird out, cannot touch it, goes to pieces, stands there helpless. Sound of a knob turning in the other room.* MRS. HALE *snatches the box and puts it in the pocket of her big coat. Enter* COUNTY ATTORNEY *and* SHERIFF.]

365 COUNTY ATTORNEY [*facetiously*] Well, Henry, at least we found out that she was not going to quilt it. She was going to—what is it you call it, ladies?

MRS. HALE [*her hand against her pocket*] We call it—knot it, Mr. Henderson.

Curtain.

LUIGI PIRANDELLO

1867–1937

WHEN Pirandello received the Nobel Prize in Literature in 1934, at the age of sixty-seven, he was widely known as the author of intricate philosophical comedies. One in particular, SIX CHARACTERS IN SEARCH OF AN AUTHOR (1921), had catapulted him onto the international scene in the early 1920s, leading to acclaimed performances all over Europe and the Americas. Like his contemporaries GEORGE BERNARD SHAW for the English-speaking world and Maurice Maeterlinck for the French-speaking world, Pirandello became the Italian representative of the New Drama. Pirandello's worldwide success occurred relatively late in his life, at the end of a busy writing career that included hundreds of short stories, dozens of early plays, and a handful of novels as well as essays, a dissertation in linguistics, and several film scripts. Outside Italy, however, Pirandello's name remained tied to the invention of a new, intellectual drama thriving on arguments, paradoxes, and inversions. These plays, of which *Six Characters* is the best known, apply their wit to the theater itself, turning actors, directors, and dramatic authors into the material from which to fashion outrageous plots and far-fetched conceits. Somehow, Pirandello managed to transform himself from an author of local and rather traditional novellas and plays into the most

fashionable and advanced European dramatist of his age.

Luigi Pirandello was born into a nineteenth-century Sicily where a small landowning class lorded over impoverished peasants. It was a society with many lingering feudal structures and a deeply traditional literature and culture to go with it. Pirandello himself was rather fortunate, since his father was quite wealthy and was therefore capable of financing Pirandello's studies in Rome, his doctorate at the University of Bonn, and his early career as a writer. Despite his cosmopolitan education, however, Pirandello did not reject the social values of Sicily and agreed to an arranged marriage to Antonietta Portulano, the daughter of one of his father's business partners, whom he barely knew. His marriage of 1894, business interests, the sulfur mine—these were the pillars of Pirandello's life. But they did not last. His father's fortune and his wife's dowry were heavily invested in a mine that was flooded in 1903, and everything was lost. In the meantime, Pirandello had begun teaching at a women's college in Rome, an occupation he continued until his international breakthrough in the early twenties. Just as the economic foundations of his life crumbled, so did the personal ones. His wife was subject to increasingly pathological fits of jealousy and other delusional behavior, and Pirandello retired more and more from social life, maintaining his three children and suffering from an untenable domestic arrangement until Antonietta was eventually committed to a mental institution in 1914.

In the early twentieth century, Pirandello withdrew from life, but he also became a prolific writer of short stories, with which he supplemented his teacher's income. Over the years, he perfected his command of the genre and reissued selected short stories in a collection, *Novellas for a Year* (15 vols., 1922–37), that still enjoys great popularity in Italy. Pirandello's later mastery of drama can be traced back to these works. Like drama, the short story is a genre that requires economy and constraint and is often built around very few scenes and exchanges. Pirandello would frequently recycle his short stories in his dramas, including *Six Characters*.

The world in which Pirandello had grown up had fallen to pieces, but it continued to make itself felt in his literary work. His short stories, novels, and plays often revolve around closed family structures made insufferable by arranged marriages, jealousy, and betrayal. They are set in deeply patriarchal worlds in which women are seen as mothers, virgins, or whores. Even when Pirandello shows the extent to which these roles lead to pathologies, he held on to them to the end. His acclaimed comedies, such as *Six Characters* and *Henry IV* (1922), with their plays-within-the-play, philosophizing characters, and modern structures, contain under their surface the traditional plots of marriage and fertility, jealousy and adultery that are premised on the most traditional of family roles. Pirandello could never quite let go of Sicily—even during his time in Germany, when he studied philology and philosophy at Bonn, he chose as his dissertation subject the Sicilian dialects of his home region.

A similar fascination with Sicily also prompted Pirandello to turn from the short story to drama. After having become acquainted with a Sicilian dialect theater group headed by the charismatic Angelo Musco, Pirandello started writing dialect plays of high passion and melodrama. It was a traditionalist and provincial begin-

ning for the future modern dramatist, but it gave him a first taste of the pleasures of the theater, which would come to full fruition in his most successful plays. Musco's group acted in a style reminiscent of the commedia dell'arte, the tradition of improvised theater based on fixed types that are often accentuated with masks. Pirandello continued to use this technique later in his career: for example, in *Six Characters,* where a number of actors wear such masks. Indeed, it was Carlo Goldoni (1707–1793), the playwright most closely associated with commedia dell'arte, rather than HENRIK IBSEN, Shaw, or any of the other modern dramatists, who was Pirandello's favorite playwright. Pirandello's best and best-known dialect play, *Liolà* (1916), whose plot is taken entirely from the first chapters of his novel *The Late Mattia Pascal* (1904), is representative of this phase of his work in that it revolves around fertility, adultery, and the necessity of producing an heir. Yet all these subjects are presented in a particular form of comedy. In a long essay written to qualify for his teaching position, Pirandello had defined humor as the collision of ideals and harsh reality, as a sentiment of contradiction, as a moment when one position merges with its opposite, and as an art of quick reversals and inversions. This theory of humor underlies much of Pirandello's later drama.

Despite some considerable success in the theater, however, Pirandello still viewed it as a secondary art form. He put actors in the same category as illustrators of novels or translators—merely necessary but lamentable vehicles for bringing works of literature to the public. But over time, he became more interested in theatrical representation as well as in modernist forms of literature and drama. The first of his modernist plays, *It Is So! (If You Think So)* (1917), introduced the philosophizing *raisonneur*—a character that comments on the main action of the play, expressing skepticism about the truth of appearances. More important than the validity of this skepticism as a philosophical position is its close relation to Pirandello's theory of humor, which is premised on sudden reversals and quick changes from one appearance to the next. Many of his later plays, including *Six Characters,*

Henry IV, and *Each in His Own Way* (1923), exploit philosophical relativism as a vehicle for a comedy, and they often rely on the figure of the *raisonneur*. Because of the prominence of this figure in many of his plays, Pirandello's works are sometimes considered too theoretical or intellectual, too dependent on words and conceits. But in his most successful plays, Pirandello manages to draw these explanatory figures into the action, exposing their own blindness, missteps, and mistakes. After decades of writing more or less realistic literature set in Sicily and Rome, Pirandello found that the theater formed the perfect setting and subject matter for his art.

The best-known and most cunning of these plays about theater is *Six Characters*. Here Pirandello highlights the difference between the fixed dramatic text and its ever-changing performances by staging a conflict between two groups: a set of characters and the actors who want to impersonate these characters according to the traditions and rules of theatrical representation. Even though the charac-

ters are putatively searching for an author who will write down their story, that story already exists within them. The real conflict breaks out not over how to transform these characters into a play but over how to bring the story that they represent onto the stage. The title, in this sense, is a misnomer, one that can be explained by the history of the play's composition; like many of Pirandello's dramas, it originated as a short story. In fact, it originated as three short stories, all of which featured "characters" appearing before an author and demanding to be turned into literature: "Character" (1906), "A Character's Tragedy" (1911), and "Interview of Characters" (1915). But once this conceit is transported to the theater, characters and actors engage in a struggle over the question of what it means to stage a play. While the characters demand absolute fidelity to their story, the director and the actors recast that story into one suitable for the theater. They simplify the plot, reduce the number of scenes, and do everything necessary for an audience to be able to follow the play.

A family of characters is searching for an author in Robert Brustein's adaptation of Pirandello's *Six Characters in Search of an Author*, performed at the American Repertory Theater in Cambridge, Massachusetts, in 1996.

Having characters appear onstage as characters and not as full-fledged persons creates a number of interesting problems and conundrums, which Pirandello exploits to the full. Since the story is enclosed inside these characters, they have to tell their story to the director and the actors so that it can be brought to the stage. Most of the narration is done by the father, another version of Pirandello's *raisonneur* figure; he also explains the predicament of the actors, who are caught in their roles and hope to find release through an author. Far from being detached observers, however, these characters, including the father, are fully immersed in their story and therefore lack the capacity to tell it coherently and succinctly. Every time they begin to narrate what happened and how it happened, they "fall into character," as the common theatrical idiom has it—that is, they stop narrating and start feeling and enacting their plight. Indeed, they are entirely trapped inside their story and are forced to live it over and over again. It is only at the very end of the play, after many conflicts between characters and actors, that the audience can surmise that story's contours.

But living the story is one thing, playing it is another. While the characters *feel* their passions, the actors need to *represent* them. The director and the actors in this play argue directly against the common critique of acting as falsifying the author's intentions (a position Pirandello himself had maintained early in his career)—or, more precisely, they prove the necessity of such falsifications in the interest of art. *Six Characters* is thus essentially a play about acting, about theater, about the rules and integrity of theatrical representation. As eccentric and unusual as this piece of metatheater may be, the actual story inside the characters is strikingly traditional. It is precisely the kind of story that had populated Pirandello's earlier works, featuring an adulterous affair, a separation between husband and wife, the threat of incest, and rivalries between stepsiblings, as well as hatred and shame. *Six Characters* is metatheater, but metatheater with a traditional, melodramatic core.

The difference between the unchanging eternal play to which the characters are tied and its variations every time they relive it on the stage was something Pirandello had absorbed from the Italian critic Adriano Tilgher. Tilgher supplied Pirandello with an aesthetic philosophy, borrowed from such theorists as Henri Bergson (1859–1941) and Friedrich Nietzsche (1844–1900), according to which life is a perpetual chaos onto which the human mind seeks to impose order and form. Art, in Tilgher's view, is the highest imposition of form onto life, connecting the ever-changing with eternal and ideal forms. Pirandello realized that this difference between eternal works of art and ever-changing life corresponded directly to the relation between a fixed literary text and its ever-new performances through live actors. This insight was put into practice most brilliantly in Pirandello's plays about the theater. Some of these metatheatrical pieces—*Six Characters, Each in His Own Way,* and *Tonight We Improvise* (1930)—actually take place in the theater, but many others that draw on the same aesthetic theory do not.

Six Characters, and Pirandello's metatheater more generally, has a more sinister, political side, which is often ignored: it supplied the language in which Pirandello formulated his strong and unwavering allegiance to Benito Mussolini and Italian fascism. Pirandello favored a powerful leader who could stand above the chaos of democratic multiplicity and lead the country with a strong and fatherly hand. In Mussolini he got precisely the leader he was looking for. He met Mussolini in 1923 and immediately began to heap praise on him in the right-wing press, in the precise terms of his aesthetic doctrine—namely, as a strong leader capable of imposing onto the chaos of the nation a single and eternal form. Pirandello thus envisioned Mussolini as the artist of the Italian nation. The playwright who often declared that his art had nothing to do with his politics here treated politics as if it were nothing but an extension of art.

Pirandello's antidemocratic and profascist sympathies were not isolated moments of enthusiasm but were deeply felt. Indeed, he made his strongest gesture of support for fascism at a time of the movement's greatest weakness, after fascist supporters had brutally murdered a socialist member of parliament, Giacomo Matteotti. Rather than being outraged at this level of brutality, as many otherwise sympathetic to fascism were, Pirandello publicly declared his allegiance to the National Fascist Party and finally applied for membership. This political dimension may also account for a somewhat puzzling aspect of Pirandello's work: its violence. Even and especially his most philosophical and metatheatrical plays end with acts of extreme violence; *Six Characters*, for instance, culminates in two sudden deaths, one a suicide. This unexpectedly violent turn in an otherwise talkative and intellectual play corresponds structurally to the fascist doctrine of action: talking is what democracy practices in parliament and it must be ended by pure and bloody acts. It is as if Pirandello felt that his verbose and witty plays likewise needed to be concluded with bloodshed so that mere talking could stop and real action could start.

In addition to Pirandello's genuine attraction to fascism, there was also a mercenary element to his relationship with Mussolini—he hoped that the fascist leader would establish a national theater and place him in charge of it. After his success with *Six Characters*, which received multiple stagings by Europe's most innovative directors, Pirandello founded a theater of his own, the Teatro d'Arte. Although Mussolini never gave sufficient funds to satisfy Pirandello's ambitious plans for a national theater, he supplied enough to enable Pirandello's theater company to tour Europe and the Americas with *Six Characters* and other plays, thereby functioning, as Pirandello never tired of telling Mussolini, as cultural ambassadors for fascist Italy. These tours also exposed Pirandello to Europe's most innovative directors, such as the Russian Nikolai Evreinov and the Austrian Max Reinhardt, who had perfected new forms of spectacular theater. Indeed, one of Pirandello's last pieces of metatheater set in a theater, *Tonight We Improvise*, contains a parody of Max Reinhardt as a director disrespectful of the playwright and interested only in creating spectacles.

It was during his own work as director and producer that Pirandello in 1925 met the young actress Marta Abba, whom he fell in love with and continued to adore for the rest of his life. It was for her that he wrote his final plays, all of which feature strong female protagonists, such as the utopian *The New Colony* (1928) or his last play, *The Mountain Giants* (1937), a metatheatrical work that features a group of actors and magicians living in a remote mountain region. After a tumultuous life of personal tragedy, political entanglement, and artistic fame, Pirandello ended with a eulogy to the art that he had first rejected but that turned out to be his calling: the theater.   M.P.

Six Characters in Search of an Author[1]

CHARACTERS OF THE PLAY-IN-THE-MAKING

The FATHER
The MOTHER
The SON, aged 22
The STEPDAUGHTER, 18

The BOY, 14
The LITTLE GIRL, 4
  (these two last do not speak)
Then, called into being:
  MADAM PACE

1. Translated by Eric Bentley.

ACTORS IN THE COMPANY

The DIRECTOR
(DIRETTORE-CAPOCOMICO)[2]
LEADING LADY
LEADING MAN
SECOND ACTRESS
INGENUE
JUVENILE LEAD
Other actors and actresses

STAGE MANAGER
PROMPTER
PROPERTY MAN
TECHNICIAN
Director's SECRETARY
STAGE DOOR MAN
STAGE CREW

THE PLACE: *The stage of a playhouse.*[3]

When the audience arrives in the theater, the curtain is raised; and the stage, as normally in the daytime, is without wings or scenery and almost completely dark and empty. From the beginning we are to receive the impression of an unrehearsed performance.

Two stairways, left and right respectively, connect the stage with the auditorium. Onstage the dome of the prompter's box[4] has been placed on one side of the box itself. On the other side, at the front of the stage, a small table and an armchair with its back to the audience, for the DIRETTORE-CAPOCOMICO [DIRECTOR].

Two other small tables of different sizes with several chairs around them have also been placed at the front of the stage, ready as needed for the rehearsal. Other chairs here and there, left and right, for the actors, and at the back, a piano, on one side and almost hidden.

As soon as the houselights dim, the TECHNICIAN *is seen entering at the door onstage. He is wearing a blue shirt, and a tool bag hangs from his belt. From a corner at the back he takes several stage braces,[5] then arranges them on the floor downstage, and kneels down to hammer some nails in. At the sound of the hammering, the* STAGE MANAGER *comes running from the door that leads to the dressing rooms.*

STAGE MANAGER   Oh! What are you doing?

TECHNICIAN   What am I doing? Hammering.

STAGE MANAGER   At this hour? [*He looks at the clock.*] It's ten-thirty already. The Director will be here any moment. For the rehearsal.

5 TECHNICIAN   I gotta have time to work, too, see.

STAGE MANAGER   You will have. But not now.

TECHNICIAN   When?

STAGE MANAGER   Not during rehearsal hours. Now move along, take all this stuff away, and let me set the stage for the second act of, um, *The Game of* 10 *Role Playing.*[6]

---

2. Pirandello here combines the modern 20th-century role of director (*direttore* in Italian) with the older position of actor-manager (or "chief actor," *capocomico* in Italian), who fulfilled the function of supervising a theatrical production.

3. The play has neither acts nor scenes. The performance should be interrupted twice; first—without any lowering of the curtain—when the Director and the chief among the Characters retire to put the scenario together and the Actors leave the stage; second when

the Technician lets the curtain down by mistake [Pirandello's note].

4. A box in the apron or on the side of a stage, opening toward the actors, that houses someone with a script (sitting below the stage) who is ready to prompt the actors when they forget their lines.

5. Braces used to support a stage set from behind.

6. *Il Gioco delle Parti* (1918), a stage adaptation of Pirandello's own novella.

[*Muttering, grumbling, the* TECHNICIAN *picks up the stage braces and goes away. Meanwhile, from the door onstage, the* ACTORS OF THE COMPANY *start coming in, both men and women, one at a time at first, then in twos, at random, nine or ten of them, the number one would expect as the cast in rehearsals of Pirandello's play "The Game of Role Playing," which is the order of the day. They enter, greet the* STAGE MANAGER *and each other, all saying good-morning to all. Several go to their dressing rooms. Others, among them the* PROMPTER, *who has a copy of the script rolled up under his arm, stay onstage, waiting for the* DIRECTOR *to begin the rehearsal. Meanwhile, either seated in conversational groups, or standing, they exchange a few words among themselves. One lights a cigarette, one complains about the part he has been assigned, one reads aloud to his companions items of news from a theater journal. It would be well if both the Actresses and the Actors wore rather gay and brightly colored clothes and if this first improvised scene* [scena a soggetto] *combined vivacity with naturalness. At a certain point, one of the actors can sit down at the piano and strike up a dance tune. The younger actors and actresses start dancing.*]

STAGE MANAGER [*clapping his hands to call them to order*] All right, that's enough of that. The Director's here.

[*The noise and the dancing stop at once. The Actors turn and look toward the auditorium from the door of which the* DIRECTOR *is now seen coming. A bowler hat on his head, a walking stick under his arm, and a big cigar in his mouth, he walks down the aisle and, greeted by the Actors, goes onstage by one of the two stairways. The* SECRETARY *hands him his mail: several newspapers and a script in a wrapper.*]

DIRECTOR Letters?

SECRETARY None. That's all the mail there is.

15 DIRECTOR [*handing him the script*] Take this to my room. [*Then, looking around and addressing himself to the* STAGE MANAGER] We can't see each other in here. Want to give us a little light?

STAGE MANAGER OK.

[*He goes to give the order, and shortly afterward, the whole left side of the stage where the Actors are is lit by a vivid white light. Meanwhile, the* PROMPTER *has taken up his position in his box. He uses a small lamp and has the script open in front of him.*]

DIRECTOR [*clapping his hands*] Very well, let's start. [*To the* STAGE MANAGER]

20 Someone missing?

STAGE MANAGER The Leading Lady.

DIRECTOR As usual! [*He looks at the clock.*] We're ten minutes late already. Fine her for that, would you, please? Then she'll learn to be on time.

[*He has not completed his rebuke when the voice of the* LEADING LADY *is heard from the back of the auditorium.*]

LEADING LADY No, no, for heaven's sake! I'm here! I'm here! [*She is dressed all in white with a big, impudent hat on her head and a cute little dog in her arms. She runs down the aisle and climbs one of the sets of stairs in great haste.*]

25 DIRECTOR You've sworn an oath always to keep people waiting.

LEADING LADY You must excuse me. Just couldn't find a taxi. But you haven't even begun, I see. And I'm not on right away. [*Then, calling the* STAGE MANAGER *by name, and handing the little dog over to him*] Would you please shut him in my dressing room?

30 DIRECTOR [*grumbling*]   And the little dog to boot! As if there weren't enough
    dogs around here. [*He claps his hands again and turns to the* PROMPTER.]
    Now then, the second act of *The Game of Role Playing*. [*As he sits down in
    his armchair*] Quiet, gentlemen. Who's onstage?

> [*The Actresses and Actors clear the front of the stage and go and sit on
> one side, except for the three who will start the rehearsal and the* LEAD-
> ING LADY *who, disregarding the* DIRECTOR's *request, sits herself down at
> one of the two small tables.*]

DIRECTOR [*to the* LEADING LADY]   You're in this scene, are you?
35 LEADING LADY   Me? No, no.
DIRECTOR [*irritated*]   Then how about getting up, for Heaven's sake?

> [*The* LEADING LADY *rises and goes and sits beside the other Actors who
> have already gone to one side.*]

DIRECTOR [*to the* PROMPTER]   Start, start.
PROMPTER [*reading from the script*]   "In the house of Leone Gala. A strange
    room, combined study and dining room."
40 DIRECTOR [*turning to the* STAGE MANAGER]   We'll use the red room.
STAGE MANAGER [*making a note on a piece of paper*]   Red room. Very good.
PROMPTER [*continuing to read from the script*]   "The table is set and the desk
    has books and papers on it. Shelves with books on them, and cupboards
    with lavish tableware. Door in the rear through which one goes to Leone's
45 bedroom. Side door on the left through which one goes to the kitchen. The
    main entrance is on the right."
DIRECTOR [*rising and pointing*]   All right, now listen carefully. That's the main
    door. This is the way to the kitchen. [*Addressing himself to the Actor playing
    the part of Socrates*] You will come on and go out on this side. [*To the* STAGE
50 MANAGER] The compass at the back. And curtains. [*He sits down again.*]
STAGE MANAGER [*making a note*]   Very good.
PROMPTER [*reading as before*]   "Scene One. Leone Gala, Guido Venanzi,
    Filippo called Socrates." [*To the* DIRECTOR] Am I supposed to read the stage
    directions, too?
55 DIRECTOR   Yes, yes, yes! I've told you that a hundred times!
PROMPTER [*reading as before*]   "At the rise of the curtain, Leone Gala, wear-
    ing a chef's hat and apron, is intent on beating an egg in a saucepan with a
    wooden spoon. Filippo, also dressed as a cook, is beating another egg.
    Guido Venanzi, seated, is listening."
60 LEADING ACTOR [*to the* DIRECTOR]   Excuse me, but do I really have to wear a
    chef's hat?
DIRECTOR [*annoyed by this observation*]   I should say so! It's in the script.
    [*And he points at it.*]
LEADING ACTOR   But it's ridiculous, if I may say so.
DIRECTOR [*leaping to his feet, furious*]   "Ridiculous, ridiculous!" What do you
65 want me to do? We never get a good play from France any more, so we're
    reduced to producing plays by Pirandello, a fine man and all that, but nei-
    ther the actors, the critics, nor the audience are ever happy with his plays,
    and if you ask me, he does it all on purpose. [*The Actors laugh. And now he
    rises and coming over to the* LEADING ACTOR *shouts.*] A cook's hat, yes, my
70 dear man! And you beat eggs. And you think you have nothing more on
    your hands than the beating of eggs? Guess again. You symbolize the shell
    of those eggs. [*The Actors resume their laughing, and start making ironical*

comments among themselves.] Silence! And pay attention while I explain.
[*Again addressing himself to the* LEADING ACTOR] Yes, the shell: that is to say,
75   the empty *form* of reason without the *content* of instinct, which is blind.
You are reason, and your wife is instinct in the game of role playing. You
play the part assigned you, and you're your own puppet—of your own free
will. Understand?

LEADING ACTOR [*extending his arms, palms upward*]   Me? No.

80   DIRECTOR [*returning to his place*]   Nor do I. Let's go on. Wait and see what I
do with the ending. [*In a confidential tone*] I suggest you face three-
quarters front. Otherwise, what with the abstruseness of the dialogue, and
an audience that can't hear you, good-bye play! [*Again clapping*] Now,
again, order! Let's go.

85   PROMPTER   Excuse me, sir, may I put the top back on the prompter's box?
There's rather a draft.

DIRECTOR   Yes, yes, do that.

[*The* STAGE DOOR MAN *has entered the auditorium in the meanwhile, his
braided cap on his head. Proceeding down the aisle, he goes up onstage
to announce to the* DIRECTOR *the arrival of the Six Characters, who have
also entered the auditorium, and have started following him at a certain
distance, a little lost and perplexed, looking around them.*

*Whoever is going to try and translate this play into scenic terms must
take all possible measures not to let these Six Characters get confused
with the Actors of the Company. Placing both groups correctly, in accordance with the stage directions, once the Six are onstage, will certainly
help, as will lighting the two groups in contrasting colors. But the most
suitable and effective means to be suggested here is the use of special
masks for the Characters: masks specially made of material which doesn't
go limp when sweaty and yet masks which are not too heavy for the Actors
wearing them, cut out and worked over so they leave eyes, nostrils, and
mouth free. This will also bring out the inner significance of the play. The
Characters in fact should not be presented as ghosts but as created realities, unchanging constructs of the imagination, and therefore more solidly
real than the Actors with their fluid naturalness. The masks will help to
give the impression of figures constructed by art, each one unchangeably
fixed in the expression of its own fundamental sentiment, thus:*

remorse in the case of the FATHER; *revenge in the case of the* STEP-
DAUGHTER; *disdain in the case of the* SON; *grief in the case of the*
MOTHER, *who should have wax tears fixed in the rings under her eyes and
on her cheeks, as with the sculpted and painted images of the* mater dolo-
rosa[7] *in church. Their clothes should be of special material and design,
without extravagance, with rigid, full folds like a statue, in short not suggesting a material you might buy at any store in town, cut out and tai-
lored at any dressmaker's.*

The FATHER *is a man of about fifty, hair thin at the temples, but not
bald, thick mustache coiled round a still youthful mouth that is often open
in an uncertain, pointless smile. Pale, most notably on his broad forehead:
blue eyes, oval, very clear and piercing; dark jacket and light trousers: at
times gentle and smooth, at times he has hard, harsh outbursts.*

The MOTHER *seems scared and crushed by an intolerable weight of
shame and self-abasement. Wearing a thick black crepe widow's veil, she*

---

7. Grieving mother (Latin); specifically, Mary, mother of Jesus, grieving over the body of her dead
son.

is modestly dressed in black, and when she lifts the veil, the face does not show signs of suffering, and yet seems made of wax. Her eyes are always on the ground.

The STEPDAUGHTER, eighteen, is impudent, almost insolent. Very beautiful, and also in mourning, but mourning of a showy elegance. She shows contempt for the timid, afflicted, almost humiliated manner of her little brother, rather a mess of a BOY, fourteen, also dressed in black, but a lively tenderness for her little sister, a LITTLE GIRL of around four, dressed in white with a black silk sash round her waist.

The SON, twenty-two, tall, almost rigid with contained disdain for the FATHER and supercilious indifference toward the MOTHER, wears a mauve topcoat and a long green scarf wound round his neck.]

STAGE DOOR MAN [beret in hand]   Excuse me, your honor.

DIRECTOR [rudely jumping on him]   What is it now?

90 STAGE DOOR MAN [timidly]   There are some people here asking for you.

[The DIRECTOR and the Actors turn in astonishment to look down into the auditorium.]

DIRECTOR [furious again]   But I'm rehearsing here! And you know perfectly well no one can come in during rehearsal! [Turning again toward the house] Who are these people? What do they want?

THE FATHER [stepping forward, followed by the others, to one of the two little stairways to the stage]   We're here in search of an author.

95 DIRECTOR [half angry, half astounded]   An author? What author?

FATHER   Any author, sir.

DIRECTOR   There's no author here at all. It's not a new play we're rehearsing.

STEPDAUGHTER [very vivaciously as she rushes up the stairs]   Then so much the better, sir! We can be your new play!

100 ONE OF THE ACTORS [among the racy comments and laughs of the others]   Did you hear that?

FATHER [following the STEPDAUGHTER onstage]   Certainly, but if the author's not here . . . [To the DIRECTOR] Unless you'd like to be the author?

[The MOTHER, holding the LITTLE GIRL by the hand, and the BOY climb the first steps of the stairway and remain there waiting. The SON stays morosely below.]

DIRECTOR   Is this your idea of a joke?

105 FATHER   Heavens, no! Oh, sir, on the contrary: we bring you a painful drama.

STEPDAUGHTER   We can make your fortune for you.

DIRECTOR   Do me a favor, and leave. We have no time to waste on madmen.

FATHER [wounded, smoothly]   Oh, sir, you surely know that life is full of infinite absurdities which, brazenly enough, do not need to appear probable, 110 because they're true.

DIRECTOR   What in God's name are you saying?

FATHER   I'm saying it can actually be considered madness, sir, to force oneself to do the opposite: that is, to give probability to things so they will seem true. But permit me to observe that, if this is madness, it is also the 115 raison d'être of your profession.

[The Actors become agitated and indignant.]

DIRECTOR [rising and looking him over]   It is, is it? It seems to you an affair for madmen, our profession?

FATHER   Well, to make something seem true which is not true . . . without any need, sir: just for fun . . . Isn't it your job to give life onstage to crea-
120   tures of fantasy?

DIRECTOR [*immediately, making himself spokesman for the growing indignation of his Actors*]   Let me tell you something, my good sir. The actor's profession is a very noble one. If, as things go nowadays, our new playwrights give us nothing but stupid plays, with puppets in them instead of men, it is our boast, I'd have you know, to have given life—on these very boards—to
125   immortal works of art.

[*Satisfied, the Actors approve and applaud their* DIRECTOR.]

FATHER [*interrupting and bearing down hard*]   Exactly! That's just it. You have created living beings—*more* alive than those that breathe and wear clothes! Less real, perhaps; but more true! We agree completely!

[*The Actors look at each other, astounded.*]

DIRECTOR   What? You were saying just now . . .

130   FATHER   No, no, don't misunderstand me. You shouted that you hadn't time to waste on madmen. So I wanted to tell you that no one knows better than you that Nature employs the human imagination to carry her work of creation on to a higher plane!

DIRECTOR   All right, all right. But what are you getting at, exactly?

135   FATHER   Nothing, sir. I only wanted to show that one may be born to this life in many modes, in many forms: as tree, as rock, water or butterfly . . . or woman. And that . . . characters are born too.

DIRECTOR [*his amazement ironically feigned*]   And you—with these companions of yours—were born a character?

140   FATHER   Right, sir. And alive, as you see.

[*The* DIRECTOR *and the Actors burst out laughing as at a joke.*]

FATHER [*wounded*]   I'm sorry to hear you laugh, because, I repeat, we carry a painful drama within us, as you all might deduce from the sight of that lady there, veiled in black.

[*As he says this, he gives his hand to the* MOTHER *to help her up the last steps and, still holding her by the hand, he leads her with a certain tragic solemnity to the other side of the stage, which is suddenly bathed in fantastic light. The* LITTLE GIRL *and the* BOY *follow the* MOTHER; *then the* SON, *who stands on one side at the back; then the* STEPDAUGHTER *who also detaches herself from the others—downstage and leaning against the proscenium arch. At first astonished at this development, then overcome with admiration, the Actors now burst into applause as at a show performed for their benefit.*]

DIRECTOR [*bowled over at first, then indignant*]   Oh, stop this! Silence please!
145   [*Then, turning to the Characters*] And you, leave! Get out of here! [*To the* STAGE MANAGER] For God's sake, get them out!

STAGE MANAGER [*stepping forward but then stopping, as if held back by a strange dismay*]   Go! Go!

FATHER [*to the* DIRECTOR]   No, look, we, um—

DIRECTOR [*shouting*]   I tell you we've got to work!

150   LEADING MAN   It's not right to fool around like this . . .

FATHER [*resolute, stepping forward*]   I'm amazed at your incredulity! You're accustomed to seeing the created characters of an author spring to life,

aren't you, right here on this stage, the one confronting the other? Perhaps
the trouble is there's no script *there* [*Pointing to the* PROMPTER's *box*] with
155   us in it?

STEPDAUGHTER [*going right up to the* DIRECTOR, *smiling, coquettish*]   Believe
me, we really are six characters, sir. Very interesting ones at that. But lost.
Adrift.

FATHER [*brushing her aside*]   Very well: lost, adrift. [*Going right on*] In the
160   sense, that is, that the author who created us, made us live, did not wish,
or simply and materially was not able, to place us in the world of art. And
that was a real crime, sir, because whoever has the luck to be born a living
character can also laugh at death. He will never die! The man will die, the
writer, the instrument of creation; the creature will never die! And to have
165   eternal life it doesn't even take extraordinary gifts, nor the performance of
miracles. Who was Sancho Panza? Who was Don Abbondio?[8] But they live
forever because, as live germs, they have the luck to find a fertile matrix, an
imagination which knew how to raise and nourish them, make them live
through all eternity!

170   DIRECTOR   That's all well and good. But what do you people want here?

FATHER   We want to live, sir.

DIRECTOR [*ironically*]   Through all eternity?

FATHER   No, sir. But for a moment at least. In you.

AN ACTOR   Well, well, well!

175   LEADING LADY   They want to live in us.

JUVENILE LEAD [*pointing to the* STEPDAUGHTER]   Well, I've no objection, so
long as I get that one.

FATHER   Now look, look. The play is still in the making. [*To the* DIRECTOR]
But if you wish, and your actors wish, we can make it right away. Acting in
180   concert.

LEADING MAN [*annoyed*]   Concert? We don't put on concerts! We do plays,
dramas, comedies!

FATHER   Very good. That's why we came.

DIRECTOR   Well, where's the script?

185   FATHER   Inside us, sir. [*The Actors laugh.*] The drama is inside us. It *is* us.
And we're impatient to perform it. According to the dictates of the passion
within us.

STEPDAUGHTER [*scornful, with treacherous grace, deliberate impudence*]   My
passion—if you only knew, sir! My passion—for him! [*She points to the*
FATHER *and makes as if to embrace him but then breaks into a strident
laugh.*]

190   FATHER [*an angry interjection*]   You keep out of this now. And please don't
laugh that way!

STEPDAUGHTER   No? Then, ladies and gentlemen, permit me. A two months'
orphan, I shall dance and sing for you all. Watch how! [*She mischievously
starts to sing "Beware of Chu Chin Chow" by Dave Stamper, reduced to foxtrot or slow one-step by Francis Salabert:[9] the first verse, accompanied by a*

8. A rural priest in Alessandro Manzoni's
novel *I Promessi sposi* (*The Betrothed*, 1825–
27). *Sancho Panza*: the servant and companion of the title character in Miguel de
Cervantes' novel *Don Quixote* (1605, 1615).
9. A French music publisher (1884–1946);

his company released numerous recordings of
dance music in the 1920s and 1930s. "Beware
of Chu Chin Chow" (1917), with music by
Dave Stamper (1883–1963) and words by
Gene Buck and Charles Wilmott, was a popular novelty song.

step or two of dancing. While she sings and dances, the Actors, especially the young ones, as if drawn by some strange fascination, move toward her and half raise their hands as if to take hold of her. She runs away and when the Actors burst into applause she just stands there, remote, abstracted, while the DIRECTOR *protests.*]

ACTORS and ACTRESSES [*laughing and clapping*]   Brava![1] Fine! Splendid!

195 DIRECTOR [*annoyed*]   Silence! What do you think this is, a night spot? [*Taking the* FATHER *a step or two to one side, with a certain amount of consternation*] Tell me something. Is she crazy?

FATHER   Crazy? Of course not. It's much worse than that.

STEPDAUGHTER [*running over at once to the* DIRECTOR]   Worse! Worse! Not crazy but worse! Just listen: I'll play it for you right now, this drama, and at

200 a certain point you'll see me—when this dear little thing—[*She takes the* LITTLE GIRL *who is beside the* MOTHER *by the hand and leads her to the* DIRECTOR.]—isn't she darling? [*Takes her in her arms and kisses her.*] Sweetie! Sweetie! [*Puts her down again and adds with almost involuntary emotion.*] Well, when God suddenly takes this little sweetheart away from her poor mother, and that idiot there—[*Thrusting the* BOY *forward, rudely*

205 *seizing him by a sleeve*] does the stupidest of things, like the nitwit that he is, [*With a shove she drives him back toward the* MOTHER] then you will see me take to my heels. Yes, ladies and gentlemen, take to my heels! I can hardly wait for that moment. For after what happened between him and me—[*She points to the* FATHER *with a horrible wink.*] something very inti-

210 mate, you understand—I can't stay in such company any longer, witnessing the anguish of our mother on account of that fool there—[*She points to the* SON.] Just look at him, look at him!—how indifferent, how frozen, because he is the legitimate son, that's what he is, full of contempt for me, for him [*the* BOY], and for that little creature [*the* LITTLE GIRL], because we three

215 are bastards, d'you see? Bastards. [*Goes to the* MOTHER *and embraces her.*] And this poor mother, the common mother of us all, he—well, he doesn't want to acknowledge her as *his* mother too, and he looks down on her, that's what he does, looks on her as only the mother of us three bastards, the wretch! [*She says this rapidly in a state of extreme excitement. Her voice swells to the word: "bastards!" and descends again to the final "wretch," almost spitting it out.*]

220 MOTHER [*to the* DIRECTOR, *with infinite anguish*]   In the name of these two small children, sir, I implore you . . . [*She grows faint and sways.*] Oh, heavens . . .

FATHER [*rushing over to support her with almost all the Actors, who are astonished and scared*]   Please! Please, a chair, a chair for this poor widow!

ACTORS [*rushing over*]   —Is it true then?—She's *really* fainting?

225 DIRECTOR   A chair!

[*One of the Actors proffers a chair. The others stand around, ready to help. The* MOTHER, *seated, tries to stop the* FATHER *from lifting the veil that hides her face.*]

FATHER [*to the* DIRECTOR]   Look at her, look at her . . .

MOTHER   Heavens, no, stop it!

---

1. An Italian exclamation of approval, used when applauding a woman (as *bravo* is used of a man).

FATHER   Let them see you. [*He lifts her veil.*]

MOTHER [*rising and covering her face with her hands, desperate*]   Oh, sir,
230   please stop this man from carrying out his plan. It's horrible for me!

DIRECTOR [*surprised, stunned*]   I don't know where we're at! What's this all
about? [*To the* FATHER] Is this your wife?

FATHER [*at once*]   Yes, sir, my wife.

DIRECTOR   Then how is she a widow, if you're alive?

[*The Actors relieve their astonishment in a loud burst of laughter.*]

235   FATHER [*wounded, with bitter resentment*]   Don't laugh! Don't laugh like
that! Please! Just that is her drama, sir. She had another man. Another man
who should be here!

MOTHER [*with a shout*]   No! No!

STEPDAUGHTER   He had the good luck to die. Two months ago, as I told you.
240   We're still in mourning as you see.

FATHER   But he's absent, you see, not just because he's dead. He's absent—
take a look at her, sir, and you will understand at once!—Her drama wasn't
in the love of two men for whom she was incapable of feeling anything—
except maybe a little gratitude [not to me, but to him]—She is not a woman,
245   she is a mother!—And her drama—a powerful one, very powerful—is in
fact all in those four children which she bore to her two men.

MOTHER   *My* men? Have you the gall to say I wanted two men? It was him,
sir. He forced the other man on me. Compelled—yes, compelled—me to go
off with him!

250   STEPDAUGHTER [*cutting in, roused*]   It's not true!

MOTHER [*astounded*]   How d'you mean, not true?

STEPDAUGHTER   It's not true! It's not true!

MOTHER   And what can you know about it?

STEPDAUGHTER   It's not true. [*To the* DIRECTOR] Don't believe it. Know why
255   she says it? For his sake. [*Pointing to the* SON] His indifference tortures her,
destroys her. She wants him to believe that, if she abandoned him when he
was two, it was because he [*the* FATHER] compelled her to.

MOTHER [*with violence*]   He did compel me, he did compel me, as God is my
witness! [*To the* DIRECTOR] Ask him if that isn't true. [*Her husband*] Make
260   him tell him. [*The* SON] She couldn't know anything about it.

STEPDAUGHTER   With my father, while he lived, I know you were always
happy and content. Deny it if you can.

MOTHER   I don't deny it, I don't . . .

STEPDAUGHTER   He loved you, he cared for you! [*To the* BOY, *with rage*] Isn't
265   that so? Say it! Why don't you speak, you dope?

MOTHER   Leave the poor boy alone. Why d'you want to make me out ungrateful, daughter? I have no wish to offend your father! I told him [*the* FATHER]
I didn't abandon my son and my home for my own pleasure. It wasn't my
fault.

270   FATHER   That's true, sir. It was mine.

[*Pause.*]

LEADING MAN [*to his companions*]   What a show!

LEADING LADY   And *they* put it on—for us.

JUVENILE LEAD   Quite a change!

DIRECTOR [*who is now beginning to get very interested*] Let's listen to this,
275 let's listen! [*And saying this, he goes down one of the stairways into the auditorium, and stands in front of the stage, as if to receive a spectator's impression of the show.*]

SON [*without moving from his position, cold, quiet, ironic*] Oh yes, you can
now listen to the philosophy lecture. He will tell you about the Demon of
Experiment.

FATHER You are a cynical idiot, as I've told you a hundred times. [*To the*
280 DIRECTOR, *now in the auditorium*] He mocks me, sir, on account of that
phrase I found to excuse myself with.

SON [*contemptuously*] Phrases!

FATHER Phrases! Phrases! As if they were not a comfort to everyone: in the
face of some unexplained fact, in the face of an evil that eats into us, to
285 find a word that says nothing but at least quiets us down!

STEPDAUGHTER Quiets our guilt feelings too. That above all.

FATHER Our guilt feelings? Not so. I have never quieted my guilt feelings
with words alone.

STEPDAUGHTER It took a little money as well, didn't it, it took a little dough!
290 The hundred lire[2] he was going to pay me, ladies and gentlemen!

[*Movement of horror among the Actors.*]

SON [*with contempt toward the* STEPDAUGHTER] That's filthy.

STEPDAUGHTER Filthy? The dough was there. In a small pale blue envelope
on the mahogany table in the room behind the shop. Madam Pace's [*she
pronounces it "Pah-chay"*] shop. One of those Madams who lure us poor
295 girls from good families into their *ateliers* under the pretext of selling *Robes
et Manteaux*.[3]

SON And with those hundred lire he was going to pay she has bought the
right to tyrannize over us all. Only it so happens—I'd have you know—that
he never actually incurred the debt.

300 STEPDAUGHTER Oh, oh, but we were really going to it, I assure you! [*She
bursts out laughing.*]

MOTHER [*rising in protest*] Shame, daughter! Shame!

STEPDAUGHTER [*quickly*] Shame? It's my revenge! I am frantic, sir, frantic to
live it, live that scene! The room . . . here's the shop window with the coats
in it; there's the bed-sofa; the mirror; a screen; and in front of the window
305 the little mahogany table with the hundred lire in the pale blue envelope. I
can see it. I could take it. But you men should turn away now: I'm almost
naked. I don't blush any more. It's he that blushes now. [*Points to the
FATHER.*] But I assure you he was very pale, very pale, at that moment. [*To
the* DIRECTOR] You must believe me, sir.

310 DIRECTOR You lost me some time ago.

FATHER Of course! Getting it thrown at you like that! Restore a little order,
sir, and let *me* speak. And never mind this ferocious girl. She's trying to
heap opprobrium on me by withholding the relevant explanations!

STEPDAUGHTER This is no place for long-winded narratives!

315 FATHER I said—explanations.

2. Equivalent to about $50 today.
3. Dressing gowns and coats (French). *Ateliers:* workshops (French).

STEPDAUGHTER   Oh, certainly. Those that suit your turn.

[*At this point, the* DIRECTOR *returns to the stage to restore order.*]

FATHER   But that's the whole root of the evil. Words. Each of us has, inside him, a world of things—to everyone, his world of things. And how can we understand each other, sir, if, in the words I speak, I put the sense and value of things as they are inside me, whereas the man who hears them inevitably receives them in the sense and with the value they have for him, the sense and value of the world inside him? We think we understand each other but we never do. Consider: the compassion, all the compassion I feel for this woman [*the* MOTHER] has been received by her as the most ferocious of cruelties!

MOTHER   You ran me out of the house.

FATHER   Hear that? Ran her out. It *seemed to her* that I ran her out.

MOTHER   You can talk; I can't . . . But, look, sir, after he married me . . . and who knows why he did? I was poor, of humble birth . . .

FATHER   And that's why I married you for your . . . humility. I loved you for it, believing . . . [*He breaks off, seeing her gestured denials; seeing the impossibility of making himself understood by her, he opens his arms wide in a gesture of despair, and turns to the* DIRECTOR.] See that? She says No. It's scarifying, isn't it, sir, scarifying, this deafness of hers, this mental deafness! She has a heart, oh yes, where her children are concerned! But she's deaf, deaf in the brain, deaf, sir, to the point of desperation!

STEPDAUGHTER [*to the* DIRECTOR]   All right, but now make him tell you what his intelligence has ever done for us.

FATHER   If we could only foresee all the evil that can result from the good we believe we're doing!

[*At this point, the* LEADING LADY, *who has been on hot coals seeing the* LEADING MAN *flirt with the* STEPDAUGHTER, *steps forward and asks of the* DIRECTOR:]

LEADING LADY   Excuse me, is the rehearsal continuing?

DIRECTOR   Yes, of course! But let me listen a moment.

JUVENILE LEAD   This is something quite new.

INGENUE   Very interesting!

LEADING LADY   If that sort of thing interests you. [*And she darts a look at the* LEADING MAN.]

DIRECTOR [*to the* FATHER]   But you must give us *clear* explanations. [*He goes and sits down.*]

FATHER   Right. Yes. Listen. There was a man working for me. A poor man. As my secretary. Very devoted to me. Understood *her* [*the* MOTHER] very well. There was mutual understanding between them. Nothing wrong in it. They thought no harm at all. Nothing off-color about it. No, no, he knew his place, as she did. They didn't do anything wrong. Didn't even think it.

STEPDAUGHTER   So he thought it *for* them. And did it.

FATHER   It's not true! I wanted to do them some good. And myself too, oh yes, I admit. I'd got to this point, sir: I couldn't say a word to either of them but they would exchange a significant look. The one would consult the eyes of the other, asking how what I had said should be taken, if they didn't want to put me in a rage. That sufficed, you will understand, to keep me continually in a rage, in a state of unbearable exasperation.

DIRECTOR   Excuse me, why didn't you fire him, this secretary?

FATHER   Good question! That's what I did do, sir. But then I had to see that
360   poor woman remain in my house, a lost soul. Like an animal without a
master that one takes pity on and carries home.

MOTHER   No, no, it's—

FATHER   [*at once, turning to her to get it in first*]   Your son? Right?

MOTHER   He'd already snatched my son from me.

365   FATHER   But not from cruelty. Just so he'd grow up strong and healthy. In
touch with the soil.

STEPDAUGHTER [*pointing at the latter, ironic*]   And just look at him!

FATHER [*at once*]   Uh? Is it also my fault if he then grew up this way? I sent
him to a wet nurse, sir, in the country, a peasant woman. I didn't find her
370   [*the* MOTHER] strong enough, despite her humble origin. I'd married her for
similar reasons, as I said. All nonsense maybe, but there we are. I always
had these confounded aspirations toward a certain solidity, toward what is
morally sound. [*Here the* STEPDAUGHTER *bursts out laughing.*] Make her
stop that! It's unbearable!

375   DIRECTOR   Stop it. I can't hear, for Heaven's sake!

[*Suddenly, again, as the* DIRECTOR *rebukes her, she is withdrawn and
remote, her laughter cut off in the middle. The* DIRECTOR *goes down
again from the stage to get an impression of the scene.*]

FATHER   I couldn't bear to be with that woman any more. [*Points to the*
MOTHER] Not so much, believe me, because she irritated me, and even
made me feel physically ill, as because of the pain—a veritable anguish—
that I felt on her account.

380   MOTHER   And he sent me away!

FATHER.   Well provided for. And to that man. Yes, sir. So she could be free of
me.

MOTHER   And so *he* could be free.

FATHER   That, too. I admit it. And much evil resulted. But I intended good.
385   And more for her than for me, I swear it! [*He folds his arms across his chest.
Then, suddenly, turning to the* MOTHER] I never lost sight of you, never lost
sight of you till, from one day to the next, unbeknown to me, he carried you
off to another town. He noticed I was interested in her, you see, but that
was silly, because my interest was absolutely pure, absolutely without ulte-
390   rior motive. The interest I took in her new family, as it grew up, had an
unbelievable tenderness to it. Even she should bear witness to that! [*He
points to the* STEPDAUGHTER.]

STEPDAUGHTER   Oh, very much so! I was a little sweetie. Pigtails over my
shoulders. Panties coming down a little bit below my skirt. A little sweetie.
He would see me coming out of school, at the gate. He would come and
395   see me as I grew up . . .

FATHER   This is outrageous. You're betraying me!

STEPDAUGHTER   I'm not! What do you mean?

FATHER   Outrageous. Outrageous. [*Immediately, still excited, he continues in
a tone of explanation, to the* DIRECTOR.] My house, sir, when she had left it,
400   at once seemed empty. [*Points to the* MOTHER.] She was an incubus. But she
filled my house for me. Left alone, I wandered through these rooms like a
fly without a head. This fellow here [*the* SON] was raised away from home.
Somehow, when he got back, he didn't seem mine any more. Without a
mother between me and him, he grew up on his own, apart, without any

405 relationship to me, emotional or intellectual. And then—strange, sir, but true—first I grew curious, then I was gradually attracted toward *her* family, which I had brought into being. The thought of *this* family began to fill the void around me. I had to—really had to—believe she was at peace, absorbed in the simplest cares of life, lucky to be away and far removed from the

410 complicated torments of my spirit. And to have proof of this, I would go and see that little girl at the school gate.

STEPDAUGHTER   Correct! He followed me home, smiled at me and, when I was home, waved to me, like this! I would open my eyes wide and look at him suspiciously. I didn't know who it was. I told mother. And she guessed

415 right away it was him. [*The* MOTHER *nods.*] At first she didn't want to send me back to school for several days. When I did go, I saw him again at the gate—the clown!—with a brown paper bag in his hand. He came up to me, caressed me, and took from the bag a lovely big Florentine straw hat with a ring of little May roses round it—for me!

420 DIRECTOR   You're making too long a story of this.

SON [*contemptuously*]   Story is right! Fiction! Literature!

FATHER   Literature? This is life, sir. Passion!

DIRECTOR   Maybe! But not actable!

FATHER   I agree. This is all preliminary. I wouldn't *want* you to act it. As

425 you see, in fact, she [*the* STEPDAUGHTER] is no longer that little girl with pigtails—

STEPDAUGHTER   —and the panties showing below her skirt!

FATHER   The drama comes now, sir. Novel, complex—

STEPDAUGHTER [*gloomy, fierce, steps forward*]   —What my father's death

430 meant for us was—

FATHER [*not giving her time to continue*]   —poverty, sir. They returned, unbeknownst to me. She's so thickheaded. [*Pointing to the* MOTHER] It's true she can hardly write herself, but she could have had her daughter write, or her son, telling me they were in need!

435 MOTHER   But, sir, how could I have guessed he felt the way he did?

FATHER   Which is just where you always went wrong. You could never guess how I felt about anything!

MOTHER   After so many years of separation, with all that had happened . . .

FATHER   And is it my fault if that fellow carried you off as he did? [*Turning to*

440 *the* DIRECTOR] From one day to the next, as I say. He'd found some job someplace. I couldn't even trace them. Necessarily, then, my interest dwindled, with the years. The drama breaks out, sir, unforeseen and violent, at their return. When I, alas, was impelled by the misery of my still-living flesh . . . Oh, and what misery that is for a man who is alone, who has not

445 wanted to form debasing relationships, not yet old enough to do without a woman, and no longer young enough to go and look for one without shame! Misery? It's horror, horror, because no woman can give him love any more.—Knowing this, one should go without! Well, sir, on the outside, when other people are watching, each man is clothed in dignity: but, on

450 the inside, he knows what unconfessable things are going on within him. One gives way, gives way to temptation, to rise again, right afterward, of course, in a great hurry to put our dignity together again, complete, solid, a stone on a grave that hides and buries from our eyes every sign of our shame and even the very memory of it! It's like that with everybody. Only

455 the courage to say it is lacking—to say certain things.

STEPDAUGHTER   The courage to do them, though—everybody's got that.

FATHER   Everybody. But in secret. That's why it takes more courage to say
them. A man only has to say them and it's all over: he's labeled a cynic. But,
sir, he isn't! He's just like everybody else. Better! He's better because he's
460   not afraid to reveal, by the light of intelligence, the red stain of shame,
there, in the human beast, which closes its eyes to it. Woman—yes,
woman—what is she like, actually? She looks at us, inviting, tantalizing.
You take hold of her. She's no sooner in your arms than she shuts her eyes.
It is the sign of her submission. The sign with which she tells the man:
465   Blind yourself for I am blind.

STEPDAUGHTER   How about when she no longer keeps them shut? When
she no longer feels the need to hide the red stain of shame from herself by
closing her eyes, and instead, her eyes now dry and impassive, sees the
shame of the man, who has blinded himself even without love? They make
470   me vomit, all those intellectual elaborations, this philosophy that begins
by revealing the beast and then goes on to excuse it and save its soul . . . I
can't bear to hear about it! Because when a man feels obliged to *reduce*
life this way, reduce it all to "the beast," throwing overboard every vestige
of the truly human, every aspiration after chastity, all feelings of purity, of
475   the ideal, of duties, of modesty, of shame, then nothing is more contemptible, more nauseating than his wretched guilt feelings! Crocodile
tears!

DIRECTOR   Let's get to the facts, to the facts! This is just discussion.

FATHER   Very well. But a fact is like a sack. When it's empty, it won't stand
480   up. To make it stand up you must first pour into it the reasons and feelings
by which it exists. I couldn't know that—when that man died and they
returned here in poverty—she went out to work as a dressmaker to support
the children, nor that the person she went to work for was that . . . that
Madam Pace!

485   STEPDAUGHTER   A high-class dressmaker, if you'd all like to know! To all
appearances, she serves fine ladies, but then she arranges things so that
the fine ladies serve *her* . . . without prejudice to ladies not so fine!

MOTHER   Believe me, sir, I never had the slightest suspicion that that old
witch hired me because she had her eye on my daughter . . .

490   STEPDAUGHTER   Poor mama! Do you know, sir, what the woman did when I
brought her my mother's work? She would point out to me the material
she'd ruined by giving it to my mother to sew. And she deducted for that,
she deducted. And so, you understand, *I* paid, while that poor creature
thought she was making sacrifices for me and those two by sewing, even at
495   night, Madam Pace's material!

[*Indignant movements and exclamations from the* ACTORS.]

DIRECTOR [*without pause*]   And there, one day, you met—

STEPDAUGHTER [*pointing to the* FATHER]   —him, him, yes sir! An old client!
Now there's a scene for you to put on! Superb!

FATHER   Interrupted by her—the mother—

500   STEPDAUGHTER [*without pause, treacherously*]   —almost in time!—

FATHER [*shouting*]   No, no, *in* time! Because, luckily, I recognized the girl in
time. And I took them all back, sir, into my home. Now try to visualize my
situation and hers, the one confronting the other—she as you see her now,
myself unable to look her in the face any more.

505 STEPDAUGHTER It's too absurd! But—afterward—was it possible for me to be
a modest little miss, virtuous and well-bred, in accordance with those confounded aspirations toward a certain solidity, toward what is morally sound?

FATHER And therein lies the drama, sir, as far as I'm concerned: in my awareness that each of us thinks of himself as *one* but that, well, it's not true,
510 each of us is many, oh so many, sir, according to the possibilities of being
that are in us. We are one thing for this person, another for that! Already
two utterly different things! And with it all, the illusion of being always one
thing for all men, and always this one thing in every single action. It's not
true! Not true! We realize as much when, by some unfortunate chance, in
515 one or another of our acts, we find ourselves suspended, hooked. We see, I
mean, that we are not wholly in that act, and that therefore it would be
abominably unjust to judge us by that act alone, to hold us suspended,
hooked, in the pillory, our whole life long, as if our life were summed up in
that act! Now do you understand this girl's treachery? She surprised me in
520 a place, in an act, in which she should never have had to know me—I
couldn't be that way for her. And she wants to give me a reality such as I
could never had expected I would have to assume for her, the reality of a
fleeting moment, a shameful one, in my life! This, sir, this is what I feel
most strongly. And you will see that the drama will derive tremendous value
525 from this. But now add the situation of the others! His . . . [*He points to the*
SON.]

SON [*shrugging contemptuously*] Leave me out of this! It's none of my
business.

FATHER What? None of your business?

SON None. And I *want* to be left out. I wasn't made to be one of you, and
530 you know it.

STEPDAUGHTER We're common, aren't we?—And he's so refined.—But from
time to time I give him a hard, contemptuous look, and he looks down at
the ground. You may have noticed that, sir. He looks down at the ground.
For he knows the wrong he's done me.

535 SON [*hardly looking at her*] Me?

STEPDAUGHTER You! You! I'm on the streets because of you! [*A movement of
horror from the Actors*] Did you or did you not, by your attitude, deny us—I
won't say the intimacy of home but even the hospitality which puts guests
at their ease? We were the intruders, coming to invade the kingdom of your
540 legitimacy! I'd like to have you see, sir, certain little scenes between just
him and me! He says I tyrannized over them all. But it was entirely because
of his attitude that I started to exploit the situation he calls filthy, a situation which had brought me into his home with my mother, who is also *his*
mother, *as its mistress!*

545 SON [*coming slowly forward*] They can't lose, sir, three against one, an easy
game. But figure to yourself a son, sitting quietly at home, who one fine
day sees a young woman arrive, an impudent type with her nose in the air,
asking for his father, with whom she has heaven knows what business; and
then he sees her return, in the same style, accompanied by that little girl
550 over there; and finally he sees her treat his father—who can say why?—in
a very ambiguous and cool manner, demanding money, in a tone that takes
for granted that he *has* to give it, has to, is obligated—

FATHER —but I *am* obligated: it's for your mother!

SON   How would I know? When, sir, [*To the* DIRECTOR] have I ever seen her?
555   When have I ever heard her spoken of? One day I see her arrive with her
[*the* STEPDAUGHTER], with that boy, with that little girl. They say to me: "It's
your mother too, know that?" I manage to figure out from her carryings-on
[*Pointing at the* STEPDAUGHTER] why they arrived in our home from one day
to the next . . . What I'm feeling and experiencing I can't put into words,
560   and wouldn't want to. I wouldn't want to confess it, even to myself. It cannot therefore result in any action on my part. You can see that. Believe me,
sir, I'm a character that, dramatically speaking, remains unrealized. I'm out
of place in their company. So please leave me out of it all!
FATHER   What? But it's just because you're so—
565   SON [*in violent exasperation*]   —I'm so what? How would *you* know? When
did you ever care about me?
FATHER   *Touché! Touché!* But isn't even that a dramatic situation? This with-
drawnness of yours, so cruel to me, and to your mother who, on her return
home is seeing you almost for the first time, a grown man she doesn't rec-
570   ognize, though she knows you're her son . . . [*Pointing out the* MOTHER *to
the* DIRECTOR] Just look at her, she's crying.
STEPDAUGHTER [*angrily, stamping her foot*]   Like the fool she is!
FATHER [*pointing her out to the* DIRECTOR]   And she can't abide him, you
know. [*Again referring to the* SON]—He says it's none of his business. The
575   truth is he's almost the pivot of the action. Look at that little boy, clinging
to his mother all the time, scared, humiliated . . . It's all because of *him*
[*the* SON]. Perhaps the most painful situation of all is that little boy's: he
feels alien, more than all the others, and the poor little thing is so mortified, so anguished at being taken into our home—out of charity, as it
580   were . . . [*Confidentially*] He's just like his father: humble, doesn't say
anything . . .
DIRECTOR   He won't fit anyway. You've no idea what a nuisance children are
onstage.
FATHER   But he wouldn't be a nuisance for long. Nor would the little girl, no,
585   she's the first to go . . .
DIRECTOR   Very good, yes! The whole thing interests me very much indeed. I
have a hunch, a definite hunch, that there's material here for a fine play!
STEPDAUGHTER [*trying to inject herself*]   With a character like me in it!
FATHER [*pushing her to one side in his anxiety to know what the* DIRECTOR *will
decide*]   You be quiet!
590   DIRECTOR   [*going right on, ignoring the interruption*]   Yes, it's new stuff . . .
FATHER   Very new!
DIRECTOR   You had some gall, though, to come and throw it at me this
way . . .
FATHER   Well, you see, sir, born as we are to the stage . . .
595   DIRECTOR   You're amateurs, are you?
FATHER   No. I say: "born to the stage" because . . .
DIRECTOR   Oh, come on, you must have done some acting!
FATHER   No, no, sir, only as every man acts the part assigned to him—by
himself or others—in this life. In me you see passion itself, which—in
600   almost all people, as it rises—invariably becomes a bit theatrical . . .
DIRECTOR   Well, never mind! Never mind about that!—You see, my dear sir,
without the author . . . I could direct you to an author . . .

FATHER   No, no, look: you be the author!

DIRECTOR   Me? What are you talking about?

605 FATHER   Yes, you. You. Why not?

DIRECTOR   Because I've never been an author, that's why not!

FATHER   Couldn't you be one now, hm? There's nothing to it. Everyone's doing it. And your job is made all the easier by the fact that you have us— here—alive—right in front of your nose!

610 DIRECTOR   It wouldn't be enough.

FATHER   Not enough? Seeing us live our own drama . . .

DIRECTOR   I know, but you always need someone to write it!

FATHER   No. Just someone to take it down, maybe, since you have us here—in action—scene by scene. It'll be enough if we piece together a rough sketch 615 for you, then you can rehearse it.

DIRECTOR   [tempted, goes up onstage again] Well, I'm almost, almost tempted . . . Just for kicks . . . We could actually rehearse . . .

FATHER   Of course you could! What scenes you'll see emerge! I can list them for you right away.

620 DIRECTOR   I'm tempted . . . I'm tempted . . . Let's give it a try . . . Come to my office. [Turns to the Actors.] Take a break, will you? But don't go away. We'll be back in fifteen or twenty minutes. [To the FATHER] Let's see what we can do . . . Maybe we can get something very extraordinary out of all this . . .

FATHER   We certainly can. Wouldn't it be better to take them along? [He points to the Characters.]

625 DIRECTOR   Yes, let them all come. [Starts going off, then comes back to address the Actors.] Now don't forget. Everyone on time. Fifteen minutes.

[DIRECTOR and Six Characters cross the stage and disappear. The Actors stay there and look at one another in amazement.]

LEADING MAN   Is he serious? What's he going to do?

JUVENILE   This is outright insanity.

A THIRD ACTOR   We have to improvise a drama right off the bat?

630 JUVENILE LEAD   That's right. Like Commedia dell'Arte.[4]

LEADING LADY   Well, if he thinks I'm going to lend myself to that sort of thing . . .

INGENUE   Count me out.

A FOURTH ACTOR   [alluding to the Characters]   I'd like to know who those people are.

635 THE THIRD ACTOR   Who would they be? Madmen or crooks!

JUVENILE LEAD   And he's going to pay attention to them?

INGENUE   Carried away by vanity! Wants to be an author now . . .

LEADING MAN   It's out of this world. If this is what the theater is coming to, my friends . . .

640 A FIFTH ACTOR   I think it's rather fun.

THE THIRD ACTOR   Well! We shall see. We shall see. [And chatting thus among themselves, the Actors leave the stage, some using the little door at the back, others returning to their dressing rooms.]

The curtain remains raised. The performance is interrupted by a twenty-minute intermission.

Bells ring. The performance is resumed.

---

4. A traditional form of Italian comedy featuring stock characters, some in masks, who improvise dialogue.

[*From dressing rooms, from the door, and also from the house, the Actors, the* STAGE MANAGER, *the* TECHNICIAN, *the* PROMPTER, *the* PROPERTY MAN *return to the stage; at the same time the* DIRECTOR *and the Six Characters emerge from the office.*

As soon as the house lights are out, the stage lighting is as before.]

DIRECTOR   Let's go, everybody! Is everyone here? Quiet! We're beginning. [*Calls the* TECHNICIAN *by name.*]

TECHNICIAN   Here!

DIRECTOR   Set the stage for the parlor scene. Two wings and a backdrop with
645   a door in it will do, quickly please!

[*The* TECHNICIAN *at once runs to do the job, and does it while the* DIRECTOR *works things out with the* STAGE MANAGER, *the* PROPERTY MAN, *the* PROMPTER, *and the Actors. This indication of a set consists of two wings, a drop with a door in it, all in pink and gold stripes.*]

DIRECTOR [*to the* PROPERTY MAN]   See if we have some sort of bed-sofa in the prop room.

PROPERTY MAN   Yes, sir, there's the green one.

STEPDAUGHTER   No, no, not green! It was yellow, flowered, plush, and very
650   big. Extremely comfortable.

PROPERTY MAN   Well, we have nothing like that.

DIRECTOR   But it doesn't matter. Bring the one you have.

STEPDAUGHTER   Doesn't matter? Madam Pace's famous chaise longue!

DIRECTOR   This is just for rehearsal. Please don't meddle! [*To the* STAGE MAN-
655   AGER] See if we have a display case—long and rather narrow.

STEPDAUGHTER   The table, the little mahogany table for the pale blue envelope!

STAGE MANAGER [*to the* DIRECTOR]   There's the small one. Gilded.

DIRECTOR   All right. Get that one.

FATHER   A large mirror.

660 STEPDAUGHTER   And the screen. A screen, please, or what'll I do?

STAGE MANAGER   Yes, ma'am, we have lots of screens, don't worry.

DIRECTOR [*to the* STEPDAUGHTER]   A few coat hangers?

STEPDAUGHTER   A great many, yes.

DIRECTOR [*to the* STAGE MANAGER]   See how many we've got, and have them
665   brought on.

STAGE MANAGER   Right, sir, I'll see to it.

[*The* STAGE MANAGER *also hurries to do his job and while the* DIRECTOR *goes on talking with the* PROMPTER *and then with the Characters and the Actors, has the furniture carried on by stagehands and arranges it as he thinks fit.*]

DIRECTOR [*to the* PROMPTER]   Meanwhile you can get into position. Look: this is the outline of the scenes, act by act. [*He gives him several sheets of paper.*] You'll have to be a bit of a virtuoso today.

670 PROMPTER   Shorthand?

DIRECTOR [*pleasantly surprised*]   Oh, good! You know shorthand?

PROMPTER   I may not know prompting, but shorthand . . . [*Turning to a stage-hand*] Get me some paper from my room—quite a lot—all you can find!

[*The stagehand runs off and returns a little later with a wad of paper which he gives to the* PROMPTER.]

DIRECTOR [*going right on, to the* PROMPTER]   Follow the scenes line by line as
675   we play them, and try to pin down the speeches, at least the most important

ones. [*Then, turning to the Actors*] Clear the stage please, everyone! Yes, come over to this side and pay close attention. [*He indicates the left.*]

LEADING LADY   Excuse me but—

DIRECTOR [*forestalling*]   There'll be no improvising, don't fret.

680 LEADING MAN   Then what are we to do?

DIRECTOR   Nothing. For now, just stop, look, and listen. Afterward you'll be given written parts. Right now we'll rehearse. As best we can. With them doing the rehearsing for us. [*He points to the Characters.*]

FATHER [*amid all the confusion onstage, as if he'd fallen from the clouds*] We're rehearsing? How d'you mean?

685 DIRECTOR   Yes, for them. You rehearse for them. [*Indicates the Actors.*]

FATHER   But if we are the characters . . .

DIRECTOR   All right, you're characters, but, my dear sir, characters don't perform here, actors perform here. The characters are there, in the script [*He points to the PROMPTER's box.*]—when there *is* a script!

690 FATHER   Exactly! Since there isn't, and you gentlemen have the luck to have them right here, alive in front of you, those characters . . .

DIRECTOR   Oh, great! Want to do it all yourselves? Appear before the public, do the acting yourselves?

FATHER   Of course. Just as we are.

695 DIRECTOR [*ironically*]   I'll bet you'd put on a splendid show!

LEADING MAN   Then what's the use of staying?

DIRECTOR [*without irony, to the Characters*]   Don't run away with the idea that you can act! That's laughable . . . [*And in fact the Actors laugh.*] Hear that? They're laughing. [*Coming back to the point*] I was forgetting. I must

700 cast the show. It's quite easy. It casts itself. [*To the SECOND ACTRESS*] You, ma'am, will play the Mother. [*To the FATHER*] You'll have to find her a name.

FATHER   Amalia, sir.

DIRECTOR   But that's this lady's real name. We wouldn't want to call her by her real name!

705 FATHER   Why not? If that is her name . . . But of course, if it's to be this lady . . . [*He indicates the SECOND ACTRESS with a vague gesture.*] To me *she* [*the MOTHER*] is Amalia. But suit yourself . . . [*He is getting more and more confused.*] I don't know what to tell you . . . I'm beginning to . . . oh, I don't know . . . to find my own words ringing false, they sound different somehow.

710 DIRECTOR   Don't bother about that, just don't bother about it. We can always find the right sound. As for the name, if you say Amalia, Amalia it shall be; or we'll find another. For now, we'll designate the characters thus: [*To the JUVENILE LEAD*] You're the Son. [*To the LEADING LADY*] You, ma'am, are of course the Stepdaughter.

715 STEPDAUGHTER [*excitedly*]   What, what? That one there is me? [*She bursts out laughing.*]

DIRECTOR [*mad*]   What is there to laugh at?

LEADING LADY [*aroused*]   No one has ever dared laugh at me! I insist on respect—or I quit!

STEPDAUGHTER   But, excuse me, I'm not laughing at you.

720 DIRECTOR [*to the STEPDAUGHTER*]   You should consider yourself honored to be played by . . .

LEADING LADY [*without pause, contemptuously*]   —"That one there!"

STEPDAUGHTER   But I wasn't speaking of you, believe me. I was speaking of me. I don't see me in you, that's all. I don't know why . . . I guess you're just
725   not like me!

FATHER   That's it, exactly, my dear sir! What is *expressed* in us . . .

DIRECTOR   Expression, expression! You think that's your business? Not at all!

FATHER   Well, but what *we* express . . .

DIRECTOR   But you don't. You don't express. You provide us with raw mate-
730   rial. The actors give it body and face, voice and gesture. They've given expression to much loftier material, let me tell you. Yours is on such a small scale that, if it stands up onstage at all, the credit, believe me, should all go to my actors.

FATHER   I don't dare contradict you, sir, but it's terribly painful for us who
735   are as you see us—with these bodies, these faces—

DIRECTOR [*cutting in, out of patience*]   —that's where makeup comes in, my dear sir, for whatever concerns the face, the remedy is makeup!

FATHER   Yes. But the voice, gesture—

DIRECTOR   Oh, for Heaven's sake! You can't exist here! Here the actor acts
740   you, and that's that!

FATHER   I understand, sir. But now perhaps I begin to guess also why our author who saw us, alive as we are, did not want to put us onstage. I don't want to offend your actors. God forbid! But I feel that seeing myself acted . . . I don't know by whom . . .

LEADING MAN [*rising with dignity and coming over, followed by the gay young*
745   *Actresses who laugh*]   By me, if you've no objection.

FATHER [*humble, smooth*]   I'm very honored, sir. [*He bows.*] But however much art and willpower the gentleman puts into absorbing me into him- self . . . [*He is bewildered now.*]

LEADING MAN   Finish. Finish.

[*The Actresses laugh.*]

750   FATHER   Well, the performance he will give, even forcing himself with makeup to resemble me, well, with that figure [*All the Actors laugh.*] he can hardly play me as I am. I shall rather be—even apart from the face—what he interprets me to be, as he feels I am—if he feels I am anything—and not as I feel myself inside myself. And it seems to me that whoever is called
755   upon to judge us should take this into account.

DIRECTOR   So now you're thinking of what the critics will say? And I was still listening! Let the critics say what they want. We will concentrate on putting on your play! [*He walks away a little, and looks around.*] Come on, come on. Is the set ready? [*To the Actors and the Characters*] Don't clutter up the stage,
760   I want to be able to see! [*He goes down from the stage.*] Let's not lose any more time! [*To the STEPDAUGHTER*] Does the set seem pretty good to you?

STEPDAUGHTER   Oh! But I can't recognize it!

DIRECTOR   Oh my God, don't tell me we should reconstruct Madam Pace's back room for you! [*To the FATHER*] Didn't you say a parlor with flowered
765   wallpaper?

FATHER   Yes, sir. White.

DIRECTOR   It's not white. Stripes. But it doesn't matter. As for furniture we're in pretty good shape. That little table—bring it forward a bit! [*Stagehands do this. To the PROPERTY MAN*] Meanwhile you get an envelope, possibly a
770   light blue one, and give it to the gentleman. [*Indicating the FATHER*]

PROPERTY MAN   A letter envelope?

DIRECTOR and FATHER   Yes, a letter envelope.

PROPERTY MAN   I'll be right back.

> [*He exits.*]

775 DIRECTOR   Come on, come on. It's the young lady's scene first. [*The* LEADING LADY *comes forward.*] No, no, wait. I said the young lady. [*Indicating the* STEPDAUGHTER] You will just watch—

STEPDAUGHTER [*adding, without pause*]   —watch me live it!

LEADING LADY [*resenting this*]   I'll know how to live it too, don't worry, once I put myself in the role!

780 DIRECTOR [*raising his hands to his head*]   Please! No more chatter! Now, scene one. The Young Lady with Madam Pace. Oh, and how about this Madam Pace? [*Bewildered, looking around him, he climbs back onstage.*]

FATHER   She isn't with us, sir.

DIRECTOR   Then what do we do?

785 FATHER   But she's alive. She's alive too.

DIRECTOR   Fine. But where?

FATHER   I'll tell you. [*Turning to the Actresses*] If you ladies will do me the favor of giving me your hats for a moment.

THE ACTRESSES [*surprised a little, laughing a little, in chorus*]   —What?—Our
790 hats?—What does he say?—Why?—Oh, dear!

DIRECTOR   What are you going to do with the ladies' hats?

> [*The Actors laugh.*]

FATHER   Oh, nothing. Just put them on these coathooks for a minute. And would some of you be so kind as to take your coats off too?

ACTORS [*as before*]   Their coats too?—And then?—He's nuts!

795 AN ACTRESS OR TWO [*as above*]   —But why?—Just the coats?

FATHER   Just so they can be hung there for a moment. Do me this favor. Will you?

ACTRESSES [*taking their hats off, and one or two of them their coats, too, continuing to laugh, and going to hang the hats here and there on the coathooks*]   —Well, why not?—There!—This is getting to be really funny!—Are we to put them on display?

800 FATHER   Exactly! That's just right, ma'am: on display!

DIRECTOR   May one inquire *why* you are doing this?

FATHER   Yes, sir. If we set the stage better, who knows but she may come to us, drawn by the objects of her trade . . . [*Inviting them to look toward the entrance at the back*] Look! Look!

> [*The entrance at the back opens, and* MADAM PACE *walks a few paces downstage, a hag of enormous fatness with a pompous wig of carrot-colored wool and a fiery red rose on one side of it, à l'espagnole,*[5] *heavily made up, dressed with gauche elegance in garish red silk, a feathered fan in one hand and the other hand raised to hold a lighted cigarette between two fingers. At the sight of this apparition, the* DIRECTOR *and the Actors at once dash off the stage with a yell of terror, rushing down the stairs and making as if to flee up the aisle. The* STEPDAUGHTER, *on the other hand runs to* MADAM PACE—*deferentially, as to her boss.*]

---

5. Spanish-style (French).

805 STEPDAUGHTER [*running to her*]   Here she is, here she is!

FATHER [*beaming*]   It's she! What did I tell you? Here she is!

DIRECTOR [*overcoming his first astonishment, and incensed now*]   What tricks are these?

> [*The next four speeches are more or less simultaneous.*]

LEADING MAN   What goes on around here?

810 JUVENILE LEAD   Where on earth did she come from?

INGENUE   They must have been holding her in reserve.

LEADING LADY   Hocus pocus! Hocus pocus!

FATHER [*dominating these protests*]   Excuse me, though! Why, actually, would you want to destroy this prodigy in the name of vulgar truth, this miracle of
815 a reality that is born of the stage itself—called into being by the stage, drawn here by the stage, and shaped by the stage—and which has more right to live on the stage than you have because it is much truer? Which of you actresses will later re-create Madam Pace? This lady *is* Madam Pace. You must admit that the actress who re-creates her will be less true than
820 this lady—who is Madam Pace. Look: my daughter recognized her, and went right over to her. Stand and watch the scene!

> [*Hesitantly, the* DIRECTOR *and the Actors climb back onstage. But the scene between the* STEPDAUGHTER *and* MADAM PACE *has begun during the protest of the Actors and the* FATHER's *answer: sotto voce,[6] very quietly, in short naturally—as would never be possible on a stage. When, called to order by the* FATHER, *the Actors turn again to watch, they hear* MADAM PACE, *who has just placed her hand under the* STEPDAUGHTER's *chin in order to raise her head, talk unintelligibly. After trying to hear for a moment, they just give up.*]

DIRECTOR   Well?

LEADING MAN   What's she saying?

LEADING LADY   One can't hear a thing.

825 JUVENILE LEAD   Louder!

STEPDAUGHTER [*leaving* MADAM PACE, *who smiles a priceless smile, and walking down toward the Actors*]   Louder, huh? How d'you mean: louder? These aren't things that can be said louder. *I* was able to say them loudly—to shame him [*Indicating the* FATHER]—that was my revenge. For Madam, it's different, my friends: it would mean—jail.

830 DIRECTOR   Oh my God! It's like that, is it? But, my dear young lady, in the theater one must be heard. And even we couldn't hear you, right here on the stage. How about an audience out front? There's a scene to be done. And anyway you *can* speak loudly—it's just between yourselves, we won't be standing here listening like now. Pretend you're alone. In a room. The
835 back room of the shop. No one can hear you. [*The* STEPDAUGHTER *charmingly and with a mischievous smile tells him No with a repeated movement of the finger.*] Why not?

STEPDAUGHTER [*sotto voce, mysteriously*]   There's someone who'll hear if she [MADAM PACE] speaks loudly.

DIRECTOR [*in consternation*]   Is someone else going to pop up now?

> [*The Actors make as if to quit the stage again.*]

---

6. Under the voice (Italian); that is, spoken very softly, under the breath.

840 FATHER   No, no, sir. She means me. I'm to be there—behind the door—
waiting. And Madam knows. So if you'll excuse me. I must be ready for my
entrance. [*He starts to move.*]

DIRECTOR [*stopping him*]   No, wait. We must respect the exigencies of the
theater. Before you get ready—

845 STEPDAUGHTER [*interrupting him*]   Let's get on with it! I tell you I'm dying
with desire to live it, to live that scene! If he's ready, I'm more than ready!

DIRECTOR [*shouting*]   But first we have to get that scene out of you and her!
[*Indicating* MADAM PACE] Do you follow me?

STEPDAUGHTER   Oh dear, oh dear, she was telling me things you already
850 know—that my mother's work had been badly done once again, the material is ruined, and I'm going to have to bear with her if I want her to go on
helping us in our misery.

MADAM PACE [*coming forward with a great air of importance*]   Sí, sí, señor,
porque yo[7] no want profit. No advantage, no.

855 DIRECTOR [*almost scared*]   What, what? She talks like *that*?!
[*All the Actors loudly burst out laughing.*]

STEPDAUGHTER [*also laughing*]   Yes, sir, she talks like that—halfway between
Spanish and English—very funny, isn't it?

MADAM PACE   Now that is not good manners, no, that you laugh at me! Yo
hablo[8] the English as good I can, señor!

860 DIRECTOR   And it *is* good! Yes! Do talk that way, ma'am! It's a surefire effect!
There couldn't be anything better to, um, soften the crudity of the situation! Do talk that way! It's fine!

STEPDAUGHTER   Fine! Of course! To have certain propositions put to you in a
lingo like that. Surefire, isn't it? Because, sir, it seems almost a joke. When
865 I hear there's "an old señor" who wants to "have good time conmigo,"[9] I
start to laugh—don't I, Madam Pace?

MADAM PACE   Old, viejo, no. Viejito—leetle beet old, sí, darling? Better like
that: if he no give you fun, he bring you prudencia.[1]

MOTHER [*jumping up, to the stupefaction and consternation of all the Actors,
who had been taking no notice of her, and who now respond to her shouts
with a start and, smiling, try to restrain her, because she has grabbed* MADAM
PACE'*s wig and thrown it on the floor*]   Witch! Witch! Murderess! My
870 daughter!

STEPDAUGHTER [*running over to restrain her* MOTHER]   No, no, mama, no,
please!

FATHER [*running over too at the same time*]   Calm down, calm down! Sit
here.

875 MOTHER   Then send that woman away!

STEPDAUGHTER [*to the* DIRECTOR, *who also has run over*]   It's not possible, not
possible that my mother should be here!

FATHER [*also to the* DIRECTOR]   They can't be together. That's why, you see,
the woman wasn't with us when we came. Their being together would spoil
880 it, you understand.

DIRECTOR   It doesn't matter, doesn't matter at all. This is just a preliminary
sketch. Everything helps. However confusing the elements, I'll piece them

7. Yes, yes, yes, Mister, because I . . . (Span-   8. I speak (Spanish).
ish). In Pirandello's original Italian text,   9. With me (Spanish).
Madam Pace mixes Spanish and Italian.   1. Care, caution (Spanish).

together somehow. [*Turning to the* MOTHER *and sitting her down again in her place*] Come along, come along, ma'am, calm down: sit down again.

STEPDAUGHTER [*who meanwhile has moved center stage again. Turning to* MADAM PACE] All right, let's go!

MADAM PACE   Ah, no! No thank you! Yo aquí no do nada[2] with your mother present.

STEPDAUGHTER   Oh, come on! Bring in that old señor who wants to have good time conmigo! [*Turning imperiously to all the others*] Yes, we've got to have it, this scene!—Come on, let's go! [*To* MADAM PACE] You may leave.

MADAM PACE   Ah sí, I go, I go, go seguramente[3] . . . [*She makes her exit furiously, putting her wig back on, and looking haughtily at the Actors who applaud mockingly.*]

STEPDAUGHTER [*to the* FATHER]   And you can make your entrance. No need to go out and come in again. Come here. Pretend, you're already in. Right. Now I'm here with bowed head, modest, huh? Let's go! Speak up! With a different voice, the voice of someone just in off the street: "Hello, miss."

DIRECTOR [*by this time out front again*]   Now look: are you directing this, or am I? [*To the* FATHER *who looks undecided and perplexed.*] Do it, yes. Go to the back. Don't leave the stage, though. And then come forward.

[*The* FATHER *does it, almost dismayed. Very pale; but already clothed in the reality of his created life, he smiles as he approaches from the back, as if still alien to the drama which will break upon him. The Actors now pay attention to the scene which is beginning.*]

DIRECTOR [*softly, in haste, to the* PROMPTER *in the box*]   And you, be ready now, ready to write!

THE SCENE

FATHER [*coming forward, with a different voice*]   Hello, miss.

STEPDAUGHTER [*with bowed head and contained disgust*]   Hello.

FATHER [*scrutinizing her under her hat which almost hides her face and noting that she is very young, exclaims, almost to himself, a little out of complaisance and a little out of fear of compromising himself in a risky adventure*]   Oh . . . —Well, I was thinking, it wouldn't be the first time, hm? The first time you came here.

STEPDAUGHTER [*as above*]   No, sir.

FATHER   You've been here other times? [*And when the* STEPDAUGHTER *nods*] More than once? [*He waits a moment for her to answer, then again scrutinizes her under her hat; smiles; then says*] Well then, hm . . . it shouldn't any longer be so . . . May I take this hat off for you?

STEPDAUGHTER [*without pause, to forestall him, not now containing her disgust*]   No, sir, I will take it off! [*And she does so in haste, convulsed.*]

[*The* MOTHER, *watching the scene with the* SON *and with the two others, smaller and more her own, who are close to her all the time, forming a group at the opposite side of the stage from the Actors, is on tenterhooks as she follows the words and actions of* FATHER *and* STEPDAUGHTER *with varied expression: grief, disdain, anxiety, horror, now hiding her face, now emitting a moan.*]

MOTHER   Oh God! My God!

2. I do nothing here (Spanish and English).   3. Certainly (Spanish).

FATHER [*is momentarily turned to stone by the moaning; then he reassumes the previous tone*]   Now give it to me: I'll hang it up for you. [*He takes the hat from her hands.*] But I could wish for a little hat worthier of such a dear, lovely little head! Would you like to help me choose one? From the many
915   Madam has?—You wouldn't?

INGENUE [*interrupting*]   Oh now, come on, those are *our* hats!

DIRECTOR [*without pause, very angry*]   Silence, for Heaven's sake, don't try to be funny!—This is the stage. [*Turning back to the* STEPDAUGHTER] Would you begin again, please?

920 STEPDAUGHTER [*beginning again*]   No, thank you, sir.

FATHER   Oh, come on now, don't say no. Accept one from me. To please me . . . There are some lovely ones you know. And we would make Madam happy. Why else does she put them on display?

STEPDAUGHTER   No, no, sir, look: I wouldn't even be able to wear it.

925 FATHER   You mean because of what the family would think when they saw you come home with a new hat on? Think nothing of it. Know how to handle that? What to tell them at home?

STEPDAUGHTER [*breaking out, at the end of her rope*]   But that's not why, sir. I couldn't wear it because I'm . . . as you see me. You might surely have
930   noticed! [*Points to her black attire.*]

FATHER   In mourning, yes. Excuse me. It's true: I do see it. I beg your pardon. I'm absolutely mortified, believe me.

STEPDAUGHTER [*forcing herself and plucking up courage to conquer her contempt and nausea*]   Enough! Enough! It's for me to thank you, it is not for you to be mortified or afflicted. Please pay no more attention to what I
935   said. Even for me, you understand . . . [*She forces herself to smile and adds*] I need to forget I am dressed like this.

DIRECTOR [*interrupting, addressing himself to the* PROMPTER *in his box, and going up onstage again*]   Wait! Wait! Don't write. Leave that last sentence out, leave it out! [*Turning to the* FATHER *and* STEPDAUGHTER] It's going very well indeed. [*Then to the* FATHER *alone*] This is where you go into the part
940   we prepared. [*To the Actors*] Enchanting, that little hat scene, don't you agree?

STEPDAUGHTER   Oh, but the best is just coming. Why aren't we continuing?

DIRECTOR   Patience one moment. [*Again addressing himself to the Actors*] Needs rather delicate handling, of course . . .

945 LEADING MAN   —With a certain *ease*—

LEADING LADY   Obviously. But there's nothing to it. [*To the* LEADING MAN] We can rehearse it at once, can't we?

LEADING MAN   As far as I'm . . . Very well, I'll go out and make my entrance. [*And he does go out by the back door, ready to reenter.*]

DIRECTOR [*to the* LEADING LADY]   And so, look, your scene with that Madam
950   Pace is over. I'll write it up later. You are standing . . . Hey, where are you going?

LEADING LADY   Wait. I'm putting my hat back on . . . [*She does so, taking the hat from the hook.*]

DIRECTOR   Oh yes, good.—Now, you're standing here with your head bowed.

STEPDAUGHTER [*amused*]   But she's not wearing black!

955 LEADING LADY   *I shall* wear black! And I'll carry it better than you!

DIRECTOR [*to the* STEPDAUGHTER]   Keep quiet, please! Just watch. You can learn something. [*Claps his hands.*] Get going, get going! The entrance! [*And he goes back out front to get an impression of the stage.*]

[*The door at the back opens, and the* LEADING MAN *comes forward, with the relaxed, waggish manner of an elderly Don Juan.*[4] *From the first speeches, the performance of the scene by the Actors is quite a different thing, without, however, having any element of parody in it—rather, it seems corrected, set to rights. Naturally, the* STEPDAUGHTER *and the* FATHER, *being quite unable to recognize themselves in this* LEADING LADY *and* LEADING MAN *but hearing them speak their own words express in various ways, now with gestures, now with smiles, now with open pro-tests, their surprise, their wonderment, their suffering, etc., as will be seen forthwith.*

The PROMPTER's *voice is clearly heard from the box.*]

LEADING MAN   Hello, miss.

FATHER [*without pause, unable to contain himself*]   No, no!

[*The* STEPDAUGHTER, *seeing how the* LEADING MAN *makes his entrance, has burst out laughing.*]

960   DIRECTOR [*coming from the proscenium, furious*]   Silence here! And stop that laughing at once! We can't go ahead till it stops.

STEPDAUGHTER [*coming from the proscenium*]   How can I help it? This lady [*the* LEADING LADY] just stands there. If she's supposed to be me, let me tell you that if anyone said hello to me in that manner and that tone of voice,
965   I'd burst out laughing just as I actually did!

FATHER [*coming forward a little too*]   That's right . . . the manner, the tone . . .

DIRECTOR   Manner! Tone! Stand to one side now, and let me see the rehearsal.

LEADING MAN [*coming forward*]   If I'm to play an old man entering a house of
970   ill—

DIRECTOR   Oh, pay no attention, please. Just begin again. It was going fine. [*Waiting for the Actor to resume*] Now then . . .

LEADING MAN   Hello, miss.

LEADING LADY   Hello.

LEADING MAN [*re-creating the* FATHER's *gesture of scrutinizing her under her hat, but then expressing very distinctly first the complaisance and then the*
975   *fear*]   Oh . . . Well . . . I was thinking it wouldn't be the first time, I hope . . .

FATHER [*unable to help correcting him*]   Not "I hope." "Would it?" "Would it?"

DIRECTOR   He says: "would it?" A question.

980   LEADING MAN [*pointing to the* PROMPTER]   I heard: "I hope."

DIRECTOR   Same thing! "Would it." Or: "I hope." Continue, continue.—Now, maybe a bit less affected . . . Look, I'll do it for you. Watch me . . . [*Returns to the stage, then repeats the bit since the entrance*]—Hello, miss.

LEADING LADY   Hello.

985   DIRECTOR   Oh, well . . . I was thinking . . . [*Turning to the* LEADING MAN *to have him note how he has looked at the* LEADING LADY *under her hat*] Surprise . . .

---

4. That is, a great lover or seducer of women (from the legendary Spaniard of that name).

fear and complaisance. [*Then, going on, and turning to the* LEADING LADY] It wouldn't be the first time, would it? The first time you came here. [*Again turning to the* LEADING MAN *with an inquiring look*] Clear? [*To the* LEADING
990   LADY] Then you say: No, sir. [*Back to the* LEADING MAN] How shall I put it? Plasticity! [*Goes back out front.*]

LEADING LADY   No, sir.

LEADING MAN   You came here other times? More than once?

DIRECTOR   No, no, wait. [*Indicating the* LEADING LADY] First let her nod. "You
995   came here other times?"

> [*The* LEADING LADY *raises her head a little, closes her eyes painfully as if in disgust, then nods twice at the word "Down" from the* DIRECTOR.]

STEPDAUGHTER [*involuntarily*]   Oh, my God! [*And she at once puts her hand on her mouth to keep the laughter in.*]

DIRECTOR [*turning round*]   What is it?

STEPDAUGHTER [*without pause*]   Nothing, nothing.

DIRECTOR [*to the* LEADING MAN   That's your cue. Go straight on.

1000   LEADING MAN   More than once? Well then, hm . . . it shouldn't any longer be so . . . May I take this little hat off for you?

> [*The* LEADING MAN *says this last speech in such a tone and accompanies it with such a gesture that the* STEPDAUGHTER, *her hands on her mouth, much as she wants to hold herself in, cannot contain her laughter, which comes bursting out through her fingers irresistibly and very loud.*]

LEADING LADY [*returning to her place, enraged*]   Now look, I'm not going to be made a clown of by that person!

LEADING MAN   Nor am I. Let's stop.

1005   DIRECTOR [*to the* STEPDAUGHTER, *roaring*]   Stop it! Stop it!

STEPDAUGHTER   Yes, yes. Forgive me, forgive me . . .

DIRECTOR   You have no manners! You're presumptuous! So there!

FATHER [*seeking to intervene*]   That's true, yes, that's true, sir, but forgive . . .

1010   DIRECTOR [*onstage again*]   Forgive nothing! It's disgusting!

FATHER   Yes, sir. But believe me, it has such a strange effect—

DIRECTOR   Strange? Strange? What's strange about it?

FATHER   I admire your actors, sir, I really admire them, this gentleman [LEADING MAN] and that lady [LEADING LADY] but assuredly . . . well, they're
1015   not us . . .

DIRECTOR   So what? How *could* they be you, if they're the actors?

FATHER   Exactly, the actors! And they play our parts well, both of them. But of course, to us, they seem something else—that tries to be the same but simply isn't!

1020   DIRECTOR   How d'you mean: isn't? What is it then?

FATHER   Something that . . . becomes theirs. And stops being ours.

DIRECTOR   Necessarily! I explained that to you!

FATHER   Yes. I understand, I do under—

DIRECTOR   Then that will be enough! [*Turning to the Actors*] We'll be rehears-
1025   ing by ourselves as we usually do. Rehearsing with authors present has always been hell, in my experience. There's no satisfying them. [*Turning to the* FATHER *and the* STEPDAUGHTER] Come along then. Let's resume. And let's hope you find it possible not to laugh this time.

STEPDAUGHTER   Oh, no, I won't be laughing this time around. My big
moment comes up now. Don't worry!

DIRECTOR   Very well, when she says: "Please pay no more attention to what I
said . . . Even for me—you understand . . ." [*Turning to the* FATHER] You'll
have to cut right in with: "I understand, oh yes, I understand . . ." and ask
her right away—

STEPDAUGHTER [*interrupting*]   Oh? Ask me what?

DIRECTOR   —why she is in mourning.

STEPDAUGHTER   No, no, look: when I told him I needed to forget I was
dressed like this, do you know what his answer was? "Oh, good! Then let's
take that little dress right off, shall we?"

DIRECTOR   Great! Terrific! It'll knock 'em right out of their seats!

STEPDAUGHTER   But it's the truth.

DIRECTOR   Truth, is it? Well, well, well. This is the theater! Our motto is:
truth up to a certain point!

STEPDAUGHTER   Then what would you propose?

DIRECTOR   You'll see. You'll see it. Just leave me alone.

STEPDAUGHTER   Certainly not. From my nausea—from all the reasons one
more cruel than another why I am what I am, why I am "that one there"—
you'd like to cook up some romantic, sentimental concoction, wouldn't
you? He asks me why I'm in mourning, and I tell him, through my tears,
that Papa died two months ago! No, my dear sir! He has to say what he did
say: "Then let's take that little dress right off, shall we?" And I, with my
two-months mourning in my heart, went back there—you see? behind that
screen—and—my fingers quivering with shame, with loathing—I took off
my dress, took off my corset . . .

DIRECTOR [*running his hands through his hair*]   Good God, what are you
saying?

STEPDAUGHTER [*shouting frantically*]   The truth, sir, the truth!

DIRECTOR   Well, yes, of course, that must be the truth . . . and I quite understand your horror, young lady. Would you try to understand that all that is
impossible *on the stage?*

STEPDAUGHTER   Impossible? Then, thanks very much, I'm leaving.

DIRECTOR   No, no, look . . .

STEPDAUGHTER   I'm leaving, I'm leaving! You went in that room, you two, didn't
you, and figured out "what is possible on the stage"? Thanks very much. I see
it all. He wants to skip to the point where he can act out his [*Exaggerating*]
spiritual travail! But I want to play *my* drama. Mine!

DIRECTOR [*annoyed, and shrugging haughtily*]   Oh well, *your* drama. This is
not just your drama, if I may say so. How about the drama of the others?
His drama [*the* FATHER], hers [*the* MOTHER]? We can't let one character hog
the limelight, just taking the whole stage over, and overshadowing all the
others! Everything must be placed within the frame of one harmonious
picture! We must perform only what is performable! I know as well as you
do that each of us has a whole life of his own inside him and would like to
bring it all out. But the difficult thing is this: to bring out only as much as
is needed—in relation to the others—and in this to *imply* all the rest, *suggest* what remains inside! Oh, it would be nice if every character could
come down to the footlights and tell the audience just what is brewing

inside him—in a fine monologue or, if you will, a lecture! [*Good-natured, conciliatory*] Miss, you will have to *contain yourself*. And it will be in your
1080   interest. It could make a bad impression—let me warn you—this tearing fury, this desperate disgust—since, if I may say so, you confessed having been with others at Madam Pace's—before him—more than once!

STEPDAUGHTER [*lowering her head, pausing to recollect, a deeper note in her voice*] It's true. But to me the others are also *him*, all of them equally!

DIRECTOR [*not getting it*] The others? How d'you mean?

1085 STEPDAUGHTER People "go wrong." And wrong follows on the heels of wrong. Who is responsible, if not whoever it was who first brought them down? Isn't that always the case? And for me that is him. Even before I was born. Look at him, and see if it isn't so.

DIRECTOR Very good. And if he has so much to feel guilty about, can't you
1090   appreciate how it must weigh him down? So let's at least permit him to act it out.

STEPDAUGHTER And how, may I ask, how could he act out all that "noble" guilt, all those so "moral" torments, if you propose to spare him the horror of one day finding in his arms—after having bade her take off the black
1095   clothes that marked her recent loss—a woman now, and already gone wrong—that little girl, sir, that little girl whom he used to go watch coming out of school?

    [*She says these last words in a voice trembling with emotion. The* MOTHER, *hearing her say this, overcome with uncontrollable anguish, which comes out first in suffocated moans and subsequently bursts out in bitter weeping. The emotion takes hold of everyone. Long pause.*]

STEPDAUGHTER [*as soon as the* MOTHER *gives signs of calming down, somber, determined*] We're just among ourselves now. Still unknown to the public. Tomorrow you will make of us the show you have in mind. You will put
1100   it together in your way. But would you like to really see—our drama? Have it explode—the real thing?

DIRECTOR Of course. Nothing I'd like better. And I'll use as much of it as I possibly can!

STEPDAUGHTER Very well. Have this Mother here go out.

1105 MOTHER [*ceasing to weep, with a loud cry*] No, no! Don't allow this, don't allow it!

DIRECTOR I only want to take a look, ma'am.

MOTHER I can't, I just can't!

DIRECTOR But if it's already happened? Excuse me but I just don't get it.

1110 MOTHER No, no, it's happening now. It's always happening. My torment is not a pretense! I am alive and present—always, in every moment of my torment—it keeps renewing itself, it too is alive and always present. But those two little ones over there—have you heard them speak? They cannot speak, sir, not any more! They still keep clinging to me—to keep my tor-
1115   ment alive and present. For themselves they don't exist, don't exist any longer. And she [*the* STEPDAUGHTER], she just fled, ran away from me, she's lost, lost . . . If I see her before me now, it's for the same reason: to renew the torment, keep it always alive and present forever—the torment I've suffered on her account too—forever!

1120 FATHER [*solemn*] The eternal moment, sir, as I told you. She [*the* STEPDAUGHTER] is here to catch me, fix me, hold me there in the pillory, hanging there forever, hooked, in that single fleeting shameful moment of my life! She cannot give it up. And, actually, sir, *you* cannot spare me.

DIRECTOR   But I didn't say I wouldn't use that. On the contrary, it will be the
1125   nucleus of the whole first act. To the point where she [*the* MOTHER] surprises you.

FATHER   Yes, exactly. Because that is the sentence passed upon me: all our passion which has to culminate in her [*the* MOTHER'S] final cry!

STEPDAUGHTER   It still rings in my ears. It's driven me out of my mind, that
1130   cry!—You can present me as you wish, sir, it doesn't matter. Even dressed. As long as at least my arms—just my arms—are bare. Because it was like this. [*She goes to the* FATHER *and rests her head on his chest.*] I was standing like this with my head on his chest and my arms round his neck like this. Then I saw something throbbing right here on my arm. A vein. Then, as if
1135   it was just this living vein that disgusted me, I jammed my eyes shut, like this, d'you see? and buried my head on his chest. [*Turning to the* MOTHER] Scream, scream, mama! [*Buries her head on the* FATHER'S *chest and with her shoulders raised as if to avoid hearing the scream she adds in a voice stifled with torment.*] Scream as you screamed then!

MOTHER [*rushing forward to part them*]   No! My daughter! My daughter!
1140   [*Having pulled her from him*] Brute! Brute! It's my daughter, don't you see—my daughter!

DIRECTOR [*the outburst having sent him reeling to the footlights, while the Actors show dismay*]   Fine! Splendid! And now: curtain, curtain!

FATHER [*running to him, convulsed*]   Right! Yes! Because that, sir, is how it actually was!

1145   DIRECTOR [*in admiration and conviction*]   Yes, yes, of course! Curtain! Curtain!

[*Hearing this repeated cry of the* DIRECTOR, *the* TECHNICIAN *lets down the curtain, trapping the* DIRECTOR *and the* FATHER *between curtain and footlights.*]

DIRECTOR [*looking up, with raised arms*]   What an idiot! I say Curtain, meaning that's how the act should end, and they let down the actual curtain! [*He lifts a corner of the curtain so he can get back onstage. To the* FATHER] Yes, yes, fine, splendid! Absolutely surefire! Has to end that way. I can
1150   vouch for the first act. [*Goes behind the curtain with the* FATHER.]

[*When the curtain rises we see that the stagehands have struck that first "indication of a set," and have put onstage in its stead a small garden fountain. On one side of the stage, the Actors are sitting in a row, and on the other are the Characters. The* DIRECTOR *is standing in the middle of the stage, in the act of meditating with one hand, fist clenched, on his mouth.*]

DIRECTOR [*shrugging after a short pause*]   Yes, well then, let's get to the second act. Just leave it to me as we agreed beforehand and everything will be all right.

STEPDAUGHTER   Our entrance into his house [*the* FATHER] in spite of him [*the* SON].

1155   DIRECTOR [*losing patience*]   Very well. But leave it all to me, I say.

STEPDAUGHTER   In spite of him. Just let that be clear.

MOTHER [*shaking her head from her corner*]   For all the good that's come out of it . . .

STEPDAUGHTER [*turning quickly on her*]   It doesn't matter. The more damage
1160   to us, the more guilt feelings for him.

DIRECTOR [*still out of patience*]   I understand, I understand. All this will be
taken into account, especially at the beginning. Rest assured.

MOTHER [*supplicatingly*]   Do make them understand, I beg you, sir, for my
conscience' sake, for I tried in every possible way—

1165   STEPDAUGHTER [*continuing her* MOTHER's *speech, contemptuously*]   To placate
me, to advise me not to give him trouble. [*To the* DIRECTOR] Do what she
wants, do it because it's true. I enjoy the whole thing very much because,
look: the more she plays the suppliant and tries to gain entrance into his
heart, the more he holds himself aloof: he's an absentee! How I relish this!

1170   DIRECTOR   We want to get going—on the second act, don't we?

STEPDAUGHTER   I won't say another word. But to play it all in the garden, as
you want to, won't be possible.

DIRECTOR   Why won't it be possible?

STEPDAUGHTER   Because he [*the* SON] stays shut up in his room, on his own.
1175   Then again we need the house for the part about this poor bewildered little
boy, as I told you.

DIRECTOR   Quite right. But on the other hand, we can't change the scenery
in view of the audience three or four times in one act, nor can we stick up
signs—

1180   LEADING MAN   They used to at one time . . .

DIRECTOR   Yes, when the audiences were about as mature as that little girl.

LEADING LADY   They got the illusion more easily.

FATHER [*suddenly, rising*]   The illusion, please don't say illusion! Don't use
that word! It's especially cruel to us.

1185   DIRECTOR [*astonished*]   And why, if I may ask?

FATHER   Oh yes, cruel, cruel! You should understand that.

DIRECTOR   What word would you have us use anyway? The illusion of creating here for our spectators—

LEADING MAN   —By our performance—

1190   DIRECTOR   —the illusion of a reality.

FATHER   I understand, sir, but perhaps you do not understand us. Because,
you see, for you and for your actors all this—quite rightly—is a game—

LEADING LADY [*indignantly interrupting*]   Game! We are not children, sir. We
act in earnest.

1195   FATHER   I don't deny it. I just mean the game of your art which, as this gentleman rightly says, must provide a perfect illusion of reality.

DIRECTOR   Yes, exactly.

FATHER   But consider this. We [*He quickly indicates himself and the other
five Characters.*], we have no reality outside this illusion.

DIRECTOR [*astonished, looking at his Actors who remain bewildered and lost*]
1200   And that means?

FATHER [*after observing them briefly, with a pale smile*]   Just that, ladies and
gentlemen. How should we have any other reality? What for you is an illusion, to be created, is for us our unique reality. [*Short pause. He takes several short steps toward the* DIRECTOR, *and adds*] But not for us alone, of
1205   course. Think a moment. [*He looks into his eyes.*] Can you tell me who you
are? [*And he stands there pointing his first finger at him.*]

DIRECTOR [*upset, with a half-smile*]   How do you mean, who I am? I am I.

FATHER   And if I told you that wasn't true because you are me?

DIRECTOR   I would reply that you are out of your mind. [*The Actors laugh.*]

1210 FATHER   You are right to laugh: because this is a game. [*To the* DIRECTOR] And you can object that it's only in a game that that gentleman there [LEADING MAN], who is himself, must be me, who am *myself*. I've caught you in a trap, do you see that?

[*Actors start laughing again.*]

DIRECTOR [*annoyed*]   You said all this before. Why repeat it?

1215 FATHER   I won't—I didn't intend to say that. I'm inviting you to emerge from this game. [*He looks at the* LEADING LADY *as if to forestall what she might say.*] This game of art which you are accustomed to play here with your actors. Let me again ask quite seriously: Who are you?

DIRECTOR [*turning to the Actors, amazed and at the same time irritated*]   The
1220 gall of this fellow! Calls himself a character and comes here to ask me who I am!

FATHER [*dignified, but not haughty*]   A character, sir, can always ask a man who he is. Because a character really has his own life, marked with his own characteristics, by virtue of which he is always someone. Whereas, a man—
1225 I'm not speaking of you now—a man can be no one.

DIRECTOR   Oh sure. But you are asking me! And I am the manager, understand?

FATHER [*quite softly with mellifluous modesty*]   Only in order to know, sir, if you as you now are see yourself . . . for example, at a distance in time. Do you see
1230 the man you once were, with all the illusions you had then, with everything, inside you and outside, as it seemed then—as it was then for you?—Well sir, thinking back to those illusions which you don't have any more, to all those things which no longer seem to be what at one time they were for you, don't you feel, not just the boards of this stage, but the very earth beneath slipping
1235 away from you? For will not all that you feel yourself to be now, your whole reality of today, as it is now, inevitably seem an illusion tomorrow?

DIRECTOR [*who has not followed exactly, but has been staggered by the plausibilities of the argument*]   Well, well, what do you want to prove?

FATHER   Oh nothing, sir. I just wanted to make you see that if *we* [*pointing again at himself and the other Characters*] have no reality outside of illu-
1240 sion, it would be well if you should distrust your reality because, though you breathe it and touch it today, it is destined like that of yesterday to stand revealed to you tomorrow as illusion.

DIRECTOR [*deciding to mock him*]   Oh splendid! And you'll be telling me next that you and this play that you have come to perform for me are truer and
1245 more real than I am.

FATHER [*quite seriously*]   There can be no doubt of that, sir.

DIRECTOR   Really?

FATHER   I thought you had understood that from the start.

DIRECTOR   More real than me?

1250 FATHER   If your reality can change overnight . . .

DIRECTOR   Of course it can, it changes all the time, like everyone else's.

FATHER [*with a cry*]   But ours does not, sir. You see, that is the difference. It does not change, it cannot ever change or be otherwise because it is already fixed, it is what is, just that, forever—a terrible thing, sir!—an
1255 immutable reality. You should shudder to come near us.

DIRECTOR [*suddenly struck by a new idea, he steps in front of the* FATHER]
I should like to know, however, when anyone ever saw a character get out
of his part and set about expounding and explicating it, delivering lectures
on it. Can you tell me? I have never seen anything like that.

FATHER   You have never seen it, sir, because authors generally hide the tra-
1260   vail of their creations. When characters are alive and turn up, living, before
their author, all that author does is follow the words and gestures which
they propose to him. He has to want them to be as they themselves want to
be. Woe betide him if he doesn't! When a character is born, he at once
acquires such an independence, even of his own author, that the whole
1265   world can imagine him in innumerable situations other than those the
author thought to place him in. At times he acquires a meaning that the
author never dreamt of giving him.

DIRECTOR   Certainly, I know that.

FATHER   Then why all this astonishment at us? Imagine what a misfortune it
1270   is for a character such as I described to you—given life in the imagination
of an author who then wished to deny him life—and tell me frankly: isn't
such a character, given life and left without life, isn't he right to set about
doing just what we are doing now as we stand here before you, after having
done just the same—for a very long time, believe me—before *him,* trying to
1275   persuade him, trying to push him . . . I would appear before him sometimes, sometimes she [*looks at* STEPDAUGHTER] would go to him, sometimes
that poor mother . . .

STEPDAUGHTER [*coming forward as if in a trance*]   It's true. I too went there,
sir, to tempt him, many times, in the melancholy of that study of his, at the
1280   twilight hour, when he would sit stretched out in his armchair, unable to
make up his mind to switch the light on, and letting the evening shadows
invade the room, knowing that these shadows were alive with us and that
we were coming to tempt him . . . [*As if she saw herself still in that study
and felt only annoyance at the presence of all of these* Actors] Oh, if only you
1285   would all go away! Leave us alone! My mother there with her son—I with
this little girl—the boy there always alone—then I with him [*the* FATHER]—
then I by myself, I by myself . . . in those shadows. [*Suddenly she jumps up
as if she wished to take hold of herself in the vision she has of herself lighting
up the shadows and alive.*] Ah, my life! What scenes, what scenes we went
there to propose to him: I, I tempted him more than the others.

1290 FATHER   Right, but perhaps that was the trouble: you insisted too much. You
thought you could seduce him.

STEPDAUGHTER   Nonsense. He wanted me that way. [*She comes up to the*
DIRECTOR *to tell him as in confidence.*] If you ask me, sir, it was because he
was so depressed, or because he despised the theater the public knows and
1295   wants . . .

DIRECTOR   Let's continue. Let's continue, for heaven's sake. Enough theories, I'd like some facts. Give me some facts.

STEPDAUGHTER   It seems to me that we have already given you more facts
than you can handle—with our entry into his [*the* FATHER's] house! You said
1300   you couldn't change the scene every five minutes or start hanging signs.

DIRECTOR   Nor can we, of course not, we have to combine the scenes and
group them in one simultaneous close-knit action. Not your idea at all.
You'd like to see your brother come home from school and wander through

the house like a ghost, hiding behind the doors, and brooding on a plan
1305   which—how did you put it—?

STEPDAUGHTER   —shrivels him up, sir, completely shrivels him up, sir.

DIRECTOR   "Shrivels!" What a word! All right then: his growth was stunted
except for his eyes. Is that what you said?

STEPDAUGHTER   Yes, sir. Just look at him. [*She points him out next to the*
MOTHER.]

1310   DIRECTOR   Good girl. And then at the same time you want this little girl to be
playing in the garden, dead to the world. Now, the boy in the house, the girl
in the garden, is that possible?

STEPDAUGHTER   Happy in the sunshine! Yes, that is my only reward, her pleasure, her joy in that garden! After the misery, the squalor of a horrible room
1315   where we slept, all four of us, she with me: just think, of the horror of my
contaminated body next to hers! She held me tight, oh so tight with her
loving innocent little arms! In the garden she would run and take my hand
as soon as she saw me. She did not see the big flowers, she ran around
looking for the teeny ones and wanted to show them to me, oh the joy of it!

[*Saying this and tortured by the memory she breaks into prolonged desperate sobbing, dropping her head onto her arms which are spread out on
the work table. Everyone is overcome by her emotion. The* DIRECTOR *goes
to her almost paternally and says to comfort her*]

1320   DIRECTOR   We'll do the garden. We'll do the garden, don't worry, and you'll
be very happy about it. We'll bring all the scenes together in the garden.
[*Calling a* STAGEHAND *by name*] Hey, drop me a couple of trees, will you,
two small cypress trees, here in front of the fountain.

[*Two small cypress trees are seen descending from the flies.*[5] *A* STAGEHAND
runs on to secure them with nails and a couple of braces.]

DIRECTOR [*to the* STEPDAUGHTER]   Something to go on with anyway. Gives us
1325   an idea. [*Again calling the* STAGEHAND *by name*] Hey, give me a bit of sky.

STAGEHAND [*from above*]   What?

DIRECTOR   Bit of sky, a backcloth, to go behind that fountain. [*A white backdrop is seen descending from the flies.*] Not white, I said sky. It doesn't matter, leave it, I'll take care of it. [*Shouting*] Hey, Electrician, put these lights
1330   out. Let's have a bit of atmosphere, lunar atmosphere, blue background,
and give me a blue spot on that backcloth. That's right. That's enough. [*At
his command a mysterious lunar scene is created which induces the Actors to
talk and move as they would on an evening in the garden beneath the moon.*]
[*To* STEPDAUGHTER] You see? And now instead of hiding behind doors in the
house the boy could move around here in the garden and hide behind
trees. But it will be difficult, you know, to find a little girl to play the scene
1335   where she shows you the flowers. [*Turning to the* BOY] Come down this way
a bit. Let's see how this can be worked out. [*And when the* BOY *doesn't
move*] Come on, come on. [*Then dragging him forward he tries to make him
hold his head up but it falls down again every time.*] Oh dear, another problem, this boy . . . What *is* it? . . . My God, he'll have to say something . . .
[*He goes up to him, puts a hand on his shoulder and leads him behind one of
1340   the tree drops.*] Come on. Come on. Let me see. You can hide a bit here . . .
Like this . . . You can stick your head out a bit to look . . . [*He goes to one*

5. The space over the stage from which scenery and equipment can be lowered.

side to see the effect. The BOY *has scarcely run through the actions when the Actors are deeply affected; and they remain quite overwhelmed.*] Ah! Fine! Splendid! [*He turns again to the* STEPDAUGHTER.] If the little girl surprises him looking out and runs over to him, don't you think she might drag a few 1345 words out of him too?

STEPDAUGHTER [*jumping to her feet*] Don't expect him to speak while *he's* here. [*She points to the* SON.] You have to send *him* away first.

SON [*going resolutely toward one of the two stairways*] Suits me. Glad to go. Nothing I want more.

1350 DIRECTOR [*immediately calling him*] No. Where are you going? Wait.

[*The* MOTHER *rises, deeply moved, in anguish at the thought that he is really going. She instinctively raises her arms as if to halt him, yet without moving away from her position.*]

SON [*arriving at the footlights, where the* DIRECTOR *stops him*] I have absolutely nothing to do here. So let me go please. Just let me go.

DIRECTOR How do you mean, you have nothing to do?

STEPDAUGHTER [*placidly, with irony*] Don't hold him! He won't go.

1355 FATHER He has to play the terrible scene in the garden with his mother.

SON [*unhesitating, resolute, proud*] I play nothing. I said so from the start. [*To the* DIRECTOR] Let me go.

STEPDAUGHTER [*running to the* DIRECTOR *to get him to lower his arms so that he is no longer holding the* SON *back*] Let him go. [*Then turning to the* SON *as soon as the* DIRECTOR *has let him go*] Very well, go. [*The* SON *is all set to move toward the stairs but, as if held by some occult power, he cannot go down the steps. While the Actors are both astounded and deeply troubled, he moves slowly across the footlights straight to the other stairway. But having arrived there he remains poised for the descent but unable to descend. The* STEP-DAUGHTER, *who has followed him with her eyes in an attitude of defiance,* 1360 *bursts out laughing.*] He can't, you see. He can't. He has to stay here, has to. Bound by a chain, indissolubly. But if I who do take flight, sir, when that happens which has to happen, and precisely because of the hatred I feel for him, precisely so as not to see him again—very well, if *I* am still here and can bear the sight of him and his company—you can imagine 1365 whether *he* can go away. He who really must, must remain here with that fine father of his and that mother there who no longer has any other children. [*Turning again to the* MOTHER] Come on, Mother, come on. [*Turning again to the* DIRECTOR *and pointing to the* MOTHER] Look, she got up to hold him back. [*To the* MOTHER, *as if exerting a magical power over her*] Come. 1370 Come . . . [*Then to the* DIRECTOR] You can imagine how little she wants to display her love in front of your actors. But so great is her desire to get at him that—look, you see—she is even prepared to live her scene.

[*In fact the* MOTHER *has approached and no sooner has the* STEPDAUGHTER *spoken her last words than she spreads her arms to signify consent.*]

SON [*without pause*] But *I* am not, *I* am not. If I cannot go I will stay here, but I repeat: I will play nothing.

1375 FATHER [*to the* DIRECTOR, *enraged*] You can force him, sir.

SON No one can force me.

FATHER I will force you.

STEPDAUGHTER Wait, wait. First the little girl must be at the fountain. [*She runs to take the* LITTLE GIRL, *drops on her knees in front of her, takes her*

little face in her hands.] My poor little darling, you look bewildered with
1380   those lovely big eyes of yours. Who knows where you think you are? We are
on a stage my dear. What is a stage? It is a place where you play at being
serious, a place for playacting, where we will now playact. But seriously!
For real! You too . . . [*She embraces her, presses her to her bosom, and rocks
her a little.*] Oh, little darling, little darling, what an ugly play you will
1385   enact! What a horrible thing has been planned for you, the garden, the
fountain . . . All pretense, of course, that's the trouble, my sweet, everything is make-believe here, but perhaps for you, my child, a make-believe
fountain is nicer than a real one for playing in, hmm? It will be a game for
the others, but not for you, alas, because you are real, my darling, and are
1390   actually playing in a fountain that is real, beautiful, big, green with many
bamboo plants reflected in it and giving it shade. Many, many ducklings
can swim in it, breaking the shade to bits. You want to take hold of one of
these ducklings . . . [*With a shout that fills everyone with dismay*] No! No,
my Rosetta! Your mother is not looking after you because of that beast of a
1395   son. A thousand devils are loose in my head . . . and *he* . . . [*She leaves the
LITTLE GIRL and turns with her usual hostility to the BOY.*] And what are you
doing here, always looking like a beggar child? It will be your fault too if
this little girl drowns—with all your standing around like that. As if I hadn't
paid for everybody when I got you all into this house. [*Grabbing one of his
1400   arms to force him to take a hand out of his pocket*] What have you got there?
What are you hiding? Let's see this hand. [*Tears his hand out of his pocket,
and to the horror of everyone discovers that it holds a small revolver. She
looks at it for a moment as if satisfied and then says*] Ah! Where did you get
that and how? [*And as the BOY in his confusion, with his eyes staring and
vacant all the time, does not answer her*] Idiot, if I were you I wouldn't have
1405   killed myself, I would have killed one of those two—or both of them—the
father and the son! [*She hides him behind the small cypress tree from which
he had been looking out, and she takes the LITTLE GIRL and hides her in the
fountain, having her lie down in it in such a way as to be quite hidden.
Finally, the STEPDAUGHTER goes down on her knees with her face in her
hands, which are resting on the rim of the fountain.*]

DIRECTOR   Splendid! [*Turning to the SON*] And at the same time . . .

SON [*with contempt*]   And at the same time, nothing. It is not true, sir. There
was never any scene between me and her. [*He points to the MOTHER.*] Let
1410   her tell you herself how it was.

> [*Meanwhile the SECOND ACTRESS and the JUVENILE LEAD have detached
> themselves from the group of Actors. The former has started to observe
> the MOTHER, who is opposite her, very closely. And the other has started
> to observe the SON. Both are planning how they will re-create the
> roles.*]

MOTHER   Yes, it is true, sir. I had gone to his room.

SON   My room, did you hear that? Not the garden.

DIRECTOR   That is of no importance. We have to rearrange the action, I told
you that.

1415   SON [*noticing that the JUVENILE LEAD is observing him*]   What do *you* want?

JUVENILE LEAD   Nothing. I am observing you.

SON [*turning to the other side where the SECOND ACTRESS is*]   Ah, and here we
have you to re-create the role, eh? [*He points to the MOTHER.*]

DIRECTOR   Exactly, exactly. You should be grateful, it seems to me, for the
1420   attention they are giving you.

SON   Oh yes, thank you. But you still haven't understood that you cannot do
this drama. We are not inside you, not in the least, and your actors are
looking at us from the outside. Do you think it's possible for us to live
before a mirror which, not content to freeze us in the fixed image it pro-
1425   vides of our expression, also throws back at us an unrecognizable grimace
purporting to be ourselves?

FATHER   That is true. That is true. You must see that.

DIRECTOR   [*to the* JUVENILE LEAD *and the* SECOND ACTRESS]   Very well, get
away from here.

1430   SON   No good. I won't cooperate.

DIRECTOR   Just be quiet a minute and let me hear your mother. [*To the*
MOTHER]   Well? You went into his room?

MOTHER   Yes sir, into his room. I was at the end of my tether. I wanted to
pour out all of the anguish which was oppressing me. But as soon as he
1435   saw me come in—

SON   —There was no scene. I went away. I went away so there would be no
scene. Because I have never made scenes, never, understand?

MOTHER   That's true. That's how it was. Yes.

DIRECTOR   But now there's got to be a scene between you and him. It is
1440   indispensable.

MOTHER   As for me, sir, I am ready. If only you could find some way to have
me speak to him for one moment, to have me say what is in my heart.

FATHER   [*going right up to the* SON, *very violent*]   You will do it! For your
mother! For your mother!

1445   SON   [*more decisively than ever*]   I will do nothing!

FATHER   [*grabbing him by the chest and shaking him*]   By God, you will obey!
Can't you hear how she is talking to you? Aren't you her son?

SON   [*grabbing his* FATHER]   No! No! Once and for all let's have done with it!

[*General agitation. The* MOTHER, *terrified, tries to get between them to
separate them.*]

MOTHER   [*as before*]   Please, please!

1450   FATHER   [*without letting go of the* SON]   You must obey, you must obey!

SON   [*wrestling with his* FATHER *and in the end throwing him to the ground
beside the little stairway, to the horror of everyone*]   What's this frenzy that's
taken hold of you? To show your shame and ours to everyone? Have you no
restraint? I won't cooperate, I won't cooperate! And that is how I interpret
the wishes of the man who did not choose to put us onstage.

1455   DIRECTOR   But you came here.

SON   [*pointing to his* FATHER]   He came here—not me!

DIRECTOR   But aren't you here too?

SON   It was he who wanted to come, dragging the rest of us with him, and
then getting together with you to plot not only what really happened, but
1460   also—as if that did not suffice—*what did not happen.*

DIRECTOR   Then tell me. Tell me what did happen. Just tell me. You came out
of your room without saying a thing?

SON   [*after a moment of hesitation*]   Without saying a thing. In order not to
make a scene.

1465   DIRECTOR   [*driving him on*]   Very well, and then, what did you do then?

SON [*while everyone looks on in anguished attention, he moves a few steps on the front part of the stage*]   Nothing . . . crossing the garden . . . [*He stops, gloomy, withdrawn.*]

DIRECTOR [*always driving him on to speak, impressed by his reticence*]   Very well, crossing the garden?

SON [*desperate, hiding his face with one arm*]   Why do you want to make me
1470 say it, sir? It is horrible.

        [*The* MOTHER *trembles all over, and stifles groans, looking toward the fountain.*]

DIRECTOR [*softly, noticing this look of hers, turning to the* SON, *with growing apprehension*]   The little girl?

SON [*looking out into the auditorium*]   Over there—in the fountain . . .

FATHER [*on the ground, pointing compassionately toward the* MOTHER]   And she followed him, sir.

1475 DIRECTOR [*to the* SON, *anxiously*]   And then you . . .

SON [*slowly, looking straight ahead all the time*]   I ran out. I started to fish her out . . . but all of a sudden I stopped. Behind those trees I saw something that froze me: the boy, the boy was standing there, quite still. There was madness in the eyes. He was looking at his drowned sister in the fountain. [*The* STEPDAUGHTER, *who has been bent over the fountain, hiding the* LITTLE
1480 GIRL, *is sobbing desperately, like an echo from the bottom. Pause.*] I started to approach and then . . .

        [*From behind the trees where the* BOY *has been hiding, a revolver shot rings out.*]

MOTHER [*running up with a tormented shout, accompanied by the* SON *and all the Actors in a general tumult*]   Son! My son! [*And then amid the hubbub and the disconnected shouts of the others*]   Help! Help!

DIRECTOR [*amid the shouting, trying to clear a space while the* BOY *is lifted by his head and feet and carried away behind the backcloth*]   Is he wounded,
1485 is he wounded, really?

        [*Everyone except the* DIRECTOR *and the* FATHER, *who has remained on the ground beside the steps, has disappeared behind the backcloth which has served for a sky, where they can still be heard for a while whispering anxiously. Then from one side and the other of this curtain, the Actors come back onstage.*]

LEADING LADY [*reentering from the right, very much upset*]   He's dead! Poor boy! He's dead! What a terrible thing!

LEADING MAN [*reentering from the left, laughing*]   How do you mean, dead? Fiction, fiction, one doesn't believe such things.

1490 OTHER ACTORS [*on the right*]   Fiction? Reality! Reality! He is dead!

OTHER ACTORS [*on the left*]   No! Fiction! Fiction!

FATHER [*rising, and crying out to them*]   Fiction indeed! Reality, reality, gentlemen, reality! [*Desperate, he too disappears at the back.*]

DIRECTOR [*at the end of his rope*]   Fiction! Reality! To hell with all of you!
1495 Lights, lights, lights! [*At a single stroke the whole stage and auditorium is flooded with very bright light. The* DIRECTOR *breathes again, as if freed from an incubus, and they all look each other in the eyes, bewildered and lost.*] Things like this don't happen to me, they've made me lose a whole day. [*He looks at his watch.*] Go, you can all go. What could we do now anyway? It is too late to pick up the rehearsal where we left off. See you this evening. [*As*

soon as the Actors have gone he talks to the ELECTRICIAN by name.] Hey,
1500   Electrician, lights out. [He has hardly said the words when the theater is
plunged for a moment into complete darkness.] Hey, for God's sake, leave
me at least one light! I like to see where I am going!

[Immediately, from behind the backcloth, as if the wrong switch had
been pulled, a green light comes on which projects the silhouettes, clear-
cut and large, of the Characters, minus the BOY and the LITTLE GIRL.
Seeing the silhouettes, the DIRECTOR, terrified, rushes from the stage. At
the same time the light behind the backcloth goes out and the stage is
again lit in nocturnal blue as before.

Slowly, from the right side of the curtain, the SON comes forward first,
followed by the MOTHER with her arms stretched out toward him; then
from the left side, the FATHER. They stop in the middle of the stage and
stay there as if in a trance. Last of all from the right, the STEPDAUGHTER
comes out and runs toward the two stairways. She stops on the first step,
to look for a moment at the other three, and then breaks into a harsh
laugh before throwing herself down the steps; she runs down the aisle
between the rows of seats; she stops one more time and again laughs,
looking at the three who are still onstage; she disappears from the auditorium, and from the lobby her laughter is still heard. Shortly thereafter the
curtain falls.]

EUGENE O'NEILL

1888–1953

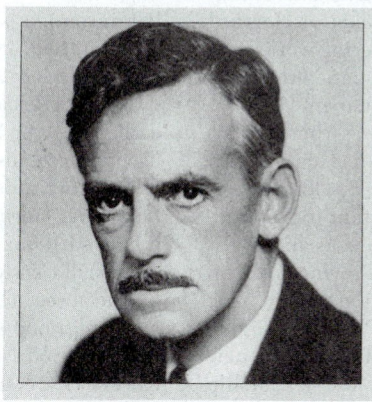

E VER since his breakthrough in the 1920s, Eugene O'Neill has been regarded as the first truly modern playwright of the United States—a status confirmed in 1936, when he became the first American dramatist to receive the Nobel Prize in Literature. O'Neill made full use of the cultural and artistic achievements of modernism. We find in his oeuvre the vernacular voices of working-class characters, typical of naturalism; the exaggerated, shrill voices of expressionism; the eruptions of repressed feelings associated with Freudian psychology; the chorus and masks of ancient tragedy that were being revived in the early twentieth century; and the multiple voices and open structures of modern ensemble pieces that have no main protagonist. In bringing the new experimental dramas of modernism to America, O'Neill drew on a panoply of styles, thereby providing in effect a condensed history of the various stages of modern drama. At the same time, however, O'Neill did more than merely channel artistic and intellectual trends invented elsewhere. He managed to create out of them original plays that capture the forces of the modern world through unusual dramatic structures as well as through deeply felt and often tragic characters. For many, O'Neill remains not only the founder of modern drama in America but also its most distinguished representative.

O'Neill was born into an Irish American family, with a dominating father who was a successful actor and a doting mother from a wealthy family. While his father's career in the theater would prove an important inspiration for the dramatist, it was also a cautionary tale. James O'Neill, born in Ireland and raised in poverty in America, had once been a rising star. Then he was offered the title role in a melodrama that would dominate the rest of his life: *The Count of Monte Cristo* (1846). He bought the rights to the work and played its wrongly accused hero more than 5,000 times, only to find that the role and its endless performances had blunted his talent, bringing him fame and financial rewards but thwarting his true artistic achievement. For much of his youth, Eugene seemed to be rebelling against parental expectations—failing to complete his freshman year at Princeton, working odd jobs, and marrying a respectable young woman, Kathleen Jenkins, against his father's wishes. Leaving behind his wife and infant son, he then went to sea as a crewman on a cargo ship; he spent considerable time on a number of freighters and passenger liners. When he returned to New York, he and his wife divorced, and he began working for the *New London Telegraph*, writing both news stories and occasional verse. Soon thereafter he was diagnosed with a life-threatening case of tuberculosis. During the months he spent at a sanatorium, 1912–13, O'Neill found a new focus: he decided to become a playwright.

His first significant teacher and champion was George Pierce Baker of Harvard University, a pioneer in offering workshop-like courses in modern dramatic literature; O'Neill attended his seminar in 1914–15. Another early supporter was the influential New York theater critic George Jean Nathan, who became O'Neill's close friend. Equally if not more important for his success was a group that formed as an experimental summer theater in Provincetown on Cape Cod and later relocated to New York City. The Provincetown Players, founded in 1915, was devoted to fostering a new American theater; under the leadership of George Cram (Jig) Cook and SUSAN GLASPELL, the group—which had its first New York City season in 1916—helped establish off-Broadway theaters as essential venues for serious drama. One of the plays featured in that first season was O'Neill's *Bound East for Cardiff* (1916); over the next ten years, the Provincetown Players staged many of his plays, some of which later moved to Broadway.

Even during this relatively stable and highly productive period of his life, O'Neill was restless. He had married Agnes Boulton in 1918, and they moved between Provincetown and New York before taking up residence in a series of houses purchased on Cape Cod, in Connecticut, and finally in Bermuda. But in 1927 he left Agnes and their two children for Carlotta Monterey, whom he married in Paris in 1929. After living in France for two years, they returned to the United States, living first in Georgia and then in California. His final decades were marred by declining health as well as by disappointment in and estrangement from his children; his eldest child, Eugene Jr., an alcoholic who failed to live up to his early promise, committed suicide in 1950; his other son, Shane, became a heroin addict; and he disowned his eighteen-year-old daughter, Oona, in 1943, after she married Charlie Chaplin, who was three times her age and was widely reputed to be a womanizer. As early as the mid-1930s O'Neill was showing signs of physical weakness, no doubt exac-

erbated by his lifelong struggles with depression and alcohol; he was too ill to attend his own Nobel Prize ceremony. By 1940, hand tremors were making it difficult for him to hold a pencil—the Parkinson-like shaking was caused by the degenerative neurological disease that ultimately led to his death at the age of sixty-five. He had stopped writing ten years earlier, in 1943. Yet in his last years of work, he produced his finest plays, *The Iceman Cometh* (written 1939; produced 1946) and *Long Day's Journey into Night* (written 1941; produced 1956).

O'Neill's early plays drew extensively on his life at sea. The one-act plays *Bound East for Cardiff* and *The Moon of the Caribbees* (1918), as well as the full-length drama *Anna Christie* (1921), are set on ships, and many of his mature later works also pay homage to the sea. These plays brought O'Neill recognition, and soon he began writing the plays with which he staked his claim to be the first modernist playwright in the United States. An expressionist play, *The Emperor Jones* (1920), is set on an island in the West Indies; it revolves around a megalomaniac ruler, with a plot inspired by Joseph Conrad's modernist story *Heart of Darkness* (1902). Indeed, O'Neill frequently drew on the techniques of novels, as is clear from his long and descriptive stage directions and characterizations. More specifically, in having characters express their secret thoughts through long asides, as he did in *Strange Interlude* (1928), he sought to introduce the new stream-of-consciousness technique of James Joyce and Virginia Woolf to drama. In some plays—such as *The Great God Brown* (1926), whose title character is an architect who ultimately assumes the persona of his rival—O'Neill relied on masks to help reveal characters' innermost thoughts and express hidden conflicts.

Though O'Neill worked with an astonishing range of theatrical styles, he concentrated on modern tragedy, a thrust that culminated in his great late plays. O'Neill owed his tragic worldview in part to his enthusiasm for the writings of Friedrich Nietzsche, who in *The Birth of Tragedy* (1872) advocated a revival of Greek tragedy, a project to which O'Neill remained dedicated throughout his career as a dramatist. Several of his most significant plays are rewritings of specific Greek tragedies; for example, *Desire under the Elms* (1924) transfers the story of the love felt for Hippolytus by his young stepmother, Phaedra, to a New England farm, and O'Neill's magisterial trilogy, *Mourning Becomes Electra* (1931), is a modern version of AESCHYLUS's plays about the house of Atreus.

THE HAIRY APE (1922) is America's quintessential expressionist play. Instead of adhering to a tight dramatic structure, it unfolds in eight disconnected scenes that track the protagonist, an industrial laborer known as Yank, from his job feeding the furnace of a steamship to his disoriented wanderings around New York City. Yank and his fellow laborers speak in various working-class and immigrant dialects, but the play does not seek to paint a naturalistic picture of working-class life in the early twentieth century. Yank's companions and, indeed, all characters act and speak in exaggerated, stylized ways. An heiress and

her chaperone, who provide a striking contrast to the noise and dirt of Yank's engine room, are described, by the playwright, as "artificial figures." Actors playing New York's high society, attending church and window-shopping on Fifth Avenue, are instructed to behave like "a procession of gaudy marionettes." And Yank acts so outlandishly brutish that he is routinely assumed to be barely human and called, beginning in the third scene, a "hairy ape."

In this scene—the play's main turning point—Yank and his world of the engine room are confronted with the world of the upper-class passengers when the young heiress demands to inspect the stokehole. As the daughter of the president of a large Steel Trust, the heiress cannot be refused, and the stewards reluctantly take her down. The encounter between Yank and the heiress, in which the laborer feels addressed as if he were a hairy ape, will forever change his life. Though he is a respected figure in the stokehold, and even

Carlotta Monterey and Louis Wolheim in the original production of O'Neill's *The Hairy Ape* in 1922. Developed by the Provincetown Players, the production later transferred to Broadway. Carlotta would go on to become O'Neill's third wife.

takes a certain pride in his place there, the heiress' reaction to him makes him question his role in life, and he begins to pick fights and finally ends up in a zoo face to face with an actual ape. The play might have followed the consequences of the encounter for the heiress as well, but O'Neill chooses not to do so, focusing the remainder of the play exclusively on Yank's futile search for a place in the world.

As a playwright mostly known for his tragedies, O'Neill has puzzled many readers by giving the play the subtitle: "A Comedy of Ancient and Modern Life." Each element of this title poses a question: Why a comedy? Why modern life? Why ancient life? Let's start with the last. By calling the Yank a "hairy ape," O'Neill wants his audience to think about the origin of the human species and wonder whether Yank is in fact more ape than man. Uneducated, instinctual, speaking in ungrammatical sentences, Yank spends the play trying to make sense of the world and his role within it, without success. Instead he finds himself on a collision with others that invariably ends with physical violence.

And yet, O'Neill has Yank assume the pose of Auguste Rodin's sculpture The Thinker at various moments of the play. There is irony in the contrast between this lowly worker and the pose, but as the play goes on the pose becomes a strangely fitting one. As the sole protagonist of the play, Yank refuses readymade explanations such as those given in the political pamphlets he receives from a labor union. Instead, he tries to think for himself. There is something uncompromising and heroic about this individual quest, even if it fails. The references to Yank as uncivilized, to the notion that his life is taking place in some sort of industrial jungle and that he himself is some sort of primate does not mean that he is at an earlier stage of human development. Rather, we see him engaged in an age-old conflict between the individual and society, an existential search for a proper place. We can see this in Yank's own words, in the phrase that expresses his highest approval: "that belongs."

Returning to the puzzle of the play's subtitle: why modern life? At least for the first few acts, Yank does belong, namely to the new world of mechanized industry, the world of steam engines and steel. While some of his fellow workers wax nostalgic about the lost world of sail ships, Yank fully identifies with the heat and energy, and the unleashing of previously unheard-of forces, that are made possible by modern furnaces. Despite his contempt for foremen and engineers, Yank encourages his workers to work harder. Shoveling coal into the hot furnace makes him feel the power that fuels modern life. It is only after his encounter with the heiress that this identification is broken. In his desperation he wants to blow up the factories owned by her father with dynamite.

Like other expressionist plays, The Hairy Ape takes the measure of modern life by honing in on the first machine age and the concentration of capital during the Gilded Age. The play satirizes the anemic heiress, drained of all vital force and energy, which the Hairy Ape enjoys in abundance (using another industrial metaphor, the heiress calls herself "a waste product in the Bessemer Process," referring to the production of steel that separates out all impure elements). Capitalists are seen as exploiters and upper-class characters as caricatures, but the international labor movement doesn't fare much better. Rather than denounce industrial capitalism as pure exploitation, The Hairy Ape seems to celebrate its power, despite its destructive potential. The play registers what is admirable about the world of steam and steel without offering solutions to the social problems it creates. This refusal to preach any particular political or social solution has allowed the play to endure and remain relevant to this day.

Why call it a comedy? O'Neill, who wrote only one other comedy—Ah Wilderness!, not one of his better-known plays—may have wanted to make sure that The Hairy Ape would not be read as a tragedy of a worker displaced by machines. Additionally, O'Neill may have sensed that the play's fascination with precisely choreographed industrial work processes might allow for physical comedy when enacted on stage, as Charlie Chaplin would do in his film, Modern Times. Finally, the play is premised on incongruous contrasts and misunderstandings, including the final one between Yank and an actual ape, whom Yank addresses like a circus announcer.

This "Comedy of Ancient and Modern Life" has enjoyed a significant afterlife on the stage. The original set was designed by Edmund Jones, the most important experimental designer of his generation, and it has been revived with some regularity since. Its unflinching diagnosis of the sublime yet dehumanizing forces of industrial production has made it of interest to directors and audiences since its premiere almost a hundred years ago. Although the play is eclipsed in popularity by O'Neill's late tragedies such as *Long Day's Journey into Night*, it stands as the pinnacle of O'Neill's experimental phase—and as the high-water mark of American expressionism.   M.P.

The Hairy Ape

CHARACTERS

ROBERT SMITH, "YANK"
PADDY
LONG
MILDRED DOUGLAS
HER AUNT

SECOND ENGINEER
A GUARD
A SECRETARY OF AN ORGANIZATION
STOKERS, LADIES, GENTLEMEN, ETC.

SCENE ONE

[SCENE: *The firemen's forecastle of a transatlantic liner an hour after sailing from New York for the voyage across. Tiers of narrow, steel bunks, three deep, on all sides. An entrance in rear. Benches on the floor before the bunks. The room is crowded with men, shouting, cursing, laughing, singing—a confused, inchoate uproar swelling into a sort of unity, a meaning—the bewildered, furious, baffled defiance of a beast in a cage. Nearly all the men are drunk. Many bottles are passed from hand to hand. All are dressed in dungaree pants, heavy ugly shoes. Some wear singlets, but the majority are stripped to the waist.*

The treatment of this scene, or of any other scene in the play, should by no means be naturalistic. The effect sought after is a cramped space in the bowels of a ship, imprisoned by white steel. The lines of bunks, the uprights supporting them, cross each other like the steel framework of a cage. The ceiling crushes down upon the men's heads. They cannot stand upright. This accentuates the natural stooping posture which shoveling coal and the resultant over-development of back and shoulder muscles have given them. The men themselves should resemble those pictures in which the appearance of Neanderthal Man is guessed at. All are hairy-chested, with long arms of tremendous power, and low, receding brows above their small, fierce, resentful eyes. All the civilized white races are represented, but except for the slight differentiation in color of hair, skin, eyes, all these men are alike.

The curtain rises on a tumult of sound. YANK *is seated in the foreground. He seems broader, fiercer, more truculent, more powerful, more sure of himself than the rest. They respect his superior strength—the grudging respect of fear. Then, too, he represents to them a self-expression, the very last word in what they are, their most highly developed individual.*]

VOICES Gif me trink dere, you!
'Ave a wet!
Salute!
Gesundheit!¹
5 Skoal!²
Drunk as a lord, God stiffen you!
Here's how!
Luck!
Pass back that bottle, damn you!
10 Pourin' it down his neck!
Ho, Froggy! Where the devil have you been?
*La Touraine*³
I hit him smash in yaw, py Gott!⁴
Jenkins—the First—he's a rotten swine—
15 And the coppers nabbed him—and I run—
I like peer better. It don't pig head gif you.
A slut, I'm sayin'! She robbed me aslape—
To hell with 'em all!
You're a bloody liar!
20 Say dot again! [*Commotion. Two men about to fight are pulled apart.*]
No scrappin' now!
Tonight—
See who's the best man!
Bloody Dutchman!
25 Tonight on the for'ard square.
I'll bet on Dutchy.
He packa da wallop, I tella you!
Shut up, Wop!
No fightin', maties. We're all chums, ain't we?
  [*A voice starts bawling a song.*]
30 "Beer, beer, glorious beer!
Fill yourselves right up to here."

YANK [*For the first time seeming to take notice of the uproar about him, turns
around threateningly—in a tone of contemptuous authority*] Choke off dat
noise! Where d'yuh get dat beer stuff? Beer, hell! Beer's for goils—and
Dutchmen. Me for somep'n wit a kick to it! Gimme a drink, one of youse
35 guys. [*Several bottles are eagerly offered. He takes a tremendous gulp of one
of them; then, keeping the bottle in his hand, glares belligerently at the
owner who hastens to acquiesce in this robbery by saying:*] All righto, Yank.
Keep it and have another. [YANK *contemptuously turns his back on the crowd
again. For a second there is an embarrassed silence. Then—*]
VOICES We must be passing the Hook.
She's beginning to roll to it.
40 Six days in hell—and then Southampton.⁵
Py Yesus, I vish somepody take my first vatch for me!

---

1. Health (German).
2. A Norwegian and Swedish toast.
3. A region in France. Here it refers to an
ocean liner of the same name.
4. By God (German).
5. A major port in southern England.

Gittin' seasick, Square-head?
Drink up and forget it!
What's in your bottle?
Gin.
Dot's nigger trink.
Absinthe? It's doped. You'll go off your chump. Froggy!
Cochon![6]
Whisky, that's the ticket!
Where's Paddy?
Going asleep.
Sing us that whisky song, Paddy.

[*They all turn to an old, wizened Irishman who is dozing, very drunk, on the benches forward. His face is extremely monkey-like with all the sad, patient pathos of that animal in his small eyes.*]

Singa da song, Caruso Pat![7]
He's gettin' old. The drink is too much for him.
He's too drunk.

PADDY [*Blinking about him, starts to his feet resentfully, swaying, holding on to the edge of a bunk*] I'm never too drunk to sing. 'Tis only when I'm dead to the world I'd be wishful to sing at all. [*With a sort of sad contempt*] "Whisky Johnny," ye want? A chanty, ye want? Now that's a queer wish from the ugly like of you, God help you. But no mather. [*He starts to sing in a thin, nasal, doleful tone.*]

    Oh, whisky is the life of man!
        Whisky! O Johnny! [*They all join in on this*]
    Oh, whisky is the life of man!
        Whisky for my Johnny! [*Again chorus*]
    Oh, whisky drove my old man mad!
        Whisky! O Johnny!
    Oh, whisky drove my old man mad!
        Whisky for my Johnny!

YANK [*Again turning around scornfully*] Aw hell! Nix on dat old sailing ship stuff! All dat bull's dead, see? And you're dead, too, yuh damned old Harp, on'y yuh don't know it. Take it easy, see. Give us a rest. Nix on de loud noise. [*With a cynical grin*] Can't youse see I'm tryin' to t'ink?

ALL [*Repeating the word after him as one with same cynical amused mockery*] Think! [*The chorused word has a brazen metallic quality as if their throats were phonograph horns. It is followed by a general uproar of hard, barking laughter.*]

VOICES Don't be cracking your head wid ut, Yank.
You gat headache, py yingo![8]
One thing about it—it rhymes with drink!
Ha, ha, ha!
Drink, don't think!
Drink, don't think!
Drink, don't think! [*A whole chorus of voices has taken up this refrain, stamping on the floor, pounding on the benches with fist.*]

6. Pig (French).
7. Enrico Caruso (1873–1921), celebrated   opera singer.
8. By Jingo, a minced oath for "By Jesus."

80 YANK [*Taking a gulp from his bottle—good-naturedly*] Aw right. Can de noise.
I got yuh de foist time. [*The uproar subsides. A very drunken sentimental
tenor begins to sing*]:

> "Far away in Canada,
> Far across the sea,
> There's a lass who fondly waits
85 > Making a home for me——"

YANK [*Fiercely contemptuous*] Shut up, yuh lousey boob![9] Where d'yuh get
dat tripe? Home? Home, hell! I'll make a home for yuh! I'll knock yuh dead.
Home! T'hell wit home! Where d'yuh get dat tripe? Dis is home, see? What
d'yuh want wit home? [*Proudly*] I runned away from mine when I was a kid.
90 On'y too glad to beat it, dat was me. Home was lickings for me, dat's all. But
yuh can bet your shoit no one ain't never licked me since! Wanter try it, any
of youse? Huh! I guess not. [*In a more placated but still contemptuous tone*]
Goils waitin' for yuh, huh? Aw, hell! Dat's all tripe. Dey don't wait for no
one. Dey'd double-cross yuh for a nickel. Dey're all tarts, get me? Treat 'em
95 rough, dat's me. To hell wit 'em. Tarts, dat's what, de whole bunch of 'em.

LONG [*Very drunk, jumps on a bench excitedly, gesticulating with a bottle in his
hand*] Listen 'ere, Comrades! Yank 'ere is right. 'E says this 'ere stinkin'
ship is our 'ome. And 'e says as 'ome is 'ell. And 'e's right! This is 'ell. We
lives in 'ell, Comrades—and right enough we'll die in it. [*Raging*] And who's
100 ter blame, I arsks yer? We ain't. We wasn't born this rotten way. All men is
born free and ekal. That's in the bleedin' Bible, maties. But what d'they
care for the Bible—them lazy, bloated swine what travels first cabin?
Them's the ones. They dragged us down'til we're on'y wage slaves in the
bowels of a bloody ship, sweatin', burnin' up, eatin' coal dust! Hit's them's
ter blame—the damned Capitalist clarss! [*There had been a gradual murmur of contemptuous resentment rising among the men until now he is interrupted by a storm of catcalls, hisses, boos, hard laughter.*]

105 VOICES Turn it off!
Shut up!
Sit down!
Closa da face!
Tamn fool! [*Etc.*]

110 YANK [*Standing up and glaring at* LONG] Sit down before I knock yuh down!
[LONG *makes haste to efface himself.* YANK *goes on contemptuously.*] De Bible,
huh? De Cap'tlist class, huh? Aw nix on dat Salvation Army–Socialist bull. Git
a soapbox! Hire a hall! Come and be saved, huh? Jerk us to Jesus, huh? Aw
g'wan! I've listened to lots of guys like you, see. Yuh're all wrong. Wanter know
115 what I t'ink? Yuh ain't no good for no one. Yuh're de bunk. Yuh ain't got no
noive, get me? Yuh're yellow, dat's what. Yellow, dat's you. Say! What's dem
slobs in de foist cabin got to do wit us? We're better men dan dey are, ain't
we? Sure! One of us guys could clean up de whole mob wit one mit. Put
one of 'em down here for one watch in de stokehole, what'd happen? Dey'd
120 carry him off on a stretcher. Dem boids don't amount to nothin'. Dey're
just baggage. Who makes dis old tub run? Ain't it us guys? Well den, we
belong, don't we? We belong and dey don't. Dat's all. [*A loud chorus of*

---

9. Stupid or foolish person (slang).

approval. YANK *goes on*] As for dis bein' hell—aw, nuts! Yuh lost your noive, dat's what. Dis is a man's job, get me? It belongs. It runs dis tub. No stiffs
125 need apply. But yuh're a stiff, see? Yuh're yellow, dat's you.

    VOICES [*With a great hard pride in them*]   Righto!

             A man's job!

             Talk is cheap, Long.

             He never could hold up his end.

130   Divil take him!

             Yank's right. We make it go.

             Py Gott, Yank say right ting!

             We don't need no one cryin' over us.

             Makin' speeches.

135   Throw him out!

             Yellow!

             Chuck him overboard!

             I'll break his jaw for him! [*They crowd around* LONG *threateningly.*]

YANK [*Half good-natured again—contemptuously*] Aw, take it easy. Leave him
140 alone. He ain't woith a punch. Drink up. Here's how, whoever owns dis. [*He takes a long swallow from his bottle. All drink with him. In a flash all is hilarious amiability again, back-slapping, loud talk, etc.*]

PADDY [*Who has been sitting in a blinking, melancholy daze—suddenly cries out in a voice full of old sorrow*] We belong to this, you're saying? We make the ship to go, you're saying? Yerra[1] then, that Almighty God have pity on us! [*His voice runs into the wail of a keen, he rocks back and forth on his bench. The men stare at him, startled and impressed in spite of themselves.*] Oh, to be back in the fine days of my youth, ochone.[2] Oh, there was
145 fine beautiful ships them days—clippers wid tall masts touching the sky— fine strong men in them—men that was sons of the sea as if 'twas the mother that bore them. Oh, the clean skins of them, and the clear eyes, the straight backs and full chests of them! Brave men they was, and bold men surely! We'd be sailing out, bound down round the Horn maybe. We'd be
150 making sail in the dawn, with a fair breeze, singing a chanty song wid no care to it. And astern the land would be sinking low and dying out, but we'd give it no heed but a laugh, and never a look behind. For the day that was, was enough, for we was free men—and I'm thinking 'tis only slaves do be giving heed to the day that's gone or the day to come—until they're old like
155 me. [*With a sort of religious exaltation*] Oh, to be scudding south again wid the power of the Trade Wind driving her on steady through the nights and the days! Full sail on her! Nights and days! Nights when the foam of the wake would be flaming wid fire, when the sky'd be blazing and winking wid stars. Or the full of the moon maybe. Then you'd see her driving through
160 the gray night, her sails stretching aloft all silver and white, not a sound on the deck, the lot of us dreaming dreams, till you'd believe 'twas no real ship at all you was on but a ghost ship like the *Flying Dutchman*[3] they say does be roaming the seas forevermore widout touching a port. And there was the days, too. A warm sun on the clean decks. Sun warming the blood of you,

---

1. Irish expression signaling a low opinion.
2. Irish expression of woe.
3. Legend of a ghost ship that can never make land.

165 and wind over the miles of shiny green ocean like strong drink to your
lungs. Work—aye, hard work—but who'd mind that at all? Sure, you worked
under the sky and 'twas work wid skill and daring to it. And wid the day
done, in the dog watch, smoking me pipe at ease, the lookout would be raising land maybe, and we'd see the mountains of South Americy wid the red
170 fire of the setting sun painting their white tops and the clouds floating by
them! [*His tone of exaltation ceases. He goes on mournfuly.*] Yerra, what's the
use of talking? 'Tis a dead man's whisper. [*To* YANK *resentfully*] 'Twas them
days men belonged to ships, not now. 'Twas them days a ship was part of the
sea, and a man was part of a ship, and the sea joined all together and made it
175 one. [*Scornfully*] Is it one wid this you'd be, Yank—black smoke from the funnels smudging the sea, smudging the decks—the bloody engines pounding
and throbbing and shaking—wid divil a sight of sun or a breath of clean air—
choking our lungs wid coal dust—breaking our backs and hearts in the hell
of the stokehole—feeding the bloody furnace—feeding our lives along wid
180 the coal, I'm thinking—caged in by steel from a sight of the sky like bloody
apes in the Zoo! [*With a harsh laugh*] Ho-ho, divil mend you! Is it to belong
to that you're wishing? Is it a flesh and blood wheel of the engines you'd be?

YANK [*Who has been listening with a contemptuous sneer, barks out the answer*]
Sure ting! Dat's me. What about it?

PADDY [*As if to himself—with great sorrow*]   Me time is past due. That a great
185 wave wid sun in the heart of it may sweep me over the side sometime I'd be
dreaming of the days that's gone!

YANK   Aw, yuh crazy Mick.[4] [*He springs to his feet and advances on* PADDY
*threateningly—then stops, fighting some queer struggle within himself—lets
his hands fall to his sides—contemptuously.*] Aw, take it easy. Yuh're aw right,
at dat. Yuh're bugs, dat's all—nutty as a cuckoo. All dat tripe yuh been
190 pullin'—Aw, dat's all right. On'y it's dead, get me? Yuh don't belong no
more, see. Yuh don't get de stuff. Yuh're too old. [*Disgustedly*] But aw say,
come up for air onct in a while, can't yuh? See what's happened since yuh
croaked. [*He suddenly bursts forth vehemently, growing more and more
excited.*] Say! Sure! Sure I meant it! What de hell—Say, lemme talk! Hey!
195 Hey, you old Harp![5] Hey, youse guys! Say, listen to me—wait a moment—I
gotta talk, see. I belong and he don't. He's dead but I'm livin'. Listen to me!
Sure I'm part of de engines! Why de hell not! Dey move, don't dey? Dey're
speed, ain't dey? Dey smash trou, don't dey? Twenty-five knots a hour!
Dat's goin' some! Dat's new stuff! Dat belongs! But him, he's too old. He
200 gets dizzy. Say, listen. All dat crazy tripe about nights and days; all dat crazy
tripe about stars and moons; all dat crazy tripe about suns and winds, fresh
air and de rest of it—Aw hell, dat's all a dope dream! Hittin' de pipe of de
past, dat's what he's doin'. He's old and don't belong no more. But me, I'm
young! I'm in de pink! I move wit it! It, get me! I mean de ting dat's de guts
205 of all dis. It ploughs trou all de tripe he's been sayin'. It blows dat up! It
knocks dat dead! It slams dat offen de face of de oith! It, get me! De
engines and de coal and de smoke and all de rest of it! He can't breathe and
swallow coal dust, but I kin, see? Dat's fresh air for me! Dat's food for me!
I'm new, get me? Hell in de stokehole? Sure! It takes a man to work in hell.
210 Hell, sure, dat's my fav'rite climate. I eat it up! I git fat on it! It's me makes

---

4. Condescending term for an Irish person.   5. Condescending term for an Irish person.

it hot! It's me makes it roar! It's me makes it move! Sure, on'y for me everyting stops. It all goes dead, get me? De noise and smoke and all de engines
movin' de woild, dey stop. Dere ain't nothin' no more! Dat's what I'm sayin'.
Everyting else dat makes de woild move, somep'n makes it move. It can't
215   move witout somep'n else, see? Den yuh get down to me. I'm at de bottom,
get me! Dere ain't nothin' foither. I'm de end! I'm de start! I start somep'n and
de woild moves! It—dat's me!—de new dat's moiderin' de old! I'm de ting in
coal dat makes it boin; I'm steam and oil for de engines; I'm de ting in noise
dat makes yuh hear it; I'm smoke and express trains and steamers and factory
220   whistles; I'm de ting in gold dat makes money! And I'm what makes iron into
steel! Steel, dat stands for de whole ting! And I'm steel—steel—steel! I'm de
muscles in steel, de punch behind it! [As he says this he pounds with his fist
against the steel bunks. All the men, roused to a pitch of frenzied self-glorification
by his speech, do likewise. There is a deafening metallic roar, through which
YANK's voice can be heard bellowing.] Slaves, hell! We run de whole woiks. All
de rich guys dat tink dey're somep'n, dey ain't nothin'! Dey don't belong. But
225   us guys, we're in de move, we're at de bottom, de whole ting is us! [PADDY from
the start of YANK's speech has been taking one gulp after another from his bottle,
at first frightenedly, as if he were afraid to listen, then desperately, as if to drown
his senses, but finally has achieved complete indifferent, even amused, drunkenness. Yank sees his lips moving. He quells the uproar with a shout.] Hey, youse
guys, take it easy! Wait a moment! De nutty Harp is sayin' somep'n.
PADDY [Is heard now—throws his head back with a mocking burst of laughter]
Ho-ho-ho-ho-ho—
YANK [Drawing back his fist, with a snarl] Aw! Look out who yuh're givin' the
230   bark!
PADDY [Begins to sing the "Miller of Dee" with enormous good nature]:

> "I care for nobody, no, not I,
> And nobody cares for me."

YANK [Good-natured himself in a flash, interrupts PADDY with a slap on the bare back
like a report] Dat's de stuff! Now yuh're gettin' wise to somep'n. Care for
nobody, dat's de dope! To hell wit 'em all! And nix on nobody else carin'. I kin care
235   for myself, get me! [Eight bells sound, muffled, vibrating through the steel walls as
if some enormous brazen gong were imbedded in the heart of the ship. All the men
jump up mechanically, file through the door silently close upon each other's heels
in what is very like a prisoners' lockstep. YANK slaps PADDY on the back.] Our watch,
yuh old Harp! [Mockingly] Come on down in hell. Eat up de coal dust. Drink
in de heat. It's it, see! Act like yuh liked it, yuh better—or croak yuhself.
PADDY [With jovial defiance] To the divil wid it! I'll not report this watch. Let
240   thim log me and be damned. I'm no slave the like of you. I'll be sittin' here
at me ease, and drinking, and thinking, and dreaming dreams.
YANK [Contemptuously] Tinkin' and dreamin', what'll that get yuh? What's
tinkin' got to do wit it? We move, don't we? Speed, ain't it? Fog, dat's all you
stand for. But we drive trou dat, don't we? We split dat up and smash
245   trou—twenty-five knots a hour! [Turns his back on PADDY scornfully] Aw,
yuh make me sick! Yuh don't belong! [He strides out the door in rear. PADDY
hums to himself, blinking drowsily.]

[Curtain]

SCENE TWO

[SCENE: *Two days out. A section of the promenade deck.* MILDRED DOUGLAS *and her aunt are discovered reclining in deck chairs. The former is a girl of twenty, slender, delicate, with a pale, pretty face marred by a self-conscious expression of disdainful superiority. She looks fretful, nervous and discontented, bored by her own anemia. Her aunt is a pompous and proud—and fat—old lady. She is a type even to the point of a double chin and lorgnettes.*[6] *She is dressed pretentiously, as if afraid her face alone would never indicate her position in life.* MILDRED *is dressed all in white.*

The impression to be conveyed by this scene is one of the beautiful, vivid life of the sea all about—sunshine on the deck in a great flood, the fresh sea wind blowing across it. In the midst of this, these two incongruous, artificial figures, inert and disharmonious, the elder like a gray lump of dough touched up with rouge, the younger looking as if the vitality of her stock had been sapped before she was conceived, so that she is the expression not of its life energy but merely of the artificialities that energy had won for itself in the spending.]

MILDRED [*Looking up with affected dreaminess*]   How the black smoke swirls back against the sky! Is it not beautiful?
AUNT [*Without looking up*]   I dislike smoke of any kind.
MILDRED   My great-grandmother smoked a pipe—a clay pipe.
5 AUNT [*Ruffling*]   Vulgar!
MILDRED   She was too distant a relative to be vulgar. Time mellows pipes.
AUNT [*Pretending boredom but irritated*]   Did the sociology you took up at college teach you that—to play the ghoul on every possible occasion, excavating old bones? Why not let your great-grandmother rest in her grave?
10 MILDRED [*Dreamily*]   With her pipe beside her—puffing in Paradise.
AUNT [*With spite*]   Yes, you are a natural born ghoul. You are even getting to look like one, my dear.
MILDRED [*In a passionless tone*]   I detest you, Aunt. [*Looking at her critically*] Do you know what you remind me of? Of a cold pork pudding against a
15 background of linoleum tablecloth in the kitchen of a—but the possibilities are wearisome. [*She closes her eyes.*]
AUNT [*With a bitter laugh*]   Merci[7] for your candor. But since I am and must be your chaperone—in appearance, at least—let us patch up some sort of armed truce. For my part you are quite free to indulge any pose of eccen-
20 tricity that beguiles you—as long as you observe the amenities—
MILDRED [*Drawling*]   The inanities?
AUNT [*Going on as if she hadn't heard*]   After exhausting the morbid thrills of social service work on New York's East Side—how they must have hated you, by the way, the poor that you made so much poorer in their own
25 eyes!—you are now bent on making your slumming international. Well, I hope Whitechapel[8] will provide the needed nerve tonic. Do not ask me to chaperone you there, however. I told your father I would not. I loathe deformity. We will hire an army of detectives and you may investigate everything—they allow you to see.
30 MILDRED [*Protesting with a trace of genuine earnestness*]   Please do not mock at my attempts to discover how the other half lives. Give me credit for some sort of groping sincerity in that at least. I would like to help them. I would like to

---

6. Hand-held spectacles.
7. Thank you (French).
8. A poor district in East London.

be of some use in the world. Is it my fault I don't know how? I would like to
be sincere, to touch life somewhere. [*With weary bitterness*] But I'm afraid I
35 have neither the vitality nor integrity. All that was burnt out in our stock
before I was born. Grandfather's blast furnaces, flaming to the sky, melting
steel, making millions—then father keeping those home fires burning, making more millions—and little me at the tail-end of it all. I'm a waste product
in the Bessemer process[9]—like the millions. Or rather, I inherit the acquired
40 trait of the by-product, wealth, but none of the energy, none of the strength of
the steel that made it. I am sired by gold and damned by it, as they say at the
race track—damned in more ways than one. [*She laughs mirthlessly*].

AUNT [*Unimpressed—superciliously*] You seem to be going in for sincerity
today. It isn't becoming to you, really—except as an obvious pose. Be as
45 artificial as you are, I advise. There's a sort of sincerity in that, you know.
And, after all, you must confess you like that better.

MILDRED [*Again affected and bored*] Yes, I suppose I do. Pardon me for my
outburst. When a leopard complains of its spots, it must sound rather grotesque. [*In a mocking tone*] Purr, little leopard. Purr, scratch, tear, kill,
50 gorge yourself and be happy—only stay in the jungle where your spots are
camouflage. In a cage they make you conspicuous.

AUNT I don't know what you are talking about.

MILDRED It would be rude to talk about anything to you. Let's just talk. [*She
looks at her wrist watch.*] Well, thank goodness, it's about time for them to
55 come for me. That ought to give me a new thrill, Aunt.

AUNT [*Affectedly troubled*] You don't mean to say you're really going? The
dirt—the heat must be frightful—

MILDRED Grandfather started as a puddler.[1] I should have inherited an
immunity to heat that would make a salamander shiver. It will be fun to
60 put it to the test.

AUNT But don't you have to have the captain's—or someone's—permission
to visit the stokehole?

MILDRED [*With a triumphant smile*] I have it—both his and the chief engineer's. Oh, they didn't want to at first, in spite of my social service creden-
65 tials. They didn't seem a bit anxious that I should investigate how the other
half lives and works on a ship. So I had to tell them that my father, the
president of Nazareth Steel, chairman of the board of directors of this line,
had told me it would be all right.

AUNT He didn't.

70 MILDRED How naïve age makes one! But I said he did, Aunt. I even said he
had given me a letter to them—which I had lost. And they were afraid to
take the chance that I might be lying. [*Excitedly*] So it's ho! for the stokehole. The second engineer is to escort me. [*Looking at her watch again*] It's
time. And here he comes, I think.

[*The SECOND ENGINEER enters. He is a husky, fine-looking man of thirty-
five or so. He stops before the two and tips his cap, visibly embarrassed
and ill-at-ease.*]

75 SECOND ENGINEER Miss Douglas?

---

9. Industrial process for making steel that
removes impurities from the iron.

1. Profession of making iron.

MILDRED   Yes. [*Throwing off her rugs and getting to her feet*] Are we all ready to start?

SECOND ENGINEER   In just a second, ma'am. I'm waiting for the Fourth. He's coming along.

MILDRED [*With a scornful smile*]   You don't care to shoulder this responsibil-
80   ity alone, is that it?

SECOND ENGINEER [*Forcing a smile*]   Two are better than one. [*Disturbed by her eyes, glances out to sea—blurts out*] A fine day we're having.

MILDRED   Is it?

SECOND ENGINEER   A nice warm breeze—

85   MILDRED   It feels cold to me.

SECOND ENGINEER   But it's hot enough in the sun—

MILDRED   Not hot enough for me. I don't like Nature. I was never athletic.

SECOND ENGINEER [*Forcing a smile*]   Well, you'll find it hot enough where you're going.

90   MILDRED   Do you mean hell?

SECOND ENGINEER [*Flabbergasted, decides to laugh*]   Ho-ho! No, I mean the stokehole.

MILDRED   My grandfather was a puddler. He played with boiling steel.

SECOND ENGINEER [*All at sea—uneasily*]   Is that so? Hum, you'll excuse me,
95   ma'am, but are you intending to wear that dress?

MILDRED   Why not?

SECOND ENGINEER   You'll likely rub against oil and dirt. It can't be helped.

MILDRED   It doesn't matter. I have lots of white dresses.

SECOND ENGINEER   I have an old coat you might throw over—

100   MILDRED   I have fifty dresses like this. I will throw this one into the sea when I come back. That ought to wash it clean, don't you think?

SECOND ENGINEER [*Doggedly*]   There's ladders to climb down that are none too clean—and dark alleyways—

MILDRED   I will wear this very dress and none other.

105   SECOND ENGINEER   No offense meant. It's none of my business. I was only warning you—

MILDRED   Warning? That sounds thrilling.

SECOND ENGINEER [*Looking down the deck—with a sigh of relief*]   There's the Fourth now. He's waiting for us. If you'll come—

110   MILDRED   Go on. I'll follow you. [*He goes.* MILDRED *turns a mocking smile on her aunt.*] An oaf—but a handsome, virile oaf.

AUNT [*Scornfully*]   Poser!

MILDRED   Take care. He said there were dark alleyways—

AUNT [*In the same tone*]   Poser!

115   MILDRED [*Biting her lips angrily*]   You are right. But would that my millions were not so anemically chaste!

AUNT   Yes, for a fresh pose I have no doubt you would drag the name of Douglas in the gutter!

MILDRED   From which it sprang. Good-by, Aunt. Don't pray too hard that I
120   may fall into the fiery furnace.

AUNT   Poser!

MILDRED [*Viciously*]   Old hag! [*She slaps her aunt insultingly across the face and walks off, laughing gaily.*]

AUNT [*Screams after her*]   I said poser!

[*Curtain*]

SCENE THREE

[SCENE: *The stokehole. In the rear, the dimly outlined bulks of the furnaces and boilers. High overhead one hanging electric bulb sheds just enough light through the murky air laden with coal dust to pile up masses of shadows everywhere. A line of men, stripped to the waist, is before the furnace doors. They bend over, looking neither to right nor left, handling their shovels as if they were part of their bodies, with a strange, awkward, swinging rhythm. They use the shovels to throw open the furnace doors. Then from these fiery round holes in the black a flood of terrific light and heat pours full upon the men who are outlined in silhouette in the crouching, inhuman attitudes of chained gorillas. The men shovel with a rhythmic motion, swinging as on a pivot from the coal which lies in heaps on the floor behind to hurl it into the flaming mouths before them. There is a tumult of noise—the brazen clang of the furnace doors as they are flung open or slammed shut, the grating, teeth-gritting grind of steel against steel, of crunching coal. This clash of sounds stuns one's ears with its rending dissonance. But there is order in it, rhythm, a mechanical regulated recurrence, a tempo. And rising above all, making the air hum with the quiver of liberated energy, the roar of leaping flames in the furnaces, the monotonous throbbing beat of the engines.*

As the curtain rises, the furnace doors are shut. The men are taking a breathing spell. One or two are arranging the coal behind them, pulling it into more accessible heaps. The others can be dimly made out leaning on their shovels in relaxed attitudes of exhaustion.]

PADDY [*From somewhere in the line—plaintively*] Yerra, will this divil's own watch nivir end? Me back is broke. I'm destroyed entirely.

YANK [*From the center of the line—with exuberant scorn*] Aw, yuh make me sick! Lie down and croak, why don't yuh? Always beefin', dat's you! Say, dis

5   is a cinch!² Dis was made for me! It's my meat, get me! [*A whistle is blown—a thin, shrill note from somewhere overhead in the darkness.* YANK *curses without resentment*] Dere's de damn engineer crackin' de whip. He tinks we're loafin'.

PADDY [*Vindictively*] God stiffen him!

YANK [*In an exultant tone of command*] Come on, youse guys! Git into de

10   game! She's gittin' hungry! Pile some grub in her! Trow it into her belly! Come on now, all of youse! Open her up!

   [*At this last all the men, who have followed his movements of getting into position, throw open their furnace doors with a deafening clang. The fiery light floods over their shoulders as they bend round for the coal. Rivulets of sooty sweat have traced maps on their backs. The enlarged muscles form bunches of high light and shadow.*]

YANK [*Chanting a count as he shovels without seeming effort*] One—two—tree—[*His voice rising exultantly in the joy of battle.*] Dat's de stuff! Let her have it! All togedder now! Sling it into her! Let her ride! Shoot de piece

15   now! Call de toin on her! Drive her into it! Feel her move! Watch her smoke! Speed, dat's her middle name! Give her coal, youse guys! Coal, dat's her booze! Drink it up, baby! Let's see yuh sprint! Dig in and gain a lap! Dere she go-o-es.

   [*This last in the chanting formula of the gallery gods at the six-day bike race.³ He slams his furnace door shut. The others do likewise with as*

2. An easy task (slang).

3. Gallery gods are the occupants of the highest and cheapest seats in a theater, or arena in this case. Six-day bike races were a popular endurance sport in the late nineteenth and early twentieth centuries.

much unison as their wearied bodies will permit. The effect is of one fiery eye after another being blotted out with a series of accompanying bangs.]

PADDY [*Groaning*]   Me back is broke. I'm bate out[3]—bate—

[*There is a pause. Then the inexorable whistle sounds again from the dim regions above the electric light. There is a growl of cursing rage from all sides.*]

20   YANK [*Shaking his fist upward—contemptuously*]   Take it easy dere, you! Who d'yuh tinks runnin' dis game, me or you? When I git ready, we move. Not before! When I git ready, get me!

VOICES [*Approvingly*]   That's the stuff!

Yank tal him, py golly!

25   Yank ain't affeerd.

Goot poy, Yank!

Give him hell!

Tell 'im 'e's a bloody swine!

Bloody slave-driver!

30   YANK [*Contemptuously*]   He ain't got no noive. He's yellow, get me? All de engineers is yellow. Dey got streaks a mile wide. Aw, to hell wit him! Let's move, youse guys. We had a rest. Come on, she needs it! Give her pep! It ain't for him. Him and his whistle, dey don't belong. But we belong, see! We gotter feed de baby! Come on!

[*He turns and flings his furnace door open. They all follow his lead. At this instant the* SECOND *and* FOURTH ENGINEERS *enter from the darkness on the left with* MILDRED *between them. She starts, turns paler, her pose is crumbling, she shivers with fright in spite of the blazing heat, but forces herself to leave the* ENGINEERS *and take a few steps near the men. She is right behind* YANK. *All this happens quickly while the men have their backs turned.*]

35   YANK   Come on, youse guys!

[*He is turning to get coal when the whistle sounds again in a peremptory, irritating note. This drives* YANK *into a sudden fury. While the other men have turned full around and stopped dumbfounded by the spectacle of* MILDRED *standing there in her white dress,* YANK *does not turn far enough to see her. Besides, his head is thrown back, he blinks upward through the murk trying to find the owner of the whistle, he brandishes his shovel murderously over his head in one hand, pounding on his chest, gorilla-like, with the other, shouting.*]

Toin off dat whistle! Come down outa dere, yuh yellow, brass-buttoned, Belfast bum, yuh! Come down and I'll knock yer brains out! Yuh lousy, stinkin', yellow mut of a Catholic-moiderin' bastard! Come down and I'll moider yuh! Pullin' dat whistle on me, huh? I'll show yuh! I'll crash yer 40   skull in! I'll drive yer teet' down yer troat! I'll slam yer nose trou de back of yer head! I'll cut yer guts out for a nickel, yuh lousy boob, yuh dirty, crummy, muck-eatin' son of a—

[*Suddenly he becomes conscious of all the other men staring at something directly behind his back. He whirls defensively with a snarling, murderous growl, crouching to spring, his lips drawn back over his teeth, his small eyes gleaming ferociously. He sees* MILDRED, *like a white apparition*

---

3. Tired (Irish slang).

in the full light from the open furnace doors. He glares into her eyes, turned to stone. As for her, during his speech she has listened, paralyzed with horror, terror, her whole personality crushed, beaten in, collapsed, by the terrific impact of this unknown, abysmal brutality, naked and shameless. As she looks at his gorilla face, as his eyes bore into hers, she utters a low, choking cry and shrinks away from him, putting both hands up before her eyes to shut out the sight of his face, to protect her own. This startles YANK *to a reaction. His mouth falls open, his eyes grow bewildered.*]

MILDRED [*About to faint—to the* ENGINEERS, *who now have her one by each arm—whimperingly*]   Take me away! Oh, the filthy beast!

[*She faints. They carry her quickly back, disappearing in the darkness at the left, rear. An iron door clangs shut. Rage and bewildered fury rush back on* YANK. *He feels himself insulted in some unknown fashion in the very heart of his pride. He roars.*]

God damn yuh! [*And hurls his shovel after them at the door which has just closed. It hits the steel bulkhead with a clang and falls clattering on the steel floor. From overhead the whistle sounds again in a long, angry, insistent command.*]

[*Curtain*]

SCENE FOUR

[SCENE: *The firemen's forecastle.* YANK's *watch has just come off duty and had dinner. Their faces and bodies shine from a soap and water scrubbing but around their eyes, where a hasty dousing does not touch, the coal dust sticks like black make-up, giving them a queer, sinister expression.* YANK *has not washed either face or body. He stands out in contrast to them, a blackened, brooding figure. He is seated forward on a bench in the exact attitude of Rodin's "The Thinker."*[4] *The others, most of them smoking pipes, are staring at* YANK, *half-apprehensively, as if fearing an outburst; half-amusedly, as if they saw a joke somewhere that tickled them.*]

VOICES   He ain't ate nothin'.
Py golly, a fallar gat gat to grub in him.
Divil a lie.
Yank feeda da fire, no feeda da face.
5   Ha-ha.
He ain't even washed hisself.
He's forgot.
Hey, Yank, you forgot to wash.

YANK [*Sullenly*]   Forgot nothin'! To hell wit washin'.

10 VOICES   It'll stick to you.
It'll get under your skin.
Give yer the bleedin' itch, that's wot.
It makes spots on you—like a leopard.
Like a piebald nigger, you mean.
15   Better wash up, Yank.
You sleep better.
Wash up, Yank.
Wash up! Wash up!

4. A sculpture by Auguste Rodin showing a muscular, naked man in the pose of a thinker.

YANK [*Resentfully*] Aw say, youse guys. Lemme alone. Can't youse see I'm
20   tryin' to tink?

ALL [*Repeating the word after him as one with cynical mockery*] Think! [*The
    word has a brazen, metallic quality as if their throats were phonograph horns.
    It is followed by a chorus of hard, barking laughter.*]

YANK [*Springing to his feet and glaring at them belligerently*] Yes, tink! Tink,
    dat's what I said! What about it?

        [*They are silent, puzzled by his sudden resentment at what used to be one
        of his jokes.* YANK *sits down again in the same attitude of "The Thinker."*]

VOICES Leave him alone.
25   He's got a grouch on.
        Why wouldn't he?

PADDY [*With a wink at the others*] Sure I know what's the matther. 'Tis aisy
    to see. He's fallen in love. I'm telling you.

ALL [*Repeating the word after him as one with cynical mockery*] Love! [*The
    word has a brazen, metallic quality as if their throats were phonograph horns.
    It is followed by a chorus of hard, barking laughter.*]

30 YANK [*With a contemptuous snort*] Love, hell! Hate, dat's what. I've fallen in
    hate, get me?

PADDY [*Philosophically*] 'Twould take a wise man to tell one from the other.
    [*With a bitter, ironical scorn, increasing as he goes on*] But I'm telling you
    it's love that's in it. Sure what else but love for us poor bastes in the stoke-
35   hole would be bringing a fine lady, dressed like a white quane, down a mile
    of ladders and steps to be havin' a look at us? [*A growl of anger goes up from
    all sides.*]

LONG [*Jumping on a bench—hectically*] Hinsultin' us! Hinsultin' us, the
    bloody cow! And them bloody engineers! What right 'as they got to be
    exhibitin' us 's if we was bleedin' monkeys in a menagerie? Did we sign for
40   hinsults to our dignity as 'onest workers? Is that in the ship's articles? You
    kin bloody well bet it ain't! But I knows why they done it. I arsked a deck
    steward 'o she was and 'e told me. 'Er old man's a bleedin' millionaire, a
    bloody Capitalist! 'E's got enuf bloody gold to sink this bleedin' ship! 'E
    makes arf the bloody steel in the world! 'E owns this bloody boat! And you
45   and me, comrades, we're 'is slaves! And the skipper and mates and engi-
    neers, they're 'is slaves! And she's 'is bloody daughter and we're all 'er
    slaves, too! And she gives 'er orders as 'ow she wants to see the bloody ani-
    mals below decks and down they takes 'er! [*There is a roar of rage from all
    sides.*]

YANK [*Blinking at him bewilderedly*] Say! Wait a moment! Is all dat straight
50   goods?

LONG Straight as string! The bleedin' steward as waits on 'em, 'e told me
    about 'er. And what're we goin' ter do, I arsks yer? 'Ave we got ter swaller 'er
    hinsults like dogs? It ain't in the ship's articles. I tell yer we got a case. We
    kin go ter law—

55 YANK [*With abysmal contempt*] Hell! Law!

ALL [*Repeating the word after him as one with cynical mockery*] Law! [*The
    word has a brazen metallic quality as if their throats were phonograph horns.
    It is followed by a chorus of hard, barking laughter.*]

LONG [*Feeling the ground slipping from under his feet—desperately*] As vot-
    ers and citizens we kin force the bloody governments—

YANK [*With abysmal contempt*]   Hell! Governments!

60 ALL [*Repeating the word after him as one with cynical mockery*]   Governments! [*The word has a brazen metallic quality as if their throats were phonograph horns. It is followed by a chorus of hard, barking laughter.*]

LONG [*Hysterically*]   We're free and equal in the sight of God—

YANK [*With abysmal contempt*]   Hell! God!

ALL [*Repeating the word after him as one with cynical mockery*]   God! [*The
word has a brazen metallic quality as if their throats were phonograph horns.
It is followed by a chorus of hard, barking laughter.*]

YANK [*Witheringly*]   Aw, join de Salvation Army!

65 ALL   Sit down! Shut up! Damn fool! Sea-lawyer! [LONG *slinks back out of
sight.*]

PADDY [*Continuing the trend of his thoughts as if he had never been interrupted—
bitterly*]   And there she was standing behind us, and the Second pointing
at us like a man you'd hear in a circus would be saying: In this cage is a
queerer kind of baboon than ever you'd find in darkest Africy. We roast
them in their own sweat—and be damned if you won't hear some of thim

70 saying they like it! [*He glances scornfully at* YANK.]

YANK [*With a bewildered uncertain growl*]   Aw!

PADDY   And there was Yank roarin' curses and turning round wid his shovel to
brain her—and she looked at him, and him at her—

YANK [*Slowly*]   She was all white. I tought she was a ghost. Sure.

75 PADDY [*With heavy, biting sarcasm*]   'Twas love at first sight, divil a doubt of
it! If you'd seen the endearin' look on her pale mug when she shriveled
away with her hands over her eyes to shut out the sight of him! Sure, 'twas
as if she'd seen a great hairy ape escaped from the Zoo!

YANK [*Stung—with a growl of rage*]   Aw!

80 PADDY   And the loving way Yank heaved his shovel at the skull of her, only
she was out the door! [*A grin breaking over his face*] 'Twas touching, I'm
telling you! It put the touch of home, swate home in the stokehole. [*There
is a roar of laughter from all.*]

YANK [*Glaring at* PADDY *menacingly*]   Aw, choke dat off, see!

PADDY [*Not heeding him—to the others*]   And her grabbin' at the Second's
85 arm for protection. [*With a grotesque imitation of a woman's voice*] Kiss me,
Engineer dear, for it's dark down here and me old man's in Wall Street
making money! Hug me tight, darlin', for I'm afeerd in the dark and me
mother's on deck makin' eyes at the skipper! [*Another roar of laughter*]

YANK [*Threateningly*]   Say! What yuh tryin' to do, kid me, yuh old Harp?

90 PADDY   Divil a bit! Ain't I wishin' myself you'd brained her?

YANK [*Fiercely*]   I'll brain her! I'll brain her yet, wait 'n' see! [*Coming over to*
PADDY—*slowly*] Say, is dat what she called me—a hairy ape?

PADDY   She looked it at you if she didn't say the word itself.

YANK [*Grinning horribly*]   Hairy ape, huh? Sure! Dat's de way she looked at
95 me, aw right. Hairy ape! So dat's me, huh? [*Bursting into rage—as if she
were still in front of him*] Yuh skinny tart! Yuh white-faced bum, yuh! I'll
show yuh who's a ape! [*Turning to the others, bewilderment seizing him
again*] Say, youse guys. I was bawlin' him out for pullin' de whistle on us.
You heard me. And den I seen youse lookin' at somep'n and I tought he'd
100 sneaked down to come up in back of me, and I hopped round to knock him
dead wit de shovel. And dere she was wit de light on her! Christ, yuh

coulda pushed me over with a finger! I was scared, get me? Sure! I tought
she was a ghost, see? She was all in white like dey wrap around stiffs. You
seen her. Kin yuh blame me? She didn't belong, dat's what. And den when
105 I come to and seen it was a real skoit and seen de way she was lookin' at
me—like Paddy said—Christ, I was sore, get me? I don't stand for dat stuff
from nobody. And I flung de shovel—on'y she'd beat it. [*Furiously*] I wished
it'd banged her! I wished it'd knocked her block off!

LONG And be 'anged for murder or 'lectrocuted? She ain't bleedin' well
110 worth it.

YANK I don't give a damn what! I'd be square wit her, wouldn't I? Tink I
wanter let her put somep'n over on me? Tink I'm goin' to let her git away
wit dat stuff? Yuh don't know me! No one ain't never put nothin' over on me
and got away wit it, see!—not dat kind of stuff—no guy and no skoit nei-
115 ther! I'll fix her! Maybe she'll come down again—

VOICE No chance, Yank. You scared her out of a year's growth.

YANK I scared her? Why de hell should I scare her? Who de hell is she? Ain't
she de same as me? Hairy ape, huh? [*With his old confident bravado*] I'll
show her I'm better'n her, if she on'y knew it. I belong and she don't, see! I
120 move and she's dead! Twenty-five knots a hour, dat's me! Dat carries her but
I make dat. She's on'y baggage. Sure! [*Again bewilderedly*] But, Christ, she
was funny lookin'! Did yuh pipe her hands? White and skinny. Yuh could see
de bones through 'em. And her mush, dat was dead white, too. And her eyes,
dey was like dey'd seen a ghost. Me, dat was! Sure! Hairy ape! Ghost, huh?
125 Look at dat arm! [*He extends his right arm, swelling out the great muscles.*]
I coulda took her wit dat, wit' just my little finger even, and broke her in
two. [*Again bewilderedly*] Say, who is dat skoit, huh? What is she? What's
she come from? Who made her? Who give her de noive to look at me like
dat? Dis ting's got my goat right. I don't get her. She's new to me. What does
130 a skoit like her mean, huh? She don't belong, get me! I can't see her. [*With
growing anger*] But one ting I'm wise to, aw right, aw right! Youse all kin bet
your shoits I'll git even wit her. I'll show her if she tinks she—She grinds de
organ and I'm on de string, huh? I'll fix her! Let her come down again and
I'll fling her in de furnace! She'll move den! She won't shiver at nothin', den!
135 Speed, dat'll be her! She'll belong den! [*He grins horribly.*]

PADDY She'll never come. She's had her belly-full, I'm telling you. She'll be
in bed now, I'm thinking, wid ten doctors and nurses feedin' her salts to
clean the fear out of her.

YANK [*Enraged*] Yuh tink I made her sick, too, do yuh? Just lookin' at me,
140 huh? Hairy ape, huh? [*In a frenzy of rage*] I'll fix her! I'll tell her where to git
off! She'll git down on her knees and take it back or I'll bust de face offen
her! [*Shaking one fist upward and beating on his chest with the other*] I'll
find yuh! I'm comin', d'yuh hear? I'll fix yuh, God damn yuh! [*He makes a
rush for the door.*]

VOICES Stop him!
145 He'll get shot!
He'll murder her!
Trip him up!
Hold him!
He's gone crazy!
150 Gott, he's strong!

> Hold him down!
> Look out for a kick!
> Pin his arms!
>
> [*They have all piled on him and, after a fierce struggle, by sheer weight of numbers have borne him to the floor just inside the door.*]

PADDY [*Who has remained detached*]   Kape him down till he's cooled off.
155   [*Scornfully*] Yerra, Yank, you're a great fool. Is it payin' attention at all you are to the like of that skinny sow widout one drop of rale blood in her?

YANK [*Frenziedly, from the bottom of the heap*]   She done me doit! She done me doit, didn't she? I'll git square wit her! I'll get her some way! Git offen me, youse guys! Lemme up! I'll show her who's a ape!

[*Curtain*]

SCENE FIVE

[SCENE: *Three weeks later. A corner of Fifth Avenue in the Fifties on a fine Sunday morning. A general atmosphere of clean, well-tidied, wide street; a flood of mellow, tempered sunshine; gentle, genteel breezes. In the rear, the show windows of two shops, a jewelry establishment on the corner, a furrier's next to it. Here the adornments of extreme wealth are tantalizingly displayed. The jeweler's window is gaudy with glittering diamonds, emeralds, rubies, pearls, etc., fashioned in ornate tiaras, crowns, necklaces, collars, etc. From each piece hangs an enormous tag from which a dollar sign and numerals in intermittent electric lights wink out the incredible prices. The same in the furrier's Rich furs of all varieties hang there bathed in a downpour of artificial light. The general effect is of a background of magnificence cheapened and made grotesque by commercialism, a background in tawdry disharmony with the clear light and sunshine on the street itself.*

Up the side street YANK *and* LONG *come swaggering.* LONG *is dressed in shore clothes, wears a black Windsor tie, cloth cap.* YANK *is in his dirty dungarees. A fireman's cap with black peak is cocked defiantly on the side of his head. He has not shaved for days and around his fierce, resentful eyes—as around those of* LONG *to a lesser degree—the black smudge of coal dust still sticks like make-up. They hesitate and stand together at the corner, swaggering, looking about them with a forced, defiant contempt.*]

LONG [*Indicating it all with an oratorical gesture*]   Well, 'ere we are. Fif' Avenoo. This 'ere's their bleedin' private lane, as yer might say. [*Bitterly*] We're trespassers 'ere. Proletarians keep orf the grass!

YANK [*Dully*]   I don't see no grass, yuh boob. [*Staring at the sidewalk*] Clean,
5   ain't it? Yuh could eat a fried egg offen it. The white wings got some job sweepin' dis up. [*Looking up and down the avenue—surlily*] Where's all de white-collar stiffs yuh said was here—and de skoits—*her* kind?

LONG   In church, blarst 'em! Arskin' Jesus to give 'em more money.

YANK   Choich, huh? I useter go to choich onct—sure—when I was a kid. Me
10   old man and woman, dey made me. Dey never went demselves, dough. Always got too big a head on Sunday mornin', dat was dem. [*With a grin*] Dey was scrappers[5] for fair, bot' of dem. On Satiday nights when dey bot' got a skinful dey could put up a bout oughter been staged at de Garden. When dey got trough dere wasn't a chair or table wit a leg under it. Or else dey

5. Individuals prone to fighting.

15 bot' jumped on me for somep'n. Dat was where I loined to take punishment. [*With a grin and a swagger*] I'm a chip offen de old block, get me?

LONG   Did yer old man follow the sea?

YANK   Naw. Worked along shore. I runned away when me old lady croaked
wit de tremens.[6] I helped at truckin' and in de market. Den I shipped in de
20 stokehole. Sure. Dat belongs. De rest was nothin'. [*Looking around him*] I
ain't never seen dis before. De Brooklyn waterfront, dat was where I was
dragged up. [*Taking a deep breath*] Dis ain't so bad at dat, huh?

LONG   Not bad? Well, we pays for it wiv our bloody sweat, if yer wants to
know!

25 YANK [*With sudden angry disgust*]   Aw, hell! I don't see no one, see—like her.
All dis gives me a pain. It don't belong. Say, ain't dere a backroom around
dis dump? Let's go shoot a ball. All dis is too clean and quiet and dolled-up,
get me? It gives me a pain.

LONG   Wait and yer'll bloody well see—

30 YANK   I don't wait for no one. I keep on de move. Say, what yuh drag me up
here for, anyway? Tryin' to kid me, yuh simp, yuh?

LONG   Yer wants to get back at 'er, don't yer? That's what yer been saying'
every bloomin' 'our since she hinsulted yer.

YANK [*Vehemently*]   Sure ting I do! Didn't I try to get even wit her in South-
35 ampton? Didn't I sneak on de dock and wait for her by de gangplank? I was
goin' to spit in her pale mug, see! Sure, right in her pop-eyes! Dat woulda
made me even, see? But no chanct. Dere was a whole army of plainclothes
bulls around. Dey spotted me and gimme de bum's rush. I never seen her.
But I'll git square wit her yet, you watch! [*Furiously*] De lousy tart! She
40 tinks she kin get away wit moider—but not wit me! I'll fix her! I'll tink of a
way!

LONG [*As disgusted as he dares to be*]   Ain't that why I brought yer up 'ere—to
show yer? Yer been lookin' at this 'ere 'ole affair wrong. Yer been actin' an'
talkin' 's if it was all a bleedin' personal matter between yer and that bloody
45 cow. I wants to convince yer she was on'y a representative of 'er clarss. I
wants to awaken yer bloody clarss consciousness. Then yer'll see it's 'er
clarss yer've got to fight, not 'er alone. There's a 'ole mob of 'em like 'er,
Gawd blind 'em!

YANK [*Spitting on his hands—belligerently*]   De more de merrier when I gits
50 started. Bring on de gang!

LONG   Yer'll see 'em in arf a mo', when that church lets out. [*He turns and
sees the window display in the two stores for the first time*] Blimey! Look at
that, will yer? [*They both walk back and stand looking in the jewelers.* LONG
flies into a fury.] Just look at this 'ere bloomin' mess! Just look at it! Look at
55 the bleedin' prices on 'em—more'n our 'ole bloody stoke-hole makes in ten
voyages sweatin' in 'ell! And they—'er and 'er bloody clarss—buys 'em for
toys to dangle on 'em! One of these 'ere would buy scoff for a starvin' family
for a year!

YANK   Aw, cut de sob stuff! T' hell wit de starvin' family! Yuh'll be passin' de
60 hat to me next. [*With naïve admiration*] Say, dem tings is pretty, huh? Bet
yuh dey'd hock for a piece of change aw right. [*Then turning away, bored*]
But, aw hell, what good are dey? Let 'er have 'em. Dey don't belong no

---

6. Delirium tremens: state of confusion induced by withdrawal of alcohol.

more'n she does. [*With a gesture of sweeping the jewelers into oblivion*] All dat don't count, get me?

65 LONG [*Who has moved to the furrier's—indignantly*]   And I s'pose this 'ere don't count neither—skins of poor, 'armless animals slaughtered so as 'er and 'ers can keep their bleedin' noses warm!

YANK [*Who has been staring at something inside—with queer excitement*] Take a slant at dat! Give it de once-over! Monkey fur—two t'ousand bucks!

70 [*Bewilderedly*] Is dat straight goods—monkey fur? What de hell—?

LONG [*Bitterly*]   It's straight enuf. [*With grim humor*] They wouldn't bloody well pay that for a 'airy ape's skin—no, nor for the 'ole livin' ape with all 'is 'ead, and body, and soul thrown in!

YANK [*Clenching his fists, his face growing pale with rage as if the skin in the window were a personal insult*]   Trowin' it up in my face! Christ! I'll
75 fix her!

LONG [*Excitedly*]   Church is out. 'Ere they come, the bleedin' swine. [*After a glance at* YANK's *lowering face—uneasily*] Easy goes, Comrade. Keep yer bloomin' temper. Remember force defeats itself. It ain't our weapon. We must impress our demands through peaceful means—the votes of the on-
80 marching proletarians of the bloody world!

YANK [*With abysmal contempt*]   Votes, hell! Votes is a joke, see. Votes for women! Let dem do it!

LONG [*Still more uneasily*]   Calm, now. Treat 'em wiv the proper contempt. Observe the bleedin' parasites but 'old yer 'orses.

85 YANK [*Angrily*]   Git away from me! Yuh're yellow, dat's what. Force, dat's me! De punch, dat's me every time, see!

> [*The crowd from church enter from the right, sauntering slowly and affectedly, their heads held stiffly up, looking neither to right nor left, talking in toneless, simpering voices. The women are rouged, calcimined, dyed, overdressed to the nth degree. The men are in Prince Alberts, high hats, spats, canes, etc. A procession of gaudy marionettes, yet with something of the relentless horror of Frankenstein monsters in their detached, mechanical unawareness.*]

VOICES   Dear Doctor Caiaphas! He is so sincere!
What was the sermon? I dozed off.
About the radicals, my dear—and the false doctrines that are
90 being preached.
We must organize a hundred per cent American bazaar.
And let everyone contribute one one-hundredth percent of their income tax.
What an original idea!
95 We can devote the proceeds to rehabilitating the veil of the temple.
But that has been done so many times.

YANK [*Glaring from one to the other of them—with an insulting snort of scorn*] Huh! Huh!

> [*Without seeming to see him, they make wide detours to avoid the spot where he stands in the middle of the sidewalk.*]

LONG [*Frightenedly*]   Keep yer bloomin' mouth shut, I tells yer.

YANK [*Viciously*]   G'wan! Tell it to Sweeney! [*He swaggers away and deliberately lurches into a top-hatted gentleman, then glares at him pugnaciously.*]
100 Say, who d'yuh tink yuh're bumpin'? Tink yuh own de oith?

GENTLEMAN [*Coldly and affectedly*]   I beg your pardon. [*He has not looked at* YANK *and passes on without a glance, leaving him bewildered.*]

LONG [*Rushing up and grabbing* YANK's *arm*]   'Ere! Come away! This wasn't what I meant. Yer'll 'ave the bloody coppers down on us.

YANK [*Savagely—giving him a push that sends him sprawling*]   G'wan!

105 LONG [*Picks himself up—hysterically*]   I'll pop orf then. This ain't what I meant. And whatever 'appens, yer can't blame me. [*He slinks off left.*]

YANK   T' hell wit youse! [*He approaches a lady—with a vicious grin and a smirking wink.*] Hello, Kiddo. How's every little ting? Got anyting on for tonight? I know an old boiler down to de docks we kin crawl into. [*The lady stalks by without a look, without a change of pace.* YANK *turns to others—insultingly.*]

110 Holy smokes, what a mug! Go hide yuhself before de horses shy at yuh. Gee, pipe de heine on dat one! Say, youse, yuh look like de stoin of a ferryboat. Paint and powder! All dolled up to kill! Yuh look like stiffs laid out for de boneyard! Aw, g'wan, de lot of youse! Yuh give me de eye-ache. Yuh don't belong, get me! Look at me, why don't youse dare? I belong, dat's me! [*Pointing to a skyscraper across the street which is in process of construction—*

115 *with bravado*] See dat building goin' up dere? See de steel work? Steel, dat's me! Youse guys live on it and tink yuh're somep'n. But I'm *in* it, see! I'm de hoistin' engine dat makes it go up! I'm it—de inside and bottom of it! Sure! I'm steel and steam and smoke and de rest of it! It moves—speed— twenty-five stories up—and me at de top and bottom—movin'! Youse simps

120 don't move. Yuh're on'y dolls I winds up to see 'm spin. Yuh're de garbage, get me—de leavins—de ashes we dump over de side! Now, what 'a'yuh gotta say? [*But as they seem neither to see nor hear him, he flies into a fury*] Bums! Pigs! Tarts! Bitches! [*He turns in a rage on the men, bumping viciously into them but not jarring them the least bit. Rather it is he who recoils after each collision. He keeps growling.*] Git off de oith! G'wan, yuh bum! Look

125 where yuh're goin,' can't yuh? Git outa here! Fight, why don't yuh? Put up yer mits! Don't be a dog! Fight or I'll knock yuh dead! [*But, without seeming to see him, they all answer with mechanical affected politeness.*] I beg your pardon. [*Then at a cry from one of the women, they all scurry to the furrier's window.*]

THE WOMAN [*Ecstatically, with a gasp of delight*]   Monkey fur! [*The whole crowd of men and women chorus after her in the same tone of affected delight.*] Monkey fur!

YANK [*With a jerk of his head back on his shoulders, as if he had received a*

130 *punch full in the face—raging*]   I see yuh, all in white! I see yuh, yuh white-faced tart, yuh! Hairy ape, huh? I'll hairy ape yuh!

> [*He bends down and grips at the street curbing as if to pluck it out and hurl it. Foiled in this, snarling with passion, he leaps to the lamp-post on the corner and tries to pull it up for a club. Just at that moment a bus is heard rumbling up. A fat, high-hatted, spatted gentleman runs out from the side street. He calls out plaintively.*]

"Bus! Bus! Stop there!"

> [*And runs full tilt into the bending, straining* YANK, *who is bowled off his balance*]

YANK [*Seeing a fight—with a roar of joy as he springs to his feet*]   At last! Bus, huh? I'll bust yuh! [*He lets drive a terrific swing, his fist landing full on the fat gentleman's face. But the gentleman stands unmoved as if nothing had happened.*]

135 GENTLEMAN I beg your pardon. [*Then irritably*] You have made me lose my bus. [*He claps his hands and begins to scream.*] Officer! Officer!

> [*Many police whistles shrill out on the instant and a whole platoon of policemen rush in on* YANK *from all sides. He tries to fight but is clubbed to the pavement and fallen upon. The crowd at the window have not moved or noticed this disturbance. The clanging gong of the patrol wagon approaches with a clamoring din.*]

[*Curtain*]

SCENE SIX

[SCENE: *Night of the following day. A row of cells in the prison on Blackwell's Island.[7] The cells extend back diagonally from right front to left rear. They do not stop, but disappear in the dark background as if they ran on, numberless, into infinity. One electric bulb from the low ceiling of the narrow corridor sheds its light through the heavy steel bars of the cell at the extreme front and reveals part of the interior.* YANK *can be seen within, crouched on the edge of his cot in the attitude of Rodin's "The Thinker." His face is spotted with black and blue bruises. A blood-stained bandage is wrapped around his head.*]

YANK [*Suddenly starting as if awakening from a dream, reaches out and shakes the bars—aloud to himself, wonderingly*] Steel. Dis is de Zoo, huh?

> [*A burst of hard, barking laughter comes from the unseen occupants of the cells, runs back down the tier, and abruptly ceases.*]

VOICES [*Mockingly*] The Zoo? That's a new name for this coop—a damn good name!

Steel, eh? You said a mouthful. This is the old iron house.

5   Who is that boob talkin'?

He's the bloke they brung in out of his head. The bulls had beat him up fierce.

YANK [*Dully*] I musta been dreamin'. I tought I was in a cage at de Zoo—but de apes don't talk, do dey?

10 VOICES [*With mocking laughter*] You're in a cage aw right.

A coop!

A pen!

A sty!

A kennel! [*Hard laughter—a pause*]

15   Say, guy! Who are you? No, never mind lying. What are you?

Yes, tell us your sad story. What's your game?

What did they jug yuh for?

YANK [*Dully*] I was a fireman—stokin' on de liners. [*Then with sudden rage, rattling his cell bars*] I'm a hairy ape, get me? And I'll bust youse all in de

20 jaw if yuh don't lay off kiddin' me.

VOICES Huh! You're a hard boiled duck, ain't you!

When you spit, it bounces! [*Laughter*]

Aw, can it. He's a regular guy. Ain't you?

What did he say he was—a ape?

---

7. Today known as Roosevelt Island, located on the East River of New York City, Blackwell's Island housed the city's main prison.

25 YANK [*Defiantly*]   Sure ting! Ain't dat what youse all are—apes? [*A silence.
    Then a furious rattling of bars from down the corridor.*]
    A VOICE [*Thick with rage*]   I'll show yuh who's a ape, yuh bum!
    VOICES Ssshh! Nix!
            Can de noise!
            Piano!
30   You'll have the guard down on us!
    YANK [*Scornfully*]   De guard? Yuh mean de keeper, don't yuh? [*Angry excla-
    mations from all the cells*]
    VOICE [*Placatingly*]   Aw, don't pay no attention to him. He's off his nut from
    the beatin'-up he got. Say, you guy! We're waitin' to hear what they landed
    you for—or ain't yuh tellin'?
35 YANK   Sure, I'll tell youse. Sure! Why de hell not? On'y—youse won't get me.
    Nobody gets me but me, see? I started to tell de Judge and all he says was:
    "Toity days to tink it over." Tink it over! Christ, dat's all I been doin' for
    weeks! [*After a pause*] I was tryin' to git even wit someone, see?—someone
    dat done me doit.
40   VOICES [*Cynically*]   De old stuff, I bet. Your goil, huh?
            Give yuh the double-cross, huh?
            That's them every time!
            Did yuh beat up de odder guy?
    YANK [*Disgustedly*]   Aw, yuh're all wrong! Sure dere was a skoit in it—but not
45 what youse mean, not dat old tripe. Dis was a new kind of skoit. She was
    dolled up all in white—in de stokehole. I tought she was a ghost. Sure. [*A
    pause*]
    VOICES [*Whispering*]   Gee, he's still nutty.
            Let him rave. It's fun listenin'.
    YANK [*Unheeding—groping in his thoughts*]   Her hands—dey was skinny and
50 white like dey wasn't real but painted on somep'n. Dere was a million miles
    from me to her—twenty-five knots a hour. She was like some dead ting de
    cat brung in. Sure, dat's what. She didn't belong. She belonged in de win-
    dow of a toy store, or on de top of a garbage can, see! Sure! [*He breaks out
    angrily*] But would yuh believe it, she had de noive to do me doit. She
55 lamped me like she was seein' somep'n broke loose from de menagerie.
    Christ, yuh'd oughter seen her eyes! [*He rattles the bars of his cell furiously.*]
    But I'll get back at her yet, you watch! And if I can't find her I'll take it out
    on de gang she runs wit. I'm wise to where dey hangs out now. I'll show her
    who belongs! I'll show her who's in de move and who ain't. You watch my
60 smoke!
    VOICES [*Serious and joking*]   Dat's de talkin'!
            Take her for all she's got!
            What was this dame, anyway? Who was she, eh?
    YANK   I dunno. First cabin stiff. Her old man's a millionaire, dey says—name
65 of Douglas.
    VOICES   Douglas? That's the president of the Steel Trust, I bet.
            Sure. I seen his mug in de papers.
            He's filthy with dough.
    VOICE   Hey, feller, take a tip from me. If you want to get back at that dame,
70 you better join the Wobblies. You'll get some action then.

YANK Wobblies? What de hell's dat?

VOICE Ain't you ever heard of the I. W. W.?[8]

YANK Naw. What is it?

VOICE A gang of blokes—a tough gang. I been readin' about 'em today in the
75 paper. The guard give me the *Sunday Times.* There's a long spiel about 'em.
It's from a speech made in the Senate by a guy named Senator Queen. [*He is
in the cell next to* YANK's. *There is a rustling of paper.*] Wait'll I see if I got light
enough and I'll read you. Listen. [*He reads*] "There is a menace existing in
this country today which threatens the vitals of our fair Republic—as foul a
80 menace against the very life-blood of the American Eagle as was the foul
conspiracy of Cataline[9] against the eagles of ancient Rome!"

VOICE [*Disgustedly*] Aw hell! Tell him to salt de tail of dat eagle!

VOICE [*Reading*] "I refer to that devil's brew of rascals, jailbirds, murderers
and cutthroats who libel all honest working men by calling themselves the
85 Industrial Workers of the World, but in the light of their nefarious plots, I
call them the Industrious *Wreckers* of the World!"

YANK [*With vengeful satisfaction*] Wreckers, dat's de right dope! Dat belongs!
Me for dem!

VOICE Ssshh! [*Reading*] "This fiendish organization is a foul ulcer on the
90 fair body of our Democracy—"

VOICE Democracy, hell! Give him the bold, fellers—the raspberry! [*They do*]

VOICE Ssshh! [*Reading*] "Like Cato[1] I say to this Senate, the I. W. W. must
be destroyed! For they represent an ever-present dagger pointed at the
heart of the greatest nation the world has ever known, where all men are
95 born free and equal, with equal opportunities to all, where the Founding
Fathers have guaranteed to each one happiness, where Truth, Honor, Liberty, Justice, and the Brotherhood of Man are a religion absorbed with
one's mother's milk, taught at our father's knee, sealed, signed, and stamped
upon in the glorious Constitution of these United States!" [*A perfect storm
of hisses, catcalls, boos, and hard laughter*]

100 VOICES [*Scornfully*] Hurrah for de Fort' of July!
Pass de hat!
Liberty!
Justice!
Honor!
105 Opportunity!
Brotherhood!

ALL [*With abysmal scorn*] Aw, hell!

VOICE Give that Queen Senator guy the bark! All togedder now—one—
two—tree—[*A terrific chorus of barking and yapping*]

110 GUARD [*From a distance*] Quiet there, youse—or I'll git the hose. [*The noise
subsides.*]

YANK [*With growling rage*] I'd like to catch dat senator guy alone for a second. I'd loin him some trute!

VOICE Ssshh! Here's where he gits down to cases on the Wobblies. [*Reads*]
"They plot with fire in one hand and dynamite in the other. They stop not

---

8. An international labor union.
9. Roman senator of the 1st century B.C. who

plotted to overthrow the Roman Republic.
1. Roman orator.

115 before murder to gain their ends, nor at the outraging of defenseless womanhood. They would tear down society, put the lowest scum in the seats of
the mighty, turn Almighty God's revealed plan for the world topsy-turvy,
and make of our sweet and lovely civilization a shambles, a desolation
where man, God's masterpiece, would soon degenerate back to the ape!"

120 VOICE [*To* YANK] Hey, you guy. There's your ape stuff again.

YANK [*With a growl of fury*] I got him. So dey blow up tings, do dey? Dey
turn tings round, do dey? Hey, lend me dat paper, will yuh?

VOICE Sure. Give it to him. On'y keep it to yourself, see. We don't wanter
listen to no more of that slop.

125 VOICE Here you are. Hide it under your mattress.

YANK [*Reaching out*] Tanks. I can't read much but I kin manage. [*He sits, the paper
in the hand at his side, in the attitude of Rodin's "The Thinker." A pause. Several
snores from down the corridor. Suddenly* YANK *jumps to his feet with a furious
groan as if some appalling thought had crashed on him—bewilderedly.*] Sure—
her old man—president of de Steel Trust—makes half de steel in de world—
steel—where I tought I belonged—drivin' trou—movin'—in dat—to make

130 her—and cage me in for her to spit on! Christ [*He shakes the bars of his cell door
till the whole tier trembles. Irritated, protesting exclamations from those awakened or trying to get to sleep.*] He made dis—dis cage! Steel! *It* don't belong,
dat's what! Cages, cells, locks, bolts, bars—dat's what it means!—holdin' me
down wit him at de top! But I'll drive trou! Fire, dat melts it! I'll be fire—under
de heap—fire dat never goes out—hot as hell—breakin' out in de night—

[*While he has been saying this last he has shaken his cell door to a clanging
accompaniment. As he comes to the "breakin' out" he seizes one bar with
both hands and, putting his two feet up against the others so that his position
is parallel to the floor like a monkey's, he gives a great wrench backwards.
The bar bends like a licorice stick under his tremendous strength. Just at this
moment the* PRISON GUARD *rushes in, dragging a hose behind him.*]

135 GUARD [*Angrily*] I'll loin youse burns to wake me up! [*Sees* YANK] Hello, it's
you, huh? Got the D.T.s.[2] hey? Well, I'll cure 'em. I'll drown your snakes for
yuh! [*Noticing the bar*] Hell, look at dat bar bended! On'y a bug is strong
enough for dat!

YANK [*Glaring at him*] Or a hairy ape, yuh big yellow bum! Look out! Here I

140 come! [*He grabs another bar*]

GUARD [*Scared now—yelling off left*] Toin de hose on, Ben!—full pressure!
And call de others—and a straitjacket!

[*The curtain is falling. As it hides* YANK *from view, there is a splattering
smash as the stream of water hits the steel of* YANK's *cell.*]

[*Curtain*]

SCENE SEVEN

[SCENE: *Nearly a month later. An I.W.W. local near the waterfront, showing the interior of a front room on the ground floor, and the street outside. Moonlight on the narrow street, buildings massed in black shadow. The interior of the room, which is
general assembly room, office, and reading room, resembles some dingy settlement
boys' club. A desk and high stool are in one corner. A table with papers, stacks of pam-*

2. Delirium Tremens.

phlets, chairs about it, is at center. The whole is decidedly cheap, banal, common-place and unmysterious as a room could well be. The secretary is perched on the stool making entries in a large ledger. An eye shade casts his face into shadows. Eight or ten men, longshoremen, iron workers, and the like, are grouped about the table. Two are playing checkers. One is writing a letter. Most of them are smoking pipes. A big sign-board is on the wall at the rear, "Industrial Workers of the World—Local No. 57."]

YANK [*Comes down the street outside. He is dressed as in Scene Five. He moves cautiously, mysteriously. He comes to a point opposite the door; tiptoes softly up to it, listens, is impressed by the silence within, knocks carefully, as if he were guessing at the password to some secret rite. Listens. No answer. Knocks again a bit louder. No answer. Knocks impatiently, much louder.*]

SECRETARY [*Turning around on his stool*]   What the hell is that—someone knocking? [*Shouts*] Come in, why don't you?
> [*All the men in the room look up.* YANK *opens the door slowly, gingerly, as if afraid of an ambush. He looks around for secret doors, mystery, is taken aback by the commonplaceness of the room and the men in it, thinks he may have gotten in the wrong place, then sees the signboard on the wall and is reassured.*]

YANK [*Blurts out*]   Hello.
MEN [*Reservedly*]   Hello.
5 YANK [*More easily*]   I tought I'd bumped into de wrong dump.
SECRETARY [*Scrutinizing him carefully*]   Maybe you have. Are you a member?
YANK   Naw, not yet. Dat's what I come for—to join.
SECRETARY   That's easy. What's your job—longshore?
YANK   Naw. Fireman—stoker on de liners.
10 SECRETARY [*With satisfaction*]   Welcome to our city. Glad to know you people are waking up at last. We haven't got many members in your line.
YANK   Naw. Dey're all dead to de woild.
SECRETARY   Well, you can help to wake 'em. What's your name? I'll make out your card.
15 YANK [*Confused*]   Name? Lemme tink.
SECRETARY [*Sharply*]   Don't you know your own name?
YANK   Sure; but I been just Yank for so long—Bob, dat's it—Bob Smith.
SECRETARY [*Writing*]   Robert Smith. [*Fills out the rest of card*] Here you are. Cost you half a dollar.
20 YANK   Is dat all—four bits? Dat's easy. [*Gives the* SECRETARY *the money*]
SECRETARY [*Throwing it in drawer*]   Thanks. Well, make yourself at home. No introductions needed. There's literature on the table. Take some of those pamphlets with you to distribute aboard ship. They may bring results. Sow the seed, only go about it right. Don't get caught and fired. We got
25 plenty out of work. What we need is men who can hold their jobs—and work for us at the same time.
YANK   Sure. [*But he still stands, embarrassed and uneasy.*]
SECRETARY [*Looking at him—curiously*]   What did you knock for? Think we had a coon in uniform to open doors?
30 YANK   Naw. I tought it was locked—and dat yuh'd wanter give me the once-over trou a peep-hole or somep'n to see if I was right.

SECRETARY [*Alert and suspicious but with an easy laugh*]   Think we were
   running a crap game? That door is never locked. What put that in your nut?

YANK [*With a knowing grin, convinced that this is all camouflage, a part of the
   secrecy*]   Dis burg is full of bulls, ain't it?

35 SECRETARY [*Sharply*]   What have the cops got to do with us? We're breaking
   no laws.

YANK [*With a knowing wink*]   Sure. Youse wouldn't for woilds. Sure. I'm wise
   to dat.

SECRETARY   You seem to be wise to a lot of stuff none of us knows about.

40 YANK [*With another wink*]   Aw, dat's aw right, see. [*Then made a bit resentful
   by the suspicious glances from all sides*] Aw, can it! Youse needn't put me
   trou de toid degree. Can't youse see I belong? Sure! I'm reg'lar. I'll stick, get
   me? I'll shoot de woiks for youse. Dat's why I wanted to join in.

SECRETARY [*Breezily, feeling him out*]   That's the right spirit. Only are you
45   sure you understand what you've joined? It's all plain and above-board;
   still, some guys get a wrong slant on us. [*Sharply*] What's your notion of the
   purpose of the I. W. W.?

YANK   Aw, I know all about it.

SECRETARY [*Sarcastically*]   Well, give us some of your valuable information.

50 YANK [*Cunningly*]   I know enough not to speak outa my toin. [*Then resentfully
   again*] Aw, say! I'm reg'lar. I'm wise to de game. I know yuh got to watch
   your step wit a stranger. For all youse know, I might be a plain-clothes dick,
   or somep'n, dat's what yuh're tinkin', huh? Aw, forget it! I belong, see? Ask
   any guy down to de docks if I don't.

55 SECRETARY   Who said you didn't?

YANK   After I'm nitiated, I'll show yuh.

SECRETARY [*Astounded*]   Inititated? There's no initiation.

YANK [*Disappointed*]   Ain't there no password—no grip nor nothin'?

SECRETARY   What'd you think this is—the Elks—or the Black Hand?

60 YANK   De Elks, hell! De Black Hand, dey're a lot of yellow back-stickin'
   Ginees. Naw, Dis is a man's gang, ain't it?

SECRETARY   You said it! That's why we stand on our two feet in the open. We
   got no secrets.

YANK [*Surprised but admiringly*]   Yuh mean to say yuh always run wide
65   open—like dis?

SECRETARY   Exactly.

YANK   Den yuh sure got your noive wit youse!

SECRETARY [*Sharply*]   Just what was it made you want to join us? Come out
   with that straight.

70 YANK   Yuh call me? Well, I got noive, too! Here's my hand. Yuh wanter blow
   tings up, don't yuh? Well, dat's me! I belong!

SECRETARY [*With pretended carelessness*]   You mean change the unequal conditions of society by legitimate direct action—or with dynamite?

YANK   Dynamite! Blow it offen de oith—steel—all de cages—all de factories,
75   steamers, buildings, jails—de Steel Trust and all dat makes it go.

SECRETARY   So—that's your idea, eh? And did you have any special job in
   that line you wanted to propose to us? [*He makes a sign to the men, who get
   up cautiously one by one and group behind* YANK.]

YANK [*Boldly*]   Sure. I'll come out wit it. I'll show youse I'm one of de gang.
   Dere's dat millionaire guy, Douglas—

80   SECRETARY   President of the Steel Trust, you mean? Do you want to assassinate him?

    YANK   Naw, dat don't get yuh nothin'. I mean blow up de factory, de woiks,
where he makes de steel. Dats what I'm after—to blow up de steel, knock
all de steel in de woild up to de moon. Dat'll fix tings! [*Eagerly, with a touch*
85   *of bravado*] I'll do it by me lonesome! I'll show yuh! Tell me where his woiks
is, how to git there, all de dope. Gimme de stuff, de old butter—and watch
me do de rest! Watch de smoke and see it move! I don't give a damn if dey
nab me—long as it's done! I'll soive life for it—and give 'em de laugh! [*Half
to himself*] And I'll write her a letter and tell her de hairy ape done it. Dat'll
90   square tings.

    SECRETARY [*Stepping away from* YANK]   Very interesting.

        [*He gives a signal. The men, huskies all, throw themselves on* YANK *and
before he knows it they have his legs and arms pinioned. But he is too
flabbergasted to make a struggle, anyway. They feel him over for
weapons.*]

    MAN   No gat, no knife. Shall we give him what's what and put the boots to
him?

    SECRETARY   No. He isn't worth the trouble we'd get into. He's too stupid.
95   [*He comes closer and laughs mockingly in* YANK's *face.*] Ho-ho! By God,
this is the biggest joke they've put up on us yet. Hey, you Joke! Who sent
you—Burns or Pinkerton? No, by God, you're such a bonehead I'll bet
you're in the Secret Service! Well, you dirty spy, you rotten agent provoca-
tor, you can go back and tell whatever skunk is paying you blood-money
100   for betraying your brothers that he's wasting his coin. You couldn't catch
a cold. And tell him that all he'll ever get on us, or ever has got, is just his
own sneaking plots that he's framed up to put us in jail. We are what our
manifesto says we are, neither more nor less—and we'll give him a copy of
that any time he calls. And as for you—[*He glares scornfully at* YANK, *who
105   is sunk in an oblivious stupor.*] Oh, hell, what's the use of talking? You're a
brainless ape.

    YANK [*Aroused by the word to fierce but futile struggles*]   What's dat, yuh
Sheeny[3] bum, yuh!

    SECRETARY   Throw him out, boys.

        [*In spite of his struggles, this is done with gusto and éclat. Propelled by
several parting kicks,* YANK *lands sprawling in the middle of the narrow
cobbled street. With a growl he starts to get up and storm the closed door,
but stops bewildered by the confusion in his brain, pathetically impotent.
He sits there, brooding, in as near to the attitude of Rodin's "Thinker" as
he can get in his position.*]

110   YANK [*Bitterly*]   So dem boids don't tink I belong, neider. Aw, to hell wit 'em!
Dey're in de wrong pew—de same old bull—soapboxes and Salvation
Army—no guts! Cut out an hour offen de job a day and make me happy!
Gimme a dollar more a day and make me happy! Tree square a day, and
cauliflowers in de front yard—ekal rights—a woman and kids—a lousy
115   vote—and I'm all fixed for Jesus, huh? Aw, hell! What does dat get yuh? Dis
ting's in your inside, but it ain't your belly. Feedin' your face—sinkers and

---

3. Derogatory term for a Jewish person.

coffee—dat don't touch it. It's way down—at de bottom. Yuh can't grab it, and yuh can't stop it. It moves, and everyting moves. It stops and de whole woild stops. Dat's me now—I don't tick, see?—I'm a busted Ingersoll,[4] dat's what. Steel was me, and I owned de woild. Now I ain't steel, and de woild owns me. Aw, hell! I can't see—it's all dark, get me? It's all wrong! [*He turns a bitter mocking face up like an ape gibbering at the moon.*] Say, youse up dere, Man in de Moon, yuh look so wise, gimme de answer, huh? Slip me de inside dope, de information right from de stable—where do I get off at, huh?

A POLICEMAN [*Who has come up the street in time to hear this last—with grim humor*]   You'll get off at the station, you boob, if you don't get up out of that and keep movin'.

YANK [*Looking up at him—with a hard, bitter laugh*]   Sure! Lock me up! Put me in a cage! Dat's de on'y answer yuh know. G'wan, lock me up!

POLICEMAN   What you been doin'?

YANK   Enuf to gimme life for! I was born, see? Sure, dat's de charge. Write it in de blotter. I was born, get me?

POLICEMAN [*Jocosely*]   God pity your old woman! [*Then matter-of-fact*] But I've no time for kidding. You're soused. I'd run you in but it's too long a walk to the station. Come on now, get up, or I'll fan your ears with this club. Beat it now! [*He hauls* YANK *to his feet.*]

YANK [*In a vague mocking tone*]   Say, where do I go from here?

POLICEMAN [*Giving him a push—with a grin, indifferently*]   Go to hell.

[*Curtain*]

SCENE EIGHT

[SCENE: *Twilight of the next day. The monkey house at the Zoo. One spot of clear gray light falls on the front of one cage so that the interior can be seen. The other cages are vague, shrouded in shadow from which chatterings pitched in a conversational tone can be heard. On the one cage a sign from which the word "gorilla" stands out. The gigantic animal himself is seen squatting on his haunches on a bench in much the same attitude as Rodin's "Thinker." *YANK *enters from the left. Immediately a chorus of angry chattering and screeching breaks out. The gorilla turns his eyes but makes no sound or move.*]

YANK [*With a hard, bitter laugh*]   Welcome to your city, huh? Hail, hail, de gang's all here!

[*At the sound of his voice the chattering dies away into an attentive silence.* YANK *walks up to the gorilla's cage and, leaning over the railing, stares in at its occupant, who stares back at him, silent and motionless. There is a pause of dead stillness. Then* YANK *begins to talk in a friendly confidential tone, half-mockingly, but with a deep undercurrent of sympathy.*]

Say, yuh're some hard-lookin' guy, ain't yuh? I seen lots of tough nuts dat de gang called gorillas, but yuh're de foist real one I ever seen. Some chest yuh got, and shoulders, and dem arms and mits! I bet yuh got a punch in eider fist dat'd knock 'em all silly!

[*This with genuine admiration. The gorilla, as if he understood, stands upright, swelling out his chest and pounding on it with his fist.* YANK *grins sympathetically.*]

---

4. Robert Ingersoll (1833–1899), American political leader known for his progressive ideas.

Sure, I get yuh. Yuh challenge de whole woild, huh? Yuh got what I was sayin'
even if yuh muffed de woids. [*Then bitterness creeping in*] And why wouldn't
yuh get me? Ain't we both members of de same club—de Hairy Apes?
[*They stare at each other—a pause—then* YANK *goes on slowly and bitterly.*]
10   So yuh're what she seen when she looked at me, de white-faced tart! I was
you to her, get me? On'y outa de cage—broke out—free to moider her, see?
Sure! Dat's what she tought. She wasn't wise dat I was in a cage, too—
worser'n yours—sure—a damn sight—'cause you got some chanct to bust
loose—but me—[*He grows confused*] Aw, hell! It's all wrong, ain't it? [*A pause*]
15   I s'pose yuh wanter know what I'm doin' here, huh? I been warmin' a bench
down to de Battery[5]—ever since last night. Sure. I seen de sun come up. Dat
was pretty, too—all red and pink and green. I was lookin' at de skyscrapers—
steel—and all de ships comin' in, sailin' out, all over de oith—and dey was
steel, too. De sun was warm, dey wasn't no clouds, and dere was a breeze
20   blowin'. Sure, it was great stuff. I got it aw right—what Paddy said about dat
bein' de right dope—on'y I couldn't get *in* it, see? I couldn't belong in dat. It
was over my head. And I kept tinkin'—and den I beat it up here to see what
youse was like. And I waited till dey was all gone to git yuh alone. Say, how
d'yuh feel sittin' in dat pen all de time, havin' to stand for 'em comin' and
25   starin' at yuh—de white-faced, skinny tarts and de boobs what marry 'em—
makin' fun of yuh, laughin' at yuh, gittin' scared of yuh—damn 'em!
[*He pounds on the rail with his fist. The gorilla rattles the bars of his cage
and snarls. All the other monkeys set up an angry chattering in the darkness.* YANK *goes on excitedly.*]

Sure! Dat's de way it hits me, too. On'y yuh're lucky, see? Yuh don't belong
wit 'em and yuh know it. But me, I belong wit 'em—but I don't, see? Dey
don't belong wit me, dat's what. Get me? Tinkin' is hard—
[*He passes one hand across his forehead with a painful gesture. The
gorilla growls impatiently.* YANK *goes on gropingly.*]

30   It's dis way, what I'm drivin' at. Youse can sit and dope dream in de past, green
woods, de jungle and de rest of it. Den yuh belong and dey don't. Den yuh kin
laugh at 'em, see? Yuh're de champ of de woild. But me—I ain't got no past to
tink in, nor nothin' dat's comin', on'y what's now—and dat don't belong. Sure,
you're de best off! Yuh can't tink, can yuh? Yuh can't talk neider. But I kin
35   make a bluff at talkin' and tinkin'—a'most git away wit it—a'most!—and dat's
where de joker comes in. [*He laughs.*] I ain't on oith and I ain't in heaven, get
me? I'm in de middle tryin' to separate 'em, takin' all de woist punches from
bot' of 'em. Maybe dat's what dey call hell, huh? But you, yuh're at de bottom.
You belong! Sure! Yuh're de on'y one in de woild dat does, yuh lucky stiff!
[*The gorilla growls proudly.*]

40   And dat's why dey gotter put yuh in a cage, see?
[*The gorilla roars angrily.*]

Sure! Yuh get me. It beats it when you try to tink it or talk it—it's way down—
deep—behind—you 'n' me we feel it. Sure! Bot' members of dis club! [*He

5. The southern tip of Manhattan.

laughs—then in a savage tone.] What de hell! T' hell wit it! A little action,
dat's our meat! Dat belongs! Knock 'em down and keep bustin' 'em till dey
croaks yuh wit a gat—wit steel! Sure! Are yuh game? Dey've looked at youse,
ain't dey—in a cage? Wanter get even? Wanter wind up like a sport 'stead of
croakin' slow in dere?

[*The gorilla roars an emphatic affirmative.* YANK *goes on with a sort of
furious exaltation.*]

Sure! Yuh're reg'lar! Yuh'll stick to de finish! Me 'n' you, huh?—bot' members of this club! We'll put up one last star bout dat'll knock 'em offen deir
seats! Dey'll have to make de cages stronger after we're trou!

[*The gorilla is straining at his bars, growling, hopping from one foot to
the other.* YANK *takes a jimmy from under his coat and forces the lock on
the cage door. He throws this open.*]

Pardon from de governor! Step out and shake hands! I'll take yuh for a walk
down Fif' Avenoo. We'll knock 'em offen de oith and croak wit de band
playin'. Come on, Brother.

[*The gorilla scrambles gingerly out of his cage. Goes to* YANK *and stands
looking at him.* YANK *keeps his mocking tone—holds out his hand.*]

Shake—de secret grip of our order.

[*Something, the tone of mockery, perhaps, suddenly enrages the animal.
With a spring he wraps his huge arms around* YANK *in a murderous hug.
There is a crackling snap of crushed ribs—a gasping cry, still mocking,
from* YANK.]

Hey, I didn't say kiss me!

[*The gorilla lets the crushed body slip to the floor; stands over it uncertainly, considering; then picks it up, throws it in the cage, shuts the door,
and shuffles off menacingly into the darkness at left. A great uproar of
frightened chattering and whimpering comes from the other cages. Then*
YANK *moves, groaning, opening his eyes, and there is silence. He mutters
painfully.*]

Say—dey oughter match him—wit Zybszko. He got me, aw right. I'm trou.
Even him didn't tink I belonged. [*Then, with sudden passionate despair*]
Christ, where do I get off at? Where do I fit in? [*Checking himself as suddenly*] Aw, what de hell! No squawkin', see! No quittin', get me! Croak wit
your boots on! [*He grabs hold of the bars of the cage and hauls himself painfully to his feet—looks around him bewilderedly—forces a mocking laugh.*]
In de cage, huh? [*In the strident tones of a circus barker*] Ladies and gents,
step forward and take a slant at de one and only—[*His voice weakened*]—
one and original—Hairy Ape from de wilds of—[*He slips in a heap on the
floor and dies. The monkeys set up a chattering, whimpering wail. And, perhaps, the Hairy Ape at last belongs.*]

[*Curtain*]

SOPHIE TREADWELL

1885–1970

I N the early-morning hours of March 20, 1927, Albert Snyder was murdered in his Queens, New York, home. His wife, Ruth, and her lover, Judd Gray, were accused of the crime, tried, and convicted. An all-male jury sentenced them both to death, and when Ruth Snyder was executed, on January 12, 1928, she became the first woman to die in the electric chair in the state of New York. Considered one of the most sensational events of the era, the murder, the arrests, the trial, the sentences, and the executions all made headlines. Almost two hundred reporters, from the mainstream press and the tabloids alike, were assigned to cover various aspects of the case. By early May 1927, these journalists had already filed approximately 1,500,000 words over the wires; the *New York Times* alone published a story, often on the front page, almost daily from the revelation of the murder through the announcement of the executions. The trial, which was the first to use microphones and speakers in the courtroom, was observed by over 1,500 people, including a number of prominent writers, artists, and public figures. The *New York Times* described the spectators as "a typical Broadway audience," and other

reports used similarly theatrical images and language to depict the trial. Author Damon Runyon is said to have deemed it "the best show in town." Thus it should not surprise us that the murder and its perpetrators became infamously popular culture referents for decades thereafter and that the crime spawned any number of fictionalizations, including the films *Double Indemnity* (1944) and *Body Heat* (1981). Journalist Sophie Treadwell, while not formally assigned to cover the story, chose to attend the proceedings; her analysis of the trial and its reportage in the media inspired her theatrical triumph, MACHINAL,[1] the first major creative work based on the Snyder murder, which premiered on Broadway in September 1928. Far from a dramatization of the case as spectacle, however, *Machinal* presents the murder as a response to modern culture and indicts life in the machine age, especially for women, as warping, oppressive, and deadly.

Sophia Anita Treadwell was born in Stockton, California, in 1885. Her father, Alfred, was of English, Spanish, and Mexican ancestry and had spent his childhood in Mexico; her mother, Nettie, had emigrated with her family to the United States

1. The definitive pronunciation of this title remains unclear. While some critics believe Treadwell was using the French word meaning *mechan-*

ical or *unconscious*, pronounced "ma'-shin-al," others argue for "mak'-i-nal" or "ma-shin'-al."

from Scotland. When Sophie was very young, Alfred left Nettie and moved to San Francisco, where he held several judicially related elected offices. Despite efforts to reunite with Alfred, Nettie was left alone to provide for herself and her daughter. These early, troubled impressions of marital and economic instability made a profound impression on the young Sophie. Yet she also felt drawn to her father and her Mexican heritage, and through his influence, she was introduced to the theater and the study of language, interests she pursued as an undergraduate at the University of California at Berkeley. During college, Sophie acted in student theatrical productions, co-edited a campus humor magazine, served as a campus reporter for the *San Francisco Examiner,* and began to experiment with creative writing in addition to pursuing her degree in French. But Treadwell also had to hold multiple jobs to pay for her education, and she suffered the first of a series of breakdowns from the strain and exhaustion of juggling all these undertakings. Indeed, Treadwell's early life was punctuated by periods of productivity and collapse, through which she may have gained an understanding of how external pressures can affect us both psychologically and physiologically—an understanding that shapes *Machinal.*

Treadwell wrote her first full-length drama, *Le Grand Prix,* in 1906–07. On the strength of this writing she received an introduction to the famous actress Helena Modjeska. The star hired Sophie to assist with the writing of her memoirs and instilled in her protégée an understanding of the importance of creative integrity for artists. Treadwell then secured a post as a feature writer and theater critic for the *San Francisco Bulletin.* While working for the paper she met fellow journalist William O. McGeehan; they married in 1910. In 1914 McGeehan took a job with the *New York Evening Journal.* When McGeehan moved east, Treadwell remained in San Francisco to pursue a major assignment: she was convinced by her editor to use her acting as well as her writing skills to go undercover as a homeless prostitute to explore what resources the city would offer her. The resulting serial, "An Outcast at the Christian Door," caused a sensation

and no doubt contributed to Treadwell's expanding feminist consciousness. In 1915 Treadwell traveled to France as one of the first accredited female journalists to cover World War I. Denied access to the front because of her gender, however, she decided to join McGeehan in New York, where she embraced a number of important feminist movements of the era, including the fight for women's suffrage and the campaign for legalized birth control. Treadwell continued to work as a theater critic and also briefly joined the Provincetown Players, home to dramatists SUSAN GLASPELL and EUGENE O'NEILL. With the Players, Treadwell participated in play selection and directed one of their productions in 1917. But she had set her dramaturgical sights on Broadway, maintaining an uncompromising commitment to playwriting for the commercial theater that incorporated formal experimentation, feminist and other progressive political concerns, and timely narratives.

In 1920–21 Treadwell covered the final phases of the Mexican Revolution for the *New York Tribune,* including an exclusive interview with revolutionary leader Pancho Villa, which provided the foundation for her first Broadway play, *Gringo* (1922). A qualified success critically, *Gringo* may have proven too complex politically for audiences or reviewers to fully appreciate. With this play, as with her later *Hope for a Harvest* (1941), Treadwell considered controversial issues still highly relevant today, including America's attitudes toward Mexico and Mexicans and its ambivalence about immigrants. Her creation of Hispanic characters and engagement with the relationship between the United States and Mexico are only now being recognized as evidence of Treadwell's early contributions to the Chicana literary tradition.

Treadwell's investment in current events and sociocultural concerns, combined with her theatrical and journalistic sensibilities, facilitated the expeditious writing of *Machinal* in early 1928. Finishing the script just a few months after the executions, Treadwell was able to take advantage of audiences' continued fixation on the recent, lurid murder. Utilizing core elements of the Snyder case, she created a piece that would be narratively familiar yet thematically and stylistically innovative. In a series of discrete scenes, *Machinal* follows the life of a young woman, whom we come to know as Helen Jones, who works in an office to support herself and her mother. Stifled by the pressures of urban life, she reluctantly accepts her employer's proposal of marriage, deciding that it may be her only alternative to a life of drudgery. The young woman soon realizes that a loveless marriage is equally suffocating, however, and she experiences a fleeting sense of freedom only in an illicit affair. Her naive efforts to secure lasting freedom fail; it is impossible for her to escape the confines of patriarchal law and society. Focusing on the young woman's efforts to untangle the thoughts and feelings she is discovering, Treadwell employed the latest trends in modernist stagecraft, engaged public fascination with emerging concepts in human psychology, and endeavored—as her manuscript notes suggest—also to reach into her spectators' "still secret places," their "consciousness."

America's interest in psychology and psychoanalysis had been piqued when Sigmund Freud and Carl Jung visited Clark University in 1909 to give a series of lectures. Jung returned to the United States in 1912 to give further lectures at Fordham University. These clinicians' theories about dreams, sexuality, the conscious and unconscious mind, and the psychiatric condition known as "hysteria"[2] were soon being disseminated, although not always accurately, in the popular media. Modernist artists and writers quickly latched on to these new notions of the psyche as resonant with their own efforts to better express human thoughts and feelings. Discussions of psychoanalysis and experiments in depicting characters' mental states soon occupied the theater. Some early dramatic efforts, such as Alice Gerstenberg's *Overtones* (1915), sought to demonstrate repressed ideas and emotions by staging characters as split selves, one "cultured," the other "primitive," played by two actors. Susan Glaspell's *The Verge* (1921) featured a central female character diagnosed with

hysteria, represented chillingly by her fractured speech and by the angles and shadows in the lighting and scenic design of her "thwarted tower" room. Eugene O'Neill's *Strange Interlude,* drafted in 1923, utilized lengthy soliloquies to express his characters' psychic struggles; the play premiered on Broadway in January 1928 and won the Pulitzer Prize for drama. *Machinal,* like *The Verge* and *Strange Interlude,* features a woman grappling with the strictures of modern life, and like Glaspell and O'Neill Treadwell sought both a dramaturgical form and a theatrical style that would complement her protagonist's sense of entrapment and desperation and represent her psychic distress.

Precisely because these efforts to represent characters' inner lives necessitated new modes of dramatic writing and staging, some American theater artists now rejected the realist style of stage impresarios like David Belasco, who was famous for the elaborate and authentic physical details of his productions' settings, and gravitated instead toward sparer modernist techniques developed in Europe. A number of international artists, writers, and intellectuals traveled to or lived in exile in New York during the war years; many Americans also encountered modernist artistry while abroad during the war. Discrete European modernist styles, which included symbolism, cubism, fauvism, and surrealism, were often interwoven by the Americans to generate new, hybrid forms. Treadwell participated in the creative fervor of the New York artists who sought to craft through these diverse stylistic influences a uniquely American avant-garde.

Following the war, American artists found in expressionism an aesthetic particularly suited to the representation of modern life. The stage version of this avant-garde form sought to externalize the subjective and internal dimensions of character, complemented by design schema that reflected this subjectivity, often by way of distorted, fragmented, or abstract sounds and images; we find these techniques readily apparent in *Machinal*. There were also

2. Frequently diagnosed in women, hysteria manifested in a range of symptoms and disorders, both physical and psychological, that are

now believed to reflect the severe sexual and social restrictions of patriarchal culture.

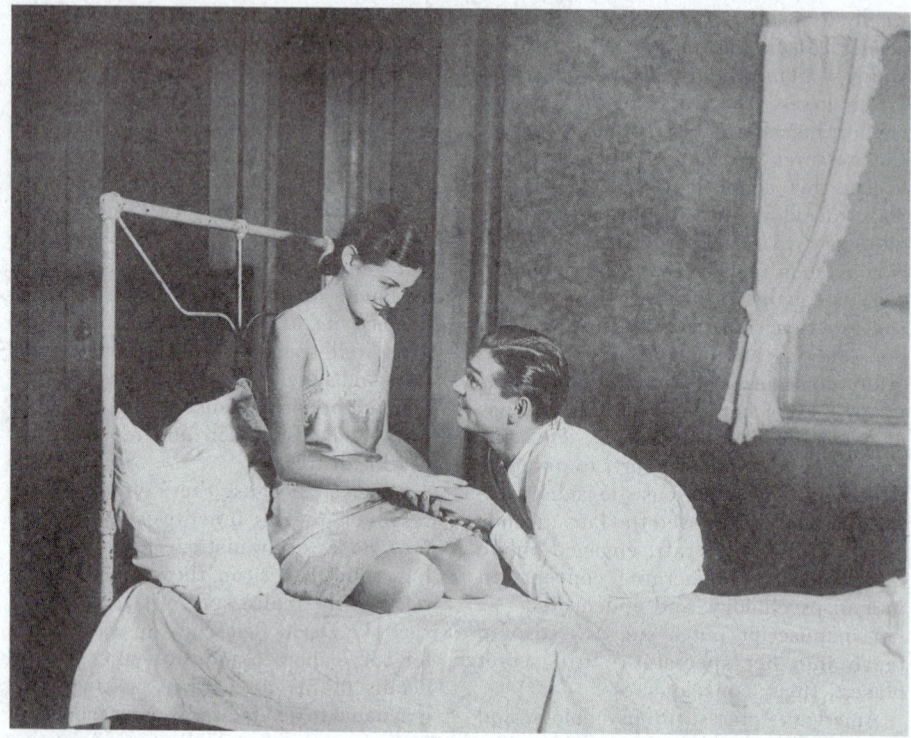

Zita Johann as Helen Jones and Clark Gable as Richard Roe in the original 1928 production of *Machinal* at the Plymouth Theater (New York).

influential expressionist productions of classical works, such as HAMLET, by directors who discovered in older plays psychic strains that were still relevant for their contemporary moment. Some initial reviewers of *Machinal*, as well as later theater historians, have suggested that Treadwell's play, rather than expanding the scope of the modernist theater, merely imitated Elmer Rice's *The Adding Machine* (1923), which utilized expressionist techniques to depict the world of Mr. Zero, a bookkeeper who kills his employer in retaliation for being replaced by an adding machine. Whereas many American expressionist productions in the 1920s were staged by noncommercial theaters, Rice's play remains important for its use of expressionism on Broadway to tell a story critical of American culture and industry. Yet the dismissal of Treadwell's work as simply derivative of Rice's is typical of the undervaluing of women's dramaturgy and creative innovation in the professional theater. Despite its artistic and commercial

success, with productions in France, Germany, England, and the Soviet Union following the Broadway premier, *Machinal* later fell into critical neglect, perhaps exacerbated by Treadwell's inability to duplicate its impact with any of her subsequent productions. Although Treadwell wrote thirty-nine plays, seven of which appeared on Broadway between 1922 and 1941, by the time of her death in 1970 her work for the theater was virtually unknown.

Scholarly efforts to identify forgotten women writers—aided immeasurably by the revival of *Machinal* at New York's Public Theatre in 1990—returned Treadwell to critical attention in the late twentieth century. This notable production then prompted a revival at the Royal National Theatre in London in 1993, and interest in Treadwell and *Machinal* blossomed. Now championed as an important feminist drama, *Machinal* has also reemerged as a pivotal text for the twentieth-century American theater. Treadwell's complex interweaving of cultural critique and stylistic innovation, coupled with her wrenching portrait of a young woman trapped in mechanized, depersonalized urban life, exemplifies the modernist notion of the *gesamtkunstwerk*, or total work of art, that in the theater reflects a synergy of narrative and theme, dramaturgical form, and production style.

Treadwell signals her affinity with expressionist techniques in the script's introductory information. The list of nameless characters, designated only by generic terms, resonates with the impersonal world they inhabit. Treadwell tells us that her central figure, the young woman, could be "any woman," suggesting that her feelings and actions are not unique; indeed, this female figure becomes threatening precisely because she is "ordinary," and thus many others could be like her. At the same time, her repeated calls for "somebody" point to the isolation of the modern individual: we are like each other, but we are also all alone.

Treadwell shifts us away from the thrall to traditional narrative by telling us what will occur: "The plot is the story of a woman who murders her husband." By so doing, Treadwell refocuses our attention to how and why this happens—questions more conducive to our active participation in the drama. *Machinal*'s episodic structure also resists that of traditional realist narrative; even more significantly, each scene occurs either before or following what in conventional plots would be considered the dramatic events: a proposal, a wedding, a birth, a moment of sexual passion, a killing. This dramaturgical strategy enables Treadwell to explore the psychic impact of such moments on her Everywoman.

In this regard Treadwell was not only sidestepping the traditional well-made play form, she was also directly critiquing the media's sensationalization of the Snyder murder. In particular, Treadwell recognized how Ruth Snyder became a product of the media, denied any personal agency or voice in her representation. Through each episode of *Machinal*, Treadwell similarly demonstrates how her protagonist is constructed by others and how modern, patriarchal culture systematically precludes any opportunity for the young woman to experience true freedom or independence.

One of the signal strengths of the play is Treadwell's ability to create this character fully despite her relative inarticulateness. In this regard, we might look to Treadwell's own recent contact with new methods in actor training as central to her dramaturgy in *Machinal*. From 1923 to 1925 Treadwell worked with Richard Boleslavski, a pupil of Konstantin Stanislavski who brought the master's acting techniques from Russia to the United States. Stanislavski's "system" provided actors with the means to decipher and then truthfully represent characters' motivations and actions. Through this training Treadwell may have grasped the critical synergy between actor and script and learned how what is unscripted, or unspoken, in the dialogue—what is otherwise known as the "subtext"—must nevertheless be clear if the actor is to understand and embody a character.

One of the hallmarks of Treadwell's expressionist concept for *Machinal* is her notion of a soundscape—the antithesis of a traditional musical score—that accompanies the dialogue and action and, perhaps even more strategically, provides the transitions between scenes. This aural text—every bit as important as the dialogic text to the play's overall theatrical effect—both complements the action and comments on it, especially as words fade out and sounds fill their place. Treadwell believed that sound has an "inherent emotional effect" in addition to its ability to foster atmosphere. In *Machinal* these are, moreover, everyday sounds, as generic as the characters who share the stage with them. Treadwell's dramatic language is everyday as well; she uses colloquial speech and current slang to create an urban American milieu easily recognizable for her Broadway audience. Yet she eschews traditional dialogic forms to strategic effect: words may be used as one part of the larger soundscape, as with the office workers' overlapping staccato speech, mechanical in its rapid-fire articulation, accompanied by the noise of the office equipment in "To Business"; or words may synecdochically reflect, as in the young woman's soliloquized syntactic gaps, the impossibility of full expression of any kind.

The play's scenic environment is generic as well, with only a minimum of furniture and props placed for each episode within a basic stage space. The set is demarcated by a larger, and then a smaller, window and by two, and then only one, entrance as the young woman's world closes in around her. Treadwell understood that lighting would also be integral to the work's impact. The unpublished production script for *Machinal* details the closing moment of the play, which some critics described as a distinct, wordless final scene following the execution and blackout: *Pause—overhead lights come on cyclorama first faint blue—then red—then pink—then amber—they are thrown up full . . . PAUSE, then . . . Curtain.*

This visual evocation of dawn must have provided some emotional balm at the same time that it left audiences with a final image of the complex interplay of technology, culture, and nature in the modern world. Almost a century later Treadwell's urgent questioning of the social, legal, and economic forces that may constrain our lives remains valid and critically important. To learn more about the staging of *Machinal* and to view photographs from select performances of the play, see the "Plays in Performance" color insert near the center of this volume.　　　　J.E.G.

Machinal

CHARACTERS

YOUNG WOMAN	MAN
TELEPHONE GIRL	ANOTHER MAN
STENOGRAPHER	WAITER
FILING CLERK	JUDGE
ADDING CLERK	LAWYER FOR DEFENSE
MOTHER	LAWYER FOR PROSECUTION
HUSBAND	COURT REPORTER
BELLBOY	BAILIFF
NURSE	REPORTER
DOCTOR	SECOND REPORTER
YOUNG MAN	THIRD REPORTER
GIRL	JAILER
MAN	MATRON
BOY	PRIEST

PLAYWRIGHT'S NOTES

THE PLOT is the story of a woman who murders her husband—an ordinary young woman, any woman.

THE PLAN is to tell this story by showing the different phases of life that the woman comes in contact with, and in none of which she finds any place, any peace. The woman is essentially soft, tender, and the life around her is essentially hard, mechanized. Business, home, marriage, having a child, seeking pleasure—all are difficult for her—mechanical, nerve nagging. Only in an illicit love does she find anything with life in it for her, and when she loses this, the desperate effort to win free to it again is her undoing.

The story is told in nine scenes. In the dialogue of these scenes there is the attempt to catch the rhythm of our common city speech, its brassy sound, its trick of repetition, etc.

Then there is, also, the use of many different sounds chosen primarily for their inherent emotional effect (steel riveting, a priest chanting, a Negro singing, jazz band, etc.), but contributing also to the creation of a background, an atmosphere.

THE HOPE is to create a stage production that will have "style," and at the same time, by the story's own innate drama, by the directness of its telling, by the variety and quick changingness of its scenes, and the excitement of its sounds, to create an interesting play.

SCENICALLY this play is planned to be handled in two basic sets (or in one set with two backs).

The first division—(The first Four Episodes)—needs an entrance at one side, and a back having a door and a large window. The door gives, in

Episode 1—to Vice President's office.

" 2— " hall.
" 3— " bathroom.
" 4— " corridor.

And the window shows, in

" 1—An opposite office.
" 2—An inner apartment court.
" 3—Window of a dance casino opposite.
" 4—Steel girders.

(Of these, only the casino window is important. Sky could be used for the others.)

The second division—(the last Five Episodes)—has the same side entrance, but the back has only one opening—for a small window (barred).

Episode 5, window is masked by electric piano.

" 6, " " disclosed (sidewalk outside).
" 7, " " curtained.
" 8, " " masked by Judge's bench.
" 9, " " disclosed (sky outside).

There is a change of furniture, and props for each episode—(only essential things, full of character).

For Episode 9, the room is closed in from the sides, and there is a place with bars and a door in it, put straight across stage down front (back far enough to leave a clear passageway in front of it).

LIGHTING concentrated and intense.—Light and shadow—bright light and darkness.—This darkness, already in the scene, grows and blacks out the light for dark stage when the scene changes are made.

OFFSTAGE VOICES

Characters in the Background
Heard, but Unseen

A Janitor
A Baby
A Boy and a Girl
A Husband and Wife
A Husband and Wife
A Radio Announcer
A Negro Singer

MECHANICAL
OFFSTAGE SOUNDS

A small jazz band
A hand organ
Steel riveting
Telegraph instruments
Aeroplane engine

MECHANICAL ONSTAGE SOUNDS

Office Machines (Typewriters, telephones, etc.)
Electric piano.

CHARACTERS

In the Background
Seen, Not Heard

(Seen, off the main set; i.e., through a window or door)

Couples of men and women dancing
A Woman in a bathrobe
A Woman in a wheel chair

A Nurse with a covered basin
A Nurse with a tray
The feet of men and women passing in the street.

Episode One

TO BUSINESS

SCENE: *An Office.*
  A Switchboard
  Filing Cabinet
  Adding Machine
  Typewriter and Table
  Manifold Machine[1]

SOUNDS: *Office Machines.*
  Typewriters
  Adding Machine
  Manifold
  Telephone Bells
  Buzzers

CHARACTERS AND THEIR MACHINES:
  A YOUNG WOMAN [*Typewriter*]
  A STENOGRAPHER [*Typewriter*]
  A FILING CLERK [*Filing cabinet and manifold*]
  AN ADDING CLERK [*Adding Machine*]
  TELEPHONE OPERATOR [*Switchboard*]

[BEFORE THE CURTAIN—*Sounds of Machines going. They continue throughout the scene, and accompany the Young Woman's thoughts after the scene is blacked out.*]

[AT THE RISE OF THE CURTAIN: *All the Machines are disclosed, and all the characters with the exception of* THE YOUNG WOMAN.]

Of these characters, THE YOUNG WOMAN, *going any day to any business. Ordinary. The confusion of her own inner thoughts, emotions, desires, dreams cuts her off from any actual adjustment to the routine of work. She gets through this routine with a very small surface of her consciousness. She is not homely and she is not pretty. She is preoccupied with herself—with her person. She has well kept hands, and a trick of constantly arranging her hair over her ears.*

The STENOGRAPHER *is the faded, efficient woman office worker. Drying, dried.*

The ADDING CLERK *is her male counterpart.*

The FILING CLERK *is a boy not grown, callow adolescence.*

The TELEPHONE GIRL, *young, cheap and amorous.*

Lights come up on office scene. Two desks R. *and* L. *Telephone booth back* R.C. *Filing cabinet back of* C. *Adding machine back* L.C.

ADDING CLERK [*in the monotonous voice of his monotonous thoughts; at his adding machine*]   2490, 28, 76, 123, 36842, 1, ¼, 37, 804, 23½, 982.

FILING CLERK [*in the same way—at his filing desk*]   Accounts—A. Bonds—B. Contracts—C. Data—D. Earnings—E.

STENOGRAPHER [*in the same way—Left*]   Dear Sir—in re—your letter—recent
5   date—will state—

TELEPHONE GIRL   Hello—Hello—George H. Jones Company good morning—hello hello—George H. Jones Company good morning—hello.

---

1. Copying machine.

FILING CLERK Market—M. Notes—N. Output—O. Profits—P.—! [*Suddenly.*] What's the matter with Q?

10 TELEPHONE GIRL Matter with it—Mr. J.—Mr. K. wants you— What you mean matter? Matter with what?

FILING CLERK Matter with Q.

TELEPHONE GIRL Well—what is? Spring 1726?

FILING CLERK I'm asking yuh——

15 TELEPHONE GIRL WELL?

FILING CLERK Nothing filed with it——

TELEPHONE GIRL Well?

FILING CLERK Look at A. Look at B. What's the matter with Q?

TELEPHONE GIRL Ain't popular. Hello—Hello—George H. Jones Company.

20 FILING CLERK Hot dog! Why ain't it?

ADDING CLERK Has it personality?

STENOGRAPHER Has it Halitosis?[2]

TELEPHONE GIRL Has it got it?

FILING CLERK Hot dog!

25 TELEPHONE GIRL What number do you want? [*Recognizing but not pleased.*] Oh—hello—sure I know who it is—tonight? Uh, uh—[*Negative, but each with a different inflection.*]—you heard me—No!

FILING CLERK Don't you like him?

STENOGRAPHER She likes 'em all.

30 TELEPHONE GIRL I do not!

STENOGRAPHER Well—pretty near all!

TELEPHONE GIRL What number do you want? Wrong number. Hello— hello—George H. Jones Company. Hello, hello—

STENOGRAPHER Memorandum—attention Mr. Smith—at a conference 35 of——

ADDING CLERK 125—83¾—22—908—34—¼—28593——

FILING CLERK Report—R, Sales—S, Trade—T.

TELEPHONE GIRL Shh—! Yes, Mr. J.—? No—Miss A. ain't in yet—I'll tell her, Mr. J.—just the minute she gets in.

40 STENOGRAPHER She's late again, huh?

TELEPHONE GIRL Out with her sweetie last night, huh?

FILING CLERK Hot dog.

ADDING CLERK She ain't got a sweetie.

STENOGRAPHER How do you know?

45 ADDING CLERK I know.

FILING CLERK Hot dog.

ADDING CLERK She lives alone with her mother.

TELEPHONE GIRL Spring 1876? Hello—Spring 1876. Spring! Hello, Spring 1876? 1876! Wrong number! Hello! Hello!

50 STENOGRAPHER Director's meeting semi-annual report card.

FILING CLERK Shipments—Sales—Schedules—S.

ADDING CLERK She doesn't belong in an office.

TELEPHONE GIRL Who does?

STENOGRAPHER I do!

55 ADDING CLERK You said it!

FILING CLERK Hot dog!

---

2. Bad breath.

TELEPHONE GIRL   Hello—hello—George H. Jones Company—hello—hello—

STENOGRAPHER   I'm efficient. She's inefficient.

FILING CLERK   She's inefficient.

60 TELEPHONE GIRL   She's got J. going.

STENOGRAPHER   Going?

TELEPHONE GIRL   Going and coming.

FILING CLERK   Hot dog.

> [*Enter* JONES.]

JONES   Good morning, everybody.

65 TELEPHONE GIRL   Good morning.

FILING CLERK   Good morning.

ADDING CLERK   Good morning.

STENOGRAPHER   Good morning, Mr. J.

JONES   Miss A. isn't in yet?

70 TELEPHONE GIRL   Not yet, Mr. J.

FILING CLERK   Not yet.

ADDING CLERK   Not yet.

STENOGRAPHER   She's late.

JONES   I just wanted her to take a letter.

75 STENOGRAPHER   I'll take the letter.

JONES   One thing at a time and that done well.

ADDING CLERK [*yessing*]   Done well.

STENOGRAPHER   I'll finish it later.

JONES   Hew to the line.

80 ADDING CLERK   Hew to the line.

STENOGRAPHER   Then I'll hurry.

JONES   Haste makes waste.

ADDING CLERK   Waste.

STENOGRAPHER   But if you're in a hurry.

85 JONES   I'm never in a hurry—That's how I get ahead! [*Laughs. They all laugh.*]
First know you're right—then go ahead.

ADDING CLERK   Ahead.

JONES [*to* TELEPHONE GIRL]   When Miss A. comes in tell her I want her to
take a letter. [*Turns to go in—then.*] It's important.

90 TELEPHONE GIRL [*making a note*]   Miss A.—important.

JONES [*starts up—then*]   And I don't want to be disturbed.

TELEPHONE GIRL   You're in conference?

JONES   I'm in conference. [*Turns—then*] Unless it's A.B.—of course.

TELEPHONE GIRL   Of course—A.B.

95 JONES [*starts—turns again; attempts to be facetious*]   Tell Miss A. the early
bird catches the worm.

> [*Exit* JONES.]

TELEPHONE GIRL   The early worm gets caught.

ADDING CLERK   He's caught.

TELEPHONE GIRL   Hooked.

100 ADDING CLERK   In the pan.

FILING CLERK   Hot dog.

STENOGRAPHER   We beg leave to announce——

> [*Enter* YOUNG WOMAN. *Goes behind telephone booth to desk* R.]

STENOGRAPHER   You're late!

FILING CLERK You're late.
105 ADDING CLERK You're late.
STENOGRAPHER And yesterday!
FILING CLERK The day before.
ADDING CLERK And the day before.
STENOGRAPHER You'll lose your job.
110 YOUNG WOMAN No!
STENOGRAPHER No?

[WORKERS *exchange glances.*]

YOUNG WOMAN I can't!
STENOGRAPHER Can't?

[*Same business.*]

FILING CLERK Rent—bills—installments—miscellaneous.
115 ADDING CLERK A dollar ten—ninety-five—3.40—35—12.60.
STENOGRAPHER Then why are you late?
YOUNG WOMAN Why?
STENOGRAPHER Excuse!
ADDING CLERK Excuse!
120 FILING CLERK Excuse.
TELEPHONE GIRL Excuse it, please.
STENOGRAPHER Why?
YOUNG WOMAN The subway?
TELEPHONE GIRL Long distance?
125 FILING CLERK Old stuff!
ADDING CLERK That stall!
STENOGRAPHER Stalled?
YOUNG WOMAN No——
STENOGRAPHER What?
130 YOUNG WOMAN I had to get out!
ADDING CLERK Out!
FILING CLERK Out?
STENOGRAPHER Out where?
YOUNG WOMAN In the air!
135 STENOGRAPHER Air?
YOUNG WOMAN All those bodies pressing.
FILING CLERK Hot dog!
YOUNG WOMAN I thought I would faint! I had to get out in the air!
FILING CLERK Give her the air.
140 ADDING CLERK Free air—
STENOGRAPHER Hot air.
YOUNG WOMAN Like I'm dying.
STENOGRAPHER Same thing yesterday. [*Pause.*] And the day before.
YOUNG WOMAN Yes—what am I going to do?
145 ADDING CLERK Take a taxi!

[THEY *laugh.*]

FILING CLERK Call a cop!
TELEPHONE GIRL Mr. J. wants you.
YOUNG WOMAN Me?
TELEPHONE GIRL You!
150 YOUNG WOMAN [*rises*] Mr. J.!

STENOGRAPHER Mr. J.

TELEPHONE GIRL He's bellowing for you!

[YOUNG WOMAN *gives last pat to her hair—goes off into door—back.*]

STENOGRAPHER [*after her*] Get it just right.

FILING CLERK She's always doing that to her hair.

155 TELEPHONE GIRL It gives a line—it gives a line—3

FILING CLERK Hot dog.

ADDING CLERK She's artistic.

STENOGRAPHER She's inefficient.

FILING CLERK She's inefficient.

160 STENOGRAPHER Mr. J. knows she's inefficient.

ADDING CLERK 46-23-84-2-2-2-1,492—678.

TELEPHONE GIRL Hello—hello—George H. Jones Company—hello—Mr. Jones? He's in conference.

STENOGRAPHER [*sarcastic*] Conference!

165 ADDING CLERK Conference.

FILING CLERK Hot dog!

TELEPHONE GIRL Do you think he'll marry her?

ADDING CLERK If she'll have him.

STENOGRAPHER If she'll have him!

170 FILING CLERK Do you think she'll have him?

TELEPHONE GIRL How much does he get?

ADDING CLERK Plenty—5,000—10,000—15,000—20,000—25,000.

STENOGRAPHER And plenty put away.

ADDING CLERK Gas Preferred—4's—steel—5's—oil—6's.

175 FILING CLERK Hot dog.

STENOGRAPHER Will she have him? Will she have him? This agreement entered into—party of the first part—party of the second part—will he have her?

TELEPHONE GIRL Well, I'd hate to get into bed with him. [*Familiar melting voice.*] Hello—humhum—hum—hum—hold the line a minute—will you—

180 hum hum. [*Professional voice.*] Hell, hello—A.B., just a minute, Mr. A.B.—Mr. J.? Mr. A.B.—go ahead, Mr. A.B. [*Melting voice.*] We were interrupted—huh—huh—huh-huhuh—hum—hum.

[*Enter* YOUNG WOMAN—*she goes to her chair, sits with folded hands.*]

FILING CLERK That's all you ever say to a guy—

STENOGRAPHER Hum—hum—or uh huh—[*Negative.*]

185 TELEPHONE GIRL That's all you have to. [*To phone.*] Hum—hum—hum hum—hum hum—

STENOGRAPHER Mostly hum hum.

ADDING CLERK You've said it!

FILING CLERK Hot dog.

190 TELEPHONE GIRL Hum hum huh hum humhumhum—tonight? She's got a date—she told me last night—humhumhuh—hum—all right. [*Disconnects.*] Too bad—my boy friend's got a friend—but my girl friend's got a date.

YOUNG WOMAN You have a good time.

TELEPHONE GIRL Big time.

195 STENOGRAPHER Small time.

ADDING CLERK A big time on the small time.

---

3. The slant or line of a woman's bobbed haircut was one of its notable features.

TELEPHONE GIRL I'd ask you, kid, but you'd be up to your neck!

STENOGRAPHERS Neckers!

ADDING CLERK Petters!

200 FILING CLERK Sweet papas.

TELEPHONE GIRL Want to come?

YOUNG WOMAN Can't.

TELEPHONE GIRL Date?

YOUNG WOMAN My mother.

205 STENOGRAPHER Worries?

TELEPHONE GIRL Nags—hello—George H. Jones Company—Oh hello—

[YOUNG WOMAN *sits before her machine—hands in lap, looking at them.*]

STENOGRAPHER Why don't you get to work?

YOUNG WOMAN [*dreaming*] What?

ADDING CLERK Work!

210 YOUNG WOMAN Can't.

STENOGRAPHER Can't?

YOUNG WOMAN My machine's out of order.

STENOGRAPHER Well, fix it!

YOUNG WOMAN I can't—got to get somebody.

215 STENOGRAPHER Somebody! Somebody! Always somebody! Here, sort the mail, then!

YOUNG WOMAN [*rises*] All right.

STENOGRAPHER And hurry! You're late.

YOUNG WOMAN [*sorting letters*] George H. Jones & Company—George H.

220 Jones Inc. George H. Jones—

STENOGRAPHER You're always late.

ADDING CLERK You'll lose your job.

YOUNG WOMAN [*hurrying*] George H. Jones—George H. Jones Personal—

TELEPHONE GIRL Don't let 'em get your goat, kid—tell 'em where to get off.

225 YOUNG WOMAN What?

TELEPHONE GIRL Ain't it all set?

YOUNG WOMAN What?

TELEPHONE GIRL You and Mr. J.

STENOGRAPHER You and the boss.

230 FILING CLERK You and the big chief.

ADDING CLERK You and the big cheese.

YOUNG WOMAN Did he tell you?

TELEPHONE GIRL I told you!

ADDING CLERK I told you!

235 STENOGRAPHER I don't believe it.

ADDING CLERK 5,000—10,000—15,000.

FILING CLERK Hot dog.

YOUNG WOMAN No—it isn't so.

STENOGRAPHER Isn't it?

240 YOUNG WOMAN No.

TELEPHONE GIRL Not yet.

ADDING CLERK But soon.

FILING CLERK Hot dog.

[*Enter* JONES.]

TELEPHONE GIRL [*busy*] George H. Jones Company—Hello—Hello.

245 STENOGRAPHER   Awaiting your answer—
ADDING CLERK   5,000—10,000—15,000—
JONES [*crossing to* YOUNG WOMAN—*puts hand on her shoulder,* ALL *stop and stare*]   That letter done?
YOUNG WOMAN   No. [*She pulls away.*]
JONES   What's the matter?
250 STENOGRAPHER   She hasn't started.
JONES   O.K.—want to make some changes.
YOUNG WOMAN   My machine's out of order.
JONES   O.K.—use the one in my room.
YOUNG WOMAN   I'm sorting the mail.
255 STENOGRAPHER [*sarcastic*]   One thing at a time!
JONES [*retreating—goes back* c.]   O.K. [*To* YOUNG WOMAN] When you're finished. [*Starts back to his room.*]
STENOGRAPHER   Haste makes waste.
JONES [*at door*]   O.K.—don't hurry.
          [*Exits.*]
260 STENOGRAPHER   Hew to the line!
TELEPHONE GIRL   He's hewing.
FILING CLERK   Hot dog.
TELEPHONE GIRL   Why did you flinch, kid?
YOUNG WOMAN   Flinch?
265 TELEPHONE GIRL   Did he pinch?
YOUNG WOMAN   No!
TELEPHONE GIRL   Then what?
YOUNG WOMAN   Nothing!—Just his hand.
TELEPHONE GIRL   Oh—just his hand—[*Shakes her head thoughtfully.*] Uhhuh.
270 [*Negative.*] Uhhuh. [*Decisively.*] No! Tell him no.
STENOGRAPHER   If she does she'll lose her job.
ADDING CLERK   Fired.
FILING CLERK   The sack!
TELEPHONE GIRL [*on the defensive*]   And if she doesn't?
275 ADDING CLERK   She'll come to work in a taxi!
TELEPHONE GIRL   Work?
FILING CLERK   No work.
STENOGRAPHER   No worry.
ADDING CLERK   Breakfast in bed.
280 STENOGRAPHER [*sarcastic*]   Did Madame ring?
FILING CLERK   Lunch in bed!
TELEPHONE GIRL   A double bed! [*In phone.*] Yes, Mr. J. [*To* YOUNG WOMAN]
J. wants you.
YOUNG WOMAN [*starts to get to her feet—but doesn't*]   I can't—I'm not
285 ready—In a minute. [*Sits staring ahead of her.*]
ADDING CLERK   5,000—10,000—15,000—
FILING CLERK   Profits—plans—purchase—
STENOGRAPHER   Call your attention our prices are fixed.
TELEPHONE GIRL   Hello—hello—George H. Jones Company—hello—hello—
YOUNG WOMAN [*thinking her thoughts aloud—to the subdued accompani-*
290 *ment of the office sounds and voices*]   Marry me—wants to marry me—
George H. Jones—George H. Jones and Company—Mrs. George H.

Jones—Mrs. George H. Jones. Dear Madame—marry—do you take this man to be your wedded husband—I do—to love honor and to love—kisses—no—I can't—George H. Jones—How would you like to marry me—What do
295 you say—Why Mr. Jones I—let me look at your little hands—you have such pretty little hands—let me hold your pretty little hands—George H. Jones—Fat hands—flabby hands—don't touch me—please—fat hands are never weary—please don't—married—all girls—most girls—married—babies—a baby—curls—little curls all over its head—George H. Jones—straight—
300 thin—bald—don't touch me—please—no—can't—must—somebody—something—no rest—must rest—no rest—must rest—no rest—late today—yesterday—before—late—subway—air—pressing—bodies pressing—bodies—trembling—air—stop—air—late—job—no job—fired—late—alarm clock—alarm clock—alarm clock—hurry—job—ma—nag—
305 nag—nag—ma—hurry—job—no job—no money—installments due—no money—money—George H. Jones—money—Mrs. George H. Jones—money—no work—no worry—free!—rest—sleep till nine—sleep till ten—sleep till noon—now you take a good rest this morning—don't get up till you want to—thank you—oh thank you—oh don't!—please don't touch me—I
310 want to rest—no rest—earn—got to earn—married—earn—no—yes—earn—all girls—most girls—ma—pa—ma—all women—most women—I can't—must—maybe—must—somebody—something—ma—pa—ma—can I, ma? Tell me, ma—something—somebody.

BLACK OUT

[*The sounds of the office machines continue until the scene lights into Episode 2,—and the office sounds become the sound of a radio (offstage).*]

Episode Two

AT HOME

SCENE: *A Kitchen.*
    Table—chairs—plates and food—Garbage can—a pair of rubber gloves.
    The door at the back now opens on a hall—the window, on an apartment house court.

CHARACTERS:
    YOUNG WOMAN
    MOTHER

OUTSIDE VOICES: *Characters heard, but not seen:*
    A JANITOR
    A BABY
    A MOTHER AND A SMALL BOY
    A YOUNG BOY AND YOUNG GIRL
    A HUSBAND AND A WIFE
    ANOTHER HUSBAND AND A WIFE

SOUNDS:
    Buzzer
    Radio [Voice of Announcer]
        [Music and Singer]

AT RISE:
    YOUNG WOMAN *and* MOTHER *eating—Radio offstage—Radio stops.*

————————————

YOUNG WOMAN Ma—I want to talk to you.

MOTHER Aren't you eating a potato?

YOUNG WOMAN No.

MOTHER Why not?

5 YOUNG WOMAN I don't want one.

MOTHER That's no reason. Here! Take one.

YOUNG WOMAN I don't want it.

MOTHER Potatoes go with stew—here!

YOUNG WOMAN Ma, I don't want it!

10 MOTHER Want it! Take it!

YOUNG WOMAN But I—oh, all right. [*Takes it—then.*] Ma, I want to ask you something.

MOTHER Eat your potato.

YOUNG WOMAN [*takes a bite—then*] Ma, there's something I want to ask
15 you—something important.

MOTHER Is it mealy?

YOUNG WOMAN S'all right. Ma—tell me.

MOTHER Three pounds for a quarter.

YOUNG WOMAN Ma—tell me—
    [*Buzzer.*]

20 MOTHER [*her dull voice brightening*] There's the garbage. [*Goes to door—or dumbwaiter⁴—opens it.*]
    [*Stop radio.*]

JANITOR'S VOICE [*offstage*] Garbage.

MOTHER [*pleased—busy*] All right. [*Gets garbage can—puts it out.* YOUNG WOMAN *walks up and down.*] What's the matter now?

YOUNG WOMAN Nothing.

25 MOTHER That jumping up from the table every night the garbage is collected! You act like you're crazy.

YOUNG WOMAN Ma, do all women—

MOTHER I suppose you think you're too nice for anything so common! Well, let me tell you, my lady, that it's a very important part of life.

30 YOUNG WOMAN I know, but, Ma, if you—

MOTHER If it weren't for garbage cans where would we be? Where would we all be? Living in filth—that's what! Filth! I should think you'd be glad! I should think you'd be grateful!

YOUNG WOMAN Oh, Ma!

35 MOTHER Well, are you?

YOUNG WOMAN Am I what?

MOTHER Glad! Grateful.

YOUNG WOMAN Yes!

MOTHER You don't act like it!

40 YOUNG WOMAN Oh, Ma, don't talk!

MOTHER You just said you wanted to talk.

YOUNG WOMAN Well now—I want to think. I got to think.

MOTHER Aren't you going to finish your potato?

YOUNG WOMAN Oh, Ma!

45 MOTHER Is there anything the matter with it?

YOUNG WOMAN No—

4. Small elevator system used to move food or other goods between floors of a building.

MOTHER   Then why don't you finish it?

YOUNG WOMAN   Because I don't want it.

MOTHER   Why don't you?

50 YOUNG WOMAN   Oh, Ma! Let me alone!

MOTHER   Well, you've got to eat! If you don't eat—

YOUNG WOMAN   Ma! Don't nag!

MOTHER   Nag! Just because I try to look out for you—nag! Just because I try
to care for you—nag! Why, you haven't sense enough to eat! What would
55 become of you I'd like to know—if I didn't nag!

[*Offstage—a sound of window opening—all these offstage sounds come
in through the court window at the back.*]

WOMAN'S VOICE   Johnny—Johnny—come in now!

A SMALL BOY'S VOICE   Oh, Ma!

WOMAN VOICE   It's getting cold.

A SMALL BOY'S VOICE   Oh, Ma!

60 WOMAN'S VOICE   You heard me! [*Sound of window slamming.*]

YOUNG WOMAN   I'm grown up, Ma.

MOTHER   Grown up! What do you mean by that?

YOUNG WOMAN   Nothing much—I guess. [*Offstage sound of baby crying.*
MOTHER *rises, clatters dishes.*] Let's not do the dishes right away, Ma. Let's
65 talk—I gotta.

MOTHER   Well, I can't talk with dirty dishes around—you may be able to
but—[*Clattering—clattering.*]

YOUNG WOMAN   Ma! Listen! Listen!—There's a man wants to marry me.

MOTHER [*stops clattering—sits*]   What man?

70 YOUNG WOMAN   He says he fell in love with my hands.

MOTHER   In love! Is that beginning again! I thought you were over that!

[*Offstage* BOY'S VOICE—*whistles—*GIRL'S VOICE *answers.*]

BOY'S VOICE   Come on out.

GIRL'S VOICE   Can't.

BOY'S VOICE   Nobody'll see you.

75 GIRL'S VOICE   I can't.

BOY'S VOICE   It's dark now—come on.

GIRL'S VOICE   Well—just for a minute.

BOY'S VOICE   Meet you round the corner.

YOUNG WOMAN   I got to get married, Ma.

80 MOTHER   What do you mean?

YOUNG WOMAN   I gotta.

MOTHER   You haven't got in trouble, have you?

YOUNG WOMAN   Don't talk like that!

MOTHER   Well, you say you got to get married—what do you mean?

85 YOUNG WOMAN   Nothing.

MOTHER   Answer me!

YOUNG WOMAN   All women get married, don't they?

MOTHER   Nonsense!

YOUNG WOMAN   You got married, didn't you?

90 MOTHER   Yes, I did!

[*Offstage voices.*]

WOMAN'S VOICE   Where you going?

MAN'S VOICE   Out.

WOMAN'S VOICE   You were out last night.

MAN'S VOICE   Was I?

95   WOMAN'S VOICE   You're always going out.

MAN'S VOICE   Am I?

WOMAN'S VOICE   Where you going?

MAN'S VOICE   Out.

[*End of offstage voices.*]

MOTHER   Who is he? Where did you come to know him?

100   YOUNG WOMAN   In the office.

MOTHER   In the office!

YOUNG WOMAN   It's Mr. J.

MOTHER   Mr. J.?

YOUNG WOMAN   The Vice-President.

105   MOTHER   Vice-President! His income must be—Does he know you've got a mother to support?

YOUNG WOMAN   Yes.

MOTHER   What does he say?

YOUNG WOMAN   All right.

110   MOTHER   How soon you going to marry him?

YOUNG WOMAN   I'm not going to.

MOTHER   Not going to!

YOUNG WOMAN   No! I'm not going to.

MOTHER   But you just said—

115   YOUNG WOMAN   I'm not going to.

MOTHER   Are you crazy?

YOUNG WOMAN   I can't, Ma! I can't!

MOTHER   Why can't you?

YOUNG WOMAN   I don't love him.

120   MOTHER   Love!—what does that amount to! Will it clothe you? Will it feed you? Will it pay the bills?

YOUNG WOMAN   No! But it's real just the same!

MOTHER   Real!

YOUNG WOMAN   If it isn't—what can you count on in life?

125   MOTHER   I'll tell you what you can count on! You can count that you've got to eat and sleep and get up and put clothes on your back and take 'em off again—that you got to get old—and that you got to die. That's what you can count on! All the rest is in your head!

YOUNG WOMAN   But Ma—didn't you love Pa?

130   MOTHER   I suppose I did—I don't know—I've forgotten—what difference does it make—now?

YOUNG WOMAN   But then!—oh Ma, tell me!

MOTHER   Tell you what?

YOUNG WOMAN   About all that—love!

[*Offstage voices.*]

135   WIFE'S VOICE   Don't.

HUSBAND'S VOICE   What's the matter—don't you want me to kiss you?

WIFE'S VOICE   Not like that.

HUSBAND'S VOICE   Like what?

WIFE'S VOICE   That silly kiss!

140 HUSBAND'S VOICE   Silly kiss?

WIFE'S VOICE   You look so silly—oh I know what's coming when you look like that—and kiss me like that—don't—go away—

[*End of off stage voices.*]

MOTHER   He's a decent man, isn't he?

YOUNG WOMAN   I don't know. How should I know—yet.

145 MOTHER   He's a Vice-President—of course he's decent.

YOUNG WOMAN   I don't care whether he's decent or not. I won't marry him.

MOTHER   But you just said you wanted to marry—

YOUNG WOMAN   Not him.

MOTHER   Who?

150 YOUNG WOMAN   I don't know—I don't know—I haven't found him yet!

MOTHER   You talk like you're crazy!

YOUNG WOMAN   Oh, Ma—tell me!

MOTHER   Tell you what?

YOUNG WOMAN   Tell me—[*Words suddenly pouring out.*] Your skin oughtn't
155   to curl—ought it—when he just comes near you—ought it? That's wrong, ain't it? You don't get over that, do you—ever, do you or do you? How is it, Ma—do you?

MOTHER   Do you what?

YOUNG WOMAN   Do you get used to, it—so after a while it doesn't matter? Or
160   don't you? Does it always matter? You ought to be in love, oughtn't you, Ma? You must be in love, mustn't you, Ma? That changes everything, doesn't it—or does it? Maybe if you just like a person it's all right—is it? When he puts a hand on me, my blood turns cold. But your blood oughtn't to run cold, ought it? His hands are—his hands are—fat, Ma—don't you
165   see—his hands are fat—and they sort of press—and they're fat—don't you see?—Don't you see?

MOTHER [*stares at her bewildered*]   See what?

YOUNG WOMAN [*rushing on*]   I've always thought I'd find somebody—somebody young—and—and attractive—with wavy hair—wavy hair—I
170   always think of children with curls—little curls all over their head—somebody young—and attractive—that I'd like—that I'd love— But I haven't found anybody like that yet—I haven't found anybody— I've hardly known anybody—you'd never let me go with anybody and—

MOTHER   Are you throwing it up to me that—

175 YOUNG WOMAN   No—let me finish, Ma! No—let me finish! I just mean I've never found anybody—anybody—nobody's ever asked me—till now—he's the only man that's ever asked me— And I suppose I got to marry somebody—all girls do—

MOTHER   Nonsense.

180 YOUNG WOMAN   But, I can't go on like this, Ma—I don't know why—but I can't—it's like I'm all tight inside—sometimes I feel like I'm stifling!— You don't know—stifling. [*Walks up and down.*] I can't go on like this much longer—going to work—coming home—going to work—coming home—I can't— Sometimes in the subway I think I'm going to die—sometimes even
185   in the office if something don't happen—I got to do something—I don't know—it's like I'll all tight inside.

MOTHER   You're crazy.

YOUNG WOMAN   Oh, Ma!

MOTHER   You're crazy!

190 YOUNG WOMAN   Ma—if you tell me that again I'll kill you! I'll kill you!

MOTHER   If that isn't crazy!

YOUNG WOMAN   I'll kill you—Maybe I am crazy—I don't know. Sometimes I think I am—the thoughts that go on in my mind—sometimes I think I am—I can't help it if I am—I do the best I can—I do the best I can and I'm
195 nearly crazy! [MOTHER *rises and sits.*] Go away! Go away! You don't know anything about anything! And you haven't got any pity—no pity—you just take it for granted that I go to work every day—and come home every night and bring my money every week—you just take it for granted—you'd let me go on forever—and never feel any pity—

[*Offstage* RADIO—*a voice singing a sentimental Mother song or popular home song.*]

[MOTHER *begins to cry—crosses to chair Left—sits.*]

200 YOUNG WOMAN   Oh Ma—forgive me! Forgive me!

MOTHER   My own child! To be spoken to like that by my own child!

YOUNG WOMAN   I didn't mean it, Ma—I didn't mean it!

[*She goes to her mother—crosses to Left.*]

MOTHER   [*clinging to her hand*]   You're all I've got in the world—and you don't want me—you want to kill me.

205 YOUNG WOMAN   No—no, I don't, Ma! I just said that!

MOTHER   I've worked for you and slaved for you!

YOUNG WOMAN   I know, Ma.

MOTHER   I brought you into the world.

YOUNG WOMAN   I know, Ma.

210 MOTHER   You're flesh of my flesh and—

YOUNG WOMAN   I know, Ma, I know.

MOTHER   And—

YOUNG WOMAN   You rest, now, Ma—you rest—

MOTHER   [*struggling*]   I got to do the dishes.

215 YOUNG WOMAN   I'll do the dishes— You listen to the music, Ma—I'll do the dishes.

[MA *sits.*]

[YOUNG WOMAN *crosses to behind screen.*]

[*Takes a pair of rubber gloves and begins to put them on.*]

[*The* MOTHER *sees them—they irritate her—there is a return of her characteristic mood.*]

MOTHER   Those gloves! I've been washing dishes for forty years and I never wore gloves! But my lady's hands! My lady's hands!

YOUNG WOMAN   Sometimes you talk to me like you're jealous, Ma.

220 MOTHER   Jealous?

YOUNG WOMAN   It's my hands got me a husband.

MOTHER   A husband? So you're going to marry him now!

YOUNG WOMAN   I suppose so.

MOTHER   If you ain't the craziest—

[*The scene blacks out.*]

[*In the darkness, the* MOTHER *song goes into jazz—very faint—as the scene lights into*]

Episode Three
HONEYMOON

SCENE: *Hotel Bedroom.*
    Bed, chair, mirror.
    The door at the back now opens on a bathroom; the window, on a dancing
    casino opposite.

CHARACTERS:
    YOUNG WOMAN
    HUSBAND
    BELLBOY

OFFSTAGE:
    *Seen but not heard—*MEN *and* WOMEN *dancing in couples.*

SOUNDS:
    A small jazz band [violin, piano, saxophone—very dim, at first, then louder].

AT RISE:
    Set dark.

BELLBOY, HUSBAND, *and* YOUNG WOMAN *enter.* BELLBOY *carries luggage. He switches
    on light by door.*

Stop music.

———————————

HUSBAND   Well, here we are.
    [*Throws hat on bed.*]
    [BELLBOY *puts luggage down, crosses to window, raises shade three inches,*
    opens window three inches.]
    [*Sounds of jazz music louder. Offstage.*]
BELLBOY [*comes to man for tip*]   Anything else, Sir?
    [*Receives tip. Exits.*]
HUSBAND   Well, here we are.
YOUNG WOMAN   Yes, here we are.
5 HUSBAND   Aren't you going to take your hat off—stay a while? [YOUNG WOMAN
    looks around as though looking for a way out, then takes off her hat, pulls the
    hair automatically around her ears.] This is all right, isn't it? Huh? Huh?
YOUNG WOMAN   It's very nice.
HUSBAND   Twelve bucks a day![5] They know how to soak you in these pleasure
    resorts. Twelve bucks! [*Music.*] Well—we'll get our money's worth out of it
10   all right. [*Goes toward bathroom.*] I'm going to wash up. [*Stops at door.*]
    Don't you want to wash up? [YOUNG WOMAN *shakes head "No".*] I do! It was
    a long trip! I want to wash up! [*Goes off—closes door. Sings in bathroom.*
    YOUNG WOMAN *goes to window—raises shade—sees the dancers going round*
    and round in couples. Music is louder. Re-enter HUSBAND.] Say, pull that
    blind down! They can see in!
15 YOUNG WOMAN   I thought you said there'd be a view of the ocean!
HUSBAND   Sure there is.
YOUNG WOMAN   I just see people—dancing.
HUSBAND   The ocean's beyond.

5. Approximately $160 in current value; in 1928 luxury hotel room rates began at $4 to $6 per night, so a $12 room rate would have been for the finest accommodations possible.

YOUNG WOMAN [*desperately*]   I was counting on seeing it!

20 HUSBAND   You'll see it tomorrow—what's eating you? We'll take in the board-walk[6]—Don't you want to wash up?

YOUNG WOMAN   No!

HUSBAND   It was a long trip. Sure you don't? [YOUNG WOMAN *shakes her head "No."* HUSBAND *takes off his coat—puts it over chair.*] Better make yourself at

25 home. I'm going to. [*She stares at him—moves away from the window.*] Say, pull down that blind! [*Crosses to chair down* L—*sits.*]

YOUNG WOMAN   It's close—don't you think it's close?

HUSBAND   Well—you don't want people looking in, do you? [*Laughs.*] Huh—huh?

30 YOUNG WOMAN   No.

HUSBAND [*laughs*]   I guess not. Huh? [*Takes off shoes.* YOUNG WOMAN *leaves the window, and crosses down to the bed.*] Say—you look a little white around the gills! What's the matter?

YOUNG WOMAN   Nothing.

35 HUSBAND   You look like you're scared.

YOUNG WOMAN   No.

HUSBAND   Nothing to be scared of. You're with your husband, you know.
    [*Takes her to chair, left.*]

YOUNG WOMAN   I know.

HUSBAND   Happy?

40 YOUNG WOMAN   Yes.

HUSBAND [*sitting*]   Then come here and give us a kiss. [*He puts her on his knee.*] That's the girlie. [*He bends her head down, and kisses her along the back of her neck.*] Like that? [*She tries to get to her feet.*] Say—stay there! What you moving for?—You know—you got to learn to relax, little girl—

45 [*Dancers go off. Dim lights. Pinches her above knee.*] Say, what you got under there?

YOUNG WOMAN   Nothing.

HUSBAND   Nothing! [*Laughs.*] That's a good one! Nothing, huh? Huh? That reminds me of the story of the pullman porter and the—what's the matter—

50 did I tell you that one?
    [*Music dims off and out.*]

YOUNG WOMAN   I don't know.

HUSBAND   The pullman porter and the tart?

YOUNG WOMAN   No.

HUSBAND   It's a good one—well—the train was just pulling out and the

55 tart—

YOUNG WOMAN   You did tell that one!

HUSBAND   About the—

YOUNG WOMAN   Yes! Yes! I remember now!

HUSBAND   About the—

60 YOUNG WOMAN   Yes!

HUSBAND   All right—if I did. You're sure it was the one about the—

YOUNG WOMAN   I'm sure.

6. Although Treadwell does not specify locations in the play, this reference to a boardwalk would have suggested Atlantic City, New Jersey, a popular tourist location accessible from New York City by train.

HUSBAND   When he asked her what she had underneath her seat and she said—

65 YOUNG WOMAN   Yes! Yes! That one!

HUSBAND   All right— But I don't believe I did. [SHE *tries to get up again, as* HE *holds her.*] You know you have got something under there—what is it?

YOUNG WOMAN   Nothing—just—just my garter.

HUSBAND   Your garter! Your garter! Say did I tell you the one about—

70 YOUNG WOMAN   Yes! Yes!

HUSBAND   [*with dignity*]   How do you know which one I meant?

YOUNG WOMAN   You told me them all!

HUSBAND   [*pulling her back to his knee*]   No, I didn't! Not by a jugful! I got a lot of 'em up my sleeve yet—that's part of what I owe my success to—my

75   ability to spring a good story—You know—you got to learn to relax, little girl—haven't you?

YOUNG WOMAN   Yes.

HUSBAND   That's one of the biggest things to learn in life. That's part of what I owe my success to. Now you go and get those heavy things off—

80   and relax.

YOUNG WOMAN   They're not heavy.

HUSBAND   You haven't got much on—have you? But you'll feel better with 'em off. [*Gets up.*] Want me to help you?

YOUNG WOMAN   No.

85 HUSBAND   I'm your husband, you know.

YOUNG WOMAN   I know.

HUSBAND   You aren't afraid of your husband, are you?

YOUNG WOMAN   No—of course not—but I thought maybe—can't we go out for a little while?

90 HUSBAND   Out? What for?

YOUNG WOMAN   Fresh air—walk—talk.

HUSBAND   We can talk here—I'll tell you all about myself. Go along now. [YOUNG WOMAN *goes toward bathroom door—gets bag.*] Where are you going?

YOUNG WOMAN   In here.

95 HUSBAND   I thought you'd want to wash up.

YOUNG WOMAN   I just want to—get ready.

HUSBAND   You don't have to go in there to take your clothes off!

YOUNG WOMAN   I want to.

HUSBAND   What for?

100 YOUNG WOMAN   I always do.

HUSBAND   What?

YOUNG WOMAN   Undress by myself.

HUSBAND   You've never been married till now—have you? [*Laughs.*] Or have you been putting something over on me?

105 YOUNG WOMAN   No.

HUSBAND   I understand—kind of modest—huh? Huh?

YOUNG WOMAN   Yes.

HUSBAND   I understand women—[*Indulgently.*] Go along. [*She goes off— starts to close door.* YOUNG WOMAN *exits.*] Don't close the door—thought you

110   wanted to talk. [*He looks around the room with satisfaction—after a pause— Rises—takes off his collar.*] You're awful quiet—what are you doing in there?

YOUNG WOMAN   Just—getting ready—

HUSBAND [*still in his mood of satisfaction*]   I'm going to enjoy life from now
    on—I haven't had such an easy time of it. I got where I am by hard work
115   and self denial—now I'm going to enjoy life—I'm going to enjoy life—I'm
    going to make up for all I missed—aren't you about ready?
YOUNG WOMAN   Not yet.
HUSBAND   Next year maybe we'll go to Paris. You can buy a lot of that French
    underwear—and Switzerland—all my life I've wanted a Swiss watch—that
120   I bought right there—I coulda' got a Swiss watch here, but I always
    wanted one that I bought right there—Isn't that funny—huh? Isn't it?
    Huh? Huh?
YOUNG WOMAN   Yes.
HUSBAND   All my life I've wanted a Swiss watch that I bought right there. All
125   my life I've counted on having that some day—more than anything—except
    one thing—you know what?
YOUNG WOMAN   No.
HUSBAND   Guess.
YOUNG WOMAN   I can't.
130 HUSBAND   Then I'm coming in and tell you.
YOUNG WOMAN   No! Please! Please don't.
HUSBAND   Well hurry up then! I thought you women didn't wear much of
    anything these days—huh? Huh? I'm coming in!
YOUNG WOMAN   No—no! Just a minute!
135 HUSBAND   All right. Just a minute!
        [YOUNG WOMAN *is silent.*]
HUSBAND [*laughs and takes out watch*]   13—14—I'm counting the seconds
    on you—that's what you said, didn't you—just a minute!—49—50—51—
    52—53—
        [*Enter* YOUNG WOMAN.]
YOUNG WOMAN [*at the door*]   Here I am.
        [*She wears a little white gown that hangs very straight. She is very still,*
        but her eyes are wide with a curious, helpless, animal terror.]
HUSBAND [*starts toward her—stops. The room is in shadow except for one dim*
140   *light by the bed. Sound of* GIRL *weeping*].   You crying? [*Sound of weeping.*]
    What you crying for? [*Crosses to her.*]
YOUNG WOMAN [*crying out*]   Ma! Ma! I want my mother!
HUSBAND   I thought you were glad to get away from her.
YOUNG WOMAN   I want her now—I want somebody.
145 HUSBAND   You got me, haven't you?
YOUNG WOMAN   Somebody—somebody—
HUSBAND   There's nothing to cry about. There's nothing to cry about.

BLACK OUT

[*The music continues until the lights go up for* EPISODE FOUR.]
[*Rhythm of the music is gradually replaced by the sound of steel riveting for* EPISODE
FOUR.]

Episode Four

MATERNAL

SCENE: *A room in a hospital. The door in the back now opens on a corridor; the
window on a tall building going up.*
> *Bed. Chair.*

CHARACTERS IN THE SCENE:
> YOUNG WOMAN
> DOCTORS
> NURSES
> HUSBAND

OUTSIDE—CORRIDOR LIFE:

CHARACTERS SEEN BUT NOT HEARD:
> WOMAN IN WHEEL CHAIR
> WOMAN IN BATHROBE
> STRETCHER WAGON
> NURSE WITH TRAY
> NURSE WITH COVERED BASIN

SOUNDS:
> [*outside window*]
> > *Riveting.*

AT RISE:
> YOUNG WOMAN *lies still in bed.*
> *The door is open.*
> *In the corridor, a stretcher wagon goes by.*
> *Enter* NURSE.

NURSE   How are you feeling today? [*No response from* YOUNG WOMAN.] Better? [*No response.*] No pain? [*No response.* NURSE *takes her watch in one
hand,* YOUNG WOMAN'S *wrist in the other—stands, then goes to chart at foot of
bed—writes.*] You're getting along fine. [*No response.*] Such a sweet baby
you have, too. [*No response.*] Aren't you glad it's a girl? [YOUNG WOMAN
5   *makes sign with her head, "No".*] You're not! Oh, my! That's no way to talk!
Men want boys—women ought to want girls. [*No response.*] Maybe you
didn't want either, eh? [YOUNG WOMAN *signs "No". Riveting machine.*] You'll
feel different when it begins to nurse. You'll just love it then. Your milk
hasn't come yet—has it? [*Sign—"No".*] It will [*Sign—"No".*] Oh, you don't
10   know Doctor! [*Goes to door—turns.*] Anything else you want? [YOUNG
WOMAN *points to window.*] Draft? [*Sign—"No".*] The noise? [YOUNG WOMAN
signs "Yes".] Oh, that can't be helped. Hospital's got to have a new wing.
We're the biggest Maternity Hospital in the world. I'll close the window,
though. [YOUNG WOMAN *signs "No".*] No?
15   YOUNG WOMAN [*whispers*]   I smell everything then.
NURSE [*starting out the door—riveting machine*]   Here's your man!
> [*Enter* HUSBAND *with large bouquet. Crosses to bed.*]
HUSBAND   Well, how are we today?
> [YOUNG WOMAN—*no response.*]
NURSE   She's getting stronger!
HUSBAND   Of course she is!
20   NURSE [*taking flowers*]   See what your husband brought you.

HUSBAND   Better put 'em in water right away. [*Exit* NURSE.] Everything O.K.?
[YOUNG WOMAN *signs "No".*] Now see here, my dear, you've got to brace up,
you know! And—and face things! Everybody's got to brace up and face
things! That's what makes the world go round. I know all you've been
25   through but—[YOUNG WOMAN *signs "No".*] Oh, yes I do! I know all about it!
I was right outside all the time! [YOUNG WOMAN *makes violent gesture of
"No". Ignoring.*] Oh yes! But you've got to brace up now! Make an effort!
Pull yourself together! Start the uphill climb! Oh I've been down—but I
haven't stayed down. I've been licked but I haven't stayed licked! I've pulled
30   myself up by my own bootstraps, and that's what you've got to do! Will
power! That's what conquers! Look at me! Now you've got to brace up!
Face the music! Stand the gaff![7] Take life by the horns! Look it in the face!
—Having a baby's natural! Perfectly natural thing—why should—

> [YOUNG WOMAN *chokes—points wildly to door. Enter* NURSE *with flowers
> in a vase.*]

NURSE   What's the matter?

35   HUSBAND   She's got that gagging again—like she had the last time I was here.

> [YOUNG WOMAN *gestures him out.*]

NURSE   Better go, sir.

HUSBAND [*at door*]   I'll be back.

> [YOUNG WOMAN *gasping and gesturing.*]

NURSE   She needs rest.

HUSBAND   Tomorrow then. I'll be back tomorrow—tomorrow and every
40   day—goodbye.

> [*Exits.*]

NURSE   You got a mighty nice husband, I guess you know that? [*Writes on
chart.*] Gagging.

> [*Corridor life*—WOMAN IN BATHROBE *passes door. Enter* DOCTOR, YOUNG
> DOCTOR, NURSE *wheeling surgeon's wagon with bottles, instruments, etc.*]

DOCTOR   How's the little lady today?

> [*Crosses to bed.*]

NURSE   She's better, Doctor.

45   DOCTOR   Of course she's better! She's all right—aren't you? [YOUNG WOMAN
does not respond.] What's the matter? Can't you talk?

> [*Drops her hand—takes chart.*]

NURSE   She's a little weak yet, Doctor.

DOCTOR [*at chart*]   Milk hasn't come yet?

NURSE   No, Doctor.

50   DOCTOR   Put the child to breast. [YOUNG WOMAN—"*No—no!*"—*Riveting
machine.*] No? Don't you want to nurse your baby? [YOUNG WOMAN *signs
"No".*] Why not? [*No response.*] These modern neurotic[8] women, eh, Doctor? What are we going to do with 'em? [YOUNG DOCTOR *laughs.* NURSE
smiles.] Bring the baby!

55   YOUNG WOMAN   No!

DOCTOR   Well—that's strong enough. I thought you were too weak to talk—
that's better. You don't want your baby?

---

7. Harsh treatment, abuse.
8. Hysteria and neuroses were seen as mod-   ern women's psychological conditions; see
introduction.

YOUNG WOMAN   No.

DOCTOR   What do you want?

60 YOUNG WOMAN   Let alone—let alone.

DOCTOR   Bring the baby.

NURSE   Yes, Doctor—she's behaved very badly every time, Doctor—very upset—maybe we better not.

DOCTOR   I decide what we better and better not here, Nurse!

65 NURSE   Yes, Doctor.

DOCTOR   Bring the baby.

NURSE   Yes, Doctor.

DOCTOR   [with chart]   Gagging—you mean nausea.

NURSE   Yes, Doctor, but—

70 DOCTOR   No buts, nurse.

NURSE   Yes, Doctor.

DOCTOR   Nausea!—Change her diet!—What is her diet?

NURSE   Liquids.

DOCTOR   Give her solids.

75 NURSE   Yes, Doctor. She says she can't swallow solids.

DOCTOR   Give her solids.

NURSE   Yes, Doctor. [Starts to go.]
          [Riveting machine.]

DOCTOR   Wait—I'll change her medicine [Takes pad and writes prescription in Latin. Hands it to NURSE.] After meals. [To door.] Bring her baby.
          [Exit DOCTOR, followed by YOUNG DOCTOR and NURSE with surgeon's wagon.]

80 NURSE   Yes, Doctor.
          [Exits.]

YOUNG WOMAN   [alone]   Let me alone—let me alone—let me alone—I've submitted to enough—I won't submit to any more—crawl off—crawl off in the dark—Vixen crawled under the bed—way back in the corner under the bed—they were all drowned—puppies don't go to heaven—heaven—golden
85 stairs—long stairs—long—too long—long golden stairs—climb those golden stairs—stairs—stairs—climb—tired—too tired—dead—no matter—nothing matters—dead—stairs—long stairs—all the dead going up—going up to be in heaven—heaven—golden stairs—all the children coming down—coming down to be born—dead going up—children coming down—
90 going up—coming down—going up—coming down—going up—coming down—going up—stop—stop—no—no traffic cop—no—no traffic cop in heaven—traffic cop—traffic cop—can't you give us a smile—tired—too tired—no matter—it doesn't matter—St. Peter—St. Peter at the gate—you can't come in—no matter—it doesn't matter—I'll rest—I'll lie down—
95 down—all written down—down in a big book[9]—no matter—it doesn't matter—I'll lie down—it weighs me—it's over me—it weighs—weighs—it's heavy—it's a heavy book—no matter—lie still—don't move—can't move—rest—forget—they say you forget—a girl—aren't you glad it's a girl—a little

9. Matthew 16.19 provides the Biblical source for popularized images of St. Peter as the keeper of the gates to heaven; Peter is often depicted with keys and with a book that lists who has earned entrance through good deeds during life.

girl—with no hair—none—little curls all over his head—a little bald girl—
100 curls—curls all over his head—what kind of hair has God? no matter—it
doesn't matter—everybody loves God—they've got to—got to—got to love
God—God is love—even if he's bad they got to love him—even if he's got
fat hands—fat hands—no no—he wouldn't be God—His hands make you
well—He lays on his hands—well—and happy—no matter—doesn't matter—
105 far—too far—tired—too tired Vixen crawled off under bed—eight—there
were eight—a woman crawled off under the bed—a woman has one—two
three four—one two three four—one two three four—two plus two is
four—two times two is four—two times four is eight Vixen had eight—one
two three four five six seven eight—eight—Puffie had eight—all drowned—
110 drowned—drowned in blood—blood—oh God! God—God never had
one—Mary had one—in a manger—the lowly manger—God's on a high
throne—far—too far—no matter—it doesn't matter—God Mary Mary God
Mary—Virgin Mary—Mary had one—the Holy Ghost—the Holy Ghost—
George H. Jones—oh don't—please don't! Let me rest—now I can rest—the
115 weight is gone—inside the weight is gone—it's only outside—outside—all
around—weight—I'm under it—Vixen crawled under the bed—there were
eight—I'll not submit any more—I'll not submit—I'll not submit—

[*The scene* BLACKS OUT. *The sound of riveting continues until it goes into
the sound of an electric piano and the scene lights up for* EPISODE FIVE.]

Episode Five

PROHIBITED[1]

SCENE: *Bar—Bottles—Tables—Chairs—Electric piano.*

SOUND: *Electric piano.*

CHARACTERS:
  MAN *behind the bar*
  POLICEMAN *at bar*
  WAITER
  At Table 1. A MAN *and a* WOMAN
  At Table 2. A MAN *and a* BOY
  At Table 3. TWO MEN *waiting for* TWO GIRLS, *who are*
  TELEPHONE GIRL *of Episode One and* YOUNG WOMAN.

AT RISE. *Everyone except the* GIRLS *on. Of the characters, the* MAN *and* WOMAN *at
Table 1 are an ordinary man and woman.* THE MAN *at Table 2 is a middle-aged
fairy;*[2] *the* BOY *is young, untouched. At Table 3,* 1ST MAN *is pleasing, common,
vigorous. He has coarse wavy hair.* 2ND MAN *is an ordinary salesman type.*

1ST MAN [*at Table 3*] I'm going to beat it.
2ND MAN Oh, for the love of Mike.

---

1. The period known as Prohibition, 1919–
33, began with the ratification of the Eighteenth Amendment to the U.S. Constitution,
which prohibited the sale or transport of alcohol, and ended with its repeal by the Twenty-
first Amendment. During this period illegal
bars known as "speakeasies" sprang up around
the country, especially in urban areas. Treadwell
slyly signals how inconsistently the law was
enforced by placing a policeman at the bar,
flouting the law he was supposed to uphold.
2. Term used to describe an effeminate homosexual male; at the time, such usage was not
necessarily derogatory.

1ST MAN   They ain't going to show.

2ND MAN   Sure they'll show.

5   1ST MAN   How do you know they'll show?

2ND MAN   I tell you you can't keep that baby away from me—just got to—[*Snaps fingers.*]—She comes running.

1ST MAN   Looks like it.

2ND MAN   [*to* WAITER—*makes sign "2", with his fingers.*]   The same.

[WAITER *goes to the bar.*]

10   MAN   [*at Table 2*]   Oh, I'm sorry I brought you here.

BOY   Why?

MAN   This Purgatory of noise! I brought you here to give you pleasure—let you taste pleasure. This sherry they have here is bottled—heaven. Wait till you taste it.

15   BOY   But I don't drink.

MAN   Drink! This isn't drink! Real amontillado³ is sunshine and orange groves—it's the Mediterranean and blue moonlight and—love? Have you ever been in love?

BOY   No.

20   MAN   Never in love with—a woman?

BOY   No—not really.

MAN   What do you mean—really?

BOY   Just—that.

MAN   Ah! [*Makes sign to* WAITER.] Two—you know what I want—Two.

[WAITER *goes to the bar.*]

25   MAN   [*at Table 1*]   Well, are you going through with it, or ain't you?

WOMAN   That's what I want to do—go through with it.

MAN   But you can't.

WOMAN   Why can't I?

MAN   How can yuh? [*Silence.*] It's nothing—most women don't think
30   anything about it—they just—Bert told me a doctor to go to—gave me the address—

WOMAN   Don't talk about it!

MAN   Got to talk about it—you got to get out of this. [*Silence*—MAN *makes sign to* WAITER.] What you having?

35   WOMAN   Nothing—I don't want anything. I had enough.

MAN   Do you good. The same?

WOMAN   I suppose so.

MAN   [*makes sign "2" to* WAITER]   The same.

[WAITER *goes to the bar.*]

———————————

[*At Table 3.*]

1ST MAN   I'm going to beat it.

40   2ND MAN   Oh say, listen! I'm counting on you to take the other one off my hands.

1ST MAN   I'm going to beat it.

2ND MAN   For the love of Mike have a heart! Listen—as a favor to me—I got to be home by six—I promised my wife—sure. That don't leave me no time

3. Type of dry sherry.

45   at all if we got to hang around—entertain some dame. You got to take her
off my hands.
1ST MAN   Maybe she won't fall for me.
2ND MAN   Sure she'll fall for you! They all fall for you—even my wife likes
you—tries to kid herself it's your brave exploits, but I know what it is—sure
50   she'll fall for you.
[Enter two girls—TELEPHONE GIRL and YOUNG WOMAN.]
GIRL [coming to Table.]   Hello—
2ND MAN [grouch]   Good night.
GIRL   Good night? What's eatin' yuh?
2ND MAN [same]   Nothin's eatin' me—thought somethin' musta swallowed
55   you.
GIRL   Why?
2ND MAN   You're late!
GIRL [unimpressed]   Oh—[Brushing it aside.]—Mrs. Jones—Mr. Smith.
2ND MAN   Meet my friend, Mr. Roe. [They all sit. To the WAITER.] The same,
60   and two more.
[WAITER goes.]
GIRL   So we kept you waiting, did we?
2ND MAN   Only about an hour.
YOUNG WOMAN   Was it that long?
2ND MAN   We been here that long—ain't we, Dick?
65   1ST MAN   Just about, Harry.
2ND MAN   For the love of God what delayed yuh?
GIRL   Tell Helen that one.
2ND MAN [to YOUNG WOMAN]   The old Irish woman that went to her first race?
Bet on the skate that came in last—she went up to the jockey and asked
70   him, "For the love of God, what delayed yuh?" [All laugh.]
YOUNG WOMAN   Why, that's kinda funny!
2ND MAN   Kinda!—What do you mean kinda?
YOUNG WOMAN   I just mean there are not many of 'em that are funny at all.
2ND MAN   Not if you haven't heard the funny ones.
75   YOUNG WOMAN   Oh I've heard 'em all.
1ST MAN   Not a laugh in a carload, eh?
GIRL   Got a cigarette?
2ND MAN [with package]   One of these?
GIRL [taking one]   Uhhuh.
[He offers the package to YOUNG WOMAN.]
80   YOUNG WOMAN [taking one]   Uhhuh.
2ND MAN [to 1ST MAN]   One of these?
1ST MAN [showing his own package]   Thanks—I like these. [He lights YOUNG
WOMAN's cigarette.]
2ND MAN [lighting GIRL's cigarette]   Well—baby—how they comin', huh?
GIRL   Couldn't be better.
85   2ND MAN   How's every little thing?
GIRL   Just great.
2ND MAN   Miss me?
GIRL   I'll say so—when did you get in?
2ND MAN   Just a coupla hours ago.

90 GIRL   Miss me?

2ND MAN   Did I? You don't know the half of it.

YOUNG WOMAN [*interrupting restlessly*]   Can we dance here?

2ND MAN   Not here.

YOUNG WOMAN   Where do we go from here?

95 2ND MAN   Where do we go from here! You just got here!

1ST MAN   What's the hurry?

2ND MAN   What's the rush?

YOUNG WOMAN   I don't know.

GIRL   Helen wants to dance.

100 YOUNG WOMAN   I just want to keep moving.

1ST MAN [*smiling*]   You want to keep moving, huh?

2ND MAN   You must be one of those restless babies! Where do we go from here!

YOUNG WOMAN   It's only some days—I want to keep moving.

105 1ST MAN   You want to keep moving, huh? [*He is staring at her smilingly.*]

YOUNG WOMAN [*nods*]   Uhhuh.

1ST MAN [*quietly*]   Stick around a while.

2ND MAN   Where do we go from here! Say, what kind of a crowd do you run with, anyway?

110 GIRL   Helen don't run with any crowd—do you, Helen?

YOUNG WOMAN [*embarrassed*] No.

1ST MAN   Well, I'm not a crowd—run with me.

2ND MAN [*gratified*]   All set, huh?—Dick was about ready to beat it.

1ST MAN   That's before I met the little lady.

[WAITER *serves drinks.*]

115 1ST MAN   Here's how.

2ND MAN   Here's to you.

GIRL   Here's looking at you.

YOUNG WOMAN   Here's—happy days.

[*They all drink.*]

1ST MAN   That's good stuff!

120 2ND MAN   Off a boat.

1ST MAN   Off a boat?

2ND MAN   They get all their stuff here—off a boat.

GIRL   That's what *they* say.

2ND MAN   No! Sure! Sure they do! Sure!

125 GIRL   It's all right with me.

2ND MAN   But they do! Sure!

GIRL   I believe you, darling!

2ND MAN   Did you miss me?

GIRL   Uhhuh. [*Affirmative.*]

130 2ND MAN   Any other daddies?

GIRL   Uhhuh. [*Negative.*]

2ND MAN   Love any daddy but daddy?

GIRL   Uhhuh. [*Negative.*]

2ND MAN   Let's beat it!

135 GIRL [*a little self-conscious before* YOUNG WOMAN]   We just got here.

2ND MAN   Don't I know it—Come on!

GIRL But—[*Indicates* YOUNG WOMAN.]

2ND MAN [*not understanding*] They're all set—aren't you?

1ST MAN [*to* YOUNG WOMAN.] Are we? [*She doesn't answer.*]

140 2ND MAN I got to be out to the house by six—come on—[*Rising—to* GIRL.] Come on, kid—let's us beat it! [GIRL *indicates* YOUNG WOMAN.] [*Now understanding—very elaborate.*] Business is business, you know! I got a lot to do yet this afternoon—thought you might go along with me—help me out—how about it?

145 GIRL [*rising, her dignity preserved*] Sure—I'll go along with you—help you out. [*Both rise.*]

2ND MAN All right with you folks?

1ST MAN All right with me.

2ND MAN All right with you? [*To* YOUNG WOMAN.]

YOUNG WOMAN All right with me.

150 2ND MAN Come on, kid. [*They rise.*] Where's the damage?[4]

1ST MAN Go on!

2ND MAN No!

1ST MAN Go on!

2ND MAN I'll match you.

155 YOUNG WOMAN Heads win!

GIRL Heads I win—tails you lose.

2ND MAN [*impatiently*] He's matching me.

1ST MAN Am I matching you or you matching me?

2ND MAN I'm matching you. [*They match.*] You're stung!

160 1ST MAN [*contentedly*] Not so you can notice it. [*Smiles at* YOUNG WOMAN.]

GIRL That's for you, Helen.

2ND MAN She ain't dumb! Come on.

GIRL [*to* 1ST MAN] You be nice to her now. She's very fastidious. —Goodbye. [*Exit* 2ND MAN *and* GIRL.]

YOUNG WOMAN I know what business is like.

165 1ST MAN You do—do yuh?

YOUNG WOMAN I used to be a business girl myself before—

1ST MAN Before what?

YOUNG WOMAN Before I quit.

1ST MAN What did you quit for?

170 YOUNG WOMAN I just quit.

1ST MAN You're married, huh?

YOUNG WOMAN Yes—I am.

1ST MAN All right with me.

YOUNG WOMAN Some men don't seem to like a woman after she's married— [WAITER *comes to the table.*]

175 1ST MAN What's the difference?

YOUNG WOMAN Depends on the man, I guess.

1ST MAN Depends on the woman, I guess. [*To* WAITER, *makes sign of "2".*] The same. [WAITER *goes to the bar.*]

---

4. The bill, or charge for the drinks.

[*At Table 1.*]

MAN   It don't amount to nothing. God! Most women just—
180 WOMAN   I know—I know—I know.
MAN   They don't think nothing of it. They just—
WOMAN   I know—I know—I know.

[*Re-enter* 2ND MAN *and* GIRL. *They go to Table 3.*]

2ND MAN   Say, I forgot—I want you to do something for me, will yuh?
1ST MAN   Sure—what is it?
185 2ND MAN   I want you to telephone me out home tomorrow—and ask me to
come into town—will yuh?
1ST MAN   Sure—why not?
2ND MAN   You know—business—get me?
1ST MAN   I get you.
190 2ND MAN   I've worked the telegraph gag to death—and my wife likes you.
1ST MAN   What's your number?
2ND MAN   I'll write it down for you.
[*Writes.*]
1ST MAN   How is your wife?
2ND MAN   She's fine.
195 1ST MAN   And the kid?
2ND MAN   Great. [*Hands him the card.*] Come on, kid. [*To* GIRL. *Turns back to*
YOUNG WOMAN.] Get this bird to tell you about himself.
GIRL   Keep him from it.
2ND MAN   Get him to tell you how he killed a couple a spig[5] down in Mexico.
200 GIRL   You been in Mexico?
2ND MAN   He just came up from there.
GIRL   Can you teach us the tango?
YOUNG WOMAN   You killed a man?
2ND MAN   Two of 'em! With a bottle! Get him to tell you—with a bottle.
205 Come on, kid. Goodbye.
[*Exit* 2ND MAN *and* GIRL.]
YOUNG WOMAN   Why did you?
1ST MAN   What?
YOUNG WOMAN   Kill 'em?
1ST MAN   To get free.
210 YOUNG WOMAN   Oh.

[*At Table 2.*]

MAN   You really must taste this—just taste it. It's a real amontillado, you
know.
BOY   Where do they get it here?
MAN   It's always down the side streets one finds the real pleasures, don't you
215 think?
BOY   I don't know.

---

5. Derogatory term, alternate of "spic," used to describe Spanish speakers or those speaking
English with a Spanish accent.

MAN   Learn. Come, taste this! Amontillado! Or don't you like amontillado?
BOY   I don't know. I never had any before.
MAN   Your first taste! How I envy you! Come, taste it! Taste it! And die.
        [BOY *tastes wine—finds it disappointing.*]
220 MAN [*gilding it*]   Poe was a lover of amontillado. He returns to it continually,
        you remember—or are you a lover of Poe?[6]
BOY   I've read a lot of him.
MAN   But are you a lover?

———————

        [*At Table 3.*]
1ST MAN   There were a bunch of bandidos—bandits, you know, took me into
225   the hills—holding me there—what was I to do? I got the two birds that
        guarded me drunk one night, and then I filled the empty bottle with small
        stones—and let 'em have it!
YOUNG WOMAN   Oh!
1ST MAN   I had to get free, didn't I? I let 'em have it—
230 YOUNG WOMAN   Oh—then what did you do?
1ST MAN   Then I beat it.
YOUNG WOMAN   Where to—?
1ST MAN   Right here. [*Pause*] Glad?
YOUNG WOMAN [*nods*]   Yes.
235 1ST MAN [*makes sign to* WAITER *of* "2"]   The same.
        [WAITER *goes to bar.*]

———————

        [*At Table 1.*]
MAN   You're just scared because this is the first time and—
WOMAN   I'm not scared.
MAN   Then what are you for Christ's sake?
WOMAN   I'm not scared. I want it—I want to have it—that ain't being scared,
240   is it?
MAN   It's being goofy.
WOMAN   I don't care.
MAN   What about your folks?
WOMAN   I don't care.
245 MAN   What about your job? [*Silence.*] You got to keep your job, haven't you?
        [*Silence.*] Haven't you?
WOMAN   I suppose so.
MAN   Well—there you are!
WOMAN [*silence—then*]   All right—let's go now— You got the address?
250 MAN   Now you're coming to.
        [*They get up and go off.*]
        [*Exit* MAN *and* WOMAN.]

———————

6. Edgar Allan Poe (1809–1849), American short story writer and poet, perhaps best known today for his contributions to the mystery genre, although here the emphasis appears to be on his verse. To be a lover of Poe, in this context, may also be code for homosexuality.

[*At Table* 3.]

YOUNG WOMAN   A bottle like that? [*She picks it up.*]

1ST MAN   Yeah—filled with pebbles.

YOUNG WOMAN   What kind of pebbles?

1ST MAN   Pebbles! Off the ground.

255   YOUNG WOMAN   Oh.

1ST MAN   Necessity, you know, mother of invention. [*As* YOUNG WOMAN *handles the bottle.*] Ain't a bad weapon—first you got a sledge hammer—then you got a knife.

YOUNG WOMAN   Oh. [*Puts bottle down.*]

260   1ST MAN   Women don't like knives, do they? [*Pours drink.*]

YOUNG WOMAN   No.

1ST MAN   Don't mind a hammer so much, though, do they?

YOUNG WOMAN   No—

1ST MAN   I didn't like it myself—any of it—but I had to get free, didn't I?

265   Sure I had to get free, didn't I? [*Drinks.*] Now I'm damn glad I did.

YOUNG WOMAN   Why?

1ST MAN   You know why. [*He puts his hand over hers.*]

[*At Table* 2.]

MAN   Let's go to my rooms—and I'll show them to you—I have a first edition of Verlaine[7] that will simply make your mouth water. [*They stand up.*]

270   Here—there's just a sip at the bottom of my glass—[BOY *takes it.*] That last sip that's sweetest—Wasn't it?

BOY [*laughs*]   And I always thought that was dregs.

[*Exit* MAN *followed by* BOY.]

[*At Table* 3.]

[*The* MAN *is holding her hand across the table.*]

YOUNG WOMAN   When you put your hand over mine! When you just touch me!

1ST MAN   Yeah? [*Pause.*] Come on, kid, let's go!

275   YOUNG WOMAN   Where?

1ST MAN   You haven't been around much, have you, kid?

YOUNG WOMAN   No.

1ST MAN   I could tell that just to look at you.

YOUNG WOMAN   You could?

280   1ST MAN   Sure I could. What are you running around with a girl like that other one for?

YOUNG WOMAN   I don't know. She seems to have a good time.

1ST MAN   So that's it?

YOUNG WOMAN   Don't she?

285   1ST MAN   Don't you?

YOUNG WOMAN   No.

1ST MAN   Never?

YOUNG WOMAN   Never.

1ST MAN   What's the matter?

---

7. Paul Verlaine (1844–1896), French symbolist poet.

290 YOUNG WOMAN   Nothing—just me, I guess.

IST MAN   You're all right.

YOUNG WOMAN   Am I?

IST MAN   Sure. You just haven't met the right guy—that's all—a girl like you—you got to meet the right guy.

295 YOUNG WOMAN   I know.

IST MAN   You're different from girls like that other one—any guy'll do her. You're different.

YOUNG WOMAN   I guess I am.

IST MAN   You didn't fall for that business gag—did you—when they went off?

300 YOUNG WOMAN   Well, I thought they wanted to be alone probably, but—

IST MAN   And how!

YOUNG WOMAN   Oh—so that's it.

IST MAN   That's it. Come along—let's go—

YOUNG WOMAN   Oh, I couldn't! Like this?

305 IST MAN   Don't you like me?

YOUNG WOMAN   Yes.

IST MAN   Then what's the matter?

YOUNG WOMAN   Do—you—like me?

IST MAN   Like yuh? You don't know the half of it—listen—you know what

310 you seem like to me?

YOUNG WOMAN   What?

IST MAN   An angel. Just like an angel.

YOUNG WOMAN   I do?

IST MAN   That's what I said! Let's go!

315 YOUNG WOMAN   Where?

IST MAN   Where do you live?

YOUNG WOMAN   Oh, we can't go to my place.

IST MAN   Then come to my place.

YOUNG WOMAN   Oh I couldn't—is it far?

320 IST MAN   Just a step—come on—

YOUNG WOMAN   Oh I couldn't—what is it—a room?

IST MAN   No—an apartment—a one-room apartment.

YOUNG WOMAN   That's different.

IST MAN   On the ground floor—no one will see you—coming or going.

325 YOUNG WOMAN [getting up]   I couldn't.

IST MAN [rises]   Wait a minute—I got to pay the damage—and I'll get a bottle of something to take along.

YOUNG WOMAN   No—don't.

IST MAN   Why not?

330 YOUNG WOMAN   Well—don't bring any pebbles.

IST MAN   Say—forget that! Will you?

YOUNG WOMAN   I just meant I don't think I'll need anything to drink.

IST MAN [leaning to her eagerly]   You like me—don't you, kid?

YOUNG WOMAN   Do you me?

335 IST MAN   Wait!

[He goes to the bar. SHE remains, her hands outstretched on the table staring ahead.]

[Enter a MAN and a GIRL. They go to one of the empty tables. The WAITER goes to them.]

MAN [*to* GIRL]   What do you want?

GIRL   Same old thing.

MAN [*to the* WAITER]   The usual. [*Makes a sign "2".*]

> [*The* 1ST MAN *crosses to* YOUNG WOMAN *with a wrapped bottle under his arm.* SHE *rises and starts out with him. As they pass the piano,* HE *stops and puts in a nickel—the music starts as they exit.*]

BLACK OUT

[*The music of the electric piano continues until the lights go up for* EPISODE SIX, *and the music has become the music of a hand organ, very very faint.*]

Episode Six

INTIMATE

SCENE: *A dark room.*

SOUNDS: *A hand organ. Footbeats, of passing feet.*

CHARACTERS:

> MAN
>
> YOUNG WOMAN

AT RISE:

> DARKNESS. *Nothing can be discerned. From the outside comes the sound of a hand organ, very faint, and the irregular rhythm of passing feet.*
> *The hand organ is playing "Cielito Lindo,"[8] that Spanish song that has been on every hand organ lately.*

———————

MAN   You're awful still, honey. What you thinking about?

WOMAN   About sea shells. [*The sound of her voice is beautiful.*]

MAN   Sheshells? Gee! I can't say it!

WOMAN   When I was little my grandmother used to have a big pink sea shell
5   on the mantle behind the stove. When we'd go to visit her they'd let me hold it, and listen. That's what I was thinking about now.

MAN   Yeah?

WOMAN   You can hear the sea in 'em, you know.

MAN   Yeah, I know.

10 WOMAN   I wonder why that is?

MAN   Search me. [*Pause.*]

WOMAN.   You going?

> [*He has moved.*]

MAN   No. I just want a cigarette.

WOMAN [*glad, relieved*]   Oh.

15 MAN   Want one?

WOMAN   No. [*Taking the match.*] Let me light it for you.

MAN   You got mighty pretty hands, honey. [*The match is out.*] This little pig went to market. This little pig stayed home. This little pig went—

WOMAN [*laughs*]   Diddle diddle dee.

> [*Laughs again.*]

20 MAN   You got awful pretty hands.

8. Famous Mexican folk song; the title is a term of endearment meaning "little heaven."

WOMAN   I used to have. But I haven't taken much care of them lately. I will now—[*Pause. The music gets clearer.*] What's that?

MAN   What?

WOMAN   That music?

25   MAN   A dago[9] hand organ. I gave him two bits the first day I got here—so he comes every day.

WOMAN   I mean—what's that he's playing?

MAN   Cielito Lindo.

WOMAN   What does that mean?

30   MAN   Little Heaven?

WOMAN   Little Heaven?

MAN   That's what lovers call each other in Spain.

WOMAN   Spain's where all the castles are, ain't it?

MAN   Yeah.

35   WOMAN   Little Heaven—sing it!

MAN   [*singing to the music of the hand organ*]   De la sierra morena viene, bajando, viene, bajando; un par de ojitos negros—cielito lindo—da contrabando.[1]

WOMAN   What does it mean?

MAN   From the high dark mountains.

40   WOMAN   From the high dark mountains—?

MAN   Oh it doesn't mean anything. It doesn't make sense. It's love. [*Taking up the song.*] Ay-ay-ay-ay.

WOMAN   I know what that means.

MAN   What?

45   WOMAN   Ay-ay-ay-ay.

[*They laugh.*]

MAN   [*taking up the song*]   Canta non llores— Sing don't cry—

WOMAN   [*taking up song*]   La-la-la-la-la-la-la-la-la-la—Little Heaven!

MAN   You got a nice voice, honey.

WOMAN   Have I?

[*Laughs—tickles him.*]

50   MAN   You bet you have—hey!

WOMAN   [*laughing*]   You ticklish?

MAN   Sure I am! Hey! [*They laugh.*] Go on, honey, sing something.

WOMAN   I couldn't.

MAN   Go on—you got a fine voice.

WOMAN   [*laughs and sings*]

55   Hey, diddle, diddle, the cat and the fiddle,
       The cow jumped over the moon
       The little dog laughed to see the sport
       And the dish ran away with the spoon—[*Both laugh.*] I never thought that had any sense before—now I get it.

60   MAN   You got me beat.

WOMAN   It's you and me.—La—lalalalalala—lalalalalala—Little Heaven. You're the dish and I'm the spoon.

MAN   You're a little spoon all right.

---

9. Slang term, usually for someone of Italian or Spanish origin.
1. "A pair of sweet little black eyes, my dar-ling, is being smuggled down from the Sierra Morena mountain range, my darling."

WOMAN   And I guess I'm the little cow that jumped over the moon. [*A pause.*]
65   Do you believe in sorta guardian angels?

MAN   What?

WOMAN   Guardian angels?

MAN   I don't know. Maybe.

WOMAN   I do. [*Taking up the song again.*] Lalalalala-lalalalala-lalalala—Little
70   Heaven. [*Talking.*] There must be something that looks out for you and brings
you your happiness, at last—look at us! How did we both happen to go to
that place today if there wasn't something!

MAN   Maybe you're right.

WOMAN   Look at us!

75   MAN   Everything's us to you, kid—ain't it?

WOMAN   Ain't it?

MAN   All right with me.

WOMAN   We belong together! We belong together! And we're going to stick
together, ain't we?

80   MAN   Sing something else.

WOMAN   I tell you I can't sing!

MAN   Sure you can!

WOMAN   I tell you I hadn't thought of singing since I was a little bit of a girl.

MAN   Well sing anyway.

85   WOMAN   [*singing*]   And every little wavelet had its night cap on—its night cap
on—its night cap on—and every little wave had its night cap on—so very
early in the morning.[2] [*Talking.*] Did you used to sing that when you were a
little kid?

MAN   Nope.

90   WOMAN   Didn't you? We used to—in the first grade—little kids—we used to
go round and round in a ring—and flop our hands up and down—supposed
to be the waves. I remember it used to confuse me—because we did just
the same thing to be little angels.

MAN   Yeah?

95   WOMAN   You know why I came here?

MAN   I can make a good guess.

WOMAN   Because you told me I looked like an angel to you! That's why I came.

MAN   Jeez, honey, all women look like angels to me—all white women. I ain't
been seeing nothing but Indians, you know, for the last couple a years.
100   Gee, when I got off the boat here the other day—and saw all the women—
gee I pretty near went crazy—talk about looking like angels—why—

WOMAN   You've had a lot of women, haven't you?

MAN   Not so many—real ones.

WOMAN   Did you—like any of 'em—better than me?

105   MAN   Nope—there wasn't one of 'em any sweeter than you, honey—not as
sweet—no—not as sweet.

WOMAN   I like to hear you say it. Say it again—

MAN   [*protesting good humoredly*]   Oh—

WOMAN   Go on—tell me again!

110   MAN   Here! [*Kisses her.*] Does that tell you?

WOMAN   Yes. [*Pause.*] We're going to stick together—always—aren't we?

2. Excerpt from "A Song for Hal" by Laura Elizabeth Howe Richards, from the collection *In My Nursery* (1890).

MAN [*honestly*] I'll have to be moving on, kid—some day, you know.

WOMAN When?

MAN Quien sabe?

115 WOMAN What does that mean?

MAN Quien sabe? You got to learn that, kid, if you're figuring on coming with me. It's the answer to everything—below the Rio Grande.[3]

WOMAN What does it mean?

MAN It means—who knows?

120 WOMAN Keen sabe?

MAN Yep—don't forget it—now.

WOMAN I'll never forget it!

MAN Quien sabe?

WOMAN And I'll never get to use it.

125 MAN Quien sabe.

WOMAN I'll never get—below the Rio Grande—I'll never get out of here.

MAN Quien sabe.

WOMAN [*change of mood*] That's right! Keen sabe? Who knows?

MAN That's the stuff.

130 WOMAN You must like it down there.

MAN I can't live anywhere else—for long.

WOMAN Why not?

MAN Oh—you're free down there! You're free!

> [*A Street Light is lit outside. The outlines of a window take form against this light. There are bars across it, and from outside it, the sidewalk cuts across almost at the top. (It is a basement room.) The constant going and coming of passing feet, (mostly feet of couples) can be dimly seen. Inside, on the ledge, there is a lily blooming in a bowl of rocks and water.*]

WOMAN What's that?

135 MAN Just the street light going on.

WOMAN Is it as late as that?

MAN Late as what?

WOMAN Dark.

MAN It's been dark for hours—didn't you know that?

140 WOMAN No!—I must go! [*Rises.*]

MAN Wait—the moon will be up in a little while—full moon.

WOMAN It isn't that! I'm late! I must go! [SHE *comes into the light. She wears a white chemise that might be the tunic of a dancer, and as she comes into the light she fastens about her waist a little skirt. She really wears almost exactly the clothes that women wear now, but the finesse of their cut, and the grace and ease with which she puts them on, must turn this episode of her dressing into a personification, an idealization of a woman clothing herself. All her gestures must be unconscious, innocent, relaxed, sure and full of natural grace. As she sits facing the window pulling on a stocking.*] What's that?

MAN What?

145 WOMAN On the window ledge.

MAN A flower.

WOMAN Who gave it to you?

MAN Nobody gave it to me. I bought it.

WOMAN For yourself?

---

3. River marking the border between Texas and Mexico.

150 MAN   Yeah—why not?

WOMAN   I don't know.

MAN   In Chinatown—made me think of Frisco where I was a kid—so I bought it.

WOMAN   Is that where you were born—Frisco?

MAN   Yep. Twin Peaks.

155 WOMAN   What's that?

MAN   A couple hills—together.

WOMAN   One for you and one for me.

MAN   I bet you'd like Frisco.

WOMAN   I know a woman went out there once!

160 MAN   The bay and the hills! Jeez, that's the life! Every Saturday we used to cross the Bay—get a couple nags[4] and just ride—over the hills. One would have a blanket on the saddle—the other, the grub. At night, we'd make a little fire and eat—and then roll up in the old blanket and—

WOMAN   Who? Who was with you?

165 MAN   [indifferently]   Anybody. [Enthusiastically.] Jeez, that dry old grass out there smells good at night—full of tar weed—you know—

WOMAN   Is that a good smell?

MAN   Tar weed? Didn't you ever smell it? [She shakes her head, "No".] Sure it's a good smell! The Bay and the hills. [She goes to the mirror of the dresser, to finish dressing. She has only a dress to put on that is in one piece—with one fastening on the side. Before slipping it on, she stands before the mirror

170 and stretches. Appreciatively but indifferently.] You look in good shape, kid. A couple of months riding over the mountains with me, you'd be great.

WOMAN   Can I?

MAN   What?

WOMAN   Some day—ride mountains with you?

175 MAN   Ride mountains? Ride donkeys!

WOMAN   It's the same thing!—with you!—Can I—some day? The high dark mountains?

MAN   Who knows?

WOMAN   It must be great!

180 MAN   You ever been off like that, kid?—high up? On top of the world?

WOMAN   Yes.

MAN   When?

WOMAN   Today.

MAN   You're pretty sweet.

185 WOMAN   I never knew anything like this way! I never knew that I could feel like this! So,—so purified! Don't laugh at me!

MAN   I ain't laughing, honey.

WOMAN   Purified.

MAN   It's a hell of a word—but I know what you mean. That's the way it

190 is—sometimes.

WOMAN [she puts on a little hat, then turns to HIM]   Well—goodbye.

MAN   Aren't you forgetting something? [Rises.]

WOMAN [she looks toward him, then throws her head slowly back, lifts her right arm—this gesture that is in so many statues of women [Volupte][5]—He comes

---

4. Horses.

5. Such imagery had recently become popular through its depiction by French painter Henri

Matisse (1869–1954) in his work Luxe, Calme, et Volupté (1904).

*out of the shadow, puts his arm around her, kisses her. Her head and arm go
further back,—then she brings her arm around with a wide encircling gesture,
her hand closes over his head, her fingers spread. Her fingers are protective,
clutching. When he releases her, her eyes are shining with tears. She turns
away. She looks back at him—and the room—and her eyes fasten on the lily*].
Can I have that?

MAN   Sure—why not?

> [*She takes it—goes. As she opens the door, the music is louder. The scene
> blacks out.*]

195 WOMAN   Goodbye. And—[*Hesitates.*] And—thank you.

MUSIC—CURTAIN—BLACK OUT

[*The music continues until the Curtain goes up for* EPISODE SEVEN—*It goes up on
silence.*]

Episode Seven

DOMESTIC

SCENE: *A Sitting Room* [*A divan—a telephone—a window.*]

CHARACTERS:

> HUSBAND
>
> YOUNG WOMAN

*They are seated on opposite ends of the divan. They are both reading papers—to
themselves.*

———————————

HUSBAND   Record production.

YOUNG WOMAN   Girl turns on gas.

HUSBAND   Sale hits a million—

YOUNG WOMAN   Woman leaves all for love—

5 HUSBAND   Market trend steady—

YOUNG WOMAN   Young wife disappears—

HUSBAND   Owns a life interest—[*Phone rings.* YOUNG WOMAN *looks toward
it.*] That's for me. [*In phone.*] Hello—oh hello, A.B. It's all settled?—
Everything signed? Good. Good! Tell R.A. to call me up. [*Closes phone—to*
10   YOUNG WOMAN.] Well, it's all settled. They signed!—aren't you interested?
Aren't you going to ask me?

YOUNG WOMAN [*by rote*]   Did you put it over?

HUSBAND   Sure I put it over.

YOUNG WOMAN   Did you swing it?

15 HUSBAND   Sure I swung it.

YOUNG WOMAN   Did they come through?

HUSBAND   Sure they came through.

YOUNG WOMAN   Did they sign?

HUSBAND   I'll say they signed.

20 YOUNG WOMAN   On the dotted line?

HUSBAND   On the dotted line.

YOUNG WOMAN   The property's yours?

HUSBAND   The property's mine. I'll put a first mortgage. I'll put a second
mortgage and the property's mine. Happy?

25 YOUNG WOMAN [*by rote*]   Happy.

HUSBAND [*going to her*]   The property's mine! It's not all that's mine! [*Pinching her cheek—happy and playful.*] I got a first mortgage on her—I got a second mortgage on her—and she's mine! [YOUNG WOMAN *pulls away swiftly.*] What's the matter?

30 YOUNG WOMAN   Nothing—what?

HUSBAND   You flinched when I touched you.

YOUNG WOMAN   No.

HUSBAND   You haven't done that in a long time.

YOUNG WOMAN   Haven't I?

35 HUSBAND   You used to do it every time I touched you.

YOUNG WOMAN   Did I?

HUSBAND   Didn't know that, did you?

YOUNG WOMAN [*unexpectedly*]   Yes. Yes, I know it.

HUSBAND   Just purity.

40 YOUNG WOMAN   No.

HUSBAND   Oh, I liked it. Purity.

YOUNG WOMAN   No.

HUSBAND   You're one of the purest women that ever lived.

YOUNG WOMAN   I'm just like anybody else only—[*Stops.*]

45 HUSBAND   Only what?

YOUNG WOMAN [*a pause*]   Nothing.

HUSBAND   It must be something.

[*Phone rings.*]

[*She gets up and goes to window.*]

HUSBAND [*in phone*]   Hello—hello, R.A.—well, I put it over—yeah, I swung it—sure they came through—did they sign? On the dotted line! The prop-

50 erty's mine. I made the proposition. I sold them the idea. Now watch me. Tell D.D. to call me up. [*Hangs up.*] That was R.A. What are you looking at?

YOUNG WOMAN   Nothing.

HUSBAND   You must be looking at something.

YOUNG WOMAN   Nothing—the moon.

55 HUSBAND   The moon's something, isn't it?

YOUNG WOMAN   Yes.

HUSBAND   What's it doing?

YOUNG WOMAN   Nothing.

HUSBAND   It must be doing something.

60 YOUNG WOMAN   It's moving—moving—

[*She comes down restlessly.*]

HUSBAND   Pull down the shade, my dear.

YOUNG WOMAN   Why?

HUSBAND   People can look in. [*Phone rings.*] Hello—hello D.D.—Yes—I put it over—they came across—I put it over on them—yep—yep—yep—I'll say

65 I am—yep—on the dotted line— Now you watch me—yep. Yep yep. Tell B.M. to phone me. [*Hangs up.*] That was D.D. [*To* YOUNG WOMAN *who has come down to davenport and picked up a paper.*] Aren't you listening?

YOUNG WOMAN   I'm reading.

HUSBAND   What you reading?

70 YOUNG WOMAN   Nothing.

HUSBAND   Must be something. [*He sits and picks up his paper.*]

YOUNG WOMAN [*reading*] Prisoner escapes—lifer breaks jail—shoots way to freedom—

HUSBAND Don't read that stuff—listen—here's a first rate editorial. I agree
75 with this. I agree absolutely. Are you listening?

YOUNG WOMAN I'm listening.

HUSBAND [*importantly*] All men are born free and entitled to the pursuit of happiness. [YOUNG WOMAN *gets up.*] My, you're nervous tonight.

YOUNG WOMAN I try not to be.

80 HUSBAND You inherit that from your mother. She was in the office today.

YOUNG WOMAN Was she?

HUSBAND To get her allowance.

YOUNG WOMAN Oh—

HUSBAND Don't you know it's the *first*.

85 YOUNG WOMAN Poor Ma.

HUSBAND What would she do without me?

YOUNG WOMAN I know. You're very good.

HUSBAND One thing—she's grateful.

YOUNG WOMAN Poor Ma—poor Ma.

90 HUSBAND She's got to have care.

YOUNG WOMAN Yes. She's got to have care.

HUSBAND A mother's a very precious thing—a good mother.

YOUNG WOMAN [*excitedly*] I try to be a good mother.

HUSBAND Of course you're a good mother.

95 YOUNG WOMAN I try! I try!

HUSBAND A mother's a very precious thing—[*Resuming his paper.*] And a child's a very precious thing. Precious jewels.

YOUNG WOMAN [*reading*] Sale of jewels and precious stones. [YOUNG WOMAN *puts her hand to throat.*]

HUSBAND What's the matter?

100 YOUNG WOMAN I feel as though I were drowning.

HUSBAND Drowning?

YOUNG WOMAN With stones around my neck.

HUSBAND You just imagine that.

YOUNG WOMAN Stifling.

105 HUSBAND You don't breathe deep enough—breathe now—look at me. [*He breathes.*] Breath is life. Life is breath.

YOUNG WOMAN [*suddenly*] And what is death?

HUSBAND [*smartly*] Just—no breath!

YOUNG WOMAN [*to herself*] Just no breath! [*Takes up paper.*]

110 HUSBAND All right?

YOUNG WOMAN All right.

HUSBAND [*reads as she stares at her paper. Looks up after a pause*] I feel cold air, my dear.

YOUNG WOMAN Cold air?

115 HUSBAND Close the window, will you?

YOUNG WOMAN It isn't open.

HUSBAND Don't you feel cold air?

YOUNG WOMAN No—you just imagine it.

HUSBAND I never imagine anything. [YOUNG WOMAN *is staring at the paper.*]

120 What are you reading?

YOUNG WOMAN   Nothing.

HUSBAND   You must be reading something.

YOUNG WOMAN   Woman finds husband dead.

HUSBAND [*uninterested*]   Oh. [*Interested.*] Here's a man says "I owe my suc-
125   cess to a yeast cake a day—my digestion is good—I sleep very well—and—
[*His wife gets up, goes toward door.*] Where you going?

YOUNG WOMAN   No place.

HUSBAND   You must be going some place.

YOUNG WOMAN   Just—to bed.

130 HUSBAND   It isn't eleven yet. Wait.

YOUNG WOMAN   Wait?

HUSBAND   It's only ten-forty-six—wait! [*Holds out his arms to her.*] Come
here!

YOUNG WOMAN [*takes a step toward him—recoils*]   Oh—I want to go away!

135 HUSBAND   Away? Where?

YOUNG WOMAN   Anywhere—away.

HUSBAND   Why, what's the matter?

YOUNG WOMAN   I'm scared.

HUSBAND   What of?

140 YOUNG WOMAN   I can't sleep—I haven't slept.

HUSBAND   That's nothing.

YOUNG WOMAN   And the moon—when it's a full moon.

HUSBAND   That's nothing.

YOUNG WOMAN   I can't sleep.

145 HUSBAND   Of course not. It's the light.

YOUNG WOMAN   I don't see it! I feel it! I'm afraid.

HUSBAND [*kindly*]   Nonsense—come here.

YOUNG WOMAN   I want to go away.

HUSBAND   But I can't get away now.

150 YOUNG WOMAN   Alone!

HUSBAND   You've never been away alone.

YOUNG WOMAN   I know.

HUSBAND   What would you do?

YOUNG WOMAN   Maybe I'd sleep.

155 HUSBAND   Now you wait.

YOUNG WOMAN [*desperately*]   Wait?

HUSBAND   We'll take a trip—we'll go to Europe—I'll get my watch—I'll get
my Swiss watch—I've always wanted a Swiss watch that I bought right
there—isn't that funny? Wait—wait. [YOUNG WOMAN *comes down to*
160   *davenport—sits.* HUSBAND *resumes his paper.*] Another revolution below the
Rio Grande.

YOUNG WOMAN   Below the Rio Grande?

HUSBAND   Yes—another—

YOUNG WOMAN   Anyone—hurt?

165 HUSBAND   No.

YOUNG WOMAN   Any Prisoners?

HUSBAND   No.

YOUNG WOMAN   All free?

HUSBAND   All free.

[*He resumes his paper.*]

[YOUNG WOMAN *sits, staring ahead of her—The music of the hand-organ sounds off very dimly, playing Cielito Lindo. Voices begin to sing it—'Ay-ay-ay-ay'—and then the words—the music and voices get louder.*]

170 THE VOICE OF HER LOVER They were a bunch of bandidos—bandits you know—holding me there—what was I to do—I had to get free—didn't I? I had to get free—

VOICES Free—free—free—

LOVER I filled an empty bottle with small stones—

175 VOICES Stones—stones—precious stones—millstones—stones—stones—millstones—

LOVER Just a bottle with small stones.

VOICES Stones—stones—small stones—

LOVER You only need a bottle with small stones.

180 VOICES Stones—stones—small stones—

VOICE OF A HUCKSTER Stones for sale—stones—stones—small stones—precious stones—

VOICES Stones—stones—precious stones—

LOVER Had to get free, didn't I? Free?

185 VOICES Free? Free?

LOVER Quien sabe? Who knows? Who knows?

VOICES Who'd know? Who'd know? Who'd know?

HUCKSTER Stones—stones—small stones—big stones—millstones—cold stones—head stones—

190 VOICES Head stones—head stones—head stones.

[*The music,—the voices—mingle—increase—the* YOUNG WOMAN *flies from her chair and cries out in terror.*]

YOUNG WOMAN Oh! Oh!

[*The scene* BLACKS OUT—*the music and the dim voices, "Stones—stones—stones," continue until the scene lights for* EPISODE EIGHT.]

Episode Eight

THE LAW

SCENE: *Courtroom.*

SOUNDS: *Clicking of telegraph instruments offstage.*

CHARACTERS:
   JUDGE
   JURY
   LAWYERS
   SPECTATORS
   REPORTERS
   MESSENGER BOYS
   LAW CLERKS
   BAILIFF
   COURT REPORTER
   YOUNG WOMAN

The words and movements of all these people except the YOUNG WOMAN *are routine—mechanical—Each is going through the motions of his own game.*

AT RISE: ALL *assembled, except* JUDGE.

[*Enter* JUDGE.]

BAILIFF [*mumbling*]   Hear ye—hear ye—hear ye!

[ALL *rise*. JUDGE *sits*. ALL *sit*.]

[LAWYER FOR DEFENSE *gets to his feet—He is the verbose, 'eloquent'—typical criminal defense lawyer.*]

[JUDGE *signs to him to wait—turns to* LAW CLERKS, *grouped at foot of the bench.*]

1ST CLERK [*handing up a paper—routine voice*]   State versus Kling—stay of execution.

JUDGE   Denied.

[1ST CLERK *goes.*]

5   2ND CLERK   Bing vs. Ding—demurrer.[6]

[JUDGE *signs.*]

[2ND CLERK *goes.*]

3RD CLERK   Case of John King—habeas corpus.[7]

[JUDGE *signs.*]

[3RD CLERK *goes.*]

[JUDGE *signs to* BAILIFF.]

BAILIFF [*mumbling*]   People of the State of———versus Helen Jones.

JUDGE [*to* LAWYER FOR THE DEFENSE]   Defense ready to proceed?

LAWYER FOR DEFENSE   We're ready, your Honor.

10   JUDGE   Proceed.

LAWYER FOR DEFENSE   Helen Jones.

BAILIFF   HELEN JONES!

[YOUNG WOMAN *rises.*]

LAWYER FOR DEFENSE   Mrs. Jones, will you take the stand?

[YOUNG WOMAN *goes to witness stand.*]

1ST REPORTER [*writing rapidly*]   The defense sprang a surprise at the opening
15   of court this morning by putting the accused woman on the stand. The
prosecution was swept off its feet by this daring defense strategy and—

[*Instruments get louder.*]

2ND REPORTER   Trembling and scarcely able to stand, Helen Jones, accused
murderess, had to be almost carried to the witness stand this morning
when her lawyer—

20   BAILIFF [*mumbling—with Bible*]   Do you swear to tell the truth, the whole
truth and nothing but the truth—so help you God?

YOUNG WOMAN   I do.

JUDGE   You may sit.

[*She sits in witness chair.*]

COURT REPORTER   What is your name?

25   YOUNG WOMAN   Helen Jones.

COURT REPORTER   Your age?

YOUNG WOMAN [*hesitates—then*]   Twenty-nine.

COURT REPORTER   Where do you live?

YOUNG WOMAN   In prison.

---

6. Form of legal objection.
7. In law, method of releasing someone from unlawful restraint.

30 LAWYER FOR DEFENSE   This is my client's legal address. [*Hands a scrap of paper.*]

LAWYER FOR PROSECUTION [*jumping to his feet*]   I object to this insinuation on the part of counsel on any illegality in the holding of this defendant in jail when the law—

LAWYER FOR DEFENSE   I made no such insinuation.

35 LAWYER FOR PROSECUTION   You implied it—

LAWYER FOR DEFENSE   I did not!

LAWYER FOR PROSECUTION   You're a—

JUDGE   Order!

BAILIFF   Order!

40 LAWYER FOR DEFENSE   Your Honor, I object to counsel's constant attempt to—

LAWYER FOR PROSECUTION   I protest—I—

JUDGE   Order!

BAILIFF   Order!

JUDGE   Proceed with the witness.

45 LAWYER FOR DEFENSE   Mrs. Jones, you are the widow of the late George H. Jones, are you not?

YOUNG WOMAN   Yes.

LAWYER FOR DEFENSE   How long were you married to the late George H. Jones before his demise?

50 YOUNG WOMAN   Six years.

LAWYER FOR DEFENSE   Six years! And it was a happy marriage, was it not? [YOUNG WOMAN *hesitates.*] Did you quarrel?

YOUNG WOMAN   No, sir.

LAWYER FOR DEFENSE   Then it was a happy marriage, wasn't it?

55 YOUNG WOMAN   Yes, sir.

LAWYER FOR DEFENSE   In those six years of married life with your late husband, the late George H. Jones, did you EVER have a quarrel?

YOUNG WOMAN   No, sir.

LAWYER FOR DEFENSE   Never one quarrel?

60 LAWYER FOR PROSECUTION   The witness has said—

LAWYER FOR DEFENSE   Six years without one quarrel! Six years! Gentlemen of the jury, I ask you to consider this fact! Six years of married life without a quarrel. [*The* JURY *grins.*] I ask you to consider it seriously! Very seriously! Who of us—and this is not intended as any reflection on the sacred institu-

65 tion of marriage—no—but!

JUDGE   Proceed with your witness.

LAWYER FOR DEFENSE   You have one child—have you not, Mrs. Jones?

YOUNG WOMAN   Yes, sir.

LAWYER FOR DEFENSE   A little girl, is it not?

70 YOUNG WOMAN.   Yes, sir.

LAWYER FOR DEFENSE   How old is she?

YOUNG WOMAN   She's five—past five.

LAWYER FOR DEFENSE   A little girl of past five. Since the demise of the late Mr. Jones you are the only parent she has living, are you not?

75 YOUNG WOMAN   Yes, sir.

LAWYER FOR DEFENSE   Before your marriage to the late Mr. Jones, you worked and supported your mother, did you not?

LAWYER FOR PROSECUTION   I object, your honor! Irrelevant—immaterial—and—

80 JUDGE   Objection sustained!

LAWYER FOR DEFENSE   In order to support your mother and yourself as a girl, you worked, did you not?

YOUNG WOMAN   Yes, sir.

LAWYER FOR DEFENSE   What did you do?

85 YOUNG WOMAN   I was a stenographer.

LAWYER FOR DEFENSE   And since your marriage you have continued as her sole support, have you not?

YOUNG WOMAN   Yes, sir.

LAWYER FOR DEFENSE   A devoted daughter, gentlemen of the jury! As well as
90   a devoted wife and a devoted mother!

LAWYER FOR PROSECUTION   Your Honor!

LAWYER FOR DEFENSE [quickly]   And now, Mrs. Jones, I will ask you—the law expects me to ask you—it demands that I ask you—did you—or did you not—on the night of June 2nd last or the morning of June 3rd last—kill
95   your husband, the late George H. Jones—did you, or did you not?

YOUNG WOMAN   I did not.

LAWYER FOR DEFENSE   You did not?

YOUNG WOMAN   I did not.

LAWYER FOR DEFENSE   Now, Mrs. Jones, you have heard the witnesses for the
100   State—They were not many—and they did not have much to say—

LAWYER FOR PROSECUTION   I object.

JUDGE   Sustained.

LAWYER FOR DEFENSE   You have heard some police and you have heard some doctors. None of whom was present! The prosecution could not furnish
105   any witness to the crime—not one witness!

LAWYER FOR PROSECUTION   Your Honor!

LAWYER FOR DEFENSE   Nor one motive.

LAWYER FOR PROSECUTION   Your Honor—I protest! I—

JUDGE   Sustained.

110 LAWYER FOR DEFENSE   But such as these witnesses were, you have heard them try to accuse you of deliberately murdering your own husband, this husband with whom, by your own statement, you had never had a quarrel— not one quarrel in six years of married life, murdering him, I say, or rather they say, while he slept, by brutally hitting him over the head with a bot-
115   tle—a bottle filled with small stones—Did you, I repeat this, or did you not?

YOUNG WOMAN   I did not.

LAWYER FOR DEFENSE   You did not! Of course you did not! [Quickly.] Now, Mrs. Jones, will you tell the jury in your own words exactly what happened
120   on the night of June 2nd or the morning of June 3rd last, at the time your husband was killed.

YOUNG WOMAN   I was awakened by hearing somebody—something—in the room, and I saw two men standing by my husband's bed.

LAWYER FOR DEFENSE   Your husband's bed—that was also your bed, was it
125   not, Mrs. Jones?

YOUNG WOMAN   Yes.

LAWYER FOR DEFENSE   You hadn't the modern idea of separate beds, had you, Mrs. Jones?

YOUNG WOMAN   Mr. Jones objected.

130 LAWYER FOR DEFENSE   I mean you slept in the same bed, did you not?

YOUNG WOMAN   Yes.

LAWYER FOR DEFENSE   Then explain just what you meant by saying 'my husband's bed.'

YOUNG WOMAN   Well—I—

135 LAWYER FOR DEFENSE   You meant his side of the bed, didn't you?

YOUNG WOMAN   Yes. His side.

LAWYER FOR DEFENSE   That is what I thought, but I wanted the jury to be
clear on that point. [*To the* JURY.] Mr. and Mrs. Jones slept in the same bed.
[*To her.*] Go on, Mrs. Jones. [*As she is silent.*] You heard a noise and—

140 YOUNG WOMAN   I heard a noise and I awoke and saw two men standing
beside my husband's side of the bed.

LAWYER FOR DEFENSE   Two men?

YOUNG WOMAN   Yes.

LAWYER FOR DEFENSE   Can you describe them?

145 YOUNG WOMAN   Not, very well—I couldn't see them very well.

LAWYER FOR DEFENSE   Could you say whether they were big or small—light
or dark, thin or—

YOUNG WOMAN   They were big dark looking men.

LAWYER FOR DEFENSE   Big dark looking men?

150 YOUNG WOMAN   Yes.

LAWYER FOR DEFENSE   And what did you do, Mrs. Jones, when you suddenly
awoke and saw two big dark looking men standing beside your bed?

YOUNG WOMAN   I didn't do anything!

LAWYER FOR DEFENSE   You didn't have time to do anything—did you?

155 YOUNG WOMAN   No. Before I could do anything—one of them raised—
something in his hand and struck Mr. Jones over the head with it.

LAWYER FOR DEFENSE   And what did Mr. Jones do?

   [SPECTATORS *laugh.*]

JUDGE   Silence.

BAILIFE   Silence.

160 LAWYER FOR DEFENSE   What did Mr. Jones do, Mrs. Jones?

YOUNG WOMAN   He gave a sort of groan and tried to raise up.

LAWYER FOR DEFENSE   Tried to raise up!

YOUNG WOMAN   Yes!

LAWYER FOR DEFENSE   And then what happened?

165 YOUNG WOMAN   The man struck him again and he fell back.

LAWYER FOR DEFENSE   I see. What did the men do then? The big dark looking
men.

YOUNG WOMAN   They turned and ran out of the room.

LAWYER FOR DEFENSE   I see. What did you do then, Mrs. Jones?

170 YOUNG WOMAN   I saw Mr. Jones was bleeding from the temple. I got towels
and tried to stop it, and then I realized he had—passed away—

LAWYER FOR DEFENSE   I see. What did you do then?

YOUNG WOMAN   I didn't know what to do. But I thought I'd better call the
police. So I went to the telephone and called the police.

175 LAWYER FOR DEFENSE   What happened then.

YOUNG WOMAN   Nothing. Nothing happened.

LAWYER FOR DEFENSE   The police came, didn't they?

YOUNG WOMAN   Yes—they came.

LAWYER FOR DEFENSE   [*quickly*]   And that is all you know concerning the
180 death of your husband in the late hours of June 2nd or the early hours of
June 3rd last, isn't it?

YOUNG WOMAN   Yes sir.

LAWYER FOR DEFENSE   All?

YOUNG WOMAN   Yes sir.

185 LAWYER FOR DEFENSE [*to* LAWYER FOR PROSECUTION]   Take the witness.

1ST REPORTER [*writing*]   The accused woman told a straightforward story of—

2ND REPORTER   The accused woman told a rambling, disconnected story of—

LAWYER FOR PROSECUTION   You made no effort to cry out, Mrs. Jones, did you, when you saw those two big dark men standing over your helpless

190 husband, did you?

YOUNG WOMAN   No sir. I didn't. I—

LAWYER FOR PROSECUTION   And when they turned and ran out of the room, you made no effort to follow them or cry out after them, did you?

YOUNG WOMAN   No sir.

195 LAWYER FOR PROSECUTION   Why didn't you?

YOUNG WOMAN   I saw Mr. Jones was hurt.

LAWYER FOR PROSECUTION   Ah! You saw Mr. Jones was hurt! You saw this— how did you see it?

YOUNG WOMAN   I just saw it.

200 LAWYER FOR PROSECUTION   Then there was a light in the room?

YOUNG WOMAN   A sort of light.

LAWYER FOR PROSECUTION   What do you mean—a sort of light? A bed light?

YOUNG WOMAN   No. No, there was no light on.

LAWYER FOR PROSECUTION   Then where did it come from—this sort of light?

205 YOUNG WOMAN   I don't know.

LAWYER FOR PROSECUTION   Perhaps—from the window.

YOUNG WOMAN   Yes—from the window.

LAWYER FOR PROSECUTION   Oh, the shade was up!

YOUNG WOMAN   No—no, the shade was down.

210 LAWYER FOR PROSECUTION   You're sure of that?

YOUNG WOMAN   Yes. Mr. Jones always wanted the shade down.

LAWYER FOR PROSECUTION   The shade was down—there was no light in the room—but the room was light—how do you explain this?

YOUNG WOMAN   I don't know.

215 LAWYER FOR PROSECUTION   You don't know!

YOUNG WOMAN   I think where the window was open—under the shade—light came in—

LAWYER FOR PROSECUTION   There is a street light there?

YOUNG WOMAN   No—there's no street light.

220 LAWYER FOR PROSECUTION   Then where did this light come from—that came in under the shade?

YOUNG WOMAN [*desperately*]   From the moon!

LAWYER FOR PROSECUTION   The moon!

YOUNG WOMAN   Yes! It was bright moon!

225 LAWYER FOR PROSECUTION   It was bright moon—you are sure of that!

YOUNG WOMAN   Yes.

LAWYER FOR PROSECUTION   How are you sure?

YOUNG WOMAN   I couldn't sleep—I never can sleep in the bright moon. I never can.

230 LAWYER FOR PROSECUTION   It was bright moon. Yet you could not see two big dark looking men—but you could see your husband bleeding from the temple.

YOUNG WOMAN   Yes sir.

LAWYER FOR PROSECUTION   And did you call a doctor?

235 YOUNG WOMAN   No.

LAWYER FOR PROSECUTION   Why didn't you?

YOUNG WOMAN   The police did.

LAWYER FOR PROSECUTION   But you didn't?

YOUNG WOMAN   No.

240 LAWYER FOR PROSECUTION   What didn't you? [*No answer.*] Why didn't you?

YOUNG WOMAN   [*whispers*]   I saw it was—useless.

LAWYER FOR PROSECUTION   Ah! You saw that! You saw that—very clearly.

YOUNG WOMAN   Yes.

LAWYER FOR PROSECUTION   And you didn't call a doctor.

245 YOUNG WOMAN   It was—useless.

LAWYER FOR PROSECUTION   What did you do?

YOUNG WOMAN   It was useless—there was no use of anything.

LAWYER FOR PROSECUTION   I asked you what you did?

YOUNG WOMAN   Nothing.

250 LAWYER FOR PROSECUTION   Nothing!

YOUNG WOMAN   I just sat there.

LAWYER FOR PROSECUTION   You sat there! A long while, didn't you?

YOUNG WOMAN   I don't know.

LAWYER FOR PROSECUTION   You don't know? [*Showing her the neck of a bro-*
255   *ken bottle.*] Mrs. Jones, did you ever see this before?

YOUNG WOMAN   I think so.

LAWYER FOR PROSECUTION   You think so.

YOUNG WOMAN   Yes.

LAWYER FOR PROSECUTION   What do you think it is?

260 YOUNG WOMAN   It think it's the bottle that was used against Mr. Jones.

LAWYER FOR PROSECUTION   Used against him—yes—that's right. You've
   guessed right. This neck and these broken pieces and these pebbles were
   found on the floor and scattered over the bed. There were no fingerprints,
   Mrs. Jones, on this bottle. None at all. Doesn't that seem strange to you?

265 YOUNG WOMAN   No.

LAWYER FOR PROSECUTION   It doesn't seem strange to you that this bottle
   held in the big dark hand of one of those big dark men left no mark! No
   print! That doesn't seem strange to you?

YOUNG WOMAN   No.

270 LAWYER FOR PROSECUTION   You are in the habit of wearing rubber gloves at
   night, Mrs. Jones—are you not? To protect—to soften your hands—are you
   not?

YOUNG WOMAN   I used to.

LAWYER FOR PROSECUTION   Used to—when was that?

275 YOUNG WOMAN   Before I was married.

LAWYER FOR PROSECUTION   And after your marriage you gave it up?

YOUNG WOMAN   Yes.

LAWYER FOR PROSECUTION   Why?

YOUNG WOMAN   Mr. Jones did not like the feeling of them.

280 LAWYER FOR PROSECUTION   You always did everything Mr. Jones wanted?

YOUNG WOMAN   I tried to—Anyway I didn't care any more—so much—about
   my hands.

LAWYER FOR PROSECUTION   I see—so after your marriage you never wore gloves at night any more?

285   YOUNG WOMAN   No.

LAWYER FOR PROSECUTION   Mrs. Jones, isn't it true that you began wearing your rubber gloves again—in spite of your husband's expressed dislike—about a year ago—a year ago this spring?

YOUNG WOMAN   No.

290   LAWYER FOR PROSECUTION   You did not suddenly begin to care particularly for your hands again—about a year ago this spring?

YOUNG WOMAN   No.

LAWYER FOR PROSECUTION   You're quite sure of that?

YOUNG WOMAN   Yes.

295   LAWYER FOR PROSECUTION   Quite sure?

YOUNG WOMAN   Yes.

LAWYER FOR PROSECUTION   Then you did not have in your possession, on the night of June 2nd last, a pair of rubber gloves?

YOUNG WOMAN   [shakes her head]   No.

300   LAWYER FOR PROSECUTION   [to JUDGE]   I'd like to introduce these gloves as evidence at this time, your Honor.

JUDGE   Exhibit 24.

LAWYER FOR PROSECUTION   I'll return to them later—now, Mrs. Jones—this nightgown—you recognize it, don't you?

305   YOUNG WOMAN   Yes.

LAWYER FOR PROSECUTION   Yours, is it not?

YOUNG WOMAN   Yes.

LAWYER FOR PROSECUTION   The one you were wearing the night your husband was murdered, isn't it?

310   YOUNG WOMAN   The night he died,—yes.

LAWYER FOR PROSECUTION   Not the one you wore under your peignoir—I believe that is what you call it, isn't it? A peignoir? When you received the police—but the one you wore before that—isn't it?

YOUNG WOMAN   Yes.

315   LAWYER FOR PROSECUTION   This was found—not where the gloves were found—no—but at the bottom of the soiled clothes hamper in the bathroom—rolled up and wet—why was it wet, Mrs. Jones?

YOUNG WOMAN   I had tried to wash it.

LAWYER FOR PROSECUTION   Wash it? I thought you had just sat?

320   YOUNG WOMAN   First—I tried to make things clean.

LAWYER FOR PROSECUTION   Why did you want to make this—clean—as you say?

YOUNG WOMAN   There was blood on it.

LAWYER FOR PROSECUTION   Spattered on it?

YOUNG WOMAN   Yes.

325   LAWYER FOR PROSECUTION   How did that happen?

YOUNG WOMAN   The bottle broke—and the sharp edge cut.

LAWYER FOR PROSECUTION   Oh, the bottle broke and the sharp edge cut!

YOUNG WOMAN   Yes. That's what they told me afterwards.

LAWYER FOR PROSECUTION   Who told you?

330   YOUNG WOMAN   The police—that's what they say happened.

LAWYER FOR PROSECUTION   Mrs. Jones, why did you try so desperately to wash that blood away—before you called the police?

LAWYER FOR DEFENSE   I object!

JUDGE   Objection overruled.

335 LAWYER FOR PROSECUTION   Why, Mrs. Jones?

YOUNG WOMAN   I don't know. It's what anyone would have done, wouldn't they?

LAWYER FOR PROSECUTION   That depends, doesn't it? [*Suddenly taking up bottle.*] Mrs. Jones—when did you first see this?

340 YOUNG WOMAN   The night my husband was—done away with.

LAWYER FOR PROSECUTION   Done away with! You mean killed?

YOUNG WOMAN   Yes.

LAWYER FOR PROSECUTION   Why don't you say killed?

YOUNG WOMAN   It sounds so brutal.

345 LAWYER FOR PROSECUTION   And you never saw this before then?

YOUNG WOMAN   No sir.

LAWYER FOR PROSECUTION   You're quite sure of that?

YOUNG WOMAN   Yes.

LAWYER FOR PROSECUTION   And these stones—when did you first see them?

350 YOUNG WOMAN   The night my husband was done away with.

LAWYER FOR PROSECUTION   Before that night your husband was murdered—you never saw them? Never before then?

YOUNG WOMAN   No sir.

LAWYER FOR PROSECUTION   You are quite sure of that!

355 YOUNG WOMAN   Yes.

LAWYER FOR PROSECUTION   Mrs. Jones, do you remember about a year ago, a year ago this spring, bringing home to your house—a lily, a Chinese water lily?

YOUNG WOMAN   No—I don't think I do.

LAWYER FOR PROSECUTION   You don't think you remember bringing home a 360 water lily growing in a bowl filled with small stones?

YOUNG WOMAN   No—No I don't.

LAWYER FOR PROSECUTION   I'll show you this bowl, Mrs. Jones. Does that refresh your memory?

YOUNG WOMAN   I remember the bowl—but I don't remember—the lily.

365 LAWYER FOR PROSECUTION   You recognize the bowl then?

YOUNG WOMAN   Yes.

LAWYER FOR PROSECUTION   It is yours, isn't it?

YOUNG WOMAN   It was in my house—yes.

LAWYER FOR PROSECUTION   How did it come there?

370 YOUNG WOMAN   How did it come there?

LAWYER FOR PROSECUTION   Yes—where did you get it?

YOUNG WOMAN   I don't remember.

LAWYER FOR PROSECUTION   You don't remember?

YOUNG WOMAN   No.

375 LAWYER FOR PROSECUTION   You don't remember about a year ago bringing this bowl into your bedroom filled with small stones and some water and a lily? You don't remember tending very carefully that lily till it died? And when it died you don't remember hiding the bowl full of little stones away on the top shelf of your closet—and keeping it there until—you don't 380 remember?

YOUNG WOMAN   No, I don't remember.

LAWYER FOR PROSECUTION   You may have done so?

YOUNG WOMAN   No—no—I didn't! I didn't! I don't know anything about all that.

385 LAWYER FOR PROSECUTION   But you do remember the bowl?

YOUNG WOMAN   Yes. It was in my house—you found it in my house.

LAWYER FOR PROSECUTION   But you don't remember the lily or the stones?

YOUNG WOMAN   No—No I don't!

> [LAWYER FOR PROSECUTION *turns to look among his papers in a brief case.*]

1ST REPORTER [*writing*]   Under the heavy artillery fire of the State's attorney's
390 brilliant cross-questioning, the accused woman's defense was badly riddled. Pale and trembling she—

2ND REPORTER [*writing*]   Undaunted by the Prosecution's machine-gun attack, the defendant was able to maintain her position of innocence in the face of rapid-fire questioning that threatened, but never seriously menaced
395 her defense. Flushed but calm she—

LAWYER FOR PROSECUTION [*producing paper*]   Your Honor, I'd like to introduce this paper in evidence at this time.

JUDGE   What is it?

LAWYER FOR PROSECUTION   It is an affidavit taken in the State of Guanajato,
400 Mexico.

LAWYER FOR DEFENSE   Mexico? Your Honor, I protest. A Mexican affidavit! Is this the United States of America or isn't it?

LAWYER FOR PROSECUTION   It's properly executed—sworn to before a notary—and certified to by an American Consul.

405 LAWYER FOR DEFENSE   Your Honor! I protest! In the name of this great United States of America—I protest—are we to permit our sacred institutions to be thus—

JUDGE   What is the purpose of this document—who signed it?

LAWYER FOR PROSECUTION   It is signed by one Richard Roe, and its purpose
410 is to refresh the memory of the witness on the point at issue—and incidentally supply a motive for this murder—this brutal and cold-blooded murder of a sleeping man by—

LAWYER FOR DEFENSE   I protest, your Honor! I object!

JUDGE   Objection sustained. Let me see the document. [*Takes paper which is
415 handed up to him—looks at it.*] Perfectly regular. Do you offer this affidavit as evidence at this time for the purpose of refreshing the memory of the witness at this time?

LAWYER FOR PROSECUTION   Yes, your Honor.

JUDGE   You may introduce the evidence.

420 LAWYER FOR DEFENSE   I object! I object to the introduction of this evidence at this time as irrelevant, immaterial, illegal, biased, prejudicial, and—

JUDGE   Objection overruled.

LAWYER FOR DEFENSE   Exception.

JUDGE   Exception noted. Proceed.

425 LAWYER FOR PROSECUTION   I wish to read the evidence to the jury at this time.

JUDGE   Proceed.

LAWYER FOR DEFENSE   I object.

JUDGE   Objection overruled.

430 LAWYER FOR DEFENSE   Exception.

JUDGE Noted.

LAWYER FOR DEFENSE Why is this witness himself not brought into court—
so he can be cross-questioned?

LAWYER FOR PROSECUTION The witness is a resident of the Republic of
435 Mexico and as such not subject to subpoena as a witness to this court.

LAWYER FOR DEFENSE If he was out of the jurisdiction of this court how did
you get this affidavit out of him?

LAWYER FOR PROSECUTION This affidavit was made voluntarily by the depo-
nent in the furtherance of justice.

440 LAWYER FOR DEFENSE I suppose you didn't threaten him with extradition on
some other trumped-up charge so that—

JUDGE Order!

BAILIFF Order!

JUDGE Proceed with the evidence.

445 LAWYER FOR PROSECUTION [reading] In the matter of the State of——vs.
Helen Jones, I Richard Roe, being of sound mind, do herein depose and
state that I know the accused, Helen Jones, and have known her for a
period of over one year immediately preceding the date of the signature on
this affidavit. That I first met the said Helen Jones in a so-called speak-easy
450 somewhere in the West 40s in New York City. That on the day I met her,
she went with me to my room, also somewhere in the West 40s in New York
City, where we had intimate relations—

YOUNG WOMAN [moans] Oh!

LAWYER FOR PROSECUTION [continues reading] —and where I gave her a
455 blue bowl filled with pebbles, also containing a flowering lily. That from the
first day we met until I departed for Mexico in the Fall, the said Helen
Jones was an almost daily visitor to my room where we continued to—

YOUNG WOMAN. No! No!

[Moans.]

LAWYER FOR PROSECUTION What is it, Mrs. Jones—what is it?

460 YOUNG WOMAN Don't read any more! No more!

LAWYER FOR PROSECUTION Why not?

YOUNG WOMAN I did it! I did it! I did it!

LAWYER FOR PROSECUTION You confess?

YOUNG WOMAN Yes—I did it!

465 LAWYER FOR DEFENSE I object, your Honor.

JUDGE You confess you killed your husband?

YOUNG WOMAN I put him out of the way—yes.

JUDGE Why?

YOUNG WOMAN To be free.

470 JUDGE To be free? Is that the only reason?

YOUNG WOMAN Yes.

JUDGE If you just wanted to be free—why didn't you divorce him?

YOUNG WOMAN Oh I couldn't do that!! I couldn't hurt him like that!

[Burst of laughter from ALL in the court. The YOUNG WOMAN stares out at
them, and then seems to go rigid.]

JUDGE Silence!

475 BAILIFF Silence!

[There is a gradual silence.]

JUDGE   Mrs. Jones, why—[YOUNG WOMAN *begins to moan—suddenly—as though the realization of her enormity and her isolation had just come upon her. It is a sound of desolation, of agony, of human woe. It continues until the end of the scene.*] Why—?

> [YOUNG WOMAN *cannot speak.*]

LAWYER FOR DEFENSE   Your Honor, I ask a recess to—

JUDGE   Court's adjourned.

> [SPECTATORS *begin to file out. The* YOUNG WOMAN *continues in the witness box, unseeing, unheeding.*]

480 1ST REPORTER   Murderess confesses.

2ND REPORTER   Paramour brings confession.

3RD REPORTER   I did it! Woman cries!

> [*There is a great burst of speed from the telegraphic instruments. They keep up a constant accompaniment to the* WOMAN'S *moans.*
>
> *The scene* BLACKS OUT *as the courtroom empties and* TWO POLICEMEN *go to stand by the woman.*]

BLACK OUT

[*The sound of the telegraph instruments continues until the scene lights into* EPISODE NINE—*and the prayers of the* PRIEST.]

Episode Nine

A MACHINE

SCENE: *A Prison Room. The front bars face the audience.* [*They are set back far enough to permit a clear passageway across the stage.*]

SOUNDS: *The voice of a Negro singing. The whir of an aeroplane flying.*

CHARACTERS:
> YOUNG WOMAN
> A PRIEST
> A JAILER
> TWO BARBERS
> A MATRON
> MOTHER
> TWO GUARDS

AT RISE:
> *In front of the bars, at one side, sits a* MAN; *at the opposite side, a* WOMAN. [*The* JAILER *and the* MATRON.]
> *Inside the bars, a* MAN *and a* WOMAN. [*The* YOUNG WOMAN *and a* PRIEST.] *The* YOUNG WOMAN *sits still with folded hands. The* PRIEST *is praying.*

PRIEST   Hear, oh Lord, my prayer; and let me cry come to Thee. Turn not away Thy face from me; in the day when I am in trouble, incline Thy ear to me. In what day soever I shall call upon Thee, hear me speedily. For my days are vanished like smoke; and my bones are grown dry, like fuel for the
5   fire. I am smitten as grass, and my heart is withered; because I forgot to eat my bread. Through the voice of my groaning, my bone hath cleaved to my flesh. I am become like to a pelican of the wilderness. I am like a night raven in the house. I have watched and become as a sparrow all alone on

the housetop. All the day long my enemies reproach me; and they that
10 praised me did swear against me. My days have declined like a shadow, and
I am withered like grass. But Thou, oh Lord, end rest forever.[8] Thou shalt
arise and have mercy, for it is time to have mercy. The time is come.

> [*Voice of* NEGRO *offstage—Begins to sing a Negro spiritual.*]

PRIEST   The Lord hath looked upon the earth, that He might hear the
groans of them that are in fetters, that He might release the children
15 of—[9]

> [VOICE OF NEGRO *grown louder.*]

JAILER   Stop that nigger yelling.

YOUNG WOMAN   No, let him sing. He helps me.

MATRON   You can't hear the Father.

YOUNG WOMAN   He helps me.

20 PRIEST   Don't I help you, daughter?

YOUNG WOMAN   I understand him. He is condemned. I understand him.

> [THE VOICE OF THE NEGRO SINGER *goes on louder, drowning out the voice
> of the* PRIEST.]

PRIEST [*chanting in Latin*]   Gratiam tuum, quaesumus, Domine, metibus nos-
tris infunde, ut qui, angelo nuntiante, Christifilii tui incarnationem cognovi-
mus, per passionem eius et crucem ad ressurectionis gloriam perducamus.
25 Per eudem Christum Dominum nostrum.[1]

> [*Enter* TWO BARBERS. *There is a rattling of keys.*]

1ST BARBER.   How is she?

MATRON   Calm.

JAILER   Quiet.

YOUNG WOMAN [*rising*]   I am ready.

30 1ST BARBER   Then sit down.

YOUNG WOMAN [*in a steady voice*]   Aren't you the death guard come to take
me?

1ST BARBER   No, we ain't the death guard. We're the barbers.

YOUNG WOMAN   The barbers.

35 MATRON   Your hair must be cut.

JAILER   Must be shaved.

BARBER   Just a patch. [*The* BARBERS *draw near her.*]

YOUNG WOMAN   No!

PRIEST   Daughter, you're ready. You know you are ready.

40 YOUNG WOMAN [*crying out*]   Not for this! Not for this!

MATRON   The rule.

JAILER   Regulations.

BARBER   Routine. [*The* BARBERS *take her by the arms.*]

YOUNG WOMAN   No! No! Don't touch me—touch me! [THEY *take her and put
45 her down in the chair, cut a patch from her hair.*] I will not be submitted—

---

8. Psalm 102.1–13, known as the Fifth Peni-
tential Psalm. "End rest forever" more commonly reads "sit enthroned forever."
9. Ibid., verses 19–20.
1. Excerpt from a Catholic prayer sequence
known as the *Angelus*: "Pour out, we pray

Lord, your grace on our hearts, so that we,
who came to know the incarnation of Christ
your Son through the angel's message, might
come, through His passion and cross, to the
glory of the resurrection. Through the same
Christ our Lord."

this indignity! No! I will not be submitted!—Leave me alone! Oh my God am I never to be let alone! Always to have to submit—to submit! No more— not now—I'm going to die—I won't submit! Not now!

BARBER [*finishing cutting a patch from her hair*]   You'll submit, my lady. Right
50   to the end, you'll submit! There, and a neat job too.

JAILER   Very neat.

MATRON   Very neat.

[*Exit* BARBERS.]

YOUNG WOMAN [*her calm shattered*]   Father, Father! Why was I born?

PRIEST   I came forth from the Father and have come into the world—I leave
55   the world and go into the Father.[2]

YOUNG WOMAN [*weeping*]   Submit! Submit! Is nothing mine? The hair on my head! The very hair on my head—

PRIEST   Praise God.

YOUNG WOMAN   Am I never to be let alone! Never to have peace! When I'm
60   dead, won't I have peace?

PRIEST   Ye shall indeed drink of my cup.[3]

YOUNG WOMAN   Won't I have peace tomorrow?

PRIEST   I shall raise Him up at the last day.[4]

YOUNG WOMAN   Tomorrow! Father! Where shall I be tomorrow?

65   PRIEST   Behold the hour cometh. Yea, is now come. Ye shall be scattered every man to his own.[5]

YOUNG WOMAN   In Hell! Father! Will I be in Hell?

PRIEST   I am the Resurrection and the Life.[6]

YOUNG WOMAN   Life has been hell to me, Father!

70   PRIEST   Life has been hell to you, daughter, because you never knew God! Gloria in excelsis Deo.[7]

YOUNG WOMAN   How could I know Him, Father? He never was around me.

PRIEST   You didn't seek Him, daughter. Seek and ye shall find.[8]

YOUNG WOMAN   I sought something—I was always seeking something.

75   PRIEST   What? What were you seeking?

YOUNG WOMAN   Peace. Rest and peace. Will I find it tonight, Father? Will I find it?

PRIEST   Trust in God.

[*A shadow falls across the passage in the front of the stage—and there is a shirring sound.*]

YOUNG WOMAN   What is that? Father! Jailer! What is that?

80   JAILER   An aeroplane.

MATRON   Aeroplane.

PRIEST   God in His Heaven.

YOUNG WOMAN   Look, Father! A man flying! He has wings! But he is not an angel!

85   JAILER   Hear his engine.

MATRON   Hear the engine.

2. John 16.28.
3. Matthew 20.23.
4. John 6.54.
5. John 16.32.

6. John 11.25.
7. "Glory to God in the highest."
8. Matthew 7.7.

YOUNG WOMAN   He has wings—but he isn't free! I've been free, Father! For one moment—down here on earth—I have been free! When I did what I did I was free! Free and not afraid! How is that, Father? How can that be?
90   A great sin—a mortal sin—for which I must die and go to hell—but it made me free! One moment I was free! How is that, Father? Tell me that?

PRIEST   Your sins are forgiven.

YOUNG WOMAN   And that other sin—that other sin—that sin of love—That's all I ever knew of Heaven—heaven on earth! How is that, Father? How can
95   that be—a sin—a mortal sin—all I know of heaven?

PRIEST   Confess to Almighty God.

YOUNG WOMAN   Oh, Father, pray for me—a prayer—that I can understand!

PRIEST   I will pray for you, daughter, the prayer of desire. Behind the King of Heaven, behold Thy Redeemer and God, Who is even now coming; pre-
100   pare thyself to receive Him with love, invite him with the ardor of thy desire; come, oh my Jesus, come to thy soul which desires Thee! Before Thou givest Thyself to me, I desire to give Thee my miserable heart. Do Thou accept it, and come quickly to take possession of it! Come my God, hasten! Delay no longer! My only and Infinite Good, my Treasure, my Life,
105   my Paradise, my Love, my all, my wish is to receive Thee with the love with which—[9]

> [Enter the MOTHER. She comes along the passage way and stops before the bars.]

YOUNG WOMAN [recoiling]   Who's that woman?

JAILER   Your mother.

MATRON   Your mother.

110 YOUNG WOMAN   She's a stranger—take her away—she's a stranger.

JAILER   She's come to say goodbye to you—

MATRON   To say goodbye.

YOUNG WOMAN   But she's never known me—never known me—ever—[To the MOTHER.] Go away! You're a stranger! Stranger! Stranger! [MOTHER
115   turns and starts away. Reaching out her hands to her.] Oh Mother! Mother!

> [They embrace through the bars.]

> [Enter TWO GUARDS.]

PRIEST   Come, daughter.

1ST GUARD   It's time.

2ND GUARD   Time.

YOUNG WOMAN   Wait! Mother, my child; my little strange child! I never knew
120   her! She'll never know me! Let her live, Mother. Let her live! Live! Tell her—

PRIEST   Come, daughter.

YOUNG WOMAN   Wait! wait! Tell her—

> [The JAILER takes the MOTHER away.]

GUARD   It's time.

YOUNG WOMAN   Wait! Wait! Tell her! Wait! Just a minute more! There's so
125   much I want to tell her—Wait—

> [The JAILER takes the MOTHER off.]

---

9 Excerpt from St. Alphonsus Liguori, *Visits to the Blessed Sacrament and the Blessed Virgin Mary* (1835); "Behind the King of Heaven" may be a mistranscription of "Behold the King of Heaven," found in some versions of this text.

[*The* TWO GUARDS *take the* YOUNG WOMAN *by the arms, and start through the door in the bars and down the passage, across stage and off.*
The PRIEST *follows; the* MATRON *follows the* PRIEST; *the* PRIEST *is praying.*
The scene BLACKS OUT.

The voice of the PRIEST *gets dimmer and dimmer.*]

PRIEST   Lord have mercy—Christ have mercy—Lord have mercy—Christ hear us! God the Father of Heaven! God the Son, Redeemer of the World, God the Holy Ghost—Holy Trinity one God—Holy Mary—Holy Mother of God—Holy Virgin of Virgins—St. Michael—St. Gabriel—St. Raphael—
[*His voice dies out.*]
[*Out of the darkness come the voices of* REPORTERS.]

130 1ST REPORTER   What time is it now?

2ND REPORTER   Time now.

3RD REPORTER   Hush.

1ST REPORTER   Here they come.

3D REPORTER   Hush.

135 PRIEST [*his voice sounds dimly—gets louder—continues until the end*]   St. Peter pray for us—St. Paul pray for us—St. James pray for us—St. John pray for us—all ye holy Angels and Archangels—all ye blessed orders of holy spirits—St. Joseph—St. John the Baptist—St. Thomas—

1ST REPORTER   Here they are!

140 2ND REPORTER   How little she looks! She's gotten smaller.

3RD REPORTER   Hush.

PRIEST   St. Phillip pray for us. All ye Holy Patriarchs and prophets—St. Phillip—St. Matthew—St. Simon—St. Thaddeus—All ye holy apostles—all ye holy disciples—all ye holy innocents—Pray for us—Pray for us—Pray for

145 us.—

1ST REPORTER   Suppose the machine shouldn't work!

2ND REPORTER   It'll work!—It always works!

3RD REPORTER   Hush!

PRIEST   Saints of God make intercession for us—Be merciful—Spare us, oh

150 Lord—be merciful—

1ST REPORTER   Her lips are moving—what is she saying?

2ND REPORTER   Nothing.

3RD REPORTER   Hush!

PRIEST   Oh Lord deliver us from all evil—from all sin—from Thy wrath—

155 from the snares of the devil—from anger and hatred and every evil will—from—

1ST REPORTER   Did you see that? She fixed her hair under the cap—pulled her hair out under the cap.

3RD REPORTER   Hush!

160 PRIEST   —Beseech Thee—hear us—that Thou would'st spare us—that Thou would'st pardon us—Holy Mary—pray for us—

2ND REPORTER   There—

YOUNG WOMAN [*calling out*]   Somebody! Somebod—
[*Her voice is cut off.*]

PRIEST   Christ have mercy—Lord have mercy—Christ have mercy—

CURTAIN

FEDERICO GARCÍA LORCA

1898–1936

WHEN Federico García Lorca was arrested and executed by fascist militia at the beginning of the Spanish Civil War, he was already the best-known Spanish poet and dramatist of his generation. During the long years of Generalissimo Franco's rule, which lasted until 1975, the memory and work of García Lorca were systematically suppressed in Spain even as he achieved worldwide fame for his poetry and his three greatest tragedies, *The Blood Wedding* (1933), *Yerma* (1934), and THE HOUSE OF BERNARDA ALBA (written 1936; produced 1945). Like other modern dramatists, such as the Irish JOHN MILLINGTON SYNGE, the Italian LUIGI PIRANDELLO, and the West Indian Derek Walcott, García Lorca used remote, rural settings for his particular brand of modern tragedy. Like them, he transformed colloquial dialects into an intensely poetic language, creating plays of unusual resonance and beauty. But García Lorca did not excel only at tragedy. Inspired by an early interest in puppet theater, he composed several plays and curtain-raisers in the crude form of the Punch and Judy show, as well as farces and other pieces of popular entertainment. He worked, throughout his short life, on a visionary piece of metatheater, which was not performed until the 1980s. And he became well known as the author of several collections of poetry,

some traditional and others daring and modernist. Despite this wide-ranging oeuvre, García Lorca will be remembered as an author of modern tragedies whose own life made him a martyr in the fight against fascism.

García Lorca was born into a small village in a relatively remote region of Andalusia, in southern Spain; his father, a farmer and landowner, had managed to amass a small fortune, enabling him to support García Lorca during his studies and early career as a writer. After undertaking his first poetic and dramatic experiments as a student in Granada, García Lorca moved to Madrid to study law. There he encountered the leading Spanish artists of his generation, including the surrealist filmmaker Luis Buñuel, the composer Manuel de Falla, and the painter Salvador Dalí. His friendship with the latter two led to artistic collaborations and exchanges. With Falla, he organized an arts festival, during which Falla performed the 1927 Spanish premiere of Igor Stravinsky's *The Soldier's Tale* (1918), and Dalí created the sets for García Lorca's historical play *Mariana Pineda* (1927). The collaborative experimental films made by Dalí and Buñuel in the late 1920s (the most famous of which is *Un Chien Andalou* [1928]) also left a lasting impact on García Lorca; he later wrote several short film scripts, including *Trip to the Moon* (written ca. 1930), as well as an homage to the American silent film star Buster Keaton in the form of a short dialogue. García Lorca was deeply involved with various experimental avant-garde movements, especially surrealism—he was a contributor to the Spanish surrealist journal *Gallo*—and he was on his way to becoming a leading experimental artist himself.

At the same time, however, García Lorca had a serious interest in an entirely different type of art: folklore. An accomplished pianist, he became familiar with the flamenco tradition by taking some guitar lessons from an aunt. His most successful book of poetry was his collection *Gypsy Ballads* (1928), and he drew on a gypsy form popular in his home region, *conte jondo* (deep song), in his *Poem of the Deep Song* (1931). Most important, he sought to revive the puppet theater. García Lorca was intrigued by the unapologetically colloquial and rough language, the sharply drawn characters, and the economy of action characteristic of this popular art form. In this fascination, he was not alone. Many modern dramatists, from Maurice Maeterlinck and William Butler Yeats to E. G. Craig and ALFRED JARRY, turned to the puppet theater for inspiration; in García Lorca's own circle, Falla had composed several operas involving puppet theater, in particular his acclaimed *Master Peter's Puppet Show* (1923). García Lorca's main work for the puppet theater, often revised and adapted to different occasions, was the *Tragicomedy of Don Cristóbal and Donna Rosita* (1921–22), which, like Jarry's UBU THE KING (1896), became an important example of the avant-garde mixture of crude puppet theater and modern drama. But García Lorca also wrote more traditional, short pieces of puppet theater—for example, *The Girl Who Waters the Basil and the Very Inquisitive Prince Cristobical* (1923), a play aimed mainly at children. Although not written explicitly for the puppet theater, several of García Lorca's comical farces—*The Shoemaker's Prodigious Wife* (1930) and *The Love of Don Perlimpín and Belisa in Her Garden* (1933) among them—are clearly influenced by the tradition of the Punch and Judy show.

Before completing *The Shoemaker's Prodigious Wife*, García Lorca took a lengthy trip to the United States, which included a semester studying at Columbia University. The most important product of his time in New York was his collection *A Poet in New York* (written 1930; published 1940), a widely read and translated homage to the city. At the same time, García Lorca started to work on his most private work, ironically titled *The Public* (written in 1930), a play depicting the homosexuality that he had to hide throughout his life. Like many writers with a secret, García Lorca had a public side and a private side, and many of his works, especially his tragedies, revolve around the differences between the two spheres.

Upon his return to Spain, García Lorca also returned to working actively in the theater. In 1931 he started the Barraca, a traveling student theater troupe that performed both the classics and several of García Lorca's own plays. With this group, García Lorca went to smaller towns and villages, trying to introduce a new theatrical culture to remote places. This enterprise was part of the spirit of progress and reform that took hold in Spain after the election of the country's first democratic-republican government in 1931. But Spanish traditionalists and defenders of established interests—monarchists, the church, landowners, and a large portion of the military—fought against the reforms and were joined by a new fascist party, the Falange. As the struggle between the republican Loyalists and the conservative Nationalists grew, García Lorca was among the many Spaniards who became more politically engaged. His political awakening and his support for the republican cause would soon have tragic consequences, forcing García Lorca into hiding and leading to his execution by a Nationalist death squad.

During the last years of his life García Lorca wrote the three tragedies for which he is mainly known today: *The Blood Wedding*, *Yerma*, and *The House of Bernarda Alba*. All are set in the rural parts of Spain that García Lorca knew from his own childhood—a world of poverty, restrictive Catholic morality, and submerged passions. The first, *The Blood Wedding*, a drama partly in prose and partly in verse, is most fully attuned to the poetic possibilities of the dialect of Andalusia. Like García Lorca's other tragedies, *The Blood Wedding* revolves around the strict moral codes and customs governing life in this world: a bride lets herself be abducted by a former admirer whom she had been forced to reject because of his poverty— with tragic consequences. The second tragedy, *Yerma*, approaches the enforced marriage of convenience from another angle. Yerma, whose name echoes the Spanish word for infertility, is interested in nothing but having children, a desire not shared by her husband. The tension between them is followed by the playwright until its climax, when in desperation she strangles her husband. The strictures of the honor code, blood revenge, and marriage expectations trap these characters into lives from which they can escape only through violence and death.

The abduction of *The Blood Wedding* and the tragedy of infertility in *Yerma* are brought to a perfect union in García Lorca's last play and masterpiece: *The House of Bernarda Alba*. Here, adherence to the strictest morality, in particular the moral codes governing women and female sexu-

ality, is ensured not by men but by a mother, Bernarda Alba, who controls her five marriageable daughters (as well as her own mother) as best she can. The oldest, the thirty-nine-year-old Angustias, is from Bernarda's first marriage and has inherited a small fortune from her deceased father. All Bernarda wants is to match Angustias with a suitable husband, and she seems to have found a halfway acceptable candidate in the much younger Pepe. But all too quickly she loses control when Pepe falls in love with her youngest daughter, Adela. When the two are discovered, the orderly world of the house of Bernarda Alba comes crashing down on its inhabitants with sudden force.

Bernarda's desire for control, which dominates the entire play, is partially motivated by misguided class arrogance: since the Albas are the richest family in the village, appearances have to be kept up—and consequently no one is good enough to marry the daughters. When it is suggested to Bernarda that she could have moved to a larger village, where she would no longer have the burden of maintaining the finest establishment, Bernarda dismisses this thought, thus showing that her aims of upholding her class position and

Penelope Wilton (right) in the title role of the 2005 National Theatre (London) production of *The House of Bernarda Alba*.

controlling her daughters are inextricably intertwined. Bernarda has so fully internalized the rules she imposes on her house—the laws of propriety, position, and social expectations—that she can no longer see their damaging effects. This damage is particularly severe for the younger daughters, but in the end all suffer: marriage and having children are the only purposes for women in this world, without which they shrivel and waste away. Like García Lorca's other plays, *The House of Bernarda Alba* takes a tragic turn precisely at the moment when these ends of matrimony and motherhood cannot be achieved. This repeated pattern suggests a critical attitude on the part of the author, who as a bohemian and homosexual certainly did not subscribe to the view of life presented by Bernarda and the other characters in his plays. García Lorca's own experience of having to hide his sexuality from a hostile world made him all too familiar with the repressive force of society that is brought to bear on these characters. At the same time, his play does not explicitly denounce the traditional moral system that informs it. Rather, *The House of Bernarda Alba* shows how the obsessive pursuit of this conservative morality invariably has tragic consequences.

Bernarda seeks to control not just whom her daughters marry but everything about their existence, down to their smallest movements and gestures. She insists, for example, on a complete separation between men and women, a separation much stricter than is customary in her community. The play opens with a funeral scene; because the men are kept outdoors, we see only the women on the stage. Indeed, the play's cast is composed exclusively of women. All their thoughts revolve around men, focusing on how much they would like to be married and how to achieve that goal. Thus, through their absence, the men dominate the play. Moreover, the play is confined entirely to the inside of the house. One is reminded here of other modern plays that emphasize even more strongly the entrapment of their protagonists in enclosed spaces: for example, Jean-Paul Sartre's *No Exit* (1944) and SAMUEL BECKETT's *Endgame* (1957). In these plays, the interior space of the house and the interior space of the theater fuse,

and that identity gives them their unique claustrophobic power. Such confinement also imposes on these plays a great economy of means—a simplicity that is the hallmark of much modernist theater, which García Lorca here anticipates.

Enclosure and the absence of men also determine the structure of the play, as the women inside the house are obsessed with trying to break through to the outside or, alternatively, to lure someone from the outside in. The one character who moves freely between the outside and inside is the old maid, La Poncia. Bernarda sends her out to inquire about daily events and, more important, about the honor and standing of the Alba family. Even though Poncia is only a maid, her mobility gives her a position of power, but she does not use that power to resist Bernarda's strict regime: she is as interested as her mistress in upholding the honor of the house. The other somewhat anomalous figure in the household, and another victim of Bernarda's regime, is her mother. At the beginning of the play, María Josefa is locked into a closet, and her unending efforts to escape her daughter's control set the scene for the rebellion of Bernarda's own daughters. They constantly spy through cracks in the door or various windows in order to have some relation with the outside world; they exhibit themselves in the windows to attract the attention of passersby; they jealously watch one another for signs of successful communication. All this we surmise only indirectly, as the daughters fight among themselves and with their mother and their maid. We are as enclosed and in the dark as Bernarda herself, who tries to understand what is going on at each moment and who desperately holds on to the vestiges of her power.

Based apparently on childhood neighbors of García Lorca, *The House of Bernarda Alba* is "intended as a photographic document." Its language is markedly different from that of his other tragedies and indeed all his previous plays. With *The House of Bernarda Alba*, García Lorca inaugurates a new style—more economical, more functional, and much less prone to lyrical interludes, songs, flights of fancy, metaphors, and rhetorical embellishments. Nor does the play seek to render the dialect of peasants. Its language, like the lives of the characters, is tightly controlled, in this regard making good its claim of photographic realism. At the same time, however, the play is subtitled "A Drama about Women in the Villages of Spain," underscoring that it has much larger scope and significance than a single photo-realist snapshot of one particular family. It is a play that aspires to tell a more general truth about an entire world.

We can only speculate about the contribution to modern drama that García Lorca could have made in this new mode had his life not been cut short, at the age of thirty-eight, by fascist violence. But even the works he was able to write are remarkable documents of a modernism that is rooted in local culture and tradition. Somehow, García Lorca was able to combine an unusual number of influences and styles. From the folk music of Andalusia and its popular puppet theater to his collaborations with avant-garde artists such as Falla and Dalí, García Lorca forged a modernist drama that sought not to overthrow tradition but instead to continue it. Given this sensibility, it is perhaps not surprising that he met with his greatest success in the most traditional art form of them all: tragedy. While other writers of modern tragedy felt that they had to battle against the long history of that form since Greek antiquity, García Lorca welcomed this legacy, which he enriched by embedding it in the rural traditions he knew best. The result was an art of tragedy that is rooted in a specific place but that also speaks eloquently to audiences around the world.   M.P.

The House of Bernarda Alba
A Drama about Women in the Villages of Spain[1]

CHARACTERS

BERNARDA (age: 60)
MARÍA JOSEFA, Bernarda's mother (age: 80)
ANGUSTIAS, Bernarda's daughter (age: 39)
MAGDALENA, Bernarda's daughter (age: 30)
AMELIA, Bernarda's daughter (age: 27)
MARTIRIO, Bernarda's daughter (age: 24)

ADELA, Bernarda's daughter (age: 20)
A SERVANT (age: 50)
LA PONCIA, a maid (age: 60)
PRUDENCIA (age: 50)
A BEGGAR WOMAN
Women in mourning

The writer states that these Three Acts are intended as a photographic document.

Act 1

[SCENE: *A very white room in* BERNARDA ALBA's *house. The walls are white. There are arched doorways with jute curtains tied back with tassels and ruffles. Wicker chairs. On the walls, pictures of unlikely landscapes full of nymphs or legendary kings.*

---

1. Translated by James Graham-Luján and Richard L. O'Connell.

It is summer. A great brooding silence fills the stage. It is empty when the curtain rises. Bells can be heard tolling outside.]

FIRST SERVANT [*entering*]   The tolling of those bells hits me right between the eyes.

PONCIA [*she enters, eating bread and sausage*]   More than two hours of mumbo jumbo. Priests are here from all the towns. The church looks beau-
5   tiful. At the first responsory for the dead,[2] Magdalena fainted.

FIRST SERVANT   She's the one who's left most alone.

PONCIA   She's the only one who loved her father. Ay! Thank God we're alone for a little. I came over to eat.

FIRST SERVANT   If Bernarda sees you . . . !

10 PONCIA   She's not eating today so she'd just as soon we'd all die of hunger! Domineering old tyrant! But she'll be fooled! I opened the sausage crock.

FIRST SERVANT [*with an anxious sadness*]   Couldn't you give me some for my little girl, Poncia?

PONCIA   Go ahead! And take a fistful of peas too. She won't know the differ-
15   ence today.

VOICE [*within*]   Bernarda!

PONCIA   There's the grandmother! Isn't she locked up tight?

FIRST SERVANT   Two turns of the key.

PONCIA   You'd better put the cross-bar up too. She's got the fingers of a
20   lock-picker!

VOICE [*within*]   Bernarda!

PONCIA [*shouting*]   She's coming! [*To the* SERVANT] Clean everything up good. If Bernarda doesn't find things shining, she'll pull out the few hairs I have left.

25 SERVANT   What a woman!

PONCIA   Tyrant over everyone around her. She's perfectly capable of sitting on your heart and watching you die for a whole year without turning off that cold little smile she wears on her wicked face. Scrub, scrub those dishes!

30 SERVANT   I've got blood on my hands from so much polishing of everything.

PONCIA   She's the cleanest, she's the decentest, she's the highest everything! A good rest her poor husband's earned!

[*The bells stop.*]

SERVANT   Did all the relatives come?

PONCIA   Just hers. His people hate her. They came to see him dead and make
35   the sign of the cross over him; that's all.

SERVANT   Are there enough chairs?

PONCIA   More than enough. Let them sit on the floor. When Bernarda's father died people stopped coming under this roof. She doesn't want them to see her in her "domain." Curse her!

40 SERVANT   She's been good to you.

PONCIA   Thirty years washing her sheets. Thirty years eating her leftovers. Nights of watching when she had a cough. Whole days peeking through a crack in the shutters to spy on the neighbors and carry her the tale. Life

---

2. A section of the Roman Catholic memorial service.

without secrets one from the other. But in spite of that—curse her! May
45   the "pain of the piercing nail"[3] strike her in the eyes.

SERVANT   Poncia!

PONCIA   But I'm a good watchdog! I bark when I'm told and bite beggars'
heels when she sics me on 'em. My sons work in her fields—both of them
already married, but one of these days I'll have enough.

50 SERVANT   And then . . . ?

PONCIA   Then I'll lock myself up in a room with her and spit in her face—a
whole year. "Bernarda, here's for this, that and the other!" Till I leave her—
just like a lizard the boys have squashed. For that's what she is—she and
her whole family! Not that I envy her her life. Five girls are left her, five
55 ugly daughters—not counting Angustias the eldest, by her first husband,
who has money—the rest of them, plenty of eyelets to embroider, plenty of
linen petticoats, but bread and grapes when it comes to inheritance.

SERVANT   Well, *I'd* like to have what they've got!

PONCIA   All we have is our hands and a hole in God's earth.

60 SERVANT   And that's the only earth they'll ever leave to us—to us who have
nothing!

PONCIA [*at the cupboard*]   This glass has some specks.

SERVANT   Neither soap nor rag will take them off.

    [*The bells toll.*]

PONCIA   The last prayer! I'm going over and listen. I certainly like the way
65 our priest sings. In the Pater Noster[4] his voice went up, and up—like a
pitcher filling with water little by little. Of course, at the end his voice
cracked, but it's glorious to hear it. No, there never was anybody like the
old Sacristan[5]—Tronchapinos. At my mother's Mass, may she rest in
peace, he sang. The walls shook—and when he said "Amen," it was as if a
70 wolf had come into the church. [*Imitating him*] A-a-a-a-men! [*She starts
coughing.*]

SERVANT   Watch out—you'll strain your windpipe!

PONCIA   I'd rather strain something else!

    [*Goes out laughing.*]

    [*The* SERVANT *scrubs. The bells toll.*]

SERVANT [*imitating the bells*]   Dong, dong, dong. Dong, dong, dong. May God
forgive him!

75 BEGGAR WOMAN [*at the door, with a little girl*]   Blessèd be God!

SERVANT   Dong, dong, dong. I hope he waits many years for us! Dong, dong,
dong.

BEGGAR [*loudly, a little annoyed*]   Blessèd be God!

SERVANT [*annoyed*]   Forever and ever![6]

80 BEGGAR   I came for the scraps.

    [*The bells stop tolling.*]

SERVANT   You can go right out the way you came in. Today's scraps are for
me.

---

3. That is, one of the nails holding Jesus to
the cross.
4. Our Father (Latin); that is, the Lord's
Prayer, which begins "Our Father which art
in heaven" (Matthew 6.9–13).

5. The church officer in charge of the sacristy, the room where vestments, sacred vessels, and valuable items are kept.
6. The formulaic responses given here and
later echo the Roman Catholic ritual of burial.

BEGGAR But you have somebody to take care of you—and my little girl and I are all alone!

85 SERVANT Dogs are alone too, and they live.

BEGGAR They always give them to me.

SERVANT Get out of here! Who let you in anyway? You've already tracked up the place.

> [The BEGGAR WOMAN and little girl leave. The SERVANT goes on scrubbing.]

90 Floors finished with oil, cupboards, pedestals, iron beds—but us servants, we can suffer in silence—and live in mud huts with a plate and a spoon. I hope someday not a one will be left to tell it.

> [The bells sound again.]

Yes, yes—ring away. Let them put you in a coffin with gold inlay and brocade to carry it on—you're no less dead than I'll be, so take what's coming to you, Antonio María Benavides—stiff in your broadcloth suit and your

95 high boots—take what's coming to you! You'll never again lift my skirts behind the corral door!

> [From the rear door, two by two, women in mourning with large shawls and black skirts and fans, begin to enter. They come in slowly until the stage is full.]

SERVANT [breaking into a wail] Oh, Antonio María Benavides, now you'll never see these walls, nor break bread in this house again! I'm the one who loved you most of all your servants. [Pulling her hair] Must I live on after

100 you've gone? Must I go on living?

> [The two hundred women finish coming in, and BERNARDA and her five daughters enter. BERNARDA leans on a cane.]

BERNARDA [to the SERVANT] Silence!

SERVANT [weeping] Bernarda!

BERNARDA Less shrieking and more work. You should have had all this cleaner for the wake. Get out. This isn't your place.

> [The SERVANT goes off crying.]

105 The poor are like animals—they seem to be made of different stuff.

FIRST WOMAN The poor feel their sorrows too.

BERNARDA But they forget them in front of a plateful of peas.

FIRST GIRL [timidly] Eating is necessary for living.

BERNARDA At your age one doesn't talk in front of older people.

110 WOMAN Be quiet, child.

BERNARDA I've never taken lessons from anyone. Sit down.

> [They sit down. Pause. Loudly.]

Magdalena, don't cry. If you want to cry, get under your bed. Do you hear me?

SECOND WOMAN [to BERNARDA] Have you started to work the fields?

115 BERNARDA Yesterday.

THIRD WOMAN The sun comes down like lead.

FIRST WOMAN I haven't known heat like this for years.

> [Pause. They all fan themselves.]

BERNARDA Is the lemonade ready?

PONCIA Yes, Bernarda.

> [She brings in a large tray full of little white jars which she distributes.]

120 BERNARDA   Give the men some.

PONCIA   They're already drinking in the patio.

BERNARDA   Let them get out the way they came in. I don't want them walking through here.

A GIRL [to ANGUSTIAS]   Pepe el Romano was with the men during the service.

125 ANGUSTIAS   There he was.

BERNARDA   His mother was there. She saw his mother. Neither she nor I saw Pepe . . .

GIRL   I thought . . .

BERNARDA   The one who *was* there was Darajalí, the widower. Very close to

130   your aunt. We all of us saw him.

SECOND WOMAN [aside, in a low voice]   Wicked, worse than wicked woman!

THIRD WOMAN   A tongue like a knife!

BERNARDA   Women in church shouldn't look at any man but the priest—and him only because he wears skirts. To turn your head is to be looking for the

135   warmth of corduroy.

FIRST WOMAN   Sanctimonious old snake!

PONCIA [between her teeth]   Itching for a man's warmth.

BERNARDA [beating with her cane on the floor]   Blessèd be God!

ALL [crossing themselves]   Forever blessèd and praised.

140 BERNARDA   Rest in peace with holy company at your head.

ALL   Rest in peace!

BERNARDA   With the Angel Saint Michael, and his sword of justice.

ALL   Rest in peace!

BERNARDA   With the key that opens, and the hand that locks.

145 ALL   Rest in peace!

BERNARDA   With the most blessèd, and the little lights of the field.

ALL   Rest in peace!

BERNARDA   With our holy charity, and all souls on land and sea.

ALL   Rest in peace!

150 BERNARDA   Grant rest to your servant, Antonio María Benavides, and give him the crown of your blessèd glory.

ALL   Amen.

BERNARDA [she rises and chants]   Requiem aeternam dona eis domine.[7]

ALL [standing and chanting in the Gregorian fashion][8]   Et lux perpetua luce

155   ab eis.

[They cross themselves.]

FIRST WOMAN   May you have health to pray for his soul.

[They start filing out.]

THIRD WOMAN   You won't lack loaves of hot bread.

SECOND WOMAN   Nor a roof for your daughters.

[They are all filing in front of BERNARDA and going out.]

[ANGUSTIAS leaves by the door to the patio.]

FOURTH WOMAN   May you go on enjoying your wedding wheat.

---

7. Grant them eternal rest, Lord (Latin); the first words of the Requiem Mass. She is answered with the next line, "And let eternal light shine on them."

8. That is, like the antiphonal plain chant whose invention is credited to Saint Gregory I (ca. 540–604).

160 PONCIA [*she enters, carrying a money bag*]   From the men—this bag of money for Masses.[9]

BERNARDA   Thank them—and let them have a glass of brandy.

GIRL [*to* MAGDALENA]   Magdalena . . .

BERNARDA [*to* MAGDALENA, *who is starting to cry*]   Sh-h-h-h!
> [*She beats with her cane on the floor.*]
> [*All the women have gone out.*]

165 BERNARDA [*to the women who have just left*]   Go back to your houses and criticize everything you've seen! I hope it'll be many years before you pass under the archway of my door again.

PONCIA   You've nothing to complain about. The whole town came.

BERNARDA   Yes, to fill my house with the sweat from their wraps and the poi-
170 son of their tongues.

AMELIA   Mother, don't talk like that.

BERNARDA   What other way is there to talk about this cursèd village with no river—this village full of wells where you drink water always fearful it's been poisoned?

175 PONCIA   Look what they've done to the floor!

BERNARDA   As though a herd of goats had passed through.
> [PONCIA *cleans the floor.*]

Adela, give me a fan.

ADELA   Take this one.
> [*She gives her a round fan with green and red flowers.*]

BERNARDA [*throwing the fan on the floor*]   Is that the fan to give to a widow?
180 Give me a black one and learn to respect your father's memory.

MARTIRIO   Take mine.

BERNARDA   And you?

MARTIRIO   I'm not hot.

BERNARDA   Well, look for another, because you'll need it. For the eight years
185 of mourning, not a breath of air will get in this house from the street. We'll act as if we'd sealed up doors and windows with bricks. That's what hap-pened in my father's house—and in my grandfather's house. Meantime, you can all start embroidering your hope-chest linens. I have twenty bolts of linen in the chest from which to cut sheets and coverlets. Magdalena
190 can embroider them.

MAGDALENA   It's all the same to me.

ADELA [*sourly*]   If you don't want to embroider them—they can go without. That way yours will look better.

MAGDALENA   Neither mine nor yours. I know I'm not going to marry. I'd
195 rather carry sacks to the mill. Anything except sit here day after day in this dark room.

BERNARDA   That's what a woman is for.

MAGDALENA   Cursèd be all women.

BERNARDA   In this house you'll do what I order. You can't run with the story
200 to your father any more. Needle and thread for women. Whiplash and

---

9. The money will be given to the church so that the priest will mention the dead man's name at Mass.

mules for men. That's the way it has to be for people who have certain obligations.

[ADELA *goes out.*]

VOICE   Bernarda! Let me out!

BERNARDA [*calling*]   Let her out now!

[*The* FIRST SERVANT *enters.*]

205 FIRST SERVANT   I had a hard time holding her. In spite of her eighty years, your mother's strong as an oak.

BERNARDA   It runs in the family. My grandfather was the same way.

SERVANT   Several times during the wake I had to cover her mouth with an empty sack because she wanted to shout out to you to give her dishwater to

210 drink at least, and some dog meat, which is what she says you feed her.

MARTIRIO   She's mean!

BERNARDA [*to* SERVANT]   Let her get some fresh air in the patio.

SERVANT   She took her rings and the amethyst earrings out of the box, put them on, and told me she wants to get married.

[*The daughters laugh.*]

215 BERNARDA   Go with her and be careful she doesn't get near the well.

SERVANT   You don't need to be afraid she'll jump in.

BERNARDA   It's not that—but the neighbors can see her there from their windows.

[*The* SERVANT *leaves.*]

MARTIRIO   We'll go change our clothes.

220 BERNARDA   Yes, but don't take the kerchiefs from your heads.

[ADELA *enters.*]

And Angustias?

ADELA [*meaningfully*]   I saw her looking out through the cracks of the back door. The men had just gone.

BERNARDA   And you, what were *you* doing at the door?

225 ADELA   I went there to see if the hens had laid.

BERNARDA   But the men had already gone!

ADELA [*meaningfully*]   A group of them were still standing outside.

BERNARDA [*furiously*]   Angustias! Angustias!

ANGUSTIAS [*entering*]   Did you want something?

230 BERNARDA   For what—and at whom—were you looking?

ANGUSTIAS   Nobody.

BERNARDA   Is it decent for a woman of your class to be running after a man the day of her father's funeral? Answer me! Whom were you looking at? [*Pause*]

ANGUSTIAS   I . . .

235 BERNARDA   Yes, you!

ANGUSTIAS   Nobody.

BERNARDA   Soft! Honeytongue!

[*She strikes her.*]

PONCIA [*running to her*]   Bernarda, calm down!

[*She holds her.* ANGUSTIAS *weeps.*]

BERNARDA   Get out of here, all of you!

[*They all go out.*]

240 PONCIA   She did it not realizing what she was doing—although it's bad, of course. It really disgusted me to see her sneak along to the patio. Then she stood at the window listening to the men's talk which, as usual, was not the sort one should listen to.

BERNARDA   That's what they come to funerals for. [*With curiosity*] What were
245   they talking about?

PONCIA   They were talking about Paca la Roseta. Last night they tied her husband up in a stall, stuck her on a horse behind the saddle, and carried her away to the depths of the olive grove.

BERNARDA   And what did she do?

250 PONCIA   She? She was just as happy—they say her breasts were exposed and Maximiliano held on to her as if he were playing a guitar. Terrible!

BERNARDA   And what happened?

PONCIA   What had to happen. They came back almost at daybreak. Paca la Roseta with her hair loose and a wreath of flowers on her head.

255 BERNARDA   She's the only bad woman we have in the village.

PONCIA   Because she's not from here. She's from far away. And those who went with her are the sons of outsiders too. The men from here aren't up to a thing like that.

BERNARDA   No, but they like to see it, and talk about it, and suck their fin-
260   gers over it.

PONCIA   They were saying a lot more things.

BERNARDA [*looking from side to side with a certain fear*]   What things?

PONCIA   I'm ashamed to talk about them.

BERNARDA   And my daughter heard them?

265 PONCIA   Of course!

BERNARDA   That one takes after her aunts: white and mealymouthed and casting sheep's eyes at any little barber's compliment. Oh, what one has to go through and put up with so people will be decent and not too wild!

PONCIA   It's just that your daughters are of an age when they ought to have
270   husbands. Mighty little trouble they give you. Angustias must be much more than thirty now.

BERNARDA   Exactly thirty-nine.

PONCIA   Imagine. And she's never had a beau . . .

BERNARDA [*furiously*]   None of them has ever had a beau and they've never
275   needed one! They get along very well.

PONCIA   I didn't mean to offend you.

BERNARDA   For a hundred miles around there's no one good enough to come near them. The men in this town are not of their class. Do you want me to turn them over to the first shepherd?

280 PONCIA   You should have moved to another town.

BERNARDA   That's it. To sell them!

PONCIA   No, Bernarda, to change . . . Of course, anyplace else, they'd be the poor ones.

BERNARDA   Hold your tormenting tongue!

285 PONCIA   One can't even talk to you. Do we, or do we not share secrets?

BERNARDA   We do not. You're a servant and I pay you. Nothing more.

PONCIA   But . . .

FIRST SERVANT [*entering*]   Don Arturo's here. He's come to see about dividing the inheritance.

290 BERNARDA   Let's go. [*To the* SERVANT] You start whitewashing the patio. [*To* LA PONCIA] And you start putting all the dead man's clothes away in the chest.

PONCIA   We could give away some of the things.

BERNARDA   Nothing—not a button even! Not even the cloth we covered his
295 face with.

> [*She goes out slowly, leaning on her cane. At the door she turns to look at the two servants. They go out. She leaves.*]
>
> [AMELIA *and* MARTIRIO *enter.*]

AMELIA   Did you take the medicine?

MARTIRIO   For all the good it'll do me.

AMELIA   But you took it?

MARTIRIO   I do things without any faith, but like clockwork.

300 AMELIA   Since the new doctor came you look livelier.

MARTIRIO   I feel the same.

AMELIA   Did you notice? Adelaida wasn't at the funeral.

MARTIRIO   I know. Her sweetheart doesn't let her go out even to the front doorstep. Before, she was gay. Now, not even powder on her face.

305 AMELIA   These days a girl doesn't know whether to have a beau or not.

MARTIRIO   It's all the same.

AMELIA   The whole trouble is all these wagging tongues that won't let us live. Adelaida has probably had a bad time.

MARTIRIO   She's afraid of our mother. Mother is the only one who knows the
310 story of Adelaida's father and where he got his lands. Every time she comes here, Mother twists the knife in the wound. Her father killed his first wife's husband in Cuba so he could marry her himself. Then he left her here and went off with another woman who already had one daughter, and then he took up with this other girl, Adelaida's mother, and married her after his
315 second wife died insane.

AMELIA   But why isn't a man like that put in jail?

MARTIRIO   Because men help each other cover up things like that and no one's able to tell on them.

AMELIA   But Adelaida's not to blame for any of that.

320 MARTIRIO   No. But history repeats itself. I can see that everything is a terrible repetition. And she'll have the same fate as her mother and grandmother— both of them wife to the man who fathered her.

AMELIA   What an awful thing!

MARTIRIO   It's better never to look at a man. I've been afraid of them since I
325 was a little girl. I'd see them in the yard, yoking the oxen and lifting grain sacks, shouting and stamping, and I was always afraid to grow up for fear one of them would suddenly take me in his arms. God has made me weak and ugly and has definitely put such things away from me.

AMELIA   Don't say that! Enrique Humanas was after you and he liked you.

330 MARTIRIO   That was just people's ideas! One time I stood in my nightgown at the window until daybreak because he let me know through his shepherd's little girl that he was going to come, and he didn't. It was all just talk. Then he married someone else who had more money than I.

AMELIA   And ugly as the devil.

335 MARTIRIO   What do men care about ugliness? All they care about is lands, yokes of oxen, and a submissive bitch who'll feed them.

AMELIA Ay!

[MAGDALENA *enters.*]

MAGDALENA What are you doing?

MARTIRIO Just here.

340 AMELIA And you?

MAGDALENA I've been going through all the rooms. Just to walk a little, and look at Grandmother's needlepoint pictures—the little woolen dog, and the black man wrestling with the lion—which we liked so much when we were children. Those were happier times. A wedding lasted ten days and evil
345 tongues weren't in style. Today people are more refined. Brides wear white veils, just as in the cities, and we drink bottled wine, but we rot inside because of what people might say.

MARTIRIO Lord knows what went on then!

AMELIA [*to* MAGDALENA] One of your shoelaces has come untied.

350 MAGDALENA What of it?

AMELIA You'll step on it and fall.

MAGDALENA One less!

MARTIRIO And Adela?

MAGDALENA Ah! She put on the green dress she made to wear for her birth-
355 day, went out to the yard, and began shouting: "Chickens! Chickens, look at me!" I had to laugh.

AMELIA If Mother had only seen her!

MAGDALENA Poor little thing! She's the youngest one of us and still has her illusions. I'd give something to see her happy.

[*Pause.* ANGUSTIAS *crosses the stage, carrying some towels.*]

360 ANGUSTIAS What time is it?

MAGDALENA It must be twelve.

ANGUSTIAS So late?

AMELIA It's about to strike.

[ANGUSTIAS *goes out.*]

MAGDALENA [*meaningfully*] Do you know what? [*Pointing after* ANGUSTIAS]

365 AMELIA No.

MAGDALENA Come on!

MARTIRIO I don't know what you're talking about!

MAGDALENA Both of you know it better than I do, always with your heads together, like two little sheep, but not letting anybody else in on it. I mean
370 about Pepe el Romano!

MARTIRIO Ah!

MAGDALENA [*mocking her*] Ah! The whole town's talking about it. Pepe el Romano is coming to marry Angustias. Last night he was walking around the house and I think he's going to send a declaration soon.

375 MARTIRIO I'm glad. He's a good man.

AMELIA Me too. Angustias is well off.

MAGDALENA Neither one of you is glad.

MARTIRIO Magdalena! What do you mean?

MAGDALENA If he were coming because of Angustias's looks, for Angustias as
380 a woman, I'd be glad too, but he's coming for her money. Even though Angustias is our sister, we're her family here and we know she's old and sickly, and always has been the least attractive one of us! Because if she

looked like a dressed-up stick at twenty, what can she look like now, now that she's forty?

385 MARTIRIO   Don't talk like that. Luck comes to the one who least expects it.

AMELIA   But Magdalena's right after all! Angustias has all her father's money; she's the only rich one in the house and that's why, now that Father's dead and the money will be divided, they're coming for her.

MAGDALENA   Pepe el Romano is twenty-five years old and the best-looking
390 man around here. The natural thing would be for him to be after you, Amelia, or our Adela, who's twenty—not looking for the least likely one in this house, a woman who, like her father, talks through her nose.

MARTIRIO   Maybe he likes that!

MAGDALENA   I've never been able to bear your hypocrisy.

395 MARTIRIO   Heavens!

[ADELA enters.]

MAGDALENA   Did the chickens see you?

ADELA   What did you want me to do?

AMELIA   If Mother sees you, she'll drag you by your hair!

ADELA   I had a lot of illusions about this dress. I'd planned to put it on the
400 day we were going to eat watermelons at the well. There wouldn't have been another like it.

MARTIRIO   It's a lovely dress.

ADELA   And one that looks very good on me. It's the best thing Magdalena's ever cut.

405 MAGDALENA   And the chickens, what did they say to you?

ADELA   They presented me with a few fleas that riddled my legs.

[They laugh.]

MARTIRIO   What you can do is dye it black.

MAGDALENA   The best thing you can do is give it to Angustias for her wedding with Pepe el Romano.

410 ADELA [with hidden emotion]   But Pepe el Romano . . .

AMELIA   Haven't you heard about it?

ADELA   No.

MAGDALENA   Well, now you know!

ADELA   But it can't be!

415 MAGDALENA   Money can do anything.

ADELA   Is that why she went out after the funeral and stood looking through the door? [Pause] And that man would . . .

MAGDALENA   Would do anything. [Pause]

MARTIRIO   What are you thinking, Adela?

420 ADELA   I'm thinking that this mourning has caught me at the worst moment of my life for me to bear it.

MAGDALENA   You'll get used to it.

ADELA [bursting out, crying with rage]   I will not get used to it! I can't be locked up. I don't want my skin to look like yours. I don't want my skin's
425 whiteness lost in these rooms. Tomorrow I'm going to put on my green dress and go walking in the streets. I want to go out!

[The FIRST SERVANT enters.]

MAGDALENA [in a tone of authority]   Adela!

SERVANT   The poor thing! How she misses her father. . . .

[*She goes out.*]

MARTIRIO   Hush!

430 AMELIA   What happens to one will happen to all of us.

[ADELA *grows calm.*]

MAGDALENA   The servant almost heard you.

SERVANT [*entering*]   Pepe el Romano is coming along at the end of the street.

[AMELIA, MARTIRIO, *and* MAGDALENA *run hurriedly.*]

MAGDALENA   Let's go see him!

[*They leave rapidly.*]

SERVANT [*to* ADELA]   Aren't you going?

435 ADELA   It's nothing to me.

SERVANT   Since he has to turn the corner, you'll see him better from the window of your room.

[*The* SERVANT *goes out.* ADELA *is left on the stage, standing doubtfully; after a moment, she also leaves rapidly, going toward her room.* BERNARDA *and* LA PONCIA *come in.*]

BERNARDA   Damned portions and shares!

PONCIA   What a lot of money is left to Angustias!

440 BERNARDA   Yes.

PONCIA   And for the others, considerably less.

BERNARDA   You've told me that three times now, when you know I don't want it mentioned! Considerably less; a lot less! Don't remind me any more.

[ANGUSTIAS *comes in, her face heavily made up.*]

ANGUSTIAS   Mother.

445 BERNARDA   Have you dared to powder your face? Have you dared to wash your face on the day of your father's death?

ANGUSTIAS   He wasn't my father. Mine died a long time ago. Have you forgotten that already?

BERNARDA   You owe more to this man, father of your sisters, than to your

450 own. Thanks to him, your fortune is intact.

ANGUSTIAS   We'll have to see about that first!

BERNARDA   Even out of decency! Out of respect!

ANGUSTIAS   Let me go out, mother!

BERNARDA   Let you go out? After I've taken that powder off your face, I will.

455 Spineless! Painted hussy! Just like your aunts!

[*She removes the powder violently with her handkerchief.*]

Now get out!

PONCIA   Bernarda, don't be so hateful!

BERNARDA   Even though my mother is crazy, I still have my five senses and I know what I'm doing.

[*They all enter.*]

460 MAGDALENA   What's going on here?

BERNARDA   Nothing's "going on here"!

MAGDALENA [*to* ANGUSTIAS]   If you're fighting over the inheritance, you're the richest one and can hang on to it all.

ANGUSTIAS   Keep your tongue in your pocketbook!

465 BERNARDA [*beating on the floor*]   Don't fool yourselves into thinking you'll sway me. Until I go out of this house feet first I'll give the orders for myself and for you!

[*Voices are heard and* MARÍA JOSEFA, BERNARDA's *mother, enters. She is very old and has decked out her head and breast with flowers.*]

MARÍA JOSEFA   Bernarda, where is my mantilla? Nothing, nothing of what I own will be for any of you. Not my rings nor my black moiré dress.[1] Because not a
470   one of you is going to marry—not a one. Bernarda, give me my necklace of pearls.

BERNARDA [*to the* SERVANT]   Why did you let her get in here?

SERVANT [*trembling*]   She got away from me!

MARÍA JOSEFA   I ran away because I want to marry—I want to get married to
475   a beautiful manly man from the shore of the sea. Because here the men run from women.

BERNARDA   Hush, hush, Mother!

MARÍA JOSEFA   No, no—I won't hush. I don't want to see these single women, longing for marriage, turning their hearts to dust; and I want to go to my
480   hometown. Bernarda, I want a man to get married to and be happy with!

BERNARDA   Lock her up!

MARÍA JOSEFA   Let me go out, Bernarda!

[*The* SERVANT *seizes* MARÍA JOSEFA.]

BERNARDA   Help her, all of you!

[*They all grab the old woman.*]

MARÍA JOSEFA   I want to get away from here! Bernarda! To get married by the
485   shore of the sea—by the shore of the sea!

Quick Curtain.

Act 2

[SCENE: *A white room in Bernarda's house. The doors on the left lead to the bedrooms.*]

[BERNARDA's *daughters are seated on low chairs, sewing.* MAGDALENA *is embroidering.* LA PONCIA *is with them.*]

ANGUSTIAS   I've cut the third sheet.

MARTIRIO   That one goes to Amelia.

MAGDALENA   Angustias, shall I put Pepe's initials here too?

ANGUSTIAS [*dryly*]   No.

5   MAGDALENA [*calling, from offstage to* ADELA]   Adela, aren't you coming?

AMELIA   She's probably stretched out on the bed.

PONCIA   Something's wrong with that one. I find her restless, trembling, frightened—as if a lizard were between her breasts.

MARTIRIO   There's nothing, more or less, wrong with her than there is with
10   all of us.

MAGDALENA   All of us except Angustias.

ANGUSTIAS   I feel fine, and anybody who doesn't like it can pop.

MAGDALENA   We all have to admit the nicest things about you are your figure and your tact.

15   ANGUSTIAS   Fortunately, I'll soon be out of this hell.

MAGDALENA   Maybe you won't get out!

MARTIRIO   Stop this talk!

---

1. A dress made of watered silk, or a fabric with a similar shimmering appearance.

ANGUSTIAS   Besides, a good dowry is better than dark eyes in one's face!

MAGDALENA   All you say just goes in one ear and out the other.

20 AMELIA [*to* LA PONCIA]   Open the patio door[2] and see if we can get a bit of a breeze.

[LA PONCIA *opens the door.*]

MARTIRIO   Last night I couldn't sleep because of the heat.

AMELIA   Neither could I.

MAGDALENA   I got up for a bit of air. There was a black storm cloud and a few
25 drops even fell.

PONCIA   It was one in the morning and the earth seemed to give off fire. I got up too. Angustias was still at the window with Pepe.

MAGDALENA [*with irony*]   That late? What time did he leave?

ANGUSTIAS   Why do you ask, if you saw him?

30 AMELIA   He must have left about one-thirty.

ANGUSTIAS   Yes. How did you know?

AMELIA   I heard him cough and heard his mare's hoofbeats.

PONCIA   But I heard him leave around four.

ANGUSTIAS   It must have been someone else!

35 PONCIA   No, I'm sure of it!

AMELIA   That's what it seemed to me, too.

MAGDALENA   That's very strange! [*Pause*]

PONCIA   Listen, Angustias, what did he say to you the first time he came by your window?

40 ANGUSTIAS   Nothing. What should he say? Just talked.

MARTIRIO   It's certainly strange that two people who never knew each other should suddenly meet at a window and be engaged.

ANGUSTIAS   Well, I didn't mind.

AMELIA   I'd have felt very strange about it.

45 ANGUSTIAS   No, because when a man comes to a window he knows, from all the busybodies who come and go and fetch and carry, that he's going to be told "yes."

MARTIRIO   All right, but he'd have to ask you.

ANGUSTIAS   Of course!

50 AMELIA [*inquisitively*]   And how did he ask you?

ANGUSTIAS   Why, no way:—"You know I'm after you. I need a good, well-brought-up woman, and that's you—if it's agreeable."

AMELIA   These things embarrass me!

ANGUSTIAS   They embarrass me too, but one has to go through it!

55 PONCIA   And did he say anything more?

ANGUSTIAS   Yes, he did all the talking.

MARTIRIO   And you?

ANGUSTIAS   I couldn't have said a word. My heart was almost coming out of my mouth. It was the first time I'd ever been alone at night with a man.

60 MAGDALENA   And such a handsome man.

ANGUSTIAS   He's not bad looking!

PONCIA   Those things happen among people who have an idea how to do things, who talk and say and move their hand. The first time my husband, Evaristo the Short-tailed, came to my window . . . Ha! Ha! Ha!

---

2. That is, the door to an inner courtyard (a common feature in Spanish residences).

65 AMELIA   What happened?

PONCIA   It was very dark. I saw him coming along and as he went by he said, "Good evening." "Good evening," I said. Then we were both silent for more than half an hour. The sweat poured down my body. Then Evaristo got nearer and nearer as if he wanted to squeeze in through the bars and said
70   in a very low voice—"Come here and let me feel you!"

[*They all laugh.* AMELIA *gets up, runs, and looks through the door.*]

AMELIA   Ay, I thought mother was coming!

MAGDALENA   What she'd have done to us!

[*They go on laughing.*]

AMELIA   Sh-h-h! She'll hear us.

PONCIA   Then he acted very decently. Instead of getting some other idea, he
75   went to raising birds, until he died. You aren't married but it's good for you to know, anyway, that two weeks after the wedding a man gives up the bed for the table, then the table for the tavern, and the woman who doesn't like it can just rot, weeping in a corner.

AMELIA   You liked it.

80 PONCIA   I learned how to handle him!

MARTIRIO   Is it true that you sometimes hit him?

PONCIA   Yes, and once I almost poked out one of his eyes!

MAGDALENA   All women ought to be like that!

PONCIA   I'm one of your mother's school. One time I don't know what he said
85   to me, and then I killed all his birds—with the pestle!

[*They laugh.*]

MAGDALENA   Adela, child! Don't miss this.

AMELIA   Adela! [*Pause*]

MAGDALENA   I'll go see!

[*She goes out.*]

PONCIA   That child is sick!

90 MARTIRIO   Of course. She hardly sleeps!

PONCIA   What *does* she do, then?

MARTIRIO   How do I know what she does?

PONCIA   You probably know better than we do, since you sleep with just a wall between you.

95 ANGUSTIAS   Envy gnaws on people.

AMELIA   Don't exaggerate.

ANGUSTIAS   I can tell it in her eyes. She's getting the look of a crazy woman.

MARTIRIO   Don't talk about crazy women. This is one place you're not allowed to say that word.

[MAGDALENA *and* ADELA *enter.*]

100 MAGDALENA   Didn't you say she was asleep?

ADELA   My body aches.

MARTIRIO [*with a hidden meaning*]   Didn't you sleep well last night?

ADELA   Yes.

MARTIRIO   Then?

105 ADELA [*loudly*]   Leave me alone. Awake or asleep, it's no affair of yours. I'll do whatever I want to with my body.

MARTIRIO   I was just concerned about you!

ADELA   Concerned? Curious! Weren't you sewing? Well, continue! I wish I were invisible so I could pass through a room without being asked where I

110   was going!

SERVANT [*entering*]   Bernarda is calling you. The man with the laces is here.

> [*All but* ADELA *and* LA PONCIA *go out, and as* MARTIRIO *leaves, she looks fixedly at* ADELA.]

ADELA   Don't look at me like that! If you want, I'll give you my eyes, for they're younger, and my back to improve that hump you have, but look the other way when I go by.

115   PONCIA   Adela, she's your sister, and the one who most loves you besides!

ADELA   She follows me everywhere. Sometimes she looks in my room to see if I'm sleeping. She won't let me breathe, and always, "Too bad about that face!" "Too bad about that body! It's going to waste!" But I won't let that happen. My body will be for whomever I choose.

120   PONCIA [*insinuatingly, in a low voice*]   For Pepe el Romano, no?

ADELA [*frightened*]   What do you mean?

PONCIA   What I said, Adela!

ADELA   Shut up!

PONCIA [*loudly*]   Don't you think I've noticed?

125   ADELA   Lower your voice!

PONCIA   Then forget what you're thinking about!

ADELA   What do you know?

PONCIA   We old ones can see through walls. Where do you go when you get up at night?

130   ADELA   I wish you were blind!

PONCIA   But my head and hands are full of eyes, where something like this is concerned. I couldn't possibly guess your intentions. Why did you sit almost naked at your window, and with the light on and the window open, when Pepe passed by the second night he came to talk with your sister?

135   ADELA   That's not true!

PONCIA   Don't be a child! Leave your sister alone. And if you like Pepe el Romano, keep it to yourself.

> [ADELA *weeps.*]

Besides, who says you can't marry him? Your sister Angustias is sickly. She'll die with her first child. Narrow waisted, old—and out of my experi-

140   ence I can tell you she'll die. Then Pepe will do what all widowers do in these parts: he'll marry the youngest and most beautiful, and that's you. Live on that hope, forget him, anything; but don't go against God's law.

ADELA   Hush!

PONCIA   I won't hush!

145   ADELA   Mind your own business. Snooper, traitor!

PONCIA   I'm going to stick to you like a shadow!

ADELA   Instead of cleaning the house and then going to bed and praying for the dead, you root around like an old sow about goings-on between men and women—so you can drool over them.

150   PONCIA   I keep watch; so people won't spit when they pass our door.

ADELA   What a tremendous affection you've suddenly conceived for my sister.

PONCIA   I don't have any affection for any of you. I want to live in a decent house. I don't want to be dirtied in my old age!

155 ADELA   Save your advice. It's already too late. For I'd leap not over you, just a servant, but over my mother to put out this fire I feel in my legs and my mouth. What can you possibly say about me? That I lock myself in my room and will not open the door? That I don't sleep? I'm smarter than you! See if you can catch the hare with your hands.

160 PONCIA   Don't defy me, Adela, don't defy me! Because I can shout, light lamps, and make bells ring.

ADELA   Bring four thousand yellow flares and set them about the walls of the yard. No one can stop what has to happen.

PONCIA   You like him that much?

165 ADELA   That much! Looking in his eyes I seem to drink his blood in slowly.

PONCIA   I won't listen to you.

ADELA   Well, you'll have to! I've been afraid of you. But now I'm stronger than you!

[ANGUSTIAS *enters.*]

ANGUSTIAS   Always arguing!

170 PONCIA   Certainly. She insists that in all this heat I have to go bring her I don't know what from the store.

ANGUSTIAS   Did you buy me the bottle of perfume?

PONCIA   The most expensive one. And the face powder. I put them on the table in your room.

[ANGUSTIAS *goes out.*]

175 ADELA   And be quiet!

PONCIA   We'll see!

[MARTIRIO *and* AMELIA *enter.*]

MARTIRIO [*to* ADELA]   Did you see the laces?

AMELIA   Angustias's, for her wedding sheets, are beautiful.

ADELA [*to* MARTIRIO, *who is carrying some lace*]   And these?

180 MARTIRIO   They're for me. For a nightgown.

ADELA [*with sarcasm*]   One needs a sense of humor around here!

MARTIRIO [*meaningfully*]   But only for me to look at. I don't have to exhibit myself before anybody.

PONCIA   No one ever sees us in our nightgowns.

185 MARTIRIO [*meaningfully, looking at* ADELA]   Sometimes they don't! But I love nice underwear. If I were rich, I'd have it made of Holland cloth.[3] It's one of the few tastes I've left.

PONCIA   These laces are beautiful for babies' caps and christening gowns. I could never afford them for my own. Now let's see if Angustias will use

190 them for hers. Once she starts having children, they'll keep her running night and day.

MAGDALENA   I don't intend to sew a stitch on them.

AMELIA   And much less bring up some stranger's children. Look how our neighbors across the road are—making sacrifices for four brats.

195 PONCIA   They're better off than you. There at least they laugh and you can hear them fight.

MARTIRIO   Well, you go work for them, then.

PONCIA   No, fate has sent me to this nunnery!

---

3. An expensive linen fabric from Holland.

[*Tiny bells are heard distantly as though through several thicknesses of wall.*]

MAGDALENA   It's the men going back to work.

200 PONCIA   It was three o'clock a minute ago.

MARTIRIO   With this sun!

ADELA [*sitting down*]   Ay! If only we could go out in the fields too!

MAGDALENA [*sitting down*]   Each class does what it has to!

MARTIRIO [*sitting down*]   That's it!

205 AMELIA [*sitting down*]   Ay!

PONCIA   There's no happiness like that in the fields right at this time of year. Yesterday morning the reapers arrived. Forty or fifty handsome young men.

MAGDALENA   Where are they from this year?

PONCIA   From far, far away. They came from the mountains! Happy! Like
210   weathered trees! Shouting and throwing stones! Last night a woman who dresses in sequins and dances, with an accordion, arrived, and fifteen of them made a deal with her to take her to the olive grove. I saw them from far away. The one who talked with her was a boy with green eyes—tight-knit as a sheaf of wheat.

215 AMELIA   Really?

ADELA   Are you sure?

PONCIA   Years ago another one of those women came here, and I myself gave my eldest son some money so he could go. Men need things like that.

ADELA   Everything's forgiven *them*.

220 AMELIA   To be born a woman's the worst possible punishment.

MAGDALENA   Even our eyes aren't our own.

[*A distant song is heard, coming nearer.*]

PONCIA   There they are. They have a beautiful song.

AMELIA   They're going out to reap now.

CHORUS
   The reapers have set out
225   Looking for ripe wheat;
   They'll carry off the hearts
   Of any girls they meet.

[*Tambourines and carrañacas*[4] *are heard. Pause. They all listen in the silence cut by the sun.*]

AMELIA   And they don't mind the sun!

MARTIRIO   They reap through flames.

230 ADELA   How I'd like to be a reaper so I could come and go as I pleased. Then we could forget what's eating at us all.

MARTIRIO   What do you have to forget?

ADELA   Each one of us has something.

MARTIRIO [*intensely*]   Each one!

235 PONCIA   Quiet! Quiet!

CHORUS [*very distantly*]
   Throw wide your doors and windows,
   You girls who live in the town
   The reaper asks you for roses
   With which to deck his crown.

4. Rattles (Spanish).

240 PONCIA What a song!

MARTIRIO [*with nostalgia*]

> Throw wide your doors and windows,
> You girls who live in the town.

ADELA [*passionately*]

> The reaper asks you for roses
> With which to deck his crown.

> [*The song grows more distant.*]

245 PONCIA Now they're turning the corner.

ADELA Let's watch them from the window of my room.

PONCIA Be careful not to open the shutters too much because they're likely to give them a push to see who's looking.

> [*The three leave.* MARTIRIO *is left sitting on the low chair with her head between her hands.*]

AMELIA [*drawing near her*] What's wrong with you?

250 MARTIRIO The heat makes me feel ill.

AMELIA And it's no more than that?

MARTIRIO I was wishing it were November, the rainy days, the frost—anything except this unending summertime.

AMELIA It'll pass and come again.

255 MARTIRIO Naturally. [*Pause*] What time did you go to sleep last night?

AMELIA I don't know. I sleep like a log. Why?

MARTIRIO Nothing. Only I thought I heard someone in the yard.

AMELIA Yes?

MARTIRIO Very late.

260 AMELIA And weren't you afraid?

MARTIRIO No. I've heard it other nights.

AMELIA We'd better watch out! Couldn't it have been the shepherds?

MARTIRIO The shepherds come at six.

AMELIA Maybe a young, unbroken mule?

265 MARTIRIO [*to herself, with double meaning*] That's it! That's it. An unbroken little mule.

AMELIA We'll have to set a watch.

MARTIRIO No. No. Don't say anything. It may be I've just imagined it.

AMELIA Maybe.

> [*Pause.* AMELIA *starts to go.*]

270 MARTIRIO Amelia!

AMELIA [*at the door*] What? [*Pause*]

MARTIRIO Nothing. [*Pause*]

AMELIA Why did you call me? [*Pause*]

MARTIRIO It just came out. I didn't mean to. [*Pause*]

275 AMELIA Lie down for a little.

ANGUSTIAS [*she bursts in furiously, in a manner that makes a great contrast with previous silence*] Where's that picture of Pepe I had under my pillow? Which one of you has it?

MARTIRIO No one.

AMELIA You'd think he was a silver St. Bartholomew.[5]

280 ANGUSTIAS Where's the picture?

---

5. That is, a silver medal depicting Bartholomew, one of the Twelve Apostles.

[PONCIA, MAGDALENA, *and* ADELA *enter.*]

ADELA What picture?

ANGUSTIAS One of you has hidden it from me.

MAGDALENA Do you have the effrontery to say that?

ANGUSTIAS I had it in my room, and now it isn't there.

285 MARTIRIO But couldn't it have jumped out into the yard at midnight? Pepe likes to walk around in the moonlight.

ANGUSTIAS Don't joke with me! When he comes I'll tell him.

PONCIA Don't do that! Because it'll turn up. [*Looking at* ADELA]

ANGUSTIAS I'd like to know which one of you has it.

290 ADELA [*looking at* MARTIRIO] Somebody has it! But not me!

MARTIRIO [*with meaning*] Of course not you!

BERNARDA [*entering, with her cane*] What scandal is this in my house in the heat's heavy silence? The neighbors must have their ears glued to the walls.

ANGUSTIAS They've stolen my sweetheart's picture!

295 BERNARDA [*fiercely*] Who? Who?

ANGUSTIAS They have!

BERNARDA Which one of you? [*Silence*] Answer me! [*Silence*] [*To* LA PONCIA] Search their rooms! Look in their beds. This comes of not tying you up with shorter leashes. But I'll teach you now! [*To* ANGUSTIAS] Are you sure?

300 ANGUSTIAS Yes.

BERNARDA Did you look everywhere?

ANGUSTIAS Yes, Mother.

[*They all stand in an embarrassed silence.*]

BERNARDA At the end of my life—to make me drink the bitterest poison a mother knows. [*To* PONCIA] Did you find it?

305 PONCIA Here it is.

BERNARDA Where did you find it?

PONCIA It was . . .

BERNARDA Say it! Don't be afraid.

PONCIA [*wonderingly*] Between the sheets in Martirio's bed.

310 BERNARDA [*to* MARTIRIO] Is that true?

MARTIRIO It's true.

BERNARDA [*advancing on her, beating her with her cane*] You'll come to a bad end yet, you hypocrite! Trouble maker!

MARTIRIO [*fiercely*] Don't hit me, Mother!

315 BERNARDA All I want to!

MARTIRIO If I let you! You hear me? Get back!

PONCIA Don't be disrespectful to your mother!

ANGUSTIAS [*holding* BERNARDA] Let her go, please!

BERNARDA Not even tears in your eyes.

320 MARTIRIO I'm not going to cry just to please you.

BERNARDA Why did you take the picture?

MARTIRIO Can't I play a joke on my sister? What else would I want it for?

ADELA [*leaping forward, full of jealousy*] It wasn't a joke! You never liked to play jokes. It was something else bursting in her breast—trying to come

325 out. Admit it openly now.

MARTIRIO Hush, and don't make me speak; for if I should speak the walls would close together one against the other with shame.

ADELA An evil tongue never stops inventing lies.

BERNARDA Adela!

330 MAGDALENA You're crazy.

AMELIA And you stone us all with your evil suspicions.

MARTIRIO But some others do things more wicked!

ADELA Until all at once they stand forth stark naked and the river carries them along.

335 BERNARDA Spiteful!

ANGUSTIAS It's not my fault Pepe el Romano chose me!

ADELA For your money.

ANGUSTIAS Mother!

BERNARDA Silence!

340 MARTIRIO For your fields and your orchards.

MAGDALENA That's only fair.

BERNARDA Silence, I say! I saw the storm coming but I didn't think it'd burst so soon. Oh, what an avalanche of hate you've thrown on my heart! But I'm not old yet—I have five chains for you, and this house my father built, so

345 not even the weeds will know of my desolation. Out of here!

> [*They go out.* BERNARDA *sits down desolately.* LA PONCIA *is standing close to the wall.* BERNARDA *recovers herself, and beats on the floor.*]

I'll have to let them feel the weight of my hand! Bernarda, remember your duty!

PONCIA May I speak?

BERNARDA Speak. I'm sorry you heard. A stranger is always out of place in a

350 family.

PONCIA What I've seen, I've seen.

BERNARDA Angustias must get married right away.

PONCIA Certainly. We'll have to get her away from here.

BERNARDA Not her, him!

355 PONCIA Of course. He's the one to get away from here. You've thought it all out.

BERNARDA I'm not thinking. There are things that shouldn't and can't be thought out. I give orders.

PONCIA And you think he'll be satisfied to go away?

360 BERNARDA [*rising*] What are you imagining now?

PONCIA He will, of course, marry Angustias.

BERNARDA Speak up! I know you well enough to see that your knife's out for me.

PONCIA I never knew a warning could be called murder.

365 BERNARDA Have you some "warning" for me?

PONCIA I'm not making any accusations, Bernarda. I'm only telling you to open your eyes and you'll see.

BERNARDA See what?

PONCIA You've always been smart, Bernarda. You've seen other people's sins

370 a hundred miles away. Many times I've thought you could read minds. But, your children are your children, and now you're blind.

BERNARDA Are you talking about Martirio?

PONCIA Well, yes—about Martirio . . . [*With curiosity*] I wonder why she hid the picture?

375 BERNARDA [*shielding her daughter*] After all, she says it was a joke. What else could it be?

PONCIA [*scornfully*] Do you believe that?

BERNARDA [*sternly*] I don't merely believe it. It's so!

PONCIA Enough of this. We're talking about your family. But if we were talk-
380 ing about your neighbor across the way, what would it be?

BERNARDA Now you're beginning to pull the point of the knife out.

PONCIA [*always cruelly*] No, Bernarda. Something very grave is happening
here. I don't want to put the blame on your shoulders, but you've never
given your daughters any freedom. Martirio is lovesick, I don't care what
385 you say. Why didn't you let her marry Enrique Humanas? Why, on the very
day he was coming to her window did you send him a message not to
come?

BERNARDA [*loudly*] I'd do it a thousand times over! My blood won't mingle
with the Humanases' while I live! His father was a shepherd.

390 PONCIA And you see now what's happening to you with these airs!

BERNARDA I have them because I can afford to. And you don't have them
because you know where you came from!

PONCIA [*with hate*] Don't remind me! I'm old now. I've always been grateful
for your protection.

395 BERNARDA [*emboldened*] You don't seem so!

PONCIA [*with hate, behind softness*] Martirio will forget this.

BERNARDA And if she doesn't—the worse for her. I don't believe this is that
"very grave thing" that's happening here. Nothing's happening here. It's
just that you wish it would! And if it should happen one day, you can be
400 sure it won't go beyond these walls.

PONCIA I'm not so sure of that! There are people in town who can also read
hidden thoughts, from afar.

BERNARDA How you'd like to see me and my daughters on our way to a
whorehouse!

405 PONCIA No one knows her own destiny!

BERNARDA I know my destiny! And my daughters'! The whorehouse was for
a certain woman, already dead. . . .

PONCIA [*fiercely*] Bernarda, respect the memory of my mother!

BERNARDA Then don't plague me with your evil thoughts! [*Pause*]

410 PONCIA I'd better stay out of everything.

BERNARDA That's what you ought to do. Work and keep your mouth shut.
The duty of all who work for a living.

PONCIA But we can't do that. Don't you think it'd be better for Pepe to marry
Martirio or . . . yes! . . . Adela?

415 BERNARDA No, I *don't* think so.

PONCIA [*with meaning*] Adela! She's Romano's real sweetheart!

BERNARDA Things are never the way we want them!

PONCIA But it's hard work to turn them from their destined course. For Pepe
to be with Angustias seems wrong to me—and to other people—and even
420 to the wind. Who knows if they'll get what they want?

BERNARDA There you go again! Sneaking up on me—giving me bad dreams.
But I won't listen to you, because if all you say should come to pass—I'd
scratch your face.

PONCIA Frighten someone else with that.

425 BERNARDA Fortunately, my daughters respect me and have never gone against
my will!

PONCIA   That's right! But, as soon as they break loose they'll fly to the rooftops!

BERNARDA   And I'll bring them down with stones!

430   PONCIA   Oh, yes! You were always the bravest one!

BERNARDA   I've always enjoyed a good fight!

PONCIA   But aren't people strange. You should see Angustias's enthusiasm for her lover, at her age! And he seems very smitten too. Yesterday my oldest son told me that when he passed by with the oxen at four-thirty in the

435   morning they were still talking.

BERNARDA   At four-thirty?

ANGUSTIAS [entering]   That's a lie!

PONCIA   That's what he told me.

BERNARDA [to ANGUSTIAS]   Speak up!

440   ANGUSTIAS   For more than a week Pepe has been leaving at one. May God strike me dead if I'm lying.

MARTIRIO [entering]   I heard him leave at four too.

BERNARDA   But did you see him with your eyes?

MARTIRIO   I didn't want to look out. Don't you talk now through the side

445   window?

ANGUSTIAS   We talk through my bedroom window.

[ADELA appears at the door.]

MARTIRIO   Then . . .

BERNARDA   What's going on here?

PONCIA   If you're not careful, you'll find out! At least Pepe was at one of your

450   windows—and at four in the morning too!

BERNARDA   Are you sure of that?

PONCIA   You can't be sure of anything in this life!

ADELA   Mother, don't listen to someone who wants us to lose everything we have.

455   BERNARDA   I know how to take care of myself! If the townspeople want to come bearing false witness against me, they'll run into a stone wall! Don't any of you talk about this! Sometimes other people try to stir up a wave of filth to drown us.

MARTIRIO   I don't like to lie.

460   PONCIA   So there must be something.

BERNARDA   There won't be anything. I was born to have my eyes always open. Now I'll watch without closing them 'til I die.

ANGUSTIAS   I have the right to know.

BERNARDA   You don't have any right except to obey. No one's going to fetch

465   and carry for me. [To LA PONCIA] And don't meddle in our affairs. No one will take a step without my knowing it.

SERVANT [entering]   There's a big crowd at the top of the street, and all the neighbors are at their doors!

BERNARDA [to PONCIA]   Run see what's happening!

[The girls are about to run out.]

470   Where are you going? I always knew you for window-watching women and breakers of your mourning. All of you, to the patio!

[They go out. BERNARDA leaves. Distant shouts are heard. MARTIRIO and ADELA enter and listen, not daring to step farther than the front door.]

MARTIRIO   You can be thankful I didn't happen to open my mouth.

ADELA   I would have spoken too.

MARTIRIO   And what were you going to say? Wanting isn't doing!

475 ADELA   I do what I can and what happens to suit me. You've wanted to, but haven't been able.

MARTIRIO   You won't go on very long.

ADELA   I'll have everything!

MARTIRIO   I'll tear you out of his arms!

480 ADELA [*pleadingly*]   Martirio, let me be!

MARTIRIO   None of us will have him!

ADELA   He wants me for his house!

MARTIRIO   I saw how he embraced you!

ADELA   I didn't want him to. It's as if I were dragged by a rope.

485 MARTIRIO   I'll see you dead first!

> [MAGADALENA *and* ANGUSTIAS *look in. The tumult is increasing. A* SERVANT *enters with* BERNARDA. PONCIA *also enters from another door.*]

PONCIA   Bernarda!

BERNARDA   What's happening?

PONCIA   Librada's daughter, the unmarried one, had a child and no one knows whose it is!

490 ADELA   A child?

PONCIA   And to hide her shame she killed it and hid it under the rocks, but the dogs, with more heart than most Christians, dug it out and, as though directed by the hand of God, left it at her door. Now they want to kill her. They're dragging her through the streets—and down the paths and across

495   the olive groves the men are coming, shouting so the fields shake.

BERNARDA   Yes, let them all come with olive whips and hoe handles—let them all come and kill her!

ADELA   No, not to kill her!

MARTIRIO   Yes—and let us go out too!

500 BERNARDA   And let whoever loses her decency pay for it!

> [*Outside a woman's shriek and a great clamor is heard.*]

ADELA   Let her escape! Don't you go out!

MARTIRIO [*looking at* ADELA]   Let her pay what she owes!

BERNARDA [*at the archway*]   Finish her before the guards come! Hot coals in the place where she sinned!

505 ADELA [*holding her belly*]   No! No!

BERNARDA   Kill her! Kill her!

Curtain.

Act 3

[SCENE: *Four white walls, lightly washed in blue, of the interior patio of* BERNARDA ALBA'S *house. The doorways, illumined by the lights inside the rooms, give a tenuous glow to the stage.*]

> [*At the center there is a table with a shaded oil lamp about which* BERNARDA *and her daughters are eating.* LA PONCIA *serves them.* PRUDENCIA *sits apart. When the curtain rises, there is a great silence interrupted only by the noise of plates and silverware.*]

PRUDENCIA   I'm going. I've made you a long visit.

> [*She rises.*]

BERNARDA   But wait, Prudencia. We never see one another.

PRUDENCIA   Have they sounded the last call to rosary?[6]

PONCIA   Not yet.

[PRUDENCIA *sits down again.*]

5 BERNARDA   And your husband, how's he getting on?

PRUDENCIA   The same.

BERNARDA   We never see him either.

PRUDENCIA   You know how he is. Since he quarrelled with his brothers over the inheritance, he hasn't used the front door. He takes a ladder and climbs
10 over the back wall.

BERNARDA   He's a real man! And your daughter?

PRUDENCIA   He's never forgiven her.

BERNARDA   He's right.

PRUDENCIA   I don't know what he told you. I suffer because of it.

15 BERNARDA   A daughter who's disobedient stops being a daughter and becomes an enemy.

PRUDENCIA   I let water run. The only consolation I've left is to take refuge in the church, but, since I'm losing my sight, I'll have to stop coming so the children won't make fun of me.

[*A heavy blow is heard against the walls.*]

20 What's that?

BERNARDA   The stallion. He's locked in the stall and he kicks against the wall of the house. [*Shouting*] Tether him and take him out in the yard! [*In a lower voice*] He must be too hot.

PRUDENCIA   Are you going to put the new mares to him?

25 BERNARDA   At daybreak.

PRUDENCIA   You've known how to increase your stock.

BERNARDA   By dint of money and struggling.

PONCIA [*interrupting*]   And she has the best herd in these parts. It's a shame that prices are low.

30 BERNARDA   Do you want a little cheese and honey?

PRUDENCIA   I have no appetite.

[*The blow is heard again.*]

PONCIA   My God!

PRUDENCIA   It quivered in my chest!

BERNARDA [*rising, furiously*]   Do I have to say things twice? Let him out to
35 roll on the straw. [*Pause. Then, as though speaking to the stableman*] Well then, lock the mares in the corral, but let him run free or he may kick down the walls.

[*She returns to the table and sits again.*]

Ay, what a life!

PRUDENCIA   You have to fight like a man.

40 BERNARDA   That's it.

[ADELA *gets up from the table.*]

Where are you going?

ADELA   For a drink of water.

6. A form of devotion that consists of a set of repeated prayers.

BERNARDA [*raising her voice*] Bring a pitcher of cool water. [*To* ADELA] You can sit down.

[ADELA *sits down.*]

45 PRUDENCIA And Angustias, when will she get married?

BERNARDA They're coming to ask for her within three days.

PRUDENCIA You must be happy.

ANGUSTIAS Naturally!

AMELIA [*to* MAGDALENA] You've spilled the salt!

50 MAGDALENA You can't possibly have worse luck than you're having.

AMELIA It always brings bad luck.

BERNARDA That's enough!

PRUDENCIA [*to* ANGUSTIAS] Has he given you the ring yet?

ANGUSTIAS Look at it.

[*She holds it out.*]

55 PRUDENCIA It's beautiful. Three pearls. In my day, pearls signified tears.

ANGUSTIAS But things have changed now.

ADELA I don't think so. Things go on meaning the same. Engagement rings should be diamonds.

PONCIA The most appropriate.

60 BERNARDA With pearls or without them, things are as one proposes.

MARTIRIO Or as God disposes.

PRUDENCIA I've been told your furniture is beautiful.

BERNARDA It cost sixteen thousand *reales*.[7]

PONCIA [*interrupting*] The best is the wardrobe with the mirror.

65 PRUDENCIA I never saw a piece like that.

BERNARDA We had chests.

PRUDENCIA The important thing is that everything be for the best.

ADELA And that you never know.

BERNARDA There's no reason why it shouldn't be.

[*Bells are heard very distantly.*]

70 PRUDENCIA The last call. [*To* ANGUSTIAS] I'll be coming back to have you show me your clothes.

ANGUSTIAS Whenever you like.

PRUDENCIA Good evening—God bless you!

BERNARDA Good-bye, Prudencia.

75 ALL FIVE DAUGHTERS [*at the same time*] God go with you!

[*Pause.* PRUDENCIA *goes out.*]

BERNARDA Well, we've eaten.

[*They rise.*]

ADELA I'm going to walk as far as the gate to stretch my legs and get a bit of fresh air.

[MAGDALENA *sits down in a low chair and leans against the wall.*]

AMELIA I'll go with you.

80 MARTIRIO I too.

---

7. Originally, silver coins (the 8-real coin was the Spanish dollar). The real was the chief unit in Spain's first decimal currency; though from 1868 until 2002 it was replaced in that role by the peseta (worth 4 reales), the term remained in common use.

ADELA [*with contained hate*]   I'm not going to get lost!

AMELIA   One needs company at night.

[*They go out.* BERNARDA *sits down.* ANGUSTIAS *is clearing the table.*]

BERNARDA   I've told you once already! I want you to talk to your sister Martirio. What happened about the picture was a joke and you must forget it.

85 ANGUSTIAS   You know she doesn't like me.

BERNARDA   Each one knows what she thinks inside. I don't pry into anyone's heart, but I want to put up a good front and have family harmony. You understand?

ANGUSTIAS   Yes.

90 BERNARDA   Then that's settled.

MAGDALENA [*she is almost asleep*]   Besides, you'll be gone in no time.

[*She falls asleep.*]

ANGUSTIAS   Not soon enough for me.

BERNARDA   What time did you stop talking last night?

ANGUSTIAS   Twelve-thirty.

95 BERNARDA   What does Pepe talk about?

ANGUSTIAS   I find him absent-minded. He always talks to me as though he were thinking of something else. If I ask him what's the matter, he answers—"We men have our worries."

BERNARDA   You shouldn't ask him. And when you're married, even less. Speak

100   if he speaks, and look at him when he looks at you. That way you'll get along.

ANGUSTIAS   But, Mother, I think he's hiding things from me.

BERNARDA   Don't try to find out. Don't ask him, and above all, never let him see you cry.

ANGUSTIAS   I should be happy, but I'm not.

105 BERNARDA   It's all the same.

ANGUSTIAS   Many nights I watch Pepe very closely through the window bars and he seems to fade away—as though he were hidden in a cloud of dust like those raised by the flocks.

BERNARDA   That's just because you're not strong.

110 ANGUSTIAS   I hope so!

BERNARDA   Is he coming tonight?

ANGUSTIAS   No, he went into town with his mother.

BERNARDA   Good, we'll get to bed early. Magdalena!

ANGUSTIAS   She's asleep.

[ADELA, MARTIRIO, *and* AMELIA *enter.*]

115 AMELIA   What a dark night!

ADELA   You can't see two steps in front of you.

MARTIRIO   A good night for robbers, for anyone who needs to hide.

ADELA   The stallion was in the middle of the corral. White. Twice as large. Filling all the darkness.

120 AMELIA   It's true. It was frightening. Like a ghost.

ADELA   The sky has stars as big as fists.

MARTIRIO   This one stared at them till she almost cracked her neck.

ADELA   Don't you like them up there?

MARTIRIO   What goes on over the roof doesn't mean a thing to me. I have my

125   hands full with what happens under it.

ADELA   Well, that's the way it goes with you!

BERNARDA   And it goes the same for you as for her.

ANGUSTIAS   Good night.

ADELA   Are you going to bed now?

130 ANGUSTIAS   Yes, Pepe isn't coming tonight.

> [*She goes out.*]

ADELA   Mother, why, when a star falls or lightning flashes, does one say:
> Holy Barbara,[8] blessed on high
> May your name be in the sky
> With holy water written high?

135 BERNARDA   The old people know many things we've forgotten.

AMELIA   I close my eyes so I won't see them.

ADELA   Not I. I like to see what's quiet and been quiet for years on end, running with fire.

MARTIRIO   But all that has nothing to do with us.

140 BERNARDA   And it's better not to think about it.

ADELA   What a beautiful night! I'd like to stay up till very late and enjoy the breeze from the fields.

BERNARDA   But we have to go to bed. Magdalena!

AMELIA   She's just dropped off.

145 BERNARDA   Magdalena!

MAGDALENA [*annoyed*]   Leave me alone!

BERNARDA   To bed!

MAGDALENA [*rising, in a bad humor*]   You don't give anyone a moment's peace!

> [*She goes off grumbling.*]

150 AMELIA   Good night!

> [*She goes out.*]

BERNARDA   You two get along, too.

MARTIRIO   How is it Angustias's sweetheart isn't coming tonight?

BERNARDA   He went on a trip.

MARTIRIO [*looking at* ADELA]   Ah!

155 ADELA   I'll see you in the morning!

> [*She goes out.* MARTIRIO *drinks some water and goes out slowly, looking at the door to the yard.* LA PONCIA *enters.*]

PONCIA   Are you still here?

BERNARDA   Enjoying this quiet and not seeing anywhere the "very grave thing" that's happening here—according to you.

PONCIA   Bernarda, let's not go any further with this.

160 BERNARDA   In this house there's no question of a yes or a no. My watchfulness can take care of anything.

PONCIA   Nothing's happening outside. That's true, all right. Your daughters act and are as though stuck in a cupboard. But neither you nor anyone else can keep watch inside a person's heart.

165 BERNARDA   My daughters breathe calmly enough.

PONCIA   That's your business, since you're their mother. I have enough to do just with serving you.

BERNARDA   Yes, you've turned quiet now.

---

8. Saint Barbara, an early Christian martyr traditionally invoked for protection from lightning. Lightning and falling stars were thought to bring bad luck, which this rhyme is meant to avert.

PONCIA   I keep my place—that's all.

170 BERNARDA   The trouble is you've nothing to talk about. If there were grass in this house, you'd make it your business to put the neighbors' sheep to pasture here.

PONCIA   I hide more than you think.

BERNARDA   Do your sons still see Pepe at four in the morning? Are they still
175 repeating this house's evil litany?

PONCIA   They say nothing.

BERNARDA   Because they can't. Because there's nothing for them to sink their teeth in. And all because my eyes keep constant watch!

PONCIA   Bernarda, I don't want to talk about this because I'm afraid of what
180 you'll do. But don't you feel so safe.

BERNARDA   Very safe!

PONCIA   Who knows, lightning might strike suddenly. Who knows but what all of a sudden, in a rush of blood, your heart might stop.

BERNARDA   Nothing will happen here. I'm on guard now against all your
185 suspicions.

PONCIA   All the better for you.

BERNARDA   Certainly, all the better!

SERVANT [entering]   I've just finished with the dishes. Is there anything else, Bernarda?

190 BERNARDA [rising]   Nothing. I'm going to get some rest.

PONCIA   What time do you want me to call you?

BERNARDA   No time. Tonight I intend to sleep well.

[She goes out.]

PONCIA   When you're powerless against the sea, it's easier to turn your back on it and not look at it.

195 SERVANT   She's so proud! She herself pulls the blindfold over her eyes.

PONCIA   I can do nothing. I tried to head things off, but now they frighten me too much. You feel this silence?—in each room there's a thunderstorm—and the day it breaks, it'll sweep all of us along with it. But I've said what I had to say.

200 SERVANT   Bernarda thinks nothing can stand against her, yet she doesn't know the strength a man has among women alone.

PONCIA   It's not all the fault of Pepe el Romano. It's true last year he was running after Adela; and she was crazy about him—but she ought to keep her place and not lead him on. A man's a man.

205 SERVANT   And some there are who believe he didn't have to talk many times with Adela.

PONCIA   That's true. [In a low voice] And some other things.

SERVANT   I don't know what's going to happen here.

PONCIA   How I'd like to sail across the sea and leave this house, this battle-
210 ground, behind!

SERVANT   Bernarda's hurrying the wedding and it's possible nothing will happen.

PONCIA   Things have gone much too far already. Adela is set no matter what comes, and the rest of them watch without rest.

215 SERVANT   Martirio too . . . ?

PONCIA   That one's the worst. She's a pool of poison. She sees El Romano is not for her, and she'd sink the world if it were in her hand to do so.

SERVANT   How bad they all are!

PONCIA   They're women without men, that's all. And in such matters even
220   blood is forgotten. Sh-h-h-h!

[*She listens.*]

SERVANT   What's the matter?

PONCIA [*she rises*]   The dogs are barking.

SERVANT   Someone must have passed by the back door.

[ADELA *enters wearing a white petticoat and corselet.*]

PONCIA   Aren't you in bed yet?

225   ADELA   I want a drink of water.

[*She drinks from a glass on the table.*]

PONCIA   I imagined you were asleep.

ADELA   I got thirsty and woke up. Aren't you two going to get some rest?

SERVANT   Soon now.

[ADELA *goes out.*]

PONCIA   Let's go.

230   SERVANT   We've certainly earned some sleep. Bernarda doesn't let me rest
the whole day.

PONCIA   Take the light.

SERVANT   The dogs are going mad.

PONCIA   They're not going to let us sleep.

[*They go out. The stage is left almost dark.* MARÍA JOSEFA *enters with a
lamb in her arms.*]

MARÍA JOSEFA [*singing*]

235   Little lamb, child of mine,
Let's go to the shore of the sea,
The tiny ant will be at his doorway,
I'll nurse you and give you your bread.
Bernarda, old leopard-face,
240   And Magdalena, hyena-face,
Little lamb . . .
Rock, rock-a-bye,
Let's go to the palms at Bethlehem's gate.

[*She laughs.*]

Neither you nor I would want to sleep
245   The door will open by itself
And on the beach we'll go and hide
In a little coral cabin.

Bernarda, old leopard-face,
And Magdalena, hyena-face,
250   Little lamb . . .
Rock, rock-a-bye,
Let's go to the palms at Bethlehem's gate.

[*She goes off singing.*]

[ADELA *enters. She looks about cautiously and disappears out the door
leading to the corral.* MARTIRIO *enters by another door and stands in*

anguished watchfulness near the center of the stage. She also is in petticoats. She covers herself with a small black scarf. MARÍA JOSEFA *crosses before her.*]

MARTIRIO Grandmother, where are you going?

MARÍA JOSEFA You are going to open the door for me? Who are you?

255 MARTIRIO How did you get out here?

MARÍA JOSEFA I escaped. You, who are you?

MARTIRIO Go back to bed.

MARÍA JOSEFA You're Martirio. Now I see you. Martirio, face of a martyr. And when are you going to have a baby? I've had this one.

260 MARTIRIO Where did you get that lamb?

MARÍA JOSEFA I know it's a lamb. But can't a lamb be a baby? It's better to have a lamb than not to have anything. Old Bernarda, leopard-face, and Magdalena, hyena-face!

MARTIRIO Don't shout.

265 MARÍA JOSEFA It's true. Everything's very dark. Just because I have white hair you think I can't have babies, but I can—babies and babies and babies. This baby will have white hair, and I'd have *this* baby, and another, and this *one* other; and with all of us with snow-white hair we'll be like the waves— one, then another, and another. Then we'll all sit down and all of us will

270 have white heads, and we'll be sea-foam. Why isn't there any sea-foam here? Nothing but mourning shrouds here.

MARTIRIO Hush, hush.

MARÍA JOSEFA When my neighbor had a baby, I'd carry her some chocolate and later she'd bring me some, and so on—always and always and always.

275 You'll have white hair, but your neighbors won't come. Now I have to go away, but I'm afraid the dogs will bite me. Won't you come with me as far as the fields? I don't like fields. I like houses, but open houses, and the neighbor women asleep in their beds with their little tiny tots, and the men outside sitting in their chairs. Pepe el Romano is a giant. All of you love

280 him. But he's going to devour you because you're grains of wheat. No, not grains of wheat. Frogs with no tongues!

MARTIRIO [*angrily*] Come, off to bed with you.

[*She pushes her.*]

MARÍA JOSEFA Yes, but then you'll open the door for me, won't you?

MARTIRIO Of course.

MARÍA JOSEFA [*weeping*]

285   Little lamb, child of mine,
          Let's go to the shore of the sea,
          The tiny ant will be at his doorway,
          I'll nurse you and give you your bread.

[MARTIRIO *locks the door through which* MARÍA JOSEFA *came out and goes to the yard door. There she hesitates, but goes two steps farther.*]

MARTIRIO [*in a low voice*] Adela!

[*Pause. She advances to the door. Then, calling*]

290 Adela!

[ADELA *enters. Her hair is disarranged.*]

ADELA And what are you looking for me for?

MARTIRIO Keep away from him.

ADELA   Who are you to tell me that?

MARTIRIO   That's no place for a decent woman.

295 ADELA   How you wish *you'd* been there!

MARTIRIO [*shouting*]   This is the moment for me to speak. This can't go on.

ADELA   This is just the beginning. I've had strength enough to push myself forward—the spirit and looks you lack. I've seen death under this roof, and gone out to look for what was mine, what belonged to me.

300 MARTIRIO   That soulless man came for another woman. You pushed yourself in front of him.

ADELA   He came for the money, but his eyes were always on me.

MARTIRIO   I won't allow you to snatch him away. He'll marry Angustias.

ADELA   You know better than I he doesn't love her.

305 MARTIRIO   I know.

ADELA   You know because you've seen—he loves me, me!

MARTIRIO [*desperately*]   Yes.

ADELA [*close before her*]   He loves me, *me!* He loves me, *me!*

MARTIRIO   Stick me with a knife if you like, but don't tell me that again.

310 ADELA   That's why you're trying to fix it so I won't go away with him. It makes no difference to you if he puts his arms around a woman he doesn't love. Nor does it to me. He could be a hundred years with Angustias, but for him to have his arms around me seems terrible to you—because you too love him! You love him!

315 MARTIRIO [*dramatically*]   Yes! Let me say it without hiding my head. Yes! My breast's bitter, bursting like a pomegranate! I love him!

ADELA [*impulsively, hugging her*]   Martirio, Martirio, I'm not to blame!

MARTIRIO   Don't put your arms around me! Don't try to smooth it over. My blood's no longer yours, and even though I try to think of you as a sister, I 320 see you as just another woman.

[*She pushes her away.*]

ADELA   There's no way out here. Whoever has to drown—let her drown. Pepe is mine. He'll carry me to the rushes along the river bank. . . .

MARTIRIO   He won't!

ADELA   I can't stand this horrible house after the taste of his mouth. I'll be 325 what he wants me to be. Everybody in the village against me, burning me with their fiery fingers; pursued by those who claim they're decent, and I'll wear, before them all, the crown of thorns that belongs to the mistress of a married man.

MARTIRIO   Hush!

330 ADELA   Yes, yes. [*In a low voice*] Let's go to bed. Let's let him marry Angustias. I don't care any more, but I'll go off alone to a little house where he'll come to see me whenever he wants, whenever he feels like it.

MARTIRIO   That'll never happen! Not while I have a drop of blood left in my body.

335 ADELA   Not just weak you, but a wild horse I could force to his knees with just the strength of my little finger.

MARTIRIO   Don't raise that voice of yours to me. It irritates me. I have a heart full of a force so evil that, without my wanting to be, I'm drowned by it.

ADELA   You show us the way to love our sisters. God must have meant to 340 leave me alone in the midst of darkness, because I can see you as I've never seen you before.

[*A whistle is heard and* ADELA *runs toward the door, but* MARTIRIO *gets in front of her.*]

MARTIRIO   Where are you going?

ADELA   Get away from that door!

MARTIRIO   Get by me if you can!

345 ADELA   Get away!

[*They struggle.*]

MARTIRIO [*shouts*]   Mother! Mother!

ADELA   Let me go!

[BERNARDA *enters. She wears petticoats and a black shawl.*]

BERNARDA   Quiet! Quiet! How poor I am without even a man to help me!

MARTIRIO [*pointing to* ADELA]   She was with him. Look at those skirts cov-
350 ered with straw!

BERNARDA [*going furiously toward* ADELA]   That's the bed of a bad woman!

ADELA [*facing her*]   There'll be an end to prison voices here!

[ADELA *snatches away her mother's cane and breaks it in two.*]

This is what I do with the tyrant's cane. Not another step. No one but Pepe
commands me!

[MAGDALENA *enters.*]

355 MAGDALENA   Adela!

[LA PONCIA *and* ANGUSTIAS *enter.*]

ADELA   I'm his. [*To* ANGUSTIAS] Know that—and go out in the yard and tell
him. He'll be master in this house.

ANGUSTIAS   My God!

BERNARDA   The gun! Where's the gun?

[*She rushes out.* LA PONCIA *runs ahead of her.* AMELIA *enters and looks on
frightened, leaning her head against the wall. Behind her comes*
MARTIRIO.]

360 ADELA   No one can hold me back!

[*She tries to go out.*]

ANGUSTIAS [*holding her*]   You're not getting out of here with your body's triumph! Thief! Disgrace of this house!

MAGDALENA   Let her go where we'll never see her again!

[*A shot is heard.*]

BERNARDA [*entering*]   Just try looking for him now!

365 MARTIRIO [*entering*]   That does away with Pepe el Romano.

ADELA   Pepe! My God! Pepe!

[*She runs out.*]

PONCIA   Did you kill him?

MARTIRIO   No. He raced away on his mare!

BERNARDA   It was my fault. A woman can't aim.

370 MAGDALENA   Then, why did you say . . . ?

MARTIRIO   For her! I'd like to pour a river of blood over her head!

PONCIA   Curse you!

MAGDALENA   Devil!

BERNARDA   Although it's better this way!

[*A thud is heard.*]

375   Adela! Adela!

PONCIA [*at her door*]   Open this door!

BERNARDA   Open! Don't think the walls will hide your shame!

SERVANT [*entering*]   All the neighbors are up!

BERNARDA [*in a low voice, but like a roar*]   Open! Or I'll knock the door
380   down!

> [*Pause. Everything is silent.*]

Adela!

> [*She walks away from the door.*]

A hammer!

> [LA PONCIA *throws herself against the door. It opens and she goes in. As
> she enters, she screams and backs out.*]

What is it?

PONCIA [*she puts her hands to her throat*]   May we never die like that!

> [*The sisters fall back. The* SERVANT *crosses herself.* BERNARDA *screams
> and goes forward.*]

385   Don't go in!

BERNARDA   No, not I! Pepe, you're running now, alive, in the darkness, under
the trees, but another day you'll fall. Cut her down! My daughter died a
virgin. Take her to another room and dress her as though she were a virgin.
No one will say anything about this! She died a virgin. Tell them, so that at
390   dawn, the bells will ring twice.

MARTIRIO   A thousand times happy she, who had him.

BERNARDA   And I want no weeping. Death must be looked at face to face.
Silence! [*To one daughter*] Be still, I said! [*To another daughter*] Tears when
you're alone! We'll drown ourselves in a sea of mourning. She, the youngest
395   daughter of Bernarda Alba, died a virgin. Did you hear me? Silence, silence,
I said. Silence!

Curtain.

BERTOLT BRECHT

1898–1956

ARGUABLY the most influential dramatist of the twentieth century, Bertolt
Brecht developed and popularized a provocative form of theater that has changed
the course of theater history. Through
dozens of plays and adaptations, elaborate theories of acting, and a whole new
approach to theatrical performance, Brecht
touched every aspect of theater making
and imposed on it his distinct style and
method. Collaborating with leading musicians, writers, actors, and designers, such
as the composers Kurt Weill and Hanns
Eisler, the writer Elisabeth Hauptmann,
the actor Helene Weigel (Brecht's wife),
and the designer Caspar Neher, Brecht
sought to combine these different arts into
a new and jarring theatrical experience. He
was also intrigued by radio and film, the
newest media at the time, and sought to
transform the theater in their light, making
sure that it would remain "up to date," as
he liked to put it. Brecht wanted to create
new theater fit for an age dominated by science and progress. The product also of an
intensely felt political and social vision,
Brecht's reform sought above all to change
the relation between theater and its audience, seeking to instill in the audience a
critical and analytical attitude. The lasting impact of his work can be measured by
the fact that the adjective *Brechtian* has
long ceased to refer to Brecht's particular

reforms and practices, and often stands for
much modernist theater in general.

Born in the city of Augsburg in southern Germany, Brecht studied philosophy
and medicine in Munich; but in 1924, he
left Munich in order to work with Max
Reinhardt, the acclaimed director of the
Deutsches Theater in Berlin. By that time,
he had already won some recognition with
a number of plays, including *Baal* (1922),
Drums in the Night (1922), and *In the
Jungle of Cities* (1923; 1927). Influenced by
the episodic structures and jagged style of
German expressionist playwrights such
as Ernst Toller (1893–1939) and Georg
Kaiser (1878–1945), these plays are set in
a world whose social fabric has broken
down; even the language spoken by the
characters is ruptured, shifting abruptly
from colloquial speech to abstract metaphysical and religious terms, never resting
in a single, stable idiom.

In the course of the 1920s, Brecht gradually moved away from the topics and the
characteristic language of his early expressionist plays, although he retained their episodic structure. Increasingly, his theater
became a vehicle for understanding, analyzing, and criticizing the social world. *Man
Equals Man* (1926) is a good example of this
change, focused as it is on the analysis of a
single problem: the transformation of a porter, Galy Gay, into a cold-blooded soldier,

or rather into a "human fighting machine," as the play puts it. A similar purpose of critical analysis informs *The Rise and Fall of the City of Mahagonny* (1927; 1930), which identifies different forms of greed and consumption in a capitalist Sodom and Gomorrah. Brecht's greatest success during this period was *The Threepenny Opera* (1928), inspired by John Gay's *Beggar's Opera* (1728). *The Threepenny Opera* depicts a reality as cold as that of *Mahagonny*: the criminal underworld of London, where the king of the beggars, Peachum, and a crook, Macheath, fight for Peachum's daughter. This criminal sphere itself is not the main object of critique, however; instead, it functions as a metaphor for the criminality of capitalism. Though never a member of the Communist Party, Brecht shared with Marxist intellectuals an interest in power relations, and he sought to expose, through his plays, the hidden mechanisms of exploitation. Theater for him had become part of the struggle for a better society.

Even though the subject matter of Brecht's plays had grown more sober during the 1920s, their form and style remained exuberant. *Man Equals Man*, *Mahagonny*, and *The Threepenny Opera*—as well as many subsequent works, including THE GOOD WOMAN OF SETZUAN (1943)—were conceived as musical plays. In some cases, the music has come to overshadow the plays themselves. The popularity of *The Threepenny Opera,* perhaps the most entertaining work of them all, was due mostly to Kurt Weill's catchy songs; the best known is "Mack the Knife," which hit the top of the American charts after being recorded in the 1950s by Louis Armstrong and by Bobby Darin. Onstage, however, Brecht did not so much use the conventions of musical theater as transform them. Rather than being smoothly integrated into these plays, the music was deliberately set apart. The same was true of the other elements of performance—dialogue, acting, set design. Brecht called this technique the

The 1957 Berliner Ensemble production, under the alternate title of *The Good Person of Szechwan*.

"separation of the elements"; it was an attempt to use the different components of performance in such a way that they would interrupt one another rather than work in unison. Brecht and his collaborators thought of the resulting productions as antioperas: operas whose components had been pulled apart and put back together in a new and startling manner.

The result was the *Verfremdungseffekt* or the "estrangement effect," the attempt to "make strange" the entire experience of watching theater (an alternate translation sometimes used, "alienation effect," misleadingly implies an alienation from nature rather than the defamiliarization emphasized by Brecht). This was the heart of the theory of drama that made Brecht famous. Instead of enchanting the audience through well-integrated, harmonious spectacles, Brecht and his collaborators meant to disentangle the different sensory experiences associated with music, acting, scene design, language, and suspenseful plots and to set them against one another. Ultimately, they envisioned estrangement as the foundation of a new relation between theatrical performance and the audience, aimed at making the audience pause, examine, reflect, and criticize—that is, to look at the performance as if from a distance. Brecht once compared this attitude to that displayed by spectators at a boxing match or a similar sporting event; such audiences examine the skill of the players, appreciating their strategies and techniques from a critical distance, rather than being drawn unreflectively into a simulated world.

The technique of estrangement also extended to acting. Whereas traditionally the actor was supposed to inhabit the role completely, Brecht wanted his actors to remind the audience that they were only playing, that they were pretending to be another person for the duration of the performance. Put in the language of the theater, this meant that actor and role were to be clearly distinguished. Accomplishing this separation was a difficult task, but Brecht helped the actors by often having them speak about the character they are impersonating in the third person—commenting on the role as if from the outside. To illustrate his ideal of estranged acting, Brecht used the example of a court-room in which witnesses are asked to demonstrate to the jury how a particular accident occurred. They take on different roles, Brecht explains, and go through the action, but do not seek to become completely absorbed in their performance. They never lose sight of their specific purpose. To encourage playgoers to shift their attention from the "what" (what happened) to the "how" (how did it happen), Brecht often gave away the plot at the beginning of each scene, sometimes writing a brief summary on a half-curtain. The audience (the "jury") was meant to analyze the events depicted onstage, focusing on how they had taken place and how they could be altered, rather than be engrossed by the suspense.

The final dimension of estrangement Brecht employed was geographic. Many of his plays are set in non-European locales: America (*Jungle of Cities; Mahagonny; St. Joan of the Stockyards* [1932]), South Asia (*Man Equals Man*), China (*The Good Woman of Setzuan*), Japan (*The Yea Sayer* [1930]). Brecht's goal here was not to represent, as accurately as possible, these different cultures. Instead he used settings that were foreign (to his German audience) to facilitate a distanced, analytical attitude toward the events depicted onstage, rather than one complicated by familiar investments and opinions. At the same time, however, Brecht was genuinely influenced by the tradition of Chinese acting and by the Japanese noh theater; his play *The Yea Sayer*, for example, is based on the noh play *Taniko* (fifteenth century).

The geographic displacement of the plays was mirrored by Brecht's later life. Fearing the rise of National Socialism, he fled first to Denmark in 1933 and then to the United States in 1941, where he tried and mostly failed to produce his plays or make a living by writing Hollywood screenplays. In 1947, as the McCarthyite anticommunist witch hunts began, Brecht was called before the House Un-American Activities Committee (HUAC); he left the United States directly after the harrowing experience, going first to Switzerland and then, in 1949, to East Germany, where he built the Berliner Ensemble into one of the premier theaters of the world. It was during the years in exile that he wrote not only some of his best-known plays, including *Mother Courage* (1941), *The Life of*

Galileo Galilei (1943), and *The Good Woman of Setzuan,* but also his adaptation of AESCHYLUS's *ANTIGONE* (1948; his other famous adaptation, of SHAKESPEARE's *Coriolanus,* was written and left incomplete in 1952). In his last years, Brecht withdrew from the public eye, though he was accompanied, as he had been throughout his life, not only by his wife, Helene Weigel, but also by a number of lovers; indeed, many of his plays were collaborations with lovers (especially Elisabeth Hauptmann). He died in East Berlin in 1956, having become the most important cultural representative of socialist East Germany.

The Good Woman of Setzuan, written between 1930 and 1942 but not published until 1953, combines many of Brecht's characteristic techniques. It is set in a remote locale, the Chinese province of Sichuan (spelled "Sezuan" by Brecht and "Setzuan" in the following translation). A prelude, interludes, and the play's scenes are organized episodically and not into a tightly constructed plot; the play is also scattered with songs, written by Paul Dessau, that interrupt the flow of the action. In accordance with Brecht's theory of acting, actors address the audience directly, commenting on the action and explaining their problems and thus destroying any illusion of realism. Brecht worked on this play over a long period of time—precisely the period in which he formulated the tenets of his theory of estrangement. It therefore became the chief representative of estranged theater, or what Brecht himself preferred to call "epic theater."

Like many of Brecht's plays, *The Good Woman of Setzuan* presents a relatively simple dilemma: the inability of the female protagonist, Shen Te, to be good in the world as it is. Brecht even uses a didactic genre, the parable, to drive this point home: three gods visit Setzuan in order to find a single good person. The only good person they can find, the only one to offer them shelter, is the prostitute Shen Te, whom they reward by giving her a considerable sum of money. They then leave her to her own devices, urging her only to remain good. Doing so, however, is not all that easy. Shen Te uses the money to buy a tobacco store. As a good person, she soon begins taking in all kinds of people in need and distributing food to the poor, until finally the tobacco store itself is in danger of failing. It is at this point that she calls on the services of Shui Ta, her hard-nosed cousin, to keep her business afloat. Immediately, Shui Ta cuts down on Shen Te's philanthropy and thus restores her business to a sound economic footing. Therein lies the play's central concern: being a good person and getting by in this world are mutually incompatible goals.

The play presents this point through an intriguing variation on the estrangement technique—Shen Te and Shui Ta are the same person and are played by the same actor. The device is revealed to the audience relatively early, when the change in costume occurs in front of the spectators' eyes; yet all but one of the other characters on the stage remain in the dark. Brecht thereby ensures that the audience has more information at its disposal than the characters and can thus observe their motivations and actions. No attention is wasted on a state of suspense, trying to discover this identity (the "what"); the focus instead is entirely on understanding why Shen Te depends on Shui Ta. Brecht employs a split character to show not psychological conflict but social conflict.

Another source of dramatic conflict is the demand made by the gods that Shen Te must be good, which fails to take into account whether she can afford goodness. The state of the world, the fact that the world as it is does not allow a person to be good and survive, does not concern them. This discrepancy between the world and the gods is mediated by a man named Wong, a water carrier. No angel himself, Wong knows what this world requires and how it forces those who live in it to behave. At the same time, he honors the gods, striving to please them as best he can, even as he recognizes the impossibility of their demands. He seeks shelter for them and tries to hide most people's indifference toward them. He is a figure of compromise and attempts to mediate the clash between the gods and the harsh realities of the world—with limited success.

Fueling this clash is not just the gods' disinterest in the world but ultimately their ignorance of it. Wong first recognizes them because their very appearance bears no traces of labor; they are creatures of leisure who know nothing of the world's

Jane Horrocks as Shen Teh / Shui Ta in a 2008 production (under the alternate title *The Good Soul of Szechuan*) staged at the Young Vic Theatre, London.

hard realities; their conception of goodness is merely a lofty ideal. In particular, the gods refuse to interfere in the area of economics, assuming instead that morality and economics have nothing to do with one another. They cling to Shen Te's goodness without recognizing that it depends on the constant interventions of her harder self, of which the gods disapprove. By revealing to the audience that Shui Ta is just the other side of Shen Te, Brecht constructs a disjunction between the audience and the gods of which only the audience is aware. The gods are thus in a position of ignorance and the audience, of knowledge.

Like Brecht's other didactic plays, *The Good Woman of Setzuan* does not offer, or preach, a particular solution to the dilemma it presents, such as a socialist society or a new conception of goodness. What it does do, however, is suggest a problem or a set of contradictions, here between the conception of goodness imposed by the gods and the (economic) requisites of the world. It is clear that such a contradiction offers two lines of attack: to get rid of the gods or to get rid of the economic system that does not allow for goodness.

These two consequences are suggested throughout, but they come to the fore in the final scene, which is a trial. Now the contradictions on which the entire play is built are brought into the open: the audience, both onstage and offstage, has to make up its mind. Indeed, trial scenes can be found frequently in Brecht's works, for they offer an opportunity to expose false morals, false laws, and other abuses. At the same time, trial scenes resonate with Brecht's ideal audience: an audience willing to make its own judgments and to come to its own conclusions.

Brecht's theater shaped many of the most important theater makers of the twentieth century, including the German experimental writers Heiner Müller and Peter Weiss, the British feminist playwright CARYL CHURCHILL, and the Brazilian political dramatist Augusto Boal. That they, despite their enormous differences, all refer to Brecht as their primary influence testifies to the long and varied impact he has had on contemporary theater the world over. This unparalleled influence was due to Brecht's ability to institute a coherent theater reform in every dimension of performance, a reform that other artists could then adopt, alter, or rebel against. But despite all his fame, Brecht did not achieve—or at least he did not fully achieve—his ultimate end: namely, to transform the theater from a vehicle of entertainment into a vehicle of critical thought. His legacy is thus an ambiguous one: he single-handedly changed the course of theater history, and yet this change fell short of his grand goal.   M.P.

The Good Woman of Setzuan[1]

CHARACTERS

WONG, *a water seller*
THREE GODS
SHEN TE, *a prostitute, later a shopkeeper*
MRS. SHIN, *former owner of Shen Te's shop*
A family of eight (HUSBAND, WIFE, BROTHER, SISTER-IN-LAW, GRANDFATHER, NEPHEW, NIECE, BOY)
An UNEMPLOYED MAN
A CARPENTER
MRS. MI TZU, *Shen Te's landlady*

Mr. SHUI TA
YANG SUN, *an unemployed pilot, later a factory manager*
An OLD WHORE
A POLICEMAN
An OLD MAN
An OLD WOMAN, *his wife*
Mr. SHU FU, *a barber*
MRS. YANG, *mother of Yang Sun*
GENTLEMEN, VOICES, PRIEST, WAITER, children (three), etc.

Prologue

At the gates of the half-Westernized city of Setzuan. Evening. WONG *the water seller*[2] *introduces himself to the audience.*

WONG   I sell water here in the city of Setzuan. It isn't easy. When water is scarce, I have long distances to go in search of it, and when it is plentiful,

1. Translated by Eric Bentley.
2. The "city of Setzuan" is Chengdu, the capital of Sichuan (Setzuan), a province in Western China. However, the Chinese setting of this play is drawn largely from Brecht's imagination, not from historical or geographical fact.

I have no income. But in our part of the world there is nothing unusual
about poverty. Many people think only the gods can save the situation. And
I hear from a cattle merchant—who travels a lot—that some of the highest
gods are on their way here at this very moment. Informed sources have it
that heaven is quite disturbed at all the complaining. I've been coming out
here to the city gates for three days now to bid these gods welcome. I want
to be the first to greet them. What about those fellows over there? No, no,
they *work*. And that one there has ink on his fingers, he's no god, he must
be a clerk from the cement factory. *Those* two are another story. They look
as though they'd like to beat you. But gods don't need to beat you, do they?
[THREE GODS *appear.*] What about those three? Old-fashioned clothes—
dust on their feet—they *must* be gods! [*He throws himself at their feet.*] Do
with me what you will, illustrious ones!

FIRST GOD [*With an ear trumpet.*]   Ah! [*He is pleased.*] So we were expected?

WONG [*Giving them water.*]   Oh, yes. And I *knew* you'd come.

FIRST GOD   We need somewhere to stay the night. You know of a place?

WONG   The whole town is at your service, illustrious ones! What sort of a
place would you like?

[*The GODS eye each other.*]

FIRST GOD   Just try the first house you come to, my son.

WONG   That would be Mr. Fo's place.

FIRST GOD   Mr. Fo.

WONG   One moment! [*He knocks at the first house.*]

VOICE FROM MR. FO'S   No!

[WONG *returns a little nervously.*]

WONG   It's too bad. Mr. Fo isn't in. And his servants don't dare do a thing
without his consent. He'll have a fit when he finds out who they turned
away, won't he?

FIRST GOD [*Smiling.*]   He will, won't he?

WONG   One moment! The next house is Mr. Cheng's. Won't he be thrilled!

FIRST GOD   Mr. Cheng.

[WONG *knocks.*]

VOICE FROM MR. CHENG'S   Keep your gods. We have our own troubles!

WONG [*Back with the GODS.*]   Mr. Cheng is very sorry, but he has a houseful
of relations. I think some of them are a bad lot, and naturally, he wouldn't
like you to see them.

THIRD GOD   Are we so terrible?

WONG   Well, only with bad people, of course. Everyone knows the province
of Kwan is always having floods.

SECOND GOD   Really? How's that?

WONG   Why, because they're so irreligious.

SECOND GOD   Rubbish. It's because they neglected the dam.

FIRST GOD [*To* SECOND.]   Sh! [*To* WONG.] You're still in hopes, aren't you, my
son?

WONG   Certainly. All Setzuan is competing for the honor! What happened up
to now is pure coincidence. I'll be back. [*He walks away, but then stands
undecided.*]

SECOND GOD   What did I tell you?

THIRD GOD   It *could* be pure coincidence.

SECOND GOD   The same coincidence in Shun, Kwan, and Setzuan? People just aren't religious any more, let's face the fact. Our mission has failed!

50 FIRST GOD   Oh come, we might run into a good person any minute.

THIRD GOD   How did the resolution read? [*Unrolling a scroll and reading from it.*] "The world can stay as it is if enough people are found [*At the word "found" he unrolls it a little more*] living lives worthy of human beings." Good people, that is. Well, what about this water seller himself? *He's* good,

55 or I'm very much mistaken.

SECOND GOD   You're very much mistaken. When he gave us a drink, I had the impression there was something odd about the cup. Well, look! [*He shows the cup to the* FIRST GOD.]

FIRST GOD   A false bottom!

SECOND GOD   The man is a swindler.

60 FIRST GOD   Very well, count *him* out. That's one man among millions. And as a matter of fact, we only need one on *our* side. These atheists are saying, "The world must be changed because no one can *be* good and *stay* good." No one, eh? I say: let us find one—just one—and we have those fellows where we want them!

65 THIRD GOD [*To* WONG.]   Water seller, is it so hard to find a place to stay?

WONG   Nothing could be easier. It's just me. I don't go about it right.

THIRD GOD   Really?

[*He returns to the others. A* GENTLEMAN *passes by.*]

WONG   Oh dear, they're catching on. [*He accosts the* GENTLEMAN.] Excuse the intrusion, dear sir, but three gods have just turned up. Three of the very

70 highest. They need a place for the night. Seize this rare opportunity—to have real gods as your guests!

GENTLEMAN [*laughing*]   A new way of finding free rooms for a gang of crooks. [*Exit* GENTLEMAN.]

WONG [*shouting at him.*]   Godless rascal! Have you no religion, gentlemen of Setzuan? [*Pause.*] Patience, illustrious ones! [*Pause.*] There's only one person

75 left. Shen Te, the prostitute. She *can't* say no. [*Calls up to a window.*] Shen Te!

[SHEN TE *opens the shutters and looks out.*]

WONG   Shen Te, it's Wong. *They're* here, and nobody wants them. Will you take them?

SHEN TE   Oh, no, Wong, I'm expecting a gentleman.

WONG   Can't you forget about him for tonight?

80 SHEN TE   The rent has to be paid by tomorrow or I'll be out on the street.

WONG   This is no time for calculation, Shen Te.

SHEN TE   Stomachs rumble even on the Emperor's birthday, Wong.

WONG   Setzuan is one big dung hill!

SHEN TE   Oh, very well! I'll hide till my gentleman has come and gone. Then

85 I'll take them. [*She disappears.*]

WONG   They mustn't see her gentleman or they'll know what she is.

FIRST GOD [*Who hasn't heard any of this.*]   I think it's hopeless.

[*They approach* WONG.]

WONG [*Jumping, as he finds them behind him.*]   A room has been found, illustrious ones! [*He wipes sweat off his brow.*]

90 SECOND GOD   Oh, good.

THIRD GOD   Let's see it.

WONG [*Nervously.*]   Just a minute. It has to be tidied up a bit.

THIRD GOD   Then we'll sit down here and wait.

WONG [*Still more nervous.*]   No, no! [*Holding himself back.*] Too much traffic,
95   you know.

THIRD GOD [*With a smile.*]   Of course, if you *want* us to move.

> [*They retire a little. They sit on a doorstep.* WONG *sits on the ground.*]

WONG [*After a deep breath.*]   You'll be staying with a single girl—the finest
human being in Setzuan!

THIRD GOD   That's nice.

100   WONG [*To the audience.*]   They gave me such a look when I picked up my
cup just now.

THIRD GOD   You're worn out, Wong.

WONG   A little, maybe.

FIRST GOD   Do people here have a hard time of it?

105   WONG   The good ones do.

FIRST GOD   What about yourself!

WONG   You mean I'm not good. That's true. And I don't have an easy time either!

> [*During this dialogue, a* GENTLEMAN *has turned up in front of Shen Te's
> House, and has whistled several times. Each time* WONG *has given a
> start.*]

THIRD GOD [*To* WONG, *softly.*]   Psst! I think he's gone now.

WONG [*Confused and surprised.*]   Ye-e-es.

> [*The* GENTLEMAN *has left now, and* SHEN TE *has come down to the street.*]

110   SHEN TE [*Softly.*]   Wong!

> [*Getting no answer, she goes off down the street.* WONG *arrives just too
> late, forgetting his carrying pole.*]

WONG [*Softly.*]   Shen Te! Shen Te! [*To himself.*] So she's gone off to earn the
rent. Oh dear, I can't go to the gods *again* with no room to offer them. Having failed in the service of the gods, I shall run to my den in the sewer pipe
down by the river and hide from their sight!

> [*He rushes off.* SHEN TE *returns, looking for him, but finding the* GODS.
> *She stops in confusion.*]

115   SHEN TE   You are the illustrious ones? My name is Shen Te. It would please
me very much if my simple room could be of use to you.

THIRD GOD   Where is the water seller, Miss . . . Shen Te?

SHEN TE   I missed him, somehow.

FIRST GOD   Oh, he probably thought you weren't coming, and was afraid of
120   telling us.

THIRD GOD [*Picking up the carrying pole.*]   We'll leave this with you. He'll be
needing it.

> [*Led by* SHEN TE, *they go into the house. It grows dark, then light. Dawn.
> Again escorted by* SHEN TE, *who leads them through the half-light with a
> little lamp, the* GODS *take their leave.*]

FIRST GOD   Thank you, thank you, dear Shen Te, for your elegant hospitality!
We shall not forget! And give our thanks to the water seller—he showed us
125   a good human being.

SHEN TE   Oh, *I'm* not good. Let me tell you something: when Wong asked me
to put you up, I hesitated.

FIRST GOD   It's all right to hesitate if you then go ahead! And in giving us that
room you did much more than you knew. You proved that good people still
130   exist, a point that has been disputed of late—even in heaven. Farewell!

SECOND GOD   Farewell!

THIRD GOD   Farewell!

SHEN TE   Stop, illustrious ones! I'm not sure you're right. I'd like to be good,
it's true, but there's the rent to pay. And that's not all: I sell myself for a living.
135   Even so I can't make ends meet, there's too much competition. I'd like to
honor my father and mother and speak nothing but the truth and not covet
my neighbor's house. I should love to stay with one man. But how? How is it
done? Even breaking a few of your commandments, I can hardly manage.

FIRST GOD [*Clearing his throat.*]   These thoughts are but, um, the misgivings
140   of an unusually good woman!

THIRD GOD   Good-bye, Shen Te! Give our regards to the water seller!

SECOND GOD   And above all: be good! Farewell!

FIRST GOD   Farewell!

THIRD GOD   Farewell!

[*They start to wave good-bye.*]

145   SHEN TE   But everything is so expensive, I don't feel sure I can do it!

SECOND GOD   That's not in our sphere. We never meddle with economics.

THIRD GOD   One moment. [*They stop.*] Isn't it true she might do better if she
had more money?

SECOND GOD   Come, come! How could we ever account for it Up Above?

150   FIRST GOD   Oh, there are ways. [*They put their heads together and confer in
dumb show. To* SHEN TE, *with embarrassment.*] As you say you can't pay your
rent, well, um, we're not paupers, so of course we *insist* on paying for our
room. [*Awkwardly thrusting money into her hands.*] There! [*Quickly.*] But
don't tell anyone! The incident is open to misinterpretation.

155   SECOND GOD   It certainly is!

FIRST GOD [*Defensively.*]   But there's no law against it! It was never decreed
that a god mustn't pay hotel bills!

[*The* GODS *leave.*]

1

*A small tobacco shop. The shop is not as yet completely furnished and hasn't started
doing business.*

SHEN TE [*To the audience.*]   It's three days now since the gods left. When they
said they wanted to pay for the room, I looked down at my hand, and there
was more than a thousand silver dollars! I bought a tobacco shop with
the money, and moved in yesterday. I don't own the building, of course, but
5   I can pay the rent, and I hope to do a lot of good here. Beginning with Mrs.
Shin, who's just coming across the square with her pot. She had the shop
before me, and yesterday she dropped in to ask for rice for her children.
[*Enter* MRS. SHIN. *Both women bow.*] How do you do, Mrs. Shin.

MRS. SHIN   How do you do, Miss Shen Te. You like your new home?

10   SHEN TE   Indeed, yes. Did your children have a good night?

MRS. SHIN   In that hovel? The youngest is coughing already.

SHEN TE   Oh, dear!

MRS. SHIN You're going to learn a thing or two in these slums.

SHEN TE Slums? That's not what you said when you sold me the shop!

15 MRS. SHIN Now don't start nagging! Robbing me and my innocent children of their home and then calling it a slum! That's the limit!

[*She weeps.*]

SHEN TE [*Tactfully.*] I'll get your rice.

MRS. SHIN And a little cash while you're at it.

SHEN TE I'm afraid I haven't sold anything yet.

20 MRS. SHIN [*Screeching.*] I've got to have it. Strip the clothes from my back and then cut my throat, will you? I know what I'll do: I'll dump my children on your doorstep! [*She snatches the pot out of* SHEN TE's *hands.*]

SHEN TE Please don't be angry. You'll spill the rice.

[*Enter an elderly* HUSBAND *and* WIFE *with their shabbily dressed* NEPHEW.]

WIFE Shen Te, dear! You've come into money, they tell me. And we haven't a 25 roof over our heads! A tobacco shop. We had one too. But it's gone. Could we spend the night here, do you think?

NEPHEW [*Appraising the shop.*] Not bad!

WIFE He's our nephew. We're inseparable!

MRS. SHIN And who are these . . . ladies and gentlemen?

30 SHEN TE They put me up when I first came in from the country. [*To the audience.*] Of course, when my small purse was empty, they put me out on the street, and they may be afraid I'll do the same to them. [*To the newcomers, kindly.*] Come in, and welcome, though I've only one little room for you—it's behind the shop.

35 HUSBAND That'll do. Don't worry.

WIFE [*Bringing* SHEN TE *some tea.*] We'll stay over here, so we won't be in your way. Did you make it a tobacco shop in memory of your first real home? We can certainly give you a hint or two! That's one reason we came.

MRS. SHIN [*To* SHEN TE.] Very nice! As long as you have a few customers too!

40 HUSBAND Sh! A customer!

[*Enter an* UNEMPLOYED MAN, *in rags.*]

UNEMPLOYED MAN Excuse me. I'm unemployed.

[MRS. SHIN *laughs.*]

SHEN TE Can I help you?

UNEMPLOYED MAN Have you any damaged cigarettes? I thought there might be some damage when you're unpacking.

45 WIFE What nerve, begging for tobacco! [*Rhetorically.*] Why don't they ask for bread?

UNEMPLOYED MAN Bread is expensive. One cigarette butt and I'll be a new man.

SHEN TE [*Giving him cigarettes.*] That's very important—to be a new man. 50 You'll be my first customer and bring me luck.

[*The* UNEMPLOYED MAN *quickly lights a cigarette, inhales, and goes off, coughing.*]

WIFE Was that right, Shen Te, dear?

MRS. SHIN If this is the opening of a shop, you can hold the closing at the end of the week.

HUSBAND I bet he had money on him.

55 SHEN TE Oh, no, he said he hadn't!

NEPHEW   How d'you know he wasn't lying?

SHEN TE [*Angrily.*]   How do you know he was?

WIFE [*Wagging her head.*]   You're too good, Shen Te, dear. If you're going to keep this shop, you'll have to learn to say no.

60 HUSBAND   Tell them the place isn't yours to dispose of. Belongs to . . . some relative who insists on all accounts being strictly in order . . .

MRS. SHIN   That's right! What do you think you are—a philanthropist?

SHEN TE [*Laughing.*]   Very well, suppose I ask you for my rice back, Mrs. Shin?

WIFE [*Combatively, at* MRS. SHIN.]   So that's *her* rice?

[*Enter the* CARPENTER, *a small man.*]

65 MRS. SHIN [*Who, at the sight of him, starts to hurry away.*]   See you tomorrow, Miss Shen Te! [*Exit* MRS. SHIN.]

CARPENTER   Mrs. Shin, it's you I want!

WIFE [*To* SHEN TE.]   Has she some claim on you?

SHEN TE   She's hungry. That's a claim.

70 CARPENTER   Are you the new tenant? And filling up the shelves already? Well, they're not yours till they're paid for, ma'am. I'm the carpenter, so I should know.

SHEN TE   I took the shop "furnishings included."

CARPENTER   You're in league with that Mrs. Shin, of course. All right. I demand 75 my hundred silver dollars.

SHEN TE   I'm afraid I haven't got a hundred silver dollars.

CARPENTER   Then you'll find it. Or I'll have you arrested.

WIFE [*Whispering to* SHEN TE.]   That relative: make it a cousin.

SHEN TE   Can't it wait till next month?

80 CARPENTER   No!

SHEN TE   Be a little patient, Mr. Carpenter, I can't settle all claims at once.

CARPENTER   Who's patient with me? [*He grabs a shelf from the wall.*] Pay up—or I take the shelves back!

WIFE   Shen Te! Dear! Why don't you let your . . . cousin settle this affair? [*To* 85 CARPENTER.] Put your claim in writing. Shen Te's cousin will see you get paid.

CARPENTER [*Derisively.*]   Cousin, eh?

HUSBAND   Cousin, yes.

CARPENTER   I know these cousins!

90 NEPHEW   Don't be silly. He's a personal friend of mine.

HUSBAND   What a man! Sharp as a razor!

CARPENTER   All right. I'll put my claim in writing. [*Puts shelf on floor, sits on it, writes out bill.*]

WIFE [*To* SHEN TE.]   He'd tear the dress off your back to get his shelves. Never recognize a claim! That's my motto.

95 SHEN TE   He's done a job, and wants something in return. It's shameful that I can't give it to him. What will the gods say?

HUSBAND   You did your bit when you took *us* in.

[*Enter the* BROTHER, *limping, and the* SISTER-IN-LAW, *pregnant.*]

BROTHER [*To* HUSBAND *and* WIFE.]   So this is where you're hiding out! There's family feeling for you! Leaving us on the corner!

100 WIFE [*Embarrassed, to* SHEN TE.]   It's my brother and his wife. [*To them.*] Now stop grumbling, and sit quietly in that corner. [*To* SHEN TE.] It can't be helped. She's in her fifth month.

SHEN TE   Oh yes. Welcome!

WIFE [*To the couple.*]   Say thank you. [*They mutter something.*] The cups are
105   there. [*To* SHEN TE.] Lucky you bought this shop when you did!

SHEN TE [*Laughing and bringing tea.*]   Lucky indeed!

[*Enter* MRS. MI TZU, *the landlady.*]

MRS. MI TZU   Miss Shen Te? I am Mrs. Mi Tzu, your landlady. I hope our relationship will be a happy one. I like to think I give my tenants modern, personalized service. Here is your lease. [*To the others, as* SHEN TE *reads the lease.*]
110   There's nothing like the opening of a little shop, is there? A moment of true
beauty! [*She is looking around.*] Not very much on the shelves, of course.
But everything in the gods' good time! Where are your references, Miss
Shen Te?

SHEN TE   Do I *have* to have references?

115 MRS. MI TZU   After all, I haven't a notion who you are!

HUSBAND   Oh, *we'd* be glad to vouch for Miss Shen Te! We'd go through fire
for her!

MRS. MI TZU   And who may *you* be?

HUSBAND [*Stammering.*]   Ma Fu, tobacco dealer.

120 MRS. MI TZU   Where is your shop, Mr. . . . Ma Fu?

HUSBAND   Well, um, I haven't got a shop—I've just sold it.

MRS. MI TZU   I see. [*To* SHEN TE.] Is there no one else that knows you?

WIFE [*Whispering to* SHEN TE.]   Your cousin! Your cousin!

MRS. MI TZU   This is a respectable house, Miss Shen Te. I never sign a lease
125   without certain assurances.

SHEN TE [*Slowly, her eyes downcast.*]   I have . . . a cousin.

MRS. MI TZU   On the square? Let's go over and see him. What does he do?

SHEN TE [*As before.*]   He lives . . . in another city.

WIFE [*Prompting.*]   Didn't you say he was in Shung?

130 SHEN TE   That's right. Shung.

HUSBAND [*Prompting.*]   I had his name on the tip of my tongue, Mr. . . .

SHEN TE [*With an effort.*]   Mr. . . . Shui . . . Ta.

HUSBAND   That's it! Tall, skinny fellow!

SHEN TE   Shui Ta!

135 NEPHEW [*To* CARPENTER.]   *You* were in touch with him, weren't you? About
the shelves?

CARPENTER [*Surlily.*]   Give him this bill. [*He hands it over.*] I'll be back in the
morning. [*Exit* CARPENTER.]

NEPHEW [*Calling after him, but with his eyes on* MRS. MI TZU.]   Don't worry!
140   Mr. Shui Ta pays on the nail!

MRS. MI TZU [*Looking closely at* SHEN TE.]   I'll be happy to make his acquaintance, Miss Shen Te. [*Exit* MRS. MI TZU.]

[*Pause.*]

WIFE   By tomorrow morning she'll know more about you than you do yourself.

SISTER-IN-LAW [*To* NEPHEW.]   This thing isn't built to last.

[*Enter* GRANDFATHER.]

145 WIFE   It's Grandfather! [*To* SHEN TE.] Such a good old soul!

[*The* BOY *enters.*]

BOY [*Over his shoulder.*]   Here they are!

WIFE   And the boy, how he's grown! But he always could eat enough for ten.

[*Enter the* NIECE.]

WIFE [*To* SHEN TE.]   Our little niece from the country. There are more of us now than in your time. The less we had, the more there were of us; the more there were of us, the less we had. Give me the key. We must protect ourselves from unwanted guests. [*She takes the key and locks the door.*] Just make yourself at home. I'll light the little lamp.

NEPHEW [*A big joke.*]   I hope her cousin doesn't drop in tonight! The strict Mr. Shui Ta!

[SISTER-IN-LAW *laughs.*]

BROTHER [*Reaching for a cigarette.*]   One cigarette more or less . . .

HUSBAND   One cigarette more or less.

[*They pile into the cigarettes. The* BROTHER *hands a jug of wine round.*]

NEPHEW   Mr. Shui Ta'll pay for it!

GRANDFATHER [*Gravely, to* SHEN TE.]   How do you do?

[SHEN TE, *a little taken aback by the belatedness of the greeting, bows. She has the carpenter's bill in one hand, the landlady's lease in the other.*]

WIFE   How about a bit of a song? To keep Shen Te's spirits up?

NEPHEW   Good idea. Grandfather: you start!

SONG OF THE SMOKE

GRANDFATHER
           I used to think (before old age beset me)
             That brains could fill the pantry of the poor.
           But where did all my cerebration get me?
           I'm just as hungry as I was before.
                So what's the use?
              See the smoke float free
              Into ever colder coldness!
              It's the same with me

HUSBAND
           The straight and narrow path leads to disaster
             And so the crooked path I tried to tread.
           That got me to disaster even faster.
             (They say we shall be happy when we're dead.)
                So what's the use?
              See the smoke float free
              Into ever colder coldness!
               It's the same with me

NIECE
           You older people, full of expectation,
             At any moment now you'll walk the plank!
           The future's for the younger generation!
             Yes, even if that future is a blank.
                So what's the use?
              See the smoke float free
              Into ever colder coldness!
               It's the same with me.

NEPHEW [*To the* BROTHER.]   Where'd you get that wine?

SISTER-IN-LAW [*Answering for the* BROTHER.]   He pawned the sack of tobacco.

HUSBAND [*Stepping in.*]   What? That tobacco was all we had to fall back on! You pig!

BROTHER   *You'd* call a man a pig because your wife was frigid! Did you refuse
190   to drink it?

> [*They fight. The shelves fall over.*]

SHEN TE [*Imploringly.*]   Oh don't! Don't break everything! Take it, take it all, but don't destroy a gift from the gods!

WIFE [*Disparagingly.*]   This shop isn't big enough. I should never have mentioned it to Uncle and the others. When *they* arrive, it's going to be disgust-
195   ingly overcrowded.

SISTER-IN-LAW   And did you hear our gracious hostess? She cools off quick!

> [*Voices outside. Knocking at the door.*]

UNCLE'S VOICE   Open the door!

WIFE   Uncle? Is that you, Uncle?

UNCLE'S VOICE   Certainly, it's me. Auntie says to tell you she'll have the chil-
200   dren here in ten minutes.

WIFE [*To* SHEN TE.]   I'll have to let him in.

SHEN TE [*Who scarcely hears her.*]

> The little lifeboat is swiftly sent down
> Too many men too greedily
205   > Hold on to it as they drown.

1a

Wong's den in a sewer pipe.

WONG [*Crouching there.*]   All quiet! It's four days now since I left the city. The gods passed this way on the second day. I heard their steps on the bridge over there. They must be a long way off by this time, so I'm safe. [*Breathing a sigh of relief, he curls up and goes to sleep. In his dream the pipe becomes transparent, and the* GODS *appear. Raising an arm, as if in self-defense.*] I know, I know, illustrious ones! I found no one to give you a
5   room—not in all Setzuan! There, it's out. Please continue on your way!

FIRST GOD [*Mildly.*]   But you did find someone. Someone who took us in for the night, watched over us in our sleep, and in the early morning lighted us down to the street with a lamp.

WONG   It was . . . Shen Te that took you in?

10 THIRD GOD   Who else?

WONG   And I ran away! "She isn't coming," I thought, "she just can't afford it."

GODS [*Singing.*]

> O you feeble, well-intentioned, and yet feeble chap
> Where there's need the fellow thinks there is no goodness!
> When there's danger he thinks courage starts to ebb away!
15   > Some people only see the seamy side!
> What hasty judgment! What premature desperation!

WONG   I'm *very* ashamed, illustrious ones.

FIRST GOD   Do us a favor, water seller. Go back to Setzuan. Find Shen Te, and give us a report on her. We hear that she's come into a little money.
20   Show interest in her goodness—for no one can be good for long if goodness is not in demand. Meanwhile we shall continue the search, and find

other good people. After which, the idle chatter about the impossibility of
goodness will stop!

[*The* GODS *vanish.*]

2

A knocking.

WIFE Shen Te! Someone at the door. Where is she anyway?

NEPHEW She must be getting the breakfast. Mr. Shui Ta will pay for it.

[*The* WIFE *laughs and shuffles to the door. Enter Mr.* SHUI TA *and the*
CARPENTER.]

WIFE Who is it?

SHUI TA I am Miss Shen Te's cousin.

5 WIFE What??

SHUI TA My name is Shui Ta.

WIFE Her cousin?

NEPHEW Her cousin?

NIECE But that was a joke. She hasn't got a cousin.

10 HUSBAND So early in the morning?

BROTHER What's all the noise?

SISTER-IN-LAW This fellow says he's her cousin.

BROTHER Tell him to prove it.

NEPHEW Right. If you're Shen Te's cousin, prove it by getting the breakfast.

SHUI TA [*Whose regime begins as he puts out the lamp to save oil; loudly, to all*
15   *present, asleep or awake.*] Would you all please get dressed! Customers
will be coming! I wish to open my shop!

HUSBAND *Your* shop? Doesn't it belong to our good friend Shen Te?

[SHUI TA *shakes his head.*]

SISTER-IN-LAW So we've been cheated. Where *is* the little liar?

SHUI TA Miss Shen Te has been delayed. She wishes me to tell you there will
20   be nothing she can do—now I am here.

WIFE [*Bowled over.*] I thought she was good!

NEPHEW Do you have to believe *him*?

HUSBAND I don't.

NEPHEW Then do something.

25 HUSBAND Certainly! I'll send out a search party at once. You, you, you, and
you, go out and look for Shen Te. [*As the* GRANDFATHER *rises and makes for
the door*] Not you, Grandfather, you and I will hold the fort.

SHUI TA You won't find Miss Shen Te. She has suspended her hospitable
activity for an unlimited period. There are too many of you. She asked me to
30   say: this is a tobacco shop, not a gold mine.

HUSBAND Shen Te never said a thing like that. Boy, food! There's a bakery on
the corner. Stuff your shirt full when they're not looking!

SISTER-IN-LAW Don't overlook the raspberry tarts.

HUSBAND And don't let the policeman see you.

[*The* BOY *leaves.*]

35 SHUI TA Don't you depend on this shop now? Then why give it a bad name
by stealing from the bakery?

NEPHEW Don't listen to him. Let's find Shen Te. She'll give him a piece of
her mind.

SISTER-IN-LAW   Don't forget to leave us some breakfast.

[BROTHER, SISTER-IN-LAW *and* NEPHEW *leave*.]

40 SHUI TA [*To the* CARPENTER.]   You see, Mr. Carpenter, nothing has changed since the poet, eleven hundred years ago, penned these lines:

> A governor was asked what was needed
> To save the freezing people in the city.
> He replied:
45 > "A blanket ten thousand feet long
> To cover the city and all its suburbs."

[*He starts to tidy up the shop.*]

CARPENTER   Your cousin owes me money. I've got witnesses. For the shelves.

SHUI TA   Yes, I have your bill. [*He takes it out of his pocket.*] Isn't a hundred silver dollars rather a lot?

50 CARPENTER   No deductions! I have a wife and children.

SHUI TA   How many children?

CARPENTER   Three.

SHUI TA   I'll make you an offer. Twenty silver dollars.

[*The* HUSBAND *laughs*.]

CARPENTER   You're crazy. Those shelves are real walnut.

55 SHUI TA   Very well, Take them away.

CARPENTER   What?

SHUI TA   They cost too much. Please take them away.

WIFE   Not bad! [*And she, too, is laughing.*]

CARPENTER [*A little bewildered.*]   Call Shen Te, someone! [*To* SHUI TA.] She's 60 good!

SHUI TA   Certainly. She's ruined.

CARPENTER [*Provoked into taking some of the shelves.*]   All right, you can keep your tobacco on the floor.

SHUI TA [*To the* HUSBAND.]   Help him with the shelves.

HUSBAND [*Grins and carries one shelf over to the door where the* CARPENTER 65 *now is.*]   Good-bye, shelves!

CARPENTER [*To the* HUSBAND.]   You dog! You want my family to starve?

SHUI TA   I repeat my offer. I have no desire to keep my tobacco on the floor. Twenty silver dollars.

CARPENTER [*With desperate aggressiveness.*]   One hundred!

[SHUI TA *shows indifference, looks through the window. The* HUSBAND *picks up several shelves.*]

70 CARPENTER [*To* HUSBAND.]   You needn't smash them against the doorpost, you idiot! [*To* SHUI TA.] These shelves were made to measure. They're no use anywhere else!

SHUI TA   Precisely.

[*The* WIFE *squeals with pleasure.*]

CARPENTER [*Giving up, sullenly.*]   Take the shelves. Pay what you want to pay.

75 SHUI TA [*Smoothly.*]   Twenty silver dollars.

[*He places two large coins on the table. The* CARPENTER *picks them up.*]

HUSBAND [*Brings the shelves back in.*]   And quite enough too!

CARPENTER [*Slinking off.*]   Quite enough to get drunk on.

HUSBAND [*Happily.*]   Well, we got rid of *him*!

WIFE [*Weeping with fun, gives a rendition of the dialogue just spoken.*] "Real
walnut," says he. "Very well, take them away," says his lordship. "I have
three children," says he. "Twenty silver dollars," says his lordship. "They're
no use anywhere else," says he. "Pre-cisely," said his lordship! [*She dissolves
into shrieks of merriment.*]

SHUI TA   And now: go!

HUSBAND   What's that?

SHUI TA   You're thieves, parasites. I'm giving you this chance. Go!

HUSBAND [*Summoning all his ancestral dignity.*]   That sort deserves no
answer. Besides, one should never shout on an empty stomach.

WIFE   Where's that boy?

SHUI TA   Exactly. The boy. I want no stolen goods in this shop. [*Very loudly.*]
I strongly advise you to leave! [*But they remain seated, noses in the air. Quietly.*] As you wish. [SHUI TA *goes to the door. A* POLICEMAN *appears.* SHUI TA
bows.] I am addressing the officer in charge of this precinct?

POLICEMAN   That's right, Mr., um, what was the name, sir?

SHUI TA   Mr. Shui Ta.

POLICEMAN   Yes, of course, sir.

[*They exchange a smile.*]

SHUI TA   Nice weather we're having.

POLICEMAN   A little on the warm side, sir.

SHUI TA   Oh, a little on the warm side.

HUSBAND [*Whispering to the* WIFE.]   If he keeps it up till the boy's back, we're
done for. [*Tries to signal* SHUI TA.]

SHUI TA [*Ignoring the signal.*]   Weather, of course, is one thing indoors,
another out on the dusty street!

POLICEMAN   Oh, quite another, sir!

WIFE [*To the* HUSBAND.]   It's all right as long as he's standing in the doorway—
the boy will see him.

SHUI TA   Step inside for a moment! It's quite cool indoors. My cousin and I
have just opened the place. And we attach the greatest importance to being
on good terms with the, um, authorities.

POLICEMAN [*Entering.*]   Thank you, Mr. Shui Ta. It *is* cool!

HUSBAND [*Whispering to the* WIFE.]   And now the boy *won't* see him.

SHUI TA [*Showing* HUSBAND *and* WIFE *to the* POLICEMAN.]   Visitors, I think my
cousin knows them. They were just leaving.

HUSBAND [*Defeated.*]   Ye-e-es, we were . . . just leaving.

SHUI TA   I'll tell my cousin you couldn't wait.

[*Noise from the street. Shouts of "Stop, Thief!"*]

POLICEMAN   What's that?

[*The* BOY *is in the doorway with cakes and buns and rolls spilling out of
his shirt. The* WIFE *signals desperately to him to leave. He gets the idea.*]

POLICEMAN   No, you don't. [*He grabs the* BOY *by the collar.*] Where's all this
from?

BOY [*Vaguely pointing.*]   Down the street.

POLICEMAN [*Grimly.*]   So that's it. [*Prepares to arrest the* BOY.]

WIFE [*Stepping in.*]   And *we* knew nothing about it. [*To the* BOY.] Nasty little
thief!

POLICEMAN [*Dryly.*]   Can you clarify the situation, Mr. Shui Ta?

[SHUI TA *is silent.*]

POLICEMAN [*Who understands silence.*]   Aha. You're all coming with me—to the station.

125 SHUI TA   I can hardly say how sorry I am that *my* establishment . . .

WIFE   Oh, he saw the boy leave not ten minutes ago!

SHUI TA   And to conceal the theft asked a policeman in?

POLICEMAN   Don't listen to her, Mr. Shui Ta, I'll be happy to relieve you of their presence one and all! [*To all three.*] Out!

[*He drives them before him.*]

130 GRANDFATHER [*Leaving last, gravely.*]   Good morning!

POLICEMAN   Good morning!

[SHUI TA, *left alone, continues to tidy up.* MRS. MI TZU *breezes in.*]

MRS. MI TZU   *You're* her cousin, are you? Then have the goodness to explain what all this means—police dragging people from a respectable house! By what right does your Miss Shen Te turn my property into a house of 135 assignation?—Well, as you see, I know all!

SHUI TA   Yes. My cousin has the worst possible reputation: that of being poor.

MRS. MI TZU   No sentimental rubbish, Mr. Shui Ta. Your cousin was a common . . .

SHUI TA   Pauper. Let's use the uglier word.

140 MRS. MI TZU   I'm speaking of her conduct, not her earnings. But there must have *been* earnings, or how did she buy all this? Several elderly gentlemen took care of it, I suppose. I repeat: this is a respectable house! I have tenants who prefer not to live under the same roof with such a person.

SHUI TA [*Quietly.*]   How much do you want?

145 MRS. MI TZU [*He is ahead of her now.*]   I beg your pardon.

SHUI TA   To reassure yourself. To reassure your tenants. How much will it cost?

MRS. MI TZU   You're a cool customer.

SHUI TA [*Picking up the lease.*]   The rent is high. [*He reads on.*] I assume it's payable by the month?

150 MRS. MI TZU   Not in her case.

SHUI TA [*Looking up.*]   What?

MRS. MI TZU   Six months' rent payable in advance. Two hundred silver dollars.

SHUI TA   Six . . . ! Sheer usury! And where am I to find it?

MRS. MI TZU   You should have thought of that before.

155 SHUI TA   Have you no heart, Mrs. Mi Tzu? It's true Shen Te acted foolishly, being kind to all those people, but she'll improve with time. I'll see to it she does. She'll work her fingers to the bone to pay her rent, and all the time be as quiet as a mouse, as humble as a fly.

MRS. MI TZU   Her social background . . .

160 SHUI TA   Out of the depths! She came out of the depths! And before she'll go back there, she'll work, sacrifice, shrink from nothing. . . . Such a tenant is worth her weight in gold, Mrs. Mi Tzu.

MRS. MI TZU   It's silver we were talking about, Mr. Shui Ta. Two hundred silver dollars or . . .

[*Enter the* POLICEMAN.]

165 POLICEMAN   Am I intruding, Mr. Shui Ta?

MRS. MI TZU   This tobacco shop is well known to the police, I see.

POLICEMAN   Mr. Shui Ta has done us a service, Mrs. Mi Tzu. I am here to present our official felicitations!

MRS. MI TZU   That means less than nothing to me, sir. Mr. Shui Ta, all I can say is: I hope your cousin will find my terms acceptable. Good day, gentlemen. [*Exit.*]

SHUI TA   Good day, ma'am.

[*Pause.*]

POLICEMAN   Mrs. Mi Tzu a bit of a stumbling block, sir?

SHUI TA   She wants six months' rent in advance.

POLICEMAN   And you haven't got it, eh? [SHUI TA *is silent.*] But surely you can get it, sir? A man like you?

SHUI TA   What about a woman like Shen Te?

POLICEMAN   You're not staying, sir?

SHUI TA   No, and I won't be back. Do you smoke?

POLICEMAN [*Taking two cigars, and placing them both in his pocket.*] Thank you, sir—I see your point, Miss Shen Te—let's mince no words—Miss Shen Te lived by selling herself. "What else could she have done?" you ask. "How else was she to pay the rent?" True. But the fact remains, Mr. Shui Ta, it is not respectable. Why not? A very deep question. But, in the first place, love—love isn't bought and sold like cigars, Mr. Shui Ta. In the second place, it isn't respectable to go waltzing off with someone that's paying his way, so to speak—it must be for love! Thirdly and lastly, as the proverb has it: not for a handful of rice but for love! [*Pause. He is thinking hard.*] "Well," you may say, "and what good is all this wisdom if the milk's already spilt?" Miss Shen Te is what she is. Is *where* she is. We have to face the fact that if she doesn't get hold of six months' rent pronto, she'll be back on the streets. The question then as I see it—everything in this world is a matter of opinion—the question as I see it is: *how* is she to get hold of this rent? How? Mr. Shui Ta: I don't know. [*Pause.*] I take that back, sir. It's just come to me. A husband. We must find her a husband!

[*Enter a little* OLD WOMAN.]

OLD WOMAN   A good cheap cigar for my husband, we'll have been married forty years tomorrow and we're having a little celebration.

SHUI TA   Forty years? And you still want to celebrate?

OLD WOMAN   As much as we can afford to. We have the carpet shop across the square. We'll be good neighbors, I hope?

SHUI TA   I hope so too.

POLICEMAN [*Who keeps making discoveries.*]   Mr. Shui Ta, you know what we need? We need capital. And how do we acquire capital? We get married.

SHUI TA [*To* OLD WOMAN.]   I'm afraid I've been pestering this gentleman with my personal worries.

POLICEMAN [*Lyrically.*]   We can't pay six months' rent, so what do we do? We marry money.

SHUI TA   That might not be easy.

POLICEMAN   Oh, I don't know. She's a good match. Has a nice, growing business. [*To the* OLD WOMAN.] What do you think?

OLD WOMAN [*Undecided.*]   Well—

POLICEMAN   Should she put an ad in the paper?

OLD WOMAN [*Not eager to commit herself.*]   Well, if *she* agrees—

POLICEMAN   I'll write it for her. *You* lend us a hand, and *we* write an ad for you! [*He chuckles away to himself, takes out his notebook, wets the stump of a pencil between his lips, and writes away.*]

SHUI TA [*Slowly.*]   Not a bad idea.

POLICEMAN   "What . . . *respectable* . . . man . . . with small capital . . . widower . . . not excluded . . . desires . . . marriage . . . into flourishing . . . tobacco shop?" And now let's add: "Am . . . pretty . . ." No! . . . "Prepossessing appearance."

SHUI TA   If you don't think that's an exaggeration?

OLD WOMAN   Oh, not a bit. I've seen her.

[*The* POLICEMAN *tears the page out of his notebook, and hands it over to* SHUI TA.]

SHUI TA [*With horror in his voice.*]   How much luck we need to keep our heads above water! How many ideas! How many friends! [*To the* POLICEMAN.] Thank you, sir, I think I see my way clear.

3

Evening in the municipal park. Noise of a plane overhead. YANG SUN, *a young man in rags, is following the plane with his eyes: one can tell that the machine is describing a curve above the park.* YANG SUN *then takes a rope out of his pocket, looking anxiously about him as he does so. He moves toward a large willow. Enter two prostitutes, one old, the other the* NIECE *whom we have already met.*

NIECE   Hello. Coming with me?

YANG SUN [*Taken aback.*]   If you'd like to buy me a dinner.

OLD WHORE   Buy you a dinner! [*To the* NIECE.] Oh, we know him—it's the unemployed pilot. Waste no time on him!

NIECE   But he's the only man left in the park. And it's going to rain.

OLD WHORE   Oh, how do you know?

[*And they pass by.* YANG SUN *again looks about him, again takes his rope, and this time throws it round a branch of the willow tree. Again he is interrupted. It is the two prostitutes returning—and in such a hurry they don't notice him.*]

NIECE   It's going to pour!

[*Enter* SHEN TE.]

OLD WHORE   There's that *gorgon* Shen Te! That *drove* your family out into the cold!

NIECE   It wasn't her. It was that cousin of hers. She offered to pay for the cakes. I've nothing against her.

OLD WHORE   I have, though. [*So that* SHEN TE *can hear.*] Now where could the little lady be off to? She may be rich now but that won't stop her snatching our young men, will it?

SHEN TE   I'm going to the tearoom by the pond.

NIECE   Is it true what they say? You're marrying a widower—with three children?

SHEN TE   Yes. I'm just going to see him.

YANG SUN [*His patience at breaking point.*]   Move on there! This is a park, not a whorehouse!

OLD WHORE   Shut your mouth!

[*But the two prostitutes leave.*]

YANG SUN   Even in the farthest corner of the park, even when it's raining, you can't get rid of them! [*He spits.*]

SHEN TE [*Overhearing this.*]   And what right have you to scold them? [*But at*
25   *this point she sees the rope.*] Oh!

YANG SUN   Well, what are you staring at?

SHEN TE   That rope. What is it for?

YANG SUN   Think! Think! I haven't a penny. Even if I had, I wouldn't spend it
on you. I'd buy a drink of water.

[*The rain starts.*]

30   SHEN TE [*Still looking at the rope.*]   What is the rope for? You mustn't!

YANG SUN   What's it to you? Clear out!

SHEN TE [*Irrelevantly.*]   It's raining.

YANG SUN   Well, don't try to come under this tree.

SHEN TE   Oh, no. [*She stays in the rain.*]

35   YANG SUN   Now go away. [*Pause.*] For one thing, I don't like your looks, you're
bowlegged.

SHEN TE [*Indignantly.*]   That's not true!

YANG SUN   Well, don't show 'em to me. Look, it's raining. You better come
under this tree.

[*Slowly, she takes shelter under the tree.*]

40   SHEN TE   Why did you want to do it?

YANG SUN   You really want to know? [*Pause.*] To get rid of you! [*Pause.*] You
know what a flyer is?

SHEN TE   Oh yes, I've met a lot of pilots. At the tearoom.

YANG SUN   You call *them* flyers? Think they know what a machine is? Just
45   'cause they have leather helmets? They gave the airfield director a bribe,
that's the way *those* fellows got up in the air! Try one of them out sometime.
"Go up to two thousand feet," tell him, "then let it fall, then pick it up
again with a flick of the wrist at the last moment." Know what he'll say to
that? "It's not in my contract." Then again, there's the landing problem. It's
50   like landing on your own backside. It's no different, planes are human.
Those fools don't understand. [*Pause.*] And I'm the biggest fool for reading
the book on flying in the Peking[3] school and skipping the page where it
says: "We've got enough flyers and we don't need you." I'm a mail pilot with
no mail. You understand that?

55   SHEN TE [*Shyly.*]   Yes, I do.

YANG SUN   No, you don't. You'd never understand that.

SHEN TE   When we were little we had a crane with a broken wing. He made
friends with us and was very good-natured about our jokes. He would strut
along behind us and call out to stop us going too fast for him. But every
60   spring and autumn when the cranes flew over the villages in great swarms,
he got quite restless. [*Pause.*] I understand that.

[*She bursts out crying.*]

YANG SUN   Don't!

SHEN TE [*Quieting down.*]   No.

YANG SUN   It's bad for the complexion.

65   SHEN TE [*Sniffing.*]   I've stopped.

---

3. That is, Beijing, the capital of China.

[*She dries her tears on her big sleeve. Leaning against the tree, but not looking at her, he reaches for her face.*]

YANG SUN You can't even wipe your own face. [*He is wiping it for her with his handkerchief. Pause.*]

SHEN TE [*Still sobbing.*] I don't know *anything*!

YANG SUN You interrupted me! What for?

SHEN TE It's such a rainy day. You only wanted to do . . . *that* because it's
70 such a rainy day. [*To the audience.*]

> In our country
> The evenings should never be somber
> High bridges over rivers
> The gray hour between night and morning
75 And the long, long winter:
> Such things are dangerous
> For, with all the misery,
> A very little is enough
> And men throw away an unbearable life.

[*Pause.*]

80 YANG SUN Talk about yourself for a change.

SHEN TE What about me? I have a shop.

YANG SUN [*Incredulous.*] You have a shop, have you? Never thought of walking the streets?

SHEN TE I did walk the streets. Now I have a shop.

85 YANG SUN [*Ironically.*] A gift of the gods, I suppose!

SHEN TE How did you know?

YANG SUN [*Even more ironical.*] One fine evening the gods turned up saying: here's some money!

SHEN TE [*Quickly.*] One fine morning.

90 YANG SUN [*Fed up.*] This isn't much of an entertainment.

[*Pause.*]

SHEN TE I can play the zither a little. [*Pause.*] And I can mimic men. [*Pause.*] I got the shop, so the first thing I did was to give my zither away. I can be as stupid as a fish now, I said to myself, and it won't matter.

> I'm rich now, I said
95 I walk alone, I sleep alone
> For a whole year, I said
> I'll have nothing to do with a man.

YANG SUN And now you're marrying one! The one at the tearoom by the pond?

[SHEN TE *is silent.*]

YANG SUN What do you know about love?

100 SHEN TE Everything.

YANG SUN Nothing. [*Pause.*] Or d'you just mean you enjoyed it?

SHEN TE No.

YANG SUN [*Again without turning to look at her, he strokes her cheek with his hand.*] You like that?

SHEN TE Yes.

105 YANG SUN [*Breaking off.*] You're easily satisfied, I must say. [*Pause.*] What a town!

SHEN TE You have no friends?

YANG SUN [*Defensively.*] Yes, I have! [*Change of tone.*] But they don't want to
hear I'm still unemployed. "What?" they ask. "Is there still water in the
sea?" You have friends?

SHEN TE [*Hesitating.*] Just a . . . cousin.

YANG SUN Watch him carefully.

SHEN TE He only came once. Then he went away. He won't be back. [YANG SUN
is looking away.] But to be without hope, they say, is to be without goodness!
[*Pause.*]

YANG SUN Go on talking. A voice is a voice.

SHEN TE Once, when I was a little girl, I fell, with a load of brushwood. An
old man picked me up. He gave me a penny too. Isn't it funny how people
who don't have very much like to give some of it away? They must like to
show what they can do, and how could they show it better than by being
kind? Being wicked is just like being clumsy. When we sing a song, or build
a machine, or plant some rice, we're being kind. You're kind.

YANG SUN You make it sound easy.

SHEN TE Oh, no. [*Little pause.*] Oh! A drop of rain!

YANG SUN Where'd you feel it?

SHEN TE Between the eyes.

YANG SUN Near the right eye? Or the left?

SHEN TE Near the left eye.

YANG SUN Oh, good. [*He is getting sleepy.*] So you're through with men,
eh?

SHEN TE [*With a smile.*] But I'm not bowlegged.

YANG SUN Perhaps not.

SHEN TE Definitely not.
[*Pause.*]

YANG SUN [*Leaning wearily against the willow.*] I haven't had a drop to
drink all day, I haven't eaten anything for *two* days. I couldn't love you if
I tried.
[*Pause.*]

SHEN TE I like it in the rain.
[*Enter* WONG *the water seller, singing.*]

THE SONG OF THE WATER SELLER IN THE RAIN

"Buy my water," I am yelling
And my fury restraining
For no water I'm selling
'Cause it's raining, 'cause it's raining!
  I keep yelling: "Buy my water!"
But no one's buying
Athirst and dying
And drinking and paying!
  Buy water!
  Buy water, you dogs!

Nice to dream of lovely weather!
Think of all the consternation

Were there no precipitation
150 Half a dozen years together!
　　Can't you hear them shrieking: "Water!"
　　Pretending they adore me?
　　They all would go down on their knees before me!
　　Down on your knees!
155 　　Go down on your knees, you dogs!

　　What are lawns and hedges thinking?
　　What are fields and forests saying?
　　"At the cloud's breast we are drinking!
　　And we've no idea who's paying!"
160 　　I keep yelling: "Buy my water!"
　　But no one's buying
　　Athirst and dying
　　And drinking and paying!
　　Buy water!
165 　　Buy water, you dogs!

[*The rain has stopped now.* SHEN TE *sees* WONG *and runs toward him.*]

SHEN TE　Wong! You're back! Your carrying pole's at the shop.

WONG　Oh, thank you, Shen Te. And how is life treating *you*?

SHEN TE　I've just met a brave and clever man. And I want to buy him a cup of your water.

170 WONG [*Bitterly.*]　Throw back your head and open your mouth and you'll have all the water you need—

SHEN TE [*Tenderly.*]
　　I want *your* water, Wong
　　The water that has tired you so
　　The water that you carried all this way
175 　　The water that is hard to sell because it's been raining.
　　I need it for the young man over there—he's a flyer!

　　A flyer is a bold man:
　　Braving the storms
　　In company with the clouds
180 　　He crosses the heavens
　　And brings to friends in faraway lands
　　The friendly mail!

[*She pays* WONG, *and runs over to* YANG SUN *with the cup. But* YANG SUN *is fast asleep.*]

SHEN TE [*Calling to* WONG, *with a laugh.*]　He's fallen asleep! Despair and rain and I have worn him out!

3a

Wong's den. The sewer pipe is transparent, and the GODS *again appear to* WONG *in a dream.*

WONG [*Radiant*]　I've seen her, illustrious ones! And she hasn't changed!

FIRST GOD　That's good to hear.

WONG She loves someone.

FIRST GOD Let's hope the experience gives her the strength to stay good!

5 WONG It does. She's doing good deeds all the time.

FIRST GOD Ah? What sort? What sort of good deeds, Wong?

WONG Well, she has a kind word for everybody.

FIRST GOD [*Eagerly.*] And then?

WONG Hardly anyone leaves her shop without tobacco in his pocket—even

10 if he can't pay for it.

FIRST GOD Not bad at all. Next?

WONG She's putting up a family of eight.

FIRST GOD [*Gleefully, to the* SECOND GOD.] Eight! [*To* WONG.] And that's not
all, of course!

15 WONG She bought a cup of water from me even though it was raining.

FIRST GOD Yes, yes, yes, all these smaller good deeds!

WONG Even they run into money. A little tobacco shop doesn't make so much.

FIRST GOD [*Sententiously.*] A prudent gardener works miracles on the smallest plot.

20 WONG She hands out rice every morning. That eats up half her earnings.

FIRST GOD [*A little disappointed.*] Well, as a beginning . . .

WONG They call her the Angel of the Slums—whatever the carpenter may say!

FIRST GOD What's this? A carpenter speaks ill of her?

WONG Oh, he only says her shelves weren't paid for in full.

SECOND GOD [*Who has a bad cold and can't pronounce his n's and m's.*]

25 What's this? Not paying a carpenter? Why was that?

WONG I suppose she didn't have the money.

SECOND GOD [*Severely.*] One pays what one owes, that's in our book of rules!
First the letter of the law, then the spirit.

WONG But it wasn't Shen Te, illustrious ones, it was her cousin. She called

30 *him* in to help.

SECOND GOD Then her cousin must never darken her threshold again!

WONG Very well, illustrious ones! But in fairness to Shen Te, let me say that
her cousin is a businessman.

FIRST GOD Perhaps we should inquire what is customary? I find business

35 quite unintelligible. But everybody's doing it. Business! Did the Seven
Good Kings do business? Did Kung the Just[4] sell fish?

SECOND GOD In any case, such a thing must not occur again!

[*The* GODS *start to leave.*]

THIRD GOD Forgive us for taking this tone with you, Wong, we haven't been
getting enough sleep. The rich recommend us to the poor, and the poor tell

40 us they haven't enough room.

SECOND GOD Feeble, feeble, the best of them!

FIRST GOD No great deeds! No heroic daring!

THIRD GOD On such a *small* scale!

SECOND GOD Sincere, yes, but what is actually *achieved*?

---

4. K'ung Futzu (Master K'ung), the Chinese
philosopher better known by his latinized
name, Confucius (551–497 B.C.E.). *Seven
Good Kings*: rulers of the first historical
dynasty of China (traditionally dated ca.
1766–ca. 1122 B.C.E.), whom the Confucian
scholar Mencius called "sage worthies."

[*One can no longer hear them.*]

45 WONG [*Calling after them.*] I've thought of something, illustrious ones: Perhaps you shouldn't ask—too—much—all—at—once!

4

The square in front of Shen Te's tobacco shop. Besides Shen Te's place, two other shops are seen: the carpet shop and a barber's. Morning. Outside Shen Te's the GRANDFATHER, *the* SISTER-IN-LAW, *the* UNEMPLOYED MAN, *and* MRS. SHIN *stand waiting.*

SISTER-IN-LAW She's been out all night again.

MRS. SHIN No sooner did we get rid of that crazy cousin of hers than Shen Te herself starts carrying on! Maybe she does give us an ounce of rice now and then, but can you depend on her? Can you depend on her?

[*Loud voices from the barber's.*]

5 VOICE OF SHU FU What are you doing in my shop? Get out—at once!

VOICE OF WONG But sir. They all let me sell . . .

[WONG *comes staggering out of the barber's shop pursued by Mr.* SHU FU, *the barber, a fat man carrying a heavy curling iron.*]

SHU FU Get out, I said! Pestering my customers with your slimy old water! Get out! Take your cup!

[*He holds out the cup.* WONG *reaches out for it. Mr.* SHU FU *strikes his hand with the curling iron, which is hot.* WONG *howls.*]

SHU FU You had it coming my man!

[*Puffing, he returns to his shop. The* UNEMPLOYED MAN *picks up the cup and gives it to* WONG.]

10 UNEMPLOYED MAN You can report that to the police.

WONG My hand! It's smashed up!

UNEMPLOYED MAN Any bones broken?

WONG I can't move my fingers.

UNEMPLOYED MAN Sit down. I'll put some water on it.

[WONG *sits.*]

15 MRS. SHIN The water won't cost you anything.

SISTER-IN-LAW You might have got a bandage from Miss Shen Te till she took to staying out all night. It's a scandal.

MRS. SHIN [*Despondently.*] If you ask me, she's forgotten we ever existed!

[*Enter* SHEN TE *down the street, with a dish of rice.*]

SHEN TE [*To the audience.*] How wonderful to see Setzuan in the early
20 morning! I always used to stay in bed with my dirty blanket over my head afraid to wake up. This morning I saw the newspapers being delivered by little boys, the streets being washed by strong men, and fresh vegetables coming in from the country on ox carts. It's a long walk from where Yang Sun lives, but I feel lighter at every step. They say you walk on air when
25 you're in love, but it's even better walking on the rough earth, on the hard cement. In the early morning, the old city looks like a great heap of rubbish! Nice, though, with all its little lights. And the sky, so pink, so transparent, before the dust comes and muddies it! What a lot you miss if you never see your city rising from its slumbers like an honest old craftsman
30 pumping his lungs full of air and reaching for his tools, as the poet says! [*Cheerfully, to her waiting guests.*] Good morning, everyone, here's your

rice! [*Distributing the rice, she comes upon* WONG.] Good morning, Wong, I'm quite lightheaded today. On my way over, I looked at myself in all the shop windows. I'd love to be beautiful.

[*She slips into the carpet shop. Mr.* SHU FU *has just emerged from his shop.*]

35 SHU FU [*To the audience.*]   It surprises me how beautiful Miss Shen Te is looking today! I never gave her a passing thought before. But now I've been gazing upon her comely form for exactly three minutes! I begin to suspect I am in love with her. She is overpoweringly attractive! [*Crossly, to* WONG.] Be off with you rascal!

[*He returns to his shop.* SHEN TE *comes back out of the carpet shop with the* OLD MAN, *its proprietor, and his wife—whom we have already met— the* OLD WOMAN. SHEN TE *is wearing a shawl. The* OLD MAN *is holding up a looking glass for her.*]

40 OLD WOMAN   Isn't it lovely? We'll give you a reduction because there's a little hole in it.

SHEN TE [*Looking at another shawl on the old woman's arm.*]   The other one's nice too.

OLD WOMAN [*Smiling.*]   Too bad there's no hole in that!

45 SHEN TE   That's right. My shop doesn't make very much.

OLD WOMAN   And your deeds eat it all up! Be more careful, my dear . . .

SHEN TE [*Trying on the shawl with the hole.*]   Just now, I'm lightheaded! Does the color suit me?

OLD WOMAN   You'd better ask a man.

50 SHEN TE [*To the* OLD MAN.]   Does the color suit me?

OLD MAN   You'd better ask your young friend.

SHEN TE   I'd like to have your opinion.

OLD MAN   It suits you very well. But wear it this way: the dull side out.

[SHEN TE *pays up.*]

OLD WOMAN   If you decide you don't like it, you can exchange it. [*She pulls*
55   SHEN TE *to one side.*]   Has he got money?

SHEN TE [*With a laugh.*]   Yang Sun? Oh, no.

OLD WOMAN   Then how're you going to pay your rent?

SHEN TE   I'd forgotten about that.

OLD WOMAN   And next Monday is the first of the month! Miss Shen Te, I've
60   got something to say to you. After we [*Indicating her husband.*] got to know you, we had our doubts about that marriage ad. We thought it would be better if you'd let *us* help you. Out of our savings. We reckon we could lend you two hundred silver dollars. We don't need anything in writing—you could pledge us your tobacco stock.

65 SHEN TE   You're prepared to lend money to a person like me?

OLD WOMAN   It's folks like you that need it. We'd think twice about lending anything to your cousin.

OLD MAN [*Coming up.*]   All settled, my dear?

SHEN TE   I wish the gods could have heard what your wife was just saying,
70   Mr. Ma. They're looking for good people who're happy—and helping me makes you happy because you know it was love that got me into difficulties!

[*The old couple smile knowingly at each other.*]

OLD MAN   And here's the money, Miss Shen Te.

[*He hands her an envelope.* SHEN TE *takes it. She bows. They bow back. They return to their shop.*]

SHEN TE [*Holding up her envelope.*] Look, Wong, here's six months' rent! Don't you believe in miracles now? And how do you like my new shawl?

75 WONG For the young fellow I saw you with in the park?

[SHEN TE *nods.*]

MRS. SHIN Never mind all that. It's time you took a look at this hand!

SHEN TE Have you hurt your hand?

MRS. SHIN That barber smashed it with his hot curling iron. Right in front of our eyes.

80 SHEN TE [*Shocked at herself.*] And I never noticed! We must get you to a doctor this minute or who knows what will happen?

UNEMPLOYED MAN It's not a doctor he should see, it's a judge. He can ask for compensation. The barber's filthy rich.

WONG You think I have a chance?

85 MRS. SHIN [*With relish.*] If it's really good and smashed. But is it?

WONG I think so. It's very swollen. Could I get a pension?

MRS. SHIN You'd need a witness.

WONG Well, you all saw it. You could all testify.

[*He looks round. The* UNEMPLOYED MAN, *the* GRANDFATHER, *and the* SISTER-IN-LAW *are all sitting against the wall of the shop eating rice. Their concentration on eating is complete.*]

SHEN TE [*To* MRS. SHIN.] You saw it yourself.

90 MRS. SHIN I want nothing to do with the police. It's against my principles.

SHEN TE [*To* SISTER-IN-LAW.] What about you?

SISTER-IN-LAW Me? I wasn't looking.

SHEN TE [*To the* GRANDFATHER, *coaxingly.*] Grandfather, *you'll* testify, won't you?

95 SISTER-IN-LAW And a lot of good that will do. He's simple-minded.

SHEN TE [*To the* UNEMPLOYED MAN.] You seem to be the only witness left.

UNEMPLOYED MAN My testimony would only hurt him. I've been picked up twice for begging.

SHEN TE
     Your brother is assaulted, and you shut your eyes?
100   He is hit, cries out in pain, and you are silent?
     The beast prowls, chooses and seizes his victim, and you say:
     "Because we showed no displeasure, he has spared us."
  If no one present will be a witness, I will. I'll say *I* saw it.

MRS. SHIN [*Solemnly.*] The name for that is perjury.

105 WONG I don't know if I can accept that. Though maybe I'll have to. [*Looking at his hand.*] Is it swollen enough, do you think? The swelling's not going down.

UNEMPLOYED MAN No, no, the swelling's holding up well.

WONG Yes. It's *more* swollen if anything. Maybe my wrist is broken after all.
110 I'd better see a judge at once.

[*Holding his hand very carefully, and fixing his eyes on it, he runs off.* MRS. SHIN *goes quickly into the barber's shop.*]

UNEMPLOYED MAN [*Seeing her.*] She is getting on the right side of Mr. Shu Fu.

SISTER-IN-LAW You and I can't change the world, Shen Te.

SHEN TE Go away! Go away all of you! [*The* UNEMPLOYED MAN, *the* SISTER-IN-LAW, *and the* GRANDFATHER *stalk off, eating and sulking. To the audience.*]

They've stopped answering
115   They stay put
They do as they're told
They don't care
Nothing can make them look up
But the smell of food.

[*Enter* MRS. YANG, *Yang Sun's mother, out of breath.*]

120 MRS. YANG   Miss Shen Te. My son has told me everything. I am Mrs. Yang, Sun's mother. Just think. He's got an offer. Of a job as a pilot. A letter has just come. From the director of the airfield in Peking!

SHEN TE   So he can fly again! Isn't that wonderful!

MRS. YANG [*Less breathlessly all the time.*]   They won't give him the job for
125   nothing. They want five hundred silver dollars.

SHEN TE   We can't let money stand in his way, Mrs. Yang!

MRS. YANG   If only you could help him out!

SHEN TE   I have the shop. I can try! [*She embraces* MRS. YANG.] I happen to have two hundred with me now. Take it. [*She gives her the old couple's*
130   *money.*] It was a loan but they said I could repay it with my tobacco stock.

MRS. YANG   And they were calling Sun the Dead Pilot of Setzuan! A friend in need!

SHEN TE   We must find another three hundred.

135 MRS. YANG   How?

SHEN TE   Let me think. [*Slowly.*] I know someone who can help. I didn't want to call on his services again, he's hard and cunning. But a flyer must fly. And I'll make this the last time.

[*Distant sound of a plane.*]

MRS. YANG   If the man you mentioned can do it . . . Oh, look, there's the
140   morning mail plane, heading for Peking!

SHEN TE   The pilot can see us, let's wave!

[*They wave. The noise of the engine is louder.*]

MRS. YANG   You know that pilot up there?

SHEN TE   Wave, Mrs. Yang! I know the pilot who will be up there. He gave up hope. But he'll do it now. One man to raise himself above the misery, above
145   us all. [*To the audience.*]

Yang Sun, my lover:
Braving the storms
In company with the clouds
Crossing the heavens
150   And bringing to friends in faraway lands
The friendly mail!

4a

In front of the inner curtain. Enter SHEN TE, *carrying Shui Ta's mask. She sings.*

THE SONG OF DEFENSELESSNESS

In our country
A useful man needs luck
Only if he finds strong backers

Can he prove himself useful.
5 The good can't defend themselves and
Even the gods are defenseless.

Oh, why don't the gods have their own ammunition
And launch against badness their own expedition
Enthroning the good and preventing sedition
10 And bringing the world to a peaceful condition?

Oh, why don't the gods do the buying and selling
Injustice forbidding, starvation dispelling
Give bread to each city and joy to each dwelling?
Oh, why don't the gods do the buying and selling?

[*She puts on Shui Ta's mask and sings in his voice.*]

15 You can only help one of your luckless brothers
By trampling down a dozen others.

Why is it the gods do not feel indignation
And come down in fury to end exploitation
Defeat all defeat and forbid desperation
20 Refusing to tolerate such toleration?

Why is it?

5

Shen Te's tobacco shop. Behind the counter, Mr. SHUI TA, *reading the paper.* MRS. SHIN *is cleaning up. She talks and he takes no notice.*

MRS. SHIN   And when certain rumors get about, what *happens* to a little place like this? It goes to pot. *I* know. So, if you want my advice, Mr. Shui Ta, find out just what has been going on between Miss Shen Te and that Yang Sun from Yellow Street. And remember: a certain interest in Miss
5 Shen Te has been expressed by the barber next door, a man with twelve houses and only one wife,[5] who, for that matter, is likely to drop off at any time. A certain interest has been expressed. He was even inquiring about her means and, if *that* doesn't prove a man is getting serious, what would?
[*Still getting no response, she leaves with her bucket.*]
YANG SUN'S VOICE   Is that Miss Shen Te's tobacco shop?
10 MRS. SHIN'S VOICE   Yes, it is, but it's Mr. Shui Ta who's here today.
[SHUI TA *runs to the mirror with the short, light steps of* SHEN TE, *and is just about to start primping, when he realizes his mistake, and turns away, with a short laugh. Enter* YANG SUN. MRS. SHIN *enters behind him and slips into the back room to eavesdrop.*]
YANG SUN   I am Yang Sun. [SHUI TA *bows.*] Is Shen Te in?
SHUI TA   No.
YANG SUN   I guess you know our relationship? [*He is inspecting the stock.*] Quite a place! And I thought she was just talking big. I'll be flying again, all
15 right. [*He takes a cigar, solicits and receives a light from* SHUI TA.] You think we can squeeze the other three hundred out of the tobacco stock?

5. Ancient Chinese law permitted a man to have more than one wife.

SHUI TA   May I ask if it is your intention to sell at once?

YANG SUN   It was decent of her to come out with the two hundred but they aren't much use with the other three hundred still missing.

20 SHUI TA   Shen Te was overhasty promising so much. She might have to sell the shop itself to raise it. Haste, they say, is the wind that blows the house down.

YANG SUN   Oh, she isn't a girl to keep a man waiting. For one thing or the other, if you take my meaning.

25 SHUI TA   I take your meaning.

YANG SUN [Leering.]   Uh, huh.

SHUI TA   Would you explain what the five hundred silver dollars are for?

YANG SUN   Want to sound me out? Very well. The director of the Peking airfield is a friend of mine from flying school. I give him five hundred: he gets
30 me the job.

SHUI TA   The price is high.

YANG SUN   Not as these things go. He'll have to fire one of the present pilots—for negligence. Only the man he has in mind isn't negligent. Not easy, you understand. You needn't mention that part of it to Shen Te.

35 SHUI TA [Looking intently at YANG SUN.]   Mr. Yang Sun, you are asking my cousin to give up her possessions, leave her friends, and place her entire fate in your hands. I presume you intend to marry her?

YANG SUN   I'd be prepared to.

[Slight pause.]

SHUI TA   Those two hundred silver dollars would pay the rent here for six
40 months. If you were Shen Te wouldn't you be tempted to continue in business?

YANG SUN   What? Can you imagine Yang Sun the flyer behind a counter? [In an oily voice.] "A strong cigar or a mild one, worthy sir?" Not in this century!

45 SHUI TA   My cousin wishes to follow the promptings of her heart, and, from her own point of view, she may even have what is called the right to love. Accordingly, she has commissioned me to help you to this post. There is nothing here that I am not empowered to turn immediately into cash. Mrs. Mi Tzu, the landlady, will advise me about the sale.

[Enter MRS. MI TZU.]

50 MRS. MI TZU   Good morning, Mr. Shui Ta, you wish to see me about the rent? As you know it falls due the day after tomorrow.

SHUI TA   Circumstances have changed, Mrs. Mi Tzu: my cousin is getting married. Her future husband here, Mr. Yang Sun, will be taking her to Peking. I am interested in selling the tobacco stock.

55 MRS. MI TZU   How much are you asking, Mr. Shui Ta?

YANG SUN   Three hundred sil—

SHUI TA   Five hundred silver dollars.

MRS. MI TZU   How much did she pay for it, Mr. Shui Ta?

SHUI TA   A thousand. And very little has been sold.

60 MRS. MI TZU   She was robbed. But I'll make you a special offer if you'll promise to be out by the day after tomorrow. Three hundred silver dollars.

YANG SUN [Shrugging.]   Take it, man, take it.

SHUI TA   It is not enough.

YANG SUN   Why not? Why not? Certainly, it's enough.

65 SHUI TA Five hundred silver dollars.

YANG SUN But why? We only need three!

SHUI TA [*To* MRS. MI TZU.] Excuse me. [*Takes* YANG SUN *on one side.*] The tobacco stock is pledged to the old couple who gave my cousin the two hundred.

70 YANG SUN Is it in writing?

SHUI TA No.

YANG SUN [*To* MRS. MI TZU.] Three hundred will do.

MRS. MI TZU Of course, I need an assurance that Miss Shen Te is not in debt.

YANG SUN Mr. Shui Ta?

75 SHUI TA She is not in debt.

YANG SUN When can you let us have the money?

MRS. MI TZU The day after tomorrow. And remember: I'm doing this because I have a soft spot in my heart for young lovers! [*Exit.*]

YANG SUN [*Calling after her.*] Boxes, jars and sacks—three hundred for the

80 lot and the pain's over! [*To* SHUI TA.] Where else can we raise money by the day after tomorrow?

SHUI TA Nowhere. Haven't you enough for the trip and the first few weeks?

YANG SUN Oh, certainly.

SHUI TA How much, exactly.

85 YANG SUN Oh, I'll dig it up, even if I have to steal it.

SHUI TA I see.

YANG SUN Well, don't fall off the roof. I'll get to Peking somehow.

SHUI TA Two people can't travel for nothing.

YANG SUN [*Not giving* SHUI TA *a chance to answer.*] I'm leaving *her* behind.

90 No millstones round *my* neck!

SHUI TA Oh.

YANG SUN Don't look at me like that!

SHUI TA How precisely is my cousin to live?

YANG SUN Oh, you'll think of something.

95 SHUI TA A small request, Mr. Yang Sun. Leave the two hundred silver dollars here until you can show me two tickets for Peking.

YANG SUN You learn to mind your own business, Mr. Shui Ta.

SHUI TA I'm afraid Miss Shen Te may not wish to sell the shop when she discovers that . . .

100 YANG SUN You don't know women. She'll want to. Even then.

SHUI TA [*A slight outburst.*] She is a human being, sir! And not devoid of common sense!

YANG SUN Shen Te is a woman: she *is* devoid of common sense. I only have to lay my hand on her shoulder, and church bells ring.

105 SHUI TA [*With difficulty.*] Mr. Yang Sun!

YANG SUN Mr. Shui Whatever-it-is!

SHUI TA My cousin is devoted to you . . . because . . .

YANG SUN Because I have my hands on her breasts. Give me a cigar. [*He takes one for himself, stuffs a few more in his pocket, then changes his mind and takes the whole box.*] Tell her I'll marry her, then bring me the three

110 hundred. Or let her bring it. One or the other. [*Exit.*]

MRS. SHIN [*Sticking her head out of the back room.*] Well, he has your cousin under his thumb, and doesn't care if all Yellow Street knows it!

SHUI TA [*Crying out.*] I've lost my shop! And he doesn't love me! [*He runs berserk through the room, repeating these lines incoherently. Then stops sud-*

denly, and addresses MRS. SHIN.] Mrs. Shin, you grew up in the gutter, like
115   me. Are we lacking in hardness? I doubt it. If you steal a penny from me,
I'll take you by the throat till you spit it out! You'd do the same to me. The
times are bad, this city is hell, but we're like ants, we keep coming, up and
up the walls, however smooth! Till bad luck comes. Being in love, for
instance. One weakness is enough, and love is the deadliest.

120 MRS. SHIN [*Emerging from the back room.*]   You should have a little talk with
Mr. Shu Fu, the barber. He's a real gentleman and just the thing for your
cousin. [*She runs off.*]

SHUI TA

A caress becomes a stranglehold
A sigh of love turns to a cry of fear
125   Why are there vultures circling in the air?
A girl is going to meet her lover.

[SHUI TA *sits down and Mr.* SHU FU *enters with* MRS. SHIN.]

SHUI TA   Mr. Shu Fu?
SHU FU   Mr. Shui Ta.

[*They both bow.*]

SHUI TA   I am told that you have expressed a certain interest in my cousin
130   Shen Te. Let me set aside all propriety and confess: she is at this moment
in grave danger.
SHU FU   Oh, dear!
SHUI TA   She has lost her shop, Mr. Shu Fu.
SHU FU   The charm of Miss Shen Te, Mr. Shui Ta, derives from the good-
135   ness, not of her shop, but of her heart. Men call her the Angel of the
Slums.
SHUI TA   Yet her goodness has cost her two hundred silver dollars in a single
day: we must put a stop to it.
SHU FU   Permit me to differ, Mr. Shui Ta. Let us, rather, open wide the gates
140   to such goodness! Every morning, with pleasure tinged by affection, I watch
her charitable ministrations. For they are hungry, and she giveth them to
eat! Four of them, to be precise. Why only four? I ask. Why not four hundred? I hear she has been seeking shelter for the homeless. What about my
humble cabins behind the cattle run? They are at her disposal. And so
145   forth. And so on. Mr. Shui Ta, do you think Miss Shen Te could be persuaded to listen to certain ideas of mine? Ideas like these?
SHUI TA   Mr. Shu Fu, she would be honored.

[*Enter* WONG *and the* POLICEMAN. *Mr.* SHU FU *turns abruptly away and
studies the shelves.*]

WONG   Is Miss Shen Te here?
SHUI TA   No.
150 WONG   I am Wong the water seller. You are Mr. Shui Ta?
SHUI TA   I am.
WONG   I am a friend of Shen Te's.
SHUI TA   An intimate friend, I hear.
WONG [*To the* POLICEMAN.]   You see? [*To* SHUI TA.] It's because of my hand.
155 POLICEMAN   He hurt his hand, sir, that's a fact.
SHUI TA [*Quickly.*]   You need a sling, I see. [*He takes a shawl from the back
room, and throws it to* WONG.]
WONG   But that's her new shawl!

SHUI TA She has no more use for it.

WONG But she bought it to please someone!

160 SHUI TA It happens to be no longer necessary.

WONG [*Making the sling.*] She is my only witness.

POLICEMAN Mr. Shui Ta, your cousin is supposed to have seen the barber hit the water seller with a curling iron.

SHUI TA I'm afraid my cousin was not present at the time.

165 WONG But she was, sir! Just ask her! Isn't she in?

SHUI TA [*Gravely.*] Mr. Wong, my cousin has her own troubles. You wouldn't wish her to add to them by committing perjury?

WONG But it was she that told me to go to the judge!

SHUI TA Was the judge supposed to heal your hand?

[*Mr.* SHU FU *turns quickly around.* SHUI TA *bows to* SHU FU, *and vice versa.*]

170 WONG [*Taking the sling off, and putting it back.*] I see how it is.

POLICEMAN Well, I'll be on my way. [*To* WONG.] And you be careful. If Mr. Shu Fu wasn't a man who tempers justice with mercy, as the saying is, you'd be in jail for libel. Be off with you!

[*Exit* WONG *followed by* POLICEMAN.]

SHUI TA Profound apologies, Mr. Shu Fu.

175 SHU FU Not at all, Mr. Shui Ta. [*Pointing to the shawl.*] The episode is over?

SHUI TA It may take her time to recover. There are some fresh wounds.

SHU FU We shall be discreet. Delicate. A short vacation could be arranged . . .

SHUI TA First of course, you and she would have to talk things over.

SHU FU At a small supper in a small, but high-class, restaurant.

180 SHUI TA I'll go and find her. [*Exit into back room.*]

MRS. SHIN [*Sticking her head in again.*] Time for congratulations, Mr. Shu Fu?

SHU FU Ah, Mrs. Shin! Please inform Miss Shen Te's guests they may take shelter in the cabins behind the cattle run!

[MRS. SHIN *nods, grinning.*]

185 SHU FU [*To the audience.*] Well? What do you think of me, ladies and gentlemen? What could a man do more? Could he be less selfish? More farsighted? A small supper in a small but . . . Does that bring rather vulgar and clumsy thoughts into your mind? Ts, ts, ts. Nothing of the sort will occur. She won't even be touched. Not even accidentally while passing the

190 salt. An exchange of ideas only. Over the flowers on the table—white chrysanthemums, by the way [*He writes down a note of this.*]—yes, over the white chrysanthemums, two young souls will . . . shall I say "find each other"? We shall NOT exploit the misfortune of others. Understanding? Yes. An offer of assistance? Certainly. But quietly. Almost inaudibly. Perhaps

195 with a single glance. A glance that could also—mean more.

MRS. SHIN [*Coming forward.*] Everything under control, Mr. Shu Fu?

SHU FU Oh, Mrs. Shin, what do you know about this worthless rascal Yang Sun?

MRS. SHIN Why, he's the most worthless rascal . . .

200 SHU FU Is he really? You're sure? [*As she opens her mouth.*] From now on, he doesn't exist! Can't be found anywhere!

[*Enter* YANG SUN.]

YANG SUN What's been going on here?

MRS. SHIN Shall I call Mr. Shui Ta, Mr. Shu Fu? He wouldn't want strangers in here!

205 SHU FU Mr. Shui Ta is in conference with Miss Shen Te. Not to be disturbed!

YANG SUN Shen Te here? I didn't see her come in. What kind of conference?

SHU FU [Not letting him enter the back room.] Patience, dear sir! And if by chance I have an inkling who you are, pray take note that Miss Shen Te and I are about to announce our engagement.

210 YANG SUN What?

MRS. SHIN You didn't expect that, did you?

[YANG SUN is trying to push past the barber into the back room when SHEN TE comes out.]

SHU FU My dear Shen Te, ten thousand apologies! Perhaps you . . .

YANG SUN What is it, Shen Te? Have you gone crazy?

SHEN TE [Breathless.] My cousin and Mr. Shu Fu have come to an under-
215 standing. They wish me to hear Mr. Shu Fu's plans for helping the poor.

YANG SUN Your cousin wants to part us.

SHEN TE Yes.

YANG SUN And you've agreed to it?

SHEN TE Yes.

220 YANG SUN They told you I was bad. [SHEN TE is silent.] And suppose I am. Does that make me need you less? I'm low, Shen Te, I have no money, I don't do the right thing but at least I put up a fight! [He is near her now, and speaks in an undertone.] Have you no eyes? Look at him. Have you forgotten already?

225 SHEN TE No.

YANG SUN How it was raining?

SHEN TE No.

YANG SUN How you cut me down from the willow tree? Bought me water? Promised me money to fly with?

230 SHEN TE [Shakily.] Yang Sun, what do you want?

YANG SUN I want you to come with me.

SHEN TE [In a small voice.] Forgive me, Mr. Shu Fu, I want to go with Mr. Yang Sun.

YANG SUN We're lovers, you know. Give me the key to the shop. [SHEN TE takes the key from around her neck. YANG SUN puts it on the counter. To MRS.
235 SHIN.] Leave it under the mat when you're through. Let's go, Shen Te.

SHU FU But this is rape! Mr. Shui Ta!!

YANG SUN [To SHEN TE.] Tell him not to shout.

SHEN TE Please don't shout for my cousin, Mr. Shu Fu. He doesn't agree with me, I know, but he's wrong. [To the audience.]

240   I want to go with the man I love
     I don't want to count the cost
     I don't want to consider if it's wise
     I don't want to know if he loves me
     I want to go with the man I love.

245 YANG SUN That's the spirit.

[And the couple leave.]

5a

In front of the inner curtain. SHEN TE *in her wedding clothes, on the way to her wedding.*

SHEN TE   Something terrible has happened. As I left the shop with Yang Sun,
I found the old carpet dealer's wife waiting on the street, trembling all over.
She told me her husband had taken to his bed—sick with all the worry and
excitement over the two hundred silver dollars they lent me. She said it
5   would be best if I gave it back now. Of course, I had to say I would. She said
she couldn't quite trust my cousin Shui Ta or even my fiancé, Yang Sun.
There were tears in her eyes. With my emotions in an uproar, I threw myself
into Yang Sun's arms, I couldn't resist him. The things he'd said to Shui Ta
had taught Shen Te nothing. Sinking into his arms, I said to myself:
10   To let no one perish, not even oneself
                 To fill everyone with happiness, even oneself
                 Is so good
How could I have forgotten those two old people? Yang Sun swept me away
like a small hurricane. But he's not a bad man, and he loves me. He'd
15   rather work in the cement factory than owe his flying to a crime. Though,
of course, flying *is* a great passion with Sun. Now, on the way to my wedding, I waver between fear and joy.

6

*The "private dining room" on the upper floor of a cheap restaurant in a poor section
of town. With* SHEN TE: *the* GRANDFATHER, *the* SISTER-IN-LAW, *the* NIECE, MRS.
SHIN, *the* UNEMPLOYED MAN. *In a corner, alone, a* PRIEST.[6] *A* WAITER *pouring wine.
Downstage,* YANG SUN *talking to his mother. He wears a dinner jacket.*

YANG SUN   Bad news, Mamma. She came right out and told me she can't sell
the shop for me. Some idiot is bringing a claim because he lent her the two
hundred she gave you.
MRS. YANG   What did you say? Of course, you can't marry her now.
5   YANG SUN   It's no use saying anything to *her*. I've sent for her cousin, Mr.
Shui Ta. He said there was nothing in writing.
MRS. YANG   Good idea. I'll go out and look for him. Keep an eye on things.
          [*Exit* MRS. YANG. SHEN TE *has been pouring wine.*]
SHEN TE [*To the audience, pitcher in hand.*]   I wasn't mistaken in him. He's
bearing up well. Though it must have been an awful blow—giving up fly-
10   ing. I do love him so. [*Calling across the room to him.*] Sun, you haven't
drunk a toast with the bride!
YANG SUN   What do we drink to?
SHEN TE   Why, to the future!
YANG SUN   When the bridegroom's dinner jacket won't be a hired one!
15   SHEN TE   But when the bride's dress will still get rained on sometimes!
YANG SUN   To everything we ever wished for!
SHEN TE   May all our dreams come true!
          [*They drink.*]

6. A Buddhist monk or priest.

YANG SUN [*With loud conviviality.*] And now, friends, before the wedding gets under way, I have to ask the bride a few questions. I've no idea what
20 kind of a wife she'll make, and it worries me. [*Wheeling on* SHEN TE.] For example. Can you make five cups of tea with three tea leaves?

SHEN TE No.

YANG SUN So I won't be getting very much tea. Can you sleep on a straw mattress the size of that book? [*He points to the large volume the* PRIEST *is reading.*]

25 SHEN TE The two of us?

YANG SUN The one of you.

SHEN TE In that case, no.

YANG SUN What a wife! I'm shocked!

[*While the audience is laughing, his mother returns. With a shrug of her shoulders, she tells* SUN *the expected guest hasn't arrived. The* PRIEST *shuts the book with a bang, and makes for the door.*]

MRS. YANG Where are *you* off to? It's only a matter of minutes.

30 PRIEST [*Watch in hand.*] Time goes on, Mrs. Yang, and I've another wedding to attend to. Also a funeral.

MRS. YANG [*Irately.*] D'you think we planned it this way? I was hoping to manage with one pitcher of wine, and we've run through two already. [*Points to empty pitcher. Loudly.*] My dear Shen Te, I don't know where
35 your cousin can be keeping himself!

SHEN TE My cousin?!

MRS. YANG Certainly. I'm old-fashioned enough to think such a close relative should attend the wedding.

SHEN TE Oh, Sun, is it the three hundred silver dollars?

40 YANG SUN [*Not looking her in the eye.*] Are you deaf? Mother says she's old-fashioned. And I say I'm considerate. We'll wait another fifteen minutes.

HUSBAND Another fifteen minutes.

MRS. YANG [*Addressing the company.*] Now you all know, don't you, that my son is getting a job as a mail pilot?

45 SISTER-IN-LAW In Peking, too, isn't it?

MRS. YANG In Peking, too! The two of us are moving to Peking!

SHEN TE Sun, tell your mother Peking is out of the question now.

YANG SUN Your cousin'll tell her. If he agrees. I don't agree.

SHEN TE [*Amazed, and dismayed.*] Sun!

50 YANG SUN I hate this godforsaken Setzuan. What people! Know what they look like when I half close my eyes? Horses! Whinnying, fretting, stamping, screwing their necks up! [*Loudly.*] And what is it the thunder says? They are su-per-flu-ous! [*He hammers out the syllables.*] They've run their last race! They can go trample themselves to death! [*Pause.*] I've got to get out
55 of here.

SHEN TE But I've promised the money to the old couple.

YANG SUN And since you always do the wrong thing, it's lucky your cousin's coming. Have another drink.

SHEN TE [*Quietly.*] My cousin can't be coming.

60 YANG SUN How d'you mean?

SHEN TE My cousin can't be where I am.

YANG SUN Quite a conundrum!

SHEN TE [*Desperately.*] Sun, I'm the one that loves you. Not my cousin. He
was thinking of the job in Peking when he promised you the old couple's
65 money—

YANG SUN Right. And that's why he's bringing the three hundred silver dollars. Here—to my wedding.

SHEN TE He is not bringing the three hundred silver dollars.

YANG SUN Huh? What makes you think that?

70 SHEN TE [*Looking into his eyes.*] He says you only bought one ticket to
Peking.

[*Short pause.*]

YANG SUN That was yesterday. [*He pulls two tickets part way out of his inside
pocket, making her look under his coat.*] Two tickets. I don't want Mother
to know. She'll get left behind. I sold her furniture to buy these tickets, so
75 you see . . .

SHEN TE But what's to become of the old couple?

YANG SUN What's to become of me? Have another drink. Or do you believe
in moderation? If I drink, I fly again. And if you drink, you may learn to
understand me.

80 SHEN TE You want to fly. But I can't help you.

YANG SUN "Here's a plane, my darling—but it's only got one wing!"

[*The* WAITER *enters.*]

WAITER Mrs. Yang!

MRS. YANG Yes?

WAITER Another pitcher of wine, ma'am?

85 MRS. YANG We have enough, thanks. Drinking makes me sweat.

WAITER Would you mind paying, ma'am?

MRS. YANG [*To everyone.*] Just be patient a few moments longer, everyone,
Mr. Shui Ta is on his way over! [*To the* WAITER.] Don't be a spoilsport.

WAITER I can't let you leave till you've paid your bill, ma'am.

90 MRS. YANG But they know me here!

WAITER That's just it.

PRIEST [*Ponderously getting up.*] I humbly take my leave. [*And he does.*]

MRS. YANG [*To the others, desperately.*] Stay where you are, everybody! The
priest says he'll be back in two minutes!

95 YANG SUN It's no good Mamma. Ladies and gentlemen, Mr. Shui Ta still
hasn't arrived and the priest has gone home. We won't detain you any
longer.

[*They are leaving now.*]

GRANDFATHER [*In the doorway, having forgotten to put his glass down.*] To the
bride! [*He drinks, puts down the glass, and follows the others.*]

[*Pause.*]

100 SHEN TE Shall I go too?

YANG SUN You? Aren't you the bride? Isn't this your wedding? [*He drags her
across the room, tearing her wedding dress.*] If we can wait, you can wait.
Mother calls me her falcon. She wants to see me in the clouds. But I think
it may be St. Nevercome's Day before she'll go to the door and see my
105 plane thunder by. [*Pause. He pretends the guests are still present.*] Why such
a lull in the conversation, ladies and gentlemen? Don't you like it here?
The ceremony is only slightly postponed—because an important guest is

expected at any moment. Also because the bride doesn't know what love is. While we're waiting, the bridegroom will sing a little song. [*He does so.*]

THE SONG OF ST. NEVERCOME'S DAY

110   On a certain day, as is generally known,
        One and all will be shouting: Hooray, hooray!
    For the beggar maid's son has a solid-gold throne
        And the day is St. Nevercome's Day
    On St. Nevercome's, Nevercome's, Nevercome's Day
115   He'll sit on his solid-gold throne

    Oh, hooray, hooray! That day goodness will pay!
        That day badness will cost you your head!
    And merit and money will smile and be funny
        While exchanging salt and bread
120   On St. Nevercome's, Nevercome's, Nevercome's Day
        While exchanging salt and bread

    And the grass, oh, the grass will look down at the sky
        And the pebbles will roll up the stream
    And all men will be good without batting an eye
125   They will make of our earth a dream
    On St. Nevercome's, Nevercome's, Nevercome's Day
        They will make of our earth a dream

    And as for me, that's the day I shall be
        A flyer and one of the best
130   Unemployed man, you will have work to do
        Washerwoman, you'll get your rest
    On St. Nevercome's, Nevercome's, Nevercome's Day
        Washerwoman, you'll get your rest

MRS. YANG   It looks like he's not coming.

    [*The three of them sit looking at the door.*]

6a

Wong's den. The sewer pipe is again transparent and again the GODS *appear to* WONG *in a dream.*

WONG   I'm so glad you've come, illustrious ones. It's Shen Te. She's in great trouble from following the rule about loving thy neighbor. Perhaps she's *too* good for this world!

FIRST GOD   Nonsense! You are eaten up by lice and doubts!

5 WONG   Forgive me, illustrious one, I only meant you might deign to intervene.

FIRST GOD   Out of the question! My colleague here intervened in some squabble or other only yesterday. [*He points to the* THIRD GOD, *who has a black eye.*] The results are before us!

10 WONG   She had to call on her cousin again. But not even he could help. I'm afraid the shop is done for.

THIRD GOD [*A little concerned.*]   Perhaps we should help after all?

FIRST GOD   The gods help those that help themselves.

WONG What if we *can't* help ourselves, illustrious ones?
    [*Slight pause.*]
15 SECOND GOD Try, anyway! Suffering ennobles!
FIRST GOD Our faith in Shen Te is unshaken!
THIRD GOD We certainly haven't found any *other* good people. You can see
    where we spend our nights from the straw on our clothes.
WONG You might help her find her way by—
20 FIRST GOD The good man finds his own way here below!
SECOND GOD The good woman too.
FIRST GOD The heavier the burden, the greater her strength!
THIRD GOD We're only onlookers, you know.
FIRST GOD And everything will be all right in the end, O ye of little faith!
    [*They are gradually disappearing through these last lines.*]

7

The yard behind Shen Te's shop. A few articles of furniture on a cart. SHEN TE *and*
MRS. SHIN *are taking the washing off the line.*

MRS. SHIN If you ask me, you should fight tooth and nail to keep the shop.
SHEN TE How can I? I have to sell the tobacco to pay back the two hundred
    silver dollars today.
MRS. SHIN No husband, no tobacco, no house and home! What are you
5   going to live on?
SHEN TE I can work. I can sort tobacco.
MRS. SHIN Hey, look, Mr. Shui Ta's trousers! He must have left here stark
    naked!
SHEN TE Oh, he may have another pair, Mrs. Shin.
10 MRS. SHIN But if he's gone for good as you say, why has he left his pants
    behind?
SHEN TE Maybe he's thrown them away.
MRS. SHIN Can I take them?
SHEN TE Oh, no.
    [*Enter Mr.* SHU FU, *running.*]
15 SHU FU Not a word! Total silence! I know all. You have sacrificed your own
    love and happiness so as not to hurt a dear old couple who had put their
    trust in you! Not in vain does this district—for all its malevolent tongues—
    call you the Angel of the Slums! That young man couldn't rise to your level,
    so you left him. And now, when I see you closing up the little shop, that
20   veritable haven of rest for the multitude, well, I cannot, I cannot let it pass.
    Morning after morning I have stood watching in the doorway not
    unmoved—while you graciously handed out rice to the wretched. Is that
    never to happen again? Is the good woman of Setzuan to disappear? If only
    you would allow *me* to assist you! Now don't say anything! No assurances,
25   no exclamations of gratitude! [*He has taken out his checkbook.*] Here! A
    blank check. [*He places it on the cart.*] Just my signature. Fill it out as you
    wish. Any sum in the world. I herewith retire from the scene, quietly, unob-
    trusively, making no claims, on tiptoe, full of veneration, absolutely self-
    lessly . . . [*He has gone.*]

30 MRS. SHIN   Well! You're saved. There's always some idiot of a man. . . . Now hurry! Put down a thousand silver dollars and let me fly to the bank before he comes to his senses.

SHEN TE   I can pay you for the washing without any check.

MRS. SHIN   What? You're not going to cash it just because you might have to
35   marry him? Are you crazy? Men like him *want* to be led by the nose! Are you still thinking of that flyer? All Yellow Street knows how he treated you!

SHEN TE   When I heard his cunning laugh, I was afraid
But when I saw the holes in his shoes, I loved him dearly.

MRS. SHIN   Defending that good-for-nothing after all that's happened!

40 SHEN TE [*Staggering as she holds some of the washing.*]   Oh!

MRS. SHIN [*Taking the washing from her, dryly.*]   So you feel dizzy when you stretch and bend? There couldn't be a little visitor on the way? If that's it, you can forget Mr. Shu Fu's blank check: it wasn't meant for a christening present!

[*She goes to the back with a basket. Shen Te's eyes follow MRS. SHIN for a moment. Then she looks down at her own body, feels her stomach, and a great joy comes into her eyes.*]

45 SHEN TE   O joy! A new human being is on the way. The world awaits him. In the cities the people say: he's got to be reckoned with, this new human being! [*She imagines a little boy to be present, and introduces him to the audience.*] This is my son, the well-known flyer!

Say: Welcome
50   To the conqueror of unknown mountains and unreachable regions
Who brings us our mail across the impassable deserts!

[*She leads him up and down by the hand.*]

Take a look at the world, my son. That's a tree. Tree, yes. Say: "Hello, tree!" And bow. Like this. [*She bows.*] Now you know each other. And, look, here comes the water seller. He's a friend, give him your hand. A cup of fresh
55   water for my little son, please. Yes, it *is* a warm day. [*Handing the cup.*] Oh dear, a policeman, we'll have to make a circle round *him*. Perhaps we can pick a few cherries over there in the rich Mr. Pung's garden. But we mustn't be seen. You want cherries? Just like children with fathers. No, no, you can't go straight at them like that. Don't pull. We must learn to be
60   reasonable. Well, have it your own way. [*She has let him make for the cherries.*] Can you reach? Where to put them? Your mouth is the best place. [*She tries one herself.*] Mmm, they're good. But the policeman, we must run! [*They run.*] Yes, back to the street. Calm now, so no one will notice us. [*Walking the street with her child, she sings.*]

Once a plum—'twas in Japan—
65   Made a conquest of a man
But the man's turn soon did come
For he gobbled up the plum

[*Enter WONG, with a child by the hand. He coughs.*]

SHEN TE   Wong!

WONG   It's about the carpenter, Shen Te. He's lost his shop, and he's been
70   drinking. His children are on the streets. This is one. Can you help?

SHEN TE [*To the child.*]   Come here, little man. [*Takes him down to the foot-lights. To the audience.*]

> > You there! A man is asking you for shelter!
> > A man of tomorrow says: what about today?
> > His friend the conqueror, whom you know,
75
> > Is his advocate!

> [*To* WONG.] He can live in Mr. Shu Fu's cabins. I may have to go there myself. I'm going to have a baby. That's a secret—don't tell Yang Sun—we'd only be in his way. Can you find the carpenter for me?

WONG   I knew you'd think of something. [*To the child.*] Good-bye, son, I'm
80 going for your father.

SHEN TE   What about your hand, Wong? I wanted to help, but my cousin . . .

WONG   Oh, I can get along with one hand, don't worry. [*He shows how he can handle his pole with his left hand alone.*]

SHEN TE   But your right hand! Look, take this cart, sell everything that's on it, and go to the doctor with the money . . .

85 WONG   She's still good. But first I'll bring the carpenter. I'll pick up the cart when I get back. [*Exit* WONG.]

SHEN TE [*To the child.*]   Sit down over here, son, till your father comes.

> [*The child sits crosslegged on the ground. Enter the* HUSBAND *and* WIFE, *each dragging a large, full sack.*]

WIFE [*Furtively.*]   You're alone, Shen Te, dear?

> [SHEN TE *nods. The* WIFE *beckons to the* NEPHEW *offstage. He comes on with another sack.*]

WIFE   Your cousin's away? [SHEN TE *nods.*] He's not coming back?

90 SHEN TE   No. I'm giving up the shop.

WIFE   That's why we're here. We want to know if we can leave these things in your new home. Will you do us this favor?

SHEN TE   Why, yes, I'd be glad to.

HUSBAND [*Cryptically.*]   And if anyone asks about them, say they're yours.

95 SHEN TE   Would anyone ask?

WIFE [*With a glance back at her husband.*]   Oh, someone might. The police, for instance. They don't seem to like us. Where can we put it?

SHEN TE   Well, I'd rather not get in any more trouble . . .

WIFE   Listen to her! The good woman of Setzuan!

> [SHEN TE *is silent.*]

100 HUSBAND   There's enough tobacco in those sacks to give us a new start in life. We could have our own tobacco factory!

SHEN TE [*Slowly.*]   You'll have to put them in the back room.

> [*The sacks are taken offstage, while the child is alone. Shyly glancing about him, he goes to the garbage can, starts playing with the contents, and eating some of the scraps. The others return.*]

WIFE   We're counting on you, Shen Te!

SHEN TE   Yes. [*She sees the child and is shocked.*]

105 HUSBAND   We'll see you in Mr. Shu Fu's cabins.

NEPHEW   The day after tomorrow.

SHEN TE   Yes. Now, go. Go! I'm not feeling well.

> [*Exeunt all three, virtually pushed off.*]

He is eating the refuse in the garbage can!
Only look at his little gray mouth!

[*Pause. Music.*]

110 As this is the world *my* son will enter
I will study to defend him.
To be good to you, my son,
I shall be a tigress to all others
If I have to.
115 And I shall have to.

[*She starts to go*]

One more time, then. I hope really the last.

[*Exit* SHEN TE, *taking Shui Ta's trousers.* MRS. SHIN *enters and watches her with marked interest. Enter the* SISTER-IN-LAW *and the* GRANDFATHER.]

SISTER-IN-LAW So it's true, the shop has closed down. And the furniture's in the back yard. It's the end of the road!

MRS. SHIN [*Pompously.*] The fruit of high living, selfishness, and sensuality!
120 Down the primrose path to Mr. Shu Fu's cabins—with you!

SISTER-IN-LAW Cabins? Rat holes! He gave them to us because his soap supplies only went moldy there!

[*Enter the* UNEMPLOYED MAN.]

UNEMPLOYED MAN Shen Te is moving?

SISTER-IN-LAW Yes. She was sneaking away.

125 MRS. SHIN She's ashamed of herself, and no wonder!

UNEMPLOYED MAN Tell her to call Mr. Shui Ta or she's done for this time!

SISTER-IN-LAW Tell her to call Mr. Shui Ta or *we're* done for this time!

[*Enter* WONG *and* CARPENTER, *the latter with a child on each hand.*]

CARPENTER So we'll have a roof over our heads for a change!

MRS. SHIN Roof? Whose roof?

130 CARPENTER Mr. Shu Fu's cabins. And we have little Feng to thank for it.
[*Feng, we find, is the name of the child already there; his father now takes him. To the other two.*] Bow to your little brother, you two!

[*The* CARPENTER *and the two new arrivals bow to Feng. Enter* SHUI TA.]

UNEMPLOYED MAN Sst! Mr. Shui Ta!

[*Pause.*]

SHUI TA And what is this crowd here for, may I ask?

WONG How do you do, Mr. Shui Ta. This is the carpenter. Miss Shen Te
135 promised him space in Mr. Shu Fu's cabins.

SHUI TA That will not be possible.

CARPENTER We can't go there after all?

SHUI TA All the space is needed for other purposes.

SISTER-IN-LAW You mean we have to get out? But we've got nowhere to go.

140 SHUI TA Miss Shen Te finds it possible to provide employment. If the proposition interests you, you may stay in the cabins.

SISTER-IN-LAW [*With distaste.*] You mean *work*? Work for Miss Shen Te?

SHUI TA Making tobacco, yes. There are three bales here already. Would you like to get them?

145 SISTER-IN-LAW [*Trying to bluster.*] We have our own tobacco! We were in the tobacco business before you were born!

SHUI TA [*To the* CARPENTER *and the* UNEMPLOYED MAN] You *don't* have your own tobacco. What about you?

> [*The* CARPENTER *and the* UNEMPLOYED MAN *get the point, and go for the sacks. Enter* MRS. MI TZU.]

MRS. MI TZU Mr. Shui Ta? I've brought you your three hundred silver dollars.

150 SHUI TA I'll sign your lease instead. I've decided not to sell.

MRS. MI TZU What? You don't need the money for that flyer?

SHUI TA No.

MRS. MI TZU And you can pay six months' rent?

SHUI TA [*Takes the barber's blank check from the cart and fills it out.*] Here is

155 a check for ten thousand silver dollars. On Mr. Shu Fu's account. Look. [*He shows her the signature on the check.*] Your six months' rent will be in your hands by seven this evening. And now, if you'll excuse me.

MRS. MI TZU So it's Mr. Shu Fu now. The flyer has been given his walking papers. These modern girls! In my day they'd have said she was flighty.

160 That poor, deserted Mr. Yang Sun!

> [*Exit* MRS. MI TZU. *The* CARPENTER *and the* UNEMPLOYED MAN *drag the three sacks back on the stage.*]

CARPENTER [*To* SHUI TA.] I don't know why I'm doing this for you.

SHUI TA Perhaps your children want to eat, Mr. Carpenter.

SISTER-IN-LAW [*Catching sight of the sacks.*] Was my brother-in-law here?

MRS. SHIN Yes, he was.

165 SISTER-IN-LAW I thought as much. I know those sacks! That's our tobacco!

SHUI TA Really? I thought it came from my back room! Shall we consult the police on the point?

SISTER-IN-LAW [*Defeated.*] No.

SHUI TA Perhaps you will show me the way to Mr. Shu Fu's cabins?

> [*Taking Feng by the hand,* SHUI TA *goes off, followed by the* CARPENTER *and his two older children, the* SISTER-IN-LAW, *the* GRANDFATHER, *and the* UNEMPLOYED MAN. *Each of the last three drags a sack. Enter* OLD MAN *and* OLD WOMAN.]

170 MRS. SHIN A pair of pants—missing from the clothes line one minute—and next minute on the honorable backside of Mr. Shui Ta.

OLD WOMAN We thought Miss Shen Te was here.

MRS. SHIN [*Preoccupied.*] Well, she's not.

OLD MAN There was something she was going to give us.

175 WONG She was going to help me too. [*Looking at his hand.*] It'll be too late soon. But she'll be back. This cousin has never stayed long.

MRS. SHIN [*Approaching a conclusion.*] No, he hasn't, has he?

7a

The Sewer Pipe: WONG *asleep. In his dream, he tells the* GODS *his fears. The* GODS *seem tired from all their travels. They stop for a moment and look over their shoulders at the water seller.*

WONG Illustrious ones. I've been having a bad dream. Our beloved Shen Te was in great distress in the rushes down by the river—the spot where the bodies of suicides are washed up. She kept staggering and holding her head down as if she was carrying something and it was dragging her down into

5 the mud. When I called out to her, she said she had to take your Book of

Rules[7] to the other side, and not get it wet, or the ink would all come off. You had talked to her about the virtues, you know, the time she gave you shelter in Setzuan.

THIRD GOD   Well, but what do you suggest, my dear Wong?

10 WONG   Maybe a little relaxation of the rules, Benevolent One, in view of the bad times.

THIRD GOD   As for instance?

WONG   Well, um, good-will, for instance, might do instead of love?

THIRD GOD   I'm afraid that would create new problems.

15 WONG   Or, instead of justice, good sportsmanship?

THIRD GOD   That would only mean more work.

WONG   Instead of honor, outward propriety?

THIRD GOD   Still more work! No, no! The rules will have to stand, my dear Wong!

[*Wearily shaking their heads, all three journey on.*]

8

Shui Ta's tobacco factory in Shu Fu's cabins. Huddled together behind bars, several families, mostly women and children. Among these people the SISTER-IN-LAW, *the* GRANDFATHER, *the* CARPENTER, *and his three children. Enter* MRS. YANG *followed by* YANG SUN.

MRS. YANG   [*To the audience.*]   There's something I just *have* to tell you: strength and wisdom are wonderful things. The strong and wise Mr. Shui Ta has transformed my son from a dissipated good-for-nothing into a model citizen. As you may have heard, Mr. Shui Ta opened a small tobacco factory
5 near the cattle runs. It flourished. Three months ago—I shall never forget it—I asked for an appointment, and Mr. Shui Ta agree to see us—me and my son. I can see him now as he came through the door to meet us. . . .

[*Enter* SHUI TA, *from a door.*]

SHUI TA   What can I do for you, Mrs. Yang?

MRS. YANG   This morning the police came to the house. We find you've brought
10 an action for breach of promise of marriage. In the name of Shen Te. You also claim that Sun came by two hundred silver dollars by improper means.

SHUI TA   That is correct.

MRS. YANG   Mr. Shui Ta, the money's all gone. When the Peking job didn't materialize, he ran through it all in three days. I know he's a good-for-nothing.
15 He sold my furniture. He was moving to Peking without me. Miss Shen Te thought highly of him at one time.

SHUI TA   What do *you* say, Mr. Yang Sun?

YANG SUN   The money's gone.

SHUI TA   [*To* MRS. YANG.]   Mrs. Yang, in consideration of my cousin's incom
20 prehensible weakness for your son, I am prepared to give him another chance. He can have a job—here. The two hundred silver dollars will be taken out of his wages.

YANG SUN   So it's the factory or jail?

SHUI TA   Take your choice.

25 YANG SUN   May I speak with Shen Te?

---

7. Reference to neo-Confucianist commentator's rigid and prescriptive interpretation of Confucius's *Analects*, especially regarding the role of women.

SHUI TA   You may not.

[*Pause.*]

YANG SUN [*Sullenly.*]   Show me where to go.

MRS. YANG   Mr. Shui Ta, you are kindness itself: the gods will reward you! [*To*
YANG SUN.] And honest work will make a man of you, my boy. [YANG SUN *follows* SHUI TA *into the factory.* MRS. YANG *comes down again to the footlights.*]

30   Actually, honest work didn't agree with him—at first. And he got no opportunity to distinguish himself till—in the third week—when the wages were
being paid . . .

[SHUI TA *has a bag of money. Standing next to his foreman—the former*
UNEMPLOYED MAN—*he counts out the wages. It is Yang Sun's turn.*]

UNEMPLOYED MAN [*Reading.*]   Carpenter, six silver dollars. Yang Sun, six silver dollars.

35 YANG SUN [*Quietly.*]   Excuse me, sir. I don't think it can be more than five.
May I see? [*He takes the foreman's list.*] It says six working days. But that's
a mistake, sir. I took a day off for court business. And I won't take what I
haven't earned, however miserable the pay is!

UNEMPLOYED MAN   Yang Sun. Five silver dollars. [*To* SHUI TA.] A rare case,
40   Mr. Shui Ta!

SHUI TA   How is it the book says six when it should say five?

UNEMPLOYED MAN   I must've made a mistake, Mr. Shui Ta. [*With a look at*
YANG SUN.] It won't happen again.

SHUI TA [*Taking* YANG SUN *aside.*]   You don't hold back, do you? You give your
45   all to the firm. You're even honest. Do the foreman's mistakes always favor
the workers?

YANG SUN   He does have . . . friends.

SHUI TA   Thank you. May I offer you any little recompense?

YANG SUN   Give me a trial period of one week, and I'll prove my intelligence
50   is worth more to you than my strength.

MRS. YANG [*Still down at the footlights.*]   Fighting words, fighting words! That
evening, I said to Sun: "If you're a flyer, then fly, my falcon! Rise in the
world!" And he got to be foreman. Yes, in Mr. Shui Ta's tobacco factory, he
worked real miracles.

[*We see* YANG SUN *with his legs apart standing behind the workers, who
are handing along a basket of raw tobacco above their heads.*]

55 YANG SUN   Faster! Faster! You, there, d'you think you can just stand around,
now you're not foreman any more? It'll be your job to lead us in song. Sing!

[UNEMPLOYED MAN *starts singing. The others join in the refrain.*]

SONG OF THE EIGHTH ELEPHANT

Chang had seven elephants—all much the same—
But then there was Little Brother
The seven, they were wild, Little Brother, he was tame
60   And to guard them Chang chose Little Brother
Run faster!
Mr. Chang has a forest park
Which must be cleared before tonight
And already it's growing dark!

65   When the seven elephants cleared that forest park
        Mr. Chang rode high on Little Brother
     While the seven toiled and moiled till dark
        On his big behind sat Little Brother
          Dig faster!
70   Mr. Chang has a forest park
        Which must be cleared before tonight
        And already it's growing dark!

     And the seven elephants workèd many an hour
        Till none of them could work another
75   Old Chang, he looked sour, on the seven he did glower
        But gave a pound of rice to Little Brother
          What was that?
          Mr. Chang has a forest park
        Which must be cleared before tonight
80   And already it's growing dark!

     And the seven elephants hadn't any tusks
        The one that had the tusks was Little Brother
     Seven are no match for one, if the one has a gun!
        How old Chang did laugh at Little Brother!
85   Keep on digging!
          Mr. Chang has a forest park
        Which must be cleared before tonight
        And already it's growing dark!

[*Smoking a cigar,* SHUI TA *strolls by.* YANG SUN, *laughing, has joined in the refrain of the third stanza and speeded up the tempo of the last stanza by clapping his hands.*]

MRS. YANG   And that's why I say: strength and wisdom are wonderful things.
90   It took the strong and wise Mr. Shui Ta to bring out the best in Yang Sun.
  A real superior man is like a bell. If you ring it, it rings, and if you don't, it
  don't, as the saying is.[8]

9

Shen Te's shop, now an office with club chairs and fine carpets. It is raining. SHUI
TA, *now fat, is just dismissing the* OLD MAN *and* OLD WOMAN. MRS. SHIN, *in obviously
new clothes, looks on, smirking.*

SHUI TA   No! I cannot tell you when we expect her back.
OLD WOMAN   The two hundred silver dollars came today. In an envelope.
  There was no letter, but it must be from Shen Te. We want to write and
  thank her. May we have her address?
5 SHUI TA   I'm afraid I haven't got it.
OLD MAN [*Pulling Old Woman's sleeve.*]   Let's be going.
OLD WOMAN   She's got to come back some time!
    [*They move off, uncertainly, worried.* SHUI TA *bows.*]

---

8. A saying by the Chinese philosopher Mo-tzu (470–391 B.C.E.).

MRS. SHIN   They lost the carpet shop because they couldn't pay their taxes. The money arrived too late.

10 SHUI TA   They could have come to me.

MRS. SHIN   People don't like coming to you.

SHUI TA [*Sits suddenly, one hand to his head.*]   I'm dizzy.

MRS. SHIN   After all, you *are* in your seventh month. But old Mrs. Shin will be there in your hour of trial! [*She cackles feebly.*]

15 SHUI TA [*In a stifled voice.*]   Can I count on that?

MRS. SHIN   We all have our price, and mine won't be too high for the great Mr. Shui Ta! [*She opens Shui Ta's collar.*]

SHUI TA   It's for the child's sake. All of this.

MRS. SHIN   "All for the child," of course.

20 SHUI TA   I'm so fat. People must notice.

MRS. SHIN   Oh no, they think it's 'cause you're rich.

SHIU TA [*More feelingly.*]   What will happen to the child?

MRS. SHIN   You ask that nine times a day. Why, it'll have the best that money can buy!

25 SHUI TA   He must never see Shui Ta.

MRS. SHIN   Oh, no. Always Shen Te.

SHUI TA   What about the neighbors? There are rumors, aren't there?

MRS. SHIN   As long as Mr. Shu Fu doesn't find out, there's nothing to worry about. Drink this.

[*Enter* YANG SUN *in a smart business suit, and carrying a businessman's briefcase.* SHUI TA *is more or less in Mrs. Shin's arms.*]

30 YANG SUN [*Surprised.*]   I guess I'm in the way.

SHUI TA [*Ignoring this, rises with an effort.*]   Till tomorrow, Mrs. Shin.

[MRS. SHIN *leaves with a smile, putting on her new gloves.*]

YANG SUN   Gloves now! She couldn't be fleecing you? And since when did *you* have a private life? [*Taking a paper from the briefcase.*] You haven't been at your best lately, and things are getting out of hand. The police want to

35 close us down. They say that at the most they can only permit twice the lawful number of workers.

SHUI TA [*Evasively.*]   The cabins are quite good enough.

YANG SUN   For the workers maybe, not for the tobacco. They're too damp. We must take over some of Mrs. Mi Tzu's buildings.

40 SHUI TA   Her price is double what I can pay.

YANG SUN   Not unconditionally. If she has me to stroke her knees she'll come down.

SHUI TA   I'll never agree to that.

YANG SUN   What's wrong? Is it the rain? You get so irritable whenever it rains.

45 SHUI TA   Never! I will never . . .

YANG SUN   Mrs. Mi Tzu'll be here in five minutes. *You* fix it. And Shu Fu will be with her. . . . What's all that noise?

[*During the above dialogue,* WONG *is heard offstage, calling: "The good Shen Te, where is she? Which of you has seen Shen Te, good people? Where is Shen Te?" A knock. Enter* WONG.]

WONG   Mr. Shui Ta, I've come to ask when Miss Shen Te will be back, it's six months now. . . . There are rumors. People say something's happened to

50 her.

SHUI TA   I'm busy. Come back next week.

WONG [*Excited.*]   In the morning there was always rice on her doorstep—for
the needy. It's been there again lately!

SHUI TA   And what do people conclude from this?

55 WONG   That Shen Te is still in Setzuan! She's been . . . [*He breaks off.*]

SHUI TA   She's been what? Mr. Wong, if you're Shen Te's friend, talk a little
less about her, that's my advice to you.

WONG   I don't want your advice! Before she disappeared, Miss Shen Te told
me something very important—she's pregnant!

60 YANG SUN   What? What was that?

SHUI TA [*Quickly.*]   The man is lying.

WONG   A good woman isn't so easily forgotten, Mr. Shui Ta.

[*He leaves.* SHUI TA *goes quickly into the back room.*]

YANG SUN [*To the audience.*]   Shen Te pregnant? So that's why. Her cousin
sent her away, so I wouldn't get wind of it. I have a son, a Yang appears on

65 the scene, and what happens? Mother and child vanish into thin air! That
scoundrel, that unspeakable . . . [*The sound of sobbing is heard from the
back room.*] What was that? Someone sobbing? Who was it? Mr. Shui Ta
the Tobacco King doesn't weep his heart out. And where does the rice
come from that's on the doorstep in the morning? [SHUI TA *returns. He goes*

70 *to the door and looks out into the rain.*] Where is she?

SHUI TA   Sh! It's nine o'clock. But the rain's so heavy, you can't hear a thing.

YANG SUN   What do you want to hear?

SHUI TA   The mail plane.

YANG SUN   What?!

75 SHUI TA   I've been told *you* wanted to fly at one time. Is that all forgotten?

YANG SUN   Flying mail is night work. I prefer the daytime. And the firm is
very dear to me—after all it belongs to my ex-fiancée, even if she's not
around. And she's not, is she?

SHUI TA   What do you mean by that?

80 YANG SUN   Oh, well, let's say I haven't altogether—lost interest.

SHUI TA   My cousin might like to know that.

YANG SUN   I might not be indifferent—if I found she was being kept under
lock and key.

SHUI TA   By whom?

85 YANG SUN   By you.

SHUI TA   What could you do about it?

YANG SUN   I could submit for discussion—my position in the firm.

SHUI TA   You are now my manager. In return for a more . . . appropriate
position, you might agree to drop the inquiry into your ex-fiancée's

90 whereabouts?

YANG SUN   I might.

SHUI TA   What position *would* be more appropriate?

YANG SUN   The one at the top.

SHUI TA   My own? [*Silence.*] And if I preferred to throw you out on your

95 neck?

YANG SUN   I'd come back on my feet. With suitable escort.

SHUI TA   The police?

YANG SUN   The police.

SHUI TA   And when the police found no one?

100 YANG SUN   I might ask them not to overlook the back room. [*Ending the pretense.*] In short, Mr. Shui Ta, my interest in this young woman has not been officially terminated. I should like to see more of her. [*Into Shui Ta's face.*] Besides, she's pregnant and needs a friend. [*He moves to the door.*] I shall talk about it with the water seller.

> [*Exit.* SHUI TA *is rigid for a moment, then he quickly goes into the back room. He returns with Shen Te's belongings: underwear, etc. He takes a long look at the shawl of the previous scene. He then wraps the things in a bundle, which, upon hearing a noise, he hides under the table. Enter* MRS. MI TZU *and Mr.* SHU FU. *They put away their umbrellas and galoshes.*]

105 MRS. MI TZU   I thought your manager was here, Mr. Shui Ta. He combines charm with business in a way that can only be to the advantage of all of us.

SHU FU   You sent for us, Mr. Shui Ta?

SHUI TA   The factory is in trouble.

110 SHU FU   It always is.

SHUI TA   The police are threatening to close us down unless I can show that the extension of our facilities is imminent.

SHU FU   Mr. Shui Ta, I'm sick and tired of your constantly expanding projects. I place cabins at your cousin's disposal; you make a factory of them. I

115 hand your cousin a check; you present it. Your cousin disappears; you find the cabins too small and start talking of yet more—

SHUI TA   Mr. Shu Fu, I'm authorized to inform you that Miss Shen Te's return is now imminent.

SHU FU   Imminent? It's becoming his favorite word.

120 MRS. MI TZU   Yes, what does it mean?

SHUI TA   Mrs. Mi Tzu, I can pay you exactly half what you asked for your buildings. Are you ready to inform the police that I am taking them over?

MRS. MI TZU   Certainly, if I can take over your manager.

SHU FU   What?

125 MRS. MI TZU   He's so efficient.

SHUI TA   I'm afraid I need Mr. Yang Sun.

MRS. MI TZU   So do I.

SHUI TA   He will call on you tomorrow.

SHU FU   So much the better. With Shen Te likely to turn up at any moment,

130 the presence of that young man is hardly in good taste.

SHUI TA   So we have reached a settlement. In what was once the good Shen Te's little shop we are laying the foundations for the great Mr. Shui Ta's twelve magnificent super tobacco markets. You will bear in mind that though they call me the Tobacco King of Setzuan, it is my cousin's interests

135 that have been served . . .

VOICES [*Off.*]   The police, the police! Going to the tobacco shop! Something must have happened!

> [*Enter* YANG SUN, WONG, *and the* POLICEMAN.]

POLICEMAN   Quiet there, quiet, quiet! [*They quiet down.*] I'm sorry, Mr. Shui Ta, but there's a report that you've been depriving Miss Shen Te of her

140 freedom. Not that I believe all I hear, but the whole city's in an uproar.

SHUI TA   That's a lie.

POLICEMAN   Mr. Yang Sun has testified that he heard someone sobbing in the back room.

SHU FU   Mrs. Mi Tzu and myself will testify that no one here has been
145 sobbing.

MRS. MI TZU   We have been quietly smoking our cigars.

POLICEMAN   Mr. Shui Ta, I'm afraid I shall have to take a look at that room. [*He does so. The room is empty.*] No one there, of course, sir.

YANG SUN   But I heard sobbing. What's that?

[*He finds the clothes.*]

150 WONG   Those are Shen Te's things. [*To crowd.*] Shen Te's clothes are here!

VOICES [*Off, in sequence.*]   Shen Te's clothes!
—They've been found under the table!
—Body of murdered girl still missing!
—Tobacco King suspected!

155 POLICEMAN   Mr. Shui Ta, unless you can tell us where the girl is, I'll have to ask you to come along.

SHUI TA   I do not know.

POLICEMAN   I can't say how sorry I am, Mr. Shui Ta. [*He shows him the door.*]

SHUI TA   Everything will be cleared up in no time. There are still judges in
160 Setzuan.

YANG SUN   I heard sobbing!

9a

Wong's den. For the last time, the GODS *appear to the water seller in his dream. They have changed and show signs of a long journey, extreme fatigue, and plenty of mishaps. The* FIRST *no longer has a hat; the* THIRD *has lost a leg; all three are barefoot.*

WONG   Illustrious ones, at last you're here. Shen Te's been gone for months and today her cousin's been arrested. They think he murdered her to get the shop. But I had a dream and in this dream Shen Te said her cousin was keeping her prisoner. You must find her for us, illustrious ones!

5 FIRST GOD   We've found very few good people anywhere, and even they didn't keep it up. Shen Te is still the only one that stayed good.

SECOND GOD   If she *has* stayed good.

WONG   Certainly she has. But she's vanished.

FIRST GOD   That's the last straw. All is lost!

10 SECOND GOD   A little moderation, dear colleague!

FIRST GOD [*Plaintively.*]   What's the good of moderation now? If she can't be found, we'll have to resign! The world is a terrible place! Nothing but misery, vulgarity, and waste! Even the countryside isn't what it used to be. The trees are getting their heads chopped off by telephone wires, and there's
15 such a noise from all the gunfire, and I can't stand those heavy clouds of smoke, and—

THIRD GOD   The place is absolutely unlivable! Good intentions bring people to the brink of the abyss, and good deeds push them over the edge. I'm afraid our book of rules is destined for the scrap heap—

20 SECOND GOD   It's people! They're a worthless lot!

THIRD GOD   The world is too cold!

SECOND GOD   It's people! They're too weak!

FIRST GOD   Dignity, dear colleagues, dignity! Never despair! As for this world, didn't we agree that we only have to find one human being who can stand
25   the place? Well, we found her. True, we lost her again. We must find her again, that's all! And at once!

[*They disappear.*]

10

Courtroom. Groups: SHU FU *and* MRS. MI TZU; YANG SUN *and* MRS. YANG; WONG, *the* CARPENTER, *the* GRANDFATHER, *the* NIECE, *the* OLD MAN, *the* OLD WOMAN; MRS. SHIN, *the* POLICEMAN; *the* UNEMPLOYED MAN, *the* SISTER-IN-LAW.

OLD MAN   So much power isn't good for one man.

UNEMPLOYED MAN   And he's going to open twelve super tobacco markets!

WIFE   One of the judges is a friend of Mr. Shu Fu's.

SISTER-IN-LAW   Another one accepted a present from Mr. Shui Ta only last
5   night. A great fat goose.

OLD WOMAN [*To* WONG]   And Shen Te is nowhere to be found.

WONG   Only the gods will ever know the truth.

POLICEMAN   Order in the court! My lords the judges!

[*Enter the* THREE GODS *in judges' robes. We overhear their conversation as they pass along the footlights to their bench.*]

THIRD GOD   We'll never get away with it, our certificates were so badly forged.
10   SECOND GOD   My predecessor's "sudden indigestion" will certainly cause comment.

FIRST GOD   But he *had* just eaten a whole goose.

UNEMPLOYED MAN   Look at that! *New* judges.

WONG   New judges. And what good ones!

[*The* THIRD GOD *hears this, and turns to smile at* WONG. *The* GODS *sit. The* FIRST GOD *beats on the bench with his gavel. The* POLICEMAN *brings in* SHUI TA, *who walks with lordly steps. He is whistled*[9] *at.*]

15   POLICEMAN [*To* SHUI TA.]   Be prepared for a surprise. The judges have been changed.

[SHUI TA *turns quickly round, looks at them, and staggers.*]

NIECE   What's the matter now?

WIFE   The great Tobacco King nearly fainted.

HUSBAND   Yes, as soon as he saw the new judges.
20   WONG   Does *he* know who they are?

[SHUI TA *picks himself up, and the proceedings open.*]

FIRST GOD   Defendant Shui Ta, you are accused of doing away with your cousin Shen Te in order to take possession of her business. Do you plead guilty or not guilty?

SHUI TA   Not guilty, my lord.
25   FIRST GOD [*Thumbing through the documents of the case.*]   The first witness is the policeman. I shall ask him to tell us something of the respective reputations of Miss Shen Te and Mr. Shui Ta.

9. Hissed.

POLICEMAN   Miss Shen Te was a young lady who aimed to please, my lord.
She liked to live and let live, as the saying goes. Mr. Shui Ta, on the other
30   hand, is a man of principle. Though the generosity of Miss Shen Te forced
him at times to abandon half measures, unlike the girl he was always on
the side of the law, my lord. One time, he even unmasked a gang of thieves
to whom his too trustful cousin had given shelter. The evidence, in short,
my lord, proves that Mr. Shui Ta was *incapable* of the crime of which he
35   stands accused!

FIRST GOD   I see. And are there others who could testify along, shall we say,
the same lines?

[SHU FU *rises.*]

POLICEMAN [*Whispering to* GODS.]   Mr. Shu Fu—a very important person.

FIRST GOD [*Inviting him to speak.*]   Mr. Shu Fu!

40   SHU FU   Mr. Shui Ta is a businessman, my lord. Need I say more?

FIRST GOD   Yes.

SHU FU   Very well, I will. He is Vice President of the Council of Commerce
and is about to be elected a Justice of the Peace. [*He returns to his seat.*
MRS. MI TZU *rises.*]

WONG   Elected! *He* gave him the job!

[*With a gesture the* FIRST GOD *asks who* MRS. MI TZU *is.*]

45   POLICEMAN   Another very important person. Mrs. Mi Tzu.

FIRST GOD [*Inviting her to speak.*]   Mrs. Mi Tzu!

MRS. MI TZU   My lord, as Chairman of the Committee on Social Work, I
wish to call attention to just a couple of eloquent facts: Mr. Shui Ta not
only has erected a model factory with model housing in our city, he is a
50   regular contributor to our home for the disabled. [*She returns to her
seat.*]

POLICEMAN [*Whispering.*]   And she's a great friend of the judge that ate the
goose!

FIRST GOD [*To the* POLICEMAN.]   Oh, thank you. What next? [*To the Court,
genially.*] Oh, yes. We should find out if any of the evidence is less favorable
55   to the defendant.

[WONG, *the* CARPENTER, *the* OLD MAN, *the* OLD WOMAN, *the* UNEMPLOYED
MAN, *the* SISTER-IN-LAW, *and the* NIECE *come forward.*]

POLICEMAN [*Whispering.*]   Just the riffraff, my lord.

FIRST GOD [*Addressing the "riffraff."*]   Well, um, riffraff—do you know anything
of the defendant, Mr. Shui Ta?

WONG   Too much, my lord.

60   UNEMPLOYED MAN   What don't we know, my lord.

CARPENTER   He ruined us.

SISTER-IN-LAW   He's a cheat.

NIECE   Liar.

WIFE   Thief.

65   BOY   Blackmailer.

BROTHER   Murderer.

FIRST GOD   Thank you. We should now let the defendant state his point of
view.

SHU TA   I only came on the scene when Shen Te was in danger of losing
70   what I had understood was a gift from the gods. Because I did the filthy

jobs which someone had to do, they hate me. My activities were restricted to the minimum, my lord.

SISTER-IN-LAW   He had us arrested!

SHUI TA   Certainly. You stole from the bakery!

75 SISTER-IN-LAW   Such concern for the bakery! You didn't want the shop for yourself, I suppose!

SHUI TA   I didn't want the shop overrun with parasites.

SISTER-IN-LAW   We had nowhere else to go.

SHUI TA   There were too many of you.

80 WONG   What about this old couple: Were *they* parasites?

OLD MAN   We lost our shop because of you!

OLD WOMAN   And we gave your cousin money!

SHUI TA   My cousin's fiancé was a flyer. The money had to go to *him*.

WONG   Did you care whether he flew or not? Did you care whether she mar-
85 ried him or not? You wanted her to marry someone else!

[*He points to* SHU FU.]

SHUI TA   The flyer unexpectedly turned out to be a scoundrel.

YANG SUN [*Jumping up.*]   Which was the reason you made him your manager?

SHUI TA   Later on he improved.

WONG   And when he improved, you sold him to her? [*He points out* MRS. MI TZU.]

90 SHUI TA   She wouldn't let me have her premises unless she had him to stroke her knees!

MRS. MI TZU   What? The man's a pathological liar. [*To him.*] Don't mention my property to me as long as you live! Murderer! [*She rustles off, in high dudgeon.*]

YANG SUN [*Pushing in.*]   My lord, I wish to speak for the defendant.

95 SISTER-IN-LAW   Naturally. He's your employer.

UNEMPLOYED MAN   And the worst slave driver in the country.

MRS. YANG   That's a lie! My lord, Mr. Shui Ta is a great man. He . . .

YANG SUN   He's this and he's that, but he is not a murderer, my lord. Just fifteen minutes before his arrest I heard Shen Te's voice in his own back
100 room.

FIRST GOD   Oh? Tell us more!

YANG SUN   I heard sobbing, my lord!

FIRST GOD   But lots of women sob, we've been finding.

YANG SUN   Could I fail to recognize her voice?

105 SHU FU   No, you made her sob so often yourself, young man!

YANG SUN   Yes. But I also made her happy. Till he [*Pointing at* SHUI TA.] decided to sell her to you!

SHUI TA   Because you didn't love her.

WONG   Oh, no: it was for the money, my lord!

110 SHUI TA   And what was the money for, my lord? For the poor! And for Shen Te so she could go on being good!

WONG   For the poor? That sent to his sweatshops? And why didn't you let Shen Te be good when you signed the big check?

SHUI TA   For the child's sake, my lord.

115 CARPENTER   What about *my* children? What did he do about them?

[SHUI TA *is silent.*]

WONG   The shop was to be a fountain of goodness. That was the gods' idea. You came and spoiled it!

SHUI TA   If I hadn't, it would have run dry!

MRS. SHIN   There's a lot in that, my lord.

120 WONG   What have you done with the good Shen Te, bad man? She *was* good, my lords, she was, I swear it! [*He raises his hand in an oath.*]

THIRD GOD   What's happened to your hand, water seller?

WONG [*Pointing to* SHUI TA.]   It's all his fault, my lord, *she* was going to send me to a doctor— [*To* SHUI TA.] You were her worst enemy!

125 SHUI TA   I was her only friend!

WONG   Where is she then? Tell us where your good friend is!

   [*The excitement of this exchange has run through the whole crowd.*]

ALL   Yes, where is she? Where is Shen Te? [*Etc.*]

SHUI TA   Shen Te . . . had to go.

WONG   Where? Where to?

130 SHUI TA   I cannot tell you! I cannot tell you!

ALL   Why? Why did she have to go away? [*Etc.*]

WONG [*Into the din with the first words, but talking on beyond the others.*] Why not, why not? Why did she have to go away?

SHUI TA [*Shouting.*]   Because you'd all have torn her to shreds, that's why! My lords, I have a request. Clear the court! When only the judges remain, 135 I will make a confession.

ALL [*Except* WONG, *who is silent, struck by the new turn of events.*]   So he's guilty! He's confessing! [*Etc.*]

FIRST GOD [*Using the gavel.*]   Clear the court!

POLICEMAN   Clear the court!

140 WONG   Mr. Shui Ta has met his match this time.

MRS. SHIN [*With a gesture toward the judges.*]   You're in for a little surprise.

   [*The court is cleared. Silence.*]

SHUI TA   Illustrious ones!

   [*The* GODS *look at each other, not quite believing their ears.*]

SHUI TA   Yes, I recognize you!

SECOND GOD [*Taking matters in hand, sternly.*]   What have you done with our 145 good woman of Setzuan?

SHUI TA   I have a terrible confession to make: I am she! [*He takes off his mask, and tears away his clothes.* SHEN TE *stands there.*]

SECOND GOD   Shen Te!

SHEN TE   Shen Te, yes. Shui Ta *and* Shen Te. Both.

      Your injunction
150   To be good and yet to live
      Was a thunderbolt:
      It has torn me in two
      I can't tell how it was
      But to be good to others
155   And myself at the same time
      I could not do it
      Your world is not an easy one, illustrious ones!

When we extend our hand to a beggar, he tears it off for us
When we help the lost, we are lost ourselves

160 And so
Since not to eat is to die
Who can long refuse to be bad?
As I lay prostrate beneath the weight of good intentions
Ruin stared me in the face

165 It was when I was unjust that I ate good meat
And hobnobbed with the mighty
Why?
Why are bad deeds rewarded?
Good ones punished?

170 I enjoyed giving
I truly wished to be the Angel of the Slums
But washed by a foster-mother in the water of the gutter
I developed a sharp eye
The time came when pity was a thorn in my side

175 And, later, when kind words turned to ashes in my mouth
And anger took over
I became a wolf
Find me guilty, then, illustrious ones,
But know:

180 All that I have done I did
To help my neighbor
To love my lover
And to keep my little one from want
For your great, godly deeds, I was too poor, too small.

[*Pause.*]

185 FIRST GOD [*Shocked.*]   Don't go on making yourself miserable, Shen Te!
We're overjoyed to have found you!

SHEN TE   I'm telling you I'm the bad man who committed all those crimes!

FIRST GOD [*Using—or failing to use—his ear trumpet.*]   The good woman who
did all those good deeds?

190 SHEN TE   Yes, but the bad man too!

FIRST GOD [*As if something had dawned.*]   Unfortunate coincidences! Heartless neighbors!

THIRD GOD [*Shouting in his ear.*]   But how is she to continue?

FIRST GOD   Continue? Well, she's a strong, healthy girl . . .

195 SECOND GOD   You didn't hear what she said!

FIRST GOD   I heard every word! She is confused, that's all! [*He begins to bluster.*] And what about this book of rules—we can't renounce our rules, can
we? [*More quietly.*] Should the world be changed? How? By whom? The
world should *not* be changed! [*At a sign from him, the lights turn pink, and
music plays.*]

200 And now the hour of parting is at hand.
Dost thou behold, Shen Te, yon fleecy cloud?
It is our chariot. At a sign from me
'Twill come and take us back from whence we came
Above the azure vault and silver stars. . . .

205 SHEN TE   No! Don't go, illustrious ones!
FIRST GOD

        Our cloud has landed now in yonder field
        From which it will transport us back to heaven.
        Farewell, Shen Te, let not thy courage fail thee. . . .

        [*Exeunt* GODS.]

SHEN TE   What about the old couple? They've lost their shop! What about
210 the water seller and his hand? And I've got to defend myself against the
barber, because I don't love him! And against Sun, because I do love him!
How? How?

        [*Shen Te's eyes follow the* GODS *as they are imagined to step into a cloud,
        which rises and moves forward over the orchestra and up beyond the
        balcony.*]

FIRST GOD [*From on high.*]   We have faith in you, Shen Te!
SHEN TE   There'll be a child. And he'll have to be fed. I can't stay here.
215 Where shall I go?
FIRST GOD   Continue to be good, good woman of Setzuan!
SHEN TE   I need my bad cousin!
FIRST GOD   But not very often!
SHEN TE   Once a week at least!
220 FIRST GOD   Once a month will be quite enough!
SHEN TE [*Shrieking.*]   No, no! Help!

        [*But the cloud continues to recede as the* GODS *sing.*]

VALEDICTORY HYMN

        What rapture, oh, it is to know
          A good thing when you see it
        And having seen a good thing, oh,
225   What rapture 'tis to flee it

        Be good, sweet maid of Setzuan
          Let Shui Ta be clever
        Departing, we forget the man
          Remember your endeavor

230   Because through all the length of days
          Her goodness faileth never
        Sing hallelujah! Make Shen Te's
          Good name live on forever!

SHEN TE   Help!

Epilogue

235   You're thinking, aren't you, that this is no right
        Conclusion to the play you've seen tonight?
        After a tale, exotic, fabulous,
        A nasty ending was slipped up on us.
        We feel deflated too. We too are nettled
240   To see the curtain down and nothing settled.
        How could a better ending be arranged?

Could one change people? Can the world be changed?
Would new gods do the trick? Will atheism?
Moral rearmament? Materialism?
It is for you to find a way, my friends,
To help good men arrive at happy ends.
You write the happy ending to the play!
There must, there must, there's got to be a way!

JEAN GENET

1910–1986

A WARD of the state, a vagabond, deserter, prostitute, thief, and convict, Jean Genet is an unlikely candidate for the role of great author. After he had served many short prison sentences for theft, a mandatory sentence of life imprisonment threatened to remove Genet from the world for good. He was hardly the first French author who was also a social outcast; indeed, in the late nineteenth century, Paul Verlaine applied the label "accursed poets" to those who—like Genet's models, Baudelaire and Rimbaud—wrote from the margins of society. It was this tradition that Genet's supporters invoked both to prevent the imposition of a life sentence in 1944 and to win an official pardon from the president of the Republic in 1949. Genet was able to live and write for the rest of his life in freedom, creating an astonishing oeuvre that included not just novels and plays but also film and ballet scripts, art criticism, and political writings.

Even though Genet was abandoned by his mother, his childhood was not one of extreme deprivation. Placed in a family in a small mountain town, Genet was a good student but began stealing; at the age of fifteen he was put in a psychiatric clinic, from which he promptly ran away. He was soon caught, spent three months in prison, and was sentenced to live in the Mettray

Reformatory, an agricultural penitentiary for adolescents. His experiences in this closed world began his lifelong fascination with life in penal institutions; here, too, his homosexuality was openly expressed. In 1929 he gained early release from Mettray by enlisting in the army, which sent him to Syria and Morocco. After deserting in 1936, he began a period of drifting through Europe and its prisons. During this phase of his life, Genet supported himself by panhandling, stealing, prostitution, and smuggling. But when he found himself again in prison in 1941, Genet did not simply sink back into the familiar routine of prison life. Instead, he began work on his first novel, *Our Lady of the Flowers* (1943), which attracted the attention of Jean Cocteau and other literary figures in Paris. The outcast was in the process of transforming himself into a writer.

Between 1942 and 1948, Genet wrote several largely autobiographical novels in quick succession: *Our Lady of the Flowers* was followed by *Miracle of the Rose* (1946), *Funeral Rites* (1947), *Querelle of Brest* (1947), and *The Thief's Journal* (1948). With the exception of *Querelle*, these novels are narrated by a figure based on Jean Genet and set in the different milieus that Genet had come to know intimately, from the reform school at Mettray and Fontevrault State Prison (*Miracle*), the bohemian and homosexual scene of Montmartre (*Our Lady*), and the German occupation of Paris (*Funeral*) to the experience of drifting through Europe (*Thief*). They are frank and often graphic in depicting the world of pimps and criminals, as well as homosexuality. Defying almost all ethical norms, these novels revel in the abject and strategically evoke disgust even as they dwell on aesthetic objects such as flowers. Like Genet's later plays, these novels pay almost fetishistic attention to body parts, individual gestures, flowers, and pieces of clothing, including and especially uniforms. Indeed, his protagonists are alternately attracted to and repulsed by figures of authority, around which many of these works revolve.

The juxtaposition of the abject and the beautiful is part of the most surprising aspect of Genet's work: its fascination with the saintly and the sacred. Raised in the Catholicism of small-town France, Genet continued to invoke such ascetic qualities as submission and self-negation, even when he associated them with such acts as passively submitting to sodomy. Nor was this language of sainthood intended as blasphemy, at least in any simple sense. Rather it works as a mode of thinking, behaving, and writing that undergirds much of Genet's work. The person who first noted this constant underlying theme was Jean-Paul Sartre, whose monumental study of Genet, *Saint Genet: Actor and Martyr* (1952), had a decisive impact on his career. That France's most eminent philosopher would dedicate a 700-page book to a relatively unknown author was remarkable—particularly since he was presented as the embodiment of Sartre's existentialist philosophy of freedom. Genet was flattered and accepted Sartre's analysis, but he also felt exposed—and he knew that he could no longer claim the role of the cultural outsider.

Even before Sartre published his study, Genet had recognized that he had exhausted the autobiographical material on which his novels had relied and decided to transform himself once more: this time into a playwright. His choice did not reflect a long-standing love for the theater; in fact, he had shown very little interest in this art form and often claimed that he did not much like it. He rarely went to rehearsals or performances of his plays, and even after he had made a name as a dramatist, he continued to consider his great models not the playwrights but the "accursed poets" Baudelaire and Rimbaud, as well as the novelist Marcel Proust. His preference for poetry and the novel over drama did not keep him from expressing intense preferences when it came to directors and their productions of his work, however. Genet strongly favored Roger Blin, for example, the director of SAMUEL BECKETT'S *WAITING FOR GODOT* (1953), and turned sharply against Peter Brook, whose earlier productions he had admired. Genet's letters to Blin offer a fascinating insight into his conception of the theater, in particular his vision of costumes and stage props.

What drove Genet to write plays was the inner logic of his literary style, built as it was around the artificial and the fake, around masks and poses, mirrors and props. Many commentators, including Sartre, had sensed something decidedly theatrical in Genet's novels from the beginning, and this theatricality now came into its own. His first play, *Deathwatch* (1947), is a transitional piece, which, like several of his novels, is set in a prison. It also anticipates the ceremonial rituals, role-playing, and manipulations that would become hallmarks of Genet's most successful plays. In *The Blacks* (1959), for example, a group of black actors puts on white masks to play the white slaveholders for whose benefit a group of black actors enact a ritualistic punishment, one that has clearly been rehearsed and performed innumerable times before. *The Blacks*, like many of Genet's plays, employs a play-within-the-play and therefore belongs to the tradition of metatheater—theater about theater. *The Balcony* (1956) is also set in a world of artifice, but of a different sort. It takes place in an elaborate brothel whose decorated rooms represent different fantasy worlds for clients who play at being a general, bishop, or judge. Around the brothel, a revolt is under way; and when the real general, bishop, and judge flee, the brothel clients take their places. In the end, it is impossible to determine what is real and what is fantasy; even the real rebellion happening outside the brothel relies on theatrical techniques to achieve its goal.

Scene from the 1948 staging of *The Maids* at Stockholm's Royal
Dramatic Theatre, starring Maj-Britt Nilsson (foreground) and Anita
Bjork (background).

The form Genet chose for this play enhances
the impression of different fake worlds col-
liding: the fantasy worlds are painted on
large screens whose arrangement repeatedly changes. Indeed, screens became
Genet's favorite device, finding their
most elaborate application in his longest
play, *The Screens* (1961), which is set in
Algeria during the struggle against
French colonialism.

Formal restraint and manipulative
games also characterize Genet's most
important play, THE MAIDS (1946), which
was his first play to be performed and the
first to bring him fame as a dramatist.
Like *Deathwatch*, which was not staged
until 1949, *The Maids* takes place in a single contained space—one room in a house
inhabited by two maids, who are sisters,
and their mistress, Madame. The atmosphere is one of complete control: everything in this household is precisely
proscribed, and the maids are trained to

obey Madame's every order. But once
Madame is out of the house—as is the
case for most of the play—things change.
The two maids then engage in an elaborate game in which one of them plays
Madame and the other plays a maid. They
push this role-playing so far that even the
one pretending to be a maid usually acts
as her sister, not herself; thus both play
roles. In fact, role-playing is the main
focus of this drama. Only well into the
action do we recognize that what appeared
to be an exchange between Madame and
her maid was just such a game, a play-
within-the-play that is interrupted by the
ringing of an alarm clock.

At first sight, the maids seem to be
engaging in this game merely to pass the
time while Madame is away. One of its
important components, and the main
source of pleasure for those engaged in it, is
the handling of clothing and accessories—
the simple act of getting dressed and

undressed. The two sisters relish taking out Madame's beautiful dresses, jewelry, and flowers and putting them on. Like so much of Genet's work, *The Maids* seems baroque in its delight in elaborate attire and the energy spent on getting a bow right or a piece of jewelry placed at just the perfect spot. The excessive beauty of Madame's clothes stands in stark contrast to the maids' ordinary garb and their ugly kitchen gloves. Clearly, the maids seek to escape their utilitarian everyday life through this game of dressing up. Genet here transposes his fetishistic attention to clothes and objects onto the stage, creating a theater of objects, of stage props, and of costumes.

The game of dressing up as Madame is more than a benign diversion, however. It becomes increasingly obvious that it is full of violence, a violence that the maid playing Madame directs toward her sister playing "maid." The maids appear to be willfully reenacting their daily suffering, the countless humiliations to which they are subjected. As in many of Genet's novels and plays, the infliction of pain causes a strange kind of pleasure, bringing the game nearer to a sadomasochistic ritual. The maids clearly delight not just in humiliating one another but also in being humiliated, in deliciously and elaborately enacting the power games usually played by Madame with them. Their play focuses on the disturbing connection between power, domination, and pleasure. Here, as elsewhere in Genet's work, it is difficult to find human relations among equals. He always constructs constellations that are infused with authority, even as he subverts that authority.

As the play progresses, it becomes evident that the maids' role-playing is indeed such an act of subversion: the maids are plotting a revolt, for what they are rehearsing is the killing of Madame. At this point, *The Maids* turns into a kind of murder mystery revolving around the question of whether the sisters will be able to carry out their plan. A forged letter that leads to the temporary arrest of Madame's lover and withheld information about a phone call are some of the ingredients of this suspenseful dimension of the play. Indeed, *The Maids* is partly based on the famous murder case of Lea and Christine Papin, who brutally murdered their employer and her daughter in Le Mans, France, in 1933.

Yet ultimately, Genet cares little about the historical case or the murder mystery. Each merely serves as a vehicle that can carry his primary interest in theater and theatricality. Like Genet's other plays, *The Maids* is a particular brand of metatheater: nothing on the stage can be taken at face value, not even the actors, who may be playing any number of roles. In this sense, Genet's theater is the opposite of naturalism, which emphasizes authentic decoration and acting. To increase the sense of artifice, Genet originally envisioned that the three women be played—and played badly—by adolescent boys. An unauthorized, though widely noted, 1965 production of *The Maids* by the experimental American company Living Theatre took up this suggestion and presented the play with an all-male cast to stunning effect.

The games and role-playing of Genet's play call to mind a number of cultural practices, including the ceremonies and rituals of the Catholic mass as well as children's games. Genet was an avid reader of Friedrich Nietzsche (1844–1900), the philosopher who insisted on the seriousness of children's games and who also envisioned a renewal of Western theater by returning it to its roots in ancient Greek ritual. Among the many theorists of the early twentieth century who took up Nietzsche's vision was Antonin Artaud, whose so-called Theater of Cruelty is often compared to Genet's. In the eyes of many, Genet was the playwright who finally fulfilled these dreams. In a note, Genet even imagined a performance of *The Maids* at Epidaurus, the largest and best-preserved classical Greek theater. Whereas Genet's novels were steeped in the language of saintliness, his plays translate this religious vocabulary into ritual.

After winning early fame with his novels and later succeeding with drama, Genet published no literary works for decades. He stopped writing about revolutions and freedom struggles to become an activist, speaking in support of and even living with such groups as the Palestine Liberation Organization and, in the United States, the Black Panthers. In September 1982, Genet was one of the first Westerners to set foot in Shatila, a UN-sanctioned refugee camp for Palestinians near Beirut, after the Israeli army allowed the Lebanese Christian militia to enter Sabra and Shatila and to massacre hundreds of their inhabitants—a criminal act that shocked the world. More broadly, Genet incorporated these experiences into his last great work of literature, *Prisoner of Love* (1986), an autobiographical account of his time with the Palestinians and the Panthers. This meditation on the troubling relationship between revolutionary struggles and theatricality made use of many of his earlier styles and forms.

Dramatizing the intimate if contentious links between theater, power, and revolution is Genet's most significant achieve-

ment. His plays embody two seemingly contradictory impulses: on the one hand, they are deeply immersed in the theater, in artificiality and role-play; on the other hand, they refuse to turn away from the world in order to celebrate the theater, as many metaplays do. Instead, they manage to turn theatricality into an effective tool for analyzing power—its attractions, its erotic charge, and its violence. Genet, who himself suffered from the tyranny and brutality of prison wardens, army superiors, and police, did not denounce the exploitation of power directly. But his plays are profound indictments of authoritarian behavior of every kind. They also seek to plant in the audience the seeds of rebellion that may bring authoritarianism to an end.   M.P.

The Maids[1]

CHARACTERS

SOLANGE ⎱ Two housemaids, sisters, thirty to thirty-five
CLAIRE   ⎰   years old. Solange is the elder.
MADAME   Their mistress. She is about twenty-five.

MADAME's *bedroom. Louis-Quinze furniture,[2] Lace. Rear, a window opening on the front of the house opposite. Right, a bed. Left, a door and a dressing table. Flowers in profusion. The time is evening.*

> [CLAIRE, *wearing a slip, is standing with her back to the dressing table. Her gestures—arm extended—and tone are exaggeratedly tragic.*]

CLAIRE Those gloves! Those eternal gloves! I've told you time and again to leave them in the kitchen. You probably hope to seduce the milkman with them. No, no, don't lie; that won't get you anywhere! Hang them over the sink. When *will* you understand that this room is not to be sullied. Every-
5   thing, yes, everything that comes out of the kitchen is spit! So stop it! [*During this speech,* SOLANGE *has been playing with a pair of rubber gloves and observing her gloved hands, which are alternately spread fanwise and folded*

---

1. Translated by Bernard Frechtman.
2. The richly ornamental style of furniture and

decoration common during the reign of Louis XV (r. 1715–74). *Quinze:* fifteen (French).

in the form of a bouquet.] Make yourself quite at home. Preen like a peacock. And above all, don't hurry, we've plenty of time. Go!

> [SOLANGE's *posture changes and she leaves humbly, holding the rubber gloves with her fingertips.* CLAIRE *sits down at the dressing table. She sniffs at the flowers, runs her hand over the toilet articles, brushes her hair, pats her face.*]

Get my dress ready. Quick! Time presses. Are you there? [*She turns round.*] Claire! Claire!

> [SOLANGE *enters.*]

10 SOLANGE I beg Madame's pardon, I was preparing her tea. [*She pronounces it "tay."*]

CLAIRE Lay out my things. The white spangled dress. The fan. The emeralds.

SOLANGE Very well, Madame. All Madame's jewels?

CLAIRE Put them out and I shall choose. And, of course, my patent-
15 leather slippers. The ones you've had your eye on for years. [SOLANGE *takes a few jewel boxes from the closet, opens them, and lays them out on the bed.*] For your wedding, no doubt. Admit he seduced you! Just look at you! How big you are! Admit it! [SOLANGE *squats on the rug, spits on the patent-leather slippers, and polishes them.*] I've told you, Claire, without spit. Let it sleep in you, my child, let it stagnate. Ah! Ah! [*She giggles*
20 *nervously.*] May the lost wayfarer drown in it. Ah! Ah! You *are* hideous. Lean forward and look at yourself in my shoes. Do you think I find it pleasant to know that my foot is shrouded by the veils of your saliva? By the mists of your swamps?

SOLANGE [*on her knees, and very humble*] I wish Madame to be lovely.

25 CLAIRE I shall be. [*She primps in front of the mirror.*] You hate me, don't you? You crush me with your attentions and your humbleness; you smother me with gladioli and mimosa. [*She stands up and, lowering her tone*] There are too many flowers. The room is needlessly cluttered. It's *impossible.* [*She looks at herself again in the glass.*] I shall be lovely. Lovelier than you'll ever
30 be. With a face and body like that, you'll never seduce Mario. [*Dropping the tragic tone*] A ridiculous young milkman despises us, and if we're going to have a kid by him—

SOLANGE Oh! I've never—

CLAIRE [*resuming*] Be quiet, you fool. My dress!

35 SOLANGE [*she looks in the closet, pushing aside a few dresses*] The red dress. Madame will wear the red dress.

CLAIRE I said the white dress, the one with spangles.

SOLANGE [*firmly*] I'm sorry. Madame will wear the scarlet velvet dress this evening.

40 CLAIRE [*naively*] Ah? Why?

SOLANGE [*coldly*] It's impossible to forget Madame's bosom under the velvet folds. And the jet brooch, when Madame was sighing and telling Monsieur[3] of my devotion! Your widowhood really requires that you be entirely in black.

CLAIRE Eh?

45 SOLANGE Need I say more? A word to the wise—

---

3. Mister (French); literally, "my lord" (as *madame* is "my lady"), and thus used alone as a courtesy title.

CLAIRE   Ah! So you want to talk. . . . Very well. Threaten me. Insult your
mistress, Solange. You want to talk about Monsieur's misfortunes, don't
you? Fool. It was hardly the moment to allude to him, but I can turn this
matter to fine account! You're smiling? Do you doubt it?

50 SOLANGE   The time is not yet ripe to unearth—

CLAIRE   What a word! My infamy? My infamy! To unearth!

SOLANGE   Madame!

CLAIRE   Am I to be at your mercy for having denounced Monsieur to the
police, for having sold him? And yet I'd have done even worse, or better.

55 You think I haven't suffered? Claire, I forced my hand to pen the letter—
without mistakes in spelling or syntax, without crossing anything out—the
letter that sent my lover to prison. And you, instead of standing by me, you
mock me. You force your colors on me! You speak of widowhood! He isn't
dead. Claire, Monsieur will be led from prison to prison, perhaps even to

60 Devil's Island,[4] where I, his mistress, mad with grief, shall follow him. I
shall be in the convoy. I shall share his glory. You speak of widowhood and
deny me the white gown—the mourning of queens. You're unaware of that,
Claire—

SOLANGE [coldly]   Madame will wear the red dress.

65 CLAIRE [simply]   Quite. [Severely] Hand me the dress. Oh! I'm so alone and
friendless. I can see in your eyes that you loathe me. You don't care what
happens to me.

SOLANGE   I'll follow you everywhere. I love you.

CLAIRE   No doubt. As one loves a mistress. You love and respect me. And

70 you're hoping for a legacy, a codicil in your favor—

SOLANGE   I'd do all in my power—

CLAIRE [ironically]   I know. You'd go through fire for me. [SOLANGE helps
CLAIRE put on her dress.] Fasten it. Don't pull so hard. Don't try to bind me.
[SOLANGE kneels at CLAIRE's feet and arranges the folds of the dress.] Avoid

75 pawing me. You smell like an animal. You've brought those odors from
some foul attic, where the lackeys visit us at night. The maid's room! The
garret! [Graciously] Claire, if I speak of the smell of garrets, it is for memory's sake. And of the twin beds where two sisters fall asleep, dreaming of
one another. There, [She points to a spot in the room.] there, the two iron

85 beds with the night table between them. There, [She points to a spot opposite.] the pinewood dresser with the little altar to the Holy Virgin![5] That's
right, isn't it?

SOLANGE   We're so unhappy. I could cry! If you go on—

CLAIRE   It is right, isn't it! Let's skip the business of your prayers and kneeling.

85 I won't even mention the paper flowers. . . . [She laughs.] Paper flowers! And
the branch of holy boxwood! [She points to the flowers in the room.] Just look
at these flowers open in my honor! Claire, am I not a lovelier Virgin?

SOLANGE [as if in adoration]   Be quiet—

CLAIRE   And there, [She points to a very high spot at the window.] that notori-

90 ous skylight from which a half-naked milkman jumps to your bed!

SOLANGE   Madame is forgetting herself, Madame—

---

4. The notorious French penal colony;
located several miles off the shore of French
Guiana, on the northern coast of South
America, it operated from 1852 to 1952.
5. That is, the Virgin Mary; the mother of
Jesus.

CLAIRE And what about your hands? Don't *you* forget your hands. How often have I [*She hesitates.*] murmured: they befoul the sink.

SOLANGE The fall!

95 CLAIRE Eh?

SOLANGE [*arranging the dress on* CLAIRE's *hips*] The fall of your dress. I'm arranging your fall from grace.

CLAIRE Get away, you bungler! [*She kicks* SOLANGE *in the temple with her Louis-Quinze heel.* SOLANGE, *who is kneeling, staggers and draws back.*]

SOLANGE Oh! Me a burglar?

100 CLAIRE I said bungler; and if you must whimper, do it in your garret. Here, in my bedroom, I will have only noble tears. A time will come when the hem of my gown will be studded with them, but those will be precious tears. Arrange my train, you clod.

SOLANGE [*in ecstasy*] Madame's being carried away!

105 CLAIRE By the devil! He's carrying me away in his fragrant arms. He's lifting me up, I leave the ground, I'm off. . . . [*She stamps with her heel.*] And I stay behind. Get my necklace! But hurry, we won't have time. If the gown's too long, make a hem with some safety pins. [SOLANGE *gets up and goes to take the necklace from a jewel case, but* CLAIRE *rushes ahead of her and seizes the jewels. Her fingers graze those of* SOLANGE, *and she recoils in horror.*] Keep your hands off mine! I can't stand your touching me. Hurry up!

110 SOLANGE There's no need to overdo it. Your eyes are ablaze.

CLAIRE [*shocked astonishment*] What's that you said?

SOLANGE Limits, boundaries, Madame. Frontiers are not conventions but laws. Here, my lands; there, your shore—

CLAIRE What language, my dear. Claire, do you mean that I've already

115 crossed the seas? Are you offering me the dreary exile of your imagination? You're taking revenge, aren't you? You feel the time coming when, no longer a maid—

SOLANGE You see straight through me. You divine my thoughts.

CLAIRE [*increasingly carried away*] —the time coming when, no longer a

120 maid, you become vengeance itself, but, Claire, don't forget—Claire, are you listening?—don't forget, it was the maid who hatched schemes of vengeance, and I—Claire, you're not listening.

SOLANGE [*absent-mindedly*] I'm listening.

CLAIRE And I contain within me both vengeance and the maid and give

125 them a chance for life, a chance for salvation. Claire, it's a burden, it's terribly painful to be a mistress, to contain all the springs of hatred, to be the dunghill on which you grow. You want to see me naked every day. I *am* beautiful, am I not? And the desperation of my love makes me even more so, but you have no idea what strength I need!

130 SOLANGE [*contemptuously*] Your lover!

CLAIRE My unhappy lover heightens my nobility. Yes. Yes, my child. All that you'll ever know is your own baseness.

SOLANGE That'll do! Now hurry! Are you ready?

CLAIRE Are you?

135 SOLANGE [*she steps back to the wardrobe*] I'm ready.—I'm tired of being an object of disgust. I hate you, too. I despise you. I hate your scented bosom. Your . . . *ivory* bosom! Your . . . *golden* thighs! Your . . . *amber* feet! I hate you! [*She spits on the red dress.*]

CLAIRE [*aghast*]   Oh! . . . Oh! . . . But . . .

140 SOLANGE [*walking up to her*]   Yes, my proud beauty. You think you can always
do just as you like. You think you can deprive me forever of the beauty
of the sky, that you can choose your perfumes and powders, your nail polish
and silk and velvet and lace, and deprive *me* of them? That you can steal
the milkman from me? Admit it! Admit about the milkman. His youth and
145 vigor excite you, don't they? Admit about the milkman. For Solange says: to
hell with you!

CLAIRE [*panic-stricken*]   Claire! Claire!

SOLANGE   Eh?

CLAIRE [*in a murmur*]   Claire, Solange, Claire.

150 SOLANGE   Ah! Yes, Claire, Claire says: to hell with you! Claire is here, more
dazzling than ever. Radiant! [*She slaps* CLAIRE.]

CLAIRE   Oh! . . . Oh! Claire . . . You . . . Oh!

SOLANGE   Madame thought she was protected by her barricade of flowers,
saved by some special destiny, by a sacrifice. But she reckoned without a
155 maid's rebellion. Behold her wrath, Madame. She turns your pretty
speeches to nought. She'll cut the ground from under your fine adventure.
Your Monsieur was just a cheap thief, and you—

CLAIRE   I forbid you! Confound your impudence!

SOLANGE   Twaddle! She forbids me! It's Madame who's confounded. Her
160 face is all convulsed. Would you like a mirror? Here. [*She hands* CLAIRE *a
mirror.*]

CLAIRE [*regarding herself with satisfaction*]   I see the marks of a slap, but now
I'm more beautiful than ever!

SOLANGE   Yes, a slap!

CLAIRE   Danger is my halo, Claire; and you, you dwell in darkness. . . .

165 SOLANGE   But the darkness is dangerous.—I know. I've heard all that before.
I can tell by your face what I'm supposed to answer. So I'll finish it up.
Now, here are the two maids, the faithful servants! They're standing in
front of you. Despise them. Look more beautiful.—We no longer fear you.
We're merged, enveloped in our fumes, in our revels, in our hatred of you.
170 The mold is setting. We're taking shape, Madame. Don't laugh—ah! above
all, don't laugh at my grandiloquence. . . .

CLAIRE   Get out!

SOLANGE   But only to be of further service to Madame! I'm going back to my
kitchen, back to my gloves and the smell of my teeth. To my belching sink.
175 You have your flowers, I my sink. I'm the maid. You, at least, you can't
defile me. But! But! . . . [*She advances on* CLAIRE, *threateningly.*] But before
I go back, I'm going to finish the job. [*Suddenly an alarm clock goes off.
SOLANGE stops. The two actresses, in a state of agitation, run together. They
huddle and listen.*] Already?

CLAIRE   Let's hurry! Madame'll be back. [*She starts to unfasten her dress.*]
180 Help me. It's over already. And you didn't get to the end.

SOLANGE [*helping her. In a sad tone of voice*]   The same thing happens every
time. And it's all your fault, you're never ready. I can't finish you off.

CLAIRE   We waste too much time with the preliminaries. But we've still . . .

SOLANGE [*as she helps* CLAIRE *out of her dress*]   Watch at the window.

185 CLAIRE   We've still got a little time left. I set the clock so we'd be able to put
the things in order. [*She drops wearily into the armchair.*]

SOLANGE [*gently*]   It's so close this evening. It's been close all day.

CLAIRE [*gently*]   Yes.

SOLANGE   Is that what's killing us, Claire?

190 CLAIRE   Yes.

SOLANGE   It's time now.

CLAIRE   Yes. [*She gets up wearily.*] I'm going to make the tea.

SOLANGE   Watch at the window.

CLAIRE   There's time. [*She wipes her face.*]

195 SOLANGE   Still looking at yourself . . . Claire, dear . . .

CLAIRE   Let me alone. I'm exhausted.

SOLANGE [*sternly*]   Watch at the window. Thanks to you, the whole place is
   in a mess again. And I've got to clean Madame's gown. [*She stares at her
   sister.*] Well, what's the matter with you? You can be like me now. Be your-

200   self again. Come on, Claire, be my sister again.

CLAIRE   I'm finished. That light's killing me. Do you think the people
   opposite . . .

SOLANGE   Who cares! You don't expect us to . . . [*She hesitates.*] organize
   things in the dark? Have a rest. Shut your eyes. Shut your eyes, Claire.

205 CLAIRE [*she puts on her short black dress*]   Oh! When I say I'm exhausted, it's
   just a way of talking. Don't use it to pity me. Stop trying to dominate me.

SOLANGE   I've never tried to dominate you. I only want you to rest. You'll help
   me more by resting.

CLAIRE   I understand, don't explain.

210 SOLANGE   Yes, I will explain. It was you who started it. When you mentioned
   the milkman. You think I couldn't see what you were driving at? If Mario—

CLAIRE   Oh!

SOLANGE   If the milkman says indecent things to me, he does to you, too.
   But you loved mingling. . . .

215 CLAIRE [*shrugging her shoulders*]   You'd better see whether everything's in
   order. Look, the key of the secretary[6] was like this [*She arranges the key.*]
   and, as Monsieur says—

SOLANGE [*violently*]   You loved mingling your insults—

CLAIRE   He's always finding the maids' hairs all over the pinks and roses!

220 SOLANGE   And things about our private life with—

CLAIRE   With? With? With what? Say it! Go on, name it! The ceremony?
   Besides, we've no time to start a discussion now. She'll be back, back, back!
   But, Solange, this time we've got her. I envy you; I wish I could have seen
   the expression on her face when she heard about her lover's arrest. For

225   once in my life, I did a good job. You've got to admit it. If it weren't for me,
   if it hadn't been for my anonymous letter, you'd have missed a pretty sight:
   the lover handcuffed and Madame in tears. It's enough to kill her. This
   morning she could hardly stand up.

SOLANGE   Fine. She can drop dead! And I'll inherit! Not to have to set foot

230   again in that filthy garret, with those two idiots, that cook and that butler.

CLAIRE   I really liked our garret.

SOLANGE   Just to contradict me. Don't start getting sentimental about it. I
   loathe it and I see it as it really is, bare and mean. And shabby. But what of
   it! We're just scum!

---

6. A writing desk, usually topped by a cabinet.

235 CLAIRE Ah! No, don't start that again. Better watch at the window. I can't
see a thing. It's too dark outside.

SOLANGE Let me talk. Let me get it out of my system. I liked the garret
because it was plain and I didn't have to put on a show. No hangings to
push aside, no rugs to shake, no furniture to caress—with my eyes or with
240 a rag, no mirrors, no balcony. Nothing forced us to make pretty gestures.
Don't worry, you'll be able to go on playing queen, playing at Marie Antoi-
nette,[7] strolling about the apartment at night.

CLAIRE You're mad! I've never strolled about the apartment.

SOLANGE [*ironically*] Oh, no. Mademoiselle has never gone strolling!
245 Wrapped in the curtains or the lace bedcover. Oh no! Looking at herself in
the mirrors, strutting on the balcony at two in the morning, and greeting
the populace which has turned out to parade beneath her windows. Never,
oh no, never.

CLAIRE But, Solange—

250 SOLANGE It's too dark at night for spying on Madame, and you thought you
were invisible on your balcony. What do you take me for? Don't try to tell
me you walk in your sleep. At the stage we've reached you can admit it.

CLAIRE But, Solange, you're shouting. Please, please lower your voice.
Madame may come in without making a sound. . . . [*She runs to the window and lifts the curtain.*]

255 SOLANGE All right, I've had my say. Let go of the curtains. Oh, I can't stand
the way you lift them. Let go of them. It upsets me; that's how Monsieur
did it when he was spying on the police, the morning he was arrested.

CLAIRE So you're scared now? The slightest gesture makes you feel like a
murderer trying to slip away by the service stairway.

260 SOLANGE Go on, be sarcastic, work me up! Go on, be sarcastic! Nobody
loves me! Nobody loves us!

CLAIRE *She* does, *she* loves us. She's kind. Madame is kind! Madame adores
us.

SOLANGE She loves us the way she loves her armchair. Not even *that* much!
265 Like her bidet, rather. Like her pink enamel toilet seat. And we, can't love
one another. Filth . . .

CLAIRE Ah! . . .

SOLANGE . . . doesn't love filth. D'you think I'm going to put up with it, that
I'm going to keep playing this game and then at night go back to my folding
270 cot? The game! Will we even be able to go on with it? And if I have to stop
spitting on someone who calls me Claire, I'll simply choke! My spurt of
saliva is my spray of diamonds!

CLAIRE [*she stands up and cries*] Speak more softly, please, please. Speak—
speak of Madame's kindness.

275 SOLANGE Her kindness, is it? It's easy to be kind, and smiling, and sweet—ah!
that sweetness of hers!—when you're beautiful and rich. But what if you're
only a maid? The best you can do is to give yourself airs while you're doing
the cleaning or washing up. You twirl a feather duster like a fan. You make
fancy gestures with the dishcloth. Or like *you*, you treat yourself to histori-
280 cal parades in Madame's apartment.

---

7. As the wife of Louis XVI, the queen of France (1755–1793), legendary for her extravagance. She
and her husband were executed by the revolutionary government in 1793.

CLAIRE Solange! You're starting again! What are you trying to do? We'll never calm down if you talk like that! I could say a thing or two about you.

SOLANGE You? You?

CLAIRE Yes, me. If I wanted to. Because, after all . . .

285 SOLANGE All? After all? What are you insinuating? It was you who started talking about that man. Claire, I hate you.

CLAIRE Same to you and more! But if I wanted to provoke you, I wouldn't have to use the milkman as an excuse. I've got something better on you and you know it.

290 SOLANGE Who's going to get the better of who? Eh? Well, say something?

CLAIRE Go on, start it! You hit first. It's you who're backing out, Solange. You don't dare accuse me of the worst: my letters. Pages and pages of them. The garret was littered with them. I invented the most fantastic stories and you used them for your own purposes. You frittered away my frenzy. Yester-

295 day, when you were Madame, I could see how delighted you were at the chance they gave you to stow away on the *Lamartiniere*,[8] to flee France in the company of your lover—

SOLANGE Claire—

CLAIRE Your lover, to Devil's Island, to Guiana. You were delighted that my

300 letters allowed you to be the prostitute kneeling at the feet of the thief. You were happy to sacrifice yourself, to bear the cross of the impenitent thief, to wipe his face, to stand by him, to take his place in the galleys so that he could rest. And you felt yourself growing. Your brow rose higher than mine, it rose above the palm trees.

305 SOLANGE But what about you, just before, when you were talking about following him. . . .

CLAIRE Right. I don't deny it. I took up where you left off. But with less violence than you. Even in the garret, amidst all the letters, you started swaying back and forth with the pitching of the boat.

310 SOLANGE You didn't see yourself—

CLAIRE I did. I'm more sensible than you. You're the one who concocted the story. Turn your head. Ha! If only you could see yourself, Solange. Your face is still lit up by the sun setting through the virgin forest! You're planning his escape! [*She laughs nervously.*] You certainly do work yourself up!

315 But don't let it worry you; it would be cruel to disturb your blissful voyage. I hate you for other reasons, and you know what they are.

SOLANGE [*lowering her voice*] I'm not afraid of you. I know you hate me and that you're a sneak, but be careful now. I'm older than you.

CLAIRE So what?—Older! And stronger too? You're trying to put me off by

320 making me talk about that man. Hmph! You think I haven't found you out? You tried to kill her.

SOLANGE Are you accusing me?

CLAIRE Don't deny it. I saw you.

[*A long silence.*]

And I was frightened. Frightened, Solange. Through her, it was me you

325 were aiming at. I'm the one who's in danger. When we finish the ceremony, I'll protect my neck.

[*A long silence.* SOLANGE *shrugs her shoulders.*]

8. A prison ship.

SOLANGE [*with decision*] Is that all? Yes, I did try. I wanted to free you. I
couldn't bear it any longer. It made me suffocate to see you suffocating, to
see you turning red and green, rotting away in that woman's bittersweet-
ness. Blame me for it, you're right. I loved you too much. Had I killed her,
you'd have been the first to denounce me. You'd have turned me over to the
police, yes, you.

CLAIRE [*she seizes her by the wrists*] Solange. . . .

SOLANGE [*freeing herself*] What are *you* afraid of? It's *my* concern.

CLAIRE Solange, my little sister, she'll be back soon.

SOLANGE I didn't kill anyone. I was a coward, you realize. I did the best I
could, but she turned over in her sleep. [*Rising exaltation*] She was breathing softly. She swelled out the sheets: it was Madame.

CLAIRE Stop it.

SOLANGE Now you want to stop me. You wanted to know, didn't you. Well,
wait, I've got some more to tell you. You'll see what your sister's made of.
What stuff she's made of. What a servant girl really is. I wanted to strangle
her—

CLAIRE Let me alone. Think of what comes after.

SOLANGE Nothing comes after. I'm sick and tired of kneeling in pews. In
church I'd have had the red velvet of abbesses or the stone of the penitents,
but my bearing at least would have been noble. Look, just look at how she
suffers. How she suffers in beauty. Grief transfigures her, doesn't it? Beau-
tifies her? When she learned that her lover was a thief, she stood up to the
police. She exulted. Now she is forlorn and splendid, supported under each
arm by two devoted servants whose hearts bleed to see her grief. Did you
see it? Her grief sparkling with the glint of her jewels, with the satin of her
gowns, in the glow of the chandelier! Claire, I wanted to make up for the
poverty of my grief by the splendor of my crime. Afterward, I'd have set fire
to the lot.

CLAIRE Solange, calm down. The fire might not have caught. You'd have
been found out. You know what happens to incendiaries.

SOLANGE I know everything. I kept my eye and ear to the keyhole. No servant ever listened at doors as I did. I know everything. Incendiary! It's a
splendid title.

CLAIRE Be quiet. I'm stifling. You're stifling me. [*She wants to open the window.*] Oh! Let's have some air!

SOLANGE Get away from the window. Open the anteroom and the kitchen
doors. [CLAIRE *opens both doors.*] Go and see whether the water's boiling.

CLAIRE All alone?

SOLANGE Wait, all right, wait till she comes. She's bringing her stars, her
tears, her smiles, her sighs. She'll corrupt us with her sweetness.

    [*The telephone rings. The two sisters listen.*]

CLAIRE [*at the telephone*] Monsieur? It's Monsieur! . . . This is Claire, Monsieur. . . . [SOLANGE *wants to hear too, but* CLAIRE *pushes her away.*] Very
well. I'll inform Madame. Madame will be overjoyed to hear that Monsieur
is free. . . . Yes, Monsieur. . . . Very well. . . . Good-by, Monsieur. [*She
wants to hang up, but her hand trembles, and she lays the receiver on the
table.*]

SOLANGE Is he out?

CLAIRE The judge let him out on bail.

SOLANGE   Well, you've done a fine job. My compliments. Your denunciations,
375   your letters, it's working out beautifully. And if they recognize your handwriting, it'll be perfect.

CLAIRE   Please, please, don't overwhelm me. Since you're so clever, you
should have managed your business with Madame. But you were afraid.
The bed was warm. The air thick with perfume. It was Madame! We've got
380   to carry on with the same kind of life. With the same old game. But, you
poor wretch! Even the game is dangerous. I'm sure we've left traces. We
leave them every time. I see a host of traces I'll never be able to cover up.
And she, she walks about in her tamed menagerie. She unravels the clues.
She points to our traces with the tip of her pink toe. She discovers us, one
385   by one. Madame jeers at us. And it's your fault. All's lost because you
lacked strength.

SOLANGE   I can still find whatever strength I need.

CLAIRE   Where? Where? You've been outstripped by *me*. You don't live above
the treetops. A milkman passing through your mind gets you all flustered.

390   SOLANGE   It was because I couldn't see her face, Claire. Because I was so
close to Madame, so close to her sleep. I lost my strength. In order to get
at her throat, I'd have had to lift the sheet from her heaving bosom.

CLAIRE [*ironically*]   And the sheets were warm. The night dark. That kind of
thing has to be done in broad daylight. You're incapable of it. It's too terri-
395   ble a deed. But *I* can manage it.

SOLANGE   Claire!

CLAIRE   Where you botched it, *I'll* succeed.

SOLANGE [*she runs a comb through her hair*]   Claire, don't get carried away,
don't be rash—

400   CLAIRE   What makes you think I'm being rash? First of all, don't mix your
hairpins up with mine! You . . . Oh! All right, mix your muck with mine.
Mix it! Mix your rags with my tatters! Mix it all up. It'll stink of the maids.
So Monsieur won't have any trouble discovering us. And we'll die in a flood
of shame. [*Suddenly calm*] I'm capable of anything, you know.

405   SOLANGE   The sleeping pills.

CLAIRE   Yes. Let's talk calmly. I'm strong. You tried to dominate me. . . .

SOLANGE   But, Claire—

CLAIRE [*calmly*]   I beg your pardon, but I know what I'm saying. I've made
up my mind. I'm ready. I'm tired of it all. Tired of being the spider, the
410   umbrella case, the shabby, godless nun, without a family! I'm tired of
having a stove for an altar. I'm that disagreeable, sullen, smelly girl. To
you, too.

SOLANGE   Claire . . . we're both nervous. [*Anxiously*] Where's Madame? I
can't stand it any more either. I can't stand our being so alike, I can't stand
415   my hands, my black stockings, my hair. I'm not reproaching you for anything, my little sister. I understand that your strolls through the apartment
helped ease the strain.

CLAIRE [*irritated*]   Ah! Stop it!

SOLANGE   I want to help you. I want to comfort you, but I know I disgust
420   you. I'm repulsive to you. And I know it because you disgust me. When
slaves love one another, it's not love.

CLAIRE   And me, I'm sick of seeing my image thrown back at me by a mirror,
like a bad smell. You're my bad smell. Well, I'm ready. Ready to bite. I'll
have my crown and I shall stroll about the apartment.

425 SOLANGE   That's not reason enough to kill her.

CLAIRE   Really? Why, please? For what other reason? Where and when could we find a better excuse? Ah, so it's not enough, not enough to be raped by a milkman who goes blithely through our garrets? Tonight Madame will witness our shame. Bursting with laughter, laughing until
430 the tears roll down her face, with her flabby sighs. No. I shall have my crown. I shall be the poisoner that you failed to be. It's my turn now to dominate you!

SOLANGE   But I never . . .

CLAIRE   Hand me the towel! Hand me the clothespins! Peel the onions! Scrape the carrots! Scrub the tiles! It's over. Over. Ah! I almost forgot! Turn
435 off the tap! It's over. [*Exalted*] I'll run the world!

SOLANGE   My little baby sister!

CLAIRE   You'll help me.

SOLANGE   You won't know what gestures to make. Things are more serious, Claire, and simpler too.

440 CLAIRE [*exalted*]   We've read the story of Sister Holy Cross of the Blessed Valley who poisoned twenty-seven Arabs. She walked without shoes, with her feet all stiff. She was lifted up, carried off to the crime. We've read the story of Princess Albanarez who caused the death of her lover and her husband. She uncorked the bottle and made a big sign of the cross over the
445 goblet. As she stood before the corpses, she saw only death and, off in the distance, the fleet image of herself being carried by the wind. She made all the gestures of earthly despair. In the book about the Marquise de Venosa, the one who poisoned her children, we're told that, as she approached the bed, her arms were supported by the ghost of her lover.[9]

450 SOLANGE   Baby sister, my angel!

CLAIRE   I'll be supported by the sturdy arms of the milkman. I'll lean my left hand on the back of his neck. He won't flinch. You'll help me. And, far away, Solange, if we have to go far away, if I have to leave for Devil's Island, you'll come with me. You'll board the boat. The flight you were planning for
455 him can be used for me. We shall be that eternal couple, Solange, the two of us, the eternal couple of the criminal and the saint. We'll be saved, Solange, saved, I swear to you! [*She falls on* MADAME's *bed.*]

SOLANGE   Be calm. You're going to sleep. I'll carry you upstairs.

CLAIRE   Let me alone. Turn out the light. Please turn out the light. [SOLANGE *turns out the light.*]

460 SOLANGE   Rest. Rest, little sister. [*She kneels, removes* CLAIRE's *shoes, kisses her feet.*] Be calm, my darling. [*She caresses her.*] Put your feet on my shoulders. There. Close your eyes.

CLAIRE [*she sighs*]   I'm ashamed, Solange.

SOLANGE [*very gently*]   Don't talk. Leave things to me. I'm going to put you to
465 bed and, when you fall asleep, I'll carry you upstairs, to the garret. I'll undress you and put you into your little cot. Sleep. I'll be here.

CLAIRE   I'm ashamed, Solange.

SOLANGE   Sh! Let me tell you a story.

CLAIRE [*simply*]   Solange.

470 SOLANGE   My angel?

CLAIRE   Solange, listen . . .

SOLANGE   Sleep. [*A long silence*]

---

9. These stories were apparently invented by Genet.

CLAIRE   You have lovely hair. You have such lovely hair. Hers—

SOLANGE   Don't talk about her any more.

475 CLAIRE   Hers is false. [*A long silence*] Do you remember? Under the tree, just the two of us? Our feet in the sun? Solange?

SOLANGE   I'm here. Sleep. I'm your big sister.

[*Silence. A moment later* CLAIRE *gets up.*]

CLAIRE   No! No weakness! Put the light on! Put it on! Quick! It's too great a moment! [SOLANGE *puts the light on.*] Stand up. And let's eat. What's in the

480 kitchen? Eh? We've got to eat. To be strong. Come along, you'll advise me. The phenobarbital.[1]

SOLANGE   I'm too exhausted. Yes, the phenobarbital.

CLAIRE   The phenobarbital! Don't make such a face. We must be joyous. And sing. Let's sing! Sing, the way you'll sing when you go begging in the courts

485 and embassies! Laugh! [*They burst out laughing.*] Otherwise, it'll be so tragic that we'll go flying out the window. Shut the window. [SOLANGE, *laughing, shuts the window.*] Murder is a thing that's . . . unspeakable!

SOLANGE   Let's sing! We'll carry her off to the woods, and under the fir trees we'll cut her to bits by the light of the moon. And we'll sing. We'll bury her

490 beneath the flowers, in our flower beds, and at night—we'll water her *toes* with a little *hose!* [*The front doorbell rings.*]

CLAIRE   It's Madame!

SOLANGE   It must be her! Straighten the bed. [*She seizes her sister by the wrists.*] Claire, are you sure you can go through with it?

495 CLAIRE   How many do we need?

SOLANGE   About ten. Put ten pills into her tea. Will you do it?

CLAIRE   [*she frees herself, goes to tidy the bed, stares at it for a moment*]   Yes. I've got the tube in my pocket.

[*Exit* SOLANGE, *left.* CLAIRE *continues tidying the room and leaves right. A few seconds elapse. A burst of nervous laughter backstage.* MADAME, *in a fur coat, enters laughing, with* SOLANGE *behind her.*]

MADAME   There's no end to it! Such horrible gladioli, such a sickly pink, and

500 mimosa! They probably hunt through the market before dawn to get them cheaper. [SOLANGE *helps her off with her coat.*]

SOLANGE   Madame wasn't too cold?

MADAME   Yes, Solange, I was very cold. I've been trailing through corridors all night long. I've been seeing frozen men and stony faces, but I did man-

505 age to catch a glimpse of Monsieur. From a distance. I waved to him. I've only just left the wife of a magistrate. Claire!

SOLANGE   She's preparing Madame's tea.

MADAME   I wish she'd hurry. I'm ashamed to ask for tea when Monsieur is all alone, without a thing, without food, without cigarettes.

510 SOLANGE   But Monsieur won't stay there long. They'll see right away that he's not guilty.

MADAME   Guilty or not, I shall never desert him, never. You see, Solange, it's at times like this that you realize how much you love someone. I don't think he's guilty either, but if he were, I'd become his accomplice. I'd fol-

515 low him to Devil's Island, to Siberia.[2]

---

1. A barbiturate, prescribed as an anticonvul-sant and, formerly, as a sedative.
2. A region used as a place of exile and penal colonies, first by czarist Russia and then, beginning in the 1930s, by the Soviet Union.

SOLANGE   There's no need to get panicky. I've seen worse cases acquitted. There was a trial in Bordeaux[3]—

MADAME   Do you go to trials? You?

SOLANGE   I read the crime news. It was about a man who—

520 MADAME   You can't compare Monsieur's case. He's been accused of the most idiotic thefts. I know he'll get out of it. All I mean is that, as a result of this preposterous affair, I've come to realize how deeply attached I am to him. Of course, none of this is serious, but if it were, Solange, it would be a joy for me to bear his cross. I'd follow him from place to place, from prison to
525   prison, on foot if need be, as far as the penal colony.

SOLANGE   They wouldn't let you. Only bandits' wives, or their sisters, or their mothers, are allowed to follow them.

MADAME   A condemned man is no longer a bandit. And then I'd force my way in, past the guards. [*Suddenly conquettish*] And, Solange, I'd be utterly
530   fearless. I'd use my weapons. What do you take me for?

SOLANGE   Madame mustn't get such ideas into her head. You must rest.

MADAME   I'm not tired. You treat me like an invalid. You're always ready to coddle me and pamper me as if I were dying. Thank God, I've got my wits about me. I'm ready for the fight. [*She looks at* SOLANGE *and, feeling that*
535   *she has hurt her, adds, with a smile*] Come, come, don't make such a face. [*With sudden violence*] All right, it's true! There are times when you're so sweet that I simply can't stand it. It crushes me, stifles me! And those flowers which are there for the very opposite of a celebration!

SOLANGE   If Madame means that we lack discretion . . .

540 MADAME   But I didn't mean anything of the kind, my dear girl. It's just that I'm so upset. You see what a state I'm in.

SOLANGE   Would Madame like to see the day's accounts?

MADAME   You certainly picked the right time. You must be mad. Do you think I could look at figures now? Show them to me tomorrow.

545 SOLANGE [*putting away the fur cape*]   The lining's torn. I'll take it to the furrier tomorrow.

MADAME   If you like. Though it's hardly worthwhile. I'm giving up my wardrobe. Besides, I'm an old woman.

SOLANGE   There go those gloomy ideas again.

550 MADAME   I'm thinking of going into mourning. Don't be surprised if I do. How can I lead a worldly life when Monsieur is in prison? If you find the house too sad . . .

SOLANGE   We'll never desert Madame.

MADAME   I know you won't, Solange. You've not been too unhappy with me,
555   have you?

SOLANGE   Oh!

MADAME   When you needed anything, I saw that you got it. With my old gowns alone you both could have dressed like princesses. Besides . . . [*She goes to the closet and looks at her dresses.*] of what use will they be to me?
560   I'm through with finery and all that goes with it.

          [CLAIRE *enters carrying the tea.*]

CLAIRE   The tea is ready.

MADAME   Farewell to parties and dances and the theater. You'll inherit all that.

CLAIRE   Madame is losing her self-control. She must pull herself together.

3. A major city in the Aquitaine region of southwestern France.

SOLANGE   The tea is ready.

565   MADAME   Put it down. I'm going to bed. It's all over. [*She runs her hand over the red velvet dress.*] My lovely "Fascination," the loveliest of them all. [*She takes it down and runs her hand over it.*] It was designed for me by Chanel.[4] Specially. Here, you may have it. It's yours. [*She gives it to* CLAIRE *and searches in the closet.*]

CLAIRE   For me?

570   MADAME   [*smiling sadly*]   Of course. I said so, didn't I?

SOLANGE   Madame is very kind. [*To* CLAIRE] You might thank Madame. You've been admiring it so long.

CLAIRE   It's so beautiful. I'll never dare wear it.

MADAME   You can have it altered. There's enough velvet in the train alone for

575   the sleeves. And for you, Solange, I'm going to give you. . . . What shall I give you? Here, this coat. [*She hands* SOLANGE *the magnificent fur cape.*]

CLAIRE   Oh! the fur cape!

SOLANGE   [*thrilled*]   Oh! Madame . . . never . . . Madame's too kind.

MADAME   No, no, don't thank me. It's such a pleasure to make people happy.

580   Now I'm going to get undressed. [*She looks at the telephone.*] Who left the receiver off?

CLAIRE   It was Monsieur. . . . [*She stops suddenly.*]

MADAME   [*dumbfounded*]   Eh? Monsieur? [CLAIRE *is silent.*] What do you mean? Speak up!

585   SOLANGE   [*slowly and as if in spite of herself*]   When Monsieur rang up.

MADAME   What are you talking about? Monsieur phoned?

SOLANGE   We wanted to surprise Madame. Monsieur's out on bail. He's waiting for Madame at the Hong-Kong Bar.

MADAME   [*rising to her feet*]   And you didn't say anything! Go get a taxi! Sol-

590   ange, quick, quick, get me a taxi. And hurry up. Go on, run. [*She pushes* SOLANGE *out of the room.*] My furs! Quick, quick! You're both mad. You let me go on talking. You really are mad. Or am *I* going mad! [*She puts on her fur coat. To* CLAIRE] When did he phone?

CLAIRE   [*in a toneless voice*]   Five minutes before Madame came in.

595   MADAME   But you should have told me. And this cold tea! I'll never be able to wait for Solange to get back! Oh! What did he say?

CLAIRE   What I've just told you. He was very calm.

MADAME   Ah, him, he always is. He'd be utterly unconcerned if he were condemned to death. The man's unique! What else did he say?

600   CLAIRE   Nothing. He said the judge was letting him out.

MADAME   How can anyone leave police headquarters at midnight? Do judges work as late as that?

CLAIRE   Sometimes, much later.

MADAME   Much later? How do *you* know that?

605   CLAIRE   I read *True Detective*.[5] I know those things.

MADAME   [*astonished*]   Oh you do? You really are an odd little girl, Claire. She *might* hurry. [*She looks at her wristwatch.*] You won't forget to have the lining of my coat sewn?

CLAIRE   I'll take it to the furrier tomorrow. [*A long silence*]

4. Coco Chanel (1883–1971), prominent French fashion designer.
5. The earliest magazine of this title, which claimed to present true stories of crime, was published in the United States (1924–95).

610 MADAME   What about the accounts? The day's accounts. Let me see them.
I've got time!

CLAIRE   Solange attends to that.

MADAME   That's right. I'm all in a dither. I'll look at them tomorrow. [*Staring at* CLAIRE] Come a little closer! Come here! Why . . . you've got makeup on!
615 [*Laughing*] Why Claire, you've been putting makeup on!

CLAIRE [*very embarrassed*]   Madame . . .

MADAME   Ah, don't lie! Besides, you've every right to. Live, my child, live. In whose honor is it? Eh? Got a crush on someone? Own up!

CLAIRE   I put a little powder on. . . .

620 MADAME   That's not powder, it's makeup. But there's nothing wrong in that, you're still young. Make yourself attractive. Smarten up. [*She puts a flower in* CLAIRE's *hair. She looks at her wristwatch.*] What *can* she be doing? It's midnight and she's not back!

CLAIRE   There aren't many taxis at this hour. She probably had to run to the
625 cab-stand.

MADAME   You think so? I've lost track of time. I'm wild with happiness. Monsieur ringing up at a time like that! And that he's free.

CLAIRE   Madame ought to sit down. I'll go and heat up the tea. [*She starts to leave.*]

MADAME   Don't bother, I'm not thirsty. It's champagne we'll be drinking
630 tonight. You can be sure we won't be coming home.

CLAIRE   Really, just a little tea . . .

MADAME [*laughing*]   I'm nervous enough as it is. I don't want you and Solange to wait up for us. Go upstairs and get to bed right away. [*Suddenly she sees the alarm clock.*] But . . . That alarm clock, what's that doing here?
635 Where does it come from?

CLAIRE [*very embarrassed*]   The alarm clock? It's the kitchen clock.

MADAME   It is? I've never seen it before.

CLAIRE [*she takes the alarm clock*]   It belongs on the shelf. It's always been there.

640 MADAME [*smiling*]   It's true I'm something of a stranger in the kitchen. You're at home there. It's your domain. You're its sovereigns. But, I wonder why you brought it in here?

CLAIRE   It was Solange, for the cleaning. She'd never dare trust the big clock.

MADAME   How odd.

[CLAIRE *goes out carrying the alarm clock.*]

645 How odd. [*She looks at her wristwatch.*] She's certainly taking her time. You can find taxis at every street corner. [*She sits down at her dressing table. She looks at herself in the mirror and talks to herself.*] And what about you, you fool, will you be beautiful enough to receive him? No wrinkles, eh? It's been such a long separation, it'll have been like a thousand years! Eh? Let's
650 see, now. Gay? Wistful? Idiot, you idiot, there I go talking to myself. Happiness makes me giddy. And Solange not back yet. All those flowers! Those girls do worship me, but—[*She looks at the top of the dressing table and blows at the powder.*] but they haven't dusted the dressing table. Their housekeeping is the most extraordinary combination of luxury and filth.

[*As she utters the last sentence,* CLAIRE *enters the room on tiptoe. She stands silently behind* MADAME *who suddenly notices her in the mirror.*]

655 Eh? I'm raving, Claire, my mind's wandering. Forgive me. Today's been too
dreadful.

CLAIRE   Isn't Madame satisfied with our work?

MADAME [*smiling*]   But I am, Claire. Delighted. In seventh heaven.

CLAIRE   Madame's making fun of us.

660 MADAME [*laughing*]   Oh, stop nagging me. After what I've been through
today, I've got a right to be out of sorts. In the first place, there's that business of the letters to the police. . . . I wonder who could have sent them. I
suppose you wouldn't have any idea?

CLAIRE   Does Madame mean . . . ?

665 MADAME   I don't mean anything. I'd like to know, that's all. I've been groping
around the whole day long as if I were blind. I felt like the police hunting
in the bushes for a girl's corpse.

CLAIRE   That's all over with. Monsieur is free.

MADAME   Thank heavens. Which still doesn't account for those letters. What
670 *can* she be doing? She's been gone an hour. Why didn't you tell me at once
that Monsieur had phoned? He'll be furious.

CLAIRE   We were terribly afraid of alarming Madame, of giving her a shock.

MADAME   That was very bright. You're quietly killing me with flowers and
kindness. One fine day I'll be found dead beneath the roses. Claire, what
675 do you think of this coiffure? Do you like it?

CLAIRE   If I might venture . . .

MADAME   Eh? If you might venture? Well, venture. I've full confidence in
your opinion. Well? What do you think of it?

CLAIRE   If I might be so bold as to make a suggestion, Madame's hair would
680 look fluffier worn over the forehead.

MADAME   Are you sure?

CLAIRE   It would soften Madame's face.

MADAME   Like that? You're right. You *are* a bright girl, Claire. You know,
Claire, I've always thought you had a great deal of taste and that you were
685 meant for better things.

CLAIRE   I'm not complaining.

MADAME   No, no, I know. But after all, you *are* more sensitive than the others. I realize that it's not much fun living with them. Fortunately you're
with your sister. You're a family. But with a bit of luck you—

690 CLAIRE   Oh! If I had wanted to!

MADAME   I don't doubt it! [*She listens.*] Listen! [*She stands up.*] Listen! A car.
It's her. Ah! [*She looks at herself again in the mirror.*]

CLAIRE   Madame should have some tea because of the cold.

MADAME [*laughing*]   You're trying to kill me with your tea and your flowers
695 and your suggestions. You're too much for me, Claire. No. I've never felt so
alive. Oh! And served in the best tea set, the *very best* set! Such pomp! Such
elegance! [*She wants to leave, but* CLAIRE *stands between her and the door.*]

CLAIRE [*imploringly*]   Madame *must* drink it. Otherwise . . .

[SOLANGE *dashes in. She pushes her sister aside and turns to* MADAME.]

MADAME   Well!

700 SOLANGE [*surprised*]   Ah! Madame's still here. I've looked everywhere. No
one wanted to come as late as this!

MADAME   Did you get a taxi?

SOLANGE   It's here, Madame. It's downstairs, Madame.

MADAME Let's hurry. So it's understood, you're to go upstairs and to bed.
705   And tomorrow morning we'll just sleep and sleep and sleep. Claire, come
    and close the door behind me. And you're not to latch it.

>   [*She leaves, followed by* CLAIRE. SOLANGE *is left alone.* CLAIRE *returns.*
>   *The two sisters look at one another.*]

SOLANGE [*ironically*] You certainly did a fine job. And you sneered at me.
CLAIRE Don't. I tried so hard not to say it, but I just couldn't help myself.
SOLANGE Didn't she drink it? [CLAIRE *shakes her head "no."*] Obviously. It
710   was to be expected.
CLAIRE I'd have liked to see *you* in my place. [*She remains motionless for a*
    moment and then starts walking toward the kitchen.]
SOLANGE Where are you going?
CLAIRE [*without turning around and in a weary voice*] To sleep!

>   [*She leaves.*]

SOLANGE Claire! [*Silence*] Claire! [*She goes to the door and calls her.*] Claire,
715   I'm calling you.
CLAIRE [*offstage*] Who cares?
SOLANGE [*facing the door at the right*] Come here. Do you hear me? Come
    here.

>   [CLAIRE *comes in untying her apron.*]

CLAIRE [*very wearily*] What do you want? Is it my fault? The "tay"—as she
720   says—was ready. I put in the pills. She wouldn't drink it!
SOLANGE And so you think we're just going to sit here and shake? [*She stares*
    hard at her sister.] They'll both be back tomorrow, drunk probably and
    vicious, like conquerors. They'll know where the letters came from. They—I
    hate her. [CLAIRE *shrugs her shoulders.*] Oh, I hate her! I loathe her. And
725   you, you just stand there! Didn't you see how she sparkled? How disgust-
    ingly happy she was? *Her* joy feeds on *our* shame. Her carnation is the red
    of our shame. Her dress . . . [*She kicks at the red velvet dress.*] It's the red of
    our shame. Her furs . . . Ah! She took back her furs! And you just stand
    there! You don't scream. Are you dead?
730 CLAIRE What do you want me to do? She got away from us. You came back
    too soon.
SOLANGE She gets away and you just stand there!
CLAIRE What do you want to do? Make a scene? Eh? [*She screams in the face*
    of SOLANGE, *who remains motionless.*] You want to make a scene? Answer.
735   Answer. Well, answer. We've got time. We've got all night.
SOLANGE [*in a very calm tone*] Let's get on with it.
CLAIRE What's the hurry? No, we'll take our time. Shall we? [*She unties her*
    apron.]
SOLANGE Keep your apron on. It's your turn.
CLAIRE No, that doesn't matter.
740 SOLANGE It's my turn to be Madame.
CLAIRE Take the apron.
SOLANGE But Claire . . .
CLAIRE [*simply*] I'm used to it. Here. [*She delicately hands the apron to* SOL-
    ANGE.] Do you think I've really got too much rouge on?
745 SOLANGE Rouge? Yes, there's some rouge left. . . . But you're not rouged.
    You're all made-up.
CLAIRE That's what she said.

SOLANGE   That's all over. [*She grabs the apron.*] Forced to wear that! But I
         want to be a real maid. [*She ties the strings behind her back.*] Put out the
750   light.
CLAIRE [*timidly*]   You . . . You don't want us to . . . to organize things in the
         dark?
SOLANGE   Do as I say. [*She puts out the light. The room is in semi-darkness.*
         The two sisters look at one another and speak, without moving.]
CLAIRE   Oh! Let's wait a little while, Solange. Suppose she comes back?
755   Madame might have forgotten something. At times like that one always
         forgets . . . one's bag, or money, or . . .
SOLANGE   Naive!
CLAIRE [*muttering*]   She left in such a hurry. It's a trap. Madame suspects
         something.
760 SOLANGE [*shrugging her shoulders*]   What? For instance?
CLAIRE   She's suspicious. We're being watched. . . .
SOLANGE   What of it? We're beyond that!
CLAIRE [*she wants to gain time*]   You're not listening to me, Solange. I assure
         you, I feel something, I feel it. Listen, we're being spied on. I'm sure she'll
765   come back unexpectedly. She'll have forgotten her handkerchief. Or her
         gloves. [SOLANGE *shrugs her shoulders.*] Or her compact, God knows what.
         But I feel there's something here, Solange—something in this room—that
         can record our gestures and play them back. Remember, Madame told us
         not to latch the front door. . . .
770 SOLANGE   You're raving.
CLAIRE   I'm not! No! Please, wait, please, it's so serious. Suppose she came
         back. . . .
SOLANGE   Too bad for her!
CLAIRE   You're growing terrible, Solange. You've got an answer for every-
775   thing. At least . . .
SOLANGE   What?
CLAIRE [*timidly*]   At least . . . suppose we said a prayer?
SOLANGE   Do you dare bring God . . .
CLAIRE   But to the Holy . . .
780 SOLANGE   Bring the *Mother* of God into the ceremony? Really, you've got
         more nerve than I thought. You've no shame.
CLAIRE   More softly, Solange, the walls are thin.
SOLANGE [*less loudly*]   You're going mad, Claire. It's God who's listening to
         us. We know that it's for Him that the last act is to be performed, but we
785   mustn't forewarn Him. We'll play it to the hilt.
CLAIRE   Not so loud!
SOLANGE   The walls are His ears.
CLAIRE   Then I'll put on the white dress.
SOLANGE   If you like. It makes no difference. But hurry up! Let's drop the
790   preliminaries and get on with it. We've long since stopped needing the
         twists and turns and the lies. Let's get right into the transformation. Hurry
         up! Hurry up! I can't stand the shame and humiliation any longer. Who
         cares if the world listens to us and smiles and shrugs its shoulders and says
         I'm crazy and envious! I'm quivering, I'm shuddering with pleasure. Claire,
795   I'm going to whinny with joy!

[*During this speech,* CLAIRE *has taken down the white dress and, hidden behind a screen, has put it on over her black dress whose black sleeves show.*]

CLAIRE [*appearing, all in white, with an imperious voice*]   Begin!

SOLANGE [*ecstatically*]   You're beautiful!

CLAIRE   Skip that. You said we're skipping the prelude. Start the insults.

SOLANGE   I'll never be able to. You dazzle me.

800 CLAIRE   I said the insults! Let them come, let them unfurl, let them drown me, for, as you well know, I loathe servants. A vile and odious breed, I loathe them. They're not of the human race. Servants ooze. They're a foul effluvium drifting through our rooms and hallways, seeping into us, entering our mouths, corrupting us. I vomit you!

805 SOLANGE   Go on. [*Silence.* CLAIRE *coughs.*] Go on! I'm getting there, I'm getting there!

CLAIRE   I know they're necessary, just as gravediggers and scavengers and policemen are necessary. Nevertheless, they're a putrid lot.

SOLANGE   Go on, go on!

810 CLAIRE   Your frightened guilty faces, your puckered elbows, your outmoded clothes, your wasted bodies, only fit for our castoffs! You're our distorting mirrors, our loathsome vent, our shame, our dregs!

SOLANGE   Go on, go on!

CLAIRE   Please hurry. Please! I can't go on. You're . . . you're . . . My God, I 815 can't think of anything. My mind's a blank. I've run out of insults. Claire, you exhaust me.

SOLANGE   Stop. I've got there. It's my turn.—Madame had her billing and cooing, her lovers, her milkman. . . .

CLAIRE   Solange . . .

820 SOLANGE   Silence! Her morning milkman, her messenger of dawn, her handsome clarion, her pale and charming lover. That's over. [*She takes down a riding whip.*] Take your place for the ball.

CLAIRE   What are you doing?

SOLANGE [*solemnly*]   I'm checking the flow. Down on your knees!

825 CLAIRE   Solange . . .

SOLANGE   Down on your knees! [CLAIRE *hesitates and kneels.*] Ah! Ah! You were so beautiful, the way you wrung your precious arms! Your tears, your petals oozed down your lovely face. Ah! Ah! Down! [CLAIRE *does not move.*] Down! [SOLANGE *strikes her.*] Get down! [CLAIRE *lies down.*] Ah! You amuse 830 me, my dear! Crawl! Crawl, I say, like a worm! And you were going to follow in the wake of the boats, to cross the sea to aid and comfort your handsome exile! Look at yourself again! That role is only for the fairest of the fair. The guards would snicker. People would point at you. Your lover would hang his head in shame! And are you strong enough? Strong enough to carry his 835 bag? And spry enough, Madame, spry enough on your feet? Don't worry. I'm not jealous. I don't need that thief where I'm going. No, Madame. I myself am both the thief and his slavish shadow. I move alone toward the brightest shores.

CLAIRE   I'm losing him!

840 SOLANGE   Aren't I enough for you?

CLAIRE   Solange, please, I'm sinking.

SOLANGE   Sink! But rise again to the surface. I know what my final destiny is
       to be. I've reached shelter. I can be bountiful. [*She takes a breath.*] Stand
       up! I'll marry you standing up! Ah! Ah! Groveling on the rug at a man's feet.
845   What a sorry, facile gesture. The great thing is to end in beauty. How are
       you going to get up?
CLAIRE [*getting up slowly and clumsily*]   You're killing me.
SOLANGE [*ironically*]   Careful now, watch your movements.
CLAIRE [*on her feet*]   We're out of our depth. We must go to bed. My throat's—
850 SOLANGE [*striding up to her*]   Madame has a very lovely throat. The throat of
       a queen. [CLAIRE *moves back to the kitchen door.*] Of a dove. Come, my
       turtle dove!
CLAIRE [*she withdraws farther back, putting her hands to her neck as if to pro-
       tect it*]   It's late.
SOLANGE   Never too late.
855 CLAIRE   Madame . . .
SOLANGE   . . . is drinking champagne with Monsieur who has returned from
       the dead.
CLAIRE   She'll be back any moment. Let me go.
SOLANGE   Stop worrying. She's waltzing! She's waltzing! She's guzzling fine
860   wine! She's delirious.
CLAIRE   Let's get out of here, Solange. I tell you we're in danger.
SOLANGE   Go into the vestry.[6] [*She points to the kitchen door.*] Go on in.
       You've got to finish the linoleum.
CLAIRE [*she screams in a hollow voice*]   Help!
865 SOLANGE   Don't yell! It's useless. Death is present, and is stalking you. Don't
       yell! I, who kept you the way they keep kittens for drowning. I, yes I, who
       trimmed my belly with pins to stab all the foetuses I threw into the gutter!
       In order to keep you, to have *you* alive!
CLAIRE [*running about the room*]   Solange, Solange, come to yourself!
870 SOLANGE [*running after her*]   To *yourself*!
CLAIRE [*in a dull voice*]   Help!
SOLANGE   Stop yelling! No one can hear you! We're both beyond the pale.
CLAIRE   Solange . . .
SOLANGE   Everyone's listening, but no one will hear.
875 CLAIRE   I'm ill. . . .
SOLANGE   You'll be taken care of there.
CLAIRE   I'm ill . . . I . . . I'm going to be sick. . . . [*She seems to be gagging.*]
SOLANGE [*she approaches her and says sympathetically*]   Really? Are you really
       ill? Claire, are you really feeling ill?
880 CLAIRE   I'm, I'm going to—
SOLANGE   Not here, Claire, hold it in. [*She supports her.*] Not here, please,
       please. Come. Lean on me. There. Walk gently. We'll be better off there,
       in our flowered domain. I have such sure ways of putting an end to all
       suffering.
          [*They leave by the kitchen door. The stage remains empty for a few sec-
          onds. A gust of wind opens the unlocked window. Enter* SOLANGE, *right,
          wearing her short black dress. Throughout the scene she will seem to be
          addressing characters who are imaginary, though present.*]

6. A room in a church.

885 SOLANGE   Madame . . . At last! Madame is dead! . . . laid out on the linoleum . . . strangled by the dish-gloves. What? Oh, Madame may remain
seated. . . . Madame may call me Mademoiselle[7] Solange. . . . Exactly. It's
because of what I've done. Madame and Monsieur will call me Mademoiselle Solange Lemercier. . . . Madame should have taken off that black
890 dress. It's grotesque. [*She imitates* MADAME'S *voice.*] So I'm reduced to
wearing mourning for my maid. As I left the cemetery all the servants of
the neighborhood marched past me as if I were a member of the family. I've
so often been part of the family. Death will see the joke through to the bitter end. . . . What? Oh! Madame needn't feel sorry for me. I'm Madame's
895 equal and I hold my head high. . . . Oh! And there are things Monsieur
doesn't realize. He doesn't know that he used to obey our orders. [*She
laughs.*] Ah! Ah! Monsieur was a tiny little boy. Monsieur toed the line
when we threatened. No, Inspector, no . . . I won't talk! I won't say a word.
I refuse to speak about our complicity in this murder. . . . The dresses? Oh,
900 Madame could have kept them. My sister and I had our own. Those we
used to put on at night, in secret. Now, I have my own dress, and I'm your
equal. I wear the red garb of criminals. Monsieur's laughing at me? He's
smiling at me. Monsieur thinks I'm mad. He's thinking maids should have
better taste than to make gestures reserved for Madame! Monsieur really
905 forgives me? Monsieur is the soul of kindness. He'd like to vie with me in
grandeur. But I've scaled the fiercest heights. Madame now sees my loneliness—at last! Yes, I am alone. And fearsome. I might say cruel things, but I
can be kind. . . . Madame will get over her fright. She'll get over it well
enough. What with her flowers and perfumes and gowns and jewels and
910 lovers. As for me, I've my sister. . . . Yes. I dare speak of these things. I do,
Madame. There's nothing I won't dare. And who could silence me, who?
Who would be so bold as to say to me: "My dear child!" I've been a servant.
Well and good. I've made the gestures a servant must make. I've smiled at
Madame. I've bent down to make the bed, bent down to scrub the tiles,
915 bent down to peel vegetables, to listen at doors, to glue my eye to keyholes!
But now I stand upright. And firm. I'm the strangler. Mademoiselle Solange, the one who strangled her sister! . . . Me be still? Madame is delicate, really. But I pity Madame. I pity Madame's whiteness, her satiny skin,
and her little ears, and little wrists. . . . Eh? I'm the black crow. . . . Oh!
920 Oh! I have my judges. I belong to the police. Claire? She was really very
fond of Madame. . . . YOUR dresses again! And THAT white dress, THAT
one, which I forbade her to put on, the one you wore the night of the
Opera Ball, the night you poked fun at her, because she was sitting in the
kitchen admiring a photo of Gary Cooper[8] . . . Madame will remember.
925 Madame will remember her gentle irony, the maternal grace with which
she took the magazine from us, and smiled. Nor will Madame forget that
she called her Clarinette.[9] Monsieur laughed until the tears rolled down
his cheeks. . . . Eh? Who am I? The monstrous soul of servantdom! . . .
No, Inspector, I'll explain nothing in their presence. That's *our* business. It
930 would be a fine thing if masters could pierce the shadows where servants
live. . . . That, my child, is our darkness, ours. [*She lights a cigarette and*

---

7. That is, use the respectful title "Miss"
rather than her first name alone (as servants
were addressed).

8. An American film star (1901–1961).
9. In French, *-ette* is a feminine diminutive
("little one").

smokes clumsily. The smoke makes her cough.] Neither you nor anyone else will be told anything. Just tell yourselves that this time Solange has gone through with it. . . . You see her dressed in red. She is going out. [*She goes to the window, opens it, and steps out on the balcony. Facing the night, with her back to the audience, she delivers the following speech. A slight breeze makes the curtains stir.*] Going out. Descending the great stairway. Accompanied by the police. Out on your balconies to see her making her way among the shadowy penitents! It's noon. She's carrying a nine-pound torch. The hangman follows close behind. He's whispering sweet nothings in her ear. Claire! The hangman's by my side! Now take your hand off my waist. He's trying to kiss me! Let go of me! Ah! Ah! [*She laughs.*] The hangman's trifling with me. She will be led in procession by all the maids of the neighborhood, by all the servants who accompanied Claire to her final resting place. They'll all be wearing crowns, flowers, streamers, banners. They'll toll the bell. The funeral will unfold its pomp. It's beautiful, isn't it? First come the butlers, in full livery, but without silk lining. They're wearing their crowns. Then come the footmen, the lackeys in knee breeches and white stockings. They're wearing their crowns. Then come the valets, and then the chambermaids wearing our colors. Then the porters. And then come the delegations from heaven. And I'm leading them. The hangman's lulling me. I'm being acclaimed. I'm pale and I'm about to die. . . . [*She returns to the room.*] And what flowers! They gave her such a lovely funeral, didn't they? Oh! Claire, poor little Claire! [*She bursts into tears and collapses into an armchair*] What? [*She gets up.*] It's no use, Madame, I'm obeying the police. They're the only ones who understand me. They too belong to the world of outcasts, the world you touch only with tongs.

[*Visible only to the audience,* CLAIRE, *during the last few moments, has been leaning with her elbows against the jamb of the kitchen door and listening to her sister.*]

Now we are Mademoiselle Solange Lemercier, that Lemercier woman. The famous criminal. And above all, Monsieur need not be uneasy. I'm not a maid. I have a noble soul. . . . [*She shrugs her shoulders.*] No, no, not another word, my dear fellow. Ah, Madame's not forgetting what I've done for her. . . . No, no she must not forget my devotion. . . .

[*Meanwhile* CLAIRE *enters through the door at the left. She is wearing the white dress.*]

And in spite of my forbidding it, Madame continues to stroll about the apartment. She will please sit down . . . and listen to me. . . . [*To* CLAIRE] Claire . . . we're raving!

CLAIRE [*complainingly,* MADAME's *voice*] You're talking far too much, my child. Far too much. Shut the window. [SOLANGE *shuts the window.*] Draw the curtains. Very good, Claire!

SOLANGE   It's late. Everyone's in bed. . . . We're playing an idiotic game.

CLAIRE [*she signals with her hand for silence*] Claire, pour me a cup of tea.

SOLANGE   But . . .

CLAIRE   I said a cup of tea.

SOLANGE   We're dead tired. We've got to stop. [*She sits down in an armchair.*]

CLAIRE   Ah, by no means! Poor servant girl, you think you'll get out of it as easily as that? It would be too simple to conspire with the wind, to make the night one's accomplice. Solange, you will contain me within you. Now pay close attention.

SOLANGE   Claire . . .

CLAIRE   Do as I tell you. I'm going to help you. I've decided to take the lead. Your role is to keep me from backing out, nothing more.

SOLANGE   What more do you want? We're at the end. . . .

980 CLAIRE   We're at the very beginning.

SOLANGE   They'll be coming. . . .

CLAIRE   Forget about them. We're alone in the world. Nothing exists but the altar where one of the two maids is about to immolate herself—

SOLANGE   But—

985 CLAIRE   Be still. It will be your task, yours alone, to keep us both alive. You must be very strong. In prison no one will know that I'm with you, secretly. On the sly.

SOLANGE   I'll never be able . . .

CLAIRE   Please, stand up straight. Up straight, Solange! Claire! Darling, 990 stand straight now. Up straight. Pull yourself together.

SOLANGE   You're overwhelming me.

CLAIRE   A staff! A standard! Claire, up straight! I call upon you to represent me—

SOLANGE   I've been working too hard. I'm exhausted.

995 CLAIRE   To represent me in the world. [*She tries to lift her sister and keep her on her feet.*] My darling, stand up straight.

SOLANGE   Please, I beg of you.

CLAIRE [*domineeringly*]   I beg of you, stand up straight. Solemnly, Claire! Pretty does it, pretty does it! Up Claire! Up on your paws! [*She holds her by 1000 the wrists and lifts her from her chair.*] Up on your paws! Now then! Up! Up!

SOLANGE   You don't realize the danger—

CLAIRE   But, Solange, you're immortal! Repeat after me—

SOLANGE   Talk. But not so loud.

CLAIRE [*mechanically*]   Madame must have her tea.

1005 SOLANGE [*firmly*]   No, I won't.

CLAIRE [*holding her by the wrists*]   You bitch! Repeat. Madame must have her tea.

SOLANGE   I've just been through such a lot. . . .

CLAIRE [*more firmly*]   Madame will have her tea. . . .

1010 SOLANGE   Madame will have her tea. . . .

CLAIRE   Because she must sleep . . .

SOLANGE   Because she must sleep . . .

CLAIRE   And I must stay awake.

SOLANGE   And I must stay awake.

1015 CLAIRE [*she lies down on* MADAME'*s bed*]   Don't interrupt again. I repeat. Are you listening? Are you obeying? [SOLANGE *nods "yes."*] I repeat: My tea!

SOLANGE [*hesitating*]   But . . .

CLAIRE   I say: my tea.

SOLANGE   But, Madame.

1020 CLAIRE   Good. Continue.

SOLANGE   But, Madame, it's cold.

CLAIRE   I'll drink it anyway. Let me have it. [SOLANGE *brings the tray.*] And you've poured it into the best, the finest tea set. [*She takes the cup and drinks, while* SOLANGE, *facing the audience, delivers the end of her speech.*]

SOLANGE   The orchestra is playing brilliantly. The attendant is raising the red 1025 velvet curtain. He bows. Madame is descending the stairs. Her furs brush against the green plants. Madame steps into the car. Monsieur is whispering sweet nothings in her ear. She would like to smile, but she is dead. She rings the bell. The porter yawns. He opens the door. Madame goes up the stairs. She enters her apartment—but, Madame is dead. Her two maids are alive: they've just risen up, free, from Madame's icy form. All the maids were present at her side—not they themselves, but rather the hellish agony of their names. And all that remains of them to float about Madame's airy corpse is the delicate perfume of the holy maidens which they were in secret. We are beautiful, joyous, drunk, and free!

Curtain.

TENNESSEE WILLIAMS

1911–1983

When Tennessee Williams's play *The Glass Menagerie* premiered in 1944, American drama found itself at a crossroads. EUGENE O'NEILL, whose plays helped establish the American theater as a serious artistic medium, had been absent from the stage since 1934, and the drama of social protest that dominated the 1930s was eclipsed by the outbreak of World War II. American society was undergoing a transition, as traditional values and institutions were shaken by the mid-twentieth century's accelerating economic and social transformations. In this theatrical and social climate, the plays of Williams and ARTHUR MILLER restored the centrality of theater to the nation's cultural life. But whereas Miller's *All My Sons* (1947) and *DEATH OF A SALESMAN* (1949) concentrated on the ethical conflicts of individuals and society, Williams's drama explored the deeper (and often darker) regions of America's psyche: the psychological fault lines between convention and romantic individualism; the dynamics of sexuality, violence, and alienation; and the place of art and the artist's visionary temperament in a society seen as increasingly hostile to the imagination. Drawn to characters who cling to failing illusions—outsiders who have difficulty fitting in the modern world—Williams pioneered a lyrical dramatic style that confronted but also transcended the harsh realities of contemporary life. In plays such as *The Glass Menagerie*, *A STREETCAR NAMED DESIRE* (1947), and *Cat on a Hot Tin Roof* (1955), the clash of cultures, generations, and psyches is marked by a lyricism reminiscent of the works of ANTON CHEKHOV (1860–1904) and FEDERICO GARCÍA LORCA (1898–1936). After Williams's death, the playwright DAVID MAMET called these plays "the greatest dramatic poetry in the American language."

Williams was, before all else, a Southern writer; like his fellow twentieth-century authors William Faulkner, Eudora Welty, and Flannery O'Connor, he explored the region's self-defining myths and codes of behavior, its changing economy, and its multiple—often conflicting—cultures. The playwright was born Thomas Lanier Williams III on March 26, 1911, in Columbus, Mississippi, to Edwina Dakin Williams, the daughter of an Episcopal minister, and Cornelius Coffin Williams, a shoe salesman from east Tennessee. (The playwright would later change his first name to Tennessee in recognition of his paternal ancestors.) Although he suffered a near-fatal bout of diphtheria at the age of five that kept him out of school, his childhood in Mississippi was an idyllic one. But the idyll ended in 1918 when his father moved the family to St. Louis to take a managerial position at the International Shoe Company. Living in what he later recalled as "a perpetually dim little apartment in a wilderness of identical brick and concrete structures with no grass and no trees nearer than the park," mocked by other children for their southern accents, Williams and his sister Rose (with whom he was very close) found themselves isolated and unhappy in this harsh urban setting. The situation at home was hardly better: his parents quarreled frequently, and his relationship with his father was strained.

Williams began writing at the age of twelve and saw his first article published in a popular magazine at the age of sixteen. He attended the University of Missouri from 1929 to 1932 and majored in journalism, but his father withdrew him from college after he failed a mandatory ROTC course. For the next several years, he worked at his father's company while writing stories at night. Williams eventually attended Washington University in St. Louis and the University of Iowa, where he earned a B.A. in English in 1938. During these years Williams turned his attention to playwriting. A year after his first play—a farce about sailors titled *Cairo! Shanghai! Bombay!*—was produced in a backyard theater in 1935, Williams became involved with the Mummers, a semiprofessional St. Louis theater group specializing in plays of social protest. The country was in the throes of the Depression, and the theater had become an outlet for expressing social and political discontent. Clifford Odets's *Waiting for Lefty* took the theater world by storm in 1935, and the Federal Theatre Project (part of the New Deal's Works Progress Administration) was popularizing the multimedia "Living Newspaper" format as a way of commenting on poverty and other social issues. Reflecting this theatrical climate, Williams's drama during these years was socially and politically engaged. In 1937 the Mummers produced *Candles to the Sun*, a play about Alabama coal miners, and *Fugitive Kind*, which explored the hardships of Depression America through a group of characters living in a St. Louis flophouse. Williams also completed *Not About Nightingales*, a play about prison conditions that he had started at the University of Iowa; the Mummers considered this play, but it would not be produced until 1998.

Buoyed by the local success of these plays, Williams submitted three works to a playwriting competition sponsored by the Group Theater, one of the leading American theater companies of the 1930s. He also moved to New Orleans for two months, a city to which he would return throughout his career and to which he would later refer as his "spiritual home." Williams received a special prize from the Group Theater for a collection of one-act plays and subsequently won a Rockefeller Foundation fellowship, which he used to write *The Battle of Angels*. The Theater Guild of New York produced this play in Boston in 1940, but the production was condemned by spectators and critics.

Over the next four years Williams held a variety of jobs, including a two-month scriptwriting stint for MGM in Hollywood, and he worked on a number of other writing projects. One of these, a play titled *The Gentleman Caller*, would earn Williams the fame that had eluded him in Boston. Under the revised title *The Glass Menagerie*, this play opened in Chicago in December 1944. Response was initially lukewarm, but the glowing review by a prominent Chicago theater critic led to sold-out houses. After transferring to Broadway in March 1945, the play ran for 561 performances and won the New York Drama Critics' Circle Award for Best Play. Williams's most deeply autobiographical drama—its narrator, Tom Wingfield, is modeled on Williams himself, and Tom's sister Laura is a portrait of Rose Williams—*The Glass Menagerie* was important to American theater (and to the playwright's subsequent career) as much for its technical and stylistic innovations as for its subject matter. Seeking to express the fluidity of memory in theatrical terms, Williams employs setting, music, and light in ways that blur the lines between realism and expressionism. The playwright's production notes to *The Glass Menagerie* call for "a new, plastic theatre which must take the place of the exhausted theatre of realistic conventions if the theatre is to resume vitality as a part of our culture." Such a theater must not escape reality; rather, the use of expressionistic and poetic devices allows fuller access to the truth. "[T]ruth, life, or reality," Williams wrote, "is an organic thing which the poetic imagination can represent or suggest, in essence, only through transformation, through changing into other forms than those which were merely present in appearance."

The success of *The Glass Menagerie* catapulted Williams to the forefront of public attention and generated a celebrity toward which he remained profoundly ambivalent. His reputation as one of America's leading dramatists was underscored by the success of his next play, *A Streetcar Named Desire*. Williams had conceived the play's outlines in the early 1940s and had written a number of early versions: *Blanche's Chair on the Moon*, *The Moth*, *The Primary Colors*, and *The Poker Night* were among the titles he tried. The completed *Streetcar Named Desire* opened on December 3, 1947, at the Ethel Barrymore Theater in New York in a production directed by Elia Kazan. Starring a little-known actor, Marlon Brando, in the role of Stanley Kowalski, the play ran for 855 performances over the next two years and was awarded a Pulitzer Prize and the New York Drama Critics' Circle Award. The 1951

film version of *Streetcar* (also directed by Kazan) was equally celebrated. In addition to receiving a number of major revivals, *A Streetcar Named Desire* has been translated into nearly twenty-five languages and staged around the world.

During the decade and a half after *A Streetcar Named Desire*, Williams had a string of plays produced on Broadway: *The Rose Tattoo* (1951), *Camino Real* (1953), *Cat on a Hot Tin Roof* (1955, Pulitzer Prize), *Orpheus Descending* (1957), *Suddenly Last Summer* (1958), *Sweet Bird of Youth* (1959), and *The Night of the Iguana* (1961). Although Williams continued to write plays in the 1960s and 1970s—including *In the Bar of a Tokyo Hotel* (1969), *The Two-Character Play/Out Cry* (1967, 1971), *The Red Devil Battery Sign* (1975), and *Clothes for a Summer Hotel* (1980)—his dramatic work after *Night of the Iguana* failed to receive the acclaim of his earlier plays. Convinced for most of his life that he would die young, Tennessee Williams passed away at the age of seventy-one on February 25, 1983.

Final scene from the original 1947 Broadway production of *A Streetcar Named Desire*.

A *Streetcar Named Desire* is set in the French Quarter of New Orleans, a city known for its international influences (French, Spanish, Caribbean) as well as its theatricalized ceremonies and celebrations and its bohemian subculture. The play is full of references to the city's sites and institutions; indeed, the streetcar named Desire, which brings Blanche DuBois to her sister's apartment in the play's opening scene, did run through the French Quarter in the 1940s. At the same time, Williams's New Orleans is as much an atmosphere as an actual location. Like the blues music rising from a nearby bar, the turquoise evening sky that opens the play "invests the scene with a kind of lyricism and gracefully attenuates the atmosphere of decay." Throughout *A Streetcar Named Desire*, the play's setting embodies moods and states of mind, accentuating points of crisis and imbuing realism with expressionism's more subjective reach. The apartment of Stanley and Stella Kowalski reflects this shifting border between inside and outside. Obscured in darkness when the play's action takes place outside, it appears as an interior acting space when the lighting changes. Its back wall consists of a scrim (or see-through fabric), which appears solid when lit from the front but transparent when lit from behind, allowing a view of the alley beyond the apartment.

Reviewers and scholars who have written about *A Streetcar Named Desire* have focused, for the most part, on the characters of Stanley and Blanche. While such an emphasis risks obscuring the important roles of other characters (particularly Stella and Stanley's friend Mitch), the interaction between Stanley and Blanche represents one of the great *agones,* or dramatic conflicts, in Western drama. The two characters are, in many ways, dramatic antitheses. From his initial appearance, Stanley is defined by his rough manners, working-class pride, and sexual confidence. Polish American by birth, he inhabits a neighbor-

Vivien Leigh as Blanche DuBois and Marlon Brando as Stanley Kowalski in Elia Kazan's 1951 film adaptation of *A Streetcar Named Desire.*

hood defined by its relaxed—at times violent—behavior and its ethnic and racial mix. Stanley's is a male-centered world of poker nights, Jax beer, and sexual pleasure; as Williams writes in introducing the character, "Since earliest manhood the center of his being has been pleasure with women, the giving and taking of it, not with weak indulgence, dependently, but with the power and pride of a richly feathered male bird among hens." Given to explosive outbursts but also a man of shrewdness and calculation, he defends his territory with a fierceness that masks an awareness of his own limitations. His charismatic yet threatening presence in Williams's play derives from the aggressive masculinity that he wears like a badge. In this mode of interacting with others he contrasts markedly with Mitch, a man of sensitivity and deep emotional attachments who lives with his mother.

Unlike Stanley, Blanche comes from a plantation world of landed wealth, breeding, and sexual decorum, a world (encapsulated in the plantation's name, Belle Reve—French for "beautiful dream") that was, in reality, already yielding in the 1940s to a newly industrializing South. With her white suit, bodice, and gloves, Blanche's mothlike appearance in the opening scene is incongruous with her urban surroundings. Whereas Stanley represents the vitality, dynamism, and swagger of a country emerging from World War II, Blanche represents more traditional ideals of culture, civilization, and manners. Yet even as Blanche articulates these ideals, the audience is aware that they have failed her. Belle Reve has been lost to the sexual appetites and financial improvidence of its inhabitants, and the history of decline and death that Blanche recounts is gothic in tone. Traumatized by the suicide of her homosexual husband years earlier, Blanche has led a life of promiscuity and fleeting encounters. As age begins to threaten her attractiveness, her efforts to maintain the southern belle image that she was raised to project grow more strained. Standing as the centerpiece of Williams's theatrical world, Blanche becomes stage manager in her own right, controlling the lighting by which she is seen and adding music, decorating the Kowalski apartment,

and dressing herself and applying makeup in order to play the starring role in her interactions with others. "I don't want realism. I want magic!" she tells Mitch, and these words capture her increasingly desperate faith in the compensatory power of illusion. Her attempts to maintain this illusion and the accompanying struggle to hold together the different parts of her personality break down the lines between her subjective life and the ever more hostile surroundings in which she finds herself. Of all the characters, it is Blanche who is most closely linked to the expressionistic devices of *A Streetcar Named Desire*. In the play's early scenes she hears the Varsouviana polka that was playing the night her husband shot himself; and as the play progresses, the lighting and sound effects of the stage increasingly mirror her mental and emotional turmoil.

In the aftermath of Stanley's violent outburst at the poker night he hosts for his friends in scene 3, Blanche pleads with Stella to choose tenderness and civilization over the bestiality and violence that Stanley embodies: *"Don't—don't hang back with the brutes!"* By framing the choice of values so explicitly, Blanche seeks to triumph over Stanley in the battle for Stella's love and allegiance. But the claims presented by the characters engage the audience's sympathies as well. Though scholars and reviewers have often sided with Stanley or Blanche in their assessments of the play's central confrontation, such judgments violate the complex balances and counterpoints that Williams establishes. In their sympathies, audiences must come to terms with competing social and moral codes, and they must deal with the fact that Williams's character portrayals amplify and change as the play progresses. For his part, while Williams condemned what he called "the ravishment of the tender, the sensitive, the delicate, by the savage and brutal forces of modern society," his sympathies extended in both directions: "[Blanche] was broken on the rock of the world; I find her a sympathetic character, but I also find Stanley sympathetic."

With its exploration of traditional and contemporary gender roles and its juxtaposition of the old South with the new, *A Streetcar Named Desire* offers a powerful portrait of the changing social landscape of postwar America. In keeping with this achievement, its characters, actions, and lines of dialogue became potent cultural symbols in the decades that followed. Brando's Stanley—memorialized by the widely successful film adaptation—became an image of masculinity for a generation that also worshipped such male icons as John Wayne, Elvis Presley, and James Dean. Subsequent actors playing Stanley have had to work to free their role from this mesmerizing performance. But the figure of Blanche DuBois—introduced on stage by Jessica Tandy and popularized on screen by Vivien Leigh—may be more resonant in the latter half of the twentieth century and the early years of the twenty-first. Embodying the strains in female social roles during the supposed return to normalcy following World War II, Blanche serves as an image of the conflicted place of both women and men in a society in which expected ideals and behaviors no longer match the realities of contemporary gender relations. Like Stanley, she deals with the realities of desire—physical and emotional—that fly in the face of death itself. That she cannot control her journey on the streetcar named Desire says as much about the society she inhabits as it does her precarious psyche. Though the contemporary world is no longer that of postwar America, issues of sexuality remain pressing in both traditional and cosmopolitan societies. When the drag queen Prior Walters quotes Blanche in TONY KUSHNER's ANGELS IN AMERICA (1991–92), he acknowledges the line between Williams's female protagonist—trapped between roles—and a more contemporary field of sexual identities. To learn more about the staging of A Streetcar Named Desire and to view photographs from select performances of the play, see the "Plays in Performance" color insert near the center of this volume.

S.G.

A Streetcar Named Desire

And so it was I entered the broken world
To trace the visionary company of love, its voice
An instant in the wind (I know not whither hurled)
But not for long to hold each desperate choice.
"The Broken Tower" by Hart Crane[1]

CHARACTERS

BLANCHE	PABLO
STELLA	A NEGRO WOMAN
STANLEY	A DOCTOR
MITCH	A NURSE
EUNICE	A YOUNG COLLECTOR
STEVE	A MEXICAN WOMAN

1. American poet (1899–1932); "The Broken Tower" was the last poem Crane wrote before committing suicide at the age of 32.

Scene 1

The exterior of a two-story corner building on a street in New Orleans which is named Elysian Fields and runs between the L & N tracks[2] and the river. The section is poor but, unlike corresponding sections in other American cities, it has a raffish charm. The houses are mostly white frame, weathered grey, with rickety outside stairs and galleries and quaintly ornamented gables. This building contains two flats, upstairs and down. Faded white stairs ascend to the entrances of both.

It is first dark of an evening early in May. The sky that shows around the dim white building is a peculiarly tender blue, almost a turquoise, which invests the scene with a kind of lyricism and gracefully attenuates the atmosphere of decay. You can almost feel the warm breath of the brown river beyond the river warehouses with their faint redolences of bananas and coffee. A corresponding air is evoked by the music of Negro entertainers at a barroom around the corner. In this part of New Orleans you are practically always just around the corner, or a few doors down the street, from a tinny piano being played with the infatuated fluency of brown fingers. This "blue piano" expresses the spirit of the life which goes on here.

Two women, one white and one colored, are taking the air on the steps of the building. The white woman is EUNICE, *who occupies the upstairs flat; the colored woman a neighbor, for New Orleans is a cosmopolitan city where there is a relatively warm and easy intermingling of races in the old part of town.*

Above the music of the "blue piano" the voices of people on the street can be heard overlapping.

> [*Two men come around the corner,* STANLEY KOWALSKI *and* MITCH. *They are about twenty-eight or thirty years old, roughly dressed in blue denim work clothes.* STANLEY *carries his bowling jacket and a red-stained package from a butcher's. They stop at the foot of the steps.*]

STANLEY [*bellowing*]   Hey, there! Stella, baby!

> [STELLA *comes out on the first floor landing, a gentle young woman, about twenty-five, and of a background obviously quite different from her husband's.*]

STELLA [*mildly*]   Don't holler at me like that. Hi, Mitch.

STANLEY   Catch!

STELLA   What?

5 STANLEY   Meat!

> [*He heaves the package at her. She cries out in protest but manages to catch it: then she laughs breathlessly. Her husband and his companion have already started back around the corner.*]

STELLA [*calling after him*]   Stanley! Where are you going?

STANLEY   Bowling!

STELLA   Can I come watch?

STANLEY   Come on.

> [*He goes out.*]

10 STELLA   Be over soon. [*To the white woman*] Hello, Eunice. How are you?

EUNICE   I'm all right. Tell Steve to get him a poor boy's sandwich[3] 'cause nothing's left here.

---

2. Tracks used by trains of the Louisville and Nashville Railroad—formerly a major freight and passenger company in the southeastern United States. *Elysian Fields:* a street just north of the French Quarter, the oldest neighborhood of New Orleans; also, in classical mythology, the abode of the blessed dead.

3. A po'boy, the Gulf Coast version of a submarine sandwich, featuring beef, shrimp, or other fillings in a hollowed-out loaf of French bread.

[*They all laugh; the* COLORED WOMAN *does not stop.* STELLA *goes out.*]

COLORED WOMAN   What was that package he th'ew at 'er? [*She rises from steps, laughing louder.*]

EUNICE   You hush, now!

15 NEGRO WOMAN   Catch *what*!

[*She continues to laugh.* BLANCHE *comes around the corner, carrying a valise. She looks at a slip of paper, then at the building, then again at the slip and again at the building. Her expression is one of shocked disbelief. Her appearace is incongruous to this setting. She is daintily dressed in a white suit with a fluffy bodice, necklace and earrings of pearl, white gloves and hat, looking as if she were arriving at a summer tea or cocktail party in the garden district.*[4] *She is about five years older than* STELLA. *Her delicate beauty must avoid a strong light. There is something about her uncertain manner, as well as her white clothes, that suggests a moth.*]

EUNICE [*finally*]   What's the matter, honey? Are you lost?

BLANCHE [*with faintly hysterical humor*]   They told me to take a streetcar named Desire, and then transfer to one called Cemeteries[5] and ride six blocks and get off at—Elysian Fields!

20 EUNICE   That's where you are now.

BLANCHE   At Elysian Fields?

EUNICE   This here is Elysian Fields.

BLANCHE   They mustn't have—understood—what number I wanted . . .

EUNICE   What number you lookin' for?

[BLANCHE *wearily refers to the slip of paper.*]

25 BLANCHE   Six thirty-two.

EUNICE   You don't have to look no further.

BLANCHE [*uncomprehendingly*]   I'm looking for my sister, Stella DuBois. I mean—Mrs. Stanley Kowalski.

EUNICE   That's the party.—You just did miss her, though.

30 BLANCHE   This—can this be—her home?

EUNICE   She's got the downstairs here and I got the up.

BLANCHE   Oh. She's—out?

EUNICE   You noticed that bowling alley around the corner?

BLANCHE   I'm—not sure I did.

35 EUNICE   Well, that's where she's at, watchin' her husband bowl. [*There is a pause.*] You want to leave your suitcase here an' go find her?

BLANCHE   No.

NEGRO WOMAN   I'll go tell her you come.

BLANCHE   Thanks.

40 NEGRO WOMAN   You welcome.

[*She goes out.*]

EUNICE   She wasn't expecting you?

BLANCHE   No. No, not tonight.

EUNICE   Well, why don't you just go in and make yourself at home till they get back.

45 BLANCHE   How could I—do that?

EUNICE   We own this place so I can let you in.

4. An elegant New Orleans neighborhood known for its Greek Revival and Italianate architecture.
5. Streetcar routes in New Orleans at the time the play was written; the Desire line, which went through the French Quarter, was replaced by a bus in 1948.

[*She gets up and opens the downstairs door. A light goes on behind the blind, turning it light blue.* BLANCHE *slowly follows her into the downstairs flat. The surrounding areas dim out as the interior is lighted.*]

[*Two rooms can be seen, not too clearly defined. The one first entered is primarily a kitchen but contains a folding bed to be used by* BLANCHE. *The room beyond this is a bedroom. Off this room is a narrow door to a bathroom.*]

EUNICE [*defensively, noticing* BLANCHE'*s look*] It's sort of messed up right now but when it's clean it's real sweet.

BLANCHE Is it?

50 EUNICE Uh-huh, I think so. So you're Stella's sister?

BLANCHE Yes. [*Wanting to get rid of her*] Thanks for letting me in.

EUNICE *Por nada,*[6] as the Mexicans say, *por nada!* Stella spoke of you.

BLANCHE Yes?

EUNICE I think she said you taught school.

55 BLANCHE Yes.

EUNICE And you're from Mississippi, huh?

BLANCHE Yes.

EUNICE She showed me a picture of your home-place, the plantation.

BLANCHE Belle Reve?[7]

60 EUNICE A great big place with white columns.

BLANCHE Yes . . .

EUNICE A place like that must be awful hard to keep up.

BLANCHE If you will excuse me, I'm just about to drop.

EUNICE Sure, honey. Why don't you set down?

65 BLANCHE What I meant was I'd like to be left alone.

EUNICE [*offended*] Aw. I'll make myself scarce, in that case.

BLANCHE I didn't mean to be rude, but—

EUNICE I'll drop by the bowling alley an' hustle her up.

[*She goes out the door.*]

[BLANCHE *sits in a chair very stiffly with her shoulders slightly hunched and her legs pressed close together and her hands tightly clutching her purse as if she were quite cold. After a while the blind look goes out of her eyes and she begins to look slowly around. A cat screeches. She catches her breath with a startled gesture. Suddenly she notices something in a half-opened closet. She springs up and crosses to it, and removes a whiskey bottle. She pours a half tumbler of whiskey and tosses it down. She carefully replaces the bottle and washes out the tumbler at the sink. Then she resumes her seat in front of the table.*]

BLANCHE [*faintly to herself*] I've got to keep hold of myself!

[STELLA *comes quickly around the corner of the building and runs to the door of the downstairs flat.*]

70 STELLA [*calling out joyfully*] Blanche!

[*For a moment they stare at each other. Then* BLANCHE *springs up and runs to her with a wild cry.*]

BLANCHE Stella, oh, Stella, Stella! Stella for Star![8]

[*She begins to speak with feverish vivacity as if she feared for either of them to stop and think. They catch each other in a spasmodic embrace.*]

6. It's nothing (Spanish).
7. Beautiful Dream (French).

8. *Stella* means "star" in Latin.

BLANCHE   Now, then, let me look at you. But don't you look at me, Stella, no, no, no, not till later, not till I've bathed and rested! And turn that over-light off! Turn that off! I won't be looked at in this merciless glare! [STELLA
75   *laughs and complies.*] Come back here now! Oh, my baby! Stella! Stella for Star! [*She embraces her again.*] I thought you would never come back to this horrible place! What am I saying? I didn't mean to say that. I meant to be nice about it and say—Oh, what a convenient location and such—Ha-a-ha! Precious lamb! You haven't said a *word* to me.

80 STELLA   You haven't given me a chance to, honey! [*She laughs, but her glance at* BLANCHE *is a little anxious.*]

BLANCHE   Well, now you talk. Open your pretty mouth and talk while I look around for some liquor! I know you must have some liquor on the place! Where could it be, I wonder? Oh, I spy, I spy!

     [*She rushes to the closet and removes the bottle; she is shaking all over and panting for breath as she tries to laugh. The bottle nearly slips from her grasp.*]

STELLA [*noticing*]   Blanche, you sit down and let me pour the drinks. I don't
85   know what we've got to mix with. Maybe a coke's[9] in the icebox. Look'n see, honey, while I'm—

BLANCHE   No coke, honey, not with my nerves tonight! Where—where—where is—?

STELLA   Stanley? Bowling! He loves it. They're having a—found some
90   soda!—tournament . . .

BLANCHE   Just water, baby, to chase it! Now don't get worried, your sister hasn't turned into a drunkard, she's just all shaken up and hot and tired and dirty! You sit down, now, and explain this place to me! What are you doing in a place like this?

95 STELLA   Now, Blanche—

BLANCHE   Oh, I'm not going to be hypocritical, I'm going to be honestly critical about it! Never, never, never in my worst dreams could I picture—Only Poe! Only Mr. Edgar Allan Poe!—could do it justice! Out there I suppose is the ghoul-haunted woodland of Weir![1] [*She laughs.*]

100 STELLA   No, honey, those are the L & N tracks.

BLANCHE   No, now seriously, putting joking aside. Why didn't you tell me, why didn't you write me, honey, why didn't you let me know?

STELLA [*carefully, pouring herself a drink*]   Tell you what, Blanche?

BLANCHE   Why, that you had to live in these conditions!

105 STELLA   Aren't you being a little intense about it? It's not that bad at all! New Orleans isn't like other cities.

BLANCHE   This has got nothing to do with New Orleans. You might as well say—forgive me, blessed baby! [*She suddenly stops short.*] The subject is closed!

110 STELLA [*a little drily*]   Thanks.

     [*During the pause,* BLANCHE *stares at her. She smiles at* BLANCHE.]

BLANCHE [*looking down at her glass, which shakes in her hand*]   You're all I've got in the world, and you're not glad to see me!

---

9. In the South, *coke* is often used as a generic term for any soft drink.
1. The setting of the gothic ballad "Ulalume"
(1847), by Poe, the American short story writer and poet (1809–1849).

STELLA [*sincerely*] Why, Blanche, you know that's not true.

BLANCHE No?—I'd forgotten how quiet you were.

115 STELLA You never did give me a chance to say much, Blanche. So I just got in the habit of being quiet around you.

BLANCHE [*vaguely*] A good habit to get into . . . [*Then, abruptly*] You haven't asked me how I happened to get away from the school before the spring term ended.

120 STELLA Well, I thought you'd volunteer that information—if you wanted to tell me.

BLANCHE You thought I'd been fired?

STELLA No, I—thought you might have—resigned . . .

BLANCHE I was so exhausted by all I'd been through my—nerves broke.

125 [*Nervously tamping cigarette*] I was on the verge of—lunacy, almost! So Mr. Graves—Mr. Graves is the high school superintendent—he suggested I take a leave of absence. I couldn't put all of those details into the wire[2] . . . [*She drinks quickly.*] Oh, this buzzes right through me and feels so *good*!

STELLA Won't you have another?

130 BLANCHE No, one's my limit.

STELLA Sure?

BLANCHE You haven't said a word about my appearance.

STELLA You look just fine.

BLANCHE God love you for a liar! Daylight never exposed so total a ruin! But

135 you—you've put on some weight, yes, you're just as plump as a little partridge! And it's so becoming to you!

STELLA Now, Blanche—

BLANCHE Yes, it is, it is or I wouldn't say it! You just have to watch around the hips a little. Stand up.

140 STELLA Not now.

BLANCHE You hear me? I said stand up! [STELLA *complies reluctantly.*] You messy child, you, you've spilt something on that pretty white lace collar! About your hair—you ought to have it cut in a feather bob with your dainty features. Stella, you have a maid, don't you?

145 STELLA No. With only two rooms it's—

BLANCHE What? *Two* rooms, did you say?

STELLA This one and— [*She is embarrassed.*]

BLANCHE The other one? [*She laughs sharply. There is an embarrassed silence.*] I am going to take just one little tiny nip more, sort of to put the

150 stopper on, so to speak. . . . Then put the bottle away so I won't be tempted. [*She rises.*] I want you to look at *my* figure! [*She turns around.*] You know I haven't put on one ounce in ten years, Stella? I weigh what I weighed the summer you left Belle Reve. The summer Dad died and you left us . . .

155 STELLA [*a little wearily*] It's just incredible, Blanche, how well you're looking.

[*They both laugh uncomfortably.*]

BLANCHE But, Stella, there's only two rooms, I don't see where you're going to put me!

STELLA We're going to put you in here.

2. Telegram.

160 BLANCHE   What kind of bed's this—one of those collapsible things?
            [*She sits on it.*]
STELLA   Does it feel all right?
BLANCHE [*dubiously*]   Wonderful, honey. I don't like a bed that gives much.
    But there's no door between the two rooms, and Stanley—will it be decent?
STELLA   Stanley is Polish, you know.
165 BLANCHE   Oh, yes. They're something like Irish, aren't they?
STELLA   Well—
BLANCHE   Only not so—highbrow? [*They both laugh again in the same way.*]
    I brought some nice clothes to meet all your lovely friends in.
STELLA   I'm afraid you won't think they are lovely.
170 BLANCHE   What are they like?
STELLA   They're Stanley's friends.
BLANCHE   Polacks?
STELLA   They're a mixed lot, Blanche.
BLANCHE   Heterogeneous—types?
175 STELLA   Oh, yes. Yes, types is right!
BLANCHE   Well—anyhow—I brought nice clothes and I'll wear them. I guess
    you're hoping I'll say I'll put up at a hotel, but I'm not going to put up at a
    hotel. I want to be *near* you, got to be *with* somebody, I *can't be alone!*
    Because—as you must have noticed—I'm—*not* very *well* . . . [*Her voice
    drops and her look is frightened.*]
180 STELLA   You seem a little bit nervous or overwrought or something.
BLANCHE   Will Stanley like me, or will I be just a visiting in-law, Stella? I
    couldn't stand that.
STELLA   You'll get along fine together, if you'll just try not to—well—compare
    him with men that we went out with at home.
185 BLANCHE   Is he so—different?
STELLA   Yes. A different species.
BLANCHE   In what way; what's he like?
STELLA   Oh, you can't describe someone you're in love with! Here's a picture
    of him! [*She hands a photograph to* BLANCHE.]
190 BLANCHE   An officer?
STELLA   A Master Sergeant in the Engineers' Corps.[3] Those are decorations!
BLANCHE   He had those on when you met him?
STELLA   I assure you I wasn't just blinded by all the brass.
BLANCHE   That's not what I—
195 STELLA   But of course there were things to adjust myself to later on.
BLANCHE   Such as his civilian background! [STELLA *laughs uncertainly.*] How
    did he take it when you said I was coming?
STELLA   Oh, Stanley doesn't know yet.
BLANCHE [*frightened*]   You—haven't told him?
200 STELLA   He's on the road a good deal.
BLANCHE   Oh. Travels?
STELLA   Yes.
BLANCHE   Good. I mean—isn't it?
STELLA [*half to herself*]   I can hardly stand it when he is away for a night . . .

---

3. A branch of the U.S. Army that provides construction and engineering services in support of
combat soldiers and federal agencies.

205 BLANCHE   Why, Stella!

STELLA   When he's away for a week I nearly go wild!

BLANCHE   Gracious!

STELLA   And when he comes back I cry on his lap like a baby . . . [*She smiles to herself.*]

BLANCHE   I guess that is what is meant by being in love . . . [STELLA *looks up*
210   *with a radiant smile.*] Stella—

STELLA   What?

BLANCHE   [*in an uneasy rush*]   I haven't asked you the things you probably
thought I was going to ask. And so I'll expect you to be understanding
about what *I* have to tell *you.*

215 STELLA   What, Blanche? [*Her face turns anxious.*]

BLANCHE   Well, Stella—you're going to reproach me, I know that you're
bound to reproach me—but before you do—take into consideration—you
left! I stayed and struggled! You came to New Orleans and looked out for
yourself! *I* stayed at *Belle Reve* and tried to hold it together! I'm not mean
220   ing this in any reproachful way, but *all* the burden descended on *my*
shoulders.

STELLA   The best I could do was make my own living, Blanche.

[*Blanche begins to shake again with intensity.*]

BLANCHE   I know, I know. But you are the one that abandoned Belle Reve,
not I! I stayed and fought for it, bled for it, almost died for it!

225 STELLA   Stop this hysterical outburst and tell me what's happened? What do
you mean fought and bled? What kind of—

BLANCHE   I knew you would, Stella. I knew you would take this attitude
about it!

STELLA   About—what?—please!

230 BLANCHE   [*slowly*]   The loss—the loss . . .

STELLA   Belle Reve? Lost, is it? No!

BLANCHE   Yes, Stella.

[*They stare at each other across the yellow-checked linoleum of the table.*
BLANCHE *slowly nods her head and* STELLA *looks slowly down at her*
hands folded on the table. The music of the "blue piano" grows louder.
BLANCHE *touches her handkerchief to her forehead.*]

STELLA   But how did it go? What happened?

BLANCHE   [*springing up*]   You're a fine one to ask me how it went!

230 STELLA   Blanche!

BLANCHE   You're a fine one to sit there *accusing me* of it!

STELLA   *Blanche!*

BLANCHE   I, I, *I* took the blows in my face and my body! All of those deaths!
The long parade to the graveyard! Father, Mother! Margaret, that dreadful
240   way! So big with it, it couldn't be put in a coffin! But had to be burned like
rubbish! You just came home in time for the funerals, Stella. And funerals
are pretty compared to deaths. Funerals are quiet, but deaths—not always.
Sometimes their breathing is hoarse, and sometimes it rattles, and sometimes they even cry out to you, "Don't let me go!" Even the old, sometimes,
245   say, "Don't let me go." As if you were able to stop them! But funerals are
quiet, with pretty flowers. And, oh, what gorgeous boxes they pack them
away in! Unless you were there at the bed when they cried out, "Hold me!"
you'd never suspect there was the struggle for breath and bleeding. You

didn't dream, but I saw! *Saw! Saw!* And now you sit there telling me with
250 your eyes that I let the place go! How in hell do you think all that sickness
and dying was paid for? Death is expensive, Miss Stella! And old Cousin
Jessie's right after Margaret's, hers! Why, the Grim Reaper had put up his
tent on our doorstep! . . . Stella. Belle Reve was his headquarters! Honey—
that's how it slipped through my fingers! Which of them left us a fortune?
255 Which of them left a cent of insurance even? Only poor Jessie—one hundred to pay for her coffin. That was all, Stella! And I with my pitiful salary
at the school. Yes, accuse me! Sit there and stare at me, thinking I let the
place go! *I* let the place go? Where were *you*! In bed with your—Polack!
STELLA [*springing*] Blanche! You be still! That's enough! [*She starts out.*]
260 BLANCHE Where are you going?
STELLA I'm going into the bathroom to wash my face.
BLANCHE Oh, Stella, Stella, you're crying!
STELLA Does that surprise you?
BLANCHE Forgive me—I didn't mean to—

> [*The sound of men's voices is heard.* STELLA *goes into the bathroom, clos-
> ing the door behind her. When the men appear, and* BLANCHE *realizes it
> must be* STANLEY *returning, she moves uncertainly from the bathroom
> door to the dressing table, looking apprehensively toward the front door.*
> STANLEY *enters, followed by* STEVE *and* MITCH. STANLEY *pauses near his
> door,* STEVE *by the foot of the spiral stair, and* MITCH *is slightly above and
> to the right of them, about to go out. As the men enter, we hear some of
> the following dialogue.*]

265 STANLEY Is that how he got it?
STEVE Sure that's how he got it. He hit the old weather-bird for 300 bucks
on a six-number-ticket.[4]
MITCH Don't tell him those things; he'll believe it.

> [MITCH *starts out.*]

STANLEY [*restraining* MITCH] Hey, Mitch—come back here.

> [BLANCHE, *at the sound of voices, retires in the bedroom. She picks up*
> STANLEY's *photo from dressing table, looks at it, puts it down. When* STAN-
> LEY *enters the apartment, she darts and hides behind the screen at the
> head of bed.*]

270 STEVE [*to* STANLEY *and* MITCH] Hey, are we playin' poker tomorrow?
STANLEY Sure—at Mitch's.
MITCH [*hearing this, returns quickly to the stair rail*] No—not at my place.
My mother's still sick!
STANLEY Okay, at my place . . . [MITCH *starts out again.*] But you bring the
275 beer!

> [MITCH *pretends not to hear—calls out "Goodnight, all," and goes out,
> singing.*]

EUNICE [*heard from above*] Break it up down there! I made the spaghetti
dish and ate it myself.
STEVE [*going upstairs*] I told you and phoned you we was playing. [*To the
men*] Jax beer![5]

---

4. That is, he won $300 on a six-number lottery
ticket. *Hit the old weather-bird*: got extraordinarily lucky (as one would have to be to shoot
at and hit an ornamental weather vane, which

traditionally was shaped like a rooster).
5. Made by the Jackson Brewing Company of
New Orleans until 1974. The brewery sponsored a bowling team in nearby St. Charles.

280 EUNICE   You never phoned me once.

STEVE   I told you at breakfast—and phoned you at lunch . . .

EUNICE   Well, never mind about that. You just get yourself home here once in a while.

STEVE   You want it in the papers?

[*More laughter and shouts of parting come from the men.* STANLEY *throws the screen door of the kitchen open and comes in. He is of medium height, about five feet eight or nine, and strongly, compactly built. Animal joy in his being is implicit in all his movements and attitudes. Since earliest manhood the center of his life has been pleasure with women, the giving and taking of it, not with weak indulgence, dependently, but with the power and pride of a richly feathered male bird among hens. Branching out from this complete and satisfying center are all the auxiliary channels of his life, such as his heartiness with men, his appreciation of rough humor, his love of good drink and food and games, his car, his radio, everything that is his, that bears his emblem of the gaudy seed-bearer. He sizes women up at a glance, with sexual classifications, crude images flashing into his mind and determining the way he smiles at them.*]

285 BLANCHE   [*drawing involuntarily back from his stare*]   You must be Stanley. I'm Blanche.

STANLEY   Stella's sister?

BLANCHE   Yes.

STANLEY   H'lo. Where's the little woman?

290 BLANCHE   In the bathroom.

STANLEY   Oh. Didn't know you were coming in town.

BLANCHE   I—uh—

STANLEY   Where you from, Blanche?

BLANCHE   Why, I—live in Laurel.[6]

[*He has crossed to the closet and removed the whiskey bottle.*]

295 STANLEY   In Laurel, huh? Oh, yeah. Yeah, in Laurel, that's right. Not in my territory. Liquor goes fast in hot weather.

[*He holds the bottle to the light to observe its depletion.*]

Have a shot?

BLANCHE   No, I—rarely touch it.

STANLEY   Some people rarely touch it, but it touches them often.

300 BLANCHE   [*faintly*]   Ha-ha.

STANLEY   My clothes're stickin' to me. Do you mind if I make myself comfortable? [*He starts to remove his shirt.*]

BLANCHE   Please, please do.

STANLEY   Be comfortable is my motto.

305 BLANCHE   It's mine, too. It's hard to stay looking fresh. I haven't washed or even powdered my face and—here you are!

STANLEY   You know you can catch cold sitting around in damp things, especially when you been exercising hard like bowling is. You're a teacher, aren't you?

310 BLANCHE   Yes.

STANLEY   What do you teach, Blanche?

BLANCHE   English.

6. A town in southeast Mississippi, about 135 miles from New Orleans.

STANLEY   I never was a very good English student. How long you here for, Blanche?

315 BLANCHE   I—don't know yet.

STANLEY   You going to shack up here?

BLANCHE   I thought I would if it's not inconvenient for you all.

STANLEY   Good.

BLANCHE   Traveling wears me out.

320 STANLEY   Well, take it easy.

[*A cat screeches near the window.* BLANCHE *spring up.*]

BLANCHE   What's that?

STANLEY   Cats . . . Hey, Stella!

STELLA [*faintly, from the bathroom*]   Yes, Stanley.

STANLEY   Haven't fallen in, have you? [*He grins at* BLANCHE. *She tries unsuc-*
325 *cessfully to smile back. There is a silence.*] I'm afraid I'll strike you as being the unrefined type. Stella's spoke of you a good deal. You were married once, weren't you?

[*The music of the polka rises up, faint in the distance.*]

BLANCHE   Yes. When I was quite young.

STANLEY   What happened?

330 BLANCHE   The boy—the boy died. [*She sinks back down.*] I'm afraid I'm— going to be sick!

[*Her head falls on her arms.*]

Scene 2

It is six o'clock the following evening. BLANCHE *is bathing.* STELLA *is completing her toilette.* BLANCHE's *dress, a flowered print, is laid out on* STELLA's *bed.*

STANLEY *enters the kitchen from outside, leaving the door open on the perpetual "blue piano" around the corner.*

STANLEY   What's all this monkey doings?

STELLA   Oh, Stan! [*She jumps up and kisses him, which he accepts with lordly composure.*] I'm taking Blanche to Galatoire's[7] for supper and then to a show, because it's your poker night.

5 STANLEY   How about my supper, huh? I'm not going to no Galatoire's for supper!

STELLA   I put you a cold plate on ice.

STANLEY   Well, isn't that just dandy!

STELLA   I'm going to try to keep Blanche out till the party breaks up because
10 I don't know how she would take it. So we'll go to one of the little places in the Quarter[8] afterward and you'd better give me some money.

STANLEY   Where is she?

STELLA   She's soaking in a hot tub to quiet her nerves. She's terribly upset.

STANLEY   Over what?

15 STELLA   She's been through such an ordeal.

STANLEY   Yeah?

STELLA   Stan, we've—lost Belle Reve!

STANLEY   The place in the country?

7. An elegant restaurant on Bourbon Street, specializing in French Creole cuisine.   8. The French Quarter.

STELLA Yes.

20 STANLEY How?

STELLA [*vaguely*] Oh, it had to be—sacrificed or something. [*There is a pause while* STANLEY *considers.* STELLA *is changing into her dress.*] When she comes in be sure to say something nice about her appearance. And, oh! Don't mention the baby. I haven't said anything yet, I'm waiting until she

25 gets in a quieter condition.

STANLEY [*ominously*] So?

STELLA And try to understand her and be nice to her, Stan.

BLANCHE [*singing in the bathroom*] "From the land of the sky blue water, They brought a captive maid!"[9]

30 STELLA She wasn't expecting to find us in such a small place. You see I'd tried to gloss things over a little in my letters.

STANLEY So?

STELLA And admire her dress and tell her she's looking wonderful. That's important with Blanche. Her little weakness!

35 STANLEY Yeah. I get the idea. Now let's skip back a little to where you said the country place was disposed of.

STELLA Oh!—yes . . .

STANLEY How about that? Let's have a few more details on that subjeck.

STELLA It's best not to talk much about it until she's calmed down.

40 STANLEY So that's the deal, huh? Sister Blanche cannot be annoyed with business details right now!

STELLA You saw how she was last night.

STANLEY Uh-hum, I saw how she was. Now let's have a gander at the bill of sale.

45 STELLA I haven't seen any.

STANLEY She didn't show you no papers, no deed of sale or nothing like that, huh?

STELLA It seems like it wasn't sold.

STANLEY Well, what in hell was it then, give away? To charity?

50 STELLA Shhh! She'll hear you.

STANLEY I don't care if she hears me. Let's see the papers!

STELLA There weren't any papers, she didn't show any papers, I don't care about papers.

STANLEY Have you ever heard of the Napoleonic code?[1]

55 STELLA No, Stanley, I haven't heard of the Napoleonic code and if I have, I don't see what it—

STANLEY Let me enlighten you on a point or two, baby.

STELLA Yes?

STANLEY In the state of Louisiana we have the Napoleonic code according

60 to which what belongs to the wife belongs to the husband and vice versa. For instance if I had a piece of property, or you had a piece of property—

9. From "From the Land of the Sky-Blue Water" (1908), by Nelle Richmond Eberhart and Charles Wakefield Cadman, a song popularized by the Andrews Sisters in the late 1930s.

1. The civil law code established in France under Napoleon in 1804 and adopted by most other European countries. In 1808, after Louisiana had been purchased from France but before it became a state, it adopted a version of the Napoleonic code; all other U.S. states follow the British common law model.

STELLA   My head is swimming!

STANLEY   All right. I'll wait till she gets through soaking in a hot tub and then
I'll inquire if *she* is acquainted with the Napoleonic code. It looks to me
65   like you have been swindled, baby, and when you're swindled under the
Napoleonic code I'm swindled *too*. And I don't like to be *swindled*.

STELLA   There's plenty of time to ask her questions later but if you do now
she'll go to pieces again. I don't understand what happened to Belle Reve
but you don't know how ridiculous you are being when you suggest that my
70   sister or I or anyone of our family could have perpetrated a swindle on anyone else.

STANLEY   Then where's the money if the place was sold?

STELLA   Not sold—*lost, lost!*

[*He stalks into bedroom, and she follows him.*]

Stanley!

[*He pulls open the wardrobe trunk standing in middle of room and jerks
out an armful of dresses.*]

75   STANLEY   Open your eyes to this stuff! You think she got them out of a
teacher's pay?

STELLA   Hush!

STANLEY   Look at these feathers and furs that she come here to preen herself
in! What's this here? A solid-gold dress, I believe! And this one! What is
80   these here? Fox-pieces! [*He blows on them.*] Genuine fox fur-pieces, a half
a mile long! Where are your fox-pieces, Stella? Bushy snow-white ones, no
less! Where are your white fox-pieces?

STELLA   Those are inexpensive summer furs that Blanche has had a long
time.

85   STANLEY   I got an acquaintance who deals in this sort of merchandise. I'll
have him in here to appraise it. I'm willing to bet you there's thousands of
dollars invested in this stuff here!

STELLA   Don't be such an idiot, Stanley!

[*He hurls the furs to the day bed. Then he jerks open small drawer in the
trunk and pulls up a fistful of costume jewelry.*]

STANLEY   And what have we here? The treasure chest of a pirate!

90   STELLA   Oh, Stanley!

STANLEY   Pearls! Ropes of them! What is this sister of yours, a deep-sea
diver? Bracelets of solid gold, too! Where are your pearls and gold
bracelets?

STELLA   Shhh! Be still, Stanley!

95   STANLEY   And diamonds! A crown for an empress!

STELLA   A rhinestone tiara she wore to a costume ball.

STANLEY   What's rhinestone?

STELLA   Next door to glass.

STANLEY   Are you kidding? I have an acquaintance that works in a jewelry
100   store. I'll have him in here to make an appraisal of this. Here's your plantation, or what was left of it, here!

STELLA   You have no idea how stupid and horrid you're being! Now close that
trunk before she comes out of the bathroom!

[*He kicks the trunk partly closed and sits on the kitchen table.*]

STANLEY   The Kowalskis and the DuBoises have different notions.

105 STELLA [*angrily*]   Indeed they have, thank heavens!—*I'm* going outside.

> [*She snatches up her white hat and gloves and crosses to the outside door.*]

You come out with me while Blanche is getting dressed.

STANLEY   Since when do you give me orders?

STELLA   Are you going to stay here and insult her?

STANLEY   You're damn tootin' I'm going to stay here.

> [STELLA *goes out to the porch.* BLANCHE *comes out of the bathroom in a red satin robe.*]

110 BLANCHE [*airily*]   Hello, Stanley! Here I am, all freshly bathed and scented, and feeling like a brand-new human being!

> [*He lights a cigarette.*]

STANLEY   That's good.

BLANCHE [*drawing the curtains at the windows*]   Excuse me while I slip on my pretty new dress!

115 STANLEY   Go right ahead, Blanche.

> [*She closes the drapes between the rooms.*]

BLANCHE   I understand there's to be a little card party to which we ladies are cordially *not* invited!

STANLEY [*ominously*]   Yeah?

> [BLANCHE *throws off her robe and slips into a flowered print dress.*]

BLANCHE   Where's Stella?

120 STANLEY   Out on the porch.

BLANCHE   I'm going to ask a favor of you in a moment.

STANLEY   What could that be, I wonder?

BLANCHE   Some buttons in back! You may enter!

> [*He crosses through drapes with a smoldering look.*]

How do I look?

125 STANLEY   You look all right.

BLANCHE   Many thanks! Now the buttons!

STANLEY   I can't do nothing with them.

BLANCHE   You men with your big clumsy fingers. May I have a drag on your cig?

130 STANLEY   Have one for yourself.

BLANCHE   Why, thanks! . . . It looks like my trunk has exploded.

STANLEY   Me an' Stella were helping you unpack.

BLANCHE   Well, you certainly did a fast and thorough job of it!

STANLEY   It looks like you raided some stylish shops in Paris.

135 BLANCHE   Ha-ha! Yes—clothes are my passion!

STANLEY   What does it cost for a string of fur-pieces like that?

BLANCHE   Why, those were a tribute from an admirer of mine!

STANLEY   He must have had a lot of—admiration!

BLANCHE   Oh, in my youth I excited some admiration. But look at me now!

140 [*She smiles at him radiantly.*] Would you think it possible that I was once considered to be—attractive?

STANLEY   Your looks are okay.

BLANCHE   I was fishing for a compliment, Stanley.

STANLEY   I don't go in for that stuff.

145 BLANCHE   What—stuff?

STANLEY   Compliments to women about their looks. I never met a woman that didn't know if she was good-looking or not without being told, and some of them give themselves credit for more than they've got. I once went out with a doll who said to me, "I am the glamorous type, I am the glamor
150   ous type!" I said, "So what?"

BLANCHE   And what did she say then?

STANLEY   She didn't say nothing. That shut her up like a clam.

BLANCHE   Did it end the romance?

STANLEY   It ended the conversation—that was all. Some men are took in by
155   this Hollywood glamor stuff and some men are not.

BLANCHE   I'm sure you belong in the second category.

STANLEY   That's right.

BLANCHE   I cannot imagine any witch of a woman casting a spell over you.

STANLEY   That's—right.

160   BLANCHE   You're simple, straightforward and honest, a little bit on the primitive side I should think. To interest you a woman would have to— [*She pauses with an indefinite gesture.*]

STANLEY   [*slowly*]   Lay . . . her cards on the table.

BLANCHE   [*smiling*]   Well, I never cared for wishy-washy people. That was why, when you walked in here last night, I said to myself—"My sister has
165   married a man!"—Of course that was all that I could tell about you.

STANLEY   [*booming*]   Now let's cut the re-bop![2]

BLANCHE   [*pressing hands to her ears*]   Ouuuuu!

STELLA   [*calling from the steps*]   Stanley! You come out here and let Blanche finish dressing!

170   BLANCHE   I'm through dressing, honey.

STELLA   Well, you come out, then.

STANLEY   Your sister and I are having a little talk.

BLANCHE   [*lightly*]   Honey, do me a favor. Run to the drugstore and get me a lemon Coke with plenty of chipped ice in it!—Will you do that for me,
175   sweetie?

STELLA   [*uncertainly*]   Yes.

[*She goes around the corner of the building.*]

BLANCHE   The poor little thing was out there listening to us, and I have an idea she doesn't understand you as well as I do. . . . All right; now, Mr. Kowalski, let us proceed without any more double-talk. I'm ready to answer
180   all questions. I've nothing to hide. What is it?

STANLEY   There is such a thing in this state of Louisiana as the Napoleonic code, according to which whatever belongs to my wife is also mine—and vice versa.

BLANCHE   My, but you have an impressive judicial air!

[*She sprays herself with her atomizer; then playfully sprays him with it. He seizes the atomizer and slams it down on the dresser. She throws back her head and laughs.*]

185   STANLEY   If I didn't know that you was my wife's sister I'd get ideas about you!

BLANCHE   Such as what!

---

2. Nonsense (a variant of *bebop* or *bop*, the virtuosic jazz of the late 1940s and a term meaning "glib or deceptive talk").

STANLEY   Don't play so dumb. You know what!

BLANCHE [*she puts the atomizer on the table*]   All right. Cards on the table.

190   That suits me. [*She turns to* STANLEY.] I know I fib a good deal. After all, a
woman's charm is fifty per cent illusion, but when a thing is important I
tell the truth, and this is the truth: I haven't cheated my sister or you or
anyone else as long as I have lived.

STANLEY   Where's the papers? In the trunk?

195   BLANCHE   Everything that I own is in that trunk.

> [STANLEY *crosses to the trunk, shoves it roughly open and begins to open
> compartments.*]

BLANCHE   What in the name of heaven are you thinking of! What's in the
back of that little boy's mind of yours? That I am absconding with something, attempting some kind of treachery on my sister?—Let me do that! It
will be faster and simpler . . . [*She crosses to the trunk and takes out a box.*]

200   I keep my papers mostly in this tin box. [*She opens it.*]

STANLEY   What's them underneath? [*He indicates another sheaf of paper.*]

BLANCHE   These are love-letters, yellowing with antiquity, all from one boy.
[*He snatches them up. She speaks fiercely.*] Give those back to me!

STANLEY   I'll have a look at them first!

205   BLANCHE   The touch of your hands insults them!

STANLEY   Don't pull that stuff!

> [*He rips off the ribbon and starts to examine them.* BLANCHE *snatches
> them from him, and they cascade to the floor.*]

BLANCHE   Now that you've touched them I'll burn them!

STANLEY [*staring, baffled*]   What in hell are they?

BLANCHE [*on the floor gathering them up*]   Poems a dead boy wrote. I hurt

210   him the way that you would like to hurt me, but you can't! I'm not young
and vulnerable any more. But my young husband was and I—never mind
about that! Just give them back to me!

STANLEY   What do you mean by saying you'll have to burn them?

BLANCHE   I'm sorry, I must have lost my head for a moment. Everyone has

215   something he won't let others touch because of their—intimate nature . . .

> [*She now seems faint with exhaustion and she sits down with the strong
> box and puts on a pair of glasses and goes methodically through a large
> stack of papers.*]

Ambler & Ambler. Hmmmmm. . . . Crabtree. . . . More Ambler & Ambler.

STANLEY   What is Ambler & Ambler?

BLANCHE   A firm that made loans on the place.

STANLEY   Then it *was* lost on a mortgage?

220   BLANCHE [*touching her forehead*]   That must've been what happened.

STANLEY   I don't want no ifs, ands or buts! What's all the rest of them papers?

> [*She hands him the entire box. He carries it to the table and starts to
> examine the papers.*]

BLANCHE [*picking up a large envelope containing more papers*]   There are
thousands of papers, stretching back over hundreds of years, affecting
Belle Reve as, piece by piece, our improvident grandfathers and father and

225   uncles and brothers exchanged the land for their epic fornications—to put
it plainly! [*She removes her glasses with an exhausted laugh.*] The four-letter
word deprived us of our plantation, till finally all that was left—and Stella
can verify that!—was the house itself and about twenty acres of ground,

including a graveyard, to which now all but Stella and I have retreated.
[*She pours the contents of the envelope on the table.*] Here all of them are, all papers! I hereby endow you with them! Take them, peruse them—commit them to memory, even! I think it's wonderfully fitting that Belle Reve should finally be this bunch of old papers in your big, capable hands! . . . I wonder if Stella's come back with my lemon Coke . . . [*She leans back and closes her eyes.*]

STANLEY I have a lawyer acquaintance who will study these out.

BLANCHE Present them to him with a box of aspirin tablets.

STANLEY [*becoming somewhat sheepish*] You see, under the Napoleonic code—a man has to take an interest in his wife's affairs—especially now that she's going to have a baby.

[BLANCHE *opens her eyes. The "blue piano" sounds louder.*]

BLANCHE Stella? Stella going to have a baby? [*Dreamily*] I didn't know she was going to have a baby!

[*She gets up and crosses to the outside door.* STELLA *appears around the corner with a carton from the drugstore.*]

[STANLEY *goes into the bedroom with the envelope and the box.*]

[*The inner rooms fade to darkness and the outside wall of the house is visible.* BLANCHE *meets* STELLA *at the foot of the steps to the sidewalk.*]

BLANCHE Stella, Stella for Star! How lovely to have a baby! It's all right. Everything's all right.

STELLA I'm sorry he did that to you.

BLANCHE Oh, I guess he's just not the type that goes for jasmine perfume, but maybe he's what we need to mix with our blood now that we've lost Belle Reve. We thrashed it out. I feel a bit shaky, but I think I handled it nicely, I laughed and treated it all as a joke. [STEVE *and* PABLO *appear, carrying a case of beer.*] I called him a little boy and laughed and flirted. Yes, I was flirting with your husband! [*As the men approach*] The guests are gathering for the poker party. [*The two men pass between them, and enter the house.*] Which way do we go now, Stella—this way?

STELLA No, this way. [*She leads* BLANCHE *away.*]

BLANCHE [*laughing*] The blind are leading the blind![3]

[*A tamale* VENDOR *is heard calling.*]

VENDOR'S VOICE Red-hot!

Scene 3
The Poker Night[4]

*There is a picture of Van Gogh's of a billiard-parlor at night.[5] The kitchen now suggests that sort of lurid nocturnal brilliance, the raw colors of childhood's spectrum. Over the yellow linoleum of the kitchen table hangs an electric bulb with a vivid green glass shade. The poker players—*STANLEY, STEVE, MITCH, *and* PABLO—*wear colored shirts, solid blue, a purple, a red-and-white check, a light green, and they are men at the peak of their physical manhood, as coarse and direct and powerful as the primary colors. There are vivid slices of watermelon on the table, whiskey bottles*

---

3. See Matthew 15.14: "And if the blind lead the blind, both shall fall into the ditch."
4. "The Poker Night" was Williams's working title for *A Streetcar Named Desire.*
5. *The Night Café* (1888), by the Dutch painter Vincent Van Gogh (1853–1890).

and glasses. The bedroom is relatively dim with only the light that spills between the portieres[6] and through the wide window on the street. For a moment, there is absorbed silence as a hand is dealt.

STEVE   Anything wild this deal?

PABLO   One-eyed jacks are wild.

STEVE   Give me two cards.

PABLO   You, Mitch?

5 MITCH   I'm out.

PABLO   One.

MITCH   Anyone want a shot?

STANLEY   Yeah. Me.

PABLO   Why don't somebody go to the Chinaman's and bring back a load of
10   chop suey?

STANLEY   When I'm losing you want to eat! Ante up! Openers? Openers! Get y'r ass off the table, Mitch. Nothing belongs on a poker table but cards, chips, and whiskey.

[*He lurches up and tosses some watermelon rinds to the floor.*]

MITCH   Kind of on your high horse, ain't you?

15 STANLEY   How many?

STEVE   Give me three.

STANLEY   One.

MITCH   I'm out again. I oughta go home pretty soon.

STANLEY   Shut up.

20 MITCH   I gotta sick mother. She don't go to sleep until I come in at night.

STANLEY   Then why don't you stay home with her?

MITCH   She says to go out, so I go, but I don't enjoy it. All the while I keep wondering how she is.

STANLEY   Aw, for the sake of Jesus, go home, then!

25 PABLO   What've you got?

STEVE   Spade flush.

MITCH   You all are married. But I'll be alone when she goes.—I'm going to the bathroom.

STANLEY   Hurry back and we'll fix you a sugar-tit.[7]

30 MITCH   Aw, go rut. [*He crosses through the bedroom into the bathroom.*]

STEVE   [*dealing a hand*]   Seven card stud. [*Telling his joke as he deals.*] This ole farmer is out in back of his house sittin' down th'owing corn to the chickens when all at once he hears a loud cackle and this young hen comes lickety split around the side of the house with the rooster right behind her
35   and gaining on her fast.

STANLEY   [*impatient with the story*]   Deal!

STEVE   But when the rooster catches sight of the farmer th'owing the corn he puts on the brakes and lets the hen get away and starts pecking corn. And the old farmer says, "Lord God, I hopes I never gits *that* hongry!"

[STEVE *and* PABLO *laugh. The sisters appear around the corner of the building.*]

40 STELLA   The game is still going on.

BLANCHE   How do I look?

STELLA   Lovely, Blanche.

6. Heavy curtains hung across a doorway.   7. A pacifier dipped in sugar.

BLANCHE   I feel so hot and frazzled. Wait till I powder before you open the
    door. Do I look done in?

45 STELLA   Why no. You are as fresh as a daisy.

BLANCHE   One that's been picked a few days.

    [STELLA *opens the door and they enter.*]

STELLA   Well, well, well. I see you boys are still at it!

STANLEY   Where you been?

STELLA   Blanche and I took in a show. Blanche, this is Mr. Gonzales and Mr.
50   Hubbell.

BLANCHE   Please don't get up.

STANLEY   Nobody's going to get up, so don't be worried.

STELLA   How much longer is this game going to continue?

STANLEY   Till we get ready to quit.

55 BLANCHE   Poker is so fascinating. Could I kibitz?

STANLEY   You could not. Why don't you women go up and sit with Eunice?

STELLA   Because it is nearly two-thirty. [BLANCHE *crosses into the bedroom and
    partially closes the portieres.*] Couldn't you call it quits after one more hand?

    [*A chair scrapes.* STANLEY *gives a loud whack of his hand on her thigh.*]

STELLA [*sharply*]   That's not fun, Stanley.

    [*The men laugh.* STELLA *goes into the bedroom.*]

60 STELLA   It makes me so mad when he does that in front of people.

BLANCHE   I think I will bathe.

STELLA   Again?

BLANCHE   My nerves are in knots. Is the bathroom occupied?

STELLA   I don't know.

    [BLANCHE *knocks.* MITCH *opens the door and comes out, still wiping his
    hands on a towel.*]

65 BLANCHE   Oh!—good evening.

MITCH   Hello. [*He stares at her.*]

STELLA   Blanche, this is Harold Mitchell. My sister, Blanche DuBois.

MITCH [*with awkward courtesy*]   How do you do, Miss DuBois.

STELLA   How is your mother now, Mitch?

70 MITCH   About the same, thanks. She appreciated your sending over that
    custard.—Excuse me, please.

    [*He crosses slowly back into the kitchen, glancing back at* BLANCHE *and
    coughing a little shyly. He realizes he still has the towel in his hands and
    with an embarrassed laugh hands it to* STELLA. BLANCHE *looks after him
    with a certain interest.*]

BLANCHE   That one seems—superior to the others.

STELLA   Yes, he is.

BLANCHE   I thought he had a sort of sensitive look.

75 STELLA   His mother is sick.

BLANCHE   Is he married?

STELLA   No.

BLANCHE   Is he a wolf?

STELLA   Why, Blanche! [BLANCHE *laughs.*] I don't think he would be.

80 BLANCHE   What does—what does he do?

    [*She is unbuttoning her blouse.*]

STELLA   He's on the precision bench in the spare parts department. At the plant Stanley travels for.

BLANCHE   Is that something much?

STELLA   No. Stanley's the only one of his crowd that's likely to get anywhere.

85 BLANCHE   What makes you think Stanley will?

STELLA   Look at him.

BLANCHE   I've looked at him.

STELLA   Then you should know.

BLANCHE   I'm sorry, but I haven't noticed the stamp of genius even on Stan-
90 ley's forehead.

[*She takes off the blouse and stands in her pink silk brassiere and white skirt in the light through the portieres. The game has continued in undertones.*]

STELLA   It isn't on his forehead and it isn't genius.

BLANCHE   Oh. Well, what is it, and where? I would like to know.

STELLA   It's a drive that he has. You're standing in the light, Blanche!

BLANCHE   Oh, am I!

[*She moves out of the yellow streak of light. Stella has removed her dress and put on a light blue satin kimona.*[8]]

95 STELLA [*with girlish laughter*]   You ought to see their wives.

BLANCHE [*laughingly*]   I can imagine. Big, beefy things, I suppose.

STELLA   You know that one upstairs? [*More laughter*] One time [*Laughing*] the plaster—[*Laughing*] cracked—

STANLEY   You hens cut out that conversation in there!

100 STELLA   You can't hear us.

STANLEY   Well, you can hear me and I said to hush up!

STELLA   This is my house and I'll talk as much as I want to!

BLANCHE   Stella, don't start a row.

STELLA   He's half drunk!—I'll be out in a minute.

[*She goes into the bathroom.* BLANCHE *rises and crosses leisurely to a small white radio and turns it on.*]

105 STANLEY   Awright, Mitch, you in?

MITCH   What? Oh!—No, I'm out!

[BLANCHE *moves back into the streak of light. She raises her arms and stretches, as she moves indolently back to the chair.*]

[*Rhumba music comes over the radio.* MITCH *rises at the table.*]

STANLEY   Who turned that on in there?

BLANCHE   I did. Do you mind?

STANLEY   Turn it off!

110 STEVE   Aw, let the girls have their music.

PABLO   Sure, that's good, leave it on!

STEVE   Sounds like Xavier Cugat![9]

[STANLEY *jumps up and, crossing to the radio, turns it off. He stops short at the sight of* BLANCHE *in the chair. She returns his look without flinching. Then he sits again at the poker table.*]

[*Two of the men have started arguing hotly.*]

8. Kimono.
9. The Cuban American bandleader (1900–   1990) whose hits of the 1930s won him the
      nickname "Rhumba King."

STEVE   I didn't hear you name it.

PABLO   Didn't I name it, Mitch?

115 MITCH   I wasn't listenin'.

PABLO   What were you doing, then?

STANLEY   He was looking through them drapes. [*He jumps up and jerks roughly at curtains to close them.*] Now deal the hand over again and let's play cards or quit. Some people get ants[1] when they win.

[*MITCH rises as STANLEY returns to his seat.*]

120 STANLEY   [*yelling*]   Sit down!

MITCH   I'm going to the "head."[2] Deal me out.

PABLO   Sure he's got ants now. Seven five-dollar bills in his pants pocket folded up tight as spitballs.

STEVE   Tomorrow you'll see him at the cashier's window getting them 125 changed into quarters.

STANLEY   And when he goes home he'll deposit them one by one in a piggy bank his mother give him for Christmas. [*Dealing*] This game is Spit in the Ocean.

[*MITCH laughs uncomfortably and continues through the portieres. He stops just inside.*]

BLANCHE   [*softly*]   Hello! The Little Boys' Room is busy right now.

130 MITCH   We've—been drinking beer.

BLANCHE   I hate beer.

MITCH   It's—a hot weather drink.

BLANCHE   Oh, I don't think so; it always makes me warmer. Have you got any cigs? [*She has slipped on the dark red satin wrapper.*]

135 MITCH   Sure.

BLANCHE   What kind are they?

MITCH   Luckies.

BLANCHE   Oh, good. What a pretty case. Silver?

MITCH   Yes. Yes; read the inscription.

140 BLANCHE   Oh, is there an inscription? I can't make it out. [*He strikes a match and moves closer.*] Oh! [*Reading with feigned difficulty.*]

"And if God choose,
I shall but love thee better—after—death!"

Why, that's from my favorite sonnet by Mrs. Browning![3]

145 MITCH   You know it?

BLANCHE   Certainly I do!

MITCH   There's a story connected with that inscription.

BLANCHE   It sounds like a romance.

MITCH   A pretty sad one.

150 BLANCHE   Oh?

MITCH   The girl's dead now.

BLANCHE   [*in a tone of deep sympathy*]   Oh!

---

1. Antsy.
2. Navy slang for a ship's toilet.
3. The English poet Elizabeth Barrett Browning (1806–1861). She is best known for her *Sonnets from the Portuguese* (1850), a

sequence of love poems written before her marriage to Robert Browning; Blanche quotes from the most famous of them, Sonnet XLIII ("How do I love thee? Let me count the ways").

MITCH   She knew she was dying when she give me this. A very strange girl, very sweet—very!

155 BLANCHE   She must have been fond of you. Sick people have such deep, sincere attachments.

MITCH   That's right, they certainly do.

BLANCHE   Sorrow makes for sincerity, I think.

MITCH   It sure brings it out in people.

160 BLANCHE   The little there is belongs to people who have experienced some sorrow.

MITCH   I believe you are right about that.

BLANCHE   I'm positive that I am. Show me a person who hasn't known any sorrow and I'll show you a shuperficial—Listen to me! My tongue is a

165 little—thick! You boys are responsible for it. The show let out at eleven and we couldn't come home on account of the poker game so we had to go somewhere and drink. I'm not accustomed to having more than one drink. Two is the limit—and *three*! [*She laughs.*] Tonight I had three.

STANLEY   Mitch!

170 MITCH   Deal me out. I'm talking to Miss—

BLANCHE   DuBois.

MITCH   Miss DuBois?

BLANCHE   It's a French name. It means woods and Blanche means white, so the two together mean white woods. Like an orchard in spring! You can

175 remember it by that.

MITCH   You're French?

BLANCHE   We are French by extraction. Our first American ancestors were French Huguenots.[4]

MITCH   You are Stella's sister, are you not?

180 BLANCHE   Yes, Stella is my precious little sister. I call her little in spite of the fact she's somewhat older than I. Just slightly. Less than a year. Will you do something for me?

MITCH   Sure. What?

BLANCHE   I bought this adorable little colored paper lantern at a Chinese

185 shop on Bourbon.[5] Put it over the light bulb! Will you, please?

MITCH   Be glad to.

BLANCHE   I can't stand a naked light bulb, any more than I can a rude remark or a vulgar action.

MITCH   [*adjusting the lantern*]   I guess we strike you as being a pretty rough

190 bunch.

BLANCHE   I'm very adaptable—to circumstances.

MITCH   Well, that's a good thing to be. You are visiting Stanley and Stella?

BLANCHE   Stella hasn't been so well lately, and I came down to help her for a while. She's very run down.

195 MITCH   You're not—?

BLANCHE   Married? No, no. I'm an old maid schoolteacher!

MITCH   You may teach school but you're certainly not an old maid.

---

4. French Protestants, repeatedly persecuted by the Catholic monarchy. Many Huguenots emigrated to the American colonies after Louis XIV's Edict of Fontainebleau declared Protestantism illegal in 1685.
5. Bourbon Street, the center of the French Quarter's nightlife.

BLANCHE   Thank you, sir! I appreciate your gallantry!

MITCH   So you are in the teaching profession?

200   BLANCHE   Yes. Ah, yes . . .

MITCH   Grade school or high school or—

STANLEY [*bellowing*]   Mitch!

MITCH   *Coming!*

BLANCHE   Gracious, what lung-power! . . . I teach high school. In Laurel.

205   MITCH   What do you teach? What subject?

BLANCHE   Guess!

MITCH   I bet you teach art or music? [BLANCHE *laughs delicately.*] Of course I could be wrong. You might teach arithmetic.

BLANCHE   Never arithmetic, sir; never arithmetic! [*With a laugh*] I don't even
210   know my multiplication tables! No, I have the misfortune of being an English instructor. I attempt to instill a bunch of bobby-soxers and drug-store Romeos with reverence for Hawthorne and Whitman and Poe![6]

MITCH   I guess that some of them are more interested in other things.

BLANCHE   How very right you are! Their literary heritage is not what most of
215   them treasure above all else! But they're sweet things! And in the spring, it's touching to notice them making their first discovery of love! As if nobody had ever known it before!

> [*The bathroom door opens and* STELLA *comes out.* BLANCHE *continues talking to* MITCH.]

Oh! Have you finished? Wait—I'll turn on the radio.

> [*She turns the knobs on the radio and it begins to play "Wien, Wien, nur du allein."*[7] BLANCHE *waltzes to the music with romantic gestures.* MITCH *is delighted and moves in awkward imitation like a dancing bear.*]

> [STANLEY *stalks fiercely through the portieres into the bedroom. He crosses to the small white radio and snatches it off the table. With a shouted oath, he tosses the instrument out the window.*]

STELLA   *Drunk—drunk—animal thing, you!* [*She rushes through to the poker*
220   *table.*] All of you—please go home! If any of you have one spark of decency in you—

BLANCHE [*wildly*]   Stella, watch out, he's—

> [STANLEY *charges after* STELLA.]

MEN [*feebly*]   Take it easy, Stanley. Easy, fellow.—Let's all—

STELLA   You lay your hands on me and I'll—

> [*She backs out of sight. He advances and disappears. There is the sound of a blow.* STELLA *cries out.* BLANCHE *screams and runs into the kitchen. The men rush forward and there is grappling and cursing. Something is overturned with a crash.*]

225   BLANCHE [*shrilly*]   My sister is going to have a baby!

MITCH   This is terrible.

---

6. Classic American authors: Nathaniel Hawthorne (1804–1864), Walt Whitman (1819–
1892), and Edgar Allan Poe. *Bobby-soxers and
drugstore Romeos:* teenage boys and girls.
"Bobby-soxer" was a term first applied to the
girls in ankle socks who cried and swooned at
Frank Sinatra's concerts in the early 1940s;
and boys were "drugstore Romeos" because

drugstores usually had soda fountains, where
teenagers socialized.
7. "Vienna, Vienna, only you alone" (German); from the popular waltz "Wien, du Stadt
meiner Träume" ("Vienna, You City of My
Dreams," 1914), by the Austrian composer
Rudolf Sieczynski.

BLANCHE   Lunacy, absolute lunacy!

MITCH   Get him in here, men.

> [STANLEY *is forced, pinioned by the two men, into the bedroom. He nearly throws them off. Then all at once he subsides and is limp in their grasp.*]

> [*They speak quietly and lovingly to him and he leans his face on one of their shoulders.*]

230 STELLA [*in a high, unnatural voice, out of sight*]   I want to go away, I want to go away!

MITCH   Poker shouldn't be played in a house with women.

> [BLANCHE *rushes into the bedroom.*]

BLANCHE   I want my sister's clothes! We'll go to that woman's upstairs!

MITCH   Where is the clothes?

BLANCHE [*opening the closet*]   I've got them! [*She rushes through to* STELLA.]

235 Stella, Stella, precious! Dear, dear little sister, don't be afraid!

> [*With her arms around* STELLA, BLANCHE *guides her to the outside door and upstairs.*]

STANLEY [*dully*]   What's the matter; what's happened?

MITCH   You just blew your top, Stan.

PABLO   He's okay, now.

STEVE   Sure, my boy's okay!

240 MITCH   Put him on the bed and get a wet towel.

PABLO   I think coffee would do him a world of good, now.

STANLEY [*thickly*]   I want water.

MITCH   Put him under the shower!

> [*The men talk quietly as they lead him to the bathroom.*]

STANLEY   Let the rut go of me, you sons of bitches!

> [*Sounds of blows are heard. The water goes on full tilt.*]

245 STEVE   Let's get quick out of here!

> [*They rush to the poker table and sweep up their winings on their way out.*]

MITCH [*sadly but firmly*]   Poker should not be played in a house with women.

> [*The door closes on them and the place is still. The Negro entertainers in the bar around the corner play "Paper Doll"[8] slow and blue. After a moment Stanley comes out of the bathroom dripping water and still in his clinging wet polka-dot drawers.*]

STANLEY   Stella! [*There is a pause.*] My baby doll's left me!

> [*He breaks into sobs. Then he goes to the phone and dials, still shuddering with sobs.*]

Eunice? I want my baby! [*He waits a moment; then he hangs up and dials again.*] Eunice! I'll keep on ringin' until I talk with my baby!

> [*An indistinguishable shrill voice is heard. He hurls phone to floor. Dissonant brass and piano sounds as the rooms dim out to darkness and the outer walls appear in the night light. The "blue piano" plays for a brief interval.*]

> [*Finally,* STANLEY *stumbles half-dressed out to the porch and down the wooden steps to the pavement before the building. There he throws back his head like a baying hound and bellows his wife's name: "Stella! Stella, sweetheart! Stella!"*]

---

8. A song written by Johnny S. Black in 1915; the Mills Brothers' 1943 version was a huge hit.

250 STANLEY   Stell-*lahhhhh!*

EUNICE [*calling down from the door of her upper apartment*]   Quit that howling out there an' go back to bed!

STANLEY   I want my baby down here. Stella, Stella!

EUNICE   She ain't comin' down so you quit! Or you'll git th' law on you!

255 STANLEY   Stella!

EUNICE   You can't beat on a woman an' then call 'er back! She won't come! And her goin' t' have a baby! . . . You stinker! You whelp of a Polack, you! I hope they do haul you in and turn the fire hose on you, same as the last time!

260 STANLEY [*humbly*]   Eunice, I want my girl to come down with me!

EUNICE   Hah! [*She slams her door.*]

STANLEY [*with heaven-splitting violence*]   *STELL-LAHHHHH!*

[*The low-tone clarinet moans. The door upstairs opens again.* STELLA *slips down the rickety stairs in her robe. Her eyes are glistening with tears and her hair loose about her throat and shoulders. They stare at each other. Then they come together with low, animal moans. He falls to his knees on the steps and presses his face to her belly, curving a little with maternity. Her eyes go blind with tenderness as she catches his head and raises him level with her. He snatches the screen door open and lifts her off her feet and bears her into the dark flat.*]

[BLANCHE *comes out on the upper landing in her robe and slips fearfully down the steps.*]

BLANCHE   Where is my little sister? Stella? Stella?

[*She stops before the dark entrance of her sister's flat. Then catches her breath as if struck. She rushes down to the walk before the house. She looks right and left as if for a sanctuary.*]

[*The music fades away.* MITCH *appears from around the corner.*]

MITCH   Miss DuBois?

265 BLANCHE   Oh!

MITCH   All quiet on the Potomac[9] now?

BLANCHE   She ran downstairs and went back in there with him.

MITCH   Sure she did.

BLANCHE   I'm terrified!

270 MITCH   Ho-ho! There's nothing to be scared of. They're crazy about each other.

BLANCHE   I'm not used to such—

MITCH   Naw, it's a shame this had to happen when you just got here. But don't take it serious.

275 BLANCHE   Violence! Is so—

MITCH   Set down on the steps and have a cigarette with me.

BLANCHE   I'm not properly dressed.

MITCH   That don't make no difference in the Quarter.

BLANCHE   Such a pretty silver case.

280 MITCH   I showed you the inscription, didn't I?

9. Because of the inaction of the Union general George McClellan in 1861–62, newspaper correspondents frequently reported "All quiet on the Potomac"; it became a bitter catchphrase, featured in ballads and a popular song.

BLANCHE   Yes. [*During the pause, she looks up at the sky.*] There's so much—so much confusion in the world . . . [*He coughs diffidently.*] Thank you for being so kind! I need kindness now.

Scene 4

It is early the following morning. There is a confusion of street cries like a choral chant.

STELLA *is lying down in the bedroom. Her face is serene in the early morning sunlight. One hand rests on her belly, rounding slightly with new maternity. From the other dangles a book of colored comics. Her eyes and lips have that almost narcotized tranquility that is in the faces of Eastern idols.*

The table is sloppy with remains of breakfast and the debris of the preceding night, and STANLEY's *gaudy pyjamas lie across the threshold of the bathroom. The outside door is slightly ajar on a sky of summer brilliance.*

BLANCHE *appears at this door. She has spent a sleepless night and her appearance entirely contrasts with Stella's. She presses her knuckles nervously to her lips as she looks through the door, before entering.*

BLANCHE   Stella?
STELLA [*stirring lazily*]   Hmmh?
>[BLANCHE *utters a moaning cry and runs into the bedroom, throwing herself down beside* STELLA *in a rush of hysterical tenderness.*]

BLANCHE   Baby, my baby sister!
STELLA [*drawing away from her*]   Blanche, what is the matter with you?
>[BLANCHE *straightens up slowly and stands beside the bed looking down at her sister with knuckles pressed to her lips.*]

5   BLANCHE   He's left?
STELLA   Stan? Yes.
BLANCHE   Will he be back?
STELLA   He's gone to get the car greased. Why?
BLANCHE   Why! I've been half crazy, Stella! When I found out you'd been
10   insane enough to come back in here after what happened—I started to rush in after you!
STELLA   I'm glad you didn't.
BLANCHE   What were you thinking of? [STELLA *makes an indefinite gesture.*] Answer me! What? What?
15   STELLA   Please, Blanche! Sit down and stop yelling.
BLANCHE   All right, Stella. I will repeat the question quietly now. How could you come back in this place last night? Why, you must have slept with him!
>[STELLA *gets up in a calm and leisurely way.*]

STELLA   Blanche, I'd forgotten how excitable you are. You're making much too much fuss about this.
20   BLANCHE   Am I?
STELLA   Yes, you are, Blanche. I know how it must have seemed to you and I'm awful sorry it had to happen, but it wasn't anything as serious as you seem to take it. In the first place, when men are drinking and playing poker anything can happen. It's always a powder-keg. He didn't know what he
25   was doing. . . . He was as good as a lamb when I came back and he's really very, very ashamed of himself.

BLANCHE   And that—that makes it all right?

STELLA   No, it isn't all right for anybody to make such a terrible row, but—people do sometimes. Stanley's always smashed things. Why, on our wed-ding night—soon as we came in here—he snatched off one of my slippers and rushed about the place smashing light bulbs with it.

BLANCHE   He did—*what?*

STELLA   He smashed all the light bulbs with the heel of my slipper! [*She laughs.*]

BLANCHE   And you—you *let* him? Didn't *run*, didn't *scream?*

STELLA   I was—sort of—thrilled by it. [*She waits for a moment.*] Eunice and you had breakfast?

BLANCHE   Do you suppose I wanted any breakfast?

STELLA   There's some coffee left on the stove.

BLANCHE   You're so—matter-of-fact about it, Stella.

STELLA   What other can I be? He's taken the radio to get it fixed. It didn't land on the pavement so only one tube[1] was smashed.

BLANCHE   And you are standing there smiling!

STELLA   What do you want me to do?

BLANCHE   Pull yourself together and face the facts.

STELLA   What are they, in your opinion?

BLANCHE   In my opinion? You're married to a madman!

STELLA   No!

BLANCHE   Yes, you are, your fix is worse than mine is! Only you're not being sensible about it. I'm going to *do* something. Get hold of myself and make myself a new life!

STELLA   Yes?

BLANCHE   But you've given in. And that isn't right, you're not old! You can get out.

STELLA [*slowly and emphatically*]   I'm not in anything I want to get out of.

BLANCHE [*incredulously*]   What—Stella?

STELLA   I said I am not in anything that I have a desire to get out of. Look at the mess in this room! And those empty bottles! They went through two cases last night! He promised this morning that he was going to quit having these poker parties, but you know how long such a promise is going to keep. Oh, well, it's his pleasure, like mine is movies and bridge. People have got to tolerate each other's habits, I guess.

BLANCHE   I don't understand you. [STELLA *turns toward her.*] I don't under-stand your indifference. Is this a Chinese philosophy you've—cultivated?

STELLA   Is what—what?

BLANCHE   This—shuffling about and mumbling—'One tube smashed—beer bottles—mess in the kitchen!'—as if nothing out of the ordinary has hap-pened! [STELLA *laughs uncertainly and picking up the broom, twirls it in her hands.*]

BLANCHE   Are you deliberately shaking that thing in my face?

STELLA   No.

BLANCHE   Stop it. Let go of that broom. I won't have you cleaning up for him!

STELLA   Then who's going to do it? Are you?

BLANCHE   I? I!

---

1. Vacuum tube (used in radios before the invention of transistors).

STELLA No, I didn't think so.

BLANCHE Oh, let me think, if only my mind would function! We've got to get
75   hold of some money, that's the way out!

STELLA I guess that money is always nice to get hold of.

BLANCHE Listen to me. I have an idea of some kind. [*Shakily she twists a
cigarette into her holder.*] Do you remember Shep Huntleigh? [STELLA
shakes her head.] Of course you remember Shep Huntleigh. I went out
80   with him at college and wore his pin[2] for a while. Well—

STELLA Well?

BLANCHE I ran into him last winter. You know I went to Miami during the
Christmas holidays?

STELLA No.

85 BLANCHE Well, I did. I took the trip as an investment, thinking I'd meet
someone with a million dollars.

STELLA Did you?

BLANCHE Yes. I ran into Shep Huntleigh—I ran into him on Biscayne Boulevard, on Christmas Eve, about dusk . . . getting into his car—Cadillac
90   convertible; must have been a block long!

STELLA I should think it would have been—inconvenient in traffic!

BLANCHE You've heard of oil wells?

STELLA Yes—remotely.

BLANCHE He has them, all over Texas. Texas is literally spouting gold in his
95   pockets.

STELLA My, my.

BLANCHE Y'know how indifferent I am to money. I think of money in terms
of what it does for you. But he could do it, he could certainly do it!

STELLA Do what, Blanche?

100 BLANCHE Why—set us up in a—shop!

STELLA What kind of a shop?

BLANCHE Oh, a—shop of some kind! He could do it with half what his wife
throws away at the races.

STELLA He's married?

105 BLANCHE Honey, would I be here if the man weren't married? [STELLA
laughs a little. BLANCHE *suddenly springs up and crosses to phone. She speaks
shrilly.*] How do I get Western Union?[3]—Operator! Western Union!

STELLA That's a dial phone,[4] honey.

BLANCHE I can't dial, I'm too—

STELLA Just dial O.

110 BLANCHE O?

STELLA Yes, "O" for Operator! [BLANCHE *considers a moment; then she puts
the phone down.*]

BLANCHE Give me a pencil. Where is a slip of paper? I've got to write it
down first—the message, I mean . . .

[*She goes to the dressing table, and grabs up a sheet of Kleenex and an
eyebrow pencil for writing equipment.*]

---

2. A fraternity pin, worn as a sign that a couple
were "going steady."
3. The dominant American telegraph company for most of the twentieth century.

4. Though dial telephones came into use in the
1930s, in some parts of the country (rural Mississippi presumably among them) operators
placed all calls for another decade or more.

Let me see now . . . [*She bites the pencil.*] 'Darling Shep. Sister and I in
115   desperate situation.'

STELLA   I beg your pardon!

BLANCHE   'Sister and I in desperate situation. Will explain details later.
Would you be interested in—?' [*She bites the pencil again.*] 'Would you
be—interested—in . . .' [*She smashes the pencil on the table and springs
120   up.*] You never get anywhere with direct appeals!

STELLA [*with a laugh*]   Don't be so ridiculous, darling!

BLANCHE   But I'll think of something, I've *got* to think of—*something!* Don't,
don't laugh at me, Stella! Please, please don't—I—I want you to look at the
contents of my purse! Here's what's in it! [*She snatches her purse open.*]
125   Sixty-five measly cents in coin of the realm!

STELLA [*crossing to bureau*]   Stanley doesn't give me a regular allowance, he
likes to pay bills himself, but—this morning he gave me ten dollars to
smooth things over. You take five of it, Blanche, and I'll keep the rest.

BLANCHE   Oh, no. No, Stella.

130 STELLA [*insisting*]   I know how it helps your morale just having a little pocket
money on you.

BLANCHE   No, thank you—I'll take to the streets!

STELLA   Talk sense! How did you happen to get so low on funds?

BLANCHE   Money just goes—it goes places. [*She rubs her forehead.*] Some
135   time today I've got to get hold of a Bromo![5]

STELLA   I'll fix you one now.

BLANCHE   Not yet—I've got to keep thinking!

STELLA   I wish you'd just let things go, at least for a—while . . .

BLANCHE   Stella, I can't live with him! You can, he's your husband. But how
140   could I stay here with him, after last night, with just those curtains between
us?

STELLA   Blanche, you saw him at his worst last night.

BLANCHE   On the contrary, I saw him at his best! What such a man has to
offer is animal force and he gave a wonderful exhibition of that! But the
145   only way to live with such a man is to—go to bed with him! And that's your
job—not mine!

STELLA   After you've rested a little, you'll see it's going to work out. You don't
have to worry about anything while you're here. I mean—expenses . . .

BLANCHE   I have to plan for us both, to get us both—out!

150 STELLA   You take it for granted that I am in something that I want to get out of.

BLANCHE   I take it for granted that you still have sufficient memory of Belle
Reve to find this place and these poker players impossible to live with.

STELLA   Well, you're taking entirely too much for granted.

BLANCHE   I can't believe you're in earnest.

155 STELLA   No?

BLANCHE   I understand how it happened—a little. You saw him in uniform,
an officer, not here but—

STELLA   I'm not sure it would have made any difference where I saw him.

BLANCHE   Now don't say it was one of those mysterious electric things
160   between people! If you do I'll laugh in your face.

---

5. Bromo-Seltzer, a headache remedy and antacid introduced in 1891; its effervescent granules
are dissolved in water.

STELLA   I am not going to say anything more at all about it!

BLANCHE   All right, then, don't!

STELLA   But there are things that happen between a man and a woman in the dark—that sort of make everything else seem—unimportant. [*Pause*]

165 BLANCHE   What you are talking about is brutal desire—just—Desire!—the name of that rattletrap streetcar that bangs through the Quarter, up one old narrow street and down another . . .

STELLA   Haven't you ever ridden on that streetcar?

BLANCHE   It brought me here.—Where I'm not wanted and where I'm
170   ashamed to be . . .

STELLA   Then don't you think your superior attitude is a bit out of place?

BLANCHE   I am not being or feeling at all superior, Stella. Believe me I'm not! It's just this. This is how I look at it. A man like that is someone to go out with—once—twice—three times when the devil is in you. But live with?
175   Have a child by?

STELLA   I have told you I love him.

BLANCHE   Then I *tremble* for you! I just—*tremble* for you.. . . .

STELLA   I can't help your trembling if you insist on trembling!

   [*There is a pause.*]

BLANCHE   May I—speak—*plainly*?

180 STELLA   Yes, do. Go ahead. As plainly as you want to.

   [*Outside, a train approaches. They are silent till the noise subsides. They are both in the bedroom.*]

   [*Under cover of the train's noise* STANLEY *enters from outside. He stands unseen by the women, holding some packages in his arms, and overhears their following conversation. He wears an undershirt and grease-stained seersucker pants.*]

BLANCHE   Well—if you'll forgive me—he's *common*!

STELLA   Why, yes, I suppose he is.

BLANCHE   Suppose! You can't have forgotten that much of our bringing up, Stella, that you just *suppose* that any part of a gentleman's in his nature!
185   *Not one particle, no!* Oh, if he was just—*ordinary*! Just *plain*—but good and wholesome, but—*no*. There's something downright—*bestial*—about him! You're hating me saying this, aren't you?

STELLA   [*coldly*]   Go on and say it all, Blanche.

BLANCHE   He acts like an animal, has an animal's habits! Eats like one,
190   moves like one, talks like one! There's even something—subhuman—something not quite to the stage of humanity yet! Yes, something—apelike about him, like one of those pictures I've seen in—anthropological studies! Thousands and thousands of years have passed him right by, and there he is—Stanley Kowalski—survivor of the Stone Age! Bearing the raw meat home
195   from the kill in the jungle! And you—*you* here—*waiting* for him! Maybe he'll strike you or maybe grunt and kiss you! That is, if kisses have been discovered yet! Night falls and the other apes gather! There in the front of the cave, all grunting like him, and swilling and gnawing and hulking! His poker night!—you call it—this party of apes! Somebody growls—some
200   creature snatches at something—the fight is on! *God!* Maybe we are a long way from being made in God's image, but Stella—my sister—there has been *some* progress since then! Such things as art—as poetry and music—such kinds of new light have come into the world since then! In some kinds

of people some tenderer feelings have had some little beginning! That we have got to make *grow!* And *cling* to, and hold as our flag! In this dark march toward whatever it is we're approaching. . . . *Don't—don't hang back with the brutes!*

[*Another train passes outside.* STANLEY *hesitates, licking his lips. Then suddenly he turns stealthily about and withdraws through front door. The women are still unaware of his presence. When the train has passed he calls through the closed front door.*]

STANLEY Hey! Hey, Stella!

STELLA [*who has listened gravely to* BLANCHE] Stanley!

BLANCHE Stell, I—

[*But* STELLA *has gone to the front door.* STANLEY *enters casually with his packages.*]

STANLEY Hiyuh, Stella. Blanche back?

STELLA Yes, she's back.

STANLEY Hiyuh, Blanche. [*He grins at her.*]

STELLA You must've got under the car.

STANLEY Them darn mechanics at Fritz's don't know their ass fr'm—*Hey!*

[STELLA *has embraced him with both arms, fiercely, and full in the view of* BLANCHE. *He laughs and clasps her head to him. Over her head he grins through the curtains at* BLANCHE.]

[*As the lights fade away, with a lingering brightness on their embrace, the music of the "blue piano" and trumpet and drums is heard.*]

Scene 5

BLANCHE *is seated in the bedroom fanning herself with a palm leaf as she reads over a just-completed letter. Suddenly she bursts into a peal of laughter.* STELLA *is dressing in the bedroom.*

STELLA What are you laughing at, honey?

BLANCHE Myself, myself, for being such a liar! I'm writing a letter to Shep. [*She picks up the letter.*] "Darling Shep. I am spending the summer on the wing, making flying visits here and there. And who knows, perhaps I shall take a sudden notion to *swoop* down on *Dallas!* How would you feel about that? Ha-ha! [*She laughs nervously and brightly, touching her throat as if actually talking to Shep.*] Forewarned is forearmed, as they say!"—How does that sound?

STELLA Uh-huh . . .

BLANCHE [*going on nervously*] "Most of my sister's friends go north in the summer but some have homes on the Gulf and there has been a continued round of entertainments, teas, cocktails, and luncheons—"

[*A disturbance is heard upstairs at the Hubbells' apartment.*]

STELLA Eunice seems to be having some trouble with Steve.

[EUNICE'S *voice shouts in terrible wrath.*]

EUNICE I heard about you and that blonde!

STEVE That's a damn lie!

EUNICE You ain't pulling the wool over my eyes! I wouldn't mind if you'd stay down at the Four Deuces, but you always going up.

STEVE Who ever seen me up?

EUNICE I seen you chasing her 'round the balcony—I'm gonna call the vice squad!

STEVE   Don't you throw that at me!

EUNICE [*shrieking*]   You hit me! I'm gonna call the police!

> [*A clatter of aluminum striking a wall is heard, followed by a man's angry roar, shouts and overturned furniture. There is a crash; then a relative hush.*]

BLANCHE [*brightly*]   Did he *kill* her?

> [EUNICE *appears on the steps in daemonic disorder.*]

STELLA   No! She's coming downstairs.

25 EUNICE   Call the police, I'm going to call the police! [*She rushes around the corner.*]

> [*They laugh lightly.* STANLEY *comes around the corner in his green and scarlet silk bowling shirt. He trots up the steps and bangs into the kitchen.* BLANCHE *registers his entrance with nervous gestures.*]

STANLEY   What's a matter with Eun-uss?

STELLA   She and Steve had a row. Has she got the police?

STANLEY   Naw. She's gettin' a drink.

STELLA   That's much more practical!

> [STEVE *comes down nursing a bruise on his forehead and looks in the door.*]

30 STEVE   She here?

STANLEY   Naw, naw. At the Four Deuces.

STEVE   That rutting hunk! [*He looks around the corner a bit timidly, then turns with affected boldness and runs after her.*]

BLANCHE   I must jot that down in my notebook. Ha-ha! I'm compiling a notebook of quaint little words and phrases I've picked up here.

35 STANLEY   You won't pick up nothing here you ain't heard before.

BLANCHE   Can I count on that?

STANLEY   You can count on it up to five hundred.

BLANCHE   That's a mighty high number. [*He jerks open the bureau drawer, slams it shut and throws shoes in a corner. At each noise* BLANCHE *winces slightly. Finally she speaks.*] What sign were you born under?

40 STANLEY [*while he is dressing*]   Sign?

BLANCHE   Astrological sign. I bet you were born under Aries. Aries people are forceful and dynamic. They dote on noise! They love to bang things around! You must have had lots of banging around in the army and now that you're out, you make up for it by treating inanimate objects with such

45 a fury!

> [STELLA *has been going in and out of closet during this scene. Now she pops her head out of the closet.*]

STELLA   Stanley was born just five minutes after Christmas.

BLANCHE   Capricorn—the Goat!

STANLEY   What sign were *you* born under?

BLANCHE   Oh, my birthday's next month, the fifteenth of September; that's

50 under Virgo.

STANLEY   What's Virgo?

BLANCHE   Virgo is the Virgin.

STANLEY [*contemptuously*]   Hah! [*He advances a little as he knots his tie.*] Say, do you happen to know somebody named Shaw?

> [*Her face expresses a faint shock. She reaches for the cologne bottle and dampens her handkerchief as she answers carefully.*]

55 BLANCHE   Why, everybody knows somebody named Shaw!

STANLEY   Well, this somebody named Shaw is under the impression he met you in Laurel, but I figure he must have got you mixed up with some other party because this other party is someone he met at a hotel called the Flamingo.

[BLANCHE *laughs breathlessly as she touches the cologne-dampened handkerchief to her temples.*]

60 BLANCHE   I'm afraid he does have me mixed up with this "other party." The Hotel Flamingo is not the sort of establishment I would dare to be seen in!

STANLEY   You know of it?

BLANCHE   Yes, I've seen it and smelled it.

STANLEY   You must've got pretty close if you could smell it.

65 BLANCHE   The odor of cheap perfume is penetrating.

STANLEY   That stuff you use is expensive?

BLANCHE   Twenty-five dollars an ounce! I'm nearly out. That's just a hint if you want to remember my birthday! [*She speaks lightly but her voice has a note of fear.*]

STANLEY   Shaw must've got you mixed up. He goes in and out of Laurel all
70   the time so he can check on it and clear up any mistake.

[*He turns away and crosses to the portieres.* BLANCHE *closes her eyes as if faint. Her hand trembles as she lifts the handkerchief again to her forehead.*]

[STEVE *and* EUNICE *come around corner.* STEVE's *arm is around* EUNICE's *shoulder and she is sobbing luxuriously and he is cooing love-words. There is a murmur of thunder as they go slowly upstairs in a tight embrace.*]

STANLEY [*to* STELLA]   I'll wait for you at the Four Deuces!

STELLA   Hey! Don't I rate one kiss?

STANLEY   Not in front of your sister.

[*He goes out.* BLANCHE *rises from her chair. She seems faint; looks about her with an expression of almost panic.*]

BLANCHE   Stella! What have you heard about me?

75 STELLA   Huh?

BLANCHE   What have people been telling you about me?

STELLA   Telling?

BLANCHE   You haven't heard any—unkind—gossip about me?

STELLA   Why, no, Blanche, of course not!

80 BLANCHE   Honey, there was—a good deal of talk in Laurel.

STELLA   About *you,* Blanche?

BLANCHE   I wasn't so good the last two years or so, after Belle Reve had started to slip through my fingers.

STELLA   All of us do things we—

85 BLANCHE   I never was hard or self-sufficient enough. When people are soft—soft people have got to shimmer and glow—they've got to put on soft colors, the colors of butterfly wings, and put a—paper lantern over the light. . . . It isn't enough to be soft. You've got to be soft *and attractive.* And I—I'm fading now! I don't know how much longer I can turn the trick.

[*The afternoon has faded to dusk.* STELLA *goes into the bedroom and turns on the light under the paper lantern. She holds a bottled soft drink in her hand.*]

90 BLANCHE   Have you been listening to me?

STELLA   I don't listen to you when you are being morbid! [*She advances with the bottled Coke.*]

BLANCHE [*with abrupt change to gaiety*]   Is that Coke for me?

STELLA   Not for anyone else!

BLANCHE   Why, you precious thing, you! Is it just Coke?

95 STELLA [*turning*]   You mean you want a shot in it!

BLANCHE   Well, honey, a shot never does a Coke any harm! Let me! You mustn't wait on me!

STELLA   I like to wait on you, Blanche. It makes it seem more like home. [*She goes into the kitchen, finds a glass and pours a shot of whiskey into it.*]

BLANCHE   I have to admit I love to be waited on . . .

[*She rushes into the bedroom.* STELLA *goes to her with the glass.* BLANCHE *suddenly clutches* STELLA'S *free hand with a moaning sound and presses the hand to her lips.* STELLA *is embarrassed by her show of emotion.* BLANCHE *speaks in a choked voice.*]

100   You're—you're—so *good* to me! And I—

STELLA   Blanche.

BLANCHE   I know, I won't! You hate me to talk sentimental! But honey, *believe* I feel things more than I *tell* you! I *won't* stay long! I won't, I *promise* I—

STELLA   Blanche!

105 BLANCHE [*hysterically*]   I won't, I promise, *I'll* go! Go *soon*! I will *really*! I *won't* hang around until he—throws me out . . .

STELLA   Now will you stop talking foolish?

BLANCHE   Yes, honey. Watch how you pour—that fizzy stuff foams over!

[BLANCHE *laughs shrilly and grabs the glass, but her hand shakes so it almost slips from her grasp.* STELLA *pours the Coke into the glass. It foams over and spills.* BLANCHE *gives a piercing cry.*]

STELLA [*shocked by the cry*]   Heavens!

110 BLANCHE   Right on my pretty white skirt!

STELLA   Oh . . . Use my hanky. Blot gently.

BLANCHE [*slowly recovering*]   I know—gently—gently . . .

STELLA   Did it stain?

BLANCHE   Not a bit. Ha-ha! Isn't that lucky? [*She sits down shakily, taking a grateful drink. She holds the glass in both hands and continues to laugh a little.*]

115 STELLA   Why did you scream like that?

BLANCHE   I don't know why I screamed! [*Continuing nervously*] Mitch—Mitch is coming at seven. I guess I am just feeling nervous about our relations. [*She begins to talk rapidly and breathlessly.*] He hasn't gotten a thing but a good-night kiss, that's all I have given him, Stella. I want his respect.

120   And men don't want anything they get too easy. But on the other hand men lose interest quickly. Especially when the girl is over—thirty. They think a girl over thirty ought to—the vulgar term is—"put out." . . . And I—I'm not "putting out." Of course he—he doesn't know—I mean I haven't informed him—of my real age!

125 STELLA   Why are you sensitive about your age?

BLANCHE   Because of hard knocks my vanity's been given. What I mean is—he thinks I'm sort of—prim and proper, you know! [*She laughs out sharply.*] I want to *deceive* him enough to make him—want me . . .

STELLA   Blanche, do you want *him*?

130 BLANCHE   I want to *rest!* I want to breathe quietly again! Yes—I *want* Mitch . . . *very badly!* Just think! If it happens! I can leave here and not be anyone's problem . . .

[STANLEY *comes around the corner with a drink under his belt.*]

STANLEY [*bawling*]   Hey, Steve! Hey, Eunice! Hey, Stella!

[*There are joyous calls from above. Trumpet and drums are heard from around the corner.*]

STELLA [*kissing* BLANCHE *impulsively*]   It *will* happen!

135 BLANCHE [*doubtfully*]   It will?

STELLA   It *will!* [*She goes across into the kitchen, looking back at* BLANCHE.] It will, honey, *it will.* . . . But don't take another drink! [*Her voice catches as she goes out the door to meet her husband.*]

[BLANCHE *sinks faintly back in her chair with her drink.* EUNICE *shrieks with laughter and runs down the steps.* STEVE *bounds after her with goat-like screeches and chases her around corner.* STANLEY *and* STELLA *twine arms as they follow, laughing.*]

[*Dusk settles deeper. The music from the Four Deuces is slow and blue.*]

BLANCHE   Ah, me, ah, me, ah, me . . .

[*Her eyes fall shut and the palm leaf fan drops from her fingers. She slaps her hand on the chair arm a couple of times. There is a little glimmer of lightning about the building.*]

[*A* YOUNG MAN *comes along the street and rings the bell.*]

BLANCHE   Come in.

[*The* YOUNG MAN *appears through the portieres. She regards him with interest.*]

140 BLANCHE   Well, well! What can I do for *you?*

YOUNG MAN   I'm collecting for *The Evening Star.*

BLANCHE   I didn't know that stars took up collections.

YOUNG MAN   It's the paper.

BLANCHE   I know, I was joking—feebly! Will you—have a drink?

145 YOUNG MAN   No, ma'am. No, thank you. I can't drink on the job.

BLANCHE   Oh, well, now, let's see. . . . No, I don't have a dime! I'm not the lady of the house. I'm her sister from Mississippi. I'm one of those poor relations you've heard about.

YOUNG MAN   That's all right. I'll drop by later. [*He starts to go out. She approaches a little.*]

150 BLANCHE   Hey! [*He turns back shyly. She puts a cigarette in a long holder.*] Could you give me a light? [*She crosses toward him. They meet at the door between the two rooms.*]

YOUNG MAN   Sure. [*He takes out a lighter.*] This doesn't always work.

BLANCHE   It's temperamental? [*It flares.*] Ah!—thank you. [*He starts away again.*] Hey! [*He turns again, still more uncertainly. She goes close to him.*]

155 Uh—what time is it?

YOUNG MAN   Fifteen of seven, ma'am.

BLANCHE   So late? Don't you just love these long rainy afternoons in New Orleans when an hour isn't just an hour—but a little piece of eternity dropped into your hands—and who knows what to do with it? [*She touches

160 his shoulders.*] You—uh—didn't get wet in the rain?

YOUNG MAN   No, ma'am. I stepped inside.

BLANCHE   In a drugstore? And had a soda?

YOUNG MAN   Uh-huh.

BLANCHE   Chocolate?

165 YOUNG MAN   No, ma'am. Cherry.

BLANCHE [*laughing*]   Cherry!

YOUNG MAN   A cherry soda.

BLANCHE   You make my mouth water. [*She touches his cheek lightly, and smiles. Then she goes to the trunk.*]

YOUNG MAN   Well, I'd better be going—

170 BLANCHE [*stopping him*]   Young man!

[*He turns. She takes a large, gossamer scarf from the trunk and drapes it about her shoulders.*]

[*In the ensuing pause, the "blue piano" is heard. It continues through the rest of this scene and the opening of the next. The young man clears his throat and looks yearningly at the door.*]

Young man! Young, young, young man! Has anyone ever told you that you look like a young Prince out of the Arabian Nights?[6]

[*The* YOUNG MAN *laughs uncomfortably and stands like a bashful kid.* BLANCHE *speaks softly to him.*]

Well, you do, honey lamb! Come here. I want to kiss you, just once, softly and sweetly on your mouth!

[*Without waiting for him to accept, she crosses quickly to him and presses her lips to his.*]

175 Now run along, now, quickly! It would be nice to keep you, but I've got to be good—and keep my hands off children.

[*He stares at her a moment. She opens the door for him and blows a kiss at him as he goes down the steps with a dazed look. She stands there a little dreamily after he has disappeared. Then* MITCH *appears around the corner with a bunch of roses.*]

BLANCHE [*gaily*]   Look who's coming! My Rosenkavalier! Bow to me first . . . now present them! *Ahhhh—Merciiii!*[7]

[*She looks at him over them, coquettishly pressing them to her lips. He beams at her self-consciously.*]

Scene 6

It is about two A.M. *on the same evening. The outer wall of the building is visible.* BLANCHE *and* MITCH *come in. The utter exhaustion which only a neurasthenic personality[8] can know is evident in* BLANCHE*'s voice and manner.* MITCH *is stolid but depressed. They have probably been out to the amusement park on Lake Pontchartrain, for* MITCH *is bearing, upside down, a plaster statuette of Mae West,[9] the sort of prize won at shooting galleries and carnival games of chance.*

6. That is, *The Thousand and One Nights*, a collection of ancient tales in Arabic, arranged in its present form in the 15th century.

7. Thank you (French). *Rosenkavalier:* literally, "Knight of the Rose" (German), an allusion to Richard Strauss's romantic opera *Der Rosenkavalier* (1911).

8. Someone suffering from neurasthenia, a psychological disorder characterized by ner-vous exhaustion. A common clinical diagnosis during the late 19th century, the term is no longer in scientific use.

9. An American actress of burlesque shows, stage, and screen (1893–1980), famous for her sexual double entendres. *Lake Pontchartrain:* the large, shallow lake immediately north of New Orleans.

BLANCHE [*stopping lifelessly at the steps*] Well—

[MITCH *laughs uneasily.*]

Well . . .

MITCH I guess it must be pretty late—and you're tired.

BLANCHE Even the hot tamale man has deserted the street, and he hangs on
5 till the end. [MITCH *laughs uneasily again.*] How will you get home?

MITCH I'll walk over to Bourbon and catch an owl-car.[1]

BLANCHE [*laughing grimly*] Is that streetcar named Desire still grinding
along the tracks at this hour?

MITCH [*heavily*] I'm afraid you haven't gotten much fun out of this evening,
10 Blanche.

BLANCHE I spoiled it for *you*.

MITCH No, you didn't, but I felt all the time that I wasn't giving you
much—entertainment.

BLANCHE I simply couldn't rise to the occasion. That was all. I don't think
15 I've ever tried so hard to be gay and made such a dismal mess of it. I get ten
points for trying!—I *did* try.

MITCH Why did you try if you didn't feel like it, Blanche?

BLANCHE I was just obeying the law of nature.

MITCH Which law is that?

20 BLANCHE The one that says the lady must entertain the gentleman—or no
dice! See if you can locate my door key in this purse. When I'm so tired my
fingers are all thumbs!

MITCH [*rooting in her purse*] This it?

BLANCHE No, honey, that's the key to my trunk which I must soon be
25 packing.

MITCH You mean you are leaving here soon?

BLANCHE I've outstayed my welcome.

MITCH This it?

[*The music fades away.*]

BLANCHE Eureka! Honey, you open the door while I take a last look at the
30 sky. [*She leans on the porch rail. He opens the door and stands awkwardly
behind her.*] I'm looking for the Pleiades, the Seven Sisters,[2] but these girls
are not out tonight. Oh, yes they are, there they are! God bless them! All in
a bunch going home from their little bridge party. . . . Y' get the door open?
Good boy! I guess you—want to go now . . .

[*He shuffles and coughs a little.*]

35 MITCH Can I—uh—kiss you—good night?

BLANCHE Why do you always ask me if you may?

MITCH I don't know whether you want me to or not.

BLANCHE Why should you be so doubtful?

MITCH That night when we parked by the lake and I kissed you, you—

40 BLANCHE Honey, it wasn't the kiss I objected to. I liked the kiss very much.
It was the other little—familiarity—that I—felt obliged to—discourage. . . .
I didn't resent it! Not a bit in the world! In fact, I was somewhat flattered
that you—desired me! But, honey, you know as well as I do that a single

---

1. A late-night streetcar (i.e., for "night
owls").
2. In Greek mythology, the Pleiades are the
seven daughters of Atlas who were changed
into a cluster of stars in the constellation
Taurus.

45 girl, a girl alone in the world, has got to keep a firm hold on her emotions
or she'll be lost!

MITCH [*solemnly*] Lost?

BLANCHE I guess you are used to girls that like to be lost. The kind that get
lost immediately, on the first date!

MITCH I like you to be exactly the way that you are, because in all my—
50 experience—I have never known anyone like you.

> [BLANCHE *looks at him gravely; then she bursts into laughter and then
> claps a hand to her mouth.*]

MITCH Are you laughing at me?

BLANCHE No, honey. The lord and lady of the house have not yet returned,
so come in. We'll have a nightcap. Let's leave the lights off. Shall we?

MITCH You just—do what you want to.

> [BLANCHE *precedes him into the kitchen. The outer wall of the building
> disappears and the interiors of the two rooms can be dimly seen.*]

55 BLANCHE [*remaining in the first room*] The other room's more comfortable—go
on in. This crashing around in the dark is my search for some liquor.

MITCH You want a drink?

BLANCHE I want *you* to have a drink! You have been so anxious and solemn
all evening, and so have I; we have both been anxious and solemn and now
60 for these few last remaining moments of our lives together—I want to create—*joie de vivre!*[3] I'm lighting a candle.

MITCH That's good.

BLANCHE We are going to be very Bohemian. We are going to pretend that
we are sitting in a little artists' cafe on the Left Bank[4] in Paris! [*She lights a
65 candle stub and puts it in a bottle.*] *Je suis la Dame aux Camellias! Vous
êtes—Armand!*[5] Understand French?

MITCH [*heavily*] Naw. Naw, I—

BLANCHE *Voulez-vous couchez avec moi ce soir? Vous ne comprenez pas? Ah,
quelle dommage!*[6] I mean it's a damned good thing. . . . I've found some
70 liquor! Just enough for two shots without any dividends, honey . . .

MITCH [*heavily*] That's—good.

> [*She enters the bedroom with the drinks and the candle.*]

BLANCHE Sit down! Why don't you take off your coat and loosen your collar?

MITCH I better leave it on.

BLANCHE No. I want you to be comfortable.

75 MITCH I am ashamed of the way I perspire. My shirt is sticking to me.

BLANCHE Perspiration is healthy. If people didn't perspire they would die in
five minutes. [*She takes his coat from him.*] This is a nice coat. What kind
of material is it?

MITCH They call that stuff alpaca.

3. Joy of life (French).
4. A neighborhood on the western ("left")
bank of the river Seine, known for cultural
and intellectual activities.
5. I am the Lady of the Camellias. You are—
Armand! (French). The reference is to Alexandre Dumas's novel *La Dame aux camélias*
(1848), the tragic story of Marguerite
Gautier, a Parisian courtesan who falls in love

with Armand Duval, a respectable member
of middle-class society, and dies of consumption. Dumas's 1852 theatrical adaptation of
this novel (often titled *Camille* in English)
was highly popular with late 19th-century
audiences.
6. Would you like to go to bed with me
tonight? You don't understand? Ah, what a
shame! (French).

80 BLANCHE   Oh. Alpaca.

MITCH   It's very light-weight alpaca.

BLANCHE   Oh. Light-weight alpaca.

MITCH   I don't like to wear a wash-coat[7] even in summer because I sweat through it.

85 BLANCHE   Oh.

MITCH   And it don't look neat on me. A man with a heavy build has got to be careful of what he puts on him so he don't look too clumsy.

BLANCHE   You are not too heavy.

MITCH   You don't think I am?

90 BLANCHE   You are not the delicate type. You have a massive bone-structure and a very imposing physique.

MITCH   Thank you. Last Christmas I was given a membership to the New Orleans Athletic Club.

BLANCHE   Oh, good.

95 MITCH   It was the finest present I ever was given. I work out there with the weights and I swim and I keep myself fit. When I started there, I was getting soft in the belly but now my belly is hard. It is so hard now that a man can punch me in the belly and it don't hurt me. Punch me! Go on! See? [*She pokes lightly at him.*]

BLANCHE   Gracious. [*Her hand touches her chest.*]

100 MITCH   Guess how much I weigh, Blanche?

BLANCHE   Oh, I'd say in the vicinity of—one hundred and eighty?

MITCH   Guess again.

BLANCHE   Not that much?

MITCH   No. More.

105 BLANCHE   Well, you're a tall man and you can carry a good deal of weight without looking awkward.

MITCH   I weigh two hundred and seven pounds and I'm six feet one and one half inches tall in my bare feet—without shoes on. And that is what I weigh stripped.

110 BLANCHE   Oh, my goodness, me! It's awe-inspiring.

MITCH [*embarrassed*]   My weight is not a very interesting subject to talk about. [*He hesitates for a moment.*] What's yours?

BLANCHE   My weight?

MITCH   Yes.

115 BLANCHE   Guess!

MITCH   Let me lift you.

BLANCHE   Samson![8] Go on, lift me. [*He comes behind her and puts his hands on her waist and raises her lightly off the ground.*] Well?

MITCH   You are light as a feather.

120 BLANCHE   Ha-ha! [*He lowers her but keeps his hands on her waist.* BLANCHE *speaks with an affectation of demureness.*] You may release me now.

MITCH   Huh?

BLANCHE [*gaily*]   I said unhand me, sir. [*He fumblingly embraces her. Her voice sounds gently reproving.*] Now, Mitch. Just because Stanley and Stella

125   aren't at home is no reason why you shouldn't behave like a gentleman.

---

7. A light washable jacket, here made of a silky wool.

8. An Israelite hero of great strength (see Judges 13–16).

MITCH   Just give me a slap whenever I step out of bounds.

BLANCHE   That won't be necessary. You're a natural gentleman, one of the very few that are left in the world. I don't want you to think that I am severe and old maid school-teacherish or anything like that. It's just—well—

130 MITCH   Huh?

BLANCHE   I guess it is just that I have—old-fashioned ideals! [*She rolls her eyes, knowing he cannot see her face.* MITCH *goes to the front door. There is a considerable silence between them.* BLANCHE *sighs and* MITCH *coughs self-consciously.*]

MITCH [*finally*]   Where's Stanley and Stella tonight?

BLANCHE   They have gone out. With Mr. and Mrs. Hubbell upstairs.

MITCH   Where did they go?

135 BLANCHE   I think they were planning to go to a midnight prevue at Loew's State.

MITCH   We should all go out together some night.

BLANCHE   No. That wouldn't be a good plan.

MITCH   Why not?

140 BLANCHE   You are an old friend of Stanley's?

MITCH   We was together in the Two-forty-first.[9]

BLANCHE   I guess he talks to you frankly?

MITCH   Sure.

BLANCHE   Has he talked to you about me?

145 MITCH   Oh—not very much.

BLANCHE   The way you say that, I suspect that he has.

MITCH   No, he hasn't said much.

BLANCHE   But what he *has* said. What would you say his attitude toward me was?

150 MITCH   Why do you want to ask that?

BLANCHE   Well—

MITCH   Don't you get along with him?

BLANCHE   What do you think?

MITCH   I don't think he understands you.

155 BLANCHE   That is putting it mildly. If it weren't for Stella about to have a baby, I wouldn't be able to endure things here.

MITCH   He isn't—nice to you?

BLANCHE   He is insufferably rude. Goes out of his way to offend me.

MITCH   In what way, Blanche?

160 BLANCHE   Why, in every conceivable way.

MITCH   I'm surprised to hear that.

BLANCHE   Are you?

MITCH   Well, I—don't see how anybody could be rude to you.

BLANCHE   It's really a pretty frightful situation. You see, there's no privacy

165 here. There's just these portieres between the two rooms at night. He stalks through the rooms in his underwear at night. And I have to ask him to close the bathroom door. That sort of commonness isn't necessary. You probably wonder why I don't move out. Well, I'll tell you frankly. A teacher's salary is barely sufficient for her living expenses. I didn't save a penny last year and

170 so I had to come here for the summer. That's why I have to put up with my

9. The 241st Battalion of the Army Corps of Engineers.

sister's husband. And he has to put up with me, apparently so much against his wishes. . . . Surely he must have told you how much he hates me!

MITCH   I don't think he hates you.

BLANCHE   He hates me. Or why would he insult me? The first time I laid
175   eyes on him I thought to myself, that man is my executioner! That man will destroy me, unless—

MITCH   Blanche—

BLANCHE   Yes, honey?

MITCH   Can I ask you a question?

180 BLANCHE   Yes. What?

MITCH   How old are you?

[She makes a nervous gesture.]

BLANCHE   Why do you want to know?

MITCH   I talked to my mother about you and she said, "How old is Blanche?" And I wasn't able to tell her. [There is another pause.]

185 BLANCHE   You talked to your mother about me?

MITCH   Yes.

BLANCHE   Why?

MITCH   I told my mother how nice you were, and I liked you.

BLANCHE   Were you sincere about that?

190 MITCH   You know I was.

BLANCHE   Why did your mother want to know my age?

MITCH   Mother is sick.

BLANCHE   I'm sorry to hear it. Badly?

MITCH   She won't live long. Maybe just a few months.

195 BLANCHE   Oh.

MITCH   She worries because I'm not settled.

BLANCHE   Oh.

MITCH   She wants me to be settled down before she—[His voice is hoarse and he clears his throat twice, shuffling nervously around with his hands in and out of his pockets.]

BLANCHE   You love her very much, don't you?

200 MITCH   Yes.

BLANCHE   I think you have a great capacity for devotion. You will be lonely when she passes on, won't you? [MITCH clears his throat and nods.] I understand what that is.

MITCH   To be lonely?

205 BLANCHE   I loved someone, too, and the person I loved I lost.

MITCH   Dead? [She crosses to the window and sits on the sill, looking out. She pours herself another drink.] A man?

BLANCHE   He was a boy, just a boy, when I was a very young girl. When I was sixteen, I made the discovery—love. All at once and much, much too com-
210   pletely. It was like you suddenly turned a blinding light on something that had always been half in shadow, that's how it struck the world for me. But I was unlucky. Deluded. There was something different about the boy, a nervousness, a softness and tenderness which wasn't like a man's, although he wasn't the least bit effeminate-looking—still—that thing was there. . . .
215   He came to me for help. I didn't know that. I didn't find out anything till after our marriage when we'd run away and come back and all I knew was I'd failed him in some mysterious way and wasn't able to give the help he

needed but couldn't speak of! He was in the quicksands and clutching at me—but I wasn't holding him out, I was slipping in with him! I didn't know that. I didn't know anything except I loved him unendurably but without being able to help him or help myself. Then I found out. In the worst of all possible ways. By coming suddenly into a room that I thought was empty—which wasn't empty, but had two people in it . . . the boy I had married and an older man who had been his friend for years . . .

> [*A locomotive is heard approaching outside. She claps her hands to her ears and crouches over. The headlight of the locomotive glares into the room as it thunders past. As the noise recedes she straightens slowly and continues speaking.*]

Afterward we pretended that nothing had been discovered. Yes, the three of us drove out to Moon Lake Casino,[1] very drunk and laughing all the way.

> [*Polka music sounds, in a minor key faint with distance.*]

We danced the Varsouviana![2] Suddenly in the middle of the dance the boy I had married broke away from me and ran out of the casino. A few moments later—a shot!

> [*The polka stops abruptly.*]

> [BLANCHE *rises stiffly. Then, the polka resumes in a major key.*]

I ran out—all did!—all ran and gathered about the terrible thing at the edge of the lake! I couldn't get near for the crowding. Then somebody caught my arm. "Don't go any closer! Come back! You don't want to see!" See? See what! Then I heard voices say—Allan! Allan! The Grey boy! He'd stuck the revolver into his mouth, and fired—so that the back of his head had been—blown away!

> [*She sways and covers her face.*]

It was because—on the dance floor—unable to stop myself—I'd suddenly said—"I saw! I know! You disgust me . . ." And then the searchlight which had been turned on the world was turned off again and never for one moment since has there been any light that's stronger than this—kitchen— candle . . .

> [MITCH *gets up awkwardly and moves toward her a little. The polka music increases.* MITCH *stands beside her.*]

MITCH [*drawing her slowly into his arms*] You need somebody. And I need somebody, too. Could it be—you and me, Blanche?

> [*She stares at him vacantly for a moment. Then with a soft cry huddles in his embrace. She makes a sobbing effort to speak but the words won't come. He kisses her forehead and her eyes and finally her lips. The polka tune fades out. Her breath is drawn and released in long, grateful sobs.*]

BLANCHE Sometimes—there's God—so quickly!

Scene 7

It is late afternoon in mid-September.

The portieres are open and a table is set for a birthday supper, with cake and flowers. STELLA *is completing the decorations as* STANLEY *comes in.*

---

1. A popular night spot and casino during the 1940s, located in Dundee, Mississippi.   2. A jaunty polka dance.

STANLEY   What's all this stuff for?

STELLA   Honey, it's Blanche's birthday.

STANLEY   She here?

STELLA   In the bathroom.

5 STANLEY [*mimicking*]   "Washing out some things"?

STELLA   I reckon so.

STANLEY   How long she been in there?

STELLA   All afternoon.

STANLEY [*mimicking*]   "Soaking in a hot tub"?

10 STELLA   Yes.

STANLEY   Temperature 100 on the nose, and she soaks herself in a hot tub.

STELLA   She says it cools her off for the evening.

STANLEY   And you run out an' get her cokes, I suppose? And serve 'em to Her Majesty in the tub? [STELLA *shrugs*.] Set down here a minute.

15 STELLA   Stanley, I've got things to do.

STANLEY   Set down! I've got th' dope on your big sister, Stella.

STELLA   Stanley, stop picking on Blanche.

STANLEY   That girl calls *me* common!

STELLA   Lately you been doing all you can think of to rub her the wrong way,
20   Stanley, and Blanche is sensitive and you've got to realize that Blanche and I grew up under very different circumstances than you did.

STANLEY   So I been told. And told and told and told! You know she's been feeding us a pack of lies here?

STELLA   No, I don't, and—

25 STANLEY   Well, she has, however. But now the cat's out of the bag! I found out some things!

STELLA   What—things?

STANLEY   Things I already suspected. But now I got proof from the most reliable sources—which I have checked on!

[BLANCHE *is singing in the bathroom a saccharine popular ballad which is used contrapuntally with Stanley's speech.*]

30 STELLA [*to STANLEY*]   Lower your voice!

STANLEY   Some canary bird, huh!

STELLA   Now please tell me quietly what you think you've found out about my sister.

STANLEY   Lie Number One: All this squeamishness she puts on! You should
35   just know the line she's been feeding to Mitch. He thought she had never been more than kissed by a fellow! But Sister Blanche is no lily! Ha-ha! Some lily she is!

STELLA   What have you heard and who from?

STANLEY   Our supply-man down at the plant has been going through Laurel
40   for years and he knows all about her and everybody else in the town of Laurel knows all about her. She is as famous in Laurel as if she was the President of the United States, only she is not respected by any party! This supply-man stops at a hotel called the Flamingo.

BLANCHE [*singing blithely*]

"Say, it's only a paper moon, Sailing over a cardboard sea—But it
45   wouldn't be make-believe If you believed in me!"[3]

---

3. From "It's Only a Paper Moon" (lyrics by Yip Harburg and Billy Rose, music by Harold Arlen), used in the film *Take a Chance* (1933).

STELLA   What about the—Flamingo?

STANLEY   She stayed there, too.

STELLA   My sister lived at Belle Reve.

STANLEY   This is after the home-place had slipped through her lily-white fingers! She moved to the Flamingo! A second-class hotel which has the advantage of not interfering in the private social life of the personalities there! The
Flamingo is used to all kinds of goings-on. But even the management of the
Flamingo was impressed by Dame Blanche! In fact they was so impressed by
Dame Blanche that they requested her to turn in her room key—for permanently! This happened a couple of weeks before she showed here.

BLANCHE [*singing*]

"It's a Barnum and Bailey world,[4] Just as phony as it can be—
But it wouldn't be make-believe If you believed in me!"

STELLA   What—contemptible—lies!

STANLEY   Sure, I can see how you would be upset by this. She pulled the
wool over your eyes as much as Mitch's!

STELLA   It's pure invention! There's not a word of truth in it and if I were a
man and this creature had dared to invent such things in my presence—

BLANCHE [*singing*]

"Without your love,
It's a honky-tonk parade!
Without your love,
It's a melody played In a penny arcade . . ."

STANLEY   Honey, I told you I thoroughly checked on these stories! Now wait
till I finished. The trouble with Dame Blanche was that she couldn't put on
her act any more in Laurel! They got wised up after two or three dates with
her and then they quit, and she goes on to another, the same old line, same
old act, same old hooey! But the town was too small for this to go on forever! And as time went by she became a town character. Regarded as not
just different but downright loco—nuts.

[STELLA *draws back.*]

And for the last year or two she has been washed up like poison. That's why
she's here this summer, visiting royalty, putting on all this act—because
she's practically told by the mayor to get out of town! Yes, did you know
there was an army camp near Laurel and your sister's was one of the places
called "Out-of-Bounds"?

BLANCHE

"It's only a paper moon, Just as phony as it can be—
But it wouldn't be make-believe If you believed in me!"

STANLEY   Well, so much for her being such a refined and particular type of
girl. Which brings us to Lie Number Two.

STELLA   I don't want to hear any more!

STANLEY   She's not going back to teach school! In fact I am willing to bet
you that she never had no idea of returning to Laurel! She didn't resign

4. That is, a circus performance. P. T. Barnum (1810–1891) and James A. Bailey (1847–1906)
merged their circuses in 1881.

temporarily from the high school because of her nerves! No, siree, Bob! She didn't. They kicked her out of that high school before the spring term ended—and I hate to tell you the reason that step was taken! A seventeen-year-old boy—she'd gotten mixed up with!

BLANCHE

90   "It's a Barnum and Bailey world, Just as phony as it can be—"

> [*In the bathroom the water goes on loud; little breathless cries and peals of laughter are heard as if a child were frolicking in the tub.*]

STELLA   This is making me—sick!

STANLEY   The boy's dad learned about it and got in touch with the high school superintendent. Boy, oh, boy, I'd like to have been in that office when Dame Blanche was called on the carpet! I'd like to have seen her try-
95   ing to squirm out of that one! But they had her on the hook good and proper that time and she knew that the jig was all up! They told her she better move on to some fresh territory. Yep, it was practickly a town ordinance passed against her!

> [*The bathroom door is opened and* BLANCHE *thrusts her head out, holding a towel about her hair.*]

BLANCHE   Stella!

100 STELLA [*faintly*]   Yes, Blanche?

BLANCHE   Give me another bath-towel to dry my hair with. I've just washed it.

STELLA   Yes, Blanche. [*She crosses in a dazed way from the kitchen to the bathroom door with a towel.*]

BLANCHE   What's the matter, honey?

STELLA   Matter? Why?

105 BLANCHE   You have such a strange expression on your face!

STELLA   Oh—[*She tries to laugh.*] I guess I'm a little tired!

BLANCHE   Why don't you bathe, too, soon as I get out?

STANLEY [*calling from the kitchen*]   How soon is that going to be?

BLANCHE   Not so terribly long! Possess your soul in patience![5]

110 STANLEY   It's not my soul, it's my kidneys I'm worried about!

> [BLANCHE *slams the door.* STANLEY *laughs harshly.* STELLA *comes slowly back into the kitchen.*]

STANLEY   Well, what do you think of it?

STELLA   I don't believe all of those stories and I think your supply-man was mean and rotten to tell them. It's possible that some of the things he said are partly true. There are things about my sister I don't approve of—things
115   that caused sorrow at home. She was always—flighty!

STANLEY   Flighty!

STELLA   But when she was young, very young, she married a boy who wrote poetry. . . . He was extremely good-looking. I think Blanche didn't just love him but worshipped the ground he walked on! Adored him and thought
120   him almost too fine to be human! But then she found out—

STANLEY   What?

STELLA   This beautiful and talented young man was a degenerate. Didn't your supply-man give you that information?

STANLEY   All we discussed was recent history. That must have been a pretty
125   long time ago.

---

5. "In your patience possess ye your souls" (Luke 21.19).

STELLA   Yes, it was—a pretty long time ago . . .

[STANLEY *comes up and takes her by the shoulders rather gently. She gently withdraws from him. Automatically she starts sticking little pink candles in the birthday cake.*]

STANLEY   How many candles you putting in that cake?

STELLA   I'll stop at twenty-five.

STANLEY   Is company expected?

130 STELLA   We asked Mitch to come over for cake and ice-cream.

[STANLEY *looks a little uncomfortable. He lights a cigarette from the one he has just finished.*]

STANLEY   I wouldn't be expecting Mitch over tonight.

[STELLA *pauses in her occupation with candles and looks slowly around at* STANLEY.]

STELLA   *Why?*

STANLEY   Mitch is a buddy of mine. We were in the same outfit together—
Two-forty-first Engineers. We work in the same plant and now on the same
135   bowling team. You think I could face him if—

STELLA   Stanley Kowalski, did you—did you repeat what that—?

STANLEY   You're goddam right I told him! I'd have that on my conscience the
rest of my life if I knew all that stuff and let my best friend get caught!

STELLA   Is Mitch through with her?

140 STANLEY   Wouldn't you be if—?

STELLA   I said, *Is Mitch through with her?*

[BLANCHE's *voice is lifted again, serenely as a bell. She sings "But it wouldn't be make-believe If you believed in me."*]

STANLEY   No, I don't think he's necessarily through with her—just wised up!

STELLA   Stanley, she thought Mitch was—going to—going to marry her. I
was hoping so, too.

145 STANLEY   Well, he's not going to marry her. Maybe he *was,* but he's not going
to jump in a tank with a school of sharks—now! [*He rises.*] Blanche! Oh,
Blanche! Can I please get in my bathroom? [*There is a pause.*]

BLANCHE   Yes, indeed, sir! Can you wait one second while I dry?

STANLEY   Having waited one hour I guess one second ought to pass in a
150   hurry.

STELLA   And she hasn't got her job? Well, what will she do!

STANLEY   She's not stayin' here after Tuesday. You know that, don't you? Just
to make sure I bought her ticket myself. A bus ticket?

STELLA   In the first place, Blanche wouldn't go on a bus.

155 STANLEY   She'll go on a bus and like it.

STELLA   No, she won't, no, she won't, Stanley!

STANLEY   *She'll go!* Period. P.S. She'll go *Tuesday!*

STELLA [*slowly*]   What'll—she—do? What on earth will she—*do!*

STANLEY   Her future is mapped out for her.

160 STELLA   What do you mean?

[BLANCHE *sings.*]

STANLEY   Hey, canary bird! Toots! Get *OUT* of the *BATHROOM!*

[*The bathroom door flies open and* BLANCHE *emerges with a gay peal of laughter, but as* STANLEY *crosses past her, a frightened look appears in her face, almost a look of panic. He doesn't look at her but slams the bathroom door shut as he goes in.*]

BLANCHE [*snatching up a hairbrush*]   Oh, I feel so good after my long, hot
bath, I feel so good and cool and—rested!

STELLA [*sadly and doubtfully from the kitchen*]   Do you, Blanche?

165 BLANCHE [*brushing her hair vigorously*]   Yes, I do, so refreshed! [*She tinkles her
highball glass.*] A hot bath and a long, cold drink always give me a brand new
outlook on life! [*She looks through the portieres at* STELLA, *standing between
them, and slowly stops brushing.*] Something has happened!—What is it?

STELLA [*turning away quickly*]   Why, nothing has happened, Blanche.

170 BLANCHE   You're lying! Something has!

> [*She stares fearfully at* STELLA, *who pretends to be busy at the table. The
> distant piano goes into a hectic breakdown.*]

Scene 8

Three-quarters of an hour later.

*The view through the big windows is fading gradually into a still-golden dusk. A
torch of sunlight blazes on the side of a big water-tank or oil-drum across the empty
lot toward the business district which is now pierced by pinpoints of lighted windows or windows reflecting the sunset.*

The three people are completing a dismal birthday supper. STANLEY *looks sullen.*
STELLA *is embarrassed and sad.* BLANCHE *has a tight, artificial smile on her drawn
face. There is a fourth place at the table which is left vacant.*

BLANCHE [*suddenly*]   Stanley, tell us a joke, tell us a funny story to make us
all laugh. I don't know what's the matter, we're all so solemn. Is it because
I've been stood up by my beau?

> [STELLA *laughs feebly.*]

It's the first time in my entire experience with men, and I've had a good
5   deal of all sorts, that I've actually been stood up by anybody! Ha-ha! I don't
know how to take it. . . . Tell us a funny little story, Stanley! Something to
help us out.

STANLEY   I didn't think you liked my stories, Blanche.

BLANCHE   I like them when they're amusing but not indecent.

10 STANLEY   I don't know any refined enough for your taste.

BLANCHE   Then let me tell one.

STELLA   Yes, you tell one, Blanche. You used to know lots of good stories.

> [*The music fades.*]

BLANCHE   Let me see, now. . . . I must run through my repertoire! Oh, yes—I
love parrot stories! Do you all like parrot stories? Well, this one's about the
15   old maid and the parrot. This old maid, she had a parrot that cursed a blue
streak and knew more vulgar expressions than Mr. Kowalski!

STANLEY   Huh.

BLANCHE   And the only way to hush the parrot up was to put the cover back
on its cage so it would think it was night and go back to sleep. Well, one
20   morning the old maid had just uncovered the parrot for the day—when
who should she see coming up the front walk but the preacher! Well, she
rushed back to the parrot and slipped the cover back on the cage and then
she let in the preacher. And the parrot was perfectly still, just as quiet as a
mouse, but just as she was asking the preacher how much sugar he wanted
25   in his coffee—the parrot broke the silence with a loud—[*She whistles.*]—
and said—"God *damn*, but that was a short day!"

[*She throws back her head and laughs.* STELLA *also makes an ineffectual effort to seem amused.* STANLEY *pays no attention to the story but reaches way over the table to spear his fork into the remaining chop which he eats with his fingers.*]

BLANCHE   Apparently Mr. Kowalski was not amused.

STELLA   Mr. Kowalski is too busy making a pig of himself to think of anything else!

30 STANLEY   That's right, baby.

STELLA   Your face and your fingers are disgustingly greasy. Go and wash up and then help me clear the table.

[*He hurls a plate to the floor.*]

STANLEY   That's how I'll clear the table! [*He seizes her arm.*] Don't ever talk that way to me! "Pig—Polack—disgusting—vulgar—greasy!"—them kind
35 of words have been on your tongue and your sister's too much around here! What do you two think you are? A pair of queens? Remember what Huey Long said—"Every Man is a King!"[6] And I am the king around here, so don't forget it! [*He hurls a cup and saucer to the floor.*] My place is cleared! You want me to clear your places?

[STELLA *begins to cry weakly.* STANLEY *stalks out on the porch and lights a cigarette.*]

[*The Negro entertainers around the corner are heard.*]

40 BLANCHE   What happened while I was bathing? What did he tell you, Stella?

STELLA   Nothing, nothing, nothing!

BLANCHE   I think he told you something about Mitch and me! You know why Mitch didn't come but you won't tell me! [STELLA *shakes her head helplessly.*] I'm going to call him!

45 STELLA   I wouldn't call him, Blanche.

BLANCHE   I am, I'm going to call him on the phone.

STELLA [*miserably*]   I wish you wouldn't.

BLANCHE   I intend to be given some explanation from someone!

[*She rushes to the phone in the bedroom.* STELLA *goes out on the porch and stares reproachfully at her husband. He grunts and turns away from her.*]

STELLA   I hope you're pleased with your doings. I never had so much trouble
50 swallowing food in my life, looking at that girl's face and the empty chair! [*She cries quietly.*]

BLANCHE [*at the phone*]   Hello. Mr. Mitchell, please.... Oh.... I would like to leave a number if I may. Magnolia 9047. And say it's important to call.... Yes, very important.... Thank you. [*She remains by the phone with a lost, frightened look.*]

[STANLEY *turns slowly back toward his wife and takes her clumsily in his arms.*]

STANLEY   Stell, it's gonna be all right after she goes and after you've had the
55 baby. It's gonna be all right again between you and me the way that it was. You remember that way that it was? Them nights we had together? God, honey, it's gonna be sweet when we can make noise in the night the way

---

6. The slogan used by the populist Democrat Long (1893–1935) in his successful campaigns for governor of and then senator from Louisiana.

that we used to and get the colored lights going with nobody's sister behind the curtains to hear us!

[*Their upstairs neighbors are heard in bellowing laughter at something.* STANLEY *chuckles.*]

60 Steve an' Eunice . . .

STELLA Come on back in. [*She returns to the kitchen and starts lighting the candles on the white cake.*] Blanche?

BLANCHE Yes. [*She returns from the bedroom to the table in the kitchen.*] Oh, those pretty, pretty little candles! Oh, don't burn them, Stella.

65 STELLA I certainly will.

[STANLEY *comes back in.*]

BLANCHE You ought to save them for baby's birthdays. Oh, I hope candles are going to glow in his life and I hope that his eyes are going to be like candles, like two blue candles lighted in a white cake!

STANLEY [*sitting down*] What poetry!

70 BLANCHE [*she pauses reflectively for a moment*] I shouldn't have called him.

STELLA There's lots of things could have happened.

BLANCHE There's no excuse for it, Stella. I don't have to put up with insults. I won't be taken for granted.

STANLEY Goddamn, it's hot in here with the steam from the bathroom.

75 BLANCHE I've said I was sorry three times. [*The piano fades out.*] I take hot baths for my nerves. Hydrotherapy, they call it. You healthy Polack, without a nerve in your body, of course you don't know what anxiety feels like!

STANLEY I am not a Polack. People from Poland are Poles, not Polacks. But what I am is a one-hundred-per-cent American, born and raised in the great-
80 est country on earth and proud as hell of it, so don't ever call me a Polack.

[*The phone rings.* BLANCHE *rises expectantly.*]

BLANCHE Oh, that's for me, I'm sure.

STANLEY *I'm* not sure. Keep your seat. [*He crosses leisurely to phone.*] H'lo. Aw, yeh, hello, Mac.

[*He leans against wall, staring insultingly in at* BLANCHE. *She sinks back in her chair with a frightened look.* STELLA *leans over and touches her shoulder.*]

BLANCHE Oh, keep your hands off me, Stella. What is the matter with you?
85 Why do you look at me with that pitying look?

STANLEY [*bawling*] QUIET IN THERE!—We've got a noisy woman on the place.—Go on, Mac. At Riley's? No, I don't wanta bowl at Riley's. I had a little trouble with Riley last week. I'm the team captain, ain't I? All right, then, we're not gonna bowl at Riley's, we're gonna bowl at the West Side or
90 the Gala! All right, Mac. See you!

[*He hangs up and returns to the table.* BLANCHE *fiercely controls herself, drinking quickly from her tumbler of water. He doesn't look at her but reaches in a pocket. Then he speaks slowly and with false amiability.*]

Sister Blanche, I've got a little birthday remembrance for you.

BLANCHE Oh, have you, Stanley? I wasn't expecting any, I—I don't know why Stella wants to observe my birthday! I'd much rather forget it—when you—reach twenty-seven! Well—age is a subject that you'd prefer
95 to—ignore!

STANLEY Twenty-seven?

BLANCHE [*quickly*]   What is it? Is it for *me*?

[*He is holding a little envelope toward her.*]

STANLEY   Yes, I hope you like it!

BLANCHE   Why, why—Why, it's a—

100 STANLEY   Ticket! Back to Laurel! On the Greyhound![7] Tuesday!

[*The Varsouviana music steals in softly and continues playing.* STELLA *rises abruptly and turns her back.* BLANCHE *tries to smile. Then she tries to laugh. Then she gives both up and springs from the table and runs into the next room. She clutches her throat and then runs into the bathroom. Coughing, gagging sounds are heard.*]

Well!

STELLA   You didn't need to do that.

STANLEY   Don't forget all that I took off her.

STELLA   You needn't have been so cruel to someone alone as she is.

105 STANLEY   Delicate piece she is.

STELLA   She is. She was. You didn't know Blanche as a girl. Nobody, nobody, was tender and trusting as she was. But people like you abused her, and forced her to change.

[*He crosses into the bedroom, ripping off his shirt, and changes into a brilliant silk bowling shirt. She follows him.*]

Do you think you're going bowling now?

110 STANLEY   Sure.

STELLA   You're not going bowling. [*She catches hold of his shirt.*] Why did you do this to her?

STANLEY   I done nothing to no one. Let go of my shirt. You've torn it.

STELLA   I want to know why. Tell me why.

115 STANLEY   When we first met, me and you, you thought I was common. How right you was, baby. I was common as dirt. You showed me the snapshot of the place with the columns. I pulled you down off them columns and how you loved it, having them colored lights going! And wasn't we happy together, wasn't it all okay till she showed here?

[STELLA *makes a slight movement. Her look goes suddenly inward as if some interior voice had called her name. She begins a slow, shuffling progress from the bedroom to the kitchen, leaning and resting on the back of the chair and then on the edge of a table with a blind look and listening expression. Stanley, finishing with his shirt, is unaware of her reaction.*]

120 And wasn't we happy together? Wasn't it all okay? Till she showed here. Hoity-toity, describing me as an ape. [*He suddenly notices the change in* STELLA.] Hey, what is it, Stell? [*He crosses to her.*]

STELLA [*quietly*]   Take me to the hospital.

[*He is with her now, supporting her with his arm, murmuring indistinguishably as they go outside.*]

Scene 9

A while later that evening. BLANCHE *is seated in a tense hunched position in a bedroom chair that she has recovered with diagonal green and white stripes. She has on her scarlet satin robe. On the table beside chair is a bottle of liquor and a glass. The rapid, feverish polka tune, the "Varsouviana," is heard. The music is in her mind;*

7. That is, the long-distance bus.

she is drinking to escape it and the sense of disaster closing in on her, and she seems to whisper the words of the song. An electric fan is turning back and forth across her.

MITCH *comes around the corner in work clothes: blue denim shirt and pants. He is unshaven. He climbs the steps to the door and rings.* BLANCHE *is startled.*

BLANCHE Who is it, please?

MITCH [*hoarsely*] Me. Mitch.

[*The polka tune stops.*]

BLANCHE Mitch!—Just a minute.

[*She rushes about frantically, hiding the bottle in a closet, crouching at the mirror and dabbing her face with cologne and powder. She is so excited that her breath is audible as she dashes about. At last she rushes to the door in the kitchen and lets him in.*]

5   Mitch!—Y'know, I really shouldn't let you in after the treatment I have received from you this evening! So utterly uncavalier! But hello, beautiful!

[*She offers him her lips. He ignores it and pushes past her into the flat. She looks fearfully after him as he stalks into the bedroom.*]

My, my, what a cold shoulder! And such uncouth apparel! Why, you haven't even shaved! The unforgivable insult to a lady! But I forgive you. I forgive you because it's such a relief to see you. You've stopped that polka tune that I had caught in my head. Have you ever had anything caught in your head?

10   No, of course you haven't, you dumb angel-puss, you'd never get anything awful caught in your head!

[*He stares at her while she follows him while she talks. It is obvious that he has had a few drinks on the way over.*]

MITCH Do we have to have that fan on?

BLANCHE No!

MITCH I don't like fans.

15 BLANCHE Then let's turn it off, honey. I'm not partial to them!

[*She presses the switch and the fan nods slowly off. She clears her throat uneasily as* MITCH *plumps himself down on the bed in the bedroom and lights a cigarette.*]

I don't know what there is to drink. I—haven't investigated.

MITCH I don't want Stan's liquor.

BLANCHE It isn't Stan's. Everything here isn't Stan's. Some things on the premises are actually mine! How is your mother? Isn't your mother well?

20 MITCH Why?

BLANCHE Something's the matter tonight, but never mind. I won't cross-examine the witness. I'll just—[*She touches her forehead vaguely. The polka tune starts up again.*]—pretend I don't notice anything different about you! That—music again . . .

25 MITCH What music?

BLANCHE The "Varsouviana"! The polka tune they were playing when Allan—Wait!

[*A distant revolver shot is heard.* BLANCHE *seems relieved.*]

There now, the shot! It always stops after that.

[*The polka music dies out again.*]

Yes, now it's stopped.

30 MITCH Are you boxed out of your mind?

BLANCHE   I'll go and see what I can find in the way of—[*She crosses into the closet, pretending to search for the bottle.*] Oh, by the way, excuse me for not being dressed. But I'd practically given you up! Had you forgotten your invitation to supper?

35 MITCH   I wasn't going to see you any more.

BLANCHE   Wait a minute. I can't hear what you're saying and you talk so little that when you do say something, I don't want to miss a single syllable of it. . . . What am I looking around here for? Oh, yes—liquor! We've had so much excitement around here this evening that I *am* boxed out of my

40 mind! [*She pretends suddenly to find the bottle. He draws his foot up on the bed and stares at her contemptuously.*] Here's something. Southern Comfort![8] What is that, I wonder?

MITCH   If you don't know, it must belong to Stan.

BLANCHE   Take your foot off the bed. It has a light cover on it. Of course you

45 boys don't notice things like that. I've done so much with this place since I've been here.

MITCH   I bet you have.

BLANCHE   You saw it before I came. Well, look at it now! This room is almost—dainty! I want to keep it that way. I wonder if this stuff ought to be

50 mixed with something? Ummm, it's sweet, so sweet! It's terribly, terribly sweet! Why, it's a *liqueur*, I believe! Yes, that's what it *is*, a liqueur! [MITCH *grunts.*] I'm afraid you won't like it, but try it, and maybe you will.

MITCH   I told you already I don't want none of his liquor and I mean it. You ought to lay off his liquor. He says you been lapping it up all summer like a

55 wild cat!

BLANCHE   What a fantastic statement! Fantastic of him to say it, fantastic of you to repeat it! I won't descend to the level of such cheap accusations to answer them, even!

MITCH   Huh.

60 BLANCHE   What's in your mind? I see something in your eyes!

MITCH [*getting up*]   It's dark in here.

BLANCHE   I like it dark. The dark is comforting to me.

MITCH   I don't think I ever seen you in the light. [BLANCHE *laughs breathlessly.*] That's a fact!

65 BLANCHE   Is it?

MITCH   I've never seen you in the afternoon.

BLANCHE   Whose fault is that?

MITCH   You never want to go out in the afternoon.

BLANCHE   Why, Mitch, you're at the plant in the afternoon!

70 MITCH   Not Sunday afternoon. I've asked you to go out with me sometimes on Sundays but you always make an excuse. You never want to go out till after six and then it's always some place that's not lighted much.

BLANCHE   There is some obscure meaning in this but I fail to catch it.

MITCH   What it means is I've never had a real good look at you, Blanche.

75 Let's turn the light on here.

BLANCHE [*fearfully*]   Light? Which light? What for?

MITCH   This one with the paper thing on it. [*He tears the paper lantern off the light bulb. She utters a frightened gasp.*]

---

8. A flavored whiskey liqueur.

BLANCHE   What did you do that for?

MITCH   So I can take a look at you good and plain!

80 BLANCHE   Of course you don't really mean to be insulting!

MITCH   No, just realistic.

BLANCHE   I don't want realism. I want magic! [MITCH *laughs.*] Yes, yes, magic!
I try to give that to people. I misrepresent things to them. I don't tell truth,
I tell what *ought* to be truth. And if that is sinful, then let me be damned
85   for it!—*Don't turn the light on!*

> [MITCH *crosses to the switch. He turns the light on and stares at her. She
> cries out and covers her face. He turns the light off again.*]

MITCH [*slowly and bitterly*]   I don't mind you being older than what I thought.
But all the rest of it—Christ! That pitch about your ideals being so old-
fashioned and all the malarkey that you've dished out all summer. Oh, I
knew you weren't sixteen any more. But I was a fool enough to believe you
90   was straight.

BLANCHE   Who told you I wasn't—"straight"? My loving brother-in-law. And
you believed him.

MITCH   I called him a liar at first. And then I checked on the story. First I
asked our supply-man who travels through Laurel. And then I talked directly
95   over long-distance to this merchant.

BLANCHE   Who is this merchant?

MITCH   Kiefaber.

BLANCHE   The merchant Kiefaber of Laurel! I know the man. He whistled at
me. I put him in his place. So now for revenge he makes up stories about
100   me.

MITCH   Three people, Kiefaber, Stanley, and Shaw, swore to them!

BLANCHE   Rub-a-dub-dub, three men in a tub![9] And such a filthy tub!

MITCH   Didn't you stay at a hotel called The Flamingo?

BLANCHE   Flamingo? No! Tarantula was the name of it! I stayed at a hotel
105   called The Tarantula Arms!

MITCH [*stupidly*]   Tarantula?

BLANCHE   Yes, a big spider! That's where I brought my victims. [*She pours
herself another drink.*] Yes, I had many intimacies with strangers. After the
death of Allan—intimacies with strangers was all I seemed able to fill my
110   empty heart with. . . . I think it was panic, just panic, that drove me from
one to another, hunting for some protection—here and there, in the most—
unlikely places—even, at last, in a seventeen-year-old boy but—somebody
wrote the superintendent about it—"This woman is morally unfit for her
position!"

> [*She throws back her head with convulsive, sobbing laughter. Then she
> repeats the statement, gasps, and drinks.*]

115   True? Yes, I suppose—unfit somehow—anyway. . . . So I came here. There
was nowhere else I could go. I was played out. You know what played out
is? My youth was suddenly gone up the water-spout, and—I met you. You
said you needed somebody. Well, I needed somebody, too. I thanked God
for you, because you seemed to be gentle—a cleft in the rock of the world
120   that I could hide in! But I guess I was asking, hoping—too much! Kiefaber,
Stanley, and Shaw have tied an old tin can to the tail of the kite.

9. A reference to the nursery rhyme.

[*There is a pause.* MITCH *stares at her dumbly.*]

MITCH   You lied to me, Blanche.

BLANCHE   Don't say I lied to you.

MITCH   Lies, lies, inside and out, all lies.

125   BLANCHE   Never inside, I didn't lie in my heart . . .

[*A vendor comes around the corner. She is a blind* MEXICAN WOMAN *in a dark shawl, carrying bunches of those gaudy tin flowers that lower-class Mexicans display at funerals and other festive occasions. She is calling barely audibly. Her figure is only faintly visible outside the building.*]

MEXICAN WOMAN   Flores. Flores. Flores para los muertos.[1] Flores. Flores.

BLANCHE   What? Oh! Somebody outside . . . [*She goes to the door, opens it and stares at the* MEXICAN WOMAN.]

MEXICAN WOMAN [*she is at the door and offers* BLANCHE *some of her flowers*] Flores? Flores para los muertos?

BLANCHE [*frightened*]   No, no! Not now! Not now!

[*She darts back into the apartment, slamming the door.*]

130   MEXICAN WOMAN [*she turns away and starts to move down the street*]   Flores para los muertos.

[*The polka tune fades in.*]

BLANCHE [*as if to herself*]   Crumble and fade and—regrets—recriminations . . . "If you'd done this, it wouldn't've cost me that!"

MEXICAN WOMAN   Corones[2] para los muertos. Corones . . .

135   BLANCHE   Legacies! Huh. . . . And other things such as bloodstained pillowslips—"Her linen needs changing"—"Yes, Mother. But couldn't we get a colored girl to do it?" No, we couldn't of course. Everything gone but the—

MEXICAN WOMAN   Flores.

BLANCHE   Death—I used to sit here and she used to sit over there and death

140   was as close as you are. . . . We didn't dare even admit we had ever heard of it!

MEXICAN WOMAN   Flores para los muertos, flores—flores . . .

BLANCHE   The opposite is desire. So do you wonder? How could you possibly wonder! Not far from Belle Reve, before we had lost Belle Reve, was a

145   camp where they trained young soldiers. On Saturday nights they would go in town to get drunk—

MEXICAN WOMAN [*softly*]   Corones . . .

BLANCHE   —and on the way back they would stagger onto my lawn and call—"Blanche! Blanche!"—the deaf old lady remaining suspected noth-

150   ing. But sometimes I slipped outside to answer their calls. . . . Later the paddy-wagon would gather them up like daisies . . . the long way home . . .

[*The* MEXICAN WOMAN *turns slowly and drifts back off with her soft mournful cries.* BLANCHE *goes to the dresser and leans forward on it. After a moment,* MITCH *rises and follows her purposefully. The polka music fades away. He places his hands on her waist and tries to turn her about.*]

BLANCHE   What do you want?

MITCH [*fumbling to embrace her*]   What I been missing all summer.

BLANCHE   Then marry me, Mitch!

155   MITCH   I don't think I want to marry you any more.

BLANCHE   No?

---

1. Flowers for the dead (Spanish).   2. Crowns (Spanish); wreaths of flowers.

MITCH [*dropping his hands from her waist*]   You're not clean enough to bring in the house with my mother.

BLANCHE   Go away, then. [*He stares at her.*] Get out of here quick before I start screaming fire! [*Her throat is tightening with hysteria.*] Get out of here quick before I start screaming fire.

160

[*He still remains staring. She suddenly rushes to the big window with its pale blue square of the soft summer light and cries wildly.*]

Fire! Fire! Fire!

[*With a startled gasp,* MITCH *turns and goes out the outer door, clatters awkwardly down the steps and around the corner of the building.* BLANCHE *staggers back from the window and falls to her knees. The distant piano is slow and blue.*]

Scene 10

It is a few hours later that night.

BLANCHE *has been drinking fairly steadily since* MITCH *left. She has dragged her wardrobe trunk into the center of the bedroom. It hangs open with flowery dresses thrown across it. As the drinking and packing went on, a mood of hysterical exhilaration came into her and she has decked herself out in a somewhat soiled and crumpled white satin evening gown and a pair of scuffed silver slippers with brilliants[3] set in their heels.*

Now she is placing the rhinestone tiara on her head before the mirror of the dressing-table and murmuring excitedly as if to a group of spectral admirers.

BLANCHE   How about taking a swim, a moonlight swim at the old rock quarry? If anyone's sober enough to drive a car! Ha-ha! Best way in the world to stop your head buzzing! Only you've got to be careful to dive where the deep pool is—if you hit a rock you don't come up till tomorrow. . . .

[*Tremblingly she lifts the hand mirror for a closer inspection. She catches her breath and slams the mirror face down with such violence that the glass cracks. She moans a little and attempts to rise.*]

[STANLEY *appears around the corner of the building. He still has on the vivid green silk bowling shirt. As he rounds the corner the honky-tonk music is heard. It continues softly throughout the scene.*]

[*He enters the kitchen, slamming the door. As he peers in at* BLANCHE, *he gives a low whistle. He has had a few drinks on the way and has brought some quart beer bottles home with him.*]

5   BLANCHE   How is my sister?

STANLEY   She is doing okay.

BLANCHE   And how is the baby?

STANLEY [*grinning amiably*]   The baby won't come before morning so they told me to go home and get a little shut-eye.

10   BLANCHE   Does that mean we are to be alone in here?

STANLEY   Yep. Just me and you, Blanche. Unless you got somebody hid under the bed. What've you got on those fine feathers for?

BLANCHE   Oh, that's right. You left before my wire came.

STANLEY   You got a wire?

15   BLANCHE   I received a telegram from an old admirer of mine.

---

3. Sparkling gems.

STANLEY   Anything good?

BLANCHE   I think so. An invitation.

STANLEY   What to? A fireman's ball?

BLANCHE [*throwing back her head*]   A cruise of the Caribbean on a yacht!

20 STANLEY   Well, well. What do you know?

BLANCHE   I have never been so surprised in my life.

STANLEY   I guess not.

BLANCHE   It came like a bolt from the blue!

STANLEY   Who did you say it was from?

25 BLANCHE   An old beau of mine.

STANLEY   The one that give you the white fox-pieces?

BLANCHE   Mr. Shep Huntleigh. I wore his ATO[4] pin my last year at college. I
hadn't seen him again until last Christmas. I ran in to him on Biscayne
Boulevard. Then—just now—this wire—inviting me on a cruise of the
30 Caribbean! The problem is clothes. I tore into my trunk to see what I have
that's suitable for the tropics!

STANLEY   And come up with that—gorgeous—diamond—tiara?

BLANCHE   This old relic? Ha-ha! It's only rhinestones.

STANLEY   Gosh. I thought it was Tiffany diamonds.[5] [*He unbuttons his shirt.*]

35 BLANCHE   Well, anyhow, I shall be entertained in style.

STANLEY   Uh-huh. It goes to show, you never know what is coming.

BLANCHE   Just when I thought my luck had begun to fail me—

STANLEY   Into the picture pops this Miami millionaire.

BLANCHE   This man is not from Miami. This man is from Dallas.

40 STANLEY   This man is from Dallas?

BLANCHE   Yes, this man is from Dallas where gold spouts out of the ground!

STANLEY   Well, just so he's from somewhere! [*He starts removing his shirt.*]

BLANCHE   Close the curtains before you undress any further.

STANLEY [*amiably*]   This is all I'm going to undress right now. [*He rips the
45 sack off a quart beer bottle.*] Seen a bottle-opener?

[*She moves slowly toward the dresser, where she stands with her hands
knotted together.*]

I used to have a cousin who could open a beer bottle with his teeth. [*Pounding the bottle cap on the corner of table.*] That was his only accomplishment,
all he could do—he was just a human bottle-opener. And then one time, at
a wedding party, he broke his front teeth off! After that he was so ashamed
50 of himself he used t' sneak out of the house when company came . . .

[*The bottle cap pops off and a geyser of foam shoots up.* STANLEY *laughs
happily, holding up the bottle over his head.*]

Ha-ha! Rain from heaven! [*He extends the bottle toward her.*] Shall we bury
the hatchet and make it a loving-cup? Huh?

BLANCHE   No, thank you.

STANLEY   Well, it's a red-letter night for us both. You having an oil millionaire
55 and me having a baby.

[*He goes to the bureau in the bedroom and crouches to remove something from the bottom drawer.*]

4. The fraternity Alpha Tau Omega.
5. That is, diamonds from the famous jewelry store in New York.

BLANCHE [*drawing back*]   What are you doing in here?

STANLEY   Here's something I always break out on special occasions like this. The silk pyjamas I wore on my wedding night!

BLANCHE   Oh.

60 STANLEY   When the telephone rings and they say, "You've got a son!" I'll tear this off and wave it like a flag! [*He shakes out a brilliant pyjama coat.*] I guess we are both entitled to put on the dog.[6] [*He goes back to the kitchen with the coat over his arm.*]

BLANCHE   When I think of how divine it is going to be to have such a thing as privacy once more—I could weep with joy!

65 STANLEY   This millionaire from Dallas is not going to interfere with your privacy any?

BLANCHE   It won't be the sort of thing you have in mind. This man is a gentleman and he respects me. [*Improvising feverishly.*] What he wants is my companionship. Having great wealth sometimes makes people lonely! A 70 cultivated woman, a woman of intelligence and breeding, can enrich a man's life—immeasurably! I have those things to offer, and this doesn't take them away. Physical beauty is passing. A transitory possession. But beauty of the mind and richness of the spirit and tenderness of the heart— and I have all of those things—aren't taken away, but grow! Increase with 75 the years! How strange that I should be called a destitute woman! When I have all of these treasures locked in my heart. [*A choked sob comes from her.*] I think of myself as a very, very rich woman! But I have been foolish— casting my pearls before swine![7]

STANLEY   Swine, huh?

80 BLANCHE   Yes, swine! Swine! And I'm thinking not only of you but of your friend, Mr. Mitchell. He came to see me tonight. He dared to come here in his work clothes! And to repeat slander to me, vicious stories that he had gotten from you! I gave him his walking papers. . . .

STANLEY   You did, huh?

85 BLANCHE   But then he came back. He returned with a box of roses to beg my forgiveness! He implored my forgiveness. But some things are not forgivable. Deliberate cruelty is not forgivable. It is the one unforgivable thing in my opinion and it is the one thing of which I have never, never been guilty. And so I told him, I said to him, "Thank you," but it was foolish of me to 90 think that we could ever adapt ourselves to each other. Our ways of life are too different. Our attitudes and our backgrounds are incompatible. We have to be realistic about such things. So farewell, my friend! And let there be no hard feelings . . .

STANLEY   Was this before or after the telegram came from the Texas oil 95 millionaire?

BLANCHE   What telegram? No! No, after! As a matter of fact, the wire came just as—

STANLEY   As a matter of fact there wasn't no wire at all!

BLANCHE   Oh, oh!

100 STANLEY   There isn't no millionaire! And Mitch didn't come back with roses 'cause I know where he is—

BLANCHE   Oh!

---

6. That is, put on uncharacteristic stylishness, show off.

7. An allusion to Jesus's Sermon on the Mount (Matthew 7.6).

STANLEY   There isn't a goddam thing but imagination!

BLANCHE   Oh!

105 STANLEY   And lies and conceit and tricks!

BLANCHE   Oh!

STANLEY   And look at yourself! Take a look at yourself in that worn-out Mardi Gras[8] outfit, rented for fifty cents from some rag-picker! And with the crazy crown on! What queen do you think you are?

110 BLANCHE   Oh—God . . .

STANLEY   I've been on to you from the start! Not once did you pull any wool over this boy's eyes! You come in here and sprinkle the place with powder and spray perfume and cover the lightbulb with a paper lantern, and lo and behold the place has turned into Egypt and you are the Queen of the Nile!
115 Sitting on your throne and swilling down my liquor! I say—Ha!—Ha! Do you hear me? Ha—ha—ha! [*He walks into the bedroom.*]

BLANCHE   Don't come in here!

> [*Lurid reflections appear on the walls around* BLANCHE. *The shadows are of a grotesque and menacing form. She catches her breath, crosses to the phone and jiggles the hook.* STANLEY *goes into the bathroom and closes the door.*]

Operator, operator! Give me long-distance, please. . . . I want to get in touch with Mr. Shep Huntleigh of Dallas. He's so well known he doesn't
120 require any address. Just ask anybody who—Wait!!—No, I couldn't find it right now. . . . Please understand, I—No! No, wait! . . . One moment! Someone is—Nothing! Hold on, please!

> [*She sets the phone down and crosses warily into the kitchen. The night is filled with inhuman voices like cries in a jungle.*]
>
> [*The shadows and lurid reflections move sinuously as flames along the wall spaces.*]
>
> [*Through the back wall of the rooms, which have become transparent, can be seen the sidewalk. A prostitute has rolled[9] a drunkard. He pursues her along the walk, overtakes her and there is a struggle. A policeman's whistle breaks it up. The figures disappear.*]
>
> [*Some moments later the* NEGRO WOMAN *appears around the corner with a sequined bag which the prostitute had dropped on the walk. She is rooting excitedly through it.*]
>
> [BLANCHE *presses her knuckles to her lips and returns slowly to the phone. She speaks in a hoarse whisper.*]

BLANCHE   Operator! Operator! Never mind long-distance. Get Western Union. There isn't time to be—Western—Western Union!

> [*She waits anxiously.*]

125 Western Union? Yes! I—want to—Take down this message! "In desperate, desperate circumstances! Help me! Caught in a trap. Caught in—" Oh!

> [*The bathroom door is thrown open and* STANLEY *comes out in the brilliant silk pyjamas. He grins at her as he knots the tasseled sash about his waist. She gasps and backs away from the phone. He stares at her for a*

---

8. Fat Tuesday (French), or Shrove Tuesday, the final day before Lent, traditionally a time of penitence and prayer for Christians, begins. In many places it is celebrated with merrymaking and parades; the festivities are particularly famous and extensive in New Orleans.

9. Robbed (by going through the pockets of someone drunk, unconscious, or asleep).

count of ten. Then a clicking becomes audible from the telephone, steady and rasping.]

STANLEY You left th' phone off th' hook.

[He crosses to it deliberately and sets it back on the hook. After he has replaced it, he stares at her again, his mouth slowly curving into a grin, as he weaves between BLANCHE and the outer door.]

[The barely audible "blue piano" begins to drum up louder. The sound of it turns into the roar of an approaching locomotive. BLANCHE crouches, pressing her fists to her ears until it has gone by.]

BLANCHE [finally straightening] Let me—let me get by you!

STANLEY Get by me? Sure. Go ahead. [He moves back a pace in the doorway.]

130 BLANCHE You—you stand over there! [She indicates a further position.]

STANLEY [grinning] You got plenty of room to walk by me now.

BLANCHE Not with you there! But I've got to get out somehow!

STANLEY You think I'll interfere with you? Ha-ha!

[The "blue piano" goes softly. She turns confusedly and makes a faint gesture. The inhuman jungle voices rise up. He takes a step toward her, biting his tongue which protrudes between his lips.]

STANLEY [softly] Come to think of it—maybe you wouldn't be bad to—
135 interfere with . . .

[BLANCHE moves backward through the door into the bedroom.]

BLANCHE Stay back! Don't you come toward me another step or I'll—

STANLEY What?

BLANCHE Some awful thing will happen! It will!

STANLEY What are you putting on now?

[They are now both inside the bedroom.]

140 BLANCHE I warn you, don't, I'm in danger!

[He takes another step. She smashes a bottle on the table and faces him, clutching the broken top.]

STANLEY What did you do that for?

BLANCHE So I could twist the broken end in your face!

STANLEY I bet you would do that!

BLANCHE I would! I will if you—

145 STANLEY Oh! So you want some roughhouse! All right, let's have some roughhouse!

[He springs toward her, overturning the table. She cries out and strikes at him with the bottle top but he catches her wrist.]

Tiger—tiger! Drop the bottle-top! Drop it! We've had this date with each other from the beginning!

[She moans. The bottle-top falls. She sinks to her knees. He picks up her inert figure and carries her to the bed. The hot trumpet and drums from the Four Deuces sound loudly.]

Scene 11

It is some weeks later. STELLA is packing BLANCHE's things. Sound of water can be heard running in the bathroom.

The portieres are partly open on the poker players—STANLEY, STEVE, MITCH, and PABLO—who sit around the table in the kitchen. The atmosphere of the kitchen is now the same raw, lurid one of the disastrous poker night.

The building is framed by the sky of turquoise. STELLA *has been crying as she arranges the flowery dresses in the open trunk.*

EUNICE *comes down the steps from her flat above and enters the kitchen. There is an outburst from the poker table.*

STANLEY   Drew to an inside straight and made it, by God.

PABLO   *Maldita sea tu suerto!*

STANLEY   Put it in English, greaseball.

PABLO   I am cursing your rutting luck.

5 STANLEY   [*prodigiously elated*]   You know what luck is? Luck is believing you're lucky. Take at Salerno.[1] I believed I was lucky. I figured that 4 out of 5 would not come through but I would . . . and I did. I put that down as a rule. To hold front position in this rat race you've got to believe you are lucky.

10 MITCH   You . . . you . . . you. . . . Brag . . . brag . . . bull . . . bull.

[STELLA *goes into the bedroom and starts folding a dress.*]

STANLEY   What's the matter with him?

EUNICE   [*walking past the table*]   I always did say that men are callous things with no feelings, but this does beat anything. Making pigs of yourselves. [*She comes through the portieres into the bedroom.*]

STANLEY   What's the matter with her?

15 STELLA   How is my baby?

EUNICE   Sleeping like a little angel. Brought you some grapes. [*She puts them on a stool and lowers her voice.*] Blanche?

STELLA   Bathing.

EUNICE   How is she?

20 STELLA   She wouldn't eat anything but asked for a drink.

EUNICE   What did you tell her?

STELLA   I—just told her that—we'd made arrangements for her to rest in the country. She's got it mixed in her mind with Shep Huntleigh.

[BLANCHE *opens the bathroom door slightly.*]

BLANCHE   Stella.

25 STELLA   Yes, Blanche?

BLANCHE   If anyone calls while I'm bathing take the number and tell them I'll call right back.

STELLA   Yes.

BLANCHE   That cool yellow silk—the bouclé.[2] See if it's crushed. If it's not too crushed I'll wear it and on the lapel that silver and turquoise pin in the shape of a seahorse. You will find them in the heart-shaped box I keep my accessories in. And Stella . . . Try and locate a bunch of artificial violets in that box, too, to pin with the seahorse on the lapel of the jacket.

[*She closes the door.* STELLA *turns to* EUNICE.]

STELLA   I don't know if I did the right thing.

35 EUNICE   What else could you do?

STELLA   I couldn't believe her story and go on living with Stanley.

EUNICE   Don't ever believe it. Life has got to go on. No matter what happens, you've got to keep on going.

---

1. A city in southern Italy on the Gulf of Salerno, an important beachhead in the Allied invasion of Italy during World War II.

2. A rough-textured fabric made of looped yarn.

[*The bathroom door opens a little.*]

BLANCHE [*looking out*]   Is the coast clear?

40 STELLA   Yes, Blanche. [*To* EUNICE] Tell her how well she's looking.

BLANCHE   Please close the curtains before I come out.

STELLA   They're closed.

STANLEY   —How many for you?

PABLO   —Two.

45 STEVE   —Three.

[BLANCHE *appears in the amber light of the door. She has a tragic radi-*
ance in her red satin robe following the sculptural lines of her body. The
"Varsouviana" rises audibly as BLANCHE *enters the bedroom.*]

BLANCHE [*with faintly hysterical vivacity*]   I have just washed my hair.

STELLA   Did you?

BLANCHE   I'm not sure I got the soap out.

EUNICE   Such fine hair!

50 BLANCHE [*accepting the compliment*]   It's a problem. Didn't I get a call?

STELLA   Who from, Blanche?

BLANCHE   Shep Huntleigh . . .

STELLA   Why, not yet, honey!

BLANCHE   How strange! I—

[*At the sound of* BLANCHE's *voice* MITCH's *arm supporting his cards has*
sagged and his gaze is dissolved into space. STANLEY *slaps him on the*
shoulder.]

55 STANLEY   Hey, Mitch, come to!

[*The sound of this new voice shocks* BLANCHE. *She makes a shocked ges-*
ture, forming his name with her lips. STELLA *nods and looks quickly*
away. BLANCHE *stands quite still for some moments—the silver-backed*
mirror in her hand and a look of sorrowful perplexity as though all
human experience shows on her face. BLANCHE *finally speaks but with*
sudden hysteria.]

BLANCHE   What's going on here?

[*She turns from* STELLA *to* EUNICE *and back to* STELLA. *Her rising voice*
penetrates the concentration of the game. MITCH *ducks his head lower*
but STANLEY *shoves back his chair as if about to rise.* STEVE *places a*
restraining hand on his arm.]

BLANCHE [*continuing*]   What's happened here? I want an explanation of
what's happened here.

STELLA [*agonizingly*]   Hush! Hush!

60 EUNICE   Hush! Hush! Honey.

STELLA   Please, Blanche.

BLANCHE   Why are you looking at me like that? Is something wrong with me?

EUNICE   You look wonderful, Blanche. Don't she look wonderful?

STELLA   Yes.

65 EUNICE   I understand you are going on a trip.

STELLA   Yes, Blanche *is*. She's going on a vacation.

EUNICE   I'm green with envy.

BLANCHE   Help me, help me get dressed!

STELLA [*handing her dress*]   Is this what you—

70 BLANCHE   Yes, it will do! I'm anxious to get out of here—this place is a trap!

EUNICE   What a pretty blue jacket.

STELLA   It's lilac colored.

BLANCHE   You're both mistaken. It's Della Robbia blue.[3] The blue of the robe in the old Madonna pictures. Are these grapes washed?

[*She fingers the bunch of grapes which* EUNICE *had brought in.*]

75 EUNICE   Huh?

BLANCHE   Washed, I said. Are they washed?

EUNICE   They're from the French Market.[4]

BLANCHE   That doesn't mean they've been washed. [*The cathedral bells chime.*] Those cathedral bells—they're the only clean thing in the Quarter.

80   Well, I'm going now. I'm ready to go.

EUNICE [*whispering*]   She's going to walk out before they get here.

STELLA   Wait, Blanche.

BLANCHE   I don't want to pass in front of those men.

EUNICE   Then wait'll the game breaks up.

85 STELLA   Sit down and . . .

[BLANCHE *turns weakly, hesitantly about. She lets them push her into a chair.*]

BLANCHE   I can smell the sea air. The rest of my time I'm going to spend on the sea. And when I die, I'm going to die on the sea. You know what I shall die of? [*She plucks a grape.*] I shall die of eating an unwashed grape one day out on the ocean. I will die—with my hand in the hand of some nice-looking ship's doctor, a very young one with a small blond mustache and a big silver watch. "Poor lady," they'll say, "the quinine[5] did her no good. That unwashed grape has transported her soul to heaven." [*The cathedral chimes are heard.*] And I'll be buried at sea sewn up in a clean white sack and dropped overboard—at noon—in the blaze of summer—and into an ocean

95   as blue as [*Chimes again*] my first lover's eyes!

[*A* DOCTOR *and a* MATRON *have appeared around the corner of the building and climbed the steps to the porch. The gravity of their profession is exaggerated—the unmistakable aura of the state institution with its cynical detachment. The* DOCTOR *rings the doorbell. The murmur of the game is interrupted.*]

EUNICE [*whispering to* STELLA]   That must be them.

[STELLA *presses her fists to her lips.*]

BLANCHE [*rising slowly*]   What is it?

EUNICE [*affectedly casual*]   Excuse me while I see who's at the door.

STELLA   Yes.

[EUNICE *goes into the kitchen.*]

100 BLANCHE [*tensely*]   I wonder if it's for me.

[*A whispered colloquy takes place at the door.*]

EUNICE [*returning, brightly*]   Someone is calling for Blanche.

BLANCHE   It is for me, then! [*She looks fearfully from one to the other and then to the portieres. The "Varsouviana" faintly plays.*] Is it the gentleman I was expecting from Dallas?

105 EUNICE   I think it is, Blanche.

---

3. The distinctive blue backgrounds of the reliefs made first by the Florentine sculptor Luca della Robbia (ca. 1400–1482) and then by his descendants. The color blue is symbolic of heaven and is associated with fidelity, chastity, and modesty.

4. A city market—partly open-air, partly enclosed—in the French Quarter, on the bank of the Mississippi, since 1791.

5. A salt used to treat malaria and reduce fever.

BLANCHE   I'm not quite ready.

STELLA   Ask him to wait outside.

BLANCHE   I . . .

[EUNICE *goes back to the portieres. Drums sound very softly.*]

STELLA   Everything packed?

110 BLANCHE   My silver toilet articles are still out.

STELLA   Ah!

EUNICE [*returning*]   They're waiting in front of the house.

BLANCHE   They! Who's "they"?

EUNICE   There's a lady with him.

115 BLANCHE   I cannot imagine who this "lady" could be! How is she dressed?

EUNICE   Just—just a sort of a—plain-tailored outfit.

BLANCHE   Possibly she's— [*Her voice dies out nervously.*]

STELLA   Shall we go, Blanche?

BLANCHE   Must we go through that room?

120 STELLA   I will go with you.

BLANCHE   How do I look?

STELLA   Lovely.

EUNICE [*echoing*]   Lovely.

[BLANCHE *moves fearfully to the portieres.* EUNICE *draws them open for her.* BLANCHE *goes into the kitchen.*]

BLANCHE [*to the men*]   Please don't get up. I'm only passing through.

[*She crosses quickly to outside door.* STELLA *and* EUNICE *follow. The poker players stand awkwardly at the table—all except* MITCH, *who remains seated, looking down at the table.* BLANCHE *steps out on a small porch at the side of the door. She stops short and catches her breath.*]

125 DOCTOR   How do you do?

BLANCHE   You are not the gentleman I was expecting. [*She suddenly gasps and starts back up the steps. She stops by* STELLA, *who stands just outside the door, and speaks in a frightening whisper.*] That man isn't Shep Huntleigh.

[*The "Varsouviana" is playing distantly.*]

[STELLA *stares back at* BLANCHE. EUNICE *is holding* STELLA's *arm. There is a moment of silence—no sound but that of* STANLEY *steadily shuffling the cards.*]

[BLANCHE *catches her breath again and slips back into the flat. She enters the flat with a peculiar smile, her eyes wide and brilliant. As soon as her sister goes past her,* STELLA *closes her eyes and clenches her hands.* EUNICE *throws her arms comfortingly about her. Then she starts up to her flat.* BLANCHE *stops just inside the door.* MITCH *keeps staring down at his hands on the table, but the other men look at her curiously. At last she starts around the table toward the bedroom. As she does,* STANLEY *suddenly pushes back his chair and rises as if to block her way. The* MATRON *follows her into the flat.*]

STANLEY   Did you forget something?

BLANCHE [*shrilly*]   Yes! Yes, I forgot something!

[*She rushes past him into the bedroom. Lurid reflections appear on the walls in odd, sinuous shapes. The "Varsouviana" is filtered into a weird distortion, accompanied by the cries and noises of the jungle.* BLANCHE *seizes the back of a chair as if to defend herself.*]

130 STANLEY [*sotto voce*[6]] Doc, you better go in.

DOCTOR [*sotto voce, motioning to the* MATRON] Nurse, bring her out.

> [*The* MATRON *advances on one side,* STANLEY *on the other. Divested of all the softer properties of womanhood, the* MATRON *is a peculiarly sinister figure in her severe dress. Her voice is bold and toneless as a fire-bell.*]

MATRON Hello, Blanche.

> [*The greeting is echoed and re-echoed by other mysterious voices behind the walls, as if reverberated through a canyon of rock.*]

STANLEY She says that she forgot something.

> [*The echo sounds in threatening whispers.*]

MATRON That's all right.

135 STANLEY What did you forget, Blanche?

BLANCHE I—I—

MATRON It don't matter. We can pick it up later.

STANLEY Sure. We can send it along with the trunk.

BLANCHE [*retreating in panic*] I don't know you—I don't know you. I want to

140 be—left alone—please!

MATRON Now, Blanche!

ECHOES [*rising and falling*] Now, Blanche—now, Blanche—now, Blanche!

STANLEY You left nothing here but spilt talcum and old empty perfume bottles—unless it's the paper lantern you want to take with you. You want

145 the lantern?

> [*He crosses to dressing table and seizes the paper lantern, tearing it off the light bulb, and extends it toward her. She cries out as if the lantern was herself. The* MATRON *steps boldly toward her. She screams and tries to break past the* MATRON. *All the men spring to their feet.* STELLA *runs out to the porch, with* EUNICE *following to comfort her, simultaneously with the confused voices of the men in the kitchen.* STELLA *rushes into* EUNICE'S *embrace on the porch.*]

STELLA Oh, my God, Eunice help me! Don't let them do that to her, don't let them hurt her! Oh, God, oh, please God, don't hurt her! What are they doing to her? What are they doing? [*She tries to break from* EUNICE'S *arms.*]

EUNICE No, honey, no, no, honey. Stay here. Don't go back in there. Stay

150 with me and don't look.

STELLA What have I done to my sister? Oh, God, what have I done to my sister?

EUNICE You done the right thing, the only thing you could do. She couldn't stay here; there wasn't no other place for her to go.

> [*While* STELLA *and* EUNICE *are speaking on the porch the voices of the men in the kitchen overlap them.* MITCH *has started toward the bedroom.* STANLEY *crosses to block him.* STANLEY *pushes him aside.* MITCH *lunges and strikes at* STANLEY. STANLEY *pushes* MITCH *back. Mitch collapses at the table, sobbing.*]

> [*During the preceding scenes, the* MATRON *catches hold of* BLANCHE'S *arm and prevents her flight.* BLANCHE *turns wildly and scratches at the* MATRON. *The heavy woman pinions her arms.* BLANCHE *cries out hoarsely and slips to her knees.*]

---

6. Under his breath, in an undertone (Italian).

155 MATRON   These fingernails have to be trimmed. [*The* DOCTOR *comes into the room and she looks at him.*] Jacket,[7] Doctor?

DOCTOR   Not unless necessary.

[*He takes off his hat and now he becomes personalized. The unhuman quality goes. His voice is gentle and reassuring as he crosses to* BLANCHE *and crouches in front of her. As he speaks her name, her terror subsides a little. The lurid reflections fade from the walls, the inhuman cries and noises die out and her own hoarse crying is calmed.*]

DOCTOR   Miss DuBois.

[*She turns her face to him and stares at him with desperate pleading. He smiles; then he speaks to the* MATRON.]

It won't be necessary.

160 BLANCHE [*faintly*]   Ask her to let go of me.

DOCTOR [*to the* MATRON]   Let go.

[*The* MATRON *releases her.* BLANCHE *extends her hands toward the* DOCTOR. *He draws her up gently and supports her with his arm and leads her through the portieres.*]

BLANCHE [*holding tight to his arm*]   Whoever you are—I have always depended on the kindness of strangers.

[*The poker players stand back as* BLANCHE *and the* DOCTOR *cross the kitchen to the front door. She allows him to lead her as if she were blind. As they go out on the porch,* STELLA *cries out her sister's name from where she is crouched a few steps up on the stairs.*]

STELLA   Blanche! Blanche, Blanche!

[BLANCHE *walks on without turning, followed by the* DOCTOR *and the* MATRON. *They go around the corner of the building.*]

[EUNICE *descends to* STELLA *and places the child in her arms. It is wrapped in a pale blue blanket. Stella accepts the child, sobbingly.* EUNICE *continues downstairs and enters the kitchen where the men, except for* STANLEY, *are returning silently to their places about the table.* STANLEY *has gone out on the porch and stands at the foot of the steps looking at* STELLA.]

165 STANLEY [*a bit uncertainly*]   Stella?

[*She sobs with inhuman abandon. There is something luxurious in her complete surrender to crying now that her sister is gone.*]

STANLEY [*voluptuously, soothingly*]   Now, honey. Now, love. Now, now, love. [*He kneels beside her and his fingers find the opening of her blouse.*] Now, now, love. Now, love. . . .

[*The luxurious sobbing, the sensual murmur fade away under the swelling music of the "blue piano" and the muted trumpet.*]

STEVE   This game is seven-card stud.

Curtain.

---

7. Straitjacket.

ARTHUR MILLER

1915–2005

IN A career that lasted sixty-one years and garnered national and international acclaim, Arthur Miller established himself as one of the American theater's most visible and publicly engaged playwrights. He was born two years before the United States' entry into World War I, and his political and artistic convictions were forged in the crucible of national crisis: the Great Depression, World War II, McCarthyism. While Miller felt the impact of these turbulent years in very personal ways—like EUGENE O'NEILL and TENNESSEE WILLIAMS, he is a deeply autobiographical playwright—his plays situate the personal within social realms where the individual is defined as an ethical and moral agent. The son of an Eastern European Jewish immigrant, Miller grew up in a country struggling to come to terms with its national identity, with the social contracts that underlie this identity, and with the increasing tension between its various animating myths and ideologies. Following what the playwright called "the age-old tradition of theatre as a civic art," Miller's plays trace the fault lines running through social psyche of twentieth-century America.

In plays such as *DEATH OF A SALESMAN* (1949), Miller determined many of the directions that postwar American drama would follow. But the roots of his drama

and the central experiences to which it gives form lie in the century's earlier decades. Miller was born in Manhattan on October 17, 1915, to Isadore Miller, a clothing manufacturer, and his wife, Augusta Barnett Miller. The family lived in an apartment on the edge of Harlem overlooking Central Park and enjoyed an affluent life during Miller's childhood. When his father's business failed in 1928, however, they were forced to move to a small house in Brooklyn. The stock market crash in 1929 and the Depression years that followed deepened the future playwright's awareness of the narrow line separating success and failure and the discrepancy between myth and reality in the American capitalist system. Attending high school in Brooklyn, Miller played on the football team but was an average student; for two years after he graduated he held a series of jobs, including deliveryman for his father and sales clerk in an auto parts warehouse in Manhattan. Having saved enough money to attend college, Miller applied and was accepted to the University of Michigan in 1934.

In Ann Arbor, Miller wrote for the school newspaper, majored in English, and began writing drama. He studied playwriting with the English professor Kenneth Rowe and became aware of Clifford Odets, the author of *Waiting for Lefty*

(1935), and other dramatists who made the theater an instrument of social protest during the 1930s. His first two plays won the university's prestigious Avery Hopwood Award in drama in successive years, and he won the Theatre Guild Bureau of New Plays award in 1937. After graduating in June of that year, Miller went to New York to work with the Federal Theatre Project, which was established in 1935 to offer employment to promising young playwrights as part of the New Deal's Works Progress Administration. When the program was abolished by Congress in 1939, he worked in a series of jobs, sold a number of radio scripts, and published *Situation Normal* (1944), a work of military reportage, and *Focus* (1945), a novel dealing with anti-Semitism. At that time, he was living in Brooklyn Heights with his first wife, Mary Grace Slattery, and their two children.

Miller's emergence onto the New York theater scene came in November 1944, when his play *The Man Who Had All the Luck* was produced on Broadway. Although this production received some favorable notice, most reviews were negative, and it closed after only four performances. Three more years would elapse before Miller found Broadway success with *All My Sons* (1947). This play—which is about Joe Keller, a manufacturer of airplane engines, and the disclosure that he had sold defective airplane parts that led to the death of twenty-one pilots and, indirectly, his eldest son—won the New York Drama Critics' Circle Award and was made into a movie in 1948. Its critical and financial success would pale, of course, next to the acclaim that greeted Miller's next play. After a brief preview run in Philadelphia, *Death of a Salesman* opened on February 10, 1949, at Broadway's Morosco Theater in a production directed by Elia Kazan (who had also directed *All My Sons*) and starring Lee J. Cobb as the aging salesman Willy Loman. Hailed by many reviewers as one of the finest plays to emerge in the American theater, *Salesman* won the Critics' Circle Award and the inaugural Pulitzer Prize for Drama. The play ran for 742 productions on Broadway, and by early 1950 eleven foreign productions had opened in Europe, South America, and Israel.

The success of *Salesman* catapulted Miller into the ranks of America's leading writers. But the country itself, growing increasingly obsessed with what it perceived as the Communist threat to its way of life, was undergoing a different kind of transformation. In response to the heightened paranoia of the postwar Red Scare, Miller wrote a play about the 1692 witch persecutions in Salem, Massachusetts. *The Crucible* (1953) is the story of John Proctor, a Salem individualist who struggles with questions of guilt, responsibility, and moral conduct as the witch hunt develops and he is accused. Miller himself was subpoenaed to appear before the House Un-American Activities Committee in June 1956; and while he was forthright in answering questions concerning his own brief involvement with so-called subversive organizations during the war, he, like Proctor, refused to provide the names of others who attended meetings of Communist writers. As a result, he was found guilty of contempt of Congress in May 1957, a conviction that was reversed the following year by the U.S. Court of Appeals.

In the decade after *The Crucible*, Miller wrote several important plays for the theater, including *A View from the Bridge* (1955), *After the Fall* (1964), and *Incident at Vichy* (1964). *After the Fall*, Miller's most autobiographical play, drew on the playwright's often troubled marriage (1956–61) with his second wife, the film star Marilyn Monroe. He married Inge Morath, an Austrian-born photographer, in 1962 (they had two children, and they remained together until Inge's death in 2002). After a four-year break from playwriting—during which he was appointed president of PEN, an international organization that fights censorship and other political pressures on writers—Miller returned to the theater in 1968 with *The Price*, which ran on Broadway for more than a year. But the American theater was changing, and in ways that proved less hospitable to Miller's drama of the individual, society, and the ethical life. Miller wrote a number of plays after *The*

The set, designed by Jo Mielziner, for the original 1949 Broadway production of *Death of a Salesman* at the Morosco Theater in New York.

Price—including *The Creation of the World and Other Business* (1972), *The Archbishop's Ceiling* (1977), *The American Clock* (1980), *The Last Yankee* (1991; 1993), *The Ride Down Mt. Morgan* (1991), *Broken Glass* (1994), *Mr. Peters' Connections* (1998), and *Resurrection Blues* (2002)—but these later works received a mixed reception from American reviewers.

Death of a Salesman is one of the most widely known and influential plays of the twentieth-century theater, and in its narrative techniques and stagecraft, it represents an important development in Miller's career. His preceding play, *All My Sons*, which hinges on the gradual revelation of past events, follows the cause-and-effect structure of discovery and consequence that he admired in the plays of HENRIK IBSEN. In *Salesman*, in contrast, the playwright sought to capture the lived experience of time, with its fluid boundaries between past and present, inner world and outer world. He wanted a play, he later wrote, that would "cut through time like a knife through a layer cake or a road through a mountain revealing its geologic layers, and instead of one incident in one time-frame succeeding another, display past and present concurrently, with neither one ever coming to a stop." Miller's initial image of the set was of a face as tall as the proscenium arch that would open up to reveal the inside of a man's head, a conception captured in his early working title: *The Inside of His Head*. But as the play developed—and as he incorporated the theatrical contributions of Kazan and the stage designer, Jo Mielziner—Miller abandoned such an expressionistic approach for the mode of subjective realism that Mielziner had pioneered in productions of Tennessee Williams's *A Glass Menagerie* (1945) and *A STREETCAR NAMED DESIRE* (1947).

By drawing on realist stagecraft while simultaneously transcending it, subjective realism renders porous the boundaries between internal and external reality.

Death of a Salesman takes place in the house and backyard of the Loman family in midcentury Brooklyn. Surrounding this area, marked by a harsh orange glow, loom the towering shapes of city buildings. The house itself, which creates an impression of fragility, is indicated only in outline, with imaginary walls, a one-dimensional roofline, and minimal furnishings. An apron that curves into the audience provides the setting for other city scenes and for Willy Loman's memories and imaginings. When the play's action takes place in the present, characters observe the conventions of realistic time and space, entering the house only through its doors. When the scene shifts to the past, however, characters walk through the imaginary walls as if they didn't exist. In keeping with Willy's memories of a more pastoral Brooklyn when the neighborhood was covered with elms, the surrounding buildings recede and the stage is lit with a pattern of leaves during those scenes when Willy relives his past.

Even before Miller wrote *Death of a Salesman* in the spring of 1948, the figure of the salesman occupied an important place in his life and imagination. His father had worked as a salesman for Miller's grandfather's company, traveling around the country selling coats, and two of his uncles—both of whom lived with their families in Brooklyn, where Miller visited them before his own family moved to the borough—were career salesmen. The traveling salesmen whom Miller knew embodied the entrepreneurial dreams and haunting failures that marked American capitalism. "[T]hese men lived like artists," Miller declared, "like actors whose product is first of all themselves, forever imagining triumphs in a world that either ignores them or denies their presence altogether." While working for his father in the early 1930s, Miller wrote a short story, "In Memoriam," that was based on a salesman in his father's business who had committed suicide by throwing himself in front of a New York elevated train.

In the twenty-four hours during which the play takes place, Willy Loman searches for some way of reconciling the aspirations that have shaped his life with what he fears is the failure of that life. More than sixty years old, he can no longer earn his keep as a traveling salesman, his sons have not fulfilled the dreams he held for them, and the contradictions that have defined his personality are becoming increasingly apparent. Faced with a desperate present, he seeks refuge in a past that is the product more of nostalgia than of accurate recall. The "remembered" scenes with his family a quarter century earlier, in which he basks in his sons' adoration, are clearly idealized, polished and buffed like his old car. The glow of this past is the glow of an America with a limitless panorama of opportunity and promise, a place where the sky's the limit and all things are possible for a man with personal magnetism. This America has roots in the nineteenth-century frontier: specifically, the American West, where Willy's father sold flutes with his family in a covered wagon, and the territories—Alaska and Africa—where his brother Ben earned a fortune. "[T]hat's the wonder, the wonder of this country," Willy rhapsodizes, "that a man can end with diamonds here on the basis of being liked!" These myths of individualism and success are epitomized in Dave Singleman, a salesman of the previous generation who, after a successful career spent crisscrossing the country, winning customers and making friends, dies "the death of a salesman"—in green velvet slippers in the smoking car of a train—and is fondly remembered by hundreds of salesmen and buyers at his funeral.

Willy holds fiercely to this entrepreneurial dream and all it entails—competition, consumerism, status, the marketing of oneself as a commodity—as if his faith in the American dream guaranteed him a place within it. His slogans about success and popularity are repeated like mantras. But the discrepancies between myth and reality, as well as the contradictions between different facets of the myth itself, create powerful ironies. Willy buys the refrigerator that has the "biggest ads" but finds it in constant need of repairs. He boasts of his popularity on the road—"I can park my car in any street in New England, and the cops protect it like their own"—but minutes later confides to his wife that prospective customers laugh at him behind his back. Willy champions his sons Biff and Happy over their neighbor Bernard, but it is the latter who achieves economic and social success. Once a promising high school football star, Biff drifts from job to job, compulsively stealing things in a self-destructive flight from himself. And the ironically named Happy, who works as an assistant manager, womanizes as a way of bolstering his self-image. Willy has tried to imbue his sons with the secrets of success, but what they inherit from him are the pathological undersides of the ethic he advocates.

To the director and drama critic Harold Clurman, *Death of a Salesman* represents a challenge to the American dream, or at least the capitalist version of it: "[S]ince the Civil War, and particularly since 1900, the American dream has become distorted by the dream of business success." From a Marxist perspective, Willy's tragedy reflects the logic of commodification, whereby the value of something is what it can sell for. Alienated from the work of his hands and the genuineness of relationships, this salesman is worth, in the end, only the dollar amount of the insurance policy on his life. Reacting to this component of Miller's critique, one right-wing publication called *Death of a Salesman* "a time bomb expertly placed under the edifice of Americanism." But Miller's attitude toward the capitalist culture that produced Willy Loman was ambivalent. As he himself pointed out, the most decent person in the play is Charley, a successful businessman, and the dreams that he and his son hold come to pass, as far as we can see. And while Biff Loman finds himself by rejecting his father's aspirations—"He had the wrong dreams"—Charley offers an alternative perspective: "A salesman is got to dream, boy. It comes with the territory."

Willy Loman (played by Lee Cobb, center) in a "memory" scene with his boys Happy (left; played by Cameron Mitchell) and Biff (right; played by Arthur Kennedy), from the 1949 Broadway production of *Death of a Salesman*.

The last words in *Salesman* belong to Linda Loman, and her presence underscores the centrality of family to Miller's tragedy. *Death of a Salesman* was written and produced in the years immediately after World War II, and its dramatic concerns reflect pressures on the institution of the family that mounted in the postwar United States: urbanization, the emergence (and increasing isolation) of the nuclear family, and a hardening of gender roles that would continue into the 1950s. Miller registers the impact of these forces on the relationships within the Loman family, particularly those between fathers and sons. The sense of need that drives Willy—he confesses to feeling "kind of temporary about [him]self"—is linked to his having been abandoned by his father at an early age, and he turns to his brother Ben as a surrogate for that missing paternal presence. Looking to the generation ahead, he seeks to consolidate through his two sons what identity he does possess. Despite the heightened images of male accomplishment throughout the play—high school football hero, wilderness explorer, business tycoon, ladies' man—masculinity, for Miller, is a source of anxiety, and the struggles, exaggerations, and rule breaking in which Willy engages are compensations for his failure to live up to these images. Emphasizing this dynamic, feminists and other analysts have drawn attention to Linda's role within the play. Some critics view her as a source of Willy's problems, arguing that she fails to understand him, encourages him in self-deception or illusion, or interjects materialistic values of her own. Others see her as a source of strength, acting forcefully at a number of moments while trying to balance the claims of reality with her husband's need for self-esteem. In the eyes of one of the play's early reviewers, the single-mindedness of Linda's love holds the play together; more recently, a number of feminist critics have contended that her characterization is circumscribed by the roles available to her in the masculine value system that dominates Miller's play.

In a 1999 essay commemorating the play's fiftieth anniversary, Miller described what he considered to be the power of *Death of a Salesman*: "Being human—a father, mother, son—is something most of us fail at most of the time, and a little mercy is eminently in order given the societies we live in, which purport to be stable and sound as mountains when in fact they are all trembling in a fast wind blowing mindlessly around the earth." In countries as remote from postwar America as Communist China (where *Salesman* was produced to great acclaim in 1983), the play has spoken to the dreams and anxieties of the late twentieth- and early twenty-first-century world. Indeed, as national economies become part of an ever-expanding global capitalism—and developed nations deal with outsourced labor, international finance markets, and the loss of blue-collar jobs—its insistence on the dignity of the individual is as urgent as ever.   S.G.

Death of a Salesman

CHARACTERS

WILLY LOMAN	UNCLE BEN
LINDA	HOWARD WAGNER
BIFF	JENNY
HAPPY	STANLEY
BERNARD	MISS FORSYTHE
THE WOMAN	LETTA
CHARLEY	

The action takes place in Willy Loman's house and yard and in various places he visits in the New York and Boston of today.

Act 1

A melody is heard, played upon a flute. It is small and fine, telling of grass and trees and the horizon. The curtain rises.

Before us is the Salesman's house. We are aware of towering, angular shapes behind it, surrounding it on all sides. Only the blue light of the sky falls upon the house and forestage; the surrounding area shows an angry glow of orange. As more light appears, we see a solid vault of apartment houses around the small, fragile-seeming home. An air of the dream clings to the place, a dream rising out of reality. The kitchen at center seems actual enough, for there is a kitchen table with three chairs, and a refrigerator. But no other fixtures are seen. At the back of the kitchen there is a draped entrance, which leads to the living room. To the right of the kitchen, on a level raised two feet, is a bedroom furnished only with a brass bed-stead and a straight chair. On a shelf over the bed a silver athletic trophy stands. A window opens onto the apartment house at the side.

Behind the kitchen, on a level raised six and a half feet, is the boys' bedroom, at present barely visible. Two beds are dimly seen, and at the back of the room a dor-mer window. (This bedroom is above the unseen living room.) At the left a stairway curves up to it from the kitchen.

The entire setting is wholly, or, in some places, partially transparent. The roofline of the house is one-dimensional; under and over it we see the apartment buildings. Before the house lies an apron,[1] curving beyond the forestage into the orchestra. This forward area serves as the backyard as well as the locale of all WILLY's imagin-ings and of his city scenes. Whenever the action is in the present the actors observe the imaginary wall-lines, entering the house only through its door at the left. But in the scenes of the past these boundaries are broken, and characters enter or leave a room by stepping "through" a wall onto the forestage.

From the right, WILLY LOMAN, the Salesman, enters, carrying two large sample cases. The flute plays on. He hears but is not aware of it. He is past sixty years of age, dressed quietly. Even as he crosses the stage to the doorway of the house, his

---

1. The foremost part of the stage, in front of the proscenium arch.

exhaustion is apparent. He unlocks the door, comes into the kitchen, and thankfully lets his burden down, feeling the soreness of his palms. A word-sigh escapes his lips—it might be "Oh, boy, oh, boy." He closes the door, then carries his cases out into the living room, through the draped kitchen doorway.

LINDA, *his wife, has stirred in her bed at the right. She gets out and puts on a robe, listening. Most often jovial, she has developed an iron repression of her exceptions to Willy's behavior—she more than loves him, she admires him, as though his mercurial nature, his temper, his massive dreams and little cruelties, served her only as sharp reminders of the turbulent longings within him, longings which she shares but lacks the temperament to utter and follow to their end.*

LINDA [*hearing* WILLY *outside the bedroom, calls with some trepidation*]   Willy!

WILLY   It's all right. I came back.

LINDA   Why? What happened? [*Slight pause*] Did something happen, Willy?

WILLY   No, nothing happened.

5 LINDA   You didn't smash the car, did you?

WILLY [*with casual irritation*]   I said nothing happened. Didn't you hear me?

LINDA   Don't you feel well?

WILLY   I'm tired to the death. [*The flute has faded away. He sits on the bed beside her, a little numb.*] I couldn't make it. I just couldn't make it, Linda.

10 LINDA [*very carefully, delicately*]   Where were you all day? You look terrible.

WILLY   I got as far as a little above Yonkers. I stopped for a cup of coffee. Maybe it was the coffee.

LINDA   What?

WILLY [*after a pause*]   I suddenly couldn't drive any more. The car kept going

15 off onto the shoulder, y'know?

LINDA [*helpfully*]   Oh. Maybe it was the steering again. I don't think Angelo knows the Studebaker.

WILLY   No, it's me, it's me. Suddenly I realize I'm goin' sixty miles an hour and I don't remember the last five minutes. I'm—I can't seem to—keep my

20 mind to it.

LINDA   Maybe it's your glasses. You never went for your new glasses.

WILLY   No, I see everything. I came back ten miles an hour. It took me nearly four hours from Yonkers.

LINDA [*resigned*]   Well, you'll just have to take a rest, Willy, you can't

25 continue this way.

WILLY   I just got back from Florida.

LINDA   But you didn't rest your mind. Your mind is overactive, and the mind is what counts, dear.

WILLY   I'll start out in the morning. Maybe I'll feel better in the morning.

30 [*She is taking off his shoes.*] These goddam arch supports are killing me.

LINDA   Take an aspirin. Should I get you an aspirin? It'll soothe you.

WILLY [*with wonder*]   I was driving along, you understand? And I was fine. I was even observing the scenery. You can imagine, me looking at scenery, on the road every week of my life. But it's so beautiful up there, Linda, the

35 trees are so thick, and the sun is warm. I opened the windshield and just let the warm air bathe over me. And then all of a sudden I'm goin' off the road! I'm tellin' ya, I absolutely forgot I was driving. If I'd've gone the other way over the white line I might've killed somebody. So I went on again—and five minutes later I'm dreamin' again, and I nearly—[*He presses two fingers

40 against his eyes.*] I have such thoughts, I have such strange thoughts.

LINDA   Willy, dear. Talk to them again. There's no reason why you can't work in New York.

WILLY   They don't need me in New York. I'm the New England man. I'm vital in New England.

45 LINDA   But you're sixty years old. They can't expect you to keep traveling every week.

WILLY   I'll have to send a wire to Portland. I'm supposed to see Brown and Morrison tomorrow morning at ten o'clock to show the line. Goddammit, I could sell them! [*He starts putting on his jacket.*]

50 LINDA   [*taking the jacket from him*]   Why don't you go down to the place tomorrow and tell Howard you've simply got to work in New York? You're too accommodating, dear.

WILLY   If old man Wagner was alive I'd a been in charge of New York now! That man was a prince, he was a masterful man. But that boy of his, that

55   Howard, he don't appreciate. When I went north the first time, the Wagner Company didn't know where New England was!

LINDA   Why don't you tell those things to Howard, dear?

WILLY   [*encouraged*]   I will, I definitely will. Is there any cheese?

LINDA   I'll make you a sandwich.

60 WILLY   No, go to sleep. I'll take some milk. I'll be up right away. The boys in?

LINDA   They're sleeping. Happy took Biff on a date tonight.

WILLY   [*interested*]   That so?

LINDA   It was so nice to see them shaving together, one behind the other, in the bathroom. And going out together. You notice? The whole house smells

65   of shaving lotion.

WILLY   Figure it out. Work a lifetime to pay off a house. You finally own it, and there's nobody to live in it.

LINDA   Well, dear, life is a casting off. It's always that way.

WILLY   No, no, some people—some people accomplish something. Did Biff

70   say anything after I went this morning?

LINDA   You shouldn't have criticized him, Willy, especially after he just got off the train. You mustn't lose your temper with him.

WILLY   When the hell did I lose my temper? I simply asked him if he was making any money. Is that a criticism?

75 LINDA   But, dear, how could he make any money?

WILLY   [*worried and angered*]   There's such an undercurrent in him. He became a moody man. Did he apologize when I left this morning?

LINDA   He was crestfallen, Willy. You know how he admires you. I think if he finds himself, then you'll both be happier and not fight any more.

80 WILLY   How can he find himself on a farm? Is that a life? A farmhand? In the beginning, when he was young, I thought, well, a young man, it's good for him to tramp around, take a lot of different jobs. But it's more than ten years now and he has yet to make thirty-five dollars[2] a week!

LINDA   He's finding himself, Willy.

85 WILLY   Not finding yourself at the age of thirty-four is a disgrace!

LINDA   Shh!

WILLY   The trouble is he's lazy, goddammit!

LINDA   Willy, please!

2. The equivalent of about $358 in 2017.

WILLY   Biff is a lazy bum!

90 LINDA   They're sleeping. Get something to eat. Go on down.

WILLY   Why did he come home? I would like to know what brought him home.

LINDA   I don't know. I think he's still lost, Willy. I think he's very lost.

WILLY   Biff Loman is lost. In the greatest country in the world a young man
95 with such—personal attractiveness, gets lost. And such a hard worker.
There's one thing about Biff—he's not lazy.

LINDA   Never.

WILLY   [*with pity and resolve*]   I'll see him in the morning; I'll have a nice talk
with him. I'll get him a job selling. He could be big in no time. My God!
100 Remember how they used to follow him around in high school? When he
smiled at one of them their faces lit up. When he walked down the
street . . . [*He loses himself in reminiscences.*]

LINDA   [*trying to bring him out of it*]   Willy, dear, I got a new kind of American-
type cheese today. It's whipped.

105 WILLY   Why do you get American when I like Swiss?

LINDA   I just thought you'd like a change—

WILLY   I don't want a change! I want Swiss cheese. Why am I always being
contradicted?

LINDA   [*with a covering laugh*]   I thought it would be a surprise.

110 WILLY   Why don't you open a window in here, for God's sake?

LINDA   [*with infinite patience*]   They're all open, dear.

WILLY   The way they boxed us in here. Bricks and windows, windows and
bricks.

LINDA   We should've bought the land next door.

115 WILLY   The street is lined with cars. There's not a breath of fresh air in the
neighborhood. The grass don't grow any more, you can't raise a carrot in
the backyard. They should've had a law against apartment houses. Remember those two beautiful elm trees out there? When I and Biff hung the
swing between them?

120 LINDA   Yeah, like being a million miles from the city.

WILLY   They should've arrested the builder for cutting those down. They
massacred the neighborhood. [*Lost*] More and more I think of those days,
Linda. This time of year it was lilac and wisteria. And then the peonies
would come out, and the daffodils. What fragrance in this room!

125 LINDA   Well, after all, people had to move somewhere.

WILLY   No, there's more people now.

LINDA   I don't think there's more people. I think—

WILLY   There's more people! That's what's ruining this country! Population is
getting out of control. The competition is maddening! Smell the stink from
130 that apartment house! And another one on the other side . . . How can they
whip cheese?

[*On* WILLY'S *last line,* BIFF *and* HAPPY *raise themselves up in their beds,
listening.*]

LINDA   Go down, try it. And be quiet.

WILLY   [*turning to* LINDA, *guiltily*]   You're not worried about me, are you,
sweetheart?

135 BIFF   What's the matter?

HAPPY   Listen!

LINDA You've got too much on the ball to worry about.

WILLY You're my foundation and my support, Linda.

LINDA Just try to relax, dear. You make mountains out of molehills.

140 WILLY I won't fight with him any more. If he wants to go back to Texas, let him go.

LINDA He'll find his way.

WILLY Sure. Certain men just don't get started till later in life. Like Thomas Edison, I think. Or B. F. Goodrich.[3] One of them was deaf. [*He starts for* 145 *the bedroom doorway.*] I'll put my money on Biff.

LINDA And Willy—if it's warm Sunday we'll drive in the country. And we'll open the windshield, and take lunch.

WILLY No, the windshields don't open on the new cars.

LINDA But you opened it today.

150 WILLY Me? I didn't. [*He stops.*] Now isn't that peculiar! Isn't that a remarkable—[*He breaks off in amazement and fright as the flute is heard distantly.*]

LINDA What, darling?

WILLY That is the most remarkable thing.

LINDA What, dear?

155 WILLY I was thinking of the Chevvy. [*Slight pause*] Nineteen twenty-eight . . . when I had that red Chevvy—[*Breaks off.*] That funny? I coulda sworn I was driving that Chevvy today.

LINDA Well, that's nothing. Something must've reminded you.

WILLY Remarkable. Ts. Remember those days? The way Biff used to simo- 160 nize[4] that car? The dealer refused to believe there was eighty thousand miles on it. [*He shakes his head.*] Heh! [*To* LINDA] Close your eyes, I'll be right up. [*He walks out of the bedroom.*]

HAPPY [*to* BIFF] Jesus, maybe he smashed up the car again!

LINDA [*calling after* WILLY] Be careful on the stairs, dear! The cheese is on 165 the middle shelf! [*She turns, goes over to the bed, takes his jacket, and goes out of the bedroom.*]

> [*Light has risen on the boys' room. Unseen,* WILLY *is heard talking to himself, "Eighty thousand miles," and a little laugh.* BIFF *gets out of bed, comes downstage a bit, and stands attentively.* BIFF *is two years older than his brother* HAPPY, *well built, but in these days bears a worn air and seems less self-assured. He has succeeded less, and his dreams are stronger and less acceptable than* HAPPY'S. HAPPY *is tall, powerfully made. Sexuality is like a visible color on him, or a scent that many women have discovered. He, like his brother, is lost, but in a different way, for he has never allowed himself to turn his face toward defeat and is thus more confused and hard-skinned, although seemingly more content.*]

HAPPY [*getting out of bed*] He's going to get his license taken away if he keeps that up. I'm getting nervous about him, y'know, Biff?

BIFF His eyes are going.

---

3. An American industrialist (1851–1888); his first investment venture into rubber manufacturing failed, but in 1870 he helped form the company that soon bore only his name. The legendary American inventor Edison (1847–1931) is most famous for creating the phonograph and the first commercially viable incandescent lightbulb; his rapid rise to success and early hearing loss are well-known chapters in his life story.

4. To polish (the Simoniz brand of car wax was first sold in 1935).

HAPPY   No, I've driven with him. He sees all right. He just doesn't keep his
170   mind on it. I drove into the city with him last week. He stops at a green
    light and then it turns red and he goes. [*He laughs.*]

BIFF   Maybe he's color-blind.

HAPPY   Pop? Why he's got the finest eye for color in the business. You know
    that.

175 BIFF [*sitting down on his bed*]   I'm going to sleep.

HAPPY   You're not still sour on Dad, are you, Biff?

BIFF   He's all right, I guess.

WILLY [*underneath them, in the living room*]   Yes, sir, eighty thousand miles—
    eighty-two thousand!

180 BIFF You smoking?

HAPPY [*holding out a pack of cigarettes*]   Want one?

BIFF [*taking a cigarette*]   I can never sleep when I smell it.

WILLY   What a simonizing job, heh!

HAPPY [*with deep sentiment*]   Funny, Biff, y'know? Us sleeping in here again?
185   The old beds. [*He pats his bed affectionately.*] All the talk that went across
    those two beds, huh? Our whole lives.

BIFF   Yeah. Lotta dreams and plans.

HAPPY [*with a deep and masculine laugh*]   About five hundred women would
    like to know what was said in this room.

    [*They share a soft laugh.*]

190 BIFF Remember that big Betsy something—what the hell was her name—
    over on Bushwick Avenue?[5]

HAPPY [*combing his hair*]   With the collie dog!

BIFF   That's the one. I got you in there, remember?

HAPPY   Yeah, that was my first time—I think. Boy, there was a pig! [*They
195   laugh, almost crudely.*] You taught me everything I know about women.
    Don't forget that.

BIFF   I bet you forgot how bashful you used to be. Especially with girls.

HAPPY   Oh, I still am, Biff.

BIFF   Oh, go on.

200 HAPPY I just control it, that's all. I think I got less bashful and you got more
    so. What happened, Biff? Where's the old humor, the old confidence? [*He
    shakes* BIFF's *knee.* BIFF *gets up and moves restlessly about the room.*] What's
    the matter?

BIFF   Why does Dad mock me all the time?

205 HAPPY He's not mocking you, he—

BIFF   Everything I say there's a twist of mockery on his face. I can't get near
    him.

HAPPY   He just wants you to make good, that's all. I wanted to talk to you
    about Dad for a long time, Biff. Something's—happening to him. He—
210   talks to himself.

BIFF   I noticed that this morning. But he always mumbled.

HAPPY   But not so noticeable. It got so embarrassing I sent him to Florida.
    And you know something? Most of the time he's talking to you.

BIFF   What's he say about me?

5. A major thoroughfare in Brooklyn, New York.

215 HAPPY I can't make it out.

BIFF What's he say about me?

HAPPY I think the fact that you're not settled, that you're still kind of up in the air . . .

BIFF There's one or two other things depressing him, Happy.

220 HAPPY What do you mean?

BIFF Never mind. Just don't lay it all to me.

HAPPY But I think if you just got started—I mean—is there any future for you out there?

BIFF I tell ya, Hap, I don't know what the future is. I don't know—what I'm

225 supposed to want.

HAPPY What do you mean?

BIFF Well, I spent six or seven years after high school trying to work myself up. Shipping clerk, salesman, business of one kind or another. And it's a measly manner of existence. To get on that subway on the hot mornings in

230 summer. To devote your whole life to keeping stock, or making phone calls, or selling or buying. To suffer fifty weeks of the year for the sake of a two-week vacation, when all you really desire is to be outdoors, with your shirt off. And always to have to get ahead of the next fella. And still—that's how you build a future.

235 HAPPY Well, you really enjoy it on a farm? Are you content out there?

BIFF [with rising agitation] Hap, I've had twenty or thirty different kinds of jobs since I left home before the war, and it always turns out the same. I just realized it lately. In Nebraska when I herded cattle, and the Dakotas, and Arizona, and now in Texas. It's why I came home now, I guess,

240 because I realized it. This farm I work on, it's spring there now, see? And they've got about fifteen new colts. There's nothing more inspiring or— beautiful than the sight of a mare and a new colt. And it's cool there now, see? Texas is cool now, and it's spring. And whenever spring comes to where I am, I suddenly get the feeling, my God, I'm not gettin' anywhere!

245 What the hell am I doing, playing around with horses, twenty-eight dollars a week! I'm thirty-four years old, I oughta be makin' my future. That's when I come running home. And now, I get here, and I don't know what to do with myself. [After a pause] I've always made a point of not wasting my life, and every time I come back here I know that all I've done is to waste

250 my life.

HAPPY You're a poet, you know that, Biff? You're a—you're an idealist!

BIFF No, I'm mixed up very bad. Maybe I oughta get married. Maybe I oughta get stuck into something. Maybe that's my trouble. I'm like a boy. I'm not married, I'm not in business, I just—I'm like a boy. Are you content,

255 Hap? You're a success, aren't you? Are you content?

HAPPY Hell, no!

BIFF Why? You're making money, aren't you?

HAPPY [moving about with energy, expressiveness] All I can do now is wait for the merchandise manager to die. And suppose I get to be merchandise

260 manager? He's a good friend of mine, and he just built a terrific estate on Long Island. And he lived there about two months and sold it, and now he's building another one. He can't enjoy it once it's finished. And I know that's just what I would do. I don't know what the hell I'm workin' for. Sometimes

I sit in my apartment—all alone. And I think of the rent I'm paying. And it's
265 crazy. But then, it's what I always wanted. My own apartment, a car, and
plenty of women. And still, goddammit, I'm lonely.

BIFF [*with enthusiasm*] Listen, why don't you come out West with me?

HAPPY You and I, heh?

BIFF Sure, maybe we could buy a ranch. Raise cattle, use our muscles. Men
270 built like we are should be working out in the open.

HAPPY [*avidly*] The Loman Brothers, heh?

BIFF [*with vast affection*] Sure, we'd be known all over the counties!

HAPPY [*enthralled*] That's what I dream about, Biff. Sometimes I want to
just rip my clothes off in the middle of the store and outbox that goddam
275 merchandise manager. I mean I can outbox, outrun, and outlift anybody in
that store, and I have to take orders from those common, petty sons-of-
bitches till I can't stand it any more.

BIFF I'm tellin' you, kid, if you were with me I'd be happy out there.

HAPPY [*enthused*] See, Biff, everybody around me is so false that I'm con-
280 stantly lowering my ideals . . .

BIFF Baby, together we'd stand up for one another, we'd have someone to
trust.

HAPPY If I were around you—

BIFF Hap, the trouble is we weren't brought up to grub for money. I don't
285 know how to do it.

HAPPY Neither can I!

BIFF Then let's go!

HAPPY The only thing is—what can you make out there?

BIFF But look at your friend. Builds an estate and then hasn't the peace of
290 mind to live in it.

HAPPY Yeah, but when he walks into the store the waves part in front of him.
That's fifty-two thousand dollars a year coming through the revolving door,
and I got more in my pinky finger than he's got in his head.

BIFF Yeah, but you just said—

295 HAPPY I gotta show some of those pompous, self-important executives over
there that Hap Loman can make the grade. I want to walk into the store
the way he walks in. Then I'll go with you, Biff. We'll be together yet,
I swear. But take those two we had tonight. Now weren't they gorgeous
creatures?

300 BIFF Yeah, yeah, most gorgeous I've had in years.

HAPPY I get that anytime I want, Biff. Whenever I feel disgusted. The only
trouble is, it gets like bowling or something. I just keep knockin' them over
and it doesn't mean anything. You still run around a lot?

BIFF Naa. I'd like to find a girl—steady, somebody with substance.

305 HAPPY That's what I long for.

BIFF Go on! You'd never come home.

HAPPY I would! Somebody with character, with resistance! Like Mom,
y'know? You're gonna call me a bastard when I tell you this. That girl Charlotte I was with tonight is engaged to be married in five weeks. [*He tries on
his new hat.*]

310 BIFF No kiddin'!

HAPPY Sure, the guy's in line for the vice-presidency of the store. I don't
know what gets into me, maybe I just have an overdeveloped sense of

competition or something, but I went and ruined her, and furthermore I
can't get rid of her. And he's the third executive I've done that to. Isn't that
315 a crummy characteristic? And to top it all, I go to their weddings! [*Indignantly, but laughing*] Like I'm not supposed to take bribes. Manufacturers
offer me a hundred-dollar bill now and then to throw an order their way.
You know how honest I am, but it's like this girl, see. I hate myself for it.
Because I don't want the girl, and, still, I take it and—I love it!

320 BIFF   Let's go to sleep.

HAPPY   I guess we didn't settle anything, heh?

BIFF   I just got one idea that I think I'm going to try.

HAPPY   What's that?

BIFF   Remember Bill Oliver?

325 HAPPY   Sure, Oliver is very big now. You want to work for him again?

BIFF   No, but when I quit he said something to me. He put his arm on my
shoulder, and he said, "Biff, if you ever need anything, come to me."

HAPPY   I remember that. That sounds good.

BIFF   I think I'll go to see him. If I could get ten thousand or even seven or
330 eight thousand dollars I could buy a beautiful ranch.

HAPPY   I bet he'd back you. 'Cause he thought highly of you, Biff. I mean,
they all do. You're well liked, Biff. That's why I say to come back here, and
we both have the apartment. And I'm tellin' you, Biff, any babe you
want . . .

335 BIFF   No, with a ranch I could do the work I like and still be something. I
just wonder though. I wonder if Oliver still thinks I stole that carton of
basketballs.

HAPPY   Oh, he probably forgot that long ago. It's almost ten years. You're too
sensitive. Anyway, he didn't really fire you.

340 BIFF   Well, I think he was going to. I think that's why I quit. I was never sure
whether he knew or not. I know he thought the world of me, though. I was
the only one he'd let lock up the place.

WILLY [*below*]   You gonna wash the engine, Biff?

HAPPY   Shh!

> [BIFF *looks at* HAPPY, *who is gazing down, listening.* WILLY *is mumbling
> in the parlor.*]

345 HAPPY   You hear that?

> [*They listen.* WILLY *laughs warmly.*]

BIFF [*growing angry*]   Doesn't he know Mom can hear that?

WILLY   Don't get your sweater dirty, Biff!

> [*A look of pain crosses* BIFF's *face.*]

HAPPY   Isn't that terrible? Don't leave again, will you? You'll find a job here.
You gotta stick around. I don't know what to do about him, it's getting
350 embarrassing.

WILLY   What a simonizing job!

BIFF   Mom's hearing that!

WILLY   No kiddin', Biff, you got a date? Wonderful!

HAPPY   Go on to sleep. But talk to him in the morning, will you?

355 BIFF [*reluctantly getting into bed*]   With her in the house. Brother!

HAPPY [*getting into bed*]   I wish you'd have a good talk with him.

> [*The light on their room begins to fade.*]

BIFF [*to himself in bed*] That selfish, stupid . . .

HAPPY Sh . . . Sleep, Biff.

> [*Their light is out. Well before they have finished speaking,* WILLY'*s form is dimly seen below in the darkened kitchen. He opens the refrigerator, searches in there, and takes out a bottle of milk. The apartment houses are fading out, and the entire house and surroundings become covered with leaves. Music insinuates itself as the leaves appear.*]

360 WILLY Just wanna be careful with those girls, Biff, that's all. Don't make any promises. No promises of any kind. Because a girl, y'know, they always believe what you tell 'em, and you're very young, Biff, you're too young to be talking seriously to girls.

> [*Light rises on the kitchen.* WILLY, *talking, shuts the refrigerator door and comes downstage to the kitchen table. He pours milk into a glass. He is totally immersed in himself, smiling faintly.*]

WILLY Too young entirely, Biff. You want to watch your schooling first. Then when you're all set, there'll be plenty of girls for a boy like you. [*He smiles*
365 *broadly at a kitchen chair.*] That so? The girls pay for you? [*He laughs.*] Boy, you must really be makin' a hit.

> [WILLY *is gradually addressing—physically—a point offstage, speaking through the wall of the kitchen, and his voice has been rising in volume to that of a normal conversation.*]

WILLY I been wondering why you polish the car so careful. Ha! Don't leave the hubcaps, boys. Get the chamois to the hubcaps. Happy, use newspaper on the windows, it's the easiest thing. Show him how to do it, Biff! You see,
370 Happy? Pad it up, use it like a pad. That's it, that's it, good work. You're doin' all right, Hap. [*He pauses, then nods in approbation for a few seconds, then looks upward.*] Biff, first thing we gotta do when we get time is clip that big branch over the house. Afraid it's gonna fall in a storm and hit the roof. Tell you what. We get a rope and sling her around, and then we climb
375 up there with a couple of saws and take her down. Soon as you finish the car, boys, I wanna see ya. I got a surprise for you, boys.

BIFF [*offstage*] Whatta ya got, Dad?

WILLY No, you finish first. Never leave a job till you're finished—remember that. [*Looking toward the "big trees"*] Biff, up in Albany I saw a beautiful
380 hammock. I think I'll buy it next trip, and we'll hang it right between those two elms. Wouldn't that be something? Just swingin' there under those branches. Boy, that would be . . .

> [YOUNG BIFF *and* YOUNG HAPPY *appear from the direction* WILLY *was addressing.* HAPPY *carries rags and a pail of water.* BIFF, *wearing a sweater with a block "S," carries a football.*]

BIFF [*pointing in the direction of the car offstage*] How's that, Pop, professional?

385 WILLY Terrific. Terrific job, boys. Good work, Biff.

HAPPY Where's the surprise, Pop?

WILLY In the back seat of the car.

HAPPY Boy! [*He runs off.*]

BIFF What is it, Dad? Tell me, what'd you buy?

390 WILLY [*laughing, cuffs him*] Never mind, something I want you to have.

BIFF [*turns and starts off*] What is it, Hap?

HAPPY [*offstage*] It's a punching bag!

BIFF   Oh, Pop!

WILLY   It's got Gene Tunney's[6] signature on it!

[HAPPY *runs onstage with a punching bag.*]

395   BIFF   Gee, how'd you know we wanted a punching bag?

WILLY   Well, it's the finest thing for the timing.

HAPPY [*lies down on his back and pedals with his feet*]   I'm losing weight, you notice, Pop?

WILLY [*to* HAPPY]   Jumping rope is good too.

400   BIFF   Did you see the new football I got?

WILLY [*examining the ball*]   Where'd you get a new ball?

BIFF   The coach told me to practice my passing.

WILLY   That so? And he gave you the ball, heh?

BIFF   Well, I borrowed it from the locker room. [*He laughs confidentially.*]

405   WILLY [*laughing with him at the theft*]   I want you to return that.

HAPPY   I told you he wouldn't like it!

BIFF [*angrily*]   Well, I'm bringing it back!

WILLY [*stopping the incipient argument, to* HAPPY]   Sure, he's gotta practice with a regulation ball, doesn't he? [*To* BIFF] Coach'll probably congratulate

410   you on your initiative!

BIFF   Oh, he keeps congratulating my initiative all the time, Pop.

WILLY   That's because he likes you. If somebody else took that ball there'd be an uproar. So what's the report, boys, what's the report?

BIFF   Where'd you go this time, Dad? Gee, we were lonesome for you.

415   WILLY [*pleased, puts an arm around each boy and they come down to the apron*]   Lonesome, heh?

BIFF   Missed you every minute.

WILLY   Don't say? Tell you a secret, boys. Don't breathe it to a soul. Someday I'll have my own business, and I'll never have to leave home any more.

HAPPY   Like Uncle Charley, heh?

420   WILLY   Bigger than Uncle Charley! Because Charley is not—liked. He's liked, but he's not—well liked.

BIFF   Where'd you go this time, Dad?

WILLY   Well, I got on the road, and I went north to Providence. Met the Mayor.

425   BIFF   The Mayor of Providence!

WILLY   He was sitting in the hotel lobby.

BIFF   What'd he say?

WILLY   He said, "Morning!" And I said, "You got a fine city here, Mayor." And then he had coffee with me. And then I went to Waterbury. Waterbury is a

430   fine city. Big clock city, the famous Waterbury clock. Sold a nice bill[7] there. And then Boston—Boston is the cradle of the Revolution. A fine city. And a couple of other towns in Mass., and on to Portland and Bangor and straight home!

BIFF   Gee, I'd love to go with you sometime, Dad.

435   WILLY   Soon as summer comes.

HAPPY   Promise?

---

6. James Joseph Tunney (1897–1978), an American boxer who was undefeated world heavyweight champion, 1926–28.

7. That is, a bill of goods; a consignment of merchandise.

WILLY   You and Hap and I, and I'll show you all the towns. America is full of beautiful towns and fine, upstanding people. And they know me, boys, they know me up and down New England. The finest people. And when I bring
440   you fellas up, there'll be open sesame for all of us, 'cause one thing, boys: I have friends. I can park my car in any street in New England, and the cops protect it like their own. This summer, heh?

BIFF and HAPPY [*together*]   Yeah! You bet!

WILLY   We'll take our bathing suits.

445   HAPPY   We'll carry your bags, Pop!

WILLY   Oh, won't that be something! Me comin' into the Boston stores with you boys carryin' my bags. What a sensation!

[BIFF *is prancing around, practicing passing the ball.*]

WILLY   You nervous, Biff, about the game?

BIFF   Not if you're gonna be there.

450   WILLY   What do they say about you in school, now that they made you captain?

HAPPY   There's a crowd of girls behind him every time the classes change.

BIFF [*taking* WILLY's *hand*]   This Saturday, Pop, this Saturday—just for you, I'm going to break through for a touchdown.

455   HAPPY   You're supposed to pass.

BIFF   I'm takin' one play for Pop. You watch me, Pop, and when I take off my helmet, that means I'm breakin' out. Then you watch me crash through that line!

WILLY [*kisses* BIFF]   Oh, wait'll I tell this in Boston!

[BERNARD *enters in knickers. He is younger than* BIFF, *earnest and loyal, a worried boy.*]

460   BERNARD   Biff, where are you? You're supposed to study with me today.

WILLY   Hey, looka Bernard. What're you lookin' so anemic about, Bernard?

BERNARD   He's gotta study, Uncle Willy. He's got Regents[8] next week.

HAPPY [*tauntingly, spinning* BERNARD *around*]   Let's box, Bernard!

BERNARD   Biff! [*He gets away from* HAPPY.] Listen, Biff, I heard Mr. Birnbaum
465   say that if you don't start studyin' math he's gonna flunk you, and you won't graduate. I heard him!

WILLY   You better study with him, Biff. Go ahead now.

BERNARD   I heard him!

BIFF   Oh, Pop, you didn't see my sneakers! [*He holds up a foot for* WILLY *to look at.*]

470   WILLY   Hey, that's a beautiful job of printing!

BERNARD [*wiping his glasses*]   Just because he printed University of Virginia on his sneakers doesn't mean they've got to graduate him, Uncle Willy!

WILLY [*angrily*]   What're you talking about? With scholarships to three universities they're gonna flunk him?

475   BERNARD   But I heard Mr. Birnbaum say—

WILLY   Don't be a pest, Bernard! [*To his boys*] What an anemic!

BERNARD   Okay, I'm waiting for you in my house, Biff.

[BERNARD *goes off. The Lomans laugh.*]

WILLY   Bernard is not well liked, is he?

8. That is, Regents examinations: tests in specific subject areas administered by the state of New York to all students in public high schools.

BIFF   He's liked, but he's not well liked.

480 HAPPY   That's right, Pop.

WILLY   That's just what I mean. Bernard can get the best marks in school, y'understand, but when he gets out in the business world, y'understand, you are going to be five times ahead of him. That's why I thank Almighty God you're both built like Adonises.[9] Because the man who makes an
485 appearance in the business world, the man who creates personal interest, is the man who gets ahead. Be liked and you will never want. You take me, for instance. I never have to wait in line to see a buyer. "Willy Loman is here!" That's all they have to know, and I go right through.

BIFF   Did you knock them dead, Pop?

490 WILLY   Knocked 'em cold in Providence, slaughtered 'em in Boston.

HAPPY   [*on his back, pedaling again*]   I'm losing weight, you notice, Pop?

[LINDA *enters, as of old, a ribbon in her hair, carrying a basket of washing.*]

LINDA   [*with youthful energy*]   Hello, dear!

WILLY   Sweetheart!

LINDA   How'd the Chevvy run?

495 WILLY   Chevrolet, Linda, is the greatest car ever built. [*To the boys*] Since when do you let your mother carry wash up the stairs?

BIFF   Grab hold there, boy!

HAPPY   Where to, Mom?

LINDA   Hang them up on the line. And you better go down to your friends,
500 Biff. The cellar is full of boys. They don't know what to do with themselves.

BIFF   Ah, when Pop comes home they can wait!

WILLY   [*laughs appreciatively*]   You better go down and tell them what to do, Biff.

BIFF   I think I'll have them sweep out the furnace room.

505 WILLY   Good work, Biff.

BIFF   [*goes through wall-line of kitchen to doorway at back and calls down*] Fellas! Everybody sweep out the furnace room! I'll be right down!

VOICES   All right! Okay, Biff.

BIFF   George and Sam and Frank, come out back! We're hangin' up the wash! Come on, Hap, on the double! [*He and* HAPPY *carry out the basket.*]

510 LINDA   The way they obey him!

WILLY   Well, that's training, the training. I'm tellin' you, I was sellin' thousands and thousands, but I had to come home.

LINDA   Oh, the whole block'll be at that game. Did you sell anything?

WILLY   I did five hundred gross in Providence and seven hundred gross in
515 Boston.

LINDA   No! Wait a minute, I've got a pencil. [*She pulls pencil and paper out of her apron pocket.*] That makes your commission . . . Two hundred—my God! Two hundred and twelve dollars!

WILLY   Well, I didn't figure it yet, but . . .

520 LINDA   How much did you do?

WILLY   Well, I—I did—about a hundred and eighty gross in Providence. Well, no—it came to—roughly two hundred gross on the whole trip.

LINDA   [*without hesitation*]   Two hundred gross. That's . . . [*She figures.*]

9. In Greek mythology, Adonis was a beautiful youth.

WILLY   The trouble was that three of the stores were half closed for inventory
525   in Boston. Otherwise I woulda broke records.
LINDA   Well, it makes seventy dollars and some pennies. That's very good.
WILLY   What do we owe?
LINDA   Well, on the first there's sixteen dollars on the refrigerator—
WILLY   Why sixteen?
530 LINDA   Well, the fan belt broke, so it was a dollar eighty.
WILLY   But it's brand new.
LINDA   Well, the man said that's the way it is. Till they work themselves in,
y'know.

[*They move through the wall-line into the kitchen.*]

WILLY   I hope we didn't get stuck on that machine.
535 LINDA   They got the biggest ads of any of them!
WILLY   I know, it's a fine machine. What else?
LINDA   Well, there's nine-sixty for the washing machine. And for the vacuum
cleaner there's three and a half due on the fifteenth. Then the roof, you got
twenty-one dollars remaining.
540 WILLY   It don't leak, does it?
LINDA   No, they did a wonderful job. Then you owe Frank for the carburetor.
WILLY   I'm not going to pay that man! That goddam Chevrolet, they ought to
prohibit the manufacture of that car!
LINDA   Well, you owe him three and a half. And odds and ends, comes to
545   around a hundred and twenty dollars by the fifteenth.
WILLY   A hundred and twenty dollars! My God, if business don't pick up I
don't know what I'm gonna do!
LINDA   Well, next week you'll do better.
WILLY   Oh, I'll knock 'em dead next week. I'll go to Hartford. I'm very well
550   liked in Hartford. You know, the trouble is, Linda, people don't seem to
take to me.

[*They move onto the forestage.*]

LINDA   Oh, don't be foolish.
WILLY   I know it when I walk in. They seem to laugh at me.
LINDA   Why? Why would they laugh at you? Don't talk that way, Willy.

[*WILLY moves to the edge of the stage. LINDA goes into the kitchen and
starts to darn stockings.*]

555 WILLY   I don't know the reason for it, but they just pass me by. I'm not noticed.
LINDA   But you're doing wonderful, dear. You're making seventy to a hundred
dollars a week.
WILLY   But I gotta be at it ten, twelve hours a day. Other men—I don't
know—they do it easier. I don't know why—I can't stop myself—I talk too
560   much. A man oughta come in with a few words. One thing about Charley.
He's a man of few words, and they respect him.
LINDA   You don't talk too much, you're just lively.
WILLY [*smiling*]   Well, I figure, what the hell, life is short, a couple of jokes.
[*To himself*] I joke too much! [*The smile goes.*]
565 LINDA   Why? You're—
WILLY   I'm fat. I'm very—foolish to look at, Linda. I didn't tell you, but
Christmastime I happened to be calling on F. H. Stewart's, and a salesman
I know, as I was going in to see the buyer I heard him say something

about—walrus. And I—I cracked him right across the face. I won't take
570 that. I simply will not take that. But they do laugh at me. I know that.

LINDA Darling . . .

WILLY I gotta overcome it. I know I gotta overcome it. I'm not dressing to
advantage, maybe.

LINDA Willy, darling, you're the handsomest man in the world—

575 WILLY Oh, no, Linda.

LINDA To me you are. [*Slight pause*] The handsomest.

> [*From the darkness is heard the laughter of a woman.* WILLY *doesn't turn
> to it, but it continues through* LINDA'S *lines.*]

LINDA And the boys, Willy. Few men are idolized by their children the way
you are.

> [*Music is heard as behind a scrim, to the left of the house,* THE WOMAN,
> *dimly seen, is dressing.*]

WILLY [*with great feeling*] You're the best there is, Linda, you're a pal, you
580 know that? On the road—on the road I want to grab you sometimes and
just kiss the life outa you.

> [*The laughter is loud now, and he moves into a brightening area at the
> left, where* THE WOMAN *has come from behind the scrim and is standing,
> putting on her hat, looking into a "mirror" and laughing.*]

WILLY 'Cause I get so lonely—especially when business is bad and there's
nobody to talk to. I get the feeling that I'll never sell anything again, that I
won't make a living for you, or a business, a business for the boys. [*He talks
through* THE WOMAN'S *subsiding laughter;* THE WOMAN *primps at the "mir-
585 ror."*] There's so much I want to make for—

THE WOMAN Me? You didn't make me, Willy. I picked you.

WILLY [*pleased*] You picked me?

THE WOMAN [*who is quite proper-looking,* WILLY'S *age*] I did. I've been sitting
at that desk watching all the salesmen go by, day in, day out. But you've got
590 such a sense of humor, and we do have such a good time together, don't
we?

WILLY Sure, sure. [*He takes her in his arms.*] Why do you have to go now?

THE WOMAN It's two o'clock . . .

WILLY No, come on in! [*He pulls her.*]

595 THE WOMAN . . . my sisters'll be scandalized. When'll you be back?

WILLY Oh, two weeks about. Will you come up again?

THE WOMAN Sure thing. You do make me laugh. It's good for me. [*She
squeezes his arm, kisses him.*] And I think you're a wonderful man.

WILLY You picked me, heh?

600 THE WOMAN Sure. Because you're so sweet. And such a kidder.

WILLY Well, I'll see you next time I'm in Boston.

THE WOMAN I'll put you right through to the buyers.

WILLY [*slapping her bottom*] Right. Well, bottoms up!

THE WOMAN [*slaps him gently and laughs*] You just kill me, Willy. [*He sud-
605 denly grabs her and kisses her roughly.*] You kill me. And thanks for the
stockings. I love a lot of stockings. Well, good night.

WILLY Good night. And keep your pores open!

THE WOMAN Oh, Willy!

> [THE WOMAN *bursts out laughing, and* LINDA'S *laughter blends in.* THE
> WOMAN *disappears into the dark. Now the area at the kitchen table*

brightens. LINDA *is sitting where she was at the kitchen table, but now is mending a pair of her silk stockings.*]

LINDA   You are, Willy. The handsomest man. You've got no reason to feel that—

610 WILLY [*coming out of* THE WOMAN's *dimming area and going over to* LINDA]   I'll make it all up to you, Linda, I'll—

LINDA   There's nothing to make up, dear. You're doing fine, better than—

WILLY [*noticing her mending*]   What's that?

LINDA   Just mending my stockings. They're so expensive—

615 WILLY [*angrily, taking them from her*]   I won't have you mending stockings in this house! Now throw them out!

[LINDA *puts the stockings in her pocket.*]

BERNARD [*entering on the run*]   Where is he? If he doesn't study!

WILLY [*moving to the forestage, with great agitation*]   You'll give him the answers!

620 BERNARD   I do, but I can't on a Regents! That's a state exam! They're liable to arrest me!

WILLY   Where is he? I'll whip him, I'll whip him!

LINDA   And he'd better give back that football, Willy, it's not nice.

WILLY   Biff! Where is he? Why is he taking everything?

625 LINDA   He's too rough with the girls, Willy. All the mothers are afraid of him!

WILLY   I'll whip him!

BERNARD   He's driving the car without a license!

[THE WOMAN's *laugh is heard.*]

WILLY   Shut up!

LINDA   All the mothers—

630 WILLY   Shut up!

BERNARD [*backing quietly away and out*]   Mr. Birnbaum says he's stuck up.

WILLY   Get outa here!

BERNARD   If he doesn't buckle down he'll flunk math! [*He goes off.*]

LINDA   He's right, Willy, you've gotta—

635 WILLY [*exploding at her*]   There's nothing the matter with him! You want him to be a worm like Bernard? He's got spirit, personality . . .

[*As he speaks,* LINDA, *almost in tears, exits into the living room.* WILLY *is alone in the kitchen, wilting and staring. The leaves are gone. It is night again, and the apartment houses look down from behind.*]

WILLY   Loaded with it. Loaded! What is he stealing? He's giving it back, isn't he? Why is he stealing? What did I tell him? I never in my life told him anything but decent things.

[HAPPY *in pajamas has come down the stairs;* WILLY *suddenly becomes aware of* HAPPY's *presence.*]

640 HAPPY   Let's go now, come on.

WILLY [*sitting down at the kitchen table*]   Huh! Why did she have to wax the floors herself? Everytime she waxes the floors she keels over. She knows that!

HAPPY   Shh! Take it easy. What brought you back tonight?

645 WILLY   I got an awful scare. Nearly hit a kid in Yonkers. God! Why didn't I go to Alaska with my brother Ben that time! Ben! That man was a genius, that man was success incarnate! What a mistake! He begged me to go.

HAPPY   Well, there's no use in—

WILLY   You guys! There was a man started with the clothes on his back and
650   ended up with diamond mines!

HAPPY   Boy, someday I'd like to know how he did it.

WILLY   What's the mystery? The man knew what he wanted and went out and
got it! Walked into a jungle, and comes out, the age of twenty-one, and he's
rich! The world is an oyster, but you don't crack it open on a mattress!

655   HAPPY   Pop, I told you I'm gonna retire you for life.

WILLY   You'll retire me for life on seventy goddam dollars a week? And your
women and your car and your apartment, and you'll retire me for life!
Christ's sake, I couldn't get past Yonkers today! Where are you guys, where
are you? The woods are burning! I can't drive a car!

[CHARLEY *has appeared in the doorway. He is a large man, slow of speech,
laconic, immovable. In all he says, despite what he says, there is pity, and,
now, trepidation. He has a robe over pajamas, slippers on his feet. He
enters the kitchen.*]

660   CHARLEY   Everything all right?

HAPPY   Yeah, Charley, everything's . . .

WILLY   What's the matter?

CHARLEY   I heard some noise. I thought something happened. Can't we do
something about the walls? You sneeze in here, and in my house hats blow
665   off.

HAPPY   Let's go to bed, Dad. Come on.

[CHARLEY *signals to* HAPPY *to go.*]

WILLY   You go ahead, I'm not tired at the moment.

HAPPY [*to* WILLY]   Take it easy, huh? [*He exits.*]

WILLY   What're you doin' up?

670   CHARLEY [*sitting down at the kitchen table opposite* WILLY]   Couldn't sleep
good. I had a heartburn.

WILLY   Well, you don't know how to eat.

CHARLEY   I eat with my mouth.

WILLY   No, you're ignorant. You gotta know about vitamins and things like
675   that.

CHARLEY   Come on, let's shoot. Tire you out a little.

WILLY [*hesitantly*]   All right. You got cards?

CHARLEY [*taking a deck from his pocket*]   Yeah, I got them. Someplace. What
is it with those vitamins?

680   WILLY [*dealing*]   They build up your bones. Chemistry.

CHARLEY   Yeah, but there's no bones in a heartburn.

WILLY   What are you talkin' about? Do you know the first thing about it?

CHARLEY   Don't get insulted.

WILLY   Don't talk about something you don't know anything about.

[*They are playing. Pause.*]

685   CHARLEY   What're you doin' home?

WILLY   A little trouble with the car.

CHARLEY   Oh. [*Pause*] I'd like to take a trip to California.

WILLY   Don't say.

CHARLEY   You want a job?

690   WILLY   I got a job, I told you that. [*After a slight pause*] What the hell are you
offering me a job for?

CHARLEY   Don't get insulted.

WILLY   Don't insult me.

CHARLEY   I don't see no sense in it. You don't have to go on this way.

695 WILLY   I got a good job. [*Slight pause*] What do you keep comin' in here for?

CHARLEY   You want me to go?

WILLY [*after a pause, withering*] I can't understand it. He's going back to Texas again. What the hell is that?

CHARLEY   Let him go.

700 WILLY   I got nothin' to give him, Charley, I'm clean, I'm clean.

CHARLEY   He won't starve. None a them starve. Forget about him.

WILLY   Then what have I got to remember?

CHARLEY   You take it too hard. To hell with it. When a deposit bottle is broken you don't get your nickel back.

705 WILLY   That's easy enough for you to say.

CHARLEY   That ain't easy for me to say.

WILLY   Did you see the ceiling I put up in the living room?

CHARLEY   Yeah, that's a piece of work. To put up a ceiling is a mystery to me. How do you do it?

710 WILLY   What's the difference?

CHARLEY   Well, talk about it.

WILLY   You gonna put up a ceiling?

CHARLEY   How could I put up a ceiling?

WILLY   Then what the hell are you bothering me for?

715 CHARLEY   You're insulted again.

WILLY   A man who can't handle tools is not a man. You're disgusting.

CHARLEY   Don't call me disgusting. Willy.

[UNCLE BEN, *carrying a valise and an umbrella, enters the forestage from around the right corner of the house. He is a stolid man, in his sixties, with a mustache and an authoritative air. He is utterly certain of his destiny, and there is an aura of far places about him. He enters exactly as* WILLY *speaks.*]

WILLY   I'm getting awfully tired, Ben.

[BEN's *music is heard.* BEN *looks around at everything.*]

CHARLEY   Good, keep playing; you'll sleep better. Did you call me Ben?

[BEN *looks at his watch.*]

720 WILLY   That's funny. For a second there you reminded me of my brother Ben.

BEN   I only have a few minutes. [*He strolls, inspecting the place.* WILLY *and* CHARLEY *continue playing.*]

CHARLEY   You never heard from him again, heh? Since that time?

WILLY   Didn't Linda tell you? Couple of weeks ago we got a letter from his wife in Africa. He died.

725 CHARLEY   That so.

BEN [*chuckling*]   So this is Brooklyn, eh?

CHARLEY   Maybe you're in for some of his money.

WILLY   Naa, he had seven sons. There's just one opportunity I had with that man . . .

730 BEN   I must make a train, William. There are several properties I'm looking at in Alaska.

WILLY   Sure, sure! If I'd gone with him to Alaska that time, everything would've been totally different.

CHARLEY   Go on, you'd froze to death up there.

735 WILLY   What're you talking about?

BEN   Opportunity is tremendous in Alaska, William. Surprised you're not up there.

WILLY   Sure, tremendous.

CHARLEY   Heh?

740 WILLY   There was the only man I ever met who knew the answers.

CHARLEY   Who?

BEN   How are you all?

WILLY [taking a pot,[1] smiling]   Fine, fine.

CHARLEY   Pretty sharp tonight.

745 BEN   Is Mother living with you?

WILLY   No, she died a long time ago.

CHARLEY   Who?

BEN   That's too bad. Fine specimen of a lady, Mother.

WILLY [to Charley]   Heh?

750 BEN   I'd hoped to see the old girl.

CHARLEY   Who died?

BEN   Heard anything from Father, have you?

WILLY [unnerved]   What do you mean, who died?

CHARLEY [taking a pot]   What're you talkin' about?

755 BEN [looking at his watch]   William, it's half-past eight!

WILLY [as though to dispel his confusion he angrily stops CHARLEY's hand]   That's my build![2]

CHARLEY   I put the ace—

WILLY   If you don't know how to play the game I'm not gonna throw my money away on you!

760 CHARLEY [rising]   It was my ace, for God's sake!

WILLY   I'm through, I'm through!

BEN   When did Mother die?

WILLY   Long ago. Since the beginning you never knew how to play cards.

CHARLEY [picks up the cards and goes to the door]   All right! Next time I'll
765   bring a deck with five aces.

WILLY   I don't play that kind of game!

CHARLEY [turning to him]   You ought to be ashamed of yourself!

WILLY   Yeah?

CHARLEY   Yeah! [He goes out.]

770 WILLY [slamming the door after him]   Ignoramus!

BEN [as WILLY comes toward him through the wall-line of the kitchen]   So you're William.

WILLY [shaking BEN's hand]   Ben! I've been waiting for you so long! What's the answer? How did you do it?

775 BEN   Oh, there's a story in that.

[LINDA enters the forestage, as of old, carrying the wash basket.]

LINDA   Is this Ben?

BEN [gallantly]   How do you do, my dear.

LINDA   Where've you been all these years? Willy's always wondered why you—

---

1. The bets at stake in a hand of casino, the card game they are playing.

2. Casino players must take in builds (cards that combine to form a declared total) to win.

780 WILLY [*pulling* BEN *away from her impatiently*]   Where is Dad? Didn't you follow him? How did you get started?

BEN   Well, I don't know how much you remember.

WILLY   Well, I was just a baby, of course, only three or four years old—

BEN   Three years and eleven months.

785 WILLY   What a memory, Ben!

BEN   I have many enterprises, William, and I have never kept books.

WILLY   I remember I was sitting under the wagon in—was it Nebraska?

BEN   It was South Dakota, and I gave you a bunch of wild flowers.

WILLY   I remember you walking away down some open road.

790 BEN [*laughing*]   I was going to find Father in Alaska.

WILLY   Where is he?

BEN   At that age I had a very faulty view of geography, William. I discovered after a few days that I was heading due south, so instead of Alaska, I ended up in Africa.

795 LINDA   Africa!

WILLY   The Gold Coast!³

BEN   Principally diamond mines.

LINDA   Diamond mines!

BEN   Yes, my dear. But I've only a few minutes—

800 WILLY   No! Boys! Boys! [YOUNG BIFF *and* HAPPY *appear.*] Listen to this. This is your Uncle Ben, a great man! Tell my boys, Ben!

BEN   Why, boys, when I was seventeen I walked into the jungle, and when I was twenty-one I walked out. [*He laughs.*] And by God I was rich.

WILLY [*to the boys*]   You see what I been talking about? The greatest things can happen!

805 BEN [*glancing at his watch*]   I have an appointment in Ketchikan Tuesday week.⁴

WILLY   No, Ben! Please tell about Dad. I want my boys to hear. I want them to know the kind of stock they spring from. All I remember is a man with a

810 big beard, and I was in Mamma's lap, sitting around a fire, and some kind of high music.

BEN   His flute. He played the flute.

WILLY   Sure, the flute, that's right!

[*New music is heard, a high, rollicking tune.*]

BEN   Father was a very great and a very wild-hearted man. We would start in

815 Boston, and he'd toss the whole family into the wagon, and then he'd drive the team right across the country; through Ohio, and Indiana, Michigan, Illinois, and all the Western states. And we'd stop in the towns and sell the flutes that he'd made on the way. Great inventor, Father. With one gadget he made more in a week than a man like you could make in a lifetime.

820 WILLY   That's just the way I'm bringing them up, Ben—rugged, well liked, all-around.

BEN   Yeah? [*To* BIFF] Hit that, boy—hard as you can. [*He pounds his stomach.*]

BIFF   Oh, no, sir!

3. The region of West Africa that is now Ghana (still a British colony in 1949); industrial diamonds are one of its major exports.

4. That is, in Ketchikan, Alaska, one week from Tuesday.

BEN [*taking boxing stance*]   Come on, get to me! [*He laughs.*]

825 WILLY   Go to it, Biff! Go ahead, show him!

BIFF   Okay! [*He cocks his fists and starts in.*]

LINDA [*to Willy*]   Why must he fight, dear?

BEN [*sparring with* BIFF]   Good boy! Good boy!

WILLY   How's that, Ben, heh?

830 HAPPY   Give him the left, Biff!

LINDA   Why are you fighting?

BEN   Good boy! [*Suddenly comes in, trips* BIFF, *and stands over him, the point of his umbrella poised over* BIFF's *eye.*]

LINDA   Look out, Biff!

BIFF   Gee!

835 BEN [*patting* BIFF's *knee*]   Never fight fair with a stranger, boy. You'll never get out of the jungle that way. [*Taking* LINDA's *hand and bowing*] It was an honor and a pleasure to meet you, Linda.

LINDA [*withdrawing her hand coldly, frightened*]   Have a nice—trip.

BEN [*to* WILLY]   And good luck with your—what do you do?

840 WILLY   Selling.

BEN   Yes. Well . . . [*He raises his hand in farewell to all.*]

WILLY   No, Ben, I don't want you to think . . . [*He takes* BEN's *arm to show him.*] It's Brooklyn, I know, but we hunt too.

BEN   Really, now.

845 WILLY   Oh, sure, there's snakes and rabbits and—that's why I moved out here. Why, Biff can fell any one of these trees in no time! Boys! Go right over to where they're building the apartment house and get some sand. We're gonna rebuild the entire front stoop right now! Watch this, Ben!

BIFF   Yes, sir! On the double, Hap!

850 HAPPY [*as he and* BIFF *run off*]   I lost weight, Pop, you notice?

[CHARLEY *enters in knickers, even before the boys are gone.*]

CHARLEY   Listen, if they steal any more from that building the watchman'll put the cops on them!

LINDA [*to Willy*]   Don't let Biff . . .

[BEN *laughs lustily.*]

WILLY   You shoulda seen the lumber they brought home last week. At least a

855 dozen six-by-tens worth all kinds a money.

CHARLEY   Listen, if that watchman—

WILLY   I gave them hell, understand. But I got a couple of fearless characters there.

CHARLEY   Willy, the jails are full of fearless characters.

860 BEN [*clapping* WILLY *on the back, with a laugh at* CHARLEY]   And the stock exchange, friend!

WILLY [*joining in Ben's laughter*]   Where are the rest of your pants?

CHARLEY   My wife bought them.

WILLY   Now all you need is a golf club and you can go upstairs and go to

865 sleep. [*To* BEN] Great athlete! Between him and his son Bernard they can't hammer a nail!

BERNARD [*rushing in*]   The watchman's chasing Biff!

WILLY [*angrily*]   Shut up! He's not stealing anything!

LINDA [*alarmed, hurrying off left*]   Where is he? Biff, dear! [*She exits.*]

870 WILLY [*moving toward the left, away from* BEN] There's nothing wrong.
What's the matter with you?

BEN Nervy boy. Good!

WILLY [*laughing*] Oh, nerves of iron, that Biff!

CHARLEY Don't know what it is. My New England man comes back and he's
875 bleedin', they murdered him up there.

WILLY It's contacts, Charley, I got important contacts!

CHARLEY [*sarcastically*] Glad to hear it, Willy. Come in later, we'll shoot a
little casino. I'll take some of your Portland money. [*He laughs at Willy and
exits.*]

WILLY [*turning to* BEN] Business is bad, it's murderous. But not for me, of
880 course.

BEN I'll stop by on my way back to Africa.

WILLY [*longingly*] Can't you stay a few days? You're just what I need, Ben,
because I—I have a fine position here, but I—well, Dad left when I was
such a baby and I never had a chance to talk to him and I still feel—kind of
885 temporary about myself.

BEN I'll be late for my train.

[*They are at opposite ends of the stage.*]

WILLY Ben, my boys—can't we talk? They'd go into the jaws of hell for me,
see, but I—

BEN William, you're being first-rate with your boys. Outstanding, manly
890 chaps!

WILLY [*hanging on to his words*] Oh, Ben, that's good to hear! Because sometimes I'm afraid that I'm not teaching them the right kind of—Ben, how
should I teach them?

BEN [*giving great weight to each word, and with a certain vicious audacity*]
William, when I walked into the jungle, I was seventeen. When I walked
895 out I was twenty-one. And, by God, I was rich! [*He goes off into the darkness
around the right corner of the house.*]

WILLY . . . was rich! That's just the spirit I want to imbue them with! To
walk into a jungle! I was right! I was right! I was right!

[BEN *is gone, but* WILLY *is still speaking to him as* LINDA, *in nightgown
and robe, enters the kitchen, glances around for* WILLY, *then goes to the
door of the house, looks out and sees him. Comes down to his left. He
looks at her.*]

LINDA Willy, dear? Willy?

WILLY I was right!

900 LINDA Did you have some cheese? [*He can't answer.*] It's very late, darling.
Come to bed, heh?

WILLY [*looking straight up*] Gotta break your neck to see a star in this yard.

LINDA You coming in?

WILLY Whatever happened to that diamond watch fob? Remember? When
905 Ben came from Africa that time? Didn't he give me a watch fob with a diamond in it?

LINDA You pawned it, dear. Twelve, thirteen years ago. For Biff's radio correspondence course.

WILLY Gee, that was a beautiful thing. I'll take a walk.

910 LINDA But you're in your slippers.

WILLY [*starting to go around the house at the left*]   I was right! I was! [*Half to* LINDA, *as he goes, shaking his head*] What a man! There was a man worth talking to. I was right!

LINDA [*calling after* WILLY]   But in your slippers, Willy!

[WILLY *is almost gone when* BIFF, *in his pajamas, comes down the stairs and enters the kitchen.*]

915 BIFF   What is he doing out there?

LINDA   Sh!

BIFF   God Almighty, Mom, how long has he been doing this?

LINDA   Don't, he'll hear you.

BIFF   What the hell is the matter with him?

920 LINDA   It'll pass by morning.

BIFF   Shouldn't we do anything?

LINDA   Oh, my dear, you should do a lot of things, but there's nothing to do, so go to sleep.

[HAPPY *comes down the stair and sits on the steps.*]

HAPPY   I never heard him so loud, Mom.

925 LINDA   Well, come around more often; you'll hear him. [*She sits down at the table and mends the lining of* WILLY'S *jacket.*]

BIFF   Why didn't you ever write me about this, Mom?

LINDA   How would I write to you? For over three months you had no address.

BIFF   I was on the move. But you know I thought of you all the time. You know that, don't you, pal?

930 LINDA   I know, dear, I know. But he likes to have a letter. Just to know that there's still a possibility for better things.

BIFF   He's not like this all the time, is he?

LINDA   It's when you come home he's always the worst.

BIFF   When I come home?

935 LINDA   When you write you're coming, he's all smiles, and talks about the future, and—he's just wonderful. And then the closer you seem to come, the more shaky he gets, and then, by the time you get here, he's arguing, and he seems angry at you. I think it's just that maybe he can't bring himself to—to open up to you. Why are you so hateful to each other? Why is 940 that?

BIFF [*evasively*]   I'm not hateful, Mom.

LINDA   But you no sooner come in the door than you're fighting!

BIFF   I don't know why. I mean to change. I'm tryin', Mom, you understand?

LINDA   Are you home to stay now?

945 BIFF   I don't know. I want to look around, see what's doin'.

LINDA   Biff, you can't look around all your life, can you?

BIFF   I just can't take hold, Mom. I can't take hold of some kind of a life.

LINDA   Biff, a man is not a bird, to come and go with the springtime.

BIFF   Your hair . . . [*He touches her hair.*] Your hair got so gray.

950 LINDA   Oh, it's been gray since you were in high school. I just stopped dyeing it, that's all.

BIFF   Dye it again, will ya? I don't want my pal looking old. [*He smiles.*]

LINDA   You're such a boy! You think you can go away for a year and . . . You've got to get it into your head now that one day you'll knock on this door and 955 there'll be strange people here—

BIFF   What are you talking about? You're not even sixty, Mom.

LINDA   But what about your father?

BIFF [*lamely*]   Well, I meant him too.

HAPPY   He admires Pop.

960 LINDA   Biff, dear, if you don't have any feeling for him, then you can't have any feeling for me.

BIFF   Sure I can, Mom.

LINDA   No. You can't just come to see me, because I love him. [*With a threat, but only a threat, of tears*] He's the dearest man in the world to me, and I

965   won't have anyone making him feel unwanted and low and blue. You've got to make up your mind now, darling, there's no leeway any more. Either he's your father and you pay him that respect, or else you're not to come here. I know he's not easy to get along with—nobody knows that better than me—but . . .

970 WILLY [*from the left, with a laugh*]   Hey, hey, Biffo!

BIFF [*starting to go out after* WILLY]   What the hell is the matter with him? [HAPPY *stops him.*]

LINDA   Don't—don't go near him!

BIFF   Stop making excuses for him! He always, always wiped the floor with you. Never had an ounce of respect for you.

975 HAPPY   He's always had respect for—

BIFF   What the hell do you know about it?

HAPPY [*surlily*]   Just don't call him crazy!

BIFF   He's got no character—Charley wouldn't do this. Not in his own house—spewing out that vomit from his mind.

980 HAPPY   Charley never had to cope with what he's got to.

BIFF   People are worse off than Willy Loman. Believe me, I've seen them!

LINDA   Then make Charley your father, Biff. You can't do that, can you? I don't say he's a great man. Willy Loman never made a lot of money. His name was never in the paper. He's not the finest character that ever lived.

985   But he's a human being, and a terrible thing is happening to him. So attention must be paid. He's not to be allowed to fall into his grave like an old dog. Attention, attention must be finally paid to such a person. You called him crazy—

BIFF   I didn't mean—

990 LINDA   No, a lot of people think he's lost his—balance. But you don't have to be very smart to know what his trouble is. The man is exhausted.

HAPPY   Sure!

LINDA   A small man can be just as exhausted as a great man. He works for a company thirty-six years this March, opens up unheard-of territories to

995   their trademark, and now in his old age they take his salary away.

HAPPY [*indignantly*]   I didn't know that, Mom.

LINDA   You never asked, my dear! Now that you get your spending money someplace else you don't trouble your mind with him.

HAPPY   But I gave you money last—

1000 LINDA   Christmastime, fifty dollars! To fix the hot water it cost ninety-seven fifty! For five weeks he's been on straight commission, like a beginner, an unknown!

BIFF   Those ungrateful bastards!

LINDA Are they any worse than his sons? When he brought them business,
1005 when he was young, they were glad to see him. But now his old friends, the
old buyers that loved him so and always found some order to hand him in
a pinch—they're all dead, retired. He used to be able to make six, seven
calls a day in Boston. Now he takes his valises out of the car and puts them
back and takes them out again and he's exhausted. Instead of walking he
1010 talks now. He drives seven hundred miles, and when he gets there no one
knows him any more, no one welcomes him. And what goes through a
man's mind, driving seven hundred miles home without having earned a
cent? Why shouldn't he talk to himself? Why? When he has to go to Charley and borrow fifty dollars a week and pretend to me that it's his pay? How
1015 long can that go on? How long? You see what I'm sitting here and waiting
for? And you tell me he has no character? The man who never worked a day
but for your benefit? When does he get the medal for that? Is this his
reward—to turn around at the age of sixty-three and find his sons, who he
loved better than his life, one a philandering bum—
1020 HAPPY Mom!
LINDA That's all you are, my baby! [*To* BIFF] And you! What happened to the
love you had for him? You were such pals! How you used to talk to him on
the phone every night! How lonely he was till he could come home to you!
BIFF All right, Mom. I'll live here in my room, and I'll get a job. I'll keep
1025 away from him, that's all.
LINDA No, Biff. You can't stay here and fight all the time.
BIFF He threw me out of this house, remember that.
LINDA Why did he do that? I never knew why.
BIFF Because I know he's a fake and he doesn't like anybody around who
1030 knows!
LINDA Why a fake? In what way? What do you mean?
BIFF Just don't lay it all at my feet. It's between me and him—that's all I
have to say. I'll chip in from now on. He'll settle for half my paycheck. He'll
be all right. I'm going to bed. [*He starts for the stairs.*]
1035 LINDA He won't be all right.
BIFF [*turning on the stairs, furiously*] I hate this city and I'll stay here. Now
what do you want?
LINDA He's dying, Biff.
[HAPPY *turns quickly to her, shocked.*]
BIFF [*after a pause*] Why is he dying?
1040 LINDA He's been trying to kill himself.
BIFF [*with great horror*] How?
LINDA I live from day to day.
BIFF What're you talking about?
LINDA Remember I wrote you that he smashed up the car again? In February?
1045 BIFF Well?
LINDA The insurance inspector came. He said that they have evidence. That
all these accidents in the last year—weren't—weren't—accidents.
HAPPY How can they tell that? That's a lie.
LINDA It seems there's a woman . . . [*She takes a breath as*]
1050 BIFF [*sharply but contained*] What woman? ⎫
LINDA [*simultaneously*]   . . . and this woman . . . ⎭

LINDA What?

BIFF Nothing. Go ahead.

LINDA What did you say?

1055 BIFF Nothing. I just said what woman?

HAPPY What about her?

LINDA Well, it seems she was walking down the road and saw his car. She says that he wasn't driving fast at all, and that he didn't skid. She says he came to that little bridge, and then deliberately smashed into the railing, and it was only the shallowness of the water that saved him.

1060

BIFF Oh, no, he probably just fell asleep again.

LINDA I don't think he fell asleep.

BIFF Why not?

LINDA Last month . . . [*With great difficulty*] Oh, boys, it's so hard to say a thing like this! He's just a big stupid man to you, but I tell you there's more good in him than in many other people. [*She chokes, wipes her eyes.*] I was looking for a fuse. The lights blew out, and I went down the cellar. And behind the fuse box—it happened to fall out—was a length of rubber pipe—just short.

1065

1070 HAPPY No kidding?

LINDA There's a little attachment on the end of it. I knew right away. And sure enough, on the bottom of the water heater there's a new little nipple on the gas pipe.

HAPPY [*angrily*] That—jerk.

1075 BIFF Did you have it taken off?

LINDA I'm—I'm ashamed to. How can I mention it to him? Every day I go down and take away that little rubber pipe. But, when he comes home, I put it back where it was. How can I insult him that way? I don't know what to do. I live from day to day, boys. I tell you, I know every thought in his mind. It sounds so old-fashioned and silly, but I tell you he put his whole life into you and you've turned your backs on him. [*She is bent over in the chair, weeping, her face in her hands.*] Biff, I swear to God! Biff, his life is in your hands!

1080

HAPPY [*to* BIFF] How do you like that damned fool!

1085 BIFF [*kissing her*] All right, pal, all right. It's all settled now. I've been remiss. I know that, Mom. But now I'll stay, and I swear to you, I'll apply myself. [*Kneeling in front of her, in a fever of self-reproach*] It's just—you see, Mom, I don't fit in business. Not that I won't try. I'll try, and I'll make good.

HAPPY Sure you will. The trouble with you in business was you never tried to please people.

1090

BIFF I know, I—

HAPPY Like when you worked for Harrison's. Bob Harrison said you were tops, and then you go and do some damn fool thing like whistling whole songs in the elevator like a comedian.

1095 BIFF [*against* HAPPY] So what? I like to whistle sometimes.

HAPPY You don't raise a guy to a responsible job who whistles in the elevator!

LINDA Well, don't argue about it now.

HAPPY Like when you'd go off and swim in the middle of the day instead of taking the line around.

1100

BIFF [*his resentment rising*] Well, don't you run off? You take off sometimes, don't you? On a nice summer day?

HAPPY   Yeah, but I cover myself!

LINDA   Boys!

1105 HAPPY   If I'm going to take a fade⁵ the boss can call any number where I'm supposed to be and they'll swear to him that I just left. I'll tell you something that I hate to say, Biff, but in the business world some of them think you're crazy.

BIFF [*angered*]   Screw the business world!

1110 HAPPY   All right, screw it! Great, but cover yourself!

LINDA   Hap, Hap!

BIFF   I don't care what they think! They've laughed at Dad for years, and you know why? Because we don't belong in this nuthouse of a city! We should be mixing cement on some open plain, or—or carpenters. A carpenter is

1115   allowed to whistle!

[WILLY *walks in from the entrance of the house, at left.*]

WILLY   Even your grandfather was better than a carpenter. [*Pause. They watch him.*] You never grew up. Bernard does not whistle in the elevator, I assure you.

BIFF [*as though to laugh* WILLY *out of it*]   Yeah, but you do, Pop.

1120 WILLY   I never in my life whistled in an elevator! And who in the business world thinks I'm crazy?

BIFF   I didn't mean it like that, Pop. Now don't make a whole thing out of it, will ya?

WILLY   Go back to the West! Be a carpenter, a cowboy, enjoy yourself!

1125 LINDA   Willy, he was just saying—

WILLY   I heard what he said!

HAPPY [*trying to quiet* WILLY]   Hey, Pop, come on now . . .

WILLY [*continuing over* HAPPY'*s line*]   They laugh at me, heh? Go to Filene's, go to the Hub,⁶ go to Slattery's, Boston. Call out the name Willy Loman

1130   and see what happens! Big shot!

BIFF   All right, Pop.

WILLY   Big!

BIFF   All right!

WILLY   Why do you always insult me?

1135 BIFF   I didn't say a word. [*To* LINDA] Did I say a word?

LINDA   He didn't say anything, Willy.

WILLY [*going to the doorway of the living room*]   All right, good night, good night.

LINDA   Willy, dear, he just decided . . .

1140 WILLY [*to* BIFF]   If you get tired hanging around tomorrow, paint the ceiling I put up in the living room.

BIFF   I'm leaving early tomorrow.

HAPPY   He's going to see Bill Oliver, Pop.

WILLY [*interestedly*]   Oliver? For what?

1145 BIFF [*with reserve, but trying, trying*]   He always said he'd stake me. I'd like to go into business, so maybe I can take him up on it.

LINDA   Isn't that wonderful?

WILLY   Don't interrupt. What's wonderful about it? There's fifty men in the City of New York who'd stake him. [*To* BIFF] Sporting goods?

---

5. Disappear.
6. Boston (label given the Massachusetts State House in 1858 by Oliver Wendell Holmes).

1150 BIFF   I guess so. I know something about it and—

WILLY   He knows something about it! You know sporting goods better than Spalding,[7] for God's sake! How much is he giving you?

BIFF   I don't know, I didn't even see him yet, but—

WILLY   Then what're you talkin' about?

1155 BIFF [*getting angry*]   Well, all I said was I'm gonna see him, that's all!

WILLY [*turning away*]   Ah, you're counting your chickens again.

BIFF [*starting left for the stairs*]   Oh, Jesus, I'm going to sleep!

WILLY [*calling after him*]   Don't curse in this house!

BIFF [*turning*]   Since when did you get so clean?

1160 HAPPY [*trying to stop them*]   Wait a . . .

WILLY   Don't use that language to me! I won't have it!

HAPPY [*grabbing* BIFF, *shouts*]   Wait a minute! I got an idea. I got a feasible idea. Come here, Biff, let's talk this over now, let's talk some sense here. When I was down in Florida last time, I thought of a great idea to sell

1165   sporting goods. It just came back to me. You and I, Biff—we have a line, the Loman Line. We train a couple of weeks, and put on a couple of exhibitions, see?

WILLY   That's an idea!

HAPPY   Wait! We form two basketball teams, see? Two water-polo teams. We

1170   play each other. It's a million dollars' worth of publicity. Two brothers, see? The Loman Brothers. Displays in the Royal Palms—all the hotels. And banners over the ring and the basketball court: "Loman Brothers." Baby, we could sell sporting goods!

WILLY   That is a one-million-dollar idea!

1175 LINDA   Marvelous!

BIFF   I'm in great shape as far as that's concerned.

HAPPY   And the beauty of it is, Biff, it wouldn't be like a business. We'd be out playin' ball again . . .

BIFF [*enthused*]   Yeah, that's . . .

1180 WILLY   Million-dollar . . .

HAPPY   And you wouldn't get fed up with it, Biff. It'd be the family again. There'd be the old honor, and comradeship, and if you wanted to go off for a swim or somethin'—well, you'd do it! Without some smart cooky gettin' up ahead of you!

1185 WILLY   Lick the world! You guys together could absolutely lick the civilized world.

BIFF   I'll see Oliver tomorrow. Hap, if we could work that out . . .

LINDA   Maybe things are beginning to—

WILLY [*wildly enthused, to* LINDA]   Stop interrupting! [*To* BIFF] But don't wear

1190   sport jacket and slacks when you see Oliver.

BIFF   No, I'll—

WILLY   A business suit, and talk as little as possible, and don't crack any jokes.

BIFF   He did like me. Always liked me.

1195 LINDA   He loved you!

---

7. The sporting goods company named after the American baseball star A. G. Spalding (1850–1915), who founded it.

WILLY [*to* LINDA]   Will you stop! [*To* BIFF] Walk in very serious. You are not
applying for a boy's job. Money is to pass. Be quiet, fine, and serious.
Everybody likes a kidder, but nobody lends him money.

HAPPY   I'll try to get some myself, Biff. I'm sure I can.

1200 WILLY   I see great things for you kids, I think your troubles are over. But
remember, start big and you'll end big. Ask for fifteen. How much you
gonna ask for?

BIFF   Gee, I don't know—

WILLY   And don't say "Gee." "Gee" is a boy's word. A man walking in for fif
1205 teen thousand dollars does not say "Gee!"

BIFF   Ten, I think, would be top though.

WILLY   Don't be so modest. You always started too low. Walk in with a big
laugh. Don't look worried. Start off with a couple of your good stories to
lighten things up. It's not what you say, it's how you say it—because per
1210 sonality always wins the day.

LINDA   Oliver always thought the highest of him—

WILLY   Will you let me talk?

BIFF   Don't yell at her, Pop, will ya?

WILLY [*angrily*]   I was talking, wasn't I?

1215 BIFF   I don't like you yelling at her all the time, and I'm tellin' you, that's all.

WILLY   What're you, takin' over this house?

LINDA   Willy—

WILLY [*turning on her*]   Don't take his side all the time, goddammit!

BIFF [*furiously*]   Stop yelling at her!

1220 WILLY [*suddenly pulling on his cheek, beaten down, guilt ridden*]   Give my
best to Bill Oliver—he may remember me. [*He exits through the living room
doorway.*]

LINDA [*her voice subdued*]   What'd you have to start that for? [BIFF *turns
away.*] You see how sweet he was as soon as you talked hopefully? [*She goes
over to* BIFF.] Come up and say good night to him. Don't let him go to bed
1225 that way.

HAPPY   Come on, Biff, let's buck him up.

LINDA   Please, dear. Just say good night. It takes so little to make him happy.
Come. [*She goes through the living room doorway, calling upstairs from
within the living room.*] Your pajamas are hanging in the bathroom, Willy!

1230 HAPPY [*looking toward where* LINDA *went out*]   What a woman! They broke
the mold when they made her. You know that, Biff?

BIFF   He's off salary. My God, working on commission!

HAPPY   Well, let's face it: he's no hot-shot selling man. Except that sometimes, you have to admit, he's a sweet personality.

1235 BIFF [*deciding*]   Lend me ten bucks, will ya? I want to buy some new ties.

HAPPY   I'll take you to a place I know. Beautiful stuff. Wear one of my striped
shirts tomorrow.

BIFF   She got gray. Mom got awful old. Gee, I'm gonna go in to Oliver tomorrow and knock him for a—

1240 HAPPY   Come on up. Tell that to Dad. Let's give him a whirl. Come on.

BIFF [*steamed up*]   You know, with ten thousand bucks, boy!

HAPPY [*as they go into the living room*]   That's the talk, Biff, that's the first
time I've heard the old confidence out of you! [*From within the living room,*

fading off] You're gonna live with me, kid, and any babe you want just say
1245   the word . . . [*The last lines are hardly heard. They are mounting the stairs to
their parents' bedroom.*]

LINDA [*entering her bedroom and addressing* WILLY, *who is in the bathroom.
She is straightening the bed for him.*]   Can you do anything about the
shower? It drips.

WILLY [*from the bathroom*]   All of a sudden everything falls to pieces! Goddam plumbing, oughta be sued, those people. I hardly finished putting it in
1250   and the thing . . . [*His words rumble off.*]

LINDA   I'm just wondering if Oliver will remember him. You think he might?

WILLY [*coming out of the bathroom in his pajamas*]   Remember him? What's
the matter with you, you crazy? If he'd've stayed with Oliver he'd be on top
by now! Wait'll Oliver gets a look at him. You don't know the average cali-
1255   ber any more. The average young man today—[*He is getting into bed.*]—is
got a caliber of zero. Greatest thing in the world for him was to bum
around.

         [BIFF *and* HAPPY *enter the bedroom. Slight pause.*]

WILLY [*stops short, looking at* BIFF]   Glad to hear it, boy.

HAPPY   He wanted to say good night to you, sport.

1260 WILLY [*to* BIFF]   Yeah. Knock him dead, boy. What'd you want to tell me?

BIFF   Just take it easy, Pop. Good night. [*He turns to go.*]

WILLY [*unable to resist*]   And if anything falls off the desk while you're talking
to him—like a package or something—don't you pick it up. They have
office boys for that.

1265 LINDA   I'll make a big breakfast—

WILLY   Will you let me finish? [*To* BIFF] Tell him you were in the business in
the West. Not farm work.

BIFF   All right, Dad.

LINDA   I think everything—

1270 WILLY [*going right through her speech*]   And don't undersell yourself. No less
than fifteen thousand dollars.

BIFF [*unable to bear him*]   Okay. Good night, Mom. [*He starts moving.*]

WILLY   Because you got a greatness in you, Biff, remember that. You got all
kinds a greatness . . . [*He lies back, exhausted.* BIFF *walks out.*]

1275 LINDA [*calling after Biff*]   Sleep well, darling!

HAPPY   I'm gonna get married, Mom. I wanted to tell you.

LINDA   Go to sleep, dear.

HAPPY [*going*]   I just wanted to tell you.

WILLY   Keep up the good work. [HAPPY *exits.*] God . . . remember that Ebbets
1280   Field[8] game? The championship of the city?

LINDA   Just rest. Should I sing to you?

WILLY   Yeah. Sing to me. [LINDA *hums a soft lullaby.*] When that team came
out—he was the tallest, remember?

LINDA   Oh, yes. And in gold.

         [BIFF *enters the darkened kitchen, takes a cigarette, and leaves the house.
He comes downstage into a golden pool of light. He smokes, staring at the
night.*]

8. Brooklyn's baseball stadium, home of the Dodgers before the team's move to Los Angeles in
1957. Football was also played there.

1285 WILLY   Like a young god. Hercules[9]—something like that. And the sun, the sun all around him. Remember how he waved to me? Right up from the field, with the representatives of three colleges standing by? And the buyers I brought, and the cheers when he came out—Loman, Loman, Loman! God Almighty, he'll be great yet. A star like that, magnificent, can never
1290 really fade away!

> [*The light on* WILLY *is fading. The gas heater begins to glow through the kitchen wall, near the stairs, a blue flame beneath red coils.*]

LINDA [*timidly*]   Willy dear, what has he got against you?
WILLY   I'm so tired. Don't talk any more.

> [BIFF *slowly returns to the kitchen. He stops, stares toward the heater.*]

LINDA   Will you ask Howard to let you work in New York?
WILLY   First thing in the morning. Everything'll be all right.

> [BIFF *reaches behind the heater and draws out a length of rubber tubing. He is horrified and turns his head toward* WILLY's *room, still dimly lit, from which the strains of* LINDA's *desperate but monotonous humming rise.*]

1295 WILLY [*staring through the window into the moonlight*]   Gee, look at the moon moving between the buildings!

> [BIFF *wraps the tubing around his hand and quickly goes up the stairs.*]

Curtain.

Act 2

Music is heard, gay and bright. The curtain rises as the music fades away. WILLY, *in shirt sleeves, is sitting at the kitchen table, sipping coffee, his hat in his lap.* LINDA *is filling his cup when she can.*

WILLY   Wonderful coffee. Meal in itself.
LINDA   Can I make you some eggs?
WILLY   No. Take a breath.
LINDA   You look so rested, dear.
5 WILLY   I slept like a dead one. First time in months. Imagine, sleeping till ten on a Tuesday morning. Boys left nice and early, heh?
LINDA   They were out of here by eight o'clock.
WILLY   Good work!
LINDA   It was so thrilling to see them leaving together. I can't get over the
10 shaving lotion in this house!
WILLY [*smiling*]   Mmm—
LINDA   Biff was very changed this morning. His whole attitude seemed to be hopeful. He couldn't wait to get downtown to see Oliver.
WILLY   He's heading for a change. There's no question, there simply are cer-
15 tain men that take longer to get—solidified. How did he dress?
LINDA   His blue suit. He's so handsome in that suit. He could be a—anything in that suit!

> [WILLY *gets up from the table.* LINDA *holds his jacket for him.*]

WILLY   There's no question, no question at all. Gee, on the way home tonight I'd like to buy some seeds.

---

9. In classical mythology, the greatest of all heroes (a son of Zeus, king of the gods, and the mortal Alcmene).

20 LINDA [*laughing*]   That'd be wonderful. But not enough sun gets back there. Nothing'll grow any more.

WILLY   You wait, kid, before it's all over we're gonna get a little place out in the country, and I'll raise some vegetables, a couple of chickens . . .

LINDA   You'll do it yet, dear.

[WILLY *walks out of his jacket.* LINDA *follows him.*]

25 WILLY   And they'll get married, and come for a weekend. I'd build a little guest house. 'Cause I got so many fine tools, all I'd need would be a little lumber and some peace of mind.

LINDA [*joyfully*]   I sewed the lining . . .

WILLY   I could build two guest houses, so they'd both come. Did he decide

30 how much he's going to ask Oliver for?

LINDA [*getting him into the jacket*]   He didn't mention it, but I imagine ten or fifteen thousand. You going to talk to Howard today?

WILLY   Yeah. I'll put it to him straight and simple. He'll just have to take me off the road.

35 LINDA   And Willy, don't forget to ask for a little advance, because we've got the insurance premium. It's the grace period now.

WILLY   That's a hundred . . . ?

LINDA   A hundred and eight, sixty-eight. Because we're a little short again.

WILLY   Why are we short?

40 LINDA   Well, you had the motor job on the car . . .

WILLY   That goddam Studebaker!

LINDA   And you got one more payment on the refrigerator . . .

WILLY   But it just broke again!

LINDA   Well, it's old, dear.

45 WILLY   I told you we should've bought a well-advertised machine. Charley bought a General Electric and it's twenty years old and it's still good, that son-of-a-bitch.

LINDA   But, Willy—

WILLY   Whoever heard of a Hastings refrigerator? Once in my life I would

50 like to own something outright before it's broken! I'm always in a race with the junkyard! I just finished paying for the car and it's on its last legs. The refrigerator consumes belts like a goddam maniac. They time those things. They time them so when you finally paid for them, they're used up.

LINDA [*buttoning up his jacket as he unbuttons it*]   All told, about two hun-

55 dred dollars would carry us, dear. But that includes the last payment on the mortgage. After this payment, Willy, the house belongs to us.

WILLY   It's twenty-five years!

LINDA   Biff was nine years old when we bought it.

WILLY   Well, that's a great thing. To weather a twenty-five year mortgage is—

60 LINDA   It's an accomplishment.

WILLY   All the cement, the lumber, the reconstruction I put in this house! There ain't a crack to be found in it any more.

LINDA   Well, it served its purpose.

WILLY   What purpose? Some stranger'll come along, move in, and that's that.

65 If only Biff would take this house, and raise a family . . . [*He starts to go.*] Good-by, I'm late.

LINDA [*suddenly remembering*]   Oh, I forgot! You're supposed to meet them for dinner.

WILLY   Me?

70 LINDA   At Frank's Chop House on Forty-eighth near Sixth Avenue.

WILLY   Is that so! How about you?

LINDA   No, just the three of you. They're gonna blow you to a big meal![1]

WILLY   Don't say! Who thought of that?

LINDA   Biff came to me this morning, Willy, and he said, "Tell Dad, we want
75   to blow him to a big meal." Be there six o'clock. You and your two boys are
going to have dinner.

WILLY   Gee whiz! That's really somethin'. I'm gonna knock Howard for a
loop, kid. I'll get an advance, and I'll come home with a New York job. Goddammit, now I'm gonna do it!

80 LINDA   Oh, that's the spirit, Willy!

WILLY   I will never get behind a wheel the rest of my life!

LINDA   It's changing, Willy, I can feel it changing!

WILLY   Beyond a question. G'by, I'm late. [*He starts to go again.*]

LINDA   [*calling after him as she runs to the kitchen table for a handkerchief*]
You got your glasses?

85 WILLY   [*feels for them, then comes back in*]   Yeah, yeah, got my glasses.

LINDA   [*giving him the handkerchief*]   And a handkerchief.

WILLY   Yeah, handkerchief.

LINDA   And your saccharine?

WILLY   Yeah, my saccharine.

90 LINDA   Be careful on the subway stairs.

> [*She kisses him, and a silk stocking is seen hanging from her hand.* WILLY
> *notices it.*]

WILLY   Will you stop mending stockings? At least while I'm in the house. It
gets me nervous. I can't tell you. Please.

> [LINDA *hides the stocking in her hand as she follows* WILLY *across the
> forestage in front of the house.*]

LINDA   Remember, Frank's Chop House.

WILLY   [*passing the apron*]   Maybe beets would grow out there.

95 LINDA   [*laughing*]   But you tried so many times.

WILLY   Yeah. Well, don't work hard today. [*He disappears around the right
corner of the house.*]

LINDA   Be careful!

> [*As* WILLY *vanishes, Linda waves to him. Suddenly the phone rings. She
> runs across the stage and into the kitchen and lifts it.*]

LINDA   Hello? Oh, Biff! I'm so glad you called, I just . . . Yes, sure, I just told
him. Yes, he'll be there for dinner at six o'clock, I didn't forget. Listen, I was
100   just dying to tell you. You know that little rubber pipe I told you about?
That he connected to the gas heater? I finally decided to go down the cellar
this morning and take it away and destroy it. But it's gone! Imagine? He
took it away himself, it isn't there! [*She listens*]. When? Oh, then you took
it. Oh—nothing, it's just that I'd hoped he'd taken it away himself. Oh, I'm
105   not worried, darling, because this morning he left in such high spirits, it
was like the old days! I'm not afraid any more. Did Mr. Oliver see you? . . . .
Well, you wait there then. And make a nice impression on him, darling.
Just don't perspire too much before you see him. And have a nice time with

---

1. That is, treat him to dinner, spending extravagantly on it.

Dad. He may have big news too! . . . That's right, a New York job. And be
sweet to him tonight, dear. Be loving to him. Because he's only a little boat
looking for a harbor. [*She is trembling with sorrow and joy.*] Oh, that's wonderful, Biff, you'll save his life. Thanks, darling. Just put your arm around
him when he comes into the restaurant. Give him a smile. That's the
boy . . . Good-by, dear. . . . You got your comb? . . . That's fine. Good-by,
Biff dear.

[*In the middle of her speech,* HOWARD WAGNER, *thirty-six, wheels in a
small typewriter table on which is a wire-recording machine[2] and proceeds to plug it in. This is on the left forestage. Light slowly fades on*
LINDA *as it rises on* HOWARD. HOWARD *is intent on threading the machine
and only glances over his shoulder as* WILLY *appears.*]

WILLY   Pst! Pst!

HOWARD   Hello, Willy, come in.

WILLY   Like to have a little talk with you, Howard.

HOWARD   Sorry to keep you waiting. I'll be with you in a minute.

WILLY   What's that, Howard?

HOWARD   Didn't you ever see one of these? Wire recorder.

WILLY   Oh. Can we talk a minute?

HOWARD   Records things. Just got delivery yesterday. Been driving me crazy,
the most terrific machine I ever saw in my life. I was up all night with it.

WILLY   What do you do with it?

HOWARD   I bought it for dictation, but you can do anything with it. Listen
to this. I had it home last night. Listen to what I picked up. The first one
is my daughter. Get this. [*He flicks the switch and "Roll out the Barrel"[3] is
heard being whistled.*] Listen to that kid whistle.

WILLY   That is lifelike, isn't it?

HOWARD   Seven years old. Get that tone.

WILLY   Ts, ts. Like to ask a little favor if you . . .

[*The whistling breaks off, and the voice of* HOWARD's *daughter is heard.*]

HIS DAUGHTER   "Now you, Daddy."

HOWARD   She's crazy for me! [*Again the same song is whistled.*] That's me!
Ha! [*He winks.*]

WILLY   You're very good!

[*The whistling breaks off again. The machine runs silent for a moment.*]

HOWARD   Sh! Get this now, this is my son.

HIS SON   "The capital of Alabama is Montgomery; the capital of Arizona is
Phoenix; the capital of Arkansas is Little Rock; the capital of California is
Sacramento . . ." [*And on, and on.*]

HOWARD [*holding up five fingers*]   Five years old, Willy!

WILLY   He'll make an announcer some day!

HIS SON [*continuing*]   "The capital . . ."

HOWARD   Get that—alphabetical order! [*The machine breaks off suddenly.*]
Wait a minute. The maid kicked the plug out.

WILLY   It certainly is a—

HOWARD   Sh, for God's sake!

2. The earliest practical magnetic sound
recording machine, first commercially available after World War II (soon made obsolete
by the tape recorder).

3. "The Beer Barrel Polka" (music written
1927; English lyrics written 1939), a song that
became very popular during World War II.

HIS SON "It's nine o'clock, Bulova watch time.[4] So I have to go to sleep."

WILLY That really is—

150 HOWARD Wait a minute! The next is my wife.

[*They wait.*]

HOWARD'S VOICE "Go on, say something." [*Pause*] "Well, you gonna talk?"

HIS WIFE "I can't think of anything."

HOWARD'S VOICE "Well, talk—it's turning."

HIS WIFE [*shyly, beaten*] "Hello." [*Silence*] "Oh, Howard, I can't talk into
155 this . . ."

HOWARD [*snapping the machine off*] That was my wife.

WILLY That is a wonderful machine. Can we—

HOWARD I tell you, Willy, I'm gonna take my camera, and my bandsaw, and
all my hobbies, and out they go. This is the most fascinating relaxation I
160 ever found.

WILLY I think I'll get one myself.

HOWARD Sure, they're only a hundred and a half. You can't do without it.
Supposing you wanna hear Jack Benny,[5] see? But you can't be at home at
that hour. So you tell the maid to turn the radio on when Jack Benny
165 comes on, and this automatically goes on with the radio . . .

WILLY And when you come home you . . .

HOWARD You can come home twelve o'clock, one o'clock, anytime you like,
and you get yourself a Coke and sit yourself down, throw the switch, and
there's Jack Benny's program in the middle of the night!

170 WILLY I'm definitely going to get one. Because lots of time I'm on the road,
and I think to myself, what I must be missing on the radio!

HOWARD Don't you have a radio in the car?

WILLY Well, yeah, but who ever thinks of turning it on?

HOWARD Say, aren't you supposed to be in Boston?

175 WILLY That's what I want to talk to you about, Howard. You got a minute?
[*He draws a chair in from the wing.*]

HOWARD What happened? What're you doing here?

WILLY Well . . .

HOWARD You didn't crack up again, did you?

WILLY Oh, no. No . . .

180 HOWARD Geez, you had me worried there for a minute. What's the trouble?

WILLY Well, tell you the truth, Howard. I've come to the decision that I'd
rather not travel any more.

HOWARD Not travel! Well, what'll you do?

WILLY Remember, Christmastime, when you had the party here? You said
185 you'd try to think of some spot for me here in town.

HOWARD With us?

WILLY Well, sure.

HOWARD Oh, yeah, yeah. I remember. Well, I couldn't think of anything for
you, Willy.

190 WILLY I tell ya, Howard. The kids are all grown up, y'know. I don't need
much any more. If I could take home—well, sixty-five dollars a week, I
could swing it.

---

4. A phrase used for years in Bulova's radio advertisements, beginning in 1926.

5. American comedian and actor (Benjamin Kubelsky, 1894–1974), host of a popular comedy show on radio (1932–55) and television (1950–65).

HOWARD   Yeah, but Willy, see I—

WILLY   I tell ya why, Howard. Speaking frankly and between the two of us,
195   y'know—I'm just a little tired.

HOWARD   Oh, I could understand that, Willy. But you're a road man, Willy,
and we do a road business. We've only got a half-dozen salesmen on the
floor here.

WILLY   God knows, Howard, I never asked a favor of any man. But I was with
200   the firm when your father used to carry you in here in his arms.

HOWARD   I know that, Willy, but—

WILLY   Your father came to me the day you were born and asked me what I
thought of the name of Howard, may he rest in peace.

HOWARD   I appreciate that, Willy, but there just is no spot here for you. If I
205   had a spot I'd slam you right in, but I just don't have a single solitary spot.

   [*He looks for his lighter.* WILLY *has picked it up and gives it to him.
   Pause.*]

WILLY [*with increasing anger*]   Howard, all I need to set my table is fifty dollars a week.

HOWARD   But where am I going to put you, kid?

WILLY   Look, it isn't a question of whether I can sell merchandise, is it?

210   HOWARD   No, but it's a business, kid, and everybody's gotta pull his own
weight.

WILLY [*desperately*]   Just let me tell you a story, Howard—

HOWARD   'Cause you gotta admit, business is business.

WILLY [*angrily*]   Business is definitely business, but just listen for a minute.
215   You don't understand this. When I was a boy—eighteen, nineteen—I was
already on the road. And there was a question in my mind as to whether
selling had a future for me. Because in those days I had a yearning to go to
Alaska. See, there were three gold strikes in one month in Alaska, and I felt
like going out. Just for the ride, you might say.

220   HOWARD [*barely interested*]   Don't say.

WILLY   Oh, yeah, my father lived many years in Alaska. He was an adventurous man. We've got quite a little streak of self-reliance in our family. I
thought I'd go out with my older brother and try to locate him, and maybe
settle in the North with the old man. And I was almost decided to go, when
225   I met a salesman in the Parker House.[6] His name was Dave Singleman.
And he was eighty-four years old, and he'd drummed merchandise in
thirty-one states. And old Dave, he'd go up to his room, y'understand, put
on his green velvet slippers—I'll never forget—and pick up his phone and
call the buyers, and without ever leaving his room, at the age of eighty-four,
230   he made his living. And when I saw that, I realized that selling was the
greatest career a man could want. 'Cause what could be more satisfying
than to be able to go, at the age of eighty-four, into twenty or thirty different cities, and pick up a phone, and be remembered and loved and helped
by so many different people? Do you know? when he died—and by the way
235   he died the death of a salesman, in his green velvet slippers in the smoker[7]
of the New York, New Haven and Hartford, going into Boston—when he
died, hundreds of salesmen and buyers were at his funeral. Things were

6. A venerable Boston luxury hotel.
7. The smoking car on a train (Willy names the specific railroad).

sad on a lotta trains for months after that. [*He stands up.* HOWARD *has not looked at him.*] In those days there was personality in it, Howard. There
240 was respect, and comradeship, and gratitude in it. Today, it's all cut and dried, and there's no chance for bringing friendship to bear—or personality. You see what I mean? They don't know me any more.

HOWARD [*moving away, to the right*]   That's just the thing, Willy.

WILLY   If I had forty dollars a week—that's all I'd need. Forty dollars,
245 Howard.

HOWARD   Kid, I can't take blood from a stone, I—

WILLY [*desperation is on him now*]   Howard, the year Al Smith was nominated,[8] your father came to me and—

HOWARD [*starting to go off*]   I've got to see some people, kid.

250 WILLY [*stopping him*]   I'm talking about your father! There were promises made across this desk! You mustn't tell me you've got people to see—I put thirty-four years into this firm, Howard, and now I can't pay my insurance! You can't eat the orange and throw the peel away—a man is not a piece of fruit! [*After a pause*] Now pay attention. Your father—in 1928 I had a big
255 year. I averaged a hundred and seventy dollars a week in commissions.

HOWARD [*impatiently*]   Now, Willy, you never averaged—

WILLY [*banging his hand on the desk*]   I averaged a hundred and seventy dollars a week in the year of 1928! And your father came to me—or rather, I was in the office here—it was right over this desk—and he put his hand on
260 my shoulder—

HOWARD [*getting up*]   You'll have to excuse me, Willy, I gotta see some people. Pull yourself together. [*Going out*] I'll be back in a little while.

> [*On* HOWARD'*s exit, the light on his chair grows very bright and strange.*]

WILLY   Pull myself together! What the hell did I say to him? My God, I was yelling at him! How could I! [WILLY *breaks off, staring at the light, which occupies the chair, animating it. He approaches this chair, standing across*
265 *the desk from it.*] Frank, Frank, don't you remember what you told me that time? How you put your hand on my shoulder, and Frank . . . [*He leans on the desk and as he speaks the dead man's name he accidentally switches on the recorder, and instantly.*]

HOWARD'S SON   ". . . of New York is Albany. The capital of Ohio is Cincinnati, the capital of Rhode Island is . . ." [*The recitation continues.*]

WILLY [*leaping away with fright, shouting*]   Ha! Howard! Howard! Howard!

270 HOWARD [*rushing in*]   What happened?

WILLY [*pointing at the machine, which continues nasally, childishly, with the capital cities*]   Shut it off! Shut it off!

HOWARD [*pulling the plug out*]   Look, Willy . . .

WILLY [*pressing his hands to his eyes*]   I gotta get myself some coffee. I'll get some coffee . . .

> [WILLY *starts to walk out.* HOWARD *stops him.*]

275 HOWARD [*rolling up the cord*]   Willy, look . . .

WILLY   I'll go to Boston.

HOWARD   Willy, you can't go to Boston for us.

WILLY   Why can't I go?

---

8. That is, in 1928; Smith (1873–1944) was the Democratic Party's presidential nominee.

HOWARD   I don't want you to represent us. I've been meaning to tell you for
280   a long time now.
WILLY   Howard, are you firing me?
HOWARD   I think you need a good long rest, Willy.
WILLY   Howard—
HOWARD   And when you feel better, come back, and we'll see if we can work
285   something out.
WILLY   But I gotta earn money, Howard. I'm in no position to—
HOWARD   Where are your sons? Why don't your sons give you a hand?
WILLY   They're working on a very big deal.
HOWARD   This is no time for false pride, Willy. You go to your sons and you
290   tell them that you're tired. You've got two great boys, haven't you?
WILLY   Oh, no question, no question, but in the meantime . . .
HOWARD   Then that's that, heh?
WILLY   All right, I'll go to Boston tomorrow.
HOWARD   No, no.
295   WILLY   I can't throw myself on my sons. I'm not a cripple!
HOWARD   Look, kid, I'm busy this morning.
WILLY   [grasping HOWARD's arm]   Howard, you've got to let me go to Boston!
HOWARD   [hard, keeping himself under control]   I've got a line of people to see
this morning. Sit down, take five minutes, and pull yourself together, and
300   then go home, will ya? I need the office, Willy. [He starts to go, turns,
remembering the recorder, starts to push off the table holding the recorder.]
Oh, yeah. Whenever you can this week, stop by and drop off the samples.
You'll feel better, Willy, and then come back and we'll talk. Pull yourself
together, kid, there's people outside.

> [HOWARD exits, pushing the table off left. WILLY stares into space,
> exhausted. Now the music is heard—BEN's music—first distantly, then
> closer, closer. As WILLY speaks, BEN enters from the right. He carries valise
> and umbrella.]

WILLY   Oh, Ben, how did you do it? What is the answer? Did you wind up
305   the Alaska deal already?
BEN   Doesn't take much time if you know what you're doing. Just a short
business trip. Boarding ship in an hour. Wanted to say good-by.
WILLY   Ben, I've got to talk to you.
BEN   [glancing at his watch]   Haven't the time, William.
310   WILLY   [crossing the apron to Ben]   Ben, nothing's working out. I don't know
what to do.
BEN   Now, look here, William. I've bought timberland in Alaska and I need a
man to look after things for me.
WILLY   God, timberland! Me and my boys in those grand outdoors!
315   BEN   You've a new continent at your doorstep, William. Get out of these cities, they're full of talk and time payments and courts of law. Screw on your
fists and you can fight for a fortune up there.
WILLY   Yes, yes! Linda, Linda!

> [LINDA enters as of old, with the wash.]

LINDA   Oh, you're back?
320   BEN   I haven't much time.
WILLY   No, wait! Linda, he's got a proposition for me in Alaska.
LINDA   But you've got—[To BEN] He's got a beautiful job here.

WILLY   But in Alaska, kid, I could—

LINDA   You're doing well enough, Willy!

325   BEN [to LINDA]   Enough for what, my dear?

LINDA [frightened of BEN and angry at him]   Don't say those things to him! Enough to be happy right here, right now. [To WILLY, while BEN laughs] Why must everybody conquer the world? You're well liked, and the boys love you, and someday—[To BEN]—why, old man Wagner told him just the other day

330   that if he keeps it up he'll be a member of the firm, didn't he, Willy?

WILLY   Sure, sure. I am building something with this firm, Ben, and if a man is building something he must be on the right track, mustn't he?

BEN   What are you building? Lay your hand on it. Where is it?

WILLY [hesitantly]   That's true, Linda, there's nothing.

335   LINDA   Why? [To BEN] There's a man eighty-four years old—

WILLY   That's right, Ben, that's right. When I look at that man I say, what is there to worry about?

BEN   Bah!

WILLY   It's true, Ben. All he has to do is go into any city, pick up the phone,

340   and he's making his living and you know why?

BEN [picking up his valise]   I've got to go.

WILLY [holding BEN back]   Look at this boy!

[BIFF, in his high school sweater, enters carrying suitcase. HAPPY carries BIFF's shoulder guards, gold helmet, and football pants.]

WILLY   Without a penny to his name, three great universities are begging for him, and from there the sky's the limit, because it's not what you do, Ben.

345   It's who you know and the smile on your face! It's contacts, Ben, contacts! The whole wealth of Alaska passes over the lunch table at the Commodore Hotel, and that's the wonder, the wonder of this country, that a man can end with diamonds here on the basis of being liked! [He turns to BIFF.] And that's why when you get out on that field today it's important. Because

350   thousands of people will be rooting for you and loving you. [To BEN, who has again begun to leave] And Ben! when he walks into a business office his name will sound out like a bell and all the doors will open to him! I've seen it, Ben, I've seen it a thousand times! You can't feel it with your hand like timber, but it's there!

355   BEN   Good-by, William.

WILLY   Ben, am I right? Don't you think I'm right? I value your advice.

BEN   There's a new continent at your doorstep, William. You could walk out rich. Rich! [He is gone.]

WILLY   We'll do it here, Ben! You hear me? We're gonna do it here!

[YOUNG BERNARD rushes in. The gay music of the Boys is heard.]

360   BERNARD   Oh, gee, I was afraid you left already!

WILLY   Why? What time is it?

BERNARD   It's half-past one!

WILLY   Well, come on, everybody! Ebbets Field next stop! Where's the pennants? [He rushes through the wall-line of the kitchen and out into the living room.]

365   LINDA [to BIFF]   Did you pack fresh underwear?

BIFF [who has been limbering up]   I want to go!

BERNARD   Biff, I'm carrying your helmet, ain't I?

HAPPY   No, I'm carrying the helmet.

BERNARD Oh, Biff, you promised me.

370 HAPPY I'm carrying the helmet.

BERNARD How am I going to get in the locker room?

LINDA Let him carry the shoulder guards. [*She puts her coat and hat on in the kitchen*.]

BERNARD Can I, Biff? 'Cause I told everybody I'm going to be in the locker room.

375 HAPPY In Ebbets Field it's the clubhouse.

BERNARD I meant the clubhouse. Biff!

HAPPY Biff!

BIFF [*grandly, after a slight pause*] Let him carry the shoulder guards.

HAPPY [*as he gives* BERNARD *the shoulder guards*] Stay close to us now.

[WILLY *rushes in with the pennants*.]

380 WILLY [*handing them out*] Everybody wave when Biff comes out on the field. [HAPPY *and* BERNARD *run off*.] You set now, boy?

[*The music has died away*.]

BIFF Ready to go, Pop. Every muscle is ready.

WILLY [*at the edge of the apron*] You realize what this means?

BIFF That's right, Pop.

385 WILLY [*feeling* BIFF's *muscle*] You're comin' home this afternoon captain of the All-Scholastic Championship Team of the City of New York.

BIFF I got it, Pop. And remember, pal, when I take off my helmet, that touchdown is for you.

WILLY Let's go! [*He is starting out, with his arm around Biff, when* CHARLEY

390 *enters, as of old, in knickers*.] I got no room for you, Charley.

CHARLEY Room? For what?

WILLY In the car.

CHARLEY You goin' for a ride? I wanted to shoot some casino.

WILLY [*furiously*] Casino! [*Incredulously*] Don't you realize what today is?

395 LINDA Oh, he knows, Willy. He's just kidding you.

WILLY That's nothing to kid about!

CHARLEY No. Linda, what's goin' on?

LINDA He's playing in Ebbets Field.

CHARLEY Baseball in this weather?

400 WILLY Don't talk to him. Come on, come on! [*He is pushing them out*.]

CHARLEY Wait a minute, didn't you hear the news?

WILLY What?

CHARLEY Don't you listen to the radio? Ebbets Field just blew up.

WILLY You go to hell! [CHARLEY *laughs. Pushing them out*] Come on, come

405 on! We're late.

CHARLEY [*as they go*] Knock a homer, Biff, knock a homer!

WILLY [*the last to leave, turning to* CHARLEY] I don't think that was funny, Charley. This is the greatest day of his life.

CHARLEY Willy, when are you going to grow up?

410 WILLY Yeah, heh? When this game is over, Charley, you'll be laughing out of the other side of your face. They'll be calling him another Red Grange.[9] Twenty-five thousand a year.

9. Harold Edward Grange (1903–1991), a football player who was a three-time All-American halfback at the University of Illinois (1923–25); after starting for the Chicago Bears, he became a sportscaster.

CHARLEY [*kidding*]   Is that so?

WILLY   Yeah, that's so.

415 CHARLEY   Well, then, I'm sorry, Willy. But tell me something.

WILLY   What?

CHARLEY   Who is Red Grange?

WILLY   Put up your hands. Goddam you, put up your hands!

> [CHARLEY, *chuckling, shakes his head and walks away, around the left corner of the stage.* WILLY *follows him. The music rises to a mocking frenzy.*]

WILLY   Who the hell do you think you are, better than everybody else? You

420   don't know everything, you big, ignorant, stupid . . . Put up your hands!

> [*Light rises, on the right side of the forestage, on a small table in the reception room of* CHARLEY's *office. Traffic sounds are heard.* BERNARD, *now mature, sits whistling to himself. A pair of tennis rackets and an overnight bag are on the floor beside him.*]

WILLY [*offstage*]   What are you walking away for? Don't walk away! If you're going to say something say it to my face! I know you laugh at me behind my back. You'll laugh out of the other side of your goddam face after this game. Touchdown! Touchdown! Eighty thousand people! Touchdown! Right

425   between the goal posts.

> [BERNARD *is a quiet, earnest, but self-assured young man.* WILLY's *voice is coming from right upstage now.* BERNARD *lowers his feet off the table and listens.* JENNY, *his father's secretary, enters.*]

JENNY [*distressed*]   Say, Bernard, will you go out in the hall?

BERNARD   What is that noise? Who is it?

JENNY   Mr. Loman. He just got off the elevator.

BERNARD [*getting up*]   Who's he arguing with?

430 JENNY   Nobody. There's nobody with him. I can't deal with him any more, and your father gets all upset everytime he comes. I've got a lot of typing to do, and your father's waiting to sign it. Will you see him?

WILLY [*entering*]   Touchdown! Touch—[*He sees* JENNY.] Jenny, Jenny, good to see you. How're ya? Workin'? Or still honest?

435 JENNY   Fine. How've you been feeling?

WILLY   Not much any more, Jenny. Ha, ha! [*He is surprised to see the rackets.*]

BERNARD   Hello, Uncle Willy.

WILLY [*almost shocked*]   Bernard! Well, look who's here! [*He comes quickly, guiltily, to* BERNARD *and warmly shakes his hand.*]

BERNARD   How are you? Good to see you.

440 WILLY   What are you doing here?

BERNARD   Oh, just stopped by to see Pop. Get off my feet till my train leaves. I'm going to Washington in a few minutes.

WILLY   Is he in?

BERNARD   Yes, he's in his office with the accountant. Sit down.

445 WILLY [*sitting down*]   What're you going to do in Washington?

BERNARD   Oh, just a case I've got there, Willy.

WILLY   That so? [*Indicating the rackets*] You going to play tennis there?

BERNARD   I'm staying with a friend who's got a court.

WILLY   Don't say. His own tennis court. Must be fine people, I bet.

450 BERNARD   They are, very nice. Dad tells me Biff's in town.

WILLY [*with a big smile*]   Yeah, Biff's in. Working on a very big deal, Bernard.

BERNARD   What's Biff doing?

WILLY   Well, he's been doing very big things in the West. But he decided to establish himself here. Very big. We're having dinner. Did I hear your wife
455   had a boy?

BERNARD   That's right. Our second.

WILLY   Two boys! What do you know!

BERNARD   What kind of a deal has Biff got?

WILLY   Well, Bill Oliver—very big sporting-goods man—he wants Biff very
460   badly. Called him in from the West. Long distance, carte blanche, special deliveries. Your friends have their own private tennis court?

BERNARD   You still with the old firm, Willy?

WILLY [after a pause]   I'm—I'm overjoyed to see how you made the grade, Bernard, overjoyed. It's an encouraging thing to see a young man really—
465   really—Looks very good for Biff—very—[He breaks off, then] Bernard— [He is so full of emotion, he breaks off again.]

BERNARD   What is it, Willy?

WILLY [small and alone]   What—what's the secret?

BERNARD   What secret?

WILLY   How—how did you? Why didn't he ever catch on?
470   BERNARD   I wouldn't know that, Willy.

WILLY [confidentially, desperately]   You were his friend, his boyhood friend. There's something I don't understand about it. His life ended after that Ebbets Field game. From the age of seventeen nothing good ever happened to him.
475   BERNARD   He never trained himself for anything.

WILLY   But he did, he did. After high school he took so many correspondence courses. Radio mechanics; television; God knows what, and never made the slightest mark.

BERNARD [taking off his glasses]   Willy, do you want to talk candidly?
480   WILLY [rising, faces BERNARD]   I regard you as a very brilliant man, Bernard. I value your advice.

BERNARD   Oh, the hell with the advice, Willy. I couldn't advise you. There's just one thing I've always wanted to ask you. When he was supposed to graduate, and the math teacher flunked him—
485   WILLY   Oh, that son-of-a-bitch ruined his life.

BERNARD   Yeah, but, Willy, all he had to do was go to summer school and make up that subject.

WILLY   That's right, that's right.

BERNARD   Did you tell him not to go to summer school?
490   WILLY   Me? I begged him to go. I ordered him to go!

BERNARD   Then why wouldn't he go?

WILLY   Why? Why! Bernard, that question has been trailing me like a ghost for the last fifteen years. He flunked the subject, and laid down and died like a hammer hit him!
495   BERNARD   Take it easy, kid.

WILLY   Let me talk to you—I got nobody to talk to. Bernard, Bernard, was it my fault? Y'see? It keeps going around in my mind, maybe I did something to him. I got nothing to give him.

BERNARD   Don't take it so hard.
500   WILLY   Why did he lay down? What is the story there? You were his friend!

BERNARD   Willy, I remember, it was June, and our grades came out. And he'd flunked math.

WILLY   That son-of-a-bitch!

BERNARD   No, it wasn't right then. Biff just got very angry, I remember, and
505   he was ready to enroll in summer school.

WILLY [*surprised*]   He was?

BERNARD   He wasn't beaten by it at all. But then, Willy, he disappeared from
the block for almost a month. And I got the idea that he'd gone up to New
England to see you. Did he have a talk with you then?

[WILLY *stares in silence.*]

510   BERNARD   Willy?

WILLY [*with a strong edge of resentment in his voice*]   Yeah, he came to Boston. What about it?

BERNARD   Well, just that when he came back—I'll never forget this, it always
mystifies me. Because I'd thought so well of Biff, even though he'd always
515   taken advantage of me. I loved him, Willy, y'know? And he came back after
that month and took his sneakers—remember those sneakers with "University of Virginia" printed on them? He was so proud of those, wore them
every day. And he took them down in the cellar, and burned them up in the
furnace. We had a fist fight. It lasted at least half an hour. Just the two of
520   us, punching each other down the cellar, and crying right through it. I've
often thought of how strange it was that I knew he'd given up his life. What
happened in Boston, Willy?

[WILLY *looks at him as at an intruder.*]

BERNARD   I just bring it up because you asked me.

WILLY [*angrily*]   Nothing. What do you mean, "What happened?" What's
525   that got to do with anything?

BERNARD   Well, don't get sore.

WILLY   What are you trying to do, blame it on me? If a boy lays down is that
my fault?

BERNARD   Now, Willy, don't get—

530   WILLY   Well, don't—don't talk to me that way! What does that mean, "What
happened?"

[CHARLEY *enters. He is in his vest, and he carries a bottle of bourbon.*]

CHARLEY   Hey, you're going to miss that train. [*He waves the bottle.*]

BERNARD   Yeah, I'm going. [*He takes the bottle.*] Thanks, Pop. [*He picks up
his rackets and bag.*] Good-by, Willy, and don't worry about it. You know, "If
535   at first you don't succeed . . ."

WILLY   Yes, I believe in that.

BERNARD   But sometimes, Willy, it's better for a man just to walk away.

WILLY   Walk away?

BERNARD   That's right.

540   WILLY   But if you can't walk away?

BERNARD [*after a slight pause*]   I guess that's when it's tough. [*Extending his
hand*] Good-by, Willy.

WILLY [*shaking* BERNARD'*s hand*]   Good-by, boy.

CHARLEY [*an arm on* BERNARD'*s shoulder*]   How do you like this kid? Gonna
545   argue a case in front of the Supreme Court.

BERNARD [*protesting*]   Pop!

WILLY [*genuinely shocked, pained, and happy*]   No! The Supreme Court!

BERNARD   I gotta run. 'By, Dad!

CHARLEY   Knock 'em dead, Bernard!

[BERNARD *goes off.*]

550 WILLY [*as* CHARLEY *takes out his wallet*]   The Supreme Court! And he didn't even mention it!

CHARLEY [*counting out money on the desk*]   He don't have to—he's gonna do it.

WILLY   And you never told him what to do, did you? You never took any interest in him.

555 CHARLEY   My salvation is that I never took any interest in anything. There's some money—fifty dollars. I got an accountant inside.

WILLY   Charley, look . . . [*With difficulty*] I got my insurance to pay. If you can manage it—I need a hundred and ten dollars.

[CHARLEY *doesn't reply for a moment; merely stops moving.*]

WILLY   I'd draw it from my bank but Linda would know, and I . . .

560 CHARLEY   Sit down, Willy.

WILLY [*moving toward the chair*]   I'm keeping an account of everything, remember. I'll pay every penny back. [*He sits.*]

CHARLEY   Now listen to me, Willy.

WILLY   I want you to know I appreciate . . .

565 CHARLEY [*sitting down on the table*]   Willy, what're you doin'? What the hell is goin' on in your head?

WILLY   Why? I'm simply . . .

CHARLEY   I offered you a job. You can make fifty dollars a week. And I won't send you on the road.

570 WILLY   I've got a job.

CHARLEY   Without pay? What kind of a job is a job without pay? [*He rises.*] Now, look, kid, enough is enough. I'm no genius but I know when I'm being insulted.

WILLY   Insulted!

575 CHARLEY   Why don't you want to work for me?

WILLY   What's the matter with you? I've got a job.

CHARLEY   Then what're you walkin' in here every week for?

WILLY [*getting up*]   Well, if you don't want me to walk in here—

CHARLEY   I am offering you a job.

580 WILLY   I don't want your goddam job!

CHARLEY   When the hell are you going to grow up?

WILLY [*furiously*]   You big ignoramus, if you say that to me again I'll rap you one! I don't care how big you are! [*He's ready to fight.*]

[*Pause.*]

CHARLEY [*kindly, going to him*]   How much do you need, Willy?

585 WILLY   Charley, I'm strapped, I'm strapped. I don't know what to do. I was just fired.

CHARLEY   Howard fired you?

WILLY   That snotnose. Imagine that? I named him. I named him Howard.

CHARLEY   Willy, when're you gonna realize that them things don't mean any-
590 thing? You named him Howard, but you can't sell that. The only thing you got in this world is what you can sell. And the funny thing is that you're a salesman, and you don't know that.

WILLY   I've always tried to think otherwise, I guess. I always felt that if a man was impressive, and well liked, that nothing—

595 CHARLEY   Why must everybody like you? Who liked J. P. Morgan?[1] Was he impressive? In a Turkish bath he'd look like a butcher. But with his pockets on he was very well liked. Now listen, Willy, I know you don't like me, and nobody can say I'm in love with you, but I'll give you a job because—just for the hell of it, put it that way. Now what do you say?

600 WILLY   I—I just can't work for you, Charley.

CHARLEY   What're you, jealous of me?

WILLY   I can't work for you, that's all, don't ask me why.

CHARLEY   [*angered, takes out more bills*]   You been jealous of me all your life, you damned fool! Here, pay your insurance. [*He puts the money in* WILLY's *hand.*]

605 WILLY   I'm keeping strict accounts.

CHARLEY   I've got some work to do. Take care of yourself. And pay your insurance.

WILLY   [*moving to the right*]   Funny, y'know? After all the highways, and the trains, and the appointments, and the years, you end up worth more dead
610 than alive.

CHARLEY   Willy, nobody's worth nothin' dead. [*After a slight pause*] Did you hear what I said?

[WILLY *stands still, dreaming.*]

CHARLEY   Willy!

WILLY   Apologize to Bernard for me when you see him. I didn't mean to
615 argue with him. He's a fine boy. They're all fine boys, and they'll end up big—all of them. Someday they'll all play tennis together. Wish me luck, Charley. He saw Bill Oliver today.

CHARLEY   Good luck.

WILLY   [*on the verge of tears*]   Charley, you're the only friend I got. Isn't that a
620 remarkable thing? [*He goes out.*]

CHARLEY   Jesus!

[CHARLEY *stares after him a moment and follows. All light blacks out. Suddenly raucous music is heard, and a red glow rises behind the screen at right.* STANLEY, *a young waiter, appears, carrying a table, followed by* HAPPY, *who is carrying two chairs.*]

STANLEY   [*putting the table down*]   That's all right, Mr. Loman, I can handle it myself. [*He turns and takes the chairs from* HAPPY *and places them at the table.*]

HAPPY   [*glancing around*]   Oh, this is better.

625 STANLEY   Sure, in the front there you're in the middle of all kinds a noise. Whenever you got a party, Mr. Loman, you just tell me and I'll put you back here. Y'know, there's a lotta people they don't like it private, because when they go out they like to see a lotta action around them because they're sick and tired to stay in the house by theirself. But I know you, you ain't from
630 Hackensack.[2] You know what I mean?

HAPPY   [*sitting down*]   So how's it coming, Stanley?

STANLEY   Ah, it's a dog's life. I only wish during the war they'd a took me in the Army. I coulda been dead by now.

---

1. American financier, industrialist, and philanthropist (1837–1913); he amassed an enormous fortune.

2. A mainly working-class town in northern New Jersey, several miles from Manhattan.

HAPPY My brother's back, Stanley.

635 STANLEY Oh, he come back, heh? From the Far West.

HAPPY Yeah, big cattle man, my brother, so treat him right. And my father's coming too.

STANLEY Oh, your father too!

HAPPY You got a couple of nice lobsters?

640 STANLEY Hundred per cent, big.

HAPPY I want them with the claws.

STANLEY Don't worry, I don't give you no mice. [HAPPY *laughs*.] How about some wine? It'll put a head on the meal.

HAPPY No. You remember, Stanley, that recipe I brought you from overseas?

645 With the champagne in it?

STANLEY Oh, yeah, sure. I still got it tacked up yet in the kitchen. But that'll have to cost a buck apiece anyways.

HAPPY That's all right.

STANLEY What'd you, hit a number[3] or somethin'?

650 HAPPY No, it's a little celebration. My brother is—I think he pulled off a big deal today. I think we're going into business together.

STANLEY Great! That's the best for you. Because a family business, you know what I mean?—that's the best.

HAPPY That's what I think.

655 STANLEY 'Cause what's the difference? Somebody steals? It's in the family. Know what I mean? [*Sotto voce*[4]] Like this bartender here. The boss is goin' crazy what kinda leak he's got in the cash register. You put it in but it don't come out.

HAPPY [*raising his head*] Sh!

660 STANLEY What?

HAPPY You notice I wasn't lookin' right or left, was I?

STANLEY No.

HAPPY And my eyes are closed.

STANLEY So what's the—?

665 HAPPY Strudel's comin'.

STANLEY [*catching on, looks around*] Ah, no, there's no—

[*He breaks off as a furred, lavishly dressed girl enters and sits at the next table. Both follow her with their eyes.*]

STANLEY Geez, how'd ya know?

HAPPY I got radar or something. [*Staring directly at her profile*] Oooooooo . . . Stanley.

670 STANLEY I think that's for you, Mr. Loman.

HAPPY Look at that mouth. Oh, God. And the binoculars.

STANLEY Geez, you got a life, Mr. Loman.

HAPPY Wait on her.

STANLEY [*going to the girl's table*] Would you like a menu, ma'am?

675 GIRL I'm expecting someone, but I'd like a—

HAPPY Why don't you bring her—excuse me, miss, do you mind? I sell champagne, and I'd like you to try my brand. Bring her a champagne, Stanley.

---

3. That is, win in an illegal lottery.
4. Under the voice (Italian); that is, spoken very softly, under the breath.

GIRL   That's awfully nice of you.

680 HAPPY   Don't mention it. It's all company money. [*He laughs.*]

GIRL   That's a charming product to be selling, isn't it?

HAPPY   Oh, gets to be like everything else. Selling is selling, y'know.

GIRL   I suppose.

HAPPY   You don't happen to sell, do you?

685 GIRL   No, I don't sell.

HAPPY   Would you object to a compliment from a stranger? You ought to be on a magazine cover.

GIRL [*looking at him a little archly*]   I have been.

[STANLEY *comes in with a glass of champagne.*]

HAPPY   What'd I say before, Stanley? You see? She's a cover girl.

690 STANLEY   Oh, I could see, I could see.

HAPPY [*to the* GIRL]   What magazine?

GIRL   Oh, a lot of them. [*She takes the drink.*] Thank you.

HAPPY   You know what they say in France, don't you? "Champagne is the drink of the complexion"—Hya, Biff!

[BIFF *has entered and sits with* HAPPY.]

695 BIFF   Hello, kid. Sorry I'm late.

HAPPY   I just got here. Uh, Miss—?

GIRL   Forsythe.

HAPPY   Miss Forsythe, this is my brother.

BIFF   Is Dad here?

700 HAPPY   His name is Biff. You might've heard of him. Great football player.

GIRL   Really? What team?

HAPPY   Are you familiar with football?

GIRL   No, I'm afraid I'm not.

HAPPY   Biff is quarterback with the New York Giants.

705 GIRL   Well, that is nice, isn't it? [*She drinks.*]

HAPPY   Good health.

GIRL   I'm happy to meet you.

HAPPY   That's my name. Hap. It's really Harold, but at West Point they called me Happy.

710 GIRL [*now really impressed*]   Oh, I see. How do you do? [*She turns her profile.*]

BIFF   Isn't Dad coming?

HAPPY   You want her?

BIFF   Oh, I could never make that.

HAPPY   I remember the time that idea would never come into your head.

715 Where's the old confidence, Biff?

BIFF   I just saw Oliver—

HAPPY   Wait a minute. I've got to see that old confidence again. Do you want her? She's on call.[5]

BIFF   Oh, no. [*He turns to look at the* GIRL.]

720 HAPPY   I'm telling you. Watch this. [*Turning to the* GIRL] Honey? [*She turns to him.*] Are you busy?

GIRL   Well, I am . . . but I could make a phone call.

---

5. That is, a call girl, a prostitute.

HAPPY Do that, will you, honey? And see if you can get a friend. We'll be here for a while. Biff is one of the greatest football players in the country.

725 GIRL [*standing up*] Well, I'm certainly happy to meet you.

HAPPY Come back soon.

GIRL I'll try.

HAPPY Don't try, honey, try hard.

> [*The* GIRL *exits.* STANLEY *follows, shaking his head in bewildered admiration.*]

HAPPY Isn't that a shame now? A beautiful girl like that? That's why I can't

730 get married. There's not a good woman in a thousand. New York is loaded with them, kid!

BIFF Hap, look—

HAPPY I told you she was on call!

BIFF [*strangely unnerved*] Cut it out, will ya? I want to say something to you.

735 HAPPY Did you see Oliver?

BIFF I saw him all right. Now look, I want to tell Dad a couple of things and I want you to help me.

HAPPY What? Is he going to back you?

BIFF Are you crazy? You're out of your goddam head, you know that?

740 HAPPY Why? What happened?

BIFF [*breathlessly*] I did a terrible thing today, Hap. It's been the strangest day I ever went through. I'm all numb, I swear.

HAPPY You mean he wouldn't see you?

BIFF Well, I waited six hours for him, see? All day. Kept sending my name in.

745 Even tried to date his secretary so she'd get me to him, but no soap.

HAPPY Because you're not showin' the old confidence, Biff. He remembered you, didn't he?

BIFF [*stopping* HAPPY *with a gesture*] Finally, about five o'clock, he comes out. Didn't remember who I was or anything. I felt like such an idiot, Hap.

750 HAPPY Did you tell him my Florida idea?

BIFF He walked away. I saw him for one minute. I got so mad I could've torn the walls down! How the hell did I ever get the idea I was a salesman there? I even believed myself that I'd been a salesman for him! And then he gave me one look and—I realized what a ridiculous lie my whole life has been!

755 We've been talking in a dream for fifteen years. I was a shipping clerk.

HAPPY What'd you do?

BIFF [*with great tension and wonder*] Well, he left, see. And the secretary went out. I was all alone in the waiting-room. I don't know what came over me, Hap. The next thing I know I'm in his office—paneled walls, every-

760 thing. I can't explain it. I—Hap, I took his fountain pen.

HAPPY Geez, did he catch you?

BIFF I ran out. I ran down all eleven flights. I ran and ran and ran.

HAPPY That was an awful dumb—what'd you do that for?

BIFF [*agonized*] I don't know, I just—wanted to take something, I don't

765 know. You gotta help me, Hap, I'm gonna tell Pop.

HAPPY You crazy? What for?

BIFF Hap, he's got to understand that I'm not the man somebody lends that kind of money to. He thinks I've been spiting him all these years and it's eating him up.

770 HAPPY   That's just it. You tell him something nice.

BIFF   I can't.

HAPPY   Say you got a lunch date with Oliver tomorrow.

BIFF   So what do I do tomorrow?

HAPPY   You leave the house tomorrow and come back at night and say Oliver
775   is thinking it over. And he thinks it over for a couple of weeks, and gradually it fades away and nobody's the worse.

BIFF   But it'll go on forever!

HAPPY   Dad is never so happy as when he's looking forward to something!

[WILLY *enters.*]

HAPPY   Hello, scout!

780 WILLY   Gee, I haven't been here in years!

[STANLEY *has followed* WILLY *in and sets a chair for him.* STANLEY *starts
off but* HAPPY *stops him.*]

HAPPY   Stanley!

[STANLEY *stands by, waiting for an order.*]

BIFF [*going to* WILLY *with guilt, as to an invalid*]   Sit down, Pop. You want a
drink?

WILLY   Sure, I don't mind.

785 BIFF   Let's get a load on.

WILLY   You look worried.

BIFF   N-no. [*To* STANLEY] Scotch all around. Make it doubles.

STANLEY   Doubles, right. [*He goes.*]

WILLY   You had a couple already, didn't you?

790 BIFF   Just a couple, yeah.

WILLY   Well, what happened, boy? [*Nodding affirmatively, with a smile*]
Everything go all right?

BIFF [*takes a breath, then reaches out and grasps* WILLY's *hand*]   Pal . . . [*He is
smiling bravely, and* WILLY *is smiling too.*] I had an experience today.

795 HAPPY   Terrific, Pop.

WILLY   That so? What happened?

BIFF [*high, slightly alcoholic, above the earth*]   I'm going to tell you everything from first to last. It's been a strange day. [*Silence. He looks around,
composes himself as best he can, but his breath keeps breaking the rhythm of
his voice.*] I had to wait quite a while for him, and—

800 WILLY   Oliver?

BIFF   Yeah, Oliver. All day, as a matter of cold fact. And a lot of—instances—
facts, Pop, facts about my life came back to me. Who was it, Pop? Who
ever said I was a salesman with Oliver?

WILLY   Well, you were.

805 BIFF   No, Dad, I was a shipping clerk.

WILLY   But you were practically—

BIFF [*with determination*]   Dad, I don't know who said it first, but I was
never a salesman for Bill Oliver.

WILLY   What're you talking about?

810 BIFF   Let's hold on to the facts tonight, Pop. We're not going to get anywhere
bullin' around. I was a shipping clerk.

WILLY [*angrily*]   All right, now listen to me—

BIFF   Why don't you let me finish?

WILLY   I'm not interested in stories about the past or any crap of that kind
815   because the woods are burning, boys, you understand? There's a big blaze
going on all around. I was fired today.

BIFF [*shocked*]   How could you be?

WILLY   I was fired, and I'm looking for a little good news to tell your mother,
because the woman has waited and the woman has suffered. The gist of it
820   is that I haven't got a story left in my head, Biff. So don't give me a lecture
about facts and aspects. I am not interested. Now what've you got to say to
me?

> [STANLEY *enters with three drinks. They wait until he leaves.*]

WILLY   Did you see Oliver?

BIFF   Jesus, Dad!

825   WILLY   You mean you didn't go up there?

HAPPY   Sure he went up there.

BIFF   I did. I—saw him. How could they fire you?

WILLY [*on the edge of his chair*]   What kind of a welcome did he give you?

BIFF   He won't even let you work on commission?

830   WILLY   I'm out! [*Driving*] So tell me, he gave you a warm welcome?

HAPPY   Sure, Pop, sure!

BIFF [*driven*]   Well, it was kind of—

WILLY   I was wondering if he'd remember you. [*To* HAPPY] Imagine, man
doesn't see him for ten, twelve years and gives him that kind of a
835   welcome!

HAPPY   Damn right!

BIFF [*trying to return to the offensive*]   Pop, look—

WILLY   You know why he remembered you, don't you? Because you impressed
him in those days.

840   BIFF   Let's talk quietly and get this down to the facts, huh?

WILLY [*as though* BIFF *had been interrupting*]   Well, what happened? It's
great news, Biff. Did he take you into his office or'd you talk in the waiting
room?

BIFF   Well, he came in, see, and—

845   WILLY [*with a big smile*]   What'd he say? Betcha he threw his arm around
you.

BIFF   Well, he kinda—

WILLY   He's a fine man. [*To* HAPPY] Very hard man to see, y'know.

HAPPY [*agreeing*]   Oh, I know.

850   WILLY [*to Biff*]   Is that where you had the drinks?

BIFF   Yeah, he gave me a couple of—no, no!

HAPPY [*cutting in*]   He told him my Florida idea.

WILLY   Don't interrupt. [*To* BIFF] How'd he react to the Florida idea?

BIFF   Dad, will you give me a minute to explain?

855   WILLY   I've been waiting for you to explain since I sat down here! What happened? He took you into his office and what?

BIFF   Well—I talked. And—and he listened, see.

WILLY   Famous for the way he listens, y'know. What was his answer?

BIFF   His answer was—[*He breaks off, suddenly angry.*] Dad, you're not let-
860   ting me tell you what I want to tell you!

WILLY [*accusing, angered*]   You didn't see him, did you?

BIFF   I did see him!

WILLY What'd you insult him or something? You insulted him, didn't you?

BIFF Listen, will you let me out of it, will you just let me out of it!

865 HAPPY What the hell!

WILLY Tell me what happened!

BIFF [*to* HAPPY] I can't talk to him!

> [*A single trumpet note jars the ear. The light of green leaves stains the house, which holds the air of night and a dream.* YOUNG BERNARD *enters and knocks on the door of the house.*]

YOUNG BERNARD [*frantically*] Mrs. Loman, Mrs. Loman!

HAPPY Tell him what happened!

870 BIFF [*to* HAPPY] Shut up and leave me alone!

WILLY No, no! You had to go and flunk math!

BIFF What math? What're you talking about?

YOUNG BERNARD Mrs. Loman, Mrs. Loman!

> [LINDA *appears in the house, as of old.*]

WILLY [*wildly*] Math, math, math!

875 BIFF Take it easy, Pop!

YOUNG BERNARD Mrs. Loman!

WILLY [*furiously*] If you hadn't flunked you'd've been set by now!

BIFF Now, look, I'm gonna tell you what happened, and you're going to listen to me.

880 YOUNG BERNARD Mrs. Loman!

BIFF I waited six hours—

HAPPY What the hell are you saying?

BIFF I kept sending in my name but he wouldn't see me. So finally he . . .

> [*He continues unheard as light fades low on the restaurant.*]

YOUNG BERNARD Biff flunked math!

885 LINDA No!

YOUNG BERNARD Birnbaum flunked him! They won't graduate him!

LINDA But they have to. He's gotta go to the university. Where is he? Biff! Biff!

YOUNG BERNARD No, he left. He went to Grand Central.[6]

890 LINDA Grand—You mean he went to Boston!

YOUNG BERNARD Is Uncle Willy in Boston?

LINDA Oh, maybe Willy can talk to the teacher. Oh, the poor, poor boy!

> [*Light on house area snaps out.*]

BIFF [*at the table, now audible, holding up a gold fountain pen*] . . . so I'm washed up with Oliver, you understand? Are you listening to me?

895 WILLY [*at a loss*] Yeah, sure. If you hadn't flunked—

BIFF Flunked what? What're you talking about?

WILLY Don't blame everything on me! I didn't flunk math—you did! What pen?

HAPPY That was awful dumb, Biff, a pen like that is worth—

900 WILLY [*seeing the pen for the first time*] You took Oliver's pen?

BIFF [*weakening*] Dad, I just explained it to you.

WILLY You stole Bill Oliver's fountain pen!

BIFF I didn't exactly steal it! That's just what I've been explaining to you!

6. Grand Central Terminal, one of New York City's two main railroad stations.

HAPPY   He had it in his hand and just then Oliver walked in, so he got ner-
905 vous and stuck it in his pocket!

WILLY   My God, Biff!

BIFF   I never intended to do it, Dad!

OPERATOR'S VOICE   Standish Arms, good evening!

WILLY [*shouting*]   I'm not in my room!

910 BIFF [*frightened*]   Dad, what's the matter? [*He and* HAPPY *stand up.*]

OPERATOR   Ringing Mr. Loman for you!

WILLY   I'm not there, stop it!

BIFF [*horrified, gets down on one knee before* WILLY]   Dad, I'll make good, I'll
  make good. [WILLY *tries to get to his feet.* BIFF *holds him down.*] Sit down
915 now.

WILLY   No, you're no good, you're no good for anything.

BIFF   I am, Dad, I'll find something else, you understand? Now don't worry
  about anything. [*He holds up* WILLY's *face.*] Talk to me, Dad.

OPERATOR   Mr. Loman does not answer. Shall I page him?

920 WILLY [*attempting to stand, as though to rush and silence the* OPERATOR]   No,
  no, no!

HAPPY   He'll strike something, Pop.

WILLY   No, no . . .

BIFF [*desperately, standing over* WILLY]   Pop, listen! Listen to me! I'm telling
925 you something good. Oliver talked to his partner about the Florida idea.
  You listening? He—he talked to his partner, and he came to me . . . I'm
  going to be all right, you hear? Dad, listen to me, he said it was just a question of the amount!

WILLY   Then you . . . got it?

930 HAPPY   He's gonna be terrific, Pop!

WILLY [*trying to stand*]   Then you got it, haven't you? You got it! You got it!

BIFF [*agonized, holds* WILLY *down*]   No, no. Look, Pop. I'm supposed to have
  lunch with them tomorrow. I'm just telling you this so you'll know that I
  can still make an impression, Pop. And I'll make good somewhere, but I
935 can't go tomorrow, see?

WILLY   Why not? You simply—

BIFF   But the pen, Pop!

WILLY   You give it to him and tell him it was an oversight!

HAPPY   Sure, have lunch tomorrow!

940 BIFF   I can't say that—

WILLY   You were doing a crosswood puzzle and accidentally used his pen!

BIFF   Listen, kid, I took those balls years ago, now I walk in with his fountain
  pen? That clinches it, don't you see? I can't face him like that! I'll try
  elsewhere.

945 PAGE'S VOICE   Paging Mr. Loman!

WILLY   Don't you want to be anything?

BIFF   Pop, how can I go back?

WILLY   You don't want to be anything, is that what's behind it?

BIFF [*now angry at* WILLY *for not crediting his sympathy*]   Don't take it that
950 way! You think it was easy walking into that office after what I'd done to
  him? A team of horses couldn't have dragged me back to Bill Oliver!

WILLY   Then why'd you go?

BIFF   Why did I go? Why did I go! Look at you! Look at what's become of you!

PLALYS IN PERFORMANCE

HEDDA GABLER

Cate Blanchett in the title role of the Sydney Theatre Company's 2006 production of *Hedda Gabler* at the Brooklyn Academy of Music. © 2006 Richard Termine

Hedda Gabler is a role that most actresses dream of performing during their careers. What makes the character so appealing? At a glance, Hedda appears self-absorbed and intent on manipulating everyone around her out of sheer boredom. But she would not have endured as one of the most fascinating characters in dramatic literature if she were so easily explained. Just what exactly motivates her often destructive actions remains opaque, leaving room for great actresses to present their own interpretations.

Complex characters like Hedda Gabler, whose layers must be carefully uncovered in performance, are a hallmark of realism, a style of drama that emerged at the end of the nineteenth century. Realist drama seeks to reproduce the rich details of three-dimensional characters and their everyday lives. Henrik Ibsen, the "father of modern drama," was at the forefront of this development. He also paid particular attention to female roles because of his engagement with women's struggles and the various accommodations women were forced to make in order to survive the rigid strictures of late nineteenth-century Victorian society.

What are the strictures that Hedda rebels against? Is she a victim of a society that permits expression of her wild, passionate nature only by riding a horse or living vicariously through men? Or is she a case study in pathological behavior? Is she a woman whose only pleasure is derived from the manipulation and control of others? Is her need to control a counterbalance to the lack of control she has over her own life?

From the play's opening scene, it is evident that Hedda is suffocating under the weight of social convention and yearns to break free. Like a caged animal, she moves about the stage looking for an escape from the married life she has chosen; her disdain for Aunt Juliane is palpable, as is her disgust for George Tesman and his petty, academic "specialization." Judge Brack, with his detached sophistication, offers Hedda the possibility of an equally matched playmate. However, even this arrangement becomes intolerable once Brack blackmails Hedda with the facts surrounding Eilert Løvborg's death, and Hedda's complicity in that death gives Brack the upper hand in their intellectual contest. Only Løvborg, the brilliant but debauched visionary, had the passion and courage that Hedda so desperately craves for herself.

Actresses who play Hedda Gabler must embrace her as both victimizer and victim. Not only does she prey upon others, but she is preyed upon. Capturing these facets in performance requires a careful balancing act and is a challenge to which great actresses must rise.

———————

One of the most recent actresses to join the long list of Hedda interpreters is film star Cate Blanchett, in the Sydney Theatre Company's production at New York's Brooklyn Academy of Music in 2006. The production, as well as the lithe and luminous Blanchett, met with mixed reviews. While some critics praised Blanchett's physical energy, which clearly articulated Hedda's pent-up frustration, others remarked that her performance was "brittle" and "mannered" and did not fully explore Hedda's vulnerability. According to one reviewer, the actress did not provide anything for "an audience to identify or at least sympathize with."[1] Some of the production's problems were attributed to Andrew Upton's adaptation of the play. Although Ibsen uses the term "cold" to describe Hedda, Upton's version and Robyn Nevin's directing turned her into, as Les Gutman put it, a "bitch on wheels." It was the production's direction that drew the most criticism. Gutman, writing for *CurtainUp*, described it as "the most muddled *Hedda* I've experienced."[2] Ben Brantley's review for the *New York Times* remarked that "this production is possessed by the restlessness of artists determined to shake the dust off a familiar classic by applying the equivalent of a motorized rug beater."[3] Looking back at the

1. David Rooney, "Hedda Gabler," *Variety*, Mar. 2, 2006.
2. Les Gutman, "Hedda Gabler," *CurtainUp*, 2006, curtainup.com/heddabam.html (accessed 4/16/13).
3. Ben Brantley, "A Heroine in a Hurry, via Ibsen," *New York Times*, Mar. 3, 2006.

Director Ivo van Hove's 2004 production of *Hedda Gabler* for the New York Theatre Workshop, featuring Elizabeth Marvel in the title role. Photo © Joan Marcus

performance several years later, however, he came to a different conclusion, regarding Blanchett's interpretation of Hedda as full of "energy and audacity and, yes, fearlessness."

In contrast to Nevin's direction, Dutch director Ivo van Hove's 2004 production for the New York Theatre Workshop received nearly unanimous praise. The set was updated to a contemporary loft, and Hedda was clad in a pink satin slip for most of the show. By modernizing the play, van Hove was able to find "a little bit of Hedda in all of us."[4]

Although van Hove's Hedda did not have the star power of Cate Blanchett, the versatile actress Elizabeth Marvel provided a powerful interpretation of the character. Rather than a caged panther waiting to pounce on her next victim, Marvel's Hedda vacillated between desperate woman and spoiled brat. She was the personification of depression as she alternated between languid toying with and maniacal pounding on the piano. The piano and her father's pistols were the only vestiges of her higher aspirations in this otherwise mundane atmosphere.

The other characters were given a fresh spin as well. Tesman was less the nerd and more the boyish innocent; Aunt Juliane was no shrinking violet; and Judge Brack was a sadistic adversary. Contrary to Ibsen's last line, "People just don't act that way!" Marvel and van Hove's production seems to be saying that we all "act that way" to a degree. **M.P.**

---

4. Charles Isherwood, "A Hedda for Self-Absorbed Modern Times," *New York Times*, Sept. 22, 2004.

A STREETCAR NAMED DESIRE

The stage history of Tennessee Williams's *A Streetcar Named Desire* is dominated by director Elia Kazan's 1947 Broadway production, which ran for 855 performances with the relatively unknown Marlon Brando as Stanley Kowalski, Jessica Tandy as Blanche DuBois, Kim Hunter as Stella Kowalski, and Karl Malden as Mitch. Featuring Jo Mielziner's stage design and the jazzy/bluesy music of Alex North, the production was characterized by a lyrical, occasionally jarring blend of realism and expressionism, a style that offers external representations of internal states of mind. The same team collaborated on the 1951 Warner Bros. film of *Streetcar*, with Vivien Leigh (who had starred in the London stage premiere) replacing Tandy as Blanche. The film, which was nominated for twelve Academy Awards and has been seen by many more viewers than all the theater productions combined, reinforced the cultural status of Williams's play. Much of the play's celebrity resulted from the iconic portrayals of its principal actors. Brooding and emotionally explosive, Brando's Stanley was a figure of imposing, confident sexuality. Clad in a tight white T-shirt or stripped to his waist during certain scenes, he exhibited a physical magnetism that allowed him to dominate those around him. He was certainly unrefined—eating his dinner from his plate with his fingers in scene 2 and delivering his lines throughout the play in a half-mumbled, half-slurred manner—but he proved a cunning adversary when threatened.

Tandy's Blanche, by contrast, was high-bred, fragile, and sensitive. Struggling on the edge of breakdown, she was clearly a woman afraid of her surroundings and her own inner turmoil. While many reviewers praised her performance, others felt that the pathetic tone she established for her character shifted the audience's sympathies disproportionately to Stanley. When Leigh took over the role for the film version, her stronger, more resourceful Blanche matched Brando's Stanley in intensity and force of will. She flirted shamelessly with Stanley, but retained her dignity, assertiveness, and intrinsic theatricality even as her underlying panic increased. The fact that Leigh, a British actor, had also portrayed Scarlett O'Hara in the 1939 film *Gone with the Wind* gave her performance of Blanche additional resonance—as if the cinema's most famous southern belle was trying, twelve years later, to maintain the performance of aristocratic youth against the ravages of time, change, and loss of innocence.

Subsequent *Streetcars* have had to contend with the overwhelming influence of the original stage production and the film. Although many fine productions of Williams's play appeared in the decades immediately following the Broadway, it is arguably not until recent years that we have seen transformative new productions of *Streetcar*. One of the most remarkable of these was the 2009 Sydney Theatre Company production, which starred Joel Edgerton as Stanley and Cate Blanchett as Blanche. Under the direction of Swedish actor and film director Liv Ullmann, this *Streetcar* focused on the play's poetic and psychological complexities. The

Jessica Tandy, who originated the role of Blanche DuBois on Broadway in 1947, balanced Blanche's selfishness with her sympathetic qualities. Marlon Brando's Stanley set the standard for all subsequent Stanleys. Photo © John Springer Collection / Getty Images

Cate Blanchett as Blanche DuBois and Joel Edgerton as Stanley Kowalski in the Sydney Theatre Company's 2009 production of *A Streetcar Named Desire*. Photo © 2009 Richard Termine

stripped-down setting reinforced this focus. Gone were the diaphanous walls that let in the sights and sounds of New Orleans and blurred the line between reality and Blanche's disintegrating psyche; the only exterior fixture was the fire escape leading up to the Hubbells' second-story apartment, and the building itself was constructed from black cinder block. The interior of the Kowalskis' apartment was cramped and dingy. Freed in this way from the scenic lyricism that marked earlier *Streetcars*, the Sydney production focused on the characters and their relationships. In a widely praised performance, Blanchett portrayed Blanche as a haunted figure who marshals her remaining dignity in the interactions that bring about her collapse. The production opened with Blanche sitting nervously on the side of the stage and ended with her being led off dressed only in her slip. Although Blanche's heartbreaking downfall was at the center of this production, Blanchett also brought out the humor in some of Blanche's lines as well as the sexuality that charges her interactions with men. In one of the many moments that captured the psychological and sexual stakes among Williams's characters, Blanchett sat on a bedroom side table, legs propped defiantly and seductively on the floor, blocking Edgerton's path to the radio. Reviewer Adam Green described Edgerton's performance: "With his braying laugh and wailing cry, this Stanley is an overgrown boy whose childish insistence on getting his way and very grown-up strength make him a dangerous opponent."[1] While Edgerton's athletic and youthful Stanley may have lacked Brando's magnetism, he was a formidable figure nonetheless; broad-shouldered and compact, he became the epitome of remorseless, predatory resentment as the play went on.

In 2012 Emily Mann directed a multiracial cast that included African American actors Blair Underwood as Stanley and Nicole Ari Parker as Blanche in a Broadway revival of *A Streetcar Named Desire*. References to Stanley's Polish background were cut from the script in order to facilitate this casting. This production stressed the vibrancy and sexual energy of Williams's New Orleans. The play's skeletal wooden set was bathed at times in blue and rose light, and the production opened with a festive yet haunting jazz funeral. Under Mann's direction,

Stanley (Blair Underwood) confronts Blanche (Nicole Ari Parker) in the 2012 Broadhurst Theatre production of *A Streetcar Named Desire*, directed by Emily Mann. Photo © Ken Howard

1. Adam Green, rev. of the Sydney Theatre Company production of *A Streetcar Named Desire*, *Vogue*, Nov. 3, 2009.

the actors engaged in physical contact at every opportunity, and Daphne Rubin-Vega's Stella was sensual and energetic. Underwood's physically imposing Stanley was cocky and aggressive, and he asserted his sexuality with an intensity bordering on violence. Parker's Blanche had a confidence of her own; used to getting her way with men, she displayed a sharp wit and obvious sense of manipulation. Reviewer Elisabeth Vincentelli described her as "[t]all and lithe . . . less fading flower than resilient reed."[2] While this portrayal brought out the shrewd survivor in Blanche's character, it also made her breakdown at the play's end more shocking than tragic. Not surprisingly, some reviewers felt that her performance—and Mann's production as a whole—sacrificed psychological complexity for emotion and sensuality.

S.G.

2. Elisabeth Vincentelli, rev. of the Broadhurst Theatre production of *A Streetcar Named Desire*, *New York Post*, Apr. 22, 2012.

A RAISIN IN THE SUN

When *A Raisin in the Sun* opened at the Ethel Barrymore Theatre on March 11, 1959, it was hailed by audiences and critics alike. The production, which starred Sidney Poitier, Claudia McNeil, Ruby Dee, and Diana Sands, ran for 530 performances, won the New York Drama Critics Circle Award for Best Play, and formed the basis for the 1961 Columbia Pictures film. Appearing as it did at the height of the United States civil rights movement, the play's African American perspective on life in segregated America dominated reviews and initiated other discussions of its significance. Reviewer Harold Clurman praised Hansberry's portrait of "the aspirations, anxieties, ambitions, and contradictory pressures" facing urban African Americans, and other reviewers similarly hailed its truthfulness to African American experience and its complex characterizations.[1] Some critics felt that Hansberry's portrayal of aspiration and courage was universal rather than racially specific, implying—as one critic stated—that the characters of *Raisin* were "real people" who only happened to be "colored people."[2] Such responses contributed to the opinion of some later commentators that Hansberry's play was "safe" for white audiences because its characters aspired to lives just like theirs.

This charge, which was made by writers such as playwright Amiri Baraka, reflected the emergence of more radically confrontational African American political and artistic currents during the 1960s. It also reflected the fact that some

1. Harold Clurman, rev. of the 1959 Ethel Barrymore Theatre production of *A Raisin in the Sun*, *The Nation*, Apr. 4, 1959.
2. Henry Hewes, rev. of the 1959 Ethel Barrymore Theatre production of *A Raisin in the Sun*, *Saturday Review*, Apr. 4, 1959.

Phylicia Rashad as Lena Younger, Audra McDonald as Ruth Younger, and Sanaa Nathan as Beneatha Younger in the 2004 production of *A Raisin in the Sun* at New York's Royale Theater. Photo © Joan Marcus

of Hansberry's most pointed attacks on American racism were omitted from the Broadway production and the 1961 film. This material was restored when *A Raisin in the Sun* was revived in 1986 by New York's Roundabout Theatre Company. With the distance afforded by twenty-seven years and the omitted lines and scenes returned to the script, Hansberry's passionate account of the African American spirit combatting the assaults on its dignity rang clearly. Baraka, for one, was moved to rescind his earlier criticism, admitting that he and others who rallied to the call of Malcolm X "missed the essence of the work—that Hansberry had created a family engaged in the same class struggle and ideological struggle as existed in the movement itself and among the people."[3] The continuing power of Hansberry's play was underscored in the 1989 American Playhouse television production, which was based on the Roundabout production and featured Danny Glover's electrifying performance as Walter Lee Younger.

With its psychological complexity, emotional range, and rich dialogue, *A Raisin in the Sun* has been a showcase for established and aspiring African American actors. From the play's original cast through the performers of the present century, *Raisin* has rewarded outstanding ensemble acting as well as nuanced individual performances. In return, actors and directors have offered changing interpretations of one of the most frequently produced plays of the last sixty years. Two contemporary revivals directed by Kenny Leon, one of the country's leading African American directors, demonstrate the different ways in which Hansberry's master-

3. Amiri Baraka, "A Braver Play Than Some of Us Knew," *Los Angeles Times*, March 22, 1987.

piece has been given theatrical life. The first production, mounted at New York's Royale Theatre for the play's fortieth anniversary, was noted for the director's decision to cast rap artist Sean ("Diddy") Combs as Walter Lee and actors Phylicia Rashad, Audra McDonald, and Sanaa Nathan as Lena, Ruth, and Beneatha. In choosing Combs, Leon clearly intended to draw a connection between Walter Lee's rage against racial inequality and the assertiveness of a contemporary urban generation, but the choice of an untrained actor proved to be a liability in the opinion of many who saw the production. Combs's performance, reviewers felt, failed to capture the energy and emotional variety of Hansberry's character. During the scene in which the family learns that Walter has lost the money his mother entrusted him with, Combs sat dejectedly with his head between his knees instead of performing his character's anguish. What distinguished the 2004 revival were its female actors, particularly Rashad and McDonald, both of whom received Tony Awards for their performances. Rashad's matriarch carried a lifetime of experiences, and as she navigated the play's emotional terrain she displayed spiritedness, faith, and heartbreak in equal measure. McDonald conveyed a similar range in her performance of Ruth. Sassy yet deeply in love with her discounted husband, she struggled against weariness and disappointment; one reviewer described her as "a life force on the verge of extinction."[4]

When Leon returned to *A Raisin in the Sun* ten years later for a production at the Broadway theater where it had premiered fifty-five years earlier, he addressed the 2004 production's imbalance between Walter Lee and the women who surround him by casting Denzel Washington as the play's male lead. While Washington was fifty-nine, a quarter century older than Hansberry's male lead, the age discrepancy receded as soon as he took the stage. Washington played Walker Lee with boyish charm and an easy casualness that erupted in bitterness when his plans for a new life came crashing down on him. In the role of Ruth, Sophie Okonedo countered his energy with an affecting performance of physical and emotional exhaustion. In the play's opening moments, for example, Okonedo stood motionless against the kitchen counter, summoning the resources to get through another day. LaTanya Richardson Jackson portrayed Lena's sharper edges—an irritability that accompanied her love for her children, for example—while Anika Noni Rose was widely praised for her energetic, youthful performance as Beneatha. What most impressed reviewers about this revival, though, was Leon's ability to integrate its acting performances into a collective accomplishment. As one critic wrote, "Denzel Washington is the star attraction, but it's the harmonious balance of an impeccably matched ensemble that makes Kenny Leon's lovingly staged revival of *A Raisin in the Sun* so alive with authentic feeling."[5]

4. Ben Brantley, rev. of the 2004 Royale Theatre production of *A Raisin in the Sun, New York Times,* Apr. 27, 2004.
5. David Rooney, rev. of the 2014 Ethel Barrymore Theatre production of *A Raisin in the Sun, Hollywood Reporter,* Apr. 3, 2014.

Denzel Washington as Walter Lee Younger in the 2014 production of *A Raisin in the Sun* at New York's Ethel Barrymore Theatre. Photo © Sara Krulwich / The New York Times / Redux

ANGELS IN AMERICA

The kind of theater in which a play is produced can have a significant impact on audience response. Different theatrical spaces not only make different stagings possible, they also affect the audience's sense of intimacy with, or distance from, the action. Black box theaters, where the audience may be seated just inches from the actors, are frequently used for plays with smaller casts and more modest sets, while plays with greater technical demands may require a proscenium stage. Yet such creative considerations must often give way to even more essential production issues, specifically financial ones. Indeed, the costs of presenting and the potential revenue to be earned from live theater can be *the* determining factors for where a work is produced, or if it can be produced at all. Theater companies, whether not-for-profit or commercial, can rarely afford to take major financial risks, especially with new scripts that have no track record of audience success. Tony Kushner's journey to Broadway with *Angels in America, Part I: Millennium Approaches* exemplifies the complexities of new play development for an emerging playwright and also illustrates how dynamic creative teams can help a play succeed in very different kinds of theaters.

Before *Angels* saw production of any kind, the script went through an extensive developmental process of readings and workshops, in partnership with the New York Theatre Workshop, San Francisco's Eureka Theatre, and the Mark Taper Forum in Los Angeles. According to Bruce Weber, writing for the *New York Times*, the Taper alone spent $80,000 for its 1990 workshop performances;[1] the Eureka undertook seventeen readings of the complete work, which helped Kushner refine the play's second part, *Perestroika*. The Taper workshop, attended by Richard Eyre, artistic director of England's Royal National Theatre, led to the London production in January 1992. The overwhelming success of *Angels* at this important theater heightened the interest of New York producers, for whom the play now appeared commercially viable for a Broadway run. Kushner then had to decide whether to have his New York opening first in Greenwich Village at the not-for-profit Public Theater, amid the gay community so central to the play, or to opt directly for Broadway. Kushner chose the latter, in order to make his work available to an even wider audience and to secure the kind of exposure and creative support he felt the commercial producers could offer. The Broadway production was capitalized at $2.2 million; its weekly operating costs were about $180,000. Kushner insisted, however, that reduced-price tickets be made available for audiences who might not otherwise be able to see the show. Thus the producers knew that they would have to secure a long run even to recoup their initial investment. Ultimately, with a movie sale and touring revenues, on top of sus-

1. Bruce Weber, "Angels' Angels," *New York Times Magazine*, Apr. 25, 1993.

Sean Chapman as Prior and Nancy Crane as the Angel in the 1992 London premiere of *Angels in America* at the Royal National Theatre. Photo © John Haynes / Lebrecht Music & Arts

tained audience ticket demand following its triumph at the Tony Awards,[2] *Angels* became a financial success.

Significantly, different teams of directors and designers worked on each of the productions, bringing distinct visions to each staging. The fact that the play worked so effectively in such varied locations as London's Cottesloe Theatre (essentially a black box space) and Broadway's Walter Kerr Theatre (a proscenium space that seats almost a thousand) speaks to the collective talents of these artists, all of whom helped realize the power of Kushner's script in different ways. Some of the play's challenges include how to represent its multiple locations and how to accomplish its frequent scene shifts without halting the action or narrative momentum. At the Cottesloe, director Declan Donnellan and scenic designer Nick Ormerod used a large background image of stars and stripes to symbolize America. For critic Michael Billington of the *Guardian*, their staging achieved "a breathtaking fluidity" as the actors simply moved essential furniture pieces and props on and off to maintain the flow.[3] In the climactic final moment, according to Frank Rich of the *New York Times*, "Old Glory explodes in a burst of lightning" as the Angel crashes in.[4] At the Mark Taper Forum, director Oskar Eustis and scenic designer John Conklin "sought a unifying image that would evoke Americana." As Arnold Aronson explains in his discussion of the design, they installed a "façade of a house that combined elements of a New England meetinghouse with Jeffersonian classicism" against the theater's back wall. Yet, as Aronson further details, this symbolic amalgam of American architecture also included "a jagged split down the center" to represent "'an ideal that was cracked.' The Angel flew in through this crack in the wall, rather than through the ceiling, which did not exist in this production." On Broadway, however, director George C. Wolfe and scenic designer Robin Wagner "opted for neutrality rather than visual metaphor." For Aronson, "unity was achieved by the proscenium arch itself and ever-changing configurations of black velour flats in chrome frames."[5] This creative team was also able to utilize the technological capabilities of a Broadway house to enhance the show's pacing. The theater had a winch system that allowed platforms with set pieces "to glide on and off the stage with seeming ease as other units flew in or out. . . . Action or dialogue could start as one wagon rolled on while another rolled off." Sufficient fly space made the Angel's crash through the Walter Kerr stage ceiling truly spectacular.

Throughout this development and production process in the United States, several key cast members remained in place: Stephen Spinella as Prior Walter, Kathleen Chalfant as Hannah Pitt, and Ellen McLaughlin as the Angel. The

2. *Millennium Approaches* won both the Pulitzer Prize for Drama and the Tony Award for Best Play in 1993, among numerous other awards.

3. Michael Billington, "Nation Built on Guilt," *Guardian*, Jan. 25, 1992.

4. Frank Rich, "The Reaganite Ethos, with Roy Cohn as a Dark Metaphor," *New York Times*, Mar. 5, 1992.

5. Arnold Aronson, "Design for *Angels in America*: Envisioning the Millennium," *Approaching the Millennium: Essays on "Angels in America*," eds. Deborah R. Geis and Steven F. Kruger (Ann Arbor: University of Michigan Press, 1997).

The 1993 Broadway debut of *Angels in America*. Photo © Joan Marcus

continuity provided by these actors must surely have anchored the productions and contributed markedly to their success in so many different theaters and with so many creative teams. Yet some critics who saw the play in both small and large venues also expressed a preference for the simpler productions on smaller stages, which made the theatrical experience more immediate. Michael Feingold of the *Village Voice* felt Wolfe's production exuded "flat, neat efficiency."[6] And Frank Rich clearly preferred the National's version to that of the Taper, which he deemed "plodding."[7] Yet, despite such quibbles, critics unanimously championed Kushner's writing and the scope of the drama. As Malcolm Rutherford of London's *Financial Times* concluded, "You should see this play, for even if you loathe it, you will love discussing it afterwards."[8]

J.E.G.

6. Michael Feingold, "Building the Monolith," *Village Voice*, May 18, 1993.
7. Frank Rich, "Marching out of the Closet, into History," *New York Times*, Nov. 10, 1992.
8. Malcolm Rutherford, "Arts: A Drama out of a Crisis," *Financial Times*, Jan. 25, 1992.

[*Off left,* THE WOMAN *laughs.*]

WILLY   Biff, you're going to go to that lunch tomorrow, or—

955   BIFF   I can't go. I've got no appointment!

HAPPY   Biff, for . . . !

WILLY   Are you spiting me?

BIFF   Don't take it that way! Goddammit!

WILLY   [*strikes* BIFF *and falters away from the table*]   You rotten little louse! Are

960   you spiting me?

THE WOMAN   Someone's at the door, Willy!

BIFF   I'm no good, can't you see what I am?

HAPPY   [*separating them*]   Hey, you're in a restaurant! Now cut it out, both of
you! [*The girls enter.*] Hello, girls, sit down.

[THE WOMAN *laughs, off left.*]

965   MISS FORSYTHE   I guess we might as well. This is Letta.

THE WOMAN   Willy, are you going to wake up?

BIFF   [*ignoring* WILLY]   How're ya, miss, sit down. What do you drink?

MISS FORSYTHE   Letta might not be able to stay long.

LETTA   I gotta get up very early tomorrow. I got jury duty. I'm so excited!

970   Were you fellows ever on a jury?

BIFF   No, but I been in front of them! [*The girls laugh.*] This is my father.

LETTA   Isn't he cute? Sit down with us, Pop.

HAPPY   Sit him down, Biff!

BIFF   [*going to him*]   Come on, slugger, drink us under the table. To hell with

975   it! Come on, sit down, pal.

[*On* BIFF's *last insistence,* WILLY *is about to sit.*]

THE WOMAN   [*now urgently*]   Willy, are you going to answer the door!

[THE WOMAN's *call pulls* WILLY *back. He starts right, befuddled.*]

BIFF   Hey, where are you going?

WILLY   Open the door.

BIFF   The door?

980   WILLY   The washroom . . . the door . . . where's the door?

BIFF   [*leading* WILLY *to the left*]   Just go straight down.

[WILLY *moves left.*]

THE WOMAN   Willy, Willy, are you going to get up, get up, get up, get up?

[WILLY *exits left.*]

LETTA   I think it's sweet you bring your daddy along.

MISS FORSYTHE   Oh, he isn't really your father!

985   BIFF   [*at left, turning to her resentfully*]   Miss Forsythe, you've just seen a
prince walk by. A fine, troubled prince. A hard-working, unappreciated
prince. A pal, you understand? A good companion. Always for his boys.

LETTA   That's so sweet.

HAPPY   Well, girls, what's the program? We're wasting time. Come on, Biff.

990   Gather round. Where would you like to go?

BIFF   Why don't you do something for him?

HAPPY   Me!

BIFF   Don't you give a damn for him, Hap?

HAPPY   What're you talking about? I'm the one who—

995   BIFF   I sense it, you don't give a good goddam about him. [*He takes the
rolled-up hose from his pocket and puts it on the table in front of* HAPPY.]

Look what I found in the cellar, for Christ's sake. How can you bear to let it go on?

HAPPY Me? Who goes away? Who runs off and—

BIFF Yeah, but he doesn't mean anything to you. You could help him—I can't! Don't you understand what I'm talking about? He's going to kill himself, don't you know that?

HAPPY Don't I know it! Me!

BIFF Hap, help him! Jesus . . . help him . . . Help me, help me, I can't bear to look at his face! [*Ready to weep, he hurries out, up right.*]

HAPPY [*starting after him*] Where are you going?

MISS FORSYTHE What's he so mad about?

HAPPY Come on, girls, we'll catch up with him.

MISS FORSYTHE [*as Happy pushes her out*] Say, I don't like that temper of his!

HAPPY He's just a little overstrung, he'll be all right!

WILLY [*off left, as* THE WOMAN *laughs*] Don't answer! Don't answer!

LETTA Don't you want to tell your father—

HAPPY No, that's not my father. He's just a guy. Come on, we'll catch Biff, and, honey, we're going to paint this town! Stanley, where's the check! Hey, Stanley!

[*They exit.* STANLEY *looks toward left.*]

STANLEY [*calling to* HAPPY *indignantly*] Mr. Loman! Mr. Loman!

[STANLEY *picks up a chair and follows them off. Knocking is heard off left.* THE WOMAN *enters, laughing.* WILLY *follows her. She is in a black slip; he is buttoning his shirt. Raw, sensuous music accompanies their speech.*]

WILLY Will you stop laughing? Will you stop?

THE WOMAN Aren't you going to answer the door? He'll wake the whole hotel.

WILLY I'm not expecting anybody.

THE WOMAN Whyn't you have another drink, honey, and stop being so damn self-centered?

WILLY I'm so lonely.

THE WOMAN You know you ruined me, Willy? From now on, whenever you come to the office, I'll see that you go right through to the buyers. No waiting at my desk any more, Willy. You ruined me.

WILLY That's nice of you to say that.

THE WOMAN Gee, you are self-centered! Why so sad? You are the saddest, self-centeredest soul I ever did see-saw. [*She laughs. He kisses her.*] Come on inside, drummer[7] boy. It's silly to be dressing in the middle of the night. [*As knocking is heard*] Aren't you going to answer the door?

WILLY They're knocking on the wrong door.

THE WOMAN But I felt the knocking. And he heard us talking in here. Maybe the hotel's on fire!

WILLY [*his terror rising*] It's a mistake.

THE WOMAN Then tell him to go away!

WILLY There's nobody there.

THE WOMAN It's getting on my nerves, Willy. There's somebody standing out there and it's getting on my nerves!

7. A commercial traveler, a salesman.

WILLY [*pushing her away from him*]   All right, stay in the bathroom here,
1040   and don't come out. I think there's a law in Massachusetts about it,[8] so
don't come out. It may be that new room clerk. He looked very mean.
So don't come out. It's a mistake, there's no fire.

> [*The knocking is heard again. He takes a few steps away from her, and
> she vanishes into the wing. The light follows him, and now he is facing
> YOUNG BIFF, who carries a suitcase. Biff steps toward him. The music is
> gone.*]

BIFF   Why didn't you answer?

WILLY   Biff! What are you doing in Boston?

1045   BIFF   Why didn't you answer? I've been knocking for five minutes, I called
you on the phone—

WILLY   I just heard you. I was in the bathroom and had the door shut. Did
anything happen home?

BIFF   Dad—I let you down.

1050   WILLY   What do you mean?

BIFF   Dad . . .

WILLY   Biffo, what's this about? [*Putting his arm around* BIFF] Come on, let's
go downstairs and get you a malted.

BIFF   Dad, I flunked math.

1055   WILLY   Not for the term?

BIFF   The term. I haven't got enough credits to graduate.

WILLY   You mean to say Bernard wouldn't give you the answers?

BIFF   He did, he tried, but I only got a sixty-one.

WILLY   And they wouldn't give you four points?

1060   BIFF   Birnbaum refused absolutely. I begged him, Pop, but he won't give me
those points. You gotta talk to him before they close the school. Because if
he saw the kind of man you are, and you just talked to him in your way, I'm
sure he'd come through for me. The class came right before practice, see,
and I didn't go enough. Would you talk to him? He'd like you, Pop. You
1065   know the way you could talk.

WILLY   You're on. We'll drive right back.

BIFF   Oh, Dad, good work! I'm sure he'll change it for you!

WILLY   Go downstairs and tell the clerk I'm checkin' out. Go right down.

BIFF   Yes, sir! See, the reason he hates me, Pop—one day he was late for
1070   class so I got up at the blackboard and imitated him. I crossed my eyes and
talked with a lithp.

WILLY [*laughing*]   You did? The kids like it?

BIFF   They nearly died laughing!

WILLY   Yeah? What'd you do?

1075   BIFF   The thquare root of thixty twee is . . . [WILLY *bursts out laughing;* BIFF
joins him.] And in the middle of it he walked in!

> [WILLY *laughs and* THE WOMAN *joins in offstage.*]

WILLY [*without hesitation*]   Hurry downstairs and—

BIFF   Somebody in there?

WILLY   No, that was next door.

> [THE WOMAN *laughs offstage.*]

---

8. That is, adultery, which is a felony in Massachusetts, though this law was rarely enforced even
in the 1940s.

1080 BIFF   Somebody got in your bathroom!

WILLY   No, it's the next room, there's a party—

THE WOMAN [*enters, laughing. She lisps this*]   Can I come in? There's something in the bathtub, Willy, and it's moving!

[WILLY *looks at* BIFF, *who is staring open-mouthed and horrified at* THE
WOMAN.]

WILLY   Ah—you better go back to your room. They must be finished painting
1085   by now. They're painting her room so I let her take a shower here. Go back,
go back . . . [*He pushes her.*]

THE WOMAN [*resisting*]   But I've got to get dressed, Willy, I can't—

WILLY   Get out of here! Go back, go back . . . [*Suddenly striving for the ordinary*] This is Miss Francis, Biff, she's a buyer. They're painting her room.
1090   Go back, Miss Francis, go back . . .

THE WOMAN   But my clothes, I can't go out naked in the hall!

WILLY [*pushing her offstage*]   Get outa here! Go back, go back!

[BIFF *slowly sits down on his suitcase as the argument continues
offstage.*]

THE WOMAN   Where's my stockings? You promised me stockings, Willy!

WILLY   I have no stockings here!

1095 THE WOMAN   You had two boxes of size nine sheers for me, and I want them!

WILLY   Here, for God's sake, will you get outa here!

THE WOMAN [*enters holding a box of stockings*]   I just hope there's nobody in
the hall. That's all I hope. [*To* BIFF] Are you football or baseball?

BIFF   Football.

1100 THE WOMAN [*angry, humiliated*]   That's me too. G'night. [*She snatches her
clothes from* WILLY, *and walks out.*]

WILLY [*after a pause*]   Well, better get going. I want to get to the school first
thing in the morning. Get my suits out of the closet. I'll get my valise. [BIFF
doesn't move.] What's the matter? [BIFF *remains motionless, tears falling.*]
She's a buyer. Buys for J. H. Simmons. She lives down the hall—they're
1105   painting. You don't imagine—[*He breaks off. After a pause*] Now listen, pal,
she's just a buyer. She sees merchandise in her room and they have to keep
it looking just so . . . [*Pause. Assuming command*] All right, get my suits.
[BIFF *doesn't move.*] Now stop crying and do as I say. I gave you an order.
Biff, I gave you an order! Is that what you do when I give you an order?
1110   How dare you cry! [*Putting his arm around Biff*] Now look, Biff, when you
grow up you'll understand about these things. You mustn't—you mustn't
overemphasize a thing like this. I'll see Birnbaum first thing in the
morning.

BIFF   Never mind.

1115 WILLY [*getting down beside* BIFF]   Never mind! He's going to give you those
points. I'll see to it.

BIFF   He wouldn't listen to you.

WILLY   He certainly will listen to me. You need those points for the U. of
Virginia.

1120 BIFF   I'm not going there.

WILLY   Heh? If I can't get him to change that mark you'll make it up in summer school. You've got all summer to—

BIFF [*his weeping breaking from him*]   Dad . . .

WILLY [*infected by it*]   Oh, my boy . . .

1125   BIFF   Dad . . .

WILLY   She's nothing to me, Biff. I was lonely, I was terribly lonely.

BIFF   You—you gave her Mama's stockings! [*His tears break through and he rises to go.*]

WILLY [*grabbing for* BIFF]   I gave you an order!

BIFF   Don't touch me, you—liar!

1130   WILLY   Apologize for that!

BIFF   You fake! You phony little fake! You fake! [*Overcome, he turns quickly and weeping fully goes out with his suitcase.* WILLY *is left on the floor on his knees.*]

WILLY   I gave you an order! Biff, come back here or I'll beat you! Come back here! I'll whip you!

[STANLEY *comes quickly in from the right and stands in front of* WILLY.]

WILLY [*shouts at Stanley*]   I gave you an order . . .

1135   STANLEY   Hey, let's pick it up, pick it up, Mr. Loman. [*He helps* WILLY *to his feet.*] Your boys left with the chippies.[9] They said they'll see you home.

[*A second waiter watches some distance away.*]

WILLY   But we were supposed to have dinner together.

[*Music is heard,* WILLY's *theme.*]

STANLEY   Can you make it?

WILLY   I'll—sure, I can make it. [*Suddenly concerned about his clothes*] Do

1140   I—I look all right?

STANLEY   Sure, you look all right. [*He flicks a speck off* WILLY's *lapel.*]

WILLY   Here—here's a dollar.

STANLEY   Oh, your son paid me. It's all right.

WILLY [*putting it in* STANLEY's *hand*]   No, take it. You're a good boy.

1145   STANLEY   Oh, no, you don't have to . . .

WILLY   Here—here's some more, I don't need it any more. [*After a slight pause*] Tell me—is there a seed store in the neighborhood?

STANLEY   Seeds? You mean like to plant?

[*As* WILLY *turns,* STANLEY *slips the money back into his jacket pocket.*]

WILLY   Yes. Carrots, peas . . .

1150   STANLEY   Well, there's hardware stores on Sixth Avenue, but it may be too late now.

WILLY [*anxiously*]   Oh, I'd better hurry, I've got to get some seeds. [*He starts off to the right.*] I've got to get some seeds, right away. Nothing's planted. I don't have a thing in the ground.

[WILLY *hurries out as the light goes down.* STANLEY *moves over to the right after him, watches him off. The other waiter has been staring at* WILLY.]

1155   STANLEY [*to the waiter*]   Well, whatta you looking at?

[*The waiter picks up the chairs and moves off right.* STANLEY *takes the table and follows him. The light fades on this area. There is a long pause, the sound of the flute coming over. The light gradually rises on the kitchen, which is empty.* HAPPY *appears at the door of the house, followed by* BIFF. HAPPY *is carrying a large bunch of long-stemmed roses. He enters the kitchen, looks around for* LINDA. *Not seeing her, he turns to* BIFF, *who is just outside the house door, and makes a gesture with his hands, indicating "Not here, I guess." He looks into the living room and freezes.*]

---

9. Tramps, prostitutes.

Inside, LINDA, *unseen, is seated,* WILLY's *coat on her lap. She rises ominously and quietly and moves toward* HAPPY, *who backs up into the kitchen, afraid.*]

HAPPY   Hey, what're you doing up? [LINDA *says nothing but moves toward him implacably.*] Where's Pop? [*He keeps backing to the right, and now* LINDA *is in full view in the doorway to the living room.*] Is he sleeping?

LINDA   Where were you?

1160   HAPPY [*trying to laugh it off*]   We met two girls, Mom, very fine types. Here, we brought you some flowers. [*Offering them to her*] Put them in your room, Ma.

[*She knocks them to the floor at* BIFF's *feet. He has now come inside and closed the door behind him. She stares at* BIFF, *silent.*]

HAPPY   Now what'd you do that for? Mom, I want you to have some flowers—

LINDA [*cutting* HAPPY *off, violently to* BIFF]   Don't you care whether he lives
1165   or dies?

HAPPY [*going to the stairs*]   Come upstairs, Biff.

BIFF [*with a flare of disgust, to* HAPPY]   Go away from me! [*To* LINDA] What do you mean, lives or dies? Nobody's dying around here, pal.

LINDA   Get out of my sight! Get out of here!

1170   BIFF   I wanna see the boss.

LINDA   You're not going near him!

BIFF   Where is he? [*He moves into the living room and* LINDA *follows.*]

LINDA [*shouting after* BIFF]   You invite him for dinner. He looks forward to it all day—[BIFF *appears in his parents' bedroom, looks around, and exits.*]—
1175   and then you desert him there. There's no stranger you'd do that to!

HAPPY   Why? He had a swell time with us. Listen, when I—[LINDA *comes back into the kitchen.*]—desert him I hope I don't outlive the day!

LINDA   Get out of here!

HAPPY   Now look, Mom . . .

1180   LINDA   Did you have to go to women tonight? You and your lousy rotten whores!

[BIFF *reenters the kitchen.*]

HAPPY   Mom, all we did was follow Biff around trying to cheer him up! [*To* BIFF] Boy, what a night you gave me!

LINDA   Get out of here, both of you, and don't come back! I don't want you
1185   tormenting him any more. Go on now, get your things together! [*To* BIFF] You can sleep in his apartment. [*She starts to pick up the flowers and stops herself.*] Pick up this stuff, I'm not your maid any more. Pick it up, you bum, you!

[HAPPY *turns his back to her in refusal.* BIFF *slowly moves over and gets down on his knees, picking up the flowers.*]

LINDA   You're a pair of animals! Not one, not another living soul would have
1190   had the cruelty to walk out on that man in a restaurant!

BIFF [*not looking at her*]   Is that what he said?

LINDA   He didn't have to say anything. He was so humiliated he nearly limped when he came in.

HAPPY   But, Mom, he had a great time with us—

1195   BIFF [*cutting him off violently*]   Shut up!

[*Without another word,* HAPPY *goes upstairs.*]

LINDA   You! You didn't even go in to see if he was all right!

BIFF [*still on the floor in front of* LINDA, *the flowers in his hand; with self-loathing*] No. Didn't. Didn't do a damned thing. How do you like that, heh? Left him babbling in a toilet.

LINDA You louse. You . . .

1200 BIFF Now you hit it on the nose! [*He gets up, throws the flowers in the waste-basket.*] The scum of the earth, and you're looking at him!

LINDA Get out of here!

BIFF I gotta talk to the boss, Mom. Where is he?

LINDA You're not going near him. Get out of this house!

1205 BIFF [*with absolute assurance, determination*] No. We're gonna have an abrupt conversation, him and me.

LINDA You're not talking to him!

[*Hammering is heard from outside the house, off right.* BIFF *turns toward the noise.*]

LINDA [*suddenly pleading*] Will you please leave him alone?

BIFF What's he doing out there?

1210 LINDA He's planting the garden!

BIFF [*quietly*] Now? Oh, my God!

[BIFF *moves outside,* LINDA *following. The light dies down on them and comes up on the center of the apron as* WILLY *walks into it. He is carrying a flashlight, a hoe, and a handful of seed packets. He raps the top of the hoe sharply to fix it firmly, and then moves to the left, measuring off the distance with his foot. He holds the flashlight to look at the seed packets, reading off the instructions. He is in the blue of night.*]

WILLY Carrots . . . quarter-inch apart. Rows . . . one-foot rows. [*He measures it off.*] One foot. [*He puts down a package and measures off.*] Beets. [*He puts down another package and measures again.*] Lettuce. [*He reads the*

1215 *package, puts it down.*] One foot—[*He breaks off as* BEN *appears at the right and moves slowly down to him.*] What a proposition, ts, ts. Terrific, terrific. 'Cause she's suffered, Ben, the woman has suffered. You understand me? A man can't go out the way he came in, Ben, a man has got to add up to something. You can't, you can't—[BEN *moves toward him as though to inter-*

1220 *rupt.*] You gotta consider, now. Don't answer so quick. Remember, it's a guaranteed twenty-thousand-dollar proposition. Now look, Ben, I want you to go through the ins and outs of this thing with me. I've got nobody to talk to, Ben, and the woman has suffered, you hear me?

BEN [*standing still, considering*] What's the proposition?

1225 WILLY It's twenty thousand dollars on the barrelhead. Guaranteed, gilt-edged, you understand?

BEN You don't want to make a fool of yourself. They might not honor the policy.

WILLY How can they dare refuse? Didn't I work like a coolie to meet every

1230 premium on the nose? And now they don't pay off? Impossible!

BEN It's called a cowardly thing, William.

WILLY Why? Does it take more guts to stand here the rest of my life ringing up a zero?

BEN [*yielding*] That's a point, William. [*He moves, thinking, turns.*] And

1235 twenty thousand—that *is* something one can feel with the hand, it is there.

WILLY [*now assured, with rising power*] Oh, Ben, that's the whole beauty of it! I see it like a diamond, shining in the dark, hard and rough, that I can pick up and touch in my hand. Not like—like an appointment! This would

not be another damned-fool appointment, Ben, and it changes all the
aspects. Because he thinks I'm nothing, see and so he spites me. But the
funeral—[*Straightening up*] Ben, that funeral will be massive! They'll come
from Maine, Massachusetts, Vermont, New Hampshire! All the old-timers
with the strange license plates—that boy will be thunder-struck, Ben,
because he never realized—I am known! Rhode Island, New York, New
Jersey—I am known, Ben, and he'll see it with his eyes once and for all.
He'll see what I am, Ben! He's in for a shock, that boy!

BEN [*coming down to the edge of the garden*] He'll call you a coward.

WILLY [*suddenly fearful*] No, that would be terrible.

BEN Yes. And a damned fool.

WILLY No, no, he mustn't, I won't have that! [*He is broken and desperate.*]

BEN He'll hate you, William.

> [*The gay music of the Boys is heard.*]

WILLY Oh, Ben, how do we get back to all the great times? Used to be so full
of light, and comradeship, the sleigh-riding in winter, and the ruddiness on
his cheeks. And always some kind of good news coming up, always something nice coming up ahead. And never even let me carry the valises in the
house, and simonizing, simonizing that little red car! Why, why can't I give
him something and not have him hate me?

BEN Let me think about it. [*He glances at his watch.*] I still have a little time.
Remarkable proposition, but you've got to be sure you're not making a fool
of yourself.

> [BEN *drifts off upstage and goes out of sight.* BIFF *comes down from the left.*]

WILLY [*suddenly conscious of* BIFF, *turns and looks up at him, then begins picking up the packages of seeds in confusion*] Where the hell is that seed?
[*Indignantly*] You can't see nothing out here! They boxed in the whole goddam neighborhood!

BIFF There are people all around here. Don't you realize that?

WILLY I'm busy. Don't bother me.

BIFF [*taking the hoe from* WILLY] I'm saying good-by to you, Pop. [WILLY
looks at him, silent, unable to move.] I'm not coming back any more.

WILLY You're not going to see Oliver tomorrow?

BIFF I've got no appointment, Dad.

WILLY He put his arm around you, and you've got no appointment?

BIFF Pop, get this now, will you? Everytime I've left it's been a fight that sent
me out of here. Today I realized something about myself and I tried to
explain it to you and I—I think I'm just not smart enough to make any
sense out of it for you. To hell with whose fault it is or anything like that.
[*He takes* WILLY'S *arm.*] Let's just wrap it up, heh? Come on in, we'll tell
Mom. [*He gently tries to pull* WILLY *to left.*]

WILLY [*frozen, immobile, with guilt in his voice*] No, I don't want to see her.

BIFF Come on! [*He pulls again, and* WILLY *tries to pull away.*]

WILLY [*highly nervous*] No, no, I don't want to see her.

BIFF [*tries to look into* WILLY'S *face, as if to find the answer there*] Why don't
you want to see her?

WILLY [*more harshly now*] Don't bother me, will you?

BIFF What do you mean, you don't want to see her? You don't want them
calling you yellow, do you? This isn't your fault; it's me, I'm a bum. Now
come inside! [WILLY *strains to get away.*] Did you hear what I said to you?

[WILLY *pulls away and quickly goes by himself into the house.* BIFF *follows.*]

LINDA [*to* WILLY]   Did you plant, dear?

BIFF [*at the door, to* LINDA]   All right, we had it out. I'm going and I'm not writing any more.

LINDA [*going to* WILLY *in the kitchen*]   I think that's the best way, dear. 'Cause there's no use drawing it out, you'll just never get along.

1290

[WILLY *doesn't respond.*]

BIFF   People ask where I am and what I'm doing, you don't know, and you don't care. That way it'll be off your mind and you can start brightening up again. All right? That clears it, doesn't it? [WILLY *is silent, and* BIFF *goes to him.*] You gonna wish me luck, scout? [*He extends his hand.*] What do you say?

1295

LINDA   Shake his hand, Willy.

WILLY [*turning to her, seething with hurt*]   There's no necessity to mention the pen at all, y'know.

BIFF [*gently*]   I've got no appointment, Dad.

1300 WILLY [*erupting fiercely*]   He put his arm around . . . ?

BIFF   Dad, you're never going to see what I am, so what's the use of arguing? If I strike oil I'll send you a check. Meantime forget I'm alive.

WILLY [*to* LINDA]   Spite, see?

BIFF   Shake hands, Dad.

1305 WILLY   Not my hand.

BIFF   I was hoping not to go this way.

WILLY   Well, this is the way you're going. Good-by.

[BIFF *looks at him a moment, then turns sharply and goes to the stairs.*]

WILLY [*stops him with*]   May you rot in hell if you leave this house!

BIFF [*turning*]   Exactly what is it that you want from me?

1310 WILLY   I want you to know, on the train, in the mountains, in the valleys, wherever you go, that you cut down your life for spite!

BIFF   No, no.

WILLY   Spite, spite, is the word of your undoing! And when you're down and out, remember what did it. When you're rotting somewhere beside the rail-

1315 road tracks, remember, and don't you dare blame it on me!

BIFF   I'm not blaming it on you!

WILLY   I won't take the rap for this, you hear?

[HAPPY *comes down the stairs and stands on the bottom step, watching.*]

BIFF   That's just what I'm telling you!

WILLY [*sinking into a chair at the table, with full accusation*]   You're trying to

1320 put a knife in me—don't think I don't know what you're doing!

BIFF   All right, phony! Then let's lay it on the line. [*He whips the rubber tube out of his pocket and puts it on the table.*]

HAPPY   You crazy—

LINDA   Biff! [*She moves to grab the hose, but* BIFF *holds it down with his hand.*]

BIFF   Leave it there! Don't move it!

1325 WILLY [*not looking at it*]   What is that?

BIFF   You know goddam well what that is.

WILLY [*caged, wanting to escape*]   I never saw that.

BIFF   You saw it. The mice didn't bring it into the cellar! What is this sup-
posed to do, make a hero out of you? This supposed to make me sorry for
1330   you?
WILLY   Never heard of it.
BIFF   There'll be no pity for you, you hear it? No pity!
WILLY [to LINDA]   You hear the spite!
BIFF   No, you're going to hear the truth—what you are and what I am!
1335   LINDA   Stop it!
WILLY   Spite!
HAPPY [coming down toward BIFF]   You cut it now!
BIFF [to HAPPY]   The man don't know who we are! The man is gonna know!
[To WILLY] We never told the truth for ten minutes in this house!
1340   HAPPY   We always told the truth!
BIFF [turning on him]   You big blow, are you the assistant buyer? You're one
of the two assistants to the assistant, aren't you?
HAPPY   Well, I'm practically—
BIFF   You're practically full of it! We all are! And I'm through with it. [To
1345   WILLY] Now hear this, Willy, this is me.
WILLY   I know you!
BIFF   You know why I had no address for three months? I stole a suit in Kan-
sas City and I was in jail. [To LINDA, who is sobbing] Stop crying. I'm
through with it.
        [LINDA turns away from them, her hands covering her face.]
1350   WILLY   I suppose that's my fault!
BIFF   I stole myself out of every good job since high school!
WILLY   And whose fault is that?
BIFF   And I never got anywhere because you blew me so full of hot air I
could never stand taking orders from anybody! That's whose fault it is!
1355   WILLY   I hear that!
LINDA   Don't, Biff!
BIFF   It's goddam time you heard that! I had to be boss big shot in two weeks,
and I'm through with it!
WILLY   Then hang yourself! For spite, hang yourself!
1360   BIFF   No! Nobody's hanging himself, Willy! I ran down eleven flights with a
pen in my hand today. And suddenly I stopped, you hear me? And in the
middle of that office building, do you hear this? I stopped in the middle of
that building and I saw—the sky. I saw the things that I love in this world.
The work and the food and time to sit and smoke. And I looked at the pen
1365   and said to myself, what the hell am I grabbing this for? Why am I trying to
become what I don't want to be? What am I doing in an office, making a
contemptuous, begging fool of myself, when all I want is out there, waiting
for me the minute I say I know who I am! Why can't I say that, Willy? [He
tries to make WILLY face him, but WILLY pulls away and moves to the left.]
WILLY [with hatred, threateningly]   The door of your life is wide open!
1370   BIFF   Pop! I'm a dime a dozen, and so are you!
WILLY [turning on him now in an uncontrolled outburst]   I am not a dime a
dozen! I am Willy Loman, and you are Biff Loman!
        [BIFF starts for WILLY, but is blocked by HAPPY. In his fury, BIFF seems on
        the verge of attacking his father.]

BIFF I am not a leader of men, Willy, and neither are you. You were never anything but a hard-working drummer who landed in the ash can like all the rest of them! I'm one dollar an hour, Willy! I tried seven states and couldn't raise it. A buck an hour! Do you gather my meaning? I'm not bringing home any prizes any more, and you're going to stop waiting for me to bring them home!

WILLY [*directly to* BIFF] You vengeful, spiteful mut!

[BIFF *breaks from* HAPPY. WILLY, *in fright, starts up the stairs.* BIFF *grabs him.*]

BIFF [*at the peak of his fury*] Pop, I'm nothing! I'm nothing, Pop. Can't you understand that? There's no spite in it any more. I'm just what I am, that's all.

[BIFF's *fury has spent itself, and he breaks down, sobbing, holding on to* WILLY, *who dumbly fumbles for* BIFF's *face.*]

WILLY [*astonished*] What're you doing? What're you doing? [*To* LINDA] Why is he crying?

BIFF [*crying, broken*] Will you let me go, for Christ's sake? Will you take that phony dream and burn it before something happens? [*Struggling to contain himself, he pulls away and moves to the stairs.*] I'll go in the morning. Put him—put him to bed. [*Exhausted,* BIFF *moves up the stairs to his room.*]

WILLY [*after a long pause, astonished, elevated*] Isn't that—isn't that remarkable? Biff—he likes me!

LINDA He loves you, Willy!

HAPPY [*deeply moved*] Always did, Pop.

WILLY Oh, Biff! [*Staring wildly*] He cried! Cried to me. [*He is choking with his love, and now cries out his promise*] That boy—that boy is going to be magnificent!

[BEN *appears in the light just outside the kitchen.*]

BEN Yes, outstanding, with twenty thousand behind him.

LINDA [*sensing the racing of his mind, fearfully, carefully*] Now come to bed, Willy. It's all settled now.

WILLY [*finding it difficult not to rush out of the house*] Yes, we'll sleep. Come on. Go to sleep, Hap.

BEN And it does take a great kind of a man to crack the jungle.

[*In accents of dread,* BEN's *idyllic music starts up.*]

HAPPY [*his arm around* LINDA] I'm getting married, Pop, don't forget it. I'm changing everything. I'm gonna run that department before the year is up. You'll see, Mom. [*He kisses her.*]

BEN The jungle is dark but full of diamonds, Willy.

[WILLY *turns, moves, listening to* BEN.]

LINDA Be good. You're both good boys, just act that way, that's all.

HAPPY Night, Pop. [*He goes upstairs.*]

LINDA [*to* WILLY] Come, dear.

BEN [*with greater force*] One must go in to fetch a diamond out.

WILLY [*to* LINDA, *as he moves slowly along the edge of the kitchen, toward the door*] I just want to get settled down, Linda. Let me sit alone for a little.

LINDA [*almost uttering her fear*] I want you upstairs.

WILLY [*taking her in his arms*] In a few minutes, Linda. I couldn't sleep right now. Go on, you look awful tired. [*He kisses her.*]

BEN   Not like an appointment at all. A diamond is rough and hard to the
1415   touch.

WILLY   Go on now. I'll be right up.

LINDA   I think this is the only way, Willy.

WILLY   Sure, it's the best thing.

BEN   Best thing!

1420 WILLY   The only way. Everything is gonna be—go on, kid, get to bed. You
look so tired.

LINDA   Come right up.

WILLY   Two minutes.

> [LINDA *goes into the living room, then reappears in her bedroom.* WILLY
> *moves just outside the kitchen door.*]

WILLY   Loves me. [*Wonderingly*] Always loved me. Isn't that a remarkable
1425   thing? Ben, he'll worship me for it!

BEN [*with promise*]   It's dark there, but full of diamonds.

WILLY   Can you imagine that magnificence with twenty thousand dollars in
his pocket?

LINDA [*calling from her room*]   Willy! Come up!

1430 WILLY [*calling into the kitchen*]   Yes! Yes. Coming! It's very smart, you realize
that, don't you, sweetheart? Even Ben sees it. I gotta go, baby. 'By! 'By!
[*Going over to Ben, almost dancing*] Imagine? When the mail comes he'll
be ahead of Bernard again!

BEN   A perfect proposition all around.

1435 WILLY   Did you see how he cried to me? Oh, if I could kiss him, Ben!

BEN   Time, William, time!

WILLY   Oh, Ben, I always knew one way or another we were gonna make it,
Biff and I!

BEN [*looking at his watch*]   The boat. We'll be late. [*He moves slowly off into
the darkness.*]

1440 WILLY [*elegiacally, turning to the house*]   Now when you kick off, boy, I want
a seventy-yard boot, and get right down the field under the ball, and when
you hit, hit low and hit hard, because it's important, boy. [*He swings around
and faces the audience.*] There's all kinds of important people in the stands,
and the first thing you know . . . [*Suddenly realizing he is alone*] Ben! Ben,
1445   where do I . . . ? [*He makes a sudden movement of search.*] Ben, how do
I . . . ?

LINDA [*calling*]   Willy, you coming up?

WILLY [*uttering a gasp of fear, whirling about as if to quiet her*]   Sh! [*He turns
around as if to find his way; sounds, faces, voices, seem to be swarming in
upon him and he flicks at them, crying*] Sh! Sh! [*Suddenly music, faint and
high, stops him. It rises in intensity, almost to an unbearable scream. He goes
1450   up and down on his toes, and rushes off around the house.*] Shhh!

LINDA   Willy?

> [*There is no answer.* LINDA *waits.* BIFF *gets up off his bed. He is still in his
> clothes.* HAPPY *sits up.* BIFF *stands listening.*]

LINDA [*with real fear*]   Willy, answer me! Willy!

> [*There is the sound of a car starting and moving away at full speed.*]

LINDA   No!

BIFF [*rushing down the stairs*]   Pop!

[*As the car speeds off, the music crashes down in a frenzy of sound, which becomes the soft pulsation of a single cello string.* BIFF *slowly returns to his bedroom. He and* HAPPY *gravely don their jackets.* LINDA *slowly walks out of her room. The music has developed into a dead march. The leaves of day are appearing over everything.* CHARLEY *and* BERNARD, *somberly dressed, appear and knock on the kitchen door.* BIFF *and* HAPPY *slowly descend the stairs to the kitchen as* CHARLEY *and* BERNARD *enter. All stop a moment when* LINDA, *in clothes of mourning, bearing a little bunch of roses, comes through the draped doorway into the kitchen. She goes to* CHARLEY *and takes his arm. Now all move toward the audience, through the wall-line of the kitchen. At the limit of the apron,* LINDA *lays down the flowers, kneels, and sits back on her heels. All stare down at the grave.*]

Requiem[1]

CHARLEY It's getting dark, Linda.

[LINDA *doesn't react. She stares at the grave.*]

BIFF How about it, Mom? Better get some rest, heh? They'll be closing the gate soon.

[LINDA *makes no move. Pause.*]

HAPPY [*deeply angered*] He had no right to do that. There was no necessity
5   for it. We would've helped him.

CHARLEY [*grunting*] Hmmm.

BIFF Come along, Mom.

LINDA Why didn't anybody come?

CHARLEY It was a very nice funeral.

10 LINDA But where are all the people he knew? Maybe they blame him.

CHARLEY Naa. It's a rough world, Linda. They wouldn't blame him.

LINDA I can't understand it. At this time especially. First time in thirty-five years we were just about free and clear. He only needed a little salary. He was even finished with the dentist.

15 CHARLEY No man only needs a little salary.

LINDA I can't understand it.

BIFF There were a lot of nice days. When he'd come home from a trip; or on Sundays, making the stoop; finishing the cellar; putting on the new porch; when he built the extra bathroom; and put up the garage. You know some-
20 thing, Charley, there's more of him in that front stoop than in all the sales he ever made.

CHARLEY Yeah. He was a happy man with a batch of cement.

LINDA He was so wonderful with his hands.

BIFF He had the wrong dreams. All, all, wrong.

25 HAPPY [*almost ready to fight* BIFF] Don't say that!

BIFF He never knew who he was.

CHARLEY [*stopping* HAPPY's *movement and reply. To* BIFF] Nobody dast blame this man. You don't understand: Willy was a salesman. And for a salesman, there is no rock bottom to the life. He don't put a bolt to a nut, he don't tell
30 you the law or give you medicine. He's a man way out there in the blue, riding on a smile and a shoeshine. And when they start not smiling back—

---

1. In Roman Catholicism, a special mass for the repose of departed souls; also, a musical setting for such a mass, and by extension any solemn dirge or chant for the dead.

that's an earthquake. And then you get yourself a couple of spots on your hat, and you're finished. Nobody dast blame this man. A salesman is got to dream, boy. It comes with the territory.

35 BIFF   Charley, the man didn't know who he was.

HAPPY [*infuriated*]   Don't say that!

BIFF   Why don't you come with me, Happy?

HAPPY   I'm not licked that easily. I'm staying right in this city, and I'm gonna beat this racket! [*He looks at* BIFF, *his chin set.*] The Loman Brothers!

40 BIFF   I know who I am, kid.

HAPPY   All right, boy. I'm gonna show you and everybody else that Willy Loman did not die in vain. He had a good dream. It's the only dream you can have—to come out number-one man. He fought it out here, and this is where I'm gonna win it for him.

45 BIFF [*with a hopeless glance at* HAPPY, *bends toward his mother*]   Let's go, Mom.

LINDA   I'll be with you in a minute. Go on, Charley. [*He hesitates.*] I want to, just for a minute. I never had a chance to say good-by.

> [CHARLEY *moves away, followed by* HAPPY. BIFF *remains a slight distance up and left of* LINDA. *She sits there, summoning herself. The flute begins, not far away, playing behind her speech.*]

LINDA   Forgive me, dear. I can't cry. I don't know what it is, but I can't cry. I
50   don't understand it. Why did you ever do that? Help me, Willy, I can't cry. It seems to me that you're just on another trip. I keep expecting you. Willy, dear, I can't cry. Why did you do it? I search and search and I search, and I can't understand it, Willy. I made the last payment on the house today. Today, dear. And there'll be nobody home. [*A sob rises in her throat.*] We're
55   free and clear. [*Sobbing more fully, released*] We're free. [BIFF *comes slowly toward her.*] We're free . . . We're free . . .

> [BIFF *lifts her to her feet and moves out up right with her in his arms.* LINDA *sobs quietly.* BERNARD *and* CHARLEY *come together and follow them, followed by* HAPPY. *Only the music of the flute is left on the darkening stage as over the house the hard towers of the apartment buildings rise into sharp focus, and*]

The curtain falls.

CRITICAL PERSPECTIVE

ARTHUR MILLER

Shortly after the opening of DEATH OF A SALESMAN at New York's Morosco Theatre on February 10, 1949, the *New York Times* published an essay by Arthur Miller titled "Tragedy and the Common Man." Without mentioning his play by name, Miller justified the choice of Willy Loman, an everyday salesman, as the protagonist of his modern tragedy. The prevailing view of tragedy at the time, derived from Aristotle's fourth-century B.C.E. treatise the *Poetics*, was that only kings, princes, and others of elevated social standing could be its protagonists. Against this view, Miller argues that all individuals, regardless of class or social standing, are capable of heroic self-assertion in the face of what threatens their dignity. Seven years after American vice president Henry A. Wallace proclaimed the dawning of the "Century of the Common Man" and composer Aaron Copeland's *Fanfare for the Common Man* premiered in Cincinnati, Miller adapted one of the defining features of classical tragedy to a democratic age.   S.G.

"TRAGEDY AND THE COMMON MAN"

In this age few tragedies are written. It has often been held that the lack is due to a paucity of heroes among us, or else that modern man has had the blood drawn out of his organs of belief by the skepticism of science, and the heroic attack on life cannot feed on an attitude of reserve and circumspection. For one reason or another, we are often held to be below tragedy—or tragedy above us. The inevitable conclusion is, of course, that the tragic mode is archaic, fit only for the very highly placed, the kings or the kingly, and where this admission is not made in so many words it is most often implied.

I believe that the common man is as apt a subject for tragedy in its highest sense as kings were. On the face of it this ought to be obvious in the light of modern psychiatry, which bases its analysis upon classic formulations, such as the Oedipus and Orestes complexes,[1] for instances,

---

1. Coined by psychiatrist Frederic Wertham to describe a son's unconscious desire to kill his mother. Orestes, according to Greek mythology, killed his mother, Clytemnestra, in retribution for the murder of his father, Agamemnon, king of Mycenea. *Oedipus complex*: term proposed by Sigmund Freud, founder of psychoanalysis, for a son's unconscious rivalry with his father for possession of his mother. Oedipus, king of Thebes in Greek mythology, unknowingly killed his father and married his mother, bearing children with her.

which were enacted by royal beings, but which apply to everyone in similar emotional situations.

More simply, when the question of tragedy in art is not at issue, we never hesitate to attribute to the well-placed and the exalted the very same mental processes as the lowly. And finally, if the exaltation of tragic action were truly a property of the high-bred character alone, it is inconceivable that the mass of mankind should cherish tragedy above all other forms, let alone be capable of understanding it.

As a general rule, to which there may be exceptions unknown to me, I think the tragic feeling is evoked in us when we are in the presence of a character who is ready to lay down his life, if need be, to secure one thing—his sense of personal dignity. From Orestes to Hamlet, Medea to Macbeth,[2] the underlying struggle is that of the individual attempting to gain his "rightful" position in his society.

Sometimes he is one who has been displaced from it, sometimes one who seeks to attain it for the first time, but the fateful wound from which the inevitable events spiral is the wound of indignity, and its dominant force is indignation. Tragedy, then, is the consequence of a man's total compulsion to evaluate himself justly.

In the sense of having been initiated by the hero himself, the tale always reveals what has been called his "tragic flaw,"[3] a failing that is not peculiar to grand or elevated characters. Nor is it necessarily a weakness. The flaw, or crack in the character, is really nothing—and need be nothing—but his inherent unwillingness to remain passive in the face of what he conceives to be a challenge to his dignity, his image of his rightful status. Only the passive, only those who accept their lot without active retaliation, are "flawless." Most of us are in that category.

But there are among us today, as there always have been, those who act against the scheme of things that degrades them, and in the process of action everything we have accepted out of fear or insensitivity or ignorance is shaken before us and examined, and from this total onslaught by an individual against the seemingly stable cosmos surrounding us—from this total examination of the "unchangeable" environment—comes the terror and the fear that is classically associated with tragedy.

More important, from this total questioning of what has previously been unquestioned, we learn. And such a process is not beyond the common man. In revolutions around the world, these past thirty years, he has demonstrated again and again this inner dynamic of all tragedy.

Insistence upon the rank of the tragic hero, or the so-called nobility of his character, is really but a clinging to the outward forms of tragedy. If rank or nobility of character was indispensable, then it would follow that the problems of those with rank were the particular problems of

2. Shakespeare's *Macbeth* was first performed in 1606. Orestes appears in plays by the 5th-century B.C.E. dramatists Aeschylus, Sophocles, and Euripides. Medea is the protagonist of a play by Euripides. Shakespeare's *Hamlet* was first performed in 1600–01.

3. A character flaw or error of judgment that brings about the downfall of a tragic protagonist.

tragedy. But surely the right of one monarch to capture the domain from another no longer raises our passions; nor are our concepts of justice what they were to the mind of an Elizabethan king.

The quality in such plays that does shake us, however, derives from the underlying fear of being displaced, the disaster inherent in being torn away from our chosen image of what and who we are in this world. Among us today this fear is as strong, and perhaps stronger, than it ever was. In fact, it is the common man who knows this fear best.

Now, if it is true that tragedy is the consequence of a man's total compulsion to evaluate himself justly, his destruction in the attempt posits a wrong or an evil in his environment. And this is precisely the morality of tragedy and its lesson. The discovery of the moral law, which is what the enlightenment of tragedy consists of, is not the discovery of some abstract or metaphysical quantity.

The tragic right[4] is a condition of life, a condition in which the human personality is able to flower and realize itself. The wrong is the condition which suppresses man, perverts the flowing out of his love and creative instinct. Tragedy enlightens—and it must, in that it points the heroic finger at the enemy of man's freedom. The thrust for freedom is the quality in tragedy which exalts. The revolutionary questioning of the stable environment is what terrifies. In no way is the common man debarred from such thoughts or such actions.

Seen in this light, our lack of tragedy may be partially accounted for by the turn which modern literature has taken toward the purely psychiatric view of life, or the purely sociological. If all our miseries, our indignities, are born and bred within our minds, then all action, let alone the heroic action, is obviously impossible.

And if society alone is responsible for the cramping of our lives, then the protagonist must needs be so pure and faultless as to force us to deny his validity as a character. From neither of these views can tragedy derive, simply because neither represents a balanced concept of life. Above all else, tragedy requires the finest appreciation by the writer of cause and effect.

No tragedy can therefore come about when its author fears to question absolutely everything, when he regards any institution, habit or custom as being either everlasting, immutable or inevitable. In the tragic view the need of man to wholly realize himself is the only fixed star, and whatever it is that hedges his nature and lowers it is ripe for attack and examination. Which is not to say that tragedy must preach revolution.

The Greeks could probe the very heavenly origin of their ways and return to confirm the rightness of laws. And Job[5] could face God in

---

4. I.e., what tragedy affirms in the human spirit.

5. Central figure in the Old Testament book of Job. A devout and prosperous man, Job loses his possessions, children, and physical health in a series of calamities through which God allows Satan to test Job's righteousness. Refusing to curse God for the misfortunes that have befallen him, Job is rewarded with a life even richer than the one he lost.

anger, demanding his right and end in submission. But for a moment everything is in suspension, nothing is accepted, and in this stretching and tearing apart of the cosmos, in the very action of so doing, the character gains "size," the tragic stature which is spuriously attached to the royal or the highborn in our minds. The commonest of men may take on that stature to the extent of his willingness to throw all he has into the contest, the battle to secure his rightful place in his world.

There is a misconcepion of tragedy with which I have been struck in review after review, and in many conversations with writers and readers alike. It is the idea that tragedy is of necessity allied to pessimism. Even the dictionary says nothing more about the word than that it means a story with a sad or unhappy ending. This impression is so firmly fixed that I almost hesitate to claim that in truth tragedy implies more optimism in its author than does comedy, and that its final result ought to be the reinforcement of the onlooker's brightest opinions of the human animal.

For, if it is true to say that in essence the tragic hero is intent upon claiming his whole due as a personality, and if this struggle must be total and without reservation, then it automatically demonstrates the indestructible will of man to achieve his humanity.

The possibility of victory must be there in tragedy. Where pathos[6] rules, where pathos is finally derived, a character has fought a battle he could not possibly have won. The pathetic is achieved when the protagonist is, by virtue of his witlessness, his insensitivity or the very air he gives off, incapable of grappling with a much superior force.

Pathos truly is the mode for the pessimist. But tragedy requires a nicer balance between what is possible and what is impossible. And it is curious, although edifying, that the plays we revere, century after century, are the tragedies. In them, and in them alone, lies the belief—optimistic, if you will, in the perfectibility of man.

It is time, I think, that we who are without kings, took up this bright thread of our history and followed it to the only place it can possibly lead in our time—the heart and spirit of the average man.

6. That which evokes pity.

TAWFIQ AL-HAKIM

1898–1987

COMMONLY regarded as the founder of modern Egyptian drama, Tawfiq al-Hakim is a towering literary figure in Egypt and the Arab world. His diverse literary output includes plays, short stories, poems, autobiographies, essays, and novels, but his reputation rests mostly on his dramatic work. Driven by what he called a "creative panic" to explore new artistic terrain and new modes of expression, al-Hakim continuously examined fresh perspectives and challenged the social and artistic status quo. Throughout his long life, al-Hakim was also involved in the intellectual and political ferment of his country, and by the 1980s, he was widely revered as a sage and elder statesman as well as one of the most prominent Arab writers. Produced domestically and internationally, such plays as SONG OF DEATH (1950) address the shifting cultural and political landscapes of twentieth-century Egypt and the broader Arab world.

Born to a rural upper-middle-class family, al-Hakim was pushed by his parents to become a lawyer. In 1920, he was sent to live with his uncles in Cairo to finish his undergraduate studies in law, but al-Hakim spent this unsupervised time attending plays and getting to know Cairo's theatrical community. Before long, he started writing musicals and farces—the most popular theatrical forms at that time—for the well-known 'Ukasha Brothers Troupe. Between 1920 and 1925, he wrote four plays: three of them were adaptations of French plays and the fourth, al-Mar'ah al-Jadida (The Modern Woman, 1923), was an original play inspired by the nascent feminist movement in Egypt. Though al-Hakim had assumed a pseudonym, hoping to avoid his parents' disapproval, they discovered his increasingly active participation in Cairo's theater world. After al-Hakim finished his licence en droit (bachelor's in law) in 1925 at Cairo University, his father attempted to break his son's attachment to the theater by sending him to France to obtain a doctorate in law. But the move only encouraged the young playwright, for in Paris al-Hakim had the opportunity to attend the plays of such modern European dramatists as HENRIK IBSEN, Maurice Maeterlinck, GEORGE BERNARD SHAW, Jean Cocteau, and LUIGI PIRANDELLO. He found himself drawn to the intellectual content in these plays and to the craftsmanship of the European stage. Al-Hakim also read widely during this time in philosophy, poetry, and fiction. Among the writers who affected him deeply were LOPE DE VEGA, JOHANN WOLFGANG VON GOETHE, Edgar Allan Poe, Arthur Rimbaud, Friedrich Nietzsche, and Andre Gide. Al-Hakim's time in Paris profoundly expanded his aesthetic and creative consciousness, transforming him into a full-fledged writer and intellectual.

Realizing after a few years that his son was not going to earn his doctorate, al-Hakim's father summoned him back to Cairo and encouraged him to become a public prosecutor in the Egyptian provinces. Upon his return to Cairo in 1928, al-Hakim embarked on an important new stage in his playwriting career, as he ceased to collaborate with popular theater troupes. Determined that Arab theater not remain an ephemeral art form, al-Hakim set out to write serious plays that would help establish an Arab dramatic literary heritage. In choosing this path, he was consciously working against the long-held belief in Egypt and the Arab world more generally that theater was a popular form, not high literature, and that plays therefore need not be preserved for future generations or even published at all. Most of Egypt's theater producers were convinced that to achieve commercial success, they must stage popular drama, in colloquial language. At the same time, Egypt's cultural elite scorned any texts not written in classical Arabic, a language in which few were proficient; they viewed colloquial texts as beneath the dignity of the Arabic literary canon. Consequently, though theater was a vital part of popular culture, Egypt had no written dramatic literary tradition to speak of.

In choosing to write plays in a literary mode, al-Hakim thus filled a glaring gap in modern Arabic literature. His plays of the 1930s were inspired by history, Greek and Arab mythology, folklore, and religion and were written in the classical Arabic known as *Fusha*: they belonged to what he called the "theater of ideas" (or "theater of the mind"). Al-Hakim considered these plays—among them *Ahl al-Kahf* (*People of the Cave*, 1933), *Shahrazad* (1934), *Praxagora* (1939; enlarged, 1954), *Pygmalion* (1942), *Sulayman al-Hakim* (*Solomon the Wise*, 1943), and *Al-Malik Udib* (*King Oedipus*, 1949)—works to be read, not staged; he insisted that they should be categorized as dramatic literature, not theatrical pieces.

The earliest of these plays, *People of the Cave*, was both a turning point in al-Hakim's career and a milestone in Egyptian and Arab drama. Based on a Christian tale retold in the Qur'an, *People of the Cave* tells the story of three Christian converts who seek refuge in a cave in order to escape the wrath of a brutal king who is persecuting converts. The three characters and a dog sleep there for three hundred years. When they rise from their long slumber, they realize that the world around them has changed. Overwhelmed by these changes and aware that they have become representatives of the past, the characters decide to retreat to the cave. Addressed to Egyptians unsure of how to respond to a rapidly changing modern world, al-Hakim's play suggests that if nations do not modernize, they perish. The intellectual content of this play (as well as others that al-Hakim wrote during the early 1930s) and the classical Arabic language in which it was written gained the approval of Egypt's literary and intellectual elite, who praised al-Hakim for winning drama a place in the canon of Arabic literature. In recognition of its importance, *People of the Cave* was the first play staged at Egypt's National Theater when it opened in 1935. Though the play's use of classical Arabic—and its division into four very long acts—guaranteed that *People of the Cave* would not appeal to a broad audience, it remains a touchstone in Egyptian cultural memory.

Al-Hakim continued to compose philosophy-steeped plays through the 1940s, but in the 1950s, he started to write in a more populist vein. This shift in al-Hakim's career was tied in part to political changes in the country. In 1952, a peaceful coup d'état led by Gamal Abdel Nasser transformed Egypt from a 150-year-old monarchy into a socialist republic. Nasser and his allies instituted educational and cultural reforms designed to publicize and promote the socialist principles of the new republic. Many Egyptian authors, including the novelist Naguib Mahfouz (who would win the Nobel Prize in Literature in 1988), supported Nasser's reforms and embraced a "social realist" style that reflected his ideology.

Under the leadership of the Ministry of Culture, those engaged in the performance arts turned away from the adaptations of Western plays, musicals, and farces that had dominated the pre-Nasser period and directed their efforts toward establishing a national literary dramatic canon. While the National Theater continued to provide a venue for classic Arab plays and world classics in translation, additional theaters were built that featured other kinds of performance: the Puppet Theater for children's drama, the Pocket Theater for experimental drama, the Balloon Theater for ballet and folkloric dance, and the Modern Theater for contemporary texts. A number of new initiatives were also undertaken to support artists, such as artist-in-residence programs, and prizes were granted to honor excellence in the arts. Al-Hakim himself received two important playwriting awards in the 1950s.

During this decade of social and political reform, both Nasser's government and the creative community were mainly concerned with giving artistic expression to the lives of the masses. The young playwrights who emerged in the postrevolutionary period with the state's encouragement and financial support generally advocated commitment to social change. The dramas (and films) that they produced during this period focused on social issues, the family, and the place of the new postcolonial Egyptian in the world, and did so in a realist and naturalistic vein. Playwrights and intellectuals during the 1950s paid equal attention to the remaking of Egyptian theater arts and of Arab theater more generally. For most Egyptian intellectuals, this work of creating a uniquely Arab theater depended on their establishing a connection to the Arab past—a period of intellectual and cultural flowering that, they believed, was cut off by European colonialism. As part of this cultural effort, many playwrights, including al-Hakim, incorporated Arab history and folklore into their plays.

The issue of language played a central role in this nationalist project. Wanting both to reach a wide audience and to help shape the identity of Egyptian and Arab theater, al-Hakim realized that the long-standing dispute over the use of classical versus colloquial language in drama had to be resolved if Arab theater was to continue developing at all. His solution was a new stage language, which he called "the third language." He proposed that writers com-

pose plays in a style that could both entertain and serve literature, accessible to the layperson as well as the intellectual; such a style could accommodate realist topics and express a variety of themes, including tragic ones. The language of these plays was similar to classical Arabic, or *Fusha,* but with some concessions to everyday speech. By writing in this modified version of *Fusha* rather than the local Egyptian dialect, al-Hakim also ensured that his plays could be understood in all of the Standard Arabic–speaking countries that constitute the Arab world. Al-Hakim's approach could easily be adapted to Arabic's many local dialects, and by the 1960s, the period many consider the heyday of Arab drama, a number of other playwrights had taken it up.

In his introduction to *Masrah al-Mujtama (Theater of Social Themes,* 1950), a collection of short plays from this period that contains some of his most widely read and produced works, al-Hakim emphasizes that every play in the volume—even ones whose plots seem to be far-fetched—authentically reflects Egyptian social realities in the 1940s and 1950s. One central reality is the place of women in traditional Arab society. Three plays in the collection underscore women's power and represent female characters in nonstereotypical ways: *Urid Hadha'l-Rajul (I Want This Man), al-Na'iba al-Muhtarama (The Honorable Lady Member of Parliament),* and *Ughiniyyat al-Mawt (Song of Death),* which is included here. In keeping with the dictates of social realism, al-Hakim wished to depict the opportunities for education and work that became increasingly available to women during the 1940s and 1950s. Although feminist and other critics have taken issue with aspects of his representation of women—arguing, for instance, that these characters are given to irrationality and often pursue domestic bliss more avidly than independence—the works in this collection explore the social, familial, and psychological demands with which Arab women contend and the conflicting roles they have traditionally assumed.

No play of al-Hakim's more powerfully captures the pressures of tradition on women—and on Egyptian society as a whole—than *Song of Death,* whose well-crafted structure and poignant, tragic tone have won it praise as one of the finest modern Arabic plays. An unsparing critique of brutal village customs and the tyranny of traditional gender roles, *Song of Death* takes as its subject the long-standing peasant tradition of blood revenge. For centuries, cycles of blood revenge were the undisputed law of the land for country folk in Egypt, and since the beginning of the twentieth century, governments have combated the deeply ingrained belief that the murder of a family member should be punished privately, not by the state's justice system. As a public prosecutor who had confronted this provincial mind-set directly, al-Hakim strongly believed that private vengeance was a barbaric and regressive custom—a tradition that had to end if society was to move forward. *Song of Death* was his attempt in dramatic form to address his professional and humanistic concerns about this destructive tradition.

Al-Hakim's play takes place in a peasant house in Upper Egypt, the region of the Nile Valley that stretches south of Cairo. Asakir, a widow, has spent seventeen years yearning for retribution for the death of her husband, murdered by a member of a rival family as part of a generations-long blood feud. As the play opens, she is awaiting the arrival of her son, Ilwan, who was sent away as a child and raised as a student at one of Cairo's oldest theology schools (housed in an ancient mosque), with the expectation that he will take the weapon with which his father was killed and exact vengeance. When Ilwan arrives and challenges the cycle of violence, maintaining that the law is more important, his refusal to meet traditional expectations precipitates an equally devastating tragedy, and Asakir must face the consequences of her commitment to retribution and family honor. *Song of Death* embeds its story of vengeance and loss in the images and remembered sounds of rural Egyptian life: a reference to walls painted in mud, the joyful trilling of women, ritual gestures.

Hard and single-minded, the figure of Asakir dominates the play. With "a memory that can never forget and a heart that cannot relent," she has put her implacable fantasy of revenge before maternal and other feelings. The events of the past have shaped her view of the world, but the hardness to which she has given herself also reflects the social role that she, as woman and mother, has been asked to assume. The deliberately masculine name Asakir (which means "soldiers" in Arabic) indicates that although she is a woman, she is expected to act as a man. In peasant societies, such as the one depicted in the play, masculinity has historically signified strength and status; thus, sons have been valued more than daughters. This power imbalance forces women to act in conformity with masculine ways—to teach their sons to be "men" and to inspire their daughters to become more like men (by giving them ruthless-sounding names, for instance). Women in such communities are responsible for upholding the laws of their village and passing them down to their children. As *Song of Death* illustrates, women also play central roles in preserving and defending family honor.

But such hardening comes with a price. What makes Asakir such a richly dramatic figure is the conflict between her consuming desire for vengeance and the emotional bond that connects her, despite her struggles to escape it, to her son, Ilwan. Asakir is portrayed as both nurturing and controlling, but her excessive determination to take revenge for her husband's murder turns her into a tragic figure: her single-minded focus on killing drives all tenderness from her motherly love, leaving her with nothing but hatred on her mind and in her heart. By upholding the code that requires sons to avenge their fathers, she places the imperatives of the past over life in the present. In the play's climactic scene, as her desires pull her in opposite directions, Asakir confronts the grim logic of her vengeance in a growing spectacle of loss.

Song of Death delves deeply into the particularities of Egyptian rural life and exposes universal human flaws, such as excessive hatred, adherence to illogical traditions, and the blindness caused by anger and pride. Its themes are as relevant to our contemporary world as to al-Hakim's Egypt in 1950. Because of its poignant message—its insistence on the need to put an end to violence between nations and to the cycles of grievance that perpetuate this violence—it continues to be staged by Arab directors. The local and universal layers of *Song of Death* suggest why al-Hakim's name remains synonymous with modern Arab theater and why his concerns, vision, and tireless experimentation are still points of reference for emerging dramatic voices in the Arab world.   DINA AHMED AMIN

Song of Death[1]

CHARACTERS[2]

ASAKIR, a widowed peasant woman
MABRUKA, her sister-in-law
SIMEIDA, son of Mabruka
ILWAN, son of Asakir

[*A peasant hut in an Upper Egyptian village.*[3] ASAKIR *and* MABRUKA, *both dressed in black, are sitting near the entrance, with heads bowed in silence. Close by them a calf and a kid are seen eating herbage and dried clover. The whistle of a train is heard.*]

MABRUKA [*raising her head*]   There's the train.

ASAKIR [*without moving*]   Do you think he has come on it?

MABRUKA   Didn't he say he would, in his letter? Sheikh[4] Isnawi, the schoolteacher, read it out for us yesterday.

5   ASAKIR   Are you sure you've told no one at all that he's my son?

MABRUKA   Do you think I've gone mad? Your son Ilwan died when he was a mere child of two. He was drowned in the sluice of the waterwheel.[5] The whole village knows that.

ASAKIR   But *they* no longer believe it.

10   MABRUKA   Who are "they"? The Tahawis?

ASAKIR   Didn't your son Simeida tell you what he heard in the market the other day?

MABRUKA   No. What did he hear?

ASAKIR   He heard someone say to a group of people, "Either the Azizes have
15   no more men left among them or else they're concealing a man in order to take revenge, a man closer to the victim then his nephew Simeida." And who but a man's own son can be any closer than his nephew?

---

1. Translated by Mustafa Badawi; revised by Andrew Parkin and Mahmoud Manzalaoui.
2. The characters' names in this play, like most Arabic names, have specific meanings: *Asakir*, "army of soldiers"; *Mabruka*, "blessed"; *Simeida*, "stiff" or "stonelike"; *Ilwan*, "transcendent" or "sublime."
3. That is, a village in the less populous

southern region of Egypt, up the Nile River from Cairo.
4. An honorary title given to teachers in provincial religious schools (and to graduates of al-Azhar University). The local schoolteacher reads the letter to Asakir and Mabruka because they are illiterate.
5. An irrigation device.

MABRUKA   Oh yes: Simeida told me about that. If it hadn't been for this rumor he would never have been able to hold up his head in the village.

20 ASAKIR   Well, let them know now that the dead man's son is still alive. We've no fear for him now that he's a grown man. I'm not the one who is afraid now. It's them that fear keeps awake of a night. Hurry up, train, and bring him soon. I've waited a long time—seventeen years, I've counted them hour by hour. Seventeen whole years and I've milked them out of Time's

25 udders, drop after drop, with all the hard tugging you'd need if you were milking a cow that's far gone in her age.

MABRUKA [listening to a far-off sound]   There's the train arrived in the station. He'll find my son Simeida waiting to meet him.

ASAKIR [as if talking to herself]   That's right.

30 MABRUKA [turning to her]   What's the matter with you, Asakir? You're trembling.

ASAKIR [as if to herself]   Simeida's song will tell me.

MABRUKA   Tell you?

ASAKIR   That he's come.

35 MABRUKA   Did you tell my son to sing as a sign that Ilwan was here?

ASAKIR   Yes, as soon as they set foot across the village bounds.

MABRUKA   Patience, Asakir. Be patient. The worst is over now.

ASAKIR   It's not fear nor weakness that I'm feeling now.

MABRUKA   The fearsome days have now gone. Gone forever, they are. I shan't

40 ever forget the day when you hid your son Ilwan—and he a mere child of two then—hid him in the flour basket and carried him under cover of darkness out of the village. Took him all the way to Cairo, and gave him into the care of that kinsman of yours, the flour merchant who kept shop in the spice dealer's row near the mosque of our blessed Hussein.[6]

45 ASAKIR   Bring him up as a butcher, I said to him. Let him learn to use the knife like a master.

MABRUKA   But he never did as you asked him.

ASAKIR   He did that! Soon as he was seven years old he placed him in a butcher's shop. But run away, he did, some time later.

50 MABRUKA   And went into the Holy al-Azhar[7] as a student.

ASAKIR   That's it. When I visited him last year I saw him in his gown and turban[8] looking most dignified. I said to him, "If only your father could have seen you looking like that, he'd have been mighty proud." But they didn't spare him to enjoy watching his son grow up.

55 MABRUKA   Wouldn't it have been better if he'd stayed on in the butcher's shop?

ASAKIR   What makes you say that, Mabruka?

MABRUKA   I don't know. It's only a thought that came into my head.

ASKIR   I reckon I know your thought.

60 MABRUKA   What is it, then, Asakir?

---

6. That is, the ancient mosque and shrine of Hussein (also spelled al-Husayn, ca. 629–680), the grandson of the Prophet Muhammad, in the heart of old Cairo.
7. That is, Cairo's al-Azhar University; estab-

lished in 975, it is one of the oldest universities in the world and a leading center for the study of Islam and the Arabic language.
8. Attire worn by students and graduates of al-Azhar, highly respected as clerics and scholars.

ASAKIR It grieves you to see my son in gown and turban while yours goes on wearing his woolly skull cap and his smock.[9]

MABRUKA By the memory of the dear departed, I give you my oath, nothing of the kind was in my mind.

65 ASAKIR Why then don't you like Ilwan to be at the Holy al-Azhar?

MABRUKA I give you my oath, it isn't that I don't like it, it's just that I'm afraid . . .

ASAKIR Afraid?

MABRUKA That he might not be such a master at wielding his knife.

70 ASAKIR Set your mind at rest, Mabruka. When you see Ilwan now, a full-grown man, you'll realize that he has the lean, strong-thewed arm of the Aziz family.

MABRUKA [listening to the train whistle] The train's moving out of the station now.

75 ASAKIR Let it go where it will, so long as it's brought us Ilwan to force the murderer's soul out of his body, and to leave him for the farm dogs in scattered gobbets of flesh.

MABRUKA What if he hasn't come?

ASAKIR Why do you say that, Mabruka?

80 MABRUKA I don't know. Just a feeling I've got.

ASAKIR What would stop him coming?

MABRUKA What would drive him to leave Cairo and the city life and the Holy al-Azhar and come to this—?

ASAKIR This is where he was born, where blood is calling out to him.

85 MABRUKA Our village is a long, long way away from Cairo! Can blood make itself heard as far as the cities?

ASAKIR Do you really think he hasn't come?

MABRUKA I know no more about it than you do.

ASAKIR And what about the letter that the schoolmaster read out to us?

90 MABRUKA Don't you recall his words: "I hope to come if my circumstances allow it." Who knows whether or not his circumstances have allowed it?

ASAKIR Don't dampen my spirits, Mabruka. Don't dash my hope. I've just heard the train whistle turning into trills[1] of joy in my heart, announcing that the end of this long mourning is near. Ilwan not come? What would

95 become of me if that were true? And how much longer would I have to wait then?

MABRUKA The station isn't so far from here, nor the main road. If he'd arrived, Simeida would be singing now.

ASAKIR Perhaps they're taking their time, chatting. After all, they haven't

100 seen each other for more than three years . . . since your son was in Cairo last during the Fair of the Blessed Hussein.[2]

MABRUKA If he'd come my son's heart would have brimmed over with joy and he'd have started his singing even before he'd reached the main road.

ASAKIR Perhaps he's forgotten to sing.

105 MABRUKA It's impossible: he can't forget.

9. That is, wearing attire typical of peasants.
1. High-pitched sounds traditionally made by women to express joy on such happy occasions as weddings, pregnancy announcements, and the births of children.
2. In the Islamic world, fairs are popular festivals in honor of venerated religious figures.

ASAKIR [*listening*]   I can hear no one singing.

MABRUKA [*listening*]   Nor I neither.

ASAKIR [*continuing to listen*]   There's no one singing, not even a shepherd
lad. There's not a single creature singing, not even the owl over the
110 ruins. You're right, Mabruka. He hasn't come.

MABRUKA [*as if to herself*]   My heart tells me things.

ASAKIR   No, not yours—mine. Mine, that's as secret as the grave, as hard as
rock, is now beginning to tell me things.

MABRUKA   What things?

115 ASAKIR   Things that will happen.

MABRUKA   Do tell me.

ASAKIR [*listening intently*]   Hush! Listen, listen. Can you not hear, Mabruka?
Can you not hear?

MABRUKA   Simeida singing.

120 ASAKIR   The heavens be thanked for that!

[*They listen for a while to* SIMEIDA's *song, which grows increasingly clear.*]

SIMEIDA [*sings*]

> O my dear one,
> Your bitter voice accuses:
> Repentance and excuses
> Were all I ever gave!
125 > You reproached me then the more,
> And out of grief
> My clothes
> To shreds I tore.
> When they told me of your father,
130 > It was my silent shame
> Which set unmanly cheeks aflame,
> Where eyes ran dry
> And made a desert of my face.

ASAKIR   He's come, Ilwan is here! And now it's off with the shirt of my shame
135 and on with my garment of honor.

MABRUKA   And now we can hold the true rites[3] over the body of the dear
one—and may he rest in peace.

ASAKIR   And sacrifice to his spirit the kid and the calf.

MABRUKA   O joy! O happiness! [*Makes as though to give out a loud trill.*]

140 ASAKIR [*restrains her*]   Not now. Otherwise we'll be known to the world too
early.

MABRUKA   Your hours are numbered, Suweilam Tahawi![4]

[*A knock on the door.* ASAKIR *rushes to open it:* SIMEIDA *appears carrying
a bag.*]

SIMEIDA   I have brought you Sheikh Ilwan. [*Puts the bag on the floor and is
soon followed in by* ILWAN.]

ASAKIR [*with open arms*]   Ilwan, my son.

145 ILWAN [*kisses her head*]   Mother.

---

3. By village custom, a person killed in a
blood feud is not officially mourned until his
family has avenged his death.

4. Either the man or the son of the man who
killed Asakir's husband.

ASAKIR [*to her son*]   Say your greetings to your Aunt Mabruka.

ILWAN [*turns to* MABRUKA]   Are you well, Aunt Mabruka?

MABRUKA   You can see for yourself, Ilwan. You are our only hope now.

SIMEIDA   Let us go home now, Mother.

150 MABRUKA   Come. It's close now, Asakir—the hour of relief.

> [MABRUKA *and* SIMEIDA *go out*.]

ASAKIR   You must be hungry, Ilwan. I've a bowl of sour milk.

ILWAN   Thank you, Mother. No, I'm not hungry. I had some hard-boiled eggs and some barley cake on the train.

ASAKIR   You'll be thirsty then?

155 ILWAN   No, not thirsty either.

ASAKIR   Of course you haven't come here for food or drink. You've come to eat of his flesh and drink of his blood.

ILWAN [*as if in a trance*]   I have come here to do something truly great, Mother.

160 ASAKIR   I know, I know, my son. Wait till I bring you something: something you've never set your eyes on before. [*Rushes to an inner room where she disappears for a while*.]

ILWAN [*casting a look around the room*]   My eyes can still see animals and their droppings in your houses. The dirty water jar, firewood, and dried stalks of maize forming a shaky roof.

ASAKIR [*emerges from the inner room holding a saddlebag which she lays before
165   her son*]   Here. For seventeen years I have kept these things for you.

ILWAN [*looks at the saddlebag without moving*]   What is this?

ASAKIR   The saddlebag that your father's body was sent to me in, carried on his donkey. In this pouch I found his severed head, and in the other one the rest of his body, hacked to pieces. With his own knife they stabbed him
170   to death—the knife he was carrying, then they put knife and body in the saddlebag. See, here is the knife. I left the blood on it until it's turned to rust as you can see. As for the donkey that brought me the body of your murdered father, tracing its steps back to this house by force of habit, with its head bowed down, as if it was grieving over its master—I couldn't keep
175   it alive for you. It couldn't endure for all these years: it's died.

ILWAN   Who did this?

ASAKIR   Suweilam Tahawi.

ILWAN   How do you know?

ASAKIR   The whole village knows.

180 ILWAN   I know you've told me that. You've told that name to me over and over again, whenever you came to visit me in Cairo. I was too young to think then or to argue. But now my reason needs to be satisfied. What's the evidence? Did the police ever look into the crime?

ASAKIR   Look into the crime?

185 ILWAN   Yes. What did you say to the Public Prosecutor?

ASAKIR   Public Prosecutor? The shame of it! We say anything to the Public Prosecutor? We the Azizes do that? Did even the Tahawis ever do that?

ILWAN   Didn't the Public Prosecutor ask you any questions?

ASAKIR   Of course. But we said we knew nothing about the business, that
190   we'd seen no corpse. Meantime we had buried your father in secret under cover of darkness.

ILWAN [*as if addressing himself*]   So that we may exact requital with our own hands.

ASAKIR   With the selfsame knife that stabbed your father.

195 ILWAN   And the murderer?

ASAKIR   Alive and hearty. There's not a saint or a holy man in the neighborhood but whose shrine I visited. I held on to the railings of their sanctuary, uncovered my head and heaped dust from their ground over my hair,[5] and I prayed to them to beseech our God for me that He might prolong the 200 slayer's days until you, my son, should take his life—with your own hands.

ILWAN   Are you sure, Mother, that he was the murderer?

ASAKIR   We've no enemies beside the Tahawis.

ILWAN   But how do you know it was Suweilam himself who did it?

ASAKIR   Because he believed it was your father who'd murdered his father.

205 ILWAN   And is that true? Did my father kill his father?

ASAKIR   God alone knows.

ILWAN   But what started this family feud in the first place?

ASAKIR   I don't know. Nobody knows. It's something far gone in the past. All that we know is that there's always been blood spilt between us.

210 ILWAN   The cause may well be that one of our calves happened to drink from a water-channel in a field that belonged to their ancestors!

ASAKIR   God alone knows. As for us mortals, all that we know is that between the Azizes and Tahawis rivers of blood have flowed.

ILWAN   Rivers that water neither crop nor fruit.

215 ASAKIR   Rivers that stopped flowing only with the death of your father. And that because of your tender age. Years then went past dry as the thirsty season, and people whispered lies and false rumors, while I was writhing in the flames of my hidden anger, waiting for this hour. And now the hour has come, so get up, son, and put out my fire and slake my thirst for the blood 220 of Suweilam Tahawi.

ILWAN   Has this Suweilam Tahawi got a son?

ASAKIR   Yes. Fourteen years old.

ILWAN   So I have no more than another four or five years to live.

ASAKIR   What is it you are saying?

225 ILWAN   . . . Only until he grows strong enough to do to me what I am supposed to do to his father.

ASAKIR   Do you fear for your life, Ilwan?

ILWAN   And what about you, Mother? Do you fear for my life?

ASAKIR   The Lord be my witness, how I fear for every hair on your head.

230 ILWAN   You really care about my life, Mother?

ASAKIR   Has my life any worth without yours? Or for that matter, the lives of all the Azizes? It's your life alone has made it possible for every one of us to live through the past seventeen years.

ILWAN [*bows his head*]   I see.

235 ASAKIR   How often we suffered shame and humiliation. But as soon as your image crossed our minds our energy would revive, our resolution would strengthen and we were united in the hope that we placed upon you.

ILWAN [*his head still bowed and as if talking to himself*]   You certainly need my life.

---

5. A traditional gesture of abasement and supplication.

240 ASAKIR   Even your father's funeral waits for you, Ilwan. These sacrifices here
       are ready for the slaughter. My lamentation which I've been choking down
       in my throat all these years is waiting for you to set it free. My frock, which
       I've kept myself from tearing open all that time, is waiting for you,[6] too.
       Everything in our existence is dead. Stagnant. Looking to you to breathe
245   life into it.
      ILWAN   Is this how life is breathed into you?
      ASAKIR   Yes, Ilwan. Bring the appointed hour closer. Be quick, for we've been
       waiting for it for so long.
      ILWAN [in wonder]   The appointed hour?
250 ASAKIR   I've forgotten nothing. Even the stone to whet the rusty knife I've
       brought for you and hidden in this room.
      ILWAN   But how am I to know this Suweilam? I've never set eyes on him in
       the whole of my life.
      ASAKIR   Simeida will show you where to find him. He'll point him out to you.
255 ILWAN [looks at his clothes]   Am I to commit this deed while I'm dressed in
       this way?
      ASAKIR   Take off those clothes. I've a cloak that belonged to your father. I've
       kept it for you. [She turns to go into the inner room.]
      ILWAN [stops her]   Just a minute, Mother. Why the hurry?
260 ASAKIR   Every breath Suweilam draws while you are here is a gift which you
       are granting to him.
      ILWAN   And what harm is there in that?
      ASAKIR   It's taken from our breaths; it's drawn out of our well-being. Against
       our wishes we were forced to extend his life by as much as nearly brought
265   us to the grave. Look at your mother, Ilwan. I was a young woman when
       your father died. But look what all those years have done to me. It is as if
       they were forty years, not seventeen. The sap of my youth has dried up and
       my bones have grown weak. All I have left is a memory that can never for-
       get and a heart that cannot relent.
270 ILWAN [as if to himself]   What a price it costs to avenge one's blood.
      ASAKIR [uncomprehending]   What did you say, Ilwan?
      ILWAN   I said that God the Mighty Avenger is merciful to us: He offers to
       relieve us of this burden without any cost to us.
      ASAKIR [in a suspicious tone]   What do you mean?
275 ILWAN   Nothing, Mother, nothing.
      ASAKIR [decisively]   Take off those clothes. I'll bring you the cloak and
       sharpen the knife for you myself.
      ILWAN   Isn't there a mosque nearby?
      ASAKIR   We've only a little chapel next to Sheikh Isnawi's schoolhouse.
280 ILWAN [moving]   I'll go there and say my evening prayers.
      ASAKIR   At this hour?
      ILWAN   I think the sun is about to set.[7]
      ASAKIR   Do you want to be seen in the mosque by everyone in the village?
      ILWAN   That would be the best opportunity for my purpose.
285 ASAKIR [stares him in the face]   Have you gone mad, Ilwan?

6. In Egyptian villages, the tearing of one's
outer garments is a ritualized expression of
extreme grief.
7. Every healthy adult Muslim is required to

pray five times daily—at dawn, at midday, in
late afternoon, at sunset, and at night before
retiring—and it is better to pray in a mosque
than alone.

ILWAN It's most important for me to meet the villagers. Haven't I just told
you that I have come to do something truly great?

ASAKIR [*as if mocking him*] I shouldn't imagine you'll want to reveal to the
village the reason for your coming here?

290 ILWAN It's essential to let them all hear what I have to tell.

ASAKIR Ilwan, my son! What is it that I hear you say? Are you serious? Are
you in your right mind? What is it that you want to tell them?

ILWAN [*as if in a dream*] I'll tell them what I have come here to say. I have
often thought about my village and its people, in spite of the long time I've
295 been away from it. There, at al-Azhar, when the classes were over, we—the
students, that is—we'd gather together and read the newspapers. And we'd
think of the places we'd come from. We were very homesick. And we often
worried about when our people in the countryside would be able to live like
human beings, in clean houses where they wouldn't share their meals with
300 animals. When the roofs of their houses would be something better than
dry stalks of cotton and maize, and the walls painted with something better
than mud and the droppings of their beasts. When the water pot would
disappear and there would be clean piped water in the house. When electric lights would replace the oil lamp. Was that too much to ask for our
305 people? Don't they have the same rights as others?

ASAKIR [*as if uncomprehending*] What is all this you're saying, Ilwan?

ILWAN This is what the people of the village ought to know. And those of us
who were educated in Cairo—it's our duty to make them see and realize
their human rights. It shouldn't be difficult for them to achieve this aim: if
310 only they would unite, join hands, and co-operate. They ought to set up a
council. Elect a council, that's it, from amongst themselves. And they
could tax those who had money enough to pay. They'd form a team of able-
bodied men to spend those long hours when there's nothing doing in making dykes and bridges and other constructive things. Not wasting time in
315 squabbles and feuds. Why, if they worked together like that, if they would
only make the effort, we'd make this a model village. And it would soon be
an example for all the other villages in the country to follow.

ASAKIR You're talking the language of books. You can keep that for later. For
when you have your evening talk with Sheikh Muhammad Isnawi. He can
320 understand it—I can't. As for the present, there's something more important that we've to do, Ilwan.

ILWAN [*shocked*] What is it that's more important?

ASAKIR No. Don't go to the mosque to pray tonight. Else our plan might fail.
Pray here tonight, if you wish to. Go and take off those clothes. I'll fetch
325 water from the water pot for you to prepare for your prayers.[8] Put on the
cloak and help me sharpen the knife.

ILWAN [*his head bowed, whispers*] Your mercy, O God, Your favor and
forgiveness!

ASAKIR What are you saying, Ilwan?

330 ILWAN [*raises his head*] I am saying that I have come here only to make you
see and realize what life is, to bring you life.

ASAKIR And that's exactly what we've been waiting for patiently for all these
long nights. For seventeen years all the Azizes have been dead, waiting for
your return to bring life back to them.

8. In Islam, ritual washing before prayer is obligatory.

335 ILWAN [*whispers with his head bowed down*]   God! What am I to do with
these people?

ASAKIR   What is wrong with you, Ilwan? You keep bowing your head. Come
on. Get up. Don't waste any more time.

ILWAN [*raises his head and takes courage*]   Mother, I will not kill.

340 ASAKIR [*tries to conceal her distress*]   What do I hear?

ILWAN   I will not kill.

ASAKIR [*in a rough voice*]   The blood of your father!

ILWAN   It's you yourselves who left it spilt and wasted by hiding the crime
from the government. It's up to the authorities to punish.

345 ASAKIR [*beside herself*]   The blood of your father!

ILWAN   My hand wasn't made to destroy a human being.

ASAKIR [*as if in a trance*]   The blood of your father!

ILWAN [*alarmed at her condition*]   Mother, Mother: what is the matter with
you?

350 ASAKIR [*as if she can see nobody in front of her*]   The blood of your father!
Seventeen years. The blood of your father. Seventeen years . . . !

ILWAN   Mother, calm yourself. Of course it's a shock to you. But you must
realize that I could never be an assassin and use my knife on a man.

ASAKIR [*whispers as if out of her mind*]   Seventeen years . . . Vengeance for
355 your father's murder . . . . Seventeen years . . .

ILWAN [*as if to himself*]   Mother, I know that you've stood it patiently for so
long. If only this patience and endurance of yours were given up to a useful
cause you would perform miracles! But you must understand that I—

ASAKIR [*with a quaver in her throat*]   The blood of your father!

360 ILWAN [*rushes towards her, alarmed*]   Mother! Mother! Mother!

ASAKIR [*recovers awareness of her surroundings*]   Who are you?

ILWAN   Your son, Ilwan. Your son.

ASAKIR [*screams*]   Son? *My* son? No, no! Never, never, never!

ILWAN [*astonished*]   Mother!

365 ASAKIR   I'm not your mother. I don't know you. No son has ever been born
out of my womb. No son have I ever given birth to.

ILWAN [*pleading*]   Please, Mother! Try to understand that I—

ASAKIR   Out of my house . . . God's curse be upon you to the Day of Judgment. Out of my house.

370 ILWAN   Mother!

ASAKIR [*screams*]   Out of my house . . . or else I'll ask the help of our men to
throw you out. We still have men. There are still men among the Azizes.
But you—you're not one of them. Out of my house with you.

ILWAN [*picks up his bag*]   I'll go to the station and go back to where I came
375 from. And I'll pray to God that your disturbed soul may find peace, and that
I may see you in Cairo soon to explain my way of looking at things, in quiet,
far away from here. Goodbye, Mother.

> [*He leaves. His mother remains motionless in her place. After a while,*
> SIMEIDA *enters, first putting his head round the door, then gently pushing*
> *it open.*]

SIMEIDA   Was it you screaming, Aunt Asakir?

ASAKIR [*with determination: she is fully recovered now*]   Come here, Simeida.

380 SIMEIDA [*looks round*]   Where's Ilwan? Where's your son?

ASAKIR   I have no son. I never bore a son.

SIMEIDA   What are you saying, Aunt Asakir?

ASAKIR   If I had a son he'd now be avenging his father's murder.

SIMEIDA   Where has he gone?

385 ASAKIR   To the station. On his way back to Cairo.

SIMEIDA   My mother was right. As soon as she saw him just now, she said, as
we were leaving, "That turbaned preacher will never kill Suweilam Tahawi."

ASAKIR   I wish my womb had been torn to shreds before it brought such a
son into the world!

390 SIMEIDA   Don't upset yourself, Aunt. There are still men among the Azizes.

ASAKIR   Our hope is now in you, Simeida.

SIMEIDA   A nephew can stand in for a son.

ASAKIR   But in this case the son's alive. It's his duty before anybody else, to
avenge the shedding of his father's blood. He's alive. Alive. He's about

395 amongst the living.

SIMEIDA   Just try to tell yourself that he's dead.

ASAKIR   I wish he had really died, drowned in the sluice of the waterwheel
when he was a child. We would then never have had to wait all those years,
writhing and roasting on the live coals of our pent-up anger, waiting to no

400 purpose. I wish he had truly died. We would have been able to live honor-
ably then, and not be wearing our garment of shame. But he is alive, and it
has been broadcast in the market places and in the whole neighborhood
that he is alive. Oh, the shame. The ignominy. The disgrace!

SIMEIDA   Aunt, don't be so upset.

405 ASAKIR   It's impossible not to be upset by a disgrace like this. Carrying such
a shame, life will be impossible. How can I go on living in this village now
that people know that I have a son like this. How many a mouth'll spit
whenever his name is mentioned. From all directions the cry will be heard:
"Cursed be the womb that brought him forth!" Yes, this womb [*striking her*

410 *belly hard and wildly*]. A curse on this womb. All the women of the village
will mock it: even the ugly, the dim-witted, the barren. This womb . . . this
womb . . . this womb.

SIMEIDA [*tries to stop her*]   Aunt Asakir, don't punish yourself so!

ASAKIR   Fetch the knife, Simeida, fetch the knife, and rip it open.

415 SIMEIDA   Have you gone mad?

ASAKIR [*screams*]   Simeida: are you a man?

SIMEIDA [*looks at her intently*]   What is it you want?

ASAKIR   Stop your cousin's disgrace.

SIMEIDA   Ilwan's?

420 ASAKIR   And his mother's, your Aunt Asakir's. Prevent her shame.

SIMEIDA   How?

ASAKIR [*takes the knife from the saddle bag*]   Kill him with this knife.

SIMEIDA   Kill who?

ASAKIR   Ilwan. Dig this knife into his heart.

425 SIMEIDA   I kill Ilwan? Your son?

ASAKIR   Yes. Kill him. Send him to join the dead.

SIMEIDA   Pull yourself together, Aunt.

ASAKIR   Do this, Simeida . . . for my sake and for his!

SIMEIDA   For his sake!

430 ASAKIR   Yes. Better for him and better for me that it should be said he was
killed, than for folk to say that he fled from his duty of avenging his father's
murder.

SIMEIDA   My own cousin!

ASAKIR   If you're a man, Simeida, you must never let him bring shame upon
435   the Azizes. Never again will you be able to carry yourself like a man. Men
will whisper and laugh behind their hands at you and point at you in the
marketplace, and say: "There goes no more than a woman and one who's
given shelter to another mere woman, at that."

SIMEIDA [*to himself*]   A woman!

440   ASAKIR   If the Tahawis had such a son they'd never have let him live for an
hour.

SIMEIDA [*to himself*]   A woman—giving shelter to another woman!

ASAKIR   Yes, that's so; that'll be you if you allow him to behave as he means
to.

445   SIMEIDA [*stretches out his hand resolutely*]   Give me the knife.

ASAKIR [*hands him the knife*]   Here it is. But wait till I wash the dried blood
and the rust off its blade.

SIMEIDA [*impatiently*]   Give it to me, before he slips away by the evening
train.

450   ASAKIR [*gives him the knife eagerly and forcefully*]   Take it. Let his blood
wash away the blood of his father that's dried upon the blade.

SIMEIDA [*goes off with the knife*]   If I manage to kill him, you'll at hear my
voice raised in song at the outskirts of the village, Aunt.

[*Exit quickly.* ASAKIR *remains alone, fixed to the spot like a statue, gazing
motionless and absently. After a while,* MABRUKA *appears, carrying a
water pitcher on her head.*]

MABRUKA [*puts down the pitcher*]   I've brought some dried fish for Sheikh
455   Ilwan.

ASAKIR [*turns to her slowly*]   May your life be longer than his,[9] Mabruka.

MABRUKA   Who are you talking about?

ASAKIR   Ilwan.

MABRUKA   Your son?

460   ASAKIR   He's no longer mine; he belongs to the dust.

MABRUKA   What are you saying, Asakir? I left him with you only a moment
ago. Where is he?

ASAKIR   Gone to the station on his way back to where he came from. Giving
his back to the duty of avenging his father's murder.

465   MABRUKA [*her head bowed down*]   Just as my heart has been telling me.

ASAKIR   Your prophecy has come true, Mabruka.

MABRUKA   If only he had never come.

ASAKIR   Seventeen years we've been waiting.

MABRUKA   Every year you used to say, "He's growing." You measured him by
470   the handspan as if he were a shoot of maize. But then, when he grew tall
and his cob was ripe, you stripped him, only to find that there was no grain
on the cob.

ASAKIR   It wouldn't have been such a disaster if he were no more than a bare
cob. We never expected any material gain through him. We expected him
475   to give us back our dignity—that was all. How proud I was of him, Mabruka,
how often I boasted about him to you. I thought I'd brought forth the son
who'd cleanse the stain off the honor of the family. And how has he turned

9. According to funeral etiquette throughout   deceased family; the customary response is
the Arab world, the blessing "May you live   "May your life be longer than his."
long after the departed one" is directed to the

out now? The very son I've given birth to, the son I took great care to hide
like a treasure in a crock of clay—he's no more than a stain on our tree, like
a blight overtaking a cotton plant. God's mercy be on your soul, my husband: they spilt your blood and it has not been avenged. I've given you a
son who brings comfort to your enemies and makes them gloat.

MABRUKA   Oh shame, shame on the Azizes!

ASAKIR   If he stays alive. But before long he'll be buried in the earth.

MABRUKA [*turns round suddenly*]   Where's Simeida?

        [*The whistling of a train is heard.*]

ASAKIR [*listening intently*]   Hush! There's the evening train entering the
station.

MABRUKA   Asakir, where's Simeida?

ASAKIR [*still listening intently*]   Be quiet. Now, at this instant, at this very
instant.

MABRUKA [*astonished*]   What happens at this instant?

ASAKIR [*as if to herself*]   Do you think the train has carried him off? Or has
he been carried off by—

MABRUKA   If he's gone to the station, as you say, he must have got on the
train. All these curses you are heaping on his head will do no good.

ASAKIR   Do you really think he has got on the train?

MABRUKA   What could have stopped him?

ASAKIR [*slipping out the answer*]   Simeida!

MABRUKA   Simeida? Did he go after him to stop him leaving?

ASAKIR   Yes.

MABRUKA   When did he go?

ASAKIR   A short while before you came.

MABRUKA   I shouldn't think he could have overtaken him.

ASAKIR [*sighs in relief*]   Do you really think so?

MABRUKA   Unless he ran very fast.

        [*The train whistle is heard again.*]

ASAKIR [*listens intently*]   There, the train is leaving the station.

MABRUKA [*stares at her*]   What's wrong with you, Asakir? Why have you gone
so pale?

ASAKIR   What does your heart tell you, Mabruka?

MABRUKA   It tells me that he has gone.

ASAKIR   Gone. Gone—where?

MABRUKA   Where he came from.

ASAKIR   What do you mean?

MABRUKA [*watches her*]   Why is your breast heaving like that?

ASAKIR [*in a whisper, her eyes wandering*]   Gone where he came from!

MABRUKA   Do you still hope for some good from him?

ASAKIR   No.

MABRUKA   You must think of him as if he'd never been.

ASAKIR [*as if to herself*]   Yes. His death is less shameful than his life.

MABRUKA   And thank God that he's far away.

ASAKIR [*to herself*]   Is he on the train now?

MABRUKA   Who knows? Perhaps Simeida was able to catch him up and persuade him not to go: perhaps he'll bring him back now.

ASAKIR [*as if dreaming*]   Bring him back now?

525 MABRUKA   Why not? If Simeida ran really fast he wouldn't have missed the
        train.
     ASAKIR [*whispers*]   . . . Was able to catch him up . . .
     MABRUKA   And it may not be long before we see them coming back again
        together.
530 ASAKIR [*to herself*]   No. This time Simeida will be coming alone.
     MABRUKA [*watches her anxiously*]   Your face, Asakir: it fills me with terror.
     ASAKIR [*listens intently*]   Hush! Listen! Listen! Can't you hear anything?
     MABRUKA   No. What do you want me to hear?
     ASAKIR   Singing.
535 MABRUKA   No, I cannot hear any singing.
     ASAKIR [*with relief*]   Nor can I.
     MABRUKA   Did Simeida tell you he was going to sing?
     ASAKIR [*to herself, anxiously*]   Perhaps he hasn't reached the edge of the vil-
        lage yet.
540 MABRUKA   I should imagine he has, by now.
     ASAKIR [*breathing more freely*]   And he is not singing!
     MABRUKA   Now the blood has come back to your cheeks.
     ASAKIR [*whispers*]   He hasn't caught him up.
     MABRUKA   You'd rather he didn't come back, Asakir, wouldn't you? You'd
545   rather the train carried him away from this village. So would I. I'd much
        rather he returned to his Cairo, to his preachers and the other students.
        He doesn't belong to us, nor we to him. He's done well to leave us so soon,
        before the people of the village could meet him and get to know what we
        know about him. [ASAKIR *listens to a distant sound.*] You're not listening to
550   me, Asakir. Don't you think I'm right?
     ASAKIR [*in a rough, alarmed voice*]   No, no, I can't hear anything!
     MABRUKA [*listens*]   It is Simeida singing. [*Turns, alarmed, to* ASAKIR, *whose
        eyes have glazed over.*] Asakir! Asakir! What's wrong? You scare me!
     SIMEIDA [*outside, sings*]

              O my dear one,
555   Your bitter voice accuses:
              Repentance and excuses
              Were all I ever gave!
              You reproached me then the more,
              And out of grief
560   My clothes
              To shreds I tore.
              When they told me of your father,
              It was my silent shame
              Which set unmanly cheeks aflame,
565   Where eyes ran dry
              And made a desert of my face.

     ASAKIR [*pulls herself together, to stop herself from collapsing, but lets slip a faint
        choking cry like a death rattle*]   My son!

                         Curtain.

SAMUEL BECKETT

1906–1989

THE career of Samuel Beckett, one of the modern period's most influential dramatists, bridges the most important artistic currents of the early and late twentieth century. A member of the novelist James Joyce's literary circle in Paris during the late 1920s and early 1930s, Beckett was one of the last of the high modernists, and his drama and fiction mark the twilight of a movement that produced such works as Joyce's *Ulysses* and T. S. Eliot's *The Waste Land* (both published in 1922). A writer who lived in France most of his life (and who often composed in French), he also continued a tradition of modern Irish playwriting that flourished in the plays of William Butler Yeats and JOHN MILLINGTON SYNGE. Even as they are rooted in the past, however, Beckett's works opened paths for later twentieth-century writers. His trailblazing is particularly evident in the theater, whose boundaries Beckett's plays extended in radically individual ways. WAITING FOR GODOT, which premiered in Paris in 1953 and became a symbol of the crisis of meaning in post–World War II Europe, stands as the landmark play of contemporary drama. With its drama of nonaction announcing the exhaustion of traditional dramatic structures, *Waiting for Godot*—like Beckett's other plays—inaugurated new theatrical possibilities for dramatists as diverse

as HAROLD PINTER, SAM SHEPARD, ATHOL FUGARD, and CARYL CHURCHILL.

Samuel Barclay Beckett was born in 1906 to an affluent Protestant family who lived in the Dublin suburb of Foxrock. His date of birth is listed on his birth certificate as May 13, though he was actually born on April 13 (Beckett relished the fact that this date coincided not only with Friday the thirteenth but also with Good Friday). Beckett was educated in Portora Royal School in County Fermanagh, the alma mater of his fellow Irish writer OSCAR WILDE, and Trinity College, Dublin, where he excelled as a student while studying Dante as well as English and French literature. Upon graduation, Beckett taught French in Belfast for two terms; he then was chosen to represent Trinity as *lecteur* in English at the Ecole Normale Supérieure in Paris, and he began this two-year position in 1928. It was in Paris that Beckett met Joyce, who was at work on his final novel, *Finnegans Wake* (1939), and who became a powerful influence on the younger Irishman. Beckett's own career as a writer was launched with an essay on Joyce's work (published in 1929 as the lead essay in a collection of essays on *Finnegans Wake*, then known as *Work in Progress*) and a poetic parody of the seventeenth-century French philosopher Descartes titled *Whoroscope*, which was published in 1930. In 1930, Beckett also wrote a study of Marcel Proust, the French author whose novel *Remembrance of Things Past* (1913–27) explores questions of time, memory, and human consciousness that would prove central to Beckett's later writing.

After completing his term as *lecteur,* Beckett spent seven years living in Dublin, Paris, and London before returning to France for good in 1937. In addition to *Proust,* which appeared in 1931, these years saw the publication of a collection of short stories, *More Kicks Than Pricks* (1934), and the novel *Murphy* (1938). Twenty years after the end of World War I, war was on the horizon again; and when Germany invaded France in 1940 Beckett joined the French Resistance, typing and translating information concerning German troop movements. As a result of his activities he was forced to flee Paris in 1942; he spent the rest of the war in hiding in Roussillon, in the Vichy-controlled south of France, where he wrote the novel *Watt* (published in 1953).

The period immediately after World War II was, for Beckett, a time of enormous creativity. In fiction, Beckett wrote a trilogy that helped revolutionize the novel form: *Molloy* (1951), *Malone Dies* (1951), and *The Unnamable* (1953). Composed originally in French, then translated (primarily by Beckett) into English, these novels establish deeply self-referential narrative worlds; they explore the limits of fiction, as consciousness engages in an increasingly urgent struggle with the language in which it seeks to articulate itself. It was in part to escape the constrictions of language in these novels that Beckett turned to the stage. In 1948–49, between completing the second and third novels in his trilogy, Beckett wrote *En attendant Godot*—soon to be translated by the author himself as *Waiting for Godot*—"as a relaxation, to get away from the awful prose I was writing at the time." It was not his first play. *Eleuthéria,* a drawing room play that was written in January 1947 but never published or produced during Beckett's lifetime, gave little indication of what he would achieve less than two years later. When *Godot* opened at the 230-seat Théâtre de Babylone in Paris on January 5, 1953, audiences were confronted by a radically new conception of drama. Over the course of two acts that mix vaudeville routines with metaphysical speculation, two tramps wait on a country road for a figure—referred to as Godot—who never arrives. *Waiting for Godot,* which ran for more than 100 performances, became an immediate cause célèbre, and critics struggled to come to terms with its reduced but undeniably powerful dramatic vision. Beckett's "tragicomedy" was soon produced in Berlin (1953), London (1955), and Miami (the United States premiere, 1956); in the decades since, it has received theatrical productions all over the world.

In the plays that followed *Godot,* Beckett continued his theatrical innovations as he explored the human predicament. The action of *Endgame* (1957), one of Beckett's most bleakly comic plays, is restricted to a room set against a postapocalyptic landscape; its characters, positioned like pieces in the terminal stage of a chess match, play out their diminished existence within a world that is winding down. *Krapp's Last Tape* (1958) explores the existence of the individual in time as its lone protagonist plays the recorded voices of his earlier selves. In *Happy Days* (1961), a woman buried in a mound up to her waist—then neck—plays with the objects and words that are all that is left of her world. *Play* (1963) offers one of Beckett's most arresting stage images: three characters, entombed up to their necks in urns, recount the details of a love triangle in alternating confessional fragments. In the late 1950s and early 1960s, he also wrote several plays for radio—including *All That Fall,* which was broadcast by the British Broadcasting Company in 1957—that allowed him to experiment with the staging of disembodied voices.

Following the principle that less is more, Beckett's drama from *Godot* to *Play* is increasingly minimalistic, with its characters progressively immobilized and its dialogue transformed into interiorized monologues. Through that process, this drama laid the foundation for his remarkable plays of the 1970s and 1980s, where character and setting are more radically reduced and even the human body is subject to fragmentation. The protagonist of *Not I* (1972) is a mouth: illuminated at a height of eight feet above the stage floor, it narrates the disconnected pieces of a life that it refuses to acknowledge as its own. A companion play, *That Time* (1976), features a suspended head listening to the voices of intersecting memories. Inhabiting an increasingly spectral space, the figures who people these and other late Beckett plays— *Footfalls* (1976), · *Rockaby* (1981), *Ohio Impromptu* (1981), and *What Where* (1983), to name some of the most prominent— encounter the voices of their own ghosted lives within a field of emptiness and silence. This deepening minimalism also characterizes Beckett's late plays for television, a medium whose dramatic possibilities first interested him in the 1960s. His television plays of the 1970s and 1980s—including *Ghost Trio* (1977), . . . *but the clouds* . . . (1977), and *Nacht und Träume* (1983)— exploit the medium's technical possibilities in order to achieve unearthly, and deeply lyrical, visual landscapes. By the 1970s, Beckett's dramatic writing—and his continuing work in fiction—had garnered an international reputation; he received the Nobel Prize in Literature in 1969, and he was revered as one of the greatest living writers until his death in 1989. Since then, his plays have continued to be produced around the world.

Waiting for Godot, the play that launched Beckett's career in the theater, reflects the intellectual and artistic climate of a Europe still recovering from the devastation of World War II. In the aftermath of the war's unprecedented horrors, a number of Continental dramatists rejected dramatic coherence and logic and the centuries-old tradition of rationality on which they stood. In 1961 the critic Martin Esslin coined the influential phrase "Theater of the Absurd" to describe the drama of Beckett, Eugène Ionesco, JEAN GENET, and others. Philosophically akin to the writings of Albert Camus, Jean-Paul Sartre, and other existential philosophers who were writing about human existence in a world without meaning, the Theater of the Absurd, according to Esslin, sought to convey this human condition in nontraditional dramatic forms. In *The Myth of Sisyphus* (1942), Albert Camus wrote:

A world that can be explained by reasoning, however faulty, is a familiar world. But in a universe that is suddenly deprived of illusions and of light, man feels a stranger. His is an irremediable exile, because he is deprived of memories of a lost homeland as much as he lacks the hope of a promised land to come. This divorce between man and his life, the actor and his setting, truly constitutes the feeling of Absurdity.

Playing out the implications of Camus' theatrical metaphor, Beckett dismantles the elements, or meaning structures, that have sustained and defined dramatic literature. In place of a plot that might organize onstage incidents in relation to each other and that generates movement toward a conclusion, *Waiting for Godot* is organized around activities—pacing, speaking, remembering, falling down—that refuse to cohere into a beginning, middle, and end. Instead of presenting dramatic action, Beckett dramatizes the condition of waiting, a quintessential nonaction that depends on forces and events beyond the acting subject. Time, for its part, loses what claim it has to linearity and becomes disconnected and unknowable. The amount of time that elapses between acts 1 and 2 of *Godot* remains mysterious: the latter act seems to take place the next day, but the lone onstage tree has sprouted leaves—a change that suggests a longer temporal span—and neither Vladimir (Didi) nor Estragon (Gogo), the play's protagonists, can determine how much time has passed. The play's minimalist setting—"A country road. A tree."—is equally indeterminate. Unlike the coherent settings of such modern dramatists as HENRIK IBSEN or GEORGE BERNARD SHAW, Beckett's setting is a kind of nonplace. Uncongenial, not humanized in any way, it is obviously a stage, and an empty one at that. The world beyond the stage is even more frightening and unknown. The characters make references to more idyllic times and places—climbing the Eiffel Tower in the 1890s, grape harvesting near the Rhône—but it is barely conceivable that these realms could be continuous with the inert, radically reduced world the text describes.

Like all of Beckett's characters, Vladimir and Estragon try to understand this world and to come to terms with their own being (or nonbeing) as its inhabitants. Waiting for a figure whose arrival might give meaning to their lives, the two ponder their condition while devising strategies to pass the time. It is worth noting, in this regard, that the play's original French title—*En attendant Godot*—translates into English more accurately as "While waiting for Godot," a participial phrase that shifts attention from the act of waiting to what one does to kill time during that time of waiting. Didi and Gogo develop routines—putting on boots, engaging in crosstalk "canters," even (they fantasize) hanging themselves—that provide distractions from the tedium of waiting. Much of the crosstalk and many of the routines that these tramps devise recall vaudeville and music hall entertainment, clown performances, and the silent films of Charlie Chaplin; indeed, the many visual gags (pants falling down, pratfalls, exchanges of hats) of *Waiting for Godot* help explain why this play has attracted many of the theater's finest comic actors. But there is no mistaking either the urgency of the characters' attempts to distract themselves through such activities or the high stakes for these figures whose very reality and purpose elude their grasp. As Estragon says to Vladimir, "We always find something, eh Didi, to give us the impression we exist?" The absurdity of their predicament and the meaninglessness of their existence repeatedly interrupt their attempts at play, particularly at those times when language gives way to silence. In such moments, as Beckett wrote in his study of Proust, "the boredom of living is replaced by the suffering of being." After one particularly long silence, Vladimir's anguish is undisguisable: "Say something! . . . Say anything at all!"

The two tramps' greatest distraction in each of the two acts is the arrival and departure of Pozzo and Lucky, whose master-slave relationship is reflected in the rope that connects them. Pozzo, a former landowner, seeks to dominate the stage and those around him with oratorical declamations and physical assertions of power. The ironically named Lucky, his servant, carries his bags like a packhorse and submits to Pozzo's abuse. Lucky remains silent until commanded to "think" near the end of the first act, at which point he delivers a disjointed monologue consisting of quasi-philosophical and quasi-theological discourse, arcane and invented references, and sexual/scatological wordplay. This monologue, which teases the audience with fragmentary structures and half-meanings amid its barrage of apparent nonsense, offers a mock-academic portrayal of an intellectual tradition whose religious and rational frameworks have imploded. The very notion of an originative thinking subject is undermined by Lucky's performance. His torrent of words issues forth—involuntarily, it seems—like water from a faucet, and it is turned off just as mechanically when Vladimir wrestles away his hat.

Pozzo and Lucky cross the stage in each act, moving on a linear course between unknown points. In this regard, they differ from Vladimir and Estragon, who return to the same point each evening, who mark the boundaries of their familiar space by marking the edges of the stage, and whose existence is one of familiarities and recurrences. Pozzo and Lucky undergo catastrophic changes between acts—Pozzo becomes blind, and Lucky loses the ability to speak—while the two tramps seem largely unchanged. Like the German drinking song that Vladimir sings to open it—in which a dog's death is recounted in an endlessly repeating narrative—the play's second act recapitulates many of the situations, actions, and changes of the first act. At the same time, it is not an exact repetition. The scholar Vivian Mercier may have characterized *Godot*, famously, as "a play in which nothing happens, twice," but the shape and feel of nothing assume different forms in the two acts. The second act is noticeably darker than the first, the comic efforts of its central figures more strained. Time for Didi and Gogo is a process of diminishment, in which "lessness" (to borrow a title from one of Beckett's late prose pieces) makes itself felt with increasing force. The carrot of act 1 is gone in act 2. Even memory seems to weaken between acts. The two characters labor to remember what happened in act 1, and the uncertainty that they confront renders their lives even more out of their control.

And what about Godot, the object of their waiting? Scholars have speculated on the origins of this name—Godeau is the name of an absent character in a Balzac novel, and *godillot* and *godasse* are French slang terms for "boot"—but whatever echoes the name may carry, the identity of this figure remains, in the end, unknowable. A frequent assumption by spectators, readers, and critics is that Godot represents the Christian God and that his absence marks the twentieth-century historical moment when the Age of Faith had passed and the idea of God no longer served, in the minds of leading artists and intellectuals, as the foundation of moral order. The play is filled, to be sure, with Christian references and allusions: Didi and Gogo speak of the two thieves who were crucified on either side of Jesus, and references to crucifixion, salvation, and other Christian motifs occur throughout. But the name "Godot" is not linguistically identical with "God"; and as Beckett himself noted, this resemblance is wholly absent from the text in French, the play's original language.

Patrick Stewart (left) as Vladimir and Ian McKellen as Estragon in the 2009 production of *Waiting for Godot* at the Theatre Royal Haymarket (London), directed by Sean Mathias.

Beckett also said that if he knew who Godot was, he would have said so in the play. In the absence of such direct identification, we can conclude little more than the following: Godot is that for which Didi and Gogo wait, the absent promise on which they pin their desires for meaningfulness and purpose. Does he really exist? Though his repeated failure to arrive may suggest that he doesn't, the entrance of a boy who brings a message from him at the end of each act undermines even this potential certainty. Beckett once stated, not surprisingly, that his favorite word was "perhaps."

Against their uncertainty and disappointment, the dignity of these two tramps lies in their insistence on keeping their appointment and their refusal to succumb to despair, close though they may come to it. They also have the presence of each other and their shared familiarity, which keeps them together even though they ask themselves, in moments of weariness, whether they should part. Finally, they have the consolation of language, which finds poetry in the most painful of recognitions: "Astride of a grave and a difficult birth. Down in the hole, lingeringly, the gravedigger puts on the forceps. We have time to grow old. The air is full of our cries." In its gritty lyricism and daringly innovative use of the stage, this most original of plays offers a theatrically rich portrayal of boredom, anguish, hope, and resiliency. In urging his London audience to see *Waiting for Godot*, Harold Hobson, one of the play's first English reviewers, captured its haunting power for a generation that had experienced nothing like it: "At the worst you will discover a curiosity, a four-leaved clover, a black tulip; at the best, something that will securely lodge in a corner of your mind for as long as you live."

S.G.

Waiting for Godot
A Tragicomedy in Two Acts[1]

CHARACTERS

ESTRAGON	POZZO
VLADIMIR	A BOY
LUCKY	

Act 1

A country road. A tree.
Evening.

[ESTRAGON, *sitting on a low mound, is trying to take off his boot. He pulls at it with both hands, panting. He gives up, exhausted, rests, tries again. As before.*]

[*Enter* VLADIMIR.]

ESTRAGON [*giving up again*]   Nothing to be done.
VLADIMIR [*advancing with short, stiff strides, legs wide apart*]   I'm beginning to come round to that opinion. All my life I've tried to put it from me, saying,

---

1. Translated from the original French text by the author.

Vladimir, be reasonable, you haven't yet tried everything. And I resumed the
5   struggle. [*He broods, musing on the struggle. Turning to* ESTRAGON.] So there
you are again.

ESTRAGON   Am I?

VLADIMIR   I'm glad to see you back. I thought you were gone for ever.

ESTRAGON   Me too.

10 VLADIMIR   Together again at last! We'll have to celebrate this. But how? [*He
reflects.*] Get up till I embrace you.

ESTRAGON [*irritably*]   Not now, not now.

VLADIMIR [*hurt, coldly*]   May one enquire where His Highness spent the night?

ESTRAGON   In a ditch.

15 VLADIMIR [*admiringly*]   A ditch! Where?

ESTRAGON [*without gesture*]   Over there.

VLADIMIR   And they didn't beat you?

ESTRAGON   Beat me? Certainly they beat me.

VLADIMIR   The same lot as usual?

20 ESTRAGON   The same? I don't know.

VLADIMIR   When I think of it . . . all these years . . . but for me . . . where
would you be . . . [*Decisively*] You'd be nothing more than a little heap of
bones at the present minute, no doubt about it.

ESTRAGON   And what of it?

25 VLADIMIR [*gloomily*]   It's too much for one man. [*Pause. Cheerfully.*] On the
other hand what's the good of losing heart now, that's what I say. We should
have thought of it a million years ago, in the nineties.[2]

ESTRAGON   Ah stop blathering and help me off with this bloody thing.

VLADIMIR   Hand in hand from the top of the Eiffel Tower, among the first.
30 We were respectable in those days. Now it's too late. They wouldn't even let
us up. [ESTRAGON *tears at his boot.*] What are you doing?

ESTRAGON   Taking off my boot. Did that never happen to you?

VLADIMIR   Boots must be taken off every day, I'm tired telling you that. Why
don't you listen to me?

35 ESTRAGON [*feebly*]   Help me!

VLADIMIR   It hurts?

ESTRAGON [*angrily*]   Hurts! He wants to know if it hurts!

VLADIMIR [*angrily*]   No one ever suffers but you. I don't count. I'd like to
hear what you'd say if you had what I have.

40 ESTRAGON   It hurts?

VLADIMIR [*angrily*]   Hurts! He wants to know if it hurts!

ESTRAGON [*pointing*]   You might button it all the same.

VLADIMIR [*stooping*]   True. [*He buttons his fly.*] Never neglect the little things
of life.

45 ESTRAGON   What do you expect, you always wait till the last moment.

VLADIMIR [*musingly*]   The last moment . . . [*He meditates.*] Hope deferred
maketh the something sick, who said that?[3]

ESTRAGON   Why don't you help me?

VLADIMIR   Sometimes I feel it coming all the same. Then I go all queer. [*He
takes off his hat, peers inside it, feels about inside it, shakes it, puts it on*

---

2. That is, the 1890s.

3. "Hope deferred maketh the heart sick: but

when the desire cometh, it is a tree of life"
(Proverbs 13.12).

50 *again.*] How shall I say? Relieved and at the same time . . . [*He searches for the word.*] . . . appalled. [*With emphasis*] AP-PALLED. [*He takes off his hat again, peers inside it.*] Funny. [*He knocks on the crown as though to dislodge a foreign body, peers into it again, puts it on again.*] Nothing to be done. [ESTRAGON *with a supreme effort succeeds in pulling off his boot. He peers inside it, feels about inside it, turns it upside down, shakes it, looks on the ground to see if anything has fallen out, finds nothing, feels inside it again, staring sightlessly before him.*] Well?

55 ESTRAGON   Nothing.

VLADIMIR   Show.

ESTRAGON   There's nothing to show.

VLADIMIR   Try and put it on again.

ESTRAGON [*examining his foot*]   I'll air it for a bit.

60 VLADIMIR   There's man all over for you, blaming on his boots the faults of his feet. [*He takes off his hat again, peers inside it, feels about inside it, knocks on the crown, blows into it, puts it on again.*] This is getting alarming. [*Silence. Vladimir deep in thought, Estragon pulling at his toes.*] One of the thieves was saved.[4] [*Pause*] It's a reasonable percentage. [*Pause*] Gogo.

65 ESTRAGON   What?

VLADIMIR   Suppose we repented.

ESTRAGON   Repented what?

VLADIMIR   Oh . . . [*He reflects.*] We wouldn't have to go into the details.

ESTRAGON   Our being born?

[VLADIMIR *breaks into a hearty laugh which he immediately stifles, his hand pressed to his pubis, his face contorted.*]

70 VLADIMIR   One daren't even laugh any more.

ESTRAGON   Dreadful privation.

VLADIMIR   Merely smile. [*He smiles suddenly from ear to ear, keeps smiling, ceases as suddenly.*] It's not the same thing. Nothing to be done. [*Pause*] Gogo.

75 ESTRAGON [*irritably*]   What is it?

VLADIMIR   Did you ever read the Bible?

ESTRAGON   The Bible . . . [*He reflects.*] I must have taken a look at it.

VLADIMIR   Do you remember the Gospels?

ESTRAGON   I remember the maps of the Holy Land. Coloured they were. Very
80 pretty. The Dead Sea[5] was pale blue. The very look of it made me thirsty. That's where we'll go, I used to say, that's where we'll go for our honeymoon. We'll swim. We'll be happy.

VLADIMIR   You should have been a poet.

ESTRAGON   I was. [*Gesture towards his rags*] Isn't that obvious?

[*Silence.*]

85 VLADIMIR   Where was I . . . How's your foot?

ESTRAGON   Swelling visibly.

VLADIMIR   Ah yes, the two thieves. Do you remember the story?

---

4. That is, one of the two thieves crucified at the same time as Jesus. One of the Gospels describes one thief railing at him and the other asking to be remembered in heaven. To the second thief Jesus replied, "Verily I say unto thee, today shalt thou be with me in paradise" (Luke 23.43).

5. A salt lake, about 45 miles long and up to 10 miles wide, on the boundary between Israel and Jordan.

ESTRAGON   No.

VLADIMIR   Shall I tell it to you?

90 ESTRAGON   No.

VLADIMIR   It'll pass the time. [*Pause*] Two thieves, crucified at the same time as our Saviour. One—

ESTRAGON   Our what?

VLADIMIR   Our Saviour. Two thieves. One is supposed to have been saved

95   and the other . . . [*He searches for the contrary of saved.*] . . . damned.

ESTRAGON   Saved from what?

VLADIMIR   Hell.

ESTRAGON   I'm going.

  [*He does not move.*]

VLADIMIR   And yet . . . [*Pause*] . . . how is it—this is not boring you I hope—-

100   how is it that of the four Evangelists only one speaks of a thief being saved. The four of them were there—or thereabouts—and only one speaks of a thief being saved. [*Pause*] Come on, Gogo, return the ball, can't you, once in a way?

ESTRAGON   [*with exaggerated enthusiasm*]   I find this really most extraordi

105   narily interesting.

VLADIMIR   One out of four. Of the other three two don't mention any thieves at all and the third says that both of them abused him.[6]

ESTRAGON   Who?

VLADIMIR   What?

110 ESTRAGON   What's all this about? Abused who?

VLADIMIR   The Saviour.

ESTRAGON   Why?

VLADIMIR   Because he wouldn't save them.

ESTRAGON   From hell?

115 VLADIMIR   Imbecile! From death.

ESTRAGON   I thought you said hell.

VLADIMIR   From death, from death.

ESTRAGON   Well what of it?

VLADIMIR   Then the two of them must have been damned.

120 ESTRAGON   And why not?

VLADIMIR   But one of the four says that one of the two was saved.

ESTRAGON   Well? They don't agree and that's all there is to it.

VLADIMIR   But all four were there. And only one speaks of a thief being saved. Why believe him rather than the others?

125 ESTRAGON   Who believes him?

VLADIMIR   Everybody. It's the only version they know.

ESTRAGON   People are bloody ignorant apes.

  [*He rises painfully, goes limping to extreme left, halts, gazes into distance off with his hand screening his eyes, turns, goes to extreme right, gazes into distance. *VLADIMIR* watches him, then goes and picks up the boot, peers into it, drops it hastily.*]

VLADIMIR   Pah!

  [*He spits. *ESTRAGON* moves to center, halts with his back to auditorium.*]

6. See Matthew 27.44. Both Mark (15.27) and John (who calls them simply "two others"; 19.18) mention the thieves.

ESTRAGON   Charming spot. [*He turns, advances to front, halts facing audito*
130   *rium.*] Inspiring prospects. [*He turns to* VLADIMIR.] Let's go.
VLADIMIR   We can't.
ESTRAGON   Why not?
VLADIMIR   We're waiting for Godot.
ESTRAGON [*despairingly*]   Ah! [*Pause*] You're sure it was here?
135 VLADIMIR   What?
ESTRAGON   That we were to wait.
VLADIMIR   He said by the tree. [*They look at the tree.*] Do you see any others?
ESTRAGON   What is it?
VLADIMIR   I don't know. A willow.[7]
140 ESTRAGON   Where are the leaves?
VLADIMIR   It must be dead.
ESTRAGON   No more weeping.
VLADIMIR   Or perhaps it's not the season.
ESTRAGON   Looks to me more like a bush.
145 VLADIMIR   A shrub.
ESTRAGON   A bush.
VLADIMIR   A—. What are you insinuating? That we've come to the wrong
place?
ESTRAGON   He should be here.
150 VLADIMIR   He didn't say for sure he'd come.
ESTRAGON   And if he doesn't come?
VLADIMIR   We'll come back tomorrow.
ESTRAGON   And then the day after tomorrow.
VLADIMIR   Possibly.
155 ESTRAGON   And so on.
VLADIMIR   The point is—
ESTRAGON   Until he comes.
VLADIMIR   You're merciless.
ESTRAGON   We came here yesterday.
160 VLADIMIR   Ah no, there you're mistaken.
ESTRAGON   What did we do yesterday?
VLADIMIR   What did we do yesterday?
ESTRAGON   Yes.
VLADIMIR   Why . . . [*Angrily*] Nothing is certain when you're about.
165 ESTRAGON   In my opinion we were here.
VLADIMIR [*looking round*]   You recognize the place?
ESTRAGON   I didn't say that.
VLADIMIR   Well?
ESTRAGON   That makes no difference.
170 VLADIMIR   All the same . . . that tree . . . [*Turning towards auditorium*] that
bog . . .
ESTRAGON   You're sure it was this evening?
VLADIMIR   What?
ESTRAGON   That we were to wait.
175 VLADIMIR   He said Saturday. [*Pause*] I think.

7. A tree associated with mourning.

ESTRAGON   You think.

VLADIMIR   I must have made a note of it. [*He fumbles in his pockets, bursting with miscellaneous rubbish.*]

ESTRAGON [*very insidious*]   But what Saturday? And is it Saturday? Is it not rather Sunday? [*Pause*] Or Monday? [*Pause*] Or Friday?

VLADIMIR [*looking wildly about him, as though the date was inscribed in the landscape*]   It's not possible!

ESTRAGON   Or Thursday?

VLADIMIR   What'll we do?

ESTRAGON   If he came yesterday and we weren't here you may be sure he won't come again today.

VLADIMIR   But you say we were here yesterday.

ESTRAGON   I may be mistaken. [*Pause*] Let's stop talking for a minute, do you mind?

VLADIMIR [*feebly*]   All right. [ESTRAGON *sits down on the mound.* VLADIMIR *paces agitatedly to and fro, halting from time to time to gaze into distance off.* ESTRAGON *falls asleep.* VLADIMIR *halts finally before* ESTRAGON.] Gogo! . . . Gogo! . . . GOGO!

[ESTRAGON *wakes with a start.*]

ESTRAGON [*restored to the horror of his situation*]   I was asleep! [*Despairingly*] Why will you never let me sleep?

VLADIMIR   I felt lonely.

ESTRAGON   I had a dream.

VLADIMIR   Don't tell me!

ESTRAGON   I dreamt that—

VLADIMIR   DON'T TELL ME!

ESTRAGON [*gesture towards the universe*]   This one is enough for you? [*Silence*] It's not nice of you, Didi. Who am I to tell my private nightmares to if I can't tell them to you?

VLADIMIR   Let them remain private. You know I can't bear that.

ESTRAGON [*coldly*]   There are times when I wonder if it wouldn't be better for us to part.

VLADIMIR   You wouldn't go far.

ESTRAGON   That would be too bad, really too bad. [*Pause*] Wouldn't it, Didi, be really too bad? [*Pause*] When you think of the beauty of the way. [*Pause*] And the goodness of the wayfarers. [*Pause. Wheedling.*] Wouldn't it, Didi?

VLADIMIR   Calm yourself.

ESTRAGON [*voluptuously*]   Calm . . . calm . . . The English say cawm. [*Pause*] You know the story of the Englishman in the brothel?

VLADIMIR   Yes.

ESTRAGON   Tell it to me.

VLADIMIR   Ah stop it!

ESTRAGON   An Englishman having drunk a little more than usual proceeds to a brothel. The bawd asks him if he wants a fair one, a dark one or a red-haired one. Go on.

VLADIMIR   STOP IT!

[*Exit* VLADIMIR *hurriedly.* ESTRAGON *gets up and follows him as far as the limit of the stage. Gestures of* ESTRAGON *like those of a spectator encouraging a pugilist. Enter* VLADIMIR. *He brushes past* ESTRAGON, *crosses the stage with bowed head.* ESTRAGON *takes a step towards him, halts.*]

ESTRAGON [*gently*] You wanted to speak to me? [*Silence.* ESTRAGON *takes a step forward.*] You had something to say to me? [*Silence. Another step forward.*] Didi . . .

VLADIMIR [*without turning*] I've nothing to say to you.

ESTRAGON [*step forward*] You're angry? [*Silence. Step forward.*] Forgive me. [*Silence. Step forward.* ESTRAGON *lays his hand on* VLADIMIR's *shoulder.*] Come, Didi. [*Silence*] Give me your hand. [VLADIMIR *half turns.*] Embrace me! [VLADIMIR *stiffens.*] Don't be stubborn! [VLADIMIR *softens. They embrace.* ESTRAGON *recoils.*] You stink of garlic!

VLADIMIR It's for the kidneys. [*Silence.* ESTRAGON *looks attentively at the tree.*] What do we do now?

ESTRAGON Wait.

VLADIMIR Yes, but while waiting.

ESTRAGON What about hanging ourselves?

VLADIMIR Hmm. It'd give us an erection.

ESTRAGON [*highly excited*] An erection!

VLADIMIR With all that follows. Where it[8] falls mandrakes grow. That's why they shriek when you pull them up. Did you not know that?

ESTRAGON Let's hang ourselves immediately!

VLADIMIR From a bough? [*They go towards the tree.*] I wouldn't trust it.

ESTRAGON We can always try.

VLADIMIR Go ahead.

ESTRAGON After you.

VLADIMIR No no, you first.

ESTRAGON Why me?

VLADIMIR You're lighter than I am.

ESTRAGON Just so!

VLADIMIR I don't understand.

ESTRAGON Use your intelligence, can't you?

[VLADIMIR *uses his intelligence.*]

VLADIMIR [*finally*] I remain in the dark.

ESTRAGON This is how it is. [*He reflects.*] The bough . . . the bough . . . [*Angrily*] Use your head, can't you?

VLADIMIR You're my only hope.

ESTRAGON [*with effort*] Gogo light—bough not break—Gogo dead. Didi heavy—bough break—Didi alone. Whereas—

VLADIMIR I hadn't thought of that.

ESTRAGON If it hangs you it'll hang anything.

VLADIMIR But am I heavier than you?

ESTRAGON So you tell me. I don't know. There's an even chance. Or nearly.

VLADIMIR Well? What do we do?

ESTRAGON Don't let's do anything. It's safer.

VLADIMIR Let's wait and see what he says.

ESTRAGON Who?

VLADIMIR Godot.

ESTRAGON Good idea.

---

8. That is, semen. The mandrake, whose root sometimes splits in a way that resembles a man's body, was long believed to be inhabited by a demon (its shriek at being uprooted was said to be fatal). The idea that mandrakes grow from the semen of hanged men was widespread in Europe in the Middle Ages.

VLADIMIR   Let's wait till we know exactly how we stand.

ESTRAGON   On the other hand it might be better to strike the iron before it freezes.[9]

265 VLADIMIR   I'm curious to hear what he has to offer. Then we'll take it or leave it.

ESTRAGON   What exactly did we ask him for?

VLADIMIR   Were you not there?

ESTRAGON   I can't have been listening.

270 VLADIMIR   Oh . . . Nothing very definite.

ESTRAGON   A kind of prayer.

VLADIMIR   Precisely.

ESTRAGON   A vague supplication.

VLADIMIR   Exactly.

275 ESTRAGON   And what did he reply?

VLADIMIR   That he'd see.

ESTRAGON   That he couldn't promise anything.

VLADIMIR   That he'd have to think it over.

ESTRAGON   In the quiet of his home.

280 VLADIMIR   Consult his family.

ESTRAGON   His friends.

VLADIMIR   His agents.

ESTRAGON   His correspondents.

VLADIMIR   His books.

285 ESTRAGON   His bank account.

VLADIMIR   Before taking a decision.[1]

ESTRAGON   It's the normal thing.

VLADIMIR   Is it not?

ESTRAGON   I think it is.

290 VLADIMIR   I think so too.

[Silence.]

ESTRAGON [anxious]   And we?

VLADIMIR   I beg your pardon?

ESTRAGON   I said, And we?

VLADIMIR   I don't understand.

295 ESTRAGON   Where do we come in?

VLADIMIR   Come in?

ESTRAGON   Take your time.

VLADIMIR   Come in? On our hands and knees.

ESTRAGON   As bad as that?

300 VLADIMIR   Your Worship wishes to assert his prerogatives?

ESTRAGON   We've no rights any more?

[Laugh of VLADIMIR, stifled as before, less the smile.]

VLADIMIR   You'd make me laugh if it wasn't prohibited.

ESTRAGON   We've lost our rights?

VLADIMIR [distinctly]   We got rid of them.

---

9. A version of the proverb "Strike while the iron is hot," whose earliest attribution is to Publilius Syrus (1st c. B.C.E.).

1. That is, making a decision (a British idiom).

[*Silence. They remain motionless, arms dangling, heads sunk, sagging at the knees.*]

305 ESTRAGON [*feebly*]   We're not tied? [*Pause*] We're not—
VLADIMIR   Listen!

[*They listen, grotesquely rigid.*]

ESTRAGON   I hear nothing.
VLADIMIR   Hsst! [*They listen.* ESTRAGON *loses his balance, almost falls. He clutches the arm of* VLADIMIR *who totters. They listen, huddled together.*] Nor I.

[*Sighs of relief. They relax and separate.*]

310 ESTRAGON   You gave me a fright.
VLADIMIR   I thought it was he.
ESTRAGON   Who?
VLADIMIR   Godot.
ESTRAGON   Pah! The wind in the reeds.
315 VLADIMIR   I could have sworn I heard shouts.
ESTRAGON   And why would he shout?
VLADIMIR   At his horse.

[*Silence.*]

ESTRAGON [*violently*]   I'm hungry!
VLADIMIR   Do you want a carrot?
320 ESTRAGON   Is that all there is?
VLADIMIR   I might have some turnips.
ESTRAGON   Give me a carrot. [VLADIMIR *rummages in his pockets, takes out a turnip and gives it to* ESTRAGON *who takes a bite out of it. Angrily.*] It's a turnip!
325 VLADIMIR   Oh pardon! I could have sworn it was a carrot. [*He rummages again in his pockets, finds nothing but turnips.*] All that's turnips. [*He rummages.*] You must have eaten the last. [*He rummages.*] Wait, I have it. [*He brings out a carrot and gives it to* ESTRAGON.] There, dear fellow. [ESTRAGON *wipes the carrot on his sleeve and begins to eat it.*] Make it last, that's the
330 end of them.
ESTRAGON [*chewing*]   I asked you a question.
VLADIMIR   Ah.
ESTRAGON   Did you reply?
VLADIMIR   How's the carrot?
335 ESTRAGON   It's a carrot.
VLADIMIR   So much the better, so much the better. [*Pause.*] What was it you wanted to know?
ESTRAGON   I've forgotten. [*Chews.*] That's what annoys me. [*He looks at the carrot appreciatively, dangles it between finger and thumb.*] I'll never forget
340 this carrot. [*He sucks the end of it meditatively.*] Ah yes, now I remember.
VLADIMIR   Well?
ESTRAGON [*his mouth full, vacuously*]   We're not tied?
VLADIMIR   I don't hear a word you're saying.
ESTRAGON [*chews, swallows*]   I'm asking you if we're tied.
345 VLADIMIR   Tied?
ESTRAGON   Ti-ed.
VLADIMIR   How do you mean tied?

ESTRAGON   Down.

VLADIMIR   But to whom? By whom?

350 ESTRAGON   To your man.

VLADIMIR   To Godot? Tied to Godot! What an idea! No question of it. [*Pause*] For the moment.

ESTRAGON   His name is Godot?

VLADIMIR   I think so.

355 ESTRAGON   Fancy that. [*He raises what remains of the carrot by the stub of leaf, twirls it before his eyes.*] Funny, the more you eat the worse it gets.

VLADIMIR   With me it's just the opposite.

ESTRAGON   In other words?

VLADIMIR   I get used to the muck as I go along.

360 ESTRAGON   [*after prolonged reflection*]   Is that the opposite?

VLADIMIR   Question of temperament.

ESTRAGON   Of character.

VLADIMIR   Nothing you can do about it.

ESTRAGON   No use struggling.

365 VLADIMIR   One is what one is.

ESTRAGON   No use wriggling.

VLADIMIR   The essential doesn't change.

ESTRAGON   Nothing to be done. [*He proffers the remains of the carrot to* VLADIMIR.] Like to finish it?

[*A terrible cry, close at hand.* ESTRAGON *drops the carrot. They remain motionless, then together make a sudden rush towards the wings.* ESTRAGON *stops halfway, runs back, picks up the carrot, stuffs it in his pocket, runs to rejoin* VLADIMIR *who is waiting for him, stops again, runs back, picks up his boot, runs to rejoin* VLADIMIR. *Huddled together, shoulders hunched, cringing away from the menace, they wait.*]

[*Enter* POZZO *and* LUCKY. POZZO *drives* LUCKY *by means of a rope passed round his neck, so that* LUCKY *is the first to enter, followed by the rope which is long enough to let him reach the middle of the stage before* POZZO *appears.* LUCKY *carries a heavy bag, a folding stool, a picnic basket and a greatcoat,* POZZO *a whip.*]

370 POZZO   [*off*]   On! [*Crack of whip.* POZZO *appears. They cross the stage.* LUCKY *passes before* VLADIMIR *and* ESTRAGON *and exit.* POZZO *at the sight of* VLADIMIR *and* ESTRAGON *stops short. The rope tautens.* POZZO *jerks at it violently.*] Back!

[*Noise of* LUCKY *falling with all his baggage.* VLADIMIR *and* ESTRAGON *turn towards him, half wishing half fearing to go to his assistance.* VLADIMIR *takes a step towards Lucky,* ESTRAGON *holds him back by the sleeve.*]

VLADIMIR   Let me go!

ESTRAGON   Stay where you are!

POZZO   Be careful! He's wicked. [VLADIMIR *and* ESTRAGON *turn towards* 375 POZZO.] With strangers.

ESTRAGON   [*undertone*]   Is that him?

VLADIMIR   Who?

ESTRAGON   [*trying to remember the name*]   Er . . .

VLADIMIR   Godot?

380 ESTRAGON   Yes.

POZZO   I present myself: Pozzo.

VLADIMIR [*to* ESTRAGON] Not at all!

ESTRAGON He said Godot.

VLADIMIR Not at all!

385 ESTRAGON [*timidly, to* POZZO] You're not Mr. Godot, Sir?

POZZO [*terrifying voice*] I am Pozzo! [*Silence*] Pozzo! [*Silence*] Does that name mean nothing to you? [*Silence*] I say does that name mean nothing to you?

[VLADIMIR *and* ESTRAGON *look at each other questioningly.*]

ESTRAGON [*pretending to search*] Bozzo . . . Bozzo . . .

390 VLADIMIR [*ditto*] Pozzo . . . Pozzo . . .

POZZO PPPOZZZO!

ESTRAGON Ah! Pozzo . . . let me see . . . Pozzo . . .

VLADIMIR Is it Pozzo or Bozzo?

ESTRAGON Pozzo . . . no . . . I'm afraid I . . . no . . . I don't seem to . . .

[POZZO *advances threateningly.*]

395 VLADIMIR [*conciliating*] I once knew a family called Cozzo. The mother had the clap.[2]

ESTRAGON [*hastily*] We're not from these parts, Sir.

POZZO [*halting*] You are human beings none the less. [*He puts on his glasses.*] As far as one can see. [*He takes off his glasses.*] Of the same species as 400 myself. [*He bursts into an enormous laugh.*] Of the same species as Pozzo! Made in God's image!

VLADIMIR Well you see—

POZZO [*peremptory*] Who is Godot?

ESTRAGON Godot?

405 POZZO You took me for Godot.

VLADIMIR Oh no, Sir, not for an instant, Sir.

POZZO Who is he?

VLADIMIR Oh he's a . . . he's a kind of acquaintance.

ESTRAGON Nothing of the kind, we hardly know him.

410 VLADIMIR True . . . we don't know him very well . . . but all the same . . .

ESTRAGON Personally I wouldn't even know him if I saw him.

POZZO You took me for him.

ESTRAGON [*recoiling before* POZZO] That's to say . . . you understand . . . the dusk . . . the strain . . . waiting . . . I confess . . . I imagined . . . for a 415 second . . .

POZZO Waiting? So you were waiting for him?

VLADIMIR Well you see—

POZZO Here? On my land?

VLADIMIR We didn't intend any harm.

420 ESTRAGON We meant well.

POZZO The road is free to all.

VLADIMIR That's how we looked at it.

POZZO It's a disgrace. But there you are.

ESTRAGON Nothing we can do about it.

425 POZZO [*with magnanimous gesture*] Let's say no more about it. [*He jerks the rope.*] Up pig! [*Pause*] Every time he drops he falls asleep. [*Jerks the rope.*] Up hog! [*Noise of* LUCKY *getting up and picking up his baggage.* POZZO *jerks*

---

2. Gonorrhea (slang).

the rope.] Back! [*Enter* LUCKY *backwards.*] Stop! [LUCKY *stops.*] Turn! [LUCKY
turns. *To* VLADIMIR *and* ESTRAGON, *affably.*] Gentlemen, I am happy to have
430   met you. [*Before their incredulous expression*] Yes yes, sincerely happy. [*He
jerks the rope.*] Closer! [LUCKY *advances.*] Stop! [LUCKY *stops.*] Yes, the road
seems long when one journeys all alone for . . . [*He consults his watch.*] . . .
yes . . . [*He calculates.*] . . . yes, six hours, that's right, six hours on end,
and never a soul in sight. [*To* LUCKY] Coat! [LUCKY *puts down the bag,
435   advances, gives the coat, goes back to his place, takes up the bag.*] Hold that!
[POZZO *holds out the whip.* LUCKY *advances and, both his hands being occupied, takes the whip in his mouth, then goes back to his place.* POZZO *begins
to put on his coat, stops.*] Coat! [LUCKY *puts down bag, basket and stool,
advances, helps* POZZO *on with his coat, goes back to his place and takes up
bag, basket and stool.*] Touch of autumn in the air this evening. [POZZO *finishes buttoning his coat, stoops, inspects himself, straightens up.*] Whip!
[LUCKY *advances, stoops,* POZZO *snatches the whip from his mouth,* LUCKY
goes back to his place.*] Yes, gentlemen, I cannot go for long without the
440   society of my likes [*He puts on his glasses and looks at the two likes.*] even
when the likeness is an imperfect one. [*He takes off his glasses.*] Stool!
[LUCKY *puts down bag and basket, advances, opens stool, puts it down, goes
back to his place, takes up bag and basket.*] Closer! [LUCKY *puts down bag
and basket, advances, moves stool, goes back to his place, takes up bag and
basket.* POZZO *sits down, places the butt of his whip against* LUCKY's *chest and
pushes.*] Back! [LUCKY *takes a step back.*] Further! [LUCKY *takes another step
back.*] Stop! [LUCKY *stops. To* VLADIMIR *and* ESTRAGON.] That is why, with
445   your permission, I propose to dally with you a moment, before I venture
any further. Basket! [LUCKY *advances, gives the basket, goes back to his
place.*] The fresh air stimulates the jaded appetite. [*He opens the basket,
takes out a piece of chicken and a bottle of wine.*] Basket! [LUCKY *advances,
picks up the basket and goes back to his place.*] Further! [LUCKY *takes a step
450   back.*] He stinks. Happy days!

> [*He drinks from the bottle, puts it down and begins to eat. Silence.*
> VLADIMIR *and* ESTRAGON, *cautiously at first, then more boldly, begin to
> circle about* LUCKY, *inspecting him up and down.* POZZO *eats his chicken
> voraciously, throwing away the bones after having sucked them.* LUCKY
> *sags slowly, until bag and basket touch the ground, then straightens up
> with a start and begins to sag again. Rhythm of one sleeping on his feet.*]

ESTRAGON   What ails him?
VLADIMIR   He looks tired.
ESTRAGON   Why doesn't he put down his bags?
VLADIMIR   How do I know? [*They close in on him.*] Careful!
455 ESTRAGON   Say something to him.
VLADIMIR   Look!
ESTRAGON   What?
VLADIMIR [*pointing*]   His neck!
ESTRAGON [*looking at the neck*]   I see nothing.
460 VLADIMIR   Here.

> [ESTRAGON *goes over beside* VLADIMIR.]

ESTRAGON   Oh I say!
VLADIMIR   A running sore!
ESTRAGON   It's the rope.

VLADIMIR It's the rubbing.

465 ESTRAGON It's inevitable.

VLADIMIR It's the knot.

ESTRAGON It's the chafing.

[*They resume their inspection, dwell on the face.*]

VLADIMIR [*grudgingly*] He's not bad looking.

ESTRAGON [*shrugging his shoulders, wry face*] Would you say so?

470 VLADIMIR A trifle effeminate.

ESTRAGON Look at the slobber.

VLADIMIR It's inevitable.

ESTRAGON Look at the slaver.[3]

VLADIMIR Perhaps he's a halfwit.

475 ESTRAGON A cretin.

VLADIMIR [*looking closer*] Looks like a goiter.

ESTRAGON [*ditto*] It's not certain.

VLADIMIR He's panting.

ESTRAGON It's inevitable.

480 VLADIMIR And his eyes!

ESTRAGON What about them?

VLADIMIR Goggling out of his head.

ESTRAGON Looks at his last gasp to me.

VLADIMIR It's not certain. [*Pause*] Ask him a question.

485 ESTRAGON Would that be a good thing?

VLADIMIR What do we risk?

ESTRAGON [*timidly*] Mister . . .

VLADIMIR Louder.

ESTRAGON [*louder*] Mister . . .

490 POZZO Leave him in peace! [*They turn towards* POZZO *who, having finished eating, wipes his mouth with the back of his hand.*] Can't you see he wants to rest? Basket! [*He strikes a match and begins to light his pipe.* ESTRAGON *sees the chicken bones on the ground and stares at them greedily. As* LUCKY *does not move* POZZO *throws the match angrily away and jerks the rope.*] Basket! [LUCKY *starts, almost falls, recovers his senses, advances, puts the bottle in the basket and goes back to his place.* ESTRAGON *stares at the bones.* POZZO *strikes another match and lights his pipe.*] What can you expect, it's 495 not his job. [*He pulls at his pipe, stretches out his legs.*] Ah! That's better.

ESTRAGON [*timidly*] Please Sir . . .

POZZO What is it, my good man?

ESTRAGON Er . . . you've finished with the . . . er . . . you don't need the . . . er . . . bones, Sir?

500 VLADIMIR [*scandalized*] You couldn't have waited?

POZZO No no, he does well to ask. Do I need the bones? [*He turns them over with the end of his whip.*] No, personally I do not need them any more. [ESTRAGON *takes a step towards the bones.*] But . . . [ESTRAGON *stops short.*] . . . but in theory the bones go to the carrier. He is therefore the one 505 to ask. [ESTRAGON *turns towards* LUCKY, *hesitates.*] Go on, go on, don't be afraid, ask him, he'll tell you.

---

3. Saliva falling from the mouth.

[ESTRAGON *goes towards* LUCKY, *stops before him.*]

ESTRAGON   Mister . . . excuse me, Mister . . .

POZZO   You're being spoken to, pig! Reply! [*To* ESTRAGON] Try him again.

ESTRAGON   Excuse me, Mister, the bones, you won't be wanting the bones?

[LUCKY *looks long at* ESTRAGON.]

510 POZZO [*in raptures*]   Mister! [LUCKY *bows his head.*] Reply! Do you want them or don't you? [*Silence of* LUCKY. *To* ESTRAGON.] They're yours. [ESTRAGON *makes a dart at the bones, picks them up and begins to gnaw them.*] I don't like it. I've never known him refuse a bone before. [*He looks anxiously at* LUCKY.] Nice business it'd be if he fell sick on me! [*He puffs at his pipe.*]

515 VLADIMIR [*exploding*]   It's a scandal!

[*Silence. Flabbergasted,* ESTRAGON *stops gnawing, looks at* POZZO *and* VLADIMIR *in turn.* POZZO *outwardly calm.* VLADIMIR *embarrassed.*]

POZZO [*to* VLADIMIR]   Are you alluding to anything in particular?

VLADIMIR [*stutteringly resolute*]   To treat a man . . . [*Gesture towards* LUCKY] . . . like that . . . I think that . . . no . . . a human being . . . no . . . it's a scandal!

520 ESTRAGON [*not to be outdone*]   A disgrace! [*He resumes his gnawing.*]

POZZO   You are severe. [*To* VLADIMIR] What age are you, if it's not a rude question? [*Silence*] Sixty? Seventy? [*To* ESTRAGON] What age would you say he was?

ESTRAGON   Eleven.

525 POZZO   I am impertinent. [*He knocks out his pipe against the whip, gets up.*] I must be getting on. Thank you for your society. [*He reflects.*] Unless I smoke another pipe before I go. What do you say? [*They say nothing.*] Oh I'm only a small smoker, a very small smoker, I'm not in the habit of smoking two pipes one on top of the other, it makes [*Hand to heart, sighing*] my

530 heart go pit-a-pat. [*Silence*] It's the nicotine, one absorbs it in spite of one's precautions. [*Sighs*] You know how it is. [*Silence*] But perhaps you don't smoke? Yes? No? It's of no importance. [*Silence*] But how am I to sit down now, without affectation, now that I have risen? Without appearing to— how shall I say—without appearing to falter. [*To* VLADIMIR] I beg your par-

535 don? [*Silence*] Perhaps you didn't speak? [*Silence*] It's of no importance. Let me see . . . [*He reflects.*]

ESTRAGON   Ah! That's better. [*He puts the bones in his pocket.*]

VLADIMIR   Let's go.

ESTRAGON   So soon?

540 POZZO   One moment! [*He jerks the rope.*] Stool! [*He points with his whip.* LUCKY *moves the stool.*] More! There! [*He sits down.* LUCKY *goes back to his place.*] Done it! [*He fills his pipe.*]

VLADIMIR [*vehemently*]   Let's go!

POZZO   I hope I'm not driving you away. Wait a little longer, you'll never

545 regret it.

ESTRAGON [*sensing charity*]   We're in no hurry.

POZZO [*having lit his pipe*]   The second is never so sweet . . . [*He takes the pipe out of his mouth, contemplates it.*] . . . as the first I mean. [*He puts the pipe back in his mouth.*] But it's sweet just the same.

550 VLADIMIR   I'm going.

POZZO   He can no longer endure my presence. I am perhaps not particularly human, but who cares? [*To* VLADIMIR] Think twice before you do anything

rash. Suppose you go now while it is still day, for there is no denying it is still day. [*They all look up at the sky.*] Good. [*They stop looking at the sky.*]
555 What happens in that case—[*He takes the pipe out of his mouth, examines it.*]—I'm out—[*He relights his pipe.*]—in that case—[*Puff*]—in that case—[*Puff*]—what happens in that case to your appointment with this . . . Godet . . . Godot . . . Godin . . . anyhow you see who I mean, who has your future in his hands . . . [*Pause*] . . . at least your immediate future?
560 VLADIMIR   Who told you?
POZZO   He speaks to me again! If this goes on much longer we'll soon be old friends.
ESTRAGON   Why doesn't he put down his bags?
POZZO   I too would be happy to meet him. The more people I meet the hap
565 pier I become. From the meanest creature one departs wiser, richer, more conscious of one's blessings. Even you . . . [*He looks at them ostentatiously in turn to make it clear they are both meant.*] . . . even you, who knows, will have added to my store.
ESTRAGON   Why doesn't he put down his bags?
570 POZZO   But that would surprise me.
VLADIMIR   You're being asked a question.
POZZO [*delighted*]   A question! Who? What? A moment ago you were calling me Sir, in fear and trembling. Now you're asking me questions. No good will come of this!
575 VLADIMIR [*to* ESTRAGON]   I think he's listening.
ESTRAGON [*circling about* LUCKY]   What?
VLADIMIR   You can ask him now. He's on the alert.
ESTRAGON   Ask him what?
VLADIMIR   Why he doesn't put down his bags.
580 ESTRAGON   I wonder.
VLADIMIR   Ask him, can't you?
POZZO [*who has followed these exchanges with anxious attention, fearing lest the question get lost*]   You want to know why he doesn't put down his bags, as you call them.
VLADIMIR   That's it.
585 POZZO [*to* ESTRAGON]   You are sure you agree with that?
ESTRAGON   He's puffing like a grampus.[4]
POZZO   The answer is this. [*To* ESTRAGON] But stay still, I beg of you, you're making me nervous!
VLADIMIR   Here.
590 ESTRAGON   What is it?
VLADIMIR   He's about to speak.

[ESTRAGON *goes over beside* VLADIMIR. *Motionless, side by side, they wait.*]

POZZO   Good. Is everybody ready? Is everybody looking at me? [*He looks at* LUCKY, *jerks the rope.* LUCKY *raises his head.*] Will you look at me, pig! [LUCKY *looks at him.*] Good. [*He puts the pipe in his pocket, takes out a little vaporizer and sprays his throat, puts back the vaporizer in his pocket, clears his throat, spits, takes out the vaporizer again, sprays his throat again, puts
595 back the vaporizer in his pocket.*] I am ready. Is everybody listening? Is everybody ready? [*He looks at them all in turn, jerks the rope.*] Hog! [LUCKY

4. A variety of dolphin.

raises his head.] I don't like talking in a vacuum. Good. Let me see. [*He reflects.*]

ESTRAGON   I'm going.

POZZO   What was it exactly you wanted to know?

600 VLADIMIR   Why he—

POZZO [*angrily*]   Don't interrupt me! [*Pause. Calmer.*] If we all speak at once we'll never get anywhere. [*Pause.*] What was I saying? [*Pause. Louder.*] What was I saying?

> [VLADIMIR *mimics one carrying a heavy burden.* POZZO *looks at him, puzzled.*]

ESTRAGON [*forcibly*]   Bags. [*He points at* LUCKY.] Why? Always hold. [*He sags,*
605 *panting.*] Never put down. [*He opens his hands, straightens up with relief.*] Why?

POZZO   Ah! Why couldn't you say so before? Why he doesn't make himself comfortable? Let's try and get this clear. Has he not the right to? Certainly he has. It follows that he doesn't want to. There's reasoning for you. And
610 why doesn't he want to? [*Pause*] Gentlemen, the reason is this.

VLADIMIR [*to* ESTRAGON]   Make a note of this.

POZZO   He wants to impress me, so that I'll keep him.

ESTRAGON   What?

POZZO   Perhaps I haven't got it quite right. He wants to mollify me, so that
615 I'll give up the idea of parting with him. No, that's not exactly it either.

VLADIMIR   You want to get rid of him?

POZZO   He wants to cod[5] me, but he won't.

VLADIMIR   You want to get rid of him?

POZZO   He imagines that when I see how well he carries I'll be tempted to
620 keep him on in that capacity.

ESTRAGON   You've had enough of him?

POZZO   In reality he carries like a pig. It's not his job.

VLADIMIR   You want to get rid of him?

POZZO   He imagines that when I see him indefatigable I'll regret my deci
625 sion. Such is his miserable scheme. As though I were short of slaves! [*All three look at* LUCKY.] Atlas, son of Jupiter![6] [*Silence*] Well, that's that I think. Anything else?

> [*Vaporizer.*]

VLADIMIR   You want to get rid of him?

POZZO   Remark that I might just as well have been in his shoes and he in
630 mine. If chance had not willed otherwise. To each one his due.

VLADIMIR   You waagerrim?

POZZO   I beg your pardon?

VLADIMIR   You want to get rid of him?

POZZO   I do. But instead of driving him away as I might have done, I mean
635 instead of simply kicking him out on his arse, in the goodness of my heart I am bringing him to the fair, where I hope to get a good price for him. The truth is you can't drive such creatures away. The best thing would be to kill them.

---

5. Play a joke on, tease; or, perhaps, a short-ened version of *coddle*.
6. In classical mythology, Atlas's father was the Titan Iapetus, not Jupiter; as punishment for leading the Titans in their war against the Olympian gods, Atlas was condemned to hold the heavens on his shoulders.

[LUCKY *weeps.*]

ESTRAGON   He's crying!

640 POZZO   Old dogs have more dignity. [*He proffers his handkerchief to* ESTRAGON.] Comfort him, since you pity him. [ESTRAGON *hesitates.*] Come on. [ESTRAGON *takes the handkerchief.*] Wipe away his tears, he'll feel less forsaken.

[ESTRAGON *hesitates.*]

VLADIMIR   Here, give it to me, I'll do it.

[ESTRAGON *refuses to give the handkerchief. Childish gestures.*]

645 POZZO   Make haste, before he stops. [ESTRAGON *approaches* LUCKY *and makes to wipe his eyes.* LUCKY *kicks him violently in the shins.* ESTRAGON *drops the handkerchief, recoils, staggers about the stage howling with pain.*] Hanky!

[LUCKY *puts down bag and basket, picks up handkerchief and gives it to* POZZO, *goes back to his place, picks up bag and basket.*]

ESTRAGON   Oh the swine! [*He pulls up the leg of his trousers.*] He's crippled me!

POZZO   I told you he didn't like strangers.

650 VLADIMIR [*to* ESTRAGON]   Show. [ESTRAGON *shows his leg. To* POZZO, *angrily*] He's bleeding!

POZZO   It's a good sign.

ESTRAGON [*on one leg*]   I'll never walk again!

VLADIMIR [*tenderly*]   I'll carry you. [*Pause*] If necessary.

655 POZZO   He's stopped crying. [*To* ESTRAGON] You have replaced him as it were. [*Lyrically*] The tears of the world are a constant quantity. For each one who begins to weep somewhere else another stops. The same is true of the laugh. [*He laughs.*] Let us not then speak ill of our generation, it is not any unhappier than its predecessors. [*Pause*] Let us not speak well of it either.
660 [*Pause*] Let us not speak of it at all. [*Pause. Judiciously.*] It is true the population has increased.

VLADIMIR   Try and walk.

[ESTRAGON *takes a few limping steps, stops before* LUCKY *and spits on him, then goes and sits down on the mound.*]

POZZO   Guess who taught me all these beautiful things. [*Pause. Pointing to* LUCKY] My Lucky!

665 VLADIMIR [*looking at the sky*]   Will night never come?

POZZO   But for him all my thoughts, all my feelings, would have been of common things. [*Pause. With extraordinary vehemence.*] Professional worries! [*Calmer*] Beauty, grace, truth of the first water,[7] I knew they were all beyond me. So I took a knook.[8]

670 VLADIMIR [*startled from his inspection of the sky*]   A knook?

POZZO   That was nearly sixty years ago . . . [*He consults his watch.*] . . . yes, nearly sixty. [*Drawing himself up proudly*] You wouldn't think it to look at me, would you? Compared to him I look like a young man, no? [*Pause*] Hat!

7. Of the highest quality (formerly, a technical term used of diamonds).
8. A coinage of Beckett's, possibly echoing *knut* (the Russian word for "whip"). In a passage from the original French version that Beckett did not include in his English trans- lation, Pozzo expounds on the word to Vladimir as follows: "You are not from these parts. Are you so out of touch with the times? Years ago people used to have jesters. Now they have knouks. Those who are able to afford them."

[LUCKY *puts down the basket and takes off his hat. His long white hair falls about his face. He puts his hat under his arm and picks up the basket.*] Now
675   look. [POZZO *takes off his hat.*[9] *He is completely bald. He puts on his hat again.*] Did you see?

VLADIMIR   And now you turn him away? Such an old and faithful servant!

ESTRAGON   Swine!

        [POZZO *more and more agitated.*]

VLADIMIR   After having sucked all the good out of him you chuck him away
680   like a . . . like a banana skin. Really . . .

POZZO [*groaning, clutching his head*]   I can't bear it . . . any longer . . . the way he goes on . . . you've no idea . . . it's terrible . . . he must go . . . [*He waves his arms.*] . . . I'm going mad . . . [*He collapses, his head in his hands.*] . . . I can't bear it . . . any longer . . .

        [*Silence. All look at* POZZO.]

685 VLADIMIR   He can't bear it.

ESTRAGON   Any longer.

VLADIMIR   He's going mad.

ESTRAGON   It's terrible.

VLADIMIR [*to* LUCKY]   How dare you! It's abominable! Such a good master!
690   Crucify him like that! After so many years! Really!

POZZO [*sobbing*]   He used to be so kind . . . so helpful . . . and entertaining . . . my good angel . . . and now . . . he's killing me.

ESTRAGON [*to* VLADIMIR]   Does he want to replace him?

VLADIMIR   What?

695 ESTRAGON   Does he want someone to take his place or not?

VLADIMIR   I don't think so.

ESTRAGON   What?

VLADIMIR   I don't know.

ESTRAGON   Ask him.

700 POZZO [*calmer*]   Gentlemen, I don't know what came over me. Forgive me. Forget all I said. [*More and more his old self*] I don't remember exactly what it was, but you may be sure there wasn't a word of truth in it. [*Drawing himself up, striking his chest*] Do I look like a man that can be made to suffer? Frankly? [*He rummages in his pockets.*] What have I done with my
705   pipe?

VLADIMIR   Charming evening we're having.

ESTRAGON   Unforgettable.

VLADIMIR   And it's not over.

ESTRAGON   Apparently not.

710 VLADIMIR   It's only beginning.

ESTRAGON   It's awful.

VLADIMIR   Worse than the pantomime.

ESTRAGON   The circus.

VLADIMIR   The music-hall.

715 ESTRAGON   The circus.

POZZO   What can I have done with that briar?[1]

ESTRAGON   He's a scream. He's lost his dudeen.[2] [*Laughs noisily.*]

---

9. All four wear bowlers [Beckett's note].
1. That is, his pipe made from briar wood.

2. A short-stemmed clay tobacco pipe (Irish Gaelic).

VLADIMIR   I'll be back. [*He hastens towards the wings.*]

ESTRAGON   End of the corridor, on the left.

720 VLADIMIR   Keep my seat. [*Exit* VLADIMIR.]

POZZO [*on the point of tears*]   I've lost my Kapp and Peterson![3]

ESTRAGON [*convulsed with merriment*]   He'll be the death of me!

POZZO   You didn't see by any chance—. [*He misses* VLADIMIR.] Oh! He's gone! Without saying goodbye! How could he! He might have waited!

725 ESTRAGON   He would have burst.

POZZO   Oh! [*Pause*] Oh well then of course in that case . . .

ESTRAGON   Come here.

POZZO   What for?

ESTRAGON   You'll see.

730 POZZO   You want me to get up?

ESTRAGON   Quick! [POZZO *gets up and goes over beside* ESTRAGON. ESTRAGON *points off.*] Look!

POZZO [*having put on his glasses*]   Oh I say!

ESTRAGON   It's all over.

[*Enter* VLADIMIR, *somber. He shoulders* LUCKY *out of his way, kicks over the stool, comes and goes agitatedly.*]

735 POZZO   He's not pleased.

ESTRAGON [*to* VLADIMIR]   You missed a treat. Pity.

[VLADIMIR *halts, straightens the stool, comes and goes, calmer.*]

POZZO   He subsides. [*Looking round*] Indeed all subsides. A great calm descends. [*Raising his hand*] Listen! Pan sleeps.[4]

VLADIMIR   Will night never come?

[*All three look at the sky.*]

740 POZZO   You don't feel like going until it does?

ESTRAGON   Well you see—

POZZO   Why it's very natural, very natural. I myself in your situation, if I had an appointment with a Godin . . . Godet . . . Godot . . . anyhow you see who I mean, I'd wait till it was black night before I gave up. [*He looks at the stool.*] I'd very much like to sit down, but I don't quite know how to go about it.

745

ESTRAGON   Could I be of any help?

POZZO   If you asked me perhaps.

ESTRAGON   What?

750 POZZO   If you asked me to sit down.

ESTRAGON   Would that be a help?

POZZO   I fancy so.

ESTRAGON   Here we go. Be seated, Sir, I beg of you.

POZZO   No no, I wouldn't think of it! [*Pause. Aside.*] Ask me again.

755 ESTRAGON   Come come, take a seat I beseech you, you'll get pneumonia.

POZZO   You really think so?

ESTRAGON   Why it's absolutely certain.

---

3. A brand of pipe. Kapp and Peterson were Dublin's most renowned manufacturers and purveyors of smoking pipes and other tobacco products.

4. Pan, the Greek god of pastures, flocks, and wild places, was said to sleep at noon; to accommodate him, all of nature fell quiet.

POZZO   No doubt you are right. [*He sits down.*] Done it again! [*Pause*] Thank
you, dear fellow. [*He consults his watch.*] But I must really be getting along,
if I am to observe my schedule.

VLADIMIR   Time has stopped.

POZZO [*cuddling his watch to his ear*]   Don't you believe it, Sir, don't you
believe it. [*He puts his watch back in his pocket.*] Whatever you like, but
not that.

ESTRAGON [*to* POZZO]   Everything seems black to him today.

POZZO   Except the firmament. [*He laughs, pleased with this witticism.*] But I
see what it is, you are not from these parts, you don't know what our twi-
lights can do. Shall I tell you? [*Silence.* ESTRAGON *is fiddling with his boot
again,* VLADIMIR *with his hat.*] I can't refuse you. [*Vaporizer*] A little attention, if you please. [VLADIMIR *and* ESTRAGON *continue their fiddling,* LUCKY
is half asleep. POZZO *cracks his whip feebly.*] What's the matter with this
whip? [*He gets up and cracks it more vigorously, finally with success.* LUCKY
jumps. VLADIMIR'S *hat,* ESTRAGON'S *boot,* LUCKY'S *hat, fall to the ground.* POZZO
throws down the whip.] Worn out, this whip. [*He looks at* VLADIMIR *and*
ESTRAGON.] What was I saying?

VLADIMIR   Let's go.

ESTRAGON   But take the weight off your feet, I implore you, you'll catch your
death.

POZZO   True. [*He sits down. To* ESTRAGON.] What is your name?

ESTRAGON   Adam.

POZZO [*who hasn't listened*]   Ah yes! The night. [*He raises his head.*] But be a
little more attentive, for pity's sake, otherwise we'll never get anywhere.
[*He looks at the sky.*] Look! [*All look at the sky except* LUCKY *who is dozing off
again.* POZZO *jerks the rope.*] Will you look at the sky, pig! [LUCKY *looks at the
sky.*] Good, that's enough. [*They stop looking at the sky.*] What is there so
extraordinary about it? Qua[5] sky. It is pale and luminous like any sky at this
hour of the day. [*Pause*] In these latitudes. [*Pause*] When the weather is
fine. [*Lyrical*] An hour ago [*He looks at his watch, prosaic.*] roughly [*Lyrical*]
after having poured forth even since [*He hesitates, prosaic.*] say ten o'clock
in the morning [*Lyrical*] tirelessly torrents of red and white light it begins
to lose its effulgence, to grow pale [*Gesture of the two hands lapsing by
stages*] pale, ever a little paler, a little paler until [*Dramatic pause, ample
gesture of the two hands flung wide apart*] pppfff! finished! it comes to rest.
But—[*Hand raised in admonition*]—but behind this veil of gentleness and
peace night is charging [*Vibrantly*] and will burst upon us [*Snaps his fin
gers.*] pop! like that! [*His inspiration leaves him.*] just when we least expect
it. [*Silence. Gloomily.*] That's how it is on this bitch of an earth.

  [*Long silence.*]

ESTRAGON   So long as one knows.

VLADIMIR   One can bide one's time.

ESTRAGON   One knows what to expect.

VLADIMIR   No further need to worry.

ESTRAGON   Simply wait.

---

5. As (a term common in philosophical discourse).

VLADIMIR   We're used to it. [*He picks up his hat, peers inside it, shakes it, puts it on.*]

POZZO   How did you find me? [VLADIMIR *and* ESTRAGON *look at him blankly.*] Good? Fair? Middling? Poor? Positively bad?

805 VLADIMIR [*first to understand*]   Oh very good, very very good.

POZZO [*to* ESTRAGON]   And you, Sir?

ESTRAGON   Oh tray bong, tray tray tray bong.[6]

POZZO [*fervently*]   Bless you, gentlemen, bless you! [*Pause*] I have such need of encouragement! [*Pause*] I weakened a little towards the end, you didn't
810   notice?

VLADIMIR   Oh perhaps just a teeny weeny little bit.

ESTRAGON   I thought it was intentional.

POZZO   You see my memory is defective.
             [*Silence.*]

ESTRAGON   In the meantime nothing happens.

815 POZZO   You find it tedious?

ESTRAGON   Somewhat.

POZZO [*to* VLADIMIR]   And you, Sir?

VLADIMIR   I've been better entertained.
             [*Silence.* POZZO *struggles inwardly.*]

POZZO   Gentlemen, you have been . . . civil to me.

820 ESTRAGON   Not at all!

VLADIMIR   What an idea!

POZZO   Yes yes, you have been correct. So that I ask myself is there anything I can do in my turn for these honest fellows who are having such a dull, dull time.

825 ESTRAGON   Even ten francs would be a help.

VLADIMIR   We are not beggars!

POZZO   Is there anything I can do, that's what I ask myself, to cheer them up? I have given them bones, I have talked to them about this and that, I have explained the twilight, admittedly. But is it enough, that's what tor-
830   tures me, is it enough?

ESTRAGON   Even five.

VLADIMIR [*to* ESTRAGON, *indignantly*]   That's enough!

ESTRAGON   I couldn't accept less.

POZZO   Is it enough? No doubt. But I am liberal. It's my nature. This eve-
835   ning. So much the worse for me. [*He jerks the rope.* LUCKY *looks at him.*] For I shall suffer, no doubt about that. [*He picks up the whip.*] What do you prefer? Shall we have him dance, or sing, or recite, or think, or—

ESTRAGON   Who?

POZZO   Who! You know how to think, you two?

840 VLADIMIR   He thinks?

POZZO   Certainly. Aloud. He even used to think very prettily once, I could listen to him for hours. Now . . . [*He shudders.*] So much the worse for me. Well, would you like him to think something for us?

6. "Oui! Tray bong!" (which plays on the French phrase *oui très bon*—"yes, very good") was the title of a late 19th-century song made popular in English music halls by Charles Chaplin Sr., father of the famous film actor.

ESTRAGON   I'd rather he'd dance, it'd be more fun.

845 POZZO   Not necessarily.

ESTRAGON   Wouldn't it, Didi, be more fun?

VLADIMIR   I'd like well to hear him think.

ESTRAGON   Perhaps he could dance first and think afterwards, if it isn't too much to ask him.

850 VLADIMIR [to POZZO]   Would that be possible?

POZZO   By all means, nothing simpler. It's the natural order. [He laughs briefly.]

VLADIMIR   Then let him dance.

    [Silence.]

POZZO   Do you hear, hog?

ESTRAGON   He never refuses?

855 POZZO   He refused once. [Silence] Dance, misery!

    [LUCKY puts down bag and basket, advances towards front, turns to POZZO. LUCKY dances. He stops.]

ESTRAGON   Is that all?

POZZO   Encore!

    [LUCKY executes the same movements, stops.]

ESTRAGON   Pooh! I'd do as well myself. [He imitates LUCKY, almost falls.] With a little practice.

860 POZZO   He used to dance the farandole, the fling, the brawl, the jig, the fandango and even the hornpipe.[7] He capered. For joy. Now that's the best he can do. Do you know what he calls it?

ESTRAGON   The Scapegoat's Agony.

VLADIMIR   The Hard Stool.

865 POZZO   The Net. He thinks he's entangled in a net.

VLADIMIR [squirming like an aesthete]   There's something about it . . .

    [LUCKY makes to return to his burdens.]

POZZO   Woaa!

    [LUCKY stiffens.]

ESTRAGON   Tell us about the time he refused.

POZZO   With pleasure, with pleasure. [He fumbles in his pockets.] Wait. [He
870 fumbles.] What have I done with my spray? [He fumbles.] Well now isn't that . . . [He looks up, consternation on his features. Faintly.] I can't find my pulverizer![8]

ESTRAGON [faintly]   My left lung is very weak! [He coughs feebly. In ringing tones.] But my right lung is as sound as a bell!

875 POZZO [normal voice]   No matter! What was I saying. [He ponders.] Wait. [Ponders.] Well now isn't that . . . [He raises his head.] Help me!

ESTRAGON   Wait!

VLADIMIR   Wait!

POZZO   Wait!

    [All three take off their hats simultaneously, press their hands to their foreheads, concentrate.]

---

7. All energetic dances, associated (respectively) with Provence, the Scottish highlands, France, Ireland, Spain, and England.

8. That is, his vaporizer, mentioned earlier.

880 ESTRAGON [*triumphantly*]   Ah!

VLADIMIR   He has it.

POZZO [*impatient*]   Well?

ESTRAGON   Why doesn't he put down his bags?

VLADIMIR   Rubbish!

885 POZZO   Are you sure?

VLADIMIR   Damn it haven't you already told us?

POZZO   I've already told you?

ESTRAGON   He's already told us?

VLADIMIR   Anyway he has put them down.

890 ESTRAGON [*glance at Lucky*]   So he has. And what of it?

VLADIMIR   Since he has put down his bags it is impossible we should have asked why he does not do so.

POZZO   Stoutly reasoned!

ESTRAGON   And why has he put them down?

895 POZZO   Answer us that.

VLADIMIR   In order to dance.

ESTRAGON   True!

POZZO   True!

[*Silence. They put on their hats.*]

ESTRAGON   Nothing happens, nobody comes, nobody goes, it's awful!

900 VLADIMIR [*to* POZZO]   Tell him to think.

POZZO   Give him his hat.

VLADIMIR   His hat?

POZZO   He can't think without his hat.

VLADIMIR [*to* ESTRAGON]   Give him his hat.

905 ESTRAGON   Me! After what he did to me! Never!

VLADIMIR   I'll give it to him. [*He does not move.*]

ESTRAGON [*to* POZZO]   Tell him to go and fetch it.

POZZO   It's better to give it to him.

VLADIMIR   I'll give it to him.

[*He picks up the hat and tenders it at arm's length to* LUCKY, *who does not move.*]

910 POZZO   You must put it on his head.

ESTRAGON [*to* POZZO]   Tell him to take it.

POZZO   It's better to put it on his head.

VLADIMIR   I'll put it on his head.

[*He goes round behind* LUCKY, *approaches him cautiously, puts the hat on his head and recoils smartly.* LUCKY *does not move. Silence.*]

ESTRAGON   What's he waiting for?

915 POZZO   Stand back! [VLADIMIR *and* ESTRAGON *move away from* LUCKY. POZZO *jerks the rope.* LUCKY *looks at* POZZO.] Think, pig! [*Pause.* LUCKY *begins to dance.*] Stop! [LUCKY *stops.*] Forward! [LUCKY *advances.*] Stop! [LUCKY *stops.*] Think!

[*Silence.*]

LUCKY   On the other hand with regard to—

920 POZZO   Stop! [LUCKY *stops.*] Back! [LUCKY *moves back.*] Stop! [LUCKY *stops.*] Turn! [LUCKY *turns towards auditorium.*] Think!

LUCKY   Given the existence as uttered forth in the public works of Puncher
and Wattmann[9] of a personal God quaquaquaqua with white beard
quaquaquaqua outside time without extension who from the heights of
925   divine apathia divine athambia divine aphasia[1] loves us dearly with some
exceptions for reasons unknown but time will tell and

[VLADIMIR   suffers like the divine Miranda[2] with those who for reasons
and   unknown but time will tell are plunged in torment plunged in
ESTRAGON   fire whose fire flames if that continues and who can doubt it will
930   all   fire the firmament that is to say blast hell to heaven so blue still
attention,   and calm so calm with a calm which even though intermittent
POZZO   is better than nothing but not so fast and considering what is
dejected   more that as a result of the labors left unfinished crowned by the
and   Acacacacademy of Anthropopopometry of Essy-in-Possy[3] of
935   disgusted.]   Testew and Cunard it is established beyond all doubt all other
doubt than that which clings to the labors of men that as a
[VLADIMIR   result of the labors unfinished of Testew and Cunard it is
and   established as hereinafter but not so fast for reasons unknown
ESTRAGON   that as a result of the public works of Puncher and Wattmann
940   begin to   it is established beyond all doubt that in view of the labors of
protest,   Fartov and Belcher left unfinished for reasons unknown of
POZZO's   Testew and Cunard left unfinished it is established what many
sufferings   deny that man in Possy of Testew and Cunard that man in Essy
increase.]   that man in short that man in brief in spite of the strides of
945   alimentation and defecation wastes and pines wastes and pines
[VLADIMIR   and concurrently simultaneously what is more for reasons
and   unknown in spite of the strides of physical culture the practice
ESTRAGON   of sports such as tennis football running cycling swimming
attentive   flying floating riding gliding conating camogie[4] skating tennis of
950   again,   all kinds dying flying sports of all sorts autumn summer winter
POZZO   winter tennis of all kinds hockey of all sorts penicillin and
more and   succedanea[5] in a word I resume flying gliding golf over nine
more   and eighteen holes tennis of all sorts in a word for reasons
agitated   unknown in Feckham Peckham Fulham Clapham[6] namely
955   and   concurrently simultaneously what is more for reasons unknown
groaning.]   but time will tell fades away I resume Fulham Clapham in a
word the dead loss per head since the death of Bishop

	Berkeley[7] being to the tune of one inch four ounce per head
	approximately by and large more or less to the nearest decimal
960 [VLADIMIR	good measure round figures stark naked in the stockinged feet
and	in Connemara[8] in a word for reasons unknown no matter what
ESTRAGON	matter the facts are there and considering what is more much
protest	more grave that in the light of the labors lost of Steinweg
violently.	and Peterman it appears what is more much more grave that
965 POZZO	in the light the light the light of the labors lost of Steinweg
jumps up,	and Peterman that in the plains in the mountains by the
pulls on	seas by the rivers running water running fire the air is the
the rope.	same and then the earth namely the air and then the earth
General	in the great cold the great dark the air and the earth abode
970 *outcry.*	of stones in the great cold alas alas in the year of their Lord
LUCKY *pulls*	six hundred and something the air the earth the sea the earth
on the rope,	abode of stones in the great deeps the great cold on sea on
staggers,	land and in the air I resume for reasons unknown in spite of the
shouts his	tennis the facts are there but time will tell I resume alas alas
975 *text. All*	on on in short in fine on on abode of stones who can doubt it I
three throw	resume but not so fast I resume the skull fading fading fading
themselves	and concurrently simultaneously what is more for reasons
on LUCKY	unknown in spite of the tennis on on the beard the flames
who	the tears the stones so blue so calm alas alas on on the skull
980 *struggles*	the skull the skull the skull in Connemara in spite of the
and shouts	tennis the labors abandoned left unfinished graver still abode
his text.]	of stones in a word I resume alas alas abandoned unfinished
	the skull the skull in Connemara in spite of the tennis the skull
	alas the stones Cunard [*Mêlée, final vociferations*] tennis . . . the
985	stones . . . so calm . . . Cunard . . . unfinished . . .

POZZO His hat!

> [VLADIMIR *seizes* LUCKY'S *hat. Silence of* LUCKY. *He falls. Silence. Panting of the victors.*]

ESTRAGON Avenged!

> [VLADIMIR *examines the hat, peers inside it.*]

POZZO Give me that! [*He snatches the hat from* VLADIMIR, *throws it on the ground, tramples on it.*] There's an end to his thinking!

990 VLADIMIR But will he be able to walk?

POZZO Walk or crawl! [*He kicks* LUCKY.] Up pig!

ESTRAGON Perhaps he's dead.

VLADIMIR You'll kill him.

POZZO Up scum! [*He jerks the rope.*] Help me!

995 VLADIMIR How?

POZZO Raise him up!

> [VLADIMIR *and* ESTRAGON *hoist* LUCKY *to his feet, support him an instant, then let him go. He falls.*]

ESTRAGON He's doing it on purpose!

---

7. George Berkeley (1685–1753), Irish idealist philosopher and bishop in the Church of Ireland. Berkeley's theory, which held that the world exists only insofar as it is perceived by the senses, is summed up in his Latin dictum *Esse est percipi* (To be is to be perceived).
8. A region of Galway in western Ireland.

POZZO   You must hold him. [*Pause*] Come on, come on, raise him up.
ESTRAGON   To hell with him!
1000 VLADIMIR   Come on, once more.
ESTRAGON   What does he take us for?

[*They raise* LUCKY, *hold him up.*]

POZZO   Don't let him go! [VLADIMIR *and* ESTRAGON *totter.*] Don't move! [POZZO *fetches bag and basket and brings them towards* LUCKY.] Hold him tight! [*He puts the bag in* LUCKY's *hand.* LUCKY *drops it immediately.*] Don't let him go! [*He puts back the bag in* LUCKY's *hand. Gradually, at the feel of the bag,*
1005   LUCKY *recovers his senses and his fingers finally close round the handle.*] Hold him tight! [*As before with basket*] Now! You can let him go. [VLADIMIR *and* ESTRAGON *move away from* LUCKY *who totters, reels, sags, but succeeds in remaining on his feet, bag and basket in his hands.* POZZO *steps back, cracks his whip.*] Forward! [LUCKY *totters forward.*] Back! [LUCKY *totters back.*] Turn! [LUCKY *turns.*] Done it! He can walk. [*Turning to* VLADIMIR *and* ESTRAGON] Thank you, gentlemen, and let me . . . [*He fumbles in his pock-*
1010   *ets*] . . . let me wish you . . . [*Fumbles.*] . . . wish you . . . [*Fumbles.*] . . . what have I done with my watch? [*Fumbles.*] A genuine half-hunter, gentlemen, with deadbeat escapement![9] [*Sobbing.*] Twas my granpa gave it to me! [*He searches on the ground,* VLADIMIR *and* ESTRAGON *likewise.* POZZO *turns over with his foot the remains of* LUCKY's *hat.*] Well now isn't that just—
VLADIMIR   Perhaps it's in your fob.[1]
1015 POZZO   Wait! [*He doubles up in an attempt to apply his ear to his stomach, listens. Silence.*] I hear nothing. [*He beckons them to approach.* VLADIMIR *and* ESTRAGON *go over to him, bend over his stomach.*] Surely one should hear the tick-tick.
VLADIMIR   Silence!

[*All listen, bent double.*]

1020 ESTRAGON   I hear something.
POZZO   Where?
VLADIMIR   It's the heart.
POZZO [*disappointed*]   Damnation!
VLADIMIR   Silence!
1025 ESTRAGON   Perhaps it has stopped.

[*They straighten up.*]

POZZO   Which of you smells so bad?
ESTRAGON   He has stinking breath and I have stinking feet.
POZZO   I must go.
ESTRAGON   And your half-hunter?
1030 POZZO   I must have left it at the manor.

[*Silence.*]

ESTRAGON   Then adieu.
POZZO   Adieu.
VLADIMIR   Adieu.
POZZO   Adieu.

---

9. The mechanism in watches that regulates the movement of the hands, here "deadbeat" because it does not recoil. *Half-hunter:* a kind of pocket watch featuring a metal case with a small glass window through which the hands are visible.

1. A small pocket, originally in the waistband (also known as a "watch pocket").

[*Silence. No one moves.*]

1035 VLADIMIR Adieu.

POZZO Adieu.

ESTRAGON Adieu.

[*Silence.*]

POZZO And thank you.

VLADIMIR Thank *you*.

1040 POZZO Not at all.

ESTRAGON Yes yes.

POZZO No no.

VLADIMIR Yes yes.

ESTRAGON No no.

[*Silence.*]

1045 POZZO I don't seem to be able . . . [*Long hesitation*] . . . to depart.

ESTRAGON Such is life.

[POZZO *turns, moves away from* LUCKY *towards the wings, paying out the rope as he goes.*]

VLADIMIR You're going the wrong way.

POZZO I need a running start. [*Having come to the end of the rope, i.e. off stage, he stops, turns and cries.*] Stand back! [VLADIMIR *and* ESTRAGON *stand*

1050 *back, look towards* POZZO. *Crack of whip.*] On! On!

ESTRAGON On!

VLADIMIR On!

[LUCKY *moves off.*]

POZZO Faster! [*He appears, crosses the stage preceded by* LUCKY. VLADIMIR *and* ESTRAGON *wave their hats. Exit* LUCKY.] On! On! [*On the point of disappearing in his turn he stops and turns. The rope tautens. Noise of* LUCKY *falling*

1055 *off.*] Stool! [VLADIMIR *fetches stool and gives it to* POZZO *who throws it to* LUCKY.] Adieu!

VLADIMIR ⎫
ESTRAGON ⎭ [*waving*] Adieu! Adieu!

POZZO Up! Pig! [*Noise of* LUCKY *getting up.*] On! [*Exit* POZZO.] Faster! On! Adieu! Pig! Yip! Adieu!

[*Long silence.*]

1060 VLADIMIR That passed the time.

ESTRAGON It would have passed in any case.

VLADIMIR Yes, but not so rapidly.

[*Pause.*]

ESTRAGON What do we do now?

VLADIMIR I don't know.

1065 ESTRAGON Let's go.

VLADIMIR We can't.

ESTRAGON Why not?

VLADIMIR We're waiting for Godot.

ESTRAGON [*despairingly*] Ah!

[*Pause.*]

1070 VLADIMIR How they've changed!

ESTRAGON Who?

VLADIMIR   Those two.

ESTRAGON   That's the idea, let's make a little conversation.

VLADIMIR   Haven't they?

1075 ESTRAGON   What?

VLADIMIR   Changed.

ESTRAGON   Very likely. They all change. Only we can't.

VLADIMIR   Likely! It's certain. Didn't you see them?

ESTRAGON   I suppose I did. But I don't know them.

1080 VLADIMIR   Yes you do know them.

ESTRAGON   No I don't know them.

VLADIMIR   We know them, I tell you. You forget everything. [*Pause. To himself.*] Unless they're not the same . . .

ESTRAGON   Why didn't they recognize us then?

1085 VLADIMIR   That means nothing. I too pretended not to recognize them. And then nobody ever recognizes us.

ESTRAGON   Forget it. What we need—ow! [VLADIMIR *does not react.*] Ow!

VLADIMIR   [*to himself*]   Unless they're not the same . . .

ESTRAGON   Didi! It's the other foot! [*He goes hobbling towards the mound.*]

1090 VLADIMIR   Unless they're not the same . . .

BOY   [*off*]   Mister!

[ESTRAGON *halts. Both look towards the voice.*]

ESTRAGON   Off we go again.

VLADIMIR   Approach, my child.

[*Enter* BOY, *timidly. He halts.*]

BOY   Mister Albert . . . ?

1095 VLADIMIR   Yes.

ESTRAGON   What do you want?

VLADIMIR   Approach!

[*The* BOY *does not move.*]

ESTRAGON   [*forcibly*]   Approach when you're told, can't you?

[*The* BOY *advances timidly, halts.*]

VLADIMIR   What is it?

1100 BOY   Mr. Godot . . .

VLADIMIR   Obviously . . . [*Pause*] Approach.

ESTRAGON   [*violently*]   Will you approach! [*The* BOY *advances timidly.*] What kept you so late?

VLADIMIR   You have a message from Mr. Godot?

1105 BOY   Yes Sir.

VLADIMIR   Well, what is it?

ESTRAGON   What kept you so late?

[*The* BOY *looks at them in turn, not knowing to which he should reply.*]

VLADIMIR   [*to* ESTRAGON]   Let him alone.

ESTRAGON   [*violently*]   You let me alone. [*Advancing, to the* BOY] Do you know

1110 what time it is?

BOY   [*recoiling*]   It's not my fault, Sir.

ESTRAGON   And whose is it? Mine?

BOY   I was afraid, Sir.

ESTRAGON   Afraid of what? Of us? [*Pause*] Answer me!

1115 VLADIMIR   I know what it is, he was afraid of the others.

ESTRAGON How long have you been here?

BOY A good while, Sir.

VLADIMIR You were afraid of the whip?

BOY Yes Sir.

1120 VLADIMIR The roars?

BOY Yes Sir.

VLADIMIR The two big men.

BOY Yes Sir.

VLADIMIR Do you know them?

1125 BOY No Sir.

VLADIMIR Are you a native of these parts? [*Silence*] Do you belong to these parts?

BOY Yes Sir.

ESTRAGON That's all a pack of lies. [*Shaking the* BOY *by the arm*] Tell us the

1130 truth!

BOY [*trembling*] But it is the truth, Sir!

VLADIMIR Will you let him alone! What's the matter with you? [ESTRAGON *releases the* BOY, *moves away, covering his face with his hands.* VLADIMIR *and the* BOY *observe him.* ESTRAGON *drops his hands. His face is convulsed.*] What's the matter with you?

ESTRAGON I'm unhappy.

1135 VLADIMIR Not really! Since when?

ESTRAGON I'd forgotten.

VLADIMIR Extraordinary the tricks that memory plays!

[ESTRAGON *tries to speak, renounces, limps to his place, sits down and begins to take off his boots. To* BOY]

Well?

BOY Mr. Godot—

1140 VLADIMIR I've seen you before, haven't I?

BOY I don't know, Sir.

VLADIMIR You don't know me?

BOY No Sir.

VLADIMIR It wasn't you came yesterday?

1145 BOY No Sir.

VLADIMIR This is your first time?

BOY Yes Sir.

[*Silence.*]

VLADIMIR Words words. [*Pause*] Speak.

BOY [*in a rush*] Mr. Godot told me to tell you he won't come this evening but

1150 surely tomorrow.

[*Silence.*]

VLADIMIR Is that all?

BOY Yes Sir.

[*Silence.*]

VLADIMIR You work for Mr. Godot?

BOY Yes Sir.

1155 VLADIMIR What do you do?

BOY I mind the goats, Sir.

VLADIMIR Is he good to you?

BOY Yes Sir.

VLADIMIR He doesn't beat you?

1160 BOY No Sir, not me.

VLADIMIR Whom does he beat?

BOY He beats my brother, Sir.

VLADIMIR Ah, you have a brother?

BOY Yes Sir.

1165 VLADIMIR What does he do?

BOY He minds the sheep, Sir.

VLADIMIR And why doesn't he beat you?

BOY I don't know, Sir.

VLADIMIR He must be fond of you.

1170 BOY I don't know, Sir.

[Silence.]

VLADIMIR Does he give you enough to eat? [*The* BOY *hesitates.*] Does he feed you well?

BOY Fairly well, Sir.

VLADIMIR You're not unhappy? [*The* BOY *hesitates.*] Do you hear me?

1175 BOY Yes Sir.

VLADIMIR Well?

BOY I don't know, Sir.

VLADIMIR You don't know if you're unhappy or not?

BOY No Sir.

1180 VLADIMIR You're as bad as myself. [*Silence*] Where do you sleep?

BOY In the loft, Sir.

VLADIMIR With your brother?

BOY Yes Sir.

VLADIMIR In the hay?

1185 BOY Yes Sir.

[*Silence.*]

VLADIMIR All right, you may go.

BOY What am I to tell Mr. Godot, Sir?

VLADIMIR Tell him . . . [*He hesitates.*] . . . tell him you saw us. [*Pause*] You did see us, didn't you?

1190 BOY Yes Sir.

[*He steps back, hesitates, turns and exits running. The light suddenly fails. In a moment it is night. The moon rises at back, mounts in the sky, stands still, shedding a pale light on the scene.*]

VLADIMIR At last! [ESTRAGON *gets up and goes towards* VLADIMIR, *a boot in each hand. He puts them down at edge of stage, straightens and contemplates the moon.*] What are you doing?

ESTRAGON Pale for weariness.

VLADIMIR Eh?

1195 ESTRAGON Of climbing heaven and gazing on the likes of us.

VLADIMIR Your boots, what are you doing with your boots?

ESTRAGON [*turning to look at the boots*] I'm leaving them there. [*Pause*] Another will come, just as . . . as . . . as me, but with smaller feet, and they'll make him happy.

1200 VLADIMIR But you can't go barefoot!

ESTRAGON   Christ did.

VLADIMIR   Christ! What has Christ got to do with it? You're not going to compare yourself to Christ!

ESTRAGON   All my life I've compared myself to him.

1205 VLADIMIR   But where he lived it was warm, it was dry!

ESTRAGON   Yes. And they crucified quick.

   [Silence.]

VLADIMIR   We've nothing more to do here.

ESTRAGON   Nor anywhere else.

VLADIMIR   Ah Gogo, don't go on like that. Tomorrow everything will be

1210   better.

ESTRAGON   How do you make that out?

VLADIMIR   Did you not hear what the child said?

ESTRAGON   No.

VLADIMIR   He said that Godot was sure to come tomorrow. [Pause] What do

1215   you say to that?

ESTRAGON   Then all we have to do is to wait on here.

VLADIMIR   Are you mad? We must take cover. [He takes ESTRAGON by the arm.] Come on.

   [He draws ESTRAGON after him. ESTRAGON yields, then resists. They halt.]

ESTRAGON   [looking at the tree]   Pity we haven't got a bit of rope.

1220 VLADIMIR   Come on. It's cold.

   [He draws ESTRAGON after him. As before.]

ESTRAGON   Remind me to bring a bit of rope tomorrow.

VLADIMIR   Yes. Come on.

   [He draws him after him. As before.]

ESTRAGON   How long have we been together all the time now?

VLADIMIR   I don't know. Fifty years maybe.

1225 ESTRAGON   Do you remember the day I threw myself into the Rhône?[2]

VLADIMIR   We were grape harvesting.

ESTRAGON   You fished me out.

VLADIMIR   That's all dead and buried.

ESTRAGON   My clothes dried in the sun.

1230 VLADIMIR   There's no good harking back on that. Come on.

   [He draws him after him. As before.]

ESTRAGON   Wait!

VLADIMIR   I'm cold!

ESTRAGON   Wait! [He moves away from VLADIMIR.] I sometimes wonder if we wouldn't have been better off alone, each one for himself. [He crosses the

1235   stage and sits down on the mound.] We weren't made for the same road.

VLADIMIR   [without anger]   It's not certain.

ESTRAGON   No, nothing is certain.

   [VLADIMIR slowly crosses the stage and sits down beside ESTRAGON.]

VLADIMIR   We can still part, if you think it would be better.

ESTRAGON   It's not worthwhile now.

   [Silence.]

2. A major river in southeastern France.

1240 VLADIMIR No, it's not worthwhile now.

　　　[*Silence.*]

ESTRAGON Well, shall we go?

VLADIMIR Yes, let's go.

　　　[*They do not move.*]

Curtain.

Act 2

Next day. Same time.

Same place.

　　　[ESTRAGON's *boots front center, heels together, toes splayed.* LUCKY's *hat at same place.*]

　　　[*The tree has four or five leaves.*]

　　　[*Enter* VLADIMIR *agitatedly. He halts and looks long at the tree, then suddenly begins to move feverishly about the stage. He halts before the boots, picks one up, examines it, sniffs it, manifests disgust, puts it back carefully. Comes and goes. Halts extreme right and gazes into distance off, shading his eyes with his hand. Comes and goes. Halts extreme left, as before. Comes and goes. Halts suddenly and begins to sing loudly.*]

VLADIMIR A dog came in—

　　　[*Having begun too high he stops, clears his throat, resumes.*]

　　　A dog came in the kitchen

　　　And stole a crust of bread.

　　　Then cook up with a ladle

5　　　And beat him till he was dead.

　　　Then all the dogs came running

　　　And dug the dog a tomb—

　　　[*He stops, broods, resumes.*]

　　　Then all the dogs came running

　　　And dug the dog a tomb

10　　And wrote upon the tombstone

　　　For the eyes of dogs to come:

　　　A dog came in the kitchen

　　　And stole a crust of bread.

　　　Then cook up with a ladle

15　　And beat him till he was dead.

　　　Then all the dogs came running

　　　And dug the dog a tomb—

　　　[*He stops, broods, resumes.*]

　　　Then all the dogs came running

　　　And dug the dog a tomb—

　　　[*He stops, broods. Softly.*]

20　　And dug the dog a tomb . . .

[*He remains a moment silent and motionless, then begins to move fever-ishly about the stage. He halts before the tree, comes and goes, before the boots, comes and goes, halts extreme right, gazes into distance, extreme left, gazes into distance. Enter* ESTRAGON *right, barefoot, head bowed. He slowly crosses the stage.* VLADIMIR *turns and sees him.*]

VLADIMIR   You again! [ESTRAGON *halts but does not raise his head.* VLADIMIR *goes towards him.*] Come here till I embrace you.

ESTRAGON   Don't touch me!

[VLADIMIR *holds back, pained.*]

VLADIMIR   Do you want me to go away? [*Pause*] Gogo! [*Pause.* VLADIMIR
25   *observes him attentively.*] Did they beat you? [*Pause*] Gogo! [ESTRAGON *remains silent, head bowed.*] Where did you spend the night?

ESTRAGON   Don't touch me! Don't question me! Don't speak to me! Stay with me!

VLADIMIR   Did I ever leave you?

30 ESTRAGON   You let me go.

VLADIMIR   Look at me. [ESTRAGON *does not raise his head. Violently.*] Will you look at me!

[ESTRAGON *raises his head. They look long at each other, then suddenly embrace, clapping each other on the back. End of the embrace.* ESTRAGON, *no longer supported, almost falls.*]

ESTRAGON   What a day!

VLADIMIR   Who beat you? Tell me.

35 ESTRAGON   Another day done with.

VLADIMIR   Not yet.

ESTRAGON   For me it's over and done with, no matter what happens. [*Silence*] I heard you singing.

VLADIMIR   That's right, I remember.

40 ESTRAGON   That finished me. I said to myself, He's all alone, he thinks I'm gone for ever, and he sings.

VLADIMIR   One is not master of one's moods. All day I've felt in great form. [*Pause*] I didn't get up in the night, not once!

ESTRAGON [*sadly*]   You see, you piss better when I'm not there.

45 VLADIMIR   I missed you . . . and at the same time I was happy. Isn't that a queer thing?

ESTRAGON [*shocked*]   Happy?

VLADIMIR   Perhaps it's not quite the right word.

ESTRAGON   And now?

50 VLADIMIR   Now? . . . [*Joyous*] There you are again . . . [*Indifferent*] There we are again . . . [*Gloomy*] There I am again.

ESTRAGON   You see, you feel worse when I'm with you. I feel better alone too.

VLADIMIR [*vexed*]   Then why do you always come crawling back?

ESTRAGON   I don't know.

55 VLADIMIR   No, but I do. It's because you don't know how to defend yourself. I wouldn't have let them beat you.

ESTRAGON   You couldn't have stopped them.

VLADIMIR   Why not?

ESTRAGON   There was ten of them.

60 VLADIMIR   No, I mean before they beat you. I would have stopped you from doing whatever it was you were doing.

ESTRAGON   I wasn't doing anything.

VLADIMIR   Then why did they beat you?

ESTRAGON   I don't know.

65 VLADIMIR   Ah no, Gogo, the truth is there are things escape you that don't escape me, you must feel it yourself.

ESTRAGON   I tell you I wasn't doing anything.

VLADIMIR   Perhaps you weren't. But it's the way of doing it that counts, the way of doing it, if you want to go on living.

70 ESTRAGON   I wasn't doing anything.

VLADIMIR   You must be happy too, deep down, if you only knew it.

ESTRAGON   Happy about what?

VLADIMIR   To be back with me again.

ESTRAGON   Would you say so?

75 VLADIMIR   Say you are, even if it's not true.

ESTRAGON   What am I to say?

VLADIMIR   Say, I am happy.

ESTRAGON   I am happy.

VLADIMIR   So am I.

80 ESTRAGON   So am I.

VLADIMIR   We are happy.

ESTRAGON   We are happy. [*Silence*] What do we do now, now that we are happy?

VLADIMIR   Wait for Godot. [ESTRAGON *groans. Silence.*] Things have changed
85   here since yesterday.

ESTRAGON   And if he doesn't come.

VLADIMIR [*after a moment of bewilderment*]   We'll see when the time comes. [*Pause*] I was saying that things have changed here since yesterday.

ESTRAGON   Everything oozes.

90 VLADIMIR   Look at the tree.

ESTRAGON   It's never the same pus from one second to the next.

VLADIMIR   The tree, look at the tree.

[ESTRAGON *looks at the tree.*]

ESTRAGON   Was it not there yesterday?

VLADIMIR   Yes of course it was there. Do you not remember? We nearly
95   hanged ourselves from it. But you wouldn't. Do you not remember?

ESTRAGON   You dreamt it.

VLADIMIR   Is it possible you've forgotten already?

ESTRAGON   That's the way I am. Either I forget immediately or I never forget.

100 VLADIMIR   And Pozzo and Lucky, have you forgotten them too?

ESTRAGON   Pozzo and Lucky?

VLADIMIR   He's forgotten everything!

ESTRAGON   I remember a lunatic who kicked the shins off me. Then he played the fool.

105 VLADIMIR   That was Lucky.

ESTRAGON   I remember that. But when was it?

VLADIMIR   And his keeper, do you not remember him?

ESTRAGON   He gave me a bone.

VLADIMIR   That was Pozzo.

110 ESTRAGON   And all that was yesterday, you say?

VLADIMIR   Yes of course it was yesterday.

ESTRAGON   And here where we are now?

VLADIMIR   Where else do you think? Do you not recognize the place?

ESTRAGON [*suddenly furious*]   Recognize! What is there to recognize? All my
115   lousy life I've crawled about in the mud! And you talk to me about scenery!
[*Looking wildly about him*] Look at this muckheap! I've never stirred from it!

VLADIMIR   Calm yourself, calm yourself.

ESTRAGON   You and your landscapes! Tell me about the worms!

VLADIMIR   All the same, you can't tell me that this [*Gesture*] bears any resem
120   blance to . . . [*He hesitates.*] . . . to the Mâcon country[3] for example. You
can't deny there's a big difference.

ESTRAGON   The Mâcon country! Who's talking to you about the Mâcon
country?

VLADIMIR   But you were there yourself, in the Mâcon country.

125   ESTRAGON   No I was never in the Mâcon country! I've puked my puke of a
life away here, I tell you! Here! In the Cackon country!

VLADIMIR   But we were there together, I could swear to it! Picking grapes for
a man called . . . [*He snaps his fingers.*] . . . can't think of the name of the
man, at a place called . . . [*Snaps his fingers.*] . . . can't think of the name of
130   the place, do you not remember?

ESTRAGON [*a little calmer*]   It's possible. I didn't notice anything.

VLADIMIR   But down there everything is red!

ESTRAGON [*exasperated*]   I didn't notice anything, I tell you!
[*Silence.* VLADIMIR *sighs deeply.*]

VLADIMIR   You're a hard man to get on with, Gogo.

135   ESTRAGON   It'd be better if we parted.

VLADIMIR   You always say that and you always come crawling back.

ESTRAGON   The best thing would be to kill me, like the other.

VLADIMIR   What other? [*Pause*] What other?

ESTRAGON   Like billions of others.

140   VLADIMIR [*sententious*]   To every man his little cross. [*He sighs.*] Till he dies.
[*Afterthought*] And is forgotten.

ESTRAGON   In the meantime let us try and converse calmly, since we are
incapable of keeping silent.

VLADIMIR   You're right, we're inexhaustible.

145   ESTRAGON   It's so we won't think.

VLADIMIR   We have that excuse.

ESTRAGON   It's so we won't hear.

VLADIMIR   We have our reasons.

ESTRAGON   All the dead voices.

150   VLADIMIR   They make a noise like wings.

ESTRAGON   Like leaves.

VLADIMIR   Like sand.

ESTRAGON   Like leaves.
[*Silence.*]

VLADIMIR   They all speak at once.

155   ESTRAGON   Each one to itself.
[*Silence.*]

3. A wine-producing district in the Bourgogne region of east-central France.

VLADIMIR   Rather they whisper.
ESTRAGON   They rustle.
VLADIMIR   They murmur.
ESTRAGON   They rustle.
            [*Silence.*]
160 VLADIMIR   What do they say?
ESTRAGON   They talk about their lives.
VLADIMIR   To have lived is not enough for them.
ESTRAGON   They have to talk about it.
VLADIMIR   To be dead is not enough for them.
165 ESTRAGON   It is not sufficient.
            [*Silence.*]
VLADIMIR   They make a noise like feathers.
ESTRAGON   Like leaves.
VLADIMIR   Like ashes.
ESTRAGON   Like leaves.
            [*Long silence.*]
170 VLADIMIR   Say something!
ESTRAGON   I'm trying.
            [*Long silence.*]
VLADIMIR [*in anguish*]   Say anything at all!
ESTRAGON   What do we do now?
VLADIMIR   Wait for Godot.
175 ESTRAGON   Ah!
            [*Silence.*]
VLADIMIR   This is awful!
ESTRAGON   Sing something.
VLADIMIR   No no! [*He reflects.*] We could start all over again perhaps.
ESTRAGON   That should be easy.
180 VLADIMIR   It's the start that's difficult.
ESTRAGON   You can start from anything.
VLADIMIR   Yes, but you have to decide.
ESTRAGON   True.
            [*Silence.*]
VLADIMIR   Help me!
185 ESTRAGON   I'm trying.
            [*Silence.*]
VLADIMIR   When you seek you hear.
ESTRAGON   You do.
VLADIMIR   That prevents you from finding.
ESTRAGON   It does.
190 VLADIMIR   That prevents you from thinking.
ESTRAGON   You think all the same.
VLADIMIR   No no, impossible.
ESTRAGON   That's the idea, let's contradict each other.
VLADIMIR   Impossible.
195 ESTRAGON   You think so?
VLADIMIR   We're in no danger of ever thinking any more.

	ESTRAGON	Then what are we complaining about?
	VLADIMIR	Thinking is not the worst.
	ESTRAGON	Perhaps not. But at least there's that.
200	VLADIMIR	That what?
	ESTRAGON	That's the idea, let's ask each other questions.
	VLADIMIR	What do you mean, at least there's that?
	ESTRAGON	That much less misery.
	VLADIMIR	True.
205	ESTRAGON	Well? If we gave thanks for our mercies?
	VLADIMIR	What is terrible is to *have* thought.
	ESTRAGON	But did that ever happen to us?
	VLADIMIR	Where are all these corpses from?
	ESTRAGON	These skeletons.
210	VLADIMIR	Tell me that.
	ESTRAGON	True.
	VLADIMIR	We must have thought a little.
	ESTRAGON	At the very beginning.
	VLADIMIR	A charnel-house! A charnel-house!⁴
215	ESTRAGON	You don't have to look.
	VLADIMIR	You can't help looking.
	ESTRAGON	True.
	VLADIMIR	Try as one may.
	ESTRAGON	I beg your pardon?
220	VLADIMIR	Try as one may.
	ESTRAGON	We should turn resolutely towards Nature.
	VLADIMIR	We've tried that.
	ESTRAGON	True.
	VLADIMIR	Oh it's not the worst, I know.
225	ESTRAGON	What?
	VLADIMIR	To have thought.
	ESTRAGON	Obviously.
	VLADIMIR	But we could have done without it.
	ESTRAGON	Que voulez-vous?⁵
230	VLADIMIR	I beg your pardon?
	ESTRAGON	Que voulez-vous.
	VLADIMIR	Ah! que voulez-vous. Exactly.

[*Silence.*]

	ESTRAGON	That wasn't such a bad little canter.
	VLADIMIR	Yes, but now we'll have to find something else.
235	ESTRAGON	Let me see. [*He takes off his hat, concentrates.*]
	VLADIMIR	Let me see. [*He takes off his hat, concentrates. Long silence.*] Ah!

[*They put on their hats, relax.*]

	ESTRAGON	Well?
	VLADIMIR	What was I saying, we could go on from there.
	ESTRAGON	What were you saying when?
240	VLADIMIR	At the very beginning.

4. A building or vault in which the bodies or
bones of the dead are placed.

5. What do you want? (French).

ESTRAGON   The very beginning of WHAT?

VLADIMIR   This evening . . . I was saying . . . I was saying . . .

ESTRAGON   I'm not a historian.

VLADIMIR   Wait . . . we embraced . . . we were happy . . . happy . . . what do
245 we do now that we're happy . . . go on waiting . . . waiting . . . let me
think . . . it's coming . . . go on waiting . . . now that we're happy . . . let
me see . . . ah! The tree!

ESTRAGON   The tree?

VLADIMIR   Do you not remember?

250 ESTRAGON   I'm tired.

VLADIMIR   Look at it.

[*They look at the tree.*]

ESTRAGON   I see nothing.

VLADIMIR   But yesterday evening it was all black and bare. And now it's covered with leaves.

255 ESTRAGON   Leaves?

VLADIMIR   In a single night.

ESTRAGON   It must be the Spring.

VLADIMIR   But in a single night!

ESTRAGON   I tell you we weren't here yesterday. Another of your nightmares.

260 VLADIMIR   And where were we yesterday evening according to you?

ESTRAGON   How would I know? In another compartment. There's no lack of
void.

VLADIMIR   [*sure of himself*]   Good. We weren't here yesterday evening. Now
what did we do yesterday evening?

265 ESTRAGON   Do?

VLADIMIR   Try and remember.

ESTRAGON   Do . . . I suppose we blathered.

VLADIMIR   [*controlling himself*]   About what?

ESTRAGON   Oh . . . this and that I suppose, nothing in particular. [*With
270 assurance*] Yes, now I remember, yesterday evening we spent blathering
about nothing in particular. That's been going on now for half a century.

VLADIMIR   You don't remember any fact, any circumstance?

ESTRAGON   [*weary*]   Don't torment me, Didi.

VLADIMIR   The sun. The moon. Do you not remember?

275 ESTRAGON   They must have been there, as usual.

VLADIMIR   You didn't notice anything out of the ordinary?

ESTRAGON   Alas!

VLADIMIR   And Pozzo? And Lucky?

ESTRAGON   Pozzo?

280 VLADIMIR   The bones.

ESTRAGON   They were like fishbones.

VLADIMIR   It was Pozzo gave them to you.

ESTRAGON   I don't know.

VLADIMIR   And the kick.

285 ESTRAGON   That's right, someone gave me a kick.

VLADIMIR   It was Lucky gave it to you.

ESTRAGON   And all that was yesterday?

VLADIMIR   Show your leg.

ESTRAGON Which?

290 VLADIMIR Both. Pull up your trousers. [ESTRAGON *gives a leg to* VLADIMIR, *staggers.* VLADIMIR *takes the leg. They stagger.*] Pull up your trousers.

ESTRAGON I can't.

[VLADIMIR *pulls up the trousers, looks at the leg, lets it go.* ESTRAGON *almost falls.*]

VLADIMIR The other. [ESTRAGON *gives the same leg.*] The other, pig! [ESTRAGON *gives the other leg. Triumphantly.*] There's the wound! Beginning to fester!

295 ESTRAGON And what about it?

VLADIMIR [*letting go the leg*] Where are your boots?

ESTRAGON I must have thrown them away.

VLADIMIR When?

ESTRAGON I don't know.

300 VLADIMIR Why?

ESTRAGON [*exasperated*] I don't know why I don't know!

VLADIMIR No, I mean why did you throw them away?

ESTRAGON [*exasperated*] Because they were hurting me!

VLADIMIR [*triumphantly, pointing to the boots*] There they are! [ESTRAGON
305 *looks at the boots.*] At the very spot where you left them yesterday!

[ESTRAGON *goes towards the boots, inspects them closely.*]

ESTRAGON They're not mine.

VLADIMIR [*stupefied*] Not yours!

ESTRAGON Mine were black. These are brown.

VLADIMIR You're sure yours were black?

310 ESTRAGON Well they were a kind of grey.

VLADIMIR And these are brown. Show.

ESTRAGON [*picking up a boot*] Well they're a kind of green.

VLADIMIR Show. [ESTRAGON *hands him the boot.* VLADIMIR *inspects it, throws
it down angrily.*] Well of all the—

315 ESTRAGON You see, all that's a lot of bloody—

VLADIMIR Ah! I see what it is. Yes, I see what's happened.

ESTRAGON All that's a lot of bloody—

VLADIMIR It's elementary. Someone came and took yours and left you his.

ESTRAGON Why?

320 VLADIMIR His were too tight for him, so he took yours.

ESTRAGON But mine were too tight.

VLADIMIR For you. Not for him.

ESTRAGON [*having tried in vain to work it out*] I'm tired! [*Pause*] Let's go.

VLADIMIR We can't.

325 ESTRAGON Why not?

VLADIMIR We're waiting for Godot.

ESTRAGON Ah! [*Pause. Despairing*] What'll we do, what'll we do!

VLADIMIR There's nothing we can do.

ESTRAGON But I can't go on like this!

330 VLADIMIR Would you like a radish?

ESTRAGON Is that all there is?

VLADIMIR There are radishes and turnips.

ESTRAGON Are there no carrots?

VLADIMIR No. Anyway you overdo it with your carrots.

335 ESTRAGON Then give me a radish. [VLADIMIR *fumbles in his pockets, finds nothing but turnips, finally brings out a radish and hands it to* ESTRAGON *who examines it, sniffs it.*] It's black!

VLADIMIR It's a radish.

ESTRAGON I only like the pink ones, you know that!

VLADIMIR Then you don't want it?

340 ESTRAGON I only like the pink ones!

VLADIMIR Then give it back to me. [ESTRAGON *gives it back.*]

ESTRAGON I'll go and get a carrot. [*He does not move.*]

VLADIMIR This is becoming really insignificant.

ESTRAGON Not enough.

   [*Silence.*]

345 VLADIMIR What about trying them.

ESTRAGON I've tried everything.

VLADIMIR No, I mean the boots.

ESTRAGON Would that be a good thing?

VLADIMIR It'd pass the time. [ESTRAGON *hesitates.*] I assure you, it'd be an 350 occupation.

ESTRAGON A relaxation.

VLADIMIR A recreation.

ESTRAGON A relaxation.

VLADIMIR Try.

355 ESTRAGON You'll help me?

VLADIMIR I will of course.

ESTRAGON We don't manage too badly, eh Didi, between the two of us?

VLADIMIR Yes yes. Come on, we'll try the left first.

ESTRAGON We always find something, eh Didi, to give us the impression we 360 exist?

VLADIMIR [*impatiently*] Yes yes, we're magicians. But let us persevere in what we have resolved, before we forget. [*He picks up a boot.*] Come on, give me your foot. [ESTRAGON *raises his foot.*] The other, hog! [ESTRAGON *raises the other foot.*] Higher! [*Wreathed together they stagger about the* 365 *stage.* VLADIMIR *succeeds finally in getting on the boot.*] Try and walk. [ESTRAGON *walks.*] Well?

ESTRAGON It fits.

VLADIMIR [*taking string from his pocket*] We'll try and lace it.

ESTRAGON [*vehemently*] No no, no laces, no laces!

370 VLADIMIR You'll be sorry. Let's try the other. [*As before*] Well?

ESTRAGON [*grudgingly*] It fits too.

VLADIMIR They don't hurt you?

ESTRAGON Not yet.

VLADIMIR Then you can keep them.

375 ESTRAGON They're too big.

VLADIMIR Perhaps you'll have socks some day.

ESTRAGON True.

VLADIMIR Then you'll keep them?

ESTRAGON That's enough about these boots.

380 VLADIMIR Yes, but—

ESTRAGON [*violently*] Enough! [*Silence*] I suppose I might as well sit down. [*He looks for a place to sit down, then goes and sits down on the mound.*]

VLADIMIR   That's where you were sitting yesterday evening.

ESTRAGON   If I could only sleep.

VLADIMIR   Yesterday you slept.

385 ESTRAGON   I'll try. [*He resumes his foetal posture, his head between his knees.*]

VLADIMIR   Wait. [*He goes over and sits down beside* ESTRAGON *and begins to sing in a loud voice.*]

Bye bye bye bye
Bye bye—

ESTRAGON [*looking up angrily*]   Not so loud!

VLADIMIR [*softly*]

390
Bye bye bye bye
Bye bye bye bye
Bye bye bye bye
Bye bye . . .

[ESTRAGON *sleeps.* VLADIMIR *gets up softly, takes off his coat and lays it across* ESTRAGON's *shoulders, then starts walking up and down, swinging his arms to keep himself warm.* ESTRAGON *wakes with a start, jumps up, casts about wildly.* VLADIMIR *returns to him, puts his arms round him.*]

There . . . there . . . Didi is there . . . don't be afraid . . .

395 ESTRAGON   Ah!

VLADIMIR   There . . . there . . . it's all over.

ESTRAGON   I was falling—

VLADIMIR   It's all over, it's all over.

ESTRAGON   I was on top of a—

400 VLADIMIR   Don't tell me! Come, we'll walk it off.

[*He takes* ESTRAGON *by the arm and walks him up and down until* ESTRAGON *refuses to go any further.*]

ESTRAGON   That's enough. I'm tired.

VLADIMIR   You'd rather be stuck there doing nothing?

ESTRAGON   Yes.

VLADIMIR   Please yourself.

[*He releases* ESTRAGON, *picks up his coat and puts it on.*]

405 ESTRAGON   Let's go.

VLADIMIR   We can't.

ESTRAGON   Why not?

VLADIMIR   We're waiting for Godot.

ESTRAGON   Ah! [VLADIMIR *walks up and down.*] Can you not stay still?

410 VLADIMIR   I'm cold.

ESTRAGON   We came too soon.

VLADIMIR   It's always at nightfall.

ESTRAGON   But night doesn't fall.

VLADIMIR   It'll fall all of a sudden, like yesterday.

415 ESTRAGON   Then it'll be night.

VLADIMIR   And we can go.

ESTRAGON   Then it'll be day again. [*Pause. Despairing.*] What'll we do, what'll we do!

VLADIMIR [*halting, violently*]   Will you stop whining! I've had about my bellyful of your lamentations!

ESTRAGON   I'm going.

VLADIMIR [*seeing* LUCKY's *hat*]   Well!

ESTRAGON   Farewell.

VLADIMIR   Lucky's hat. [*He goes towards it.*] I've been here an hour and never saw it. [*Very pleased*] Fine!

ESTRAGON   You'll never see me again.

VLADIMIR   I knew it was the right place. Now our troubles are over. [*He picks up the hat, contemplates it, straightens it.*] Must have been a very fine hat. [*He puts it on in place of his own which he hands to* ESTRAGON.] Here.

ESTRAGON   What?

VLADIMIR   Hold that.

[ESTRAGON *takes* VLADIMIR's *hat.* VLADIMIR *adjusts* LUCKY's *hat on his head.* ESTRAGON *puts on* VLADIMIR's *hat in place of his own which he hands to* VLADIMIR. VLADIMIR *takes* ESTRAGON's *hat.* ESTRAGON *adjusts* VLADIMIR's *hat on his head.* VLADIMIR *puts on* ESTRAGON's *hat in place of* LUCKY's *which he hands to* ESTRAGON. ESTRAGON *takes* LUCKY's *hat.* VLADIMIR *adjusts* ESTRAGON's *hat on his head.* ESTRAGON *puts on* LUCKY's *hat in place of* VLADIMIR's *which he hands to* VLADIMIR. VLADIMIR *takes his hat.* ESTRAGON *adjusts* LUCKY's *hat on his head.* VLADIMIR *puts on his hat in place of* ESTRAGON's *which he hands to* ESTRAGON. ESTRAGON *takes his hat.* VLADIMIR *adjusts his hat on his head.* ESTRAGON *puts on his hat in place of* LUCKY's *which he hands to* VLADIMIR. VLADIMIR *takes* LUCKY's *hat.* ESTRAGON *adjusts his hat on his head.* VLADIMIR *puts on* LUCKY's *hat in place of his own which he hands to* ESTRAGON. ESTRAGON *takes* VLADIMIR's *hat.* VLADIMIR *adjusts* LUCKY's *hat on his head.* ESTRAGON *hands* VLADIMIR's *hat back to* VLADIMIR *who takes it and hands it back to* ESTRAGON *who takes it and hands it back to* VLADIMIR *who takes it and throws it down.*]

How does it fit me?

ESTRAGON   How would I know?

VLADIMIR   No, but how do I look in it? [*He turns his head coquettishly to and fro, minces like a mannequin.*]

ESTRAGON   Hideous.

VLADIMIR   Yes, but not more so than usual?

ESTRAGON   Neither more nor less.

VLADIMIR   Then I can keep it. Mine irked me. [*Pause*] How shall I say? [*Pause*] It itched me. [*He takes off* LUCKY's *hat, peers into it, shakes it, knocks on the crown, puts it on again.*]

ESTRAGON   I'm going.

[*Silence.*]

VLADIMIR   Will you not play?

ESTRAGON   Play at what?

VLADIMIR   We could play at Pozzo and Lucky.

ESTRAGON   Never heard of it.

VLADIMIR   I'll do Lucky, you do Pozzo. [*He imitates* LUCKY *sagging under the weight of his baggage.* ESTRAGON *looks at him with stupefaction.*] Go on.

ESTRAGON   What am I to do?

VLADIMIR   Curse me!

ESTRAGON [*after reflection*]   Naughty!

450 VLADIMIR Stronger!

ESTRAGON Gonococcus! Spirochete![6]

[VLADIMIR *sways back and forth, doubled in two.*]

VLADIMIR Tell me to think.

ESTRAGON What?

VLADIMIR Say, Think, pig!

455 ESTRAGON Think, pig!

[*Silence.*]

VLADIMIR I can't!

ESTRAGON That's enough of that.

VLADIMIR Tell me to dance.

ESTRAGON I'm going.

460 VLADIMIR Dance, hog! [*He writhes. Exit* ESTRAGON *left, precipitately.*] I can't!
[*He looks up, misses* ESTRAGON.] Gogo! [*He moves wildly about the stage.
Enter* ESTRAGON *left, panting. He hastens towards* VLADIMIR, *falls into his
arms.*] There you are again at last!

ESTRAGON I'm accursed!

VLADIMIR Where were you? I thought you were gone for ever.

465 ESTRAGON They're coming!

VLADIMIR Who?

ESTRAGON I don't know.

VLADIMIR How many?

ESTRAGON I don't know.

470 VLADIMIR [*triumphantly*] It's Godot! At last! Gogo! It's Godot! We're saved!
Let's go and meet him! [*He drags* ESTRAGON *towards the wings.* ESTRAGON
resists, pulls himself free, exit right.] Gogo! Come back! [VLADIMIR *runs to
extreme left, scans the horizon. Enter* ESTRAGON *right, he hastens towards*
VLADIMIR, *falls into his arms.*] There you are again again!

ESTRAGON I'm in hell!

475 VLADIMIR Where were you?

ESTRAGON They're coming there too!

VLADIMIR We're surrounded! [ESTRAGON *makes a rush towards back.*] Imbecile! There's no way out there. [*He takes* ESTRAGON *by the arm and drags
him towards front. Gesture towards front.*] There! Not a soul in sight! Off
480 you go! Quick! [*He pushes* ESTRAGON *towards auditorium.* ESTRAGON *recoils
in horror.*] You won't? [*He contemplates auditorium.*] Well I can understand
that. Wait till I see. [*He reflects.*] Your only hope left is to disappear.

ESTRAGON Where?

VLADIMIR Behind the tree. [ESTRAGON *hesitates.*] Quick! Behind the tree.
[ESTRAGON *goes and crouches behind the tree, realizes he is not hidden,
485 comes out from behind the tree.*] Decidedly this tree will not have been the
slightest use to us.

ESTRAGON [*calmer*] I lost my head. Forgive me. It won't happen again. Tell
me what to do.

VLADIMIR There's nothing to do.

490 ESTRAGON You go and stand there. [*He draws* VLADIMIR *to extreme right and
places him with his back to the stage.*] There, don't move, and watch out.

---

6. Bacteria that cause venereal diseases. The gonococcus bacterium is associated with gonorrhea; the spirochete, with syphilis as well as other diseases.

[VLADIMIR *scans horizon, screening his eyes with his hand.* ESTRAGON *runs and takes up same position extreme left. They turn their heads and look at each other.*] Back to back like in the good old days. [*They continue to look at each other for a moment, then resume their watch. Long silence.*] Do you see anything coming?

495 VLADIMIR [*turning his head.*]　What?

ESTRAGON [*louder*]　Do you see anything coming?

VLADIMIR　No.

ESTRAGON　Nor I.

　　　　[*They resume their watch. Silence.*]

VLADIMIR　You must have had a vision.

500 ESTRAGON [*turning his head*]　What?

VLADIMIR [*louder*]　You must have had a vision.

ESTRAGON　No need to shout!

　　　　[*They resume their watch. Silence.*]

VLADIMIR
ESTRAGON }[*turning simultaneously*]　Do you—

VLADIMIR　Oh pardon!

505 ESTRAGON　Carry on.

VLADIMIR　No no, after you.

ESTRAGON　No no, you first.

VLADIMIR　I interrupted you.

ESTRAGON　On the contrary.

　　　　[*They glare at each other angrily.*]

510 VLADIMIR　Ceremonious ape!

ESTRAGON　Punctilious pig!

VLADIMIR　Finish your phrase, I tell you!

ESTRAGON　Finish your own!

　　　　[*Silence. They draw closer, halt.*]

VLADIMIR　Moron!

515 ESTRAGON　That's the idea, let's abuse each other.

　　　　[*They turn, move apart, turn again and face each other.*]

VLADIMIR　Moron!

ESTRAGON　Vermin!

VLADIMIR　Abortion!

ESTRAGON　Morpion![7]

520 VLADIMIR　Sewer-rat!

ESTRAGON　Curate!

VLADIMIR　Cretin!

ESTRAGON [*with finality*]　Crritic!

VLADIMIR　Oh! [*He wilts, vanquished, and turns away.*]

525 ESTRAGON　Now let's make it up.

VLADIMIR　Gogo!

ESTRAGON　Didi!

VLADIMIR　Your hand!

ESTRAGON　Take it!

530 VLADIMIR　Come to my arms!

7. Crab louse (a French word, obsolete in English).

ESTRAGON   Your arms?

VLADIMIR   My breast!

ESTRAGON   Off we go!

[*They embrace. They separate. Silence.*]

VLADIMIR   How time flies when one has fun!

[*Silence.*]

535 ESTRAGON   What do we do now?

VLADIMIR   While waiting.

ESTRAGON   While waiting.

[*Silence.*]

VLADIMIR   We could do our exercises.

ESTRAGON   Our movements.

540 VLADIMIR   Our elevations.

ESTRAGON   Our relaxations.

VLADIMIR   Our elongations.

ESTRAGON   Our relaxations.

VLADIMIR   To warm us up.

545 ESTRAGON   To calm us down.

VLADIMIR   Off we go.

[VLADIMIR *hops from one foot to the other.* ESTRAGON *imitates him.*]

ESTRAGON [*stopping*]   That's enough. I'm tired.

VLADIMIR [*stopping*]   We're not in form. What about a little deep breathing?

ESTRAGON   I'm tired breathing.

550 VLADIMIR   You're right. [*Pause*] Let's just do the tree, for the balance.

ESTRAGON   The tree?

[VLADIMIR *does the tree, staggering about on one leg.*]

VLADIMIR [*stopping*]   Your turn.

[ESTRAGON *does the tree, staggers.*]

ESTRAGON   Do you think God sees me?

VLADIMIR   You must close your eyes.

[ESTRAGON *closes his eyes, staggers worse.*]

555 ESTRAGON [*stopping, brandishing his fists, at the top of his voice*]   God have
pity on me!

VLADIMIR [*vexed*]   And me?

ESTRAGON   On me! On me! Pity! On me!

[*Enter* POZZO *and* LUCKY. POZZO *is blind.* LUCKY *burdened as before. Rope
as before, but much shorter, so that* POZZO *may follow more easily.* LUCKY
wearing a different hat. At the sight of VLADIMIR *and* ESTRAGON *he stops
short.* POZZO, *continuing on his way, bumps into him.*]

VLADIMIR   Gogo!

560 POZZO [*clutching on to* LUCKY *who staggers*]   What is it? Who is it?

[LUCKY *falls, drops everything and brings down* POZZO *with him. They lie
helpless among the scattered baggage.*]

ESTRAGON   Is it Godot?

VLADIMIR   At last! [*He goes towards the heap.*] Reinforcements at last!

POZZO   Help!

ESTRAGON   Is it Godot?

565 VLADIMIR   We were beginning to weaken. Now we're sure to see the evening
out.

POZZO   Help!

ESTRAGON   Do you hear him?

VLADIMIR   We are no longer alone, waiting for the night, waiting for Godot,
570   waiting for . . . waiting. All evening we have struggled, unassisted. Now it's
over. It's already tomorrow.

POZZO   Help!

VLADIMIR   Time flows again already. The sun will set, the moon rise, and we
away . . . from here.

575 POZZO   Pity!

VLADIMIR   Poor Pozzo!

ESTRAGON   I knew it was him.

VLADIMIR   Who?

ESTRAGON   Godot.

580 VLADIMIR   But it's not Godot.

ESTRAGON   It's not Godot?

VLADIMIR   It's not Godot.

ESTRAGON   Then who is it?

VLADIMIR   It's Pozzo.

585 POZZO   Here! Here! Help me up!

VLADIMIR   He can't get up.

ESTRAGON   Let's go.

VLADIMIR   We can't.

ESTRAGON   Why not?

590 VLADIMIR   We're waiting for Godot.

ESTRAGON   Ah!

VLADIMIR   Perhaps he has another bone for you.

ESTRAGON   Bone?

VLADIMIR   Chicken. Do you not remember?

595 ESTRAGON   It was him?

VLADIMIR   Yes.

ESTRAGON   Ask him.

VLADIMIR   Perhaps we should help him first.

ESTRAGON   To do what?

600 VLADIMIR   To get up.

ESTRAGON   He can't get up?

VLADIMIR   He wants to get up.

ESTRAGON   Then let him get up.

VLADIMIR   He can't.

605 ESTRAGON   Why not?

VLADIMIR   I don't know.

[POZZO *writhes, groans, beats the ground with his fists.*]

ESTRAGON   We should ask him for the bone first. Then if he refuses we'll
leave him there.

VLADIMIR   You mean we have him at our mercy?

610 ESTRAGON   Yes.

VLADIMIR   And that we should subordinate our good offices to certain
conditions?

ESTRAGON   What?

VLADIMIR   That seems intelligent all right. But there's one thing I'm afraid of.

615 POZZO   Help!

ESTRAGON   What?

VLADIMIR   That Lucky might get going all of a sudden. Then we'd be
ballocksed.[8]

ESTRAGON   Lucky?

620 VLADIMIR   The one that went for you yesterday.

ESTRAGON   I tell you there was ten of them.

VLADIMIR   No, before that, the one that kicked you.

ESTRAGON   Is he there?

VLADIMIR   As large as life. [*Gesture towards* LUCKY.] For the moment he is
625 inert. But he might run amuck any minute.

POZZO   Help!

ESTRAGON   And suppose we gave him a good beating the two of us?

VLADIMIR   You mean if we fell on him in his sleep?

ESTRAGON   Yes.

630 VLADIMIR   That seems a good idea all right. But could we do it? Is he really
asleep? [*Pause*] No, the best would be to take advantage of Pozzo's calling
for help—

POZZO   Help!

VLADIMIR   To help him—

635 ESTRAGON   We help *him*?

VLADIMIR   In anticipation of some tangible return.

ESTRAGON   And suppose he—

VLADIMIR   Let us not waste our time in idle discourse! [*Pause. Vehemently.*] Let
us do something, while we have the chance! It is not every day that we are
640 needed. Not indeed that we personally are needed. Others would meet the
case equally well, if not better. To all mankind they were addressed, those
cries for help still ringing in our ears! But at this place, at this moment of
time, all mankind is us, whether we like it or not. Let us make the most of it,
before it is too late! Let us represent worthily for once the foul brood to which
645 a cruel fate consigned us! What do you say? [ESTRAGON *says nothing.*] It is true
that when with folded arms we weigh the pros and cons we are no less a
credit to our species. The tiger bounds to the help of his congeners[9] without
the least reflexion, or else he slinks away into the depths of the thickets. But
that is not the question. What are we doing here, *that* is the question. And we
650 are blessed in this, that we happen to know the answer. Yes, in this immense
confusion one thing alone is clear. We are waiting for Godot to come—

ESTRAGON   Ah!

POZZO   Help!

VLADIMIR   Or for night to fall. [*Pause*] We have kept our appointment and
655 that's an end to that. We are not saints, but we have kept our appointment.
How many people can boast as much?

ESTRAGON   Billions.

VLADIMIR   You think so?

ESTRAGON   I don't know.

660 VLADIMIR   You may be right.

POZZO   Help!

VLADIMIR   All I know is that the hours are long, under these conditions, and
constrain us to beguile them with proceedings which—how shall I say—

---

8. Ruined, screwed (slang).   9. Members of his class or kind.

which may at first sight seem reasonable, until they become a habit. You
665 may say it is to prevent our reason from foundering. No doubt. But has it
not long been straying in the night without end of the abyssal depths?
That's what I sometimes wonder. You follow my reasoning?

ESTRAGON [*aphoristic for once*]   We are all born mad. Some remain so.

POZZO   Help! I'll pay you!

670 ESTRAGON   How much?

POZZO   One hundred francs!

ESTRAGON   It's not enough.

VLADIMIR   I wouldn't go so far as that.

ESTRAGON   You think it's enough?

675 VLADIMIR   No, I mean so far as to assert that I was weak in the head when I
came into the world. But that is not the question.

POZZO   Two hundred!

VLADIMIR   We wait. We are bored. [*He throws up his hand.*] No, don't protest,
we are bored to death, there's no denying it. Good. A diversion comes along
680 and what do we do? We let it go to waste. Come, let's get to work! [*He
advances towards the heap, stops in his stride.*] In an instant all will vanish
and we'll be alone once more, in the midst of nothingness! [*He broods.*]

POZZO   Two hundred!

VLADIMIR   We're coming!

[*He tries to pull* POZZO *to his feet, fails, tries again, stumbles, falls, tries to
get up, fails.*]

685 ESTRAGON   What's the matter with you all?

VLADIMIR   Help!

ESTRAGON   I'm going.

VLADIMIR   Don't leave me! They'll kill me!

POZZO   Where am I?

690 VLADIMIR   Gogo!

POZZO   Help!

VLADIMIR   Help!

ESTRAGON   I'm going.

VLADIMIR   Help me up first, then we'll go together.

695 ESTRAGON   You promise?

VLADIMIR   I swear it!

ESTRAGON   And we'll never come back?

VLADIMIR   Never!

ESTRAGON   We'll go to the Pyrenees.[1]

700 VLADIMIR   Wherever you like.

ESTRAGON   I've always wanted to wander in the Pyrenees.

VLADIMIR   You'll wander in them.

ESTRAGON [*recoiling*]   Who farted?

VLADIMIR   Pozzo.

705 POZZO   Here! Here! Pity!

ESTRAGON   It's revolting!

VLADIMIR   Quick! Give me your hand!

ESTRAGON   I'm going. [*Pause. Louder.*] I'm going.

1. The mountain range on the border between Spain and France, extending from the Atlantic
Ocean to the Mediterranean Sea.

VLADIMIR   Well I suppose in the end I'll get up by myself. [*He tries, fails.*] In
710   the fullness of time.

ESTRAGON   What's the matter with you?

VLADIMIR   Go to hell.

ESTRAGON   Are you staying there?

VLADIMIR   For the time being.

715   ESTRAGON   Come on, get up, you'll catch a chill.

VLADIMIR   Don't worry about me.

ESTRAGON   Come on, Didi, don't be pig-headed!

> [*He stretches out his hand which* VLADIMIR *makes haste to seize.*]

VLADIMIR   Pull!

> [ESTRAGON *pulls, stumbles, falls. Long silence.*]

POZZO   Help!

720   VLADIMIR   We've arrived.

POZZO   Who are you?

VLADIMIR   We are men.

> [*Silence.*]

ESTRAGON   Sweet mother earth!

VLADIMIR   Can you get up?

725   ESTRAGON   I don't know.

VLADIMIR   Try.

ESTRAGON   Not now, not now.

> [*Silence.*]

POZZO   What happened?

VLADIMIR [*violently*]   Will you stop it, you! Pest! He can think of nothing but
730   himself!

ESTRAGON   What about a little snooze?

VLADIMIR   Did you hear him? He wants to know what happened!

ESTRAGON   Don't mind him. Sleep.

> [*Silence.*]

POZZO   Pity! Pity!

735   ESTRAGON [*with a start*]   What is it?

VLADIMIR   Were you asleep?

ESTRAGON   I must have been.

VLADIMIR   It's this bastard Pozzo at it again.

ESTRAGON   Make him stop it. Kick him in the crotch.

740   VLADIMIR [*striking Pozzo*]   Will you stop it! Crablouse! [POZZO *extricates himself with cries of pain and crawls away. He stops, saws the air blindly, calling
for help.* VLADIMIR, *propped on his elbow, observes his retreat.*] He's off!
[POZZO *collapses.*] He's down!

ESTRAGON   What do we do now?

VLADIMIR   Perhaps I could crawl to him.

745   ESTRAGON   Don't leave me!

VLADIMIR   Or I could call to him.

ESTRAGON   Yes, call to him.

VLADIMIR   Pozzo! [*Silence*] Pozzo! [*Silence*] No reply.

ESTRAGON   Together.

750   VLADIMIR } Pozzo! Pozzo!
ESTRAGON

VLADIMIR   He moved.

ESTRAGON   Are you sure his name is Pozzo?

VLADIMIR [*alarmed*]   Mr. Pozzo! Come back! We won't hurt you!

[*Silence.*]

ESTRAGON   We might try him with other names.

755 VLADIMIR   I'm afraid he's dying.

ESTRAGON   It'd be amusing.

VLADIMIR   What'd be amusing?

ESTRAGON   To try him with other names, one after the other. It'd pass the time. And we'd be bound to hit on the right one sooner or later.

760 VLADIMIR   I tell you his name is Pozzo.

ESTRAGON   We'll soon see. [*He reflects.*] Abel! Abel!

POZZO   Help!

ESTRAGON   Got it in one!

VLADIMIR   I begin to weary of this motif.

765 ESTRAGON   Perhaps the other is called Cain.² Cain! Cain!

POZZO   Help!

ESTRAGON   He's all humanity. [*Silence*] Look at the little cloud.

VLADIMIR [*raising his eyes*]   Where?

ESTRAGON   There. In the zenith.³

770 VLADIMIR   Well? [*Pause*] What is there so wonderful about it?

[*Silence.*]

ESTRAGON   Let's pass on now to something else, do you mind?

VLADIMIR   I was just going to suggest it.

ESTRAGON   But to what?

VLADIMIR   Ah!

[*Silence.*]

775 ESTRAGON   Suppose we got up to begin with?

VLADIMIR   No harm trying.

[*They get up.*]

ESTRAGON   Child's play.

VLADIMIR   Simple question of will-power.

ESTRAGON   And now?

780 POZZO   Help!

ESTRAGON   Let's go.

VLADIMIR   We can't.

ESTRAGON   Why not?

VLADIMIR   We're waiting for Godot.

785 ESTRAGON   Ah! [*Despairing*] What'll we do, what'll we do!

POZZO   Help!

VLADIMIR   What about helping him?

ESTRAGON   What does he want?

VLADIMIR   He wants to get up.

790 ESTRAGON   Then why doesn't he?

VLADIMIR   He wants us to help him to get up.

ESTRAGON   Then why don't we? What are we waiting for?

2. In the Bible, the first murderer (a son of Adam and Eve); after Cain killed his brother Abel, God made him "a fugitive and a vaga- bond" (Genesis 4.12).

3. Literally, the point of the sky directly overhead.

[They help POZZO *to his feet, let him go. He falls.]*

VLADIMIR   We must hold him. [*They get him up again.* POZZO *says between them, his arms round their necks.*] Feeling better?

795 POZZO   Who are you?

VLADIMIR   Do you not recognize us?

POZZO   I am blind.

[*Silence.*]

ESTRAGON   Perhaps he can see into the future.

VLADIMIR   Since when?

800 POZZO   I used to have wonderful sight—but are you friends?

ESTRAGON [*laughing noisily*]   He wants to know if we are friends!

VLADIMIR   No, he means friends of his.

ESTRAGON   Well?

VLADIMIR   We've proved we are, by helping him.

805 ESTRAGON   Exactly. Would we have helped him if we weren't his friends?

VLADIMIR   Possibly.

ESTRAGON   True.

VLADIMIR   Don't let's quibble about that now.

POZZO   You are not highwaymen?

810 ESTRAGON   Highwaymen! Do we look like highwaymen?

VLADIMIR   Damn it can't you see the man is blind!

ESTRAGON   Damn it so he is. [*Pause*] So he says.

POZZO   Don't leave me!

VLADIMIR   No question of it.

815 ESTRAGON   For the moment.

POZZO   What time is it?

VLADIMIR [*inspecting the sky*]   Seven o'clock . . . eight o'clock . . .

ESTRAGON   That depends what time of year it is.

POZZO   Is it evening?

[*Silence.* VLADIMIR *and* ESTRAGON *scrutinize the sunset.*]

820 ESTRAGON   It's rising.

VLADIMIR   Impossible.

ESTRAGON   Perhaps it's the dawn.

VLADIMIR   Don't be a fool. It's the west over there.

ESTRAGON   How do you know?

825 POZZO [*anguished*]   Is it evening?

VLADIMIR   Anyway it hasn't moved.

ESTRAGON   I tell you it's rising.

POZZO   Why don't you answer me?

ESTRAGON   Give us a chance.

830 VLADIMIR [*reassuring*]   It's evening, Sir, it's evening, night is drawing nigh. My friend here would have me doubt it and I must confess he shook me for a moment. But it is not for nothing I have lived through this long day and I can assure you it is very near the end of its repertory. [*Pause*] How do you feel now?

835 ESTRAGON   How much longer are we to cart him around. [*They half release him, catch him again as he falls.*] We are not caryatids![4]

VLADIMIR   You were saying your sight used to be good, if I heard you right.

4. In architecture, draped female figures that act as supporting columns.

POZZO   Wonderful! Wonderful, wonderful sight!
       [*Silence.*]
ESTRAGON [*irritably*]   Expand! Expand!
840 VLADIMIR   Let him alone. Can't you see he's thinking of the days when
       he was happy. [*Pause*] *Memoria praeteritorum bonorum*[5]—that must be
       unpleasant.
ESTRAGON   We wouldn't know.
VLADIMIR   And it came on you all of a sudden?
845 POZZO   Quite wonderful!
VLADIMIR   I'm asking you if it came on you all of a sudden.
POZZO   I woke up one fine day as blind as Fortune.[6] [*Pause*] Sometimes I
       wonder if I'm not still asleep.
VLADIMIR   And when was that?
850 POZZO   I don't know.
VLADIMIR   But no later than yesterday—
POZZO [*violently*]   Don't question me! The blind have no notion of time. The
       things of time are hidden from them too.
VLADIMIR   Well just fancy that! I could have sworn it was just the opposite.
855 ESTRAGON   I'm going.
POZZO   Where are we?
VLADIMIR   I couldn't tell you.
POZZO   It isn't by any chance the place known as the Board?[7]
VLADIMIR   Never heard of it.
860 POZZO   What is it like?
VLADIMIR [*looking round*]   It's indescribable. It's like nothing. There's noth-
       ing. There's a tree.
POZZO   Then it's not the Board.
ESTRAGON [*sagging*]   Some diversion!
865 POZZO   Where is my menial?
VLADIMIR   He's about somewhere,
POZZO   Why doesn't he answer when I call?
VLADIMIR   I don't know. He seems to be sleeping. Perhaps he's dead.
POZZO   What happened exactly?
870 ESTRAGON   Exactly!
VLADIMIR   The two of you slipped. [*Pause*] And fell.
POZZO   Go and see is he hurt.
VLADIMIR   We can't leave you.
POZZO   You needn't both go.
875 VLADIMIR [*to* ESTRAGON]   You go.
ESTRAGON   After what he did to me? Never!
POZZO   Yes yes, let your friend go, he stinks so. [*Silence.*] What is he waiting
       for?
VLADIMIR   What you waiting for?
880 ESTRAGON   I'm waiting for Godot.
       [*Silence.*]

---

5. Memory of past goods (Latin); a phrase
quoted from St. Thomas Aquinas, *Summa
Theologica* (1269–73), 2.2.36.1.
6. The Roman goddess Fortuna, the personi-

fication of fortune, was sometimes depicted
wearing a blindfold.
7. The stage itself is often referred to as "the
boards."

VLADIMIR   What exactly should he do?

POZZO   Well to begin with he should pull on the rope, as hard as he likes so long as he doesn't strangle him. He usually responds to that. If not he should give him a taste of his boot, in the face and the privates as far as

885   possible.

VLADIMIR [*to* ESTRAGON]   You see, you've nothing to be afraid of. It's even an opportunity to revenge yourself.

ESTRAGON   And if he defends himself?

POZZO   No no, he never defends himself.

890   VLADIMIR   I'll come flying to the rescue.

ESTRAGON   Don't take your eyes off me. [*He goes towards* LUCKY.]

VLADIMIR   Make sure he's alive before you start. No point in exerting yourself if he's dead.

ESTRAGON [*bending over* LUCKY]   He's breathing.

895   VLADIMIR   Then let him have it.

> [*With sudden fury* ESTRAGON *starts kicking* LUCKY, *hurling abuse at him as he does so. But he hurts his foot and moves away, limping and groaning.* LUCKY *stirs.*]

ESTRAGON   Oh the brute!

> [*He sits down on the mound and tries to take off his boot. But he soon desists and disposes himself for sleep, his arms on his knees and his head on his arms.*]

POZZO   What's gone wrong now?

VLADIMIR   My friend has hurt himself.

POZZO   And Lucky?

900   VLADIMIR   So it is he?

POZZO   What?

VLADIMIR   It is Lucky?

POZZO   I don't understand.

VLADIMIR   And you are Pozzo?

905   POZZO   Certainly I am Pozzo.

VLADIMIR   The same as yesterday?

POZZO   Yesterday?

VLADIMIR   We met yesterday. [*Silence*] Do you not remember?

POZZO   I don't remember having met anyone yesterday. But tomorrow I won't

910   remember having met anyone today. So don't count on me to enlighten you.

VLADIMIR   But—

POZZO   Enough! Up pig!

VLADIMIR   You were bringing him to the fair to sell him. You spoke to us. He

915   danced. He thought. You had your sight.

POZZO   As you please. Let me go! [VLADIMIR *moves away.*] Up! [LUCKY *gets up, gathers up his burdens.*]

VLADIMIR   Where do you go from here.

POZZO   On. [LUCKY, *laden down, takes his place before* POZZO.] Whip! [LUCKY *puts everything down, looks for whip, finds it, puts it into* POZZO's *hand, takes up everything again.*] Rope!

> [LUCKY *puts everything down, puts end of rope into* POZZO's *hand, takes up everything again.*]

920   VLADIMIR   What is there in the bag?

POZZO   Sand. [*He jerks the rope.*] On!

VLADIMIR   Don't go yet.

POZZO   I'm going.

VLADIMIR   What do you do when you fall far from help?

925 POZZO   We wait till we can get up. Then we go on. On!

VLADIMIR   Before you go tell him to sing.

POZZO   Who?

VLADIMIR   Lucky.

POZZO   To sing?

930 VLADIMIR   Yes. Or to think. Or to recite.

POZZO   But he is dumb.

VLADIMIR   Dumb!

POZZO   Dumb. He can't even groan.

VLADIMIR   Dumb! Since when?

935 POZZO   [*suddenly furious*]   Have you not done tormenting me with your
accursed time! It's abominable! When! When! One day, is that not enough
for you, one day he went dumb, one day I went blind, one day we'll go deaf,
one day we were born, one day we shall die, the same day, the same second,
is that not enough for you? [*Calmer*] They give birth astride of a grave, the
940 light gleams an instant, then it's night once more. [*He jerks the rope.*] On!

[*Exeunt*[8] *Pozzo and Lucky. Vladimir follows them to the edge of the
stage, looks after them. The noise of falling, reinforced by mimic of Vladimir, announces that they are down again. Silence. Vladimir goes towards
Estragon, contemplates him a moment, then shakes him awake.*]

ESTRAGON   [*wild gestures, incoherent words. Finally*]   Why will you never let
me sleep?

VLADIMIR   I felt lonely.

ESTRAGON   I was dreaming I was happy.

945 VLADIMIR   That passed the time.

ESTRAGON   I was dreaming that—

VLADIMIR   [*violently*]   Don't tell me! [*Silence*] I wonder is he really blind.

ESTRAGON   Blind? Who?

VLADIMIR   Pozzo.

950 ESTRAGON   Blind?

VLADIMIR   He told us he was blind.

ESTRAGON   Well what about it?

VLADIMIR   It seemed to me he saw us.

ESTRAGON   You dreamt it. [*Pause*] Let's go. We can't. Ah! [*Pause*] Are you sure
955 it wasn't him?

VLADIMIR   Who?

ESTRAGON   Godot.

VLADIMIR   But who?

ESTRAGON   Pozzo.

960 VLADIMIR   Not at all! [*Less sure*] Not at all! [*Still less sure*] Not at all!

ESTRAGON   I suppose I might as well get up. [*He gets up painfully.*] Ow! Didi!

VLADIMIR   I don't know what to think any more.

ESTRAGON   My feet! [*He sits down again and tries to take off his boots.*] Help
me!

8. [They] exit (Latin).

965 VLADIMIR   Was I sleeping, while the others suffered? Am I sleeping now? Tomorrow, when I wake, or think I do, what shall I say of today? That with Estragon my friend, at this place, until the fall of night, I waited for Godot? That Pozzo passed, with his carrier, and that he spoke to us? Probably. But in all that what truth will there be? [ESTRAGON, *having struggled with his*
970 *boots in vain, is dozing off again.* VLADIMIR *looks at him.*] He'll know nothing. He'll tell me about the blows he received and I'll give him a carrot. [*Pause*] Astride of a grave and a difficult birth. Down in the hole, lingeringly, the grave-digger puts on the forceps.[9] We have time to grow old. The air is full of our cries. [*He listens.*] But habit is a great deadener. [*He looks*
975 *again at* ESTRAGON.] At me too someone is looking, of me too someone is saying, He is sleeping, he knows nothing, let him sleep on. [*Pause*] I can't go on! [*Pause*] What have I said?

> [*He goes feverishly to and fro, halts finally at extreme left, broods. Enter* BOY *right. He halts. Silence.*]

BOY   Mister . . . [VLADIMIR *turns.*] Mister Albert . . .
VLADIMIR   Off we go again. [*Pause*] Do you not recognize me?
980 BOY   No Sir.
VLADIMIR   It wasn't you came yesterday.
BOY   No Sir.
VLADIMIR   This is your first time.
BOY   Yes Sir.

> [*Silence.*]

985 VLADIMIR   You have a message from Mr. Godot.
BOY   Yes Sir.
VLADIMIR   He won't come this evening.
BOY   No Sir.
VLADIMIR   But he'll come tomorrow.
990 BOY   Yes Sir.
VLADIMIR   Without fail.
BOY   Yes Sir.

> [*Silence.*]

VLADIMIR   Did you meet anyone?
BOY   No Sir.
995 VLADIMIR   Two other . . . [*He hesitates.*] . . . men?
BOY   I didn't see anyone, Sir.

> [*Silence.*]

VLADIMIR   What does he do, Mr. Godot? [*Silence*] Do you hear me?
BOY   Yes Sir.
VLADIMIR   Well?
1000 BOY   He does nothing, Sir.

> [*Silence*]

VLADIMIR   How is your brother?
BOY   He's sick, Sir.
VLADIMIR   Perhaps it was he came yesterday.
BOY   I don't know, Sir.

> [*Silence*]

---

9. An instrument for grasping (obstetrical forceps help pull a baby from the birth canal).

1005 VLADIMIR [*softly*]   Has he a beard, Mr. Godot?

BOY   Yes Sir.

VLADIMIR   Fair or . . . [*He hesitates.*] . . . or black?

BOY   I think it's white, Sir.

[*Silence.*]

VLADIMIR   Christ have mercy on us!

[*Silence.*]

1010 BOY   What am I to tell Mr. Godot, Sir?

VLADIMIR   Tell him . . . [*He hesitates.*] . . . tell him you saw me and that . . . [*He hesitates.*] . . . that you saw me. [*Pause.* VLADIMIR *advances, the* BOY *recoils.* VLADIMIR *halts, the* BOY *halts. With sudden violence.*] You're sure you saw me, you won't come and tell me tomorrow that you never saw me!

[*Silence.* VLADIMIR *makes a sudden spring forward, the* BOY *avoids him and exit running. Silence. The sun sets, the moon rises. As in Act 1.* VLADI-MIR *stands motionless and bowed.* ESTRAGON *wakes, takes off his boots, gets up with one in each hand and goes and puts them down center front, then goes towards* VLADIMIR.]

1015 ESTRAGON   What's wrong with you?

VLADIMIR   Nothing.

ESTRAGON   I'm going.

VLADIMIR   So am I.

ESTRAGON   Was I long asleep?

1020 VLADIMIR   I don't know.

[*Silence.*]

ESTRAGON   Where shall we go?

VLADIMIR   Not far.

ESTRAGON   Oh yes, let's go far away from here.

VLADIMIR   We can't.

1025 ESTRAGON   Why not?

VLADIMIR   We have to come back tomorrow.

ESTRAGON   What for?

VLADIMIR   To wait for Godot.

ESTRAGON   Ah! [*Silence.*] He didn't come?

1030 VLADIMIR   No.

ESTRAGON   And now it's too late.

VLADIMIR   Yes, now it's night.

ESTRAGON   And if we dropped him? [*Pause*] If we dropped him?

VLADIMIR   He'd punish us. [*Silence. He looks at the tree.*] Everything's dead

1035 but the tree.

ESTRAGON [*looking at the tree*]   What is it?

VLADIMIR   It's the tree.

ESTRAGON   Yes, but what kind?

VLADIMIR   I don't know. A willow.

[ESTRAGON *draws* VLADIMIR *towards the tree. They stand motionless before it. Silence.*]

1040 ESTRAGON   Why don't we hang ourselves?

VLADIMIR   With what?

ESTRAGON   You haven't got a bit of rope?

VLADIMIR   No.

ESTRAGON   Then we can't.

[*Silence.*]

1045   VLADIMIR   Let's go.

ESTRAGON   Wait, there's my belt.

VLADIMIR   It's too short.

ESTRAGON   You could hang on to my legs.

VLADIMIR   And who'd hang on to mine?

1050   ESTRAGON   True.

VLADIMIR   Show all the same. [ESTRAGON *loosens the cord that holds up his trousers which, much too big for him, fall about his ankles. They look at the cord.*] It might do at a pinch. But is it strong enough?

ESTRAGON   We'll soon see. Here.

[*They each take an end of the cord and pull. It breaks. They almost fall.*]

VLADIMIR   Not worth a curse.

[*Silence.*]

1055   ESTRAGON   You say we have to come back tomorrow?

VLADIMIR   Yes.

ESTRAGON   Then we can bring a good bit of rope.

VLADIMIR   Yes.

[*Silence.*]

ESTRAGON   Didi.

1060   VLADIMIR   Yes.

ESTRAGON   I can't go on like this.

VLADIMIR   That's what you think.

ESTRAGON   If we parted? That might be better for us.

VLADIMIR   We'll hang ourselves tomorrow. [*Pause*] Unless Godot comes.

1065   ESTRAGON   And if he comes?

VLADIMIR   We'll be saved.

[VLADIMIR *takes off his hat* (LUCKY's), *peers inside it, feels about inside it, shakes it, knocks on the crown, puts it on again.*]

ESTRAGON   Well? Shall we go?

VLADIMIR   Pull on your trousers.

ESTRAGON   What?

1070   VLADIMIR   Pull on your trousers.

ESTRAGON   You want me to pull off my trousers?

VLADIMIR   Pull ON your trousers.

ESTRAGON [*realizing his trousers are down*]   True. [*He pulls up his trousers.*]

VLADIMIR   Well? Shall we go?

1075   ESTRAGON   Yes, let's go.

[*They do not move.*]

Curtain.

CRITICAL PERSPECTIVE

MARTIN ESSLIN

The critic and dramatist Martin Esslin is most famous for having coined the term "Theatre of the Absurd," with which he describes the work of mid-century playwrights such as SAMUEL BECKETT, Eugène Ionesco, and Arthur Adamov. These authors confront a world that is apparently devoid of meaning, and their dramas address the failures of language and logic that arise from this confrontation. Esslin identifies the existential philosophy of Albert Camus and Jean-Paul Sartre at the heart of this new form of drama and argues that the dramatists of the Theatre of the Absurd are in fact more faithful proponents of existential philosophy than were Camus and Sartre in their own works for the theater because they presented this con-dition not just thematically but also in the absurdist form and language of their work.

In this selection, Esslin discusses a production of Beckett's WAITING FOR GODOT that was staged at the San Quentin penitentiary in 1957, which received a strong positive response from the prison inmates. Esslin uses *Godot*'s production history to argue for the universal human appeal of the play, which had often been dismissed by audiences and critics as esoteric and avant-garde. Esslin goes on to identify important distinctions between the Theatre of the Absurd, the existentialist theater, and the poetic avant-garde theater, all of which flourished in and around Paris during the 1950s and 1960s.　　　　　M.P.

---

from *The Theatre of the Absurd*

INTRODUCTION

On 19 November 1957, a group of worried actors were preparing to face their audience. The actors were members of the company of the San Francisco Actors' Workshop. The audience consisted of fourteen hundred convicts at the San Quentin penitentiary. No live play had been performed at San Quentin since Sarah Bernhardt[1] appeared there in 1913. Now, forty-four years later, the play that had been chosen, largely

---

1. A French stage and film actress (1844–1923), among the most famous performers of her age.

because no woman appeared in it, was Samuel Beckett's *Waiting for Godot*.

No wonder the actors and Herbert Blau, the director, were apprehensive. How were they to face one of the toughest audiences in the world with a highly obscure, intellectual play that had produced near riots among a good many highly sophisticated audiences in Western Europe? Herbert Blau decided to prepare the San Quentin audience for what was to come. He stepped on to the stage and addressed the packed, darkened North Dining Hall—a sea of flickering matches that the convicts tossed over their shoulders after lighting their cigarettes. Blau compared the play to a piece of jazz music 'to which one must listen for whatever one may find in it'. In the same way, he hoped, there would be some meaning, some personal significance for each member of the audience in *Waiting for Godot*.

The curtain parted. The play began. And what had bewildered the sophisticated audiences of Paris, London, and New York was immediately grasped by an audience of convicts. As the writer of 'Memos of a first-nighter' put it in the columns of the prison paper, the *San Quentin News*:

> The trio of muscle-men, biceps overflowing . . . parked all 642 lbs on the aisle and waited for the girls and funny stuff. When this didn't appear they audibly fumed and audibly decided to wait until the house lights dimmed before escaping. They made one error. They listened and looked two minutes too long—and stayed. Left at the end. All shook . . .[2]

Or as the writer of the lead story of the same paper reported, under the headline, 'San Francisco Group Leaves S.Q. Audience Waiting for Godot':

> From the moment Robin Wagner's thoughtful and limbo-like set was dressed with light, until the last futile and expectant handclasp was hesitantly activated between the two searching vagrants, the San Francisco company had its audience of captives in its collective hand. . . . Those that had felt a less controversial vehicle should be attempted as a first play here had their fears allayed a short five minutes after the Samuel Beckett piece began to unfold.[3]

A reporter from the San Francisco *Chronicle* who was present noted that the convicts did not find it difficult to understand the play. One prisoner told him, 'Godot is society.' Said another: 'He's the outside.'[4] A teacher at the prison was quoted as saying, 'They know what is meant by waiting . . . and they knew if Godot finally came, he would only be a disappointment.'[5] The leading article of the prison paper showed how clearly the writers had understood the meaning of the play:

2. *San Quentin News,* San Quentin, Calif., 28 November 1957 [Esslin's note].

3. Ibid. [Esslin's note].

4. *Theatre Arts,* New York, July 1958 [Esslin's note].

5. Ibid. [Esslin's note].

It was an expression, symbolic in order to avoid all personal error, by an author who expected each member of his audience to draw his own conclusions, make his own errors. It asked nothing in point, it forced no dramatized moral on the viewer, it held out no specific hope. . . . We're still waiting for Godot, and shall continue to wait. When the scenery gets too drab and the action too slow, we'll call each other names and swear to part forever—but then, there's no place to go![6]

It is said that Godot himself, as well as turns of phrase and characters from the play, has since become a permanent part of the private language, the institutional mythology of San Quentin.

Why did a play of the supposedly esoteric avant-garde make so immediate and so deep an impact on an audience of convicts? Because it confronted them with a situation in some ways analogous to their own? Perhaps. Or perhaps because they were unsophisticated enough to come to the theatre without any preconceived notions and ready-made expectations, so that they avoided the mistake that trapped so many established critics who condemned the play for its lack of plot, development, characterization, suspense, or plain common sense. Certainly the prisoners of San Quentin could not be suspected of the sin of intellectual snobbery, for which a sizeable proportion of the audiences of *Waiting for Godot* have often been reproached; of pretending to like a play they did not even begin to understand, just to appear in the know.

The reception of *Waiting for Godot* at San Quentin, and the wide acclaim given to plays by Ionesco, Adamov, Pinter,[7] and others, testify that these plays, which are so often superciliously dismissed as nonsense or mystification, *have* something to say and *can* be understood. Most of the incomprehension with which plays of this type are still being received by critics and theatrical reviewers, most of the bewilderment they have caused and to which they still give rise, come from the fact that they are part of a new and still developing stage convention that has not yet been generally understood and has hardly even been defined. Inevitably, plays written in this new convention will, when judged by the standards and criteria of another, be regarded as impertinent and outrageous impostures. If a good play must have a cleverly constructed story, these have no story or plot to speak of; if a good play is judged by subtlety of characterization and motivation, these are often without recognizable characters and present the audience with almost mechanical puppets; if a good play has to have a fully explained theme, which is neatly exposed and finally solved, these often have neither a beginning nor an end; if a good play is to hold the mirror up to nature and portray the manners and mannerisms of the age in finely observed sketches, these seem often to be reflections of

---

6. *San Quentin News,* 28 November 1957 [Esslin's note].

7. Eugène Ionesco (1909–1994), French and Romanian playwright; Arthur Adamov (1908–1970), Russian playwright; and Harold Pinter (1930–2008), British playwright—considered by Esslin to be among the foremost representatives of the Theatre of the Absurd.

dreams and nightmares; if a good play relies on witty repartee and pointed dialogue, these often consist of incoherent babblings.

But the plays we are concerned with here pursue ends quite different from those of the conventional play and therefore use quite different methods. They can be judged only by the standards of the Theatre of the Absurd.

It must be stressed, however, that the dramatists whose work is here discussed do not form part of any self-proclaimed or self-conscious school or movement. On the contrary, each of the writers in question is an individual who regards himself as a lone outsider, cut off and isolated in his private world. Each has his own personal approach to both subject-matter and form; his own roots, sources, and background. If they also, very clearly and in spite of themselves, have a good deal in common, it is because their work most sensitively mirrors and reflects the preoccupations and anxieties, the emotions and thinking of many of their contemporaries in the Western world.

This is not to say that their works are representative of mass attitudes. It is an oversimplification to assume that any age presents a homogeneous pattern. Ours being, more than most others, an age of transition, it displays a bewilderingly stratified picture: medieval beliefs still held and overlaid by eighteenth-century rationalism and mid-nineteenth-century Marxism, rocked by sudden volcanic eruptions of prehistoric fanaticisms and primitive tribal cults. Each of these components of the cultural pattern of the age finds its own artistic expression. The Theatre of the Absurd, however, can be seen as the reflection of what seems to be the attitude most genuinely representative of our own time.

The hallmark of this attitude is its sense that the certitudes and unshakable basic assumptions of former ages have been swept away, that they have been tested and found wanting, that they have been discredited as cheap and somewhat childish illusions. The decline of religious faith was masked until the end of the Second World War by the substitute religions of faith in progress, nationalism, and various totalitarian fallacies. All this was shattered by the war. By 1942, Albert Camus[8] was calmly putting the question why, since life had lost all meaning, man should not seek escape in suicide. In one of the great, seminal heart-searchings of our time, *The Myth of Sisyphus,* Camus tried to diagnose the human situation in a world of shattered beliefs:

> A world that can be explained by reasoning, however faulty, is a familiar world. But in a universe that is suddenly deprived of illusions and of light, man feels a stranger. His is an irremediable exile, because he is deprived of memories of a lost homeland as much as he lacks the hope of a promised land to come. This divorce between man and his life, the actor and his setting, truly constitutes the feeling of Absurdity.[9]

8. French writer and philosopher (1913–1960) associated with the philosophical movements of existentialism and absurdism.

9. Albert Camus, *Le Mythe de Sisyphe* (Paris: Gallimard, 1942), p. 18 [Esslin's note].

'Absurd' originally means 'out of harmony', in a musical context. Hence its dictionary definition: 'out of harmony with reason or propriety; incongruous, unreasonable, illogical'. In common usage, 'absurd' may simply mean 'ridiculous', but this is not the sense in which Camus uses the word, and in which it is used when we speak of the Theatre of the Absurd. In an essay on Kafka, Ionesco defined his understanding of the term as follows: 'Absurd is that which is devoid of purpose. . . . Cut off from his religious, metaphysical, and transcendental roots, man is lost; all his actions become senseless, absurd, useless.'[1]

This sense of metaphysical anguish at the absurdity of the human condition is, broadly speaking, the theme of the plays of Beckett, Adamov, Ionesco, Genet, and the other writers. But it is not merely the subject-matter that defines what is here called the Theatre of the Absurd. A similar sense of the senselessness of life, of the inevitable devaluation of ideals, purity, and purpose, is also the theme of much of the work of dramatists like Giraudoux, Anouilh, Salacrou, Sartre,[2] and Camus himself. Yet these writers differ from the dramatists of the Absurd in an important respect: they present their sense of the irrationality of the human condition in the form of highly lucid and logically constructed reasoning, while the Theatre of the Absurd strives to express its sense of the senselessness of the human condition and the inadequacy of the rational approach by the open abandonment of rational devices and discursive thought. While Sartre or Camus express the new content in the old convention, the Theatre of the Absurd goes a step further in trying to achieve a unity between its basic assumptions and the form in which these are expressed. In some senses, the *theatre* of Sartre and Camus is less adequate as an expression of the *philosophy* of Sartre and Camus—in artistic, as distinct from philosophic, terms—than the Theatre of the Absurd.

If Camus argued that in our disillusioned age the world has ceased to make sense, he did so in the elegantly rationalistic and discursive style of an eighteenth-century moralist, in well-constructed and polished plays. If Sartre argues that existence comes before essence and that human personality can be reduced to pure potentiality and the freedom to choose itself anew at any moment, he presents his ideas in plays based on brilliantly drawn characters who remain wholly consistent and thus reflect the old convention that each human being has a core of immutable, unchanging essence—in fact, an immortal soul. And the beautiful phrasing and argumentative brilliance of both Sartre and Camus in their relentless probing still, by implication, proclaim a tacit conviction that logical discourse can offer valid solutions, that the analysis of language will lead to the uncovering of basic concepts—Platonic ideas.

1. Eugène Ionesco, *'Dans les armes de la ville', Cahiers de la Compagnie Madeleine Renaud—Jean-Louis Barrault,* Paris, no. 20, October 1957 [Esslin's note].
2. Jean-Paul Sartre (1905–1980), French philosopher and cultural figure who was a major proponent of the philosophical movement of existentialism. Hippolyte Jean Giraudoux (1882–1944), French novelist and playwright. Jean Anouilh (1910–1987), French dramatist. Armand Salacrou (1899–1989), French dramatist.

This is an inner contradiction that the dramatists of the Absurd are trying, by instinct and intuition rather than by conscious effort, to overcome and resolve. The Theatre of the Absurd has renounced arguing *about* the absurdity of the human condition; it merely *presents* it in being—that is, in terms of concrete stage images. This is the difference between the approach of the philosopher and that of the poet; the difference, to take an example from another sphere, between the *idea* of God in the works of Thomas Aquinas or Spinoza and the *intuition* of God in those of St John of the Cross or Meister Eckhart—the difference between theory and experience.

It is this striving for an integration between the subject-matter and the form in which it is expressed that separates the Theatre of the Absurd from the Existentialist theatre.

It must also be distinguished from another important, and parallel, trend in the contemporary French theatre, which is equally preoccupied with the absurdity and uncertainty of the human condition: the 'poetic avant-garde' theatre of dramatists like Michel de Ghelderode, Jacques Audiberti, Georges Neveux, and, in the younger generation, Georges Schehadé, Henri Pichette, and Jean Vauthier, to name only some of its most important exponents. This is an even more difficult dividing line to draw, for the two approaches overlap a good deal. The 'poetic avant-garde' relies on fantasy and dream reality as much as the Theatre of the Absurd does; it also disregards such traditional axioms as that of the basic unity and consistency of each character or the need for a plot. Yet basically the 'poetic avant-garde' represents a different mood; it is more lyrical, and far less violent and grotesque. Even more important is its different attitude toward language: the 'poetic avant-garde' relies to a far greater extent on consciously 'poetic' speech; it aspires to plays that are in effect poems, images composed of a rich web of verbal associations.

The Theatre of the Absurd, on the other hand, tends toward a radical devaluation of language, toward a poetry that is to emerge from the concrete and objectified images of the stage itself. The element of language still plays an important part in this conception, but what *happens* on the stage transcends, and often contradicts, the *words* spoken by the characters. In Ionesco's *The Chairs,* for example, the poetic content of a powerfully poetic play does not lie in the banal words that are uttered but in the fact that they are spoken to an ever-growing number of empty chairs.

The Theatre of the Absurd is thus part of the 'anti-literary' movement of our time, which has found its expression in abstract painting, with its rejection of 'literary' elements in pictures; or in the 'new novel' in France, with its reliance on the description of objects and its rejection of empathy and anthropomorphism. It is no coincidence that, like all these movements and so many of the efforts to create new forms of expression in all the arts, the Theatre of the Absurd should be centred in Paris.

*   *   *

EDWARD ALBEE

1928–2016

Iᴺ January 1960, a previously unknown playwright, Edward Albee, emerged on the nascent off-Broadway theater scene with THE ZOO STORY. Paired in performance with SAMUEL BECKETT's *Krapp's Last Tape*, Albee's play more than held its own, despite the attention focused on a new work by Beckett, author of the controversial theatrical sensation, WAITING FOR GODOT (1953). Indeed, for some early reviewers, Albee's piece merited the greater scrutiny, precisely because his was a new American voice, immediately identified for its potential to make a significant impact on U.S. theater. The prominent critic Harold Clurman announced in *The Nation* that *The Zoo Story* interested him "more than any other new American play" he'd recently seen, and he hoped that Albee had "the stuff" to overcome "the various impediments that usually face our promising dramatists." These obstacles were increasingly logistical: Broadway had been hit hard by the Great Depression and World War II, and production costs had risen sharply while the number of theaters had shrunk by half, making it nearly impossible for an untried playwright to secure a production. At the same time, the mainstays of the midcentury commercial theater, including EUGENE O'NEILL, ARTHUR MILLER, and TENNESSEE WILLIAMS, appeared to have their best work behind

them. Their writing seemed not to be addressing the social and political issues that concerned the current "beat" generation. The playwrights of this younger demographic, influenced by postwar European artistic and intellectual trends, were actively seeking to express their ideas in alternative dramatic forms and at alternative venues, like Greenwich Village's Provincetown Playhouse, where *The Zoo Story* saw its U.S. premiere. Quickly established as a sensation in its own right, Albee's drama was revived eight times over the next six years, becoming the defining off-Broadway play of the decade. *The Zoo Story* not only launched Albee, it also remains one of the most significant works of his career, which spanned almost sixty years, until his death in 2016 at age eighty-eight.

Shortly after his birth in March 1928, Edward F. Albee III was adopted into an established New York theatrical family. Edward's adoptive grandfather, for whom he was named, had been a partner in one of the most successful vaudeville theater syndicates in the United States. His adoptive father, Reed Albee, retired from theater management around the time of Edward's birth. Reed and his wife, Louise, raised Edward in suburban Larchmont, New York, in an atmosphere of great financial privilege; by all reports, however, the Albees were emotionally distant parents who entrusted their son primarily to the care of a nurse.

Albee's checkered adolescence featured enrollment in and early departure from a series of private schools; he ultimately graduated from Choate, an elite college-preparatory school in Connecticut, where he had finally thrived intellectually and begun to write avidly. But further academic engagement eluded him. After brief, unsuccessful stints at both Trinity College and Columbia University, Albee took up residence in Greenwich Village in 1949, where he became part of the circle of painters, writers, composers, and other artists who were contributing to the development of a new avant-garde in the 1950s. He absorbed the cultural outpourings of that decade, especially its music and theater, attending productions by playwrights such as Eugene O'Neill, Tennessee Williams, JEAN GENET, and T. S. Eliot. Albee continued to experiment with poetry, fiction, essays, and drama, but he focused on plays only after receiving some modest encouragement from an early mentor—Thornton Wilder, author of the quintessential American drama *Our Town* (1938). To support himself, Albee worked at a series of service-sector jobs, enjoying most a stint as a Western Union telegram deliverer that introduced him to a wide range of New York neighborhoods and their residents—an experience that would soon inform his dramaturgy. He claimed to have "liberated" a typewriter from the Western Union office, and shortly before his thirtieth birthday drafted *The Zoo Story* in what he described as a moment of creative "explosion."

Since that breakthrough, Albee's record of continued productivity and achievement stands unmatched in American theater. In 1961, Albee composed *Who's Afraid of Virginia Woolf*, which took Broadway by storm the following year: it won the Tony and the New York Drama Critics' Circle Award for Best Play as well as the Outer Critics Circle Award for Playwright of the Season. *Virginia Woolf* and *The Zoo Story* remain among the most frequently revived and best-known of all his plays. Albee received his first Pulitzer Prize for Drama in 1967 with *A Delicate Balance*. He won subsequent Pulitzers in 1975 for *Seascape* and

in 1994 for *Three Tall Women*. His 2002 play *The Goat* earned the Tony Award for Best Play, and he also received a series of lifetime achievement recognitions, including a special Tony Award, The Edward MacDowell Medal, and a Pioneer Award from the Lambda Literary Foundation.

Albee's remarkable theatrical career nevertheless began quite circuitously. Initially (and ironically, given Clurman's subsequent comments), although read and praised by various other writers, directors, and agents, *The Zoo Story* could not secure a New York production. The one-act work depicts an encounter—at first innocuous but ultimately disastrous—between two men in Central Park, Jerry, an eccentric loner who has just been to the zoo, and Peter, a successful if conventional publishing executive. The play opens with a light tone and seemingly innocuous exchanges and exposition that echo conventions of dramatic realism. These give way, however, to sardonic humor, an adventurous use of extended monologue, and increasingly fraught dialogue that, taken together, convey a sense of both menace and isolation in contemporary urban society. These tonal and dramaturgical shifts, coupled with the absence of a typical, realist plot and the play's violent conclusion no doubt made it difficult for potential producers to see the work as commercially viable, despite its compelling theme. Although shortly after its premiere he parodically alluded to *The Zoo Story* as "DILEMMA, DERELICTION AND DEATH," in an early interview Albee, with a nod to the beast lurking within us all, gestured toward a more serious message: "We must try to claw our way into compassion."

While Albee was making efforts in New York to find *The Zoo Story* a theatrical home, his partner at the time, composer William Flanagan, through contacts abroad, facilitated the script's consideration by colleagues in Europe. The play made its way to the drama department at S. Fischer Verlag, the German publisher of Eugene O'Neill, Tennessee Williams, and Thornton Wilder. The department head was so impressed with the script that she brought it to the director of the Schiller Theater in Berlin, who paired it with *Krapp's Last Tape* and premiered both works in German in

1959. In the meantime, Albee had obtained representation by the William Morris Agency, and through the efforts of his agent, the script was finally optioned and a New York production arranged. The same double bill, which had been enthusiastically received in Germany, then premiered (in the original English) at the Provincetown Playhouse.

As theater historians have since noted, this location was auspicious, for not only did *The Zoo Story* revitalize American drama by helping to bolster the off-Broadway theater movement of the 1960s, but it also heralded a renewal of the one-act dramatic form which, decades earlier, had been promoted on that very same stage by the Provincetown Players—home to SUSAN

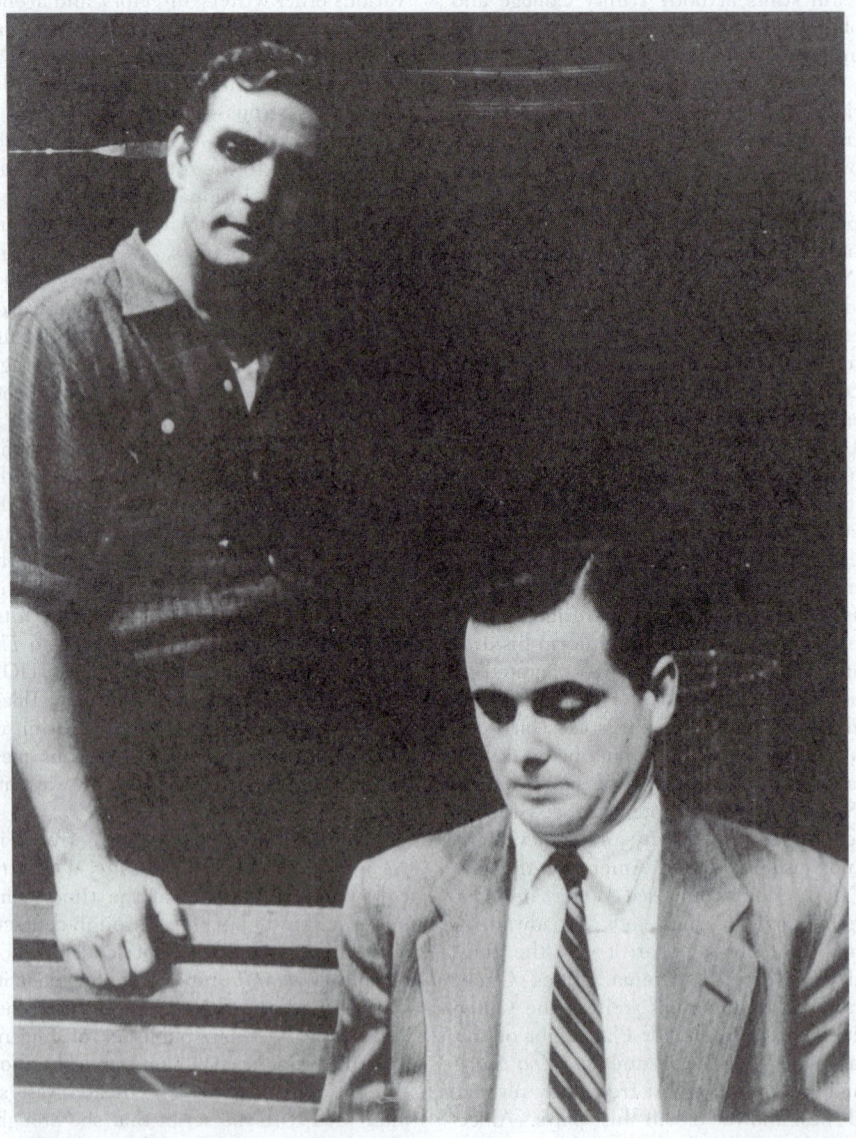

Peter Mark Richman as Jerry and William Daniels as Peter in the 1960 production of *Zoo Story* at the Provincetown Playhouse.

GLASPELL and Eugene O'Neill. As a critic in *Theatre Magazine* noted in 1916, "The one-act play is . . . especially suited to our national temperament" because it provides exactly what the public craves: the "tenseness of interest at an emotional height, [and] an irresistible focusing of interest and emotion upon a particular situation" accomplished through a vitalized "exposition and psychological explanation." Almost fifty years later, *The Zoo Story* offers those very dramaturgical qualities.

Ironically, one of the excuses Albee was initially given for the rejection of *The Zoo Story* was that only full-length plays were theatrically viable. This remained a sore point for him, as he considered all his plays, regardless of their playing time, "'full-length' in that they are full to their lengths." He further noted, "The one-act form is often scorned as being minor, or superficial, or some such nonsense, by people who forget that *Oedipus Rex* is a one-act play, as are many of Beckett's masterpieces." Fortunately, visionary director Alan Schneider, who had already emerged as a leading interpreter of Samuel Beckett and would soon become Albee's close collaborator, felt that *The Zoo Story* was "the most original and powerful American work" he'd recently encountered. Within theatre circles, any equivocation on the form was no doubt put to rest by cultural critic Norman Mailer, who, at an early private performance for members of the influential Actors Studio, exuberantly pronounced *Zoo Story* "the best fucking one-act play I've ever seen!"

Although the New York theater critics were not as ebullient as Mailer, Albee received praise from the *New York Post* for the "power, skill and freshness" of his writing, while the *New York Times* called *The Zoo Story* "original and engrossing." The reviewer for *Variety* believed that Albee demonstrated "an impressive grasp of what makes effective theatre," a perspective echoed in the *Village Voice*: Albee "knows how to handle a situation and dialogue and bring you deftly to the edge of your seat." Detractors argued that the drama's ending was too melodramatic, however, and some reviews reflected undisguised homophobia toward the play and toward Albee as a writer. One befuddled critic simply opined that "the only sense I could draw from it is the conviction that one shouldn't talk to strangers in Central Park."

Yet the most influential early assessment of Albee as an important, emerging voice for the American theater came not from the U.S. press, but from a critic based in England, Martin Esslin, who was soon to become one of the most important figures in twentieth-century drama studies. Esslin's groundbreaking volume, *The Theatre of the Absurd* (1961), shaped the West's understanding of the contemporary stage, offering a powerful reading of postwar dramaturgy. Quoting Romanian-French playwright Eugène Ionesco, Esslin defined "the Absurd" as "'that which is devoid of purpose,'" a condition that leaves us adrift, "cut off from . . . religious, metaphysical, and transcendental roots." The result is a feeling that our "actions become senseless, absurd, useless.'" For Esslin then, "the Theatre of the Absurd strives to express its sense of the senselessness of the human condition and the inadequacy of the rational approach by the open abandonment of rational devices and discursive thought." He focuses his discussion on dramatists such as Beckett, Ionesco, PINTER, and Genet, arguing that there are, by contrast, a "dearth of examples" of U.S. writers working in this mode, because the "feeling of deep disillusionment, the draining away of the sense of meaning and purpose in life" better characterized Europe after the Second World War. However, he singles out Albee as an exception, offering a detailed consideration of his early works. Praising him for his "promising and brilliant first example of an American contribution" to this mode, Esslin groups Albee with the Absurdists "precisely because his work attacks the very foundations of American optimism."

A number of critics and scholars embraced this reading, noting Albee's debt to one of Esslin's quintessential Absurdist works, *Waiting for Godot*, in terms of the interplay between Albee's characters Peter and Jerry, the absence of a traditional plot, and his spare setting, comprising only two park benches and a backdrop of "foliage, trees, sky." Other scholars rejected the Absurdist label for *The Zoo Story*, however, Christopher Bigsby most compellingly, who argued that the play was instead a blend of impressionism and realism, "an articulate assertion of the need to break out of an isolation which is socially rather than metaphysically derived, which is self-imposed rather than determined." Over the years, Albee was repeatedly asked by interviewers to provide his own analysis of this stylistic debate; although he acknowledged that he "write[s] about man's absurd position in a world that makes no sense," he nevertheless described the play, and successful American theater generally, as "naturalistic."

Regardless of which form(s) one sees in *The Zoo Story*, how one perceives the interaction of Jerry and Peter is integral to an understanding of the play. On the most basic level, Albee presents us with two characters who have different goals: Peter's plan for the afternoon is to read—to engage alone with the written word. Jerry, however, wants to talk—to connect with another person through speech. These fundamentally different objectives shape the dialogue and drive the action; Jerry pushes Peter to answer his questions and listen to his stories, especially that of "Jerry and the Dog." A disturbing but also darkly comic narrative about Jerry's life in a run-down rooming house, and his attempts to establish a relationship with his landlady's "black monster of a beast," the monologue additionally functions, as Albee scholar Philip C. Kolin notes, as metatheatre, with Jerry taking on the roles of actor, director, and playwright through his storytelling. This tale not only occupies the play's center and about a fourth of its length, but it also serves as a microcosm of the work overall in its revelation of failed efforts at communication and the retaliative action that can result when one feels thwarted and alone.

Understandably, given its textual placement and length, the story is seen by scholars as thematically integral to the play, and tied to Jerry's decision to visit the Central Park Zoo "to find out more about the way people exist with animals, and the way animals exist with each other, and with people too." But how, exactly, we are to interpret the monologue's meaning in the context of the play overall has prompted much critical debate, especially in light of Jerry's climactic goading of Peter to wield a knife on which Jerry then impales himself. One line of interpretation, first proffered by the reviewer

for the *New Yorker*, suggests that we might "relate Jerry and Peter to a pair of celebrated figures from the New Testament." Such readings have described the drama as a morality play, and see the story of the dog, or the work generally, as a parable. In these analyses, scholars identify Jerry as a Christ figure sacrificing himself for the modern Everyman who has lost contact with humanity. Peter, notably, denies Jerry three times in the play's later moments, echoing the Gospels. Albee's dialogue certainly supports such a reading, at times even assuming a biblical tone in lines such as Jerry's "I came unto you . . . and you have comforted me" and Peter's repeated cries of "Oh my God" at the play's conclusion.

When queried about such interpretations, Albee acknowledged that he "put an awful lot more Christian symbolism into my plays than I am consciously aware of," but wryly noted that if critics "make you seem far more interesting than you consciously *were*, you incorporate those things as part of your original intention. Naturally." Although he expressed some ambivalence about his early religious education, Albee said that he had "always been very interested in Jesus Christ," whom he considered "the only substantial and good Marxist I know about." Interestingly, relatively few Albee scholars other than Bigsby have acknowledged that *The Zoo Story* indeed invites a Marxist analysis, given the glaring economic disparities that separate the characters' worlds. Noting that "all plays are political, way deep down underneath," Albee also admitted that he "write[s] angry plays." While he didn't "set out to write plays as a social critic" he nevertheless aligned himself with the image of a playwright "as a man out-of-step with his society. A man who feels primarily that his plays should not have had to have been written." Many Albee critics have thus seen parallels between the tenor and impact of his writing and that of British playwrights like John Osborne, whose *Look Back in Anger* (1956) had marked a comparable, recent turning point for the English stage. In this regard, Kolin observes that Albee "pummeled American conformity with scathing satire and ideological fervor."

Jerry's jesting critique of Peter's comfortable, clichéd middle-class existence, as he elicits details of Peter's family, pets, and possessions, comes to stand in stark contrast to the images of "the colored queen, the Puerto Rican family, the person in the front room whom I've never seen, the woman who cries deliberately behind her closed door, and the rest of the people in all rooming-houses, everywhere" with whom Jerry identifies and through whom we understand the gulf separating America's social classes. Yet, as critics have noted and Albee also admitted, as remarkable and complex as Jerry is, *The Zoo Story* "didn't do a full job on the character of Peter." After considering this problem for decades, Albee finally decided to revisit and expand Peter's story, writing a new one-act play "about Peter before he meets Jerry . . . at home with his wife, Ann, and how this affects his reaction to Jerry—to the extent that it *does*." The new piece, *Homelife*, was commissioned and premiered by the Hartford Stage Company in 2004. The combined work, comprising *Homelife* as act one and *The Zoo Story* as act two, was initially called *Peter and Jerry*, but was renamed *At Home at the Zoo*, perhaps after *New York Times* critic Jane Gordon noted that, especially in light of the title, Ann appears "inconsequential." As has been true throughout Albee's career, the critics were divided over this new work, but Albee championed both *Homelife* and *At Home at the Zoo*, and maintained that on some subconscious level the entire work must have been in his mind from the beginning.

Over the years, Albee tinkered with *The Zoo Story*, making small but significant changes in the script to streamline and clarify the action and update some details. Peter's annual salary, for example, increases from $18,000 in the first version to "around" $200,000. Albee also cut some of the more obvious foreshadowing from early in the play, along with some repetition in Jerry's long monologue. Albee considered the version included here, which dates from 1999, "definitive," although he made some further changes for *At Home at the Zoo*, such as the substitution of "black" for "colored" to describe the "queen" who lives next to Jerry. Such emendations exemplify Albee's dramaturgical process of alert engagement with his culture and his audiences, even with regard to work from the earliest period of his professional career.

Critics and scholars alike consider Edward Albee the most important and influential playwright of his generation. While Albee always graciously accepted such accolades, he was also resolute about the goals for his work: "I dismiss all labels. Theater of the Absurd. Angry Young Man. Playwright of Protest. Labels are so facile, and they're a substitute for conscientious analysis so much of the time." He steadfastly maintained that "the responsibility of the writer is to be a sort of demonic social critic—to present the world and people in it as he sees it and say, 'Do you like it? If you don't like it, change it.'"   J.E.G.

The Zoo Story
A Play in One Scene

PETER

A man in his early forties, neither fat nor gaunt, neither handsome nor homely. He wears tweeds, smokes a pipe, carries horn-rimmed glasses. Although he is moving into middle age, his dress and his manner would suggest a man younger.

JERRY

A man in his late thirties, not poorly dressed, but carelessly. What was once a trim and lightly muscled body has begun to go to fat; and while he is no longer hand-some, it is evident that he once was. His fall from physical grace should not suggest debauchery; he has, to come closest to it, a great weariness.

THE SCENE

It is Central Park; a Sunday afternoon in summer; the present. There are two park benches, one toward either side of the stage; they both face the audience. Behind them foliage, trees, sky. At the beginning, Peter is seated on one of the benches.

> [*As the curtain rises,* PETER *is seated on the bench stage-right. He is read-ing a book. He stops reading, cleans his glasses, goes back to reading.* JERRY *enters.*]

JERRY   I've been to the zoo. [PETER *doesn't notice.*] I said, I've been to the zoo. MISTER, I'VE BEEN TO THE ZOO![1]

PETER   Hm? . . . What? . . . I'm sorry, were you talking to me?

JERRY   I went to the zoo, and then I walked until I came here. Have I been
5   walking north?

PETER [*Puzzled*]   North? Why . . . I . . . I think so. Let me see.

JERRY [*Pointing past the audience*]   Is that Fifth Avenue?

PETER   Why yes; yes, it is.

JERRY   And what is that cross street there; that one, to the right?

10 PETER   That? Oh, that's Seventy-fourth Street.

JERRY   And the zoo is around Sixty-fifth Street; so, I've been walking north.

PETER [*Anxious to get back to his reading*]   Yes, it would seem so.

JERRY   Good old north.

PETER [*Lightly, by reflex*]   Ha, ha.

15 JERRY [*After a slight pause*]   But not due north.

PETER   I . . . well, no, not due north; but, we . . . call it north. It's northerly.

---

1. The Central Park Zoo is located near the southeast corner of the park. The zoo occupies 6.5 acres, and its main entrance is on 5th Avenue near 64th Street.

JERRY [*Watches as* PETER, *anxious to dismiss him, prepares his pipe*]   Well,
   boy; *you're* not going to get lung cancer, are you?

PETER [*Looks up, a little annoyed, then smiles*]   No, sir. Not from this.

20 JERRY   No, sir. What you'll probably get is cancer of the mouth, and then
   you'll have to wear one of those things Freud[2] wore after they took one
   whole side of his jaw away. What do they call those things?

PETER [*Uncomfortable*]   A prosthesis?

JERRY   The very thing! A prosthesis. You're an educated man, aren't you? Are
25   you a doctor?

PETER   Oh, no; no. I read about it somewhere; *Time* magazine, I think. [*He
   turns to his book.*]

JERRY   Well, *Time* magazine isn't for blockheads.

PETER   No, I suppose not.

JERRY [*After a pause*]   Boy, I'm glad that's Fifth Avenue there.

30 PETER [*Vaguely*]   Yes.

JERRY   I don't like the west side of the park much.

PETER   Oh? [*Then, slightly wary, but interested*] Why?

JERRY [*Offhand*]   I don't know.

PETER   Oh. [*He returns to his book.*]

JERRY [*He stands for a few seconds, looking at* PETER; *who finally looks up*
35   *again, puzzled.*]   Do you mind if we talk?

PETER [*Obviously minding*]   Why . . . no, no.

JERRY   Yes you do; you do.

PETER [*Puts his book down, his pipe out and away, smiling*]   No, really; I don't
   mind.

40 JERRY   Yes you do.

PETER [*Finally decided*]   No; I don't mind at all, really.

JERRY   It's . . . it's a nice day.

PETER [*Stares unnecessarily at the sky*]   Yes. Yes, it is; lovely.

JERRY   I've been to the zoo.

45 PETER   Yes, I think you said so . . . didn't you?

JERRY   I bet you've got TV, huh?

PETER   Why yes, we have two; one for the children.

JERRY   You're married!

PETER [*With pleased emphasis*]   Why, certainly.

50 JERRY   It isn't a law, for God's sake.

PETER   No . . . no, of course not.

JERRY   And you have a wife.

PETER [*Bewildered by the seeming lack of communication*]   Yes!

JERRY   And you have children.

55 PETER   Yes; two.

JERRY   Boys?

PETER   No, girls . . . both girls.

JERRY   But you wanted boys.

PETER   Well . . . naturally, every man wants a son, but . . .

60 JERRY [*Lightly mocking*]   But that's the way the cookie crumbles?

2. Sigmund Freud (1856–1936), psychiatrist and psychoanalytic theorist who developed oral
cancer from smoking in 1923. He had several surgeries, but the cancer metastasized and was
ultimately fatal.

PETER [*Annoyed*]   I wasn't going to say that.

JERRY   And you're not going to have any more kids, are you?

PETER [*A bit distantly*]   No. No more. [*Then back, and irksome*] Why did you say that? How would you know about that?

65 JERRY   The way you cross your legs, perhaps; something in the voice. Or maybe I'm just guessing. Is it your wife?

PETER [*Furious*]   That's none of your business! [*A silence*] Do you understand? [JERRY *nods.* PETER *is quiet now.*] Well, you're right. We'll have no more children.

70 JERRY [*Softly*]   That *is* the way the cookie crumbles.

PETER [*Forgiving*]   Yes . . . I guess so.

JERRY   Do you mind if I ask you questions?

PETER   Oh, not really.

JERRY   I'll tell you why I do it; I don't talk to many people—except to say like:
75 give me a beer, or where's the john, or what time does the feature go on, or keep your hands to yourself, buddy. You know—things like that.

PETER   I must say I don't . . .

JERRY   But every once in a while I like to talk to somebody, really *talk*; like to get to know somebody, know all about him.

80 PETER [*Lightly laughing, still a little uncomfortable*]   And am I the guinea pig for today?

JERRY   On a sun-drenched Sunday afternoon like this? Who better than a nice married man with two daughters and . . . uh . . . a dog? [PETER *shakes his head.*]   No? Two dogs. [PETER *shakes his head again.*] Hm. No dogs? [PETER
85 *shakes his head, sadly.*] Oh, that's a shame. But you look like an animal man. CATS? [PETER *nods his head, ruefully.*] Cats! But, that can't be your idea. No, sir. Your wife and daughters? [PETER *nods his head.*] Is there anything else I should know?

PETER [*He has to clear his throat.*]   There are . . . there are two parakeets.
90 One . . . uh . . . one for each of my daughters.

JERRY   Birds.

PETER   My daughters keep them in a cage in their bedroom.

JERRY   Do they carry disease? The birds.

PETER   I don't believe so.

95 JERRY   That's too bad. If they did you could set them loose in the house and the cats could eat them and die, maybe. [PETER *looks blank for a moment, then laughs.*] And what else? What do you do to support your enormous household?

PETER   I . . . uh . . . I have an executive position with a . . . a small publishing house. We . . . uh . . . we publish textbooks.

100 JERRY   That sounds nice; very nice. What do you make?

PETER [*Still cheerful*]   Now look here!

JERRY   Oh, come on.

PETER   Well, I make around two hundred thousand a year[3] but I don't carry more than forty dollars at any one time . . . in case you're a . . . a holdup
105 man . . . ha, ha, ha.

JERRY [*Ignoring the above*]   Where do you live? [PETER *is reluctant.*] Oh, look; I'm not going to rob you, and I'm not going to kidnap your parakeets, your cats, or your daughters.

3. In the original version, Peter's salary was $18,000. Both that figure and its updated counterpart appear to be higher than is standard for the profession at the time.

PETER [*Too loud*]   I live between Lexington and Third Avenue, on Seventy-
110   fourth Street.[4]

JERRY   That wasn't so hard, was it?

PETER   I didn't mean to seem . . . ah . . . it's that you don't really carry on a
conversation; you just ask questions. And I'm . . . I'm normally . . . uh . . .
reticent. Why do you just stand there?

115 JERRY   Say, what's the dividing line between upper-middle-middle-class and
lower-upper-middle-class?

PETER   My dear fellow, I . . .

JERRY   Don't my dear fellow me.

PETER [*Unhappily*]   Was I patronizing? I believe I was; I'm sorry. But, you see
120   your question about the classes bewildered me.

JERRY   And when you're bewildered you become patronizing?

PETER   I . . . I don't express myself too well, sometimes. [*He attempts a joke
on himself.*] I'm in publishing, not writing.

JERRY [*Amused, but not at the humor*]   So be it. The truth *is: I* was being
125   patronizing.

PETER   Oh, now; you needn't say that.

> [*It is at this point that* JERRY *may begin to move about the stage with
> slowly increasing determination and authority, but pacing himself, so
> that the long speech about the dog comes at the high point of the arc.*]

JERRY   All right. Who are your favorite writers? Baudelaire and Stephen
King?[5]

PETER [*Wary*]   Well, I like a great many writers; I have a considerable catho-
130   licity of taste, if I may say so. Those two men are fine, each in his way.
[*Warming up*] Baudelaire, of course . . . uh . . . is by far the finer of the two,
but Stephen King has a place . . . in our . . . uh . . . national . . .

JERRY   Skip it.

PETER   I . . . sorry.

135 JERRY   Do you know what I did before I went to the zoo today? I walked all
the way up Fifth Avenue from Washington Square; all the way.[6]

PETER   Oh; you live in Greenwich Village! [*This seems to enlighten* PETER.]

JERRY   No, I don't. I took the subway down to the Village so I could walk all
the way up Fifth Avenue to the zoo. It's one of those things a person has to
140   do; sometimes a person has to go a very long distance out of his way to
come back a short distance correctly.

PETER [*Almost pouting*]   Oh, I thought you lived in Greenwich Village.

JERRY   What were you trying to do? Make sense out of things? Bring order? The
old pigeonhole bit? Well, that's easy; I'll tell you. I live in a four-story brown-
145   stone roominghouse on the Upper West Side between Columbus Avenue and
Central Park West. I live on the top floor; rear; west. It's a laughably small
room, and one of my walls is made of beaverboard;[7] this beaverboard separates

---

4. Peter's address is on the Upper East Side of
Manhattan, which is considered a prosperous
neighborhood.
5. In the original version, the authors here
were Baudelaire and J. P. Marquand. Albee
updated the latter to James Michener, and
then again to Stephen King, to keep the
popular fiction authorship current. Charles

Baudelaire (1821–1867), French modernist
poet, best known for the verse collection *Les
Fleurs du Mal.*
6. Washington Square is located in Greenwich Village; the walk from there up 5th Avenue to Central Park is about four miles.
7. An inexpensive building material made from
compressed wood fibers.

my room from another laughably small room, so I assume that the two rooms were once one room, a small room, but not necessarily laughable. The
150 room beyond my beaverboard wall is occupied by a colored queen who always keeps his door open; well, not always but *always* when he's plucking his eyebrows, which he does with Buddhist concentration. This colored queen has rotten teeth, which is rare, and he has a Japanese kimono, which is also pretty rare; and he wears this kimono to and from the john in the hall, which is
155 pretty frequent. I mean, he goes to the john a lot. He never bothers me, and he never brings anyone up to his room. All he does is pluck his eyebrows, wear his kimono and go to the john. Now, the two front rooms on my floor are a little larger, I guess; but they're pretty small, too. There's a Puerto Rican family in one of them, a husband, a wife, and some kids; I don't know how
160 many. These people entertain a lot. And in the other front room, there's somebody living there, but I don't know who it is. I've never seen who it is. Never. Never ever.

PETER [*Embarrassed*] Why . . . why do you live there?

JERRY [*From a distance again*] I don't know.

165 PETER It doesn't sound like a very nice place . . . where you live.

JERRY Well, no; it isn't an apartment in the East Seventies. But, then again, I don't have one wife, two daughters, two cats and two parakeets. What I do have, I have toilet articles, a few clothes, a hot plate that I'm not supposed to have, a can opener, one that works with a key, you know; a knife, two
170 forks, and two spoons, one small, one large; three plates, a cup, a saucer, a drinking glass, two picture frames, both empty, eight or nine books, a pack of pornographic playing cards, regular deck, an old Western Union typewriter that prints nothing but capital letters, and a small strongbox without a lock which has in it . . . what? Rocks! Some rocks . . . sea-rounded rocks
175 I picked up on the beach when I was a kid. Under which . . . weighed down . . . are some letters . . . please letters . . . please why don't you do this, and please when will you do that letters. And when letters, too. When will you write? When will you come? When? These letters are from more recent years.

PETER [*Stares glumly at his shoes, then*] About those two empty picture
180 frames . . . ?

JERRY I don't see why they need any explanation at all. Isn't it clear? I don't have pictures of anyone to put in them.

PETER Your parents . . . perhaps . . . a girl friend . . .

JERRY You're a very sweet man, and you're possessed of a truly enviable inno-
185 cence. But good old Mom and good old Pop are dead . . . you know? . . . I'm broken up about it, too . . . I mean really. BUT. That particular vaudeville act is playing the cloud circuit now, so I don't see how I can look at them, all neat and framed. Besides, or, rather to be pointed about it, good old Mom walked out on good old Pop when I was ten and a half years old; she embarked on
190 an adulterous turn of our southern states . . . a journey of a year's duration . . . and her most constant companion . . . among others, among many others . . . was a Mr. Barleycorn.[8] At least, that's what good old Pop told me after he went down . . . came back . . . brought her body north. We'd received the

---

8. Jerry may be suggesting that she was an alcoholic, as beer and other distilled liquors are made from barley.

news between Christmas and New Year's, you see, that good old Mom had
195   parted with the ghost in some dump in Alabama. And, without the ghost . . .
she was less welcome. I mean, what was she? A stiff . . . a northern stiff. At
any rate, good old Pop celebrated the New Year for an even two weeks and
then slapped into the front of a somewhat moving city omnibus, which sort of
cleaned things out family-wise. Well no; then there was Mom's sister, who
200   was given neither to sin nor the consolations of the bottle. I moved in on her,
and my memory of her is slight excepting I remember still that she did all
things dourly: sleeping, eating, working, praying. She dropped dead on the
stairs to her apartment, my apartment then, too, on the afternoon of my high
school graduation. A terribly middle-European joke, if you ask me.
205 PETER   Oh, my; oh, my.
  JERRY   Oh, your what? But that was a long time ago, and I have no feeling
about any of it that I care to admit to myself. Perhaps you can see, though,
why good old Mom and good old Pop are frameless. What's your name?
Your first name?
210 PETER   I'm Peter.
  JERRY   I'd forgotten to ask you. I'm Jerry.
  PETER [*With a slight, nervous laugh*]   Hello, Jerry.
  JERRY [*Nods his hello*]   And let's see now; what's the point of having a girl's
picture, especially in two frames? I have two picture frames, you remember.
215   I never see the pretty little ladies more than once, and most of them wouldn't
be caught in the same room with a camera. It's odd, and I wonder if it's sad.
  PETER   The girls?
  JERRY   No. I wonder if it's sad that I never see the little ladies more than
once. I've never been able to have sex with, or, how is it put? . . . make love
220   to anybody more than once. Once; that's it. . . . Oh, wait; for a week and a
half, when I was fifteen and I hang my head in shame that puberty was
late . . . I was a h-o-m-o-s-e-x-u-a-l. I mean, I was queer . . . [*Very fast*] . . .
queer, queer, queer . . . with bells ringing, banners snapping in the wind.
And for those eleven days, I met at least twice a day with the park superin-
225   tendent's son . . . a Greek boy, whose birthday was the same as mine,
except he was a year older. I think I was very much in love . . . maybe just
with sex. But that was the jazz of a very special hotel, wasn't it? And now;
oh, do I love the little ladies; really, I love them. For about an hour.
  PETER   Well, it seems perfectly simple to me . . .
230 JERRY [*Angry*]   Look! Are you going to tell me to get married and have
parakeets?
  PETER [*Angry himself*]   Forget the parakeets! And stay single if you want to.
It's no business of mine. I didn't start this conversation in the . . .
  JERRY   All right, all right. I'm sorry. All right? You're not angry?
235 PETER [*Laughing*]   No, I'm not angry.
  JERRY [*Relieved*]   Good. [*Now back to his previous tone*] Interesting that you
asked me about the picture frames. I would have thought that you would
have asked me about the pornographic playing cards.
  PETER [*With a knowing smile*]   Oh, I've seen those cards.
240 JERRY   That's not the point. [*Laughs*] I suppose when you were a kid you and
your pals passed them around, or you had a pack of your own.
  PETER   Well, I guess a lot of us did.
  JERRY   And you threw them away just before you got married.

PETER Oh, now; look here. I didn't *need* anything like that when I got older.

245 JERRY No?

PETER [*Embarrassed*] I'd rather not talk about these things.

JERRY So? Don't. Besides. I wasn't trying to plumb your post-adolescent sexual life and hard times; what I wanted to get at is the value difference between pornographic playing cards when you're a kid, and pornographic

250 playing cards when you're older. It's that when you're a kid you use the cards as a substitute for a real experience, and when you're older you use real experience as a substitute for the fantasy. But I imagine you'd rather hear about what happened at the zoo.

PETER [*Enthusiastic*] Oh, yes; the zoo. [*Then, awkward*] That is . . . if you . . .

255 JERRY Let me tell you about why I went . . . well, let me tell you some things. I've told you about the fourth floor of the roominghouse where I live. I think the rooms are better as you go down, floor by floor. I guess they are; I don't know. I don't know any of the people on the third and second floors. Oh, wait! I do know that there's a lady living on the third floor, in the front. I know

260 because she cries all the time. Whenever I go out or come back in, whenever I pass her door, I always hear her crying, muffled, but . . . very determined. Very determined indeed. But the one I'm getting to, and all about the dog, is the landlady. I don't like to use words that are too harsh in describing people. I don't like to. But the landlady is a fat, ugly, mean, stupid, unwashed, misan-

265 thropic, cheap, drunken bag of garbage. And you may have noticed that I very seldom use profanity, so I can't describe her as well as I might.

PETER You describe her . . . vividly.

JERRY Well, thanks. Anyway, she has a dog, and I will tell you about the dog, and she and her dog are the gatekeepers of my dwelling. The woman is bad

270 enough; she leans around in the entrance hall, spying to see that I don't bring in things or people, and when she's had her mid-afternoon pint of lemon-flavored gin she always stops me in the hall, and grabs ahold of my coat or my arm, and she presses her disgusting body up against me to keep me in a corner so she can talk to me. The smell of her body and her breath . . . you can't

275 imagine it . . . and somewhere, somewhere in the back of that pea-sized brain of hers, an organ developed just enough to let her eat, drink, and emit, she has some foul parody of sexual desire. And I, Peter, I am the object of her sweaty lust.

PETER That's disgusting. That's . . . horrible.

280 JERRY But I have found a way to keep her off. When she talks to me, when she presses herself to my body and mumbles about her room and how I should come there, I merely say: but, Love; wasn't yesterday enough for you, and the day before? Then she puzzles, she makes slits of her tiny eyes, she sways a little, and then, Peter . . . and it is at this moment that I think I

285 might be doing some good in that tormented house . . . a simple-minded smile begins to form on her unthinkable face, and she giggles and groans as she thinks about yesterday and the day before; as she believes and relives what never happened. Then, she motions to that black monster of a dog she has, and she goes back to her room. And I am safe until our next meeting.

290 PETER It's so . . . unthinkable. I find it hard to believe that people such as that really *are*.

JERRY [*Lightly mocking*] It's for reading about, isn't it?

PETER [*Seriously*]   Yes.

JERRY   And fact is better left to fiction. You're right, Peter. Well, what I have
295   been meaning to tell you about is the dog; I shall, now.

PETER [*Nervously*]   Oh, yes; the dog.

JERRY   Don't go. You're not thinking of going, are you?

PETER   Well . . . no, I don't think so.

JERRY [*As if to a child*]   Because after I tell you about the dog, do you know
300   what then? Then . . . then I'll tell you about what happened at the zoo.

PETER [*Laughing faintly*]   You're . . . you're full of stories, aren't you?

JERRY   You don't *have* to listen. Nobody is holding you here; remember that.
       Keep that in your mind.

PETER [*Irritably*]   I know that.
305   JERRY   You do? Good.

> [*The following long speech, it seems to me, should be done with a great
> deal of action, to achieve a hypnotic effect on* PETER, *and on the audi-
> ence, too. Some specific actions have been suggested, but the director
> and the actor playing Jerry might best work it out for themselves.*]

ALL RIGHT. [*As if reading from a huge billboard*] THE STORY OF JERRY
AND THE DOG! [*Natural again*] What I am going to tell you has something
to do with how sometimes it's necessary to go a long distance out of the way
in order to come back a short distance correctly; or, maybe I only think that
310   it has something to do with that. But, it's why I went to the zoo today, and
why I walked north . . . northerly, rather . . . until I came here. All right. The
dog, I think I told you, is a black monster of a beast: an oversized head, tiny,
tiny ears, and eyes . . . bloodshot, infected, maybe; and a body you can see
the ribs through the skin. The dog is black, all black; all black except for the
315   bloodshot eyes, and . . . yes . . . and an open sore on its . . . *right* forepaw;
that is red, too. And, oh yes; the poor monster, and I do believe it's an old
dog . . . it's certainly a misused one . . . almost always has an erection . . . of
sorts. That's red, too. And . . . what else? . . . oh, yes; there's a gray-yellow-
white color, too, when he bares his fangs. Like this: Grrrrrr! Which is what
320   he did when he saw me for the first time . . . the day I moved in. I worried
about that animal the very first minute I met him. Now, animals don't take to
me like Saint Francis[9] had birds hanging off him all the time. What I mean
is: Animals are indifferent to me . . . like people [*He smiles slightly*] . . . most
of the time. But this dog wasn't indifferent. From the very beginning he'd
325   snarl and then go for me, to get one of my legs. Not like he was rabid, you
know; he was sort of a stumbly dog, but he wasn't half-assed, either. It was a
good, stumbly run; but I always got away. He got a piece of my trouser leg,
look, you can see right here, where it's mended; he got that the second day I
lived there; but, I kicked free and got upstairs fast, so that was that. [*Puzzles*]
330   I still don't know to this day how the other roomers manage it, but you know
what I *think*: I think it had to do only with me. Cozy. So. Anyway, this went
on for over a week, whenever I came in; but never when I went out. That's
funny. Or, it *was* funny. I could pack up and live in the street for all the dog
cared. Well, I thought about it up in my room one day, one of the times after
335   I'd bolted upstairs, and I made up my mind. I decided: First, I'll kill the dog

9. St. Francis of Assisi (1182–1226), frequently associated and depicted with animals and nature.

with kindness, and if that doesn't work . . . I'll just kill him. [PETER *winces*] Don't react, Peter; just listen. So, the next day I went out and bought a bag of hamburgers, medium rare, no catsup, no onion; and on the way home I threw away all the rolls and kept just the meat.

[*Action for the following, perhaps*]

340 When I got back to the roominghouse the dog was waiting for me. I half opened the door that led into the entrance hall, and there he was; waiting for me. It figured. I went in, very cautiously, and I had the hamburgers, you remember; I opened the bag, and I set the meat down about twelve feet from where the dog was snarling at me. Like so! He snarled; stopped snarling;
345 sniffed; moved slowly; then faster; then faster toward the meat. Well, when he got to it he stopped, and he looked at me. I smiled; but tentatively, you understand. He turned his face back to the hamburgers, smelled, sniffed some more, and then . . . RRRAAAAGGGGGHHHH, like that . . . he tore into them. It was as if he had never eaten anything in his life before, except
350 like garbage. Which might very well have been the truth. I don't think the landlady ever eats anything but garbage. But. He ate all the hamburgers, almost all at once, making sounds in his throat like a woman. *Then*, when he'd finished the meat, the hamburger, and tried to eat the paper, too, he sat down and smiled. I think he smiled; I know cats do. It was a very gratifying
355 few moments. Then, BAM, he snarled and made for me again. He didn't get me this time, either. So, I got upstairs, and I lay down on my bed and started to think about the dog again. To be truthful, I was offended, and I was damn mad, too. It was six perfectly good hamburgers with not enough pork in them to make it disgusting. I was offended. But, after a while, I decided to try it for
360 a few more days. If you think about it, this dog had what amounted to an antipathy toward me; really. And, I wondered if I mightn't overcome this antipathy. So, I tried it for five more days, but it was always the same: snarl, sniff, move; faster; stare; gobble; RAAGGGHHH; smile; snarl; BAM. Well, now; by this time Columbus Avenue was strewn with hamburger rolls and I
365 was less offended than disgusted. So, I decided to kill the dog.

[PETER *raises a hand in protest.*]

Oh, don't be so alarmed, Peter; I didn't succeed. The day I tried to kill the dog I bought only one hamburger and what I thought was a murderous portion of rat poison. When I bought the hamburger I asked the man not to bother with the roll, all I wanted was the meat. I expected some reaction from him, like:
370 we don't sell no hamburgers without rolls; or, wha' d'ya wanna do, eat it out'a ya han's? But no; he smiled benignly, wrapped up the hamburger in waxed paper, and said. A bite for ya pussy-cat? I wanted to say: No, not really; it's part of a plan to poison a dog I know. But, you can't say "a dog I know" without sounding funny; so I said, a little too loud, I'm afraid, and too formally: YES,
375 A BITE FOR MY PUSSY-CAT. People looked up. It always happens when I try to simplify things; people look up. But that's neither hither nor thither. So. On my way back to the roominghouse, I kneaded the hamburger and the rat poison together between my hands, at that point feeling as much sadness as disgust. I opened the door to the entrance hall, and there the monster was,
380 waiting to take the offering and then jump me. Poor bastard; he never learned that the moment he took to smile before he went for me gave me time enough to get out of range. BUT, there he was; malevolence with an erection, waiting.

I put the poison patty down, moved toward the stairs and watched. The poor
animal gobbled the food down as usual, smiled, which made me almost sick,
385 and then, BAM. But, I sprinted up the stairs, as usual, and the dog didn't get
me, as usual. AND IT CAME TO PASS THAT THE BEAST WAS DEATHLY
ILL. I knew this because he no longer attended me, and because the landlady
sobered up. She stopped me in the hall the same evening of the attempted
murder and confided the information that God had struck her puppy-dog a
390 surely fatal blow. She had forgotten her bewildered lust, and her eyes were
wide open for the first time. They looked like the dog's eyes. She sniveled and
implored me to pray for the animal. I wanted to say to her: Madam, I have
myself to pray for, the colored queen, the Puerto Rican family, the person in
the front room whom I've never seen, the woman who cries deliberately
395 behind her closed door, and the rest of the people in all roominghouses,
everywhere; besides, Madam, I don't understand how to pray. But . . . to simplify things . . . I told her I would pray. She looked up. She said that I was a
liar, and that I probably wanted the dog to die. I told her, and there was so
much truth here, that I didn't want the dog to die. I didn't, and not just
400 because I'd poisoned him. I'm afraid that I must tell you I wanted the dog to
live so that I could see what our new relationship might come to.

> [PETER *indicates his increasing displeasure and slowly growing
> antagonism.*]

Please understand, Peter; that sort of thing is important. You must believe
me; it is important. We have to know the effect of our actions. [*Another deep
sigh*] Well, anyway; the dog recovered. I have no idea why, unless he was a
405 descendant of the puppy that guarded the gates of hell[1] or some such resort.
I'm not up on my mythology. [*He pronounces the word myth-o-logy.*] Are you?

> [PETER *sets to thinking, but* JERRY *goes on.*]

At any rate, and you've missed the eight-thousand-dollar question, Peter; at
any rate, the dog recovered his health and the landlady recovered her thirst,
in no way altered by the bow-wow's deliverance. When I came home from a
410 movie that was playing on Forty-second Street[2] a movie I'd seen, or one that
was very much like one or several I'd seen, after the landlady told me pup-
pykins was better, I was so hoping for the dog to be waiting for me. I was . . .
well, how would you put it . . . enticed? . . . fascinated? . . . no, I don't think
so . . . heart-shatteringly anxious, that's it; I was heart-shatteringly anxious to
415 confront my friend again.

> [PETER *reacts scoffingly.*]

Yes, Peter; friend. That's the only word for it. I was heart-shatteringly et
cetera to confront my doggy friend again. I came in the door and advanced,
unafraid, to the center of the entrance hall. The beast was there . . . looking
at me. And, you know, he looked better for his scrape with the nevermind. I
420 stopped; I looked at him; he looked at me. I think . . . I think we stayed a
long time that way . . . still, stone-statue . . . just looking at one another. I
looked more into his face than he looked into mine. I mean, I can concentrate longer at looking into a dog's face than a dog can concentrate at looking

---

1. In classical mythology Cerberus was a mul-
tiheaded dog who guarded the entrance to
hell so that no living person could enter and
so the dead could not escape.
2. In the late 1950s 42nd Street had a number of X-rated movie theaters.

into mine, or into anybody else's face, for that matter. But during that twenty
seconds or two hours that we looked into each other's face, we made contact.
Now, here is what I had wanted to happen: I loved the dog now, and I wanted
him to love me. I had tried to love, and I had tried to kill, and both had been
unsuccessful by themselves. I hoped . . . and I don't really know why I
expected the dog to understand anything, much less my motivations . . . I
hoped that the dog would understand.

> [PETER *seems to be hypnotized.*]

It's just . . . it's just that . . . [JERRY *is abnormally tense, now.*] . . . it's just that if
you can't deal with people, you have to make a start somewhere. WITH ANI-
MALS! [*Much faster now, and like a conspirator*] Don't you see? A person has
to have some way of dealing with SOMETHING. If not with people . . . if not
with people . . . SOMETHING. With a bed, with a cockroach, with a mirror . . . no, that's too hard, that's one of the last steps. With a cockroach, with
a . . . with a . . . with a carpet, a roll of toilet paper . . . no, not that, either . . .
that's a mirror, too; always check bleeding. You see how hard it is to find
things? With a street corner, and too many lights, all colors reflecting on the
oily-wet streets . . . with a wisp of smoke, a wisp . . . of smoke . . . with . . .
with pornographic playing cards, with a strongbox . . . WITHOUT A
LOCK . . . with love, with vomiting, with crying, with fury because the pretty
little ladies aren't pretty little ladies, with making money with your body
which is an act of love and I could prove it, with howling because you're alive;
with God. How about that? WITH GOD WHO IS A COLORED QUEEN
WHO WEARS A KIMONO AND PLUCKS HIS EYEBROWS, WHO IS A
WOMAN WHO CRIES WITH DETERMINATION BEHIND HER
CLOSED DOOR . . . with God who, I'm told, turned his back on the whole
thing some time ago . . . with . . . someday, with people. [JERRY *sighs the next
word heavily.*] People. With an idea; a concept. And where better, where ever
better in this humiliating excuse for a jail, where better to communicate one
single, simple-minded idea than in an entrance hall? Where? It would be A
START! Where better to make a beginning . . . to understand and just possibly be understood . . . a beginning of an understanding, than with . . .

> [*Here* JERRY *seems to fall into almost grotesque fatigue.*]

than with A DOG. Just that; a dog.

> [*Here there is a silence that might be prolonged for a moment or so; then*
> JERRY *wearily finishes his story.*]

A dog. It seemed like a perfectly sensible idea. Man is a dog's best friend,
remember. So: the dog and I looked at each other. I longer than the dog. And
what I saw then has been the same ever since. Whenever the dog and I see
each other we both stop where we are. We regard each other with a mixture
of sadness and suspicion, and then we feign indifference. We walk past each
other safely; we have an understanding. It's very sad, but you'll have to admit
that it is an understanding. We had made many attempts at contact, and we
had failed. The dog has returned to garbage, and I to solitary but free passage.
I have not returned. I mean to say. I have *gained* solitary free passage, if that
much further loss can be said to be gain. I have learned that neither kindness
nor cruelty by themselves, independent of each other, creates any effect
beyond themselves; and I have learned that the two combined, together, at

the same time, are the teaching emotion. And what is gained is loss. And what
has been the result: the dog and I have attained a compromise; more of a
470 bargain, really. We neither love nor hurt because we do not try to reach each
other. And, *was* trying to feed the dog an act of love? And, perhaps, was the
dog's attempt to bite me *not* an act of love? If we can so misunderstand, well
then, why have we invented the word love in the first place?

> [*There is silence.* JERRY *moves to* PETER's *bench and sits down beside him.
> This is the first time that* JERRY *has sat down during the play.*]

The Story of Jerry and the Dog: the end.

> [PETER *is silent.*]

475 Well, Peter? [JERRY *is suddenly cheerful.*] Well, Peter? Do you think I could
sell that story to the *Reader's Digest* and make a couple of hundred bucks
for *The Most Unforgettable Character I've Ever Met?*[3] Huh?

> [JERRY *is animated, but* PETER *is disturbed.*]

Oh, come on now, Peter; tell me what you think.

PETER [*Numb*] I . . . I don't understand what . . . I don't think I . . . [*Now,*
480 *almost tearfully*] Why did you tell me all of this?

JERRY Why not?

PETER I DON'T UNDERSTAND!

JERRY [*Furious, but whispering*] That's a lie.

PETER No. No, it's not.

485 JERRY [*Quietly*] I tried to explain it to you as I went along. I went slowly; it
all has to do with . . .

PETER I DON'T WANT TO HEAR ANY MORE. I don't understand you, or
your landlady, or her dog . . .

JERRY Her dog! I thought it was my . . . No. No, you're right. It *is* her dog.
490 [*Looks at* PETER *intently, shaking his head*] I don't know what I was thinking
about; of course you don't understand. [*In a monotone, wearily*] I don't live in
your block; I'm not married to two parakeets, or whatever your setup is. I am
a *permanent transient,* and my home is the sickening roominghouses on the
West Side of New York City, which is the greatest city in the world. Amen.

495 PETER I'm . . . I'm sorry; I didn't mean to . . .

JERRY Forget it. I suppose you don't quite know what to make of me, eh?

PETER [*A joke*] We get all kinds in publishing. [*Chuckles*]

JERRY You're a funny man. [*He forces a laugh.*] You know that? You're a
very . . . a richly comic person.

500 PETER [*Modestly, but amused*] Oh, now, not really. [*Still chuckling*]

JERRY Peter, do I annoy you, or confuse you?

PETER [*Lightly*] Well, I must confess that this wasn't the kind of afternoon
I'd anticipated.

JERRY You mean, I'm not the gentleman you were expecting.

505 PETER I wasn't expecting anybody.

JERRY No, I don't imagine you were. But I'm here, and I'm not leaving.

PETER [*Consulting his watch*] Well, you may not be, but I must be getting
home now.

JERRY Oh, come on; stay a while longer.

---

3. Mass-market magazine, first published in 1922, best known for its book excerpts, information
and humor sections, and first-person essays.

510 PETER   I really should get home; you see . . .

JERRY [*Tickles* PETER's *ribs with his fingers*]   Oh, come on.

PETER [*He is very ticklish; as* JERRY *continues to tickle him his voice becomes falsetto.*] No, I . . . OHHHHH! Don't do that. Stop, Stop. Ohhh, no, no.

JERRY   Oh, come on.

PETER [*As* JERRY *tickles*]   Oh, hee, hee, hee. I must go. I . . . hee, hee, hee. After 515   all, stop, stop, hee, hee, hee, after all, the parakeets will be getting dinner ready soon. Hee, hee. And the cats are setting the table. Stop, stop, and, and . . . [PETER *is beside himself now*] and we're having . . . hee, hee . . . uh . . . ho, ho, ho.

> [JERRY *stops tickling* PETER, *but the combination of the tickling and his own mad whimsy has* PETER *laughing almost hysterically. As his laughter continues, then subsides,* JERRY *watches him, with a curious fixed smile.*]

JERRY   Peter?

520 PETER   Oh, ha, ha, ha, ha, ha. What? What?

JERRY   Listen, now.

PETER   Oh, ho, ho. What . . . what is it, Jerry? Oh, my.

JERRY [*Mysteriously*]   Peter, do you want to know what happened at the zoo?

PETER   Ah, ha, ha. The what? Oh, yes; the zoo. Oh, ho, ho. Well, I had my 525   own zoo there for a moment with . . . hee, hee, the parakeets getting dinner ready, and the . . . ha, ha, whatever it was, the . . .

JERRY [*Calmly*]   Yes, that was very funny, Peter. I wouldn't have expected it. But do you want to hear about what happened at the zoo, or not?

PETER   Yes. Yes, by all means; tell me what happened at the zoo. Oh, my. I 530   don't know what happened to me.

JERRY   Now I'll let you in on what happened at the zoo; but first, I should tell you why I went to the zoo. I went to the zoo to find out more about the way people exist with animals, and the way animals exist with each other, and with people too. It probably wasn't a fair test, what with everyone separated 535   by bars from everyone else, the animals for the most part from each other, and always the people from the animals. But, if it's a zoo, that's the way it is. [*He pokes* PETER *on the arm.*] Move over.

PETER [*Friendly*]   I'm sorry, haven't you enough room? [*He shifts a little.*]

JERRY [*Smiling slightly*]   Well, all the animals are there, and all the people 540   are there, and it's Sunday and all the children are there. [*He pokes* PETER *again.*] Move over.

PETER [*Patiently, still friendly*]   All right.

> [*He moves some more, and* JERRY *has all the room he might need.*]

JERRY   And it's a hot day, so all the stench is there, too, and all the balloon sellers, and all the ice cream sellers, and all the seals are barking, and all 545   the birds are screaming [*Pokes* PETER *harder.*] Move over!

PETER [*Beginning to be annoyed*]   Look here, you have more than enough room! [*But he moves more, and is now fairly cramped at one end of the bench*]

JERRY   And I am there, and it's feeding time at the lions' house, and the lion keeper comes into the lion cage, one of the lion cages, to feed one of the 550   lions. [*Punches* PETER *on the arm, hard*] MOVE OVER!

PETER [*Very annoyed*]   I can't move over any more, and stop hitting me. What's the matter with you?

JERRY   Do you want to hear the story? [*Punches* PETER's *arm again*]

PETER [*Flabbergasted*]   I'm not so sure! I certainly don't want to be punched
555   in the arm.

JERRY [*Punches* PETER's *arm again*]   Like that?

PETER   Stop it! What's the matter with you?

JERRY   I'm crazy, you bastard.

PETER   That isn't funny.

560 JERRY   Listen to me, Peter. I want this bench. You go sit on the bench over
there, and if you're good I'll tell you the rest of the story.

PETER [*Flustered*]   But . . . whatever for? What *is* the matter with you?
Besides, I see no reason why I should give up this bench. I sit on this bench
almost every Sunday afternoon, in good weather. It's secluded here; there's
565   never anyone sitting here, so I have it all to myself.

JERRY [*Softly*]   Get off this bench, Peter; I want it.

PETER [*Almost whining*]   No.

JERRY   I said I want this bench, and I'm going to have it. Now get over there.

PETER   People can't have everything they want. You should know that; it's a
570   rule; people can have some of the things they want, but they can't have
everything.

JERRY [*Laughs*]   Imbecile! You're slow-witted!

PETER   Stop that!

JERRY   You're a vegetable! Go lie down on the ground.

575 PETER [*Intense*]   Now *you* listen to me. I've put up with you all afternoon.

JERRY   Not really.

PETER   LONG ENOUGH. I've put up with you long enough. I've listened to
you because you seemed . . . well, because I thought you wanted to talk to
somebody.

580 JERRY   You put things well; economically, and, yet . . . oh, what is the word I
want to put justice to your . . . JESUS, you make me sick . . . get off here
and give me my bench.

PETER   MY BENCH!

JERRY [*Pushes* PETER *almost, but not quite, off the bench*]   Get out of my
585   sight.

PETER [*Regaining his position*]   God da . . . mn you. That's enough! I've had
enough of you. I will not give up this bench; you can't have it, and that's
that. Now, go away.

[JERRY *snorts but does not move.*]

Go away, I said.

[JERRY *does not move.*]

590   Get away from here. If you don't move on . . . you're a bum . . . that's what
you are . . . If you don't move on, I'll get a policeman here and make
you go.

[JERRY *laughs, stays.*]

I warn you, I'll call a policeman.

JERRY [*Softly*]   You won't find a policeman around here, they're all over on
595   the west side of the park chasing fairies down from trees or out of the
bushes.[4] That's all they do. That's their function. So scream your head off;
it won't do you any good.

---

4. Central Park was long known as a meeting spot for gay men.

PETER   POLICE! I warn you, I'll have you arrested. POLICE! [*Pause*] I said
POLICE! [*Pause*] I feel ridiculous.

600 JERRY   You look ridiculous: a grown man screaming for the police on a bright
Sunday afternoon in the park with nobody harming you. If a policeman *did*
fill his quota and come sludging over this way he'd probably take you in as
a nut.

PETER   [*With disgust and impotence*]   Great God, I just came here to read,
605 and now you want me to give up the bench. You're mad.

JERRY   Hey, I got news for you, as they say. I'm on your precious bench, and
you're never going to have it for yourself again.

PETER   [*Furious*]   Look, you; get off my bench. I don't care if it makes any
sense or not. I want this bench to myself; I want you OFF IT!

610 JERRY   [*Mocking*]   Aw . . . look who's mad.

PETER   GET OUT!

JERRY   No.

PETER   I WARN YOU!

JERRY   Do you know how ridiculous you look *now*?

615 PETER   [*His fury and self-consciousness have possessed him.*]   It doesn't matter.
[*He is almost crying.*] GET AWAY FROM MY BENCH!

JERRY   Why? You have everything in the world you want; you've told me
about your home, and your family, and *your own* little zoo. You have everything, and now you want this bench. Are these the things men fight for?
620 Tell me, Peter, is this bench, this iron and this wood, is this your honor? Is
this the thing in the world you'd fight for? Can you think of anything more
absurd?

PETER   Absurd? Look, I'm not going to talk to you about honor, or even try to
explain it to you. Besides, it isn't a question of honor; but even if it were,
625 you wouldn't understand.

JERRY   [*Contemptuously*]   You don't even know what you're saying, do you?
This is probably the first time in your life you've had anything more trying
to face than changing your cats' toilet box. Stupid! Don't you have any idea,
not even the slightest, what other people *need*?

630 PETER   Oh, boy, listen to you; well, you don't need this bench. That's for
sure.

JERRY   Yes; yes, I do.

PETER   [*Quivering*]   I've come here for years; I have hours of great pleasure,
great satisfaction, right here. And that's important to a man. I'm a respon-
635 sible person, and I'm a GROWNUP. This is my bench, and you have no
right to take it away from me.

JERRY   Fight for it, then. Defend yourself; defend your bench.

PETER   You've *pushed* me to it. Get up and fight.

JERRY   Like a man?

640 PETER   [*Still angry*]   Yes, like a man, if you insist on mocking me even
further.

JERRY   I'll have to give you credit for one thing: you *are* a vegetable, and a
slightly nearsighted one, I think . . .

PETER   THAT'S ENOUGH. . . .

645 JERRY   . . . but, you know, as they say on TV all the time—you know—and I
mean this, Peter, you have a certain dignity; it surprises me . . .

PETER   STOP!

JERRY [*Rises lazily*]   Very well, Peter, we'll battle for the bench, but we're not evenly matched.

> [*He takes out and clicks open an ugly-looking knife.*]

PETER [*Suddenly awakening to the reality of the situation*]

650   You *are* mad! You're stark raving mad! YOU'RE GOING TO KILL ME!

> [*But before* PETER *has time to think what to do,* JERRY *tosses the knife at* PETER's *feet*]

JERRY   There you go. Pick it up. You have the knife and we'll be more evenly matched.

PETER [*Horrified*]   No!

JERRY [*Rushes over to* PETER, *grabs him by the collar;* PETER *rises; their faces almost touch*]

Now you pick up that knife and you fight with me. You fight for your self-
655   respect; you fight for that goddamned bench.

PETER [*Struggling*]   No! Let . . . let go of me! He . . . Help!

JERRY [*Slaps* PETER *on each "fight"*]   You fight, you miserable bastard; fight for that bench; fight for your manhood, you pathetic little vegetable. [*Spits in* PETER's *face*] You couldn't even get your wife with a male child.

660   PETER [*Breaks away, enraged*]   It's a matter of genetics, not manhood, you . . . you monster.

> [*He darts down, picks up the knife and backs off a little; he is breathing heavily.*]

I'll give you one last chance; get out of here and leave me alone!

> [*He holds the knife with a firm arm, but far in front of him, not to attack, but to defend.*]

JERRY [*Sigh's heavily*]   So, be it!

> [*With a rush he charges* PETER *and impales himself on the knife. Tableau: For just a moment, complete silence,* JERRY *impaled on the knife at the end of* PETER's *still firm arm. Then* PETER *screams, pulls away, leaving the knife in* JERRY. JERRY *is motionless, on point. Then he, too, screams, and it must be the sound of an infuriated and fatally wounded animal. With the knife in him, he stumbles back to the bench that* PETER *had vacated. He crumbles there, sitting, facing* PETER, *his eyes wide in agony, his mouth open.*]

PETER [*Whispering*]   Oh my God, oh my God, oh my God. . . .

> [*He repeats these words many times, very rapidly.*]

JERRY [JERRY *is dying; but now his expression seems to change. His features relax, and while his voice varies, sometimes wrenched with pain, for the most part he seems removed from his dying. He smiles.*]

665   Peter, thank you, Peter. I mean that now; thank you very much.

> [PETER's *mouth drops open. He cannot move; he is transfixed.*]

I came unto you [*He laughs, so faintly.*] and you have comforted me. Dear Peter.

PETER [*Almost fainting*]   Oh my God!

JERRY   You'd better go now. Somebody might come by, and you don't want to
670   be here when anyone comes.

PETER [*Does not move, but begins to weep*]   Oh my God, oh my God.

JERRY   And Peter, I'll tell you something now; you're not really a vegetable; it's all right, you're an animal. You're an animal, too. But you'd better hurry now, Peter. Hurry, you'd better go . . . see?

[JERRY *takes a handkerchief and with great effort and pain wipes the knife handle clean of fingerprints.*]

675   Hurry away, Peter.

[PETER *begins to stagger away.*]

Wait . . . wait, Peter. Take your book . . . book. Right here . . . beside me . . . on your bench . . . my bench, rather. Come . . . take your book.

[PETER *starts for the book, but retreats.*]

Hurry . . . Peter.

[PETER *rushes to the bench, grabs the book, retreats.*]

Very good, Peter . . . very good. Now . . . hurry away.

[PETER *hesitates for a moment, then flees, stage-left.*]

680   Hurry away. . . . [*His eyes are closed now.*] Hurry away, your parakeets are making the dinner . . . the cats . . . are setting the table . . .

PETER [*Offstage*]

[*A pitiful howl*]

OH MY GOD!

JERRY [*His eyes still closed, he shakes his head and speaks; a combination of scornful mimicry and supplication.*]

Oh . . . my . . . God.

[*He is dead.*]

Curtain.

LORRAINE HANSBERRY

1930–1965

When Lorraine Hansberry's play *A RAISIN IN THE SUN* opened at New York's Ethel Barrymore Theatre on March 11, 1959, the United States was in the midst of the civil rights movement. Coming almost a century after the Emancipation Proclamation (1863), this movement sought to end segregation and other forms of racial discrimination that remained deeply entrenched in American society since the late nineteenth century. In 1954, the U.S. Supreme Court ruled in *Brown v. Board of Education of Topeka* that state laws establishing separate public schools based on race were unconstitutional. Widespread resistance to school integration in the South and elsewhere in the country was forcefully represented by Arkansas Governor Orval Faubus ordering the Arkansas National Guard to block black students' entry to Little Rock High School in 1957. In 1955 Rosa Parks sparked the Montgomery Bus Boycott by refusing to yield her bus seat to a white passenger, and in 1958 black students organized sit-ins to protest segregated seating policies at lunch counters in Oklahoma City. Lorraine Hansberry, who grew up in Chicago, Illinois, knew that the hardships and indignities of segregation were not restricted to the South. In *A Raisin in the Sun*, the first play by an African American woman to be produced on Broadway, she portrayed the lives of those confronting

these realities with unprecedented richness and dramatic energy. In the words of novelist James Baldwin, "[N]ever before, in the entire history of the American theater, had so much of the truth of black people's lives been seen on the stage." In the second decade of a new millennium, it remains one of the most frequently produced plays in the American theater.

The youngest of four children, Lorraine Vivian Hansberry was born on May 19, 1930, to Nannie Perry Hansberry, a former schoolteacher, and Carl Hansberry, a successful realtor. Both her parents, who had moved to Chicago as part of the Great Migration that brought southern African Americans to northern cities in the early and mid-twentieth century, were political leaders in the predominantly African American area of Chicago's South Side known as the "Black Belt." Because of the Hansberrys' public profile, their home served as a center for black cultural and political life, and the family's guests included noted author, editor, and activist W. E. B. Du Bois; actor and singer Paul Robeson; musician Duke Ellington; poet and dramatist Langston Hughes; and track-and-field athlete Jesse Owens. Another visitor was Carl's brother William Leo Hansberry, a highly respected professor of African history at Howard University in Washington, D.C., and a prominent advocate for the study of

African history and culture. He sometimes brought along his African-born students when he visited the Hansberry
household.

Though the Hansberrys were well-to-do
by the standards of their community, Lorraine was exposed to the poverty and what
she later described as "the scars, the marks
that the ghettoized child carries through
life" at school. When she was eight years
old, the harshness of discrimination was
brought home with terrifying directness when her father had a friend purchase
a home for the family in an all-white neighborhood. Like other white neighborhoods
in the South Side, the one Carl Hansberry
chose was protected by a "restrictive cove-
nant," a contractual agreement among
property owners that prohibited selling or
leasing property to African Americans.
When members of the neighborhood realized that a black family had moved in, their
hostility became violent. Lorraine later
wrote about a mob hurling a brick through
the window of their house with such force
that it nearly hit her; in an equally arresting image, she described her mother patrol-
ling their house at night with a loaded gun.
The family was eventually forced to vacate
the house when the neighborhood improvement association filed an injunction that
was upheld by the Illinois Supreme Court.
Carl Hansberry appealed the injunction,
and it was overturned on a technicality by
the U.S. Supreme Court in the case *Hansberry v. Lee* (1940). The victory, which was
a watershed in the battle over housing discrimination, took its toll on the Hansberrys. Carl Hansberry, who lost a great deal
of money during the appeal and was embittered by this latest ordeal in a life spent
combatting racial injustice, died six years
later from a cerebral hemorrhage. As
Lorraine later wrote, "American racism
helped kill him."

In high school Hansberry excelled in
English and history, and was elected president of her high school debate team.
She was introduced to SHAKESPEARE and
attended her first plays. Upon graduation
she attended the largely white University of
Wisconsin rather than an all-black university like Howard. One afternoon during her
first year she wandered into a rehearsal of
Irish dramatist Sean O'Casey's 1924 play
Juno and the Paycock. Captivated by the

melody and force of expression in O'Casey's
language, she sensed a power that she
would later strive to attain in her own dramatic writing. Pursuing her interest in
drama, she attended other plays, hung
around with actors, and studied set design;
theater, she came to realize, "embraces
everything I like all at one time." Hansberry was also politically active during this
period, working on the presidential campaign of Progressive Henry Wallace and
serving as campus chair of the Young Pro-
gressives of America. At the end of her
sophomore year, she decided to move to
New York City in order "to pursue an education of a different kind." After spending
the summer of 1950 taking classes at the
New School for Social Research, Hansberry
moved there for good in 1951.

New York exerted a profound influence
on Hansberry's political education and on
her career as an activist and writer. Shortly
after arriving, she began working for the
radical black monthly magazine *Freedom*,
which was co-founded by Paul Robeson and
Louis Burnham. During her five-year association with the magazine Hansberry wrote
articles on a range of topics and issues,
including the independence movement in
Ghana; the 1951 "Sojourners for Truth"
conference in Washington, D.C., which was
attended by 132 black women; and the
deplorable conditions in Harlem public
schools. She traveled to Mississippi with a
delegation of women to protest the impend-
ing execution of a young black man accused
of rape and flew to Uruguay to deliver a
speech at a peace conference on behalf of
Robeson, whose passport had been confiscated by the U.S. State Department because
of his political views. At a demonstration at
New York University protesting the exclusion of blacks from the school's basketball
team, she met Robert Nemiroff, a graduate
student and aspiring writer-editor of
Russian-Jewish descent. The two were married in 1953. That same year she resigned
her job as associate editor at *Freedom*,
though she continued to write articles for
that and other radical publications, and she
held a series of jobs until 1956, when she
was able to devote her time entirely to writing. Nemiroff and Hansberry divorced in
1964, but remained close.

One of the projects that Hansberry had
been working on was a play about the

housing segregation her family had experienced in Chicago. In the fall of 1957 Hansberry read the first draft of *A Raisin in the Sun* to music publisher Philip Rose at a dinner gathering. Rose, who would become one of New York's leading theater producers based in part on his association with *Raisin*, was so impressed by the play that he optioned it for Broadway. Over the next year, Rose raised money for the production, and in early 1959 tryouts of the play were held in New Haven, Philadelphia, and Chicago. When the play finally found a New York home and opened at the Ethel Barrymore Theatre on March 11 it was acclaimed by critics and audiences, and Lorraine Hansberry became a household name overnight. Directed by Lloyd Richards with a cast that featured Sidney Poitier, Claudia McNeil, Ruby Dee, Diana Sands, and Lou Gossett Jr., *Raisin in the Sun* ran for 530 performances. It won the New York Drama Critics Circle Award for Best Musical of the year, making Hansberry the youngest playwright, the fifth woman, and the first African American to win this prestigious award. Columbia Pictures purchased the movie rights to the play, and the following year Hansberry submitted two screenplays. These screenplays included a number of additions that heightened the play's racial issues, but the screenplays were rejected by the studio, which wanted a version closer to the stage play. The film, which was released in 1961 with most of its original cast, received a special award at the Cannes Film Festival and was nominated for a Best Screenplay Award by the Screen Writers Guild. After Hansberry's untimely death at the age of thirty-four, the play saw two more successful adaptations: a 1973 musical entitled *Raisin*, which won the Tony Award for Best Musical, and a 1989 television production featuring Danny Glover as Walter Lee Younger.

In addition to her continuing public life as a socially engaged writer and activist, Hansberry completed a number of other dramatic projects in the early 1960s. In 1960 she was commissioned to write an antebellum slavery drama as part of a five-part NBC series commemorating the Civil War Centennial. She completed the play, entitled *The Drinking Gourd*, but the studio executives decided that it was too violent and controversial and shelved it along with the projected series. During this time she began an ambitious play entitled *Les Blancs* (*The Whites*), which centered on an anticolonial uprising in an unnamed African country. She also wrote a post-nuclear holocaust television play entitled *What Use Are Flowers?*, the beginnings of a play about the Haitian revolutionary Toussaint L'Ouverture, and *The Sign in Sidney Brustein's Window*, a play about a white Greenwich Village intellectual and the women and men in his life. Although this last play addresses issues of social and personal commitment, it received mixed reviews when it opened at New York's Longacre Theatre on October 15, 1964. *The Sign in Sidney Brustein's Window* was the second, and last, of her plays to be performed during her lifetime. A year and a half before the play's opening, Hansberry was hospitalized for dizziness and nausea; after undergoing a number of tests, she was diagnosed with cancer. Though she was able to attend rehearsals of her latest play, she continued to decline and passed away on January 12, 1965, four months short of her thirty-fifth birthday. Nemiroff, whom Hansberry had designated her literary executor, ensured that her dramatic career did not end with her death. He compiled the play *To Be Young, Gifted, and Black*, a work that chronicles Hansberry's life, using excerpts from her published and unpublished writings. It became the longest-running play of the 1968–69 off-Broadway season and toured the country to strong reviews. In 1970, a completed version of *Les Blancs* was produced on Broadway. That play, *The Drinking Gourd*, and *What Use Are Flowers?* were published in 1972 as *Les Blancs: The Collected Last Plays of Lorraine Hansberry*.

It is remarkable that a dramatist with so short a career could have such an impact on the American theater. *A Raisin in the Sun*, Hansberry's masterpiece, electrified its audience, black and white, by presenting the human registers of a nation at a profound racial crossroads. Like ARTHUR MILLER'S *DEATH OF A SALESMAN* (1949), to which Hansberry compared her play, *Raisin* locates its action in the American family, but it does so with deep sensitivity to the particular social and psychological pressures faced by mid-twentieth-century African Americans. The play is set in Chicago's South Side at some point between 1945 and 1959, and it portrays a segregated urban environment that had changed little since Hansberry's childhood in the 1930s. The legal enforcement of racially restricted covenants was declared unconstitutional by the Supreme Court in 1948, but Chicago witnessed some of the nation's most violent confrontations during the 1950s when African Americans attempted to move into white neighborhoods. Houses were bombed, property vandalized, and black property owners terrorized; in some instances police escorts were required when black residents left their houses to run errands or attend churches. According to Stephen Grant Meyer's book *As Long as They Don't Move Next Door: Segregation and Racial Conflict in American Neighborhoods*, during the years 1956–58 over 250 incidents of racial violence were reported in Chicago, many connected with housing, and the city saw thirty-eight incidents of arson, most of them on the periphery of the Black Belt and other African American residential areas. For their part, African Americans who lived in the South Side's segregated neighborhoods continued to live in crowded, substandard conditions.

These conditions are evident in the setting for *A Raisin in the Sun*. Lena (Mama) and Big Walter Younger rented the small apartment when they were married while planning to buy a two-story house within a year, but their dream never materialized, and the apartment now also houses their daughter, Beneatha; their son, Walter Lee; his wife, Ruth; and their son, Travis. Now that Big Walter has died, Mama and Beneatha share a bed, and Travis sleeps on the roll-out couch. The Younger family share the bathroom down the hall with their neighbors. Inside the apartment, the carpet is worn, as is the upholstery on the living-room couch, and the only natural light that reaches them comes through a single kitchen window. Their neighborhood is infested with rats, and they have to spray their apartment to keep the roaches at bay.

The title of Hansberry's play is taken from Langston Hughes's poem "Harlem." "What happens to a dream deferred?" the poem asks: "Does it dry up / like a raisin in the sun? / Or fester like a sore— / And then run? [. . .] / Or does it explode?" As the play begins, the Youngers are awaiting the delivery of a check worth $10,000 from the life-insurance policy that Big Walter took

out in order to protect his family. Big Walter's memory hovers over his family and the play as a whole. "[H]ardheaded, mean, kind of wild with women" (according to Lena), he worked himself to death trying to care for the children he loved. "Seem like God didn't see fit to give the black man nothing but dreams," he would say, "but He did give us children to make them dreams seem worth while." While Big Walter's dream of providing his family with the life that he and Lena envisioned gave way to discouragement, his death—and the insurance payment he provided—offers hope for the dreams of those who survive him.

These dreams are different, though, and much of the play's dramatic tension derives from this difference. Lena and Ruth, both of whom work as domestics, desire to escape the confinement of their lives and living environment. Lena wants a house with a yard where she can keep a garden. Ruth wants a life where her son can have a nurturing childhood instead of a childhood spent chasing down rats in the street and where she and her husband can rekindle their romance. Beneatha, who attends college with the financial support of her family, wants to be a doctor and fix people who are sick or injured. Walter Lee's dream is expansive in a different way. He wants what he sees when he chauffeurs white men around and observes them making deals in restaurants: access to a capitalist system that allows men to make something of themselves and their lives. His desire to invest in a liquor store with two friends represents what he sees as his best chance in segregated Chicago to take charge of his fortunes. When Lena announces that she has used a portion of the insurance money to make a down payment on a house in the all-white neighborhood of Clybourne Park, he experiences this as rejection.

Lena is the matriarch of her family, but her children belong to a different generation and hold values that seem alien to the earlier African American world she represents. "You my children," she says, "but how different we done become." Beneatha, like Hansberry herself at an earlier age, is restless with ideas and the desire to find herself. Caught between George Murchison, a well-off suitor who scorns what he considers pretentiousness, and Joseph Asagai, a Nigerian student who urges her to recognize her roots in Africa, she is drawn to the latter. Asagai is the voice of an Africa embarking on independence after a history of colonial rule: in 1957 Ghana became the third sub-Saharan country (after Ethiopia and Liberia) to gain independence, and two years after *A Raisin in the Sun*'s premiere it had been joined by eighteen others, including Nigeria. As Beneatha and her brother demonstrate in one of the play's most electric scenes, the call of Africa is strong in Hansberry's play. Even though the realities that Asagai describes there are different from those in Chicago's South Side, the juxtaposition of these two worlds establishes a parallel between the civil rights movement and Africa's campaigns for independence and self-determination.

Walter Lee's struggle to achieve self-identity is more desperate than his sister's, caught up as it is in notions of what it means to be a man in a society that consistently thwarts his dreams of financial success and

independence. He believes in the American Dream, its vision of material success all the more irresistible in a decade that followed the Depression and World War II. While his uncritical endorsement of this dream is questioned in the play, we should remind ourselves that its promise of self-determination is the same that brought Big Walter, Lena, and their generation from their southern past to the North's industrialized economy. Walter Lee sees his chance at the American Dream as a way of avoiding the disappointed life his father led and validating his own roles as husband, father, son, and brother. The fact that his aspirations distance him from his wife and family is one of the play's central tensions. When Walter is given a chance to act on his dreams, *A Raisin in the Sun* moves through a series of defining moments. These moments resonate today as they did over fifty years ago with their portrait of resilience, courage, apprehension, and possibility.

Ruby Dee as Ruth Younger, Sidney Poitier as Walter Lee, and Diana Sands as Beneatha in the 1959 production of *A Raisin in the Sun* at Broadway's Ethel Barrymore Theatre.

When the civil rights movement assumed more radical forms in the 1960s with the Black Arts movement, the Black Power movement, and the black nationalism of Malcolm X and others, some in the African American community viewed Hansberry's play as too conventional in form and assimilationist (that is, too sympathetic to the idea of African Americans integrating into white society and its values). What this attitude missed was Hansberry's keen insight into the internal and external costs of segregation and her commitment to the African American struggle for equality. These aspects of the play became even more evident when later editions of the play restored material that had been cut in earlier productions. After seeing a 1986 revival of the play, playwright Amiri Baraka, one of the play's earlier detractors, wrote, "We missed the essence of the work: that Hansberry had created a family engaged in the same class and ideological struggles as existed in the movement—and within individuals." *A Raisin in the Sun*, he acknowledged, "has the life that only classics can maintain." s.g.

A Raisin in the Sun

What happens to a dream deferred?
Does it dry up
Like a raisin in the sun?
Or fester like a sore—
And then run?
Does it stink like rotten meat
Or crust and sugar over—
Like a syrupy sweet?

Maybe it just sags
Like a heavy load.

Or *does it explode?*

LANGSTON HUGHES[1]

CHARACTERS

RUTH YOUNGER
TRAVIS YOUNGER
WALTER LEE YOUNGER (BROTHER)
BENEATHA YOUNGER
LENA YOUNGER (MAMA)

JOSEPH ASAGAI
GEORGE MURCHISON
KARL LINDNER
BOBO
MOVING MEN

The action of the play is set in Chicago's Southside, sometime between World War II and the present.[2]

1. Hughes's poem, entitled "Harlem (A Dream Deferred)," was published in 1951.
2. That is, between 1945 and the late 1950s. *Southside*: since the early 20th century, the southern area of Chicago has been home to a majority of the city's African American population.

ACT I

Scene One

The YOUNGER *living room would be a comfortable and well-ordered room if it were not for a number of indestructible contradictions to this state of being. Its furnishings are typical and undistinguished and their primary feature now is that they have clearly had to accommodate the living of too many people for too many years—and they are tired. Still, we can see that at some time, a time probably no longer remembered by the family (except perhaps for* MAMA), *the furnishings of this room were actually selected with care and love and even hope—and brought to this apartment and arranged with taste and pride.*

That was a long time ago. Now the once loved pattern of the couch upholstery has to fight to show itself from under acres of crocheted doilies[3] and couch covers which have themselves finally come to be more important than the upholstery. And here a table or a chair has been moved to disguise the worn places in the carpet; but the carpet has fought back by showing its weariness, with depressing uniformity, elsewhere on its surface.

Weariness has, in fact, won in this room. Everything has been polished, washed, sat on, used, scrubbed too often. All pretenses but living itself have long since vanished from the very atmosphere of this room.

Moreover, a section of this room, for it is not really a room unto itself, though the landlord's lease would make it seem so, slopes backward to provide a small kitchen area, where the family prepares the meals that are eaten in the living room proper, which must also serve as dining room. The single window that has been provided for these "two" rooms is located in this kitchen area. The sole natural light the family may enjoy in the course of a day is only that which fights its way through this little window.

At left, a door leads to a bedroom which is shared by MAMA *and her daughter,* BENEATHA. *At right, opposite, is a second room (which in the beginning of the life of this apartment was probably a breakfast room) which serves as a bedroom for* WALTER *and his wife,* RUTH.

Time: Sometime between World War II and the present.

Place: Chicago's Southside.

At Rise: It is morning dark in the living room. TRAVIS *is asleep on the make-down bed at center. An alarm clock sounds from within the bedroom at right, and presently* RUTH *enters from that room and closes the door behind her. She crosses sleepily toward the window. As she passes her sleeping son she reaches down and shakes him a little. At the window she raises the shade and a dusky Southside morning light comes in feebly. She fills a pot with water and puts it on to boil. She calls to the boy, between yawns, in a slightly muffled voice.*

RUTH *is about thirty. We can see that she was a pretty girl, even exceptionally so, but now it is apparent that life has been little that she expected, and disappointment has already begun to hang in her face. In a few years, before thirty-five even, she will be known among her people as a "settled woman."*

She crosses to her son and gives him a good, final, rousing shake.

RUTH   Come on now, boy, it's seven thirty! [*Her son sits up at last, in a stupor of sleepiness*] I say hurry up, Travis! You ain't the only person in the world got to use a bathroom! [*The child, a sturdy, handsome little boy of ten or eleven, drags*

---

3. Round, ornamental cloths or mats often draped over furniture to hide wear and damage.

himself out of the bed and almost blindly takes his towels and "today's clothes" from drawers and a closet and goes out to the bathroom, which is in an outside hall and which is shared by another family or families on the same floor. RUTH *crosses to the bedroom door at right and opens it and calls in to her husband.*]
Walter Lee! . . . It's after seven thirty! Lemme see you do some waking up in

5   there now! [*She waits.*] You better get up from there, man! It's after seven thirty I tell you. [*She waits again.*] All right, you just go ahead and lay there and next thing you know Travis be finished and Mr. Johnson'll be in there and you'll be fussing and cussing round here like a madman! And be late too! [*She waits, at the end of patience.*] Walter Lee—it's time for you to GET UP!

> [*She waits another second and then starts to go into the bedroom, but is apparently satisfied that her husband has begun to get up. She stops, pulls the door to, and returns to the kitchen area. She wipes her face with a moist cloth and runs her fingers through her sleep-disheveled hair in a vain effort and ties an apron around her housecoat. The bedroom door at right opens and her husband stands in the doorway in his pajamas, which are rumpled and mismated. He is a lean, intense young man in his middle thirties, inclined to quick nervous movements and erratic speech habits— and always in his voice there is a quality of indictment.*]

10   WALTER   Is he out yet?

RUTH   What you mean *out*? He ain't hardly got in there good yet.

WALTER [*Wandering in, still more oriented to sleep than to a new day*]   Well, what was you doing all that yelling for if I can't even get in there yet? [*Stopping and thinking*] Check coming today?

15   RUTH   They *said* Saturday and this is just Friday and I hopes to God you ain't going to get up here first thing this morning and start talking to me 'bout no money—'cause I 'bout don't want to hear it.

WALTER   Something the matter with you this morning?

RUTH   No—I'm just sleepy as the devil. What kind of eggs you want?

20   WALTER   Not scrambled. [RUTH *starts to scramble eggs.*]   Paper come? [RUTH *points impatiently to the rolled up* Tribune[4] *on the table, and he gets it and spreads it out and vaguely reads the front page.*] Set off another bomb[5] yesterday.

RUTH [*Maximum indifference*]   Did they?

WALTER [*Looking up*]   What's the matter with you?

25   RUTH   Ain't nothing the matter with me. And don't keep asking me that this morning.

WALTER   Ain't nobody bothering you. [*Reading the news of the day absently again*] Say Colonel McCormick[6] is sick.

RUTH [*Affecting tea-party interest*]   Is he now? Poor thing.

30   WALTER [*Sighing and looking at his watch*]   Oh, me. [*He waits.*] Now what is that boy doing in that bathroom all this time? He just going to have to start getting up earlier. I can't be being late to work on account of him fooling around in there.

RUTH [*Turning on him*]   Oh, no he ain't going to be getting up no earlier no

35   such thing! It ain't his fault that he can't get to bed no earlier nights

---

4. The *Chicago Tribune*, major daily newspaper founded in 1847.
5. Reference to above-ground nuclear weapon testing, which the United States con-

ducted between 1945 and 1963.
6. Robert Rutherford McCormick (1880–1955), editor and publisher of the *Chicago Tribune*.

'cause he got a bunch of crazy good-for-nothing clowns sitting up running
their mouths in what is supposed to be his bedroom after ten o'clock at
night . . .

WALTER   That's what you mad about, ain't it? The things I want to talk about
40   with my friends just couldn't be important in your mind, could they?

> [*He rises and finds a cigarette in her handbag on the table and crosses to
> the little window and looks out, smoking and deeply enjoying this first
> one.*]

RUTH [*Almost matter of factly, a complaint too automatic to deserve emphasis*]   Why you always got to smoke before you eat in the morning?

WALTER [*At the window*]   Just look at 'em down there . . . Running and racing to work . . . [*He turns and faces his wife and watches her a moment at
the stove, and then, suddenly*] You look young this morning, baby.

45   RUTH [*Indifferently*]   Yeah?

WALTER   Just for a second—stirring them eggs. Just for a second it was—you
looked real young again. [*He reaches for her; she crosses away. Then, drily:*]
It's gone now—you look like yourself again!

RUTH   Man, if you don't shut up and leave me alone.

50   WALTER [*Looking out to the street again*]   First thing a man ought to learn in
life is not to make love to no colored woman first thing in the morning. You
all some eeeevil people at eight o'clock in the morning.

> [TRAVIS *appears in the hall doorway, almost fully dressed and quite wide
> awake now, his towels and pajamas across his shoulders. He opens the
> door and signals for his father to make the bathroom in a hurry.*]

TRAVIS [*Watching the bathroom*]   Daddy, come on!

> [WALTER *gets his bathroom utensils and flies out to the bathroom.*]

RUTH   Sit down and have your breakfast, Travis.

55   TRAVIS   Mama, this is Friday. [*Gleefully*] Check coming tomorrow, huh?

RUTH   You get your mind off money and eat your breakfast.

TRAVIS [*Eating*]   This is the morning we supposed to bring the fifty cents to
school.

RUTH   Well, I ain't got no fifty cents this morning.

60   TRAVIS   Teacher say we have to.

RUTH   I don't care what teacher say. I ain't got it. Eat your breakfast, Travis.

TRAVIS   I *am* eating.

RUTH   Hush up now and just eat!

> [*The boy gives her an exasperated look for her lack of understanding, and
> eats grudgingly.*]

TRAVIS   You think Grandmama would have it?

65   RUTH   No! And I want you to stop asking your grandmother for money, you
hear me?

TRAVIS [*Outraged*]   Gaaaleee! I don't ask her, she just gimme it sometimes!

RUTH   Travis Willard Younger—I got too much on me this morning to be—

TRAVIS   Maybe Daddy—

70   RUTH   Travis!

> [*The boy hushes abruptly. They are both quiet and tense for several
> seconds.*]

TRAVIS [*Presently*]   Could I maybe go carry some groceries in front of the
supermarket for a little while after school then?

RUTH   Just hush, I said. [*Travis jabs his spoon into his cereal bowl viciously; and rests his head in anger upon his fists*] If you through eating, you can get
75   over there and make up your bed.

[*The boy obeys stiffly and crosses the room, almost mechanically, to the bed and more or less folds the bedding into a heap, then angrily gets his books and cap.*]

TRAVIS [*Sulking and standing apart from her unnaturally*]   I'm gone.

RUTH [*Looking up from the stove to inspect him automatically*]   Come here. [*He crosses to her and she studies his head.*] If you don't take this comb and fix this here head, you better! [TRAVIS *puts down his books with a great sigh of oppression, and crosses to the mirror. His mother mutters under her breath*
80   *about his "slubbornness"*] 'Bout to march out of here with that head looking just like chickens slept in it! I just don't know where you get your slubborn ways . . . And get your jacket, too. Looks chilly out this morning.

TRAVIS [*With conspicuously brushed hair and jacket*]   I'm gone.

RUTH   Get carfare and milk money—[*Waving one finger*]—and not a single
85   penny for no caps, you hear me?

TRAVIS [*With sullen politeness*]   Yes'm.

[*He turns in outrage to leave. His mother watches after him as in his frustration he approaches the door almost comically. When she speaks to him, her voice has become a very gentle tease.*]

RUTH [*Mocking; as she thinks he would say it.*]   Oh, Mama makes me so mad sometimes, I don't know what to do! [*She waits and continues to his back as he stands stock-still in front of the door*] I wouldn't kiss that woman good-bye for
90   nothing in this world this morning! [*The boy finally turns around and rolls his eyes at her, knowing the mood has changed and he is vindicated; he does not, however, move toward her yet.*] Not for nothing in this world! [*She finally laughs aloud at him and holds out her arms to him and we see that it is a way between them, very old and practiced. He crosses to her and allows her to embrace him warmly but keeps his face fixed with masculine rigidity. She holds him back from her presently and looks at him and runs her fingers over the features of his face. With utter gentleness—*] Now—whose little old angry man are you?

TRAVIS [*The masculinity and gruffness start to fade at last.*]   Aw
95   gaalee—Mama . . .

RUTH [*Mimicking*]   Aw gaaaaalleeeee, Mama! [*She pushes him, with rough playfulness and finality, toward the door.*] Get on out of here or you going to be late.

TRAVIS [*In the face of love, new aggressiveness*]   Mama, could I *please* go carry
100   groceries?

RUTH   Honey, it's starting to get so cold evenings.

WALTER [*Coming in from the bathroom and drawing a make-believe gun from a make-believe holster and shooting at his son*] What is it he wants to do?

RUTH   Go carry groceries after school at the supermarket.

WALTER   Well, let him go . . .

105   TRAVIS [*Quickly, to the ally*]   I *have* to—she won't gimme the fifty cents . . .

WALTER [*To his wife only*]   Why not?

RUTH [*Simply, and with flavor*]   'Cause we don't have it.

WALTER [*To RUTH only*]   What you tell the boy things like that for? [*Reaching down into his pants with a rather important gesture*] Here, son—

[*He hands the boy the coin, but his eyes are directed to his wife's.* TRAVIS *takes the money happily.*]

110 TRAVIS Thanks, Daddy.

[*He starts out.* RUTH *watches both of them with murder in her eyes.* WALTER *stands and stares back at her with defiance, and suddenly reaches into his pocket again on an afterthought.*]

WALTER [*Without even looking at his son, still staring hard at his wife*] In fact, here's another fifty cents . . . Buy yourself some fruit today—or take a taxi-cab to school or something!

TRAVIS Whoopee—

[*He leaps up and clasps his father around the middle with his legs, and they face each other in mutual appreciation; slowly* WALTER LEE *peeks around the boy to catch the violent rays from his wife's eyes and draws his head back as if shot.*]

115 WALTER You better get down now—and get to school, man.

TRAVIS [*At the door*] O.K. Good-bye.

[*He exits*]

WALTER [*After him, pointing with pride*] That's *my* boy. [*She looks at him in disgust and turns back to her work.*] You know what I was thinking 'bout in the bathroom this morning?

120 RUTH No.

WALTER How come you always try to be so pleasant!

RUTH What is there to be pleasant 'bout!

WALTER You want to know what I was thinking 'bout in the bathroom or not!

RUTH I know what you thinking 'bout.

125 WALTER [*Ignoring her*] 'Bout what me and Willy Harris was talking about last night.

RUTH [*Immediately—a refrain*] Willy Harris is a good-for-nothing loudmouth.

WALTER Anybody who talks to me has got to be a good-for-nothing loud-

130 mouth, ain't he? And what you know about who is just a good-for-nothing loudmouth? Charlie Atkins was just a "good-for-nothing loudmouth" too, wasn't he! When he wanted me to go in the dry-cleaning business with him. And now—he's grossing a hundred thousand a year. A hundred thousand dollars a year! You still call *him* a loudmouth!

135 RUTH [*Bitterly*] Oh, Walter Lee . . .

[*She folds her head on her arms over the table.*]

WALTER [*Rising and coming to her and standing over her*] You tired, ain't you? Tired of everything. Me, the boy, the way we live—this beat-up hole—everything. Ain't you? [*She doesn't look up, doesn't answer.*] So tired—moaning and groaning all the time, but you wouldn't do nothing to help,

140 would you? You couldn't be on my side that long for nothing, could you?

RUTH Walter, please leave me alone.

WALTER A man needs for a woman to back him up . . .

RUTH Walter—

WALTER Mama would listen to you. You know she listen to you more than

145 she do me and Bennie. She think more of you. All you have to do is just sit down with her when you drinking your coffee one morning and talking 'bout things like you do and—[*He sits down beside her and demonstrates*

graphically what he thinks her methods and tone should be.]—you just sip your coffee, see, and say easy like that you been thinking 'bout that deal Walter Lee is so interested in, 'bout the store and all, and sip some more coffee, like what you saying ain't really that important to you—And the next thing you know, she be listening good and asking you questions and when I come home—I can tell her the details. This ain't no fly-by-night proposition, baby. I mean we figured it out, me and Willy and Bobo.

RUTH [*With a frown*] Bobo?

WALTER Yeah. You see, this little liquor store we got in mind cost seventy-five thousand and we figured the initial investment on the place be 'bout thirty thousand, see. That be ten thousand each. Course, there's a couple of hundred you got to pay so's you don't spend your life just waiting for them clowns to let your license get approved—

RUTH You mean graft?[7]

WALTER [*Frowning impatiently*] Don't call it that. See there, that just goes to show you what women understand about the world. Baby, don't *nothing* happen for you in this world 'less you pay *somebody* off!

RUTH Walter, leave me alone! [*She raises her head and stares at him vigorously—then says, more quietly*] Eat your eggs, they gonna be cold.

WALTER [*Straightening up from her and looking off*] That's it. There you are. Man say to his woman: I got me a dream. His woman say: Eat your eggs. [*Sadly, but gaining in power*] Man say: I got to take hold of this here world, baby! And a woman will say: Eat your eggs and go to work. [*Passionately now*] Man say: I got to change my life, I'm choking to death, baby! And his woman say—[*In utter anguish as he brings his fists down on his thighs*]— Your eggs is getting cold!

RUTH [*Softly*] Walter, that ain't none of our money.

WALTER [*Not listening at all or even looking at her*] This morning, I was lookin' in the mirror and thinking about it . . . I'm thirty-five years old; I been married eleven years and I got a boy who sleeps in the living room— [*Very, very quietly*]—and all I got to give him is stories about how rich white people live . . .

RUTH Eat your eggs, Walter.

WALTER [*Slams the table and jumps up*] —DAMN MY EGGS—DAMN ALL THE EGGS THAT EVER WAS!

RUTH Then go to work.

WALTER [*Looking up at her*] See—I'm trying to talk to you 'bout myself— [*Shaking his head with the repetition*]—and all you can say is eat them eggs and go to work.

RUTH [*Wearily*] Honey, you never say nothing new. I listen to you every day, every night and every morning, and you never say nothing new. [*Shrugging*] So you would rather *be* Mr. Arnold than be his chauffeur. So—I would *rather* be living in Buckingham Palace.[8]

WALTER That is just what is wrong with the colored woman in this world . . . Don't understand about building their men up and making 'em feel like they somebody. Like they can do something.

RUTH [*Drily, but to hurt*] There *are* colored men who do things.

7. That is, gaining profit by dishonest means.
8. London residence of the British monarch.

195 WALTER   No thanks to the colored woman.

RUTH   Well, being a colored woman, I guess I can't help myself none.

[*She rises and gets the ironing board and sets it up and attacks a huge pile of rough-dried clothes, sprinkling them in preparation for the ironing and then rolling them into tight fat balls.*]

WALTER [*Mumbling*]   We one group of men tied to a race of women with small minds!

[*His sister* BENEATHA *enters. She is about twenty, as slim and intense as her brother. She is not as pretty as her sister-in-law, but her lean, almost intellectual face has a handsomeness of its own. She wears a bright-red flannel nightie, and her thick hair stands wildly about her head. Her speech is a mixture of many things; it is different from the rest of the family's insofar as education has permeated her sense of English—and perhaps the Midwest rather than the South has finally—at last—won out in her inflection; but not altogether, because over all of it is a soft slurring and transformed use of vowels which is the decided influence of the Southside. She passes through the room without looking at either* RUTH *or* WALTER *and goes to the outside door and looks, a little blindly, out to the bathroom. She sees that it has been lost to the Johnsons. She closes the door with a sleepy vengeance and crosses to the table and sits down a little defeated.*]

BENEATHA   I am going to start timing those people.

200 WALTER   You should get up earlier.

BENEATHA [*Her face in her hands. She is still fighting the urge to go back to bed.*]   Really—would you suggest dawn? Where's the paper?

WALTER [*Pushing the paper across the table to her as he studies her almost clinically, as though he has never seen her before*]   You a horrible-looking chick at this hour.

BENEATHA [*Drily*]   Good morning, everybody.

205 WALTER [*Senselessly*]   How is school coming?

BENEATHA [*In the same spirit*]   Lovely. Lovely. And you know, biology is the greatest. [*Looking up at him*] I dissected something that looked just like you yesterday.

WALTER   I just wondered if you've made up your mind and everything.

210 BENEATHA [*Gaining in sharpness and impatience*]   And what did I answer yesterday morning—and the day before that?

RUTH [*From the ironing board, like someone disinterested and old*]   Don't be so nasty, Bennie.

BENEATHA [*Still to her brother*]   And the day before that and the day before

215 that!

WALTER [*Defensively*]   I'm interested in you. Something wrong with that? Ain't many girls who decide—

WALTER *and* BENEATHA [*In unison*]   —"to be a doctor."

[*Silence*]

WALTER   Have we figured out yet just exactly how much medical school is

220 going to cost?

RUTH   Walter Lee, why don't you leave that girl alone and get out of here to work?

BENEATHA [*Exits to the bathroom and bangs on the door*]   Come on out of there, please!

[*She comes back into the room.*]

225 WALTER [*Looking at his sister intently*] You know the check is coming tomorrow.

BENEATHA [*Turning on him with a sharpness all her own*] That money belongs to Mama, Walter, and it's for her to decide how she wants to use it. I don't care if she wants to buy a house or a rocket ship or just nail it up some-
230 where and look at it. It's hers. Not ours—hers.

WALTER [*Bitterly*] Now ain't that fine! You just got your mother's interest at heart, ain't you, girl? You such a nice girl—but if Mama got that money she can always take a few thousand and help you through school too—can't she?

235 BENEATHA I have never asked anyone around here to do anything for me!

WALTER No! And the line between asking and just accepting when the time comes is big and wide—ain't it!

BENEATHA [*With fury*] What do you want from me, Brother—that I quit school or just drop dead, which!

240 WALTER I don't want nothing but for you to stop acting holy 'round here. Me and Ruth done made some sacrifices for you—why can't you do something for the family?

RUTH Walter, don't be dragging me in it.

WALTER You are in it—Don't you get up and go work in somebody's kitchen
245 for the last three years to help put clothes on her back?

RUTH Oh, Walter—that's not fair . . .

WALTER It ain't that nobody expects you to get on your knees and say thank you, Brother; thank you, Ruth; thank you, Mama—and thank you, Travis, for wearing the same pair of shoes for two semesters—

250 BENEATHA [*Dropping to her knees*] Well—I *do*—all right?—thank everybody! And forgive me for ever wanting to be anything at all! [*Pursuing him on her knees across the floor*] FORGIVE ME, FORGIVE ME, FORGIVE ME!

RUTH Please stop it! Your mama'll hear you.

WALTER Who the hell told you you had to be a doctor? If you so crazy 'bout
255 messing 'round with sick people—then go be a nurse like other women—or just get married and be quiet . . .

BENEATHA Well—you finally got it said . . . It took you three years but you finally got it said. Walter, give up; leave me alone—it's Mama's money.

WALTER *He was my father, too!*

260 BENEATHA So what? He was mine, too—and Travis' grandfather—but the insurance money belongs to Mama. Picking on me is not going to make her give it to you to invest in any liquor stores—[*Underbreath, dropping into a chair*]—and I for one say, God bless Mama for that!

WALTER [*To* RUTH] See—did you hear? Did you hear!

265 RUTH Honey, please go to work.

WALTER Nobody in this house is ever going to understand me.

BENEATHA Because you're a nut.

WALTER Who's a nut?

BENEATHA You—you are a nut. Thee is mad, boy.

270 WALTER [*Looking at his wife and his sister from the door, very sadly*] The world's most backward race of people, and that's a fact.

BENEATHA [*Turning slowly in her chair*] And then there are all those proph-ets who would lead us out of the wilderness—[WALTER *slams out of the house.*]—into the swamps!

275   RUTH   Bennie, why you always gotta be pickin' on your brother? Can't you be a little sweeter sometimes? [*Door opens.* WALTER *walks in. He fumbles with his cap, starts to speak, clears throat, looks everywhere but at* RUTH. *Finally:*]

WALTER [*To* RUTH]   I need some money for carfare.

RUTH [*Looks at him, then warms; teasing, but tenderly*]   Fifty cents? [*She goes to her bag and gets money.*] Here—take a taxi!

[WALTER *exits.* MAMA *enters. She is a woman in her early sixties, full-bodied and strong. She is one of those women of a certain grace and beauty who wear it so unobtrusively that it takes a while to notice. Her dark-brown face is surrounded by the total whiteness of her hair, and, being a woman who has adjusted to many things in life and overcome many more, her face is full of strength. She has, we can see, wit and faith of a kind that keep her eyes lit and full of interest and expectancy. She is, in a word, a beautiful woman. Her bearing is perhaps most like the noble bearing of the women of the Hereros of Southwest Africa[9]—rather as if she imagines that as she walks she still bears a basket or a vessel upon her head. Her speech, on the other hand, is as careless as her carriage is precise—she is inclined to slur everything—but her voice is perhaps not so much quiet as simply soft.*]

280   MAMA   Who that 'round here slamming doors at this hour?

[*She crosses through the room, goes to the window, opens it, and brings in a feeble little plant growing doggedly in a small pot on the windowsill. She feels the dirt and puts it back out.*]

RUTH   That was Walter Lee. He and Bennie was at it again.

MAMA   My children and they tempers. Lord, if this little old plant don't get more sun than it's been getting it ain't never going to see spring again. [*She turns from the window.*] What's the matter with you this morning, Ruth?

285   You looks right peaked. You aiming to iron all them things? Leave some for me. I'll get to 'em this afternoon. Bennie honey, it's too drafty for you to be sitting 'round half dressed. Where's your robe?

BENEATHA   In the cleaners.

MAMA   Well, go get mine and put it on.

290   BENEATHA   I'm not cold, Mama, honest.

MAMA   I know—but you so thin . . .

BENEATHA [*Irritably*]   Mama, I'm not cold.

MAMA [*Seeing the make-down bed as* TRAVIS *has left it*]   Lord have mercy, look at that poor bed. Bless his heart—he tries, don't he?

[*She moves to the bed* TRAVIS *has sloppily made up.*]

295   RUTH   No—he don't half try at all 'cause he knows you going to come along behind him and fix everything. That's just how come he don't know how to do nothing right now—you done spoiled that boy so.

MAMA [*Folding bedding*]   Well—he's a little boy. Ain't supposed to know 'bout housekeeping. My baby, that's what he is. What you fix for his breakfast

300   this morning?

RUTH [*Angrily*]   I feed my son, Lena!

MAMA   I ain't meddling—[*Underbreath; busy-bodyish*] I just noticed all last week he had cold cereal, and when it starts getting this chilly in the fall a child ought to have some hot grits or something when he goes out in the cold—

---

9. Bantu-speaking ethnic group prevalent in modern-day Namibia.

305 RUTH [*Furious*] I gave him hot oats—is that all right!

MAMA I ain't meddling. [*Pause*] Put a lot of nice butter on it? [RUTH *shoots her an angry look and does not reply.*] He likes lots of butter.

RUTH [*Exasperated*] Lena—

MAMA [*To* BENEATHA. MAMA *is inclined to wander conversationally some-times.*] What was you and your brother fussing 'bout this morning?

310 BENEATHA It's not important, Mama.

[*She gets up and goes to look out at the bathroom, which is apparently free, and she picks up her towels and rushes out.*]

MAMA What was they fighting about?

RUTH Now you know as well as I do.

MAMA [*Shaking her head*] Brother still worrying hisself sick about that money?

RUTH You know he is.

315 MAMA You had breakfast?

RUTH Some coffee.

MAMA Girl, you better start eating and looking after yourself better. You almost thin as Travis.

RUTH Lena—

320 MAMA Un-hunh?

RUTH What are you going to do with it?

MAMA Now don't you start, child. It's too early in the morning to be talking about money. It ain't Christian.

RUTH It's just that he got his heart set on that store—

325 MAMA You mean that liquor store that Willy Harris want him to invest in?

RUTH Yes—

MAMA We ain't no business people, Ruth. We just plain working folks.

RUTH Ain't nobody business people till they go into business. Walter Lee say colored people ain't never going to start getting ahead till they start gambling

330 on some different kinds of things in the world—investments and things.

MAMA What done got into you, girl? Walter Lee done finally sold you on investing.

RUTH No. Mama, something is happening between Walter and me. I don't know what it is—but he needs something—something I can't give him any

335 more. He needs this chance, Lena.

MAMA [*Frowning deeply*] But liquor, honey—

RUTH Well—like Walter say—I spec people going to always be drinking themselves some liquor.

MAMA Well—whether they drinks it or not ain't none of my business. But

340 whether I go into business selling it to 'em *is*, and I don't want that on my ledger this late in life. [*Stopping suddenly and studying her daughter-in-law*] Ruth Younger, what's the matter with you today? You look like you could fall over right there.

RUTH I'm tired.

345 MAMA Then you better stay home from work today.

RUTH I can't stay home. She'd be calling up the agency[1] and screaming at them, "My girl didn't come in today—send me somebody! My girl didn't come in!" Oh, she just have a fit . . .

MAMA Well, let her have it. I'll just call her up and say you got the flu—

---

1. Staffing agency.

350 RUTH [*Laughing*]   Why the flu?

MAMA   'Cause it sounds respectable to 'em. Something white people get, too. They know 'bout the flu. Otherwise they think you been cut up or something when you tell 'em you sick.

RUTH   I got to go in. We need the money.

355 MAMA   Somebody would of thought my children done all but starved to death the way they talk about money here late. Child, we got a great big old check coming tomorrow.

RUTH [*Sincerely, but also self-righteously*]   Now that's your money. It ain't got nothing to do with me. We all feel like that—Walter and Bennie and me—

360 even Travis.

MAMA [*Thoughtfully, and suddenly very far away*]   Ten thousand dollars—

RUTH   Sure is wonderful.

MAMA   Ten thousand dollars.

RUTH   You know what you should do, Miss Lena? You should take yourself a

365 trip somewhere. To Europe or South America or someplace—

MAMA [*Throwing up her hands at the thought*]   Oh, child!

RUTH   I'm serious. Just pack up and leave! Go on away and enjoy yourself some. Forget about the family and have yourself a ball for once in your life—

MAMA [*Drily*]   You sound like I'm just about ready to die. Who'd go with me?

370 What I look like wandering 'round Europe by myself?

RUTH   Shoot—these here rich white women do it all the time. They don't think nothing of packing up they suitcases and piling on one of them big steamships and—swoosh!—they gone, child.

MAMA   Something always told me I wasn't no rich white woman.

375 RUTH   Well—what are you going to do with it then?

MAMA   I ain't rightly decided. [*Thinking. She speaks now with emphasis.*] Some of it got to be put away for Beneatha and her schoolin'—and ain't nothing going to touch that part of it. Nothing. [*She waits several seconds, trying to make up her mind about something, and looks at* RUTH *a little tentatively before going on.*] Been thinking that we maybe could meet the notes[2] on a little old

380 two-story somewhere, with a yard where Travis could play in the summertime, if we use part of the insurance for a down payment and everybody kind of pitch in. I could maybe take on a little day work again, few days a week—

RUTH [*Studying her mother-in-law furtively and concentrating on her ironing, anxious to encourage without seeming to*]   Well, Lord knows, we've put enough rent into this here rat trap to pay for four houses by now . . .

MAMA [*Looking up at the words "rat trap" and then looking around and leaning

385 back and sighing—in a suddenly reflective mood—*]   "Rat trap"—yes, that's all it is. [*Smiling*] I remember just as well the day me and Big Walter moved in here. Hadn't been married but two weeks and wasn't planning on living here no more than a year. [*She shakes her head at the dissolved dream.*] We was going to set away, little by little, don't you know, and buy a little place out

390 in Morgan Park. We had even picked out the house. [*Chuckling a little*] Looks right dumpy today. But Lord, child, you should know all the dreams I had 'bout buying that house and fixing it up and making me a little garden in the back—[*She waits and stops smiling.*] And didn't none of it happen.

[*Dropping her hands in a futile gesture*]

---

2. That is, make monthly house payments.

RUTH [*Keeps her head down, ironing*]   Yes, life can be a barrel of disappoint-
395   ments, sometimes.

MAMA   Honey, Big Walter would come in here some nights back then and
slump down on that couch there and just look at the rug, and look at me and
look at the rug and then back at me—and I'd know he was down then . . .
really down. [*After a second very long and thoughtful pause; she is seeing back
400   to times that only she can see*] And then, Lord, when I lost that baby—little
Claude—I almost thought I was going to lose Big Walter too. Oh, that man
grieved hisself! He was one man to love his children.

RUTH   Ain't nothin' can tear at you like losin' your baby.

MAMA   I guess that's how come that man finally worked hisself to death like
405   he done. Like he was fighting his own war with this here world that took
his baby from him.

RUTH   He sure was a fine man, all right. I always liked Mr. Younger.

MAMA   Crazy 'bout his children! God knows there was plenty wrong with
Walter Younger—hard-headed, mean, kind of wild with women—plenty
410   wrong with him. But he sure loved his children. Always wanted them to
have something—be something. That's where Brother gets all these
notions, I reckon. Big Walter used to say, he'd get right wet in the eyes
sometimes, lean his head back with the water standing in his eyes and say,
"Seem like God didn't see fit to give the black man nothing but dreams—
415   but He did give us children to make them dreams seem worth while." [*She
smiles.*] He could talk like that, don't you know.

RUTH   Yes, he sure could. He was a good man, Mr. Younger.

MAMA   Yes, a fine man—just couldn't never catch up with his dreams,
that's all.

[BENEATHA *comes in, brushing her hair and looking up to the ceiling,
where the sound of a vacuum cleaner has started up.*]

420   BENEATHA   What could be so dirty on that woman's rugs that she has to
vacuum them every single day?

RUTH   I wish certain young women 'round here who I could name would
take inspiration about certain rugs in a certain apartment I could also
mention.

425   BENEATHA [*Shrugging*]   How much cleaning can a house need, for Christ's
sakes.

MAMA [*Not liking the Lord's name used thus*]   Bennie!

RUTH   Just listen to her—just listen!

BENEATHA   Oh, God!

430   MAMA   If you use the Lord's name just one more time—

BENEATHA [*A bit of a whine*]   Oh, Mama—

RUTH   Fresh—just fresh as salt, this girl!

BENEATHA [*Drily*]   Well—if the salt loses its savor[3]—

MAMA   Now that will do. I just ain't going to have you 'round here reciting
435   the scriptures in vain—you hear me?

BENEATHA   How did I manage to get on everybody's wrong side by just walking into a room?

RUTH   If you weren't so fresh—

---

3. "You are the salt of the earth. But if the salt lose its savor, wherewith shall it be salted? It is
good for nothing any more but to be cast out, and to be trodden on by men" (Matthew 5.13).

BENEATHA   Ruth, I'm twenty years old.

440 MAMA   What time you be home from school today?

BENEATHA   Kind of late. [*With enthusiasm*] Madeline is going to start my guitar lessons today.

> [MAMA *and* RUTH *look up with the same expression.*]

MAMA   Your *what* kind of lessons?

BENEATHA   Guitar.

445 RUTH   Oh, Father!

MAMA   How come you done taken it in your mind to learn to play the guitar?

BENEATHA   I just want to, that's all.

MAMA [*Smiling*]   Lord, child, don't you know what to do with yourself? How
450 long it going to be before you get tired of this now—like you got tired of that little play-acting group you joined last year? [*Looking at* RUTH] And what was it the year before that?

RUTH   The horseback-riding club for which she bought that fifty-five-dollar riding habit that's been hanging in the closet ever since!

455 MAMA [*To* BENEATHA]   Why you got to flit so from one thing to another, baby?

BENEATHA [*Sharply*]   I just want to learn to play the guitar. Is there anything wrong with that?

MAMA   Ain't nobody trying to stop you. I just wonders sometimes why you has to flit so from one thing to another all the time. You ain't never done
460 nothing with all that camera equipment you brought home—

BENEATHA   I don't flit! I—I experiment with different forms of expression—

RUTH   Like riding a horse?

BENEATHA   —People have to express themselves one way or another.

MAMA   What is it you want to express?

465 BENEATHA [*Angrily*]   Me! [MAMA *and* RUTH *look at each other and burst into raucous laughter.*] Don't worry—I don't expect you to understand.

MAMA [*To change the subject*]   Who you going out with tomorrow night?

BENEATHA [*With displeasure*]   George Murchison again.

MAMA [*Pleased*]   Oh—you getting a little sweet on him?

470 RUTH   You ask me, this child ain't sweet on nobody but herself— [*Underbreath*] Express herself!

> [*They laugh*]

BENEATHA   Oh—I like George all right, Mama. I mean I like him enough to go out with him and stuff, but—

RUTH [*For devilment*]   What does *and stuff* mean?

475 BENEATHA   Mind your own business.

MAMA   Stop picking at her now, Ruth. [*She chuckles—then a suspicious sudden look at her daughter as she turns in her chair for emphasis.*] What DOES it mean?

BENEATHA [*Wearily*]   Oh, I just mean I couldn't ever really be serious about
480 George. He's—he's so shallow.

RUTH   Shallow—what do you mean he's shallow? He's *rich!*

MAMA   Hush, Ruth.

BENEATHA   I know he's rich. He knows he's rich, too.

RUTH   Well—what other qualities a man got to have to satisfy you, little
485 girl?

BENEATHA You wouldn't even begin to understand. Anybody who married Walter could not possibly understand.

MAMA [*Outraged*] What kind of way is that to talk about your brother?

BENEATHA Brother is a flip—let's face it.

490 MAMA [*To* RUTH, *helplessly*] What's a flip?

RUTH [*Glad to add kindling*] She's saying he's crazy.

BENEATHA Not crazy. Brother isn't really crazy yet—he—he's an elaborate neurotic.

MAMA Hush your mouth!

495 BENEATHA As for George. Well. George looks good—he's got a beautiful car and he takes me to nice places and, as my sister-in-law says, he is probably the richest boy I will ever get to know and I even like him sometimes—but if the Youngers are sitting around waiting to see if their little Bennie is going to tie up the family with the Murchisons, they are wasting their time.

500 RUTH You mean you wouldn't marry George Murchison if he asked you someday? That pretty, rich thing? Honey, I knew you was odd—

BENEATHA No I would not marry him if all I felt for him was what I feel now. Besides, George's family wouldn't really like it.

MAMA Why not?

505 BENEATHA Oh, Mama—The Murchisons are honest-to-God-real-*live*-rich colored people, and the only people in the world who are more snobbish than rich white people are rich colored people. I thought everybody knew that. I've met Mrs. Murchison. She's a scene!

MAMA You must not dislike people 'cause they well off, honey.

510 BENEATHA Why not? It makes just as much sense as disliking people 'cause they are poor, and lots of people do that.

RUTH [*A wisdom-of-the-ages manner. To* MAMA] Well, she'll get over some of this—

BENEATHA Get over it? What are you talking about, Ruth? Listen, I'm going

515 to be a doctor. I'm not worried about who I'm going to marry yet—if I ever get married.

MAMA *and* RUTH If!

MAMA Now, Bennie—

BENEATHA Oh, I probably will . . . but first I'm going to be a doctor, and George,

520 for one, still thinks that's pretty funny. I couldn't be bothered with that. I am going to be a doctor and everybody around here better understand that!

MAMA [*Kindly*] 'Course you going to be a doctor, honey, God willing.

BENEATHA [*Drily*] God hasn't got a thing to do with it.

MAMA Beneatha—that just wasn't necessary.

525 BENEATHA Well—neither is God. I get sick of hearing about God.

MAMA Beneatha!

BENEATHA I mean it! I'm just tired of hearing about God all the time. What has He got to do with anything? Does he pay tuition?

MAMA You 'bout to get your fresh little jaw slapped!

530 RUTH That's just what she needs, all right!

BENEATHA Why? Why can't I say what I want to around here, like everybody else?

MAMA It don't sound nice for a young girl to say things like that—you wasn't brought up that way. Me and your father went to trouble to get you and

535 Brother to church every Sunday.

BENEATHA   Mama, you don't understand. It's all a matter of ideas, and God is just one idea I don't accept. It's not important. I am not going out and be immoral or commit crimes because I don't believe in God. I don't even think about it. It's just that I get tired of Him getting credit for all the things the human race achieves through its own stubborn effort. There simply is no blasted God—there is only man and it is *he* who makes miracles!

[MAMA *absorbs this speech, studies her daughter and rises slowly and crosses to* BENEATHA *and slaps her powerfully across the face. After, there is only silence and the daughter drops her eyes from her mother's face, and* MAMA *is very tall before her.*]

MAMA   Now—you say after me, in my mother's house there is still God. [*There is a long pause and* BENEATHA *stares at the floor wordlessly.* MAMA *repeats the phrase with precision and cool emotion.*] In my mother's house there is still God.

BENEATHA   In my mother's house there is still God.

[*A long pause*]

MAMA   [*Walking away from* BENEATHA, *too disturbed for triumphant posture. Stopping and turning back to her daughter.*]   There are some ideas we ain't going to have in this house. Not long as I am at the head of this family.

BENEATHA   Yes, ma'am.

[MAMA *walks out of the room.*]

RUTH   [*Almost gently, with profound understanding*]   You think you a woman, Bennie—but you still a little girl. What you did was childish—so you got treated like a child.

BENEATHA   I see. [*Quietly*] I also see that everybody thinks it's all right for Mama to be a tyrant. But all the tyranny in the world will never put a God in the heavens!

[*She picks up her books and goes out. Pause.*]

RUTH   [*Goes to* MAMA's *door*]   She said she was sorry.

MAMA   [*Coming out, going to her plant*]   They frightens me, Ruth. My children.

RUTH   You got good children, Lena. They just a little off sometimes—but they're good.

MAMA   No—there's something come down between me and them that don't let us understand each other and I don't know what it is. One done almost lost his mind thinking 'bout money all the time and the other done commence to talk about things I can't seem to understand in no form or fashion. What is it that's changing, Ruth.

RUTH   [*Soothingly, older than her years*]   Now . . . you taking it all too seriously. You just got strong-willed children and it takes a strong woman like you to keep 'em in hand.

MAMA   [*Looking at her plant and sprinkling a little water on it*]   They spirited all right, my children. Got to admit they got spirit—Bennie and Walter. Like this little old plant that ain't never had enough sunshine or nothing— and look at it . . .

[*She has her back to* RUTH, *who has had to stop ironing and lean against something and put the back of her hand to her forehead.*]

RUTH   [*Trying to keep* MAMA *from noticing*]   You . . . sure . . . loves that little old thing, don't you? . . .

MAMA   Well, I always wanted me a garden like I used to see sometimes at the back of the houses down home. This plant is close as I ever got to having

one. [*She looks out of the window as she replaces the plant*] Lord, ain't noth-
575 ing as dreary as the view from this window on a dreary day, is there? Why
ain't you singing this morning, Ruth? Sing that "No Ways Tired."[4] That song
always lifts me up so—[*She turns at last to see that* RUTH *has slipped quietly to
the floor, in a state of semiconsciousness.*] Ruth! Ruth honey—what's the
matter with you . . . Ruth!

Curtain

Scene Two

*It is the following morning; a Saturday morning, and house cleaning is in progress
at the* YOUNGERS. *Furniture has been shoved hither and yon and* MAMA *is giving the
kitchen-area walls a washing down.* BENEATHA, *in dungarees, with a handkerchief
tied around her face, is spraying insecticide into the cracks in the walls. As they
work, the radio is on and a Southside disk-jockey program is inappropriately filling
the house with a rather exotic saxophone blues.* TRAVIS, *the sole idle one, is leaning
on his arms, looking out of the window.*

TRAVIS   Grandmama, that stuff Bennie is using smells awful. Can I go down-
stairs, please?
MAMA   Did you get all them chores done already? I ain't seen you doing
much.
5 TRAVIS   Yes'm—finished early. Where did Mama go this morning?
MAMA [*Looking at* BENEATHA]   She had to go on a little errand.
    [*The phone rings.* BENEATHA *runs to answer it and reaches it before* WAL-
    TER, *who has entered from bedroom.*]
TRAVIS   Where?
MAMA   To tend to her business.
BENEATHA   Haylo . . . [*Disappointed*] Yes, he is. [*She tosses the phone to* WAL-
10 TER, *who barely catches it.*] It's Willie Harris again.
WALTER [*As privately as possible under* MAMA'S *gaze*]   Hello, Willie. Did you get
    the papers from the lawyer? . . . No, not yet. I told you the mailman doesn't
    get here till ten-thirty . . . No, I'll come there . . . Yeah! Right away. [*He hangs
    up and goes for his coat.*]
BENEATHA   Brother, where did Ruth go?
15 WALTER [*As he exits*]   How should I know!
TRAVIS   Aw come on, Grandma. Can I go outside?
MAMA   Oh, I guess so. You stay right in front of the house, though, and keep
    a good lookout for the postman.
TRAVIS   Yes'm. [*He darts into bedroom for stickball and bat, reenters, and sees*
    BENEATHA *on her knees spraying under sofa with behind upraised. He edges*
20 *closer to the target, takes aim, and lets her have it. She screams.*] Leave them
    poor little cockroaches alone, they ain't bothering you none! [*He runs as
    she swings the spray gun at him viciously and playfully.*] Grandma! Grandma!
MAMA   Look out there, girl, before you be spilling some of that stuff on that
    child!
25 TRAVIS [*Safely behind the bastion of* MAMA]   That's right—look out, now! [*He
    exits*]
BENEATHA [*Drily*]   I can't imagine that it would hurt him—it has never hurt
    the roaches.

4. "I Don't Feel No Ways Tired" (African American spiritual).

MAMA   Well, little boys' hides ain't as tough as Southside roaches. You better get over there behind the bureau. I seen one marching out of there like
30   Napoleon[5] yesterday.

BENEATHA   There's really only one way to get rid of them, Mama—

MAMA   How?

BENEATHA   Set fire to this building! Mama, where did Ruth go?

MAMA   [*Looking at her with meaning*]   To the doctor, I think.

35   BENEATHA   The doctor? What's the matter? [*They exchange glances.*] You don't think—

MAMA   [*With her sense of drama*]   Now I ain't saying what I think. But I ain't never been wrong 'bout a woman neither.

[*The phone rings.*]

BENEATHA   [*At the phone*]   Hay-lo . . . [*Pause, and a moment of recognition*]
40   Well—when did you get back! . . . And how was it? . . . Of course I've missed you—in my way . . . This morning? No . . . house cleaning and all that and Mama hates it if I let people come over when the house is like this . . . You *have*? Well, that's different . . . What is it—Oh, what the hell, come on over . . . Right, see you then. *Arrivederci.*[6]

[*She hangs up.*]

45   MAMA   [*Who has listened vigorously, as is her habit.*]   Who is that you inviting over here with this house looking like this? You ain't got the pride you was born with!

BENEATHA   Asagai doesn't care how houses look, Mama—he's an intellectual.

MAMA   *Who?*

50   BENEATHA   Asagai—Joseph Asagai. He's an African boy I met on campus. He's been studying in Canada all summer.

MAMA   What's his name?

BENEATHA   Asagai, Joseph. Ah-sah-guy . . . He's from Nigeria.

MAMA   Oh, that's the little country that was founded by slaves way back . . .

55   BENEATHA   No, Mama—that's Liberia.

MAMA   I don't think I never met no African before.

BENEATHA   Well, do me a favor and don't ask him a whole lot of ignorant questions about Africans. I mean, do they wear clothes and all that—

MAMA   Well, now, I guess if you think we so ignorant 'round here maybe you
60   shouldn't bring your friends here—

BENEATHA   It's just that people ask such crazy things. All anyone seems to know about when it comes to Africa is Tarzan[7]—

MAMA   [*Indignantly*]   Why should I know anything about Africa?

BENEATHA   Why do you give money at church for the missionary work?

65   MAMA   Well, that's to help save people.

BENEATHA   You mean save them from *heathenism*—

MAMA   [*Innocently*]   Yes.

BENEATHA   I'm afraid they need more salvation from the British and the French.[8]

[RUTH *comes in forlornly and pulls off her coat with dejection. They both turn to look at her.*]

---

5. That is, like Napoleon Bonaparte (1769–1821) French military leader who rose to power during the French Revolution.
6. Goodbye (Italian).
7. Fictional character raised in the African

jungle by apes in Edgar Rice Burroughs's 1912 novel, *Tarzan of the Apes.*
8. Colonial powers on the African continent from the late 1800s until the end of African independence.

RUTH [*Dispiritedly*]   Well, I guess from all the happy faces—everybody knows.

70 BENEATHA   You pregnant?

MAMA   Lord have mercy, I sure hope it's a little old girl. Travis ought to have a sister.

> [BENEATHA *and* RUTH *give her a hopeless look for this grandmotherly enthusiasm.*]

BENEATHA   How far along are you?

RUTH   Two months.

75 BENEATHA   Did you mean to? I mean did you plan it or was it an accident?

MAMA   What do you know about planning or not planning?

BENEATHA   Oh, Mama.

RUTH [*Wearily*]   She's twenty years old, Lena.

BENEATHA   Did you plan it, Ruth?

80 RUTH   Mind your own business.

BENEATHA   It is my business—where is he going to live, on the *roof?* [*There is silence following the remark as the three women react to the sense of it.*] Gee—I didn't mean that, Ruth, honest. Gee, I don't feel like that at all. I—I think it is wonderful.

RUTH [*Dully*]   Wonderful.

85 BENEATHA   Yes—really. [*There is a sudden commotion from the street and she goes to the window to look out.*] What on earth is going on out there? These kids. [*There are, as she throws open the window, the shouts of children rising up from the street. She sticks her head out to see better and calls out.*] TRAVIS! TRAVIS . . . WHAT ARE YOU DOING DOWN THERE? [*She sees.*]

90 Oh Lord, they're chasing a rat!

> [RUTH *covers her face with hands and turns away.*]

MAMA [*Angrily*]   Tell that youngun to get himself up here, at once!

BENEATHA   TRAVIS . . . YOU COME UPSTAIRS . . . AT ONCE!

RUTH [*Her face twisted*]   Chasing a rat. . . .

MAMA [*Looking at* RUTH, *worried*]   Doctor say everything going to be all

95 right?

RUTH [*Far away*]   Yes—she says everything is going to be fine . . .

MAMA [*Immediately suspicious*]   "She"—What doctor you went to?

> [RUTH *just looks at* MAMA *meaningfully and* MAMA *opens her mouth to speak as* TRAVIS *bursts in.*]

TRAVIS [*Excited and full of narrative, coming directly to his mother*]   Mama, you should of seen the rat . . . Big as a cat, honest! [*He shows an exagger-*

100 *ated size with his hands.*] Gaaleee, that rat was really cuttin' and Bubber caught him with his heel and the janitor, Mr. Barnett, got him with a stick—and then they got him in a corner and—BAM! BAM! BAM!—and he was still jumping around and bleeding like everything too—there's rat blood all over the street—

> [RUTH *reaches out suddenly and grabs her son without even looking at him and clamps her hand over his mouth and holds him to her.* MAMA *crosses to them rapidly and takes the boy from her.*]

105 MAMA   You hush up now . . . talking all that terrible stuff. . . . [TRAVIS *is staring at his mother with a stunned expression.* BENEATHA *comes quickly and takes him away from his grandmother and ushers him to the door.*]

BENEATHA You go back outside and play . . . but not with any rats. [*She pushes him gently out the door with the boy straining to see what is wrong with his mother.*]

MAMA [*Worriedly hovering over* RUTH] Ruth honey—what's the matter with you—you sick?

[RUTH *has her fists clenched on her thighs and is fighting hard to suppress a scream that seems to be rising in her.*]

BENEATHA What's the matter with her, Mama?

110 MAMA [*Working her fingers in* RUTH'S *shoulders to relax her*] She be all right. Women gets right depressed sometimes when they get her way. [*Speaking softly, expertly, rapidly*] Now you just relax. That's right . . . just lean back, don't think 'bout nothing at all . . . nothing at all—

RUTH I'm all right . . .

[*The glassy-eyed look melts and then she collapses into a fit of heavy sobbing. The bell rings.*]

115 BENEATHA Oh, my God—that must be Asagai.

MAMA [*To* RUTH] Come on now, honey. You need to lie down and rest awhile . . . then have some nice hot food.

[*They exit,* RUTH'S *weight on her mother-in-law.* BENEATHA, *herself profoundly disturbed, opens the door to admit a rather dramatic-looking young man with a large package.*]

ASAGAI Hello, Alaiyo—

BENEATHA [*Holding the door open and regarding him with pleasure*] Hello . . .
120 [*Long pause*] Well—come in. And please excuse everything. My mother was very upset about my letting anyone come here with the place like this.

ASAGAI [*Coming into the room*] You look disturbed too . . . Is something wrong?

BENEATHA [*Still at the door, absently*] Yes . . . we've all got acute ghetto-itis. [*She smiles and comes toward him, finding a cigarette and sitting.*] So—sit down! No!
125 Wait! [*She whips the spray gun off sofa where she had left it and puts the cushions back. At last perches on arm of sofa. He sits.*] So, how was Canada?

ASAGAI [*A sophisticate*] Canadian.

BENEATHA [*Looking at him*] Asagai, I'm very glad you are back.

ASAGAI [*Looking back at her in turn*] Are you really?

130 BENEATHA Yes—very.

ASAGAI Why?—you were quite glad when I went away. What happened?

BENEATHA You went away.

ASAGAI Ahhhhhhhh.

BENEATHA Before—you wanted to be so serious before there was time.

135 ASAGAI How much time must there be before one knows what one feels?

BENEATHA [*Stalling this particular conversation. Her hands pressed together, in a deliberately childish gesture.*] What did you bring me?

ASAGAI [*Handing her the package*] Open it and see.

BENEATHA [*Eagerly opening the package and drawing out some records and the colorful robes of a Nigerian woman*] Oh, Asagai! . . . You got them for me! . . . How beautiful . . . and the records too! [*She lifts out the robes and runs to the mirror with them and holds the drapery up in front of herself.*]

140 ASAGAI [*Coming to her at the mirror*] I shall have to teach you how to drape it properly. [*He flings the material about her for the moment and stands back*

to look at her.] Ah—Oh-pay-gay-day, oh-gbah-mu-shay. [A Yoruba[9] exclamation for admiration] You wear it well . . . very well . . . mutilated hair[1] and all.

145 BENEATHA [Turning suddenly]   My hair—what's wrong with my hair?

ASAGAI [Shrugging]   Were you born with it like that?

BENEATHA [Reaching up to touch it]   No . . . of course not.

[She looks back to the mirror, disturbed.]

ASAGAI [Smiling]   How then?

BENEATHA   You know perfectly well how . . . as crinkly as yours . . . that's
150   how.

ASAGAI   And it is ugly to you that way?

BENEATHA [Quickly]   Oh, no—not ugly . . . [More slowly, apologetically] But it's so hard to manage when it's, well—raw.

ASAGAI   And so to accommodate that—you mutilate it every week?

155 BENEATHA   It's not mutilation!

ASAGAI [Laughing aloud at her seriousness]   Oh . . . please! I am only teasing you because you are so very serious about these things. [He stands back from her and folds his arms across his chest as he watches her pulling at her hair and frowning in the mirror.] Do you remember the first time you met me at school? . . . [He laughs.] You came up to me and you said—and I
160   thought you were the most serious little thing I had ever seen—you said: [He imitates her.] "Mr. Asagai—I want very much to talk with you. About Africa. You see, Mr. Asagai, I am looking for my identity!"

[He laughs.]

BENEATHA [Turning to him, not laughing]   Yes—

[Her face is quizzical, profoundly disturbed]

ASAGAI [Still teasing and reaching out and taking her face in his hands and turning her profile to him]   Well . . . it is true that this is not so much a
165   profile of a Hollywood queen as perhaps a queen of the Nile[2]—[A mock dismissal of the importance of the question] But what does it matter? Assimilationism[3] is so popular in your country.

BENEATHA [Wheeling, passionately, sharply]   I am not an assimilationist!

ASAGAI [The protest hangs in the room for a moment and ASAGAI studies her, his laughter fading.]   Such a serious one. [There is a pause.] So—you like the
170   robes? You must take excellent care of them—they are from my sister's personal wardrobe.

BENEATHA [With incredulity]   You—you sent all the way home—for me?

ASAGAI [With charm]   For you—I would do much more . . . Well, that is what I came for. I must go.

175 BENEATHA   Will you call me Monday?

ASAGAI   Yes . . . We have a great deal to talk about. I mean about identity and time and all that.

BENEATHA   Time?

ASAGAI   Yes. About how much time one needs to know what one feels.

---

9. West African ethnic group centered in Nigeria and Benin.
1. That is, relaxed and straightened.
2. That is, like Cleopatra, Ptolemaic queen of

Egypt between 51 and 30 B.C.E.
3. The ideal of integrating minority groups into a dominant culture.

180 BENEATHA You see! You never understood that there is more than one kind of feeling which can exist between a man and a woman—or, at least, there should be.

ASAGAI [*Shaking his head negatively but gently*] No. Between a man and a woman there need be only one kind of feeling. I have that for you . . . Now
185 even . . . right this moment . . .

BENEATHA I know—and by itself—it won't do. I can find that anywhere.

ASAGAI For a woman it should be enough.

BENEATHA I know—because that's what it says in all the novels that men write. But it isn't. Go ahead and laugh—but I'm not interested in being
190 someone's little episode in America or—[*With feminine vengeance*]—one of them! [ASAGAI *has burst into laughter again.*] That's funny as hell, huh!

ASAGAI It's just that every American girl I have known has said that to me. White—black—in this you are all the same. And the same speech, too!

BENEATHA [*Angrily*] Yuk, yuk, yuk!

195 ASAGAI It's how you can be sure that the world's most liberated women are not liberated at all. You all talk about it too much!

[MAMA *enters and is immediately all social charm because of the presence of a guest.*]

BENEATHA Oh—Mama—this is Mr. Asagai.

MAMA How do you do?

ASAGAI [*Total politeness to an elder*] How do you do, Mrs. Younger. Please
200 forgive me for coming at such an outrageous hour on a Saturday.

MAMA Well, you are quite welcome. I just hope you understand that our house don't always look like this. [*Chatterish*] You must come again. I would love to hear all about—[*Not sure of the name*]—your country. I think it's so sad the way our American Negroes don't know nothing about Africa
205 'cept Tarzan and all that. And all that money they pour into these churches when they ought to be helping you people over there drive out them French and Englishmen done taken away your land.

[*The mother flashes a slightly superior look at her daughter upon completion of the recitation.*]

ASAGAI [*Taken aback by this sudden and acutely unrelated expression of sympathy*] Yes . . . yes . . .

MAMA [*Smiling at him suddenly and relaxing and looking him over*] How
210 many miles is it from here to where you come from?

ASAGAI Many thousands.

MAMA [*Looking at him as she would* WALTER] I bet you don't half look after yourself, being away from your mama either. I spec you better come 'round here from time to time to get yourself some decent home-cooked meals . . .

215 ASAGAI [*Moved*] Thank you. Thank you very much. [*They are all quiet, then*—] Well . . . I must go. I will call you Monday, Alaiyo.

MAMA What's that he call you?

ASAGAI Oh—"Alaiyo." I hope you don't mind. It is what you would call a nickname, I think. It is a Yoruba word. I am a Yoruba.

220 MAMA [*Looking at* BENEATHA] I—I thought he was from—[*Uncertain*]

ASAGAI [*Understanding*] Nigeria is my country. Yoruba is my tribal origin—

BENEATHA You didn't tell us what Alaiyo means . . . for all I know, you might be calling me Little Idiot or something . . .

ASAGAI   Well . . . let me see . . . I do not know how just to explain it . . . The
225   sense of a thing can be so different when it changes languages.

BENEATHA   You're evading.

ASAGAI   No—really it is difficult . . . [*Thinking*] It means . . . it means One for
Whom Bread—Food—Is Not Enough. [*He looks at her.*] Is that all right?

BENEATHA [*Understanding, softly*]   Thank you.

230   MAMA [*Looking from one to the other and not understanding any of it*]   Well . . .
that's nice . . . You must come see us again—Mr.——

ASAGAI   Ah-sah-guy . . .

MAMA   Yes . . . Do come again.

ASAGAI   Good-bye.

[*He exits*]

235   MAMA [*After him*]   Lord, that's a pretty thing just went out here! [*Insinuatingly, to her daughter*] Yes, I guess I see why we done commence to get so
interested in Africa 'round here. Missionaries my aunt Jenny!

[*She exits*]

BENEATHA   Oh, Mama! . . .

[*She picks up the Nigerian dress and holds it up to her in front of the
mirror again. She sets the headdress on haphazardly and then notices her
hair again and clutches at it and then replaces the headdress and frowns
at herself. Then she starts to wriggle in front of the mirror as she thinks a
Nigerian woman might.* TRAVIS *enters and stands regarding her.*]

TRAVIS   What's the matter, girl, you cracking up?

240   BENEATHA   Shut up.

[*She pulls the headdress off and looks at herself in the mirror and
clutches at her hair again and squinches her eyes as if trying to imagine
something. Then, suddenly, she gets her raincoat and kerchief and hurriedly prepares for going out.*]

MAMA [*Coming back into the room*]   She's resting now. Travis, baby, run next
door and ask Miss Johnson to please let me have a little kitchen cleanser.
This here can is empty as Jacob's kettle.

TRAVIS   I just came in.

245   MAMA   Do as you told. [*He exits and she looks at her daughter.*] Where you
going?

BENEATHA [*Halting at the door*]   To become a queen of the Nile!

[*She exits in a breathless blaze of glory.* RUTH *appears in the bedroom
doorway.*]

MAMA   Who told you to get up?

RUTH   Ain't nothing wrong with me to be lying in no bed for. Where did Ben-
250   nie go?

MAMA [*Drumming her fingers*]   Far as I could make out—to Egypt. [RUTH *just
looks at her.*] What time is it getting to?

RUTH   Ten twenty. And the mailman going to ring that bell this morning just
like he done every morning for the last umpteen years.

[TRAVIS *comes in with the cleanser can.*]

255   TRAVIS   She say to tell you that she don't have much.

MAMA [*Angrily*]   Lord, some people I could name sure is tight-fisted! [*Directing her grandson*] Mark two cans of cleanser down on the list there. If she

that hard up for kitchen cleanser, I sure don't want to forget to get her none!

260 RUTH   Lena—maybe the woman is just short on cleanser—

MAMA [*Not listening*]   —Much baking powder as she done borrowed from me all these years, she could of done gone into the baking business!

> [*The bell sounds suddenly and sharply and all three are stunned—serious and silent—mid-speech. In spite of all the other conversations and distractions of the morning, this is what they have been waiting for, even* TRAVIS *who looks helplessly from his mother to his grandmother.* RUTH *is the first to come to life again.*]

RUTH [*To* TRAVIS]   Get down them steps, boy!

> [TRAVIS *snaps to life and flies out to get the mail.*]

MAMA [*Her eyes wide, her hand to her breast*]   You mean it done really come?

265 RUTH [*Excited*]   Oh, Miss Lena!

MAMA [*Collecting herself*]   Well . . . I don't know what we all so excited about 'round here for. We known it was coming for months.

RUTH   That's a whole lot different from having it come and being able to hold it in your hands . . . a piece of paper worth ten thousand dollars . . . [TRAVIS *bursts back into the room. He holds the envelope high above his head, like a little dancer, his face is radiant and he is breathless. He moves to his grandmother with sudden slow ceremony and puts the envelope into her*

270 *hands. She accepts it, and then merely holds it and looks at it.*] Come on! Open it . . . Lord have mercy, I wish Walter Lee was here!

TRAVIS   Open it, Grandmama!

MAMA [*Staring at it*]   Now you all be quiet. It's just a check.

RUTH   Open it . . .

275 MAMA [*Still staring at it*]   Now don't act silly . . . We ain't never been no people to act silly 'bout no money—

RUTH [*Swiftly*]   We ain't never had none before—OPEN IT!

> [MAMA *finally makes a good strong tear and pulls out the thin blue slice of paper and inspects it closely. The boy and his mother study it raptly over* MAMA's *shoulders.*]

MAMA   Travis! [*She is counting off with doubt.*] Is that the right number of zeros?

280 TRAVIS   Yes'm . . . ten thousand dollars. Gaalee, Grandmama, you rich.

MAMA [*She holds the check away from her, still looking at it. Slowly her face sobers into a mask of unhappiness.*]   Ten thousand dollars. [*She hands it to* RUTH.] Put it away somewhere, Ruth. [*She does not look at* RUTH; *her eyes seem to be seeing something somewhere very far off.*] Ten thousand dollars they give you. Ten thousand dollars.

285 TRAVIS [*To his mother, sincerely*]   What's the matter with Grandmama—don't she want to be rich?

RUTH [*Distractedly*]   You go on out and play now, baby. [TRAVIS *exits.* MAMA *starts wiping dishes absently, humming intently to herself.* RUTH *turns to her, with kind exasperation.*] You've gone and got yourself upset.

MAMA [*Not looking at her*]   I spec if it wasn't for you all . . . I would just put

290 that money away or give it to the church or something.

RUTH   Now what kind of talk is that. Mr. Younger would just be plain mad if he could hear you talking foolish like that.

MAMA [*Stopping and staring off*] Yes . . . he sure would. [*Sighing*] We got enough to do with that money, all right. [*She halts then, and turns and looks at her daughter-in-law hard;* RUTH *avoids her eyes and* MAMA *wipes her hands*
295 *with finality and starts to speak firmly to* RUTH.] Where did you go today, girl?

RUTH To the doctor.

MAMA [*Impatiently*] Now, Ruth . . . you know better than that. Old Doctor Jones is strange enough in his way but there ain't nothing 'bout him make somebody slip and call him "she"—like you done this morning.

300 RUTH Well, that's what happened—my tongue slipped.

MAMA You went to see that woman, didn't you?

RUTH [*Defensively, giving herself away*] What woman you talking about?

MAMA [*Angrily*] That woman who—

[WALTER *enters in great excitement.*]

WALTER Did it come?

305 MAMA [*Quietly*] Can't you give people a Christian greeting before you start asking about money?

WALTER [*To* RUTH] Did it come? [RUTH *unfolds the check and lays it quietly before him, watching him intently with thoughts of her own.* WALTER *sits down and grasps it close and counts off the zeros.*] Ten thousand dollars—[*He turns suddenly, frantically to his mother and draws some papers out of his breast pocket.*] Mama—look. Old Willy Harris put everything on paper—

310 MAMA Son—I think you ought to talk to your wife . . . I'll go on out and leave you alone if you want—

WALTER I can talk to her later—Mama, look—

MAMA Son—

WALTER WILL SOMEBODY PLEASE LISTEN TO ME TODAY!

315 MAMA [*Quietly*] I don't 'low no yellin' in this house, Walter Lee, and you know it—[WALTER *stares at them in frustration and starts to speak several times.*] And there ain't going to be no investing in no liquor stores.

WALTER But, Mama, you ain't even looked at it.

MAMA I don't aim to have to speak on that again. [*A long pause*]

320 WALTER You ain't looked at it and you don't aim to have to speak on that again? You ain't even looked at it and *you* have decided—[*Crumpling his papers*] Well, *you* tell that to my boy tonight when you put him to sleep on the living-room couch . . . [*Turning to* MAMA *and speaking directly to her*] Yeah—and tell it to my wife, Mama, tomorrow when she has to go out of
325 here to look after somebody else's kids. And tell it to *me*, Mama, every time we need a new pair of curtains and I have to watch *you* go out and work in somebody's kitchen. Yeah, you tell me then! [WALTER *starts out.*]

RUTH Where you going?

WALTER I'm going out!

330 RUTH Where?

WALTER Just out of this house somewhere—

RUTH [*Getting her coat*] I'll come too.

WALTER I don't want you to come!

RUTH I got something to talk to you about, Walter.

335 WALTER That's too bad.

MAMA [*Still quietly*] Walter Lee—[*She waits and he finally turns and looks at her.*] Sit down.

WALTER I'm a grown man, Mama.

MAMA Ain't nobody said you wasn't grown. But you still in my house and my
340 presence. And as long as you are—you'll talk to your wife civil. Now sit
down.

RUTH [*Suddenly*] Oh, let him go on out and drink himself to death! He
makes me sick to my stomach! [*She flings her coat against him and exits to
bedroom.*]

WALTER [*Violently flinging the coat after her*] And you turn mine too, baby!
345 [*The door slams behind her.*] That was my biggest mistake—

MAMA [*Still quietly*] Walter, what is the matter with you?

WALTER Matter with me? Ain't nothing the matter with *me*!

MAMA Yes there is. Something eating you up like a crazy man. Something
more than me not giving you this money. The past few years I been watch-
350 ing it happen to you. You get all nervous acting and kind of wild in the
eyes—[WALTER *jumps up impatiently at her words.*] I said sit there now, I'm
talking to you!

WALTER Mama—I don't need no nagging at me today.

MAMA Seem like you getting to a place where you always tied up in some
355 kind of knot about something. But if anybody ask you 'bout it you just yell
at 'em and bust out the house and go out and drink somewheres. Walter
Lee, people can't live with that. Ruth's a good, patient girl in her way—but
you getting to be too much. Boy, don't make the mistake of driving that girl
away from you.

360 WALTER Why—what she do for me?

MAMA She loves you.

WALTER Mama—I'm going out. I want to go off somewhere and be by myself
for a while.

MAMA I'm sorry 'bout your liquor store, son. It just wasn't the thing for us to
365 do. That's what I want to tell you about—

WALTER I got to go out, Mama—
[*He rises.*]

MAMA It's dangerous, son.

WALTER What's dangerous?

MAMA When a man goes outside his home to look for peace.

370 WALTER [*Beseechingly*] Then why can't there never be no peace in this
house then?

MAMA You done found it in some other house?

WALTER No—there ain't no woman! Why do women always think there's a
woman somewhere when a man gets restless. [*Picks up the check*] Do you
375 know what this money means to me? Do you know what this money can do
for us? [*Puts it back*] Mama—Mama—I want so many things . . .

MAMA Yes, son—

WALTER I want so many things that they are driving me kind of crazy . . .
Mama—look at me.

380 MAMA I'm looking at you. You a good-looking boy. You got a job, a nice wife,
a fine boy and—

WALTER A job. [*Looks at her*] Mama, a job? I open and close car doors all day
long. I drive a man around in his limousine and I say, "Yes, sir; no, sir; very
good, sir; shall I take the Drive, sir?" Mama, that ain't no kind of job . . .
385 that ain't nothing at all. [*Very quietly*] Mama, I don't know if I can make
you understand.

MAMA Understand what, baby?

WALTER [*Quietly*] Sometimes it's like I can see the future stretched out in
front of me—just plain as day. The future, Mama. Hanging over there at
390 the edge of my days. Just waiting for me—a big, looming blank space—full
of *nothing*. Just waiting for *me*. But it don't have to be. [*Pause. Kneeling
beside her chair.*] Mama—sometimes when I'm downtown and I pass them
cool, quiet-looking restaurants where them white boys are sitting back and
talking 'bout things . . . sitting there turning deals worth millions of dol-
395 lars . . . sometimes I see guys don't look much older than me—

MAMA Son—how come you talk so much 'bout money?

WALTER [*With immense passion*] Because it is life, Mama!

MAMA [*Quietly*] Oh—[*Very quietly*] So now it's life. Money is life. Once
upon a time freedom used to be life—now it's money. I guess the world
400 really do change . . .

WALTER No—it was always money, Mama. We just didn't know about it.

MAMA No . . . something has changed. [*She looks at him.*] You something
new, boy. In my time we was worried about not being lynched and getting
to the North if we could and how to stay alive and still have a pinch of dig-
405 nity too . . . Now here come you and Beneatha—talking 'bout things we
ain't never even thought about hardly, me and your daddy. You ain't satisfied or proud of nothing we done. I mean that you had a home; that we
kept you out of trouble till you was grown; that you don't have to ride to
work on the back of nobody's streetcar—You my children—but how differ-
410 ent we done become.

WALTER [*A long beat. He pats her hand and gets up.*] You just don't understand, Mama, you just don't understand.

MAMA Son—do you know your wife is expecting another baby? [WALTER
stands, stunned, and absorbs what his mother has said.] That's what she
415 wanted to talk to you about. [WALTER *sinks down into a chair.*] This ain't for
me to be telling—but you ought to know. [*She waits.*] I think Ruth is thinking 'bout getting rid of that child.

WALTER [*Slowly understanding*] No—no—Ruth wouldn't do that.

MAMA When the world gets ugly enough—a woman will do anything for her
420 family. *The part that's already living.*

WALTER You don't know Ruth, Mama, if you think she would do that.

[RUTH *opens the bedroom door and stands there a little limp.*]

RUTH [*Beaten*] Yes I would too, Walter. [*Pause*] I gave her a five-dollar down
payment.

[*There is total silence as the man stares at his wife and the mother stares
at her son.*]

MAMA [*Presently*] Well—[*Tightly*] Well—son, I'm waiting to hear you say
425 something . . . [*She waits.*] I'm waiting to hear how you be your father's
son. Be the man he was . . . [*Pause. The silence shouts.*] Your wife say she
going to destroy your child. And I'm waiting to hear you talk like him and
say we a people who give children life, not who destroys them—[*She rises.*]
I'm waiting to see you stand up and look like your daddy and say we done
430 give up one baby to poverty and that we ain't going to give up nary another
one . . . I'm waiting.

WALTER Ruth—[*He can say nothing.*]

MAMA   If you a son of mine, tell her! [WALTER *picks up his keys and his coat and walks out. She continues, bitterly.*] You . . . you are a disgrace to your
435   father's memory. Somebody get me my hat!

Curtain

ACT II

Scene One

Time: Later the same day.

At rise: RUTH *is ironing again. She has the radio going. Presently* BENEATHA'S *bedroom door opens and* RUTH'S *mouth falls and she puts down the iron in fascination.*

RUTH   What have we got on tonight!

BENEATHA [*Emerging grandly from the doorway so that we can see her thoroughly robed in the costume Asagai brought*]   You are looking at what a well-dressed Nigerian woman wears—[*She parades for* RUTH, *her hair completely hidden by the headdress; she is coquettishly fanning herself with an ornate oriental fan, mistakenly more like Butterfly*[4] *than any Nigerian that ever was.*] Isn't it beautiful? [*She promenades to the radio and, with an arro-*
5   *gant flourish, turns off the good loud blues that is playing.*] Enough of this assimilationist junk! [RUTH *follows her with her eyes as she goes to the phonograph and puts on a record and turns and waits ceremoniously for the music to come up. Then, with a shout—*] OCOMOGOSIAY!

[RUTH *jumps. The music comes up, a lovely Nigerian melody.* BENEATHA *listens, enraptured, her eyes far away—"back to the past." She begins to dance.* RUTH *is dumbfounded*].

RUTH   What kind of dance is that?

BENEATHA   A folk dance.

10   RUTH [*Pearl Bailey*][5]   What kind of folks do that, honey?

BENEATHA   It's from Nigeria. It's a dance of welcome.

RUTH   Who you welcoming?

BENEATHA   The men back to the village.

RUTH   Where they been?

15   BENEATHA   How should I know—out hunting or something. Anyway, they are coming back now . . .

RUTH   Well, that's good.

BENEATHA [*With the record*]
Alundi, alundi
Alundi alunya
20   *Jop pu a jeepua*
Ang gu soooooooooo

Ai yai yae . . .
Ayehaye—alundi . . .

[WALTER *comes in during this performance; he has obviously been drinking. He leans against the door heavily and watches his sister, at first with*

4. Title character of Giacomo Puccini's 1904 opera *Madame Butterfly*, which is set in Japan.

5. Prominent African American entertainer and singer (1918–1990) known for her wry humor.

*distaste. Then his eyes look off—"back to the past"—as he lifts both his
fists to the roof, screaming.*]

WALTER YEAH . . . AND ETHIOPIA STRETCH FORTH HER HANDS
25 AGAIN![6] . . .

RUTH [*Drily, looking at him*] Yes—and Africa sure is claiming her own
tonight. [*She gives them both up and starts ironing again.*]

WALTER [*All in a drunken, dramatic shout*] Shut up! . . . I'm digging them
drums . . . them drums move me! . . . [*He makes his weaving way to his
30 wife's face and leans in close to her.*] In my *heart of hearts*—[*He thumps his
chest.*]—I am much warrior!

RUTH [*Without even looking up*] In your heart of hearts you are much
drunkard.

WALTER [*Coming away from her and starting to wander around the room,
shouting*] Me and Jomo . . . [*Intently, in his sister's face. She has stopped
35 dancing to watch him in this unknown mood.*] That's my man, Kenyatta.[7]
[*Shouting and thumping his chest.*] FLAMING SPEAR! HOT DAMN! [*He
is suddenly in possession of an imaginary spear and actively spearing enemies
all over the room.*] OCOMOGOSIAY . . .

BENEATHA [*To encourage WALTER, thoroughly caught up with this side of
him*] OCOMOGOSIAY, FLAMING SPEAR!

40 WALTER THE LION IS WAKING . . . OWIMOWEH! [*He pulls his shirt
open and leaps up on the table and gestures with his spear.*]

BENEATHA OWIMOWEH!

WALTER [*On the table, very far gone, his eyes pure glass sheets. He sees what we
cannot, that he is a leader of his people, a great chief, a descendant of
Chaka,[8] and that the hour to march has come.*] Listen, my black brothers—

BENEATHA OCOMOGOSIAY!

WALTER —Do you hear the waters rushing against the shores of the coast
45 lands—

BENEATHA OCOMOGOSIAY!

WALTER —Do you hear the screeching of the cocks in yonder hills beyond
where the chiefs meet in council for the coming of the mighty war—

BENEATHA OCOMOGOSIAY!

[*And now the lighting shifts subtly to suggest the world of WALTER's imagination, and the mood shifts from pure comedy. It is the inner WALTER
speaking: the Southside chauffeur has assumed an unexpected majesty.*]

50 WALTER —Do you hear the beating of the wings of the birds flying low over
the mountains and the low places of our land—

BENEATHA OCOMOGOSIAY!

WALTER —Do you hear the singing of the women, singing the war songs of
our fathers to the babies in the great houses? Singing the sweet war songs!
55 [*The doorbell rings.*] OH, DO YOU HEAR, MY BLACK BROTHERS!

BENEATHA [*Completely gone*] We hear you, Flaming Spear—

[*RUTH shuts off the phonograph and opens the door. GEORGE MURCHISON
enters.*]

6. "Princes shall come out of Egypt; Ethiopia
shall soon stretch out her hands unto God"
(Psalms 68.31). Ethiopia is located in the
horn of Africa.
7. Jomo Kenyatta (1894–1978), African
political leader and nationalist, first president

of Kenya (1964–78) after it gained independence from Great Britain.
8. Zulu chief (1787–1828), also known as
"Shaka," one of the most powerful warrior-
leaders of the Zulu Kingdom in southern
Africa.

WALTER   Telling us to prepare for the GREATNESS OF THE TIME! [*Lights back to normal. He turns and sees* GEORGE.] Black Brother!

[*He extends his hand for the fraternal clasp.*]

GEORGE   Black Brother, hell!

60 RUTH [*Having had enough, and embarrassed for the family*]   Beneatha, you got company—what's the matter with you? Walter Lee Younger, get down off that table and stop acting like a fool . . .

[WALTER *comes down off the table suddenly and makes a quick exit to the bathroom.*]

RUTH   He's had a little to drink . . . I don't know what her excuse is.

GEORGE [*To* BENEATHA]   Look honey, we're going *to* the theatre—we're not 65 going to be *in* it . . . so go change, huh?

[BENEATHA *looks at him and slowly, ceremoniously, lifts her hands and pulls off the headdress. Her hair is close-cropped and unstraightened.* GEORGE *freezes mid-sentence and* RUTH'S *eyes all but fan out of her head.*]

GEORGE   What in the name of—

RUTH [*Touching* BENEATHA'S *hair*]   Girl, you done lost your natural mind!? Look at your head!

GEORGE   What have you done to your head—I mean your hair!

70 BENEATHA   Nothing—except cut it off.

RUTH   Now that's the truth—it's what ain't been done to it! You expect this boy to go out with you with your head all nappy like that?

BENEATHA [*Looking at* GEORGE]   That's up to George. If he's ashamed of his heritage—

75 GEORGE   Oh, don't be so proud of yourself, Bennie—just because you look eccentric.

BENEATHA   How can something that's natural be eccentric?

GEORGE   That's what being eccentric means—being natural. Get dressed.

BENEATHA   I don't like that, George.

80 RUTH   Why must you and your brother make an argument out of everything people say?

BENEATHA   Because I hate assimilationist Negroes!

RUTH   Will somebody please tell me what assimila-whoever means!

GEORGE   Oh, it's just a college girl's way of calling people Uncle Toms[9]—but 85 that isn't what it means at all.

RUTH   Well, what does it mean?

BENEATHA [*Cutting* GEORGE *off and staring at him as she replies to* RUTH]   It means someone who is willing to give up his own culture and submerge himself completely in the dominant, and in this case *oppressive* culture!

90 GEORGE   Oh, dear, dear, dear! Here we go! A lecture on the African past! On our Great West African Heritage! In one second we will hear all about the great Ashanti empires; the great Songhay civilizations; and the great sculpture of Bénin—and then some poetry in the Bantu[1]—and the whole monologue will

---

9. Disparaging term for African Americans who act subservient to white people, based on the slave in Harriet Beecher Stowe's 1852 novel *Uncle Tom's Cabin.*

1. Language family shared by ethnic groups living in central and southern Africa. *Ashanti:* precolonial empire occupying what is now Ghana in the 18th and 19th centuries. *Songhay:* precolonial empire occupying an area from Nigeria and Mali to the Atlantic Ocean in the 15th and 16th centuries. *Bénin:* precolonial kingdom located in present-day Benin and Nigeria between the 13th and 19th centuries and famous for its magnificently executed brass sculptures and plaques.

end with the word *heritage!* [*Nastily*] Let's face it, baby, your heritage is nothing but a bunch of raggedy-assed spirituals and some grass huts!

BENEATHA   GRASS HUTS! [RUTH *crosses to her and forcibly pushes her toward
the bedroom.*] See there . . . you are standing there in your splendid ignorance talking about people who were the first to smelt iron on the face of
the earth! [RUTH *is pushing her through the door.*] The Ashanti were per
forming surgical operations when the English—[RUTH *pulls the door to,
with* BENEATHA *on the other side, and smiles graciously at* GEORGE. BENEATHA
opens the door and shouts the end of the sentence defiantly at GEORGE.]—
were still tattooing themselves with blue dragons![2] [*She goes back inside.*]

RUTH   Have a seat, George [*They both sit.* RUTH *folds her hands rather primly
on her lap, determined to demonstrate the civilization of the family.*] Warm,
ain't it? I mean for September. [*Pause*] Just like they always say about Chicago weather: If it's too hot or cold for you, just wait a minute and it'll
change. [*She smiles happily at this cliché of clichés.*] Everybody say it's got
to do with them bombs and things they keep setting off. [*Pause*] Would you
like a nice cold beer?

GEORGE   No, thank you. I don't care for beer. [*He looks at his watch.*] I hope
she hurries up.

RUTH   What time is the show?

GEORGE   It's an eight-thirty curtain. That's just Chicago, though. In New
York standard curtain time is eight forty.

    [*He is rather proud of this knowledge.*]

RUTH [*Properly appreciating it*]   You get to New York a lot?

GEORGE [*Offhand*]   Few times a year.

RUTH   Oh—that's nice. I've never been to New York.

    [WALTER *enters. We feel he has relieved himself, but the edge of unreality
    is still with him.*]

WALTER   New York ain't got nothing Chicago ain't. Just a bunch of hustling
people all squeezed up together—being "Eastern."

    [*He turns his face into a screw of displeasure.*]

GEORGE   Oh—you've been?

WALTER   *Plenty* of times.

RUTH [*Shocked at the lie*]   Walter Lee Younger!

WALTER [*Staring her down*]   Plenty! [*Pause*] What we got to drink in this
house? Why don't you offer this man some refreshment. [*To* GEORGE] They
don't know how to entertain people in this house, man.

GEORGE   Thank you—I don't really care for anything.

WALTER [*Feeling his head; sobriety coming*]   Where's Mama?

RUTH   She ain't come back yet.

WALTER [*Looking* MURCHISON *over from head to toe, scrutinizing his carefully
casual tweed sports jacket over cashmere V-neck sweater over soft eyelet shirt
and tie, and soft slacks, finished off with white buckskin shoes*] Why all you
college boys wear them faggoty-looking white shoes?

RUTH   Walter Lee!

    [GEORGE MURCHISON *ignores the remark.*]

---

2. Reference to the blue tattoos worn by Celtic warriors in the British Isles, made using woad,
a plant that produces blue dye.

WALTER [*To* RUTH] Well, they look crazy as hell—white shoes, cold as it is.

RUTH [*Crushed*] You have to excuse him—

WALTER No he don't! Excuse me for what? What you always excusing me for! I'll excuse myself when I needs to be excused! [*A pause*] They look as 135 funny as them black knee socks Beneatha wears out of here all the time.

RUTH It's the college *style*, Walter.

WALTER Style, hell. She looks like she got burnt legs or something!

RUTH Oh, Walter—

WALTER [*An irritable mimic*] Oh, Walter! Oh, Walter! [*To* MURCHISON] How's 140 your old man making out? I understand you all going to buy that big hotel on the Drive?[3] [*He finds a beer in the refrigerator, wanders over to* MURCHISON, *sipping and wiping his lips with the back of his hand, and straddling a chair backwards to talk to the other man.*] Shrewd move. Your old man is all right, man. [*Tapping his head and half winking for emphasis*] I mean he knows how to operate. I mean he thinks *big*, you know what I mean, I mean for a *home*, 145 you know? But I think he's kind of running out of ideas now. I'd like to talk to him. Listen, man, I got some plans that could turn this city upside down. I mean think like he does. *Big*. Invest big, gamble big, hell, lose *big* if you have to, you know what I mean. It's hard to find a man on this whole Southside who understands my kind of thinking—you dig? [*He scrutinizes* MURCHI-SON *again, drinks his beer, squints his eyes and leans in close, confidential, man* 150 *to man*] Me and you ought to sit down and talk sometimes, man. Man, I got me some ideas . . .

GEORGE [*With boredom*] Yeah—sometimes we'll have to do that, Walter.

WALTER [*Understanding the indifference, and offended*] Yeah—well, when you get the time, man. I know you a busy little boy.

155 RUTH Walter, please—

WALTER [*Bitterly, hurt*] I know ain't nothing in this world as busy as you colored college boys with your fraternity pins and white shoes . . .

RUTH [*Covering her face with humiliation*] Oh, Walter Lee—

WALTER I see you all all the time—with the books tucked under your arms— 160 going to your [*British A*—*a mimic*] "clahsses." And for what! What the hell you learning over there? Filling up your heads—[*Counting off on his fingers*]—with the sociology and the psychology—but they teaching you how to be a man? How to take over and run the world? They teaching you how to run a rubber plantation or a steel mill? Naw—just to talk proper and 165 read books and wear them faggoty-looking white shoes . . .

GEORGE [*Looking at him with distaste, a little above it all*] You're all wacked up with bitterness, man.

WALTER [*Intently, almost quietly, between the teeth, glaring at the boy*] And you—ain't you bitter, man? Ain't you just about had it yet? Don't you see no 170 stars gleaming that you can't reach out and grab? You happy?—You contented son-of-a-bitch—you happy? You got it made? Bitter? Man, I'm a volcano. Bitter? Here I am a giant—surrounded by ants! Ants who can't even understand what it is the giant is talking about.

RUTH [*Passionately and suddenly*] Oh, Walter—ain't you with nobody!

175 WALTER [*Violently*] No! 'Cause ain't nobody with me! Not even my own mother!

---

3. Lake Shore Drive, an expressway that runs through Chicago along the Lake Michigan shore.

RUTH   Walter, that's a terrible thing to say!

> [BENEATHA *enters, dressed for the evening in a cocktail dress and earrings, hair natural*]

GEORGE   Well—hey—[*Crosses to* BENEATHA; *thoughtful, with emphasis, since this is a reversal*] You look great!

180   WALTER   [*Seeing his sister's hair for the first time*]   What's the matter with your head?

BENEATHA   [*Tired of the jokes now*]   I cut it off, Brother.

WALTER   [*Coming close to inspect it and walking around her*]   Well, I'll be damned. So that's what they mean by the African bush . . .

185   BENEATHA   Ha ha. Let's go, George.

GEORGE   [*Looking at her*]   You know something? I like it. It's sharp. I mean it really is. [*Helps her into her wrap*]

RUTH   Yes—I think so, too. [*She goes to the mirror and starts to clutch at her hair.*]

WALTER   Oh no! You leave yours alone, baby. You might turn out to have a

190   pin-shaped head or something!

BENEATHA   See you all later.

RUTH   Have a nice time.

GEORGE   Thanks. Good night. [*Half out the door, he reopens it. To* WALTER] Good night, Prometheus![4]

> [BENEATHA *and* GEORGE *exit*]

195   WALTER   [*To* RUTH]   Who is Prometheus?

RUTH   I don't know. Don't worry about it.

WALTER   [*In fury, pointing after* GEORGE]   See there—they get to a point where they can't insult you man to man—they got to go talk about something ain't nobody never heard of!

200   RUTH   How do you know it was an insult? [*To humor him*] Maybe Prometheus is a nice fellow.

WALTER   Prometheus! I bet there ain't even no such thing! I bet that simpleminded clown—

RUTH   Walter—

> [*She stops what she is doing and looks at him.*]

205   WALTER   [*Yelling*]   Don't start!

RUTH   Start what?

WALTER   Your nagging! Where was I? Who was I with? How much money did I spend?

RUTH   [*Plaintively*]   Walter Lee—why don't we just try to talk about it . . .

210   WALTER   [*Not listening*]   I been out talking with people who understand me. People who care about the things I got on my mind.

RUTH   [*Wearily*]   I guess that means people like Willy Harris.

WALTER   Yes, people like Willy Harris.

RUTH   [*With a sudden flash of impatience*]   Why don't you all just hurry up

215   and go into the banking business and stop talking about it!

WALTER   Why? You want to know why? 'Cause we all tied up in a race of people that don't know how to do nothing but moan, pray and have babies!

> [*The line is too bitter even for him and he looks at her and sits down.*]

---

4. Titan in Greek mythology who stole fire from the gods and gave it to humans.

RUTH   Oh, Walter . . . [*Softly*] Honey, why can't you stop fighting me?

WALTER [*Without thinking*]   Who's fighting you? Who even cares about you?
[*This line begins the retardation of his mood.*]

220 RUTH   Well—[*She waits a long time, and then with resignation starts to put away her things.*] I guess I might as well go on to bed . . . [*More or less to herself*] I don't know where we lost it . . . but we have . . . [*Then, to him*] I—I'm sorry about this new baby, Walter. I guess maybe I better go on and do what I started . . . I guess I just didn't realize how bad things was with 225 us . . . I guess I just didn't really realize—[*She starts out to the bedroom and stops.*] You want some hot milk?

WALTER   Hot milk?

RUTH   Yes—hot milk.

WALTER   Why hot milk?

230 RUTH   'Cause after all that liquor you come home with you ought to have something hot in your stomach.

WALTER   I don't want no milk.

RUTH   You want some coffee then?

WALTER   No, I don't want no coffee. I don't want nothing hot to drink.
235 [*Almost plaintively*] Why you always trying to give me something to eat?

RUTH [*Standing and looking at him helplessly*]   What else can I give you, Walter Lee Younger?

[*She stands and looks at him and presently turns to go out again. He lifts his head and watches her going away from him in a new mood which began to emerge when he asked her "Who cares about you?"*]

WALTER   It's been rough, ain't it, baby? [*She hears and stops but does not turn around and he continues to her back.*] I guess between two people there 240 ain't never as much understood as folks generally thinks there is. I mean like between me and you—[*She turns to face him*] How we gets to the place where we scared to talk softness to each other. [*He waits, thinking hard himself.*] Why you think it got to be like that? [*He is thoughtful, almost as a child would be.*] Ruth, what is it gets into people ought to be close?

245 RUTH   I don't know, honey. I think about it a lot.

WALTER   On account of you and me, you mean? The way things are with us. The way something done come down between us.

RUTH   There ain't so much between us, Walter . . . Not when you come to me and try to talk to me. Try to be with me . . . a little even.

250 WALTER [*Total honesty*]   Sometimes . . . sometimes . . . I don't even know how to try.

RUTH   Walter—

WALTER   Yes?

RUTH [*Coming to him, gently and with misgiving, but coming to him*]   Honey . . . 255 life don't have to be like this. I mean sometimes people can do things so that things are better . . . You remember how we used to talk when Travis was born . . . about the way we were going to live . . . the kind of house . . . [*She is stroking his head.*] Well, it's all starting to slip away from us . . .

[*He turns her to him and they look at each other and kiss, tenderly and hungrily. The door opens and* MAMA *enters—*WALTER *breaks away and jumps up. A beat.*]

WALTER   Mama, where have you been?

260 MAMA   My—them steps is longer than they used to be. Whew! [*She sits down and ignores him.*] How you feeling this evening, Ruth?

[RUTH *shrugs, disturbed at having been interrupted and watching her husband knowingly.*]

WALTER   Mama, where have you been all day?

MAMA [*Still ignoring him and leaning on the table and changing to more comfortable shoes*]   Where's Travis?

RUTH   I let him go out earlier and he ain't come back yet. Boy, is he going to
265 get it!

WALTER   Mama!

MAMA [*As if she has heard him for the first time*]   Yes, son?

WALTER   Where did you go this afternoon?

MAMA   I went downtown to tend to some business that I had to tend to.

270 WALTER   What kind of business?

MAMA   You know better than to question me like a child, Brother.

WALTER [*Rising and bending over the table*]   Where were you, Mama? [*Bringing his fists down and shouting*] Mama, you didn't go do something with that insurance money, something crazy?

[*The front door opens slowly, interrupting him, and* TRAVIS *peeks his head in, less than hopefully.*]

275 TRAVIS [*To his mother*]   Mama, I—

RUTH   "Mama I" nothing! You're going to get it, boy! Get on in that bedroom and get yourself ready!

TRAVIS   But I—

MAMA   Why don't you all never let the child explain hisself.

280 RUTH   Keep out of it now, Lena.

[MAMA *clamps her lips together, and* RUTH *advances toward her son menacingly.*]

RUTH   A thousand times I have told you not to go off like that—

MAMA [*Holding out her arms to her grandson*]   Well—at least let me tell him something. I want him to be the first one to hear . . . Come here, Travis. [*The boy obeys, gladly.*] Travis—[*She takes him by the shoulder and looks
285 into his face.*]—you know that money we got in the mail this morning?

TRAVIS   Yes'm—

MAMA   Well—what you think your grandmama gone and done with that money?

TRAVIS   I don't know, Grandmama.

290 MAMA [*Putting her finger on his nose for emphasis*]   She went out and she bought you a house! [*The explosion comes from* WALTER *at the end of the revelation and he jumps up and turns away from all of them in a fury.* MAMA *continues, to* TRAVIS.] You glad about the house? It's going to be yours when you get to be a man.

TRAVIS   Yeah—I always wanted to live in a house.

295 MAMA   All right, gimme some sugar then—[TRAVIS *puts his arms around her neck as she watches her son over the boy's shoulder. Then, to* TRAVIS, *after the embrace.*] Now when you say your prayers tonight, you thank God and your grandfather—'cause it was him who give you the house—in his way.

RUTH [*Taking the boy from* MAMA *and pushing him toward the bedroom*]   Now you get out of here and get ready for your beating.

300 TRAVIS Aw, Mama—

RUTH Get on in there—[*Closing the door behind him and turning radiantly to her mother-in-law*] So you went and did it!

MAMA [*Quietly, looking at her son with pain*] Yes, I did.

RUTH [*Raising both arms classically*] PRAISE GOD! [*Looks at* WALTER *a*
305 *moment, who says nothing. She crosses rapidly to her husband*] Please, honey—let me be glad . . . you be glad too. [*She has laid her hands on his shoulders, but he shakes himself free of her roughly, without turning to face her.*] Oh Walter . . . a home . . . *a home.* [*She comes back to* MAMA.] Well— where is it? How big is it? How much it going to cost?

MAMA Well—

310 RUTH When we moving?

MAMA [*Smiling at her*] First of the month.

RUTH [*Throwing back her head with jubilance*] Praise God!

MAMA [*Tentatively, still looking at her son's back turned against her and*
RUTH] It's—it's a nice house too . . . [*She cannot help speaking directly to him. An imploring quality in her voice, her manner, makes her almost like a girl now.*] Three bedrooms—nice big one for you and Ruth. . . . Me and
315 Beneatha still have to share our room, but Travis have one of his own—and [*With difficulty*] I figure if the—new baby—is a boy, we could get one of them double-decker outfits . . . And there's a yard with a little patch of dirt where I could maybe get to grow me a few flowers . . . And a nice big basement . . .

320 RUTH Walter honey, be glad—

MAMA [*Still to his back, fingering things on the table*] 'Course I don't want to make it sound fancier than it is . . . It's just a plain little old house—but it's made good and solid—and it will be *ours.* Walter Lee—it makes a differ- ence in a man when he can walk on floors that belong to *him* . . .

325 RUTH Where is it?

MAMA [*Frightened at this telling*] Well—well—it's out there in Clybourne Park—

[RUTH's *radiance fades abruptly, and* WALTER *finally turns slowly to face his mother with incredulity and hostility.*]

RUTH Where?

MAMA [*Matter-of-factly*] Four o six Clybourne Street, Clybourne Park.

330 RUTH Clybourne Park? Mama, there ain't no colored people living in Clybourne Park.

MAMA [*Almost idiotically*] Well, I guess there's going to be some now.

WALTER [*Bitterly*] So that's the peace and comfort you went out and bought for us today!

335 MAMA [*Raising her eyes to meet his finally*] Son—I just tried to find the nic- est place for the least amount of money for my family.

RUTH [*Trying to recover from the shock*] Well—well—'course I ain't one never been 'fraid of no crackers,[5] mind you—but—well, wasn't there no other houses nowhere?

340 MAMA Them houses they put up for colored in them areas way out all seem to cost twice as much as other houses. I did the best I could.

RUTH [*Struck senseless with the news, in its various degrees of goodness and trouble, she sits a moment, her fists propping her chin in thought, and then*

5. Pejorative term for poor white people, especially rural Southerners.

she starts to rise, bringing her fists down with vigor, the radiance spreading from cheek to cheek again.] Well—well!—All I can say is—if this is my time in life—MY TIME—to say good-bye—[*And she builds with momentum as she starts to circle the room with an exuberant, almost tearfully happy release*]—to these goddamned cracking walls!—[*She pounds the walls.*]—

345 and these marching roaches!—[*She wipes at an imaginary army of marching roaches.*]—and this cramped little closet which ain't now or never was no kitchen! . . . then I say it loud and good, HALLELUJAH! AND GOOD-BYE MISERY . . . I DON'T NEVER WANT TO SEE YOUR UGLY FACE AGAIN! [*She laughs joyously, having practically destroyed the apartment, and flings her arms up and lets them come down happily, slowly, reflectively, over her abdomen, aware for the first time perhaps that the life therein pulses*

350 *with happiness and not despair.*] Lena?

MAMA [*Moved, watching her happiness*] Yes, honey?

RUTH [*Looking off*] Is there—is there a whole lot of sunlight?

MAMA [*Understanding*] Yes, child, there's a whole lot of sunlight.

[*Long pause*]

RUTH [*Collecting herself and going to the door of the room* TRAVIS *is in*] Well—I

355 guess I better see 'bout Travis. [*To* MAMA] Lord, I sure don't feel like whipping nobody today!

[*She exits*]

MAMA [*The mother and son are left alone now and the mother waits a long time, considering deeply, before she speaks.*] Son—you—you understand what I done, don't you? [WALTER *is silent and sullen.*] I—I just seen my family falling apart today . . . just falling to pieces in front of my eyes . . . We couldn't

360 of gone on like we was today. We was going backwards 'stead of forwards—talking 'bout killing babies and wishing each other was dead . . . When it gets like that in life—you just got to do something different, push on out and do something bigger . . . [*She waits.*] I wish you say something, son . . . I wish you'd say how deep inside you you think I done the right thing—

WALTER [*Crossing slowly to his bedroom door and finally turning there and*

365 *speaking measuredly*] What you need me to say you done right for? *You* the head of this family. You run our lives like you want to. It was your money and you did what you wanted with it. So what you need for me to say it was all right for? [*Bitterly, to hurt her as deeply as he knows is possible*] So you butchered up a dream of mine—you—who always talking 'bout

370 your children's dreams . . .

MAMA Walter Lee—

[*He just closes the door behind him.* MAMA *sits alone, thinking heavily.*]

Curtain

Scene Two

Time: Friday night. A few weeks later.

At rise: Packing crates mark the intention of the family to move. BENEATHA *and* GEORGE *come in, presumably from an evening out again.*

GEORGE O.K. . . . O.K., whatever you say . . . [*They both sit on the couch. He tries to kiss her. She moves away.*] Look, we've had a nice evening; let's not spoil it, huh? . . .

[*He again turns her head and tries to nuzzle in and she turns away from him, not with distaste but with momentary lack of interest; in a mood to pursue what they were talking about.*]

BENEATHA I'm *trying* to talk to you.

5 GEORGE We always talk.

BENEATHA Yes—and I love to talk.

GEORGE [*Exasperated; rising*] I know it and I don't mind it sometimes . . . I want you to cut it out, see—The moody stuff, I mean. I don't like it. You're a nice-looking girl . . . all over. That's all you need, honey, forget the atmo-
10 sphere. Guys aren't going to go for the atmosphere—they're going to go for what they see. Be glad for that. Drop the Garbo routine.[6] It doesn't go with you. As for myself, I want a nice—[*Groping*]—simple [*Thoughtfully*]—sophisticated girl . . . not a poet—O.K.?

[*He starts to kiss her, she rebuffs him again and he jumps up.*]

BENEATHA Why are you angry, George?

15 GEORGE Because this is stupid! I don't go out with you to discuss the nature of "quiet desperation"[7] or to hear all about your thoughts—because the world will go on thinking what it thinks regardless—

BENEATHA Then why read books? Why go to school?

GEORGE [*With artificial patience, counting on his fingers*] It's simple. You
20 read books—to learn facts—to get grades—to pass the course—to get a degree. That's all—it has nothing to do with thoughts.

[*A long pause*]

BENEATH I see. [*He starts to sit.*] Good night, George.

[GEORGE *looks at her a little oddly, and starts to exit. He meets* MAMA *coming in.*]

GEORGE Oh—hello, Mrs. Younger.

MAMA Hello, George, how you feeling?

25 GEORGE Fine—fine, how are you?

MAMA Oh, a little tired. You know them steps can get you after a day's work. You all have a nice time tonight?

GEORGE Yes—a fine time. A fine time.

MAMA Well, good night.

30 GEORGE Good night. [*He exits.* MAMA *closes the door behind her.*] Hello, honey. What you sitting like that for?

BENEATH I'm just sitting.

MAMA Didn't you have a nice time?

BENEATHA No.

35 MAMA No? What's the matter?

BENEATHA Mama, George is a fool—honest. [*She rises.*]

MAMA [*Hustling around unloading the packages she has entered with. She stops*] Is he, baby?

BENEATH Yes.

[BENEATHA *makes up* TRAVIS' *bed as she talks.*]

MAMA You sure?

40 BENEATHA Yes.

---

6. Greta Garbo (1905–1990), Swedish American film actress known for her remoteness and mystique.

7. From Henry David Thoreau's *Walden* (1854): "The mass of men lead lives of quiet desperation."

MAMA   Well—I guess you better not waste your time with no fools.

[BENEATHA *looks up at her mother, watching her put groceries in the refrigerator. Finally she gathers up her things and starts into the bedroom. At the door she stops and looks back at her mother.*]

BENEATHA   Mama—

MAMA   Yes, baby—

BENEATHA   Thank you.

45 MAMA   For what?

BENEATHA   For understanding me this time.

[*She exits quickly and the mother stands, smiling a little, looking at the place where* BENEATHA *just stood.* RUTH *enters.*]

RUTH   Now don't you fool with any of this stuff, Lena—

MAMA   Oh, I just thought I'd sort a few things out. Is Brother here?

RUTH   Yes.

50 MAMA [*With concern*]   Is he—

RUTH [*Reading her eyes*]   Yes.

[MAMA *is silent and someone knocks on the door.* MAMA *and* RUTH *exchange weary and knowing glances and* RUTH *opens it to admit the neighbor,* MRS. JOHNSON,[8] *who is a rather squeaky wide-eyed lady of no particular age, with a newspaper under her arm.*]

MAMA [*Changing her expression to acute delight and a ringing cheerful greeting*]   Oh—hello there, Johnson.

JOHNSON [*This is a woman who decided long ago to be enthusiastic about EVERYTHING in life and she is inclined to wave her wrist vigorously at the height of her exclamatory comments.*]   Hello there, yourself! H'you this evening, Ruth?

55 RUTH [*Not much of a deceptive type*]   Fine, Mis' Johnson, h'you?

JOHNSON   Fine. [*Reaching out quickly, playfully, and patting* RUTH's *stomach*] Ain't you starting to poke out none yet! [*She mugs with delight at the overfamiliar remark and her eyes dart around looking at the crates and packing preparation;* MAMA's *face is a cold sheet of endurance.*]   Oh, ain't we getting ready 'round here, though! Yessir! Lookathere! I'm telling you the Youngers

60   is really getting ready to "move on up a little higher!"—Bless God!

MAMA [*A little drily, doubting the total sincerity of the Blesser*]   Bless God.

JOHNSON   He's good, ain't He?

MAMA   Oh yes, He's good.

JOHNSON   I mean sometimes He works in mysterious ways . . . but He works,

65   don't He!

MAMA [*The same*]   Yes, he does.

JOHNSON   I'm just soooooo happy for y'all. And this here child—[*About* RUTH] looks like she could just pop open with happiness, don't she. Where's all the rest of the family?

70 MAMA   Bennie's gone to bed—

JOHNSON   Ain't no . . . [*The implication is pregnancy.*] sickness done hit you—I hope . . . ?

MAMA   No—she just tired. She was out this evening.

---

8. This character and the scene of her visit were cut from the original production and early editions of the play.

JOHNSON [*All is a coo, an emphatic coo*]   Aw—ain't that lovely. She still going
out with the little Murchison boy?

MAMA [*Drily*]   Ummmm huh.

JOHNSON   That's lovely. You sure got lovely children, Younger. Me and Isaiah
talks all the time 'bout what fine children you was blessed with. We sure
do.

MAMA   Ruth, give Mis' Johnson a piece of sweet potato pie and some milk.

JOHNSON   Oh honey, I can't stay hardly a minute—I just dropped in to see if
there was anything I could do. [*Accepting the food easily*] I guess y'all seen
the news what's all over the colored paper[9] this week . . .

MAMA   No—didn't get mine yet this week.

JOHNSON [*Lifting her head and blinking with the spirit of catastrophe*]   You
mean you ain't read 'bout them colored people that was bombed out their
place out there?

> [RUTH *straightens with concern and takes the paper and reads it.* JOHN-
> SON *notices her and feeds commentary.*]

JOHNSON   Ain't it something how bad these here white folks is getting here in
Chicago! Lord, getting so you think you right down in Mississippi! [*With a
tremendous and rather insincere sense of melodrama*] 'Course I thinks it's
wonderful how our folks keeps on pushing out. You hear some of these
Negroes 'round here talking 'bout how they don't go where they ain't
wanted and all that—but not me, honey! [*This is a lie.*] Wilhemenia Othella
Johnson goes anywhere, any time she feels like it! [*With head movement for
emphasis*] Yes I do! Why if we left it up to these here crackers, the poor niggers wouldn't have nothing—[*She clasps her hand over her mouth.*] Oh, I
always forgets you don't 'low that word in your house.

MAMA [*Quietly, looking at her*]   No—I don't 'low it.

JOHNSON [*Vigorously again*]   Me neither! I was just telling Isaiah yesterday
when he come using it in front of me—I said, "Isaiah, it's just like Mis'
Younger says all the time—"

MAMA   Don't you want some more pie?

JOHNSON   No—no thank you; this was lovely. I got to get on over home and
have my midnight coffee. I hear some people say it don't let them sleep but
I finds I can't close my eyes right lessen I done had that laaaast cup of coffee . . . [*She waits. A beat. Undaunted.*] My Goodnight coffee, I calls it!

MAMA [*With much eye-rolling and communication between herself and
RUTH*]   Ruth, why don't you give Mis' Johnson some coffee.

> [RUTH *gives* MAMA *an unpleasant look for her kindness.*]

JOHNSON [*Accepting the coffee*]   Where's Brother tonight?

MAMA   He's lying down.

JOHNSON   Mmmmmm, he sure gets his beauty rest, don't he? Good-looking
man. Sure is a good-looking man! [*Reaching out to pat* RUTH's *stomach
again*] I guess that's how come we keep on having babies around here. [*She
winks at* MAMA.] One thing 'bout Brother, he always know how to have a
good time. And soooooo ambitious! I bet it was his idea y'all moving out to
Clybourne Park. Lord—I bet this time next month y'all's names will have
been in the papers plenty—[*Holding up her hands to mark off each word of*

---

9. Most likely the *Chicago Defender*, one of the United States' leading black metropolitan
newspapers.

the headline she can see in front of her] "NEGROES INVADE CLY-
BOURNE PARK—BOMBED!"

MAMA [*She and* RUTH *look at the woman in amazement.*]   We ain't exactly
120   moving out there to get bombed.

JOHNSON   Oh, honey—you know I'm praying to God every day that don't
nothing like that happen! But you have to think of life like it is—and these
here Chicago peckerwoods[1] is some baaaad peckerwoods.

MAMA [*Wearily*]   We done thought about all that Mis' Johnson.

> [BENEATHA *comes out of the bedroom in her robe and passes through to*
> *the bathroom.* MRS. JOHNSON *turns.*]

125   JOHNSON   Hello there, Bennie!

BENEATHA [*Crisply*]   Hello, Mrs. Johnson.

JOHNSON   How is school?

BENEATHA [*Crisply*]   Fine, thank you. [*She goes out.*]

JOHNSON [*Insulted*]   Getting so she don't have much to say to nobody.

130   MAMA   The child was on her way to the bathroom.

JOHNSON   I know—but sometimes she act like ain't got time to pass the time
of day with nobody ain't been to college. Oh—I ain't criticizing her none.
It's just—you know how some of our young people gets when they get a
little education. [MAMA *and* RUTH *say nothing, just look at her.*] Yes—well.
135   Well, I guess I better get on home. [*Unmoving*] 'Course I can understand
how she must be proud and everything—being the only one in the family to
make something of herself. I know just being a chauffeur ain't never satisfied Brother none. He shouldn't feel like that, though. Ain't nothing wrong
with being a chauffeur.

140   MAMA   There's plenty wrong with it.

JOHNSON   What?

MAMA   Plenty. My husband always said being any kind of a servant wasn't a
fit thing for a man to have to be. He always said a man's hands was made to
make things, or to turn the earth with—not to drive nobody's car for 'em—
145   or—[*She looks at her own hands.*] carry they slop jars.[2] And my boy is just
like him—he wasn't meant to wait on nobody.

JOHNSON [*Rising, somewhat offended*]   Mmmmmmmmm. The Youngers is
too much for me! [*She looks around.*] You sure one proud-acting bunch of
colored folks. Well—I always thinks like Booker T. Washington[3] said that
150   time—"Education has spoiled many a good plow hand"—

MAMA   Is that what old Booker T. said?

JOHNSON   He sure did.

MAMA   Well, it sounds just like him. The fool.

JOHNSON [*Indignantly*]   Well—he was one of our great men.

155   MAMA   Who said so?

JOHNSON [*Nonplussed*]   You know, me and you ain't never agreed about some
things, Lena Younger. I guess I better be going—

RUTH [*Quickly*]   Good night.

---

1. Pejorative term for poor whites.
2. Chamber pots, used for discarding human
and other waste.
3. Educator and reformer (1856–1915) who
was born into slavery but became one of the

most respected African American men of his
time. Washington's position that African
Americans were better served by vocational
training than by higher education proved controversial with many of his contemporaries.

JOHNSON   Good night. Oh—[*Thrusting it at her*] You can keep the paper!
160   [*With a trill*] 'Night.
MAMA   Good night, Mis' Johnson.

    [MRS. JOHNSON *exits*]

RUTH   If ignorance was gold . . .
MAMA   Shush. Don't talk about folks behind their backs.
RUTH   You do.
165 MAMA   I'm old and corrupted. [BENEATHA *enters*] You was rude to Mis' John-
    son, Beneatha, and I don't like it at all.
BENEATHA [*At her door*]   Mama, if there are two things we, as a people, have
    got to overcome, one is the Ku Klux Klan[4]—and the other is Mrs. Johnson.
    [*She exits*]
MAMA   Smart aleck.

    [*The phone rings*]

170 RUTH   I'll get it.
MAMA   Lord, ain't this a popular place tonight.
RUTH [*At the phone*]   Hello—Just a minute. [*Goes to door*] Walter, it's
    Mrs. Arnold. [*Waits. Goes back to the phone. Tense.*] Hello. Yes, this is his
    wife speaking . . . He's lying down now. Yes . . . well, he'll be in tomorrow.
175   He's been very sick. Yes—I know we should have called, but we were so
    sure he'd be able to come in today. Yes—yes, I'm very sorry. Yes . . . Thank
    you very much. [*She hangs up.* WALTER *is standing in the doorway of the
    bedroom behind her.*] That was Mrs. Arnold.
WALTER [*Indifferently*]   Was it?
180 RUTH   She said if you don't come in tomorrow that they are getting a new
    man . . .
WALTER   Ain't that sad—ain't that crying sad.
RUTH   She said Mr. Arnold has had to take a cab for three days . . . Walter,
    you ain't been to work for three days! [*This is a revelation to her.*] Where
185   you been, Walter Lee Younger? [WALTER *looks at her and starts to laugh.*]
    You're going to lose your job.
WALTER   That's right . . . [*He turns on the radio.*]
RUTH   Oh, Walter, and with your mother working like a dog every day—

    [*A steamy, deep blues pours into the room*]

WALTER   That's sad too—Everything is sad.
190 MAMA   What you been doing for these three days, son?
WALTER   Mama—you don't know all the things a man what got leisure can
    find to do in this city . . . What's this—Friday night? Well—Wednesday I bor-
    rowed Willy Harris' car and I went for a drive . . . just me and myself and I
    drove and drove . . . Way out . . . way past South Chicago, and I parked the
195   car and I sat and looked at the steel mills all day long. I just sat in the car and
    looked at them big black chimneys for hours. Then I drove back and I went
    to the Green Hat. [*Pause*] And Thursday—Thursday I borrowed the car again
    and I got in it and I pointed it the other way and I drove the other way—for
    hours—way, way up to Wisconsin, and I looked at the farms. I just drove and
200   looked at the farms. Then I drove back and I went to the Green Hat. [*Pause*]
    And today—today I didn't get the car. Today I just walked. All over the South-

---

4. Post–Civil War white supremacist organization responsible for violence and intimidation
against African Americans.

side. And I looked at the Negroes and they looked at me and finally I just sat down on the curb at Thirty-ninth and South Parkway and I just sat there and watched the Negroes go by. And then I went to the Green Hat. You all sad?

205 You all depressed? And you know where I am going right now—

[RUTH *goes out quietly.*]

MAMA   Oh, Big Walter, is this the harvest of our days?

WALTER   You know what I like about the Green Hat? I like this little cat they got there who blows a sax . . . He blows. He talks to me. He ain't but 'bout five feet tall and he's got a conked head[5] and his eyes is always closed and

210 he's all music—

MAMA [*Rising and getting some papers out of her handbag*]   Walter—

WALTER   And there's this other guy who plays the piano . . . and they got a sound. I mean they can work on some music . . . They got the best little combo in the world in the Green Hat . . . You can just sit there and drink

215 and listen to them three men play and you realize that don't nothing matter worth a damn, but just being there—

MAMA   I've helped do it to you, haven't I, son? Walter I been wrong.

WALTER   Naw—you ain't never been wrong about nothing, Mama.

MAMA   Listen to me, now. I say I been wrong, son. That I been doing to you

220 what the rest of the world been doing to you. [*She turns off the radio*] Walter—[*She stops and he looks up slowly at her and she meets his eyes pleadingly*] What you ain't never understood is that I ain't got nothing, don't own nothing, ain't never really wanted nothing that wasn't for you. There ain't nothing as precious to me . . . There ain't nothing worth holding on to,

225 money, dreams, nothing else—if it means—if it means it's going to destroy my boy. [*She takes an envelope out of her handbag and puts it in front of him and he watches her without speaking or moving.*] I paid the man thirty-five hundred dollars down on the house. That leaves sixty-five hundred dollars. Monday morning I want you to take this money and take three thousand dol-

230 lars and put it in a savings account for Beneatha's medical schooling. The rest you put in a checking account—with your name on it. And from now on any penny that come out of it or that go in it is for you to look after. For you to decide. [*She drops her hands a little helplessly.*] It ain't much, but it's all I got in the world and I'm putting it in your hands. I'm telling you to be the

235 head of this family from now on like you supposed to be.

WALTER [*Stares at the money*]   You trust me like that, Mama?

MAMA   I ain't never stop trusting you. Like I ain't never stop loving you.

[*She goes out, and* WALTER *sits looking at the money on the table. Finally, in a decisive gesture, he gets up, and, in mingled joy and desperation, picks up the money. At the same moment,* TRAVIS *enters for bed.*]

TRAVIS   What's the matter, Daddy? You drunk?

WALTER [*Sweetly, more sweetly than we have ever known him*]   No, Daddy

240 ain't drunk. Daddy ain't going to never be drunk again. . . .

TRAVIS   Well, good night, Daddy.

[*The* FATHER *has come from behind the couch and leans over, embracing his son.*]

WALTER   Son, I feel like talking to you tonight.

TRAVIS   About what?

5. Men's hairstyle in which the hair is straightened, usually by chemical means.

WALTER   Oh, about a lot of things. About you and what kind of man you
245   going to be when you grow up. . . . Son—son, what do you want to be when
you grow up?

TRAVIS   A bus driver.

WALTER [*Laughing a little*]   A what? Man, that ain't nothing to want to be!

TRAVIS   Why not?

250   WALTER   'Cause, man—it ain't big enough—you know what I mean.

TRAVIS   I don't know then. I can't make up my mind. Sometimes Mama asks
me that too. And sometimes when I tell her I just want to be like you—she
says she don't want me to be like that and sometimes she says she does. . . .

WALTER [*Gathering him up in his arms*]   You know what, Travis? In seven
255   years you going to be seventeen years old. And things is going to be very
different with us in seven years, Travis. . . . One day when you are seventeen I'll come home—home from my office downtown somewhere—

TRAVIS   You don't work in no office, Daddy.

WALTER   No—but after tonight. After what your daddy gonna do tonight,
260   there's going to be offices—a whole lot of offices. . . .

TRAVIS   What you gonna do tonight, Daddy?

WALTER   You wouldn't understand yet, son, but your daddy's gonna make a
transaction . . . a business transaction that's going to change our lives. . . .
That's how come one day when you 'bout seventeen years old I'll come home
265   and I'll be pretty tired, you know what I mean, after a day of conferences and
secretaries getting things wrong the way they do . . .'cause an executive's life
is hell, man—[*The more he talks the farther away he gets.*] And I'll pull the car
up on the driveway . . . just a plain black Chrysler, I think, with white walls—
no—black tires. More elegant. Rich people don't have to be flashy . . . though
270   I'll have to get something a little sportier for Ruth—maybe a Cadillac convertible to do her shopping in. . . . And I'll come up the steps to the house
and the gardener will be clipping away at the hedges and he'll say, "Good
evening, Mr. Younger." And I'll say, "Hello, Jefferson, how are you this evening?" And I'll go inside and Ruth will come downstairs and meet me at the
275   door and we'll kiss each other and she'll take my arm and we'll go up to your
room to see you sitting on the floor with the catalogues of all the great
schools in America around you. . . . All the great schools in the world! And—
and I'll say, all right son—it's your seventeenth birthday, what is it you've
decided? . . . Just tell me where you want to go to school and you'll *go*. Just
280   tell me, what it is you want to be—and you'll *be* it. . . . Whatever you want to
be—Yessir! [*He holds his arms open for* TRAVIS.]   You just name it, son . . .
[TRAVIS *leaps into them.*] and I hand you the world!

> [WALTER's *voice has risen in pitch and hysterical promise and on the last
> line he lifts* TRAVIS *high.*]

Blackout

Scene Three

Time: Saturday, moving day, one week later.

Before the curtain rises, RUTH's *voice, a strident, dramatic church alto, cuts
through the silence.*

*It is, in the darkness, a triumphant surge, a penetrating statement of expecta-
tion: "Oh, Lord, I don't feel no ways tired! Children, oh, glory hallelujah!"*

As the curtain rises we see that RUTH *is alone in the living room, finishing up the family's packing. It is moving day. She is nailing crates and tying cartons.* BENEATHA *enters, carrying a guitar case, and watches her exuberant sister-in-law.*

RUTH   Hey!

BENEATHA [*Putting away the case*]   Hi.

RUTH [*Pointing at a package*]   Honey—look in that package there and see what I found on sale this morning at the South Center. [RUTH *gets up and moves to*
5   *the package and draws out some curtains*] Lookahere—hand-turned hems!

BENEATHA   How do you know the window size out there?

RUTH [*Who hadn't thought of that*]   Oh—Well, they bound to fit something in the whole house. Anyhow, they was too good a bargain to pass up. [RUTH *slaps her head, suddenly remembering something.*] Oh, Bennie—I meant to
10   put a special note on that carton over there. That's your mama's good china and she wants 'em to be very careful with it.

BENEATHA   I'll do it.

[BENEATHA *finds a piece of paper and starts to draw large letters on it.*]

RUTH   You know what I'm going to do soon as I get in that new house?

BENEATHA   What?

15   RUTH   Honey—I'm going to run me a tub of water up to here . . . [*With her fingers practically up to her nostrils*] And I'm going to get in it—and I am going to sit . . . and sit . . . and sit in that hot water and the first person who knocks to tell me to hurry up and come out—

BENEATHA   Gets shot at sunrise.

20   RUTH [*Laughing happily*]   You said it, sister! [*Noticing how large* BENEATHA *is absent-mindedly making the note*] Honey, they ain't going to read that from no airplane.

BENEATHA [*Laughing herself*]   I guess I always think things have more emphasis if they are big, somehow.

25   RUTH [*Looking up at her and smiling*]   You and your brother seem to have that as a philosophy of life. Lord, that man—done changed so 'round here. You know—you know what we did last night? Me and Walter Lee?

BENEATHA   What?

RUTH [*Smiling to herself*]   We went to the movies. [*Looking at* BENEATHA *to*
30   *see if she understands*] We went to the movies. You know the last time me and Walter went to the movies together?

BENEATHA   No.

RUTH   Me neither. That's how long it been. [*Smiling again*] But we went last night. The picture wasn't much good, but that didn't seem to matter. We
35   went—and we held hands.

BENEATHA   Oh, Lord!

RUTH   We held hands—and you know what?

BENEATHA   What?

RUTH   When we come out of the show it was late and dark and all the stores
40   and things was closed up . . . and it was kind of chilly and there wasn't many people on the streets . . . and we was still holding hands, me and Walter.

BENEATHA   You're killing me.

[WALTER *enters with a large package. His happiness is deep in him; he cannot keep still with his newfound exuberance. He is singing and wiggling and snapping his fingers. He puts his package in a corner and puts a phonograph record, which he has brought in with him, on the record player. As the music, soulful and sensuous, comes up he dances over to* RUTH *and tries to get her to dance with him. She gives in at last to his raunchiness and in a fit of giggling allows herself to be drawn into his mood. They dip and she melts into his arms in a classic, body-melding "slow drag."*]

BENEATHA [*Regarding them a long time as they dance, then drawing in her breath for a deeply exaggerated comment which she does not particularly mean*] Talk about—oldddddddddd-fashionedddddddd—Negroes!

WALTER [*Stopping momentarily*] What kind of Negroes? [*He says this in fun. He is not angry with her today, nor with anyone. He starts to dance with his wife again.*]

45 BENEATHA Old-fashioned.

WALTER [*As he dances with* RUTH] You know, when these New Negroes have their convention—[*Pointing at his sister*]—that is going to be the chairman of the Committee on Unending Agitation. [*He goes on dancing, then stops*] Race, race, race! . . . Girl, I do believe you are the first person in the history 50 of the entire human race to successfully brainwash yourself. [BENEATHA *breaks up and he goes on dancing. He stops again, enjoying his tease.*] Damn, even the N double A C P[6] takes a holiday sometimes! [BENEATHA *and* RUTH *laugh. He dances with* RUTH *some more and starts to laugh and stops and pantomimes someone over an operating table.*] I can just see that chick someday looking down at some poor cat on an operating table and before 55 she starts to slice him, she says . . . [*Pulling his sleeves back maliciously*] "By the way, what are your views on civil rights down there? . . ."

[*He laughs at her again and starts to dance happily. The bell sounds.*]

BENEATHA Sticks and stones may break my bones but . . . words will never hurt me!

[BENEATHA *goes to the door and opens it as* WALTER *and* RUTH *go on with the clowning.* BENEATHA *is somewhat surprised to see a quiet-looking middle-aged white man in a business suit holding his hat and a briefcase in his hand and consulting a small piece of paper.*]

MAN Uh—how do you do, miss. I am looking for a Mrs.—[*He looks at the 60 slip of paper.*] Mrs. Lena Younger? [*He stops short, struck dumb at the sight of the oblivious* WALTER *and* RUTH.]

BENEATHA [*Smoothing her hair with slight embarrassment*] Oh—yes, that's my mother. Excuse me [*She closes the door and turns to quiet the other two.*] Ruth! Brother! [*Enunciating precisely but soundlessly: "There's a white man at the door!" They stop dancing,* RUTH *cuts off the phonograph,* BENEATHA *opens the door. The man casts a curious quick glance at all of them.*] Uh—- 65 come in please.

MAN [*Coming in*] Thank you.

BENEATHA My mother isn't here just now. Is it business?

MAN Yes . . . well, of a sort.

WALTER [*Freely, the Man of the House*] Have a seat. I'm Mrs. Younger's son. 70 I look after most of her business matters.

[RUTH *and* BENEATHA *exchange amused glances.*]

---

6. The National Association for the Advancement of Colored People, an African American civil rights organization, was founded in 1909.

MAN [*Regarding* WALTER, *and sitting*]   Well—My name is Karl Lindner . . .

WALTER [*Stretching out his hand*]   Walter Younger. This is my wife—[RUTH
nods politely.]—and my sister.

LINDNER   How do you do.

WALTER [*Amiably, as he sits himself easily on a chair, leaning forward on his
knees with interest and looking expectantly into the newcomer's face*]   What
can we do for you, Mr. Lindner!

LINDNER [*Some minor shuffling of the hat and briefcase on his knees*]   Well—I
am a representative of the Clybourne Park Improvement Association—

WALTER [*Pointing*]   Why don't you sit your things on the floor?

LINDNER   Oh—yes. Thank you. [*He slides the briefcase and hat under the
chair.*] And as I was saying—I am from the Clybourne Park Improvement
Association and we have had it brought to our attention at the last meeting
that you people—or at least your mother—has bought a piece of residential
property at—[*He digs for the slip of paper again.*]—four o six Clybourne
Street. . . .

WALTER   That's right. Care for something to drink? Ruth, get Mr. Lindner a
beer.

LINDNER [*Upset for some reason*]   Oh—no, really. I mean thank you very
much, but no thank you.

RUTH [*Innocently*]   Some coffee?

LINDNER   Thank you, nothing at all.

[BENEATHA *is watching the man carefully.*]

LINDNER   Well, I don't know how much you folks know about our organization. [*He is a gentle man; thoughtful and somewhat labored in his manner.*] It is one of these community organizations set up to look after—oh,
you know, things like block upkeep and special projects and we also have
what we call our New Neighbors Orientation Committee . . .

BENEATHA [*Drily*]   Yes—and what do they do?

LINDNER [*Turning a little to her and then returning the main force to* WAL-
TER]   Well—it's what you might call a sort of welcoming committee, I
guess. I mean they, we—I'm the chairman of the committee—go around
and see the new people who move into the neighborhood and sort of give
them the lowdown on the way we do things out in Clybourne Park.

BENEATHA [*With appreciation of the two meanings, which escape* RUTH *and*
WALTER]   Un-huh.

LINDNER   And we also have the category of what the association calls—[*He
looks elsewhere.*]—uh—special community problems . . .

BENEATHA   Yes—and what are some of those?

WALTER   Girl, let the man talk.

LINDNER [*With understated relief*]   Thank you. I would sort of like to explain
this thing in my own way. I mean I want to explain to you in a certain way.

WALTER   Go ahead.

LINDNER   Yes. Well. I'm going to try to get right to the point. I'm sure we'll all
appreciate that in the long run.

BENEATHA   Yes.

WALTER   Be still now!

LINDNER   Well—

RUTH [*Still innocently*]   Would you like another chair—you don't look
comfortable.

LINDNER [*More frustrated than annoyed*]   No, thank you very much. Please. Well—to get right to the point I—[*A great breath, and he is off at last*] I am sure you people must be aware of some of the incidents which have hap-
120 pened in various parts of the city when colored people have moved into certain areas—[BENEATHA *exhales heavily and starts tossing a piece of fruit up and down in the air.*] Well—because we have what I think is going to be a unique type of organization in American community life—not only do we deplore that kind of thing—but we are trying to do something about it. [BENEATHA *stops tossing and turns with a new and quizzical interest to the man.*] We feel—[*gaining confidence in his mission because of the interest in the faces of*
125 *the people he is talking to*]—we feel that most of the trouble in this world, when you come right down to it—[*He hits his knee for emphasis.*]—most of the trouble exists because people just don't sit down and talk to each other.

RUTH [*Nodding as she might in church, pleased with the remark*] You can say that again, mister.

130 LINDNER [*More encouraged by such affirmation*]   That we don't try hard enough in this world to understand the other fellow's problem. The other guy's point of view.

RUTH   Now that's right.

[BENEATHA *and* WALTER *merely watch and listen with genuine interest.*]

LINDNER   Yes—that's the way we feel out in Clybourne Park. And that's why I
135 was elected to come here this afternoon and talk to you people. Friendly like, you know, the way people should talk to each other and see if we couldn't find some way to work this thing out. As I say, the whole business is a matter of *caring* about the other fellow. Anybody can see that you are a nice family of folks, hard working and honest I'm sure. [BENEATHA *frowns slightly, quizzi-*
140 *cally, her head tilted regarding him.*] Today everybody knows what it means to be on the outside of *something*. And of course, there is always somebody who is out to take advantage of people who don't always understand.

WALTER   What do you mean?

LINDNER   Well—you see our community is made up of people who've worked
145 hard as the dickens for years to build up that little community. They're not rich and fancy people; just hard-working, honest people who don't really have much but those little homes and a dream of the kind of community they want to raise their children in. Now, I don't say we are perfect and there is a lot wrong in some of the things they want. But you've got to admit that a
150 man, right or wrong, has the right to want to have the neighborhood he lives in a certain kind of way. And at the moment the overwhelming majority of our people out there feel that people get along better, take more of a common interest in the life of the community, when they share a common background. I want you to believe me when I tell you that race prejudice simply
155 doesn't enter into it. It is a matter of the people of Clybourne Park believing, rightly or wrongly, as I say, that for the happiness of all concerned that our Negro families are happier when they live in their *own* communities.

BENEATHA [*With a grand and bitter gesture*]   This, friends, is the Welcoming Committee!

160 WALTER [*Dumbfounded, looking at* LINDNER]   Is this what you came marching all the way over here to tell us?

LINDNER   Well, now we've been having a fine conversation. I hope you'll hear me all the way through.

WALTER [*Tightly*] Go ahead, man.

165 LINDNER You see—in the face of all the things I have said, we are prepared
to make your family a very generous offer . . .

BENEATHA Thirty pieces[7] and not a coin less!

WALTER Yeah?

LINDNER [*Putting on his glasses and drawing a form out of the briefcase*] Our
170 association is prepared, through the collective effort of our people, to buy
the house from you at a financial gain to your family.

RUTH Lord have mercy, ain't this the living gall!

WALTER All right, you through?

LINDNER Well, I want to give you the exact terms of the financial
175 arrangement—

WALTER We don't want to hear no exact terms of no arrangements. I want to
know if you got any more to tell us 'bout getting together?

LINDNER [*Taking off his glasses*] Well—I don't suppose that you feel . . .

WALTER Never mind how I feel—you got any more to say 'bout how people
180 ought to sit down and talk to each other? . . . Get out of my house, man.

[*He turns his back and walks to the door.*]

LINDNER [*Looking around at the hostile faces and reaching and assembling his
hat and briefcase*] Well—I don't understand why you people are reacting
this way. What do you think you are going to gain by moving into a neighborhood where you just aren't wanted and where some elements—well—
people can get awful worked up when they feel that their whole way of life
185 and everything they've ever worked for is threatened.

WALTER Get out.

LINDNER [*At the door, holding a small card*] Well—I'm sorry it went like this.

WALTER Get out.

LINDNER [*Almost sadly regarding WALTER*] You just can't force people to
190 change their hearts, son.

[*He turns and put his card on a table and exits.* WALTER *pushes the door
to with stinging hatred, and stands looking at it.* RUTH *just sits and*
BENEATHA *just stands. They say nothing.* MAMA *and* TRAVIS *enter.*]

MAMA Well—this all the packing got done since I left out of here this morning. I testify before God that my children got all the energy of the *dead*!
What time the moving men due?

BENEATHA Four o'clock. You had a caller, Mama.

[*She is smiling, teasingly*]

195 MAMA Sure enough—who?

BENEATHA [*Her arms folded saucily*] The Welcoming Committee.

[WALTER *and* RUTH *giggle.*]

MAMA [*Innocently*] Who?

BENEATHA The Welcoming Committee. They said they're sure going to be
glad to see you when you get there.

200 WALTER [*Devilishly*] Yeah, they said they can't hardly wait to see your face.

[*Laughter*]

MAMA [*Sensing their facetiousness*] What's the matter with you all?

---

7. In Matthew 25.15, the amount of silver that Judas Iscariot was paid to betray Jesus to the
chief priests of Jerusalem.

WALTER   Ain't nothing the matter with us. We just telling you 'bout the gentleman who came to see you this afternoon. From the Clybourne Park
Improvement Association.

205 MAMA   What he want?

RUTH [*In the same mood as* BENEATHA *and* WALTER]   To welcome you, honey.

WALTER   He said they can't hardly wait. He said the one thing they don't
have, that they just *dying* to have out there is a fine family of fine colored
people! [*To* RUTH *and* BENEATHA] Ain't that right!

210 RUTH [*Mockingly*]   Yeah! He left his card—

BENEATHA [*Handing card to* MAMA]   In case.

> [MAMA *reads and throws it on the floor—understanding and looking off as
> she draws her chair up to the table on which she has put her plant and
> some sticks and some cord.*]

MAMA   Father, give us strength. [*Knowingly—and without fun*] Did he threaten
us?

BENEATHA   Oh—Mama—they don't do it like that any more. He talked
215 Brotherhood. He said everybody ought to learn how to sit down and hate
each other with good Christian fellowship.

> [*She and* WALTER *shake hands to ridicule the remark.*]

MAMA [*Sadly*]   Lord, protect us . . .

RUTH   You should hear the money those folks raised to buy the house from
us. All we paid and then some.

220 BENEATHA   What they think we going to do—eat 'em?

RUTH   No, honey, marry 'em.

MAMA [*Shaking her head*]   Lord, Lord, Lord . . .

RUTH   Well—that's the way the crackers crumble. [*A beat*] Joke.

BENEATHA [*Laughingly noticing what her mother is doing*]   Mama, what are
225 you doing?

MAMA   Fixing my plant so it won't get hurt none on the way . . .

BENEATHA   Mama, you going to take *that* to the new house?

MAMA   Un-huh—

BENEATHA   That raggedy-looking old thing?

230 MAMA [*Stopping and looking at her*]   It expresses ME!

RUTH [*With delight, to* BENEATHA]   So there, Miss Thing!

> [WALTER *comes to* MAMA *suddenly and bends down behind her and
> squeezes her in his arms with all his strength. She is overwhelmed by the
> suddenness of it and, though delighted, her manner is like that of* RUTH
> *and* TRAVIS.]

MAMA   Look out now, boy! You make me mess up my thing here!

WALTER [*His face lit, he slips down on his knees beside her, his arms still about
her*]   Mama . . . you know what it means to climb up in the chariot?

MAMA [*Gruffly, very happy*]   Get on away from me now . . .

235 RUTH [*Near the gift-wrapped package, trying to catch* WALTER'S *eye*]   Psst—

WALTER   What the old song say, Mama . . .

RUTH   Walter—Now?

> [*She is pointing at the package.*]

WALTER [*Speaking the lines, sweetly, playfully, in his mother's face*]
I got wings . . . you got wings . . .
All God's children got wings . . .

240 MAMA   Boy—get out of my face and do some work . . .

WALTER
When I get to heaven gonna put on my wings,
Gonna fly all over God's heaven . . .

BENEATHA [*Teasingly, from across the room*]   Everybody talking 'bout heaven ain't going there!

245 WALTER [*To* RUTH, *who is carrying the box across to them*]   I don't know, you think we ought to give her that . . . Seems to me she ain't been very appreciative around here.

MAMA [*Eyeing the box, which is obviously a gift*]   What is that?

WALTER [*Taking it from* RUTH *and putting it on the table in front of* MAMA]   Well—what you all think? Should we give it to her?

250 RUTH   Oh—she was pretty good today.

MAMA   I'll good you—
[*She turns her eyes to the box again.*]

BENEATHA   Open it, Mama.
[*She stands up, looks at it, turns and looks at all of them, and then presses her hands together and does not open the package.*]

WALTER [*Sweetly*]   Open it, Mama. It's for you. [MAMA *looks in his eyes. It is the first present in her life without its being Christmas. Slowly she opens her package and lifts out, one by one, a brand-new sparkling set of gardening tools.* WALTER *continues, prodding.*] Ruth made up the note—read it . . .

255 MAMA [*Picking up the card and adjusting her glasses*]   "To our own Mrs. Miniver[8]—Love from Brother, Ruth and Beneatha." Ain't that lovely . . .

TRAVIS [*Tugging at his father's sleeve*]   Daddy, can I give her mine now?

WALTER   All right, son. [TRAVIS *flies to get his gift.*]

MAMA   Now I don't have to use my knives and forks no more . . .

260 WALTER   Travis didn't want to go in with the rest of us, Mama. He got his own. [*Somewhat amused*] We don't know what it is . . .

TRAVIS [*Racing back in the room with a large hatbox and putting it in front of his grandmother*]   Here!

MAMA   Lord have mercy, baby. You done gone and bought your grandmother a hat?

265 TRAVIS [*Very proud*]   Open it!
[*She does and lifts out an elaborate, but very elaborate, wide gardening hat, and all the adults break up at the sight of it.*]

RUTH   Travis, honey, what is that?

TRAVIS [*Who thinks it is beautiful and appropriate*]   It's a gardening hat! Like the ladies always have on in the magazines when they work in their gardens.

270 BENEATHA [*Giggling fiercely*]   Travis—we were trying to make Mama Mrs. Miniver—not Scarlett O'Hara![9]

MAMA [*Indignantly*]   What's the matter with you all! This here is a beautiful hat! [*Absurdly*] I always wanted me one just like it!
[*She pops it on her head to prove it to her grandson, and the hat is ludicrous and considerably oversized.*]

---

8. Courageous British housewife in a 1942 film with the same name.
9. Spirited heroine of *Gone with the Wind*, a 1939 film adapted from Margaret Mitchell's 1936 romantic novel set during the American Civil War.

RUTH   Hot dog! Go, Mama!

275 WALTER [*Doubled over with laughter*]   I'm sorry, Mama—but you look like
you ready to go out and chop you some cotton sure enough!

[*They all laugh except* MAMA, *out of deference to* TRAVIS' *feelings.*]

MAMA [*Gathering the boy up to her*]   Bless your heart—this is the prettiest
hat I ever owned—[WALTER, RUTH and BENEATHA *chime in—noisily, festively
and insincerely congratulating* TRAVIS *on his gift.*] What are we all standing

280 around here for? We ain't finished packin' yet. Bennie, you ain't packed one
book.

[*The bell rings.*]

BENEATHA   That couldn't be the movers . . . it's not hardly two good yet—

[BENEATHA *goes into her room.* MAMA *starts for door.*]

WALTER [*Turning, stiffening*]   Wait—wait—I'll get it.

[*He stands and looks at the door.*]

MAMA   You expecting company, son?

285 WALTER [*Just looking at the door*]   Yeah—yeah . . .

[MAMA *looks at* RUTH, *and they exchange innocent and unfrightened
glances.*]

MAMA [*Not understanding*]   Well, let them in, son.

BENEATHA [*From her room*]   We need some more string.

MAMA   Travis—you run to the hardware and get me some string cord.

[MAMA *goes out and* WALTER *turns and looks at* RUTH. TRAVIS *goes to a
dish for money*]

RUTH   Why don't you answer the door, man?

290 WALTER [*Suddenly bounding across the floor to embrace her*]   'Cause sometimes it hard to let the future begin!

[*Stooping down in her face*]

I got wings! You got wings!
All God's children got wings!

[*He crosses to the door and throws it open. Standing there is a very slight
little man in a not too prosperous business suit and with haunted frightened eyes and a hat pulled down tightly, brim up, around his forehead.*
TRAVIS *passes between the men and exits.* WALTER *leans deep in the man's
face, still in his jubilance.*]

When I get to heaven gonna put on my wings,
295 Gonna fly all over God's heaven . . .

[*The little man just stares at him.*]

Heaven—

[*Suddenly he stops and looks past the little man into the empty hallway.*]
Where's Willy, man?

BOBO   He ain't with me.

WALTER [*Not disturbed*]   Oh—come on in. You know my wife.

BOBO [*Dumbly, taking off his hat*]   Yes—h'you, Miss Ruth.

300 RUTH [*Quietly, a mood apart from her husband already, seeing* BOBO]   Hello,
Bobo.

WALTER   You right on time today . . . Right on time. That's the way! [*He slaps* BOBO *on his back.*] Sit down . . . lemme hear.

> [RUTH *stands stiffly and quietly in back of them, as though somehow she senses death, her eyes fixed on her husband.*]

BOBO [*His frightened eyes on the floor, his hat in his hands*]   Could I please
305   get a drink of water, before I tell you about it, Walter Lee?

> [WALTER *does not take his eyes off the man.* RUTH *goes blindly to the tap and gets a glass of water and brings it to* BOBO.]

WALTER   There ain't nothing wrong, is there?

BOBO   Lemme tell you—

WALTER   Man—didn't nothing go wrong?

BOBO   Lemme tell you—Walter Lee. [*Looking at* RUTH *and talking to her*
310   *more than to* WALTER] You know how it was. I got to tell you how it was. I mean first I got to tell you how it was all the way . . . I mean about the money I put in, Walter Lee . . .

WALTER [*With taut agitation now*]   What about the money you put in?

BOBO   Well—it wasn't much as we told you—me and Willy—[*He stops.*] I'm
315   sorry, Walter. I got a bad feeling about it. I got a real bad feeling about it . . .

WALTER   Man, what you telling me about all this for? . . . Tell me what happened in Springfield[1] . . .

BOBO   Springfield.

RUTH [*Like a dead woman*]   What was supposed to happen in Springfield?

320   BOBO [*To her*]   This deal that me and Walter went into with Willy—Me and Willy was going to go down to Springfield and spread some money 'round so's we wouldn't have to wait so long for the liquor license . . . That's what we were going to do. Everybody said that was the way you had to do, you understand, Miss Ruth?

325   WALTER   Man—what happened down there?

BOBO [*A pitiful man, near tears*]   I'm trying to tell you, Walter.

WALTER [*Screaming at him suddenly*]   THEN TELL ME, GODDAMMIT . . . WHAT'S THE MATTER WITH YOU?

BOBO   Man . . . I didn't go to no Springfield, yesterday.

330   WALTER [*Halted, life hanging in the moment*]   Why not?

BOBO [*The long way, the hard way to tell*]   'Cause I didn't have no reasons to . . .

WALTER   Man, what are you talking about!

BOBO   I'm talking about the fact that when I got to the train station yesterday morning—eight o'clock like we planned . . . Man—*Willy didn't never show up.*

335   WALTER   Why . . . where was he . . . where is he?

BOBO   That's what I'm trying to tell you . . . I don't know . . . I waited six hours . . . I called his house . . . and I waited . . . six hours . . . I waited in that train station six hours . . . [*Breaking into tears*] That was all the extra money I had in the world . . . [*Looking up at* WALTER *with the tears running*
340   *down his face*] Man, *Willy is gone.*

WALTER   Gone, what you mean Willy is gone? Gone where? You mean he went by himself. You mean he went off to Springfield by himself—to take care of getting the license—[*Turns and looks anxiously at* RUTH] You mean maybe he didn't want too many people in on the business down there? [*Looks to* RUTH
345   *again, as before*] You know Willy got his own ways. [*Looks back to* BOBO]

---

1. Illinois state capital.

Maybe you was late yesterday and he just went on down there without you. Maybe—maybe—he's been callin' you at home tryin' to tell you what happened or something. Maybe—maybe—he just got sick. He's somewhere—he's got to be somewhere. We just got to find him—me and you got to find him. [*Grabs* BOBO *senselessly by the collar and starts to shake him*] We got to!

BOBO [*In sudden angry, frightened agony*] What's the matter with you, Walter! *When a cat take off with your money he don't leave you no road maps!*

WALTER [*Turning madly, as though he is looking for* WILLY *in the very room*] Willy! . . . Willy . . . don't do it . . . Please don't do it . . . Man, not with that money . . . Man, please, not with that money . . . Oh, God . . . Don't let it be true . . . [*He is wandering around, crying out for* WILLY *and looking for him or perhaps for help from God*] Man . . . I trusted you . . . Man, I put my life in your hands . . . [*He starts to crumple down on the floor as* RUTH *just covers her face in horror.* MAMA *opens the door and comes into the room, with* BENEATHA *behind her.*] Man . . . [*He starts to pound the floor with his fists, sobbing wildly.*] THAT MONEY IS MADE OUT OF MY FATHER'S FLESH—

BOBO [*Standing over him helplessly*] I'm sorry, Walter . . . [*Only* WALTER'S *sobs reply.* BOBO *puts on his hat*] I had my life staked on this deal, too . . .
> [*He exits*]

MAMA [*To* WALTER] Son—[*She goes to him, bends down to him, talks to his bent head.*] Son . . . Is it gone? Son, I gave you sixty-five hundred dollars. Is it gone? All of it? Beneatha's money too?

WALTER [*Lifting his head slowly*] Mama . . . I never . . . went to the bank at all . . .

MAMA [*Not wanting to believe him*] You mean . . . your sister's school money . . . you used that too . . . Walter? . . .

WALTER Yessss! All of it . . . It's all gone . . .
> [*There is total silence.* RUTH *stands with her face covered with her hands;* BENEATHA *leans forlornly against a wall, fingering a piece of red ribbon from the mother's gift.* MAMA *stops and looks at her son without recognition and then, quite without thinking about it, starts to beat him senselessly in the face.* BENEATHA *goes to them and stops it.*]

BENEATHA Mama!
> [MAMA *stops and looks at both of her children and rises slowly and wanders vaguely, aimlessly away from them.*]

MAMA I seen . . . him . . . night after night . . . come in . . . and look at that rug . . . and then look at me . . . the red showing in his eyes . . . the veins moving in his head . . . I seen him grow thin and old before he was forty . . . working and working and working like somebody's old horse . . . killing himself . . . and you—you give it all away in a day—[*She raises her arms to strike him again.*]

BENEATHA Mama—

MAMA Oh, God . . . [*She looks up to Him.*] Look down here—and show me the strength.

BENEATHA Mama—

MAMA [*Folding over*] Strength . . .

BENEATHA [*Plaintively*] Mama . . .

MAMA Strength!

Curtain

ACT III

An hour later.

   At curtain, there is a sullen light of gloom in the living room, gray light not unlike that which began the first scene of Act One. At left we can see WALTER *within his room, alone with himself. He is stretched out on the bed, his shirt out and open, his arms under his head. He does not smoke, he does not cry out, he merely lies there, looking up at the ceiling, much as if he were alone in the world.*

   In the living room BENEATHA *sits at the table, still surrounded by the now almost ominous packing crates. She sits looking off. We feel that this is a mood struck perhaps an hour before, and it lingers now, full of the empty sound of profound disappointment. We see on a line from her brother's bedroom the sameness of their attitudes. Presently the bell rings and* BENEATHA *rises without ambition or interest in answering. It is* ASAGAI, *smiling broadly, striding into the room with energy and happy expectation and conversation.*

ASAGAI   I came over . . . I had some free time. I thought I might help with the packing. Ah, I like the look of packing crates! A household in preparation for a journey! It depresses some people . . . but for me . . . it is another feeling. Something full of the flow of life, do you understand? Movement,
5   progress . . . It makes me think of Africa.
BENEATHA   Africa!
ASAGAI   What kind of a mood is this? Have I told you how deeply you move me?
BENEATHA   He gave away the money, Asagai . . .
10 ASAGAI   Who gave away what money?
BENEATHA   The insurance money. My brother gave it away.
ASAGAI   Gave it away?
BENEATHA   He made an investment! With a man even Travis wouldn't have trusted with his most worn-out marbles.
15 ASAGAI   And it's gone?
BENEATHA   Gone!
ASAGAI   I'm very sorry . . . And you, now?
BENEATHA   Me? . . . Me? . . . Me, I'm nothing . . . Me. When I was very small . . . we used to take our sleds out in the wintertime and the only hills
20   we had were the ice-covered stone steps of some houses down the street. And we used to fill them in with snow and make them smooth and slide down them all day . . . and it was very dangerous, you know . . . far too steep . . . and sure enough one day a kid named Rufus came down too fast and hit the sidewalk and we saw his face just split open right there in front
25   of us . . . And I remember standing there looking at his bloody open face thinking that was the end of Rufus. But the ambulance came and they took him to the hospital and they fixed the broken bones and they sewed it all up . . . and the next time I saw Rufus he just had a little line down the middle of his face . . . I never got over that . . .
30 ASAGAI   What?
BENEATHA   That that was what one person could do for another, fix him up— sew up the problem, make him all right again. That was the most marvelous thing in the world . . . I wanted to do that. I always thought it was the

one concrete thing in the world that a human being could do. Fix up the
35   sick, you know—and make them whole again. This was truly being God . . .

ASAGAI   You wanted to be God?

BENEATHA   No—I wanted to cure. It used to be so important to me. I wanted
to cure. It used to matter. I used to care. I mean about people and how
their bodies hurt . . .

40 ASAGAI   And you've stopped caring?

BENEATHA   Yes—I think so.

ASAGAI   Why?

BENEATHA   [*Bitterly*] Because it doesn't seem deep enough, close enough to
what ails mankind! It was a child's way of seeing things—or an idealist's.

45 ASAGAI   Children see things very well sometimes—and idealists even better.

BENEATHA   I know that's what you think. Because you are still where I left
off. You with all your talk and dreams about Africa! You still think you can
patch up the world. Cure the Great Sore of Colonialism—[*Loftily, mocking
it*] with the Penicillin of Independence—!

50 ASAGAI   Yes!

BENEATHA   Independence *and then what?* What about all the crooks and
thieves and just plain idiots who will come into power and steal and plun-
der the same as before—only now they will be black and do it in the name
of the new Independence—WHAT ABOUT THEM?!

55 ASAGAI   That will be the problem for another time. First we must get there.

BENEATHA   And where does it end?

ASAGAI   End? Who even spoke of an end? To life? To living?

BENEATHA   An end to misery! To stupidity! Don't you see there isn't any real
progress, Asagai, there is only one large circle that we march in, around
60   and around, each of us with our own little picture in front of us—our own
little mirage that we think is the future.

ASAGAI   That is the mistake.

BENEATHA   What?

ASAGAI   What you just said about the circle. It isn't a circle—it is simply a
long line—as in geometry, you know, one that reaches into infinity. And
65   because we cannot see the end—we also cannot see how it changes. And it
is very odd but those who see the changes—who dream, who will not give
up—are called idealists . . . and those who see only the circle we call *them*
the "realists"!

BENEATHA   Asagai, while I was sleeping in that bed in there, people went out
70   and took the future right out of my hands! And nobody asked me, nobody
consulted me—they just went out and changed my life!

ASAGAI   Was it your money?

BENEATHA   What?

ASAGAI   Was it your money he gave away?

75 BENEATHA   It belonged to all of us.

ASAGAI   But did you earn it? Would you have had it at all if your father had
not died?

BENEATHA   No.

ASAGAI   Then isn't there something wrong in a house—in a world—where all
80   dreams, good or bad, must depend on the death of a man? I never thought
to see *you* like this, Alaiyo. You! Your brother made a mistake and you are
grateful to him so that now you can give up the ailing human race on

account of it! You talk about what good is struggle, what good is anything! Where are we all going and why are we bothering!

85 BENEATHA AND YOU CANNOT ANSWER IT!

ASAGAI [*Shouting over her*] I LIVE THE ANSWER! [*Pause*] In my village at home it is the exceptional man who can even read a newspaper . . . or who ever sees a book at all. I will go home and much of what I will have to say will seem strange to the people of my village. But I will teach and work and

90 things will happen, slowly and swiftly. At times it will seem that nothing changes at all . . . and then again the sudden dramatic events which make history leap into the future. And then quiet again. Retrogression even. Guns, murder, revolution. And I even will have moments when I wonder if the quiet was not better than all that death and hatred. But I will look

95 about my village at the illiteracy and disease and ignorance and I will not wonder long. And perhaps . . . perhaps I will be a great man . . . I mean perhaps I will hold on to the substance of truth and find my way always with the right course . . . and perhaps for it I will be butchered in my bed some night by the servants of empire . . .

100 BENEATHA *The martyr!*

ASAGAI [*He smiles.*] . . . or perhaps I shall live to be a very old man, respected and esteemed in my new nation . . . And perhaps I shall hold office and this is what I'm trying to tell you, Alaiyo: Perhaps the things I believe now for my country will be wrong and outmoded, and I will not understand and

105 do terrible things to have things my way or merely to keep my power. Don't you see that there will be young men and women—not British soldiers then, but my own black countrymen—to step out of the shadows some evening and slit my then useless throat? Don't you see they have always been there . . . that they always will be. And that such a thing as my own death

110 will be an advance? They who might kill me even . . . actually replenish all that I was.

BENEATHA Oh, Asagai, I know all that.

ASAGAI Good! Then stop moaning and groaning and tell me what you plan to do.

115 BENEATHA Do?

ASAGAI I have a bit of a suggestion.

BENEATHA What?

ASAGAI [*Rather quietly for him*] That when it is all over—that you come home with me—

120 BENEATHA [*Staring at him and crossing away with exasperation*] Oh— Asagai—at this moment you decide to be romantic!

ASAGAI [*Quickly understanding the misunderstanding*] My dear, young creature of the New World—I do not mean across the city—I mean across the ocean: home—to Africa.

BENEATHA [*Slowly understanding and turning to him with murmured amaze-

125 ment*] To Africa?

ASAGAI Yes! . . . [*Smiling and lifting his arms playfully*] Three hundred years later the African Prince rose up out of the seas and swept the maiden back across the middle passage over which her ancestors had come—

BENEATHA [*Unable to play*] To—to Nigeria?

130 ASAGAI Nigeria, Home. [*Coming to her with genuine romantic flippancy*] I will show you our mountains and our stars; and give you cool drinks from

gourds and teach you the old songs and the ways of our people—and, in time, we will pretend that—[*Very softly*]—you have only been away for a day. Say that you'll come [*He swings her around and takes her full in his arms in a kiss which proceeds to passion.*]

135 BENEATHA [*Pulling away suddenly*] You're getting me all mixed up—

ASAGAI Why?

BENEATHA Too many things—too many things have happened today. I must sit down and think. I don't know what I feel about anything right this minute.

> [*She promptly sits down and props her chin on her fist.*]

140 ASAGAI [*Charmed*] All right, I shall leave you. No—don't get up. [*Touching her, gently, sweetly*] Just sit awhile and think . . . Never be afraid to sit awhile and think. [*He goes to door and looks at her.*] How often I have looked at you and said, "Ah—so this is what the New World hath finally wrought . . ."

> [*He exits.* BENEATHA *sits on alone. Presently* WALTER *enters from his room and starts to rummage through things, feverishly looking for something. She looks up and turns in her seat.*]

145 BENEATHA [*Hissingly*] Yes—just look at what the New World hath wrought! . . . Just look! [*She gestures with bitter disgust.*] There he is! Monsieur le petit bourgeois noir[2]—himself! There he is—Symbol of a Rising Class! Entrepreneur! Titan of the system! [WALTER *ignores her completely and continues frantically and destructively looking for something and hurling things to floor and tearing things out of their place in his search.* BENEATHA *ignores the eccentricity of his actions and goes on with the monologue of insult.*] Did you dream of yachts on Lake Michigan, Brother? Did you see

150 yourself on that Great Day sitting down at the Conference Table, surrounded by all the mighty bald-headed men in America? All halted, waiting, breathless, waiting for your pronouncements on industry? Waiting for you—Chairman of the Board! [WALTER *finds what he is looking for—a small piece of white paper—and pushes it in his pocket and puts on his coat and rushes out without ever having looked at her. She shouts after him.*] I look at

155 you and I see the final triumph of stupidity in the world!

> [*The door slams and she returns to just sitting again.* RUTH *comes quickly out of* MAMA'S *room.*]

RUTH Who was that?

BENEATHA Your husband.

RUTH Where did he go?

BENEATHA Who knows—maybe he has an appointment at U.S. Steel.

160 RUTH [*Anxiously, with frightened eyes*] You didn't say nothing bad to him, did you?

BENEATHA Bad? Say anything bad to him? No—I told him he was a sweet boy and full of dreams and everything is strictly peachy keen, as the ofay[3] kids say!

> [MAMA *enters from her bedroom. She is lost, vague, trying to catch hold, to make some sense of her former command of the world, but it still eludes her. A sense of waste overwhelms her gait; a measure of apology*

---

2. Mr. Little Black Middle-Class (French).
3. Pejorative term for white people.

rides on her shoulders. She goes to her plant, which has remained on the table, looks at it, picks it up and takes it to the window-sill and sits it outside, and she stands and looks at it a long moment. Then she closes the window, straightens her body with effort and turns around to her children.]

165 MAMA   Well—ain't it a mess in here, though? [*A false cheerfulness, a beginning of something*] I guess we all better stop moping around and get some work done. All this unpacking and everything we got to do. [RUTH *raises her head slowly in response to the sense of the line; and* BENEATHA *in similar manner turns very slowly to look at her mother.*] One of you all better call the moving people and tell 'em not to come.

170 RUTH   Tell 'em not to come?

MAMA   Of course, baby. Ain't no need in 'em coming all the way here and having to go back. They charges for that too. [*She sits down, fingers to her brow, thinking.*] Lord, ever since I was a little girl, I always remembers people saying, "Lena—Lena Eggleston, you aims too high all the time. You needs to

175 slow down and see life a little more like it is. Just slow down some." That's what they always used to say down home—"Lord, that Lena Eggleston is a high-minded thing. She'll get her due one day!"

RUTH   No, Lena . . .

MAMA   Me and Big Walter just didn't never learn right.

180 RUTH   Lena, no! We gotta go. Bennie—tell her . . . [*She rises and crosses to* BENEATHA *with her arms outstretched.* BENEATHA *doesn't respond.*] Tell her we can still move . . . the notes ain't but a hundred and twenty-five a month. We got four grown people in this house—we can work . . .

MAMA [*To herself*]   Just aimed too high all the time—

RUTH [*Turning and going to* MAMA *fast—the words pouring out with urgency*
185 *and desperation*]   Lena—I'll work . . . I'll work twenty hours a day in all the kitchens in Chicago . . . I'll strap my baby on my back if I have to and scrub all the floors in America and wash all the sheets in America if I have to—but we got to MOVE! We got to get OUT OF HERE!!

[MAMA *reaches out absently and pats* RUTH's *hand.*]

MAMA   No—I sees things differently now. Been thinking 'bout some of the
190 things we could do to fix this place up some. I seen a secondhand bureau over on Maxwell Street just the other day that could fit right there. [*She points to where the new furniture might go.* RUTH *wanders away from her.*] Would need some new handles on it and then a little varnish and it look like something brand-new. And—we can put up them new curtains in the kitchen . . . Why this place be looking fine. Cheer us all up so that we forget
195 trouble ever come . . . [*To* RUTH] And you could get some nice screens to put up in your room 'round the baby's bassinet . . . [*She looks at both of them, pleadingly.*] Sometimes you just got to know when to give up some things . . . and hold on to what you got. . . .

[WALTER *enters from the outside, looking spent and leaning against the door, his coat hanging from him.*]

MAMA   Where you been, son?

200 WALTER [*Breathing hard*]   Made a call.

MAMA   To who, son?

WALTER   To The Man. [*He heads for his room.*]

MAMA   What man, baby?

WALTER [*Stops in the door*]   The Man, Mama. Don't you know who The
205   Man is?

RUTH   Walter Lee?

WALTER   *The Man.* Like the guys in the streets say—The Man. Captain
Boss—Mistuh Charley . . . Old Cap'n Please Mr. Bossman . . .

BENEATHA [*Suddenly*]   Lindner!

210   WALTER   That's right! That's good. I told him to come right over.

BENEATHA [*Fiercely, understanding*]   For what? What do you want to see him
for!

WALTER [*Looking at his sister*]   We going to do business with him.

MAMA   What you talking 'bout, son?

215   WALTER   Talking 'bout life, Mama. You all always telling me to see life like it is.
Well—I laid in there on my back today . . . and I figured it out. Life just like
it is. Who gets and who don't get. [*He sits down with his coat on and laughs.*]
Mama, you know it's all divided up. Life is. Sure enough. Between the takers
and the "tooken." [*He laughs.*] I've figured it out finally. [*He looks around at*
220   *them.*] Yeah. Some of us always getting "tooken." [*He laughs.*] People like
Willy Harris, they don't never get "tooken." And you know why the rest of us
do? 'Cause we all mixed up. Mixed up bad. We get to looking 'round for the
right and the wrong; and we worry about it and cry about it and stay up
nights trying to figure out 'bout the wrong and the right of things all the
225   time . . . And all the time, man, them takers is out there operating, just taking and taking. Willy Harris? Shoot—Willy Harris don't even count. He don't
even count in the big scheme of things. But I'll say one thing for old Willy
Harris . . . he's taught me something. He's taught me to keep my eye on what
counts in this world. Yeah—[*Shouting out a little*] Thanks, Willy!

230   RUTH   What did you call that man for, Walter Lee?

WALTER   Called him to tell him to come on over to the show. Gonna put on
a show for the man. Just what he wants to see. You see, Mama, the man
came here today and he told us that them people out there where you want
us to move—well they so upset they willing to pay us *not* to move! [*He*
235   *laughs again.*] And—and oh, Mama you would of been proud of the way me
and Ruth and Bennie acted. We told him to get out . . . Lord have mercy!
We told the man to get out! Oh, we was some proud folks this afternoon,
yeah. [*He lights a cigarette.*] We were still full of that old-time stuff . . .

RUTH [*Coming toward him slowly*]   You talking 'bout taking them people's
240   money to keep us from moving in that house?

WALTER   I ain't just talking 'bout it, baby—I'm telling you that's what's going
to happen!

BENEATHA   Oh, God! Where is the bottom! Where is the real honest-to-God
bottom so he can't go any farther!

245   WALTER   See—that's the old stuff. You and that boy that was here today. You
all want everybody to carry a flag and a spear and sing some marching
songs, huh? You wanna spend your life looking into things and trying to
find the right and the wrong part, huh? Yeah. You know what's going to happen to that boy someday—he'll find himself sitting in a dungeon, locked in
250   forever—and the takers will have the key! Forget it, baby! There ain't no
causes—there ain't nothing but taking in this world, and he who takes
most is smartest—and it don't make a damn bit of difference *how*.

MAMA   You making something inside me cry, son. Some awful pain inside me.

WALTER   Don't cry, Mama. Understand. That white man is going to walk in that
255   door able to write checks for more money than we ever had. It's important to
him and I'm going to help him . . . I'm going to put on the show, Mama.

MAMA   Son—I come from five generations of people who was slaves and
sharecroppers—but ain't nobody in my family never let nobody pay 'em no
money that was a way of telling us we wasn't fit to walk the earth. We ain't
260   never been that poor. [*Raising her eyes and looking at him*] We ain't never
been that—dead inside.

BENEATHA   Well—we are dead now. All the talk about dreams and sunlight
that goes on in this house. It's all dead now.

WALTER   What's the matter with you all! I didn't make this world! It was give
265   to me this way! Hell, yes, I want me some yachts someday! Yes, I want to
hang some real pearls 'round my wife's neck. Ain't she supposed to wear no
pearls? Somebody tell me—tell me, who decides which women is suppose
to wear pearls in this world. I tell you I am a *man*—and I think my wife
should wear some pearls in this world!

[*This last line hangs a good while and* WALTER *begins to move about the
room. The word "Man" has penetrated his consciousness; he mumbles it
to himself repeatedly between strange agitated pauses as he moves about.*]

270   MAMA   Baby, how you going to feel on the inside?

WALTER   Fine! . . . Going to feel fine . . . a man . . .

MAMA   You won't have nothing left then, Walter Lee.

WALTER [*Coming to her*]   I'm going to feel fine, Mama. I'm going to look that
son-of-a-bitch in the eyes and say—[*He falters.*]—and say, "All right,
275   Mr. Lindner—[*He falters even more.*]—that's *your* neighborhood out there! You
got the right to keep it like you want! You got the right to have it like you want!
Just write the check and—the house is yours." And—and I am going to say—
[*His voice almost breaks.*] "And you—you people just put the money in my
hand and you won't have to live next to this bunch of stinking niggers! . . ." [*He
280   straightens up and moves away from his mother, walking around the room.*] And
maybe—maybe I'll just get down on my black knees . . . [*He does so;* RUTH *and*
BENNIE *and* MAMA *watch him in frozen horror.*] "Captain, Mistuh, Bossman—
[*Groveling and grinning and wringing his hands in profoundly anguished imitation of the slowwitted movie stereotype*] A-hee-hee-hee! Oh, yassuh boss!
Yasssssuh! Great white—[*Voice breaking, he forces himself to go on*]—Father,
285   just gi' ussen de money, fo' God's sake, and we's—we's ain't gwine come out
deh and dirty up yo' white folks neighborhood . . ." [*He breaks down completely.*] And I'll feel fine! Fine! FINE! [*He gets up and goes into the bedroom.*]

BENEATHA   That is not a man. That is nothing but a toothless rat.

MAMA   Yes—death done come in this here house. [*She is nodding, slowly,
290   reflectively.*] Done come walking in my house on the lips of my children.
You what supposed to be my beginning again. You—what supposed to be
my harvest. [*To* BENEATH] You—you mourning your brother?

BENEATHA   He's no brother of mine.

MAMA   What you say?

295   BENEATHA   I said that that individual in that room is no brother of mine.

MAMA   That's what I thought you said. You feeling like you better than he is
today? [BENEATHA *does not answer.*] Yes? What you tell him a minute ago?
That he wasn't a man? Yes? You give him up for me? You done wrote his
epitaph too—like the rest of the world? Well, who give you the privilege?

300 BENEATHA   Be on my side for once! You saw what he just did, Mama! You saw
       him—down on his knees. Wasn't it you who taught me to despise any man
       who would do that? Do what he's going to do?

MAMA   Yes—I taught you that. Me and your daddy. But I thought I taught
       you something else too . . . I thought I taught you to love him.

305 BENEATHA   Love him? There is nothing left to love.

MAMA   There is *always* something left to love. And if you ain't learned that, you
       ain't learned nothing. [*Looking at her*] Have you cried for that boy today? I
       don't mean for yourself and for the family 'cause we lost the money. I mean for
       him: what he been through and what it done to him. Child, when do you think
310   is the time to love somebody the most? When they done good and made things
       easy for everybody? Well then, you ain't through learning—because that ain't
       the time at all. It's when he's at his lowest and can't believe in hisself 'cause the
       world done whipped him so! When you starts measuring somebody, measure
       him right, child, measure him right. Make sure you done taken into account
315   what hills and valleys he come through before he got to wherever he is.
       [TRAVIS *bursts into the room at the end of the speech, leaving the door
       open.*]

TRAVIS   Grandmama—the moving men are downstairs! The truck just pulled up.

MAMA [*Turning and looking at him*]   Are they, baby? They downstairs?
       [*She sighs and sits.* LINDNER *appears in the doorway. He peers in and
       knocks lightly, to gain attention, and comes in. All turn to look at him.*]

LINDNER [*Hat and briefcase in hand*]   Uh—hello . . .
       [RUTH *crosses mechanically to the bedroom door and opens it and lets it
       swing open freely and slowly as the lights come up on* WALTER *within,
       still in his coat, sitting at the far corner of the room. He looks up and out
       through the room to* LINDNER.]

RUTH   He's here.
       [*A long minute passes and* WALTER *slowly gets up.*]

LINDNER [*Coming to the table with efficiency, putting his briefcase on the table
320   and starting to unfold papers and unscrew fountain pens*]   Well, I certainly
       was glad to hear from you people. [WALTER *has begun the trek out of the
       room, slowly and awkwardly, rather like a small boy, passing the back of his
       sleeve across his mouth from time to time.*] Life can really be so much sim-
       pler than people let it be most of the time. Well—with whom do I negoti-
       ate? You, Mrs. Younger, or your son here? [MAMA *sits with her hands folded
       on her lap and her eyes closed as* WALTER *advances.* TRAVIS *goes closer to*
325   LINDNER *and looks at the papers curiously.*] Just some official papers, sonny.

RUTH   Travis, you go downstairs—

MAMA [*Opening her eyes and looking into* WALTER'S]   No. Travis, you stay right
       here. And you make him understand what you doing, Walter Lee. You teach
       him good. Like Willy Harris taught you. You show where our five generations
330   done come to. [WALTER *looks from her to the boy, who grins at him innocently.*]
       Go ahead, son—[*She folds her hands and closes her eyes.*] Go ahead.

WALTER [*At last crosses to* LINDNER, *who is reviewing the contract.*]   Well,
       Mr. Lindner. [BENEATHA *turns away.*] We called you—[*There is a profound,
       simple groping quality in his speech.*]—because, well, me and my family [*He
335   looks around and shifts from one foot to the other.*] Well—we are very plain
       people . . .

LINDNER   Yes—

WALTER   I mean—I have worked as a chauffeur most of my life—and my
wife here, she does domestic work in people's kitchens. So does my mother.
340   I mean—we are plain people . . .

LINDNER   Yes, Mr. Younger—

WALTER   [*Really like a small boy, looking down at his shoes and then up at the
man*]   And—uh—well, my father, well, he was a laborer most of his life. . . .

LINDNER   [*Absolutely confused*]   Uh, yes—yes, I understand. [*He turns back
to the contract.*]

WALTER   [*A beat; staring at him*]   And my father—[*With sudden intensity*] My
345   father almost *beat a man to death* once because this man called him a bad
name or something, you know what I mean?

LINDNER   [*Looking up, frozen*]   No, no, I'm afraid I don't—

WALTER   [*A beat. The tension hangs; then* WALTER *steps back from it.*]   Yeah.
Well—what I mean is that we come from people who had a lot of *pride.* I
350   mean—we are very proud people. And that's my sister over there and she's
going to be a doctor—and we are very proud—

LINDNER   Well—I am sure that is very nice, but—

WALTER   What I am telling you is that we called you over here to tell you that
we are very proud and that this—[*Signaling to* TRAVIS] Travis, come here.
355   [TRAVIS *crosses and* WALTER *draws him before him facing the man.*] This is
my son, and he makes the sixth generation of our family in this country.
And we have all thought about your offer—

LINDNER   Well, good . . . good—

WALTER   And we have decided to move into our house because my father—
360   my father—he earned it for us brick by brick. [MAMA *has her eyes closed and
is rocking back and forth as though she were in church, with her head nodding the Amen yes.*] We don't want to make no trouble for nobody or fight
no causes, and we will try to be good neighbors. And that's *all* we got to say
about that. [*He looks the man absolutely in the eyes.*] We don't want your
money. [*He turns and walks away.*]

365 LINDNER   [*Looking around at all of them*]   I take it then—that you have decided to occupy . . .

BENEATHA   That's what the man said.

LINDNER   [*To* MAMA *in her reverie*]   Then I would like to appeal to you,
Mrs. Younger. You are older and wiser and understand things better I am
370   sure . . .

MAMA   I am afraid you don't understand. My son said we was going to move
and there ain't nothing left for me to say. [*Briskly*] You know how these
young folks is nowadays, mister. Can't do a thing with 'em! [*As he opens his
mouth, she rises*] Good-bye.

375 LINDNER   [*Folding up his materials*]   Well—if you are that final about it . . .
there is nothing left for me to say. [*He finishes, almost ignored by the family,
who are concentrating on* WALTER LEE. *At the door* LINDNER *halts and looks
around.*] I sure hope you people know what you're getting into.

         [*He shakes his head and exits.*]

RUTH   [*Looking around and coming to life*]   Well, for God's sake—if the moving men are here—LET'S GET THE HELL OUT OF HERE!

380 MAMA   [*Into action*]   Ain't it the truth! Look at all this here mess. Ruth, put
Travis' good jacket on him . . . Walter Lee, fix your tie and tuck your shirt
in, you look like somebody's hoodlum! Lord have mercy, where is my plant?
[*She flies to get it amid the general bustling of the family, who are deliber-*

ately trying to ignore the nobility of the past moment.] You all start on
down . . . Travis child, don't go empty-handed . . . Ruth, where did I put
that box with my skillets in it? I want to be in charge of it myself . . . I'm
going to make us the biggest dinner we ever ate tonight . . . Beneatha,
what's the matter with them stockings? Pull them things up, girl . . .

[*The family starts to file out as two moving men appear and begin to carry
out the heavier pieces of furniture, bumping into the family as they move
about.*]

BENEATHA Mama, Asagai asked me to marry him today and go to Africa—

MAMA [*In the middle of her getting-ready activity*] He did? You ain't old
enough to marry nobody—[*Seeing the moving men lifting one of her chairs
precariously*] Darling, that ain't no bale of cotton, please handle it so we
can sit in it again! I had that chair twenty-five years . . .

[*The movers sigh with exasperation and go on with their work.*]

BENEATHA [*Girlishly and unreasonably trying to pursue the conversation*] To
go to Africa, Mama—be a doctor in Africa . . .

MAMA [*Distracted*] Yes, baby—

WALTER *Africa!* What he want you to go to Africa for?

BENEATHA To practice there . . .

WALTER Girl, if you don't get all them silly ideas out your head! You better
marry yourself a man with some loot . . .

BENEATHA [*Angrily, precisely as in the first scene of the play*] What have you
got to do with who I marry!

WALTER Plenty. Now I think George Murchison—

BENEATHA *George Murchison!* I wouldn't marry him if he was Adam and I
was Eve!

[WALTER *and* BENEATHA *go out yelling at each other vigorously and the
anger is loud and real till their voices diminish.* RUTH *stands at the door
and turns to* MAMA *and smiles knowingly.*]

MAMA [*Fixing her hat at last*] Yeah—they something all right, my children . . .

RUTH Yeah—they're something. Let's go, Lena.

MAMA [*Stalling, starting to look around at the house*] Yes—I'm coming. Ruth—

RUTH Yes?

MAMA [*Quietly, woman to woman*] He finally come into his manhood today,
didn't he? Kind of like a rainbow after the rain . . .

RUTH [*Biting her lip lest her own pride explode in front of* MAMA] Yes, Lena.

[WALTER'S *voice calls for them raucously.*]

WALTER [*Off stage*] Y'all come on! These people charges by the hour, you know!

MAMA [*Waving* RUTH *out vaguely*] All right, honey—go on down. I be down
directly.

[RUTH *hesitates, then exits.* MAMA *stands, at last alone in the living room,
her plant on the table before her as the lights start to come down. She looks
around at all the walls and ceilings and suddenly, despite herself, while the
children call below, a great heaving thing rises in her and she puts her fist
to her mouth to stifle it, takes a final desperate look, pulls her coat about
her, pats her hat and goes out. The lights dim down. The door opens and
she comes back in, grabs her plant, and goes out for the last time.*]

Curtain

HAROLD PINTER

1930–2008

Harold Pinter, who won the Nobel Prize in Literature in 2005, is, in the opinion of many, the most important British dramatist since GEORGE BERNARD SHAW. Despite the obvious differences between the playwrights, they shared a similar relationship to the theater and society of their times. An Irishman and outsider to the English stage at the turn of the twentieth century, Shaw turned one of its dominant genres, the well-made play, into a mode of ironic social drama recalling the socially conscious realist plays of HENRIK IBSEN that he had championed. Likewise Pinter, a Jewish, working-class outsider from London's East End, remade the dominant conventions of the London stage after World War II—those of psychological realism and the drawing-room play—into vehicles of modern tragicomedy. Although both the playwright and his work lacked Shaw's didacticism, Pinter became a leading figure in the movement for a new British drama in the late 1950s and 1960s. More than those of any other playwright associated with that movement, Pinter's plays moved the British theater nearer to the Absurdist vision of SAMUEL BECKETT and the Continental avant-garde.

Beginning with his first play, *The Room* (1957), and continuing with *The Birthday Party* (1958), *The Caretaker* (1960), and *THE HOMECOMING* (1965), Pinter developed a dramaturgy so distinctive it has earned the label "Pinteresque." Employing a mix of familiar and indecipherable dramatic events, the Pinteresque is associated with the following elements: a sparsely furnished room; an ongoing and precarious balance of power—physical, verbal, and psychological—between the inhabitants of the room; and the entrance of an outsider who disturbs the balance, provoking power struggles that issue in a violent or near-violent denouement. The term "Pinteresque" also refers to Pinter's characteristic use of dramatic language. In Pinter's plays, every line (and every silence) serves to maintain, disturb, or renegotiate the balance of power between characters. Speech often reflects a need for dominance and displaces a physical violence that would break out if that need were not contained or redirected. The dialogue is marked by patterns of verbal repetition, crosstalk (characters speaking "past" or "around" each other), outbursts of uneasy garrulity (trivial banter, jokes, anecdotes, philosophical ruminations), and, above all, Pinter's signature pauses and silences. The patterns emerge from what Pinter called the "desire for verification"—the speaker's desire to have an assertion, and often his or her very sense of identity, affirmed by the other character. Silence is pivotal in this cat-and-mouse game as characters refuse or become unable to say what they think or feel or to verify what their interlocutor has asserted. Early in his career, Pinter wrote: "The speech we hear . . . is a necessary avoidance, a violent, sly, and anguished or mocking smoke screen which keeps the other in its place. When true silence falls we are still left with the echo but are nearer nakedness. One way of looking at speech is to say that it is a constant stratagem to cover nakedness."

The facts of Pinter's early life provide clues to his obsession with violence and the power of language to embody and repress it. Born in 1930, Pinter grew up in Hackney, a run-down working-class area in London's East End. His father was a women's tailor, and his ancestors were Jews who had escaped pogroms in Poland and Ukraine. At the start of World War II, the ten-year-old Pinter was sent to the countryside to escape the German bombing of London, though he returned home a year later and experienced the Blitz firsthand. While Pinter was a teenager, a fascist movement led by Sir Oswald Mosley was active in the East End. Pinter and his friends, many of whom were Jewish, regularly encountered gangs of young toughs who were roaming the streets with broken milk bottles and threatening to attack Jews and Communists. They escaped assault by engaging gang members in verbal banter, using language to defer violence in a manner that would become typical in Pinter's plays.

During 1944–47 Pinter attended Hackney Downs, the local all-boys grammar school, where he was an accomplished runner, cricketer, and soccer player. He also wrote poetry, acted in productions of SHAKESPEARE, and developed a close circle of friends who shared his interests in art and literature. After graduation, Pinter trained as an actor at the Royal Academy of Dramatic Art (RADA) and the Central School of Speech and Drama, both in London. In the 1950s, he acted in provincial repertory theaters, most notably Andrew McMaster's Shakespearean touring company; there he met his first wife, Vivien Merchant, who became a leading interpreter of his female characters in the 1960s and early 1970s. (They divorced in 1980, and Pinter married the novelist and historian Lady Antonia Fraser.) During this time, Pinter wrote steadily: poems, short stories, and a semiautobiographical novel, *The Dwarfs* (published 1990). He turned to playwriting in 1957 after being invited to write a play for the Bristol University Drama Department. The resulting one act, *The Room,* was performed in the Sunday Times Student Drama Festival and received an enthusiastic review from the influential *Times* critic Harold Hobson. The review brought Pinter to the attention of the West End producer Michael Codron, who staged Pinter's first full-length play, *The Birthday Party,* in 1958. The daily reviewers (with the exception of Hobson) attacked the play, but it caught the interest of critics and directors in the United States and Germany as well as in Britain. In 1959–60 Pinter premiered two additional works: a one act, *The Dumb Waiter* (1959), and a second full-length play, *The Caretaker.* More naturalistic than his previous plays, *The Caretaker* was Pinter's first critical success, winning prestigious prizes in London and New York and solidifying his reputation as a major if controversial dramatist.

In the late 1950s and early 1960s several other young authors—most notably John Osborne, Arnold Wesker, and John Arden—received widespread critical attention for plays that decried the rise of social affluence and complacency in Britain after the war. Dubbed the "Angry Young Men" by the press, these playwrights offered both innovative naturalistic depictions of British working-class life and epic historical dramas that used the past to mirror present-day political concerns. Unlike the Angry Young Men, Pinter never sought to lead a theatrical movement or advocate a new kind of drama. Pinter's early plays reflect the realities of working-class life in their settings, characters, and language; yet social class is not so much a dramatic focus of the plays as an aspect of the sense of identity over which Pinter's characters struggle. Although Pinter himself was a man of strong political beliefs—a conscientious objector during the Cold War, he published scathing essays on American and British military interventions in the Balkans and the Middle East during the 1990s and 2000s—it was not until the 1980s that Pinter's plays expressed explicitly political subjects. Even then, though, the political represents one facet of a power dynamic that operates at all levels of human relationship—physical, emotional, and psychological as well as political.

Both *The Room* and *The Birthday Party* present mundane situations that disintegrate into scenes of ominous danger. The latter opens with a breakfast at a seaside boardinghouse, as the landlady fusses over her husband and a young boarder. The domestic scene is disturbed when two men visit the boarder and interrogate him with unanswerable questions; in the end, they take him away. These plays turn a seemingly familiar situation into something mystifying and inexplicable: characters and their pasts are not revealed but instead are shown to be perplexing, beyond explanation. In *The Caretaker,* and to even greater effect in *The Homecoming*, the tensions between the familiar and the inexplicable remain constant while the dramatic action grows more complex. In *The Caretaker,* a young man takes in an elderly homeless man to serve as "caretaker" of the apartment that the young man shares with his brother; the three men become entwined in a territorial struggle that ends when one of them is evicted and humiliated. In *The Homecoming,* a philosophy professor returns from an American university to his working-class home in London, where he introduces his father, brothers, and uncle to his English-born wife. The struggles that ensue among the men are heightened by sexual tension between the men and the wife, by the couple's deployment of the higher social position to which they have risen, and by the tough "male" occupations (boxer, pimp) of the brothers. In both plays, the territorial struggle for dominance within the room is wedded to intricate psychological encounters that occur over issues of class, education, age, sex, and gender.

This deepening of Pinter's psychological exploration in *The Caretaker* and *The Homecoming* anticipated the tone and focus of Pinter's major plays of the 1970s: *Old Times* (1971), *No Man's Land* (1975), and *Betrayal* (1978). Abandoning the physically menacing environments of the earlier works, these plays dwell more deeply on the remembered past and the impor-

tance of memory to self-identity. Though they are grounded in realistic portrayals of the English middle class, the plays unfold in a fragmented, dreamlike manner. *Betrayal,* for example, traces the relationship between two old university friends and a woman who is the wife of one and the lover of the other. The play presents the development of these relationships over many years but does so in reverse chronological order; it thereby highlights the duplicities, both small and large, on which friendship, marriage, and infidelity are founded. In their use of time-jumping and time-eliding strategies more common to film, these plays exhibit the impact of Pinter's work as a screenwriter on his playwriting. That career included screen adaptations of his plays and novels by other authors (notably, John Fowles's *The French Lieutenant's Woman* [1969; film, 1981] and Margaret Atwood's *The Handmaid's Tale* [1985; film, 1990]). In bringing works of fiction to the screen, Pinter exploited the structural flexibility of film to find a cinematic equivalent of the novel's complex point of view and use of time. The playwright's foremost achievement in this regard is his adaptation of *Remembrance of Things Past* (1913–27), Marcel Proust's fictional reminiscence of childhood, love, and sexual awakening, on which Pinter worked in the years between *Old Times* and *No Man's Land.* While this film was never produced, a dramatic adaptation was staged in 2000 at the Royal National Theatre in London.

Although Pinter's exploration of memory continued in *Family Voices* (1981), *Victoria Station* (1982), and *A Kind of Alaska* (1982), the 1980s saw a shift in his dramatic writing to more directly political situations and issues. In *One for the Road* (1984), *Mountain Language* (1988), and *Party Time* (1991), which deal with government torture, class inequality, and other human rights abuses, the violence that lurks beneath the surface of Pinter's earlier plays is given specific institutional contexts. Pinter's final plays—*Moonlight* (1993), *Ashes to Ashes* (1996), and *Celebration* (1999)—revisit the subject of memory while conveying the political overtones that marked his work in the 1980s. As these very different plays indicate, the "Pinteresque" is a resilient and adaptable dramatic mode, and Pinter's dramaturgy of minimal words and maximal silence continues, like that of Beckett, to speak to the anxieties of contemporary life.

The Homecoming is Harold Pinter's best-known play. Initially produced by the Royal Shakespeare Company at London's Aldwych Theatre on June 3, 1965, the play has been staged a number of times over the years, including a 1967 Broadway production (which won four Tony Awards) and a highly acclaimed New York revival forty years later. Since its opening, The Homecoming has also been one of Pinter's most analyzed plays, as critics, theater artists, audiences, and readers try to come to terms with its unexpected, often shocking, action. Teddy, a professor of philosophy, brings his wife, Ruth, from the United States, where they live with three children, to introduce her to his North London family. But the family he rejoins is anything but benign. On the play's emotionally barren set, his father, Max, a former butcher, lashes out bitterly against his other two sons—Lenny, a small-time pimp, and Joey, an aspiring boxer—and against his brother Sam, who

works as a chauffeur. Throughout the play's opening scenes, the four seek dominance over each other with aggressive, animal-like territoriality. When Ruth arrives with Teddy, the men alternate between treating her as a target of hostility and welcoming her as "kith" and "kin." Under the eye of her impassive husband, the males make increasingly open sexual advances on Ruth and end with the proposition that she stay with them as part of the family. The terms of this proposition, Ruth's response to it, and Teddy's calm departure represent the final outrages in this disturbing, savagely funny play.

As the metaphors of butchering and boxing indicate, The Homecoming is pervaded with violence and the threat of violence. Max lectures Joey on boxing: "[Y]ou've got to learn how to defend yourself, and you've got to learn how to attack." But with the exception of one explosive onstage moment this violence is exerted through language. As Austin Quigley notes in his influential study The Pinter Problem, the dialogue in a play like The Homecoming is "interrelational" rather than referential. Words (and their absence), in other words, are a form of

A 2011 production of The Homecoming at the American Conservatory Theatre (San Francisco), featuring (left to right) Andrew Polk as Lenny, Anthony Fusco as Teddy, and René Augesen as Ruth.

action taken on others rather than a medium for referring to reality. When Max attempts to talk with Lenny in the play's opening scene, his silence in response to much of what he is told has the effect of leaving his father unacknowledged and exposed. Their subsequent conversation shifts the balance of power with the precision of a sparring match. When Sam enters, followed by Joey, the dynamics change yet again. Sam boasts about his reputation as a chauffeur, but Max changes the subject in order to target his brother's vulnerability: "It's funny you never got married, isn't it? A man with all your gifts." Reading and acting out exchanges such as this, one needs to pay attention to the subtextual meaning of words, to the intentions beneath what is spoken that accomplish something other than what the words purport to say. One should also pay attention to the pauses and silences, those moments when characters are brought up short, words fail, and the hostile intimacy that binds these characters is open to view.

Underlying the play's territorial struggles is the assertion of masculine power: power over women, power over other men, power over each other. Max, a failing patriarch, claims to have been one of the "worst hated men in the West End of London" when he prowled the city in his prime with his friend MacGregor. In the play's second act Lenny recounts the story that he and Joey picked up two women, chased away their escorts, and had sex with them, bordering on rape, in the rubble of a bombed site. But their pose of aggressive, even violent, masculinity masks a much more complex psychodynamic terrain, one defined—indeed dominated—by the memory of Max's deceased wife, Jessie. What kind of wife and mother Jessie was is difficult to determine: Max remembers her at one point as a woman "with a will of iron, a heart of gold, and a mind" but shortly after refers to her as "a slutbitch of a wife." Sam, we learn, drove Jessie and MacGregor around in the backseat of his car, and in his references to this he taunts Max with what he claims to know. Remembered in the conflicting roles of mother and whore, the absent Jessie embodies an

unsteady emotional landscape of domesticity, maternal love, sexuality, and betrayal. The family that remains negotiates this landscape with a male assertiveness made all the fiercer by the wounds they harbor.

This is the world that Ruth enters when she and Teddy arrive in the play's first act. The details of Ruth's past are themselves sketchy. She refers to having worked as a photographic "model for the body," but exactly what this entailed and how she met Teddy are never disclosed. She is clearly unhappy with her life as a professor's wife in the United States, and she seems on more familiar ground when she takes a walk alone at night after they arrive. She is also surprisingly adept at dealing with the reception she receives. When Lenny encounters Ruth alone after her walk, he questions the nature of her relationship with his brother, refers to the fact that he's in his pajamas and she's fully dressed, and subjects her to two long stories that end with physical violence to women. In addition, when Max finds out that she spent the night in his house, he refers to her as a "stinking pox-ridden slut." But Ruth skillfully establishes her control of these situations. In a series of brilliant moves, she turns the tables on Lenny in their nighttime exchange, asserting her sexuality and calling his bluff as a misogynistic aggressor. And in her interactions with Max and the others she quickly asserts her role as a member of the family, occupying the place vacated by the deceased Jessie. While her decision at the end of the play comes as a shock, it is consistent with her newfound authority. Like the Old Testament Ruth, who returned with her mother-in-law, Naomi, to Bethlehem after the death of her husband and remarried one of Naomi's kinsmen, she undergoes a homecoming of her own.

As *The Homecoming*'s interactions take their course, no character appears more enigmatic than Teddy. Why does Teddy bring his wife home to this environment, and why does he respond to the play's developments as he does? When the subject of his critical works comes up, he characterizes them in terms of an intellectual stance that doesn't get lost in the objects and encounters of the world: "It's a question of how far you can operate on things and not in things." Teddy's seeming detachment from the events that transpire represents, in his eyes, a triumph in the play's survival-of-the-fittest struggle. But passivity can be its own form of aggression, and Teddy is very much a product of this violent, wounded family. As *The Homecoming* moves to its almost inconceivable conclusion, one wonders if Teddy and his own three sons are destined to repeat the cycle he knows so well.

ART BORRECA, S.G.

The Homecoming

CHARACTERS

MAX, *a man of seventy*
LENNY, *a man in his early thirties*
SAM, *a man of sixty-three*

JOEY, *a man in his middle twenties*
TEDDY, *a man in his middle thirties*
RUTH, *a woman in her early thirties*

An old house in North London.[1]

A large room, extending the width of the stage.

The back wall, which contained the door, has been removed. A square arch shape remains. Beyond it, the hall. In the hall a staircase, ascending U.L., *well in view. The front door* U.R. *A coatstand, hooks, etc.*

In the room a window, R. *Odd tables, chairs. Two large armchairs. A large sofa,* L. *Against* R. *wall a large sideboard,*[2] *the upper half of which contains a mirror.* U.L., *a radiogram.*[3]

Act One

Evening.

LENNY *is sitting on the sofa with a newspaper, a pencil in his hand. He wears a dark suit. He makes occasional marks on the back page.*

MAX *comes in, from the direction of the kitchen. He goes to sideboard, opens top drawer, rummages in it, closes it.*

He wears an old cardigan[4] *and a cap, and carries a stick.*[5]

He walks downstage, stands, looks about the room.

MAX   What have you done with the scissors?

[*Pause.*]

---

1. Area of London north of the River Thames. Demographically diverse, North London includes well-established Jewish and nonwhite communities.
2. Piece of furniture, typically placed against a wall, that is used for serving and displaying food.
3. Piece of furniture that combines a radio and a gramophone (record player).
4. Sweater that fastens in the front.
5. That is, walking stick or cane.

I said I'm looking for the scissors. What have you done with them?

[*Pause.*]

Did you hear me? I want to cut something out of the paper.

LENNY   I'm reading the paper.

5   MAX   Not that paper. I haven't even read that paper. I'm talking about last Sunday's paper. I was just having a look at it in the kitchen.

[*Pause.*]

Do you hear what I'm saying? I'm talking to you! Where's the scissors?

LENNY [*looking up, quietly*]   Why don't you shut up, you daft prat?[6]

[MAX *lifts his stick and points it at him.*]

MAX   Don't you talk to me like that. I'm warning you.

[*He sits in large armchair.*]

10   There's an advertisement in the paper about flannel vests. Cut price. Navy surplus. I could do with a few of them.

[*Pause.*]

I think I'll have a fag.[7] Give me a fag.

[*Pause.*]

I just asked you to give me a cigarette.

[*Pause.*]

Look what I'm lumbered[8] with.

[*He takes a crumpled cigarette from his pocket.*]

15   I'm getting old, my word of honour.

[*He lights it.*]

You think I wasn't a tearaway?[9] I could have taken care of you, twice over. I'm still strong. You ask your Uncle Sam what I was. But at the same time I always had a kind heart. Always.

[*Pause.*]

I used to knock about with[1] a man called MacGregor. I called him Mac.

20   You remember Mac? Eh?

[*Pause.*]

Huhh! We were two of the worst hated men in the West End of London.[2] I tell you, I still got the scars. We'd walk into a place, the whole room'd stand up, they'd make way to let us pass. You never heard such silence. Mind you, he was a big man, he was over six foot tall. His family were all

25   MacGregors, they came all the way from Aberdeen,[3] but he was the only one they called Mac.

[*Pause.*]

He was very fond of your mother, Mac was. Very fond. He always had a good word for her.

---

6. Idiot or fool (British), originally slang for "buttocks."
7. Cigarette (slang).
8. Burdened or encumbered.
9. Petty thief or hooligan (British slang).
1. Associate with.

2. Fashionable area of central London known for its government buildings and monuments, upscale shopping, theaters, and other cultural attractions.
3. City in northeast Scotland.

[*Pause.*]

Mind you, she wasn't such a bad woman. Even though it made me sick just
30 to look at her rotten stinking face, she wasn't such a bad bitch. I gave her
the best bleeding years of my life, anyway.

LENNY Plug it, will you, you stupid sod,[4] I'm trying to read the paper.

MAX Listen! I'll chop your spine off, you talk to me like that! You understand? Talking to your lousy filthy father like that!

35 LENNY You know what, you're getting demented.

[*Pause.*]

What do you think of Second Wind for the three-thirty?[5]

MAX Where?

LENNY Sandown Park.[6]

MAX Don't stand a chance.

40 LENNY Sure he does.

MAX Not a chance.

LENNY He's the winner.

[LENNY *ticks the paper.*]

MAX He talks to me about horses.

[*Pause.*]

I used to live on the course. One of the loves of my life. Epsom? I knew it
45 like the back of my hand. I was one of the best-known faces down at the
paddock. What a marvellous open-air life.

[*Pause.*]

He talks to me about horses. You only read their names in the papers.
But I've stroked their manes, I've held them, I've calmed them down
before a big race. I was the one they used to call for. Max, they'd say,
50 there's a horse here, he's highly strung, you're the only man on the
course who can calm him. It was true. I had a . . . I had an instinctive
understanding of animals. I should have been a trainer. Many times I
was offered the job—you know, a proper post, by the Duke of . . . I forget his name . . . one of the Dukes. But I had family obligations, my
55 family needed me at home.

[*Pause.*]

The times I've watched those animals thundering past the post. What an
experience. Mind you, I didn't lose, I made a few bob[7] out of it, and you
know why? Because I always had the smell of a good horse. I could smell
him. And not only the colts but the fillies. Because the fillies are more
60 highly strung than the colts, they're more unreliable, did you know that?
No, what do you know? Nothing. But I was always able to tell a good filly
by one particular trick. I'd look her in the eye. You see? I'd stand in front of
her and look her straight in the eye, it was a kind of hypnotism, and by the

---

4. That is, "sodomite," or homosexual (British
slang).
5. Name of a racehorse running in the 3:30
P.M. race.
6. Like Epsom Downs, referred to several
lines later, a horse-racing track on the outskirts of London.
7. Shilling. Before the decimalization of British currency in 1971, a shilling was equivalent to 12 pence (or pennies), and one pound
was equivalent to 20 shillings.

look deep down in her eye I could tell whether she was a stayer[8] or not. It
was a gift. I had a gift.

[*Pause.*]

And he talks to me about horses.

LENNY   Dad, do you mind if I change the subject?

[*Pause.*]

I want to ask you something. That dinner we had before, what was the
name of it? What do you call it?

[*Pause.*]

Why don't you buy a dog? You're a dog cook. Honest. You think you're cooking for a lot of dogs.

MAX   If you don't like it get out.

LENNY   I am going out. I'm going out to buy myself a proper dinner.

MAX   Well, get out! What are you waiting for?

[LENNY *looks at him.*]

LENNY   What did you say?

MAX   I said shove off out of it, that's what I said.

LENNY   You'll go before me, Dad, if you talk to me in that tone of voice.

MAX   Will I, you bitch?

[MAX *grips his stick.*]

LENNY   Oh, Daddy, you're not going to use your stick on me, are you? Eh?
Don't use your stick on me, Daddy. No, please. It wasn't my fault, it was one
of the others. I haven't done anything wrong, Dad, honest. Don't clout[9] me
with that stick, Dad.

[*Silence.*]

[MAX *sits hunched.* LENNY *reads the paper.*]

[SAM *comes in the front door. He wears a chauffeur's uniform. He hangs
his hat on a hook in the hall and comes into the room. He goes to a chair,
sits in it and sighs.*]

Hullo, Uncle Sam.

SAM   Hullo.

LENNY   How are you, Uncle?

SAM   Not bad. A bit tired.

LENNY   Tired? I bet you're tired. Where you been?

SAM   I've been to London Airport.[1]

LENNY   All the way up to London Airport? What, right up the M4?[2]

SAM   Yes, all the way up there.

LENNY   Tch, tch, tch. Well, I think you're entitled to be tired, Uncle.

SAM   Well, it's the drivers.

LENNY   I know. That's what I'm talking about. I'm talking about the drivers.

SAM   Knocks you out.

[*Pause.*]

MAX   I'm here, too, you know.

---

8. Horse-racing term for a horse that races
well over long distances.
9. Strike or hit.
1. Heathrow Airport was known as the Lon-

don Airport until 1966.
2. A major motorway (highway) that runs
east-west between London and South Wales.

[SAM *looks at him.*]

I said I'm here, too. I'm sitting here.

SAM   I know you're here.

[*Pause.*]

SAM   I took a Yankee[3] out there today . . . to the Airport.

LENNY   Oh, a Yankee, was it?

100 SAM   Yes, I been with him all day. Picked him up at the Savoy at half past twelve, took him to the Caprice[4] for his lunch. After lunch I picked him up again, took him down to a house in Eaton Square[5]—he had to pay a visit to a friend there—and then round about tea-time[6] I took him right the way out to the Airport.

105 LENNY   Had to catch a plane there, did he?

SAM   Yes. Look what he gave me. He gave me a box of cigars.

[SAM *takes a box of cigars from his pocket.*]

MAX   Come here. Let's have a look at them.

[SAM *shows* MAX *the cigars.* MAX *takes one from the box, pinches it and sniffs it.[7]*]

It's a fair cigar.

SAM   Want to try one?

[MAX *and* SAM *light cigars.*]

110 You know what he said to me? He told me I was the best chauffeur he'd ever had. The best one.

MAX   From what point of view?

SAM   Eh?

MAX   From what point of view?

115 LENNY   From the point of view of his driving, Dad, and his general sense of courtesy, I should say.

MAX   Thought you were a good driver, did he, Sam? Well, he gave you a first-class cigar.

SAM   Yes, he thought I was the best he'd ever had. They all say that, you 120 know. They won't have anyone else, they only ask for me. They say I'm the best chauffeur in the firm.

LENNY   I bet the other drivers tend to get jealous, don't they, Uncle?

SAM   They do get jealous. They get very jealous.

MAX   Why?

[*Pause.*]

125 SAM   I just told you.

MAX   No, I just can't get it clear, Sam. Why do the other drivers get jealous?

SAM   Because (a) I'm the best driver, and because . . . (b) I don't take liberties.

[*Pause.*]

---

3. That is, an American.

4. Le Caprice is an upscale restaurant, and the Savoy is a well-known luxury hotel. Both are located in London's West End.

5. Residential square in London's West End that is one of the city's most exclusive and fashionable neighborhoods.

6. Small meal taken in the afternoon, traditionally consisting of tea and lighter fare such as small sandwiches, scones, or small cakes.

7. Pinching a cigar is the most common method of testing the cigar's quality. The feel of the cigar can indicate whether or not it has been stored at the proper humidity.

I don't press myself on people, you see. These big businessmen, men of
affairs, they don't want the driver jawing[8] all the time, they like to sit in the
back, have a bit of peace and quiet. After all, they're sitting in a Humber
Super Snipe,[9] they can afford to relax. At the same time, though, this is
what really makes me special . . . I do know how to pass the time of day
when required.

    [*Pause.*]

For instance, I told this man today I was in the second world war. Not the
first. I told him I was too young for the first. But I told him I fought in the
second.

    [*Pause.*]

So did he, it turned out.

    [LENNY *stands, goes to the mirror and straightens his tie.*]

LENNY He was probably a colonel, or something, in the American Air Force.
SAM Yes.
LENNY Probably a navigator, or something like that, in a Flying Fortress.[1]
Now he's most likely a high executive in a worldwide group of aeronautical
engineers.
SAM Yes.
LENNY Yes, I know the kind of man you're talking about.

    [LENNY *goes out, turning to his right.*]

SAM After all, I'm experienced. I was driving a dust cart[2] at the age of nineteen. Then I was in long-distance haulage. I had ten years as a taxi-driver
and I've had five as a private chauffeur.
MAX It's funny you never got married, isn't it? A man with all your gifts.

    [*Pause.*]

Isn't it? A man like you?
SAM There's still time.
MAX Is there?

    [*Pause.*]

SAM You'd be surprised.
MAX What you been doing, banging away at your lady customers, have you?
SAM Not me.
MAX In the back of the Snipe? Been having a few crafty reefs[3] in a layby,[4]
have you?
SAM Not me.
MAX On the back seat? What about the armrest, was it up or down?
SAM I've never done that kind of thing in my car.
MAX Above all that kind of thing, are you, Sam?
SAM Too true.
MAX Above having a good bang on the back seat, are you?
SAM Yes, I leave that to others.

---

8. Speaking aimlessly or babbling.
9. Six-cylinder luxury vehicle produced in
England by Humber Motor Cars between
1938 and 1967.
1. American-designed bomber aircraft. "Flying
Fortress" bombers were instrumental in World
War II campaigns against German targets.

2. Garbage truck.
3. Fondling, petting, or groping (British slang).
The term also has homosexual connotations.
4. Paved area next to a major roadway where
travelers can park and rest. On larger roadways
these areas can include public facilities.

165 MAX   You leave it to others? What others? You paralysed prat!

SAM   I don't mess up my car! Or my . . . . my boss's car! Like other people.

MAX   Other people? What other people?

> [*Pause.*]

What other people?

> [*Pause.*]

SAM   Other people.

> [*Pause.*]

170 MAX   When you find the right girl, Sam, let your family know, don't forget, we'll give you a number one send-off, I promise you. You can bring her to live here, she can keep us all happy. We'd take it in turns to give her a walk round the park.

SAM   I wouldn't bring her here.

175 MAX   Sam, it's your decision. You're welcome to bring your bride here, to the place where you live, or on the other hand you can take a suite at the Dorchester.[5] It's entirely up to you.

SAM   I haven't got a bride.

> [SAM *stands, goes to the sideboard, takes an apple from the bowl, bites into it.*]

Getting a bit peckish.[6]

> [*He looks out of the window.*]

180 Never get a bride like you had, anyway. Nothing like your bride . . . going about these days. Like Jessie.

> [*Pause.*]

After all, I escorted her once or twice, didn't I? Drove her round once or twice in my cab. She was a charming woman.

> [*Pause.*]

All the same, she was your wife. But still . . . they were some of the most

185 delightful evenings I've ever had. Used to just drive her about. It was my pleasure.

MAX [*softly, closing his eyes*]   Christ.

SAM   I used to pull up at a stall[7] and buy her a cup of coffee. She was a very nice companion to be with.

> [*Silence.*]
> [JOEY *comes in the front door. He walks into the room, takes his jacket off, throws it on a chair and stands.*]
> [*Silence.*]

190 JOEY   Feel a bit hungry.

SAM   Me, too.

MAX   Who do you think I am, your mother? Eh? Honest. They walk in here every time of the day and night like bloody[8] animals. Go and find yourself a mother.

> [LENNY *walks into the room, stands.*]

195 JOEY   I've been training down at the gym.

SAM   Yes, the boy's been working all day and training all night.

---

5. Another luxury hotel in the West End of London.
6. Hungry.

7. Stand where food and beverages are sold.
8. A mild oath, usually used as an intensifier (British).

MAX What do you want, you bitch? You spend all the day sitting on your arse at London Airport, buy yourself a jamroll.[9] You expect me to sit here waiting to rush into the kitchen the moment you step in the door? You've been
200 living sixty-three years, why don't you learn to cook?

SAM I can cook.

MAX Well, go and cook!

[*Pause.*]

LENNY What the boys want, Dad, is your own special brand of cooking, Dad.
That's what the boys look forward to. The special understanding of food,
205 you know, that you've got.

MAX Stop calling me Dad. Just stop all that calling me Dad, do you understand?

LENNY But I'm your son. You used to tuck me up in bed every night. He
tucked you up, too, didn't he, Joey?

[*Pause.*]

210 He used to like tucking up his sons.

[LENNY *turns and goes towards the front door.*]

MAX Lenny.

LENNY [*turning*] What?

MAX I'll give you a proper tuck up one of these nights, son. You mark my word.

[*They look at each other.*]
[LENNY *opens the front door and goes out.*]
[*Silence.*]

JOEY I've been training with Bobby Dodd.[1]

[*Pause.*]

215 And I had a good go at the bag as well.[2]

[*Pause.*]

I wasn't in bad trim.[3]

MAX Boxing's a gentleman's game.

[*Pause.*]

I'll tell you what you've got to do. What you've got to do is you've got to
learn how to defend yourself, and you've got to learn how to attack. That's
220 your only trouble as a boxer. You don't know how to defend yourself, and
you don't know how to attack.

[*Pause.*]

Once you've mastered those arts you can go straight to the top.

[*Pause.*]

JOEY I've got a pretty good idea . . . of how to do that.

[JOEY *looks round for his jacket, picks it up, goes out of the room and up
the stairs.*]
[*Pause.*]

MAX Sam . . . why don't you go, too, eh? Why don't you just go upstairs?
225 Leave me quiet. Leave me alone.

SAM I want to make something clear about Jessie, Max. I want to. I do.
When I took her out in the cab, round the town, I was taking care of her,

---

9. That is, jelly roll.
1. Unknown reference.

2. Punching bag.
3. That is, in bad physical condition.

for you. I was looking after her for you, when you were busy, wasn't I? I was showing her the West End.

> [*Pause.*]

230 You wouldn't have trusted any of your other brothers. You wouldn't have trusted Mac, would you? But you trusted me. I want to remind you.

> [*Pause.*]

Old Mac died a few years ago, didn't he? Isn't he dead?

> [*Pause.*]

He was a lousy stinking rotten loudmouth. A bastard uncouth sodding[4] runt. Mind you, he was a good friend of yours.

> [*Pause.*]

235 MAX Eh, Sam . . .

SAM What?

MAX Why do I keep you here? You're just an old grub.

SAM Am I?

MAX You're a maggot.

240 SAM Oh yes?

MAX As soon as you stop paying your way here, I mean when you're too old to pay your way, you know what I'm going to do? I'm going to give you the boot.

SAM You are, eh?

245 MAX Sure. I mean, bring in the money and I'll put up with you. But when the firm gets rid of you—you can flake off.

SAM This is my house as well, you know. This was our mother's house.

MAX One lot after the other. One mess after the other.

SAM Our father's house.

250 MAX Look what I'm lumbered with. One cast-iron bunch of crap after another. One flow of stinking pus after another.

> [*Pause.*]

Our father? I remember him. Don't worry. You kid yourself. He used to come over to me and look down at me. My old man did. He'd bend right over me, then he'd pick me up. I was only that big. Then he'd dandle[5] me. Give me the
255 bottle. Wipe me clean. Give me a smile. Pat me on the bum. Pass me around, pass me from hand to hand. Toss me up in the air. Catch me coming down. I remember my father.

> [BLACKOUT.]
> [LIGHTS UP.]
> [*Night.*]
> [TEDDY *and* RUTH *stand at the threshold of the room.*]
> [*They are both well dressed in light summer suits and light raincoats.*]
> [*Two suitcases are by their side.*]
> [*They look at the room.* TEDDY *tosses the key in his hand, smiles.*]

TEDDY Well, the key worked.

> [*Pause.*]

They haven't changed the lock.

> [*Pause.*]

---

4. An oath, derived from "sod."   5. Playfully bounce up and down on one knee.

260 RUTH   No one's here.

TEDDY [*looking up*]   They're asleep.

[*Pause.*]

RUTH   Can I sit down?

TEDDY   Of course.

RUTH   I'm tired.

[*Pause.*]

265 TEDDY   Then sit down.

[*She does not move.*]

That's my father's chair.

RUTH   That one?

TEDDY [*smiling*]   Yes, that's it. Shall I go up and see if my room's still there?

RUTH   It can't have moved.

270 TEDDY   No, I mean if my bed's still there.

RUTH   Someone might be in it.

TEDDY   No. They've got their own beds.

[*Pause.*]

RUTH   Shouldn't you wake someone up? Tell them you're here?

TEDDY   Not at this time of night. It's too late.

[*Pause.*]

275 Shall I go up?

[*He goes into the hall, looks up the stairs, comes back.*]

Why don't you sit down?

[*Pause.*]

I'll just go up . . . have a look.

[*He goes up the stairs, stealthily.*]
[RUTH *stands, then slowly walks across the room.*]
[TEDDY *returns.*]

It's still there. My room. Empty. The bed's there. What are you doing?

[*She looks at him.*]

Blankets, no sheets. I'll find some sheets. I could hear snores. Really.

280 They're all still here, I think. They're all snoring up there. Are you cold?

RUTH   No.

TEDDY   I'll make something to drink, if you like. Something hot.

RUTH   No, I don't want anything.

[TEDDY *walks about.*]

TEDDY   What do you think of the room? Big, isn't it? It's a big house. I mean,

285 it's a fine room, don't you think? Actually there was a wall, across there . . .
with a door. We knocked it down . . . years ago . . . . to make an open living
area. The structure wasn't affected, you see. My mother was dead.

[RUTH *sits.*]

Tired?

RUTH   Just a little.

290 TEDDY   We can go to bed if you like. No point in waking anyone up now. Just go
to bed. See them all in the morning . . . see my father in the morning. . . .

[*Pause.*]

RUTH   Do you want to stay?

TEDDY   Stay?

　　　　[*Pause.*]

We've come to stay. We're bound to stay . . . for a few days.

295 RUTH   I think . . . the children . . . might be missing us.

TEDDY   Don't be silly.

RUTH   They might.

TEDDY   Look, we'll be back in a few days, won't we?

　　　　[*He walks about the room.*]

Nothing's changed. Still the same.

　　　　[*Pause.*]

300   Still, he'll get a surprise in the morning, won't he? The old man. I think you'll like him very much. Honestly. He's a . . . well, he's old, of course. Getting on.

　　　　[*Pause.*]

I was born here, do you realize that?

RUTH   I know.

　　　　[*Pause.*]

305 TEDDY   Why don't you go to bed? I'll find some sheets. I feel . . . wide awake, isn't it odd? I think I'll stay up for a bit. Are you tired?

RUTH   No.

TEDDY   Go to bed. I'll show you the room.

RUTH   No, I don't want to.

310 TEDDY   You'll be perfectly all right up there without me. Really you will. I mean, I won't be long. Look, it's just up there. It's the first door on the landing. The bathroom is right next door. You . . . need some rest, you know.

　　　　[*Pause.*]

I just want to . . . walk about for a few minutes. Do you mind?

RUTH   Of course I don't.

315 TEDDY   Well . . . Shall I show you the room?

RUTH   No, I'm happy at the moment.

TEDDY   You don't have to go to bed. I'm not saying you have to. I mean, you can stay up with me. Perhaps I'll make a cup of tea or something. The only thing is we don't want to make too much noise, we don't want to wake any-

320   one up.

RUTH   I'm not making any noise.

TEDDY   I know you're not.

　　　　[*He goes to her.*]

[*Gently.*] Look, it's all right, really. I'm here. I mean . . . I'm with you. There's no need to be nervous. Are you nervous?

325 RUTH   No.

TEDDY   There's no need to be.

　　　　[*Pause.*]

They're very warm people, really. Very warm. They're my family. They're not ogres.

　　　　[*Pause.*]

Well, perhaps we should go to bed. After all, we have to be up early, see

330   Dad. Wouldn't be quite right if he found us in bed, I think. [*He chuckles.*] Have to be up before six, come down, say hullo.

[*Pause.*]

RUTH I think I'll have a breath of air.

TEDDY Air?

[*Pause.*]

What do you mean?

335 RUTH [*standing*] Just a stroll.

TEDDY At this time of night? But we've . . . only just got here. We've got to go to bed.

RUTH I just feel like some air.

TEDDY But I'm going to bed.

340 RUTH That's all right.

TEDDY But what am I going to do?

[*Pause.*]

The last thing I want is a breath of air. Why do you want a breath of air?

RUTH I just do.

TEDDY But it's late.

345 RUTH I won't go far. I'll come back.

[*Pause.*]

TEDDY I'll wait up for you.

RUTH Why?

TEDDY I'm not going to bed without you.

RUTH Can I have the key?

[*He gives it to her.*]

350 Why don't you go to bed?

[*He puts his arms on her shoulders and kisses her.*]
[*They look at each other, briefly. She smiles.*]

I won't be long.

[*She goes out of the front door.*]
[TEDDY *goes to the window, peers out after her, half turns from the window, stands, suddenly chews his knuckles.*]
[LENNY *walks into the room from* U.L. *He stands. He wears pyjamas and dressing-gown.*[6] *He watches* TEDDY.]
[TEDDY *turns and sees him.*]
[*Silence.*]

TEDDY Hullo, Lenny.

LENNY Hullo, Teddy.

[*Pause.*]

TEDDY I didn't hear you come down the stairs.

355 LENNY I didn't.

[*Pause.*]

I sleep down here now. Next door. I've got a kind of study, workroom cum[7] bedroom next door now, you see.

TEDDY Oh. Did I . . . wake you up?

LENNY No. I just had an early night tonight. You know how it is. Can't sleep. Keep waking up.

360 [*Pause.*]

6. Robe or housecoat.   7. With (Latin).

TEDDY   How are you?

LENNY   Well, just sleeping a bit restlessly, that's all. Tonight, anyway.

TEDDY   Bad dreams?

LENNY   No, I wouldn't say I was dreaming. It's not exactly a dream. It's just
365   that something keeps waking me up. Some kind of tick.

TEDDY   A tick?

LENNY   Yes.

TEDDY   Well, what is it?

LENNY   I don't know.

> [*Pause.*]

370 TEDDY   Have you got a clock in your room?

LENNY   Yes.

TEDDY   Well, maybe it's the clock.

LENNY   Yes, could be, I suppose.

> [*Pause.*]

Well, if it's the clock I'd better do something about it. Stifle it in some way,
375   or something.

> [*Pause.*]

TEDDY   I've . . . just come back for a few days.

LENNY   Oh yes? Have you?

> [*Pause.*]

TEDDY   How's the old man?

LENNY   He's in the pink.[8]

> [*Pause.*]

380 TEDDY   I've been keeping well.

LENNY   Oh, have you?

> [*Pause.*]

Staying the night then, are you?

TEDDY   Yes.

LENNY   Well, you can sleep in your old room.

385 TEDDY   Yes, I've been up.

LENNY   Yes, you can sleep there.

> [LENNY *yawns.*]

Oh well.

TEDDY   I'm going to bed.

LENNY   Are you?

390 TEDDY   Yes, I'll get some sleep.

LENNY   Yes, I'm going to bed, too.

> [TEDDY *picks up the cases.*]

I'll give you a hand.

TEDDY   No, they're not heavy.

> [TEDDY *goes into the hall with the cases.*]
> [LENNY *turns out the light in the room.*]
> [*The light in the hall remains on.*]
> [LENNY *follows into the hall.*]

LENNY   Nothing you want?

---

8. In perfect health and high spirits.

395 TEDDY   Mmmm?

LENNY   Nothing you might want, for the night? Glass of water, anything like that?

TEDDY   Any sheets anywhere?

LENNY   In the sideboard in your room.

400 TEDDY   Oh, good.

LENNY   Friends of mine occasionally stay there, you know, in your room, when they're passing through this part of the world.

[LENNY *turns out the hall light and turns on the first landing*[9] *light.*]

[TEDDY *begins to walk up the stairs.*]

TEDDY   Well, I'll see you at breakfast, then.

LENNY   Yes, that's it. Ta-ta.

[TEDDY *goes upstairs.*]
[LENNY *goes off* L.]
[*Silence.*]
[*The landing light goes out.*]
[*Slight night light in the hall and room.*]
[LENNY *comes back into the room, goes to the window and looks out.*]
[*He leaves the window and turns on a lamp.*]
[*He is holding a small clock.*]
[*He sits, places the clock in front of him, lights a cigarette and sits.*]
[RUTH *comes in the front door.*]
[*She stands still.* LENNY *turns his head, smiles. She walks slowly into the room.*]

405 LENNY   Good evening.

RUTH   Morning, I think.

LENNY   You're right there.

[*Pause.*]

My name's Lenny. What's yours?

RUTH   Ruth.

[*She sits, puts her coat collar around her.*]

410 LENNY   Cold?

RUTH   No.

LENNY   It's been a wonderful summer, hasn't it? Remarkable.

[*Pause.*]

Would you like something? Refreshment of some kind? An aperitif,[1] anything like that?

415 RUTH   No, thanks.

LENNY   I'm glad you said that. We haven't got a drink in the house. Mind you, I'd soon get some in, if we had a party or something like that. Some kind of celebration . . . you know.

[*Pause.*]

You must be connected with my brother in some way. The one who's been
420 abroad.

RUTH   I'm his wife.

---

9. That is, the light at the top of the first stairwell.

1. Drink served before a meal and typically intended to whet the appetite.

LENNY   Eh listen, I wonder if you can advise me. I've been having a bit of a
rough time with this clock. The tick's been keeping me up. The trouble is
I'm not all that convinced it was the clock. I mean there are lots of things
which tick in the night, don't you find that? All sorts of objects, which, in
the day, you wouldn't call anything else but commonplace. They give you
no trouble. But in the night any given one of a number of them is liable to
start letting out a bit of a tick. Whereas you look at these objects in the day
and they're just commonplace. They're as quiet as mice during the daytime. So . . . all things being equal . . . this question of me saying it was the
clock that woke me up, well, that could very easily prove something of a
false hypothesis.

> [*He goes to the sideboard, pours from a jug into a glass, takes the glass to*
> RUTH.]

Here you are. I bet you could do with this.

RUTH   What is it?

LENNY   Water.

> [*She takes it, sips, places the glass on a small table by her chair.*]
> [LENNY *watches her.*]

Isn't it funny? I've got my pyjamas on and you're fully dressed?

> [*He goes to the sideboard and pours another glass of water.*]

Mind if I have one? Yes, it's funny seeing my old brother again after all
these years. It's just the sort of tonic my Dad needs, you know. He'll be
chuffed[2] to his bollocks[3] in the morning, when he sees his eldest son. I was
surprised myself when I saw Teddy, you know. Old Ted. I thought he was in
America.

RUTH   We're on a visit to Europe.

LENNY   What, both of you?

RUTH   Yes.

LENNY   What, you sort of live with him over there, do you?

RUTH   We're married.

LENNY   On a visit to Europe, eh? Seen much of it?

RUTH   We've just come from Italy.

LENNY   Oh, you went to Italy first, did you? And then he brought you over
here to meet the family, did he? Well, the old man'll be pleased to see you,
I can tell you.

RUTH   Good.

LENNY   What did you say?

RUTH   Good.

> [*Pause.*]

LENNY   Where'd you go to in Italy?

RUTH   Venice.

LENNY   Not dear old Venice? Eh? That's funny. You know, I've always had a
feeling that if I'd been a soldier in the last war—say in the Italian
campaign[4]—I'd probably have found myself in Venice. I've always had that

---

2. Pleased.
3. Testicles (slang).
4. Pivotal World War II campaign (1943–45)

in which British, American, and Canadian
forces converged upon and defeated German
forces in Italy.

460 feeling. The trouble was I was too young to serve, you see. I was only a
child, I was too small, otherwise I've got a pretty shrewd idea I'd probably
have gone through Venice. Yes, I'd almost certainly have gone through it
with my battalion. Do you mind if I hold your hand?

RUTH   Why?

465 LENNY   Just a touch.

[*He stands and goes to her.*]

Just a tickle.

RUTH   Why?

[*He looks down at her.*]

LENNY   I'll tell you why.

[*Slight pause.*]

One night, not too long ago, one night down by the docks, I was standing
470 alone under an arch, watching all the men jibbing the boom,[5] out in the
harbour, and playing about with the yardarm,[6] when a certain lady came up
to me and made me a certain proposal. This lady had been searching for
me for days. She'd lost track of my whereabouts. However, the fact was she
eventually caught up with me, and when she caught up with me she made
475 me this certain proposal. Well, this proposal wasn't entirely out of order
and normally I would have subscribed to it. I mean I would have subscribed to it in the normal course of events. The only trouble was she was
falling apart with the pox.[7] So I turned it down. Well, this lady was very
insistent and started taking liberties with me down under this arch, liber-
480 ties which by any criterion I couldn't be expected to tolerate, the facts
being what they were, so I clumped her one.[8] It was on my mind at the
time to do away with her, you know, to kill her, and the fact is, that as kill-
ings go, it would have been a simple matter, nothing to it. Her chauffeur,
who had located me for her, he'd popped round the corner to have a drink,
485 which just left this lady and myself, you see, alone, standing underneath
this arch, watching all the steamers steaming up, no one about, all quiet on
the Western Front,[9] and there she was up against this wall—well, just sliding down the wall, following the blow I'd given her. Well, to sum up, everything was in my favour, for a killing. Don't worry about the chauffeur. The
490 chauffeur would never have spoken. He was an old friend of the family.
But . . . in the end I thought . . . Aaah, why go to all the bother . . . you
know, getting rid of the corpse and all that, getting yourself into a state of
tension. So I just gave her another belt in the nose and a couple of turns of
the boot and sort of left it at that.

495 RUTH   How did you know she was diseased?

LENNY   How did I know?

---

5. Nautical term that describes shifting the
sail of a sailboat so that the wind hits the sail
from the opposite side, thereby causing the
boom (the bar on the bottom of the sail) to
swing to the other side and the boat to change
directions.
6. Horizontal bar perpendicular to the main
mast from which sails are hung.

7. Syphilis (slang).
8. Hit her.
9. Title of a 1929 novel by German World
War I veteran Erich Maria Remarque, which
details the horrors of combat trauma endured
by soldiers of war as they try to reenter civilian life. "Western Front" refers to the battle
line in western Europe.

[*Pause.*]

I decided she was.

[*Silence.*]

You and my brother are newly-weds, are you?

RUTH   We've been married six years.

500   LENNY   He's always been my favourite brother, old Teddy. Do you know that? And my goodness we are proud of him here, I can tell you. Doctor of Philosophy and all that . . . leaves quite an impression. Of course, he's a very sensitive man, isn't he? Ted. Very. I've often wished I was as sensitive as he is.

505   RUTH   Have you?

LENNY   Oh yes. Oh yes, very much so. I mean, I'm not saying I'm not sensitive. I am. I could just be a bit more so, that's all.

RUTH   Could you?

LENNY   Yes, just a bit more so, that's all.

[*Pause.*]

510   I mean, I am very sensitive to atmosphere, but I tend to get desensitized, if you know what I mean, when people make unreasonable demands on me. For instance, last Christmas I decided to do a bit of snow-clearing for the Borough Council,[1] because we had a heavy snow over here that year in Europe. I didn't have to do this snow-clearing—I mean I wasn't financially embarrassed in any way—it just appealed to me, it appealed to something inside me. What I anticipated with a good deal of pleasure was the brisk cold bite in the air in the early morning. And I was right. I had to get my snowboots on and I had to stand on a corner, at about five-thirty in the morning, to wait for the lorry[2] to pick me up, to take me to the allotted area. Bloody freezing. Well, the lorry came, I jumped on the tailboard,[3] headlights on, dipped,[4] and off we went. Got there, shovels up, fags on, and off we went, deep into the December snow, hours before cockcrow.[5] Well, that morning, while I was having my mid-morning cup of tea in a neighbouring cafe, the shovel standing by my chair, an old lady approached me and asked me if I would give her a hand with her iron mangle.[6] Her brother-in-law, she said, had left it for her, but he'd left it in the wrong room, he'd left it in the front room. Well, naturally, she wanted it in the back room. It was a present he'd given her, you see, a mangle, to iron out the washing. But he'd left it in the wrong room, he'd left it in the front room, well that was a silly place to leave it, it couldn't stay there. So I took time off to give her a hand. She only lived up the road. Well, the only trouble was when I got there I couldn't move this mangle. It must have weighed about half a ton. How this brother-in-law got it up there in the first place I can't even begin to envisage. So there I was, doing a bit of shoulders on with the mangle, risking a rupture, and this old lady just standing there, waving me on,

515

520

525

530

535

1. Local authority.
2. Truck (British).
3. Board on the back of a truck, usually attached by hinges, intended to assist in loading and unloading.
4. Lowered (British). Headlight beams are generally lowered at night or during inclem-

ent weather in order to avoid glare.
5. That is, dawn.
6. A laundry machine with heavy rollers, designed to wring water from laundered items. An iron mangle can also serve as a heavy-service flatiron.

not even lifting a little finger to give me a helping hand. So after a few minutes I said to her, now look here, why don't you stuff this iron mangle up your
arse? Anyway, I said, they're out of date, you want to get a spin drier. I had a
good mind to give her a workover there and then, but as I was feeling jubilant
540   with the snow-clearing I just gave her a short-arm jab to the belly and jumped
on a bus outside. Excuse me, shall I take this ashtray out of your way?

RUTH   It's not in my way.

LENNY   It seems to be in the way of your glass. The glass was about to fall. Or
the ashtray. I'm rather worried about the carpet. It's not me, it's my father.
545   He's obsessed with order and clarity. He doesn't like mess. So, as I don't
believe you're smoking at the moment, I'm sure you won't object if I move the
ashtray.

> [*He does so.*]

And now perhaps I'll relieve you of your glass.

RUTH   I haven't quite finished.

550 LENNY   You've consumed quite enough, in my opinion.

RUTH   No, I haven't.

LENNY   Quite sufficient, in my own opinion.

RUTH   Not in mine, Leonard.

> [*Pause.*]

LENNY   Don't call me that, please.

555 RUTH   Why not?

LENNY   That's the name my mother gave me.

Just give me the glass.

RUTH   No.

> [*Pause.*]

LENNY   I'll take it, then.

560 RUTH   If you take the glass . . . I'll take you.

> [*Pause.*]

LENNY   How about me taking the glass without you taking me?

RUTH   Why don't I just take you?

> [*Pause.*]

LENNY   You're joking.

> [*Pause.*]

You're in love, anyway, with another man. You've had a secret liaison with
565   another man. His family didn't even know. Then you come here without a
word of warning and start to make trouble.

> [*She picks up the glass and lifts it towards him.*]

RUTH   Have a sip. Go on. Have a sip from my glass.

> [*He is still.*]

Sit on my lap. Take a long cool sip.

> [*She pats her lap. Pause.*]
> [*She stands, moves to him with the glass.*]

Put your head back and open your mouth.

570 LENNY   Take that glass away from me.

RUTH   Lie on the floor. Go on. I'll pour it down your throat.

LENNY   What are you doing, making me some kind of proposal?

[*She laughs shortly, drains the glass.*]

RUTH   Oh, I was thirsty.

[*She smiles at him, puts the glass down, goes into the hall and up the stairs.*]

[*He follows into the hall and shouts up the stairs.*]

LENNY   What was that supposed to be? Some kind of proposal?

[*Silence.*]

[*He comes back into the room, goes to his own glass, drains it.*]

[*A door slams upstairs.*]

[*The landing light goes on.*]

[MAX *comes down the stairs, in pyjamas and cap. He comes into the room.*]

575   MAX   What's going on here? You drunk?

[*He stares at* LENNY.]

What are you shouting about? You gone mad?

[LENNY *pours another glass of water.*]

Prancing about in the middle of the night shouting your head off. What are you, a raving lunatic?

LENNY   I was thinking aloud.

580   MAX   Is Joey down here? You been shouting at Joey?

LENNY   Didn't you hear what I said, Dad? I said I was thinking aloud.

MAX   You were thinking so loud you got me out of bed.

LENNY   Look, why don't you just . . . pop off,[7] eh?

MAX   Pop off? He wakes me up in the middle of the night, I think we got

585   burglars here, I think he's got a knife stuck in him, I come down here, he tells me to pop off.

[LENNY *sits down.*]

He was talking to someone. Who could he have been talking to? They're all asleep. He was having a conversation with someone. He won't tell me who it was. He pretends he was thinking aloud. What are you doing, hiding

590   someone here?

LENNY   I was sleepwalking. Get out of it, leave me alone, will you?

MAX   I want an explanation, you understand? I asked you who you got hiding here.

[*Pause.*]

LENNY   I'll tell you what, Dad, since you're in the mood for a bit of a . . .

595   chat, I'll ask you a question. It's a question I've been meaning to ask you for some time. That night . . . you know . . . the night you got me[8] . . . that night with Mum, what was it like? Eh? When I was just a glint in your eye.[9] What was it like? What was the background to it? I mean, I want to know the real facts about my background. I mean, for instance, is it a fact that

600   you had me in mind all the time, or is it a fact that I was the last thing you had in mind?

[*Pause.*]

I'm only asking this in a spirit of inquiry, you understand that, don't you? I'm curious. And there's lots of people of my age share that curiosity, you know

7. Die (slang).
8. That is, when I was conceived.

9. That is, before my conception.

that, Dad? They often ruminate, sometimes singly, sometimes in groups, about the true facts of that particular night—the night they were made in the image of those two people *at it*.[1] It's a question long overdue, from my point of view, but as we happen to be passing the time of day here tonight I thought I'd pop it to you.

[*Pause.*]

MAX You'll drown in your own blood.

LENNY If you prefer to answer the question in writing I've got no objection.

[MAX *stands.*]

I should have asked my dear mother. Why didn't I ask my dear mother? Now it's too late. She's passed over to the other side.

[MAX *spits at him.*]

[LENNY *looks down at the carpet.*]

Now look what you've done. I'll have to Hoover[2] that in the morning, you know.

[MAX *turns and walks up the stairs.*]
[LENNY *sits still.*]
[BLACKOUT.]
[LIGHTS UP.]

Morning.

JOEY *in front of the mirror. He is doing some slow limbering-up exercises. He stops, combs his hair, carefully. He then shadowboxes, heavily, watching himself in the mirror.*

MAX *comes in from* U.L.

Both MAX *and* JOEY *are dressed.* MAX *watches* JOEY *in silence.* JOEY *stops shadowboxing, picks up a newspaper and sits.*

Silence.

MAX I hate this room.

[*Pause.*]

It's the kitchen I like. It's nice in there. It's cosy.

[*Pause.*]

But I can't stay in there. You know why? Because he's always washing up in there, scraping the plates, driving me out of the kitchen, that's why.

JOEY Why don't you bring your tea in here?

MAX I don't want to bring my tea in here. I hate it here. I want to drink my tea in there.

[*He goes into the hall and looks towards the kitchen.*]

What's he doing in there?

[*He returns.*]

What's the time?

JOEY Half past six.

MAX Half past six.

[*Pause.*]

I'm going to see a game of football this afternoon.[3] You want to come?

[*Pause.*]

1. Having sexual intercourse.   3. Soccer (British).
2. That is, vacuum.

I'm talking to you.

JOEY   I'm training this afternoon. I'm doing six rounds with Blackie.

MAX   That's not till five o'clock. You've got time to see a game of football
630   before five o'clock. It's the first game of the season.

JOEY   No, I'm not going.

MAX   Why not?

>   [*Pause.*]
>   [MAX *goes into the hall.*]

Sam! Come here!

>   [MAX *comes back into the room.*]
>   [SAM *enters with a cloth.*]

SAM   What?

635 MAX   What are you doing in there?

SAM   Washing up.

MAX   What else?

SAM   Getting rid of your leavings.

MAX   Putting them in the bin,[4] eh?

640 SAM   Right in.

MAX   What point you trying to prove?

SAM   No point.

MAX   Oh yes, you are. You resent making my breakfast, that's what it is, isn't
it? That's why you bang round the kitchen like that, scraping the frying-
645   pan, scraping all the leavings into the bin, scraping all the plates, scraping
all the tea out of the teapot . . . that's why you do that, every single stinking morning. I know. Listen, Sam. I want to say something to you. From
my heart.

>   [*He moves closer.*]

I want you to get rid of these feelings of resentment you've got towards me.
650   I wish I could understand them. Honestly, have I ever given you cause?
Never. When Dad died he said to me, Max, look after your brothers. That's
exactly what he said to me.

SAM   How could he say that when he was dead?

MAX   What?

655 SAM   How could he speak if he was dead?

>   [*Pause.*]

MAX   Before he died, Sam. Just before. They were his last words. His last
sacred words, Sammy. A split second after he said those words . . . he was a
dead man. You think I'm joking? You think when my father spoke—on his
death-bed—I wouldn't obey his words to the last letter? You hear that, Joey?
660   He'll stop at nothing. He's even prepared to spit on the memory of our Dad.
What kind of a son were you, you wet wick?[5] You spent half your time doing
crossword puzzles! We took you into the butcher's shop, you couldn't even
sweep the dust off the floor. We took MacGregor into the shop, he could
run the place by the end of a week. Well, I'll tell you one thing. I respected
665   my father not only as a man but as a number one butcher! And to prove
it I followed him into the shop. I learned to carve a carcass at his knee. I

---

4. Trashcan.
5. Penis (slang); by extension, feeble or effeminate male.

commemorated his name in blood. I gave birth to three grown men! All on
my own bat.[6] What have you done?

[*Pause.*]

What have you done? You tit!

670 SAM   Do you want to finish the washing up? Look, here's the cloth.

MAX   So try to get rid of these feelings of resentment, Sam. After all, we are
brothers.

SAM   Do you want the cloth? Here you are. Take it.

[TEDDY *and* RUTH *come down the stairs. They walk across the hall and
stop just inside the room.*]
[*The others turn and look at them.* JOEY *stands.*]
[TEDDY *and* RUTH *are wearing dressing-gowns.*]
[*Silence.*]
[TEDDY *smiles.*]

TEDDY   Hullo . . . Dad . . . We overslept.

[*Pause.*]

675   What's for breakfast?

[*Silence.*]
[TEDDY *chuckles.*]

Huh. We overslept.

[MAX *turns to* SAM.]

MAX   Did you know he was here?

SAM   No.

[MAX *turns to* JOEY.]

MAX   Did you know he was here?

[*Pause.*]

680   I asked you if you knew he was here.

JOEY   No.

MAX   Then who knew?

[*Pause.*]

Who knew?

[*Pause.*]

I didn't know.

685 TEDDY   I was going to come down, Dad, I was going to . . . be here, when you
came down.

[*Pause.*]

How are you?

[*Pause.*]

Uh . . . look, I'd . . . like you to meet . . .

MAX   How long you been in this house?

690 TEDDY   All night.

MAX   All night? I'm a laughing-stock. How did you get in?

TEDDY   I had my key.

[MAX *whistles and laughs.*]

MAX   Who's this?

6. Through my own efforts.

TEDDY   I was just going to introduce you.

695 MAX   Who asked you to bring tarts[7] in here?

TEDDY   Tarts?

MAX   Who asked you to bring dirty tarts into this house?

TEDDY   Listen, don't be silly—

MAX   You been here all night?

700 TEDDY   Yes, we arrived from Venice—

MAX   We've had a smelly scrubber[8] in my house all night. We've had a stinking pox-ridden slut in my house all night.

TEDDY   Stop it! What are you talking about?

MAX   I haven't seen the bitch for six years, he comes home without a word,
705   he brings a filthy scrubber off the street, he shacks up in my house!

TEDDY   She's my wife! We're married!

[Pause.]

MAX   I've never had a whore under this roof before. Ever since your mother
died. My word of honour. [To JOEY.] Have you ever had a whore here? Has
Lenny ever had a whore here? They come back from America, they bring
710   the slopbucket[9] with them. They bring the bedpan with them. [To TEDDY.]
Take that disease away from me. Get her away from me.

TEDDY   She's my wife.

MAX [to JOEY]   Chuck them out.

[Pause.]

A Doctor of Philosophy. Sam, you want to meet a Doctor of Philosophy?
715   [To JOEY.] I said chuck them out.

[Pause.]

What's the matter? You deaf?

JOEY   You're an old man. [To TEDDY.] He's an old man.

[LENNY walks into the room, in a dressing-gown.]
[He stops.]
[They all look round.]
[MAX turns back, hits JOEY in the stomach with all his might. JOEY con-
torts, staggers across the stage. MAX, with the exertion of the blow, begins
to collapse. His knees buckle. He clutches his stick.]
[SAM moves forward to help him.]
[MAX hits him across the head with his stick. SAM sits, head in hands.]
[JOEY, hands pressed to his stomach, sinks down at the feet of RUTH.]
[She looks down at him.]
[LENNY and TEDDY are still.]
[JOEY slowly stands. He is close to RUTH. He turns from RUTH, looks round
at MAX.]
[SAM clutches his head.]
[MAX breathes heavily, very slowly gets to his feet.]
[JOEY moves to him.]
[They look at each other.]
[Silence.]
[MAX moves past JOEY, walks towards RUTH. He gestures with his stick.]

MAX   Miss.

7. Loose or immoral woman; prostitute (slang).
8. Prostitute (slang).
9. Bucket for collecting mud or liquid refuse;
also used to collect food waste for pigs or
other farm animals.

[RUTH *walks towards him.*]

RUTH   Yes?

[*He looks at her.*]

720 MAX   You a mother?

RUTH   Yes.

MAX   How many you got?

RUTH   Three.

[*He turns to* TEDDY.]

MAX   All yours, Ted?

[*Pause.*]

725   Teddy, why don't we have a nice cuddle and kiss, eh? Like the old days? What about a nice cuddle and kiss, eh?

TEDDY   Come on, then.

[*Pause.*]

MAX   You want to kiss your old father? Want a cuddle with your old father?

TEDDY   Come on, then.

[TEDDY *moves a step towards him.*]

730   Come on.

[*Pause.*]

MAX   You still love your old Dad, eh?

[*They face each other.*]

TEDDY   Come on, Dad. I'm ready for the cuddle.

[MAX *begins to chuckle, gurgling.*]
[*He turns to the family and addresses them.*]

MAX   He still loves his father!

Curtain

Act Two

Afternoon.

MAX, TEDDY, LENNY *and* SAM *are about the stage, lighting cigars.*

JOEY *comes in from* U.L. *with a coffee tray, followed by* RUTH. *He puts the tray down.* RUTH *hands coffee to all the men. She sits with her cup.* MAX *smiles at her.*

RUTH   That was a very good lunch.

MAX   I'm glad you liked it. [*To the others.*] Did you hear that? [*To* RUTH.] Well, I put my heart and soul into it, I can tell you. [*He sips.*] And this is a lovely cup of coffee.

5 RUTH   I'm glad.

[*Pause.*]

MAX   I've got the feeling you're a first-rate cook.

RUTH   I'm not bad.

MAX   No, I've got the feeling you're a number one cook. Am I right, Teddy?

TEDDY   Yes, she's a very good cook.

[*Pause.*]

10 MAX   Well, it's a long time since the whole family was together, eh? If only your mother was alive. Eh, what do you say, Sam? What would Jessie say if she was alive? Sitting here with her three sons. Three fine grown-up lads.

And a lovely daughter-in-law. The only shame is her grandchildren aren't here. She'd have petted them and cooed over them, wouldn't she, Sam?
15 She'd have fussed over them and played with them, told them stories, tickled them—I tell you she'd have been hysterical. [*To* RUTH.] Mind you, she taught those boys everything they know. She taught them all the morality they know. I'm telling you. Every single bit of the moral code they live by— was taught to them by their mother. And she had a heart to go with it. What
20 a heart. Eh, Sam? Listen, what's the use of beating round the bush? That woman was the backbone to this family. I mean, I was busy working twenty-four hours a day in the shop, I was going all over the country to find meat, I was making my way in the world, but I left a woman at home with a will of iron, a heart of gold and a mind. Right, Sam?

[*Pause.*]
25 What a mind.

[*Pause.*]

Mind you, I was a generous man to her. I never left her short of a few bob. I remember one year I entered into negotiations with a top-class group of butchers with continental connections. I was going into association with them. I remember the night I came home, I kept quiet. First of all I gave
30 Lenny a bath, then Teddy a bath, then Joey a bath. What fun we used to have in the bath, eh, boys? Then I came downstairs and I made Jessie put her feet up on a pouffe[1]—what happened to that pouffe, I haven't seen it for years— she put her feet up on the pouffe and I said to her, Jessie, I think our ship is going to come home,[2] I'm going to treat you to a couple of items, I'm going
35 to buy you a dress in pale corded blue silk, heavily encrusted in pearls, and for casual wear, a pair of pantaloons[3] in lilac flowered taffeta.[4] Then I gave her a drop of cherry brandy. I remember the boys came down, in their pyjamas, all their hair shining, their faces pink, it was before they started shaving, and they knelt down at our feet, Jessie's and mine. I tell you, it was like
40 Christmas.

[*Pause.*]

RUTH   What happened to the group of butchers?
MAX   The group? They turned out to be a bunch of criminals like everyone else.

[*Pause.*]

This is a lousy cigar.

[*He stubs it out.*]
[*He turns to* SAM.]
45 What time you going to work?
SAM   Soon.
MAX   You've got a job on this afternoon, haven't you?
SAM   Yes, I know.
MAX   What do you mean, you know? You'll be late. You'll lose your job? What
50 are you trying to do, humiliate me?

---

1. Low-cushioned ottoman or padded seat without a back.
2. Popular phrase indicating the expectation of good fortune.
3. Long, loose pants.
4. Light fabric made from silk or synthetic fibers.

SAM Don't worry about me.

MAX It makes the bile come up in my mouth. The bile—you understand? [*To* RUTH.] I worked as a butcher all my life, using the chopper and the slab, the slab, you know what I mean, the chopper and the slab! To keep my
55 family in luxury. Two families! My mother was bedridden, my brothers were all invalids. I had to earn the money for the leading psychiatrists. I had to read books! I had to study the disease, so that I could cope with an emergency at every stage. A crippled family, three bastard sons, a slutbitch of a wife—don't talk to me about the pain of childbirth—I suffered the pain,
60 I've still got the pangs—when I give a little cough my back collapses—and here I've got a lazy idle bugger of a brother won't even get to work on time. The best chauffeur in the world. All his life he's sat in the front seat giving lovely hand signals. You call that work? This man doesn't know his gearbox from his arse!

65 SAM You go and ask my customers! I'm the only one they ever ask for.

MAX What do the other drivers do, sleep all day?

SAM I can only drive one car. They can't all have me at the same time.

MAX Anyone could have you at the same time. You'd bend over[5] for half a dollar on Blackfriars Bridge.[6]

70 SAM Me!

MAX For two bob and a toffee apple.[7]

SAM He's insulting me. He's insulting his brother. I'm driving a man to Hampton Court[8] at four forty-five.

MAX Do you want to know who could drive? MacGregor! MacGregor was a
75 driver.

SAM Don't you believe it.

[MAX *points his stick at* SAM.]

MAX He didn't even fight in the war. This man didn't even fight in the bloody war!

SAM I did!

80 MAX Who did you kill?

[*Silence.*]

[SAM *gets up, goes to* RUTH, *shakes her hand and goes out of the front door.*]

[MAX *turns to* TEDDY.]

Well, how you been keeping, son?

TEDDY I've been keeping very well, Dad.

MAX It's nice to have you with us, son.

TEDDY It's nice to be back, Dad.

[*Pause.*]

85 MAX You should have told me you were married, Teddy. I'd have sent you a present. Where was the wedding, in America?

TEDDY No. Here. The day before we left.

MAX Did you have a big function?

---

5. That is, submit sexually.
6. Bridge spanning the River Thames, open to pedestrian and motor traffic.
7. Apple covered in toffee on a stick.

8. Sixteenth-century royal palace in the Greater London county of Middlesex. Hampton Court Palace is open to the public.

TEDDY No, there was no one there.

90 MAX You're mad. I'd have given you a white wedding. We'd have had the cream of the cream here. I'd have been only too glad to bear the expense, my word of honour.

[*Pause.*]

TEDDY You were busy at the time. I didn't want to bother you.

MAX But you're my own flesh and blood. You're my first born. I'd have
95 dropped everything. Sam would have driven you to the reception in the Snipe, Lenny would have been your best man, and then we'd have all seen you off on the boat. I mean, you don't think I disapprove of marriage, do you? Don't be daft. [*To* RUTH.] I've been begging my two youngsters for years to find a nice feminine girl with proper credentials—it makes life worth liv-
100 ing. [*To* TEDDY.] Anyway, what's the difference, you did it, you made a wonderful choice, you've got a wonderful family, a marvellous career . . . so why don't we let bygones be bygones?

[*Pause.*]

You know what I'm saying? I want you both to know that you have my blessing.

105 TEDDY Thank you.

MAX Don't mention it. How many other houses in the district have got a Doctor of Philosophy sitting down drinking a cup of coffee?

[*Pause.*]

RUTH I'm sure Teddy's very happy . . . to know that you're pleased with me.

[*Pause.*]

110 I think he wondered whether you would be pleased with me.

MAX But you're a charming woman.

[*Pause.*]

RUTH I was . . .

MAX What?

[*Pause.*]

What she say?

[*They all look at her.*]

115 RUTH I was . . . different . . . when I met Teddy . . . first.

TEDDY No you weren't. You were the same.

RUTH I wasn't.

MAX Who cares? Listen, live in the present, what are you worrying about? I mean, don't forget the earth's about five thousand million years old, at
120 least. Who can afford to live in the past?

[*Pause.*]

TEDDY She's a great help to me over there. She's a wonderful wife and mother. She's a very popular woman. She's got lots of friends. It's a great life, at the University . . . you know . . . it's a very good life. We've got a lovely house . . . we've got all . . . we've got everything we want. It's a very stimulating
125 environment.

[*Pause.*]

My department . . . is highly successful.

[*Pause.*]

We've got three boys, you know.

MAX　All boys? Isn't that funny, eh? You've got three, I've got three. You've got three nephews, Joey. Joey! You're an uncle, do you hear? You could teach
130　them how to box.

[*Pause.*]

JOEY [*to* RUTH]　I'm a boxer. In the evenings, after work. I'm in demolition in the daytime.

RUTH　Oh?

JOEY　Yes. I hope to be full time, when I get more bouts.

135　MAX [*to* LENNY]　He speaks so easily to his sister-in-law, do you notice? That's because she's an intelligent and sympathetic woman.

[*He leans to her.*]

Eh, tell me, do you think the children are missing their mother?

[*She looks at him.*]

TEDDY　Of course they are. They love her. We'll be seeing them soon.

[*Pause.*]

LENNY [*to* TEDDY]　Your cigar's gone out.

140　TEDDY　Oh, yes.

LENNY　Want a light?

TEDDY　No. No.

[*Pause.*]

So has yours.

LENNY　Oh, yes.

[*Pause.*]

145　Eh, Teddy, you haven't told us much about your Doctorship of Philosophy. What do you teach?

TEDDY　Philosophy.

LENNY　Well, I want to ask you something. Do you detect a certain logical incoherence in the central affirmations of Christian theism?[9]

150　TEDDY　That question doesn't fall within my province.[1]

LENNY　Well, look at it this way . . . you don't mind my asking you some questions, do you?

TEDDY　If they're within my province.

LENNY　Well, look at it this way. How can the unknown merit reverence? In
155　other words, how can you revere that of which you're ignorant? At the same time, it would be ridiculous to propose that what we *know* merits reverence. What we know merits any one of a number of things, but it stands to reason reverence isn't one of them. In other words, apart from the known and the unknown, what else is there?

[*Pause.*]

160　TEDDY　I'm afraid I'm the wrong person to ask.

LENNY　But you're a philosopher. Come on, be frank. What do you make of all this business of being and not-being?[2]

---

9. Christian worldview that centers on the belief in one God.
1. Area of expertise.
2. Reference to Jean-Paul Sartre's 1943

Being and Nothingness, which addresses the issues of consciousness and free will. Sartre's treatise was an important work of existential philosophy.

TEDDY   What do you make of it?

LENNY   Well, for instance, take a table. Philosophically speaking. What is it?

165 TEDDY   A table.

LENNY   Ah. You mean it's nothing else but a table. Well, some people would envy your certainty, wouldn't they, Joey? For instance, I've got a couple of friends of mine, we often sit round the Ritz Bar[3] having a few liqueurs, and they're always saying things like that, you know, things like: Take a table,

170   take it. All right, I say, *take* it, *take* a table, but once you've taken it, what you going to do with it? Once you've got hold of it, where you going to take it?

MAX   You'd probably sell it.

LENNY   You wouldn't get much for it.

175 JOEY   Chop it up for firewood.

> [LENNY *looks at him and laughs.*]

RUTH   Don't be too sure though. You've forgotten something. Look at me. I . . . move my leg. That's all it is. But I wear . . . underwear . . . which moves with me . . . it . . . captures your attention. Perhaps you misinterpret. The action is simple. It's a leg . . . moving. My lips move. Why don't

180   you restrict . . . your observations to that? Perhaps the fact that they move is more significant . . . than the words which come through them. You must bear that . . . possibility . . . in mind.

> [*Silence.*]
> [TEDDY *stands.*]

I was born quite near here.

> [*Pause.*]

Then . . . six years ago, I went to America.

> [*Pause.*]

185 It's all rock. And sand. It stretches . . . so far . . . everywhere you look. And there's lots of insects there.

> [*Pause.*]

And there's lots of insects there.

> [*Silence.*]
> [*She is still.*]
> [MAX *stands.*]

MAX   Well, it's time to go to the gym. Time for your workout, Joey.

LENNY [*standing*]   I'll come with you.

> [JOEY *sits looking at* RUTH.]

190 MAX   Joe.

> [JOEY *stands. The three go out.*]
> [TEDDY *sits by* RUTH, *holds her hand.*]
> [*She smiles at him.*]
> [*Pause.*]

TEDDY   I think we'll go back. Mmnn?

---

3. The Ritz Hotel in London's West End is known for its ornate restaurant, bar, and tea room.

[*Pause.*]

Shall we go home?

RUTH   Why?

TEDDY   Well, we were only here for a few days, weren't we? We might as
195   well . . . cut it short, I think.

RUTH   Why? Don't you like it here?

TEDDY   Of course I do. But I'd like to go back and see the boys now.

[*Pause.*]

RUTH   Don't you like your family?

TEDDY   Which family?

200 RUTH   Your family here.

TEDDY   Of course I like them. What are you talking about?

[*Pause.*]

RUTH   You don't like them as much as you thought you did?

TEDDY   Of course I do. Of course I . . . like them. I don't know what you're
talking about.

[*Pause.*]

205   Listen. You know what time of the day it is there now, do you?

RUTH   What?

TEDDY   It's morning. It's about eleven o'clock.

RUTH   Is it?

TEDDY   Yes, they're about six hours behind us . . . I mean . . . behind
210   the time here. The boys'll be at the pool . . . now . . . swimming. Think
of it. Morning over there. Sun. We'll go anyway, mmnn? It's so clean there.

RUTH   Clean.

TEDDY   Yes.

RUTH   Is it dirty here?

215 TEDDY   No, of course not. But it's cleaner there.

[*Pause.*]

Look, I just brought you back to meet the family, didn't I? You've met them,
we can go. The fall semester will be starting soon.

RUTH   You find it dirty here?

TEDDY   I didn't say I found it dirty here.

[*Pause.*]

220   I didn't say that.

[*Pause.*]

Look. I'll go and pack. You rest for a while. Will you? They won't be back
for at least an hour. You can sleep. Rest. Please.

[*She looks at him.*]

You can help me with my lectures when we get back. I'd love that. I'd be so
grateful for it, really. We can bathe till October. You know that. Here, there's
225   nowhere to bathe, except the swimming bath[4] down the road. You know
what it's like? It's like a urinal. A filthy urinal!

[*Pause.*]

You liked Venice, didn't you? It was lovely, wasn't it? You had a good week.
I mean . . . I took you there. I can speak Italian.

---

4. That is, swimming pool. To "bathe," in this instance, is to swim.

RUTH   But if I'd been a nurse in the Italian campaign I would have been
230   there before.

>   [*Pause.*]

TEDDY   You just rest. I'll go and pack.

>   [TEDDY *goes out and up the stairs.*]
>   [*She closes her eyes.*]
>   [LENNY *appears from* U.L.]
>   [*He walks into the room and sits near her.*]
>   [*She opens her eyes.*]
>   [*Silence.*]

LENNY   Well, the evenings are drawing in.

RUTH   Yes, it's getting dark.

>   [*Pause.*]

LENNY   Winter'll soon be upon us. Time to renew one's wardrobe.

>   [*Pause.*]

235   RUTH   That's a good thing to do.

LENNY   What?

>   [*Pause.*]

RUTH   I always . . .

>   [*Pause.*]

Do you like clothes?

LENNY   Oh, yes. Very fond of clothes.

>   [*Pause.*]

240   RUTH   I'm fond . . .

>   [*Pause.*]

What do you think of my shoes?

LENNY   They're very nice.

RUTH   No, I can't get the ones I want over there.

LENNY   Can't get them over there, eh?

245   RUTH   No . . . you don't get them there.

>   [*Pause.*]

I was a model before I went away.

LENNY   Hats?

>   [*Pause.*]

I bought a girl a hat once. We saw it in a glass case, in a shop. I tell you what
it had. It had a bunch of daffodils on it, tied with a black satin bow, and then
250   it was covered with a cloche[5] of black veiling. A cloche. I'm telling you. She
was made for it.

RUTH   No . . . I was a model for the body. A photographic model for the body.

LENNY   Indoor work?

RUTH   That was before I had . . . all my children.

>   [*Pause.*]

255   No, not always indoors.

>   [*Pause.*]

5. Close-fitting, bell-shaped woman's hat.

Once or twice we went to a place in the country, by train. Oh, six or seven times. We used to pass a . . . a large white water tower. This place . . . this house . . . was very big . . . the trees . . . there was a lake, you see . . . we used to change and walk down towards the lake . . . we went down a path . . . on stones . . . there were . . . on this path. Oh, just . . . wait . . . yes . . . when we changed in the house we had a drink. There was a cold buffet.

[*Pause.*]

Sometimes we stayed in the house but . . . most often . . . we walked down to the lake . . . and did our modelling there.

[*Pause.*]

Just before we went to America I went down there. I walked from the station to the gate and then I walked up the drive. There were lights on . . . I stood in the drive . . . the house was very light.

[TEDDY *comes down the stairs with the cases. He puts them down, looks at* LENNY.]

TEDDY What have you been saying to her?

[*He goes to* RUTH.]

Here's your coat.

[LENNY *goes to the radiogram and puts on a record of slow jazz.*]

Ruth. Come on. Put it on.

LENNY [*to* RUTH] What about one dance before you go?

TEDDY We're going.

LENNY Just one.

TEDDY No. We're going.

LENNY Just one dance, with her brother-in-law, before she goes.

[LENNY *bends to her.*]

Madam?

[RUTH *stands. They dance, slowly.*]

[TEDDY *stands, with* RUTH'S *coat.*]

[MAX *and* JOEY *come in the front door and into the room. They stand.*]

[LENNY *kisses* RUTH. *They stand, kissing.*]

JOEY Christ, she's wide open. Dad, look at that.

[*Pause.*]

She's a tart.

[*Pause.*]

Old Lenny's got a tart in here.

[JOEY *goes to them. He takes* RUTH'S *arm. He smiles at* LENNY. *He sits with* RUTH *on the sofa, embraces and kisses her.*]

[*He looks up at* LENNY.]

Just up my street.

[*He leans her back until she lies beneath him. He kisses her.*]

[*He looks up at* TEDDY *and* MAX.]

It's better than a rubdown,[6] this.

[LENNY *sits on the arm of the sofa. He caresses* RUTH'S *hair as* JOEY *embraces her.*]

[MAX *comes forward, looks at the cases.*]

6. Brisk massage used to increase circulation and relax the muscles, often administered by trainers or therapists.

MAX   You going, Teddy? Already?

    [*Pause.*]

Well, when you coming over again, eh? Look, next time you come over, don't forget to let us know beforehand whether you're married or not. I'll always be glad to meet the wife. Honest. I'm telling you.

    [JOEY *lies heavily on* RUTH.]
    [*They are almost still.*]
    [LENNY *caresses her hair.*]

285   Listen, you think I don't know why you didn't tell me you were married? I know why. You were ashamed. You thought I'd be annoyed because you married a woman beneath you. You should have known me better. I'm broad-minded. I'm a broadminded man.

    [*He peers to see* RUTH's *face under* JOEY, *turns back to* TEDDY.]

Mind you, she's a lovely girl. A beautiful woman. And a mother too. A
290   mother of three. You've made a happy woman out of her. It's something to be proud of. I mean, we're talking about a woman of quality. We're talking about a woman of feeling.

    [JOEY *and* RUTH *roll off the sofa on to the floor.*]
    [JOEY *clasps her.* LENNY *moves to stand above them. He looks down on them. He touches* RUTH *gently with his foot.*]
    [RUTH *suddenly pushes* JOEY *away.*]
    [*She stands up.*]
    [JOEY *gets to his feet, stares at her.*]

RUTH   I'd like something to eat. [*To* LENNY.] I'd like a drink. Did you get any drink?

295 LENNY   We've got drink.

RUTH   I'd like one, please.

LENNY   What drink?

RUTH   Whisky.

LENNY   I've got it.

    [*Pause.*]

300 RUTH   Well, get it.

    [LENNY *goes to the sideboard, takes out bottle and glasses.*]
    [JOEY *moves towards her.*]

Put the record off.

    [*He looks at her, turns, puts the record off.*]

I want something to eat.

    [*Pause.*]

JOEY   I can't cook. [*Pointing to* MAX.] He's the cook.

    [LENNY *brings her a glass of whisky.*]

LENNY   Soda on the side?

305 RUTH   What's this glass? I can't drink out of this. Haven't you got a tumbler?[7]

LENNY   Yes.

RUTH   Well, put it in a tumbler.

    [*He takes the glass back, pours whisky into a tumbler, brings it to her.*]

---

7. Flat-bottomed drinking glass used for serving whiskey.

LENNY   On the rocks? Or as it comes?[8]

310   RUTH   Rocks? What do you know about rocks?

LENNY   We've got rocks. But they're frozen stiff in the fridge.

[RUTH *drinks.*]

[LENNY *looks round at the others.*]

Drinks all round?

[*He goes to the sideboard and pours drinks.*]

[JOEY *moves closer to* RUTH.]

JOEY   What food do you want?

[RUTH *walks round the room.*]

RUTH [*to* TEDDY]   Have your family read your critical works?

315   MAX   That's one thing I've never done. I've never read one of his critical works.

TEDDY   You wouldn't understand them.

[LENNY *hands drinks all round.*]

JOEY   What sort of food do you want? I'm not the cook, anyway.

LENNY   Soda, Ted? Or as it comes?

320   TEDDY   You wouldn't understand my works. You wouldn't have the faintest idea of what they were about. You wouldn't appreciate the points of reference. You're way behind. All of you. There's no point in my sending you my works. You'd be lost. It's nothing to do with the question of intelligence. It's a way of being able to look at the world. It's a question of how far you can
325   operate on things and not in things. I mean it's a question of your capacity to ally the two, to relate the two, to balance the two. To see, to be able to *see*! I'm the one who can see. That's why I can write my critical works. Might do you good . . . have a look at them . . . see how certain people can view . . . things . . . how certain people can maintain . . . intellectual equi-
330   librium. Intellectual equilibrium. You're just objects. You just . . . move about. I can observe it. I can see what you do. It's the same as I do. But you're lost in it. You won't get me being . . . I won't be lost in it.

[BLACKOUT.]
[LIGHTS UP.]
[*Evening.*]
[TEDDY *sitting, in his coat, the cases by him.* SAM.]
[*Pause.*]

SAM   Do you remember MacGregor, Teddy?

TEDDY   Mac?

335   SAM   Yes.

TEDDY   Of course I do.

SAM   What did you think of him? Did you take to him?

TEDDY   Yes. I liked him. Why?

[*Pause.*]

SAM   You know, you were always my favourite, of the lads. Always.

[*Pause.*]

---

8. Served without anything else. "On the rocks": over ice. Like "frozen stiff," these phrases carry sexual connotations.

340 When you wrote to me from America I was very touched, you know. I mean
you'd written to your father a few times but you'd never written to me. But
then, when I got that letter from you . . . well, I was very touched. I never
told him. I never told him I'd heard from you.

[*Pause.*]

[*Whispering.*] Teddy, shall I tell you something? You were always your
345 mother's favourite. She told me. It's true. You were always the . . . you were
always the main object of her love.

[*Pause.*]

Why don't you stay for a couple more weeks, eh? We could have a few
laughs.

[LENNY *comes in the front door and into the room.*]

LENNY   Still here, Ted? You'll be late for your first seminar.

[*He goes to the sideboard, opens it, peers in it, to the right and the left,
stands.*]

350 Where's my cheese-roll?[9]

[*Pause.*]

Someone's taken my cheese-roll. I left it there. [*To* SAM.] You been
thieving?

TEDDY   I took your cheese-roll, Lenny.

[*Silence.*]

[SAM *looks at them, picks up his hat and goes out of the front door.*]

[*Silence.*]

LENNY   You took my cheese-roll?

355 TEDDY   Yes.

LENNY   I made that roll myself. I cut it and put the butter on. I sliced a
piece of cheese and put it in between. I put it on a plate and I put it in the
sideboard. I did all that before I went out. Now I come back and you've
eaten it.

360 TEDDY   Well, what are you going to do about it?

LENNY   I'm waiting for you to apologize.

TEDDY   But I took it deliberately, Lenny.

LENNY   You mean you didn't stumble on it by mistake?

TEDDY   No, I saw you put it there. I was hungry, so I ate it.

[*Pause.*]

365 LENNY   Barefaced audacity.

[*Pause.*]

What led you to be so . . . vindictive against your own brother? I'm bowled
over.[1]

[*Pause.*]

Well, Ted, I would say this is something approaching the naked truth, isn't
it? It's a real cards on the table[2] stunt. I mean, we're in the land of no holds

---

9. A slice of bread covered in cheese, rolled
up, then toasted in the oven or held in place
with toothpicks.
1. Surprised, overwhelmed.
2. "Cards on the table" refers to the moment

at the end of a card game when players reveal
their hand by laying their cards face up on
the table. The phrase is commonly used to
refer to the moment when a truth is revealed.

370 barred[3] now. Well, how else can you interpret it? To pinch[4] your younger brother's specially made cheese-roll when he's out doing a spot of work, that's not equivocal, it's unequivocal.

[*Pause.*]

Mind you, I will say you do seem to have grown a bit sulky during the last six years. A bit sulky. A bit inner. A bit less forthcoming. It's funny, because I'd

375 have thought that in the United States of America, I mean with the sun and all that, the open spaces, on the old campus, in your position, lecturing, in the centre of all the intellectual life out there, on the old campus, all the social whirl, all the stimulation of it all, all your kids and all that, to have fun with, down by the pool, the Greyhound buses and all that, tons of iced

380 water, all the comfort of those Bermuda shorts and all that, on the old campus, no time of the day or night you can't get a cup of coffee or a Dutch gin,[5] I'd have thought you'd have grown more forthcoming, not less. Because I want you to know that you set a standard for us, Teddy. Your family looks up to you, boy, and you know what it does? It does its best to follow the

385 example you set. Because you're a great source of pride to us. That's why we were so glad to see you come back, to welcome you back to your birthplace. That's why.

[*Pause.*]

No, listen, Ted, there's no question that we live a less rich life here than you do over there. We live a closer life. We're busy, of course. Joey's busy with his

390 boxing, I'm busy with my occupation, Dad still plays a good game of poker, and he does the cooking as well, well up to his old standard, and Uncle Sam's the best chauffeur in the firm. But nevertheless we do make up a unit, Teddy, and you're an integral part of it. When we all sit round the backyard having a quiet gander[6] at the night sky, there's always an empty chair stand-

395 ing in the circle, which is in fact yours. And so when you at length return to us, we do expect a bit of grace, a bit of je ne sais quoi,[7] a bit of generosity of mind, a bit of liberality of spirit, to reassure us. We do expect that. But do we get it? Have we got it? Is that what you've given us?

[*Pause.*]

TEDDY Yes.

[JOEY *comes down the stairs and into the room, with a newspaper.*]

400 LENNY [*to* JOEY] How'd you get on?

JOEY Er . . . not bad.

LENNY What do you mean?

[*Pause.*]

What do you mean?

JOEY Not bad.

405 LENNY I want to know what you *mean*—by not bad.

JOEY What's it got to do with you?

3. Wrestling term indicating that all moves will be considered legal.
4. Steal.
5. English term for Jenever, a strong Dutch liqueur flavored with juniper berries.

6. Look.
7. "I don't know what" (French), commonly used to indicate an indescribable special quality.

LENNY   Joey, you tell your brother everything.

> [*Pause.*]

JOEY   I didn't get all the way.

LENNY   You didn't get all the way?

> [*Pause.*]

410   [*With emphasis.*] You didn't get all the way?

But you've had her up there for two hours.

JOEY   Well?

LENNY   You didn't get all the way and you've had her up there for two hours!

JOEY   What about it?

> [LENNY *moves closer to him.*]

415   LENNY   What are you telling me?

JOEY   What do you mean?

LENNY   Are you telling me she's a tease?

> [*Pause.*]

She's a tease!

> [*Pause.*]

What do you think of that, Ted? Your wife turns out to be a tease. He's had

420   her up there for two hours and he didn't go the whole hog.[8]

JOEY   I didn't say she was a tease.

LENNY   Are you joking? It sounds like a tease to me, don't it to you, Ted?

TEDDY   Perhaps he hasn't got the right touch.

LENNY   Joey? Not the right touch? Don't be ridiculous. He's had more dolly[9]

425   than you've had cream cakes.[1] He's irresistible. He's one of the few and far

between. Tell him about the last bird[2] you had, Joey.

> [*Pause.*]

JOEY   What bird?

LENNY   The last bird! When we stopped the car . . .

JOEY   Oh, that . . . yes . . . well, we were in Lenny's car one night last week . . .

430   LENNY   The Alfa.[3]

JOEY   And er . . . bowling down the road . . .

LENNY   Up near the Scrubs.[4]

JOEY   Yes, up over by the Scrubs . . .

LENNY   We were doing a little survey of North Paddington.[5]

435   JOEY   And er . . . it was pretty late, wasn't it?

LENNY   Yes, it was late. Well?

> [*Pause.*]

JOEY   And then we . . . well, by the kerb,[6] we saw this parked car . . . with a

couple of girls in it.

LENNY   And their escorts.

440   JOEY   Yes, there were two geezers[7] in it. Anyway . . .

> [*Pause.*]

---

8. That is, complete the act of sexual intercourse.

9. Attractive young woman (slang).

1. Cakes filled and often topped with cream or custard.

2. Woman (slang).

3. Alfa Romeo, an expensive Italian sports car.

4. Wormwood Scrubs is a large area of open land in West London.

5. Borough in west-central London, located several miles from Wormwood Scrubs.

6. Curb.

7. Guys, men (British).

What we do then?

LENNY We stopped the car and got out!

JOEY Yes . . . we got out . . . and we told the . . . two escorts . . . to go away . . . which they did . . . and then we . . . got the girls out of the car . . .

445 LENNY We didn't take them over the Scrubs.

JOEY Oh, no. Not over the Scrubs. Well, the police would have noticed us there . . . you see. We took them over a bombed site.[8]

LENNY Rubble. In the rubble.

JOEY Yes, plenty of rubble.

[Pause.]

450 Well . . . you know . . . then we had them.

LENNY You've missed out the best bit. He's missed out the best bit!

JOEY What bit?

LENNY [to TEDDY] His bird says to him, I don't mind, she says, but I've got to have some protection. I've got to have some contraceptive protection. I

455 haven't got any contraceptive protection, old Joey says to her. In that case I won't do it, she says. Yes you will, says Joey, never mind about the contraceptive protection.

[LENNY laughs.]

Even my bird laughed when she heard that. Yes, even she gave out a bit of a laugh. So you can't say old Joey isn't a bit of a knockout when he gets going,

460 can you? And here he is upstairs with your wife for two hours and he hasn't even been the whole hog. Well, your wife sounds like a bit of a tease to me, Ted. What do you make of it, Joey? You satisfied? Don't tell me you're satisfied without going the whole hog?

[Pause.]

JOEY I've been the whole hog plenty of times. Sometimes . . . you can be

465 happy . . . and not go the whole hog. Now and again . . . you can be happy . . . without going any hog.

[LENNY stares at him.]

[MAX and SAM come in the front door and into the room.]

MAX Where's the whore? Still in bed? She'll make us all animals.

LENNY The girl's a tease.

MAX What?

470 LENNY She's had Joey on a string.

MAX What do you mean?

TEDDY He had her up there for two hours and he didn't go the whole hog.

[Pause.]

MAX My Joey? She did that to my boy?

[Pause.]

To my youngest son? Tch, tch, tch, tch. How you feeling, son? Are you all

475 right?

JOEY Sure I'm all right.

MAX [to TEDDY] Does she do that to you, too?

---

8. Remnant of the heavy German bombing of London and other British cities during World War II.

TEDDY No.

LENNY He gets the gravy.[9]

480 MAX You think so?

JOEY No he don't.

[*Pause.*]

SAM He's her lawful husband. She's his lawful wife.

JOEY No he don't! He don't get no gravy! I'm telling you. I'm telling all of you. I'll kill the next man who says he gets the gravy.

485 MAX Joey . . . what are you getting so excited about? [*To* LENNY.] It's because he's frustrated. You see what happens?

JOEY Who is?

MAX Joey. No one's saying you're wrong. In fact everyone's saying you're right.

[*Pause.*]

[MAX *turns to the others.*]

You know something? Perhaps it's not a bad idea to have a woman in the

490 house. Perhaps it's a good thing. Who knows? Maybe we should keep her.

[*Pause.*]

Maybe we'll ask her if she wants to stay.

[*Pause.*]

TEDDY I'm afraid not, Dad. She's not well, and we've got to get home to the children.

MAX Not well? I told you, I'm used to looking after people who are not so

495 well. Don't worry about that. Perhaps we'll keep her here.

[*Pause.*]

SAM Don't be silly.

MAX What's silly?

SAM You're talking rubbish.

MAX Me?

500 SAM She's got three children.

MAX She can have more! Here. If she's so keen.

TEDDY She doesn't want any more.

MAX What do you know about what she wants, eh, Ted?

TEDDY [*smiling*] The best thing for her is to come home with me, Dad. Really.

505 We're married, you know.

[MAX *walks about the room, clicks his fingers.*]

MAX We'd have to pay her, of course. You realize that? We can't leave her walking about without any pocket money. She'll have to have a little allowance.

JOEY Of course we'll pay her. She's got to have some money in her pocket.

MAX That's what I'm saying. You can't expect a woman to walk about without

510 a few bob to spend on a pair of stockings.

[*Pause.*]

LENNY Where's the money going to come from?

MAX Well, how much is she worth? What we talking about, three figures?

LENNY I asked you where the money's going to come from. It'll be an extra mouth to feed. It'll be an extra body to clothe. You realize that?

9. Reaps the benefit (here, sexually).

515 JOEY   I'll buy her clothes.

LENNY   What with?

JOEY   I'll put in a certain amount out of my wages.

MAX   That's it. We'll pass the hat round. We'll make a donation. We're all grown-up people, we've got a sense of responsibility. We'll all put a little in
520   the hat. It's democratic.

LENNY   It'll come to a few quid,[1] Dad.

    [Pause.]

I mean, she's not a woman who likes walking around in second-hand goods. She's up to the latest fashion. You wouldn't want her walking about in clothes which don't show her off at her best, would you?

525 MAX   Lenny, do you mind if I make a little comment? It's not meant to be critical. But I think you're concentrating too much on the economic considerations. There are other considerations. There are the human considerations. You understand what I mean? There are the human considerations. Don't forget them.

530 LENNY   I won't.

MAX   Well don't.

    [Pause.]

Listen, we're bound to treat her in something approximating, at least, to the manner in which she's accustomed. After all, she's not someone off the street, she's my daughter-in-law!

535 JOEY   That's right.

MAX   There you are, you see. Joey'll donate, Sam'll donate. . . .

    [SAM looks at him.]

I'll put in a few bob out of my pension, Lenny'll cough up. We're laughing. What about you, Ted? How much you going to put in the kitty?[2]

TEDDY   I'm not putting anything in the kitty.

540 MAX   What? You won't even help to support your own wife? I thought he was a son of mine. You lousy stinkpig. Your mother would drop dead if she heard you take that attitude.

LENNY   Eh, Dad.

    [LENNY walks forward.]

I've got a better idea.

545 MAX   What?

LENNY   There's no need for us to go to all this expense. I know these women. Once they get started they ruin your budget. I've got a better idea. Why don't I take her up with me to Greek Street?[3]

    [Pause.]

MAX   You mean put her on the game?[4]

    [Pause.]

1. British pounds (currency).
2. In a card game, the pool into which players contribute a pre-agreed-upon amount to begin the betting. The term also refers, as here, to a general pool of money to which the members of a group contribute.
3. Street in the fashionable West End neighborhood of Soho. The street is famous for its restaurants and nightclubs and has been a primary location for London's sex trade. The Street Offences Act of 1959 meant that prostitutes could no longer solicit clients in the street, and as a result, many of the homes and businesses on Greek Street in the 1960s served as a front for brothels.
4. That is, put her on the market as a prostitute.

550   We'll put her on the game. That's a stroke of genius, that's a marvellous idea. You mean she can earn the money herself—on her back?

LENNY   Yes.

MAX   Wonderful. The only thing is, it'll have to be short hours. We don't want her out of the house all night.

555 LENNY   I can limit the hours.

MAX   How many?

LENNY   Four hours a night.

MAX [*dubiously*]   Is that enough?

LENNY   She'll bring in a good sum for four hours a night.

560 MAX   Well, you should know. After all, it's true, the last thing we want to do is wear the girl out. She's going to have her obligations this end as well. Where you going to put her in Greek Street?

LENNY   It doesn't have to be right in Greek Street, Dad. I've got a number of flats[5] all around that area.

565 MAX   You have? Well, what about me? Why don't you give me one?

LENNY   You're sexless.

JOEY   Eh, wait a minute, what's all this?

MAX   I know what Lenny's saying. Lenny's saying she can pay her own way. What do you think, Teddy? That'll solve all our problems.

570 JOEY   Eh, wait a minute. I don't want to share her.

MAX   What did you say?

JOEY   I don't want to share her with a lot of yobs![6]

MAX   Yobs! You arrogant git![7] What arrogance. [*To* LENNY.] Will you be supplying her with yobs?

575 LENNY   I've got a very distinguished clientèle, Joey. They're more distinguished than you'll ever be.

MAX   So you can count yourself lucky we're including you in.

JOEY   I didn't think I was going to have to share her!

MAX   Well, you *are* going to have to share her! Otherwise she goes straight

580 back to America. You understand?

[*Pause.*]

It's tricky enough as it is, without you shoving your oar in. But there's something worrying me. Perhaps she's not so up to the mark.[8] Eh? Teddy, you're the best judge. Do you think she'd be up to the mark?

[*Pause.*]

I mean what about all this teasing? Is she going to make a habit of it? That'll

585 get us nowhere.

[*Pause.*]

TEDDY   It was just love play . . . I suppose . . . that's all I suppose it was.

MAX   Love play? Two bleeding hours? That's a bloody long time for love play!

LENNY   I don't think we've got anything to worry about on that score, Dad.

MAX   How do you know?

590 LENNY   I'm giving you a professional opinion.

---

5. Apartments or suite of rooms on one floor of a building.

6. Thugs or hooligans (British slang). The word was coined in the 18th century by spell-ing "boy" backward.

7. Worthless or contemptible person.

8. That is, up to standard.

[LENNY *goes to* TEDDY.]

LENNY   Listen, Teddy, you could help us, actually. If I were to send you some cards, over to America . . . you know, very nice ones, with a name on, and a telephone number, very discreet, well, you could distribute them . . . to various parties, who might be making a trip over here. Of course, you'd get a
595   little percentage out of it.

MAX   I mean, you needn't tell them she's your wife.

LENNY   No, we'd call her something else. Dolores, or something.

MAX   Or Spanish Jacky.

LENNY   No, you've got to be reserved about it, Dad. We could call her some-
600   thing nice . . . like Cynthia . . . or Gillian.

[*Pause.*]

JOEY   Gillian.

[*Pause.*]

LENNY   No, what I mean, Teddy, you must know lots of professors, heads of departments, men like that. They pop over here for a week at the Savoy, they need somewhere they can go to have a nice quiet poke.[9] And of course
605   you'd be in a position to give them inside information.

MAX   Sure. You can give them proper data. You know, the kind of thing she's willing to do. How far she'd be prepared to go with their little whims and fancies. Eh, Lenny? To what extent she's various. I mean if you don't know who does?

[*Pause.*]

610   I bet you before two months we'd have a waiting list.

LENNY   You could be our representative in the States.

MAX   Of course. We're talking in international terms! By the time we've finished Pan-American'll[1] give us a discount.

[*Pause.*]

TEDDY   She'd get old . . . very quickly.

615   MAX   No . . . not in this day and age! With the health service?[2] Old! How could she get old? She'll have the time of her life.

[RUTH *comes down the stairs, dressed.*]
[*She comes into the room.*]
[*She smiles at the gathering, and sits.*]
[*Silence.*]

TEDDY   Ruth . . . the family have invited you to stay, for a little while longer. As a . . . as a kind of guest. If you like the idea I don't mind. We can manage very easily at home . . . until you come back.

620   RUTH   How very nice of them.

[*Pause.*]

MAX   It's an offer from our heart.

RUTH   It's very sweet of you.

MAX   Listen . . . it would be our pleasure.

[*Pause.*]

9. Sexual intercourse (slang).
1. Leading international air carrier that went bankrupt in 1991.

2. The National Health Service, which was founded in 1948, provides free access to health care for residents of the United Kingdom.

RUTH   I think I'd be too much trouble.

625 MAX   Trouble? What are you talking about? What trouble? Listen, I'll tell you something. Since poor Jessie died, eh, Sam? we haven't had a woman in the house. Not one. Inside this house. And I'll tell you why. Because their mother's image was so dear any other woman would have . . . tarnished it. But you . . . Ruth . . . you're not only lovely and beautiful, but you're kin.[3] You're
630 kith.[4] You belong here.

[*Pause.*]

RUTH   I'm very touched.

MAX   Of course you're touched. I'm touched.

[*Pause.*]

TEDDY   But Ruth, I should tell you . . . that you'll have to pull your weight a little, if you stay. Financially. My father isn't very well off.

635 RUTH [*to* MAX]   Oh, I'm sorry.

MAX   No, you'd just have to bring in a little, that's all. A few pennies. Nothing much. It's just that we're waiting for Joey to hit the top as a boxer. When Joey hits the top . . . well . . .

[*Pause.*]

TEDDY   Or you can come home with me.

640 LENNY   We'd get you a flat.

[*Pause.*]

RUTH   A flat?

LENNY   Yes.

RUTH   Where?

LENNY   In town.

[*Pause.*]

645   But you'd live here, with us.

MAX   Of course you would. This would be your home. In the bosom of the family.

LENNY   You'd just pop up to the flat a couple of hours a night, that's all.

MAX   Just a couple of hours, that's all. That's all.

650 LENNY   And you make enough money to keep you going here.

[*Pause.*]

RUTH   How many rooms would this flat have?

LENNY   Not many.

RUTH   I would want at least three rooms and a bathroom.

LENNY   You wouldn't need three rooms and a bathroom.

655 MAX   She'd need a bathroom.

LENNY   But not three rooms.

[*Pause.*]

RUTH   Oh, I would. Really.

LENNY   Two would do.

RUTH   No. Two wouldn't be enough.

[*Pause.*]

660   I'd want a dressing-room, a rest-room, and a bedroom.

[*Pause.*]

3. Family, blood relations.
4. Acquaintances, friends, or fellow countrymen.

LENNY   All right, we'll get you a flat with three rooms and a bathroom.

RUTH   With what kind of conveniences?

LENNY   All conveniences.

RUTH   A personal maid?

665 LENNY   Of course.

[Pause.]

We'd finance you, to begin with, and then, when you were established, you could pay us back, in instalments.

RUTH   Oh, no, I wouldn't agree to that.

LENNY   Oh, why not?

670 RUTH   You would have to regard your original outlay simply as a capital investment.[5]

[Pause.]

LENNY   I see. All right.

RUTH   You'd supply my wardrobe, of course?

LENNY   We'd supply everything. Everything you need.

675 RUTH   I'd need an awful lot. Otherwise I wouldn't be content.

LENNY   You'd have everything.

RUTH   I would naturally want to draw up an inventory of everything I would need, which would require your signatures in the presence of witnesses.

LENNY   Naturally.

680 RUTH   All aspects of the agreement and conditions of employment would have to be clarified to our mutual satisfaction before we finalized the contract.

LENNY   Of course.

[Pause.]

RUTH   Well, it might prove a workable arrangement.

LENNY   I think so.

685 MAX   And you'd have the whole of your daytime free, of course. You could do a bit of cooking here if you wanted to.

LENNY   Make the beds.

MAX   Scrub the place out a bit.

TEDDY   Keep everyone company.

[SAM comes forward.]

690 SAM [in one breath]   MacGregor had Jessie in the back of my cab as I drove them along.

[He croaks and collapses.]
[He lies still.]
[They look at him.]

MAX   What's he done? Dropped dead?

LENNY   Yes.

MAX   A corpse? A corpse on my floor? Get him out of here! Clear him out of
695   here!

[JOEY bends over SAM.]

JOEY   He's not dead.

LENNY   He probably was dead, for about thirty seconds.

---

5. One-time expense, or initial outlay, meant to increase a business's assets, as opposed to an operational expense, which would be the daily cost of maintaining and operating a business.

MAX   He's not even dead!

       [LENNY *looks down at* SAM.]

LENNY   Yes, there's still some breath there.

700   MAX [*pointing at* SAM]   You know what that man had?

LENNY   Has.

MAX   Has! A diseased imagination.

       [*Pause.*]

RUTH   Yes, it sounds a very attractive idea.

MAX   Do you want to shake on it now, or do you want to leave it till later?

705   RUTH   Oh, we'll leave it till later.

       [TEDDY *stands.*]

       [*He looks down at* SAM.]

TEDDY   I was going to ask him to drive me to London Airport.

       [*He goes to the cases, picks one up.*]

Well, I'll leave your case, Ruth. I'll just go up the road to the Underground.[6]

MAX   Listen, if you go the other way, first left, first right, you remember, you might find a cab passing there.

710   TEDDY   Yes, I might do that.

MAX   Or you can take the tube to Piccadilly Circus,[7] won't take you ten minutes, and pick up a cab from there out to the Airport.

TEDDY   Yes, I'll probably do that.

MAX   Mind you, they'll charge you double fare. They'll charge you for the

715   return trip. It's over the six-mile limit.

TEDDY   Yes. Well, bye-bye, Dad. Look after yourself.

       [*They shake hands.*]

MAX   Thanks, son. Listen. I want to tell you something. It's been wonderful to see you.

       [*Pause.*]

TEDDY   It's been wonderful to see you.

720   MAX   Do your boys know about me? Eh? Would they like to see a photo, do you think, of their grandfather?

TEDDY   I know they would.

       [MAX *brings out his wallet.*]

MAX   I've got one on me. I've got one here. Just a minute. Here you are. Will they like that one?

725   TEDDY [*taking it*]   They'll be thrilled.

       [*He turns to* LENNY.]

Good-bye, Lenny.

       [*They shake hands.*]

LENNY   Ta-ta, Ted. Good to see you. Have a good trip.

TEDDY   Bye-bye, Joey.

       [JOEY *does not move.*]

JOEY   Ta-ta.

---

6. London's major rail transportation system. While some lines have aboveground sections, most of the rail system is underground.

7. Bustling, well-known intersection in London's West End.

[TEDDY *goes to the front door.*]

730 RUTH Eddie.

[TEDDY *turns.*]
[*Pause.*]

Don't become a stranger.

[TEDDY *goes, shuts the front door.*]
[*Silence.*]
[*The three men stand.*]
[RUTH *sits relaxed in her chair.*]
[SAM *lies still.*]
[JOEY *walks slowly across the room.*]
[*He kneels at her chair.*]
[*She touches his head, lightly.*]
[*He puts his head in her lap.*]
[MAX *begins to move above them, backwards and forwards.*]
[LENNY *stands still.*]
[MAX *turns to* LENNY.]

MAX I'm too old, I suppose. She thinks I'm an old man.

[*Pause.*]

I'm not such an old man.

[*Pause.*]

[*To* RUTH.] You think I'm too old for you?

[*Pause.*]

735 Listen. You think you're just going to get that big slag[8] all the time? You think
you're just going to have him . . . you're going to just have him all the time?
You're going to have to work! You'll have to take them on, you understand?

[*Pause.*]

Does she realize that?

[*Pause.*]

Lenny, do you think she understands . . .

[*He begins to stammer.*]

740 What . . . what . . . what . . . we're getting at? What . . . we've got in mind?
Do you think she's got it clear?

[*Pause.*]

I don't think she's got it clear.

[*Pause.*]

You understand what I mean? Listen, I've got a funny idea she'll do the
dirty on us, you want to bet? She'll use us, she'll make use of us, I can tell
745 you! I can smell it! You want to bet?

[*Pause.*]

She won't . . . be adaptable!

[*He falls to his knees, whimpers, begins to moan and sob.*]
[*He stops sobbing, crawls past* SAM'S *body round her chair, to the other
side of her.*]

I'm not an old man.

[*He looks up at her.*]

---

8. Prostitute or promiscuous woman (slang), particularly derogatory when applied, as here, to a man.

Do you hear me?
>[*He raises his face to her.*]

Kiss me.
>[*She continues to touch* JOEY'S *head, lightly.*]
>[LENNY *stands, watching.*]

Curtain

WOLE SOYINKA

b. 1934

An active writer for more than five decades, Wole Soyinka is widely regarded as Africa's foremost dramatist and one of the most compelling contemporary writers in English more generally, a judgment affirmed by his being awarded the Nobel Prize in Literature in 1986. Though he is also an accomplished poet, novelist, and essayist, Soyinka's worldwide acclaim rests mainly on his dramatic oeuvre. His plays make use of the rituals and festivals of Nigeria's Yoruba culture and are marked by Nigeria's volatile history, but they also reflect the influences of other cultures, such as that of classical Greece. Soyinka has been one of the continent's most outspoken critics of abuses of power, in Nigeria and elsewhere, even as he has crafted plays that cannot be tied to a particular political creed. For many, his most significant achievement is the creation of a new form of tragedy that draws on both Western and Yoruba traditions, a form that is perhaps most fully realized in DEATH AND THE KING'S HORSEMAN (1975).

During Soyinka's formative years, Nigeria was in its last decades of British rule. Consequently, Soyinka received a traditional education in English, first at an elite grammar school and then at Government College, Ibadan, where he excelled in the study of various Western literatures, including French and Greek. He continued his education in England, where he studied drama at the University of Leeds. In Leeds and later in London, Soyinka also intensified his engagement with the theater and wrote his first plays, which helped win him a research grant and begin his swift rise as a dramatist. He returned to Nigeria in 1960, the year of its independence from Britain and the start of a period of intense conflict between different regions of the country. Over the next few years, Soyinka founded theater groups; wrote fiction and verse as well as plays for stage, television, and radio; and taught as a university lecturer in English. At the same time, he attempted to prevent the civil war that ultimately broke out in 1967 when the southeast of Nigeria declared its independence as Biafra; these efforts led to his imprisonment. He spent much of his two years of detention in solitary confinement, an experience he later described in one of his autobiographical prose works, *The Man Died: Prison Notes of Wole Soyinka* (1972). His subsequent career has been marked by a series of exiles and returns. Soyinka has taught at the University of Cambridge and Yale University and has directed shows in Europe and the United States, but his most sustained project has been the fostering of Nigeria's literary culture and democracy.

The clearest indications of Soyinka's changing attitude toward nationalism and cultural autonomy can be found in his essays. Writing in the sixties, Soyinka was often critical of those seeking an "authentic" culture that existed before Europeans colonized Africa and focused instead on cultural mixture. By the 1970s, however, he had turned more fully to Yoruba culture—to which he was exposed early, despite his mother's fervent Christianity—as a resource for drama. In the 1980s, as Soyinka once more became disenchanted with Nigeria's political realities, he placed less emphasis on Yoruba culture. His critical writings thus chart a path through the cultural struggles of a former colony dealing with an imposed culture that has now fused with local ones; after the terrible experience of colonialism, Western and indigenous cultures had become permanently intertwined. Soyinka's relation to colonialism was further complicated by his decision to write in English, albeit an English shot through with metaphors, idioms, and sayings from Yoruba. At various times in his career, he advocated the use of Swahili throughout the continent as a lingua franca to replace the languages of Africa's former European colonizers, but this proposal won few followers.

Soyinka's oeuvre oscillates between tradition and modernity. His earliest plays, *The Swamp Dwellers* (1958) and *The Lion and the Jewel* (1959), present a critique of traditional Yoruba practices and social structures as they come under increasing pressure from forces of modernization both from within and from without. Each play contains a village priest or ruler who opposes modernization and who cunningly seeks to hold on to vestiges of power predicated on the old ways. Soyinka clearly does not endorse this defensive rejection of modernization, although he recognizes the pain that accompanied the transformation of the Nigerian hinterland. Ultimately, these plays satirize the attempt to preserve the old at all cost. A similar critique is developed in *The Trials of Brother Jero* (1960) and *Jero's Metamorphosis* (1973), two plays that revolve around a pseudo-prophet who attracts followers solely for his own economic gain and who is ready to employ every trick possible to outsmart his rivals. In other works, Soyinka is more fully concerned with the social reality of the

outcast. In *The Road* (1965), one of his best plays, a number of lowlifes are assembled around a figure called Professor, who is akin to the sham prophet Jero. As Professor ekes out a living by forging documents, he is also engaged in an unlikely quest for spiritual enlightenment. These plays show that modernity is not something imposed onto Yoruba culture from the outside but a force at work within it.

Some of Soyinka's plays aim squarely at Nigerian politics—for example, *From Zia, with Love* (1992), which harshly indicts the dictatorship—but his best-known plays avoid direct political engagement, seeking instead to weave together different cultures and traditions. In his drama, Soyinka has continually insisted on the affinities between Greek and Yoruba tragedy. Most significantly, he has related the Yoruba god Ogun, the deity to whom he himself feels closest, to the Greek god Dionysus, who is connected with the origins of Greek tragedy. This attempt to forge new forms of tragedy out of Western and African traditions led to a long-standing controversy between Soyinka and a group of Nigerian intellectuals and critics—dubbed by Soyinka the "Leftocracy"—who accused him of seeking universal human meaning while ignoring the specifics of Nigeria's political and social situation after independence.

The tensions between political drama and tragedy as well as the tensions between the use of Western and Yoruba traditions are most visible in Soyinka's adaptations of EURIPIDES' *THE BACCHAE* (406 B.C.E.) and of BERTOLT BRECHT's *The Threepenny Opera* (1928). *The Bacchae of Euripides* (1973) provided Soyinka with an occasion to gauge the similarities and differences between Greek and Yoruba myths. Soyinka's Dionysus is less vindictive than Euripides', and his play displays a broader social range (its chorus is made up of slaves). Yet he shares with Euripides the attempt to connect drama to its lost origin in ritual. Brecht's *Threepenny Opera* is much more overtly political; *Opera Wonyosi* (1977) replaces the underworld of London, which Brecht himself had borrowed from the eighteenth-century British playwright John Gay, with a politically corrupt West Africa. In both adaptations, Soyinka demonstrates the power of translation and transposition, encouraging cultural mixture and cross-fertilization in a way that respects the integrity of different traditions and practices.

Soyinka's project of inventing a new tragic form culminates in *Death and the King's Horseman*, a play based on a historical incident. In 1946, a British colonial district officer interrupted the ritual suicide of a village notable, the King's Horseman—a suicide prescribed by the Yoruba religious and social system—without realizing how his interference would affect the village and, most important, the King's Horseman's son, who is also his protégé. This historical incident thus ties the officer, the King's Horseman, and his son in an inextricable and fatal knot. The officer himself is presented as a relatively two-dimensional figure, distinguished mainly by his colonial arrogance: Simon Pilkings interferes with local customs without knowing anything about their role in the social order or their religious significance. As a result, some critics have read the play as a defense of Yoruba customs. In his author's note, however, Soyinka takes issue with all readings that reduce the play to a simple "clash of cultures"; indeed, the play spends considerable energy trying—and failing—to bridge the gulf between them.

The two cultures are connected by various mediating figures, who participate in or have knowledge of both worlds. The officer, for example, depends on his Yoruba employees for information about local customs and religion. While Pilkings, who arrogantly dismisses their culture, often finds it difficult to interpret what his informants say, his wife is somewhat more open-minded and thus more aware of the inescapable cultural clash. The most competent intermediary is Olunde, the son of Elesin, the King's Horseman. Sent by Pilkings to England to study medicine against his father's wishes, Olunde has now returned for his father's burial. Although he is Westernized (as evidenced by the suit he wears), he does not dismiss the requirement that his father commit suicide, knowing how deeply the ritual is woven into the social fabric of the village. In eloquently criticizing the folly of the colonial officer's attempt to stop the ritual, he serves as an authoritative commentator on the play's main conflict. Events take a tragic turn at precisely the moment when the son feels forced to abandon his role as mediator and instead become a participant.

Nonso Amozie as the King's Horseman in Rufus Norris's 2013 production of *Death and the King's Horseman* at the National Theatre in London.

Even as Soyinka emphasizes the significance of the Yoruba custom and Elesin's social position, he also highlights the customs and social rituals of the British colonizers. Jane, the colonial officer's wife, approvingly recounts the story of a British captain's suicide, condoned because it was deemed heroic. At the same time, Soyinka contrasts Yoruba dances with a masque held by the British, who dress in costumes to attend a ball that evokes European court culture and its rigid hierarchies. Each culture thus has a place for suicide and for masked dance. To intertwine the two cultures even more closely, Soyinka has each imitate the other. At one point, a group of village women and girls mock the idioms and intonation of their colonial rulers. At another, we see the Pilkingses appear in sacred costumes associated with the Yoruba dead, mimicking ritual movements (as best they can) to amuse their European audience.

Soyinka's interest in different forms of ritual is part of an undertaking that informs his entire oeuvre, including *Death and the King's Horseman*: the creation of a total theater. Like many other theater artists of the nineteenth and twentieth centuries, Soyinka employs as many different modes of expression as possible, seeking to bring together song, poetry, dance, speech, ritual, and music. In this play, we encounter a variety of sounds and instruments—for example, the royal drums, which weave together the traditional rhythms of wedding and death and delineate the play's tragic trajectory; different dance interludes, including the gripping suicidal dance of the King's Horseman; and different Western musical pieces, such as the tango blaring from a gramophone at the colonial officer's house and a band playing "Rule Britannia" in honor of the Prince, who is visiting the colony. But unlike some makers of total theater, Soyinka is not interested in unifying these various traditions of music, dance, and theater into one seamless whole. Rather, the play thrives on their collisions, interchanges, and mutual imitations.

The different forms of ceremony, ritual, and dance that make up this complex play are mirrored and reinforced by its unusual language and poetry. Certain Yoruba songs that accompany the play's central event, the ritual suicide, are rendered in poetic English. Like all of the utterances of the non-British characters, they are informed by the syntax, idioms, expressions, proverbs, and metaphors of Yoruba. The result is a multilayered English that takes on deeper meaning as it draws on the Yoruba world—its flora, fauna, social structure, and cosmology. The play juxtaposes and blends different languages as thoroughly as it intermingles different forms of theater and performance.

This commingling is perhaps the most important feature of *Death and the King's Horseman*. For while the play certainly shows the violence that occurs at a moment of cultural contact between the British and Yoruba cultures, it refuses to blame all problems on their clash. Each culture has internal tensions. Thus Yoruba culture, for Soyinka, is never simply an authentic and monolithic given that is then, in a second step, set against the putatively modern British culture. He instead views Yoruba culture as having itself undergone a process of modernization, making it a culture compatible with the international, cosmopolitan world represented by Olunde, the most articulate figure in the play. At the same time, Soyinka points to tradition and even ritualistic aspects of British culture. In this way, both Yoruba culture and British culture are divided between tradition and modernization, though Soyinka never lets us forget which one has suppressed and belittled the other.

The attempt to show the different forms of modernization at work in Yoruba and British culture stands behind the mythic construction of this tragedy, which rests on the assumption that the Yoruba gods and the Greek gods are somehow compatible or comparable. It was a project conceived as a response to the more simplistic forms of postcolonial nationalism, which took shape as incipient nations sought to create distinct national traditions in isolation. At the same time, Soyinka is trying to dismantle the vestiges of colonialism—specifically, the assumption that Western culture has a unique claim to being modern and that in order for Yoruba culture to become modern it would have to adapt Western customs, religion, and culture.

Death and the King's Horseman has sometimes been accused of nostalgically privileging the Yoruba ritual by contrasting it favorably with the ignorance of the colonial officer, but Soyinka's complex mixing of the different ritualistic practices shows that no false nostalgia is in fact at work. Like many other works of modernism written by former colonizers and colonized alike, his plays display not just a fascination with premodern mythology and ritual but also an awareness that such myths and rituals can never be recovered in the present.

Just as Richard Wagner sought to relate his operatic artwork of the future to a mythic German past and James Joyce fashioned his groundbreaking novel after Homer, so Soyinka's play gains its strength by invoking but not embracing different ritual practices. While its characters accept and perform the ritual, Soyinka's play itself is and remains a modern work, albeit one with living roots in the past.   M.P.

Death and the King's Horseman

Dedicated
In Affectionate Greeting
to
My Father, Ayodele
who lately danced, and joined the Ancestors.

Author's Note

This play is based on events which took place in Oyo,[1] ancient Yoruba city of Nigeria, in 1946. That year, the lives of Elesin (Olori Elesin), his son, and the Colonial District Officer intertwined with the disastrous results set out in the play. The changes I have made are in matters of detail, sequence, and of course characterisation. The action has also been set back two or three years to while the war was still on,[2] for minor reasons of dramaturgy.

The factual account still exists in the archives of the British Colonial Administration. It has already inspired a fine play in Yoruba (Oba Wàjà[3]) by Duro Ladipo. It has also misbegotten a film by some German television company.

The bane of themes of this genre is that they are no sooner employed creatively than they acquire the facile tag of 'clash of cultures', a prejudicial label which, quite apart from its frequent misapplication, presupposes a potential equality *in every given situation* of the alien culture and the indigenous, on the actual soil of the latter. (In the area of misapplication, the overseas prize for illiteracy and mental conditioning undoubtedly goes to the blurb-writer for the American edition of my novel *Season of Anomy*[4] who unblushingly declares that this work portrays the 'clash between old values and new ways, between western methods and African traditions'!) It is thanks to this kind of perverse mentality that I find it necessary to caution the would-be producer of this play against a sadly familiar reductionist tendency, and to direct his vision instead to the far more difficult and risky task of eliciting the play's threnodic[5] essence.

1. A city in western Nigeria, about 100 miles north of Lagos.
2. That is, World War II.
3. *The King Is Dead* (1964).

4. Published in New York in 1974 (London, 1973).
5. Resembling a threnody, or song of lament for the dead.

One of the more obvious alternative structures of the play would be to make the District Officer the victim of a cruel dilemma. This is not to my taste and it is not by chance that I have avoided dialogue or situation which would encourage this. No attempt should be made in production to suggest it. The Colonial Factor is an incident, a catalytic incident merely. The confrontation in the play is largely metaphysical, contained in the human vehicle which is Elesin and the universe of the Yoruba mind—the world of the living, the dead and the unborn, and the numinous passage which links all: transition. *Death and the King's Horseman* can be fully realised only through an evocation of music from the abyss of transition.   W.S.

CHARACTERS

PRAISE-SINGER
ELESIN, Horseman of the King
IYALOJA, 'Mother' of the market
SIMON PILKINGS, District Officer
JANE PILKINGS, his wife
SERGEANT AMUSA
JOSEPH, houseboy to the Pilkingses
BRIDE
H.R.H. THE PRINCE
THE RESIDENT[6]
AIDE-DE-CAMP
OLUNDE, eldest son of Elesin

DRUMMERS, WOMEN, YOUNG GIRLS, DANCERS AT THE BALL

The play should run without an interval. For rapid scene changes, one adjustable outline set is very appropriate.

Act 1

A passage through a market in its closing stages. The stalls are being emptied, mats folded. A few WOMEN *pass through on their way home, loaded with baskets. On a cloth-stand, bolts of cloth are taken down, display pieces folded and piled on a tray.* ELESIN OBA *enters along a passage before the market, pursued by his* DRUMMERS *and* PRAISE-SINGERS. *He is a man of enormous vitality, speaks, dances, and sings with that infectious enjoyment of life which accompanies all his actions.*

PRAISE-SINGER   Elesin o! Elesin Oba! Howu![7] What tryst is this the cockerel goes to keep with such haste that he must leave his tail behind?
ELESIN [*slows down a bit, laughing*]   A tryst where the cockerel needs no adornment.
5 PRAISE-SINGER   O-oh, you hear that my companions? That's the way the world goes. Because the man approaches a brand-new bride he forgets the long faithful mother of his children.[8]
ELESIN   When the horse sniffs the stable does he not strain at the bridle? The market is the long-suffering home of my spirit and the women are

---

6. The ranking British officer in a province.
7. Why have you come? (Yoruba greeting). *Oba*: king (Yoruba).

8. Traditionally, Yoruba men had multiple wives.

10   packing up to go. That Esu[9]-harassed day slipped into the stewpot while we
    feasted. We ate it up with the rest of the meat. I have neglected my women.

PRAISE-SINGER We know all that. Still it's no reason for shedding your tail on
    this day of all days. I know the women will cover you in damask and *alari*[1]
    but when the wind blows cold from behind, that's when the fowl knows his
15   true friends.

ELESIN Olohun-iyo![2]

PRAISE-SINGER Are you sure there will be one like me on the other side?

ELESIN Olohun-iyo!

PRAISE-SINGER Far be it for me to belittle the dwellers of that place but, a
20   man is either born to his art or he isn't. And I don't know for certain that
    you'll meet my father, so who is going to sing these deeds in accents that
    will pierce the deafness of the ancient ones. I have prepared my going—just
    tell me: Olohun-iyo, I need you on this journey and I shall be behind you.

ELESIN You're like a jealous wife. Stay close to me, but only on this side. My
25   fame, my honour are legacies to the living; stay behind and let the world
    sip its honey from your lips.

PRAISE-SINGER Your name will be like the sweet berry a child places under
    his tongue to sweeten the passage of food. The world will never spit it out.

ELESIN Come then. This market is my roost. When I come among the
30   women I am a chicken with a hundred mothers. I become a monarch
    whose palace is built with tenderness and beauty.

PRAISE-SINGER They love to spoil you but beware. The hands of women also
    weaken the unwary.

ELESIN This night I'll lay my head upon their lap and go to sleep. This night
35   I'll touch feet with their feet in a dance that is no longer of this earth. But
    the smell of their flesh, their sweat, the smell of indigo[3] on their cloth, this
    is the last air I wish to breathe as I go to meet my great forebears.

PRAISE-SINGER In their time the world was never tilted from its groove, it
    shall not be in yours.

40 ELESIN The gods have said No.

PRAISE-SINGER In their time the great wars came and went, the little wars
    came and went; the white slavers came and went, they took away the heart
    of our race, they bore away the mind and muscle of our race. The city fell
    and was rebuilt; the city fell and our people trudged through mountain and
45   forest to found a new home but—Elesin Oba do you hear me?

ELESIN I hear your voice Olohun-iyo.

PRAISE-SINGER Our world was never wrenched from its true course.

ELESIN The gods have said No.

PRAISE-SINGER There is only one home to the life of a river-mussel; there is
50   only one home to the life of a tortoise; there is only one shell to the soul of
    man; there is only one world to the spirit of our race. If that world leaves its
    course and smashes on boulders of the great void, whose world will give us
    shelter?

ELESIN It did not in the time of my forebears, it shall not in mine.

55 PRAISE-SINGER The cockerel must not be seen without his feathers.

---

9. The Yoruba trickster god.
1. A rich, woven cloth, brightly coloured
[Soyinka]. *Damask:* a lustrous patterned fabric.

2. Praise-singer (Yoruba).
3. A costly blue dye made from plants and
used by royalty in Africa.

ELESIN   Nor will the Not-I bird[4] be much longer without his nest.

PRAISE-SINGER [*stopped in his lyric stride*]   The Not-I bird, Elesin?

ELESIN   I said, the Not-I bird.

PRAISE-SINGER   All respect to our elders but, is there really such a bird?

60 ELESIN   What! Could it be that he failed to knock on your door?

PRAISE-SINGER [*smiling*]   Elesin's riddles are not merely the nut in the kernel that breaks human teeth; he also buries the kernel in hot embers and dares a man's fingers to draw it out.

ELESIN   I am sure he called on you, Olohun-iyo. Did you hide in the loft and
65 push out the servant to tell him you were out?

[ELESIN *executes a brief, half-taunting dance. The* DRUMMER *moves in and draws a rhythm out of his steps.* ELESIN *dances towards the market-place as he chants the story of the Not-I bird, his voice changing dexterously to mimic his characters. He performs like a born raconteur, infecting his retinue with his humour and energy. More* WOMEN *arrive during his recital, including* IYALOJA.]

Death came calling.
Who does not know his rasp of reeds?
A twilight whisper in the leaves before
The great araba[5] falls? Did you hear it?
70 Not I! swears the farmer. He snaps
His fingers round his head, abandons
A hard-worn harvest and begins
A rapid dialogue with his legs.

'Not I,' shouts the fearless hunter, 'but—
75 It's getting dark, and this night-lamp
Has leaked out all its oil. I think
It's best to go home and resume my hunt
Another day.' But now he pauses, suddenly
Lets out a wail: 'Oh foolish mouth, calling
80 Down a curse on your own head! Your lamp
Has leaked out all its oil, has it?'
Forwards or backwards now he dare not move.
To search for leaves and make *etutu*[6]
On that spot? Or race home to the safety
85 Of his hearth? Ten market-days have passed
My friends, and still he's rooted there
Rigid as the plinth of Orayan.[7]

The mouth of the courtesan barely
Opened wide enough to take a ha'penny *robo*[8]
90 When she wailed: 'Not I.' All dressed she was
To call upon my friend the Chief Tax Officer.
But now she sends her go-between instead:

---

4. A bird whose call resembles the Yoruba phrase that means "not I."
5. A silk-cotton tree (Yoruba), which yields the fiber kapok.
6. Placatory rites or medicine [Soyinka].
7. A tall landmark in Ile-Ife, ancestral home

of the Yoruba. Orayan was a son of Oduduwa, first Yoruba king, and progenitor of all subsequent kings.
8. A delicacy made from crushed melon seeds, fried in tiny balls [Soyinka].

'Tell him I'm ill: my period has come suddenly
But not—I hope—my time.'

95   Why is the pupil crying?
His hapless head was made to taste
The knuckles of my friend the Mallam.[9]
'If you were then reciting the Koran
Would you have ears for idle noises
100 Darkening the trees, you child of ill omen?'
He shuts down school before its time
Runs home and rings himself with amulets.

And take my good kinsman Ifawomi.
His hands were like a carver's, strong
105 And true. I saw them
Tremble like wet wings of a fowl
One day he cast his time-smoothed *opele*[1]
Across the divination board. And all because
The supplicant looked him in the eye and asked,
110 'Did you hear that whisper in the leaves?'
'Not I,' was his reply; 'perhaps I'm growing deaf—
Good-day.' And Ifa spoke no more that day
The priest locked fast his doors,
Sealed up his leaking roof—but wait!
115 This sudden care was not for Fawomi
But for Osanyin,[2] courier-bird of Ifa's
Heart of wisdom. I did not know a kite
Was hovering in the sky
And Ifa now a twittering chicken in
120 The brood of Fawomi the Mother Hen.

Ah, but I must not forget my evening
Courier from the abundant palm, whose groan
Became Not I, as he constipated down
A wayside bush. He wonders if Elegbara[3]
125 Has tricked his buttocks to discharge
Against a sacred grove. Hear him
Mutter spells to ward off penalties
For an abomination he did not intend.
If any here
130 Stumbles on a gourd of wine, fermenting
Near the road, and nearby hears a stream
Of spells issuing from a crouching form,
Brother to a *sigidi*,[4] bring home my wine,
Tell my tapper[5] I have ejected

---

9. A teacher of Islamic doctrine (Hausa).
1. String of beads used in Ifa divination
[Soyinka].
2. Patron deity of diviners. *Fawomi*: a reference to Ifa, the Yoruba god of divination.
3. Another name for Esu, the trickster god.

4. A squat, carved figure, endowed with the powers of an incubus [Soyinka], which is a demon that lies on people in their sleep.
5. The person who collects the sap of palm trees, which is fermented into wine.

135   Fear from home and farm. Assure him,
      All is well.

PRAISE-SINGER   In your time we do not doubt the peace of farmstead and home,
    the peace of road and hearth, we do not doubt the peace of the forest.
ELESIN   There was fear in the forest too.
140   Not-I was lately heard even in the lair
    Of beasts. The hyena cackled loud Not I,
    The civet[6] twitched his fiery tail and glared:
    Not I. Not-I became the answering-name
    Of the restless bird, that little one
145   Whom Death found nesting in the leaves
    When whisper of his coming ran
    Before him on the wind. Not-I
    Has long abandoned home. This same dawn
    I heard him twitter in the gods' abode.
150   Ah, companions of this living world
    What a thing this is, that even those
    We call immortal
    Should fear to die.
IYALOJA   But you, husband of multitudes?
155 ELESIN   I, when that Not-I bird perched
    Upon my roof, bade him seek his nest again,
    Safe, without care or fear. I unrolled
    My welcome mat for him to see. Not-I
    Flew happily away, you'll hear his voice
160   No more in this lifetime—You all know
    What I am.
PRAISE-SINGER   That rock which turns its open lodes
    Into the path of lightning. A gay
    Thoroughbred whose stride disdains
165   To falter though an adder reared
    Suddenly in his path.
ELESIN   My rein is loosened.
    I am master of my Fate. When the hour comes
    Watch me dance along the narrowing path
170   Glazed by the soles of my great precursors.
    My soul is eager. I shall not turn aside.
WOMEN   You will not delay?
ELESIN   Where the storm pleases, and when, it directs
    The giants of the forest. When friendship summons
175   Is when the true comrade goes.
WOMEN   Nothing will hold you back?
ELESIN   Nothing. What! Has no one told you yet?
    I go to keep my friend and master company.
    Who says the mouth does not believe in
180   'No, I have chewed all that before?' I say I have.
    The world is not a constant honey-pot.

---

6. A weasel-like carnivorous mammal (especially the species native to Africa).

Where I found little I made do with little.
Where there was plenty I gorged myself.
My master's hands and mine have always
185 Dipped together and, home or sacred feast,
The bowl was beaten bronze, the meats
So succulent our teeth accused us of neglect.
We shared the choicest of the season's
Harvest of yams. How my friend would read
190 Desire in my eyes before I knew the cause—
However rare, however precious, it was mine.

WOMEN   The town, the very land was yours.

ELESIN   The world was mine. Our joint hands
Raised houseposts of trust that withstood
195 The siege of envy and the termites of time.
But the twilight hour brings bats and rodents—
Shall I yield them cause to foul the rafters?

PRAISE-SINGER   Elesin Oba! Are you not that man who
Looked out of doors that stormy day
200 The god of luck limped by, drenched
To the very lice that held
His rags together? You took pity upon
His sores and wished him fortune.
Fortune was footloose this dawn, he replied,
205 Till you trapped him in a heartfelt wish
That now returns to you. Elesin Oba!
I say you are that man who
Chanced upon the calabash[7] of honour
You thought it was palm wine and
210 Drained its contents to the final drop.

ELESIN   Life has an end. A life that will outlive
Fame and friendship begs another name.
What elder takes his tongue to his plate,
Licks it clean of every crumb? He will encounter
215 Silence when he calls on children to fulfill
The smallest errand! Life is honour.
It ends when honour ends.

WOMEN   We know you for a man of honour.

ELESIN   Stop! Enough of that!

WOMEN   [puzzled, they whisper among themselves, turning mostly to IYALOJA]
220 What is it? Did we say something to give offence? Have we slighted him in
some way?

ELESIN   Enough of that sound I say. Let me hear no more in that vein. I've
heard enough.

IYALOJA   We must have said something wrong. [Comes forward a little.]
225 Elesin Oba, we ask forgiveness before you speak.

ELESIN   I am bitterly offended.

IYALOJA   Our unworthiness has betrayed us. All we can do is ask your forgiveness. Correct us like a kind father.

---

7. A drinking vessel made from a gourd.

ELESIN This day of all days . . .

230 IYALOJA It does not bear thinking. If we offend you now we have mortified the gods. We offend heaven itself. Father of us all, tell us where we went astray. [*She kneels, the other women follow.*]

ELESIN Are you not ashamed? Even a tear-veiled
    Eye preserves its function of sight.
235 Because my mind was raised to horizons
    Even the boldest man lowers his gaze
    In thinking of, must my body here
    Be taken for a vagrant's?

IYALOJA Horseman of the King, I am more baffled than ever.

240 PRAISE-SINGER The strictest father unbends his brow when the child is penitent, Elesin. When time is short, we do not spend it prolonging the riddle. Their shoulders are bowed with the weight of fear lest they have marred your day beyond repair. Speak now in plain words and let us pursue the ailment to the home of remedies.

245 ELESIN Words are cheap. 'We know you for
    A man of honour.' Well tell me, is this how
    A man of honour should be seen?
    Are these not the same clothes in which
    I came among you a full half-hour ago?

        [*He roars with laughter and the* WOMEN, *relieved, rise and rush into stalls
        to fetch rich cloths.*]

250 WOMEN The gods are kind. A fault soon remedied is soon forgiven. Elesin Oba, even as we match our words with deed, let your heart forgive us completely.

ELESIN You who are breath and giver of my being
    How shall I dare refuse you forgiveness
255 Even if the offence were real.

IYALOJA [*dancing round him. Sings*]
    He forgives us. He forgives us.
    What a fearful thing it is when
    The voyager sets forth
    But a curse remains behind.

260 WOMEN For a while we truly feared
    Our hands had wrenched the world adrift
    In emptiness.

IYALOJA Richly, richly, robe him richly
    The cloth of honour is *alari*
265 *Sanyan* is the band of friendship
    Boa-skin[8] makes slippers of esteem

WOMEN For a while we truly feared
    Our hands had wrenched the world adrift
    In emptiness.

270 PRAISE-SINGER He who must, must voyage forth
    The world will not roll backwards
    It is he who must, with one
    Great gesture overtake the world.

---

8. That is, snakeskin. *Sanyan:* a richly valued woven cloth [Soyinka].

WOMEN   For a while we truly feared
275   Our hands had wrenched the world
       In emptiness.

PRAISE-SINGER   The gourd you bear is not for shirking.
       The gourd is not for setting down
       At the first crossroad or wayside grove.
280   Only one river may know its contents.

WOMEN   We shall all meet at the great market[9]
       We shall all meet at the great market
       He who goes early takes the best bargains
       But we shall meet, and resume our banter.

[ELESIN *stands resplendent in rich clothes, cap, shawl, etc. His sash is of a bright red alari cloth. The* WOMEN *dance round him. Suddenly, his attention is caught by an object offstage.*]

285 ELESIN   The world I know is good.

WOMEN   We know you'll leave it so.

ELESIN   The world I know is the bounty
       Of hives after bees have swarmed.
       No goodness teems with such open hands
290   Even in the dreams of deities.

WOMEN   And we know you'll leave it so.

ELESIN   I was born to keep it so. A hive
       Is never known to wander. An anthill
       Does not desert its roots. We cannot see
295   The still great womb of the world—
       No man beholds his mother's womb—
       Yet who denies it's there? Coiled
       To the navel of the world is that
       Endless cord that links us all
300   To the great origin. If I lose my way
       The trailing cord will bring me to the roots.

WOMEN   The world is in your hands.

[*The earlier distraction, a beautiful* YOUNG GIRL, *comes along the passage through which* ELESIN *first made his entry.*]

ELESIN   I embrace it. And let me tell you, women—
       I like this farewell that the world designed,
305   Unless my eyes deceive me, unless
       We are already parted, the world and I,
       And all that breeds desire is lodged
       Among our tireless ancestors. Tell me friends,
       Am I still earthed in that beloved market
310   Of my youth? Or could it be my will
       Has outleapt the conscious act and I have come
       Among the great departed?

PRAISE-SINGER   Elesin-Oba why do your eyes roll like a bush-rat who sees his fate like his father's spirit, mirrored in the eye of a snake? And all these
315 questions! You're standing on the same earth you've always stood upon. This voice you hear is mine, Oluhun-iyo, not that of an acolyte in heaven.

---

9. That is, in the afterlife.

ELESIN   How can that be? In all my life
    As Horseman of the King, the juiciest
    Fruit on every tree was mine. I saw,
320   I touched, I wooed, rarely was the answer No.
    The honour of my place, the veneration I
    Received in the eye of man or woman
    Prospered my suit and
    Played havoc with my sleeping hours.
325   And they tell me my eyes were a hawk
    In perpetual hunger. Split an iroko[1] tree
    In two, hide a woman's beauty in its heartwood
    And seal it up again—Elesin, journeying by,
    Would make his camp beside that tree
330   Of all the shades in the forest.
PRAISE-SINGER   Who would deny your reputation, snake-on-the-loose in dark
    passages of the market! Bed-bug who wages war on the mat and receives
    the thanks of the vanquished! When caught with his bride's own sister he
    protested—but I was only prostrating myself to her as becomes a grateful in-
335   law. Hunter who carries his powder-horn on the hips and fires crouching or
    standing! Warrior who never makes that excuse of the whining coward—but
    how can I go to battle without my trousers?—trouserless or shirtless it's all
    one to him. Oka[2]-rearing-from-a-camouflage-of-leaves, before he strikes the
    victim is already prone! Once they told him, Howu, a stallion does not feed
340   on the grass beneath him: he replied, true, but surely he can roll on it!
WOMEN   Ba-a-a-ba O!
PRAISE-SINGER   Ah, but listen yet. You know there is the leaf-nibbling grub
    and there is the cola-chewing beetle; the leaf-nibbling grub lives on the
    leaf, the cola-chewing beetle lives in the colanut. Don't we know what our
345   man feeds on when we find him cocooned in a woman's wrapper?
ELESIN   Enough, enough, you all have cause
    To know me well. But, if you say this earth
    Is still the same as gave birth to those songs,
    Tell me who was that goddess through whose lips
350   I saw the ivory pebbles of Oya's[3] river-bed.
    Iyaloja, who is she? I saw her enter
    Your stall; all your daughters I know well.
    No, not even Ogun[4]-of-the-farm toiling
    Dawn till dusk on his tuber patch
355   Not even Ogun with the finest hoe he ever
    Forged at the anvil could have shaped
    That rise of buttocks, not though he had
    The richest earth between his fingers.
    Her wrapper was no disguise
360   For thighs whose ripples shamed the river's

---

1. A large tree of the mulberry family, sometimes called African teak; according to Yoruba folklore, its denser, multicolored heartwood is inhabited by an impish spirit.
2. A snake.
3. The goddess of the Niger River and of winds.

4. The god of iron and war and patron of blacksmiths. Soyinka compares him to various gods and figures from Greek myth—Apollo, Prometheus, and especially Dionysus, the god of fertility and wine and patron of theater.

Coils around the hills of Ilesi.[5] Her eyes
Were new-laid eggs glowing in the dark.
Her skin . . .

IYALOJA   Elesin Oba . . .

365 ELESIN   What! Where do you all say I am?

IYALOJA   Still among the living.

ELESIN   And that radiance which so suddenly
Lit up this market I could boast
I knew so well?

370 IYALOJA   Has one step already in her husband's home. She is betrothed.

ELESIN [*irritated*]   Why do you tell me that?

[IYALOJA *falls silent. The* WOMEN *shuffle uneasily.*]

IYALOJA   Not because we dare give you offence Elesin. Today is your day and
the whole world is yours. Still, even those who leave town to make a new
dwelling elsewhere like to be remembered by what they leave behind.

375 ELESIN   Who does not seek to be remembered?
Memory is Master of Death, the chink
In his armour of conceit. I shall leave
That which makes my going the sheerest
Dream of an afternoon. Should voyagers
380 Not travel light? Let the considerate traveller
Shed, of his excessive load, all
That may benefit the living.

WOMEN [*relieved*]   Ah Elesin Oba, we knew you for a man of honour.

ELESIN   Then honour me. I deserve a bed of honour to lie upon.

385 IYALOJA   The best is yours. We know you for a man of honour. You are not one
who eats and leaves nothing on his plate for children. Did you not say it
yourself? Not one who blights the happiness of others for a moment's
pleasure.

ELESIN   Who speaks of pleasure? O women, listen!
390 Pleasure palls. Our acts should have meaning.
The sap of the plantain never dries.
You have seen the young shoot swelling
Even as the parent stalk begins to wither.
Women, let my going be likened to
395 The twilight hour of the plantain.

WOMEN   What does he mean Iyaloja? This language is the language of our
elders, we do not fully grasp it.

IYALOJA   I dare not understand you yet Elesin.

ELESIN   All you who stand before the spirit that dares
400 The opening of the last door of passage,
Dare to rid my going of regrets! My wish
Transcends the blotting out of thought
In one mere moment's tremor of the senses.
Do me credit. And do me honour.
405 I am girded for the route beyond
Burdens of waste and longing.
Then let me travel light. Let

5. A town in western Nigeria.

Seed that will not serve the stomach
On the way remain behind. Let it take root
410 In the earth of my choice, in this earth
I leave behind.
IYALOJA [*turns to* WOMEN]   The voice I hear is already touched by the waiting
fingers of our departed. I dare not refuse.
WOMEN   But Iyaloja . . .
415 IYALOJA   The matter is no longer in our hands.
WOMAN   But she is betrothed to your own son. Tell him.
IYALOJA   My son's wish is mine. I did the asking for him, the loss can be remedied. But who will remedy the blight of closed hands on the day when all
should be openness and light? Tell him, you say! You wish that I burden
420 him with knowledge that will sour his wish and lay regrets on the last
moments of his mind. You pray to him who is your intercessor to the
world—don't set this world adrift in your own time; would you rather it was
my hand whose sacrilege wrenched it loose?
WOMAN   Not many men will brave the curse of a dispossessed husband.
425 IYALOJA   Only the curses of the departed are to be feared. The claims of one
whose foot is on the threshold of their abode surpasses even the claims of
blood. It is impiety even to place hindrances in their ways.
ELESIN   What do my mothers say? Shall I step
Burdened into the unknown?
430 IYALOJA   Not we, but the very earth says No. The sap in the plantain does not
dry. Let grain that will not feed the voyager at his passage drop here and
take root as he steps beyond this earth and us. Oh you who fill the home
from hearth to threshold with the voices of children, you who now bestride
the hidden gulf and pause to draw the right foot across and into the
435 resting-home of the great forebears, it is good that your loins be drained
into the earth we know, that your last strength be ploughed back into the
womb that gave you being.
PRAISE-SINGER   Iyaloja, mother of multitudes in the teeming market of the
world, how your wisdom transfigures you!
440 IYALOJA [*smiling broadly, completely reconciled*]   Elesin, even at the narrow
end of the passage I know you will look back and sigh a last regret for the
flesh that flashed past your spirit in flight. You always had a restless eye.
Your choice has my blessing. [*To the* WOMEN] Take the good news to our
daughter and make her ready. [*Some* WOMEN *go off.*]
445 ELESIN   Your eyes were clouded at first.
IYALOJA   Not for long. It is those who stand at the gateway of the great
change to whose cry we must pay heed. And then, think of this—it makes
the mind tremble. The fruit of such a union is rare. It will be neither of this
world nor of the next. Nor of the one behind us. As if the timelessness of
450 the ancestor world and the unborn have joined spirits to wring an issue of
the elusive being of passage . . . Elesin!
ELESIN   I am here. What is it?
IYALOJA   Did you hear all I said just now?
ELESIN   Yes.
455 IYALOJA   The living must eat and drink. When the moment comes, don't turn
the food to rodents' droppings in their mouth. Don't let them taste the ashes
of the world when they step out at dawn to breathe the morning dew.

ELESIN   This doubt is unworthy of you Iyaloja.

IYALOJA   Eating the awusa nut[6] is not so difficult as drinking water afterwards.

460   ELESIN   The waters of the bitter stream are honey to a man
Whose tongue has savoured all.

IYALOJA   No one knows when the ants desert their home; they leave the
mound intact. The swallow is never seen to peck holes in its nest when it is
time to move with the season. There are always throngs of humanity
465   behind the leave-taker. The rain should not come through the roof for
them, the wind must not blow through the walls at night.

ELESIN   I refuse to take offence.

IYALOJA   You wish to travel light. Well, the earth is yours. But be sure the
seed you leave in it attracts no curse.

470   ELESIN   You really mistake my person Iyaloja.

IYALOJA   I said nothing. Now we must go prepare your bridal chamber. Then
these same hands will lay your shrouds.

ELESIN   [*exasperated*]   Must you be so blunt? [*Recovers.*]   Well, weave your
shrouds, but let the fingers of my bride seal my eyelids with earth and wash
475   my body.

IYALOJA   Prepare yourself Elesin.

[*She gets up to leave. At that moment the* WOMEN *return, leading
the* BRIDE. ELESIN's *face glows with pleasure. He flicks the sleeves
of his agbada[7] with renewed confidence and steps forward to meet
the group. As the girl kneels before* IYALOJA, *lights fade out on the
scene.*]

Act 2

*The verandah of the District Officer's bungalow. A tango is playing from an old
hand-cranked gramophone and, glimpsed through the wide windows and doors
which open onto the forestage verandah are the shapes of* SIMON PILKINGS *and his
wife,* JANE, *tangoing in and out of shadows in the living room. They are wearing
what is immediately apparent as some form of fancy dress.[8] The dance goes on for
some moments and then the figure of a* 'NATIVE ADMINISTRATION' POLICEMAN *emerges
and climbs up the steps onto the verandah. He peeps through and observes the
dancing couple, reacting with what is obviously a long-standing bewilderment. He
stiffens suddenly, his expression changes to one of disbelief and horror. In his excitement he upsets a flowerpot and attracts the attention of the couple. They stop
dancing.*

PILKINGS   Is there anyone out there?

JANE   I'll turn off the gramophone.

PILKINGS   [*approaching the verandah*]   I'm sure I heard something fall over.
[*The* CONSTABLE *retreats slowly, open-mouthed as* PILKINGS *approaches the
verandah.*] Oh it's you Amusa. Why didn't you just knock instead of knock-
5   ing things over?

AMUSA   [*stammers badly and points a shaky finger at his dress*]   Mista Pirinkin . . . Mista Pirinkin . . .

PILKINGS   What is the matter with you?

---

6. A walnutlike seed that is eaten or used to
produce oil. Raw, it has a bitter flavor.
7. A flowing, wide-sleeved robe worn by

important men.
8. That is, costumes.

JANE [*emerging*]   Who is it dear? Oh, Amusa . . .

10 PILKINGS   Yes it's Amusa, and acting most strangely.

AMUSA [*his attention now transferred to* MRS PILKINGS]   Mammadam . . . you too!

PILKINGS   What the hell is the matter with you man!

JANE   Your costume darling. Our fancy dress.

15 PILKINGS   Oh hell, I'd forgotten all about that. [*Lifts the face mask over his head showing his face. His wife follows suit.*]

JANE   I think you've shocked his big pagan heart bless him.

PILKINGS   Nonsense, he's a Moslem. Come on Amusa, you don't believe in all this nonsense do you? I thought you were a good Moslem.

AMUSA   Mista Pirinkin, I beg you sir, what you think you do with that dress?
20   It belong to dead cult, not for human being.

PILKINGS   Oh Amusa, what a let down you are. I swear by you at the club you know—thank God for Amusa, he doesn't believe in any mumbo-jumbo. And now look at you!

AMUSA   Mista Pirinkin, I beg you, take it off. Is not good for man like you to
25   touch that cloth.

PILKINGS   Well, I've got it on. And what's more Jane and I have bet on it we're taking first prize at the ball. Now, if you can just pull yourself together and tell me what you wanted to see me about . . .

AMUSA   Sir, I cannot talk this matter to you in that dress. I no fit.

30 PILKINGS   What's that rubbish again?

JANE   He is dead earnest too Simon. I think you'll have to handle this delicately.

PILKINGS   Delicately my . . . ! Look here Amusa, I think this little joke has gone far enough hm? Let's have some sense. You seem to forget that you are a police officer in the service of His Majesty's Government. I order you
35   to report your business at once or face disciplinary action.

AMUSA   Sir, it is a matter of death. How can man talk against death to person in uniform of death? Is like talking against government to person in uniform of police. Please sir, I go and come back.

PILKINGS [*roars*]   Now! [AMUSA *switches his gaze to the ceiling suddenly, remains mute.*]

40 JANE   Oh Amusa, what is there to be scared of in the costume? You saw it confiscated last month from those *egungun*[9] men who were creating trouble in town. You helped arrest the cult leaders yourself—if the juju[1] didn't harm you at the time how could it possibly harm you now? And merely by looking at it?

45 AMUSA [*without looking down*]   Madam, I arrest the ringleaders who make trouble but me I no touch *egungun*. That *egungun* itself, I no touch. And I no abuse 'am. I arrest ringleader but I treat *egungun* with respect.

PILKINGS   It's hopeless. We'll merely end up missing the best part of the ball. When they get this way there is nothing you can do. It's simply hammering
50   against a brick wall. Write your report or whatever it is on that pad Amusa and take yourself out of here. Come on Jane. We only upset his delicate sensibilities by remaining here.

[AMUSA *waits for them to leave, then writes in the notebook, somewhat laboriously. Drumming from the direction of the town wells up.* AMUSA

9. Ancestral masquerade [Soyinka]. The spirits of the dead are believed to temporarily

possess those wearing these costumes.
1. Magic associated with fetish objects.

listens, makes a movement as if he wants to recall PILKINGS *but changes his mind. Completes his note and goes. A few moments later* PILKINGS *emerges, picks up the pad and reads.*]

PILKINGS Jane!

JANE [*from the bedroom*] Coming darling. Nearly ready.

55 PILKINGS Never mind being ready, just listen to this.

JANE What is it?

PILKINGS Amusa's report. Listen. 'I have to report that it come to my information that one prominent chief, namely, the Elesin Oba, is to commit
death tonight as a result of native custom. Because this is criminal offence

60 I await further instruction at charge office. Sergeant Amusa.'

[JANE *comes out onto the verandah while he is reading.*]

JANE Did I hear you say commit death?

PILKINGS Obviously he means murder.

JANE You mean a ritual murder?

PILKINGS Must be. You think you've stamped it all out but it's always lurking

65 under the surface somewhere.

JANE Oh. Does it mean we are not getting to the ball at all?

PILKINGS No-o. I'll have the man arrested. Everyone remotely involved. In
any case there may be nothing to it. Just rumours.

JANE Really? I thought you found Amusa's rumours generally reliable.

70 PILKINGS That's true enough. But who knows what may have been giving
him the scare lately. Look at his conduct tonight.

JANE [*laughing*] You have to admit he had his own peculiar logic. [*Deepens
her voice.*] How can man talk against death to person in uniform of death?
[*Laughs.*] Anyway, you can't go into the police station dressed like that.

75 PILKINGS I'll send Joseph with instructions. Damn it, what a confounded
nuisance!

JANE But don't you think you should talk first to the man, Simon?

PILKINGS Do you want to go to the ball or not?

JANE Darling, why are you getting rattled? I was only trying to be intelligent. It

80 seems hardly fair just to lock up a man—and a chief at that—simply on the
er . . . what is the legal word again?—uncorroborated word of a sergeant.

PILKINGS Well, that's easily decided. Joseph!

JOSEPH [*from within*] Yes master.

PILKINGS You're quite right of course, I am getting rattled. Probably the

85 effect of those bloody drums. Do you hear how they go on and on?

JANE I wondered when you'd notice. Do you suppose it has something to do
with this affair?

PILKINGS Who knows? They always find an excuse for making a noise . . .
[*Thoughtfully*] Even so . . .

90 JANE Yes Simon?

PILKINGS It's different Jane. I don't think I've heard this particular—sound—
before. Something unsettling about it.

JANE I thought all bush drumming sounded the same.

PILKINGS Don't tease me now Jane. This may be serious.

95 JANE I'm sorry. [*Gets up and throws her arms around his neck. Kisses him.
The* HOUSEBOY *enters, retreats and knocks.*]

PILKINGS [*wearily*] Oh, come in Joseph! I don't know where you pick up all
these elephantine notions of tact. Come over here.

JOSEPH   Sir?

PILKINGS   Joseph, are you a Christian or not?

100 JOSEPH   Yessir.

PILKINGS   Does seeing me in this outfit bother you?

JOSEPH   No sir, it has no power.

PILKINGS   Thank God for some sanity at last. Now Joseph, answer me on the honour of a Christian—what is supposed to be going on in town tonight?

105 JOSEPH   Tonight sir? You mean the chief who is going to kill himself?

PILKINGS   What?

JANE   What do you mean, kill himself?

PILKINGS   You do mean he is going to kill somebody don't you?

JOSEPH   No master. He will not kill anybody and no one will kill him. He will
110   simply die.

JANE   But why Joseph?

JOSEPH   It is native law and custom. The King die last month. Tonight is his burial. But before they can bury him, the Elesin must die so as to accompany him to heaven.

115 PILKINGS   I seem to be fated to clash more often with that man than with any of the other chiefs.

JOSEPH   He is the King's Chief Horseman.

PILKINGS   [in a resigned way]   I know.

JANE   Simon, what's the matter?

120 PILKINGS   It would have to be him!

JANE   Who is he?

PILKINGS   Don't you remember? He's that chief with whom I had a scrap some three or four years ago. I helped his son get to a medical school in England, remember? He fought tooth and nail to prevent it.

125 JANE   Oh now I remember. He was that very sensitive young man. What was his name again?

PILKINGS   Olunde. Haven't replied to his last letter come to think of it. The old pagan wanted him to stay and carry on some family tradition or the other. Honestly I couldn't understand the fuss he made. I literally had to
130   help the boy escape from close confinement and load him onto the next boat. A most intelligent boy, really bright.

JANE   I rather thought he was much too sensitive you know. The kind of person you feel should be a poet munching rose petals in Bloomsbury.[2]

PILKINGS   Well, he's going to make a first-class doctor. His mind is set on
135   that. And as long as he wants my help he is welcome to it.

JANE   [after a pause]   Simon.

PILKINGS   Yes?

JANE   This boy, he was the eldest son wasn't he?

PILKINGS   I'm not sure. Who could tell with that old ram?

140 JANE   Do you know, Joseph?

JOSEPH   Oh yes madam. He was the eldest son. That's why Elesin cursed master good and proper. The eldest son is not supposed to travel away from the land.

---

2. The district of central London in which the British Museum and the University of London are located; it has long been associated with art and literary culture, notably the Pre-Raphaelites in the 19th century and Virginia Woolf and the "Bloomsbury Group" in the 20th.

JANE [*giggling*]   Is that true Simon? Did he really curse you good and proper?

145 PILKINGS   By all accounts I should be dead by now.

JOSEPH   Oh no, master is white man. And good Christian. Black man juju can't touch master.

JANE   If he was his eldest, it means that he would be the Elesin to the next king. It's a family thing isn't it Joseph?

150 JOSEPH   Yes madam. And if this Elesin had died before the King, his eldest son must take his place.

JANE   That would explain why the old chief was so mad you took the boy away.

PILKINGS   Well it makes me all the more happy I did.

155 JANE   I wonder if he knew.

PILKINGS   Who? Oh, you mean Olunde?

JANE   Yes. Was that why he was so determined to get away? I wouldn't stay if I knew I was trapped in such a horrible custom.

PILKINGS [*thoughtfully*]   No, I don't think he knew. At least he gave no indi-
160   cation. But you couldn't really tell with him. He was rather close[3] you know, quite unlike most of them. Didn't give much away, not even to me.

JANE   Aren't they all rather close, Simon?

PILKINGS   These natives here? Good gracious. They'll open their mouths and yap with you about their family secrets before you can stop them. Only the
165   other day . . .

JANE   But Simon, do they really give anything away? I mean, anything that really counts. This affair for instance, we didn't know they still practised that custom did we?

PILKINGS   Ye-e-es, I suppose you're right there. Sly, devious bastards.

170 JOSEPH [*stiffly*]   Can I go now master? I have to clean the kitchen.

PILKINGS   What? Oh, you can go. Forgot you were still there.

[JOSEPH *goes.*]

JANE   Simon, you really must watch your language. Bastard isn't just a simple swear-word in these parts, you know.

PILKINGS   Look, just when did you become a social anthropologist, that's
175   what I'd like to know.

JANE   I'm not claiming to know anything. I just happen to have overheard quarrels among the servants. That's how I know they consider it a smear.

PILKINGS   I thought the extended family system took care of all that. Elastic family, no bastards.

180 JANE [*shrugs*]   Have it your own way.

[*Awkward silence. The drumming increases in volume.* JANE *gets up suddenly, restless.*]

That drumming Simon, do you think it might really be connected with this ritual? It's been going on all evening.

PILKINGS   Let's ask our native guide. Joseph! Just a minute Joseph. [JOSEPH
reenters.] What's the drumming about?

185 JOSEPH   I don't know master.

PILKINGS   What do you mean you don't know? It's only two years since your conversion. Don't tell me all that holy water nonsense also wiped out your tribal memory.

---

3. Secretive, taciturn.

JOSEPH [*visibly shocked*]   Master!

190 JANE   Now you've done it.

PILKINGS   What have I done now?

JANE   Never mind. Listen Joseph, just tell me this. Is that drumming connected with dying or anything of that nature?

JOSEPH   Madam, this is what I am trying to say: I am not sure. It sounds like
195   the death of a great chief and then, it sounds like the wedding of a great chief. It really mix me up.

PILKINGS   Oh get back to the kitchen. A fat lot of help you are.

JOSEPH   Yes master. [*Goes.*]

JANE   Simon . . .

200 PILKINGS   Alright, alright. I'm in no mood for preaching.

JANE   It isn't my preaching you have to worry about, it's the preaching of the missionaries who preceded you here. When they make converts they really convert them. Calling holy water nonsense to our Joseph is really like insulting the Virgin Mary before a Roman Catholic. He's going to hand in
205   his notice tomorrow you mark my word.

PILKINGS   Now you're being ridiculous.

JANE   Am I? What are you willing to bet that tomorrow we are going to be without a steward-boy? Did you see his face?

PILKINGS   I am more concerned about whether or not we will be one native
210   chief short by tomorrow. Christ! Just listen to those drums. [*He strides up and down, undecided.*]

JANE   [*getting up*]   I'll change and make us some supper.

PILKINGS   What's that?

JANE   Simon, it's obvious we have to miss this ball.

PILKINGS   Nonsense. It's the first bit of real fun the European club has man-
215   aged to organise for over a year, I'm damned if I'm going to miss it. And it is a rather special occasion. Doesn't happen every day.

JANE   You know this business has to be stopped Simon. And you are the only man who can do it.

PILKINGS   I don't have to stop anything. If they want to throw themselves off
220   the top of a cliff or poison themselves for the sake of some barbaric custom what is that to me? If it were ritual murder or something like that I'd be duty-bound to do something. I can't keep an eye on all the potential suicides in this province. And as for that man—believe me it's good riddance.

225 JANE   [*laughs*]   I know you better than that Simon. You are going to have to do something to stop it—after you've finished blustering.

PILKINGS   [*shouts after her*]   And suppose after all it's only a wedding. I'd look a proper fool if I interrupted a chief on his honeymoon, wouldn't I? [*Resumes his angry stride, slows down.*] Ah well, who can tell what those chiefs actually
230   do on their honeymoon anyway? [*He takes up the pad and scribbles rapidly on it.*] Joseph! Joseph! Joseph! [*Some moments later* JOSEPH *puts in a sulky appearance.*] Did you hear me call you? Why the hell didn't you answer?

JOSEPH   I didn't hear master.

PILKINGS   You didn't hear me! How come you are here then?

235 JOSEPH   [*stubbornly*]   I didn't hear master.

PILKINGS   [*controls himself with an effort*]   We'll talk about it in the morning. I want you to take this note directly to Sergeant Amusa. You'll find him at

the charge office.[4] Get on your bicycle and race there with it. I expect you
back in twenty minutes exactly. Twenty minutes, is that clear?

240 JOSEPH Yes master. [*Going*]

PILKINGS Oh er . . . Joseph.

JOSEPH Yes master?

PILKINGS [*between gritted teeth*] Er . . . forget what I said just now. The holy
water is not nonsense. *I* was talking nonsense.

245 JOSEPH Yes master. [*Goes.*]

JANE [*pokes her head round the door*] Have you found him?

PILKINGS Found who?

JANE Joseph. Weren't you shouting for him?

PILKINGS Oh yes, he turned up finally.

250 JANE You sounded desperate. What was it all about?

PILKINGS Oh nothing. I just wanted to apologise to him. Assure him that the
holy water isn't really nonsense.

JANE Oh? And how did he take it?

PILKINGS Who the hell gives a damn! I had a sudden vision of our Very Rev-
255 erend MacFarlane drafting another letter of complaint to the Resident
about my unchristian language towards his parishioners.

JANE Oh I think he's given up on you by now.

PILKINGS Don't be too sure. And anyway, I wanted to make sure Joseph
didn't 'lose' my note on the way. He looked sufficiently full of the holy cru-
260 sade to do some such thing.

JANE If you've finished exaggerating, come and have something to eat.

PILKINGS No, put it all away. We can still get to the ball.

JANE Simon . . .

PILKINGS Get your costume back on. Nothing to worry about. I've instructed
265 Amusa to arrest the man and lock him up.

JANE But that station is hardly secure Simon. He'll soon get his friends to help
him escape.

PILKINGS A-ah, that's where I have out-thought you. I'm not having him put
in the station cell. Amusa will bring him right here and lock him up in my
270 study. And he'll stay with him till we get back. No one will dare come here
to incite him to anything.

JANE How clever of you darling. I'll get ready.

PILKINGS Hey.

JANE Yes darling.

275 PILKINGS I have a surprise for you. I was going to keep it until we actually
got to the ball.

JANE What is it?

PILKINGS You know the Prince[5] is on a tour of the colonies don't you? Well,
he docked in the capital only this morning but he is already at the Residency.
280 He is going to grace the ball with his presence later tonight.

JANE Simon! Not really.

PILKINGS Yes he is. He's been invited to give away the prizes and he has
agreed. You must admit old Engleton is the best Club Secretary we ever
had. Quick off the mark that lad.

4. Police station.
5. Prince Henry, duke of Gloucester (1900–
1974), the uncle of the future Queen Elizabeth

II, toured Ceylon (Sri Lanka), India, and North
Africa in 1942.

285 JANE   But how thrilling.

PILKINGS   The other provincials are going to be damned envious.

JANE   I wonder what he'll come as.

PILKINGS   Oh I don't know. As a coat-of-arms perhaps. Anyway it won't be anything to touch this.

290 JANE   Well that's lucky. If we are to be presented I won't have to start looking for a pair of gloves. It's all sewn on.

PILKINGS [*laughing*]   Quite right. Trust a woman to think of that. Come on, let's get going.

JANE [*rushing off*]   Won't be a second. [*Stops.*] Now I see why you've been so
295   edgy all evening. I thought you weren't handling this affair with your usual brilliance—to begin with that is.

PILKINGS [*his mood is much improved*]   Shut up woman and get your things on.

JANE   Alright boss, coming.

> [PILKINGS *suddenly begins to hum the tango to which they were dancing before. Starts to execute a few practice steps. Lights fade.*]

Act 3

A swelling, agitated hum of women's voices rises immediately in the background. The lights come on and we see the frontage of a converted cloth stall in the market. The floor leading up to the entrance is covered in rich velvets and woven cloth. The WOMEN *come on stage, borne backwards by the determined progress of Sergeant* AMUSA *and his two* CONSTABLES *who already have their batons out and use them as a pressure against the* WOMEN. *At the edge of the cloth-covered floor however the* WOMEN *take a determined stand and block all further progress of the men. They begin to tease them mercilessly.*

AMUSA   I am tell you women for last time to commot my road.[6] I am here on official business.

WOMAN   Official business you white man's eunuch? Official business is taking place where you want to go and it's a business you wouldn't under-
5   stand.

WOMAN [*makes a quick tug at the* CONSTABLE'S *baton*]   That doesn't fool anyone you know. It's the one you carry under your government knickers[7] that counts. [*She bends low as if to peep under the baggy shorts. The embarrassed* CONSTABLE *quickly puts his knees together. The* WOMEN *roar.*]

WOMAN   You mean there is nothing there at all?

10 WOMAN   Oh there was something. You know that handbell which the white-man uses to summon his servants . . . ?

AMUSA [*he manages to preserve some dignity throughout*]   I hope you women know that interfering with officer in execution of his duty is criminal offence.

15 WOMAN   Interfere? He says we're interfering with him. You foolish man we're telling you there's nothing to interfere with.

AMUSA   I am order you now to clear the road.

---

6. Come out of my road (pidgin English); that is, get out of my way.

7. Woman's underpants; here, a contemptu-ous reference to the khaki shorts worn by colonial policemen.

WOMAN   What road? The one your father built?

WOMAN   You are a Policeman not so? Then you know what they call trespass-
20   ing in court. Or—[*Pointing to the cloth-lined steps*]—do you think that kind
of road is built for every kind of feet.

WOMAN   Go back and tell the white man who sent you to come himself.

AMUSA   If I go I will come back with reinforcement. And we will all return
carrying weapons.

25 WOMAN   Oh, now I understand. Before they can put on those knickers the
white man first cuts off their weapons.

WOMAN   What a cheek! You mean you come here to show power to women
and you don't even have a weapon.

AMUSA [*shouting above the laughter*]   For the last time I warn you women to
30   clear the road.

WOMAN   To where?

AMUSA   To that hut. I know he dey dere.

WOMAN   Who?

AMUSA   The chief who call himself Elesin Oba.

35 WOMAN   You ignorant man. It is not he who calls himself Elesin Oba, it is his
blood that says it. As it called out to his father before him and will to his
son after him. And that is in spite of everything your white man can do.

WOMAN   Is it not the same ocean that washes this land and the white man's
land? Tell your white man he can hide our son away as long as he likes.
40   When the time comes for him, the same ocean will bring him back.

AMUSA   The government say dat kin' ting[8] must stop.

WOMAN   Who will stop it? You? Tonight our husband and father will prove
himself greater than the laws of strangers.

AMUSA   I tell you nobody go prove anyting tonight or anytime. Is ignorant
45   and criminal to prove dat kin' prove.

IYALOJA [*entering, from the hut. She is accompanied by a group of* YOUNG GIRLS
who have been attending the BRIDE]   What is it Amusa? Why do you come
here to disturb the happiness of others.

AMUSA   Madame Iyaloja, I glad you come. You know me, I no like trouble but
duty is duty. I am here to arrest Elesin for criminal intent. Tell these
50   women to stop obstructing me in the performance of my duty.

IYALOJA   And you? What gives you the right to obstruct our leader of men in
the performance of his duty?

AMUSA   What kin' duty be dat one Iyaloja.

IYALOJA   What kin' duty? What kin' duty does a man have to his new bride?

AMUSA [*bewildered, looks at the* WOMEN *and at the entrance to the hut*]
55   Iyaloja, is it wedding you call dis kin' ting?

IYALOJA   You have wives haven't you? Whatever the white man has done to
you he hasn't stopped you having wives. And if he has, at least he is married. If you don't know what a marriage is, go and ask him to tell you.

AMUSA   This no to wedding.

60 IYALOJA   And ask him at the same time what he would have done if anyone
had come to disturb him on his wedding night.

AMUSA   Iyaloja, I say dis no to wedding.

8. That kind of thing (pidgin English).

IYALOJA You want to look inside the bridal chamber? You want to see for yourself how a man cuts the virgin knot?

65 AMUSA Madam . . .

WOMAN Perhaps his wives are still waiting for him to learn.

AMUSA Iyaloja, make you tell dese women make den no insult me again. If I hear dat kin' insult once more . . .

GIRL [pushing her way through] You will do what?

70 GIRL He's out of his mind. It's our mothers you're talking to, do you know that? Not to any illiterate villager you can bully and terrorise. How dare you intrude here anyway?

GIRL What a cheek, what impertinence!

GIRL You've treated them too gently. Now let them see what it is to tamper
75 with the mothers of this market.

GIRL Your betters dare not enter the market when the women say no!

GIRL Haven't you learnt that yet, you jester in khaki and starch?

IYALOJA Daughters . . .

GIRL No no Iyaloja, leave us to deal with him. He no longer knows his
80 mother, we'll teach him.

> [With a sudden movement they snatch the batons of the two CONSTABLES. They begin to hem them in.]

GIRL What next? We have your batons? What next? What are you going to do?

> [With equally swift movements they knock off their hats.]

GIRL Move if you dare. We have your hats, what will you do about it? Didn't the white man teach you to take off your hats before women?

IYALOJA It's a wedding night. It's a night of joy for us. Peace . . .

85 GIRL Not for him. Who asked him here?

GIRL Does he dare go to the Residency without an invitation?

GIRL Not even where the servants eat the left-overs.

GIRL [in turn. In an 'English' accent] Well well it's Mister Amusa. Were you invited? [Play-acting to one another. The older WOMEN encourage them with their titters.]

90 —Your invitation card please?

—Who are you? Have we been introduced?

—And who did you say you were?

—Sorry, I didn't quite catch your name.

—May I take your hat?

95 —If you insist. May I take yours? [Exchanging the POLICEMEN's hats]

—How very kind of you.

—Not at all. Won't you sit down?

—After you.

—Oh no.

100 —I insist.

—You're most gracious.

—And how do you find the place?

—The natives are alright.

—Friendly?

105 —Tractable.

—Not a teeny-weeny bit restless?

—Well, a teeny-weeny bit restless.

—One might even say, difficult?

—Indeed one might be tempted to say, difficult.
110 —But you do manage to cope?
—Yes indeed I do. I have a rather faithful ox called Amusa.
—He's loyal?
—Absolutely.
—Lay down his life for you what?
115 —Without a moment's thought.
—Had one like that once. Trust him with my life.
—Mostly of course they are liars.
—Never known a native to tell the truth.
—Does it get rather close[9] around here?
120 —It's mild for this time of the year.
—But the rains may still come.
—They are late this year aren't they?
—They are keeping African time.
—Ha ha ha ha
125 —Ha ha ha ha
—The humidity is what gets me.
—It used to be whisky.
—Ha ha ha ha
—Ha ha ha ha
130 —What's your handicap old chap?
—Is there racing by golly?
—Splendid golf course, you'll like it.
—I'm beginning to like it already.
—And a European club, exclusive.
135 —You've kept the flag flying.
—We do our best for the old country.
—It's a pleasure to serve.
—Another whisky old chap?
—You are indeed too too kind.
140 —Not at all sir. Where is that boy? [*With a sudden bellow*] Sergeant!
AMUSA [*snaps to attention*] Yessir!
              [*The* WOMEN *collapse with laughter.*]
GIRL   Take your men out of here.
AMUSA [*realising the trick, he rages from loss of face*] I'm give you warning . . .
GIRL   Alright then. Off with his knickers! [*They surge slowly forward.*]
145 IYALOJA   Daughters, please.
AMUSA [*squaring himself for defence*] The first woman wey touch me . . .
IYALOJA   My children, I beg of you . . .
GIRL   Then tell him to leave this market. This is the home of our mothers.
    We don't want the eater of white left-overs at the feast their hands have
150 prepared.
IYALOJA   You heard them Amusa. You had better go.
GIRL   Now!
AMUSA [*commencing his retreat*] We dey go now, but make you no say we no
    warn you.
155 GIRL   Now!

9. Stifling, hot.

GIRL Before we read the riot act[1]—you should know all about that.

AMUSA Make we go. [*They depart, more precipitately.*]

[*The* WOMEN *strike their palms across in the gesture of wonder.*]

WOMEN Do they teach you all that at school?

WOMAN And to think I nearly kept Apinke away from the place.

WOMAN Did you hear them? Did you see how they mimicked the white man?

WOMAN The voices exactly. Hey, there are wonders in this world!

IYALOJA Well, our elders have said it: Dada may be weak, but he has a younger sibling who is truly fearless.[2]

WOMAN The next time the white man shows his face in this market I will set Wuraola[3] on his tail.

[*A* WOMAN *bursts into song and dance of euphoria—'Tani l'awa o l'ogbeja? Kayi! A l'ogbeja. Omo Kekere l'ogbeja.'*[4] *The rest of the* WOMEN *join in, some placing the* GIRLS *on their back like infants, others dancing round them. The dance becomes general, mounting in excitement.* ELESIN *appears, in wrapper only. In his hands a white velvet cloth folded loosely as if it held some delicate object. He cries out.*]

ELESIN Oh you mothers of beautiful brides! [*The dancing stops. They turn and see him, and the object in his hands.* IYALOJA *approaches and gently takes the cloth from him.*] Take it. It is no mere virgin stain, but the union of life and the seeds of passage. My vital flow, the last from this flesh is intermingled with the promise of future life. All is prepared. Listen! [*A steady drum-beat from the distance.*] Yes. It is nearly time. The King's dog has been killed. The King's favourite horse is about to follow his master. My brother chiefs know their task and perform it well. [*He listens again.*]

[*The* BRIDE *emerges, stands shyly by the door. He turns to her.*]

Our marriage is not yet wholly fulfilled. When earth and passage wed, the consummation is complete only when there are grains of earth on the eyelids of passage. Stay by me till then. My faithful drummers, do me your last service. This is where I have chosen to do my leave-taking, in this heart of life, this hive which contains the swarm of the world in its small compass. This is where I have known love and laughter away from the palace. Even the richest food cloys when eaten days on end; in the market, nothing ever cloys. Listen. [*They listen to the drums.*] They have begun to seek out the heart of the King's favourite horse. Soon it will ride in its bolt of raffia[5] with the dog at its feet. Together they will ride on the shoulders of the King's grooms through the pulse centres of the town. They know it is here I shall await them. I have told them. [*His eyes appear to cloud. He passes his hand over them as if to clear his sight. He gives a faint smile.*] It promises well; just then I felt my spirit's eagerness. The kite[6] makes for wide spaces and the wind creeps up behind its tail;

1. The act of Parliament (1716) that enabled local authorities to declare a group unlawfully assembled; before the law could be enforced, a proclamation ordering them to disperse had to be read.
2. Dada, the mythical king of Oyo and god of vegetables, abdicated in favor of his fierce younger brother Shango, who was god of lightning.
3. A common Yoruba girl's name; it means "rich gold."
4. Who says we haven't a defender? Silence! We have our defenders. Little children are our champions [Soyinka's translation].
5. The fiber of raffia palms, used to fringe the masks of *egungun* and make their skirts.
6. One of a number of birds in the family that includes hawks.

190 can the kite say less than—thank you, the quicker the better? But wait a while my spirit. Wait. Wait for the coming of the courier of the King. Do you know, friends, the horse is born to this one destiny, to bear the burden that is man upon its back. Except for this night, this night alone when the spotless stallion will ride in triumph on the back of man. In the time of my father I witnessed the strange sight. Perhaps tonight also I shall see it for the last time. If they arrive before the drums beat for me, I shall tell them to let the Alafin[7]

195 know I follow swiftly. If they come after the drums have sounded, why then, all is well for I have gone ahead. Our spirits shall fall in step along the great passage. [*He listens to the drums. He seems again to be falling into a state of semi-hypnosis; his eyes scan the sky but it is in a kind of daze. His voice is a little breathless.*] The moon has fed, a glow from its full stomach fills the sky and air, but I cannot tell where is that gateway through which I must pass. My

200 faithful friends, let our feet touch together this last time, lead me into the other market with sounds that cover my skin with down yet make my limbs strike earth like a thoroughbred. Dear mothers, let me dance into the passage even as I have lived beneath your roofs. [*He comes down progressively among them. They make way for him, the* DRUMMERS *playing. His dance is one of solemn, regal motions, each gesture of the body is made with a solemn finality. The* WOMEN *join him, their steps a somewhat more fluid version of his. Beneath the* PRAISE-SINGER'*s exhortations the women dirge* 'Alẹ lẹ lẹ, awo mi lọ.'[8]]

PRAISE-SINGER   Elesin Alafin, can you hear my voice?

205 ELESIN   Faintly, my friend, faintly.

PRAISE-SINGER   Elesin Alafin, can you hear my call?

ELESIN   Faintly my king, faintly.

PRAISE-SINGER   Is your memory sound Elesin?
    Shall my voice be a blade of grass and

210   Tickle the armpit of the past?

ELESIN   My memory needs no prodding but
    What do you wish to say to me?

PRAISE-SINGER   Only what has been spoken. Only what concerns
    The dying wish of the father of all.

215 ELESIN   It is buried like seed-yam in my mind.
    This is the season of quick rains, the harvest
    Is this moment due for gathering.

PRAISE-SINGER   If you cannot come, I said, swear
    You'll tell my favourite horse. I shall

220   Ride on through the gates alone.

ELESIN   Elesin's message will be read
    Only when his loyal heart no longer beats.

PRAISE-SINGER   If you cannot come Elesin, tell my dog.
    I cannot stay the keeper too long

225   At the gate.

ELESIN   A dog does not outrun the hand
    That feeds it meat. A horse that throws its rider
    Slows down to a stop. Elesin Alafin

---

7. The title of the paramount king of the Yoruba (that is, the deceased king); thus "Elesin Alafin," below, means "King's Horseman."

8. Night has fallen, the seasoned initiate is leaving (Yoruba).

Trusts no beasts with messages between
230   A king and his companion.
PRAISE-SINGER   If you get lost my dog will track
    The hidden path to me.
ELESIN   The seven-way crossroads[9] confuses
    Only the stranger. The Horseman of the King
235   Was born in the recesses of the house.
PRAISE-SINGER   I know the wickedness of men. If there is
    Weight on the loose end of your sash, such weight
    As no mere man can shift; if your sash is earthed
    By evil minds who mean to part us at the last . . .
240 ELESIN   My sash is of the deep purple *alari*;
    It is no tethering-rope. The elephant
    Trails no tethering-rope; that king
    Is not yet crowned who will peg an elephant—
    Not even you my friend and King.
245 PRAISE-SINGER   And yet this fear will not depart from me
    The darkness of this new abode is deep—
    Will your human eyes suffice?
ELESIN   In a night which falls before our eyes
    However deep, we do not miss our way.
250 PRAISE-SINGER   Shall I now not acknowledge I have stood
    Where wonders met their end? The elephant deserves
    Better than that we say 'I have caught
    A glimpse of something'. If we see the tamer
    Of the forest let us say plainly, we have seen
255   An elephant.
ELESIN [*his voice is drowsy*]
    I have freed myself of earth and now
    It's getting dark. Strange voices guide my feet.
PRAISE-SINGER   The river is never so high that the eyes
    Of a fish are covered. The night is not so dark
260   That the albino[1] fails to find his way. A child
    Returning homewards craves no leading by the hand.
    Gracefully does the mask regain his grove at the end of the day . . .
    Gracefully. Gracefully does the mask dance
    Homeward at the end of the day, gracefully . . .
    [ELESIN'S *trance appears to be deepening, his steps heavier.*]
265 IYALOJA   It is the death of war that kills the valiant,
    Death of water is how the swimmer goes
    It is the death of markets that kills the trader
    And death of indecision takes the idle away
    The trade of the cutlass blunts its edge
270   And the beautiful die the death of beauty.
    It takes an Elesin to die the death of death . . .
    Only Elesin . . . dies the unknowable death of death . . .

---

9. A symbol of confusion; in Yoruba folklore, the trickster god, Esu Elegba, is often found at such a crossroads.

1. Yoruba view albinism as a handicap (while believing that handicapped people are sacred to the creator of humans).

Gracefully, gracefully does the horseman regain
The stables at the end of day, gracefully . . .

275 PRAISE-SINGER   How shall I tell what my eyes have seen? The Horseman gal-
lops on before the courier, how shall I tell what my eyes have seen? He says
a dog may be confused by new scents of beings he never dreamt of, so he
must precede the dog to heaven. He says a horse may stumble on strange
boulders and be lamed, so he races on before the horse to heaven. It is
280 best, he says, to trust no messenger who may falter at the outer gate; oh
how shall I tell what my ears have heard? But do you hear me still Elesin,
do you hear your faithful one?

[ELESIN *in his motions appears to feel for a direction of sound, subtly, but*
he only sinks deeper into his trance-dance.]

Elesin Alafin, I no longer sense your flesh. The drums are changing now
but you have gone far ahead of the world. It is not yet noon in heaven; let
285 those who claim it is begin their own journey home. So why must you rush
like an impatient bride: why do you race to desert your Olohun-iyo?

[ELESIN *is now sunk fully deep in his trance, there is no longer sign of any*
awareness of his surroundings.]

Does the deep voice of *gbedu*[2] cover you then, like the passage of royal elephants? Those drums that brook no rivals, have they blocked the passage to
your ears that my voice passes into wind, a mere leaf floating in the night? Is
290 your flesh lightened Elesin, is that lump of earth I slid between your slippers to
keep you longer slowly sifting from your feet? Are the drums on the other side
now tuning skin to skin with ours in *osugbo?*[3] Are there sounds there I cannot
hear, do footsteps surround you which pound the earth like *gbedu*, roll like
thunder round the dome of the world? Is the darkness gathering in your head
295 Elesin? Is there now a streak of light at the end of the passage, a light I dare
not look upon? Does it reveal whose voices we often heard, whose touches we
often felt, whose wisdoms come suddenly into the mind when the wisest have
shaken their heads and murmured: It cannot be done? Elesin Alafin, don't
think I do not know why your lips are heavy, why your limbs are drowsy as palm
300 oil in the cold of harmattan.[4] I would call you back but when the elephant
heads for the jungle, the tail is too small a handhold for the hunter that would
pull him back. The sun that heads for the sea no longer heeds the prayers of
the farmer. When the river begins to taste the salt of the ocean, we no longer
know what deity to call on, the river-god or Olokun.[5] No arrow flies back to the
305 string, the child does not return through the same passage that gave it birth.
Elesin Oba, can you hear me at all? Your eyelids are glazed like a courtesan's, is
it that you see the dark groom and master of life? And will you see my father?
Will you tell him that I stayed with you to the last? Will my voice ring in your
ears awhile, will you remember Olohun-iyo even if the music on the other side
310 surpasses his mortal craft? But will they know you over there? Have they eyes
to gauge your worth, have they the heart to love you, will they know what thoroughbred prances towards them in caparisons[6] of honour? If they do not Elesin, if any there cuts your yam with a small knife, or pours you wine in a

---

2. A deep-timbred royal drum [Soyinka].
3. Secret "executive" cult of the Yoruba; its
meeting place [Soyinka].
4. A dry, dust-bearing seasonal wind that blows

into West Africa from the Sahara Desert.
5. The god of the ocean.
6. Ornamental cloths spread over the saddle
or harness of horses.

315 small calabash, turn back and return to welcoming hands. If the world were not greater than the wishes of Olohun-iyo, I would not let you go . . .

[*He appears to break down.* ELESIN *dances on, completely in a trance. The dirge wells up louder and stronger.* ELESIN's *dance does not lose its elasticity but his gestures become, if possible, even more weighty. Lights fade slowly on the scene.*]

Act 4

A Masque.[7] *The front side of the stage is part of a wide corridor around the great hall of the Residency extending beyond vision into the rear and wings. It is redolent of the tawdry decadence of a far-flung but key imperial frontier. The couples in a variety of fancy-dress are ranged around the walls, gazing in the same direction. The guest-of-honour is about to make an appearance. A portion of the local police brass band with its white conductor is just visible. At last, the entrance of Royalty. The band plays 'Rule Britannia',*[8] *badly, beginning long before he is visible. The couples bow and curtsey as he passes by them. Both he and his companions are dressed in seventeenth-century European costume. Following behind are the* RESIDENT *and his partner similarly attired. As they gain the end of the hall where the orchestra dais begins the music comes to an end. The* PRINCE *bows to the guests. The band strikes up a Viennese waltz and the* PRINCE *formally opens the floor. Several bars later the* RESIDENT *and his companion follow suit. Others follow in appropriate pecking order. The orchestra's waltz rendition is not of the highest musical standard.*

Some time later the PRINCE *dances again into view and is settled into a corner by the* RESIDENT *who then proceeds to select couples as they dance past for introduction, sometimes threading his way through the dancers to tap the lucky couple on the shoulder. Desperate efforts from many to ensure that they are recognised in spite of, perhaps, their costume. The ritual of introductions soon takes in* PILKINGS *and his wife. The* PRINCE *is quite fascinated by their costume and they demonstrate the adaptations they have made to it, pulling down the mask to demonstrate how the egungun normally appears, then showing the various press-button controls they have innovated for the face flaps, the sleeves, etc. They demonstrate the dance steps and the guttural sounds made by the egungun, harass other dancers in the hall,* MRS PILKINGS *playing the 'restrainer'*[9] *to* PILKINGS' *manic darts. Everyone is highly entertained, the Royal Party especially who lead the applause.*

At this point a liveried footman comes in with a note on a salver and is intercepted almost absent-mindedly by the RESIDENT *who takes the note and reads it. After polite coughs he succeeds in excusing the* PILKINGS *from the* PRINCE *and takes them aside. The* PRINCE *considerately offers the* RESIDENT's *wife his hand and dancing is resumed.*

On their way out the RESIDENT *gives an order to his* AIDE-DE-CAMP. *They come into the side corridor where the* RESIDENT *hands the note to* PILKINGS.

RESIDENT   As you see it says 'emergency' on the outside. I took the liberty of opening it because His Highness was obviously enjoying the entertainment. I didn't want to interrupt unless really necessary.

PILKINGS   Yes, yes of course, sir.

5 RESIDENT   Is it really as bad as it says? What's it all about?

PILKINGS   Some strange custom they have sir. It seems because the King is dead some important chief has to commit suicide.

---

7. That is, a masquerade, or elaborate masked ball (a European entertainment).
8. A patriotic song (1740); its words, taken from James Thomson's poem of the same

title, are set to music by Thomas Arne.
9. The person who exercises a restraining influence on the wild movements of the main dancer.

RESIDENT   The King? Isn't it the same one who died nearly a month ago?

PILKINGS   Yes sir.

10 RESIDENT   Haven't they buried him yet?

PILKINGS   They take their time about these things, sir. The preburial ceremonies last nearly thirty days. It seems tonight is the final night.

RESIDENT   But what has it got to do with the market women? Why are they
rioting? We've waived that troublesome tax haven't we?

15 PILKINGS   We don't quite know that they are exactly rioting yet sir. Sergeant
Amusa is sometimes prone to exaggerations.

RESIDENT   He sounds desperate enough. That comes out even in his rather
quaint grammar. Where is the man anyway? I asked my aide-de-camp to
bring him here.

20 PILKINGS   They are probably looking in the wrong verandah. I'll fetch him
myself.

RESIDENT   No no you stay here. Let your wife go and look for them. Do you
mind my dear . . . ?

JANE   Certainly not, your Excellency. [*Goes.*]

25 RESIDENT   You should have kept me informed, Pilkings. You realise how
disastrous it would have been if things had erupted while His Highness
was here.

PILKINGS   I wasn't aware of the whole business until tonight sir.

RESIDENT   Nose to the ground Pilkings, nose to the ground. If we all let
30 these little things slip past us where would the empire be eh? Tell me that.
Where would we all be?

PILKINGS [*low voice*]   Sleeping peacefully at home I bet.

RESIDENT   What did you say Pilkings?

PILKINGS   It won't happen again sir.

35 RESIDENT   It mustn't Pilkings. It mustn't. Where is that damned sergeant? I
ought to get back to His Highness as quickly as possible and offer him
some plausible explanation for my rather abrupt conduct. Can you think of
one, Pilkings?

PILKINGS   You could tell him the truth, sir.

40 RESIDENT   I could? No no no Pilkings, that would never do. What! Go and
tell him there is a riot just two miles away from him? This is supposed to be
a secure colony of His Majesty, Pilkings.

PILKINGS   Yes, sir.

RESIDENT   Ah, there they are. No, these are not our native police. Are these
45 the ring-leaders of the riot?

PILKINGS   Sir, these are my police officers.

RESIDENT   Oh, I beg your pardon officers. You do look a little . . . I say, isn't
there something missing in their uniform? I think they used to have some
rather colourful sashes. If I remember rightly I recommended them myself
50 in my young days in the service. A bit of colour always appeals to the
natives, yes, I remember putting that in my report. Well well well, where
are we? Make your report man.

PILKINGS [*moves close to* AMUSA, *between his teeth*]   And let's have no more
superstitious nonsense from you Amusa or I'll throw you in the guardroom
55 for a month and feed you pork![1]

RESIDENT   What's that? What has pork to do with it?

---

1. The eating of pork is forbidden to Muslims by the Qur'an.

PILKINGS   Sir, I was just warning him to be brief. I'm sure you are most anxious to hear his report.

RESIDENT   Yes yes yes of course. Come on man, speak up. Hey, didn't we give them some colourful fez hats with all those wavy things, yes, pink tassels . . .

PILKINGS   Sir, I think if he was permitted to make his report we might find that he lost his hat in the riot.

RESIDENT   Ah yes indeed. I'd better tell His Highness that. Lost his hat in the riot, ha ha. He'll probably say well, as long as he didn't lose his head. [*Chuckles to himself.*] Don't forget to send me a report first thing in the morning young Pilkings.

PILKINGS   No sir.

RESIDENT   And whatever you do, don't let things get out of hand. Keep a cool head and—nose to the ground Pilkings. [*Wanders off in the general direction of the hall.*]

PILKINGS   Yes, sir.

AIDE-DE-CAMP   Would you be needing me sir?

PILKINGS   No thanks Bob. I think His Excellency's need of you is greater than ours.

AIDE-DE-CAMP   We have a detachment of soldiers from the capital sir. They accompanied His Highness up here.

PILINGS   I doubt if it will come to that but, thanks, I'll bear it in mind. Oh, could you send an orderly with my cloak.

AIDE-DE-CAMP   Very good sir. [*Goes.*]

PILKINGS   Now sergeant.

AMUSA   Sir . . . [*Makes an effort, stops dead. Eyes to the ceiling.*]

PILKINGS   Oh, not again.

AMUSA   I cannot against death to dead cult. This dress get power of dead.

PILKINGS   Alright, let's go. You are relieved of all further duty Amusa. Report to me first thing in the morning.

JANE   Shall I come Simon?

PILKINGS   No, there's no need for that. If I can get back later I will. Otherwise get Bob to bring you home.

JANE   Be careful Simon . . . I mean, be clever.

PILKINGS   Sure I will. You two, come with me. [*As he turns to go, the clock in the Residency begins to chime.* PILKINGS *looks at his watch then turns, horror-stricken, to stare at his wife. The same thought clearly occurs to her. He swallows hard. An orderly brings his cloak.*] It's midnight. I had no idea it was that late.

JANE   But surely . . . they don't count the hours the way we do. The moon, or something . . .

PILKINGS   I am . . . not so sure.

[*He turns and breaks into a sudden run. The two* CONSTABLES *follow, also at a run.* AMUSA, *who has kept his eyes on the ceiling throughout waits until the last of the footsteps has faded out of hearing. He salutes suddenly, but without once looking in the direction of the woman.*]

AMUSA   Goodnight madam.

JANE   Oh. [*She hesitates.*] Amusa . . . [*He goes off without seeming to have heard.*] Poor Simon . . . [*A figure emerges from the shadows, a young black man dressed in a sober western suit. He peeps into the hall, trying to make out the figures of the dancers.*] Who is that?

100 OLUNDE [*emerging into the light*] I didn't mean to startle you madam. I am
    looking for the District Officer.

JANE Wait a minute . . . don't I know you? Yes, you are Olunde, the young
    man who . . .

OLUNDE Mrs Pilkings! How fortunate. I came here to look for your husband.

105 JANE Olunde! Let's look at you. What a fine young man you've become.
    Grand but solemn. Good God, when did you return? Simon never said a
    word. But you do look well Olunde. Really!

OLUNDE You are . . . well, you look quite well yourself Mrs Pilkings. From
    what little I can see of you.

110 JANE Oh, this. It's caused quite a stir I assure you, and not all of it very
    pleasant. You are not shocked I hope?

OLUNDE Why should I be? But don't you find it rather hot in there? Your
    skin must find it difficult to breathe.

JANE Well, it is a little hot I must confess, but it's all in a good cause.

115 OLUNDE What cause Mrs Pilkings?

JANE All this. The ball. And His Highness being here in person and all that.

OLUNDE [*mildly*] And that is the good cause for which you desecrate an
    ancestral mask?

JANE Oh, so you are shocked after all. How disappointing.

120 OLUNDE No I am not shocked Mrs Pilkings. You forget that I have now spent
    four years among your people. I discovered that you have no respect for
    what you do not understand.

JANE Oh. So you've returned with a chip on your shoulder. That's a pity
    Olunde. I am sorry.

    [*An uncomfortable silence follows.*]

125 I take it then that you did not find your stay in England altogether edifying.

OLUNDE I don't say that. I found your people quite admirable in many ways,
    their conduct and courage in this war[2] for instance.

JANE Ah yes, the war. Here of course it is all rather remote. From time to
    time we have a black-out drill just to remind us that there is a war on. And
130 the rare convoy passes through on its way somewhere or on manoeuvres.
    Mind you there is the occasional bit of excitement like that ship that was
    blown up in the harbour.[3]

OLUNDE Here? Do you mean through enemy action?

JANE Oh no, the war hasn't come that close. The captain did it himself. I
135 don't quite understand it really. Simon tried to explain. The ship had to be
    blown up because it had become dangerous to the other ships, even to the
    city itself. Hundreds of the coastal population would have died.

OLUNDE Maybe it was loaded with ammunition and had caught fire. Or
    some of those lethal gases they've been experimenting on.

140 JANE Something like that. The captain blew himself up with it. Deliberately.
    Simon said someone had to remain on board to light the fuse.

OLUNDE It must have been a very short fuse.

JANE [*shrugs*] I don't know much about it. Only that there was no other way
    to save lives. No time to devise anything else. The captain took the decision
145 and carried it out.

2. That is, World War II.
3. Perhaps a reference to a tragic incident that
involved no heroism: on December 5, 1942,
when three British naval trawlers were moored
in the harbor at Lagos, an oil spill caught fire.
The ships exploded, killing about 200 men.

OLUNDE   Yes . . . I quite believe it. I met men like that in England.

JANE   Oh just look at me! Fancy welcoming you back with such morbid news. Stale too. It was at least six months ago.

OLUNDE   I don't find it morbid at all. I find it rather inspiring. It is an affir-
150 mative commentary on life.

JANE   What is?

OLUNDE   That captain's self-sacrifice.

JANE   Nonsense. Life should never be thrown deliberately away.

OLUNDE   And the innocent people round the harbour?

155 JANE   Oh, how does one know? The whole thing was probably exaggerated anyway.

OLUNDE   That was a risk the captain couldn't take. But please Mrs Pilkings, do you think you could find your husband for me? I have to talk to him.

JANE   Simon? Oh. [*As she recollects for the first time the full significance of*
160 OLUNDE*'s presence.*] Simon is . . . there is a little problem in town. He was sent for. But . . . when did you arrive? Does Simon know you're here?

OLUNDE   [*suddenly earnest*]   I need your help Mrs Pilkings. I've always found you somewhat more understanding than your husband. Please find him for me and when you do, you must help me talk to him.

165 JANE   I'm afraid I don't quite . . . follow you. Have you seen my husband already?

OLUNDE   I went to your house. Your houseboy told me you were here. [*He smiles.*] He even told me how I would recognise you and Mr Pilkings.

JANE   Then you must know what my husband is trying to do for you.

170 OLUNDE   For me?

JANE   For you. For your people. And to think he didn't even know you were coming back! But how do you happen to be here? Only this evening we were talking about you. We thought you were still four thousand miles away.

OLUNDE   I was sent a cable.

175 JANE   A cable? Who did? Simon? The business of your father didn't begin till tonight.

OLUNDE   A relation sent it weeks ago, and it said nothing about my father. All it said was, Our King is dead. But I knew I had to return home at once so as to bury my father. I understood that.

180 JANE   Well, thank God you don't have to go through that agony. Simon is going to stop it.

OLUNDE   That's why I want to see him. He's wasting his time. And since he has been so helpful to me I don't want him to incur the enmity of our people. Especially over nothing.

185 JANE   [*sits down open-mouthed*]   You . . . you Olunde!

OLUNDE   Mrs Pilkings, I came home to bury my father. As soon as I heard the news I booked my passage home. In fact we were fortunate. We trav-elled in the same convoy as your Prince, so we had excellent protection.

JANE   But you don't think your father is also entitled to whatever protection
190 is available to him?

OLUNDE   How can I make you understand? He *has* protection. No one can undertake what he does tonight without the deepest protection the mind can conceive. What can you offer him in place of his peace of mind, in place of the honour and veneration of his own people? What would you
195 think of your Prince if he refused to accept the risk of losing his life on this voyage? This . . . showing-the-flag tour of colonial possessions.

JANE   I see. So it isn't just medicine you studied in England.

OLUNDE   Yet another error into which your people fall. You believe that everything which appears to make sense was learnt from you.

200 JANE   Not so fast Olunde. You have learnt to argue I can tell that, but I never said you made sense. However clearly you try to put it, it is still a barbaric custom. It is even worse—it's feudal! The king dies and a chieftain must be buried with him. How feudalistic can you get!

OLUNDE   [*waves his hand towards the background. The* PRINCE *is dancing past again—to a different step—and all the guests are bowing and curtseying as he passes*]   And this? Even in the midst of a devastating war, look at that.
205   What name would you give to that?

JANE   Therapy, British style. The preservation of sanity in the midst of chaos.

OLUNDE   Others would call it decadence. However, it doesn't really interest me. You white races know how to survive; I've seen proof of that. By all logical and natural laws this war should end with all the white races wiping
210   out one another, wiping out their so-called civilisation for all time and reverting to a state of primitivism the like of which has so far only existed in your imagination when you thought of us. I thought all that at the beginning. Then I slowly realised that your greatest art is the art of survival. But at least have the humility to let others survive in their own way.

215 JANE   Through ritual suicide?

OLUNDE   Is that worse than mass suicide? Mrs Pilkings, what do you call what those young men are sent to do by their generals in this war? Of course you have also mastered the art of calling things by names which don't remotely describe them.

220 JANE   You talk! You people with your long-winded, roundabout way of making conversation.

OLUNDE   Mrs Pilkings, whatever we do, we never suggest that a thing is the opposite of what it really is. In your newsreels I heard defeats, thorough, murderous defeats described as strategic victories. No wait, it wasn't just
225   on your newsreels. Don't forget I was attached to hospitals all the time. Hordes of your wounded passed through those wards. I spoke to them. I spent long evenings by their bedsides while they spoke terrible truths of the realities of that war. I know now how history is made.

JANE   But surely, in a war of this nature, for the morale of the nation you
230   must expect . . .

OLUNDE   That a disaster beyond human reckoning be spoken of as a triumph? No. I mean, is there no mourning in the home of the bereaved that such blasphemy is permitted?

JANE   [*after a moment's pause*]   Perhaps I can understand you now. The time
235   we picked for you was not really one for seeing us at our best.

OLUNDE   Don't think it was just the war. Before that even started I had plenty of time to study your people. I saw nothing, finally, that gave you the right to pass judgement on other peoples and their ways. Nothing at all.

JANE   [*hesitantly*]   Was it the . . . colour thing? I know there is some
240   discrimination.

OLUNDE   Don't make it so simple, Mrs Pilkings. You make it sound as if when I left, I took nothing at all with me.

JANE   Yes . . . and to tell the truth, only this evening, Simon and I agreed that we never really knew what you left with.

245 OLUNDE   Neither did I. But I found out over there. I am grateful to your
country for that. And I will never give it up.

JANE   Olunde please . . . promise me something. Whatever you do, don't
throw away what you have started to do. You want to be a doctor. My husband and I believe you will make an excellent one, sympathetic and compe-
250 tent. Don't let anything make you throw away your training.

OLUNDE [*genuinely surprised*]   Of course not. What a strange idea. I intend
to return and complete my training. Once the burial of my father is over.

JANE   Oh, please . . . !

OLUNDE   Listen! Come outside. You can't hear anything against that music.

255 JANE   What is it?

OLUNDE   The drums. Can you hear the changes? Listen.

[*The drums come over, still distant but more distinct. There is a change
of rhythm, it rises to a crescendo and then, suddenly, it is cut off. After a
silence, a new beat begins, slow and resonant.*]

There, it's all over.

JANE   You mean he's . . .

OLUNDE   Yes, Mrs Pilkings, my father is dead. His will-power has always
260 been enormous; I know he is dead.

JANE [*screams*]   How can you be so callous! So unfeeling! You announce your
father's own death like a surgeon looking down on some strange . . . stranger's body! You're just a savage like all the rest.

AIDE-DE-CAMP [*rushing out*]   Mrs Pilkings. Mrs Pilkings. [*She breaks down,
265 sobbing.*] Are you all right, Mrs Pilkings?

OLUNDE   She'll be all right. [*Turns to go.*]

AIDE-DE-CAMP   Who are you? And who the hell asked your opinion?

OLUNDE   You're quite right, nobody. [*Going*]

AIDE-DE-CAMP   What the hell! Did you hear me ask you who you were?

270 OLUNDE   I have business to attend to.

AIDE-DE-CAMP   I'll give you business in a moment you impudent nigger.
Answer my question!

OLUNDE   I have a funeral to arrange. Excuse me. [*Going*]

AIDE-DE-CAMP   I said stop! Orderly!

275 JANE   No, no, don't do that. I'm alright. And for heaven's sake don't act so
foolishly. He's a family friend.

AIDE-DE-CAMP   Well he'd better learn to answer civil questions when he's
asked them. These natives put a suit on and they get high opinions of
themselves.

280 OLUNDE   Can I go now?

JANE   No no don't go. I must talk to you. I'm sorry about what I said.

OLUNDE   It's nothing, Mrs Pilkings. And I'm really anxious to go. I couldn't
see my father before, it's forbidden for me, his heir and successor, to set
eyes on him from the moment of the King's death. But now . . . I would
285 like to touch his body while it is still warm.

JANE   You will. I promise I shan't keep you long. Only, I couldn't possibly let
you go like that. Bob, please excuse us.

AIDE-DE-CAMP   If you're sure . . .

JANE   Of course I'm sure. Something happened to upset me just then, but
290 I'm alright now. Really.

[*The* AIDE-DE-CAMP *goes, somewhat reluctantly.*]

OLUNDE   I mustn't stay long.

JANE   Please, I promise not to keep you. It's just that . . . oh you saw yourself what happens to one in this place. The Resident's man thought he was being helpful, that's the way we all react. But I can't go in among that crowd just now and if I stay by myself somebody will come looking for me. Please, just say something for a few moments and then you can go. Just so I can recover myself.

OLUNDE   What do you want me to say?

JANE   Your calm acceptance for instance, can you explain that? It was so unnatural. I don't understand that at all. I feel a need to understand all I can.

OLUNDE   But you explained it yourself. My medical training perhaps. I have seen death too often. And the soldiers who returned from the front, they died on our hands all the time.

JANE   No. It has to be more than that. I feel it has to do with the many things we don't really grasp about your people. At least you can explain.

OLUNDE   All these things are part of it. And anyway, my father has been dead in my mind for nearly a month. Ever since I learnt of the King's death. I've lived with my bereavement so long now that I cannot think of him alive. On that journey on the boat, I kept my mind on my duties as the one who must perform the rites over his body. I went through it all again and again in my mind as he himself had taught me. I didn't want to do anything wrong, something which might jeopardise the welfare of my people.

JANE   But he had disowned you. When you left he swore publicly you were no longer his son.

OLUNDE   I told you, he was a man of tremendous will. Sometimes that's another way of saying stubborn. But among our people, you don't disown a child just like that. Even if I had died before him I would still be buried like his eldest son. But it's time for me to go.

JANE   Thank you. I feel calmer. Don't let me keep you from your duties.

OLUNDE   Goodnight, Mrs Pilkings.

JANE   Welcome home. [*She holds out her hand. As he takes it footsteps are heard approaching the drive. A short while later a woman's sobbing is also heard.*]

PILKINGS [*off*]   Keep them here till I get back. [*He strides into view, reacts at the sight of* OLUNDE *but turns to his wife.*] Thank goodness you're still here.

JANE   Simon, what happened?

PILKINGS   Later Jane, please. Is Bob still here?

JANE   Yes, I think so. I'm sure he must be.

PILKINGS   Try and get him out here as quickly as you can. Tell him it's urgent.

JANE   Of course. Oh Simon, you remember . . .

PILKINGS   Yes yes. I can see who it is. Get Bob out here. [*She runs off.*] At first I thought I was seeing a ghost.

OLUNDE   Mr Pilkings, I appreciate what you tried to do. I want you to believe that. I can tell you it would have been a terrible calamity if you'd succeeded.

PILKINGS [*opens his mouth several times, shuts it*]   You . . . said what?

OLUNDE   A calamity for us, the entire people.

PILKINGS [*sighs*]   I see. Hm.

OLUNDE   And now I must go. I must see him before he turns cold.

PILKINGS   Oh ah . . . em . . . but this is a shock to see you. I mean er thinking all this while you were in England and thanking God for that.

340 OLUNDE   I came on the mail boat. We travelled in the Prince's convoy.

PILKINGS   Ah yes, a-ah, hm . . . er well . . .

OLUNDE   Goodnight. I can see you are shocked by the whole business. But you must know by now there are things you cannot understand—or help.

PILKINGS   Yes. Just a minute. There are armed policemen that way and they
345   have instructions to let no one pass. I suggest you wait a little. I'll er . . . give you an escort.

OLUNDE   That's very kind of you. But do you think it could be quickly arranged?

PILKINGS   Of course. In fact, yes, what I'll do is send Bob over with some men to the er . . . place. You can go with them. Here he comes now. Excuse
350   me a minute.

AIDE-DE-CAMP   Anything wrong sir?

PILKINGS   [takes him to one side]   Listen Bob, that cellar in the disused annexe of the Residency, you know, where the slaves were stored before being taken down to the coast . . .

355 AIDE-DE-CAMP   Oh yes, we use it as a storeroom for broken furniture.

PILKINGS   But it's still got the bars on it?

AIDE-DE-CAMP   Oh yes, they are quite intact.

PILKINGS   Get the keys please. I'll explain later. And I want a strong guard over the Residency tonight.

360 AIDE-DE-CAMP   We have that already. The detachment from the coast . . .

PILKINGS   No, I don't want them at the gates of the Residency. I want you to deploy them at the bottom of the hill, a long way from the main hall so they can deal with any situation long before the sound carries to the house.

AIDE-DE-CAMP   Yes of course.

365 PILKINGS   I don't want His Highness alarmed.

AIDE-DE-CAMP   You think the riot will spread here?

PILKINGS   It's unlikely but I don't want to take a chance. I made them believe I was going to lock the man up in my house, which was what I had planned to do in the first place. They are probably assailing it by now. I took a
370   roundabout route here so I don't think there is any danger at all. At least not before dawn. Nobody is to leave the premises of course—the native employees I mean. They'll soon smell something is up and they can't keep their mouths shut.

AIDE-DE-CAMP   I'll give instructions at once.

375 PILKINGS   I'll take the prisoner down myself. Two policemen will stay with him throughout the night. Inside the cell.

AIDE-DE-CAMP   Right sir. [Salutes and goes off at the double.]

PILKINGS   Jane. Bob is coming back in a moment with a detachment. Until he gets back please stay with Olunde. [He makes an extra warning gesture with his eyes.]

380 OLUNDE   Please, Mr Pilkings . . .

PILKINGS   I hate to be stuffy old son, but we have a crisis on our hands. It has to do with your father's affair if you must know. And it happens also at a time when we have His Highness here. I am responsible for security so you'll simply have to do as I say. I hope that's understood. [Marches off quickly, in the direction from which he made his first appearance.]

385 OLUNDE   What's going on? All this can't be just because he failed to stop my father killing himself.

JANE   I honestly don't know. Could it have sparked off a riot?

OLUNDE   No. If he'd succeeded that would be more likely to start the riot. Perhaps there were other factors involved. Was there a chieftancy dispute?

390 JANE   None that I know of.

ELESIN [*an animal bellow from off*]   Leave me alone! Is it not enough that you have covered me in shame! White man, take your hand from my body!

> [OLUNDE *stands frozen to the spot.* JANE, *understanding at last, tries to move him.*]

JANE   Let's go in. It's getting chilly out here.

PILKINGS [*off*]   Carry him.

395 ELESIN   Give me back the name you have taken away from me you ghost from the land of the nameless!

PILKINGS   Carry him! I can't have a disturbance here. Quickly! stuff up his mouth.

JANE   Oh God! Let's go in. Please Olunde. [OLUNDE *does not move.*]

400 ELESIN   Take your albino's[4] hand from me you . . .

> [*Sounds of a struggle. His voice chokes as he is gagged.*]

OLUNDE [*quietly*]   That was my father's voice.

JANE   Oh you poor orphan, what have you come home to?

> [*There is a sudden explosion of rage from offstage and powerful steps come running up the drive.*]

PILKINGS   You bloody fools, after him!

> [*Immediately* ELESIN, *in handcuffs, comes pounding in the direction of* JANE *and* OLUNDE, *followed some moments afterwards by* PILKINGS *and the* CONSTABLES. ELESIN, *confronted by the seeming statue of his son, stops dead.* OLUNDE *stares above his head into the distance. The* CONSTABLES *try to grab him.* JANE *screams at them.*]

JANE   Leave him alone! Simon, tell them to leave him alone.

405 PILKINGS   All right, stand aside you. [*Shrugs.*] Maybe just as well. It might help to calm him down.

> [*For several moments they hold the same position.* ELESIN *moves a step forward, almost as if he's still in doubt.*]

ELESIN   Olunde? [*He moves his head, inspecting him from side to side.*] Olunde! [*He collapses slowly at* OLUNDE's *feet.*] Oh son, don't let the sight of your father turn you blind!

OLUNDE [*he moves for the first time since he heard his voice, brings his head
410 slowly down to look on him*]   I have no father, eater of left-overs.

> [*He walks slowly down the way his father had run. Light fades out on* ELESIN, *sobbing into the ground.*]

Act 5

A wide iron-barred gate stretches almost the whole width of the cell in which ELE-SIN *is imprisoned. His wrists are encased in thick iron bracelets, chained together; he stands against the bars, looking out. Seated on the ground to one side on the outside is his recent bride, her eyes bent perpetually to the ground. Figures of the two* GUARDS *can be seen deeper inside the cell, alert to every movement* ELESIN *makes.* PILKINGS *now in a police officer's uniform, enters noiselessly, observes him a while. Then he coughs ostentatiously and approaches. Leans against the bars near a*

---

4. A term of abuse when applied to a white person.

corner, his back to ELESIN. *He is obviously trying to fall in mood with him. Some moments' silence.*

PILKINGS   You seem fascinated by the moon.

ELESIN *[after a pause]*   Yes, ghostly one. Your twin-brother up there engages my thoughts.

PILKINGS   It is a beautiful night.

5 ELESIN   Is that so?

PILKINGS   The light on the leaves, the peace of the night . . .

ELESIN   The night is not at peace, District Officer.

PILKINGS   No? I would have said it was. You know, quiet . . .

ELESIN   And does quiet mean peace for you?

10 PILKINGS   Well, nearly the same thing. Naturally there is a subtle difference . . .

ELESIN   The night is not at peace, ghostly one. The world is not at peace. You have shattered the peace of the world for ever. There is no sleep in the world tonight.

15 PILKINGS   It is still a good bargain if the world should lose one night's sleep as the price of saving a man's life.

ELESIN   You did not save my life, District Officer. You destroyed it.

PILKINGS   Now come on . . .

ELESIN   And not merely my life but the lives of many. The end of the night's
20 work is not over. Neither this year nor the next will see it. If I wished you well, I would pray that you do not stay long enough on our land to see the disaster you have brought upon us.

PILKINGS   Well, I did my duty as I saw it. I have no regrets.

ELESIN   No. The regrets of life always come later.

     [Some moments' pause.]

25 You are waiting for dawn white man. I hear you saying to yourself: only so many hours until dawn and then the danger is over. All I must do is to keep him alive tonight. You don't quite understand it all but you know that tonight is when what ought to be must be brought about. I shall ease your mind even more, ghostly one. It is not an entire night but a moment of the
30 night, and that moment is past. The moon was my messenger and guide. When it reached a certain gateway in the sky, it touched that moment for which my whole life has been spent in blessings. Even I do not know the gateway. I have stood here and scanned the sky for a glimpse of that door but, I cannot see it. Human eyes are useless for a search of this nature. But
35 in the house of *osugbo*, those who keep watch through the spirit recognised the moment, they sent word to me through the voice of our sacred drums to prepare myself. I heard them and I shed all thoughts of earth. I began to follow the moon to the abode of the gods . . . servant of the white king, that was when you entered my chosen place of departure on feet of
40 desecration.

PILKINGS   I'm sorry, but we all see our duty differently.

ELESIN   I no longer blame you. You stole from me my first-born, sent him to your country so you could turn him into something in your own image. Did you plan it all beforehand? There are moments when it seems part of a
45 larger plan. He who must follow my footsteps is taken from me, sent across the ocean. Then, in my turn, I am stopped from fulfilling my destiny. Did

you think it all out before, this plan to push our world from its course and sever the cord that links us to the great origin?

PILKINGS You don't really believe that. Anyway, if that was my intention with your son, I appear to have failed.

ELESIN You did not fail in the main thing ghostly one. We know the roof covers the rafters, the cloth covers blemishes; who would have known that the white skin covered our future, preventing us from seeing the death our enemies had prepared for us. The world is set adrift and its inhabitants are lost. Around them, there is nothing but emptiness.

PILKINGS Your son does not take so gloomy a view.

ELESIN Are you dreaming now, white man? Were you not present at the reunion of shame? Did you not see when the world reversed itself and the father fell before his son, asking forgiveness?

PILKINGS That was in the heat of the moment. I spoke to him and . . . if you want to know, he wishes he could cut out his tongue for uttering the words he did.

ELESIN No. What he said must never be unsaid. The contempt of my own son rescued something of my shame at your hands. You have stopped me in my duty but I know now that I did give birth to a son. Once I mistrusted him for seeking the companionship of those my spirit knew as enemies of our race. Now I understand. One should seek to obtain the secrets of his enemies. He will avenge my shame, white one. His spirit will destroy you and yours.

PILKINGS That kind of talk is hardly called for. If you don't want my consolation . . .

ELESIN No white man, I do not want your consolation.

PILKINGS As you wish. Your son, anyway, sends his consolation. He asks your forgiveness. When I asked him not to despise you his reply was: I cannot judge him, and if I cannot judge him, I cannot despise him. He wants to come to you and say goodbye and to receive your blessing.

ELESIN Goodbye? Is he returning to your land?

PILKINGS Don't you think that's the most sensible thing for him to do? I advised him to leave at once, before dawn, and he agrees that is the right course of action.

ELESIN Yes, it is best. And even if I did not think so, I have lost the father's place of honour. My voice is broken.

PILKINGS Your son honours you. If he didn't he would not ask your blessing.

ELESIN No. Even a thoroughbred is not without pity for the turf he strikes with his hoof. When is he coming?

PILKINGS As soon as the town is a little quieter. I advised it.

ELESIN Yes white man, I am sure you advised it. You advise all our lives although on the authority of what gods, I do not know.

PILKINGS [opens his mouth to reply, then appears to change his mind. Turns to go. Hesitates and stops again] Before I leave you, may I ask just one thing of you?

ELESIN I am listening.

PILKINGS I wish to ask you to search the quiet of your heart and tell me—do you not find great contradictions in the wisdom of your own race?

ELESIN Make yourself clear, white one.

PILKINGS   I have lived among you long enough to learn a saying or two. One
came to my mind tonight when I stepped into the market and saw what
was going on. You were surrounded by those who egged you on with song
100   and praises. I thought, are these not the same people who say: the elder
grimly approaches heaven and you ask him to bear your greetings yonder;
do you really think he makes the journey willingly? After that, I did not
hesitate.

> [*A pause.* ELESIN *sighs. Before he can speak a sound of running feet is
> heard.*]

JANE [*off*]   Simon! Simon!
105   PILKINGS   What on earth . . . ! [*Runs off.*]

> [ELESIN *turns to his new wife, gazes on her for some moments.*]

ELESIN   My young bride, did you hear the ghostly one? You sit and sob in
your silent heart but say nothing to all this. First I blamed the white man,
then I blamed my gods for deserting me. Now I feel I want to blame you for
the mystery of the sapping of my will. But blame is a strange peace offering
110   for a man to bring a world he has deeply wronged, and to its innocent
dwellers. Oh little mother, I have taken countless women in my life but you
were more than a desire of the flesh. I needed you as the abyss across
which my body must be drawn, I filled it with earth and dropped my seed
in it at the moment of preparedness for my crossing. You were the final gift
115   of the living to their emissary to the land of the ancestors, and perhaps
your warmth and youth brought new insights of this world to me and
turned my feet leaden on this side of the abyss. For I confess to you, daughter, my weakness came not merely from the abomination of the white man
who came violently into my fading presence, there was also a weight of
120   longing on my earth-held limbs. I would have shaken it off, already my foot
had begun to lift but then, the white ghost entered and all was defiled.

> [*Approaching voices of* PILKINGS *and his wife.*]

JANE   Oh Simon, you will let her in won't you?
PILKINGS   I really wish you'd stop interfering.

> [*They come into view.* JANE *is in a dressing-gown.* PILKINGS *is holding a
> note to which he refers from time to time.*]

JANE   Good gracious, I didn't initiate this. I was sleeping quietly, or trying to
125   anyway, when the servant brought it. It's not my fault if one can't sleep
undisturbed even in the Residency.
PILKINGS   He'd have done the same thing if we were sleeping at home so
don't sidetrack the issue. He knows he can get round[5] you or he wouldn't
send you the petition in the first place.
130   JANE   Be fair Simon. After all he was thinking of your own interests. He is
grateful you know, you seem to forget that. He feels he owes you something.
PILKINGS   I just wish they'd leave this man alone tonight, that's all.
JANE   Trust him Simon. He's pledged his word it will all go peacefully.
PILKINGS   Yes, and that's the other thing. I don't like being threatened.
135   JANE   Threatened? [*Takes the note.*] I didn't spot any threat.
PILKINGS   It's there. Veiled, but it's there. The only way to prevent serious
rioting tomorrow—what a cheek!

5. That is, circumvent, cajole.

JANE   I don't think he's threatening you Simon.

PILKINGS   He's picked up the idiom alright. Wouldn't surprise me if he's been
140   mixing with commies or anarchists over there. The phrasing sounds too good
to be true. Damn! If only the Prince hadn't picked this time for his visit.

JANE   Well, even so Simon, what have you got to lose? You don't want a riot
on your hands, not with the Prince here.

PILKINGS [*going up to* ELESIN]   Let's see what he has to say. Chief Elesin, there
145   is yet another person who wants to see you. As she is not a next-of-kin I don't
really feel obliged to let her in. But your son sent a note with her, so it's up to
you.

ELESIN   I know who that must be. So she found out your hiding-place. Well,
it was not difficult. My stench of shame is so strong, it requires no hunter's
150   dog to follow it.

PILKINGS   If you don't want to see her, just say so and I'll send her packing.

ELESIN   Why should I not want to see her? Let her come. I have no more
holes in my rag of shame. All is laid bare.

PILKINGS   I'll bring her in. [*Goes off.*]

155   JANE [*hesitates, then goes to* ELESIN]   Please, try and understand. Everything
my husband did was for the best.

ELESIN [*he gives her a long strange stare, as if he is trying to understand who she
is*]   You are the wife of the District Officer?

JANE   Yes. My name, is Jane.

ELESIN   That is my wife sitting down there. You notice how still and silent she
160   sits? My business is with your husband.

[PILKINGS *returns with* IYALOJA.]

PILKINGS   Here she is. Now first I want your word of honour that you will try
nothing foolish.

ELESIN   Honour? White one, did you say you wanted my word of honour?

PILKINGS   I know you to be an honourable man. Give me your word of honour
165   you will receive nothing from her.

ELESIN   But I am sure you have searched her clothing as you would never
dare touch your own mother. And there are these two lizards of yours who
roll their eyes even when I scratch.

PILKINGS   And I shall be sitting on that tree trunk watching even how you
170   blink. Just the same I want your word that you will not let her pass anything to you.

ELESIN   You have my honour already. It is locked up in that desk in which
you will put away your report of this night's events. Even the honour of my
people you have taken already; it is tied together with those papers of
175   treachery which make you masters in this land.

PILKINGS   Alright. I am trying to make things easy but if you must bring in
politics we'll have to do it the hard way. Madam, I want you to remain
along this line and move no nearer to the cell door. Guards! [*They spring to
attention.*] If she moves beyond this point, blow your whistle. Come on
180   Jane. [*They go off.*]

IYALOJA   How boldly the lizard struts before the pigeon when it was the eagle
itself he promised us he would confront.

ELESIN   I don't ask you to take pity on me Iyaloja. You have a message for
me or you would not have come. Even if it is the curses of the world,
185   I shall listen.

IYALOJA You made so bold with the servant of the white king who took your side against death. I must tell your brother chiefs when I return how bravely you waged war against him. Especially with words.

ELESIN I more than deserve your scorn.

190 IYALOJA [*with sudden anger*] I warned you, if you must leave a seed behind, be sure it is not tainted with the curses of the world. Who are you to open a new life when you dared not open the door to a new existence? I say who are you to make so bold? [*The* BRIDE *sobs and* IYALOJA *notices her. Her contempt noticeably increases as she turns back to* ELESIN.] Oh you self-vaunted

195 stem of the plantain, how hollow it all proves. The pith is gone in the parent stem, so how will it prove with the new shoot? How will it go with that earth that bears it? Who are you to bring this abomination on us!

ELESIN My powers deserted me. My charms, my spells, even my voice lacked strength when I made to summon the powers that would lead me

200 over the last measure of earth into the land of the fleshless. You saw it, Iyaloja. You saw me struggle to retrieve my will from the power of the stranger whose shadow fell across the doorway and left me floundering and blundering in a maze I had never before encountered. My senses were numbed when the touch of cold iron came upon my wrists. I could do noth-

205 ing to save myself.

IYALOJA You have betrayed us. We fed you sweetmeats such as we hoped awaited you on the other side. But you said No, I must eat the world's leftovers. We said you were the hunter who brought the quarry down; to you belonged the vital portions of the game. No, you said, I am the hunter's dog

210 and I shall eat the entrails of the game and the faeces of the hunter. We said you were the hunter returning home in triumph, a slain buffalo pressing down on his neck; you said wait, I first must turn up this cricket hole with my toes. We said yours was the doorway at which we first spy the tapper when he comes down from the tree, yours was the blessing of the twi-

215 light wine, the purl[6] that brings night spirits out of doors to steal their portion before the light of day. We said yours was the body of wine whose burden shakes the tapper like a sudden gust on his perch. You said, No, I am content to lick the dregs from each calabash when the drinkers are done. We said, the dew on earth's surface was for you to wash your feet

220 along the slopes of honour. You said No, I shall step in the vomit of cats and the droppings of mice; I shall fight them for the left-overs of the world.

ELESIN Enough Iyaloja, enough.

IYALOJA We called you leader and oh, how you led us on. What we have no intention of eating should not be held to the nose.

225 ELESIN Enough, enough. My shame is heavy enough.

IYALOJA Wait. I came with a burden.

ELESIN You have more than discharged it.

IYALOJA I wish I could pity you.

ELESIN I need neither your pity nor the pity of the world. I need understand-

230 ing. Even I need to understand. You were present at my defeat. You were part of the beginnings. You brought about the renewal of my tie to earth, you helped in the binding of the cord.

6. A liquor made by infusing bitter herbs in beer or ale. *Twilight wine:* that is, the finest wine; palm wine tapped before dawn is believed to be especially fresh and potent.

IYALOJA   I gave you warning. The river which fills up before our eyes does not
sweep us away in its flood.

235   ELESIN   What were warnings beside the moist contact of living earth between
my fingers? What were warnings beside the renewal of famished embers
lodged eternally in the heart of man. But even that, even if it overwhelmed
one with a thousandfold temptations to linger a little while, a man could
overcome it. It is when the alien hand pollutes the source of will, when a
240   stranger force of violence shatters the mind's calm resolution, this is when
a man is made to commit the awful treachery of relief, commit in his
thought the unspeakable blasphemy of seeing the hand of the gods in this
alien rupture of his world. I know it was this thought that killed me, sapped
my powers and turned me into an infant in the hands of unnamable
245   strangers. I made to utter my spells anew but my tongue merely rattled in
my mouth. I fingered hidden charms and the contact was damp; there was
no spark left to sever the life-strings that should stretch from every finger-
tip. My will was squelched in the spittle of an alien race, and all because I
had committed this blasphemy of thought—that there might be the hand
250   of the gods in a stranger's intervention.

IYALOJA   Explain it how you will, I hope it brings you peace of mind. The
bush-rat fled his rightful cause, reached the market and set up a lamentation.
'Please save me!'—are these fitting words to hear from an ancestral mask?
'There's a wild beast at my heels' is not becoming language from a hunter.

255   ELESIN   May the world forgive me.

IYALOJA   I came with a burden I said. It approaches the gates which are so
well guarded by those jackals whose spittle will from this day be on your
food and drink. But first, tell me, you who were once Elesin Oba, tell me,
you who know so well the cycle of the plantain: is it the parent shoot which
260   withers to give sap to the younger or, does your wisdom see it running the
other way?

ELESIN   I don't see your meaning Iyaloja?

IYALOJA   Did I ask you for a meaning? I asked a question. Whose trunk withers to give sap to the other? The parent shoot or the younger?

265   ELESIN   The parent.

IYALOJA   Ah. So you do know that. There are sights in this world which say
different Elesin. There are some who choose to reverse the cycle of our
being. Oh, you emptied bark that the world once saluted for a pith-laden
being, shall I tell you what the gods have claimed of you?

[*In her agitation she steps beyond the line indicated by* PILKINGS *and the
air is rent by piercing whistles. The two* GUARDS *also leap forward and
place safe-guarding hands on* ELESIN. IYALOJA *stops, astonished.* PILKINGS
comes racing in, followed by JANE.]

270   PILKINGS   What is it? Did they try something?

GUARD   She stepped beyond the line.

ELESIN [*in a broken voice*]   Let her alone. She meant no harm.

IYALOJA   Oh Elesin, see what you've become. Once you had no need to open
your mouth in explanation because evil-smelling goats, itchy of hand and
275   foot, had lost their senses. And it was a brave man indeed who dared lay
hands on you because Iyaloja stepped from one side of the earth onto
another. Now look at the spectacle of your life. I grieve for you.

PILKINGS   I think you'd better leave. I doubt you have done him much good by coming here. I shall make sure you are not allowed to see him again. In
280   any case we are moving him to a different place before dawn, so don't bother to come back.

IYALOJA   We foresaw that. Hence the burden I trudged here to lay beside your gates.

PILKINGS   What was that you said?

285   IYALOJA   Didn't our son explain? Ask that one. He knows what it is. At least we hope the man we once knew as Elesin remembers the lesser oaths he need not break.

PILKINGS   Do you know what she is talking about?

ELESIN   Go to the gates, ghostly one. Whatever you find there, bring it to me.

290   IYALOJA   Not yet. It drags behind me on the slow, weary feet of women. Slow as it is Elesin, it has long overtaken you. It rides ahead of your laggard will.

PILKINGS   What is she saying now? Christ! Must your people forever speak in riddles?

ELESIN   It will come white man, it will come. Tell your men at the gates to let
295   it through.

PILKINGS   [dubiously]   I'll have to see what it is.

IYALOJA   You will. [Passionately] But this is one oath he cannot shirk. White one, you have a king here, a visitor from your land. We know of his presence here. Tell me, were he to die would you leave his spirit roaming restlessly on
300   the surface of earth? Would you bury him here among those you consider less than human? In your land have you no ceremonies of the dead?

PILKINGS   Yes. But we don't make our chiefs commit suicide to keep him company.

IYALOJA   Child, I have not come to help your understanding. [Points to ELE-
305   SIN.] This is the man whose weakened understanding holds us in bondage to you. But ask him if you wish. He knows the meaning of a king's passage; he was not born yesterday. He knows the peril to the race when our dead father, who goes as intermediary, waits and waits and knows he is betrayed. He knows when the narrow gate was opened and he knows it will not stay
310   for laggards who drag their feet in dung and vomit, whose lips are reeking of the left-overs of lesser men. He knows he has condemned our King to wander in the void of evil with beings who are enemies of life.

PILKINGS   Yes er . . . but look here . . .

IYALOJA   What we ask is little enough. Let him release our King so he can
315   ride on homewards alone. The messenger is on his way on the backs of women. Let him send word through the heart that is folded up within the bolt. It is the least of all his oaths, it is the easiest fulfilled.

[The AIDE-DE-CAMP runs in.]

PILKINGS   Bob?

AIDE-DE-CAMP   Sir, there's a group of women chanting up the hill.

320   PILKINGS   [rounding on IYALOJA]   If you people want trouble . . .

JANE   Simon, I think that's what Olunde referred to in his letter.

PILKINGS   He knows damned well I can't have a crowd here! Damn it, I explained the delicacy of my position to him. I think it's about time I got him out of town. Bob, send a car and two or three soldiers to bring him in.
325   I think the sooner he takes his leave of his father and gets out the better.

IYALOJA   Save your labour white one. If it is the father of your prisoner you
want, Olunde, he who until this night we knew as Elesin's son, he comes
soon himself to take his leave. He has sent the women ahead, so let them in.

[PILKINGS *remains undecided.*]

AIDE-DE-CAMP   What do we do about the invasion? We can still stop them far
330   from here.

PILKINGS   What do they look like?

AIDE-DE-CAMP   They're not many. And they seem quite peaceful.

PILKINGS   No men?

AIDE-DE-CAMP   Mm, two or three at the most.

335 JANE   Honestly, Simon, I'd trust Olunde. I don't think he'll deceive you about
their intentions.

PILKINGS   He'd better not. Alright then, let them in Bob. Warn them to control themselves. Then hurry Olunde here. Make sure he brings his baggage
because I'm not returning him into town.

340 AIDE-DE-CAMP   Very good, sir. [*Goes.*]

PILKINGS [*to* IYALOJA]   I hope you understand that if anything goes wrong it
will be on your head. My men have orders to shoot at the first sign of
trouble.

IYALOJA   To prevent one death you will actually make other deaths? Ah, great
345   is the wisdom of the white race. But have no fear. Your Prince will sleep
peacefully. So at long last will ours. We will disturb you no further, servant
of the white King. Just let Elesin fulfil his oath and we will retire home and
pay homage to our King.

JANE   I believe her Simon, don't you?

350 PILKINGS   Maybe.

ELESIN   Have no fear ghostly one. I have a message to send my King and
then you have nothing more to fear.

IYALOJA   Olunde would have done it. The chiefs asked him to speak the
words but he said no, not while you lived.

355 ELESIN   Even from the depths to which my spirit has sunk, I find some joy
that this little has been left to me.

[*The* WOMEN *enter, intoning the dirge 'Alẹ lẹ lẹ' and swaying from side to
side. On their shoulders is borne a longish object roughly like a cylindri-
cal bolt, covered in cloth. They set it down on the spot where* IYALOJA
had stood earlier, and form a semi-circle round it. The PRAISE-SINGER
and DRUMMER *stand on the inside of the semi-circle but the drum is
not used at all. The* DRUMMER *intones under the* PRAISE-SINGER's
invocations.]

PILKINGS [*as they enter*]   What is *that*?

IYALOJA   The burden you have made white one, but we bring it in peace.

PILKINGS   I said *what* is it?

360 ELESIN   White man, you must let me out. I have a duty to perform.

PILKINGS   I most certainly will not.

ELESIN   There lies the courier of my King. Let me out so I can perform what
is demanded of me.

PILKINGS   You'll do what you need to do from inside there or not at all. I've
365   gone as far as I intend to with this business.

ELESIN   The worshipper who lights a candle in your church to bear a message
to his god bows his head and speaks in a whisper to the flame. Have I not

seen it ghostly one? His voice does not ring out to the world. Mine are no words for anyone's ears. They are not words even for the bearers of this
370 load. They are words I must speak secretly, even as my father whispered them in my ears and I in the ears of my first-born. I cannot shout them to the wind and the open night-sky.

JANE   Simon . . .

PILKINGS   Don't interfere. Please!

375 IYALOJA   They have slain the favourite horse of the King and slain his dog. They have borne them from pulse to pulse centre of the land receiving prayers for their King. But the rider has chosen to stay behind. Is it too much to ask that he speak his heart to heart of the waiting courier? [PILK-INGS *turns his back on her.*] So be it, Elesin Oba, you see how even the
380 mere leavings are denied you. [*She gestures to the* PRAISE-SINGER.]

PRAISE-SINGER   Elesin Oba! I call you by that name only this last time. Remember when I said, if you cannot come, tell my horse. [*Pause.*] What? I cannot hear you? I said, if you cannot come, whisper in the ears of my horse. Is your tongue severed from the roots Elesin? I can hear no response.
385 I said, if there are boulders you cannot climb, mount my horse's back, this spotless black stallion, he'll bring you over them. [*Pauses.*] Elesin Oba, once you had a tongue that darted like a drummer's stick. I said, if you get lost my dog will track a path to me. My memory fails me but I think you replied: My feet have found the path, Alafin.

[*The dirge rises and falls.*]

390 I said at the last, if evil hands hold you back, just tell my horse there is weight on the hem of your smock. I dare not wait too long.

[*The dirge rises and falls.*]

There lies the swiftest-ever messenger of a king, so set me free with the errand of your heart. There lie the head and heart of the favourite of the gods, whisper in his ears. Oh my companion, if you had followed when you
395 should, we would not say that the horse preceded its rider. If you had fol-lowed when it was time, we would not say the dog has raced beyond and left his master behind. If you had raised your will to cut the thread of life at the summons of the drums, we would not say your mere shadow fell across the gateway and took its owner's place at the banquet. But the hunter, laden with
400 slain buffalo, stayed to root in the cricket's hole with his toes. What now is left? If there is a dearth of bats, the pigeon must serve us for the offering. Speak the words over your shadow which must now serve in your place.

ELESIN   I cannot approach. Take off the cloth. I shall speak my message from heart to heart of silence.

405 IYALOJA [*moves forward and removes the covering*]   Your courier Elesin, cast your eyes on the favoured companion of the King.

[*Rolled up in the mat, his head and feet showing at either end, is the body of* OLUNDE.]

There lies the honour of your household and of our race. Because he could not bear to let honour fly out of doors, he stopped it with his life. The son has proved the father, Elesin, and there is nothing left in your mouth to
410 gnash but infant gums.

PRAISE-SINGER   Elesin, we placed the reins of the world in your hands yet you watched it plunge over the edge of the bitter precipice. You sat with

folded arms while evil strangers tilted the world from its course and crashed it beyond the edge of emptiness—you muttered, there is little that one man
415 can do, you left us floundering in a blind future. Your heir has taken the burden on himself. What the end will be, we are not gods to tell. But this young shoot has poured its sap into the parent stalk, and we know this is not the way of life. Our world is tumbling in the void of strangers, Elesin.

> [ELESIN *has stood rock-still, his knuckles taut on the bars, his eyes glued to the body of his son. The stillness seizes and paralyses everyone, including* PILKINGS *who has turned to look. Suddenly* ELESIN *flings one arm round his neck, once, and with the loop of the chain, strangles himself in a swift, decisive pull. The* GUARDS *rush forward to stop him but they are only in time to let his body down.* PILKINGS *has leapt to the door at the same time and struggles with the lock. He rushes within, fumbles with the handcuffs and unlocks them, raises the body to a sitting position while he tries to give resuscitation. The* WOMEN *continue their dirge, unmoved by the sudden event.*]

IYALOJA   Why do you strain yourself? Why do you labour at tasks for which
420 no one, not even the man lying there, would give you thanks? He is gone at last into the passage but oh, how late it all is. His son will feast on the meat and throw him bones. The passage is clogged with droppings from the King's stallion; he will arrive all stained in dung.

PILKINGS [*in a tired voice*]   Was this what you wanted?

425 IYALOJA   No child, it is what you brought to be, you who play with strangers' lives, who even usurp the vestments of our dead, yet believe that the stain of death will not cling to you. The gods demanded only the old expired plantain but you cut down the sap-laden shoot to feed your pride. There is your board, filled to overflowing. Feast on it. [*She screams at him suddenly,*
430 *seeing that* PILKINGS *is about to close* ELESIN'S *staring eyes.*] Let him alone! However sunk he was in debt he is no pauper's carrion abandoned on the road. Since when have strangers donned clothes of indigo before the bereaved cries out his loss?

> [*She turns to the* BRIDE *who has remained motionless throughout.*]

Child.

> [*The girl takes up a little earth, walks calmly into the cell and closes* ELESIN'S *eyes. She then pours some earth over each eyelid and comes out again.*]

435 IYALOJA   Now forget the dead, forget even the living. Turn your mind only to the unborn.

> [*She goes off, accompanied by the* BRIDE. *The dirge rises in volume and the* WOMEN *continue their sway. Lights fade to a black-out.*]

The End

SAM SHEPARD
1943–2017

SAM Shepard wrote plays about power—about individuals' attempts to gain or exert power over one another physically, emotionally, spiritually, psychologically. Embracing the age-old precept that all drama arises from conflict and the battle for control, he placed primal, agonistic struggles between characters at the core of his dramaturgy. Moreover, Shepard saw power as an important issue for American culture, and his plays are littered with mythic figures, historical characters, and social and cultural institutions that are popularly seen as exemplars of strength and dominance. He gravitated to the genres to which an audience responds most powerfully—live theater, with its immediate force, and film, whose characters are larger than life. His Pulitzer Prize–winning drama BURIED CHILD (1978) exemplifies Shepard's ability to showcase potent symbols of American life while also questioning the deeply troubled structures of family and community in which they are embedded.

Samuel ("Steve") Shepard Rogers was born on November 5, 1943, in Fort Sheridan, Illinois—an army base where his mother lived while his father, a pilot, was serving overseas. In the early years of his life, the family moved often; but after his father left the military in 1949, they settled in California—first in South Pasadena, then on an avocado ranch in Duarte.

A fascination with popular images of the West, of southern California, and of the American heartland animates many of his works, including *Cowboys #2* (1967), *The Unseen Hand* (1969), *Angel City* (1976), and *The Sad Lament of Pecos Bill on the Eve of Killing His Wife* (1976).

After graduating from high school, Shepard spent some time at a local junior college, where he drifted into acting. Shepard read SAMUEL BECKETT's WAITING FOR GODOT (1952) and was struck by its freedom from conventional theatrical form and language, although he maintained that he did not understand the play. When a touring group, the Bishop's Company Repertory Players, advertised local auditions, Shepard decided to join them. On the road, he changed his name from Steve Rogers to Sam Shepard, thereby crystallizing the new identity that he was creating separate from the one associated with his family. The process of self-discovery and self-fashioning later became a central motif in his work; it was often connected with an artist figure trying to find an identity within society, as vividly exemplified in *The Tooth of Crime* (1972).

When the Players reached New York City, Shepard stayed behind. There he became involved with the downtown art scene, especially its music and the off-off-Broadway theaters that were beginning to emerge. Shepard's first two plays, *Cowboys* and *The Rock Garden*, were produced in 1964. Although they were roundly panned by the uptown critics, the pieces were championed by the *Village Voice*'s reviewer, Michael Smith, who saw Shepard as a new, exciting talent. Buoyed by Smith's support, Shepard began churning out plays, and in 1966 he garnered three Obies (annual awards for excellence in off-off- and off-Broadway theater). Between 1964 and 1971, nearly twenty Shepard dramas opened in New York, and small theaters around the country began to produce his plays as well. Shepard is unique among major American dramatists for rising to prominence with a series of one-act plays and for a career constituted almost entirely of regional and off- or off-off-Broadway productions. The 1996 staging of *Buried Child* (in a newly revised version) was the first full production of a Shepard drama on Broadway.

In 1969, Shepard married the actress O-Lan Jones, and their son was born in 1970. Their marriage was turbulent from the start, with a number of separations; after an intense relationship with the rock musician and poet Patti Smith ended, and seeking to escape what he saw as the impersonality and materialism of New York City, in 1971 Shepard moved with his family to London. During three years there, he gained invaluable perspective on his country and its culture as well as on his own writing. Resettling with his family in California, Shepard formed a fruitful, lasting association with San Francisco's Magic Theater, where he began to hone his skills as a director of his own work. He also reengaged with acting, and his featured appearance in *Days of Heaven* (1978) launched what has become a highly successful film career. During the filming of *Frances* (1982), he met Jessica Lange and began living with her soon thereafter (he and O-Lan divorced in 1984); together they had two children.

Shepard never felt an obligation to conform to prevailing ideas of what American dramaturgy should be. Indeed, he claimed in a 1974 interview (reprinted in *American Dreams: The Imagination of Sam Shepard* [1981]) that he "didn't have any idea about how to shape an action into what is seen" and that the "so-called originality of the early work just comes from ignorance." Yet critics suspect that Shepard's early artistic persona may have been just that—a pose that suited his public image as an unintentional iconoclast. They have subsequently identified, through Shepard's interviews and correspondence, his wide array of influences from the nineteenth century (notably, the French symbolist poets and Fyodor Dostoyevsky) and the twentieth century—BERTOLT BRECHT, TENNESSEE WILLIAMS, Jack Kerouac, Lawrence Ferlinghetti, EDWARD ALBEE, the beat poets, Carlos Casteneda, and Werner Herzog, among others.

The development of Shepard's dramaturgy in effect inverts the history of modern drama; over the span of his career, his plays have moved from postmodernism and absurdism through expressionism to a modified realism. They fall into roughly three groups: the one-act abstract collages of the 1960s, the works focusing on artist figures of the early to mid-1970s, and the dramas written since 1974, when Shepard turned his attention to the American family. The plays within these relatively neat periods are highly complex pieces, which have consistently resisted interpreters' efforts to pin down their "meaning." Shepard's dramas do not rely on logic, cohesion, and order, and they cannot be easily categorized by form, style, or technique.

Shepard emerged as the contemporary American dramatist most fully engaged in examining national identity through the trope of the Anglo-American family, a stand-in—with all its dysfunctionality and decay—for the United States itself. *Curse of the Starving Class* (1977), *Buried Child, True West* (1980), *Fool for Love* (1983), and *A Lie of the Mind* (1985) are often discussed together as family dramas. Shepard himself observed that his fascination with the family puts his work squarely within the American dramatic tradition that embraces such canonical works as EUGENE O'NEILL's *Long Day's Journey into Night* (1957), ARTHUR MILLER's *DEATH OF A SALESMAN* (1949), and Tennessee Williams's *The Glass Menagerie* (1945). Though Shepard's plays rarely display the theatrical conventions we associate with "kitchen sink" and "dining room table" dramaturgy, they resemble the form in their direct focus on the domestic milieu. Each conveys the deeply problematic nature of familial relationships, while also showing flashes of bizarre humor and inexplicable love. Shepard admitted, in the interview reprinted in *American Dreams,* that this new form for his work "could be called realism," but he insisted that it was not "the kind of realism where husbands and wives squabble and that kind of stuff." Critics and scholars have instead labeled his approach a type of "subverted" realism that freely borrows elements from styles quite foreign to traditional realism: the perverse grotesqueries of American gothic, for example, or the discontinuity and pastiche so common in postmodern artistry.

Buried Child uses a "homecoming" structure to reunite three generations of family members. Vince and his girlfriend, Shelly, decide to stop at the rural farm of his grandparents while en route to New Mexico to visit Vince's father, Tilden. They do not know that the psychologically damaged Tilden has preceded them and is living in his childhood home with his aging parents—the decaying alcoholic Dodge

and vague yet controlling Halie—as well as his menacing amputee brother Bradley. When Vince arrives, no one, inexplicably, seems to recognize him, and he must grapple with the increasingly bizarre comments and behavior of people whom he thought he knew. Mysterious references to a child buried in the fields behind the house only complicate Vince's efforts to comprehend what has happened in his family, who he really is, and what place he holds in the world he has entered.

In *Buried Child,* Shepard refined the style and tone of the family environment first explored in *Curse of the Starving Class.* The aging patriarch, the ineffective mother, and the estranged, psychologically or physically wounded children all come together in a sordid world of incest, abuse, and neglect. As an outsider, Shelly may *perhaps* be a more objective witness through whose eyes we can better understand and evaluate the familial machinations. She at first believes that the house is "like a Norman Rockwell cover or something," but the facade of idealized American family life soon shatters. The mystery of the titular

Vince (Christopher McCann) torments Bradley (William M. Carr) as Shelly (Mary McDonnell) looks on in the background, in the 1979 Circle Repertory production of *Buried Child.*

buried child—whose it is, what happened to it, and what it symbolizes for Vince's family and, by analogy, for the American family—is interwoven with Shepard's portrait of home life in the heartland, which never can match its Rockwellian exterior.

Replete with symbolic harvests of carrots and corn, *Buried Child* points toward Shepard's understanding of the plight of America's family farms and his awareness of the economic pressures faced more generally by the working class. Unlike many of his colleagues from the 1960s, Shepard was not usually perceived as a political playwright; yet the mood and tone of many of his works, including *Buried Child*, suggest a political consciousness that is integral to his identity as an American writer. Shepard was also deeply concerned with what he saw as an American ethos of violence, closely related to the struggles for power within his plays. Violence appears imminent throughout *Buried Child*, as characters' verbal, psychological, and, at moments, physical aggression toward each other punctuates both dialogue and action. As Shepard explained in a 1984 *New York Times* interview, he saw such violence as tied to gender roles:

> I think there's something about American violence that to me is very touching. In full force it's very ugly, but there's also something very moving about it, because it has to do with humiliation. There's some hidden, deeply rooted thing in the Anglo male American that has to do with inferiority, that has to do with not being a man, and always, continually having to act out some idea of manhood that invariably is violent. This sense of failure runs very deep—maybe it has to do with the frontier being systematically taken away, with the guilt of having gotten this country by wiping out a native race of people, with the whole Protestant work ethic. I can't put my finger on it, but it's the source of a lot of intrigue for me.

It is no coincidence that each of the men in *Buried Child* is profoundly damaged and is grappling with just such senses of inferiority and impotence. Shepard intuits a direct connection between larger cultural and economic forces and patterns of American identity, particularly those of American men. He traces a line of influence between the participation of members of his father's generation in World War II and their inability to reintegrate neatly into American life on their return. Shepard saw such men, like Dodge, as "lost children" who, unable to cope with their postwar roles, withdraw from their families and from society. Yet Shepard's representations of women are much more conventional and less nuanced. His work has been criticized for this comparative imbalance of complexity; the women in his plays often appear to be ciphers—opaque figures who lack an inner life. Halie and Shelly reflect a dramaturgical ambivalence toward female sexuality and the struggles for power between the sexes.

In his collection of short stories, poems, and autobiographical reveries *Motel Chronicles* (1982), Shepard provides a memory of visiting his grandparents in Illinois that seems to have informed his creation of *Buried Child*. Yet this "chronicle" appears in a work that hovers between autobiography and fiction and puts into question the truth and value of memory—issues central to *Buried Child* as well. In an interview published in *The Cambridge Companion to Sam Shepard* in 2002, Shepard discussed his ongoing compulsion to explore familial dynamics. Musing on the inescapability of one's ties to family, Shepard confirmed his career-long interest "in the family's biological connections and how those patterns of behavior are passed on." Perhaps alluding to the speech at the end of the play in which Vince explains to Shelly what he has realized about his connections to his ancestors, Shepard describes how every individual is "intimately, inevitably, and entirely connected to who brought you into the world—through a long, long chain, regardless of whether you knew them face to face or not." Shepard believed, moreover, that "the disaster inherent in this thing called the American Family is very very resonant now with audiences" and accounts for the continued interest in his family plays from the late 1970s and early 1980s.

The ambivalence of Shepard's relationship with American literary traditions reverberates on other levels as well. Shepard's conflicted representation of the American heartland in *Buried Child* resonates both with the trope of American pastoralism—a new Eden in the New World, fruitful and abundant—and with its opposite, an infertile wasteland that is decaying before our eyes. At the same time, these oppositional images of the land evoke a pattern of death and rebirth that strongly influenced many modernist writers: the myth of the Corn King.

The Corn King was a figure of ancient ritual. According to *The Golden Bough* (1890; 3d ed., 1911–14), James Frazer's massive comparative study of myth and religion, almost all the world's mythologies feature a priest-king who embodies the life and fertility of his kingdom; his decline would weaken the land. Thus, he must be ritually killed, so that a new king can assume the same role and the land can be reborn in spring. This dying and resurrected god found in ancient religions and fertility cults has obvious parallels with Christianity, and in *From Ritual to Romance* (1920) Jesse Weston argued that key elements of the Arthurian Grail legend—notably, the healing of a barren land and wounded king—are rooted in such religions. The medieval Grail stories also involve a questing knight who must overcome obstacles and respond to seemingly unanswerable questions.

Shepard's literal use of corn; the symbolic burial (under vegetables and Shelly's coat) and actual death of the patriarch, Dodge; and Vince's claiming of his ancestral home evoke this mythic backdrop, into which is woven the biblical story of the prodigal son. Yet Shepard's dark rendition of these tales reveals his ambivalence about the cultural power of myths and the traditions they embody.

Shepard's original version of *Buried Child* exemplifies the qualities of his most powerful dramas: lyrical, imagistic, fragmented, nonlinear. But in the mid-1990s Shepard decided to revisit this play to "follow through [on] . . . certain questions that were ignited" in the original. As he explained in *American Theatre* magazine at that time, he was seeking not to resolve all the play's mysteries but to ensure that nothing was "gratuitously ambiguous." While the new production of *Buried Child* was enthusiastically received by reviewers, most critics view the revised script, like his revision of *The Tooth of Crime* (1996), as weaker than the original. In rewriting *Buried Child,* Shepard made the work more realistic and literal. He trimmed some of its notable monologues, including Dodge's recital of his will and Halie's description of their dead son Ansel's wedding; other cuts in the dialogue curtail the presentation of Shelly.

In executing these changes, Shepard may have been trying to alter the tempo of these works. As he noted in the 2002 interview, "writing is very rhythmic"; he had "always been fascinated by the rhythm of language, and language is musical . . . particularly written language when it's spoken." Indeed, Shepard's command of language may well be his greatest strength as a dramatist. Each of his characters has an utterly distinctive voice. In a 1977 essay, "Language, Visualization and the Inner Library" (reprinted in *American Dreams*), Shepard defined words "as tools of imagery in motion." He believed that

> the power of words . . . isn't so much in the delineation of a character's social circumstances as it is in the capacity to evoke visions in the eye of the audience . . . words as living incantations and not as symbols. Taken in this way, the organization of living, breathing words as they hit the air between the actor and the audience actually possesses the power to change our chemistry.

Shepard functioned as an alchemist for the contemporary American theater, transforming and recasting our very sense of what can be seen, heard, and imagined onstage.   J.E.G.

Buried Child

While the rain of your fingertips falls,
while the rain of your bones falls,
and your laughter and marrow fall down,
you come flying.　　　—Pablo Neruda[1]

CHARACTERS

DODGE, in his seventies
HALIE, his wife, mid-sixties
TILDEN, their oldest son
BRADLEY, their next oldest son,
　an amputee

VINCE, Tilden's son
SHELLY, Vince's girlfriend
FATHER DEWIS, a Protestant minister

Act 1

SCENE: *Day. Old wooden staircase down left with pale, frayed carpet laid down on the steps. The stairs lead offstage left up into the wings with no landing. Up right is an old, dark green sofa with the stuffing coming out in spots. Stage right of the sofa is an upright lamp with a faded yellow shade and a small night table with several small bottles of pills on it. Down right of the sofa, with the screen facing the sofa, is a large, old-fashioned brown T.V. A flickering blue light comes from the screen, but no image, no sound. In the dark, the light of the lamp and the T.V. slowly brighten in the black space. The space behind the sofa, upstage, is a large, screened-in porch with a board floor. A solid interior door to stage right of the sofa, leading into the room onstage; and another screen door up left, leading from the porch to the out-side. Beyond that are the shapes of dark elm trees.*

Gradually the form of DODGE *is made out, sitting on the couch, facing the T.V., the blue light flickering on his face. He wears a well-worn T-shirt, suspenders, khaki work pants, and brown slippers. He's covered himself in an old brown blan-ket. He's very thin and sickly looking, in his late seventies. He just stares at the T.V. More light fills the stage softly. The sound of light rain.* DODGE *slowly tilts his head back and stares at the ceiling for a while, listening to the rain. He lowers his head again and stares at the T.V. He turns his head slowly to the left and stares at the cushion of the sofa next to the one he's sitting on. He pulls his left arm out from under the blanket, slides his hand under the cushion, and pulls out a bottle of whiskey. He looks down left toward the staircase, listens, then uncaps the bot-tle, takes a long swig, and caps it again. He puts the bottle back under the cushion and stares at the T.V. He starts to cough slowly and softly. The coughing gradually builds. He holds one hand to his mouth and tries to stifle it. The coughing gets louder, then suddenly stops when he hears the sound of his wife's voice coming from the top of the staircase.*

---

1. Chilean poet and politician (1904–1973); the epigraph is from his elegy "Alberto Rojas Jimé-nez Comes Flying" (1934).

HALIE'S VOICE   Dodge?

[DODGE *just stares at the T.V. Long pause. He stifles two short coughs.*]

HALIE'S VOICE   Dodge! You want a pill, Dodge?

[*He doesn't answer. Takes the bottle out again and takes another long swig. Puts the bottle back, stares at T.V., pulls blanket up around his neck.*]

HALIE'S VOICE   You know what it is, don't you? It's the rain! Weather. That's it. Every time. Every time you get like this, it's the rain. No sooner does the
5 rain start then you start. [*Pause*] Dodge?

[*He makes no reply. Pulls a pack of cigarettes out from his sweater and lights one. Stares at T.V. Pause.*]

HALIE'S VOICE   You should see it coming down up here. Just coming down in sheets. Blue sheets. The bridge is pretty near flooded. What's it like down there? Dodge?

[DODGE *turns his head back over his left shoulder and takes a look out through the porch. He turns back to the T.V.*]

DODGE [*to himself*]   Catastrophic.

10 HALIE'S VOICE   What? What'd you say, Dodge?

DODGE [*louder*]   It looks like rain to me! Plain old rain!

HALIE'S VOICE   Rain? Of course it's rain! Are you having a seizure or something! Dodge? [*Pause*] I'm coming down there in about five minutes if you don't answer me!

15 DODGE   Don't come down.

HALIE'S VOICE   What!

DODGE [*louder*]   Don't come down!

[*He has another coughing attack. Stops.*]

HALIE'S VOICE   You should take a pill for that! I don't see why you just don't take a pill. Be done with it once and for all. Put a stop to it.

[*He takes bottle out again. Another swig. Returns bottle.*]

20 HALIE'S VOICE   It's not Christian, but it works, It's not necessarily Christian, that is. We don't know. There's some things the ministers can't even answer. I, personally, can't see anything wrong with it. Pain is pain. Pure and simple. Suffering is a different matter. That's entirely different. A pill seems as good an answer as any. Dodge? [*Pause*] Dodge, are you watching
25 baseball?

DODGE   No.

HALIE'S VOICE   What?

DODGE [*louder*]   No!

HALIE'S VOICE   What're you watching? You shouldn't be watching anything
30 that'll get you excited! No horse racing!

DODGE   They don't race on Sundays.

HALIE'S VOICE   What?

DODGE [*louder*]   They don't race on Sundays!

HALIE'S VOICE   Well they shouldn't race on Sundays.

35 DODGE   Well they don't!

HALIE'S VOICE   Good. I'm amazed they still have that kind of legislation. That's amazing.

DODGE   Yeah, it's amazing.

HALIE'S VOICE   What?

40 DODGE [*louder*]   It is amazing!

HALIE'S VOICE   It is. It truly is. I would've thought these days they'd be racing on Christmas even. A big flashing Christmas tree right down at the finish line.

DODGE [*shakes his head*]   No.

HALIE'S VOICE   They used to race on New Year's! I remember that.

45 DODGE   They never raced on New Year's!

HALIE'S VOICE   Sometimes they did.

DODGE   They never did!

HALIE'S VOICE   Before we were married they did!

> [DODGE *waves his hand in disgust at the staircase. Leans back in sofa. Stares at T.V.*]

HALIE'S VOICE   I went once. With a man.

50 DODGE [*mimicking her*]   Oh, a "man."

HALIE'S VOICE   What?

DODGE   Nothing!

HALIE'S VOICE   A wonderful man. A breeder.

DODGE   A what?

55 HALIE'S VOICE   A breeder! A horse breeder! Thoroughbreds.

DODGE   Oh, Thoroughbreds. Wonderful.

HALIE'S VOICE   That's right. He knew everything there was to know.

DODGE   I bet he taught you a thing or two huh? Gave you a good turn around the old stable!

60 HALIE'S VOICE   Knew everything there was to know about horses. We won bookoos[2] of money that day.

DODGE   What?

HALIE'S VOICE   Money! We won every race I think.

DODGE   Bookoos?

65 HALIE'S VOICE   Every single race.

DODGE   Bookoos of money?

HALIE'S VOICE   It was one of those kind of days.

DODGE   New Year's!

HALIE'S VOICE   Yes! It might've been Florida. Or California! One of those two.

70 DODGE   Can I take my pick?

HALIE'S VOICE   It was Florida!

DODGE   Aha!

HALIE'S VOICE   Wonderful! Absolutely wonderful! The sun was just gleaming. Flamingos. Bougainvilleas. Palm trees.

75 DODGE [*to himself, mimicking her*]   Bougainvilleas. Palm trees.

HALIE'S VOICE   Everything was dancing with life! There were all kinds of people from everywhere. Everyone was dressed to the nines. Not like today. Not like they dress today.

DODGE   When was this anyway?

80 HALIE'S VOICE   This was long before I knew you.

DODGE   Must've been.

HALIE'S VOICE   Long before. I was escorted.

DODGE   To Florida?

HALIE'S VOICE   Yes. Or it might've been California. I'm not sure which.

85 DODGE   All that way you were escorted?

---

2. Mock French, playing on *beaucoup* (much; a great deal).

HALIE'S VOICE   Yes.

DODGE   And he never laid a finger on you I suppose? [*Long silence*] Halie?
[*No answer. Long pause.*]

HALIE'S VOICE   Are you going out today?

DODGE [*gesturing toward rain*]   In this?

90 HALIE'S VOICE   I'm just asking a simple question.

DODGE   I rarely go out in the bright sunshine, why would I go out in this?

HALIE'S VOICE   I'm just asking because I'm not doing any shopping today. And
if you need anything you should ask Tilden.

DODGE   Tilden's not here!

95 HALIE'S VOICE   He's in the kitchen.
[DODGE *looks toward stage left, then back toward T.V.*]

DODGE   All right.

HALIE'S VOICE   What?

DODGE [*louder*]   All right!

HALIE'S VOICE   Don't scream. It'll only get your coughing started.

100 DODGE   All right.

HALIE'S VOICE   Just tell Tilden what you want and he'll get it. [*Pause*] Bradley
should be over later.

DODGE   Bradley?

HALIE'S VOICE   Yes. To cut your hair.

105 DODGE   My hair? I don't need my hair cut!

HALIE'S VOICE   It won't hurt!

DODGE   I don't need it!

HALIE'S VOICE   It's been more than two weeks Dodge.

DODGE   I don't need it!

110 HALIE'S VOICE   I have to meet Father Dewis for lunch.

DODGE   You tell Bradley that if he shows up here with those clippers, I'll kill
him!

HALIE'S VOICE   I won't be very late. No later than four at the very latest.

DODGE   You tell him! Last time he left me almost bald! And I wasn't even
115 awake! I was sleeping! I woke up and he'd already left!

HALIE'S VOICE   That's not my fault!

DODGE   You put him up to it!

HALIE'S VOICE   I never did!

DODGE   You did too! You had some fancy, stupid meeting planned! Time to
120 dress up the corpse for company! Lower the ears a little! Put up a little
front! Surprised you didn't tape a pipe to my mouth while you were at it!
That woulda' looked nice! Huh? A pipe? Maybe a bowler hat! Maybe a copy
of The Wall Street Journal casually placed on my lap!

HALIE'S VOICE   You always imagine the worst things of people!

125 DODGE   That's not the worst! That's the least of the worst!

HALIE'S VOICE   I don't need to hear it! All day long I hear things like that and
I don't need to hear more.

DODGE   You better tell him!

HALIE'S VOICE   You tell him yourself! He's your own son. You should be able
130 to talk to your own son.

DODGE   Not while I'm sleeping! He cut my hair while I was sleeping!

HALIE'S VOICE   Well he won't do it again.

DODGE   There's no guarantee.

HALIE'S VOICE   I promise he won't do it without your consent.

135 DODGE [*after pause*]   There's no reason for him to even come over here.

HALIE'S VOICE   He feels responsible.

DODGE   For my hair?

HALIE'S VOICE   For your appearance.

DODGE   My appearance is out of his domain! It's even out of mine! In fact,
140   it's disappeared! I'm an invisible man!

HALIE'S VOICE   Don't be ridiculous.

DODGE   He better not try it. That's all I've got to say.

HALIE'S VOICE   Tilden will watch out for you.

DODGE   Tilden won't protect me from Bradley!

145 HALIE'S VOICE   Tilden's the oldest. He'll protect you.

DODGE   Tilden can't even protect himself!

HALIE'S VOICE   Not so loud! He'll hear you. He's right in the kitchen.

DODGE [*yelling off left*]   Tilden!

HALIE'S VOICE   Dodge, what are you trying to do?

150 DODGE [*yelling off left*]   Tilden, get in here!

HALIE'S VOICE   Why do you enjoy stirring things up?

DODGE   I don't enjoy anything!

HALIE'S VOICE   That's a terrible thing to say.

DODGE   Tilden!

155 HALIE'S VOICE   That's the kind of statement that leads people right to the end
    of their rope.

DODGE   Tilden!

HALIE'S VOICE   It's no wonder people turn to Christ!

DODGE   TILDEN!!

160 HALIE'S VOICE   It's no wonder the messengers of God's word are shouted
    down in public places!

DODGE   TILDEN!!!!

[DODGE *goes into a violent, spasmodic coughing attack as* TILDEN *enters
from stage left, his arms loaded with fresh ears of corn.* TILDEN *is* DODGE's
*oldest son, late forties, wears heavy construction boots, covered with mud,
dark green work pants, a plaid shirt, and a faded brown windbreaker. He
has a butch haircut, wet from the rain. Something about him is profoundly burned out and displaced. He stops center stage with the ears of
corn in his arms and just stares at* DODGE *until he slowly finishes his
coughing attack.* DODGE *looks up at him slowly. He stares at the corn.
Long pause as they watch each other.*]

HALIE'S VOICE   Dodge, if you don't take that pill nobody's going to force you.

[*The two men ignore the voice.*]

DODGE [*to* TILDEN]   Where'd you get that?

165 TILDEN   Picked it.

DODGE   You picked all that?

[TILDEN *nods.*]

DODGE   You expecting company?

TILDEN   No.

DODGE   Where'd you pick it from?

170 TILDEN   Right out back.

DODGE   Out back where?

TILDEN   Right out in back.

DODGE There's nothing out there!

TILDEN There's corn.

175 DODGE There hasn't been corn out there since about nineteen thirty-five! That's the last time I planted corn out there!

TILDEN It's out there now.

DODGE [yelling at stairs] Halie!

HALIE'S VOICE Yes dear!

180 DODGE Tilden's brought a whole bunch of corn in here! There's no corn out in back is there?

TILDEN [to himself] There's tons of corn.

HALIE'S VOICE Not that I know of!

DODGE That's what I thought.

185 HALIE'S VOICE Not since about nineteen thirty-five!

DODGE [to TILDEN] That's right. Nineteen thirty-five.

TILDEN It's out there now.

DODGE You go and take that corn back to wherever you got it from!

TILDEN [after pause, staring at DODGE] It's picked. I picked it all in the rain.

190 Once it's picked you can't put it back.

DODGE I haven't had trouble with neighbors here for fifty-seven years. I don't even know who the neighbors are! And I don't wanna know! Now go put that corn back where it came from!

[TILDEN stares at DODGE then walks slowly over to him and dumps all the corn on DODGE's lap and steps back. DODGE stares at the corn then back to TILDEN. Long pause.]

DODGE Are you having trouble here, Tilden! Are you in some kind of trouble?

195 TILDEN I'm not in any trouble.

DODGE You can tell me if you are. I'm still your father.

TILDEN I know you're still my father.

DODGE I know you had a little trouble back in New Mexico. That's why you came out here.

200 TILDEN I never had any trouble.

DODGE Tilden, your mother told me all about it.

TILDEN What'd she tell you?

[TILDEN pulls some chewing tobacco out of his jacket and bites off a plug.]

DODGE I don't have to repeat what she told me! She told me all about it!

TILDEN Can I bring my chair in from the kitchen?

205 DODGE What?

TILDEN Can I bring in my chair from the kitchen?

DODGE Sure. Bring your chair in.

[TILDEN exits left. DODGE pushes all the corn off his lap onto the floor. He pulls the blanket off angrily and tosses it at one end of the sofa, pulls out the bottle and takes another swig. TILDEN enters again from left with a milking stool and a pail. DODGE hides the bottle quickly under the cushion before TILDEN see it. TILDEN sets the stool down by the sofa, sits on it, puts the pail in front of him on the floor. TILDEN starts picking up the ears of corn one at a time and husking them. He throws the husks and silk in the center of the stage and drops the ears into the pail each time he cleans one. He repeats this process as they talk.]

DODGE [after pause] Sure is nice-looking corn.

TILDEN   It's the best.

210   DODGE   Hybrid?

TILDEN   What?

DODGE   Some kinda fancy hybrid?

TILDEN   You planted it. I don't know what it is.

DODGE   [*pause*]   Tilden, look, you can't stay here forever. You know that, don't

215   you?

TILDEN   [*spits in spittoon*]   I'm not.

DODGE   I know you're not. I'm not worried about that. That's not the reason
I brought it up.

TILDEN   What's the reason?

220   DODGE   The reason is I'm wondering what you're gonna do.

TILDEN   You're not worried about me, are you?

DODGE   I'm not worried about you.

TILDEN   You weren't worried about me when I wasn't here. When I was in
New Mexico.

225   DODGE   No, I wasn't worried about you then either.

TILDEN   You shoulda worried about me then.

DODGE   Why's that? You didn't do anything down there, did you?

TILDEN   I didn't do anything.

DODGE   Then why should I have worried about you?

230   TILDEN   Because I was lonely.

DODGE   Because you were lonely?

TILDEN   Yeah. I was more lonely than I've ever been before.

DODGE   Why was that?

TILDEN   [*pause*]   Could I have some of that whiskey you've got?

235   DODGE   What whiskey? I haven't got any whiskey.

TILDEN   You've got some under the sofa.

DODGE   I haven't got anything under the sofa! Now mind your own damn
business! Jesus God, you come into the house outa the middle of nowhere,
haven't heard or seen you in twenty years and suddenly you're making

240   accusations.

TILDEN   I'm not making accusations.

DODGE   You're accusing me of hoarding whiskey under the sofa!

TILDEN   I'm not accusing you.

DODGE   You just got through telling me I had whiskey under the sofa!

245   HALIE'S VOICE   Dodge?

DODGE   [*to* TILDEN]   Now she knows about it!

TILDEN   She doesn't know about it.

HALIE'S VOICE   Dodge, are you talking to yourself down there?

DODGE   I'm talking to Tilden!

250   HALIE'S VOICE   Tilden's down there?

DODGE   He's right here!

HALIE'S VOICE   What?

DODGE   [*louder*]   He's right here!

HALIE'S VOICE   What's he doing?

255   DODGE   [*to* TILDEN]   Don't answer her.

TILDEN   [*to* DODGE]   I'm not doing anything wrong.

DODGE   I know you're not.

HALIE'S VOICE   What's he doing down there!

DODGE [*to* TILDEN]   Don't answer.

260 TILDEN   I'm not.

HALIE'S VOICE   Dodge!

> [*The men sit in silence.* DODGE *lights a cigarette.* TILDEN *keeps husking corn, spits tobacco now and then in spittoon.*]

HALIE'S VOICE   Dodge! He's not drinking anything, is he? You see to it that he doesn't drink anything! You've gotta watch out for him. It's our responsibility. He can't look after himself any more, so we have to do it. Nobody else

265 will do it. We can't just send him away somewhere. If we had lots of money we could send him away. But we don't. We never will. That's why we have to stay healthy. You and me. Nobody's going to look after us. Bradley can't look after us. Bradley can hardly look after himself. I was always hoping that Tilden would look out for Bradley when they got older. After Bradley

270 lost his leg. Tilden's the oldest. I always thought he'd be the one to take responsibility. I had no idea in the world that Tilden would be so much trouble. Who would've dreamed. Tilden was an All-American, don't forget. Don't forget that. Fullback. Or quarterback. I forget which.

TILDEN [*to himself*]   Fullback. [*Still husking*]

275 HALIE'S VOICE   Then when Tilden turned out to be so much trouble, I put all my hopes on Ansel. Of course Ansel wasn't as handsome, but he was smart. He was the smartest probably. I think he probably was. Smarter than Bradley, that's for sure. Didn't go and chop his leg off with a chain saw. Smart enough not to go and do that. I think he was smarter than

280 Tilden too. Especially after Tilden got in all that trouble. Doesn't take brains to go to jail. Anybody knows that. Course then when Ansel died that left us all alone. Same as being alone. No different. Same as if they'd all died. He was the smartest. He could've earned lots of money. Lots and lots of money.

> [HALIE *enters slowly from the top of the staircase as she continues talking. Just her feet are seen at first as she makes her way down the stairs, a step at a time. She appears dressed completely in black, as though in mourning. Black handbag, hat with a veil, and pulling on elbow length black gloves. She is about sixty-five with pure white hair. She remains absorbed in what she's saying as she descends the stairs and doesn't really notice the two men who continue sitting there as they were before she came down, smoking and husking.*]

285 HALIE   He would've took care of us, too. He would've seen to it that we were repaid. He was like that. He was a hero. Don't forget that. A genuine hero. Brave. Strong. And very intelligent. Ansel could've been a great man. One of the greatest. I only regret that he didn't die in action. It's not fitting for a man like that to die in a motel room. A soldier. He could've won a medal.

290 He could've been decorated for valor. I've talked to Father Dewis about putting up a plaque for Ansel. He thinks it's a good idea. He agrees. He knew Ansel when he used to play basketball. Went to every game. Ansel was his favorite player. He even recommended to the City Council that they put up a statue of Ansel. A big, tall statue with a basketball in one

295 hand and a rifle in the other. That's how much he thinks of Ansel.

> [HALIE *reaches the stage and begins to wander around, still absorbed in pulling on her gloves, brushing lint off her dress and continuously talking to herself as the men just sit.*]

HALIE   Of course, he'd still be alive today if he hadn't married into the Catholics. The Mob. How in the world he never opened his eyes to that is beyond me. Just beyond me. Everyone around him could see the truth. Even Tilden. Tilden told him time and again. Catholic women are the Devil incarnate. He wouldn't listen. He was blind with love. Blind. I knew. Everyone knew. The wedding was more like a funeral. You remember? All those Italians. All that horrible black, greasy hair. The smell of cheap cologne. I think even the priest was wearing a pistol. When he gave her the ring I knew he was a dead man. I knew it. As soon as he gave her the ring. But then it was the honeymoon that killed him. The honeymoon. I knew he'd never come back from the honeymoon. I kissed him and he felt like a corpse. All white. Cold. Icy blue lips. He never used to kiss like that. Never before. I knew then that she'd cursed him. Taken his soul. I saw it in her eyes. She smiled at me with that Catholic sneer of hers. She told me with her eyes that she'd murder him in his bed. Murder my son. She told me. And there was nothing I could do. Absolutely nothing. He was going with her, thinking he was free. Thinking it was love. What could I do? I couldn't tell him she was a witch. I couldn't tell him that. He'd have turned on me. Hated me. I couldn't stand him hating me and then dying before he ever saw me again. Hating me in his deathbed. Hating me and loving her! How could I do that? I had to let him go. I had to. I watched him leave. I watched him throw gardenias as he helped her into the limousine. I watched his face disappear behind the glass.

> [*She stops abruptly and stares at the corn husks. She looks around the space as though just waking up. She turns and looks hard at* TILDEN *and* DODGE *who continue sitting calmly. She looks again at the corn husks.*]

HALIE [*pointing to the husks*]   What's this in my house! [*Kicks husks.*] What's all this!

> [TILDEN *stops husking and stares at her.*]

HALIE [*to* DODGE]   And you encourage him!

> [DODGE *pulls blanket over him again.*]

DODGE   You're going out in the rain?

HALIE   It's not raining.

> [TILDEN *starts husking again.*]

DODGE   Not in Florida it's not.

HALIE   We're not in Florida!

DODGE   It's not raining at the racetrack.

HALIE   Have you been taking those pills? Those pills always make you talk crazy. Tilden, has he been taking those pills?

TILDEN   He hasn't took anything.

HALIE [*to* DODGE]   What've you been taking?

DODGE   It's not raining in California or Florida or the racetrack. Only in Illinois. This is the only place it's raining. All over the rest of the world it's bright golden sunshine.

> [HALIE *goes to the night table next to the sofa and checks the bottle of pills.*]

HALIE   Which ones did you take? Tilden, you must've seen him take something.

TILDEN   He never took a thing.

HALIE   Then why's he talking crazy?

TILDEN   I've been here the whole time.

HALIE   Then you've both been taking something!

340 TILDEN   I've just been husking the corn.

HALIE   Where'd you get that corn anyway? Why is the house suddenly full of corn?

DODGE   Bumper crop!

HALIE [*moving center*]   We haven't had corn here for over thirty years.

345 TILDEN   The whole back lot's full of corn. Far as the eye can see.

DODGE [*to* HALIE]   Things keep happening while you're upstairs, ya know. The world doesn't stop just because you're upstairs. Corn keeps growing. Rain keeps raining.

HALIE   I'm not unaware of the world around me! Thank you very much. It
350   so happens that I have an overall view from the upstairs. The backyard's in plain view of my window. And there's no corn to speak of. Absolutely none!

DODGE   Tilden wouldn't lie. If he says there's corn, there's corn.

HALIE   What's the meaning of this corn Tilden!

355 TILDEN   It's a mystery to me. I was out in back there. And the rain was coming down. And I didn't feel like coming back inside. I didn't feel the cold so much. I didn't mind the wet. So I was just walking. I was muddy but I didn't mind the mud so much. And I looked up. And I saw this stand of corn. In fact I was standing in it. So, I was standing in it.

360 HALIE   There isn't any corn outside, Tilden! There's no corn! Now, you must've either stolen this corn or you bought it.

DODGE   He doesn't have any money.

HALIE [*to* TILDEN]   So you stole it!

TILDEN   I didn't steal it. I don't want to get kicked out of Illinois. I was kicked
365   out of New Mexico and I don't want to get kicked out of Illinois.

HALIE   You're going to get kicked out of this house, Tilden, if you don't tell me where you got that corn!

[TILDEN *starts crying softly to himself but keeps husking corn. Pause.*]

DODGE [*to* HALIE]   Why'd you have to tell him that? Who cares where he got the corn? Why'd you have to go and tell him that?

370 HALIE [*to* DODGE]   It's your fault you know! You're the one that's behind all this! I suppose you thought it'd be funny! Some joke! Cover the house with corn husks. You better get this cleaned up before Bradley sees it.

DODGE   Bradley's not getting in the front door!

HALIE [*kicking husks, striding back and forth*]   Bradley's going to be very
375   upset when he sees this. He doesn't like to see the house in disarray. He can't stand it when one thing is out of place. The slightest thing. You know how he gets.

DODGE   Bradley doesn't even live here!

HALIE   It's his home as much as ours. He was born in this house!

380 DODGE   He was born in a hog wallow.

HALIE   Don't you say that! Don't you ever say that!

DODGE   He was born in a goddamn hog wallow! That's where he was born and that's where he belongs! He doesn't belong in this house!

HALIE [*she stops*]   I don't know what's come over you, Dodge. I don't know
385   what in the world's come over you. You've become an evil man. You used to be a good man.

DODGE   Six of one, a half dozen of another.

HALIE   You sit here day and night, festering away! Decomposing! Smelling up the house with your putrid body! Hacking your head off till all hours of the morning! Thinking up mean, evil, stupid things to say about your own flesh and blood!

DODGE   He's not my flesh and blood! My flesh and blood's buried in the backyard!

[*They freeze. Long pause. The men stare at her.*]

HALIE [*quietly*]   That's enough, Dodge. That's quite enough. I'm going out now. I'm going to have lunch with Father Dewis. I'm going to ask him about a monument. A statue. At least a plaque.

[*She crosses to the door up right. She stops.*]

HALIE   If you need anything, ask Tilden. He's the oldest. I've left some money on the kitchen table.

DODGE   I don't need anything.

HALIE   No, I suppose not. [*She opens the door and looks out through porch.*] Still raining. I love the smell just after it stops. The ground. I won't be too late.

[*She goes out door and closes it. She's still visible on the porch as she crosses toward stage left screen door. She stops in the middle of the porch, speaks to DODGE but doesn't turn to him.*]

HALIE   Dodge, tell Tilden not to go out in the back lot any more. I don't want him back there in the rain.

DODGE   You tell him. He's sitting right here.

HALIE   He never listens to me Dodge. He's never listened to me in the past.

DODGE   I'll tell him.

HALIE   We have to watch him just like we used to now. Just like we always have. He's still a child.

DODGE   I'll watch him.

HALIE   Good.

[*She crosses to screen door, left, takes an umbrella off a hook and goes out the door. The door slams behind her. Long pause. TILDEN husks corn, stares at pail. DODGE lights a cigarette, stares at T.V.*]

TILDEN [*still husking*]   You shouldn't a told her that.

DODGE [*staring at T.V.*]   What?

TILDEN   What you told her. You know.

DODGE   What do you know about it?

TILDEN   I know. I know all about it. We all know.

DODGE   So what difference does it make? Everybody knows, everybody's forgot.

TILDEN   She hasn't forgot.

DODGE   She should've forgot.

TILDEN   It's different for a woman. She couldn't forget that. How could she forget that?

DODGE   I don't want to talk about it!

TILDEN   What do you want to talk about?

DODGE   I don't want to talk about anything! I don't want to talk about troubles or what happened fifty years ago or thirty years ago or the racetrack or Florida or the last time I seeded the corn! I don't want to talk!

TILDEN   You don't wanna die do you?

DODGE	No, I don't wanna die either.
TILDEN	Well, you gotta talk or you'll die.
430 DODGE	Who told you that?
TILDEN	That's what I know. I found that out in New Mexico. I thought I was dying but I just lost my voice.
DODGE	Were you with somebody?
TILDEN	I was alone. I thought I was dead.
435 DODGE	Might as well have been. What'd you come back here for?
TILDEN	I didn't know where to go.
DODGE	You're a grown man. You shouldn't be needing your parents at your age. It's unnatural. There's nothing we can do for you now anyway. Couldn't you make a living down there? Couldn't you find some way to make a liv-
440	ing? Support yourself? What'd'ya come back here for? You expect us to feed you forever?
TILDEN	I didn't know where else to go.
DODGE	I never went back to my parents. Never. Never even had the urge. I was independent. Always independent. Always found a way.
445 TILDEN	I didn't know what to do. I couldn't figure anything out.
DODGE	There's nothing to figure out. You just forge ahead. What's there to figure out?

[TILDEN *stands.*]

TILDEN	I don't know.
DODGE	Where are you going?
450 TILDEN	Out back.
DODGE	You're not supposed to go out there. You heard what she said. Don't play deaf with me!
TILDEN	I like it out there.
DODGE	In the rain?
455 TILDEN	Especially in the rain. I like the feeling of it. Feels like it always did.
DODGE	You're supposed to watch out for me. Get me things when I need them.
TILDEN	What do you need?
DODGE	I don't need anything! But I might. I might need something any sec-
460	ond. Any second now. I can't be left alone for a minute!

[DODGE *starts to cough.*]

TILDEN	I'll be right outside. You can just yell.
DODGE	[*between coughs*] No! It's too far! You can't go out there! It's too far! You might not ever hear me!
TILDEN	[*moving to pills*] Why don't you take a pill? You want a pill?

[DODGE *coughs more violently, throws himself back against sofa, clutches his throat.* TILDEN *stands by helplessly.*]

465 DODGE	Water! Get me some water!

[TILDEN *rushes off left.* DODGE *reaches out for the pills, knocking some bottles to the floor, coughing in spasms. He grabs a small bottle, takes out pills and swallows them.* TILDEN *rushes back on with a glass of water.* DODGE *takes it and drinks, his coughing subsides.*]

TILDEN	You all right now?

[DODGE *nods. Drinks more water.* TILDEN *moves in closer to him.* DODGE *sets glass of water on the night table. His coughing is almost gone.*]

TILDEN   Why don't you lay down for a while? Just rest a little.

[TILDEN *helps* DODGE *lay down on the sofa. Covers him with blanket.*]

DODGE   You're not going outside are you?

TILDEN   No.

470 DODGE   I don't want to wake up and find you not here.

TILDEN   I'll be here.

[TILDEN *tucks blanket around* DODGE.]

DODGE   You'll stay right here?

TILDEN   I'll stay in my chair.

DODGE   That's not a chair. That's my old milking stool.

475 TILDEN   I know.

DODGE   Don't call it a chair.

TILDEN   I won't.

[TILDEN *tries to take* DODGE's *baseball cap off.*]

DODGE   What're you doing! Leave that on me! Don't take that offa me! That's my cap!

[TILDEN *leaves the cap on* DODGE.]

480 TILDEN   I know.

DODGE   Bradley'll shave my head if I don't have that on. That's my cap.

TILDEN   I know it is.

DODGE   Don't take my cap off.

TILDEN   I won't.

485 DODGE   You stay right here now.

TILDEN [*sits on stool*]   I will.

DODGE   Don't go outside. There's nothing out there.

TILDEN   I won't.

DODGE   Everything's in here. Everything you need. Money's on the table.

490   T.V. Is the T.V. on?

TILDEN   Yeah.

DODGE   Turn it off! Turn the damn thing off! What's it doing on?

TILDEN [*shuts off T.V., light goes out*]   You left it on.

DODGE   Well turn it off.

495 TILDEN [*sits on stool again*]   It's off.

DODGE   Leave it off.

TILDEN   I will.

DODGE   When I fall asleep you can turn it on.

TILDEN   Okay.

500 DODGE   You can watch the ball game. Red Sox. You like the Red Sox don't you?

TILDEN   Yeah.

DODGE   You can watch the Red Sox. Pee Wee Reese.[3] Pee Wee Reese. You remember Pee Wee Reese?

505 TILDEN   No.

DODGE   Was he with the Red Sox?

---

3. An American baseball player (1918–1999); the All-Star shortstop played for the Brooklyn (later Los Angeles) Dodgers (1940–42, 1946–58), but he was originally drafted by the Boston Red Sox.

TILDEN   I don't know.

DODGE   Pee Wee Reese. [*Falling asleep*] You can watch the Cardinals. You remember Stan Musial.[4]

510 TILDEN   No.

DODGE   Stan Musial. [*Falling into sleep*] Bases loaded. Top a' the sixth. Bases loaded. Runner on first and third. Big fat knuckle ball. Floater. Big as a blimp. Cracko! Ball just took off like a rocket. Just pulverized. I marked it. Marked it with my eyes. Straight between the clock and the Burma Shave

515 ad.[5] I was the first kid out there. First kid. I had to fight hard for that ball. I wouldn't give it up. They almost tore the ears right off me. But I wouldn't give it up.

> [DODGE *falls into deep sleep.* TILDEN *just sits staring at him for a while. Slowly he leans toward the sofa, checking to see if* DODGE *is well asleep. He reaches slowly under the cushion and pulls out the bottle of booze.* DODGE *sleeps soundly.* TILDEN *stands quietly, staring at* DODGE *as he uncaps the bottle and takes a long drink. He caps the bottle and sticks it in his hip pocket. He looks around at the husks on the floor and then back to* DODGE. *He moves center stage and gathers an armload of corn husks then crosses back to the sofa. He stands holding the husks over* DODGE *and looking down at him he gently spreads the corn husks over the whole length of* DODGE's *body. He stands back and looks at* DODGE. *Pulls out bottle, takes another drink, returns bottle to his hip pocket. He gathers more husks and repeats the procedure until the floor is clean of corn husks and* DODGE *is completely covered in them except for his head.* TILDEN *takes another long drink, stares at* DODGE *sleeping, then quietly exits stage left. Long pause as the sound of rain continues.* DODGE *sleeps on. The figure of* BRADLEY *appears up left, outside the screen porch door. He holds a wet newspaper over his head as a protection from the rain. He seems to be struggling with the door then slips and almost falls to the ground.* DODGE *sleeps on, undisturbed.*]

BRADLEY   Sonuvabitch! Sonuvagoddamnbitch!

> [BRADLEY *recovers his footing and makes it through the screen door onto the porch. He throws the newspaper down, shakes the water out of his hair, and brushes the rain off of his shoulders. He is a big man dressed in a gray sweat shirt, black suspenders, baggy dark blue pants, and black janitor's shoes. His left leg is wooden, having been amputated above the knee. He moves with an exaggerated, almost mechanical limp. The squeaking sounds of leather and metal accompany his walk coming from the harness and hinges of the false leg. His arms and shoulders are extremely powerful and muscular due to a lifetime dependency on the upper torso doing all the work for the legs. He is about five years younger than* TILDEN. *He moves laboriously to the stage right door and enters, closing the door behind him. He doesn't notice* DODGE *at first. He moves toward the staircase.*]

BRADLEY [*calling to upstairs*]   Mom!

> [*He stops and listens. Turns upstage and sees* DODGE *sleeping. Notices corn husks. He moves slowly toward sofa. Stops next to pail and looks into it. Looks at husks.* DODGE *stays asleep. Talks to himself.*]

---

4. An American outfielder and first baseman (1920–2013); one of the greatest hitters in baseball history, he played his entire career for the St. Louis Cardinals (1941–63).

5. Burma-Shave was a brand of brushless shaving cream, introduced in 1925. (Dodge is recalling a home run, apparently hit into the outfield bleachers.)

520 BRADLEY   What in the hell is this?

[*He looks at* DODGE's *sleeping face and shakes his head in disgust. He pulls out a pair of black electric hair clippers from his pocket. Unwinds the cord and crosses to the lamp. He jabs his wooden leg behind the knee, causing it to bend at the joint and awkwardly kneels to plug the cord into a floor outlet. He pulls himself to his feet again by using the sofa as leverage. He moves to* DODGE's *head and again jabs his false leg. Goes down on one knee. He violently knocks away some of the corn husks then jerks off* DODGE's *baseball cap and throws it down center stage.* DODGE *stays asleep.* BRADLEY *switches on the clippers. Lights start dimming.* BRADLEY *cuts* DODGE's *hair while he sleeps. Lights dim slowly to black with the sound of clippers and rain.*]

Act 2

SCENE: *Same set as act 1. Night. Sounds of rain.* DODGE *still asleep on sofa. His hair is cut extremely short and in places the scalp is cut and bleeding. His cap is still center stage. All the corn and husks, pail, and milking stool have been cleared away. The lights come up to the sound of a young girl laughing off stage left.* DODGE *remains asleep.* SHELLY *and* VINCE *appear up left outside the screen porch door sharing the shelter of* VINCE's *overcoat above their heads.* SHELLY *is about nineteen, black hair, very beautiful. She wears tight jeans, high heels, purple T-shirt, and a short rabbit-fur coat. Her makeup is exaggerated and her hair has been curled.* VINCE *is* TILDEN's *son, about twenty-two, wears a plaid shirt, jeans, dark glasses, cowboy boots, and carries a black saxophone case. They shake the rain off themselves as they enter the porch through the screen door.*

SHELLY [*laughing, gesturing to house*]   This is it? I don't believe this is it!
VINCE   This is it.
SHELLY   This is the house?
VINCE   This is the house.
5 SHELLY   I don't believe it!
VINCE   How come?
SHELLY   It's like a Norman Rockwell[6] cover or something.
VINCE   What's a' matter with that? It's American.
SHELLY   Where's the milkman and the little dog? What's the little dog's
10   name? Spot. Spot and Jane. Dick and Jane and Spot.[7]
VINCE   Knock it off.
SHELLY   Dick and Jane and Spot and Mom and Dad and Junior and Sissy!
[*She laughs. Slaps her knee.*]
VINCE   Come on! It's my heritage. What dya' expect?
[*She laughs more hysterically, out of control.*]

6. An American illustrator (1894–1978) best known for his covers for the *Saturday Evening Post* magazine, which appeared from 1916 through the early 1960s. Rockwell's drawings often featured realistic yet humorous and wholesome images of small-town American life.
7. Names from the famous Dick and Jane readers; created in 1930 for Scott, Foresman and Company, they were widely used throughout the United States up to the 1970s. The illustrated books, designed to teach children to read by repeating a limited number of carefully chosen words, depicted an idealized white, middle-class family.

SHELLY   "And Tuffy and Toto and Dooda and Bonzo[8] all went down one day
15   to the corner grocery store to buy a big bag of licorice for Mr. Marshall's
pussy cat!"

[*She laughs so hard she falls to her knees holding her stomach.* VINCE
stands there looking at her.]

VINCE   Shelly will you get up!

[*She keeps laughing. Staggers to her feet. Turning in circles holding her
stomach.*]

SHELLY [*continuing her story in kid's voice*]   "Mr. Marshall was on vacation.
He had no idea that the four little boys had taken such a liking to his little
20   kitty cat."

VINCE   Have some respect would ya'!

SHELLY [*trying to control herself*]   I'm sorry.

VINCE   Pull yourself together.

SHELLY [*salutes him*]   Yes sir.

[*She giggles.*]

25 VINCE   Jesus Christ, Shelly.

SHELLY [*pause, smiling*]   And Mr. Marshall—

VINCE   Cut it out.

[*She stops. Stands there staring at him. Stifles a giggle.*]

VINCE [*after pause*]   Are you finished?

SHELLY   Oh brother!

30 VINCE   I don't wanna go in there with you acting like an idiot.

SHELLY   Thanks.

VINCE   Well, I don't.

SHELLY   I won't embarrass you. Don't worry.

VINCE   I'm not worried.

35 SHELLY   You are too.

VINCE   Shelly look, I just don't wanna go in there with you giggling your head
off. They might think something's wrong with you.

SHELLY   There is.

VINCE   There is not!

40 SHELLY   Something's definitely wrong with me.

VINCE   There is not!

SHELLY   There's something wrong with you too.

VINCE   There's nothing wrong with me either!

SHELLY   You wanna know what's wrong with you?

45 VINCE   What?

[SHELLY *laughs.*]

VINCE [*crosses back left toward screen door*]   I'm leaving!

---

8. A reference to the Bonzo Dog Doo-Dah
Band, created by British art students in the
1960s; the Bonzos played a mixture of jazz
and psychedelic rock and performed regularly
on a BBC children's series, *Do Not Adjust
Your Set* (1967–69). (Bonzo was also a chim-
panzee in *Bedtime for Bonzo*, a 1951 film

starring Ronald Reagan.) *Tuffy:* a baby mouse
featured in the *Tom and Jerry* cartoon series
(begun in the 1940s). *Toto:* Dorothy's dog in
The Wizard of Oz (1939), the movie musical
adapted from L. Frank Baum's novel *The Wonderful Wizard of Oz* (1900) and its sequels.

SHELLY [*stops laughing*] Wait! Stop! Stop! [VINCE *stops.*] What's wrong with you is that you take the situation too seriously.

VINCE I just don't want to have them think that I've suddenly arrived out of
50 the middle of nowhere completely deranged.

SHELLY What do you want them to think then?

VINCE [*pause*] Nothing. Let's go in.

[*He crosses porch toward stage right interior door.* SHELLY *follows him. The stage right door opens slowly.* VINCE *sticks his head in, doesn't notice* DODGE *sleeping. Calls out toward staircase.*]

VINCE Grandma!

[SHELLY *breaks into laughter, unseen behind* VINCE. VINCE *pulls his head back outside and pulls door shut. We hear their voices again without seeing them.*]

SHELLY'S VOICE [*stops laughing*] I'm sorry. I'm sorry Vince. I really am. I
55 really am sorry. I won't do it again. I couldn't help it.

VINCE'S VOICE It's not all that funny.

SHELLY'S VOICE I know it's not. I'm sorry.

VINCE'S VOICE I mean this is a tense situation for me! I haven't seen them for over six years. I don't know what to expect.

60 SHELLY'S VOICE I know. I won't do it again.

VINCE'S VOICE Can't you bite your tongue or something?

SHELLY'S VOICE Just don't say "Grandma," okay? [*She giggles, stops.*] I mean if you say "Grandma" I don't know if I can stop myself.

VINCE'S VOICE Well try!

65 SHELLY'S VOICE Okay. Sorry.

[*Door opens again.* VINCE *sticks his head in then enters.* SHELLY *follows behind him.* VINCE *crosses to staircase, sets down saxophone case and overcoat, looks up staircase.* SHELLY *notices* DODGE's *baseball cap. Crosses to it. Picks it up and puts it on her head.* VINCE *goes up the stairs and disappears at the top.* SHELLY *watches him then turns and sees* DODGE *on the sofa. She takes off the baseball cap.*]

VINCE'S VOICE [*from above stairs*] Grandma!

[SHELLY *crosses over to* DODGE *slowly and stands next to him. She stands at his head, reaches out slowly and touches one of the cuts. The second she touches his head,* DODGE *jerks up to a sitting position on the sofa, eyes open.* SHELLY *gasps.* DODGE *looks at her, sees his cap in her hands, quickly puts his hand to his bare head. He glares at* SHELLY *then whips the cap out of her hands and puts it on.* SHELLY *backs away from him.* DODGE *stares at her.*]

SHELLY I'm uh—with Vince.

[DODGE *just glares at her.*]

SHELLY He's upstairs.

[DODGE *looks at the staircase then back to* SHELLY.]

SHELLY [*calling upstairs*] Vince!

70 VINCE'S VOICE Just a second!

SHELLY You better get down here!

VINCE'S VOICE Just a minute! I'm looking at the pictures.

[DODGE *keeps staring at her.*]

SHELLY [*to* DODGE] We just got here. Pouring rain on the freeway so we thought we'd stop by. I mean Vince was planning on stopping anyway. He
75 wanted to see you. He said he hadn't seen you in a long time.

[*Pause.* DODGE *just keeps staring at her.*]

SHELLY We were going all the way through to New Mexico. To see his father.
I guess his father lives out there. We thought we'd stop by and see you on
the way. Kill two birds with one stone, you know? [*She laughs,* DODGE
stares, she stops laughing.] I mean Vince has this thing about his family

80 now. I guess it's a new thing with him. I kind of find it hard to relate to. But
he feels it's important. You know. I mean he feels he wants to get to know
you all again. After all this time.

[*Pause.* DODGE *just stares at her. She moves nervously to staircase and
yells up to* VINCE.]

SHELLY Vince will you come down here please!

[VINCE *comes halfway down the stairs.*]

VINCE I guess they went out for a while.

[SHELLY *points to sofa and* DODGE. VINCE *turns and sees* DODGE. *He
comes all the way down staircase and crosses to* DODGE. SHELLY *stays
behind near staircase, keeping her distance.*]

85 VINCE Grandpa?

[DODGE *looks up at him, not recognizing him.*]

DODGE Did you bring the whiskey?

[VINCE *looks back at* SHELLY *then back to* DODGE.]

VINCE Grandpa, it's Vince. I'm Vince. Tilden's son. You remember?

[DODGE *stares at him.*]

DODGE You didn't do what you told me. You didn't stay here with me.

VINCE Grandpa, I haven't been here until just now. I just got here.

90 DODGE You left. You went outside like we told you not to do. You went out
there in back. In the rain.

[VINCE *looks back at* SHELLY. *She moves slowly toward sofa.*]

SHELLY Is he okay?

VINCE I don't know. [*Takes off his shades.*] Look, Grandpa, don't you remember me? Vince. Your Grandson.

[DODGE *stares at him then takes off his baseball cap.*]

95 DODGE [*points to his head*] See what happens when you leave me alone? See
that? That's what happens.

[VINCE *looks at his head.* VINCE *reaches out to touch his head.* DODGE
slaps his hand away with the cap and puts it back on his head.]

VINCE What's going on Grandpa? Where's Halie?

DODGE Don't worry about her. She won't be back for days. She says she'll be
back but she won't be. [*He starts laughing.*] There's life in the old girl yet!
[*Stops laughing.*]

100 VINCE How did you do that to your head?

DODGE I didn't do it! Don't be ridiculous!

VINCE Well who did then?

[*Pause.* DODGE *stares at* VINCE.]

DODGE Who do you think did it? Who do you think?

[SHELLY *moves toward* VINCE.]

SHELLY Vince, maybe we oughta' go. I don't like this. I mean this isn't my

105 idea of a good time.

VINCE [*to* SHELLY]   Just a second. [*To* DODGE] Grandpa, look, I just got here. I just now got here. I haven't been here for six years. I don't know anything that's happened.

[*Pause.* DODGE *stares at him.*]

DODGE   You don't know anything?

110 VINCE   No.

DODGE   Well that's good. That's good. It's much better not to know anything. Much, much better.

VINCE   Isn't there anybody here with you?

[DODGE *turns slowly and looks off to stage left.*]

DODGE   Tilden's here.

115 VINCE   No, Grandpa, Tilden's in New Mexico. That's where I was going. I'm going out there to see him.

[DODGE *turns slowly back to* VINCE.]

DODGE   Tilden's here.

[VINCE *backs away and joins* SHELLY. DODGE *stares at them.*]

SHELLY   Vince, why don't we spend the night in a motel and come back in the morning? We could have breakfast. Maybe everything would be
120 different.

VINCE   Don't be scared. There's nothing to be scared of. He's just old.

SHELLY   I'm not scared!

DODGE   You two are not my idea of the perfect couple!

SHELLY [*after pause*]   Oh really? Why's that?

125 VINCE   Shh! Don't aggravate him.

DODGE   There's something wrong between the two of you. Something not compatible.

VINCE   Grandpa, where did Halie go? Maybe we should call her.

DODGE   What are you talking about? Do you know what you're talking
130 about? Are you just talking for the sake of talking? Lubricating the gums?

VINCE   I'm trying to figure out what's going on here!

DODGE   Is that it?

VINCE   Yes. I mean I expected everything to be different.

135 DODGE   Who are you to expect anything? Who are you supposed to be?

VINCE   I'm Vince! Your Grandson!

DODGE   Vince. My Grandson.

VINCE   Tilden's son.

DODGE   Tilden's son, Vince.

140 VINCE   You haven't seen me for a long time.

DODGE   When was the last time?

VINCE   I don't remember.

DODGE   You don't remember?

VINCE   No.

145 DODGE   You don't remember. How am I supposed to remember if you don't remember?

SHELLY   Vince, come on. This isn't going to work out.

VINCE [*to* SHELLY]   Just take it easy.

SHELLY   I'm taking it easy! He doesn't even know who you are!

150 VINCE [*crossing toward* DODGE]   Grandpa, look—

DODGE   Stay where you are! Keep your distance!

[VINCE *stops. Looks back at* SHELLY *then to* DODGE.]

SHELLY   Vince, this is really making me nervous. I mean he doesn't even want us here. He doesn't even like us.

DODGE   She's a beautiful girl.

155 VINCE   Thanks.

DODGE   Very Beautiful Girl.

SHELLY   Oh my God.

DODGE [*to* SHELLY]   What's your name?

SHELLY   Shelly.

160 DODGE   Shelly. That's a man's name isn't it?

SHELLY   Not in this case.

DODGE [*to* VINCE]   She's a smart-ass too.

SHELLY   Vince! Can we go?

DODGE   She wants to go. She just got here and she wants to go.

165 VINCE   This is kind of strange for her.

DODGE   She'll get used to it. [*To* SHELLY] What part of the country do you come from?

SHELLY   Originally?

DODGE   That's right. Originally. At the very start.

170 SHELLY   L.A.

DODGE   L.A. Stupid country.

SHELLY   I can't stand this Vince! This is really unbelievable!

DODGE   It's stupid! L.A. is stupid! So is Florida! All those Sunshine States. They're all stupid. Do you know why they're stupid?

175 SHELLY   Illuminate me.

DODGE   I'll tell you why. Because they're full of smart-asses! That's why.

[SHELLY *turns her back to* DODGE, *crosses to staircase and sits on bottom step.*]

DODGE [*to* VINCE]   Now she's insulted.

VINCE   Well you weren't very polite.

DODGE   She's insulted! Look at her! In my house she's insulted! She's over
180   there sulking because I insulted her!

SHELLY [*to* VINCE]   This is really terrific. This is wonderful. And you were worried about me making the right first impression!

DODGE [*to* VINCE]   She's a fireball isn't she? Regular fireball. I had some a' them in my day. Temporary stuff. Never lasted more than a week.

185 VINCE   Grandpa—

DODGE   Stop calling me Grandpa will ya'! It's sickening. "Grandpa." I'm nobody's Grandpa!

[DODGE *starts feeling around under the cushion for the bottle of whiskey.* SHELLY *gets up from the staircase.*]

SHELLY [*to* VINCE]   Maybe you've got the wrong house. Did you ever think of that? Maybe this is the wrong address!

190 VINCE   It's not the wrong address! I recognize the yard.

SHELLY   Yeah but do you recognize the people? He says he's not your Grandfather.

DODGE [*digging for bottle*]   Where's that bottle!

VINCE   He's just sick or something. I don't know what's happened to him.

195 DODGE   Where's my goddamn bottle!

> [DODGE *gets up from sofa and starts tearing the cushions off it and throwing them downstage, looking for the whiskey.*]

SHELLY   Can't we just drive on to New Mexico? This is terrible, Vince! I don't want to stay here. In this house. I thought it was going to be turkey dinners and apple pie and all that kinda stuff.

VINCE   Well I hate to disappoint you!

200 SHELLY   I'm not disappointed! I'm fuckin' terrified! I wanna' go!

> [DODGE *yells toward stage left.*]

DODGE   Tilden! Tilden!

> [DODGE *keeps ripping away at the sofa looking for his bottle, he knocks over the night stand with the bottles.* VINCE *and* SHELLY *watch as he starts ripping the stuffing out of the sofa.*]

VINCE [*to* SHELLY]   He's lost his mind or something. I've got to try to help him.

SHELLY   You help him! I'm leaving!

> [SHELLY *starts to leave.* VINCE *grabs her. They struggle as* DODGE *keeps ripping away at the sofa and yelling.*]

DODGE   Tilden! Tilden get your ass in here! Tilden!

205 SHELLY   Let go of me!

VINCE   You're not going anywhere! You're going to stay right here!

SHELLY   Let go of me you sonuvabitch! I'm not your property!

> [*Suddenly* TILDEN *walks on from stage left just as he did before. This time his arms are full of carrots.* DODGE, VINCE, *and* SHELLY *stop suddenly when they see him. They all stare at* TILDEN *as he crosses slowly center stage with the carrots and stops.* DODGE *sits on sofa, exhausted.*]

DODGE [*panting, to* TILDEN]   Where in the hell have you been?

TILDEN   Out back.

210 DODGE   Where's my bottle?

TILDEN   Gone.

> [TILDEN *and* VINCE *stare at each other.* SHELLY *backs away.*]

DODGE [*to* TILDEN]   You stole my bottle!

VINCE [*to* TILDEN]   Dad?

> [TILDEN *just stares at* VINCE.]

DODGE   You had no right to steal my bottle! No right at all!

215 VINCE [*to* TILDEN]   It's Vince. I'm Vince.

> [TILDEN *stares at* VINCE *then looks at* DODGE *then turns to* SHELLY.]

TILDEN [*after pause*]   I picked these carrots. If anybody wants any carrots, I picked 'em.

SHELLY [*to* VINCE]   This is your father?

VINCE [*to* TILDEN]   Dad, what're you doing here?

> [TILDEN *just stares at* VINCE, *holding carrots,* DODGE *pulls the blanket back over himself.*]

220 DODGE [*to* TILDEN]   You're going to have to get me another bottle! You gotta get me a bottle before Halie comes back! There's money on the table. [*Points to stage left kitchen.*]

TILDEN [*shaking his head*]   I'm not going down there. Into town.

> [SHELLY *crosses to* TILDEN. TILDEN *stares at her.*]

SHELLY [*to* TILDEN]   Are you Vince's father?

TILDEN [*to* SHELLY]   Vince?

225 SHELLY [*pointing to* VINCE]   This is supposed to be your son! Is he your son? Do you recognize him! I'm just along for the ride here. I thought everybody knew each other!

> [TILDEN *stares at* VINCE. DODGE *wraps himself up in the blanket and sits on sofa staring at the floor.*]

TILDEN   I had a son once but we buried him.

> [DODGE *quickly looks at* TILDEN. SHELLY *looks to* VINCE.]

DODGE   You shut up about that! You don't know anything about that!

230 VINCE   Dad, I thought you were in New Mexico. We were going to drive down there and see you.

TILDEN   Long way to drive.

DODGE [*to* TILDEN]   You don't know anything about that! That happened before you were born! Long before!

235 VINCE   What's happened, Dad? What's going on here? I thought everything was all right. What's happened to Halie?

TILDEN   She left.

SHELLY [*to* TILDEN]   Do you want me to take those carrots for you?

> [TILDEN *stares at her. She moves in close to him. Holds out her arms.* TILDEN *stares at her arms then slowly dumps the carrots into her arms.* SHELLY *stands there holding the carrots.*]

TILDEN [*to* SHELLY]   You like carrots?

240 SHELLY   Sure. I like all kinds of vegetables.

DODGE [*to* TILDEN]   You gotta get me a bottle before Halie comes back!

> [DODGE *hits sofa with his fist.* VINCE *crosses up to* DODGE *and tries to console him.* SHELLY *and* TILDEN *stay facing each other.*]

TILDEN [*to* SHELLY]   Backyard's full of carrots. Corn. Potatoes.

SHELLY   You're Vince's father, right?

TILDEN   All kinds of vegetables. You like vegetables?

245 SHELLY [*laughs*]   Yeah. I love vegetables.

TILDEN   We could cook these carrots ya' know. You could cut 'em up and we could cook 'em.

SHELLY   All right.

TILDEN   I'll get you a pail and a knife.

250 SHELLY   Okay.

TILDEN   I'll be right back. Don't go.

> [TILDEN *exits offstage left.* SHELLY *stands center, arms full of carrots.* VINCE *stands next to* DODGE. SHELLY *looks toward* VINCE *then down at the carrots.*]

DODGE [*to* VINCE]   You could get me a bottle. [*Pointing off left*] There's money on the table.

VINCE   Grandpa why don't you lay down for a while?

255 DODGE   I don't wanna lay down for a while! Every time I lay down something happens! [*Whips off his cap, points at his head.*] Look what happens! That's what happens! [*Pulls his cap back on.*] You go lie down and see what happens to you! See how you like it! They'll steal your bottle! They'll cut your hair! They'll murder your children! That's what'll happen.

260 VINCE   Just relax for a while.

DODGE [*pause*]   You could get me a bottle ya' know. There's nothing stopping you from getting me a bottle.

SHELLY   Why don't you get him a bottle, Vince? Maybe it would help everybody identify each other.

265 DODGE [*pointing to* SHELLY]   There, see? She thinks you should get me a bottle.

[VINCE *crosses to* SHELLY.]

VINCE   What're you doing with those carrots.

SHELLY   I'm waiting for your father.

DODGE   She thinks you should get me a bottle!

VINCE   Shelly put the carrots down will ya'! We gotta deal with the situation
270 here! I'm gonna need your help.

SHELLY   I'm helping.

VINCE   You're only adding to the problem! You're making things worse! Put
the carrots down!

[VINCE *tries to knock the carrots out of her arms. She turns away from
him, protecting the carrots.*]

SHELLY   Get away from me! Stop it!

[VINCE *stands back from her. She turns to him still holding the carrots.*]

275 VINCE [*to* SHELLY]   Why are you doing this! Are you trying to make fun of
me? This is my family you know!

SHELLY   You coulda' fooled me! I'd just as soon not be here myself. I'd just as
soon be a thousand miles from here. I'd rather be anywhere but here.
You're the one who wants to stay. So I'll stay. I'll stay and I'll cut the carrots.
280 And I'll cook the carrots. And I'll do whatever I have to do to survive. Just
to make it through this.

VINCE   Put the carrots down Shelly.

[TILDEN *enters from left with pail, milking stool, and a knife. He sets the
stool and pail center stage for* SHELLY. SHELLY *looks at* VINCE *then sits
down on stool, sets the carrots on the floor and takes the knife from* TIL-
DEN. *She looks at* VINCE *again then picks up a carrot, cuts the ends off,
scrapes it and drops it in pail. She repeats this,* VINCE *glares at her. She
smiles.*]

DODGE   She could get me a bottle. She's the type a' girl that could get me a
bottle. Easy. She'd go down there. Slink up to the counter. They'd probably
285 give her two bottles for the price of one. She could do that.

[SHELLY *laughs. Keeps cutting carrots.* VINCE *crosses up to* DODGE, *looks
at him.* TILDEN *watches* SHELLY's *hands. Long pause.*]

VINCE [*to* DODGE]   I haven't changed that much. I mean physically. Physically I'm just about the same. Same size. Same weight. Everything's the
same.

[DODGE *keeps staring at* SHELLY *while* VINCE *talks to him.*]

DODGE   She's a beautiful girl. Exceptional.

[VINCE *moves in front of* DODGE *to block his view of* SHELLY. DODGE *keeps
craning his head around to see her as* VINCE *demonstrates tricks from his
past.*]

290 VINCE   Look. Look at this. Do you remember this? I used to bend my thumb
behind my knuckles. You remember? I used to do it at the dinner table.

[VINCE *bends a thumb behind his knuckles for* DODGE *and holds it out to
him.* DODGE *takes a short glance, then looks back at* SHELLY. VINCE *shifts
position and shows him something else.*]

VINCE   What about this?

[VINCE *curls his lips back and starts drumming on his teeth with his fingernails making little tapping sounds.* DODGE *watches a while.* TILDEN *turns toward the sound.* VINCE *keeps it up. He sees* TILDEN *taking notice and crosses to* TILDEN *as he drums on his teeth.* DODGE *turns T.V. on. Watches it.*]

VINCE You remember this Dad?

[VINCE *keeps on drumming for* TILDEN. TILDEN *watches a while, fascinated, then turns back to* SHELLY. VINCE *keeps up the drumming on his teeth, crosses back to* DODGE *doing it.* SHELLY *keeps working on carrots, talking to* TILDEN.]

SHELLY [*to* TILDEN] He drives me crazy with that sometimes.

295 VINCE [*to* DODGE] I know! Here's one you'll remember. You used to kick me out of the house for this one.

[VINCE *pulls his shirt out of his belt and holds it tucked under his chin with his stomach exposed. He grabs the flesh on either side of his belly button and pushes it in and out to make it look like a mouth talking. He watches his belly button and makes a deep-sounding cartoon voice to synchronize with the movement. He demonstrates it to* DODGE, *then crosses down to* TILDEN *doing it. Both* DODGE *and* TILDEN *take short, uninterested glances then ignore him.*]

VINCE [*deep cartoon voice*] "Hello. How are you? I'm fine. Thank you very much. It's so good to see you looking well this fine Sunday morning. I was going down to the hardware store to fetch a pail of water."

300 SHELLY Vince, don't be pathetic will ya'!

[VINCE *stops. Tucks his shirt back in.*]

SHELLY Jesus Christ. They're not gonna play. Can't you see that?

[SHELLY *keeps cutting carrots.* VINCE *slowly moves toward* TILDEN. TILDEN *keeps watching* SHELLY. DODGE *watches T.V.*]

VINCE [*to* SHELLY] I don't get it. I really don't get it. Maybe it's me. Maybe I forgot something.

DODGE [*from sofa*] You forgot to get me a bottle! That's what you forgot. Anybody in this house could get me a bottle. Anybody! But nobody will. Nobody understands the urgency! Peelin' carrots is more important. Playin' piano on your teeth! Well I hope you all remember this when you get up in years. When you find yourself immobilized. Dependent on the whims of others.

[VINCE *moves up toward* DODGE. *Pause as he looks at him.*]

310 VINCE I'll get you a bottle.

DODGE You will?

VINCE Sure.

[SHELLY *stands holding knife and carrot.*]

SHELLY You're not going to leave me here are you?

VINCE [*moving to her*] You suggested it! You said, "why don't I go get him a bottle." So I'll go get him a bottle!

SHELLY But I can't stay here.

VINCE What is going on! A minute ago you were ready to cut carrots all night!

SHELLY That was only if you stayed. Something to keep me busy, so I wouldn't be so nervous. I don't want to stay here alone.

320 DODGE Don't let her talk you out of it! She's a bad influence. I could see it the minute she stepped in here.

SHELLY [*to* DODGE]   You were asleep!

TILDEN [*to* SHELLY]   Don't you want to cut carrots any more?

SHELLY   Sure. Sure I do.

> [SHELLY *sits back down on stool and continues cutting carrots. Pause.* VINCE *moves around, stroking his hair, staring at* DODGE *and* TILDEN. VINCE *and* SHELLY *exchange glances.* DODGE *watches T.V.*]

325 VINCE   Boy! This is amazing. This is truly amazing. [*Keeps moving around.*] What is this anyway? Am I in a time warp or something? Have I committed an unpardonable offence? It's true, I'm not married. [SHELLY *looks at him, then back to carrots.*] But I'm also not divorced. I have been known to plunge into sinful infatuation with the Alto Saxophone. Sucking on num-
330 ber 5 reeds[9] deep into the wee, wee hours.

SHELLY   Vince, what are you doing that for? They don't care about any of that. They just don't recognize you, that's all.

VINCE   How could they not recognize me! How in the hell could they not recognize me! I'm their son!

335 DODGE [*watching T.V.*]   You're no son of mine. I've had sons in my time and you're not one of 'em.

> [*Long pause.* VINCE *stares at* DODGE *then looks at* TILDEN. *He turns to* SHELLY.]

VINCE   Shelly, I gotta go out for a while. I just gotta go out. I'll get a bottle and I'll come right back. You'll be o.k. here. Really.

SHELLY   I don't know if I can handle this, Vince.

340 VINCE   I just gotta think or something. I don't know. I gotta put this all together.

SHELLY   Can't we just go?

VINCE   No! I gotta find out what's going on.

SHELLY   Look, you think you're bad off, what about me? Not only don't they
345 recognize me but I've never seen them before in my life. I don't know who these guys are. They could be anybody!

VINCE   They're not anybody!

SHELLY   That's what you say.

VINCE   They're my family for Christ's sake! I should know who my own fam-
350 ily is! Now give me a break. It won't take that long. I'll just go out and I'll come right back. Nothing'll happen. I promise.

> [SHELLY *stares at him. Pause.*]

SHELLY   All right.

VINCE   Thanks. [*He crosses up to* DODGE.] I'm gonna go out now, Grandpa, and I'll pick you up a bottle. Okay?

355 DODGE   Change of heart huh? [*Pointing off left*] Money's on the table. In the kitchen.

> [VINCE *moves toward* SHELLY.]

VINCE [*to* SHELLY]   You be all right?

SHELLY [*cutting carrots*]   Sure. I'm fine. I'll just keep real busy while you're gone.

> [VINCE *looks at* TILDEN *who keeps staring down at* SHELLY's *hands.*]

---

9. The number assigned to a woodwind reed refers to its hardness (5 is extremely hard).

360 DODGE   Persistence see? That's what it takes. Persistence. Persistence, forti-
tude, and determination. Those are the three virtues. You stick with those
three and you can't go wrong.

VINCE [*to* TILDEN]   You want anything, Dad?

TILDEN [*looks up at* VINCE]   Me?

365 VINCE   From the store? I'm gonna get Grandpa a bottle.

TILDEN   He's not supposed to drink. Halie wouldn't like it.

VINCE   He wants a bottle.

TILDEN   He's not supposed to drink.

DODGE [*to* VINCE]   Don't negotiate with him! Don't make any transactions
370   until you've spoken to me first! He'll steal you blind!

VINCE [*to* DODGE]   Tilden says you're not supposed to drink.

DODGE   Tilden's lost his marbles! Look at him! He's around the bend. Take a
look at him.

   [VINCE *stares at* TILDEN. TILDEN *watches* SHELLY's *hands as she keeps cutting carrots.*]

DODGE   Now look at me. Look here at me!

   [VINCE *looks back to* DODGE.]

375 DODGE   Now, between the two of us, who do you think is more trustworthy?
Him or me? Can you trust a man who keeps bringing in vegetables from
out of nowhere? Take a look at him.

   [VINCE *looks back at* TILDEN.]

SHELLY   Go get the bottle, Vince.

VINCE [*to* SHELLY]   You sure you'll be all right?

380 SHELLY   I'll be fine. I feel right at home now.

VINCE   You do?

SHELLY   I'm fine. Now that I've got the carrots everything is all right.

VINCE   I'll be right back.

   [VINCE *crosses stage left.*]

DODGE   Where are you going?

385 VINCE   I'm going to get the money.

DODGE   Then where are you going?

VINCE   Liquor store.

DODGE   Don't go anyplace else. Don't go off someplace and drink. Come
right back here.

390 VINCE   I will.

   [VINCE *exits stage left.*]

DODGE [*calling after* VINCE]   You've got responsibility now! And don't go out
the back way either! Come out through this way! I wanna' see you when
you leave! Don't go out the back!

VINCE'S VOICE [*off left*]   I won't!

   [DODGE *turns and looks at* TILDEN *and* SHELLY.]

395 DODGE   Untrustworthy. Probably drown himself if he went out the back. Fall
right in a hole. I'd never get my bottle.

SHELLY   I wouldn't worry about Vince. He can take care of himself.

DODGE   Oh he can, huh? Independent.

   [VINCE *comes on again from stage left with two dollars in his hand. He
   crosses stage right past* DODGE.]

DODGE [*to* VINCE]   You got the money?

400 VINCE   Yeah. Two bucks.

DODGE   Two bucks. Two bucks is two bucks. Don't sneer.

VINCE   What kind do you want?

DODGE   Whiskey! Gold Star Sour Mash. Use your own discretion.

VINCE   Okay.

[VINCE *crosses to stage right door. Opens it. Stops when he hears* TILDEN.]

405 TILDEN [*to* VINCE]   You drove all the way from New Mexico?

[VINCE *turns and looks at* TILDEN. *They stare at each other.* VINCE *shakes his head, goes out the door, crosses porch, and exits out screen door.* TILDEN *watches him go. Pause.*]

SHELLY   You really don't recognize him? Either one of you?

[TILDEN *turns again and stares at* SHELLY's *hands as she cuts carrots.*]

DODGE [*watching T.V.*]   Recognize who?

SHELLY   Vince.

DODGE   What's to recognize?

[DODGE *lights a cigarette, coughs slightly, and stares at T.V.*]

410 SHELLY   It'd be cruel if you recognized him and didn't tell him. Wouldn't be fair.

[DODGE *just stares at T.V., smoking.*]

TILDEN   I thought I recognized him. I thought I recognized something about him.

SHELLY   You did?

415 TILDEN   I thought I saw a face inside his face.

SHELLY   Well it was probably that you saw what he used to look like. You haven't seen him for six years.

TILDEN   I haven't?

SHELLY   That's what he says.

[TILDEN *moves around in front of her as she continues with carrots.*]

420 TILDEN   Where was it I saw him last?

SHELLY   I don't know. I've only known him for a few months. He doesn't tell me everything.

TILDEN   He doesn't?

SHELLY   Not stuff like that.

425 TILDEN   What does he tell you?

SHELLY   You mean in general?

TILDEN   Yeah.

[TILDEN *moves around behind her.*]

SHELLY   Well he tells me all kinds of things.

TILDEN   Like what?

430 SHELLY   I don't know! I mean I can't just come right out and tell you how he feels.

TILDEN   How come?

[TILDEN *keeps moving around her slowly in a circle.*]

SHELLY   Because it's stuff he told me privately!

TILDEN   And you can't tell me?

435 SHELLY   I don't even know you!

DODGE   Tilden, go out in the kitchen and make me some coffee! Leave the girl alone.

SHELLY [*to* DODGE]   He's all right.

[TILDEN *ignores* DODGE, *keeps moving around* SHELLY. *He stares at her hair and coat.* DODGE *stares at T.V.*]

TILDEN   You mean you can't tell me anything?

440 SHELLY   I can tell you some things. I mean we can have a conversation.

TILDEN   We can?

SHELLY   Sure. We're having a conversation right now.

TILDEN   We are?

SHELLY   Yes. That's what we're doing.

445 TILDEN   But there's certain things you can't tell me, right?

SHELLY   Right.

TILDEN   There's certain things I can't tell you either.

SHELLY   How come?

TILDEN   I don't know. Nobody's supposed to hear it.

450 SHELLY   Well, you can tell me anything you want to.

TILDEN   I can?

SHELLY   Sure.

TILDEN   It might not be very nice.

SHELLY   That's all right. I've been around.

455 TILDEN   It might be awful.

SHELLY   Well, can't you tell me anything nice?

[TILDEN *stops in front of her and stares at her coat.* SHELLY *looks back at him. Long pause.*]

TILDEN [*after pause*] Can I touch your coat?

SHELLY   My coat? [*She looks at her coat then back to* TILDEN.] Sure.

TILDEN   You don't mind?

460 SHELLY   No. Go ahead.

[SHELLY *holds her arm out for* TILDEN *to touch.* DODGE *stays fixed on T.V.* TILDEN *moves in slowly toward* SHELLY, *staring at her arm. He reaches out very slowly and touches her arm, feels the fur gently then draws his hand back.* SHELLY *keeps her arm out.*]

SHELLY   It's rabbit.

TILDEN   Rabbit.

[*He reaches out again very slowly and touches the fur on her arm then pulls back his hand again.* SHELLY *drops her arm.*]

SHELLY   My arm was getting tired.

TILDEN   Can I hold it?

465 SHELLY [*pause*] The coat? Sure.

[SHELLY *takes off her coat and hands it to* TILDEN. TILDEN *takes it slowly, feels the fur, then puts it on.* SHELLY *watches as* TILDEN *strokes the fur slowly. He smiles at her. She goes back to cutting carrots.*]

SHELLY   You can have it if you want.

TILDEN   I can?

SHELLY   Yeah. I've got a raincoat in the car. That's all I need.

TILDEN   You've got a car?

470 SHELLY   Vince does.

[TILDEN *walks around stroking the fur and smiling at the coat.* SHELLY *watches him when he's not looking.* DODGE *sticks with T.V., stretches out on sofa wrapped in blanket.*]

TILDEN [*as he walks around*] I had a car once! I had a white car! I drove. I went everywhere. I went to the mountains. I drove in the snow.

SHELLY   That must've been fun.

TILDEN [*still moving, feeling coat*]   I drove all day long sometimes. Across the
475   desert. Way out across the desert. I drove past towns. Anywhere. Past palm
       trees. Lightning. Anything. I would drive through it. I would drive through
       it and I would stop and I would look around and I would drive on. I would
       get back in and drive! I loved to drive. There was nothing I loved more.
       Nothing I dreamed of was better than driving.

480   DODGE [*eyes on T.V.*]   Pipe down would ya'!

[TILDEN *stops. Stares at* SHELLY.]

SHELLY   Do you do much driving now?

TILDEN   Now? Now? I don't drive now.

SHELLY   How come?

TILDEN   I'm grown up now.

485   SHELLY   Grown up?

TILDEN   I'm not a kid.

SHELLY   You don't have to be a kid to drive.

TILDEN   It wasn't driving then.

SHELLY   What was it?

490   TILDEN   Adventure. I went everywhere.

SHELLY   Well you can still do that.

TILDEN   Not now.

SHELLY   Why not?

TILDEN   I just told you. You don't understand anything. If I told you some-
495   thing you wouldn't understand it.

SHELLY   Told me what?

TILDEN   Told you something that's true.

SHELLY   Like what?

TILDEN   Like a baby. Like a little tiny baby.

500   SHELLY   Like when you were little?

TILDEN   If I told you you'd make me give your coat back.

SHELLY   I won't. I promise. Tell me.

TILDEN   I can't. Dodge won't let me.

SHELLY   He won't hear you. It's okay.

[*Pause.* TILDEN *stares at her. Moves slightly toward her.*]

505   TILDEN   We had a baby. [*Motioning to* DODGE] He did. Dodge did. Could pick
       it up with one hand. Put it in the other. Little baby. Dodge killed it.

[SHELLY *stands.*]

TILDEN   Don't stand up. Don't stand up!

[SHELLY *sits again.* DODGE *sits up on sofa and looks at them.*]

TILDEN   Dodge drowned it.

SHELLY   Don't tell me any more! Okay?

[TILDEN *moves closer to her.* DODGE *takes more interest.*]

510   DODGE   Tilden? You leave that girl alone!

TILDEN [*pays no attention*]   Never told Halie. Never told anybody. Just
       drowned it.

DODGE [*shuts off T.V.*]   Tilden!

TILDEN   Nobody could find it. Just disappeared. Cops looked for it. Neigh-
515   bors. Nobody could find it.

[DODGE *struggles to get up from sofa.*]

DODGE   Tilden, what're you telling her! Tilden!

[DODGE SHELLY. *keeps struggling until he's standing.*]

TILDEN   Finally everybody just gave up. Just stopped looking. Everybody had a different answer. Kidnap. Murder. Accident. Some kind of accident.

[DODGE *struggles to walk toward* TILDEN *and falls.* TILDEN *ignores him.*]

DODGE   Tilden you shut up! You shut up about it!

[DODGE *starts coughing on the floor.* SHELLY *watches him from the stool.*]

520   TILDEN   Little tiny baby just disappeared. It's not hard. It's so small. Almost invisible.

[SHELLY *makes a move to help* DODGE. TILDEN *firmly pushes her back down on the stool.* DODGE *keeps coughing.*]

TILDEN   He said he had his reasons. Said it went a long way back. But he wouldn't tell anybody.

DODGE   Tilden! Don't tell her anything! Don't tell her!

525   TILDEN   He's the only one who knows where it's buried. The only one. Like a secret buried treasure. Won't tell any of us. Won't tell me or mother or even Bradley. Especially Bradley. Bradley tried to force it out of him but he wouldn't tell. Wouldn't even tell why he did it. One night he just did it.

[DODGE's *coughing subsides.* SHELLY *stays on stool staring at* DODGE. TILDEN *slowly takes* SHELLY's *coat off and holds it out to her. Long pause.* SHELLY *sits there trembling.*]

TILDEN   You probably want your coat back now.

[SHELLY *stares at coat but doesn't move to take it. The sound of* BRADLEY's *leg squeaking is heard off left. The others onstage remain still.* BRADLEY *appears up left outside the screen door wearing a yellow rain slicker. He enters through screen door, crosses porch to stage right door and enters stage. Closes door. Takes off rain slicker and shakes it out. He sees all the others and stops.* TILDEN *turns to him.* BRADLEY *stares at* SHELLY. DODGE *remains on floor.*]

530   BRADLEY   What's going on here? [*Motioning to* SHELLY] Who's that?

[SHELLY *stands, moves back away from* BRADLEY *as he crosses toward her. He stops next to* TILDEN. *He sees coat in* TILDEN's *hand and grabs it away from him.*]

BRADLEY   Who's she supposed to be?

TILDEN   She's driving to New Mexico.

[BRADLEY *stares at her.* SHELLY *is frozen.* BRADLEY *limps over to her with the coat in his fist. He stops in front of her.*]

BRADLEY [*to* SHELLY, *after pause*]   Vacation?

[SHELLY *shakes her head "no," trembling.*]

BRADLEY [*to* SHELLY, *motioning to* TILDEN]   You taking him with you?

[SHELLY *shakes her head "no."* BRADLEY *crosses back to* TILDEN.]

535   BRADLEY   You oughta'. No use leaving him here. Doesn't do a lick a' work. Doesn't raise a finger. [*Stopping, to* TILDEN] Do ya'? [*To* SHELLY] 'Course he used to be an All-American. Quarterback or Fullback or somethin'. He tell you that?

[SHELLY *shakes her head "no."*]

BRADLEY   Yeah, he used to be a big deal. Wore lettermen's sweaters. Had
540   medals hanging all around his neck. Real purty. Big deal. [*He laughs to him-*

self, notices DODGE *on floor, crosses to him, stops.*] This one too. [*To* SHELLY] You'd never think it to look at him would ya'? All bony and wasted away.

[SHELLY *shakes her head again.* BRADLEY *stares at her, crosses back to her, clenching the coat in his fist. He stops in front of* SHELLY.]

BRADLEY   Women like that kinda' thing don't they?

SHELLY   What?

545 BRADLEY   Importance. Importance in a man?

SHELLY   I don't know.

BRADLEY   Yeah. You know, you know. Don't give me that. [*Moves closer to* SHELLY.] You're with Tilden?

SHELLY   No.

550 BRADLEY   [*turning to* TILDEN]   Tilden! She with you?

[TILDEN *doesn't answer. Stares at floor.*]

BRADLEY   Tilden!

[TILDEN *suddenly bolts and runs off up stage left.* BRADLEY *laughs. Talks to* SHELLY. DODGE *starts moving his lips silently as though talking to someone invisible on the floor.*]

BRADLEY   [*laughing*]   Scared to death! He was always scared!

[BRADLEY *stops laughing. Stares at* SHELLY.]

BRADLEY   You're scared too, right? [*Laughs again.*] You're scared and you don't even know me. [*Stops laughing.*] You don't gotta be scared.

[SHELLY *looks at* DODGE *on the floor.*]

555 SHELLY   Can't we do something for him?

BRADLEY   [*looking at* DODGE]   We could shoot him. [*Laughs.*] We could drown him! What about drowning him?

SHELLY   Shut up!

[BRADLEY *stops laughing. Moves in closer to* SHELLY. *She freezes.* BRADLEY *speaks slowly and deliberately.*]

BRADLEY   Hey! Missus. Don't talk to me like that. Don't talk to me in that
560 tone a' voice. There was a time when I had to take that tone a' voice from pretty near everyone. [*Motioning to* DODGE] Him, for one! Him and that half brain that just ran outa' here. They don't talk to me like that now. Not any more. Everything's turned around now. Full circle. Isn't that funny?

SHELLY   I'm sorry.

565 BRADLEY   Open your mouth.

SHELLY   What?

BRADLEY   [*motioning for her to open her mouth*]   Open up.

[*She opens her mouth slightly.*]

BRADLEY   Wider.

[*She opens her mouth wider.*]

BRADLEY   Keep it like that.

[*She does. Stares at* BRADLEY. *With his free hand he puts his fingers into her mouth. She tries to pull away.*]

570 BRADLEY   Just stay put!

[*She freezes. He keeps his fingers in her mouth. Stares at her. Pause. He pulls his hand out. She closes her mouth, keeps her eyes on him.* BRAD-LEY *smiles. He looks at* DODGE *on the floor and crosses over to him.* SHELLY *watches him closely.* BRADLEY *stands over* DODGE *and smiles at*

SHELLY. *He holds her coat up in both hands over* DODGE, *keeps smiling at* SHELLY. *He looks down at* DODGE *then drops the coat so that it lands on* DODGE *and covers his head.* BRADLEY *keeps his hands up in the position of holding the coat, looks over at* SHELLY *and smiles. The lights black out.*]

Act 3

SCENE: *Same set. Morning. Bright sun. No sound of rain. Everything has been cleared up again. No sign of carrots. No pail. No stool.* VINCE'S *saxophone case and overcoat are still at the foot of the staircase.* BRADLEY *is asleep on the sofa under* DODGE'S *blanket. His head toward stage left.* BRADLEY'S *wooden leg is leaning against the sofa right by his head. The shoe is left on it. The harness hangs down.* DODGE *is sitting on the floor, propped up against the T.V. set facing stage left wearing his baseball cap.* SHELLY'S *rabbit fur coat covers his chest and shoulders. He stares off toward stage left. He seems weaker and more disoriented. The lights rise slowly to the sound of birds and remain for a while in silence on the two men.* BRADLEY *sleeps very soundly.* DODGE *hardly moves.* SHELLY *appears from stage left with a big smile, slowly crossing toward* DODGE *balancing a steaming cup of broth in a saucer.* DODGE *just stares at her as she gets closer to him.*

SHELLY [*as she crosses*]   This is going to make all the difference in the world, Grandpa. You don't mind me calling you Grandpa do you? I mean I know you minded when Vince called you that but you don't even know him.

DODGE   He skipped town with my money ya' know. I'm gonna hold you as
5   collateral.

SHELLY   He'll be back. Don't you worry.

[*She kneels down next to* DODGE *and puts the cup and saucer in his lap.*]

DODGE   It's morning already! Not only didn't I get my bottle but he's got my two bucks!

SHELLY   Try to drink this, okay? Don't spill it.

10 DODGE   What is it?

SHELLY   Beef bouillon. It'll warm you up.

DODGE   Bouillon! I don't want any goddamn bouillon! Get that stuff away from me!

SHELLY   I just got through making it.

15 DODGE   I don't care if you just spent all week making it! I ain't drinking it!

SHELLY   Well, what am I supposed to do with it then? I'm trying to help you out. Besides, it's good for you.

DODGE   Get it away from me!

[SHELLY *stands up with cup and saucer.*]

DODGE   What do you know what's good for me anyway?

[*She looks at* DODGE *then turns away from him, crossing to staircase, sits on bottom step and drinks the bouillon.* DODGE *stares at her.*]

20 DODGE   You know what'd be good for me?

SHELLY   What?

DODGE   A little massage. A little contact.

SHELLY   Oh no. I've had enough contact for a while. Thanks anyway.

[*She keeps sipping bouillon, stays sitting. Pause as* DODGE *stares at her.*]

DODGE   Why not? You got nothing better to do. That fella's not gonna be back
25   here. You're not expecting him to show up again are you?

SHELLY   Sure. He'll show up. He left his horn here.

DODGE   His horn? [*Laughs.*] You're his horn!

SHELLY   Very funny.

DODGE   He's run off with my money? He's not coming back here.

30 SHELLY   He'll be back.

DODGE   You're a funny chicken, you know that?

SHELLY   Thanks.

DODGE   Full of faith. Hope. Faith and hope. You're all alike you hopers. If it's not God then it's a man. If it's not a man then it's a woman. If it's not a

35   woman then it's the land or the future of some kind. Some kind of future.

[*Pause.*]

SHELLY [*looking toward porch*]   I'm glad it stopped raining.

DODGE [*looks toward porch then back to her*]   That's what I mean. See, you're glad it stopped raining. Now you think everything's gonna be different. Just 'cause the sun comes out.

40 SHELLY   It's already different. Last night I was scared.

DODGE   Scared a' what?

SHELLY   Just scared.

DODGE   Bradley? [*Looks at* BRADLEY.] He's a pushover. 'Specially now. All ya' gotta' do is take his leg and throw it out the back door. Helpless. Totally

45   helpless.

[SHELLY *turns and stares at* BRADLEY's *wooden leg then looks at* DODGE. *She sips bouillon.*]

SHELLY   You'd do that?

DODGE   Me? I've hardly got the strength to breathe.

SHELLY   But you'd actually do it if you could?

DODGE   Don't be so easily shocked, girlie. There's nothing a man can't do.

50   You dream it up and he can do it. Anything.

SHELLY   You've tried I guess.

DODGE   Don't sit there sippin' your bouillon and judging me! This is my house!

SHELLY   I forgot.

DODGE   You forgot? Whose house did you think it was?

55 SHELLY   Mine.

[DODGE *just stares at her. Long pause. She sips from cup.*]

SHELLY   I know it's not mine but I had that feeling.

DODGE   What feeling?

SHELLY   The feeling that nobody lives here but me. I mean everybody's gone. You're here, but it doesn't seem like you're supposed to be. [*Pointing to*

60   BRADLEY] Doesn't seem like he's supposed to be here either. I don't know what it is. It's the house or something. Something familiar. Like I know my way around here. Did you ever get that feeling?

[DODGE *stares at her in silence. Pause.*]

DODGE   No. No, I never did.

[SHELLY *gets up. Moves around space holding cup.*]

SHELLY   Last night I went to sleep up there in that room.

65 DODGE   What room?

SHELLY   That room up there with all the pictures. All the crosses on the wall.

DODGE   Halie's room?

SHELLY Yeah. Whoever "Halie" is.

DODGE She's my wife.

70 SHELLY So you remember her?

DODGE Whad'ya mean! 'Course I remember her! She's only been gone for a day—half a day. However long it's been.

SHELLY Do you remember her when her hair was bright red? Standing in front of an apple tree?

75 DODGE What is this, the third degree or something! Who're you to be askin' me personal questions about my wife!

SHELLY You never look at those pictures up there?

DODGE What pictures!

SHELLY Your whole life's up there hanging on the wall. Somebody who looks 80 just like you. Somebody who looks just like you used to look.

DODGE That isn't me! That never was me! This is me. Right here. This is it. The whole shootin' match, sittin' right in front of you.

SHELLY So the past never happened as far as you're concerned?

DODGE The past? Jesus Christ. The past. What do you know about the past?

85 SHELLY Not much. I know there was a farm.

[*Pause.*]

DODGE A farm?

SHELLY There's a picture of a farm. A big farm. A bull. Wheat. Corn.

DODGE Corn?

SHELLY All the kids are standing out in the corn. They're all waving these big 90 straw hats. One of them doesn't have a hat.

DODGE Which one was that?

SHELLY There's a baby. A baby in a woman's arms. The same woman with the red hair. She looks lost standing out there. Like she doesn't know how she got there.

95 DODGE She knows! I told her a hundred times it wasn't gonna' be the city! I gave her plenty a' warning.

SHELLY She's looking down at the baby like it was somebody else's. Like it didn't even belong to her.

DODGE That's about enough outa' you! You got some funny ideas. Some 100 damn funny ideas. You think just because people propagate they have to love their offspring? You never seen a bitch eat her puppies? Where are you from anyway?

SHELLY L.A. We already went through that.

DODGE That's right, L.A. I remember.

105 SHELLY Stupid country.

DODGE That's right! No wonder.

[*Pause.*]

SHELLY What's happened to this family anyway?

DODGE You're in no position to ask! What do you care? You some kinda' Social Worker?

110 SHELLY I'm Vince's friend.

DODGE Vince's friend! That's rich. That's really rich. "Vince"! "Mr. Vince"! "Mr. Thief" is more like it! His name doesn't mean a hoot in hell to me. Not a tinkle in the well. You know how many kids I've spawned? Not to mention Grand kids and Great Grand kids and Great Great Grand kids after them?

115 SHELLY   And you don't remember any of them?

DODGE   What's to remember? Halie's the one with the family album. She's the one you should talk to. She'll set you straight on the heritage if that's what you're interested in. She's traced it all the way back to the grave.

SHELLY   What do you mean?

120 DODGE   What do you think I mean? How far back can you go? A long line of corpses! There's not a living soul behind me. Not a one. Who's holding me in their memory? Who gives a damn about bones in the ground?

SHELLY   Was Tilden telling the truth?

[DODGE *stops short. Stares at* SHELLY. *Shakes his head. He looks off stage left.*]

SHELLY   Was he?

[DODGE's *tone changes drastically.*]

125 DODGE   Tilden? [*Turns to* SHELLY, *calmly.*] Where is Tilden?

SHELLY   Last night. Was he telling the truth about the baby?

[*Pause.*]

DODGE [*turns toward stage left*]   What's happened to Tilden? Why isn't Tilden here?

SHELLY   Bradley chased him out.

130 DODGE [*looking at* BRADLEY *asleep*]   Bradley? Why is he on my sofa? [*Turns back to* SHELLY.] Have I been here all night? On the floor?

SHELLY   He wouldn't leave. I hid outside until he fell asleep.

DODGE   Outside? Is Tilden outside? He shouldn't be out there in the rain. He'll get himself into trouble. He doesn't know his way around here any
135   more. Not like he used to. He went out West and got himself into trouble. Got himself into bad trouble. We don't want any of that around here.

SHELLY   What did he do?

[*Pause.*]

DODGE [*quietly stares at* SHELLY]   Tilden? He got mixed up. That's what he did. We can't afford to leave him alone. Not now.

[*Sound of* HALIE *laughing comes from off left.* SHELLY *stands, looking in direction of voice, holding cup and saucer, doesn't know whether to stay or run.*]

140 DODGE [*motioning to* SHELLY]   Sit down! Sit back down!

[SHELLY *sits. Sounds of* HALIE's *laughter again.*]

DODGE [*to* SHELLY *in a heavy whisper, pulling coat up around him*]   Don't leave me alone now! Promise me? Don't go off and leave me alone. I need somebody here with me. Tilden's gone now and I need someone. Don't leave me! Promise!

145 SHELLY [*sitting*]   I won't.

[HALIE *appears outside the screen porch door, up left with* FATHER DEWIS. *She is wearing a bright yellow dress, no hat, white gloves and her arms are full of yellow roses.* FATHER DEWIS *is dressed in traditional black suit, white clerical collar, and shirt. He is a very distinguished gray-haired man in his sixties. They are both slightly drunk and feeling giddy. As they enter the porch through the screen door,* DODGE *pulls the rabbit fur coat over his head and hides.* SHELLY *stands again.* DODGE *drops the coat and whispers intensely to* SHELLY. *Neither* HALIE *nor* FATHER DEWIS *are aware of the people inside the house.*]

DODGE [*to* SHELLY *in a strong whisper*]   You promised!

[SHELLY *sits on stairs again.* DODGE *pulls coat back over his head.* HALIE *and* FATHER DEWIS *talk on the porch as they cross toward stage right interior door.*]

HALIE   Oh Father! That's terrible! That's absolutely terrible. Aren't you afraid of being punished?

[*She giggles.*]

DEWIS   Not by the Italians. They're too busy punishing each other.

[*They both break out in giggles.*]

150 HALIE   What about God?

DEWIS   Well, prayerfully, God only hears what he wants to. That's just between you and me of course. In our heart of hearts we know we're every bit as wicked as the Catholics.

[*They giggle again and reach the stage right door.*]

HALIE   Father, I never heard you talk like this in Sunday sermon.

155 DEWIS   Well, I save all my best jokes for private company. Pearls before swine[1] you know.

[*They enter the room laughing and stop when they see* SHELLY. SHELLY *stands.* HALIE *closes the door behind* FATHER DEWIS. DODGE'S *voice is heard under the coat, talking to* SHELLY.]

DODGE [*under coat, to* SHELLY]   Sit down, sit down! Don't let 'em buffalo you!

[SHELLY *sits on stair again.* HALIE *looks at* DODGE *on the floor then looks at* BRADLEY *asleep on sofa and sees his wooden leg. She lets out a shriek of embarrassment for* FATHER DEWIS.]

HALIE   Oh my gracious! What in the name of Judas Priest is going on in this house!

[*She hands over the roses to* FATHER DEWIS.]

160 HALIE   Excuse me Father.

[HALIE *crosses to* DODGE, *whips the coat off him, and covers the wooden leg with it.* BRADLEY *stays asleep.*]

HALIE   You can't leave this house for a second without the Devil blowing in through the front door!

DODGE   Gimme back that coat! Gimmie back that goddamn coat before I freeze to death!

165 HALIE   You're not going to freeze! The sun's out in case you hadn't noticed!

DODGE   Gimme back that coat! That coat's for live flesh not dead wood!

[HALIE *whips the blanket off* BRADLEY *and throws it on* DODGE. DODGE *covers his head again with blanket.* BRADLEY'S *amputated leg can be faked by having half of it under a cushion of the sofa. He's fully clothed.* BRADLEY *sits up with a jerk when the blanket comes off him.*]

HALIE [*as she tosses blanket*]   Here! Use this! It's yours anyway! Can't you take care of yourself for once!

BRADLEY [*yelling at* HALIE]   Gimme that blanket! Gimme back that blanket!

170 That's my blanket!

---

1. See Matthew 7.6: "Give not that which is holy unto the dogs, neither cast ye your pearls before swine, lest they trample them under their feet, and turn again and rend you."

[HALIE *crosses back toward* FATHER DEWIS *who just stands there with the roses.* BRADLEY *thrashes helplessly on the sofa trying to reach blanket.* DODGE *hides himself deeper in blanket.* SHELLY *looks on from staircase, still holding cup and saucer.*]

HALIE   Believe me, Father, this is not what I had in mind when I invited you in.

DEWIS   Oh, no apologies please. I wouldn't be in the ministry if I couldn't face real life.

[*He laughs self-consciously.* HALIE *notices* SHELLY *again and crosses over to her.* SHELLY *stays sitting.* HALIE *stops and stares at her.*]

175   BRADLEY   I want my blanket back! Gimme my blanket!

[HALIE *turns toward* BRADLEY *and silences him.*]

HALIE   Shut up, Bradley! Right this minute! I've had enough!

[BRADLEY *slowly recoils, lies back down on sofa, turns his back toward* HALIE, *and whimpers softly.* HALIE *directs her attention to* SHELLY *again. Pause.*]

HALIE [*to* SHELLY]   What're you doing with my cup and saucer?

SHELLY [*looking at cup, back to* HALIE]   I made some bouillon for Dodge.

HALIE   For Dodge?

180   SHELLY   Yeah.

HALIE   Well, did he drink it?

SHELLY   No.

HALIE   Did you drink it?

SHELLY   Yes.

[HALIE *stares at her. Long pause. She turns abruptly away from* SHELLY *and crosses back to* FATHER DEWIS.]

185   HALIE   Father, there's a stranger in my house. What would you advise? What would be the Christian thing?

DEWIS [*squirming*]   Oh, well. . . . I. . . . I really—

HALIE   We still have some whiskey, don't we?

[DODGE *slowly pulls the blanket down off his head and looks toward* FATHER DEWIS. SHELLY *stands.*]

SHELLY   Listen, I don't drink or anything. I just—

[HALIE *turns toward* SHELLY *viciously.*]

190   HALIE   You sit back down!

[SHELLY *sits again on stair.* HALIE *turns again to* DEWIS.]

HALIE   I think we have plenty of whiskey left! Don't we Father?

DEWIS   Well, yes. I think so. You'll have to get it. My hands are full.

[HALIE *giggles. Reaches into* DEWIS's *pockets, searching for bottle. She smells the roses as she searches.* DEWIS *stands stiffly.* DODGE *watches* HALIE *closely as she looks for bottle.*]

HALIE   The most incredible things, roses! Aren't they incredible, Father?

DEWIS   Yes. Yes they are.

195   HALIE   They almost cover the stench of sin in this house. Just magnificent! The smell. We'll have to put some at the foot of Ansel's statue. On the day of the unveiling.

[HALIE *finds a silver flask of whiskey in* DEWIS's *vest pocket. She pulls it out.* DODGE *looks on eagerly.* HALIE *crosses to* DODGE, *opens the flask, and takes a sip.*]

HALIE [*to* DODGE]   Ansel's getting a statue, Dodge. Did you know that? Not a plaque but a real live statue. A full bronze. Tip to toe. A basketball in one
200   hand and a rifle in the other.

BRADLEY [*his back to* HALIE]   He never played basketball!

HALIE   You shut up, Bradley! You shut up about Ansel! Ansel played basketball better than anyone! And you know it! He was an All-American! There's no reason to take the glory away from others.

> [HALIE *turns away from* BRADLEY, *crosses back toward* DEWIS *sipping on the flask and smiling.*]

205 HALIE [*to* DEWIS]   Ansel was a great basketball player. One of the greatest.

DEWIS   I remember Ansel.

HALIE   Of course! You remember. You remember how he could play. [*She turns toward* SHELLY.] Of course, nowadays they play a different brand of basketball. More vicious. Isn't that right, dear?

210 SHELLY   I don't know.

> [HALIE *crosses to* SHELLY, *sipping on flask. She stops in front of* SHELLY.]

HALIE   Much, much more vicious. They smash into each other. They knock each other's teeth out. There's blood all over the court. Savages.

> [HALIE *takes the cup from* SHELLY *and pours whiskey into it.*]

HALIE   They don't train like they used to. Not at all. They allow themselves to run amuck. Drugs and women. Women mostly.

> [HALIE *hands the cup of whiskey back to* SHELLY *slowly.* SHELLY *takes it.*]

215 HALIE   Mostly women. Girls. Sad, pathetic little girls. [*She crosses back to* FATHER DEWIS.] It's just a reflection of the times, don't you think Father? An indication of where we stand?

DEWIS   I suppose so, yes.

HALIE   Yes. A sort of a bad omen. Our youth becoming monsters.

220 DEWIS   Well, I uh—

HALIE   Oh you can disagree with me if you want to, Father. I'm open to debate. I think argument only enriches both sides of the question don't you? [*She moves toward* DODGE.] I suppose, in the long run, it doesn't matter. When you see the way things deteriorate before your very eyes. Everything
225   running downhill. It's kind of silly to even think about youth.

DEWIS   No, I don't think so. I think it's important to believe in certain things.

HALIE   Yes. Yes, I know what you mean. I think that's right. I think that's true. [*She looks at* DODGE.] Certain basic things. We can't shake certain basic things. We might end up crazy. Like my husband. You can see it in his
230   eyes. You can see how mad he is.

> [DODGE *covers his head with the blanket again.* HALIE *takes a single rose from* DEWIS *and moves slowly over to* DODGE.]

HALIE   We can't not believe in something. We can't stop believing. We just end up dying if we stop. Just end up dead.

> [HALIE *throws the rose gently onto* DODGE's *blanket. It lands between his knees and stays there. Long pause as* HALIE *stares at the rose.* SHELLY *stands suddenly.* HALIE *doesn't turn to her but keeps staring at rose.*]

SHELLY [*to* HALIE]   Don't you wanna' know who I am! Don't you wanna know what I'm doing here! I'm not dead!

> [SHELLY *crosses toward* HALIE. HALIE *turns slowly toward her.*]

235 HALIE   Did you drink your whiskey?

SHELLY   No! And I'm not going to either!

HALIE   Well that's a firm stand. It's good to have a firm stand.

SHELLY   I don't have any stand at all. I'm just trying to put all this together.

[HALIE *laughs and crosses back to* DEWIS.]

HALIE [*to* DEWIS]   Surprises, surprises! Did you have any idea we'd be return-
240   ing to this?

SHELLY   I came here with your Grandson for a little visit! A little innocent friendly visit.

HALIE   My Grandson?

SHELLY   Yes! That's right. The one no one remembers.

245 HALIE [*to* DEWIS]   This is getting a little far-fetched.

SHELLY   I told him it was stupid to come back here. To try to pick up from where he left off.

HALIE   Where was that?

SHELLY   Wherever he was when he left here! Six years ago! Ten years ago!
250   Whenever it was. I told him nobody cares.

HALIE   Didn't he listen?

SHELLY   No! No he didn't. We had to stop off at every tiny little meatball town that he remembered from his boyhood! Every stupid little donut shop he ever kissed a girl in. Every Drive-In. Every Drag Strip. Every football
255   field he ever broke a bone on.

HALIE [*suddenly alarmed, to* DODGE]   Where's Tilden?

SHELLY   Don't ignore me!

HALIE   Dodge! Where's Tilden gone?

[SHELLY *moves violently toward* HALIE.]

SHELLY [*to* HALIE]   I'm talking to you!

[BRADLEY *sits up fast on the sofa,* SHELLY *backs away.*]

260 BRADLEY [*to* SHELLY]   Don't you yell at my mother!

HALIE   Dodge! [*She kicks* DODGE.] I told you not to let Tilden out of your sight! Where's he gone to?

DODGE   Gimme a drink and I'll yell ya'.

DEWIS   Halie, maybe this isn't the right time for a visit.

[HALIE *crosses back to* DEWIS.]

265 HALIE [*to* DEWIS]   I never should've left! I never, never should've left! Tilden could be anywhere by now! Anywhere! He's not in control of his faculties. Dodge knew that. I told him when I left here. I told him specifically to watch out for Tilden.

[BRADLEY *reaches down, grabs* DODGE's *blanket, and yanks it off him. He lays down on sofa and pulls the blanket over his head.*]

DODGE   He's got my blanket again! He's got my blanket!

270 HALIE [*turning to* BRADLEY]   Bradley! Bradley, put that blanket back!

[HALIE *moves toward* BRADLEY. SHELLY *suddenly throws the cup and saucer against the stage right door.* DEWIS *ducks. The cup and saucer smash into pieces.* HALIE *stops, turns toward* SHELLY. *Everyone freezes.* BRADLEY *slowly pulls his head out from under blanket, looks toward stage right door, then to* SHELLY. SHELLY *stares at* HALIE. DEWIS *cowers with roses.* SHELLY *moves slowly toward* HALIE. *Long pause.* SHELLY *speaks softly.*]

SHELLY [*to* HALIE]   I don't like being ignored. I don't like being treated like I'm not here. I didn't like it when I was a kid and I still don't like it.

BRADLEY [*sitting up on sofa*]   We don't have to tell you anything, girl. Not a
  thing. You're not the police are you? You're not the government. You're just
275   some prostitute that Tilden brought in here.
HALIE   Language! I won't have that language in my house!
SHELLY [*to* BRADLEY]   You stuck your hand in my mouth and you call me a
  prostitute!
HALIE   Bradley! Did you put your hand in her mouth? I'm ashamed of you. I
280   can't leave you alone for a minute.
BRADLEY   I never did. She's lying!
DEWIS   Halie, I think I'll be running along now. I'll just put the roses in the
  kitchen.

  [DEWIS *moves toward stage left.* HALIE *stops him.*]

HALIE   Don't go now, Father! Not now.
285   BRADLEY   I never did anything, Mom! I never touched her! She proposi-
  tioned me! And I turned her down. I turned her down flat!

  [SHELLY *suddenly grabs her coat off the wooden leg and takes both the leg
  and coat down stage, away from* BRADLEY.]

BRADLEY   Mom! Mom! She's got my leg! She's taken my leg! I never did anything to her! She's stolen my leg!

  [BRADLEY *reaches pathetically in the air for his leg.* SHELLY *sets it down
  for a second, puts on her coat fast, and picks the leg up again.* DODGE
  starts coughing softly.]

HALIE [*to* SHELLY]   I think we've had about enough of you young lady. Just
290   about enough. I don't know where you came from or what you're doing
  here but you're no longer welcome in this house.
SHELLY [*laughs, holds leg*]   No longer welcome!
BRADLEY   Mom! That's my leg! Get my leg back! I can't do anything without
  my leg.

  [BRADLEY *keeps making whimpering sounds and reaching for his leg.*]

295   HALIE   Give my son back his leg. Right this very minute!

  [DODGE *starts laughing softly to himself in between coughs.*]

HALIE [*to* DEWIS]   Father, do something about this would you! I'm not about
  to be terrorized in my own house!
BRADLEY   Gimme back my leg!
HALIE   Oh, shut up Bradley! Just shut up! You don't need your leg now! Just
300   lay down and shut up!

  [BRADLEY *whimpers. Lays down and pulls blanket around him. He keeps
  one arm outside blanket, reaching out toward his wooden leg.* DEWIS *cautiously approaches* SHELLY *with the roses in his arms.* SHELLY *clutches the
  wooden leg to her chest as though she's kidnapped it.*]

DEWIS [*to* SHELLY]   Now, honestly dear, wouldn't it be better to try to talk
  things out? To try to use some reason?
SHELLY   There isn't any reason here! I can't find a reason for anything.
DEWIS   There's nothing to be afraid of. These are all good people. All righ-
305   teous people.
SHELLY   I'm not afraid!
DEWIS   But this isn't your house. You have to have some respect.
SHELLY   You're the strangers here, not me.
HALIE   This has gone far enough!

310 DEWIS Halie, please. Let me handle this.

SHELLY Don't come near me! Don't anyone come near me. I don't need any words from you. I'm not threatening anybody. I don't even know what I'm doing here. You all say you don't remember Vince, okay, maybe you don't. Maybe it's Vince that's crazy. Maybe he's made this whole family thing up.
315 I don't even care any more. I was just coming along for the ride. I thought it'd be a nice gesture. Besides, I was curious. He made all of you sound familiar to me. Every one of you. For every name, I had an image. Every time he'd tell me a name, I'd see the person. In fact, each of you was so clear in my mind that I actually believed it was you. I really believed when I walked
320 through that door that the people who lived here would turn out to be the same people in my imagination. But I don't recognize any of you. Not one. Not even the slightest resemblance.

DEWIS Well you can hardly blame others for not fulfilling your hallucination.

SHELLY It was no hallucination! It was more like a prophecy. You believe in
325 prophecy, don't you?

HALIE Father, there's no point in talking to her any further. We're just going to have to call the police.

BRADLEY No! Don't get the police in here. We don't want the police in here. This is our home.

330 SHELLY That's right. Bradley's right. Don't you usually settle your affairs in private? Don't you usually take them out in the dark? Out in the back?

BRADLEY You stay out of our lives! You have no business interfering!

SHELLY I don't have any business period. I got nothing to lose.

[*She moves around, staring at each of them.*]

BRADLEY You don't know what we've been through. You don't know anything!

335 SHELLY I know you've got a secret. You've all got a secret. It's so secret in fact, you're all convinced it never happened.

[HALIE *moves to* DEWIS.]

HALIE Oh, my God, Father!

DODGE [*laughing to himself*] She thinks she's going to get it out of us. She thinks she's going to uncover the truth of the matter. Like a detective or
340 something.

BRADLEY I'm not telling her anything! Nothing's wrong here! Nothing's ever been wrong! Everything's the way it's supposed to be! Nothing ever happened that's bad! Everything is all right here! We're all good people!

DODGE She thinks she's gonna suddenly bring everything out into the open
345 after all these years.

DEWIS [*to* SHELLY] Can't you see that these people want to be left in peace? Don't you have any mercy? They haven't done anything to you.

DODGE She wants to get to the bottom of it. [*To* SHELLY] That's it, isn't it? You'd like to get right down to bedrock? You want me to tell ya'? You want
350 me to tell ya' what happened? I'll tell ya'. I might as well.

BRADLEY No! Don't listen to him. He doesn't remember anything!

DODGE I remember the whole thing from start to finish. I remember the day he was born.

[*Pause.*]

HALIE Dodge, if you tell this thing—if you tell this, you'll be dead to me.
355 You'll be just as good as dead.

DODGE   That won't be such a big change, Halie. See this girl, this girl here, she wants to know. She wants to know something more. And I got this feeling that it doesn't make a bit difference. I'd sooner tell it to a stranger than anybody else.

360 BRADLEY [*to* DODGE]   We made a pact! We made a pact between us! You can't break that now!

DODGE   I don't remember any pact.

BRADLEY [*to* SHELLY]   See, he doesn't remember anything. I'm the only one in the family who remembers. The only one. And I'll never tell you!

365 SHELLY   I'm not so sure I want to find out now.

DODGE [*laughing to himself*]   Listen to her! Now she's runnin' scared!

SHELLY   I'm not scared!

[DODGE *stops laughing, long pause.* DODGE *stares at her.*]

DODGE   You're not huh? Well, that's good. Because I'm not either. See, we were a well-established family once. Well-established. All the boys were 370 grown. The farm was producing enough milk to fill Lake Michigan twice over. Me and Halie here were pointed toward what looked like the middle part of our life. Everything was settled with us. All we had to do was ride it out. Then Halie got pregnant again. Outa' the middle a' nowhere, she got pregnant. We weren't planning on havin' any more boys. We had enough 375 boys already. In fact, we hadn't been sleepin' in the same bed for about six years.

HALIE [*moving toward stairs*]   I'm not listening to this! I don't have to listen to this!

DODGE [*stops* HALIE]   Where are you going! Upstairs! You'll just be listenin' to 380 it upstairs! You go outside, you'll be listenin' to it outside. Might as well stay here and listen to it.

[HALIE *stays by stairs.*]

BRADLEY   If I had my leg you wouldn't be saying this. You'd never get away with it if I had my leg.

DODGE [*pointing to* SHELLY]   She's got your leg. [*Laughs*] She's gonna keep 385 your leg too. [*To* SHELLY] She wants to hear this. Don't you?

SHELLY   I don't know.

DODGE   Well even if ya' don't I'm gonna' tell ya'. [*Pause*] Halie had this kid. This baby boy. She had it. I let her have it on her own. All the other boys I had had the best doctors, best nurses, everything. This one I let her have by 390 herself. This one hurt real bad. Almost killed her, but she had it anyway. It lived, see. It lived. It wanted to grow up in this family. It wanted to be just like us. It wanted to be a part of us. It wanted to pretend that I was its father. She wanted me to believe in it. Even when everyone around us knew. Everyone. All our boys knew. Tilden knew.

395 HALIE   You shut up! Bradley, make him shut up!

BRADLEY   I can't.

DODGE   Tilden was the one who knew. Better than any of us. He'd walk for miles with that kid in his arms. Halie let him take it. All night sometimes. He'd walk all night out there in the pasture with it. Talkin' to it. Singin' to 400 it. Used to hear him singing to it. He'd make up stories. He'd tell that kid all kinds a' stories. Even when he knew it couldn't understand him. Couldn't understand a word he was sayin'. Never would understand him. We couldn't let a thing like that continue. We couldn't allow that to grow up right in the

middle of our lives. It made everything we'd accomplished look like it
405 was nothin'. Everything was cancelled out by this one mistake. This one
weakness.

SHELLY   So you killed him?

DODGE   I killed it. I drowned it. Just like the runt of a litter. Just drowned it.

[HALIE *moves toward* BRADLEY.]

HALIE [*to* BRADLEY]   Ansel would've stopped him! Ansel would've stopped
410 him from telling these lies! He was a hero! A man! A whole man! What's
happened to the men in this family! Where are the men!

[*Suddenly* VINCE *comes crashing through the screen porch door up left,
tearing it off its hinges. Everyone but* DODGE *and* BRADLEY *back away from
the porch and stare at* VINCE *who has landed on his stomach on the porch
in a drunken stupor. He is singing loudly to himself and hauls himself
slowly to his feet. He has a paper shopping bag full of empty booze bottles.
He takes them out one at a time as he sings and smashes them at the opposite end of the porch, behind the solid interior door, stage right.* SHELLY
moves slowly toward stage right, holding wooden leg and watching VINCE.]

VINCE [*singing loudly as he hurls bottles*]   "From the Halls of Montezuma to
the Shores of Tripoli. We will fight our country's battles on the land and on
the sea."[2]

[*He punctuates the words "Montezuma," "Tripoli," "battles," and "sea"
with a smashed bottle each. He stops throwing for a second, stares toward
stage right of the porch, shades his eyes with his hand as though looking
across to a battlefield, then cups his hands around his mouth and yells
across the space of the porch to an imaginary army. The others watch in
terror and expectation.*]

415 VINCE [*to imagined army*]   Have you had enough over there! 'Cause there's a
lot more here where that came from! [*Pointing to paper bag full of bottles*]
A helluva lot more! We got enough over here to blow ya' from here to
Kingdomcome!

[*He takes another bottle, makes high whistling sound of a bomb and
throws it toward stage right porch. Sound of bottle smashing against wall.
This should be the actual smashing of bottles and not tape sound. He
keeps yelling and heaving bottles one after another.* VINCE *stops for a
while, breathing heavily from exhaustion. Long silence as the others
watch him.* SHELLY *approaches tentatively in* VINCE'S *direction, still holding* BRADLEY'S *wooden leg.*]

SHELLY [*after silence*]   Vince?

[VINCE *turns toward her. Peers through screen.*]

420 VINCE   Who? What? Vince who? Who's that in there?

[VINCE *pushes his face against the screen from the porch and stares in at
everyone.*]

DODGE   Where's my goddamn bottle!

VINCE [*looking in at* DODGE]   What? Who is that?

---

2. The opening of the official anthem of the
U.S. Marine Corps (author unknown; the
music is from a song in the 1867 revision of
Geneviève de Brabant [1859], a comic opera
by Jacques Offenbach). The first line refers,
respectively, to the capture of Mexico City's
Castle of Chapultepec (the Halls of Montezuma) in the Mexican-American War (1846–
48) and to the 1801–05 war against the
Barbary pirates of North Africa, who were
based largely in Tripoli (in northwest Libya).

DODGE It's me! Your Grandfather! Don't play stupid with me! Where's my
two bucks!

425 VINCE Your two bucks?

> [HALIE *moves away from* DEWIS, *upstage, peers out at* VINCE, *trying to
> recognize him.*]

HALIE Vincent? Is that you, Vincent?

> [SHELLY *stares at* HALIE *then looks out at* VINCE.]

VINCE [*from porch*] Vincent who? What is this! Who are you people?

SHELLY [*to* HALIE] Hey, wait a minute. Wait a minute! What's going on?

HALIE [*moving closer to porch screen*] We thought you were a murderer or
430 something. Barging in through the door like that.

VINCE I am a murderer! Don't underestimate me for a minute! I'm the Midnight Strangler! I devour whole families in a single gulp!

> [VINCE *grabs another bottle and smashes it on the porch.* HALIE *backs away.*]

SHELLY [*approaching* HALIE] You mean you know who he is?

HALIE Of course I know who he is! That's more than I can say for you.

435 BRADLEY [*sitting up on sofa*] You get off our front porch you creep! What're
you doing out there breaking bottles? Who are these foreigners anyway!
Where did they come from?

VINCE Maybe I should come in there and break them!

HALIE [*moving toward porch*] Don't you dare! Vincent, what's got into you!
440 Why are you acting like this?

VINCE Maybe I should come in there and usurp your territory!

> [HALIE *turns back toward* DEWIS *and crosses to him.*]

HALIE [*to* DEWIS] Father, why are you just standing around here when everything's falling apart? Can't you rectify this situation?

> [DODGE *laughs, coughs.*]

DEWIS I'm just a guest here, Halie. I don't know what my position is exactly.
445 This is outside my parish anyway.

> [VINCE *starts throwing more bottles as things continue.*]

BRADLEY If I had my leg I'd rectify it! I'd rectify him all over the goddamn
highway! I'd pull his ears out if I could reach him!

> [BRADLEY *sticks his fist through the screening of the porch and reaches
> out for* VINCE, *grabbing at him and missing.* VINCE *jumps away from*
> BRADLEY'S *hand.*]

VINCE Aaaah! Our lines have been penetrated! Tentacled animals! Beasts
from the deep!

> [VINCE *strikes out at* BRADLEY'S *hand with a bottle.* BRADLEY *pulls his
> hand back inside.*]

450 SHELLY Vince! Knock it off will ya'! I want to get out of here!

> [VINCE *pushes his face against screen, looks in at* SHELLY.]

VINCE [*to* SHELLY] Have they got you prisoner in there, dear? Such a sweet
young thing too. All her life in front of her. Nipped in the bud.

SHELLY I'm coming out there, Vince! I'm coming out there and I want us to
get in the car and drive away from here. Anywhere. Just away from here.

> [SHELLY *moves toward* VINCE'S *saxophone case and overcoat. She sets
> down the wooden leg, downstage left, and picks up the saxophone case
> and overcoat.* VINCE *watches her through the screen.*]

455 VINCE [*to* SHELLY]   We'll have to negotiate. Make some kind of a deal. Prisoner exchange or something. A few of theirs for one of ours. Small price to pay if you ask me.

> [SHELLY *crosses toward stage right door with overcoat and case.*]

SHELLY   Just go and get the car! I'm coming out there now. We're going to leave.

460 VINCE   Don't come out here! Don't you dare come out here!

> [SHELLY *stops short of the door, stage right.*]

SHELLY   How come?

VINCE   Off limits! Verboten![3] This is taboo territory. No man or woman has ever crossed the line and lived to tell the tale!

SHELLY   I'll take my chances.

> [SHELLY *moves to stage right door and opens it.* VINCE *pulls out a big folding hunting knife and pulls open the blade. He jabs the blade into the screen and starts cutting a hole big enough to climb through.* BRADLEY *cowers in a corner of the sofa as* VINCE *rips at the screen.*]

465 VINCE [*as he cuts screen*]   Don't come out here! I'm warning you! You'll disintegrate!

> [DEWIS *takes* HALIE *by the arm and pulls her toward staircase.*]

DEWIS   Halie, maybe we should go upstairs until this blows over.

HALIE   I don't understand it. I just don't understand it. He was the sweetest little boy!

> [DEWIS *drops the roses beside the wooden leg at the foot of the staircase then escorts* HALIE *quickly up the stairs.* HALIE *keeps looking back at* VINCE *as they climb the stairs.*]

470 HALIE   There wasn't a mean bone in his body. Everyone loved Vincent. Everyone. He was the perfect baby.

DEWIS   He'll be all right after a while. He's just had a few too many that's all.

HALIE   He used to sing in his sleep. He'd sing. In the middle of the night. The sweetest voice. Like an angel. [*She stops for a moment.*] I used to lie
475 awake listening to it. I used to lie awake thinking it was all right if I died. Because Vincent was an angel. A guardian angel. He'd watch over us. He'd watch over all of us.

> [DEWIS *takes her all the way up the stairs. They disappear above.* VINCE *is now climbing through the porch screen onto the sofa.* BRADLEY *crashes off the sofa, holding tight to his blanket, keeping it wrapped around him.* SHELLY *is outside on the porch.* VINCE *holds the knife in his teeth once he gets the hole wide enough to climb through.* BRADLEY *starts crawling slowly toward his wooden leg, reaching out for it.*]

DODGE [*to* VINCE]   Go ahead! Take over the house! Take over the whole goddamn house! You can have it! It's yours. It's been a pain in the neck ever
480 since the very first mortgage. I'm gonna die any second now. Any second. You won't even notice. So I'll settle my affairs once and for all.

> [As DODGE *proclaims his last will and testament,* VINCE *climbs into the room, knife in mouth, and strides slowly around the space, inspecting his inheritance. He casually notices* BRADLEY *as he crawls toward his leg.* VINCE *moves to the leg and keeps pushing it with his foot so that it's out*

---

3. Forbidden! (German).

of BRADLEY'S *reach, then goes on with his inspection. He picks up the roses and carries them around smelling them.* SHELLY *can be seen outside on the porch, moving slowly center and staring in at* VINCE. VINCE *ignores her.*]

DODGE: The house goes to my Grandson, Vincent. All the furnishings, accoutrements, and paraphernalia therein. Everything tacked to the walls or otherwise resting under this roof. My tools—namely my band saw, my
485 Skilsaw,[4] my drill press, my chain saw, my lathe, my electric sander, all go to my eldest son, Tilden. That is, if he ever shows up again. My shed and gasoline-powered equipment, namely my tractor, my dozer,[5] my hand tiller plus all the attachments and riggings for the above-mentioned machinery, namely my spring-tooth harrow,[6] my deep plows, my disk plows, my automatic
490 fertilizing equipment, my reaper, my swathe, my seeder, my John Deere Harvester, my posthole digger, my jackhammer, my lathe—[*To himself*] Did I mention my lathe? I already mentioned my lathe—my Bennie Good-man[7] records, my harnesses, my bits, my halters, my brace, my rough rasp, my forge, my welding equipment, my shoeing nails, my levels and bevels,
495 my milking stool—no, not my milking stool—my hammers and chisels, my hinges, my cattle gates, my barbed wire, self-tapping augers, my horsehair ropes, and all related materials are to be pushed into a gigantic heap and set ablaze in the very center of my fields. When the blaze is at its highest, preferably on a cold, windless night, my body is to be pitched into the
500 middle of it and burned till nothing remains but ash.

    [*Pause.* VINCE *takes the knife out of his mouth and smells the roses. He's facing toward audience and doesn't turn around to* SHELLY. *He folds up knife and pockets it.*]

SHELLY [*from porch*] I'm leaving, Vince. Whether you come or not, I'm leaving.
VINCE [*smelling roses*] Just put my horn on the couch there before you take off.
SHELLY [*moving toward hole in screen*] You're not coming?

    [VINCE *stays downstage, turns and looks at her.*]

505 VINCE I just inherited a house.
SHELLY [*through hole, from porch*] You want to stay here?
VINCE [*as he pushes* BRADLEY'S *leg out of reach*] I've gotta carry on the line. I've gotta see to it that things keep rolling.

    [BRADLEY *looks up at him from floor, keeps pulling himself toward his leg.* VINCE *keeps moving it.*]

SHELLY What happened to you Vince? You just disappeared.
510 VINCE [*pause, delivers speech front*] I was gonna run last night. I was gonna run and keep right on running. I drove all night. Clear to the Iowa border. The old man's two bucks sitting right on the seat beside me. It never stopped raining the whole time. Never stopped once. I could see myself in the windshield. My face. My eyes. I studied my face. Studied everything
515 about it. As though I was looking at another man. As though I could see his whole race behind him. Like a mummy's face. I saw him dead and alive at

---

4. Circular saw (a brand name).
5. That is, bulldozer.
6. An implement, pulled by a tractor, that breaks up soil and levels it before planting.

7. That is, Benny Goodman (1909–1986), American jazz clarinetist, composer, and bandleader.

the same time. In the same breath. In the windshield, I watched him breathe as though he was frozen in time. And every breath marked him. Marked him forever without him knowing. And then his face changed. His face became his father's face. Same bones. Same eyes. Same nose. Same breath. And his father's face changed to his Grandfather's face. And it went on like that. Changing. Clear on back to faces I'd never seen before but still recognized. Still recognized the bones underneath. The eyes. The breath. The mouth. I followed my family clear into Iowa. Every last one. Straight into the Corn Belt and further. Straight back as far as they'd take me. Then it all dissolved. Everything dissolved.

[SHELLY *stares at him for a while then reaches through the hole in the screen and sets the saxophone case and* VINCE's *overcoat on the sofa. She looks at* VINCE *again.*]

SHELLY   Bye Vince.

[*She exits left off the porch.* VINCE *watches her go.* BRADLEY *tries to make a lunge for his wooden leg.* VINCE *quickly picks it up and dangles it over* BRADLEY's *head like a carrot.* BRADLEY *keeps making desperate grabs at the leg.* DEWIS *comes down the staircase and stops halfway, staring at* VINCE *and* BRADLEY. VINCE *looks up at* DEWIS *and smiles. He keeps moving backwards with the leg toward upstage left as* BRADLEY *crawls after him.*]

VINCE [*to* DEWIS *as he continues torturing* BRADLEY]   Oh, excuse me Father. Just getting rid of some of the vermin in the house. This is my house now, ya' know? All mine. Everything. Except for the power tools and stuff. I'm gonna get all new equipment anyway. New plows, new tractor, everything. All brand-new. [VINCE *teases* BRADLEY *closer to the up left corner of the stage.*] Start right off on the ground floor.

[VINCE *throws* BRADLEY's *wooden leg far off stage left.* BRADLEY *follows his leg offstage, pulling himself along on the ground, whimpering. As* BRADLEY *exits* VINCE *pulls the blanket off him and throws it over his own shoulder. He crosses toward* DEWIS *with the blanket and smells the roses.* DEWIS *comes to the bottom of the stairs.*]

DEWIS   You'd better go up and see your Grandmother.

VINCE [*looking up stairs, back to* DEWIS]   My Grandmother? There's nobody else in this house. Except for you. And you're leaving aren't you?

[DEWIS *crosses toward stage right door. He turns back to* VINCE.]

DEWIS   She's going to need someone. I can't help her. I don't know what to do. I don't know what my position is. I just came in for some tea. I had no idea there was any trouble. No idea at all.

[VINCE *just stares at him.* DEWIS *goes out the door, crosses porch, and exits left.* VINCE *listens to him leaving. He smells roses, looks up the staircase, then smells roses again. He turns and looks upstage at* DODGE. *He crosses up to him and bends over looking at* DODGE's *open eyes.* DODGE *is dead. His death should have come completely unnoticed. Vince lifts the blanket, then covers his head. He sits on the sofa, smelling roses and staring at* DODGE's *body. Long pause.* VINCE *places the roses on* DODGE's *chest, then lays down on the sofa, arms folded behind his head, staring at the ceiling. His body is in the same relationship to* DODGE's. *After a while* HALIE's *voice is heard coming from above the staircase. The lights start to dim almost imperceptibly as* HALIE *speaks.* VINCE *keeps staring at the ceiling.*]

540 HALIE'S VOICE   Dodge? Is that you Dodge? Tilden was right about the corn
you know. I've never seen such corn. Have you taken a look at it lately? Tall
as a man already. This early in the year. Carrots too. Potatoes. Peas. It's like
a paradise out there, Dodge. You oughta' take a look. A miracle. I've never
seen it like this. Maybe the rain did something. Maybe it was the rain.

> [As HALIE *keeps talking offstage,* TILDEN *appears from stage left, dripping
> with mud from the knees down. His arms and hands are covered with
> mud. In his hands he carries the corpse of a small child at chest level,
> staring down at it. The corpse mainly consists of bones wrapped in
> muddy, rotten cloth. He moves slowly downstage toward the staircase,
> ignoring* VINCE *on the sofa.* VINCE *keeps staring at the ceiling as though*
> TILDEN *wasn't there. As* HALIE'S VOICE *continues,* TILDEN *slowly makes his
> way up the stairs. His eyes never leave the corpse of the child. The lights
> keep fading.*]

545 HALIE'S VOICE   Good hard rain. Takes everything straight down deep to the
roots. The rest takes care of itself. You can't force a thing to grow. You can't
interfere with it. It's all hidden. It's all unseen. You just gotta wait till it
pops up out of the ground. Tiny little shoot. Tiny little white shoot. All
hairy and fragile. Strong though. Strong enough to break the earth even.
550 It's a miracle, Dodge. I've never seen a crop like this in my whole life.
Maybe it's the sun. Maybe that's it. Maybe it's the sun.

> [TILDEN *disappears above. Silence. Lights go to black.*]

CARYL CHURCHILL

b. 1938

IN May 1982, shortly before English dramatist Caryl Churchill won the OBIE Award[1] for Best Playwriting for *CLOUD NINE* (1979), *Ms.* magazine published a feature story on the socialist feminist writer and her enthusiastically received play—a groundbreaking, antic exposé of patriarchal culture and imperialist ideology in both the Victorian and contemporary eras. Just over a year later, having earned the same accolade for *Top Girls* (1982)—a clear-eyed examination of feminism and women's lives in the "me decade"— Churchill agreed to be interviewed for *Vogue* magazine. There, she was dubbed "Britain's top girl playwright," albeit with less irony than was embedded in Churchill's own use of the phrase. These two articles from the early 1980s, printed in ideologically antithetical locations, nevertheless demonstrated Churchill's burgeoning international prominence as a writer and public figure; they also spoke to the growing appeal of her perennially *topical* dramaturgy to disparate audiences. At the same time, the features confirmed that feminism was a movement of note for those with serious sociopolitical commitments as well as those with an interest in current cultural trends. Indeed, following the volatile suffrage and women's rights campaigns of the late nineteenth through early twentieth centuries, the final two decades of the twentieth century were marked globally by the rise of and attention to what is now called "second wave" feminism. These more recent struggles reflect women's renewed efforts to achieve greater financial, educational, legal, and social equality. Through this movement, we have come to recognize the existence of multiple "feminisms," which embrace the range of women's racial and ethnic identities, gender roles and sexual orientations, and class positions, all of which inform their relationship to society. Churchill's plays from this period compellingly dramatize women's historical conflicts with and current resistance to patriarchal culture. They brought a female playwright's voice into a theater dominated by male dramatists and also helped launch the influential field of feminist theater theory and criticism. Her subsequent writing has expanded her topical and stylistic reach even further; she remains among the most influential, productive, and innovative of contemporary dramatists, consistently challenging theater artists and audiences alike since the 1970s with her politically charged and technically adventurous dramaturgy.

1. The OBIE Awards are given annually by *The Village Voice* for excellence in off-Broadway theater.

Caryl Churchill came of age at a potent, transitional period in English theater, the era of the "angry young men" like John Osborne, whose *Look Back in Anger* (1956) voiced hostility toward the British class system. Born in London in 1938, Churchill spent part of her childhood in Canada but returned to England in 1955; in 1957 she went to Oxford, studying English language and literature. At the university she began writing plays that were produced by student theater groups. Shortly after graduation she married David Harter, a lawyer. The couple had three children in the 1960s, and Churchill speaks frankly of her struggles in attempting simultaneously to continue writing and to fulfill her family obligations. She was initially politicized not by the broader social movements of that tumultuous era but by "being discontent with [her] own way of life—of being a barrister's wife and just being at home with small children." She started composing radio plays, because working in that form afforded her both the flexibility required by her family life and a respectable outlet for her work that was relatively accessible. As Churchill later noted in an interview, it was a time when world-renowned dramatist "[SAMUEL] BECKETT was on the radio" and when the medium was perceived as "the way to break in" to professional playwriting.

In 1972 the first of Churchill's several television plays was produced and *Owners* was staged at London's Royal Court Theatre, a venue known for its commitment to new playwrights. Two years later Churchill became the first woman to be offered a playwriting residency with the Royal Court; more than a dozen of her plays have premiered there, including *Top Girls, Serious Money* (1987), and *A Number* (2002). Another professional relationship that was to profoundly influence Churchill's work began in 1976, when she became involved with the Joint Stock Company. This theater collective was committed to a collaborative production process and creative political engagement, and Churchill's affiliation with it facilitated the creation of *Cloud Nine*, her first commercially successful play.

During the late 1970s Churchill also worked closely with the socialist-feminist theater group Monstrous Regiment, which took its name from a sixteenth-century misogynist pamphlet by John Knox that inveighs against the "monstrous regiment of women." The group collaborated with her in staging several pieces; one of these was *Vinegar Tom* (1976), a gripping historical drama about the persecution of women accused of witchcraft. Over the next decade, Churchill catapulted to international renown; *Top Girls, Cloud Nine, Fen* (1983), and *Serious Money* were among her plays produced throughout the English-speaking world as well as in Europe, Asia, and Latin America. She received the Susan Smith Blackburn Prize for both *Fen* and *Serious Money* and the Laurence Olivier Award (the British equivalent of the Tony Award) for *Serious Money*.

Churchill has repeatedly harnessed the power of live performance to engage audiences in meaningful political debate. Together with Mark Wing-Davey, the artistic director of London's Central School of Speech and Drama, she brought students from that professional conservatory to Romania to work with students from the Caragiale Institute of Theatre and Cinema in Bucharest in developing a piece dealing with the fall of Nicolae Ceauşescu and the impact of his policies on the lives of Romanian citizens. The resulting drama, *Mad Forest* (1990), captures the complexities of life under and after an oppressive political regime. *The Skriker* (1994) weaves the dark world of folktale magic together with a hard-edged consideration of contemporary female adolescence and our natural environment as it blurs the boundaries of drama and dance. In *Far Away* (2000) Churchill creates an apocalyptic vision of a land torn apart by conflict so profound it beggars description. And *A Number* brings us into a frightening and all-too-conceivable world where scientific advances challenge long-held assumptions about individuals' autonomy and humanity. Working in a country where theater has long reflected and affected national culture and discourse, Churchill has embraced the stage for expressing her deeply held social convictions. For decades, her plays have conveyed with growing urgency and intensity the potential devastation—sociological, economic, environmental, and political—

that those with power can wreak on the individual and on society.

Cloud Nine exemplifies these concerns through its interweaving of the past and the present (as of 1979). While its two acts are set a century apart, many of the characters we meet in act 1 also appear in act 2, having aged only twenty-five years. Churchill uses this chronological compression to demonstrate both the tenacity of historical perspectives and the potential for their gradual change. She simultaneously distances her audiences from both eras, allowing for greater objectivity and critique. Churchill scholars have identified this device as a form of Brechtian estrangement, referencing the techniques BERTOLT BRECHT championed for a politically engaged theater. While Churchill has not explicitly identified Brecht as an influence for *Cloud Nine*, she has acknowledged that English theater artists of the 1970s had absorbed his ideas, which became more widely known there following the tour of Brecht's Berliner Ensemble in 1956. A number of Brecht's plays were then staged in England in the 1960s, and British theater artists—especially those who shared Brecht's socialist beliefs—soon began to utilize Brechtian acting and dramaturgical techniques in their own work. Critics suggest that, both performatively and thematically, *Cloud Nine* engages Brechtian theatrical strategies.

Employing the conceit of the family as a microcosm of society, Churchill explores in *Cloud Nine* the nexus of the personal and the political as she traces the lives of Clive, a British colonial administrator, his wife, Betty, their children, Edward and Victoria, and their household staff, extended family, and friends. Throughout, the characters negotiate their relations with each other in a culture defined by white male supremacy and heteronormativity—a culture resisted more strongly as the play progresses. Act 1, set in Africa, provides comically exaggerated, yet still disturbing, images of compulsory heterosexuality and British imperial practices. We watch *paterfamilias* Clive blithely embody the sexual double standard and impose traditional gender roles on all around him, while he simultaneously endeavors to suppress native resistance to British rule. Act 2,

set in England, shows less parodically the lingering influence of such oppression as Betty, Edward, and Victoria struggle toward independent identities and new notions of what constitutes a family.

A number of Churchill's early dramatic themes, especially her critique of patriarchy and its construction and control of female identity, emerged through the creation of *Cloud Nine*. Some of her signature dramaturgical techniques coalesced at this time as well, including her nonnaturalistic and nonlinear narrative style and her use of cross-gender/race casting and double casting. In act 1, for example, Betty is played by a male actor because, as she explains, "I am a man's creation as you see, / And what men want is what I want to be." Their black servant, Joshua, is played by a white actor for comparable reasons: "My skin is black but oh my soul is white. / I hate my tribe. My master is my light." *Cloud Nine*'s seven actors all play multiple roles, but Churchill provides options as to how this doubling occurs. Which roles the actors portray thus affects how we see the characters and their interrelationships; this happens because, for the audience, the actors will carry from one role to the next a resonance of their previous characters. Thus if the actor playing Clive in act 1 becomes the child Cathy in act 2, that will impact the audience differently than if the actor who played Joshua in act 1 becomes this same little girl.

The origins of these noteworthy components of Churchill's playwriting can be traced to various theatrical influences explored with the Joint Stock Theatre Company during its creative process. Logistical constraints with the company, such as the fact that it had no black actors at the time, were also significant: Churchill, the actors, and Joint Stock's director, Max Stafford-Clark, began with a workshop involving research, improvisation, and discussion around the topic of sexual politics. Churchill then used the fruits of that exploratory process to draft her script. The play's title emerged from an interview with an older woman who employed the phrase to describe physical intimacy with her husband, while some of the actors' discoveries about themselves and their attitudes toward gender roles

Bo Poraj as Betty and James Fleet as Clive in the 2007 Almeida Theatre (London) production of *Cloud Nine*.

and sexual identities helped give shape to the plot. According to Churchill, Kate Millet's groundbreaking feminist literary study *Sexual Politics* (1970) informed their thinking, as did the work of French dramatist JEAN GENET, whose plays *THE MAIDS* (1947), *The Balcony* (1957), *The Blacks* (1958), and *The Screens* (1961), already published in English, had also all been revived in England in the 1970s. Churchill credits Genet with articulating "the parallel between colonial and sexual repression"—one of the main themes in *Cloud Nine*. *The Screens*, Genet's critique of French colonialism, may have been important both thematically and theatrically, as it requires actors "to play five or six roles, male or female." In other writing, Genet envisioned his female characters "performed by adolescent boys." He

also stated that he "would bring this [casting] to the attention of the spectators by means of a placard which would remain nailed to . . . the sets during the entire performance." Such directives, similar to Brecht's alienation effect, not only disrupt any semblance of theatrical realism but also call audiences' attention to the separation between actor and role. The English theater, of course, also has a long history of cross-gender casting, which includes performances by the all-male troupes of SHAKESPEARE's day. The Victorian tradition of an actress playing a young male character, known as a "principal boy," still defines the casting of Peter Pan and similarly shapes the portrayal of *Cloud Nine*'s Edward. Similarly, the tradition of "dame" roles, which use male actors for comic portraits of female characters, may have informed the creation of Cathy in Churchill's so-called "reversal" of Edward.[2]

In *The Blacks*, subtitled "a clown show," Genet instructs some of the characters in the all-black cast to wear white masks to highlight the dominant culture's notions of racial identity. In this regard Genet, like Churchill and the Joint Stock Company, was influenced by Francophone writer Frantz Fanon (1925–61), whose seminal work *Black Skin, White Masks* (1952) suggests that "what is called the black soul is a construction by white folk." Thus the embodiment of Joshua by a white actor in *Cloud Nine* neatly wedded Fanon's theory with theatrical necessity. But because the colonial context in Africa is so strongly defined by issues of race, Churchill's effort to create a synergy with the colonial context of Northern Ireland in act 2 has not always been seen as successful. In particular, she has been criticized for a simplified notion of racial identity, her failure to consider the complex position of black women experiencing both imperial and patriarchal oppression, and her generalizing of African colonization. Her critique of England's ongoing imperialist enterprise, embodied by the ghost of a British soldier just killed in Belfast, only briefly informs the second act. Rather, as critics have noted, Churchill's use of colonialism as a metaphor for sex and gender repression emerges as the dominant structuring device for *Cloud Nine* overall.

Through the Joint Stock workshop process Churchill discovered that many of the actors had experienced, during their childhoods and young adulthoods, the tenacity of Victorian ideas about gender and sexuality. Traditional notions of what it means to be the ideal wife and mother, for example—what Coventry Patmore (1823–96) famously called "The Angel in the House" in his poem of that title (1854/1862)—can create conflicts for women who experience other kinds of desires or may have different life goals. Churchill's script both satirizes and critiques such proscriptive notions of femininity and masculinity at the same time that she demonstrates the challenges of breaking free of their constraints. When it premiered, *Cloud Nine* also stood out for its frank and objective depiction of gay and lesbian sexualities. Yet critics have subsequently noted how, in performance, *Cloud Nine* may actually, albeit unintentionally, reinforce heteronormativity. When in act 1 the governess Ellen expresses her love and desire for Betty, or the explorer Harry accepts the sexual overtures of Edward, the attractions the audience observes occur between a man and a woman—the sexes of the actors in those roles. Moreover, the casting of Edward may mirror stereotypical notions of gay male identity as feminine. Any sexual encounters between homosexual characters played by actors of the same sex, such as that between Harry and Joshua, only happen offstage. Such critical realizations exemplify the challenges facing artists who wish to tackle complex theoretical and sociological precepts while they also craft creative, innovative work. Yet despite these valid concerns, *Cloud Nine* remains one of the most influential of Churchill's plays and among her most widely produced. Indeed, precisely because of her standing in the contemporary theater, Churchill's dramas continue to fascinate artists and scholars alike. Her works provide vivid characters and memorable narratives that bring to life her social and political convictions. For over forty years Caryl Churchill has offered audiences worldwide plays that stimulate, provoke, and entertain.

J.E.G.

---

2. Dame roles are, traditionally, older female figures, but Churchill's comedic style with Cathy is comparable.

Cloud Nine

Except for Cathy, characters in Act Two are played by actors of their own sex.

Act One takes place in a British colony in Africa in Victorian times. Act Two takes place in London in 1979. But for the characters it is twenty-five years later.

Act One

SCENE ONE: *Low bright sun. Veranda. Flagpole with Union Flag. The family*—CLIVE, BETTY, EDWARD, VICTORIA, MAUD, ELLEN, JOSHUA.

ALL [*sing*]　Come gather, sons of England, come gather in your pride.
　　Now meet the world united, now face it side by side;
　　Ye who the earth's wide corners, from veldt to prairie, roam.
　　From bush and jungle muster all who call old England 'home'.
5　　Then gather round for England,
　　Rally to the flag,
　　From north and south and east and west
　　Come one and all for England![1]
CLIVE　This is my family. Though far from home
10　　We serve the Queen wherever we may roam.
　　I am a father to the natives here,
　　And father to my family so dear.
　　　　[*He presents* BETTY. *She is played by a man.*]
　　My wife is all I dreamt a wife should be,
　　And everything she is she owes to me.
15　BETTY　I live for Clive. The whole aim of my life
　　Is to be what he looks for in a wife.
　　I am a man's creation as you see,

---

1. Lyric from 1902, by Anthony Wilkin.

And what men want is what I want to be.

[CLIVE *presents* JOSHUA. *He is played by a white.*]

CLIVE   My boy's a jewel. Really has the knack.
20   You'd hardly notice that the fellow's black.

JOSHUA   My skin is black but oh my soul is white.
           I hate my tribe. My master is my light.
           I only live for him. As you can see,
           What white men want is what I want to be.

[CLIVE *presents* EDWARD. *He is played by a woman.*]

25 CLIVE   My son is young. I'm doing all I can
           To teach him to grow up to be a man.

EDWARD   What father wants I'd dearly like to be.
           I find it rather hard as you can see.

[CLIVE *presents* VICTORIA, *who is a dummy,* MAUD, *and* ELLEN.]

CLIVE   No need for any speeches by the rest.
30   My daughter, mother-in-law, and governess.

ALL [*sing*]   O'er countless numbers she, our Queen,
           Victoria reigns supreme;
           O'er Africa's sunny plains, and o'er
           Canadian frozen stream;
35   The forge of war shall weld the chains of brotherhood secure;
           So to all time in ev'ry clime our Empire shall endure.

           Then gather round for England,
           Rally to the flag,
           From north and south and east and west
40   Come one and all for England!

[*All go except* BETTY. CLIVE *comes.*]

BETTY   Clive?
CLIVE   Betty. Joshua!

[JOSHUA *comes with a drink for* CLIVE.]

BETTY   I thought you would never come. The day's so long without you.
CLIVE   Long ride in the bush.
45 BETTY   Is anything wrong? I heard drums.
CLIVE   Nothing serious. Beauty is a damned good mare. I must get some new
           boots sent from home. These ones have never been right. I have a blister.
BETTY   My poor dear foot.
CLIVE   It's nothing.
50 BETTY   Oh but it's sore.
CLIVE   We are not in this country to enjoy ourselves. Must have ridden fifty
           miles. Spoke to three different headmen who would all gladly chop off
           each other's heads and wear them round their waists.
BETTY   Clive!
55 CLIVE   Don't be squeamish, Betty, let me have my joke. And what has my little
           dove done today?
BETTY   I've read a little.
CLIVE   Good. Is it good?
BETTY   It's poetry.
60 CLIVE   You're so delicate and sensitive.

BETTY And I played the piano. Shall I send for the children?

CLIVE Yes, in a minute. I've a piece of news for you.

BETTY Good news?

CLIVE You'll certainly think it's good. A visitor.

65 BETTY From home?

CLIVE No. Well of course originally from home.

BETTY Man or woman?

CLIVE Man.

BETTY I can't imagine.

70 CLIVE Something of an explorer. Bit of a poet. Odd chap but brave as a lion. And a great admirer of yours.

BETTY What do you mean? Whoever can it be?

CLIVE With an H and a B. And does conjuring tricks for little Edward.

BETTY That sounds like Mr Bagley.

75 CLIVE Harry Bagley.

BETTY He certainly doesn't admire me, Clive, what a thing to say. How could I possibly guess from that. He's hardly explored anything at all, he's just been up a river, he's done nothing at all compared to what you do. You should have said a heavy drinker and a bit of a bore.

80 CLIVE But you like him well enough. You don't mind him coming?

BETTY Anyone at all to break the monotony.

CLIVE But you have your mother. You have Ellen.

BETTY Ellen is a governess. My mother is my mother.

CLIVE I hoped when she came to visit she would be company for you.

85 BETTY I don't think mother is on a visit. I think she lives with us.

CLIVE I think she does.

BETTY Clive you are so good.

CLIVE But are you bored my love?

BETTY It's just that I miss you when you're away. We're not in this country to
90 enjoy ourselves. If I lack society that is my form of service.

CLIVE That's a brave girl. So today has been, all right? No fainting? No hysteria?[2]

BETTY I have been very tranquil.

CLIVE Ah what a haven of peace to come home to. The cool, the calm, the
95 beauty.

BETTY There is one thing, Clive, if you don't mind.

CLIVE What can I do for you, my dear?

BETTY It's about Joshua.

CLIVE I wouldn't leave you alone here with a quiet mind if it weren't for
100 Joshua.

BETTY Joshua doesn't like me.

CLIVE Joshua has been my boy for eight years. He has saved my life. I have saved his life. He is devoted to me and to mine. I have said this before.

BETTY He is rude to me. He doesn't do what I say. Speak to him.

105 CLIVE Tell me what happened.

BETTY He said something improper.

CLIVE Well, what?

---

2. Churchill alludes here parodically to Sigmund Freud (1856–1939), whose theory of female hysteria influenced feminist notions of the patriarchal suppression of women.

BETTY   I don't like to repeat it.

CLIVE   I must insist.

110 BETTY   I had left my book inside on the piano. I was in the hammock. I asked him to fetch it.

CLIVE   And did he not fetch it?

BETTY   Yes, he did eventually.

CLIVE   And what did he say?

115 BETTY   Clive.

CLIVE   Betty.

BETTY   He said Fetch it yourself. You've got legs under that dress.

CLIVE   Joshua!

[JOSHUA *comes.*]

Joshua, madam says you spoke impolitely to her this afternoon.

120 JOSHUA   Sir?

CLIVE   When she asked you to pass her book from the piano.

JOSHUA   She has the book, sir.

BETTY   I have the book now, but when I told you

CLIVE   Betty, please, let me handle this. You didn't pass it at once?

125 JOSHUA   No sir, I made a joke first.

CLIVE   What was that?

JOSHUA   I said my legs were tired, sir. That was funny because the book was very near, it would not make my legs tired to get it.

BETTY   That's not true.

130 JOSHUA   Did madam hear me wrong?

CLIVE   She heard something else.

JOSHUA   What was that, madam?

BETTY   Never mind.

CLIVE   Now Joshua, it won't do you know. Madam doesn't like that kind of
135   joke. You must do what madam says, just do what she says and don't answer back. You know your place, Joshua. I don't have to say any more.

JOSHUA   No sir.

BETTY   I expect an apology.

JOSHUA   I apologise, madam.

140 CLIVE   There now. It won't happen again, my dear. I'm very shocked Joshua, very shocked.

[CLIVE *winks at* JOSHUA, *unseen by* BETTY.]

[JOSHUA *goes.*]

CLIVE   I think another drink, and send for the children, and isn't that Harry riding down the hill? Wave, wave. Just in time before dark. Cuts it fine, the blighter. Always a hothead, Harry.

145 BETTY   Can he see us?

CLIVE   Stand further forward. He'll see your white dress.
There, he waved back.

BETTY   Do you think so? I wonder what he saw.
Sometimes sunset is so terrifying I can't bear to look.

150 CLIVE   It *makes me* proud. Elsewhere in the empire the sun is rising.

BETTY   Harry looks so small on the hillside.

[ELLEN *comes.*]

ELLEN   Shall I bring the children?

BETTY   Shall Ellen bring the children?

CLIVE   Delightful.

155 BETTY   Yes, Ellen, make sure they're warm. The night air is deceptive. Victoria was looking pale yesterday.

CLIVE   My love.

[MAUD *comes from inside the house.*]

MAUD   Are you warm enough Betty?

BETTY   Perfectly.

160 MAUD   The night air is deceptive.

BETTY   I'm quite warm. I'm too warm.

MAUD   You're not getting a fever, I hope? She's not strong, you know, Clive. I
don't know how long you'll keep her in this climate.

CLIVE   I look after Her Majesty's domains. I think you can trust me to look

165   after my wife.

[ELLEN *comes carrying* VICTORIA, *aged 2.*]
[EDWARD, *aged 9, lags behind.*]

BETTY   Victoria, my pet, say good evening to Papa.

[CLIVE *takes* VICTORIA *on his knee.*]

CLIVE   There's my sweet little Vicky. What have we done today?

BETTY   She wore Ellen's hat.

CLIVE   Did she wear Ellen's big hat like a lady. What a pretty.

170 BETTY   And Joshua gave her a piggy back. Tell Papa. Horsey with Joshy?

ELLEN   She's tired.

CLIVE   Nice Joshy played horsey. What a big strong Joshy. Did you have a gallop? Did you make him stop and go? Not very chatty tonight are we?

BETTY   Edward, say good evening to Papa.

175 CLIVE   Edward my boy. Have you done your lessons well?

EDWARD   Yes Papa.

CLIVE   Did you go riding?

EDWARD   Yes Papa.

CLIVE   What's that you're holding?

180 BETTY   It's Victoria's doll. What are you doing with it, Edward?

EDWARD   Minding her.

BETTY   Well I should give it to Ellen quickly. You don't want Papa to see you
with a doll.

CLIVE   No, we had you with Victoria's doll once before, Edward.

185 ELLEN   He's minding it for Vicky. He's not playing with it.

BETTY   He's not playing with it, Clive. He's minding it for Vicky.

CLIVE   Ellen minds Victoria, let Ellen mind the doll.

ELLEN   Come, give it to me.

[ELLEN *takes the doll.*]

EDWARD   Don't pull her about. Vicky's very fond of her. She likes me to have

190   her.

BETTY   He's a very good brother.

CLIVE   Yes, it's manly of you Edward, to take care of your little sister. We'll
say no more about it. Tomorrow I'll take you riding with me and Harry
Bagley. Would you like that?

195 EDWARD   Is he here?

CLIVE   He's just arrived. There Betty, take Victoria now. I must go and welcome Harry.

[CLIVE *tosses* VICTORIA *to* BETTY, *who gives her to* ELLEN.]

EDWARD   Can I come, Papa?

BETTY   Is he warm enough?

200 EDWARD   Am I warm enough?

CLIVE   Never mind the women, Ned. Come and meet Harry.

[*They go. The women are left. There is a silence.*]

MAUD   I daresay Mr Bagley will be out all day and we'll see nothing of
him.

BETTY   He plays the piano. Surely he will sometimes stay at home with
205   us.

MAUD   We can't expect it. The men have their duties and we have ours.

BETTY   He won't have seen a piano for a year. He lives a very rough life.

ELLEN   Will it be exciting for you, Betty?

MAUD   Whatever do you mean, Ellen?

210 ELLEN   We don't have very much society.

BETTY   Clive is my society.

MAUD   It's time Victoria went to bed.

ELLEN   She'd like to stay up and see Mr Bagley.

MAUD   Mr Bagley can see her tomorrow.

[ELLEN *goes.*]

215 MAUD   You let that girl forget her place, Betty.

BETTY   Mother, she is governess to my son. I know what her place is. I think
my friendship does her good. She is not very happy.

MAUD   Young women are never happy.

BETTY   Mother, what a thing to say.

220 MAUD   Then when they're older they look back and see that comparatively
speaking they were ecstatic.

BETTY   I'm perfectly happy.

MAUD   You are looking very pretty tonight. You were such a success as a
young girl. You have made a most fortunate marriage. I'm sure you will be
225   an excellent hostess to Mr Bagley.

BETTY   I feel quite nervous at the thought of entertaining.

MAUD   I can always advise you if I'm asked.

BETTY   What a long time they're taking. I always seem to be waiting for
the men.

230 MAUD   Betty you have to learn to be patient. I am patient. My mama was very
patient.

[CLIVE *approaches, supporting* MRS SAUNDERS.]

CLIVE   It is a pleasure. It is an honour. It is positively your duty to seek my
help. I would be hurt, I would be insulted by any show of independence.
Your husband would have been one of my dearest friends if he had lived.
235   Betty, look who has come, Mrs Saunders. She has ridden here all alone,
amazing spirit. What will you have? Tea or something stronger? Let her lie
down, she is overcome. Betty, you will know what to do.

[MRS SAUNDERS *lies down.*]

MAUD   I knew it. I heard drums. We'll be killed in our beds.

CLIVE   Now, please, calm yourself.

240 MAUD   I am perfectly calm. I am just outspoken. If it comes to being killed I
shall take it as calmly as anyone.

CLIVE   There is no cause for alarm. Mrs Saunders has been alone since her husband died last year, amazing spirit. Not surprisingly, the strain has told. She has come to us as her nearest neighbours.

245 MAUD   What happened to make her come?

CLIVE   This is not an easy country for a woman.

MAUD   Clive, I heard drums. We are not children.

CLIVE   Of course you heard drums. The tribes are constantly at war, if the term is not too grand to grace their squabbles. Not unnaturally Mrs

250 Saunders would like the company of white women. The piano. Poetry.

BETTY   We are not her nearest neighbours.

CLIVE   We are among her nearest neighbours and I was a dear friend of her late husband. She knows that she will find a welcome here. She will not be disappointed. She will be cared for.

255 MAUD   Of course we will care for her.

BETTY   Victoria is in bed. I must go and say goodnight. Mother, please, you look after Mrs Saunders.

CLIVE   Harry will be here at once.

[BETTY goes.]

MAUD   How rash to go out after dark without a shawl.

260 CLIVE   Amazing spirit. Drink this.

MRS SAUNDERS   Where am I?

MAUD   You are quite safe.

MRS SAUNDERS   Clive? Clive? Thank God. This is very kind. How do you do? I am sorry to be a nuisance. Charmed. Have you a gun? I have a gun.

265 CLIVE   There is no need for guns I hope. We are all friends here.

MRS SAUNDERS   I think I will lie down again.

[HARRY BAGLEY and EDWARD have approached.]

MAUD   Ah, here is Mr Bagley.

EDWARD   I gave his horse some water.

CLIVE   You don't know Mrs Saunders, do you Harry? She has at present col-

270 lapsed, but she is recovering thanks to the good offices of my wife's mother who I think you've met before. Betty will be along in a minute. Edward will go home to school shortly. He is quite a young man since you saw him.

HARRY   I hardly knew him.

MAUD   What news have you for us, Mr Bagley?

275 CLIVE   Do you know Mrs Saunders, Harry? Amazing spirit.

EDWARD   Did you hardly know me?

HARRY   Of course I knew you. I mean you have grown.

EDWARD   What do you expect?

HARRY   That's quite right, people don't get smaller.

280 MAUD   Edward. You should be in bed.

EDWARD   No, I'm not tired, I'm not tired am I Uncle Harry?

HARRY   I don't think he's tired.

CLIVE   He is overtired. It is past his bedtime. Say goodnight.

EDWARD   Goodnight, sir.

285 CLIVE   And to your grandmother.

EDWARD   Goodnight, Grandmother.

[EDWARD goes.]

MAUD   Shall I help Mrs Saunders indoors? I'm afraid she may get a chill.

CLIVE   Shall I give her an arm?

MAUD   How kind of you Clive. I think I am strong enough.

[MAUD *helps* MRS SAUNDERS *into the house.*]

290   CLIVE   Not a word to alarm the women.

HARRY   Absolutely.

CLIVE   I did some good today I think. Kept up some alliances. There's a lot of affection there.

HARRY   They're affectionate people. They can be very cruel of course.

295   CLIVE   Well they are savages.

HARRY   Very beautiful people many of them.

CLIVE   Joshua! [*To* HARRY.] I think we should sleep with guns.

HARRY   I haven't slept in a house for six months. It seems extremely safe.

[JOSHUA *comes.*]

CLIVE   Joshua, you will have gathered there's a spot of bother. Rumours of
300   this and that. You should be armed I think.

JOSHUA   There are many bad men, sir. I pray about it. Jesus will protect us.

CLIVE   He will indeed and I'll also get you a weapon. Betty, come and keep Harry company. Look in the barn, Joshua, every night.

[CLIVE *and* JOSHUA *go.* BETTY *comes.*]

HARRY   I wondered where you were.

305   BETTY   I was singing lullabies.

HARRY   When I think of you I always think of you with Edward in your lap.

BETTY   Do you think of me sometimes then?

HARRY   You have been thought of where no white woman has ever been thought of before.

310   BETTY   It's one way of having adventures. I suppose I will never go in person.

HARRY   That's up to you.

BETTY   Of course it's not. I have duties.

HARRY   Are you happy, Betty?

BETTY   Where have you been?

315   HARRY   Built a raft and went up the river. Stayed with some people. The king is always very good to me. They have a lot of skulls around the place but not white men's I think. I made up a poem one night. If I should die in this forsaken spot, There is a loving heart without a blot, Where I will live—and so on.

BETTY   When I'm near you it's like going out into the jungle. It's like going up
320   the river on a raft. It's like going out in the dark.

HARRY   And you are safety and light and peace and home.

BETTY   But I want to be dangerous.

HARRY   Clive is my friend.

BETTY   I am your friend.

325   HARRY   I don't like dangerous women.

BETTY   Is Mrs Saunders dangerous?

HARRY   Not to me. She's a bit of an old boot.

[JOSHUA *comes, unobserved.*]

BETTY   Am I dangerous?

HARRY   You are rather.

330   BETTY   Please like me.

HARRY   I worship you.

BETTY   Please want me.

HARRY   I don't want to want you. Of course I want you.

BETTY   What are we going to do?

335 HARRY   I should have stayed on the river. The hell with it.

> [*He goes to take her in his arms, she runs away into the house.* HARRY *stays where he is. He becomes aware of* JOSHUA.]

HARRY   Who's there?

JOSHUA   Only me sir.

HARRY   Got a gun now have you?

JOSHUA   Yes sir.

340 HARRY   Where's Clive?

JOSHUA   Going round the boundaries sir.

HARRY   Have you checked there's nobody in the barns?

JOSHUA   Yes sir.

HARRY   Shall we go in a barn and fuck? It's not an order.

345 JOSHUA   That's all right, yes.

> [*They go off.*]

SCENE TWO: *An open space some distance from the house.* MRS SAUNDERS *alone, breathless. She is carrying a riding crop.* CLIVE *arrives.*

CLIVE   Why? Why?

MRS SAUNDERS   Don't fuss, Clive, it makes you sweat.

CLIVE   Why ride off now? Sweat, you would sweat if you were in love with somebody as disgustingly capricious as you are. You will be shot with poi-
350 soned arrows. You will miss the picnic. Somebody will notice I came after you.

MRS SAUNDERS   I didn't want you to come after me. I wanted to be alone.

CLIVE   You will be raped by cannibals.

MRS SAUNDERS   I just wanted to get out of your house.

355 CLIVE   My God, what women put us through. Cruel, cruel. I think you are the sort of woman who would enjoy whipping somebody. I've never met one before.

MRS SAUNDERS   Can I tell you something, Clive?

CLIVE   Let me tell you something first. Since you came to the house I have
360 had an erection twenty-four hours a day except for ten minutes after the time we had intercourse.

MRS SAUNDERS   I don't think that's physically possible.

CLIVE   You are causing me appalling physical suffering. Is this the way to treat a benefactor?

365 MRS SAUNDERS   Clive, when I came to your house the other night I came because I was afraid. The cook was going to let his whole tribe in through the window.

CLIVE   I know that, my poor sweet. Amazing—

MRS SAUNDERS   I came to you although you are not my nearest neighbour—

370 CLIVE   Rather than to the old major of seventy-two.

MRS SAUNDERS   Because the last time he came to visit me I had to defend myself with a shotgun and I thought you would take no for an answer.

CLIVE   But you've already answered yes.

MRS SAUNDERS   I answered yes once. Sometimes I want to say no.

375 CLIVE   Women, my God. Look the picnic will start, I have to go to the picnic. Please Caroline—

MRS SAUNDERS   I think I will have to go back to my own house.

CLIVE   Caroline, if you were shot with poisoned arrows do you know what
          I'd do? I'd fuck your dead body and poison myself. Caroline, you smell
380   amazing. You terrify me. You are dark like this continent. Mysterious.
          Treacherous. When you rode to me through the night. When you fainted
          in my arms. When I came to you in your bed, when I lifted the mosquito
          netting, when I said let me in, let me in. Oh don't shut me out, Caroline,
          let me in.

          [*He has been caressing her feet and legs. He disappears completely under
          her skirt.*]

385 MRS SAUNDERS   Please stop. I can't concentrate. I want to go home. I wish
          I didn't enjoy the sensation because I don't like you, Clive. I do like
          living in your house where there's plenty of guns. But I don't like you at
          all. But I do like the sensation. Well I'll have it then. I'll have it, I'll have
          it—

          [*Voices are heard singing 'The First Noel'.*]

390   Don't stop. Don't stop.

          [CLIVE *comes out from under her skirt.*]

CLIVE   The Christmas picnic. I came.
MRS SAUNDERS   I didn't.
CLIVE   I'm all sticky.
MRS SAUNDERS   What about me? Wait.
395 CLIVE   All right, are you? Come on. We mustn't be found.
MRS SAUNDERS   Don't go now.
CLIVE   Caroline, you are so voracious. Do let go. Tidy yourself up. There's a
          hair in my mouth.

          [CLIVE *and* MRS SAUNDERS *go off.* BETTY *and* MAUD *come, with* JOSHUA
          carrying hamper.]

MAUD   I never would have thought a guinea fowl could taste so like a
400   turkey.
BETTY   I had to explain to Cook three times.
MAUD   You did very well dear.

          [JOSHUA *sits apart with gun.* EDWARD *and* HARRY *with* VICTORIA *on his
          shoulder, singing 'The First Noel'.* MAUD *and* BETTY *are unpacking the
          hamper.* CLIVE *arrives separately.*]

MAUD   This tablecloth was one of my mama's.
BETTY   Uncle Harry playing horsey.
405 EDWARD   Crackers crackers.[3]
BETTY   Not yet, Edward.
CLIVE   And now the moment we have all been waiting for.

          [CLIVE *opens champagne. General acclaim.*]

          Oh dear, stained my trousers, never mind.
EDWARD   Can I have some?
410 MAUD   Oh no Edward, not for you.
CLIVE   Give him half a glass.
MAUD   If your father says so.

---

3. Traditional British Christmas favor made
of stiff paper tubes filled with a paper crown
and small toys, covered with colored paper.
When the paper wrapping is pulled at both
ends, the tube makes a cracking noise and
splits open to release the contents.

CLIVE   All rise please. To Her Majesty Queen Victoria, God bless her, and
    her husband and all her dear children.

415 ALL   The Queen.

EDWARD   Crackers crackers.

        [*General cracker pulling, hats.* CLIVE *and* HARRY *discuss champagne.*]

HARRY   Excellent, Clive, wherever did you get it?

CLIVE   I know a chap in French Equatorial Africa.

EDWARD   I won, I won Mama.

        [ELLEN *arrives.*]

420 BETTY   Give a hat to Joshua, he'd like it.

        [EDWARD *takes hat to* JOSHUA. BETTY *takes a ball from the hamper and
        plays catch with* ELLEN. *Murmurs of surprise and congratulation from
        the men as they catch the ball.*]

EDWARD   Mama, don't play. You know you can't catch a ball.

BETTY   He's perfectly right. I can't throw either.

        [BETTY *sits down.* ELLEN *has the ball.*]

EDWARD   Ellen, don't you play either. You're no good. You spoil it.

        [EDWARD *takes* VICTORIA *from* HARRY *and gives her to* ELLEN. *He takes the
        ball and throws it to* HARRY. HARRY, CLIVE *and* EDWARD *play ball.*]

BETTY   Ellen come and sit with me. We'll be spectators and clap.

        [EDWARD *misses the ball.*]

425 CLIVE   Butterfingers.

EDWARD   I'm not.

HARRY   Throw straight now.

EDWARD   I did, I did.

CLIVE   Keep your eye on the ball.

430 EDWARD   You can't throw.

CLIVE   Don't be a baby.

EDWARD   I'm not, throw a hard one, throw a hard one—

CLIVE   Butterfingers. What will Uncle Harry think of you?

EDWARD   It's your fault. You can't throw. I hate you.

        [*He throws the ball wildly in the direction of* JOSHUA.]

435 CLIVE   Now you've lost the ball. He's lost the ball.

EDWARD   It's Joshua's fault. Joshua's butterfingers.

CLIVE   I don't think I want to play any more. Joshua, find the ball will you?

EDWARD   Yes, please play. I'll find the ball. Please play.

CLIVE   You're so silly and you can't catch. You'll be no good at cricket.

440 MAUD   Why don't we play hide-and-seek?

EDWARD   Because it's a baby game.

BETTY   You've hurt Edward's feelings.

CLIVE   A boy has no business having feelings.

HARRY   Hide-and-seek. I'll be it. Everybody must hide. This is the base, you

445   have to get home to base.

EDWARD   Hide-and-seek, hide-and-seek.

HARRY   Can we persuade the ladies to join us?

MAUD   I'm playing. I love games.

BETTY   I always get found straight away.

450 ELLEN   Come on, Betty, do. Vicky wants to play.

EDWARD   You won't find me ever.

[*They all go except* CLIVE, HARRY, JOSHUA.]

HARRY   It is safe, I suppose?

CLIVE   They won't go far. This is very much my territory and it's broad daylight. Joshua will keep an open eye.

455 HARRY   Well I must give them a hundred. You don't know what this means to
me, Clive. A chap can only go on so long alone. I can climb mountains and
go down rivers, but what's it for? For Christmas and England and games and
women singing. This is the empire, Clive. It's not me putting a flag in new
lands. It's you. The empire is one big family. I'm one of its black sheep, Clive.

460   And I know you think my life is rather dashing. But I want you to know I
admire you. This is the empire, Clive, and I serve it. With all my heart.

CLIVE   I think that's about a hundred.

HARRY   Ready or not, here I come!

[*He goes.*]

CLIVE   Harry Bagley is a fine man, Joshua. You should be proud to know him.

465   He will be in history books.

JOSHUA   Sir, while we are alone.

CLIVE   Joshua of course, what is it? You always have my ear. Any time.

JOSHUA   Sir, I have some information. The stable boys are not to be trusted.
They whisper. They go out at night. They visit their people. Their people

470   are not my people. I do not visit my people.

CLIVE   Thank you, Joshua. They certainly look after Beauty. I'll be sorry to
have to replace them.

JOSHUA   They carry knives.

CLIVE   Thank you, Joshua.

475 JOSHUA   And, sir.

CLIVE   I appreciate this, Joshua, very much.

JOSHUA   Your wife.

CLIVE   Ah, yes?

JOSHUA   She also thinks Harry Bagley is a fine man.

480 CLIVE   Thank you, Joshua.

JOSHUA   Are you going to hide?

CLIVE   Yes, yes I am. Thank you. Keep your eyes open Joshua.

JOSHUA   I do, sir.

[CLIVE *goes.* JOSHUA *goes.* HARRY *and* BETTY *race back to base.*]

BETTY   I can't run, I can't run at all.

485 HARRY   There, I've caught you.

BETTY   Harry, what are we going to do?

HARRY   It's impossible, Betty.

BETTY   Shall we run away together?

[MAUD *comes.*]

MAUD   I give up. Don't catch me. I have been stung.

490 HARRY   Nothing serious I hope.

MAUD   I have ointment in my bag. I always carry ointment. I shall just sit
down and rest. I am too old for all this fun. Hadn't you better be seeking,
Harry?

[HARRY *goes.* MAUD *and* BETTY *are alone for some time. They don't speak.*]
[HARRY *and* EDWARD *race back.*]

EDWARD   I won, I won, you didn't catch me.

495 HARRY   Yes I did.

EDWARD   Mama, who was first?

BETTY   I wasn't watching. I think it was Harry.

EDWARD   It wasn't Harry. You're no good at judging. I won, didn't I Grandma?

MAUD   I expect so, since it's Christmas.

500 EDWARD   I won, Uncle Harry. I'm better than you.

BETTY   Why don't you help Uncle Harry look for the others?

EDWARD   Shall I?

HARRY   Yes, of course.

BETTY   Run along then. He's just coming.

> [EDWARD goes.]

505   Harry, I shall scream.

HARRY   Ready or not here I come.

> [HARRY runs off.]

BETTY   Why don't you go back to the house, Mother, and rest your insect bite?

MAUD   Betty, my duty is here. I don't like what I see. Clive wouldn't like it,

510   Betty. I am your mother.

BETTY   Clive gives you a home because you are my mother.

> [HARRY comes back.]

HARRY   I can't find anyone else. I'm getting quite hot.

BETTY   Sit down a minute.

HARRY   I can't do that I'm he. How's your sting?

515 MAUD   It seems to be swelling up.

BETTY   Why don't you go home and rest? Joshua will go with you. Joshua!

HARRY   I could take you back.

MAUD   That would be charming.

BETTY   You can't go. You're he.

> [JOSHUA comes.]

520 BETTY   Joshua, my mother wants to go back to the house. Will you go with her please.

JOSHUA   Sir told me I have to keep an eye.

BETTY   I am telling you to go back to the house. Then you can come back here and keep an eye.

525 MAUD   Thank you Betty. I know we have our little differences, but I always want what is best for you.

> [JOSHUA and MAUD go.]

HARRY   Don't give way. Keep calm.

BETTY   I shall kill myself.

HARRY   Betty, you are a star in my sky. Without you I would have no sense of

530   direction. I need you, and I need you where you are, I need you to be Clive's wife. I need to go up rivers and know you are sitting here thinking of me.

BETTY   I want more than that. Is that wicked of me?

HARRY   Not wicked, Betty. Silly.

> [EDWARD calls in the distance.]

535 EDWARD   Uncle Harry, where are you?

BETTY   Can't we ever be alone?

HARRY   You are a mother. And a daughter. And a wife.

BETTY   I think I shall go and hide again.

> [BETTY *goes.* HARRY *goes.* CLIVE *chases* MRS SAUNDERS *across the stage.*]
> [EDWARD *and* HARRY *call in the distance.*]

EDWARD   Uncle Harry!

540   HARRY   Edward!

> [EDWARD *comes.*]

EDWARD   Uncle Harry!

> [HARRY *comes.*]

There you are. I haven't found anyone have you?

HARRY   I wonder where they all are.

EDWARD   Perhaps they're lost for ever. Perhaps they're dead. There's trouble
545   going on isn't there, and nobody says because of not frightening the women
and children.

HARRY   Yes, that's right.

EDWARD   Do you think we'll be killed in our beds?

HARRY   Not very likely.

550   EDWARD   I can't sleep at night. Can you?

HARRY   I'm not used to sleeping in a house.

EDWARD   If I'm awake at night can I come and see you? I won't wake you up.
I'll only come in if you're awake.

HARRY   You should try to sleep.

555   EDWARD   I don't mind being awake because I make up adventures. Once
we were on a raft going down to the rapids. We've lost the paddles
because we used them to fight off the crocodiles. A crocodile comes at
me and I stab it again and again and the blood is everywhere and it tips
up the raft and it has you by the leg and it's biting your leg right off and I
560   take my knife and stab it in the throat and rip open its stomach and it lets
go of you but it bites my hand but it's dead. And I drag you onto the river
bank and I'm almost fainting with pain and we lie there in each other's
arms.

HARRY   Have I lost my leg?

565   EDWARD   I forgot about the leg by then.

HARRY   Hadn't we better look for the others?

EDWARD   Wait I've got something for you. It was in Mama's box but she
never wears it.

> [EDWARD *gives* HARRY *a necklace.*]

You don't have to wear it either but you might like it to look at.

570   HARRY   It's beautiful. But you'll have to put it back.

EDWARD   I wanted to give it to you.

HARRY   You did. It can go back in the box. You still gave it to me. Come on
now, we have to find the others.

EDWARD   Harry, I love you.

575   HARRY   Yes I know. I love you too.

EDWARD   You know what we did when you were here before. I want to do it
again. I think about it all the time. I try to do it to myself but it's not as
good. Don't you want to any more?

HARRY   I do, but it's a sin and a crime and it's also wrong.

580   EDWARD   But we'll do it anyway won't we?

HARRY   Yes of course.

EDWARD   I wish the others would all be killed. Take it out now and let me see it.

HARRY   No.

EDWARD   Is it big now?

585   HARRY   Yes.

EDWARD   Let me touch it.

HARRY   No.

EDWARD   Just hold me.

HARRY   When you can't sleep.

590   EDWARD   We'd better find the others then. Come on.

HARRY   Ready or not, here we come.

[*They go out with whoops and shouts.* BETTY *and* ELLEN *come.*]

BETTY   Ellen, I don't want to play any more.

ELLEN   Nor do I, Betty.

BETTY   Come and sit here with me. Oh Ellen, what will become of me?

595   ELLEN   Betty, are you crying? Are you laughing?

BETTY   Tell me what you think of Harry Bagley.

ELLEN   He's a very fine man.

BETTY   No, Ellen, what you really think.

ELLEN   I think you think he's very handsome.

600   BETTY   And don't you think he is? Oh Ellen, you're so good and I'm so wicked.

ELLEN   I'm not so good as you think.

[EDWARD *comes.*]

EDWARD   I've found you.

ELLEN   We're not hiding Edward.

EDWARD   But I found you.

605   ELLEN   We're not playing, Edward, now run along.

EDWARD   Come on, Ellen, do play. Come on, Mama.

ELLEN   Edward, don't pull your mama like that.

BETTY   Edward, you must do what your governess says. Go and play with Uncle Harry.

610   EDWARD   Uncle Harry!

[EDWARD *goes.*]

BETTY   Ellen, can you keep a secret?

ELLEN   Oh yes, yes please.

BETTY   I love Harry Bagley. I want to go away with him. There, I've said it, it's true.

615   ELLEN   How do you know you love him?

BETTY   I kissed him.

ELLEN   Betty.

BETTY   He held my hand like this. Oh I want him to do it again. I want him to stroke my hair.

620   ELLEN   Your lovely hair. Like this, Betty?

BETTY   I want him to put his arm around my waist.

ELLEN   Like this, Betty?

BETTY   Yes, oh I want him to kiss me again.

ELLEN   Like this Betty?

[ELLEN *kisses* BETTY.]

625   BETTY   Ellen, whatever are you doing? It's not a joke.

ELLEN   I'm sorry, Betty. You're so pretty. Harry Bagley doesn't deserve you. You wouldn't really go away with him?

BETTY   Oh Ellen, you don't know what I suffer. You don't know what love is. Everyone will hate me, but it's worth it for Harry's love.

630 ELLEN   I don't hate you, Betty, I love you.

BETTY   Harry says we shouldn't go away. But he says he worships me.

ELLEN   I worship you Betty.

BETTY   Oh Ellen, you are my only friend.

[*They embrace. The others have all gathered together.*]
[MAUD *has rejoined the party, and* JOSHUA.]

CLIVE   Come along everyone, you mustn't miss Harry's conjuring trick.

[BETTY *and* ELLEN *go to join the others.*]

635 MAUD   I didn't want to spoil the fun by not being here.

HARRY   What is it that flies all over the world and is up my sleeve?

[HARRY *produces a Union Flag from up his sleeve.*[4] *General acclaim.*]

CLIVE   I think we should have some singing now. Ladies, I rely on you to lead the way.

ELLEN   We have a surprise for you. I have taught Joshua a Christmas carol.

640 He has been singing it at the piano but I'm sure he can sing it unaccompanied, can't you, Joshua?

JOSHUA   In the deep midwinter
Frosty wind made moan,
Earth stood hard as iron,

645 Water like a stone.
Snow had fallen snow on snow
Snow on snow,
In the deep midwinter
Long long ago.

650 What can I give him
Poor as I am?
If I were a shepherd
I would bring a lamb.
If I were a wise man

655 I would do my part.
What I can I give him?
Give my heart.[5]

SCENE THREE: *Inside the house.* BETTY, MRS SAUNDERS, MAUD *with* VICTORIA. *The blinds are down so the light isn't bright though it is day outside.* CLIVE *looks in.*

CLIVE   Everything all right? Nothing to be frightened of.

[CLIVE *goes. Silence.*]

---

4. The flag of England, also known as the Union Jack.

5. Excerpt from a Christina Rossetti (1830–1894) lyric, "A Christmas Carol" (1872), set to music in 1906 by Gustav Holst (1874–1934).

MAUD   Clap hands, Daddy comes, with his pockets full of plums. All for
660   Vicky.

        [*Silence.*]

MRS SAUNDERS   Who actually does the flogging?

MAUD   I don't think we want to imagine.

MRS SAUNDERS   I imagine Joshua.

BETTY   Yes I think it would be Joshua. Or would Clive do it himself?

665 MRS SAUNDERS   Well we can ask them afterwards.

MAUD   I don't like the way you speak of it, Mrs Saunders.

MRS SAUNDERS   How should I speak of it?

MAUD   The men will do it in the proper way, whatever it is. We have our own
     part to play.

670 MRS SAUNDERS   Harry Bagley says they should just be sent away. I don't think
     he likes to see them beaten.

BETTY   Harry is so tender-hearted. Perhaps he is right.

MAUD   Harry Bagley is not altogether— He has lived in this country a long
     time without any responsibilities. It is part of his charm but it hasn't
675   improved his judgement. If the boys were just sent away they would go back
     to the village and make more trouble.

MRS SAUNDERS   And what will they say about us in the village if they've been
     flogged?

BETTY   Perhaps Clive should keep them here.

680 MRS SAUNDERS   That is never wise.

BETTY   Whatever shall we do?

MAUD   I don't think it is up to us to wonder. The men don't tell us what is
     going on among the tribes, so how can we possibly make a judgement?

MRS SAUNDERS   I know a little of what is going on.

685 BETTY   Tell me what you know. Clive tells me nothing.

MAUD   You would not want to be told about it, Betty. It is enough for you that
     Clive knows what is happening. Clive will know what to do. Your father
     always knew what to do.

BETTY   Are you saying you would do something different, Caroline?

690 MRS SAUNDERS   I would do what I did at my own home. I left. I can't see any
     way out except to leave. I will leave here. I will keep leaving everywhere I
     suppose.

MAUD   Luckily this household has a head. I am squeamish myself. But luck-
     ily Clive is not.

695 BETTY   You are leaving here then, Caroline?

MRS SAUNDERS   Not immediately. I'm sorry.

        [*Silence.*]

I wonder if it's over.

        [EDWARD *comes in.*]

BETTY   Shouldn't you be with the men, Edward?

EDWARD   I didn't want to see any more. They got what they deserved. Uncle
700   Harry said I could come in.

MRS SAUNDERS   I never allowed the servants to be beaten in my own house.
     I'm going to find out what's happening.

        [MRS SAUNDERS *goes out.*]

BETTY   Will she go and look?

MAUD   Let Mrs Saunders be a warning to you, Betty. She is alone in the
705   world. You are not, thank God. Since your father died, I know what it is to
be unprotected. Vicky is such a pretty little girl. Clap hands, Daddy comes,
with his pockets full of plums. All for Vicky.

> [EDWARD, *meanwhile, has found the doll and is playing clap hands with
> her.*]

BETTY   Edward, what have you got there?

EDWARD   I'm minding her.

710   BETTY   Edward, I've told you before, dolls are for girls.

MAUD   Where is Ellen? She should be looking after Edward. [*She goes to the
door.*] Ellen! Betty, why do you let that girl mope about in her own room?
That's not what she's come to Africa for.

BETTY   You must never let the boys at school know you like dolls. Never,
715   never. No one will talk to you, you won't be on the cricket team, you won't
grow up to be a man like your papa.

EDWARD   I don't want to be like Papa. I hate Papa.

MAUD   Edward! Edward!

BETTY   You're a horrid wicked boy and Papa will beat you. Of course you
720   don't hate him, you love him. Now give Victoria her doll at once.

EDWARD   She's not Victoria's doll, she's my doll. She doesn't love Victoria
and Victoria doesn't love her. Victoria never even plays with her.

MAUD   Victoria will learn to play with her.

EDWARD   She's mine and she loves me and she won't be happy if you take her
725   away, she'll cry, she'll cry, she'll cry.

> [BETTY *takes the doll away, slaps him, bursts into tears.*]
> [ELLEN *comes in.*]

BETTY   Ellen, look what you've done. Edward's got the doll again. Now,
Ellen, will you please do your job.

ELLEN   Edward, you are a wicked boy. I am going to lock you in the nursery
until supper time. Now go upstairs this minute.

> [*She slaps* EDWARD, *who bursts into tears and goes out.*]

730   I do try to do what you want. I'm so sorry.

> [ELLEN *bursts into tears and goes out.*]

MAUD   There now, Vicky's got her baby back. Where did Vicky's naughty baby
go? Shall we smack her? Just a little smack. [MAUD *smacks the doll hard.*]
There, now she's a good baby. Clap hands, Daddy comes, with his pockets
full of plums. All for Vicky's baby. When I was a child we honoured our
735   parents. My mama was an angel.

> [JOSHUA *comes in. He stands without speaking.*]

BETTY   Joshua?

JOSHUA   Madam?

BETTY   Did you want something?

JOSHUA   Sent to see the ladies are all right, madam.

> [MRS SAUNDERS *comes in.*]

740   MRS SAUNDERS   We're very well thank you, Joshua, and how are you?

JOSHUA   Very well thank you, Mrs Saunders.

MRS SAUNDERS   And the stable boys?

JOSHUA   They have had justice, madam.

MRS SAUNDERS   So I saw. And does your arm ache?

745 MAUD   This is not a proper conversation, Mrs Saunders.

MRS SAUNDERS   You don't mind beating your own people?

JOSHUA   Not my people, madam.

MRS SAUNDERS   A different tribe?

JOSHUA   Bad people.

[HARRY *and* CLIVE *come in.*]

750 CLIVE   Well this is all very gloomy and solemn. Can we have the shutters open? The heat of the day has gone, we could have some light, I think. And cool drinks on the verandah, Joshua. Have some lemonade yourself. It is most refreshing. [*Sunlight floods in as the shutters are opened.*]

[EDWARD *comes.*]

EDWARD   Papa, Papa, Ellen tried to lock me in the nursery. Mama is going to
755 tell you of me. I'd rather tell you myself. I was playing with Vicky's doll again and I know it's very bad of me. And I said I didn't want to be like you and I said I hated you. And it's not true and I'm sorry, I'm sorry and please beat me and forgive me.

CLIVE   Well there's a brave boy to own up. You should always respect and
760 love me, Edward, not for myself, I may not deserve it, but as I respected and loved my own father, because he was my father. Through our father we love our Queen and our God, Edward.[6] Do you understand? It is something men understand.

EDWARD   Yes Papa.

765 CLIVE   Then I forgive you and shake you by the hand. You spend too much time with the women. You may spend more time with me and Uncle Harry, little man.

EDWARD   I don't like women. I don't like dolls Papa, and I love you, Uncle Harry.

770 CLIVE   There's a fine fellow. Let us go out onto the verandah.

[*They all start to go.* EDWARD *takes* HARRY's *hand and goes with him.* CLIVE *draws* BETTY *back. They embrace.*]

BETTY   Poor Clive.

CLIVE   It was my duty to have them flogged. For you and Edward and Victoria, to keep you safe.

BETTY   It is terrible to feel betrayed.

775 CLIVE   You can tame a wild animal only so far. They revert to their true nature and savage your hand. Sometimes I feel the natives are the enemy. I know that is wrong. I know I have a responsibility towards them, to care for them and bring them all to be like Joshua. But there is something dangerous. Implacable. This whole continent is my enemy. I am pitching my
780 whole mind and will and reason and spirit against it to tame it, and I sometimes feel it will break over me and swallow me up.

BETTY   Clive, Clive, I am here. I have faith in you.

CLIVE   Yes, I can show you my moments of weakness, Betty, because you are my wife and because I trust you. I trust you, Betty, and it would break my

---

6. Churchill alludes here to the notion of the "Great Chain of Being," explicated by E. M. W. Tillyard in *The Elizabethan World Picture* (1943). Tillyard traces this notion of continu- ous ties from the lowest forms on earth up to God back to the medieval period and establishes its flourishing in Renaissance culture.

785 heart if you did not deserve that trust. Harry Bagley is my friend. It would break my heart if he did not deserve my trust.

BETTY I'm sorry, I'm sorry. Forgive me. It is not Harry's fault, it is all mine. Harry is noble. He has rejected me. It is my wickedness. I get bored, I get restless, I imagine things. There is something so wicked in me, Clive.

790 CLIVE I have never thought of you having the weakness of your sex, only the good qualities.

BETTY I am bad, bad, bad—

CLIVE You are thoughtless, Betty, that's all. Women can be treacherous and evil. They are darker and more dangerous than men. The family protects us

795 from that, you protect me from that. You are not that sort of woman. You are not unfaithful to me, Betty. I can't believe you are. It would hurt me so much to cast you off. That would be my duty.

BETTY No, no, no.

CLIVE Joshua has seen you kissing.

800 BETTY Forgive me.

CLIVE But I don't want to know about it. I don't want to know. I wonder of course, I wonder constantly. If Harry Bagley was not my friend I would shoot him. If I shot you every British man and woman would applaud me. But no. It was a moment of passion such as women are too weak to

805 resist. But you must resist it, Betty, or it will destroy us. We must fight against it. We must resist this dark female lust, Betty, or it will swallow us up.[7]

BETTY I do, I do resist. Help me. Forgive me.

CLIVE Yes I do forgive you. But I can't feel the same about you as I did. You

810 are still my wife and we still have duties to the household.

[*They go out arm in arm. As soon as they have gone* EDWARD *sneaks back to get the doll, which has been dropped on the floor. He picks it up and comforts it.* JOSHUA *comes through with a tray of drinks.*]

JOSHUA Baby. Sissy. Girly.

[JOSHUA *goes.* BETTY *calls from off.*]

BETTY Edward?

[BETTY *comes in.*]

There you are my darling. Come, Papa wants us all to be together. Uncle Harry is going to tell how he caught a crocodile. Mama's sorry she smacked you.

[*They embrace.* JOSHUA *comes in again, passing through.*]

815 BETTY Joshua, fetch me some blue thread from my sewing box. It is on the piano.

JOSHUA You've got legs under that skirt.

BETTY Joshua.

JOSHUA And more than legs.

820 BETTY Edward, are you going to stand there and let a servant insult your mother?

EDWARD Joshua, get my mother's thread.

JOSHUA Oh little Eddy, playing at master. It's only a joke.

EDWARD Don't speak to my mother like that again.

---

7. Churchill alludes here parodically to traditional Western patriarchal notions of female lasciviousness, which originate with the story of Eve in the Book of Genesis.

825 JOSHUA   Ladies have no sense of humour. You like a joke with Joshua.

EDWARD   You fetch her sewing at once, do you hear me? You move when I speak to you, boy.

JOSHUA   Yes sir, master Edward sir.

[JOSHUA *goes.*]

BETTY   Edward, you were wonderful.

[*She goes to embrace him but he moves away.*]

830 EDWARD   Don't touch me.

ALL [*sing 'A Boy's Best Friend'*]

While plodding on our way, the toilsome road of life,
How few the friends that daily there we meet.
Not many will stand by in trouble and strife,
With counsel and affection ever sweet.
835 But there is one whose smile will ever on us beam,
Whose love is dearer far than any other;
And wherever we may turn
This lesson we will learn
A boy's best friend is his mother.

840 Then cherish her with care
And smooth her silv'ry hair,
When gone you will never get another.
And wherever we may turn
This lesson we shall learn,
845 A boy's best friend is his mother.[8]

SCENE FOUR: *The verandah as in Scene One. Early morning. Nobody there.* JOSHUA *comes out of the house slowly and stands for some time doing nothing.* EDWARD *comes out.*

EDWARD   Tell me another bad story, Joshua. Nobody else is even awake yet.

JOSHUA   First there was nothing and then there was the great goddess. She was very large and she had golden eyes and she made the stars and the sun and the earth. But soon she was miserable and lonely and she cried like a 850 great waterfall and her tears made all the rivers in the world. So the great spirit sent a terrible monster, a tree with hundreds of eyes and a long green tongue, and it came chasing after her and she jumped into a lake and the tree jumped in after her, and she jumped right up into the sky. And the tree couldn't follow, he was stuck in the mud. So he picked up a big handful of 855 mud and he threw it at her, up among the stars, and it hit her on the head. And she fell down onto the earth into his arms and the ball of mud is the moon in the sky. And then they had children which is all of us.

EDWARD   It's not true, though.

JOSHUA   Of course it's not true. It's a bad story. Adam and Eve is true. God 860 made man white like him and gave him the bad woman who liked the snake and gave us all this trouble.

[CLIVE *and* HARRY *come out.*]

CLIVE   Run along now, Edward. No, you may stay. You mustn't repeat anything you hear to your mother or your grandmother or Ellen.

8. Lyric from 1897, by Joseph D. Skelly.

EDWARD   Or Mrs Saunders?

865   CLIVE   Mrs Saunders is an unusual woman and does not require protection
        in the same way. Harry, there was trouble last night where we expected it.
        But it's all over now. Everything is under control but nobody should leave
        the house today I think.

HARRY   Casualties?

870   CLIVE   No, none of the soldiers hurt thank God. We did a certain amount of
        damage, set a village on fire and so forth.

HARRY   Was that necessary?

CLIVE   Obviously, it was necessary, Harry, or it wouldn't have happened. The
        army will come and visit, no doubt. You'll like that, eh, Joshua, to see the
875   British army? And a treat for you, Edward, to see the soldiers. Would you
        like to be a soldier?

EDWARD   I'd rather be an explorer.

CLIVE   Ah, Harry, like you, you see. I didn't know an explorer at his age.
        Breakfast, I think, Joshua.

        [CLIVE *and* JOSHUA *go in.* HARRY *is following.*]

880   EDWARD   Uncle.

        [HARRY *stops.*]

        Harry, why won't you talk to me?

HARRY   Of course I'll talk to you.

EDWARD   If you won't be nice to me I'll tell father.

HARRY   Edward, no, not a word, never, not to your mother, nobody, please.
885   Edward, do you understand? Please.

EDWARD   I won't tell. I promise I'll never tell. I've cut my finger and sworn.

HARRY   There's no need to get so excited Edward. We can't be together all
        the time. I will have to leave soon anyway, and go back to the river.

EDWARD   You can't, you can't go. Take me with you.

890   ELLEN   Edward!

HARRY   I have my duty to the Empire.

        [HARRY *goes in.* ELLEN *comes out.*]

ELLEN   Edward, breakfast time. Edward.

EDWARD   I'm not hungry.

ELLEN   Betty, please come and speak to Edward.

        [BETTY *comes.*]

895   BETTY   Why, what's the matter?

ELLEN   He won't come in for breakfast.

BETTY   Edward, I shall call your father.

EDWARD   You can't make me eat.

        [*He goes in.* BETTY *is about to follow.*]

ELLEN   Betty.

        [BETTY *stops.*]

900   Betty, when Edward goes to school will I have to leave?

BETTY   Never mind, Ellen dear, you'll get another place. I'll give you an excel-
        lent reference.

ELLEN   I don't want another place, Betty. I want to stay with you for ever.

BETTY   If you go back to England you might get married, Ellen. You're quite
905   pretty, you shouldn't despair of getting a husband.

ELLEN   I don't want a husband. I want you.

BETTY   Children of your own, Ellen, think.

ELLEN   I don't want children, I don't like children. I just want to be alone with you, Betty, and sing for you and kiss you because I love you, Betty.

910 BETTY   I love you too, Ellen. But women have their duty as soldiers have. You must be a mother if you can.

ELLEN   Betty, Betty, I love you so much. I want to stay with you for ever, my love for you is eternal, stronger than death. I'd rather die than leave you, Betty.

915 BETTY   No you wouldn't, Ellen, don't be silly. Come, don't cry. You don't feel what you think you do. It's the loneliness here and the climate is very confusing. Come and have breakfast, Ellen dear, and I'll forget all about it.

[ELLEN goes. CLIVE comes.]

BETTY   Clive, please forgive me.

CLIVE   Will you leave me alone?

[BETTY goes back into the house. HARRY comes.]

920   Women, Harry. I envy you going into the jungle, a man's life.

HARRY   I envy you.

CLIVE   Harry, I know you do. I have spoken to Betty.

HARRY   I assure you, Clive—

CLIVE   Please say nothing about it.

925 HARRY   My friendship for you—

CLIVE   Absolutely. I know the friendship between us, Harry, is not something that could be spoiled by the weaker sex. Friendship between men is a fine thing. It is the noblest form of relationship.

HARRY   I agree with you.

930 CLIVE   There is the necessity of reproduction. The family is all important. And there is the pleasure. But what we put ourselves through to get the pleasure, Harry. When I heard about our fine fellows last night fighting those savages to protect us I thought yes, that is what I aspire to. I tell you Harry, in confidence, I suddenly got out of Mrs Saunders' bed and came

935   out here on the verandah and looked at the stars.

HARRY   I couldn't sleep last night either.

CLIVE   There is something dark about women, that threatens what is best in us. Between men that light burns brightly.

HARRY   I didn't know you felt like that.

940 CLIVE   Women are irrational, demanding, inconsistent, treacherous, lustful, and they smell different from us.

HARRY   Clive—

CLIVE   Think of the comradeship of men, Harry, sharing adventures, sharing danger, risking their lives together.

[HARRY takes hold of CLIVE.]

945 CLIVE   What are you doing?

HARRY   Well, you said—

CLIVE   I said what?

HARRY   Between men.

[CLIVE is speechless.]

I'm sorry, I misunderstood, I would never have dreamt, I thought—

950 CLIVE   My God, Harry, how disgusting.

HARRY   You will not betray my confidence.

CLIVE   I feel contaminated.

HARRY   I struggle against it. You cannot imagine the shame. I have tried everything to save myself.

955 CLIVE   The most revolting perversion. Rome fell, Harry, and this sin can destroy an empire.[9]

HARRY   It is not a sin, it is a disease.

CLIVE   A disease more dangerous than diphtheria. Effeminacy is contagious. How I have been deceived. Your face does not look degenerate.[1] Oh Harry,
960   how did you sink to this?

HARRY   Clive, help me, what am I to do?

CLIVE   You have been away from England too long,

HARRY   Where can I go except into the jungle to hide?

CLIVE   You don't do it with the natives, Harry? My God, what a betrayal of
965   the Queen.

HARRY   Clive, I am like a man born crippled. Please help me.

CLIVE   You must repent.

HARRY   I have thought of killing myself.

CLIVE   That is a sin too.

970 HARRY   There is no way out. Clive, I beg of you, do not betray my confidence.

CLIVE   I cannot keep a secret like this. Rivers will be named after you, it's unthinkable. You must save yourself from depravity. You must get married. You are not unattractive to women. What a relief that you and Betty were
975   not after all—good God, how disgusting. Now Mrs Saunders. She's a woman of spirit, she could go with you on your expeditions.

HARRY   I suppose getting married wouldn't be any worse than killing myself.

CLIVE   Mrs Saunders! Mrs Saunders! Ask her now, Harry. Think of England.

[MRS SAUNDERS *comes.* CLIVE *withdraws.*]

[HARRY *goes up to* MRS SAUNDERS.]

980 HARRY   Mrs Saunders, will you marry me?

MRS SAUNDERS   Why?

HARRY   We are both alone.

MRS SAUNDERS   I choose to be alone, Mr Bagley. If I can look after myself, I'm sure you can. Clive, I have something important to tell you. I've just
985   found Joshua putting earth on his head. He tells me his parents were killed last night by the British soldiers. I think you owe him an apology on behalf of the Queen.

CLIVE   Joshua! Joshua!

MRS SAUNDERS   Mr Bagley, I could never be a wife again. There is only one
990   thing about marriage that I like.

[JOSHUA *comes.*]

CLIVE   Joshua, I am horrified to hear what has happened. Good God.

MRS SAUNDERS   His father was shot. His mother died in the blaze.

[MRS SAUNDERS *goes.*]

---

9. Allusion to Edward Gibbon's *The History of the Decline and Fall of the Roman Empire* (1776–89), which chronicled the end of Roman supremacy through moral decay and ebbing manliness.

1. Allusion to Max Nordau's influential study *Degeneration* (1892), translated from German to English in 1895.

CLIVE   Joshua, do you want a day off? Do you want to go to your people?

JOSHUA   Not my people, sir.

995 CLIVE   But you want to go to your parents' funeral?

JOSHUA   No sir.

CLIVE   Yes, Joshua, yes, your father and mother. I'm sure they were loyal to the Crown. I'm sure it was all a terrible mistake.

JOSHUA   My mother and father were bad people.

1000 CLIVE   Joshua, no.

JOSHUA   You are my father and mother.

CLIVE   Well really. I don't know what to say. That's very decent of you. Are you sure there's nothing I can do? You can have the day off you know.

[BETTY *comes out followed by* EDWARD.]

BETTY   What's the matter? What's happening?

1005 CLIVE   Something terrible has happened. No, I mean some relatives of Joshua's met with an accident.

JOSHUA   May I go sir?

CLIVE   Yes, yes of course. Good God, what a terrible thing. Bring us a drink will you Joshua?

[JOSHUA *goes*.]

1010 EDWARD   What? What?

BETTY   Edward, go and do your lessons.

EDWARD   What is it, Uncle Harry?

HARRY   Go and do your lessons.

ELLEN   Edward, come in here at once.

1015 EDWARD   What's happened, Uncle Harry?

[HARRY *has moved aside*. EDWARD *follows him*.]

[ELLEN *comes out*.]

HARRY   Go away. Go inside. Ellen!

ELLEN   Go inside, Edward. I shall tell your mother.

BETTY   Go inside, Edward at once. I shall tell your father.

CLIVE   Go inside, Edward. And Betty you go inside too.

[BETTY, EDWARD *and* ELLEN *go*. MAUD *comes out*.]

1020 Go inside. And Ellen, you come outside.

[ELLEN *comes out*.]

Mr Bagley has something to say to you.

HARRY   Ellen. I don't suppose you would marry me?

ELLEN   What if I said yes?

CLIVE   Run along now, you two want to be alone.

[HARRY *and* ELLEN *go out*. JOSHUA *brings* CLIVE *a drink*.]

1025 JOSHUA   The governess and your wife, sir.

CLIVE   What's that, Joshua?

JOSHUA   She talks of love to your wife, sir. I have seen them. Bad women.

CLIVE   Joshua, you go too far. Get out of my sight.

SCENE FIVE: *The verandah. A table with a white cloth. A wedding cake and a large knife. Bottles and glasses.* JOSHUA *is putting things on the table.* EDWARD *has the doll.* JOSHUA *sees him with it. He holds out his hand.* EDWARD *gives him the doll.* JOSHUA *takes the knife and cuts the doll open and shakes the sawdust out of it.* JOSHUA *throws the doll under the table.*

MAUD   Come along Edward, this is such fun.

     [*Everyone enters, triumphal arch for* HARRY *and* ELLEN.]

1030   Your mama's wedding was a splendid occasion, Edward. I cried and cried.

     [ELLEN *and* BETTY *go aside.*]

ELLEN   Betty, what happens with a man? I don't know what to do.

BETTY   You just keep still.

ELLEN   And what does he do?

1035 BETTY   Harry will know what to do.

ELLEN   And is it enjoyable?

BETTY   Ellen, you're not getting married to enjoy yourself.

ELLEN   Don't forget me, Betty.

     [ELLEN *goes.*]

BETTY   I think my necklace has been stolen Clive. I did so want to wear it at

1040   the wedding.

EDWARD   It was Joshua. Joshua took it.

CLIVE   Joshua?

EDWARD   He did, he did, I saw him with it.

HARRY   Edward, that's not true.

1045 EDWARD   It is, it is.

HARRY   Edward, I'm afraid you took it yourself.

EDWARD   I did not.

HARRY   I have seen him with it.

CLIVE   Edward, is that true? Where is it? Did you take your mother's neck-

1050   lace? And to try and blame Joshua, good God.

     [EDWARD *runs off.*]

BETTY   Edward, come back. Have you got my necklace?

HARRY   I should leave him alone. He'll bring it back.

BETTY   I wanted to wear it. I wanted to look my best at your wedding.

HARRY   You always look your best to me.

1055 BETTY   I shall get drunk.

     [MRS SAUNDERS *comes.*]

MRS SAUNDERS   The sale of my property is completed. I shall leave tomorrow.

CLIVE   That's just as well. Whose protection will you seek this time?

MRS SAUNDERS   I shall go to England and buy a farm there. I shall introduce threshing machines.

1060 CLIVE   Amazing spirit.

     [*He kisses her.* BETTY *launches herself on* MRS SAUNDERS. *They fall to the ground.*]

   Betty—Caroline—I don't deserve this—Harry, Harry.

     [HARRY *and* CLIVE *separate them.* HARRY *holding* MRS SAUNDERS, CLIVE BETTY.]

   Mrs Saunders, how can you abuse my hospitality? How dare you touch my wife? You must leave here at once.

BETTY   Go away, go away. You are a wicked woman.

1065 MAUD   Mrs Saunders, I am shocked. This is your hostess.

CLIVE   Pack your bags and leave the house this instant.

MRS SAUNDERS   I was leaving anyway. There's no place for me here. I have made arrangements to leave tomorrow, and tomorrow is when I will leave. I wish you joy, Mr Bagley.

[MRS SAUNDERS *goes.*]

1070 CLIVE   No place for her anywhere I should think. Shocking behaviour.

BETTY   Oh Clive, forgive me, and love me like you used to.

CLIVE   Were you jealous my dove? My own dear wife!

MAUD   Ah, Mr Bagley, one flesh, you see.

[EDWARD *comes back with the necklace.*]

CLIVE   Good God, Edward, it's true.

1075 EDWARD   I was minding it for Mama because of the troubles.

CLIVE   Well done, Edward, that was very manly of you. See Betty? Edward was protecting his mama's jewels from the rebels. What a hysterical fuss over nothing. Well done, little man. It is quite safe now. The bad men are dead. Edward, you may do up the necklace for Mama.

[EDWARD *does up* BETTY's *necklace, supervised by* CLIVE. JOSHUA *is drinking steadily.* ELLEN *comes back.*]

1080 MAUD   Ah, here's the bride. Come along, Ellen, you don't cry at your own wedding, only at other people's.

CLIVE   Now, speeches, speeches. Who is going to make a speech? Harry, make a speech.

HARRY   I'm no speaker. You're the one for that.

1085 ALL   Speech, speech.

HARRY   My dear friends—what can I say—the empire—the family—the married state to which I have always aspired—your shining example of domestic bliss—my great good fortune in winning Ellen's love—happiest day of my life.

[*Applause.*]

1090 CLIVE   Cut the cake, cut the cake.

[HARRY *and* ELLEN *take the knife to cut the cake.* HARRY *steps on the doll under the table.*]

HARRY   What's this?

ELLEN   Oh look.

BETTY   Edward.

EDWARD   It was Joshua. It was Joshua. I saw him.

1095 CLIVE   Don't tell lies again.

[*He hits* EDWARD *across the side of the head.*]

Unaccustomed as I am to public speaking—

[*Cheers.*]

Harry, my friend. So brave and strong and supple. Ellen, from 'neath her veil so shyly peeking. I wish you joy. A toast—the happy couple. Dangers are past. Our enemies are killed. Put your arm around her, Harry, have a

1100 kiss—All murmuring of discontent is stilled. Long may you live in peace and joy and bliss.

[*While he is speaking,* JOSHUA *raises his gun to shoot* CLIVE. *Only* EDWARD *sees. He does nothing to warn the others. He put his hands over his ears.*]

[BLACK.]

Act Two

SCENE ONE

GERRY   The train from Victoria to Clapham still has those compartments without a corridor. As soon as I got on the platform I saw who I wanted. Slim hips, tense shoulders, trying not to look at anyone. I put my hand on my packet just long enough so that he couldn't miss it. The train came in.
5   You don't want to get in too fast or some straight dumbo might get in with you. I sat by the window. I couldn't see where the fuck he'd got to. Then just as the whistle went he got in. Great. It's a six-minute journey so you can't start anything you can't finish. I stared at him and he unzipped his flies. Then he stopped. So I stood up and took my cock out. He took me in
10   his mouth and shut his eyes tight. He was sort of mumbling it about as if he wasn't sure what to do, so I said, A bit tighter son and he said Sorry and then got on with it. He was jerking off with his left hand, and I could see he'd got a fair-sized one. I wished he'd keep still so I could see his watch. I was getting really turned on. What if we pulled into Clapham Junction
15   now. Of course by the time we sat down again the train was just slowing up. I felt wonderful. Then he started talking. It's better if nothing is said. Once you find he's a librarian in Walthamstow[2] with a special interest in science fiction and lives with his aunt, then forget it. He said I hope you don't think I do this all the time. I said I hope you will from now on. He
20   said he would if I was on the train, but why don't we go out for a meal? I opened the door before the train stopped. I told him I lived with somebody. I don't want to know. He was jogging sideways to keep up. He said What's your phone number, you're my ideal physical type, what sign of the zodiac are you? Where do you live? Where are you going now? It's not fair. I saw
25   him at Victoria a couple of months later and I went straight down to the end of the platform and I picked up somebody really great who never said a word, just smiled.

Winter afternoon. Inside the hut of a one o'clock club,[3] a children's play centre in a park, VICTORIA *and* LIN, *mothers.* CATHY, LIN's *daughter, aged 4, played by a man, clinging to* LIN. VICTORIA *reading a book.*

CATHY   Yum yum bubblegum.
        Stick it up your mother's bum.
30   When it's brown
        Pull it down
        Yum yum bubblegum.
LIN   Like your shoes, Victoria.
CATHY   Jack be nimble, Jack be quick,
35   Jack jump over the candlestick.
        Silly Jack, he should jump higher,
        Goodness gracious, great balls of fire.
LIN   Cathy, do stop. Do a painting.
CATHY   You do a painting.
40 LIN   You do a painting.

---

2. Suburban community in the northeast part of London.
3. Public spaces, often connected with parks or recreation centers, where parents or caregivers can bring young children for play and supervised activities.

CATHY   What shall I paint?

LIN   Paint a house.

CATHY   No.

LIN   Princess.

45 CATHY   No.

LIN   Pirates.

CATHY   Already done that.

LIN   Spacemen.

CATHY   I never paint spacemen. You know I never.

50 LIN   Paint a car crash and blood everywhere.

CATHY   No, don't tell me. I know what to paint.

LIN   Go on then. You need an apron, where's an apron. Here.

CATHY   Don't want an apron.

LIN   Lift up your arms. There's a good girl.

55 CATHY   I don't want to paint.

LIN   Don't paint. Don't paint.

CATHY   What shall I do? You paint. What shall I do Mum?

VICTORIA   There's nobody on the big bike, Cathy, quick.

[CATHY *goes out.* VICTORIA *is watching the children playing outside.*]

VICTORIA   Tommy, it's Jimmy's gun. Let him have it. What the hell.

[*She goes on reading. She reads while she talks.*]

60 LIN   I don't know how you can concentrate.

VICTORIA   You have to or you never do anything.

LIN   Yeah well. It's really warm in here, that's one thing. It's better than standing out there. I got chilblains[4] last winter.

VICTORIA   It is warm.

65 LIN   I suppose Tommy doesn't let you read much. I expect he talks to you while you're reading.

VICTORIA   Yes, he does.

LIN   I didn't get very far with that book you lent me.

VICTORIA   That's all right.

70 LIN   I was glad to have it, though. I sit with it on my lap while I'm watching telly. Well, Cathy's off. She's frightened I'm going to leave her. It's the baby-minder[5] didn't work out when she was two, she still remembers. You can't get them used to other people if you're by yourself. It's no good blaming me. She clings round my knees every morning up the nursery[6] and they don't say anything but they make you feel you're making her do it. But I'm desperate for her to go to school. I did cry when I left her the first day. You wouldn't, you're too fucking sensible. You'll call the teacher by her first name. I really fancy you.

VICTORIA   What?

80 LIN   Put your book down will you for five minutes. You didn't hear a word I said.

VICTORIA   I don't get much time to myself.

LIN   Do you ever go to the movies?

VICTORIA   Tommy's very funny who he's left with. My mother babysits sometimes.

85

4. Inflammation from exposure to cold.   6. As in nursery school or preschool.
5. Babysitter.

LIN   Your husband could babysit.

VICTORIA   But then we couldn't go to the movies.

LIN   You could go to the movies with me.

VICTORIA   Oh I see.

90   LIN   Couldn't you?

VICTORIA   Well yes, I could.

LIN   Friday night?

VICTORIA   What film are we talking about?

LIN   Does it matter what film?

95   VICTORIA   Of course it does.

LIN   You choose then. Friday night.

> [CATHY *comes in with gun, shoots them saying kiou kiou kiou, and runs off again.*]

Not in a foreign language, OK. You don't go to the movies to read.

> [LIN *watches the children playing outside.*]

Don't hit him, Cathy, kill him. Point the gun, kiou, kiou, kiou. That's the way.

VICTORIA   They've just banned war toys in Sweden.

100   LIN   The kids'll just hit each other more.

VICTORIA   Well, psychologists do differ in their opinions as to whether or not aggression is innate.

LIN   Yeah?

VICTORIA   I'm afraid I do let Tommy play with guns and just hope he'll get it

105   out of his system and not end up in the army.

LIN   I've got a brother in the army.

VICTORIA   Oh I'm sorry. Whereabouts is he stationed?

LIN   Belfast.[7]

VICTORIA   Oh dear.

110   LIN   I've got a friend who's Irish and we went on a Troops Out march.[8] Now my dad won't speak to me.

VICTORIA   I don't get on too well with my father either.

LIN   And your husband? How do you get on with him?

VICTORIA   Oh, fine. Up and down. You know. Very well. He helps with the

115   washing up and everything.

LIN   I left mine two years ago. He let me keep Cathy and I'm grateful for that.

VICTORIA   You shouldn't be grateful.

LIN   I'm a lesbian.

120   VICTORIA   You still shouldn't be grateful.

LIN   I'm grateful he didn't hit me harder than he did.

VICTORIA   I suppose I'm very lucky, with Martin.

LIN   Don't get at me about how I bring up Cathy, OK?

VICTORIA   I didn't.

125   LIN   Yes you did. War toys. I'll give her a rifle for Christmas and blast Tommy's pretty head off for a start.

> [VICTORIA *goes back to her book.*]

I hate men.

---

7. Capital of Northern Ireland, central to the ongoing conflict between loyalist forces that support the British government and republican forces that support an end to British rule.
8. Movement supporting the end of British military involvement in Northern Ireland.

VICTORIA   You have to look at it in a historical perspective in terms of learnt
behaviour since the industrial revolution.

130 LIN   I just hate the bastards.

VICTORIA   Well it's a point of view.

[*By now* CATHY *has come back in and started painting in many colours,
without an apron.* EDWARD *comes in.*]

EDWARD   Victoria, mother's in the park. She's walking round all the paths
very fast.

VICTORIA   By herself.

135 EDWARD   I told her you were here.

VICTORIA   Thanks.

EDWARD   Come on.

VICTORIA   Ten minutes talking to my mother and I have to spend two hours
in a hot bath.

[VICTORIA *goes out.*]

140 LIN   Shit, Cathy, what about an apron. I don't mind you having paint on your
frock but if it doesn't wash off just don't tell me you can't wear a frock with
paint on, OK?

CATHY   OK.

LIN   You're gay, aren't you?

145 EDWARD   I beg your pardon?

LIN   I really fancy your sister. I thought you'd understand. You do but you
can go on pretending you don't, I don't mind. That's lovely Cathy, I like the
green bit.

EDWARD   Don't go around saying that. I might lose my job.

150 LIN   The last gardener was ever so straight. He used to flash at all the little
girls.

EDWARD   I wish you hadn't said that about me. It's not true.

LIN   It's not true and I never said it and I never thought it and I never will
think it again.

155 EDWARD   Someone might have heard you.

LIN   Shut up about it then.

[BETTY *and* VICTORIA *come up.*]

BETTY   It's quite a nasty bump.

VICTORIA   He's not even crying.

BETTY   I think that's very worrying. You and Edward always cried. Perhaps
160 he's got concussion.

VICTORIA   Of course he hasn't Mummy.

BETTY   That other little boy was very rough. Should you speak to somebody
about him?

VICTORIA   Tommy was hitting him with a spade.

165 BETTY   Well he's a real little boy. And so brave not to cry. You must watch him
for signs of drowsiness. And nausea. If he's sick in the night, phone an
ambulance. Well, you're looking very well darling, a bit tired, a bit peaky. I
think the fresh air agrees with Edward. He likes the open-air life because
of growing up in Africa. He misses the sunshine, don't you, darling? We'll
170 soon have Edward back on his feet. What fun it is here.

VICTORIA   This is Lin. And Cathy.

BETTY   Oh Cathy what a lovely painting. What is it? Well I think it's a house
on fire. I think all that red is a fire. Is that right? Or do I see legs, is it a

175 horse? Can I have the lovely painting or is it for Mummy? Children have such imagination, it makes them so exhausting. [*To* LIN.] I'm sure you're wonderful, just like Victoria. I had help with my children. One does need help. That was in Africa of course so there wasn't the servant problem. This is my son Edward. This is—

EDWARD   Lin.

180 BETTY   Lin, this is Lin. Edward is doing something such fun, he's working in the park as a gardener. He does look exactly like a gardener.

EDWARD   I am a gardener.

BETTY   He's certainly making a stab at it. Well it will be a story to tell. I expect he will write a novel about it, or perhaps a television series. Well what a

185 pretty child Cathy is. Victoria was a pretty child just like a little doll—you can't be certain how they'll grow up. I think Victoria's very pretty but she doesn't make the most of herself, do you darling, it's not the fashion I'm told but there are still women who dress out of *Vogue*, well we hope that's not what Martin looks for, though in many ways I wish it was, I don't know

190 what it is Martin looks for and nor does he I'm afraid poor Martin. Well I am rattling on. I like your skirt dear but your shoes won't do at all. Well do they have lady gardeners, Edward, because I'm going to leave your father and I think I might need to get a job, not a gardener really of course. I haven't got green fingers I'm afraid, everything I touch shrivels straight up. Vicky gave

195 me a poinsettia last Christmas and the leaves all fell off on Boxing Day.[9] Well good heavens, look what's happened to that lovely painting.

   [CATHY *has slowly and carefully been going over the whole sheet with black paint. She has almost finished.*]

LIN   What you do that for silly? It was nice.

CATHY   I like your earrings.

VICTORIA   Did you say you're leaving Daddy?

200 BETTY   Do you darling? Shall I put them on you? My ears aren't pierced, I never wanted that, they just clip on the lobe.

LIN   She'll get paint on you, mind.

BETTY   There's a pretty girl. It doesn't hurt does it? Well you'll grow up to know you have to suffer a little bit for beauty.

205 CATHY   Look mum I'm pretty, I'm pretty, I'm pretty.

LIN   Stop showing off Cathy.

VICTORIA   It's time we went home. Tommy, time to go home. Last go then, all right.

EDWARD   Mum did I hear you right just now?

210 CATHY   I want my ears pierced.

BETTY   Ooh, not till you're big.

CATHY   I know a girl got her ears pierced and she's three. She's got real gold.

BETTY   I don't expect she's English, darling. Can I give her a sweetie? I know they're not very good for the teeth, Vicky gets terribly cross with me. What

215 does Mummy say?

LIN   Just one, thank you very much.

CATHY   I like your beads.

BETTY   Yes they are pretty. Here you are.

   [*It is the necklace from Act One.*]

---

9. December 26; traditionally, the day for boxing up Christmas gifts.

CATHY   Look at me, look at me. Vicky, Vicky look at me.
220 LIN   You look lovely, come on now.
CATHY   And your hat, and your hat.
LIN   No, that's enough.
BETTY   Of course she can have my hat.
CATHY   Yes, yes, hat, hat. Look look look.
225 LIN   That's enough, please, stop it now. Hat off, bye-bye hat.
CATHY   Give me my hat.
LIN   Bye-bye beads.
BETTY   It's just fun.
LIN   It's very nice of you.
230 CATHY   I want my beads.
LIN   Where's the other earring?
CATHY   I want my beads.

> [CATHY *has the other earring in her hand. Meanwhile* VICTORIA *and*
> EDWARD *look for it.*]

EDWARD   Is it on the floor?
VICTORIA   Don't step on it.
235 EDWARD   Where?
CATHY   I want my beads. I want my beads.
LIN   You'll have a smack.

> [LIN *gets the earring from* CATHY.]

CATHY   I want my beads.
BETTY   Oh dear oh dear. Have you got the earring? Thank you darling.
240 CATHY   I want my beads, you're horrid, I hate you, Mum, you smell.
BETTY   This is the point you see where one had help. Well it's been lovely
    seeing you dears and I'll be off again on my little walk.
VICTORIA   You're leaving him? Really?
BETTY   Yes you hear a'right, Vicky, yes. I'm finding a little flat, that will be
245   fun. Bye-bye Tommy, Granny's going now. Tommy don't hit that little girl,
    say goodbye to Granny.

> [BETTY *goes.*]

VICTORIA   Fucking hell.
EDWARD   Puking Jesus.
LIN   That was news was it, leaving your father?
250 EDWARD   They're going to want so much attention.
VICTORIA   Does everybody hate their mothers?
EDWARD   Mind you, I wouldn't live with him.
LIN   Stop snivelling, pigface. Where's your coat? Be quiet now and we'll have
    doughnuts for tea and if you keep on we'll have dogshit on toast.

> [CATHY *laughs so much she lies on the floor.*]

255 VICTORIA   Tommy, you've had two last goes. Last last last last go.
LIN   Not that funny, come on, coat on.
EDWARD   Can I have your painting?
CATHY   What for?
EDWARD   For a friend of mine.
260 CATHY   What's his name?
EDWARD   Gerry.
CATHY   How old is he?

EDWARD   Thirty-two.

CATHY   You can if you like. I don't care. Kiou kiou kiou kiou.

[CATHY *goes out.* EDWARD *takes the painting and goes out.*]

265   LIN   Will you have sex with me?

VICTORIA   I don't know what Martin would say. Does it count as adultery with a woman?

LIN   You'd enjoy it.

SCENE TWO: *Spring. Swing, bench, pond nearby.* EDWARD *is gardening.* GERRY *is sitting on a bench.*

EDWARD   I sometimes pretend we don't know each other. And you've come to
270   the park to eat your sandwiches and look at me.

GERRY   That would be more interesting, yes. Come and sit down.

EDWARD   If the superintendent comes I'll be in trouble. It's not my dinner time yet. Where were you last night? I think you owe me an explanation. We always do tell each other everything.

275   GERRY   Is that a rule?

EDWARD   It's what we agreed.

GERRY   It's a habit we've got into. Look, I was drunk. I woke up at four o'clock on somebody's floor. I was sick. I hadn't any money for a cab. I went back to sleep.

280   EDWARD   You could have phoned.

GERRY   There wasn't a phone.

EDWARD   Sorry.

GERRY   There was a phone and I didn't phone you. Leave it alone, Eddy, I'm warning you.

285   EDWARD   What are you going to do to me, then?

GERRY   I'm going to the pub.

EDWARD   I'll join you in ten minutes.

GERRY   I didn't ask you to come.

[EDWARD *goes.* CATHY *is on the swing.*]

CATHY   Batman and Robin
290   Had a batmobile.
         Robin done a fart
         And paralysed the wheel.
         The wheel couldn't take it,
         The engine fell apart,
295   All because of Robin
         And his supersonic fart.

[CATHY *goes.* MARTIN, VICTORIA *and* BETTY *walking slowly.*]

MARTIN   Tom!

BETTY   He'll fall in.

VICTORIA   No he won't.

300   MARTIN   Don't go too near the edge, Tom. Throw the bread from there. The ducks can get it.

BETTY   I'll never be able to manage. If I can't even walk down the street by myself. Everything looks so fierce.

VICTORIA   Just watch Tommy feeding the ducks.

305 BETTY   He's going to fall in. Make Martin make him move back.

VICTORIA   He's not going to fall in.

BETTY   It's since I left your father.

VICTORIA   Mummy, it really was the right decision.

BETTY   Everything comes at me from all directions. Martin despises me.

310 VICTORIA   Of course he doesn't Mummy.

BETTY   Of course he does.

MARTIN   Throw the bread. That's the way. The duck can get it. Quack quack
quack quack quack.

BETTY   I don't want to take pills. Lin says you can't trust doctors.

315 VICTORIA   You're not taking pills. You're doing very well.

BETTY   But I'm so frightened.

VICTORIA   What are you frightened of?

BETTY   Victoria, you always ask that as if there was suddenly going to be an
answer.

320 VICTORIA   Are you all right sitting there?

BETTY   Yes, yes. Go and be with Martin.

[VICTORIA *joins* MARTIN. BETTY *stays sitting on the bench.*]

MARTIN   You take the job, you go to Manchester. You turn it down, you stay
in London. People are making decisions like this every day of the week. It
needn't be for more than a year. You get long vacations. Our relationship
325 might well stand the strain of that, and if it doesn't we're better out of it. I
don't want to put any pressure on you. I'd just like to know so we can sell the
house. I think we're moving into an entirely different way of life if you go to
Manchester because it won't end there. We could keep the house as security
for Tommy but he might as well get used to the fact that life nowadays is
330 insecure. You should ask your mother what she thinks and then do the opposite. I could just take that room in Barbara's house, and then we could babysit for each other. You think that means I want to fuck Barbara. I don't. Well
I do, but I won't. And even if I did, what's a fuck between friends? Who are
we meant to do it with, strangers? Whatever you want to do, I'll be delighted.
335 If you could just let me know what it is I'm to be delighted about. Don't cry
again, Vicky, I'm not the sort of man who makes women cry.

[LIN *has come in and sat down with* BETTY.]

[CATHY *joins them. She is wearing a pink dress and carrying a rifle.*]

LIN   I've bought her three new frocks. She won't wear jeans to school any
more because Tracy and Mandy called her a boy.

CATHY   Tracy's got a perm.

340 LIN   You should have shot them.

CATHY   They're coming to tea and we've got to have trifle. Not trifle you
make, trifle out of a packet.[1] And you've got to wear a skirt. And tights.

LIN   Tracy's mum wears jeans.

CATHY   She does not. She wears velvet.

345 BETTY   Well I think you look very pretty. And if that gun has caps in it please
take it a long way away.

CATHY   It's got red caps. They're louder.

---

1. Traditional English layered dessert made with sponge cake, jam, custard, and whipped cream.
The packet version includes cake and mixes for the other components.

MARTIN   Do you think you're well enough to do this job? You don't have to do
it. No one's going to think any the less of you if you stay here with me.
There's no point being so liberated you make yourself cry all the time. You
stay and we'll get everything sorted out. What it is about sex, when we talk
while it's happening I get to feel it's like a driving lesson. Left, right, a little
faster, carry on, slow down—

[CATHY *shoots* VICTORIA.]

CATHY   You're dead Vicky.
VICTORIA   Aaaargh.
CATHY   Fall over.
VICTORIA   I'm not falling over, the ground's wet.
CATHY   You're dead.
VICTORIA   Yes, I'm dead.
CATHY   The Dead Hand Gang fall over. They said I had to fall over in the
mud or I can't play. That duck's a mandarin.
MARTIN   Which one? Look, Tommy?
CATHY   That's a diver. It's got a yellow eye and it dives. That's a goose. Tommy
doesn't know it's a goose, he thinks it's a duck. The babies get eaten by wea-
sels. Kiou kiou.

[CATHY *goes.*]

MARTIN   So I lost my erection last night, not because I'm not prepared to
talk, it's just that taking in technical information is a different part of the
brain and also I don't like to feel that you do it better to yourself. I have
read the Hite Report.[2] I do know that women have to learn to get their
pleasure despite our clumsy attempts at expressing undying devotion and
ecstasy, and that what we spent our adolescence thinking was an animal
urge we had to suppress is in fact a fine art we have to acquire. I'm not like
whatever percentage of American men have become impotent as a direct
result of women's liberation, which I am totally in favour of, more I sometimes think than you are yourself. Nor am I one of your villains who sticks
it in, bangs away, and falls asleep. My one aim is to give you pleasure. My
one aim is to give you rolling orgasms like I do other women. So why the
hell don't you have them? My analysis for what it's worth is that despite all
my efforts you still feel dominated by me. I in fact think it's very sad that
you don't feel able to take that job. It makes me feel very guilty. I don't want
you to do it just because I encourage you to do it. But don't you think you'd
feel better if you did take the job? You're the one who's talked about freedom. You're the one who's experimenting with bisexuality, and I don't stop
you, I think women have something to give each other. You seem to need
the mutual support. You find me too overwhelming. So follow it through,
go away, leave me and Tommy alone for a bit, we can manage perfectly well
without you. I'm not putting any pressure on you but I don't think you're
being a whole person. God knows I do everything I can to make you stand
on your own two feet. Just be yourself. You don't seem to realise how
insulting it is to me that you can't get yourself together.

[MARTIN *and* VICTORIA *go.*]

2. Shere Hite's influential 1976 study of female sexuality.

BETTY   You must be very lonely yourself with no husband. You don't miss him?

LIN   Not really, no.

BETTY   Maybe you like being on your own.

395 LIN   I'm seeing quite a lot of Vicky. I don't live alone. I live with Cathy.

BETTY   I would have been frightened when I was your age. I thought, the poor children, their mother all alone.

LIN   I've a lot of friends.

BETTY   I find when I'm making tea I put out two cups. It's strange not having

400   a man in the house. You don't know who to do things for.

LIN   Yourself.

BETTY   Oh, that's very selfish.

LIN   Have you any women friends?

BETTY   I've never been so short of men's company that I've had to bother

405   with women.

LIN   Don't you like women?

BETTY   They don't have such interesting conversations as men. There has never been a woman composer of genius. They don't have a sense of humour. They spoil things for themselves with their emotions. I can't say I do like

410   women very much, no.

LIN   But you're a woman.

BETTY   There's nothing says you have to like yourself.

LIN   Do you like me?

BETTY   There's no need to take it personally, Lin.

      [MARTIN *and* VICTORIA *come back.*]

415 MARTIN   Do you know if you put cocaine on your prick you can keep up it all night? The only thing is of course it goes numb so you don't feel anything. But you would, that's the main thing. I just want to make you happy.

BETTY   Vicky, I'd like to go home.

VICTORIA   Yes, Mummy, of course.

420 BETTY   I'm sorry, dear.

VICTORIA   I think Tommy would like to stay out a bit longer.

LIN   Hello, Martin. We do keep out of each other's way.

MARTIN   I think that's the best thing to do.

BETTY   Perhaps you'd walk home with me, Martin. I do feel safer with a man.

425   The park is so large the grass seems to tilt.

MARTIN   Yes, I'd like to go home and do some work. I'm writing a novel about women from the women's point of view.

      [MARTIN *and* BETTY *go.* LIN *and* VICTORIA *are alone. They embrace.*]

VICTORIA   Why the hell can't he just be a wife and come with me? Why does Martin make me tie myself in knots? No wonder we can't just have a simple

430   fuck. No, not Martin, why do I make myself tie myself in knots. It's got to stop, Lin. I'm not like that with you. Would you love me if I went to Manchester?

LIN   Yes.

VICTORIA   Would you love me if I went on a climbing expedition in the Andes mountains?

435 LIN   Yes.

VICTORIA   Would you love me if my teeth fell out?

LIN   Yes.

VICTORIA   Would you love me if I loved ten other people?

LIN   And me?

440 VICTORIA   Yes.

LIN   Yes.

VICTORIA   And I feel apologetic for not being quite so subordinate as I was. I am more intelligent than him. I am brilliant.

LIN   Leave him Vic. Come and live with me.

445 VICTORIA   Don't be silly

LIN   Silly, Christ, don't then. I'm not asking because I need to live with someone. I'd enjoy it, that's all, we'd both enjoy it. Fuck you. Cathy, for fuck's sake stop throwing stones at the ducks. The man's going to get you.

VICTORIA   What man? Do you need a man to frighten your child with?

450 LIN   My mother said it.

VICTORIA   You're so inconsistent, Lin.

LIN   I've changed who I sleep with, I can't change everything.

VICTORIA   Like when I had to stop you getting a job in a boutique and collaborating with sexist consumerism.

455 LIN   I should have got that job, Cathy would have liked it. Why shouldn't I have some decent clothes? I'm sick of dressing like a boy, why can't I look sexy, wouldn't you love me?

VICTORIA   Lin, you've no analysis.

LIN   No but I'm good at kissing aren't I? I give Cathy guns, my mum didn't
460   give me guns. I dress her in jeans, she wants to wear dresses. I don't know. I can't work it out I don't want to. You read too many books, you get at me all the time, you're worse to me than Martin is to you, you piss me off, my brother's been killed. I'm sorry to win the argument that way but there it is.

465 VICTORIA   What do you mean win the argument?

LIN   I mean be nice to me.

VICTORIA   In Belfast?

LIN   I heard this morning. Don't don't start. I've hardly seen him for two years. I rung my father. You'd think I shot him myself. He doesn't want me
470   to go to the funeral.

[CATHY approaches.]

VICTORIA   What will you do?

LIN   Go of course.

CATHY   What is it? Who's killed? What?

LIN   It's Bill. Your uncle. In the army. Bill that gave you the blue teddy.

475 CATHY   Can I have his gun?

LIN   It's time we went home. Time you went to bed.

CATHY   No it's not.

LIN   We go home and you have tea and you have a bath and you go to bed.

CATHY   Fuck off.

480 LIN   Cathy, shut up.

VICTORIA   It's only half past five, why don't we—

LIN   I'll tell you why she has to go to bed—

VICTORIA   She can come home with me.

LIN   Because I want her out the fucking way.

485 VICTORIA   She can come home with me.

CATHY   I'm not going to bed.

LIN   I want her home with me not home with you, I want her in bed, I want
     today over.

CATHY   I'm not going to bed.

> [LIN *hits* CATHY, CATHY *cries.*]

490 LIN   And shut up or I'll give you something to cry for.

CATHY   I'm not going to bed.

VICTORIA   Cathy—

LIN   You keep out of it.

VICTORIA   Lin for God's sake.

> [*They are all shouting.* CATHY *runs off.* LIN *and* VICTORIA *are silent. Then
> they laugh and embrace.*]

495 LIN   Where's Tommy?

VICTORIA   What? Didn't he go with Martin?

LIN   Did he?

VICTORIA   God oh God.

LIN   Cathy! Cathy!

500 VICTORIA   I haven't thought about him. How could I not think about him?
     Tommy!

LIN   Cathy! Come on, quick, I want some help.

VICTORIA   Tommy! Tommy!

> [CATHY *comes back.*]

LIN   Where's Tommy? Have you seen him? Did he go with Martin? Do you
505   know where he is?

CATHY   I showed him the goose. We went in the bushes.

LIN   Then what?

CATHY   I came back on the swing.

VICTORIA   And Tommy? Where was Tommy?

510 CATHY   He fed the ducks.

LIN   No that was before.

CATHY   He did a pee in the bushes. I helped him with his trousers.

VICTORIA   And after that?

CATHY   He fed the ducks.

515 VICTORIA   No no.

CATHY   He liked the ducks. I expect he fell in.

LIN   Did you see him fall in?

VICTORIA   Tommy! Tommy!

LIN   What's the last time you saw him?

520 CATHY   He did a pee.

VICTORIA   Mummy said he would fall in. Oh God, Tommy!

LIN   We'll go round the pond. We'll go opposite ways round the pond.

ALL [*shout*]   Tommy!

> [VICTORIA *and* LIN *go off opposite sides.* CATHY *climbs the bench.*]

CATHY   Georgie Best superstar
525   Walks like a woman and wears a bra.
     There he is! I see him! Mum! Vicky! There he is!
     He's in the bushes.

> [LIN *comes back.*]

LIN   Come on Cathy love, let's go home.

CATHY   Vicky's got him.

530 LIN   Come on.
CATHY   Is she cross?
LIN   No. Come on.
CATHY   I found him.
LIN   Yes. Come on.

[CATHY *gets off the bench.* CATHY *and* LIN *hug.*]

535 CATHY   I'm watching telly.
LIN   OK.
CATHY   After the news.
LIN   OK.
CATHY   I'm not going to bed.
540 LIN   Yes you are.
CATHY   I'm not going to bed now.
LIN   Not now but early.
CATHY   How early?
LIN   Not late.
545 CATHY   How not late?
LIN   Early.
CATHY   How early?
LIN   Not late.

[*They go off together.* GERRY *comes on. He waits.* EDWARD *comes.*]

EDWARD   I've got some fish for dinner. I thought I'd make a cheese sauce.
550 GERRY   I won't be in.
EDWARD   Where are you going?
GERRY   For a start I'm going to a sauna. Then I'll see.
EDWARD   All right. What time will you be back? We'll eat then.
GERRY   You're getting like a wife.
555 EDWARD   I don't mind that.
GERRY   Why don't I do the cooking some time?
EDWARD   You can if you like. You're just not as good at it that's all. Do it
   tonight.
GERRY   I won't be in tonight.
560 EDWARD   Do it tomorrow. If we can't eat it we can always go to a restaurant.
GERRY   Stop it.
EDWARD   Stop what?
GERRY   Just be yourself.
EDWARD   I don't know what you mean. Everyone's always tried to stop me
565   being feminine and now you are too.
GERRY   You're putting it on.
EDWARD   I like doing the cooking. I like being fucked. You do like me like
   this really.
GERRY   I'm bored, Eddy.
570 EDWARD   Go to the sauna.
GERRY   And you'll stay home and wait up for me.
EDWARD   No, I'll go to bed and read a book.
GERRY   Or knit. You could knit me a pair of socks.
EDWARD   I might knit. I like knitting.
575 GERRY   I don't mind if you knit. I don't want to be married.
EDWARD   I do.
GERRY   Well I'm divorcing you.

EDWARD   I wouldn't want to keep a man who wants his freedom.

GERRY   Eddy, do stop playing the injured wife, it's not funny.

580   EDWARD   I'm not playing. It's true.

GERRY   I'm not the husband so you can't be the wife.

EDWARD   I'll always be here, Gerry, if you want to come back. I know you men like to go off by yourselves. I don't think I could love deeply more than once. But I don't think I can face life on my own so don't leave it too long 585   or it may be too late.

GERRY   What are you trying to turn me into?

EDWARD   A monster, darling, which is what you are.

GERRY   I'll collect my stuff from the flat in the morning.

[GERRY *goes.* EDWARD *sits on the bench. It gets darker.* VICTORIA *comes.*]

VICTORIA   Tommy dropped a toy car somewhere, you haven't seen it? It's red. 590   He says it's his best one. Oh the hell with it. Martin's reading him a story. There, isn't it quiet?

[*They sit on the bench, holding hands.*]

EDWARD   I like women.

VICTORIA   That should please Mother.

EDWARD   No listen Vicky. I'd rather be a woman. I wish I had breasts like 595   that, I think they're beautiful. Can I touch them?

VICTORIA   What, pretending they're yours?

EDWARD   No, I know it's you.

VICTORIA   I think I should warn you I'm enjoying this.

EDWARD   I'm sick of men.

600   VICTORIA   I'm sick of men.

EDWARD   I think I'm a lesbian.

SCENE THREE: *The park. Summer night.* VICTORIA, LIN *and* EDWARD *drunk.*

LIN   Where are you?

VICTORIA   Come on.

EDWARD   Do we sit in a circle?

605   VICTORIA   Sit in a triangle.

EDWARD   You're good at mathematics. She's good at mathematics.

VICTORIA   Give me your hand. We all hold hands.

EDWARD   Do you know what to do?

LIN   She's making it up.

610   VICTORIA   We start off by being quiet.

EDWARD   What?

LIN   Hush.

EDWARD   Will something appear?

VICTORIA   It was your idea.

615   EDWARD   It wasn't my idea. It was your book.

LIN   You said call up the goddess.

EDWARD   I don't remember saying that.

LIN   We could have called her on the telephone.

EDWARD   Don't be so silly, this is meant to be frightening.

620   LIN   Kiss me.

VICTORIA   Are we going to do it?

LIN   We're doing it.

VICTORIA   A ceremony.

LIN   It's very sexy, you said it is. You said the women were priests in the
625   temples and fucked all the time. I'm just helping.

VICTORIA   As long as it's sacred.

LIN   It's very sacred.

VICTORIA   Innin, Innana, Nana, Nut, Anat, Anahita, Istar, Isis.[3]

LIN   I can't remember all that.

630   VICTORIA   Lin! Innin, Innana, Nana, Nut, Anat, Anahita, Istar, Isis.

> [LIN *and* EDWARD *join in and continue the chant under* VICTORIA's
> *speech.*]

Goddess of many names, oldest of the old, who walked in chaos and created life, hear us calling you back through time, before Jehovah, before
Christ, before men drove you out and burnt your temples, hear us, Lady,
give us back what we were, give us the history we haven't had, make us the
635   women we can't be.

ALL   Innin, Innana, Nana, Nut, Anat, Anahita, Istar, Isis.

> [*Chant continues under other speeches.*]

LIN   Come back, goddess.

VICTORIA   Goddess of the sun and the moon her brother, little goddess of
Crete with snakes in your hands.

640   LIN   Goddess of breasts.

VICTORIA   Goddess of cunts.

LIN   Goddess of fat bellies and babies. And blood blood blood.

> [*Chant continues.*]

I see her.

EDWARD   What?

> [*They stop chanting.*]

645   LIN   I see her. Very tall. Snakes in her hands. Light light light—look out! Did
I give you a fright?

EDWARD   I was terrified.

VICTORIA   Don't spoil it Lin.

LIN   It's all out of a book.

650   VICTORIA   Innin Innana I can't do it now. I was really enjoying myself.

LIN   She won't appear with a man here.

VICTORIA   They had men, they had sons and lovers.

EDWARD   They had eunuchs.

LIN   Don't give us ideas.

655   VICTORIA   There's Attis and Tammuz, they're torn to pieces.[4]

EDWARD   Tear me to pieces, Lin.

VICTORIA   The priestess chose a lover for a year and he was king because she
chose him and then he was killed at the end of the year.

EDWARD   Hurray.

---

3. Mythological goddesses from various
ancient cultures. Innin, Innana, and Nana
are all names for the Sumerian goddess of
fertility and sexual love; Istar is the Akkadian
name and Anahita the Persian name for the
same goddess. Anat is the Egyptian war goddess; Isis is the Egyptian mother goddess; and
Nut is the Egyptian sky goddess.
4. Attis was a Phrygian semideity associated
with castration; he was also a vegetation god.
Tammuz was his Sumerian counterpart, consort of Innana.

660 VICTORIA   And the women had the children and nobody knew it was done by fucking so they didn't know about their fathers and nobody cared who the father was and the property was passed down through the maternal line—

LIN   Don't turn it into a lecture, Vicky, it's meant to be an orgy.

VICTORIA   It never hurts to understand the theoretical background. You can't
665   separate fucking and economics.

LIN   Give us a kiss.

EDWARD   Shut up, listen.

LIN   What?

EDWARD   There's somebody there.

670 LIN   Where?

EDWARD   There.

VICTORIA   The priestesses used to make love to total strangers.

LIN   Go on then, I dare you.

EDWARD   Go on, Vicky.

675 VICTORIA   He won't know it's a sacred rite in honour of the goddess.

EDWARD   We'll know.

LIN   We can tell him.

EDWARD   It's not what he thinks, it's what we think.

LIN   Don't tell him till after, he'll run a mile.

680 VICTORIA   Hello. We're having an orgy. Do you want me to suck your cock?

[*The stranger approaches. It is* MARTIN.]

MARTIN   There you are. I've been looking everywhere. What the hell are you doing. Do you know what the time is? You're all pissed out of your minds.

[*They leap on* MARTIN, *and pull him down and start to make love to him.*]

Well that's all right. If all we're talking about is having a lot of sex there's no problem. I was all for the sixties when liberation just meant fucking.

[*Another stranger approaches.*]

685 LIN   Hey you, come here. Come and have sex with us.

VICTORIA   Who is it?

[*The stranger is a* SOLDIER.]

LIN   It's my brother.

EDWARD   Lin, don't.

LIN   It's my brother.

690 VICTORIA   It's her sense of humour, you get used to it.

LIN   Shut up Vicky, it's my brother. Isn't it? Bill?

SOLDIER   Yes it's me.

LIN   And you are dead.

SOLDIER   Fucking dead all right yeah.

695 LIN   Have you come back to tell us something?

SOLDIER   No I've come for a fuck. That was the worst thing in the fucking army. Never fucking let out. Can't fucking talk to Irish girls. Fucking bored out of my fucking head. That or shit scared. For five minutes I'd be glad I wasn't bored, then I was fucking scared. Then we'd come in and I'd be glad I wasn't scared and then I was fucking bored. Spend the day reading fuck-
700   ing porn and the fucking night wanking. Man's nicking life in the fucking army? No fun when the fucking kids hate you. I got so I fucking wanted to kill someone and I got fucking killed myself and I want a fuck.

LIN   I miss you. Bill. Bill.

      [LIN *collapses.* SOLDIER *goes.* VICTORIA *comforts* LIN.]

705 EDWARD   Let's go home.

LIN   Victoria, come home with us. Victoria's coming to live with me and Edward.

MARTIN   Tell me about it in the morning.

LIN   It's true.

710 VICTORIA   It is true.

MARTIN   Tell me when you're sober.

      [EDWARD, LIN, VICTORIA *go off together.*]

      [MARTIN *goes off alone.* GERRY *comes on.*]

GERRY   I come here sometimes at night and pick somebody up. Sometimes I come here at night and don't pick anybody up. I do also enjoy walking about at night. There's never any trouble finding someone. I can have sex any 715 time. You might not find the type you most fancy every day of the week, but there's plenty of people about who just enjoy having a good time. I quite like living alone. If I live with someone I get annoyed with them. Edward always put on Capital Radio[5] when he got up. The silence gets wasted. I wake up at four o'clock sometimes. Birds. Silence. If I bring somebody home I never 720 let them stay the night. Edward! Edward!

      [EDWARD *from Act One comes on.*]

EDWARD   Gerry, I love you.

GERRY   Yes, I know. I love you, too.

EDWARD   You know what we did? I want to do it again. I think about it all the time. Don't you want to any more?

725 GERRY   Yes, of course.

ALL   [*sing 'Cloud Nine'*]

      It'll be fine when you reach Cloud Nine.

      Mist was rising and the night was dark.
      Me and my baby took a walk in the park.
      He said Be mine and you're on Cloud Nine.

730   Better watch out when you're on Cloud Nine.

      Smoked some dope on the playground swings
      Higher and higher on true love's wings
      He said Be mine and you're on Cloud Nine.

      Twenty-five years on the same Cloud Nine.

735   Who did she meet on her first blind date?
      The guys were no surprise but the lady was great
      They were women in love, they were on Cloud Nine.

      Two the same, they were on Cloud Nine.

      The bride was sixty-five, the groom was seventeen,
740   They fucked in the back of the black limousine.
      It was divine in the silver Cloud Nine.

      Simply divine in their silver Cloud Nine.

---

5. United Kingdom hit music station.

The wife's lover's children and my lover's wife,
Cooking in my kitchen, confusing my life.
745   And it's upside down when you reach Cloud Nine.

Upside down when you reach Cloud Nine.[6]

SCENE FOUR: *The park. Afternoon in late summer.* MARTIN, CATHY, EDWARD.

CATHY   Under the bramble bushes,
Under the sea boom boom boom,
True love for you my darling,
750   True love for me my darling,
When we are married,
We'll raise a family.
Boy for you, girl for me,
Boom tiddley oom boom.[7]
755   SEXY.

EDWARD   You'll have Tommy and Cathy tonight then OK? Tommy's still on antibiotics, do make him finish the bottle, he takes it in Ribena.[8] It's no good in orange, he spits it out. Remind me to give you Cathy's swimming things.

760 CATHY   I did six strokes, didn't I Martin? Did I do a width? How many strokes is a length? How many miles is a swimming pool? I'm going to take my bronze and silver and gold and diamond.

MARTIN   Is Tommy still wetting the bed?

EDWARD   Don't get angry with him about it.

765 MARTIN   I just need to go to the launderette so I've got a spare sheet. Of course I don't get fucking angry, Eddy, for God's sake. I don't like to say he is my son but he is my son. I'm surprised I'm not wetting the bed myself.

CATHY   I don't wet the bed ever. Do you wet the bed Martin?

MARTIN   No.

770 CATHY   You said you did.

        [BETTY *comes.*]

BETTY   I do miss the sun living in England but today couldn't be more beautiful. You appreciate the weekend when you're working. Betty's been at work this week, Cathy. It's terribly tiring, Martin, I don't know how you've done it all these years. And the money, I feel like a child with money, Clive always
775   paid everything but I do understand it perfectly well. Look, Cathy, let me show you my money.

CATHY   I'll count it. Let me count it. What's that?

BETTY   Five pounds. Five and five is—?

CATHY   One two three—

780 BETTY   Five and five is ten, and five—

CATHY   If I get it right can I have one?

EDWARD   No you can't.

        [CATHY *goes on counting the money.*]

BETTY   I never like to say anything, Martin, or you'll think I'm being a mother-in-law.

---

6. Churchill and Andy Roberts composed this song for the play.
7. Traditional English children's rhymed clap-

ping game.
8. Popular British fruit beverage, traditionally made from black currants.

785 EDWARD   Which you are.

BETTY   Thank you, Edward, I'm not talking to you. Martin, I think you're being wonderful. Vicky will come back. Just let her stay with Lin till she sorts herself out. It's very nice for a girl to have a friend, I had friends at school, that was very nice. But I'm sure Lin and Edward don't want her with

790 them all the time. I'm not at all shocked that Lin and Edward aren't married and she already has a child, we all know first marriages don't always work out. But really Vicky must be in the way. And poor little Tommy. I hear he doesn't sleep properly and he's had a cough.

MARTIN   No, he's fine, Betty, thank you.

795 CATHY   My bed's horrible. I want to sleep in the big bed with Lin and Vicky and Eddy and I do get in if I've got a bad dream, and my bed's got a bump right in my back. I want to sleep in a tent.

BETTY   Well Tommy has got a nasty cough, Martin, whatever you say.

EDWARD   He's over that. He's got some medicine.

800 MARTIN   He takes it in Ribena.

BETTY   Well I'm glad to hear it. Look what a lot of money, Cathy, and I sit behind a desk on my own and I answer the telephone and keep the doctor's appointment book and it really is great fun.

CATHY   Can we go camping, Martin, in a tent? We could take the Dead Hand

805 Gang.

BETTY   Not those big boys, Cathy? They're far too big and rough for you. They climb back into the park after dark. I'm sure Mummy doesn't let you play with them, does she Edward? Well I don't know.

[*Ice-cream bells.*]

CATHY   Ice cream. Martin you promised. I'll have a double ninety-nine. No

810 I'll have a shandy lolly.[9] Betty, you have a shandy lolly and I'll have a lick. No, you have a double ninety-nine and I'll have the chocolate.

[MARTIN, CATHY *and* BETTY *go, leaving* EDWARD. GERRY *comes.*]

GERRY   Hello, Eddy. Thought I might find you here.

EDWARD   Gerry.

GERRY   Not working today then?

815 EDWARD   I don't work here any more.

GERRY   Your mum got you into a dark suit?

EDWARD   No of course not. I'm on the dole.[1] I am working, though, I do housework.

GERRY   Whose wife are you now then?

820 EDWARD   Nobody's. I don't think like that any more. I'm living with some women.

GERRY   What women?

EDWARD   It's my sister, Vic, and her lover. They go out to work and I look after the kids.

825 GERRY   I thought for a moment you said you were living with women.

EDWARD   We do sleep together, yes.

GERRY   I was passing the park anyway so I thought I'd look in. I was in the sauna the other night and I saw someone who looked like you but it wasn't. I had sex with him anyway.

9. Nonalcoholic beer and lemon-flavored pop-sicle; a double ninety-nine is a vanilla soft-serve   cone with two flaky chocolate bars inserted.
1. Public assistance or welfare.

830 EDWARD   I do go to the sauna sometimes.

> [CATHY *comes, gives* EDWARD *an ice cream, goes.*]

GERRY   I don't think I'd like living with children. They make a lot of noise don't they?

EDWARD   I tell them to shut up and they shut up. I wouldn't want to leave them at the moment.

835 GERRY   Look why don't we go for a meal some time?

EDWARD   Yes I'd like that. Where are you living now?

GERRY   Same place.

EDWARD   I'll come round for you tomorrow night about 7.30.

GERRY   Great.

> [EDWARD *goes.* HARRY *comes.* HARRY *and* GERRY *pick each other up. They go off.* BETTY *comes back.*]

840 BETTY   No, the ice cream was my treat, Martin. Off you go. I'm going to have a quiet sit in the sun.

> [MAUD *comes.*]

MAUD   Let Mrs Saunders be a warning to you, Betty. I know what it is to be unprotected.

BETTY   But Mother, I have a job. I earn money.

845 MAUD   I know we have our little differences but I always want what is best for you.

> [ELLEN *comes.*]

ELLEN   Betty, what happens with a man?

BETTY   You just keep still.

ELLEN   And is it enjoyable? Don't forget me, Betty.

> [MAUD *and* ELLEN *go.*]

850 BETTY   I used to think Clive was the one who liked sex. But then I found I missed it. I used to touch myself when I was very little, I thought I'd invented something wonderful. I used to do it to go to sleep with or to cheer myself up, and one day it was raining and I was under the kitchen table, and my mother saw me with my hand under my dress rubbing away, and she dragged

855 me out so quickly I hit my head and it bled and I was sick, and nothing was said, and I never did it again till this year. I thought if Clive wasn't looking at me there wasn't a person there. And one night in bed in my flat I was so frightened I started touching myself. I thought my hand might go through into space. I touched my face, it was there, my arm, my breast, and my hand

860 went down where I thought it shouldn't, and I thought well there is some-body there. It felt very sweet, it was a feeling from very long ago, it was very soft, just barely touching, and I felt myself gathering together more and more and I felt angry with Clive and angry with my mother and I went on and on defying them, and there was this vast feeling growing in me and all round me

865 and they couldn't stop me and no one could stop me and I was there and coming and coming. Afterwards I thought I'd betrayed Clive. My mother would kill me. But I felt triumphant because I was a separate person from them. And I cried because I didn't want to be. But I don't cry about it any more. Sometimes I do it three times in one night and it really is great fun.

> [VICTORIA *and* LIN *come in.*]

870 VICTORIA   So I said to the professor, I don't think this is an occasion for invoking the concept of structural causality—oh hello Mummy.

BETTY   I'm going to ask you a question, both of you. I have a little money from your grandmother. And the three of you are living in that tiny flat with two children. I wonder if we could get a house and all live in it together? It

875   would give you more room.

VICTORIA   But I'm going to Manchester anyway.

LIN   We'd have a garden, Vicky.

BETTY   You do seem to have such fun all of you.

VICTORIA   I don't want to.

880   BETTY   I didn't think you would.

LIN   Come on, Vicky, she knows we sleep together, and Eddy.

BETTY   I think I've known for quite a while but I'm not sure. I don't usually think about it, so I don't know if I know about it or not.

VICTORIA   I don't want to live with my mother.

885   LIN   Don't think of her as your mother, think of her as Betty.

VICTORIA   But she thinks of herself as my mother.

BETTY   I am your mother.

VICTORIA   But Mummy we don't even like each other.

BETTY   We might begin to.

[CATHY *comes on howling with a nosebleed.*]

890   LIN   Oh Cathy what happened?

BETTY   She's been assaulted.

VICTORIA   It's a nosebleed.

CATHY   Took my ice cream.

LIN   Who did?

895   CATHY   Took my money.

[MARTIN *comes.*]

MARTIN   Is everything all right?

LIN   I thought you were looking after her.

CATHY   They hit me. I can't play. They said I'm a girl.

BETTY   Those dreadful boys, the gang, the Dead Hand.

900   MARTIN   What do you mean you thought I was looking after her?

LIN   Last I saw her she was with you getting an ice cream. It's your afternoon.

MARTIN   Then she went off to play. She goes off to play. You don't keep an eye on her every minute.

905   LIN   She doesn't get beaten up when I'm looking after her.

CATHY   Took my money.

MARTIN   Why the hell should I look after your child anyway? I just want Tommy. Why should he live with you and Vicky all week?

LIN   I don't mind if you don't want to look after her but don't say you will and

910   then this happens.

VICTORIA   When I get to Manchester everything's going to be different anyway, Lin's staying here, and you're staying here, we're all going to have to sit down and talk it through.

MARTIN   I'd really enjoy that.

915   CATHY   Hit me on the face.

LIN   You were the one looking after her and look at her now, that's all.

MARTIN   I've had enough of you telling me.

LIN   Yes you know it all.

MARTIN   Now stop it. I work very hard at not being like this, I could do with
920   some credit.

LIN   OK you're quite nice, try and enjoy it. Don't make me sorry for you,
       Martin, it's hard for me too. We've better things to do than quarrel. I've got
       to go and sort those little bastards out for a start. Where are they, Cathy?

CATHY   Don't kill them, Mum, hit them. Give them a nosebleed, Mum.
         [LIN *goes.*]

930   VICTORIA   Tommy's asleep in the pushchair. We'd better wake him up or he
       won't sleep tonight.

MARTIN   Sometimes I keep him up watching television till he falls asleep on
       the sofa so I can hold him. Come on, Cathy, we'll get another ice cream.

CATHY   Chocolate sauce and nuts.

930   VICTORIA   Betty, would you like an ice cream?

BETTY   No thank you, the cold hurts my teeth, but what a nice thought,
       Vicky, thank you.
         [VICTORIA *goes.* BETTY *alone.* GERRY *comes.*]
       I think you used to be Edward's flatmate.

GERRY   You're his mother. He's talked about you.

935   BETTY   Well never mind children are always wrong about their parents. It's a
       great problem knowing where to live and who to share with. I live by myself
       just now.

GERRY   Good, so do I. You can do what you like.

BETTY   I don't really know what I like.

940   GERRY   You'll soon find out.

BETTY   What do you like?

GERRY   Waking up at four in the morning.

BETTY   I like listening to music in bed and sometimes for supper I just have
       a big piece of bread and dip it in very hot lime pickle. So you don't get
945   lonely by yourself? Perhaps you have a lot of visitors. I've been thinking I
       should have some visitors, I could give a little dinner party. Would you
       come? There wouldn't just be bread and lime pickle.

GERRY   Thank you very much.

BETTY   Or don't wait to be asked to dinner. Just drop in informally. I'll give
950   you the address shall I? I don't usually give strange men my address but
       then you're not a strange man, you're a friend of Edward's. I suppose I
       seem a different generation to you but you are older than Edward. I was
       married for so many years it's quite hard to know how to get acquainted.
       But if there isn't a right way to do things you have to invent one. I always
955   thought my mother was far too old to be attractive but when you get to an
       age yourself it feels quite different.

GERRY   I think you could be quite attractive.

BETTY   If what?

GERRY   If you stop worrying.

960   BETTY   I think when I do more about things I worry about them less. So per-
       haps you could help me do more.

GERRY   I might be going to live with Edward again.

BETTY   That's nice, but I'm rather surprised if he wants to share a flat. He's
       rather involved with a young woman he lives with, or two young women, I
965   don't understand Edward but never mind.

GERRY   I'm very involved with him.

BETTY   I think Edward did try to tell me once but I didn't listen. So what I'm
being told now is that Edward is 'gay' is that right? And you are too. And
I've been making rather a fool of myself. But Edward does also sleep with
970   women.

GERRY   He does, yes, I don't.

BETTY   Well people always say it's the mother's fault but I don't intend to
start blaming myself. He seems perfectly happy.

GERRY   I could still come and see you.

975   BETTY   So you could, yes. I'd like that. I've never tried to pick up a man
before.

GERRY   Not everyone's gay.

BETTY   No, that's lucky isn't it.

[GERRY *goes.* CLIVE *comes.*]

CLIVE   You are not that sort of woman, Betty. I can't believe you are. I can't
980   feel the same about you as I did. And Africa is to be Communist I suppose.
I used to be proud to be British. There was a high ideal. I came out onto
the verandah and looked at the stars.

[CLIVE *goes.* BETTY *from Act One comes.* BETTY *and* BETTY *embrace.*]

ATHOL FUGARD

b. 1932

I N Athol Fugard's *Sorrows and Rejoicings* (2001), a poet's death gives his friends an occasion to ponder the conflicted role of the white, liberal writer in contemporary South Africa. One character observes that the late author "was meant to be a poet, not a politician," but another disagrees: "And he would have told you that in this country you can't separate the two." Fugard might have been describing himself, for the politics of South Africa—specifically, his opposition to the practice of racial segregation known as apartheid—cannot be separated from his life's work; it has driven his creativity. Though critics may disagree on the political impact and efficacy of Fugard's dramaturgy, especially in a post-apartheid era, all acknowledge Fugard's place as one of the leading dramatists of the late twentieth century: a writer whose work has been produced to acclaim around the world and who has fostered global understanding of his country and its people.

Harold Athol Lannigan Fugard (called "Hally" as a boy) describes himself as being of "mixed descent." His mother, Elizabeth Magdalena Potgieter, was of Afrikaner heritage—that is, she was descended from the Dutch who were the original European settlers in South Africa—while his father, Harold David, was of Anglo-Irish stock. Fugard grew up in a polyglot environment, speaking both Afrikaans (one of the coun-

try's official languages, derived from Dutch) and English, and he was also exposed to African languages (mainly Xhosa). He writes in English but uses a South African idiom richly peppered with words and phrases from other tongues in the region.

In 1935, Fugard's family moved to Port Elizabeth, a coastal city in the Eastern Cape. Fugard's father, a musician who had been crippled in youth and who suffered from chronic pain and alcoholism, became incapable of supporting his family. Fugard's mother, their financial mainstay, first ran the Jubilee Hotel (a small boardinghouse) and then the Saint George's Park Tea Room, both of which feature in *"MASTER HAROLD" . . . AND THE BOYS* (1982). At the Port Elizabeth Technical College, Fugard studied automobile mechanics and experimented with amateur dramatics and creative writing. He won a scholarship to the University of Cape Town; there he pursued studies in social anthropology and philosophy and first encountered the existentialist writings of Albert Camus and Jean-Paul Sartre, both of whom have strongly influenced his dramaturgy. In 1953, he decided to hitchhike with a friend north through Africa, and he left the university without a degree. Arriving penniless in Port Sudan, he signed on as the captain's personal servant aboard a British tramp steamer. Fugard maintains that his experience as the only white crew member, living and working closely with men of other races, liberated him from his boyhood prejudices.

Upon his return to South Africa in 1954, Fugard wrote briefly for the *Port Elizabeth Evening Post* before settling in Cape Town to work in broadcast journalism. There he met Sheila Meiring, an actor (and later a poet and novelist); they married in 1956. Meiring encouraged his latent interest in theater and directed some of his early one-act plays for amateur groups. Watching productions of imported English dramas, Fugard had recognized the need for writers to tell South Africa's own stories on stage. In notebooks (published in 1983), in which he recorded ideas for future writing and thoughts about his experiences, he explained that he believes his "life's work was possibly just to witness as truthfully as I could, the nameless and destitute (desperate) of this one little corner of the world." By "witness," Fugard means not just to observe but also to provide oral or written evidence of what he has observed—sharing with others faithful images of his region and those who live there.

The couple moved to Johannesburg in 1958. Working as a clerk in a local court, where violations of South Africa's "pass law" were tried, Fugard saw the apartheid system in action. During this same period, his encounter with the artists and culture of Sophiatown, a black township on the outskirts of Johannesburg that was "open"—that is, it could be entered by whites without a special permit—proved instrumental in the development of his dramaturgy. Fugard wrote his first full-length plays, *No-Good Friday* (1958) and *Nongogo* (1959), about blacks living in Johannesburg and its environs. The plays were performed by amateur casts and directed by the playwright. Both featured the actor Zakes Mokae, whom Fugard had met in Sophiatown and who soon became one of his most important collaborators and closest friends. Fugard would later cast Mokae as Sam in the world premiere of *"MASTER HAROLD" . . . and the boys*.

Several years later, Fugard co-founded an amateur theater group called the Serpent Players, based in the black township near Port Elizabeth. Fugard directed its productions of Machiavelli (*The Man-*

drake), GEORG BÜCHNER, Camus, Sartre, SAMUEL BECKETT, and WOLE SOYINKA, all amid increasing police scrutiny of its activities. When two black actors were arrested and sent to Robben Island, a jail for political dissidents, one of them chose to perform there a version of SOPHOCLES' *ANTIGONE* (ca. 441 B.C.E.)—an incident that inspired a series of original pieces developed by Fugard and the Serpent Players. *Sizwe Bansi Is Dead* (1972) and *The Island* (1973), both co-written with John Kani and Winston Ntshona, soon provided international audiences gripping representations of the inequities and inhumanity of the apartheid regime. Fugard's growing international reputation helped foster strong ties with several theater companies abroad, including London's National Theatre and New Haven's Yale Repertory Theatre. He turned to the latter when, in 1982, he chose for the first time to stage the world premiere of one of his works outside South Africa. According to Fugard, *"MASTER HAROLD" . . . and the boys*—a play based on memories of his childhood relationships with his family and with a black man who worked for them—was too personal for him to produce at home before testing the work's broader appeal elsewhere.

Set on a rainy afternoon in the Saint George's Park Tea Room, *"MASTER HAROLD"* opens on the daily routine of two black employees, Sam and Willie, who await the arrival from school of the white owner's teenage son, Hally. Sam and Willie are practicing for an upcoming ballroom dance competition—an event that Hally later will realize could serve as the topic of an assigned school essay. As Hally settles in, doing his homework and reminiscing with the men about their years of service to his family, he receives a phone call from his mother: his father, a disabled alcoholic, is unexpectedly being discharged from the hospital. Hally's ambivalence about this news and the impact his father's release will have on his family life triggers emotions he cannot control and actions that will haunt him ever after. Simultaneously establishing their own dignity and maturity, as well as their deep affection for the troubled youth, the black men serve as witnesses for Hally, whose struggle to decide what kind of man he will be has just begun.

Sahr Ngaujah as Willie, Noah Robbins as Hally, and Leon Addison Brown as Sam in the 2016 production of *"MASTER HAROLD"* . . . *and the Boys* at the Signature Theatre in New York. The play was directed by Athol Fugard.

Fugard's ability to truthfully represent the motivations and perspectives of each of his characters at critical junctures—no matter how difficult or ugly—is a hallmark of his dramaturgy. He creates great intimacy with small casts, a technique that is often compared to that of Beckett. Most of Fugard's plays feature only two or three characters, reflecting as well a stylistic predilection for the "poor theatre" championed by Jerzy Grotowski, whose theory Fugard explicitly embraces, along with Grotowski's concept of an actor-centered theater devoid of the trappings of the commercial stage. In finally writing this autobiographical drama—this portrait of the artist as a young man (or, as he has said, a young fool)—Fugard explores the universal tropes of conflict between fathers and sons and exposes personal and political realities specific to his native country.

Fugard places *"MASTER HAROLD"* in 1950, just when the South African government enacted the Population Registration Act and the Group Areas Act, legislation that classified and separated its residents by race. Although the autobiographical

events chronicled by the play had actually occurred earlier, his decision to advance Hally's age from boyhood to adolescence allows Fugard to set him at the cusp of adulthood—the moment when an individual's identity and ideas about the world solidify—at a time of enormous political change. The play's title—and Fugard has been extremely clear about the importance of his capitalization and punctuation—highlights the ironies inherent in the ages and races of these characters as individuals and as South Africans. Hally has yet to grasp, for example, that Willie's agonizing choice between using his coins to play music to which he can practice ballroom dancing or to pay for bus fare home has everything to do with the laws that forced blacks to live in areas far removed from their places of employment. Fugard wants us to see this pivotal historic moment as having both microcosmic and macrocosmic consequences—we cannot separate the story of these three people from the world we now inhabit.

Fugard weaves together these stories of individuals and a nation in three scenes demarcated by two telephone calls. The play is, structurally, a long one act, running about 100 minutes in performance, with no intermission to relieve its growing tension. Confined to a single set, the action onstage occurs in real time; neither the audience nor the characters can escape the inexorable momentum of the conflict. Fugard also frames the action with separate glimpses of the lives of Sam and Willie; as characters, the men must have the independence and agency necessary to resist both the political context that would deny them those capacities and the narrative traditions that normalize blacks' marginality.

As the three characters discuss "social reformers" and "men of magnitude" from Hally's lessons, such men as Abraham Lincoln and Charles Darwin, the first scene foregrounds historic figures whose achievements resonate with the play's own societal concerns. This conversation later intertwines with Hally's personal memories, especially the story of a kite that Sam once made for him. Sam emerges as an unheralded man of magnitude for the troubled boy—someone who has affected him profoundly but whose story would not appear in any textbook. Fugard uses this same tale to develop Hally's conflicting allegiance to his two "fathers" and, ultimately, his passage from youthful obliviousness to a more mature recognition of the significance of apartheid. Sam interprets for Hally the current meaning of the whites-only area in which the boy had rested after their kite flying: "You don't *have* to sit up there by yourself. You know what that bench means now, and you can leave it any time you choose. All you've got to do is stand up and walk away from it."

Hally cannot walk away from his conflicted relationship to his biological father, however, and Fugard uses the trope of mobility to connect Hally's personal dilemma with the metaphoric narratives of the kite and the ballroom competition. The miracle of the kite's flight and the beauty of the dancers' movement stand in stark contrast to Hally's perceptions of his father's disability, yet we also see these same stories of physical triumph from the perspectives of Sam and Willie, who are crippled by social forces beyond their control. In the play's closing moments, Fugard may be using ballroom dance to suggest hope not only on a global but also on a local scale. A final glimpse of Sam and Willie dancing a slow foxtrot seems to hint at a better future if South Africa's disenfranchised majority can work together to bring it about. Such an interpretation may account for why the play was initially banned from production in South Africa. While officials pointed to what they called obscene language in the script and not its political content in justifying their decision, they also maintained that they did not know the drama was by Fugard, despite the wide publicity surrounding its premiere and its enthusiastic critical reception in the United States. Because of the work's literary merit, the ban was soon lifted; ironically, this governmental response to "MASTER HAROLD" had the immediate effect of drawing international attention to the work and its contemporary relevance.

Fugard no longer considers himself a dissident writer, driven by the necessity to give voice to a silenced majority. Yet he feels a continuing challenge to "witness" his country and its people as they confront new questions about their identity and their past. He holds fast to the idea that the theater can be a force for change and maintains his commitment "to entertain in order to make a difference" worldwide.   J.E.G.

"MASTER HAROLD"
. . . and the boys

CHARACTERS

HALLY
SAM
WILLIE

The St. George's Park Tea Room on a wet and windy Port Elizabeth[1] afternoon.

Tables and chairs have been cleared and are stacked on one side except for one which stands apart with a single chair. On this table a knife, fork, spoon, and side plate in anticipation of a simple meal, together with a pile of comic books.

Other elements: a serving counter with a few stale cakes under glass and a not very impressive display of sweets, cigarettes and cool drinks, etc.; a few cardboard advertising handouts—Cadbury's Chocolate, Coca-Cola—and a blackboard on which an untrained hand has chalked up the prices of Tea, Coffee, Scones, Milkshakes—all flavors—and Cool Drinks; a few sad ferns in pots; a telephone; an old-style jukebox.

There is an entrance on one side and an exit into a kitchen on the other.

Leaning on the solitary table, his head cupped in one hand as he pages through one of the comic books, is SAM. *A black man in his mid-forties. He wears the white coat of a waiter. Behind him on his knees, mopping down the floor with a bucket of water and a rag, is* WILLIE. *Also black and about the same age as* SAM. *He has his sleeves and trousers rolled up.*

The year: 1950.

WILLIE [*singing as he works*]
"She was scandalizin' my name,[2]
She took my money
She called me honey
But she was scandalizin' my name.
5 Called it love but was playin' a game . . ."

[*He gets up and moves the bucket. Stands thinking for a moment, then, raising his arms to hold an imaginary partner, he launches into an intricate ballroom dance step. Although a mildly comic figure, he reveals a reasonable degree of accomplishment.*]

Hey, Sam.

[SAM, *absorbed in the comic book, does not respond.*]

Hey, Boet[3] Sam!

---

1. A city on the southeastern coast of South Africa; it has been Fugard's primary residence since 1935 and is the setting for a number of his plays.
2. "Scandalizing My Name," recorded by Thomas Wayne (1959); a rhythm-and-blues version of "Scandalize My Name," a black gospel song recorded by Paul Robeson in the 1930s.
3. Brother (Afrikaans), a term here used in the sense of friendship.

[SAM *looks up.*]

I'm getting it. The quickstep. Look now and tell me. [*He repeats the step.*] Well?

10 SAM [*encouragingly*]   Show me again.

WILLIE   Okay, count for me.

SAM   Ready?

WILLIE   Ready.

SAM   Five, six, seven, eight . . . [WILLIE *starts to dance.*] A-n-d one two three
15 four . . . and one two three four. . . . [*Ad libbing as* WILLIE *dances*] Your shoulders, Willie . . . your shoulders! Don't look down! Look happy, Willie! Relax, Willie!

WILLIE [*desperate but still dancing*]   I am relax.

SAM   No, you're not.

20 WILLIE [*he falters*]   Ag no man, Sam! Mustn't talk. You make me make mistakes.

SAM   But you're too stiff.

WILLIE   Yesterday I'm not straight . . . today I'm too stiff!

SAM   Well, you are. You asked me and I'm telling you.

25 WILLIE   Where?

SAM   Everywhere. Try to glide through it.

WILLIE   Glide?

SAM   Ja,[4] make it smooth. And give it more style. It must look like you're enjoying yourself.

30 WILLIE [*emphatically*]   I wasn't.

SAM   Exactly.

WILLIE   How can I enjoy myself? Not straight, too stiff and now it's also glide, give it more style, make it smooth. . . . Haai! Is hard to remember all those things, Boet Sam.

35 SAM   That's your trouble. You're trying too hard.

WILLIE   I try hard because it *is* hard.

SAM   But don't let me see it. The secret is to make it look easy. Ballroom must look happy, Willie, not like hard work. It must . . . Ja! . . . it must look like romance.

40 WILLIE   Now another one! What's romance?

SAM   Love story with happy ending. A handsome man in tails, and in his arms, smiling at him, a beautiful lady in evening dress!

WILLIE   Fred Astaire, Ginger Rogers.[5]

SAM   You got it. Tapdance or ballroom, it's the same. Romance. In two weeks'
45 time when the judges look at you and Hilda, they must see a man and a woman who are dancing their way to a happy ending. What I saw was you holding her like you were frightened she was going to run away.

WILLIE   Ja! Because that is what she wants to do! I got no romance left for Hilda any more, Boet Sam.

50 SAM   Then pretend. When you put your arms around Hilda, imagine she is Ginger Rogers.

WILLIE   With no teeth? You try.

---

4. Yes (Afrikaans).
5. Famous dance partners in movie musicals; the American actors Astaire (1899–1987) and

Rogers (1911–1995) starred together in ten films (1933–39, 1949).

SAM   Well, just remember, there's only two weeks left.

WILLIE   I know, I know! [*To the jukebox*] I do it better with music. You got
55   sixpence for Sarah Vaughan?[6]

SAM   That's a slow foxtrot. You're practicing the quickstep.

WILLIE   I'll practice slow foxtrot.

SAM [*shaking his head*]   It's your turn to put money in the jukebox.

WILLIE   I only got bus fare to go home. [*He returns disconsolately to his
60   work.*] Love story and happy ending! She's doing it all right, Boet Sam, but
is not me she's giving happy endings. Fuckin' whore! Three nights now she
doesn't come practice. I wind up gramophone, I get record ready and I sit
and wait. What happens? Nothing. Ten o'clock I start dancing with my pillow. You try and practice romance by yourself, Boet Sam. Struesgod,[7] she
65   doesn't come tonight I take back my dress and ballroom shoes and I find
me new partner. Size twenty-six. Shoes size seven. And now she's also making trouble for me with the baby again. Reports me to Child Wellfed, that
I'm not giving her money. She lies! Every week I am giving her money for
milk. And how do I know is my baby? Only his hair looks like me. She's fuck-
70   ing around all the time I turn my back. Hilda Samuels is a bitch! [*Pause*] Hey,
Sam!

SAM   Ja.

WILLIE   You listening?

SAM   Ja.

75   WILLIE   So what you say?

SAM   About Hilda?

WILLIE   Ja.

SAM   When did you last give her a hiding?

WILLIE [*reluctantly*]   Sunday night.

80   SAM   And today is Thursday.

WILLIE [*he knows what's coming*]   Okay.

SAM   Hiding on Sunday night, then Monday, Tuesday and Wednesday she
doesn't come to practice . . . and you are asking me why?

WILLIE   I said okay, Boet Sam!

85   SAM   You hit her too much. One day she's going to leave you for good.

WILLIE   So? She makes me the hell-in[8] too much.

SAM [*emphasizing his point*]   *Too* much and *too* hard. You had the same trouble with Eunice.

WILLIE   Because she also make the hell-in, Boet Sam. She never got the
90   steps right. Even the waltz.

SAM   Beating her up every time she makes a mistake in the waltz? [*Shaking
his head*] No, Willie! That takes the pleasure out of ballroom dancing.

WILLIE   Hilda is not too bad with the waltz, Boet Sam. Is the quickstep
where the trouble starts.

95   SAM [*teasing him gently*]   How's your pillow with the quickstep?

WILLIE [*ignoring the tease*]   Good! And why? Because it got no legs. That's
her trouble. She can't move them quick enough, Boet Sam. I start the

---

6. An American jazz vocalist and pianist
(1924–1990).
7. As true as God (Afrikaans); that is, "I swear."

8. That is, she drives me crazy (South African
slang).

record and before halfway Count Basie[9] is already winning. Only time we catch up with him is when gramophone runs down.

> [SAM *laughs.*]

100   Haaikona,[1] Boet Sam, is not funny.

SAM [*snapping his fingers*]   I got it! Give her a handicap.

WILLIE   What's that?

SAM   Give her a ten-second start and then let Count Basie go. Then I put my money on her. Hot favorite in the Ballroom Stakes: Hilda Samuels ridden
105   by Willie Malopo.

WILLIE [*turning away*]   I'm not talking to you no more.

SAM [*relenting*]   Sorry, Willie . . .

WILLIE   It's finish between us.

SAM   Okay, okay . . . I'll stop.

110 WILLIE   You can also fuck off.

SAM   Willie, listen! I want to help you!

WILLIE   No more jokes?

SAM   I promise.

WILLIE   Okay. Help me.

115 SAM [*his turn to hold an imaginary partner*]   Look and learn. Feet together. Back straight. Body relaxed. Right hand placed gently in the small of her back and wait for the music. Don't start worrying about making mistakes or the judges or the other competitors. It's just you, Hilda, and the music, and you're going to have a good time. What Count Basie do you play?

120 WILLIE   "You the cream in my coffee, you the salt in my stew."[2]

SAM   Right. Give it to me in strict tempo.[3]

WILLIE   Ready?

SAM   Ready.

WILLIE   A-n-d . . . [*Singing*]

125   "You the cream in my coffee.

You the salt in my stew.

You will always be my necessity.

I'd be lost without you. . . ." (*etc.*)

> [SAM *launches into the quickstep. He is obviously a much more accomplished dancer than* WILLIE. HALLY *enters. A seventeen-year-old white boy. Wet raincoat and school case. He stops and watches* SAM. *The demonstration comes to an end with a flourish. Applause from* HALLY *and* WILLIE.]

HALLY   Bravo! No question about it. First place goes to Mr. Sam Semela.

130 WILLIE [*in total agreement*]   You was gliding with style, Boet Sam.

HALLY [*cheerfully*]   How's it, chaps?

SAM   Okay, Hally.

WILLIE [*springing to attention like a soldier and saluting*]   At your service, Master[4] Harold!

---

9. William "Count" Basie (1904–1984), American pianist, arranger, and composer who was one of the most influential bandleaders of the 20th century.
1. An exclamation of strong negation (Xhosa).
2. From "You're the Cream in My Coffee" (1928; music by Ray Henderson, lyrics by

Buddy G. DeSylva and Lew Brown).
3. That is, with an unvarying beat, so that it can be danced to more easily.
4. In Britain, the traditional courtesy title of a young gentleman not considered old enough to be called "Mister."

135 HALLY   Not long to the big event, hey!
     SAM   Two weeks.
     HALLY   You nervous?
     SAM   No.
     HALLY   Think you stand a chance?
140 SAM   Let's just say I'm ready to go out there and dance.
     HALLY   It looked like it. What about you, Willie?

          [WILLIE *groans.*]

     What's the matter?
     SAM   He's got leg trouble.
     HALLY   [*innocently*]   Oh, sorry to hear that, Willie.
145 WILLIE   Boet Sam! You promised. [WILLIE *returns to his work.*]

          [HALLY *deposits his school case and takes off his raincoat. His clothes are
          a little neglected and untidy: black blazer with school badge, gray flannel
          trousers in need of an ironing, khaki shirt and tie, black shoes.* SAM *has
          fetched a towel for* HALLY *to dry his hair.*]

     HALLY   God, what a lousy bloody day. It's coming down cats and dogs out
     there. Bad for business, chaps . . . [*Conspiratorial whisper*] . . . but it also
     means we're in for a nice quiet afternoon.
     SAM   You can speak loud. Your Mom's not here.
150 HALLY   Out shopping?
     SAM   No. The hospital.
     HALLY   But it's Thursday. There's no visiting on Thursday afternoons. Is my
     Dad okay?
     SAM   Sounds like it. In fact, I think he's going home.
155 HALLY   [*stopped short by* SAM's *remark*]   What do you mean?
     SAM   The hospital phoned.
     HALLY   To say what?
     SAM   I don't know. I just heard your Mom talking.
     HALLY   So what makes you say he's going home?
160 SAM   It sounded as if they were telling her to come and fetch him.

          [HALLY *thinks about what* SAM *has said for a few seconds.*]

     HALLY   When did she leave?
     SAM   About an hour ago. She said she would phone you. Want to eat?

          [HALLY *doesn't respond.*]

     Hally, want your lunch?
     HALLY   I suppose so. [*His mood has changed.*] What's on the menu? . . . as if
165 I don't know.
     SAM   Soup, followed by meat pie and gravy.
     HALLY   Today's?
     SAM   No.
     HALLY   And the soup?
170 SAM   Nourishing pea soup.
     HALLY   Just the soup. [*The pile of comic books on the table*] And these?
     SAM   For your Dad. Mr. Kempston brought them.
     HALLY   You haven't been reading them, have you?
     SAM   Just looking.
175 HALLY   [*examining the comics*]   Jungle Jim . . . Batman and Robin . . . Tar-
     zan . . . God, what rubbish! Mental pollution. Take them away.

[SAM *exits waltzing into the kitchen.* HALLY *turns to* WILLIE.]

HALLY   Did you hear my Mom talking on the telephone, Willie?

WILLIE   No, Master Hally. I was at the back.

HALLY   And she didn't say anything to you before she left?

180 WILLIE   She said I must clean the floors.

HALLY   I mean about my Dad.

WILLIE   She didn't say nothing to me about him, Master Hally.

HALLY [*with conviction*]   No! It can't be. They said he needed at least another three weeks of treatment. Sam's definitely made a mistake. [*Rummages through his school case, finds a book and settles down at the table to read.*]

185 So, Willie!

WILLIE   Yes, Master Hally! Schooling okay today?

HALLY   Yes, okay. . . . [*He thinks about it.*] . . . No, not really. Ag, what's the difference? I don't care. And Sam says you've got problems.

WILLIE   Big problems.

190 HALLY   Which leg is sore?

[WILLIE *groans.*]

Both legs.

WILLIE   There is nothing wrong with my legs. Sam is just making jokes.

HALLY   So then you *will* be in the competition.

WILLIE   Only if I can find me a partner.

195 HALLY   But what about Hilda?

SAM [*returning with a bowl of soup*]   She's the one who's got trouble with her legs.

HALLY   What sort of trouble, Willie?

SAM   From the way he describes it, I think the lady has gone a bit lame.

200 HALLY   Good God! Have you taken her to see a doctor?

SAM   I think a vet would be better.

HALLY   What do you mean?

SAM   What do you call it again when a racehorse goes very fast?

HALLY   Gallop?

205 SAM   That's it!

WILLIE   Boet Sam!

HALLY   "A gallop down the homestretch to the winning post." But what's that got to do with Hilda?

SAM   Count Basie always gets there first.

[WILLIE *lets fly with his slop rag. It misses* SAM *and hits* HALLY.]

210 HALLY [*furious*]   For Christ's sake, Willie! What the hell do you think you're doing!

WILLIE   Sorry, Master Hally, but it's him. . . .

HALLY   Act your bloody age! [*Hurls the rag back at* WILLIE.] Cut out the nonsense now and get on with your work. And you too, Sam. Stop fooling around.

[SAM *moves away.*]

215 No. Hang on. I haven't finished! Tell me exactly what my Mom said.

SAM   I have. "When Hally comes, tell him I've gone to the hospital and I'll phone him."

HALLY   She didn't say anything about taking my Dad home?

SAM   No. It's just that when she was talking on the phone . . .

220 HALLY [*interrupting him*]   No, Sam. They can't be discharging him. She
would have said so if they were. In any case, we saw him last night and he
wasn't in good shape at all. Staff nurse even said there was talk about taking more X-rays. And now suddenly today he's better? If anything, it sounds
more like a bad turn to me . . . which I sincerely hope it isn't. Hang on . . .
225 how long ago did you say she left?

SAM   Just before two . . . [*His wristwatch*] . . . hour and a half.

HALLY   I know how to settle it. [*Behind the counter to the telephone. Talking
as he dials*] Let's give her ten minutes to get to the hospital, ten minutes to
load him up, another ten, at the most, to get home, and another ten to get
230 him inside. Forty minutes. They should have been home for at least half an
hour already. [*Pause—he waits with the receiver to his ear.*] No reply, chaps.
And you know why? Because she's at his bedside in hospital helping him
pull through a bad turn. You definitely heard wrong.

SAM   Okay.

> [*As far as* HALLY *is concerned, the matter is settled. He returns to his
> table, sits down and divides his attention between the book and his soup.*
> SAM *is at his school case and picks up a textbook.*]

235 *Modern Graded Mathematics for Standards*[5] *Nine and Ten*. [*Opens it at random and laughs at something he sees.*] Who is this supposed to be?

HALLY   Old fart-face Prentice.

SAM   Teacher?

HALLY   Thinks he is. And believe me, that is not a bad likeness.

240 SAM   Has he seen it?

HALLY   Yes.

SAM   What did he say?

HALLY   Tried to be clever, as usual. Said I was no Leonardo da Vinci[6] and
that bad art had to be punished. So, six of the best, and his are bloody
245 good.

SAM   On your bum?

HALLY   Where else? The days when I got them on my hands are gone forever,
Sam.

SAM   With your trousers down!

250 HALLY   No. He's not quite that barbaric.

SAM   That's the way they do it in jail.

HALLY [*flicker of morbid interest*]   Really?

SAM   Ja. When the magistrate sentences you to "strokes with a light cane."

HALLY   Go on.

255 SAM   They make you lie down on a bench. One policeman pulls down your
trousers and holds your ankles, another one pulls your shirt over your head
and holds your arms . . .

HALLY   Thank you! That's enough.

SAM   . . . and the one that gives you the strokes talks to you gently and for a
260 long time between each one. [*He laughs.*]

HALLY   I've heard enough, Sam! Jesus! It's a bloody awful world when you
come to think of it. People can be real bastards.

---

5. That is, grades.
6. Italian artist (1452–1519), famous for his
precisely rendered drawings as well as his
paintings.

SAM   That's the way it is, Hally.

HALLY   It doesn't *have* to be that way. There is something called progress,
265   you know. We don't exactly burn people at the stake any more.

SAM   Like Joan of Arc.[7]

HALLY   Correct. If she was captured today, she'd be given a fair trial.

SAM   And then the death sentence.

HALLY   [*a world-weary sigh*]   I know, I know! I oscillate between hope and
270   despair for this world as well, Sam. But things will change, you wait and
see. One day somebody is going to get up and give history a kick up the
backside and get it going again.

SAM   Like who?

HALLY   [*after thought*]   They're called social reformers. Every age, Sam, has
275   got its social reformer. My history book is full of them.

SAM   So where's ours?

HALLY   Good question. And I hate to say it, but the answer is: I don't know.
Maybe he hasn't even been born yet. Or is still only a babe in arms at his
mother's breast. God, what a thought.

280   SAM   So we just go on waiting.

HALLY   Ja, looks like it. [*Back to his soup and the book*]

SAM   [*reading from the textbook*]   "Introduction: In some mathematical problems only the magnitude . . ." [*He mispronounces the word "magnitude."*]

HALLY   [*correcting him without looking up*]   Magnitude.

285   SAM   What's it mean?

HALLY   How big it is. The size of the thing.

SAM   [*reading*]   ". . . magnitude of the quantities is of importance. In other
problems we need to know whether these quantities are negative or positive. For example, whether there is a debit or credit bank balance . . ."

290   HALLY   Whether you're broke or not.

SAM   ". . . whether the temperature is above or below Zero . . ."

HALLY   Naught degrees. Cheerful state of affairs! No cash and you're freezing to death. Mathematics won't get you out of that one.

SAM   "All these quantities are called . . ." [*Spelling the word*] . . . s-c-a-l . . .

295   HALLY   Scalars.

SAM   Scalars! [*Shaking his head with a laugh*] You understand all that?

HALLY   [*turning a page*]   No. And I don't intend to try.

SAM   So what happens when the exams come?

HALLY   Failing a maths exam isn't the end of the world, Sam. How many
300   times have I told you that examination results don't measure intelligence?

SAM   I would say about as many times as you've failed one of them.

HALLY   [*mirthlessly*]   Ha, ha, ha.

SAM   [*simultaneously*]   Ha, ha, ha.

HALLY   Just remember Winston Churchill[8] didn't do particularly well at
305   school.

SAM   You've also told me that one many times.

HALLY   Well, it just so happens to be the truth.

---

7. The French saint and national heroine
(ca. 1412–1431); she successfully led French
troops against the English, but was captured
and burned at the stake after being charged
with heresy and witchcraft.

8. British statesman and author (1874–1965);
as prime minister (1940–45, 1951–55) he
was a highly effective leader during World
War II.

SAM [*enjoying the word*]   Magnitude! Magnitude! Show me how to use it.

HALLY [*after thought*]   An intrepid social reformer will not be daunted by the
310   magnitude of the task he has undertaken.

SAM [*impressed*]   Couple of jaw-breakers in there!

HALLY   I gave you three for the price of one. Intrepid, daunted, and magnitude. I did that once in an exam. Put five of the words I had to explain in
one sentence. It was half a page long.

315 SAM   Well, I'll put my money on you in the English exam.

HALLY   Piece of cake. Eighty percent without even trying.

SAM [*another textbook from* HALLY's *case*]   And history?

HALLY   So-so. I'll scrape through. In the fifties if I'm lucky.

SAM   You didn't do too badly last year.

320 HALLY   Because we had World War One. That at least had some action. You
try to find that in the South African Parliamentary system.

SAM [*reading from the history textbook*]   "Napoleon[9] and the principle of
equality." Hey! This sounds interesting. "After concluding peace with Britain in 1802, Napoleon used a brief period of calm to in-sti-tute . . ."

325 HALLY   Introduce.

SAM   ". . . many reforms. Napoleon regarded all people as equal before the
law and wanted them to have equal opportunities for advancement. All ves-
ti-ges of the feu-dal system with its oppression of the poor were abolished."
Vestiges, feudal system, and abolished. I'm all right on oppression.

330 HALLY   I'm thinking. He swept away . . . abolished . . . the last remains . . .
vestiges . . . of the bad old days . . . feudal system.

SAM   Ha! There's the social reformer we're waiting for. He sounds like a man
of some magnitude.

HALLY   I'm not so sure about that. It's a damn good title for a book, though.
335   A man of magnitude!

SAM   He sounds pretty big to me, Hally.

HALLY   Don't confuse historical significance with greatness. But maybe I'm
being a bit prejudiced. Have a look in there and you'll see he's two chapters
long. And hell! . . . has he only got dates, Sam, all of which you've got to
340   remember! This campaign and that campaign, and then, because of all the
fighting, the next thing is we get Peace Treaties all over the place. And
what's the end of the story? Battle of Waterloo, which he loses. Wasn't
worth it. No, I don't know about him as a man of magnitude.

SAM   Then who would you say was?

345 HALLY   To answer that, we need a definition of greatness, and I suppose that
would be somebody who . . . somebody who benefited all mankind.

SAM   Right. But like who?

HALLY [*he speaks with total conviction*]   Charles Darwin.[1] Remember him?
That big book from the library. *The Origin of the Species.*

350 SAM   Him?

HALLY   Yes. For his Theory of Evolution.

SAM   You didn't finish it.

9. Napoleon Bonaparte (1769–1821), the
French general who in 1804 declared himself
emperor of France; he undertook domestic
reforms as well as military conquest (he was
finally defeated at Waterloo in 1815).

1. British naturalist (1809–1882), author of
the groundbreaking treatise *On the Origin of
Species by Means of Natural Selection* (1859).
Chapter 3 of the work is titled "Struggle for
Existence."

HALLY   I ran out of time. I didn't finish it because my two weeks was up. But I'm going to take it out again after I've digested what I read. It's safe. I've
355   hidden it away in the Theology section. Nobody ever goes in there. And anyway who are you to talk? You hardly even looked at it.

SAM   I tried. I looked at the chapters in the beginning and I saw one called "The Struggle for an Existence." Ah ha, I thought. At last! But what did I get? Something called the mistiltoe which needs the apple tree and there's
360   too many seeds and all are going to die except one . . . !² No, Hally.

HALLY [*intellectually outraged*]   What do you mean, No! The poor man had to start somewhere. For God's sake, Sam, he revolutionized science. Now we know.

SAM   What?

365 HALLY   Where we come from and what it all means.

SAM   And that's a benefit to mankind? Anyway, I still don't believe it.

HALLY   God, you're impossible. I showed it to you in black and white.

SAM   Doesn't mean I got to believe it.

HALLY   It's the likes of you that kept the Inquisition³ in business. It's called
370   bigotry. Anyway, that's my man of magnitude. Charles Darwin! Who's yours?

SAM [*without hesitation*]   Abraham Lincoln.⁴

HALLY   I might have guessed as much. Don't get sentimental, Sam. You've never been a slave, you know. And anyway we freed your ancestors here in
375   South Africa long before the Americans. But if you want to thank somebody on their behalf, do it to Mr. William Wilberforce.⁵ Come on. Try again. I want a real genius. [*Now enjoying himself, and so is* SAM. HALLY *goes behind the counter and helps himself to a chocolate.*]

SAM   William Shakespeare.

HALLY [*no enthusiasm*]   Oh. So you're also one of them,⁶ are you? You're bas-
380   ing that opinion on only one play, you know. You've only read my *Julius Caesar* and even I don't understand half of what they're talking about. They should do what they did with the old Bible: bring the language up to date.

SAM   That's all you've got. It's also the only one *you've* read.

HALLY   I know. I admit it. That's why I suggest we reserve our judgment until
385   we've checked up on a few others. I've got a feeling, though, that by the end of this year one is going to be enough for me, and I can give you the names of twenty-nine other chaps in the Standard Nine class of the Port Elizabeth Technical College who feel the same. But if you want him, you can have him. My turn now. [*Pacing*] This is a damned good exercise, you

2. In two dense sentences, Darwin mentions mistletoe and apple trees to distinguish parasitism and competition.
3. A tribunal of the Roman Catholic Church, established in 1233 to investigate heresy; over the centuries, a number of philosophers and scientists (including Galileo) were tried by its officers.
4. The sixteenth president of the United States (1809–1865; president, 1861–65), known as the "Great Emancipator" because of his proclamation freeing the slaves who were living in states that were in rebellion against the federal government.
5. British politician and opponent of slavery (1759–1833); days before his death, Parliament passed an act outlawing slavery throughout most of the British Empire, including the Cape Colony (later to become part of South Africa).
6. That is, one of the many who regard Shakespeare (1564–1616) as the greatest dramatist of all time. *Julius Caesar* was first performed in 1599.

390   know! It started off looking like a simple question and here it's got us really probing into the intellectual heritage of our civilization.

SAM   So who is it going to be?

HALLY   My next man . . . and he gets the title on two scores: social reform and literary genius . . . is Leo Nikolaevich Tolstoy.[7]

395 SAM   That Russian.

HALLY   Correct. Remember the picture of him I showed you?

SAM   With the long beard.

HALLY [*trying to look like Tolstoy*]   And those burning, visionary eyes. My God, the face of a social prophet if ever I saw one! And remember my words

400   when I showed it to you? Here's a *man*, Sam!

SAM   Those were words, Hally.

HALLY   Not many intellectuals are prepared to shovel manure with the peasants and then go home and write a "little book" called *War and Peace*. Incidentally, Sam, he was somebody else who, to quote, ". . . did not distinguish

405   himself scholastically."

SAM   Meaning?

HALLY   He was also no good at school.

SAM   Like you and Winston Churchill.

HALLY [*mirthlessly*]   Ha, ha, ha.

410 SAM [*simultaneously*]   Ha, ha, ha.

HALLY   Don't get clever, Sam. That man freed his serfs of his own free will.

SAM   No argument. He was a somebody, all right. I accept him.

HALLY   I'm sure Count Tolstoy will be very pleased to hear that. Your turn. Shoot. [*Another chocolate from behind the counter*] I'm waiting, Sam.

415 SAM   I've got him.

HALLY   Good. Submit your candidate for examination.

SAM   Jesus.

HALLY [*stopped dead in his tracks*]   Who?

SAM   Jesus Christ.

420 HALLY   Oh, come on, Sam!

SAM   The Messiah.

HALLY   Ja, but still . . . No, Sam. Don't let's get started on religion. We'll just spend the whole afternoon arguing again. Suppose I turn around and say Mohammed?

425 SAM   All right.

HALLY   You can't have them both on the same list!

SAM   Why not? You like Mohammed, I like Jesus.

HALLY   I *don't* like Mohammed. I never have. I was merely being hypothetical. As far as I'm concerned, the Koran is as bad as the Bible. No. Religion

430   is out! I'm not going to waste my time again arguing with you about the existence of God. You know perfectly well I'm an atheist . . . and I've got homework to do.

SAM   Okay, I take him back.

HALLY   You've got time for one more name.

---

7. Russian novelist and philosopher (1828–1910), born into the nobility (he inherited an estate that included hundreds of serfs); one of his masterpieces is *War and Peace* (1863–69).

435 SAM [*after thought*]   I've got one I know we'll agree on. A simple straightforward great Man of Magnitude . . . and no arguments. And *he* really *did*
benefit all mankind.

HALLY   I wonder. After your last contribution I'm beginning to doubt whether
anything in the way of an intellectual agreement is possible between the
440 two of us. Who is he?

SAM   Guess.

HALLY   Socrates? Alexandre Dumas? Karl Marx? Dostoevsky? Nietzsche?[8]

[SAM *shakes his head after each name.*]

Give me a clue.

SAM   The letter P is important . . .

445 HALLY   Plato!

SAM   . . . and his name begins with an F.

HALLY   I've got it. Freud[9] and Psychology.

SAM   No. I didn't understand him.

HALLY   That makes two of us.

450 SAM   Think of mouldy apricot jam.

HALLY [*after a delighted laugh*]   Penicillin and Sir Alexander Fleming![1] And
the title of the book: *The Microbe Hunters.* [*Delighted.*] Splendid, Sam!
Splendid. For once we are in total agreement. The major breakthrough in
medical science in the Twentieth Century. If it wasn't for him, we might
455 have lost the Second World War. It's deeply gratifying, Sam, to know that I
haven't been wasting my time in talking to you. [*Strutting around proudly*]
Tolstoy may have educated his peasants, but I've educated you.

SAM   Standard Four to Standard Nine.

HALLY   Have we been at it as long as that?

460 SAM   Yep. And my first lesson was geography.

HALLY [*intrigued*]   Really? I don't remember.

SAM   My room there at the back of the old Jubilee Boarding House. I had
just started working for your Mom. Little boy in short trousers walks in one
afternoon and asks me seriously: "Sam, do you want to see South Africa?"
465 Hey man! Sure I wanted to see South Africa!

HALLY   Was that me?

SAM   . . . So the next thing I'm looking at a map you had just done for homework. It was your first one and you were very proud of yourself.

HALLY   Go on.

470 SAM   Then came my first lesson. "Repeat after me, Sam: Gold in the Transvaal, mealies in the Free State, sugar in Natal and grapes in the Cape."[2] I
still know it!

---

8. A mixture of philosophers—the Greek
Socrates (469–399 B.C.E.), who is featured in
the dialogues of Plato (427–347 B.C.E.), and
the Germans Karl Marx (1818–1883) and
Friedrich Nietzsche (1844–1900)—and novelists: the French Dumas père (1802–1870)
and fils (1824–1895), and the Russian Fyodor
Dostoyevsky (1821–1881).
9. Sigmund Freud (1856–1939), the Austrian
founder of psychoanalysis.

1. A Scottish bacteriologist (1881–1955); in
1928, he discovered penicillin, the first effective antibiotic. Fleming is one of the scientists
featured in Paul de Kruif's *Microbe Hunters*
(1926).
2. In 1950, the four provinces of South Africa
were the Transvaal, the Orange Free State,
Natal, and the Cape Province. *Mealies:* maize
(U.S. corn), the principal staple of southern
Africa.

HALLY   Well, I'll be buggered.[3] So that's how it all started.

SAM   And your next map was one with all the rivers and the mountains they
475   came from. The Orange, the Vaal, the Limpopo, the Zambezi . . .

HALLY   You've got a phenomenal memory!

SAM   You should be grateful. That is why you started passing your exams. You
tried to be better than me.

[*They laugh together.* WILLIE *is attracted by the laughter and joins them.*]

HALLY   The old Jubilee Boarding House. Sixteen rooms with board and lodg-
480   ing, rent in advance and one week's notice. I haven't thought about it for
donkey's years[4] . . . and I don't think that's an accident. God, was I glad
when we sold it and moved out. Those years are not remembered as the
happiest ones of an unhappy childhood.

WILLIE [*knocking on the table and trying to imitate a woman's voice*]   "Hally,
485   are you there?"

HALLY   Who's that supposed to be?

WILLIE   "What you doing in there, Hally? Come out at once!"

HALLY [*to* SAM]   What's he talking about?

SAM   Don't you remember?

490   WILLIE   "Sam, Willie . . . is he in there with you boys?"

SAM   Hiding away in our room when your mother was looking for you.

HALLY [*another good laugh*]   Of course! I used to crawl and hide under your
bed! But finish the story, Willie. Then what used to happen? You chaps
would give the game away by telling her I was in there with you. So much
495   for friendship.

SAM   We couldn't lie to her. She knew.

HALLY   Which meant I got another rowing[5] for hanging around the "servants'
quarters." I think I spent more time in there with you chaps than anywhere
else in that dump. And do you blame me? Nothing but bloody misery wher
500   ever you went. Somebody was always complaining about the food, or my
mother was having a fight with Micky Nash because she'd caught her with
a petty officer in her room. Maud Meiring was another one. Remember
those two? They were prostitutes, you know. Soldiers and sailors from the
troopships. Bottom fell out of the business when the war ended. God, the
505   flotsam and jetsam that life washed up on our shores! No joking, if it wasn't
for your room, I would have been the first certified[6] ten-year-old in medical
history. Ja, the memories are coming back now. Walking home from school
and thinking: "What can I do this afternoon?" Try out a few ideas, but
sooner or later I'd end up in there with you fellows. I bet you I could still
510   find my way to your room with my eyes closed. [*He does exactly that.*] Down
the corridor . . . telephone on the right, which my Mom keeps locked
because somebody is using it on the sly and not paying . . . past the kitchen
and unappetizing cooking smells . . . around the corner into the backyard,
hold my breath again because there are more smells coming when I pass
515   your lavatory, then into that little passageway, first door on the right and
into your room. How's that?

SAM   Good. But, as usual, you forgot to knock.

---

3. That is, I'll be damned (slang).   5. Scolding.
4. That is, a very long time (British slang).   6. Officially declared insane.

HALLY   Like that time I barged in and caught you and Cynthia . . . at it. Remember? God, was I embarrassed! I didn't know what was going on at first.

520 SAM   Ja, that taught you a lesson.

HALLY   And about a lot more than knocking on doors, I'll have you know, and I don't mean geography either. Hell, Sam, couldn't you have waited until it was dark?

SAM   No.

525 HALLY   Was it that urgent?

SAM   Yes, and if you don't believe me, wait until your time comes.

HALLY   No, thank you. I am not interested in girls. [*Back to his memories . . . Using a few chairs he re-creates the room as he lists the items.*] A gray little room with a cold cement floor. Your bed against that wall . . . and I now
530 know why the mattress sags so much! . . . Willie's bed . . . it's propped up on bricks because one leg is broken . . . that wobbly little table with the washbasin and jug of water . . . Yes! . . . stuck to the wall above it are some pin-up pictures from magazines. Joe Louis[7] . . .

WILLIE   Brown Bomber. World Title. [*Boxing pose*] Three rounds and knockout.

535 HALLY   Against who?

SAM   Max Schmeling.

HALLY   Correct. I can also remember Fred Astaire and Ginger Rogers, and Rita Hayworth[8] in a bathing costume which always made me hot and bothered when I looked at it. Under Willie's bed is an old suitcase with all his
540 clothes in a mess, which is why I never hide there. Your things are neat and tidy in a trunk next to your bed, and on it there is a picture of you and Cynthia in your ballroom clothes, your first silver cup for third place in a competition and an old radio which doesn't work any more. Have I left out anything?

545 SAM   No.

HALLY   Right, so much for the stage directions. Now the characters. [SAM *and* WILLIE *move to their appropriate positions in the bedroom.*] Willie is in bed, under his blankets with his clothes on, complaining nonstop about something, but we can't make out a word of what he's saying because he's
550 got his head under the blankets as well. You're on your bed trimming your toenails with a knife—not a very edifying sight—and as for me . . . What am I doing?

SAM   You're sitting on the floor giving Willie a lecture about being a good loser while you get the checkerboard and pieces ready for a game. Then
555 you go to Willie's bed, pull off the blankets and make him play with you first because you know you're going to win, and that gives you the second game with me.

HALLY   And you certainly were a bad loser, Willie!

WILLIE   Haai!

560 HALLY   Wasn't he, Sam? And so slow! A game with you almost took the whole afternoon. Thank God I gave up trying to teach you how to play chess.

WILLIE   You and Sam cheated.

---

7. A black American boxer (1914–1981); he was world heavyweight champion when he knocked out the German champion, Max Schmeling (1905–2005), in the first round of
their celebrated 1938 rematch (Schmeling had knocked him out in a 1936 fight).
8. American movie star (1918–1987), a leading sex symbol of the 1940s.

HALLY   I never saw Sam cheat, and mine were mostly the mistakes of youth.

WILLIE   Then how is it you two was always winning?

565 HALLY   Have you ever considered the possibility, Willie, that it was because we were better than you?

WILLIE   Every time better?

HALLY   Not every time. There were occasions when we deliberately let you win a game so that you would stop sulking and go on playing with us. Sam

570   used to wink at me when you weren't looking to show me it was time to let you win.

WILLIE   So then you two didn't play fair.

HALLY   It was for your benefit, Mr. Malopo, which is more than being fair. It was an act of self-sacrifice. [*To* SAM] But you know what my best memory

575   is, don't you?

SAM   No.

HALLY   Come on, guess. If your memory is so good, you must remember it as well.

SAM   We got up to a lot of tricks in there, Hally.

580 HALLY   This one was special, Sam.

SAM   I'm listening.

HALLY   It started off looking like another of those useless nothing-to-do afternoons. I'd already been down to Main Street looking for adventure, but nothing had happened. I didn't feel like climbing trees in the Donkin

585   Park[9] or pretending I was a private eye and following a stranger . . . so as usual: See what's cooking in Sam's room. This time it was you on the floor. You had two thin pieces of wood and you were smoothing them down with a knife. It didn't look particularly interesting, but when I asked you what you were doing, you just said, "Wait and see, Hally. Wait . . . and see" . . .

590   in that secret sort of way of yours, so I knew there was a surprise coming. You teased me, you bugger, by being deliberately slow and not answering my questions!

            [SAM *laughs.*]

And whistling while you worked away! God, it was infuriating! I could have brained you! It was only when you tied them together in a cross and put

595   that down on the brown paper that I realized what you were doing. "Sam is making a kite?" And when I asked you and you said "Yes" . . . ! [*Shaking his head with disbelief*] The sheer audacity of it took my breath away. I mean, seriously, what the hell does a black man know about flying a kite? I'll be honest with you, Sam, I had no hopes for it. If you think I was excited and

600   happy, you got another guess coming. In fact, I was shit-scared that we were going to make fools of ourselves. When we left the boarding house to go up onto the hill, I was praying quietly that there wouldn't be any other kids around to laugh at us.

SAM   [*enjoying the memory as much as* HALLY]   Ja, I could see that.

605 HALLY   I made it obvious, did I?

SAM   Ja. You refused to carry it.

HALLY   Do you blame me? Can you remember what the poor thing looked like? Tomato-box wood and brown paper! Flour and water for glue! Two of

---

9. That is, the Donkin Reserve, a park established in Port Elizabeth in 1820.

my mother's old stockings for a tail, and then all those bits and pieces of
610   string you made me tie together so that we could fly it! Hell, no, that was
now only asking for a miracle to happen.

SAM   Then the big argument when I told you to hold the string and run with
it when I let go.

HALLY   I was prepared to run, all right, but straight back to the boarding
615   house.

SAM   [*knowing what's coming*]   So what happened?

HALLY   Come on, Sam, you remember as well as I do.

SAM   I want to hear it from you.

[HALLY *pauses. He wants to be as accurate as possible.*]

HALLY   You went a little distance from me down the hill, you held it up ready
620   to let it go. . . . "This is it," I thought. "Like everything else in my life, here
comes another fiasco." Then you shouted, "Go, Hally!" and I started to run.
[*Another pause*] I don't know how to describe it, Sam. Ja! The miracle happened! I was running, waiting for it to crash to the ground, but instead suddenly there was something alive behind me at the end of the string, tugging
625   at it as if it wanted to be free. I looked back . . . [*Shakes his head.*] . . . I still
can't believe my eyes. It was flying! Looping around and trying to climb
even higher into the sky. You shouted to me to let it have more string. I did,
until there was none left and I was just holding that piece of wood we had
tied it to. You came up and joined me. You were laughing.

630   SAM   So were you. And shouting, "It works, Sam! We've done it!"

HALLY   And we had! I was so proud of us! It was the most splendid thing I
had ever seen. I wished there were hundreds of kids around to watch us.
The part that scared me, though, was when you showed me how to make it
dive down to the ground and then just when it was on the point of crash-
635   ing, swoop up again!

SAM   You didn't want to try yourself.

HALLY   Of course not! I would have been suicidal if anything had happened
to it. Watching you do it made me nervous enough. I was quite happy just
to see it up there with its tail fluttering behind it. You left me after that,
640   didn't you? You explained how to get it down, we tied it to the bench so that
I could sit and watch it, and you went away. I wanted you to stay, you know.
I was a little scared of having to look after it by myself.

SAM   [*quietly*]   I had work to do, Hally.

HALLY   It was sort of sad bringing it down, Sam. And it looked sad again
645   when it was lying there on the ground. Like something that had lost its
soul. Just tomato-box wood, brown paper and two of my mother's old stockings! But, hell, I'll never forget that first moment when I saw it up there. I
had a stiff neck the next day from looking up so much.

[SAM *laughs.* HALLY *turns to him with a question he never thought of asking before.*]

Why did you make that kite, Sam?

650   SAM   [*evenly*]   I can't remember.

HALLY   Truly?

SAM   Too long ago, Hally.

HALLY   Ja, I suppose it was. It's time for another one, you know.

SAM   Why do you say that?

655   HALLY   Because it feels like that. Wouldn't be a good day to fly it, though.

SAM   No. You can't fly kites on rainy days.

HALLY [*he studies* SAM. *Their memories have made him conscious of the man's presence in his life*]   How old are you, Sam?

SAM   Two score and five.

HALLY   Strange, isn't it?

660 SAM   What?

HALLY   Me and you.

SAM   What's strange about it?

HALLY   Little white boy in short trousers and a black man old enough to be his father flying a kite. It's not every day you see that.

665 SAM   But why strange? Because the one is white and the other black?

HALLY   I don't know. Would have been just as strange, I suppose, if it had been me and my Dad . . . cripple man and a little boy! Nope! There's no chance of me flying a kite without it being strange. [*Simple statement of fact—no self-pity*] There's a nice little short story there. "The Kite-Flyers."

670 But we'd have to find a twist in the ending.

SAM   Twist?

HALLY   Yes. Something unexpected. The way it ended with us was too straightforward . . . me on the bench and you going back to work. There's no drama in that.

675 WILLIE   And me?

HALLY   You?

WILLIE   Yes me.

HALLY   You want to get into the story as well, do you? I got it! Change the title: "Afternoons in Sam's Room" . . . expand it and tell all the stories. It's on

680 its way to being a novel. Our days in the old Jubilee. Sad in a way that they're over. I almost wish we were still in that little room.

SAM   We're still together.

HALLY   That's true. It's just that life felt the right size in there . . . not too big and not too small. Wasn't so hard to work up a bit of courage. It's got so

685 bloody complicated since then.

[*The telephone rings.* SAM *answers it.*]

SAM   St. George's Park Tea Room . . . Hello, Madam . . . Yes, Madam, he's here. . . . Hally, it's your mother.

HALLY   Where is she phoning from?

SAM   Sounds like the hospital. It's a public telephone.

690 HALLY [*relieved*]   You see! I told you. [*The telephone*] Hello, Mom . . . Yes . . . Yes no fine. Everything's under control here. How's things with poor old Dad? . . . Has he had a bad turn? . . . What? . . . Oh, God! . . . Yes, Sam told me, but I was sure he'd made a mistake. But what's this all about, Mom? He didn't look at all good last night. How can he get better so quickly? . . .

695 Then very obviously you must say no. Be firm with him. You're the boss. . . . You know what it's going to be like if he comes home. . . . Well then, don't blame me when I fail my exams at the end of the year. . . . Yes! How am I expected to be fresh for school when I spend half the night massaging his gammy[1] leg? . . . So am I! . . . So tell him a white lie. Say Dr. Colley wants

700 more X-rays of his stump. Or bribe him. We'll sneak in double tots of brandy in future. . . . What? . . . Order him to get back into bed at once! If

---

1. Game; lame.

he's going to behave like a child, treat him like one. . . . All right, Mom! I was just trying to . . . I'm sorry. . . . I said I'm sorry. . . . Quick, give me your number. I'll phone you back. [*He hangs up and waits a few seconds.*] Here
705   we go again! [*He dials.*] I'm sorry, Mom. . . . Okay . . . But now listen to me carefully. All it needs is for you to put your foot down. Don't take no for an answer. . . . Did you hear me? And whatever you do, don't discuss it with him. . . . Because I'm frightened you'll give in to him. . . . Yes, Sam gave me lunch. . . . I ate all of it! . . . No, Mom not a soul. It's still raining here. . . .
710   Right, I'll tell them. I'll just do some homework and then lock up. . . . But remember now, Mom. Don't listen to anything he says. And phone me back and let me know what happens. . . . Okay. Bye, Mom. [*He hangs up. The men are staring at him.*] My Mom says that when you're finished with the floors you must do the windows. [*Pause*] Don't misunderstand me, chaps.
715   All I want is for him to get better. And if he was, I'd be the first person to say: "Bring him home." But he's not, and we can't give him the medical care and attention he needs at home. That's what hospitals are there for. [*Brusquely*] So don't just stand there! Get on with it!

    [SAM *clears* HALLY's *table.*]

You heard right. My Dad wants to go home.
720 SAM   Is he better?
HALLY [*sharply*]   No! How the hell can he be better when last night he was groaning with pain? This is not an age of miracles!
SAM   Then he should stay in hospital.
HALLY [*seething with irritation and frustration*]   Tell me something I don't
725   know, Sam. What the hell do you think I was saying to my Mom? All I can say is fuck-it-all.
SAM   I'm sure he'll listen to your Mom.
HALLY   You don't know what she's up against. He's already packed his shaving kit and pajamas and is sitting on his bed with his crutches, dressed and
730   ready to go. I know him when he gets in that mood. If she tries to reason with him, we've had it. She's no match for him when it comes to a battle of words. He'll tie her up in knots. [*Trying to hide his true feelings*]
SAM   I suppose it gets lonely for him in there.
HALLY   With all the patients and nurses around? Regular visits from the Sal
735   vation Army? Balls! It's ten times worse for him at home. I'm at school and my mother is here in the business all day.
SAM   He's at least got you at night.
HALLY [*before he can stop himself*]   And we've got him! Please! I don't want to talk about it any more. [*Unpacks his school case, slamming down books on*
740   *the table.*] Life is just a plain bloody mess, that's all. And people are fools.
SAM   Come on, Hally.
HALLY   Yes, they are! They bloody well deserve what they get.
SAM   Then don't complain.
HALLY   Don't try to be clever, Sam. It doesn't suit you. Anybody who thinks
745   there's nothing wrong with this world needs to have his head examined. Just when things are going along all right, without fail someone or something will come along and spoil everything. Somebody should write that down as a fundamental law of the Universe. The principle of perpetual disappointment. If there is a God who created this world, he should scrap it
750   and try again.

SAM   All right, Hally, all right. What you got for homework?

HALLY   Bullshit, as usual. [*Opens an exercise book and reads.*] "Write five hundred words describing an annual event of cultural or historical significance."

755 SAM   That should be easy enough for you.

HALLY   And also plain bloody boring. You know what he wants, don't you? One of their useless old ceremonies. The commemoration of the landing of the 1820 Settlers,[2] or if it's going to be culture, Carols by Candlelight every Christmas.

760 SAM   It's an impressive sight. Make a good description, Hally. All those candles glowing in the dark and the people singing hymns.

HALLY   And it's called religious hysteria. [*Intense irritation*] Please, Sam! Just leave me alone and let me get on with it. I'm not in the mood for games this afternoon. And remember my Mom's orders . . . you're to help Willie with

765 the windows. Come on now, I don't want any more nonsense in here.

SAM   Okay, Hally, okay.

[HALLY *settles down to his homework; determined preparations . . . pen, ruler, exercise book, dictionary, another cake . . . all of which will lead to nothing.*]

[SAM *waltzes over to* WILLIE *and starts to replace tables and chairs. He practices a ballroom step while doing so.* WILLIE *watches. When* SAM *is finished,* WILLIE *tries.*] Good! But just a little bit quicker on the turn and only move in to her after she's crossed over. What about this one?

[*Another step. When* SAM *is finished,* WILLIE *again has a go.*]

Much better. See what happens when you just relax and enjoy yourself?

770 Remember that in two weeks' time and you'll be all right.

WILLIE   But I haven't got partner, Boet Sam.

SAM   Maybe Hilda will turn up tonight.

WILLIE   No, Boet Sam. [*Reluctantly*] I gave her a good hiding.

SAM   You mean a bad one.

775 WILLIE   Good bad one.

SAM   Then you mustn't complain either. Now you pay the price for losing your temper.

WILLIE   I also pay two pounds ten shilling entrance fee.

SAM   They'll refund you if you withdraw now.

780 WILLIE [*appalled*]   You mean, don't dance?

SAM   Yes.

WILLIE   No! I wait too long and I practice too hard. If I find me new partner, you think I can be ready in two weeks? I ask Madam for my leave now and we practice every day.

785 SAM   Quickstep non-stop for two weeks. World record, Willie, but you'll be mad at the end.

WILLIE   No jokes, Boet Sam.

SAM   I'm not joking.

WILLIE   So then what?

790 SAM   Find Hilda. Say you're sorry and promise you won't beat her again.

WILLIE   No.

---

2. That is, the founders of Port Elizabeth, which was established to strengthen the Cape Colony against the Xhosa people to the east.

SAM   Then withdraw. Try again next year.

WILLIE   No.

SAM   Then I give up.

795 WILLIE   Haaikona, Boet Sam, you can't.

SAM   What do you mean, I can't? I'm telling you: I give up.

WILLIE   [*adamant*] No! [*Accusingly*] It was you who start me ballroom dancing.

SAM   So?

800 WILLIE   Before that I use to be happy. And is you and Miriam who bring me to Hilda and say here's partner for you.

SAM   What are you saying, Willie?

WILLIE   You!

SAM   But me what? To blame?

805 WILLIE   Yes.

SAM   Willie . . . ? [*Bursts into laughter.*]

WILLIE   And now all you do is make jokes at me. You wait. When Miriam leaves you is my turn to laugh. Ha! Ha! Ha!

SAM   [*he can't take* WILLIE *seriously any longer*]   She can leave me tonight! I

810 know what to do. [*Bowing before an imaginary partner*] May I have the pleasure? [*He dances and sings.*]

"Just a fellow with his pillow . . .

Dancin' like a willow . . .

In an autumn breeze . . ."

815 WILLIE   There you go again!

[SAM *goes on dancing and singing.*]

Boet Sam!

SAM   There's the answer to your problem! Judges' announcement in two weeks' time: "Ladies and gentlemen, the winner in the open section . . . Mr. Willie Malopo and his pillow!"

[*This is too much for a now really angry* WILLIE. *He goes for* SAM, *but the latter is too quick for him and puts* HALLY'S *table between the two of them.*]

820 HALLY   [*exploding*]   For Christ's sake, you two!

WILLIE   [*still trying to get at* SAM]   I donner[3] you, Sam! Struesgod!

SAM   [*still laughing*]   Sorry, Willie . . . Sorry . . .

HALLY   Sam! Willie! [*Grabs his ruler and gives* WILLIE *a vicious whack on the bum.*] How the hell am I supposed to concentrate with the two of you

825 behaving like bloody children!

WILLIE   Hit him too!

HALLY   Shut up, Willie.

WILLIE   He started jokes again.

HALLY   Get back to your work. You too, Sam. [*His ruler*] Do you want

830 another one, Willie?

[SAM *and* WILLIE *return to their work.* HALLY *uses the opportunity to escape from his unsuccessful attempt at homework. He struts around like a little despot, ruler in hand, giving vent to his anger and frustration.*]

Suppose a customer had walked in then? Or the Park Superintendent. And seen the two of you behaving like a pair of hooligans. That would have

---

3. Beat up (slang).

been the end of my mother's license, you know. And your jobs! Well, this is
the end of it. From now on there will be no more of your ballroom non-
835   sense in here. This is a business establishment, not a bloody New Brighton[4]
dancing school. I've been far too lenient with the two of you. [*Behind the
counter for a green cool drink and a dollop of ice cream. He keeps up his
tirade as he prepares it.*] But what really makes me bitter is that I allow you
chaps a little freedom in here when business is bad and what do you do
with it? The foxtrot! Specially you, Sam. There's more to life than trotting
840   around a dance floor and I thought at least you knew it.

SAM   It's a harmless pleasure, Hally. It doesn't hurt anybody.

HALLY   It's also a rather simple one, you know.

SAM   You reckon so? Have you ever tried?

HALLY   Of course not.

845 SAM   Why don't you? Now.

HALLY   What do you mean? Me dance?

SAM   Yes. I'll show you a simple step—the waltz—then you try it.

HALLY   What will that prove?

SAM   That it might not be as easy as you think.

850 HALLY   I didn't say it was easy. I said it was simple—like in simple-minded,
meaning mentally retarded. You can't exactly say it challenges the intellect.

SAM   It does other things.

HALLY   Such as?

SAM   Make people happy.

855 HALLY [*the glass in his hand*]   So do American cream sodas with ice cream.
For God's sake, Sam, you're not asking me to take ballroom dancing serious, are you?

SAM   Yes.

HALLY [*sigh of defeat*]   Oh, well, so much for trying to give you a decent edu-
860   cation. I've obviously achieved nothing.

SAM   You still haven't told me what's wrong with admiring something that's
beautiful and then trying to do it yourself.

HALLY   Nothing. But we happen to be talking about a foxtrot, not a thing of
beauty.

865 SAM   But that is just what I'm saying. If you were to see two champions
doing, two masters of the art . . . !

HALLY   Oh, God, I give up. So now it's also art!

SAM   Ja.

HALLY   There's a limit, Sam. Don't confuse art and entertainment.

870 SAM   So then what is art?

HALLY   You want a definition?

SAM   Ja.

HALLY [*he realizes he has got to be careful. He gives the matter a lot of thought
before answering*]   Philosophers have been trying to do that for centuries.
What is Art? What is Life? But basically I suppose it's . . . the giving of
875   meaning to matter.

SAM   Nothing to do with beautiful?

HALLY   It goes beyond that. It's the giving of form to the formless.

SAM   Ja, well, maybe it's not art, then. But I still say it's beautiful.

4. A suburb of Port Elizabeth (a black township).

HALLY   I'm sure the word you mean to use is entertaining.

880   SAM [*adamant*]   No. Beautiful. And if you want proof, come along to the Centenary Hall in New Brighton in two weeks' time.

[*The mention of the Centenary Hall draws* WILLIE *over to them.*]

HALLY   What for? I've seen the two of you prancing around in here often enough.

SAM [*he laughs*]   This isn't the real thing, Hally. We're just playing around in
885   here.

HALLY   So? I can use my imagination.

SAM   And what do you get?

HALLY   A lot of people dancing around and having a so-called good time.

SAM   That all?

890   HALLY   Well, basically it is that, surely.

SAM   No, it isn't. Your imagination hasn't helped you at all. There's a lot more to it than that. We're getting ready for the championships, Hally, not just another dance. There's going to be a lot of people, all right, and they're going to have a good time, but they'll only be spectators, sitting around and
895   watching. It's just the competitors out there on the dance floor. Party decorations and fancy lights all around the walls! The ladies in beautiful evening dresses!

HALLY   My mother's got one of those, Sam, and, quite frankly, it's an embarrassment every time she wears it.

900   SAM [*undeterred*]   Your imagination left out the excitement.

[HALLY *scoffs.*]

Oh, yes. The finalists are not going to be out there just to have a good time. One of those couples will be the 1950 Eastern Province Champions. And your imagination left out the music.

WILLIE   Mr. Elijah Gladman Guzana and his Orchestral Jazzonions.

905   SAM   The sound of the big band, Hally. Trombone, trumpet, tenor and alto sax. And then, finally, your imagination also left out the climax of the evening when the dancing is finished, the judges have stopped whispering among themselves and the Master of Ceremonies collects their scorecards and goes up onto the stage to announce the winners.

910   HALLY   All right. So you make it sound like a bit of a do. It's an occasion. Satisfied?

SAM [*victory*]   So you admit that!

HALLY   Emotionally yes, intellectually no.

SAM   Well, I don't know what you mean by that, all I'm telling you is that it is
915   going to be *the* event of the year in New Brighton. It's been sold out for two weeks already. There's only standing room left. We've got competitors coming from Kingwilliamstown, East London, Port Alfred.[5]

[HALLY *starts pacing thoughtfully.*]

HALLY   Tell me a bit more.

SAM   I thought you weren't interested . . . intellectually.

920   HALLY [*mysteriously*]   I've got my reasons.

SAM   What do you want to know?

HALLY   It takes place every year?

---

5. East London is a coastal city, not far from King William's Town and about 150 miles east of Port Elizabeth; Port Alfred is a small town halfway between East London and Port Elizabeth.

SAM   Yes. But only every third year in New Brighton. It's East London's turn to have the championships next year.

925 HALLY   Which, I suppose, makes it an even more significant event.

SAM   Ah ha! We're getting somewhere. Our "occasion" is now a "significant event."

HALLY   I wonder.

SAM   What?

930 HALLY   I wonder if I would get away with it.

SAM   But what?

HALLY   [*to the table and his exercise book*]   "Write five hundred words describing an annual event of cultural or historical significance." Would I be stretching poetic license a little too far if I called your ballroom champion-
935 ships a cultural event?

SAM   You mean . . . ?

HALLY   You think we could get five hundred words out of it, Sam?

SAM   Victor Sylvester[6] has written a whole book on ballroom dancing.

WILLIE   You going to write about it, Master Hally?

940 HALLY   Yes, gentlemen, that is precisely what I am considering doing. Old Doc Bromely—he's my English teacher—is going to argue with me, of course. He doesn't like natives. But I'll point out to him that in strict anthropological terms the culture of a primitive black society includes its dancing and singing. To put my thesis in a nutshell: The war-dance has been replaced
945 by the waltz. But it still amounts to the same thing: the release of primitive emotions through movement. Shall we give it a go?

SAM   I'm ready.

WILLIE   Me also.

HALLY   Ha! This will teach the old bugger a lesson. [*Decision taken*[7]] Right.
950 Let's get ourselves organized. [*This means another cake on the table. He sits.*] I think you've given me enough general atmosphere, Sam, but to build the tension and suspense I need facts. [*Pencil poised*]

WILLIE   Give him facts, Boet Sam.

HALLY   What you called the climax . . . how many finalists?

955 SAM   Six couples.

HALLY   [*making notes*]   Go on. Give me the picture.

SAM   Spectators seated right around the hall. [WILLIE *becomes a spectator.*]

HALLY   . . . and it's a full house.

SAM   At one end, on the stage, Gladman and his Orchestral Jazzonions. At
960 the other end is a long table with the three judges. The six finalists go onto the dance floor and take up their positions. When they are ready and the spectators have settled down, the Master of Ceremonies goes to the microphone. To start with, he makes some jokes to get the people laughing . . .

HALLY   Good touch! [*As he writes*] ". . . creating a relaxed atmosphere which
965 will change to one of tension and drama as the climax is approached."

SAM   [*onto a chair to act out the M.C.*]   "Ladies and gentlemen, we come now to the great moment you have all been waiting for this evening. . . . The finals of the 1950 Eastern Province Open Ballroom Dancing Champion-

---

6. An English dancer and bandleader (1900–1978), who helped popularize ballroom dancing worldwide—notably, in *Modern Ballroom* *Dancing* (1927); by 1952, it was already in its 45th edition.
7. Made.

ships. But first let me introduce the finalists! Mr. and Mrs. Welcome Tcha-
970   balala from Kingwilliamstown . . ."

WILLIE [*he applauds after every name*]   Is when the people clap their hands
and whistle and make a lot of noise, Master Hally.

SAM   "Mr. Mulligan Njikelane and Miss Nomhle Nkonyeni of Grahamstown;
Mr. and Mrs. Norman Nchinga from Port Alfred; Mr. Fats Bokolane and Miss
975   Dina Plaatjies from East London; Mr. Sipho Dugu and Mrs. Mable Magada
from Peddie; and from New Brighton our very own Mr. Willie Malopo and
Miss Hilda Samuels."

> [WILLIE *can't believe his ears. He abandons his role as spectator and
> scrambles into position as a finalist.*]

WILLIE   Relaxed and ready to romance!

SAM   The applause dies down. When everybody is silent, Gladman lifts up
980   his sax, nods at the Orchestral Jazzonions . . .

WILLIE   Play the jukebox please, Boet Sam!

SAM   I also only got bus fare, Willie.

HALLY   Hold it, everybody. [*Heads for the cash register behind the counter.*]
How much is in the till, Sam?

985   SAM   Three shillings. Hally . . . your Mom counted it before she left.

> [HALLY *hesitates.*]

HALLY   Sorry, Willie. You know how she carried on the last time I did it. We'll
just have to pool our combined imaginations and hope for the best. [*Returns
to the table.*] Back to work. How are the points scored, Sam?

SAM   Maximum of ten points each for individual style, deportment, rhythm,
990   and general appearance.

WILLIE   Must I start?

HALLY   Hold it for a second, Willie. And penalties?

SAM   For what?

HALLY   For doing something wrong. Say you stumble or bump into some-
995   body . . . do they take off any points?

SAM [*aghast*]   Hally . . . !

HALLY   When you're dancing. If you and your partner collide into another
couple.

> [HALLY *can get no further.* SAM *has collapsed with laughter. He explains
> to* WILLIE.]

SAM   If me and Miriam bump into you and Hilda . . .

> [WILLIE *joins him in another good laugh.*]

1000   Hally, Hally . . . !

HALLY [*perplexed*]   Why? What did I say?

SAM   There's no collisions out there, Hally. Nobody trips or stumbles or
bumps into anybody else. That's what that moment is all about. To be one
of those finalists on that dance floor is like . . . like being in a dream about
1005   a world in which accidents don't happen.

HALLY [*genuinely moved by* SAM's *image*]   Jesus, Sam! That's beautiful!

WILLIE [*can endure waiting no longer*]   I'm starting! [WILLIE *dances while*
SAM *talks.*]

SAM   Of course it is. That's what I've been trying to say to you all afternoon.
And it's beautiful because that is what we want life to be like. But instead,
1010   like you said, Hally, we're bumping into each other all the time. Look at the

three of us this afternoon: I've bumped into Willie, the two of us have
bumped into you, you've bumped into your mother, she bumping into your
Dad. . . . None of us knows the steps and there's no music playing. And it
doesn't stop with us. The whole world is doing it all the time. Open a newspaper and what do you read? America has bumped into Russia, England is
bumping into India, rich man bumps into poor man. Those are big collisions, Hally. They make for a lot of bruises. People get hurt in all that
bumping, and we're sick and tired of it now. It's been going on for too long.
Are we never going to get it right? . . . Learn to dance life like champions
instead of always being just a bunch of beginners at it?

HALLY [*deep and sincere admiration of the man*]   You've got a vision, Sam!

SAM   Not just me. What I'm saying to you is that everybody's got it. That's
why there's only standing room left for the Centenary Hall in two weeks'
time. For as long as the music lasts, we are going to see six couples get it
right, the way we want life to be.

HALLY   But is that the best we can do, Sam . . . watch six finalists dreaming
about the way it should be?

SAM   I don't know. But it starts with that. Without the dream we won't know
what we're going for. And anyway I reckon there are a few people who have
got past just dreaming about it and are trying for something real. Remember that thing we read once in the paper about the Mahatma Gandhi?[8]
Going without food to stop those riots in India?

HALLY   You're right. He certainly was trying to teach people to get the steps
right.

SAM   And the Pope.

HALLY   Yes, he's another one. Our old General Smuts[9] as well, you know.
He's also out there dancing. You know, Sam, when you come to think of it,
that's what the United Nations boils down to . . . a dancing school for
politicians!

SAM   And let's hope they learn.

HALLY [*a little surge of hope*]   You're right. We mustn't despair. Maybe there's
some hope for mankind after all. Keep it up, Willie. [*Back to his table with
determination*] This is a lot bigger than I thought. So what have we got?
Yes, our title: "A World Without Collisions."

SAM   That sounds good! "A World Without Collisions."

HALLY   Subtitle: "Global Politics on the Dance Floor." No. A bit too heavy,
hey? What about "Ballroom Dancing as a Political Vision"?

[*The telephone rings. SAM answers it.*]

SAM   St. George's Park Tea Room . . . Yes, Madam . . . Hally, it's your Mom.

HALLY [*back to reality*]   Oh, God, yes! I'd forgotten all about that. Shit!
Remember my words, Sam? Just when you're enjoying yourself, someone
or something will come along and wreck everything.

8. Indian political activist and religious leader
(1869–1948) who used nonviolent resistance
and fasting in his struggle against British
imperial rule; when violence between Muslims and Hindus erupted before the partition
of the Indian subcontinent into India and
Pakistan, he undertook lengthy fasts (the last
ended with his assassination).

9. Jan Christian Smuts (1870–1950), a South
African statesman and soldier who helped
found the Union of South Africa (1910) as a
self-governing nation within the British Commonwealth. He twice served as its prime
minister (1919–24, 1939–48), and he championed the creation of both the League of
Nations and the United Nations.

SAM   You haven't heard what she's got to say yet.

HALLY   Public telephone?

SAM   No.

1055 HALLY   Does she sound happy or unhappy?

SAM   I couldn't tell. [*Pause*] She's waiting, Hally.

HALLY [*to the telephone*]   Hello, Mom . . . No, everything is okay here. Just
doing my homework. . . . What's your news? . . . You've what? . . . [*Pause.
He takes the receiver away from his ear for a few seconds. In the course of*
HALLY's *telephone conversation,* SAM *and* WILLIE *discretely position the
stacked tables and chairs.* HALLY *places the receiver back to his ear.*] Yes, I'm
1060 still here. Oh, well, I give up now. Why did you do it, Mom? . . . Well, I just
hope you know what you've let us in for. . . . [*Loudly*] I said I hope you
know what you've let us in for! It's the end of the peace and quiet we've
been having. [*Softly*] Where is he? [*Normal voice*] He can't hear us from in
there. But for God's sake, Mom, what happened? I told you to be firm with
1065 him. . . . Then you and the nurses should have held him down, taken his
crutches away. . . . I know only too well he's my father! . . . I'm not being
disrespectful, but I'm sick and tired of emptying stinking chamberpots full
of phlegm and piss. . . . Yes, I do! When you're not there, he asks *me* to do
it. . . . If you really want to know the truth, that's why I've got no appetite
1070 for my food. . . . Yes! There's a lot of things you don't know about. For your
information, I still haven't got that science textbook I need. And you know
why? He borrowed the money you gave me for it. . . . Because I didn't want
to start another fight between you two. . . . He says that every time. . . . All
right, Mom! [*Viciously*] Then just remember to start hiding your bag away
1075 again, because he'll be at your purse before long for money for booze. And
when he's well enough to come down here, you better keep an eye on the
till as well, because that is also going to develop a leak. . . . Then don't
complain to me when he starts his old tricks. . . . Yes, you do. I get it from
you on one side and from him on the other, and it makes life hell for me.
1080 I'm not going to be the peacemaker any more. I'm warning you now: when
the two of you start fighting again, I'm leaving home. . . . Mom, if you start
crying, I'm going to put down the receiver. . . . Okay . . . [*Lowering his
voice to a vicious whisper*] Okay, Mom. I heard you. [*Desperate*] No. . . .
Because I don't want to. I'll see him when I get home! Mom! . . . [*Pause.
When he speaks again, his tone changes completely. It is not simply pretense.
1085 We sense a genuine emotional conflict.*] Welcome home, chum! . . . What's
that? . . . Don't be silly, Dad. You being home is just about the best news in
the world. . . . I bet you are. Bloody depressing there with everybody going
on about their ailments, hey! . . . How you feeling? . . . Good . . . Here as
well, pal. Coming down cats and dogs. . . . That's right. Just the day for a
1090 kip and a toss in your old Uncle Ned.[1] . . . Everything's just hunky-dory on
my side, Dad. . . . Well, to start with, there's a nice pile of comics for you
on the counter. . . . Yes, old Kemple brought them in. *Batman and Robin,
Submariner* . . . just your cup of tea . . . I will. . . . Yes, we'll spin a few
yarns tonight. . . . Okay, chum, see you in a little while. . . . No, I promise.
1095 I'll come straight home. . . . [*Pause—his mother comes back on the phone.*]
Mom? Okay. I'll lock up now. . . . What? . . . Oh, the brandy . . . Yes, I'll

---

1. That is, a nap (kip, toss) in your bed ("Uncle Ned" in Cockney rhyming slang).

remember! . . . I'll put it in my suitcase now, for God's sake. I know well enough what will happen if he doesn't get it. . . . [*Places a bottle of brandy on the counter.*] I *was* kind to him, Mom. I didn't say anything nasty! . . . All right. Bye. [*End of telephone conversation. A desolate* HALLY *doesn't move. A strained silence.*]

SAM [*quietly*]   That sounded like a bad bump, Hally.

HALLY [*having a hard time controlling his emotions. He speaks carefully*] Mind your own business, Sam.

SAM   Sorry. I wasn't trying to interfere. Shall we carry on? Hally? [*He indicates the exercise book. No response from* HALLY.]

WILLIE [*also trying*]   Tell him about when they give out the cups, Boet Sam.

SAM   Ja! That's another big moment. The presentation of the cups after the winners have been announced. You've got to put that in.

[*Still no response from* HALLY.]

WILLIE   A big silver one, Master Hally, called floating trophy for the champions.

SAM   We always invite some big-shot personality to hand them over. Guest of honor this year is going to be His Holiness Bishop Jabulani of the All African Free Zionist Church.

[HALLY *gets up abruptly, goes to his table and tears up the page he was writing on.*]

HALLY   So much for a bloody world without collisions.

SAM   Too bad. It was on its way to being a good composition.

HALLY   Let's stop bullshitting ourselves, Sam.

SAM   Have we been doing that?

HALLY   Yes! That's what all our talk about a decent world has been . . . just so much bullshit.

SAM   We did say it was still only a dream.

HALLY   And a bloody useless one at that. Life's a fuck-up and it's never going to change.

SAM   Ja, maybe that's true.

HALLY   There's no maybe about it. It's a blunt and brutal fact. All we've done this afternoon is waste our time.

SAM   Not if we'd got your homework done.

HALLY   I don't give a shit about my homework, so, for Christ's sake, just shut up about it. [*Slamming books viciously into his school case*] Hurry up now and finish your work. I want to lock up and get out of here. [*Pause*] And then go where? Home-sweet-fucking-home. Jesus, I hate that word.

[HALLY *goes to the counter to put the brandy bottle and comics in his school case. After a moment's hesitation, he smashes the bottle of brandy. He abandons all further attempts to hide his feelings.* SAM *and* WILLIE *work away as unobtrusively as possible.*]

Do you want to know what is really wrong with your lovely little dream, Sam? It's not just that we are all bad dancers. That does happen to be perfectly true, but there's more to it than just that. You left out the cripples.

SAM   Hally!

HALLY [*now totally reckless*]   Ja! Can't leave them out, Sam. That's why we always end up on our backsides on the dance floor. They're also out there dancing . . . like a bunch of broken spiders trying to do the quickstep! [*An ugly attempt at laughter*] When you come to think of it, it's a bloody comical sight. I mean, it's bad enough on two legs . . . but one and a pair of crutches! Hell, no, Sam. That's guaranteed to turn that dance floor into a shambles. Why you shaking your head? Picture it, man. For once this afternoon let's use our imaginations sensibly.

1140 SAM   Be careful, Hally.

HALLY   Of what? The truth? I seem to be the only one around here who is prepared to face it. We've had the pretty dream, it's time now to wake up and have a good long look at the way things really are. Nobody knows the steps, there's no music, the cripples are also out there tripping up every-1145 body and trying to get into the act, and it's all called the All-Comers-How-to-Make-a-Fuckup-of-Life Championships. [*Another ugly laugh*] Hang on, Sam! The best bit is still coming. Do you know what the winner's trophy is? A beautiful big chamber-pot with roses on the side, and it's full to the brim with piss. And guess who I think is going to be this year's winner.

1150 SAM   [*almost shouting*]   Stop now!

HALLY   [*suddenly appalled by how far he has gone*]   Why?

SAM   Hally? It's your father you're talking about.

HALLY   So?

SAM   Do you know what you've been saying?

[HALLY *can't answer. He is rigid with shame.* SAM *speaks to him sternly.*]

1155   No, Hally, you mustn't do it. Take back those words and ask for forgiveness! It's a terrible sin for a son to mock his father with jokes like that. You'll be punished if you carry on. Your father is your father, even if he is a . . . cripple man.

WILLIE   Yes, Master Hally. Is true what Sam say.

1160 SAM   I understand how you are feeling, Hally, but even so . . .

HALLY   No, you don't!

SAM   I think I do.

HALLY   And I'm telling you you don't. Nobody does. [*Speaking carefully as his shame turns to rage at* SAM] It's your turn to be careful, Sam. Very careful! 1165 You're treading on dangerous ground. Leave me and my father alone.

SAM   I'm not the one who's been saying things about him.

HALLY   What goes on between me and my Dad is none of your business!

SAM   Then don't tell me about it. If that's all you've got to say about him, I don't want to hear.

[*For a moment* HALLY *is at loss for a response.*]

1170 HALLY   Just get on with your bloody work and shut up.

SAM   Swearing at me won't help you.

HALLY   Yes, it does! Mind your own fucking business and shut up!

SAM   Okay. If that's the way you want it, I'll stop trying.

[*He turns away. This infuriates* HALLY *even more.*]

HALLY   Good. Because what you've been trying to do is meddle in something 1175 you know nothing about. All that concerns you in here, Sam, is to try and do what you get paid for—keep the place clean and serve the customers. In plain words, just get on with your job. My mother is right. She's always warning me about allowing you to get too familiar. Well, this time you've gone too far. It's going to stop right now.

[*No response from* SAM.]

1180   You're only a servant in here, and don't forget it.

[*Still no response.* HALLY *is trying hard to get one.*]

And as far as my father is concerned, all you need to remember is that he is your boss.

SAM [*needled at last*]   No, he isn't. I get paid by your mother.

HALLY   Don't argue with me, Sam!

1185 SAM   Then don't say he's my boss.

HALLY   He's a white man and that's good enough for you.

SAM   I'll try to forget you said that.

HALLY   Don't! Because you won't be doing me a favor if you do. I'm telling you to remember it.

> [*A pause.* SAM *pulls himself together and makes one last effort.*]

1190 SAM   Hally, Hally . . . ! Come on now. Let's stop before it's too late. You're right. We *are* on dangerous ground. If we're not careful, somebody is going to get hurt.

HALLY   It won't be me.

SAM   Don't be so sure.

1195 HALLY   I don't know what you're talking about, Sam.

SAM   Yes, you do.

HALLY [*furious*]   Jesus, I wish you would stop trying to tell me what I do and what I don't know.

> [SAM *gives up. He turns to* WILLIE.]

SAM   Let's finish up.

1200 HALLY   Don't turn your back on me! I haven't finished talking.

> [*He grabs* SAM *by the arm and tries to make him turn around.* SAM *reacts with a flash of anger.*]

SAM   Don't do that, Hally! [*Facing the boy*] All right, I'm listening. Well? What do you want to say to me?

HALLY [*pause as* HALLY *looks for something to say*]   To begin with, why don't you also start calling me Master Harold, like Willie.

1205 SAM   Do you mean that?

HALLY   Why the hell do you think I said it?

SAM   And if I don't?

HALLY   You might just lose your job.

SAM [*quietly and very carefully*]   If you make me say it once, I'll never call
1210 you anything else again.

HALLY   So? [*The boy confronts the man.*] Is that meant to be a threat?

SAM   Just telling you what will happen if you make me do that. You must decide what it means to you.

HALLY   Well, I have. It's good news. Because that is exactly what Master
1215 Harold wants from now on. Think of it as a little lesson in respect, Sam, that's long overdue, and I hope you remember it as well as you do your geography. I can tell you now that somebody who will be glad to hear I've finally given it to you will be my Dad. Yes! He agrees with my Mom. He's always going on about it as well. "You must teach the boys to show you
1220 more respect, my son."

SAM   So now you can stop complaining about going home. Everybody is going to be happy tonight.

HALLY   That's perfectly correct. You see, you mustn't get the wrong idea about me and my Dad, Sam. We also have our good times together. Some
1225 bloody good laughs. He's got a marvelous sense of humor. Want to know

what our favorite joke is? He gives out a big groan, you see, and says: "It's not fair, is it, Hally?" Then I have to ask: "What, chum?" And then he says: "A nigger's arse"[2] . . . and we both have a good laugh.

[*The men stare at him with disbelief.*]

What's the matter, Willie? Don't you catch the joke? You always were a bit slow on the uptake. It's what is called a pun. You see, fair means both light in color and to be just and decent. [*He turns to* SAM.] I thought *you* would catch it, Sam.

SAM   Oh ja, I catch it all right.

HALLY   But it doesn't appeal to your sense of humor.

SAM   Do you really laugh?

HALLY   Of course.

SAM   To please him? Make him feel good?

HALLY   No, for heaven's sake! I laugh because I think it's a bloody good joke.

SAM   You're really trying hard to be ugly, aren't you? And why drag poor old Willie into it? He's done nothing to you except show you the respect you want so badly. That's also not being fair, you know . . . and *I* mean just or decent.

WILLIE   It's all right, Sam. Leave it now.

SAM   It's me you're after. You should just have said "Sam's arse" . . . because that's the one you're trying to kick. Anyway, how do you know it's not fair? You've never seen it. Do you want to? [*He drops his trousers and underpants and presents his backside for* HALLY's *inspection.*] Have a good look. A real Basuto[3] arse . . . which is about as nigger as they can come. Satisfied? [*Trousers up*] Now you can make your Dad even happier when you go home tonight. Tell him I showed you my arse and he is quite right. It's not fair. And if it will give him an even better laugh next time, I'll also let *him* have a look. Come, Willie, let's finish up and go.

[SAM *and* WILLIE *start to tidy up the tea room.* HALLY *doesn't move. He waits for a moment when* SAM *passes him.*]

HALLY [*quietly*]   Sam . . .

[SAM *stops and looks expectantly at the boy.* HALLY *spits in his face. A long and heartfelt groan from* WILLIE. *For a few seconds* SAM *doesn't move.*]

SAM [*taking out a handkerchief and wiping his face*]   It's all right, Willie.

[*To* HALLY.]

Ja, well, you've done it . . . Master Harold. Yes, I'll start calling you that from now on. It won't be difficult any more. You've hurt yourself, Master Harold. I saw it coming. I warned you, but you wouldn't listen. You've just hurt yourself *bad.* And you're a coward, Master Harold. The face you should be spitting in is your father's . . . but you used mine, because you think you're safe inside your fair skin . . . and this time I don't mean just or decent. [*Pause, then moving violently towards* HALLY] Should I hit him, Willie?

WILLIE [*stopping* SAM]   No, Boet Sam.

SAM [*violently*]   Why not?

WILLIE   It won't help, Boet Sam.

2. In editions and performances outside the United States, Fugard replaces "nigger's" with "kaffir's," a term that in South Africa conveys   comparable insult and contempt.
3. One of the principal tribal groups of southern Africa.

SAM   I don't want to help! I want to hurt him.

WILLIE   You also hurt yourself.

SAM   And if he had done it to you, Willie?

WILLIE   Me? Spit at me like I was a dog? [*A thought that had not occurred to*
1270   *him before. He looks at* HALLY.] Ja. Then I want to hit him. I want to hit him
hard!

> [*A dangerous few seconds as the men stand staring at the boy.* WILLIE
> *turns away, shaking his head.*]

But maybe all I do is go cry at the back. He's little boy, Boet Sam. Little
white boy. Long trousers now, but he's still little boy.

SAM   [*his violence ebbing away into defeat as quickly as it flooded*] You're
1275   right. So go on, then: groan again, Willie. You do it better than me. [*To*
HALLY] You don't know all of what you've just done . . . Master Harold. It's
not just that you've made me feel dirtier than I've ever been in my life . . . I
mean, how do I wash off yours and your father's filth? . . . I've also failed. A
long time ago I promised myself I was going to try and do something, but
1280   you've just shown me . . . Master Harold . . . that I've failed. [*Pause*] I've
also got a memory of a little white boy when he was still wearing short
trousers and a black man, but they're not flying a kite. It was the old Jubilee days,[4] after dinner one night. I was in my room. You came in and just
stood against the wall, looking down at the ground, and only after I'd asked
1285   you what you wanted, what was wrong, I don't know how many times, did
you speak and even then so softly I almost didn't hear you. "Sam, please
help me to go and fetch my Dad." Remember? He was dead drunk on the
floor of the Central Hotel Bar. They'd phoned for your Mom, but you were
the only one at home. And do you remember how we did it? You went in
1290   first by yourself to ask permission for me to go into the bar. Then I loaded
him onto my back like a baby and carried him back to the boarding house
with you following behind carrying his crutches. [*Shaking his head as he
remembers*] A crowded Main Street with all the people watching a little
white boy following his drunk father on a nigger's back! I felt for that little
1295   boy . . . Master Harold. I felt for him. After that we still had to clean him
up, remember? He'd messed in his trousers, so we had to clean him up and
get him into bed.

HALLY   [*great pain*] I love him, Sam.

SAM   I know you do. That's why I tried to stop you from saying these things
1300   about him. It would have been so simple if you could have just despised
him for being a weak man. But he's your father. You love him and you're
ashamed of him. You're ashamed of so much! . . . And now that's going to
include yourself. That was the promise I made to myself: to try and stop
that happening. [*Pause*] After we got him to bed you came back with me to
1305   my room and sat in a corner and carried on just looking down at the
ground. And for days after that! You hadn't done anything wrong, but you
went around as if you owed the world an apology for being alive. I didn't
like seeing that! That's not the way a boy grows up to be a man! . . . But the
one person who should have been teaching you what that means was the
1310   cause of your shame. If you really want to know, that's why I made you that
kite. I wanted you to look up, be proud of something, of yourself . . . [*Bitter*

---

4. That is, when they were living in the old Jubilee Boarding House.

smile at the memory] . . . and you certainly were that when I left you with it up there on the hill. Oh, ja . . . something else! . . . If you ever do write it as a short story, there *was* a twist in our ending. I couldn't sit down there and stay with you. It was a "Whites Only" bench. You were too young, too excited to notice then. But not any more. If you're not careful . . . Master Harold . . . you're going to be sitting up there by yourself for a long time to come, and there won't be a kite in the sky. [SAM *has got nothing more to say. He exits into the kitchen, taking off his waiter's jacket.*]

WILLIE   Is bad. Is all all bad in here now.

HALLY [*books into his school case, raincoat on*]   Willie . . . [*It is difficult to speak.*] Will you lock up for me and look after the keys?

WILLIE   Okay.

> [SAM *returns.* HALLY *goes behind the counter and collects the few coins in the cash register. As he starts to leave* . . .]

SAM   Don't forget the comic books.

> [HALLY *returns to the counter and puts them in his case. He starts to leave again.*]

SAM [*to the retreating back of the boy*]   Stop . . . Hally . . .

> [HALLY *stops, but doesn't turn to face him.*]

Hally . . . I've got no right to tell you what being a man means if I don't behave like one myself, and I'm not doing so well at that this afternoon. Should we try again, Hally?

HALLY   Try what?

SAM   Fly another kite, I suppose. It worked once, and this time I need it as much as you do.

HALLY   It's still raining, Sam. You can't fly kites on rainy days, remember.

SAM   So what do we do? Hope for better weather tomorrow?

HALLY [*helpless gesture*]   I don't know. I don't know anything any more.

SAM   You sure of that, Hally? Because it would be pretty hopeless if that was true. It would mean nothing has been learnt in here this afternoon, and there was a hell of a lot of teaching going on . . . one way or the other. But anyway, I don't believe you. I reckon there's one thing you know. You don't *have* to sit up there by yourself. You know what that bench means now, and you can leave it any time you choose. All you've got to do is stand up and walk away from it.

> [HALLY *leaves.* WILLIE *goes up quietly to* SAM.]

WILLIE   Is okay, Boet Sam. You see. Is . . . [*He can't find any better words.*] . . . is going to be okay tomorrow. [*Changing his tone*] Hey, Boet Sam! [*He is trying hard.*] You right. I think about it and you right. Tonight I find Hilda and say sorry. And make promise I won't beat her no more. You hear me, Boet Sam?

SAM   I hear you, Willie.

WILLIE   And when we practice I relax and romance with her from beginning to end. Non-stop! You watch! Two weeks' time: "First prize for promising newcomers: Mr. Willie Malopo and Miss Hilda Samuels." [*Sudden impulse*] To hell with it! I walk home. [*He goes to the jukebox, puts in a coin and selects a record. The machine comes to life in the gray twilight, blushing its way through a spectrum of soft, romantic colors.*] How did you say it, Boet Sam? Let's dream. [WILLIE *sways with the music and gestures for* SAM *to dance.*]

[*Sarah Vaughan sings.*[5]]

"Little man you're crying,
I know why you're blue,

1355   Someone took your kiddy car away;
     Better go to sleep now,
Little man you've had a busy day."   [*etc. etc.*]

     You lead. I follow.

     [*The men dance together.*]

"Johnny won your marbles,

1360   Tell you what we'll do;
     Dad will get you new ones right away;
     Better go to sleep now,
     Little man you've had a busy day."

5. "Little Man You've Had a Busy Day" (1934; by Al Hoffman, Maurice Sigler, and Mabel Wayne), recorded by Sarah Vaughan and the Count Basie Orchestra in 1961.

MARÍA IRENE FORNÉS

b. 1930

María Irene Fornés emerged on the burgeoning off-off-Broadway scene of the early 1960s as a vibrant new voice for the American theater. Since that revolutionary time, she has retained a commitment to exploration and innovation while rejecting commercialism in the arts. Long considered one of the leading figures in the American alternative theater movement and a finalist for the Pulitzer Prize for Drama in 1988, Fornés has also become one of the country's foremost directors and playwriting teachers. Her play *MUD* (1983), dating from the middle period of her career, exemplifies the spare, evocative, and emotionally raw style of writing that has become the hallmark of her dramaturgy. Her focus on the elemental forces driving human behavior and her concern with such social structures as class and gender come together in this powerful and disturbing drama.

Fornés was born in Cuba in 1930, a time of economic depression and political instability. Her father, Carlos, was a civil engineer but was often out of work; her mother, Carmen, was a former teacher; and together they shared with their six children their enthusiasm for politics, ideas, and the arts. In the early 1940s, Carmen attempted to move the family to the United States, but obtaining visas during wartime was difficult. After Carlos's unexpected death in 1945, she suceeded in emigrating to New York City with her two youngest children; one of them was María Irene.

Fornés soon became more interested in painting than in pursuing her formal education; after briefly studying abstract art, in 1954 she moved to Europe to paint. That same year, she saw the world premiere in Paris of SAMUEL BECKETT's groundbreaking drama *En Attendant Godot* (*WAITING FOR GODOT*)—a play that she claims moved her deeply and changed her life, though she did not understand French. Fornés had had little prior exposure to the theater, and she maintains that the only play she had read before embarking on her own theatrical career was HENRIK IBSEN's *HEDDA GABLER* (1890). In 1957 she returned to the United States to pursue work as a textile designer. For a while she rented an apartment with Susan Sontag, soon to become one of America's foremost cultural critics, and the two women challenged each other to write. After some early efforts translating family letters from Spanish to English and putting them in dramatic form (*The Widow*, 1961), Fornés became obsessed with the idea of writing another play; in the space of a few weeks, she produced *Tango Palace* (originally titled *There! You Died!*, 1963). In its existential struggle between characters, this piece clearly reflects the impact of

Beckett's dramaturgy—an influence that is still strong in *Mud*.

Deceptively simple in its narrative arc, *Mud* chronicles the evolving relationships between three characters: Mae, Lloyd, and Henry. Locked in a cycle of interdependency and conflict, Mae and Lloyd can barely survive on what Mae earns by taking in ironing, and Lloyd's illness has added to the strain. Mae strives for a better life, seeing education as a means of self-improvement. She gravitates toward Henry, with whom she feels she can genuinely communicate. The dynamic shifts when Henry becomes incapacitated and Mae and Lloyd decide they must care for him. The men then begin to make increasing demands on Mae, both emotionally and financially, driving the play to its crisis and devastating conclusion.

The focus in *Mud* on both the intense dynamics between and the complex inner lives of the characters reflects Fornés's formative early exposure to "the Method," an approach to acting that had enormous influence in the United States. It was promoted by the director Lee Strasberg, who had derived his concepts about acting in large part from the "System" of the legendary Russian director and actor Konstantin Stanislavsky, and in the late 1950s, Fornés joined the playwriting unit of Strasberg's Actors Studio. She quickly grasped the principle at the core of the Method: to access and embody the truth of a character in any drama, regardless of how that drama is written or staged. Although these techniques are often associated with theatrical realism, a piece like *Mud*, which is stripped of the usual trappings of the realist stage, demonstrates how closely these concepts of emotional and psychological truth dovetail with Fornés's abstract, imagistic naturalism. Her early training as a visual artist, too, has significantly shaped her dramaturgy, which has been described as "a form of painting with words." Interestingly, some critics have also noted Brechtian elements—which are often seen as diametrically opposed to Method techniques—in her productions. Fornés has never claimed BERTOLT BRECHT as an influence, however; indeed, this interpretation may owe more to the political dimensions of her themes and to her frank, seemingly matter-of-fact depictions of violence—evident in *Mud* and a number of her other plays—than to her own conscious choices as a dramatist or as a director.

Experimentation with form, parody of popular entertainment styles, and humorous social critique distinguish the first phase of Fornés's theatrical career. But her style and tone changed markedly with *Fefu and Her Friends* (1977), and we can

Clare Barron as Mae and Julian Farhat as Lloyd in the 2013 Masrah Ensemble production of *Mud* in Lebanon, directed by Eyad Houssami.

see her further refinement of this new kind of dramaturgy in *Mud*. A richer, more complex work than any of her previous pieces, *Fefu* breaks new ground in its concentration on female characters and their thoughts, feelings, and interrelationships; its relative disinterest in traditional plot; and its innovative environmental staging. *Mud* expands this focus on character to encompass men as well, within a narrative similarly lacking in traditional stage action or a realist stage milieu.

Critics have noted the transition from Fornés's use of irony and playfulness as vehicles for social and political critique to the more somber tone of *Fefu* and *Mud*. We might attribute this change in part to Fornés's sense that her earlier styles were inadequate to address profound events such as the war in Vietnam and to her growing recognition of gender and class inequities in contemporary society. A number of her plays after *Fefu*, especially *The Conduct of Life* (1985), treat sexual and political violence while displaying her ongoing commitment to an evenhanded and truthful representation of all her characters' complex motivations and responses, no matter how disturbing these may be.

Fornés developed and premiered *Mud* at the Padua Hills Playwrights Festival in southern California. This locale had a profound and tangible impact on the piece: the outdoor venue informed the play's structure (as shown most obviously in the freezes between scenes, made necessary by the lack of blackouts) and its palette—the sky became more gray as the day wore on, and Fornés opted to maintain this effect through the costuming and lighting in subsequent productions. The theater's location may have been equally influential in suggesting the symbolism of earth, dirt, and mud that permeates the play, as well as its setting, "a wooden room which sits on an earth promontory." External circumstances strongly affected the piece in other ways. According to Fornés, because an older actor whom she had initially envisioned as a father for Mae was unavailable, she had to rethink the role for a younger actor—and thus Henry was created. She further explains that her discovery at a local flea market of an inexpensive set of farm tools and an ironing board decided both the play's rural

setting and Mae's occupation. Such seemingly random events have shaped Fornés's entire career, leading critics to liken her work to the "found art" movement.

Mud ultimately reveals both Fornés's deep sensitivity to the disenfranchised and her refusal to soft-pedal the stark realities of their lives. Yet this play, which remains one of Fornés's favorites—she has called it "a little jewel"—has also proven controversial; critics have expressed considerable ambivalence about the elemental interrelationship of Mae, Lloyd, and Henry and the choices each makes to survive. The character of Mae has come under particular scrutiny and has been condemned for the gender-coded, menial work she performs and the brutality she experiences. In response, Fornés has faulted critics for making judgments about her writing based on erroneous assumptions and preconceived ideas, particularly regarding gender roles and the responsibilities of women playwrights in depicting female identity. In her essay "Creative Danger," Fornés remarks of her characters:

> These people are too poor to indulge in bizarre ego games. They have a reality to deal with, which is poverty. That is the way things have worked out for them. The concepts of sex roles and role playing are a luxury, an indulgence that requires a degree of affluence. . . . If you reversed the sexes in *Mud*, you would see that Mae's nature is more male than female in terms of dominance, and that the men's natures are more female in terms of tenderness and acceptance. . . . But the attention to sex roles, protest against sex roles, defense against the guilt that results from that protest, all these things keep us from seeing a work with a full perspective. They prevent us from seeing characters as human beings; we see them rather as party members.

At the same time, Fornés has acknowledged the aptness of other critical observations on her work, especially that it is always about immigrants, because all her plays in some way "deal with a person going to another world."

A closely related concern is with language acquisition—a process of which Fornés is acutely aware, both as a nonnative speaker of English and as a translator of plays by such Spanish dramatists as FEDERICO GARCÍA LORCA and PEDRO CALDERÓN DE LA BARCA. Language is equally at stake for her characters who, in a broader sense, must discover themselves in words. In her plays, Fornés consistently foregrounds the interrelationship of language, thought, and action. The struggle for verbal expression thus emerges as a core element of her dramaturgy, represented with aching beauty and clarity through Mae's study of starfish in *Mud*. Mae's quest for language and learning also reflects Fornés's revision of the Western philosophical tradition that links masculinity with thought and femininity with emotion. Fornés explained in an interview that "what's wonderful about Mae is her love for knowledge" and that,

ultimately, "what is important about this play is that Mae is the central character . . . simply because she is the *center* of the play." Fornés concludes that "it is because of that mind, Mae's mind, *a woman's mind,* that the play exists. To me that is an . . . important step toward redeeming women's position in the world." Such insights into the significance of her own contributions as a dramatist demonstrate the importance of avoiding entanglements in narrow debates about Fornés's work. Attempts to reduce her writing to such binaries as feminist/not feminist describe only the most obvious aspects of its characters or action. Fornés has revealed how deep the foundations of her characters are laid, and we must tunnel down just as far to understand the fundamental human truths she dramatizes.　　　　　　　　　　　　　J.E.G.

Mud

CHARACTERS

MAE　A spirited young woman. She is single-minded and determined, a believer. She is mid-twenties.

LLOYD　A simple and good-hearted young man. He is ungainly and unkempt. His shoulders slope, his stomach protrudes, some of his teeth are missing. At the start of the play, illness contributes to his poor appearance. He is mid-twenties.

HENRY　A large man. He has a natural sense of dignity, a philosophical mind. He can barely read. He is mid-fifties.

The set is a wooden room which sits on an earth promontory. The promontory is five feet high and covers the same periphery as the room. The wood has the color and texture of bone that has dried in the sun. It is ashen and cold. The earth in the promontory is red and soft and so is the earth around it. There is no greenery. Behind the promontory there is a vast blue sky. On the back wall of the room there is an oversized fireplace which is the same color and texture as the walls and floor. On each side of the fireplace there are narrow doors. The door to the right leads to the exterior. There is a blue sky. The one to the left leads to a dark corridor. In the center of the room there is a kitchen table. There is a chair on each end. Down right there is an ironing board. There is an iron on it and a pair of trousers. Against the back wall on the left there is another chair. After the first scene these three chairs will always be placed around the table and will be referred to as right, center, and left. Against the right wall there is a bench. On it there is a pile of unpressed trousers. On the table there is a pile of pressed trousers. Under the bench, there is a bundle of women's clothes and a pair of old, flat women's shoes. Inside the fireplace there are two cardboard boxes. One is full and tied with a string, the other is empty. On the mantelpiece there are, from right to left: a brown paper bag with a pamphlet in it, a pot with three metal plates and three spoons stacked upon it, a plate with broken bread, a pitcher with milk, a textbook, a notebook and pencil, a dish with string beans, a folded newspaper, and a box with pills. Between the fireplace and the door to the left there are an ax and a rifle.

Offstage there is an empty box the same size as the box tied with a string. The following props are carried by the actors as they enter to perform the scene:

MAE: *2 bundles of clothes and a loose clean rag.*

LLOYD: *3 coins, a prescription note, and a cup with oatmeal and a spoon.*

HENRY: *lipstick wrapped in paper, a small mirror, a notebook, bills and pencil, loose coins, a tin cup of milk, and a wad of bills.*

At the end of each scene a freeze is indicated. These freezes will last eight seconds which will create the effect of a still photograph. When the freeze is broken, the actors will make the necessary set changes and proceed to perform the following scene.

Act 1

Scene 1

> [LLOYD *sits left. He is unwashed and unshaven. He has a fever. He is clumsy and badly coordinated.* MAE *is at the ironing board. She is unkempt.*]

LLOYD   You think you learn a lot at school?

MAE   I do.

LLOYD   What do you learn?

MAE   Subjects.

5 LLOYD   What is subjects?

MAE   Different things.

LLOYD   What things?

MAE   You want to know?

LLOYD   What are they?

10 MAE   Arithmetic.

LLOYD   Big deal arithmetic. I know arithmetic.

MAE   I'll bet.

LLOYD   Don't talk back to me. I'll kick your ass.

MAE   Fuck you, Lloyd. I'm telling you about arithmetic and you talk to me
15 like that? You're a moron. I won't tell you anything.

LLOYD   Oh, no?

MAE   No.

LLOYD   So what's arithmetic?

MAE   Fuck you. I'm not telling you.

20 LLOYD [*moving toward her*]   I'll fuck you till you're blue in the face! [*He stops
and starts back to the chair.*] I don't even want to fuck you.

MAE   You can't, that's why. You can't get it up.

LLOYD   Oh yeah? I got it up yesterday!

MAE   When!

25 LLOYD   Afternoon!

MAE   Never saw it.

LLOYD   You weren't here.

MAE   Where was I?

LLOYD   At school. You missed it. I got it up.

30   MAE   Who with?

LLOYD   Fuck you. I'm not telling you.

MAE   Who with?

LLOYD   With myself.—I don't need someone. I got it up right here. [*Pointing*
      to the wall] See that? I did that! From here. I didn't give it to you or anyone.

35   [*Pantomiming an erection and ejaculation*] I held it as long as I wanted.
      Then I gave it to the wall. [*Pointing to a spot on the wall*] See. Fuck you,
      Mae.

MAE   Fuck you, Lloyd.

LLOYD   So tell me!

40   MAE   Tell you what.

LLOYD   What's arithmetic?

MAE   It's numbers.

LLOYD   Oh yeah!

MAE   Yeah!

45   LLOYD   Why didn't you say it's numbers!—I know numbers.

MAE   You don't know numbers.

LLOYD   Yes I do. [*He stands.*] I'm Lloyd. I have two pigs. My mother died. I
      was seven. My father left. He is dead. [*He gets three coins from his pocket.*]
      This is money. It's mine. It's three nickels. I'm Lloyd. That's arithmetic.

50   MAE   That is not arithmetic.

LLOYD   Why not?

MAE   It isn't.

LLOYD   [*he returns to the chair*]   It's numbers!

MAE   Arithmetic is more!

55   LLOYD   What more!

MAE   A lot more!—Multiplication!

LLOYD   Come here! [*She puts the iron down.*]

MAE   What for!

LLOYD   I'm going to show you something.

60   MAE   [*she walks to him*]   What!

LLOYD   [*in one move he takes her hand, crosses his left leg, and puts her hand on
      his crotch*]   Feel it!

MAE   What?

LLOYD   It! It! Touch it!

MAE   I'm touching it!

65   LLOYD   Do something to it!

MAE   What!

LLOYD   Anything, stupid!

MAE   Let go of my hand!

LLOYD   [*pressing her tighter*]   What hand?

70   MAE   Let go, you jerk! You stink! You smell bad!

LLOYD   So what!

MAE   You're disgusting!

LLOYD   No kidding!

MAE   Let go! [*She steps on his foot.*]

75 LLOYD   Shit! [*She goes back to the ironing board.*] I'll kick your ass! [*He feels his genitals.*] Shit, it's gone!

MAE   What's gone! You can't get it up! You have some sickness there! [*Short pause*] You should go to a doctor.

LLOYD   Didn't I say I got it up yesterday!

80 MAE   Yes. You did.

LLOYD   OK! So I did!—So where's dinner!

MAE   I don't know where's dinner.

LLOYD   You know where's dinner!

MAE   You know where's dinner!

85 LLOYD   Yeah, where's dinner! Dinner's in a pot on the stove! Dinner's on the table! It's in the cupboard! It's dried up in the pot! Dinner is somewhere! It's spilled on the floor! Where's dinner! [*There is a pause.*] Where's dinner! [*She continues ironing.*] Come here!

MAE   Fuck you.

90 LLOYD   You're a whore!

MAE   I'm pressing, jerk! What are you doing! I'm pressing. What are you doing! [*He looks away.*] I'm pressing what are you doing! You're a jerk. [*She continues ironing.*] I work. See, I work. I'm working. I learned to work. I wake up and I work. Open my eyes and I work. I work. What do you do! Yeah, what 95 do you do!—*Work!*

LLOYD   So what. [*He sits in a corner on the floor.*]

MAE   What do you do when you open your eyes. I work, jerk. You're a pig. You'll die like a pig in the mud. You'll rot there in the mud. No one will bury you. Your skin will bloat. In the mud. Then, it will get blue like rotten meat 100 and it will bloat even more. And you will get so rotten that the dogs will puke when they come near you. Even flies won't go near you. You'll just lay there and rot. [*She irons.*] I'm going to die in a hospital. In white sheets. You hear? [*She looks front.*] Clean feet. Injections. That's how I'm going to die. I'm going to die clean. I'm going to school and I'm learning things. You're 105 stupid. I'm not. When I finish school I'm leaving. You hear that? You can stay in the mud. [*She irons.*] Did you pick the corn?

LLOYD   What corn?

MAE   The corn I told you to pick.

LLOYD   There is no corn.

110 MAE   How come there is no corn.

LLOYD   The groundhog ate it.

MAE   You let him eat it.

LLOYD   I didn't.

MAE   You didn't watch it.

115 LLOYD   I came in to sleep. I had to sleep.

MAE   You can sleep in the field.

LLOYD   It's wet there! It's cold! I'm sick! You sleep there!

MAE   I work here, not in the field.

LLOYD   I'll work here. You work there.

120 MAE [*harshly*]   I wish you went to the doctor.—You're not going to get well if you don't. When I leave you'll starve.

LLOYD   I'll find food.

MAE   Where?

LLOYD   Anywhere. There's food.

125 MAE   Where.

LLOYD   There's pigslop.

MAE   What pigslop? There won't be any pigslop. Not if you don't grow something to put in it!

     [*Pause.*]

LLOYD   I did it to Betsy.

130 MAE   You did.

LLOYD   Yeah.—I felt bad.—My head hurt.—I went to her. She's nice. She lets me eat her food.—I did it to her.—I got it up. I got it in her all the way.—It didn't hurt.

MAE   No kidding.

135 LLOYD   It didn't hurt.

MAE   You don't fuck pigs.

LLOYD   She liked it.

MAE   I'll bet.

LLOYD   What do you mean?

140 MAE   Did you get clean before you did it?

LLOYD   What for? I'm clean.

MAE   No you're not. You stink.

LLOYD   She didn't mind.

MAE   [*she places the ironing board alongside the right wall and places the garment she has pressed on top of the other pressed clothes*]   I'm taking these

145 up now. We'll walk to the clinic. You have to see a doctor. [*She starts putting on her shoes.*] Put on your shoes, Lloyd.—I'll walk there with you. I know you won't get there if I don't go with you. Get moving, Lloyd. [*She takes the clothes and goes to the door.*] Come on. [*He doesn't move.*] Let's go, Lloyd. [*He stands and goes for the ax. He holds the ax as he waits for her to exit.*] You're not going to the clinic with an ax.

150 LLOYD   [*he goes to the chair still holding the ax and sits*]   Why not.

MAE   You can't.

LLOYD   I'll take my knife, then.

MAE   You can't take your knife either.

LLOYD   I won't go then.

     [*They freeze.*]

Scene 2

     [MAE *takes a brown paper bag from the mantelpiece, opens the right door, steps on the threshold, and turns front as if she had just come from the outside. She has an air of serenity.* LLOYD *sits on the left. His appearance has worsened.*]

MAE   I went to the clinic, Lloyd. And I told them what you have.

LLOYD   What did you tell them?

MAE   [*stepping into the room*]   I told them you're sick. And I told them what you have.

5 LLOYD   What did they say?

MAE   They said you have to go there. [*As she gets the chair from the left corner and places it center*] You have to go to the clinic. They won't give you medicine till you go.

LLOYD   I'm not going.

10 MAE   They have to give you a test. They can't give you medicine till they find
out what you have. They said you may have something bad.

LLOYD   What.

MAE [*she sits*]   They didn't say. [*She takes a pamphlet out of the paper bag.*]
They gave me this book.

15 LLOYD   What does it say?

MAE [*she places the paper bag on the mantelpiece*]   I couldn't read it. I tried
to read it but I can't. I got Henry to read it for you. He's outside.

LLOYD   Why can't you read it?

MAE   It's too difficult.

20 LLOYD   All that time at school and you can't read.

MAE   I tried to read it and it was too difficult. That's why I got Henry to read
it because it was too difficult for me. It is advanced. I'm not advanced yet.
I'm intermediate. I can read a lot of things but not this.—I'm going to let
Henry in.

25 LLOYD [*reproachfully*]   I wish you could have read it.

MAE   Me too. I wish I could have read it. [*She opens the door and walks to the
left of the center chair.*] Come in, Henry. [HENRY *enters and stands by the fireplace. He places his left hand on the mantelpiece.*] Sit down, Henry. [HENRY
sits on the center chair. MAE *closes the door.*] Here's Henry, Lloyd. He's going

30   to read for you.

HENRY   Are you drunk, Lloyd? You look drunk.

MAE [*sitting on the right*]   He's sick. He has a fever.

HENRY   Has he been drinking?

LLOYD   I am not drunk.

35 HENRY   What's wrong with him?

MAE   He's sick.

HENRY   Remember Ron, what happened to him.

LLOYD   What happened to him?

HENRY   He died.—And what did he die of?

40 LLOYD   He drank till he died.

MAE   His liver failed him.

HENRY   Why did his liver fail him? Alcohol.—Why did he drink? He drank
because he owned alcohol. And why did he own alcohol? He owned alcohol
because he owned a pharmacy. And why did that lead a man to drinking?

45   Because he kept alcohol in the pharmacy.—There you have two things:
alcohol and time to do nothing. So what happens? You drink yourself to
death.—So, you have alcohol, you drink it. You don't have alcohol, you don't
drink it. You have money to buy alcohol, you buy it. You don't have money
to buy it, you don't buy it.—Does Lloyd have alcohol, Mae?

50 MAE   He has no money to buy it.

HENRY   If Lloyd had money he would drink. He'd be a drunk.

MAE   Yes, he would.

HENRY   If he's not a drunk it's because he's poor.

MAE   He is.—This is the book, Henry.

HENRY [HENRY *puts on his glasses. He reads each section first to himself in a low
voice. Then he reads it out loud stumbling through the words at a high
55   speed.*]   Prostatitis and Prostatosis. Acute and chronic bacterial infection
of the prostrate[1] gland: symptoms, diagnosis, and treatment. [*He wets his*

---

1. Henry's misreading for "prostate."

finger and turns the page.] Common symptoms of acute prostatitis and bacterial prostatosis are: febrile illness, back pains, perineal pain, irritative voiding, aching of the perineum, sexual pain, sexual impotency, painful
60 ejaculation, and intermittent disureah,[2] or bloody ejaculation.

LLOYD   What does that mean?

HENRY   I don't know what it means, Lloyd. These are medical terms. It needs study. This may require the use of a dictionary—a special dictionary. One that has medical terms—technical terms—probably a dictionary that would
65 have all kinds of technical terms—from hardware and construction terms to scientific terms—like physics. There are such dictionaries. [*Short pause*] You look swollen, Lloyd.

MAE   He is swollen.

HENRY   And your color is poor.

70 MAE   Show him your tongue, Lloyd. His tongue is white and his breath smells bad.

[LLOYD *opens his mouth.* HENRY *looks at* LLOYD'S *tongue.*]

HENRY   What is wrong with you?

MAE   I want him to go to the doctor but he won't.

HENRY   Why won't you go to the doctor, Lloyd.

75 LLOYD   I don't want to go.

MAE   He will stay here and rot.

LLOYD   I won't rot. I said I'd go. You said I couldn't go.

MAE   He wanted to go up with an ax. He's an animal. You don't go to the clinic with an ax. You can't do that.

80 HENRY   Why would you do that, Lloyd?

LLOYD   I didn't do it. I never went.

HENRY   He does smell bad.

MAE   He's rotting away and he won't do anything about it. You better dig your grave while you can, Lloyd. Because I'm not going to do it for you. I told
85 him to find a spot and dig it. It takes a strong person to dig that deep. I can't do it. I wouldn't, even if I could. [*Pause*] Would you like some bread, Henry? I got some butter.

HENRY   Yes, thank you.

MAE   Would you like some dinner? We have soup.

90 HENRY   Yes, thank you.

MAE   Stay then, I haven't started it yet.

HENRY   I will, thank you.

[*They freeze.*]

Scene 3

[MAE *places the pamphlet on the mantelpiece, then takes the pot, plates, and spoons and places them on the table. They each take a spoon and plate, then they pass them to* MAE, *who holds the plates in her hands as if she were about to put them away.* LLOYD *lies on the floor, under the table, facing front.* HENRY *moves his chair slightly to the left. He and* MAE *have been talking. They both speak with philosophical objectivity.*]

HENRY   Soon everything will be used only once. We will use things once. We will need to do that as our time will be of value and it will not be feasible to

---

2. Dysuria; that is, painful or difficult urination.

spend it caring for things: washing them, mending them, repairing them. We will use a car till it breaks down. Then, we will discard it. A radio or any machine or appliance will be discarded as soon as it breaks down. We will make a call on the telephone and a new one will be delivered. Already we see places that use paper cups, paper plates, paper towels.—Our time will not be wasted and we will choose how to spend it.

MAE   I don't think I'll be wanted in such a world.

HENRY   Why not?

MAE   . . . Oh. [*Pause*] In such a world a person must be of value.

HENRY   Oh?

MAE   I feel I am hollow . . . and offensive. [*As* MAE *places the dishes on the mantelpiece*]

HENRY   Why is that?

MAE   I think most people are.

HENRY   What do you mean?—Explain what you mean.

MAE   I don't think I can.

HENRY   I am not offensive. I don't think I am offensive. I think I am a decent man.

MAE   You are decent, Henry. I know you are, and so is Lloyd in his own way.

HENRY   Then, what do you mean when you say we are offensive?

MAE   I mean that we are base, and that we spend our lives with small things.

HENRY   I don't feel I do that.

MAE   Don't be offended, Henry. You are not base. Of all the people I know you are the finest. You are the person I respect and I feel most proud to know.—[*She begins to look at him fixedly, possessed by fervor.*] I have no one to talk to. And sometimes I feel hollow and base. And I feel I don't have a mind. But when I talk to you I do. I feel I have a mind. Why is that? [*She moves closer to him.*] Why is it that some people make you feel stupid and some people make you feel smart. Not smart, because I am not smart. But some people make you feel that you have something inside you. Inside your head. [*She moves closer.*] Why is it that you can talk, Henry, and Lloyd cannot talk? Why is that? What I'm saying, Henry, is that I want you. That I want you here with me. That I love you.

HENRY   Mae, this is unexpected.

MAE   It is unexpected, Henry.

HENRY   I have nothing to offer you.

MAE   Yes, you do. I want you.

HENRY   Me?

MAE   [*she starts to move her head toward him slowly and intensely*]   I want your mind.

HENRY   . . . My mind?

MAE   [*still moving her head toward him*]   I want it. [*She kisses him intensely. They look at each other.*]

HENRY   Did you feel my mind?

MAE   Yes. I did. [*She kisses him again.*] I did. I want you here.

HENRY   Here?

MAE   I want you here.

HENRY   To live here?

MAE   If you will.

    [*They freeze.*]

Scene 4

[HENRY *exits.* MAE *places the spoons and pot on the mantelpiece. Then, she takes off her shoes, places a pair of trousers on the ironing board, and puts out the ironing board.* LLOYD *gets the box with the string from the fireplace and stands down left holding it.* MAE *irons.*]

MAE   Just put it down. [*He stands still. She continues ironing.*] Put it down Lloyd. [*He stands still.*] Henry is going to stay here with us. He is going to live here. He needs a place and I want him to stay here. You can learn from Henry. If you want to, he can teach you how to read. Put the box down. I'll
5   take it up to the bedroom. Henry's going to sleep in the bedroom. He has a bad back and he needs to sleep in the bed. You can sleep here.—Get papers from the shed and lay them on the floor. I'll get you a blanket.—I'll take it up now. [*She takes the box from* LLOYD *and exits left. He is distraught. He sits on the chair on the left and cries. He puts his head on the table and freezes.*]

Scene 5

[MAE *places the ironing board against the wall.* LLOYD *places the pitcher of milk and the plate with bread on the table.* MAE *gets the plates and spoons. She places the spoons in the center and lays each plate in front of her.* HENRY *enters and sits center.* LLOYD *sits left.* LLOYD *and* HENRY *take a spoon each.* MAE *serves bread onto the plates, pours milk on the bread, and passes two plates to* HENRY, *who passes one to* LLOYD *and keeps the second for himself.* MAE *sits. They start eating.*]

MAE   Do you say grace before a meal, Henry?

HENRY   I do sometimes.

MAE   Would you say grace?

HENRY   I will, if you want me to.

5 MAE   I do.

HENRY [*crosses his hands*]   Oh, give thanks unto the Lord, for he is good: for his mercy endures forever. For he satisfies the longing soul, and fills the hungry soul with goodness.

MAE   We never said grace in this house. My father never did and I never
10   learned how and neither did Lloyd.—Lloyd did you hear that? Henry said grace. I feel grace in my heart. I feel fresh inside as if a breeze had just gone inside my heart. What was it you said, Henry? What were these words. I don't retain the words. I never do. I find it hard to retain words I learn. It is hard for me to do the work at school. I can work on my feet all day at the
15   ironing board. I can make myself do it, even if I am tired. But I cannot make myself retain what I learn. I have no memory. The teacher says I have no memory. And it's true I don't. I don't remember the things I learn too well. Not enough to pass the test. But I rejoice with the knowledge that I get. Not everything, but most things, make me feel joyful. Do you feel that way, Henry?

20 HENRY   I am not sure. I like to know things. But if I didn't remember what I learned, I don't think I would feel any pleasure.—If I didn't remember things, I would feel that I don't know them. I like to learn things so I can live according to them, according to my knowledge. What would be the use of knowing things if they don't serve you, if they don't help you shape your life.—Lloyd,
25   do you take pleasure in learning if you forget what you have learned?

[LLOYD *looks at* MAE, *then at* HENRY *again.*]

MAE   Lloyd doesn't like learning things.

LLOYD   I like learning things.

MAE   Why don't you then?

LLOYD   What is it I haven't learned?

[MAE *and* HENRY *look at each other.*]

30   MAE   Henry, would you say grace again?

HENRY   Again?

MAE   Is that wrong?

HENRY   No. Oh, give thanks unto the Lord, for he is good: for his mercy endures forever. For he satisfies the longing soul, and fills the hungry soul 35   with goodness. [MAE *sobs.*] Why are you crying?

MAE   I am a hungry soul. I am a longing soul. I am an empty soul. [*She cries.*] I cry with joy. It satisfies me to hear words that speak so lovingly to my soul. [MAE *eats.* LLOYD *eats.* HENRY *watches* MAE.] Don't be afraid to eat from our dishes, Henry. They are clean.

[*They freeze.*]

Scene 6

[LLOYD *places his plate and spoon over* HENRY'S. HENRY *places the pitcher and bread plate on the mantelpiece and exits.* MAE *places the plates and spoons on the mantelpiece and gets the textbook. She sits center and reads with difficulty. She follows the written words with the fingers of both hands. Her reading is inspired.* LLOYD *listens to her and stares at the book.*]

MAE   The starfish is an animal, not a fish. He is called a fish because he lives in the water. The starfish cannot live out of the water. If he is moist and in the shade he may be able to live out of the water for a day. Starfish eat old and dead sea animals. They keep the water clean. A starfish has five arms 5   like a star. That is why it is called a starfish. Each of the arms of the starfish has an eye in the end. These eyes do not look like our eyes. A starfish's eye cannot see. But they can tell if it is night or day. If a starfish loses an arm he can grow a new one. This takes about a year. A starfish can live five or ten years or perhaps more, no one really knows.

[LLOYD *slaps the book off the table.* MAE *slaps* LLOYD. *They freeze.*]

Scene 7

[LLOYD *picks up the book and places it on the down-left corner of the table. He places the left chair against the wall and sits.* MAE *takes a notebook and pencil from the mantelpiece. She takes the book and stands on the up-right side of the table copying from the book.* HENRY *enters and stands on the up-left corner.*]

HENRY   What is Lloyd to you? [*There is a pause.*] He's a man and he's not a blood relative. So what is he to you?

MAE   Lloyd? [*Pause*] He is like family.

HENRY   But he is not.—Everyone knows he is not. What is he?

5   MAE   I don't know what you call what he is. If I were to ask myself I would not know what to answer.—He is not with me. You know he is not. He sleeps down here.

HENRY   I feel I am offending him. And he is offending me. So what is he.

MAE [*sitting on the right facing front*] What can I do, Henry, I don't want you
to be offended. There's nothing I can do and there's nothing you can do
and there is nothing Lloyd can do. He's always been here, since he was
little. My dad brought him in. He said that Lloyd was a good boy and that
he could keep me company. He said he was old and tired and he didn't
understand what a young person like me was like. That he had no patience
left and he was weary of life and he had no more desire to make things
work. He didn't want to listen to me talk and he felt sorry to see me sad and
lonely. He didn't want to be mean to me, but he didn't have the patience.
He was sick. My dad was good but he was sad and hopeless and when my
mom died he went to hell with himself. He got sick and died and he left
Lloyd here and Lloyd and I took care of each other. I don't know what we
are. We are related but I don't know what to call it. We are not brother and
sister. We are like animals who grow up together and mate. We were mates
till you came here, but not since then. I could not be his mate again, not
while you are here. I am not an animal. I care about things, Henry, I do. I
know some things that I never learned. It's just that I don't know what they
are. I cannot grasp them. [*She goes on her knees as her left shoulder leans on
the corner of the table.*] I don't want to live like a dog. [*Pause*] Lloyd is good,
Henry. And this is his home. [*Pause. She looks up.*] When you came here I
thought heaven had come to this place, and I still feel so. How can there be
offense here for you?

[*They freeze.*]

Scene 8

[LLOYD *places his chair by the table and exits.* MAE *places the notebook,
pencil, and textbook on the mantelpiece. She places the dish with string
beans center and sits. She snaps beans.* HENRY *walks behind* MAE *and covers
her eyes. He takes a small package from his pocket and puts it in the bowl.*]

MAE What is it? [*He uncovers her eyes. She unwraps the package. It is a lipstick.*] Lipstick . . . [HENRY *pushes the lipstick out of the tube. He takes a
mirror out of his pocket and holds it in front of her.*] A mirror. [*She holds the
mirror and puts on lipstick. She puckers her lips. He kisses her.*] Oh, Henry.

[*They freeze.*]

Scene 9

[MAE *places the lipstick, mirror, and dish with string beans on the mantelpiece. She places the textbook center and sits.* HENRY *places the paper
and lipstick cover on the mantelpiece. He takes the newspaper, turns the
left chair toward the down-left corner, and sits to read, leaning his elbow
on the table.* LLOYD *sits on the floor, down of the right chair with his arm
leaning on it.*]

MAE [*reading*] This is a hermit crab. He is called a hermit because he lives
in empty shells that once belonged to other animals. When he is little he
likes to crawl into the shells of water snails. When he grows larger he finds
a larger shell. Often he tries several shells before he finds the one that fits.
Sometimes he wants the shell of another hermit crab and then there is a
fight. Sometimes the owner is pulled out. Sometimes the owner wins and
stays.

[LLOYD *lifts himself up to look at* HENRY. *He mouths a curse.* MAE *turns to look at* LLOYD, *then looks at* HENRY. HENRY *turns to look at* MAE, *then he looks at* LLOYD. *They freeze.*]

Act 2

Scene 10

[HENRY *enters left carrying a notebook, pencil, and a few bills. He sits left. He transfers figures from the bills to the ledger.* LLOYD *enters right. He stands up-center. He reaches into his pocket for a medical prescription and stretches his arm in* HENRY's *direction. He sits to the right. The italicized words represent a stuttering.*]

LLOYD   They gave me *this.*

HENRY   [*reads what's on the paper while still in* LLOYD's *hand. He returns to his papers.*]   That's the prescription for your medicine.

LLOYD   They said I should buy *this.* [*Pause*] They said I should *buy* it.

HENRY   Did you?

5 LLOYD   No.

HENRY   Why not.

LLOYD   I went to the *clinic.*

HENRY   [*without looking at him*]   I'm glad you did.

LLOYD   It took a *while.* I thought they *kept* me a long time. I went *early* and
10   just came back.

HENRY   How do you feel?

LLOYD   I don't feel *better.*—I feel *worse.*

HENRY   Why is that?

LLOYD   They have *instruments* there. They *stuck instruments* in me.

15 HENRY   What did they say?

LLOYD   I have to take *medicine—pills.* I have to *buy* them. They said I have
    to *swallow* the pills.

HENRY   I'm glad you went.

LLOYD   [*stretches his arm to show* HENRY *the prescription*]   They gave me *this.*
20   They said I should *buy* this. [*He puts the prescription on the table.*] They
    said I should *buy* it.

HENRY   [*with contained anger*]   You should get the medicine, Lloyd. You
    should take it and get it over with. You should take the medication and get
    well. You should not walk around with an illness that's eating your insides.
25   Get the medicine. Do as you are told.

[*They freeze.*]

Scene 11

[HENRY *exits.* LLOYD *takes the box of pills from the mantelpiece and empties it on the table. He sits center.* MAE *enters right, wiping her wet hands
with her skirt. She sits right.* LLOYD *puts a pill in his mouth. A moment
later he spits it.*]

MAE   What are they?

LLOYD   Pills.

MAE   Lloyd . . . What are you doing? [*He cleans his tongue.*] Does it taste bad?

LLOYD   Yeah.

5 MAE   [*she picks up the pill and sits*]   Try it again. [*He puts it in his mouth.*]
    Swallow it. [*He swallows and chokes. She stands by him and pushes the pill*

down his throat. She looks at him.] Did you swallow it? [*She looks at him.*] What do you feel? [*He makes a face. She sits and puts the pills in the box.*] How did you get them?

10 LLOYD [*defensively*]   I bought them.—I took the money.—From Henry.— From his trousers.—I took the money from his trousers.—I don't care.—He owes me money.—For rent.—For my bed.—He took my bed.—Like a crab.—He got into my bed like a crab.—I took it.—I didn't steal it, because it belonged to me.—Because I needed to get my medicine.—And he never

15 gave me what he owed me.—I had to ask him for it.—And he never gave it to me.—I asked him.—And he never gave it to me.—And he came here only to take things from me.—Like a crab.

> [HENRY *enters left. He is in his underwear. He carries his pants over his left arm. He holds a change purse in his right hand. He walks down left and stands there. He is stunned.*]

HENRY   Someone took money from my purse.—There is less money here than I should have.—Some of the money I had is gone.

20 MAE   Lloyd took it.

HENRY [*he sits*]   Well, tell him to give it back.

MAE   He took it for his medicine.

HENRY   He went to my purse and took it?

MAE   He needed money for his medicine. [*Pause*] Would you let Lloyd have

25 that money?

HENRY   Have Lloyd have my money?

> [*Pause.*]

MAE   He'll pay it back.

HENRY   How will he pay it back?

MAE [*to* LLOYD]   . . . Lloyd . . . ? [LLOYD *looks at* MAE.]

30 HENRY   How will he pay it back. How will Lloyd get money to pay me back? [*Pause*] How much money did he take?

MAE   . . . Lloyd . . . ?

LLYOD   I don't know how much I took.

HENRY   How will he pay it back if he doesn't know how much he took?

35 [*Pause*] Tell him I want to know how much he took.

LLOYD   I went to the clinic.—And they put those instruments in me.—And they said I had to buy that medicine.—And I couldn't find someone to help me buy that medicine.—I went to the pharmacy.—And they said I had to pay for it.—And Henry had money but he wouldn't pay for it.—And he took

40 my bed.—And he can take anything he wants from me.—And I had to buy that medicine.—So I took the money from him.

HENRY   Ask him when he took it.

LLOYD   I took it while he slept.

HENRY   How much did he take?

> [*Pause.*]

45 MAE   Lloyd can't count, Henry.

HENRY [*he takes money out of the purse, puts it on the table and counts it. He does mental subtraction.*]   Tell him he took one fifty four. [MAE *looks at* LLOYD.] Is that what he spent? Does he still have any of that money? [LLOYD *reaches into his pocket.*] Tell him to put it on the table. [LLOYD *does.* HENRY *counts the money, then does mental subtraction. He puts the coins in the purse and goes to the door.*] Tell him he owes me one thirty eight. And tell

50   him I wish he'll pay it back. [*He exits.* MAE *goes to the door and looks in the direction* HENRY *has walked. They freeze.*]

Scene 12

[MAE *puts a pair of trousers on the ironing board and puts the ironing board out.* LLOYD *places the box of pills on the mantelpiece and stands on top of the table.*]

LLOYD   There is a reason why it happened to him and not to me.

MAE   I wish it had happened to you.

LLOYD   Ha!—It couldn't have happened to me. I'm strong. He's weak and old. That's why he fell. [*Doing an exaggerated demonstration of someone*
5   *walking on dangerous ground*] I can walk on wet stones and I don't fall. Look. I can run on wet stones. I can stand on my own two feet. Look! [*He jumps to the floor and stands with his feet apart.*] Try and push me. Go on. Push me. [*She ignores him. He jumps on the table in a prone position with his legs crossed and his hands under his head.*] I wish he had drowned. I
10   wish he had fallen in the water and drowned. He's old. His legs couldn't hold him. That's why he fell. [*He jumps to the floor and runs across jumping up in the air making sounds as he goes up and down. He does this several times, then holds an athletic pose.*] Can he do that?

MAE [*still ironing*]   No, he can't. He's paralyzed. He may be a cripple. You know he can't do that!

15 LLOYD [*lies on the table with his hands under his head*]   He couldn't do it before he fell. That's why he fell. He's old. He was falling apart. That's why he fell. Now he can't even move.—Look! [*He does several cartwheels.*] Can he do that?

MAE   No, he can't.

LLOYD [*sits on the table with his arms and legs in a bodybuilder's pose*]   He has no
20   muscle. I wouldn't fall if I had to walk on wet stones. I can run on wet stones. Like this. [*He demonstrates.*] I wish he had fell in the water. I wish he had drowned. So now he can't walk. [*Short pause*] Who's going to take care of him?

MAE   We are.

[LLOYD *exits right. The sound of vomiting is heard. She freezes.*]

Scene 13

[MAE *puts the ironing board alongside the wall.* LLOYD *enters left with the cup with oatmeal and the spoon. He places the right chair away from the table.* HENRY *enters. He sits on the chair to the right. His left side is paralyzed and deformed. His trousers are rolled to his knees. He is bare-chested and wears a kitchen towel as a bib. He wears a necktie under the towel. He holds a tin cup of milk in his left hand.* LLOYD *is perched against the table next to* HENRY. *He feeds oatmeal to him.* HENRY *moves the oatmeal around his mouth, then he lets it dribble out or he spits it.* HENRY'S *speech is incomprehensible.*]

LLOYD   Stop it! [*Scooping the spilled oatmeal from* HENRY'S *chin and bib and putting it back in his mouth*] Stop doing that.—Don't do that. [HENRY *lets the oatmeal out.*] You just quit that.—Chew it.—Swallow it. [HENRY *lets the oatmeal out.* LLOYD *starts scooping it.*] Stop that! Stop doing that! You better
5   stop that, Henry.— [HENRY *lets the oatmeal out.*] Quit that. You just quit that. [HENRY *slaps the cup of milk and spills it on the floor.*] That is it, Henry. [*Taking* HENRY'S *bib off.*] You get your own food.

HENRY It spilled!

LLOYD You did it on purpose.

10 HENRY It spilled.

LLOYD No, it didn't. You spilled it.

HENRY Clean it!

LLOYD No, I won't. You clean it. I saw you do it. You clean it.

HENRY Clean it!

15 LLOYD I won't clean it. You clean it.

HENRY Clean it!

LLOYD You clean it!

HENRY Mae . . . ! [*Pause*] Mae . . . ! [*Pause*] Mae . . . !

MAE [*enters. She carries a bundle of clothes and a cleaning rag.*] What is it?

20 HENRY [*pointing to the milk*] Look!

MAE What happened? (MAE *puts the clothes on the bench and stands by* HENRY *with the rag.*)

HENRY He spilled it!

LLOYD I didn't spill it! He spilled it!

MAE So clean it up!

25 HENRY Clean it!

LLOYD I'm going to kill him.

MAE Kill him if you want.—He can't talk straight any more. [*She starts wiping the oatmeal off* HENRY.] Clean up the milk!

HENRY Clean it!

[LLOYD *takes* HENRY's *bib and starts wiping the milk.*]

30 MAE Did you feed the pigs?

LLOYD Yeah.

MAE Did Henry eat?

LLOYD He spilled the milk.

MAE Did he eat! [LLOYD *doesn't answer.*] Did he eat! [*Pause*] Did you eat,

35 Henry?

HENRY I ate.

MAE He ate. Why didn't you say he ate. [MAE *walks to the left door and opens it.*]

LLOYD I'm going to kill him.

MAE [*stands on the threshold and turns to* LLOYD] So kill him.

[*They freeze.*]

Scene 14

[MAE *exits.* LLOYD *places the bib, the oatmeal cup and spoon, and the tin cup on the mantelpiece. He takes the textbook and sits center. He attempts to read. He first makes the sound of the letter. Then, he speaks the name of the letter and traces it with his finger on the table. Then, he puts the sounds of the letters together.* HENRY *sits to the right facing front. He mimics* LLOYD's *effort and laughs in silent convulsions.*]

LLOYD S.

HENRY S.

LLOYD T. St.

HENRY T. St.

5 LLOYD A.

HENRY A.

LLOYD Stop that!

HENRY   A.

LLOYD   Stop it, Henry!

10   HENRY   A.

LLOYD   R. Ar.

HENRY   R. Ar.

LLOYD   Sta.

HENRY   Sta.

15   LLOYD   Star.

[*The left door opens.* MAE *stands outside and looks in.*]

HENRY   Star.

LLOYD   F.

HENRY   F.

LLOYD   I. Fi.

20   HENRY   I. Fi.

LLOYD   S. Fis.

HENRY   S. Fis.

LLOYD   Stop it. Cut it out. Fish.

HENRY   Fish.

[MAE *enters left. She carries a bundle of clothes.*]

25   LLOYD   Fish.

HENRY   Fish.

MAE   Someone took my money. Who did? [*Neither looks at her.*] Who did!— Did you, Lloyd!

LLOYD   I didn't. Fish.

30   HENRY   Fish.

MAE   Did Henry? Did you take the money, Henry? [*She closes the door.*] Answer me. Did you take the money! Someone took it! You took it, Lloyd. Hand it over.

LLOYD   I didn't take it.

35   MAE   Hand it over.

LLOYD   I didn't take it!

MAE   Who took it then!

LLOYD   Henry took it.

MAE   [*to* LLOYD]   He didn't take it. He can't walk.

40   LLOYD   Yes, he can. You know he can. Walk, Henry. Show Mae how you can walk. Walk! He can walk.

MAE   [*enraged*]   Walk!

HENRY   I can't walk.

LLOYD   You can walk!

45   MAE   Don't say he can walk, Lloyd. He can't walk. He didn't take the money. [*She notices the book.*] What are you doing with my book? [*He lowers his head. She is perplexed.*] What are you doing? [*She takes the book and holds it protectively.*] Don't mess my book.

HENRY   He was messing it. [*He laughs.*]

50   MAE   Shut up, Henry.

HENRY   He was saying "Fish." [*He laughs.*]

MAE   Everything turns bad for me.

[*They freeze.*]

Scene 15

[LLOYD *exits.* MAE *places the book on the mantelpiece and stands by the down-right corner of the table.* HENRY *walks to the left and sits. His hand is inside his fly. He handles himself.*]

HENRY   Mae. I still feel desire.—I am sexual.—I have not lost my sexuality.—Mae, make love to me. [MAE *doesn't answer. He continues touching himself.*] You are my wife. I want you. I feel the same desires. I feel the same needs. I have not changed. [*He holds on to the table and begins to stand.*] Mae, I

5   have not stopped wanting you.—I can make love to you.—I can satisfy you. [*Supporting himself on the table, he slides toward her.*] I am potent.—I can make you happy. Kiss me, Mae.— [*He grabs her wrist.*] Tell me you still love me. Kiss me. Let me feel you close to me.—You think a cripple has no feelings.—I'm not crippled in my parts.—It gets hard. [*He puts his right*

10   *arm around her waist.*] Mae, I love you. [*He holds her tighter. He starts moving his pelvis against her.*] I'm coming. . . . [*He starts sliding down to the floor.*] I'm coming. . . . I'm coming. . . . I'm coming. . . . I'm coming. . . . [*He collapses. She falls on the chair. She stands and leans against the table.*]

MAE   You can walk, Henry. You took my money.

[*They freeze.*]

Scene 16

[MAE *exits left.* HENRY *is on the floor trying to sit on the chair.* LLOYD *enters right. He helps* HENRY *up and closes his fly.* MAE *enters with* HENRY'S *box and lifts it up in the air.*]

HENRY   Don't, Mae.

MAE [*throwing the box at him*]   Get out!

[LLOYD *exits right.*]

HENRY   Don't throw things at me, Mae!

MAE   You took the money!

5   HENRY   You hurt me, Mae! You threw that box at me and hurt me!

MAE   You took the money!

HENRY   I didn't take it!

MAE   You took it! Where is it? [*She moves toward him.*]

HENRY   I didn't take it!

[MAE *reaches in his right pocket. She pulls out a wad of bills. She grabs his necktie, turns it back, and pulls it down.* LLOYD *puts his head in through the left door and begins to enter.* MAE *and* LLOYD *speak the following speeches at the same time.*]

10   MAE   I feed you and I take care of you! And you steal from me? You eat my food and you sleep in my bed and you steal from me! You're a pig, Henry. You're worse than Lloyd!

LLOYD   Kill him, Mae! Kill him! Kill him! [*He climbs on the table on all fours.*] He's no good! Kill him, Mae! He's no good! He's a thief!

[HENRY *falls off the chair.* MAE *falls on her knees next to him.* LLOYD *jumps off the table. He lets out a hysterical laugh.*]

15   LLOYD   Look he's bleeding! [*He chants and dances.*] Henry's bleeding! Henry's bleeding! Henry's bleeding!

MAE   Shut up, Lloyd!

[*There is silence.*]

HENRY   It was my money. Lloyd never paid me. He never paid me. He never
   paid me what he owed me.

20 MAE   You could have let him have it. Just because he takes care of you. You
   could have let him have your money. He takes care of you.

HENRY   He never paid me.

MAE [*she looks up to the sky*]   Can't I have a decent life? [*There is a pause.*]

LLOYD   But I love you, Mae.

25 HENRY   I love you, Mae.

   [*They freeze.*]

Scene 17

[LLOYD *places the box inside the fireplace. He closes the left door.* MAE
*gets the empty box from the fireplace and places it on the right chair. She
places the bundle of women's clothes from under the bench on the table.
She is packing clothes in the box.* LLOYD *stands up-left. He watches her.*
HENRY *sits left.*]

MAE [*as she packs*]   I'm leaving, Lloyd. I'm going somewhere else. I'm leaving you and Henry. Both of you are no good. I got rotten luck. I work too
   hard and the two of you keep sucking my blood. I'm going to look for a
   better place to be. [LLOYD *sits on the chair upstage of the table.*] Just a place
5 where the two of you are not sucking my blood. I'm going to find myself a
   job. And a room to live in. Far away from you. Where I don't have my
   blood sucked.

LLOYD   Don't go, Mae.

HENRY   Don't go.

10 MAE   I'm going and that's that.

LLOYD   Where are you going?

MAE   I don't know, Lloyd. I'm just going.

LLOYD   I'll do what you say.

MAE   I don't care what you do. [*Closing the box*] You do what you want.
15 Henry too. I don't care what he does.

LLOYD   Stay, Mae.

HENRY   Please.

MAE   I'm going. You take care of Henry, Lloyd. [*She goes to the door.*]

LLOYD   Don't go, Mae.

20 HENRY   Please.

MAE   Goodbye.

   [*She exits through the right door and closes the door.* LLOYD *is still for a few
   seconds. He then runs to the door, knocking down his chair. He exits.*]

LLOYD [*shouting*]   Mae . . . ! [HENRY *makes a plaintive sound.*] Mae . . . !

HENRY   Mae . . . !

LLOYD [*offstage*]   Mae . . . ! [HENRY *makes a plaintive sound.*] Stop, Mae!

25 HENRY   Stop!

   [LLOYD *enters running. He takes the rifle.* HENRY *makes incoherent
   sounds.* LLOYD *exits running.*]

LLOYD   Mae . . . ! Stop . . . ! Stop, Mae!

HENRY   Mae . . . !

LLOYD   Mae, stop . . . !

HENRY   Mae . . . !

30 LLOYD   Mae! Mae! Mae!

     [A shot is heard. There is silence. Another shot is heard.]

HENRY *[plaintively]*   . . . Mae . . .

     [LLOYD appears in threshold carrying MAE. She is drenched in blood and
     unconscious. LLOYD turns to HENRY.]

LLOYD   She's not leaving, Henry.

     [HENRY lets out a whimper. LLOYD places MAE on the table. MAE begins to
     move.]

MAE   Like the starfish, I live in the dark and my eyes see only a faint light. It
is faint and yet it consumes me. I long for it. I thirst for it. I would die for
35 it. Lloyd, I am dying.

     [MAE collapses. LLOYD sobs. HENRY lets out a plaintive cry. They freeze.]

          End.

DAVID MAMET

b. 1947

EVER since his first great success with *American Buffalo* (1975), David Mamet has been the principal dramatist of a ruthless modern world in which individuals struggle for survival and dominance. Whether depicting the world of small-time crooks or of real estate salesmen, Mamet's plays center on fast-talking, street-smart characters seeking an edge to get ahead. In the end, his plays show how profoundly capitalism has shaped America, affecting not just the lives of individual characters but also their social relations; he is the poet of what might be called capitalist existentialism. Rather than denouncing the world he depicts as immoral, Mamet observes its workings with a detached fascination that is imbued with sympathy. He is also one of the few major dramatists to be equally at home in the theater and in film. His first well-known work for the cinema was an adaptation of James Cain's 1934 novel, *The Postman Always Rings Twice* (1981), and he has since turned several of his own plays into films, written original screenplays, and directed successful features, notably *The House of Games* (1987), *Homicide* (1991), and *The Spanish Prisoner* (1997). With new plays and films coming out every few years, Mamet has reached the prime of his career, and he may yet have surprises and new breakthroughs in store for us.

Born into a Jewish family in a suburb of Chicago, Mamet was introduced to drama at an early age, acting in small parts for an uncle who produced radio and television programs for the Chicago Board of Rabbis. In 1998 Mamet commemorated the urban milieu of his youth with the plays that make up *The Old Neighborhood*. After high school he attended Goddard College in Vermont. During his junior year he studied at New York's Neighborhood Playhouse with Sanford Meisner, a master teacher of naturalist acting who influenced Mamet as a director as well as a playwright. After graduation he taught drama for a year at Marlboro College in Vermont, returning a year later to Goddard as an artist-in-residence. There Mamet founded the St. Nicholas Theatre Company with William H. Macy and other actors who would become prominent interpreters of his plays—which would be produced by that company, following its revival after he moved back to Chicago.

Mamet's earliest plays—*Lakeboat* (1970), *Duck Variations* (1972), and *Sexual Perversity in Chicago* (1974)—exemplify his most typical form: the two-person dialogue. These early plays are essentially strings of episodes; Mamet shows little interest in constructing an arc of action, in building up tensions that lead to a climactic event whose consequences are then developed toward their logical conclusion. The propulsive force instead is the spoken word, the chatter of his characters as they reminisce, brag, lie, conceal, bully, and offend one another in a series of conversations. It is difficult to identify a thematic interest or project, since the plays' settings seem to be little more than an excuse for exploring the particular everyday idiom of the characters—often lowlifes—who inhabit this or that subgroup or profession. Mamet works in the tradition of naturalism in that he preserves these characters' mistakes and colloquialisms, their repetitions, interruptions, and incomplete sentences. But he also manages to turn this ordinary idiom into a rhythmic, almost poetic language and transforms everyday dialogue into a literary style. In the process, his characters often become brilliant users and abusers of language, expert storytellers and manipulators of words who enjoy their mastery as much as Mamet does his.

Mamet found this dominance of speech over action in the three writers whom he considers his primary influences: HAROLD PINTER, SAMUEL BECKETT, and the nineteenth-century German dramatist Heinrich von Kleist. From Pinter, he learned to write elliptical dialogues, full of interruptions and silences; from Beckett, he learned that a play can be sustained by cyclical and meandering exchanges that accomplish nothing and that have to begin anew in each act; and from Kleist, he learned to use language ruthlessly and strategically. A fourth influence was ANTON CHEKHOV, whose work Mamet came to know intimately through his fine adaptations of *THE CHERRY ORCHARD* (1987), *The Three Sisters* (1992), and *Uncle Vanya* (1989). Like Mamet's, Chekhov's plays are based not on action but on the rhythms of speech, the endless repetitions of phrases through which provincial characters express and repress their ideas and desires.

Mamet broke through as a dramatist when he related his interest in language and dialogue to the larger structures of life in the United States—specifically, to the nature and effects of capitalism—in *American Buffalo*. The play examines capitalist individualism at the local level: a pawn shop inhabited by a few small-time crooks. *American Buffalo* presents a world

of exchanges of commodities that are all more or less worthless. The characters are planning to steal the coin collection of someone who had earlier bought a buffalo head nickel at the shop, but their inability to determine (with the help of an outdated book) the value of another old coin suggests that the robbery would be pointless even if pulled off successfully. The men exploit one another's weak spots, play on each other's fears and desires, manipulate and lie for their piece of an increasingly worthless pie. Yet even as they present themselves as ready to sacrifice anything for a good deal, they also exhibit moments of sentimentality that belie their tough-talking poses. A work treating the same subject on a grander scale was *The Water Engine* (1977), which Mamet originally wrote as a radio play (perhaps a natural medium for a writer who emphasizes language) and later adapted to the stage. *The Water Engine* is set at the Chicago World's Fair of 1934, an awe-inspiring display of American ingenuity in the midst of the Great Depression. Running through the play is a chain letter, representing the pyramid scheme that in Mamet's view epitomizes the greed and exploitation inherent to capitalism.

The inability to assign value—indeed, the general untrustworthiness of all products of capitalism—has increasingly emerged as Mamet's most important theme. Nearly all of his work written since the 1980s seems to suggest, in one way or another, that you can't trust what people say, you can't trust what they do, and things are not what they seem to be, but he has explored this idea most fully in his films. Whereas many of his plays revolve around proposed actions that never take place and schemes that never quite work out, his films (especially *Homicide*, *A House of Games*, and *The Spanish Prisoner*) devise plans of astonishing complexity, with layers of feints, baits, and trickery that are masterminded by a single, perfect plotter.

The three pillars of Mamet's work—dialogue, capitalism, and the con game—jointly sustain what is to date his masterwork: *GLENGARRY GLEN ROSS* (1983). Like his earlier plays, it is set in a limited, enclosed world, here a small real estate office that sells worthless property in Florida with Scottish-sounding names. Mamet knew this world firsthand, for he had briefly worked in a real estate office in Chicago. The entire play proceeds at a breakneck speed, drawing its electricity from ruthless, winner-takes-all capitalism: the best salesman of the month gets a Cadillac; the second-best receives steak knives, and the two lowest performers will be fired. The salesmen are thus reduced to competitors in a high-stakes game that leaves no time for anything besides cut-throat business. Like many of Mamet's other plays, *Glengarry* presents an all-male world from which private lives have all but disappeared. Despite his declared sympathy for his salesmen and the ingenuity they exhibit in their struggle, the play excoriates the system that has produced them.

In choosing salesmen as his protagonists, Mamet joined a line of prominent twentieth-century dramatists—EUGENE O'NEILL, in *The Iceman Cometh* (1946), and ARTHUR MILLER, in *DEATH OF A SALESMAN* (1949) notable among them—who call into question America's capitalist dream. But unlike Miller, who famously turned his play into a general parable by deliberately not specifying the products sold by Willy Loman, Mamet details what is being sold and for how much. At the same time, however, none of the commodities that circulate through this play, from the Cadillac and the steak knives to the Florida property, have any genuine utility. None of the salesmen even pretend that he wants, let alone needs, the Cadillac or the steak knives, and we know that their whole enterprise is fraudulent. They are selling real estate that could hardly be less real: not only is it worthless, but even the buyers seem to have no need for it.

While *Glengarry* is a play about capitalism, it is also something of a detective story: the real estate office is broken into and valuable customer information is stolen. In the second act, the play thus turns, at least on the surface, into a whodunit. Most of the characters have a motive for the robbery, since they are all victims of the cruel system in which they are forced to operate, and one salesman's mistake that reveals his guilt coincides with the play's end. But it is important to realize that the detective plot is ultimately only a frame, not integral to the central theme.

The set and cast of the original 1983 production of *Glengarry Glen Ross* at the Cottlesloe Theatre, London.

Unlike Mamet's films, which concentrate on elaborate cons and schemes, this play uses the burglary, a crime haplessly executed and quickly solved, merely as a backdrop for a study in the language of salesmanship. It is steeped in the peculiar idiom of the salesmen—"sits" or meetings with clients, "cold calls," and the "closing" of deals. The play's epigraph is "always be closing," which is explained as a "practical sales maxim." The most important bit of jargon, used innumerable times, is "leads": the names and addresses of potential buyers, ranked according to the likelihood that they will pan out. As in Mamet's early works, the first act of *Glengarry Glen Ross* is structured around a series of dialogues, which again display the playwright's linguistic virtuosity. The characters' rapid-fire delivery of their distinctive slang makes no concessions to the audience. They are, after all, masters of the pitch, of using language to get their way by alternately threatening, pleading with, begging, and pleasing their interlocutors. More fully here than in any other play, Mamet captures the rhythms of everyday speech, filled with interruptions and awkward transitions. Indeed, one is hard-pressed to find a complete sentence. The characters constantly interrupt one another and themselves; they test words and phrases, modifying and replacing them to suit their interlocutor's reaction. It is a kind of linguistic dance that is as expert as it is ruthless.

The play is all talk, but the talk is never innocent—words are weapons. The first to speak is Levene, a salesman who is falling behind in his rate of closed deals and who therefore no longer gets the "premium leads." Desperately trying to improve his standing, he attempts to persuade his boss, Williamson, to give him some of those hot leads on the sly. He pleads and seeks to arouse pity by mentioning his daughter; he appeals to Williamson's own greed, his good judgment, his expertise, and his management style. Williamson can hardly break in with a word of his own, but Levene's verbal torrent has no effect. The next scene features the two men whose sales are lowest, Aaronow and Moss. After drawing Aaronow into a harangue about the real estate office and its managers, bad leads, and fickle clients, Moss skillfully sets a

verbal trap for his interlocutor. Building on a general remark—someone should punish the management for giving the salesmen bad leads—he begins to spin out a plot to steal the leads from the office and then sell them to a rival firm. Aaronow finds himself unwittingly drawn into this scheme when Moss convinces him that the mere act of listening has made him an accomplice. Even more subtle and successful in his strategic talking is the protagonist of the third dialogue, the top salesman Roma, who cajoles his hapless victim into buying worthless property.

In the second act, one-on-one conversations are replaced with an ensemble piece, as different interactions occur simultaneously on the stage. While the salesmen are being cross-examined by a detective who is trying to solve the burglary, Roma's latest buyer comes into the office to cancel the deal. To distract him, Levene and Roma put on an act that is reminiscent of Mamet's metatheatrical plays, such as *A Life in the Theatre* (1977). This scene is an homage to the salesmen, the artists of deception. We see them stage a veritable play within the play, a dazzling performance that exhibits their skillful improvisation and linguistic ingenuity. These are the skills that the salesmen have developed on the street and that set them apart from the office manager, whose interruption undercuts and undoes their act. The Jewish and Italian salesmen and the WASP manager are also set on opposite sides of an ethnic divide. Indeed, ethnic divides consistently inform Mamet's plays, which use ethnicity not as a central theme but as one more occasion for slurs, one more occasion to explore different dialects and modes of speech, one more social reality that is subsumed into the overpowering need to find a way of getting the good lead, to learn how to pitch the next sale, and to close the best deal.

The intersection of language, deception, and power is Mamet's great theme, which continues to inform his most recent plays—most notably *Oleanna* (1991), whose series of encounters between a professor and his student develops into a vicious cycle of attack and counterattack. More recently, Mamet has turned away from contemporary America to write plays set in historically and therefore linguistically remote eras: *Boston Marriage* (1999) in late nineteenth-century Boston and *Faustus* (2004) in the Middle Ages. Critics and audiences have generally not considered these historical experiments equal to Mam-et's earlier works. But whether Mamet persists in a historical vein or returns to the contemporary subjects that brought him fame, his future plays will most likely continue to be meditations on the power and the futility of the spoken word.   M.P.

Glengarry Glen Ross

CHARACTERS

WILLIAMSON, BAYLEN, ROMA, LINGK   Men in their early forties
LEVENE, MOSS, AARONOW   Men in their fifties

THE SCENE
The three scenes of Act 1 take place in a Chinese restaurant.
Act 2 takes place in a real estate office.

ALWAYS BE CLOSING.
Practical Sales Maxim

Act 1

Scene 1

[*A booth at a Chinese restaurant,* WILLIAMSON *and* LEVENE *are seated at the booth.*]

LEVENE   John . . . John . . . John. Okay. John. John. Look: [*Pause*] The Glengarry Highland's leads,[1] you're sending Roma out. Fine. He's a good man. We know what he is. He's fine. All I'm saying, you look at the *board,* he's throwing . . . wait, wait, wait, he's throwing them *away,* he's throwing the leads away. All that
5   I'm saying, that you're wasting leads. I don't want to tell you your *job.* All that I'm saying, things get *set,* I know they do, you get a certain *mindset.* . . . A guy gets a reputation. We know how this . . . all I'm saying, put a *closer* on the job. There's more than one man for the . . . Put a . . . wait a second, put a *proven man out* . . . and you watch, now *wait* a second—and you watch your *dollar*
10   volumes. . . . You start closing them for *fifty* 'stead of *twenty-five* . . . you put a *closer* on the . . .

---

1. Contact information about potential clients that might lead to a sale.

WILLIAMSON   Shelly, you blew the last . . .

LEVENE   No. John. No. Let's wait, let's back up here, I did . . . will you
please? Wait a second. Please. I didn't "blow" them. No. I didn't "blow"
them. No. One kicked *out*,[2] one I closed . . .

WILLIAMSON   . . . you didn't close . . .

LEVENE   . . . I, if you'd *listen* to me. Please. I *closed* the cocksucker. His *ex*,
John, his *ex*, I didn't know he was married . . . he, the *judge* invalidated
the . . .

WILLIAMSON   Shelly . . .

LEVENE   . . . and what is that, John? What? Bad *luck*. That's all it is. I pray
in your *life* you will never find it runs in streaks. That's what it does, that's
all it's doing. Streaks. I pray it misses you. That's all I want to say.

WILLIAMSON   [*pause*]   What about the other two?

LEVENE   What two?

WILLIAMSON   Four. You had four leads. One kicked out, one the *judge*, you
say . . .

LEVENE   . . . you want to see the court records? John? Eh? You want to go
down . . .

WILLIAMSON   . . . no . . .

LEVENE   . . . do you want to go down*town* . . . ?

WILLIAMSON   . . . no . . .

LEVENE   . . . then . . .

WILLIAMSON   . . . I only . . .

LEVENE   . . . then what is this "you *say*" shit, what is that? [*Pause*] What is
that . . . ?

WILLIAMSON   All that I'm saying . . .

LEVENE   What is this "you *say*"? A deal kicks out . . . I got to *eat*. Shit, Williamson, *shit*. You . . . Moss . . . Roma . . . look at the *sheets* . . . look at the
sheets. Nineteen *eighty*, eighty-*one* . . . eighty-*two* . . . six months of eighty-
two . . . who's there? Who's up there?

WILLIAMSON   Roma.

LEVENE   Under him?

WILLIAMSON   Moss.

LEVENE   Bull*shit*. John. Bull*shit*. April, September 1981. It's *me*. It isn't
fucking Moss. Due respect, he's an *order* taker, John. He *talks*, he talks a
good game, look at the *board*, and it's *me*, John, it's me . . .

WILLIAMSON   Not lately it isn't.

LEVENE   Lately kiss my ass lately. That isn't how you build an org . . . talk,
talk to Murray. Talk to Mitch. When we were on Peterson, who paid for his
fucking *car*? You talk to him. The *Seville*[3] . . . ? He came in, "You bought
that for me Shelly." Out of *what*? Cold *calling*.[4] *Nothing*. Sixty-*five*, when
we were there, with Glen *Ross* Farms? You call 'em downtown. What was
that? *Luck*? That was "luck"? *Bull*shit, John. You're burning my ass, I can't
get a fucking *lead* . . . you think that was luck. My stats for those years?

2. That is, fell through (without necessarily
involving a real estate "kick-out clause," which
allows the seller to continue to seek another
purchaser while a potential buyer attempts to
sell his or her current house).

3. The Cadillac Seville, a name reintroduced
in 1975 for the division's smallest but most
expensive model.
4. That is, telephoning potential customers
without having any lead or prior contact.

Bull*shit* . . . over that period of time . . . ? Bull*shit*. It wasn't luck. It was *skill*. You want to throw that away, John . . . ? You want to throw that away?

WILLIAMSON   It isn't me . . .

LEVENE   . . . it isn't you . . . ? Who *is* it? Who is this I'm talking to? I need
60   the *leads* . . .

WILLIAMSON   . . . after the thirtieth . . .

LEVENE   Bull*shit* the thirtieth, I don't get on the board the thirtieth, they're going to can my ass. I need the leads. I need them now. Or I'm gone, and you're going to miss me, John, I swear to you.

65 WILLIAMSON   Murray . . .

LEVENE   . . . you *talk* to Murray . . .

WILLIAMSON   I have. And my job is to marshal those leads . . .

LEVENE   Marshal the leads . . . marshal the leads? What the fuck, what bus did *you* get off of, we're here to fucking *sell*. *Fuck* marshaling the leads.
70   What the fuck talk is that? What the fuck talk is that? Where did you learn that? In school? [*Pause*] That's "talk," my friend, that's "talk." Our job is to *sell*. I'm the *man* to sell. I'm getting garbage. [*Pause*] You're giving it to me, and what I'm saying is it's *fucked*.

WILLIAMSON   You're saying that I'm fucked.

75 LEVENE   Yes. [*Pause*] I am. I'm sorry to antagonize you.

WILLIAMSON   Let me . . .

LEVENE   . . . and I'm going to get bounced and you're . . .

WILLIAMSON   . . . let me . . . are you listening to me . . . ?

LEVENE   Yes.

80 WILLIAMSON   Let me tell you something, Shelly. I do what I'm hired to do. I'm . . . wait a second. I'm *hired* to watch the leads. I'm given . . . hold on, I'm given a *policy*. *My* job is to *do that*. What I'm *told*. That's it. You, wait a second, *anybody* falls below a certain mark I'm not *permitted* to give them the premium leads.

85 LEVENE   Then how do they come up above that mark? With *dreck*[5] . . . ? That's *nonsense*. Explain this to me. 'Cause it's a waste, and it's a stupid waste. I want to tell you something . . .

WILLIAMSON   You know what those leads cost?

LEVENE   The premium leads. Yes. I know what they cost. John. Because I, *I*
90   generated the dollar revenue sufficient to *buy* them. Nineteen senny-*nine*, you know what I made? Senny-*nine*? Ninety-six thousand dollars. John? For *Murray* . . . For *Mitch* . . . look at the sheets . . .

WILLIAMSON   Murray said . . .

LEVENE   *Fuck* him. *Fuck* Murray. John? You know? You tell him I said so.
95   What does *he* fucking know? He's going to have a "sales" contest . . . you know what our sales contest used to be? *Money*. A *fortune*. Money lying on the ground. Murray? When was the last time *he* went out on a sit?[6] Sales contest? It's *laughable*. It's cold out there now, John. It's tight. Money is *tight*. This ain't sixty-five.[7] It ain't. It just ain't. See? See? Now, I'm a good
100   *man*—but I need a . . .

WILLIAMSON   Murray said . . .

---

5. Crap (Yiddish).
6. A face-to-face meeting with clients.

7. That is, 1965, remembered as a time of economic expansion and easy sales.

LEVENE   John. John . . .

WILLIAMSON   Will you please wait a second. Shelly. Please. Murray told me: the hot leads . . .

105   LEVENE   . . . ah, *fuck* this . . .

WILLIAMSON   The . . . Shelly? [*Pause*] The hot leads are assigned according to the board. During the contest. *Period.* Anyone who beats fifty per . . .

LEVENE   That's fucked. That's fucked. You don't look at the fucking *percentage.* You look at the *gross.*

110   WILLIAMSON   Either way. You're out.

LEVENE   I'm out.

WILLIAMSON   Yes.

LEVENE   I'll tell you why I'm out. I'm *out,* you're giving me toilet paper. John. I've *seen* those leads. I saw them when I was at Homestead, we pitched

115   those cocksuckers Rio Rancho nineteen sixty-*nine* they wouldn't buy. They couldn't buy a fucking *toaster.* They're *broke,* John. They're cold. They're deadbeats, you can't judge on that. Even so. Even so. Alright. Fine. Fine. Even so. I go in, FOUR FUCKING LEADS they got their money in a *sock.* They're fucking *Polacks,*[8] John. Four leads. I close two. *Two.* Fifty per . . .

120   WILLIAMSON   . . . they kicked out.

LEVENE   They *all* kick out. You run in *streaks,* pal. *Streaks.* I'm . . . I'm . . . don't look at the *board,* look at *me.* Shelly Levene. *Anyone. Ask* them on Western. Ask Getz at Homestead. Go ask Jerry Graff. You know who I am . . . I NEED A SHOT. I got to get on the fucking board. Ask them. *Ask* them. Ask

125   them who ever picked up a check I was flush. Moss, Jerry Graff, Mitch himself . . . Those guys *lived* on the business I brought in. They *lived* on it . . . and so did Murray, John. You were here you'd of benefited from it too. And now I'm saying this. Do I want charity? Do I want *pity?* I want *sits.* I want leads don't come right out of a *phone book.* Give me a lead hotter than that,

130   I'll go in and close it. Give me a chance. That's all I want. I'm going to *get* up on that fucking board and all I want is a chance. It's a *streak* and I'm going to turn it around. [*Pause*] I need your help. [*Pause*]

WILLIAMSON   I can't do it, Shelly. [*Pause*]

LEVENE   Why?

135   WILLIAMSON   The leads are assigned randomly . . .

LEVENE   *Bullshit, bullshit,* you assign them. . . . What are you *telling* me?

WILLIAMSON   . . . apart from the top men on the contest board.

LEVENE   Then put me on the board.

WILLIAMSON   You start closing again, you'll *be* on the board.

140   LEVENE   I can't close these leads, John. No one can. It's a joke. John, look, just give me a hot lead. Just give me two of the premium leads. As a "test," alright? As a "test" and I promise you . . .

WILLIAMSON   I can't do it, Shel. [*Pause*]

LEVENE   I'll give you ten percent. [*Pause*]

145   WILLIAMSON   Of what?

LEVENE   Of my end what I close.

WILLIAMSON   And what if you don't close.

LEVENE   I *will* close.

8. People of Polish descent (derogatory).

WILLIAMSON   What if you *don't* close . . . ?

150 LEVENE   I *will* close.

WILLIAMSON   What if you *don't?* Then I'm *fucked.* You see . . . ? Then it's *my* job. That's what I'm *telling* you.

LEVENE   I *will* close. John, John, ten percent. I can get hot. You *know* that . . .

WILLIAMSON   Not lately you can't . . .

155 LEVENE   Fuck that. That's defeatist. Fuck that. Fuck it. . . . Get on my side. *Go* with me. Let's *do* something. You want to run this office, *run* it.

WILLIAMSON   Twenty percent. [*Pause*]

LEVENE   Alright.

WILLIAMSON   And fifty bucks a lead.

160 LEVENE   John. [*Pause*] Listen. I want to talk to you. Permit me to do this a second. I'm older than you. A man acquires a reputation. On the street. What he does when he's *up,* what he does otherwise. . . . I said "ten," you said "no." You said "twenty." I said "fine," I'm not going to fuck with you, how can I beat that, you tell me? . . . Okay. Okay. We'll . . . Okay. Fine.

165 We'll . . . Alright, twenty percent, and fifty bucks a lead. That's fine. For now. That's fine. A month or two we'll talk. A month from now. Next month. After the thirtieth. [*Pause*] We'll talk.

WILLIAMSON   What are we going to say?

LEVENE   No. You're right. That's for later. We'll talk in a month. What have

170 you got? I want two sits. Tonight.

WILLIAMSON   I'm not sure I have two.

LEVENE   I saw the board. You've got *four* . . .

WILLIAMSON [*snaps*]   I've got *Roma.* Then I've got Moss . . .

LEVENE   *Bullshit.* They ain't been in the office yet. Give 'em some stiff. We

175 have a deal or not? Eh? Two sits. The Des Plaines. Both of 'em, six and ten, you can do it . . . six and ten . . . eight and eleven, I don't give a shit, you set 'em up? Alright? The two sits in Des Plaines.

WILLIAMSON   Alright.

LEVENE   Good. Now we're talking. [*Pause*]

180 WILLIAMSON   A hundred bucks. [*Pause*]

LEVENE   Now? [*Pause*] Now?

WILLIAMSON   Now. [*Pause*] *Yes* . . . When?

LEVENE   Ah, *shit,* John. [*Pause*]

WILLIAMSON   I wish I could.

185 LEVENE   You fucking asshole. [*Pause*] I haven't got it. [*Pause*] I haven't got it, John. [*Pause*] I'll pay you tomorrow. [*Pause*] I'm coming in here with the sales, I'll pay you *tomorrow.* [*Pause*] I haven't *got* it, when I pay, the *gas* . . . I get back the hotel, I'll bring it in tomorrow.

WILLIAMSON   Can't do it.

190 LEVENE   I'll give you thirty on them now, I'll bring the rest tomorrow. I've got it at the hotel. [*Pause*] John? [*Pause*] We do that, for chrissake?

WILLIAMSON   No.

LEVENE   I'm asking you. As a favor to me? [*Pause*] John. [*Long pause*] John: my *daughter* . . .

195 WILLIAMSON   I can't do it, Shelly.

LEVENE   Well, I want to tell you something, fella, wasn't long I could pick up the phone, call *Murray* and I'd have your job. You know that? Not too *long* ago. For what? For *nothing.* "Mur, this new kid burns my ass." "Shelly, he's

out." You're gone before I'm back from lunch. I bought him a trip to
200   Bermuda once . . .

WILLIAMSON   I have to go . . . [*Gets up.*]

LEVENE   Wait. Alright. Fine. [*Starts going in pocket for money.*] The one. Give
me the lead. Give me the one lead. The best one you have.

WILLIAMSON   I can't split them. [*Pause*]

205 LEVENE   Why?

WILLIAMSON   Because I say so.

LEVENE [*pause*]   Is that it? Is that *it?* You want to do business that way . . . ?

[WILLIAMSON *gets up, leaves money on the table.*]

LEVENE   You want to do business that way . . . ? Alright. Alright. Alright.
Alright. What is there on the other list . . . ?

210 WILLIAMSON   You want something off the B list?

LEVENE   *Yeah.* Yeah.

WILLIAMSON   Is that what you're saying?

LEVENE   That's what I'm saying. Yeah. [*Pause*] I'd like something off the
other list. Which, very least, that I'm entitled to. If I'm still *working* here,
215   which for the moment I guess that I am. [*Pause*] What? I'm sorry I spoke
harshly to you.

WILLIAMSON   That's alright.

LEVENE   The deal still stands, our other thing.

[WILLIAMSON *shrugs. Starts out of the booth.*]

LEVENE   Good. Mmm. I, you know, I left my wallet back at the hotel.

Scene 2

[*A booth at the restaurant.* MOSS *and* AARONOW *seated. After the meal.*]

MOSS   Polacks and deadbeats.

AARONOW   . . . Polacks . . .

MOSS   Deadbeats *all.*

AARONOW   . . . they hold on to their money . . .

5 MOSS   All of 'em. They, *hey:* it happens to us all.

AARONOW   Where am I going to work?

MOSS   You have to cheer up, George, you aren't out yet.

AARONOW   I'm not?

MOSS   You missed a fucking sale. Big deal. A deadbeat Polack. Big deal. How
10   you going to sell 'em in the *first* place . . . ? Your mistake, you shoun'a took
the lead.

AARONOW   I had to.

MOSS   You had to, yeah. Why?

AARONOW   To get on the . . .

15 MOSS   To get on the board. Yeah. How you goan'a get on the board sell'n a
Polack? And I'll tell you, I'll tell you what *else.* You listening? I'll tell you
what else: don't ever try to sell an Indian.

AARONOW   I'd never try to sell an Indian.

MOSS   You get those names come up, you ever get 'em, "Patel"?

20 AARONOW   Mmm . . .

MOSS   You ever get 'em?

AARONOW   Well, I think I had one once.

MOSS   You did?

AARONOW   I . . . I don't know.

25 MOSS   You had one you'd know it. *Patel.* They keep coming up. I don't know. They like to talk to salesmen. [*Pause*] They're *lonely,* something. [*Pause*] They like to feel *superior,* I don't know. Never bought a fucking thing. You're sitting down "The Rio Rancho *this,* the blah blah blah," "The Mountain View—" "Oh yes. My brother told me that. . . ." They got a grapevine.

30 Fuckin' Indians, George. Not my cup of tea. Speaking of which I want to tell you something: [*Pause*] I never got a cup of tea with them. You see them in the restaurants. A supercilious race. What is this *look* on their face all the time? I don't know. [*Pause*] I don't know. Their broads all look like they just got fucked with a dead *cat, I* don't know. [*Pause*] I don't know. I don't

35 like it. Christ . . .

AARONOW   What?

MOSS   The whole fuckin' thing . . . The pressure's just too great. You're ab . . . you're absolu . . . they're too important. All of them. You go in the door. I . . . "I got to *close* this fucker, or I don't eat lunch," "or I don't win the

40 *Cadillac.* . . ." We fuckin' work too hard. You work too hard. We all, I remember when we were at Platt . . . huh? Glen Ross Farms . . . *didn't* we sell a bunch of that . . . ?

AARONOW   They came in and they, you know . . .

MOSS   Well, they fucked it up.

45 AARONOW   They did.

MOSS   They killed the goose.[9]

AARONOW   They did.

MOSS   And now . . .

AARONOW   We're stuck with *this* . . .

50 MOSS   We're stuck with *this* fucking shit . . .

AARONOW   . . . *this* shit . . .

MOSS   It's too . . .

AARONOW   It is.

MOSS   Eh?

55 AARONOW   It's too . . .

MOSS   You get a bad month, all of a . . .

AARONOW   You're on this . . .

MOSS   All of, they got you on this "board . . ."

AARONOW   I, I . . . I . . .

60 MOSS   Some *contest* board . . .

AARONOW   I . . .

MOSS   It's not right.

AARONOW   It's not.

MOSS   No. [*Pause*]

65 AARONOW   And it's not right to the *customers.*

MOSS   I know it's not. I'll tell you, you got, you know, you got . . . what did I learn as a kid on Western? Don't sell a guy one car. Sell him *five* cars over fifteen years.

AARONOW   That's right?

70 MOSS   Eh . . . ?

---

9. That is, the goose that laid the golden eggs; in the fable about this goose, greed leads to over-reaching and the subsequent loss of easy profit.

AARONOW   That's right?

MOSS   Goddamn right, that's right. Guys come on: "Oh, the blah blah blah, *I* know what I'll do: I'll go in and rob everyone blind and go to Argentina cause nobody ever *thought* of this before."

75 AARONOW   . . . that's right . . .

MOSS   Eh?

AARONOW   No. That's absolutely right.

MOSS   And so they kill the goose. I, I, I'll . . . and a fuckin' *man,* worked all his *life* has got to . . .

80 AARONOW   . . . that's right . . .

MOSS   . . . cower in his boots . . .

AARONOW   [*simultaneously with "boots"*]   Shoes, boots, yes . . .

MOSS   For some fuckin' "Sell ten thousand and you win the steak knives . . ."

AARONOW   For some *sales* pro . . .

85 MOSS   . . . sales promotion, "You *lose,* then we fire your . . ." No. It's *medieval* . . . it's wrong. "Or we're going to fire your ass." It's wrong.

AARONOW   Yes.

MOSS   Yes, it is. And you know who's responsible?

AARONOW   Who?

90 MOSS   You know who it is. It's Mitch. And Murray. 'Cause it doesn't have to be this way.

AARONOW   No.

MOSS   Look at Jerry Graff. He's *clean,* he's doing business for *himself,* he's got his, that *list* of his with the *nurses* . . . see? You see? That's *thinking.* Why

95   take ten percent? A ten percent comm . . . why are we giving the rest away? What are we giving ninety per . . . for *nothing.* For some jerk sit in the office tell you "Get out there and close." "Go win the Cadillac." Graff. He goes out and *buys.* He pays top dollar for the . . . you see?

AARONOW   Yes.

100 MOSS   That's *thinking.* Now, he's got the leads, he goes in business for *himself.* He's . . . that's what I . . . that's *thinking!* "Who? Who's got a steady *job,* a couple bucks nobody's touched, who?"

AARONOW   Nurses.

MOSS   So Graff buys a fucking list of nurses, one grand—if he paid two I'll

105   eat my hat—four, five thousand nurses, and he's going *wild* . . .

AARONOW   He is?

MOSS   He's doing *very* well.

AARONOW   I heard that they were running cold.

MOSS   The nurses?

110 AARONOW   Yes.

MOSS   You hear a *lot* of things. . . . He's doing very well. He's doing *very* well.

AARONOW   With River Oaks?

MOSS   River Oaks, Brook Farms. *All* of that shit. Somebody told me, you know what he's clearing *himself?* Fourteen, fifteen grand[1] a *week.*

115 AARONOW   Himself?

MOSS   That's what I'm *saying.* Why? The *leads.* He's got the good leads . . . what are we, we're sitting in the shit here. Why? We have to go to *them* to

---

1. Equivalent to about $36,000 or $39,000 in 2017.

get them. Huh. Ninety percent our sale, we're *paying* to the *office* for the *leads.*

120 AARONOW The leads, the overhead, the telephones, there's *lots* of things.

MOSS What do you need? A *telephone,* some broad to say "Good morning," nothing . . . nothing . . .

AARONOW No, it's not that simple, Dave . . .

MOSS *Yes. It is. It is* simple, and you know what the hard part is?

125 AARONOW What?

MOSS Starting up.

AARONOW What hard part?

MOSS Of doing the thing. The dif . . . the difference. Between me and Jerry Graff. Going to business for yourself. The hard part is . . . you know what

130 it is?

AARONOW What?

MOSS Just the *act.*

AARONOW What act?

MOSS To say "I'm going on my own." 'Cause what you do, George, let me tell

135 you what you do: you find yourself in *thrall* to someone else. And we *enslave* ourselves. To *please.* To win some fucking *toaster* . . . to . . . to . . . and the guy who got there first made *up* those . . .

AARONOW That's right . . .

MOSS He made *up* those rules, and we're working for *him.*

140 AARONOW That's the truth . . .

MOSS That's the *God's* truth. And it gets me depressed. I *swear* that it does. At MY AGE. To see a goddamn: "Somebody wins the Cadillac this month. P.S. Two guys get fucked."

AARONOW *Huh.*

145 MOSS You don't *ax* your sales force.

AARONOW No.

MOSS You . . .

AARONOW You . . .

MOSS You *build* it!

150 AARONOW That's what I . . .

MOSS You fucking *build* it! Men come . . .

AARONOW Men come *work* for you . . .

MOSS . . . you're absolutely right.

AARONOW They . . .

155 MOSS They have . . .

AARONOW When they . . .

MOSS Look look look look, when they *build* your business, then you can't fucking turn around, *enslave* them, treat them like *children,* fuck them up the ass, leave them to fend for themselves . . . no. [*Pause*] No. [*Pause*]

160 You're absolutely right, and I want to tell you something.

AARONOW What?

MOSS I want to tell you what somebody should do.

AARONOW What?

MOSS Someone should stand up and strike *back.*

165 AARONOW What do you mean?

MOSS *Somebody* . . .

AARONOW Yes . . . ?

MOSS   Should do something to *them*.

AARONOW   What?

170 MOSS   Something. To pay them back. [*Pause*] Someone, someone should hurt them. Murray and Mitch.

AARONOW   Someone should hurt them.

MOSS   Yes.

AARONOW [*pause*]   How?

175 MOSS   How? Do something to hurt them. Where they live.

AARONOW   What? [*Pause*]

MOSS   Someone should rob the office.

AARONOW   Huh.

MOSS   That's what I'm *saying*. We were, if we were that kind of guys, to knock

180   it off, and *trash* the joint, it looks like robbery, and *take* the fuckin' leads out of the files . . . go to Jerry Graff. [*Long pause*]

AARONOW   What could somebody get for them?

MOSS   What could we *get* for them? I don't know. Buck a *throw* . . . buck-a-half a throw . . . I don't know. . . . Hey, who knows what they're worth,

185   what do they *pay* for them? All told . . . must be, I'd . . . three bucks a throw . . . *I* don't know.

AARONOW   How many leads have we got?

MOSS   The *Glengarry* . . . the premium leads . . . ? I'd say we got five thousand. Five. Five thousand leads.

190 AARONOW   And you're saying a fella could take and sell these leads to Jerry Graff.

MOSS   Yes.

AARONOW   How do you know he'd buy them?

MOSS   Graff? Because I worked for him.

195 AARONOW   You haven't talked to him.

MOSS   No. What do you mean? Have I talked to him about *this*? [*Pause*]

AARONOW   Yes. I mean are you actually *talking* about this, or are we just . . .

MOSS   No, we're just . . .

AARONOW   We're just "*talking*" about it.

200 MOSS   We're just *speaking* about it. [*Pause*] As an *idea*.

AARONOW   As an idea.

MOSS   Yes.

AARONOW   We're not actually *talking* about it.

MOSS   No.

205 AARONOW   Talking about it as a . . .

MOSS   *No.*

AARONOW   As a *robbery*.

MOSS   As a "robbery"?! No.

AARONOW   *Well.* Well . . .

210 MOSS   *Hey.* [*Pause*]

AARONOW   So all this, um, you didn't, actually, you didn't actually go talk to Graff.

MOSS   Not actually, no. [*Pause*]

AARONOW   You didn't?

215 MOSS   No. Not actually.

AARONOW   Did you?

MOSS   What did I say?

AARONOW   What did you say?

MOSS   Yes. [*Pause*] I said, "Not actually." The fuck *you* care, George? We're
220   just *talking* . . .

AARONOW   We are?

MOSS   Yes. [*Pause*]

AARONOW   Because, because, you know, it's a *crime*.

MOSS   That's right. It's a crime. It is a crime. It's also very safe.

225 AARONOW   You're actually *talking* about this?

MOSS   That's right. [*Pause*]

AARONOW   You're going to steal the leads?

MOSS   Have I said that? [*Pause*]

AARONOW   Are you? [*Pause*]

230 MOSS   Did I say that?

AARONOW   Did you talk to Graff?

MOSS   Is that what I said?

AARONOW   What did he say?

MOSS   What did he say? He'd *buy* them. [*Pause*]

235 AARONOW   You're going to steal the leads and sell the leads to him? [*Pause*]

MOSS   Yes.

AARONOW   What will he pay?

MOSS   A buck a shot.

AARONOW   For five thousand?

240 MOSS   However they are, that's the deal. A buck a throw. Five thousand dollars. Split it half and half.

AARONOW   You're saying "me."

MOSS   Yes. [*Pause*] Twenty-five hundred apiece. One night's work, and the
job with Graff. Working the premium leads. [*Pause*]

245 AARONOW   A job with Graff.

MOSS   Is that what I said?

AARONOW   He'd give me a job.

MOSS   He would take you on. Yes. [*Pause*]

AARONOW   Is that the truth?

250 MOSS   Yes. It is, George. [*Pause*] Yes. It's a big decision. [*Pause*] And it's a big
reward. [*Pause*] It's a big reward. For one night's work. [*Pause*] But it's got
to be tonight.

AARONOW   What?

MOSS   What? What? The *leads*.

255 AARONOW   You have to steal the leads tonight?

MOSS   That's *right*, the guys are moving them downtown. After the thirtieth.
Murray and Mitch. After the contest.

AARONOW   You're, you're saying so you have to go in there tonight and . . .

MOSS   You . . .

260 AARONOW   I'm sorry?

MOSS   You. [*Pause*]

AARONOW   Me?

MOSS   You have to go in. [*Pause*] You have to get the leads. [*Pause*]

AARONOW   I do?

265 MOSS   Yes.

AARONOW   I . . .

MOSS   It's not something for nothing, George, I took you in on this, you have
 to go. That's your thing. I've made the deal with Graff. I can't go. I can't go
 in, I've spoken on this too much. I've got a big mouth. [*Pause*] "The fucking
270 leads" et cetera, blah blah blah ". . . the fucking tight-ass company . . ."
AARONOW   They'll know when you go over to Graff . . .
MOSS   What will they know? That I stole the leads? I *didn't* steal the leads,
 I'm going to the *movies* tonight with a friend, and then I'm going to the
 Como Inn. Why did I go to Graff? I got a better deal. *Period.* Let 'em prove
275 something. They can't prove anything that's not the case. [*Pause*]
AARONOW   *Dave.*
MOSS   Yes.
AARONOW   You want me to break into the office tonight and steal the leads?
MOSS   Yes. [*Pause*]
280 AARONOW   No.
MOSS   Oh, yes, George.
AARONOW   What does that mean?
MOSS   Listen to this. I have an alibi, I'm going to the Como Inn, why? Why?
 The place gets robbed, they're going to come looking for *me*. Why? Because
285 I probably did it. Are you going to turn me in? [*Pause*] George? Are you
 going to turn me in?
AARONOW   What if you don't get caught?
MOSS   They come to you, you going to turn me in?
AARONOW   Why would they come to me?
290 MOSS   They're going to come to *everyone*.
AARONOW   Why would I *do* it?
MOSS   You wouldn't, George, that's why I'm talking to you. Answer me. They
 come to you. You going to turn me in?
AARONOW   No.
295 MOSS   Are you sure?
AARONOW   Yes. I'm sure.
MOSS   Then listen to this: I have to get those leads tonight. That's something
 I have to do. If I'm not at the *movies* . . . if I'm not eating over at the inn . . .
 if you don't do this, then *I* have to come in here . . .
300 AARONOW   . . . you don't have to come in . . .
MOSS   . . . and *rob* the place . . .
AARONOW   . . . I thought that we were only talking . . .
MOSS   . . . they *take* me, then. They're going to ask me who were my
 accomplices.
305 AARONOW   *Me?*
MOSS   Absolutely.
AARONOW   That's ridiculous.
MOSS   Well, to the law, you're an accessory. Before the fact.
AARONOW   I didn't ask to be.
310 MOSS   Then tough luck, George, because you are.
AARONOW   Why? *Why,* because you only *told* me about it?
MOSS   That's right.
AARONOW   Why are you doing this to me, Dave. Why are you talking this way
 to me? I don't understand. Why are you doing this at *all* . . . ?
315 MOSS   That's none of your fucking business . . .

AARONOW Well, well, well, *talk* to me, we sat down to eat *dinner*, and here I'm a *criminal* . . .

MOSS You *went* for it.

AARONOW In the abstract . . .

320 MOSS So I'm making it concrete.

AARONOW Why?

MOSS Why? Why *you* going to give me five grand?

AARONOW Do you need five grand?

MOSS Is that what I just said?

325 AARONOW You need money? Is that the . . .

MOSS Hey, hey, let's just keep it simple, what I need is not the . . . what do *you* need . . . ?

AARONOW What is the five grand? [*Pause*] What is the, you said that we were going to *split* five . . .

330 MOSS I lied. [*Pause*] Alright? My end is *my* business. Your end's twenty-five. In or out. You tell me, you're out you take the consequences.

AARONOW I do?

MOSS Yes. [*Pause*]

AARONOW And why is that?

335 MOSS Because you listened.

Scene 3

[*The restaurant.* ROMA *is seated alone at the booth.* LINGK *is at the booth next to him.* ROMA *is talking to him.*]

ROMA . . . all train compartments smell vaguely of shit. It gets so you don't mind it. That's the worst thing that I can confess. You know how long it took me to get there? A long time. When you *die* you're going to regret the things you don't do. You think you're *queer* . . . ? I'm going to tell you some-
5 thing: we're *all* queer. You think that you're a *thief*? So *what*? You get befuddled by a middle-class morality . . . ? Get *shut* of it. Shut it out. You cheated on your wife . . . ? You *did* it, *live* with it. [*Pause*] You fuck little girls, so *be* it. There's an absolute morality? May *be*. And *then* what? If you *think* there is, then *be* that thing. Bad people go to hell? I don't *think* so. If
10 you think that, act that way. A hell exists on earth? Yes. I won't live in it. That's *me*. You ever take a dump made you feel you'd just slept for twelve hours . . . ?

LINGK Did I . . . ?

ROMA Yes.

15 LINGK I don't know.

ROMA Or a *piss* . . . ? A great meal fades in reflection. Everything else gains. You know why? 'Cause it's only food. This shit we eat, it keeps us going. But it's only food. The great fucks that you may have had. What do you remember about them?

20 LINGK What do I . . . ?

ROMA Yes.

LINGK Mmmm . . .

ROMA I don't know. For *me*, I'm saying, what it is, it's probably not the orgasm. Some broads, forearms on your neck, something her *eyes* did. There was a
25 *sound* she made . . . or, me, lying, in the, I'll tell you: me lying in bed; the

next day she brought me café au lait. She gives me a cigarette, my balls feel like concrete. Eh? What I'm saying, what is our life? [*Pause*] It's looking forward or it's looking back. And that's our life. That's *it*. Where is the *moment*? [*Pause*] And what is it that we're afraid of? Loss. What else?
30 [*Pause*] The *bank* closes. We get *sick,* my wife died on a plane, the stock market collapsed . . . the house burnt down . . . what of these happen . . . ? None of 'em. We worry anyway. What does this mean? I'm not *secure.* How can I be secure? [*Pause*] Through amassing wealth beyond all measure? No. And what's beyond all measure? That's a sickness. That's a trap. There
35 is no measure. Only greed. How can we act? The right way, we would say, to deal with this: "There is a one-in-a-million chance that so and so will happen. . . . *Fuck* it, it won't happen to *me.* . . ." No. We know that's not the right way I think. [*Pause*] We say the *correct* way to deal with this is "There is one-in-so-and-so chance this will happen . . . God *protect* me. I
40 am powerless, let it not happen to me. . . ." But no to *that.* I say. There's something else. What is it? "If it happens, AS IT MAY for that is not within our powers, I will *deal* with it, just as I do *today* with what draws my concern today." I say *this* is how we must act. I do those things which seem correct to me *today.* I trust myself. And if security concerns me, I do that
45 which *today* I think will make me secure. And every day I *do* that, when that day *arrives* that I need a reserve, (a) odds are that I have it, and (b) the *true* reserve that I have is the strength that I have of *acting each day* without fear. [*Pause*] According to the dictates of my mind. [*Pause*] Stocks, bonds, objects of art, real estate. Now: what are they? [*Pause*] An opportu
50 nity. To what? To make money? Perhaps. To *lose* money? Perhaps. To "indulge" and to "learn" about ourselves? Perhaps. *So fucking what?* What *isn't*? They're an *opportunity.* That's all. They're an *event.* A guy comes up to you, you make a call, you send in a brochure, it doesn't matter, "There're these *properties* I'd like for you to see." What does it mean? What you *want*
55 it to mean. [*Pause*] Money? [*Pause*] If that's what it signifies to you. Security? [*Pause*] Comfort? [*Pause*] All it is is THINGS THAT HAPPEN TO YOU. [*Pause*] That's all it is. How are they different? [*Pause*] Some poor newly married guy gets run down by a cab. Some *busboy* wins the lottery. [*Pause*] All it is, it's a carnival. What's special . . . what *draws* us? [*Pause*]
60 We're all different. [*Pause*] We're not the same. [*Pause*] We are not the same. [*Pause*] Hmmm. [*Pause. Sighs.*] It's been a long day. [*Pause*] What are you drinking?

LINGK   Gimlet.

ROMA   Well, let's have a couple more. My name is Richard Roma, what's
65 yours?

LINGK   Lingk. James Lingk.

ROMA   James. I'm glad to meet you. [*They shake hands.*] I'm glad to meet you, James. [*Pause*] I want to show you something. [*Pause*] It might mean *nothing* to you . . . and it might not. I don't know. I don't know any more.
70 [*Pause. He takes out a small map and spreads it on a table.*] What is that? Florida. Glengarry Highlands. Florida. "Florida. *Bullshit.*" And maybe that's true; and that's what *I* said: but look *here*: what is this? This is a piece of land. Listen to what I'm going to tell you now:

Act 2

[*The real estate office. Ransacked. A broken plate-glass window boarded up, glass all over the floor.* AARONOW *and* WILLIAMSON *standing around, smoking.*]

[*Pause.*]

AARONOW   People used to say that there are numbers of such magnitude that multiplying them by two made no difference. [*Pause*]

WILLIAMSON   Who used to say that?

AARONOW   In school. [*Pause*]

[BAYLEN, *a detective, comes out of the inner office.*]

5 BAYLEN   Alright . . . ?

[ROMA *enters from the street.*]

ROMA   *Williamson . . . Williamson,* they stole the *contracts* . . . ?

BAYLEN   Excuse me, sir . . .

ROMA   Did they get my contracts?

WILLIAMSON   They got . . .

10 BAYLEN   Excuse me, fella.

ROMA   . . . did they . . .

BAYLEN   Would you excuse us, please . . . ?

ROMA   Don't *fuck* with me, fella. I'm talking about a fuckin' Cadillac car that you owe me . . .

15 WILLIAMSON   They didn't get your contract. I filed it before I left.

ROMA   They didn't get my contracts?

WILLIAMSON   They—excuse me . . .

[*He goes back into inner room with the detective.*]

ROMA   Oh, *fuck. Fuck.* [*He starts kicking the desk.*] FUCK FUCK FUCK! WILLIAMSON!!! WILLIAMSON!!! [*Goes to the door* WILLIAMSON *went into,*
20 *tries the door; it's locked.*] OPEN THE FUCKING . . . WILLIAMSON . . .

BAYLEN [*coming out*]   Who are you?

[WILLIAMSON *comes out.*]

WILLIAMSON   They didn't get the contracts.

ROMA   Did they . . .

WILLIAMSON   They got, listen to me . . .

25 ROMA   Th . . .

WILLIAMSON   Listen to me: They got *some* of them.

ROMA   Some of them . . .

BAYLEN   Who told you . . . ?

ROMA   Who told me wh . . . ? You've got a fuckin', you've . . . a . . . who is
30 this . . . ? You've got a board-up on the window. . . . *Moss* told me.

BAYLEN [*looking back toward the inner office*]   Moss . . . Who told him?

ROMA   How the fuck do *I* know? [*To* WILLIAMSON] *What . . . talk* to me.

WILLIAMSON   They took *some* of the con . . .

ROMA   . . . some of the contracts . . . Lingk. James Lingk. I closed . . .

35 WILLIAMSON   You closed him yesterday.

ROMA   *Yes.*

WILLIAMSON   It went down. I filed it.

ROMA   You did?

WILLIAMSON   Yes.

40 ROMA   Then I'm over the fucking top and you owe me a Cadillac.

WILLIAMSON   I . . .

ROMA   And I don't want any fucking shit and I don't give a shit, Lingk puts
me over the top, you filed it, that's fine, any other shit kicks out *you* go back.
You . . . *you* reclose it, 'cause I *closed* it and you . . . you owe me the car.

45 BAYLEN   Would you excuse us, please.

AARONOW   I, um, and may . . . maybe they're in . . . they're in . . . you should,
John, if we're ins . . .

WILLIAMSON   I'm sure that we're insured, George . . .

    [*Going back inside.*]

ROMA   Fuck insured. You owe me a car.

50 BAYLEN [*stepping back into the inner room*]   Please don't leave. I'm going to
talk to you. What's your name?

ROMA   Are you talking to me? [*Pause*]

BAYLEN   Yes. [*Pause*]

ROMA   My name is Richard Roma.

    [BAYLEN *goes back into the inner room.*]

55 AARONOW   I, you know, they should be insured.

ROMA   What do *you* care . . . ?

AARONOW   Then, you know, they wouldn't be so ups . . .

ROMA   Yeah. That's swell. Yes. You're right. [*Pause*] How are you?

AARONOW   I'm fine. You mean the *board?* You mean the *board* . . . ?

60 ROMA   I don't . . . yes. Okay, the board.

AARONOW   I'm, I'm, I'm, I'm fucked on the board. *You.* You see how . . . I . . .
[*Pause*] I can't . . . my mind must be in other places. 'Cause I can't do
any . . .

ROMA   *What?* You can't do any *what?* [*Pause*]

65 AARONOW   I can't close 'em.

ROMA   Well, they're old. I saw the shit that they were giving you.

AARONOW   Yes.

ROMA   Huh?

AARONOW   Yes. They are old.

70 ROMA   They're ancient.

AARONOW   Clear . . .

ROMA   Clear Meadows. That shit's dead. [*Pause*]

AARONOW   It *is* dead.

ROMA   It's a waste of time.

75 AARONOW   Yes. [*Long pause*] I'm no fucking good.

ROMA   That's . . .

AARONOW   Everything I . . . *you* know . . .

ROMA   That's not . . . Fuck that shit, George. You're a, *hey,* you had a bad
month. You're a good man, George.

80 AARONOW   I am?

ROMA   You hit a bad streak. We've all . . . look at this: fifteen units Mountain
View, the fucking things get stole.

AARONOW   He said he filed . . .

ROMA   He filed half of them, he filed the *big* one. All the little ones, I have, I

85   have to go back and . . . ah, *fuck,* I got to go out like a fucking schmuck[2]

2. Jerk; dick (Yiddish).

hat in my hand and reclose the . . . [*Pause*] I mean, talk about a bad streak. That would sap *anyone's* self confi . . . I got to go out and reclose all my . . . Where's the phones?

AARONOW   They stole . . .

90 ROMA   They stole the . . .

AARONOW   What. What kind of outfit are we running where . . . where anyone . . .

ROMA [*to himself*]   They stole the phones.

AARONOW   Where criminals can come in here . . . they take the . . .

95 ROMA   They stole the phones. They stole the leads. They're . . . *Christ.* [*Pause*] What am I going to do this month? Oh, *shit* . . . [*Starts for the door.*]

AARONOW   You think they're going to catch . . . where are you going?

ROMA   Down the street.

WILLIAMSON [*sticking his head out of the door*]   Where are you going?

100 ROMA   To the restaura . . . what do you fucking . . . ?

WILLIAMSON   Aren't you going out today?

ROMA   With what? [*Pause*] With what, John, they took the leads . . .

WILLIAMSON   I have the stuff from last year's . . .

ROMA   Oh. Oh. Oh, your "nostalgia" file, that's fine. No. Swell. 'Cause I don't

105 have to . . .

WILLIAMSON   . . . you want to go out today . . . ?

ROMA   'Cause I don't have to *eat* this month. No. Okay. *Give* 'em to me . . . [*To himself*] Fucking Mitch and Murray going to shit a br . . . what am I going to *do* all . . .

[WILLIAMSON *starts back into the office. He is accosted by* AARONOW.]

110 AARONOW   Were the leads . . .

ROMA   . . . what am I going to *do* all month . . . ?

AARONOW   Were the leads insured?

WILLIAMSON   I don't know, George, why?

AARONOW   'Cause, you know, 'cause they weren't, I know that Mitch and

115 Murray uh . . . [*Pause*]

WILLIAMSON   What?

AARONOW   That they're going to be upset.

WILLIAMSON   That's right. [*Going back into his office. Pause. To* ROMA] You want to go out today . . . ?

[*Pause.* WILLIAMSON *returns to his office.*]

120 AARONOW   He said we're all going to have to go talk to the guy.

ROMA   What?

AARONOW   He said we . . .

ROMA   To the cop?

AARONOW   Yeah.

125 ROMA   Yeah. That's swell. *Another* waste of time.

AARONOW   A waste of time? Why?

ROMA   *Why?* 'Cause they aren't going to find the guy.

AARONOW   The cops?

ROMA   Yes. The cops. No.

130 AARONOW   They aren't?

ROMA   No.

AARONOW   Why don't you think so?

ROMA   Why? Because they're *stupid.* "Where were you last night . . ."

AARONOW   Where were you?

135   ROMA   Where was *I*?

AARONOW   Yes.

ROMA   I was at home, where were *you*?

AARONOW   At home.

ROMA   *See . . . ?* Were you the guy who broke in?

140   AARONOW   Was *I*?

ROMA   Yes.

AARONOW   No.

ROMA   Then don't sweat it, George, you know why?

AARONOW   No.

145   ROMA   You have nothing to hide.

AARONOW   [*pause*]   When I talk to the police, I get nervous.

ROMA   Yeah. You know who doesn't?

AARONOW   No, who?

ROMA   Thieves.

150   AARONOW   Why?

ROMA   They're inured to it.

AARONOW   You think so?

ROMA   Yes. [*Pause*]

AARONOW   But what should I *tell* them?

155   ROMA   The truth, George. Always tell the truth. It's the easiest thing to remember.

[WILLIAMSON *comes out of the office with leads.* ROMA *takes one, reads it.*]

ROMA   *Patel?* Ravidam *Patel?* How am I going to make a living on these deadbeat *wogs?*[3] Where did you get this, from the *morgue?*

WILLIAMSON   If you don't want it, give it back.

160   ROMA   I don't "want" it, if you catch my drift.

WILLIAMSON   I'm giving you *three* leads. You . . .

ROMA   What's the fucking point in *any* case . . . ? What's the *point.* I got to argue with *you,* I got to knock heads with the *cops,* I'm busting my *balls,* sell you *dirt* to fucking *deadbeats* money in the *mattress,* I come back you

165   can't even manage to keep the contracts safe, I have to go back and close them *again.* . . . What the fuck am I wasting my time, fuck this shit. I'm going out and reclose last week's . . .

WILLIAMSON   The word from Murray is: leave them alone. If we need a new signature he'll go out himself, he'll be the *president,* just come *in,* from out

170   of *town* . . .

ROMA   Okay, okay, okay, gimme this shit. Fine. [*Takes the leads.*]

WILLIAMSON   Now, I'm giving you three . . .

ROMA   Three? I count *two.*

WILLIAMSON   Three.

175   ROMA   Patel? Fuck *you.* Fuckin' *Shiva*[4] handed him a million dollars, told him "sign the deal," he wouldn't sign. And Vishnu, too. Into the bargain.

---

3. Dark-skinned people, especially South Asians (a pejorative term, mainly British).
4. One of the most important gods of Hindu-

ism, as is Vishnu; they are identified, respectively, with destruction and preservation.

Fuck *that,* John. You know your business, I know mine. Your business is being an *asshole,* and I find out whose fucking *cousin* you are, I'm going to go to him and figure out a way to have your *ass* . . . fuck you—I'll wait for
180   the new leads.

> [SHELLY LEVENE *enters.*]

LEVENE   Get the *chalk.* Get the *chalk* . . . get the *chalk!* I closed 'em! I *closed* the cocksucker. Get the chalk and put me on the *board.* I'm going to Hawaii! Put me on the Cadillac board, Williamson! Pick up the fuckin' chalk. Eight units. Mountain View . . .

185 ROMA   You sold eight Mountain View?

LEVENE   You bet your ass. Who wants to go to lunch? Who wants to go to lunch? I'm buying. [*Slaps contract down on Williamson's desk.*] Eighty-two fucking grand. And twelve grand in commission. John. [*Pause*] On fucking deadbeat magazine subscription leads.

190 WILLIAMSON   Who?

LEVENE   [*pointing to contract*]   *Read* it. Bruce and Harriett Nyborg. [*Looking around*] What happened here?

AARONOW   Fuck. I had them on River Glen.

> [LEVENE *looks around.*]

LEVENE   What happened?

195 WILLIAMSON   Somebody broke in.

ROMA   Eight units?

LEVENE   That's right.

ROMA   *Shelly* . . . !

LEVENE   Hey, big fucking deal. Broke a bad streak . . .

200 AARONOW   Shelly, the Machine, Levene.

LEVENE   You . . .

AARONOW   That's great.

LEVENE   Thank you, George.

> [BAYLEN *sticks his head out of the room; calls in,* "Aaronow." AARONOW *goes into the side room.*]

LEVENE   Williamson, get on the phone, call Mitch . . .

205 ROMA   They took the phones . . .

LEVENE   They . . .

BAYLEN   *Aaronow* . . .

ROMA   They took the typewriters, they took the leads, they took the *cash,* they took the *contracts* . . .

210 LEVENE   Wh . . . wh . . . Wha . . . ?

AARONOW   We had a robbery.

> [*Goes into the inner room.*]

LEVENE   [*pause*]   When?

ROMA   Last night, this morning. [*Pause*]

LEVENE   They took the leads?

215 ROMA   Mmm.

> [MOSS *comes out of the interrogation.*]

MOSS   Fuckin' asshole.

ROMA   What, they beat you with a rubber bat?

MOSS   Cop couldn't find his dick two hands and a map. Anyone talks to this guy's an *asshole* . . .

220 ROMA   You going to turn State's?[5]

MOSS   Fuck you, Ricky. I ain't going out today. I'm going home. I'm going home because nothing's *accomplished* here. . . . Anyone *talks* to this guy is . . .

ROMA   Guess what the Machine did?

225 MOSS   Fuck the Machine.

ROMA   Mountain View. Eight units.

MOSS   Fuckin' cop's got no right talk to me that way. I didn't rob the place . . .

ROMA   You hear what I said?

MOSS   Yeah. He closed a deal.

230 ROMA   Eight units. Mountain View.

MOSS [*to* LEVENE]   You did that?

LEVENE   Yeah. [*Pause*]

MOSS   Fuck you.

ROMA   Guess who?

235 MOSS   When . . .

LEVENE   Just now.

ROMA   Guess who?

MOSS   You just this morning . . .

ROMA   Harriet and blah blah Nyborg.

240 MOSS   You did that?

LEVENE   Eighty-two thousand dollars. [*Pause*]

MOSS   Those fuckin' *deadbeats* . . .

LEVENE   My ass. I told 'em. [*To* ROMA] Listen to this: I said . . .

MOSS   Hey, I don't want to hear your fucking war stories . . .

245 ROMA   Fuck *you*, Dave . . .

LEVENE   "You have to believe in your*self* . . . you"—look—"alright . . . ?"

MOSS [*to* WILLIAMSON]   Give me some leads. I'm going out . . . I'm getting out of . . .

LEVENE   ". . . you have to believe in your*self* . . ."

250 MOSS   Na, fuck the leads, I'm going home.

LEVENE   "Bruce, Harriet . . . Fuck *me*, believe in your*self* . . ."

ROMA   We haven't got a lead . . .

MOSS   Why not?

ROMA   They took 'em . . .

255 MOSS   Hey, they're fuckin' garbage any case. . . . This whole goddamn . . .

LEVENE   ". . . You look around, you say, 'This one has so-and-so, and I have nothing . . .'"

MOSS   *Shit.*

LEVENE   "'*Why?* Why don't I get the opportunities . . . ?'"

260 MOSS   And did they steal the contracts . . . ?

ROMA   Fuck *you* care . . . ?

LEVENE   "I want to tell you something, Harriett . . ."

MOSS   . . . the fuck is *that* supposed to mean . . . ?

LEVENE   Will you shut up, I'm telling you this . . .

[AARONOW *sticks his head out.*]

265 AARONOW   Can we get some coffee . . . ?

---

5. That is, "turn state's evidence," a phrase applied to the actions of an accomplice who supplies prosecutors with evidence in return for a reduction in charges or in sentence.

MOSS How ya doing? [*Pause*]

AARONOW Fine.

MOSS Uh-huh.

AARONOW If anyone's going, I could use some coffee.

270 LEVENE "You *do* get the . . ." [*To* ROMA] Huh? Huh?

MOSS *Fuck* is that supposed to mean?

LEVENE "You *do* get the opportunity. . . . You *get* them. As *I* do, as *anyone* does . . ."

MOSS Ricky? . . . That I don't care they stole the contracts? [*Pause*]

275 LEVENE I got 'em in the kitchen. I'm eating her crumb cake.

MOSS What does that mean?

ROMA It *means*, Dave, you haven't closed a good one in a month, none of my business, you want to push me to answer you. [*Pause*] And so you haven't got a contract to get stolen or so forth.

280 MOSS You have a mean streak in you, Ricky, you know that . . . ?

LEVENE Rick. Let me tell you. Wait, we're in the . . .

MOSS Shut the fuck up. [*Pause*] Ricky. You have a mean streak in you. . . . [*To* LEVENE] And what the fuck are *you* babbling about . . . ? [*To* ROMA] Bring that shit up. Of my volume. You were on a bad one and I brought it 285 up to *you* you'd harbor it. [*Pause*] You'd harbor it a long long while. And you'd be right.

ROMA Who said "Fuck the Machine"?

MOSS "*Fuck the Machine*"? "*Fuck the Machine*"? What is this. *Courtesy* class . . . ? You're *fucked*, Rick—are you fucking *nuts*? You're hot, so you 290 think you're the *ruler* of this place . . . ?! You want to . . .

LEVENE Dave . . .

MOSS . . . Shut up. Decide who should be dealt with how? Is that the thing? I come into the fuckin' office today, I get humiliated by some jagoff[6] cop. I get accused of . . . I get this *shit* thrown in my face by you, you genuine 295 shit, because you're top name on the board . . .

ROMA Is that what I did? Dave? I humiliated you? My *God* . . . I'm *sorry* . . .

MOSS Sittin' on top of the *world*, sittin' on top of the *world*, everything's fucking *peach*fuzz . . .

ROMA Oh, and I don't get a moment to spare for a bust-out *humanitarian* 300 down on his luck lately. Fuck *you*, Dave, you know you got a big *mouth*, and *you* make a close the whole *place* stinks with your *farts* for a week. "How much you just ingested," what a big *man* you are, "Hey, let me buy you a pack of gum. I'll show you how to *chew* it." Your *pal* closes, all that comes out of your mouth is *bile*, how fucked *up* you are . . .

305 MOSS *Who's* my pal . . . ? And what are you, Ricky, huh, what are you, Bishop *Sheean*?[7] Who the fuck are *you*, Mr. Slick . . . ? What are you, friend to the *workingman*? Big deal. Fuck *you*, you got the memory a fuckin' *fly*. I never liked you.

ROMA What is this, your farewell speech?

310 MOSS I'm going home.

6. Jack-off, jerk-off.
7. Archbishop Fulton Sheen (1895–1979), one of the first religious figures to have regular broadcasts on radio (1930–52) and on television (1952–57, 1961–68); he popularized Roman Catholic teachings and offered Catholic interpretations of current events.

ROMA   Your farewell to the troops?

MOSS   I'm not going home. I'm going to Wis*cons*in.

ROMA   Have a good trip.

MOSS   [*simultaneously with "trip"*]   And fuck *you*. Fuck the *lot* of you. Fuck
315   you *all*.

[MOSS *exits. Pause.*]

ROMA   [*to* LEVENE]   You were saying? [*Pause*] Come on. Come on, you got them
in the kitchen, you got the stats spread out, you're in your shirtsleeves, you
can *smell* it. Huh? Snap out of it, you're eating her *crumb* cake. [*Pause*]

LEVENE   I'm eating her *crumb* cake . . .

320   ROMA   How was it . . . ?

LEVENE   From the store.

ROMA   Fuck *her* . . .

LEVENE   "What we have to do is *admit* to ourself that we see that opportunity . . . and *take* it. [*Pause*] And that's it." And we *sit* there. [*Pause*] I got
325   the pen out . . .

ROMA   "Always be closing . . ."

LEVENE   That's what I'm *saying*. The *old* ways. The *old* ways . . . convert the
motherfucker . . . *sell* him . . . *sell* him . . . *make him sign the check*. [*Pause*]
The . . . Bruce, Harriett . . . the kitchen, blah: they got their money in *gov-
330   ernment* bonds. . . . I say *fuck* it, we're going to go the whole route. I plat it
out[8] eight units. Eighty-two grand. I tell them. "This is now. This is that
thing that you've been dreaming of, you're going to find that suitcase on
the train, the guy comes in the door, the bag that's full of money. This is it,
Harriett . . ."

335   ROMA   [*reflectively*]   Harriett . . .

LEVENE   *Bruce* . . . "I don't want to fuck *around* with you. I don't want to go
round this, and *pussyfoot* around the thing, you have to look back on this. I
do, too. I came here to do good for you and me. For *both* of us. Why take
an interim position? *The only arrangement I'll accept* is full investment.
340   Period. The whole eight units. I know that you're saying 'be safe,' I know
what you're saying. I know if I left you to yourselves, you'd say 'come back
tomorrow,' and when I walked out that door, you'd make a cup of *coffee* . . .
you'd sit *down* . . . and you'd think 'let's be safe . . .' and not to disappoint
me you'd go *one* unit or maybe two, because you'd become scared because
345   you'd met possi*bility*. But this won't do, and that's not the subject. . . ."
Listen to this, I actually said this. "That's not the subject of our *evening*
together." Now I handed them the pen. I held it in my hand. I turned the
contract, eight units eighty-two grand. "Now I want you to sign." [*Pause*] I
sat there. Five minutes. Then, I sat there, Ricky, *twenty-two minutes* by the
350   kitchen *clock*. [*Pause*] Twenty-two minutes by the kitchen clock. Not a
word, not a *motion*. What am I thinking? "My arm's getting tired?" *No*. I *did*
it. I *did* it. Like in the *old* days, Ricky. Like I was taught . . . Like, like, like
I *used* to do . . . I did it.

ROMA   Like you taught me . . .

355   LEVENE   Bullshit, you're . . . No. That's raw . . . well, if I *did*, then I'm *glad* I
did. I, *well*. I locked on them. All on them, nothing on me. All my thoughts

8. That is, map out land into individual lots for development.

are on them. I'm holding the last thought that I spoke: "Now is the time."
[*Pause*] They signed, Ricky. It was *great*. It was fucking great. It was like
they wilted all at once. No *gesture* . . . nothing. Like together. They, I swear
360 to God, they both kind of *imperceptibly slumped*. And he reaches and takes
the pen and signs, he passes it to her, she signs. It was so fucking solemn.
I just let it sit. I nod like this. I nod again. I grasp his hands. I shake his
hands. I grasp *her* hands. I nod at her like this. "Bruce . . . Harriett . . ."
I'm beaming at them. I'm nodding like this. I point back in the living room,
365 back to the sideboard. [*Pause*] *I didn't fucking know there was a sideboard*
there!! He goes back, he brings us a drink. Little shot glasses. A pattern in
'em. And we toast. In silence. [*Pause*]

ROMA   That was a great sale, Shelly. [*Pause*]

LEVENE   Ah, fuck. Leads! Leads! Williamson! [WILLIAMSON *sticks his head out*
370 *of the office.*] Send me *out*! Send me *out*!

WILLIAMSON   The leads are coming.

LEVENE   *Get* 'em to me!

WILLIAMSON   I talked to Murray and Mitch an hour ago. They're coming in,
you understand they're a bit *upset* over this morning's . . .

375 LEVENE   Did you tell 'em my sale?

WILLIAMSON   How could I tell 'em your sale? Eh? I don't have a tel . . . I'll
tell 'em your sale when they bring in the leads. Alright? Shelly. Alright? We
had a little . . . You closed a deal. You made a good sale. Fine.

LEVENE   It's better than a good sale. It's a . . .

380 WILLIAMSON   Look: I have a lot of things on my mind, they're coming in,
alright, they're very upset, I'm trying to make some *sense* . . .

LEVENE   All that I'm *telling* you: that one thing you can tell them it's a
remarkable sale.

WILLIAMSON   The only thing remarkable is who you made it to.

385 LEVENE   What does *that* fucking mean?

WILLIAMSON   That if the sale sticks, it will be a miracle.

LEVENE   Why should the sale not stick? Hey, *fuck* you. That's what I'm saying. You have no idea of your job. A man's his job and you're *fucked* at
yours. You hear what I'm saying to you? Your "end of month board . . ." You
390 can't run an office. I don't care. You don't know what it *is*, you don't have
the *sense*, you don't have the *balls*. You ever been on a sit? *Ever*? Has this
cocksucker ever been . . . you ever sit down with a cust . . .

WILLIAMSON   I were you, I'd calm down, Shelly.

LEVENE   *Would* you? *Would* you . . . ? Or you're gonna *what*, fire me?

395 WILLIAMSON   It's not impossible.

LEVENE   On an eighty-thousand dollar *day*? And it ain't even *noon*.

ROMA   You closed 'em today?

LEVENE   Yes. I did. This *morning*. [*To* WILLIAMSON] What I'm *saying* to you:
things can *change*. You *see*? This is where you fuck *up*, because this is some-
400 thing you don't *know*. You can't look down the *road*. And see what's *coming*.
Might be someone *else*, John. It might be someone *new*, eh? Someone *new*.
And you can't look *back*. 'Cause you don't know *history*. You ask them.
When we were at Rio Rancho, who was top man? A month . . . ? Two
months . . . ? Eight months in twelve for three years in a row. You know
405 what that means? You know what that means? Is that *luck*? Is that some,
some, some purloined leads? That's *skill*. That's *talent*, that's, that's . . .

ROMA   . . . *yes* . . .

LEVENE   . . . and you don't *remember*. 'Cause you weren't *around*. That's
cold *calling*. Walk up to the door. I don't even know their *name*. I'm selling
410   something they don't even *want*. You talk about soft sell . . . before we had
a name for it . . . before we called it anything, we did it.

ROMA   That's right, Shel.

LEVENE   And, and, and, I *did* it. And I put a kid through *school*. She . . .
and . . . Cold *calling*, fella. Door to door. But you don't know. You don't
415   know. You never heard of a *streak*. You never heard of "marshaling your sales
force. . . ." What are you, you're a *secretary*, John. Fuck *you*. That's my message to you. Fuck you and kiss my ass. You don't like it, I'll go talk to Jerry
Graff. Period. Fuck you. Put me on the board. And I want three worthwhile leads today and I don't want any bullshit about them and I want 'em
420   close together 'cause I'm going to hit them all today. That's all I have to say
to you.

ROMA   He's right, Williamson.

[WILLIAMSON *goes into a side office. Pause.*]

LEVENE   It's not right. I'm sorry, and I'll tell you who's to blame is Mitch and
Murray.

[ROMA *sees something outside the window.*]

425 ROMA [*sotto*⁹]   Oh, Christ.

LEVENE   The hell with him. We'll go to lunch, the leads won't be up for . . .

ROMA   You're a client. I just sold you five waterfront Glengarry Farms. I rub
my head, throw me the cue "Kenilworth."

LEVENE   What is it?

430 ROMA   Kenilw . . .

[LINGK *enters the office.*]

ROMA [*to* LEVENE]   I own the property, my *mother* owns the property, I put her
into it. I'm going to show you on the plats. You look when you get home A–3
through A–14 and 26 through 30. You take your time and if you still feel.

LEVENE   No, Mr. Roma. I don't need the time, I've made a lot of *investments*
435   in the last . . .

LINGK   I've got to talk to you.

ROMA [*looking up*]   Jim! What are you doing here? Jim Lingk, D. Ray
Morton . . .

LEVENE   Glad to meet you.

440 ROMA   I just put Jim into Black Creek . . . are you acquainted with . . .

LEVENE   No . . . Black *Creek*. Yes. In *Florida?*

ROMA   Yes.

LEVENE   I wanted to *speak* with you about . . .

ROMA   Well, we'll do that this weekend.

445 LEVENE   My *wife* told me to look into . . .

ROMA   *Beautiful.* Beautiful rolling land. I was telling Jim and Jinny, Ray, I
want to tell you something. [*To* LEVENE] You, Ray, you eat in a lot of restaurants. I know you do. . . . [*To* LINGK] Mr. Morton's with American
Express . . . he's . . . [*To* LEVENE] I can tell Jim what you do . . . ?

450 LEVENE   Sure.

_____

9. That is, sotto voce: softly, under the breath (literally, "under the voice"; Italian).

ROMA   Ray is director of all European sales and services for American Ex . . . [*To* LEVENE] But I'm saying you haven't had a *meal* until you've tasted . . . I was at the Lingks' last . . . as a matter of fact, what was that service feature you were talking about . . . ?

455   LEVENE   Which . . .

ROMA   "Home Cooking" . . . what did you call it, you said it . . . it was a tag phrase that you had . . .

LEVENE   Uh . . .

ROMA   Home . . .

460   LEVENE   Home cooking . . .

ROMA   The monthly interview . . . ?

LEVENE   Oh! For the *magazine* . . .

ROMA   Yes. Is this something that I can talk ab . . .

LEVENE   Well, it isn't coming *out* until the February iss . . . *sure*. Sure, go

465   ahead, Ricky.

ROMA   You're sure?

LEVENE   [*nods*]   Go ahead.

ROMA   Well, Ray was eating at one of his company's men's home in France . . . the man's French, isn't he?

470   LEVENE   No, his *wife* is.

ROMA   Ah. Ah, his wife is. Ray: what *time* do you have . . . ?

LEVENE   Twelve-fifteen.

ROMA   Oh! My God . . . I've got to get you on the *plane!*

LEVENE   Didn't I say I was taking the two o' . . .

475   ROMA   No. You said the one. That's why you said we couldn't talk till Kenilworth.

LEVENE   Oh, my God, you're right! I'm on the one. . . . [*Getting up*] Well, let's *scoot* . . .

LINGK   I've got to talk to you . . .

480   ROMA   I've got to get Ray to O'Hare[1] . . . [*To* LEVENE] Come on, let's hustle. . . . [*Over his shoulder*] John! Call American Express in *Pittsburgh* for Mr. Morton, will you, tell them he's on the one o'clock. [*To* LINGK] I'll see you. . . . Christ, I'm sorry you came all the way in. . . . I'm running Ray over to O'Hare. . . . You wait here, I'll . . . no. [*To* LEVENE] I'm meeting your

485   man at the bank. . . . [*To* LINGK] I wish you'd phoned. . . . I'll tell you, wait: are you and Jinny going to be home tonight? [*Rubs forehead.*]

LINGK   I . . .

LEVENE   Rick.

ROMA   What?

490   LEVENE   *Kenilworth* . . . ?

ROMA   I'm sorry . . . ?

LEVENE   *Kenilworth.*

ROMA   Oh, God . . . Oh, God . . . [ROMA *takes* LINGK *aside, sotto.*] Jim, excuse me. . . . Ray, I told you, who he is is *the* senior vice-president American

495   Express. His family owns 32 per. . . . Over the past years I've sold him . . . I can't tell you the dollar amount, but *quite* a lot of land. I promised five *weeks* ago that I'd go to the wife's birthday party in Kenilworth tonight. [*Sighs.*] I *have* to go. You understand. They treat me like a member of the

1. Chicago's main airport.

500 family, so I have to go. It's funny, you know, you get a picture of the Corporation-Type Company Man, all business . . . this man, *no*. We'll go out to his home sometime. Let's see. [*He checks his datebook.*] Tomorrow. No. Tomorrow, I'm in L.A. . . . *Monday* . . . I'll take you to lunch, where would you like to go?

LINGK   My wife . . . [ROMA *rubs his head.*]

505 LEVENE [*standing in the door*]   Rick . . . ?

ROMA   I'm sorry, Jim. I can't talk now. I'll call you tonight . . . I'm sorry. I'm coming, Ray. [*Starts for the door.*]

LINGK   My wife said I have to cancel the deal.

ROMA   It's a common reaction, Jim. I'll tell you what it is, and I know that 510 that's why you married her. One of the reasons is *prudence*. It's a sizable investment. One thinks *twice* . . . it's also something *women* have. It's just a reaction to the size of the investment. *Monday,* if you'd invite me for dinner again . . . [*To* LEVENE] This woman can *cook* . . .

LEVENE [*simultaneously*]   I'm sure she can . . .

515 ROMA [*to* LINGK]   We're going to talk. I'm going to *tell* you something. Because [*Sotto*] there's something about your acreage I want you to know. I can't talk about it now. I really shouldn't. And, in fact, by *law,* I . . . [*Shrugs, resigned.*] The man next to you, he bought his lot at forty-*two*, he phoned to say that he'd *already* had an offer . . . [ROMA *rubs his head.*]

520 LEVENE   Rick . . . ?

ROMA   I'm coming, Ray . . . what a day! I'll call you this evening, Jim. I'm sorry you had to come in . . . Monday, lunch.

LINGK   My wife . . .

LEVENE   Rick, we really have to go.

525 LINGK   My wife . . .

ROMA   Monday.

LINGK   She called the consumer . . . the attorney, I don't know. The attorney gen . . . they said we have three days . . .

ROMA   *Who* did she call?

530 LINGK   I don't know, the attorney gen . . . the . . . some consumer office, umm . . .

ROMA   Why did she do *that,* Jim?

LINGK   I don't know. [*Pause*] They said we have three days. [*Pause*] They said we have three days.

535 ROMA   Three days.

LINGK   To . . . you know. [*Pause*]

ROMA   No, I don't know. *Tell* me.

LINGK   To change our minds.

ROMA   Of *course* you have three days. [*Pause*]

540 LINGK   So we can't talk *Monday.* [*Pause*]

ROMA   Jim, Jim, you saw my book . . . I *can't, you* saw my book . . .

LINGK   But we have to *before* Monday. To get our money ba . . .

ROMA   Three *business* days. They mean three *business* days.

LINGK   Wednesday, Thursday, Friday.

545 ROMA   I don't understand.

LINGK   That's what they are. Three business . . . if I wait till Monday, my time limit runs out.

ROMA   You don't count Saturday.

LINGK   I'm not.

550   ROMA   No, I'm saying you don't include Saturday . . . in your three days. It's not a *business* day.

LINGK   But I'm not *counting* it. [*Pause*] Wednesday. Thursday. Friday. So it would have elapsed.

ROMA   What would have elapsed?

555   LINGK   If we wait till Mon . . .

ROMA   When did you write the check?

LINGK   Yest . . .

ROMA   What was yesterday?

LINGK   Tuesday.

560   ROMA   And when was that check cashed?

LINGK   I don't know.

ROMA   What was the *earliest* it could have been cashed? [*Pause*]

LINGK   I don't know.

ROMA   *Today.* [*Pause*] *Today.* Which, in any case, it was not, as there were a
565   couple of points on the agreement I wanted to go over with you in any case.

LINGK   The check wasn't cashed?

ROMA   I just called downtown, and it's on their desk.

LEVENE   Rick . . .

ROMA   One moment, I'll be right with you. [*To* LINGK] In fact, a . . . *one*
570   point, which I spoke to you of which [*Looks around.*] I can't talk to you about here.

[*Detective puts his head out of the doorway.*]

BAYLEN   Levene!!!

LINGK   I, I . . .

ROMA   Listen to me, the *statute*, it's for your protection. I have no complaints
575   with that, in fact, I was a member of the board when we *drafted* it, so quite
the *opposite*. It *says* that you can change your mind three working days
from the time the deal is closed.

BAYLEN   Levene!

ROMA   Which, wait a second, which is not until the check is cashed.

580   BAYLEN   Levene!!

[AARONOW *comes out of the detective's office.*]

AARONOW   I'm *through,* with *this* fucking meshugaas.[2] No one should talk to
a man that way. How are you *talking* to me that . . . ?

BAYLEN   Levene! [WILLIAMSON *puts his head out of the office.*]

AARONOW   . . . how can you *talk* to me that . . . that . . .

585   LEVENE [*to* ROMA]   Rick, I'm going to flag a cab.

AARONOW   I didn't rob . . .

[WILLIAMSON *sees* LEVENE.]

WILLIAMSON   Shelly: get in the office.

AARONOW   I didn't . . . why should I . . . "Where were you last . . ." Is anybody listening to me . . . ? Where's Moss . . . ? Where . . . ?

590   BAYLEN   Levene? [*To* WILLIAMSON] Is this Lev . . . [BAYLEN *accosts* LINGK.]

LEVENE [*taking* BAYLEN *into the office*]   Ah. Ah. Perhaps I can advise you on
that. . . . [*To* ROMA *and* LINGK, *as he exits*] *Excuse* us, will you . . . ?

---

2. Insanity, nonsense (Yiddish; usually spelled *mishegoss*).

AARONOW [*simultaneous with* LEVENE's *speech above*] . . . Come in here . . . I *work* here, I don't come in here to be *mistreated* . . .

595 WILLIAMSON Go to *lunch,* will you . . .

AARONOW I want to *work* today, that's why I came . . .

WILLIAMSON The leads come in, I'll let . . .

AARONOW . . . that's why I came in. I thought I . . .

WILLIAMSON Just go to lunch.

600 AARONOW I don't *want* to go to lunch.

WILLIAMSON Go to lunch, George.

AARONOW Where does he get off to talk that way to a working man? It's not . . .

WILLIAMSON [*buttonholes him*] Will you take it outside, we have people try-
605 ing to do *business* here . . .

AARONOW That's what, that's what, that's what *I* was trying to do. [*Pause*] That's why I came in . . . I meet *gestapo*[3] tac . . .

WILLIAMSON [*going back into his office*] Excuse me . . .

AARONOW I meet *gestapo* tactics . . . I meet *gestapo* tactics. . . . That's not
610 right. . . . No man has the right to . . . "Call an attorney," that means you're guilt . . . you're under sus . . . "Co . . .," he says, "cooperate" or we'll go downtown. *That's* not . . . as long as I've . . .

WILLIAMSON [*bursting out of his office*] Will you get out of here. Will you get *out* of here. Will you. I'm trying to run an *office* here. Will you go to lunch?
615 Go to lunch. Will you go to lunch?

> [*Retreats into office.*]

ROMA [*to* AARONOW] Will you excuse . . .

AARONOW Where did Moss . . . ? I . . .

ROMA Will you excuse us please?

AARONOW Uh, uh, did he go to the restaurant? [*Pause*] I . . . I . . .

> [*Exits.*]

620 ROMA I'm *very* sorry, Jimmy. I apologize to you.

LINGK It's not me, it's my wife.

ROMA [*pause*] What is?

LINGK I told you.

ROMA Tell me again.

625 LINGK What's going on here?

ROMA Tell me again. Your wife.

LINGK I told you.

ROMA You tell me again.

LINGK She wants her money back.

630 ROMA We're going to speak to her.

LINGK No. She told me "right now."

ROMA We'll speak to her, Jim . . .

LINGK She won't listen.

> [*Detective sticks his head out.*]

BAYLEN *Roma.*

635 LINGK She told me if not, I have to call the State's attorney.

---

3. A secret police using terrorist methods (the shortened form of the Nazis' Geheime Staatspo-
lizei, or Secret State Police).

ROMA No, no. That's just something she "said." We don't have to do that.

LINGK She told me I *have* to.

ROMA No, Jim.

LINGK I *do.* If I don't get my *money* back . . .

[WILLIAMSON *points out* ROMA *to* BAYLEN.]

640 BAYLEN Roma! [*To* ROMA] I'm talking to you . . .

ROMA I've . . . look. [*Generally*] Will someone get this guy off my back.

BAYLEN You have a problem?

ROMA Yes, I have a problem. Yes, I *do,* my fr . . . It's not me that ripped the joint off, I'm doing *business.* I'll be with you in a *while.* You got it . . . ?

645 [*Looks back.* LINGK *is heading for the door.*] Where are you going?

LINGK I'm . . .

ROMA Where are you going . . . ? This is *me.* . . . This is Ricky, Jim. Jim, any-thing you *want,* you *want* it, you *have* it. You understand? This is *me.* Some-thing *upset* you. Sit down, now sit down. You tell me what it is. [*Pause*] Am

650 I going to help you fix it? You're goddamned right I am. Sit down. Tell you something . . . ? *Sometimes* we need someone from *outside.* It's . . . no, sit down. . . . Now *talk* to me.

LINGK I can't negotiate.

ROMA What does that mean?

655 LINGK That . . .

ROMA . . . what, what, *say* it. Say it to me . . .

LINGK I . . .

ROMA What . . . ?

LINGK I . . .

660 ROMA What . . . ? Say the words.

LINGK I don't have the *power.* [*Pause*] I said it.

ROMA What power?

LINGK The power to negotiate.

ROMA To negotiate what? [*Pause*] To negotiate what?

665 LINGK *This.*

ROMA What, "this"? [*Pause*]

LINGK The deal.

ROMA The "deal," *Forget* the deal. *Forget* the deal, you've got something on your mind, Jim, what is it?

670 LINGK [*rising*] I can't talk to you, *you* met my wife, I . . . [*Pause*]

ROMA What? [*Pause*] What? [*Pause*] What, Jim: I tell you what, let's get out of here . . . let's go get a drink.

LINGK She told me not to talk to you.

ROMA Let's . . . no one's going to know, let's go around the *corner* and we'll

675 get a drink.

LINGK She told me I had to get back the check or call the State's att . . .

ROMA *Forget* the deal, Jimmy. [*Pause*] *Forget* the deal . . . you know me. The deal's *dead.* Am I talking about the *deal?* That's *over.* Please. Let's talk about *you.* Come on. [*Pause.* ROMA *rises and starts walking toward the front door.*]

680 Come on. [*Pause*] Come on, Jim. [*Pause*] I want to tell you something. Your life is your own. You have a contract with your wife. You have certain things you do *jointly,* you have a *bond* there . . . and there are *other* things. Those things are yours. You needn't feel *ashamed,* you needn't feel that you're being *untrue* . . . or that she would abandon you if she knew. This is your

685   life. [*Pause*] *Yes.* Now I want to *talk* to you because you're obviously upset
     and that *concerns* me. Now let's go. Right now.
         [LINGK *gets up and they start for the door.*]

     BAYLEN [*sticks his head out of the door*]   Roma . . .

     LINGK   . . . and . . . and . . . [*Pause*]

     ROMA   What?

690   LINGK   And the check is . . .

     ROMA   What did I *tell* you? [*Pause*] What did I say about the three days . . . ?

     BAYLEN   Roma, would you, I'd like to get some lunch . . .

     ROMA   I'm talking with Mr. Lingk. If you please, I'll be back in. [*Checks
     watch.*] I'll be back in a while. . . . I told you, check with Mr. Williamson.

695   BAYLEN   The people downtown said . . .

     ROMA   You call them again. Mr. Williamson . . . !

     WILLIAMSON   Yes.

     ROMA   Mr. Lingk and I are going to . . .

     WILLIAMSON   Yes. Please. Please. [*To* LINGK] The police [*Shrugs.*] can be . . .

700   LINGK   What are the police doing?

     ROMA   It's nothing.

     LINGK   What are the *police* doing here . . . ?

     WILLIAMSON   We had a slight burglary last night.

     ROMA   It was nothing . . . I was assuring Mr. Lingk . . .

705   WILLIAMSON   Mr. Lingk. James Lingk. Your contract went out. Nothing to . . .

     ROMA   John . . .

     WILLIAMSON   Your contract went out to the bank.

     LINGK   You cashed the check?

     WILLIAMSON   We . . .

710   ROMA   . . . Mr. Williamson . . .

     WILLIAMSON   Your check was cashed yesterday afternoon. And we're com-
     pletely insured, as you know, in *any* case. [*Pause*]

     LINGK [*To* ROMA]   You cashed the check?

     ROMA   Not to my knowledge, no . . .

715   WILLIAMSON   I'm sure we can . . .

     LINGK   Oh, Christ . . . [*Starts out the door.*] Don't follow me. . . . Oh, Christ.
     [*Pause. To* ROMA.] I know I've let you down. I'm sorry. For . . . Forgive . . .
     for . . . I don't know any more. [*Pause*] Forgive me. [LINGK *exits. Pause.*]

     ROMA [*To* WILLIAMSON]   You stupid fucking cunt. *You,* Williamson . . . I'm

720   talking to *you,* shithead. . . . You just cost me *six thousand dollars.* [*Pause*]
     Six thousand dollars. And one Cadillac. That's right. What are you going to
     do about it? What are you going to do about it, asshole. You fucking *shit.*
     Where did you learn your *trade.* You stupid fucking *cunt.* You *idiot.* Who-
     ever told you you could work with *men?*

725   BAYLEN   Could I . . .

     ROMA   I'm going to have your *job,* shithead. I'm going *downtown* and talk to
     Mitch and Murray, and I'm going to Lemkin. I don't care *whose* nephew
     you are, who you know, whose dick you're sucking on. You're going *out,* I
     swear to you, you're going . . .

730   BAYLEN   Hey, fella, let's get this done . . .

     ROMA   Anyone in this office lives on their *wits.* . . . [*To* BAYLEN] I'm going to
     be with you in a second. [*To* WILLIAMSON] What you're hired for is to *help*
     us—does that seem clear to you? To *help* us. *Not* to fuck us up . . . to help

men who are going *out* there to try to earn a *living.* You *fairy.* You company
735 man . . . I'll tell you something else. I hope you knocked the joint off, I can
tell our friend here something might help him catch you. [*Starts into the
room.*] You want to learn the first rule you'd know if you ever spent a day in
your life . . . you never open your mouth till you know what the shot is.
[*Pause*] You fucking *child* . . .

          [ROMA *goes to the inner room.*]

740 LEVENE   You *are* a shithead, Williamson . . . [*Pause*]

WILLIAMSON   Mmm.

LEVENE   You can't think on your feet you should keep your mouth closed.
[*Pause*] You hear me? I'm *talking* to you. Do you hear me . . . ?

WILLIAMSON   Yes. [*Pause*] I hear you.

745 LEVENE   You can't learn that in an office. Eh? He's right. You have to learn it
on the streets. You can't *buy* that. You have to *live* it.

WILLIAMSON   Mmm.

LEVENE   *Yes. Mmm. Yes. Precisely. Precisely.* 'Cause your partner *depends* on
it. [*Pause*] I'm *talking* to you, I'm trying to tell you something.

750 WILLIAMSON   You are?

LEVENE   Yes, I am.

WILLIAMSON   What are you trying to tell me?

LEVENE   What Roma's trying to tell you. What I told you yesterday. Why you
don't belong in this business.

755 WILLIAMSON   Why I don't . . .

LEVENE   You listen to me, someday you might say, "Hey . . ." No, fuck that,
you just listen what I'm going to say: your partner *depends* on you. Your
partner . . . a man who's your "partner" *depends* on you . . . you have to go
with him and *for* him . . . or you're shit, you're *shit,* you can't exist alone . . .

760 WILLIAMSON   [*brushing past him*]   Excuse me . . .

LEVENE   . . . excuse you, *nothing,* you be as cold as you want, but you just
fucked a good man out of six thousand dollars and his goddamn bonus
'cause you didn't know the *shot,* if you can do that and you aren't man
enough that it gets you, then I don't know what, if you can't take *something*
765 from that . . . [*Blocking his way*] you're *scum,* you're fucking white-bread.[4]
You be as cold as you want. A *child* would know it, he's right. [*Pause*] You're
going to make something up, be sure it will *help* or keep your mouth
closed. [*Pause*]

WILLIAMSON   Mmm. [LEVENE *lifts up his arm.*]

770 LEVENE   Now I'm done with you. [*Pause*]

WILLIAMSON   How do you know I made it up?

LEVENE   [*pause*]   What?

WILLIAMSON   How do you know I made it up?

LEVENE   What are you talking about?

775 WILLIAMSON   You said, "You don't make something up unless it's sure to
help." [*Pause*] How did you know that I made it up?

LEVENE   What are you talking about?

WILLIAMSON   I told the customer that his contracts had gone to the bank.

LEVENE   Well, hadn't it?

---

4. That is, typical of the bland, white middle class.

780 WILLIAMSON   No. [*Pause*] It hadn't.

LEVENE   Don't *fuck* with me, John, don't *fuck* with me . . . what are you saying?

WILLIAMSON   Well, I'm saying this, Shel: usually I take the contracts to the bank. Last night I didn't. How did you know that? One night in a year I left

785 a contract on my desk. Nobody knew that but *you*. Now how did you know that? [*Pause*] You want to talk to me, you want to talk to someone *else* . . . because this is *my* job. This is my job on the line, and you are going to *talk* to me. Now how did you know that contract was on my desk?

LEVENE   You're so full of shit.

790 WILLIAMSON   You robbed the office.

LEVENE [*laughs*]   Sure! I robbed the office. Sure.

WILLIAMSON   What'd you do with the leads? [*Pause. Points to the detective's room.*] You want to go in there? I tell him what I know, he's going to dig up *something*. . . . You got an alibi last night? You better have one. What did

795 you do with the leads? If you tell me what you did with the leads, we can talk.

LEVENE   I don't know what you are saying.

WILLIAMSON   If you tell me where the leads are, I won't turn you in. If you *don't*, I am going to tell the cop you stole them, Mitch and Murray will see

800 that you go to jail. Believe me they will. Now, what did you do with the leads? I'm walking in that door—you have five seconds to tell me: or you are going to jail.

LEVENE   I . . .

WILLIAMSON   I don't care. You understand? *Where are the leads?* [*Pause*]

805 Alright. [WILLIAMSON *goes to open the office door.*]

LEVENE   I sold them to Jerry Graff.

WILLIAMSON   How much did you get for them? [*Pause*] How much did you get for them?

LEVENE   Five thousand. I kept half.

810 WILLIAMSON   Who kept the other half? [*Pause*]

LEVENE   Do I have to tell you? [*Pause.* WILLIAMSON *starts to open the door.*] Moss.

WILLIAMSON   *That* was easy, *wasn't* it? [*Pause*]

LEVENE   It was his idea.

815 WILLIAMSON   *Was* it?

LEVENE   I . . . I'm sure he got more than the five, actually.

WILLIAMSON   Uh-huh?

LEVENE   He told me my share was twenty-five.

WILLIAMSON   Mmm.

820 LEVENE   Okay: I . . . look: I'm going to make it worth your while. I am. I turned this thing around. I closed the *old* stuff, I can do it again. *I'm* the one's going to close 'em. *I* am! *I* am! 'Cause I turned this thing a . . . I can do *that*, I can do *anyth* . . . last night. I'm going to tell you, I was ready to Do the Dutch.[5] Moss gets me, "Do this, we'll get well. . . ." Why not. Big

825 fuckin' deal. I'm halfway hoping to get caught. To put me out of my . . . [*Pause*] But it *taught* me something. What it taught me, that you've got to

5. Commit suicide.

get *out* there. Big deal. So I wasn't cut out to be a thief. I was cut out to be a salesman. And now I'm back, and I got my *balls* back . . . and, you know, John, you have the *advantage* on me now. Whatever it takes to make it
830 right, we'll make it right. We're going to make it right.

WILLIAMSON I want to tell you something, Shelly. You have a big mouth. [*Pause*]

LEVENE What?

WILLIAMSON You've got a big mouth, and now I'm going to show you an even bigger one. [*Starts toward the detective's door.*]

835 LEVENE Where are you going, John? . . . you can't do that, you don't want to do that . . . hold, hold on . . . hold on . . . wait . . . wait . . . wait . . . [*Pulls money out of his pockets.*] Wait . . . uh, look . . . [*Starts splitting money.*] Look, twelve, twenty, two, twen . . . twenty-five hundred, it's . . . take it. [*Pause*] Take it all. . . . [*Pause*] Take it!

840 WILLIAMSON No, I don't think so, Shel.

LEVENE I . . .

WILLIAMSON No, I think I don't want your money. I think you fucked up my office. And I think you're going away.

LEVENE I . . . what? Are you, are you, that's why . . . ? Are you nuts? I'm . . .
845 I'm going to *close* for you, I'm going to . . . [*Thrusting money at him.*] Here, here, I'm going to *make* this office . . . I'm going to be back there Number One. . . . Hey, hey, hey! This is only the beginning. . . . List . . . list . . . listen. Listen. Just one moment. List . . . here's what . . . here's what we're going to do. Twenty percent. I'm going to give you twenty percent of my sales. . . .
850 [*Pause*] Twenty percent. [*Pause*] For as long as I am with the firm. [*Pause*] Fifty percent. [*Pause*] You're going to be my partner. [*Pause*] Fifty percent. Of all my sales.

WILLIAMSON What sales?

LEVENE What sales . . . ? I just *closed* eighty-two *grand*. . . . Are you fuckin' . . .
855 I'm *back* . . . I'm *back*, this is only the beginning.

WILLIAMSON Only the beginning . . .

LEVENE Abso . . .

WILLIAMSON Where have you been, Shelly? Bruce and Harriett Nyborg. Do you want to see the *memos* . . . ? They're nuts . . . they used to call in every
860 week. When I was with Webb. And we were selling Arizona . . . they're nuts . . . did you see how they were *living*? How can you delude yours . . .

LEVENE I've got the check . . .

WILLIAMSON Forget it. Frame it. It's worthless. [*Pause*]

LEVENE The check's no good?

865 WILLIAMSON You stick around I'll pull the memo for you. [*Starts for the door.*] I'm busy now . . .

LEVENE Their check's no good? They're nuts . . . ?

WILLIAMSON Call up the bank. *I* called them.

LEVENE You did?

870 WILLIAMSON I called them when we had the lead . . . four months ago. [*Pause*] The people are insane. They just like talking to salesmen. [WIL-LIAMSON *starts for door.*]

LEVENE Don't.

WILLIAMSON I'm sorry.

LEVENE *Why?*

875 WILLIAMSON   Because I don't like you.

LEVENE   John: John: . . . my *daughter* . . .

WILLIAMSON   Fuck you.

[ROMA *comes out of the detective's door.* WILLIAMSON *goes in.*]

ROMA [*To* BAYLEN] Asshole . . . [*To* LEVENE] Guy couldn't find his fuckin' couch the *living room* . . . Ah, Christ . . . what a day, what a day . . . I

880 haven't even had a cup of *coffee.* . . . Jagoff John opens his mouth he blows my Cadillac. . . . [*Sighs.*] I swear . . . it's not a world of men . . . it's not a world of men, Machine . . . it's a world of clock-watchers, bureaucrats, officeholders . . . what it is, it's a fucked-up world . . . there's no adventure *to* it. [*Pause*] Dying breed. Yes it is. [*Pause*] We are the members of a dying

885 breed. That's . . . that's . . . that's why we have to stick together. Shel: I want to talk to you. I've wanted to talk to you for some time. For a long time, actually. I said, "The Machine, there's a man I would work with. There's a man. . . ." You know? I never said a thing. I should have, don't know why I didn't. And that shit you were slinging on my guy today was *so*

890 good . . . it . . . it was, and, excuse me, 'cause it isn't even my place to say it. It was admirable . . . it was the old stuff. Hey, I've been on a hot streak, so *what?* There's things that I could learn from you. You eat today?

LEVENE   Me.

ROMA   Yeah.

895 LEVENE   Mm.

ROMA   Well, you want to swing by the Chinks,[6] watch me eat, we'll talk?

LEVENE   I think I'd better stay here for a while.

[BAYLEN *sticks his head out of the room.*]

BAYLEN   Mr. *Levene* . . . ?

ROMA   You're done, come down and let's . . .

900 BAYLEN   Would you come in here, please?

ROMA   And let's put this together. Okay? Shel? Say okay. [*Pause*]

LEVENE [*softly, to himself*]   Huh.

BAYLEN   Mr. Levene, I think we have to talk.

ROMA   I'm going to the Chinks. You're done, come down, we're going to

905 smoke a cigarette.

LEVENE   I . . .

BAYLEN [*comes over*]   . . . Get in the room.

ROMA   Hey, hey, hey, *easy,* friend. That's the "Machine." That is Shelly "The Machine" Lev . . .

910 BAYLEN   Get in the goddamn room. [BAYLEN *starts manhandling* SHELLY *into the room.*]

LEVENE   Ricky, I . . .

ROMA   Okay, okay, I'll be at the resta . . .

LEVENE   Ricky . . .

BAYLEN   "Ricky" can't help you, pal.

915 LEVENE   . . . I only want to . . .

BAYLEN   Yeah. What do you want? You want to *what?*

[*He pushes* LEVENE *into the room, closes the door behind him. Pause.*]

6. That is, the Chinese restaurant (*Chinks* is a derogatory term for the Chinese).

ROMA   Williamson: listen to me: when the *leads* come in . . . listen to me: when the *leads* come in I want my top two off the list. For *me*. My usual two. Anything you give *Levene* . . .

920 WILLIAMSON   . . . I wouldn't worry about it.

ROMA   Well I'm *going* to worry about it, and so are you, so shut up and *listen*. [*Pause*] I GET HIS ACTION. My stuff is *mine*, whatever *he* gets for himself, I'm talking half. You put me in with him.

> [AARONOW *enters.*]

AARONOW   Did they . . . ?

925 ROMA   You understand?

AARONOW   Did they catch . . . ?

ROMA   Do you understand? My stuff is mine, his stuff is ours. I'm taking half of his commissions—now, *you* work it out.

WILLIAMSON   Mmm.

930 AARONOW   Did they find the guy who broke into the office yet?

ROMA   No. *I* don't know. [*Pause*]

AARONOW   Did the leads come in yet?

ROMA   No.

AARONOW [*settling into a desk chair*]   Oh, God, I hate this job.

935 ROMA [*simultaneous with "job," exiting the office*]   I'll be at the restaurant.

AUGUST WILSON

1945–2005

OF the many African American dramatists who have written for the theater
since LORRAINE HANSBERRY's acclaimed *A
RAISIN IN THE SUN* (1959), none has enjoyed
more popular and critical success than
August Wilson. *Ma Rainey's Black Bottom*
(1984), the first of Wilson's plays to reach
Broadway, won the New York Drama Critics' Circle Award for best new play; *FENCES*
(1985) received numerous honors, including the Tony Award for Best Play and the
Pulitzer Prize; and *The Piano Lesson* (1987)
won Wilson another Drama Critics' Circle
Award and a second Pulitzer. Subsequent
plays, which continued Wilson's stated project of dramatizing African American history throughout the twentieth century one
decade at a time, have also received widespread acclaim. Few dramatists, white or
black, have matched Wilson's historical and
sociological ambition or so minutely examined the dynamics, memories, and traumas
that constitute the twentieth-century African American community.

Wilson was born Frederick August Kittel on April 27, 1945, in the Hill District, a
largely African American neighborhood of
Pittsburgh, where all but one of his major
plays are set. The fourth of six children, he
was the son of a black mother and a white
German baker who was absent throughout
his childhood. The family had little money,
relying mainly on welfare and on Daisy

Wilson Kittel's earnings as a janitor. When
his father, whose name he bore, died in
1965, the future writer began calling himself August Wilson, thereby choosing to
identify with the African American side of
his family. By that point in his life, Wilson
had had ample opportunity to learn what
such an identity meant in the civil rights–
era United States. In 1959 his mother and
her second husband, a black man named
David Bedford who worked in the city
Sewer Department and would provide a
model for Troy in *Fences*, had moved the
family to a predominantly white neighborhood. Wilson's teenage years took him from
one high school to another until, the target
of racist remarks and ostracism, he dropped
out of school for good in tenth grade when
a teacher accused him of plagiarism, insisting that his paper on Napoleon was so good
that one of his sisters must have written it.

Unwilling to tell his parents what he
had done, Wilson spent much of his free
time in a public library; there, in the "Negro
Section," he discovered the works of such
African American writers as Langston
Hughes, Ralph Ellison, and James Baldwin. Wilson later recalled in an interview
that he derived comfort from the fact that
black people wrote books, adding that he
"used to dream about being part of the Harlem Renaissance." After serving one year
in the U.S. Army and spending two years

working odd jobs, he took major steps toward realizing his ambition in 1965 when he moved from his mother's house into a rooming house back in the Hill District, bought himself a typewriter, and changed his name. The move immersed Wilson in a culturally and socially vibrant African American community, and from the musicians, artists, ex-convicts, and workers he encountered he absorbed the personalities, behaviors, and stories that would later appear in his plays. Wilson also learned the rich and varied vernacular of this black community, marked by cadences and idioms that mixed northern and southern, urban and rural.

Wilson's early years as a writer coincided with a shift in politics and culture as the forms of social and artistic protest that characterized the late 1950s and early 1960s were replaced by the more radicalized politics of black separatism, cultural nationalism, and the black power movement. By 1965 the playwright Amiri Baraka, who had begun his career as the Beat poet LeRoi Jones, had written such incendiary plays as *Dutchman* (1964) and *The Slave* (1964) and was calling for a "Black Revolutionary Theater." Wilson was deeply influenced by black cultural nationalism and its project of celebrating African American culture and developing institutions where this culture could be nurtured and shared within the black community. In 1968 he co-founded the Black Horizons Theater in Pittsburgh to raise black consciousness and help politicize the community. The new theater put on the plays of Baraka and other playwrights of the Black Arts movement, and Wilson tried his hand at playwriting for the first time.

These attempts at one-act dramas were not successful; indeed, not until the mid-1970s would Wilson devote himself seriously to the theater. A 1976 work based on the life and death of 1920s blues musician Blind Lemon Jefferson, *The Homecoming*, became Wilson's first produced play, and other playscripts followed; they included a 1977 musical satire about the white nineteenth-century rustler Black Bart and *Jitney!* (1979), a play set in a gypsy cab station in his native Pittsburgh. In 1978 Wilson moved to St. Paul, Minnesota, where he became associated with the Playwright's

Center in Minneapolis; among other jobs, he wrote short educational plays for a theater troupe affiliated with the Science Museum of Minnesota. The breakthrough for this relatively unknown playwright came when he developed early material he had written on Ma Rainey into *Ma Rainey's Black Bottom* and submitted the completed play to the Eugene O'Neill Theater Center's Playwright's Conference in Connecticut. The play was accepted for staged reading, and Wilson was introduced to Lloyd Richards, who would serve as his mentor and director in subsequent projects. After a process of workshop revisions, *Ma Rainey* premiered at the Yale Repertory Theatre in April 1984 and moved to Broadway in October of the same year.

As *Ma Rainey* was winning praise among the theatergoing public, Wilson's *Fences* and an early version of *Joe Turner's Come and Gone* had already been presented in staged readings and workshops. By that time, Wilson was fully embarked on the project that he would complete twenty years later: tracing the history of twentieth-century black America through a cycle of ten plays set in each decade of the century. The result is a remarkable panorama of modern African American history. *Ma Rainey's Black Bottom*, the only play in the cycle not set in Pittsburgh, takes place in a Chicago recording studio in 1927. Most of the action of *Fences* takes place in Troy Maxson's backyard in 1957, while *Joe Turner's Come and Gone* (1986) is set in a boardinghouse in 1911. *The Piano Lesson* (1987), which deals with the conflict between brother and sister over a 135-year-old piano that has been central to their family's history, takes place in 1936. *Two Trains Running* (1990) is set in a Pittsburgh restaurant in 1969; *Seven Guitars* (1996) deals with the causes and repercussions of a young guitar player's death in 1948. A revised version of *Jitney* (which premiered in 1996) takes place in 1977, and *King Hedley II* (1999) explores the breakdown of the black family and community in the 1980s. *Gem of the Ocean* (2003), which is set in 1904, is dominated by the figure of Aunt Ester, a 287-year-old community elder and seer who arrived on the first shipload of American slaves in 1619. *Radio Golf*, which premiered six months before Wilson's death from cancer in 2005, centers on a plan to redevelop Pittsburgh's Hill District proposed in the 1990s.

With its broad historical ambitions, Wilson's history of a people invites comparison to the cycle plays of the medieval mystery guilds presented at York, Wakefield, and elsewhere. Wilson's plays similarly stand firmly on their own yet acquire wider meanings when viewed or read in relation to each other. The historical backdrop, or metanarrative, of these plays is certainly epic in scope. Like Hansberry, Wilson takes on the legacy of the Great Migration—the movement of black Americans who left the poverty and economic limitations of the Mississippi Delta and other parts of the South for Chicago, Cleveland, New York, and other northern cities in the largest demographic shift in U.S. history. Though this migration spanned the years between 1900 and 1970 (the year that black Americans started returning to the South), its peak came during World War I and the 1920s. In his brief introduction to *Fences*, Wilson describes how the "descendants of African slaves," pursuing the same hopes and dreams as European immigrants, found a very different reception in the cities of the North and how hard they worked to make their lives, now spent "in shallow, ramshackle houses made of sticks and tar paper," into something free and dignified. Plays such as *Joe Turner's Come and Gone*, *Fences*, and *The Piano Lesson* examine the impact of the Great Migration on the generations that undertook it and those that followed. In doing so, they also look back to a past whose traumas and histories constitute the horizons of urban African American racial memory: the life of southern sharecroppers during Reconstruction, when the hopes of emancipation confronted the realities of socialized racism; the uncountable brutalities of slavery; the hardships of the Middle Passage; and, at the farthest reach, Africa and its forms of community, culture, and identity. As Wilson himself has commented, "When your back is pressed to the wall you go to the deepest part of yourself, and there's a response—it's your great ancestors talking. It's blood memory."

Their identities fragmented to varying degrees, Wilson's characters carry this history with them in the form of conflicting needs, drives, and behaviors. Such conflicts particularly affect Wilson's male characters. Negotiating their way through a society uncomfortable with their presence, they move, often compulsively, from place to place, relationship to relationship, seeking a haven in the world and some balm for their restless psyches. They fall in and out of jobs and end up so regularly in jail (or the "workhouse") that being arrested becomes a kind of initiation ritual. All of Wilson's characters, male and female, are haunted by the experiences of their parents and ancestors, and they seek, in sometimes self-defeating and contradictory ways, to escape or redeem this inheritance. In *The Piano Lesson*, Berniece and Boy Willie struggle for control of the family piano, each with a different understanding of what its painful history means to the present: Boy Willie wants to sell the piano and put the money toward purchasing the plantation where their great-grandparents had worked as slaves, while Berniece is equally determined to preserve the representations of family members that their great-grandfather had carved into the piano's legs after the relatives had been sold away. The siblings' struggle with the past comes to a head when Boy Willie fights the ghost of Sutter, the slave owner who controlled their ancestors' fate, in the play's final scene.

Wilson's dual interests in the present and the historical memories that inform it have driven certain stylistic and formal choices in the composition of his plays. Though he was influenced by Baraka's writing, Wilson chose not to employ the confrontational aesthetic of the Black Revolutionary Theater movement in his own drama. Nor has he pursued the antitheatrical styles and techniques through which some other contemporary black playwrights (such as Adrienne Kennedy, Ntozake Shange, and SUZAN-LORI PARKS) subvert the representational conventions that have traditionally governed the staging of African Americans. Wilson's drama draws on realism as an aesthetic; stylistically, his plays resemble those of EUGENE O'NEILL, ARTHUR MILLER, and others in the American mainstream. Yet at the same time that Wilson's plays display an almost ethnographic attention to the lives of his characters, detailing their material world and social codes with a range and specificity that recall the nineteenth-century realist novel, their realism is neither simple nor seamless. Wilson's settings—a backyard, a drawing room, a cab station—are based in the everyday, but they are invested with memory, history, and myth. For one thing, the dramatic present of Wilson's plays is expanded through the act of storytelling as characters narrate individual and family history, legends, and dreams. Several scholars have noted the similarities between Wilson's raconteurs and the West African griot, or storyteller, who preserved and transmitted the oral tradition of families and communities. In their access to traumatic memory and visionary revelation, these characters—such as Herald Loomis in *Joe Turner's Come and Gone,* with his trancelike vision of bones rising from the ocean waves and re-forming as bodies on the shore—introduce myth and the supernatural to Wilson's plays. In this respect, they are related to other figures created by Wilson whose presence unsettles the boundaries of realism—characters such as Aunt Ester, the centuries-old seer who has a presence, onstage and off, in several of his plays; Hedley in *Seven Guitars,* who is obsessed by visions about his dead father and the belief that he will father the Messiah; and Troy Maxson's brother Gabe in *Fences,* who, having suffered a brain injury in World War II, carries a trumpet and believes that he is the archangel Gabriel. Traversed by characters such as these, history in August Wilson's twentieth-century chronicle becomes actual and mythic at the same time.

There is certainly something mythic and outsized about the protagonist of *Fences,* Wilson's most widely known play. The name "Troy" calls to mind the embattled city of Homer's *Iliad,* while "Maxson" (Max-son) evokes the idea of patrilineal succession so central to heroic sagas. Like Babe Ruth, Josh Gibson, and the other baseball legends in whose company he places himself, Troy is larger than life; as Wilson notes, "[t]ogether with his blackness, his largeness informs his sensibilities and the choices he has made in his life." In a play profoundly concerned with space, ownership, and boundaries, Troy's presence dominates the stage even when

he is absent from a particular scene; as a glance at the character list indicates, the other characters are defined primarily in terms of their relationship to him. Boasting that he "wrestled with Death" when he was seriously ill in the hospital, Troy displays the same indomitability in his job as a garbage collector, confronting his boss to ask why only whites drive the trucks while blacks lift the garbage. His passions in life are women and baseball, and it is not always clear which comes first. Troy learned baseball while in prison for killing a man, and upon his release he played in the Negro League, the circuit of teams for black ballplayers; none played in the major leagues until Jackie Robinson joined the Brooklyn Dodgers in 1947. Negro League teams, which often drew crowds as large as those that watched

James Earl Jones as Troy in the world premiere of *Fences* at the Yale Repertory Theatre, 1985.

their white counterparts, featured some of the best players in the history of the sport—including Josh Gibson, the so-called black Babe Ruth, who played for the powerful Homestead Grays, based in a steel mill town adjacent to Pittsburgh. As the archetypal American pastime, baseball serves as a powerful symbol in *Fences* of the exclusion of black Americans from the country's social and cultural institutions. Unfortunately for Troy, by the time baseball's color line had been breached and black players gradually began playing for major league teams, he was too old to be one of them. At age fifty-three, he carries his baseball past with him as a bitter reminder of racial oppression and as a metaphor of his battles against an antagonistic life: for him, "Death ain't nothing but a fastball on the outside corner."

Troy's personality was forged in his relationship with his father, an embittered and abusive sharecropper who towered over his children and drove Troy away with a particularly ugly explosion of violence. From his father Troy learns responsibility, but it is a responsibility born of hardness, not love. When applied to his two sons, it is accompanied by a rigid sense of authority and a demand that they live their lives with the pressure-forged self-denial he has been forced to accept in his. In different ways, both Lyons (who aspires to be a musician) and Cory (a high school football star) resist this narrow definition of life's possibilities. Cory's desire to win a scholarship to play football in college reflects the changing place of black athletes in American sports: in 1957, the year the play opens, the running back Jim Brown was declared the National Football League's Most Valuable Player and the Milwaukee Braves won the World Series, defeating the New York Yankees behind the hitting of Hank Aaron (who would eventually break Babe Ruth's revered lifetime home run record). As Troy's wife Rose explains to him, "The world's changing around you and you can't even see it." But Troy is the product of a different world. Unable to perceive an alternative to the father-son struggle that he himself was forced to endure and scarred by the deprivations he faced, Troy becomes the father he ran away from, standing in the way of a younger generation's new opportunities and driving away those he loves. Resenting the

self-sacrifice, suffering, and disappointment that he has nonetheless worked into a code of living, he betrays his younger son, wife, and brother.

With its psychologically embattled patriarch, urban backyard setting, and other details of plot and action, *Fences* bears more than casual resemblance to Arthur Miller's *DEATH OF A SALESMAN* (1949). Like the earlier play, *Fences* revolves around questions of masculinity: what the social performance of maleness consists of, how it is transmitted (or not transmitted) from fathers to sons, how it relates to social models of femaleness. Their economic and social disempowerment has made the task of fulfilling traditional male roles particularly fraught for African American men. Like Biff Loman, Cory must negotiate the boundaries of his own identity and thereby become a man, in the shadow of his father's frustrated and defensive masculinity: "It would wrap around you and lay there until you couldn't tell which one was you any more." He is not alone in struggling against Troy. Rose, one of only two female characters in the play, must confront her failure to meet all of her husband's needs and affirm, in the process, her own need for selfhood. Critics have been divided over the status of the women Wilson created, who inhabit a dramatic world whose orientation is largely determined by male preoccupations. To what extent is Rose's character defined in terms of and limited by the support—psychological, domestic, sexual—that she provides her husband? To what extent, conversely, does she succeed in articulating an autonomous set of experiences, desires, and identity boundaries?

Against these psychological and sociological backdrops, the play's title resonates in complex ways. Designed both to keep people in and to keep them out, the backyard fence represents the many ways in which society and the human mind establish boundaries around psyches, social units, races, genders. The play's principal characters think about fences differently. Rose, who builds fences in order to "keep people in," desires a space where her family can remain protected and whole. Troy, on the other hand, constructs fences against those aspects of life that threaten his view of the world and himself. In so doing, he establishes barriers between himself and those who love him, denying himself the possibilities of growth, intimacy, and pride in the son who has tried so hard to live up to his expectations. Alone in the play's penultimate scene, all Troy can do is swing his bat, hoping to clear the fences—hit a home run—in one last act of solitary heroism.   S.G.

Fences

When the sins of our fathers visit us
We do not have to play host.
We can banish them with forgiveness
As God, in His Largeness and Laws.

—AUGUST WILSON

CHARACTERS

TROY MAXSON
JIM BONO, Troy's friend
ROSE, Troy's wife
LYONS, Troy's oldest son by previous marriage
GABRIEL, Troy's brother
CORY, Troy and Rose's son
RAYNELL, Troy's daughter

Setting

The setting is the yard which fronts the only entrance to the MAXSON household, an ancient two-story brick house set back off a small alley in a big-city neighborhood. The entrance to the house is gained by two or three steps leading to a wooden porch badly in need of paint.

A relatively recent addition to the house and running its full width, the porch lacks congruence. It is a sturdy porch with a flat roof. One or two chairs of dubious value sit at one end where the kitchen window opens onto the porch. An old-fashioned icebox stands silent guard at the opposite end.

The yard is a small dirt yard, partially fenced, except for the last scene, with a wooden sawhorse, a pile of lumber, and other fence-building equipment set off to the side. Opposite is a tree from which hangs a ball made of rags. A baseball bat leans against the tree. Two oil drums serve as garbage receptacles and sit near the house at right to complete the setting.

The Play

Near the turn of the century, the destitute of Europe sprang on the city with tenacious claws and an honest and solid dream. The city devoured them. They swelled its belly until it burst into a thousand furnaces and sewing machines, a thousand butcher shops and bakers' ovens, a thousand churches and hospitals and funeral parlors and moneylenders. The city grew. It nourished itself and offered each man a partnership limited only by his talent, his guile, and his willingness and capacity for hard work. For the immigrants of Europe, a dream dared and won true.

The descendants of African slaves were offered no such welcome or participation. They came from places called the Carolinas and the Virginias, Georgia, Alabama, Mississippi, and Tennessee. They came strong, eager, searching. The city rejected them and they fled and settled along the riverbanks and under bridges in shallow, ramshackle houses made of sticks and tar paper. They collected rags and wood. They sold the use of their muscles and their bodies. They cleaned houses and washed clothes, they shined shoes, and in quiet desperation and vengeful pride, they stole, and lived in pursuit of their own dream. That they could breathe free, finally, and stand to meet life with the force of dignity and whatever eloquence the heart could call upon.

By 1957, the hard-won victories of the European immigrants had solidified the industrial might of America. War had been confronted and won with new energies that used loyalty and patriotism as its fuel. Life was rich, full, and flourishing. The Milwaukee Braves won the World Series, and the hot winds of change that would make the sixties a turbulent, racing, dangerous, and provocative decade had not yet begun to blow full.

1.1

It is 1957. TROY *and* BONO *enter the yard, engaged in conversation.* TROY *is fifty-three years old, a large man with thick, heavy hands; it is this largeness that he strives to fill out and make an accommodation with. Together with his blackness, his largeness informs his sensibilities and the choices he has made in his life.*

Of the two men, BONO *is obviously the follower. His commitment to their friendship of thirty-odd years is rooted in his admiration of* TROY's *honesty, capacity for hard work, and his strength, which* BONO *seeks to emulate.*

It is Friday night, payday, and the one night of the week the two men engage in a ritual of talk and drink. TROY *is usually the most talkative and at times he can be crude and almost vulgar, though he is capable of rising to profound heights of expression. The men carry lunch buckets and wear or carry burlap aprons and are dressed in clothes suitable to their jobs as garbage collectors.*

BONO   Troy, you ought to stop that lying!

TROY   I ain't lying! The nigger had a watermelon this big. [*He indicates with his hands.*] Talking about . . . "What watermelon, Mr. Rand?" I liked to fell out![1] "What watermelon, Mr. Rand?" . . . And it sitting there big as life.

5   BONO   What did Mr. Rand say?

TROY   Ain't said nothing. Figure if the nigger too dumb to know he carrying a watermelon, he wasn't gonna get much sense out of him. Trying to hide that great big old watermelon under his coat. Afraid to let the white man see him carry it home.

10   BONO   I'm like you . . . I ain't got no time for them kind of people.

TROY   Now what he look like getting mad cause he see the man from the union talking to Mr. Rand?

BONO   He come to me talking about . . . "Maxson gonna get us fired." I told him to get away from me with that. He walked away from me calling you a

15   troublemaker. What Mr. Rand say?

TROY   Ain't said nothing. He told me to go down the Commissioner's office next Friday. They called me down there to see them.

BONO   Well, as long as you got your complaint filed, they can't fire you. That's what one of them white fellows tell me.

20   TROY   I ain't worried about them firing me. They gonna fire me cause I asked a question? That's all I did. I went to Mr. Rand and asked him, "Why? Why

1. I nearly fell out of my tree; that is, I was amazed.

you got the white mens driving and the colored lifting?" Told him, "What's the matter, don't I count? You think only white fellows got sense enough to drive a truck. That ain't no paper job! Hell, anybody can drive a truck. How
25   come you got all whites driving and the colored lifting? He told me, "Take it to the union." Well, hell, that's what I done! Now they wanna come up with this pack of lies.

BONO   I told Brownie if the man come and ask him any questions . . . just tell the truth! It ain't nothing but something they done trumped up on you
30   cause you filed a complaint on them.

TROY   Brownie don't understand nothing. All I want them to do is change the job description. Give everybody a chance to drive the truck. Brownie can't see that. He ain't got that much sense.

BONO   How you figure he be making out with that gal be up at Taylors' all the
35   time . . . that Alberta gal?

TROY   Same as you and me. Getting just as much as we is. Which is to say nothing.

BONO   It is, huh? I figure you doing a little better than me . . . and I ain't saying what I'm doing.

40 TROY   Aw, nigger, look here . . . I know you. If you had got anywhere near that gal, twenty minutes later you be looking to tell somebody. And the first one you gonna tell . . . that you gonna want to brag to . . . is gonna be me.

BONO   I ain't saying that. I see where you be eyeing her.

TROY   I eye all the women. I don't miss nothing. Don't never let nobody tell
45   you Troy Maxson don't eye the women.

BONO   You been doing more than eyeing her. You done bought her a drink or two.

TROY   Hell yeah, I bought her a drink! What that mean? I bought you one, too. What that mean cause I buy her a drink? I'm just being polite.

50 BONO   It's alright to buy her one drink. That's what you call being polite. But when you wanna be buying two or three . . . that's what you call eyeing her.

TROY   Look here, as long as you known me . . . you ever known me to chase after women?

BONO   Hell yeah! Long as I done known you. You forgetting I knew you when.

55 TROY   Naw, I'm talking about since I been married to Rose?

BONO   Oh, not since you been married to Rose. Now, that's the truth, there. I can say that.

TROY   Alright then! Case closed.

BONO   I see you be walking up around Alberta's house. You supposed to be at
60   Taylors' and you be walking up around there.

TROY   What you watching where I'm walking for? I ain't watching after you.

BONO   I seen you walking around there more than once.

TROY   Hell, you liable to see me walking anywhere! That don't mean nothing cause you see me walking around there.

65 BONO   Where she come from anyway? She just kinda showed up one day.

TROY   Tallahassee. You can look at her and tell she one of them Florida gals. They got some big healthy women down there. Grow them right up out the ground. Got a little bit of Indian in her. Most of them niggers down in Florida got some Indian in them.

70 BONO   I don't know about that Indian part. But she damn sure big and healthy. Woman wear some big stockings. Got them great big old legs and hips as wide as the Mississippi River.

TROY   Legs don't mean nothing. You don't do nothing but push them out of
the way. But them hips cushion the ride!

75 BONO   Troy, you ain't got no sense.

TROY   It's the truth! Like you riding on Goodyears![2]

[ROSE *enters from the house. She is ten years younger than* TROY, *her
devotion to him stems from her recognition of the possibilities of her life
without him: a succession of abusive men and their babies, a life of party-
ing and running the streets, the Church, or aloneness with its attendant
pain and frustration. She recognizes* TROY's *spirit as a fine and illuminating one and she either ignores or forgives his faults, only some of which
she recognizes. Though she doesn't drink, her presence is an integral part
of the Friday night rituals. She alternates between the porch and the
kitchen, where supper preparations are under way.*]

ROSE   What you all out here getting into?

TROY   What you worried about what we getting into for? This is men talk,
woman.

80 ROSE   What I care what you all talking about? Bono, you gonna stay for
supper?

BONO   No, I thank you, Rose. But Lucille say she cooking up a pot of
pigfeet.

TROY   Pigfeet! Hell, I'm going home with you! Might even stay the night if
85 you got some pigfeet. You got something in there to top them pigfeet, Rose?

ROSE   I'm cooking up some chicken. I got some chicken and collard greens.

TROY   Well, go on back in the house and let me and Bono finish what we was
talking about. This is men talk. I got some talk for you later. You know what
kind of talk I mean. You go on and powder it up.

90 ROSE   Troy Maxson, don't you start that now!

TROY   [*puts his arm around her*]   Aw, woman . . . come here. Look here,
Bono . . . when I met this woman . . . I got out that place, say, "Hitch up
my pony, saddle up my mare . . . there's a woman out there for me somewhere. I looked here. Looked there. Saw Rose and latched on to her." I
95 latched on to her and told her—I'm gonna tell you the truth—I told her,
"Baby, I don't wanna marry, I just wanna be your man." Rose told me . . .
tell him what you told me, Rose.

ROSE   I told him if he wasn't the marrying kind, then move out the way so
the marrying kind could find me.

100 TROY   That's what she told me. "Nigger, you in my way. You blocking the
view! Move out the way so I can find me a husband." I thought it over two
or three days. Come back—

ROSE   Ain't no two or three days nothing. You was back the same night.

TROY   Come back, told her . . . "Okay, baby . . . but I'm gonna buy me a
105 banty[3] rooster and put him out there in the backyard . . . and when he see
a stranger come, he'll flap his wings and crow . . ." Look here, Bono, I
could watch the front door by myself . . . it was that back door I was worried about.

ROSE   Troy, you ought not talk like that. Troy ain't doing nothing but telling
110 a lie.

TROY   Only thing is . . . when we first got married . . . forget the rooster . . .
we ain't had no yard!

2. That is, on automobile tires.
3. That is, bantam, or small (a term applied to several breeds of domestic fowl).

BONO   I hear you tell it. Me and Lucille was staying down there on Logan
Street. Had two rooms with the outhouse in the back. I ain't mind the outhouse none. But when that goddamn wind blow through there in the winter . . . that's what I'm talking about! To this day I wonder why in the hell I
ever stayed down there for six long years. But see, I didn't know I could do
no better. I thought only white folks had inside toilets and things.

ROSE   There's a lot of people don't know they can do no better than they doing
now. That's just something you got to learn. A lot of folks still shop at Bella's.

TROY   Ain't nothing wrong with shopping at Bella's. She got fresh food.

ROSE   I ain't said nothing about if she got fresh food. I'm talking about what
she charge. She charge ten cents more than the A&P.[4]

TROY   The A&P ain't never done nothing for me. I spends my money where
I'm treated right. I go down to Bella, say, "I need a loaf of bread, I'll pay you
Friday." She give it to me. What sense that make when I got money to go
and spend it somewhere else and ignore the person who done right by me?
That ain't in the Bible.

ROSE   We ain't talking about what's in the Bible. What sense it make to shop
there when she overcharge?

TROY   You shop where you want to. I'll do my shopping where the people
been good to me.

ROSE   Well, I don't think it's right for her to overcharge. That's all I was saying.

BONO   Look here . . . I got to get on. Lucille going be raising all kind of hell.

TROY   Where you going, nigger? We ain't finished this pint. Come here, finish this pint.

BONO   Well, hell, I am . . . if you ever turn the bottle loose.

TROY   [hands him the bottle]   The only thing I say about the A&P is I'm glad
Cory got that job down there. Help him take care of his school clothes and
things. Gabe done moved out and things getting tight around here. He got
that job. . . . He can start to look out for himself.

ROSE   Cory done went and got recruited by a college football team.

TROY   I told that boy about that football stuff. The white man ain't gonna let
him get nowhere with that football. I told him when he first come to me
with it. Now you come telling me he done went and got more tied up in it.
He ought to go and get recruited in how to fix cars or something where he
can make a living.

ROSE   He ain't talking about making no living playing football. It's just something the boys in school do. They gonna send a recruiter by to talk to you.
He'll tell you he ain't talking about making no living playing football. It's a
honor to be recruited.

TROY   It ain't gonna get him nowhere. Bono'll tell you that.

BONO   If he be like you in the sports . . . he's gonna be alright. Ain't but two
men ever played baseball as good as you. That's Babe Ruth and Josh Gibson.[5] Them's the only two men ever hit more home runs than you.

---

4. The dominant U.S. supermarket chain in the 1950s.

5. Respectively, the most famous white and black hitters of the 20th century. Ruth (1895–1948), who played with the N.Y. Yankees for most of his career (1914–35), held the major-league record for home runs in a season (60) for 34 years and the lifetime home run record (714) for 39; Gibson (1911–1947; catcher, 1930–46), who played mainly for the Home-stead Grays (near Pittsburgh) in the Negro League, was known as "the black Babe Ruth"; it is estimated that in his career he hit more than 800 home runs, 75 of them in a single season.

TROY   What it ever get me? Ain't got a pot to piss in or a window to throw it
out of.

ROSE   Times have changed since you was playing baseball, Troy. That was
before the war. Times have changed a lot since then.

160   TROY   How in hell they done changed?

ROSE   They got lots of colored boys playing ball now.[6] Baseball and football.

BONO   You right about that, Rose. Times have changed, Troy. You just come
along too early.

TROY   There ought not never have been no time called too early! Now you

165   take that fellow . . . what's that fellow they had playing right field for the
Yankees back then? You know who I'm talking about, Bono. Used to play
right field for the Yankees.

ROSE   Selkirk?[7]

TROY   Selkirk! That's it! Man batting .269, understand? .269. What kind of

170   sense that make? I was hitting .432 with thirty-seven home runs! Man batting .269 and playing right field for the Yankees! I saw Josh Gibson's daughter yesterday. She walking around with raggedy shoes on her feet. Now I
bet you Selkirk's daughter ain't walking around with raggedy shoes on her
feet! I bet you that!

175   ROSE   They got a lot of colored baseball players now. Jackie Robinson was
the first. Folks had to wait for Jackie Robinson.

TROY   I done seen a hundred niggers play baseball better than Jackie Robinson. Hell, I know some teams Jackie Robinson couldn't even make! What
you talking about Jackie Robinson. Jackie Robinson wasn't nobody.[8] I'm

180   talking about if you could play ball then they ought to have let you play.
Don't care what color you were. Come telling me I come along too early. If
you could play . . . then they ought to have let you play.

[TROY *takes a long drink from the bottle.*]

ROSE   You gonna drink yourself to death. You don't need to be drinking like
that.

185   TROY   Death ain't nothing. I done seen him. Done wrassled with him. You
can't tell me nothing about death. Death ain't nothing but a fastball on the
outside corner. And you know what I'll do to that! Lookee here, Bono . . .
am I lying? You get one of them fastballs, about waist high, over the outside
corner of the plate where you can get the meat of the bat on it . . . and

190   good god! You can kiss it goodbye. Now, am I lying?

BONO   Naw, you telling the truth there. I seen you do it.

TROY   If I'm lying . . . that 450 feet worth of lying![9] [*Pause*] That's all death is
to me. A fastball on the outside corner.

---

6. Until 1947, when Jackie Robinson (1919–
1972) began playing for the Brooklyn Dodgers, no "colored" athletes had been allowed to
play in baseball's minor or major leagues since
the late 19th century. Initially, professional
football had a few black players (1920–34),
but none subsequently played for the National
Football League until 1946, when four were
signed.
7. George Selkirk (1908–1987), who became
the Yankees' right fielder in 1935 after Ruth

retired; he batted .269 in 1940 (his average
was above .300 five times in the 1930s).
8. Robinson was in fact Rookie of the Year, a
six-time All-Star, and the 1949 National
League MVP, outstanding as both a fielder
and a hitter with a career batting average
of .311.
9. A ball hit this distance would be an impressive home run in any ballpark (at its deepest,
no fence is more than 435 feet from home
plate).

ROSE   I don't know why you want to get on talking about death.

195 TROY   Ain't nothing wrong with talking about death. That's part of life. Everybody gonna die. You gonna die, I'm gonna die. Bono's gonna die. Hell, we all gonna die.

ROSE   But you ain't got to talk about it. I don't like to talk about it.

TROY   You the one brought it up. Me and Bono was talking about baseball . . . you tell me I'm gonna drink myself to death. Ain't that right, Bono? You know I don't drink this but one night out of the week. That's Friday night. I'm gonna drink just enough to where I can handle it. Then I cuts it loose. I leave it alone. So don't you worry about me drinking myself to death. 'Cause I ain't worried about Death. I done seen him. I done wrestled

205   with him.

Look here, Bono . . . I looked up one day and Death was marching straight at me. Like Soldiers on Parade! The Army of Death was marching straight at me. The middle of July, 1941. It got real cold just like it be winter. It seem like Death himself reached out and touched me on the shoul-

210   der. He touch me just like I touch you. I got cold as ice and Death standing there grinning at me.

ROSE   Troy, why don't you hush that talk.

TROY   I say . . . What you want, Mr. Death? You be wanting me? You done brought your army to be getting me? I looked him dead in the eye. I wasn't

215   fearing nothing. I was ready to tangle. Just like I'm ready to tangle now. The Bible say be ever vigilant.[1] That's why I don't get but so drunk. I got to keep watch.

ROSE   Troy was right down there in Mercy Hospital. You remember he had pneumonia? Laying there with a fever talking plumb out of his head.

220 TROY   Death standing there staring at me . . . carrying that sickle in his hand. Finally he say, "You want bound over for another year?" See, just like that . . . "You want bound over[2] for another year?" I told him, "Bound over hell! Let's settle this now!"

It seem like he kinda fell back when I said that, and all the cold went out

225   of me. I reached down and grabbed that sickle and threw it just as far as I could throw it . . . and me and him commenced to wrestling.

We wrestled for three days and three nights. I can't say where I found the strength from. Every time it seemed like he was gonna get the best of me, I'd reach way down deep inside myself and find the strength to do

230   him one better.

ROSE   Every time Troy tell that story he find different ways to tell it. Different things to make up about it.

TROY   I ain't making up nothing. I'm telling you the facts of what happened. I wrestled with Death for three days and three nights and I'm standing here

235   to tell you about it.

[Pause.]

Alright. At the end of the third night we done weakened each other to where we can't hardly move. Death stood up, throwed on his robe . . . had him a white robe with a hood on it. He throwed on that robe and went off

---

1. "Be sober, be vigilant; because your adversary the devil, as a roaring lion, walketh about, seeking whom he may devour" (1 Peter 5.8).

2. That is, agreeing to one more year of servitude, as if he were a sharecropper.

to look for his sickle. Say, "I'll be back." Just like that. "I'll be back." I told
240   him, say, "Yeah, but . . . you gonna have to find me!" I wasn't no fool. I
wasn't going looking for him. Death ain't nothing to play with. And I know
he's gonna get me. I know I got to join his army . . . his camp followers. But
as long as I keep my strength and see him coming . . . as long as I keep up
my vigilance . . . he's gonna have to fight to get me. I ain't going easy.

245 BONO   Well, look here, since you got to keep up your vigilance . . . let me
have the bottle.

TROY   Aw hell, I shouldn't have told you that part. I should have left out that
part.

ROSE   Troy be talking that stuff and half the time don't even know what he
250   be talking about.

TROY   Bono know me better than that.

BONO   That's right. I know you. I know you got some Uncle Remus[3] in your
blood. You got more stories than the devil got sinners.

TROY   Aw hell, I done seen him too! Done talked with the devil.

255 ROSE   Troy, don't nobody wanna be hearing all that stuff.

> [LYONS *enters the yard from the street. Thirty-four years old,* TROY'S *son by
> a previous marriage, he sports a neatly trimmed goatee, sport coat, white
> shirt, tieless and buttoned at the collar. Though he fancies himself a musi-
> cian, he is more caught up in the rituals and "idea" of being a musician
> than in the actual practice of the music. He has come to borrow money
> from* TROY, *and while he knows he will be successful, he is uncertain as to
> what extent his lifestyle will be held up to scrutiny and ridicule.*]

LYONS   Hey, Pop.

TROY   What you come "Hey, Popping" me for?

LYONS   How you doing, Rose?

> [*He kisses her.*]

  Mr. Bono. How you doing?

260 BONO   Hey, Lyons . . . how you been?

TROY   He must have been doing alright. I ain't seen him around here last
week.

ROSE   Troy, leave your boy alone. He come by to see you and you wanna start
all that nonsense.

265 TROY   I ain't bothering Lyons. [*Offers him the bottle.*] Here . . . get you a
drink. We got an understanding. I know why he come by to see me and he
know I know.

LYONS   Come on, Pop . . . I just stopped by to say hi . . . see how you was
doing.

270 TROY   You ain't stopped by yesterday.

ROSE   You gonna stay for supper, Lyons? I got some chicken cooking in the
oven.

LYONS   No, Rose . . . thanks. I was just in the neighborhood and thought I'd
stop by for a minute.

275 TROY   You was in the neighborhood alright, nigger. You telling the truth
there. You was in the neighborhood cause it's my payday.

LYONS   Well, hell, since you mentioned it . . . let me have ten dollars.

---

3. The fictional narrator of popular black folktales compiled by the white humorist Joel Chandler
Harris, beginning with *Uncle Remus: His Songs and Sayings* (1881).

TROY   I'll be damned! I'll die and go to hell and play blackjack with the devil
        before I give you ten dollars.

280 BONO   That's what I wanna know about . . . that devil you done seen.

LYONS   What . . . Pop done seen the devil? You too much, Pops.

TROY   Yeah, I done seen him. Talked to him too!

ROSE   You ain't seen no devil. I done told you that man ain't had nothing to do
        with the devil. Anything you can't understand, you want to call it the devil.

285 TROY   Look here, Bono . . . I went down to see Hertzberger about some fur-
        niture. Got three rooms for two-ninety-eight. That what it say on the radio.
        "Three rooms . . . two-ninety-eight." Even made up a little song about it.
        Go down there . . . man tell me I can't get no credit. I'm working every day
        and can't get no credit. What to do? I got an empty house with some rag-
290   gedy furniture in it. Cory ain't got no bed. He's sleeping on a pile of rags
        on the floor. Working every day and can't get no credit. Come back
        here—Rose'll tell you—madder than hell. Sit down . . . try to figure what
        I'm gonna do. Come a knock on the door. Ain't been living here but three
        days. Who know I'm here? Open the door . . . devil standing there bigger
295   than life. White fellow . . . got on good clothes and everything. Standing
        there with a clipboard in his hand. I ain't had to say nothing. First words
        come out of his mouth was . . . "I understand you need some furniture and
        can't get no credit." I liked to fell over. He say "I'll give you all the credit you
        want, but you got to pay the interest on it." I told him, "Give me three
300   rooms worth and charge whatever you want." Next day a truck pulled up
        here and two men unloaded them three rooms. Man what drove the truck
        give me a book. Say send ten dollars, first of every month to the address in
        the book and everything will be alright. Say if I miss a payment the devil
        was coming back and it'll be hell to pay. That was fifteen years ago. To this
305   day . . . the first of the month I send my ten dollars, Rose'll tell you.

ROSE   Troy lying.

TROY   I ain't never seen that man since. Now you tell me who else that could
        have been but the devil? I ain't sold my soul or nothing like that, you
        understand. Naw, I wouldn't have truck with the devil about nothing like
310   that. I got my furniture and pays my ten dollars the first of the month just
        like clockwork.

BONO   How long you say you been paying this ten dollars a month?

TROY   Fifteen years!

BONO   Hell, ain't you finished paying for it yet? How much the man done
315   charged you?

TROY   Aw hell, I done paid for it. I done paid for it ten times over! The fact is
        I'm scared to stop paying it.

ROSE   Troy lying. We got that furniture from Mr. Glickman. He ain't paying
        no ten dollars a month to nobody.

320 TROY   Aw hell, woman. Bono know I ain't that big a fool.

LYONS   I was just getting ready to say . . . I know where there's a bridge for
        sale.[4]

---

4. To sell the Brooklyn Bridge proverbially
demonstrates both the seller's powers of persuasion and the buyer's gullibility (a couple of
turn-of-the-century confidence men did manage to pull off this swindle).

TROY   Look here, I'll tell you this . . . it don't matter to me if he was the devil.
It don't matter if the devil give credit. Somebody has got to give it.

325 ROSE   It ought to matter. You going around talking about having truck with
the devil . . . God's the one you gonna have to answer to. He's the one
gonna be at the Judgment.

LYONS   Yeah, well, look here, Pop . . . let me have that ten dollars. I'll give it
back to you. Bonnie got a job working at the hospital.

330 TROY   What I tell you, Bono? The only time I see this nigger is when he
wants something. That's the only time I see him.

LYONS   Come on, Pop, Mr. Bono don't want to hear all that. Let me have the
ten dollars. I told you Bonnie working.

TROY   What that mean to me? "Bonnie working." I don't care if she working.

335 Go ask her for the ten dollars if she working. Talking about "Bonnie working." Why ain't you working?

LYONS   Aw, Pop, you know I can't find no decent job. Where am I gonna get
a job at? You know I can't get no job.

TROY   I told you I know some people down there. I can get you on the rub-

340 bish if you want to work. I told you that the last time you came by here
asking me for something.

LYONS   Naw, Pop . . . thanks. That ain't for me. I don't wanna be carrying
nobody's rubbish. I don't wanna be punching nobody's time clock.

TROY   What's the matter, you too good to carry people's rubbish? Where you

345 think that ten dollars you talking about come from? I'm just supposed to
haul people's rubbish and give my money to you cause you too lazy to work.
You too lazy to work and wanna know why you ain't got what I got.

ROSE   What hospital Bonnie working at? Mercy?

LYONS   She's down at Passavant working in the laundry.

350 TROY   I ain't got nothing as it is. I give you that ten dollars and I got to eat
beans the rest of the week. Naw . . . you ain't getting no ten dollars here.

LYONS   You ain't got to be eating no beans. I don't know why you wanna say
that.

TROY   I ain't got no extra money. Gabe done moved over to Miss Pearl's pay-

355 ing her the rent and things done got tight around here. I can't afford to be
giving you every payday.

LYONS   I ain't asked you to give me nothing. I asked you to loan me ten dollars. I know you got ten dollars.

TROY   Yeah, I got it. You know why I got it? Cause I don't throw my money

360 away out there in the streets. You living the fast life . . . wanna be a musician . . . running around in them clubs and things . . . then, you learn to
take care of yourself. You ain't gonna find me going and asking nobody for
nothing. I done spent too many years without.

LYONS   You and me is two different people, Pop.

365 TROY   I done learned my mistake and learned to do what's right by it. You still
trying to get something for nothing. Life don't owe you nothing. You owe it
to yourself. Ask Bono. He'll tell you I'm right.

LYONS   You got your way of dealing with the world . . . I got mine. The only
thing that matters to me is the music.

370 TROY   Yeah, I can see that! It don't matter how you gonna eat . . . where your
next dollar is coming from. You telling the truth there.

LYONS   I know I got to eat. But I got to live too. I need something that gonna help me to get out of the bed in the morning. Make me feel like I belong in the world. I don't bother nobody. I just stay with my music cause that's the only way I can find to live in the world. Otherwise there ain't no telling what I might do. Now I don't come criticizing you and how you live. I just come by to ask you for ten dollars. I don't wanna hear all that about how I live.

TROY   Boy, your mama did a hell of a job raising you.

LYONS   You can't change me, Pop. I'm thirty-four years old. If you wanted to change me, you should have been there when I was growing up. I come by to see you . . . ask for ten dollars and you want to talk about how I was raised. You don't know nothing about how I was raised.

ROSE   Let the boy have ten dollars, Troy.

TROY [*to* LYONS]   What the hell you looking at me for? I ain't got no ten dollars. You know what I do with my money. [*To* ROSE] Give him ten dollars if you want him to have it.

ROSE   I will. Just as soon as you turn it loose.

TROY [*handing* ROSE *the money*]   There it is. Seventy-six dollars and forty-two cents. You see this, Bono? Now, I ain't gonna get but six of that back.

ROSE   You ought to stop telling that lie. Here, Lyons.

[*She hands him the money.*]

LYONS   Thanks, Rose. Look . . . I got to run . . . I'll see you later.

TROY   Wait a minute. You gonna say, "Thanks, Rose," and ain't gonna look to see where she got that ten dollars from? See how they do me, Bono?

LYONS   I know she got it from you, Pop. Thanks. I'll give it back to you.

TROY   There he go telling another lie. Time I see that ten dollars . . . he'll be owing me thirty more.

LYONS   See you, Mr. Bono.

BONO   Take care, Lyons!

LYONS   Thanks, Pop. I'll see you again.

[LYONS *exits the yard.*]

TROY   I don't know why he don't go and get him a decent job and take care of that woman he got.

BONO   He'll be alright, Troy. The boy is still young.

TROY   The *boy* is thirty-four years old.

ROSE   Let's not get off into all that.

BONO   Look here . . . I got to be going. I got to be getting on. Lucille gonna be waiting.

TROY [*puts his arm around* ROSE]   See this woman, Bono? I love this woman. I love this woman so much it hurts. I love her so much . . . I done run out of ways of loving her. So I got to go back to basics. Don't you come by my house Monday morning talking about time to go to work . . .'cause I'm still gonna be stroking!

ROSE   Troy! Stop it now!

BONO   I ain't paying him no mind, Rose. That ain't nothing but gin-talk. Go on, Troy. I'll see you Monday.

TROY   Don't you come by my house, nigger! I done told you what I'm gonna be doing.

[*The lights go down to black.*]

1.2

The lights come up on ROSE *hanging up clothes. She hums and sings softly to herself. It is the following morning.*

ROSE [*sings*]

Jesus, be a fence all around me every day

Jesus, I want you to protect me as I travel on my way.

Jesus, be a fence all around me every day.[5]

[TROY *enters from the house.*]

ROSE [*continued*]

Jesus, I want you to protect me

As I travel on my way.

5 [*To* TROY] 'Morning. You ready for breakfast? I can fix it soon as I finish hanging up these clothes?

TROY   I got the coffee on. That'll be alright. I'll just drink some of that this morning.

10 ROSE   That 651 hit yesterday.[6] That's the second time this month. Miss Pearl hit for a dollar . . . seem like those that need the least always get lucky. Poor folks can't get nothing.

TROY   Them numbers don't know nobody. I don't know why you fool with them. You and Lyons both.

15 ROSE   It's something to do.

TROY   You ain't doing nothing but throwing your money away.

ROSE   Troy, you know I don't play foolishly. I just play a nickel here and a nickel there.

TROY   That's two nickels you done thrown away.

20 ROSE   Now I hit sometimes . . . that makes up for it. It always comes in handy when I do hit. I don't hear you complaining then.

TROY   I ain't complaining now. I just say it's foolish. Trying to guess out of six hundred ways which way the number gonna come. If I had all the money niggers, these Negroes, throw away on numbers for one week—just one

25 week—I'd be a rich man.

ROSE   Well, you wishing and calling it foolish ain't gonna stop folks from playing numbers. That's one thing for sure. Besides . . . some good things come from playing numbers. Look where Pope done bought him that restaurant off of numbers.

30 TROY   I can't stand niggers like that. Man ain't had two dimes to rub together. He walking around with his shoes all run over bumming money for cigarettes. Alright. Got lucky there and hit the numbers . . .

ROSE   Troy, I know all about it.

TROY   Had good sense, I'll say that for him. He ain't throwed his money away.

35 I seen niggers hit the numbers and go through two thousand dollars in four days. Man brought him that restaurant down there . . . fixed it up real nice . . . and then didn't want nobody to come in it! A Negro go in there

5. Traditional gospel song.
6. A reference to playing the numbers, a form
of illegal gambling that was popular before
the advent of legal state-run lotteries.

and can't get no kind of service. I seen a white fellow come in there and order a bowl of stew. Pope picked all the meat out the pot for him. Man ain't
40 had nothing but a bowl of meat! Negro come behind him and ain't got nothing but the potatoes and carrots. Talking about what numbers do for people, you picked a wrong example. Ain't done nothing but make a worser fool out of him than he was before.

ROSE   Troy, you ought to stop worrying about what happened at work
45 yesterday.

TROY   I ain't worried. Just told me to be down there at the Commissioner's office on Friday. Everybody think they gonna fire me. I ain't worried about them firing me. You ain't got to worry about that.

[*Pause.*]

Where's Cory? Cory in the house? [*Calls.*] Cory?

50 ROSE   He gone out.

TROY   Out, huh? He gone out cause he know I want him to help me with this fence. I know how he is. That boy scared of work.

[GABRIEL *enters. He comes halfway down the alley and, hearing* TROY's *voice, stops.*]

TROY [*continues*]   He ain't done a lick of work in his life.

ROSE   He had to go to football practice. Coach wanted them to get in a little
55 extra practice before the season start.

TROY   I got his practice . . . running out of here before he get his chores done.

ROSE   Troy, what is wrong with you this morning? Don't nothing set right with you. Go on back in there and go to bed . . . get up on the other side.

60 TROY   Why something got to be wrong with me? I ain't said nothing wrong with me.

ROSE   You got something to say about everything. First it's the numbers . . . then it's the way the man runs his restaurant . . . then you done got on Cory. What's it gonna be next? Take a look up there and see if the weather
65 suits you . . . or is it gonna be how you gonna put up the fence with the clothes hanging in the yard.

TROY   You hit the nail on the head then.

ROSE   I know you like I know the back of my hand. Go on in there and get you some coffee . . . see if that straighten you up. Cause you ain't right this
70 morning.

[TROY *starts into the house and sees* GABRIEL. GABRIEL *starts singing.* TROY's *brother, he is seven years younger than* TROY. *Injured in World War II, he has a metal plate in his head. He carries an old trumpet tied around his waist and believes with every fiber of his being that he is the Archangel Gabriel. He carries a chipped basket[7] with an assortment of discarded fruits and vegetables he has picked up in the strip district and which he attempts to sell.*]

GABRIEL [*singing*]

Yes, ma'am, I got plums
You ask me how I sell them
Oh ten cents apiece

---

7. That is, a chip basket, made from roughly joined strips of split wood.

Three for a quarter
75   Come and buy now
'Cause I'm here today
And tomorrow I'll be gone

[GABRIEL *enters.*]

Hey, Rose!
ROSE   How you doing, Gabe?
80   GABRIEL   There's Troy . . . Hey, Troy!
TROY   Hey, Gabe.

[*Exit into kitchen.*]

ROSE [*to* GABRIEL]   What you got there?
GABRIEL   You know what I got, Rose. I got fruits and vegetables.
ROSE [*looking in basket*]   Where's all these plums you talking about?
85   GABRIEL   I ain't got no plums today, Rose. I was just singing that. Have some
tomorrow. Put me in a big order for plums. Have enough plums tomorrow
for St. Peter and everybody.

[TROY *reenters from kitchen, crosses to steps.*]

[*To* ROSE] Troy's mad at me.
TROY   I ain't mad at you. What I got to be mad at you about? You ain't done
90   nothing to me.
GABRIEL   I just moved over to Miss Pearl's to keep out from in your way. I
ain't mean no harm by it.
TROY   Who said anything about that? I ain't said anything about that.
GABRIEL   You ain't mad at me, is you?
95   TROY   Naw . . . I ain't mad at you, Gabe. If I was mad at you I'd tell you
about it.
GABRIEL   Got me two rooms. In the basement. Got my own door too. Wanna
see my key? [*He holds up a key.*] That's my own key! Ain't nobody else got a
key like that. That's my key! My two rooms!
100   TROY   Well, that's good, Gabe. You got your own key . . . that's good.
ROSE   You hungry, Gabe? I was just fixing to cook Troy his breakfast.
GABRIEL   I'll take some biscuits. You got some biscuits? Did you know when
I was in heaven . . . every morning me and St. Peter would sit down by the
gate and eat some big fat biscuits? Oh, yeah! We had us a good time. We'd
105   sit there and eat us them biscuits and then St. Peter would go off to sleep
and tell me to wake him up when it's time to open the gates for the
judgment.
ROSE   Well, come on . . . I'll make up a batch of biscuits.

[ROSE *exits into the house.*]

GABRIEL   Troy . . . St. Peter got your name in the book. I seen it. It say . . .
110   Troy Maxson. I say . . . I know him! He got the same name like what I got.
That's my brother!
TROY   How many times you gonna tell me that, Gabe?
GABRIEL   Ain't got my name in the book. Don't have to have my name. I done
died and went to heaven. He got your name though. One morning St. Peter
115   was looking at his book . . . marking it up for the judgment . . . and he let
me see your name. Got it in there under M. Got Rose's name . . . I ain't seen
it like I seen yours . . . but I know it's in there. He got a great big book. Got

everybody's name what was ever been born. That's what he told me. But I seen your name. Seen it with my own eyes.

120 TROY   Go on in the house there. Rose going to fix you something to eat.

GABRIEL   Oh, I ain't hungry. I done had breakfast with Aunt Jemimah.[8] She come by and cooked me up a whole mess of flapjacks. Remember how we used to eat them flapjacks?

TROY   Go on in the house and get you something to eat now.

125 GABRIEL   I got to go sell my plums. I done sold some tomatoes. Got me two quarters. Wanna see? [*He shows* TROY *his quarters.*] I'm gonna save them and buy me a new horn so St. Peter can hear me when it's time to open the gates.

[GABRIEL *stops suddenly. Listens.*]

Hear that? That's the hellhounds. I got to chase them out of here. Go on
130   get out of here! Get out!

[GABRIEL *exits singing.*]

Better get ready for the judgment
Better get ready for the judgment
My Lord is coming down

[ROSE *enters from the house.*]

TROY   He gone off somewhere.

GABRIEL   [*offstage*]

135   Better get ready for the judgment
Better get ready for the judgment morning
Better get ready for the judgment
My God is coming down

ROSE   He ain't eating right. Miss Pearl say she can't get him to eat nothing.

140 TROY   What you want me to do about it, Rose? I done did everything I can for the man. I can't make him get well. Man got half his head blown away . . . what you expect?

ROSE   Seem like something ought to be done to help him.

TROY   Man don't bother nobody. He just mixed up from that metal plate he
145   got in his head. Ain't no sense for him to go back into the hospital.

ROSE   Least he be eating right. They can help him take care of himself.

TROY   Don't nobody wanna be locked up, Rose. What you wanna lock him up for? Man go over there and fight the war . . . messin' around with them Japs, get half his head blown off . . . and they give him a lousy three thou
150   sand dollars. And I had to swoop down on that.

ROSE   Is you fixing to go into that again?

TROY   That's the only way I got a roof over my head . . . cause of that metal plate.

ROSE   Ain't no sense you blaming yourself for nothing. Gabe wasn't in no
155   condition to manage that money. You done what was right by him. Can't nobody say you ain't done what was right by him. Look how long you took

---

8. Stereotypical "mammy" from a minstrel song; in 1893 the name and image were trademarked by a pancake mix company, which for decades hired women to portray the character.

care of him . . . till he wanted to have his own place and moved over there with Miss Pearl.

TROY   That ain't what I'm saying, woman! I'm just stating the facts. If my
160   brother didn't have that metal plate in his head . . . I wouldn't have a pot to piss in or a window to throw it out of. And I'm fifty-three years old. Now see if you can understand that!

[TROY *gets up from the porch and starts to exit the yard.*]

ROSE   Where you going off to? You been running out of here every Saturday for weeks. I thought you was gonna work on this fence?

165   TROY   I'm gonna walk down to Taylors'. Listen to the ball game. I'll be back in a bit. I'll work on it when I get back.

[*He exits the yard. The lights go to black.*]

1.3

The lights come up on the yard. It is four hours later. ROSE *is taking down the clothes from the line.* CORY *enters carrying his football equipment.*

ROSE   Your daddy like to had a fit with you running out of here this morning without doing your chores.

CORY   I told you I had to go to practice.

ROSE   He say you were supposed to help him with this fence.

5   CORY   He been saying that the last four or five Saturdays, and then he don't never do nothing, but go down to Taylors'. Did you tell him about the recruiter?

ROSE   Yeah, I told him.

CORY   What he say?

10   ROSE   He ain't said nothing too much. You get in there and get started on your chores before he gets back. Go on and scrub down them steps before he gets back here hollering and carrying on.

CORY   I'm hungry. What you got to eat, Mama?

ROSE   Go on and get started on your chores. I got some meat loaf in there.
15   Go on and make you a sandwich . . . and don't leave no mess in there.

[CORY *exits into the house,* ROSE *continues to take down the clothes.* TROY *enters the yard and sneaks up and grabs her from behind.*]

Troy! Go on, now. You liked to scared me to death. What was the score of the game? Lucille had me on the phone and I couldn't keep up with it.

TROY   What I care about the game? Come here, woman. [*He tries to kiss her.*]

ROSE   I thought you went down Taylors' to listen to the game. Go on, Troy!
20   You supposed to be putting up this fence.

TROY [*attempting to kiss her again.*]   I'll put it up when I finish with what is at hand.

ROSE   Go on, Troy. I ain't studying you.[9]

TROY [*chasing after her*]   I'm studying you . . . fixing to do my homework!

25   ROSE   Troy, you better leave me alone.

TROY   Where's Cory? That boy brought his butt home yet?

ROSE   He's in the house doing his chores.

TROY [*calling*]   Cory! Get your butt out here, boy!

---

9. That is, paying any attention to you.

[ROSE *exits into the house with the laundry.* TROY *goes over to the pile of wood, picks up a board, and starts sawing.* CORY *enters from the house.*]

TROY   You just now coming in here from leaving this morning?

30 CORY   Yeah, I had to go to football practice.

TROY   Yeah, what?

CORY   Yessir.

TROY   I ain't but two seconds off you noway. The garbage sitting in there overflowing . . . you ain't done none of your chores . . . and you come in
35 here talking about "Yeah."

CORY   I was just getting ready to do my chores now, Pop . . .

TROY   Your first chore is to help me with this fence on Saturday. Everything else come after that. Now get that saw and cut them boards.

[CORY *takes the saw and begins cutting the boards.* TROY *continues working. There is a long pause.*]

CORY   Hey, Pop . . . why don't you buy a TV?

40 TROY   What I want with a TV? What I want one of them for?

CORY   Everybody got one. Earl, Ba Bra . . . Jesse!

TROY   I ain't asked you who had one. I say what I want with one?

CORY   So you can watch it. They got lots of things on TV. Baseball games and everything. We could watch the World Series.

45 TROY   Yeah . . . and how much this TV cost?

CORY   I don't know. They got them on sale for around two hundred dollars.[1]

TROY   Two hundred dollars, huh?

CORY   That ain't that much, Pop.

TROY   Naw, it's just two hundred dollars. See that roof you got over your
50 head at night? Let me tell you something about that roof. It's been over ten years since that roof was last tarred. See now . . . the snow come this winter and sit up there on that roof like it is . . . and it's gonna seep inside. It's just gonna be a little bit . . . ain't gonna hardly notice it. Then the next thing you know, it's gonna be leaking all over the house. Then the wood rot
55 from all that water and you gonna need a whole new roof. Now, how much you think it cost to get that roof tarred?

CORY   I don't know.

TROY   Two hundred and sixty-four dollars . . . cash money. While you thinking about a TV, I got to be thinking about the roof . . . and whatever else go
60 wrong around here. Now if you had two hundred dollars, what would you do . . . fix the roof or buy a TV?

CORY   I'd buy a TV. Then when the roof started to leak . . . when it needed fixing . . . I'd fix it.

TROY   Where you gonna get the money from? You done spent it for a TV. You
65 gonna sit up and watch the water run all over your brand new TV.

CORY   Aw, Pop. You got money. I know you do.

TROY   Where I got it at, huh?

CORY   You got it in the bank.

TROY   You wanna see my bankbook? You wanna see that seventy-three dollars
70 and twenty-two cents I got sitting up in there?

CORY   You ain't got to pay for it all at one time. You can put a down payment on it and carry it on home with you.

---

1. Equivalent to about $1,700 in 2017.

TROY   Not me. I ain't gonna owe nobody nothing if I can help it. Miss a payment and they come and snatch it right out your house. Then what you
75   got? Now, soon as I get two hundred dollars clear, then I'll buy a TV. Right
now, as soon as I get two hundred and sixty-four dollars, I'm gonna have
this roof tarred.

CORY   Aw . . . Pop!

TROY   You go on and get you two hundred dollars and buy one if ya want it. I
80   got better things to do with my money.

CORY   I can't get no two hundred dollars. I ain't never seen two hundred
dollars.

TROY   I'll tell you what . . . you get you a hundred dollars and I'll put the
other hundred with it.

85   CORY   Alright, I'm gonna show you.

TROY   You gonna show me how you can cut them boards right now.

[CORY *begins to cut the boards. There is a long pause.*]

CORY   The Pirates won today. That makes five in a row.

TROY   I ain't thinking about the Pirates. Got an all-white team. Got that
boy . . . that Puerto Rican boy . . . Clemente.[2] Don't even half-play him.
90   That boy could be something if they give him a chance. Play him one day
and sit him on the bench the next.

CORY   He gets a lot of chances to play.

TROY   I'm talking about playing regular. Playing every day so you can get your
timing. That's what I'm talking about.

95   CORY   They got some white guys on the team that don't play every day. You
can't play everybody at the same time.

TROY   If they got a white fellow sitting on the bench . . . you can bet your last
dollar he can't play! The colored guy got to be twice as good before he get
on the team. That's why I don't want you to get all tied up in them sports.
100   Man on the team and what it get him? They got colored on the team and
don't use them. Same as not having them. All them teams the same.

CORY   The Braves got Hank Aaron and Wes Covington.[3] Hank Aaron hit two
home runs today. That makes forty-three.

TROY   Hank Aaron ain't nobody. That's what you supposed to do. That's how
105   you supposed to play the game. Ain't nothing to it. It's just a matter of timing . . . getting the right follow-through. Hell, I can hit forty-three home
runs right now!

CORY   Not off no major-league pitching, you couldn't.

TROY   We had better pitching in the Negro leagues. I hit seven home runs off
110   of Satchel Paige.[4] You can't get no better than that!

---

2. Roberto Clemente (1934–1972), a Hall of
Fame outfielder who played for the Pittsburgh Pirates between 1955 and his death in
a plane crash; he was a twelve-time All-Star
and four-time National League batting champion. He played in 111 (of 162) games in
1957.
3. Aaron (b. 1934), who spent all but the last
two years of his major-league career (1954–76)
with the Milwaukee (later Atlanta) Braves,
was one of the greatest baseball players of all

time; his best-known achievement was breaking Ruth's lifetime home run record, eventually hitting 755; in 1957 he hit 44 home runs.
Covington (1932–2011), who played for the
Braves (1956–61) and five other teams (1961–
66), was integral to the Braves' 1957 run to
the World Series.
4. The legendary Negro League pitcher (1906–
1982); he began playing in the mid-1920s,
and between 1948 and 1965 played for several major-league teams.

CORY   Sandy Koufax.[5] He's leading the league in strikeouts.

TROY   I ain't thinking of no Sandy Koufax.

CORY   You got Warren Spahn and Lew Burdette.[6] I bet you couldn't hit no home runs off of Warren Spahn.

115   TROY   I'm through with it now. You go on and cut them boards. [*Pause*] Your mama tell me you done got recruited by a college football team? Is that right?

CORY   Yeah. Coach Zellman say the recruiter gonna be coming by to talk to you. Get you to sign the permission papers.

120   TROY   I thought you supposed to be working down there at the A&P. Ain't you suppose to be working down there after school?

CORY   Mr. Stawicki say he gonna hold my job for me until after the football season. Say starting next week I can work weekends.

TROY   I thought we had an understanding about this football stuff? You sup-
125   pose to keep up with your chores and hold that job down at the A&P. Ain't been around here all day on a Saturday. Ain't none of your chores done . . . and now you telling me you done quit your job.

CORY   I'm gonna be working weekends.

TROY   You damn right you are! And ain't no need for nobody coming around
130   here to talk to me about signing nothing.

CORY   Hey, Pop . . . you can't do that. He's coming all the way from North Carolina.

TROY   I don't care where he coming from. The white man ain't gonna let you get nowhere with that football noway. You go on and get your book-learning
135   so you can work yourself up in that A&P or learn how to fix cars or build houses or something, get you a trade. That way you have something can't nobody take away from you. You go on and learn how to put your hands to some good use. Besides hauling people's garbage.

CORY   I get good grades, Pop. That's why the recruiter wants to talk with you.
140   You got to keep up your grades to get recruited. This way I'll be going to college. I'll get a chance . . .

TROY   First you gonna get your butt down there to the A&P and get your job back.

CORY   Mr. Stawicki done already hired somebody else cause I told him I was
145   playing football.

TROY   You a bigger fool than I thought . . . to let somebody take away your job so you can play some football. Where you gonna get your money to take out your girlfriend and whatnot? What kind of foolishness is that to let somebody take away your job?

150   CORY   I'm still gonna be working weekends.

TROY   Naw . . . naw. You getting your butt out of here and finding you another job.

---

5. A Hall of Fame pitcher (b. 1935), for the Brooklyn (later Los Angeles) Dodgers (1955–66).

6. The Braves' left-handed and right-handed pitching aces in 1957. Spahn (1921–2003), a Hall of Famer, played all but the final year of his career (1942–65) with the Boston (later Milwaukee) Braves; Burdette (1926–2007), the MVP of the 1957 World Series, played mainly for the Braves (1951–63) but for four other teams as well (1950, 1963–67).

CORY   Come on, Pop! I got to practice. I can't work after school and play football too. The team needs me. That's what Coach Zellman say . . .

155   TROY   I don't care what nobody else say. I'm the boss . . . you understand? I'm the boss around here. I do the only saying what counts.

CORY   Come on, Pop!

TROY   I asked you . . . did you understand?

CORY   Yeah . . .

160   TROY   What?!

CORY   Yessir.

TROY   You go on down there to that A&P and see if you can get your job back. If you can't do both . . . then you quit the football team. You've got to take the crookeds with the straights.

165   CORY   Yessir. [*Pause*] Can I ask you a question?

TROY   What the hell you wanna ask me? Mr. Stawicki the one you got the questions for.

CORY   How come you ain't never liked me?

TROY   Liked you? Who the hell say I got to like you? What law is there say I

170   got to like you? Wanna stand up in my face and ask a damn fool-ass question like that. Talking about liking somebody. Come here, boy, when I talk to you.

[CORY *comes over to where* TROY *is working. He stands slouched over and* TROY *shoves him on his shoulder.*]

Straighten up, goddammit! I asked you a question . . . what law is there say I got to like you?

175   CORY   None.

TROY   Well, alright then! Don't you eat every day? [*Pause*] Answer me when I talk to you! Don't you eat every day?

CORY   Yeah.

TROY   Nigger, as long as you in my house, you put that sir on the end of it

180   when you talk to me!

CORY   Yes . . . sir.

TROY   You eat every day.

CORY   Yessir!

TROY   Got a roof over your head.

185   CORY   Yessir!

TROY   Got clothes on your back.

CORY   Yessir.

TROY   Why you think that is?

CORY   Cause of you.

190   TROY   Aw, hell I know it's 'cause of me . . . but why do you think that is?

CORY   [*hesitant*]   Cause you like me.

TROY   Like you? I go out of here every morning . . . bust my butt . . . putting up with them crackers[7] every day . . . cause I like you? You about the biggest fool I ever saw. [*Pause*] It's my job. It's my responsibility! You under-

195   stand that? A man got to take care of his family. You live in my house . . . sleep you behind on my bedclothes . . . fill you belly up with my food . . . cause you my son. You my flesh and blood. Not 'cause I like you! Cause it's

---

7. Poor whites (derogatory term).

my duty to take care of you. I owe a responsibility to you! Let's get this straight right here . . . before it go along any further . . . I ain't got to like 200 you. Mr. Rand don't give me my money come payday cause he likes me. He gives me cause he owe me. I done give you everything I had to give you. I gave you your life! Me and your mama worked that out between us. And liking your black ass wasn't part of the bargain. Don't you try and go through life worrying about if somebody like you or not. You best be mak 205 ing sure they doing right by you. You understand what I'm saying, boy?

CORY   Yessir.

TROY   Then get the hell out of my face, and get on down to that A&P.

> [ROSE *has been standing behind the screen door for much of the scene.*
> *She enters as* CORY *exits.*]

ROSE   Why don't you let the boy go ahead and play football, Troy? Ain't no harm in that. He's just trying to be like you with the sports.

210 TROY   I don't want him to be like me! I want him to move as far away from my life as he can get. You the only decent thing that ever happened to me. I wish him that. But I don't wish him a thing else from my life. I decided seventeen years ago that boy wasn't getting involved in no sports. Not after what they did to me in the sports.

215 ROSE   Troy, why don't you admit you was too old to play in the major leagues? For once . . . why don't you admit that?

TROY   What do you mean too old? Don't come telling me I was too old. I just wasn't the right color. Hell, I'm fifty-three years old and can do better than Selkirk's .269 right now!

220 ROSE   How's was you gonna play ball when you were over forty? Sometimes I can't get no sense out of you.

TROY   I got good sense, woman. I got sense enough not to let my boy get hurt over playing no sports. You been mothering that boy too much. Worried about if people like him.

225 ROSE   Everything that boy do . . . he do for you. He wants you to say "Good job, son." That's all.

TROY   Rose, I ain't got time for that. He's alive. He's healthy. He's got to make his own way. I made mine. Ain't nobody gonna hold his hand when he get out there in that world.

230 ROSE   Times have changed from when you was young, Troy. People change. The world's changing around you and you can't even see it.

TROY [*slow, methodical*]   Woman . . . I do the best I can do. I come in here every Friday. I carry a sack of potatoes and a bucket of lard. You all line up at the door with your hands out. I give you the lint from my pockets. I give 235 you my sweat and my blood. I ain't got no tears.[8] I done spent them. We go upstairs in that room at night . . . and I fall down on you and try to blast a hole into forever. I get up Monday morning . . . find my lunch on the table. I go out. Make my way. Find my strength to carry me through to the next Friday. [*Pause*] That's all I got, Rose. That's all I got to give. I can't give 240 nothing else.

> [TROY *exits into the house. The lights go down to black.*]

---

8. An allusion to a famous wartime declaration to the British Parliament by Prime Minister Winston Churchill in May 1940: "I have nothing to offer but blood, toil, tears, and sweat."

1.4

It is Friday. Two weeks later. CORY *starts out of the house with his football equipment. The phone rings.*

CORY [*calling*] I got it! [*He answers the phone and stands in the screen door talking.*] Hello? Hey, Jesse. Naw . . . I was just getting ready to leave now.

ROSE [*calling*] Cory!

5 CORY I told you, man, them spikes is all tore up. You can use them if you want, but they ain't no good. Earl got some spikes.

ROSE [*calling*] Cory!

CORY [*calling to* ROSE] Mam? I'm talking to Jesse. [*Into phone*] When she say that? [*Pause*] Aw, you lying, man. I'm gonna tell her you said that.

10 ROSE [*calling*] Cory, don't you go nowhere!

CORY I got to go to the game, Ma! [*Into the phone*] Yeah, hey, look, I'll talk to you later. Yeah, I'll meet you over Earl's house. Later. Bye, Ma.

[CORY *exists the house and starts out the yard.*]

ROSE Cory, where you going off to? You got that stuff all pulled out and thrown all over your room.

15 CORY [*in the yard*] I was looking for my spikes. Jesse wanted to borrow my spikes.

ROSE Get up there and get that cleaned up before your daddy get back in here.

CORY I got to go to the game! I'll clean it up *when I get back.*

[CORY *exits.*]

20 ROSE That's all he need to do is see that room all messed up.

[ROSE *exits into the house.* TROY *and* BONO *enter the yard.* TROY *is dressed in clothes other than his work clothes.*]

BONO He told him the same thing he told you. Take it to the union.

TROY Brownie ain't got that much sense. Man wasn't thinking about nothing. He wait until I confront them on it . . . then he wanna come crying seniority. [*Calls*] Hey, Rose!

25 BONO I wish I could have seen Mr. Rand's face when he told you.

TROY He couldn't get it out of his mouth! Liked to bit his tongue! When they called me down there to the Commissioner's office . . . he thought they was gonna fire me. Like everybody else.

BONO I didn't think they was gonna fire you. I thought they was gonna put you on the warning paper.

30 TROY Hey, Rose! [*To* BONO] Yeah, Mr. Rand like to bit his tongue.

[TROY *breaks the seal on the bottle, takes a drink, and hands it to* BONO.]

BONO I see you run right down to Taylors' and told that Alberta gal.

TROY [*calling*] Hey Rose! [*To* BONO] I told everybody. Hey, Rose! I went down there to cash my check.

35 ROSE [*entering from the house*] Hush all that hollering, man! I know you out here. What they say down there at the Commissioner's office?

TROY You supposed to come when I call you, woman. Bono'll tell you that. [*To* BONO] Don't Lucille come when you call her?

ROSE Man, hush your mouth. I ain't no dog . . . talk about "come when you call me."

TROY [*puts his arm around* ROSE]   You hear this, Bono? I had me an old dog used to get uppity like that. You say, "C'mere, Blue!" . . . and he just lay there and look at you. End up getting a stick and chasing him away trying to make him come.

45   ROSE   I ain't studying you and your dog. I remember you used to sing that old song.

TROY [*he sings*]

> Hear it ring! Hear it ring!
> I had a dog his name was Blue.[9]

ROSE   Don't nobody wanna hear you sing that old song.

50   TROY [*sings*]   You know Blue was mighty true.

ROSE   Used to have Cory running around here singing that song.

BONO   Hell, I remember that song myself.

TROY [*sings*]

> You know Blue was a good old dog.
> Blue treed a possum in a hollow log.

55   That was my daddy's song. My daddy made up that song.

ROSE   I don't care who made it up. Don't nobody wanna hear you sing it.

TROY [*makes a song like calling a dog*]   Come here, woman.

ROSE   You come in here carrying on, I reckon they ain't fired you. What they say down there at the Commissioner's office?

60   TROY   Look here, Rose . . . Mr. Rand called me into his office today when I got back from talking to them people down there . . . it come from up top . . . he called me in and told me they was making me a driver.

ROSE   Troy, you kidding!

TROY   No I ain't. Ask Bono.

65   ROSE   Well, that's great, Troy. Now you don't have to hassle them people no more.

[LYONS *enters from the street.*]

TROY   Aw hell, I wasn't looking to see you today. I thought you was in jail. Got it all over the front page of the *Courier*[1] about them raiding Sefus' place . . . where you be hanging out with all them thugs.

70   LYONS   Hey, Pop . . . that ain't got nothing to do with me. I don't go down there gambling. I go down there to sit in with the band. I ain't got nothing to do with the gambling part. They got some good music down there.

TROY   They got some rogues . . . is what they got.

LYONS   How you been, Mr. Bono? Hi, Rose.

75   BONO   I see where you playing down at the Crawford Grill tonight.

ROSE   How come you ain't brought Bonnie like I told you. You should have brought Bonnie with you, she ain't been over in a month of Sundays.

LYONS   I was just in the neighborhood . . . thought I'd stop by.

TROY   Here he come . . .

80   BONO   Your daddy got a promotion on the rubbish. He's gonna be the first

---

9. A variation on "Old Blue," a traditional African American folk song.
1. The *Pittsburgh Courier,* one of the top-

selling African American newspapers in the mid-20th century.

colored driver. Ain't got to do nothing but sit up there and read the paper like them white fellows.

LYONS Hey, Pop . . . if you knew how to read you'd be alright.

BONO Naw . . . naw . . . you mean if the nigger knew how to drive he'd be all
85 right. Been fighting with them people about driving and ain't even got a license. Mr. Rand know you ain't got no driver's license?

TROY Driving ain't nothing. All you do is point the truck where you want it to go. Driving ain't nothing.

BONO Do Mr. Rand know you ain't got no driver's license? That's what I'm
90 talking about. I ain't asked if driving was easy. I asked if Mr. Rand know you ain't got no driver's license.

TROY He ain't got to know. The man ain't got to know my business. Time he find out, I have two or three driver's licenses.

LYONS [going into his pocket] Say, look here, Pop . . .

95 TROY I knew it was coming. Didn't I tell you, Bono? I know what kind of "Look here, Pop" that was. The nigger fixing to ask me for some money. It's Friday night. It's my payday. All them rogues down there on the avenue . . . the ones that ain't in jail . . . and Lyons is hopping in his shoes to get down there with them.

100 LYONS See, Pop . . . if you give somebody else a chance to talk sometime, you'd see that I was fixing to pay you back your ten dollars like I told you. Here . . . I told you I'd pay you when Bonnie got paid.

TROY Naw . . . you go ahead and keep that ten dollars. Put it in the bank. The next time you feel like you wanna come by here and ask me for some-
105 thing . . . you go on down there and get that.

LYONS Here's your ten dollars, Pop. I told you I don't want you to give me nothing. I just wanted to borrow ten dollars.

TROY Naw . . . you go on and keep that for the next time you want to ask me.

LYONS Come on, Pop . . . here go your ten dollars.

110 ROSE Why don't you go on and let the boy pay you back, Troy?

LYONS Here you go, Rose. If you don't take it I'm gonna have to hear about it for the next six months.

[He hands her the money.]

ROSE You can hand yours over here too, Troy.

TROY You see this, Bono. You see how they do me.

115 BONO Yeah, Lucille do me the same way.

[GABRIEL is heard singing offstage. He enters.]

GABRIEL Better get ready for the Judgment! Better get ready for . . . Hey! . . . Hey! . . . There's Troy's boy!

LYONS How you doing, Uncle Gabe?

GABRIEL Lyons . . . The King of the Jungle! Rose . . . hey, Rose. Got a flower
120 for you. [He takes a rose from his pocket.] Picked it myself. That's the same rose like you is!

ROSE That's right nice of you, Gabe.

LYONS What you been doing, Uncle Gabe?

GABRIEL Oh, I been chasing hellhounds and waiting on the time to tell St.
125 Peter to open the gates.

LYONS You been chasing hellhounds, huh? Well . . . you doing the right thing, Uncle Gabe. Somebody got to chase them.

GABRIEL   Oh, yeah . . . I know it. The devil's strong. The devil ain't no pushover. Hellhounds snipping at everybody's heels. But I got my trumpet wait-
130   ing on the judgment time.

LYONS   Waiting on the Battle of Armageddon,[2] huh?

GABRIEL   Ain't gonna be too much of a battle when God get to waving that
Judgment sword. But the people's gonna have a hell of a time trying to get
into heaven if them gates ain't open.

135   LYONS [*putting his arm around* GABRIEL]   You hear this, Pop. Uncle Gabe,
you alright!

GABRIEL [*laughing with* LYONS]   Lyons! King of the Jungle.

ROSE   You gonna stay for supper, Gabe. Want me to fix you a plate?

GABRIEL   I'll take a sandwich, Rose. Don't want no plate. Just wanna eat with
140   my hands. I'll take a sandwich.

ROSE   How about you, Lyons? You staying? Got some short ribs cooking.

LYONS   Naw, I won't eat nothing till after we finished playing. [*Pause*] You
ought to come down and listen to me play, Pop.

TROY   I don't like that Chinese music. All that noise.

145   ROSE   Go on in the house and wash up, Gabe . . . I'll fix you a sandwich.

GABRIEL [*to* LYONS, *as he exits*]   Troy's mad at me.

LYONS   What you mad at Uncle Gabe for, Pop?

ROSE   He thinks Troy's mad at him cause he moved over to Miss Pearl's.

TROY   I ain't mad at the man. He can live where he want to live at.

150   LYONS   What he move over there for? Miss Pearl don't like nobody.

ROSE   She don't mind him none. She treats him real nice. She just don't
allow all that singing.

TROY   She don't mind that rent he be paying . . . that's what she don't mind.

ROSE   Troy, I ain't going through that with you no more. He's over there
155   cause he want to have his own place. He can come and go as he please.

TROY   Hell, he could come and go as he please here. I wasn't stopping him. I
ain't put no rules on him.

ROSE   It ain't the same thing, Troy. And you know it.

[GABRIEL *comes to the door.*]

Now, that's the last I wanna hear about that. I don't wanna hear nothing
160   else about Gabe and Miss Pearl. And next week . . .

GABRIEL   I'm ready for my sandwich, Rose.

ROSE   And next week . . . when that recruiter come from that school . . . I
want you to sign that paper and go on and let Cory play football. Then
that'll be the last I have to hear about that.

165   TROY [*to* ROSE *as she exits into the house*]   I ain't thinking about Cory nothing.

LYONS   What . . . Cory got recruited? What school he going to?

TROY   That boy walking around here smelling his piss . . . thinking he's
grown. Thinking he's gonna do what he want, irrespective of what I say.
Look here, Bono . . . I left the Commissioner's office and went down to the
170   A&P . . . that boy ain't working down there. He lying to me. Telling me he
got his job back . . . telling me he working weekends . . . telling me he working after school . . . Mr. Stawicki tell me he ain't working down there at all!

---

2. The final battle between the forces of God and of evil, as described in the New Testament's
book of Revelation (see 16.16).

LYONS   Cory just growing up. He's just busting at the seams trying to fill out
your shoes.

175 TROY   I don't care what he's doing. When he get to the point where he wanna
disobey me . . . then it's time for him to move on. Bono'll tell you that. I bet
he ain't never disobeyed his daddy without paying the consequences.

BONO   I ain't never had a chance. My daddy came on through . . . but I ain't
never knew him to see him . . . or what he had on his mind or where he

180 went. Just moving on through. Searching out the New Land. That's what
the old folks used to call it. See a fellow moving around from place to
place . . . woman to woman . . . called it searching out the New Land. I
can't say if he ever found it. I come along, didn't want no kids. Didn't know
if I was gonna be in one place long enough to fix on them right as their

185 daddy. I figured I was going searching too. As it turned out I been hooked
up with Lucille near about as long as your daddy been with Rose. Going on
sixteen years.

TROY   Sometimes I wish I hadn't known my daddy. He ain't cared nothing
about no kids. A kid to him wasn't nothing. All he wanted was for you to

190 learn how to walk so he could start you to working. When it come time for
eating . . . he ate first. If there was anything left over, that's what you got.
Man would sit down and eat two chickens and give you the wing.

LYONS   You ought to stop that, Pop. Everybody feed their kids. No matter
how hard times is . . . everybody care about their kids. Make sure they have

195 something to eat.

TROY   The only thing my daddy cared about was getting them bales of cotton
in to Mr. Lubin. That's the only thing that mattered to him. Sometimes I
used to wonder why he was living. Wonder why the devil hadn't come and
got him. "Get them bales of cotton in to Mr. Lubin" and find out he owe

200 him money[3] . . .

LYONS   He should have just went on and left when he saw he couldn't get
nowhere. That's what I would have done.

TROY   How he gonna leave with eleven kids? And where he gonna go? He
ain't knew how to do nothing but farm. No, he was trapped and I think he

205 knew it. But I'll say this for him . . . he felt a responsibility toward us.
Maybe he ain't treated us the way I felt he should have . . . but without
that responsibility he could have walked off and left us . . . made his own
way.

BONO   A lot of them did. Back in those days what you talking about . . . they

210 walk out their front door and just take on down one road or another and
keep on walking.

LYONS   There you go! That's what I'm talking about.

BONO   Just keep on walking till you come to something else. Ain't you never
heard of nobody having the walking blues? Well, that's what you call it

215 when you just take off like that.

TROY   My daddy ain't had them walking blues! What you talking about? He
stayed right there with his family. But he was just as evil as he could be. My

3. Under the sharecropping system that arose
in the South after the Civil War, tenant farmers received their seed, tools, food and clothing, and housing on credit from landowners;
after harvesting the cotton, they had to repay
these charges from their share of the value of
the crop.

mama couldn't stand him. Couldn't stand that evilness. She run off when I was about eight. She sneaked off one night after he had gone to sleep. Told me she was coming back for me. I ain't never seen her no more. All his women run off and left him. He wasn't good for nobody.

When my turn come to head out, I was fourteen and got to sniffing around Joe Canewell's daughter. Had us an old mule we called Greyboy. My daddy sent me out to do some plowing and I tied up Greyboy and went to fooling around with Joe Canewell's daughter. We done found us a nice little spot, got real cozy with each other. She about thirteen and we done figured we was grown anyway . . . so we down there enjoying ourselves . . . ain't thinking about nothing. We didn't know Greyboy had got loose and wandered back to the house and my daddy was looking for me. We down there by the creek enjoying ourselves when my daddy come up on us. Surprised us. He had them leather straps off the mule and commenced to whupping me like there was no tomorrow. I jumped up, mad and embarrassed. I was scared of my daddy. When he commenced to whupping on me . . . quite naturally I run to get out of the way.

[*Pause.*]

Now I thought he was mad cause I ain't done my work. But I see where he was chasing me off so he could have the gal for himself. When I see what the matter of it was, I lost all fear of my daddy. Right there is where I become a man . . . at fourteen years of age.

[*Pause.*]

Now it was my turn to run him off. I picked up them same reins that he had used on me. I picked up them reins and commenced to whupping on him. The gal jumped up and run off . . . and when my daddy turned to face me, I could see why the devil had never come to get him . . . cause he was the devil himself. I don't know what happened. When I woke up, I was laying right there by the creek, and Blue . . . this old dog we had . . . was licking my face. I thought I was blind. I couldn't see nothing. Both my eyes were swollen shut. I layed there and cried. I didn't know what I was gonna do. The only thing I knew was the time had come for me to leave my daddy's house. And right there the world suddenly got big. And it was a long time before I could cut it down to where I could handle it.

Part of that cutting down was when I got to the place where I could feel him kicking in my blood and knew that the only thing that separated us was the matter of a few years.

[GABRIEL *enters from the house with a sandwich.*]

LYONS   What you got there, Uncle Gabe?

GABRIEL   Got me a ham sandwich. Rose gave me a ham sandwich.

TROY   I don't know what happened to him. I done lost touch with everybody except Gabriel. But I hope he's dead. I hope he found some peace.

LYONS   That's a heavy story, Pop. I didn't know you left home when you was fourteen.

TROY   And didn't know nothing. The only part of the world I knew was the forty-two acres of Mr. Lubin's land. That's all I knew about life.

LYONS   Fourteen's kinda young to be out on your own. [*Phone rings.*] I don't even think I was ready to be out on my own at fourteen. I don't know what I would have done.

TROY   I got up from the creek and walked on down to Mobile. I was through
265   with farming. Figured I could do better in the city. So I walked the two
        hundred miles to Mobile.

LYONS   Wait a minute . . . you ain't walked no two hundred miles, Pop. Ain't
        nobody gonna walk no two hundred miles. You talking about some walking
        there.

270 BONO   That's the only way you got anywhere back in them days.

LYONS   Shhh. Damn if I wouldn't have hitched a ride with somebody!

TROY   Who you gonna hitch it with? They ain't had no cars and things like
        they got now. We talking about 1918.

ROSE [*entering*]   What you all out here getting into?

275 TROY [*to* ROSE]   I'm telling Lyons how good he got it. He don't know nothing
        about this I'm talking.

ROSE   Lyons, that was Bonnie on the phone. She say you supposed to pick
        her up.

LYONS   Yeah, okay, Rose.

280 TROY   I walked on down to Mobile and hitched up with some of them fellows
        that was heading this way. Got up here and found out . . . not only couldn't
        you get a job . . . you couldn't find no place to live. I thought I was in free-
        dom. Shhh. Colored folks living down there on the riverbanks in whatever
        kind of shelter they could find for themselves. Right down there under the
285   Brady Street Bridge. Living in shacks made of sticks and tar paper. Messed
        around there and went from bad to worse. Started stealing. First it was
        food. Then I figured, hell, if I steal money I can buy me some food. Buy me
        some shoes too! One thing led to another. Met your mama. I was young
        and anxious to be a man. Met your mama and had you. What I do that for?
290   Now I got to worry about feeding you and her. Got to steal three times as
        much. Went out one day looking for somebody to rob . . . that's what I was,
        a robber. I'll tell you the truth. I'm ashamed of it today. But it's the truth.
        Went to rob this fellow . . . pulled out my knife . . . and he pulled out a
        gun. Shot me in the chest. It felt just like somebody had taken a hot brand-
295   ing iron and laid it on me. When he shot me I jumped at him with my
        knife. They told me I killed him and they put me in the penitentiary and
        locked me up for fifteen years. That's where I met Bono. That's where I
        learned how to play baseball. Got out that place and your mama had taken
        you and went on to make life without me. Fifteen years was a long time for
300   her to wait. But that fifteen years cured me of that robbing stuff. Rose'll tell
        you. She asked me when I met her if I had gotten all that foolishness out of
        my system. And I told her, "Baby, it's you and baseball all what count with
        me." You hear me, Bono? I meant it too. She say, "Which one comes first?"
        I told her, "Baby, ain't no doubt it's baseball . . . but you stick and get old
305   with me and we'll both outlive this baseball." Am I right, Rose? And it's true.

ROSE   Man, hush your mouth. You ain't said no such thing. Talking about,
        "Baby, you know you'll always be number one with me." That's what you
        was talking.

TROY   You hear that, Bono. That's why I love her.

310 BONO   Rose'll keep you straight. You get off the track, she'll straighten you up.

ROSE   Lyons, you better get on up and get Bonnie. She waiting on you.

LYONS [*gets up to go*]   Hey, Pop, why don't you come on down to the Grill and
        hear me play?

TROY   I ain't going down there. I'm too old to be sitting around in them clubs.

315 BONO   You got to be good to play down at the Grill.

LYONS   Come on, Pop . . .

TROY   I got to get up in the morning.

LYONS   You ain't got to stay long.

TROY   Naw, I'm gonna get my supper and go on to bed.

320 LYONS   Well, I got to go. I'll see you again.

TROY   Don't you come around my house on my payday.

ROSE   Pick up the phone and let somebody know you coming. And bring Bonnie with you. You know I'm always glad to see her.

LYONS   Yeah, I'll do that, Rose. You take care now. See you, Pop. See you, Mr.

325 Bono. See you, Uncle Gabe.

GABRIEL   Lyons! King of the Jungle!

[LYONS *exits.*]

TROY   Is supper ready, woman? Me and you got some business to take care of. I'm gonna tear it up too.

ROSE   Troy, I done told you now!

330 TROY [*puts his arm around* BONO]   Aw hell, woman . . . this is Bono. Bono like family. I done known this nigger since . . . how long I done know you?

BONO   It's been a long time.

TROY   I done known this nigger since Skippy was a pup.[4] Me and him done been through some times.

335 BONO   You sure right about that.

TROY   Hell, I done know him longer than I known you. And we still standing shoulder to shoulder. Hey, look here, Bono . . . a man can't ask for no more than that. [*Drinks to him.*] I love you, nigger.

BONO   Hell, I love you too . . . but I got to get home see my woman. You got

340 yours in hand. I got to go get mine.

[BONO *starts to exit as* CORY *enters the yard, dressed in his football uniform. He gives* TROY *a hard, uncompromising look.*]

CORY   What you do that for, Pop?

[*He throws his helmet down in the direction of* TROY.]

ROSE   What's the matter? Cory . . . what's the matter?

CORY   Papa done went up to the school and told Coach Zellman I can't play football no more. Wouldn't even let me play the game. Told him to tell the

345 recruiter not to come.

ROSE   Troy . . .

TROY   What you Troying me for. Yeah, I did it. And the boy know why I did it.

CORY   Why you wanna do that to me? That was the one chance I had.

ROSE   Ain't nothing wrong with Cory playing football, Troy.

350 TROY   The boy lied to me. I told the nigger if he wanna play football . . . to keep up his chores and hold down that job at the A&P. That was the conditions. Stopped down there to see Mr. Stawicki . . .

CORY   I can't work after school during the football season, Pop! I tried to tell you that Mr. Stawicki's holding my job for me. You don't never want to lis

355 ten to nobody. And then you wanna go and do this to me!

4. That is, for a very long time (folk expression).

TROY   I ain't done nothing to you. You done it to yourself.

CORY   Just cause you didn't have a chance! You just scared I'm gonna be better than you, that's all.

TROY   Come here.

360 ROSE   Troy . . .

> [CORY *reluctantly crosses over to* TROY.]

TROY   Alright! See. You done made a mistake.

CORY   I didn't even do nothing!

TROY   I'm gonna tell you what your mistake was. See . . . you swung at the ball and didn't hit it. That's strike one. See, you in the batter's box now. You

365 swung and you missed. That's strike one. Don't you strike out!

> [*Lights fade to black.*]

2.1

The following morning. CORY *is at the tree hitting the ball with the bat. He tries to mimic* TROY, *but his swing is awkward, less sure.* ROSE *enters from the house.*

ROSE   Cory, I want you to help me with this cupboard.

CORY   I ain't quitting the team. I don't care what Poppa say.

ROSE   I'll talk to him when he gets back. He had to go see about your Uncle Gabe. The police done arrested him. Say he was disturbing the peace. He'll

5 be back directly. Come on in here and help me clean out the top of this cupboard.

> [CORY *exits into the house.* ROSE *sees* TROY *and* BONO *coming down the alley.*]

Troy . . . what they say down there?

TROY   Ain't said nothing. I give them fifty dollars and they let him go. I'll talk to you about it. Where's Cory?

10 ROSE   He's in there helping me clean out these cupboards.

TROY   Tell him to get his butt out here.

> [TROY *and* BONO *go over to the pile of wood.* BONO *picks up the saw and begins sawing.*]

TROY [*to* BONO]   All they want is the money. That makes six or seven times I done went down there and got him. See me coming they stick out their hands.

15 BONO   Yeah. I know what you mean. That's all they care about . . . that money. They don't care about what's right. [*Pause*] Nigger, why you got to go and get some hard wood? You ain't doing nothing but building a little old fence. Get you some soft pine wood. That's all you need.

TROY   I know what I'm doing. This is outside wood. You put pine wood inside

20 the house. Pine wood is inside wood. This here is outside wood. Now you tell me where the fence is gonna be?

BONO   You don't need this wood. You can put it up with pine wood and it'll stand as long as you gonna be here looking at it.

TROY   How you know how long I'm gonna be here, nigger? Hell, I might just

25 live forever. Live longer than old man Horsely.

BONO   That's what Magee used to say.

TROY   Magee's a damn fool. Now you tell me who you ever heard of gonna pull their own teeth with a pair of rusty pliers.

BONO   The old folks . . . my granddaddy used to pull his teeth with pliers.
30   They ain't had no dentists for the colored folks back then.

TROY   Get clean pliers! You understand? Clean pliers! Sterilize them! Besides
we ain't living back then. All Magee had to do was walk over to Doc
Goldblum's.

BONO   I see where you and that Tallahassee gal . . . that Alberta . . . I see
35   where you all done got tight.

TROY   What you mean "got tight"?

BONO   I see where you be laughing and joking with her all the time.

TROY   I laughs and jokes with all of them, Bono. You know me.

BONO   That ain't the kind of laughing and joking I'm talking about.

[CORY *enters from the house.*]

40   CORY   How you doing, Mr. Bono?

TROY   Cory? Get that saw from Bono and cut some wood. He talking about
the wood's too hard to cut. Stand back there, Jim, and let that young boy
show you how it's done.

BONO   He's sure welcome to it.

[CORY *takes the saw and begins to cut the wood.*]

45   Whew-e-e! Look at that. Big old strong boy. Look like Joe Louis.[5] Hell,
must be getting old the way I'm watching that boy whip through that wood.

CORY   I don't see why Mama want a fence around the yard noways.

TROY   Damn if I know either. What the hell she keeping out with it? She ain't
got nothing nobody want.

50   BONO   Some people build fences to keep people out . . . and other people
build fences to keep people in. Rose wants to hold on to you all. She loves
you.

TROY   Hell, nigger, I don't need nobody to tell me my wife loves me, Cory . . .
go on in the house and see if you can find that other saw.

55   CORY   Where's it at?

TROY   I said find it! Look for it till you find it!

[CORY *exists into the house.*]

What's that supposed to mean? Wanna keep us in?

BONO   Troy . . . I done known you seem like damn near my whole life. You
and Rose both. I done know both of you all for a long time. I remember
60   when you met Rose. When you was hitting them baseball out the park. A
lot of them old gals was after you then. You had the pick of the litter. When
you picked Rose, I was happy for you. That was the first time I knew you
had any sense. I said . . . My man Troy knows what he's doing . . . I'm
gonna follow this nigger . . . he might take me somewhere. I been follow-
65   ing you too. I done learned a whole heap of things about life watching you.
I done learned how to tell where the shit lies. How to tell it from the
alfalfa. You done learned me a lot of things. You showed me how to not
make the same mistakes . . . to take life as it comes along and keep putting
one foot in front of the other. [*Pause*] Rose a good woman, Troy.

70   TROY   Hell, nigger, I know she a good woman. I been married to her for eighteen years. What you got on your mind, Bono?

---

5. American boxer (1914–1981); as world heavyweight champion (1937–49), he was the most
famous black man in the United States.

BONO I just say she a good woman. Just like I say anything. I ain't got to have nothing on my mind.

TROY You just gonna say she a good woman and leave it hanging out there like that? Why you telling me she a good woman?

BONO She loves you, Troy. Rose loves you.

TROY You saying I don't measure up. That's what you trying to say. I don't measure up cause I'm seeing this other gal. I know what you trying to say.

BONO I know what Rose means to you, Troy. I'm just trying to say I don't want to see you mess up.

TROY Yeah, I appreciate that, Bono. If you was messing around on Lucille I'd be telling you the same thing.

BONO Well, that's all I got to say. I just say that because I love you both.

TROY Hell, you know me . . . I wasn't out there looking for nothing. You can't find a better woman than Rose. I know that. But seems like this woman just stuck onto me where I can't shake her loose. I done wrestled with it, tried to throw her off me . . . but she just stuck on tighter. Now she's stuck on for good.

BONO You's in control . . . that's what you tell me all the time. You responsible for what you do.

TROY I ain't ducking the responsibility of it. As long as it sets right in my heart . . . then I'm okay. Cause that's all I listen to. It'll tell me right from wrong every time. And I ain't talking about doing Rose no bad turn. I love Rose. She done carried me a long ways and I love and respect her for that.

BONO I know you do. That's why I don't want to see you hurt her. But what you gonna do when she find out? What you got then? If you try and juggle both of them . . . sooner or later you gonna drop one of them. That's common sense.

TROY Yeah, I hear what you saying, Bono. I been trying to figure a way to work it out.

BONO Work it out right, Troy. I don't want to be getting all up between you and Rose's business . . . but work it so it come out right.

TROY Aw hell, I get all up between you and Lucille's business. When you gonna get that woman that refrigerator she been wanting? Don't tell me you ain't got no money now. I know who your banker is. Mellon[6] don't need that money bad as Lucille want that refrigerator. I'll tell you that.

BONO Tell you what I'll do . . . when you finish building this fence for Rose . . . I'll buy Lucille that refrigerator.

TROY You done stuck your foot in your mouth now!

[TROY *grabs up a board and begins to saw.* BONO *starts to walk out the yard.*]

Hey, nigger . . . where you going?

BONO I'm going home. I know you don't expect me to help you now. I'm protecting my money. I wanna see you put that fence up by yourself. That's what I want to see. You'll be here another six months without me.

TROY Nigger, you ain't right.

BONO When it comes to my money . . . I'm right as fireworks on the Fourth of July.

TROY Alright, we gonna see now. You better get out your bankbook.

[BONO *exits, and* TROY *continues to work.* ROSE *enters from the house.*]

---

6. Mellon National Bank, founded in Pittsburgh in 1870 by Thomas Mellon.

ROSE   What they say down there? What's happening with Gabe?

TROY   I went down there and got him out. Cost me fifty dollars. Say he was
120   disturbing the peace. Judge set up a hearing for him in three weeks. Say to
       show cause why he shouldn't be recommitted.

ROSE   What was he doing that cause them to arrest him?

TROY   Some kids was teasing him and he run them off home. Say he was
       howling and carrying on. Some folks seen him and called the police. That's
125   all it was.

ROSE   Well, what's you say? What'd you tell the judge?

TROY   Told him I'd look after him. It didn't make no sense to recommit the
       man. He stuck out his big greasy palm and told me to give him fifty dollars
       and take him on home.

130 ROSE   Where's he at now? Where'd he go off to?

TROY   He's gone on about his business. He don't need nobody to hold his
       hand.

ROSE   Well, I don't know. Seem like that would be the best place for him if
       they did put him into the hospital. I know what you're gonna say. But that's
135   what I think would be best.

TROY   The man done had his life ruined fighting for what? And they wanna
       take and lock him up. Let him be free. He don't bother nobody.

ROSE   Well, everybody got their own way of looking at it I guess. Come on
       and get your lunch. I got a bowl of lima beans and some cornbread in the
140   oven. Come on get something to eat. Ain't no sense you fretting over Gabe.
                [ROSE *turns to go into the house.*]

TROY   Rose . . . got something to tell you.

ROSE   Well, come on . . . wait till I get this food on the table.

TROY   Rose!
                [*She stops and turns around.*]
       I don't know how to say this. [*Pause*] I can't explain it none. It just sort of
145   grows on you till it gets out of hand. It starts out like a little bush . . . and
       the next think you know it's a whole forest.

ROSE   Troy . . . what is you talking about?

TROY   I'm talking, woman, let me talk. I'm trying to find a way to tell you . . .
       I'm gonna be a daddy. I'm gonna be somebody's daddy.

150 ROSE   Troy . . . you're not telling me this? You're gonna be . . . what?

TROY   Rose . . . now . . . see . . .

ROSE   You telling me you gonna be somebody's daddy? You telling your *wife*
       this?
                [GABRIEL *enters from the street. He carries a rose in his hand.*]

GABRIEL   Hey, Troy! Hey, Rose!

155 ROSE   I have to wait eighteen years to hear something like this.

GABRIEL   Hey, Rose . . . I got a flower for you. [*He hands it to her.*] That's a
       rose. Same rose like you is.

ROSE   Thanks, Gabe.

GABRIEL   Troy, you ain't mad at me is you? Them bad mens come and put me
160   away. You ain't mad at me is you?

TROY   Naw, Gabe, I ain't mad at you.

ROSE   Eighteen years and you wanna come with this.

GABRIEL   [*takes a quarter out of his pocket*]   See what I got? Got a brand new
       quarter.

165 TROY   Rose . . . it's just . . .

ROSE   Ain't nothing you can say, Troy. Ain't no way of explaining that.

GABRIEL   Fellow that give me this quarter had a whole mess of them. I'm gonna keep this quarter till it stop shining.

ROSE   Gabe, go on in the house there. I got some watermelon in the frigidaire.
170   Go on and get you a piece.

GABRIEL   Say, Rose . . . you know I was chasing hellhounds and them bad mens come and get me and take me away. Troy helped me. He come down there and told them they better let me go before he beat them up. Yeah, he did!

175 ROSE   You go on and get you a piece of watermelon, Gabe. Them bad mens is gone now.

GABRIEL   Okay, Rose . . . gonna get me some watermelon. The kind with the stripes on it.

[GABRIEL *exits into the house.*]

ROSE   Why, Troy? Why? After all these years to come dragging this in to me
180   now. It don't make no sense at your age. I could have expected this ten or fifteen years ago, but not now.

TROY   Age ain't got nothing to do with it, Rose.

ROSE   I done tried to be everything a wife should be. Everything a wife could be. Been married eighteen years and I got to live to see the day you tell me
185   you been seeing another woman and done fathered a child by her. And you know I ain't never wanted no half nothing in my family. My whole family is half. Everybody got different fathers and mothers . . . my two sisters and my brother. Can't hardly tell who's who. Can't never sit down and talk about Papa and Mama. It's your papa and your mama and my papa and my mama . . .

190 TROY   Rose . . . stop it now.

ROSE   I ain't never wanted that for none of my children. And now you wanna drag your behind in here and tell me something like this.

TROY   You ought to know. It's time for you to know.

ROSE   Well, I don't want to know, goddamn it!

195 TROY   I can't just make it go away. It's done now. I can't wish the circum-stance of the thing away.

ROSE   And you don't want to either. Maybe you want to wish me and my boy away. Maybe that's what you want? Well, you can't wish us away. I've got eighteen years of my life invested in you. You ought to have stayed upstairs
200   in my bed where you belong.

TROY   Rose . . . now listen to me . . . we can get a handle on this thing. We can talk this out . . . come to an understanding.

ROSE   All of a sudden it's "we." Where was "we" at when you was down there rolling around with some godforsaken woman? "We" should have come to
205   an understanding before you started making a damn fool of yourself. You're a day late and a dollar short when it comes to an understanding with me.

TROY   It's just . . . She gives me a different idea . . . a different understanding about myself. I can step out of this house and get away from the pressures and problems . . . be a different man. I ain't got to wonder how I'm gonna
210   pay the bills or get the roof fixed. I can just be a part of myself that I ain't never been.

ROSE   What I want to know . . . is do you plan to continue seeing her. That's all you can say to me.

TROY   I can sit up in her house and laugh. Do you understand what I'm say-
215   ing. I can laugh out loud . . . and it feels good. It reaches all the way down
to the bottom of my shoes. [*Pause*] Rose, I can't give that up.

ROSE   Maybe you ought to go on and stay down there with her . . . if she a
better woman than me.

TROY   It ain't about nobody being a better woman or nothing. Rose, you ain't
220   the blame. A man couldn't ask for no woman to be a better wife than you've
been. I'm responsible for it. I done locked myself into a pattern trying to
take care of you all that I forgot about myself.

ROSE   What the hell was I there for? That was my job, not somebody else's.

TROY   Rose, I done tried all my life to live decent . . . to live a clean . . .
225   hard . . . useful life. I tried to be a good husband to you. In every way I
knew how. Maybe I come into the world backwards, I don't know. But . . .
you born with two strikes on you before you come to the plate. You got to
guard it closely . . . always looking for the curve ball on the inside corner.
You can't afford to let none get past you. You can't afford a call strike.[7]
230   If you going down . . . you going down swinging. Everything lined up
against you. What you gonna do. I fooled them, Rose. I bunted. When I
found you and Cory and a halfway decent job . . . I was safe. Couldn't
nothing touch me. I wasn't gonna strike out no more. I wasn't going back
to the penitentiary. I wasn't gonna lay in the streets with a bottle of wine. I
235   was safe. I had me a family. A job. I wasn't gonna get that last strike. I was
on first looking for one of them boys to knock me in. To get me home.

ROSE   You should have stayed in my bed, Troy.

TROY   Then when I saw that gal . . . she firmed up my backbone. And I got to
thinking that if I tried . . . I just might be able to steal second. Do you
240   understand after eighteen years I wanted to steal second.

ROSE   You should have held me tight. You should have grabbed me and held
on.

TROY   I stood on first base for eighteen years and I thought . . . well, goddamn it . . . go on for it!

245 ROSE   We're not talking about baseball! We're talking about you going off to
lay in bed with another woman . . . and then bring it home to me. That's
what we're talking about. We ain't talking about no baseball.

TROY   Rose, you're not listening to me. I'm trying the best I can to explain it
to you. It's not easy for me to admit that I been standing in the same place
250   for eighteen years.

ROSE   I been standing with you! I been right here with you, Troy. I got a life
too. I gave eighteen years of my life to stand in the same spot with you.
Don't you think I ever wanted other things? Don't you think I had dreams
and hopes? What about my life? What about me? Don't you think it ever
255   crossed my mind to want to know other men? That I wanted to lay up
somewhere and forget about my responsibilities? That I wanted someone
to make me laugh so I could feel good? You not the only one who's got
wants and needs. But I held on to you, Troy. I took all my feelings, my
wants and needs, my dreams . . . and I buried them inside you. I planted a
260   seed and watched and prayed over it. I planted myself inside you and

---

7. That is, a called strike: a pitch at which the batter fails to swing that the umpire judges to have
been within the strike zone.

waited to bloom. And it didn't take me no eighteen years to find out the soil was hard and rocky and it wasn't never gonna bloom.

But I held on to you, Troy. I held you tighter. You was my husband. I owed you everything I had. Every part of me I could find to give you. And
265 upstairs in that room . . . with the darkness falling in on me . . . I gave everything I had to try and erase the doubt that you wasn't the finest man in the world. And wherever you was going . . . I wanted to be there with you. Cause you was my husband. Cause that's the only way I was gonna survive as your wife. You always talking about what you give . . . and what
270 you don't have to give. But you take too. You take . . . and don't even know nobody's giving!

[ROSE *turns to exit into the house;* TROY *grabs her arm.*]

TROY You say I take and don't give!
ROSE Troy! You're hurting me!
TROY You say I take and don't give.
275 ROSE Troy . . . you're hurting my arm! Let go!
TROY I done give you everything I got. Don't you tell that lie on me.
ROSE Troy!
TROY Don't you tell that lie on me!

[CORY *enters from the house.*]

CORY Mama!
280 ROSE Troy. You're hurting me.
TROY Don't you tell me about no taking and giving.

[CORY *comes up behind* TROY *and grabs him.* TROY, *surprised, is thrown off balance just as* CORY *throws a glancing blow that catches him on the chest and knocks him down.* TROY *is stunned, as is* CORY.]

ROSE Troy. Troy. No!

[TROY *gets to his feet and starts at* CORY.]

Troy . . . no. Please! Troy!

[ROSE *pulls on* TROY *to hold him back.* TROY *stops himself.*]

TROY [*to* CORY] Alright. That's strike two. You stay away from around me,
285 boy. Don't you strike out. You living with a full count. Don't you strike out.

[TROY *exits out the yard as the lights go down.*]

2.2

It is six months later, early afternoon. TROY *enters from the house and starts to exit the yard.* ROSE *enters from the house.*

ROSE Troy, I want to talk to you.
TROY All of a sudden, after all this time, you want to talk to me, huh? You ain't wanted to talk to me for months. You ain't wanted to talk to me last night. You ain't wanted no part of me then. What you wanna talk to me
5 about now?
ROSE Tomorrow's Friday.
TROY I know what day tomorrow is. You think I don't know tomorrow's Friday? My whole life I ain't done nothing but look to see Friday coming and you got to tell me it's Friday.
10 ROSE I want to know if you're coming home.

TROY   I always come home, Rose. You know that. There ain't never been a
night I ain't come home.

ROSE   That ain't what I mean . . . and you know it. I want to know if you're
coming straight home after work.

15 TROY   I figure I'd cash my check . . . hang out at Taylors' with the boys . . .
maybe play a game of checkers . . .

ROSE   Troy, I can't live like this. I won't live like this. You livin' on borrowed
time with me. It's been going on six months now you ain't been coming
home.

20 TROY   I be here every night. Every night of the year. That's 365 days.

ROSE   I want you to come home tomorrow after work.

TROY   Rose . . . I don't mess up my pay. You know that now. I take my pay and
I give it to you. I don't have no money but what you give me back. I just
want to have a little time to myself . . . a little time to enjoy life.

25 ROSE   What about me? When's my time to enjoy life?

TROY   I don't know what to tell you, Rose. I'm doing the best I can.

ROSE   You ain't been home from work but time enough to change your
clothes and run out . . . and you wanna call that the best you can do?

TROY   I'm going over to the hospital to see Alberta. She went into the hospital
30 this afternoon. Look like she might have the baby early. I won't be gone long.

ROSE   Well, you ought to know. They went over to Miss Pearl's and got Gabe
today. She said you told them to go ahead and lock him up.

TROY   I ain't said no such thing. Whoever told you that is telling a lie. Pearl
ain't doing nothing but telling a big fat lie.

35 ROSE   She ain't had to tell me. I read it on the papers.

TROY   I ain't told them nothing of the kind.

ROSE   I saw it right there on the papers.

TROY   What it say, huh?

ROSE   It said you told them to take him.

40 TROY   Then they screwed that up, just the way they screw up everything. I
ain't worried about what they got on the paper.

ROSE   Say the government send part of his check to the hospital and the
other part to you.

TROY   I ain't got nothing to do with that if that's the way it works. I ain't
45 made up the rules about how it work.

ROSE   You did Gabe just like you did Cory. You wouldn't sign the paper for
Cory . . . but you signed for Gabe. You signed that paper.

[*The telephone is heard ringing inside the house.*]

TROY   I told you I ain't signed nothing, woman! The only thing I signed was
the release form. Hell, I can't read, I don't know what they had on that
50 paper! I ain't signed nothing about sending Gabe away.

ROSE   I said send him to the hospital . . . you said let him be free . . . now
you done went down there and signed him to the hospital for half his
money. You went back on yourself, Troy. You gonna have to answer for that.

TROY   See now . . . you been over there talking to Miss Pearl. She done got
55 mad cause she ain't getting Gabe's rent money. That's all it is. She's liable
to say anything.

ROSE   Troy, I seen where you signed the paper.

TROY   You ain't seen nothing I signed. What she doing got papers on my
brother anyway? Miss Pearl telling a big fat lie. And I'm gonna tell her

60   about it too! You ain't seen nothing I signed. Say . . . you ain't seen nothing
      I signed.

          [ROSE *exits into the house to answer the telephone. Presently she returns.*]

ROSE   Troy . . . that was the hospital. Alberta had the baby.

TROY   What she have? What is it?

ROSE   It's a girl.

65 TROY   I better get on down to the hospital to see her.

ROSE   Troy . . .

TROY   Rose . . . I got to go see her now. That's only right . . . what's the mat-
        ter . . . the baby's alright, ain't it?

ROSE   Alberta died having the baby.

70 TROY   Died . . . you say she's dead? Alberta's dead?

ROSE   They said they done all they could. They couldn't do nothing for her.

TROY   The baby? How's the baby?

ROSE   They say it's healthy. I wonder who's gonna bury her.

TROY   She had family, Rose. She wasn't living in the world by herself.

75 ROSE   I know she wasn't living in the world by herself.

TROY   Next thing you gonna want to know if she had any insurance.

ROSE   Troy, you ain't got to talk like that.

TROY   That's the first thing that jumped out your mouth. "Who's gonna bury
        her?" Like I'm fixing to take on that task for myself.

80 ROSE   I am your wife. Don't push me away.

TROY   I ain't pushing nobody away. Just give me some space. That's all. Just
        give me some room to breathe.

          [ROSE *exits into the house.* TROY *walks about the yard.*]

TROY [*with a quiet rage that threatens to consume him*]   Alright . . . Mr. Death.
        See now . . . I'm gonna tell you what I'm gonna do. I'm gonna take and build

85   me a fence around this yard. See? I'm gonna build me a fence around what
        belongs to me. And then I want you to stay on the other side. See? You stay
        over there until you're ready for me. Then you come on. Bring your army.
        Bring your sickle. Bring your wrestling clothes. I ain't gonna fall down on my
        vigilance this time. You ain't gonna sneak up on me no more. When you ready

90   for me . . . when the top of your list say Troy Maxson . . . that's when you
        come around here. You come up and knock on the front door. Ain't nobody
        else got nothing to do with this. This is between you and me. Man to man.
        You stay on the other side of that fence until you ready for me. Then you
        come up and knock on the front door. Anytime you want. I'll be ready for you.

          [*The lights go down to black.*]

2.3

The lights come up on the porch. It is late evening three days later. ROSE *sits listening to the ball game waiting for* TROY. *The final out of the game is made and* ROSE
switches off the radio. TROY *enters the yard carrying an infant wrapped in blankets.
He stands back from the house and calls.*

          [ROSE *enters and stands on the porch. There is a long, awkward silence,
          the weight of which grows heavier with each passing second.*]

TROY   Rose . . . I'm standing here with my daughter in my arms. She ain't
        but a wee bittie little old thing. She don't know nothing about grownups'
        business. She innocent . . . and she ain't got no mama.

ROSE   What you telling me for, Troy?

[*She turns and exits into the house.*]

5 TROY   Well . . . I guess we'll just sit out here on the porch.

[*He sits down on the porch. There is an awkward indelicateness about the way he handles the baby. His largeness engulfs and seems to swallow it. He speaks loud enough for* ROSE *to hear.*]

A man's got to do what's right for him. I ain't sorry for nothing I done. It felt right in my heart.

[*To the baby*]

What you smiling at? Your daddy's a big man. Got these great big old hands. But sometimes he's scared. And right now your daddy's scared cause
10 we sitting out here and ain't got no home. Oh, I been homeless before. I ain't had no little baby with me. But I been homeless. You just be out on the road by your lonesome and you see one of them trains coming and you just kinda go like this . . .

[*He sings as a lullaby.*]

Please, Mr. Engineer let a man ride the line
15 Please, Mr. Engineer let a man ride the line
I ain't got no ticket please let me ride the blinds[8]

[ROSE *enters from the house.* TROY *hearing her steps behind him, stands and faces her.*]

She's my daughter, Rose. My own flesh and blood. I can't deny her no more than I can deny them boys. [*Pause*] You and them boys is my family. You and them and this child is all I got in the world. So I guess what I'm saying
20 is . . . I'd appreciate it if you'd help me take care of her.

ROSE   Okay, Troy . . . you're right. I'll take care of your baby for you . . . cause . . . like you say . . . she's innocent . . . and you can't visit the sins of the father upon the child. A motherless child has got a hard time.

[*She takes the baby from him.*]

From right now . . . this child got a mother. But you a womanless man.

[ROSE *turns and exits into the house with the baby. Lights go down to black.*]

2.4

It is two months later. LYONS *enters from the street. He knocks on the door and calls.*

LYONS   Hey, Rose! [*Pause*] Rose!

ROSE [*from inside the house*]   Stop that yelling. You gonna wake up Raynell. I just got her to sleep.

LYONS   I just stopped by to pay Papa this twenty dollars I owe him. Where's
5 Papa at?

ROSE   He should be here in a minute. I'm getting ready to go down to the church. Sit down and wait on him.

LYONS   I got to go pick up Bonnie over her mother's house.

ROSE   Well, sit it down there on the table. He'll get it.

---

8. Baggage cars with no end doors. This is a traditional blues song, with lyrics adapted by Wilson.

10 LYONS [*enters the house and sets the money on the table*] Tell Papa I said thanks. I'll see you again.

ROSE Alright, Lyons. We'll see you.

[LYONS *starts to exit as* CORY *enters.*]

CORY Hey, Lyons.

LYONS What's happening, Cory. Say man, I'm sorry I missed your gradua-
15 tion. You know I had a gig and couldn't get away. Otherwise, I would have been there, man. So what you doing?

CORY I'm trying to find a job.

LYONS Yeah I know how that go, man. It's rough out here. Jobs are scarce.

CORY Yeah, I know.

20 LYONS Look here, I got to run. Talk to Papa . . . he know some people. He'll be able to help get you a job. Talk to him . . . see what he say.

CORY Yeah . . . alright, Lyons.

LYONS You take care. I'll talk to you soon. We'll find some time to talk.

[LYONS *exits the yard.* CORY *wanders over to the tree, picks up the bat and assumes a batting stance. He studies an imaginary pitcher and swings. Dissatisfied with the result, he tries again.* TROY *enters. They eye each other for a beat.* CORY *puts the bat down and exits the yard.* TROY *starts into the house as* ROSE *exits with* RAYNELL. *She is carrying a cake.*]

TROY I'm coming in and everybody's going out.

25 ROSE I'm taking this cake down to the church for the bakesale. Lyons was by to see you. He stopped by to pay you your twenty dollars. It's laying in there on the table.

TROY [*going into his pocket*] Well . . . here go this money.

ROSE Put it in there on the table, Troy. I'll get it.

30 TROY What time you coming back?

ROSE Ain't no use in you studying me. It don't matter what time I come back.

TROY I just asked you a question, woman. What's the matter . . . can't I ask you a question?

ROSE Troy, I don't want to go into it. Your dinner's in there on the stove. All
35 you got to do is heat it up. And don't you be eating the rest of them cakes in there. I'm coming back for them. We having a bakesale at the church tomorrow.

[ROSE *exits the yard.* TROY *sits down on the steps, takes a pint bottle from his pocket, opens it and drinks. He begins to sing.*]

TROY
Hear it ring! Hear it ring!
Had an old dog his name was Blue
40 You know Blue was mighty true
You know Blue as a good old dog
Blue trees a possum in a hollow log
You know from that he was a good old dog

[BONO *enters the yard.*]

BONO Hey, Troy.

45 TROY Hey, what's happening, Bono?

BONO I just thought I'd stop by to see you.

TROY What you stop by and see me for? You ain't stopped by in a month of Sundays. Hell, I must owe you money or something.

BONO   Since you got your promotion I can't keep up with you. Used to see
50   you everyday. Now I don't even know what route you working.

TROY   They keep switching me around. Got me out in Greentree[9] now . . .
hauling white folks' garbage.

BONO   Greentree, huh? You lucky, at least you ain't got to be lifting them barrels. Damn if they ain't getting heavier. I'm gonna put in my two years and
55   call it quits.

TROY   I'm thinking about retiring myself.

BONO   You got it easy. You can *drive* for another five years.

TROY   It ain't the same, Bono. It ain't like working the back of the truck. Ain't
got nobody to talk to . . . feel like you working by yourself. Naw, I'm think-
60   ing about retiring. How's Lucille?

BONO   She alright. Her arthritis get to acting up on her sometime. Saw Rose
on my way in. She going down to the church, huh?

TROY   Yeah, she took up going down there. All them preachers looking for
somebody to fatten their pockets. [*Pause*] Got some gin here.

65   BONO   Naw, thanks. I just stopped by to say hello.

TROY   Hell, nigger . . . you can take a drink. I ain't never known you to say no
to a drink. You ain't got to work tomorrow.

BONO   I just stopped by. I'm fixing to go over to Skinner's. We got us a domino game going over his house every Friday.

70   TROY   Nigger, you can't play no dominoes. I used to whup you four games
out of five.

BONO   Well, that learned me. I'm getting better.

TROY   Yeah? Well, that's alright.

BONO   Look here . . . I got to be getting on. Stop by sometime, huh?

75   TROY   Yeah, I'll do that, Bono. Lucille told Rose you bought her a new
refrigerator.

BONO   Yeah, Rose told Lucille you had finally built your fence . . . so I figured we'd call it even.

TROY   I knew you would.

80   BONO   Yeah . . . okay. I'll be talking to you.

TROY   Yeah, take care, Bono. Good to see you. I'm gonna stop over.

BONO   Yeah. Okay, Troy.

[BONO *exits.* TROY *drinks from the bottle.*]

TROY

Old Blue died and I dig his grave
Let him down with a golden chain
85   Every night when I hear old Blue bark
I know Blue treed a possum in Noah's Ark.
Hear it ring! Hear it ring!

[CORY *enters the yard. They eye each other for a beat.* TROY *is sitting in the
middle of the steps.* CORY *walks over.*]

CORY   I got to get by.

TROY   Say what? What's you say?

90   CORY   You in my way. I got to get by.

9. That is, Green Tree, an affluent suburb of Pittsburgh.

TROY   You got to get by where? This is my house. Bought and paid for. In full. Took me fifteen years. And if you wanna go in my house and I'm sitting on the steps . . . you say excuse me. Like your mama taught you.

CORY   Come on, Pop . . . I got to get by.

[CORY *starts to maneuver his way past* TROY. TROY *grabs his leg and shoves him back.*]

95   TROY   You just gonna walk over top of me?

CORY   I live here too!

TROY [*advancing toward him*]   You just gonna walk over top of me in my own house?

CORY   I ain't scared of you.

100   TROY   I ain't asked if you was scared of me. I asked you if you was fixing to walk over top of me in my own house? That's the question. You ain't gonna say excuse me? You just gonna walk over top of me?

CORY   If you wanna put it like that.

TROY   How else am I gonna put it?

105   CORY   I was walking by you to go into the house cause you sitting on the steps drunk, singing to yourself. You can put it like that.

TROY   Without saying excuse me???

[CORY *doesn't respond.*]

I asked you a question. Without saying excuse me???

CORY   I ain't got to say excuse me to you. You don't count around here no more.

110   TROY   Oh, I see . . . I don't count around here no more. You ain't got to say excuse me to your daddy. All of a sudden you done got so grown that your daddy don't count around here no more . . . Around here in his own house and yard that he done paid for with the sweat of his brow. You done got so grown to where you gonna take over. You gonna take over my house. Is that

115   right? You gonna wear my pants. You gonna go in there and stretch out on my bed. You ain't got to say excuse me cause I don't count around here no more. Is that right?

CORY   That's right. You always talking this dumb stuff. Now, why don't you just get out my way.

120   TROY   I guess you got someplace to sleep and something to put in your belly. You got that, huh? You got that? That's what you need. You got that, huh?

CORY   You don't know what I got. You ain't got to worry about what I got.

TROY   You right! You one hundred percent right! I done spent the last seventeen years worrying about what you got. Now it's your turn, see? I'll tell you

125   what to do. You grown . . . we done established that. You a man. Now, let's see you act like one. Turn your behind around and walk out this yard. And when you get out there in the alley . . . you can forget about this house. See? Cause this is my house. You go on and be a man and get your own house. You can forget about this. Cause this is mine. You go on and get

130   yours cause I'm through with doing for you.

CORY   You talking about what you did for me . . . what'd you ever give me?

TROY   Them feet and bones! That pumping heart, nigger! I give you more than anybody else is ever gonna give you.

CORY   You ain't never gave me nothing! You ain't never done nothing but hold

135   me back. Afraid I was gonna be better than you. All you ever did was try and make me scared of you. I used to tremble every time you called my

name. Every time I heard your footsteps in the house. Wondering all the time . . . what's Papa gonna say if I do this? . . . What's he gonna say if I do that? . . . What's Papa gonna say if I turn on the radio? And Mama, too . . .

140   she tries . . . but she's scared of you.

TROY   You leave your mama out of this. She ain't got nothing to do with this.

CORY   I don't know how she stand you . . . after what you did to her.

TROY   I told you to leave your mama out of this!

[*He advances toward* CORY.]

CORY   What you gonna do . . . give me a whupping? You can't whup me no

145   more. You're too old. You just an old man.

TROY [*shoves him on his shoulder*]   Nigger! That's what you are. You just another nigger on the street to me!

CORY   You crazy! You know that?

TROY   Go on now! You got the devil in you. Get on away from me!

150 CORY   You just a crazy old man . . . talking about I got the devil in me.

TROY   Yeah, I'm crazy! If you don't get on the other side of that yard . . . I'm gonna show you how crazy I am! Go on . . . get the hell out of my yard.

CORY   It ain't your yard. You took Uncle Gabe's money he got from the army to buy this house and then you put him out.

155 TROY [*advances on* CORY]   Get your black ass out of my yard!

[TROY's *advance backs* CORY *up against the tree.* CORY *grabs up the bat.*]

CORY   I ain't going nowhere! Come on . . . put me out! I ain't scared of you.

TROY   That's my bat!

CORY   Come on!

TROY   Put my bat down!

160 CORY   Come on, put me out.

[CORY *swings at* TROY, *who backs across the yard.*]

What's the matter? You so bad . . . put me out!

[TROY *advances toward* CORY.]

CORY [*backing up*]   Come on! Come on!

TROY   You're gonna have to use it! You wanna draw that bat back on me . . . you're gonna have to use it.

165 CORY   Come on! . . . Come on!

[CORY *swings the bat at* TROY *a second time. He misses.* TROY *continues to advance toward him.*]

TROY   You're gonna have to kill me! You wanna draw that bat back on me. You're gonna have to kill me.

[CORY, *backed up against the tree, can go no farther.* TROY *taunts him. He sticks out his head and offers him a target.*]

Come on! Come on!

[CORY *is unable to swing the bat.* TROY *grabs it.*]

TROY   Then I'll show you.

[CORY *and* TROY *struggle over the bat. The struggle is fierce and fully engaged.* TROY *ultimately is the stronger, and takes the bat from* CORY *and stands over him ready to swing. He stops himself.*]

170   Go on and get away from around my house.

[CORY *stung by his defeat, picks himself up, walks slowly out of the yard and up the alley.*]

CORY   Tell Mama I'll be back for my things.
TROY   They'll be on the other side of that fence.

[CORY *exits.*]

TROY   I can't taste nothing. Helluljah! I can't taste nothing no more. [TROY *assumes a batting posture and begins to taunt Death, the fastball on the outside corner.*] Come on! It's between you and me now! Come on! Anytime
175   you want! Come on! I be ready for you . . . but I ain't gonna be easy.

[*The lights go down on the scene.*]

2.5

The time is 1965. The lights come up in the yard. It is the morning of TROY's *funeral. A funeral plaque with a light hangs beside the door. There is a small garden plot off to the side. There is noise and activity in the house as* ROSE, GABRIEL, *and* BONO *have gathered. The door opens and* RAYNELL, *seven years old, enters dressed in a flannel nightgown. She crosses to the garden and pokes around with a stick.* ROSE *calls from the house.*

ROSE   Raynell!
RAYNELL   Mam?
ROSE   What you doing out there?
RAYNELL   Nothing.

[ROSE *comes to the door.*]

5   ROSE   Girl, get in here and get dressed. What you doing?
RAYNELL   Seeing if my garden growed.
ROSE   I told you it ain't gonna grow overnight. You got to wait.
RAYNELL   It don't look like it never gonna grow. Dag!
ROSE   I told you a watched pot never boils. Get in here and get dressed.
10   RAYNELL   This ain't even no pot, Mama.
ROSE   You just have to give it a chance. It'll grow. Now you come on and do what I told you. We got to be getting ready. This ain't no morning to be playing around. You hear me?
RAYNELL   Yes, mam.

[ROSE *exits into the house.* RAYNELL *continues to poke at her garden with a stick.* CORY *enters. He is dressed in a Marine corporal's uniform, and carries a duffel bag. His posture is that of a military man, and his speech has a clipped sternness.*]

15   CORY [*to* RAYNELL]   Hi. [*Pause*] I bet your name is Raynell.
RAYNELL   Uh huh.
CORY   Is your mama home?

[RAYNELL *runs up on the porch and calls through the screen door.*]

RAYNELL   Mama . . . there's some man out here. Mama?

[ROSE *comes to the door.*]

ROSE   Cory? Lord have mercy! Look here, you all!

[ROSE *and* CORY *embrace in a tearful reunion as* BONO *and* LYONS *enter from the house dressed in funeral clothes.*]

20   BONO   Aw, looka here . . .
ROSE   Done got all grown up!
CORY   Don't cry, Mama. What you crying about?
ROSE   I'm just so glad you made it.

CORY   Hey Lyons. How you doing, Mr. Bono.

[LYONS *goes to embrace* CORY.]

25 LYONS   Look at you, man. Look at you. Don't he look good, Rose. Got them
Corporal stripes.

ROSE   What took you so long.

CORY   You know how the Marines are, Mama. They got to get all their paperwork straight before they let you do anything.

30 ROSE   Well, I'm sure glad you made it. They let Lyons come. Your Uncle
Gabe's still in the hospital. They don't know if they gonna let him out or
not. I just talked to them a little while ago.

LYONS   A Corporal in the United States Marines.

BONO   Your daddy knew you had it in you. He used to tell me all the time.

35 LYONS   Don't he look good, Mr. Bono?

BONO   Yeah, he remind me of Troy when I first met him. [*Pause*] Say, Rose,
Lucille's down at the church with the choir. I'm gonna go down and get the
pallbearers lined up. I'll be back to get you all.

ROSE   Thanks, Jim.

40 CORY   See you, Mr. Bono.

LYONS   [*with his arm around* RAYNELL] Cory . . . look at Raynell. Ain't she
precious? She gonna break a whole lot of hearts.

ROSE   Raynell, come and say hello to your brother. This is your brother,
Cory. You remember Cory.

45 RAYNELL   No, Mam.

CORY   She don't remember me, Mama.

ROSE   Well, we talk about you. She heard us talk about you. [*To* RAYNELL]
This is your brother, Cory. Come on and say hello.

RAYNELL   Hi.

50 CORY   Hi. So you're Raynell. Mama told me a lot about you.

ROSE   You all come on into the house and let me fix you some breakfast.
Keep up your strength.

CORY   I ain't hungry, Mama.

LYONS   You can fix me something, Rose. I'll be in there in a minute.

55 ROSE   Cory, you sure you don't want nothing. I know they ain't feeding you
right.

CORY   No, Mama . . . thanks. I don't feel like eating. I'll get something later.

ROSE   Raynell . . . get on upstairs and get that dress on like I told you.

[ROSE *and* RAYNELL *exit into the house.*]

LYONS   So . . . I hear you thinking about getting married.

60 CORY   Yeah, I done found the right one, Lyons. It's about time.

LYONS   Me and Bonnie been split up about four years now. About the time
Papa retired. I guess she just got tired of all them changes I was putting her
through. [*Pause*] I always knew you was gonna make something out yourself. Your head was always in the right direction. So . . . you gonna stay
65 in . . . make it a career . . . put in your twenty years?[1]

CORY   I don't know. I got six already, I think that's enough.

LYONS   Stick with Uncle Sam and retire early. Ain't nothing out here. I guess
Rose told you what happened with me. They got me down the workhouse.
I thought I was being slick cashing other people's checks.

---

1. The minimum years of service required for retirement benefits.

70 CORY   How much time you doing?

LYONS   They give me three years. I got that beat now. I ain't got but nine
more months. It ain't so bad. You learn to deal with it like anything else.
You got to take the crookeds with the straights. That's what Papa used to
say. He used to say that when he struck out. I seen him strike out three
75   times in a row . . . and the next time up he hit the ball over the grandstand.
Right out there in Homestead Field. He wasn't satisfied hitting in the
seats . . . he want to hit it over everything! After the game he had two hundred people standing around waiting to shake his hand. You got to take the
crookeds with the straights. Yeah, Papa was something else.

80 CORY   You still playing?

LYONS   Cory . . . you know I'm gonna do that. There's some fellows down
there we got us a band . . . we gonna try and stay together when we get
out . . . but yeah, I'm still playing. It still helps me to get out of bed in the
morning. As long as it do that I'm gonna be right there playing and trying to
85   make some sense out of it.

ROSE [calling]   Lyons, I got these eggs in the pan.

LYONS   Let me go on and get these eggs, man. Get ready to go bury Papa.
[Pause] How you doing? You doing alright?

> [CORY nods. LYONS touches him on the shoulder and they share a moment
> of silent grief. LYONS exits into the house. CORY wanders about the yard.
> RAYNELL enters.]

RAYNELL   Hi.

90 CORY   Hi.

RAYNELL   Did you used to sleep in my room?

CORY   Yeah . . . that used to be my room.

RAYNELL   That's what Papa call it. "Cory's room." It got your football in the
closet.

> [ROSE comes to the door.]

95 ROSE   Raynell, get in there and get them good shoes on.

RAYNELL   Mama, can't I wear these? Them other one hurt my feet.

ROSE   Well, they just gonna have to hurt your feet for a while. You ain't said
they hurt your feet when you went down to the store and got them.

RAYNELL   They didn't hurt then. My feet done got bigger.

100 ROSE   Don't you give me no backtalk now. You get in there and get them
shoes on.

> [RAYNELL exits into the house.]

Ain't too much changed. He still got that piece of rag tied to that tree. He
was out here swinging that bat. I was just ready to go back in the house. He
swung that bat and then he just fell over. Seem like he swung it and stood
105   there with this grin on his face . . . and then he just fell over. They carried
him on down to the hospital, but I knew there wasn't no need . . . why
don't you come on in the house?

CORY   Mama . . . I got something to tell you. I don't know how to tell you
this . . . but I've got to tell you . . . I'm not going to Papa's funeral.

110 ROSE   Boy, hush your mouth. That's your daddy you talking about. I don't
want hear that kind of talk this morning. I done raised you to come to this?
You standing there all healthy and grown talking about you ain't going to
your daddy's funeral?

CORY   Mama . . . listen . . .

115 ROSE   I don't want to hear it, Cory. You just get that thought out of your
head.
CORY   I can't drag Papa with me everywhere I go. I've got to say no to him.
One time in my life I've got to say no.
ROSE   Don't nobody have to listen to nothing like that. I know you and your
120 daddy ain't seen eye to eye, but I ain't got to listen to that kind of talk this
morning. Whatever was between you and your daddy . . . the time has
come to put it aside. Just take it and set it over there on the shelf and forget
about it. Disrespecting your daddy ain't gonna make you a man, Cory. You
got to find a way to come to that on your own. Not going to your daddy's
125 funeral ain't gonna make you a man.
CORY   The whole time I was growing up . . . living in his house . . . Papa was
like a shadow that followed you everywhere. It weighed on you and sunk
into your flesh. It would wrap around you and lay there until you couldn't
tell which one was you any more. That shadow digging in your flesh. Trying
130 to crawl in. Trying to live through you. Everywhere I looked, Troy Maxson
was staring back at me . . . hiding under the bed . . . in the closet. I'm just
saying I've got to find a way to get rid of that shadow, Mama.
ROSE   You just like him. You got him in you good.
CORY   Don't tell me that, Mama.
135 ROSE   You Troy Maxson all over again.
CORY   I don't want to be Troy Maxson. I want to be me.
ROSE   You can't be nobody but who you are, Cory. That shadow wasn't nothing but you growing into yourself. You either got to grow into it or cut it
down to fit you. But that's all you got to make life with. That's all you got to
140 measure yourself against that world out there. Your daddy wanted you to be
everything he wasn't . . . and at the same time he tried to make you into
everything he was. I don't know if he was right or wrong . . . but I do know
he meant to do more good than he meant to do harm. He wasn't always
right. Sometimes when he touched he bruised. And sometimes when he
145 took me in his arms he cut.
When I first met your daddy I thought . . . Here is a man I can lay down
with and make a baby. That's the first thing I thought when I seen him. I
was thirty years old and had done seen my share of men. But when he
walked up to me and said, "I can dance a waltz that'll make you dizzy," I
150 thought, Rose Lee, here is a man that you can open yourself up to and be
filled to bursting. Here is a man that can fill all them empty spaces you
been tipping around the edges of. One of them empty spaces was being
somebody's mother.
I married your daddy and settled down to cooking his supper and keep-
155 ing clean sheets on the bed. When your daddy walked through the house
he was so big he filled it up. That was my first mistake. Not to make him
leave some room for me. For my part in the matter. But at that time I
wanted that. I wanted a house that I could sing in. And that's what your
daddy gave me. I didn't know to keep up his strength I had to give up little
160 pieces of mine. I did that. I took on his life as mine and mixed up the
pieces so that you couldn't hardly tell which was which any more. It was my
choice. It was my life and I didn't have to live it like that. But that's what
life offered me in the way of being a woman and I took it. I grabbed hold of
it with both hands.

165 　　By the time Raynell came into the house, me and your daddy had done lost touch with one another. I didn't want to make my blessing off of nobody's misfortune . . . but I took on to Raynell like she was all them babies I had wanted and never had.

　　　　[*The phone rings.*]

170 Like I'd been blessed to relive a part of my life. And if the Lord see fit to keep up my strength . . . I'm gonna do her just like your daddy did you . . . I'm gonna give her the best of what's in me.

RAYNELL [*entering, still with her old shoes*]　Mama . . . Reverend Tollivier on the phone.

　　　　[ROSE *exits into the house.*]

RAYNELL　Hi.

175 CORY　Hi.

RAYNELL　You in the Army or the Marines?

CORY　Marines.

RAYNELL　Papa said it was the Army. Did you know Blue?

CORY　Blue? Who's Blue?

180 RAYNELL　Papa's dog what he sing about all the time.

CORY [*singing*]
　　Hear it ring! Hear it ring!
　　I had a dog his name was Blue
　　You know Blue was mighty true
　　You know Blue was a good old dog
185　　Blue treed a possum in a hollow log
　　You know from that he was a good old dog.
　　Hear it ring! Hear it ring!

　　　　[RAYNELL *joins in singing.*]

CORY and RAYNELL
　　Blue treed a possum out on a limb
　　Blue looked at me and I looked at him
190　　Grabbed that possum and put him in a sack
　　Blue stayed there till I came back
　　Old Blue's feets was big and round
　　Never allowed a possum to touch the ground.

　　Old Blue died and I dug his grave
195　　I dug his grave with a silver spade
　　Let him down with a golden chain
　　And every night I call his name
　　Go on Blue, you good dog you
　　Go on Blue, you good dog you

RAYNELL
200　　Blue laid down and died like a man
　　Blue laid down and died . . .

BOTH
　　Blue laid down and died like a man
　　Now he's treeing possums in the Promised Land
　　I'm gonna tell you this to let you know
205　　Blue's gone where the good dogs go

When I hear old Blue bark
When I hear old Blue bark
Blue treed a possum in Noah's Ark.
Blue treed a possum in Noah's Ark.

[ROSE *comes to the screen door.*]

210 ROSE   Cory, we gonna be ready to go in a minute.

CORY [*to* RAYNELL]   You go on in the house and change them shoes like Mama told you so we can go to Papa's funeral.

RAYNELL   Okay, I'll be back.

[RAYNELL *exits into the house.* CORY *gets up and crosses over to the tree.* ROSE *stands in the screen door watching him.* GABRIEL *enters from the alley.*]

GABRIEL [*calling*]   Hey, Rose!

215 ROSE   Gabe?

GABRIEL   I'm here, Rose. Hey Rose, I'm here!

[ROSE *enters from the house.*]

ROSE   Lord . . . Look here, Lyons!

LYONS   See, I told you, Rose . . . I told you they'd let him come.

CORY   How you doing, Uncle Gabe?

220 LYONS   How you doing, Uncle Gabe?

GABRIEL   Hey, Rose. It's time. It's time to tell St. Peter to open the gates. Troy, you ready? You ready, Troy. I'm gonna tell St. Peter to open the gates. You get ready now.

[*Gabriel, with great fanfare, braces himself to blow. The trumpet is without a mouthpiece. He puts the end of it into his mouth and blows with great force, like a man who has been waiting some twenty-odd years for this single moment. No sound comes out of the trumpet. He braces himself and blows again with the same result. A third time he blows. There is a weight of impossible description that falls away and leaves him bare and exposed to a frightful realization. It is a trauma that a sane and normal mind would be unable to withstand. He begins to dance. A slow, strange dance, eerie and life-giving. A dance of atavistic signature and ritual.* LYONS *attempts to embrace him.* GABRIEL *pushes* LYONS *away. He begins to howl in what is an attempt at song, or perhaps a song turning back into itself in an attempt at speech. He finishes his dance and the gates of heaven stand open as wide as God's closet.*]

That's the way that go!

Blackout.

CRITICAL PERSPECTIVE

AUGUST WILSON

In June 1996, playwright August Wilson (1945–2005) delivered the keynote address for the national conference of the Theatre Communications Group (TCG), a not-for-profit resource, publishing, and advocacy organization for the American theater. Wilson, who had already twice earned the Pulitzer Prize for drama (*FENCES*, 1985; *The Piano Lesson*, 1990), took this opportunity to speak to the audience of leading theater professionals about issues he felt were central to the future of the American theater. His speech, titled "The Ground on Which I Stand," singled out the writing of preeminent theater critic Robert Brustein (b. 1927) for what Wilson argued was Brustein's "presumption of inferiority of the work of minority artists." Brustein, who did not attend the TCG conference, soon learned of Wilson's remarks, and subsequently published a response, "Subsidized Separatism." The fierce dispute between the two writers continued over the coming months, culminating in a public debate, sponsored by TCG and held in New York City in January 1997, moderated by theater artist Anna Deavere Smith.

In this selection, taken from the version of the original speech that Wilson revised and published in book form in 2001, he positions himself in a political and theatrical tradition with roots in the Black Power movement of the 1960s. He identifies key issues for black artists in the American professional theater, including the practice of "colorblind casting," the aesthetic criteria critics like Brustein use to assess the dramaturgy of African American playwrights, and the financial structure of subsidies that Wilson believes disproportionately supports white dramatists and the theaters that produce their work. Grounded in questions of cultural power and access to resources, Wilson's essay is an impassioned call for a fundamental rethinking of race and American theater.   J.E.G.

---

from "The Ground on Which I Stand"

I wish to make it clear from the outset that I do not have a mandate to speak for anyone. There are many intelligent blacks working in the American theatre who speak in a loud and articulate voice. It would be the greatest of presumptions to say that I speak for them. I speak only for myself and those who may think as I do.

I have come here today to make a testimony, to talk about the ground on which I stand and all the many grounds on which I and my ancestors have toiled, and the ground of theatre on which my fellow artists and I have labored to bring forth its fruits, its daring and its sometimes lacerating, and often healing, truths.

*   *   *

In one guise, the ground I stand on has been pioneered by the Greek dramatists—by Euripides, Aeschylus and Sophocles—by William Shakespeare, by Shaw, Ibsen and Chekov, Eugene O'Neill, Arthur Miller, Tennessee Williams. In another guise, the ground that I stand on has been pioneered by my grandfather, by Nat Turner, by Denmark Vesey, by Martin Delaney, Marcus Garvey and the Honorable Elijah Muhammad. That is the ground of the affirmation of the value of one's being, an affirmation of his worth in the face of this society's urgent and sometimes profound denial. It was this ground as a young man coming into manhood searching for something to dedicate my life to that I discovered the Black Power Movement of the '60s. I felt it a duty and an honor to participate in that historic moment. As a people who had arrived in America chained and malnourished in the hold of a 350-foot Portuguese, Dutch or English sailing ship, we were now seeking ways to alter our relationship to the society in which we live—and, perhaps more important, searching for ways to alter the shared expectations of ourselves as a community of people.

I find it curious but no small accident that I seldom hear those words "Black Power" spoken, and when mention is made of that part of black history in America, whether in the press or in conversation, reference is made to the Civil Rights Movement as though the Black Power Movement—an important social movement by America's ex-slaves—had in fact never happened. But the Black Power Movement of the '60s was [in fact] a reality; it was the kiln in which I was fired, and has much to do with the person I am today and the ideas and attitudes that I carry as part of my consciousness.

I mention this because it is difficult to disassociate my concerns with theatre from the concerns of my life as a black man, and it is difficult to disassociate one part of my life from another. I have strived to live it all seamless—art and life together, inseparable and indistinguishable. The ideas I discovered and embraced in my youth when my idealism was full blown I have not abandoned in middle age when idealism is something less than blooming, but wisdom is starting to bud. The ideas of self-determination, self-respect and self-defense that governed my life in the '60s I find just as valid and self-urging in 1996. The need to alter our relationship to the society and to alter the shared expectations of ourselves as a racial group I find of greater urgency now than it was then.

I am what is known, at least among the followers and supporters of the ideas of Marcus Garvey, as a "race man." That is simply that I believe that race matters—that is the largest, most identifiable and most important part of our personality. It is the largest category of identification because it is the one that most influences your perception of yourself, and it is the one to which others in the world of men most respond. Race is also an important part of the American landscape, as America is made up of an amalgamation of races from all parts of the globe. Race is also the product of a shared gene pool that allows for group identification, and it is an organizing principle around which cultures are formed. When I say culture I am speaking about the behavior patterns, the arts, beliefs, institutions and all other products of human work and thought as expressed by a particular community of people.

There are some people who will say that black Americans do not have a culture—that cultures are reserved for other people, most notably Europeans of various ethnic groupings, and that black Americans make up a sub-group of American culture that is derived from the European origins of its majority population. But black Americans are Africans, and there are many histories and many cultures on the African continent.

Those who would deny black Americans their culture would also deny them their history and the inherent values that are a part of all human life.

Growing up in my mother's house at 1727 Bedford Avenue in Pittsburgh, PA, I learned the language, the eating habits, the religious beliefs, the gestures, the notions of common sense, attitudes towards sex, concepts of beauty and justice, and the responses to pleasure and pain . . . that my mother had learned from her mother, and which you could trace back to the first African who set foot on the continent. It is this culture that stands today on these shores today as a testament to the resiliency of the African-American spirit.

The term black or African-American not only denotes race, it denotes condition, and carries with it the vestige of slavery and the social segregation and abuse of opportunity so vivid in our memory. That this abuse of opportunity and truncation of possibility is continuing and is so pervasive in our society in 1996 says much about who we are and much about the work that is necessary to alter our perceptions of each other and to effect meaningful prosperity for all.

The problematic nature of the relationship between whites and blacks has for too long led us astray from the fulfillment of our possibilities as a society. We stare at each other across a divide of economics and privilege that has become an encumbrance on black Americans' ability to prosper and on the collective will and spirit of our national purpose.

I speak about economics and privilege, one significant fact affects us all in the American theatre: of the sixty-six LORT[1] theatres, there is one that can be considered black. From this it could be falsely assumed that

---

1. League of Resident Theatres, the national association of professional, not-for-profit theater companies in the United States, whose members are sometimes referred to as "regional theaters."

there aren't sufficient numbers of blacks working in the American theatre to sustain and support more theatres.

If you do not know, I will tell you: black theatre in America is alive, it is vibrant, it is vital . . . it just isn't funded.

Black theatre doesn't share in the economics that would allow it to support its artists and supply them with meaningful avenues to develop their talent and broadcast and disseminate ideas crucial to its growth. The economics are reserved as privilege to the overwhelming abundance of institutions that preserve, promote and perpetuate white culture.

That is not a complaint. That is an advertisement. Since the funding sources, both public and private, do not publicly carry avowed missions of exclusion and segregated support, this is obviously either a glaring case of oversight, or we the proponents of black theatre have not made our presence or our needs known. I hope here tonight to correct both of those oversights and assumptions.

I do not have the time in this short talk to reiterate the long and distinguished history of black theatre—often accomplished amid adverse and hostile conditions—but I would like to take the time to mark a few high points.

There are and have always been two distinct and parallel traditions in black art: that is, art that is conceived and designed to entertain white society, and art that feeds the spirit and celebrates the life of black America by designing its strategies for survival and prosperity.

An important part of black theatre that is often ignored but is seminal to its tradition is its origins on the slave plantations of the South. Summoned to the "big house" to entertain the slave owner and his guests, the slave began a tradition of theatre as entertainment for whites that reached its pinnacle in the heyday of the Harlem Renaissance.[2] This entertainment for whites consisted of whatever the slave imagined or knew that his master wanted to see and hear. This tradition has its present-life counterpart in the crossover artists that slant their material for white consumption.

The second tradition occurred when the African in the confines of the slave quarters sought to invest his spirit with the strength of his ancestors by conceiving in his art, in his song and dance, a world in which he was the spiritual center, and his existence was a manifest act of the creator from whom life flowed. He could then create art that was functional and furnished him with a spiritual temperament necessary for his survival as property and the dehumanizing status that was attendant to that.

I stand myself and my art squarely on the self-defining ground of the slave quarters, and find the ground to be hallowed and made fertile by the blood and bones of the men and women who can be described as warriors on the cultural battlefield that affirmed their self-worth. As there is no

2. Cultural movement of the 1920s, centered in the Harlem section of Manhattan, which promoted the artistry and intellectual inquiry of African Americans.

idea that cannot be contained by black life, these men and women found themselves to be sufficient and secure in their art and their instructions.

It was this high ground of self-determination that the black playwrights of the '60s marked out for themselves. Ron Milner; Ed Bullins; Philip Hayes Dean; Richard Wesley; Lonne Elder, III; Sonia Sanchez; Barbara Ann Teer and Amiri Baraka were among those playwrights who were particularly vocal and whose talents confirmed their presence in the society, and altered the American theatre, its meaning, its craft and its history. This brilliant explosion of black arts and letters in the '60s remains for me the hallmark and the signpost that points the way to our contemporary work on the same ground. Black playwrights everywhere remain indebted to them for their brave and courageous forays into an area that is marked with land mines and the shadows of snipers—those who would reserve the territory of arts and letters and the American theatre as their own special province and point blacks toward the ball fields and the bandstands.

That black theatre today comes under such assaults should surprise no one, as we are on the verge of reclaiming and reexamining the purpose and pillars of our art and laying out new directions for its expansion. And as such we make a target for cultural imperialists who seek to empower and propagate their ideas about the world as the only valid ideas, and see blacks as woefully deficient not only in arts and letters but in the abundant gifts of humanity.

In the nineteenth century, the lack of education, the lack of contact with different cultures, the expensive and slow methods of travel and communication fostered such ideas, and the breeding ground of ignorance and racial intolerance promoted them.

The King's English and the lexicon of a people given to such ignorance and intolerance did not do much to dispel such obvious misconceptions, but provided them with a home. I cite *Webster's Third New International Dictionary:*

> "BLACK: outrageously wicked, dishonorable, connected with the devil, menacing, sullen, hostile, unqualified, illicit, illegal, violators of public regulations, affected by some undesirable condition . . ." etc.

> "WHITE: free from blemish, moral stain or impurity; outstandingly righteous, innocent; not marked by malignant influence; notably auspicious, fortunate, decent; a sterling man."

Such is the linguistic environment that informs the distance that separates blacks and whites in America and which the cultural imperialists, who cannot imagine a life existing and flourishing outside their benevolent control, embraces.

Robert Brustein,[3] writing in an article/review titled "Unity from Diversity" [*The New Republic*, July 19–26, 1993], is apparently disturbed that

---

3. American theater critic and the founding artistic director of the Yale Repertory Theatre and the American Repertory Theater (b. 1927).

"there is a tremendous outpouring of work by minority artists" which he attributes to cultural diversity. He writes that the practice of extending invitations to a national banquet from which a lot of hungry people have long been excluded is a practice that can lead to confused standards. He goes on to establish a presumption of inferiority of the work of minority artists: "Funding agencies have started substituting sociological criteria for aesthetic criteria in their grant procedures, indicating that 'elitist' notions like quality and excellence are no longer functional." He goes on to say: "It's disarming in all senses of the word to say that we don't share common experiences that are measurable by common standards. But the growing number of truly talented artists with more universal interests suggests that we may soon be in a position to return to a single value system."

Brustein's surprisingly sophomoric assumption that this tremendous outpouring of work by minority artists leads to confusing standards and that funding agencies have started substituting sociological for aesthetic criteria, leaving aside notions like quality and excellence, shows him to be a victim of nineteenth-century thinking and the linguistic environment that posits blacks as unqualified. Quite possibly this tremendous outpouring of works by minority artists may lead to a *raising* of standards and a *raising* of the levels of excellence, but Mr. Brustein cannot allow that possibility.

To suggest that funding agencies are rewarding inferior work by pursuing sociological criteria only serves to call into question the tremendous outpouring of plays by white playwrights who benefit from funding given to the sixty-six LORT theatres.

Are those theatres funded on sociological or aesthetic criteria? Do we have sixty-six excellent theatres? Or do those theatres benefit from the sociological advantage that they are run by whites and cater to largely white audiences?

The truth is that often where there are aesthetic criteria of excellence, it is the sociological criteria that have traditionally excluded blacks. I say raise the standards and remove the sociological conditions of race as privilege, and we will meet you at the crossroads, in equal numbers prepared to do the work of extending and developing the common ground of the American theatre.

We are capable of work of the highest order; we can answer to the high standards of world-class art. And anyone who doubts our capabilities at this late stage is being intellectually dishonest.

We can meet on the common ground of theatre as a field of work and endeavor. But we cannot meet on the common ground of experience.

Where is the common ground in the horrifics of lynching? Where is the common ground in the maim of the policeman's bullet? Where is the common ground in the hull of a slave ship or the deck of a slave ship with its refreshments of air and expanse?

We will not be denied our history.

We have voice and we have temper. We are too far along this road from the loss of our political will, we are too far along the road of reassembling ourselves, too far along the road to regaining spiritual health to allow such transgression of our history to go unchallenged.

The commonalties that we share are the commonalities of culture. We decorate our houses. That is something we do in common. We do it differently because we value different things. We have different manners and different values of social intercourse. We have different ideas of what a party is.

There are some commonalities to our different ideas. We both offer food and drink to our guests, but because we have different culinary values, different culinary histories, we offer different food and drink to our guests. As an example, in our culinary history, we have learned to make do with the feet and ears and tails and intestines of the pig rather than the loin and the ham and the bacon. Because of our different histories with the same animal, we have different culinary ideas. But we share a common experience with the pig as opposed to say Muslims and Jews, who do not share that experience.

We can meet on the common ground of the American theatre.

We cannot share a single value system if that value system consists of the values of white Americans based on their European ancestors. We reject that as Cultural Imperialism. We need a value system that includes our contributions as Africans in America. Our agendas are as valid as yours. We may disagree, we may forever be on opposite sides of aesthetics, but we can only share a value system that is inclusive of all Americans and recognizes their unique and valuable contributions.

The ground together: We must develop the ground together. We reject the idea of equality among equals, but we say rather the equality of all men.

The common values of the American theatre that we can share are plot . . . dialogue . . . characterization . . . design. How we both make use of them will be determined by who we are and what ground we are standing on and what our cultural values are.

Theatre is part of art history in terms of its craft and dramaturgy, but it is part of social history in terms of how it is financed and governed. By making money available to theatres willing to support colorblind casting,[4] the financiers and governors have signaled not only their unwillingness to support black theatre but their willingness to fund dangerous and divisive assaults against it. Colorblind casting is an aberrant idea that has never had any validity other than as a tool of the Cultural Imperialists who view their American culture, rooted in the icons of European culture, as beyond reproach in its perfection. It is inconceivable to them that life could be lived and enriched without knowing Shakespeare or Mozart. Their gods, their manners, their being, are the only true and correct representations of humankind. They refuse to recognize black conduct and manners as

---

4. Sometimes also called "non-traditional casting," the practice of selecting actors for roles based on their performance skills, rather than their race, thereby theoretically providing traditionally underrepresented actors with a wider range of opportunities, especially in plays that have historically been cast exclusively with white actors.

part of a system that is fueled by its own philosophy, mythology, history, creative motif, social organization and ethos. The idea that blacks have their own way of responding to the world, their own values, style, linguistics, their own religion and aesthetics, is unacceptable to them.

For a black actor to stand on the stage as part of a social milieu that has denied him his gods, his culture, his humanity, his mores, his ideas of himself and the world he lives in, is to be in league with a thousand naysayers who wish to corrupt the vigor and spirit of his heart.

To cast us in the role of mimics is to deny us our own competence.

Our manners, our style, our approach to language, our gestures, and our bodies are not for rent. The history of our bodies—the maimings, the lashings, the lynchings, the body that is capable of inspiring profound rage and pungent cruelty—is not for rent. Nor is the meaning of our history or our bodies for rent.

To mount an all-black production of a *Death of a Salesman*[5] or any other play conceived for white actors as an investigation of the human condition through the specifics of white culture is to deny us our own humanity, our own history, and the need to make our own investigations from the cultural ground on which we stand as black Americans. It is an assault on our presence, and our difficult but honorable history in America; and it is an insult to our intelligence, our playwrights, and our many and varied contributions to the society and the world at large.

The idea of colorblind casting is the same idea of assimilation that black Americans have been rejecting for the past 380 years. For the record, we reject it again. We reject any attempt to blot us out, to reinvent our history and ignore our presence or to maim our spiritual product. We must not continue to meet on this path. We will not deny our history, and we will not allow it to be made to be of little consequence, to be ignored or misinterpreted.

In an effort to spare us the burden of being "affected by an undesirable condition" and as a gesture of benevolence, many whites (like the proponents of colorblind casting) say, "Oh, I don't see color." We want you to see us. We are black and beautiful. We are not patrons of the linguistic environment that would have us as "unqualified," and "violators of public regulations." We are not ashamed. We have an honorable history in the world of men. We come from a long line of honorable people with complex codes of ethics and social discourse, who devised myths and systems of cosmology and systems of economics, and who were themselves part of a long social and political history. We are not ashamed, and we do not need you to be ashamed for us. Nor do we need the recognition of our blackness to be couched in abstract phrases like "artist of color." Who are you talking about? A Japanese artist? An Eskimo? A Filipino? A Mexican? A Cambodian? A Nigerian? Are we to suppose that one white person balances out the rest of humanity lumped together as

---

5. Arthur Miller's 1949 play won the Pulitzer Prize for Drama (see p. 827).

nondescript "people of color"? We reject that. We are unique, and we are specific.

We do not need colorblind casting; we need theatres. We need theatres to develop our playwrights. We need those misguided financial resources to be put to better use. Without theatres we cannot develop our talents. If we cannot develop our talents, then everyone suffers: our writers, the theatre, the audience. Actors are deprived of material, and our communities are deprived of the jobs in support of the art—the company manager, the press coordinator, the electricians, the carpenters, the concessionaires, the people that work in wardrobe, the box-office staff, the ushers and the janitors. We need some theatres. We have only one life to develop our talent, to fulfill our potential as artists. One life, and it is short, and the lack of the means to develop our talent is an encumbrance on that life.

We did not sit on the sidelines while the immigrants of Europe, through hard work, skill, cunning, guile and opportunity, built America into an industrial giant of the twentieth century. It was our labor that provided the capital. It was our labor in the shipyards and the stockyards and the coal mines and the steel mills. Our labor built the roads and the railroads. And when America was challenged, we strode on the battlefield, our boots strapped on and our blood left to soak into the soil of places whose names we could not pronounce, against an enemy whose only crime was ideology. We left our blood in France and Korea and the Philippines and Vietnam, and our only reward has been the deprivation of possibility and the denial of our moral personality.

It cannot continue. The ground together: The American ground on which I stand and which my ancestors purchased with their perseverance, with their survival, with their manners and with their faith.

It cannot continue, as well as other assaults upon our presence and our history cannot continue: When the *New York Times* publishes an article on pop singer Michael Bolton and lists as his influences four white singers, and then as an afterthought tosses in the phrase "and the great black rhythm and blues singers," it cannot be anything but purposeful with intent to maim. These great black rhythm and blues singers are reduced to an afterthought on the verge of oblivion—one stroke of the editor's pen and the history of American music is revised, and Otis Redding, Jerry Butler and Rufus Thomas are consigned to the dustbin of history while Joe Cocker, Mick Jagger and Rod Stewart are elevated to the status of the originators and creators of a vital art that is a product of our spiritual travails; and the history of music becomes a fabrication, a blatant forgery which under the hallowed auspices of the *New York Times* is presented as the genuine article.

We cannot accept these assaults. We must defend and protect our spiritual fruits. To ignore these assaults would make us derelict in our duties. We cannot accept them. Our political capital will not permit them.

So much of what makes this country rich in art and all manners of spiritual life is the contributions that we as African Americans have made. We cannot allow others to have authority over our cultural and spiritual products. We reject, without reservation, any attempt by anyone to rewrite our history so as to deny us the rewards of our spiritual labors, and to become the cultural custodians of our art, our literature and our lives. To give expression to the spirit that has been shaped and fashioned by our history is of necessity to give voice and vent to the history itself.

It must remain for us a history of triumph.

The time has come for black playwrights to confer with one another, to come together to meet each other face to face, to address questions of aesthetics and ways to defend ourselves from the naysayers who would trumpet our talents as insufficient to warrant the same manner of investigation and exploration as the majority. We need to develop guidelines for the protection of our cultural property, our contributions and the influence they accrue. It is time we took the responsibility for our talents in our own hands. We cannot depend on others. We cannot depend on the directors, the managers or the actors to do the work we should be doing for ourselves. It is our lives, our talent and the pursuit of our fulfillment that are being encumbered by false ideas and perceptions of ourselves.

It is time to embrace the political dictates of our history and answer the challenge to our duties. And I further think we should confer in a city in our ancestral homeland in the southern part of the United States in 1998, so that we may enter the millennium united and prepared for a long future of prosperity.

From the hull of a ship to self-determining, self-respecting people. That is the journey we are making.

We are robust in spirit, we are bright with laughter, and we are bold in imagination. Our blood is soaked into the soil and our bones lie scattered the whole way across the Atlantic Ocean, as Hansel's crumbs, to mark our way back home.

We are no longer in the House of Bondage, and soon we will no longer be victims of the counting houses who hold from us ways to develop and support our talents and our expressions of life and its varied meanings. Assaults upon the body politic that demean and ridicule and depress the value and worth of our existence, that seek to render it immobile and to extinguish the flame of freedom lit eons ago by our ancestors upon another continent, must be met with a fierce and uncompromising defense.

If you are willing to accept it, it is your duty to affirm and urge that defense, and that respect and that determination.

And I must mention here, with all due respect to W. E. B. DuBois,[6] that the concept of a "talented tenth" creates an artificial superiority. It is a fallacy and a dangerous idea that only serves to divide us further. I am not willing to throw away as untalented ninety percent of my blood; I am not

---

6. African American writer and cultural theorist (1869–1963), whose notion of the "talented tenth" promoted educational and other opportunities for the elite of the African American community, such that these individuals could then provide leadership for all African Americans.

willing to dismiss the sons and daughters of those people who gave more than lip service to the will to live and made it a duty to prosper in spirit, if not in provision. All God's children got talent. It is a dangerous idea to set one part of the populace above and aside from the other. We do a grave disservice to ourselves not to seek out and embrace and enable all of our human resources as a people. All blacks in America with very few exceptions—*with very few exceptions*—no matter what our status, no matter the size of our bank accounts, no matter how many and what kind of academic degrees we can place beside our names, no matter the furnishings and square footage of our homes, the length of our closets and the quality of the wool and cotton that hangs there—we all in America originated from the same place: the slave plantations of the South. We all share a common past, and despite how some of us might think and how it might look, we all share a common present and will share a common future.

We can make a difference. Artists, playwrights, actors—we can be the spearhead of a movement to reignite and reunite our people's positive energy for a political and social change that is reflective of our spiritual truths rather than economic fallacies. Our talents, our truths, our belief in ourselves is all in our hands. What we make of it will emerge from the self as a baptismal spray that names and defines. What we do now becomes history by which our grandchildren will judge us.

We are not off on a tangent. The foundation of the American theatre is the foundation of European theatre that begins with the great Greek dramatists; it is based on the proscenium stage and the poetics of Aristotle. This is the theatre that we have chosen to work in. And we embrace the values of that theatre but reserve the right to amend, to explore, and to add our African consciousness and our African aesthetic to the art we produce.

To pursue our cultural expression does not separate us. We are not separatists, as Mr. Brustein asserts. We are Americans trying to fulfill our talents. We are not the servants at the party. We are not apprentices in the kitchens. We are not the stable boys to the king's huntsmen. We are Africans. We are Americans. The irreversible sweep of history has decreed that. We are artists who seek to develop our talents and give expression to our personalities. We bring advantage to the common ground that is the American theatre.

All theatres depend on an audience for a dialogue. To the American theatre, subscription audiences are its life blood. But the subscription audience holds theatres hostage to the mediocrity of its tastes, and impedes the further development of an audience for the work that we do. While intentional or not, it serves to keep blacks out of the theatre. A subscription audience becomes not a support system but makes the patrons members of a club to which the theatre serves as a clubhouse. It is an irony that the people who can most afford a full-price ticket get discounts for subscribing, while the single-ticket buyer who cannot afford a subscription is charged the additional burden of support to offset the subscription-buyer's discount. It is a system that is in need of overhaul to provide not only a more equitable access to tickets but access to influence as well.

I look for and challenge students of arts management to be bold in their exploration of new systems of funding theatres, including profit-making institutions and ventures, and I challenge black artists and audiences to scale the walls erected by theatre subscriptions to gain access to this vital area of spiritual enlightenment and enrichment that is the theatre.

All theatregoers have opinions about the work they witness. Critics have an informed opinion. Sometimes it may be necessary for them to gather more information to become more informed. As playwrights grow and develop, as the theatre changes, the critic has an important responsibility to guide and encourage that growth. However, in the discharge of their duties, it may be necessary for them to also grow and develop. A stagnant body of critics, operating from the critical criteria of forty years ago, makes for a stagnant theatre without the fresh and abiding influence of contemporary ideas. It is the critics who should be in the forefront of developing new tools for analysis necessary to understand new influences.

The critic who can recognize a German neo-romantic influence should also be able to recognize an American influence from blues or black church rituals, or any other contemporary American influence.

The true critic does not sit in judgment. Rather he seeks to inform his reader, instead of adopting a posture of self-conscious importance in which he sees himself a judge and final arbiter of a work's importance or value.

We stand on the verge of an explosion of playwriting talent that will challenge our critics. As American playwrights absorb the influence of television and use new avenues of approach to the practice of their craft, they will grow to be wildly inventive and imaginative in creating dramas that will guide and influence contemporary life for years to come.

Theatre can do that. It can disseminate ideas, it can educate even the miseducated, because it is art—and all art reaches across that divide that makes order out of chaos, and embraces the truth that overwhelms with its presence, and connects man to something larger than himself and his imagination.

Theatre asserts that all of human life is universal. Love, Honor, Duty, Betrayal belong and pertain to every culture and every race. The way they are acted out on the playing field may be different, but betrayal is betrayal whether you are a South Sea Islander, a Mississippi farmer or an English baron. All of human life is universal, and it is theatre that illuminates and confers upon the universal the ability to speak for all men.

The ground together: We have to do it together. We cannot permit our lives to waste away, our talents unchallenged. We cannot permit a failure to our duty. We are brave and we are boisterous, our mettle is proven, and we are dedicated.

The ground together: the ground of the American theatre on which I am proud to stand . . . the ground which our artistic ancestors purchased with their endeavors . . . with their pursuit of the American spirit and its ideals.

I believe in the American theatre. I believe in its power to inform about the human condition, I believe in its power to heal, "to hold the mirror as 'twere up to nature," to the truths we uncover, to the truths we wrestle from uncertain and sometimes unyielding realities. All of art is a search for ways of being, of living life more fully. We who are capable of those noble pursuits should challenge the melancholy and barbaric, to bring the light of angelic grace, peace, prosperity and the unencumbered pursuit of happiness to the ground on which we all stand. Thank you.

DAVID HENRY HWANG

b. 1957

From the Filipinos who escaped from a Spanish galleon in 1763 and established villages in the Louisiana bayous to the Chinese laborers who built the transcontinental railroad in the nineteenth century to the Cambodians who fled the killing fields of the Khmer Rouge in the 1970s, Asians have come to America and have been an integral part of American history. As the United States expanded westward, a country that had defined itself in relation to Europe (and, through the institution of slavery, to Africa) found itself increasingly engaged with the Pacific region. In the Spanish-American War (1898), the United States annexed Hawaii, was granted protectorship over Guam and the Philippines, and thereby extended a colonial arm across the Pacific Ocean. As American contacts with Asia and its people deepened, popular perceptions of the East vacillated between fascination with the exotic and mysterious "Orient" and fear of the "Yellow Peril" posed by races seemingly alien to American national identity. Even as the vogue for Chinese and Japanese design flourished in the late nineteenth and early twentieth centuries, the U.S. Congress passed laws limiting Asian immigration.

Against this historical backdrop, contemporary Asian Americans—a term that generally includes those who claim origin or ancestry from East Asia, Southeast Asia, or the Indian subcontinent—have often found themselves caught between identities. Racially linked to countries with which those in later generations have had little or no contact, they inhabit a culture that has traditionally represented Asians and those of Asian descent through stereotypes: submissive lotus blossom, dragon lady, evil genius, exotic dancer, obedient servant, warmonger. In recent years Asian American writers have challenged these stereotypes by depicting the experience of themselves and their communities in its human complexity, and the drama of David Henry Hwang and other Asian American playwrights has given this experience a powerful voice in the American theater. Since Hwang first came to the attention of the theatrical world in the late 1970s, he has written plays exploring the complicated relationship of Chinese Americans to their familial, cultural, and spiritual roots. With his 1988 play M. BUTTERFLY—the most critically and commercially successful play ever written by an Asian American—Hwang broadened his gaze to include the intricate (mis)perceptions that characterize the East in the Western imagination.

David Henry Hwang (pronounced "Wong") was born on August 11, 1957, in San Gabriel, California, a wealthy suburb of Los Angeles. His father, who emigrated from Shanghai and—later—Taiwan, was a successful accountant and businessman, and his mother, who was born in southern China to a family that had been converted to fundamentalist Christianity and was raised in the Philippines, was a talented pianist. Hwang would explore this family heritage in his 1996 play *Golden Child,* which is based on the story of his great-grandfather who brought Christianity to his family in China. Because of his mother's religious background and his father's desire to assimilate in his adopted country, the family did not celebrate Chinese holidays or raise their children with an awareness of their Chinese heritage. It wasn't until he was a college student that Hwang became interested in knowing more about his roots. As a child Hwang studied violin and excelled in debating, and his talents earned him admission to an exclusive preparatory school in Hollywood Hills. Hwang would later credit music and debate as important influences on his playwriting: "Music really helps in terms of developing structure and dramatic growth, and jazz in particular helps with theatrical improvisation. . . . And my early interest in debate no doubt contributed to my theatrical interest in the opposition of ideas and the interplay of ideas in many plays."

Hwang enrolled at Stanford University in 1975 in order to study law, but by his sophomore year he decided that he wanted to write plays. When his creative writing professor explained to him that he lacked an adequate understanding of theater, he immersed himself in drama by attending the theater and reading as many plays as he could. He was particularly drawn to the drama of SAM SHEPARD, several of whose plays premiered during this time at the Magic Theater in nearby San Francisco. In 1978 Hwang had the opportunity to study playwriting with Shepard and the Cuban American playwright MARÍA IRENE FORNÉS at the Padua Hills Playwrights Festival workshop in Claremont, California; it was during this workshop that he conceived the idea of his first play, *FOB.* The play, whose title is the acronym popularly applied to new immigrants—standing for the condescending label "fresh off the boat"—centers on the interaction of three characters: Grace, a first-generation Chi-

nese American; her cousin Dale, a second-generation Chinese American; and Steve, a wealthy immigrant who has just arrived from Hong Kong. Set in the back room of a California restaurant, *FOB* explores the conflicts that immigrants experience as they struggle to assimilate into their new country while also retaining their cultural identity. Though its dialogue and action are clearly influenced by Shepard's plays of the 1970s, the play reveals a highly original dramatic sensibility. In addition to offering carefully drawn psychological portraits, the play dramatizes the confrontation between realism and myth. Steve imagines himself to be the Chinese god Gwan Gung, while Grace identifies with Fa Mu Lan, the mythic "woman warrior" who is the spiritual center of Maxine Hong Kingston's 1976 novel by the same name. When the two engage in a ritualized battle in the play's second act, the realistic present gives way to the timeless space of myth.

FOB was first performed in the lounge of Hwang's Stanford dorm in March 1979 as part of a festival of student plays and musicals. Hwang also submitted the play to the Eugene O'Neill National Playwrights Conference in Connecticut, where it was selected and produced that summer. After attracting the interest of Joseph Papp, producer of the off-Broadway New York Public Theater, *FOB* was produced in New York the following year and received enthusiastic reviews. As the play moved from its college production to the Public Theater, it underwent a significant change in its theatrical style. Papp and others who read the play felt that the ritualized sequence in the play's second act should be staged using the movements and visual approach of the Peking (or Beijing) Opera, a highly stylized form of Chinese theater involving drama, music, mime, dance, and acrobatics. The addition of stage conventions from Chinese opera established a theatrical equivalent to the confrontation of East and West within the play's action, and it launched Hwang's interest in the fusion of Eastern and Western theatrical traditions that would culminate seven years later in *M. Butterfly.*

After the success of *FOB,* which won an Obie Award for Best New American Play, Hwang spent a year in the Yale School of

Drama graduate playwriting program. During that time he wrote *The Dance and the Railroad*, which was produced in New York in 1981. Set during an 1867 strike by Chinese laborers working on the first transcontinental railroad, this two-character play dramatizes the plight of early immigrants who pursued the promise of America while living as "coolies" in an alien land. Through the character of Lone, who trained in Chinese opera and practices his craft on a mountainside at the end of each day's work, the play also expands Hwang's use of Asian theatrical traditions to explore the clash of East and West. *The Dance and the Railroad*, which enjoyed widespread critical acclaim, was followed by a series of plays whose reviews were more mixed: *Family Devotions* (1981); *The House of Sleeping Beauties* and *The Sound of a Voice*, two one-act plays produced in 1983 under the title *Sound and Beauty*; and *Rich Relations* (1986). Hwang's next play, however, would overshadow all his earlier triumphs and disappointments. After a brief preview at the National Theater in Washington, D.C., *M. Butterfly* opened at Broadway's Eugene O'Neill Theatre on March 20, 1988. Lavishly staged, the play was an enormous popular and critical success; indeed, it became one of the most commercially successful nonmusical plays in Broadway history and won a number of awards, including the Tony, Drama Desk, and Outer Critics Circle awards for Best Play. In the years since *M. Butterfly*, Hwang has done collaborative work—including a musical drama titled *1000 Airplanes on the Roof* (1988) with the composer Philip Glass—produced television scripts, and written a number of screenplays and libretti. In 2001 Hwang's updated text for the 1958 Richard Rodgers and Oscar Hammerstein II's musical *Flower Drum Song* was staged in Los Angeles before moving to Broadway. He has also continued to write dramatic works. In 1996 Hwang received an Obie Award for *Golden Child* (discussed above). Recent plays include *Yellow Face* (2007), which addresses the issue of cross-racial casting; *Chinglish* (2011), a comedy about an American businessman in China; and *Kung Fu* (2014), a play about martial artist and actor Bruce Lee. The latter was named Best New American Play of the year by *TIME* magazine.

M. Butterfly, like many of Hwang's other plays, is characterized by a blending of history and imagination. In May 1986 Hwang heard about an incident reported earlier that month in the *New York Times*. A former French diplomat named Bernard Boursicot and a Chinese opera star named Shi Pei Pu had been arrested and tried for espionage in Paris after a twenty-year sexual relationship during which Boursicot passed government information to Shi, who then passed it on to the Communist Chinese government. During the trial it was revealed that Boursicot had believed his lover—a man who played women's roles in Chinese and Western opera—was a woman and had conducted what he thought was a heterosexual affair. Boursicot explained that he had never seen "her" naked: "He was very shy. I thought it was a Chinese custom." Intrigued by the theatrical possibilities of so incredible a story, Hwang began working on a play. The crucial moment in conceiving this new work came when he realized that the French diplomat had fallen in love not with a person but with a stereotype of Asian women. "I was driving down Santa Monica Boulevard one afternoon, and asked myself, 'What did Boursicot think he was getting in this Chinese actress?' The answer came to me clearly: 'He probably thought he had found Madame Butterfly.'"

Although Hwang had not yet seen or listened to Giacomo Puccini's opera by that name, he was familiar with the stereotype represented by its delicate, self-sacrificing heroine. *Madame Butterfly* (*Madama* in the original Italian), which premiered in Milan in 1904, was based on a 1900 one-act play by the American playwright and producer David Belasco that Puccini had seen in London (Belasco's play was itself based on a 1898 short story by John Luther Long). Both play and opera tell the story of Cio-Cio-San, a Japanese geisha known as Madame Butterfly, and the American naval lieutenant named Pinkerton who marries her during one of his tours of duty to Japan. He then leaves with his ship, and although he fails to return the following year as promised, Cio-Cio-San waits faithfully, refusing the marriage proposal of a wealthy Japanese man. When Pinkerton finally does come

John Lithgow, center, as Rene Gallimard, and B. D. Wong, right, as
Song Liling, in the 1988 Broadway production of *M. Butterfly*.

back to Japan, several years later, he is
accompanied by a new American wife;
Butterfly takes her own life, leaving behind
a child that Pinkerton and his wife will
bring back to the United States. In its portrait of a submissive and feminized Asia,
Madame Butterfly exemplifies the Western
fantasy of the East as an exotic realm that
displays its mysteries for the West to
admire, collect, and dominate. Such a conception of the "Orient," as Edward Said
argued in his influential book *Orientalism*
(1978), is a Western invention, reflecting
an "imaginative geography" rather than
the actual sociocultural geography of Asia
and its peoples. The operations of such
myths, Said claimed, can be felt not only in

the representations of Asians by Europeans and North Americans but in the military and political relationships between
West and East that form part of the history
of imperialism.

In writing what he has called a "decon-
structivist *Madame Butterfly*," Hwang
established a series of parallels and counterpoints between Puccini's opera, contemporary history, and a fictionalized
version of the Boursicot story. Rene Gallimard, the diplomat of Hwang's play,
relives the events of his past from the cell
of a Paris prison, a nightly ritual in which
he seeks the understanding, and perhaps
envy, of his audience for having loved and
been loved by "the Perfect Woman." In

order to justify his belief and the actions, he recounts the story of *Madame Butterfly*—the opera in which he first saw the singer Song Liling perform—and identifies himself with Puccini's Pinkerton in his quest for the feminine ideal of beauty and submissiveness. The power of this myth is only deepened when Song challenges its premises: "It's one of your favorite fantasies, isn't it? The submissive Oriental woman and the cruel white man." In the following scenes Gallimard pursues the fantasy of Pinkerton and Butterfly, exulting in his apparent power over his mistress and in his initiation, after an unpromising sexual past, into the privileges of maleness.

One of the central themes of *M. Butterfly*, Hwang suggested in a 1989 interview, is "the nature of seduction, in the sense that to some degree we seduce ourselves." On the collective as well as the individual level, the West's self-seducing perceptions of the East are intimately connected to male perceptions of the female. As Song explains when he is asked about Gallimard's delusion by a Paris judge, "One, . . . when he finally met his fantasy woman, he wanted more than anything to believe that she was, in fact, a woman. And second, I am an Oriental. And being an Oriental, I could never be completely a man." Such thinking, the play suggests, accounts for the West's historic diplomatic and military failings in its encounters with the East. Advising the French ambassador about the Americans' prospects in neighboring Vietnam, Gallimard offers the disastrously misguided prediction that "Orientals will always submit to a greater force."

Hwang's exploration of seduction and misperception also extends to the play's interaction with its audience. On the level of theatrical form, *M. Butterfly* achieves an intricate counterpointing of Eastern and Western characters, impersonations, and styles. A French diplomat taking on the role of an American lieutenant interacts with a Chinese performer playing a Japanese heroine from an opera written by an Italian. Visually and aurally, the play juxtaposes the operatic traditions of Europe with the stage conventions and music of Chinese opera, complicating the audience's point of view with a sometimes jarring cultural fusion of East and West. Moreover, as a commentary on the fluidity of roles and identities, *M. Butterfly* challenges the seemingly clear-cut categories of male and female. Hwang replaced the *Madame* of Puccini's title with the letter *M.*, which stands for *Monsieur* in French but in English is more ambiguous in its gender reference. Even spectators who know the story on which the play is based can find themselves seduced by Song's performance as a woman. Accordingly, when Song removes "her" costume and makeup near the play's end, the audience witnesses the uncanny crossing of gender boundaries. When, in the play's unexpected final scene, Gallimard turns the tables on Song and rescues his fantasy from the harsh light of reality, these boundaries are rendered even more fluid and indeterminate.

M. Butterfly has not been without its critics in the Asian American community, a number of whom have charged Hwang with falling into stereotypes of his own concerning the East and indulging the theatrical exoticism that his play otherwise faults. Yet despite such critiques, the play established Hwang as one of the leading American playwrights of his generation and the most successful figure in Asian American theater. By bringing the lives and experiences of Asian Americans into the theatrical mainstream, he has helped expose the prejudices, misconceptions, and idealized images that have limited the representations of Asianness within and beyond the borders of the United States. Just as important, he has served as the voice of a new generation of Asian Americans who find themselves pulled between cultures and who must come to terms with their histories, myths, and traditions while making their lives in a country half a world away from their ancestors' home.   S.G.

M. Butterfly

CHARACTERS

KUROGO[1]   GIRL in magazine
RENE GALLIMARD / PINKERTON   COMRADE CHIN / SUZUKI
SONG LILING / BUTTERFLY   HELGA
WOMAN at party   SHU-FANG
MAN 1   M. TOULON
MAN 2   RENEE
MARC / CONSUL SHARPLESS   JUDGE

Playwright's Notes

*A former French diplomat and a Chinese opera singer have been sentenced
to six years in jail for spying for China after a two-day trial that traced a story
of clandestine love and mistaken sexual identity. . . . Mr. Boursicot was
accused of passing information to China after he fell in love with Mr. Shi,
whom he believed for twenty years to be a woman.*

—The New York Times, *May 11, 1986*

This play was suggested by international newspaper accounts of a recent
espionage trial. For purposes of dramatization, names have been changed,
characters created, and incidents devised or altered, and this play does
not purport to be a factual record of real events or real people.

*I could escape this feeling
With my China girl . . .* [2]
—DAVID BOWIE & IGGY POP

SETTING: *The action of the play takes place in a Paris prison in the present, and in
recall, during the decade 1960 to 1970 in Beijing, and from 1966 to the present in
Paris.*

1.1

M. GALLIMARD's *prison cell. Paris. Present.*

Lights fade up to reveal RENE GALLIMARD, *65, in a prison cell. He wears a comfortable bathrobe, and looks old and tired. The sparsely furnished cell contains a
wooden crate upon which sits a hot plate with a kettle, and a portable tape recorder.*
GALLIMARD *sits on the crate staring at the recorder, a sad smile on his face.*

1. In traditional Japanese theater, black-clad
stage attendants (treated as invisible).
2. From "China Girl," co-written by the
English rock musician David Bowie (1947–

2016) and the American rock singer Iggy
Pop (b. 1947); first released on Pop's album
The Idiot (1977), it became a hit on Bowie's
album *Let's Dance* (1983).

Upstage SONG, *who appears as a beautiful woman in traditional Chinese garb, dances a traditional piece from the Peking Opera,[3] surrounded by the percussive clatter of Chinese music.*

Then, slowly, lights and sound cross-fade; the Chinese opera music dissolves into a Western opera, the "Love Duet" from Puccini's Madame Butterfly.[4] SONG continues dancing, now to the Western accompaniment. Though her movements are the same, the difference in music now gives them a balletic quality.

GALLIMARD *rises, and turns upstage towards the figure of SONG, who dances without acknowledging him.*

GALLIMARD   Butterfly, Butterfly . . .

> [*He forces himself to turn away, as the image of SONG fades out, and talks to us.*]

GALLIMARD   The limits of my cell are as such: four-and-a-half meters by five. There's one window against the far wall; a door, very strong, to protect me from autograph hounds. I'm responsible for the tape recorder, the hot
5   plate, and this charming coffee table.

   When I want to eat, I'm marched off to the dining room—hot, steaming slop appears on my plate. When I want to sleep, the lightbulb turns itself off—the work of fairies. It's an enchanted space I occupy. The French—we know how to run a prison.

10   But, to be honest, I'm not treated like an ordinary prisoner. Why? Because I'm a celebrity. You see, I make people laugh.

   I never dreamed this day would arrive. I've never been considered witty or clever. In fact, as a young boy, in an informal poll among my grammar school classmates, I was voted "least likely to be invited to a party." It's a title
15   I managed to hold onto for many years. Despite some stiff competition.

   But now, how the tables turn! Look at me: the life of every social function in Paris. Paris? Why be modest? My fame has spread to Amsterdam, London, New York. Listen to them! In the world's smartest parlors. I'm the one who lifts their spirits!

> [*With a flourish, GALLIMARD directs our attention to another part of the stage.*]

1.2

A party. Present.

Lights go up on a chic-looking parlor, where a well-dressed trio, two men and one woman, make conversation. GALLIMARD also remains lit; he observes them from his cell.

WOMAN   And what of Gallimard?
MAN 1   Gallimard?
MAN 2   Gallimard!
GALLIMARD [*to us*]   You see? They're all determined to say my name, as if it
5   were some new dance.
WOMAN   He still claims not to believe the truth.

---

3. Chinese opera is a highly stylized art form involving drama, song, mime, dance, and acrobatics. *Peking*: former Westernization of Beijing.
4. That is, *Madama Butterfly* (1904), an Italian opera composed by Giacoppi Puccini (1858–1924) with a libretto by Luigi Illica (1857–1919) and Giuseppi Giacosa (1847–1906); it is one of the most frequently performed of all operas.

MAN 1   What? Still? Even since the trial?

WOMAN   Yes. Isn't it mad?

MAN 2 [*laughing*]   He says . . . it was dark . . . and she was very modest!

[*The trio break into laughter.*]

10 MAN 1   So—what? He never touched her with his hands?

MAN 2   Perhaps he did, and simply misidentified the equipment. A compelling case for sex education in the schools.

WOMAN   To protect the National Security—the Church can't argue with
that.

15 MAN 1   That's impossible! How could he not know?

MAN 2   Simple ignorance.

MAN 1   For twenty years?

MAN 2   Time flies when you're being stupid.

WOMAN   Well, I thought the French were ladies' men.

20 MAN 2   It seems Monsieur Gallimard was overly anxious to live up to his
national reputation.

WOMAN   Well, he's not very good-looking.

MAN 1   No, he's not.

MAN 2   Certainly not.

25 WOMAN   Actually, I feel sorry for him.

MAN 2   A toast! To Monsieur Gallimard!

WOMAN   Yes! To Gallimard!

MAN 1   To Gallimard!

MAN 2   Vive la différence!⁵

[*They toast, laughing. Lights down on them.*]

1.3

M. GALLIMARD's *cell.*

GALLIMARD [*smiling*]   You see? They toast me. I've become patron saint of the
socially inept. Can they really be so foolish? Men like that—they should be
scratching at my door, begging to learn my secrets! For I, Rene Gallimard,
you see, I have known, and been loved by . . . the Perfect Woman.

5   Alone in this cell, I sit night after night, watching our story play through
my head, always searching for a new ending, one which redeems my honor,
where she returns at last to my arms. And I imagine you—my ideal audience—
who come to understand and even, perhaps just a little, to envy me.

[*He turns on his tape recorder. Over the house speakers, we hear the
opening phrases of* Madame Butterfly.]

GALLIMARD   In order for you to understand what I did and why, I must intro-
10   duce you to my favorite opera: *Madame Butterfly.* By Giacomo Puccini. First
produced at La Scala, Milan, in 1904, it is now beloved throughout the
Western world.

[*As* GALLIMARD *describes the opera, the tape segues in and out to sections
he may be describing.*]

GALLIMARD   And why not? Its heroine, Cio-Cio-San, also known as Butterfly,
is a feminine ideal, beautiful and brave. And its hero, the man for whom

---

5. Long live the difference (French), an expression that specifically celebrates the difference
between the sexes.

15 she gives up everything, is—[*He pulls out a naval officer's cap from under his crate, pops it on his head, and struts about.*]—not very good-looking, not too bright, and pretty much a wimp: Benjamin Franklin Pinkerton of the U.S. Navy. As the curtain rises, he's just closed on two great bargains: one on a house, the other on a woman—call it a package deal.

20 Pinkerton purchased the rights to Butterfly for one hundred yen—in modern currency, equivalent to about . . . sixty-six cents. So, he's feeling pretty pleased with himself as Sharpless, the American consul, arrives to witness the marriage.

[MARC, *wearing an official cap to designate* SHARPLESS, *enters and plays the character.*]

SHARPLESS/MARC   Pinkerton!

25 PINKERTON/GALLIMARD   Sharpless! How's it hangin'? It's a great day, just great. Between my house, my wife, and the rickshaw[6] ride in from town, I've saved nineteen cents just this morning.

SHARPLESS   Wonderful. I can see the inscription on your tombstone already: "I saved a dollar, here I lie." [*He looks around.*] Nice house.

30 PINKERTON   It's artistic. Artistic, don't you think? Like the way the shoji[7] screens slide open to reveal the wet bar and disco mirror ball? Classy, huh? Great for impressing the chicks.

SHARPLESS   "Chicks"? Pinkerton, you're going to be a married man!

PINKERTON   Well, sort of.

35 SHARPLESS   What do you mean?

PINKERTON   This country—Sharpless, it is okay. You got all these geisha[8] girls running around—

SHARPLESS   I know! I live here!

PINKERTON   Then, you know the marriage laws, right? I split for one month,
40 it's annulled!

SHARPLESS   Leave it to you to read the fine print. Who's the lucky girl?

PINKERTON   Cio-Cio-San. Her friends call her Butterfly. Sharpless, she eats out of my hand!

SHARPLESS   She's probably very hungry.

45 PINKERTON   Not like American girls. It's true what they say about Oriental girls. They want to be treated bad!

SHARPLESS   Oh, please!

PINKERTON   It's true!

SHARPLESS   Are you serious about this girl?

50 PINKERTON   I'm marrying her, aren't I?

SHARPLESS   Yes—with generous trade-in terms.

PINKERTON   When I leave, she'll know what it's like to have loved a real man. And I'll even buy her a few nylons.

SHARPLESS   You aren't planning to take her with you?

55 PINKERTON   Huh? Where?

SHARPLESS   Home!

PINKERTON   You mean, America? Are you crazy? Can you see her trying to buy rice in St. Louis?

SHARPLESS   So, you're not serious.

---

6. That is, *jinrikisha* (Japanese), a light, two-wheeled passenger vehicle drawn by one or two men.
7. Paper screens used as walls, partitions, or sliding doors (Japanese).
8. In traditional Japanese society, professional women trained from childhood to entertain men with singing, dancing, and conversation.

[*Pause.*]

60 PINKERTON/GALLIMARD [*as* PINKERTON] Consul, I am a sailor in port. [*As* GAL-
LIMARD] They then proceed to sing the famous duet, "The Whole World
Over."[9]

> [*The duet plays on the speakers.* GALLIMARD, *as* PINKERTON, *lip-syncs his
> lines from the opera.*]

GALLIMARD To give a rough translation: "The whole world over, the Yankee
travels, casting his anchor wherever he wants. Life's not worth living unless
65 he can win the hearts of the fairest maidens, then hotfoot it off the premises ASAP." [*He turns towards* MARC.] In the preceding scene, I played
Pinkerton, the womanizing cad, and my friend Marc from school . . . [MARC
bows grandly for our benefit.] played Sharpless, the sensitive soul of reason.
In life, however, our positions were usually—no, always—reversed.

1.4

Ecole Nationale. Aix-en-Provence.[1] *1947.*

GALLIMARD No, Marc, I think I'd rather stay home.
MARC Are you crazy?! We are going to Dad's condo in Marseille![2] You know
what happened last time?
GALLIMARD Of course I do.
5 MARC Of course you don't! You never know. . . . They stripped, Rene!
GALLIMARD Who stripped?
MARC The girls!
GALLIMARD Girls? Who said anything about girls?
MARC Rene, we're a buncha university guys goin' up to the woods. What are
10 we gonna do—talk philosophy?
GALLIMARD What girls? Where do you get them?
MARC Who cares? The point is, they come. On trucks. Packed in like sar-
dines. The back flips open, babes hop out, we're ready to roll.
GALLIMARD You mean, they just—?
15 MARC Before you know it, every last one of them—they're stripped and
splashing around my pool. There's no moon out, they can't see what's going
on, their boobs are flapping, right? You close your eyes, reach out—it's grab
bag, get it? Doesn't matter whose ass is between whose legs, whose teeth
are sinking into who. You're just in there, going at it, eyes closed, on and on
20 for as long as you can stand. [*Pause*] Some fun, huh?
GALLIMARD What happens in the morning?
MARC In the morning, you're ready to talk some philosophy. [*Beat*[3]] So how
'bout it?
GALLIMARD Marc, I can't . . . I'm afraid they'll say no—the girls. So I never
25 ask.
MARC You don't have to ask! That's the beauty—don't you see? They don't
have to say yes. It's perfect for a guy like you, really.
GALLIMARD You go ahead . . . I may come later.

---

9. "Dovunque al mondo" is in fact an aria sung
by Pinkerton.
1. A city in southern France, about 20 miles
north of Marseille. Among its universities is
the École Nationale Supérieure d'Arts et
Métiers (National School of Arts and Trades),
an elite school of engineering.
2. France's second-largest city, an important
commercial and industrial center on the
Mediterranean coast.
3. Pause (theater term).

MARC   Hey, Rene—it doesn't matter that you're clumsy and got zits—they're
30 not looking!
GALLIMARD   Thank you very much.
MARC   Wimp.

> [MARC *walks over to the other side of the stage, and starts waving and
> smiling at women in the audience.*]

GALLIMARD   [*to us*]   We now return to my version of *Madame Butterfly* and
the events leading to my recent conviction for treason.

> [GALLIMARD *notices* MARC *making lewd gestures.*]

35 GALLIMARD   Marc, what are you doing?
MARC   Huh? [*Sotto voce*[4]] Rene, there're a lotta great babes out there.
They're probably lookin' at me and thinking, "What a dangerous guy."
GALLIMARD   Yes—how could they help but be impressed by your cool
sophistication?

> [GALLIMARD *pops the* SHARPLESS *cap on* MARC's *head, and points him off-
> stage.* MARC *exits, leering.*]

1.5

M. GALLIMARD's *cell.*

GALLIMARD   Next, Butterfly makes her entrance. We learn her age—fifteen . . .
but very mature for her years.

> [*Lights come up on the area where we saw* SONG *dancing at the top of the
> play. She appears there again, now dressed as Madame* BUTTERFLY, *mov-
> ing to the "Love Duet."*[5] GALLIMARD *turns upstage slightly to watch,
> transfixed.*]

GALLIMARD   But as she glides past him, beautiful, laughing softly behind her
fan, don't we who are men sigh with hope? We, who are not handsome, nor
5   brave, nor powerful, yet somehow believe, like Pinkerton, that we deserve
a Butterfly. She arrives with all her possessions in the folds of her sleeves,
lays them all out, for her man to do with as he pleases. Even her life
itself—she bows her head as she whispers that she's not even worth the
hundred yen he paid for her. He's already given too much, when we know
10   he's really had to give nothing at all.

> [*Music and lights on* SONG *out.* GALLIMARD *sits at his crate.*]

GALLIMARD   In real life, women who put their total worth at less than sixty-
six cents are quite hard to find. The closest we come is in the pages of
these magazines. [*He reaches into his crate, pulls out a stack of girlie magazines, and begins flipping through them.*] Quite a necessity in prison. For
15   three or four dollars, you get seven or eight women.

I first discovered these magazines at my uncle's house. One day, as a boy
of twelve. The first time I saw them in his closet . . . all lined up—my body
shook. Not with lust—no, with power. Here were women—a shelfful—who
would do exactly as I wanted.

> [*The "Love Duet" creeps in over the speakers. Special*[6] *comes up, reveal-
> ing, not* SONG *this time, but a pinup girl in a sexy negligee, her back to
> us.* GALLIMARD *turns upstage and looks at her.*]

---

4. Under the voice (Italian); that is, spoken
very softly, under the breath.
5. "Viene la sera" ("Evening Is Falling"), a
duet sung by Pinkerton and Butterfly at the

end of act 1 of *Madama Butterfly.*
6. A stage light used at designated moments
during a play for specific, highly theatrical
effects.

20 GIRL   I know you're watching me.

GALLIMARD   My throat . . . it's dry.

GIRL   I leave my blinds open every night before I go to bed.

GALLIMARD   I can't move.

GIRL   I leave my blinds open and the lights on.

25 GALLIMARD   I'm shaking. My skin is hot, but my penis is soft. Why?

GIRL   I stand in front of the window.

GALLIMARD   What is she going to do?

GIRL   I toss my hair, and I let my lips part . . . barely.

GALLIMARD   I shouldn't be seeing this. It's so dirty. I'm so bad.

30 GIRL   Then, slowly, I lift off my nightdress.

GALLIMARD   Oh, god. I can't believe it. I can't—

GIRL   I toss it to the ground.

GALLIMARD   Now, she's going to walk away. She's going to—

GIRL   I stand there, in the light, displaying myself.

35 GALLIMARD   No. She's—why is she naked?

GIRL   To you.

GALLIMARD   In front of a window? This is wrong. No—

GIRL   Without shame.

GALLIMARD   No, she must . . . like it.

40 GIRL   I like it.

GALLIMARD   She . . . she wants me to see.

GIRL   I want you to see.

GALLIMARD   I can't believe it! She's getting excited!

GIRL   I can't see you. You can do whatever you want.

45 GALLIMARD   I can't do a thing. Why?

GIRL   What would you like me to do . . . next?

[*Lights go down on her. Music off. Silence, as* GALLIMARD *puts away his magazines. Then he resumes talking to us.*]

GALLIMARD   Act Two begins with Butterfly staring at the ocean. Pinkerton's been called back to the U.S., and he's given his wife a detailed schedule of his plans. In the column marked "return date," he's written "when the
50 robins nest." This failed to ignite her suspicions. Now, three years have passed without a peep from him. Which brings a response from her faithful servant, Suzuki.

[COMRADE CHIN *enters, playing* SUZUKI.]

SUZUKI   Girl, he's a loser. What'd he ever give you? Nineteen cents and those ugly Day-Glo stockings? Look, it's finished! Kaput! Done! And you should
55 be glad! I mean, the guy was a woofer![7] He tried before, you know—before he met you, he went down to geisha central and plunked down his spare change in front of the usual candidates—everyone else gagged! These are hungry prostitutes, and they were not interested, get the picture? Now, stop slathering when an American ship sails in, and let's make some
60 bucks—I mean, yen! We are broke!
    Now, what about Yamadori? Hey, hey—don't look away—the man is a prince—figuratively, and, what's even better, literally. He's rich, he's handsome, he says he'll die if you don't marry him—and he's even willing to overlook the little fact that you've been deflowered all over the place by a
65 foreign devil. What do you mean, "But he's Japanese?" You're Japanese! You

7. That is, a dog, an ugly person (slang).

think you've been touched by the whitey god? He was a sailor with dirty hands!

[SUZUKI *stalks offstage.*]

GALLIMARD She's also visited by Consul Sharpless, sent by Pinkerton on a minor errand.

[MARC *enters, as* SHARPLESS.]

70 SHARPLESS I hate this job.

GALLIMARD This Pinkerton—he doesn't show up personally to tell his wife he's abandoning her. No, he sends a government diplomat . . . at taxpayer's expense.

SHARPLESS Butterfly? Butterfly? I have some bad—I'm going to be ill. But-
75 terfly, I came to tell you—

GALLIMARD Butterfly says she knows he'll return and if he doesn't she'll kill herself rather than go back to her own people. [*Beat*] This causes a lull in the conversation.

SHARPLESS Let's put it this way . . .

80 GALLIMARD Butterfly runs into the next room, and returns holding—

[*Sound cue: a baby crying.* SHARPLESS, *"seeing" this, backs away.*]

SHARPLESS Well, good. Happy to see things going so well. I suppose I'll be going now. Ta ta. Ciao. [*He turns away. Sound cue out.*] I hate this job. [*He exits.*]

GALLIMARD At that moment, Butterfly spots in the harbor an American ship—the *Abramo Lincoln!*[8]

[*Music cue: "The Flower Duet."*[9] SONG, *still dressed as* BUTTERFLY, *changes into a wedding kimono, moving to the music.*]

85 GALLIMARD This is the moment that redeems her years of waiting. With Suzuki's help, they cover the room with flowers—

[CHIN, *as* SUZUKI, *trudges onstage and drops a lone flower without much enthusiasm.*]

GALLIMARD —and she changes into her wedding dress to prepare for Pinker-ton's arrival.

[SUZUKI *helps* BUTTERFLY *change.* HELGA *enters, and helps* GALLIMARD *change into a tuxedo.*]

GALLIMARD I married a woman older than myself—Helga.
90 HELGA My father was ambassador to Australia. I grew up among criminals and kangaroos.[1]

GALLIMARD Hearing that brought me to the altar—

[HELGA *exits.*]

GALLIMARD —where I took a vow renouncing love. No fantasy woman would ever want me, so, yes, I would settle for a quick leap up the career ladder.
95 Passion, I banish, and in its place—practicality!

But my vows had long since lost their charm by the time we arrived in China. The sad truth is that all men want a beautiful woman, and the uglier the man, the greater the want.

---

8. Abraham Lincoln (Italian).
9. "Tutti i fior?" ("All the Flowers"), a duet sung by Butterfly and her servant Suzuki in act 2 of *Madama Butterfly* at the point in the story narrated here by Gallimard.

1. Australia was originally used by Great Brit-ain as a penal colony, and a sizable portion of the early settlers were convicts transported between 1788 and 1868.

[SUZUKI *makes final adjustments of* BUTTERFLY's *costume, as does* GALLI-MARD *of his tuxedo.*]

GALLIMARD   I married late, at age thirty-one. I was faithful to my marriage for eight years. Until the day when, as a junior-level diplomat in puritanical Peking, in a parlor at the German ambassador's house, during the "Reign of a Hundred Flowers,"[2] I first saw her . . . singing the death scene from *Madame Butterfly.*

[SUZUKI *runs offstage.*]

1.6

German ambassador's house. Beijing. 1960.

*The upstage special area now becomes a stage. Several chairs face upstage, repre-senting seating for some twenty guests in the parlor. A few "diplomats"—*RENEE, MARC, TOULON—*in formal dress enter and take seats.*

GALLIMARD *also sits down, but turns towards us and continues to talk. Orchestral accompaniment on the tape is now replaced by a simple piano.* SONG *picks up the death scene from the point where* BUTTERFLY *uncovers the hara-kiri[3] knife.*

GALLIMARD   The ending is pitiful. Pinkerton, in an act of great courage, stays home and sends his American wife to pick up Butterfly's child. The truth, long deferred, has come up to her door.

[SONG, *playing* BUTTERFLY, *sings the lines from the opera in her own voice—which, though not classical, should be decent.*]

SONG   "Con onor muore / chi non puo serbar / vita con onore."

5 GALLIMARD [*simultaneously*]   "Death with honor / Is better than life / Life with dishonor."

[*The stage is illuminated; we are now completely within an elegant dip-lomat's residence.* SONG *proceeds to play out an abbreviated death scene. Everyone in the room applauds.* SONG, *shyly, takes her bows. Others in the room rush to congratulate her.* GALLIMARD *remains with us.*]

GALLIMARD   They say in opera the voice is everything. That's probably why I'd never before enjoyed opera. Here . . . here was a Butterfly with little or no voice—but she had the grace, the delicacy . . . I believed this girl. I believed

10 her suffering. I wanted to take her in my arms—so delicate, even I could protect her, take her home, pamper her until she smiled.

[*Over the course of the preceding speech,* SONG *has broken from the upstage crowd and moved directly upstage of* GALLIMARD.]

SONG   Excuse me. Monsieur . . . ?

[GALLIMARD *turns upstage, shocked.*]

GALLIMARD   Oh! Gallimard. Mademoiselle . . . ? A beautiful . . .

SONG   Song Liling.

15 GALLIMARD   A beautiful performance.

SONG   Oh, please.

GALLIMARD   I usually—

SONG   You make me blush. I'm no opera singer at all.

GALLIMARD   I usually don't like *Butterfly.*

2. The so-called Hundred Flowers Campaign, a brief period (1956–57) during which the Communist authorities allowed intellectuals greater freedom of thought and speech.
3. Ritual suicide by disembowelment (Japanese).

20 SONG I can't blame you in the least.

GALLIMARD I mean, the story—

SONG Ridiculous.

GALLIMARD I like the story, but . . . what?

SONG Oh, you like it?

25 GALLIMARD I . . . what I mean is, I've always seen it played by huge women in so much bad makeup.

SONG Bad makeup is not unique to the West.

GALLIMARD But, who can believe them?

SONG And you believe me?

30 GALLIMARD Absolutely. You were utterly convincing. It's the first time—

SONG Convincing? As a Japanese woman? The Japanese used hundreds of our people for medical experiments during the war,[4] you know. But I gather such an irony is lost on you.

GALLIMARD No! I was about to say, it's the first time I've seen the beauty of
35 the story.

SONG Really?

GALLIMARD Of her death. It's a . . . a pure sacrifice. He's unworthy, but what can she do? She loves him . . . so much. It's a very beautiful story.

SONG Well, yes, to a Westerner.

40 GALLIMARD Excuse me?

SONG It's one of your favorite fantasies, isn't it? The submissive Oriental woman and the cruel white man.

GALLIMARD Well, I didn't quite mean . . .

SONG Consider it this way: what would you say if a blonde homecoming
45 queen fell in love with a short Japanese businessman? He treats her cruelly, then goes home for three years, during which time she prays to his picture and turns down marriage from a young Kennedy.[5] Then, when she learns he has remarried, she kills herself. Now, I believe you would consider this girl to be a deranged idiot, correct? But because it's an Oriental who kills
50 herself for a Westerner—ah!—you find it beautiful.

[Silence.]

GALLIMARD Yes . . . well . . . I see your point . . .

SONG I will never do Butterfly again, Monsieur Gallimard. If you wish to see some real theatre, come to the Peking Opera sometime. Expand your mind.

[SONG walks offstage.]

GALLIMARD [to us] So much for protecting her in my big Western arms.

1.7

M. GALLIMARD's apartment. Beijing. 1960.

GALLIMARD changes from his tux into a casual suit. HELGA enters.

GALLIMARD The Chinese are an incredibly arrogant people.

HELGA They warned us about that in Paris, remember?

---

4. The Japanese conducted gruesome medical experiments on Chinese prisoners and civilians during their World War II–era occupation of China (1937–45).
5. A member of the Massachusetts political family whose best-known members are President John F. Kennedy (1917–1963), Senator Robert F. Kennedy (1925–1968), and Senator Edward Kennedy (1932–2009).

GALLIMARD Even Parisians consider them arrogant. That's a switch.

HELGA What is it that Madame Su says? "We are a very old civilization." I never know if she's talking about her country or herself.

GALLIMARD I walk around here, all I hear every day, everywhere is how *old* this culture is. The fact that "old" may be synonymous with "senile" doesn't occur to them.

HELGA You're not going to change them. "East is east, west is west, and . . ."[6] whatever that guy said.

GALLIMARD It's just that—silly. I met . . . at Ambassador Koening's tonight—you should've been there.

HELGA Koening? Oh god, no. Did he enchant you all again with the history of Bavaria?[7]

GALLIMARD No. I met, I suppose, the Chinese equivalent of a diva.[8] She's a singer in the Chinese opera.

HELGA They have an opera, too? Do they sing in Chinese? Or maybe—in Italian?

GALLIMARD Tonight, she did sing in Italian.

HELGA How'd she manage that?

GALLIMARD She must've been educated in the West before the Revolution.[9] Her French is very good also. Anyway, she sang the death scene from *Madame Butterfly*.

HELGA *Madame Butterfly*! Then I should have come. [*She begins humming, floating around the room as if dragging long kimono sleeves.*] Did she have a nice costume? I think it's a classic piece of music.

GALLIMARD That's what *I* thought, too. Don't let her hear you say that.

HELGA What's wrong?

GALLIMARD Evidently the Chinese hate it.

HELGA She hated it, but she performed it anyway? Is she perverse?

GALLIMARD They hate it because the white man gets the girl. Sour grapes if you ask me.

HELGA Politics again? Why can't they just hear it as a piece of beautiful music? So, what's in their opera?

GALLIMARD I don't know. But, whatever it is, I'm sure it must be *old*.

[HELGA *exits.*]

1.8

Chinese opera house and the streets of Beijing. 1960.

The sound of gongs clanging fills the stage.

GALLIMARD My wife's innocent question kept ringing in my ears. I asked around, but no one knew anything about the Chinese opera. It took four weeks, but my curiosity overcame my cowardice. This Chinese diva—this unwilling Butterfly—what did she do to make her so proud?

6. "Oh, East is East, and West is West, and never the twain shall meet," from the poem "The Ballad of East and West" (1889) by the British writer Rudyard Kipling (1865–1936).
7. Germany's southernmost state, which was an independent kingdom until 1871.
8. A female opera star of the most glamorous and imperious sort (literally, "goddess"; Italian).
9. The civil war between the Nationalist government, led by Chiang Kai-shek, and the Communist rebels, led by Mao Zedong, which ended with the establishment of the People's Republic of China under Mao in 1949.

5   The room was hot, and full of smoke. Wrinkled faces, old women, teeth missing—a man with a growth on his neck, like a human toad. All smiling, pipes falling from their mouths, cracking nuts between their teeth, a live chicken pecking at my foot—all looking, screaming, gawking . . . at her.

> [*The upstage area is suddenly hit with a harsh white light. It has become the stage for the Chinese opera performance. Two dancers enter, along with* SONG. GALLIMARD *stands apart, watching.* SONG *glides gracefully amidst the two dancers. Drums suddenly slam to a halt.* SONG *strikes a pose, looking straight at* GALLIMARD. *Dancers exit. Light change. Pause, then* SONG *walks right off the stage and straight up to* GALLIMARD.]

SONG   Yes. You. White man. I'm looking straight at you.

10 GALLIMARD   Me?

SONG   You see any other white men? It was too easy to spot you. How often does a man in my audience come in a tie?

> [SONG *starts to remove her costume. Underneath, she wears simple baggy clothes. They are now backstage. The show is over.*]

SONG   So, you are an adventurous imperialist?

GALLIMARD   I . . . thought it would further my education.

15 SONG   It took you four weeks. Why?

GALLIMARD   I've been busy.

SONG   Well, education has always been undervalued in the West, hasn't it?

GALLIMARD [*laughing*]   I don't think it's true.

SONG   No, you wouldn't. You're a Westerner. How can you objectively judge

20   your own values?

GALLIMARD   I think it's possible to achieve some distance.

SONG   Do you? [*Pause*] It stinks in here. Let's go.

GALLIMARD   These are the smells of your loyal fans.

SONG   I love them for being my fans, I hate the smell they leave behind. I too

25   can distance myself from my people. [*She looks around, then whispers in his ear.*] "Art for the masses"[1] is a shitty excuse to keep artists poor. [*She pops a cigarette in her mouth.*] Be a gentleman, will you? And light my cigarette.

> [GALLIMARD *fumbles for a match.*]

GALLIMARD   I don't . . . smoke.

SONG [*lighting her own*]   Your loss. Had you lit my cigarette, I might have

30   blown a puff of smoke right between your eyes. Come.

> [*They start to walk about the stage. It is a summer night on the Beijing streets. Sounds of the city play on the house speakers.*]

SONG   How I wish there were even a tiny cafe to sit in. With cappuccinos, and men in tuxedos and bad expatriate jazz.

GALLIMARD   If my history serves me correctly, you weren't even allowed into the clubs in Shanghai[2] before the Revolution.

35 SONG   Your history serves you poorly, Monsieur Gallimard. True, there were signs reading "No dogs and Chinamen." But a woman, especially a delicate Oriental woman—we always go where we please. Could you imagine it otherwise? Clubs in China filled with pasty, big-thighed white women, while

---

1. A Communist slogan advocating a proletarian (working-class) art in place of the so-called elite art of Western capitalism.
2. The largest city in China; as one of the five ports opened to foreign trade and to foreign residents in the 19th century, it became the country's economic and cultural center until investment from overseas was halted by the Communist victory.

thousands of slender lotus blossoms[3] wait just outside the door? Never. The
40 clubs would be empty. [*Beat*] We have always held a certain fascination for
you Caucasian men, have we not?

GALLIMARD   But . . . that fascination is imperialist, or so you tell me.

SONG   Do you believe everything I tell you? Yes. It is always imperialist. But
sometimes . . . sometimes, it is also mutual. Oh—this is my flat.

45 GALLIMARD   I didn't even—

SONG   Thank you. Come another time and we will further expand your mind.

> [SONG *exits.* GALLIMARD *continues roaming the streets as he speaks to us.*]

GALLIMARD   What was that? What did she mean, "Sometimes . . . it is mutual?"
Women do not flirt with me. And I normally can't talk to them. But tonight,
I held up my end of the conversation.

1.9

GALLIMARD's *bedroom. Beijing. 1960.*

> HELGA *enters.*

HELGA   You didn't tell me you'd be home late.

GALLIMARD   I didn't intend to. Something came up.

HELGA   Oh? Like what?

GALLIMARD   I went to the . . . to the Dutch ambassador's home.

5 HELGA   Again?

GALLIMARD   There was a reception for a visiting scholar. He's writing a six-
volume treatise on the Chinese revolution. We all gathered that meant he'd
have to live here long enough to actually write six volumes, and we all
expressed our deepest sympathies.

10 HELGA   Well, I had a good night too. I went with the ladies to a martial arts
demonstration. Some of those men—when they break those thick boards—
[*She mimes fanning herself.*] whoo-whoo!

> [HELGA *exits. Lights dim.*]

GALLIMARD   I lied to my wife. Why? I've never had any reason to lie before.
But what reason did I have tonight? I didn't do anything wrong. That night, I
15 had a dream. Other people, I've been told, have dreams where angels appear.
Or dragons, or Sophia Loren[4] in a towel. In my dream, Marc from school
appeared.

> [MARC *enters, in a nightshirt and cap.*]

MARC   Rene! You met a girl!

> [GALLIMARD *and* MARC *stumble down the Beijing streets. Night sounds
> over the speakers.*]

GALLIMARD   It's not that amazing, thank you.

20 MARC   No! It's so monumental, I heard about it halfway around the world in
my sleep!

GALLIMARD   I've met girls before, you know.

MARC   Name one. I've come across time and space to congratulate you. [*He
hands* GALLIMARD *a bottle of wine.*]

---

3. That is, Asian women. The lotus blossom
symbolized the practice of footbinding, which
was highly eroticized in traditional Chinese
culture.

4. An Italian actress (b. 1934), famous for her
beauty and viewed as an international sex
symbol.

GALLIMARD   Marc, this is expensive.

25   MARC   On those rare occasions when you become a formless spirit, why not steal the best?

> [MARC *pops open the bottle, begins to share it with* GALLIMARD.]

GALLIMARD   You embarrass me. She . . . there's no reason to think she likes me.

MARC   "Sometimes, it is mutual"?

30   GALLIMARD   Oh.

MARC   "Mutual"? "Mutual"? What does that mean?

GALLIMARD   You heard!

MARC   It means the money is in the bank, you only have to write the check!

GALLIMARD   I am a married man!

35   MARC   And an excellent one too. I cheated after . . . six months. Then again and again, until now—three hundred girls in twelve years.

GALLIMARD   I don't think we should hold that up as a model.

MARC   Of course not! My life—it is disgusting! Phooey! Phooey! But, you— you are the model husband.

40   GALLIMARD   Anyway, it's impossible. I'm a foreigner.

MARC   Ah, yes. She cannot love you, it is taboo, but something deep inside her heart . . . she cannot help herself . . . she must surrender to you. It is her destiny.

GALLIMARD   How do you imagine all this?

45   MARC   The same way you do. It's an old story. It's in our blood. They fear us, Rene. Their women fear us. And their men—their men hate us. And, you know something? They are all correct.

> [*They spot a light in a window.*]

MARC   There! There, Rene!

GALLIMARD   It's her window.

50   MARC   Late at night—it burns. The light—it burns for you.

GALLIMARD   I won't look. It's not respectful.

MARC   We don't have to be respectful. We're foreign devils.

> [*Enter* SONG, *in a sheer robe. The "One Fine Day"* [5] *aria creeps in over the speakers. With her back to us,* SONG *mimes attending to her toilette. Her robe comes loose, revealing her white shoulders.*]

MARC   All your life you've waited for a beautiful girl who would lay down for you. All your life you've smiled like a saint when it's happened to every
55   other man you know. And you see them in magazines and you see them in movies. And you wonder, what's wrong with me? Will anyone beautiful ever want me? As the years pass, your hair thins and you struggle to hold onto even your hopes. Stop struggling, Rene. The wait is over. [*He exits.*]

GALLIMARD   Marc? Marc?

> [*At that moment,* SONG, *her back still towards us, drops her robe. A second of her naked back, then a sound cue: a phone ringing, very loud. Blackout, followed in the next beat by a special up on the bedroom area, where a phone now sits.* GALLIMARD *stumbles across the stage and picks up the phone. Sound cue out. Over the course of his conversation, area lights fill in the vicinity of his bed. It is the following morning.*]

---

5. "Un bel dì vedremo" ("One Fine Day We Shall See"), an aria sung by Butterfly in act 2 of *Madama Butterfly.*

60 GALLIMARD   Yes? Hello?

SONG [*offstage*]   Is it very early?

GALLIMARD   Why, yes.

SONG [*offstage*]   How early?

GALLIMARD   It's . . . it's 5:30. Why are you—?

65 SONG [*offstage*]   But it's light outside. Already.

GALLIMARD   It is. The sun must be in confusion today.

> [*Over the course of* SONG's *next speech, her upstage special comes up again. She sits in a chair, legs crossed, in a robe, telephone to her ear.*]

SONG   I waited until I saw the sun. That was as much discipline as I could manage for one night. Do you forgive me?

GALLIMARD   Of course . . . for what?

70 SONG   Then I'll ask you quickly. Are you really interested in the opera?

GALLIMARD   Why, yes. Yes I am.

SONG   Then come again next Thursday. I am playing *The Drunken Beauty.*[6] May I count on you?

GALLIMARD   Yes. You may.

75 SONG   Perfect. Well, I must be getting to bed. I'm exhausted. It's been a very long night for me.

> [SONG *hangs up; special on her goes off.* GALLIMARD *begins to dress for work.*]

1.10

SONG LILING's *apartment. Beijing. 1960.*

GALLIMARD   I returned to the opera that next week, and the week after that . . . she keeps our meetings so short—perhaps fifteen, twenty minutes at most. So I am left each week with a thirst which is intensified. In this way, fifteen weeks have gone by. I am starting to doubt the words of my

5 friend Marc. But no, not really. In my heart, I know she has . . . an interest in me. I suspect this is her way. She is outwardly bold and outspoken, yet her heart is shy and afraid. It is the Oriental in her at war with her Western education.

SONG [*offstage*]   I will be out in an instant. Ask the servant for anything you

10 want.

GALLIMARD   Tonight, I have finally been invited to enter her apartment. Though the idea is almost beyond belief, I believe she is afraid of me.

> [GALLIMARD *looks around the room. He picks up a picture in a frame, studies it. Without his noticing,* SONG *enters, dressed elegantly in a black gown from the twenties. She stands in the doorway looking like Anna May Wong.*[7]]

SONG   That is my father.

GALLIMARD [*surprised*]   Mademoiselle Song . . .

> [*She glides up to him, snatches away the picture.*]

6. A traditional Chinese opera about an imperial concubine during the Tang dynasty (set ca. 750 C.E.). Enraged that the emperor has chosen to visit a new concubine, his previous favorite drinks herself into a state of gaiety and then despondency. *The Drunken Beauty* (or *The Drunken Concubine*) was made famous by the Beijing Opera star Mei Lanfang (1894–1961), a man who specialized in female roles.

7. A Chinese American actress (1905–1961), the first Asian woman to become a film star; she often played temptresses or exotic villainesses in the 1920s and 1930s.

15   SONG   It is very good that he did not live to see the Revolution. They would, no doubt, have made him kneel on broken glass.[8] Not that he didn't deserve such a punishment. But he is my father. I would've hated to see it happen.

GALLIMARD   I'm very honored that you've allowed me to visit your home.

    [SONG *curtsies.*]

SONG   Thank you. Oh! Haven't you been poured any tea?

20   GALLIMARD   I'm really not—

SONG   [*to her offstage servant*]   Shu-Fang! Cha! Kwai-lah![9] [*To* GALLIMARD] I'm sorry. You want everything to be perfect—

GALLIMARD   Please.

SONG   —and before the evening even begins—

25   GALLIMARD   I'm really not thirsty.

SONG   —It's ruined.

GALLIMARD   [*sharply*]   Mademoiselle Song!

    [SONG *sits down.*]

SONG   I'm sorry.

GALLIMARD   What are you apologizing for now?

    [*Pause;* SONG *starts to giggle.*]

30   SONG   I don't know!

    [GALLIMARD *laughs.*]

GALLIMARD   Exactly my point.

SONG   Oh, I am silly. Lightheaded. I promise not to apologize for anything else tonight, do you hear me?

GALLIMARD   That's a good girl.

    [SHU-FANG, *a servant girl, comes out with a tea tray and starts to pour.*]

35   SONG   [*to* SHU-FANG]   No! I'll pour myself for the gentleman!

    [SHU-FANG, *staring at* GALLIMARD, *exits.*]

SONG   No, I . . . I don't even know why I invited you up.

GALLIMARD   Well, I'm glad you did.

    [SONG *looks around the room.*]

SONG   There is an element of danger to your presence.

GALLIMARD   Oh?

40   SONG   You must know.

GALLIMARD   It doesn't concern me. We both know why I'm here.

SONG   It doesn't concern me either. No . . . well perhaps . . .

GALLIMARD   What?

SONG   Perhaps I am slightly afraid of scandal.

45   GALLIMARD   What are we doing?

SONG   I'm entertaining you. In my parlor.

GALLIMARD   In France, that would hardly—

SONG   France. France is a country living in the modern era. Perhaps even ahead of it. China is a nation whose soul is firmly rooted two thousand 50   years in the past. What I do, even pouring the tea for you now . . . it has . . . implications. The walls and windows say so. Even my own heart, strapped inside this Western dress . . . even it says things—things I don't care to hear.

---

8. A punishment inflicted by the Communists on those viewed as "class enemies."   9. Tea, quickly, please! (Chinese).

[SONG *hands* GALLIMARD *a cup of tea.* GALLIMARD *puts his hand over both the teacup and* SONG'S *hand.*]

GALLIMARD   This is a beautiful dress.

55 SONG   Don't.

GALLIMARD   What?

SONG   I don't even know if it looks right on me.

GALLIMARD   Believe me—

SONG   You are from France. You see so many beautiful women.

60 GALLIMARD   France? Since when are the European women—?

SONG   Oh! What am I trying to do, anyway?!

[SONG *runs to the door, composes herself, then turns towards* GALLIMARD.]

SONG   Monsieur Gallimard, perhaps you should go.

GALLIMARD   But . . . why?

SONG   There's something wrong about this.

65 GALLIMARD   I don't see what.

SONG   I feel . . . I am not myself.

GALLIMARD   No. You're nervous.

SONG   Please. Hard as I try to be modern, to speak like a man, to hold a Western woman's strong face up to my own . . . in the end, I fail. A small,
70 frightened heart beats too quickly and gives me away. Monsieur Gallimard, I'm a Chinese girl. I've never . . . never invited a man up to my flat before. The forwardness of my actions makes my skin burn.

GALLIMARD   What are you afraid of? Certainly not me, I hope.

SONG   I'm a modest girl.

75 GALLIMARD   I know. And very beautiful. [*He touches her hair.*]

SONG   Please—go now. The next time you see me, I shall again be myself.

GALLIMARD   I like you the way you are right now.

SONG   You are a cad.

GALLIMARD   What do you expect? I'm a foreign devil.

[GALLIMARD *walks downstage.* SONG *exits.*]

80 GALLIMARD [*to us*]   Did you hear the way she talked about Western women? Much differently than the first night. She does—she feels inferior to them—and to me.

1.11

The French embassy. Beijing. 1960.

GALLIMARD *moves towards a desk.*

GALLIMARD   I determined to try an experiment. In *Madame Butterfly*, Cio-Cio-San fears that the Western man who catches a butterfly will pierce its heart with a needle, then leave it to perish. I began to wonder: had I, too, caught a butterfly who would writhe on a needle?

[MARC *enters, dressed as a bureaucrat, holding a stack of papers. As* GAL-LIMARD *speaks,* MARC *hands papers to him. He peruses, then signs, stamps, or rejects them.*]

5 GALLIMARD   Over the next five weeks, I worked like a dynamo. I stopped going to the opera, I didn't phone or write her. I knew this little flower was waiting for me to call, and, as I wickedly refused to do so, I felt for the first time that rush of power—the absolute power of a man.

[MARC *continues acting as the bureaucrat, but he now speaks as himself.*]

MARC   Rene! It's me!

10 GALLIMARD   Marc—I hear your voice everywhere now. Even in the midst of work.

MARC   That's because I'm watching you—all the time.

GALLIMARD   You were always the most popular guy in school.

MARC   Well, there's no guarantee of failure in life like happiness in high
15   school. Somehow I knew I'd end up in the suburbs working for Renault[1]
    and you'd be in the Orient picking exotic women off the trees. And they say
    there's no justice.

GALLIMARD   That's why you were my friend?

MARC   I gave you a little of my life, so that now you can give me some of
20   yours. [*Pause*] Remember Isabelle?

GALLIMARD   Of course I remember! She was my first experience.

MARC   We all wanted to ball her. But she only wanted me.

GALLIMARD   I had her.

MARC   Right. You balled her.

25 GALLIMARD   You were the only one who ever believed me.

MARC   Well, there's a good reason for that. [*Beat*] C'mon. You must've guessed.

GALLIMARD   You told me to wait in the bushes by the cafeteria that night.
    The next thing I knew, she was on me. Dress up in the air.

MARC   She never wore underwear.

30 GALLIMARD   My arms were pinned to the dirt.

MARC   She loved the superior position. A girl ahead of her time.

GALLIMARD   I looked up, and there was this woman . . . bouncing up and
    down on my loins.

MARC   Screaming, right?

35 GALLIMARD   Screaming, and breaking off the branches all around me, and
    pounding my butt up and down into the dirt.

MARC   Huffing and puffing like a locomotive.

GALLIMARD   And in the middle of all this, the leaves were getting into my
    mouth, my legs were losing circulation, I thought, "God. So this is *it*?"

40 MARC   You thought that?

GALLIMARD   Well, I was worried about my legs falling off.

MARC   You didn't have a good time?

GALLIMARD   No, that's not what I—I had a great time!

MARC   You're sure?

45 GALLIMARD   Yeah. Really.

MARC   'Cuz I wanted you to have a good time.

GALLIMARD   I did.

    [*Pause.*]

MARC   Shit. [*Pause*] When all is said and done, she was kind of a lousy lay,
    wasn't she? I mean, there was a lot of energy there, but you never knew
50   what she was doing with it. Like when she yelled "I'm coming!"—hell, it
    was so loud, you wanted to go "Look, it's not that big a deal."

GALLIMARD   I got scared. I thought she meant someone was actually coming.
    [*Pause*] But, Marc?

MARC   What?

1. A French automobile manufacturing company.

55 GALLIMARD   Thanks.

MARC   Oh, don't mention it.

GALLIMARD   It was my first experience.

MARC   Yeah. You got her.

GALLIMARD   I got her.

60 MARC   Wait! Look at that letter again!

> [GALLIMARD *picks up one of the papers he's been stamping, and rereads it.*]

GALLIMARD [*to us*]   After six weeks, they began to arrive. The letters.

> [*Upstage special on* SONG, *as Madame* BUTTERFLY. *The scene is underscored by the "Love Duet."*]

SONG   Did we fight? I do not know. Is the opera no longer of interest to you? Please come—my audiences miss the white devil in their midst.

> [GALLIMARD *looks up from the letter, towards us.*]

GALLIMARD [*to us*]   A concession, but much too dignified. [*Beat; he discards
65   the letter.*] I skipped the opera again that week to complete a position paper on trade.

> [*The bureaucrat hands him another letter.*]

SONG   Six weeks have passed since last we met. Is this your practice—to leave friends in the lurch? Sometimes I hate you, sometimes I hate myself, but always I miss you.

70 GALLIMARD [*to us*]   Better, but I don't like the way she calls me "friend." When a woman calls a man her "friend," she's calling him a eunuch or a homosexual. [*Beat; he discards the letter.*] I was absent from the opera for the seventh week, feeling a sudden urge to clean out my files.

> [*Bureaucrat hands him another letter.*]

SONG   Your rudeness is beyond belief. I don't deserve this cruelty. Don't
75   bother to call. I'll have you turned away at the door.

GALLIMARD [*to us*]   I didn't. [*He discards the letter; bureaucrat hands him another.*] And then finally, the letter that concluded my experiment.

SONG   I am out of words. I can hide behind dignity no longer. What do you want? I have already given you my shame.

> [GALLIMARD *gives the letter back to* MARC, *slowly. Special on* SONG *fades out.*]

80 GALLIMARD [*to us*]   Reading it, I became suddenly ashamed. Yes, my experiment had been a success. She was turning on my needle. But the victory seemed hollow.

MARC   Hollow?! Are you crazy?

GALLIMARD   Nothing, Marc. Please go away.

85 MARC [*exiting, with papers*]   Haven't I taught you anything?

GALLIMARD   "I have already given you my shame." I had to attend a reception that evening. On the way, I felt sick. If there is a God, surely he would punish me now. I had finally gained power over a beautiful woman, only to abuse it cruelly. There must be justice in the world. I had the strange feel-
90   ing that the ax would fall this very evening.

1.12

Ambassador TOULON's *residence. Beijing. 1960.*

> *Sound cue: party noises. Light change. We are now in a spacious residence.* TOULON, *the French ambassador, enters and taps* GALLIMARD *on the shoulder.*

TOULON   Gallimard? Can I have a word? Over here.

GALLIMARD [*to us*]   Manuel Toulon. French ambassador to China. He likes to think of us all as his children. Rather like God.

TOULON   Look, Gallimard, there's not much to say. I've liked you. From the
5   day you walked in. You were no leader, but you were tidy and efficient.

GALLIMARD   Thank you, sir.

TOULON   Don't jump the gun. Okay, our needs in China are changing. It's embarrassing that we lost Indochina.[2] Someone just wasn't on the ball there. I don't mean you personally, of course.

10   GALLIMARD   Thank you, sir.

TOULON   We're going to be doing a lot more information-gathering in the future. The nature of our work here is changing. Some people are just going to have to go. It's nothing personal.

GALLIMARD   Oh.

15   TOULON   Want to know a secret? Vice-Consul LeBon is being transferred.

GALLIMARD [*to us*]   My immediate superior!

TOULON   And most of his department.

GALLIMARD [*to us*]   Just as I feared! God has seen my evil heart—

TOULON   But not you.

20   GALLIMARD [*to us*]   —and he's taking her away just as . . . [*To* TOULON] Excuse me, sir?

TOULON   Scare you? I think I did. Cheer up, Gallimard. I want you to replace LeBon as vice-consul.

GALLIMARD   You—? Yes, well, thank you, sir.

25   TOULON   Anytime.

GALLIMARD   I . . . accept with great humility.

TOULON   Humility won't be part of the job. You're going to coordinate the revamped intelligence division. Want to know a secret? A year ago, you would've been out. But the past few months, I don't know how it hap-
30   pened, you've become this new aggressive confident . . . thing. And they also tell me you get along with the Chinese. So I think you're a lucky man, Gallimard. Congratulations.

[*They shake hands.* TOULON *exits. Party noises out.* GALLIMARD *stumbles across a darkened stage.*]

GALLIMARD   Vice-consul? Impossible! As I stumbled out of the party, I saw it written across the sky: There is no God. Or, no—say that there is a God.
35   But that God . . . understands. Of course! God who creates Eve to serve Adam, who blesses Solomon with his harem but ties Jezebel to a burning bed[3]—that God is a man. And he understands! At age thirty-nine, I was suddenly initiated into the way of the world.

---

2. That is, French Indochina, a colony established in the late 19th century that comprised present-day Laos, Cambodia, and Vietnam. It was "lost" with the French defeat at the Battle of Dien Bien Phu in 1954, ending an insurgency that had begun with Vietnam's declaration of independence in 1945.

3. A series of biblical references: see Genesis 2.21–23 and 1 Corinthians 11.8–9 (the creation of Eve), 1 Kings 11.1–3 (Solomon's wives and concubines), and Revelation 2.20–23 (the punishment of Jezebel for harlotry, as described here).

1.13

SONG LILING's *apartment. Beijing. 1960.*

SONG *enters, in a sheer dressing gown.*

SONG   Are you crazy?

GALLIMARD   Mademoiselle Song—

SONG   To come here—at this hour? After . . . after eight weeks?

GALLIMARD   It's the most amazing—

5 SONG   You bang on my door? Scare my servants, scandalize the neighbors?

GALLIMARD   I've been promoted. To vice-consul.

      [*Pause.*]

SONG   And what is that supposed to mean to me?

GALLIMARD   Are you my Butterfly?

SONG   What are you saying?

10 GALLIMARD   I've come tonight for an answer: are you my Butterfly?

SONG   Don't you know already?

GALLIMARD   I want you to say it.

SONG   I don't want to say it.

GALLIMARD   So, that is your answer?

15 SONG   You know how I feel about—

GALLIMARD   I do remember one thing.

SONG   What?

GALLIMARD   In the letter I received today.

SONG   Don't.

20 GALLIMARD   "I have already given you my shame."

SONG   It's enough that I even wrote it.

GALLIMARD   Well, then—

SONG   I shouldn't have it splashed across my face.

GALLIMARD   —if that's all true—

25 SONG   Stop!

GALLIMARD   Then what is one more short answer?

SONG   I don't want to!

GALLIMARD   Are you my Butterfly? [*Silence; he crosses the room and begins to touch her hair.*] I want from you honesty. There should be nothing false between us. No false pride.

30   [*Pause.*]

SONG   Yes, I am. I am your Butterfly.

GALLIMARD   Then let me be honest with you. It is because of you that I was promoted tonight. You have changed my life forever. My little Butterfly, there should be no more secrets: I love you.

      [*He starts to kiss her roughly. She resists slightly.*]

35 SONG   No . . . no . . . gently . . . please, I've never . . .

GALLIMARD   No?

SONG   I've tried to appear experienced, but . . . the truth is . . . no.

GALLIMARD   Are you cold?

SONG   Yes. Cold.

40 GALLIMARD   Then we will go very, very slowly.

      [*He starts to caress her; her gown begins to open.*]

SONG   No . . . let me . . . keep my clothes . . .

GALLIMARD   But . . .

SONG   Please . . . it all frightens me. I'm a modest Chinese girl.

GALLIMARD   My poor little treasure.

45 SONG   I am your treasure. Though inexperienced, I am not . . . ignorant.
They teach us things, our mothers, about pleasing a man.

GALLIMARD   Yes?

SONG   I'll do my best to make you happy. Turn off the lights.

> [GALLIMARD *gets up and heads for a lamp.* SONG, *propped up on one
> elbow, tosses her hair back and smiles.*]

SONG   Monsieur Gallimard?

50 GALLIMARD   Yes, Butterfly?

SONG   "Vieni, vieni!"[4]

GALLIMARD   "Come, darling."

SONG   "Ah! Dolce notte!"

GALLIMARD   "Beautiful night."

55 SONG   "Tutto estatico d'amor ride il ciel!"

GALLIMARD   "All ecstatic with love, the heavens are filled with laughter."

> [*He turns off the lamp. Blackout.*]

2.1

M. GALLIMARD's *cell. Paris. Present.*

Lights up on GALLIMARD. *He sits in his cell, reading from a leaflet.*

GALLIMARD   This, from a contemporary critic's commentary on *Madame Butterfly:* "Pinkerton suffers from . . . being an obnoxious bounder whom every
man in the audience itches to kick." Bully for us men in the audience!
Then, in the same note: "Butterfly is the most irresistibly appealing of Puc-
5   cini's 'Little Women.' Watching the succession of her humiliations is like
watching a child under torture." [*He tosses the pamphlet over his shoulder.*]
I suggest that, while we men may all want to kick Pinkerton, very few of us
would pass up the opportunity to *be* Pinkerton.

> [GALLIMARD *moves out of his cell.*]

2.2

GALLIMARD *and* BUTTERFLY's *flat. Beijing. 1960.*

We are in a simple but well-decorated parlor. GALLIMARD *moves to sit on a sofa,
while* SONG, *dressed in a chong sam,[5] enters and curls up at his feet.*

GALLIMARD   [*to us*]   We secured a flat on the outskirts of Peking. Butterfly, as
I was calling her now, decorated our "home" with Western furniture and
Chinese antiques. And there, on a few stolen afternoons or evenings each
week, Butterfly commenced her education.

5   SONG   The Chinese men—they keep us down.

GALLIMARD   Even in the "New Society"?[6]

---

4. Song's Italian lines ending this scene,
translated by Gallimard, are drawn from
the "Love Duet" finale of act 1 of *Madama
Butterfly.*
5. That is, a cheongsam (literally, "long gown"),

a traditional Chinese dress with a high collar
and a slit skirt.
6. In his essay "On New Democracy" (1940),
Mao Zedong called for "a new society and a
new state for the Chinese nation."

SONG   In the "New Society," we are all kept ignorant equally. That's one of the exciting things about loving a Western man. I know you are not threatened by a woman's education.

10 GALLIMARD   I'm no saint, Butterfly.

SONG   But you come from a progressive society.

GALLIMARD   We're not always reminding each other how "old" we are, if that's what you mean.

SONG   Exactly. We Chinese—once, I suppose, it is true, we ruled the world.
15 But so what? How much more exciting to be part of the society ruling the world today. Tell me—what's happening in Vietnam?[7]

GALLIMARD   Oh, Butterfly—you want me to bring my work home?

SONG   I want to know what you know. To be impressed by my man. It's not the particulars so much as the fact that you're making decisions which
20 change the shape of the world.

GALLIMARD   Not the world. At best, a small corner.

[TOULON *enters, and sits at a desk upstage.*]

2.3

French embassy. Beijing. 1961.

GALLIMARD *moves downstage, to* TOULON's *desk.* SONG *remains upstage, watching.*

TOULON   And a more troublesome corner is hard to imagine.

GALLIMARD   So, the Americans plan to begin bombing?

TOULON   This is very secret, Gallimard: yes. The Americans don't have an embassy here.[8] They're asking us to be their eyes and ears. Say Jack Ken-
5 nedy signed an order to bomb North Vietnam, Laos.[9] How would the Chinese react?

GALLIMARD   I think the Chinese will squawk—

TOULON   Uh-huh.

GALLIMARD   —but, in their hearts, they don't even like Ho Chi Minh.[1]

[*Pause.*]

10 TOULON   What a bunch of jerks. Vietnam was *our* colony. Not only didn't the Americans help us fight to keep them, but now, seven years later, they've come back to grab the territory for themselves. It's very irritating.

GALLIMARD   With all due respect, sir, why should the Americans have won our war for us back in '54 if we didn't have the will to win it ourselves?

7. On gaining its independence in 1954, Vietnam was divided into two countries: the Communist-controlled Democratic Republic of Vietnam (North Vietnam) and the U.S.-backed Republic of Vietnam (South Vietnam). In the late 1950s Communist insurgents in the South (the Viet Cong), aided by the North, launched a guerrilla war seeking the reunification of Vietnam.

8. The United States did not establish official diplomatic relations with the People's Republic of China until 1979.

9. While campaigning for the presidency in 1960, Kennedy pledged to increase U.S. military assistance to South Vietnam in its struggle

against the armed insurgency supported by the North. In 1961 his administration signed a military and economic aid treaty with South Vietnam, leading to large increases in the number of U.S. military advisers in the country (U.S. air strikes against North Vietnam and Laos would not begin until 1964).

1. Vietnamese nationalist (1890–1969), a Communist who led the struggle for independence; after the country's partition in 1954, he became president of North Vietnam. In the early 1950s China had sent military advisers and weapons to the Vietnamese insurgents, and it supported the North in its war with the South.

15 TOULON   You're kidding, aren't you?
[*Pause.*]

GALLIMARD   The Orientals simply want to be associated with whoever shows the most strength and power. You live with the Chinese, sir. Do you think they like Communism?

TOULON   I live in China. Not with the Chinese.

20 GALLIMARD   Well, I—

TOULON   *You* live with the Chinese.

GALLIMARD   Excuse me?

TOULON   I can't keep a secret.

GALLIMARD   What are you saying?

25 TOULON   Only that I'm not immune to gossip. So, you're keeping a native mistress. Don't answer. It's none of my business. [*Pause*] I'm sure she must be gorgeous.

GALLIMARD   Well . . .

TOULON   I'm impressed. You have the stamina to go out into the streets and 30 hunt one down. Some of us have to be content with the wives of the expatriate community.

GALLIMARD   I do feel . . . fortunate.

TOULON   So, Gallimard, you've got the inside knowledge—what *do* the Chinese think?

35 GALLIMARD   Deep down, they miss the old days. You know, cappuccinos, men in tuxedos—

TOULON   So what do we tell the Americans about Vietnam?

GALLIMARD   Tell them there's a natural affinity between the West and the Orient.

40 TOULON   And that you speak from experience?

GALLIMARD   The Orientals are people too. They want the good things we can give them. If the Americans demonstrate the will to win, the Vietnamese will welcome them into a mutually beneficial union.

TOULON   I don't see how the Vietnamese can stand up to American 45 firepower.

GALLIMARD   Orientals will always submit to a greater force.

TOULON   I'll note your opinions in my report. The Americans always love to hear how "welcome" they'll be. [*He starts to exit.*]

GALLIMARD   Sir?

50 TOULON   Mmmm?

GALLIMARD   This . . . rumor you've heard.

TOULON   Uh-huh?

GALLIMARD   How . . . widespread do you think it is?

TOULON   It's only widespread within this embassy. Where nobody talks 55 because everybody is guilty. We were worried about you, Gallimard. We thought you were the only one here without a secret. Now you go and find a lotus blossom . . . and top us all. [*He exits.*]

GALLIMARD [*to us*]   Toulon knows! And he approves! I was learning the benefits of being a man. We form our own clubs, sit behind thick doors, 60 smoke—and celebrate the fact that we're still boys. [*He starts to move downstage, towards* SONG.] So, over the—

[*Suddenly* COMRADE CHIN *enters.* GALLIMARD *backs away.*]

GALLIMARD [*to* SONG]   No! Why does she have to come in?

SONG   Rene, be sensible. How can they understand the story without her? Now, don't embarrass yourself.

[GALLIMARD *moves down center.*]

65 GALLIMARD [*to us*]   Now, you will see why my story is so amusing to so many people. Why they snicker at parties in disbelief. Please—try to understand it from my point of view. We are all prisoners of our time and place. [*He exits.*]

2.4

GALLIMARD *and* BUTTERFLY'S *flat. Beijing. 1961.*

SONG [*to us*]   1961. The flat Monsieur Gallimard rented for us. An evening after he has gone.

CHIN   Okay, see if you can find out when the Americans plan to start bombing Vietnam. If you can find out what cities, even better.

5 SONG   I'll do my best, but I don't want to arouse his suspicions.

CHIN   Yeah, sure, of course. So, what else?

SONG   The Americans will increase troops in Vietnam to 170,000 soldiers with 120,000 militia and 11,000 American advisors.

CHIN [*writing*]   Wait, wait. 120,000 militia and—

10 SONG   —11,000 American—

CHIN   —American advisors. [*Beat*] How do you remember so much?

SONG   I'm an actor.

CHIN   Yeah. [*Beat*] Is that how come you dress like that?

SONG   Like what, Miss Chin?

15 CHIN   Like that dress! You're wearing a dress. And every time I come here, you're wearing a dress. Is that because you're an actor? Or what?

SONG   It's a . . . disguise, Miss Chin.

CHIN   Actors, I think they're all weirdos. My mother tells me actors are like gamblers or prostitutes or—

20 SONG   It helps me in my assignment.

[*Pause.*]

CHIN   You're not gathering information in any way that violates Communist Party principles, are you?

SONG   Why would I do that?

CHIN   Just checking. Remember: when working for the Great Proletarian

25 State, you represent our Chairman Mao[2] in every position you take.

SONG   I'll try to imagine the Chairman taking my positions.

CHIN   We all think of him this way. Good-bye, comrade.[3] [*She starts to exit.*] Comrade?

SONG   Yes?

30 CHIN   Don't forget: there is no homosexuality in China!

SONG   Yes, I've heard.

CHIN   Just checking. [*She exits.*]

---

2. Mao Zedong (1893–1976) was chairman of the Central Committee of the Chinese Communist Party from 1945 until his death. *Proletarian state:* a transitional stage in the proletarian (i.e., working-class) revolution that Karl Marx and Friedrich Engels, in *Man-* *ifesto of the Communist Party* (1848), envisioned as necessary to overthrow capitalism and bring about a classless society.

3. Customary form of address among Communists.

SONG [*to us*]   What passes for a woman in modern China.

    [GALLIMARD *sticks his head out from the wings.*]

GALLIMARD   Is she gone?

35 SONG   Yes, Rene. Please continue in your own fashion.

2.5

Beijing. 1961–63.

   GALLIMARD *moves to the couch where* SONG *still sits. He lies down in her lap, and she strokes his forehead.*

GALLIMARD [*to us*]   And so, over the years 1961, '62, '63, we settled into our routine, Butterfly and I. She would always have prepared a light snack and then, ever so delicately, and only if I agreed, she would start to pleasure me. With her hands, her mouth . . . too many ways to explain, and too sad, given

5   my present situation. But mostly we would talk. About my life. Perhaps there is nothing more rare than to find a woman who passionately listens.

    [SONG *remains upstage, listening, as* HELGA *enters and plays a scene downstage with* GALLIMARD.]

HELGA   Rene, I visited Dr. Bolleart this morning.

GALLIMARD   Why? Are you ill?

HELGA   No, no. You see, I wanted to ask him . . . that question we've been

10   discussing.

GALLIMARD   And I told you, it's only a matter of time. Why did you bring a doctor into this? We just have to keep trying—like a crapshoot, actually.

HELGA   I went, I'm sorry. But listen: he says there's nothing wrong with me.

GALLIMARD   You see? Now, will you stop—?

15 HELGA   Rene, he says he'd like you to go in and take some tests.

GALLIMARD   Why? So he can find there's nothing wrong with both of us?

HELGA   Rene, I don't ask for much. One trip! One visit! And then, whatever you want to do about it—you decide.

GALLIMARD   You're assuming he'll find something defective!

20 HELGA   No! Of course not! Whatever he finds—if he finds nothing, we decide what to do about nothing! But go!

GALLIMARD   If he finds nothing, we keep trying. Just like we do now.

HELGA   But at least we'll know! [*Pause*] I'm sorry. [*She starts to exit.*]

GALLIMARD   Do you really want me to see Dr. Bolleart?

25 HELGA   Only if you want a child, Rene. We have to face the fact that time is running out. Only if you want a child. [*She exits.*]

GALLIMARD [*to* SONG]   I'm a modern man, Butterfly. And yet, I don't want to go. It's the same old voodoo. I feel like God himself is laughing at me if I can't produce a child.

30 SONG   You men of the West—you're obsessed by your odd desire for equality. Your wife can't give you a child, and *you're* going to the doctor?

GALLIMARD   Well, you see, she's already gone.

SONG   And because this incompetent can't find the defect, you now have to subject yourself to him? It's unnatural.

35 GALLIMARD   Well, what is the "natural" solution?

SONG   In Imperial China, when a man found that one wife was inadequate, he turned to another—to give him his son.

GALLIMARD   What do you—? I can't . . . marry you, yet.

40 SONG   Please. I'm not asking you to be my husband. But I am already your wife.

GALLIMARD   Do you want to . . . have my child?

SONG   I thought you'd never ask.

GALLIMARD   But, your career . . . your—

SONG   Phooey on my career! That's your Western mind, twisting itself into strange shapes again. Of course I love my career. But what would I love
45 most of all? To feel something inside me—day and night—something I know is yours. [*Pause*] Promise me . . . you won't go to this doctor. Who is this Western quack to set himself as judge over the man I love? I know who is a man, and who is not. [*She exits.*]

GALLIMARD [*to us*]   Dr. Bolleart? Of course I didn't go. What man would?

2.6

Beijing. 1963.

Party noises over the house speakers. RENEE *enters, wearing a revealing gown.*

GALLIMARD   1963. A party at the Austrian embassy. None of us could remember the Austrian ambassador's name, which seemed somehow appropriate. [*To* RENEE] So, I tell the Americans, Diem[4] must go. The U.S. wants to be respected by the Vietnamese, and yet they're propping up this
5 nobody seminarian as her president. A man whose claim to fame is his sister-in-law[5] imposing fanatic "moral order" campaigns? Oriental women— when they're good, they're very good, but when they're bad, they're Christians.

RENEE   Yeah.

10 GALLIMARD   And what do you do?

RENEE   I'm a student. My father exports a lot of useless stuff to the Third World.

GALLIMARD   How useless?

RENEE   You know. Squirt guns, confectioner's sugar, hula hoops[6] . . .

15 GALLIMARD   I'm sure they appreciate the sugar.

RENEE   I'm here for two years to study Chinese.

GALLIMARD   Two years?

RENEE   That's what everybody says.

GALLIMARD   When did you arrive?

20 RENEE   Three weeks ago.

GALLIMARD   And?

RENEE   I like it. It's primitive, but . . . well, this is the place to learn Chinese, so here I am.

GALLIMARD   Why Chinese?

25 RENEE   I think it'll be important someday.

4. Ngo Dinh Diem (1901–1963); as a boy, he studied in a French Catholic school and briefly entered a monastery. With U.S. support, he became prime minister of Vietnam in 1954 and president of South Vietnam in 1955. His authoritarian and corrupt rule made him widely unpopular, and he was ousted and murdered by a group of generals who had been assured that the United States would not interfere with a coup.
5. Tran Le Xian (1924–2011), the wife of
Diem's brother and chief adviser, Ngo Dinh Nhu; she was known as Madame Nhu. Because Diem was unmarried, she was in effect the country's first lady. A passionate convert to Roman Catholicism, she worked for laws banning divorce, contraception, brothels, and the like and encouraged the persecution of Buddhists.
6. Hula Hoops were a brief U.S. craze in 1958, when 25 million were sold in four months.

GALLIMARD   You do?

RENEE   Don't ask me when, but . . . that's what I think.

GALLIMARD   Well, I agree with you. One hundred percent. That's very farsighted.

30 RENEE   Yeah. Well of course, my father thinks I'm a complete weirdo.

GALLIMARD   He'll thank you someday.

RENEE   Like when the Chinese start buying hula hoops?

GALLIMARD   There're a billion bellies out there.

RENEE   And if they end up taking over the world—well, then I'll be lucky to
35   know Chinese too, right?

> [*Pause.*]

GALLIMARD   At this point, I don't see how the Chinese can possibly take—

RENEE   You know what I *don't* like about China?

GALLIMARD   Excuse me? No—what?

RENEE   Nothing to do at night.

40 GALLIMARD   You come to parties at embassies like everyone else.

RENEE   Yeah, but they get out at ten. And then what?

GALLIMARD   I'm afraid the Chinese idea of a dance hall is a dirt floor and a man with a flute.

RENEE   Are you married?

45 GALLIMARD   Yes. Why?

RENEE   You wanna . . . fool around?

> [*Pause.*]

GALLIMARD   Sure.

RENEE   I'll wait for you outside. What's your name?

GALLIMARD   Gallimard. Rene.

50 RENEE   Weird. I'm Renee too. [*She exits.*]

GALLIMARD [*to us*]   And so, I embarked on my first extra-extramarital affair. Renee was picture perfect. With a body like those girls in the magazines. If I put a tissue paper over my eyes, I wouldn't have been able to tell the difference. And it was exciting to be with someone who wasn't afraid to be
55   seen completely naked. But is it possible for a woman to be *too* uninhibited, *too* willing, so as to seem almost too . . . masculine?

> [*Chuck Berry*[7] *blares from the house speakers, then comes down in volume as* RENEE *enters, toweling her hair.*]

RENEE   You have a nice weenie.

GALLIMARD   What?

RENEE   Penis. You have a nice penis.

60 GALLIMARD   Oh. Well, thank you. That's very . . .

RENEE   What—can't take a compliment?

GALLIMARD   No, it's very . . . reassuring.

RENEE   But most girls don't come out and say it, huh?

GALLIMARD   And also . . . what did you call it?

65 RENEE   Oh. Most girls don't call it a "weenie," huh?

GALLIMARD   It sounds very—

RENEE   Small, I know.

---

7. An African American songwriter, guitarist, and singer (1926–2017), a pioneer of rock music whose hits include "Roll Over Beethoven" (1956) and "Johnny B. Goode" (1958).

GALLIMARD   I was going to say, "young."

RENEE   Yeah. Young, small, same thing. Most guys are pretty, uh, sensitive
about that. Like, you know, I had a boyfriend back home in Denmark. I got
mad at him once and called him a little weeniehead. He got so mad! He
said at least I should call him a great big weeniehead.

GALLIMARD   I suppose I just say "penis."

RENEE   Yeah. That's pretty clinical. There's "cock," but that sounds like a
chicken. And "prick" is painful, and "dick" is like you're talking about
someone who's not in the room.

GALLIMARD   Yes. It's a . . . bigger problem than I imagined.

RENEE   I—I think maybe it's because I really don't know what to do with
them—that's why I call them "weenies."

GALLIMARD   Well, you did quite well with . . . mine.

RENEE   Thanks, but I mean, really *do* with them. Like, okay, have you ever
looked at one? I mean, really?

GALLIMARD   No, I suppose when it's part of you, you sort of take it for
granted.

RENEE   I guess. But, like, it just hangs there. This little . . . flap of flesh. And
there's so much fuss that we make about it. Like, I think the reason we
fight wars is because we wear clothes. Because no one knows—between
the men, I mean—who has the bigger . . . weenie. So, if I'm a guy with a
small one, I'm going to build a really big building or take over a really big
piece of land or write a really long book so the other men don't know, right?
But, see, it never really works, that's the problem. I mean, you conquer the
country, or whatever, but you're still wearing clothes, so there's no way to
prove absolutely whose is bigger or smaller. And that's what we call a civilized society. The whole world run by a bunch of men with pricks the size
of pins. [*She exits.*]

GALLIMARD   [*to us*]   This was simply not acceptable.

[*A high-pitched chime rings through the air.* SONG, *dressed as* BUTTERFLY,
*appears in the upstage special. She is obviously distressed. Her body
swoons as she attempts to clip the stems of flowers she's arranging in a
vase.*]

GALLIMARD   But I kept up our affair, wildly, for several months. Why? I
believe because of Butterfly. She knew the secret I was trying to hide. But,
unlike a Western woman, she didn't confront me, threaten, even pout. I
remembered the words of Puccini's *Butterfly*:

SONG   "Noi siamo gente avvezza / alle piccole cose / umili e silenziose."[8]

GALLIMARD   "I come from a people / Who are accustomed to little / Humble
and silent." I saw Pinkerton and Butterfly, and what she would say if he
were unfaithful . . . nothing. She would cry, alone, into those wildly soft
sleeves, once full of possessions, now empty to collect her tears. It was her
tears and her silence that excited me, every time I visited Renee.

TOULON   [*offstage*]   Gallimard!

[TOULON *enters.* GALLIMARD *turns towards him. During the next section,*
SONG, *up center, begins to dance with the flowers. It is a drunken dance,
where she breaks small pieces off the stems.*]

---

8. Lines from the aria "Vogliatemi bene" ("Ah, Love Me a Little"), sung by Butterfly in the opera's
first act.

TOULON   They're killing him.

GALLIMARD   Who? I'm sorry? What?

110 TOULON   Bother you to come over at this late hour?

GALLIMARD   No . . . of course not.

TOULON   Not after you hear my secret. Champagne?

GALLIMARD   Um . . . thank you.

TOULON   You're surprised. There's something that you've wanted, Gallimard.

115   No, not a promotion. Next time. Something in the world. You're not aware
    of this, but there's an informal gossip circle among intelligence agents. And
    some of ours heard from some of the Americans—

GALLIMARD   Yes?

TOULON   That the U.S. will allow the Vietnamese generals to stage a coup . . .

120   and assassinate President Diem.[9]

> [*The chime rings again.* TOULON *freezes.* GALLIMARD *turns upstage and
> looks at* BUTTERFLY, *who slowly and deliberately clips a flower off its stem.*
> GALLIMARD *turns back towards* TOULON.]

GALLIMARD   I think . . . that's a very wise move!

> [TOULON *unfreezes.*]

TOULON   It's what you've been advocating. A toast?

GALLIMARD   Sure. I consider this a vindication.

TOULON   Not exactly. "To the test. Let's hope you pass."

> [*They drink. The chime rings again.* TOULON *freezes.* GALLIMARD *turns
> upstage, and* SONG *clips another flower.*]

125 GALLIMARD [*to* TOULON]   The test?

TOULON [*unfreezing*]   It's a test of everything you've been saying. I personally
    think the generals probably will stop the Communists. And you'll be a hero.
    But if anything goes wrong, then your opinions won't be worth a pig's ear. I'm
    sure that won't happen. But sometimes it's easier when they don't listen to you.

130 GALLIMARD   They're your opinions too, aren't they?

TOULON   Personally, yes.

GALLIMARD   So we agree.

TOULON   But my opinions aren't on that report. Yours are. Cheers.

> [TOULON *turns away from* GALLIMARD *and raises his glass. At that instant*
> SONG *picks up the vase and hurls it to the ground. It shatters.* SONG *sinks
> down amidst the shards of the vase, in a calm, childlike trance. She sings
> softly, as if reciting a child's nursery rhyme.*]

SONG [*repeat as necessary*]   "The whole world over, the white man travels,

135   setting anchor, wherever he likes. Life's not worth living, unless he finds,
    the finest maidens, of every land . . ."[1]

> [GALLIMARD *turns downstage towards us.* SONG *continues singing.*]

GALLIMARD   I shook as I left his house. That coward! That worm! To put the
    burden for his decisions on my shoulders!

    I started for Renee's. But no, that was all I needed. A schoolgirl who

140   would question the role of the penis in modern society. What I wanted was

---

9. See the first note of this scene.

1. A translation of lines sung by Pinkerton in the first act of *Madama Butterfly*.

revenge. A vessel to contain my humiliation. Though I hadn't seen her in several weeks, I headed for Butterfly's.

[GALLIMARD *enters* SONG's *apartment.*]

SONG   Oh! Rene . . . I was dreaming!

GALLIMARD   You've been drinking?

145 SONG   If I can't sleep, then yes, I drink. But then, it gives me these dreams which—Rene, it's been almost three weeks since you visited me last.

GALLIMARD   I know. There's been a lot going on in the world.

SONG   Fortunately I am drunk. So I can speak freely. It's not the world, it's you and me. And an old problem. Even the softest skin becomes like
150   leather to a man who's touched it too often. I confess I don't know how to stop it. I don't know how to become another woman.

GALLIMARD   I have a request.

SONG   Is this a solution? Or are you ready to give up the flat?

GALLIMARD   It may be a solution. But I'm sure you won't like it.

155 SONG   Oh well, that's very important. "Like it?" Do you think I "like" lying here alone, waiting, always waiting for your return? Please—don't worry about what I may not "like."

GALLIMARD   I want to see you . . . naked.

[*Silence.*]

SONG   I thought you understood my modesty. So you want me to—what—
160   strip? Like a big cowboy girl? Shiny pasties on my breasts? Shall I fling my kimono over my head and yell "ya-hoo" in the process? I thought you respected my shame!

GALLIMARD   I believe you gave me your shame many years ago.

SONG   Yes—and it is just like a white devil to use it against me. I can't believe
165   it. I thought myself so repulsed by the passive Oriental and the cruel white man. Now I see—we are always most revolted by the things hidden within us.

GALLIMARD   I just mean—

SONG   Yes?

170 GALLIMARD   —that it will remove the only barrier left between us.

SONG   No, Rene. Don't couch your request in sweet words. Be yourself—a cad—and know that my love is enough, that I submit—submit to the worst you can give me. [*Pause*] Well, come. Strip me. Whatever happens, know that you have willed it. Our love, in your hands. I'm helpless before my man.

[GALLIMARD *starts to cross the room.*]

175 GALLIMARD   Did I not undress her because I knew, somewhere deep down, what I would find? Perhaps. Happiness is so rare that our mind can turn somersaults to protect it.

At the time, I only knew that I was seeing Pinkerton stalking towards his Butterfly, ready to reward her love with his lecherous hands. The image
180   sickened me, pulled me to my knees, so I was crawling towards her like a worm. By the time I reached her, Pinkerton . . . had vanished from my heart. To be replaced by something new, something unnatural, that flew in the face of all I'd learned in the world—something very close to love.

[*He grabs her around the waist; she strokes his hair.*]

GALLIMARD   Butterfly, forgive me.

185   SONG   Rene . . .

GALLIMARD   For everything. From the start.

SONG   I'm . . .

GALLIMARD   I want to—

SONG   I'm pregnant. [*Beat*] I'm pregnant. [*Beat*] I'm pregnant.

      [*Beat.*]

190   GALLIMARD   I want to marry you!

2.7

GALLIMARD *and* BUTTERFLY's *flat. Beijing. 1963.*

    Downstage, SONG *paces as* COMRADE CHIN *reads from her notepad. Upstage,* GAL-LIMARD *is still kneeling. He remains on his knees throughout the scene, watching it.*

SONG   I need a baby.

CHIN [*from pad*]   He's been spotted going to a dorm.

SONG   I need a baby.

CHIN   At the Foreign Language Institute.

5   SONG   I need a baby.

CHIN   The room of a Danish girl . . . What do you mean, you need a baby?!

SONG   Tell Comrade Kang—last night, the entire mission, it could've ended.

CHIN   What do you mean?

SONG   Tell Kang—he told me to strip.

10   CHIN   *Strip?!*

SONG   Write!

CHIN   I tell you, I don't understand nothing about this case any more. Nothing.

SONG   He told me to strip, and I took a chance. Oh, we Chinese, we know

15   how to gamble.

CHIN [*writing*]   " . . . told him to strip."

SONG   My palms were wet, I had to make a split-second decision.

CHIN   Hey! Can you slow down?!

      [*Pause.*]

SONG   You write faster, I'm the artist here. Suddenly, it hit me—"All he wants

20   is for her to submit. Once a woman submits, a man is always ready to become 'generous.'"

CHIN   You're just gonna end up with rough notes.

SONG   And it worked! He gave in! Now, if I can just present him with a baby. A Chinese baby with blond hair—he'll be mine for life!

25   CHIN   Kang will never agree! The trading of babies has to be a counterrevolutionary[2] act!

SONG   Sometimes, a counterrevolutionary act is necessary to counter a counterrevolutionary act.

      [*Pause.*]

CHIN   Wait.

30   SONG   I need one . . . in seven months. Make sure it's a boy.

CHIN   This doesn't sound like something the Chairman would do. Maybe you'd better talk to Comrade Kang yourself.

---

2. That is, undermining the goals of the Revolution of 1949.

SONG   Good. I will.

    [CHIN *gets up to leave.*]

SONG   Miss Chin? Why, in the Peking Opera, are women's roles played by
35   men?

CHIN   I don't know. Maybe, a reactionary remnant of male—

SONG   No. [*Beat*] Because only a man knows how a woman is supposed to
    act.

    [CHIN *exits.* SONG *turns upstage, towards* GALLIMARD.]

GALLIMARD [*calling after* CHIN]   Good riddance! [*To* SONG] I could forget all
40   that betrayal in an instant, you know. If you'd just come back and become
    Butterfly again.

SONG   Fat chance. You're here in prison, rotting in a cell. And I'm on a plane,
    winging my way back to China. Your President pardoned me of our treason,
    you know.

45 GALLIMARD   Yes, I read about that.

SONG   Must make you feel . . . lower than shit.

GALLIMARD   But don't you, even a little bit, wish you were here with me?

SONG   I'm an artist, Rene. You were my greatest . . . acting challenge. [*She
    laughs.*] It doesn't matter how rotten I answer, does it? You still adore me.
50   That's why I love you, Rene. [*She points to us.*] So—you were telling your
    audience about the night I announced I was pregnant.

    [GALLIMARD *puts his arms around* SONG's *waist. He and* SONG *are in the
    positions they were in at the end of Scene 6.*]

2.8

Same.

GALLIMARD   I'll divorce my wife. We'll live together here, and then later in
    France.

SONG   I feel so . . . ashamed.

GALLIMARD   Why?

5 SONG   I had begun to lose faith. And now, you shame me with your
    generosity.

GALLIMARD   Generosity? No, I'm proposing for very selfish reasons.

SONG   Your apologies only make me feel more ashamed. My outburst a
    moment ago!

10 GALLIMARD   Your outburst? What about my request?!

SONG   You've been very patient dealing with my . . . eccentricities. A Western
    man, used to women freer with their bodies—

GALLIMARD   It was sick! Don't make excuses for me.

SONG   I have to. You don't seem willing to make them for yourself.

    [*Pause.*]

15 GALLIMARD   You're crazy.

SONG   I'm happy. Which often looks like crazy.

GALLIMARD   Then make me crazy. Marry me.

    [*Pause.*]

SONG   No.

GALLIMARD   What?

20 SONG   Do I sound silly, a slave, if I say I'm not worthy?

GALLIMARD   Yes. In fact you do. No one has loved me like you.

SONG   Thank you. And no one ever will. I'll see to that.

GALLIMARD   So what is the problem?

SONG   Rene, we Chinese are realists. We understand rice, gold, and guns.
You are a diplomat. Your career is skyrocketing. Now, what would happen if
you divorced your wife to marry a Communist Chinese actress?

GALLIMARD   That's not being realistic. That's defeating yourself before you
begin.

SONG   We must conserve our strength for the battles we can win.

GALLIMARD   That sounds like a fortune cookie!

SONG   Where do you think fortune cookies come from?

GALLIMARD   I don't care.

SONG   You do. So do I. And we should. That is why I say I'm not worthy. I'm
worthy to love and even to be loved by you. But I am not worthy to end the
career of one of the West's most promising diplomats.

GALLIMARD   It's not that great a career! I made it sound like more than it is!

SONG   Modesty will get you nowhere. Flatter yourself, and you flatter me.
I'm flattered to decline your offer. [*She exits.*]

GALLIMARD [*to us*]   Butterfly and I argued all night. And, in the end, I left,
knowing I would never be her husband. She went away for several
months—to the countryside, like a small animal. Until the night I received
her call.

[*A baby's cry from offstage.* SONG *enters, carrying a child.*]

SONG   He looks like you.

GALLIMARD   Oh! [*Beat; he approaches the baby.*] Well, babies are never very
attractive at birth.

SONG   Stop!

GALLIMARD   I'm sure he'll grow more beautiful with age. More like his
mother.

SONG   "Chi vide mai / a bimbo del Giappon . . ."[3]

GALLIMARD   "What baby, I wonder, was ever born in Japan"—or China, for
that matter—

SONG   ". . . occhi azzurrini?"

GALLIMARD   "With azure eyes"—they're actually sort of brown, wouldn't you
say?

SONG   "E il labbro."

GALLIMARD: "And such lips!" [*He kisses* SONG.] And such lips.

SONG   "E i ricciolini d'oro schietto?"

GALLIMARD   "And such a head of golden"—if slightly patchy—"curls?"

SONG   I'm going to call him "Peepee."

GALLIMARD   Darling, could you repeat that because I'm sure a rickshaw just
flew by overhead.

SONG   You heard me.

GALLIMARD   "Song Peepee"? May I suggest Michael, or Stephan, or Adolph?

SONG   You may, but I won't listen.

GALLIMARD   You can't be serious. Can you imagine the time this child will
have in school?

SONG   In the West, yes.

---

3. These lines and those that follow are sung by Butterfly in act 2 of *Madama Butterfly*.

GALLIMARD   It's worse than naming him Ping Pong or Long Dong[4] or—

SONG   But he's never going to live in the West, is he?

[Pause.]

70 GALLIMARD   That wasn't my choice.

SONG   It is mine. And this is my promise to you: I will raise him, he will be our child, but he will never burden you outside of China.

GALLIMARD   Why do you make these promises? I want to be burdened! I want a scandal to cover the papers!

75 SONG [to us]   Prophetic.

GALLIMARD   I'm serious.

SONG   So am I. His name is as I registered it. And he will never live in the West.

[SONG exits with the child.]

GALLIMARD [to us]   It is possible that her stubbornness only made me want
80   her more. That drawing back at the moment of my capitulation was the most brilliant strategy she could have chosen. It is possible. But it is also possible that by this point she could have said, could have done . . . anything, and I would have adored her still.

2.9

Beijing. 1966.

A driving rhythm of Chinese percussion fills the stage.

GALLIMARD   And then, China began to change. Mao became very old, and his cult became very strong. And, like many old men, he entered his second childhood. So he handed over the reins of state to those with minds like his own. And children ruled the Middle Kingdom[5] with complete caprice. The
5   doctrine of the Cultural Revolution[6] implied continuous anarchy. Contact between Chinese and foreigners became impossible. Our flat was confiscated. Her fame and my money now counted against us.

[*Two dancers in Mao suits and red-starred caps enter, and begin crudely mimicking revolutionary violence, in an agitprop[7] fashion.*]

GALLIMARD   And somehow the American war went wrong too. Four hundred thousand dollars were being spent for every Viet Cong killed; so General
10   Westmoreland's[8] remark that the Oriental does not value life the way

4. Penis (slang).

5. The Chinese name for China (in Mandarin, *Zongguo,* "central state"), first used in the 11th century.

6. The Great Proletarian Cultural Revolution (1966–76), a campaign launched by Mao to rekindle revolutionary fervor by removing so-called counterrevolutionary elements from the Communist Party and society in general. Repeated purges led by the Red Guards—a mass movement composed mainly of students and of young people from the countryside, who subscribed wholeheartedly to Mao's new cult of personality—were aimed at bureaucrats, teachers and intellectuals, and writers and artists. The result was factionalism, violence, and chaos.

7. Agitation and propaganda, usually on behalf of communism and conveyed through the arts or literature (from the name of the department of the Russian Communist Party responsible for such activities).

8. William Westmoreland (1914–2005), commander of American military operations in Vietnam (1964–68) and U.S. Army chief of staff (1968–72); in the documentary *Hearts and Minds* (1974) he said, "The Oriental doesn't put the same high price on life as does the Westerner. Life is plentiful, life is cheap in the Orient."

Americans do was oddly accurate. Why weren't the Vietnamese people giving in? Why were they content instead to die and die and die again?

[TOULON *enters.*]

TOULON Congratulations, Gallimard.

GALLIMARD Excuse me, sir?

15 TOULON Not a promotion. That was last time. You're going home.

GALLIMARD What?

TOULON Don't say I didn't warn you.

GALLIMARD I'm being transferred . . . because I was wrong about the American war?[9]

20 TOULON Of course not. We don't care about the Americans. We care about your mind. The quality of your analysis. In general, everything you've predicted here in the Orient . . . just hasn't happened.

GALLIMARD I think that's premature.

TOULON Don't force me to be blunt. Okay, you said China was ready to open

25 to Western trade. The only thing they're trading out there are Western heads. And, yes, you said the Americans would succeed in Indochina. You were kidding, right?

GALLIMARD I think the end is in sight.

TOULON Don't be pathetic. And don't take this personally. You were wrong.

30 It's not your fault.

GALLIMARD But I'm going home.

TOULON Right. Could I have the number of your mistress? [*Beat*] Joke! Joke! Eat a croissant for me.

[TOULON *exits.* SONG, *wearing a Mao suit,*[1] *is dragged in from the wings as part of the upstage dance. They "beat" her, then lampoon the acrobatics of the Chinese opera, as she is made to kneel onstage.*]

GALLIMARD [*simultaneously*] I don't care to recall how Butterfly and I said our

35 hurried farewell. Perhaps it was better to end our affair before it killed her.

[GALLIMARD *exits.* COMRADE CHIN *walks across the stage with a banner reading: "The Actor Renounces His Decadent Profession!" She reaches the kneeling* SONG. *Percussion stops with a thud. Dancers strike poses.*]

CHIN Actor-oppressor, for years you have lived above the common people and looked down on their labor. While the farmer ate millet—

SONG I ate pastries from France and sweetmeats from silver trays.

CHIN And how did you come to live in such an exalted position?

40 SONG I was a plaything for the imperialists!

CHIN What did you do?

SONG I shamed China by allowing myself to be corrupted by a foreigner . . .

CHIN What does this mean? The People demand a full confession!

SONG I engaged in the lowest perversions with China's enemies!

---

9. After the Tonkin Gulf Resolution (1964) gave the president authority to "take all necessary measures" to defend U.S. forces "and to prevent further aggression," the first U.S. combat troops arrived in South Vietnam, joining 16,000 military advisers. By the end of 1966 close to 400,000 troops were in Vietnam; troop strength peaked in 1968 at 540,000. The last American forces left in 1973, and South Vietnam fell to the North in 1975.

1. A suit like that worn by Mao at the ceremony founding the People's Republic of China—with a high, buttoned collar and four external pockets. It was especially common during the Cultural Revolution.

45 CHIN   What perversions? Be more clear!

SONG   I let him put it up my ass!

> [*Dancers look over, disgusted.*]

CHIN   Aaaa-ya! How can you use such sickening language?!

SONG   My language . . . is only as foul as the crimes I committed . . .

CHIN   Yeah. That's better. So—what do you want to do now?

50 SONG   I want to serve the people.

> [*Percussion starts up, with Chinese strings.*]

CHIN   What?

SONG   I want to serve the people!

> [*Dancers regain their revolutionary smiles, and begin a dance of victory.*]

CHIN   What?!

SONG   I want to serve the people!!

> [*Dancers unveil a banner: "The Actor Is Rehabilitated!"* SONG *remains kneeling before* CHIN, *as the dancers bounce around them, then exit. Music out.*]

2.10

A commune. Hunan Province.[2] *1970.*

CHIN   How you planning to do that?

SONG   I've already worked four years in the fields of Hunan, Comrade Chin.[3]

CHIN   So? Farmers work all their lives. Let me see your hands.

> [SONG *holds them out for her inspection.*]

CHIN   Goddamn! Still so smooth! How long does it take to turn you actors
5   into good anythings? Hunh. You've just spent too many years in luxury to
be any good to the Revolution.

SONG   I served the Revolution.

CHIN   Serve the Revolution? Bullshit! You wore dresses! Don't tell me—I was
there. I saw you! You and your white vice-consul! Stuck up there in your
10   flat, living off the People's Treasury! Yeah, I knew what was going on! You
two . . . homos! Homos! Homos! [*Pause; she composes herself.*] Ah! Well . . .
you will serve the people, all right. But not with the Revolution's money.
This time, you use your own money.

SONG   I have no money.

15 CHIN   Shut up! And you won't stink up China any more with your pervert
stuff. You'll pollute the place where pollution begins—the West.

SONG   What do you mean?

CHIN   Shut up! You're going to France. Without a cent in your pocket. You
find your consul's house, you make him pay your expenses—

20 SONG   No.

CHIN   And you give us weekly reports! Useful information!

SONG   That's crazy. It's been four years.

CHIN   Either that, or back to rehabilitation center!

---

2. In southern China. *Commune:* the basic unit of China's collectivized system of agriculture (introduced in 1958 and abandoned in 1981).

3. During the Cultural Revolution, many deemed counterrevolutionary were sent to the countryside in order to be "rehabilitated" through hard labor and political reindoctrination.

SONG   Comrade Chin, he's not going to support me! Not in France! He's a
25   white man! I was just his plaything—

CHIN   Oh yuck! Again with the sickening language? Where's my stick?

SONG   You don't understand the mind of a man.

[*Pause.*]

CHIN   Oh no? No I don't? Then how come I'm married, huh? How come I
got a man? Five, six years ago, you always tell me those kind of things, I felt
30   very bad. But not now! Because what does the Chairman say? He tells us
I'm now the smart one, you're now the nincompoop! *You're* the blackhead,
the harebrain, the nitwit! You think you're so smart? You understand "The
Mind of a Man"? Good! Then *you* go to France and be a pervert for Chairman Mao!

[CHIN *and* SONG *exit in opposite directions.*]

2.11

Paris. 1968–70.

GALLIMARD *enters.*

GALLIMARD   And what was waiting for me back in Paris? Well, better Chinese
food than I'd eaten in China. Friends and relatives. A little accounting,
regular schedule, keeping track of traffic violations in the suburbs. . . . And
the indignity of students shouting the slogans of Chairman Mao at me—in
5   French.[4]

HELGA   Rene? Rene? [*She enters, soaking wet.*] I've had a . . . a problem.
[*She sneezes.*]

GALLIMARD   You're wet.

HELGA   Yes, I . . . coming back from the grocer's. A group of students, waving
red flags, they—

[GALLIMARD *fetches a towel.*]

10   HELGA   —they ran by, I was caught up along with them. Before I knew what
was happening—

[GALLIMARD *gives her the towel.*]

HELGA   Thank you. The police started firing water cannons at us. I tried to
shout, to tell them I was the wife of a diplomat, but—you know how it
is . . . [*Pause*] Needless to say, I lost the groceries. Rene, what's happening
15   to France?

GALLIMARD   What's—? Well, nothing, really.

HELGA   Nothing?! The storefronts are in flames, there's glass in the streets,
buildings are toppling—and I'm wet!

GALLIMARD   Nothing! . . . that I care to think about.

20   HELGA   And is that why you stay in this room?

GALLIMARD   Yes, in fact.

HELGA   With the incense burning? You know something? I hate incense. It
smells so sickly sweet.

GALLIMARD   Well, I hate the French. Who just smell—period!

4. In May 1968 student demonstrations against the French government's heavy-handed response to earlier protests grew into a massive uprising, joined by a general strike of millions of workers, seeking to end the administration of President Charles de Gaulle. The students were a mixture of radicals and leftists, including anarchists, Marxists, Trotskyites, and Maoists.

25 HELGA   And the Chinese were better?

GALLIMARD   Please—don't start.

HELGA   When we left, this exact same thing, the riots—

GALLIMARD   No, no . . .

HELGA   Students screaming slogans, smashing down doors—

30 GALLIMARD   Helga—

HELGA   It was all going on in China, too. Don't you remember?!

GALLIMARD   Helga! Please! [*Pause*] You have never understood China, have
you? You walk in here with these ridiculous ideas, that the West is falling
apart, that China was spitting in our faces. You come in, dripping of the
35   streets, and you leave water all over my floor. [*He grabs* HELGA's *towel,
begins mopping up the floor.*]

HELGA   But it's the truth!

GALLIMARD   Helga, I want a divorce.

[*Pause;* GALLIMARD *continues, mopping the floor.*]

HELGA   I take it back. China is . . . beautiful. Incense, I like incense.

GALLIMARD   I've had a mistress.

40 HELGA   So?

GALLIMARD   For eight years.

HELGA   I knew you would. I knew you would the day I married you. And now
what? You want to marry her?

GALLIMARD   I can't. She's in China.

45 HELGA   I see. You want to leave. For someone who's not here, is that right?

GALLIMARD   That's right.

HELGA   You can't live with her, but still you don't want to live with me.

GALLIMARD   That's right.

[*Pause.*]

HELGA   Shit. How terrible that I can figure that out. [*Pause.*] I never thought
50   I'd say it. But, in China, I was happy. I knew, in my own way, I knew that
you were not everything you pretended to be. But the pretense—going on
your arm to the embassy ball, visiting your office and the guards saying,
"Good morning, good morning, Madame Gallimard"—the pretense . . .
was very good indeed. [*Pause*] I hope everyone is mean to you for the rest
55   of your life. [*She exits.*]

GALLIMARD [*to us*]   Prophetic.

[MARC *enters with two drinks.*]

GALLIMARD [*to* MARC]   In China, I was different from all other men.

MARC   Sure. You were white. Here's your drink.

GALLIMARD   I felt . . . touched.

60 MARC   In the head? Rene, I don't want to hear about the Oriental love goddess. Okay? One night—can we just drink and throw up without a lot of
conversation?

GALLIMARD   You still don't believe me, do you?

MARC   Sure I do. She was the most beautiful, et cetera, et cetera, blasé blasé.

[*Pause.*]

65 GALLIMARD   My life in the West has been such a disappointment.

MARC   Life in the West is like that. You'll get used to it. Look, you're driving
me away. I'm leaving. Happy, now? [*He exits, then returns.*] Look, I have a
date tomorrow night. You wanna come? I can fix you up with—

GALLIMARD   Of course. I would love to come.

     [*Pause.*]

70 MARC   Uh—on second thought, no. You'd better get ahold of yourself first.

     [*He exits;* GALLIMARD *nurses his drink.*]

GALLIMARD [*to us*]   This is the ultimate cruelty, isn't it? That I can talk and talk and to anyone listening, it's only air—too rich a diet to be swallowed by a mundane world. Why can't anyone understand? That in China, I once loved, and was loved by, very simply, the Perfect Woman.

     [SONG *enters, dressed as* BUTTERFLY *in wedding dress.*]

75 GALLIMARD [*to* SONG]   Not again. My imagination is hell. Am I asleep this time? Or did I drink too much?

SONG   Rene?

GALLIMARD   God, it's too painful! That you speak?

SONG   What are you talking about? Rene—touch me.

80 GALLIMARD   Why?

SONG   I'm real. Take my hand.

GALLIMARD   Why? So you can disappear again and leave me clutching at the air? For the entertainment of my neighbors who—?

     [SONG *touches* GALLIMARD.]

SONG   Rene?

     [GALLIMARD *takes* SONG's *hand. Silence.*]

85 GALLIMARD   Butterfly? I never doubted you'd return.

SONG   You hadn't . . . forgotten—?

GALLIMARD   Yes, actually, I've forgotten everything. My mind, you see—there wasn't enough room in this hard head—not for the world *and* for you. No, there was only room for one. [*Beat*] Come, look. See? Your bed has been

90 waiting, with the Klimt[5] poster you like, and—see? The xiang lu [incense burner] you gave me?

SONG   I . . . I don't know what to say.

GALLIMARD   There's nothing to say. Not at the end of a long trip. Can I make you some tea?

95 SONG   But where's your wife?

GALLIMARD   She's by my side. She's by my side at last.

     [GALLIMARD *reaches to embrace* SONG. SONG *sidesteps, dodging him.*]

GALLIMARD   Why?!

SONG [*to us*]   So I did return to Rene in Paris. Where I found—

GALLIMARD   Why do you run away? Can't we show them how we embraced

100 that evening?

SONG   Please. I'm talking.

GALLIMARD   You have to do what I say! I'm conjuring you up in *my* mind!

SONG   Rene, I've never done what you've said. Why should it be any different in your mind? Now split—the story moves on, and I must change.

105 GALLIMARD   I welcomed you into my home! I didn't have to, you know! I could've left you penniless on the streets of Paris! But I took you in!

SONG   Thank you.

GALLIMARD   So . . . please . . . don't change.

---

5. Gustav Klimt (1862–1918), an Austrian painter associated with exoticism and eroticism.

SONG   You know I have to. You know I will. And anyway, what difference does
110   it make? No matter what your eyes tell you, you can't ignore the truth. You
       already know too much.

         [GALLIMARD *exits.* SONG *turns to us.*]

SONG   The change I'm going to make requires about five minutes. So I
       thought you might want to take this opportunity to stretch your legs, enjoy
       a drink, or listen to the musicians. I'll be here, when you return, right
115   where you left me.

         [SONG *goes to a mirror in front of which is a wash basin of water. She starts
         to remove her makeup as stagelights go to half and houselights come up.*]

3.1

A courthouse in Paris. 1986.

As he promised, SONG *has completed the bulk of his transformation, onstage by
the time the houselights go down and the stagelights come up full. He removes his
wig and kimono, leaving them on the floor. Underneath, he wears a well-cut suit.*

SONG   So I'd done my job better than I had a right to expect. Well, give him
       some credit, too. He's right—I was in a fix when I arrived in Paris. I walked
       from the airport into town, then I located, by blind groping, the Chinatown
       district. Let me make one thing clear: whatever else may be said about the
5   Chinese, they are stingy! I slept in doorways three days until I could find a
       tailor who would make me this kimono on credit. As it turns out, maybe I
       didn't even need it. Maybe he would've been happy to see me in a simple
       shift and mascara. But . . . better safe than sorry.
         That was 1970, when I arrived in Paris. For the next fifteen years, yes, I
10   lived a very comfy life. Some relief, believe me, after four years on a fuck-
       ing commune in Nowheresville, China. Rene supported the boy and me,
       and I did some demonstrations around the country as part of my "cultural
       exchange" cover. And then there was the spying.

         [SONG *moves upstage, to a chair.* TOULON *enters as a judge, wearing the
         appropriate wig and robes. He sits near* SONG. *It's 1986, and* SONG *is tes-
         tifying in a courtroom.*]

SONG   Not much at first. Rene had lost all his high-level contacts. Comrade
15   Chin wasn't very interested in parking-ticket statistics. But finally, at my
       urging, Rene got a job as a courier, handling sensitive documents. He'd
       photograph them for me, and I'd pass them on to the Chinese embassy.
JUDGE   Did he understand the extent of his activity?
SONG   He didn't ask. He knew that I needed those documents, and that was
20   enough.
JUDGE   But he must've known he was passing classified information.
SONG   I can't say.
JUDGE   He never asked what you were going to do with them?
SONG   Nope.
         [*Pause.*]
25 JUDGE   There is one thing that the court—indeed, that all of France—would
       like to know.
SONG   Fire away.
JUDGE   Did Monsieur Gallimard know you were a man?

SONG   Well, he never saw me completely naked. Ever.

30 JUDGE   But surely, he must've . . . how can I put this?

SONG   Put it however you like. I'm not shy. He must've felt around?

JUDGE   Mmmmm.

SONG   Not really. I did all the work. He just laid back. Of course we did enjoy more . . . complete union, and I suppose he *might* have wondered why I was

35   always on my stomach, but. . . . But what you're thinking is: "Of course a wrist must've brushed . . . a hand hit . . . over twenty years!" Yeah. Well, Your Honor, it was my job to make him think I was a woman. And chew on this: it wasn't all that hard. See, my mother was a prostitute along the Bundt[6] before the Revolution. And, uh, I think it's fair to say she learned a

40   few things about Western men. So I borrowed her knowledge. In service to my country.

JUDGE   Would you care to enlighten the court with this secret knowledge? I'm sure we're all very curious.

SONG   I'm sure you are. [*Pause*] Okay, Rule One is: Men always believe what

45   they want to hear. So a girl can tell the most obnoxious lies and the guys will believe them every time—"This is my first time"—"That's the biggest I've ever seen"—or *both,* which, if you really think about it, is not possible in a single lifetime. You've maybe heard those phrases a few times in your own life, yes, Your Honor?

50 JUDGE   It's not my life, Monsieur Song, which is on trial today.

SONG   Okay, okay, just trying to lighten up the proceedings. Tough room.

JUDGE   Go on.

SONG   Rule Two: As soon as a Western man comes into contact with the East—he's already confused. The West has sort of an international rape

55   mentality towards the East. Do you know rape mentality?

JUDGE   Give us your definition, please.

SONG   Basically, "Her mouth says no, but her eyes say yes."
        The West thinks of itself as masculine—big guns, big industry, big money—so the East is feminine—weak, delicate, poor . . . but good at art,

60   and full of inscrutable wisdom—the feminine mystique.
        Her mouth says no, but her eyes say yes. The West believes the East, deep down, *wants* to be dominated—because a woman can't think for herself.

JUDGE   What does this have to do with my question?

SONG   You expect Oriental countries to submit to your guns, and you expect

65   Oriental women to be submissive to your men. That's why you say they make the best wives.

JUDGE   But why would that make it possible for you to fool Monsieur Gallimard? Please—get to the point.

SONG   One, because when he finally met his fantasy woman, he wanted

70   more than anything to believe that she was, in fact, a woman. And second, I am an Oriental. And being an Oriental, I could never be completely a man.

        [*Pause.*]

JUDGE   Your armchair political theory is tenuous, Monsieur Song.

---

6. That is, the Bund, a thoroughfare along the Huangpu River in the former Shanghai International Settlement; before the Revolution, it was lined with financial institutions, hotels, and clubs as well as wharves (*bund* is the name often given in the Far East to an embanked street along a river or sea).

SONG   You think so? That's why you'll lose in all your dealings with the East.

75 JUDGE   Just answer my question: did he know you were a man?

      [*Pause.*]

SONG   You know, Your Honor, I never asked.

3.2

Same.

Music from the "Death Scene" from Butterfly blares over the house speakers. It is the loudest thing we've heard in this play.

GALLIMARD *enters, crawling towards* SONG's *wig and kimono.*

GALLIMARD   Butterfly? Butterfly?

      [SONG *remains a man, in the witness box, delivering a testimony we do not hear.*]

GALLIMARD [*to us*] In my moment of greatest shame, here, in this courtroom—with that . . . person up there, telling the world. . . . What strikes me especially is how shallow he is, how glib and obsequious . . .

5 completely . . . without substance! The type that prowls around discos with a gold medallion, stinking of garlic. So little like my Butterfly.

      Yet even in this moment my mind remains agile, flip-flopping like a man on a trampoline. Even now, my picture dissolves, and I see that . . . witness . . . talking to me.

      [SONG *suddenly stands straight up in his witness box, and looks at* GALLIMARD.]

10 SONG   Yes. You. White man.

      [SONG *steps out of the witness box, and moves downstage towards* GALLI-MARD. *Light change.*]

GALLIMARD [*to* SONG] Who? Me?

SONG   Do you see any other white men?

GALLIMARD   Yes. There're white men all around. This is a French courtroom.

SONG   So you are an adventurous imperialist. Tell me, why did it take you so

15 long? To come back to this place?

GALLIMARD   What place?

SONG   This theatre in China. Where we met many years ago.

GALLIMARD [*to us*] And once again, against my will, I am transported.

      [*Chinese opera music comes up on the speakers.* SONG *begins to do opera moves, as he did the night they met.*]

SONG   Do you remember? The night you gave your heart?

20 GALLIMARD   It was a long time ago.

SONG   Not long enough. A night that turned your world upside down.

GALLIMARD   Perhaps.

SONG   Oh, be honest with me. What's another bit of flattery when you've already given me twenty years' worth? It's a wonder my head hasn't swollen

25 to the size of China.

GALLIMARD   Who's to say it hasn't?

SONG   Who's to say? And what's the shame? In pride? You think I could've pulled this off if I wasn't already full of pride when we met? No, not just pride. Arrogance. It takes arrogance, really—to believe you can will, with

30 your eyes and your lips, the destiny of another. [*He dances.*] C'mon. Admit it. You still want me. Even in slacks and a button-down collar.

GALLIMARD   I don't see what the point of—

SONG   You don't? Well maybe, Rene, just maybe—I want you.

GALLIMARD   You do?

35 SONG   Then again, maybe I'm just playing with you. How can you tell? [*Reprising his feminine character, he sidles up to* GALLIMARD.] "How I wish there were even a small cafe to sit in. With men in tuxedos, and cappuccinos, and bad expatriate jazz." Now you want to kiss me, don't you?

GALLIMARD [*pulling away*]   What makes you—?

40 SONG   —so sure? See? I take the words from your mouth. Then I wait for you to come and retrieve them. [*He reclines on the floor.*]

GALLIMARD   Why?! Why do you treat me so cruelly?

SONG   Perhaps I *was* treating you cruelly. But now—I'm being nice. Come here, my little one.

45 GALLIMARD   I'm not your little one!

SONG   My mistake. It's I who am *your* little one, right?

GALLIMARD   Yes, I—

SONG   So come get your little one. If you like. I may even let you strip me.

GALLIMARD   I mean, you were! Before . . . but not like this!

50 SONG   I was? Then perhaps I still am. If you look hard enough. [*He starts to remove his clothes.*]

GALLIMARD   What—what are you doing?

SONG   Helping you to see through my act.

GALLIMARD   Stop that! I don't want to! I don't—

SONG   Oh, but you asked me to strip, remember?

55 GALLIMARD   What? That was years ago! And I took it back!

SONG   No. You postponed it. Postponed the inevitable. Today, the inevitable has come calling.

[*From the speakers, cacophony:* BUTTERFLY *mixed in with Chinese gongs.*]

GALLIMARD   No! Stop! I don't want to see!

SONG   Then look away.

60 GALLIMARD   You're only in my mind! All this is in my mind! I order you! To stop!

SONG   To what? To strip? That's just what I'm—

GALLIMARD   No! Stop! I want you—!

SONG   You want me?

GALLIMARD   To stop!

65 SONG   You know something, Rene? Your mouth says no, but your eyes say yes. Turn them away. I dare you.

GALLIMARD   I don't have to! Every night, you say you're going to strip, but then I beg you and you stop!

SONG   I guess tonight is different.

70 GALLIMARD   Why? Why should that be?

SONG   Maybe I've become frustrated. Maybe I'm saying "Look at me, you fool!" Or maybe I'm just feeling . . . sexy. [*He is down to his briefs.*]

GALLIMARD   Please. This is unnecessary. I know what you are.

SONG   Do you? What am I?

75 GALLIMARD   A—a man.

SONG   You don't really believe that.

GALLIMARD   Yes I do! I knew all the time somewhere that my happiness was temporary, my love a deception. But my mind kept the knowledge at bay. To make the wait bearable.

80   SONG   Monsieur Gallimard—the wait is over.

> [SONG *drops his briefs. He is naked. Sound cue out. Slowly, we and* SONG *come to the realization that what we had thought to be* GALLIMARD's *sobbing is actually his laughter.*]

GALLIMARD   Oh god! What an idiot! Of course!

SONG   Rene—what?

GALLIMARD   Look at you! You're a man! [*He bursts into laughter again.*]

SONG   I fail to see what's so funny!

85   GALLIMARD   "You fail to see—!" I mean, you never did have much of a sense of humor, did you? I just think it's ridiculously funny that I've wasted so much time on just a man!

SONG   Wait. I'm not "just a man."

GALLIMARD   No? Isn't that what you've been trying to convince me of?

90   SONG   Yes, but what I mean—

GALLIMARD   And now, I finally believe you, and you tell me it's not true? I think you must have some kind of identity problem.

SONG   Will you listen to me?

GALLIMARD   Why?! I've been listening to you for twenty years. Don't I deserve
95   a vacation?

SONG   I'm not just any man!

GALLIMARD   Then, what exactly are you?

SONG   Rene, how can you ask—? Okay, what about this?

> [*He picks up* BUTTERFLY's *robes, starts to dance around. No music.*]

GALLIMARD   Yes, that's very nice. I have to admit.

> [SONG *holds out his arm to* GALLIMARD.]

100   SONG   It's the same skin you've worshiped for years. Touch it.

GALLIMARD   Yes, it does feel the same.

SONG   Now—close your eyes.

> [SONG *covers* GALLIMARD's *eyes with one hand. With the other,* SONG *draws* GALLIMARD's *hand up to his face.* GALLIMARD, *like a blind man, lets his hands run over* SONG's *face.*]

GALLIMARD   This skin, I remember. The curve of her face, the softness of her cheek, her hair against the back of my hand . . .

105   SONG   I'm your Butterfly. Under the robes, beneath everything, it was always me. Now, open your eyes and admit it—you adore me. [*He removes his hand from* GALLIMARD's *eyes.*]

GALLIMARD   You, who knew every inch of my desires—how could you, of all people, have made such a mistake?

SONG   What?

110   GALLIMARD   You showed me your true self. When all I loved was the lie. A perfect lie, which you let fall to the ground—and now, it's old and soiled.

SONG   So—you never really loved me? Only when I was playing a part?

GALLIMARD   I'm a man who loved a woman created by a man. Everything else—simply falls short.

> [*Pause.*]

115   SONG   What am I supposed to do now?

GALLIMARD   You were a fine spy, Monsieur Song, with an even finer accomplice. But now I believe you should go. Get out of my life!

SONG   Go where? Rene, you can't live without me. Not after twenty years.

GALLIMARD   I certainly can't live with you—not after twenty years of betrayal.

120 SONG   Don't be so stubborn! Where will you go?

GALLIMARD   I have a date . . . with my Butterfly.

SONG   So, throw away your pride. And come . . .

GALLIMARD   Get away from me! Tonight, I've finally learned to tell fantasy from reality. And, knowing the difference, I choose fantasy.

125 SONG   *I'm* your fantasy!

GALLIMARD   You? You're as real as hamburger. Now get out! I have a date with my Butterfly and I don't want your body polluting the room! [*He tosses* SONG's *suit at him.*] Look at these—you dress like a pimp.

SONG   Hey! These are Armani slacks[7] and—! [*He puts on his briefs and*
130   *slacks.*] Let's just say . . . I'm disappointed in you, Rene. In the crush of your adoration, I thought you'd become something more. More like . . . a woman.

But no. Men. You're like the rest of them. It's all in the way we dress, and make up our faces, and bat our eyelashes. You really have so little
135   imagination!

GALLIMARD   You, Monsieur Song? Accuse me of too little imagination? You, if anyone, should know—I am pure imagination. And in imagination I will remain. Now get out!

[GALLIMARD *bodily removes* SONG *from the stage, taking his kimono.*]

SONG   Rene! I'll never put on those robes again! You'll be sorry!

140 GALLIMARD [*to* SONG]   I'm already sorry! [*Looking at the kimono in his hands*] Exactly as sorry . . . as a Butterfly.

3.3

M. GALLIMARD's *prison cell. Paris. Present.*

GALLIMARD   I've played out the events of my life night after night, always searching for a new ending to my story, one where I leave this cell and return forever to my Butterfly's arms.

Tonight I realize my search is over. That I've looked all along in the
5   wrong place. And now, to you, I will prove that my love was not in vain—by returning to the world of fantasy where I first met her.

[*He picks up the kimono; dancers enter.*]

GALLIMARD   There is a vision of the Orient that I have. Of slender women in chong sams and kimonos who die for the love of unworthy foreign devils. Who are born and raised to be the perfect women. Who take whatever
10   punishment we give them, and bounce back, strengthened by love, unconditionally. It is a vision that has become my life.

[*Dancers bring the wash basin to him and help him make up his face.*]

GALLIMARD   In public, I have continued to deny that Song Liling is a man. This brings me headlines, and is a source of great embarrassment to my French colleagues, who can now be sent into a coughing fit by the mere
15   mention of Chinese food. But alone, in my cell, I have long since faced the truth.

And the truth demands a sacrifice. For mistakes made over the course of a lifetime. My mistakes were simple and absolute—the man I loved was a

---

7. That is, expensive designer clothing. Giorgio Armani (b. 1934) is an Italian designer of relaxed but luxurious clothes for men and women.

cad, a bounder. He deserved nothing but a kick in the behind, and instead
20 I gave him . . . all my love.

    Yes—love. Why not admit it all? That was my undoing, wasn't it? Love
warped my judgment, blinded my eyes, rearranged the very lines on my
face . . . until I could look in the mirror and see nothing but . . . a woman.

    [Dancers help him put on the BUTTERFLY *wig.]*

GALLIMARD   I have a vision. Of the Orient. That, deep within its almond
25 eyes, there are still women. Women willing to sacrifice themselves for the
love of a man. Even a man whose love is completely without worth.

    [Dancers assist GALLIMARD *in donning the kimono. They hand him a
knife.]*

GALLIMARD   Death with honor is better than life . . . life with dishonor. *[He
sets himself center stage, in a seppuku[8] position.]* The love of a Butterfly can
withstand many things—unfaithfulness, loss, even abandonment. But how
30 can it face the one sin that implies all others? The devastating knowledge
that, underneath it all, the object of her love was nothing more, nothing
less than . . . a man. *[He sets the tip of the knife against his body.]* It is 19__.
And I have found her at last. In a prison on the outskirts of Paris. My name
is Rene Gallimard—also known as Madame Butterfly.

    *[*GALLIMARD *turns upstage and plunges the knife into his body, as music
from the "Love Duet" blares over the speakers. He collapses into the arms
of the dancers, who lay him reverently on the floor. The image holds for
several beats. Then a tight special up on* SONG, *who stands as a man, staring at the dead* GALLIMARD. *He smokes a cigarette; the smoke filters up
through the lights. Two words leave his lips.]*

35 SONG   Butterfly? Butterfly?

    [Smoke rises as lights fade slowly to black.]

---

8. Ritual suicide by disembowelment (Japanese); synonymous with hara-kiri.

TONY KUSHNER

b. 1956

WHEN *MILLENNIUM APPROACHES*, Part One of *ANGELS IN AMERICA*, opened on Broadway in 1993, Tony Kushner was hailed as the savior of serious American theater. Since the 1970s skyrocketing production costs had made it all but impossible for an ambitious nonmusical drama to survive on Broadway. Not only did Kushner defy those odds, he did so with a work of enormous scope and ambition. *Angels in America* is a two-part epic drama exploring personal identity, sexual orientation, political responsibility, AIDS, Mormonism, Judaism, and Reagan-era conservatism within an eclectic dramaturgy that mixes realism, surrealism, and the spectacular. *Millennium Approaches* received numerous awards, including the Tony Award for Best Play and the Pulitzer Prize for Drama; not surprisingly, its sequel, *Perestroika,* was similarly acclaimed. Critics compared the play to such landmark works as TENNESSEE WILLIAMS'S *A STREETCAR NAMED DESIRE* (1947) and ARTHUR MILLER'S *DEATH OF A SALESMAN* (1949). In the ensuing years, additional North American and European productions of *Angels in America* have established Kushner's reputation as the preeminent American dramatist of his generation.

The success of *Angels* also made Kushner one of the most widely known gay artists and activists of the 1990s and early 2000s.

Born in 1956 in New York City to parents who were classical musicians and raised in Lake Charles, Louisiana, Kushner became aware of his homosexuality by the age of ten. Because of the social stigma attached to being gay, he felt unable to acknowledge his sexual orientation openly, even to his politically liberal parents. Like Joe in *Angels,* Kushner came out to his mother in a telephone call—made from a pay phone on the morning of his first graduate class at New York University (where he completed a master of fine arts in directing in 1984). Kushner's mentor at NYU was Carl Weber, a highly reputed scholar, director, and former assistant of BERTOLT BRECHT's at the Berliner Ensemble. After graduation Kushner worked as a director at the Repertory Theatre of St. Louis and the New York Theatre Workshop. His first major play, *A Bright Room Called Day,* premiered in San Francisco in 1987 and was produced by the New York Shakespeare Festival in 1991. In 1990 Kushner received a commission to develop *Angels in America* for the Eureka Theatre in San Francisco, where *Millennium Approaches* premiered in 1991. The play subsequently moved to the Mark Taper Forum in Los Angeles, where it was performed with *Perestroika* in 1992. Both plays were produced in London at the National Theater in 1992; in New York, *Millennium Approaches* opened in 1993 and *Perestroika* in 1994. In the years following the success of *Angels in America* Kushner wrote a number of adaptations and plays, including *Slavs! Thinking about the Longstanding Problems of Virtue and Happiness* (1994), which features scenes that the playwright had originally intended for *Angels; Henry Box Brown, or The Mirror of Slavery* (1998), the story of an American slave who mailed himself to freedom in 1848; and the musical *Caroline, or Change* (2002). Kushner's 2001 play *Homebody/Kabul* is set in Afghanistan in 1998, during the rule of the oppressive Taliban government. *Angels in America* was made into a highly acclaimed film for television in 2003. His translation of Bertolt Brecht's *Mother Courage and Her Children* premiered in 2006, and his play *The Intelligent Homosexual's Guide to Capitalism and Socialism with a Key to the Scriptures* opened at the Guthrie Theater in Minneapolis in 2009. Among his work for cinema, Kushner wrote the screenplay for Steven Spielberg's film *Lincoln* (2012).

Labeled by Kushner "a gay fantasia on national themes," *Angels* joined a number of other plays that deal with the experience of gay men in contemporary America. Although issues of homosexuality pervade the drama of Williams and EDWARD ALBEE, the emergence of openly gay drama can be dated to 1968 and the off-Broadway production of Mart Crowley's *The Boys in the Band*. Crowley's play gave the mainstream theater its first view inside "the closet" of gay life: in this case, a Manhattan birthday party at which a group of gay men descend into alcohol-fueled self-loathing. The writing and production of gay plays accelerated in the wake of two events: the Stonewall Riots of June 1969 and the onset of the AIDS crisis in the early 1980s. In the 1960s the police in New York often raided bars frequented by homosexuals—who were arrested for being "disorderly"—but late on June 26, 1969, gay and lesbian patrons of Greenwich Village's Stonewall Inn resisted arrest, spawning a riot; violent protests followed for several more nights. This uprising was instrumental in sparking a new phase of the gay rights movement; its emergence was accompanied by plays that depicted the personal and sexual struggles of gay male characters. Key works of the time include Martin Sherman's *Passing By* (1974) and *Bent* (1979), Lanford Wilson's *Fifth of July* (1978), Robert Patrick's *T-Shirts* (1978), and Harvey Fierstein's *Torch Song Trilogy* (1981).

In the 1980s "AIDS plays" expanded on the conventions of earlier gay drama to explore the impact on individuals, relationships, and families of a new and devastating epidemic. Works such as Larry Kramer's *The Normal Heart* (1985) and William Hoffman's *As Is* (1985) were aggressive in expressing their anger at the relative lack of concern displayed by the Reagan administration and by Americans generally. Even more forcefully than the plays of the 1970s, AIDS plays challenged heterosexual audiences to empathize with gay characters as individuals entitled to equal rights and opportunities within society.

Despite their dramatic power, none of these plays received the attention won by *Angels in America*. The particular acclaim that greeted Kushner's play resulted, in part, from the way in which its characters, themes, and issues address the question of American national identity. This focus on Americanness invites comparison between *Angels* and Miller's *Death of a Salesman*. Produced just four years after the end of World War II, *Salesman* exposed the false myths of the "American Dream" and the vulnerability of the self-made man whose success in business and access to the good life rest on his personal charm. Produced near the end of the twentieth century, *Angels in America* likewise reveals a fundamental social betrayal—in this case, of America's founding ideals of freedom and equality. Miller's play is grounded in the history of European immigration to the United States and in the Great Depression; Kushner's is tied to the legacy of the civil rights movement in the 1960s, the rise of the gay rights movement, and the conservative backlash against both in the 1980s and early 1990s.

Yet whereas *Salesman* critiques American society through the lens of liberal humanism, *Angels* explores how those in power legislate and enforce normative assumptions about sex and sexuality, gender, race, and class. In its affirmation of social pluralism, the play embraces a decidedly postmodern understanding of identity and history. Narratives, myths,

and themes that have traditionally constituted "America"—the Founding Fathers,
manifest destiny, "the melting pot," the
American family—no longer fit the changing demographics and experiences of contemporary life as Kushner dramatizes
them. In one of the opening scenes of *Millennium Approaches,* Harper Pitt—one
of the play's visionaries—speaks of "beautiful systems dying, old fixed orders spiraling apart." Characters in *Angels in
America* must rethink their identities and
that of their nation within new relationships and psychological frameworks, rein-
terpreting the myths of America in light
of more pluralistic social realities. On the
eve of the third millennium, Kushner
suggests, the question of what it means to
be an American must be answered in
ways that are at once collective and deeply
individual.

The political and social breadth of
Angels in America is matched by its stylistic
expansiveness. Whereas *Death of a Salesman* helped define the tradition of American poetic realism, innovatively combining
naturalistic and expressionistic elements,
Angels employs an extraordinary collage of
theatrical styles—from realism to surrealism, tragedy to farce, Brechtian political
theater to the gay performance traditions
of camp and drag. Ranging from the
broadly political to the intensely personal
and spiritual, the play balances intimately
crafted scenes with an overarching epic
structure, blending psychological realism
together with nonrealistic dream scenes
and heightened theatrical spectacle. While
interweaving these styles and structures,
the play also intercuts story lines cinemati-
cally, thereby encouraging the audience to
see the life of each character in relation to
society and to understand that such supposedly "personal" matters as sex and love
are inherently political. Coining the label
"Theatre of the Fabulous" for this stylistic
collage, Kushner has stressed the theatrical nature of the play's scenes and effects.
In his "playwright's notes," he comments,
"The moments of magic . . . are to be fully
realized, as bits of wonderful *theatrical*
illusion—which means it's OK if the wires
show, and maybe it's good that they do, but
the magic should at the same time be thoroughly amazing."

Even as *Angels in America* has one foot
in the miraculous, its other is firmly
planted in the actual. Kushner's play is set
in the mid-1980s during the Reagan presidency, and its cast includes characters
drawn from modern American history.
Most important among these is Roy Cohn,
who served as chief counsel to Senator
Joseph McCarthy during the Senate's anticommunist investigations of the 1950s and
who, earlier, as an assistant U.S. attorney
in New York, played a key role in the most
sensational and controversial case of the
decade's Red Scare: the prosecution of
Julius and Ethel Rosenberg, a Jewish couple accused of helping to pass secrets of
American nuclear research to the Soviet
Union. They were convicted in 1951 and
executed in 1953. Though Cohn's investi-
gative methods were ultimately exposed
as unethical, and perhaps illegal, he went
on to become a powerful attorney in Washington, D.C., and New York, giving behind-
the-scenes advice to FBI Chief J. Edgar
Hoover as well as to judges, mayors, and
presidents. Throughout his career he repudiated his familial and cultural roots, striving to become the reverse of what he was:
the son of a Jewish, liberal, Democratic
New York state supreme court judge. Cohn
died from AIDS in 1986 but sought, to the
very end, to hide his homosexuality, insisting that his ailment was "liver cancer."

Kushner juxtaposes Cohn's life with the
lives of two fictional couples, one homosexual and the other heterosexual, who
represent ordinary, young middle-class
Americans living in New York in the mid-
1980s. The homosexual couple are Louis,
who works as a word processor in an office
located in Roy's building, and Prior, a drag
queen who has recently learned he is HIV-
positive. When Prior develops full-blown
AIDS, Louis's commitment to him and to
their relationship shrinks as he confronts
his fears of death and emotional pain. The
heterosexual couple are Joe and Harper,
Mormons who have moved from Utah to
New York City to further Joe's legal career;
Joe has become Roy's protégé, the object
of his professional mentoring and almost
paternal love. Joe and Harper's marriage
is brought to a crisis by Roy's offer to place
Joe in a job in Washington, D.C.—a position that will enable him to block Roy's

threatened disbarment—and by Joe's homosexuality, with which he has struggled all his life and which he must eventually acknowledge to himself and his wife. As the play unfolds, shifting focus from one story to another, the choices and actions of these characters shed light on each other. The audience sees Prior's experience of AIDS against Roy's denial of the disease, Joe's personal and professional integrity against Roy's dishonesty, Louis's abandonment of his partner against Joe's rejection of Harper, and Joe's emerging awareness of

his homosexuality against Roy's repression of his own. By thus placing characters side by side, Kushner reveals their social interconnectedness and makes them symbolic of contradictions at the heart of the United States as a nation.

Joe's and Harper's Mormonism serves as one of a number of intellectual and spiritual backdrops to *Angels in America*. The one Christian religion indigenous to the United States, the Church of Jesus Christ of Latter-day Saints was founded in response to what its adherents view as a

The 2003 miniseries of *Angels in America*, produced by HBO and directed by Mike Nichols, managed to translate the play's theatricality onto the small screen.

revelation that revised established Christian belief; it developed fully only after its first members journeyed to the edges of the frontier in search of the Promised Land. The metaphor of building on a past, of migrating, of crossing personal and ideological boundaries on the way to some anticipated rebirth or revelation recurs throughout *Angels:* in the opening monologue on Jewish emigration to the United States, in Joe's awakening to his sexuality, in Louis's movement away from Prior and toward Joe, and in Harper's and Prior's visions. Indeed, Kushner makes the stage itself a frontier, filling it with diverse styles that he synthesizes into a vision of social theater. As it moves between realism and nonrealism, between epic theater and spectacle, the play explores the limits of theatrical representation; at the outer reaches of those limits are the play's split scenes and dream scenes, which address social and spiritual dissolution and redemption.

Written as the cold war ended and in the waning years of the twentieth century, *Millennium Approaches* is charged with millenarian apprehension toward an unknown future. Apocalyptic foreboding occurs throughout the play, from Harper's fears about the vanishing ozone layer to terror at the pestilential specter of AIDS. *Perestroika,* the concluding part of *Angels in America,* lightens this tone somewhat, as it affirms life, community, and the possibility of personal, social, and spiritual progress. Like Kushner himself, who found himself anointed as a theatrical prophet while he moved steadily on with his writing and his activism, the play's characters seek ways to confront the world's problems while cultivating a vision of humanity's underlying grace. But though the two-part drama moves in the direction of healing, the most memorable moment in Kushner's theatrical epic is the spectacular conclusion of *Millennium Approaches.* Terrifying, beautiful, yet ambiguous, this final scene reflects the longings and fears, the restless spirituality, and the sense of the unknown that mark the turn of the millennium. To learn more about the staging of *Angels in America* and to view photographs from select performances of the play, see the "Plays in Performance" color insert near the center of this volume.

ART BORRECA

Angels in America
A Gay Fantasia on National Themes

PART ONE:

MILLENNIUM APPROACHES

CHARACTERS

ROY M. COHN,[1] a successful New York lawyer and unofficial power broker.
JOSEPH PORTER PITT, chief clerk for Justice Theodore Wilson of the Federal Court of Appeals, Second Circuit.
HARPER AMATY PITT, Joe's wife, an agoraphobic with a mild Valium[2] addiction.

1. A Jewish, New York–born lawyer (1927–1986) who attracted public attention and controversy throughout his career, most notoriously as chief counsel (1953–54) to the Permanent Subcommittee on Investigations, which, under the chairmanship of Senator Joseph McCarthy, hunted for Communists in the government and U.S. Army.
2. Diazepam (trademark), a tranquilizer that in the 1980s was the most frequently prescribed drug in the United States.

LOUIS IRONSON, a word processor working for the Second Circuit Court of Appeals.

PRIOR WALTER, Louis's boyfriend. Occasionally works as a club designer or caterer, otherwise lives very modestly but with great style off a small trust fund.

HANNAH PORTER PITT, Joe's mother, currently residing in Salt Lake City, living off her deceased husband's army pension.

BELIZE, a former drag queen and former lover of Prior's. A registered nurse. Belize's name was originally Norman Arriaga; Belize is a drag name that stuck.

THE ANGEL, four divine emanations, Fluor, Phosphor, Lumen, and Candle;[3] manifest in One: the Continental Principality of America. She has magnificent steel-gray wings.

Other Characters in Part One

RABBI ISIDOR CHEMELWITZ, an orthodox Jewish rabbi, played by the actor playing HANNAH.

MR. LIES, Harper's imaginary friend, a travel agent, who in style of dress and speech suggests a jazz musician; he always wears a large lapel badge emblazoned "IOTA" (The International Order of Travel Agents). He is played by the actor playing BELIZE.

THE MAN IN THE PARK, played by the actor playing PRIOR.

THE VOICE, the voice of THE ANGEL.

HENRY, ROY's doctor, played by the actor playing HANNAH.

EMILY, a nurse, played by the actor playing THE ANGEL.

MARTIN HELLER, a Reagan Administration Justice Department flackman, played by the actor playing HARPER.

SISTER ELLA CHAPTER, a Salt Lake City real estate saleswoman, played by the actor playing THE ANGEL.

PRIOR 1, the ghost of a dead Prior Walter from the 13th century, played by the actor playing JOE. He is a blunt, gloomy medieval farmer with a guttural Yorkshire accent.

PRIOR 2, the ghost of a dead Prior Walter from the 17th century, played by the actor playing ROY. He is a Londoner, sophisticated, with a High British accent.

THE ESKIMO, played by the actor playing JOE.

THE WOMAN IN THE SOUTH BRONX, played by the actor playing THE ANGEL.

ETHEL ROSENBERG,[4] played by the actor playing HANNAH.

Playwright's Notes

A DISCLAIMER: Roy M. Cohn, the character, is based on the late Roy M. Cohn (1927–1986), who was all too real; for the most part the acts attributed to the character Roy, such as his illegal conferences with Judge Kaufman during the trial of Ethel Rosenberg, are to be found in the historical record. But this Roy is a work of dramatic fiction; his words are my invention, and liberties have been taken.

3. All terms having to do with light: *fluor,* or fluorite, is a mineral whose crystals can exhibit luminescence; *phosphor,* or phosphorus, also emits light; and *lumen* (literally, "light" in Latin) and *candle* are both measures of light (of its intensity and flux, respectively).

4. A Jewish, New York–born Communist (1915–1953); along with her husband, Julius, she was tried and executed for conspiring to give the Soviet Union information about the atomic bomb. As an assistant in the U.S. Attorney's office in New York, Roy Cohn played a prominent role in her 1951 trial.

A NOTE ABOUT THE STAGING: The play benefits from a pared-down style of presentation, with minimal scenery and scene shifts done rapidly (no blackouts!), employing the cast as well as stagehands—which makes for an actor-driven event, as this must be. The moments of magic—the appearance and disappearance of Mr. Lies and the ghosts, the Book hallucination, and the ending—are to be fully realized, as bits of wonderful *theatrical illusion*—which means it's OK if the wires show, and maybe it's good that they do, but the magic should at the same time be thoroughly amazing.

> In a murderous time
> the heart breaks and breaks
> and lives by breaking.
> —Stanley Kunitz[5]
> "The Testing-Tree"

Act 1: Bad News

[*October–November 1985*]

Scene 1

[*The last days of October.* RABBI ISIDOR CHEMELWITZ *alone onstage with a small coffin. It is a rough pine box with two wooden pegs, one at the foot and one at the head, holding the lid in place. A prayer shawl embroidered with a Star of David is draped over the lid, and by the head a yarzheit[6] candle is burning.*]

RABBI ISIDOR CHEMELWITZ [*he speaks sonorously, with a heavy Eastern European accent, unapologetically consulting a sheet of notes for the family names*] Hello and good morning. I am Rabbi Isidor Chemelwitz of the Bronx Home for Aged Hebrews. We are here this morning to pay respects at the passing of Sarah Ironson, devoted wife of Benjamin Ironson, also deceased, loving and caring mother of her sons Morris, Abraham, and Samuel, and her daughters Esther and Rachel; beloved grandmother of Max, Mark, Louis, Lisa, Maria . . . uh . . . Lesley, Angela, Doris, Luke, and Eric. [*Looks more closely at paper.*] Eric? This is a Jewish name? [*Shrugs.*] Eric. A large and loving family. We assemble that we may mourn collectively this good and righteous woman. [*He looks at the coffin.*]

This woman. I did not know this woman. I cannot accurately describe her attributes, nor do justice to her dimensions. She was . . . Well, in the Bronx Home of Aged Hebrews are many like this, the old, and to many I speak but not to be frank with this one. She preferred silence. So I do not know her and yet I know her. She was . . . [*He touches the coffin.*] . . . not a person but a whole kind of person, the ones who crossed the ocean, who brought with us to America the villages of Russia and Lithuania—and how we struggled, and how we fought, for the family, for the Jewish home, so that you would not grow up *here,* in this strange place, in the melting pot where nothing melted. Descendants of this immigrant woman, you do not

5. An American poet (1905–2006); "The Testing-Tree" is the title poem of a collection published in 1971.
6. Anniversary (Yiddish); on the anniversary

of a relative's death, observant Jews light a memorial candle at home and in their synagogue.

20 grow up in America, you and your children and their children with the goyische[7] names. You do not live in America. No such place exists. Your clay is the clay of some Litvak shtetl,[8] your air the air of the steppes— because she carried the old world on her back across the ocean, in a boat, and she put it down on Grand Concourse Avenue, or in Flatbush,[9] and she

25 worked that earth into your bones, and you pass it to your children, this ancient, ancient culture and home. [*Little pause*]

You can never make that crossing that she made, for such Great Voyages in this world do not any more exist. But every day of your lives the miles that voyage between that place and this one you cross. Every day. You

30 understand me? In you that journey is.

So . . .

She was the last of the Mohicans,[1] this one was. Pretty soon . . . all the old will be dead.

Scene 2

[*Same day.* ROY *and* JOE *in* ROY's *office.* ROY *at an impressive desk, bare except for a very elaborate phone system, rows and rows of flashing buttons which bleep and beep and whistle incessantly, making chaotic music underneath* ROY's *conversations.* JOE *is sitting, waiting.* ROY *conducts business with great energy, impatience, and sensual abandon: gesticulating, shouting, cajoling, crooning, playing the phone, receiver and hold button, with virtuosity and love.*]

ROY [*hitting a button*]   Hold. [*To* JOE] I wish I was an octopus, a fucking octopus. Eight loving arms and all those suckers. Know what I mean?

JOE   No, I . . .

ROY [*gesturing to a deli platter of little sandwiches on his desk*]   You want lunch?

5 JOE   No, that's OK really I just . . .

ROY [*hitting a button*]   Ailene? Roy Cohn. Now what kind of a greeting is. . . . I thought we were friends, Ai . . . Look Mrs. Soffer you don't have to get . . . You're upset. You're yelling. You'll aggravate your condition, you shouldn't yell, you'll pop little blood vessels in your face if you yell. . . . No

10 that was a joke, Mrs. Soffer, I was joking. . . . I already apologized sixteen times for that, Mrs. Soffer, you . . . [*While she's fulminating,* ROY *covers the mouthpiece with his hand and talks to* JOE.] This'll take a minute, *eat* already, what is this tasty sandwich here it's— [*He takes a bite of a sandwich.*] Mmmmm, liver or some . . . Here.

[*He pitches the sandwich to* JOE, *who catches it and returns it to the platter.*]

15 ROY [*back to Mrs. Soffer*]   Uh huh, uh huh. . . . No, I already told you, it wasn't a vacation, it was business, Mrs. Soffer, I have clients in Haiti, Mrs. Soffer, I . . . Listen, Ailene, YOU THINK I'M THE ONLY GODDAM LAWYER IN HISTORY EVER MISSED A COURT DATE? Don't make such a big fucking . . . Hold. [*He hits the hold button.*] You HAG!

7. Non-Jewish, Gentile (Yiddish; sometimes pejorative).
8. Lithuanian village (Yiddish).
9. Two middle-class areas of New York City to which Jews moved in large numbers in the

1920s and 1930s (in the Bronx and in Brooklyn, respectively).
1. That is, the last of her kind—an allusion to James Fenimore Cooper's novel *The Last of the Mohicans* (1826).

20 JOE   If this is a bad time . . .

ROY   *Bad* time? This is a *good* time! [*Button*] Baby doll, get me . . . Oh fuck,
wait . . . [*Button, button*] Hello? Yah. Sorry to keep you holding, Judge
Hollins, I . . . Oh *Mrs.* Hollins, sorry dear deep voice you got. Enjoying
your visit? [*Hand over mouthpiece again, to* JOE] She sounds like a truck-
25   driver and he sounds like Kate Smith,[2] very confusing. Nixon[3] appointed
him, all the geeks are Nixon appointees . . . [*To Mrs. Hollins*] Yeah yeah
right good so how many tickets dear? Seven. For what, *Cats, 42nd Street,*
what? No you wouldn't like *La Cage,*[4] trust me, I know. Oh for godsake . . .
Hold. [*Button, button*] Baby doll, seven for *Cats* or something, anything
30   hard to get, I don't give a fuck what and neither will they. [*Button; to* JOE]
You see *La Cage?*

JOE   No, I . . .

ROY   Fabulous. Best thing on Broadway. Maybe ever. [*Button*] Who? Aw,
Jesus H. Christ, Harry, *no*, Harry, Judge John Francis Grimes, Manhattan
35   Family Court. Do I have to do every goddam thing myself? *Touch* the bastard, Harry, and don't call me on this line again, I told you not to . . .

JOE [*starting to get up*]   Roy, uh, should I wait outside or . . .

ROY [*to* JOE]   Oh sit. [*To Harry*] You hold. I pay you to hold fuck you Harry
you jerk. [*Button*] Half-wit dick-brain. [*Instantly philosophical*] I see the
40   universe, Joe, as a kind of sandstorm in outer space with winds of mega-
hurricane velocity, but instead of grains of sand it's shards and splinters of
glass. You ever feel that way? Ever have one of those days?

JOE   I'm not sure I . . .

ROY   So how's life in Appeals?[5] How's the Judge?

45 JOE   He sends his best.

ROY   He's a good man. Loyal. Not the brightest man on the bench, but he
has manners. And a nice head of silver hair.

JOE   He gives me a lot of responsibility.

ROY   Yeah, like writing his decisions and signing his name.

50 JOE   Well . . .

ROY   He's a nice guy. And you cover admirably.

JOE   Well, thanks, Roy, I . . .

ROY [*button*]   Yah? Who is *this?* Well who the fuck are *you?* Hold— [*Button*]
Harry? Eighty-seven grand, something like that. Fuck him. Eat me. New
55   Jersey, chain of porno film stores in, uh, Weehawken.[6] That's—Harry, that's
the beauty of the law. [*Button*] So, baby doll, what? *Cats?* Bleah. [*Button*]

2. A popular American singer (1907–1986),
best known for her rendition of Irving Berlin's "God Bless America" (1918); her career
peaked in the 1940s, but her robust voice
made her a star of radio and television from
the 1930s to the 1960s.

3. Richard M. Nixon (1913–1994), thirty-
seventh president of the United States (1969–
74); Nixon rose to national prominence in the
1940s as an ardently anticommunist Republican congressman on the House Committee
on Un-American Activities.

4. Long-running musicals on Broadway in the
1980s: *Cats* (1982–2000; lyrics by T. S. Eliot

and Trevor Nunn, music by Andrew Lloyd
Webber); *42nd Street* (1980–89; book by
Mark Bramble and Michael Stewart, lyrics by
Al Dubin, music by Harry Warren); and *La
Cage aux Folles* (1983–87; book by Harvey
Fierstein, lyrics and music by Jerry Herman),
which presents the interactions between a
gay couple (the manager and the star of a
drag nightclub), the manager's son, and the
conservative parents of the son's fiancée.

5. The U.S. Court of Appeals, where Joe is a
lawyer holding a senior administrative position.

6. A town directly across the Hudson River
from New York City.

Cats! It's about cats. Singing cats, you'll love it. Eight o'clock, the theatre's always at eight. [*Button*] Fucking tourists. [*Button, then to* JOE] Oh live a little, Joe, *eat* something for Christ sake—

60 JOE   Um, Roy, could you . . .

ROY   What? [*To Harry*] Hold a minute. [*Button*] Mrs. Soffer? Mrs. . . . [*Button*] God-fucking-dammit to hell, where is . . .

JOE [*overlapping*]   Roy, I'd really appreciate it if . . .

ROY [*overlapping*]   Well she was here a minute ago, baby doll, see if . . .

[*The phone starts making three different beeping sounds, all at once.*]

65 ROY [*smashing buttons*]   Jesus fuck this goddam thing . . .

JOE [*overlapping*]   I really wish you wouldn't . . .

ROY [*overlapping*]   Baby doll? Ring the *Post*[7] get me Suzy see if . . .

[*The phone starts whistling loudly.*]

ROY   CHRIST!

JOE   *Roy.*

70 ROY [*into receiver*]   Hold. [*Button; to* JOE] *What?*

JOE   Could you please not take the Lord's name in vain? [*Pause*] I'm sorry. But please. At least while I'm . . .

ROY [*laughs, then*]   Right. Sorry. Fuck.

Only in America. [*Punches a button.*] Baby doll, tell 'em all to fuck off.

75 Tell 'em I died. You handle Mrs. Soffer. Tell her it's on the way. Tell her I'm schtupping[8] the judge. I'll call her back. I *will* call her. I *know* how much I borrowed. She's got four hundred times that stuffed up her . . . Yeah, tell her I said that. [*Button. The phone is silent.*]

So, Joe.

80 JOE   I'm sorry Roy, I just . . .

ROY   No no no no, principles count, I respect principles, I'm not religious but I like God and God likes me. Baptist, Catholic?

JOE   Mormon.

ROY   Mormon. Delectable. Absolutely. Only in America. So, Joe. Whattya

85 think?

JOE   It's . . . well . . .

ROY   Crazy life.

JOE   Chaotic.

ROY   Well but God bless chaos. Right?

90 JOE   Ummm . . .

ROY   Huh. Mormons. I knew Mormons, in, um, Nevada.

JOE   Utah, mostly.

ROY   No, these Mormons were in Vegas.

So. So, how'd you like to go to Washington and work for the Justice

95 Department?

JOE   Sorry?

ROY   How'd you like to go to Washington and work for the Justice Department? All I gotta do is pick up the phone, talk to Ed, and you're in.

JOE   In . . . what, exactly?

---

7. The *New York Post,* which by the 1980s had become a conservative tabloid.

8. Aggressively pushing, ingratiating himself with; fucking (from Yiddish).

100 ROY Associate Assistant Something Big. Internal Affairs, heart of the woods, something nice with clout.

JOE Ed . . . ?

ROY Meese.[9] The Attorney General.

JOE Oh.

105 ROY I just have to pick up the phone . . .

JOE I have to think.

ROY Of course. [*Pause*]
It's a great time to be in Washington, Joe.

JOE Roy, it's incredibly exciting . . .

110 ROY And it would mean something to me. You understand?

[*Little pause.*]

JOE I . . . can't say how much I appreciate this Roy, I'm sort of . . . well, stunned, I mean . . . Thanks, Roy. But I have to give it some thought. I have to ask my wife.

ROY Your wife. Of course.

115 JOE But I really appreciate . . .

ROY Of course. Talk to your wife.

Scene 3

[*Later that day.* HARPER *at home, alone. She is listening to the radio and talking to herself, as she often does. She speaks to the audience.*]

HARPER People who are lonely, people left alone, sit talking nonsense to the air, imagining . . . beautiful systems dying, old fixed orders spiraling apart . . .

When you look at the ozone layer, from outside, from a spaceship, it looks like a pale blue halo, a gentle, shimmering aureole encircling the atmosphere encircling the earth. Thirty miles above our heads, a thin layer of three-atom oxygen molecules, product of photosynthesis, which explains the fussy vegetable preference for visible light, its rejection of darker rays and emanations. Danger from without. It's a kind of gift, from God, the crowning touch to the creation of the world: guardian angels, hands linked, make a spherical net, a blue-green nesting orb, a shell of safety for life itself. But everywhere, things are collapsing, lies surfacing, systems of defense giving way.[1] . . . This is why, Joe, this is why I shouldn't be left alone. [*Little pause*]

I'd like to go traveling. Leave you behind to worry. I'll send postcards with strange stamps and tantalizing messages on the back. "Later maybe." "Nevermore . . ."

[MR. LIES, *a travel agent, appears.*]

HARPER Oh! You startled me!

MR. LIES Cash, check, or credit card?

HARPER I remember you. You're from Salt Lake. You sold us the plane tickets when we flew here. What are you doing in Brooklyn?

9. Edwin Meese III (b. 1931), who served as attorney general (1985–88) under President Ronald Reagan (1911–2004; 40th president, 1981–89).

1. Beginning in the 1970s, scientists began to warn that industrial pollutants such as chlorofluorocarbons (CFCs) might concentrate in the stratosphere and deplete the ozone there, which affords protection against harmful high-energy radiation. The first "ozone hole"—a seasonal depletion—was discovered above Antarctica in 1985, and subsequent research confirmed the widespread loss of ozone.

20 MR. LIES   You said you wanted to travel . . .

HARPER   And here you are. How thoughtful.

MR. LIES   Mr. Lies. Of the International Order of Travel Agents. We mobilize the globe, we set people adrift, we stir the populace and send nomads eddying across the planet. We are adepts of motion, acolytes of the flux.
25   Cash, check, or credit card. Name your destination.

HARPER   Antarctica, maybe. I want to see the hole in the ozone. I heard on the radio . . .

MR. LIES   [*he has a computer terminal in his briefcase*]   I can arrange a guided tour. Now?

30 HARPER   Soon. Maybe soon. I'm not safe here you see. Things aren't right with me. Weird stuff happens . . .

MR. LIES   Like?

HARPER   Well, like you, for instance. Just appearing. Or last week . . . well never mind.
35   People are like planets, you need a thick skin. Things get to me, Joe stays away and now. . . . Well look. My dreams are talking back to me.

MR. LIES   It's the price of rootlessness. Motion sickness. The only cure: to keep moving.

HARPER   I'm undecided. I feel . . . that something's going to give. It's 1985.
40   Fifteen years till the third millennium. Maybe Christ will come again. Maybe seeds will be planted, maybe there'll be harvests then, maybe early figs to eat, maybe new life, maybe fresh blood, maybe companionship and love and protection, safety from what's outside, maybe the door will hold, or maybe . . . maybe the troubles[2] will come, and the end will come, and the
45   sky will collapse and there will be terrible rains and showers of poison light, or maybe my life is really fine, maybe Joe loves me and I'm only crazy thinking otherwise, or maybe not, maybe it's even worse than I know, maybe . . . I want to know, maybe I don't. The suspense, Mr. Lies, it's killing me.

MR. LIES   I suggest a vacation.

50 HARPER   [*hearing something*]   That was the elevator. Oh God, I should fix myself up, I . . . You have to go, you shouldn't be here . . . you aren't even real.

MR. LIES   Call me when you decide . . .

HARPER   Go!

[*The travel agent vanishes as* JOE *enters.*]

JOE   Buddy?
55   Buddy? Sorry I'm late. I was just . . . out. Walking. Are you mad?

HARPER   I got a little anxious.

JOE   Buddy kiss.

[*They kiss.*]

JOE   Nothing to get anxious about.
      So. So how'd you like to move to Washington?

---

2. That is, the apocalyptic "end times" foretold in the New Testament's book of Revelation.

Scene 4

[*Same day.* LOUIS *and* PRIOR *outside the funeral home, sitting on a bench, both dressed in funereal finery, talking. The funeral service for Sarah Ironson has just concluded and* LOUIS *is about to leave for the cemetery.*]

LOUIS My grandmother actually saw Emma Goldman[3] speak. In Yiddish. But all Grandma could remember was that she spoke well and wore a hat. What a weird service. That rabbi . . .

PRIOR A definite find. Get his number when you go to the graveyard. I want
5 him to bury me.

LOUIS Better head out there. Everyone gets to put dirt on the coffin once it's lowered in.

PRIOR Oooh. Cemetery fun. Don't want to miss that.

LOUIS It's an old Jewish custom to express love. Here, Grandma, have a
10 shovelful. Latecomers run the risk of finding the grave completely filled.
    She was pretty crazy. She was up there in that home for ten years, talking to herself. I never visited. She looked too much like my mother.

PRIOR [*hugs him*] Poor Louis. I'm sorry your grandma is dead.

LOUIS Tiny little coffin, huh?
15   Sorry I didn't introduce you to. . . . I always get so closety[4] at these family things.

PRIOR Butch.[5] You get butch. [*Imitating*] "Hi Cousin Doris, you don't remember me I'm Lou, Rachel's boy." Lou, not Louis, because if you say Louis they'll hear the sibilant S.

20 LOUIS I don't have a . . .

PRIOR I don't blame you, hiding. Bloodlines. Jewish curses are the worst. I personally would dissolve if anyone ever looked me in the eye and said "Feh."[6] Fortunately WASPs don't say "Feh." Oh and by the way, darling, cousin Doris is a dyke.

25 LOUIS No.
    Really?

PRIOR You don't notice anything. If I hadn't spent the last four years fellating you I'd swear you were straight.

LOUIS You're in a pissy mood. Cat still missing?
    [*Little pause.*]

30 PRIOR Not a furball in sight. It's your fault.

LOUIS It is?

PRIOR I warned you, Louis. Names are important. Call an animal "Little Sheba"[7] and you can't expect it to stick around. Besides, it's a dog's name.

LOUIS I wanted a dog in the first place, not a cat. He sprayed my books.

35 PRIOR He was a female cat.

---

3. A Lithuanian-born American anarchist and writer (1869–1940); she championed socialism and women's rights in the United States, Russia, and Britain. Though Goldman's primary languages were Russian and German, she gave speeches in Yiddish—the lingua franca of Jews from central and eastern Europe—to reach the largest audience possible.

4. That is, secretive about his homosexuality.
5. Assertively masculine.
6. A Yiddish interjection that expresses disgust or displeasure.
7. A reference to *Come Back, Little Sheba*, a 1952 film (dir. Daniel Mann) based on William Inge's 1950 play, which takes its title from the call for a lost dog.

LOUIS   Cats are stupid, high-strung predators. Babylonians sealed them up in bricks. Dogs have brains.

PRIOR   Cats have intuition.

LOUIS   A sharp dog is as smart as a really dull two-year-old child.

40 PRIOR   Cats know when something's wrong.

LOUIS   Only if you stop feeding them.

PRIOR   They know. That's why Sheba left, because she knew.

LOUIS   Knew what?

　　　　[*Pause.*]

PRIOR   I did my best Shirley Booth[8] this morning, floppy slippers, housecoat,
45　　curlers, can of Little Friskies; "Come back, Little Sheba, come back. . . ."
　　To no avail. Le chat, elle ne reviendra jamais, jamais[9] . . .

　　　　[*He removes his jacket, rolls up his sleeve, shows* LOUIS *a dark-purple spot
　　on the underside of his arm near the shoulder.*] See.

LOUIS   That's just a burst blood vessel.

PRIOR   Not according to the best medical authorities.

50 LOUIS   What? [*Pause*]
　　Tell me.

PRIOR   K.S.,[1] baby. Lesion number one. Lookit. The wine-dark kiss of the angel of death.

LOUIS   [*very softly, holding* PRIOR's *arm*]   Oh please . . .

55 PRIOR   I'm a lesionnaire. The Foreign Lesion. The American Lesion. Lesionnaire's disease.

LOUIS   Stop.

PRIOR   My troubles are lesion.

LOUIS   Will you *stop.*

60 PRIOR   Don't you think I'm handling this well?
　　I'm going to die.

LOUIS   Bullshit.

PRIOR   Let go of my arm.

LOUIS   No.

65 PRIOR   Let go.

LOUIS   [*grabbing* PRIOR, *embracing him ferociously*]   No.

PRIOR   I can't find a way to spare you baby. No wall like the wall of hard scientific fact. K.S. Wham. Bang your head on that.

LOUIS   Fuck you. [*Letting go*] Fuck you fuck you fuck you.

70 PRIOR   Now that's what I like to hear. A mature reaction.
　　Let's go see if the cat's come home.
　　Louis?

LOUIS   When did you find this?

PRIOR   I couldn't tell you.

75 LOUIS   Why?

PRIOR   I was scared, Lou.

LOUIS   Of what?

PRIOR   That you'll leave me.

LOUIS   Oh.

8. An American actor (1898–1992); she starred in the stage and film versions of *Come Back, Little Sheba.*

9. The cat, she will never, ever come back (French).

1. That is, Kaposi's sarcoma, a type of lesion associated with AIDS; it was one of the first recognized signs of HIV infection.

[Little pause.]

80 PRIOR   Bad timing, funeral and all, but I figured as long as we're on the subject of death . . .

LOUIS   I have to go bury my grandma.

PRIOR   Lou?

[Pause.]

Then you'll come home?

85 LOUIS   Then I'll come home.

Scene 5

[Same day, later on. Split scene: JOE *and* HARPER *at home;* LOUIS *at the cemetery with* RABBI ISIDOR CHEMELWITZ *and the little coffin.]*

HARPER   Washington?

JOE   It's an incredible honor, buddy, and . . .

HARPER   I have to think.

JOE   Of course.

5 HARPER   Say no.

JOE   You said you were going to think about it.

HARPER   I don't want to move to Washington.

JOE   Well I do.

HARPER   It's a giant cemetery, huge white graves and mausoleums everywhere.

10 JOE   We could live in Maryland. Or Georgetown.

HARPER   We're happy here.

JOE   That's not really true, buddy, we . . .

HARPER   Well happy enough! Pretend-happy. That's better than nothing.

JOE   It's time to make some changes, Harper.

15 HARPER   No changes. Why?

JOE   I've been chief clerk for four years. I make twenty-nine thousand dollars a year. That's ridiculous. I graduated fourth in my class and I make less than anyone I know. And I'm . . . I'm tired of being a clerk, I want to go where something good is happening.

20 HARPER   Nothing good happens in Washington. We'll forget church teachings and buy furniture at . . . at *Conran's* and become yuppies.[2] I have too much to do here.

JOE   Like what?

HARPER   I *do* have things . . .

25 JOE   What things?

HARPER   I have to finish painting the bedroom.

JOE   You've been painting in there for over a year.

HARPER   I know, I . . . It just isn't done because I never get time to finish it.

JOE   Oh that's . . . that doesn't make sense. You have all the time in the
30   world. You could finish it when I'm at work.

HARPER   I'm afraid to go in there alone.

JOE   Afraid of what?

HARPER   I heard someone in there. Metal scraping on the wall. A man with a knife, maybe.

---

2. A term that came into widespread use in the 1980s. *Conran's:* New York retailer of contemporary home furnishings marketed to young urban professionals.

35 JOE   There's no one in the bedroom, Harper.

HARPER   Not now.

JOE   Not this morning either.

HARPER   How do you know? You were at work this morning. There's something creepy about this place. Remember *Rosemary's Baby?*[3]

40 JOE   *Rosemary's Baby?*

HARPER   Our apartment looks like that one. Wasn't that apartment in
Brooklyn?

JOE   No, it was . . .

HARPER   Well, it looked like this. It did.

45 JOE   Then let's move.

HARPER   Georgetown's worse. *The Exorcist* was in Georgetown.[4]

JOE   The devil, everywhere you turn, huh, buddy.

HARPER   Yeah. Everywhere.

JOE   How many pills today, buddy?

50 HARPER   None. One. Three. Only three.

LOUIS   [*pointing at the coffin*]   Why are there just two little wooden pegs
holding the lid down?

RABBI ISIDOR CHEMELWITZ   So she can get out easier if she wants to.

LOUIS   I hope she stays put.

55   I pretended for years that she was already dead. When they called to say
she had died it was a surprise. I abandoned her.

RABBI ISIDOR CHEMELWITZ   "Sharfer vi di tson fun a shlang iz an umdankbar
kind!"

LOUIS   I don't speak Yiddish.

60 RABBI ISIDOR CHEMELWITZ   Sharper than the serpent's tooth is the ingrati-
tude of children. Shakespeare. *Kenig Lear.*[5]

LOUIS   Rabbi, what does the Holy Writ say about someone who abandons
someone he loves at a time of great need?

RABBI ISIDOR CHEMELWITZ   Why would a person do such a thing?

65 LOUIS   Because he has to.

Maybe because this person's sense of the world, that it will change for
the better with struggle, maybe a person who has this neo-Hegelian positivist sense of constant historical progress towards happiness or perfection or
something,[6] who feels very powerful because he feels connected to these

70   forces, moving uphill all the time . . . maybe that person can't, um, incorporate sickness into his sense of how things are supposed to go. Maybe

3. A horror film directed by Roman Polanski
(1968), based on a best-selling novel by Ira
Levin (1967), in which a young couple move
into a Manhattan apartment building inhabited by Satan worshippers.

4. An affluent neighborhood in Washington,
D.C., that was the setting of *The Exorcist*
(1973; dir. William Friedkin), a horror film
adapted from William Peter Blatty's best-
selling novel (1971) about a twelve-year-old
girl possessed by the devil.

5. That is, *King Lear* (Yiddish); the line
paraphrases Shakespeare's play (1605),
1.4.265–66.

6. The German philosopher Georg Wilhelm
Friedrich Hegel (1770–1831), who saw in
culture and civilization the logical development of consciousness, has traditionally been
viewed as an idealist (i.e., his theory is not
connected to external reality or the senses);
but his belief in the dialectical process—that
a thesis inevitably generates its antithesis,
and their interaction results in a new
synthesis—can lead to such positivist philosophies (i.e., systems of thought focused on
observable phenomena) as the dialectical
materialism connected with Marxism.

vomit . . . and sores and disease . . . really frighten him, maybe . . . he isn't so good with death.

RABBI ISIDOR CHEMELWITZ   The Holy Scriptures have nothing to say about such a person.

LOUIS   Rabbi, I'm afraid of the crimes I may commit.

RABBI ISIDOR CHEMELWITZ   Please, mister. I'm a sick old rabbi facing a long drive home to the Bronx. You want to confess, better you should find a priest.

LOUIS   But I'm not a Catholic, I'm a Jew.

RABBI ISIDOR CHEMELWITZ   Worse luck for you, bubbulah.[7] Catholics believe in forgiveness. Jews believe in Guilt. [*He pats the coffin tenderly.*]

LOUIS   You just make sure those pegs are in good and tight.

RABBI ISIDOR CHEMELWITZ   Don't worry, mister. The life she had, she'll stay put. She's better off.

JOE   Look, I know this is scary for you. But try to understand what it means to me. Will you try?

HARPER   Yes.

JOE   Good. Really try.

I think things are starting to change in the world.

HARPER   But I don't want . . .

JOE   Wait. For the good. Change for the good. America has rediscovered itself. Its sacred position among nations. And people aren't ashamed of that like they used to be. This is a great thing. The truth restored. Law restored. That's what President Reagan's done, Harper. He says "Truth exists and can be spoken proudly." And the country responds to him. We become better. More good. I need to be a part of that, I need something big to lift me up. I mean, six years ago the world seemed in decline, horrible, hopeless, full of unsolvable problems and crime and confusion and hunger and . . .

HARPER   But it still seems that way. More now than before. They say the ozone layer is . . .

JOE   Harper . . .

HARPER   And today out the window on Atlantic Avenue there was a schizophrenic traffic cop who was making these . . .

JOE   Stop it! I'm trying to make a point.

HARPER   So am I.

JOE   You aren't even making sense, you . . .

HARPER   My point is the world seems just as . . .

JOE   It only seems that way to you because you never go out in the world, Harper, and you have emotional problems.

HARPER   I do so get out in the world.

JOE   You don't. You stay in all day, fretting about imaginary . . .

HARPER   I get out. I do. You don't know what I do.

JOE   You don't stay in all day.

HARPER   No.

JOE   Well. . . . Yes you do.

HARPER   That's what you think.

JOE   Where do you go?

HARPER   Where do *you* go? When you walk.

---

7. Literally, "little grandmother" (Yiddish); a term of endearment, often applied to children.

120   [*Pause, then angrily*] And I DO NOT have emotional problems.

JOE   I'm sorry.

HARPER   And if I do have emotional problems it's from living with you. Or . . .

JOE   I'm sorry buddy, I didn't mean to . . .

125 HARPER   Or if you do think I do then you should never have married me. You have all these secrets and lies.

JOE   I want to be married to you, Harper.

HARPER   You shouldn't. You never should. [*Pause*]

Hey buddy. Hey buddy.

130 JOE   Buddy kiss . . .

      [*They kiss.*]

HARPER   I heard on the radio how to give a blowjob.

JOE   What?

HARPER   You want to try?

JOE   You really shouldn't listen to stuff like that.

135 HARPER   Mormons can give blowjobs.

JOE   *Harper.*

HARPER [*imitating his tone*]   *Joe.*

It was a little Jewish lady with a German accent.[8]

This is a good time. For me to make a baby.

      [*Little pause.* JOE *turns away.*]

140 HARPER   Then they went on to a program about holes in the ozone layer. Over Antarctica. Skin burns, birds go blind, icebergs melt. The world's coming to an end.

Scene 6

[*First week of November. In the men's room of the offices of the Brooklyn Federal Court of Appeals;* LOUIS *is crying over the sink;* JOE *enters.*]

JOE   Oh, um . . . Morning.

LOUIS   Good morning, counselor.

JOE [*he watches* LOUIS *cry*]   Sorry, I . . . I don't know your name.

LOUIS   Don't bother. Word processor. The lowest of the low.

5 JOE [*holding out hand*]   Joe Pitt. I'm with Justice Wilson . . .

LOUIS   Oh, I know that. Counselor Pitt. Chief Clerk.

JOE   Were you . . . are you OK?

LOUIS   Oh, yeah. Thanks. What a nice man.

JOE   Not so nice.

10 LOUIS   What?

JOE   Not so nice. Nothing. You sure you're . . .

LOUIS   Life sucks shit. Life . . . just sucks shit.

JOE   What's wrong?

LOUIS   Run in my nylons.

15 JOE   Sorry . . . ?

LOUIS   Forget it. Look, thanks for asking.

8. Ruth Westheimer (b. 1928), the German-born psychologist and sex therapist who, as "Dr. Ruth," began hosting the radio call-in program *Sexually Speaking* in New York in 1980; it became hugely successful and was soon followed by a cable television program, *The Dr. Ruth Show.*

JOE   Well . . .

LOUIS   I mean it really is nice of you. [*He starts crying again.*]
Sorry, sorry, sick friend . . .

20   JOE   Oh, I'm sorry.

LOUIS   Yeah, yeah, well, that's sweet.
Three of your colleagues have preceded you to this baleful sight and
you're the first one to ask. The others just opened the door, saw me, and
fled. I hope they had to pee real bad.

25   JOE   [*handing him a wad of toilet paper*]   They just didn't want to intrude.

LOUIS   Hah. Reaganite heartless macho asshole lawyers.[9]

JOE   Oh, that's unfair.

LOUIS   What is? Heartless? Macho? Reaganite? Lawyer?

JOE   I voted for Reagan.

30   LOUIS   You did?

JOE   Twice.

LOUIS   Twice? Well, oh boy. A Gay Republican.

JOE   Excuse me?

LOUIS   Nothing.

35   JOE   I'm not . . .
Forget it.

LOUIS   Republican? Not Republican? Or . . .

JOE   What?

LOUIS   What?

40   JOE   Not gay. I'm not gay.

LOUIS   Oh. Sorry.
[*Blows his nose loudly.*] It's just . . .

JOE   Yes?

LOUIS   Well, sometimes you can tell from the way a person sounds that . . . I
mean you *sound* like a . . .

45   JOE   No I don't. Like what?

LOUIS   Like a Republican.

[*Little pause.* JOE *knows he's being teased;* LOUIS *knows he knows.* JOE
decides to be a little brave.]

JOE   [*making sure no one else is around*]   Do I? Sound like a . . . ?

LOUIS   What? Like a . . . ? Republican, or . . . ? Do I?

JOE   Do you what?

50   LOUIS   Sound like a . . . ?

JOE   Like a . . . ?
I'm . . . confused.

LOUIS   Yes.
My name is Louis. But all my friends call me Louise. I work in Word

55   Processing. Thanks for the toilet paper.

[LOUIS *offers* JOE *his hand,* JOE *reaches,* LOUIS *feints and pecks* JOE *on the
cheek, then exits.*]

---

9. Court of appeals judges and district court
judges are presidential appointees who, after
confirmation, hold their positions for life, and
they generally hire subordinates who share
their legal philosophies. During his two terms
as president, Reagan appointed almost 400
federal judges.

Scene 7

[*A week later. Mutual dream scene.* PRIOR *is at a fantastic makeup table, having a dream, applying the face.* HARPER *is having a pill-induced hallucination. She has these from time to time. For some reason,* PRIOR *has appeared in this one. Or* HARPER *has appeared in* PRIOR's *dream. It is bewildering.*]

PRIOR [*alone, putting on makeup, then examining the results in the mirror; to the audience*] "I'm ready for my closeup, Mr. DeMille."[1]

One wants to move through life with elegance and grace, blossoming infrequently but with exquisite taste, and perfect timing, like a rare bloom, a zebra orchid. . . . One wants. . . . But one so seldom gets what one wants, does one? No. One does not. One gets fucked. Over. One . . . dies at thirty, robbed of . . . decades of majesty.

Fuck this shit. Fuck this shit.

[*He almost crumbles; he pulls himself together; he studies his handiwork in the mirror.*] I look like a corpse. A corpsette. Oh my queen; you know you've hit rock-bottom when even drag is a drag.

[HARPER *appears.*]

HARPER   Are you. . . . Who are you?

PRIOR   Who are you?

HARPER   What are you doing in my hallucination?

PRIOR   I'm not in your hallucination. You're in my dream.

HARPER   You're wearing makeup.

PRIOR   So are you.

HARPER   But you're a man.

PRIOR [*feigning dismay, shock, he mimes slashing his throat with his lipstick and dies, fabulously tragic. Then*]   The hands and feet give it away.

HARPER   There must be some mistake here. I don't recognize you. You're not. . . . Are you my . . . some sort of imaginary friend?

PRIOR   No. Aren't you too old to have imaginary friends?

HARPER   I have emotional problems. I took too many pills. Why are you wearing makeup?

PRIOR   I was in the process of applying the face, trying to make myself feel better—I swiped the new fall colors at the Clinique counter at Macy's.[2] [*Showing her*]

HARPER   You stole these?

PRIOR   I was out of cash; it was an emotional emergency!

HARPER   Joe will be so angry. I promised him. No more pills.

PRIOR   These pills you keep alluding to?

HARPER   Valium. I take Valium. Lots of Valium.

PRIOR   And you're dancing as fast as you can.[3]

HARPER   I'm not *addicted*. I don't believe in addiction, and I never . . . well, I *never* drink. And I *never* take drugs.

---

1. The final line of *Sunset Boulevard* (1950; dir. Billy Wilder), spoken by Gloria Swanson as the delusional former silent-movie star Norma Desmond, is "All right, Mr. DeMille, I'm ready for my closeup." The pioneering film director Cecil B. DeMille (1881–1959) plays himself in the film.

2. A chain of department stores; its flagship store is in New York City at Herald Square. *Clinique*: an upscale brand of cosmetics.

3. A play on *I'm Dancing as Fast as I Can* (1982; dir. Jack Hofsiss), a film adapted from Barbara Gordon's best-selling 1972 memoir about Valium addiction.

PRIOR   Well, smell *you*, Nancy Drew.[4]

HARPER   Except Valium.

35 PRIOR   Except Valium; in wee fistfuls.

HARPER   It's terrible. Mormons are not supposed to be addicted to anything. I'm a Mormon.

PRIOR   I'm a homosexual.

HARPER   Oh! In my church we don't believe in homosexuals.

40 PRIOR   In my church we don't believe in Mormons.

HARPER   What church do . . . oh! [*She laughs.*] I get it.

I don't understand this. If I didn't ever see you before and I don't think I did then I don't think you should be here, in this hallucination, because in my experience the mind, which is where hallucinations come from,
45 shouldn't be able to make up anything that wasn't there to start with, that didn't enter it from experience, from the real world. Imagination can't create anything new, can it? It only recycles bits and pieces from the world and reassembles them into visions. . . . Am I making sense right now?

PRIOR   Given the circumstances, yes.

50 HARPER   So when we think we've escaped the unbearable ordinariness and, well, untruthfulness of our lives, it's really only the same old ordinariness and falseness rearranged into the appearance of novelty and truth. Nothing unknown is knowable. Don't you think it's depressing?

PRIOR   The limitations of the imagination?

55 HARPER   Yes.

PRIOR   It's something you learn after your second theme party: It's All Been Done Before.

HARPER   The world. Finite. Terribly, terribly. . . . Well . . .
This is the most depressing hallucination I've ever had.

60 PRIOR   Apologies. I do try to be amusing.

HARPER   Oh, well, don't apologize, you . . . I can't expect someone who's really sick to entertain me.

PRIOR   How on earth did you know . . .

HARPER   Oh that happens. This is the very threshhold of revelation some-
65 times. You can see things . . . how sick you are. Do you see anything about me?

PRIOR   Yes.

HARPER   What?

PRIOR   You are amazingly unhappy.

70 HARPER   Oh big deal. You meet a Valium addict and you figure out she's unhappy. That doesn't count. Of course I . . . Something else. Something surprising.

PRIOR   Something surprising.

HARPER   Yes.

75 PRIOR   Your husband's a homo.

[*Pause.*]

HARPER   Oh, ridiculous.

[*Pause, then very quietly*] *Really?*

PRIOR [*shrugs*]   Threshhold of revelation.

---

4. A schoolyard taunt; Nancy Drew, a wholesome teenage detective, is the heroine of a popular series that the Stratemeyer syndicate began publishing in 1930.

HARPER   Well I don't like your revelations. I don't think you intuit well at all. Joe's a very normal man, he . . .

80   Oh God. Oh God. He . . . Do homos take, like, lots of long walks?

PRIOR   Yes. We do. In stretch pants with lavender coifs. I just looked at you, and there was . . .

HARPER   A sort of blue streak of recognition.

PRIOR   Yes.

85 HARPER   Like you knew me incredibly well.

PRIOR   Yes.

HARPER   Yes.

I have to go now, get back, something just . . . fell apart.

Oh God, I feel so sad . . .

90 PRIOR   I . . . I'm sorry. I usually say, "Fuck the truth," but mostly, the truth fucks you.

HARPER   I see something else about you . . .

PRIOR   Oh?

HARPER   Deep inside you, there's a part of you, the most inner part, entirely
95 free of disease. I can see that.

PRIOR   Is that . . . That isn't true.

HARPER   Threshhold of revelation.

Home . . .

[*She vanishes.*]

PRIOR   People come and go so quickly here . . .
100   [*To himself in the mirror*] I don't think there's any uninfected part of me. My heart is pumping polluted blood. I feel dirty.

[*He begins to wipe makeup off with his hands, smearing it around. A large gray feather falls from up above. PRIOR stops smearing the makeup and looks at the feather. He goes to it and picks it up.*]

A VOICE [*it is an incredibly beautiful voice*]   Look up!

PRIOR [*looking up, not seeing anyone*]   Hello?

A VOICE   Look up!

105 PRIOR   Who is that?

A VOICE   Prepare the way!

PRIOR   I don't see any . . .

[*There is a dramatic change in lighting, from above.*]

A VOICE

Look up, look up,
prepare the way
110   the infinite descent
A breath in air
floating down
Glory to . . .
[*Silence.*]

PRIOR   Hello? Is that it? Helloooo!
115   What the fuck . . . ? [*He holds himself.*]

Poor me. Poor poor me. Why me? Why poor poor me? Oh I don't feel good right now. I really don't.

Scene 8

[*That night. Split scene:* HARPER *and* JOE *at home;* PRIOR *and* LOUIS *in bed.*]

HARPER   Where were you?

JOE   Out.

HARPER   Where?

JOE   Just out. Thinking.

5 HARPER   It's late.

JOE   I had a lot to think about.

HARPER   I burned dinner.

JOE   Sorry.

HARPER   Not my dinner. My dinner was fine. Your dinner. I put it back in the
10   oven and turned everything up as high as it could go and I watched till it
    burned black. It's still hot. Very hot. Want it?

JOE   You didn't have to do that.

HARPER   I know. It just seemed like the kind of thing a mentally deranged
    sex-starved pill-popping housewife would do.

15 JOE   Uh huh.

HARPER   So I did it. Who knows any more what I have to do?

JOE   How many pills?

HARPER   A bunch. Don't change the subject.

JOE   I won't talk to you when you . . .

20 HARPER   No. No. Don't do that! I'm . . . I'm fine, pills are not the problem,
    not our problem, I WANT TO KNOW WHERE YOU'VE BEEN! I WANT
    TO KNOW WHAT'S GOING ON!

JOE   Going on with what? The job?

HARPER   Not the job.

25 JOE   I said I need more time.

HARPER   Not the job!

JOE   Mr. Cohn, I talked to him on the phone, he said I had to hurry . . .

HARPER   Not the . . .

JOE   But I can't get you to talk sensibly about anything so . . .

30 HARPER   SHUT UP!

JOE   Then what?

HARPER   Stick to the subject.

JOE   I don't know what that is. You have something you want to ask me? Ask
    me. Go.

35 HARPER   I . . . can't. I'm scared of you.

JOE   I'm tired, I'm going to bed.

HARPER   Tell me without making me ask. Please.

JOE   This is crazy, I'm not . . .

HARPER   When you come through the door at night your face is never exactly
40   the way I remembered it. I get surprised by something . . . mean and hard
    about the way you look. Even the weight of you in the bed at night, the way
    you breathe in your sleep seems unfamiliar.
        You terrify me.

JOE [*cold*]   I know who you are.

45 HARPER   Yes. I'm the enemy. That's easy. That doesn't change.
        You think you're the only one who hates sex; I do; I hate it with you; I do.
    I dream that you batter away at me till all my joints come apart, like wax,

and I fall into pieces. It's like a punishment. It was wrong of me to marry you. I knew you . . . [*She stops herself.*] It's a sin, and it's killing us both.

50 JOE I can always tell when you've taken pills because it makes you red-faced and sweaty and frankly that's very often why I don't want to . . .

HARPER Because . . .

JOE Well, you aren't pretty. Not like this.

HARPER I have something to ask you.

55 JOE Then ASK! ASK! What in hell are you . . .

HARPER Are you a homo? [*Pause*]

Are you? If you try to walk out right now I'll put your dinner back in the oven and turn it up so high the whole building will fill with smoke and everyone in it will asphyxiate. So help me God I will.

60 Now answer the question.

JOE What if I . . .

[*Small pause.*]

HARPER Then tell me, please. And we'll see.

JOE No. I'm not.

I don't see what difference it makes.

65 LOUIS Jews don't have any clear textual guide to the afterlife; even that it exists. I don't think much about it. I see it as a perpetual rainy Thursday afternoon in March. Dead leaves.

PRIOR Eeeugh. Very Greco-Roman.[5]

LOUIS Well, for us it's not the verdict that counts, it's the act of judgment.

70 That's why I could never be a lawyer. In court all that matters is the verdict.

PRIOR You could never be a lawyer because you are oversexed. You're too distracted.

LOUIS Not distracted; *ab*stracted. I'm trying to make a point:

PRIOR Namely:

75 LOUIS It's the judge in his or her chambers, weighing, books open, pondering the evidence, ranging freely over categories: good, evil, innocent, guilty; the judge in the chamber of circumspection, not the judge on the bench with the gavel. The shaping of the law, not its execution.

PRIOR The point, dear, the point . . .

80 LOUIS That it should be the questions and shape of a life, its total complexity gathered, arranged, and considered, which matters in the end, not some stamp of salvation or damnation which disperses all the complexity in some unsatisfying little decision—the balancing of the scales . . .

PRIOR I like this; very zen; it's . . . reassuringly incomprehensible and use-
85 less. We who are about to die thank you.[6]

LOUIS You are not about to die.

PRIOR It's not going well, really . . . two new lesions. My leg hurts. There's protein in my urine, the doctor says, but who knows what the fuck that portends. Anyway it shouldn't be there, the protein. My butt is chapped
90 from diarrhea and yesterday I shat blood.

LOUIS I really hate this. You don't tell me . . .

---

5. An adjective apparently intended to evoke stoicism and austerity.
6. An echo of "We who are about to die greet you," popularly believed to be the salute of Roman gladiators to the emperor. *Zen:* exhibiting the calm associated with this meditative Japanese school of Buddhism.

PRIOR   You get too upset, I wind up comforting you. It's easier . . .

LOUIS   Oh thanks.

PRIOR   If it's bad I'll tell you.

95 LOUIS   Shitting blood sounds bad to me.

PRIOR   And I'm telling you.

LOUIS   And I'm handling it.

PRIOR   Tell me some more about justice.

LOUIS   I *am* handling it.

100 PRIOR   Well Louis you win Trooper of the Month.

[LOUIS *starts to cry.*]

PRIOR   I take it back. You aren't Trooper of the Month.
This isn't working . . .
Tell me some more about justice.

LOUIS   You are not about to die.

105 PRIOR   Justice . . .

LOUIS   . . . is an immensity, a confusing vastness. Justice is God.
Prior?

PRIOR   Hmmm?

LOUIS   You love me.

110 PRIOR   Yes.

LOUIS   What if I walked out on this?
Would you hate me forever?

[PRIOR *kisses* LOUIS *on the forehead.*]

PRIOR   Yes.

JOE   I think we ought to pray. Ask God for help. Ask him together . . .

115 HARPER   God won't talk to me. I have to make up people to talk to me.

JOE   You have to keep asking.

HARPER   I forgot the question.
Oh yeah. God, is my husband a . . .

JOE [*scary*]   Stop it. Stop it. I'm warning you.

120   Does it make any difference? That I might be one thing deep within, no matter how wrong or ugly that thing is, so long as I have fought, with everything I have, to kill it. What do you want from me? What do you want from me, Harper? More than that? For God's sake, there's nothing left, I'm a shell. There's nothing left to kill.

125   As long as my behavior is what I know it has to be. Decent. Correct. That alone in the eyes of God.

HARPER   No, no, not that, that's Utah talk, Mormon talk, I hate it, Joe, tell me, say it . . .

JOE   All I will say is that I am a very good man who has worked very hard to

130   become good and you want to destroy that. You want to destroy me, but I am not going to let you do that.

[*Pause.*]

HARPER   I'm going to have a baby.

JOE   Liar.

HARPER   You liar.

135   A baby born addicted to pills. A baby who does not dream but who hallucinates, who stares up at us with big mirror eyes and who does not know who we are.

[*Pause.*]

JOE   Are you really . . .

HARPER   No. Yes. No. Yes. Get away from me.

140   Now we both have a secret.

PRIOR   One of my ancestors was a ship's captain who made money bringing whale oil to Europe and returning with immigrants—Irish mostly, packed in tight, so many dollars per head. The last ship he captained foundered off the coast of Nova Scotia in a winter tempest and sank to the bottom. He

145   went down with the ship—*la Grande Geste*[7]—but his crew took seventy women and kids in the ship's only longboat, this big, open rowboat, and when the weather got too rough, and they thought the boat was over-crowded, the crew started lifting people up and hurling them into the sea. Until they got the ballast right. They walked up and down the longboat,

150   eyes to the waterline, and when the boat rode low in the water they'd grab the nearest passenger and throw them into the sea. The boat was leaky, see; seventy people; they arrived in Halifax with nine people on board.

LOUIS   Jesus.

PRIOR   I think about that story a lot now. People in a boat, waiting, terrified,

155   while implacable, unsmiling men, irresistibly strong, seize . . . maybe the person next to you, maybe you, and with no warning at all, with time only for a quick intake of air you are pitched into freezing, turbulent water and salt and darkness to drown.

I like your cosmology, baby. While time is running out I find myself

160   drawn to anything that's suspended, that lacks an ending—but it seems to me that it lets you off scot-free.

LOUIS   What do you mean?

PRIOR   No judgment, no guilt or responsibility.

LOUIS   For me.

165   PRIOR   For anyone. It was an editorial "you."

LOUIS   Please get better. Please.

Please don't get any sicker.

Scene 9

[*Third week in November.* ROY *and* HENRY, *his doctor, in* HENRY's *office.*]

HENRY   Nobody knows what causes it. And nobody knows how to cure it. The best theory is that we blame a retrovirus, the Human Immunodeficiency Virus. Its presence is made known to us by the useless antibodies which appear in reaction to its entrance into the bloodstream through a cut, or an

5   orifice. The antibodies are powerless to protect the body against it. Why, we don't know. The body's immune system ceases to function. Sometimes the body even attacks itself. At any rate it's left open to a whole horror house of infections from microbes which it usually defends against.

Like Kaposi's sarcomas. These lesions. Or your throat problem. Or the

10   glands.

We think it may also be able to slip past the blood-brain barrier[8] into the brain. Which is of course very bad news.

---

7. The grand gesture (French); by tradition, the captain is the last to leave a sinking ship.
8. The physical structure and system of cel-lular transport mechanisms that prevent harmful chemicals in the bloodstream from reaching the brain.

And it's fatal in we don't know what percent of people with suppressed immune responses.

[*Pause.*]

15 ROY This is very interesting, Mr. Wizard,[9] but why the fuck are you telling me this?

[*Pause.*]

HENRY Well, I have just removed one of three lesions which biopsy results will probably tell us is a Kaposi's sarcoma lesion. And you have a pronounced swelling of glands in your neck, groin, and armpits—lymphadenopathy[1] is
20 another sign. And you have oral candidiasis[2] and maybe a little more fungus under the fingernails of two digits on your right hand. So that's why . . .

ROY This disease . . .

HENRY Syndrome.

ROY Whatever. It afflicts mostly homosexuals and drug addicts.

25 HENRY Mostly. Hemophiliacs are also at risk.

ROY Homosexuals and drug addicts. So why are you implying that I . . .
[*Pause*]
What are you implying, Henry?

HENRY I don't . . .

ROY I'm not a drug addict.

30 HENRY Oh come on Roy.

ROY What, what, come on Roy what? Do you think I'm a junkie, Henry, do you see tracks?

HENRY This is absurd.

ROY Say it.

35 HENRY Say what?

ROY Say, "Roy Cohn, you are a . . ."

HENRY Roy.

ROY "You are a . . ." Go on. Not "Roy Cohn you are a drug fiend." "Roy Marcus Cohn, you are a . . ."
40 Go on, Henry, it starts with an "H."

HENRY Oh I'm not going to . . .

ROY *With an "H,"* Henry, and it isn't "Hemophiliac." Come on . . .

HENRY What are you doing, Roy?

ROY No, say it. I mean it. Say: "Roy Cohn, you are a homosexual." [*Pause*]
45 And I will proceed, systematically, to destroy your reputation and your practice and your career in New York State, Henry. Which you know I can do.

[*Pause.*]

HENRY Roy, you have been seeing me since 1958. Apart from the facelifts I have treated you for everything from syphilis . . .

ROY From a whore in Dallas.

50 HENRY From syphilis to venereal warts. In your rectum. Which you may have gotten from a whore in Dallas, but it wasn't a female whore.

[*Pause.*]

ROY So say it.

---

9. The host of *Watch Mr. Wizard* (1951–65), a television show that explained science to children (revived on cable as *Mr. Wizard's World*, 1983–90).

1. An abnormal enlargement of the lymph nodes.
2. An infection of the mouth by the yeastlike fungus *Candida albicans*.

HENRY   Roy Cohn, you are . . .

You have had sex with men, many many times, Roy, and one of them, or
55 any number of them, has made you very sick. You have AIDS.[3]

ROY   AIDS.

Your problem, Henry, is that you are hung up on words, on labels, that
you believe they mean what they seem to mean. AIDS. Homosexual. Gay.
Lesbian. You think these are names that tell you who someone sleeps with,
60 but they don't tell you that.

HENRY   No?

ROY   No. Like all labels they tell you one thing and one thing only: where does
an individual so identified fit in the food chain, in the pecking order? Not ideology, or sexual taste, but something much simpler: clout. Not who I fuck or
65 who fucks me, but who will pick up the phone when I call, who owes me favors.
This is what a label refers to. Now to someone who does not understand this,
homosexual is what I am because I have sex with men. But really this is wrong.
Homosexuals are not men who sleep with other men. Homosexuals are men
who in fifteen years of trying cannot get a pissant antidiscrimination bill
70 through City Council. Homosexuals are men who know nobody and who
nobody knows. Who have zero clout. Does this sound like me, Henry?

HENRY   No.

ROY   No. I have clout. A lot. I can pick up this phone, punch fifteen numbers, and you know who will be on the other end in under five minutes,
75 Henry?

HENRY   The President.

ROY   Even better, Henry. His wife.

HENRY   I'm impressed.

ROY   I don't want you to be impressed. I want you to understand. This is not
80 sophistry. And this is not hypocrisy. This is reality. I have sex with men. But
unlike nearly every other man of whom this is true, I bring the guy I'm
screwing to the White House and President Reagan smiles at us and
shakes his hand. Because *what* I am is defined entirely by *who* I am. Roy
Cohn is not a homosexual. Roy Cohn is a heterosexual man, Henry, who
85 fucks around with guys.

HENRY   OK, Roy.

ROY   And what is my diagnosis, Henry?

HENRY   You have AIDS, Roy.

ROY   No, Henry, no. AIDS is what homosexuals have. I have liver cancer.

[*Pause.*]

90 HENRY   Well, whatever the fuck you have, Roy, it's very serious, and I haven't
got a damn thing for you. The NIH in Bethesda has a new drug called AZT[4]
with a two-year waiting list that not even I can get you onto. So get on the
phone, Roy, and dial the fifteen numbers, and tell the First Lady you need
in on an experimental treatment for liver cancer, because you can call it
95 any damn thing you want, Roy, but what it boils down to is very bad news.

3. Acquired immune deficiency syndrome
was first recognized in 1981.
4. Azidothymidine or zidovudine, an antiviral
drug that was the first approved (in 1987) to
treat AIDS; that the government accelerate
the testing process required for its approval

was a major demand of early AIDS activists.
NIH: the National Institutes of Health, the
federal agency primarily responsible for supporting and conducting medical research; its
headquarters are in Bethesda, Maryland.

Act 2: In Vitro

[*December 1985–January 1986*]

Scene 1

[*Night, the third week in December.* PRIOR *alone on the floor of his bedroom; he is much worse.*]

PRIOR   Louis, Louis, please wake up, oh God.

[LOUIS *runs in.*]

PRIOR   I think something horrible is wrong with me I can't breathe . . .

LOUIS [*starting to exit*]   I'm calling the ambulance.

PRIOR   No, wait, I . . .

5 LOUIS   *Wait?* Are you fucking crazy? Oh God you're on fire, your head is on fire.

PRIOR   It hurts, it hurts . . .

LOUIS   I'm calling the ambulance.

PRIOR   I don't want to go to the hospital, I don't want to go to the hospital

10 please let me lie here, just . . .

LOUIS   No, no, God, Prior, stand up . . .

PRIOR   DON'T TOUCH MY LEG!

LOUIS   We have to . . . oh God this is so crazy.

PRIOR   I'll be OK if I just lie here Lou, really, if I can only sleep a little . . .

[LOUIS *exits.*]

15 PRIOR   Louis?

NO! NO! Don't call, you'll send me there and I won't come back, please, please Louis I'm begging, baby, please . . .

[*Screams.*] LOUIS!!

LOUIS [*from off; hysterical*]   WILL YOU SHUT THE FUCK UP!

20 PRIOR [*trying to stand*]   Aaah. I have . . . to go to the bathroom. Wait. Wait, just . . . oh. Oh God. [*He shits himself.*]

LOUIS [*Entering*]   Prior? They'll be here in . . .

Oh my God.

PRIOR   I'm sorry, I'm sorry.

25 LOUIS   What did . . . ? What?

PRIOR   I had an accident.

[LOUIS *goes to him.*]

LOUIS   This is blood.

PRIOR   Maybe you shouldn't touch it . . . me. . . . I . . . [*He faints.*]

LOUIS [*quietly*]   Oh help. Oh help. Oh God oh God oh God help me I can't I

30 can't I can't.

Scene 2

[*Same night.* HARPER *is sitting at home, all alone, with no lights on. We can barely see her.* JOE *enters, but he doesn't turn on the lights.*]

JOE   Why are you sitting in the dark? Turn on the light.

HARPER   *No.* I heard the sounds in the bedroom again. I know someone was in there.

JOE   No one was.

5 HARPER   Maybe actually in the bed, under the covers with a knife.

Oh, boy. Joe. I, um, I'm thinking of going away. By which I mean: I think I'm going off again. You . . . you know what I mean?

JOE   Please don't. Stay. We can fix it. I pray for that. This is my fault, but I can correct it. You have to try too . . .

[*He turns on the light. She turns it off again.*]

10 HARPER   When you pray, what do you pray for?

JOE   I pray for God to crush me, break me up into little pieces and start all over again.

HARPER   Oh. Please. Don't pray for that.

JOE   I had a book of Bible stories when I was a kid. There was a picture I'd
15 look at twenty times every day: Jacob wrestles with the angel.[5] I don't really remember the story, or why the wrestling—just the picture. Jacob is young and very strong. The angel is . . . a beautiful man, with golden hair and wings, of course. I still dream about it. Many nights. I'm . . . It's me. In that struggle. Fierce, and unfair. The angel is not human, and it holds nothing
20 back, so how could anyone human win, what kind of a fight is that? It's not just. Losing means your soul thrown down in the dust, your heart torn out from God's. But you can't not lose.

HARPER   In the whole entire world, you are the only person, the only person I love or have ever loved. And I love you terribly. Terribly. That's what's so
25 awfully, irreducibly real. I can make up anything but I can't dream that away.

JOE   Are you . . . are you really going to have a baby?

HARPER   It's my time, and there's no blood. I don't really know. I suppose it wouldn't be a great thing. Maybe I'm just not bleeding because I take too
30 many pills. Maybe I'll give birth to a pill. That would give a new meaning to pill-popping, huh?

I think you should go to Washington. Alone. Change, like you said.

JOE   I'm not going to leave you, Harper.

HARPER   Well maybe not. But I'm going to leave you.

Scene 3

[*One AM, the next morning.* LOUIS *and a nurse,* EMILY, *are sitting in* PRIOR'*s room in the hospital.*]

EMILY   He'll be all right now.

LOUIS   No he won't.

EMILY   No. I guess not. I gave him something that makes him sleep.

LOUIS   Deep asleep?

5 EMILY   Orbiting the moons of Jupiter.

LOUIS   A good place to be.

EMILY   Anyplace better than here. You his . . . uh?

LOUIS   Yes. I'm his uh.

EMILY   This must be hell for you.

10 LOUIS   It is. Hell. The After Life. Which is not at all like a rainy afternoon in March, by the way, Prior. A lot more vivid than I'd expected. Dead leaves, but the crunchy kind. Sharp, dry air. The kind of long, luxurious dying feeling that breaks your heart.

EMILY   Yeah, well we all get to break our hearts on this one.

5. See Genesis 32.24–30.

15   He seems like a nice guy. Cute.
     LOUIS   Not like this.
          Yes, he is. Was. Whatever.
     EMILY   Weird name. Prior Walter. Like, "The Walter before this one."
     LOUIS   Lots of Walters before this one. Prior is an old old family name in an
20   old old family. The Walters go back to the Mayflower and beyond. Back to
     the Norman Conquest. He says there's a Prior Walter stitched into the
     Bayeux tapestry.[6]
     EMILY   Is that impressive?
     LOUIS   Well, it's old. Very old. Which in some circles equals impressive.
25   EMILY   Not in my circle. What's the name of the tapestry?
     LOUIS   The Bayeux tapestry. Embroidered by La Reine Mathilde.[7]
     EMILY   I'll tell my mother. She embroiders. Drives me nuts.
     LOUIS   Manual therapy for anxious hands.
     EMILY   Maybe you should try it.
30   LOUIS   Mathilde stitched while William the Conqueror was off to war. She
     was capable of . . . more than loyalty. Devotion.
          She waited for him, she stitched for years. And if he had come back bro-
     ken and defeated from war, she would have loved him even more. And if he
     had returned mutilated, ugly, full of infection and horror, she would still
35   have loved him; fed by pity, by a sharing of pain, she would love him even
     more, and even more, and she would never, never have prayed to God,
     please let him die if he can't return to me whole and healthy and able to live
     a normal life. . . . If he had died, she would have buried her heart with him.
          So what the fuck is the matter with me? [Little pause]
40   Will he sleep through the night?
     EMILY   At least.
     LOUIS   I'm going.
     EMILY   It's one AM. Where do you have to go at . . .
     LOUIS   I know what time it is. A walk. Night air, good for the . . . The park.
45   EMILY   Be careful.
     LOUIS   Yeah. Danger.
          Tell him, if he wakes up and you're still on, tell him goodbye, tell him I
     had to go.

Scene 4

[An hour later. Split scene: JOE and ROY in a fancy (straight) bar; LOUIS
and a MAN in the Rambles[8] in Central Park. JOE and ROY are sitting at the
bar; the place is brightly lit. JOE has a plate of food in front of him but he
isn't eating. ROY occasionally reaches over the table and forks small bites
off JOE's plate. ROY is drinking heavily, JOE not at all. LOUIS and the MAN
are eyeing each other, each alternating interest and indifference.]

JOE   The pills were something she started when she miscarried or . . . no,
     she took some before that. She had a really bad time at home, when she

---

6. An embroidery, 230 feet long, that chronicles the invasion and conquest of England by
the Normans in 1066 (preserved in the Bayeux Museum in northern France). *Mayflower*: the ship that in 1620 brought the
English founders of the Plymouth Colony to
Massachusetts.
7. Queen Matilda (French; ca. 1031–1083),

the wife of William the Conqueror (ca. 1028–
1087); the tradition that attributes the creation of the Bayeux tapestry to her has little
foundation.
8. A wooded section in New York's Central
Park, designed as a wild garden; for much of
the 20th century, the Ramble was notorious
as an area for homosexual cruising.

was a kid, her home was really bad. I think a lot of drinking and physical
stuff. She doesn't talk about that, instead she talks about . . . the sky falling
down, people with knives hiding under sofas. Monsters. Mormons. Everyone thinks Mormons don't come from homes like that, we aren't supposed
to behave that way, but we do. It's not lying, or being two-faced. Everyone
tries very hard to live up to God's strictures, which are very . . . um . . .

ROY   Strict.

JOE   I shouldn't be bothering you with this.

ROY   No, please. Heart to heart. Want another. . . . What is that, seltzer?[9]

JOE   The failure to measure up hits people very hard. From such a strong
desire to be good they feel very far from goodness when they fail.
    What scares me is that maybe what I really love in her is the part of her
that's farthest from the light, from God's love; maybe I was drawn to that in
the first place. And I'm keeping it alive because I need it.

ROY   Why would you need it?

JOE   There are things. . . . I don't know how well we know ourselves. I mean,
what if? I know I married her because she . . . because I loved it that she
was always wrong, always doing something wrong, like one step out of step.
In Salt Lake City that stands out. I never stood out, on the outside, but
inside, it was hard for me. To pass.

ROY   Pass?

JOE   Yeah.

ROY   Pass as what?

JOE   Oh. Well. . . . As someone cheerful and strong. Those who love God with
an open heart unclouded by secrets and struggles are cheerful; God's easy
simple love for them shows in how strong and happy they are. The saints.[1]

ROY   But you had secrets? Secret struggles . . .

JOE   I wanted to be one of the elect, one of the Blessed. You feel you ought
to be, that the blemishes are yours by choice, which of course they aren't.
Harper's sorrow, that really deep sorrow, she didn't choose that. But it's
there.

ROY   You didn't put it there.

JOE   No.

ROY   You sound like you think you did.

JOE   I am responsible for her.

ROY   Because she's your wife.

JOE   That. And I do love her.

ROY   Whatever. She's your wife. And so there are obligations. To her. But
also to yourself.

JOE   She'd fall apart in Washington.

ROY   Then let her stay here.

JOE   She'll fall apart if I leave her.

ROY   Then bring her to Washington.

JOE   I just can't, Roy. She needs me.

ROY   Listen, Joe. I'm the best divorce lawyer in the business.

       [*Little pause.*]

JOE   Can't Washington wait?

---

9. Observant Mormons do not drink alcohol
or caffeine (or smoke).

1. That is, Mormons, members of what is

officially called the Church of Jesus Christ of
Latter-day Saints (the LDS Church).

ROY You do what you need to do, Joe. What *you* need. *You*. Let her life go
50   where it wants to go. You'll both be better for that. *Somebody* should get
     what they want.

MAN What do you want?

LOUIS I want you to fuck me, hurt me, make me bleed.

MAN I want to.

55 LOUIS Yeah?

MAN I want to hurt you.

LOUIS Fuck me.

MAN Yeah?

LOUIS Hard.

60 MAN Yeah? You been a bad boy?

     [*Pause.* LOUIS *laughs, softly.*]

LOUIS Very bad. Very bad.

MAN You need to be punished, boy?

LOUIS Yes. I do.

MAN Yes what?

     [*Little pause.*]

65 LOUIS Um, I . . .

MAN Yes *what*, boy?

LOUIS Oh. Yes sir.

MAN I want you to take me to your place, boy.

LOUIS No, I can't do that.

70 MAN No *what*?

LOUIS No sir, I can't, I . . .
     I don't live alone, sir.

MAN Your lover know you're out with a man tonight, boy?

LOUIS No sir, he . . .

75   My lover doesn't know.

MAN Your lover know you . . .

LOUIS Let's change the subject, OK? Can we go to your place?

MAN I live with my parents.

LOUIS Oh.

80 ROY Everyone who makes it in this world makes it because somebody older
     and more powerful takes an interest. The most precious asset in life, I
     think, is the ability to be a good son. You have that, Joe. Somebody who can
     be a good son to a father who pushes them farther than they would other-
     wise go. I've had many fathers, I owe my life to them, powerful, powerful
85   men. Walter Winchell, Edgar Hoover. Joe McCarthy most of all.[2] He val-

---

2. The historical Cohn, through his work on the Permanent Subcommittee on Investigations, is most closely identified with McCarthy (1908–1957), who as senator from Wisconsin (1947–57) gained national attention with his sensational and unsubstantiated claims that the State Department and other parts of the government had been infiltrated by Communists. Winchell (1897–1972) wrote a hugely popular gossip column (begun in 1924); he lost influence after he allied himself with McCarthy's anticommunist witch hunt. Hoover (1895–1972), early in his career (during the first Red Scare, 1919–20), was placed in charge of investigating suspected alien radicals; in 1924, he became director of the Bureau of Investigation (renamed the Federal Bureau of Investigation in 1935), amassing enormous and virtually unchecked power during his forty-eight years in that position. A believer in a worldwide communist conspiracy, he too was an ally of McCarthy; rumors that he was a homosexual circulated for decades.

ued me because I am a good lawyer, but he loved me because I was and am a good son. He was a very difficult man, very guarded and cagey; I brought out something tender in him. He would have died for me. And me for him. Does this embarrass you?

90 JOE I had a hard time with my father.

ROY Well sometimes that's the way. Then you have to find other fathers, substitutes, I don't know. The father-son relationship is central to life. Women are for birth, beginning, but the father is continuance. The son offers the father his life as a vessel for carrying forth his father's dream.

95 Your father's living?

JOE Um, dead.

ROY He was . . . what? A difficult man?

JOE He was in the military. He could be very unfair. And cold.

ROY But he loved you.

100 JOE I don't know.

ROY No, no, Joe, he did, I know this. Sometimes a father's love has to be very, very hard, unfair even, cold to make his son grow strong in a world like this. This isn't a good world.

MAN Here, then.

105 LOUIS I. . . . Do you have a rubber?

MAN I don't use rubbers.

LOUIS You should. [*He takes one from his coat pocket.*] Here.

MAN I don't use them.

LOUIS Forget it, then. [*He starts to leave.*]

110 MAN No, wait.

Put it on me. Boy.

LOUIS Forget it, I have to get back. Home. I must be going crazy.

MAN Oh come on please he won't find out.

LOUIS It's cold. Too cold.

115 MAN It's never too cold, let me warm you up. Please?

[*They begin to fuck.*]

MAN Relax.

LOUIS [*a small laugh*] Not a chance.

MAN It . . .

LOUIS What?

120 MAN I think it broke. The rubber. You want me to keep going?

[*Little pause*] Pull out? Should I . . .

LOUIS Keep going.

Infect me.

I don't care. I don't care.

[*Pause. The* MAN *pulls out.*]

125 MAN I . . . um, look, I'm sorry, but I think I want to go.

LOUIS Yeah.

Give my best to mom and dad.

[*The* MAN *slaps him.*]

LOUIS Ow!

[*They stare at each other.*]

LOUIS It was a joke.

[*The* MAN *leaves.*]

130 ROY   How long have we known each other?

JOE   Since 1980.

ROY   Right. A long time. I feel close to you, Joe. Do I advise you well?

JOE   You've been an incredible friend, Roy, I . . .

ROY   I want to be family. Familia, as my Italian friends call it. La Familia. A
135   lovely word. It's important for me to help you, like I was helped.

JOE   I owe practically everything to you, Roy.

ROY   I'm dying, Joe. Cancer.

JOE   Oh my God.

ROY   Please. Let me finish.

140   Few people know this and I'm telling you this only because . . . I'm not afraid of death. What can death bring that I haven't faced? I've lived; life is the worst. [*Gently mocking himself*] Listen to me, I'm a philosopher.

    Joe. You must do this. You must must must. Love; that's a trap. Responsibility; that's a trap too. Like a father to a son I tell you this: Life is full of
145   horror; nobody escapes, nobody; save yourself. Whatever pulls on you, whatever needs from you, threatens you. Don't be afraid; people are so afraid; don't be afraid to live in the raw wind, naked, alone. . . . Learn at least this: What you are capable of. Let nothing stand in your way.

Scene 5

[*Three days later.* PRIOR *and* BELIZE *in* PRIOR's *hospital room.* PRIOR *is very sick but improving.* BELIZE *has just arrived.*]

PRIOR   Miss Thing.

BELIZE   Ma cherie bichette.[3]

PRIOR   Stella.

BELIZE   Stella for star.[4] Let me see. [*Scrutinizing* PRIOR] You look like shit,
5   why yes indeed you do, comme la merde![5]

PRIOR   Merci.[6]

BELIZE   [*taking little plastic bottles from his bag, handing them to* PRIOR]   Not to despair, Belle Reeve.[7] Lookie! Magic goop!

PRIOR   [*opening a bottle, sniffing*]   Pooh! What kinda crap is that?

10 BELIZE   Beats me. Let's rub it on your poor blistered body and see what it does.

PRIOR   This is not Western medicine, these bottles . . .

BELIZE   Voodoo cream. From the botanica 'round the block.

PRIOR   And you a registered nurse.

BELIZE   [*sniffing it*]   Beeswax and cheap perfume. Cut with Jergen's Lotion.
15   Full of good vibes and love from some little black Cubana witch in Miami.

PRIOR   Get that trash away from me, I am immune-suppressed.

BELIZE   I *am* a health professional. I *know* what I'm doing.

PRIOR   It stinks. Any word from Louis?

    [*Pause.* BELIZE *starts giving* PRIOR *a gentle massage.*]

20 PRIOR   Gone.

---

3. My dear little darling (French).
4. A line spoken by Blanche DuBois to her sister Stella in Tennessee Williams's *A Streetcar Named Desire* (1947). (*Stella* means "star" in Latin.)

5. Like shit! (French).
6. Thanks (French).
7. In *A Streetcar Named Desire*, Belle Reve (Beautiful Dream; French) is the name of Blanche and Stella's ancestral home.

BELIZE   He'll be back. I know the type. Likes to keep a girl on edge.

PRIOR   It's been . . .

> [*Pause.*]

BELIZE [*trying to jog his memory*]   How long?

PRIOR   I don't remember.

25 BELIZE   How long have you been here?

PRIOR [*getting suddenly upset*]   I don't remember, I don't give a fuck. I want
Louis. I want my fucking boyfriend, where the fuck is he? I'm dying, I'm
dying, where's Louis?

BELIZE   Shhhh, shhh . . .

30 PRIOR   This is a very strange drug, this drug. Emotional lability, for starters.

BELIZE   Save a tab or two for me.

PRIOR   Oh no, not this drug, ce n'est pas pour la joyeux noël et la bonne
année, this drug she is serious poisonous chemistry, ma pauvre bichette.[8]
And not just disorienting. I hear things. Voices.

35 BELIZE   Voices.

PRIOR   A voice.

BELIZE   Saying what?

> [*Pause.*]

PRIOR   I'm not supposed to tell.

BELIZE   You better tell the doctor. Or I will.

40 PRIOR   No no don't. Please. I want the voice; it's wonderful. It's all that's
keeping me alive. I don't want to talk to some intern about it.
You know what happens? When I hear it, I get hard.

BELIZE   Oh my.

PRIOR   Comme ça.[9] [*He uses his arm to demonstrate.*] And you know I am
45   slow to rise.

BELIZE   My jaw aches at the memory.

PRIOR   And would you deny me this little solace—betray my concupiscence
to Florence Nightingale's storm troopers?[1]

BELIZE   Perish the thought, ma bébé.[2]

50 PRIOR   They'd change the drug just to spoil the fun.

BELIZE   You and your boner can depend on me.

PRIOR   Je t'adore, ma belle nègre.[3]

BELIZE   All this girl-talk shit is politically incorrect, you know. We should
have dropped it back when we gave up drag.

55 PRIOR   I'm sick, I get to be politically incorrect if it makes me feel better. You
sound like Lou. [*Little pause*]
Well, at least I have the satisfaction of knowing he's in anguish somewhere. I loved his anguish. Watching him stick his head up his asshole and
eat his guts out over some relatively minor moral conundrum—it was the
60   best show in town. But Mother warned me: if they get overwhelmed by the
little things . . .

BELIZE   They'll be belly-up bustville when something big comes along.

PRIOR   Mother warned me.

---

8. It doesn't give you a merry Christmas and a
happy New Year . . . my poor little darling
(French).
9. Like that (French).
1. That is, nurses; Nightingale (1820–1910),
an English reformer whose work organizing a

unit of nurses during the Crimean War won
her international fame, is credited with
founding modern nursing.
2. My baby, my child (French).
3. I adore you, my beautiful Negro (French).

BELIZE   And they do come along.

65 PRIOR   But I didn't listen.

BELIZE   No. [*Doing Hepburn*][4] Men are beasts.

PRIOR [*also Hepburn*]   The absolute lowest.

BELIZE   I have to go. If I want to spend my whole lonely life looking after white people I can get underpaid to do it.

70 PRIOR   You're just a Christian martyr.

BELIZE   Whatever happens, baby, I will be here for you.

PRIOR   Je t'aime.[5]

BELIZE   Je t'aime. Don't go crazy on me, girlfriend, I already got enough crazy queens for one lifetime. For two. I can't be bothering with dementia.

75 PRIOR   I promise.

BELIZE [*touching him; softly*]   Ouch.

PRIOR   Ouch. Indeed.

BELIZE   Why'd they have to pick on you?
    And eat more, girlfriend, you really do look like shit.

        [BELIZE *leaves.*]

80 PRIOR [*after waiting a beat*]   He's gone.
    Are you still . . .

VOICE   I can't stay. I will return.

PRIOR   Are you one of those "Follow me to the other side" voices?

VOICE   No. I am no nightbird. I am a messenger . . .

85 PRIOR   You have a beautiful voice, it sounds . . . like a viola, like a perfectly tuned, tight string, balanced, the truth. . . . Stay with me.

VOICE   Not now. Soon I will return, I will reveal myself to you; I am glorious, glorious; my heart, my countenance, and my message. You must prepare.

PRIOR   For what? I don't want to . . .

90 VOICE   No death, no:
    A marvelous work and a wonder[6] we undertake, an edifice awry we sink plumb and straighten, a great Lie we abolish, a great error correct, with the rule, sword, and broom of Truth!

PRIOR   What are you talking about, I . . .

VOICE

95 I am on my way; when I am manifest, our Work begins:
    Prepare for the parting of the air,
    The breath, the ascent,
    Glory to . . .

Scene 6

[*The second week of January.* MARTIN, ROY, *and* JOE *in a fancy Manhattan restaurant.*]

MARTIN   It's a revolution in Washington, Joe. We have a new agenda and finally a real leader. They got back the Senate[7] but we have the courts. By the nineties the Supreme Court will be block-solid Republican appointees, and the Federal bench—Republican judges like land mines, everywhere,

---

4. That is, the American stage and film star Katharine Hepburn (1907–2003), who often portrayed independent women.
5. I love you (French).
6. See Isaiah 29.14.

7. Majority control of the U.S. Senate shifted to the Democrats in the 1986 election (Republicans gained majorities in both the House and the Senate in 1994).

5 everywhere they turn. Affirmative action? Take it to court. Boom! Land mine. And we'll get our way on just about everything: abortion, defense, Central America, family values, a live investment climate. We have the White House locked till the year 2000. And beyond. A permanent fix on the Oval Office? It's possible. By '92 we'll get the Senate back, and in ten years 10 the South is going to give us the House. It's really the end of Liberalism. The end of New Deal Socialism.[8] The end of ipso facto secular human-ism.[9] The dawning of a genuinely American political personality. Modeled on Ronald Wilson Reagan.

JOE It sounds great, Mr. Heller.

15 MARTIN Martin. And Justice is the hub. Especially since Ed Meese took over. He doesn't specialize in Fine Points of the Law. He's a flatfoot, a cop. He reminds me of Teddy Roosevelt.[1]

JOE I can't wait to meet him.

MARTIN Too bad, Joe, he's been dead for sixty years!

[*There is a little awkwardness.* JOE *doesn't respond.*]

20 MARTIN Teddy Roosevelt. You said you wanted to. . . . Little joke. It reminds me of the story about the . . .

ROY [*smiling, but nasty*] Aw shut the fuck up Martin.

[*To* JOE] You see that? Mr. Heller here is one of the mighty, Joseph, in D.C. he sitteth on the right hand of the man who sitteth on the right hand 25 of The Man.[2] And yet I can say "shut the fuck up" and he will take no offense. Loyalty. He . . .

Martin?

MARTIN Yes, Roy?

ROY Rub my back.

30 MARTIN Roy . . .

ROY No no really, a sore spot, I get them all the time now, these . . . Rub it for me darling, would you do that for me?

[MARTIN *rubs* ROY's *back. They both look at* JOE.]

ROY [*to* JOE] How do you think a handful of Bolsheviks turned St. Peters-burg into Leningrad in one afternoon? *Comrades.* Who do for each other. 35 Marx and Engels. Lenin and Trotsky. Josef Stalin and Franklin Delano Roosevelt.[3]

[MARTIN *laughs.*]

8. That is, the government programs promoting economic and social welfare (and thus labeled "socialist" by opponents) of the type first insti-tuted during the New Deal, the name given by Franklin Delano Roosevelt (1882–1945; 32nd president, 1933–45) to his domestic reform ini-tiatives. These programs include Social Secu-rity, banking reform, and the minimum wage.
9. A philosophy that locates value in human reason and interests, rejecting religion and the supernatural.
1. Theodore Roosevelt (1858–1919), twenty-sixth president of the United States (1901–09); between 1895 and 1897, he served as president of the New York City Board of Police Commissioners.
2. Compare Colossians 3.1 ("Christ sitteth on the right hand of God").
3. That is, symbiosis—even between sup-posed adversaries—is the key to success. The German political philosopher Karl Marx (1818–1883) and the German socialist Fried-rich Engels (1820–1895) co-wrote the *Mani-festo of the Communist Party* (1848); the Russian revolutionaries Vladimir Lenin (1870–1924) and Leon Trotsky (1879–1940) led the Bolshevik faction of socialists that tri-umphed in the October Revolution of 1917 (Saint Petersburg, which was a focal point of revolutionary activity, had been given the less Germanic name Petrograd in 1914; it was renamed Leningrad after Lenin died, but its original name was restored in 1991); the dic-tator Joseph Stalin (1879–1953), who con-trolled the Soviet Union from Lenin's death until his own death, and President Roosevelt became allies in World War II. *Comrades:* form of address used among Communists.

ROY *Comrades*, right Martin?

MARTIN This man, Joe, is a Saint of the Right.

JOE I know, Mr. Heller, I . . .

40 ROY And you see what I mean, Martin? He's special, right?

MARTIN Don't embarrass him, Roy.

ROY Gravity, decency, smarts! His strength is as the strength of ten because his heart is pure![4] *And* he's a Royboy, one hundred percent.

MARTIN We're on the move, Joe. On the move.

45 JOE Mr. Heller, I . . .

MARTIN [*ending backrub*] We can't wait any longer for an answer.
[*Little pause.*]

JOE Oh. Um, I . . .

ROY Joe's a married man, Martin.

MARTIN Aha.

50 ROY With a wife. She doesn't care to go to D.C., and so Joe cannot go. And keeps us dangling. We've seen that kind of thing before, haven't we? These men and their wives.

MARTIN Oh yes. Beware.

JOE I really can't discuss this under . . .

55 MARTIN Then *don't* discuss. Say yes, Joe.

ROY Now.

MARTIN Say yes I will.

ROY Now.
Now. I'll hold my breath till you do, I'm turning blue waiting. . . . *Now*,
60 goddammit!

MARTIN Roy, calm down, it's not . . .

ROY Aw, fuck it. [*He takes a letter from his jacket pocket, hands it to* JOE.]
Read. Came today.
[JOE *reads the first paragraph, then looks up.*]

JOE Roy. This is . . . Roy, this is terrible.

65 ROY You're telling me.
A letter from the New York State Bar Association, Martin.
They're gonna try and disbar me.

MARTIN Oh my.

JOE Why?

70 ROY Why, Martin?

MARTIN Revenge.

ROY The whole Establishment. Their little rules. Because I know no rules. Because I don't see the Law as a dead and arbitrary collection of anti-quated dictums, thou shall, thou shalt not, because, because I know the
75 Law's a pliable, breathing, sweating . . . *organ*, because, because . . .

MARTIN Because he borrowed half a million from one of his clients.[5]

ROY Yeah, well, there's that.

MARTIN *And* he forgot to *return* it.

JOE Roy, that's . . . You borrowed money from a client?

80 ROY I'm deeply ashamed.

---

4. Paraphrase of a couplet from "Sir Galahad" (1842), by Alfred, Lord Tennyson.
5. Cohn was in fact disbarred in 1986 for unethical conduct, which included borrowing $109,000 from a client and not repaying her.

[*Little pause.*]

JOE [*very sympathetic*]   Roy, you know how much I admire you. Well I mean I know you have unorthodox ways, but I'm sure you only did what you thought at the time you needed to do. And I have faith that . . .

ROY   Not so damp, please. I'll deny it was a loan. She's got no paperwork.
85   Can't prove a fucking thing.

[*Little pause.* MARTIN *studies the menu.*]

JOE [*handing back the letter, more official in tone*]   Roy I really appreciate your telling me this, and I'll do whatever I can to help.

ROY [*holding up a hand, then, carefully*]   I'll tell you what you can do.

I'm about to be tried, Joe, by a jury that is not a jury of my peers. The
90   disbarment committee: genteel gentleman Brahmin[6] lawyers, country-club men. I offend them, to these men . . . I'm what, Martin, some sort of filthy little Jewish troll?

MARTIN   Oh well, I wouldn't go so far as . . .

ROY   Oh well I would.
95   Very fancy lawyers, these disbarment committee lawyers, fancy lawyers with fancy corporate clients and complicated cases. Antitrust suits. Deregulation. Environmental control. Complex cases like these need Justice Department cooperation like flowers need the sun. Wouldn't you say that's an accurate assessment, Martin?

100   MARTIN   I'm not here, Roy. I'm not hearing any of this.

ROY   No. Of course not.

Without the light of the sun, Joe, these cases, and the fancy lawyers who represent them, will wither and die.

A well-placed friend, someone in the Justice Department, say, can turn
105   off the sun. Cast a deep shadow on my behalf. Make them shiver in the cold. If they overstep. They would fear that.

[*Pause.*]

JOE   Roy. I don't understand.

ROY   You do.

[*Pause.*]

JOE   You're not asking me to . . .

110   ROY   Sssshhhh. Careful.

JOE [*a beat,*[7] *then*]   Even if I said yes to the job, it would be illegal to interfere. With the hearings. It's unethical. No. I can't.

ROY   Un-ethical.

Would you excuse us, Martin?

115   MARTIN   Excuse you?

ROY   Take a walk, Martin. For real.

[MARTIN *leaves.*]

ROY   Un-ethical. Are you trying to embarrass me in front of my friend?

JOE   Well it is unethical, I can't . . .

ROY   Boy, you are really something. What the fuck do you think this is, Sun-
120   day School?

JOE   No, but Roy this is . . .

---

6. That is, of high social standing (Brahmans are Hindus of the highest caste).   7. Pause (theater term).

ROY   This is . . . this is gastric juices churning, this is enzymes and acids, this is intestinal is what this is, bowel movement and blood-red meat—this stinks, this is *politics,* Joe, the game of being alive. And you think you're. . . .

125   What? Above that? Above alive is what? Dead! In the clouds! You're on earth, goddammit! Plant a foot, stay awhile.

        I'm sick. They smell I'm weak. They want blood this time. I must have eyes in Justice. In Justice you will protect me.

JOE   Why can't Mr. Heller . . .

130   ROY   Grow up, Joe. The administration can't get involved.

JOE   But I'd be part of the administration. The same as him.

ROY   Not the same. Martin's Ed's man. And Ed's Reagan's man. So Martin's Reagan's man.

        And you're mine. [*Little pause. He holds up the letter.*] This will never be.

135   Understand me? [*He tears the letter up.*]

        I'm gonna be a lawyer, Joe, I'm gonna be a lawyer, Joe, I'm gonna be a goddam motherfucking legally licensed member of the bar lawyer, just like my daddy was,[8] till my last bitter day on earth, Joseph, until the day I die.

        [MARTIN *returns.*]

ROY   Ah, Martin's back.

140   MARTIN   So are we agreed?

ROY   Joe?

        [*Little pause.*]

JOE   I will think about it.

        [*To* ROY.] I will.

ROY   Huh.

145   MARTIN   It's the fear of what comes after the doing that makes the doing hard to do.

ROY   Amen.

MARTIN   But you can almost always live with the consequences.

Scene 7

[*That afternoon. On the granite steps outside the Hall of Justice, Brooklyn. It is cold and sunny. A Sabrett[9] wagon is selling hot dogs. Louis, in a shabby overcoat, is sitting on the steps contemplatively eating one. Joe enters with three hot dogs and a can of Coke.*]

JOE   Can I . . . ?

LOUIS   Oh sure. Sure. Crazy cold sun.

JOE [*sitting*]   Have to make the best of it.

        How's your friend?

5   LOUIS   My . . . ? Oh. He's worse. My friend is worse.

JOE   I'm sorry.

LOUIS   Yeah, well. Thanks for asking. It's nice. You're nice. I can't believe you voted for Reagan.

JOE   I hope he gets better.

10   LOUIS   Reagan?

JOE   Your friend.

LOUIS   He won't. Neither will Reagan.

8. Albert Cohn (1885–1959) was a New York state supreme court justice, appointed by Governor Franklin Delano Roosevelt.
9. A New York–based hot dog company.

JOE   Let's not talk politics, OK?

LOUIS [*pointing to* JOE's *lunch*]   You're eating *three* of those?

15 JOE   Well . . . I'm . . . hungry.

LOUIS   They're really terrible for you. Full of rat-poo and beetle legs and wood shavings 'n' shit.

JOE   Huh.

LOUIS   And . . . um . . . irridium, I think. Something toxic.[1]

20 JOE   You're eating one.

LOUIS   Yeah, well, the shape, I can't help myself, plus I'm *trying* to commit suicide, what's your excuse?

JOE   I don't have an excuse. I just have Pepto-Bismol.[2]

[JOE *takes a bottle of Pepto-Bismol and chugs it.* LOUIS *shudders audibly.*]

JOE   Yeah I know but then I wash it down with Coke.

[*He does this.* LOUIS *mimes barfing in* JOE's *lap.* JOE *pushes* LOUIS's *head away.*]

25 JOE   Are you *always* like this?

LOUIS   I've been worrying a lot about his kids.

JOE   Whose?

LOUIS   Reagan's. Maureen and Mike and little orphan Patti and Miss Ron Reagan Jr.,[3] the you-should-pardon-the-expression heterosexual.

30 JOE   Ron Reagan Jr. is *not* . . . You shouldn't just make these assumptions about people. How do you know? About him? What he is? You don't know.

LOUIS [*doing Tallulah*[4]]   Well darling he never sucked *my* cock but . . .

JOE   Look, if you're going to get vulgar . . .

LOUIS   No no really I mean . . . What's it like to be the child of the Zeitgeist?

35 To have the American Animus as your dad? It's not really a *family,* the Reagans, I read *People,*[5] there aren't any connections there, no love, they don't ever even speak to each other except through their agents. So what's it like to be Reagan's kid? Enquiring minds want to know.

JOE   You can't believe everything you . . .

40 LOUIS [*looking away*]   But . . . I think we all know what that's like. Nowadays. No connections. No responsibilities. All of us . . . falling through the cracks that separate what we owe to our selves and . . . and what we owe to love.

JOE   You just. . . . Whatever you feel like saying or doing, you don't care, you just . . . do it.

45 LOUIS   Do what?

JOE   It. Whatever. Whatever it is you want to do.

LOUIS   Are you trying to tell me something?

[*Little pause, sexual. They stare at each other.* JOE *looks away.*]

JOE   No, I'm just observing that you . . .

LOUIS   Impulsive.

---

1. Many hot dogs contain preservatives that can be toxic in large quantities (*iridium* is a rare metallic element).

2. A product used to treat various kinds of minor digestive distress.

3. Ronald Reagan's children from his first marriage, to Jane Wyman (Maureen [1941–2001] and Michael [b. 1945]), and his second marriage, to Nancy Davis (Patti [b. 1952] and Ron [b. 1958]). Patti's estrangement from her parents made her an "orphan."

4. Imitating the husky, drawled "darling" with which the American stage and film star Tallulah Bankhead (1902–1968) customarily addressed people.

5. An American magazine that focuses on celebrities and human interest stories; it began publication in 1974.

50 JOE   Yes, I mean it must be scary, you . . .

LOUIS [*Shrugs*]   Land of the free. Home of the brave. Call me irresponsible.[6]

JOE   It's kind of terrifying.

LOUIS   Yeah, well, freedom is. Heartless, too.

JOE   Oh you're not heartless.

55 LOUIS   You don't know.

   Finish your weenie.

   [*He pats* JOE *on the knee, starts to leave.*]

JOE   Um . . .

   [LOUIS *turns, looks at him.* JOE *searches for something to say.*]

JOE   Yesterday was Sunday but I've been a little unfocused recently and I
   thought it was Monday. So I came here like I was going to work. And the
60   whole place was empty. And at first I couldn't figure out why, and I had this
   moment of incredible . . . fear and also . . . It just flashed through my
   mind: The whole Hall of Justice, it's empty, it's deserted, it's gone out of
   business. Forever. The people that make it run have up and abandoned it.

LOUIS [*looking at the building*]   Creepy.

65 JOE   Well yes but. I felt that I was going to scream. Not because it was
   creepy, but because the emptiness felt so *fast*.

   And . . . well, good. A . . . happy scream.

   I just wondered what a thing it would be . . . if overnight everything you
   owe anything to, justice, or love, had really gone away. Free.

70   It would be . . . heartless terror. Yes. Terrible, and . . .

   Very great. To shed your skin, every old skin, one by one and then walk
   away, unencumbered, into the morning. [*Little pause. He looks at the
   building.*]

   I can't go in there today.

75 LOUIS   Then don't.

JOE [*not really hearing* LOUIS]   I can't go in, I need . . .

   [*He looks for what he needs. He takes a swig of Pepto-Bismol.*] I can't *be*
   this any more. I need . . . a change, I should just . . .

LOUIS [*not a come-on, necessarily; he doesn't want to be alone*]   Want some
80   company? For whatever?

   [*Pause.* JOE *looks at* LOUIS *and looks away, afraid.* LOUIS *shrugs.*]

LOUIS   Sometimes, even if it scares you to death, you have to be willing to
   break the law. Know what I mean?

   [*Another little pause.*]

JOE   Yes.

   [*Another little pause.*]

LOUIS   I moved out. I moved out on my . . .

85   I haven't been sleeping well.

JOE   Me neither.

   [LOUIS *goes up to* JOE, *licks his napkin and dabs at* JOE's *mouth.*]

LOUIS   Antacid moustache.

   [*Points to the building.*]   Maybe the court won't convene. Ever again.
   Maybe we are free. To do whatever.

6. The opening phrase and the title of a 1963
song (music by Jimmy Van Heusen, lyrics by
Sammy Cahn). "O'er the land of the free, and
the home of the brave" is the closing phrase of
the refrain of "The Star-Spangled Banner," the
U.S. national anthem (words by Francis Scott
Key, 1814).

90   Children of the new morning, criminal minds. Selfish and greedy and loveless and blind. Reagan's children.

You're scared. So am I. Everybody is in the land of the free. God help us all.

Scene 8

[*Late that night.* JOE *at a payphone phoning* HANNAH *at home in Salt Lake City.*]

JOE   Mom?

HANNAH   Joe?

JOE   Hi.

HANNAH   You're calling from the street. It's . . . it must be four in the morning.
5   What's happened?

JOE   Nothing, nothing, I . . .

HANNAH   It's Harper. Is Harper. . . . Joe? Joe?

JOE   Yeah, hi. No, Harper's fine. Well, no, she's . . . not fine. How are you, Mom?

10   HANNAH   What's happened?

JOE   I just wanted to talk to you. I, uh, wanted to try something out on you.

HANNAH   Joe, you haven't . . . have you been drinking, Joe?

JOE   Yes ma'am. I'm drunk.

HANNAH   That isn't like you.

15   JOE   No. I mean, who's to say?

HANNAH   Why are you out on the street at four AM? In that crazy city. It's dangerous.

JOE   Actually, Mom, I'm not on the street. I'm near the boathouse in the park.

HANNAH   What park?

20   JOE   Central Park.

HANNAH   CENTRAL PARK! Oh my Lord. What on earth are you doing in Central Park at this time of night? Are you . . .

Joe, I think you ought to go home right now. Call me from home. [*Little pause*] Joe?

25   JOE   I come here to watch, Mom. Sometimes. Just to watch.

HANNAH   Watch what? What's there to watch at four in the . . .

JOE   Mom, did Dad love me?

HANNAH   What?

JOE   Did he?

30   HANNAH   You ought to go home and call from there.

JOE   Answer.

HANNAH   Oh now really. This is maudlin. I don't like this conversation.

JOE   Yeah, well, it gets worse from here on.

[*Pause.*]

HANNAH   Joe?

35   JOE   Mom. Momma. I'm a homosexual, Momma.

Boy, did that come out awkward. [*Pause*] Hello? Hello?

I'm a homosexual. [*Pause*] Please, Momma. Say something.

HANNAH   You're old enough to understand that your father didn't love you without being ridiculous about it.

40   JOE   What?

HANNAH   You're ridiculous. You're being ridiculous.

JOE   I'm . . .

What?

HANNAH   You really ought to go home now to your wife. I need to go to bed.

45   This phone call. . . . We will just forget this phone call.

JOE   Mom.

HANNAH   No more talk. Tonight. This . . .

[*Suddenly very angry*] Drinking is a sin! A sin! I raised you better than that. [*She hangs up.*]

Scene 9

[*The following morning, early. Split scene:* HARPER *and* JOE *at home;* LOUIS *and* PRIOR *in* PRIOR'S *hospital room.* JOE *and* LOUIS *have just entered. This should be fast and obviously furious; overlapping is fine; the proceedings may be a little confusing but not the final results.*]

HARPER   Oh God. Home. The moment of truth has arrived.

JOE   Harper.

LOUIS   I'm going to move out.

PRIOR   The fuck you are.

5   JOE   Harper. Please listen. I still love you very much. You're still my best buddy; I'm not going to leave you.

HARPER   No, I don't like the sound of this. I'm leaving.

LOUIS   I'm leaving.

I already have.

10   JOE   Please listen. Stay. This is really hard. We have to talk.

HARPER   We are talking. Aren't we. Now please shut up. OK?

PRIOR   Bastard. Sneaking off while I'm flat out here, that's low. If I could get up now I'd beat the holy shit out of you.

JOE   Did you take pills? How many?

15   HARPER   No pills. Bad for the . . . [*Pats stomach.*]

JOE   You aren't pregnant. I called your gynecologist.

HARPER   I'm seeing a new gynecologist.

PRIOR   You have no right to do this.

LOUIS   Oh, that's ridiculous.

20   PRIOR   No right. It's criminal.

JOE   Forget about that. Just listen. You want the truth. This is the truth.

I knew this when I married you. I've known this I guess for as long as I've known anything, but . . . I don't know, I thought maybe that with enough effort and will I could change myself . . . but I can't . . .

25   PRIOR   Criminal.

LOUIS   There oughta be a law.

PRIOR   There is a law. You'll see.

JOE   I'm losing ground here, I go walking, you want to know where I walk, I . . . go to the park, or up and down 53rd Street, or places where . . . And

30   I keep swearing I won't go walking again, but I just can't.

LOUIS   I need some privacy.

PRIOR   That's new.

LOUIS   Everything's new, Prior.

JOE   I try to tighten my heart into a knot, a snarl, I try to learn to live dead,

35   just numb, but then I see someone I want, and it's like a nail, like a hot spike right through my chest, and I know I'm losing.

PRIOR   Apartment too small for three? Louis and Prior comfy but not Louis and Prior and Prior's disease?

LOUIS   Something like that.

40   I won't be judged by you. This isn't a crime, just—the inevitable consequence of people who run out of—whose limitations . . .

PRIOR   Bang bang bang. The court will come to order.

LOUIS   I mean let's talk practicalities, schedules; I'll come over if you want, spend nights with you when I can, I can . . .

45 PRIOR   Has the jury reached a verdict?

LOUIS   I'm doing the best I can.

PRIOR   Pathetic. Who cares?

JOE   My whole life has conspired to bring me to this place, and I can't despise my whole life. I think I believed when I met you I could save you, you at

50   least if not myself, but . . .

        I don't have any sexual feelings for you, Harper. And I don't think I ever did.

        [*Little pause.*]

HARPER   I think you should go.

JOE   Where?

55 HARPER   Washington. Doesn't matter.

JOE   What are you talking about?

HARPER   Without me.

        Without me, Joe. Isn't that what you want to hear?

        [*Little pause.*]

JOE   Yes.

60 LOUIS   You can love someone and fail them. You can love someone and not be able to . . .

PRIOR   You *can*, theoretically, yes. A person can, maybe an editorial "you" can love, Louis, but not *you*, specifically you, I don't know, I think you are excluded from that general category.

65 HARPER   You were going to save me, but the whole time you were spinning a lie. I just don't understand that.

PRIOR   A person could theoretically love and maybe many do but we both know now you can't.

LOUIS   I do.

70 PRIOR   You can't even say it.

LOUIS   I love you, Prior.

PRIOR   I repeat. Who cares?

HARPER   This is so scary, I want this to stop, to go back . . .

PRIOR   We have reached a verdict, your honor. This man's heart is deficient.

75   He loves, but his love is worth nothing.

JOE   Harper . . .

HARPER   Mr. Lies, I want to get away from here. Far away. Right now. Before he starts talking again. Please, please . . .

JOE   As long as I've known you Harper you've been afraid of . . . of men hid-

80   ing under the bed, men hiding under the sofa, men with knives.

PRIOR [*shattered; almost pleading; trying to reach him*]   I'm dying! You stupid fuck! Do you know what that is! Love! Do you know what love means? We lived together four-and-a-half years, you animal, you idiot.

LOUIS   I have to find some way to save myself.

85 JOE   Who are these men? I never understood it. Now I know.

HARPER   What?

JOE   It's me.

HARPER   It is?

PRIOR   GET OUT OF MY ROOM!

90 JOE   I'm the man with the knives.

HARPER   You are?

PRIOR   If I could get up now I'd kill you. I would. Go away. Go away or I'll
    scream.

HARPER   Oh God . . .

95 JOE   I'm sorry . . .

HARPER   It is you.

LOUIS   Please don't scream.

PRIOR   Go.

HARPER   I recognize you now.

100 LOUIS   Please . . .

JOE   Oh. Wait, I . . . Oh!

    [*He covers his mouth with his hand, gags, and removes his hand, red with
    blood.*] I'm bleeding.

        [PRIOR *screams.*]

HARPER   Mr. Lies.

MR. LIES [*appearing, dressed in Antarctic explorer's apparel*]   Right here.

105 HARPER   I want to go away. I can't see him any more.

MR. LIES   Where?

HARPER   Anywhere. Far away.

MR. LIES   Absolutamento.

        [HARPER *and* MR. LIES *vanish.* JOE *looks up, sees that she's gone.*]

PRIOR [*closing his eyes*]   When I open my eyes you'll be gone.

        [LOUIS *leaves.*]

110 JOE   Harper?

PRIOR [*opening his eyes*]   Huh. It worked.

JOE [*calling*]   Harper?

PRIOR   I hurt all over. I wish I was dead.

Scene 10

[*The same day, sunset.* HANNAH *and* SISTER ELLA CHAPTER, *a real estate
saleswoman,* HANNAH PITT'*s closest friend, in front of* HANNAH'*s house in
Salt Lake City.*]

SISTER ELLA CHAPTER   Look at that view! A view of heaven. Like the living
    city of heaven,[7] isn't it, it just fairly glimmers in the sun.

HANNAH   Glimmers.

SISTER ELLA CHAPTER   Even the stone and brick it just glimmers and glitters

5   like heaven in the sunshine. Such a nice view you get, perched up on a
    canyon rim. Some kind of beautiful place.

HANNAH   It's just Salt Lake, and you're selling the house *for* me, not *to* me.

---

7. As the headquarters of the LDS Church, Salt Lake City contains an enormous temple and
many church-related buildings.

SISTER ELLA CHAPTER   I like to work up an enthusiasm for my properties.

HANNAH   Just get me a good price.

10   SISTER ELLA CHAPTER   Well, the market's off.

HANNAH   At least fifty.

SISTER ELLA CHAPTER   Forty'd be more like it.

HANNAH   Fifty.

SISTER ELLA CHAPTER   Wish you'd wait a bit.

15   HANNAH   Well I can't.

SISTER ELLA CHAPTER   Wish you would. You're about the only friend I got.

HANNAH   Oh well now.

SISTER ELLA CHAPTER   Know why I decided to like you? I decided to like you
'cause you're the only unfriendly Mormon I ever met.

20   HANNAH   Your wig is crooked.

SISTER ELLA CHAPTER   Fix it.

[HANNAH *straightens* SISTER ELLA's *wig.*]

SISTER ELLA CHAPTER   New York City. All they got there is tiny rooms.
I always thought: People ought to stay put. That's why I got my license to
sell real estate. It's a way of saying: Have a house! Stay put! It's a way of
25   saying traveling's no good. Plus I needed the cash. [*She takes a pack of cigarettes out of her purse, lights one, offers pack to* HANNAH.]

HANNAH   Not out here, anyone could come by.
There's been days I've stood at this ledge and thought about stepping over.
It's a hard place, Salt Lake: baked dry. Abundant energy; not much intel-
ligence. That's a combination that can wear a body out. No harm looking
30   someplace else. I don't need much room.
My sister-in-law Libby thinks there's radon gas[8] in the basement.

SISTER ELLA CHAPTER   Is there gas in the . . .

HANNAH   Of course not. Libby's a fool.

SISTER ELLA CHAPTER   'Cause I'd have to include that in the description.

35   HANNAH   There's no gas, Ella. [*Little pause.*] Give a puff. [*She takes a furtive
drag of* ELLA's *cigarette.*] Put it away now.

SISTER ELLA CHAPTER   So I guess it's goodbye.

HANNAH   You'll be all right, Ella, I wasn't ever much of a friend.

SISTER ELLA CHAPTER   I'll say something but don't laugh, OK?
40   This is the home of saints, the godliest place on earth, they say, and I
think they're right. That mean there's no evil here? No. Evil's everywhere.
Sin's everywhere. But this . . . is the spring of sweet water in the desert, the
desert flower. Every step a Believer takes away from here is a step fraught
with peril. I fear for you, Hannah Pitt, because you are my friend. Stay put.
45   This is the right home of saints.

HANNAH   Latter-day saints.

SISTER ELLA CHAPTER   Only kind left.

HANNAH   But still. Late in the day . . . for saints and everyone. That's all.
That's all.

50   Fifty thousand dollars for the house, Sister Ella Chapter; don't undersell. It's an impressive view.

---

8. A naturally occurring radioactive gas that can cause lung cancer.

Act 3: Not-Yet-Conscious, Forward Dawning

[*January 1986*]

Scene 1

[*Late night, three days after the end of Act 2. The stage is completely dark.* PRIOR *is in bed in his apartment, having a nightmare. He wakes up, sits up, and switches on a nightlight. He looks at his clock. Seated by the table near the bed is a man dressed in the clothing of a 13th-century British squire.*]

PRIOR [*terrified*]   Who are you?

PRIOR 1   My name is Prior Walter.

      [*Pause.*]

PRIOR   My name is Prior Walter.

PRIOR 1   I know that.

5 PRIOR   Explain.

PRIOR 1   You're alive. I'm not. We have the same name. What do you want me to explain?

PRIOR   A ghost?

PRIOR 1   An ancestor.

10 PRIOR   Not *the* Prior Walter? The Bayeux tapestry Prior Walter?

PRIOR 1   His great-great grandson. The fifth of the name.

PRIOR   I'm the thirty-fourth, I think.

PRIOR 1   Actually the thirty-second.

PRIOR   Not according to Mother.

15 PRIOR 1   She's including the two bastards, then; I say leave them out. I say no room for bastards. The little things you swallow . . .

PRIOR   Pills.

PRIOR 1   Pills. For the pestilence. I too . . .

PRIOR   Pestilence. . . . You too what?

20 PRIOR 1   The pestilence[9] in my time was much worse than now. Whole villages of empty houses. You could look outdoors and see Death walking in the morning, dew dampening the ragged hem of his black robe. Plain as I see you now.

PRIOR   You died of the plague.

25 PRIOR 1   The spotty monster. Like you, alone.

PRIOR   I'm not alone.

PRIOR 1   You have no wife, no children.

PRIOR   I'm gay.

PRIOR 1   So? Be gay, dance in your altogether for all I care, what's that to do
30 with not having children?

PRIOR   Gay homosexual, not bonny, blithe and[1] . . . never mind.

PRIOR 1   I had twelve. When I died.

      [*The second ghost appears, this one dressed in the clothing of an elegant 17th-century Londoner.*]

PRIOR 1 [*pointing to* PRIOR 2]   And I was three years younger than him.

      [PRIOR *sees the new ghost, screams.*]

---

9. Bubonic plague, or the Black Death; it killed more than one-third of the population of Asia and Europe in the 1300s.
1. An allusion to the nursery rhyme that begins "Monday's child is fair of face"; one version ends "But the child born on the Sabbath Day / Is bonny and blithe and good and gay."

PRIOR   Oh God another one.

35 PRIOR 2   Prior Walter. Prior to you by some seventeen others.

PRIOR 1   He's counting the bastards.

PRIOR   Are we having a convention?

PRIOR 2   We've been sent to declare her fabulous incipience. They love a well-paved entrance with lots of heralds, and . . .

40 PRIOR 1   The messenger come. Prepare the way. The infinite descent, a breath in air . . .

PRIOR 2   They chose us, I suspect, because of the mortal affinities. In a family as long-descended as the Walters there are bound to be a few carried off by plague.

45 PRIOR 1   The spotty monster.

PRIOR 2   Black Jack.[2] Came from a water pump, half the city of London, can you imagine? His came from fleas. Yours, I understand, is the lamentable consequence of venery . . .

PRIOR 1   Fleas on rats, but who knew that?

50 PRIOR   Am I going to die?

PRIOR 2   We aren't allowed to discuss . . .

PRIOR 1   When you do, you don't get ancestors to help you through it. You may be surrounded by children but you die alone.

PRIOR   I'm afraid.

55 PRIOR 1   You should be. There aren't even torches, and the path's rocky, dark, and steep.

PRIOR 2   Don't alarm him. There's good news before there's bad.
     We two come to strew rose petal and palm leaf before the triumphal procession. Prophet. Seer. Revelator. It's a great honor for the family.

60 PRIOR 1   He hasn't got a family.

PRIOR 2   I meant for the Walters, for the family in the larger sense.

PRIOR [*singing*]
     All I want is a room somewhere,
     Far away from the cold night air . . . [3]

PRIOR 2 [*putting a hand on* PRIOR'*s forehead*]   Calm, calm, this is no brain
65 fever . . .

          [PRIOR *calms down, but keeps his eyes closed. The lights begin to change.*
          Distant Glorious Music.]

PRIOR 1 [*low chant*]
     Adonai, Adonai,
     Olam ha-yichud,
     Zefirot, Zazahot,
     Ha-adam, ha-gadol[4]
70   Daughter of Light,

2. Another name for bubonic plague. The worst epidemic to devastate London killed up to 100,000, or one-fifth of the city's population, in 1665–66.
3. The opening lines of "Wouldn't It Be Loverly?"—a song from Alan Jay Lerner and Frederick Loewe's musical *My Fair Lady* (1956).
4. Hebrew terms associated with the Kabbalah, a tradition of mystical interpretation of the Hebrew Bible, though *Adonai* is a com-

mon way of referring to the Lord. *Olam ha-yichud*: the world of unification (i.e., unified by God); *Zefirot*: the divine emanations that represent the aspects of God visible in the world (usually *sefirot*); *Zazahot*: the three "brightnesses" (*Tzachtzachot*, often called the "splendors") that precede and govern the emanations of the sefirot; *Ha-adam, ha-gadol*: the heavenly man (literally, "the great man"; see Joshua 14.15).

Daughter of Splendors,
Fluor! Phosphor!
Lumen! Candle!

PRIOR 2 [*simultaneously*]
75 Even now,
From the mirror-bright halls of heaven,
Across the cold and lifeless infinity of space,
The Messenger comes
Trailing orbs of light,
Fabulous, incipient,
80 Oh Prophet,
To you . . .

PRIOR 1 and PRIOR 2
Prepare, prepare,
The Infinite Descent,
A breath, a feather,
85 Glory to . . .
[*They vanish.*]

Scene 2

[*The next day. Split scene:* LOUIS *and* BELIZE *in a coffee shop.* PRIOR *is at the outpatient clinic at the hospital with* EMILY, *the nurse; she has him on a pentamidine[5] IV drip.*]

LOUIS Why has democracy succeeded in America? Of course by succeeded I mean comparatively, not literally, not in the present, but what makes for the prospect of some sort of radical democracy spreading outward and growing up? Why does the power that was once so carefully preserved at
5 the top of the pyramid by the original framers of the Constitution seem drawn inexorably downward and outward in spite of the best effort of the Right to stop this? I mean it's the really hard thing about being Left in this country, the American Left can't help but trip over all these petrified little fetishes: freedom, that's the worst; you know, *Jeane Kirkpatrick*[6] for God's
10 sake will go on and on about freedom and so what does that mean, the word freedom, when she talks about it, or human rights; you have Bush[7] talking about human rights, and so what are these people talking about, they might as well be talking about the mating habits of Venusians, these people don't begin to know what, ontologically, freedom is or human rights,
15 like they see these bourgeois property-based Rights-of-Man-type rights[8] but that's not enfranchisement, not democracy, not what's implicit, what's potential within the idea, not the idea with blood in it. That's just liberalism, the worst kind of liberalism, really, bourgeois tolerance, and what I

---

5. Pentamidine isethionate, a drug that fights AIDS-related pneumonia.
6. An American professor of political science (1926–2006), selected by Reagan to be U.S. ambassador to the United Nations (1981–85); she criticized the Carter administration's emphasis on human rights, arguing for U.S. support of authoritarian regimes that oppose revolutionary totalitarian (Commu-

nist) regimes.
7. George H. W. Bush (b. 1924), vice president under Ronald Reagan (1981–89) and president (1989–93).
8. An allusion to the property-based political theory of the British philosopher John Locke (1632–1704), which influenced the framers of the U.S. Constitution.

think is that what AIDS shows us is the limits of tolerance, that it's not
20 enough to be tolerated, because when the shit hits the fan you find out
how much tolerance is worth. Nothing. And underneath all the tolerance is
intense, passionate hatred.

BELIZE Uh huh.

LOUIS Well don't you think that's true?

25 BELIZE Uh huh. It is.

LOUIS *Power* is the object, not being tolerated. Fuck assimilation. But I
mean in spite of all this the thing about America, I think, is that ultimately
we're different from every other nation on earth, in that, with people here
of every race, we can't. . . . Ultimately what defines us isn't race, but poli-
30 tics. Not like any European country where there's an insurmountable fact
of a kind of racial, or ethnic, monopoly, or monolith, like all Dutchmen, I
mean Dutch people, are well, Dutch, and the Jews of Europe were never
Europeans, just a small problem. Facing the monolith. But here there are
so many small problems, it's really just a collection of small problems, the
35 monolith is missing. Oh, I mean, of course I suppose there's the monolith
of White America. White Straight Male America.

BELIZE Which is not unimpressive, even among monoliths.

LOUIS Well, no, but when the race thing gets taken care of, and I don't mean
to minimalize how major it is, I mean I know it is, this is a really, really
40 incredibly racist country but it's like, well, the British. I mean, all these
blue-eyed pink people. And it's just weird, you know, I mean I'm not all that
Jewish-looking, or . . . well, maybe I am but, you know, in New York, everyone is . . . well, not everyone, but so many are but so but in England, in
London I walk into bars and I feel like Sid the Yid, you know I mean like
45 Woody Allen in *Annie Hall*, with the payess and the gabardine coat,[9] like
never, never anywhere so much—I mean, not actively despised, not like
they're Germans, who I think are still terribly anti-Semitic, and racist too,
I mean black-racist, they pretend otherwise but, anyway, in London, there's
just . . . and at one point I met this black gay guy from Jamaica who talked
50 with a lilt but he said his family'd been living in London since before the
Civil War—the American one[1]—and how the English never let him forget
for a minute that he wasn't blue-eyed and pink and I said yeah, me too,
these people are anti-Semites and he said yeah but the British Jews have
the clothing business all sewed up and blacks there can't get a foothold.
55 And it was an incredibly awkward moment of just . . . I mean here we were,
in this bar that was gay but it was a *pub*, you know, the beams and the plaster and those horrible little, like, two-day-old fish and egg sandwiches—
and just so British, so *old*, and I felt, well, there's no way out of this
because both of us are, right now, too much immersed in this history, hope
60 is dissolved in the sheer age of this place, where race is what counts and
there's no real hope of change—it's the racial destiny of the Brits that matters to them, not their political destiny, whereas in America . . .

BELIZE Here in America race doesn't count.

---

9. In *Annie Hall* (1977), directed by and starring Allen (b. 1935), a Jew born in New York
City, Allen's character imagines that his girlfriend's midwestern family sees him as a
Hasid, wearing the tight-woven wool coat and

payess (side curls; Yiddish) characteristic of
that ultraorthodox Jewish sect. *Yid:* Jew
(pejorative).
1. That is, not the English Civil War
(1642–48).

LOUIS   No, no, that's not . . . I mean you *can't* be hearing that . . .

65 BELIZE   I . . .

LOUIS   It's—look, race, yes, but ultimately race here is a political question, right? Racists just try to use race here as a tool in a political struggle. It's not really about race. Like the spiritualists try to use that stuff, are you enlightened, are you centered, channeled, whatever, this reaching out for a
70 spiritual past in a country where no indigenous spirits exist—only the Indians, I mean Native American spirits and we killed them off so now, there are no gods here, no ghosts and spirits in America, there are no angels in America, no spiritual past, no racial past, there's only the political, and the decoys and the ploys to maneuver around the inescapable battle of politics,
75 the shifting downwards and outwards of political power to the people . . .

BELIZE   POWER to the People![2] AMEN! [*Looking at his watch*] OH MY GOODNESS! Will you look at the time, I gotta . . .

LOUIS   Do you. . . . You think this is, what, racist or naive or something?

BELIZE   Well it's certainly *something*. Look, I just remembered I have an
80 appointment . . .

LOUIS   What? I mean I really don't want to, like, speak from some position of privilege and . . .

BELIZE   I'm sitting here, thinking, eventually he's *got* to run out of steam, so I let you rattle on and on saying about maybe seven or eight things I find
85 really offensive.

LOUIS   What?

BELIZE   But I know you, Louis, and I know the guilt fueling this peculiar tirade is obviously already swollen bigger than your hemorrhoids.

LOUIS   I don't have hemorrhoids.

90 BELIZE   I hear different. May I finish?

LOUIS   Yes, but I don't have hemorrhoids.

BELIZE   So finally, when I . . .

LOUIS   Prior told you, he's an asshole, he shouldn't have . . .

BELIZE   You promised, Louis. Prior is not a subject.

95 LOUIS   You brought him up.

BELIZE   I brought up hemorrhoids.

LOUIS   So it's indirect. Passive-aggressive.

BELIZE   Unlike, I suppose, banging me over the head with your theory that America doesn't have a race problem.

100 LOUIS   Oh be fair I never said that.

BELIZE   Not exactly, but . . .

LOUIS   I said . . .

BELIZE   . . . but it was close enough, because if it'd been that blunt I'd've just walked out and . . .

105 LOUIS   You deliberately misinterpreted! I . . .

BELIZE   Stop interrupting! I haven't been able to . . .

LOUIS   Just let me . . .

BELIZE   NO! What, *talk*? You've been running your mouth nonstop since I got here, yaddadda yaddadda blah blah blah, up the hill, down the hill,
110 playing with your MONOLITH . . .

---

2. A slogan of the 1960s, associated both with student protesters and with the militant Black Panthers.

LOUIS [*overlapping*] Well, you could have joined in at any time instead of . . .

BELIZE [*continuing over* LOUIS] . . . and girlfriend it is truly an *awesome* spectacle but I got better things to do with my time than sit here listening
115 to this racist bullshit just because I feel sorry for you that . . .

LOUIS I am not a racist!

BELIZE Oh come on . . .

LOUIS So maybe I am a racist but . . .

BELIZE Oh I really hate that! It's no fun picking on you Louis; you're so
120 guilty, it's like throwing darts at a glob of jello, there's no satisfying hits, just quivering, the darts just blop in and vanish.

LOUIS I just think when you are discussing lines of oppression it gets very complicated and . . .

BELIZE Oh is that a fact? You know, we black drag queens have a rather inti-
125 mate knowledge of the complexity of the lines of . . .

LOUIS *Ex*–black drag queen.

BELIZE Actually ex-ex.

LOUIS You're doing drag again?

BELIZE I don't . . . Maybe. I don't have to tell you. Maybe.

130 LOUIS I think it's sexist.

BELIZE I didn't ask you.

LOUIS Well it is. The gay community, I think, has to adopt the same attitude towards drag as black women have to take towards black women blues singers.

135 BELIZE Oh my we *are* walking dangerous tonight.

LOUIS Well, it's all internalized oppression, right, I mean the masochism, the stereotypes, the . . .

BELIZE Louis, are you deliberately trying to make me hate you?

LOUIS No, I . . .

140 BELIZE I mean, are you deliberately transforming yourself into an arro-gant, sexual-political Stalinist-slash-racist flag-waving thug for my benefit?

[*Pause.*]

LOUIS You know what I think?

BELIZE What?

145 LOUIS You hate me because I'm a Jew.

BELIZE I'm leaving.

LOUIS It's true.

BELIZE You have no basis except your . . .

    Louis, it's good to know you haven't changed; you are still an honorary
150 citizen of the Twilight Zone,[3] and after your pale, pale white polemics on behalf of racial insensitivity you have a flaming *fuck* of a lot of nerve calling me an anti-Semite. Now I really gotta go.

LOUIS You called me Lou the Jew.

BELIZE That was a joke.

155 LOUIS I didn't think it was funny. It was hostile.

BELIZE It was three years ago.

LOUIS So?

BELIZE You just called yourself Sid the Yid.

---

3. That is, in the fantasy world of *The Twilight Zone* (1959–64), Rod Serling's television series.

LOUIS   That's not the same thing.

160 BELIZE   Sid the Yid is different from Lou the Jew.

LOUIS   Yes.

BELIZE   Someday you'll have to explain that to me, but right now . . .
You hate me because you hate black people.

LOUIS   I do not. But I do think most black people are anti-Semitic.

165 BELIZE   "Most black people." *That's* racist, Louis, and *I* think most Jews . . .

LOUIS   Louis Farrakhan.[4]

BELIZE   Ed Koch.[5]

LOUIS   Jesse Jackson.[6]

BELIZE   Jackson. Oh really, Louis, this is . . .

170 LOUIS   Hymietown! Hymietown!

BELIZE   Louis, you voted for Jesse Jackson. You send checks to the Rainbow
Coalition.

LOUIS   I'm ambivalent. The checks bounced.

BELIZE   All your checks bounce, Louis; you're ambivalent about everything.

175 LOUIS   What's that supposed to mean?

BELIZE   You may be dumber than shit but I refuse to believe you can't figure
it out. Try.

LOUIS   I was never ambivalent about Prior. I love him. I do. I really do.

BELIZE   Nobody said different.

180 LOUIS   Love and ambivalence are . . . Real love isn't ambivalent.

BELIZE   "Real love isn't ambivalent." I'd swear that's a line from my favorite
bestselling paperback novel, *In Love with the Night Mysterious*,[7] except I
don't think you ever read it.

[*Pause.*]

LOUIS   I never read it, no.

185 BELIZE   You ought to. Instead of spending the rest of your life trying to get
through *Democracy in America*.[8] It's about this white woman whose Daddy
owns a plantation in the Deep South in the years before the Civil War—the
American one—and her name is Margaret, and she's in love with her
Daddy's number-one slave, and his name is Thaddeus, and she's married
190 but her white slave-owner husband has AIDS: Antebellum Insufficiently
Developed Sexorgans. And there's a lot of hot stuff going down when Margaret and Thaddeus can catch a spare torrid ten under the cotton-picking
moon, and then of course the Yankees come, and they set the slaves free,
and the slaves string up old Daddy, and so on. Historical fiction. Some-
195 where in there I recall Margaret and Thaddeus find the time to discuss the

4. A black religious leader (b. 1933), who in 1977 became leader of the Nation of Islam (Black Muslims); beginning in the 1980s, he received public censure for statements viewed as anti-Semitic and antiwhite.

5. Jewish New York politician (1924–2013); though popular as mayor (1978–89), early in his administration he angered black political leaders by reorganizing the city's poverty pro-grams, and in the 1980s he became a vocal critic of Farrakhan and Jesse Jackson.

6. A black civil rights leader (b. 1941), who ran for president in 1984 and 1988; the 1984 rev-elation that he had called New York "Hymie-

town," together with his association—soon disavowed—with Farrakhan, damaged his rep-utation with Jews. After the 1984 campaign, he turned his informal "rainbow coalition" of minorities into a national social justice organization.

7. A line from Cole Porter's 1948 song "So in Love" (whose refrain begins "So taunt me and hurt me, / Deceive me, desert me, / I'm yours 'til I die"); no such novel exists.

8. Alexis de Tocqueville's classic study of Americans and their system of government (2 vols., 1835–40).

nature of love; her face is reflecting the flames of the burning plantation— you know, the way white people do—and his black face is dark in the night and she says to him, "Thaddeus, real love isn't ever ambivalent."

[*Little pause.* EMILY *enters and turns off IV drip.*]

BELIZE   Thaddeus looks at her; he's contemplating her thesis; and he isn't
200   sure he agrees.

EMILY   [*removing IV drip from* PRIOR'S *arm*]   Treatment number . . . [*Consulting chart*] four.

PRIOR   Pharmaceutical miracle. Lazarus[9] breathes again.

LOUIS   Is he. . . . How bad is he?

205   BELIZE   You want the laundry list?

EMILY   Shirt off, let's check the . . .

[PRIOR *takes his shirt off. She examines his lesions.*]

BELIZE   There's the weight problem and the shit problem and the morale problem.

EMILY   Only six. That's good. Pants.

[*He drops his pants. He's naked. She examines.*]

210   BELIZE   And. He thinks he's going crazy.

EMILY   Looking good. What else?

PRIOR   Ankles sore and swollen, but the leg's better. The nausea's mostly gone with the little orange pills. BM's pure liquid but not bloody any more, for now, my eye doctor says everything's OK, for now, my dentist says
215   "Yuck!" when he sees my fuzzy tongue, and now he wears little condoms on his thumb and forefinger. And a mask. So what? My dermatologist is in Hawaii and my mother . . . well leave my mother out of it. Which is usually where my mother is, out of it. My glands are like walnuts, my weight's holding steady for week two, and a friend died two days ago of bird tuber-
220   culosis;[1] bird tuberculosis; that scared me and I didn't go to the funeral today because he was an Irish Catholic and it's probably open casket and I'm afraid of . . . something, the bird TB or seeing him or . . . So I guess I'm doing OK. Except for of course I'm going nuts.

EMILY   We ran the toxoplasmosis series[2] and there's no indication . . .

225   PRIOR   I know, I know, but I feel like something terrifying is on its way, you know, like a missile from outer space, and it's plummeting down towards the earth, and I'm ground zero, and . . . I am generally known where I am known as one cool, collected queen. And I am ruffled.

EMILY   There's really nothing to worry about. I think that shochen bamro-
230   mim hamtzeh menucho nechono al kanfey haschino.[3]

PRIOR   What?

EMILY   Everything's fine. Bemaalos k'doshim ut'horim kezohar horokeea mazhirim . . .

---

9. Jesus's resurrection of Lazarus from the dead is described in John 11.1–44.

1. A hard-to-treat form of tuberculosis that is common in AIDS patients.

2. A series of tests for toxoplasmosis, one of the infections commonly associated with AIDS; it often affects the brain.

3. This line begins transliterated Hebrew taken from the prayer traditionally recited at funerals for the soul of the departed; the translation is "[God, full of compassion,] who dwells on high, grant true rest upon the wings of your Divine Presence, in the exalted spheres of the holy and pure, who shine as the brightness of the heavens, to the soul of Prior, who has gone to his eternal rest, for charity has been donated in remembrance of his soul."

PRIOR   Oh I don't understand what you're . . .

235 EMILY   Es nishmas Prior sheholoch leolomoh, baavur shenodvoo z'dokoh b'ad hazkoras nishmosoh.

PRIOR   Why are you doing that?! Stop it! Stop it!

EMILY   Stop what?

PRIOR   You were just . . . weren't you just speaking in Hebrew or something.

240 EMILY   *Hebrew?* [*Laughs.*] I'm basically Italian-American. No. I didn't speak in Hebrew.

PRIOR   Oh no, oh God please I really think I . . .

EMILY   Look, I'm sorry, I have a waiting room full of . . . I think you're one of the lucky ones, you'll live for years, probably—you're pretty healthy for
245 someone with no immune system. Are you seeing someone? Loneliness is a danger. A therapist?

PRIOR   No, I don't need to see anyone, I just . . .

EMILY   Well think about it. You aren't going crazy. You're just under a lot of stress. No wonder . . . [*She starts to write in his chart.*]

> [*Suddenly there is an astonishing blaze of light, a huge chord sounded by a gigantic choir, and a great book with steel pages mounted atop a molten-red pillar pops up from the stage floor. The book opens; there is a large Aleph[4] inscribed on its pages, which bursts into flames. Immediately the book slams shut and disappears instantly under the floor as the lights become normal again.* EMILY *notices none of this, writing.* PRIOR *is agog.*]

250 EMILY   [*laughing, exiting*]   Hebrew . . .

> [PRIOR *flees.*]

LOUIS   Help me.

BELIZE   I beg your pardon?

LOUIS   You're a nurse, give me something, I . . . don't know what to do any more, I . . . Last week at work I screwed up the Xerox machine like perma-
255 nently and so I . . . then I tripped on the subway steps and my glasses broke and I cut my forehead, here, see, and now I can't see much and my forehead . . . it's like the Mark of Cain,[5] stupid, right, but it won't heal and every morning I see it and I think, Biblical things, Mark of Cain, Judas Iscariot and his silver and his noose,[6] people who . . . in betraying what
260 they love betray what's truest in themselves, I feel . . . nothing but cold for myself, just cold, and every night I miss him, I miss him so much but then . . . those sores, and the smell and . . . where I thought it was going. . . . I could be . . . I could be sick too, maybe I'm sick too. I don't know.
265 Belize. Tell him I love him. Can you do that?

BELIZE   I've thought about it for a very long time, and I still don't understand what love is. Justice is simple. Democracy is simple. Those things are unambivalent. But love is very hard. And it goes bad for you if you violate the hard law of love.

270 LOUIS   I'm dying.

---

4. The first letter of the Hebrew alphabet.
5. According to Genesis (4.1–16), the first son of Adam and Eve, whose forehead was marked by God after he killed Abel, his brother.

6. For the story of the betrayal of Jesus by Judas Iscariot, his disciple, for thirty pieces of silver, and Judas's subsequent suicide by hanging, see Matthew 26.14–15, 27.3–5.

BELIZE   He's dying. You just wish you were.

Oh cheer up, Louis. Look at that heavy sky out there.

LOUIS   Purple.

BELIZE   *Purple?* Boy, what kind of a homosexual are you, anyway? That's not
275 purple, Mary, that color up there is [*Very grand*] mauve.

All day today it's felt like Thanksgiving. Soon, this . . . ruination will be
blanketed white. You can smell it—can you smell it?

LOUIS   Smell what?

BELIZE   Softness, compliance, forgiveness, grace.

280 LOUIS   No . . .

BELIZE   I can't help you learn that. I can't help you, Louis. You're not my
business. [*He exits.*]

[LOUIS *puts his head in his hands, inadvertently touching his cut forehead.*]

LOUIS   Ow FUCK! [*He stands slowly, looks towards where* BELIZE *exited.*]
Smell what?

[*He looks both ways to be sure no one is watching, then inhales deeply, and*
285 *is surprised.*] Huh. Snow.

Scene 3

[*Same day.* HARPER *in a very white, cold place, with a brilliant blue sky
above; a delicate snowfall. She is dressed in a beautiful snowsuit. The
sound of the sea, faint.*]

HARPER   Snow! Ice! Mountains of ice! Where am I? I . . .

I feel better, I do,

I . . . feel better. There are ice crystals in my lungs, wonderful and sharp.
And the snow smells like cold, crushed peaches. And there's something . . .
5 some current of blood in the wind, how strange, it has that iron taste.

MR. LIES   Ozone.

HARPER   Ozone! Wow! Where am I?

MR. LIES   The Kingdom of Ice, the bottommost part of the world.

HARPER [*looking around, then realizing*]   Antarctica. This is Antarctica!

10 MR. LIES   Cold shelter for the shattered. No sorrow here, tears freeze.

HARPER   Antarctica, Antarctica, oh boy oh boy, LOOK at this, I . . . Wow, I
must've really snapped the tether, huh?

MR. LIES   Apparently . . .

HARPER   That's great. I want to stay here forever. Set up camp. Build things.
15 Build a city, an enormous city made up of frontier forts, dark wood and
green roofs and high gates made of pointed logs and bonfires burning on
every street corner. I should build by a river. Where are the forests?

MR. LIES   No timber here. Too cold. Ice, no trees.

HARPER   Oh details! I'm sick of details! I'll plant them and grow them. I'll live
20 off caribou fat, I'll melt it over the bonfires and drink it from long, curved
goat-horn cups. It'll be great. I want to make a new world here. So that I
never have to go home again.

MR. LIES   As long as it lasts. Ice has a way of melting . . .

HARPER   No. Forever. I can have anything I want here—maybe even com-
25 panionship, someone who has . . . desire for me. You, maybe.

MR. LIES   It's against the by-laws of the International Order of Travel Agents
to get involved with clients. Rules are rules. Anyway, I'm not the one you
really want.

HARPER There isn't anyone . . . maybe an Eskimo. Who could ice-fish for
30   food. And help me build a nest for when the baby comes.

MR. LIES There are no Eskimo in Antarctica. And you're not really pregnant.
You made that up.

HARPER Well all of this is made up. So if the snow feels cold I'm pregnant.
Right? Here, I can be pregnant. And I can have any kind of a baby I want.

35 MR. LIES This is a retreat, a vacuum, its virtue is that it lacks everything;
deep-freeze for feelings. You can be numb and safe here, that's what you
came for. Respect the delicate ecology of your delusions.

HARPER You mean like no Eskimo in Antarctica.

MR. LIES Correcto. Ice and snow, no Eskimo. Even hallucinations have laws.

40 HARPER Well then who's that?

[*The Eskimo appears.*]

MR. LIES An Eskimo.

HARPER An antarctic Eskimo. A fisher of the polar deep.

MR. LIES There's something wrong with this picture.

[*The Eskimo beckons.*]

HARPER I'm going to like this place. It's my own National Geographic Spe-
45   cial![7] Oh! Oh! [*She holds her stomach.*] I think . . . I think I felt her kicking.
Maybe I'll give birth to a baby covered with thick white fur, and that way
she won't be cold. My breasts will be full of hot cocoa so she doesn't get
chilly. And if it gets really cold, she'll have a pouch I can crawl into. Like a
marsupial. We'll mend together. That's what we'll do; we'll mend.

Scene 4

[*Same day. An abandoned lot in the South Bronx. A homeless* WOMAN *is
standing near an oil drum in which a fire is burning. Snowfall. Trash
around.* HANNAH *enters dragging two heavy suitcases.*]

HANNAH Excuse me? I said excuse me? Can you tell me where I am? Is this
Brooklyn? Do you know a Pineapple Street?[8] Is there some sort of bus or
train or . . . ?

   I'm lost, I just arrived from Salt Lake. City. Utah? I took the bus that I
5   was told to take and I got off—well it was the very last stop, so I had to get
off, and I *asked* the driver was this Brooklyn, and he nodded yes but he was
from one of those foreign countries where they think it's good manners to
nod at everything even if you have no idea what it is you're nodding at, and
in truth I think he spoke no English at all, which I think would make him
10   ineligible for employment on public transportation. The public being
English-speaking, mostly. Do you speak English?

[*The* WOMAN *nods.*]

HANNAH I was supposed to be met at the airport by my son. He didn't show
and I don't wait more than three and three-quarters hours for *anyone*. I
should have been patient, I guess, I . . . Is this . . .

15 WOMAN Bronx.

HANNAH Is that . . . The *Bronx*? Well how in the name of Heaven did I get to
the Bronx when the bus driver said . . .

7. That is, like the television programs—
mainly documentaries featuring the exploration of the natural world—produced by the
National Geographic Society since 1964.
8. A street in Brooklyn Heights, a historic
district of Brooklyn.

WOMAN [*talking to herself*]   Slurp slurp slurp will you STOP that disgusting slurping! YOU DISGUSTING SLURPING FEEDING ANIMAL! Feeding
20   yourself, just feeding yourself, what would it matter, to you or to ANYONE, if you just stopped. Feeding. And DIED?

[*Pause.*]

HANNAH   Can you just tell me where I . . .

WOMAN   Why was the Kosciuszko Bridge[9] named after a Polack?

HANNAH   I don't know what you're . . .

25   WOMAN   That was a joke.

HANNAH   Well what's the punchline?

WOMAN   I don't know.

HANNAH [*looking around desperately*]   Oh for pete's sake, is there anyone else who . . .

30   WOMAN [*again, to herself*]   Stand further off you fat loathsome whore, you can't have any more of this soup, slurp slurp slurp you animal, and the—I know you'll just go pee it all away and where will you do that? Behind what bush? It's FUCKING COLD out here and I . . .

Oh that's right, because it was supposed to have been a tunnel!
35   That's not very funny.

Have you read the prophecies of Nostradamus?[1]

HANNAH   Who?

WOMAN   Some guy I went out with once somewhere, Nostradamus. Prophet, outcast, eyes like . . . Scary shit, he . . .

40   HANNAH   Shut up. Please. Now I want you to stop jabbering for a minute and pull your wits together and tell me how to get to Brooklyn. Because you know! And you are going to tell me! Because there is no one else around to tell me and I am wet and cold and I am very angry! So I am sorry you're psychotic but just make the effort—take a deep breath—DO IT!

[HANNAH *and the* WOMAN *breathe together.*]

45   HANNAH   That's good. Now exhale.

[*They do.*]

HANNAH   Good. Now how do I get to Brooklyn?

WOMAN   Don't know. Never been. Sorry. Want some soup?

HANNAH   Manhattan? Maybe you know . . . I don't suppose you know the location of the Mormon Visitor's[2] . . .

50   WOMAN   65th and Broadway.

HANNAH   How do you . . .

WOMAN   Go there all the time. Free movies. Boring, but you can stay all day.

HANNAH   Well. . . . So how do I . . .

WOMAN   Take the D Train.[3] Next block make a right.

55   HANNAH   Thank you.

WOMAN   Oh yeah. In the new century I think we will all be insane.

---

9. A bridge that connects the Bronx and Queens (a borough that, like Brooklyn, is on Long Island); it is named for Tadeusz Kościuszko (1746–1817), a Polish military engineer who fought with distinction in America's Continental Army in the Revolutionary War.

1. Michel de Nostredame (1503–1566), a French astrologer and physician whose *Prophesies* (1555), a collection of predictions about the future, has long found a receptive audience.

2. The Mormon Visitors' Center.

3. A subway line that, in the Bronx, runs along the Grand Concourse; it extends to Brooklyn.

Scene 5

[*Same day.* JOE *and* ROY *in the study of* ROY's *brownstone.* ROY *is wearing an elegant bathrobe. He has made a considerable effort to look well. He isn't well, and he hasn't succeeded much in looking it.*]

JOE   I can't. The answer's no. I'm sorry.

ROY   Oh, well, apologies . . .

   I can't see that there's anyone asking for apologies.

      [*Pause.*]

JOE   I'm sorry, Roy.

5 ROY   Oh, well, apologies.

JOE   My wife is missing, Roy. My mother's coming from Salt Lake to . . . to help look, I guess. I'm supposed to be at the airport now, picking her up but . . . I just spent two days in a hospital, Roy, with a bleeding ulcer, I was spitting up blood.

10 ROY   Blood, huh? Look, I'm very busy here and . . .

JOE   It's just a job.

ROY   A job? A *job*? *Washington!* Dumb Utah Mormon hick shit!

JOE   Roy . . .

ROY   *WASHINGTON!* When Washington called me I was younger than you,

15   you think I said "Aw fuck no I can't go I got two fingers up my asshole and a little moral nosebleed to boot!" When Washington calls you my pretty young punk friend you go or you can go fuck yourself sideways 'cause the train has pulled out of the station, and you are *out*, nowhere, out in the cold. Fuck you, Mary Jane, get outta here.

20 JOE   Just let me . . .

ROY   Explain? Ephemera. You broke my heart. Explain that. Explain that.

JOE   I love you, Roy.

   There's so much that I want, to be . . . what you see in me, I want to be a participant in the world, in your world, Roy, I want to be capable of that,

25   I've tried, really I have but . . . I can't do this. Not because I don't believe in you, but because I believe in you so much, in what you stand for, at heart, the order, the decency. I would give anything to protect you, but . . . There are laws I can't break. It's too ingrained. It's not me. There's enough damage I've already done.

30   Maybe you were right, maybe I'm dead.

ROY   You're not dead, boy, you're a sissy.

   You love me; that's moving, I'm moved. It's nice to be loved. I warned you about her, didn't I, Joe? But you don't listen to me, why, because you say Roy is smart and Roy's a friend but Roy . . . well, he isn't nice, and you

35   wanna be nice. Right? A nice, nice man! [*Little pause*]

   You know what my greatest accomplishment was, Joe, in my life, what I am able to look back on and be proudest of? And I have helped make Presidents and unmake them and mayors and more goddam judges than anyone in NYC ever—AND several million dollars, tax-free—and what do you

40   think means the most to me?

   You ever hear of Ethel Rosenberg? Huh, Joe, huh?

JOE   Well, yeah, I guess I . . . Yes.

ROY   Yes. Yes. You have heard of Ethel Rosenberg. Yes. Maybe you even read about her in the history books.

45   If it wasn't for me, Joe, Ethel Rosenberg would be alive today, writing some personal-advice column for *Ms.* magazine.[4] She isn't. Because during the trial, Joe, I was on the phone every day, talking with the judge . . .

JOE   Roy . . .

ROY   Every day, doing what I do best, talking on the telephone, making sure
50   that timid Yid nebbish[5] on the bench did his duty to America, to history. That sweet unprepossessing woman, two kids, boo-hoo-hoo, reminded us all of our little Jewish mamas—she came this close to getting life; I pleaded till I wept to put her in the chair.[6] Me. I did that. I would have fucking pulled the switch if they'd have let me. Why? Because I fucking hate trai-
55   tors. Because I fucking hate communists. Was it legal? Fuck legal. Am I a nice man? Fuck nice. They say terrible things about me in the *Nation*.[7] Fuck the *Nation*. You want to be Nice, or you want to be Effective? Make the law, or subject to it. Choose. Your wife chose. A week from today, she'll be back. SHE knows how to get what SHE wants. Maybe I ought to send
60   *her* to Washington.

JOE   I don't believe you.

ROY   Gospel.

JOE   You can't possibly mean what you're saying.

    Roy, you were the Assistant United States Attorney on the Rosenberg
65   case, ex-parte[8] communication with the judge during the trial would be . . . censurable, at least, probably conspiracy and . . . in a case that resulted in execution, it's . . .

ROY   What? Murder?

JOE   You're not well is all.

70 ROY   What do you mean, not well? Who's not well?

       [*Pause.*]

JOE   You said . . .

ROY   No I didn't. I said what?

JOE   Roy, you have cancer.

ROY   No I don't.

       [*Pause.*]

75 JOE   You told me you were dying.

ROY   What the fuck are you talking about, Joe? I never said that. I'm in per-
    fect health. There's not a goddam thing wrong with me. [*He smiles.*]
    Shake?

       [JOE *hesitates. He holds out his hand to* ROY. ROY *pulls* JOE *into a close,*
       strong clinch.]

ROY   [*more to himself than to* JOE]   It's OK that you hurt me because I love
80   you, baby Joe. That's why I'm so rough on you.

       [ROY *releases* JOE. JOE *backs away a step or two.*]

---

4. An American feminist magazine that appeared monthly from 1972 to 1987; it resumed publication in 2001.
5. A nonentity, a loser (Yiddish); the presiding judge in the Rosenbergs' trial was Irving R. Kaufman (1910–1992).
6. The electric chair, used to execute the Rosenbergs.

7. A left-liberal American journal of culture and politics, published weekly since 1865.
8. In law, proceedings conducted in the absence of and without notice to one party, a practice that is normally prohibited (literally, "from [one] side"; Latin); see Playwright's Notes.

ROY   Prodigal son.[9] The world will wipe its dirty hands all over you.

JOE   It already has, Roy.

ROY   Now go.

> [ROY *shoves* JOE, *hard.* JOE *turns to leave.* ROY *stops him, turns him around.*]

ROY [*smoothing* JOE'*s lapels, tenderly*]   I'll always be here, waiting for you . . .

85   [*Then again, with sudden violence, he pulls* JOE *close, violently.*] What did you want from me, what was all this, what do you want, treacherous ungrateful little . . .

> [JOE, *very close to belting* ROY, *grabs him by the front of his robe, and propels him across the length of the room. He holds* ROY *at arm's length, the other arm ready to hit.*]

ROY [*laughing softly, almost pleading to be hit*]   Transgress a little, Joseph.

> [JOE *releases* ROY.]

ROY   There are so many laws; find one you can break.

> [JOE *hesitates, then leaves, backing out. When* JOE *has gone,* ROY *doubles over in great pain, which he's been hiding throughout the scene with* JOE.]

90   ROY   Ah, Christ . . .

Andy! Andy! Get in here! Andy!

> [*The door opens, but it isn't* ANDY. *A small Jewish* WOMAN *dressed modestly in a fifties hat and coat stands in the doorway. The room darkens.*]

ROY   Who the fuck are you? The new nurse?

> [*The figure in the doorway says nothing. She stares at* ROY. *A pause.* ROY *looks at her carefully, gets up, crosses to her. He crosses back to the chair, sits heavily.*]

ROY   Aw, fuck. Ethel.

ETHEL ROSENBERG [*her manner is friendly, her voice is ice-cold*]   You don't

95   look good, Roy.

ROY   Well, Ethel. I don't feel good.

ETHEL ROSENBERG   But you lost a lot of weight. That suits you. You were heavy back then. Zaftig, mit[1] hips.

ROY   I haven't been that heavy since 1960. We were all heavier back then,

100   before the body thing started. Now I look like a skeleton. They stare.

ETHEL ROSENBERG   The shit's really hit the fan, huh, Roy?

> [*Little pause.* ROY *nods.*]

ETHEL ROSENBERG   Well the fun's just started.

ROY   What is this, Ethel, Halloween? You trying to scare me?

> [ETHEL *says nothing.*]

ROY   Well you're wasting your time! I'm scarier than you any day of the week!

105   So beat it, Ethel! BOOO! BETTER DEAD THAN RED![2] Somebody trying to shake me up! HAH HAH! From the throne of God in heaven to the belly of hell, you can all fuck yourselves and then go jump in the lake because I'M NOT AFRAID OF YOU OR DEATH OR HELL OR ANYTHING!

---

9. That is, the son who squanders his inheritance but is joyfully welcomed back home (see Luke 15.11–32).

1. Plump, with (Yiddish); *zaftig* usually means "buxom."

2. A slogan used in the 1950s to denounce Communists ("Reds") and leftists.

ETHEL ROSENBERG   Be seeing you soon, Roy. Julius[3] sends his regards.

110 ROY   Yeah, well send this to Julius!

> [*He flips the bird in her direction,*[4] *stands and moves towards her. Half-way across the room he slumps to the floor, breathing laboriously, in pain.*]

ETHEL ROSENBERG   You're a very sick man, Roy.

ROY   Oh God . . . ANDY!

ETHEL ROSENBERG   Hmmm. He doesn't hear you, I guess. We should call the ambulance.

115 [*She goes to the phone.*] Hah! Buttons! Such things they got now.

> What do I dial, Roy?

> [*Pause.* ROY *looks at her, then.*]

ROY   911.

ETHEL ROSENBERG [*dials the phone*]   It sings!

> [*Imitating dial tones*] La la la . . .

120 Huh.

> Yes, you should please send an ambulance to the home of Mister Roy Cohn, the famous lawyer.

> What's the address, Roy?

ROY [*a beat, then*]   244 East 87th.

125 ETHEL ROSENBERG   244 East 87th Street. No apartment number, he's got the whole building.

> My name? [*A beat*] Ethel Greenglass Rosenberg.

> [*Small smile*] Me? No I'm not related to Mr. Cohn. An old friend. [*She hangs up.*]

> They said a minute.

130 ROY   I have all the time in the world.

ETHEL ROSENBERG   You're immortal.

ROY   I'm immortal. Ethel. [*He forces himself to stand.*]

> I have *forced* my way into history. I ain't never gonna die.

ETHEL ROSENBERG [*a little laugh, then*]   History is about to crack wide open.

135 Millennium approaches.

Scene 6

> [*Late that night.* PRIOR's *bedroom.* PRIOR 1 *watching* PRIOR *in bed, who is staring back at him, terrified. Tonight* PRIOR 1 *is dressed in weird alchemical robes and hat over his historical clothing and he carries a long palm-leaf bundle.*]

PRIOR 1   Tonight's the night! Aren't you excited? Tonight she arrives! Right through the roof! Ha-adam, Ha-gadol . . .

PRIOR 2 [*appearing, similarly attired*]   Lumen! Phosphor! Fluor! Candle! An unending billowing of scarlet and . . .

5 PRIOR   Look. Garlic. A mirror. Holy water. A crucifix.[5] FUCK OFF! Get the fuck out of my room! GO!

PRIOR 1 [*to* PRIOR 2]   Hard as a hickory knob, I'll bet.

PRIOR 2   We all tumesce when they approach. We wax full, like moons.

PRIOR 1   Dance.

---

3. Julius Rosenberg (1918–1953), Ethel's husband.
4. Gives her the finger.
5. All items believed to deter vampires.

10 PRIOR   Dance?

PRIOR 1   Stand up, dammit, give us your hands, dance!

PRIOR 2   Listen . . .

[*A lone oboe begins to play a little dance tune.*]

PRIOR 2   Delightful sound. Care to dance?

PRIOR   Please leave me alone, please just let me sleep . . .

15 PRIOR 2   Ah, he wants someone familiar. A partner who knows his steps. [*To* PRIOR] Close your eyes. Imagine . . .

PRIOR   I don't . . .

PRIOR 2   Hush. Close your eyes.

[PRIOR *does.*]

PRIOR 2   Now open them.

[PRIOR *does.* LOUIS *appears. He looks gorgeous. The music builds gradually into a full-blooded, romantic dance tune.*]

20 PRIOR   Lou.

LOUIS   Dance with me.

PRIOR   I can't, my leg, it hurts at night . . .

Are you . . . a ghost, Lou?

LOUIS   No. Just spectral. Lost to myself. Sitting all day on cold park benches.

25   Wishing I could be with you. Dance with me, babe . . .

[PRIOR *stands up. The leg stops hurting. They begin to dance. The music is beautiful.*]

PRIOR 1   [*to* PRIOR 2]   Hah. Now I see why he's got no children. He's a sodomite.

PRIOR 2   Oh be quiet, you medieval gnome, and let them dance.

PRIOR 1   I'm not interfering, I've done my bit. Hooray, hooray, the messenger's

30   come, now I'm blowing off. I don't like it here.

[PRIOR 1 *vanishes.*]

PRIOR 2   The twentieth century. Oh dear, the world has gotten so terribly, terribly old.

[PRIOR 2 *vanishes.* LOUIS *and* PRIOR *waltz happily. Lights fade back to normal.* LOUIS *vanishes.*

PRIOR *dances alone.*

Then suddenly, the sound of wings fills the room.]

Scene 7

[*Split scene:* PRIOR *alone in his apartment;* LOUIS *alone in the park. Again, a sound of beating wings.*]

PRIOR   Oh don't come in here don't come in . . . LOUIS!!

No. My name is Prior Walter, I am . . . the scion of an ancient line, I am . . . abandoned I . . . no, my name is . . . is . . . Prior and I live . . . *here and now,* and . . . in the dark, in the dark, the Recording Angel opens its

5   hundred eyes and snaps the spine of the Book of Life[6] and . . . hush! Hush! I'm talking nonsense, I . . .

---

6. In Jewish tradition, the symbolic book in which all who lived are sealed each year on the Day of Atonement, Yom Kippur; in the New Testament, it contains the names of those who will not be damned on Judgment Day (Revelation 13.8, 20.12–15).

No more mad scene, hush, hush . . .

> [LOUIS *in the park on a bench.* JOE *approaches, stands at a distance. They stare at each other, then* LOUIS *turns away.*]

LOUIS   Do you know the story of Lazarus?

JOE   Lazarus?

10 LOUIS   Lazarus. I can't remember what happens, exactly.

JOE   I don't . . . Well, he was dead, Lazarus, and Jesus breathed life into him. He brought him back from death.

LOUIS   Come here often?

JOE   No. Yes. Yes.

15 LOUIS   Back from the dead. You believe that really happened?

JOE   I don't know any more what I believe.

LOUIS   This is quite a coincidence. Us meeting.

JOE   I followed you.

> From work. I . . . followed you here.

> [*Pause.*]

20 LOUIS   You followed me.

> You probably saw me that day in the washroom and thought: there's a sweet guy, sensitive, cries for friends in trouble.

JOE   Yes.

LOUIS   You thought maybe I'll cry for you.

25 JOE   Yes.

LOUIS   Well I fooled you. Crocodile tears. Nothing . . . [*He touches his heart, shrugs.*]

> [JOE *reaches tentatively to touch* LOUIS's *face.*]

LOUIS [*pulling back*]   What are you doing? Don't do that.

JOE [*withdrawing his hand*]   Sorry. I'm sorry.

LOUIS   I'm . . . just not . . . I think, if you touch me, your hand might fall off
30 or something. Worse things have happened to people who have touched me.

JOE   Please.

> Oh, boy . . .

> Can I . . .

35 I . . . want . . . to touch you. Can I please just touch you . . . um, here?
[*He puts his hand on one side of* LOUIS's *face. He holds it there.*]

> I'm going to hell for doing this.

LOUIS   Big deal. You think it could be any worse than New York City?

> [*He puts his hand on* JOE's *hand. He takes* JOE's *hand away from his face, holds it for a moment, then.*] Come on.

JOE   Where?

40 LOUIS   Home. With me.

JOE   This makes no sense. I mean I don't know you.

LOUIS   Likewise.

JOE   And what you do know about me you don't like.

LOUIS   The Republican stuff?

45 JOE   Yeah, well for starters.

LOUIS   I don't not like that. I *hate* that.

JOE   So why on earth should we . . .

> [LOUIS *goes to* JOE *and kisses him.*]

LOUIS   Strange bedfellows. I don't know. I never made it with one of the damned before.

50   I would really rather not have to spend tonight alone.

JOE   I'm a pretty terrible person, Louis.

LOUIS   Lou.

JOE   No, I really really am. I don't think I deserve being loved.

LOUIS   There? See? We already have a lot in common.

[LOUIS *stands, begins to walk away. He turns, looks back at* JOE. JOE *follows. They exit.*]

[PRIOR *listens. At first no sound, then once again, the sound of beating wings, frighteningly near.*]

55 PRIOR   That sound, that sound, it. . . . What is that, like birds or something, like a *really* big bird, I'm frightened, I . . . no, no fear, find the anger, find the . . . anger, my blood is clean, my brain is fine, I can handle pressure, I am a gay man and I am used to pressure, to trouble, I am tough and strong and. . . . Oh. Oh my goodness. I . . . [*He is washed over by an intense sexual*
60   *feeling.*] Ooohhhh. . . . I'm hot, I'm . . . so . . . aw Jeez what is going on here I . . . must have a fever I . . .

[*The bedside lamp flickers wildly as the bed begins to roll forward and back. There is a deep bass creaking and groaning from the bedroom ceiling, like the timbers of a ship under immense stress, and from above a fine rain of plaster dust.*]

PRIOR   OH!

PLEASE, OH PLEASE! Something's coming in here, I'm scared, I don't like this at all, something's approaching and I . . . OH!

[*There is a great blaze of triumphal music, heralding. The light turns an extraordinary harsh, cold, pale blue, then a rich, brilliant warm golden color, then a hot, bilious green, and then finally a spectacular royal purple. Then silence.*]

65 PRIOR [*an awestruck whisper*]   God almighty . . .
       Very Steven Spielberg.[7]

[*A sound, like a plummeting meteor, tears down from very, very far above the earth, hurtling at an incredible velocity towards the bedroom; the light seems to be sucked out of the room as the projectile approaches; as the room reaches darkness, we hear a terrifying CRASH as something immense strikes earth; the whole building shudders and a part of the bedroom ceiling, lots of plaster and lathe and wiring, crashes to the floor. And then in a shower of unearthly white light, spreading great opalescent gray-silver wings, the Angel descends into the room and floats above the bed.*]

ANGEL

Greetings, Prophet;
The Great Work begins:
The Messenger has arrived.

[*Blackout.*]

End of Part One.

7. An American film director (b. 1947), known for his use of special effects in such hits as *Close Encounters of the Third Kind* (1977), *Raiders of the Lost Ark* (1981), and *E.T.: The Extraterrestrial* (1982).

DANIEL DAVID MOSES

b. 1952

W HEN the Lakota Sioux warrior chief Sitting Bull joined Buffalo Bill's Wild West show as a "show Indian" in 1884, he entered a theatrical culture that was fascinated with North America's Native, or indigenous, people. The stereotypes used to represent these people—noble savage, treacherous heathen, idealized Indian princess, loyal sidekick, vanishing primitive— have been staples of theater, film, television, and popular culture over the last two hundred years. Indigenous playwrights and theater artists, First Nations people (as they are referred to in Canada) or Native Americans (as they are referred to in the United States), have been working in the theater since the turn of the twentieth century: Cherokee dramatist Lynn Riggs's 1930 play *Green Grow the Lilacs*, for instance, was the source for the Rodgers and Hammerstein musical *Oklahoma!*, while Chickasaw storyteller and actress Te Ata performed for President Franklin Roosevelt and other heads of state during her long career. But it was not until the 1960s and 1970s that Native people on both sides of the border began organizing theater groups to challenge the stereotypical images of Indians in the mainstream media and to support the

work of Native playwrights, actors, and theater artists who have claimed the stage as a medium for their own experiences, beliefs, histories, and identities. The theater that resulted from these efforts—including the drama of First Nations playwright Daniel David Moses—challenges prevailing histories of Native/non-Native encounters, introduces new aesthetic principles and worldviews, and examines the question of Native identity in powerful and innovative ways.

Daniel David Moses, a registered Delaware (or Lenape) Indian, was born and grew up on a farm on the Six Nations Reserve, a largely Iroquoian community along the Grand River in southern Ontario ("reserves" are the Canadian equivalent of U.S. reservations). He developed a love of language from listening to the liturgy and hymns of the Anglican mission church he attended as a child and reading traditional and contemporary literature in school. He decided in high school to become a writer and pursued this vocation while earning a college degree at York University in Toronto. His earliest writing took the form of poetry, but his passion for spoken language and the interaction of multiple voices led him to playwriting as well. "Whatever idea I have . . . I have to write until the idea can be said by the body entire," he stated in a 1991 essay. "I write words that are meant to be spoken and heard, that mean what they must in the air." While completing the MFA program in creative writing at the University of British Columbia, Moses won the program's prize for playwriting in 1977, and the collection of poetry he submitted for his thesis that year included a one-act play.

Moses's exploration of Native writing and performance deepened when he moved to Toronto in the late 1970s. He volunteered with the Association for Native Development in the Performing and Visual Arts, which had been established in 1974 to support the training of Native playwrights and theater practitioners, and joined a circle of Native writers that formed around the Ojibway writer, storyteller, and Native literature activist Lenore Keeshig-Tobias. In 1982 he met Cree-born playwright Tomson Highway, who was instrumental in the founding of Native Earth Performing Arts (NEPA), Canada's most prominent Native theater company. Along with the De-ba-jeh-mu-jig Theatre Group—a Native company whose name means "storytellers" in Cree and Ojibway and which was founded in 1984 on Manitoulin Island in Lake Huron—NEPA introduced the plays of Native dramatists to Canadian audiences. Prominent among these plays were Highway's *The Rez Sisters* (1986) and *Dry Lips Oughta Move to Kapuskasing* (1989), which received widespread acclaim and helped establish First Nations drama on the international theater scene. Highway served as artistic director of NEPA from 1986 to 1992, while Moses served as co-director from 1998 to 2000.

Moses has described the writer's task as "expressing my 'self' as a twenty-first-century First Nations person, reclaiming and reviving, for myself and my circle, what is still viable in our tradition and inventing whatever else is needed." One of the Native traditions that Moses embraced was the Trickster, a figure who appears in Native folklore under such names as Coyote, Raven, Nanabush, and Weesageechak. The Trickster is a contradictory figure, marked by duplicity as well as moral

authority; both hero and fool, the Trickster teaches the lessons of life by positive and negative example. Moses's first play, *Coyote City*, which was produced by Native Earth in 1988 and nominated for the Governor General's Literary Prize in 1991, adapts the Trickster legend to contemporary Native life. It also introduces the relationship between the human and spirit worlds that Moses would return to in later plays. *Coyote City* draws upon a Nez Perce story entitled "Coyote and the Shadow People." In this story Coyote is led by a spirit guide to an open prairie, where he encounters the ghost of his wife at night in a great lodge peopled by the dead. After visiting her and the other departed souls over a series of nights, Coyote tries to bring his wife back to the real world but loses her when he disobeys the spirit guide's instructions not to embrace her. The Coyote City of Moses's play is Toronto, where the character Lena travels to rescue her lover Johnny from the spirit world in the Silver Dollar Bar, where he was killed. The family members and other characters that pursue Lena are sharply drawn personalities, while Johnny appears as a ghostly emissary from the spirit world that looms within their everyday lives. Like Coyote, Lena fails, in the end, to rescue her lover from the realm of the dead.

In subsequent plays Moses explores twentieth- and twenty-first-century Native identities through a range of subjects and dramatic styles. His one-act play *The Dreaming Beauty* (1990) draws on the story of Sleeping Beauty to describe the rebirth of Native identity in a girl, referred to as Beauty, who has forgotten her name and cultural heritage. *Big Buck City* (1991) is the second of Moses's "city plays" exploring contemporary Native urban experience, while the third, *Kyotopolis* (1993), is a space-age fantasia set "at a variety of intersections in the global Indian village, that almost-present dream of the city of tomorrow." With *ALMIGHTY VOICE AND HIS WIFE* (1991) Moses turned his attention to frontier history—in particular, a bloody confrontation between a young Cree Native and the Royal Canadian Mounted Police in late nineteenth-century western Canada. Moses returned to the frontier and its myths in *The Moon and Dead Indians* (1993), which won the DuMaurier One-

Act Playwriting Competition and was performed with another play, *Angel of the Medicine Show*, under the title *The Indian Medicine Shows* in 1996. The combined plays, which are set in New Mexico in the late nineteenth century, won the James Buller Award for Excellence in Aboriginal Theatre. Moses's 1996 play *Brebeuf's Ghost*, which is inspired by SHAKESPEARE's *Macbeth* and the story of the French missionary Jean de Brébeuf, explores European-Native conflicts during the fur trade wars in seventeenth-century Ontario, while *Red River* (1998), which Moses co-wrote with Jim Millan, is set during the Red River Rebellion in Manitoba in 1869–70. Other works include *The Witch of Niagara* (1998), a mythic play of sickness and rebirth, and *Songs of Love and Medicine* (2005), two one-act plays with songs.

Almighty Voice and His Wife, Moses's best-known play and a staple of the contemporary Canadian repertoire, is an innovative and powerful work of Native theater. The play was first produced in Ottawa in September 1991 by the Great Canadian Theatre Company and in Toronto the following spring by Native Earth Performing Arts. A highly acclaimed revival of the play, also produced by Native Earth, opened in Toronto in 2009; this production was included in an international festival of First Nations drama, film, ceremony, and comedy at London's Riverside Studios that year and toured throughout Canada in 2010 and 2012.

The success of Moses's play about a young Cree man named Almighty Voice who was killed with his two companions in an 1897 shootout with the North-West Mounted Police owes much to its theatrically daring two-act structure. While the stripped-down first act of *Almighty Voice and His Wife* explores the resistance of Native peoples to the dispossession of their lands, lives, and freedoms, the play's theatrical second act—written in the form of a parodic minstrel show—exposes the stereotypes governing non-Native perceptions of Native identity and culture. Bracing and unsettling, the collision of perspectives in *Almighty Voice and His Wife* calls attention to the artificiality of the term "Indian" and forces the audience to examine its own racial assumptions and biases.

Moses first encountered the story of Almighty Voice in the late 1970s while working as a researcher at a First Nations educational and cultural center in Brandford, Ontario. The historical Almighty Voice (1875–97), whose Cree name was *Kisse-Manitou-Wayou* but who appears in official records as Jean Baptiste, was raised by John Sounding Sky and Spotted Calf on the One Arrow Reserve a few miles from Batoche near the South Saskatchewan River. Formerly hunters, the One Arrow Cree faced starvation and disease on the reserve, where they had settled as the result of an 1876 land treaty and found themselves ill-suited to the agricultural life. In October 1895 Almighty Voice, then in his twenties, was imprisoned in nearby Duck Lake for poaching a cow—one source says to provide meat for a wedding feast, another to feed his brother's sick child. After a guard joked that he would be hanged for stealing the cow, Almighty Voice escaped from the prison and headed toward his reservation. When he was apprehended by a sergeant in the North-West Mounted Police a week later, he shot and killed the man. Now wanted for murder, he eluded the resulting manhunt for nineteen months before being discovered with two companions on the One Arrow Reserve in May 1897. The three men were pursued and cornered in a bluff of poplar trees, where they held off a siege of rifles and field guns with their own weapons. At the end of this confrontation, six men were dead, including Almighty Voice and his two friends.

When Moses researched the story of the young Cree warrior in the late 1980s, he was struck by the mention, in some accounts of these events, of a girl who accompanied Almighty Voice when he encountered and killed the Mountie. Having also learned that Almighty Voice's fourth wife was the thirteen-year-old daughter of an Indian named Old Dust, Moses decided that these sketchy historical figures represented a single character. This character, he realized, would allow him to tell a love story along the lines of *Bonnie and Clyde* or *Romeo and Juliet* rather than "the renegade Indian one that I'd heard all too often before." Moses gave the character a name—White Girl—and a childhood spent in one of the Indian residential (or industrial) schools that were established in the nineteenth century to assimilate First Nations children into the language, culture, and Christian beliefs of non-Native Canadian society. White Girl struggles with the internalized legacy of this education and with the glass-eyed "Great White God of the ghost-men" to whom she was introduced. Act One of *Almighty Voice and His Wife* presents her relationship with Almighty Voice from their courtship to his death through a series of short scenes identified by projected titles. The staging of this act is lean and lyrical, with images and locales established through language, stage lighting, sound, and movement. The events of recorded history unfold offstage, while the stage itself is the space of more intimate interactions and loss.

Moses designed his first act so that it doesn't end with the violent death of Almighty Voice. One reason for this, he later wrote, was that he didn't want to provide the public with "yet another image of the defeated wild Indian." His original plans for continuing the play beyond the first act were to explore the reasons for Almighty Voice's death through the perspective of the Mounties, soldiers, and settlers responsible for his death. After realizing that his Native actors would have to whiten their faces in order to perform these characters, he decided to make this theatrical device central to the play's second act by employing the structure and conventions of nineteenth-century minstrelsy. Minstrel shows—which enjoyed a vogue in the United States in the 1840s, remained highly popular throughout the century, and were taken on tour to other countries (including Canada)—were formally patterned variety shows featuring songs, dances, and comic dialogues. The typical stage arrangement of these shows featured musicians and singers seated in a semicircle with two "end-men" named Tambo and Bones and an Interlocutor seated in the middle who engaged in verbal back-and-forth with the other two. Minstrel shows portrayed demeaning stereotypes of African Americans, and until later in the nineteenth century, when African American minstrel companies began performing, these stereotypes were performed by white actors whose skin was "blackened" by burnt cork or shoe polish. The tradition of blackface performance that these shows helped popularize survived into the twentieth century, as did the parallel practice of "whiteface," which was used by African American actors and entertainers performing white characters. Whitening one's face, of course, is also a standard practice in clown performance.

Whiteface and the conventions of minstrel shows allowed Moses to shift his focus from the story of Almighty Voice to the ways in which this story—and the story of all Native North Americans—has been appropriated and re-presented by white society. In a theatrical tour de force entitled "Ghost Dance," White Girl and Almighty Voice reappear in the play's second act as minstrel performers: White Girl, dressed as a Mountie, in the role of Interlocutor with the Ghost of Almighty Voice standing in for the missing Tambo and Bones. Their faces whitened, they employ a series of traditional minstrel show routines—overture, baritone solo, stump speech, walkaround, tenor solo, playlet, duet, stand-up comic exchange, and finale—in order to confront the play's audience with its equally conventionalized ways of "seeing" Native people. From their position of symbolic whiteness, they recirculate long-standing images of Native people— cigar store Indians, exotic war dances, buck and squaw, redcoats and wild Indians, urban alcoholics, Tonto, Sitting Bull—and revisit the events of the first act from a series of parodic vantage points. As Ghost recounts the events of his final hours in the act's "Overture," Interlocutor sarcastically frames his story as "the Red and White Victoria Regina Spirit Revival Show" and "a shocking but true tale of the frontier." They conduct a "martial interlude" that celebrates the Mounties responsible for Almighty Voice's death, sing a parodic Indian love song, and perform a melodramatic playlet featuring a Native woman called "Sweet Sioux." The audience may want to "know the truth, the amazing details and circumstances behind your savagely beautifully appearance," as Interlocutor tells Ghost, but what they get, instead, are culturally sanctioned misrepresentations. At the heart of these distortions is whiteness itself, that racial category that depends on racial "others" for its purity. As

Derek Garza as Ghost and P. J. Prudat as Interlocutor in the 2012 Pi Theatre (Vancouver) production of *Almighty Voice and His Wife*.

Moses has written, "White as a color only exists because some of us get told we're black or yellow or Indian. I think my ghosts exist to probe this white problem, this tonal confusion, to spook its metaphors. Maybe my ghosts are like mirrors, but from a funhouse."

The perceptions of white society pose an additional problem for the play's two characters. As the abandoned industrial school that provides the backdrop for the second act reminds us, whiteness is an internalized phenomenon as well. Underlying the act's parodic send-up of stereotypes, clichés, and performances is Ghost's attempt to return White Girl-as-Interlocutor to an awareness of her Native identity. "This is what they've done to you," he says at the end of Scene Two, looking into her eyes. Seen this way, Interlocutor's minstrel performance is an act of self-hatred that reflects her acculturation within a white perspective. The sometimes playful, sometimes painful back-and-forth between the two is a spiritual wooing in which White Girl is eventually rescued from the greatest loss of all: herself.

The result of this theatricalized encounter is a brilliant, often searing examination of Native stereotypes, a journey through the funhouse mirror of distorted images. *Almighty Voice and His Wife*, Moses writes, "works like a purging or an exorcism," and in its unique combination of lyricism and grotesque variety-show comedy it seeks to clear the channels through which Native identity is experienced and perceived. Cleansed of the poison of cultural misrepresentation, the play can end with an image of reclamation and rebirth.   s.G.

Almighty Voice and His Wife

CHARACTERS

ALMIGHTY VOICE[1]   At first a young Cree[2] man, early twenties, Kisse-Manitou-Wayou, also known as John Baptist, later his own playful GHOST.

WHITE GIRL   At first a young Cree woman, early teens, the daughter of Old Dust and the wife of Almighty Voice, later the INTERLOCUTOR.

The action of Act One incorporates historic events that happened between the end of October 1895 and May of 1897 on the Saskatchewan prairie, at and between the One Arrow and Fort a la Corne reserves.[3] Act Two occurs on the auditorium stage of the abandoned industrial school at Duck Lake.[4]

Act One

A projected title: "Act One: Running with the Moon."

Scene One

The projected title: "Scene One: Her Vision." A drum beats in night's blue darkness. The full moon sweeps down from the sky like a spotlight to show and surround WHITE GIRL, *asleep in a fetal position on the ground. The drum begins a sneak-up beat, the moon pulses in a similar rhythm.* WHITE GIRL *wakes at the quake, gets to her feet, and takes a step. The drum hesitates. A gunshot and a slanting bolt of light stop her and block out the moon. Three more shots and slanting bolts of light come in quick succession, confining her in a spectral teepee. She peers out through its skin of light at* ALMIGHTY VOICE, *a silhouette against the moon. He collapses to the beats of the drum, echoes of the gunshots.* WHITE GIRL *falls to her knees as the teepee fades and the moon bleeds.*

Scene Two

The projected title: "Scene Two: The Proposal." WHITE GIRL *is by the fire, stripping meat for drying.* ALMIGHTY VOICE *loiters at a distance.*

---

1. The historical Almighty Voice (1875–1897), a Cree warrior, lived on the One Arrow Reserve in present-day Saskatchewan. Jailed in 1895 for slaughtering a cow, he escaped and killed a member of the North-West Mounted Police (or Mountie) who had apprehended him while on the run. When he was discovered eighteen months later, he fled with his companions Little Salteau and Dubling to a bluff of poplars, where the men engaged in a gun battle with a large force of Mounties and civilians. At the end of the confrontation, six people, including Almighty Voice and his two friends, were dead. "Kisse-Manitou-Wayou" (literally "Voice of the Spirit") is Cree for "Almighty Voice."

Almighty Voice also appears in some records as Jean-Baptiste.
2. The Cree, who have historically ranged across much of North America, are Canada's largest First Nations population.
3. Canadian equivalent of the American term *reservation*. The One Arrow and Fort a la Corne reserves are located to the east and northeast of Duck Lake in central Saskatchewan. In the 1900s the present-day province of Saskatchewan was a territory in western Canada.
4. St. Michael's Indian Industrial School, a school in the Canadian residential school system, opened in the town of Duck Lake in 1892. The school was closed in 1964.

VOICE   Hiya. Hiya. Hey girl, I said, "Hiya."

GIRL   I heard you the first time. I'm working here.

VOICE   Oh ya?

GIRL   I am. And my dad doesn't like it, you talking to me.

5 VOICE   Old Dust? What's he got to worry about? He's winning over there. I'm just talking.

GIRL   It's not your talking he's worried about.

VOICE   What you talking about?

GIRL   You never mind.

10 VOICE   What you talking about, girl? Hey White Girl, what you talking about?

GIRL   My dad says you already got a wife.

VOICE   What's that got to do with anything?

GIRL   I hear you already had two others.[5]

VOICE   You don't have to believe everything you hear. White Girl, you know

15   something? I think you got pretty eyes.

GIRL   I got no time to be told my eyes are pretty.

VOICE   You're pretty fierce for a little girl.

GIRL   You should leave little girls alone, Almighty Voice.

VOICE   You're not that little, little girl.

20 GIRL   I'm working here.

VOICE   You're big enough.

GIRL   Go away.

VOICE   Is that the way they do it at that school? That's not the way my mother does it.

25 GIRL   Spotted Calf doesn't know everything.

VOICE   She knows how to strip meat. Here, let me—

GIRL   You could get cut.

VOICE   You're pretty fierce all right, little girl. You are like Spotted Calf.

GIRL   What?

30 VOICE   My mother's not as pretty as you.

GIRL   Go bother my brother for a while.

VOICE   But he's not as pretty as you.

GIRL   Sure he is. He's my brother. You know what?

VOICE   What is it, White Girl?

35 GIRL   My brother, Young Dust, he likes you.

VOICE   He's my friend.

GIRL   No, Almighty Voice, he likes you. He thinks you are the pretty one. Your wife won't kiss you? Well, my brother will.

VOICE   You're a crazy one.

40 GIRL   You're right. I am a crazy one. As long as you know. But my brother does want to kiss—

VOICE   I don't want to talk about your brother.

GIRL   Look, he's coming this way.

VOICE   What? No he's not.

45 GIRL   But Young Dust does like you.

VOICE   And I like you.

GIRL   I'm just a little girl, Almighty Voice.

VOICE   A little girl working away.

---

5. Polygamy was a common practice among First Nations peoples.

GIRL   You could get cut.
50 VOICE   I want to kiss you, White Girl.
GIRL   My father's looking at you. He sees you talking to me.
VOICE   Let him.
GIRL   You got to talk to him first, you know.
VOICE   I don't want to break that hand game up. All right, I'll go talk to him
55   first.
GIRL   Then we'll talk.
VOICE   Just talk? What will we talk about?
GIRL   The wife you have now.
VOICE   What wife?
60 GIRL   The Rump's Daughter.
VOICE   Oh ya.
GIRL   You're going to send her home to her father.
VOICE   She won't go.
GIRL   She will go. I'm going to be your wife now. Your only wife. You can't
65   feed us both. Well then, my father's waiting to talk to you. Go on.
VOICE   Crazy.

Scene Three

*A projected title: "Scene Three: The Wedding Night." A second fire in night's blue.
A gunshot and a slanting bolt of light. The reverberations become a social dance
beat on a drum and bring up the rest of the teepee of light.* WHITE GIRL *enters it and
sits. Then* ALMIGHTY VOICE *enters. The drum and teepee fade.*

VOICE   Hiya, wife. I said, "Hiya, wife."
GIRL   What can I do for my husband?
VOICE   Come here. Look at me. Leave that be.
GIRL   Does my husband want some tea?
5 VOICE   Your husband wants his blanket.
GIRL   There. Your blanket's ready for you. It's snowing out. Shall I go for
    wood to build the fire up?
VOICE   Can't you be quiet, girl?
GIRL   Shall I tell your friends to be quiet? Shall I tell them to go away?
10 VOICE   They'll go when they're full.
GIRL   Do you want more to eat, husband? I'll go get some more.
VOICE   Stay here with me. Look at me, White Girl.
GIRL   That was a wonderful cow you brought for the feast. It was so fat.
VOICE   You didn't eat much.
15 GIRL   I'm stuffed full. I have never eaten so well before, husband. Now my
    father will have to admit his daughter is well-fed. You are such a hunter.
VOICE   It was only a stupid cow. What's wrong, White Girl?
GIRL   I was thinking about my mother. She would have made him come. And
    your father. How could the Mounties take him? The day before our wedding.
20 VOICE   They're stupid. Look at me, wife.
GIRL   I don't want to be a wife. I don't want to be a woman. That school—I
    don't know how. I'm only thirteen. I'm crazy.
VOICE   You're not crazy.
GIRL   I am. I am.
25 VOICE   Come here. Let me hold you.
GIRL   No, it's too dangerous.

VOICE It's not dangerous. Hey, come on, pretend I'm your brother.

GIRL No, you're my husband. I don't want you to die.

VOICE You're not going to kill me. You're going to kiss me.

30 GIRL I have bad medicine in me. I went to that school.[6] The treaty agent[7] took me.

VOICE But you got away, girl.

GIRL School's a strange place. All made out of stone. The wind tries to get in, and can't, and cries. It's so hot and dry, your throat gets sore. You cough
35 a lot, too. I used to even cough blood. And they won't let you talk. They try to make you talk like they do. It's like stones in your mouth.

VOICE You're here now.

GIRL I liked it there.

VOICE How could you like that?

40 GIRL They said I could live there forever.

VOICE What are you talking about?

GIRL They said everybody at home had died of the smallpox.[8] They said I could live forever but I had to marry their god.

VOICE Hey, you're my wife now and I'm alive. Everybody's alive.

45 GIRL He's going to kill you. He's a jealous god.

VOICE He's another one of their lies.

GIRL They say he's everywhere. He can see everything.

VOICE He's got nothing better to do than watch us?

GIRL They say he's like a ghost.

50 VOICE Hey little girl, even your dad didn't know for sure about us and he watched you like a hawk.

GIRL Or a white bird. They say he's like a white bird.

VOICE A white bird? A white bird in here?

GIRL He made the smallpox.

55 VOICE Let's get that bird out of here! Where is it?

GIRL You crazy, he'll kill you.

VOICE Hey, little girl, I found it! [*He mocks flatulence.*]

GIRL Stop that. You're crazy.

VOICE Oh ya? Both of us? Made for each other. [*He kisses and caresses her.*]
60 Little girl, my White Girl.

GIRL Wait, husband, wait. I'm afraid.

VOICE Don't be. I'm brave now I got you for my wife.

GIRL But I'm afraid.

VOICE What is it now, girl?

65 GIRL It's the bad medicine. They gave me another name when I married their god.

---

6. Reference to the Canadian Indian residential school system, which was established in the 19th century to assimilate First Nations children into the language, culture, and Christian beliefs of Euro-Canadian society. In 1884 attendance at these schools, which were run by churches of different denominations, became mandatory for children under the age of 16.

7. Government representative appointed to implement the terms of the treaties signed between the reigning monarch of Canada and First Nations peoples. While government-native relations had been conducted through treaties since the mid-1700s, the so-called "numbered treaties" affecting western Canada were signed during the years 1871–1921.

8. Smallpox, which was brought to the Americas by European settlers, ravaged Canada's First Nations population during the 19th century.

VOICE Shut up about their god! I don't want to hear it!

GIRL They called me Marrie. It's the name of their god's mother.

VOICE What's wrong with White Girl? White Girl's a good name. They're so
70 stupid. That agent has to call me John Baptist[9] so I can get my treaty money.

GIRL John Baptist. That's the name of one of their ghosts.

VOICE I'm no ghost. I'm Almighty Voice. Why can't they say Almighty Voice?

GIRL I'll call you John Baptist too.

VOICE You're not the agent! You're my wife.

75 GIRL It's so he'll kill the ghost instead of you, husband. That god won't know
it's us if we use their names.

VOICE So I have to call my wife Marrie?

GIRL Yes. Their god won't be able to touch us. Just call me Marrie.

VOICE My crazy White Girl.

80 GIRL Call me Marrie, husband.

VOICE Marrie. Marrie, will you kiss me now?

GIRL Yes, husband.

[*They kiss, caress, and begin to undress.*]

VOICE Crazy Marrie.

GIRL John Baptist.

85 VOICE My little girl.

Scene Four

The projected title: "Scene Four: Flight." A drum beats in darkness. WHITE GIRL
pretends to sleep by the second fire. ALMIGHTY VOICE *enters at a run, drops to his
knees. The drum fades.*

VOICE White Girl, wake up.

GIRL Go away. I'm sleeping here.

VOICE Where's my Winchester?[1]

GIRL How should I know?

5 VOICE Did my mother take it?

GIRL Where have you been?

VOICE I'll be right back.

GIRL Have you been with the Rump's Daughter?

VOICE I got to get my Winchester.

10 GIRL Have you been with the Rump's Daughter?

VOICE I'll go wake my mother.

GIRL Answer me!

VOICE What?

GIRL I'm your wife now. Your only wife.

15 VOICE White Girl, I was with your brother.

GIRL You weren't with the Rump's Daughter?

VOICE We were in jail.

GIRL Jail?

VOICE That sergeant over at Duck Lake, he threw us in the guard house.

9. The historical Almighty Voice was listed on
government records as Jean-Baptiste.
1. Repeating rifle widely used throughout
western Canada and the United States during
the 19th century.

20 GIRL   But you went for treaty money.[2]

VOICE   Well the sergeant has it now. Somebody told them that cow I shot belonged to somebody.

GIRL   You're all wet. Here. Get warm.

VOICE   Hey girl, I been swimming.

25 GIRL   You got away.

VOICE   In the freezing Saskatchewan.[3]

GIRL   What about Young Dust?

VOICE   He said it was warm there.

GIRL   You shouldn't have left him there. They threw you in jail for killing that
30 cow.

VOICE   That cow belonged to the Great White Mother. This half-breed told me the guard said no way would I rot in jail like my dirty chief of a father. The guard said I'd hang for killing that cow!

GIRL   But that's crazy. They don't hang people over meat.

35 VOICE   I'm not going back to that guard house, White Girl.

GIRL   They can't take you there.

VOICE   They always come after you. My dad's in jail at Prince Albert[4] over the pieces of a plough. He hates their stupid farming, this stupid reserve. They even turn the prairie into a jail.

40 GIRL   They can't put the wind in prison.

VOICE   Sounding Sky used to mean warrior. Now it's hard labour.

GIRL   Here. Dry yourself. Get warm.

VOICE   But I got to go get my Winchester.

GIRL   You rest while I find you your Winchester. They can't cross the river so
45 quick. And you need to take some of that beef with you.

VOICE   They'll catch me with it.

GIRL   You got to eat. And the Mounties aren't going to catch us.

VOICE   But you can't come.

GIRL   I'm coming with my husband.

50 VOICE   You'll slow me down.

GIRL   No I won't.

VOICE   But there's snow coming.

GIRL   Better for us. Two can be warmer than one. You know that. Lie down.
Lie down, John Baptist. I'll get your Winchester.

55 VOICE   But White Girl, crazy one—

GIRL   Lie down, John Baptist, rest. I'll be ready soon. No, rest. Listen, John Baptist, I'm a better shot than your mother Spotted Calf. I got better eyes.

VOICE   This is crazy, girl.

GIRL   Both of us. Remember?

Scene Five

The projected title: "Scene Five: The Killing." ALMIGHTY VOICE *and* WHITE GIRL *sit by the third fire. A drifting beat comes and goes on the drum.*

GIRL   It's all gone. The beef's all gone.

VOICE   I don't really like beef.

---

2. Annual payments made to First Nations people according to land treaties made with the Canadian government.

3. South Saskatchewan River.

4. City in central Saskatchewan, located 44 kilometers (27 miles) north of Duck Lake.

GIRL   What's wrong? I didn't burn it.
VOICE   No. Cattle aren't like real meat. They're stupid.
5 GIRL   They're not buffalo.
VOICE   That's for sure. They don't taste right.
GIRL   I like it. It makes me feel full.
VOICE   I'll get something else soon. My wife's not going hungry.
GIRL   It's good to be hungry.
10 VOICE   It's better to be full.
GIRL   It reminds you you're alive. That's what my mother used to say.
VOICE   What's wrong?
GIRL   Young Dust said the snow was too deep. The treaty agent wouldn't
        send the supplies out. Last winter. My mother wouldn't eat. She wouldn't
15   eat. While I was away at that school. She used to like the way I cook.
VOICE   I do too, White Girl.
GIRL   I would have cooked for her.
VOICE   Cook for me now, White Girl.
GIRL   I didn't really want to be there. We had to eat this mush made out of
20   grass seeds.
VOICE   No meat?
GIRL   Mush.
VOICE   How about some tea then? It's hot enough. It'll make you feel full.
GIRL   That's all there is.
25 VOICE   Can we go see your father now? He likes his tea. He always has sugar.
GIRL   The ice was almost too thick this morning. I was afraid we'd have to
        melt snow.
VOICE   We better go soon.
GIRL   Snow takes too long.
30 VOICE   That sergeant's not as stupid as he looks. He'll see we doubled back.
GIRL   Do you know what glass is? Like thin ice?
VOICE   What are you talking about, White Girl?
GIRL   Some of the walls at the school were made out of it.
VOICE   Made out of what?
35 GIRL   Glass. A wall you can see through. I didn't know it was there at first, the
        wall. I tried to crawl through. I saw the sky, the grass moving. Out there. I
        banged my face. The glass broke. Sharp pieces, too. That's what this is
        from.
VOICE   A place to kiss.
40 GIRL   You know what, John Baptist? I dreamed about you. I knew you would
        come.
VOICE   What's the matter?
GIRL   I was looking at you far away. Through a glass wall!
VOICE   The soldiers, they have these clear beads they look through. Far away
45   comes real close. All the walking in between seems to disappear.
GIRL   It was like that. It was. But it was also like I was waiting in my father's
        teepee. I could see you coming, I saw the moonlight on the barrel of your
        Winchester.
VOICE   I was bringing meat, I bet, buffalo meat for my wife.
50 GIRL   No you weren't. No! Let go.
VOICE   What's the matter, White Girl?

GIRL   You shot and the teepee broke. All the sharp pieces fell down on you, worse than hail. I think it hurt you, I think you got hurt.

VOICE   Stop it, White Girl, stop it. Don't be afraid. I'm all right.

55 GIRL   That god. That god. I'm afraid.

VOICE   That stupid god can't hurt me. That god belongs in that place, in the school. You're here now, I'm here now. He's not.

GIRL   He's everywhere!

VOICE   I told you he's a lie.

60 GIRL   He's like the glass. He's hard. He cuts you down.

VOICE   I'm your husband now. I won't let him hurt you. He doesn't deserve you.

GIRL   I'm sorry. I'm sorry.

VOICE   Listen, crazy one. You married Almighty Voice, who's not afraid to say

65   his name. Let your glass god hear it. Almighty Voice!—who has listened to our fathers and heard what they say. Almighty Voice, who remembers our Creator and our people's ways. Almighty Voice knows how to fight for you. Do you hear what I'm saying? Do you?

GIRL   Yes. Yes, I do.

70 VOICE   Who is saying it?

GIRL   Almighty Voice.

VOICE   Remember who you are. Remember what your mother taught you.

GIRL   Almighty Voice, the husband of White Girl!

VOICE   I'll break your glass god for you.

75 GIRL   Keep your bad medicine!

VOICE   It's just a bad smell. A stink. Come on. I'll get the horse. Your father has the tea ready for us.

GIRL   Husband, look!

VOICE   Give me my Winchester. My wife'll have rabbit for breakfast.

[*He loads and exits.* WHITE GIRL *watches him go, then builds up the fire. She hears a noise from another direction and looks and stops. A shot. She runs toward the place where* ALMIGHTY VOICE *exited. He enters, dead rabbit in hand.*]

80   [*laughing*] Look how fat! This'll make you full.

GIRL   Husband, be quiet.

[ALMIGHTY VOICE *drops the rabbit.*]

It's the god. See his glass eye.

VOICE   It's the sergeant, White Girl. Just the stupid sergeant. What's he say?

GIRL   I can't understand him.

85 VOICE   That's that stupid half-breed with him. Stay behind me, girl.

GIRL   He wants to make peace. There's the sign.

VOICE   Get down. He's got a gun.

GIRL   Where's the half-breed going?

VOICE   Stay where you are!

90 GIRL   What about the horse?

VOICE   No time. Stay there! Where's the other one?

GIRL   I can't see. Over there.

VOICE   Circling around. Don't come any closer. [*He reloads his Winchester.*]

GIRL   Leave us alone! Go away!

95 VOICE   I'm warning you!

GIRL   Husband—

VOICE   This gun's loaded!

GIRL   —the half-breed's behind us.

VOICE   Keep close. I'm warning you! Stop there! Stay there! [*shooting*] You
100   stupid!

GIRL   One shot. One shot, Almighty Voice!

VOICE   The other one?

GIRL   I told you glass breaks.

VOICE   Gone. Scared his horse, too. He'll bring more Mounties. There will
105   be more from now on.

GIRL   Glass breaks so easily.

VOICE   Wife, look at me.

GIRL   I'm all right, husband.

VOICE   Come on.

110   GIRL   No. There will be more from now on. I'll slow you down.

VOICE   I can't leave you, girl.

GIRL   They won't hurt me. They'll be afraid to now.

VOICE   White Girl, look at me.

GIRL   They'll have to take me home. I'll tell everyone how it happened, how
115   he wouldn't listen. They'll just take me home. I'll just slow them down. We
can meet at my mother's—I mean your mother's house. My mother's gone.
She died of hunger last winter. But I'm all right, Almighty Voice. And I
know I have to go talk to your mother soon.

VOICE   What about?

120   GIRL   I want us to make her a grandchild. She has to tell me how to get ready.
Women's stuff. I know I have to eat. [*She goes and picks up the rabbit.*] You
better go now.

[ALMIGHTY VOICE *exits.* WHITE GIRL *takes the rabbit to the fire.*]

Scene Six

*The projected title: "Scene Six: Mid-Winter Moon." A martial beat on the drum as
the bloody moon rises. Then silence.* WHITE GIRL *sits near the second fire while*
ALMIGHTY VOICE *wanders between the fires.*

GIRL   Mister. Mister! Mister God! I see your glass eye. Eye-eye! Stinky
breath. It's me. Marrie! Marrie, your wife. Wife wife wife! God, look at me
like before. How they taught me at school. How how. Here's my hair. Look.
Here's my skin. How how, husband god, see what a little girl I am. Great
5   White God of the ghost men,[5] mother is here. Blood blood blood between
my thighs. Yes, gimme, gimme, gimme something sweet. Oh yes, yes, you're
rotten, rotten meat, but wifey wife will eat you up. Mister God, god, stupid
god, this is what you want! Come on! Come on, don't leave! I'm your little
squaw.[6] Eye-eye! See! Eye-eye, Mister God. Eye-eye!

10   VOICE   Don't talk, cousin. You're being stupid. No one would mistake you for
a warrior. And your woman, she's so skinny, no one would call you a hunter
either. Or a lover. Could your woman do what my woman has? Could she
look those white men in the eyes? They took her back to Duck Lake and
kept her in that guard house and she gave them lies for their lies. "Run,

5. Men with pale skin (that is, Caucasians).
6. Native woman or wife.

15 husband. We will meet later." She said that to me. Is it a surprise I think about her? I believe what she says. If she is crazy, we all should be. Not a word, Little Salteau! Who's the one who killed a Mountie.[7]

GIRL   I am the wife of Almighty Voice. You don't know my name. You don't even wonder if I have one. I'm only a crazy squaw. You're watching me but

20 you expect to see my husband. His is a name you know. Almighty Voice. John Baptist. You say these names of his over and over again, like the prayers you say to your glass-eyed god for the grace of your Great White Mother Victoria.[8] But your prayers won't make him come. Mister God Mountie, you don't know what his name means.

25 VOICE   Your sister, Young Dust, she makes me remember how my father used to talk about the buffalo. Maybe because she likes meat so much. I'd like to feed her till she's fat. My father said everyone used to be like that. Everyone used to follow the buffalo. He hates farming. A man shouldn't be a bag of bones. My mother says he gets no meat. In Prince Albert. John Sound-

30 ing Sky is in jail because his son mistook a Mountie for a cow!

GIRL   You're laughing with that half-breed.[9] "Let the crazy squaw go home. Easy to keep an eye on her there." So he unlocks the door, walks away to the fire where you play with your silver coin, your dollar. That's what you want to trade my husband's blood for. Why? What is its power? A coin is

35 not the moon. Can't you see it's dead, Mister Mountie? Cold as the bullet my husband kills rabbits or enemies with.

VOICE   So my mother Spotted Calf is alone still, running things, hating it. She says there are too many women now. I think there aren't enough men. It's like a war but no one will say so, so there's never any peace. How many

40 of our brothers are there still in Stoney Mountain?[1] How many come home in the spring? My mother says it makes her children crazy, living on snow. Maybe she's right. Come on. Let's go make some blood flow tonight!

GIRL   You've got a bad look on your face, a blindness, a glassy gaze. What are you staring at? Your silver dollar? The fire? My husband's bullet. You'll stare

45 till they all turn to glass. And what will you see through them then? That forever place you want to live,[2] the one they promised me in school? I turn here in the wind toward the river and the moon is there, a woman with better things to do. She slips away from you, going home.

Scene Seven

The projected title: "Scene Seven: Honeymoon." The drum beats. The full moon sweeps down from the sky like a spotlight to show and surround the lovers, lying together on the ground.

GIRL   Almighty Voice, come on.
VOICE   Not again.

---

7. Member of the North-West Mounted Police. The NWMP was established in 1873 to maintain order in Canada's Northwest Territories, which included the present-day province of Saskatchewan.
8. Queen Victoria I (1819–1901), who ruled the United Kingdom of Great Britain and Ireland from 1836 to 1901. Under the British North America Act, which established the Dominion of Canada in 1867, Victoria continued to serve as the country's monarch.
9. Member of the Métis, an aboriginal people of mixed European and Native ancestry.
1. Penitentiary established in 1877 in the present-day province of Manitoba.
2. The Christian heaven.

GIRL   I want to be sure.

VOICE   Let me sleep.

5   GIRL   This is the time to do it. Your mother said so.

VOICE   I don't want to know that. I don't want to do it for my mother.

GIRL   Do it for me. It's the best time now.

VOICE   I don't want to know that stuff.

GIRL   Young Dust dreamed we had a son.

10 VOICE   This is none of your brother's business.

GIRL   Come on, John Baptist.

VOICE   White Girl, we got to sleep.

GIRL   Almighty Voice, do you like my hand there?

VOICE   Don't. You keep this up, we'll fall asleep on the horse later.

15 GIRL   You fall off, you can fall on me.

VOICE   White Girl, we got to move on tonight. Little Salteau said those stu-
        pid Mounties are just south of here.

GIRL   They're hunting quail, not us. I like it here. I like how flat it is. Like your
        belly.

20 VOICE   White Girl, stop it.

GIRL   Come on, Almighty Voice.

VOICE   Do as your husband says. And don't laugh.

GIRL   The Mounties don't know we're here. Why worry?

VOICE   Go to sleep.

25 GIRL   They'll forget about you.

VOICE   I killed a Mountie. They don't give up.

GIRL   But he would have killed you.

VOICE   I know.

GIRL   Spring comes, the snow goes. Too many other things to do. Cows run-
30   ning away through the grass. Fresh meat, husband.

VOICE   Can't you be quiet, girl?

GIRL   Isn't this grass moving in the wind here on your flat prairie?

VOICE   I'm your husband, White Girl.

GIRL   Oh, your wife likes to run in the grass, Almighty Voice.

35 VOICE   Stop it. Go to sleep.

GIRL   They can't see you as long as you're with me.

VOICE   We can't hide in that grass, little girl.

GIRL   We can hide. With me you're in the dark of the moon. It's what your
        mother talks about. When we're together, it's like we're inside a bead of
40   glass made of wind. They can't get at us. It's my medicine, husband. In the
        dream—you were in the dream. That's all I can tell you.

VOICE   You fasted? When?

GIRL   The last blizzard. Your mother took me out. In that wind.

VOICE   The moon was dark then.

45 GIRL   She took me down to the river. I built a fire on the ice. She visited me
        every morning. And she sang to me.

VOICE   And she serves tea to the priest!

GIRL   And laughs at him. He expects her to give you away. That priest wants
        her to marry his god too.

50 VOICE   That's crazy.

GIRL   Instead she gets news of your father in Prince Albert.

VOICE I didn't know. What does she say about my father? Is his cough any
       better? When One Arrow[3] got back from the jail at Stoney Mountain, he
       was old. He told my father that the visions of warriors have no more power
55   against the soldiers.

GIRL   He was old, husband. He was tired.

VOICE Not even Riel's vision,[4] and he was part white.

GIRL   It's the jail, husband. They watch you all the time. You can't move.

VOICE I was there when he said it.

60 GIRL   And it's all stone.

VOICE He gave away his rifle.

GIRL   You can't see anything but stones. You can't see anything, husband.
       You forget everything.

VOICE How can you forget everything and be a man?

65 GIRL   You're not a man then. You're like a ghost. You're lost.

VOICE I want to see my father. I'm going to Prince Albert.

GIRL   That's crazy.

VOICE The Mounties won't know I'm there. Why worry?

GIRL   Your mother says someone's always watching him. You don't know that
70   place.

VOICE I'm going to talk to him.

GIRL   You have to hide. Your mother said so.

VOICE Shut up about my mother! I don't want to hear it.

GIRL   She won't let you go.

75 VOICE Am I a child again? Hiding behind women. How can you look at me?

GIRL   You're my husband.

VOICE My father is a man. John Sounding Sky still means warrior. But
       Almighty Voice?

GIRL   He's a warrior.

80 VOICE Does a warrior run away? Almighty Voice is a stupid old man, a ghost.
       He's here, there, nowhere.

GIRL   You can't go.

VOICE I should be in Prince Albert. John Sounding Sky should be at home
       with Spotted Calf.

85 GIRL   They ache to hang Almighty Voice.

VOICE What good am I here?

GIRL   I need you.

VOICE What good am I to you, White Girl?

GIRL   I don't want to be alone.

90 VOICE You can stay with my mother.

GIRL   Two women old with no men? Your mother will die like my mother did.
       You can't leave me too.

VOICE Your father will take you.

GIRL   You're sending me home?

---

3. One Arrow (ca. 1815–1886), chief of the
Willow Cree band that settled on the One
Arrow reservation. One Arrow was impris-
oned after participating in the unsuccessful
North West Rebellion of 1885.

4. Louis Riel (1844–1885), who claimed to

have had a vision in which God anointed him
a prophet, led two armed rebellions against
the Canadian government on behalf of the
Métis, an aboriginal people of mixed European and Native ancestry. Riel himself is said
to have had one-eighth Native blood.

95 VOICE   He'll get you a better husband.

GIRL   He'll get me a worse one.

VOICE   Who? Who could that be?

GIRL   Any ghost man will do. You want me to die.

VOICE   You won't die!

100 GIRL   I will. For years. Kill me now. Be good to me, husband. Kill me now
and then you can go, go and be hanged.

VOICE   You're pretty fierce, all right.

GIRL   Let go of me.

VOICE   For a little girl.

105 GIRL   I'll get you your Winchester.

VOICE   Stay here with me.

GIRL   You can kill me, husband. We'll both be dead.

VOICE   That's stupid. White Girl who has visions, stay here with me.

GIRL   What about your father?

110 VOICE   We'll find a way. My mother will help.

GIRL   You won't leave me?

VOICE   Hey, I'm here with you. In the dark of the moon. They can't get at us.

GIRL   Almighty Voice—

VOICE   Can't you be quiet, girl? Your husband doesn't want to sleep any more.

115 He likes your hand here.

Scene Eight

*A projected title: "Scene Eight: The Hunting Moon." A gunshot. The social drum.
Three more shots.* ALMIGHTY VOICE *with his Winchester at the last fire, the dead one.*
WHITE GIRL *with a baby-sized bundle in her arms, still illuminated by the moon.*

GIRL   You brought me home to your mother. It was time. Spotted Calf
expected me. She took me into her new house. Other women were waiting.
"Go away," she said. "Young Dust will bring you news." Someone, the
Rump's Daughter, might tell. It was dangerous. The Mounties—it was dan-
5   gerous. You wanted to hide under the floor, under her bed like last winter.
But she made you go. "You men shouldn't know women's stuff." You men.
Little Salteau and Dubling came along. I heard you laughing. Off you rode
to hunt somewhere, the grass new, blue-green. I saw you through the glass
in the window of that house. Going.

10 VOICE   Has he come? Tell him, wife, tell him how good a season it was everywhere along the Saskatchewan the winter before he was born. Tell him I
always found game, never got cold. Till now. Say the ghost men shivered in
their huts, too afraid of the wind to fire a shot. Tell him it can be like that
again. Tell him, girl. Do you hear me? I wish you did.

15   Tell him how we visited and people would give his mother more to eat.
Even people in the woods far up north. An old bull buffalo, chewy but
sweet. You worried it might be their last one but ate anyway. Tell him Old
Dust gave in, gave us lots of sugar for our tea, called me son, when he saw
how fat you were. One day I remember. Cold, bright. Leather stiff as
20   wood. Your belly had begun to curve. Your breath feathers,[5] or smoke that

5. Downy feathers of an eagle or other bird, often used for ceremonial purposes. These are
referred to as "breath feathers" because they move under the slightest breeze.

fell, hugged the ground. I teased you, your belly like the iron stove at the store at Duck Lake. Tight as a drum. I felt him kick then. What a thump! I knew I had a son. I wanted to dance.

> [ALMIGHTY VOICE *dances with the drum in celebration. Then, as* WHITE GIRL *speaks, his steps turn into a war dance and then into stillness. The moon around* WHITE GIRL *turns bloody.*]

GIRL   They tell me you came across another cow. They say you wanted to feast
25   me and the baby. So you shot the stupid thing. Some farmer heard your guns, didn't mind his own business. Him and his sons gave chase. I can hear you laughing, leading them into this bluff[6] of poplars. And suddenly there's Mounties, soldiers, farmers everywhere. And someone shoots someone. I hope it was that farmer. They tell me you got no food, no water all day. They
30   say someone else got shot. Maybe a Mountie. Young Dust said he heard you singing. War songs. He says you were dancing. There were ghost men all around that night. Farmers, soldiers, priests of the glass god. Over a hundred against Little Salteau, Dubling, and Almighty Voice by the end. And two big iron guns.[7] I saw them myself the second day. Spotted Calf and I stood
35   watching. I wanted you to be anywhere else. Young Dust held the baby, reminded me to feed his nephew. I didn't notice I was full, aching. I have no milk now. [*She puts her bundle down.*] That night I saw my husband Almighty Voice again against that moon I had tried to forget. Then those two guns started firing and firing. Firing and firing. It was cold and the smoke would
40   not go away. I seemed to see you sometime in the night, in the smoke, but even before morning broke, your mother was singing her death song.[8]

Scene Nine

A projected title: "Scene Nine: His Vision." The drum beats in the night. The moon is low in the sky, pulsing. ALMIGHTY VOICE *lies by the dead fire, his leg badly wounded. The spectral teepee appears and the drum goes silent. Inside the teepee are* WHITE GIRL *and her baby, mother and child, a destination.* ALMIGHTY VOICE *rises and uses his Winchester as a crutch to come to the teepee.* WHITE GIRL *comes out and shows him the baby and the baby cries. The moon turns white.* ALMIGHTY VOICE *dies.*

Act Two

A follow spot finds a title placard: "Act Two: Ghost Dance."

Scene One

The spot shifts to a second title placard:[9] "Scene One: Overture," then fades. Spectral light from the dead fire. ALMIGHTY VOICE, *now in whiteface[1] as his own* GHOST, *continues his dance of celebration around the fire inside the last crescent of the moon. Scattered around the moon's half-circle are mined stools three of which are still sturdy enough to be useful. On the one upright at the crescent's midpoint, a searching spot finds a seated figure and, finding its head, discovers white-gloved hands hiding its face. As the crescent moon fades, the hands open to reveal the white-*

---

6. Dense grove of trees.
7. Mounted artillery guns.
8. Song sung by Native individuals, especially warriors, at the approach of death.
9. This and the following scene titles refer to parts of a minstrel show, a popular 19th-

century American entertainment form that featured music, song, and comic dialogue and offered stereotypical representations of African Americans.
1. Makeup applied to make a nonwhite performer appear white.

face that masks WHITE GIRL *into the role of the* INTERLOCUTOR,[2] *a Mountie and the Master of Ceremonies. In a glance their eyes meet. Sudden light shift to variety-show lights, both the* GHOST *and the* INTERLOCUTOR *in follow spots. The* INTERLOCUTOR *adjusts her monocle.*

INTERLOCUTOR   Here, here? I said, "Here, here." Hey dead man? Hey red man! Hey Indian!

GHOST   *Awas. Si-pwete.* [*Go away. Go on.*]

INTERLOCUTOR   "Here, here," I said. What's the meaning of this? Come on,
5   use the queen's tongue,[3] or I'll sell you to a cigar store.[4]

GHOST   *Awas kititin ni-nimihiton oma ota.* [*Go away. I'm dancing here.*]

INTERLOCUTOR   You dare call these furtive foot steps, these frenzied flailings of arms like wings, dancing! Stop it. It s nonsense.

GHOST   *Awena kiya? Kekwiy ka-ayimota-man?* [*Who are you? What are you talking about?*]

10   INTERLOCUTOR   Snap out of it, Chief. [*slapping him with the gloves four times*]

GHOST   Oweeya! Oweeya! Ya! Ya! *Pakitinin awena kiya moya ki-kis-ke yimitin.* [*Ow! Ow! Ow! Ow! Let go of me. Who are you? I don't know you.*]

INTERLOCUTOR   You know very well who the hell I am. I don't have to remind you no show can begin without its master. Here, here. Stop I say. How dare you go faster.

15   GHOST   *Nahkee. Kawiya-(ekosi). Ponikawin poko ta kisisimoyan.* [*Stop. Let me alone. I have to finish my dance.*]

INTERLOCUTOR   I'll break the other leg for you, Kisse-Manitou-Wayou.

GHOST   *Tansi esi kiskeyitaman ni wiyowin?* [*How do you know my name?*]

INTERLOCUTOR   Names, names, they're all the same. Crees all wear feathers. Dead man, red man. Indian, Kisse-Manitou-Wayou, Almighty Voice. John
20   Baptist! Geronimo,[5] Tonto,[6] Calijah.[7] Or most simply, Mister Ghost.

GHOST   Ghost?

INTERLOCUTOR   Boo! Almighty Ghost, Chief. Now we're speaking English.

GHOST   What? Who are you?

INTERLOCUTOR   How.[8] You're supposed to say "How." You know. Hey Pon-
25   tiac,[9] how's the engine? Can't you stick to the script? You're too new at this ghost schtick[1] to go speaking *ad liberatum.*[2]

GHOST   Let me go. I don't know you. Let me dance.

---

2. Master of ceremonies in the minstrel show. Sitting at the center of a semicircle featuring musicians and singers, the Interlocutor engaged in comic back-and-forth with Tambo and Bones, his two "endmen."

3. That is, English.

4. Because Native Americans introduced tobacco to European settlers, wooden representations of American Indians were used as advertisements on tobacconists' shops. These figures were often referred to as "cigar store Indians."

5. Apache Indian leader (1829–1909) who fought against Mexico and the United States during the Apache Wars (1849–86).

6. Native American companion of the Lone Ranger in the mid-20th century *Lone Ranger* radio and television series.

7. "Kaw-Liga," a song about a wooden display Indian who falls in love with an Indian maid in a nearby antique shop but is too stubborn to let her know, was written by Hank Williams and Fred Rose in 1952. The song was released in January 1953 after Williams's death and spent fourteen weeks at the top of the *Billboard* country chart.

8. The word "how," which derives from interjections used by Plains Indians tribes, became a stereotypical Indian greeting in popular cinema and television.

9. Leader of the Ottawa tribe (ca. 1720–1769) who led a revolt against the British following the French and Indian War. The war that bears his name—Pontiac's Rebellion—was fought during 1763–66. Until it was discontinued in 2010, Pontiac was also an automobile brand manufactured by General Motors.

1. Stage routine, gag, or gimmick (Yiddish).

2. However you wish (the actual Latin phrase is *ad libitum*).

INTERLOCUTOR   Here here. Stop. I say. How dare you! Do I have to remind
you this colourful display, these exotic ceremonials, belong later on in the
30   program? Listen to me, Chief. One doesn't begin with a climax, an end.
Unmitigated foolishness. I'll have you know. If you begin at the end, then
where do you go? Do you know? No. Well? What have you got to say for
yourself?

GHOST   How—

35   INTERLOCUTOR   That's more like it!

GHOST   How did I get here? What's going on?

INTERLOCUTOR   What's going on! The show. The Red and White Victoria
Regina[3] Spirit Revival show! These fine, kind folks want to know the truth,
the amazing details and circumstance behind your savagely beautiful
40   appearance. They also want to be entertained and enlightened and maybe
a tiny bit thrilled, just a goose of frightened. They want to laugh and cry.
They want to know the facts. And it's up to you and me to try and lie that
convincingly. And since all the rest of our company is late for the curtain,
this is your chance, your big break for certain.

45   GHOST   No, I won't dance for you.

INTERLOCUTOR   But you have to toe the line. Chief. We all do. Here. Let me
smell your breath. Bah! Like death warmed over. I've warned you before.
You choose to booze and you're back on the street where I found you.

GHOST   Leave me alone. Go away.

50   INTERLOCUTOR   Don't you realize you could be internationally known, the
most acclaimed magic act of the century?

GHOST   What do you mean?

INTERLOCUTOR   The Vanishing Indian!

GHOST   Poof?[4]

55   INTERLOCUTOR   Forget about faggots.

GHOST   I want to know how I got here.

INTERLOCUTOR   Gutter.[5] Does that sound mean anything to you? Gutter?

GHOST   All I remember—

INTERLOCUTOR   Answer me, you sotted[6] fancy dancer.

60   GHOST   My leg was gone.

INTERLOCUTOR   Come on. Chief, be a friend.

GHOST   It was! I used a branch from a sapling.

INTERLOCUTOR   Be a pal, Chiefy, dear.

GHOST   No, it was my gun for a crutch.

65   INTERLOCUTOR   This is a bit much for this early in the proceedings.

GHOST   Sometime in the night—

INTERLOCUTOR   Wait wait wait. I'd like to apologize to the ladies in the audience and suggest that this might be a prime opportunity to make use of our
theatre's other facilities. The details of the following story may be not for the
70   faint of heart, are in fact quite gory, and ordinarily it would be our custom to
warn you and ask your permission before we proceed. However—how-ever—
as you can see, my peer here feels he must thrust the entire tale upon us.
Once again, I apologize. Thank you for your attention. All right. Proceed.

---

3. Queen Victoria (Latin).
4. As a verb, to appear or disappear like a puff
of air; as a noun, a derogatory term for a
homosexual (as is *faggot* in the following line).

5. That is, street gutter. This exchange
addresses the stereotype associating Native
people with alcoholism.
6. Affected by alcohol.

GHOST   My legs were gone.

75 INTERLOCUTOR   His leg was gone!

GHOST   I must have screamed.

INTERLOCUTOR   Talk about Wounded Knee.[7]

GHOST   But my throat was too dry.

INTERLOCUTOR   The bones were shattered, pulp. Not that that mattered.

80 GHOST   There was no sound in my mouth.

INTERLOCUTOR   Quite the comedown for Almighty Vocal Cords.

GHOST   I couldn't sing my song.

INTERLOCUTOR   Oh Lord, talented, too!

GHOST   My death song. I crawled out of the pit.

85 INTERLOCUTOR   And we're not talking orchestra pits out here in the sticks.

GHOST   We had dug it in the ground to protect us from the gunfire.

INTERLOCUTOR   Not much good compared to a couple of cannons, was it?

GHOST   There was smoke close to the ground.

INTERLOCUTOR   From the fires all around?

90 GHOST   I thought I might be able to make it across the open space.

INTERLOCUTOR   And was it really over a hundred men by then?

GHOST   Against Little Salteau, Dubling, and me.

INTERLOCUTOR   Imagine. Red coats and wild Indians. What a spectacle! Where are my glasses?

95 GHOST   It was the middle of the night. I might get by if the watch was asleep.

INTERLOCUTOR   Not on duty? Now that's not very funny.

GHOST   I had seen her watching, many times that day, beyond their lines. I got halfway across.

INTERLOCUTOR   And amazingly, no one saw him then. He might have made
100 good his escape. Think about that. However—how-ever—he was bleeding a lot. Red blood oozing from red skin. Oh what a thrill! I'm not offending you, am I?

GHOST   She came to meet me.

INTERLOCUTOR   [à la "Indian Love Call"][8]   When I'm calling you-oo-oo-oo-
105 oo-oo-oo!

GHOST   No one could see her. My wife had denied their glass-eyed god. It was her medicine to be invisible.

INTERLOCUTOR   Wish my wife could do that. That's really interesting. Kissy Kisse-Manitou-Wayou? Did you give her some tongue!

110 GHOST   She told me about my son. She told me I would not be forgotten.

INTERLOCUTOR   How can I put this delicately? Your last meeting, your last touch. Your life dribbling out of you, hot and sticky. Big strong buck like you used to be. Was it savage love? Did you have a last quickie?

GHOST   I knew I could die then.

115 INTERLOCUTOR   She was some babe, eh?

GHOST   People would remember me.

INTERLOCUTOR   Give me some of the juicy details, Chief.

GHOST   My people would remember me.

---

7. South Dakota creek where more than 200 Lakota Sioux men, women, and children were massacred by U.S. Cavalry troops on December 28, 1890.

8. Popular song from the 1924 Broadway musical *Rose-Marie*, which was made into a film starring Nellie Eddie and Jeanette Mac-Donald in 1936.

INTERLOCUTOR   One must always strive for accuracy. Do you have
120   documentation?

GHOST   I knew I could die then.

INTERLOCUTOR   Come on, Chief, speak up. Anybody got a cigar? Never mind.

GHOST   I could hear my mother, off on the hill, singing her song.

INTERLOCUTOR   Talent just runs in that family!

125   GHOST   Her death song.

INTERLOCUTOR   So does manic depression! Do we feel better now? We do
    remember you, Mister Almighty Ghost. The angry young man, the passion-
    ate lover, the wild and crazy Indian kid. A shocking but true tale of the
    frontier. Now don't you think this is just too touching, ladies and gentle-
130   men? Too much for my refined sensibilities, that's a certainty. That wasn't
    too bad, Chief, considering. And now—[*She changes the title placard.*]

Scene Two

The new placard reads "Scene Two: Baritone Solo."

INTERLOCUTOR   Ladies and gentlemen, for your further edification and
    delight, a musical selection. Mister Almighty Ghost, the famous Aborigi-
    nal[9] voice, will now render for you the sweet ballad, "Lament of the Red-
    skin Lover." Mister Ghost?

5   GHOST [*in a spotlight*]   What are you talking about?

INTERLOCUTOR   Go on, Mister Ghost. We wait upon you, sir. Sing. Sing.

GHOST   I don't know this.

INTERLOCUTOR   No memory at all? Here. It's number two on your lyric sheet,
    sir.

10   GHOST   Who are you?

INTERLOCUTOR   This is it, your last show. You're back on the street in the
    morning. The gutter? Here we go.

    [*The* INTERLOCUTOR *stands behind the* GHOST *and guides him through
    the accompanying mime.*]

GHOST [*to the tune of "Oh! Susanna"*][1]
    I track the winter prairie for the little squaw I lost.
    I'm missing all the kissing I had afore the frost.
15   I'm moping, oh I'm hoping oh, to hold her hand in mine.
    My flower of Saskatchewan, oh we were doing fine.

GHOST & INTERLOCUTOR   In our teepee, oh we were so in love,
    One Arrow was too narrow for my little squaw and me.

GHOST   I had a dream the other night, I saw her on a hill.

20   INTERLOCUTOR   My little squaw was shaking, the wind was standing still.

GHOST   The bannock bread[2] was in her mouth, and blood was in her eye.
    The moon so bright I lost my sight—

INTERLOCUTOR   —I pray she didn't die!

GHOST   On the prairie, oh how the white does blow!
25   Who makes it through the winter?
    Not my little squaw or me.

---

9. Referring to an original or earliest inhabitant of a land.
1. Popular minstrel song written by Stephen
Foster and published in 1848.

2. A fried form of flat quick bread popular
among Native North Americans. Also called
fry bread.

INTERLOCUTOR   Nicely done. Thank you, thank you, Mister Ghost. You were almost your spooky self again.

GHOST   Thank you, Mister Interlocutor.

30 INTERLOCUTOR   Buck up, Mister Ghost. Isn't this all familiar? Might not, say, Buck[3] and Squaw be the latest dance craze?

> [*The* INTERLOCUTOR *pulls the* GHOST *into a short Hollywood Indian War Dance. The* GHOST *resists. At the end the* GHOST *grabs the* INTERLOCUTOR *and looks into her eyes.*]

GHOST   This is what they've done to you.

INTERLOCUTOR   Thank you, thank you, Mister Ghost. A most original interpretation of the material. Gentle listeners, Mister Bones[4] will now perform
35   for you—

GHOST   Mister Bones? He the one with the dice?

INTERLOCUTOR   No, Mister Ghost. He s the one who's got rhythm.

GHOST   There's no one like that backstage, sir.

INTERLOCUTOR   No? Perhaps our friend Mister Tambo waits in the wings.

40 GHOST   That the Tamborine Man?[5] Not even in the flies, sir. Nor, sir, is Mister Drum lurking below the trap door.

INTERLOCUTOR   No Mister Drum? Well, Mister Ghost—no! Wait!

> [*The* GHOST *changes the placard.*]

Scene Three

The new placard reads "Scene Three: The Stump."

GHOST   Ladies and gentlemen, boys and girls, dogs and cats, we of the Pale-Faced Band of the Sweet Saskatchewaners are pleased to present for your information and concern our own Mister Interlocutor in the role of Mister Drum, a loyal citizen of our territory.

5 INTERLOCUTOR   Wait a moment, Mister Ghost. That is not my part.

GHOST   But you do know it by heart. This is your chance, sir, your big break for certain. Ladies and gentlemen, please welcome Mister Drum.

INTERLOCUTOR   Ahem. Ahem. I come before you this evening, my dear friends, full, full of concern. We have ourselves a problem, dear friends, an
10   Indian problem. Dare I say an indigent Indian problem? Dear friends, the pampered redskins, they are the bad ones. Those tribes that have been cared for as if they were our equals, they, dear friends, are the first to turn and shed the blood of their benefactors. Noisemaker[6] was petted,[7] yes, even feted,[8] my friends, and now raids our farms. Pricky Pinecone was paid
15   to come up to our fine territory and what, dear friends, is his pursuit nowadays? Carnage! Large Prairie Dog, who for years has sharpened his teeth by chewing on the bone of idleness, shows his gratitude by killing his priests for their holy wine. That is not communion, friends. Little Dump, a non-treaty Indian, has been, friends, provisioned with all necessaries and so

---

3. Native male.
4. The minstrel characters, Tambo and Bones, are named for the instruments they played (a clacking folk instrument called "bones" and a tambourine). These characters, who sat on the end of the semicircle of singers and musicians, engaged in comic banter with each other and with the Interlocutor.

5. Bob Dylan's song "Mr. Tambourine Man" was recorded and released in 1965.
6. Noisemaker: Noisemaker, Pricky Pinecone, Large Prairie Dog, and Little Dump are invented names.
7. That is, pampered and indulged.
8. Feasted (French).

20   gets to spend all his days gallivanting about the territory, shouting loudly and plotting mischief. And now, my dear friends, this Almighty Gas character joins in on the season's carnival of ruin. Oh friends, the petted Indians have proved the bad ones and this gives weight to the wise adage, friends, that the only good Indians are the dead ones.

25   GHOST   Bravo! Bravo, Mister Interlocutor, sir. Mister Drum could not have said it better.

INTERLOCUTOR   Thank you. Mister Ghost.

GHOST   No, thank you. Mister Interlocutor. I take your words to heart. My heart soars! We all thank you, sir. Don't we, ladies and gentles? Never a truer

30   word was said. It is to our great benefit to know of this dread red threat to our well-beings and livelihoods, this deadly hood, this Almighty Fart character. Dead Indians would be even better, sir, if they didn't stink that way.

INTERLOCUTOR   Thank you again, Mister Ghost, thank you again. I thank you too, ladies and gentle sirs. We will now return to the sequence of events as

35   listed in your programs.

GHOST   But sir, there's still no sign of Messers Bone. Tambo, Drum, or any one. The entire company, sir, seems to be running on Indian Time![9]

INTERLOCUTOR   Would you now consider performing, Mister Ghost, for our attentive friends, that charming curiosity you called a dance?

40   GHOST   No.

INTERLOCUTOR   Surely. Mister Ghost—

GHOST   Call me the late Almighty Voice. Call me an early redman. Call me, yes, even call me a ghost—but don't call me Shirley![1]

INTERLOCUTOR   You're the most spirited ghost I've ever met.

45   GHOST   You better believe it. There's a stir of dissatisfaction, sir, in the audience. Perhaps number seven?

INTERLOCUTOR   An excellent suggestion. Mister Ghost. An excellent selection, I assure you, my friends.

GHOST   But, sir, it calls for the entire company. And we, sir, are the skeleton

50   crew!

Scene Four

The INTERLOCUTOR changes the title placard to "Scene Four: The Walkaround."

INTERLOCUTOR   Ladies and gentlemen, for your delight and encouragement, Mister Ghost and Yours Truly will now present a martial interlude. In honour of all our heroic boys in uniform!

GHOST   I'll even honour those boys out of uniform.

5   INTERLOCUTOR   I appear first in the role of Mister Allan,[2] Leading the charge through the bluff. After the renegade!

GHOST   Hurrah! We're beating the bushes.

INTERLOCUTOR   Where are the cowards?

GHOST   Moo? Pow, pow!

---

9. The traditional Native notion of time is nonlinear; the joke here is that the company's performers cannot follow a clock.
1. Reference to a comic exchange in the 1980 movie *Airplane*, starring Lesley Nielsen: "Surely you can't be serious." "I am serious. And don't call me Shirley."
2. Inspector John B. "Bronco Jack" Allan

and Sergeant Charles Raven were wounded in the attack on the poplar bluff where Almighty Voice and his two companions were holed up. Corporal Charles Home Sterling Hockin, Postmaster Ernest Grundy, and Constable J. R. Kerr were killed during this assault.

10 INTERLOCUTOR   Ambush, vicious ambush!

GHOST   It appears Mister Allan's fallen off his horse!

INTERLOCUTOR   A bullet! A bullet shattered my arm.

GHOST   Bull! The bottle did him in.

INTERLOCUTOR   Then I take the part of the brave second-in-command, Mis-
15   ter Raven.

GHOST   Already shot on the wing.

INTERLOCUTOR   What?

GHOST   In his private parts!

INTERLOCUTOR   Not my leg?

20 GHOST   Groin, groin, gone!

INTERLOCUTOR   Oh where is the rest of my happy company?

GHOST   Retreat! Retreat! Buck up, my friend, there are but three of them.

INTERLOCUTOR   We've got them outnumbered. I, Mister Hockin, take charge.
   Surround the bluff!

25 GHOST   But are you nine and the settlers enough?

INTERLOCUTOR   Postmaster Grundy here, volunteer, sir. We'll all of us beat
   them bushes again.

GHOST   March then. March south, men. They can't hide from you.

INTERLOCUTOR   Where have they gone? We had them surrounded.

30 GHOST   This could be embarrassing.

INTERLOCUTOR   East to west now. Shoulder to shoulder.

GHOST   Nothing. No one. Again?

INTERLOCUTOR   Here we go. These darn trees.

GHOST   Unpopular poplars?

35 INTERLOCUTOR   If they weren't so green. Fire would force them out.

GHOST   Say again.

INTERLOCUTOR   Fire!

GHOST   Bang bang! Bang bang, bang bang, bang bang! The mail comes late.

INTERLOCUTOR   Why?

40 GHOST   Postmaster Grundy got shot in the gut.

INTERLOCUTOR   What about Hockin?

GHOST   His heart got broken.

INTERLOCUTOR   And Kerr?

GHOST   Sorry, sir. Retreat! Retreat!

45 INTERLOCUTOR   I don't want to wait all day and all night.

GHOST   Too late.

INTERLOCUTOR   I could have got them.

GHOST   Reinforcements arrive!

INTERLOCUTOR   I could have got them alive!

50 GHOST   So can I play the one little, two little dozen Mounties?

INTERLOCUTOR   I'll take the roles of the two big guns?

GHOST   Bang bang? Boom boom. Doom doom!

INTERLOCUTOR   As well as the crowd of concerned civilians, including the
   disappointed—

55 GHOST   —I do so much for those ungrateful wretches—

INTERLOCUTOR   —farm instructor and his friend the ever hopeful—

GHOST   —Spare the rod and spoil the child!—[3]

3. Traditional saying that reflects the belief that corporal discipline encourages proper child
behavior.

INTERLOCUTOR   —missionary priest. Well?

GHOST   It will be the least I can do then and an honour to represent the
60   man's wife and mother as well as others from the One Arrow Reserve,
Treaty Number Six.[4]

INTERLOCUTOR   Perhaps, then, you will do the parts then of the young man
and his ill-fated companions? Yes?

GHOST   No.

65   INTERLOCUTOR   Mister Ghost, sure—please listen to me and consider—

GHOST   Fuck you. I'm not going through that again for your entertainment.

INTERLOCUTOR   Mister Ghost—

GHOST   You do it.

INTERLOCUTOR   [*to the tune of "Derry Down"*][5]   Who is fighting the battle
70   for everyone—

GHOST   —is fighting the battle for everyone—

INTERLOCUTOR   —fights bloodthirsty redskins and wears a grin—

GHOST   —not afeard of anything?—

GHOST & INTERLOCUTOR
Who rides high in the saddle and shoots a gun,
75   rides high in the saddle and shoots a gun,
shoots bloodthirsty redskins and wears a grin,
not afeard of anything?
We have the guns, the guts, the wit.
We know that you are stinking shit.
80   We did it to the buffalo.
Want to be next? Yes or no?
We are the men with guns and bucks.
We know that you are stupid fucks.
We did it to the buffalo.
85   Want to be next? Yes or no?

INTERLOCUTOR
Who is fighting the battle for everyone,
is fighting the battle for everyone,
shoots bloodthirsty redskins and wears a grin,
not afeard of anything?

90   GHOST   We have the guns, the guts, the wit.
We know that you are stupid shit.
We did it to the buffalo.
Want to be next? Yes or no?

GHOST & INTERLOCUTOR
We are the men,
95   well let's say it again,
to get them heathen Indians.
We are the ones,
oh let's do it with guns,

---

4. An 1876 treaty between the Canadian monarchy and the Plains and Woods Cree tribes of central Manitoba and Saskatchewan whereby land rights to large areas of First Nations lands were ceded to the federal government. In return the government provided money, 11.5 square kilometers of land for each family of five, farming tools, fishing and hunting rights, schools on reserves, and a medicine chest for use of the tribes.
5. English folk song.

let's kill them stinking Indians.
100 We are the ones,
well let's do it with rum,
let's get them redskin Indians.
We are the men,
oh let's say it again,
105 to kill them damn dead Indians.

GHOST   Who rides high in the saddle and shoots a gun,
rides high in the saddle and shoots a gun,
shoots bloodthirsty redskins and wears a grin,
not afeard of anything?

INTERLOCUTOR
110 We have the guns, the guts, the wit.
We know that you are stinking shit.
We did it to the buffalo.
Want to be next? Yes or No?

GHOST & INTERLOCUTOR
We have the bucks and you do not.
115 Is it a wonder that you got shot?
We have the bucks and you do not.
Is it a wonder that you got shot?
We have the bucks and you do not.
Is it a wonder that you got shot?
120 We have the bucks and you do not.
Is it a wonder that you got shot?

We have the blankets and the rum.
Oh did you say that you want some?

GHOST   Well, Mister Interlocutor, how do you feel now?
125 INTERLOCUTOR   No, Mister Ghost, how do you feel now?
GHOST   Well, Mister Interlocutor, I feel somewhat like a newspaper.
INTERLOCUTOR   You feel like a newspaper? How is that, Mister Ghost?
GHOST   I'm pale as a sheet of paper.
INTERLOCUTOR   A sheet of paper? With black eyes, Mister Ghost?
130 GHOST   Every one dotted, sir.
[The INTERLOCUTOR hits the GHOST.]
And ultimately, sir, I am like a newspaper in that I am read all over[6]—the
countryside.
INTERLOCUTOR   Red all over, sir? A most colourful conceit. Bloody good, as
our cousins would have it. Newspapers are our pass to an understanding of
135 the reserve and the life of its denizens.
GHOST   And we don't have to go to the Indian agent to get them. The passes.
INTERLOCUTOR   Are you making one at me, sir? [hitting him] Did you read
how we're teaching our primitive friends agriculture?
GHOST   That'll bring them down to earth.
140 INTERLOCUTOR   And we're giving them the benefit of our modern tongue.
GHOST   They'll need no other one, our kingdom come.

---

6. What's black and white and red all over? Answer (playing on the homophones red/read): a
newspaper.

INTERLOCUTOR   Did you read how tranquil and subordinate they've become under our wise and humane government?

> [*The* GHOST *claps a "gunshot."*]

Was that a gun? A shot?

145 GHOST   Likely not. The Indian agent won't give them any more ammunition until they put in a crop.

INTERLOCUTOR   What will they eat in the meantime?

GHOST [*hitting himself*]   Off to the hoose-gow[7] with them! Lazy is as lazy does. So it says in the newspaper. Or the Bible. [*reprising "Derry Down"*]

150
> Who is shooting in battle at every one,
> is shooting in battle at everyone—

GHOST & INTERLOCUTOR
> —fights bloodthirsty redskins and wears a grin,
> not afeard of anything?—

GHOST   —We have the words, the pens, the laws.
155
> We know that treaties are for fools.
> We did it to the buffalo.
> You want to be next?

Scene Five

The GHOST *reveals the next placard: "Scene Five: Tenor Solo."*

GHOST   And now, for the particular delectation of the ladies in the audience—

INTERLOCUTOR   What are you doing?

GHOST   —Mister Interlocutor will render in his most famous transvestatory manner—

5 INTERLOCUTOR   I won't do this.

GHOST   —as the Princess Porkly Haunches,[8] he now sings "The Sioux Song."

INTERLOCUTOR   This is not a regular part of the program, ladies and gentlemen.

GHOST   And therefore we must show our gratitude to the princess. Let us
10 further encourage her, ladies and gentle sirs.

INTERLOCUTOR [*to the tune of "Amazing Grace"*][9]

> How beautiful
> A man the moon.
> I am what I am.
> I'm not above
15 A buck for love.
> What good is it? Sioux me.
>
> A sparkling place
> The city is.
> My face is my face.
20 I must go far
> Below zero.
> What good is it? Sioux me.
> My name is Sioux.

---

7. Jail (slang).
8. Invented name.
9. Widely known hymn, written by English poet and clergyman John Newton in 1779. Its lyrics speak of sin, forgiveness, and redemption.

What did I do?
25 I never ever said
That red is what
I want to drink.
It goes right to my head.

How beautiful
30 A place the past.
We are where we are.
The redskin race
Finishes last.
What good is it? Sioux me.

35 GHOST   Thank you, thank you, Mister Interlocutor. An astonishingly touching masquerade. It seemed almost real. Is this a tear here, washing the war paint?[1]

INTERLOCUTOR   Unhand me, sir. I'm not afraid of you.

GHOST   Boo is no go then. So how do you feel, Mister Interlocutor?

40 INTERLOCUTOR   I'm the Interlocutor here!

GHOST   How do you feel now?

INTERLOCUTOR   I know what to do. I know the order of the show.

GHOST   You do, do you?

INTERLOCUTOR   I want my happy company.

45 GHOST   They're even later than I am, sir. It's curtains for all of us!

INTERLOCUTOR   No, the show must go on.

GHOST   The audience is waiting. Mister Interlocutor?

INTERLOCUTOR   The playlet.

Scene Six

The INTERLOCUTOR *reveals the placard: "Scene Six: The Playlet."*

GHOST   The playlet!

INTERLOCUTOR   Ladies and gentlemen, as a public service to the citizens at the forefront of our civilization, we now present a short drama of spiritual significance.

5 GHOST   Mister Interlocutor, in the continued absence of Mister Bones, will now render the role of Sweet Sioux.

INTERLOCUTOR   I dream. I dream, I do, of the bright lights of the city. Regina,[2] she's the finest, the queen city of my dreams. But I promised Daddy, Daddy dear, I would keep up the homestead, I would be his little 10 red pioneer. This on his deathbed. Sigh. Gangrene from an arrow. Oh horror!

GHOST   Shot by me, ha ha, in error. Oops!

INTERLOCUTOR   Mister Ghost now appears, in the infelicitous absence of Mister Tambo, in the role of the villainous Chief Magistrate.

15 GHOST   Ahem. Ahem. Give me some rum or I'll shoot you in the bum. I need firewater for a starter. Then off I go on a hunt or to court. Order, order, I

---

1. Paint applied to a warrior's face and body before a battle.
2. Named in 1882 for Queen Victoria, this southern Saskatchewan city served as capital of the Canadian Northwest Territories until 1903, when it became the capital of the province of Saskatchewan.

say to the buffalo. Right between the eyes, I warn the prisoners. Tonight it's too late, too late for her.

INTERLOCUTOR   It is the eleventh hour. It is beyond my power to pay the
20   mortgage on my daddy's farm. Oh I am losing courage.

GHOST   Knocka knocka, Sweet Sioux.

INTERLOCUTOR   Who's there? At this hour.

GHOST   Knocka knocka.

INTERLOCUTOR   What would Daddy do?

25 GHOST   Answer the door.

INTERLOCUTOR   You think so?

GHOST   Knocka knocka, Sioux!

INTERLOCUTOR   Hello. Who's there?

GHOST   It is I, my dear. Your sweetheart, Chief Magistrate.

30 INTERLOCUTOR   You're no sweetheart to me.

GHOST   She's not all there up here. Sometimes she believes me.

INTERLOCUTOR   Stay away. What is it you want?

GHOST   The time is short. The deed on this land is about to come due. I was worried, my dear, about you.

35 INTERLOCUTOR   You were? Really?

GHOST   Do you have the necessary dollars?

INTERLOCUTOR   No—

GHOST   —Hooray!—

INTERLOCUTOR   —I'm sorry to say.

40 GHOST   I mean to say I'm here to help you.

INTERLOCUTOR   But at what price? A chief doesn't become magistrate without vice.

GHOST   Oh Sweet Sioux.

INTERLOCUTOR   What's a girl to do?

45 GHOST   Oh sweet Sweet Sioux.

INTERLOCUTOR   Oh, no, Chief Magistrate. I couldn't do that.

GHOST   Why not, my dear? She's done it before.

INTERLOCUTOR   I'm not that kind of girl. I only do it for love and/or marriage.

50 GHOST   Why buy the moo cow?

INTERLOCUTOR   I won't do it for meat any more.

GHOST   I'll give the deed to you.

INTERLOCUTOR   Oh no. I couldn't do that. That would make me one of those women, nothing more than a squaw.

55 GHOST   A squaw? You mean like Buck and Squaw?

[The GHOST pulls the INTERLOCUTOR into a reprise of the Hollywood Indian War Dance. The INTERLOCUTOR complies but keeps it short.]

INTERLOCUTOR   Midnight is about to strike!

GHOST   There goes the farm.

INTERLOCUTOR   But I keep my honour.

GHOST   Midnight strikes. The farm is mine. And what the hell, so are you!

60 INTERLOCUTOR   Oh no no! That would be—rape!

GHOST   Right you are! You're more intelligent than you appear.

INTERLOCUTOR   Rape, oh no!

GHOST   Oh yes, yes. Sweet Sioux! Talk about the Almighty Buck.

INTERLOCUTOR   Corporal? Corporal Coat? Mister Tambo? Mister Drum!
65   Anybody!

GHOST   There's no one here to come to your aid.

INTERLOCUTOR   Stop! Stop, I know. It is I, I, Corporal Red Coat of the
Mounted Police—[3]

GHOST   —Aye, aye!—

70 INTERLOCUTOR   —cleverly disguised as Sweet Sioux in order to tempt the
evil Chief Magistrate to show his true colours.

GHOST   Blast you, Corporal Red Coat. Talk about an Indian giver. Your feminine innocence, your eyes, had me completely convinced.

INTERLOCUTOR   It is now my duty to arrest you, Chief Magistrate.

75 GHOST   Corporal Coat, could I make you an offer?

INTERLOCUTOR   Oh more villainy. You're trying to bribe me.

GHOST   I offer you the deed to the farm for a taste of your feminine charms.

INTERLOCUTOR   How dare you, sir! Bang bang!

GHOST   Oh I am wounded, I am dying, mortifying, I am dead.

80 INTERLOCUTOR   Oh Corporal Coat.

GHOST   As my soul slips toward hell, I repent. Is it too late?

INTERLOCUTOR   Call me Red, miss.

GHOST   What a sorry end this is!

INTERLOCUTOR   I want to thank you.

85 GHOST   Jesus loves me!

INTERLOCUTOR   We can talk about that later on, Sioux.

GHOST   And suddenly my skin is white.

INTERLOCUTOR   Oh, Red, may I offer you some apple cider?

GHOST   Oh miracle! I'm heaven-sent!

90 INTERLOCUTOR   I love you.

GHOST   Or are those wedding bells I hear?

INTERLOCUTOR   I love you, too, my dear. I'm beside myself with love.

GHOST   And as I say adieu to those two united souls, choirs of angels remind
me how true it is said that the only good Indians are the ones who are
95   sainted.

INTERLOCUTOR   Bravo, Mister Ghost. What a wonderful halo.

GHOST   It's old paint, Mister Interlocutor. Bravo to you, too, sir. I love your
Sweet Sioux.

INTERLOCUTOR   As you were. Thank you, thank you, ladies and gentlemen.
100   You're too kind.

GHOST   They're deaf, dumb, and blinded by the light of the heavenly Ghost,
sir.

INTERLOCUTOR   We hope our tale encouraged all and offended none.

GHOST   There ain't no nuns I can see out there, sir.

105 INTERLOCUTOR   We give you laughter and tears. We give hope to all who toil
and are laden.

GHOST   For every girl, there is a guy.

INTERLOCUTOR   For every man, a maiden.

GHOST   For every nun, a holy Ghost.

---

3. The North-West Mounted Police wore red uniform coats.

Scene Seven

The GHOST, *on his way to the footlights, bumps into the placard stand and "Scene Seven: Duet" turns up.*

GHOST   Hi, my name's Almighty. Do you come here much?

INTERLOCUTOR   Mister Ghost, where are you going?

GHOST   I want to get in touch with the audience.

INTERLOCUTOR   Our final curtain has yet to descend, Mister Ghost.

5 GHOST   Speak for yourself. I want to make some new friends in the pit.

INTERLOCUTOR   You can't leave me too.

GHOST   Hiya. Will you help me down?

INTERLOCUTOR   Mister Ghost, I implore you.

GHOST   Mister Interlocutor, sir, or madam, I was forgetting about you.

10 INTERLOCUTOR   You can't go. I mean, we do have some few ensuing num-
    bers, Mister Ghost.

GHOST   The two of us? Go on without me.

INTERLOCUTOR   None of the rest of our happy company has come along.

GHOST   Look me in the eyes and ask.

15 INTERLOCUTOR   Please, Mister Ghost. Please.

GHOST   Mister Interlocutor, sir, how do you feel?

INTERLOCUTOR   How do I feel? With my hands! No, Mister Ghost, I feel this
    evening like the moon.

GHOST   You feel like the moon, Mister Interlocutor. How is that?

20 INTERLOCUTOR   Envious and pale of face and alone, Mister Ghost.

GHOST   I know how you feel, but you are mistaken.

INTERLOCUTOR   How am I mistaken, Mister Ghost?

GHOST   The Moon's an old woman. We call her Grandmother.[4] [*to the tune of*
    "God Save The Queen"][5]
        The Moon's an old woman
25   A very wise woman.
        She's made of light!

GHOST & INTERLOCUTOR
        She watches over us,
        Over the children
        Each of us is a child again
30   In the coldest night.

INTERLOCUTOR
        The Moon's a young woman
        A very new woman
        Made out of dark
        She's waiting for the light
35   Just as a child might
        Wrapped warmly in a blanket and
        Not at all afraid.

GHOST   Well how do you feel now. Mister Interlocutor? Mister?

---

4. Grandmother Moon, who watches over the
earth, is an important figure in Native spiritual beliefs.

5. Royal anthem of the United Kingdom and
its territories since the 1700s.

Scene Eight

The INTERLOCUTOR, *fleeing the* GHOST, *bumps into the placard stand. "Scene Eight: Stand-up" turns up.*

GHOST   Sir!

INTERLOCUTOR   Did you know, Mister Ghost, that marriage is an institution?

GHOST   Yes, sir, I had heard that said.

INTERLOCUTOR   Well, sir, so is an insane asylum! Did you know, Mister
5   Ghost, that love makes the world go round? Well, sir, so does a sock in the jaw! Which reminds me, sir. An Indian from Batoche[6] came up to me the other day and said he hadn't had a bite in days. So I bit him! Do you know, sir, how many Indians it takes to screw in a light bulb?

GHOST   What's a light bulb?

10   INTERLOCUTOR   Good one, Mister Ghost, a very good one. Well then, sir, if it's nighttime here, it must be winter in Regina. Nothing could be finah than Regina in the wintah, sir. Am I making myself clear? Does this bear repeating? Does this buffalo repeating? Almighty Gas, you say! Answer me, Mister Ghost. Answer! What! A fine time to demand a medium! It's very
15   small of you, sir. I promise you I will large this in your face if you do not choose to co-operate. Tell me, is it true that the Indian brave will marry his wife's sister so he doesn't have to break in a new mother-in-law? Does it therefore follow, sir, that our good and great Queen Victoria keeps her Prince Albert in a can?[7] That's where she keeps the Indians! Hear ye, hear
20   ye! Don't knock off her bonnet and stick her in her royal rump with a sword, sir. The word, sir, is treason. Or are you drunk? Besotted! Be seated, sir. No! Stand up! You, sir, you, I recognize you now. You're that redskin! You're that wagon burner! That feather head, Chief Bullshit. No, Chief Shitting Bull![8] Oh, no, no. Bloodthirsty savage. Yes, you're primitive, unciv-
25   ilized, a cantankerous cannibal! Unruly redman, you lack human intelligence! Stupidly stoic, sick, demented, foaming at the maws! Weirdly mad and dangerous, alcoholic, diseased, dirty, filthy, stinking, ill-fated degenerate race, vanishing, dying, lazy, mortifying, fierce, fierce and crazy, crazy, shit, shit, shit, shit . . .

30   GHOST   What's a light bulb?

INTERLOCUTOR   Who are you? Who the hell are you?

GHOST   I'm a dead Indian. I eat crow instead of buffalo.

INTERLOCUTOR   That's good. That's very good.

---

6. The Battle of Batoche in central Saskatchewan concluded the 1885 Northwest Rebellion. This series of skirmishes between the Métis—mixed-race people of First Nations and European descent—and Canadian government forces resulted in the defeat of the Métis forces.

7. American brand of tobacco first introduced in 1907. The name refers to King Edward VII (reigned 1901–10), who was known as Prince Albert before his coronation. The availability of Prince Albert in tins later provided the subject for a well-known practical joke, in which a phone caller calls a store and asks, "Do you have Prince Albert in a can?" When the person on the other line answers yes, the caller retorts, "Well, let him out!"

8. Sitting Bull, Lakota Sioux Indian chief (ca. 1831–1890) who led resistance against U.S. military and civilian encroachment on Native lands.

Scene Nine

The lights shift from variety to spectral as the spotlight finds the placard: "Scene Nine: Finale."

INTERLOCUTOR   Who am I? Do you know?
GHOST   I recognized you by your eyes.
INTERLOCUTOR   Who am I?
GHOST   White Girl, my White Girl.
5 INTERLOCUTOR   Who? Who is that?
GHOST   My fierce, crazy little girl. My wife. *Ni-wikimakan.* [*My wife.*]

> [*The* INTERLOCUTOR *touches her face with her gloved hands as the* GHOST *embraces and releases her. The spotlight finds her face as her gloved hands begin to wipe the whiteface off, unmasking the woman inside. The* GHOST *removes one glove and throws it on the dead fire, she does the same with the other. The fire rekindles.*]

Piko ta-ta-wi kisisomoyan ekwo. [*I have to go finish dancing now.*]
INTERLOCUTOR   *Patima, Kisse-Manitou-Wayou.* [*Goodbye, Almighty Voice.*]

> [*The* GHOST *goes and dances in celebration to a drum. The woman removes the rest of the whiteface and costume, becoming* WHITE GIRL *again. She gathers the costume in her arms as the spotlight drifts away to become a full moon in the night.* WHITE GIRL *lifts a baby-sized bundle to the audience as the* GHOST *continues to dance in the fading lights.*]

The end.

SUZAN-LORI PARKS

b. 1964

W HEN Suzan-Lori Parks was a senior
at Mount Holyoke College, she wrote
her first play, *The Sinner's Place*. Because,
as Parks later recalled, the play's setting
consisted of "a lot of dirt on stage which
was being dug at," the Theater Department
rejected it for production. By the time she
was awarded a Pulitzer Prize in 2002 for
her play *Topdog/Underdog*, however, Parks's
fascination with digging—turning over the
topsoil of cultural myths, sifting through
the artifacts of history, unearthing the buried voices of African Americans within
history—had established her as one of
the American theater's foremost archaeologists. "The responsibility of a writer," the
novelist James Baldwin once remarked, "is
to excavate the experience of the people
who produced him." Deeply concerned
with forebears and inheritances, Parks's
drama uncovers this experience by examining its traces and absences in the American
historical imagination. "Because so much
of African American history has been unre-
corded, dismembered, washed out," Parks
writes, "one of my tasks as playwright is
to—through literature and the special
strange relationship between theater and
real-life—locate the ancestral burial
ground, dig for bones, find bones, hear the
bones sing, write it down." By "remembering" history in the double sense of retrieving
and remaking it, Parks offers new theatrical

possibilities for staging the dialogue between
past, present, and future. Innovative (often
challenging) in language, dramatic structure, and performance, her drama remains
among the most startlingly original in the
contemporary American theater.

Suzan-Lori Parks was born in Fort
Knox, Kentucky. The daughter of an Army
colonel, she moved frequently as a child
and considered a number of places home:
Texas, California, North Carolina, Maryland, Vermont, and Germany, where she
attended German schools rather than
those for the children of American military
personnel. This experience of changing
location—of moving between places with
divergent regional and national histories
and of negotiating language differences—
clearly contributed to her interest in language and in the relationships between
geography, history, and identity. As an
undergraduate at Mount Holyoke she took
a short story writing class with James
Baldwin; after she gave an animated in-
class reading of one of her stories, he suggested that she consider playwriting. The
turn to drama was a natural one: as she
explained in a 2000 interview, she felt
while writing short stories that her characters were in the room with her, "standing right behind me, talking. Not telling
the story, but acting it out—doing it."
Despite the Theater Department's rejec-

tion of *The Sinner's Place*, Parks decided to pursue her interest in dramatic writing. Encouraged by one of her English professors, she read the plays of two pioneering African American women playwrights: Adrienne Kennedy, whose *Funnyhouse of a Negro* (1962) dramatized its protagonist's haunted consciousness on a dreamlike stage reminiscent of the stages of AUGUST STRINDBERG and JEAN GENET, and Ntozake Shange, who has explored the relationship of drama, poetry, dance, and female African American identity in *for colored girls who have considered suicide / when the rainbow is enuf* (1975) and other plays. After graduating from college in 1985 with majors in English and German, Parks studied acting for a year in London.

Upon her return to the United States, Parks quickly established herself as a playwright of note. *Betting on the Dust Commander* (1987) was produced in New York, as was *Imperceptible Mutabilities in the Third Kingdom* (1989). The latter play received an Obie (off-Broadway) Award for Best New American Play and was widely praised by critics; indeed, after seeing the play, Mel Gussow of the *New York Times* called Parks "the year's most promising playwright." *The Death of the Last Black Man in the Whole Entire World* opened the following year at the same theater, and *Devotees in the Garden of Love* was produced at the Humana Festival in Louisville in 1992. Parks's next drama, THE AMERICA PLAY, was given workshop productions in Washington and Dallas in 1993 before opening at the Yale Repertory Theatre and the New York Public Theater in 1994. In 1996, her play *Venus*—based on the life of Saartjie Baartman, a Khoisan African woman who, because of her large buttocks, was exhibited in the early 1800s in London and Paris as the "Hottentot Venus"—was produced at the Public Theater in New York and received an Obie Award for Playwriting. *In the Blood* was produced in New York in 1999, and *Fucking A* premiered in Houston in 2000; both plays were inspired by Nathaniel Hawthorne's novel *The Scarlet Letter* (1850). The Pulitzer Prize–winning *Topdog/Underdog*, which features two brothers named Lincoln and Booth, opened at the Public Theater in New York in 2001 and was subsequently taken to Broadway. Parks's most ambitious

theatrical project began in 2002, when the playwright decided to write one play every day for a year. The completed plays—some less than a page in length, others considerably longer—were performed by theater groups across the United States in 2006–07 as part of a cycle titled *365 Days/365 Plays*. More recent plays include *Father Comes Home from the Wars (Parts 1, 8 & 9)* (2009), *Father Comes Home from the Wars (Parts 1, 2 & 3)* (2014), and *The Book of Grace* (2010). Her adaptation of George and Ira Gershwin's opera *Porgy and Bess* for the musical-theater stage premiered in 2011. Parks has also written the screenplay for the film *Girl 6* (1996, directed by Spike Lee) and an adaptation of Zora Neale Hurston's 1937 novel *Their Eyes Were Watching God*, which was televised in 2005. Parks's novel *Getting Mother's Body* was published in 2003.

Intricate (sometimes dense) in texture and meaning, Parks's plays have received widespread attention for their distinctive, highly theatricalized conception of language, character, and dramatic form. As befits a dramatist whose favorite writers include the modernists William Faulkner, Virginia Woolf, and James Joyce, Parks makes intricate, highly self-conscious use of the acoustic and semantic qualities of dramatic speech. Words, Parks insists, are "spells in our mouths." Driven by the cadences, syntax, and word forms of African American dialect, distinguished by frequent wordplay and by multiple meanings, the language of Parks's drama reflects her characters' complex lives and inheritance. When one of the characters in *Imperceptible Mutabilities* says "Last night I dreamed of where I comed from. But where I comed from diduhnt look like nowhere like I been," his words evoke a collective experience of migration, relocation, and lost origins. How do contemporary African Americans, descendants of those who endured the Middle Passage in the holds of slave ships, bridge the gap between Africa and North America, between the present and the history that informs it? Like the words that Parks uses, with their "thrilling histories" and "fabulous etymologies," the characters who people her plays are indelibly marked by history. They bear names such as those in *Death of the Last Black Man in the Whole Entire World*: Black Man with Watermelon, Yes and Greens Black-Eyed Peas Cornbread, And Bigger and Bigger and Bigger, Before Columbus, and Queen-then-Pharaoh-Hatshepsut. Drawing together racial stereotypes, African history, soul food, and literary references (the character And Bigger and Bigger and Bigger, for example, is named after Bigger Thomas, the protagonist of Richard Wright's 1940 novel *Native Son*), these figures embody many of the ways in which black Americans have been represented in American history and culture.

While Parks's dramatic characters are rooted in real lives and relationships, they also function as improvised meditations, or riffs, on cultural themes and images. Not surprisingly, music—in the form of jazz, classical music, opera, and hip-hop—has played an important role in the language and structure of Parks's drama. Rejecting the linear form of traditional drama, in which action proceeds with a clear beginning, middle, and end, Parks experiments with alternative ways of structuring dramatic incidents. One of her signature devices is "repetition and revision"—the

technique, popular with jazz composers and musicians (and echoing the cadence of African American oral traditions, including preaching), of repeating a phrase over and over again while varying it slightly each time. In Parks's drama, words, exchanges, and situations return with hypnotic regularity, establishing connections and counterpoints that build with a logic as much circular as linear. "Characters refigure their words," Parks declares, "and through a refiguring of language show us that they are experiencing their situation anew." The phrase that supplies the title of *The Death of the Last Black Man in the Whole Entire World*, for instance, is spoken at a number of points in the play, and this repetition mirrors that of the action, in which the central protagonist—representing one black man and every black man—is murdered over and over again. Only in the burial scene that ends the play does this repetitive cycle in African American history attain closure.

Repetition, doubling, and, again, the remembering of history are central to *The America Play*, Parks's most frequently performed work. The play is set in a "great hole" somewhere in the American West,

Ronnie Washington (left) as the Foundling Father in a 2008 production of *The America Play* staged by the Thick Description Theater Company (San Francisco).

"an exact replica" (the stage direction indicates) "of the Great Hole of History," a fictional theme park located back East where a parade of historical figures emerge and march by for the audience's entertainment. The play's protagonist, an African American man identified by his stage name, The Foundling Father, was so entranced with the marvels of history when he visited the Great Park on his honeymoon that he became determined to re-create it. After being told that he resembled Abraham Lincoln—the two "were dead ringers, more or less"—he took to reciting speeches by the famous president in costume. When someone observed that "he played Lincoln so well that he ought to be shot," The Foundling Father devised just such an act: customers pay a penny to shoot him as he sits in Ford's Theater. One after another, they select a pistol, stand in position, and, after shooting him in the head, jump to the stage yelling "Thus to the tyrants!" or other exclamations attributed to Lincoln's assassin John Wilkes Booth (and others). The assassination is replayed over and over again while The Foundling Father recounts to the play's audience his past and his peculiar vocation.

All history repeats itself, Karl Marx famously observed: "the first time as tragedy, the second time as farce." But in an age of historical theme parks, Revolutionary and Civil War reenactments, and interactive museums (such as the Abraham Lincoln Presidential Museum in Springfield, Illinois, which opened in 2005), history is just as likely to repeat itself as theater. In *The America Play,* Parks explores the many ways in which American history—the images, texts, performances, commemorations with which we tell the story of our collective past—writes itself into the present. The Foundling Father is flanked by a pasteboard cutout and bust of Lincoln, to which he frequently gestures; he collects the pennies that bear Lincoln's profile; and he carries with him the props by which the legendary president is identified in the popular imagination: black coat, stovepipe hat, and an assortment of beards (including a blond one, which he rarely wears because it undermines the illusion). The Found-

ling Father quotes from the Gettysburg Address and retells the events of the fateful night in Ford's Theater, though the account he provides is based as much on tradition and hearsay as historical fact. Parks plays with the idea of historical accuracy in her footnotes to the play, which include humorous or speculative information (including a line that Mary Todd Lincoln "might have said . . . that night") as well as documented facts. In a play that features an actor impersonating a historical figure, a replay of this performance on television (in the play's second act), and scenes from the play that Lincoln was watching (*Our American Cousin* [1858] by Tom Taylor), history becomes the site of multiple performances and competing imitations. At times, original and copy seem indistinguishable from one another. Even the Great Hole of History reappears as a theme park somewhere else.

With its parade of well-known historical figures and deeds, the Great Hole provides a spectacle of American history as it has traditionally circulated and been known. But this hole in the ground also signals its absences and elisions. Reversing the nineteenth-century tradition of blackface—white actors blackening their faces in order to play African American characters—The Foundling Father's impersonation of Abraham Lincoln foregrounds the absence or marginalization of African Americans from this history. As he refers to himself as the "Lesser Known," in contrast to the "Great Man," The Foundling Father reflects on the discrepancy between the latter's fame and his own anonymity. A "digger" by trade, he discovers a more elevated calling by following in the Great Man's footsteps. Yet the reflected glory that he acquires by impersonating Lincoln only underscores the historical invisibility to which his racial identity has otherwise consigned him. Lincoln may have freed the slaves—but the idea of America that he represents has largely excluded African Americans from its originating myths as well as from the prevailing national identity. The Foundling Father may assume the mantle of one of his country's forefathers—but as Parks's play on his name signifies, his is an illegitimate inheritance (a *foundling* is a child of unknown parentage). When one of his customers, a woman, yells "LIES!" after jumping to the stage, her accusation strikes at the heart of the national myth—the idea of America as "a new nation, conceived in Liberty, and dedicated to the proposition that all men are created equal"—that Lincoln represents.

The search for (fore)fathers in *The America Play* extends into the play's second act, set years later, when The Foundling Father's wife, Lucy, and son Brazil look for traces of him after his death.

Marked by the rituals of grief, this act is pervaded with a sense of mourning, yet it also conveys a tone of affirmation. The Foundling Father may have "fall[en] in love with the wrong person, fall[en] in love with the wrong dream" (as Parks suggests), but his deconstructive performance of American history has been celebratory as well. By showing this history to itself through the mirror of blackness, he has claimed a space, however small, in the performance of national identity.   S.G.

The America Play

THE ROLES

Act 1:	THE FOUNDLING FATHER, AS ABRAHAM LINCOLN
	A VARIETY OF VISITORS
Act 2:	LUCY
	BRAZIL
	THE FOUNDLING FATHER, AS ABRAHAM LINCOLN
	2 ACTORS
	The Visitors in Act 1 are played by the 2 Actors who assume the roles in the passages from *Our American Cousin* in Act 2.
Place	A great hole. In the middle of nowhere. The hole is an exact replica of The Great Hole of History.

SYNOPSIS OF ACTS AND SCENES

Act 1: Lincoln Act
Act 2: The Hall of Wonders

A. Big Bang   E. Spadework
B. Echo   F. Echo
C. Archeology   G. The Great Beyond
D. Echo

Brackets in the text indicate optional cuts for production.

In the beginning, all the world was America.
                    —JOHN LOCKE[1]

1. English philosopher and political theorist (1632–1704); the quotation is from *Two Treatises of Government* (1689).

Act 1: Lincoln Act

A great hole. In the middle of nowhere. The hole is an exact replica of the Great Hole of History.

THE FOUNDLING FATHER AS ABRAHAM LINCOLN   "To stop too fearful and too faint to go."[2]

[*Rest.*[3]]

"He digged the hole and the whole held him."

[*Rest.*]

"I cannot dig, to beg I am ashamed."[4]

[*Rest.*]

5   "He went to the theatre but home went she."[5]

[*Rest.*]

Goatee. Goatee. What he sported when he died. Its not my favorite.

[*Rest.*]

"He digged the hole and the whole held him." Huh.

[*Rest.*]

There was once a man who was told that he bore a strong resemblance to Abraham Lincoln.[6] He was tall and thinly built just like the Great Man.
10   His legs were the longer part just like the Great Mans legs. His hands and feet were large as the Great Mans were large. The Lesser Known had several beards which he carried around in a box. The beards were his although he himself had not grown them on his face but since he'd secretly bought the hairs from his barber and arranged their beard shapes and since the
15   procurement and upkeep of his beards took so much work he figured that the beards were completely his. Were as authentic as he was, so to speak. His beard box was of cherry wood and lined with purple velvet. He had the initials "A.L." tooled in gold on the lid.

[*Rest.*]

While the Great Mans livelihood kept him in Big Town the Lesser Knowns
20   work kept him in Small Town. The Great Man by trade was a President. The Lesser Known was a Digger by trade. From a family of Diggers. Digged graves. He was known in Small Town to dig his graves quickly and neatly. This brought him a steady business.

[*Rest.*]

2. An example of chiasmus, by Oliver Goldsmith, cited under "chiasmus" in *Webster's Ninth New Collegiate Dictionary* (Springfield, MA: Merriam-Webster, Inc., 1983) p. 232. Notes 4 and 5 also refer to examples of chiasmus [Parks's note]. *Chiasmus*: the syntactic inversion of the second of two parallel clauses (a rhetorical figure). The example is from "The Traveller; or, A Prospect of Society" (1794), by Goldsmith (ca. 1730–1774), an Irish-born novelist, poet, and playwright.
3. Pause.
4. *A Dictionary of Modern English Usage,* H. W. Fowler (New York: Oxford University Press, 1983) p. 86 [Parks's note]. The quotation is from Luke 16.3.
5. *The New American Heritage Dictionary of the English Language,* William Morris, ed. (Boston: Houghton Mifflin Co., 1981) p. 232 [Parks's note].
6. The sixteenth president of the United States (1809–1865; president, 1861–65), a lawyer and legislator from Illinois who was born in backwoods Kentucky; he has been acclaimed for his leadership during the Civil War (1861–65) and for his role in ending slavery.

A wink to Mr. Lincolns pasteboard cutout. [*Winks at Lincoln's pasteboard cutout.*]

[*Rest.*]

25 It would be helpful to our story if when the Great Man died in death he were to meet the Lesser Known. It would be helpful to our story if, say, the Lesser Known were summoned to Big Town by the Great Mans wife: "*Emergency* oh, *Emergency,* please put the Great Man in the ground"[7] (they say the Great Mans wife was given to hysterics: one young son dead

30 others sickly:[8] even the Great Man couldnt save them: a war on then off and surrendered to: "Play Dixie I always liked that song":[9] the brother against the brother: a new nation all conceived and ready to be hatched: the Great Man takes to guffawing guffawing at thin jokes in bad plays: "You sockdologizing old man-trap!"[1] haw haw haw because he wants so very

35 badly to laugh at something and one moment guffawing and the next moment the Great Man is gunned down. In his rocker. "Useless Useless."[2] And there were bills to pay.) "*Emergency,* oh *Emergency* please put the Great Man in the ground."

[*Rest.*]

It is said that the Great Mans wife did call out and it is said that the Lesser

40 Known would [sneak away from his digging and stand behind a tree where he couldnt be seen or get up and] leave his wife and child after the blessing had been said and [the meat carved during the distribution of the vegetables it is said that he would leave his wife and his child and] standing in the kitchen or sometimes out in the yard [between the right angles of the

45 house] stand out there where he couldnt be seen standing with his ear cocked. "*Emergency,* oh *Emergency,* please put the Great Man in the ground."

[*Rest.*]

It would help if she had called out and if he had been summoned been given a ticket all bought and paid for and boarded a train in his look-alike

50 black frock coat bought on time and already exhausted. Ridiculous. If he had been summoned. [Been summoned between the meat and the vegetables and boarded a train to Big Town where he would line up and gawk at

---

7. Possibly the words of Mary Todd Lincoln [1818–1882] after the death of her husband [Parks's note].

8. Of the Lincolns' four sons—Robert (1843–1926), Edward (1846–1850), William (1850–1862), and Thomas, nicknamed Tad (1853–1871)—only Robert survived into adulthood. Mary Todd Lincoln has often been described as mentally unstable.

9. At the end of the Civil War, President Lincoln told his troops to play "Dixie," the song of the South, in tribute to the Confederacy [Parks's note]. The song was published in 1860 by the Ohio-born Daniel Decatur Emmett, who wrote songs for his blackface minstrel troupe, but his claim of authorship is disputed.

1. A very funny line from the play *Our American Cousin.* As the audience roared with laughter, Booth entered Lincoln's box and shot him dead [Parks's note]. *Our American Cousin* (1858), a comedy by the English dramatist and writer Tom Taylor. John Wilkes Booth (1838–1865), a renowned Shakespearean actor and a Southern sympathizer who led the conspiracy to assassinate Lincoln as he attended a performance less than a week after the Civil War ended.

2. The last words of President Lincoln's assassin, John Wilkes Booth [Parks's note]. After shooting Lincoln, Booth leaped to the stage and broke his leg but escaped on horseback. After soldiers and detectives found him hiding in a barn in Virginia, about 75 miles southwest of Washington, he either was shot or shot himself and died shortly thereafter.

the Great Mans corpse along with the rest of them.[3]] But none of this was meant to be.

> [*Rest.*]

55 A nod to the bust of Mr. Lincoln. [*Nods to the bust of Lincoln.*] But none of this was meant to be. For the Great Man had been murdered long before the Lesser Known had been born. How uhboutthat. [So that any calling that had been done he couldnt hear, any summoning he had hoped for he couldnt answer but somehow not even unheard and unanswered because 60 he hadnt even been there] although you should note that he talked about the murder and the mourning that followed as if he'd been called away on business at the time and because of the business had missed it. Living regretting he hadnt arrived sooner. Being told from birth practically that he and the Great Man were dead ringers, more or less, and knowing that he, 65 if he had been in the slightest vicinity back then, would have had at least a chance at the great honor of digging the Great Mans grave.

> [*Rest.*]

This beard I wear for the holidays. I got shoes to match. Rarely wear em together. It's a little *much*.

> [*Rest.*]

[His son named in a fit of meanspirit after the bad joke about fancy nuts[4] 70 and old mens toes his son looked like a nobody. Not Mr. Lincoln or the father or the mother either for that matter although the father had assumed the superiority of his own blood and hadnt really expected the mother to exert any influence.]

> [*Rest.*]

Sunday. Always slow on Sunday. I'll get thuh shoes. Youll see. A wink to Mr. 75 Lincolns pasteboard cutout. [*Winks at Lincoln's cutout.*]

> [*Rest.*]

Everyone who has ever walked the earth has a shape around which their entire lives and their posterity shapes itself. The Great Man had his log cabin into which he was born, the distance between the cabin and Big Town multiplied by the half-life, the staying power of his words and image, 80 being the true measurement of the Great Mans stature. The Lesser Known had a favorite hole. A chasm, really. Not a hole he had digged but one he'd visited. Long before the son was born. When he and his Lucy were newly wedded. Lucy kept secrets for the dead. And they figured what with his digging and her Confidence work[5] they could build a mourning business. The 85 son would be a weeper.[6] Such a long time uhgo. So long uhgo. When he and his Lucy were newly wedded and looking for some postnuptial excitement: A Big Hole. A theme park. With historical parades. The size of the hole itself was enough to impress any Digger but it was the Historicity of the place the order and beauty of the pageants which marched by them the 90 Greats on parade in front of them. From the sidelines he'd be calling "Ohwayohwhyohwayoh" and "Hello" and waving and saluting. The Hole

---

3. Thousands viewed Lincoln's body lying in state in the U.S. Capitol, and thousands more watched the train bearing him home to Springfield, Illinois, where he was buried.
4. That is, Brazil nuts, which were long

known in some regions of the United States as "nigger toes."
5. That is, her work as someone entrusted with confidential communications.
6. A hired mourner.

and its Historicity and the part he played in it all gave a shape to the life and posterity of the Lesser Known that he could never shake.

[*Rest.*]

95　Here they are. I wont put them on. I'll just hold them up. See. Too much. Told ya. [Much much later when the Lesser Known had made a name for himself he began to record his own movements. He hoped he'd be of interest to posterity. As in the Great Mans footsteps.]

[*Rest.*]

Traveling home again from the honeymoon at the Big Hole riding the train with his Lucy: wife beside him the Reconstructed Historicities he has wit-
100　nessed continue to march before him in his minds eye as they had at the Hole. Cannons wicks were lit and the rockets did blare and the enemy was slain and lay stretched out and smoldering for dead and rose up again to take their bows. On the way home again the histories paraded again on past him although it wasnt on past him at all it wasnt something he could
105　expect but again like Lincolns life not "on past" but *past. Behind him.* Like an echo in his head.

[*Rest.*]

When he got home again he began to hear the summoning. At first they thought it only an echo. Memories sometimes stuck like that and he and his Lucy had both seen visions. But after a while it only called to him. And it
110　became louder not softer but louder louder as if he were moving toward it.

[*Rest.*]

This is my fancy beard. Yellow. Mr. Lincolns hair was dark so I dont wear it much. If you deviate too much they wont get their pleasure. Thats my experience. Some inconsistencies are perpetuatable because theyre good for business. But not the yellow beard. Its just my fancy. Every once and a
115　while. Of course, his hair was dark.

[*Rest.*]

The Lesser Known left his wife and child and went out West finally. [Between the meat and the vegetables. A monumentous journey. Enduring all the elements. Without a friend in the world. And the beasts of the forest took him in. He got there and he got his plot he staked his claim he tried
120　his hand at his own Big Hole.] As it had been back East everywhere out West he went people remarked on his likeness to Lincoln. How, in a limited sort of way, taking into account of course his natural God-given limitations, how he was identical to the Great Man in gait and manner how his legs were long and torso short. The Lesser Known had by this time taken to
125　wearing a false wart on his cheek in remembrance of the Great Mans wart. When the Westerners noted his wart they pronounced the 2 men in virtual twinship.

[*Rest.*]

Goatee. Huh. Goatee.

[*Rest.*]

"He digged the Hole and the Whole held him."

[*Rest.*]

130　"I cannot dig, to beg I am ashamed."

[*Rest.*]

The Lesser Known had under his belt a few of the Great Mans words and after a day of digging, in the evenings, would stand in his hole reciting. But the Lesser Known was a curiosity at best. None of those who spoke of his virtual twinship with greatness would actually pay money to watch him be
135 that greatness. One day he tacked up posters inviting them to come and throw old food at him while he spoke. This was a moderate success. People began to save their old food "for Mr. Lincoln" they said. He took to travel- ing playing small towns. Made money. And when someone remarked that he played Lincoln so well that he ought to be shot, it was as if the Great
140 Mans footsteps had been suddenly revealed:

    [*Rest.*]

The Lesser Known returned to his hole and, instead of speeching, his act would now consist of a single chair, a rocker, in a dark box. The public was invited to pay a penny, choose from the selection of provided pistols, enter the darkened box and "Shoot Mr. Lincoln." The Lesser Known became
145 famous overnight.

    [A MAN, *as John Wilkes Booth, enters. He takes a gun and "stands in posi-*
    tion": at the left side of THE FOUNDLING FATHER, *as Abraham* LINCOLN,
    pointing the gun at THE FOUNDLING FATHER's *head*]

A MAN   Ready.
THE FOUNDLING FATHER   Haw Haw Haw Haw

    [*Rest.*]

HAW HAW HAW HAW

    [BOOTH *shoots.* LINCOLN *"slumps in his chair."* BOOTH *jumps.*]

A MAN [*theatrically*]   "Thus to the tyrants!"[7]

    [*Rest.*]

150 Hhhh. [*Exits.*]

THE FOUNDLING FATHER   Most of them do that, thuh "Thus to the tyrants!"— what they say the killer said. "Thus to the tyrants!" The killer was also heard to say "The South is avenged!"[8] Sometimes they yell that.

    [A *man, the same man as before, enters again, again as John Wilkes*
    Booth. He takes a gun and "stands in position": at the left side of THE
    FOUNDLING FATHER, *as Abraham* LINCOLN, *pointing the gun at* THE
    FOUNDLING FATHER's *head.*]

A MAN   Ready.
155 THE FOUNDLING FATHER   Haw Haw Haw Haw

    [*Rest.*]

HAW HAW HAW HAW

    [BOOTH *shoots.* LINCOLN *"slumps in his chair."* BOOTH *jumps.*]

A MAN [*theatrically*]   "The South is avenged!"

    [*Rest.*]

7. Or "Sic semper tyrannis." Purportedly, Booth's words after he slew Lincoln and leapt from the presidential box to the stage of Ford's Theatre in Washington, D.C., on 14 April 1865, not only killing the President but also interrupting a performance of *Our American Cousin,* starring Miss Laura Keene [Parks's note]. *Sic semper tyrannis:* Thus always to tyrants (Latin), adopted in 1776 as the state motto of Virginia (whose capital, Richmond, became the capital of the Confederacy). Keene (ca. 1826–1873), a London-born actress who became well-known in the United States on the stage and as a theater manager.
8. Allegedly, Booth's words [Parks's note].

Hhhh.

[*Rest.*]

Thank you.

160 THE FOUNDLING FATHER   Pleasures mine.

A MAN   Till next week.

THE FOUNDLING FATHER   Till next week.

[A MAN *exits.*]

THE FOUNDLING FATHER   Comes once a week that one. Always chooses the Derringer[9] although we've got several styles he always chooses the Der-

165 ringer. Always "The tyrants" and then "The South avenged." The ones who choose the Derringer are the ones for History. He's one for History. As it Used to Be. Never wavers. No frills. By the book. Nothing excessive.

[*Rest.*]

A nod to Mr. Lincolns bust. [*Nods to Lincoln's bust.*]

[*Rest.*]

I'll wear this one. He sported this style in the early war years. Years of

170 uncertainty. When he didnt know if the war was right when it could be said he didnt always know which side he was on not because he was a stupid man but because it was sometimes not 2 different sides at all but one great side surging toward something beyond either Northern or Southern. A beard of uncertainty. The Lesser Known meanwhile living his life long after all this

175 had happened and not knowing much about it until he was much older [(as a boy "The Civil War" was an afterschool game and his folks didnt mention the Great Mans murder for fear of frightening him)] knew only that he was a dead ringer in a family of Diggers and that he wanted to grow and have others think of him and remove their hats and touch their hearts and look

180 up into the heavens and say something about the freeing of the slaves. That is, he wanted to make a great impression as he understood Mr. Lincoln to have made.

[*Rest.*]

And so in his youth the Lesser Known familiarized himself with all aspects of the Great Mans existence. What interested the Lesser Known most was

185 the murder and what was most captivating about the murder was the 20 feet—

[A WOMAN, *as* BOOTH, *enters.*]

A WOMAN   Excuse me.

THE FOUNDLING FATHER   Not at all.

[A WOMAN, *as* BOOTH, *"stands in position."*]

THE FOUNDLING FATHER   Haw Haw Haw Haw

[*Rest.*]

190 HAW HAW HAW HAW

[BOOTH *shoots.* LINCOLN *"slumps in his chair."* BOOTH *jumps.*]

A WOMAN   "Strike the tent."[1] [*Exits.*]

---

9. A small, easily concealed pistol with a large bore, invented ca. 1852 by the American gunsmith Henry Deringer; Booth used a derringer to shoot Lincoln in the back of the head.

1. The last words of General Robert E. Lee [1807–1870], Commander of the Confederate Army [Parks's note].

THE FOUNDLING FATHER   What interested the Lesser Known most about the Great Mans murder was the 20 feet which separated the presidents box from the stage. In the presidents box sat the president his wife and their 2 friends.[2] On the stage that night was *Our American Cousin* starring Miss Laura Keene. The plot of this play is of little consequence to our story. Suffice it to say that it was thinly comedic and somewhere in the 3rd Act a man holds a gun to his head—something about despair—

> [*Rest.*]

Ladies and Gentlemen: *Our American Cousin*—

> [B WOMAN, *as* BOOTH, *enters. She "stands in position."*]

B WOMAN   Go ahead.

THE FOUNDLING FATHER   Haw Haw Haw Haw

> [*Rest.*]

HAW HAW HAW HAW

> [BOOTH *shoots.* LINCOLN *"slumps in his chair."* BOOTH *jumps.*]

B WOMAN [*rest*]   LIES!

> [*Rest.*]

L I I I I I I I I I I I I I I I I I I I I I I I I I I E S !

> [*Rest.*]

L I I I I I I I I I I I I I I I I I A R R R R R R R R R R R R R R S !

> [*Rest.*]

Lies.

> [*Rest. Exits. Reenters. Steps downstage. Rest.*]

LIES!

> [*Rest.*]

L I I I I I I I I I I I I I I I I I I I I I I I I I E S !

> [*Rest.*]

L I I I I I I I I I I I I I I I I I I A R R R R R R R R R R R R R R S !

> [*Rest.*]

Lies.

> [*Rest. Exits.*]

THE FOUNDLING FATHER [*rest*]   I think I'll wear the yellow beard. Variety. Works like uh tonic.

> [*Rest.*]

Some inaccuracies are good for business. Take the stovepipe hat! Never really worn indoors but people dont like their Lincoln hatless.

> [*Rest.*]

Mr. Lincoln my apologies. [*Nods to the bust and winks to the cutout.*]

> [*Rest.*]

[Blonde. Not bad if you like a stretch. Hmmm. Let us pretend for a moment that our beloved Mr. Lincoln was a blonde. "The sun on his fair hair looked like the sun itself."[3]—. Now. What interested our Mr. Lesser Known most was those feet between where the Great *Blonde* Man sat, in

---

2. Clara Harris (1845–1883), the daughter of a U.S. senator, and her fiancé, Major Henry Rathbone (1837–1911).

3. From "The Sun," a composition by The Foundling Father, unpublished [Parks's note].

220 his rocker, the stage, the time it took the murderer to cross that expanse, and how the murderer crossed it. He jumped. Broke his leg in the jumping. It was said that the Great Mans wife then began to scream. (She was given to hysterics several years afterward in fact declared insane did you know she ran around Big Town poor desperate for money trying to sell her cloth-
225 ing? On that sad night she begged her servant: "Bring in Taddy, Father will speak to Taddy."[4] But Father died instead unconscious. And she went mad from grief. Off her rocker. Mad Mary claims she hears her dead men. Summoning. The older son, Robert, he locked her up.[5] "*Emergency*, oh, *Emergency* please put the Great Man in the ground.")

    [*Enter* B MAN, *as* BOOTH. *He "stands in position."*]

230 THE FOUNDLING FATHER   Haw Haw Haw Haw

    [*Rest.*]

HAW HAW HAW HAW

    [BOOTH *shoots.* LINCOLN *"slumps in his chair."* BOOTH *jumps.*]

B MAN   "Now he belongs to the ages."[6]

    [*Rest.*]

Blonde?

THE FOUNDLING FATHER   (I only talk with the regulars.)

235 B MAN   He wasnt blonde. [*Exits.*]

THE FOUNDLING FATHER   A slight deafness in this ear other than that there are no side effects.

    [*Rest.*]

Hhh. Clean-shaven for a while. The face needs air. Clean-shaven as in his youth. When he met his Mary. —. Hhh. Blonde.

    [*Rest.*]

240 6 feet under is a long way to go. Imagine. When the Lesser Known left to find his way out West he figured he had dug over 7 hundred and 23 graves. 7 hundred and 23. Excluding his Big Hole. Excluding the hundreds of shallow holes he later digs the hundreds of shallow holes he'll use to bury his faux-historical knickknacks when he finally quits this business. Not
245 including those. 7 hundred and 23 graves.

    [C MAN *and* C WOMAN *enter.*]

C MAN   You allow 2 at once?

THE FOUNDLING FATHER

    [*Rest.*]

C WOMAN   We're just married. You know: newlyweds. We hope you dont mind. Us both at once.

THE FOUNDLING FATHER

    [*Rest.*]

---

4. Mary Todd Lincoln, wanting her dying husband to speak to their son Tad, might have said this that night [Parks's note]. After he was shot, Lincoln was carried to a home across the street from the theater; he died the next morning.
5. In 1875 Robert had his mother committed to an insane asylum, but she was later declared legally competent. *Hears her dead men*: from the 1850s onward, Mary Todd Lincoln became increasingly interested in spiritualism, or communication with the dead (usually attempted with the help of a medium).
6. The words of Secretary of War Edwin Stanton [1814–1869], as Lincoln died [Parks's note].

C MAN We're just married.

250 C WOMAN Newlyweds.

THE FOUNDLING FATHER

    [*Rest.*]

    [*Rest.*]

    [*They "stand in position." Both hold one gun.*]

C MAN AND C WOMAN Shoot.

THE FOUNDLING FATHER Haw Haw Haw Haw

    [*Rest.*]

HAW HAW HAW HAW

    [*Rest.*]

    [*Rest.*]

HAW HAW HAW HAW

    [*They shoot.* LINCOLN *"slumps in his chair." They jump.*]

255 C MAN Go on.

C WOMAN [*theatrically*] "Theyve killed the president!"[7]

    [*Rest. They exit.*]

THE FOUNDLING FATHER Theyll have children and theyll bring their children here. A slight deafness in this ear other than that there are no side effects. Little ringing in the ears. Slight deafness. I cant complain.

    [*Rest.*]

260 The passage of time. The crossing of space. [The Lesser Known recorded his every movement.] He'd hoped he'd be of interest in his posterity. [Once again riding in the Great Mans footsteps.] A nod to the presidents bust. [*Nods.*]

    [*Rest.*]

    [*Rest.*]

The Great Man lived in the past that is was an inhabitant of time imme-morial and the Lesser Known out West alive a resident of the present. And
265 the Great Mans deeds had transpired during the life of the Great Man somewhere in past-land that is somewhere "back there" and all this while the Lesser Known digging his holes bearing the burden of his resemblance all the while trying somehow to equal the Great Man in stature, word and deed going forward with his lesser life trying somehow to follow in the
270 Great Mans footsteps footsteps that were of course behind him. The Lesser Known trying somehow to catch up to the Great Man all this while and maybe running too fast in the wrong direction. Which is to say that maybe the Great Man had to catch him. Hhhh. Ridiculous.

    [*Rest.*]

Full fringe. The way he appears on the money.

    [*Rest.*]

275 A wink to Mr. Lincolns pasteboard cutout. A nod to Mr. Lincolns bust.

    [*Rest. Time passes. Rest.*]

---

7. The words of Mary Todd, just after Lincoln was shot [Parks's note].

When someone remarked that he played Lincoln so well that he ought to be shot it was as if the Great Mans footsteps had been suddenly revealed: instead of making speeches his act would now consist of a single chair, a rocker, in a dark box. The public was cordially invited to pay a penny, choose from a selection of provided pistols enter the darkened box and "Shoot Mr. Lincoln." The Lesser Known became famous overnight.

> [A MAN, as John Wilkes BOOTH, enters. He takes a gun and "stands in position": at the left side of THE FOUNDLING FATHER, as Abraham LINCOLN, pointing the gun at THE FOUNDLING FATHER's head.]

THE FOUNDLING FATHER   Mmm. Like clockwork.

A MAN   Ready.

THE FOUNDLING FATHER   Haw Haw Haw Haw

> [Rest.]

HAW HAW HAW HAW

> [BOOTH shoots. LINCOLN "slumps in his chair." BOOTH jumps.]

A MAN [theatrically]   "Thus to the tyrants!"

> [Rest.]

Hhhh.

LINCOLN
BOOTH
LINCOLN
BOOTH
LINCOLN
BOOTH
LINCOLN
BOOTH
LINCOLN[8]

> [BOOTH jumps.]

A MAN [theatrically]   "The South is avenged!"

> [Rest.]

Hhhh.

> [Rest.]

Thank you.

THE FOUNDLING FATHER   Pleasures mine.

A MAN   Next week then. [Exits.]

THE FOUNDLING FATHER   Little ringing in the ears. Slight deafness.

> [Rest.]

Little ringing in the ears.

> [Rest.]

A wink to the Great Mans cutout. A nod to the Great Mans bust. Once again striding in the Great Mans footsteps. Riding on in. Riding to the rescue the way they do. They both had such long legs. Such big feet. And the Greater Man had such a lead although of course somehow still "back there." If the Lesser Known had slowed down stopped moving completely

---

8. The repetition of characters' names without dialogue indicates an extended pause, or what Parks has elsewhere described as "an elongated and heightened (rest)."

300 gone in reverse died maybe the Greater Man could have caught up. Woulda had a chance. Woulda sneaked up behind him the Greater Man would have sneaked up behind the Lesser Known unbeknownst and wrestled him to the ground. Stabbed him in the back. In revenge. "Thus to the tyrants!" Shot him maybe. The Lesser Known forgets who he is and just crumples. His

305 bones cannot be found. The Greater Man continues on.

> [*Rest.*]

"*Emergency,* oh *Emergency,* please put the Great Man in the ground."

> [*Rest.*]

Only a little ringing in the ears. Thats all. Slight deafness.

> [*Rest.*]

> [*He puts on the blonde beard.*]

Huh. Whatdoyou say I wear the blonde.

> [*Rest.*]

> [*A gunshot echoes. Softly. And echoes.*]

Act 2: The Hall of Wonders

A gunshot echoes. Loudly. And echoes.
They are in a great hole. In the middle of nowhere. The hole is an exact replica
of The Great Hole of History.
A gunshot echoes. Loudly. And echoes. LUCY *with ear trumpet circulates.* BRAZIL
digs.

A. BIG BANG

LUCY   Hear that?
BRAZIL   Zit him?
LUCY   No.
BRAZIL   Oh.

> [*A gunshot echoes. Loudly. And echoes.*]

5 LUCY   Hear?
BRAZIL   Zit him?!
LUCY   Nope. Ssuhecho.
BRAZIL   Ssuhecho.
LUCY   Uh echo uh huhn. Of gunplay. Once upon uh time somebody had uh
10 little gunplay and now thuh gun goes on playing: *KER-BANG!* KERBANG-
Kerbang-kerbang-(kerbang)-((kerbang)).
BRAZIL   Thuh echoes.

> [*Rest.*]

> [*Rest.*]

LUCY   Youre stopped.
BRAZIL   Mmlistenin.
15 LUCY   Dig on, Brazil. Cant stop diggin till you dig up somethin. Your Daddy
was uh Digger.
BRAZIL   Uh huhnnn.

LUCY

BRAZIL

> [*A gunshot echoes. Loudly. And echoes. Rest. A gunshot echoes. Loudly. And echoes. Rest.*]

[LUCY   Itssalways been important in my line to distinguish. Tuh know thuh difference. Not like your Fathuh. Your Fathuh became confused. His lonely
20   death and lack of proper burial is our embarrassment. Go on: dig. Now me I need tuh know thuh real thing from thuh echo. Thuh truth from thuh hearsay.

> [*Rest.*]

Bram Price for example. His dear ones and relations told me his dying words but Bram Price hisself of course told me something quite different.

25 BRAZIL   I wept forim.

LUCY   Whispered his true secrets to me and to me uhlone.

BRAZIL   Then he died.

LUCY   Then he died.

> [*Rest.*]

Thuh things he told me I will never tell. Mr. Bram Price. Huh.

> [*Rest.*]

30   Dig on.

BRAZIL

LUCY

BRAZIL

LUCY   Little Bram Price Junior.

BRAZIL   Thuh fat one?

LUCY   Burned my eardrums. Just like his Dad did.

BRAZIL   I wailed forim.

35 LUCY   Ten days dead wept over and buried and that boy comes back. Not him though. His echo. Sits down tuh dinner and eats up everybodys food just like he did when he was livin.

> [*Rest.*]

> [*Rest.*]

Little Bram Junior. Burned my eardrums. Miz Penny Price his mother. Thuh things she told me I will never tell.

> [*Rest.*]

40   You remember her.

BRAZIL   Wore red velvet in August.

LUCY   When her 2 Brams passed she sold herself, son.

BRAZIL   O.

LUCY   Also lost her mind. —. She finally went. Like your Fathuh went, per-
45   haps. Foul play.

BRAZIL   I gnashed for her.

LUCY   You did.

BRAZIL   Couldnt choose between wailin or gnashin. Weepin sobbin or moanin. Went for gnashing. More to it. Gnashed for her and hers like I
50   have never gnashed. I woulda tore at my coat but thats extra. Chipped uh tooth. One in thuh front.

LUCY   You did your job son.

BRAZIL   I did my job.

LUCY   Confidence. Huh. Thuh things she told me I will never tell. Miz Penny
55   Price. Miz Penny Price.

[*Rest.*]

Youre stopped.

BRAZIL   Mmlistenin.

LUCY   Dig on, Brazil.

BRAZIL

LUCY

BRAZIL   We arent from these parts.

60 LUCY   No. We're not.

BRAZIL   Daddy iduhnt[9] either.

LUCY   Your Daddy iduhnt either.

[*Rest.*]

Dig on, son. —. Cant stop diggin till you dig up somethin. You dig that
something up you brush that something off you give that something uh
65   designated place. Its own place. Along with thuh other discoveries. In thuh
Hall of Wonders. Uh place in the Hall of Wonders right uhlong with thuh
rest of thuh Wonders hear?

BRAZIL   Uh huhn.

[*Rest.*]

LUCY   Bram Price Senior, son. Bram Price Senior was not thuh man he
70   claimed tuh be. Huh. Nope. Was not thuh man he claimed tuh be atall.
You ever see him in his stocking feet? Or barefoot? Course not. I guessed
before he told me. He told me then he died. He told me and I havent told
no one. I'm uh good Confidence. As Confidences go. Huh. One of thuh
best. As Confidence, mmonly contracted tuh keep quiet 12 years. After 12
75   years nobody cares. For 19 years I have kept his secret. In my bosom.

[*Rest.*]

He wore lifts in his shoes, son.

BRAZIL   Lifts?

LUCY   Lifts. Made him seem taller than he was.

BRAZIL   Bram Price Senior?

80 LUCY   Bram Price Senior wore lifts in his shoes yes he did, Brazil. I tell you
just as he told me with his last breaths on his dying bed: "Lifts." Thats all
he said. Then he died. I put thuh puzzle pieces in place. I put thuh puzzle
pieces in place. Couldnt tell no one though. Not even your Pa. "Lifts." I
never told no one son. For 19 years I have kept Brams secret in my bosom.
85   Youre thuh first tuh know. Hhh! Dig on. Dig on.

BRAZIL   Dig on.

LUCY

BRAZIL

LUCY

[*A gunshot echoes. Loudly. And echoes.*]

BRAZIL [*rest*]   Ff Pa was here weud find his bones.

9. That is, "isn't."

LUCY   Not always.

BRAZIL   Thereud be his bones and thereud be thuh Wonders surrounding his
90   bones.

LUCY   Ive heard of different.

BRAZIL   Thereud be thuh Wonders surrounding his bones and thereud be his
Whispers.

LUCY   Maybe.

95   BRAZIL   Ffhe sspast like they say he'd of parlayed to uh Confidence his last
words and dying wishes. His secrets and his dreams.

LUCY   Thats how we pass[1] back East. They could pass different out here.

BRAZIL   We got Daddys ways Daddyssgot ours. When theres no Confidence
available we just dribble thuh words out. In uh whisper.

100   LUCY   Sometimes.

BRAZIL   Thuh Confidencell gather up thuh whispers when she arrives.

LUCY   Youre uh prize, Brazil. Uh prize.]

BRAZIL

LUCY

BRAZIL

LUCY

BRAZIL   You hear him then? His whispers?

LUCY   Not exactly.

105   BRAZIL   He wuduhnt here then.

LUCY   He was here.

BRAZIL   Ffyou dont hear his whispers he wuduhnt here.

LUCY   Whispers dont always come up right away. Takes time sometimes.
Whispers could travel different out West than they do back East. Maybe
110   slower. Maybe. Whispers are secrets and often shy. We aint seen your Pa in
30 years. That could be part of it. We also could be experiencing some sort
of interference. Or some sort of technical difficulty. Ssard tuh tell.

[Rest.]

So much to live for.

BRAZIL   So much to live for.

115   LUCY   Look on thuh bright side.

BRAZIL   Look on thuh bright side. Look on thuh bright side. Loook onnnnn
thuhhhh briiiiiiiight siiiiiiiiide!!!!

LUCY   DIIIIIIIIIIIIG!

BRAZIL   Dig.

LUCY

BRAZIL

120   LUCY   Helloooo! —. Hellooooo!

BRAZIL

LUCY

BRAZIL   [We're from out East. We're not from these parts.

[Rest.]

My foe-father, her husband, my Daddy, her mate, her man, my Pa come
out here. Out West.

[Rest.]

1. Die.

Come out here all uhlone. Cleared thuh path tamed thuh wilderness dug
125 this whole Hole with his own 2 hands and et cetera.

    [*Rest.*]

Left his family behind. Back East. His Lucy and his child. He waved
"Goodbye." Left us tuh carry on. I was only 5.]

    [*Rest.*]

My Daddy was uh Digger. Shes whatcha call uh Confidence. I did thuh
weepin and thuh moanin.

    [*Rest.*]

130 His lonely death and lack of proper burial is our embarrassment.

    [*Rest.*]

Diggin was his livelihood but fakin was his callin. Ssonly natural heud
come out here and combine thuh 2. Back East he was always diggin. He
was uh natural. Could dig uh hole for uh body that passed like no one else.
Digged em quick and they looked good too. This Hole here—this large
135 one—sshis biggest venture to date. So says hearsay.

    [*Rest.*]

Uh exact replica of thuh Great Hole of History!

LUCY Sshhhhhht.

BRAZIL [*rest*] Thuh original ssback East. He and Lucy they honeymooned
there. At thuh original Great Hole. Its uh popular spot. He and Her would
140 sit on thuh lip and watch everybody who was ever anybody parade on by.
Daily parades! Just like thuh Tee Vee. Mr. George Washington, for example, thuh Fathuh of our Country hisself, would rise up from thuh dead and
walk uhround and cross thuh Delaware and say stuff!![2] Right before their
very eyes!!!!

145 LUCY Son?

BRAZIL Huh?

LUCY That iduhnt how it went.

BRAZIL Oh.

LUCY Thuh Mr. Washington me and your Daddy seen was uh lookuhlike of
150 thuh Mr. Washington of history-fame, son.

BRAZIL Oh.

LUCY Thuh original Mr. Washingtonssbeen long dead.

BRAZIL O.

LUCY That Hole back East was uh theme park son. Keep your story to scale.

155 BRAZIL K.[3]

    [*Rest.*]

Him and Her would sit by thuh lip uhlong with thuh others all in uh row
cameras clickin and theyud look down into that Hole and see—ooooo—
you name it. Ever-y-day you could look down that Hole and see—ooooo
you name it. Amerigo Vespucci hisself made regular appearances. Marcus
160 Garvey. Ferdinand and Isabella. Mary Queen of thuh Scots! Tarzan King of

---

2. Washington (1732–1799), the "Father of
our Country," the first U.S. president (1789–
97), crossed the Delaware from Pennsylvania
on December 25, 1776, to make a surprise
attack on the Hessian forces garrisoned in
Trenton, New Jersey; the attack's success was
an enormous boost to American morale early
in the Revolutionary War.
3. That is, "OK."

thuh Apes! Washington Jefferson Harding and Millard Fillmore. Mistufer
Columbus even.[4] Oh they saw all thuh greats. Parading daily in thuh Great
Hole of History.

> [*Rest.*]

My Fathuh did thuh living and thuh dead. Small-town and big-time. Mr.
165 Lincoln was of course his favorite.

> [*Rest.*]

Not only Mr. Lincoln but Mr. Lincolns last show. His last deeds. His last
laughs.

> [*Rest.*]

Being uh Digger of some renown Daddy comes out here tuh build uh like
attraction. So says hearsay. Figures theres people out here who'll enjoy
170 amusements such as them amusements He and Her enjoyed. We're all citizens of one country afterall.

> [*Rest.*]

Mmrestin.

> [*A gunshot echoes. Loudly. And echoes.*]

BRAZIL Woooo! [*Drops dead.*]
LUCY Youre fakin Mr. Brazil.
175 BRAZIL Uh uhnnn.
LUCY Tryin tuh get you some benefits.
BRAZIL Uh uhnnnnnnnnn.
LUCY I know me uh faker when I see one. Your Father was uh faker. Huh.
One of thuh best. There wuduhnt nobody your Fathuh couldnt do. Did
180 thuh living and thuh dead. Small-town and big-time. Made-up and histori-
cal. Fakin was your Daddys callin but diggin was his livelihood. Oh, back
East he was always diggin. Was uh natural. Could dig uh hole for uh body
that passed like no one else. Digged em quick and they looked good too.
You dont remember of course you dont.
185 BRAZIL I was only 5.
LUCY You were only 5. When your Fathuh spoke he'd quote thuh Greats.
Mister George Washington. Thuh Misters Roosevelt.[5] Mister Millard Fillmore. Huh. All thuh greats. You dont remember of course you dont.
BRAZIL I was only 5—
190 LUCY —only 5. Mr. Lincoln was of course your Fathuhs favorite. Wuz. Huh.
Wuz. Huh. Heresay says he's past. Your Daddy. Digged this hole then he
died. So says hearsay.

---

4. Brazil names figures who were instrumental in "discovering" America: King Ferdinand
(1452–1516) and Queen Isabella (1451–
1504), rulers of Aragón and Castile, who
underwrote the expeditions of the Italian-
born explorer Christopher Columbus (1451–
1506), two of which the Italian navigator
Amerigo Vespucci (1454–1512)—whose
accounts of his voyages to the New World led
to the lands being named "America"—helped
outfit; he also mentions presidents both
lauded—Washington and Thomas Jefferson
(1743–1826; 3rd president, 1801–09)—and
disparaged: Warren Harding (1865–1923;

29th president, 1921–23) and Millard Fillmore (1800–1874; 13th president, 1850–
53). The story of Mary, Queen of Scots
(1542–1587; r. 1542–67)—executed, after
years of imprisonment, for plotting against
England's Elizabeth I—was retold in drama
and opera, and Tarzan, a fictional character
created by Edgar Rice Burroughs in *Tarzan of
the Apes* (1912), has had a long afterlife in
print sequels, film, and comics.
5. Two U.S. presidents named Roosevelt, Theodore (1858–1919; 26th president, 1901–09)
and his distant cousin Franklin Delano (1882–
1945; 32nd president, 1933–45).

[*Rest.*]

Dig, Brazil.

BRAZIL My paw—

195 LUCY Ssonly natural that heud come out here tuh dig out one of his own.
He loved that Great Hole so. He'd stand at thuh lip of that Great Hole:
"OHWAYOHWHYOHWAYOH!"

BRAZIL "OHWAYOHWHYOHWAYOH!"

LUCY "OHWAYOHWHYOHWAYOH!" You know: hole talk. Ohwayohwhyo-
200 hwayoh, just tuh get their attention, then: "Hellooo!" He'd shout down to
em. Theyd call back "Helllllooooo!" and wave. He loved that Great Hole so.
Came out here. Digged this lookuhlike.

BRAZIL Then he died?

LUCY Then he died. Your Daddy died right here. Huh. Oh, he was uh faker.
205 Uh greaaaaat biiiiig faker too. He was your Fathuh. Thats thuh connection.
You take after him.

BRAZIL I do?

LUCY Sure. Put your paw back where it belongs. Go on—back on its stump.
—. Poke it on out of your sleeve son. There you go. I'll draw uh X for you.
210 See? Heresuh X. Huh. Dig here.

[*Rest.*]

DIG!

BRAZIL

LUCY

BRAZIL

LUCY Woah! Woah!

BRAZIL Whatchaheard?!

LUCY No tellin, son. Cant say.

[BRAZIL *digs.* LUCY *circulates.*]

215 BRAZIL [*rest. Rest*] On thuh day he claimed to be the 100th anniversary of
the founding of our country the Father took the Son out into the yard. The
Father threw himself down in front of the Son and bit into the dirt with his
teeth. His eyes leaked. "This is how youll make your mark, Son" the Father
said. The Son was only 2 then. "This is the Wail," the Father said. "There's
220 money init," the Father said. The Son was only 2 then. Quiet. On what he
claimed was the 101st anniversary the Father showed the Son "the Weep"
"the Sob" and "the Moan." How to stand just so what to do with the hands
and feet (to capitalize on what we in the business call "the Mourning
Moment"). Formal stances the Fatherd picked up at the History Hole. The
225 Son studied night and day. By candlelight. No one could best him. The money
came pouring in. On the 102nd anniversary[6] the Son was 5 and the Father
taught him "the Gnash." The day after that the Father left for out West. To
seek his fortune. In the middle of dinnertime. The Son was eating his peas.

LUCY

BRAZIL

LUCY

BRAZIL

LUCY Hellooooo! Hellooooo!

[*Rest.*]

6. Hearsay [Parks's note].

BRAZIL
LUCY
230 BRAZIL HO! [*Unearths something.*]
LUCY Whatcha got?
BRAZIL Uh Wonder!
LUCY Uh Wonder!
BRAZIL Uh Wonder: Ho!
235 LUCY Dust it off and put it over with thuh rest of thuh Wonders.
BRAZIL Uh bust.
LUCY Whose?
BRAZIL Says "A. Lincoln." A. Lincolns bust. —. Abraham Lincolns bust!!!
LUCY Howuhboutthat!

> [*Rest.*]

> [*Rest.*]

240 Woah! Woah!
BRAZIL Whatchaheard?
LUCY Uh—. Cant say.
BRAZIL Whatchaheard?!!
LUCY SSShhhhhhhhhhhhhhhhhhht!

> [*Rest.*]

245 *dig!*

B. ECHO

THE FOUNDLING FATHER Ladies and Gentlemen: *Our American Cousin*, Act
III, scene 5:
MR. TRENCHARD[7] Have you found it?
MISS KEENE I find no trace of it. [*Discovering*] What is this?!
5 MR. TRENCHARD This is the place where father kept all the old deeds.
MISS KEENE Oh my poor muddled brain! What can this mean?!
MR. TRENCHARD [*with difficulty*] I cannot survive the downfall of my house
but choose instead to end my life with a pistol to my head!

> [*Applause.*]

THE FOUNDLING FATHER OHWAYOHWHYOHWAYOH!

> [*Rest.*]

> [*Rest.*]

10 Helllooooooo!

> [*Rest.*]

Helllooooooo!

> [*Rest. Waves.*]

---

7. Asa Trenchard is the title character of *Our
American Cousin*; Laura Keene played his
cousin, Florence Trenchard. (The exchange
paraphrases one found in scene 6, but Florence is not present and the suicide is threatened in the following scene by another
character, Sir Edward Trenchard.)

C. ARCHEOLOGY

BRAZIL You hear im?

LUCY Echo of thuh first sort: thuh sound. (E.g. thuh gunplay.)

[*Rest.*]

Echo of thuh 2nd sort: thuh words. Type A: thuh words from thuh dead. Category: Unrelated.

[*Rest.*]

5 Echo of thuh 2nd sort, Type B: words less fortunate: thuh Disembodied Voice. Also known as "Thuh Whispers." Category: Related. Like your Fathuhs.

[*Rest.*]

Echo of thuh 3rd sort: thuh body itself.

[*Rest.*]

BRAZIL You hear im.

LUCY Cant say. Cant say, son.

10 BRAZIL My faux-father. Thuh one who comed out here before us. Thuh one who left us behind. Tuh come out here all uhlone. Tuh do his bit. All them who comed before us—my Daddy. He's one of them.

LUCY

[*Rest.*]

[*Rest.*]

[BRAZIL: He's one of them. All of them who comed before us—my Daddy.

[*Rest.*]

I'd say thuh creation of thuh world must uh been just like thuh clearing off
15 of this plot. Just like him diggin his Hole. I'd say. Must uh been just as dug up. And unfair.

[*Rest.*]

Peoples (or thuh what-was), just had tuh hit thuh road. In thuh beginning there was one of those voids here and then "bang" and then *voilà!*[8] And here we is.

[*Rest.*]

20 But where did those voids that was here before *we* was here go off to? Hmmm. In thuh beginning there were some of them voids here and then: KERBANG-KERBLAMMO! And now it all belongs tuh us.

LUCY

[*Rest.*]

[*Rest.*]]

BRAZIL This Hole is our inheritance of sorts. My Daddy died and left it to me and Her. And when She goes, Shes gonna give it all to me!!

25 LUCY Dig, son.

BRAZIL I'd rather dust and polish. [*Puts something on.*]

LUCY Dust and polish then. —. You dont got tuh put on that tuh do it.

BRAZIL It helps. Uh Hehm. *Uh Hehm.* WELCOME WELCOME WELCOME TUH THUH HALL OF—

30 LUCY Sssht.

BRAZIL

8. Literally, "see there" (French).

LUCY

BRAZIL   (welcome welcome welcome to thuh hall. of. wonnndersss: To our
right A Jewel Box made of cherry wood, lined in velvet, letters "A.L." carved
in gold on thuh lid: the jewels have long escaped. Over here one of Mr.
Washingtons bones, right pointer so they say; here is his likeness and here:
35   his wooden teeth.[9] Yes, uh top and bottom pair of nibblers: nibblers, lookin
for uh meal. Nibblin. I iduhnt your lunch. Quit nibblin. Quit that nibblin
you. Quit that nibblin you nibblers you nibblin nibblers you.)

LUCY   Keep it tuh scale.

BRAZIL   (Over here our newest Wonder: uh bust of Mr. Lincoln carved of
40   marble lookin like he looked in life. Right heress thuh bit from thuh mouth
of thuh mount on which some great Someone rode tuh thuh rescue. This
is all thats left. Uh glass tradin bead—one of thuh first. Here are thuh licked boots. Here, uh dried scrap of whales blubber. Uh petrified scrap of uh
great blubberer, servin to remind us that once this land was covered with
45   sea. And blubberers were Kings. In this area here are several documents:
peace pacts, writs, bills of sale, treaties, notices, handbills and circulars,
freein papers, summonses, declarations of war, addresses, title deeds,
obits, long lists of dids. And thuh medals: for bravery and honesty; for
trustworthiness and for standing straight; for standing tall; for standing
50   still. For advancing and retreating. For makin do. For skills in whittlin, for
skills in painting and drawing, for uh knowledge of sewin, of handicrafts
and building things, for leather tannin, blacksmithery, lacemakin, horseback riding, swimmin, croquet, and badminton. Community Service. For
cookin and for cleanin. For bowin and scrapin. Uh medal for fakin? Huh.
55   This could uh been his. Zsis his? This is his! This is his!!!

LUCY   Keep it tuh scale, Brazil.

BRAZIL   This could be his!

LUCY   May well be.

BRAZIL   [rest]   Whaddyahear?

60 LUCY   Bits and pieces.

BRAZIL   This could be his.

LUCY   Could well be.

BRAZIL   [rest. Rest]   waaaaaahhhhhhhhHHHHHHHHHHHHHH! HUH HEE
HUH HEE HUH HEE HUH.

65 LUCY   There there, Brazil. Dont weep.

BRAZIL   WAHHHHHHHHHHH!—imissim—WAHHHHHHHHHHHHH!

LUCY   It is an honor to be of his line. He cleared this plot for us. He was uh
Digger.

BRAZIL   Huh huh huh. Uh Digger.

70 LUCY   Mr. Lincoln was his favorite.

BRAZIL   I was only 5.

LUCY   He dug this whole Hole.

BRAZIL   Sssnuch.[1] This whole Hole.

LUCY   This whole Hole.

        [Rest.]

BRAZIL

LUCY

9. Washington's famous "wooden teeth" were
in fact dentures made of ivory and of animal
and human teeth.

1. Parks defines "Sssnuch" as "a fast reverse
snort, a big sniff (usually accompanies crying
or sneezing)."

BRAZIL
LUCY
BRAZIL
LUCY
75   I couldnt never deny him nothin.
       I gived intuh him on everything.
       Thuh moon. Thuh stars.
       Thuh bees knees. Thuh cats pyjamas.
           [*Rest.*]
BRAZIL
LUCY
BRAZIL   Anything?
80 LUCY   Stories too horrible tuh mention.
BRAZIL   His stories?
LUCY   Nope.
           [*Rest.*]
BRAZIL   Mama Lucy?
85 BRAZIL   —Imissim—.
LUCY   Whut.
LUCY   Hhh. ((dig.))

D. ECHO

THE FOUNDLING FATHER   Ladies and Gentlemen: *Our American Cousin*, Act
     III, scene 2:
MR. TRENCHARD   You crave affection, *you* do. Now I've no fortune, but I'm
     biling over with affections, which I'm ready to pour out to all of you, like
5   apple sass over roast pork.
AUGUSTA   Sir, your American talk do woo me.[2]
THE FOUNDLING FATHER [*as Mrs. Mount*]   Mr. Trenchard, you will please rec-
     ollect you are addressing my daughter and in my presence.
MR. TRENCHARD   Yes, I'm offering her my heart and hand just as she wants
10   them, with nothing in 'em.
THE FOUNDLING FATHER [*as Mrs. Mount*]   Augusta dear, to your room.
AUGUSTA   Yes, Ma, the nasty beast.
THE FOUNDLING FATHER [*as Mrs. Mount*]   I am aware, Mr. Trenchard, that you
     are not used to the manners of good society, and that, alone, will excuse the
15   impertinence of which you have been guilty.
MR. TRENCHARD   Don't know the manners of good society, eh? Wal, I guess I
     know enough to turn you inside out, old gal—you sockdologizing old
     man-trap.
           [*Laughter. Applause.*]
THE FOUNDLING FATHER   Thanks. Thanks so much. Snyder has always been a
20   very special very favorite town uh mine. Thank you thank you so very
     much. Loverly loverly evening loverly tuh be here loverly tuh be here with
     you with all of you thank you very much.
           [*Rest.*]
     Uh Hehm. I *only* do thuh greats.

2. Parks adds this line to a passage that is otherwise quoted directly from the play.

[*Rest.*]

A crowd pleaser: 4score and 7 years ago our fathers brought forth upon
this continent a new nation conceived in Liberty and dedicated to the
proposition that all men are created equal![3]

[*Applause.*]

Observe!: Indiana? Indianapolis. Louisiana? Baton Rouge. Concord? New
Hampshire. Pierre? South Dakota. Honolulu? Hawaii. Springfield? Illinois.
Frankfort? Kentucky. Lincoln? Nebraska.[4] Ha! Lickety split!

[*Applause.*]

And now, the centerpiece of the evening!!

[*Rest.*]

Uh Hehm. The Death of Lincoln!: —. The watching of the play, the laughter, the smiles of Lincoln and Mary Todd, the slipping of Booth into the
presidential box unseen, the freeing of the slaves, the pulling of the trigger,
the bullets piercing above the left ear, the bullets entrance into the great
head, the bullets lodging behind the great right eye, the slumping of Lincoln, the leaping onto the stage of Booth, the screaming of Todd, the
screaming of Todd, the screaming of Keene, the leaping onto the stage of
Booth; the screaming of Todd, the screaming of Keene, the shouting of
Booth "Thus to the tyrants!," the death of Lincoln! —And the silence of
the nation.

[*Rest.*]

Yes. —.The year was way back when. The place: our nations capitol.
4score, back in the olden days, and Mr. Lincolns great head. The the-a-ter
was "Fords." The wife "Mary Todd." Thuh freeing of the slaves and thuh
great black hole that thuh fatal bullet bored. And how that great head was
bleedin. Thuh body stretched crossways acrosst thuh bed. Thuh last words.
Thuh last breaths. And how thuh nation mourned.

[*Applause.*]

E. SPADEWORK

LUCY   Thats uh hard nut tuh crack uh hard nut tuh crack indeed.

BRAZIL   Alaska—?

LUCY   Thats uh hard nut tuh crack. Thats uh hard nut tuh crack indeed. —.
Huh. Juneau.

BRAZIL   Good!

LUCY   Go uhgain.

BRAZIL   —. Texas?

LUCY   —. Austin. Wyoming?

BRAZIL   —. —. Cheyenne. Florida?

LUCY   Tallahassee.

[*Rest.*]

Ohio.

BRAZIL   Oh. Uh. Well: Columbus. Louisiana?

3. The opening sentence of Lincoln's Gettysburg Address, delivered November 19, 1863,
in Gettysburg, Pennsylvania, at the dedication ceremony for a national cemetery on the
site of the Civil War's bloodiest battle, fought
four months earlier.
4. This list pairs states with their capitals (a
pattern that continues in the next scene).

LUCY   Baton Rouge. Arkansas.

BRAZIL   Little Rock. Jackson.

15 LUCY   Mississippi. Spell it.

BRAZIL   M-i-s-s-i-s-s-i-p-p-i!

LUCY   Huh. Youre good. Montgomery.

BRAZIL   Alabama.

LUCY   Topeka.

20 BRAZIL   Kansas?

LUCY   Kansas.

BRAZIL   Boise, Idaho?

LUCY   Boise, Idaho.

BRAZIL   Huh. Nebraska.

25 LUCY   Nebraska. Lincoln.

> [*Rest.*]

Thuh year was way back when. Thuh place: our nations capitol.

> [*Rest.*]

Your Fathuh couldnt get that story out of his head: Mr. Lincolns great head. And thuh hole thuh fatal bullet bored. How that great head was bleedin. Thuh body stretched crossways acrosst thuh bed. Thuh last words.
30 Thuh last breaths. And how thuh nation mourned. Huh. Changed your Fathuhs life.

> [*Rest.*]

Couldnt get that story out of his head. Whuduhnt my favorite page from thuh book of Mr. Lincolns life, me myself now I prefer thuh part where he gets married to Mary Todd and she begins to lose her mind (and then of
35 course where he frees all thuh slaves) but shoot, he couldnt get that story out of his head. Hhh. Changed his life.

> [*Rest.*]

BRAZIL   (wahhhhhhhh—)

LUCY   There there, Brazil.

BRAZIL   (wahhhhhh—)

40 LUCY   Dont weep. Got somethin for ya.

BRAZIL   (o)?

LUCY   Spade. —. Dont scrunch up your face like that, son. Go on. Take it.

BRAZIL   Spade?

LUCY   Spade. He woulda wanted you tuh have it.

45 BRAZIL   Daddys diggin spade? Ssnnuch.

LUCY   I swannee[5] you look more and more and more and more like him every day.

BRAZIL   His chin?

LUCY   You got his chin.

50 BRAZIL   His lips?

LUCY   You got his lips.

BRAZIL   His teeths?

LUCY   Top and bottom. In his youth. He had some. Just like yours. His frock coat. Was just like that. He had hisself uh stovepipe hat which you lack.
55 His medals—yours are for weepin his of course were for diggin.

---

5. A punning combination of *I swan* (i.e., "I declare"; dialect) and *Swannee (River),* an allusion to Stephen Foster's 1851 song "Old Folks at Home" (which presents a sentimental view of African American life in the antebellum South).

BRAZIL   And I got his spade.

LUCY   And now you got his spade.

BRAZIL   We could say I'm his spittin image.

LUCY   We could say that.

60   BRAZIL   We could say I just may follow in thuh footsteps of my foe-father.

LUCY   We could say that.

BRAZIL   Look on thuh bright side!

LUCY   Look on thuh bright side!

BRAZIL   So much tuh live for!

65   LUCY   So much tuh live for! Sweet land of—! Sweet land of—?

BRAZIL   Of liberty!

LUCY   Of liberty! Thats it thats it and *"Woah!"* Lets say I hear his words!

BRAZIL   And you could say?

LUCY   And I could say.

70   BRAZIL   Lets say you hear his words!

LUCY   *Woah!*

BRAZIL   Whatwouldhesay?!

LUCY   He'd say: "Hello." He'd say. —. "Hope you like your spade."

BRAZIL   Tell him I do.

75   LUCY   He'd say: "My how youve grown!" He'd say: "Hows your weepin?" He'd
say: —Ha! He's running through his states and capitals! Licketysplit!

BRAZIL   Howuhboutthat!

LUCY   He'd say: "Uh house divided cannot stand!" He'd say: "4score and 7
years uhgoh." Say: "Of thuh people by thuh people and for thuh people."

80   Say: "Malice toward none and charity toward all." Say: "Cheat some of
thuh people some of thuh time."[6] He'd say: (and this is only to be spoken
between you and me and him—)

BRAZIL   K.

LUCY   Lean in. Ssfor our ears and our ears uhlone.

LUCY

BRAZIL

LUCY

BRAZIL

85   BRAZIL   O.

LUCY   Howuhboutthat. And here he comes. Striding on in striding on in and
he surveys thuh situation. And he nods tuh what we found cause he knows
his Wonders. And he smiles. And he tells us of his doins all these years. And
he does his Mr. Lincoln for us. Uh great page from thuh great mans great

90   life! And you n me llsmile, cause then we'll know, more or less, exactly
where he is.

[*Rest.*]

---

6. Some of the most famous words spoken by or attributed to Lincoln, from, respectively, his speech on June 16, 1858, to the Illinois Republican State Convention in Springfield—"A house divided against itself cannot stand" (an allusion to Mark 3.25); the beginning and the end of the Gettysburg Address—"government of the people, by the people, for the people"; his second Inaugural Address, delivered March 4, 1865—"With malice toward none; with charity for all"; and (with slight variations in wording) a speech of September 8, 1858, in Clinton, Illinois, or a remark made to a caller at the White House—"You may fool all the people some of the time; you can even fool some of the people all the time; but you can't fool all of the people all the time" (this observation, which does not appear in any surviving Lincoln documents, has also been attributed to the 19th-century American showman P. T. Barnum).

BRAZIL   Lucy? Where is he?
LUCY   Lincoln?
BRAZIL   Papa.
95   LUCY   Close by, I guess. Huh. Dig.

> [BRAZIL *digs. Times passes.*]

Youre uh Digger. Youre uh Digger. Your Daddy was uh Digger and so are you.

BRAZIL   Ho!
LUCY   I couldnt never deny him nothin.
100   BRAZIL   Wonder: Ho! Wonder: Ho!
LUCY   I gived intuh him on everything.
BRAZIL   Ssuhtrumpet.
LUCY   Gived intuh him on everything.
BRAZIL   Ssuhtrumpet, Lucy.
105   LUCY   Howboutthat.
BRAZIL   Try it out.
LUCY   How uh-bout that.
BRAZIL   Anythin?
LUCY   Cant say, son. Cant say.

> [*Rest.*]

110   I couldnt never deny him nothin.
I gived intuh him on everything.
Thuh moon. Thuh stars.

BRAZIL   Ho!
LUCY   Thuh bees knees. Thuh cats pyjamas.
115   BRAZIL   Wonder: Ho! Wonder: Ho!

> [*Rest.*]

Howuhboutthat: Uh bag of pennies. Money, Lucy.

LUCY   Howuhboutthat.

> [*Rest.*]

Thuh bees knees.
Thuh cats pyjamas.
120   Thuh best cuts of meat.
My baby teeth.

BRAZIL   Wonder: Ho! Wonder: HO!
LUCY

Thuh apron from uhround my waist.
Thuh hair from off my head.

125   BRAZIL   Huh. Yellow fur.
LUCY   My mores and my folkways.
BRAZIL   Oh. Uh beard. Howuhboutthat.

> [*Rest.*]

LUCY   WOAH. WOAH!
BRAZIL   Whatchaheard?
LUCY

> [*Rest.*]
>
> [*Rest.*]

130   BRAZIL   Whatchaheard?!
LUCY   You dont wanna know.

BRAZIL

LUCY

BRAZIL

LUCY

BRAZIL   Wonder: Ho! Wonder: HO! WONDER: HO!

LUCY

     Thuh apron from uhround my waist.

     Thuh hair from off my head.

135 BRAZIL   Huh: uh Tee-Vee.

LUCY   Huh.

BRAZIL   I'll hold ontooit for uh minit.

     [*Rest.*]

LUCY

     Thuh apron from uhround my waist.

     Thuh hair from off my head.

140   My mores and my folkways.

     My rock and my foundation.

BRAZIL

LUCY

BRAZIL

LUCY   My re-memberies—you know—thuh stuff out of my head.

     [*The TV comes on.* THE FOUNDLING FATHER's *face appears.*]

BRAZIL   (ho! ho! wonder: ho!)

LUCY

     My spare buttons in their envelopes.

145   Thuh leftovers from all my unmade meals.

     Thuh letter R.

     Thuh key of G.

BRAZIL   (ho! ho! wonder: ho!)

LUCY

     All my good jokes. All my jokes that fell flat.

150   Thuh way I walked, cause you liked it so much.

     All my winnin dance steps.

     My teeth when yours runned out.

     My smile.

BRAZIL   (ho! ho! wonder: ho!)

155 LUCY   Ssssssht.

     [*Rest.*]

   Well. Its him.

F. ECHO

A gunshot echoes. Loudly. And echoes.

G. THE GREAT BEYOND

LUCY *and* BRAZIL *watch the TV: a replay of* "The Lincoln Act." THE FOUNDLING FATHER *has returned. His coffin awaits him.*

LUCY   Howuhboutthat!

BRAZIL   They just gunned him down uhgain.

LUCY   Howuhboutthat.

BRAZIL   He's dead but not really.

5 LUCY   Howuhboutthat.

BRAZIL   Only fakin. Only fakin. See? Hesupuhgain.

LUCY   What-izzysayin?

BRAZIL   Sound duhnt work.

LUCY   Zat right.

       [*Rest.*]

10 THE FOUNDLING FATHER   I believe this is the place where I do the Gettysburg
    Address, I believe.

BRAZIL

THE FOUNDLING FATHER

LUCY

BRAZIL   Woah!

LUCY   Howuhboutthat.

BRAZIL   Huh. Well.

       [*Rest.*]

15   Huh. Zit him?

LUCY   Its him.

BRAZIL   He's dead?

LUCY   He's dead.

BRAZIL   Howuhboutthat.

       [*Rest.*]

20   Shit.

LUCY

BRAZIL

LUCY

BRAZIL   Mail the in-vites?

LUCY   I did.

BRAZIL   Think theyll come?

LUCY   I do. There are hundreds upon thousands who knew of your Daddy,
25   glorified his reputation, and would like to pay their respects.

THE FOUNDLING FATHER   Howuhboutthat.

BRAZIL   Howuhboutthat!

LUCY   Turn that off, son.

       [*Rest.*]

    You gonna get in yr coffin now or later?

30 THE FOUNDLING FATHER   I'd like tuh wait uhwhile.

LUCY   Youd like tuh wait uhwhile.

BRAZIL   Mmgonna gnash for you. You know: teeth in thuh dirt, hands like
    this, then jump up rip my clothes up, you know, you know go all out.

THE FOUNDLING FATHER   Howuhboutthat. Open casket or closed?

35 LUCY   —. Closed.

       [*Rest.*]

    Turn that off, son.

BRAZIL   K.

THE FOUNDLING FATHER   Hug me.

BRAZIL   Not yet.

40 THE FOUNDLING FATHER   You?

LUCY   Gimmieuhminute.
> [*A gunshot echoes. Loudly. And echoes.*]

LUCY   That gunplay. Wierdiduhntit. Comes. And goze.
> [*They ready his coffin. He inspects it.*]

At thuh Great Hole where we honeymooned—son, at thuh Original Great Hole, you could see thuh whole world without goin too far. You could look
45 intuh that Hole and see your entire life pass before you. Not your own life but someones life from history, you know, [someone who'd done somethin of note, got theirselves known somehow, uh President or] somebody who killed somebody important, uh face on uh postal stamp, you know, someone from History. *Like* you, but *not* you. You know: *Known.*

50 THE FOUNDLING FATHER   "*Emergency,* oh, *Emergency,* please put the Great Man in the ground."

LUCY   Go on. Get in. Try it out. Ssnot so bad. See? Sstight, but private. Bought on time but we'll manage. And you got enough height for your hat.
> [*Rest.*]

THE FOUNDLING FATHER   Hug me.

55 LUCY   Not yet.

THE FOUNDLING FATHER   You?

BRAZIL   Gimmieuhminute.
> [*Rest.*]

LUCY   He loved that Great Hole so. Came out here. Digged this lookuhlike.

BRAZIL   Then he died?

60 LUCY   Then he died.

THE FOUNDLING FATHER

BRAZIL

LUCY

THE FOUNDLING FATHER

BRAZIL

LUCY

THE FOUNDLING FATHER   A monumentous occasion. I'd like to say a few words from the grave. Maybe a little conversation: Such a long story. Uhhem. I quit the business. And buried all my things. I dropped anchor: Bottomless. Your turn.

LUCY

BRAZIL

THE FOUNDLING FATHER

65 LUCY [*rest*]   Do your Lincoln for im.

THE FOUNDLING FATHER   Yeah?

LUCY   He was only 5.

THE FOUNDLING FATHER   Only 5. *Uh Hehm.* So very loverly to be here so very very loverly to be here the town of —Wonderville has always been a special
70 favorite of mine always has been a very very special favorite of mine. Now, I *only* do thuh greats. Uh hehm: I was born in a log cabin of humble parentage. But I picked up uh few things. Uh Hehm: 4score and 7 years ago our fathers—ah you know thuh rest. Lets see now. Yes. Uh house divided cannot stand! You can fool some of thuh people some of thuh time! Of
75 thuh people by thuh people and for thuh people! Malice toward none and charity toward all! Ha! The Death of Lincoln! (Highlights): Haw Haw Haw Haw

[*Rest.*]

HAW HAW HAW HAW

[*A gunshot echoes. Loudly. And echoes.* THE FOUNDLING FATHER *"slumps in his chair."*]

THE FOUNDLING FATHER

LUCY

BRAZIL

LUCY

THE FOUNDLING FATHER

BRAZIL [Izzy dead?

80 LUCY   Mmlistenin.

BRAZIL   Anything?

LUCY   Nothin.

BRAZIL [*rest*]   As a child it was her luck tuh be in thuh same room with her Uncle when he died. Her family wanted to know what he had said. What
85 his last words had been. Theyre hadnt been any. Only screaming. Or, you know, breath. Didnt have uh shape to it. Her family thought she was holding on to thuh words. For safekeeping. And they proclaimed thuh girl uh Confidence. At the age of 8. Sworn tuh secrecy. She picked up thuh tricks of thuh trade as she went uhlong.]

[*Rest.*]

90   Should I gnash now?

LUCY   Better save it for thuh guests. I guess.

[*Rest.*]

Well. Dust and polish, son. I'll circulate.

BRAZIL   Welcome Welcome Welcome to thuh hall. Of. Wonders.

[*Rest.*]

To our right A Jewel Box of cherry wood, lined in velvet, letters "A.L."
95 carved in gold on thuh lid. Over here one of Mr. Washingtons bones and here: his wooden teeth. Over here: uh bust of Mr. Lincoln carved of marble lookin like he looked in life. —More or less. And thuh medals: for bravery and honesty; for trustworthiness and for standing straight; for standing tall; for standing still. For advancing and retreating. For makin
100 do. For skills in whittlin, for skills in painting and drawing, for uh knowledge of sewin, of handicrafts and building things, for leather tannin, blacksmithery, lacemakin, horseback riding, swimmin, croquet, and badminton. Community Service. For cookin and for cleanin. For bowin and scrapin. Uh medal for fakin.

[*Rest.*]

105 To my right: our newest Wonder: One of thuh greats Hisself! Note: thuh body sitting propped upright in our great Hole. Note the large mouth opened wide. Note the top hat and frock coat, just like the greats. Note the death wound: thuh great black hole—thuh great black hole in thuh great head. —And how this great head is bleedin. —Note: thuh last words. —
110 And thuh last breaths. —And how thuh nation mourns—

[*Takes his leave.*]

PAULA VOGEL

b. 1951

ONE of the most significant contemporary American playwrights,
Paula Vogel excels both at simple dramatic
scenes—one of her plays revolves around
five elderly women sitting on a park bench—
and at highly theatrical techniques that
include actors playing multiple roles, dream
sequences, off-stage voices, and puppets.
Some plays tell a chronological story while
others jump back and forth in time; some
revolve around familiar scenes such as a
family's car ride to celebrate Christmas at
the grandparents' house, while others take
audiences on mad road trips across Europe.
But no matter which topics Vogel tackles
and which dramatic techniques she uses,
her plays bear a recognizable signature that
combines seduction, provocation, and a
light touch that keeps shocking scenes
bearable and her plays from becoming mere
political manifestos. Paula Vogel has mastered the art of seductive provocation.

Born in a suburb of Washington, D.C.,
to a Jewish father and a Catholic mother,
Paula Vogel was the youngest of three
children. When her parents split up, she
and one brother, Carl, stayed with their
mother, while her other brother, Mark,
went to live with their father. Paula graduated from high school and was accepted to
Bryn Mawr College, where she spent two
years before transferring to Catholic University to complete her Bachelor of Arts

degree in 1974. It was in high school and
college that she discovered two important
things about herself: her love for the theater, and her attraction to women. Even
though Vogel identifies not as a lesbian
playwright but as a playwright who is lesbian, the two passions together have shaped
her career in the theater.

In pursuit of that career, Vogel applied
to the Yale School of Drama, but was
rejected and instead joined the PhD program at Cornell University, where she studied dramatic literature, theory, and theater
history. Having written plays since high
school, Vogel completed her first significant play, *Desdemona*, in Ithaca in 1977. A
rewriting of SHAKESPEARE's *Othello* from
the perspective of the Moor's ill-fated wife,
Desdemona is a play inspired by Tom Stoppard's *Rosencrantz and Guildenstern are
Dead*, the paradigmatic rewriting of *HAM-
LET* from the perspective of Hamlet's two
university friends. *Desdemona* is a similar
exercise in meta-theater, one designed to
restore Desdemona to the center of the
action. But Vogel does so with a characteristic twist: rather than simply denounce the
jealous violence of Shakespeare's Othello
as unfounded, she portrays Desdemona as
a spoiled upper-class wife who works in a
brothel on the side for her own amusement.
Written mostly in a comic mode, the play
delights in class-based humor between

Desdemona's Irish maid and her rival, the brothel's Madame (whom Desdemona has befriended, much to the maid's distress). We follow Shakespeare's plot device, the handkerchief—the play is subtitled "A Play about a Handkerchief"—as the three women figure out what happened to the lost item. The play seems to be on the verge of a happy ending until the tragic violence of Shakespeare's play descends at the very end.

In its meta-theatrical aspirations, the play was clearly inspired by the critical literature and theory that Vogel was reading at Cornell. Ultimately, Vogel decided to leave the program without a dissertation and headed to New York City to focus on writing plays. However, she did eventually achieve her PhD when, in 2016, she submitted a new play and dramaturgical analysis as a thesis, and Cornell granted her a doctoral degree.

If *Desdemona* was a grad school play, Vogel's next significant drama, *The Oldest Profession*, was quintessentially New York. It is set at a single location, a bench on 72th Street and Broadway, on which we find five elderly women congregating for company and gossip. Slowly it emerges that they are not just gossiping, nor are they retired. They are working as prostitutes, as they have been for decades, catering to a dwindling number of elderly clients. Vogel's most charming play, *The Oldest Profession* does not denounce prostitution as exploitation, but rather presents these woman, and indirectly their clients, in a sympathetic light.

In 1985, Vogel was invited to become a professor of playwriting at Brown University, a position she held until 2008. During her tenure at Brown, she nurtured some of the most significant younger playwrights of the generation, including Sarah Ruhl and LYNN NOTTAGE. America was entering what some have called the Program Era, when many professional writers in the United States sought refuge within universities. Traditionally, playwrights from Shakespeare to EUGENE O'NEILL had been associated with theater companies, and this is still the case with playwrights from other theater cultures, such as CARYL CHURCHILL in the United Kingdom. But in America, most literary writers of the last sixty years

have either gone through MFA programs (or, more rarely, PhD programs) or taught in them, or both. Vogel has been a particularly important figure for the Program Era of American playwriting.

While working as a teacher of drama, Vogel also created the body of work that made her own dramatic career. In the plays she wrote for the next twenty years, she maintained an irreverent, light touch and a penchant for provocative topics. Always out to seduce audiences, she wrote *Hot 'n' Throbbing*, a play that features a female writer of pornographic film scripts who fails to control her teenage daughter's budding sexuality and does not recognize her son's voyeuristic fixation with herself. When her abusive ex-husband returns, domestic chaos reaches a new pitch, but in an erotically charged atmosphere that avoids simple moralistic disapproval. Although the play's first half is entertainingly absurd, an ugly twist at the end—the husband strangles his ex-wife to death—leaves audiences gasping. Contributing to the rollicking atmosphere are the new theatrical techniques Vogel used in this play, including a voice-over that takes on different roles and different accents. *Hot 'n' Throbbing* is a play written to denounce domestic violence without preaching simple solutions, and it shows how male sexual violence and female sexual fantasy can be intertwined. It was also written as a provocation to the new antipornography rules of the National Endowment for the Arts, which Vogel denounced, accusing fellow theater makers of complicity and self-imposed censorship.

In 1992, Vogel addressed the AIDS crisis in her play *Baltimore Waltz*. Coming after TONY KUSHNER's influential play *ANGELS IN AMERICA* (1991)—perhaps the most significant literary work about AIDS—*Baltimore Waltz* is Vogel's most personal play, a testament to her grief for her brother Carl, who died of AIDS in 1988. Despite the autobiographical dimension, *Baltimore Waltz* approaches its topic through various forms of estrangement, a technique Vogel learned from BERTOLT BRECHT as well as the Russian formalist Victor Shklovsky. In the play it is she, the sister, who falls ill, and the illness isn't AIDS but an absurd, made-up epidemic apparently contracted by using public lavatories. The two siblings find themselves on a mad trip through Europe—a trip the Vogel siblings never got to take in real life. Through estrangement, Vogel manages to extract enough comedy from the grueling situation to turn the play into an affecting piece of theater.

All of Paula Vogel's plays contain an element of the political, though electoral politics are usually only hinted at—*Baltimore Waltz*, for example, is set in the early years of Ronald Reagan's presidency. Her play *Minneola Twins* (1999), based on another pair of siblings, makes electoral politics explicit by confronting a conservative and a revolutionary twin. The play is set at various moments in American history, moving through the Eisenhower, Nixon, and the first Bush administrations, with the conservative twin implicated in an attempt to blow up a Planned Parenthood clinic. But once again, Vogel's light touch, her insistence on extending sympathy to all characters and her resistance to easy preaching, extract a farcical pleasure from the material, or rather, to use a term Vogel herself favors, an element of "camp." She credits this aesthetic to a number of sources, including the high-camp films of Baltimore native John Waters (introduced to her by her brother Carl) as well as *Mother Camp: Female Impersonators in America*, a study of 1970s gay subculture by Esther Newton.

Vogel's resistance to preaching, her empathy with all characters, and her techniques of theatrical estrangement culminate in what is, to date, her most important achievement: HOW I LEARNED TO DRIVE (1997). The play revolves around an all-American rite of passage: driving lessons. It opens with such a driving lesson and proceeds to show how the female protagonist, Li'l Bit, learns how to hold the steering wheel, how to adjust the seat and the mirrors, and to respect the car for the powerful vehicle that it is. A good learner, she gets her driver's license on the first try. By the end of the play, Li'l Bit is in the car again and says triumphantly: "Ahh . . . I adjust the seat. Fasten my seat belt. Then I check the right side mirror—check the left side. Finally, I adjust the rearview mirror. And then—I floor it." She loves driving, and leaves us with the sound of a car taking off. Her induction into adulthood has succeeded.

But Vogel didn't write a play about driving. *How I Learned to Drive* is a coming-of-age story, and the driving lessons which form the structure of the play are the vehicle by which Li'l Bit learns another aspect of adulthood: sexuality. Disturbingly, it is Li'l Bit's Uncle Peck who instructs her in both. As the play progresses, we learn that something has been going on since long before the driving lessons started and that we are being confronted with a story about pedophilia. When asked by audiences grappling with the play about her intentions, Vogel responded by saying that she wanted to show that child abuse was not primarily a problem associated with homosexuality. Twenty years later, this explanation sounds dated. Since the nineties, gay marriage has become legal (Vogel herself got married to her partner in Massachusetts in 2004) and the association of homosexuality with pedophilia has significantly receded even if it has not entirely gone away. Her other stated motivation, however, is not dated: skepticism about the culture of victimization and trauma. That culture has only grown during the twenty years since the play was first published, which makes it all the more provocative and timely.

How I Learned to Drive departs from the playbook of victimization by extending sympathy to Uncle Peck and by portraying the relationship between him and his young niece as some sort of genuine—if disturbing—love. Li'l Bit is certainly harmed by the abuse, but she is not just a helpless victim whose life has been ruined by the experience. Uncle Peck is the only member of the family who pays any attention to her, the only one to teach her how to drive (he himself has suffered an unnamed trauma during the war, which the play does not elaborate on). While exploiting his young niece's isolation in the family as well as their difference in age and experience, he nevertheless claims to be following her lead and instructions (although he doesn't always do as she asks).

Vogel tells this story through a canny set of theatrical techniques. Li'l Bit is portrayed by an adult actor in her thirties or forties, so we never see child abuse on stage; we only see an adult actor playing a younger woman, and the actions are not enacted on stage but

Elizabeth Reaser and Norbert Leo Butz in Second Stage's 2012 revival of Paula Vogel's *How I Learned to Drive*, directed by Kate Whoriskey.

described in narrative passages. Always eager to entice audiences, Vogel knows that some things are better left off-stage (the Greek word for "off-stage" is "obscene").

Vogel tells the story from Li'l Bit's perspective, significantly departing from Vladimir Nabokov's quintessential novel about pedophilia, *Lolita*, which is told from the perspective of the older male. Nor is the story told chronologically. The play begins when Li'l Bit is seventeen, then moves backward and forward, though mostly backward, in time so that the most disturbing scenes come well after we have had a chance to learn about this relationship in all its complexity. It is almost as if Vogel was easing audiences into pedophilia only to confront them with its most disturbing beginnings (just as violence descends suddenly at the end of *Desdemona* and *Hot 'n' Throbbing*). Vogel also pays homage to the great memory play of the American tradition, TENNESSEE WILLIAMS's *The Glass Menagerie*, as her scenes unfold gradually in the order Li'l Bit remembers them.

The disjointed chronology is reminiscent of theories of trauma put forward in the 1980s and 1990s. But contrary to those theories, which tended to present victims as helpless in the face of abuse, the narrator of Vogel's play is taking charge of her story, at least through the theatrical retelling we witness on stage. When, by the end of the play, we see her driving off with confidence, marked deeply by her experience and the telling of it, she is much more in control of her life than would be typical of a victim suffering from post-traumatic stress syndrome.

The relation between Li'l Bit and Uncle Peck unfolds before the background of the female protagonist's family's neglect, which Vogel enhances through another theatrical technique: all family members and other smaller roles are played by three choruses, inspired by the Greek chorus: a male chorus; a female chorus; and a teenage chorus. The chorus also voices set pieces such as corny advice on social drinking for young women—even in this play, Vogel's penchant for camp and ironic juxtaposition is not entirely absent.

The play, which won Vogel the Pulitzer Prize for Drama among many other honors, has changed over the years in production. While the original production with Mary-Louise Parker as Li'l Bit portrayed the female protagonist as fragile, a 2012 production with Elizabeth Reaser in the main role gave her a larger degree of control and showed her more in charge of her own destiny, thus moving the play even further away from the sense of victimization. No matter what theatrical choices directors and actors make, the play continues to provoke, asking audiences to grapple with vexing moral problems.

As Vogel gained prominence, her earlier plays were revived, collected in book form, and began to attract important directors. The original production of *How I Learned to Drive* was directed by Mark Brokaw at the Vineyard Theater and in New York City, and it was revived by Kate Whoriskey in 2012. In 1992 the avant-garde director Anne Bogart revived *The Baltimore Waltz*

and, two years later, premiered *Hot 'n' Throbbing* at the Hasty Pudding Theatricals festival at Harvard University. Oscar Eustis, the artistic director of the Public Theater in New York, directed the premiere of *The Long Christmas Ride Home* (2003), and Tina Landau, the first production of Vogel's play *A Civil War Christmas* (2008).

After serving as the Director of Playwriting at the Yale School of Drama for several years, Vogel stepped down from that position to focus, once again, on writing plays. She still teaches, however, and so her distinguished dual career as teacher and playwright continues undiminished. While Vogel's signature style of rough topics mixed with just enough camp will certainly be seen in her future works, Vogel is a playwright unafraid of tackling new techniques and materials, and her future plays may have surprises in store for us yet.

M.P.

How I Learned to Drive

CHARACTERS

LI'L BIT   A woman who ages forty-something to eleven years old.

PECK   Attractive man in his forties. Despite a few problems, he should be played by an actor one might cast in the role of Atticus in *To Kill a Mockingbird*.

THE GREEK CHORUS   If possible, these three members should be able to sing three-part harmony.

MALE GREEK CHORUS   Plays Grandfather, Waiter, High School Boys. Thirties–forties.

FEMALE GREEK CHORUS   Plays Mother, Aunt Mary, High School Girls. Thirty–fifty.

TEENAGE GREEK CHORUS   Plays Grandmother, High School Girls and the voice of eleven-year-old Li'l Bit. Note on the casting of this actor: I would strongly recommend casting a young woman who is "of legal age," that is, twenty-one to twenty-five years old who can look as close to eleven as possible. The contrast with the other cast members will help. If the actor is too young, the audience may feel uncomfortable.

PRODUCTION NOTES

I urge directors to use the Greek Chorus in staging as environment and, well, part of the family—with the exception of the Teenage Greek Chorus member who, after the last time she appears onstage, should perhaps disappear.

AS FOR MUSIC   Please have fun. I wrote sections of the play listening to music like Roy Orbison's "Dream Baby" and The Mamas and the Papas' "Dedicated to the One I Love." The vaudeville sections go well to the Tijuana Brass or any music that sounds like a *Laugh-In* soundtrack. Other sixties music is rife with pedophilish (?) reference: the "You're Sixteen" genre hits; The Beach Boys' "Little Surfer Girl"; Gary Puckett and the Union Gap's "This Girl Is a Woman Now"; "Come Back When You Grow Up," etc.

And whenever possible, please feel free to punctuate the action with traffic signs: "No Passing," "Slow Children," "Dangerous Curves," "One Way," and the visual signs for children, deer crossings, hills, school buses, etc.

ON TITLES   Throughout the script there are bold-faced titles. In production these should be spoken in a neutral voice (the type of voice that driver education films employ).

As the house lights dim, a Voice announces:

Safety first—You and Driver Education.

Then the sound of a key turning the ignition of a car. LI'L BIT *steps into a spotlight on the stage; "well-endowed," she is a softer-looking woman in the present time than she was at seventeen.*

LI'L BIT   Sometimes to tell a secret, you first have to teach a lesson. We're going to start our lesson tonight on an early, warm summer evening.
    In a parking lot overlooking the Beltsville Agricultural Farms in subur
5 ban Maryland.
    Less than a mile away, the crumbling concrete of U.S. One wends its way past one-room revival churches, the porno drive-in, and boarded up motels with For Sale signs tumbling down.
    Like I said, it's a warm summer evening.
10   Here on the land the Department of Agriculture owns, the smell of sleeping farm animal is thick on the air. The smells of clover and hay mix in with the smells of the leather dashboard. You can still imagine how Maryland used to be, before the malls took over. This countryside was once dotted with farmhouses—from their porches you could have witnessed the
15 Civil War raging in the front fields.
    Oh yes. There's a moon over Maryland tonight, that spills into the car where I sit beside a man old enough to be—did I mention how still the night is? Damp soil and tranquil air. It's the kind of night that makes a middle-aged man with a mortgage feel like a country boy again.
20   It's 1969. And I am very old, very cynical of the world, and I know it all. In short, I am seventeen years old, parking off a dark lane with a married man on an early summer night.

[*Lights up on two chairs facing front—or a Buick Riviera, if you will. Waiting patiently, with a smile on his face,* PECK *sits sniffing the night air.* LI'L BIT *climbs in beside him, seventeen years old and tense. Throughout the following, the two sit facing directly front. They do not touch. Their bodies remain passive. Only their facial expressions emote.*]

PECK   Ummm. I love the smell of your hair.

LI'L BIT   Uh-huh.

25 PECK   Oh, Lord. Ummmm. [*Beat*] A man could die happy like this.

LI'L BIT   Well, *don't*.

PECK   What shampoo is this?

LI'L BIT   Herbal Essence.

PECK   Herbal Essence. I'm gonna buy me some. Herbal Essence. And when
30   I'm all alone in the house, I'm going to get into the bathtub, and uncap the
       bottle and—

LI'L BIT   —Be good.

PECK   What?

LI'L BIT   Stop being . . . bad.

35 PECK   What did you think I was going to say? What do you think I'm going to
       do with the shampoo?

LI'L BIT   I don't want to know. I don't want to hear it.

PECK   I'm going to wash my hair. That's all.

LI'L BIT   Oh.

40 PECK   What did you think I was going to do?

LI'L BIT   Nothing . . . I don't know. Something . . . nasty.

PECK   With shampoo? Lord, gal—your mind!

LI'L BIT   And whose fault is it?

PECK   Not mine. I've got the mind of a boy scout.

45 LI'L BIT   Right. A horny boy scout.

PECK   Boy scouts are always horny. What do you think the first Merit Badge
       is for?

LI'L BIT   There. You're going to be nasty again.

PECK   Oh, no. I'm good. Very good.

50 LI'L BIT   It's getting late.

PECK   Don't change the subject. I was talking about how good I am. [*Beat*]
       Are you ever gonna let me show you how good I am?

LI'L BIT   Don't go over the line now.

PECK   I won't. I'm not gonna do anything you don't want me to do.

55 LI'L BIT   That's right.

PECK   And I've been good all week.

LI'L BIT   You have?

PECK   Yes. All week. Not a single drink.

LI'L BIT   Good boy.

60 PECK   Do I get a reward? For not drinking?

LI'L BIT   A small one. It's getting late.

PECK   Just let me undo you. I'll do you back up.

LI'L BIT   All right. But be quick about it. [PECK *pantomimes undoing* LI'L BIT'S
       brassiere with one hand.] You know, that's amazing. The way you can undo
65   the hooks through my blouse with one hand.

PECK   Years of practice.

LI'L BIT   You would make an incredible brain surgeon with that dexterity.

PECK   I'll bet Clyde—what's the name of the boy taking you to the prom?

LI'L BIT   Claude Souders.

70 PECK   Claude Souders. I'll bet it takes him two hands, lights on, and you helping him on to get to first base.

LI'L BIT   Maybe.

[*Beat*]

PECK   Can I . . . kiss them? Please?

LI'L BIT   I don't know.

75 PECK   Don't make a grown man beg.

LI'L BIT   Just one kiss.

PECK   I'm going to lift your blouse.

LI'L BIT   It's a little cold.

[PECK *laughs gently.*]

PECK   That's not why you're shivering. [*They sit, perfectly still, for a long moment of silence.* PECK *makes gentle, concentric circles with his thumbs in*
80 *the air in front of him.*] How does that feel?

[LI'L BIT *closes her eyes, carefully keeps her voice calm:*]

LI'L BIT   It's . . . okay.

[*Sacred music, organ music or a boys' choir swells beneath the following.*]

PECK   I tell you, you can keep all the cathedrals of Europe. Just give me a second with these—these celestial orbs—

[PECK *bows his head as if praying. But he is kissing her nipple.* LI'L BIT, *eyes still closed, rears back her head on the leather Buick car seat.*]

LI'L BIT   Uncle Peck—we've got to go. I've got graduation rehearsal at school
85 tomorrow morning. And you should get on home to Aunt Mary—

PECK   —All right, Li'l Bit.

LI'L BIT   —*Don't* call me that no more. [*Calmer*] Any more. I'm a big girl now, Uncle Peck. As you know.

[LI'L BIT *pantomimes refastening her bra behind her back.*]

PECK   That you are. Going on eighteen. Kittens will turn into cats.
90 [*Sighs*] I live all week long for these few minutes with you—you know that?

LI'L BIT   I'll drive.

[*A Voice cuts in with:*]

Idling in the Neutral Gear.

[*Sound of car revving cuts off the sacred music;* LI'L BIT, *now an adult, rises out of the car and comes to us.*]

LI'L BIT   In most families, relatives get names like "Junior," or "Brother," or "Bubba." In my family, if we call someone "Big Papa," it's not because he's

95   tall. In my family, folks tend to get nicknamed for their genitalia. Uncle
Peck, for example. My mama's adage was "the titless wonder," and my
cousin Bobby got branded for life as "B.B."

     [*In unison with* GREEK CHORUS:]

LI'L BIT   For blue balls.   GREEK CHORUS   For blue balls.

FEMALE GREEK CHORUS [*As Mother*]   And of course, we were so excited to
100   have a baby girl that when the nurse brought you in and said, "It's a girl! It's
a baby girl!" I just had to see for myself. So we whipped your diapers down
and parted your chubby little legs—and right between your legs there was—

     [PECK *has come over during the above and chimes along:*]

PECK   Just a little bit.   GREEK CHORUS   Just a little bit.

FEMALE GREEK CHORUS [*As Mother*]   And when you were born, you were so
105   tiny that you fit in Uncle Peck's outstretched hand.

     [PECK *stretches his hand out.*]

PECK   Now that's a fact. I held you, one day old, right in this hand.

     [*A traffic signal is projected of a bicycle in a circle with a diagonal red slash.*]

LI'L BIT   Even with my family background, I was sixteen or so before I realized that pedophilia did not mean people who loved to bicycle. . . .

     [*A Voice intrudes:*]

Driving in First Gear.

110 LI'L BIT   1969. A typical family dinner.

FEMALE GREEK CHORUS [*As Mother*]   Look, Grandma. Li'l Bit's getting to be
as big in the bust as you are.

LI'L BIT   Mother! Could we please change the subject?

TEENAGE GREEK CHORUS [*As Grandmother*]   Well, I hope you are buying her
115   some decent bras. I never had a decent bra, growing up in the Depression,
and now my shoulders are just crippled—crippled from the weight hanging
on my shoulders—the dents from my bra straps are big enough to put your
finger in.—Here, let me show you—

     [*As Grandmother starts to open her blouse*]

LI'L BIT   Grandma! Please don't undress at the dinner table.

120 PECK   I thought the entertainment came *after* the dinner.

LI'L BIT [*To the audience*]   This is how it always starts. My grandfather, Big
Papa, will chime in next with—

MALE GREEK CHORUS [*As Grandfather*]   Yup. If Li'l Bit gets any bigger, we're
gonna haveta buy her a wheelbarrow to carry in front of her—

125 LI'L BIT   —Damn it—

PECK   —How about those Redskins on Sunday, Big Papa?

LI'L BIT [*To the audience*]   The only sport Big Papa followed was chasing
Grandma around the house—

MALE GREEK CHORUS [*As Grandfather*]   —Or we could write to Kate Smith.
130   Ask her for somma her used brassieres she don't want any more—she could
maybe give to Li'l Bit here—

LI'L BIT   —I can't stand it. I can't.

PECK   Now, honey, that's just their way—

FEMALE GREEK CHORUS [*As Mother*]   I tell you, Grandma, Li'l Bit's at that
135   age. She's so sensitive, you can't say boo—

LI'L BIT   I'd like some privacy, that's all. Okay? Some goddamn privacy—

PECK   —Well, at least she didn't use the savior's name—

LI'L BIT [*To the audience*]   And Big Papa wouldn't let a dead dog lie. No
         sirree.

140   MALE GREEK CHORUS [*As Grandfather*]   Well, she'd better stop being so
         sensitive. 'Cause five minutes before Li'l Bit turns the corner, her tits
         turn first—

LI'L BIT [*Starting to rise from the table*]   —That's it. That's it.

PECK   Li'l Bit, you can't let him get to you. Then he wins.

LI'L BIT   I hate him. *Hate* him.

145   PECK   That's fine. But hate him and eat a good dinner at the same time.

         [LI'L BIT *calms down and sits with perfect dignity.*]

LI'L BIT   The gumbo[1] is really good, Grandma.

MALE GREEK CHORUS [*As Grandfather*]   A'course, Li'l Bit's got a big surprise
         coming for her when she goes to that fancy college this fall—

PECK   Big Papa—let it go.

150   MALE GREEK CHORUS [*As Grandfather*]   What does she need a college degree
         for? She's got all the credentials she'll need on her chest—

LI'L BIT   —Maybe I want to learn things. Read. Rise above my cracker
         background—

PECK   —Whoa, now, Li'l Bit—

155   MALE GREEK CHORUS [*As Grandfather*]   What kind of things do you want to
         read?

LI'L BIT   There's a whole semester course, for example, on Shakespeare—

         [GREEK CHORUS, *as Grandfather, laughs until he weeps*]

MALE GREEK CHORUS [*As Grandfather*]   Shakespeare. That's a good one.
         Shakespeare is really going to help you in life.

160   PECK   I think it's wonderful. And on scholarship!

MALE GREEK CHORUS [*As Grandfather*]   How is Shakespeare going to help
         her lie on her back in the dark?

         [LI'L BIT *is on her feet.*]

LI'L BIT   You're getting old, Big Papa. You are going to die—very very soon.
         Maybe even *tonight*. And when you get to heaven, God's going to be a
165   beautiful black woman in a long white robe. She's gonna look at your chart
         and say: Uh-oh. Fornication. Dog-ugly mean with blood relatives. Oh.
         Uh-oh. Voted for George Wallace. Well, one last chance: If you can name
         the play, all will be forgiven. And then she'll quote: "The quality of mercy is
         not strained." Your answer? Oh, too bad—*Merchant of Venice*: Act IV, Scene
170   iii. And then she'll send your ass to fry in hell with all the other crackers.
         Excuse me, please.

---

1. A stew from Louisiana.

[*To the audience*] And as I left the house, I would always hear Big Papa say:

MALE GREEK CHORUS [*As Grandfather*]   Lucy, your daughter's got a mouth on her. Well, no sense in wasting good gumbo. Pass me her plate, Mama.

175 LI'L BIT   And Aunt Mary would come up to Uncle Peck:

FEMALE GREEK CHORUS [*As Aunt Mary*]   Peck, go after her, will you? You're the only one she'll listen to when she gets like this.

PECK   She just needs to cool off.

FEMALE GREEK CHORUS [*As Aunt Mary*]   Please, honey—Grandma's been on
180 her feet cooking all day.

PECK   All right.

LI'L BIT   And as he left the room, Aunt Mary would say:

FEMALE GREEK CHORUS [*As Aunt Mary*]   Peck's so good with them when they get to be this age.

> [LI'L BIT *has stormed to another part of the stage, her back turned, weeping with a teenage fury.* PECK, *cautiously, as if stalking a deer, comes to her. She turns away even more. He waits a bit.*]

185 PECK   I don't suppose you're talking to family. [*No response*] Does it help that I'm in-law?

LI'L BIT   Don't you dare make fun of this.

PECK   I'm not. There's nothing funny about this. [*Beat*] Although I'll bet when Big Papa is about to meet his maker, he'll remember *The Merchant of*
190 *Venice*.

LI'L BIT   I've got to get away from here.

PECK   You're going away. Soon. Here, take this.

> [PECK *hands her his folded handkerchief.* LI'L BIT *uses it, noisily. Hands it back. Without her seeing, he reverently puts it back.*]

LI'L BIT   I hate this family.

PECK   Your grandfather's ignorant. And you're right—he's going to die soon.
195 But he's family. Family is . . . family.

LI'L BIT   Grown-ups are always saying that. Family.

PECK   Well, when you get a little older, you'll see what we're saying.

LI'L BIT   Uh-huh. So family is another acquired taste, like French kissing?

PECK   Come again?

200 LI'L BIT   You know, at first it really grosses you out, but in time you grow to like it?

PECK   Girl, you are . . . a handful.

LI'L BIT   Uncle Peck—you have the keys to your car?

PECK   Where do you want to go?

205 LI'L BIT   Just up the road.

PECK   I'll come with you.

LI'L BIT   No—please? I just need to . . . to drive for a little bit. Alone.

> [PECK *tosses her the keys.*]

PECK   When can I see you alone again?

LI'L BIT   Tonight.

> [LI'L BIT *crosses to center stage while the lights dim around her. A Voice directs:*]

210   **Shifting Forward from First to Second Gear.**

LI'L BIT   There were a lot of rumors about why I got kicked out of that fancy
school in 1970. Some say I got caught with a man in my room. Some say as
a kid on scholarship I fooled around with a rich man's daughter.

[LI'L BIT *smiles innocently at the audience.*] I'm not talking.

But the real truth was I had a constant companion in my dorm room—
215   who was less than discrete. Canadian V.O.[2] A fifth a day.

1970. A Nixon recession. I slept on the floors of friends who were out of
work themselves. Took factory work when I could find it. A string of dead-
end day jobs that didn't last very long.

What I did, most nights, was cruise the Beltway and the back roads of
220   Maryland, where there was still country, past the battlefields and farm houses.
Racing in a 1965 Mustang—and as long as I had gasoline for my car and
whiskey for me, the nights would pass. Fully tanked, I would speed past the
churches and the trees on the bend, thinking just one notch of the steering
wheel would be all it would take, and yet some . . . reflex took over. My hands
225   on the wheel in the nine and three o'clock position—I never so much as got a
ticket. He taught me well.

[*A Voice announces:*]

You and the Reverse Gear.

LI'L BIT   Back up. 1968. On the Eastern Shore. A celebration dinner.

[LI'L BIT *joins* PECK *at a table in a restaurant.*]

PECK   Feeling better, missy?
230   LI'L BIT   The bathroom's really amazing here, Uncle Peck! They have these
little soaps—instead of borax or something—and they're in the shape of
shells.
PECK   I'll have to take a trip to the gentleman's room just to see.
LI'L BIT   How did you know about this place?
235   PECK   This inn is famous on the Eastern Shore—it's been open since the
seventeenth century. And I know how you like history . . .

[LI'L BIT *is shy and pleased.*]

LI'L BIT   It's great.
PECK   And you've just done your first, legal, long-distance drive. You must be
hungry.
240   LI'L BIT   I'm starved.
PECK   I would suggest a dozen oysters to start, and the crab imperial . . . [LI'L
BIT *is genuinely agog.*] You might be interested to know the town history.
When the British sailed up this very river in the dead of night—see outside
where I'm pointing?—they were going to bombard the heck out of this town.
245   But the town fathers were ready for them. They crept up all the trees with
lanterns so that the British would think they saw the town lights and they

2. A Canadian whiskey.

aimed their cannons too high. And that's why the inn is still here for business today.

LI'L BIT   That's a great story.

250   PECK [*Casually*]   Would you like to start with a cocktail?

LI'L BIT   You're not . . . you're not going to start drinking, are you, Uncle Peck?

PECK   Not me. I told you, as long as you're with me, I'll never drink. I asked you if *you'd* like a cocktail before dinner. It's nice to have a little something with the oysters.

255   LI'L BIT   But . . . I'm not . . . legal. We could get arrested. Uncle Peck, they'll never believe I'm twenty-one!

PECK   So? Today we celebrate your driver's license—on the first try. This establishment reminds me a lot of places back home.

LI'L BIT   What does that mean?

260   PECK   In South Carolina, like here on the Eastern Shore, they're . . . [*Searches for the right euphemism*] . . . "European." Not so puritanical. And very understanding if gentlemen wish to escort very attractive young ladies who might want a before-dinner cocktail. If you want one, I'll order one.

LI'L BIT   Well—sure. Just . . . one.

[*The* FEMALE GREEK CHORUS *appears in a spot.*]

265   FEMALE GREEK CHORUS [*As Mother*]   A Mother's Guide to Social Drinking:

A lady never gets sloppy—she may, however, get tipsy and a little gay.

Never drink on an empty stomach. Avail yourself of the bread basket and generous portions of butter. *Slather* the butter on your bread.

Sip your drink, slowly, let the beverage linger in your mouth—interspersed with interesting, fascinating conversation. Sip, never . . . slurp or gulp. Your glass should always be three-quarters full when his glass is empty.

Stay away from *ladies'* drinks: drinks like pink ladies, slow gin fizzes, daiquiris, gold cadillacs, Long Island iced teas, margaritas, piña coladas, mai tais, planters punch, white Russians, black Russians, red Russians, melon balls, blue balls, hummingbirds, hemorrhages and hurricanes. In short, avoid anything with sugar, or anything with an umbrella. Get your vitamin C from *fruit*. Don't order anything with Voodoo or Vixen in the title or sexual positions in the name like Dead Man Screw or the Missionary. [*She sort of titters.*]

Believe me, they are lethal. . . . I think you were conceived after one of those.

Drink, instead, like a man: straight up or on the rocks, with plenty of water in between.

Oh, yes. And never mix your drinks. Stay with one all night long, like the man you came in with: bourbon, gin, or tequila till dawn, damn the torpedoes, full speed ahead!

[*As the* FEMALE GREEK CHORUS *retreats, the* MALE GREEK CHORUS *approaches the table as a Waiter.*]

MALE GREEK CHORUS [*As Waiter*]   I hope you all are having a pleasant evening. Is there something I can bring you, sir, before you order?

[LI'L BIT *waits in anxious fear. Carefully, Uncle* PECK *says with command:*]

PECK   I'll have a plain iced tea. The lady would like a drink, I believe.

[*The* MALE GREEK CHORUS *does a double take; there is a moment when Uncle* PECK *and he are in silent communication.*]

MALE GREEK CHORUS [*As Waiter*]   Very good. What would the . . . lady like?

290 LI'L BIT [*A bit flushed*]   Is there . . . is there any sugar in a martini?

PECK   None that I know of.

LI'L BIT   That's what I'd like then—a dry martini. And could we maybe have some bread?

PECK   A drink fit for a woman of the world. —Please bring the lady a dry

295   martini, be generous with the olives, straight up.

[*The* MALE GREEK CHORUS *anticipates a large tip.*]

MALE GREEK CHORUS [*As Waiter*]   Right away. Very good, sir.

[*The* MALE GREEK CHORUS *returns with an empty martini glass which he puts in front of* LI'L BIT.]

PECK   Your glass is empty. Another martini, madam?

LI'L BIT   Yes, thank you.

[*Peck signals the* MALE GREEK CHORUS, *who nods.*] So why did you leave

300   South Carolina, Uncle Peck?

PECK   I was stationed in D.C. after the war, and decided to stay. Go North, Young Man, someone might have said.

LI'L BIT   What did you do in the service anyway?

PECK [*Suddenly taciturn*]   I . . . I did just this and that. Nothing heroic or

305   spectacular.

LI'L BIT   But did you see fighting? Or go to Europe?

PECK   I served in the Pacific Theater. It's really nothing interesting to talk about.

LI'L BIT   It is to me. [*The Waiter has brought another empty glass.*] Oh, goody.

310   I love the color of the swizzle sticks. What were we talking about?

PECK   Swizzle sticks.

LI'L BIT   Do you ever think of going back?

PECK   To the Marines?

LI'L BIT   No—to South Carolina.

315 PECK   Well, we do go back. To visit.

LI'L BIT   No, I mean to live.

PECK   Not very likely. I think it's better if my mother doesn't have a daily reminder of her disappointment.

LI'L BIT   Are these floorboards slanted?

320 PECK   Yes, the floor is very slanted. I think this is the original floor.

LI'L BIT   Oh, good.

[*The* FEMALE GREEK CHORUS *as Mother enters swaying a little, a little past tipsy.*]

FEMALE GREEK CHORUS [*As Mother*]   Don't leave your drink unattended when you visit the ladies' room. There is such a thing as white slavery; the modus operandi is to spike an unsuspecting young girl's drink with a "mickey" when

325   she's left the room to powder her nose.

But if you feel you have had more than your sufficiency in liquor, do go to the ladies' room—often. Pop your head out of doors for a refreshing breath of the night air. If you must, wet your face and head with tap water. Don't be afraid to dunk your head if necessary. A wet woman is still less conspicuous than a drunk woman.

[*The* FEMALE GREEK CHORUS *stumbles a little; conspiratorially.*] When in the course of human events it becomes necessary, go to a corner stall and insert the index and middle finger down the throat almost to the epiglottis. Divulge your stomach contents by such persuasion, and then wait a few moments before rejoining your beau waiting for you at your table.

Oh, no. Don't be shy or embarrassed. In the very best of establishments, there's always one or two debutantes crouched in the corner stalls, their beaded purses tossed willy-nilly, sounding like cats in heat, heaving up the contents of their stomachs.

[*The* FEMALE GREEK CHORUS *begins to wander off.*] I wonder what it is they do in the men's rooms . . .

LI'L BIT So why is your mother disappointed in you, Uncle Peck?

PECK Every mother in Horry County has Great Expectations.

LI'L BIT —Could I have another mar-ti-ni, please?

PECK I think this is your last one.

[PECK *signals the Waiter. The Waiter looks at* LI'L BIT *and shakes his head no.* PECK *raises his eyebrow, raises his finger to indicate one more, and then rubs his fingers together. It looks like a secret code. The Waiter sighs, shakes his head sadly, and brings over another empty martini glass. He glares at* PECK.]

LI'L BIT The name of the county where you grew up is "Horry?" [LI'L BIT, *plastered, begins to laugh. Then she stops.*] I think your mother should be proud of you.

[PECK *signals for the check.*]

PECK Well, missy, she wanted me to do—to *be* everything my father was not. She wanted me to amount to something.

LI'L BIT But you have! You've amounted a lot. . . .

PECK I'm just a very ordinary man.

[*The Waiter has brought the check and waits.* PECK *draws out a large bill and hands it to the Waiter.* LI'L BIT *is in the soppy stage.*]

LI'L BIT I'll bet your mother loves you, Uncle Peck.

[*Peck freezes a bit. To* MALE GREEK CHORUS *as Waiter:*]

PECK Thank you. The service was exceptional. Please keep the change.

MALE GREEK CHORUS [*As Waiter, in a tone that could freeze*] Thank you, sir. Will you be needing any help?

PECK I think we can manage, thank you.

[*Just then, the* FEMALE GREEK CHORUS *as Mother lurches on stage; the* MALE GREEK CHORUS *as Waiter escorts her off as she delivers:*]

FEMALE GREEK CHORUS [*As Mother*] Thanks to judicious planning and several trips to the ladies' loo, your mother once out-drank an entire regiment of British officers on a good-will visit to Washington! Every last man of them! Milquetoasts! How'd they ever kick Hitler's cahones[3] huh? No

3. Balls, a man's testicles, borrowed from *cojones* (Spanish).

match for an American lady—I could drink every man in here under the table.

[*She delivers one last crucial hint before she is gently "bounced."*] As a last
resort, when going out for an evening on the town, be sure to wear a skin-
tight girdle—so tight that only a surgical knife or acetylene torch can get it
off you—so that if you do pass out in the arms of your escort, he'll end up
with rubber burns on his fingers before he can steal your virtue—

[*A Voice punctures the interlude with:*]

> **Vehicle Failure.**
> **Even with careful maintenance and preventive operation of your**
> **automobile, it is all too common for us to experience an unexpected**
> **breakdown. If you are driving at any speed when a breakdown**
> **occurs, you must slow down and guide the automobile to the side of**
> **the road.**

[PECK *is slowly propping up* LI'L BIT *as they work their way to his car in the parking lot of the inn.*]

PECK   How are you doing, missy?

LI'L BIT   It's so far to the car, Uncle Peck. Like the lanterns in the trees the
British fired on . . .

[LI'L BIT *stumbles.* PECK *swoops her up in his arms.*]

PECK   Okay. I think we're going to take a more direct route.
[LI'L BIT *closes her eyes.*] Dizzy? [*She nods her head.*] Don't look at the
ground. Almost there—do you feel sick to your stomach? [LI'L BIT *nods.*
They reach the "car." Peck gently deposits her on the front seat.] Just settle
here a little while until things stop spinning. [LI'L BIT *opens her eyes*]

LI'L BIT   What are we doing?

PECK   We're just going to sit here until your tummy settles down.

LI'L BIT   It's such nice upholst'ry—

PECK   Think you can go for a ride, now?

LI'L BIT   Where are you taking me?

PECK   Home.

LI'L BIT   You're not taking me—upstairs? There's no room at the inn? [LI'L BIT
giggles.]

PECK   Do you want to go upstairs? [LI'L BIT *doesn't answer.*] Or home?

LI'L BIT   —This isn't right, Uncle Peck.

PECK   What isn't right?

LI'L BIT   What we're doing. It's wrong. It's very wrong.

PECK   What are we doing? [LI'L BIT *does not answer.*] We're just going out to
dinner.

LI'L BIT   You know. It's not nice to Aunt Mary.

PECK   You let me be the judge of what's nice and not nice to my wife.

[*Beat*]

LI'L BIT   Now you're mad.

PECK   I'm not mad. It's just that I thought you . . . understood me, Li'l Bit. I
think you're the only one who does.

LI'L BIT   Someone will get hurt.

PECK   Have I forced you to do anything?

[*There is a long pause as* LI'L BIT *tries to get sober enough to think this through.*]

LI'L BIT   . . . I guess not.

PECK   We are just enjoying each other's company. I've told you, nothing is
405   going to happen between us until you want it to. Do you know that?

LI'L BIT   Yes.

PECK   Nothing is going to happen until you want it to. [*A second more, with*
PECK *staring ahead at the river while seated at the wheel of his car. Then, softly:*] Do you want something to happen?

[PECK *reaches over and strokes her face, very gently.* LI'L BIT *softens, reaches for him, and buries her head in his neck. Then she kisses him. Then she moves away, dizzy again.*]

LI'L BIT   . . . I don't know.

[PECK *smiles; this has been good news for him—it hasn't been a "no."*]

410   PECK   Then I'll wait. I'm a very patient man. I've been waiting for a long time.
I don't mind waiting.

LI'L BIT   Someone is going to get hurt.

PECK   No one is going to get hurt. [LI'L BIT *closes her eyes.*] Are you feeling sick?

LI'L BIT   Sleepy.

[*Carefully,* PECK *props* LI'L BIT *up on the seat.*]

415   PECK   Stay here a second.

LI'L BIT   Where're you going?

PECK   I'm getting something from the back seat.

LI'L BIT [*Scared; too loud*]   What? What are you going to do?

[PECK *reappears in the front seat with a lap rug.*]

PECK   Shhhh. [PECK *covers* LI'L BIT. *She calms down.*] There. Think you can
420   sleep?

[LI'L BIT *nods. She slides over to rest on his shoulder. With a look of happiness,* PECK *turns the ignition key. Beat.* PECK *leaves* LI'L BIT *sleeping in the car and strolls down to the audience. Wagner's* Flying Dutchman *comes up faintly.*

A Voice interjects:]

Idling in the Neutral Gear.

TEENAGE GREEK CHORUS   Uncle Peck Teaches Cousin Bobby How to Fish.

PECK   I get back once or twice a year—supposedly to visit Mama and the family,
but the real truth is to fish. I miss this the most of all. There's a smell in the
425   Low Country—where the swamp and fresh inlet join the saltwater—a scent
of sand and cypress, that I haven't found anywhere yet.

I don't say this very often up North because it will just play into the stereotype everyone has, but I will tell you: I didn't wear shoes in the summertime
until I was sixteen. It's unnatural down here to pen up your feet in leather. Go
430   ahead—take 'em off. Let yourself breathe—it really will make you feel better.

We're going to aim for some pompano today—and I have to tell you, they're
a very shy, mercurial fish. Takes patience, and psychology. You have to believe
it doesn't matter if you catch one or not.

Sky's pretty spectacular—there's some beer in the cooler next to the crab
435   salad I packed, so help yourself if you get hungry. Are you hungry? Thirsty?
Holler if you are.

Okay. You don't want to lean over the bridge like that—pompano feed in
shallow water, and you don't want to get too close—they're frisky and shy little
things—wait, check your line. Yep, something's been munching while we
440   were talking.

Okay, look: We take the sand flea and you take the hook like this—right
through his little sand flea rump. Sand fleas should always keep their backs to
the wall. Okay. Cast it in, like I showed you. That's great! I can taste that pompano now, sautéed with some pecans and butter, a little bourbon—now—let
445   it lie on the bottom—now, reel, jerk, reel, jerk—

Look—look at your line. There's something calling, all right. Okay, tip the
rod up—not too sharp—hook it—all right, now easy, reel and then rest—let it
play. And reel—play it out, that's right—really good! I can't believe it! It's a
pompano.—Good work! Way to go! You are an official fisherman now. Pom-
450   pano are hard to catch. We are going to have a delicious little—

What? Well, I don't know how much pain a fish feels—you can't think of
that. Oh, no, don't cry, come on now, it's just a fish—the other guys are going
to see you. —No, no, you're just real sensitive, and I think that's wonderful at
your age—look, do you want me to cut it free? You do?

455   Okay, hand me those pliers—look—I'm cutting the hook—okay? And
we're just going to drop it in—no I'm not mad. It's just for fun, okay?
There—it's going to swim back to its lady friend and tell her what a terrible
day it had and she's going to stroke him with her fins until he feels better,
and then they'll do something alone together that will make them both feel
460   good and sleepy. . . .

[PECK *bends down, very earnest*] I don't want you to feel ashamed about crying. I'm not going to tell anyone, okay? I can keep secrets. You know, men cry
all the time. They just don't tell anybody, and they don't let anybody catch
them. There's nothing you could do that would make me feel ashamed of you.
465   Do you know that? Okay. [*Peck straightens up, smiles*]

Do you want to pack up and call it a day? I tell you what—I think I can
still remember—there's a really neat tree house where I used to stay for
days. I think it's still here—it was the last time I looked. But it's a secret
place—you can't tell anybody we've gone there—least of all your mom or
470   your sisters.—This is something special just between you and me. Sound
good? We'll climb up there and have a beer and some crab salad—okay,
B.B.? Bobby? Robert . . .

[LI'L BIT *sits at a kitchen table with the two* FEMALE GREEK CHORUS
members.]

LI'L BIT [*To the audience*]   Three women, three generations, sit at the kitchen table.

475   On Men, Sex, and Women: Part I:

FEMALE GREEK CHORUS [*As Mother*]   Men only want one thing.

LI'L BIT [*Wide-eyed*]   But what? What is it they want?

FEMALE GREEK CHORUS [*As Mother*]   And once they have it, they lose all interest. So Don't Give It to Them.

480   TEENAGE GREEK CHORUS [*As Grandmother*]   I never had the luxury of the rhythm method. Your grandfather is just a big bull. A big bull. Every morning, every evening.

FEMALE GREEK CHORUS [*As Mother, whispers to* LI'L BIT]   And he used to come home for lunch every day.

485   LI'L BIT   My god, Grandma!

TEENAGE GREEK CHORUS [*As Grandmother*]   Your grandfather only cares that I do two things: have the table set and the bed turned down.

FEMALE GREEK CHORUS [*As Mother*]   And in all that time, Mother, you never have experienced—?

490   LI'L BIT [*To the audience*]   —Now my grandmother believed in all the sacraments of the church, to the day she died. She believed in Santa Claus and the Easter Bunny until she was fifteen. But she didn't believe in—

TEENAGE GREEK CHORUS [*As Grandmother*]   —Orgasm! That's just something you and Mary have made up! I don't believe you.

495   FEMALE GREEK CHORUS [*As Mother*]   Mother, it happens to women all the time—

TEENAGE GREEK CHORUS [*As Grandmother*]   —Oh, now you're going to tell me about the G force!

LI'L BIT   No, Grandma, I think that's astronauts—

500   FEMALE GREEK CHORUS [*As Mother*]   Well, Mama, after all, you were a child bride when Big Papa came and got you—you were a married woman and you still believed in Santa Claus.

TEENAGE GREEK CHORUS [*As Grandmother*]   It was legal, what Daddy and I did! I was fourteen and in those days, fourteen was a grown-up woman—

[*Big Papa shuffles in the kitchen for a cookie.*]

505   MALE GREEK CHORUS [*As Grandfather*]   —Oh, now we're off on Grandma and the Rape of the Sa-bean Women![4]

TEENAGE GREEK CHORUS [*As Grandmother*]   Well, you were the one in such a big hurry—

MALE GREEK CHORUS [*As Grandfather to* LI'L BIT]   —picked your grandmother
510   out of that herd of sisters just like a lion chooses the gazelle—the plump, slow, flaky gazelle dawdling at the edge of the herd—your sisters were too smart and too fast and too scrawny—

LI'L BIT [*To the audience*]   —The family story is that when Big Papa came for Grandma, my Aunt Lily was waiting for him with a broom—and she beat
515   him over the head all the way down the stairs as he was carrying out Grandma's hope chest—

MALE GREEK CHORUS [*As Grandfather*]   —And they were *mean*. 'Specially Lily.

---

4. A legend about the first generation of Roman men who forcibly abducted women from a neighboring tribe.

FEMALE GREEK CHORUS [*As Mother*]   Well, you were robbing the baby of the family!

520   TEENAGE GREEK CHORUS [*As Grandmother*]   I still keep a broom handy in the kitchen! And I know how to use it! So get your hand out of the cookie jar and don't you spoil your appetite for dinner—out of the kitchen!

[MALE GREEK CHORUS *as Grandfather leaves chuckling with a cookie.*]

FEMALE GREEK CHORUS [*As Mother*]   Just one thing a married woman needs to know how to use—the rolling pin or the broom. I prefer a heavy, cast-iron fry

525   pan—they're great on a man's head, no matter how thick the skull is.

TEENAGE GREEK CHORUS [*As Grandmother*]   Yes, sir, your father is ruled by only two bosses! Mr. Gut and Mr. Peter! And sometimes, first thing in the morning, Mr. Sphincter Muscle![5]

FEMALE GREEK CHORUS [*As Mother*]   It's true. Men are like children. Just like

530   little boys.

TEENAGE GREEK CHORUS [*As Grandmother*]   Men are bulls! Big bulls!

[*The* GREEK CHORUS *is getting aroused.*]

FEMALE GREEK CHORUS [*As Mother*]   They'd still be crouched on their haunches over a fire in a cave if we hadn't cleaned them up!

TEENAGE GREEK CHORUS [*As Grandmother, flushed*]   Coming in smelling of

535   sweat—

FEMALE GREEK CHORUS [*As Mother*]   —looking at those naughty pictures like boys in a dime store with a dollar in their pockets!

TEENAGE GREEK CHORUS [*As Grandmother; raucous*]   No matter to them what they smell like! They've got to have it, right then, on the spot, right

540   there! Nasty!—

FEMALE GREEK CHORUS [*As Mother*]   —Vulgar!

TEENAGE GREEK CHORUS [*As Grandmother*]   Primitive!—

FEMALE GREEK CHORUS [*As Mother*]   —Hot!—

LI'L BIT   And just about then, Big Papa would shuffle in with—

545   MALE GREEK CHORUS [*As Grandfather*]   —What are you all cackling about in here?

TEENAGE GREEK CHORUS [*As Grandmother*]   Stay out of the kitchen! This is just for girls!

[*As Grandfather leaves:*]

MALE GREEK CHORUS [*As Grandfather*]   Lucy, you'd better not be filling

550   Mama's head with sex! Every time you and Mary come over and start in about sex, when I ask a simple question like, "What time is dinner going to be ready?," Mama snaps my head off!

TEENAGE GREEK CHORUS [*As Grandmother*]   Dinner will be ready when I'm good and ready! Stay out of this kitchen!

[LI'L BIT *steps out.*

A Voice directs:]

555   **When Making a Left Turn, You Must Downshift While Going Forward.**

---

5. Muscle that surrounds a body opening such as the anus.

LI'L BIT   1979. A long bus trip to Upstate New York. I settled in to read, when
a young man sat beside me.

MALE GREEK CHORUS [*As Young Man; voice cracking*]   "What are you reading?"

560 LI'L BIT   He asked. His voice broke into that miserable equivalent of vocal
acne, not quite falsetto and not tenor, either. I glanced a side view. He was
appealing in an odd way, huge ears at a defiant angle springing forward
at ninety degrees. He must have been shaving, because his face, with a
peach sheen, was speckled with nicks and styptic. "I have a class tomorrow,"

565 I told him.

MALE GREEK CHORUS [*As Young Man*]   "You're taking a class?"

LI'L BIT   "I'm teaching a class." He concentrated on lowering his voice.

MALE GREEK CHORUS [*As Young Man*]   "I'm a senior. Walt Whitman High."

LI'L BIT   The light was fading outside, so perhaps he was—with a very high

570 voice.

I felt his "interest" quicken. Five steps ahead of the hopes in his head, I
slowed down, waited, pretended surprise, acted at listening, all the while
knowing we would get off the bus, he would just then seem to think to ask
me to dinner, he would chivalrously insist on walking me home, he would

575 continue to converse in the street until I would casually invite him up to
my room—and—I was only into the second moment of conversation and I
could see the whole evening before me.

And dramaturgically speaking, after the faltering and slightly comical "first
act," there was the very briefest of intermissions, and an extremely capable

580 and forceful and *sustained* second act. And after the second act climax and a
gentle denouement—before the post-play discussion—I lay on my back in
the dark and I thought about you, Uncle Peck. Oh. Oh—this is the allure.
Being older. Being the first. Being the translator, the teacher, the epicure,
the already jaded. This is how the giver gets taken.

585   [LI'L BIT *changes her tone.*] On Men, Sex, and Women: Part II:

[LI'L BIT *steps back into the scene as a fifteen year old, gawky and quiet,
as the gazelle at the edge of the herd.*]

TEENAGE GREEK CHORUS [*As Grandmother; to* LI'L BIT]   You're being mighty
quiet, missy. Cat Got Your Tongue?

LI'L BIT   I'm just listening. Just thinking.

TEENAGE GREEK CHORUS [*As Grandmother*]   Oh, yes, Little Miss Radar Ears?

590 Soaking it all in? Little Miss Sponge? Penny for your thoughts?

[LI'L BIT *hesitates to ask but she really wants to know.*]

LI'L BIT   Does it—when you do it—you know, theoretically when I do it and
I haven't done it before—I mean—does it hurt?

FEMALE GREEK CHORUS [*As Mother*]   Does what hurt, honey?

LI'L BIT   When a . . . when a girl does it for the first time—with a man—does

595 it hurt?

TEENAGE GREEK CHORUS [*As Grandmother; horrified*]   *That's* what you're
thinking about?

FEMALE GREEK CHORUS [*As Mother; calm*]   Well, just a little bit. Like a pinch.
And there's a little blood.

600 TEENAGE GREEK CHORUS [*As Grandmother*]   Don't tell her that! She's too
young to be thinking those things!

FEMALE GREEK CHORUS [*As Mother*]   Well, if she doesn't find out from me, where is she going to find out? In the street?

TEENAGE GREEK CHORUS [*As Grandmother*]   Tell her it hurts! It's agony! You
605   think you're going to die! Especially if you do it before marriage!

FEMALE GREEK CHORUS [*As Mother*]   Mama! I'm going to tell her the truth! Unlike you, you left me and Mary completely in the dark with fairy tales and told us to go to the priest! What does an eighty-year-old priest know about love-making with girls!

610   LI'L BIT [*Getting upset*]   It's not fair!

FEMALE GREEK CHORUS [*As Mother*]   Now, see, she's getting upset—you're scaring her.

TEENAGE GREEK CHORUS [*As Grandmother*]   Good! Let her be good and scared! It hurts! You bleed like a stuck pig! And you lay there and say, "Why,
615   O Lord, have you forsaken me?!"

LI'L BIT   It's not fair! Why does everything have to hurt for girls? Why is there always blood?

FEMALE GREEK CHORUS [*As Mother*]   It's not a lot of blood—and it feels wonderful after the pain subsides . . .

620   TEENAGE GREEK CHORUS [*As Grandmother*]   You're encouraging her to just go out and find out with the first drugstore joe who buys her a milk shake!

FEMALE GREEK CHORUS [*As Mother*]   Don't be scared. It won't hurt you—if the man you go to bed with really loves you. It's important that he loves you.

TEENAGE GREEK CHORUS [*As Grandmother*]   —Why don't you just go out and
625   rent a motel room for her, Lucy?

FEMALE GREEK CHORUS [*As Mother*]   I believe in telling my daughter the truth! We have a very close relationship! I want her to be able to ask me anything— I'm not scaring with stories about Eve's sin and snakes crawling on their bellies for eternity and women bearing children in mortal pain—

630   TEENAGE GREEK CHORUS [*As Grandmother*]   —If she stops and thinks before she takes her knickers off, maybe someone in this family will finish high school!

[*Li'l Bit knows what is about to happen and starts to retreat from the scene at this point.*]

FEMALE GREEK CHORUS [*As Mother*]   Mother! If you and Daddy had helped me—I wouldn't have had to marry that—that no-good-son-of-a—

TEENAGE GREEK CHORUS [*As Grandmother*]   —He was good enough for you
635   on a full moon! I hold you responsible!

FEMALE GREEK CHORUS [*As Mother*]   —You could have helped me! You could have told me something about the facts of life!

TEENAGE GREEK CHORUS [*As Grandmother*]   —I told you what my mother told me! A girl with her skirt up can outrun a man with his pants down!

[*The* MALE GREEK CHORUS *enters the fray;* LI'L BIT *edges further downstage.*]

640   FEMALE GREEK CHORUS [*As Mother*]   And when I turned to you for a little help, all I got afterwards was—

MALE GREEK CHORUS [*As Grandfather*]   You Made Your Bed; Now Lie On It!

[*The* GREEK CHORUS *freezes, mouths open, argumentatively.*]

LI'L BIT [*To the audience*]   Oh, please! I still can't bear to listen to it, after all these years—

[*The* MALE GREEK CHORUS *"unfreezes," but out of his open mouth, as if to his surprise, comes a base refrain from a Motown song.*]

645 MALE GREEK CHORUS   "Do-Bee-Do-Wah!"

[*The* FEMALE GREEK CHORUS *member is also surprised; but she, too, unfreezes.*]

FEMALE GREEK CHORUS   "Shoo-doo-be-doo-be-doo; shoo-doo-be-doo-be-doo."

[*The Male and Female* GREEK CHORUS *members continue with their harmony, until the Teenage member of the* CHORUS *starts in with Motown lyrics such as "Dedicated to the One I Love," or "In the Still of the Night," or "Hold Me"—any Sam Cooke will do. The three modulate down into three-part harmony, softly, until they are submerged by the actual recording playing over the radio in the car in which Uncle* PECK *sits in the driver's seat, waiting.* LI'L BIT *sits in the passenger's seat.*]

LI'L BIT   Ahh. That's better.

[*Uncle* PECK *reaches over and turns the volume down; to* LI'L BIT:]
PECK   How can you hear yourself think?

[LI'L BIT *does not answer. A Voice insinuates itself in the pause:*]

Before You Drive.
650 **Always check under your car for obstructions—broken bottles, fallen tree branches, and the bodies of small children. Each year hundreds of children are crushed beneath the wheels of unwary drivers in their own driveways. Children depend on *you* to watch them.**

[*Pause. The Voice continues:*]

You and the Reverse Gear.

[*In the following section, it would be nice to have slides of erotic photographs of women and cars: women posed over the hood; women draped along the sideboards; women with water hoses spraying the car; and the actress playing* LI'L BIT *with a Bel Air or any 1950s car one can find for the finale.*]

655 LI'L BIT   1967. In a parking lot of the Beltsville Agricultural Farms. The Initiation into a Boy's First Love.
PECK [*With a soft look on his face*]   Of course, my favorite car will always be the '56 Bel Air Sports Coupe. Chevy sold more '55s, but the '56!—a V-8 with Corvette option, 225 horsepower; went from zero to sixty miles per 660 hour in 8.9 seconds.
LI'L BIT [*To the audience*]   Long after a mother's tits, but before a woman's breasts:
PECK   Super-Turbo-Fire! What a Power Pack—mechanical lifters, twin four-barrel carbs, lightweight valves, dual exhausts—
665 LI'L BIT [*To the audience*]   After the milk but before the beer:
PECK   A specific intake manifold, higher-lift camshaft, and the tightest squeeze Chevy had ever made—

LI'L BIT [*To the audience*]   Long after he's squeezed down the birth canal but
before he's pushed his way back in: The boy falls in love with the thing that
670   bears his weight with speed.

PECK   I want you to know your automobile inside and out. —Are you there?
Li'l Bit?

[*Slides end here.*]

LI'L BIT   —What?

PECK   You're drifting. I need you to concentrate.

675   LI'L BIT   Sorry.

PECK   Okay. Get into the driver's seat. [LI'L BIT *does*] Okay. Now. Show me
what you're going to do before you start the car.

[LI'L BIT *sits, with her hands in her lap. She starts to giggle.*]

LI'L BIT   I don't know, Uncle Peck.

PECK   Now, come on. What's the first thing you're going to adjust?

680   LI'L BIT   My bra strap?—

PECK   —Li'l Bit. What's the most important thing to have control of on the
inside of the car?

LI'L BIT   That's easy. The radio. I tune the radio from Mama's old fart
tunes to—

[LI'L BIT *turns the radio up so we can hear a 1960s tune. With surprising
firmness,* PECK *commands:*]

685   PECK   —Radio off. Right now. [LI'L BIT *turns the radio off.*] When you are
driving your car, with your license, you can fiddle with the stations all you
want. But when you are driving with a learner's permit in my car, I want all
your attention to be on the road.

LI'L BIT   Yes, sir.

690   PECK   Okay. Now the seat—forward and up. [LI'L BIT *pushes it forward.*] Do
you want a cushion?

LI'L BIT   No—I'm good.

PECK   You should be able to reach all the switches and controls. Your feet
should be able to push the accelerator, brake and clutch all the way down.
695   Can you do that?

LI'L BIT   Yes.

PECK   Okay, the side mirrors. You want to be able to see just a bit of the right
side of the car in the right mirror—can you?

LI'L BIT   Turn it out more.

700   PECK   Okay. How's that?

LI'L BIT   A little more . . . Okay, that's good.

PECK   Now the left—again, you want to be able to see behind you—but the left
lane—adjust it until you feel comfortable. [LI'L BIT *does so*] Next. I want you to
check the rearview mirror. Angle it so you have a clear vision of the back. [LI'L
705   BIT *does so*] Okay. Lock your door. Make sure all the doors are locked.

LI'L BIT [*Making a joke of it*]   But then I'm locked in with you.

PECK   Don't fool.

LI'L BIT   All right. We're locked in.

PECK   We'll deal with the air vents and defroster later. I'm teaching you on a
710   manual—once you learn manual, you can drive anything. I want you to be

able to drive any car, any machine. Manual gives you *control*. In ice, if your brakes fail, if you need more power—okay? It's a little harder at first, but then it becomes like breathing. Now. Put your hands on the wheel. I never want to see you driving with one hand. Always two hands. [LI'L BIT *hesi-*
715 *tates.*] What? What is it now?

LI'L BIT   If I put my hands on the wheel—how do I defend myself?

PECK [*Softly*]   Now listen. Listen up close. We're not going to fool around with this. This is serious business. I will never touch you when you are driving a car. Understand?

720 LI'L BIT   Okay.

PECK   Hands on the nine o'clock and three o'clock position gives you maximum control and turn.

[PECK *goes silent for a while.* LI'L BIT *waits for more instruction.*]

Okay. Just relax and listen to me, Li'l Bit, okay? I want you to lift your hands for a second and look at them. [LI'L BIT *feels a bit silly, but does it.*]

725 Those are your two hands. When you are driving, your life is in your own two hands. Understand? [LI'L BIT *nods.*]

I don't have any sons. You're the nearest to a son I'll ever have—and I want to give you something. Something that really matters to me.

There's something about driving—when you're in control of the car, just
730 you and the machine and the road—that nobody can take from you. A power. I feel more myself in my car than anywhere else. And that's what I want to give to you.

There's a lot of assholes out there. Crazy men, arrogant idiots, drunks, angry kids, geezers who are blind—and you have to be ready for them. I
735 want to teach you to drive like a man.

LI'L BIT   What does that mean?

PECK   Men are taught to drive with confidence—with aggression. The road belongs to them. They drive defensively—always looking out for the other guy. Women tend to be polite—to hesitate. And that can be fatal.

740 You're going to learn to think what the other guy is going to do before he does it. If there's an accident, and ten cars pile up, and people get killed, you're the one who's gonna steer through it, put your foot on the gas if you have to, and be the only one to walk away. I don't know how long you or I are going to live, but we're for damned sure not going to die in a car.

745 So if you're going to drive with me, I want you to take this very seriously.

LI'L BIT   I will, Uncle Peck. I want you to teach me to drive.

PECK   Good. You're going to pass your test on the first try. Perfect score. Before the next four weeks are over, you're going to know this baby inside
750 and out. Treat her with respect.

LI'L BIT   Why is it a "she?"

PECK   Good question. It doesn't have to be a "she"—but when you close your eyes and think of someone who responds to your touch—someone who performs just for you and gives you what you ask for—I guess I always see
755 a "she." You can call her what you like.

LI'L BIT [*To the audience*]   I closed my eyes—and decided not to change the gender.

[*A Voice:*]

Defensive driving involves defending yourself from hazardous and sudden changes in your automotive environment. By thinking ahead, the defensive driver can adjust to weather, road conditions and road kill. Good defensive driving involves mental and physical preparation. Are you prepared?

760

[*Another Voice chimes in:*]

You and the Reverse Gear.

LI'L BIT   1966. The Anthropology of the Female Body in Ninth Grade—Or A Walk Down Mammary Lane.

765

[*Throughout the following, there is occasional rhythmic beeping, like a transmitter signalling.* LI'L BIT *is aware of it, but can't figure out where it is coming from. No one else seems to hear it.*]

MALE GREEK CHORUS   In the hallway of Francis Scott Key Middle School.

[*A bell rings; the* GREEK CHORUS *is changing classes and meets in the hall, conspiratorially.*]

TEENAGE GREEK CHORUS   She's coming!

[LI'L BIT *enters the scene; the* MALE GREEK CHORUS *member has a sudden, violent sneezing and lethal allergy attack.*]

FEMALE GREEK CHORUS   Jerome? Jerome? Are you all right?

MALE GREEK CHORUS   I—don't—know. I can't breathe—get Li'l Bit—

770 TEENAGE GREEK CHORUS   —He needs oxygen!—

FEMALE GREEK CHORUS   —Can you help us here?

LI'L BIT   What's wrong? Do you want me to get the school nurse—

[*The* MALE GREEK CHORUS *member wheezes, grabs his throat and sniffs at* LI'L BIT's *chest, which is beeping away.*]

MALE GREEK CHORUS   No—it's okay—I only get this way when I'm around an allergy trigger—

775 LI'L BIT   Golly. What are you allergic to?

MALE GREEK CHORUS [*With a sudden grab of her breast.*]   Foam rubber.

[*The* GREEK CHORUS *members break up with hilarity; Jerome leaps away from* LI'L BIT's *kicking rage with agility; as he retreats:*]

LI'L BIT   Jerome! Creep! Cretin! Cro-Magnon!

TEENAGE GREEK CHORUS   Rage is not attractive in a girl.

FEMALE GREEK CHORUS   Really. Get a Sense of Humor.

[*A Voice echoes:*]

780

Good defensive driving involves mental and physical preparation. Were You Prepared?

FEMALE GREEK CHORUS   Gym Class: In the showers.

[*The sudden sound of water; the* FEMALE GREEK CHORUS *members and* LI'L BIT, *while fully clothed, drape towels across their fronts, miming nudity. They stand, hesitate, at an imaginary shower's edge.*]

LI'L BIT   Water looks hot.

FEMALE GREEK CHORUS   Yesss. . . .

[FEMALE GREEK CHORUS *members are not going to make the first move. One dips a tentative toe under the water, clutching the towel around her.*]

785   LI'L BIT   Well, I guess we'd better shower and get out of here.

FEMALE GREEK CHORUS   Yep. You go ahead. I'm still cooling off.

LI'L BIT   Okay. —Sally? Are you gonna shower?

TEENAGE GREEK CHORUS   After you—

[LI'L BIT *takes a deep breath for courage, drops the towel and plunges in: The two* FEMALE GREEK CHORUS *members look at* LI'L BIT *in the all together, laugh, gasp and high-five each other.*]

TEENAGE GREEK CHORUS   Oh my god! Can you believe—

790   FEMALE GREEK CHORUS   Told you! It's not foam rubber! I win! Jerome owes me fifty cents!

[*A Voice editorializes:*]

Were You Prepared?

[LI'L BIT *tries to cover up; she is exposed, as suddenly 1960s Motown fills the room and we segue into:*]

FEMALE GREEK CHORUS   The Sock Hop.

[LI'L BIT *stands up against the wall with her female classmates.* TEENAGE GREEK CHORUS *is mesmerized by the music and just sways alone, lip-synching the lyrics.*]

LI'L BIT   I don't know. Maybe it's just me—but—do you ever feel like you're

795   just a walking Mary Jane joke?

FEMALE GREEK CHORUS   I don't know what you mean.

LI'L BIT   You haven't heard the Mary Jane jokes? [FEMALE GREEK CHORUS *member shakes her head no.*] Okay. "Little Mary Jane is walking through the woods, when all of a sudden this man who was hiding behind a tree

800   *jumps* out, *rips* open Mary Jane's blouse, and *plunges* his hands on her breasts. And Little Mary Jane just laughed and laughed because she knew her money was in her shoes."

[LI'L BIT *laughs; the* FEMALE GREEK CHORUS *does not.*]

FEMALE GREEK CHORUS   You're weird.

[*In another space, in a strange light, Uncle* PECK *stands and stares at* LI'L BIT's *body. He is setting up a tripod, but he just stands, appreciative, watching her.*]

LI'L BIT   Well, don't you ever feel . . . self-conscious? Like you're being

805   looked at all the time?

FEMALE GREEK CHORUS   That's not a problem for me.—Oh—look—Greg's coming over to ask you to dance.

[TEENAGE GREEK CHORUS *becomes attentive, flustered.* MALE GREEK CHO-RUS *member, as Greg, bends slightly as a very short young man, whose*

head is at LI'L BIT's *chest level. Ardent, sincere and socially inept, Greg
will become a successful gynecologist.*]

TEENAGE GREEK CHORUS [*Softly*]   Hi, Greg.

[*Greg does not hear. He is intent on only one thing.*]

MALE GREEK CHORUS [*As Greg, to* LI'L BIT]   Good Evening. Would you care to
810   dance?

LI'L BIT [*Gently*]   Thank you very much, Greg—but I'm going to sit this one
out.

MALE GREEK CHORUS [*As Greg*]   Oh. Okay. I'll try my luck later.

[*He disappears.*]

TEENAGE GREEK CHORUS   Oohhh.

[LI'L BIT *relaxes. Then she tenses, aware of* PECK's *gaze.*]

815   FEMALE GREEK CHORUS   Take pity on him. Someone should.

LI'L BIT   But he's so short.

TEENAGE GREEK CHORUS   He can't help it.

LI'L BIT   But his head comes up to [LI'L BIT *gestures.*] here. And I think he
asks me on the fast dances so he can watch me—you know—jiggle.

820   FEMALE GREEK CHORUS   I wish I had your problems.

[*The tune changes; Greg is across the room in a flash.*]

MALE GREEK CHORUS [*As Greg*]   Evening again. May I ask you for the honor
of a spin on the floor?

LI'L BIT   I'm . . . very complimented, Greg. But I . . . I just don't do fast
dances.

825   MALE GREEK CHORUS [*As Greg*]   Oh. No problem. That's okay.

[*He disappears.* TEENAGE GREEK CHORUS *watches him go.*]

TEENAGE GREEK CHORUS   That is just so—sad.

[LI'L BIT *becomes aware of* PECK *waiting.*]

FEMALE GREEK CHORUS   You know, you should take it as a compliment that
the guys want to watch you jiggle. They're guys. That's what they're supposed to do.

830   LI'L BIT   I guess you're right. But sometimes I feel like these alien life forces,
these two mounds of flesh have grafted themselves onto my chest, and they're
using me until they can "propagate" and take over the world and they'll just
keep growing, with a mind of their own until I collapse under their weight and
they suck all the nourishment out of my body and I finally just waste away

835   while they get bigger and bigger and—[LI'L BIT's *classmates are just staring at
her in disbelief.*]

FEMALE GREEK CHORUS   —You are the strangest girl I have ever met.

[LI'L BIT's *trying to joke but feels on the verge of tears.*]

LI'L BIT   Or maybe someone's implanted radio transmitters in my chest at a
frequency I can't hear, that girls can't detect, but they're sending out these
signals to men who get mesmerized, like sirens, calling them to dash them-

840   selves on these "rocks"—

[*Just then, the music segues into a slow dance, perhaps a Beach Boys tune like "Little Surfer," but over the music there's a rhythmic, hypnotic beeping transmitted, which both Greg and* PECK *hear.* LI'L BIT *hears it too, and in horror she stares at her chest. She, too, is almost hypnotized. In a trance, Greg responds to the signals and is called to her side—actually, her front. Like a zombie, he stands in front of her, his eyes planted on her two orbs.*]

MALE GREEK CHORUS [*As Greg*]   This one's a slow dance. I hope your dance card isn't . . . filled?

[LI'L BIT *is aware of* PECK; *but the signals are calling her to him. The signals are no longer transmitters, but an electromagnetic force, pulling* LI'L BIT *to his side, where he again waits for her to join him. She must get away from the dance floor.*]

LI'L BIT   Greg—you really are a nice boy. But I don't like to dance.

MALE GREEK CHORUS [*As Greg*]   That's okay. We don't have to move or any-
845   thing. I could just hold you and we could just *sway* a little—

LI'L BIT   —No! I'm sorry—but I think I have to leave; I hear someone calling me—

[LI'L BIT *starts across the dance floor, leaving Greg behind. The beeping stops. The lights change, although the music does not. As* LI'L BIT *talks to the audience, she continues to change and prepare for the coming session. She should be wearing a tight tank top or a sheer blouse and very tight pants. To the audience:*]

In every man's home some small room, some zone in his house, is set aside. It might be the attic, or the study, or a den. And there's an invisible
850   sign as if from the old treehouse: Girls Keep Out.

Here, away from female eyes, lace doilies and crochet, he keeps his manly toys: the Vargas pinups, the tackle. A scent of tobacco and WD-40.[6] [*She inhales deeply.*] A dash of his Bay Rum. Ahhh . . . [LI'L BIT *savors it for just a moment more.*]

Here he keeps his secrets: a violin or saxophone, drum set or darkroom,
855   and the stacks of *Playboy*. [*In a whisper*] Here, in my aunt's home, it was the basement. Uncle Peck's turf.

[*A Voice commands:*]

You and the Reverse Gear.

LI'L BIT   1965. The Photo Shoot.

[LI'L BIT *steps into the scene as a nervous but curious thirteen year old. Music, from the previous scene, continues to play, changing into something like Roy Orbison later—something seductive with a beat.* PECK *fiddles, all business, with his camera. As in the driving lesson, he is all competency and concentration.* LI'L BIT *stands awkwardly. He looks through the Leica camera on the tripod, adjusts the back lighting, etc.*]

PECK   Are you cold? The lights should heat up some in a few minutes—
860   LI'L BIT   —Aunt Mary is?
PECK   At the National Theatre matinee. With your mother. We have time.

6. Multipurpose oil spray.

LI'L BIT   But—what if—

PECK   —And so what if they return? I told them you and I were going to be working with my camera. They won't come down. [*Li'l Bit is quiet,*
865   *apprehensive.*]—Look, are you sure you want to do this?

LI'L BIT   I said I'd do it. But—

PECK   —I know. You've drawn the line.

LI'L BIT [*Reassured*]   That's right. No frontal nudity.

PECK   Good heavens, girl, where did you pick that up?

870 LI'L BIT [*Defensive*]   I *read.*

> [PECK *tries not to laugh.*]

PECK   And I read *Playboy* for the interviews. Okay. Let's try some different music.

> [PECK *goes to an expensive reel-to-reel and forwards. Something like "Sweet Dreams" begins to play.*]

LI'L BIT   I didn't know you listened to this.

PECK   I'm not dead, you know. I try to keep up. Do you like this song? [LI'L
875   BIT *nods with pleasure.*] Good. Now listen—at professional photo shoots, they always play music for the models. Okay? I want you to just enjoy the music. Listen to it with your body, and just—respond.

LI'L BIT   Respond to the music with my . . . body?

PECK   Right. Almost like dancing. Here—let's get you on the stool, first. [PECK *comes over and helps her up.*]

880 LI'L BIT   But nothing showing—

> [PECK *firmly, with his large capable hands, brushes back her hair, angles her face.* LI'L BIT *turns to him like a plant to the sun.*]

PECK   Nothing showing. Just a peek.

> [*He holds her by the shoulder, looking at her critically. Then he unbuttons her blouse to the midpoint, and runs his hands over the flesh of her exposed sternum, arranging the fabric, just touching her. Deliberately, calmly. Asexually.* LI'L BIT *quiets, sits perfectly still, and closes her eyes.*]

Okay?

LI'L BIT   Yes.

> [PECK *goes back to his camera.*]

PECK   I'm going to keep talking to you. Listen without responding to what
885   I'm saying; you want to *listen* to the music. Sway, move just your torso or your head—I've got to check the light meter.

LI'L BIT   But—you'll be watching.

PECK   No—I'm not here—just my voice. Pretend you're in your room all alone on a Friday night with your mirror—and the music feels good—just
890   move for me, Li'l Bit—

> [LI'L BIT *closes her eyes. At first self-conscious; then she gets more into the music and begins to sway. We hear the camera start to whir. Throughout the shoot, there can be a slide montage of actual shots of the actor playing* LI'L BIT*—interspersed with other models à la Playboy, Calvin Klein and Victoriana/Lewis Carroll's Alice Liddell.*]

That's it. That looks great. Okay. Just keep doing that. Lift your head up a bit more, good, good, just keep moving, that a girl—you're a very beautiful young woman. Do you know that? [LI'L BIT *looks up, blushes.* PECK *shoots the camera. The audience should see this shot on the screen.*]

LI'L BIT   No. I don't know that.

895 PECK   Listen to the music. [LI'L BIT *closes her eyes again.*] Well you are. For a thirteen year old, you have a body a twenty-year-old woman would die for.

LI'L BIT   The boys in school don't think so.

PECK   The boys in school are little Neanderthals in short pants. You're ten years ahead of them in maturity; it's gonna take a while for them to catch up.

> [PECK *clicks another shot; we see a faint smile on* LI'L BIT *on the screen.*]

900 Girls turn into women long before boys turn into men.

LI'L BIT   Why is that?

PECK   I don't know, Li'l Bit. But it's a blessing for men.

[LI'L BIT *turns silent.*] Keep moving. Try arching your back on the stool, hands behind you, and throw your head back. [*The slide shows a* Playboy

905 *model in this pose.*] Oohh, great. That one was great. Turn your head away, same position. [*Whir*] Beautiful.

> [LI'L BIT *looks at him a bit defiantly.*]

LI'L BIT   I think Aunt Mary is beautiful.

> [PECK *stands still.*]

PECK   My wife is a very beautiful woman. Her beauty doesn't cancel yours out. [*More casually; he returns to the camera.*] All the women in your family are

910 beautiful. In fact, I think all women are. You're not listening to the music. [PECK *shoots some more film in silence.*] All right, turn your head to the left. Good. Now take the back of your right hand and put in on your right cheek— your elbow angled up—now slowly, slowly, stroke your cheek, draw back your hair with the back of your hand. [*Another classic* Playboy *or Vargas*] Good. One

915 hand above and behind your head; stretch your body; smile. [*Another pose*] Li'l Bit. I want you to think of something that makes you laugh—

LI'L BIT   I can't think of anything.

PECK   Okay. Think of Big Papa chasing Grandma around the living room. [LI'L BIT *lifts her head and laughs. Click. We should see this shot.*] Good.

920 Both hands behind your head. Great! Hold that. [*From behind his camera*] You're doing great work. If we keep this up, in five years we'll have a really professional portfolio.

> [LI'L BIT *stops.*]

LI'L BIT   What do you mean in five years?

PECK   You can't submit work to *Playboy* until you're eighteen.—

> [PECK *continues to shoot; he knows he's made a mistake.*]

925 LI'L BIT   —Wait a minute. You're joking, aren't you, Uncle Peck?

PECK   Heck, no. You can't get into *Playboy* unless you're the very best. And you are the very best.

LI'L BIT   I would never do that!

[PECK *stops shooting. He turns off the music.*]

PECK   Why? There's nothing wrong with *Playboy*—it's a very classy maga—

930   LI'L BIT [*More upset*]   But I thought you said I should go to college!

PECK   Wait—Li'l Bit—it's nothing like that. Very respectable women model
for *Playboy*—actresses with major careers—women in college—there's an
Ivy League issue every—

LI'L BIT   —I'm never doing anything like that! You'd show other people
935   these—other *men*—these—what I'm doing.—Why would you do that?! Any
boy around here could just pick up, just go into The Stop & Go and *buy*—
Why would you ever want to—to share—

PECK   —Whoa, whoa. Just stop a second and listen to me. Li'l Bit. Listen. There's nothing wrong in what we're doing. I'm very proud of you.
940   I think you have a wonderful body and an even more wonderful mind.
And of course I want other people to *appreciate* it. It's not anything
shameful.

LI'L BIT [*Hurt*]   But this is something—that I'm only doing for you. This is
something—that you said was just between us.

945   PECK   It is. And if that's how you feel, five years from now, it will remain that
way. Okay? I know you're not going to do anything you don't feel like doing.
[*He walks back to the camera.*] Do you want to stop now? I've got just a
few more shots on this roll—

LI'L BIT   I don't want anyone seeing this.

950   PECK   I swear to you. No one will. I'll treasure this—that you're doing this
only for me.
[LI'L BIT, *still shaken, sits on the stool. She closes her eyes.*] Li'l Bit? Open
your eyes and look at me. [LI'L BIT *shakes her head no.*] Come on. Just open
your eyes, honey.

955   LI'L BIT   If I look at you—if I look at the camera: You're gonna know what I'm
thinking. You'll see right through me—

PECK   —No, I won't. I want you to look at me. All right, then. I just want you
to listen. Li'l Bit. [*She waits*] I love you. [LI'L BIT *opens her eyes; she is startled.* PECK *captures the shot. On the screen we see right though her.* PECK *says
softly.*] Do you know that? [LI'L BIT *nods her head yes.*] I have loved you
960   every day since the day you were born.

LI'L BIT   Yes.

[LI'L BIT *and* PECK *just look at each other. Beat. Beneath the shot of herself on the screen,* LI'L BIT, *still looking at her uncle, begins to unbutton
her blouse.*

A neutral Voice cuts off the above scene with:]

Implied Consent.
As an individual operating a motor vehicle in the state of Maryland,
you must abide by "Implied Consent." If you do not consent to take the
965   **blood alcohol content test, there may be severe penalties: a suspension**
of license, a fine, community service and a possible *jail* sentence.

[*The Voice shifts tone:*]

Idling in the Neutral Gear.

MALE GREEK CHORUS [*Announcing*]   Aunt Mary on behalf of her husband.

> [FEMALE GREEK CHORUS *checks her appearance, and with dignity comes to the front of the stage and sits down to talk to the audience.*]

FEMALE GREEK CHORUS [*As Aunt Mary*]   My husband was such a good man—
970   is. Is. Is such a good man. Every night, he does the dishes. The second he comes home, he's taking out the garbage, or doing yard work, lifting the heavy things I can't. Everyone in the neighborhood borrows Peck—it's true—women with husbands of their own, men who just don't have Peck's abilities—there's always a knock on our door for a jump start on cold morn-
975   ings, when anyone needs a ride, or help shoveling the sidewalk—I look out, and there Peck is, without a coat, pitching in.

I know I'm lucky. The man works from dawn to dusk. And the overtime he does every year—my poor sister. She sits every Christmas when I come to dinner with a new stole, or diamonds, or with the tickets to Bermuda.

980   I know he has troubles. And we don't talk about them. I wonder, some-times, what happened to him during the war. The men who fought World War II didn't have "rap sessions" to talk about their feelings. Men in his generation were expected to be quiet about it and get on with their lives. And sometimes I can feel him just fighting the trouble—whatever has bur-
985   rowed deeper than the scar tissue—and we don't talk about it. I know he's having a bad spell because he comes looking for me in the house, and just hangs around me until it passes. And I keep my banter light—I discuss a new recipe, or sales, or gossip—because I think domesticity can be a balm for men when they're lost. We sit in the house and listen to the peace of the
990   clock ticking in his well-ordered living room, until it passes.

[*Sharply*] I'm not a fool. I know what's going on. I wish you could feel how hard Peck fights against it—he's swimming against the tide, and what he needs is to see me on the shore, believing in him, knowing he won't go under, he won't give up—
995   And I want to say this about my niece. She's a sly one, that one is. She knows exactly what she's doing; she's twisted Peck around her little finger and thinks it's all a big secret. Yet another one who's borrowing my husband until it doesn't suit her any more.

Well. I'm counting the days until she goes away to school. And she
1000   manipulates someone else. And then he'll come back again, and sit in the kitchen while I bake, or beside me on the sofa when I sew in the evenings. I'm a very patient woman. But I'd like my husband back.

I am counting the days.

> [*A Voice repeats:*]

You and the Reverse Gear.

1005   MALE GREEK CHORUS   Li'l Bit's Thirteenth Christmas. Uncle Peck Does the Dishes. Christmas 1964.

> [PECK *stands in a dress shirt and tie, nice pants, with an apron. He is washing dishes. He's in a mood we haven't seen. Quiet, brooding.* LI'L BIT *watches him a moment before seeking him out.*]

LI'L BIT   Uncle Peck? [*He does not answer. He continues to work on the pots.*]
I didn't know where you'd gone to. [*He nods. She takes this as a sign to come in.*] Don't you want to sit with us for a while?

1010   PECK   No. I'd rather do the dishes.

[*Pause.* LI'L BIT *watches him.*]

LI'L BIT   You're the only man I know who does dishes. [PECK *says nothing.*] I think it's really nice.

PECK   My wife has been on her feet all day. So's your grandmother and your mother.

1015   LI'L BIT   I know. [*Beat*] Do you want some help?

PECK   No. [*He softens a bit towards her.*] You can help by just talking to me.

LI'L BIT   Big Papa never does the dishes. I think it's nice.

PECK   I think men should be nice to women. Women are always working for us. There's nothing particularly manly in wolfing down food and then sit-
1020   ting around in a stupor while the women clean up.

LI'L BIT   That looks like a really neat camera that Aunt Mary got you.

PECK   It is. It's a very nice one.

[*Pause, as* PECK *works on the dishes and some demon that* LI'L BIT *intuits.*]

LI'L BIT   Did Big Papa hurt your feelings?

PECK [*Tired*]   What? Oh, no—it doesn't hurt me. Family is family. I'd rather
1025   have him picking on me than—I don't pay him any mind, Li'l Bit.

LI'L BIT   Are you angry with us?

PECK   No, Li'l Bit. I'm not angry.

[*Another pause.*]

LI'L BIT   We missed you at Thanksgiving. . . . I did. I missed you.

PECK   Well, there were . . . "things" going on. I didn't want to spoil anyone's
1030   Thanksgiving.

LI'L BIT   Uncle Peck? [*Very carefully*] Please don't drink any more tonight.

PECK   I'm not . . . overdoing it.

LI'L BIT   I know. [*Beat*] Why do you drink so much?

[PECK *stops and thinks, carefully.*]

PECK   Well, Li'l Bit—let me explain it this way. There are some people who
1035   have a . . . a "fire" in the belly. I think they go to work on Wall Street or they
run for office. And then there are people who have a "fire" in their heads—
and they become writers or scientists or historians. [*He smiles a little at her.*]
You. You've got a "fire" in the head. And then there are people like me.

LI'L BIT   Where do you have . . . a fire?

1040   PECK   I have a fire in my heart. And sometimes the drinking helps.

LI'L BIT   There's got to be other things that can help.

PECK   I suppose there are.

LI'L BIT   Does it help—to talk to me?

PECK   Yes. It does. [*Quiet*] I don't get to see you very much.

1045   LI'L BIT   I know. [LI'L BIT *thinks*] You could talk to me more.

PECK   Oh?

LI'L BIT   I could make a deal with you, Uncle Peck.

PECK   I'm listening.

LI'L BIT   We could meet and talk—once a week. You could just store up
1050   whatever's bothering you during the week—and then we could talk.
PECK   Would you like that?
LI'L BIT   As long as you don't drink. I'd meet you somewhere for lunch or for
   a walk—on the weekends—as long as you stop drinking. And we could talk
   about whatever you want.
1055   PECK   You would do that for me?
LI'L BIT   I don't think I'd want Mom to know. Or Aunt Mary. I wouldn't want
   them to think—
PECK   —No. It would just be us talking.
LI'L BIT   I'll tell Mom I'm going to a girlfriend's. To study. Mom doesn't get
1060   home until six, so you can call me after school and tell me where to meet
   you.
PECK   You get home at four?
LI'L BIT   We can meet once a week. But only in public. You've got to let me—
   draw the line. And once it's drawn, you mustn't cross it.
1065   PECK   Understood.
LI'L BIT   Would that help?

[PECK *is very moved.*]

PECK   Yes. Very much.
LI'L BIT   I'm going to join the others in the living room now. [*Li'l Bit turns to go.*]
PECK   Merry Christmas, Li'l Bit.

[LI'L BIT *bestows a very warm smile on him.*]

1070   LI'L BIT   Merry Christmas, Uncle Peck.

[*A Voice dictates:*]

Shifting Forward from Second to Third Gear.

[*The Male and Female* GREEK CHORUS *members come forward.*]

MALE GREEK CHORUS   1969. Days and Gifts: A Countdown:
FEMALE GREEK CHORUS   A note. "September 3, 1969. Li'l Bit: You've only
   been away two days and it feels like months. Hope your dorm room is cozy.
1075   I'm sending you this tape cassette—it's a new model—so you'll have some
   music in your room. Also that music you're reading about for class—
   Carmina Burana. Hope you enjoy. Only ninety days to go! —Peck."
MALE GREEK CHORUS   September 22. A bouquet of roses. A note: "Miss you
   like crazy. Sixty-nine days . . ."
1080   TEENAGE GREEK CHORUS   September 25. A box of chocolates. A card: "Don't
   worry about the weight gain. You still look great. Got a post office box—
   write to me there. Sixty-six days. —Love, your candy man."
MALE GREEK CHORUS   October 16. A note: "Am trying to get through the Jane
   Austen you're reading—*Emma*—here's a book in return: *Liaisons Dangereuses*.
1085   Hope you're saving time for me." Scrawled in the margin the number: "47."
FEMALE GREEK CHORUS   November 16. "Sixteen days to go! —Hope you like
   the perfume.—Having a hard time reaching you on the dorm phone. You
   must be in the library a lot. Won't you think about me getting you your own
   phone so we can talk?"

1090 TEENAGE GREEK CHORUS   November 18. "Li'l Bit—got a package returned to
the P.O. Box. Have you changed dorms? Call me at work or write to the
P.O. Am still on the wagon. Waiting to see you. Only two weeks more!"

MALE GREEK CHORUS   November 23. A letter. "Li'l Bit. So disappointed you
couldn't come home for the turkey. Sending you some money for a nice
1095 dinner out—nine days and counting!"

GREEK CHORUS [*In unison*]   November 25th. A letter:

LI'L BIT   "Dear Uncle Peck: I am sending this to you at work. Don't come up
next weekend for my birthday. I will not be here—"

[*A Voice directs:*]

Shifting Forward from Third to Fourth Gear.

1100 MALE GREEK CHORUS   December 10, 1969. A hotel room. Philadelphia.
There is no moon tonight.

[PECK *sits on the side of the bed while* LI'L BIT *paces. He can't believe
she's in his room, but there's a desperate edge to his happiness.* LI'L BIT *is
furious, edgy. There is a bottle of champagne in an ice bucket in a very
nice hotel room.*]

PECK   Why don't you sit?

LI'L BIT   I don't want to. —What's the champagne for?

PECK   I thought we might toast your birthday—

1105 LI'L BIT   —I am so pissed off at you, Uncle Peck.

PECK   Why?

LI'L BIT   I mean, are you crazy?

PECK   What did I do?

LI'L BIT   You scared the holy crap out of me—sending me that stuff in the mail—

1110 PECK   —They were gifts! I just wanted to give you some little perks your first
semester—

LI'L BIT   —Well, what the hell were those numbers all about! Forty-four days
to go—only two more weeks. —And then just numbers—69—68—67—
like some serial killer!

1115 PECK   Li'l Bit! Whoa! This is me you're talking to—I was just trying to pick
up your spirits, trying to celebrate your birthday.

LI'L BIT   My *eighteenth* birthday. I'm not a child, Uncle Peck. You were
counting down to my eighteenth birthday.

PECK   So?

1120 LI'L BIT   So? So statutory rape is not in effect when a young woman turns
eighteen. And you and I both know it.

[PECK *is walking on ice.*]

PECK   I think you misunderstand.

LI'L BIT   I think I understand all too well. I know what you want to do five
steps ahead of you doing it. Defensive Driving 101.

1125 PECK   Then why did you suggest we meet here instead of the restaurant?

LI'L BIT   I don't want to have this conversation in public.

PECK   Fine. Fine. We have a lot to talk about.

LI'L BIT   Yeah. We do.

[LI'L BIT *doesn't want to do what she has to do.*] Could I . . . have some of
that champagne?

PECK   Of course, madam! [PECK *makes a big show of it.*] Let me do the honors. I wasn't sure which you might prefer—Taittingers or Veuve Clicquot—
so I thought we'd start out with an old standard—Perrier Jouet. [*The bottle
is popped.*]

Quick—Li'l Bit—your glass! [*Uncle* PECK *fills* LI'L BIT'*s glass. He puts the
bottle back in the ice and goes for a can of ginger ale.*] Let me get some of
this ginger ale—my bubbly—and toast you.

[*He turns and sees that* LI'L BIT *has not waited for him.*]

LI'L BIT   Oh—sorry, Uncle Peck. Let me have another. [PECK *fills her glass
and reaches for his ginger ale; she stops him.*] Uncle Peck—maybe you
should join me in the champagne.

PECK   You want me to—drink?

LI'L BIT   It's not polite to let a lady drink alone.

PECK   Well, missy, if you insist . . . [PECK *hesitates*]—Just one. It's been a while.
[PECK *fills another flute for himself.*] There. I'd like to propose a toast to you
and your birthday! [PECK *sips it tentatively.*] I'm not used to this any more.

LI'L BIT   You don't have anywhere to go tonight, do you?

[PECK *hopes this is a good sign.*]

PECK   I'm all yours. —God, it's good to see you! I've gotten so used to . . .
to . . . talking to you in my head. I'm used to seeing you every week—
there's so much—I don't quite know where to begin. How's school, Li'l Bit?

LI'L BIT   I—it's hard. Uncle Peck. Harder than I thought it would be. I'm in
the middle of exams and papers and—I don't know.

PECK   You'll pull through. You always do.

LI'L BIT   Maybe. I . . . might be flunking out.

PECK   You always think the worse, Li'l Bit, but when the going gets tough—
[LI'L BIT *shrugs and pours herself another glass.*]—Hey, honey, go easy on
that stuff, okay?

LI'L BIT   Is it very expensive?

PECK   Only the best for you. But the cost doesn't matter—champagne should
be "sipped." [LI'L BIT *is quiet*] Look—if you're in trouble in school—you can
always come back home for a while.

LI'L BIT   No— [LI'L BIT *tries not to be so harsh.*]—Thanks, Uncle Peck, but I'll
figure some way out of this.

PECK   You're supposed to get in scrapes, your first year away from home.

LI'L BIT   Right. How's Aunt Mary?

PECK   She's fine. [*Pause*] Well—how about the new car?

LI'L BIT   It's real nice. What is it, again?

PECK   It's a Cadillac El Dorado.

LI'L BIT   Oh. Well, I'm real happy for you, Uncle Peck.

PECK   I got it for you.

LI'L BIT   What?

PECK   I always wanted to get a Cadillac—but I thought, Peck, wait until Li'l
Bit's old enough—and thought maybe you'd like to drive it, too.

LI'L BIT [*Confused*]   Why would I want to drive your car?

PECK   Just because it's the best—I want you to have the best.

[*They are running out of "gas"; small talk.*]

LI'L BIT   Listen, Uncle Peck, I don't   PECK   I have been thinking of how to
know how to begin this, but—   say this in my head, over and over—

PECK   Sorry.

LI'L BIT   You first.

PECK   Well, your going away—has just made me realize how much I miss you. Talking to you and being alone with you. I've really come to depend on you, Li'l Bit. And it's been so hard to get in touch with you lately—the distance and—and you're never in when I call—I guess you've been living in the library—

LI'L BIT   —No—the problem is, I haven't been in the library—

PECK   —Well, it doesn't matter—I hope you've been missing me as much.

LI'L BIT   Uncle Peck—I've been thinking a lot about this—and I came here tonight to tell you that—I'm not doing very well. I'm getting very confused—I can't concentrate on my work—and now that I'm away—I've been going over and over it in my mind—and I don't want us to "see" each other any more. Other than with the rest of the family.

PECK [*Quiet*]   Are you seeing other men?

LI'L BIT [*Getting agitated*]   I—no, that's not the reason—I—well, yes, I am seeing other—listen, it's not really anybody's business!

PECK   Are you in love with anyone else?

LI'L BIT   That's not what this is about.

PECK   Li'l Bit—you're scared. Your mother and your grandparents have filled your head with all kinds of nonsense about men—I hear them working on you all the time—and you're scared. It won't hurt you—if the man you go to bed with really loves you. [LI'L BIT *is scared. She starts to tremble.*] And I have loved you since the day I held you in my hand. And I think everyone's just gotten you frightened to death about something that is just like breathing—

LI'L BIT   Oh, my god— [*She takes a breath.*] I can't see you any more, Uncle Peck.

[PECK *downs the rest of his champagne.*]

PECK   Li'l Bit. Listen. Open your eyes and look at me. Come on. Just open your eyes, honey. [LI'L BIT, *eyes squeezed shut, refuses.*] All right then. I just want you to listen. Li'l Bit—I'm going to ask you just this once. Of your own free will. Just lie down on the bed with me—our clothes on—just lie down with me, a man and a woman . . . and let's . . . hold one another. Nothing else. Before you say anything else. I want the chance to . . . hold you. Because sometimes the body knows things that the mind isn't listening to . . . and after I've held you, then I want you to tell me what you feel.

LI'L BIT   You'll just . . . hold me?

PECK   Yes. And then you can tell me what you're feeling.

[LI'L BIT—*half wanting to run, half wanting to get it over with, half wanting to be held by him:*]

LI'L BIT   Yes. All right. Just hold. Nothing else.

[PECK *lies down on the bed and holds his arms out to her.* LI'L BIT *lies beside him, putting her head on his chest. He looks as if he's trying to soak her into his pores by osmosis. He strokes her hair, and she lies very*

still. The MALE GREEK CHORUS *member and the* FEMALE GREEK CHORUS
member as Aunt Mary come into the room.]

MALE GREEK CHORUS   Recipe for a Southern Boy:

1215 FEMALE GREEK CHORUS [*As Aunt Mary*]   A drawl of molasses in the way he
speaks.

MALE GREEK CHORUS   A gumbo of red and brown mixed in the cream of his
skin.

[*While* PECK *lies, his eyes closed,* LI'L BIT *rises in the bed and responds to
her aunt.*]

LI'L BIT   Warm brown eyes—

1220 FEMALE GREEK CHORUS [*As Aunt Mary*]   Bedroom eyes—

MALE GREEK CHORUS   A dash of Southern Baptist Fire and Brimstone—

LI'L BIT   A curl of Elvis on his forehead—

FEMALE GREEK CHORUS [*As Aunt Mary*]   A splash of Bay Rum—

MALE GREEK CHORUS   A closely shaven beard that he razors just for you—

1225 FEMALE GREEK CHORUS [*As Aunt Mary*]   Large hands—rough hands—

LI'L BIT   Warm hands—

MALE GREEK CHORUS   The steel of the military in his walk—

LI'L BIT   The slouch of the fishing skiff in his walk—

MALE GREEK CHORUS   Neatly pressed khakis—

1230 FEMALE GREEK CHORUS [*As Aunt Mary*]   And under the wide leather of the
belt—

LI'L BIT   Sweat of cypress and sand—

MALE GREEK CHORUS   Neatly pressed khakis—

LI'L BIT   His heart beating Dixie—

1235 FEMALE GREEK CHORUS [*As Aunt Mary*]   The whisper of the zipper—you
could reach out with your hand and—

LI'L BIT   His mouth—

FEMALE GREEK CHORUS [*As Aunt Mary*]   You could just reach out and—

LI'L BIT   Hold him in your hand—

1240 FEMALE GREEK CHORUS [*As Aunt Mary*]   And his mouth—

[LI'L BIT *rises above her uncle and looks at his mouth; she starts to lower
herself to kiss him—and wrenches herself free. She gets up from the bed.*]

LI'L BIT   —I've got to get back.

PECK   Wait—Li'l Bit. Did you . . . feel nothing?

LI'L BIT [*Lying*]   No. Nothing.

PECK   Do you—do you think of me?

[*The* GREEK CHORUS *whispers:*]

1245 FEMALE GREEK CHORUS   Khakis—

MALE GREEK CHORUS   Bay Rum—

FEMALE GREEK CHORUS   The whisper of the—

LI'L BIT   —No.

[PECK, *in a rush, trembling, gets something out of his pocket.*]

PECK   I'm forty-five. That's not old for a man. And I haven't been able to do
1250 anything else but think of you. I can't concentrate on my work—Li'l Bit.
You've got to—I want you to think about what I am about to ask you.

LI'L BIT I'm listening.

[PECK *opens a small ring box.*]

PECK I want you to be my wife.

LI'L BIT This isn't happening.

1255 PECK I'll tell Mary I want a divorce. We're not blood-related. It would be legal—

LI'L BIT —What have you been thinking! You are married to my aunt, Uncle Peck. She's my family. You have—you have gone way over the line. Family is family.

1260 [*Quickly,* LI'L BIT *flies through the room, gets her coat.*] I'm leaving. Now. I am not seeing you. Again.

[PECK *lies down on the bed for a moment, trying to absorb the terrible news. For a moment, he almost curls into a fetal position.*]

I'm not coming home for Christmas. You should go home to Aunt Mary. Go home now, Uncle Peck.

[PECK *gets control, and sits, rigid.*]

Uncle Peck?—I'm sorry but I have to go.

[*Pause*]

1265 Are you all right.

[*With a discipline that comes from being told that boys don't cry,* PECK *stands upright.*]

PECK I'm fine. I just think—I need a real drink.

[*The* MALE GREEK CHORUS *has become a bartender. At a small counter, he is lining up shots for* PECK. *As* LI'L BIT *narrates, we see* PECK *sitting, carefully and calmly downing shot glasses.*]

LI'L BIT [*To the audience*] I never saw him again. I stayed away from Christmas and Thanksgiving for years after.

It took my uncle seven years to drink himself to death. First he lost his job, then his wife, and finally his driver's license. He retreated to his house, and had his bottles delivered.

[PECK *stands, and puts his hands in front of him—almost like Superman flying.*]

One night he tried to go downstairs to the basement—and he flew down the steep basement stairs. My aunt came by weekly to put food on the porch, and she noticed the mail and the papers stacked up, uncollected.

1275 They found him at the bottom of the stairs. Just steps away from his dark room.

Now that I'm old enough, there are some questions I would have liked to have asked him. Who did it to you, Uncle Peck? How old were you? Were you eleven?

[PECK *moves to the driver's seat of the car and waits.*]

1280   Sometimes I think of my uncle as a kind of Flying Dutchman. In the opera, the Dutchman is doomed to wander the sea; but every seven years he can come ashore, and if he finds a maiden who will love him of her own free will—he will be released.

And I see Uncle Peck in my mind, in his Chevy '56, a spirit driving up
1285   and down the back roads of Carolina—looking for a young girl who, of her own free will, will love him. Release him.

[*A Voice states:*]

You and the Reverse Gear.

LI'L BIT   The summer of 1962. On Men, Sex, and Women: Part III:

[LI'L BIT *steps, as an eleven year old, into:*]

FEMALE GREEK CHORUS [*As Mother*]   It is out of the question. End of
1290   Discussion.

LI'L BIT   But why?

FEMALE GREEK CHORUS [*As Mother*]   Li'l Bit—we are not discussing this. I said no.

LI'L BIT   But I could spend an extra week at the beach! You're not telling me
1295   why!

FEMALE GREEK CHORUS [*As Mother*]   Your uncle pays entirely too much attention to you.

LI'L BIT   He listens to me when I talk. And—and he talks to me. He teaches me about things. Mama—he knows an awful lot.

1300 FEMALE GREEK CHORUS [*As Mother*]   He's a small town hick who's learned how to mix drinks from Hugh Hefner.

LI'L BIT   Who's Hugh Hefner?

[*Beat*]

FEMALE GREEK CHORUS [*As Mother*]   I am not letting an eleven-year-old girl spend seven hours alone in the car with a man. . . . I don't like the way
1305   your uncle looks at you.

LI'L BIT   For god's sake, mother! Just because you've gone through a bad time with my father—you think every man is evil!

FEMALE GREEK CHORUS [*As Mother*]   Oh no, Li'l Bit—not all men. . . . We . . . we just haven't been very lucky with the men in our family.

1310 LI'L BIT   Just because you lost your husband—I still deserve a chance at having a father! Someone! A man who will look out for me! Don't I get a chance?

FEMALE GREEK CHORUS [*As Mother*]   I will feel terrible if something happens.

LI'L BIT   Mother! It's in your head! Nothing will happen! I can take care of
1315   myself. And I can certainly handle Uncle Peck.

FEMALE GREEK CHORUS [*As Mother*]   All right. But I'm warning you—if anything happens, I hold you responsible.

[LI'L BIT *moves out of this scene and toward the car.*]

LI'L BIT   1962. On the Back Roads of Carolina: The First Driving Lesson.

[*The* TEENAGE GREEK CHORUS *member stands apart on stage. She will speak all of* LI'L BIT'S *lines.* LI'L BIT *sits beside* PECK *in the front seat. She looks at him closely, remembering.*]

PECK Li'l Bit? Are you getting tired?

1320 TEENAGE GREEK CHORUS A little.

PECK It's a long drive. But we're making really good time. We can take the back road from here and see . . . a little scenery. Say—I've got an idea—[PECK *checks his rearview mirror.*]

TEENAGE GREEK CHORUS Are we stopping, Uncle Peck?

PECK There's no traffic here. Do you want to drive?

1325 TEENAGE GREEK CHORUS I can't drive.

PECK It's easy. I'll show you how. I started driving when I was your age. Don't you want to?—

TEENAGE GREEK CHORUS —But it's against the law at my age!

PECK And that's why you can't tell anyone I'm letting you do this—

1330 TEENAGE GREEK CHORUS —But—I can't reach the pedals.

PECK You can sit in my lap and steer. I'll push the pedals for you. Did your father ever let you drive his car?

TEENAGE GREEK CHORUS No way.

PECK Want to try?

1335 TEENAGE GREEK CHORUS Okay. [LI'L BIT *moves into* PECK'S *lap. She leans against him, closing her eyes.*]

PECK You're just a little thing, aren't you? Okay—now think of the wheel as a big clock—I want you to put your right hand on the clock where three o'clock would be; and your left hand on the nine—

[LI'L BIT *puts one hand to* PECK'S *face, to stroke him. Then, she takes the wheel.*]

TEENAGE GREEK CHORUS Am I doing it right?

1340 PECK That's right. Now, whatever you do, don't let go of the wheel. You tell me whether to go faster or slower—

TEENAGE GREEK CHORUS Not so fast, Uncle Peck!

PECK Li'l Bit—I need you to watch the road—

[PECK *puts his hands on* LI'L BIT'S *breasts. She relaxes against him, silent, accepting his touch.*]

TEENAGE GREEK CHORUS Uncle Peck—what are you doing?

1345 PECK Keep driving. [*He slips his hands under her blouse.*]

TEENAGE GREEK CHORUS Uncle Peck—please don't do this—

PECK —Just a moment longer . . . [PECK *tenses against* LI'L BIT.]

TEENAGE GREEK CHORUS [*Trying not to cry*] This isn't happening.

[PECK *tenses more, sharply. He buries his face in* LI'L BIT'S *neck, and moans softly. The* TEENAGE GREEK CHORUS *exits, and* LI'L BIT *steps out of the car.* PECK, *too, disappears.*

A Voice reflects:]

Driving in Today's World.

1350   LI'L BIT   That day was the last day I lived in my body. I retreated above the neck, and I've lived inside the "fire" in my head ever since.

    And now that seems like a long, long time ago. When we were both very young.

    And before you know it, I'll be thirty-five. That's getting up there for a
1355 woman. And I find myself believing in things that a younger self vowed never to believe in. Things like family and forgiveness.

    I know I'm lucky. Although I still have never known what it feels like to jog or dance. Any thing that . . . "jiggles." I do like to watch people on the dance floor, or out on the running paths, just jiggling away. And I say—
1360 good for them. [LI'L BIT *moves to the car with pleasure.*]

    The nearest sensation I feel—of flight in the body—I guess I feel when I'm driving. On a day like today. It's five A.M. The radio says it's going to be clear and crisp. I've got five hundred miles of highway ahead of me—and some back roads too. I filled the tank last night, and had the oil checked.
1365 Checked the tires, too. You've got to treat her . . . with respect.

    First thing I do is: Check under the car. To see if any two year olds or household cats have crawled beneath, and strategically placed their skulls behind my back tires. [LI'L BIT *crouches.*]

    Nope. Then I get in the car. [LI'L BIT *does so.*]
1370   I lock the doors. And turn the key. Then I adjust the most important control on the dashboard—the radio— [LI'L BIT *turns the radio on: We hear all of the* GREEK CHORUS *overlapping, and static:*]

FEMALE GREEK CHORUS [*Overlapping*]   —"You were so tiny you fit in his hand—"

MALE GREEK CHORUS [*Overlapping*]   —"How is Shakespeare gonna help her
1375 lie on her back in the—"

TEENAGE GREEK CHORUS [*Overlapping*]   —"Am I doing it right?"

> [LI'L BIT *fine-tunes the radio station. A song like "Dedicated to the One I Love" or Orbison's "Sweet Dreams" comes on, and cuts off the* GREEK CHORUS.]

LI'L BIT   Ahh . . . [*Beat*] I adjust my seat. Fasten my seat belt. Then I check the right side mirror—check the left side. [*She does*] Finally, I adjust the rearview mirror. [*As* LI'L BIT *adjusts the rearview mirror, a faint light strikes the spirit of Uncle* PECK, *who is sitting in the back seat of the car. She sees him in the mirror. She smiles at him, and he nods at her. They are happy to be going for a long drive together.* LI'L BIT *slips the car into first gear; to the*
1380 *audience:*] And then—I floor it. [*Sound of a car taking off. Blackout.*]

LYNN NOTTAGE

b. 1964

DEBAUCHED." "Defiled." "Damaged goods." "Ruined." Such terms have long been used to describe women with pre- or extra-marital sexual experience—consensual or not. Traditionally, wherever aristocratic structures of inheritance and political power have depended on the production of legitimate heirs, a woman's sexual purity—virginity before marriage, and monogamy within it—has been the primary measure of her value and of her husband's honor. Over time and beyond aristocratic contexts, female sexual purity has taken on broader religious and moral (and thus metaphoric) meaning. But in the context of war, where sexual violence against women and children is rampant, terms like "damaged goods" and "ruined" describe a literal and devastating reality. *RUINED*, Lynn Nottage's 2009 Pulitzer Prize–winning drama, confronts the dehumanizing impact of wartime atrocities against women that occurred at the end of the twentieth century in the Democratic Republic of the Congo (DRC), but whose roots stretch back into the colonial era. At the same time, *Ruined* reflects the resilience, compassion, and hope among the African people whose lives have been irrevocably affected by the conflict.

Lynn Nottage was born in 1964 to a family engaged in both the arts and politics. She grew up in Brooklyn, in the Boerum Hill neighborhood, a few city blocks north of the Gowanus Canal, a notoriously polluted waterway. Her mother Ruby was a schoolteacher and then a principal who introduced her daughter to activism at an early age; her father Walter was a psychologist, also involved with prison reform. The family valued the arts; Nottage recalls her parents throwing elaborate parties attended by writers, musicians, painters, and actors, and the family home featured an extensive collection of African American art. Nottage attended the High School of Music and Art in Harlem, intending to study piano. While there, she collaborated on a musical as part of New York's Young Playwrights Festival, and then chose to pursue English and creative writing at Brown University. In her senior year, she studied playwriting with George Bass and PAULA VOGEL, and enrolled at the Yale School of Drama for further training.

Dissatisfied with what she saw as the social irrelevance of current theater, however, after receiving her MFA in 1989 Nottage took a job with Amnesty International, focusing on public relations and outreach. During her short tenure there, the organization began to discuss the issue of female genital mutilation (sometimes referred to as "female circumcision"), but because it was considered a cultural, rather than a legal, matter, the group did not immediately perceive it as a human rights violation. Nottage felt differently; she believed that this practice, and other "cultural" practices involving women, such as bride burnings and sex trafficking, should be part of an expanded organizational mandate. At the same time that she disagreed with her colleagues about priorities, she was also frustrated by Amnesty's inability to draw sufficient public attention to *any* of its concerns. Reconsidering the potential of theater to address pressing social and political issues, she decided to return to playwriting. Since 1992, Nottage has won a number of prestigious awards for her wide-ranging, stylistically diverse, and politically forceful drama. In addition to the Pulitzer Prize for *Ruined*, these include an Obie Award, a Guggenheim Fellowship, the New York Drama Critics Circle Best Play Award, the Susan Smith Blackburn Prize, and the PEN/Laura Pels Master American Dramatist Award. In 2007, Nottage received a MacArthur Foundation "Genius" Grant.

Among Nottage's most highly regarded plays are *Crumbs from the Table of Joy* (1995), about two African American girls growing up in New York before the civil rights and women's movements changed the country's cultural and political landscape; *Las Meninas* (2002), about an illicit interracial relationship, inspired by the important 1656 Velázquez painting; *Intimate Apparel* (2003), focusing on an African American seamstress at the turn of the twentieth century; and *By the Way, Meet Vera Stark* (2011), about African American actors in 1930s Hollywood. Her most recent play, *Sweat* (2015), examines the contemporary plight of factory workers during the economic recession and earned Nottage her second Pulitzer in 2017.

Describing her dramaturgy as the "marriage of passion and purpose," Nottage often looks at "women who have been marginalized but not only marginalized, who are heroic women. I like to call them . . . 'ordinary extraordinary women.'" This same quality defines the African women of *Ruined*. Set in the Ituri Rainforest in the Eastern Congo, in the bar/brothel of the strong-willed and resourceful Mama Nadi, *Ruined* introduces a group of women victimized by war, but striving to retain dignity and agency. Navigating the tenuous neutrality that Mama Nadi mandates within her establishment, the women service both rebel forces and government soldiers, as well as the local miners and profiteers who capitalize on the conflict, at the same time that they cling to hope of a peaceful future.

Nottage wrote her first play set in Africa, *Mud, River, Stone* (1998), before she had ever visited the continent. Soon after writing this piece, however, she read Adam Hochschild's *King Leopold's Ghost: A Study of Greed, Terror and Heroism in Colonial Africa* (1998), a history of Belgium's brutal colonization of the Congo, as well as of the African Americans who exposed the atrocities being committed there and introduced the phrase "crimes against humanity" to the world. In the colonial era, competing European claims in Central Africa had led to the creation of arbitrary borders that paid little attention to indigenous land rights or existing ethnic and linguistic territories; this in turn laid the foundation for both continued international interests in the Congo region and inter- and intraregional disputes, notably between the Hutu and Tutsi ethnic groups. The extent of involvement in the lasting conflict by so many forces within Africa and beyond can, moreover, be tied directly to the region's vast natural resources, which essentially fund the ongoing military campaigns. Diamonds, gold, tin, and coltan—a mineral essential for cell phone and other electronic technologies—are mined in the area, and Nottage strategically sets *Ruined* in a part of the Congo where these minerals abound, making it a locus of combat and competing financial claims.

Nottage read Hochschild's book just as the conflict in the Congo had again been drawing international attention due to escalating casualty figures and related devastation. But the implications of these more recent attacks on women were, for Nottage, still not receiving adequate focus. In 2004, Nottage felt compelled to travel to Uganda. Inviting her collaborator, director Kate Whoriskey, to join her, Nottage worked through her Amnesty International contacts to meet with Congolese women who had fled to this neighboring country to escape the violence in their homeland.

When Nottage interviewed survivors, she acknowledged that she was surprised "by the extent to which they had been physically damaged. We know that there was emotional damage, and psychological damage, but the thing that was hardest for them to talk about was the physical damage. It made them pariahs in their own communities." It is in this sense—in the visceral, physical ways in which the women have been altered by the sexual violence inflicted on them—that Salima, Sophie, and other characters in the play are "ruined." But Nottage strove neither to sensationalize the atrocities nor craft a piece of documentary theatre. Rather, she aspired to engage her audiences emotionally, because she believes that people respond more from feeling than from being told how to feel.

This dramaturgical sensibility, Nottage realized, put her at odds with BERTOLT BRECHT's idea of intellectual distance, or alienation, that she had initially considered for this play. She and Whoriskey shared an appreciation for Brecht's Mother Courage, and Nottage's original concept for Ruined had been to adapt Brecht's play to the DRC context. But after traveling to Africa in 2004 and again in 2005 to interview Congolese women, her plan changed: "I found my play Ruined in their painful narratives, in the gentle cadences and the monumental space between their gasps and sighs. The women felt it was important to go on record, which is why my play is not about victims, but survivors."

In interviews about Ruined, Nottage recalls how she also came to have a different understanding of Brecht's title from the conversations with these survivors. The women felt they had "mother courage," which Nottage defines as "doing impossible things to survive"—"women functioning as women do and finding their strength in that." In other ways, however, Nottage's play retains Brecht's influence. The moral ambiguity of Mama Nadi, who both sexually and financially exploits young women, yet also protects them from worse abuse, emerges in her oft-cited line, "I provide a bed, food and clothing. If things are good, everyone gets a little. If things are bad, then Mama eats first." Nottage's use of song in the play may be an even clearer Brechtian element. While Nottage has described the music and dance in Ruined as typically African, the anguished, poetic lyrics she wrote, which contrast with the vibrant melodies composed by Dominic Kanza, also exemplify the tensions between music and verse found throughout Brecht's work. Brecht famously directed his actors to maintain a perceptible distance from their characters, such that audiences were aware of the dual presence of actor and role, and thus the theatricality of the event. Dramatists such as CARYL CHURCHILL have used techniques of double- and triple-casting to similar effect. The appearance of the same actors in Ruined playing multiple characters, especially soldiers on opposing sides and other men who frequent Mama Nadi's, suggests, in Brechtian fashion, both the political realities of shifting loyalties in the conflict and the interchangeability of her clients, who soon all begin to look the same.

While Ruined reflects the specific geographical, political, and sociological contexts of the war-torn Congo, critics have also noted that Nottage utilizes well-established Western dramatic conventions to ground her writing, especially those of barroom plays and brothel plays, such as EUGENE O'NEILL's The Iceman Cometh (1939) and The Web (1913). Both kinds of settings allow playwrights to bring together a group of disparate characters, often ones without strong emotional ties elsewhere, to share moments of intimacy and develop family-like kinships. Especially for audiences at greater remove from the African conflict, these more familiar dramaturgical environs help foster a sense of access to the work, despite the challenges of Nottage's narrative.

Theatre scholar Sharon Friedman, however, positions Ruined differently, amidst a still-emerging, international group of plays by female dramatists that "make visible women's war stories." These more recent dramas, by playwrights such as Judith Thompson and Danai Gurira, call attention to how official histories may misrepresent such narratives or omit them entirely. These newer plays frequently denaturalize representations of gender, race, sexuality, and class dynamics in war settings. This technique in turn allows audiences to develop "critical empathy"—an alternative to Brechtian distancing or alienation that embraces the conflicting responses viewers and readers may feel about the depiction of such atrocities as rape as a weapon of war.

Condola Rashad as Sophie, Cherise Boothe as Josephine, and Quincy Tyler Bernstine as Salima in the 2009 Manhattan Theatre Club production of *Ruined*.

Yet the emotional push-and-pull that characterizes this play, especially its alternating moments of agony and humor and its romantic conclusion, has prompted some critics to question Nottage's dramaturgical choices. Christopher Isherwood of the *New York Times* suggests that the "tidiness" of the writing "at times undercuts the play's raw power." Other reviewers wonder if the work's somewhat conventional ending undermines its political force—especially its theme of female resilience and its potential to provoke further inquiry or action on the part of its audiences. Nottage, in response, points to what she calls the "necessary optimism" of *Ruined*. She believes that many of these critics "have never been to Africa. They have never spent time with these women to understand that you can be brutalized and still find a way to heal. It was very important for me to be optimistic about that and still tell the truth."

The success of Nottage's dramaturgical strategy may indeed be measured by the global reach of the play in Africa, Europe, and elsewhere, as well as its impact beyond theater walls. Soon after she received the Pulitzer Prize—only the second that has ever gone to an African American woman playwright—Nottage was invited to Washington to speak before the United States Senate Subcommittees on African Affairs and on International Operations and Organizations, Democracy, Human Rights and Global Women's Issues, which were holding hearings focusing on the Congo and Sudan entitled "Confronting Rape and Other Forms of Violence Against Women in Conflict Zones." Summarizing her experiences in Africa and her decision to dramatize the stories she had been told there, Nottage later explained, "I cannot bear to live in a world where such horrific things are happening to my African sisters without doing whatever I can to help them. Silence is complicity. . . . Why did I go to Africa to collect their stories? Because I had to."

J.E.G.

Ruined

CHARACTERS

MAMA NADI	A madam, a businesswoman, attractive, early forties
JOSEPHINE	One of Mama's girls, early twenties
SOPHIE	One of Mama's girls, eighteen
SALIMA	One of Mama's girls, nineteen
CHRISTIAN	A traveling salesman, early forties
MR. HARARI	A Lebanese diamond merchant, early forties
JEROME KISEMBE	A rebel leader
COMMANDER OSEMBENGA	A military leader for the current government
FORTUNE	A Government Soldier, Salima's husband
SIMON	A Government Soldier, Fortune's cousin
LAURENT	A Government Soldier, Osembenga's assistant
REBEL SOLDIERS	
GOVERNMENT SOLDIERS	
AID WORKER	

SETTING

A small mining town. The Democratic Republic of Congo.

Act One
Scene 1

A small mining town. The sounds of the tropical Ituri rain forest.[1] The Demo-
cratic Republic of Congo.

    A bar, makeshift furniture and a rundown pool table. A lot of effort has gone
into making the worn bar cheerful. A stack of plastic washtubs rests in the corner.
An old car battery powers the audio system, a covered birdcage sits conspicuously
in the corner of the room.

    MAMA NADI, *early forties, an attractive woman with an arrogant stride and*
majestic air, watches CHRISTIAN, *early forties, a perpetually cheerful traveling*
salesman, knock back a Fanta. His good looks have been worn down by hard liv-
ing on the road. He wears a suit that might have been considered stylish when
new, but it's now nearly ten years old, and overly loved.

CHRISTIAN   Ah. Cold. The only cold Fanta in twenty-five kilometers. You
don't know how good this tastes.

       [MAMA *flashes a warm flirtatious smile, then pours herself a Primus beer.*][2]

MAMA   And where the hell have you been?

CHRISTIAN   It was no easy task getting here.

5 MAMA   I've been expecting you for the last three weeks. How am I supposed
to do business? No soap, no cigarettes, no condoms. Not even a half liter of
petrol for the generator.

CHRISTIAN   Why are you picking a fight with me already? I didn't create this
damn chaos. Nobody, and I'm telling you, nobody could get through on the

10 main road. Every two kilometers a boy with a Kalashnikov[3] and pockets
that need filling. Toll, tax, tariff. They invent reasons to lighten your load.

MAMA   Then why does Mr. Harari always manage to get through?

CHRISTIAN   Mr. Harari doesn't bring you things you need, does he? Mr. Harari
has interests that supercede his safety. Me, I still hope to have a family one

15 day. [*Laughs heartily*]

MAMA   And my lipstick?

CHRISTIAN   Your lipstick? Aye! Did you ask me for lipstick?

MAMA   Of course, I did, you idiot!

CHRISTIAN   Look at the way you speak to me, *chérie. Comment est-ce possi-*

20 *ble?*[4] You should be happy I made it here in one piece.

      [CHRISTIAN *produces a tube of lipstick from his pocket.*]

---

1. Located in the northeast part of the Democratic Republic of the Congo (DRC), the
region is rich in natural resources and has been
the site of ongoing conflict between warring
African groups.
2. An African brand, produced by the Bralina

Brewing Company, a subsidiary of Heineken
International.
3. An automated rifle, originally produced in
the Soviet Union, named for its designer.
4. How is this possible? *Cherie:* my dear (both
French).

Play nice, or I'll give this to Josephine. She knows just how to show her appreciation.

MAMA Yes, but you always take home a little more than you ask for with Josephine. I hope you know how to use a condom.

[CHRISTIAN *laughs.*]

25 CHRISTIAN Are you jealous?

MAMA Leave me alone, you're too predictable. [*Turns away, dismissive*]

CHRISTIAN Where are you going? Hey, hey what are you doing? [*Teasingly*] Chérie, I know you wanted me to forget, so you could yell at me, but you won't get the pleasure this time.

[CHRISTIAN *taunts her with the lipstick. Mama resists the urge to smile.*]

30 MAMA Oh shut up and give it to me.

[*He passes her the lipstick.*]

Thank you, Christian.

CHRISTIAN I didn't hear you—

MAMA Don't press your luck. And it better be red.

[MAMA *grabs a sliver of a broken mirror from behind the rough-hewn bar, and gracefully applies the lipstick.*]

CHRISTIAN You don't have to say it. I know you want a husband.

35 MAMA Like a hole in my head.

CHRISTIAN [*Reciting*]

What, is this love?
An unexpected wind,
A fluctuation,
40 Fronting the coming of a storm.
Resolve, a thorny bush
Blown asunder and swept away.

There, chérie. I give you a poem in lieu of the kiss you won't allow me.

[CHRISTIAN *laughs, warmly.* MAMA *puts out a bowl of peanuts, a peace offering.*]

MAMA Here. I saved you some groundnuts, professor.

45 CHRISTIAN That's all you saved for me?

MAMA Be smart, and I'll show you the door in one second.

[MAMA *scolds him with her eyes.*]

CHRISTIAN Ach, ach . . . why are you wearing my grandmama's face?

[CHRISTIAN *mocks her expression.* MAMA *laughs and downs her beer.*]

MAMA   You sure you don't want a beer?

CHRISTIAN   You know me better than that, chérie, I haven't had a drop of
50   liquor in four years.

MAMA [*Teasing*]   It's cold.

CHRISTIAN   Tst!

[CHRISTIAN *cracks open a few peanuts, and playfully pops them into his
mouth.*
The parrot squawks.]

What's there? In the cage?

MAMA   Oh, that, a gray parrot. Old Papa Batunga passed.
55   CHRISTIAN   When?

MAMA   Last Thursday. No one wanted the damn bird. It complains too much.

CHRISTIAN [*Amused*]   Yeah, what does it say?

[CHRISTIAN *walks to the birdcage, and peers under the covering.*]

MAMA   Who the hell knows. It speaks pygmy. Old Papa was the last of his
tribe.[5] That stupid bird was the only thing he had left to talk to.
60   CHRISTIAN [*To the bird*]   Hello?

MAMA   He believed as long as the words of the forest people were spoken,
the spirits would stay alive.

CHRISTIAN   For true?

MAMA   Yeah, well, when that bird dies this place is gonna lose part of its
65   story.

CHRISTIAN [*Poking his finger into the cage*]   What are you going to do with
him?

MAMA   Sell it. I don't want it. It stinks.

CHRISTIAN [*Still poking; to the parrot*]   Hello.
70   MAMA   Hey, hey don't put your fingers in there.

CHRISTIAN   Look. He likes me. So, Mama, you haven't asked me what else
I've brought for you? Go see. [*Quickly withdraws his finger*] Ow. Shit. He
bit me.

MAMA   Well, you shouldn't be messing with it. [*Laughs*]
75   CHRISTIAN   Ow, damn it.

MAMA [*Impatiently*]   Don't be a cry baby, what did you bring me? Well? . . .
Are you going to keep me guessing?

CHRISTIAN [*Sitting back down*]   Go on. Take a peek in the truck. And don't
say I don't think about you.
80   MAMA [*Smiling*]   How many?

CHRISTIAN   Three.

MAMA   Three? But, I can't use three right now. You know that.

CHRISTIAN   Of course you can. And I'll give you a good price if you take all of
them.

[MAMA *goes to the doorway, and peers out at the offerings, unimpressed.*]

5. Possibly a reference to the Mbuti, an ethnic group in the region, many of whose members
were displaced by conflict.

85 MAMA   I don't know. They look used. Worn.

CHRISTIAN   C'mon, Mama. Take another look. A full look. You've said it yourself business is good.

[MAMA *considers, then finally*]

MAMA   Okay, one. That one in front. [*Points into the distance*]

CHRISTIAN   Three. C'mon, don't make me travel back with them.

90 MAMA   Just one. How much?

CHRISTIAN   Do you know how difficult it was getting here? The road was
completely washed out—

MAMA   All right, all right. I don't need the whole damn saga. Just tell me,
how much for the one?

95 CHRISTIAN   The same as usual plus twenty-five, because . . . because . . . You
understand it wasn't easy to get here with the—

MAMA   I'll give you fifteen.

CHRISTIAN   Ahh! Fifteen? No. That's nothing. Twenty-two. C'mon.

MAMA   Twenty. My best offer.

[CHRISTIAN *mulls it over. He's reluctant.*]

100 CHRISTIAN   Aye. Okay. Okay. Damn it. Yes. Yes. But I expect another cold
Fanta. One from the bottom this time.

[CHRISTIAN, *defeated, exits.* MAMA *smiles victoriously, and retrieves
another soda from the cooler. She reapplies her lipstick for good measure,
then counts out her money.*
CHRISTIAN *reenters proudly bearing two cartons of Ugandan cigarettes.
A moment later two women in ragged clothing step tentatively into the
bar: Sophie, a luminous beauty with an air of defiance, and Salima, a
sturdy peasant woman whose face betrays a world-weariness. They hold
hands. Mama studies the women, then:*]

MAMA   I said one. That one.

[MAMA *points to* SOPHIE.]

CHRISTIAN   It's been a good week, and I'll tell you what, I'll give you two for
the price of one. Why not?

105 MAMA   Are you deaf? No. Tst! I don't need two more mouths to feed and
pester me.

[MAMA *continues to examine each woman.*]

CHRISTIAN   Take both. Feed them as one. Please, Mama, I'll throw in the
cigarettes for cost.

MAMA   But, I'll only pay for one.

110 CHRISTIAN   Of course. We agree, why are we arguing?

MAMA [*Yelling*]   Josephine! Josephine! Where is that stupid woman?

[JOSEPHINE, *a sexy woman in a short western-style miniskirt and high
heels appears in the beaded doorway. She surveys the new women with
obvious contempt.*]

Take them out back. Get them washed and some proper clothing.
JOSEPHINE *Kuya apa* [*Beat*] *sasa.*[6] [*Beckons to the women. They reluctantly follow*]
115 MAMA Wait.

[MAMA *gestures to* SALIMA, *who clings to* SOPHIE.]

You. Come here.

[SALIMA *doesn't move.*]

Come.

[SALIMA *clings to* SOPHIE, *then slowly walks toward* MAMA.]

What's your name?
SALIMA [*Whispers*] Salima.
120 MAMA What?
SALIMA Salima.

[MAMA *examines* SALIMA's *rough hands.*]

MAMA Rough. [*With disdain*] A digger. We'll have to do something about that.

[SALIMA *yanks her hand away.* MAMA *registers the bold gesture.*]

And you, come. [SOPHIE *walks to* MAMA.] You're a pretty thing, what's your name?
125 SOPHIE [*Gently*] Sophie.
MAMA Do you have a smile?
SOPHIE Yes.
MAMA Then let me see it.

[SOPHIE *struggles to find a halfhearted smile.*]

Good. Go get washed up.

[*A moment.*]

130 JOSEPHINE [*Snaps*] C'mon, now!

[SALIMA *looks to* SOPHIE. *The women follow behind* JOSEPHINE. SOPHIE *walks with some pain and effort.*]

MAMA Did you at least tell them this time?
CHRISTIAN Yes. They know and they came willingly.
MAMA And . . . ?
CHRISTIAN Salima is from a tiny village. No place really. She was captured
135 by rebel soldiers, *Mayi-mayi,*[7] the poor thing spent nearly five months in the bush as their concubine.

---

6. Quick; *kuya apa*: come here (both Swahili).
7. A militia group in the region.

MAMA   And what of her people?

CHRISTIAN   She says her husband is a farmer. And from what I understand, her village won't have her back. Because . . . But she's a simple girl, she doesn't
140   have much learning, I wouldn't worry about her.

MAMA   And the other?

CHRISTIAN   Sophie. Sophie is . . .

MAMA   Is what?

CHRISTIAN   . . . is . . . ruined.[8]

[*A moment*]

145   MAMA [*Enraged*]   You brought me a girl that's ruined?

CHRISTIAN   She cost you nothing.

MAMA   I paid money for her, not the other one. The other one is plain. I have half a dozen girls like her, I don't need to feed another plain girl.

CHRISTIAN   I know this, okay, don't get worked-up. Sophie is a good girl, she
150   won't trouble you.

MAMA   How do I know that?

CHRISTIAN [*Defensively*]   Because I am telling you. She's seen some very bad times.

MAMA   Yeah? And why is that my concern?

155   CHRISTIAN   Take her on, just for a month. You'll see she's a good girl. Hard worker.

[MAMA *gestures toward her own genitals.*]

MAMA   But damaged, am I right?

CHRISTIAN   Yes . . . Look, militia did ungodly things to the child, took her with . . . a bayonet and then left her for dead. And she was—

160   MAMA [*Snaps*]   I don't need to hear it. Are you done?

CHRISTIAN [*Passionately*]   Things are gonna get busy, Mama. All along the road people are talking about how this red dirt is rich with coltan.[9] Suddenly everyone has a shovel, and wants to stake a claim since that boastful pygmy dug up his fortune in the reserve. I guarantee there'll be twice as
165   many miners here by September. And you know all those bastards will be thirsty. So, take her, put her to work for you.

MAMA   And what makes you think I have any use for her?

CHRISTIAN [*Pleads*]   The girl cooks, cleans and she sings like an angel. And you . . . you haven't had nice music here since that one, that beauty
170   Camille got the AIDS.

MAMA   No. A girl like this is bad luck. I can't have it. Josephine! Josephine!

CHRISTIAN   And, Mama, she's pretty pretty. She'll keep the miners eyes happy. I promise.

MAMA   Stop it already, no. You're like a hyena. Won't you shut up, now.

[JOSEPHINE *enters, put upon*]

175   JOSEPHINE   Yes, Mama.

MAMA   Bring the girl, Sophie, back.

8. Genitally mutilated, and thus useless for purposes of prostitution.
9. Valuable mineral resource found in the Ituri region, used in cell phone and other electronic technologies.

CHRISTIAN   Wait. Give us a minute, Josephine.

[JOSEPHINE *doesn't move.*]

Mama, please. Look, okay, I'm asking you to do me this favor. I've done many things for you over the years. And I don't ask you for a lot in return. Please. The child has no place else to go.

MAMA   I'm sorry, but I'm running a business not a mission. Take her to the sisters in Bunia,[1] let her weave baskets for them. Josephine, why are you standing there like a fool . . . go get the girl.

CHRISTIAN   Wait.

JOSEPHINE [*Annoyed*]   Do you want me to stay or to go?

MAMA [*Snaps*]   Get her!

[JOSEPHINE *sucks her teeth and exits.*]

CHRISTIAN [*With a tinge of resentment*]   I remembered your lipstick and everything.

MAMA   Don't look at me that way. I open my doors, and tomorrow I'm a refugee camp overrun with suffering. Everyone has their hand open since this damned war began. I can't do it. I keep food in the mouths of eight women when half the country's starving, so don't give me shit about taking on one more girl.

CHRISTIAN   Look. Have anything you want off of my truck. Anything! I even have some . . . some Belgian chocolate.

MAMA   You won't let up. Why are you so damn concerned with this girl? Huh?

CHRISTIAN   C'mon, Mama, please.

MAMA   Chocolate. I always ask you for chocolate, and you always tell me it turns in this heat. How many times have you refused me this year. Huh? But, she must be very very important to you. I see that. Do you want to fuck her or something?

[*A moment*]

CHRISTIAN   She's my sister's only daughter. Okay? I told my family I'd find a place for her . . . And here at least I know she'll be safe. Fed.

[*He stops himself and gulps down his soda.*]

And as you know the village isn't a place for a girl who has been . . . ruined. It brings shame, dishonor to the family.

MAMA [*Ironically*]   But it's okay for her to be here, huh? I'm sorry, but, I can't. I don't have room for another broken girl.

CHRISTIAN   She eats like a bird. Nothing.

[SOPHIE *enters*]

SOPHIE   Madame.

_____

1. City in the Ituri region.

210 MAMA [*Defensively*]   It's "Mademoiselle."[2]

> [MAMA *stares at* SOPHIE, *thinking, her resolve slowly softening.*]

Come here.

> [SOPHIE *walks over to* MAMA.]

How old are you?

> [SOPHIE *meets* MAMA's *eyes.*]

SOPHIE   Eighteen.
MAMA   Yeah? Do you have a beau?
215 SOPHIE   No.

> [MAMA's *surprised by her haughtiness.*]

MAMA   Are you a student?
SOPHIE   Yes, I was to sit for the university exam.
MAMA   I bet you were good at your studies. Am I right?
SOPHIE   Yes.
220 MAMA   A *petit bureaucrat*[3] in the making.

> [SOPHIE *shifts with discomfort. Her body aches, tears escape her eyes.*
> MAMA *uses her skirt to wipe* SOPHIE's *eyes.*]

Did they hurt you badly?
SOPHIE [*Whispered*]   . . . Yes.
MAMA   I bet they did.

> [MAMA *studies* SOPHIE. *She considers, then decides:*]

Christian, go get me the chocolate.
225 CHRISTIAN   Does that mean . . . ?
MAMA   I'm doing this for you, cuz you've been good to me. [*Whispers to* CHRISTIAN] But this is the last time you bring me damaged goods. Understood? It's no good for business.
CHRISTIAN   Thank you. It's the last time. I promise. Thank you.
230 MAMA [*To* SOPHIE]   You sing?
SOPHIE [*Softly*]   Yes.
MAMA   Do you know any popular songs?
SOPHIE   Yes. A few.
CHRISTIAN   Speak up!

> [CHRISTIAN *exits*]

235 SOPHIE   Yes, Mad . . . [*Catching herself*] . . . emoiselle.
MAMA   Mama. You do math? Stuff like that?

2. An unmarried woman; *Madame*: a married woman (both French), but also a woman who oversees a brothel.

3. Literally, little bureaucrat, (French), but more colloquially, a low-level bureaucrat.

SOPHIE Yes, Mama.
MAMA Good.

[MAMA *lifts* SOPHIE's *chin with her fingers, enviously examining her face.*]

Yes, you're very pretty. I can see how that caused you problems. Do you
240 know what kind of place this is?
SOPHIE Yes, Mama. I think so.
MAMA Good.

[MAMA *carefully applies red lipstick to* SOPHIE's *mouth.*]

Then we have no problems. I expect my girls to be well behaved and clean.
That's all. I provide a bed, food and clothing. If things are good, everyone
245 gets a little. If things are bad, then Mama eats first. Am I making myself
clear?

[SOPHIE *nods.*]

Good. Red is your color.

[SOPHIE *doesn't respond.*]

Thank you, Mama.
SOPHIE Thank you, Mama.

[MAMA *pours a glass of local home-brewed liquor. She holds it out.*]

250 MAMA Here. It'll help the pain down below. I know it hurts, because it
smells like the rot of meat.[4] So wash good.

[SOPHIE *takes the glass, and slowly drinks the liquor down.*]

Don't get too dependent on drink. It'll make you sloppy, and I have no tolerance for sloppiness. Understood?

[CHRISTIAN, *put upon, reenters with a faded, but pretty, box of chocolates.*]

CHRISTIAN Handmade. Imported. *Très bon.*[5] I hope you're impressed. A Bel-
255 gian shopkeeper in Bunia ordered them. Real particular. I had a hell of a
time trying to find these Goddamn chocolates. And then, poof, she's gone.
And now I'm stuck with twenty boxes. I tried to pawn them off on Pastor
Robbins, but apparently he's on a diet.

[MAMA *opens the box, surveying the chocolates. She's in seventh heaven.*
She offers a piece to SOPHIE, *who timidly selects a piece.*]

SOPHIE *Merci.*[6]

---

4. One of the indicators of genital mutilation
is the odor it produces, often a combination
of rotting flesh, urine, and/or feces.

5. Very good (French).
6. Thank you (French).

[MAMA *bites into the chocolate.*]

260 MAMA   Mmm.

CHRISTIAN   Happy? That's what the good life in Belgium tastes like.

MAMA   Caramel. [*Savoring*] Good God, I haven't had caramel in ages. You bastard, you've been holding out on me! Mmm. Smell 'em, the smell reminds me
of my mother. She'd take me and my brothers to Kisangani.[7] And she'd buy us
265 each an enormous bag of caramels wrapped in that impossible plastic. You
know why? So we wouldn't tell my grandfather about all of the uncles she
visited in the big town. She'd sit us on the bank of the river, watching the
boats and eating sweaty caramels, while she "visited with uncles."[8] And as
long as there were sweets, we didn't breathe a word, not a murmur, to old
270 Papa.

[SOPHIE *eats her chocolate, smiling for the first time.* CHRISTIAN *reaches
for a chocolate, but* MAMA *quickly slaps his hand away.*]

CHRISTIAN   What about me?

MAMA   What about you?

CHRISTIAN   Don't I get one?

MAMA   No!

[*This amuses* SOPHIE. *She smiles.*]

275 CHRISTIAN   Why are you smiling? You're a lucky girl. You're lucky you have
such a good uncle. A lot of men would've left you for dead.

[SOPHIE'*s smile disappears.*]

MAMA   Never mind him. [*To* CHRISTIAN] Go already and bring the other stuff
in before the vultures steal it!

CHRISTIAN   Sophie. I'm . . . you . . . you be a good girl. Don't make Mama
280 angry.

SOPHIE   I won't Uncle.

[CHRISTIAN *exits, an apology in his posture.* SOPHIE *licks her chocolate-
covered fingers as the lights fade.*]

Scene 2

A month later. The bar. JOSEPHINE *cranks the generator. Colorful Christmas lights
flicker. The generator hums on. Music and lights provide a festive atmosphere.
The birdcage rests in the back of the bar. Periodically the bird makes a ruckus.*

At the bar, drunk and disheveled REBEL SOLDIERS *drain their beers and laugh
too loudly.* SALIMA, *wearing a shiny gold midriff, a colorful traditional wrap and
mismatched yellow heels, shoots pool, doing her best to ignore the occasional lustful leers of the* SOLDIERS.

---

7. Capital of the Orientale Province, southwest of the Ituri region.

8. Euphemism for the mother's work as a

prostitute, in ironic contrast to Christian's
purely biological relation to Sophie.

JEROME KISEMBE, *the rebel leader dressed in military uniform, holds court.* MAMA, *toting bowls of peanuts, wears a bright red kerchief around her neck, in recognition of the rebel leader's colors.* JOSEPHINE *dirty-dances for* MR. HARARI, *a tipsy Lebanese diamond merchant, who sports surprisingly pristine clothing. He is barefoot.*

SOPHIE *plows through an upbeat dance song, accompanied by a guitar and drums.*

SOPHIE [*Sings*]:

    The liquid night slowly pours in
    Languor peels away like a curtain
    Spirits rise and tongues loosen
    And the weary ask to be forgiven.
5   You come here to forget,
    You say drive away all regret
    And dance like it's the ending
    The ending of the war.
    The day's heavy door closes quick
10 Leaving the scold of the sun behind
    Dusk ushers in the forest's music
    And your body's free to unwind.

        [JOSEPHINE *dances for the men. They give her tips.*]

    You come here to forget,
    You say drive away all regret
15 And dance like it's the ending
    The ending of the war.
    But can the music be all forgiving
    Purge the wear and tear of the living?
    Will the sound drown out your sorrow,
20 So you'll remember nothing tomorrow?

        [*A drunk* REBEL SOLDIER *stands, and demands attention.*]

REBEL SOLDIER #1   Another! Hey!
MAMA   I hear you! I hear you!
REBEL SOLDIER #1   C'mon! Another!

        [*He clumsily slams the bottle on the counter. He gestures to* SOPHIE.]

    Psst! You! Psst! Psst!

        [*Another* REBEL SOLDIER *gives* SOPHIE *a catcall.* SOPHIE *ignores him.* REBEL SOLDIER #1 *turns his attention back to* MAMA.]

25 Her! Why won't she come talk to me?
MAMA   You want to talk to her. Behave, and let me see your money.

        [KISEMBE, *haughty, lets out a roar of a laugh.*]⁹

---

9. Fictional character whose name echoes that of General Kisempya, chief of staff for the *Forces Armées de la République Démocratique du Congo.*

REBEL SOLDIER #1   The damn beer drained my pocket. It cost too much!
You're a fucking thief!

MAMA   Then go somewhere else. And mind your tongue. [*Turns away*]

30 REBEL SOLDIER #1   Hey. Wait. Wait. I want her to talk to me. Mama, lookie!
I have this. [*Proudly displays a cloth filled with little chunks of ore*]

MAMA   What is it? Huh? Coltan? Where'd you get it?

REBEL SOLDIER #1 [*Boasting*]   From a miner on the reserve.

MAMA   He just gave it to you?

35 REBEL SOLDIER #1 [*Snickering*]   Yeah, he give it to me. Dirty poacher been
diggin' up our forest, we run 'em off. Run them good, gangsta style: "Muth-
afucka run!" Left 'em for the fucking scavengers.

> [*The* REBEL SOLDIER *strikes a hip-hop "gangsta-style" pose. The other*
> SOLDIERS *laugh.* MR. HARARI, *unamused, ever so slightly registers the con-
> versation.* MAMA *laughs.*]

MAMA   Coltan? Let me see. Ah, that's nothing, it's worthless my friend. A
month ago, yes, but now you can't get a handful of meal for it. Too many
40 prospectors. Every miner that walks in here has a bucket of it. Bring me a
gram of gold, then we talk.

REBEL SOLDIER #1   What do you mean? Liar! In the city, this would fetch me
plenty.

MAMA   This ain't the city, is it, Soldier?

> [*He aggressively grabs* MAMA's *wrist.*]

45 This is a nice place for a drink. Yeah? I don't abide by bush laws. If you
want to drink like a man, you drink like a man. You want to behave like a
gorilla, then go back into the bush.

> [*The* SOLDIERS *laugh. The* REBEL SOLDIER *unhands* MAMA.]

REBEL SOLDIER #1   C'mon, Mama, this is worth plenty! Yeah?

> [*Again, he gestures to* SOPHIE. *He's growing increasingly belligerent.*]

Bitch. Why won't she talk to me?

> [*Frustrated, he puts the cloth back in his pocket. He broods, silently
> watching* SOPHIE *sway to the music. Then all of a sudden he collects him-
> self, and drunkenly makes his way toward her.*]

50 I'll teach her manners! Respect me!

> [*He pounds his chest, another* SOLDIER *goads him on.* SOPHIE *stiffens.
> The music stops.* MAMA *quickly steps between them.*]

MAMA   But . . . as the coltan is all you have. I'll take it this time. Now go sit
down. Sit down. Please.

REBEL SOLDIER #1 [*Excited*]   Yeah? Now, I want her to talk to me! Will she
talk to me?

55 MAMA   Okay. Okay. Sit.

[*He pulls out the cloth again. He gently removes several pieces of the ore.*]

Don't be stingy. Tst! Let me see all of it.

[*He reluctantly relinquishes the weathered cloth to* MAMA.]

[*Smiling*] Salima! Salima, come!

[SALIMA *bristles at the sound of her name. She reluctantly approaches the* SOLDIER. MAMA *shows her off to him.*]

REBEL SOLDIER #1   What about her? [*Gestures to* SOPHIE]
MAMA   Salima is better dancer. [SALIMA *dances, seductively*] I promise. Okay.
60   Everyone is happy.
KISEMBE   Soldier, everyone is happy!

[SALIMA *sizes up the drunken* SOLDIER.]

SALIMA   So, "Gangsta," you wanna dance with me?

[*She places his arms around her waist. He longingly looks over at* SOPHIE, *then pulls* SALIMA *close. He leads aggressively.*]

Easy.
MAMA   Sophie.

[SOPHIE, *relieved, resumes singing.* SALIMA *and the* REBEL SOLDIER *dance.*]

65   SOPHIE [*Sings*]:
Have another beer, my friend,
Douse the fire of your fears, my friend,
Get drunk and foolish on the moment,
Brush aside the day's heavy judgment.
70   Yes, have another beer, my friend,
Wipe away the angry tears, my friend,
Get drunk and foolish on the moment,
Brush aside the day's heavy judgment.
Cuz you come here to forget,
75   You say drive away all regret,
And dance like it's the ending
The ending of the war.
The ending of the war.
The ending of the war.

[*Applause.* MR. HARARI *tips* SOPHIE. MAMA *having quenched the fire, fetches her lockbox from a hiding place beneath the counter, and puts the ore inside.*]

80   MR. HARARI   That one, she's pretty. [*Gestures to* SOPHIE]
JOSEPHINE [*With disdain*]   Sophie?! She's broken. All of the girls think she's bad luck.

[JOSEPHINE *leads* MR. HARARI *to the table. He sits.*]

MR. HARARI   What are you wearing? Where's the dress I bought you?
JOSEPHINE   If I had known you were coming, I'd have put it on.
85 MR. HARARI   Then what are you waiting for, my darling?

[JOSEPHINE *exits quickly.* MAMA, *toting her lockbox, joins* MR. HARARI *at his table.*]

MAMA   What happened to your shoes, Mr. Harari?
MR. HARARI   Your fucking country, some drunk child doing his best impersonation of a rebel soldier liberated my shoes. Every time I come here I
have to buy a new fucking pair of shoes.

[*Laughter from the pool table.*]

90 MAMA   You're lucky he only wanted your shoes. *Sante.*[1]

[*The* SOLDIER *gets too friendly with* SALIMA. *She lurches away, and falls against the pool table.*]

REBEL SOLDIER #1   Hey!
KISEMBE   Ach, ach, behave, I'm trying to play here.

[*The* SOLDIER *grabs* SALIMA *onto his lap.* MR. HARARI *weighs the situation.*]

MR. HARARI [*To* MAMA]   You took that poor man's coltan. Shame on you. He
probably doesn't know what he gave away for the taste of that woman. [*To*
95   SOLDIER] Savor it! The toll to enter that tunnel was very expensive, my
friend. [*To* MAMA] We both know how much it would fetch on the market.
MAMA   Yeah, so? Six months ago it was just more black dirt. I don't get why
everyone's crawling over each other for it.
MR. HARARI   Well, my darling, in this damnable age of the mobile phone it's
100   become quite the precious ore, no? And for whatever reason, God has seen
fit to bless your backward country with an abundance of it. Now, if that
young man had come to me, I would've given him enough money to buy
pussy for a month. Even yours. So who's the bigger thief, you or him?
MAMA   He give it to me, you saw. So, does that make me a thief or merely
105   more clever than you.

[MR. HARARI *laughs.*]

MR. HARARI   My darling, you'd do well in Kisangani.
MAMA   I do well here, and I'd get homesick in Kisangani. It's a filthy city full
of bureaucrats and thieves.
MR. HARARI   Very funny, but I imagine you'd enjoy it, terribly. And I mean
110   that as a compliment.
MAMA   Do you have a minute?
MR. HARARI   Of course.

1. Cheers (Swahili).

KISEMBE   Soldier! Soldier!

REBEL SOLDIER #2   Chief.

115 KISEMBE   Bring me my mobile! What're you, an old man? Hurry!

[MAMA *empties a bag containing stones onto a cloth on the table.*]

MAMA   What do you think? Huh?

MR. HARARI [*Referring to the diamonds*]   Just looking, I can tell you, most of these are worthless. I'm sorry.

[MAMA *takes out another stone, and places it on the table.*]

MAMA   What about that one?

[MAMA *points to the rough stone.* MR. HARARI *examines the diamond on the table, then meticulously places a loup to his eye and examines it. He looks over his shoulder.*]

120 MR. HARARI [*Whispers*]   Hm. It's a raw diamond. Where'd you get this?

MAMA   Don't you worry. I'm holding it for someone.

MR. HARARI [*Continues to examine the diamond*]   Nice. Yes, you see, there. It carries the light well.

MAMA   Yeah, yeah, but is it worth anything?

125 MR. HARARI   Well . . .

MAMA   Well . . .

MR. HARARI   Depends.

[MAMA *smiles.*]

It's raw, and the market—

MAMA   Yeah, yeah, but, what are we talking? Huh? A new generator or a plot 130 of land?

MR. HARARI [*Chuckling*]   Slow down, I can offer you a fairly good price. But, be reasonable, darling, I'm an independent with a family that doesn't appreciate how hard I work.

[MAMA *takes back the diamond.*]

MAMA   You sound like old Papa. He was like you, Mr. Harari, work too much, 135 always want more, no rest. When there was famine his bananas were rotting. He used to say as long as the forest grows a man will never starve.

MR. HARARI   Does he still have his farm?

MAMA [*Smiling to herself*]   You know better, Mr. Harari, you're in the Congo. Things slip from our fingers like butter. No. When I was eleven, this white 140 man with skin the color of wild berries turned up with a piece of paper. It say he have rights to my family land. [*With acid*] Just like that. Taken![2] And you want to hear a joke? Poor old Papa bought magic from a friend, he thought a handful of powder would give him back his land. [*Examining the diamond*]

2. Allusion to European colonialist practice of claiming territory with no regard for indigenous people's rights.

Everyone talk talk diamonds, but I . . . I want a powerful slip of paper that
says I can cut down forests and dig holes and build to the moon if I choose.
I don't want someone to turn up at my door, and take my life from me. Not
ever again. But tell, how does a woman like me get a piece of land, without
having to pick up a fucking gun?

[MR. HARARI *cautiously watches the* REBEL SOLDIERS.]

MR. HARARI   These, these idiots keep changing the damn rules on us. You file
papers, and the next day the office is burned down. You buy land, and the
next day the chief's son has built a fucking house on it. I don't know why
anybody bothers. Madness. And look at them. [*Gestures to the* REBEL SOL-
DIERS] A hungry pygmy digs a hole in the forest, and suddenly every two-bit
militia is battling for the keys to hell.

MAMA   True, chérie, but someone must provide them with beer and distractions.

[MR. HARARI *laughs.* MAMA *scoops up the stones and places them back
into her lockbox.*]

MR. HARARI   Just, be careful, where will I drink if anything happens to you?

[MR. HARARI *gives* MAMA *a friendly kiss.*]

MAMA   Don't worry about me. Everything is beautiful.

[JOSEPHINE *enters proudly sporting an elegant traditional dress.*]

JOSEPHINE   What do you think?

[MR. HARARI *shifts his gaze to* JOSEPHINE.]

MR. HARARI   Such loveliness. Doesn't she look beautiful?
MAMA   Yes, very. *Karibu.*[3]
MR. HARARI   I just might have to take you home with me.
JOSEPHINE [*Excited*]   Promise.
MR. HARARI   Of course.

[JOSEPHINE *hitches up her dress and straddles* MR. HARARI. *She kisses him.*]

KISEMBE [*Shouts*]   Mama! Mama!
MAMA   Okay, okay, chief, *sawa sawa.*[4]
KISEMBE   Two more Primus. And, Mama, why can't I get mobile service in
this pit?
MAMA   You tell me, you're important, go make it happen!
MR. HARARI   Who's that?
JOSEPHINE   Him? Jerome Kisembe, leader of the rebel militia. He's very
powerful. He have sorcerer that give him a charm so he can't be touched by
bullet. He's fearless. He is the boss man, the government and the church
and anything else he wants to be.

3. Welcome (Swahili).
4. Okay, okay (Swahili).

[MR. HARARI *studies* KISEMBE.]

Don't look so hard at a man like that.

[JOSEPHINE *grabs* MR. HARARI's *face and kisses him.* MAMA *clears the beer bottles from* KISEMBE's *table. The* SOLDIER *gropes at* SALIMA, *he nips her on the neck.*]

175 SALIMA   Ow! You jackass.

[SALIMA *pulls away from the Soldier and heads for the door.* MAMA *races after her, catching her arm forcefully.*]

MAMA   What's your problem?
SALIMA   Did you see what he did?
MAMA   You selfish girl. Now get back to him.

[MAMA *shoves* SALIMA *back toward the* SOLDIER. SOPHIE, *watching, runs over to* SALIMA.]

SOPHIE   Are you all right, Salima?
180 SALIMA   The dog bit me. [*Whispered*] I'm not going back over there.
SOPHIE   You have to.
SALIMA   He's filth! It's a man like him that—
SOPHIE   Don't. Mama's looking.
SALIMA [*Tears welling up in her eyes*]:   Do you know what he said to me—
185 SOPHIE   They'll say anything to impress a lady. Half of them are lies. Dirty fucking lies! Go back, don't listen. I'll sing the song you like.

[SOPHIE *gives* SALIMA *a kiss on the cheek.* SALIMA's *eyes shoot daggers at* MAMA, *but she reluctantly returns to the drunken* SOLDIER. SOPHIE *launches into another song.* JOSEPHINE *dirty-dances for* MR. HARARI.]

Have another beer, my friend,
Wipe away the angry tears, my friend,
Get drunk and foolish on the moment,
190 Brush aside the day's heavy judgment.
Cuz you come here to forget,
You say drive away all regret
And dance like it's the ending
And dance like it's the ending

[*The music crescendos.*]

195 The ending
The ending
The ending
And dance like it's the ending . . .

[MAMA *watches* SALIMA *like a hawk. The lights fade.*]

Scene 3

Morning. Living quarters behind the bar. Ragged wood-and-straw beds. A poster of a popular African American pop star hangs over JOSEPHINE's *bed.* SOPHIE *paints* SALIMA's *fingernails, as she peruses a worn fashion magazine.* SALIMA *shifts in place, agitated.*

SALIMA [*Impatiently*]   C'mon, c'mon, c'mon, Sophie. Finish before she comes back.

SOPHIE   Keep still, will ya. Stop moving. She's with Mr. Harari.

SALIMA   She's gonna kill me if she find out I use her nail polish.

5   SOPHIE   Well, keep it up, and she's gonna find out one of these days.

SALIMA   But, not today. So hurry!

[SOPHIE *makes a mistake with* SALIMA's *nails.* SALIMA *violently yanks her hand-away.*]

Aye girl, look what you did! *Pumbafu!*[5]

SOPHIE   What's your problem?!

SALIMA   Nothing. Nothing. I'm fine.

[SALIMA, *frustrated, stands up and walks away.*]

10   SOPHIE   Yeah? You've been short with me all morning? Don't turn away. I'm talking to you.

SALIMA   "Smile, Salima. Talk pretty." Them soldiers don't respect nothing. Them miners, they easy, they want drink, company, and it's over. But the soldiers, they want more of you, and—

15   SOPHIE   Did that man do something to hurt you?

SALIMA   You know what he say? He say fifteen Hema[6] men were shot dead and buried in their own mining pit, in mud so thick it swallow them right into the ground without mercy. He say, one man stuff the coltan into his mouth to keep the soldiers from stealing his hard work, and they split his belly open
20   with a machete. "It'll show him for stealing," he say, bragging like I should be congratulating him. And then he fucked me, and when he was finished he sat on the floor and wept. He wanted me to hold him. Comfort him.

SOPHIE   And, did you?

SALIMA   No. I'm Hema. One of those men could be my brother.

25   SOPHIE   Don't even say that.

[SALIMA *is overcome by the possibility.*]

SALIMA   I . . . I . . . miss my family. My husband. My baby—

SOPHIE   Stop it! We said we wouldn't talk about it.

SALIMA   This morning I was thinking about Beatrice and how much she liked banana. I feed her like this. I squeeze banana between my fingers and let
30   her suck them, and she'd make a funny little face. Such delight. Delight. [*Emotionally*] Delight! Delight!

SOPHIE   Shhh! Lower your voice.

5. Stupid (Swahili).
6. Ethnic group in the Ituri region.

SALIMA   Please, let me say my baby's name, Beatrice.
SOPHIE   Shhh!
35 SALIMA   I wanna go home!
SOPHIE   Now, look at me. Look here, if you leave, where will you go? Huh?
        Sleep in the bush? Scrounge for food in a stinking refugee camp.
SALIMA   But I wanna—!
SOPHIE   What? Be thrown back out there? Where will you go? Huh? Your
40   husband? Your village? How much goodness did they show you?
SALIMA   [*Wounded*]   Why did you say that?
SOPHIE   I'm sorry, but you know it's true. There is a war going on, and it isn't
        safe for a woman alone. You know that! It's better this way. Here.
SALIMA   You, you don't have to be with them. Sometimes their hands are so
45   full of rage that it hurts to be touched. This night, I look over at you sing-
        ing, and you seem almost happy like a sunbird that can fly away if you
        reach out to touch it.
SOPHIE   Is that what you think? While I'm singing, I'm praying the pain will
        be gone, but what those men did to me lives inside of my body. Every step
50   I take I feel them in me. Punishing me. And it will be that way for the rest
        of my life.

[SALIMA *touches* SOPHIE's *face.*]

SALIMA   I'm pregnant.
SOPHIE   What?
SALIMA   I'm pregnant. I can't tell Mama. [*Tears fill her eyes*]

[SOPHIE *hugs* SALIMA.]

55 SOPHIE   No. Shh. Shh. Okay. Okay.
SALIMA   She'll turn me out.

[SOPHIE *breaks away from* SALIMA *and digs in a basket for a book.*]

    What are you doing?
SOPHIE   Shh. Look, look.

[SOPHIE *pulls money from between the pages of the book and empties the
bills onto the bed.*]

SALIMA   Sophie?!
60 SOPHIE   Shhh. This is for us. We won't be here forever. Okay.
SALIMA   Where'd you get . . . the money?
SOPHIE   Don't worry. Mama may be many things, but she don't count so
        good. And when there's enough we'll get a bus to Bunia. I promise. But you
        can't say anything, not even to Josephine. Okay?
65 SALIMA   But if Mama finds out that you're—
SOPHIE   Shhh. She won't.

[JOSEPHINE, *bedraggled, enters and throws herself on the bed.*]

JOSEPHINE   What you two whispering about?

SOPHIE   Nothing.

[SOPHIE *hides the nail polish and book beneath the mattress.*]

JOSEPHINE   God, I'm starving. And there's never anything to eat. I thought
70   you were going to save me some fufu.[7]
SOPHIE   I did, I put it on the shelf under the cloth.
SALIMA   I bet that stupid monkey took it again. Pesky creature.
JOSEPHINE   It ain't the monkey, it's Emeline's nasty child. He's a menace.
That boy's buttocks would be raw if he were mine.

[JOSEPHINE *takes off her shirt, revealing an enormous disfiguring black
scar circumventing her stomach. She tries to hide it.* SOPHIE'S *eyes are
drawn to the scar.*]

75   [*To* SALIMA] But, if it's you who's been pinching my supper, don't think I
won't find out. I ain't the only one who's noticed that you getting fat fat off
the same food we eating. [*To* SOPHIE] What are you looking at? [*Tosses her
shirt to* SOPHIE] Hang up my shirt! *Sasa!*[8]

[SOPHIE *hangs* JOSEPHINE'S *shirt on a nail.*]

SALIMA   Tst. [*Whispers under her breath*]
80   JOSEPHINE   And what's wrong with her?
SALIMA   Nothing.

[JOSEPHINE *suspiciously sniffs the air. Then puts on a traditional colorful
wrap. A moment.* SALIMA *sits back on the bed.* JOSEPHINE *notices her magazine on the bed.*]

JOSEPHINE   Hey, girl, why is my fashion magazine here? Huh?
SALIMA   I . . . I had a quick look.
JOSEPHINE   What do you want with it? Can you even read?
85   SALIMA   Oh, shut your mouth, I like looking at the photographs.
JOSEPHINE   Oh, c'mon, girl, you've seen them a dozen times. It's the same
photographs that were there yesterday.
SALIMA   So why do you care if I look at them?
SOPHIE   *Atsha, makelle.*[9] Let her see it, Josephine. Let's not have the same
90   argument.
JOSEPHINE   There.
SALIMA   [*Whispered*]   Bitch.
JOSEPHINE   What?
SALIMA   Thank you.
95   JOSEPHINE   Yeah, that's what I thought.

[JOSEPHINE *tosses the magazine at* SALIMA.]

Girl, I really should charge you for all the times your dirty fingers fuss with
it. [*Sucks her teeth*]

---

7. Common African food made from boiled   8. Now (Swahili).
cassava pounded and mixed with water.   9. Stop that noise (Swahili).

SOPHIE   Oh, give us peace, she doesn't feel well.

JOSEPHINE   No?

[SALIMA, *moping, thumbs through the magazine, doing her best to ignore* JOSEPHINE.]

100 SALIMA   The only reason I don't read is cuz my younger sister get school, and I get good husband.

JOSEPHINE   So where is he?!

[SALIMA *ignores her.* JOSEPHINE *turns on the portable radio hanging over her bed.*]

ANNOUNCER [*Voice-over*]   Nous avons reçu des rapports que les bandits armés de Lendu et des groupes rivaux de Hema combattent pour la commande de la
105 ville—

SALIMA   What's he say?

SOPHIE   Lendu and Hema, fighting near Bunia.

[JOSEPHINE *quickly turns the radio dial. Congolese hip-hop music plays. She does a few quick suggestive steps, then lights a cigarette.*]

JOSEPHINE   Hey. Hey. Guess what? Guess what? I'm going to Kisangani next month.

110 SOPHIE   What?

JOSEPHINE   Mr. Harari is going to take me. Watch out, chérie, he's promised to set me up in a high-rise apartment. Don't hate, all of this fineness belongs in the city.

SOPHIE   For true?

115 JOSEPHINE   What, you think I'm lying?

SOPHIE   No, no, that's real cool, Josephine. The big town. You been?

JOSEPHINE   Me? . . . No. No. [*To* SALIMA] And I know you haven't.

SALIMA   How do you know? Huh? I was planning to go some time next year. My husband—

120 JOSEPHINE [*Sarcastically*]   What, he was going to sell his yams in the market?

SALIMA   I'll ask you not to mention my family.

JOSEPHINE   And if I do?

SALIMA   I'm asking you kindly this time.

[JOSEPHINE *recognizes the weight of her words but forges on.*]

JOSEPHINE   I'm tired of hearing about your family. [*Blows smoke at* SALIMA]

125 SALIMA   Mention them again, and I swear to God I'll beat your ass.

JOSEPHINE   Yeah?

SALIMA   Yeah. You don't know what the hell you're talking about.

JOSEPHINE   I don't? All right. I'm stupid! I don't! You are smarter than all of us. Yeah? That's what you think, huh? *Kiwele wele.*[1] You wait, girl. I'll for-
130 give you, I will, when you say, "Josephine you were so so right."

SOPHIE   Just shut up!

---

1. Dummy (Swahili).

JOSEPHINE   Hey, I'm done.

[JOSEPHINE *blows a kiss.* SALIMA, *enraged, starts for the door.*]

SOPHIE   Salima, Salima.

[SALIMA *is gone.*]

JOSEPHINE [*Taunting*]   Salima!

[JOSEPHINE *falls on the bed laughing.*]

135   SOPHIE   What's wrong with you? What did Salima do to you? You make me
sick. [*Flicks off the radio*]
JOSEPHINE   Hey, *jolie fille.*[2] [*Makes kissing sounds*]
SOPHIE   Don't talk to me.
JOSEPHINE   I can't talk to you? Who put you on the top shelf? You flutter
140   about here as if God touched only you. What you seem to forget is that this
is a whorehouse, chérie.
SOPHIE   Yeah, but, I'm not a whore.
JOSEPHINE   A mere trick of fate. I'm sorry, but let me say what we all know,
you are something worse than a whore. So many men have had you that
145   you're worthless.

[*A moment.* SOPHIE, *wounded, turns and limps away silently.*]

Am I wrong?
SOPHIE   . . . Yes.
JOSEPHINE   Am I wrong?
SOPHIE   Yes.
150   JOSEPHINE   My father was chief!

[SOPHIE *is at the door.* JOSEPHINE *confronts her.*]

My father was chief! The most important man in my village, and when the
soldiers raided us, who was kind to me? Huh? Not his second wife: "There!
She is the chief's daughter!" Or the cowards who pretended not to know
me. And did any of them bring a blanket to cover me, did anyone move to
155   help me? NO! So you see, you ain't special!

[*The lights fade.*]

Scene 4

Dusk. The generator hums. SOPHIE *sings. The bar bustles with activity:* MINERS,
PROSTITUTES, MUSICIANS *and* GOVERNMENT SOLDIERS. *Laughter. A* MINER *chats
up* SALIMA. JOSEPHINE *sits at a table with a* SOLDIER.

SOPHIE [*Sings*]

2. Pretty lady (French).

A rare bird on a limb
Sings a song heard by a few,
A few patient and distant listeners
Hear, its sweet sweet call,
5   A sound that haunts the forest,
A cry that tells a story, harmonious,
But time forgotten.
To be seen, is to be doomed
It must evade, evade capture,
10   And yet the bird
Still cries out to be heard.
And yet the bird
Still cries out to be heard.
And yet the bird
15   Still cries out to be heard.

[MAMA *enters. She feeds the parrot.*]

MAMA   Hello. Talk to me. You hungry? Yes?
CHRISTIAN [*Entering*]   Mama!

[MAMA *is surprised by* CHRISTIAN. *Her face lights up.*]

MAMA   Ah, professor!

[MAMA *cracks open a couple of sodas.* CHRISTIAN *places a box of chocolates and several cartons of cigarettes on the counter then launches into a
poem:*]

CHRISTIAN

The tidal dance,
20   A nasty tug of war,
Two equally implacable partners
Day fighting night . . .

And so forth and so on. Forgive me, I bring you an early poem, but I'm
afraid it's running away from my memory. I still hope one day you will hear
25   the music and dance with me.
MAMA [*Dismissive*]   You're a ridiculous man.

[MAMA *passes a cold soda to* CHRISTIAN. *He blows a kiss to* SOPHIE.]

CHRISTIAN   Lovely, chérie. It's what I've been waiting for.
MAMA   You're the only man I know who doesn't crave a cold beer at the end
of a long drive.
30 CHRISTIAN   Last time I had a drink, I lost several years of my life.

[MAMA *hands him a list.*]

What's this?

MAMA   A list of everything I know you forgot to bring me.

[CHRISTIAN *examines the list.*]

CHRISTIAN   What? When'd you learn to spell so good?

MAMA   Oh, close your mouth. Sophie wrote it down. She's a smart girl, been
35   helping me.

CHRISTIAN [*Teasing*]   You see how things work out. And you, you wanted to
turn her away—

MAMA   Are you finished?

[SALIMA *and the* MINER *laugh and play pool.*]

I looked out for you on Friday. What the hell happened?

40   CHRISTIAN   I had to deliver supplies to the mission. Have you heard? Pastor
Robbins been missing for a couple days.

[*The* SOLDIER *whispers something in* JOSEPHINE's *ear. She laughs loudly,
flirtatiously.*]

I told them I'd ask about.

MAMA   The white preacher? I'm not surprised. He's gotta big fucking mouth.
The mission's better off without him. The only thing that old bastard ever did
45   was pass out flaky aspirin and maybe a round of penicillin if you were dying.

CHRISTIAN   Well, the rumor is the pastor's been treating wounded rebel
soldiers.

MAMA [*Concerned*]   Really?

CHRISTIAN   That's what I'm hearing. Things are getting ugly over that way.

50   MAMA   Since when?

CHRISTIAN   Last week or so. The militias, they're battling for control of the
area. It is impossible.

MAMA   What about Yaka-yaka mine? Has the fighting scared off the miners?

CHRISTIAN   I don't know about the miners, but it's scaring me.

[SALIMA *and the* MINER *laugh.*]

55   I was just by Yaka-yaka. When I was there six months ago, It was a forest
filled with noisy birds, now it looks like God spooned out heaping mouth-
fuls of earth, and every stupid bastard is trying to get a taste of it. It's been
ugly, chérie, but never like this. Not here.

MAMA   No more talk.

[*She's spooked, but doesn't want to show it. She signals for the* MUSICIANS
to play an upbeat song. The song plays softly.]

60   There will always be squabbles, ancient and otherwise.

[JOSEPHINE *takes the* SOLDIER *to the back.*]

Me, I thank God for deep dirty holes like Yaka-yaka. In my house I try to
keep everyone happy.

CHRISTIAN   Don't fool yourself!

MAMA   Hey, hey, professor, are you worried about me?

65   CHRISTIAN   [*Gently taking Mama's hand*]   Of course, chérie. I am a family man at heart. A lover, baby. We could build a nice business together. I have friends in Kampala, I have friends in Bamako, I even have friends in Paris, the city of love.

[MAMA *laughs. She quickly withdraws her hand from* CHRISTIAN. *His affection throws her off-balance.*]

MAMA   You . . . are . . . a stupid . . . man . . . with a running tongue. And look
70   here, I have my own business, and I'm not leaving it for a jackass who doesn't have enough sense to buy a new suit.

CHRISTIAN   You are too proud and stubborn, you know that. This is a good suit, *très chic*, so what if it's old? And . . . don't pretend, chérie, eventually you'll grace me with . . . a dance.

75   MAMA   Oh, have a cold beer, it'll flush out some of your foolishness.

CHRISTIAN   Ach, ach, woman! Liquor is not a dance partner I choose.

[CHRISTIAN *does a few seductive dance steps, just then* COMMANDER OSEMBENGA, *a pompous peacock of a man in dark sunglasses, a gold chain and a jogging suit, struts into the bar. He wears a pistol in a harness. He is accompanied by a* GOVERNMENT SOLDIER *in uniform.* CHRISTIAN *nods deferentially.*]

Monsieur.

[OSEMBENGA *stands erect waiting to be acknowledged. Everyone grows silent.*]

MAMA   [*Flirtatiously*]   Good evening.

OSEMBENGA   It is now.

[*He gives the place a once-over.*]

80   MAMA   Can I get you something?

OSEMBENGA   Bring me a cold Primus. A pack of cigarettes, fresh.

[MAMA *guides* OSEMBENGA *to a chair. She signals* SOPHIE *to fetch some beer.*]

MAMA   Monsieur, I must ask you to leave your bullets at the bar, otherwise you don't come in.

OSEMBENGA   And if I choose not to.

85   MAMA   Then you don't get served. I don't want any mischief in here. Is that clear?

[OSEMBENGA, *charmed by her tenacity, laughs with the robust authority of a man in charge.*]

OSEMBENGA   Do you know who I am?

MAMA   I'm afraid you must edify me, and then forgive me, if it makes absolutely no difference. Once you step through my door, then you're in my
house. And I make the rules here.

[OSEMBENGA *chuckles to himself.*]

OSEMBENGA   All right, Mama. Forgive me.

[OSEMBENGA *makes a show of removing the bullets from his gun and
placing them on the table.*]

And who said I don't respect the rule of law?

[*The drunk* GOVERNMENT SOLDIER, *half dressed, playfully chases* JOSE-
PHINE *from the back. He spots* OSEMBENGA *and jumps to attention.*]

GOVERNMENT SOLDIER #1   Commander, beg my pardon.
OSEMBENGA   Take it easy, young man. Take it easy. We're all off duty. We're in
Mama's house. Clean up.

[OSEMBENGA *sits down. He unzips his jacket.* MAMA *opens a pack of cigarettes and passes them to* OSEMBENGA.]

MAMA   Monsieur, I don't recall seeing you here before.
OSEMBENGA   No.

[MAMA *lights* OSEMBENGA's *cigarette.*]

MAMA   What brings you to *mon*³ hotel?
OSEMBENGA   Jerome Kisembe, the rebel leader.

[OSEMBENGA *studies her face to gauge the response.*]

You know him, of course.
MAMA   I know of him. We all know of him. His name is spoken here at least
several times a day. We've felt the sting of his reputation.
OSEMBENGA   So, you do know him.
MAMA   No, as I said, I know of him. His men control the road east and the
forest to the north of here.

[OSEMBENGA *turns his attention to everyone. Scrutiny. Suspicion.*]

OSEMBENGA   Is that so?
MAMA   Yes. But you must know that.

[OSEMBENGA *speaks to* MAMA, *but he is clearly addressing everyone.*]

OSEMBENGA   This Jerome Kisembe is a dangerous man. You hide him and his
band of renegades in your villages. Give them food, and say you're protecting

3. My (French).

110 your liberator. What liberator? What will he give the people? That is what I
want to know? What has he given you, Mama? Hm? A new roof? Food?
Peace?

MAMA   I don't need a man to give me anything.

OSEMBENGA   Make a joke, but Kisembe has one goal and that is to make
115 himself rich on your back, Mama.

[OSEMBENGA *grows loud and more forthright as he speaks. The music
stops. The bar grows quiet. Tension.*]

He will burn your crops, steal your women, and make slaves of your men
all in the name of peace and reconciliation. Don't believe him. He, and
men like him, these careless militias wage a diabolical campaign. They
leave stains everywhere they go. And remember the land he claims as his
120 own, it is a national reserve, it is the people's land, our land. And yet he will
tell you the government has taken everything, though we're actually paving
the way for democracy.

MAMA   I know that, but the government needs to let him know that. But you,
I'm only seeing you for the first time. Kisembe, I hear his name every day.

125 OSEMBENGA   Then hear my name, Commander Osembenga, *banga liwa.*[4]

[*A moment.* MAMA *absorbs the news, she seems genuinely humbled.*
CHRISTIAN *backs away as if to disappear.*]

You will hear my name quite a bit from now on.

MAMA   Commander Osembenga, forgive me for not knowing your name.
Karibu. It's a pleasure to have such an important man in our company.
Allow me to pour you a glass of our very best whiskey. From the U.S. of A.

130 OSEMBENGA   Thank you. A clean glass.

MAMA   Of course. *Karibu.*

[MAMA *fetches* OSEMBENGA *a glass of whiskey. She makes a show of wiping out the cloudy glass. She pours him a generous glass of whiskey and
places the bottle in front of him.*]

[*Seductively*] We take good care of our visitors. And we offer very good
company. Clean company, not like other places. You are safe here. If you
need something, anything while—

135 OSEMBENGA   You are a practical woman. I know that you have the sense to
keep your doors closed to rebel dogs. Am I right?

[OSEMBENGA *gently takes* MAMA's *hand. She allows the intimacy.* CHRIS-
TIAN *looks on. Contempt.*]

MAMA   Of course.

[*A* MINER, *covered in mud, sneaks in.*]

Hey, hey, my friend. Wash your hands and feet in the bucket outside!

4. Fear death (Swahili).

[*The* MINER, *annoyed, scrambles out of the bar.*]

These fucking miners have no respect for nothing. I have to tell that one
every time.

[CHRISTIAN *retreats to the bar, fuming.* OSEMBENGA *takes note of him.*
CHRISTIAN *quickly averts his gaze.*]

[*Obsequiously*] Anything you need.
OSEMBENGA   I will keep that in mind.
MAMA   Ladies.

[*She beckons to* JOSEPHINE *and* SALIMA, *who join* OSEMBENGA *at the
table. The* GOVERNMENT SOLDIERS *groan.*]

JOSEPHINE   Commander.

[JOSEPHINE *places her hand on* OSEMBENGA's *thigh.*]

MAMA   Excuse me a moment.

[CHRISTIAN *grabs* MAMA's *arm as she passes.*]

CHRISTIAN   Watch that one.
MAMA   What? It's always good to have friends in the government, no?

[MAMA *clears bottles. The* MINER *reenters. He sits at the bar.*]

GOVERNMENT SOLDIER #1 [*Abandoned by* JOSEPHINE, *belligerently*]   Another.
MAMA   Show me your money.

[*The* SOLDIER *holds up his money.*]

Sophie! Sophie! What are you standing around for? I'm losing money as
you speak. Quick. Quick. Two beers.

[SOPHIE *carries two beers over to the* SOLDIER. *He places his money on
the table.* SOPHIE *picks it up and quickly slips it under her shirt. She
doesn't realize* MAMA *is watching her. The drunken* SOLDIER *grabs her
onto his lap.* CHRISTIAN *protectively rises.* SOPHIE *skillfully extracts herself from the* SOLDIER's *lap.*]

CHRISTIAN   Are you okay?
SOPHIE   Yes.

[SOPHIE, *shaken, exits.* CHRISTIAN *smiles to himself, and lights a cigarette. The drunken* SOLDIER, *annoyed, plops down next to* CHRISTIAN.]

GOVERNMENT SOLDIER #1   Ça va, Papa?
CHRISTIAN   Bien merci.[5]

5. How are you? Fine, thank you (both French).

[*The* SOLDIER *stares down* CHRISTIAN.]

GOVERNMENT SOLDIER #1   You give me a cigarette, my friend?
CHRISTIAN [*Nervously*]   Sorry, this is my last one.
GOVERNMENT SOLDIER #1   Yeah? You, buy me cigarette?
CHRISTIAN   What?
160 GOVERNMENT SOLDIER #1 [*Showing off*]   Buy me cigarette!
CHRISTIAN   Sure.

[CHRISTIAN *reluctantly digs into his pocket, and places money on the counter.* MAMA *drops a cigarette on the counter. The* SOLDIER *scoops it up triumphantly, and walks away.*]

And? Merci?

[*The* SOLDIER *stops short, and menacingly stares down* CHRISTIAN.]

OSEMBENGA   Soldier, show this good man the bush hasn't robbed you of your manners.

[*A moment*]

165 GOVERNMENT SOLDIER #1   *Merci.*

[CHRISTIAN *acknowledges* OSEMBENGA *with a polite nod.*]

OSEMBENGA   Of course.

[OSEMBENGA *smiles, and gestures to* MAMA.]

MAMA   Yes, Commander?
OSEMBENGA [*Referring to* CHRISTIAN, *whispers*]:   Who is he?
MAMA   Passing through.

[*The* SOLDIER, *embarrassed, angrily drives the* MINER *out of his bar seat. The* MINER *retreats.*]

170 OSEMBENGA   What's his business?
MAMA   Salesman. He's nobody.
OSEMBENGA   I don't trust him.
MAMA   Does he look dangerous to you?
OSEMBENGA   Everyone looks dangerous to me, until I've shared a drink with
175   them.

[OSEMBENGA *sizes up* CHRISTIAN, *deciding.*]

Give him a glass of whiskey, and tell him I hope he finds success here.

[MAMA *pours a glass of whiskey. She walks over to* CHRISTIAN.]

MAMA   Good news, the commander has bought you a drink of whiskey and hopes that you'll find prosperity.

CHRISTIAN   That's very generous, but you know I don't drink. Please, tell him
180   thanks, but no thanks.

[*A moment.*]

MAMA   The commander is buying you a drink.

[MAMA *places the glass in* CHRISTIAN's *hand. She signals to the musicians
to play.*]

Raise your glass to him, and smile.
CHRISTIAN   Thank you, but I don't drink.
MAMA [*Whispered*]   Oh, you most certainly do, today. You will drink every last
185   drop of what he offers, and when he buys you another round you'll drink
that as well. You will drink until he decides you've had enough.

[CHRISTIAN *looks over at the smiling* OSEMBENGA. *He raises his glass to*
OSEMBENGA *across the room, contemplating the drink for a long hard
moment.*]

OSEMBENGA   Drink up!
CHRISTIAN   I—
MAMA   Please. [*Whispered*] He's a very important man.
190   CHRISTIAN   Please, Mama.
MAMA   He can help us, or he can cause us many problems. It's your decision.
Remember, if you don't step on the dog's tail, he won't bite you.
OSEMBENGA   Drink up!

[*The* GOVERNMENT SOLDIERS *egg* CHRISTIAN *on. Unnerved,* CHRISTIAN,
slowly and with difficulty, drinks the liquor, wincing. OSEMBENGA *laughs.
He signals for* MAMA *to pour* CHRISTIAN *another. She does. Again, the*
SOLDIERS *cheer* CHRISTIAN *on.*]

Good. [*Shouts*] To health and prosperity!

[CHRISTIAN *contemplates the second drink.* OSEMBENGA *raises his glass.*
CHRISTIAN *nervously knocks back the second shot of whiskey, and, again,
winces.* OSEMBENGA *smiles. He signals for* MAMA *to pour another. The*
SOLDIERS *cheer.* MAMA *pours him another.*]

195   CHRISTIAN   Don't make—
MAMA   Trust me.

[*She places the glass in his hand.* CHRISTIAN *walks over to* OSEMBENGA's
*table. We aren't sure whether he is going to throw the drink in his face or
toast him. He forcefully thrusts his drink in the air. Blackout.*]

Scene 5

Morning. The bar. SOPHIE *reads from the pages of a romance novel.* JOSEPHINE
and SALIMA *sit listening, rapt. It is a refuge.*

SOPHIE [*Reading*] "The others had left the party, they were alone. She was now painfully aware that there was only the kiss left between them. She felt herself stiffen as he leaned into her. The hairs on her forearms stood on end, and the room suddenly grew several degrees warmer—"

5 JOSEPHINE Oh, kiss her!

SALIMA Shh!

SOPHIE "His lips met hers. She could taste him, smell him, and all at once her body was infused with—"

[MAMA *enters with the lockbox.* SOPHIE *protectively slips the book behind her back.* MAMA *grabs it.*]

MAMA What's this?

10 SOPHIE . . . A romance, Uncle Christian bought it.

MAMA A romance?

SOPHIE Yes.

[MAMA *examines the book. The women's eyes plead with her not to take it.*]

MAMA Josephine, we need water in the back, and Salima, the broom is waiting for you in the yard.

15 SALIMA Ah, Mama, let her finish the chapter.

MAMA Are you giving me lip? I didn't think so. Come here. Hurry.

[SALIMA *reluctantly walks over to* MAMA. MAMA *grabs her wrist and runs her hand over* SALIMA's *stomach.*]

You must be happy here. You're getting fat fat!

SALIMA I didn't notice.

MAMA Well, I have.

[SALIMA, *petrified, isn't sure where* MAMA's *going. Then:*]

20 You did good last night.

SALIMA [*Surprised*] Thank you.

[MAMA *tosses the book back to* SOPHIE.]

JOSEPHINE You don't care for romance, Mama?

MAMA Me? No, the problem is I already know how it's going to end. There'll be kissing, fucking, a betrayal, and then the woman will foolishly surrender

25 her heart to an undeserving man. Okay. Move. Move. Ach. Ach. Sophie wait.

[SALIMA *grabs the broom and exits.*]

JOSEPHINE [*Gesturing to Sophie*] What about her?

MAMA I need her help.

JOSEPHINE Tst!

MAMA You have a problem with that? You count good?

[JOSEPHINE *stares down* SOPHIE. SOPHIE *isn't having it.* MAMA *laughs.* SALIMA *pokes her head in the door.*]

30 SALIMA   Mama. Someone's coming around the bend.
MAMA [*Surprised*]   So early?
JOSEPHINE   Tst! Another stupid miner looking to get his cock wet.
SALIMA   No, I think it's Mr. Harari.
JOSEPHINE   What?
35 SALIMA   "Come with me to the city, my darling."
JOSEPHINE   Don't hate!
SOPHIE   "I'm going to buy you a palace in Lebanon, my darling."

[*This strikes a nerve.*]

JOSEPHINE   Hey, hey. At least I have somebody, I take care of him good. And
he comes back.

[JOSEPHINE *seductively approaches* SOPHIE. *She grabs her close.*]

40 Joke, laugh, *jolie fille*, but we all know a man wants a woman who's
complete.
SOPHIE   Okay, stop—
JOSEPHINE   He wants her to open up and allow him to release himself, he
wants to pour the whole world into her.
45 SOPHIE   I said stop!
JOSEPHINE   Can you be that woman?
MAMA   Let her alone. Go get the water!
JOSEPHINE   I was firstborn child! My father was chief!
MAMA   Yeah, and my father was whoever put money in my mama's pocket!
50 Chief, farmer, who the hell cares? Go!

[JOSEPHINE *storms off.* SALIMA *follows.*]

Give Josephine a good smack in the mouth, and she won't bother you no
more.

[*She plops the lockbox on the table.*]

Here. Count last night's money. Let me know how we did.

[SOPHIE *opens the lockbox.* MAMA *skillfully funnels water into a whiskey
bottle.*]

I don't know where all these men are coming from, but I'm happy for it.

[SOPHIE *pulls out the money, a worn ribbon, and then a small stone.*]

55 SOPHIE   Why do you keep this pebble?
MAMA   That? It doesn't look like anything. Stupid man give it to me to hold
for one night of company and four beers not even cold enough to quench
his thirst. He said he'd be back for it and he'd pay me. It's a raw diamond.
It probably took him a half year of sifting through mud to dig it up, and it
60 promised his simple wife a Chinese motor scooter and fabric from Senegal.
And there it is, some unfortunate woman's dream.

SOPHIE   What will you do with it?

MAMA [*Chuckling to herself*]   Do? Ha!

[MAMA *knocks back a shot of watered-down whiskey.*]

65 It still tastes like whiskey. I don't know, but as long as they are foolish enough to give it to me, I'll keep accepting it. My mother taught me that you can follow behind everyone and walk in the dust, or you can walk ahead through the unbroken thorny brush. You may get blood on your ankles, but you arrive first and not covered in the residue of others. This land is fertile and blessed in many regards, and the men ain't the only ones entitled to its
70 bounty.

SOPHIE   What if the man comes back for his stone?

MAMA   A lot of people would sell it, run away. But it is my insurance policy, it is what keeps me from becoming like them. There must always be a part of you that this war can't touch. It's a damn shame, but I keep it for that stu-
75 pid woman. Enough talk, how'd we do?

SOPHIE   Good. If we—

MAMA   We?

SOPHIE   Charged a little more for the beer, just a few more francs. By the end of the year we'll have enough to buy a new generator.

80 MAMA   Yeah? A new generator? Good. You're quick with numbers. Yes. You counted everything from last night. Your tips?

SOPHIE   Yes.

MAMA   Yes?

[*A moment.* MAMA *reaches into* SOPHIE's *chest and produces a fold of money.*]

MAMA   Is this yours?

85 SOPHIE   Yes. I was—

MAMA   Yes? So tell me what you're planning to do with my money. [*With edge*] Cuz it's my money.

SOPHIE   I—

MAMA   I,I,I . . . what?

90 SOPHIE   It's not what you think, Mama.

MAMA   No, you're not trying to run off with my money? "Take her in, give her food." Your uncle begged me. What am I supposed to do? I trust you. Everyone say, she bad luck, but I think this is a smart girl, maybe Mama won't have to do everything by herself. You read books, you speak good, like
95 white man—but is this who you want to be?

SOPHIE   I'm sorry, Mama.

MAMA   No. No. I will put you out on your ass. I will let you walk naked down that road, is that what you want? What did you think you were going to do with my money?!

[MAMA *grabs* SOPHIE, *pulls her to the door.*]

100 SOPHIE   Mama! Please! . . .

MAMA   You want to be out there? Huh? Huh? Then go! Go!

[SOPHIE *struggles, terrified.*]

Huh? What were you going to do?

SOPHIE   A man that come in here said he can help me. He said there is an operation for girls.

105   MAMA   Don't you lie to me.

SOPHIE   Listen, listen, please listen, they can repair the damage.

[*A moment.* MAMA *releases* SOPHIE.]

MAMA   An operation?

SOPHIE   Yes, he give me this paper. Look, look.

MAMA   And it can make it better?

110   SOPHIE   Yes.

[MAMA *makes a show of putting the money into her lockbox.*]

MAMA   Hm. Congratulations! You're the first girl bold enough to steal from me. [*Laughs*] Where are your books?

SOPHIE   Under my bed.

MAMA   Go bring them to me. I know you better than you think, girl.

[*The lights fade.*]

Scene 6

The bar. Morning light pours in. JOSEPHINE *struggles with a drunk* MINER. *She finally manages to push him out of the bar, then exits into the back.* SALIMA *quickly sneaks food from under the counter. She stuffs fufu into her mouth. The bird squawks as if to tell on her.*

SALIMA   Shh! Shh!

[CHRISTIAN, *winded and on edge, comes rushing into the bar. He is covered in dirt.*]

Professor!

CHRISTIAN   Get Mama!

[SALIMA *quickly exits.* CHRISTIAN *paces.* MAMA *enters.*]

MAMA   Professor! [*Beat*] What, what is it?

5   CHRISTIAN   The white pastor's dead.

MAMA   What?

[CHRISTIAN *sits, then immediately stands.*]

CHRISTIAN   He was dead for over a week before anyone found his body. He was only a hundred meters from the chapel. The cook said it was Osembenga's soldiers. They accused the pastor of aiding rebels. Do you hear what I am saying?

10

[MAMA *takes in his words, they bite her.*]

They cut him up beyond recognition. Cut out his eyes and tongue. [*Nauseated by the notion*]

MAMA   The pastor? I'm sorry to hear that.

[MAMA *pours herself a whiskey.*]

CHRISTIAN   Can I have one of those, please?

MAMA   Are you sure?

15 CHRISTIAN   Just give it to me damn it!

[MAMA *hesitantly pours* CHRISTIAN *a drink. She stares at him.*]

What?

[*He gulps it down.*]

The policeman said there were no witnesses. No one saw anything, and so there is nothing he can do. Bury him, he said. Me? I barely know the man, and people who worked with him for years were mute, no one knew any-

20 thing. He was butchered, and no one knows anything.

MAMA   Take it easy.

CHRISTIAN   These ignorant country boys, who wouldn't be able to tell left from right, they put on a uniform and suddenly they're making decisions for us. Give me another.

25 MAMA   The Fantas are cold.

CHRISTIAN   I don't want a Fanta.

[MAMA *reluctantly pours* CHRISTIAN *another drink. His hand slightly quivers as he knocks back the liquor.*]

They've killed a white man. Do you know what that means? A missionary. They're pushing this way. They won't think twice about killing us.

MAMA   A dead pastor is just another dead man, and people here see that

30 every day. I can't think about it right now. I have ten girls to feed, and a business to run.

[MAMA *buries her face in her palms, overwhelmed.*]

CHRISTIAN   Come with me, Mama. We'll go to Kinshasa[6] where there's no trouble. Between the two of us . . . The two of us. We'll open a small place. Serve food, drink, dancing.

[MAMA *isn't convinced.* CHRISTIAN *reaches for the bottle of whiskey, she snatches it away.* CHRISTIAN *slams the bar.*

Two ragged SOLDIERS, FORTUNE *and* SIMON, *enter like a whirlwind. They carry beat-up rifles and wear dirty ill-fitting uniforms. Fortune also carries an iron pot. They are on edge, which makes Mama very uneasy.*]

35 MAMA   Yes?

---

6. Capital city of the DRC.

FORTUNE   Is this the place of Mama Nadi?
MAMA   Yes, that is me. What can I do for you?
FORTUNE   We'll have a meal and a beer.
MAMA   Okay, no problem. I have fish and fufu from last night.
40 FORTUNE   Yeah. Good. Good.
MAMA   It ain't hot.
SIMON   We'll have it.

[MAMA *eyes the men suspiciously.* CHRISTIAN, *petrified, does his best to mask it.*]

MAMA   Please don't be offended, but I'll need to see your money.

[FORTUNE *removes a pile of worn bills from his pocket. The men move to sit.*]

Hey. Hey. Hey. Empty your weapons.

[*The men hesitate.*]

45 SIMON   No, our wea—
MAMA   It's the rule. If you want to be fed.

[*The men reluctantly remove their clips from their guns and hand them to* MAMA.]

FORTUNE [*To* CHRISTIAN]   Good morning.
CHRISTIAN   Good morning.
SIMON   Do you have a place for us to wash up?
50 FORTUNE   In the back maybe.

[FORTUNE *gestures toward the backdoor.*]

MAMA [*Suspicious*]   I can bring you a basin of water.

[*They sit.* SOPHIE *enters, she's surprised to find* CHRISTIAN *and the* SOLDIERS.]

SOPHIE   Uncle.
CHRISTIAN   *Bonjour, mon amour.*[7]
SOPHIE   What happened to—
55 CHRISTIAN   Shh. I'm okay.

[SOPHIE *notes the caution in his tone.*]

FORTUNE AND SIMON   Good morning. How are you?

[*The men politely rise.*]

7. Good day, my love (French).

SOPHIE [*Timidly*] Good morning.

[*The men sit.*]

MAMA Bring some water for the basin.
FORTUNE Please.

[SOPHIE *exits with the basin.* MAMA *serves beer.*]

60 Thank you.
MAMA You come from the east?
FORTUNE No.
MAMA Farmers?
FORTUNE NO! We're soldiers! We follow Commander Osembenga!

[SOPHIE *returns with the full basin, but* CHRISTIAN *signals for her to leave.* CHRISTIAN *grows increasingly nervous. He watches the men like a hawk.*]

65 MAMA Easy. I don't mean to insult you, Soldier. But you look like good men. Men who don't follow trouble.

[FORTUNE *seems reluctant to speak.*]

SIMON We are—
FORTUNE I'm told there is a woman here named Salima. Is that true?
CHRISTIAN There—
70 MAMA Why? Who is looking for her?
FORTUNE Is she here!? I asked you, is she here!?
MAMA I'd adjust your tone, mister.
FORTUNE Please, I'm looking for a woman named Salima.
MAMA I have to ask inside.

[CHRISTIAN *and* MAMA *exchange a look.*]

75 FORTUNE She's from Kaligili. She has a small scar on her right cheek. Just so.
MAMA A lot of women come and go. I'll ask around. And may I say who's looking for her?
FORTUNE Fortune, her husband.

[CHRISTIAN *registers this discovery.*]

80 MAMA Excuse me. I'll go ask inside.

[MAMA *exits.* CHRISTIAN *disappears into his drink.*]

SIMON We'll find her, Fortune. C'mon, drink up. When was your last cold beer?
FORTUNE I'm not thirsty.

[SIMON *drinks.*]

SIMON   Ah, that's nice. It's nice, man.

[FORTUNE *paces.*]

85 FORTUNE   Come on, come on, where is she?
SIMON   Be patient. Man, if she's here we'll find her.
FORTUNE   Why is it taking so long?
SIMON   Take it easy.
FORTUNE   You heard it, the man on the road described Salima. It is her.

[SIMON *laughs.*]

90 What?

[FORTUNE *paces.*]

SIMON   You say that every time. Maybe it is, maybe it isn't. We've been walk-
ing for months, and in every village there is a Salima. You are certain. So
please, don't—
MAMA [*Reemerging*]   There is no Salima here.
95 FORTUNE [*Shocked*]   What? No! She is here!
MAMA   I'm sorry, you are mistaken. You got bad information.
FORTUNE   Salima! Salima Mukengeshayi!!
MAMA   I said she is not here.
FORTUNE   You lying witch! Salima!
100 MAMA   Call me names, but there's still no Salima here. I think maybe the
woman you're looking for is dead.
FORTUNE   She is here! Goddamn you, she is here.

[FORTUNE *flips over the table.* MAMA *grabs a machete.* CHRISTIAN *brandishes the whiskey bottle like a weapon.*]

MAMA   Please, I said she is not here. And if you insist I will show you how
serious I am.
105 SIMON   We don't want trouble.
MAMA   Now go. Get out! Get the hell out of here.
FORTUNE [*Shouts*]   Tell Salima, I will be back for her!

[*The parrot raises hell.* CHRISTIAN *scolds* MAMA *with his eyes. Blackout.*]

Act Two

Scene 1

FORTUNE, *in his ill-fitting uniform, stands outside the bar, like a centurion guard-
ing the gates.*
JOSEPHINE *teases two drunk* GOVERNMENT SOLDIERS *and a* MINER. *Guitar. Drums.*
MAMA *and* SOPHIE *sing a dance song.* MR. HARARI *and* CHRISTIAN *watch. Festive.*

MAMA [*Sings*]

Hey, monsieur, come play, monsieur,
Hey, monsieur, come play, monsieur,
The Congo sky rages electric
As bullets fly like hell's rain,
5   Wild flowers wilt and the forest decays.
But here we're pouring Champagne.

MAMA AND SOPHIE [*Sing*]

Cuz a warrior knows no peace,
When a hungry lion's awake.
But when that lion's asleep,
10   The warrior is free to play.

SOPHIE [*Sings*]

Drape your weariness on my shoulder,
Sweep travel dust from your heart.
Villages die as soldiers grow bolder,
We party as the world falls apart.

MAMA AND SOPHIE [*Sing*]

15   Cuz a warrior knows no peace,
When a hungry lion's awake.
But when that lion's asleep,
The warrior is free to play.

[*The drum beats out a furious rhythm.* JOSEPHINE *answers with a dance,
which begins playfully, seductively, then slowly becomes increasingly
frenzied. She releases her anger, her pain . . . everything. She desperately
grabs at the air as if trying to hold on to something. She abruptly stops,
overwhelmed.* SOPHIE *goes to her aid.*]

MAMA AND SOPHIE [*Sing*]

Hey, monsieur, come play, monsieur,
20   Hey, monsieur, come play, monsieur,

[SOPHIE *leads a spent* JOSEPHINE *to the back.*]

MAMA:

The door never closes at Mama's place.
The door never closes at Mama's place.

[MR. HARARI *nurses a beer as he watches* SOPHIE *and* MAMA *sing.* CHRIS-
TIAN, *drunk and disheveled, struggles to remain erect.*]

MAMA [*Sings*]
The door never closes at Mama's place.

[SOLDIER *laughter. Distant gunfire.*]

Scene 2

Lights fade. The back room.

    JOSEPHINE *sleeps.* SALIMA *quickly pulls down her shirt hiding her pregnant stomach as* MAMA *enters eating a mango.*

MAMA [*To* SALIMA] Are you going to hang here in the shadows until forever? I have thirsty miners with a good day in their pockets.

SALIMA Sorry, Mama, but—

MAMA I need one of you to go make them happy, show them their hard work
5   isn't for naught. [*Clicks her tongue*] C'mon. C'mon.

SALIMA [*Whispered*] But . . .

MAMA Josephine!

JOSEPHINE Ah! Why is it always me?

    [JOSEPHINE *rises. She exits in a huff, brushing past* SOPHIE, *who is just
    entering after bathing.* SALIMA *nervously looks to the door.*]

SALIMA Is Fortune still outside?

10 MAMA Your husband? Yes. He's still standing there, he couldn't be more
    quiet than if he were a stake driven into the ground. I don't like quiet men.

SALIMA He's always been so.

MAMA Well, I wish he wouldn't be "so" outside of my door.

    [SALIMA *involuntarily smiles.*]

SALIMA Why won't he go already? I don't want him to see me.

15 SOPHIE He's not leaving until he sees you, Salima.

    [SOPHIE *dresses.*]

MAMA Ha. What for? So he can turn his lip up at her again.

SOPHIE No. C'mon, he's been out there for two nights. If he doesn't love
    you, why would he still be there.

SALIMA Yeah?

20 MAMA Tst! Both of you are so stupid. He'll see you, love will flood into his
    eyes, he'll tell you everything you want to hear, and then one morning, I
    know how it happens, he will begin to ask ugly questions, but he won't be
    able to hear the answers. And no matter what you say, he won't be satisfied.
    I know. And, chérie, don't look away from me, will you be able to tell him
25   the truth? Huh? We know, don't we? The woman he loved is dead.

SOPHIE That's not true. He—

MAMA [*To* SALIMA] He left her for dead. See. This is your home now. Mama
    takes care of you.

    [MAMA *takes* SALIMA *in her arms.*]

But if you want to go back out there, go. But they, your village, your people,
30 they won't understand. Oh, they'll say they will, but they won't. Because, you
    know, underneath everything, they will be thinking she's damaged. She's been
    had by too many men. She let them, those dirty men, touch her. She's a

whore. And Salima, are you strong enough to stomach their hate? It will be worse than anything you've felt yet.

35 SOPHIE   But he—

MAMA   I'm not being cruel, but your simple life, the one you remember, that . . . Yeah the one you're so fond of . . . it's vapor, chérie. It's gone.

[*Tears flood* SALIMA's *eyes.*]

Now, uh-uh, don't cry. We keep our faces pretty. I will send him away. Okay? Okay?

40 SALIMA   Okay.

MAMA   We'll make him go away. Yeah?

SALIMA   Okay. Good.

SOPHIE   No, Mama, please, let her at least talk to him. He wants to take her home.

45 MAMA   You read too many of those romance novels where everything is forgiven with a kiss. Enough, my miners are waiting.

[MAMA *suspiciously eyes* SALIMA's *belly and exits.*]

SOPHIE   If you don't want to see him, then at least go out there and tell him. He's been sitting outside in the rain for two days, and he's not going to leave.

SALIMA   Let him sit.

50 SOPHIE   Go, talk to him. Maybe you'll feel differently.

SALIMA   He doesn't know that I'm pregnant. When he sees me, he'll hate me all over again.

SOPHIE   You don't know that. He came all this way.

[*A moment*]

SALIMA   Stupid man. Why did he have to come?

55 SOPHIE   All you ever talk about is wanting to get away from here. Go with him, Salima. Get the hell out of here! Go!

SALIMA   He called me a filthy dog, and said I tempted them. Why else would it happen? Five months in the bush, passed between the soldiers like a wash rag. Used. I was made poison by their fingers, that is what he said. He had no 60 choice but to turn away from me, because I dishonored him.

SOPHIE   He was hurting. It was sour pride.

SALIMA   Why are you defending him!? Then you go with him!

SOPHIE   I'm not def—

SALIMA   Do you know what I was doing on that morning? [*A calm washes over* 65 *her*] I was working in our garden, picking the last of the sweet tomatoes. I put Beatrice down in the shade of a frangipani tree, because my back was giving me some trouble. Forgiven? Where was Fortune? He was in town fetching a new iron pot. "Go," I said. "Go, today, man, or you won't have dinner tonight!" I had been after him for a new pot for a month. And finally on that day the 70 damn man had to go and get it. A new pot. The sun was about to crest, but I had to put in another hour before it got too hot. It was such a clear and open sky. This splendid bird, a peacock, had come into the garden to taunt me, and was showing off its feathers. I stooped down and called to the bird: "Wssht,

Wssht." And I felt a shadow cut across my back, and when I stood four men
75   were there over me, smiling, wicked schoolboy smiles. "Yes?" I said. And the
tall soldier slammed the butt of his gun into my cheek. Just like that. It was so
quick, I didn't even know I'd fallen to the ground. Where did they come from?
How could I not have heard them?

SOPHIE   You don't have to—

80   SALIMA   One of the soldiers held me down with his foot. He was so heavy,
thick like an ox and his boot was cracked and weathered like it had been left
out in the rain for weeks. His boot was pressing my chest and the cracks in
the leather had the look of drying sorghum. His foot was so heavy, and it was
all I could see as the others . . . "took" me. My baby was crying. She was a
85   good baby. Beatrice never cried, but she was crying, screaming. "Shhh," I
said. "Shhh." And right then . . . [*Closes her eyes*] A soldier stomped on her
head with his boot. And she was quiet.

[*A moment.* SALIMA *releases:*]

Where was everybody? WHERE WAS EVERYBODY?!

[SOPHIE *hugs* SALIMA.]

SOPHIE   It's okay. Take a breath.
90   SALIMA   I fought them!
SOPHIE   I know.
SALIMA   I did!
SOPHIE   I know.
SALIMA   But they still took me from my home. They took me through the
95   bush—raiding thieves. Fucking demons! "She is for everyone, soup to be had
before dinner," that is what someone said. They tied me to a tree by my foot,
and the men came whenever they wanted soup. I make fires, I cook food, I
listen to their stupid songs. I carry bullets, I clean wounds, I wash blood from
their clothing, and, and, and . . . I lay there as they tore me to pieces, until I
100   was raw . . . five months. Five months. Chained like a goat. These men fighting . . . fighting for our liberation. Still I close my eyes and I see such terrible
things. Things I cannot stand to have in my head. How can men be this way?

[*A moment*]

It was such a clear and open sky. So, so beautiful. How could I not hear them
coming?
105   SOPHIE   Those men were on a path and we were there. It happened.
SALIMA   A peacock wandered into my garden, and the tomatoes were ripe
beyond belief. Our fields of red sorghum were so perfect, it was going to be a
fine season. Fortune thought so, too, and we could finally think about planning a trip on the ferry to visit his brother. Oh God please give me back that
110   morning. "Forget the pot, Fortune. Stay . . ." "Stay," that's what I would tell
him. What did I do, Sophie? I must have done something. How did I get in
the middle of their fight?
SOPHIE   You were picking sweet tomatoes. That's all. You didn't do anything
wrong.

[SOPHIE *kisses* SALIMA *on the cheek.*]

115 SALIMA   It isn't his baby. It's the child of a monster, and there's no telling what it will be. Now, he's willing to forgive me, and is it that simple, Sophie? But what happens when the baby is born, will he be able to forgive the child, will I? And, and . . . and even if I do, I don't think I'll be able to forgive him.

SOPHIE   You can't know that until you speak to him.

120 SALIMA   I walked into the family compound expecting wide open arms. An embrace. Five months, suffering. I suffered every single second of it. And my family gave me the back of their heads. And he, the man I loved since I was fourteen, chased me away with a green switch. He beat my ankles raw. And I dishonored him? I dishonored him?! Where was he? Buying a pot? He was 125 too proud to bear my shame . . . but not proud enough to protect me from it. Let him sit in the rain.

SOPHIE   Is that really what you want?

SALIMA   Yes.

SOPHIE   He isn't going to leave.

130 SALIMA   Then I'm sorry for him.

[*The lights shift to moonlight.*]

Scene 3

Rain, moonlight. Outside the bar, FORTUNE *stands in the rain. His posture is erect. Music and laughter pour out of the bar.* MAMA *seductively stands in the doorway. She watches* FORTUNE *for a moment.*

MAMA   The sky doesn't look like it's gonna let up for a long time. My mama used to say. "Careful of the cold rain, it carries more men to their death than a storm of arrows."

FORTUNE   Why won't you let me see her?

5 MAMA   Young man, the woman you're looking for isn't here. But if you want company, I have plenty of that. What do you like? [*Seductively*] I know the challenges of a soldier's life, I hear stories from men every day. And there's nothing better than a gentle hand to pluck out the thorns, and heal the heart.

[MAMA *runs her hand up her thigh. She laughs.* FORTUNE *turns away, disgusted.* MAMA *smiles.*]

FORTUNE   Please . . . tell my wife, I love her.

10 MAMA   Yeah. Yeah. I've heard it before. You're not the first man to come here for his wife. But, Soldier, are you sure this is the place you want to be looking for her?

FORTUNE   Here. Give this to her.

[FORTUNE *lifts an iron pot.*]

MAMA   A pot?

[MAMA *laughs.*]

15   FORTUNE   Yes, please. Just give it to her.

MAMA   Very charming. A pot. Is this how you intend to woo a woman?

[FORTUNE *shoves it into her hands.*]

You're a nice-looking young man. You seem decent. Go from here. Take care of your land and your mother.

[*Two tipsy* GOVERNMENT SOLDIERS *tumble out of the bar.*]

GOVERNMENT SOLDIER #2   Just one more time. One. More. Time.

20   GOVERNMENT SOLDIER #3   Shut up! That girl doesn't want you.

GOVERNMENT SOLDIER #2   Oh yes, she do. She don't know it, but she do.

[*Drunk,* GOVERNMENT SOLDIER #2 *crumples to the ground.* GOVERNMENT SOLDIER #3 *finds this hysterically funny.*]

MAMA [*To* FORTUNE]   Go home. Have I made myself clear?

[MAMA *goes into the bar.* FORTUNE *fumes.*]

FORTUNE [*To* SOLDIER #3]   Idiot! Pick him up! God is watching you.

[SOLDIER #3 *lifts up his friend, as* SIMON, *out of breath, comes running up to* FORTUNE. JOSEPHINE *seductively fills the doorway.*]

JOSEPHINE   Ay! Ay! Don't leave me so soon. Where are you going?

25   SIMON   Fortune! Fortune!

[*The two* SOLDIERS *disappear into the night.*]

JOSEPHINE   Come back! Let me show you something sweet and pretty. Come.

[JOSEPHINE *laughs.*]

SIMON   Fortune! [*He doubles-over out of breath.*] The commander is gathering everyone. We march out tomorrow morning. The militia is moving on the next village.

30   FORTUNE   What about Salima? I can't leave her.

SIMON   But we have our orders. We have to go.

JOSEPHINE [*Seductively*]   Hello, baby. Come say hello to me.

SIMON [*His face lights up*]   God help me, look at that sweetness.

[SIMON *licks his lips.* JOSEPHINE *does several down-and-dirty pelvic thrusts.* FORTUNE *tries not to smile.*]

Quick. Let me hold some money, so I can go inside and talk to this good-

35   time girl. C'mon, c'mon . . . c'mon, Fortune. [*To* JOSEPHINE] What's your name?

JOSEPHINE   Josephine. Come inside, baby.

FORTUNE   Don't let the witch tempt you.

[JOSEPHINE *laughs and disappears inside.*]

SIMON   Let's enjoy ourselves, man, tonight . . . At least let me have one more
40   taste of pleasure. A little taste. Just the tip of my tongue. C'mon, man, let
me hold some money.

[*Laughs*]

[FORTUNE *does not respond. He silently prays.*]

How long are you gonna do this? Huh? We've been up and down the road.
It's time to consider that maybe she's dead.
FORTUNE   Then leave!

[SIMON, *frustrated, starts to go.*]

45   SIMON   This makes no sense. You can't stay here, the rebel militia are moving
this way. And if they find you, they'll kill you. We have to go by morning,
with or without her.
FORTUNE   Go!
SIMON   Are you sure? You're becoming like Emmanuel Bwiza whose wife
50   drowned in the river when we were children. Remember, the old fool got
drunk on bitterness and lost heself. Look here, Fortune, the men are making
a joke of you. They're saying, "Why won't the man just take another woman."
"Why is he chasing a damaged girl?"

[FORTUNE *enraged, grabs* SIMON *around the neck. The friends struggle.*]

FORTUNE [*Challenges*]   Say it again!
55   SIMON   It is not me saying it. It is the other men in the brigade.
FORTUNE   Who?
SIMON   If I tell you, are you going to fight all of them?
FORTUNE   Tell me who!
SIMON   Everyone. Every damn one of them. Okay.

[FORTUNE *releases* SIMON.]

60   Man, *mavi yako!*[8] It's time to forget her. I'm your cousin, and for three months
I've been walking with you, right? Got dirty, got bloody with you. But now, I'm
begging you, stop looking. It's time.
FORTUNE   No, I've prayed on this.
SIMON   Come out of the rain. We'll go inside and spend the last of our
65   money, and forget her. C'mon, Fortune. Let's get stupid drunk. Huh? Huh?
C'mon.

[SIMON *tries to drag* FORTUNE *into the bar.* FORTUNE *resists. Fuming, he
raises his fist to* SIMON.]

8. Shit (Swahili).

If you are angry, then be angry at the men who took her. Think about how they did you, they reached right into your pocket and stole from you. I know Salima since we were children. I love her the same as you. She'd
70 want you to avenge her honor. That is the only way to heal your soul.

[FORTUNE *contemplates his words.*]

FORTUNE   Kill?
SIMON   Yes.

[FORTUNE *laughs ironically.*]

FORTUNE   We are farmers. What are we doing? They tell us shoot and we shoot. But for what are we getting? Salima? A better crop? No, man, we're
75 moving further and further away from home. I want my wife! That's all. I want my family.
SIMON   The commander gave us orders to kill all deserters.
FORTUNE   Are you going to kill me?

[*A moment.*]

SIMON   I wouldn't have said it a month ago, but I'll say it now. She's gone.

[SIMON *walks off into the darkness.* FORTUNE *stands outside the bar in the pouring rain.*
Gunfire. A firefight. The sounds of the forest.]

Scene 4

The bar. CHRISTIAN, *drunk and haggard, is in the middle of an energetic story. He stands at the bar nursing a beer.* MR. HARARI, SOPHIE *and* MAMA *stand around listening.*

CHRISTIAN [*With urgency*]   No, no, no . . . listen, listen to me, I've just come from there, and it's true. I saw a boy, take a machete to a man, sever his neck, a clean blow, and lift the head in the air like a trophy. May God be my witness. Men were hollering: "We strong warriors, we taste victory. We will kill!"
5 MAMA   Shh, keep it down?!
CHRISTIAN   Oh shit, my hand, my hand is still shaking. This . . . this man Osembenga is evil. He plays at democracy. This word we bandy about, "democracy," and the first opportunity we get, we spit on our neighbors and why? Because he has cattle and I don't. Because he is and I am not. But
10 nobody has and nobody will have, except for men like you, Mr. Harari, who have the good sense to come and go, and not give a damn.
MAMA   Oh, hush up.
CHRISTIAN   But we have to pretend that all this ugliness means nothing. We wash the blood off with buckets of frigid water, and whitewash our walls.
15 Our leaders tell us: "Follow my rules, your life will be better," their doctors say, "Take this pill, your life will be better," "Plant these seeds, your life will be better," "Read this book, your life will be better," "Kill your neighbor, your life will be better—"

MAMA   Stop. Take it outside. You know I don't allow this talk in here. My
20   doors are open to everybody. And that way trouble doesn't settle here.
CHRISTIAN   Well, someone has to say it, otherwise what? We let it go on.
Huh?
MAMA   Professor, enough! Stop it now. Leave the philosophizing and preaching to the wretched politicians. I mean it! I won't have it here!
25   CHRISTIAN   One day it will be at your door, Mama.
MAMA   And then I'll shut it. People come here to leave behind what ever
mess they've made out there. That includes you, professor.

> [*Two* REBEL SOLDIERS, *fresh from battle, appear from the back of the bar in
> various stages of undress.* JOSEPHINE *and* KISEMBE, *doped-up and on edge,
> also enter from the back.* KISEMBE *has scary unpredictable energy.* JOSE-
> PHINE *buttons his shirt. He pushes her away.*]

Sophie, turn on the music.

> [SOPHIE *turns on the radio. Congolese hip-hop music plays.* CHRISTIAN
> *attempts to disappear behind his drink.* SOPHIE *stands behind the bar, dry-
> ing glasses, trying not to be noticed.* MAMA *walks over to greet the men. The
> Parrot squawks.*]

Colonel Kisembe, I hope my girls gave you good company.
30   KISEMBE   Very. It is good to be back, Mama. Where's everyone?
MAMA   You tell me. It's been this way for a week. I haven't seen but a handful
of miners. I bake bread and it goes stale.
KISEMBE   It is Commander Osembenga. He is giving us some trouble.
CHRISTIAN   He's a crazy bastard!
35   KISEMBE   His men set fire to several of our villages, now everyone has fled
deeper into the bush.
MAMA   I saw smoke over the trees.
REBEL SOLDIER #3   The mission. They burn everything to save bullets.

> [SOPHIE *gasps and covers her mouth.*]

KISEMBE   They took machetes to anything that moves. This is their justice.

> [JOSEPHINE *spots* MR. HARARI. *She is torn about where to place her
> affection.*]

40   Believe me, when we find Osembenga and his collaborators, he will be
shown the same mercy he showed our people. It's what they deserve. [*To*
CHRISTIAN] Am I right? You? Am I right?
CHRISTIAN [*Reluctantly*]   You are right. But—
KISEMBE   I'm sorry. It's how it has to be. They have done this to us. I see you
45   agree, Mama.
MAMA   Of course.

> [*Everyone in the bar grows uneasy, afraid of* KISEMBE's *intense erratic
> energy. They're barely listening to his rhetoric, instead focused on trying
> not to set him off.*]

KISEMBE   They say we are the renegades. We don't respect the rule of law . . .
but how else do we protect ourselves against their aggression? Huh? How do
we feed our families? Ay? They bring soldiers from Uganda, drive us from our
land and make us refugees . . . and then turn us into criminals when we protest or try to protect ourselves. How can we let the government carve up our
most valuable land to serve to companies in China. It's our land. Ask the
Mbuti,[9] they can describe every inch of the forest as if it were their own
flesh. Am I telling the truth?

MAMA   Here's to the truth!

[KISEMBE, *pleased with his own words, places a cigarette in his mouth. A
young* REBEL SOLDIER *quickly lights it for him.* KISEMBE *challenges* CHRIS-
TIAN *with his eyes.* CHRISTIAN *averts his gaze. He nervously raises his glass.*]

CHRISTIAN   The truth!

[*A moment.* MR. HARARI *uses the awkward silence to interject.*]

MR. HARARI   Has, um, Osembenga shut down production at Yaka-yaka mine?

KISEMBE   And you are?

MR. HARARI   I'm sorry, Colonel, may I offer you my card?

[MR. HARARI *passes* KISEMBE *his card.* KISEMBE *examines it.*]

KISEMBE   Ha-ra-i?

MR. HARARI   Aziz Harari. Yes. Please. I handle mostly minerals, some precious stones, but I have contacts for everything. My mobile is always on.
Let me buy you a drink.

[MR. HARARI *signals* SOPHIE *to bring a bottle of whiskey over to* KISEMBE.
She pours two glasses.]

KISEMBE   Thank you.

[KISEMBE *takes the bottle of whiskey and slips the card into his pocket, by
way of dismissing* MR. HARARI, *who backs away.* MAMA *wraps her arms
around* KISEMBE'*s shoulder.*]

MAMA   Come, gentlemen. You will be treated like warriors here.

KISEMBE   I wish we could stay all night, but duty calls.

[KISEMBE *signals to his men. They follow him toward the door.*]

MAMA   No! So soon? Josephine!

[MAMA *signals to* JOSEPHINE, *who refuses to budge. Instead she sits on*
MR. HARARI'*s lap.* MR. HARARI *tenses.*]

MR. HARARI [*Whispers*]   Go!

JOSEPHINE   No.

9. See note 5, p. 1688.

[KISEMBE *and his men collect their guns and leave. A moment. A huge sigh of relief. Exhale.* CHRISTIAN *slaps his thigh and stands. He does a spot-on impersonation of the haughty swagger of the rebel leader.*]

70 CHRISTIAN "Girl. Quick. Quick. Bring me a beer, so I can wash it down with Osembenga's blood."

[SOPHIE *and* JOSEPHINE *laugh.* MR. HARARI *is too nervous to enjoy the show.*]

SOPHIE Yes, Colonel.
CHRISTIAN [*Continuing to imitate* KISEMBE] "Woman, are you addressing me as 'Colonel'?"
75 SOPHIE Yes, Colonel.
CHRISTIAN "Don't you know who I am? I am from here on in to be known as the Great Commander of All Things Wise and Wonderful, with the Heart of a Hundred Lions in Battle."
SOPHIE I'm so sorry, Great Commander of All Things Wise and . . .
80 CHRISTIAN "Wonderful with the Heart of a Hundred Lions in Battle. Don't you forget that!"

[CHRISTIAN *does a playful mocking warrior dance.* JOSEPHINE *taps out a rhythm on the counter. A Drummer joins in.* MAMA *laughs.*]

MAMA You are a fool!

[MAMA *retreats to the back with empty bottles. Unseen, the formidable* COMMANDER OSEMBENGA *and a sullen* GOVERNMENT SOLDIER, LAURENT, *enter. They wear black berets and muddy uniforms. A moment.* CHRISTIAN *stops his dance abruptly.*]

OSEMBENGA Don't stop you. Go on.
CHRISTIAN Commander Osembenga.
85 OSEMBENGA Continue.

[OSEMBENGA *smiles and claps his hands.* CHRISTIAN *continues his dance, now drained of its verve and humor.* OSEMBENGA *laughs. Then he stops clapping, releasing* CHRISTIAN *from the dance.* CHRISTIAN, *humiliated, retreats to the bar.* OSEMBENGA *acknowledges* MR. HARARI *with a polite nod.*]

Where is Mama?
SOPHIE She's in the back. [*Yells*] Mama! Mama!
OSEMBENGA [*Suspiciously*] I saw a truck leaving? Whose was it?
CHRISTIAN [*Lying*] Uh . . . aid worker.
90 OSEMBENGA Oh? Good-looking vehicle. Expensive. Eight cylinders.
CHRISTIAN Yes.
OSEMBENGA Sturdy. It looked like it could take the road during rainy season.
CHRISTIAN Probably.

[OSEMBENGA *approves.*]

95 SOPHIE   Mama!

MAMA [*Entering from off, annoyed*]   Why are you calling me?! You know I'm busy.

[MAMA *stops short when she sees* OSEMBENGA. *She conjures a warm smile.*]

[*Surprised*] Commander Osembenga. *Karibu.* [*Nervously*] We . . . how are you?

[MAMA *glances at the door.*]

OSEMBENGA   Run ragged, if the truth be told. Two Primus, cold, and a pack
100   of cigarettes.

[MAMA *directs* SOPHIE *to get the beer.* OSEMBENGA *strokes* MAMA's *back-side. She playfully swats away his hand.*]

You look good, today.

MAMA   You should have seen me yesterday.

OSEMBENGA   I wish I had, but I was otherwise engaged.

MAMA   Yeah? We heard you had some trouble. Kisembe.

105 OSEMBENGA   Is that what is being said? Not trouble! Slight irritation. But you'd
    be pleased to know, we're close to shutting down Kisembe and his militia. We
    finally have him on the run. He won't be troubling the people here very much
    longer.

MAMA   Is that so?

110 OSEMBENGA   My guess, he's heading east. He'll need to come through here.
    He can't hide from me. It's the only passable road.

MAMA   I saw smoke over the trees.

OSEMBENGA   That bastard and his cronies attacked the hospital.

MR. HARARI   The hospital? Why?

115 OSEMBENGA   Because they are imbeciles. I don't know. Looking for medi-
    cine. Speed. Morphine. Who the hell knows? They rounded-up and killed
    mostly Hema patients. [*To* SOPHIE] Tsst. Tsst. You, bring me some ground-
    nuts. [*To* MAMA] It was chaos. When we arrived we found the hospital staff
    tied by their hands and cut up like meat.

120 LAURENT   One man's heart was missing.

[SOPHIE *covers her mouth with disgust.*]

MAMA [*Disgusted*]   What?

OSEMBENGA   And he accuses us of being the barbarians? Don't worry, I've
    given my soldiers the liberty to control the situation. I am afraid this is
    what must be done. They force our hand.

[OSEMBENGA *takes sadistic delight in this notion.* SOPHIE *cringes as she
places beer and peanuts on the table for the* SOLDIERS. OSEMBENGA *grabs*
SOPHIE's *wrist, and pulls her toward him.*]

125 [*Laughing*] Come here, you pretty pretty thing. What? You don't like what
    I'm wearing?

[SOPHIE *tries to gently pry herself loose.* CHRISTIAN, *sensing tension, moves toward them.* LAURENT *rises.*]

You don't like men in uniforms? You don't like men, maybe. Is that it?

[*A moment.* SOPHIE *now struggles to free herself.*]

MAMA [*Sensing the tension*]   Sophie, come here. Let—
OSEMBENGA [*Smiling*]   Hey. We are talking. We are talking, yeah?

[OSEMBENGA *pulls* SOPHIE *onto his lap. He shoves his hand up her skirt. She gasps and struggles harder.*]

130   Am I ugly? Is that what you're trying to tell me.
SOPHIE [*Hisses*]   Let go of me!

[SOPHIE *violently pushes away from* OSEMBENGA. CHRISTIAN *rushes in to protect her, as* OSEMBENGA *lunges for her.* MAMA *blocks* OSEMBENGA's *path.* LAURENT *rises to aid* OSEMBENGA.]

MAMA   Sophie, shush! Enough. Commander, ignore her, there are other girls for you. Come. Come.
OSEMBENGA   Bring this girl around back, my men will teach her a lesson.
135   She needs proper schooling.

[LAURENT *shoves* CHRISTIAN *out of the way, and grabs* SOPHIE. *This is the first time we've seen* MAMA *scared.* SOPHIE *spits on* OSEMBENGA's *feet.*]

MAMA   Sophie.

[MAMA, *horrified, bends down and wipes the spit from* OSEMBENGA's *shoes.* OSEMBENGA *glares at* SOPHIE.]

SOPHIE [*Shouting as if possessed*]   I am dead.
MAMA   No!
SOPHIE [*Possessed*]   I am dead! Fuck a corpse! What would that make you?

[OSEMBENGA *is thrown.*]

140   OSEMBENGA   I'm trying to bring order here, and this girl spits on my feet. Do you see what I have to deal with? Do you? This is the problem.

[CHRISTIAN *quickly pulls* SOPHIE *away.*]

MAMA   Gentlemen, Commander, this is not our way . . . we want you to be comfortable and happy here, let me show you the pleasures of Mama Nadi's.

[*A moment. A standoff.*]

145   OSEMBENGA   Then, Mama, you show me.

[OSEMBENGA *checks his anger. He smiles.* MAMA *understands. She follows* OSEMBENGA *into the back.* SOPHIE *desperately scrubs her hands in the basin.* MR. HARARI *pours himself a healthy drink.*]

MR. HARARI   Okay. Let's not overreact. Everything's going to be fine.

CHRISTIAN [*Whispers*]   Sophie, are you crazy? What are you doing?

[JOSEPHINE *compassionately stops* SOPHIE, *who is scrubbing her hands raw.*]

JOSEPHINE   Stop it. Stop it. [*Hugs* SOPHIE *tightly*] Shh. Shh.

[MAMA *furiously reenters. She slaps* SOPHIE *across the face.*]

MAMA   Next time I will put you out for the vultures. I don't care if that was
150   the man who slit your mother's throat. Do you understand me? You could
have gotten all of us killed. What do you have to say to me?

SOPHIE   Sorry, Mama.

MAMA   You're lucky the commander is generous. I had to plead with him to
give you another chance. Now you go in there, and you make sure that his
155   cock is clean.[1] Am I making myself clear?

SOPHIE   Please—

MAMA   Now get outta my sight.

[MAMA *grabs* SOPHIE *and thrusts her into the back.* MR. HARARI, CHRIS-
TIAN *and* JOSEPHINE *stare at* MAMA. *A moment.* MAMA *goes behind the bar
and pours herself a drink.*]

What?

CHRISTIAN   Don't make her do that! This girl is—

160   MAMA   What if Osembenga had been more than offended. What then? Who
would protect my business if he turned on me? It is but for the grace of
God, that he didn't beat her to the ground. And now I have to give away
business to keep him and his filthy soldiers happy.

CHRISTIAN   But if—

165   MAMA   Not a word from you. You have a problem, then leave.

CHRISTIAN   "Business." When you say it, it sounds vulgar, polluted.

MAMA   Are you going to lecture me, professor? Turn your dirty finger away
from me.

[CHRISTIAN *is stung by her words.*]

CHRISTIAN   Mama?

170   MAMA   What, chérie? (*Laughs*)

CHRISTIAN [*Wounded*]   Forget it! Bring me another beer. There's my money.
[*Slams the money down on the counter*] You understand *that*, don't you? You
like that? There's your fucking money.

[MAMA *slowly picks up the money and puts it in her apron. She ceremoniously cracks open a beer and places it in front of* CHRISTIAN.]

1. Sophie must perform fellatio on Osembenga.

MAMA Drink up, you fucking drunk.
175 CHRISTIAN What's wrong with you?

> [CHRISTIAN *snatches up his beer. He drinks it down quickly and deliberately.*]

MAMA You men kill me. You come in here, drink your beer, take your pleasure, and then wanna judge the way I run my "business." The front door swings both ways. I don't force anyone's hand. My girls, Emilene, Mazima, Josephine, ask them, they'd rather be here, than back out there in their villages
180 where they are taken without regard. They're safer with me than in their own homes, because this country is picked clean, while men, poets like you, drink beer, eat nuts and look for some place to disappear. And I am without mercy, is that what you're saying? Because I give them something other than a beggar's cup. [*With ferocity*] I didn't come here as Mama Nadi, I found her the
185 same way miners find their wealth in the muck. I stumbled off of that road without two twigs to start a fire. I turned a basket of sweets and soggy biscuits into a business. I don't give a damn what any of you think. This is my place, Mama Nadi's.

> [CHRISTIAN *crosses to leave.*]

Of course.

> [MAMA's *words stop him.*]

CHRISTIAN

190 The black rope of water towing
A rusted ferry fighting the current of time,
An insatiable flow,
Drifting
Without enough kerosene to get through the dark nights,
195 The destination always a port away.

MAMA [*Spits*] It's wind. If you can't place it on a scale, it's nothing.

> [CHRISTIAN *heads for the door.*]

You'll be back when you need another beer.
CHRISTIAN I don't think so.

> [CHRISTIAN *absorbs the blow, then storms outside in a huff.* JOSEPHINE *and* MR. HARARI *exit to the back.* MAMA *is left alone to contemplate her actions.*]

Scene 5

Outside the bar. OSEMBENGA *and* LAURENT *stumble out of* MAMA NADI's *place, laughing.*

OSEMBENGA I always like the taste of something new.
FORTUNE [*Approaching them*] Commander! Commander!
OSEMBENGA Yes?

FORTUNE I'm sorry to disturb you, but I . . .
5 OSEMBENGA Yes?
FORTUNE I saw Jerome Kisembe.
OSEMBENGA Who are you?
FORTUNE I am Fortune Mukengeshayi, I'm with your brigade.
OSEMBENGA Jerome Kisembe?
10 FORTUNE Yes . . . He was inside Mama Nadi's.
OSEMBENGA Inside here?
FORTUNE Yes, I saw him. She was hiding him. I heard him say the rebels are
  heading south along this road. He will join them tomorrow.
OSEMBENGA Mama Nadi's?! Here?!
15 FORTUNE He drove south in a white truck! Please, she is holding my wife. I
  just want to get her back.
OSEMBENGA [*To* LAURENT] Quick, quick. We'll go after him. Call ahead, prepare the brigade to move out.

[*They quickly exit.*]

Scene 6

Dawn. Morning light pours into the bar. MR. HARARI *paces. His traveling bag is
perched near the door.* MAMA *wipes down the bar.*

MAMA Would you like a drink while you wait?

[*Artillery fire, closer than expected.*]

MR. HARARI Yes. Thank you. A little palm wine.

[MAMA *settles her nerves, and pours them both a palm wine.*]

MAMA It looks like it's going to rain, you might wanna wait until—
MR. HARARI I can't. Thank goodness, I found a lift with one of the aid work-
5 ers. My driver, fucking idiot, took off last night. [*Jokes*] Apparently he
  doesn't care for the sound of gunfire.
MAMA I told you, you didn't pay him enough.
MR. HARARI This fucking war, ay mother, no one owns it! It's everybody's and
  nobody's.
10 MAMA Tst!
MR. HARARI It keeps fracturing and redefining itself. Militias form overnight,
  and suddenly a drunken foot soldier with a tribal vendetta is a rebel leader,
  and in possession of half of the enriched land, but you can't reason with
  him, because he's only thinking as far as his next drink.
15 MAMA Yes, and what is new?
MR. HARARI The man I shake hands with in the morning is my enemy by sun-
  down. And why? His whims. Because?! His witch doctor says I'm the enemy. I
  don't know whose hand to grease other than the one directly in front of me. At
  least I understood Mobutu's[2] brand of chaos. Now, I'm a relative beginner, I
20 must relearn the terms every few months, and make new friends, but who? It's

2. Mobuto Sese Seko (1930–97), military dictator of Zaire (the previous name of the DRC). He was
overthrown in the First Congo War and fled the region in 1997, dying of cancer soon thereafter.

difficult to say, so I must befriend everybody and nobody. And it's utterly exhausting.

MAMA   Let all the mother-hating soldiers fight it out. Cuz, in the end, do you think that will change anything here?

25 MR. HARARI   God only knows. The main road is crowded with folks heading east. There is no shame in leaving, Mama. Part of being in business is knowing when to cut your losses and get out.

MAMA   I have the only pool table in fifty kilometers. Where will people drink if anything happens to me?

30 MR. HARARI   The commander knows Kisembe was here. Eventually you must fly your colors. Take a side.

MAMA   He pays me in gold, he pays me in coltan. What is worth more? You tell me. What is their argument? I don't know. Who will win? Who cares? There's an old proverb, "Two hungry birds fight over a kernel, just then a
35 third one swoops down and carries it off. Whoops!"

MR. HARARI   You are the most devilish of optimists. You—I don't worry so much about you. But what about a lovely girl like Sophie?

[*His words hit her.* MR. HARARI *knocks back his drink, then heads for the door, looking out for his ride.*]

Until next time!

[*Distant gunfire.* MR. HARARI *anxiously stands in the doorway.* MAMA *goes to the bar, she appears conflicted. An internal battle.*]

MAMA   Ah . . . One thing, Mr. Harari. Before you leave, can I ask you a favor?
40 MR. HARARI   Of course.

[MAMA *opens the lockbox, and carefully lays out the diamond.*]

MAMA   This.

[MR. HARARI's *eyes light up.*]

MR. HARARI   Your insurance policy.

MAMA [*With irony*]   Yes. My restaurant, my garden to dig in, and a chief's fortune of cows. [*Laughs*]

45 MR. HARARI   You are ready to sell?

MAMA   Yes. Take this. [*Hands him* SOPHIE's *piece of paper*] It has the name of a man in Bunia, a doctor. [*With urgency*] He won't trouble you with questions. Use my name.

MR. HARARI   Slow, slow, what do you want me—

50 MAMA   Just listen. I want you to take her to—

MR. HARARI [*Confused*]   Josephine? [*Genuinely surprised*] Be realistic, how would a girl like Josephine survive in the city.

MAMA   No, listen—

MR. HARARI   I can't. She is a country thing, not refined at all.

55 MAMA   No, listen . . . I'm talking about Sophie. This will raise enough money for an operation, and whatever she needs to get settled.

MR. HARARI Sophie?

MAMA Yes.

MR. HARARI Why? Operation? What?

60 MAMA It's a long conversation, and there isn't time.

MR. HARARI This is more than—

MAMA Enough for a life. I know.

MR. HARARI Are you sure? This diamond will fetch a fairly decent price, you can settle over the border in Uganda. Start fresh.

65 MAMA I have ten girls here. What will I do with them? Is there enough room for all of us in the car. No. I can't go. Since I was young, people have found reasons to push me out of my home, men have laid claim to my possessions, but I am not running now. This is my place. Mama Nadi's.

MR. HARARI But I'm not—

70 MAMA You do this for me. I don't want the other women to know. So let's do this quickly.

MR. HARARI And the doctor's name is on the paper. I'm to call when I get there.

MAMA Yes. And you give Sophie the money. The money for the stone. Under-

75 stand. Promise me. It's important. All of it.

MR. HARARI . . . Yes. Are you sure?

MAMA Yes.

[MAMA *reluctantly passes the diamond to* MR. HARARI.]

Thank you. I'll get her.

[MAMA *quickly exits.* MR. HARARI *examines the diamond. An* AID WORKER *comes rushing in.*]

AID WORKER I'm loaded. We have to go now! Now! Three vehicles are com-

80 ing in fast. We can't be here.

MR. HARARI But . . . What about—

AID WORKER [*Panicked*] Now! I can't wait. C'mon. C'mon.

[*Distant gunfire.*]

MR. HARARI I have to—

AID WORKER They'll be okay. Us, men, they'll come after us—

85 MR. HARARI One minute. [*Calling to* MAMA, *off*] Mama! Mama! Come! Mama! I—

AID WORKER I have to go! I can't wait.

[*The* AID WORKER *doesn't have time to listen. He races out. The engine revs.*]

MR. HARARI Mama! Mama!

[MR. HARARI *seems torn, a moment, then he decides. He places the diamond in his pocket and leaves. Silence. Then distant gunfire.* MAMA *enters, frantically pulling* SOPHIE.]

MAMA   When you get there, he has the money to take care of everything.
90   Settle. Make a good life, hear.
SOPHIE   Why are you doing this for me?
MAMA   Stop, don't ask me stupid questions, just go. Go!

[*She tucks a piece of paper into* SOPHIE's *hand.*]

This is my cousin's wife, all I have is her address. But a motorbike will take
you. You say that I am your friend.
95 SOPHIE   Thank you, Mama. I—
MAMA   No time. You send word through Mr. Harari. Let me know that everything goes well. Okay.

[SOPHIE *hugs* MAMA. *She exits.* MAMA, *elated, goes to pour herself a celebratory drink. She doesn't see* SOPHIE *reenter until:*]

SOPHIE   He's gone.

[*The stage is flooded with intense light. The sound of chaos, shouting,
gunfire, grows with intensity.* GOVERNMENT SOLDIERS *pour in. A siege. A
white hot flash. The generator blows! Streams of natural light pour into
the bar.* FORTUNE, COMMANDER OSEMBENGA, SIMON *and* SOLDIERS *stand
over* SOPHIE *and* MAMA.]

FORTUNE   He was here! I saw him here!

[OSEMBENGA *stands over* MAMA.]

100 OSEMBENGA   This soldier said he saw Jerome Kisembe here.
MAMA   This soldier is a liar.
FORTUNE   I swear to you! He was here with two men. The same night you
were here, Commander!
MAMA   We are friends. Why would I lie to you? This soldier has been menac-
105   ing us for days. He's crazy. A liar!
FORTUNE   This woman is the devil! She's a witch! She enchanted my wife.
OSEMBENGA   Again. Where is Kisembe?
MAMA   I don't know. Why would I play these games? Don't you think I know
better. He is a simple digger. And me, I wouldn't give him what he wants,
110   so he tells tales. Commander, we are friends. You know me. I am with you.
Of course. Come, let me get you some whiskey—
OSEMBENGA   *Funga kinua yaké!*[3]

[OSEMBENGA *signals to his* SOLDIERS. *Chaos. They find* MAMA's *lockbox,
break it open and take her money. A* SOLDIER *drags* JOSEPHINE *from the
back. They throw* MAMA, SOPHIE *and* JOSEPHINE *onto the floor.*]

MAMA   NO!
OSEMBENGA   This can stop. Tell me where I can find Kisembe.
115 MAMA   I don't know where he is.

3. Shut her mouth (Swahili).

OSEMBENGA [*Points to Josephine*]   Take that one.

> [*A* SOLDIER *grabs* JOSEPHINE. *He is ready to sexually violate her.* JOSE-
> PHINE *desperately struggles to get away. The* SOLDIER *tears away at her
> clothing. The women scream, fight.*]

JOSEPHINE   No! No! Tell him, Mama. He was here.

> [OSEMBENGA *turns his rage on* MAMA.]

MAMA   Please!

> [SALIMA *slowly enters as if in a trance. A pool of blood forms in the
> middle of her dress, blood drips down her legs.*]

SALIMA [*Screams*]   STOP! Stop it!
120 FORTUNE   Salima!
SALIMA [*Screams*]   For the love of God, stop this! Haven't you done enough
to us. Enough! Enough!

> [*The* SOLDIERS *stop abruptly, shocked by* SALIMA's *defiant voice.*]

MAMA   What did you do?!

> [FORTUNE *violently pushes the* SOLDIERS *out of the way and races to* SALIMA.]

FORTUNE   Salima! Salima!
125 SALIMA   Fortune.

> [FORTUNE *scoops* SALIMA *into his arms.* MAMA *breaks away from the*
> SOLDIERS.]

MAMA   Quick go get some hot water and cloth. Salima look at me. You have
to look at me, keep your eyes on me. Don't think of anything else. C'mon
look at me.

> [SALIMA *smiles triumphantly. She takes* FORTUNE's *hand.*]

SALIMA [*To* OSEMBENGA, *the* SOLDIERS *and* FORTUNE]   You will not fight your
130 battles on my body any more.

> [SALIMA *collapses to the floor.* FORTUNE *cradles her in his arms. She dies.
> Blackout.*]

Scene 7

The sounds of the tropical Ituri rain forest. The bar. The bird quietly chatters.
SOPHIE *methodically sweeps the dirt floor with a thatched broom.* JOSEPHINE
washes the countertop. MAMA *stands in the doorway.*

SOPHIE [*Sings*]

Have another beer, my friend,
Douse the fire of your fears, my friend,
Get drunk and foolish on the moment,
Brush aside the day's heavy judgment.

[MAMA *anxiously watches the road. Excited, she spots a passing truck.*]

SOPHIE [*Sings*]

5   Cuz you come here to forget,
       You say drive away all regret,
       And dance like it's the ending . . .

MAMA   Dust rising.
JOSEPHINE [*Eagerly*]   Who is it?
10 MAMA [*Excited*]   I don't know. Blue helmets heading north. Hello? Hello?

[MAMA *seductively waves. Nothing. Disappointed, she retreats to the table.*]

Damn them. How the hell are we supposed to do business? They're draining our blood.
JOSEPHINE   Hey, Sophie, give me a hand.

[JOSEPHINE *and* SOPHIE *pick up the basin of water and exit.* MAMA *buries
her face in her hands.* CHRISTIAN *enters. He whistles.* MAMA *looks up,
doing her best to contain her excitement.* CHRISTIAN *brushes the travel
dust from his brand-new brown suit.*]

MAMA   Look who it is. The wind could have brought me a paying customer,
15   but instead I get you.
CHRISTIAN   Lovely. I'm glad to see after all these months you haven't lost any
       of your wonderful charm. You're looking fine as ever.
MAMA   Yeah? I'm making do with nothing.

[CHRISTIAN *smiles.*]

Who'd you bribe to get past the roadblock?
20 CHRISTIAN   I have my ways, and as it turns out the officer on duty has a fond-
       ness for Nigerian soap operas and Belgian chocolates.

[MAMA *finally lets herself smile.*]

I'm surprised to find you're still here.
MAMA   Were you expecting me to disappear into the forest and live off roots
       with the Mbuti? I'm staying put. The war's on the back of the gold diggers,
25   you follow them you follow trouble. What are you wearing?
CHRISTIAN   You like?
MAMA   They didn't have your size?
CHRISTIAN   Very funny. Chérie, your eyes tell me everything I need to know.
MAMA   Tst!
30 CHRISTIAN   What you have something in your teeth?
MAMA   Business must be good. Yeah?

CHRISTIAN   No, but a man's got to have at least one smart change of clothing, even in times like these . . . I heard what happened.

[*A moment*]

MAMA   *C'est la vie.*[4] Salima was a good girl.

[SOPHIE *enters*]

35 SOPHIE   Uncle!

[*They exchange a long hug.*]

CHRISTIAN   Sophie, *mon amour.* I have something for you.
SOPHIE   *Un livre?*[5]
CHRISTIAN   . . . Yes.
SOPHIE   *Merci.*

[*He hands her a package. She rips open the brown paper. She pulls out a
handful of magazines and a book.*]

40 CHRISTIAN   And this. A letter from your mother. Don't expect too much.

[SOPHIE, *shocked, grabs the letter.*]

SOPHIE [*Overwhelmed*]   Excuse me.
CHRISTIAN   Go!

[SOPHIE *exits*]

MAMA   I'm surprised to see you. I thought you were through with me.
CHRISTIAN   I was. I didn't come here to see you.
45 MAMA [*Wounded*]   Oh?
CHRISTIAN   And—
MAMA   Yes?

[*A moment*]

. . . Hello, yes?
CHRISTIAN [*Hesitantly, but genuinely*]   I . . . debated whether even to come,
50   but damn it, I missed you.

[MAMA *laughs.*]

You have nothing to say to me?
MAMA   Do you really want me to respond to your foolishness?
CHRISTIAN [*Wounded*]   You are a mean-spirited woman. I don't know why I
expect the sun to shine where only mold thrives.

4. That's life (French).
5. A book (French).

[*His frankness catches* MAMA *off guard.*]

55 MAMA I don't like your tone.

CHRISTIAN We have unfinished "business"!

MAMA Look around, there's no business here. There's nothing left.

[CHRISTIAN *looks around. He looks at* MAMA. *He shakes his head and smiles.*]

CHRISTIAN [*Blurts*] Then, Mama, settle down with me.

MAMA Go home!

60 CHRISTIAN What?!

MAMA You heard me, go the hell home. I don't wanna hear it. I have too much on my mind for this shit.

CHRISTIAN That's all you have to say. I looked death in the eye on the river road. A boy nearly took out my liver with a bayonet. I'm serious. I drop and
65 kiss the ground that he was a romantic, and spared me when I told him I was a man on a mission.

[MAMA *cracks open a cold beer.*]

MAMA It's cold, why can't you be happy with that?

CHRISTIAN Because, it isn't what I want? Bring me a Fanta, please.

[MAMA *smiles and gets him a Fanta.*]

MAMA I'll put on some music.

70 CHRISTIAN What's the point, you never dance with me.

[MAMA *laughs.*]

MAMA Oh shut up, relax. I'll roast some groundnuts. Huh?

[*A moment*]

CHRISTIAN Why not us?

MAMA What would we do, professor? How would it work? The two of us? Imagine. You'd wander. I'd get impatient. I see how men do. We'd argue, fight
75 and I'd grow resentful. You'd grow jealous. We know this story. It's tiresome.

CHRISTIAN You know everything, don't you? And if I said, I'd stay, help you run things. Make a legitimate business. A shop. Fix the door. Hang the mirror. Protect you. Make love to you.

MAMA Do I look like I need protection?

80 CHRISTIAN No, but you look like you need someone to make love to you.

MAMA Do I now?

CHRISTIAN Yes. How long has it been, Mama, since you allowed a man to touch you? Huh? A man like me, who isn't looking through you for a way home.

[MAMA *laughs at him.*]

85 MAMA   Enough. God. You're getting pathetic.

CHRISTIAN   Maybe. But damn it against my better judgment . . . I love you.

MAMA [*With contempt*]   Love. What's the point in all this shit? Love is too fragile a sentiment for out here. Think about what happens to the things we "love." It isn't worth it. "Love." It is a poisonous word. It will change us.
90   It will cost us more than it returns. Don't you think? It'll be an unnecessary burden for people like us. And it'll eventually strangle us!

CHRISTIAN   Do you hear what you're saying?

MAMA   It's the truth. Deal with it!

CHRISTIAN   Hm . . . Why do I bother. If you can't put it on a scale it is noth-
95   ing, right?! Pardon me.

[CHRISTIAN, *flustered by her response, walks to the door.*]

MAMA   Where are you going?!

[MAMA *watches, suddenly panicked.*]

Hey! You heard me. Don't be a baby.

[CHRISTIAN *stops before exiting.*]

CHRISTIAN   We joke. It's fun. But honestly I'm worn bare. I've been driving this route a long time and I'm getting to the age where I'd like to sleep in
100   the same bed every night. I need familiar company, food that is predictable, conversation that's too easy. If you don't know what I'm talking about, then I'll go. But, please, I'd like to have the truth . . . why not us?

[*A moment.* MAMA *says nothing.* CHRISTIAN *starts to leave, but her words catch him.*]

MAMA [*With surprising vulnerability*]   I'm ruined. [*Louder*] I'm ruined.

[*He absorbs her words.*]

CHRISTIAN   God, I don't know what those men did to you, but I'm sorry for it.
105   I may be an idiot for saying so, but I think we, and I speak as a man, can do better.

[*He goes to comfort her. She pulls away until he's forced to hold her in a tight embrace.*]

MAMA   No! Don't touch me! No!

[*She struggles to free herself, but eventually succumbs to his heartfelt embrace. She breaks down in tears. He kisses her.*]

SOPHIE [*Entering*]   Oh, I'm sorry. [*Smiles to herself*]

MAMA [*Pulling away*]   Why are you standing there looking like a lost elephant.
110   SOPHIE   Sorry, Mama.

[SOPHIE *slips out.*]

MAMA   Don't think this changes anything.

CHRISTIAN   Wait there.

MAMA   Where are you going?

[CHRISTIAN *straightens his suit.*]

CHRISTIAN   I swear to you, this is the last time I'll ask.

115   A branch lists to and fro,
         An answer to the insurgent wind,
         A circle dance,
         Grace nearly broken,
         But it ends peacefully,
120   Stillness welcome.

[CHRISTIAN *holds his hand out to* MAMA. *A moment. Finally, she takes his hand. He pulls her into his arms. They begin to dance. At first she's a bit stiff and resistant, but slowly she gives in. Possibility. Guitar music: "A Rare Bird" guitar solo.* SOPHIE *drags* JOSEPHINE *into the room. They watch the pair dance.*]

JOSEPHINE [*Joyfully*]   Go, Mama.

PARROT   Mama! Primus! Mama! Primus!

[MAMA *and* CHRISTIAN *continue their measured dance. The lights slowly fade.*]

THE END

Selected Bibliographies

EDWARD ALBEE

The Zoo Story was first published in 1960 in the journal *Evergreen Review* and soon thereafter appeared in an acting edition from Dramatists Play Service, Inc., and then in a trade edition from Coward-McCann, Inc. The version published here is the one Albee deemed "definitive" when he assembled the first volume of his *Collected Plays* (2004). An updated version, now part of *At Home at the Zoo*, appears in a trade edition published in 2008. Albee's collection of essays, *Stretching My Mind* (2005), contains several pieces relevant to *Zoo Story*. Former *New York Times* theater critic Mel Gussow's biography, *Edward Albee: A Singular Journey* (1999), remains the primary source of information about Albee's life and career; obituaries and career assessments from the *New York Times* in September 2016 provide additional details. Stephen J. Bottoms's study, *Playing Underground: A Critical History of the 1960s Off-Off-Broadway Movement* (2004), Matthew Roudané's *American Drama Since 1960: A Critical History* (1996), Ruby Cohn and Bernard F. Dukore, eds., *Twentieth Century Drama: England, Ireland, the United States* (1966), and especially C. W. E. Bigsby, *A Critical Introduction to Twentieth-Century American Drama* (1984) all provide useful examinations of Albee in context. There is no recent bibliography of Albee's own writings and Albee scholarship; older volumes include Richard E. Amacher and Margaret Rule, *Edward Albee at Home and Abroad: A Bibliography* (1973), Charles Lee Green, *Edward Albee: An Annotated Bibliography 1968–1977* (1980), Rich-

ard Tyce, *Edward Albee: A Bibliography* (1986), and Scott Giantvalley, *Edward Albee: A Reference Guide* (1987). The first New York production of *Zoo Story* received coverage in all the leading daily and weekly papers; notable reviews include those by Harold Clurman, "Theatre," in the *Nation*; Donald Malcolm, "And Moreover . . ." in the *New Yorker*; Richard Watts Jr., "Two on the Aisle: An Absorbing Off-Broadway Evening" in the *New York Post*; Burm., "Beckett-Albee Dual-Bill" in *Variety*; Brooks Atkinson, "Theatre: A Double Bill Off Broadway" and "Village Vagrants: Samuel Beckett's 'Krapp's Last Tape' in Double Bill at the Provincetown," in the *New York Times*; Walter Kerr, "Off Broadway: Two One-Act Plays Given at Provincetown Playhouse" in the *New York Herald Tribune*; and Jerry Tallmer, "Edward Albee's *The Zoo Story* and Samuel Beckett's *Krapp's Last Tape*" in the *Village Voice*. Albee has given numerous interviews over the course of his career. Among those most relevant to *Zoo Story* in published volumes are: with Michael E. Rutenberg, *Edward Albee: Playwright in Protest* (1969); with Jackson R. Bryer in *The Playwright's Art: Conversations with Contemporary American Dramatists* (1995); with David Savran in *The Playwright's Voice: American Dramatists on Memory, Writing and the Politics of Culture* (1999); with Matthew Roudané in Philip C. Kolin and J. Madison Davis, eds., *Critical Essays on Edward Albee*; and throughout Philip C. Kolin, ed., *Conversations with Edward Albee* (1988). Useful interviews in newspapers and journals include: with Jerry Tallmer in the *New York Post* (1962); with David

Crespy and Lincoln Konkle in *Text and Presentation* (2013); with Robert Hurwitt in *SFGate* (2009); and with Jesse Green in the *New York Times* (2004). Toby Zinman offers a brief, synthetic overview of the play in her study *Edward Albee* (2008). Notable additional volumes on Albee include Anne Paolucci, *From Tension to Tonic: The Plays of Edward Albee* (2000); Julian N. Wasserman, *Edward Albee: An Interview and Essays* (1983); and Bruce J. Mann, ed., *Edward Albee: A Casebook* (2003). *The Cambridge Companion to Edward Albee*, ed. Stephen J. Bottoms (2005) includes a number of insightful critical discussions, while Rakesh H. Solomon's *Albee in Performance* (2010) offers invaluable portraits of Albee's work as a director. Among many articles on *Zoo Story* in scholarly journals are R. F. Dietrich, "Jesus as Narrator: Albee's Case for Fiction in *The Zoo Story*" (1977); Lucina Gabbard, "At the Zoo: From O'Neill to Albee" (1976); Rose A. Zimbardo, "Symbolism and Naturalism in Edward Albee's *The Zoo Story*" (1962); Robert B. Bennett, "Tragic Vision in *The Zoo Story*" (1977); Robert S. Wallace, "*The Zoo Story*: Albee's Attack on Fiction" (1973); and Mary M. Nilan, "Albee's *The Zoo Story*: Alienated Man and the Nature of Love" (1973). Stephen Bottoms provides updated perspectives on Martin Esslin's *The Theatre of the Absurd* in his essay "The Garden in the Machine: Edward Albee, Sam Shepard and the American Absurd," in *Rethinking the Theatre of the Absurd: Ecology, the Environment and the Greening of the Modern Stage*, eds. Carl Lavery and Clare Finburgh (2015). Alan Schneider's thoughts on Albee are contained in his memoir *Entrances: An American Director's Journey* (1985), to which Albee contributed a Preface.

TAWFIQ AL-HAKIM

In addition to the 1977 translation by M. M. Badawi included here, *Song of Death* has been translated into English by C. W. R. Long (1972) and Denys Johnson-Davies (1973). One of the most comprehensive treatments in English of Tawfiq al-Hakim and his contribution to Egyptian theater is found in Badawi's seminal work *Modern Arabic Drama in Egypt* (1987). In this study, Badawi provides a thorough overview of al-Hakim's different developmental stages as a playwright and traces his dramatic production from its earliest experiments to the last stages. *Tawfiq al-Hakim: A Reader's Guide*, ed. William Maynard Hutchins (2003), discusses al-Hakim's plays, novels, and short stories and includes an excellent annotated biography and chronology of the writer's life and work. Other studies of al-Hakim's drama include Richard Long, *Tawfiq*

al-Hakim, Playwright of Egypt* (1979); Roger Allen, "Egyptian Drama after the Revolution" (1979); Paul Starkey, "Tawfiq Al-Hakim: Leading Playwright of the Arab World" (1989); and Ali al-Ra'i, "Arab Drama Since the Thirties," in *The Cambridge History of Arabic Literature: Modern Arabic Literature*, ed. M. M. Badawi (1992). Those interested in reading more of al-Hakim's works will find Denys Johnson-Davies, ed., *The Essential Tawfiq al-Hakim: Plays, Fiction, Autobiography* (2008) an excellent resource.

SAMUEL BECKETT

Samuel Beckett's plays are published in the United States by Grove/Atlantic and in Britain by Faber and Faber. The most complete biography of Beckett, written with the author's approval, is James Knowlson, *Damned to Fame: The Life of Samuel Beckett* (1996), which has supplemented and, in the view of most Beckett scholars, superseded Deirdre Bair's earlier *Samuel Beckett: A Biography* (1978). Other important biographies written since Beckett's death include Anthony Cronin, *Samuel Beckett: The Last Modernist* (1996), and Lois Gordon, *The World of Samuel Beckett, 1906–1946* (1996). Among the many critical discussions of Beckett's work, the following are particularly useful to students of his plays: Hugh Kenner, *Samuel Beckett: A Critical Study* (1961; new ed., 1968); Eugene Webb, *The Plays of Samuel Beckett* (1972); John Fletcher and John Spurling, *Beckett: A Study of His Plays* (1972; 2d ed., 1978); Ruby Cohn, *Back to Beckett* (1973) and *Just Play: Beckett's Theater* (1980); John Pilling, *Samuel Beckett* (1976); S. E. Gontarski, *The Intent of Undoing in Samuel Beckett's Dramatic Texts* (1985); Steven Connor, *Samuel Beckett: Repetition, Theory and Text* (1988); Andrew K. Kennedy, *Samuel Beckett* (1989); Enoch Brater, *Why Beckett* (1989); David Pattie, *The Complete Critical Guide to Samuel Beckett* (2000); Rónán McDonald, *The Cambridge Introduction to Samuel Beckett* (2006); Jonathan Boulter, *Beckett: A Guide for the Perplexed* (2008); S. E. Gontarski, ed., *A Companion to Samuel Beckett* (2010); and Katherine Weiss, *The Plays of Samuel Beckett* (2013). Important collections of essays include Martin Esslin, ed., *Samuel Beckett: A Collection of Critical Essays* (1965); S. E. Gontarski, ed., *On Beckett: Essays and Criticism* (1986); Lance St. John Butler and Robin J. Davis, eds., *Rethinking Beckett: A Collection of Critical Essays* (1990); Anthony Ullman, ed., *Samuel Beckett in Context* (2013); and Dirk Van Hulle, ed., *The New Cambridge Companion to Samuel Beckett* (2015). Studies of Beckett's plays in performance include Dougald

McMillan and Martha Fehsenfeld, *Beckett in the Theatre: The Author as Practical Playwright and Director* (1988), and Jonathan Kalb, *Beckett in Performance* (1989). Linda Ben-Zvi, ed., *Women in Beckett: Performance and Critical Perspectives* (1990), explores issues of gender in Beckett's drama with an emphasis on performance.

Resources for the study of *Waiting for Godot* include the following: Ruby Cohn, ed., *Casebook on "Waiting for Godot"* (1967); Bert O. States, *The Shape of Paradox: An Essay on "Waiting for Godot"* (1978); Lawrence Graver, *Samuel Beckett, "Waiting for Godot,"* (1989; 2d ed., 2004); Thomas Cousineau, *"Waiting for Godot": Form in Movement* (1990); Steven Connor, ed., *"Waiting for Godot" and "Endgame,"* by Samuel Beckett (1992); Lois Gordon, *Reading "Godot"* (2002); Harold Bloom, ed., *Samuel Beckett's "Waiting for Godot"* (2008); and Ranjan Gosh, ed., *In Dialogue with Godot: Waiting and Other Thoughts* (2013). David Bradby, *Beckett: "Waiting for Godot"* (2001), and Jonathan Croall, *The Coming of Godot: A Short History of a Masterpiece* (2005), discuss the play's production history. Dougald McMillan and James Knowlson, eds., *The Theatrical Notebooks of Samuel Beckett,* vol. 1, *Waiting for Godot* (1993), contains the working notes that Beckett kept while directing *Godot* at Berlin's Schiller-Theater in 1975 and will be of particular interest to actors and directors of Beckett's play.

BERTOLT BRECHT

Not surprisingly, the critical literature on Brecht's life and work is extensive. The person who introduced Brecht to America was Eric Bentley, who translated many of Brecht's plays, adapted them, and wrote extensively on the author. Although his not always faithful translations have been criticized, his writings on Brecht are important milestones in Brecht criticism; they include *Bentley on Brecht* (1998; 3d ed., 2008) and *The Playwright as Thinker: A Study of Drama in Modern Times* (1967). A good biography of Brecht is still Frederic Ewen's *Bertolt Brecht: His Life, His Art, and His Times* (1967). A more recent biography, John Fuegi's controversial *Brecht and Company: Sex, Politics, and the Making of the Modern Drama* (1994), argues that much of what has been viewed as original in Brecht was noncredited work by a number of others, including several of his lovers. Though exaggerated and shrill in its claims, the book nevertheless draws needed attention to the collaborative process that was undoubtedly part of Brecht's work. A good and simple introduction to Brecht's work is John Willett's *The Theatre of Bertolt Brecht: A Study from Eight Aspects* (1959; 3d ed., 1967); Martin Esslin's *Brecht: A Choice of Evils: A Critical Study of the Man, His Work, and His Opinions* (1959; 4th ed., 1984) is more ambitious and insightful. On Brecht's exile in and influence on the theater of the United States, see James Lyon's informative *Bertolt Brecht in America* (1980). Brecht's theoretical works are collected and translated by John Willett in *Brecht on Theatre: The Development of an Aesthetic* (1964; 2d ed., 1974); a good recent study of Brecht's theater is John J. White's *Bertolt Brecht's Dramatic Theory* (2004). A theoretically challenging but intriguing discussion of Brecht is Fredric Jameson's *Brecht and Method* (1998). On the use, in *The Good Person of Szechwan,* of a Chinese setting as well as on Brecht's interest in Chinese theater, see Eric Hayot's *Chinese Dreams: Pound, Brecht, Tel Quel* (2004).

Given Brecht's immense influence on modern drama, most classic studies of that period include substantial chapters on Brecht. See, for example, Raymond Williams, *Drama from Ibsen to Brecht* (1969); Richard Gilman, *The Making of Modern Drama* (1972); and Robert Brustein, *The Theatre of Revolt: An Approach to the Modern Drama* (1964). Brecht's paradigm has also shaped studies such as Janelle Reinelt's *After Brecht: British Epic Theater* (1994) and Elin Diamond's *Unmaking Mimesis* (1997).

GEORG BÜCHNER

Despite Büchner's influence, the scholarship in English on his work is somewhat limited in its range and methodologies. Both an authoritative text of *Woyzeck* and Büchner's various drafts and insertions can be found in Walter Hinderer and Henry J. Schmidt's edition of his *Complete Works and Letters,* trans. Henry J. Schmidt (1986). Given Büchner's short life and small oeuvre, most studies of the author combine a biographical account with a discussion of his plays. The earliest such work in English, A. H. J. Knight's *Georg Büchner* (1951), provides a good overview of Büchner's varied writings, but Herbert Lindenberger's study, *Georg Büchner* (1964), is more attuned to his use and revision of literary form and genre and more fully discusses the peculiar relation of Büchner to his contemporaries and descendants. Also interested in form and style is Henry Schmidt, *Satire, Caricature and Perspectivism in the Works of Georg Büchner* (1970). A number of critics have emphasized the political and revolutionary nature of Büchner's writing, for example, Maurice Benn in *The Drama of Revolt: A Critical Study of Georg Büchner* (1976). Richard Gilman begins his influential *The Making of Modern Drama* (1974) with a chapter on Büchner. Georg Lukács, a Marxist critic and philosopher, claimed Büchner as an early communist against the attempt on the part of National Socialists to see him as a fascist, in "The Real Georg Büchner and His Fascist Misrepresentation" (1939). There is, unfortunately, little scholarship focusing on Büchner's impact on theater and performance, although Lynn Sobieski's "The Bread and Puppet Theater's 'Woyzeck'" (1981) provides an account of one of the more unusual stagings this play has received. The most comprehensive and discriminating study of Büchner in English is John Reddick's *Georg Büchner: The Shattered Whole* (1994), which carefully traces Büchner's literary development within the context of his political and scientific writings.

ANTON CHEKHOV

Numerous translations of Chekhov's plays have appeared in the past forty years, including versions by such playwrights as Michael Frayn, Trevor Griffiths, and David Mamet. While its translations are not as stageworthy as the best of these, Ronald Hingley's nine-volume edition, *The Oxford Chekhov* (1964–80), includes all of Chekhov's plays and most of his stories. Laurence Senelick's Norton Critical Edition, *Anton Chekhov's Selected Plays* (2005), contains useful annotations on *The Cherry Orchard* and other plays. Donald Rayfield's authoritative biography, *Anton Chekhov: A Life* (1997), was the first account of the playwright's life to benefit from the opening of Russian archives after the dissolution of the Soviet Union in 1991. James N. Loehlin, *The Cambridge Introduction to Chekhov* (2010), is a useful introduction to Chekhov's life and work.

The following are useful studies of Chekhov's drama: Maurice Valency, *The Breaking String: The Plays of Anton Chekhov* (1966); J. L. Styan, *Chekhov in Performance: A Commentary on the Major Plays* (1971); Richard Peace, *Chekhov: A Study of the Four Major Plays* (1983); Laurence Senelick, *Anton Chekhov* (1985); Richard Gilman, *Chekhov's Plays: An Opening into Eternity* (1995); Donald Rayfield, *Understanding Chekhov: A Critical Study of Chekhov's Prose and Drama* (1999); and Rose Whyman, *Anton Chekhov* (2011). Toby W. Clyman, ed., *A Chekhov Companion* (1985), and Vera Gottlieb and Paul Allain, eds., *The Cambridge Companion to Chekhov* (2000), contain valuable essays on Chekhov, while Harold Bloom, ed., *Anton Chekhov* (1999), reprints a number of previously published essays

on Chekhov's fiction and drama. The chapters on Chekhov in Robert Brustein, *The Theatre of Revolt: An Approach to the Modern Drama* (1964), and Richard Gilman, *The Making of Modern Drama* (1974), remain among the best discussions of the playwright's dramatic work. Donald Rayfield, *The Cherry Orchard: Catastrophe and Comedy* (1994), is a book-length study of Chekhov's final play. Laurence Senelick, *The Chekhov Theatre: A Century of the Plays in Performance* (1997), and David Allen, *Performing Chekhov* (2000), examine Chekhov's plays in performance. Ronald Meyer's "*The Cherry Orchard* in the Twenty-First Century: New Adaptations and Versions," in Angela Brinlinger and Carol Apollonio, eds., *Chekhov for the 21st Century* (2012), surveys recent translations of Chekhov's final play.

CARYL CHURCHILL

Most of Caryl Churchill's produced dramas and radio scripts to date have been published in single and/or collected volumes by Methuen and Nick Hern Books. While Churchill produced a revised version of *Cloud Nine* for its initial New York production, she has stated her preference for the British version used here. Some of her very early, unproduced pieces have not yet been made publicly available. *File on Churchill* (1989), compiled by Linda Fitzsimmons, contains much useful information on Churchill's biography and early career as well as excerpts from reviews, interviews, and other commentary. To date, there is no published biography of Churchill, although she has shared information on her life with interviewers. Among the most useful of these dialogues are Kathleen Betsko and Rachel Koenig's *Interviews with Contemporary Women Playwrights* (1987); Laurie Stone, "Caryl Churchill: Making Room at the Top" (*Village Voice*, 1 March 1983); and Lynne Truss, "A Fair Cop" (*Plays and Players*, January 1984). An interview with Judith Thurman provided the foundation for the *Ms.* article (May 1982), while prominent New York theater critic John Simon interviewed Churchill for *Vogue* (August 1983). Early full-length studies of her work include Geraldine Cousin, *Churchill: The Playwright* (1989), and Amelia Howe Kritzer, *The Plays of Caryl Churchill* (1991). Elaine Aston's *Caryl Churchill* (1997); R. Darren Gobert, *The Theatre of Caryl Churchill* (2014); and Mary Luckhurst, *Caryl Churchill* (2015) build productively on this early criticism. Janelle Reinelt's relevant scholarship includes *After Brecht: British Epic Theater* (1994) and her essay on Churchill in *Modern British Women Playwrights* (2000). Phyllis Randall's edited volume, *Caryl Churchill:*

A Casebook (1988); Elaine Aston and Elin Diamond's edited volume, *The Cambridge Companion to Caryl Churchill* (2009); Helene Keyssar's entry in *Feminist Theatre* (1984); Elin Diamond's article in *Making a Spectacle: Feminist Essays on Contemporary Women's Theatre* (1989); Austin Quigley's essay in *Feminine Focus: The New Women Playwrights* (1989); Frances Gray's entry in *British and Irish Drama Since 1960* (1993); and Lisa Merrill's piece in *Modern Dramatists: A Casebook of Major British, Irish, and American Playwrights* (2001) are all worthwhile. For an understanding of Churchill in the context of British feminist theater, see Michelene Wandor, *Carry on Understudies: Theatre and Sexual Politics* (1981); for Churchill and political theater in England, see Catherine Itzin, *Stages in the Revolution: Political Theatre in Britain Since 1968* (1980). Apollo Amoko's "Casting Aside Colonial Occupation: Intersections of Race, Sex, and Gender in *Cloud Nine* and *Cloud Nine* Criticism" (1999) and James Harding's "Cloud Cover: (Re)Dressing Desire and Comfortable Subversions in Caryl Churchill's *Cloud Nine*" (1998) provide important responses to the play's explorations of colonialism and homosexuality.

MARÍA IRENE FORNÉS

Mud was originally published in Fornés's collection *Plays* (1986), with a preface by Susan Sontag. Although there is no complete bibliography of Fornés's publications to date, many of her works are listed in Maria M. Delgado and Caridad Svich, eds., *Conducting a Life: Reflections on the Theatre of Maria Irene Fornes* (1999); Marc Robinson, ed., *The Theater of Maria Irene Fornes* (1999); and Assunta Bartolomucci Kent, *Maria Irene Fornes and Her Critics* (1996). Kent's study also contains the fullest biographical information now available on Fornés as well as a thorough secondary bibliography. Fornés's generosity to interviewers is evident in pieces found in Kathleen Betsko and Rachel Koenig, comps., *Interviews with Contemporary Women Playwrights* (1987); David Savran, ed., *In Their Own Words: Contemporary American Playwrights* (1988); and Philip C. Kolin and Colby H. Kullman, eds., *Speaking on Stage: Interviews with Contemporary American Playwrights* (1996), as well as journals; see *PAJ* (Winter 1978) and *Theater* (Winter 1985). Fornés has also written on her own work in such journal essays as "I Write These Messages That Come" (1977), in the "'Woman' Playwrights" issue of *PAJ* (1983), "Creative Danger" (1985), and in the "Ages of the Avant-Garde" issue of *PAJ* (1994).

Bonnie Marranca, the editor of *PAJ*, has long championed Fornés's career through interviews and essays, including "The Real Life of Maria Irene Fornes" (1984) and "The State of Grace: Maria Irene Fornes at Sixty-Two" (1992). Two important features on her work have appeared in the *Village Voice*: Stephanie Harrington's "Irene Fornes, Playwright: Alice and the Red Queen" (1966) and Ross Wetzsteon's "Irene Fornes: The Elements of Style" (1986).

For full-length scholarly studies of Fornés, see Kent, *Maria Irene Fornes and Her Critics*, Diane Lynn Moroff, *Fornes: Theater in the Present Tense* (1996), and Scott T. Cummings, *Maria Irene Fornes* (2013). Among the important scholarly essays on Fornés are a chapter in Marc Robinson's *The Other American Drama* (1994); Deborah R. Geis, "Wordscapes of the Body: Performative Language as *Gestus* in María Irene Fornés's Plays" (1990); Cara Gargano, "The Starfish and the Strange Attractor: Myth, Science, and Theatre as Laboratory in María Irene Fornés' 'Mud'" (1997); Lurana Donnels O'Malley, "Pressing Clothes/Snapping Beans/ Reading Books: María Irene Fornés's Women's Work" (1989); and Christine Kiebuzinska, "Traces of Brecht in María Irene Fornés' *Mud*" (1993). Delgado and Svich's edited volume contains numerous responses to Fornés's writing and teaching. For the history of off-off-Broadway and Fornés's place in it, see Stephen J. Bottoms, *Playing Underground: A Critical History of the 1960s Off-Off-Broadway Movement* (2004).

ATHOL FUGARD

For a history of South African performance traditions, see Loren Kruger, *The Drama of South Africa: Plays, Pageants and Politics Since 1910* (1999); Martin Orkin, *Drama and the South African State* (1991); and Margarete Seidenspinner, *Exploring the Labyrinth: Athol Fugard's Approach to South African Drama* (1986). Useful bibliographies and resources about Athol Fugard's plays in production include Temple Hauptfleisch, Wilma Vijoen, and Céleste Van Greunen, eds., *Athol Fugard: A Source Guide* (1982); John Read, comp., *Athol Fugard: A Bibliography* (1991); and Stephen Gray, comp., *File on Fugard* (1991). For full-length critical studies of Fugard's work, see Dennis Walder, *Athol Fugard* (1984) and *Athol Fugard* (2003); Alan Shelley, *Athol Fugard: His Plays, People, and Politics: A Critical Overview* (2009); Russell Vandenbroucke, *Truths the Hand Can Touch: The Theatre of Athol Fugard* (1985); and Albert Wertheim, *The Dramatic Art of Athol Fugard: From South Africa to the World* (2000). The work most critical of Fugard as a political writer is Robert Mshengu, "Political Theatre in South Africa and the Work of Athol Fugard" (1982). For details of Fugard's plays and perspectives post-1994, see Marcia Blumberg and Dennis Walder, eds., *South African Theatre as/and Intervention* (1999).

The standard edition of "MASTER HAROLD" is that published by Penguin in 1982. Among the essays of particular relevance to its analysis are Rob Amato, "Fugard's Confessional Analysis: 'MASTER HAROLD' . . . and the boys," in *Momentum: On Recent South African Writing*, ed. M. J. Daymond, J. U. Jacobs, and Margaret Lenta (1984); Errol Durbach, "'MASTER HAROLD' . . . and the boys: Athol Fugard and the Psychopathology of Apartheid" (1987); and J. Ellen Gainor, "'A World without Collisions': Ballroom Dance in Athol Fugard's 'MASTER HAROLD' . . . and the boys," in *Bodies of the Text: Dance as Theory, Literature as Dance*, ed. Ellen W. Goellner and Jacqueline Shea Murphy (1995). Mel Gussow's "Profiles: Witness" (1982) provides a summary of the play's autobiographical elements as well as Fugard's direction of the play in the context of his career. Fugard's *Notebooks, 1960–1977* (1983) contains details of the play's background from the playwright's perspective.

FEDERICO GARCÍA LORCA

Since many sources pertaining to García Lorca's life have been available only after the fall of the fascist regime in Spain in 1975, the most extensive biographies of the playwright were written in the past two decades. An exception to this rule is one of the first studies of García Lorca in English, Edwin Honig's *García Lorca* (1944; rev. ed., 1963), which still provides a good introduction to the writer. Of the more recent biographies, the most informative is Ian Gibson's *Federico García Lorca: A Life* (1989), which includes a detailed description of the Granada region where García Lorca grew up and where he set many of his plays. Equally readable is Leslie Stainton's *Lorca: A Dream of Life* (1998). Both biographies also give detailed accounts of García Lorca's friendship with Falla, Buñuel, and Dalí. Given García Lorca's prominence as a poet, many scholars pay less attention to the theatrical aspect of his work. The first book-length study with that focus was Robert Lima's *The Theatre of García Lorca* (1963), which provides a useful introduction to the dramatist. More theoretically sophisticated is *The Theatre of García Lorca: Text, Performance, Psychoanalysis* by Paul Julian Smith (1998), which also discusses the significance of García Lorca's homosexuality. *The Comic Spirit of Federico García Lorca* (1976), by Virginia Higginbotham, provides not only insight into García Lorca's comedies and farces but also a general history of twentieth-century theater in Spain. C. Christopher Soufas's *Audience and Authority in the Modernist Theater of Federico García Lorca* (1996) discusses from the perspective of the audience García Lorca's drama, in particular his attempt to introduce avant-garde and experimental elements into mainstream theater. Special attention to García Lorca's interest in folklore and folk music, such as flamenco, can be found in Robert Stone, *The Flamenco Tradition in the Works of Federico García Lorca and Carlos Aura: The Wounded Throat* (2004).

JEAN GENET

Jean-Paul Sartre's monumental study *Saint Genet: Actor and Martyr* (1952; trans. 1963), written early in Genet's career, casts a long shadow over all subsequent scholarship. For Sartre, Genet's life and work cannot be accounted for by the traditional forms of psychoanalytic biography or Marxist criticism but instead reflect existential choices. Richard N. Coe's *The Vision of Jean Genet* (1968) and Philip Thody's *Jean Genet: A Study of His Novels and Plays* (1968) take many strategies and topics from Sartre. This Sartrean approach of weaving together Genet's life and work was criticized in Edmund White's award-winning biography, *Genet: A Biography* (1993), which tried to disentangle the two and which demonstrated the extent to which Genet himself had been engaged in exaggerating and falsifying aspects of his life. Two influential theater historians and theorists who wrote on Genet are Robert Brustein, in his *Theatre of Revolt: An Approach to the Modern Drama* (1964), which sees Genet's works as exemplifying Artaud's Theater of Cruelty, and Martin Esslin, in *The Theatre of the Absurd* (1961; 3d ed., 1980). A second generation of scholars paid more attention to the intricate structure of Genet's works, using semiotic and structuralist methods; see, for example, Una Chaudhuri's *No Man's Stage: A Semiotic Study of Genet's Major Plays* (1986) and Laura Oswald's *Jean Genet and the Semiotics of Performance* (1989). And in *Homos* (1995), Leo Bersani uses the perspective of psychoanalysis and queer theory to analyze Genet as a gay outlaw. Directly or indirectly, these studies are indebted to another philosopher's monumental work on Genet: Jacques Derrida's *Glas* (1974; trans. 1986), which pays particular attention to Genet's language and figures, including his use of slang and the prominence of flowers. That two great twentieth-century philosophers, Sartre and Derrida, devoted considerable attention to Genet is part of his lasting legacy.

SUSAN GLASPELL

All of Glaspell's dramatic writing has been collected in *Susan Glaspell: The Complete Plays*, ed. Linda Ben-Zvi and J. Ellen Gainor (2010). C. W. E. Bigsby's selection, *Plays* (1987), reprints several of her major works (including *Trifles*) and contains a worthwhile introduction; his entry on Glaspell for the first volume of his *Critical Introduction to Twentieth-Century American Drama* (1983) is also helpful. Marcia Noe's *Susan Glaspell: Voice from the Heartland* (1983) was the first critical biography of Glaspell. More recent definitive biographies are Linda Ben-Zvi, *Susan Glaspell: Her Life and Times* (2005), and Barbara Ozieblo, *Susan Glaspell: A Critical Biography* (2000). J. Ellen Gainor, *Susan Glaspell in Context: American Theater, Culture, and Politics, 1915–48* (2001), provides readings of Glaspell's dramas within their creative, historical, and critical milieus. Linda Ben-Zvi, ed., *Susan Glaspell: Essays on Her Theater and Fiction* (1995), contains a useful section on *Trifles* and "Jury." Martha C. Carpentier and Emeline Jouve's edited collection, *On Susan Glaspell's "Trifles" and "A Jury of Her Peers": Centennial Essays, Interviews and Adaptations* (2015), includes scholarly essays, interviews with theater practitioners, and dramatic responses to Glaspell's play. Veronica Makowsky, *Susan Glaspell's Century of American Women: A Critical Interpretation of Her Work* (1993), focuses on female characters and themes in Glaspell's fiction and drama, while Kristina Hinz-Bode, *Susan Glaspell and the Anxiety of Expression: Language and Isolation in the Plays* (2006), examines issues of language and isolation in the playwright's dramas, and Noelia Hernando-Real's *Self and Space in the Theater of Susan Glaspell* (2011) offers a philosophical approach to the plays. Robert Károly Sarlós, *Jig Cook and the Provincetown Players: Theatre in Ferment* (1982), provides the broader historical background to Glaspell's early theatrical career, and Cheryl Black's *The Women of Provincetown, 1915–22* (2002) focuses on the artistry of Glaspell and her female colleagues. In *Midnight Assassin: A Murder in America's Heartland* (2005), Patricia L. Bryan and Thomas Wolf provide a historical analysis of the murder that was the source for Glaspell's play. Mary E. Papke, *Susan Glaspell: A Research and Production Sourcebook* (1993), is the most comprehensive bibliographic resource.

LORRAINE HANSBERRY

The authoritative version of *A Raisin in the Sun* is the 1988 Signet edition, which is reprinted in this anthology. This edition, which was supervised by Hansberry's executor and former husband Robert Nemiroff, includes material that was omitted in the original 1959 edition as well as staging insights from the original and subsequent productions. Hansberry's unproduced screenplay version of the play was published under the title *A Raisin in the Sun: The Unfilmed Original Screenplay* (Signet, 1994). Biographical information on Hansberry's life and an overview of her published plays can be found in Anne Cheney, *Lorraine Hansberry* (1984). Many of Hansberry's writings on her own life are included in *To Be Young, Gifted, and Black,* adapted by Robert Nemiroff (1969).

The most complete and insightful study of Hansberry's literary career is Steven R. Carter, *Hansberry's Drama: Commitment amid Complexity* (1991). In addition to consulting draft versions of *A Raisin in the Sun*, Carter discusses Hansberry's unpublished work, which underscores the range of her interests as a writer. Production information on Hansberry's plays, along with early theater reviews, scholarly articles, and books, can be found in Richard M. Leeson, *Lorraine Hansberry: A Research and Production Sourcebook* (1997). The following studies of *A Raisin in the Sun* are particularly useful: Sheri Parks, "In my Mother's House: Black Feminist Aesthetics, Television, and *A Raisin in the Sun,*" in Karen Laughlin and Catherine Schuler, eds., *Theatre and Feminist Aesthetics* (1995); Ben Keppel, *The Work of Democracy: Ralph Bunche, Kenneth B. Clark, Lorraine Hansberry, and the Cultural Politics of Race* (1995); Robin Bernstein, "Inventing a Fishbowl: White Supremacy and the Critical Reception of Lorraine Hansberry's *A Raisin in the Sun*" (1999); Margaret B. Wilkerson, "Political Radicalism and Artistic Innovation in the Works of Lorraine Hansberry," in Harry J. Elam Jr. and David Krasner, eds., *American Performance and Theater History* (2001); Lisbeth Lipari, "'Fearful of the written word': White Fear, Black Writing, and Lorraine Hansberry's *A Raisin in the Sun*" (2004); Michelle Gordon, "'Somewhat like War': The Aesthetics of Segregation, Black Liberation, and *A Raisin in the Sun*" (2008); and Kristin L. Matthews, "The Politics of 'Home' in Lorraine Hansberry's *A Raisin in the Sun*" (2008). The important role of Africa in *A Raisin in the Sun* is ably explored in Philip Uko

Effiong, *In Search of a Model for African-American Drama: A Study of Selected Plays by Lorraine Hansberry, Amiri Baraka, and Ntozake Shange* (2000) and Gĩchingiri Ndĩgĩrĩgĩ, "Discrepant Cosmopolitanisms in Lorraine Hansberry's *A Raisin in the Sun*," in Tom Spencer-Walters, ed., *Memory and the Narrative Imagination in the African and Diaspora Experience* (2011).

Rebecca Ann Rugg and Harvey Young, eds., *Reimagining "A Raisin in the Sun"* (2012) features four contemporary plays written in response to Hansberry's influential drama, including Bruce Norris's 2010 play *Clybourne Park*, which won the 2011 Pulitzer Prize for Drama.

DAVID HENRY HWANG

The standard text of *M. Butterfly* is the New American Library edition (1989), which includes Hwang's afterword on the play and its composition. The acting edition (1988) published by Dramatists Play Service contains the same afterword, as well as a discussion of the play's Broadway production and suggestions for prospective actors, directors, and designers. William C. Boles, *Understanding David Henry Hwang* (2013), is an important book-length study of Hwang's life and work, as is Esther Kim Lee, *The Theatre of David Henry Hwang* (2015). Douglas Street's brief but useful monograph *David Henry Hwang* (1989) contains biographical information on the playwright and an overview of his dramatic writing through *M. Butterfly*. William C. Boles, *Understanding David Henry Hwang* (2013), is an important book-length study of Hwang's life and work. Miles Xian Liu, ed., *Asian American Playwrights: A Bio-bibliographical Critical Sourcebook* (2002), provides biographical backgrounds, production history, and bibliographical information on the works of Hwang and other Asian American dramatists.

Important articles on *M. Butterfly* include Robert Skloot, "Breaking the Butterfly: The Politics of David Henry Hwang" (1990); Douglas Kerr, "David Henry Hwang and the Revenge of *Madame Butterfly*," in *Asian Voices in English*, ed. Mimi Chan and Roy Harris (1991); Marjorie Garber, "The Occidental Tourist: *M. Butterfly* and the Scandal of Transvestism," in *Nationalities and Sexualities*, ed. Andrew Parker, Mary Russo, Doris Sommer, and Patricia Yaeger (1992); Karen Shimakawa, "'Who's to Say?' or, Making Space for Gender and Ethnicity in *M. Butterfly*" (1993); Foong Ling Kong's "Pulling the Wings off Butterfly" (1994); and Hsiu-Chen Lin, "Staging Orientalia: Dangerous 'Authenticity' in David Henry Hwang's *M. Butterfly*" (1997). James S. Moy, *Marginal Sights: Staging the Chinese in America* (1993), and Josephine

Lee, *Performing Asian America: Race and Ethnicity on the Contemporary Stage* (1997), explore *M. Butterfly* in the context of earlier and contemporary representations of Asian Americans in theater and in American culture.

HENRIK IBSEN

Among the early reactions to Ibsen was George Bernard Shaw's *The Quintessence of Ibsenism* (1891), which emphasizes Ibsen's concern with pressing social and political issues; William Archer's essays, collected by Thomas Postlewait in *William Archer on Ibsen: The Major Essays, 1889–1919* (1984), foreground Ibsen's poetic choices and techniques. The decisive impact of Shaw and Archer is described in detail in Thomas Postlewait's *Prophet of the New Drama: William Archer and the Ibsen Campaign* (1986). Ibsen's third major early supporter was the critic Georg Brandes, who accompanied Ibsen's career with three essays, written in the 1870s, 1880s, and 1890s, collected in his *Henrik Ibsen: A Critical Study* (1899). Charles Lyons's compilation, *Critical Essays on Henrik Ibsen* (1987), includes landmark essay by Ibsen's modernist admirers, among them James Joyce, E. M. Forster, and Georg Lukàcs. The wider cultural context of Ibsen's European success, as well as a wealth of personal detail, is captured in Michael Meyer's *Ibsen: A Biography* (1971). While there have been a number of excellent studies devoted to Ibsen—for example, Michael Goldman's imaginative reading of Ibsen's subtexts and psychologies in *Ibsen: The Dramaturgy of Fear* (1999)—the most influential accounts of Ibsen's impact on modern drama are to be found in studies devoted to modern drama more generally, many of which take their point of departure from Ibsen's work. Of these, Raymond Williams's *Drama: From Ibsen to Eliot* (1952; 2nd rev. ed., 1973) is the most important, discussing Ibsen's social drama and modern tragedy. Robert Brustein's *The Theatre of Revolt: An Approach to the Modern Drama* (1964) and Richard Gilman's *The Making of Modern Drama* (1974) are classics in dating the origin of a modern revolt to Ibsen's drama, as is Peter Szondi's *The Theory of the Modern Drama* (1956; trans. 1987), which measures Ibsen against Sophocles' *Oedipus the King*. In *Ibsen and Early Modernist Theatre, 1890–1900* (1997), Kirsten Shepherd-Barr situates Ibsen in the context of theater history, and Joan Templeton's *Ibsen's Women* (1997) is the first in-depth analysis of Ibsen's construction of female characters, including Hedda Gabler. *The Cambridge Companion to Ibsen*, ed. James McFarlane (1994), provides a good introduction to recent scholarship and contemporary approaches. For a detailed comparison of different English translations of *A Doll House*, see Kristian Smidt, *Ibsen Translated: A Report on English Versions of Henrik Ibsen's Peer Gynt and A Doll's House* (2000). The best book on Ibsen is Toril Moi's *Henrik Ibsen and the Birth of Modernism: Art, Theater, Philosophy* (2006).

ALFRED JARRY

An edition of the entire Ubu cycle is to be found in *The Ubu Plays*, translated and introduced by Kenneth McLeish (1997), as well as in *The Ubu Plays*, edited and introduced by Simon Watson Taylor (1968). The lesser known of Jarry's Ubu publications as well as his own writings on the theater are available in *Selected Works of Alfred Jarry*, ed. Roger Shattuck and Simon Watson Taylor (1965). The best biographical account of Jarry's life and work is to be found in Keith Beaumont's *Alfred Jarry: A Critical and Biographical Study* (1984), which weaves Jarry's biography into a discussion of his literary works, his relation to symbolism, and his use of language and style. A close analysis of the Ubu cycle is undertaken by Judith Cooper, *Ubu Roi: An Analytical Study* (1974). Specifically attuned to Jarry's important contribution to theater history is Maurice Marc LaBelle's *Alfred Jarry, Nihilism and the Theater of the Absurd* (1980), which details Jarry's stagecraft, including his use of marionettes, sets, and masks—topics that have been at the center of attention in the much richer and more wide-ranging literature on Jarry in French. Jarry's relation to the avant-garde of the early twentieth century is the central concern of Roger Shattuck's excellent *The Banquet Year: The Origins of the Avant-Garde in France, 1885 to World War I: Alfred Jarry, Henri Rousseau, Erik Satie, and Guillaume Apollinaire* (1958; rev. ed., 1968), and Claude Schumacher's *Alfred Jarry and Guillaume Apollinaire* (1984) likewise compares Jarry to the French avant-garde poet and dramatist Apollinaire, who invented the term *surrealism*.

TONY KUSHNER

Angels in America: A Gay Fantasia on National Themes (Theatre Communications Group, 1995) is the standard edition of this two-part play. James Fisher, *The Theater of Tony Kushner: Living Past Hope* (2001) and *Understanding Tony Kushner* (2008), are full-length studies of the development of Kushner's drama in its social, theatrical, and biographical contexts. Robert Vorlicky, ed., *Tony Kushner in Conversation* (1998), is a rich collection of biographical, critical, and backstage interviews with the playwright. Deborah R. Geis and Steven F. Kruger, eds., *Approaching the Millennium: Essays on "Angels in America"* (1997); Per Brask, ed., *Essays on Kush-*

ner's *"Angels"* (1995); and James Fisher, ed., *Tony Kushner: New Essays on the Art and Politics of His Plays* (2006), provide a range of historical, critical, and theatrical perspectives on the play. In addition to the essays included in the above collections, the following articles are useful: Charles McNulty, *"Angels in America: Tony Kushner's Theses on the Philosophy of History"* (1996); Jonathan Freedman, "Angels, Monsters, and Jews: Intersections of Queer and Jewish Identity in Kushner's *Angels in America*" (1998); Daryl Ogden, "Cold War Science and the Body Politic: An Immuno/Virological Approach to *Angels in America*" (2000); Ranen Omer-Sherman, "The Fate of the Other in Tony Kushner's *Angels in America*" (2007); Cristine Hutchinson-Jones, "Center and Periphery: Mormons and American Culture in Tony Kushner's *Angels in America*," in Mark T. Decker and Michael Austin, eds., *Peculiar Portrayals: Mormons on the Page, Stage, and Screen* (2010); Stephanie Byttebier, "'It Doesn't Count If It's Easy': Facing Pain, Mediating Identity in Tony Kushner's *Angels in America*" (2011); and Katie Hogan, "Green *Angels* in America: Aesthetics of Equity" (2012).

DAVID MAMET

Although no detailed biography of David Mamet has yet been written, scholarship on Mamet has burgeoned since the early 2000s. An excellent resource is *David Mamet: A Research and Production Sourcebook*, comp. David K. Sauer and Janice A. Sauer (2003), which documents both productions and scholarship. Among the monographs on Mamet, C. W. E. Bigsby's *David Mamet* (1985) provides a good overview of the dramatist's work up to the early 1980s. More specialized in their focus are Anne Dean's *David Mamet: Language as Dramatic Action* (1990), which examines the important topic of language, and Leslie Kane's *Weasels and Wisemen: Ethics and Ethnicity in the Work of David Mamet* (1999), which analyzes the complex role of ethnicity in Mamet's work.

A number of essays offer more detailed readings of Mamet than do the available book-length studies. The collection edited by Leslie Kane, *David Mamet's "Glengarry Glen Ross": Text and Performance* (1996), includes a good analysis of Mamet's representation of capitalism, Elizabeth Kalver's "David Mamet, Jean Baudrillard and the Performance of America," as well as an interesting account of a foreign production, "A Japanese *Glengarry Glen Ross*," by Robert T. Rolf. Harold Bloom, ed., *David Mamet* (2004), features two very good essays on the relation of realism and illusion: Michael L. Quinn's "Anti-theatricality and American Ideology: Mamet's Performative

Realism" and Howard Pearce's "Plato in Hollywood: David Mamet and the Power of Illusion." The best account on realism in Mamet is David Savran's "New Realism: Mamet, Mann and Nelson," in Bruce King, ed., *Contemporary American Theatre* (1991). Robert Vorlicky has investigated the question of masculinity in Mamet in *Act Like a Man: Challenging Masculinities in American Drama* (1995). Bigsby, ed., *Cambridge Companion to David Mamet* (2004), includes essays that provide a good introduction to the work of the playwright, as does Nesta Jones and Steven Dykes, comp., *File on Mamet* (1991).

ARTHUR MILLER

Arthur Miller's *Collected Plays* (1957) contains the playwright's five major plays through 1957; *The Portable Arthur Miller* (1971; rev. ed., 2003) includes a useful selection of plays from throughout his career. Published two years before the playwright's death, Martin Gottfried's *Arthur Miller: His Life and Work* (2003) is a full-length biography of Miller. An engaging overview can also be found in Enoch Brater, *Arthur Miller: A Playwright's Life and Works* (2005). Those who want an in-depth account of the playwright's life and times through the early 1980s can consult his wide-ranging and critically acclaimed autobiography, *Timebends: A Life* (1987). Important studies of Miller's plays include Sheila Huftel, *Arthur Miller: The Burning Glass* (1965); Edward Murray, *Arthur Miller, Dramatist* (1967); Leonard Moss, *Arthur Miller* (1967; rev. ed., 1980); Benjamin Nelson, *Arthur Miller: Portrait of a Playwright* (1970); Dennis Welland, *Miller the Playwright* (1979; 3d ed., 1985); Neil Carson, *Arthur Miller* (1982; 2d ed., 2008); June Schlueter and James K. Flanagan, *Arthur Miller* (1987); David Savran, *Communist, Cowboys, and Queers: The Politics of Masculinity in the Work of Arthur Miller and Tennessee Williams* (1992); Alice Griffin, *Understanding Arthur Miller* (1996); Enoch Brater, *Arthur Miller: A Playwright's Life and Works* (2005); and three books by Christopher Bigsby: *Arthur Miller: A Critical Study* (2005), *Arthur Miller: 1915–1962* (2009), and *Arthur Miller: 1962–2005* (2011). Bigsby, ed., *The Cambridge Companion to Arthur Miller* (1997; 2d ed., 2010) includes a useful collection of essays covering Miller's career as a whole.

Miller wrote and spoke widely on his plays and his career as a writer. Collections of his essays and interviews include Robert A. Martin, ed., *The Theater Essays of Arthur Miller* (1978; rev. ed., 1996); Matthew C. Roudané, ed., *Conversations with Arthur Miller* (1987); Steven R.

Centola, ed., *Echoes down the Corridor: Collected Essays, 1944–2000* (2000); and Mel Gussow, *Conversations with Miller* (2002). Stefani Koorey, *Arthur Miller's Life and Literature: An Annotated and Comprehensive Guide* (2000), offers an extensive bibliography of books and articles on Miller's drama as well as information on Miller's life and politics, references to theater reviews, and production information on his plays. Susan C. W. Abbotson's *Critical Companion to Arthur Miller: A Literary Reference to His Life and Work* (2007) is also an important resource.

Among the collections of critical essays on *Death of a Salesman* are Gerald Weales, ed., *Death of a Salesman: Text and Criticism* (1967); Helene Wickham Koon, ed., *Twentieth-Century Interpretations of "Death of a Salesman": A Collection of Critical Essays* (1983); Harold Bloom, ed., *Arthur Miller's "Death of a Salesman"* (1988; updated, 2007) and *Willy Loman* (1991; updated, 2005); Matthew C. Roudané, ed., *Approaches to Teaching Miller's "Death of a Salesman"* (1995); Stephen A. Marino, ed., *"The 'Salesman' Has a Birthday": Essays Celebrating the Fiftieth Anniversary of Arthur Miller's "Death of a Salesman"* (2000); Eric J. Sterling, ed., *Arthur Miller's "Death of a Salesman"* (2008); and Brenda Murphy, ed., *"Death of a Salesman": Critical Insights* (2010). Stephen Marino, ed., *Arthur Miller: "Death of a Salesman"/"The Crucible"* (2015) surveys the critical tradition surrounding Miller's two most famous plays. Kay Stanton, "Women and the American Dream of *Death of a Salesman*," in June Schlueter, ed., *Feminist Rereadings of Modern American Drama* (1989), is an important feminist reading of Miller's play. Brenda Murphy, *Miller: "Death of a Salesman"* (1995), is a history of *Death of a Salesman* productions during the years 1949–89, while Miller's own *Salesman in Beijing* (1984) discusses his experiences directing the play in the People's Republic of China in 1983.

DANIEL DAVID MOSES

Almighty Voice and His Wife was originally published in 1992 by Williams-Wallace Publishers; a second edition was Playwrights Canada Press in 2009. The play has also been anthologized in *Staging Coyote's Dream: An Anthology of First Nations Drama in English*, ed. Monique Mojica and Ric Knowles (2003). The fullest biographical account of Moses's life and career can be found in Don Perkins, "Daniel David Moses," in *Twentieth-Century Canadian Writers*, volume 334 of *The Dictionary of Literary Biography* (2007). Important studies of Moses's drama and *Almighty Voice* in particular include Rob Appleford, "The Desire to Crunch Bone: Daniel David Moses and the 'True Real Indian'" (1993); Barbara Goddard, "Writing between Cultures" (1997); Ric Knowles, "'Look. Look again.': Daniel David Moses' Decolonizing Optics" (2002); Helen Gilbert, "Black and White and Re(a)d All Over Again: Indigenous Minstrelsy in Contemporary Canadian and Australian Theatre" (2003); Marc Maufort, *Transgressive Itineraries: Postcolonial Hybridizations of Dramatic Realism* (2003); and Jo-Ann Episkenew, *Taking Back Our Spirits: Indigenous Literature, Public Policy, and Healing* (2009). Tracy Lindberg and David Brundage, eds., *Daniel David Moses: Spoken and Written Explorations of his Work* (2015), collects essays and other writings devoted to Moses's literary career. *Outlaws and Lawmen of Western Canada*, ed. Art Downs (1983), is one of a number of accounts of the historical Almighty Voice. In September 1999 the Canadian Broadcast Channel aired a story entitled "Cree Prisoner Almighty Voice: Hero or Outlaw?"; this story is available in the CBC Digital Archives at www.cbc.ca/archives/categories/society/crime-justice/general-3/almighty-voice-hero-or-outlaw.html.

LYNN NOTTAGE

Ruined has been published in both an acting edition by Samuel French and a trade edition from Theatre Communications Group. The latter contains a useful introduction from director Kate Whoriskey, as well as music for the production and URLs for international agencies and human rights organizations that provide further information about and support to women in the Congo. There is, to date, no published biography of Lynn Nottage. Details of her life and career can be found in interviews with and articles on the dramatist, and in reference works such as *Current Biography Yearbook* and *Women Playwrights of Diversity: A Bio-Bibliographical Sourcebook* (1997). Among numerous interviews with the playwright, some of the most informative are the conversation with fellow playwright Nilo Cruz in *The Dramatist: The Journal of the Dramatists Guild of America, Inc.* (2010); Rosemary Tichler and Barry Jay Kaplan, eds, *The Playwright at Work: Conversations* (2012); Alexis Greene, ed., *Women Who Write Plays: Interviews with American Dramatists* (2001); Nottage's appearance on the program "Theater Talk" (https://www.youtube.com/watch?v=OrL1ENfrf4Y); Nottage's comments to the Enough Project (www.enoughproject.org); Nottage's conversation with Jeffrey Brown on the PBS Newshour (www.pbs.org); the conversation with Lawrence Goodman in the *Brown Alumni Magazine* (2010); the conversation with Jean E. Howard in *PMLA* (2014); the conversation with Celia McGee in the *New York Times* (2009); the interview by Sandra G. Shannon and related scholarly article in *Contemporary African American Women Playwrights: A Casebook* (2007); and the interview with Patrick Pacheco in the *Los Angeles Times* (2009). While there is no full-length critical study of Nottage's work, there are a number of worthwhile scholarly articles about her writing. These include Sharon Friedman, "The Gendered Terrain in Contemporary Theatre of War by Women" (2010); Randy Gener, "In Defense of 'Ruined': 5 Elements that Shape Lynn Nottage's Masterwork" (2010); Carmen Mendez Garcia, "'This is my place, Mama Nadi's': Feminine Spaces and Identity in Lynn Nottage's *Ruined*" (2012); Barbara Ozieblo, "'Pornography of Violence': Strategies of Representation in Plays by Naomi Wallace, Stefanie Zadravec, and Lynn Nottage" (2011); and Ann M. Fox, "Battles on the Body: Disability, Interpreting Dramatic Literature, and the Case of Lynn Nottage's *Ruined*" (2011). Theatrical reviews of *Ruined* also contain both useful commentary and production information; among those for the initial U.S. productions, see Chris Jones in the *Chicago Tribune* (2008); Michael Feingold in the *Village Voice* (2009); Ben Brantley in the *New York Times* (2009); Charles Isherwood in the *New York Times* (2009); Jill Dolan (www.thefeministspectator.com) (2009); and Charles McNulty in the *Los Angeles Times* (2010). Several theatres that have produced *Ruined* have helpful educational materials on their websites, including the Goodman Theatre, the La Jolla Playhouse, and the Almeida Theatre. Details of Nottage's U.S. Senate appearance were reported by Patrick Healy, "Women of 'Ruined' to Speak in Washington About Rape" (2009). Useful overview studies of the war in the Congo include Filip Reyntjens, *The Great African War: Congo and Regional Geopolitics, 1996–2006* (2009); Gerard Prunier, *Africa's World War: Congo, the Rwandan Genocide, and the Making of a Continental Catastrophe* (2009), Thomas Turner, *The Congo Wars: Conflict, Myth, and Reality* (2007); Human Rights Watch, *The War within the War: Sexual Violence against Women and Girls in Eastern Congo* (2002). Additionally, the following articles are particularly relevant to *Ruined*: Patrick Cannon, "A Feminist Response to Rape as a Weapon of War in Eastern Congo" (2012); Sara Meger, "Rape of the Congo: Understanding Sexual Violence in the Conflict in the Democratic Republic of Congo" (2010); Jill Trenholm et al, "The Global, The Ethnic, and the Gendered War: Women and Rape in Eastern Democratic Republic of Congo" (2015); Nadine Puechguirbal,

"Women and War in the Democratic Republic of the Congo" (2003); and Filip Reyntjens, "Briefing: The Second Congo War: More Than a Remake" (1999).

EUGENE O'NEILL

As befits his stature as the most significant U.S. dramatist, the critical literature on O'Neill is extensive and varied. The autobiographical character of a number of O'Neill's plays has led many critics and commentators to describe O'Neill as the tragic hero of U.S. theater. The two-volume study by Louis Sheaffer, *O'Neill: Son and Playwright* (1968) and *O'Neill: Son and Artist* (1973), remains the most informative of the several biographies, although Stephen Black's *Eugene O'Neill: Beyond Mourning and Tragedy* (1999) usefully takes O'Neill's interest in Freud and psychoanalysis as a point of departure for psychoanalytical readings of O'Neill's life and work. Travis Bogard's *Contour in Time: The Plays of Eugene O'Neill* (1972; rev. ed., 1988) is the best of the earlier analyses of the drama. Many studies tend toward idealizing their subject, presenting O'Neill's work as a heroic quest for artistic excellence. Notable exceptions to this rule are Joel Pfister's *Staging Depth: Eugene O'Neill and the Politics of Psychological Discourse* (1995), which provides historical context for the playwright's interest in psychology and interiority, and Zander Brietzke's excellent *Aesthetics of Failure: Dynamic Structure in the Plays of Eugene O'Neill* (2001), which examines the relation between O'Neill's significant failures and his stunning successes. Also useful are Kurt Eisner's *The Inner Strength of Opposites: O'Neill's Novelistic Drama and the Melodramatic Imagination* (1994), which focuses on O'Neill's novelistic techniques (including his stage directions, asides, and monologues), and Thierry Dubost's *Struggle, Defeat or Rebirth: Eugene O'Neill's Vision of Humanity* (1997).

There is a rich literature on and documentation of O'Neill's view of the theater and the staging of his plays, including Ulrich Halfmann, ed., *Eugene O'Neill: Comments on the Drama and the Theater: A Source Book* (1987), which contains early reviews as well as the playwright's letters to actors, directors, and critics; see also Mark W. Estrin, ed., *Conversations with Eugene O'Neill* (1990), and Yvonne Shafer, *Performing O'Neill: Conversations with Actors and Directors* (2000). For a description of American expressionist drama, and especially of *The Hairy Ape*, see Julia A. Walker's *Expressionism and Modernism in the American Theatre: Bodies, Voices,* *Words* (2005). For the fascination with industrial power and engines, read Anson Rabinach, *The Human Motor, Energy, Fatigue, and the Origins of Modernity* (1992).

SUZAN-LORI PARKS

The America Play is published in *The America Play and Other Works* (Theatre Communications Group, 1995). Those interested in further biographical information on Suzan-Lori Parks should consult the entry on her in *Contemporary Authors Online* (Thompson Gale, 2005). Deborah R. Geis, *Suzan-Lori Parks* (2008), is an important full-length study of Parks's plays, as is Jennifer Larson, *Understanding Suzan-Lori Parks* (2012). Philip C. Kolin and Harvey Young, eds., *Suzan Lori-Parks in Person: Interviews and Commentaries* (2014) contains interviews with Parks as well as commentaries on her work by major directors and critics. Kevin J. Wetmore Jr. and Alycia Smith-Howard, eds., *Suzan-Lori Parks: A Casebook* (2007) and Philip C. Kolin, ed., *Suzan-Lori Parks: Essays on the Plays and Other Works* (2010), are important collections of critical essays. Valuable articles on *The America Play* and Parks's career as a whole include the following: Alisa Solomon, "'Signifying on the Signifyin': The Plays of Suzan-Lori Parks" (1990); Katy Ryan, "'No Less Human': Making History in Suzan-Lori Parks's *The America Play*" (1999); Harry Elam and Alice Rayner, "Echoes from the Black (W)hole: An Examination of *The America Play* by Suzan-Lori Parks," in Jeffrey D. Mason and J. Ellen Gainor, eds., *Performing America: Cultural Nationalism in American Theater* (1999); S. E. Wilmer, "Restaging the Nation: The Work of Suzan-Lori Parks" (2000); Shawn-Marie Garrett, "The Possession of Suzan-Lori Parks" (2000); Frank Haike, "The Instability of Meaning in Suzan-Lori Parks's *The America Play*" (2002); and Heidi R. Bean, "Learning from the Dramaturg: *The America Play* in the Literature Classroom" (2015).

HAROLD PINTER

The Homecoming (Grove, 1966) is the standard edition of the play; it is reprinted in volume 3 of Harold Pinter, *Complete Works* (Grove, 1990). Michael Billington's *Harold Pinter* (2007), published in an earlier edition as *The Life and Work of Harold Pinter* (1996), is the authoritative biography, while Mel Gussow's *Conversations with Pinter* (1994) is an important collection of interviews conducted at different stages of Pinter's career. Martin Esslin, *The Peopled Wound: The Work of Harold Pinter* (1970), revised and updated as *Pinter, the Playwright* (6th ed., 2000), is a classic critical study. Other valuable book-length studies are Austin E. Quigley, *The Pinter Problem* (1975); Elin Diamond, *Pinter's Comic Play* (1985); David T. Thompson, *Pinter: The Player's Playwright* (1985); Susan Hollis Merritt, *Pinter in Play: Critical Strategies and the Plays of Harold Pinter* (1990); Marc Silverstein, *Harold Pinter and the Language of Cultural Power* (1993); Mark Batty, *Harold Pinter* (2001); Charles Grimes, *Harold Pinter's Politics: A Silence beyond Echo* (2005); Robert Gordon, *Harold Pinter: The Theatre of Power* (2012); Hanna Scolnicov, *The Experimental Plays of Harold Pinter* (2012); and Mark Taylor-Batty, *The Theatre of Harold Pinter* (2014). The following collections provide a range of critical approaches: Arthur Ganz, ed., *Pinter: A Collection of Critical Essays* (1972); Steven H. Gale, ed., *Critical Essays on Harold Pinter* (1990); Peter Raby, ed., *The Cambridge Companion to Harold Pinter* (2001); Mark Batty, *Harold Pinter* (2001); Charles Grimes, *Harold Pinter's Politics: A Silence beyond Echo* (2005); and Peter Raby, ed., *The Cambridge Companion to Harold Pinter*, 2d ed. (2009). The website www.haroldpinter.org is a compendium of information about Pinter as playwright, screenwriter, actor, director, and political activist.

John Lahr, ed., *A Casebook on Harold Pinter's The Homecoming* (1971), and Michael Scott, ed., *Harold Pinter: The Birthday Party, The Caretaker, The Homecoming: A Casebook* (1986), contain important reviews and essays on those plays. The former includes revealing interviews with director Peter Hall, designer John Bury, and two actors from the original London production. Other useful essays include Bert O. States, "Pinter's *Homecoming*: The Shock of Nonrecognition" (1968), and Vera M. Jiji, "Pinter's Four Dimensional House: *The Homecoming*" (1974). The 1997–98 issue of the *Pinter Review* includes Pinter's first draft of *The Homecoming* and Francis Gillen's article "Pinter at Work: An Introduction to the First Draft of *The Homecoming* and Its Relationship to the Completed Drama."

LUIGI PIRANDELLO

As a general overview of Pirandello's life, Gaspare Guidice's *Pirandello: A Biography* (1963; abridged trans. 1975) is more measured than Domenico Vittorini's *The Drama of Luigi Pirandello* (1935), written only one year after Pirandello had received the Nobel Prize. Because of Pirandello's place in the canon of modern drama, many of the most important commentators on modern drama have devoted essays or book chapters to his work. Among the classics in the field are Eric Bentley's *The Pirandello Commentaries* (1985) and Francis Fergusson's

The Idea of the Theater, a Study of Ten Plays: The Art of Drama in Changing Perspective (1949), which places Pirandello in relation to other modern dramatists such as George Bernard Shaw and Bertolt Brecht. The best essay on Pirandello and metatheater is by Maurizio Grande, "Pirandello and the Theatre-within-the-Theatre: Thresholds and Frames in *Cascuno a suo modo*," in Gian-Paolo Biasin, ed., *Luigi Pirandello: Contemporary Perspectives* (1999). Roger W. Oliver's *Dreams of Passion: The Theater of Luigi Pirandello* (1979) focuses on Pirandello's theory of humor and applies it to his best-known plays, including *Six Characters*. The best book-length study of Pirandello in English is Ann Hallamore Caesar's *Characters and Authors in Luigi Pirandello* (1998), which includes detailed discussions of Pirandello's aesthetic theories and also an incisive critique of his patriarchal family structures. Daniela Bini's *Pirandello and His Muse: The Plays for Marta Abba* (1998) takes a similar approach to Pirandello's late plays. Pirandello's work in the theater is captured in *Luigi Pirandello in the Theatre: A Documentary Record*, ed. Susan Bassnett and Jennifer Lorch (1993), and in A. Richard Sogliuzzo's *Luigi Pirandello, Director: The Playwright in the Theatre* (1982). The political aspects of Pirandello's work are articulated especially well by Mary Ann Frese Witt in *The Search for Modern Tragedy: Aesthetic Fascism in Italy and France* (2001).

GEORGE BERNARD SHAW

Throughout his lifetime Shaw not only tried to control the presentation of his plays, he also carefully orchestrated his public persona, essentially collaborating with, if not ghostwriting, every attempt at authorized biography. Thus Michael Holroyd's four-volume *Bernard Shaw* (1988–92) may stand for some time as the only definitive and reasonably objective study of his life and work. Shaw repeatedly revised his plays even after publication; Dan Laurence's two-volume *Bernard Shaw: A Bibliography* (1983) meticulously traces Shaw's complete oeuvre. *The Bodley Head Bernard Shaw: Collected Plays with Their Prefaces*, 7 vols. (1970–74), is considered the definitive edition. Laurence also edited Shaw's four-volume *Collected Letters* (1965–88), which shed important light on his plays and other writings; many additional edited volumes of letters between Shaw and individual correspondents have also been published. Shaw published selections from his critical and political writings during his lifetime; scholarly editions of his dramatic, art, and music criticism have appeared more recently. Major Shaw research archives, which include both published and unpublished materials, are located in the British Library, the Berg Collection of the New York Public Library, the Bernard F. Burgunder Collection at Cornell University, and the Harry Ransom Humanities Research Center at the University of Texas at Austin.

Shaw's astounding volume of writing is matched only by the vast body of critical writing about him and his work. The three-volume (to date) *G. B. Shaw: An Annotated Bibliography of Writings about Him*, comp. J. P. Wearing (1986–), provides a helpful starting point for research. T. F. Evans, ed., *Shaw: The Critical Heritage* (1976) includes excerpts from reviews of his plays. Christopher Innes, ed., *The Cambridge Companion to George Bernard Shaw* (1998), includes current essays that provide valuable overviews of major topics in Shaw scholarship and contains extensive bibliographical suggestions. Raymond Mander and Joe Mitchenson's *Theatrical Companion to Shaw: A Pictorial Record of the First Performances of the Plays of George Bernard Shaw* (1954) remains the best record of his works in performance.

Among many full-length studies worth consulting are Eric Bentley, *Bernard Shaw* (1947); Tracy C. Davis, *George Bernard Shaw and the Socialist Theatre* (1994); Bernard F. Dukore, *Bernard Shaw, Playwright: Aspects of Shavian Drama* (1973); J. Ellen Gainor, *Shaw's Daughters: Dramatic and Narrative Constructions of Gender* (1991); Arthur Ganz, *George Bernard Shaw* (1983); Martin Meisel, *Shaw and the Nineteenth-Century Theater* (1963); Margery M. Morgan, *The Shavian Playground: An Exploration of the Art of George Bernard Shaw* (1972); Alfred Turco Jr., *Shaw's Moral Vision: The Self and Salvation* (1976); and Brad Kent, ed., *George Bernard Shaw in Context* (2015). Shaw scholarship has also flourished in essay form. There are three journals entirely devoted to Shaw—the *Shavian*, the *Shaw Bulletin*, and *Shaw: The Annual of Bernard Shaw Studies*—but essays abound throughout the periodic literature as well as in anthologies. For discussions of *Pygmalion* in particular, readers may wish to consult Awam Amkpa, "Drama and the Languages of Postcolonial Desire: Bernard Shaw's *Pygmalion*" (1999); Milton Crane, "*Pygmalion*: Bernard Shaw's Dramatic Theory and Practice" (1951); J. Ellen Gainor, "Bernard Shaw and the Drama of Imperialism," in Sue-Ellen Case and Janelle Reinelt, eds., *The Performance of Power: Theatrical Discourse and Politics* (1991); Celia Marshik, "Parodying the £5 Virgin: Bernard

Shaw and the Playing of *Pygmalion*" (2000); Jean Reynolds, "Deconstructing Henry Higgins, or Eliza as Derridean 'Text'" (1994); and Jennifer Buckley, "Talking Machines: Shaw, Phonography, *Pygmalion*" (2015). Derek McGovern's essay "From Stage Play to Hybrid: Shaw's Three Editions of *Pygmalion*" (2011) compares Shaw's original text with two later revisions he wrote in response to the 1938 British film adaptation, which ended (in defiance of Shaw's screenplay) with Eliza returning to Higgins.

SAM SHEPARD

Buried Child originally appeared in the collection *Seven Plays* (1981); the revised version was published first in *American Theatre* (with an interview, 1996) and then by Dramatists Play Service, Inc. (1997). Only the revised version is now authorized for production. The most comprehensive biography to date is Don Shewey's *Sam Shepard* (1985; updated ed., 1997). Earlier biographies by Martin Tucker, *Sam Shepard* (1992), and Ellen Oumano, *Sam Shepard: The Life and Dream of an American Dreamer* (1986), are also useful. Shepard criticism mushroomed during the 1980s and 1990s with such full-length studies as Ron Mottram, *Inner Landscapes: The Theater of Sam Shepard* (1984); Lynda Hart, *Sam Shepard's Metaphorical Stages* (1987); Leslie A. Wade, *Sam Shepard and the American Theatre* (1997); Stephen J. Bottoms, *The Theatre of Sam Shepard: States of Crisis* (1998); and James A. Crank, *Understanding Sam Shepard* (2012). Johan Callen takes Shepard studies in new directions with his *Dis/figuring Sam Shepard* (2007). In addition, several essay collections contain insightful perspectives on his dramaturgy: see Kimball King, ed., *Sam Shepard: A Casebook* (1988); Bonnie Maranca, ed., *American Dreams: The Imagination of Sam Shepard* (1981), which also contains essays by and interviews with the dramatist; Leonard Wilcox, ed., *Rereading Shepard: Contemporary Critical Essays on the Plays of Sam Shepard* (1993); and Matthew Roudané, ed., *The Cambridge Companion to Sam Shepard* (2002), which contains a revealing interview with the playwright.

Richard Gilman's critical introduction to Shepard's *Seven Plays* and Ross Wetzsteon's to *Fool for Love and Other Plays* (1984) both provide invaluable commentary. John Dungan's *File on Shepard* (1989) chronicles production information and reviews. Noteworthy articles on *Buried Child* include Thomas Nash, "Sam Shepard's *Buried Child*: The Ironic Use of Folklore" (1983); Charles Whiting, "Digging Up *Buried Child*" (1988); Steven D. Putzel and Suzanne

R. Westfall, "The Back Side of Myth: Sam Shepard's Subversion of Mythic Codes in *Buried Child*" (1989); Tucker Orbison, "Authorization and Subversion of Myth in Shepard's *Buried Child*" (1994); and James R. Stacy, "Making the Grave Less Deep: A Descriptive Assessment of Sam Shepard's Revisions to *Buried Child*" (1997).

WOLE SOYINKA

For an authoritative text and extensive background readings on *Death and the King's Horseman*, consult the Norton Critical Edition, edited by Simon Gikandi (2003). The general bibliography on Soyinka's work is extensive. Book-length accounts started to appear in the early 1970s—notably, Eldred Duromsimi Jones's *The Writing of Wole Soyinka* (1973; 3d ed., 1988). A more recent study, Derek Wright's *Wole Soyinka Revisited* (1993), provides a more nuanced analysis of the dramatic works; it focuses on the different theatrical categories, particularly ritual, tragedy, and satire, that are central for understanding Soyinka's work. Ketu H. Katrak's *Wole Soyinka and Modern Tragedy* (1986) examines Soyinka's attempt to create a "Yoruba tragedy." By far the best of the critical literature on the playwright is Biodun Jeyifo's *Wole Soyinka: Politics, Poetics and Postcoloniality* (2004), which analyzes the complex relations between colonial culture, independence, and literature that mark his oeuvre. Jeyifo is among those intellectuals with whom Soyinka has heatedly debated the relation between art and politics; see, for example, Soyinka's collection of essays, *Art, Dialogue, and Outrage: Essays on Literature and Culture* (1988; rev. and expanded ed., 1993). Also useful is a collection of interviews, *Conversations with Wole Soyinka*, ed. Biodun Jeyifo (2001). Other major critics to have devoted attention to Soyinka are the philosopher Anthony Appiah, in *In My Father's House: Africa in the Philosophy of Culture* (1992), and Henry Louis Gates Jr., in "Being, the Will, and the Semantics of Death" (1981). Valuable collections of essays on Soyinka include James Gibb, ed., *Critical Perspectives on Wole Soyinka* (1980), and Biodun Jeyifo, ed., *Perspectives on Wole Soyinka: Freedom and Complexity* (2001). Jonathan Peters's *A Dance of Masks: Senghor, Achebe, Soyinka* (1978) and Kole Omotoso's *Achebe or Soyinka? A Study in Contrasts* (1996) are noteworthy comparative studies of Soyinka.

AUGUST STRINDBERG

The best biography available is Michael Meyer's *Strindberg* (1985), which seeks to distinguish between Strindberg's autobiographical novels and plays and the facts of his own life, especially his three marriages. The topic of autobiography receives special focus in Michael Robinson's *Strindberg and Autobiography: Writing and Reading a Life* (1986) and Harry G. Carlson's *Out of Inferno: Strindberg's Reawakening as an Artist* (1996). Particular attention to Strindberg the playwright is paid by Evert Sprinchorn (whose translation of *Miss Julie* in included in this volume) in *Strindberg as Dramatist* (1992) and by Egil Törnqvist, Strindberg's main Swedish interpreter, in *Strindbergian Drama: Themes and Structure* (1982). More interested in the literary and poetic dimensions of Strindberg's drama is another translator of his plays, Harry G. Carlson, in *Strindberg and the Poetry of Myth* (1982). Also commendable is Freddie Rokem's *Strindberg's Secret Codes* (2004). Given Strindberg's influence, most of the classic studies of modern drama dedicate important essays to the playwright, including Robert Brustein's *The Theatre of Revolt: An Approach to the Modern Drama* (1964), which emphasizes Strindberg's revolt against modern life, and Raymond Williams's *Drama from Ibsen to Brecht* (1968), which combines social analysis with an attention to form. An international collection of essays on Strindberg was assembled by Göran Stockenström in *Strindberg's Dramaturgy* (1988) as well as by Michael Robinson in *Studies in Strindberg* (1998). More interested in particular genres is Børge Gedsø Madsen's *Strindberg's Naturalistic Theatre: Its Relation to French Naturalism* (1962), Walter Johnson's *Strindberg and the Historical Drama* (1963), and John Ward's *The Social and Religious Plays of Strindberg* (1980). And Strindberg's influence on expressionist theater is detailed in Michael Robinson and Sven Rossel's collection *Expressionism and Modernism: New Approaches to August Strindberg* (1999). Most thoroughly dedicated to Strindberg on stage is Frederick J. Marker and Lise-Lone Marker's *Strindberg and Modernist Theatre: Post-Inferno Drama on the Stage* (2002). For analysis specifically of *Miss Julie*, see the collection edited by Egil Törnqvist and Barry Jacobs, *Strindberg's "Miss Julie": A Play and Its Transpositions* (1988).

JOHN MILLINGTON SYNGE

Synge's plays have been edited by Ann Saddlemyer in volumes 3 and 4 of J. M. Synge, *Collected Works*, ed. Robin Skelton (1962–68); the appendix to *Riders to the Sea* (in volume 3) includes a transcription of Synge's draft manuscripts. W. J. McCormack, *Fool of the Family: A Life of J. M. Synge* (2000), is an excellent recent biography of Synge, though David H. Greene and Edward M. Stephens, *J. M. Synge, 1871–1909* (1959; rev. ed., 1989), and David M. Kiely, *John Millington Synge: A Biography* (1994), are also valuable. E. H. Mikhail, ed., *J. M. Synge: Interviews and Recollections* (1977), contains first-person accounts by those who knew Synge.

The following books provide useful discussions of Synge's drama: Alan Price, *Synge and Anglo-Irish Drama* (1961); Robin Skelton, *The Writings of J. M. Synge* (1971) and *J. M. Synge and His World* (1971); Nicholas Grene, *Synge: A Critical Study of the Plays* (1975); Eugene Benson, *J. M. Synge* (1982); Mary C. King, *The Drama of J. M. Synge* (1985); Donna Gerstenberger, *John Millington Synge* (1964; rev. ed., 1990); and Declan Kiberd, *Synge and the Irish Language* (1979; 2nd ed., 1993). Among the important collections of essays on Synge are Edward A. Kopper Jr., *A J. M. Synge Literary Companion* (1988); Daniel J. Casey, *Critical Essays on John Millington Synge* (1994); and Alexander G. Gonzalez, *Assessing the Achievement of J. M. Synge* (1996). David R. Clark's edition of *Riders to the Sea* (1970) includes earlier critical essays on Synge's play.

Intellectual, cultural, and theatrical background to Synge and his art can be found in D. E. S. Maxwell, *A Critical History of Modern Irish Drama, 1891–1980* (1984); Declan Kiberd, *Inventing Ireland* (1995); Gregory Castle, *Modernism and the Celtic Revival* (2001); Mary Trotter, *Ireland's National Theaters: Political Performance and the Origins of the Irish Dramatic Movement* (2001); Ben Levitas, *The Theatre of Nation: Irish Drama and Cultural Nationalism, 1890–1916* (2002); and Brian Cliff and Nicholas Grene, eds., *Synge and Edwardian Ireland* (2012).

SOPHIE TREADWELL

Machinal was first published in John Gassner's influential anthology, *Twenty-Five Best Plays of the Modern American Theatre, Early Series* (1949). It was reprinted in Judith Barlow's *Plays by American Women, 1900–1930* (1985), the anthology that led to the play's theatrical revival in 1990 and increased scholarly interest in her writing, especially among feminist critics. A number of Treadwell's other plays are now available through the *North American Women's Drama* database, issued by Alexander Street Press. The University of Arizona Library oversees the major archive of Treadwell materials, while the Billy Rose Theatre Collection of the New York Public Library maintains production-related documents and photos.

Theater scholar Jerry Dickey is the leading authority on Sophie Treadwell; he has written extensively on her life and work and serves as the literary advisor to her estate. Among Dickey's valuable publications, see his *Sophie Treadwell: A Research and Production Sourcebook* (1997), which provides a comprehensive bibliography; "The 'Real Lives' of Sophie Treadwell: Expressionism and the Feminist Aesthetic in *Machinal* and *For Saxophone*" in Jeanne Campbell Reesman, ed., *Speaking the Other Self: American Women Writers* (1997); and "The Expressionist Moment: Sophie Treadwell" in Brenda Murphy, ed., *The Cambridge Companion to American Women Playwrights* (1999). With Barbara Ozieblo, Dickey published *Susan Glaspell and Sophie Treadwell* (2008), and with J. Ellen Gainor, he wrote "Susan Glaspell and Sophie Treadwell: Staging Feminism and Modernism, 1915–1941" in *A Companion to Twentieth-Century American Drama*, ed. David Krasner (2005). With Miriam López-Rodríguez, Dickey edited *Broadway's Bravest Woman: Selected Writings of Sophie Treadwell* (2006).

Articles of note by other scholars include Nancy Wynn, "Sophie Treadwell: Author of *Machinal*" in the *Journal of American Drama and Theatre* (1991); Ginger Strand, "Treadwell's Neologism: *Machinal*" in *Theatre Journal* (1992); and Jennifer Jones, "In Defense of the Woman: Sophie Treadwell's *Machinal*" in *Modern Drama* (1994). Useful essays in edited volumes include Barbara L. Bywaters, "Marriage, Madness, and Murder in Sophie Treadwell's *Machinal*" in June Schlueter, ed., *Modern American Drama: The Female Canon*, (1990); Kornelia Tancheva, "Sophie Treadwell's Play *Machinal*: Strategies of Reception and Interpretation" in Arthur Gewirtz and James J. Kolb, eds., *Experimenters, Rebels, and Disparate Voices: The Theatre of the 1920s Celebrates American Diversity* (2003); Richard Wattenberg, "Sophie Treadwell and the Frontier Myth: Western Motifs in *Machinal* and *Hope for a Harvest*" in Marc Maufort, ed., *Staging Difference: Cultural Pluralism in American Theatre and Drama* (1995); and Miriam López-Rodríguez, "Sophie Treadwell, Jung, and the Mandala: Acting a Gendered Identity" in Barbara Ozieblo and María Dolores Narbona-Carrión, eds., *Codifying the National Self: Spectators, Actors and the American Dramatic Text* (2006).

Ronald H. Wainscott provides a detailed and informative historical analysis of American expressionist plays and productions in *The Emergence of the Modern American Theater 1914–1929* (1997). Julia A. Walker offers an additional insightful reading of *Machinal* in her book *Expressionism and Modernism in the American Theatre: Bodies, Voices, Words* (2005).

Jennifer Parent has researched the original Broadway production in her article, "Arthur Hopkins' Production of Sophie Treadwell's *Machinal*" in *The Drama Review: TDR* (1982).

For information on Ruth Snyder and Judd Gray, see John Kobler, *The Trial of Ruth Snyder and Judd Gray* (1938) and Landis MacKellar, *The "Double Indemnity" Murder: Ruth Snyder, Judd Gray, and New York's Crime of the Century* (2006). Ann Jones's *Women Who Kill* (1980, 2009) offers a compelling feminist historical reading of Ruth Snyder's case, which Jessie Ramey extends through linguistic analysis in "The Bloody Blonde and the Marble Woman: Gender and Power in the Case of Ruth Snyder" in the *Journal of Social History* (2004). Jean Marie Lutes analyzes the role of emotion in the trial, its press coverage, and Treadwell's play in "Tears on Trial in the 1920s: Female Emotion and Style in *Chicago* and *Machinal*" in *Tulsa Studies in Women's Literature* (2011). W. David Sievers's *Freud on Broadway* (1955) remains a useful resource on psychoanalysis and psychological theory as they are represented in the American theater. For a history of American women journalists, see Ishbel Ross, *Ladies of the Press: The Story of Women in Journalism by an Insider* (1936).

PAULA VOGEL

The best general introduction to the work of Paula Vogel is the book-length study *Paula Vogel* by Joanna Mansbridge (2014). A shorter introductory overview, which does not include more recent work, can be found in Christopher Bigsby, *Contemporary American Playwrights* (1999). For further study, consult the chapter on Paula Vogel in *A Queer Sort of Materialism* (2003) by David Savran, her fellow student at Cornell and long-time colleague at Brown University. For a discussion of trauma theory in *How I Learned to Drive*, see Ann Pellegrini's "Staging Sexual Injury: *How I learned to Drive*," in Janelle G. Reinelt and Joseph R. Roach, eds., *Critical Theory and Performance* (2d ed., 2007), as well as Graley Herren's "Narrating, Witnessing, and Healing Trauma in Paula Vogel's *How I Learned to Drive*," in *Modern Drama* (2010).

OSCAR WILDE

While there is no standard edition of Oscar Wilde's plays, *"The Importance of Being Earnest" and Other Plays*, ed. David Raby (1995), is a useful collection. Richard Ellmann, *Oscar Wilde* (1987), is considered the authoritative biography. Studies of Wilde's career include Rodney Shewan, *Oscar Wilde: Art and Egotism* (1977); Regenia Gagnier, *Idylls of the Marketplace: Oscar*

Wilde and the Victorian Public (1986); Alan Sinfield, *The Wilde Century: Effeminacy, Oscar Wilde, and the Queer Moment* (1994); Josephine M. Guy and Ian Small, *Oscar Wilde's Profession: Writing and the Culture Industry in the Late Nineteenth Century* (2000); Neil Sammells, *Wilde Style: The Plays and Prose of Oscar Wilde* (2000); John Sloan, *Oscar Wilde* (2003); Paul L. Fortunato, *Modernist Aesthetics and Consumer Culture in the Writings of Oscar Wilde* (2007); Kerry Powell, *Acting Wilde: Victorian Sexuality, Theatre, and Oscar Wilde* (2009); and Ruth Robbins, *Oscar Wilde* (2011). Early critical responses to Wilde's life and work are included in Richard Ellmann, ed., *Oscar Wilde: A Collection of Critical Essays* (1969). C. George Sandulescu, ed., *Rediscovering Oscar Wilde* (1994); Peter Raby, ed., *The Cambridge Companion to Oscar Wilde* (1997); and Kerry Powell and Peter Raby, eds., *Oscar Wilde in Context* (2013) are valuable collections of essays.

Wilde's drama is the subject of Alan Bird, *The Plays of Oscar Wilde* (1977); Katharine Worth, *Oscar Wilde* (1983); Sos Eltis, *Revising Wilde: Society and Subversion in the Plays of Oscar Wilde* (1996); and Kerry Powell, *Oscar Wilde and the Theatre of the 1890s* (1990). Joseph Donohue and Ruth Berggren, eds., *Oscar Wilde's "The Importance of Being Earnest": A Reconstructive Critical Edition of the Text of the First Production at St. James's Theatre, London, 1895* (1995), provides an extensively annotated edition of Wilde's masterpiece with an exhaustive discussion of the play's composition and manuscript history.

TENNESSEE WILLIAMS

The standard collection of Tennessee Williams's plays is *The Theatre of Tennessee Williams*, published in eight volumes by New Directions (1971–81). Additional plays from Williams's early career have been published separately. Among the several biographies of Williams, the finest is Lyle Leverich's *Tom: The Unknown Tennessee Williams* (1995), which covers the playwright's life to 1945. Students interested in Williams's life as a whole might consult Ronald Hayman, *Tennessee Williams: Everyone Else Is an Audience* (1993) and theater critic John Lahr's award-winning *Tennessee Williams: Mad Pilgrimage of the Flesh* (2014). Richard F. Leavitt, ed., *The World of Tennessee Williams* (1978), includes photographs, theater programs, and other documents illustrating Williams's life and career, while Philip Kolin, ed., *The Tennessee Williams Encyclopedia* (2004), contains valuable information on the playwright's works. Kenneth Holditch and Richard Freeman

Leavitt's *Tennessee Williams and the South* (2002) discusses the profound influence of this region on Williams's work.

The following include valuable critical discussions of Williams's drama: Jac Tharpe, ed., *Tennessee Williams: A Tribute* (1977); Roger Boxill, *Tennessee Williams* (1987); Alice Griffin, *Understanding Tennessee Williams* (1995); Matthew C. Roudané, ed., *The Cambridge Companion to Tennessee Williams* (1997); Robert A. Martin, ed., *Critical Essays on Tennessee Williams* (1997); Philip C. Kolin, ed., *Tennessee Williams: A Guide to Research and Performance* (1998); Nancy M. Tischler, *Student Companion to Tennessee Williams* (2000); and Judith J. Thompson, *Tennessee Williams' Plays: Memory, Myth, and Symbol* (1987; rev. ed., 2002). One of the best discussions of Williams's dramatic career can be found in volume 2 of C. W. E. Bigsby, *A Critical Introduction to Twentieth-Century American Drama* (1984). Annette J. Saddik's *Tennessee Williams and the Theatre of Excess: The Strange, the Crazed, the Queer* (2015) focuses on the playwright's late plays but offers a fascinating perspective on his playwriting career as a whole. The influence of Williams's homosexuality on his drama is explored in David Savran, *Communists, Cowboys, and Queers: The Politics of Masculinity in the Work of Arthur Miller and Tennessee Williams* (1992), and John M. Clum, *Acting Gay: Male Homosexuality in Modern Drama* (1992; expanded ed., 1994).

The essays in Jordan Y. Miller, ed., *Twentieth Century Interpretations of "A Streetcar Named Desire"* (1971), are devoted exclusively to Williams's play, as are Thomas P. Adler, *"A Streetcar Named Desire": The Moth and the Lantern* (1990), and Philip C. Kolin, ed., *Confronting Tennessee Williams's "A Streetcar Named Desire": Essays in Critical Pluralism* (1993). Philip C. Kolin, *Williams: "A Streetcar Named Desire"* (2000), provides a history of *Streetcar* in performance, while Brenda Murphy's *Tennessee Williams and Elia Kazan: A Collaboration in the Theatre* (1992) examines the productions of *Streetcar* and other Williams plays directed by Kazan. Kazan's valuable directorial notes on *Streetcar* are excerpted in the *Twentieth Century Interpretations* collection mentioned above. Maurice Yacowar's *Tennessee Williams and Film* (1977) offers a useful discussion of the 1951 film version of Williams's play.

AUGUST WILSON

The plays of August Wilson's twentieth-century cycle were published in 2007 by Theatre Communications Group in a ten-volume collection. The best book-length studies of August Wilson's life and plays are Sandra G. Shannon, *The Dramatic Vision of August Wilson* (1995); Kim Pereira, *August Wilson and the African-American Odyssey* (1995); Peter Wolfe, *August Wilson* (1999); Harry J. Elam Jr., *The Past as Present in the Drama of August Wilson* (2004); Mary L. Bogumil, *Understanding August Wilson* (rev. ed., (2011); and Sandra G. Shannon, ed., *August Wilson's Pittsburgh Cycle: Critical Perspectives on the Plays* (2016). Harry J. Elam Jr., "August Wilson," in David Krasner, ed., *A Companion to Twentieth-Century American Drama* (2005), is a general introduction to Wilson's work, while Yvonne Shafer, *August Wilson: A Research and Production Sourcebook* (1998), and Mary Ellen Snodgrass, *August Wilson: A Literary Companion* (2004), are valuable resources for the student of Wilson's plays. Jackson R. Bryer and Mary C. Hartig, eds., *Conversations with August Wilson* (2006), contains Wilson's major interviews. Dana A. Williams and Sandra G. Shannon, eds., *August Wilson and Black Aesthetics* (2004), examines the cultural politics of Wilson as an African American writer. The essays in Alan Nadel, ed., *August Wilson: Completing the Twentieth-Century Cycle* (2010), discuss Wilson's final five plays and the overall arc of the cycle as a whole.

Three collections of essays—Marilyn Elkins, ed., *August Wilson: A Casebook* (1994); Alan Nadel, ed., *May All Your Fences Have Gates: Essays on the Drama of August Wilson* (1994); and Christopher Bigsby, ed., *The Cambridge Companion to August Wilson* (2007)—present the range of critical approaches adopted by scholars analyzing Wilson's plays. Not surprisingly, *Fences* comes in for a large share of their discussion. Joan Fishman, "Developing His Song: August Wilson's *Fences*" (in Elkins), traces the development of Wilson's dramatic text through revisions, staged readings, and productions; Michael Awkward, "'The Crookeds with the Straights': *Fences*, Race, and the Politics of Adaptation" (in Nadel), considers *Fences* in the context of Wilson's well-publicized insistence that any film production of the play be directed by an African American. Susan Koprince, "Baseball as History and Myth in August Wilson's *Fences*" (2006), discusses the role of baseball in the play, as does David Letzler, "Walking around the Fences: Troy Maxson and the Ideology of 'Going Down Swinging'" (2014).

The black feminist scholar bell hooks has challenged the portrayal of women in Wilson's *Fences* in *Yearning: Race, Gender, and Cultural Politics* (1990). Harry J. Elam Jr., "August Wilson's Women," and Missy Dehn Kubitschek,

"August Wilson's Gender Lesson" (both in Nadel), address the question of Wilson's women from feminist and other theoretical perspectives. Carla J. McDonough, *Staging Masculinity: Male Identity in Contemporary American Drama* (1997), considers the question of masculinity in Wilson's drama in the context of social issues facing urban black males.

Glossary

absurdism / Absurd, Theatre of the: phrase first coined in 1961 by theater critic Martin Esslin to describe theater set in a world without God, reason, or meaning—a world through which characters are left to stumble aimlessly. Absurdist plays transcend traditions of **realism** and frequently combine elements from theatrical movements such as **expressionism**, **surrealism**, and **symbolism** to create a **tone** or sense of atmosphere that conveys the irrational world of the play. Representative writers of the genre include SAMUEL BECKETT, Eugène Ionesco, JEAN GENET, EDWARD ALBEE, and HAROLD PINTER. ALFRED JARRY'S *UBU ROI* is a precursor to the Theater of the Absurd.

act: traditional segmentation of a play that indicates a change in time, action, or location, and helps organize a play's dramatic structure. Plays may be composed of acts that, in turn, are composed of **scenes**. The Romans were the first to divide plays into acts, although the Greeks before them broke up dramas with choral interludes. Various theatrical movements emphasized the importance of including a specified number of acts. SHAKESPEARE'S plays were divided into five acts when they were published, and thereafter the five-act structure became the model for playwrights through the end of the nineteenth century. Modern dramatists began to break the tradition at the turn of the twentieth century; contemporary plays are often divided into two acts.

acting: the portrayal of a character's words and actions by an actor. Acting requires actors to embody the personality, characteristics, and motivations of a character or individual they are portraying. A psychological or internal approach to acting asks actors to rely on personal experience and emotive response, whereas an external or physical approach asks the actor to work from the outside in, creating a physical exterior as a means of exploring the interior motivation or objective for the character.

action: the physical activity or accomplishment of a character's intentions. Actions are not the events in a **plot** but rather the force that pushes the plot along. One character's action inevitably leads to another action, which together form part of a play's overall action. Aristotle describes tragedy as "an imitation of an action," meaning that a character's choices are not simply narrated but acted out onstage.

actor: an individual who portrays a **character** in a play or theatrical entertainment. Actors in a drama represent characters through imitation, interpretation of dialogue, and interaction with other persons on the stage. The Greek playwright Thespis is credited as the first actor (and from his name we have the word *thespian* for actor) because he was the first playwright to incorporate lines of dialogue in his work.

aestheticism: term applied in nineteenth-century Europe and America to the movement that advocated the creation of "art for art's sake" (a slogan coined by the philosopher Victor Cousin). Influenced by the German Romantics such as JOHANN WOLFGANG VON GOETHE, a wide range of writers and artists adopted the philosophy because it advocated the primacy of beauty over values such as political utility, thus giving them a sense of purpose. The movement is associated with writers such as OSCAR WILDE.

agon: an ancient Greek term used to denote the fundamental conflict in any drama. *Agon* also is the term used for a theatrical convention typically associated with **Old Comedy** where the chorus is divided into two halves to debate an important idea or political question that relates to the major **themes** of the play. In ARISTOPHANES' *LYSISTRATA*, for example, the chorus is composed of a group of old men and a group of old women. The *agon* in this case provides comic fuel in the battle of the sexes.

alienation effect: *see* **estrangement effect.**

allegory: extended metaphor in which characters, objects, and actions represent abstract concepts or principles in a narrative that conveys a moral lesson. Allegorical plays were especially popular in medieval England. In *EVERYMAN*, for example, the title character is intended to represent humanity itself as he negotiates the temporal state of existence.

amphitheater: A classical Greek theater usually built into a hillside with a semicircular playing space called an ***orchestra*** surrounded by a semicircle of tiered seats. *Amphitheater* can also refer to a modern theatrical space with a similar design.

anachronism: term used to describe anything incongruous with its historical context— for instance, the presence of a telephone in medieval England. Dramatists often use anachronisms in an intentional blending of worlds, sometimes to achieve a comic effect. An unintentional anachronistic gesture or expression, however, such as the use of modern slang in historical drama, can prove distracting to spectators.

anagnorisis: the moment of recognition, or enlightenment, that is realized when a character discovers the true relation of himself or herself to the incidents in the plot and to the other characters within it. This term was first described by Aristotle in his *Poetics*.

antagonist: the person or force that opposes the **protagonist** or main character in a drama or narrative. The term derives from the Greek, meaning "opponent" or "rival."

antihero: a protagonist or central character who lacks the qualities typically associated with heroism—for example, bravery, morality, or good looks—but still manages to earn sympathy from the spectator.

anti-masque: a form of theatrical entertainment introduced by BEN JONSON in 1608 intended to contrast the beauty and style of the court **masque** with stories that included grotesque or silly characters and dances. Often, masques and anti-masques would be performed together to demonstrate the scenic designer's ability to juxtapose elegance with ugliness.

apron: the area of a stage that stretches out past the primary playing space or **proscenium arch**. The apron can be used to cover the orchestra pit in a traditional proscenium theater.

arena: a theater with seating that surrounds the playing area on all sides—sometimes referred to as "theater in the round"—to create a more intimate experience for the audience. Stage configurations for arena theaters can include circular, oval, or rectangular playing areas.

aside: a theatrical convention (commonly used in drama prior to the nineteenth century but less often afterward) in which a **character**, unnoticed by the other characters on stage, speaks frankly and directly to the audience to express a thought.

Atellan farce: a form of comic **burlesque** from Atella, a Southern town in Italy, that was performed at Roman festivals during the third through first century B.C.E. The art form is considered a precursor to *commedia dell'arte*, both of which relied heavily on improvisation by a small set of **stock characters** such as the fool, the braggart, and the comic old man.

auto sacramentale: a form of religious drama presented in Spain during the sixteenth and seventeenth centuries, similar to the morality or cycle plays of England. The plays were performed outdoors on *carros*, or wagons, as part of the Feast of **Corpus Christi**, a lengthy celebration intended to honor the redemptive power of Jesus Christ. The plays were enormously popular and commanded the attention of Spain's leading dramatists.

avant-garde: originally a military term meaning "advance guard" (French), the term was increasingly used to describe unusual and therefore advanced forms of art and theater. The concept of avant-garde art can be applied to numerous theatrical movements aligned in their rejection of social institutions and established artistic conventions, though it is also used to describe artistic experimentation in the interest of pushing the art form forward. **Symbolism**, **futurism**, **expressionism**, **Dadaism**, and **surrealism** are all examples of avant-garde movements.

bhavas: in **Sanskrit** drama, the eight fundamental human emotions (pleasure, mirth, sorrow, wrath, vigor, fear, disgust, and wonder) that are paired with *rasas*, the aesthetic experiences of the spectator or the mood of the scene in question. The various combinations of these elements create a diversity of moods and experiences that enhance the viewers' sensations when watching a play.

Black Arts Movement: cultural movement in the United States during the 1960s that sought to alter the mainstream theatrical climate by cultivating works written for and about African Americans. A number of organizations spearheaded the movement including Amiri Baraka's (1934–2014) Black Arts Repertoire Theatre, the New Lafayette Theatre, and the Negro Ensemble Company.

blackface: cosmetic technique, common in nineteenth- and early twentieth-century **minstrel** shows and vaudeville performances, by which a performer paints his or her face with dark makeup to portray an African American. Extremely popular with audiences at the time, the practice is now considered deeply offensive because it propagates stereotyped caricatures of race. In contemporary theater, the practice has occasionally been appropriated by African American playwrights and directors to call attention to issues of race.

blank verse: the verse form most like everyday speech; in English, unrhymed **iambic pentameter**. In the sixteenth century blank verse became the standard form for dramatic and epic poetry. Most of SHAKESPEARE's plays are in blank verse.

blocking: the specific movement or positioning of actors onstage intended to enhance the theatrical experience for the spectator, whether that be the realistic portrayal of a domestic conflict or an abstract idea. Blocking can also set the tone of a play or convey ideas not intrinsic to the dialogue or script. Typically, the **director** determines the blocking in a play.

bugaku: a Japanese form of mask play first imported from China and India in the seventh century that later included dances from Korea, Tibet, and Vietnam. Performances were restricted to the royal court, and the form relied on strict tradition and technique. The subjects of these plays were taken from religious texts. *Bugaku* is still performed today on important state occasions.

bunraku: an elaborate form of Japanese puppet (or doll) theater that evolved from earlier puppet and storytelling traditions in the eleventh century and is still performed today. The dramas are three acts long and explore historical or domestic themes. The puppets onstage are generally two-thirds the size of the persons manipulating them, and the puppeteers are visible to the spectators. The chief operator wears a kimono, while the other participants wear black. The narrative (or *joruri*) is delivered by a speaker who stands to the right of the stage, and the action is underscored by the music of a *samisen* (a banjolike instrument). The best-known playwright of the genre is Chikamatsu Monzaemon (1653–1725).

burlesque: a form of performance that aims to mimic and distort its subject matter for comic purpose rather than invective criticism. *The Beggar's Opera* by John Gay (1685–1732), for example, mimics and pokes fun at the seriousness of traditional opera. In late nineteenth-century America, burlesques incorporating music and elements of fantasy became a popular medium for vaudeville or variety shows featuring bawdy sexual humor.

carros: wagons used as stages for *auto sacramentales*, performances that celebrated the Feast of **Corpus Christi** in Spain.

casting: the process of deciding which **actors** are to play which parts. Casting is an important factor in the establishment of **character** on stage.

catharsis (*katharis*): the emotional release or sense of relief a spectator may feel at the end of a tragedy. In his *Poetics*, Aristotle posits that the proper aim of tragedy is to arouse feelings of pity and fear and effectively rid the body of these feelings. *Katharsis* is the term he uses to describe this purging of emotions.

character: a player or personality integral to the telling of a story. In drama, actors must demonstrate character through *mimesis* or imitation rather than narration. (*See* **stock character**.)

chorēgos: in fifth-century B.C.E. Greek theater practice, the producer appointed to a playwright by an *archōn* (government leader) who underwrote the cost of training and costuming the chorus and musicians.

chorus: in Greek drama, a group of singers and dancers who often provide **exposition** and commentary on the action in the play.

City Dionysia: One of the four civic festivals held in ancient Greece each year in honor of the god **Dionysus** that are chiefly associated with the presentation of theatrical work. In the fifth century B.C.E., the festival incorporated tragedies, satyr plays, dithyrambic contests, choruses, and later in the century, comedies. Playwrights competed in the City Dionysia for prestige and prizes awarded by the state.

classical unities: *see* **unities**.

climax: in the language of traditional dramatic theory, the point in a drama's plot that is preceded by the **rising action** and followed by the **falling action**. It is sometimes also the moment of greatest crisis for the **protagonist** and/or other characters. (*See* **plot**.)

closet dramas: plays initially meant to be performed or recited at small gatherings or read in private. During the first century B.C.E., when the Roman public lost interest in traditional comedies and tragedies, many dramatists were forced to abandon staged drama and instead wrote closet dramas for recitation at public banquets and other social events. GOETHE's *FAUST* and BÜCHNER's *WOYZECK* are later examples of closet dramas.

comedia nueva: literally, "new drama" (Spanish). The most popular dramatic form written during the **Golden Age of Spain**. In structure, the plays were composed of three acts in varying verse form that mixed both tragic and comic elements. Plots were drawn from history, mythology, legend, Italian *novelle* and other literary sources, the Bible, popular ballads, and the everyday life of country and town. Specialized subgenres included: the *comedias de capa y espada* ("cape and sword plays"), which featured stories of romance and intrigue, and *comedias de costumbres* ("comedies of manners"). LOPE DE VEGA CARPIO is one of the primary contributers to this form.

Comédie Française: the world's first national theater, established by the French monarchy. Formed by the merger of Paris's two acting companies, the company began performing in 1680 and became a dominant presence in the French theatrical industry.

comedy: from the Greek word *komos* meaning "band of revelers," comedy is a form of drama that is distinguished by humorous content and endings that are, on balance, "happy" ones. The first comic performances were entertainments associated with Greek fertility rights that later took the form of **satyr plays**. Traditional comedic structure and form can be attributed to the work of ARISTOPHANES, who incorporated bawdy jokes and songs into far-fetched scenarios with fantastical or farcical situations. The conventions of comedy vary from place to place and from one era to another, depending on the sense of humor or sensibility of the age in which it is written. Some comedies rely heavily on sharp, witty dialogue (SHERIDAN's *SCHOOL FOR SCANDAL*, for example), others on bodily humor and physical clowning (**Atellan farce** or *commedia dell'arte*), and still others on a blending of these conventions (SHAKESPEARE's comedies). No matter what theatrical conventions they employ, most comedies attempt to highlight absurdities of their society's norms and values.

comedy of character: a form of Italian comedy, conceived by Carlo Goldoni in the eighteenth century, that contradicted the popular conventions of *commedia dell'arte* and sought to embrace a more literary drama. Goldoni's comedies of character often revolve around a single **protagonist** and are noted for their realistic dialogue, plausible plots, and moralistic tone.

comedy of manners: a form of comedy that satirizes the foibles of the upper class and aristocracy by means of witty dialogue and the ridicule of social decorum. The form originated in the seventeenth century in works by MOLIÈRE and arrived in England during the Restoration in the works of WILLIAM WYCHERLEY, William Congreve (1670–1729), and others. In the late nineteenth century the form once again gained popularity in such comedies as OSCAR WILDE's *THE IMPORTANCE OF BEING EARNEST*.

commedia dell'arte: literally "comedy of professional players" (Italian). A genre of Italian theater that emerged at the end of the sixteenth century. Performance relied on the portrayal of **stock characters**—some of which were derived from Roman comic types—and the improvisation of action and dialogue from a basic plot outline. There are two categories of *commedia* characters: unmasked and masked. The unmasked roles include the young lovers (the young man described as the *innamorato* and the young woman described as the *innamorata*). The many masked roles can usually be divided into masters and servants. The masters include the *Capitano*, a braggart soldier whose romantic and military exploits are often discredited; *Pantalone*, a middle-aged or elderly merchant fond of courting young women; and *Dottore*, a pedantic show-off who often played Pantalone's friend or rival. The servant characters are typically described as *zanni*. The most popular include: *Arlecchino* or *Harlequin*, *Brighella*, and *Pulcinello*.

conflict: the central problem in the **plot**, the obstacle hindering a character from getting what he or she wants. Often, the diverging interests of the **protagonist** and **antagonist** create conflict.

context: the circumstantial or dramatic situation given to characters in a play by the playwright that can (and often does) affect the development and outcome of the drama and the decisions made by the characters.

corrales: the public theaters of Spain's **Golden Age**, similar to the open-air theaters of Elizabethan England. *Corrales* were constructed within square or rectangular courtyards. A raised stage with a permanent backdrop and upper levels was placed on one end of the courtyard with an open space, or *patio*, for standing spectators directly in front of it. On either side of the *patio* a section of ascending rows of seats known as the *gradas* extended to the second story. Above the *alojería* (or refreshment booth) at the end of the courtyard facing the stage, galleries accommodated additional spectators. Windows of buildings above the *gradas* served as box seats (*aposentos*), and additional levels of boxed seats or open galleries were available at the third- and fourth-floor levels.

Corpus Christi: a monthlong festival conceived by Pope Urban IV in 1264 to celebrate the redemptive power of the Holy Eucharist. The Corpus Christi cycle play was commissioned as a theatrical tribute to the events preceding Christ's birth as well as his life and resurrection. The church worked with secular groups in the presentation of the drama. The Latin of liturgical drama was abandoned in favor of vernacular dialogue that was spoken rather than chanted and thus could be readily understood by the audience.

crisis: *see* **climax**.

Cruelty, Theater of: term introduced in 1932 by French theorist and playwright Antonin Artaud (1896–1948) to describe his vision of theater that sought to unleash the desires of the soul and thereby to repudiate the conventionalized lifelessness of Western art and society. His purpose was to shock his audiences into recognition and to appeal to their primitive impulses.

cuckold: term used to characterize a married man whose wife has been unfaithful to him. A cuckold is often portrayed as wearing horns as an attribute of his condition.

cycle plays: also called *mystery cycles*, a form of medieval drama that coincided with the feast of **Corpus Christi**, a lengthy celebration intended to honor the redemptive power of Christ. Cycle plays were performed in the vernacular and composed of short plays presented throughout a day (or over the course of several days) that chronicled the religious history of humanity from the Creation through the Last Judgment. Most Corpus Christi plays were performed outdoors by secular groups sponsored by the guilds of varying professions. THE SECOND SHEPHERDS' PLAY is an example of a cycle play.

cyclic plot: a **plot** in which the play ends in much the same way it began, rendering the action of the play futile for the characters involved. SAMUEL BECKETT'S *WAITING FOR GODOT* has a cyclic plot.

Dadaism: a literary and artistic movement introduced by Tristan Tzara (1896–1963) in 1916 as a reaction to World War I. The principle motivation of the Dadaists was to illustrate the absurdity and chaos of the war by negating the traditional conventions of art. Performances therefore revered chaotic theory and incorporated discordant elements to showcase the inherent madness of human motivation. Their performances, or "manifestations," took place at a number of performance venues, including the Cabaret Voltaire in Zurich. Dadaism was eventually absorbed into **surrealism**.

decorum: the proper way that characters should act on stage as dictated by their disposition and social standing. This concept was central to **neoclassicism**, which flourished in continental Europe in the late sixteenth and seventeenth centuries.

denouement: in a play, the point in which the loose ends of a plot are tied up, though the dramatic conflict may not be entirely resolved.

deus ex machina: literally, "a god emerging from a machine" (Latin). The *mēchanē* or crane used for special effects in fifth-century B.C.E. Greek performance would suspend an actor in midair and propel him over the playing space. Dramatists, especially EURIPIDES, often utilized the device to introduce a god who would appear at the end of the play and resolve the plot. In *THE BACCHAE*, Dionysus emerges in the final moments to punish those who do not recognize his divinity. The term is used in contemporary criticism to describe a quick and contrived resolution to a play.

dialogue: language spoken by characters on stage. Dialogue differs from narration because it is delivered in the first person and seeks to imitate human interaction or convey the artistic purpose of the playwright. Dialogue does not necessarily need to be grounded in **realism** but must be consistent with the world of the play.

diction: the choice in language or words made by a playwright or performer in a drama to achieve a specific effect or style. *Diction* can also refer to a performer's manner of speech or rhetoric, sometimes used for character development.

Dionysus: god of wine, revelry, and fertility; son of Zeus, supreme god of ancient Greece, and Semele, a mortal woman. The origins of Greek drama are attributed to the celebrations in his honor at civic festivals called the **City Dionysia**.

director: in contemporary theater, the individual responsible for the theatrical concept of the play and its staging. In addition to **casting** actors, **blocking** the performers onstage, and running rehearsals, the director must coordinate the contributions of the whole artistic team. Directing, as a profession, has only been acknowledged in the last few centuries, but throughout history drama has relied on individuals serving in a directorial role.

dithyramb: a choral ode performed in honor of the god Dionysus, composed of an improvised story by a *koryphaios* (chorus leader) and a traditional refrain sung and danced by a chorus. In his *Poetics*, Aristotle suggests that **tragedy** emerged from the dithyramb. Arion of Lesbos (about 620 B.C.E.) often referred to as the father of dithyrambic poetry, is credited for transforming the art into a literary form and is considered the first to keep a written record of his work.

documentary theater: also referred to as "theater of fact," a form of theater that dramatizes political events (often quite recent) to explore issues of social and moral concern. Primary source material such as transcriptions of judicial proceedings, speeches, essays, newspaper articles, films, and photos are often incorporated directly into the theatrical script. Rolf Hochhuth (b. 1931) and Peter Weiss (1916–1982) were both early proponents of this form in Europe. In the United States, Emily Mann (b. 1952) and Moisés Kaufman (b. 1963) have also used the form.

domestic tragedy: a form of drama, popularized at the start of the eighteenth century in England, that deals with the fortunes of middle-class or mercantile characters rather than the upper class or aristocracy, which had been the traditional focus of **tragedy**.

downstage: the area on stage closest to the audience. (*See* **upstage**.)

dramatic irony: a plot device in which a character holds a position or has an expectation that is reversed or fulfilled in a way that the character did not expect but that we, as audience members or readers, have anticipated because our knowledge of events or individuals is more complete than the character's.

dramatic structure: a textual organization based on a series of scenes, each of which is presented vividly and in detail.

dramatis personae: literally, "people in the drama" (Latin). A character list identifying important characters and their relationships, intended to help the reader or spectator understand the actions and interactions occurring onstage. In programs or playbills given to playgoers, this list often includes the names of the actors portraying the characters.

dramatist: a playwright, someone who writes dramatic literature.

dramaturg: a theatrical professional involved in a number of activities, including the development and revival of plays. Dramaturgs are trained in dramatic theory, theater practice, and the history of drama, equipping them to serve in a number of artistic capacities. As such, production dramaturgs may serve as partner to the **director**, as a sounding board for ideas, as an extra set of eyes in the rehearsal room, and as a researcher. Many dramaturgs also serve as critics for journals and newspapers or work as literary managers in regional theaters. In opera as well as theater, dramaturgs may serve as a translator of texts or author of subtitles. The German playwright Gotthold Lessing (1729–1781) is often credited as being the first dramaturg.

dramaturgy: the art of playwriting, or the composition of a theatrical text or narrative; the mechanisms of storytelling, specifically how the structure and style of a play can inform the **themes**, **motifs**, and intent of the playwright. Dramaturgy encapsulates the building blocks of dramatic writing. Aristotle's *Poetics* is the preeminent classical examination of the constituent parts of a drama, a rhetorical investigation of the effectiveness of a play's dramaturgy.

drame bourgeois: a form of **domestic tragedy**, advocated by the French playwright and critic Denis Diderot (1713–1784), which explored social and familial problems of the middle class and departed from the restrictive tenets of **neoclassicism**. Diderot believed that "middle dramas" such as the *drame bourgeois* and comedies of virtue merited being produced in addition to traditional neoclassical comedies and tragedies.

ekkyklēma: a rolling platform used in Greek performance to reveal the body of a character killed offstage.

Elizabethan drama: a work or body of works written in England during the reign of Queen Elizabeth I (r. 1558–1603). Elizabethan plays often embody a sense of optimism and prosperity as England asserted itself as a European power. SHAKESPEARE wrote many of his plays during this period, which is why the Elizabethan age—and the age of her successor, James I (r. 1603–25), often referred to as the "Jacobean period"—is considered one of the greatest ages of dramatic innovation.

environmental theater: term coined by Richard Schechner (b. 1934) to describe a theatrical event in which the performance space is integral to the genesis of the performance and in a sense becomes a metaphor for the play itself. Also called "site-specific theater." The environment or atmosphere created by the space, whether found or transformed, should not only offer context in terms of setting but contribute to the production as a whole. The focus of the performance is intended to be flexible, in that audience members can literally see the work from a variety of viewpoints and also in many instances they can participate.

epeisodia: a sequence of episodes in a Greek tragedy in which the characters drive the action through interaction with the **chorus** and one another.

epic: a long and involved narrative poem that depicts the adventures of a central figure of grand or heroic distinction. Typically, epics are split into episodes and chronicle a journey or plight of a hero. In ancient Greece, epic poems were often recited by *rhapsodes* (professional storytellers). Homer's *Iliad* and *Odyssey* are examples of epic poems.

Epic Theater: BERTOLT BRECHT's model theater intended to serve as an alternative to Aristotelian theater with its emphasis on continuous plot and right construction. The Epic Theater addresses human reason rather than feeling, thus discouraging passivity, so that the spectator leaves the theater with a sense that the current social order is alterable and that action is necessary. Political change takes precedent over aesthetic wonder. The term *estrangement effect* (*Verfremdungseffekt* in German) refers to an important technique employed by Epic Theater practitioners because it places responsibility on the audience. Onstage events are performed in an unexpected manner, thereby provoking responses of surprise or curiosity on the audience's part and prompting a desire to elicit change.

epilogue: a concluding address by an actor or group of actors that is directed toward the audience; also an additional scene, following the resolution of a play, intended to comment on the preceding events and offer a final perspective by the author or actors.

episodic plot: a **plot** that has one or more of the following characteristics: scenes or episodes that are organized in nonsequential order; shifts in time, location, or setting; or subplots that incorporate more than one set of characters. Plays with multiple characters and **subplots** are often episodic because the structure allows the focus to shift from one narrative to another. SHAKESPEARE's plays generally incorporate episodic plots.

epistle: a literary composition in the form of a letter. BEN JONSON included an epistle in the printed version of his play *VOLPONE*.

estrangement effect: A phrase translated from the German word, *Verfremdungseffekt* (sometimes also translated as "alienation effect"), referring to an important tenet of BERTOLT BRECHT's Epic Theater that asks the audience to examine familiar, everyday events from a critical distance as if they were strange. Brecht describes his theories of estrangement as a rebuttal to the popular Aristotelian perspective that an audience derives pleasure from an empathic connection to the events performed on stage. Instead, he suggests that, in performance, an actor can alter his or her technique to illustrate ideas of broader historical or social proportions. The actor's self-awareness and awareness of the performative nature of storytelling distances the spectator from an immediate emotional response that, in turn, disrupts identification with the character and elicits instead a reaction of surprise or curiosity from an otherwise ordinary or contrived situation.

exodos: the concluding scene in a Greek tragedy where all of the characters and chorus members exit the stage.

exposition: information, often delivered near the beginning of a play, that reveals something essential for the audience's understanding of the world of the play or the story's given circumstances, as well as the basic relationships between characters or events that have taken place offstage. Exposition can provide pertinent information for all of the characters in the drama but can also be limited to a few. Sometimes the audience or reader will be given information unknown to the characters on stage (*see* **dramatic irony**).

expressionism: a literary and theatrical movement that originated in Europe just before the twentieth century but flourished from 1910 to 1925. Spurred by the overwhelming social and political upheaval of World War I, expressionist dramatists strove to emphasize the moral crisis of the modern, industrial world dominated by machines and masses of people. In expressionist plays the characters are often nameless and defined solely by their occupations. Other stylistic elements include the use of primal gesture (exaggerated emotive movement), punctuated dialogue (language that emphasizes various words or expressions), and theatrical design that includes exaggerated or distorted images. Playwrights and directors demonstrate the mood of an expressionist drama by staging the play so that it reflects the emotional perspective of the protagonist or hero. Major expressionist playwrights include Ernst Toller (1893–1939) and Georg Kaiser (1878–1945). BERTOLT BRECHT, AUGUST STRINDBERG, SUSAN GLASPELL, and EUGENE O'NEILL all experimented with expressionism during their careers as playwrights.

falling action: the portion of a play's structure, usually at or near the end, in which the complications of the **rising action** are untangled.

farce: a genre of fast-paced comedy characterized by rapid stage action, a series of misunderstandings, ludicrous characterizations, and physical humor. Farcical techniques were employed by Greek and Roman playwrights such as ARISTOPHANES and PLAUTUS, though the term *farce* itself was not used until the Middle Ages, when it came to refer to comic scenes inserted in church plays. The genre of farce flourished in medieval and Renaissance Europe, most notably in the comic improvisations of the ***commedia dell'arte***. One of the most famous later writers of farce is the French playwright Georges Feydeau (1862–1921).

Federal Theatre Project: part of the Works Progress Administration enacted by President Franklin Roosevelt in 1935, the Federal Theatre Project (FTP) was a government program that created work for theater artists, writers, musicians, and arts practitioners during the Great Depression. The program was run by Hallie Flanagan (1890–1969), who had directed the Experimental Theatre at Vassar College. In the FTP, Flanagan created a forum for socially relevant theater, including the cultivation of new works and important revivals. Famous productions included Sinclair Lewis and John Moffitt's *It Can't Happen Here* and Orson Welles's *Macbeth*. The FTP was also associated with "living newspapers," multimedia theatrical productions that examined pressing social issues. The project ended in 1939 but laid the foundation for the regional theater movement in America.

flat characters: characters in a play, often but not always minor characters, who are relatively simple; who are presented as having few, though sometimes dominant, traits; and who thus do not change much in the course of a play. (*See* **round characters**.)

foil: originally, a layer of polished metal placed beneath a gem to accentuate its brilliance; when applied to drama, a character whose qualities or traits highlight those of another. In SHAKESPEARE's *HAMLET*, for instance, Laertes serves as a foil to Hamlet because both are put in the position of avenging a murdered father.

folio: a form of publication to create books of the largest format, composed of large sheets of paper folded in half to create two leaves (*folio* is Latin for "leaves"), or four pages. SHAKESPEARE's works were published posthumously in 1623 in an edition now known as the First Folio. (*See* **quarto**.)

foreshadowing: any literary device that alludes to future occurrences in a story's plot. **Symbolic** imagery is commonly used to foreshadow events, as is the convention of narrative prophecy often employed by classical Greek dramatists.

fourth wall: theatrical term applied to the **realist** stage, where actors no longer played directly to the audience but instead focused on each other. In nineteenth-century England, the convention became increasingly popular and stage sets were designed to replicate a traditional room with three walls, the "fourth wall" (that is, the proscenium arch, or front of the stage) being open for observation of the action by the audience.

futurism: a theatrical movement conceived in 1909 by Filippo Tommaso Marinetti (1876–1944) that sought to transform humanity by rejecting the past and embracing the age of the machine. A typical futurist technique is the use of brief, simultaneous skits that depart from traditional modes of character development and often involve direct interaction or even confrontation with audience members. Futurist performances also utilized technology to create multimedia effects.

Gesamtkunstwerk: literally, "total work of art" (German), a term coined by Richard Wagner (1813–1883) in his essay *Art and Revolution*, which describes his interest in the integration of dramatic literature, music, theatrical performance, and visual elements such as set and lighting design into a new and complete synthesis.

gigaku: a form of Japanese theater introduced from China via Korea in the seventh and eighth centuries that can best be described as a Buddhist dance play. At the start of *gigaku* plays, masked figures moved in procession and then performed a number of comic scenes. Performances generally incorporated music and a number of **stock characters**.

Golden Age of Spain: a period of time during the sixteenth and seventeenth centuries that saw the expansion of Spanish global power, rivaling that of Elizabethan England, while Spanish dramatic arts and literature achieved new levels of excellence.

green room: the offstage location in the theater where actors wait before they appear onstage. (*See* **wings**.)

groundlings: an expression used during the English Elizabethan age to describe theater audience members who paid a penny to stand around the three sides of the stage in the area called the "yard."

guerrilla theater: a form of theater popularized in the United States during the 1960s that sought to confront spectators with brief, unscheduled, and often provocative performances in public spaces. Performers were interested in breaking traditional social barriers in order to convey their political messages.

hamartia: the Greek term used by Aristotle to describe a character's intellectual error or mistaken assumption that prompts the tragic outcome of his or her actions. Often described as the "tragic flaw" or self-destructive force that triggers the downfall of a socially elevated figure.

Harlem Renaissance: a movement centered on Harlem, New York, during the 1920s and 1930s, marked by a proliferation of artistic achievement by African Americans in literature and the arts. The work produced during this time explores and illuminates the black experience in America. Langston Hughes (1902–1967) and Zora Neal Hurston (1891–1960) are two of the most famous writers associated with the period.

hero/heroine: the leading male/female character in a play, often larger than life, sometimes almost godlike. (*See* **antihero**, **protagonist**, and **villain**.)

high (verbal) comedy: humorous plays that employ subtlety, wit, or the representation of refined life. (*See* **low (physical) comedy**.)

history play: a play that deals with characters, events, and subjects taken from history. SHAKESPEARE wrote a number of plays about English history, including *Richard II*, *Richard III*, and *Henry IV*, Parts 1 and 2.

histriones: the Latin term for actor. In Roman theater, *histriones* were typically male and could perform in both tragedies and comedies. Unlike Greek dramatists who often doubled as both playwright and performer, *histriones* were professional performers.

hubris: the tragic flaw of pride or arrogance that can lead a hero to disregard accepted moral codes or warnings from the gods, prompting his or her own downfall.

humors comedy: a genre of comedy popularized by BEN JONSON that drew upon the classical medical theory that an individual's temperament or psychological disposition was determined by the balance (or imbalance) of four bodily fluids (known as "humors"): black bile, phlegm, blood, and choler, or yellow bile. Characters in humors comedies are motivated by their predominant humors. A choleric (or easily angered) personality, for instance, was one reflecting a predominance of yellow bile.

hypokritēs: the Greek word for actor; literally, "the answerer."

iambic pentameter: in English verse meter, ten-syllable lines with alternating unstressed and stressed syllables, the most common poetic meter in English and a particular favorite of Elizabethan playwrights such as SHAKESPEARE: "To sleep: | perchance | to dream: | ay, there's | the rub" (*HAMLET*).

intermezzo (plural **intermezzi**): a theatrical form of entertainment first produced in fifteenth-century Italy as an interlude between **acts** of a traditional drama. The performances were generally held at court and drew allegorical or mythological parallels to those being honored. The principle convention of intermezzi was lavish **spectacle**; very little dialogue was used. Music, dance, and pantomime were employed to convey the story.

joruri: the narrative of a Japanese bunraku drama.

kabuki: a form of dramatic theater that emerged in early seventeenth-century Japan that involves music, dance, and acrobatics; ornate costumes and makeup; extensive scenery; and spectacular tricks of stage technology.

kagura: a form of early Japanese dance drama that took shape in the third century B.C.E. These performances were composed of ritual dances connected with Shintoism, an ancient Japanese religion devoted to the worship of gods and spirits representing aspects of the natural world.

katharsis: *see* **catharsis**.

komos: literally, "band of revelers" (Greek), the final song or procession in a Greek **Old Comedy**.

koryphaios: in Ancient Greece, the chorus leader who sang and danced an improvised story or hymn known as the **dithyramb**. In Greek tragedy, the *koryphaios* served as the leader of the chorus but could also actively engage with the other actors on stage.

kyogen: literally, "wild words" (Japanese), farcical sketches in **noh drama** that are performed between plays by the same actors playing the colloquial roles; also, a character in noh drama, often a servant or commoner, who speaks colloquially and acts as narrator.

laughing comedy: term championed by Oliver Goldsmith (1730–1774), who suggested that the popular sentimental comedies of eighteenth-century England were a lesser form of drama. Goldsmith endorsed a more traditional conception of comedy in his *Essay on the Theatre* by stating that "comedy should excite our laughter by ridiculously exhibiting the follies of the lower part of mankind." RICHARD BRINSLEY SHERIDAN was one of the leading proponents of laughing comedy.

lazzi (singular *lazzo*): comic bits of action and dialogue performed by **stock characters** in *commedia dell'arte*. These moments were most likely performed multiple times by the same actor in various performances, though they were intended to appear improvised.

leitmotif: the dominant recurrent element in an artistic work, generally tied to the theme or overall idea of the piece as a whole. The term also refers to the melodic passage or phrase in opera that is associated with a specific character, event, or symbol.

linear plot: a traditional plot sequence in which the incidents in the drama progress chronologically; that is, all of the events build upon one another and there are no jumps from the present to the past. The Greeks and neoclassicists adopted this structure as the template for creating effective tragedy. RACINE'S *PHÈDRE* has a linear plot.

Little Theater Movement: an early twentieth-century movement in the United States that sought to emulate the European alternative theater movement to develop and support experimental and new work without the financial and creative constraints of the commercial theater. This model allowed artists to produce their work in smaller theaters across the country. Perhaps the most famous participants in the movement were EUGENE O'NEILL and SUSAN GLASPELL, who developed their work with the Provincetown Players on Cape Cod and in New York.

liturgical drama: a form of medieval European drama that sprang from the elaboration of liturgy, or the act of public worship found in the Latin Mass. As early as 925 C.E., antiphonal **tropes**, or musical passages that incorporated the imitation of religious figures in a call-and-response dialogue, served as interpolations in religious services. These tropes, credited as the first **mimetic** performances in the church, were initially part of Easter Mass, and then were added to services held on other holy days; they also became more **dramaturgically** complex over time. Typically, liturgical plays explore the mysteries and miracles depicted in the Bible and in the lives of saints.

loges: in seventeenth-century French theaters, the division of galleries that created boxes for audience members to sit.

low (physical) comedy: humorous plays that employ **burlesque**, horseplay, or the representation of unrefined life. (*See* **high (verbal) comedy**.)

Ludi Romani: a Roman religious festival, established in the sixth century B.C.E., that was given in honor of the god Jupiter. At its inception, Ludi Romani included various types of performances such as chariot races, prizefighting, dance, and farce; later, in the mid-third century B.C.E., performances of comedies and tragedies were added to the festival.

mansions: scenic structures used in the performance of liturgical dramas and **cycle plays** during the Middle Ages. Because medieval dramas often followed the travels of a single protagonist over an extended period of time, mansions were arranged to represent the various locales and circumstances in his journey.

masque: an elaborate form of court entertainment commonly associated in England with the reigns of King James I (r. 1603–25) and Charles I (r. 1625–49). The performances sought to idealize the monarchy by drawing allegorical or mythological parallels, and masques incorporated lavish **spectacle**, music, dance, and **pantomime** to convey the story. BEN JONSON wrote a number of masques for the Stuart court, and his contemporary Inigo Jones (1573–1652) was the principal designer of these spectacles.

mattavaranis: in a traditional Indian playhouse, the downstage areas that flank the sides of the main performance space.

mēchanē: the crane used for special effects in fifth-century B.C.E. Greek performance that could lift actors in the air and propel them over the playing space. The device was commonly used in depicting the gods, but it was also employed to simulate the flight of both animals and chariots.

melodrama: originally, a drama in which music is used to heighten emotion (the Greek *melos* means "song"). As it was popularized during the nineteenth century in France, Britain, and the United States, this genre grew to be characterized by stories of adventure and intrigue calculated to provoke audiences' heightened emotional response. Melodrama offers sensational plots (rather than subtle ideas or character development) in which good inevitably triumphs over evil. *Uncle Tom's Cabin*, George L. Aiken's 1852 stage adaptation of Harriet Beecher Stowe's novel, is a well-known melodrama.

metatheater: a term coined by the critic Lionel Abel in 1963 to describe the self-conscious dramatic examination of the nature of theater itself, primarily the relationship between reality and theatrical illusion. Conscious displays of theatricality and role-playing are two prominent conventions. LUIGI PIRANDELLO and JEAN GENET are known for the use of metatheatrical techniques in their dramas.

metatragedy: a modern form of drama that reflects upon the nature of tragedy, the nature of role-playing, and the relationship between reality and theatrical illusion, often through the use of self-conscious, self-referential dramatic techniques. LUIGI PIRANDELLO's *SIX CHARACTERS IN SEARCH OF AN AUTHOR* is a prominent example of metatragedy.

method acting: a system of acting derived from the **Stanislavsky** technique and developed by Lee Strasberg in the United States beginning in the 1930s. Actors who employ "the method," as it is often called, attempt to embody the emotional life of the character by utilizing experiences from their own past to stimulate engaging, realistic performances.

Middle Comedy: a transitional form of ancient Greek comedy, sometimes said to fall between the works of ARISTOPHANES and those of Menander (ca. 342–291 B.C.E.), that focused more on contemporary life and manners than the political and social subject matter of **Old Comedy** represented by Aristophanes. The role of the **chorus** is also greatly reduced in this era.

mime: the narrative art of acting out situations and stories using gesture and expression without any dialogue; also, an actor who performs in this style. A form of Greek and

Roman performance dating back to the fifth century B.C.E., mime was used to satirize everyday situations and burlesque traditional myths.

mimēsis: the Greek word for imitation that is used to describe the artistic practice of representing reality (or creating theater). In the *Republic*, Plato argues that the mimetic arts are corruptive because they are too far removed from the truth. In the *Poetics*, on the other hand, Aristotle argues that **tragedy** is an imitation of an action in a way that is embellished and perfected.

minstrelsy: a theatrical entertainment that originated in early nineteenth-century America where white artists would perform songs, skits, and comedic numbers in **blackface** (burnt cork with which actors darkened their faces). Deeply rooted in racial stereotypes, the performances caricatured slave culture. Toward the end of the nineteenth century, black artists began to appear as minstrels themselves, sometimes actually using blackface, as minstrel shows were one of the few vehicles in which African Americans could perform on stage professionally.

miracle plays: early medieval liturgical plays that demonstrated the miracles and martyrdom of saints by way of mixed narratives which often incorporated conflict and adventure.

mise-en-scène: literally "putting onto the stage" (French), the aesthetic arrangement of a stage picture including the set, properties, and positioning of actors.

modernism: a departure from artistic tradition that took place at the end of the nineteenth century and continued through the first half of the twentieth. Reflecting the social, technological, and philosophical changes that distinguished the modern world from earlier ages, modernism featured radical experimentation in drama, literature, and the arts. Modernist authors and artists include T. S. Eliot (1888–1965), Franz Kafka (1883–1924), Virginia Woolf (1882–1941), Pablo Picasso (1881–1973), and Igor Stravinsky (1882–1971). BERTOLT BRECHT, LUIGI PIRANDELLO, and SAMUEL BECKETT are examples of modernist playwrights; Antonin Artaud's dramatic theories are modernist as well.

monologue: a long speech or narrative spoken by one character. A monologue can be addressed to another character on stage, spoken to oneself, or shared with the audience as a means of elucidating internal thoughts or desires that cannot be expressed in formal dialogue. A **soliloquy** is a form of monologue, and an **aside**, if lengthy, can be characterized as a monologue.

mood: the atmosphere or emotional state of a play's **setting** or **context**.

morality plays: a secular form of medieval drama that was popular between 1400 and 1550, predominantly in England and France. Didactic in tone and allegorical in structure, morality plays dealt with the individual's moral life, the battle between figures representing good and evil, and the journey to salvation. *EVERYMAN* is an example of a morality play, and CHRISTOPHER MARLOWE's *DOCTOR FAUSTUS* shows the influence of the morality tradition on later drama.

motif: a recurrent element in an artistic work that is generally tied to the themes or overall idea of the piece as a whole. (*See* **leitmotif**.)

motivation: the thought or desire that drives a character to actively pursue a want or need, which in acting theory is called the *objective*. A character generally has an overall objective or long-term goal in a drama but may change his or her objective, and hence motivation, from scene to scene when confronted with various obstacles.

musical: a play with musical numbers interspersed throughout. At the start of the twentieth century, musicals were largely revue shows featuring beautiful girls, lavish costumes, **sets**, and **spectacle**. *Show Boat* (1927), by Jerome Kern (1885–1945) and Oscar Hammerstein II (1895–1960), is often credited as one of the first cohesive works of musical theater. The contemporary American musical that tells a cohesive story through the integration of dialogue, dance, and song began to take shape in the 1940s and is most famously embodied in the work of Richard Rodgers (1902–1979) and Oscar Hammerstein, who together created *Oklahoma!* (1943) and *The Sound of Music* (1959), among many other musicals.

mystery cycles: *see* **cycle plays**.

nanxi: a form of drama that emerged in the southern provinces of China during the fourteenth century and has proven more influential to the modern Chinese stage than the classical ***zaju*** plays. A number of **stock character** types originated in early performances. *Nanxi* plays can contain a variable number of acts with multiple songs that draw upon regional folk music.

***nataka* plays**: a classical form of Indian theater that dramatizes the plight of exalted heroes or royalty in well-known mythological or historical stories. *Nataka* plays are composed of five to ten *arikas*, or acts, and contain a number of elements such as superhuman powers, love affairs, and the conscious employment of *rasas*, or specific emotional stimuli and audience response. The theorist Bharata prescribes the elements of Nataka plays further in the *Natyasastra*, written sometime between 300 B.C.E. and 200 C.E.

naturalism: a literary and theatrical movement that thrived in the late nineteenth century. Naturalist writers sought to depict life truthfully, objectively, and with scientific accuracy. Émile Zola notes in his *Naturalism in the Theatre* (1881) that "the physiological man of our modern works insists more and more imperiously on being determined by the setting and environment of which he is a product." In naturalism, the physiological disposition of a character is the focus of the drama, and heredity or physical environment dictates his or her fate. The concept of naturalism can also be applied to the way in which a play is staged. For example, a naturalist **set** may incorporate a real working fireplace or a faucet with running water. AUGUST STRINDBERG described his play *MISS JULIE* as a naturalistic tragedy.

neoclassicism: a seventeenth-century movement, prompted by a renewed interest in the writings of Aristotle and other classical theorists, that lasted well into the eighteenth century. Neoclassical theory emphasizes three principles of tragedy. The first and most important is *verisimilitude*, defined as the quality or appearance of truth. The second principle emphasizes *decorum*, or the proper way in which characters should act on stage as dictated by their disposition and social standing. The last principle of neoclassicism is adherence to the "three **unities**" of action, time, and place as derived from a strict interpretation of Aristotle's emphasis in his *Poetics* on the importance of a singular action depicted in a plot confined to one revolution of the sun.

nepathya: the area in a **Sanskrit** playhouse that includes the backstage area and dressing rooms.

New Comedy: a form of Greek comedy written during the Hellenistic period (336–31 B.C.E.) that focused on domestic issues such as love and familial relationships rather than political satire. In structure, New Comedies include a prologue, followed by a series of episodes and choral passages. Other characteristics of the genre include the frequent use of **stock characters**, disguise, and mistaken assumptions. The most celebrated writer of New Comedy is Menander (342–291 B.C.E.).

noh drama: a form of Japanese theater developed by Kannami Kiyotsugu (1333–1384), head of one of the country's *sarugaku noh* troupes, and his son ZEAMI MOTOKIYO (1363–1443). (The term *noh* means "skill" or "craft.") The stories of noh plays are drawn from mythology, legend, and history and are typically structured in two acts. The central character speaks in an elevated, highly literary verse. Other established roles include the main character's companion (*tsure*); a third party (*waki*), frequently a priest, who encounters the main character in the first act; and a servant or commoner (*kyogen*) who speaks colloquially. An onstage chorus sings many of the characters' lines and narrates events within the dramatic action, while three or four onstage musicians accompany the play with flute and drums. The **climax** of a noh play takes the form of a ritualized dance. Noh drama falls into five categories: plays about gods; warrior plays; plays about women, or "wig plays"; miscellaneous plays, including plays about madness and plays about the present time; and demon plays, in which the main character is a good or evil supernatural being.

Old Comedy: a form of Greek comedy most likely produced during the fifth century B.C.E. The plays of ARISTOPHANES are the only surviving examples of the genre, and it is unclear whether or not his work resembled that of his contemporaries. Aristophanic Old Comedies often revolve around a theme or problem in everyday Athenian life; in style, the plays present far-fetched or farcical situations, and they incorporate bawdy jokes and songs. In structure, Old Comedies are similar to classical Greek **tragedy**: first a choral entrance or *parodos*, then the *parabasis* or presentation of an idea followed by an *agon* or debate, and finally a series of episodes that culminate in a scene called the *komos*, where the problem is resolved and the characters exit in happy revelry.

opera: a play set to music where the dialogue is sung rather than spoken. The origins of opera date back to sixteenth-century Renaissance Italy, where a renewed interest in Greek music and its relationship to drama prompted the creation of dramatic work that was recited or chanted to musical accompaniment.

orchēstra: literally, "dancing place" (Greek), the semicircular playing space in a classical Greek theater where the chorus and actors would perform.

pantomime: both a form of silent acting that relies heavily on gesture, facial expression, and dance, and also, in England, beginning in the eighteenth century, a form of elaborate production, usually staged at Christmas, that includes ballet, music, and characters derived from the *commedia dell'arte* tradition.

parabasis: literally, "digression" (Greek), in **Old Comedy** a section of a play in which the **chorus** introduces the major problem of the play and a line of action to solve it, or directly addresses the audience with an elaborate plea to win approval for the playwright.

parodos: at the start of Greek drama, the entrance of the **chorus** that provides **exposition** and sets the **mood**. The *parodos* often follows the prologue and is one of several structural elements of Greek tragedy in the fifth century B.C.E. In **Old Comedy**, the *parodos* sets the grounds for the *agon* or debate that follows.

parody: an imitative form of comedy that spoofs or mimics the structure or content of another artistic work.

parterre: in seventeenth-century French theaters, the pit for standing spectators that was positioned directly in front of the raised **proscenium** stage.

pastiche: a dramatic, musical, or artistic work that openly imitates or borrows from the style of another. Often, the work is intended to satirize or pay homage to its source of inspiration. *Pastiche* can also refer to a hodgepodge of elements drawn from different sources.

pastoral drama: a form of drama developed and popularized during the Italian Renaissance that sought to imitate the idyllic pastoral (rural) settings of Greek mythology. Perhaps influenced by the Greek satyr plays, pastoral dramas incorporate mythic elements in their depictions of the travails of young lovers, typically shepherds.

performance art: a form of individual or collective performance that began taking shape in the United States in the 1970s and 1980s to explore abstract ideas through the instrument of the performer's body. Formal theatrical settings and accoutrements are discarded in favor of a focus on the body in its movement and form.

peripeteia: in a tragic plot, the moment in which the story's action undergoes a lasting reversal, or change in direction. Aristotle notes in the *Poetics* that the best reversals are those that transpire organically according to the logic of the action.

perspective scenery: a scenic convention first used in Italy at the beginning of the sixteenth century whereby the **scenery** on stage was painted and placed strategically to create the illusion of depth for the spectator. Generally, scenic **wings** were aligned at sharp angles on either side of the stage, and a backdrop was draped at the rear of the stage. The floor of the stage was raked upward, and the wings closest to the audience were elaborately decorated. The actors primarily performed **downstage**, so as not to disrupt the illusion.

pièce bien-fait: *see* **well-made play**.

platea: in medieval performance, a neutral acting area in the church where **liturgical dramas** were performed. *Sedes* (or "**mansions**") were localized acting sites within this space.

playwright: an individual who writes plays for the theater. The first playwrights penned dramas for the Greek religious festival the **City Dionysia** and performed in their own works.

plot: the arrangement of related incidents in a play. Plots may be simple or complex, and any single play may have more than one plot (and plays from experimental, **avant-garde**, or **postmodern** traditions may calculatedly eschew plot altogether). Among the key terms associated with plot, and useful in describing and analyzing any play's plot, are *antagonist*, *conflict*, *climax*, *denouement*, *falling action*, *motivation*, *point of attack*, *protagonist*, *resolution*, and *rising action*. Plots typically begin with a triggering moment or **point of attack** that propels a character's **motivations** or needs into action. The **hero** or **protagonist** (not necessarily an individual) is prompted to make decisions that move the story forward. The **conflict** or antagonistic elements in a plot create obstacles, and the negotiation of these obstacles becomes the **rising action** intended to create dramatic tension and keep the reader or spectator interested in the story's progression. The **climax** is the most suspenseful point in the plot and is reached when the **conflict** comes to a head, initiating the **resolution** or *denouement*.

point of attack: the triggering event or defining conflict that propels the action of the play and pushes the plot into motion. (*See* **plot**.)

poor theater: a term used to describe Polish director Jerzy Grotowski's (1933–1999) theoretical approach to creating theater. Grotowski's works were premised on the idea that theater should be stripped to its essence, focusing on the exchange of ideas from actor to audience. Without the use of traditional **sets**, **sound effects**, music, or costumes, Grotowski created highly theatrical and thought-provoking productions that relied primarily on the dedication and stamina of his ensemble of actors.

popular entertainment: a term used to describe any theatrical performance that attracts a large audience or has commercial appeal. Musical revues, pageants, and **burlesque** performances are modern forms of popular entertainment.

postcolonialism: a critical standpoint or theoretical approach to examining literature, theater, and other art forms in the context of European colonialism and its aftermath. Postcolonial analysis examines relationships between native and colonial traditions; explores the influence of imperial ideologies, power structures, and discourses on contemporary perceptions and relations; and looks for new forms of identity and cultural resistance that arise in postcolonial societies. Postcolonial writers grapple with the fusion of native traditions and those of the colonial traditions in which many of them were educated. Playwrights WOLE SOYINKA (b. 1934), Derek Wolcott (1930–2017), and ATHOL FUGARD (b. 1932) address postcolonial issues in their work.

postmodernism: a movement that emerged in the 1960s in reaction against many of the cultural and aesthetic assumptions of **modernism**. While modernists often sought a clear, cohesive artistic construction, for example, postmodern artists sought to embrace inconsistencies in style and to collapse literary boundaries. **Pastiche** is a predominant element in postmodern works of art.

prakarana **play**: a classical form of Indian theater that relies on invented stories and depicts less exalted characters than those in *nataka* **plays**. Like *nataka* plays, *prakarana* plays must be composed of five to ten *arikas*, or acts, and follow a prescriptive set of rules regarding structure and staging. The theorist Bharata describes the elements of *prakarana* plays further in the *Natyasastra*, written sometime between 300 B.C.E. and 200 C.E.

prekshagriha: as described in Bharata's *Natyasastra*, the area devoted to seating an audience in the interior of a rectangular **Sanskrit** playhouse.

presentational theater: a highly theatrical type of performance in which the performers are aware of the audience's presence. In presentational theater, the fourth wall can be broken and lines can be delivered directly to the spectators.

problem play: a late nineteenth-century and early twentieth-century form of drama that addressed social issues. The early dramas of HENRIK IBSEN and GEORGE BERNARD SHAW are examples of problem plays.

prologue: in some plays, the opening scene in which information is revealed about events that occurred prior to the play's start. Historically, the prologue has also been used to praise the playwright or entreat the good will of the audience.

properties, props: any objects used on stage by actors—for example, a pair of scissors or a hairbrush. Items that are small enough to hold are often referred to as *hand props*. Pictures and decorative set items are also considered props. Costume pieces and items rooted to the **set** or playing space itself are not props.

proscenium arch: an arch over the front of a stage; thus, a *proscenium theater* is composed of a raised stage framed by a proscenium arch with the audience seated facing the stage, observing the action as if through a picture frame. This kind of stage is characteristic of European theaters built from the late sixteenth through the nineteenth centuries (for example, the *Teatro Farnese* in Parma was completed in 1628).

protagonist: the hero or central character in a play. Derived from the ancient Greek term *protagonistes*, meaning "leading actor." In traditional drama, the protagonist often engages in conflicts with an **antagonist**.

pulpitum: in a Roman theater, the raised stage in front of the scene building.

quarto: a form of publication typically used in England at the close of the sixteenth century where pages were created by folding paper in fours. Plays of the era, such as those of SHAKESPEARE, were generally published in inexpensive quarto editions. (*See* **folio**.)

raked stage: a stage that slopes upward so that it is elevated at the back (**upstage**) and lower in the front. During the Italian Renaissance, **perspective scenery** relied on raked stages to reinforce the perception of depth. The actors primarily performed **downstage**.

ranga: the performance area in a **Sanskrit** playhouse.

rangapitha: the main performance area consisting of the most prominent performance space on the stage in a **Sanskrit** playhouse.

rangashirsha: in a **Sanskrit** performance, the retiring room, or **green room** area upstage that stretches across the width of the back wall and is fronted by the performance space; there is generally an ornamental curtain with two openings for entrances and exits that separates the *rangashirsha* from the playing area.

rasas: in **Sanskrit** drama, the cumulative stimuli and aesthetic reactions of spectators that are formed when paired with *bhavas* (emotions). There are nine basic *rasas*: erotic, comic, pathetic, furious, heroic, terrible, odious, marvelous, and peaceful. A play can incorporate many *rasas* but at its conclusion, one *rasa* must predominate to ensure a sense of balance and closure for the spectator.

realism: a literary and theatrical style that seeks to depict life as it really is without conventional artifice. The origins of realism can be traced to nineteenth-century Europe when playwrights and theater practitioners sought to move away from traditional, often melodramatic, plays and productions to create drama that appeared to that era to portray real people confronted with plausible situations. An interest in realistic staging prompted the concept of the **fourth wall**, a theatrical term that involves the use of a three-dimensional playing area where the actors' performance is focused entirely on the world of the play and the audience is a silent, unseen observer. HENRIK IBSEN wrote realistic plays, as did ANTON CHEKHOV, GEORGE BERNARD SHAW, and SUSAN GLASPELL.

repertory: a set of plays. A repertory acting company will perform a series of plays in rotation, alternating productions in a given theatrical space during a specific period of time.

resolution: the final event that resolves the fundamental conflict that had sustained the play's main action. A resolution can also be a *denouement*.

Restoration: the theatrical period (1660–1700) marked by the return of Charles II to the throne of England after the Commonwealth period. Restoration drama was written for and represented the new aristocracy, which repudiated the moral strictures of Puritanism. Restoration plays, particularly the comedies, often feature bawdy and licentious humor and situations. *THE COUNTRY WIFE* by WILLIAM WYCHERLEY and *THE ROVER* by APHRA BEHN are Restoration comedies.

revenge tragedy: a form of sensational tragedy revolving around stories of murder and revenge. Characteristics of revenge tragedy include **soliloquies**, plays within a play, and sensationalistic, even supernatural, plot twists. The Roman playwright Seneca is considered the primary influence for the genre, which flourished in England during the reigns of Elizabeth I (r. 1558–1603) and James I (r. 1603–25). THOMAS KYD'S *THE SPANISH TRAGEDY* and SHAKESPEARE'S *HAMLET* are among the best-known revenge tragedies.

rhapsōidos: in ancient Greece, a storyteller who recited mythological tales and epic poems such as Homer's *Odyssey* and *Iliad* to an audience. *Rhapsōidoi* were performed at religious festivals prior to the advent of traditional drama, which emerged sometime in the late sixth century B.C.E.

rising action: the portion of a play's structure, usually near the beginning, in which events complicate the situation that existed at the beginning of a play, intensifying the **conflict** or introducing new conflict.

romance play: a term used primarily to describe SHAKESPEARE'S later plays that mix the comic with the tragic. A romance play's action moves between **pastoral** and court or city settings and often incorporates magical elements. The reuniting of long-separated family members is also a common **motif**. Shakespeare's romance plays include *Cymbeline*, *Pericles*, *The Tempest*, and *The Winter's Tale*.

Romanticism: a literary and artistic movement that began in England and Germany around 1800 and emphasized imagination and emotion over the **neoclassical** ideals of intellect and reason. Largely influenced by the philosopher Jean-Jacques Rousseau (1712–1778), Romantic literature generally reflects a belief in the innate goodness of man in his natural state. Though there are many tenets of the movement, the fundamental interest of Romanticists was to explore the idea of truth as viewed in relation to the world and natural phenomena. Romanticists cultivated emotion and sensation, free thought and mysticism, and revolt against authority. Romantic works also reflect an interest in the melancholy state of man and his capacity for cruelty. In Germany, Romanticism was influenced by the philosophies of Immanuel Kant (1742–1804) and evolved from the **Sturm und Drang** (storm and stress) **movement** associated with the early works of Friedrich Schiller (1759–1805) and JOHANN WOLFGANG VON GOETHE.

round characters: complex characters, often major characters, who can grow and change and "surprise convincingly"—that is, act in a way that the audience does not expect from what had gone on before but now accepts as possible, even probable, and "realistic." (*See* **flat characters**.)

sarugaku: literally, "monkey entertainment" (Japanese), a form of variety theater containing comic dialogues and short skits performed at Buddhist temples. By the thirteenth century, *sarugaku* become increasingly sophisticated and was thereafter known by the name *sarugaku noh*. (The term *noh* means "skill" or "craft.")

sarugaku noh: see *sarugaku*.

Sanskrit theater: a classical form of Indian theater that dates back to approximately 100 C.E. The purpose of Sanskrit theater is to move the spectator to experience the appropriate *rasa* or sense of pleasure and delight. SHUDRAKA's *THE LITTLE CLAY CART* is a Sanskrit play. (Sanskrit is the classical language of ancient India.)

satire: a form of **comedy** that relies on wit and irony to offer social commentary through imitation and ridicule of its subject.

satyr play: in ancient Greece, a comedic **burlesque** or short satirical play that often accompanied a **tragedy** at the **City Dionysia**. In form, the plays were composed of episodes followed by choral odes and also incorporated dance. Unlike tragedies, these plays used colloquial language, lewd dialogue and gesture, and **parodies** of familiar myths and stories.

scene: traditional segmentation of a play's structure to indicate a change in time or location, to jump from one **subplot** to another, or to introduce new characters or rearrange the actors on the stage. Traditionally plays are composed of **acts**, which are then broken down into scenes. In the French tradition as practiced by MOLIÈRE and RACINE, a new scene begins whenever a character enters or exits the stage.

scène à faire: literally, "scene that must be done" (French), the obligatory **scene** that resolves the end of a **well-made play**.

scenery: the physical representation of the play's **setting** (location and time period) in a production that also serves to emphasize the aesthetic concept or atmosphere of the play. Scenery can be painted drops or flats, projections, a built environment, or even a natural environment.

sedes: literally, "mansions" (Latin), localized acting sites within the acting area of a church. (*See* *platea*.)

sentimental comedy: a genre of comedy popularized in eighteenth-century England that departed from the bawdy and titillating themes of the **Restoration** (1640–1700) and emphasized instead the simple and innate goodness of humankind. Interest in the theories of Jean-Jacques Rousseau (1712–1778) and other philosophers fueled the assumption that people could be saved from vice if instructed to follow their natural instincts. Topics such as the social order, moral elevation, and appropriate sexual behavior were often the focus of these plays. Like **domestic tragedy**, sentimental comedy often centered on and appealed to the middle class.

set: the design, decoration, and **scenery** of the stage during a play, usually meant to represent the location(s) in the drama.

setting: the time and location in which a play takes place. A play can have multiple settings and incorporate more than one time period as well.

skēnē: the wooden scene house that stood behind the *orchēstra* in a classical Greek theater. The *skēnē* is thought to have had one or more doors where actors and **chorus** members could enter and exit the playing space and make costume changes, and an upper level or roof where gods and other characters could appear. On either side of the structure were passageways where the chorus could also enter and exit. The front area of the *skēnē* was later described by historians as the *paraskēnion*. *Skēnē* is the origin of the English word "scene."

slapstick: originally, a wooden sword worn by the *commedia dell'arte* character Harlequin that figured prominently in his comedic routine. As a subgenre, slapstick is a form of physical comedy often characterized by farcical situations, crude jokes, and reckless behavior.

soliloquy: a monologue uttered by a character alone onstage that provides insight into his or her thoughts. The theatrical convention is common in plays from the Renaissance through the eighteenth century and is generally associated with SHAKESPEARE's works. The device was discarded by modern dramatists, such as AUGUST STRINDBERG, concerned with creating **realistic** depictions on stage.

sound effect: a sound recorded or created for a theatrical piece to enhance the aural dimension of the world of the play.

spectacle: generally, the element(s) in a play's production that appeal to the visual theatricality of the piece, such as costumes, **scenery**, or stage tricks. Described in Aristotle's *Poetics* as the sixth element of tragedy (after **plot**, **character**, thought, **diction**, and song), spectacle can also be defined as the aspects of performance not inherent to the written text, including all of the **props** that create atmosphere or offer visual stimulation. In modern usage, the term often implies elaborate or costly stage effects.

stage business: physical activities or gestures adapted by performers to enhance their level of characterization and help elucidate a play's subtext. Stage business is generally not included in the playwright's text but is determined by the **actor** and/or **director** during the rehearsal process.

stage directions: in the text of a play, directions or actions indicated by the playwright that describe the physical movements or emotional responses of the characters on stage. Stage directions may also note the **setting**, the physical appearance of the characters, and their relationships with one another. In a printed play, stage directions are normally italicized and enclosed in brackets so they can readily be distinguished from dialogue. EUGENE O'NEILL is famous for his lengthy and detailed stage directions.

Stanislavsky Method: an approach to realistic acting created by Russian actor and director Konstantin Stanislavsky (1863–1938) that involves the study of emotional and psychological responses and their expression through physical and vocal technique. Stanislavsky's teaching methodology and the vocabulary that characterizes it exerted a profound influence on twentieth- and twenty-first-century acting and script analysis, especially in the United States.

stasima: choral dance songs that separate a series of episodes in a Greek tragedy.

stock character: a recognizable character type that can be found in many plays. Comedies have traditionally relied on such stock characters as the braggart soldier, the miserly father, the beautiful ingénue, or the trickster servant. *Commedia dell'arte* and the *Atellan farce* relied entirely on the peculiarities of stock characters to provide inspiration for creating scenarios.

***Sturm und Drang* movement**: literally, "storm and stress" (German), a movement in theatrical writing that took place in Germany between the late 1760s and the mid-1780s. Proponents of the movement rebelled against **neoclassical** dictums and eighteenth-century rationalism with a drama that emphasized passion, inspiration, and individualism.

subplot: a secondary plot that usually shares a relationship with the main plot, either thematically or incidentally. The subplot often deals with the secondary characters in the play. (*See* **Romanticism**.)

subtext: Konstantin **Stanislavsky**'s term for unspoken text; for an actor, the internal motivations or responses never explicitly stated in the dialogue, but understood either by the audience or the characters themselves. The dramatist creates subtext to underscore the emotional or intellectual truth of a character's life that is unspoken but implied.

surrealism: an artistic movement popularized in the 1920s and embraced through the late 1930s, primarily in painting and the fine arts. Spearheaded by Andre Breton (1896–1966) in his 1924 manifesto, the tenets of surrealism were greatly influenced by Sigmund Freud's (1856–1939) theory of the unconscious, in which everyday logic is rejected for the irrational mingling of symbols and desires. The manipulation of these patterns offered artists such as Antonin Artaud (1896–1948) and Jean Cocteau (1889–1963) a forum for highly theatrical work that emphasized mythic traditions and their relationship to everyday experience.

symbol: something that represents or suggests something else through association, resemblance, or convention. For example, in many cultures the color black symbolizes death and mourning, while in certain literary traditions the moon symbolizes purity and chastity.

symbolism: generally, the use of symbols; more specifically, an artistic movement, typically associated with late nineteenth-century French poets such as Arthur Rimbaud (1854–1891), Charles Baudelaire (1821–1876), and Stéphane Mallarmé (1862–1949), that began as a revolt against the predominant realistic style of European literature. In drama, this break from **realism** applied to both the dramaturgical aspects of symbolist plays and the way in which they were staged. In form and content, symbolist playwrights strayed from the conventions of popular domestic dramas and sought to represent a sense of truth that stretched beyond the recognizable or scientific world. The use of symbols or metaphors—inherently tied to visceral response and to stories that defy time or cultural milieu—was intended to express deeper states of human consciousness. This was demonstrated through staging techniques that emphasized **mood** and atmosphere over narrative. Playwright Maurice Maeterlinck (1862–1949) is a prominent representative of this movement.

tableau (plural **tableaux**): a motionless dramatic scene created by actors to depict the appearance of a moment frozen in time. In nineteenth-century drama, tableaux were often used at the end of acts to highlight dramatic relationships and climactic action.

teichoskopeia: literally, "watching from the wall" (Greek), a stage device in classical Greek theater where characters would stand on the roof of the *skēnē* and describe battles and other scenes happening on the other side of the wall.

theater in the round: *see* **arena**.

theme: the abstract message or concept that a playwright wishes to convey by uniting the dramaturgical construction of the play with specific **motifs**, **actions**, and images.

thespian: a word meaning "actor," derived from the name of the Greek tragedian Thespis who was the first to craft a character apart from the **chorus** in his **tragedies**. For this reason he is also credited as the "father of Greek tragedy."

thrust stage: a stage that juts out into the audience so that the seats are arranged on three sides of this extended playing space; this type of stage offers a variety of viewing angles for the audience.

thymelē: in a classical Greek theater, the raised stone placed in the middle of the *orchēstra* that was used as an altar or table in performance.

Tom show: after the success of George L. Aiken's 1852 stage adaptation of Harriet Beecher Stowe's novel *Uncle Tom's Cabin*, numerous attempts to imitate or burlesque the story were made. Many of these entertainments, now referred to as Tom shows, relied on racial stereotypes and missed the moral and social objectives of the original novel.

tragedy: a form of drama that arose in ancient Greek culture, though its specific origins are still debated. The term *tragōidia*, from which the word *tragedy* evolved, refers to the ritualistic practice of dancing for the prize of a goat, or slaying a goat in honor of the gods. Tragedy may have grown out of a ritualistic practice to honor the god Dionysus. Some scholars believe that tragedy evolved from the **dithyramb**, an improvised choral ode with a traditional refrain. Though the mode and structure of tragedy has varied over the centuries to reflect the cultural beliefs and conventions of each age, the central dramatic conflict remains constant: the human being struggles to overcome some antagonistic force and is ultimately defeated. In classical Greek tragedy, the **protagonist** is a man of stature who must negotiate choice and his relationship with the gods for the good of his people, as in SOPHOCLES' *OEDIPUS THE KING*. In **modernist** drama, tragedies often reflect the struggle of the middle class to overcome societal restraints or domestic conflict, as reflected in the work of HENRIK IBSEN and later ARTHUR MILLER.

tragicomedy: the term used to describe a drama that incorporates both tragic and comedic elements. This hybrid form was popularized in the sixteenth and seventeenth centuries in such works as Giovanni Battista Guarini's pastoral play *The Faithful Shepherd* (1590) and the dramatic collaborations of Francis Beaumont (1584–1616) and John Fletcher (1579–1625). Plays written in this mode often featured tragic conflicts that resolve happily through unexpected—sometimes improbable—**plot** twists. The term *tragicomedy* has also been applied to modern and contemporary plays that do not fit the traditional categories of tragedy and comedy. SAMUEL BECKETT's *WAITING FOR GODOT*, for example, is subtitled "a tragicomedy in two acts."

tragōidia: literally, "goat song," the Greek word for **tragedy**; the word was originally associated with the ritualistic practice of dancing for the prize of a goat, or slaying a goat in honor of the gods.

trope: a musical passage that serves as an interpolation in a Christian religious service and elaborates on the liturgy. Tropes included the representation of religious figures in a call-and-response structure and became a traditional part of the Easter Mass during the

middle ages: They are commonly cited as the first examples of **mimetic** performance within the church.

unities: the principles of structure, derived from Aristotle's *Poetics*, that require a **plot**'s action to be singular, to complete itself within a twenty-four hour period, and to take place in one location. During the sixteenth century, a rigid **neoclassical** interpretation of Aristotle's writings emphasized these "three unities" of action, time, and place.

upstage: the area of the stage farthest from the audience.

venationes: a form of Roman entertainment popularized at the Colosseum in approximately 80 C.E. that involved elaborate contests to the death between animals or between men and animals.

Verfremdungseffekt: *see* **estrangement effect.**

verisimilitude: a central tenet of **neoclassicism**, defined as the quality or appearance of truth. According to the doctrine of verisimilitude, characters and events on stage must be believable; in other words, they must not tax the spectator's credulity by venturing into the fantastic or improbable.

Weimar classicism: a German artistic movement spearheaded by JOHANN WOLFGANG VON GOETHE and Friedrich Schiller (1759–1805) that sought to revive drama by returning to Greek themes and forms.

well-made play: also called *pièce bien-fait* (French), a play that relies heavily on the orchestration of highly complicated **plots** rather than characterization or **themes**. The genre dominated French theater for much of the nineteenth century; its playwrights sought to integrate conventions such as overheard conversations, mistaken identities, sudden appearances and disappearances, and other forms of confusion to create suspense and intrigue. The plays conclude with a *scène à faire* or the final confrontation of characters that resolves the play's action. Eugene Scribe (1791–1861) and Victorien Sardou (1831–1908) are the two playwrights chiefly associated with the genre.

wings: traditionally associated with the **proscenium** theater, the narrow areas off both sides of the stage, where actors wait before making an entrance into the playing space. A curtain or piece of scenery often conceals the wings. *Wings* can also refer to scenery placed on the sides of a stage.

yavanika: in **Sanskrit** theater, a curtain used to hide musicians from the audience's view.

yūgen: an aesthetic concept underlying Japanese **noh** performance that suggests beauty, grace, and an awareness of life's impermanence.

zaju: a form of drama popularized and performed in the Northern provinces of China during the Yuan Dynasty (1234–1368), considered by the Chinese as "classical" drama for its poeticism and literary merit. Earlier *zaju* entertainments of the Song Dynasty (960–1279) were primarily composed of satirical sketches and acrobatic performances. GUAN HANQING's *SNOW IN MIDSUMMER* is an example of a *zaju* play.

zanni: the servant characters in *commedia dell'arte* that include Arlecchino (or Harlequin), Brighella, and Pulcinello.

Permissions Acknowledgments

Churchill, Caryl: *Cloud Nine*, copyright ©1979, 1980, 1983, 1984, 1985 Caryl Churchill Ltd. Reprinted by arrangement with Nick Hern Books Ltd: www.nickhernbooks.co.uk Published in USA by Theatre Communications Group: www.tcg.org

Esslin, Martin: Excerpts from THE THEATRE OF THE ABSURD by Martin Esslin. Copyright © 1961 by Martin Esslin. Used by permission of Doubleday, an imprint of Knopf Doubleday Publishing Group, a division of Penguin Random House LLC. All rights reserved.

Fornés, María Irene: *Mud* from MARIA IRENE FORNES: PLAYS. Copyright © 1986 by PAJ Publications. Reprinted by permission of PAJ Publications.

Fugard, Athol: Entire play from MASTER HAROLD . . . AND THE BOYS. Copyright © 1982 by Athol Fugard. Used by permission of Alfred A. Knopf, an imprint of Knopf Doubleday Publishing Group, a division of Penguin Random House LLC. All rights reserved.

García Lorca, Federico: *La casa de Bernarda Alba/The House of Bernarda Alba* by Federico García Lorca. Copyright © Herederos de Federico García Lorca. From OBRAS COMPLETAS (Galazia-Gutenberg, 1996 edition). English-language translation by James Graham-Lujan and Richard L. O'Connell. Copyright © Herederos de Federico García Lorca and James Graham-Lujan and Richard L. O'Connell. From THREE TRAGEDIES, New Directions Publishing Company, New York. All rights reserved. Reprinted by permission of Casanovas & Lynch, Agencia Literaria, Barcelona.

Genet, Jean: *The Maids* from THE MAIDS AND DEATHWATCH, translation copyright © 1954, 1961 by Bernard Frechtman. Copyright renewed © 1982 by the Estate of Bernard Frechtman. Used by permission of Grove/Atlantic, Inc. Any third party use of this material, outside of this publication, is prohibited.

Hansberry, Lorraine: Entire Play from A RAISIN IN THE SUN by Lorraine Hansberry. Copyright © 1958 by Robert Nemiroff, as an unpublished work. Copyright © 1959, 1966, 1984 by Robert Nemiroff. Copyright renewed 1986, 1987 by Robert Nemiroff. Used by permission of Random House, an imprint and division of Penguin Random House LLC. All rights reserved.

Hughes, Langston: "Harlem (2)" from THE COLLECTED POEMS OF LANGSTON HUGHES by Langston Hughes, edited by Arnold Rampersad and David Roessel, Associate Editor. Copyright © 1994 by the Estate of Langston Hughes. Used by permission of Alfred A. Knopf, and imprint of the Knopf Doubleday Publishing Group, a division of Penguin Random House LLC. All rights reserved.

Hwang, David Henry: From M. BUTTERFLY by David Henry Hwang. Copyright © 1986, 1987, 1988 by David Henry Hwang. Used by permission of New American Library, an imprint of Penguin Publishing Group, a division of Penguin Random House LLC.

Ibsen, Henrik: *Hedda Gabler* and *A Doll House* from IBSEN VOLUME 1: FOUR MAJOR PLAYS, translated by Rick Davis and Brian Johnston. Copyright © 1995. Reprinted by permission of Smith and Kraus Publishers, Inc.

Jarry, Alfred: *Ubu the King* translated by David Ball. Copyright © 2005 by David Ball. Published by W. W. Norton & Company.

Kushner, Tony: *Angels in America: Part One: Millennium Approaches*. Copyright © 1992, 1993 by Tony Kushner. Published by Theatre Communications Group. Used by permission of Theatre Communications Group.

Mamet, David: *Glengarry Glen Ross*. Copyright © 1982, 1983 by David Mamet. Used by permission of Grove/Atlantic, Inc. Any third party use of this material, outside of this publication, is prohibited.

Miller, Arthur: *Death of a Salesman*. Copyright © 1949, renewed © 1977 by Arthur Miller. Used by permission of Viking Books, an imprint of Penguin Publishing Group, a division of Penguin Random House LLC. "Tragedy and the Common Man" from THE THEATER ESSAYS OF ARTHUR MILLER by Arthur Miller, edited by Robert A. Martin. Copyright © 1949, renewed 1977 by

Arthur Miller. Used by permission of Viking Books, an imprint of Penguin Publishing Group, a division of Penguin Random House LLC.

Moses, Daniel David: *Almighty Voice and His Wife.* Copyright © 1991 by Daniel David Moses. Reprinted by permission of Playwrights Canada Press.

Nottage, Lynn: *Ruined.* Copyright © 2009 by Lynn Nottage. Published by Theatre Communications Group. Used by permission of Theatre Communications Group.

Parks, Suzan-Lori: *The America Play* from THE AMERICA PLAY AND OTHER WORKS. Copyright © 1995 by Suzan-Lori Parks. Published by Theatre Communications Group. Used by permission of Theatre Communications Group.

Pinter, Harold: *The Homecoming.* Copyright © 1965, 1966, 1967 by H. Pinter Ltd. Used by permission of Grove/Atlantic, Inc. Any third party use of this material, outside of this publication is prohibited.

Pirandello, Luigi: *Six Characters in Search of an Author,* from PIRANDELLO'S MAJOR PLAYS, translated by Eric Bentley. Copyright © 1991. Evanston: Northwestern University Press. Used by permission.

Shepard, Sam: *Buried Child,* copyright © 1979 by Sam Shepard, from SAM SHEPARD: SEVEN PLAYS: BURIED CHILD, CURSE OF THE STARVING CLASS, THE TOOTH OF CRIME, LA TURISTA, TONGUES, SAVAGE LOVE, TRUE WEST by Sam Shepard. Used by permission of Bantam Books, an imprint of Random House, a division of Penguin Random House LLC. All rights reserved.

Soyinka, Wole: From DEATH AND THE KING'S HORSEMAN by Wole Soyinka. Copyright © 1975, 2003 by Wole Soyinka. Used by permission of W. W. Norton & Company, Inc., and Melanie Jackson Agency, LLC.

Strindberg, August: *Miss Julie* from SELECTED PLAYS, VOLUME 1, translated by Evert Sprinchorn. Copyright © 1986 by University of Minnesota Press. Reprinted by permission of University of Minnesota Press.

Treadwell, Sophie: *Machinal,* copyright © 1928 by Sophie Treadwell, renewed by Diocese of Tucson. Reprinted by permission.

Vogel, Paula: *How I Learned to Drive.* Copyright © 1997 by Paula Vogel. Published by Theatre Communications Group. Used by permission of Theatre Communications Group.

Williams, Tennessee: *A Streetcar Named Desire.* Copyright © 1947 by Tennessee Williams. CAUTION: Professionals and amateurs are hereby warned that *A Streetcar Named Desire*, being fully protected under the copyright laws of the United States of America, the British Empire including the Dominion of Canada, and all other countries of the Copyright Union, is subject to royalty. All rights, including professional, amateur, motion picture, recitation, lecturing, public reading, radio and television broadcasting, and the rights of translation into foreign languages are strictly reserved. Particular emphasis is laid on the question of readings, permission for which must be secured from the author's agent, Luis Sanjurjo, c/o International Creative Management, 40 West 57th Street, New York, NY 10019. Inquiries concerning the amateur acting rights of *A Streetcar Named Desire* should be directed to the Dramatists' Play Service, Inc., 440 Park Avenue South, New York, NY 10016, without whose permission in writing no amateur performance may be given.

Wilson, August: From FENCES by August Wilson. Copyright © 1986 by August Wilson. Used by permission of New American Library, an imprint of Penguin Publishing Group, a division of Random House LLC. From *The Ground on Which I Stand* by August Wilson. Copyright © 1996, 2001 by August Wilson. Published by Theatre Communications Group. Used by permission of Theatre Communications Group

ILLUSTRATIONS

3: Marty Nordstrom c/o the Guthrie Theater; 5: Erich Lessing/Art Resource, NY; 7: The Granger Collection, New York; 9: Theater and Playhouse by Richard and Helen Leacroft, Methuen Publishing, Ltd; 11: Vanni/Art Resource, NY; 12: Museo Capitolino, Rome, Italy/Ancient Art and Architecture Collection Ltd./The Bridgeman Art Library; 13: Scala/Art Resource, NY; 15: Kings Visualization Lab; 18: The Philadelphia Museum of Art/Art Resource, NY; 21: Princeton University Press, 1976; 23: AFP/Getty Images; 28: Theater and Playhouse by Richard and Helen Leacroft, Methuen Publishing, Ltd; 30: Wikipedia Commons; 33: Wikipedia Commons; 35: Musee de la Ville de Paris, Musee Carnavalet, Paris, France/Giraudon/The Bridgeman Art Library; 37: Lebrecht Music & Arts; 39: The Art Archive; 41: Lebrecht Music & Arts/The Image Works; 43: Kevin George/Alamy; 46: akg-Images; 47: Lebrecht Authors; 48: Private Collection/The Bridgeman Art Library; 51: Tate, London/Art Resource, NY; 53: akg-Images; 55: akg-Images; 57: Lebrecht Authors; 58: Picture Collection, The Branch Libraries, The New York Public Library, Astor, Lenox and Tilden Foundations; 61: Lebrecht Authors; 63: Lipnitzki/Roger Viollet/Getty Images; 64: Kurt Weill Foundation/Lebrecht Music & Arts; 65: The New York Public Library, Astor, Lenox and Tilden Foundations; 67: Franklin D. Roosevelt Library; 70: Lipnitzki/Roger Viollet/Getty Images; 71: Hulton-Deutsch Collection/Getty Images; 72: W. Eugene Smith/Time & Life/Getty Images; 73: Bettmann/Getty Images; 75: Julio Donoso/Sygma/Getty Images; 78: Nobby Clark/Hulton Archive/Getty Images; 87: The Granger Collection, New York; 89: Eric Hansen; 108: Strindberg Museum Stockholm/Alfredo Dagli Orti/The Art Archive; 110: Strindbergsmuseet, Stockholm; 111: Geraint Lewis; 150: Private Collection MD/The Art Archive; 152: Geraint Lewis; 155: Fales Library/New York University; 261: Culver Pictures/The Art Archive; 264: courttheatre.org; 265: Nobby Clark/ArenaPAL; 309: Cultures France; 311: Marc Charmet/The Art Archive; 345: Hulton Archive/Getty Images; 348–49: Billy Rose Theatre Division, New York Public Library for the Performing Arts, Astor, Lenox and Tilden Foundations; 391: Glasgow University Library, Dept. of Special Collections; 395: Robin Skelton, J. M. Synge and His World; Viking, 1971; 406: Culver Pictures/The Art Archive; 408: Hulton Archive/Getty Images; 473: Photo courtesy of the Berg Collection; 476: Billy Rose Theatre Collection, New York Public Library for the Performing Arts; 487: Mary Evans Picture Library/Asia Media; 489: Richard Feldman; 531: akg-Images; 533: Public Domain, Image courtesy of Beinecke Rare Book & Manuscript Library, Yale University; 565: Bachrach; 568: Martha Swope; 626: Art Resource, NY; 628: Geraint Lewis; 664: Kurt Weill Foundation/Lebrecht Music & Arts; 665: Courtesy of Inge Steinert; 668: Geraint Lewis; 723: Digital Image © Museum of Modern Art/Licensed by SCALA/Art Resource, NY; 725: akg-Images; 751: Library of Congress; 753: AP/Wide World Photos; 754: Bettmann/Getty Images; 821: AP/Wide World Photos; 823: W. Eugene Smith/Getty Images; 825: Billy Rose Collection; 897: AFP/Getty Images; 914: John Haynes/Lebrecht Music & Arts; 918: Geraint Lewis; 982: Jack Mitchell/Contributor via Getty Images; 984: Courtesy of Dr. Jeffery Kennedy; 1005: Bettmann/Getty; 1009: Bettmann/Getty; 1074: Mary Evans Picture Library; 1077: Kevin Berne/American Conservatory Theater; 1126: Hulton Archive/Getty Images; 1128: Nonso Anozie as Elesin, Horseman of the King in the National Theatre's production of Wole Soyinka's Death and the King's Horseman directed by Rufus Norris at the National Theatre in London. Photograph by Robbie Jack; 1177: Brigitte Lacombe; 1179: Gerry Goodstein; 1230: Gemma Levine/Hulton Archive/Getty Images; 1233: Geraint Lewis; 1285: Hulton Archive/Getty Images; 1287: Sara Krulwich/The New York Times/Redux; 1322: Robert Giard. © Estate of Robert Giard. Courtesy Stephen Bulger Gallery; 1323: Masrah Ensemble (Lebanon); 1344: Steve Liss/Time Life Pictures/Getty; 1346: Hulton Archive/Getty Images; 1383: AP; 1386: Yale Repertory Theatre, Yale School of Drama; 1450: Paradigm Agency requested no credit be noted; 1453: © Joan Marcus; 1502: AP/Wide World Photos; 1505: John Haynes/Lebrecht Music & Arts; 1569: John Reeves; 1573: Pi Theatre Productions/Aki Studio Theatre; 1604: © Stephanie Diani; 1606: Rick Martin; 1638: Photo by Laurie Sturdevant; 1641: Joan Marcus/ArenaPAL; 1681: Linda Nylind/eyevine/Redux Pictures; 1684: Joan Marcus.

Index